CLIFTON M. MILLER LIBRARY
Washington College
Chestertown, MD 21620

Presented By
The Raymond Clarke Estate

UNITED STATES LOCAL HISTORIES IN THE LIBRARY OF CONGRESS A BIBLIOGRAPHY

UNITED STATES LOCAL HISTORIES IN THE LIBRARY OF CONGRESS

A BIBLIOGRAPHY

Edited by

MARION J. KAMINKOW

VOLUME 1

MAGNA CARTA BOOK COMPANY
BALTIMORE, MD.
U.S.A.
1975

Copyright 1975
Magna Carta Book Company

Library of Congress catalog card number: 74-25444

ISBN: 0-910946-17-5

No part of this book nor any collection of entries
may be reproduced in any manner whatsoever.

Z
1250
.U59
1975
vol. 1

CONTENTS OF VOLUME I

Each region is preceded by its classification schedule and followed by a supplementary index of places.

1	NEW ENGLAND
45	MAINE
119	NEW HAMPSHIRE
187	VERMONT
231	MASSACHUSETTS
579	RHODE ISLAND
629	CONNECTICUT
719	MIDDLE ATLANTIC STATES
735	NEW YORK

PREFACE

This bibliography lists works on U. S. local history in the collections of the Library of Congress. It includes all the books cataloged and classified under the local history portion of the Library of Congress classification schedule (F1-975) for which cards had been filed in the Library's shelflist by mid-1972. This publication was compiled from a microfilm copy of that portion of the shelflist. The books are listed in order by their classification numbers; this provides a basic arrangement by regions of the United States, which is then subdivided by State and further subdivided by city, county, or other category.

Books on U. S. local and State history must be used at the Library of Congress because the Library does not circulate them on interlibrary loan. It is advisable to ascertain the hours of public service before visiting the Library.

In general, works on U. S. local history may be consulted only in the Library's Local History and Genealogy Room. In addition to publications on local history in the Library's general collections, an extensive reference collection arranged by State is available for consultation, as well as a card catalog similar to the shelflist mentioned above. The reference staff assists readers in identifying publications that relate to the subjects of their research, chiefly by explaining the use of indexes and catalogs.

An information sheet entitled REFERENCE SERVICES AND FACILITIES OF THE LOCAL HISTORY AND GENEALOGY ROOM is available upon request from the General Reference and Bibliography Division, Library of Congress, Washington, D. C. 20540.

EDITOR'S NOTE

The Library of Congress classification schedule has been followed in the arrangement of this bibliography. The holdings of the Library for the U. S. local history portion of the F Class are shown, providing a State-by-State listing. Hawaii, which has a DU number, is also included.

Before using the bibliography, the reader is urged to consult the classification schedule at the beginning of each region. Having found his subject, he can easily follow the numerical sequence until he reaches the desired topic. Books are listed alphabetically by author under each heading, except biographies, which are listed alphabetically by subject. Localities are listed under two classes: (1) regions, counties, etc., and (2) cities, towns, etc. In each case, they are listed alphabetically by place and then alphabetically by author. Exceptions to this rule are certain regions within a county which bear the same classification number as the county and would appear to be out of order. These regions can be found by checking the classification schedule. A supplementary index of places has been compiled by the publisher for each State.

The original wording on the Library of Congress catalog cards has not been reproduced in its entirety. The titles of the works have been abbreviated, where possible. Authors' dates, joint authors, detailed descriptions of contents, number of copies printed, etc., have been omitted. Brief descriptions of contents and important notes, such as all notes of indexes and bibliographies, have been retained. Where it exists, the Library of Congress catalog card number has been listed at the end of each item to help those who wish to purchase cards. The Library's call number is also listed uniformly on the right-hand side, where the sequence can be easily followed. This number is sometimes followed by designations indicating the location of volumes not kept in the Library's main bookstacks, e.g. L H & G (Local History and Genealogy Room) or Rare Book Coll. (Collection). If the book has been replaced by a microfilm copy, that fact is also noted.

In editing of the work, the following cards were omitted:

(1) Genealogies which also carry a CS number. These all appear in *GENEALOGIES IN THE LIBRARY OF CONGRESS; A BIBLIOGRAPHY*. (Baltimore, Magna Carta Book Co., 1972. 2 v.)

(2) Minor works which are part of a larger work in the same classification, such as articles from a State historical society journal under the classification of that state.

(3) Duplicate cards which are sometimes used where more than one subject or place is covered by a single book. These items are covered by the supplementary index for each State.

Serials and directories are always a problem in cataloging. The Library's shelflist has a card for the first issue of a serial publication, but rarely does it state the complete holdings, since many of the serials are still continuing. For this information one must consult the Library's Serial Record Division. City directories in the Library's collections are no longer classified, and the F numbers have been removed. They are now shelved in alphabetical order by locality. However, since they appear in place in the Library's shelflist, they are included here as listed. State directories, which do not have a place in the classification schedule, have been inserted after guidebooks.

Once again, the publishers wish to express their gratitude to the Library of Congress for graciously permitting the use of its catalogs and the publication of this bibliography. Thanks are also due to the librarians who compiled the card index over a period of many years, and particularly to the present staff of the Local History and Genealogy Room, whose unfailing patience and courtesy in answering the myriad questions which arose during the typing and editing lightened the task. Without their help the work could not have been accomplished.

Marion J. Kaminkow

Abbreviations used for bibliographic details and locations include the following:

Alc.	Alcove
c.	copyright (usually preceding date)
Coll.	Collection
Div.	Division
G & M	Geography & Map Division
l.	leaf or leaves
L H & G	Local History and Genealogy Room
M R R	Main Reading Room
n.p.	No place of publication given
p.	page or pages
pl.	plate or plates
port.	portrait
Pub(l).	Publisher, published by
t.-p.	title page

SELECTED BIBLIOGRAPHIES

BRADFORD, Thomas Lindsley. The bibliographer's manual of American history, containing an account of all state, territory, town and county histories relating to the United States of North America ... and with an exhaustive index to titles, and an index by states ... Ed. and rev. by Stan. V. Henkels ... Philadelphia, S. V. Henkels, 1907 - 10. 5 v. 27½ cm. Contents. - v.1. A-E. - v.2. F-L. - v.3. M-Q. - v.4. R-Z. v.5. General index. 7-23470.
    Z1250. B 85
    Geneal. Sect. Ref.

— Detroit, Gale Research Co., 1968. 5 v. 23 cm. 67-14023.
    Z1250. B 852

CLARK (Arthur H.) co., publishers, Glendale, Calif. The United States; a catalogue of books relating to the history of its various states, counties and cities and territories; arranged alphabetically by states and offered for sale at reasonable prices ... Cleveland, The Arthur H. Clark co. (1928) 4, 411 p. front. 24½ cm. 10,639 entries; priced. 28-28995 Rev.
    Z1250. Z9C6 1928a

COX LIBRARY, Tucson, Ariz. Shelf list and catalogue of the Cox Library; a collection of local histories and biographies. (Comp. by Virginia E. Laughlin and Linda J. Pixley) Tucson (1963) 309 p. 28 cm. 65-4623.
    Z1250. C 6

GRIFFIN, Appleton Prentiss Clark. ... Index of articles upon American local history in historical collections in the Boston public library. ... Boston, By order of the Trustees, 1889. vii, 225 p. 28 cm. (Boston public library. Bibliographies of special subjects, originally pub. in the Bulletins of the library. no. 3) "List of works indexed": p. iii-vii, 3 - 9. 3-1589-90.
    Z1250. G 84

— Boston ... 1889. vii, 225 p. 28½ cm. Reprinted from the Bulletins of the library. Supplemented by the author's "Index of the literature of American local history in collections published in 1890 - 95," 1896. 16-2528.
    Z1250. G841

— Index of the literature of American local history in collections published in 1890 - 95 (with some others) Boston, C. H. Heintzemann, 1896. vii, 151 p. 24 cm. 3-1589-90.
    Z1250. G 85

PERKINS, Frederic Beecher, comp. Check list for American local history. Reprinted with additions from the Bulletins of the Boston public library. (1876) Boston, Press of Rockwell & Churchill, 1876. 198 p. 23½ cm. Printed in single column, on one half of the page only. This copy interleaved with manuscript additions. 2-25233.
    Z1250. P 44
    Geneal. Sect.

PETERSON, Clarence Stewart. Consolidated bibliography of county histories in fifty States in 1961, consolidated 1935 - 1961. Baltimore, 1961. A - I, 186 p. 28 cm. 61-46792.
    Z1250. P 47

— Baltimore, Genealogical Pub. Co., 1973. 186 p. 24 cm. 73-8036 MARC.
    Z1250. P 47 1973

PETERSON, Clarence Stewart. Bibliography of local histories in the Atlantic States, 1966. (Baltimore) 1966 - 67. 2 v. 28 cm. 66-9773.
    Z1251. A8 P4

STEMMONS, John D. The United States census compendium; a directory of census records, tax lists, poll lists, petitions, directories, etc. which can be used as a census. Comp. by John "D" Stemmons. Logan, Utah, Everton Publishers (1973) iv, 144 p. maps. 29 cm. Bibliography: p. 135 - 144. 73-77805 MARC.
    Z1250. S 83

UNITED STATES. - Office of Archeology and Historic Preservation. Division of History. Preliminary bibliographical inventory of park historical and architectural studies. Comp. by Gary Christopher and Dorothy Junkin. (Washington) 1971. xiii, 169 p. 27 cm. 72-601688 MARC.
    Z1251. A2A5

ANDER, Oscar Fritiof. The cultural heritage of the Swedish immigrant; selected references. (Rock Island, Ill., Augustana College Library, 1956)   xix, 191 p.   23 cm.   (Augustana Library publications, no. 27)
57-747.
                                                               Z1361.S9A55
                                                                 L H & G

MEYNEN, Emil. Bibliographie des deutschtums der kolonialzeitlichen einwanderung in Nordamerika, insbesondere der Pennsylvanien-Deutschen und ihrer nachkommen, 1683 - 1933 ... Leipzig, O. Harrassowitz, 1937.   XXXVI, 636 p.   25 cm.   Classified, with indexes of authors and surnames.   "Benutzte bibliotheken und archive": p. (xxxv) - xxxvi.   38-7457.
                                                                  Z1371.G37M6

— (Detroit, Repub. by Gale Research Co., 1966)   xxxvi, 636 p.   24 cm.   66-25870.
                                                                Z1361.G37M6
                                                                1966

POCHMANN, Henry August. Bibliography of German culture in America to 1940 ... Arthur R. Schultz, editor. Madison, University of Wisconsin Press, 1953.   xxxii, 483 p.   23 cm.   53-12539.
                                                                 Z1361.G37P6

NEW ENGLAND

SELECTED BIBLIOGRAPHIES FOR NEW ENGLAND

BAKER, Mary Ellen. Bibliography of lists of New England soldiers. Boston, New England historic genealogical soc., 1911.   56 p.   25 cm.   (Register re-prints, ser. A, no. 36)   11-27905.   Z1251.E1B2

FORBES, Mrs. Harriette (Merrifield) comp. New England diaries, 1602 - 1800, a descriptive catalogue of diaries, orderly books and sea journals. (Topsfield, Mass.) Priv. print., 1923.   2, vii - viii, 439 p.   23½ cm.   23-15046.   Z1251.E1F6
L H & G

— New York, Russell & Russell (1967)   viii, 439 p.   23 cm.   67-28478.   Z1251.E1F6
1967

NEW ENGLAND CLASSIFICATION   F1 - F15

1		Periodicals. Societies. Collections.
	.5	Museums. Exhibitions, exhibits.
2		Gazetteers. Dictionaries. Geographic names.
	.3	Guidebooks.
3		Biography (Collective). Genealogy (Collective).
	.2	Historiography.

Historians, *see* E 175.5.

.5   Study and teaching.
4   General works. Histories.
 .3 Juvenile works.
 .5 Minor works. Pamphlets, addresses, essays, etc.
 .6   Anecdotes, legends, pageants, etc.
5   Historic monuments (General). Illustrative material.
6   Antiquities (Non-Indian).
     By period.
7   Early to 1775.

The Plymouth Company, 1606; Council for New England, 1620; United Colonies of New England, 1643–1684. Colonial life; Puritans (Cf. F 67, Puritans in Massachusetts); Pilgrims (Cf. F 68, Pilgrims in New Plymouth Colony); Thanksgiving Day in New England (Cf. E 162, Thanksgiving Day in the United States); etc.

Including individual voyagers after 1607, e. g. Bartholomew Gosnold, John Smith, George Waymouth.

Cf. BF 1575–1576, Witchcraft in New England.
  E 83.63, Pequot War, 1636–1638.
  E 83.67, King Philip's War, 1675–1676.
  E 83.72, War with eastern Indians, 1722–1726.
  E 105, Norsemen, Vinland.
  E 121–135, Early voyages before 1607.
  E 196, King William's War, 1689–1697.
  E 197, Queen Anne's War, 1702–1713.
  E 198, King George's War, 1744–1748.
  E 199, French and Indian War, 1755–1763.
  F 22, Popham Colony.

.5   Dominion of New England, 1686–1689.

Consolidation of New England colonies and regions into one province; later (1688), enlarged by the addition of New York and New Jersey.

Relations with Governor Edmund Andros; Revolution of 1689, etc.

8   1775–1865.
                    Cf. E 357.6–7, Opposition to War of 1812.
9   1865–1950.
                    New England hurricane, 1938 (use local classification number for effects of hurricane on an individual state or city); etc.
10   1951–
12   Regions, A–Z.
                    Berkshire Hills, *see* F 72.B5.
            .C7   Connecticut River and Valley.
                        Cf. F 42.C65, New Hampshire.
                        F 57.C7, Vermont.
                        F 72.C7, Massachusetts.
                        F 102.C7, Connecticut.
                    Isle of Shoals, *see* F 42.I8.
                    Merrimac River and Valley, *see* F 42.M4, New Hampshire; F 72.M6, Massachusetts.
                    White Mountains, *see* F 41.
15   Elements in the population.
            .A1   General works.
            .A2–Z   Individual elements.
                        For a list of racial, ethnic, and religious elements (with cutter numbers), *see* E 184, p. 27–29.

NEW ENGLAND
F1 - 15

PERIODICALS. SOCIETIES. COLLECTIONS.

DEXTER, Franklin Bowditch.   A selection from the miscellaneous historical papers of fifty years. New Haven, Conn.   (The Tuttle, Morehouse & Taylor company) 1918.   viii, 379 p. illus. 24 cm.   19-3940.
F1. D52

GENEALOGICAL Advertiser, The.   A quarterly magazine of family history.   v. 1-4; Mar. 1898-1901.   Cambridge, Mass., Lucy H. Greenlaw, 1898 - 1901.   4 v. ports. 24½ cm.   No more pub.   6-44022.
F1. G32

HIGGINSON, Mrs. Mary Potter (Thacher)   Seashore and prairie.   Boston, J. R. Osgood & company, 1877.   3 p, 239 p. 15½ cm.   12-34063.
F1. H63

HISTORICAL New England.   v. 1, no. 2.   Dec., 1899.   Concord, N. H., 1899.   35 cm.
F1. H75

HORTON, Howard Leavitt.   New England chronicle.   (Boston? 1950 - 58)   6 vols. illus., group ports., maps, facsims. 28 cm.   Includes bibliographies.   50-8501 rev.
F1. H8

LIBRARY of New England history.   (Boston, J. K. Wiggin & W. P. Lunt, 1865-67)   4 vols. fold. maps. 21½ x 17 cm.   No more published.   6-5565.   Includes Mourt's relation; The history of King Philip's war; The history of the eastern expeditions of 1689, etc.; Plain dealing; or, News from New England.
F1. L69

MAGAZINE of New England history.   A medium of intercommunication for historical and genealogical students.   v. 1-3; Jan., 1891 - 93.   3 vols. 24 cm.   quarterly.   R. H. Tilley, editor.   Merged into Putnam's historical magazine.   2-18690.
F1. M18

NATIONAL Society of New England women.   Constitution and by-laws.   (New York, 191-?)   29 p. illus. 12½ x 10 cm.   22-742.
F1. N27

— Yearbook.
F1. N3

— New York City colony.   Year book.   (New York)   vols. 16½ x 13 cm.   16-3019.
F1. N34

NEW ENGLAND associated California pioneers of '49, Boston ... The 43rd anniversary of the discovery of gold in California ... to be held ... Jan. 17, 1891.   Boston, C. M. Barrows & co., printers, 1891.   28 p. 22 cm.   23-14849.
F1. N36

NEW ENGLAND association of New York.   The constitution and by-laws.   (New York, 1858)   14 p. 19½ cm.   17-23113.
F1. N37

NEW ENGLAND family history ... v. 1 -   July 1907 -   New York city, H. C. Quinby, 1907.   vols. plates, ports., facsims., tables. 27 cm.   quarterly.   8-31934.
F1. N38

NEW ENGLAND galaxy, The.   v. 1 - summer 1959 -   (Sturbridge, Mass., Old Sturbridge, Inc.)
illus., ports., music. 20 cm. quarterly.   F1. N39

NEW ENGLAND historic genealogical society ... Constitution and by-laws, etc. 1858.   F1. N41
                                                                                 1876   F1. N418
                                                                                 1893   F1. N42
                                                                                 1903   F1. N421

— Circular... no. 2 - 4.   (Boston, 1846)   F1. N423

— ... incorporated 1845.   (Boston) 1905   F1. N428
                                   1906   F1. N429
                                   1907   F1. N43

— ... Officer and committees ... from its formation to May, 1859.   Compiled by J. W. Dean ...
(Boston? 1859)   F1. N444

— Lists and rolls of members.   1877   F1. N445
                                 1892   F1. N448
                                 1893   F1. N449
                                 1898   F1. N4496
                                 1898   F1. N45
                                 1903   F1. N452

— Financial statements, 1870, 1871, 1873, 1876, 1902, 1904, 1905   F1. N453

— Annual meeting; reports.   F1. N454

— Proceedings ... 1865 - 1909. Boston, The Society.   54 vols. in 11. illus., plates. 23½ x 24 cm.   Previous
to 1865 the Proceedings were published in the N.E. hist. and geneal. register.   9-902.
                                                                                           F1. N46

— Addresses ... at the annual meeting ... Boston, 1858 - 87.   F1. N465

— Narrative remarks, expository notes and historical criticisms, on the New England historical and
genealogical society ...   Albany, Munsell, printer, 1874   56 p. 22 x 17 cm. 15-9274.   F1. N4657

— A century of genealogical progress, being a history of the New England historic genealogical soc.,
1845 - 1945, by William Carroll Hill ...   Boston, 1945.   4 p., 7-90 p. plates, ports. 23½ cm. 46-5537. F1. N4658

— Miscellaneous printed matter published by this body is classified in F1. 469

— A brief history of the New England historic genealogical society ... by J. H. Sheppard ...
Albany, 1862.   17 p. 23 cm. 3-20317.   F1. N471

SLAFTER, Edmund Farwell.   The Knox manuscripts. Boston, 1881. 12 p. 25½ cm. 3-9562.   F1. N476

SLAFTER, Edmund Farwell.   Chairs of New England governors. Boston, 1885.   8 p. 25 cm. 3-32526.
                                                                                           F1. N4765

NEW ENGLAND historic genealogical society.   Dedication of the society's house ... March 18, 1871)
(Boston) 1871.   24½ cm.   F1. N4871

— Description of the ... house. (Boston, 1871?)   23½ cm.   F1. N4873

— Index to necrology ... n.p., 1882.   24½ cm.   F1. N497

— The New England historical and genealogical register. v. 1 - Jan. 1847 - Boston (etc.)
vols. ports., maps, facsims., tables. 24 cm. quarterly. Absorbed the New Hampshire repository in 1847. Slight variations in title.

NEW ENGLAND 3

Published by the New England Historic Genealogical Society. Vols. 54-77 include annual supplement to April number: Proceedings of the New England Historic Genealogical Society at the annual meeting, 1900-23. Beginning in 1924 Proceedings are incorporated into the April number. Vols. 37 - 52 (1883 - 98) include section: Genealogical gleanings in England, by H. F. Waters. Indexes: General index. Vols. 1 - 10, 1847 - 56, in v.10. Vols. 11 - 15, 1857 - 61, in v.15. Person index. Vols. 1 - 50, 1847 - 96. 3 v. Subject index. Vols. 1 - 50, 1847 - 96. 1 v. Place index. Vols. 1 - 41 (1847 - 87, in v.42. Vols. 1 - 50, 1847 - 96. 1 v. Genealogy and pedigree index. Vols. 1 - 50, 1847 - 96, in v. 50. Testators in Water's Genealogical gleanings in England. Vols. 37 - 52, 1883 - 98, in v.52. 5-16188 rev 3*   F1. N56

NEW ENGLAND notes and queries, The. (A medium of intercommunication for historical and genealogical students) v.1; Jan. - Oct. 1890. Newport, R.I., R.H. Tilley, 1890.   quarterly. No more published. 5-23361.   F1. N61

NEW ENGLAND Quarterly, The; an historical review of New England life and letters ... vol. 1 - Jan. 1928 - (Orono, Me., The University press; etc., etc., 1928. -   vols. plates, maps, facsims. 24 cm.   Indexes: vols. 1 - 10, 1928 - 37. 29-23850 (rev. '44)   F1. N62

NEW ENGLAND Society in the city of Brooklyn ... Certificate of incorporation, etc., June, 1880. 21 p. 23½ cm. 8-18976.   F1. N63

— — (As adopted May 6th, 1881)   16 p. 17 cm. 8-18977.   F1. N631

— Proceedings at the annual meeting. 1881 - 1907.   F1. N64

— — 1880 - 1895.   2 v.   23 cm.   15-25682.   F1. N643

NEW ENGLAND Society in the city of New York. Anniversary celebration. 1850 - 1906   F1. N65

— 95th annual festival. 1900.   illus. 20½ cm. CA 7-7106 unrev'd.   F1. N652

NEW ENGLAND Society orations; addresses, sermons, and poems delivered before the New England society in the city of New York, 1820 - 1885 ... New York, The Century co., 1901.   2 v. 21½ cm. 2-490.   F1. N655

NEW ENGLAND Society in the City of New York, 1805 - 1957. By Horace McK Hatch. (n. p., 1958) 80 p. illus. 23 cm. 59-27841.   F1. N657

NEW ENGLAND Society of Charleston, S.C. Rules, etc. Charleston, 1842-67.   2 v.   F1. N67

— History of ... 1819 - 1919, comp... by William Way. Charleston, The Society, 1920.   ix, 307 p. front., ports. 20 cm. 20-13997.   F1. N674

NEW ENGLAND Society of Cincinnati. Annual report ... Cincinnati, 1847-48.   2 vols.   F1. N675

— Year book. 1905   17½ cm.   F1. N676

NEW ENGLAND Society of Cleveland and the Western Reserve ... Organization, anniversary addresses and enrollment. (Cleveland) 1896.   50 p. 23½ cm.   F1. N677
                1897   39 p. 23 cm.   F1. N6772

— ... 1853 - 1910, constitution, officers, members and history. Cleveland, 1910.   63 p. front., ports. 24 cm. 11-14782   F1. N6775
                                        1915   F1. N6776
                                         1900   F1. N6778

NEW ENGLAND Society of northeastern Pennsylvania, Scranton, Pa. Proceedings at the annual dinner. Scranton, Pa., 1899 - 1900.   3 v. in 1. illus. 24 cm. CA 5-2238 unrev'd.   F1. N 68

NEW ENGLAND Society of Orange, New Jersey. Year book.   v. fold. tables, diagr. 14-18 cm. Society organized in 1870 and 1st ed. of its Constitution and by-laws pub. in that year. None issued in 1902. 19-5260.   F1. N737

— Anniversary celebration. Orange, 1895.   F1. N 74

NEW ENGLAND Society of Pennsylvania, Philadelphia, annual festival of the ... 1881 - 1909. (Philadelphia, 1881 - 1901)   27 v. port. 23 cm. x 25½ cm.   F1. N75

NEW ENGLAND society of St. Louis ... Annual reunion ... (St. Louis, 1885 - 19 -)
  v. illus., plates, fold.plans. 23½ cm. Title varies. 5-31601 rev.   F1. N76

NEW ENGLAND Society of Vineland, N.J. ... Constitution, officers and members, 1902 - 1906. Vineland, N.J. 1906.   (14) p. 19½ cm. 7-18007.   F1. N78

PURITAN society, The. (Boston, T. R. Marvin & son, printers, 1911)   8 p. 24 cm.
  F1. P97

GENEALOGICAL magazine, The. v. 1-2, July 1890 - Apr. 1892; v.3-9 (new ser., v.1-7), May 1892-Dec. 1899; v.10 - (14) (new 3d. ser., v.1-5), Apr. 1900 - Jan., 1905; (4th) ser., v.1-3, v.4, no. 1-2, Apr. 1905 - Mar. 1917. Salem, Mass., The Salem press publishing and printing company; (etc., etc., 1890 - 1903; Boston, E. Putnam, etc., 1903-17)   18 v. illus., plates (part col.) ports. facsims. tables. 23 - 27½ cm. Quarterly, July 1890 - Apr., 1892; Monthly, May 1892 - Dec. 1899; quarterly, Apr. 1900 - Jan. 1905; monthly, Apr. 1905 - Mar. 1906; quarterly, 1907; publication suspended, 1908 - 14; quarterly, Dec. 1915 - Mar. 1917. Edited by Eben Putnam et al. Absorbed the Magazine of New England history in 1893, the Genealogical bulletin in 1905. Title and imprint varies. General index to vols. I, II, III ... new ser., v.3, xxvii p.; Index to names and places. Vols. IV, V, VI ... new ser. v.6, xxxi p. Subject index ...: new ser. v.6 (4) p. 5-40829 rev.
  F1. P98

— Table of contents and index to names, volumes iii, iv, v, new series ... 1902 - 1905. Boston, E. Putnam, 1907.   2 p., 24 p. 24 cm. 5-40829 rev.   F1. P98

SOCIETY for the preservation of New England antiquities, Boston. Old-time New England; the bulletin of the Society for the preservation of New England antiquities. Boston, Mass., 19 -   v. in illus. (incl. plans) plates, ports. 24½ cm. quarterly. Title varies. 12-6618 rev.   F1. S68

PALMER, Benjamin Franklin. A poem read before the Society of the sons of New England in Pennsylvania, on the first anniversary of the society, and the two hundred and thirty-seventh anniversary of the landing of the Pilgrims at Plymouth. Philadelphia, 1859.   15 p. 23 cm. 5-10309.   F1. S69

SOCIETY of the sons of New England of the city and county of Philadelphia. Constitution and by-laws ... Philadelphia, 1845.   17 p. 19 cm. 17-25200.   F1. S693

SPONHOLTZ, Carl Louis. Founders of New England. Salem, Mass, C. L. Spondholtz (1942 - 1947)   2 v. illus., maps. 18 cm. 43-10650.
  F1. S75

YANKEE guide to the New England Countryside, The.   v. 1 -   Spring/summer 1972 -   (Dublin, N.H., Yankee, inc.)   v. illus. 28 cm. semiannual. 72-623456.   F1. Y33

NEW ENGLAND guide, The. (Concord, N.H.)   v. illus. (part col.) 28 cm. annual. Ed. and pub. by S. W. Winship. 58-46331.   F1.3.N4

GAZETTEERS. DICTIONARIES. GEOGRAPHIC NAMES.

DOUGLAS-LITHGOW, Robert Alexander. Dictionary of American-Indian place and proper names in New England. Salem, Mass., Salem press co., 1909.   xxi, 400 p. front. 23 cm. Bibliography p. (397) - 400.
  F2. D72
  L H & G

HAYWARD, John. The New England gazetteer; containing descriptions of all the states, counties and towns in New England, etc. Boston, J. Hayward; Concord, N.H., Boyd & White, 1839.   (508) p. front., plates. 20½ cm. 1-7547 rev.   F2. H42

— 5th edition. 1839.   F2. H43

— 6th edition. 1839.   F2.H431

— 8th edition. 1839.   F2.H433

NEW ENGLAND

— 9th edition. 1839   F2.H434

— 14th edition. 1841.   F2.H44

— 14th edition rev. and cor. 1841.   F2.H45

NEW ENGLAND gazetter, The, comprising a concise description of the cities, towns, county seats, villages, and post-offices... Boston, Sampson, Davenport, & co., 1885. 3 - 182 p. front. (map) 8°. 1-7552.   F2.N53

NEW ENGLAND gazetter... 1902. Boston, Sampson, Murdock & co., 1902. map. 23½ cm. The gazetteer of the "New England business directory and gazetteer" pub. separately. 2-12941.   F2.N54

GUIDEBOOKS.

AMERICAN Express Company. Travelers guide: highways and places in New England. 1967 - (New York?) Meredith Press. v. maps (part col.) 22 cm. 67-20703.   F2.3.A4

FODOR, Eugene, ed. New England: Connecticut, Rhode Island, Massachusetts, Vermont, New Hampshire, Maine. Litchfield, Conn. Fodor's Modern Guides inc. (1966) 411 p. 21 cm. (Fodor Shell travel guides U.S.A. v.1) 66-18838.   F2.3.F6

— 2nd rev. edition. New York (c.1967) 411 p. 20 cm. 67-20077.   F2.3.F6

HEPBURN, Andrew. New England, a complete guide, by Andrew Hepburn and Harlan Logan. New York, Simon and Schuster, c.1951. 108 p. illus., maps. (The American travel series 3) 51-5331.   F2.3.H4 1951

HEPBURN, Andrew. New England... New York, Travel Enterprise, c.1954. 174 p. illus. 22 cm. (The American travel series, no. 3) 54-4143.   F2.3..H4 1954

— New and rev. ed. Boston, Houghton Mifflin, c.1958. 175 p. illus., maps. 22 cm. 58-9100.   F2.3.H4 1958

HEPBURN, Andrew. Complete guide to New England. New rev. ed. Garden City, N.Y., Doubleday, 1963. 192 p. illus. 21 cm. (The American travel series) 62-11292.   F2.3.H4 1963

HEPBURN, Andrew. Rand McNally guide to New England. Chicago, Rand McNally (c.1969) 208 p. illus. 23 cm. 69-19963.   F2.3.H43

MOBIL travel guide Northeastern states, etc. New York, Simon & Schuster. 1960 - v. 21 cm. 60-51602.   F2.3.M6

REDGRAVE, William J. All of New England. Greenlawn, N.Y., Harian Publications, c.1956. 88 p. illus. 28 cm. 56-3617.   F2.3.R4 1956

— 2d ed. 1959. 88 p. illus. 59-1648. 28 cm.   F2.3.R4 1959

— 2d ed. 1960. 88 p. 28 cm.   F2.3.R4 1960

DIRECTORIES.

DIRECTORY of American society, New England. 1929 - . New York, Town topics (c.1929) v. 18½ cm. 29-3771.   F2.6.D59

CONSOLIDATED directory of New England. Boston. 1958 -   v. 23 cm. 58-19053.   F2.7.C6

GEER'S express directory and railway forwarder's guide, etc. vol. I containing the New England states.   By Geo. P. Geer.   Springfield, C. R. Chaffee & Co., 1858.   24 cm.   Directories

NEW ENGLAND business directory and gazetteer for 1856 - 19 -   Boston, Sampson & Murdock company, 1856 - 19 -   v. fold. maps. 25½ - 28½ cm. 0-2437 (rev. '26)

Directories

NEW ENGLAND mercantile union business directory, etc.   New York, Pratt & co.; Boston, L. C. & H. L. Pratt, etc.   1849.   324, 9 p. incl. tables. maps (1 fold.) 22½ cm. No more pub. 8-27441 rev.   Directories

NEW ENGLAND cities business directory.   v. 1 -   1867 -   Boston, Briggs & Co.

Directories

BIOGRAPHY (COLLECTIVE). GENEALOGY (COLLECTIVE).

BACON, Martha Sherman.   Puritan promenade.   Boston, Houghton Mifflin, 1964.   160 p. 22 cm. 64-24642.   F3. B3

BANKS, Charles Edward.   Topographical dictionary of 2885 English emigrants to New England, 1620 - 1650.   Philadelphia, Pa.   (The Bertram press) 1937.   xxxviii, 295 p. front.(port.) maps. 26 cm. 37-32156.   F3. B35
L.H. & G.

— Baltimore, Southern Book Co., 1957.   xxxviii, 295 p. maps (part fold.) 24 cm. 58-3799.   F3. B35
1957

— Baltimore, Genealogical Pub. Co., 1963.   295 p. 24 cm.   F3. B35
1963

BARKER, Shirley.   Builders of New England.   New York, Dodd, Mead (1965)   238 p. 65-21420.   F3. B37

BOULEY, Charles Henry.   Biographical sketches of the pioneer settlers of New England and their descendants in Worcester, Massachusetts.   Barre, Mass., Barre Publishers (c.1964)   xi, 643 p. 24 cm. 64-22850.   F3. B6
L.H. & G.

CUTTER, William Richard.   New England families, genealogical and memorial; a record of the achievements of her people in the making of commonwealths, etc.   New York, Lewis historical publishing company, 1913.   4 v. fronts., ports. 28 cm. Paged continuously. 14-15054.   F3. C98

— 1914.   4 v. front., plates, ports. 28 x 21½ cm. Paged continuously. Part of the material is also in the editor's "New England families. 3d series. N.Y., 1915. 17-18709.   F3. C987

— 3rd series. 1915.   4 v. front., plates, ports. 28 cm. Paged continuously. 17-3895.   F3. C99

DALL, Caroline Wells Healey.   "Mrs. C.H.A. Dall" Genealogical notes and errata ... (Boston? 1873?)   24½ cm.   F3. D14

DAVEY, Frederick Arthur.   Westward, look ...! twenty-one stories of Devon pioneers and pilgrims in New England, by F. A. Davey and S. G. Watts.   Bracknell, Town and Country Press, 1970. 56 p. illus., facsims. 16 x 23 cm. Based on a series of articles pub. in the Western morning news. 70-850417 MARC.   F3. D38

DUDLEY, Dean.   Illustrated archaeological and genealogical collections, ... illustrating the history, genealogy and archaeology of New England.   Boston, L. Prang & co., 1861.   1 p, vi pl. 36 cm. 9-22101.
F3. D 84

ELIOT, John.   A biographical dictionary, containing a brief account of the first settlers, and other eminent characters ... in New England.   Cushing & Appleton, Salem, and Edward Oliver, Boston, 1809.   viii, 511 p. 22 cm. 5-1317.   F3. E42
also in Toner Coll.

NEW ENGLAND

EMMERTON, James Arthur.   Gleanings from English records about New England families.   ... by
James A. Emmerton and Henry F. Waters.   From Hist. coll. Essex inst. Vol. xvii, no. 1.   Salem
(Mass.) Salem press, 1880.   1, 147 p. 4 fold. tab.   24½ cm.   4-11468.   F3. E54

FARMER, John.   A genealogical register of the first settlers of New England, etc.   Lancaster,
Mass., Carter, Andrews & co., 1829.   viii, 9-351 p. 25 cm.   4-13419.   F3. F23
                                                                                                   1829

— Reprinted with additions and corrections by Samuel G. Drake.   Baltimore, Genealogical Pub. Co.,
1964.   355 p. 24 cm. 64-19761.   F3. F23
                                                                                                   1964

— 1969.   viii, 351 p. 23 cm.   F3. F23
                                                                                                   1969

FORBES, Mrs. Harriette Merrifield.   Gravestones of early New England and the men who made them,
1653 - 1800.   Boston, Houghton Mifflin company, 1927.   5, 141 p. front., plates. 27 cm. 27-28096.
                                                                                                   F3. F69

HANKS, Charles Stedman.   ... The New England states ...   Boston, Geo, H. Ellis co., printers, 1904.
2, 170 p. 19 cm.   Names arranged alphabetically under each state, with local addresses. 8-16019.   F3. H24

HOWE, Mrs. Julia Ward and others.   ... Sketches of representative women of New England.   Boston,
New England historical publishing company, 1904.   3, (5) - 499 p. 73 port. 29 x 24 cm.   (New England library of
popular biographies ...) 5-11060.   F3. H85

HOWE, Mark Antony De Wolfe.   Who lived here?   A baker's dozen of historic New England houses
and their occupants.   Boston, Little Brown, 1952.   139 p. illus. 26 cm. 52-5872.   F3. H853

HOYT, Albert Harrison.   ... Necrology of New England colleges.   Boston, 18 -
1 v. 26 cm.   F3. H86

KEYES, Mrs. Frances Parkinson (Wheeler)   Pioneering people in northern New England, etc.   (Washington, D. C., Judd & Detweiler, inc., 1937)   47 p. illus. (incl. port.) 26 cm.   Contents. - Frances Parkinson - Moses
Dow, William Tarleton. - Col. Thomas Johnson. - "Master" Henry Parkinson. 38-22336.   F3. K48

LE SEUR, William W.   A selected list of names of heads of prominent families in the various cities
and towns of the New England states.   Boston, 1884.   332 p. 27½ x 23 cm. 8-15374.   F3. L62

LIVES of the chief fathers of New England.   (Boston, Massachusetts Sabbath school society. 1846 - 49)
6 v. front. (port. v.5) illus. 19 cm. Contents. - I. John Cotton. - II. John Wilson, John Norton and John Davenport. III. John Eliot.
IV. Thomas Shepard. V. Increase Mather and Sir William Phipps. VI. Thomas Hooker. 5-39201.   F3. L68

MAKERS of American history: Roger Williams, by William Gammell; Colonial governors of New
England, by Jacob Bailey Moore.   New York, The University society, inc., 1904.   356 p. incl. front.
(port.) 19 cm. Contents. - Roger Williams. John Carver, William Bradford, John Winthrop, Sir Henry Vane. John Endecott, Sir Edmund Andros.
4-35305.   F3. M23

MEN of New England, ...   Winfield Scott Downs.   New York, The American historical co. inc., (1941)
v. ports., col. coat of arms. 27½ cm. 41-7349 rev.   F3. M4

MUSSEY, June Barrows.   We were New England; Yankee life by those who lived it.   New York, Stackpole sons (c. 1937)   5, 9-411 p. incl. front. (map) illus. 23½ cm. A collection of passages from the autobiographies of New
Englanders. 37-38292.   F3. M87

— (1st Borzoi ed., rev.)   New York, A. A. Knopf, 1947.   viii, 543 p. illus. 25 cm. 47-11791*.   F3. M87

NEW ENGLAND historic genealogical society,   Memorial biographies of.   v. 1-9; 1845-97.   Boston,
1880 - 1908.   9 v. 24½ cm. No more pub. 5-41806 Additions.   F3. N54

POTTER, Gail M.   Stories behind the stones.   South Brunswick, A. S. Barnes (1969)   244 p. illus. 26 cm.
68-27250. F3.   P6

RENO, Conrad, et al.   Memoirs of the judiciary and the bar of New England for the nineteenth century, etc.   Boston, The Century memorial publishing co., 1900.   2 v. front., illus., port., facsim. 32 cm. Paged continuously. 2-11904. F3.   R41

SAVAGE, James.   A genealogical dictionary of the first settlers of New England, etc.   Baltimore, Genealogical Pub. Co., 1965.   4 v. 23 cm. 65-18541. See also F7. S26 F3.   S2

SHIPTON, Clifford Kenyon.   New England life in the 18th Century; representative biographies from Sibley's Harvard graduates.   Cambridge, Belknap Press of Harvard University Press, 1963.
xxvii, 626 p. 24 cm. 63-9562. F3.   S5

SPOFFORD, Mrs. Harriet Elizabeth (Prescott) and others.   Three heroines of New England romance.
175 p. incl. front., illus., plates. 19½ cm. Contents. - Priscilla. - Agnes Surriage. - Martha Hilton. 8-30856 rev. F3.   S85
1894

— 1895.   175 p. incl. front., illus., plates. 19½ cm. 31-19456. F3. S85
1895

SWIFT, Charles Warner, ed.   A genealogist's letter-book; correspondence of Amos Otis relative to colonial ancestry.   Yarmouthport, Mass., C. W. Swift, 1913.   3 v. 28 cm. (Library of Cape Cod history and genealogy, no. 60 - 62) 14-41. F3.   S95

WARREN, Austin.   New England saints.   Ann Arbor, University of Michigan Press (1956)
192 p. 22 cm. Includes bibliography. 56-9721. F3.   W3

WHO's who in New England; a biographical dictionary of leading living men and women ... Chicago, The A. N. Marquis company (1909) -   v. 20 - 24 cm. 9-9799 rev. F3.   W61

GENERAL WORKS. HISTORIES.

ADAMS, Hannah.   A summary history of New-England, etc.   Dedham (Mass.) 1799.   513, (3) p. 22 cm.
1-7555. F4.   A21
Office

ADAMS, Hannah.   An abridgement of the History of New-England.   Boston, 1805.   F4.   A22
iv, 185 p. 18 cm. 19-4306. Toner Coll.

— 1807.   vi, (5) - 188 p. 18 cm. 1-7556. F4.   A23

ADAMS, James Truslow.   The history of New England.   Boston, Little, Brown, and co., (1923) - 27.
3 v. fronts., plates, ports., maps (1 double) facsims. 23 cm. Bibliographical foot-notes. 30-22522 rev. F4.   A24

— 1927.   3 v. fronts., plates, ports., maps (1 double) facsims. 23 cm. 32-16986. F4. A242

— 1968 -   24 cm. 68-19139. F4. A243

BARBER, John Warner.   The history and antiquities of New England, New York and New Jersey.
Worcester (Mass.) Dorr, Howland & co., 1841.   viii, 9-576 p. front., illus., pl. 8°. 1-7557-M1. F4.   B23

BARBER, John Warner.   The history and antiquities of New England, New York, New Jersey, and Pennsylvania. ...   3rd ed.   Hartford, A. S. Stillman & son, 1856.   viii, (9) - 624 p. incl. illus., plates.
23½ cm. Earlier editions ... 1840 and 1841, do not include the history of Penna. 17-12052. F4.   B24
Toner Coll.

BEALS, Carleton.   Our Yankee heritage.   New England's contribution to American civilization.
Freeport, N. Y., Books for Libraries Press (1970, c. 1955)   311 p. 23 cm. (Essay index reprint series) 73-111814.
F4.   B4

NEW ENGLAND

BIRCH, F.H. company, Boston.   New England, the individual.   (1944)   (16) p. illus. 28½ x 22 cm.
"Text by Roy Griffith."   45-380.   F4.   B5

BLANCHARD, Fessenden Seaver.   Ghost towns of New England, their ups and downs.   New York, Dodd, Mead, 1960.   205 p.   21 cm.   60-11931.   F4.   B55

BRADFORD, Alden.   Biographical notices of distinguished men in New England, etc.   Boston, S.G. Simpkins, 1842.   464 p.   18½ cm.   4-18814.   F4.   B78

BRADFORD, Alden.   New England chronology.   Boston, S.G. Simpkins, 1843.   202 p.   18½ cm.   1-7558.   F4.   B79

BRIDGMAN, Howard Allen.   New England in the life of the world; a record of adventure and achievement.   Boston, Chicago, The Pilgrim press (c. 1920)   xiii p., 3 - 395 p. front., illus. (maps) ports. 20½ cm.
Bibliography: p. 369 - 371.   21-183.   F4.   B85

CADY, Annie Cole.   A history of New England, in words of one syllable.   Chicago, New York (etc.) Belford, Clarke, (1888)   208 p. incl. front., illus. 22 x 18 cm.   1-7559 rev.   F4.   C12

COFFIN, Robert Peter Tristram.   Life in America: New England.   Grand Rapids, Fideler Co., 1951.
128 p. illus. 28 cm. ("life in America" books)   52.770 rev.   Editions also of: 1955, 1958, 1960, 1964, 1966, 1967.   F4.   C7
— Unit of teaching pictures.   28 l., 48 pl. (in portfolio) 30 cm.   52-770 rev.   F4.   C7p

COOLIDGE, Austin Jacobs and others.   A history and description of New England, general and local.   Vol. I. Maine, N.H. and Vermont.   Boston, A.J. Coolidge, 1859.   xxvii, 1024 p. front., illus., plates (1 fold.) fold. maps. 25½ cm. "Table of historical works": p. xi - xxv.   No more pub.   1-7560.   F4.   C77

— 1864.   xxvii, 1023 p. front., illus., plates (1 fold.) fold. maps. 25 cm.   No more pub.   1-7561 rev.   F4.   C78

CRANE, Jonas.   Fighting Yankees and other yarns.   Freeport, Me., Bond Wheelwright Co. (1967)
181 p. 23 cm.   67-16828.   F4.   C82

DAVIS, William Thomas, ed.   The New England states ...   Boston, D.H. Hurd & co. (c. 1897)
4 v. ports. map (v. 4) 28 cm.   Paged continuously.   1-7562.   F4.   D26

FENNELLY, Catherine, ed.   New England character and characters as seen by contemporaries. Sturbridge, Mass., Old Sturbridge Village (1956)   32 p. illus. 22 cm.   56-4796.   F4.   F4

— 2nd ed. (1965)   45 p. 22 cm.   F4.   F4
1965

HOWARD, R., ed.   A history of New England ...   Boston, Crocker & co., 1879.   805 p. illus., plates, diagr. 29 x 22½ cm.   1-7563.   F4.   H84

— 1881.   2 v. fronts., illus. (incl. ports.) plates, diagrs. 29½ x 23½ cm. 8-14427.   F4.   H85

JOSEPH, Richard.   New England.   (Prepared with the cooperation of the American Geographical Society)   Garden City, N.Y., Doubleday (1957)   64 p. illus. (part col.) map. 21 cm.   57-2525.   F4.   J6

— (c. 1967)   64 p. 21 cm.   F4.   J6
1967

McCARTHY, Joe, et al.   New England.   New York, Time Inc. (c. 1967)   192 p. 28 cm. 67-27862.   F4.   M18

McCLINTOCK, Marshall.   The story of New England.   New York, London, Harper & brothers (1941)
39 p. illus. (part col.) 28½ x 26 cm.   41-25914.   F4.   M2

MITCHELL, Edwin Valentine.   Yankee folk.   New York, Vanguard Press (1948)   278 p. illus. 22 cm.
48-9342*.   F4.   M5

OLD Colony trust company, Boston.   New England old and new ...   (Boston) 1920.   2, (9) - 62 p. incl. illus., mounted col. plates. front. 23 cm. 20-5739.   F4. O4

— 2nd ed.   (Cambridge, Mass.) 1920.   2, (9) - 62 p. incl. illus. front. 23 cm. 21-6779.   F4. O42

PEATTIE, Roderick, ed.   The friendly mountains, Green, White, and Adirondacks.   New York, The Vanguard press (1942)   5, ix - xii p. 15 - 341 p. incl. front., 1 illus., tables, diagr. plates. 23½ cm. (American mountain series, ed. Roderick Peattie. v.2) 42-50933 rev.   F4. P4

POWELL, Lyman Pierson, ed.   ... Historic towns of New England.   New York & London, G. P. Putnam's sons, 1898.   xxi, 599 p. front., illus., plates, maps. 22 cm. Contents. - Portland, Rutland, Mass., Salem, Boston, Cambridge, Concord, Plymouth, Cape Cod towns, Deerfield, Newport, Providence, Hartford, New Haven. 1-7927*-M1.   F4. P88

QUACKENBOS, George Payn.   Special history of the New England states.   (New York, D. Appleton & co.) c. 1879.   (343) - 383 p. illus. (incl. ports.) 19 cm. "Reference books and articles": p. 383. 1-16078 Rev.   F4. Q2

ROSENBERRY, Mrs. Lois (Kimball) Mathews.   The expansion of New England ...   Boston and New York, Houghton Mifflin co., 1909.   xiv, 303 p. front., maps. 23 cm. "Bibliographical notes" at end of each chapter except i and x. 9-29148 rev.   F4. R81

— New York, Russell & Russell, 1962 (c. 1936)   xiv, 303 p. 22 cm. 61-13781.   F4. R81 1962

SNOW, Edward Rowe.   Famous New England lighthouses.   Boston, Mass., The Yankee publishing co., (1945)   5, (17) - 457 p. incl. plates (1 col.) ports. front. 23½ cm. Bibliography: p. (447) - (448) 45-37897.   F4. S58

SNOW, Edward Rowe.   Great storms and famous shipwrecks of the New England coast.   Boston, Mass., The Yankee publishing co. (1943)   6, (21) - 338 p. incl. plates, ports. col. front., maps (1 fold.) 23½ cm. Bibliographical references included in "Notes" (p. 322-329) 44-491.   F4. S6

SNOW, Edward Rowe.   Mysterious tales of the New England coast.   New York, Dodd, Mead, 1961. 310 p. 21 cm. 61-18042.   F4. S62

SOLOMON, Barbara Miller.   Ancestors and immigrants, a changing New England tradition.   Cambridge, Harvard University Press, 1956.   ix, 276 p. 22 cm. "A note on sources": p. (211) - 221. Bibliographical references included in "Notes" (p. (223) - 263) 56-10163.   F4. S67

STATE street trust company, Boston.   Towns of New England and old England, Ireland and Scotland ... connecting links.   Boston, Mass., 1920 - 21.   2 v. fronts., illus., plates. 26 cm. 20-20210. Also in Rare Book Coll. F4.S792   F4. S79

— New York, Tudor publishing co., 1936.   2 v. in 1. fronts., illus., plates, maps. 26½ cm. 38-8357.   F4. S793

WEBSTER, Clarence Mertoun.   ... Town meeting country, by Clarence M. Webster.   New York, Duell, Sloan & Pearce (1945)   ix, 246 p. 22 cm. (American folkways, ed. Erskine Caldwell) 45-2984.   F4. W4 1945

— Westport, Conn., Greenwood Press (1970, c. 1945)   ix, 246 p. 23 cm. 79-100188.   F4. W4 1970

WHITING, Edward Elwell.   Changing New England.   New York, London, The Century co. (c. 1929) x, 3-275 p. front., plates. 20 cm. 29-22115.   F4. W59

JUVENILE WORKS.

GEMMING, Elizabeth.   Getting to know New England.   N.Y., Coward-McCann (1971, c1970) 69 p. illus. 23 cm. 74-121381.   F4.3.G45

McCABE, Inger.   A week in Amy's world: New England.   (New York) Crowell-Collier Press, c. 1970) (48) p. illus. 27 cm. (A Face to face book) 69-18243.   F4.3.M28

McGOVERN, Ann.   ... If you lived in colonial times.   N.Y., Four Winds Press (c. 1964)   79 p. 16 x 22 cm.   F4.3.M3

RICH, Louise (Dickinson) The first book of New England. N.Y., F. Watts (1957)   60 p. illus. 23 cm.
57-5187.   F4.3. R5

STEARNS, Monroe. The story of New England. Illus. ... by ... many ... New England artists, as well as maps and photos. N.Y., Random House (1967)   179 p. 29 cm. 67-20387.   F4.3.S8

ANECDOTES, LEGENDS, PAGEANTS, ETC.

DRAKE, Samuel Adams. A book of New England legends and folk lore; in prose and poetry. New and rev. ed. Boston, Little, Brown, 1901. Detroit, Singing Tree Press, 1969.   xvi, 477 p. illus. 22 cm. 69-19881.   F4.6.D7

— Rev. ed. Rutland, Vt., C.E. Tuttle (1971)   xx, 477 p. illus. 18 cm. 76-157254.   F4.6.D7 1971

HANSEN, Harry, ed. New England legends and folklore; Based on writings by Samuel Adams Drake and others. New York, Hastings House (1967)   192 p. 24 cm. 67-26849.   F4.6.N4

SNOW, Edward Rowe, comp. Fantastic folklore and fact; New England tales of land and sea. New York, Dodd, Mead (1968)   x, 270 p. illus. 21 cm. 68-54451.   F4.6.S65

SHOW, Edward Rowe. True tales and curious legends; dramatic stories from the Yankee past. New York, Dodd, Mead (1969)   xiii, 273 p. illus. 21 cm. 71-95911.   F4.6.S67

STEVENS, Austin N. Mysterious New England. 1st. ed. Dublin, N.H., Yankee, inc. (1971)
319 p. illus. 25 cm. 74-172976 MARC. SEE ALSO SOME ITEMS UNDER F5 SECTION.   F4.6.S7

HISTORIC MONUMENTS (GENERAL). ILLUSTRATIVE MATERIAL.

ARNOLD, Nason H. Little known historical spots in New England ... (Worcester, Mass., 1929)
24 p. illus. 23 x 9½ cm. 29-9830.   F5. A75

BEALS, Carleton. Our Yankee heritage: New England contribution to American civilization. New York, D. McKay Co. (1955)   311 p. 22 cm. 55-14235.   F5. B4

BENTON, Josiah Henry. Warning out in New England ... 1656 - 1817. Boston, W.B. Clarke co., 1911.
3, 131 p. 25½ cm. 11-25114.   F5. B47

BLISS, William Root. The Old Colony town and other sketches. Boston and New York, Houghton, Mifflin and co., 1893.   4, 4-219 p. 20 cm. 6-44013.   F5. B64

BROOKS, Henry Mason, comp. The olden time series; gleanings chiefly from old newspapers of Boston and Salem, Mass. ... Boston, Ticknor and co., 1886.   6 v. illus. 18 cm. 14-14041.   F5. B87

BROWNE, George Waldo. Legends of New England. Manchester, N.H., Standard book co., 1925.
144 p. front., illus., plates. 19½ cm. 28-28006.   F5. B88

BROWNE, George Waldo. Real legends of New England. Chicago, A. Whitman & co. (c.1930)
264 p. incl. front., illus. 21 cm. 30-28931.   F5. B885

CHAMBERLAIN, Samuel. The New England image. New York, Hastings House (1962)   192 p. (chiefly illus.) 29 cm. 62-13290.   F5. C45

CHAMBERLAIN, Samuel. New England in color; a collection of color photographs. With introductory text and notes ... by Stewart Beach. New York, Hastings House (1969)   94 p. illus. photos. 25 cm.
(Profiles of America) 71-78250.   F5. C455

CHAMBERLAIN, Samuel. The New England scene; a camera profile. New York, Hastings House (1965)   1 v. (unpaged) 20 cm. 65-23196.   F5. C46

CHAPMAN, Edward Mortimer. New England village life, by Edward M. Chapman. Cambridge... Riverside press, 1937.   vi, 232 p. 1 illus. 24½ cm.   37-37572.   F5. C48

CLEAVELAND, Nehemiah. An address delivered before the New-England society of Brooklyn, N. Y., 1849. New York, 1850.   37 p. 22½ cm. 44-37997.   F5. C55

CRAWFORD, Mary Caroline. ... Among old New England inns. Boston, L. C. Page & co., 1907.
xiii, 381 p. front., 47 pl. 19½ cm. (Little pilgrimages) 7-36234.   F5. C 89

— Detroit, Singing Tree Press, 1970.   xiii, 381 p. illus. 23 cm. 76-107629.   F5. C 89
— Boston, L. C. Page & co., 1924.
                     xiii,   381 p. front., plates. 20½ cm.   A25-165.   F5. C894

CRAWFORD, Mary Caroline. ... The romance of old New England churches. Boston, L. C. Page & co., 1904 (1903)   3, 11 - 379 p. front., plates, ports. 18 cm. (Little pilgrimages) 3-20890. F5. C91
— (1907)   5, vii-ix, 11-377, (2) p. front., plates, ports. 19½ cm. 31-30059.   F5. C91

CRAWFORD, Mary Caroline ... The romance of old New England rooftrees... Boston, L. C. Page, 1903.
(1902)   1, x, 11-390 p. front., plates, ports. 18½ cm. (Little pilgrimages) 2-23427.   F5. C912
                                                                                              1903

CRAWFORD, Mary Caroline. Social life in old New England. Boston, Little, Brown, and co., 1914.
xiii, 515 p. front., plates, ports. 21½ cm. 14-18566.   F5. C913

EARLY, Eleanor. A New England sampler. Boston, Mass., Waverly house, 1940.
xii, 372 p. incl. front., illus. 21 cm. 40-27541.   F5. E26

EKBLAW, Walter Elmer. New England fancies. Worcester, Mass., A. J. St. Onge, 1935.   vi, 9-127 p.
front. (port.) 19½ cm. 35-7793.   F5. E54

FAIRBANKS, Charles Warren. The indebtedness of the West to New England ... Indianapolis, Press of Levey bro's & co., inc. (1903)   18 p. 23 cm. 3-29110.   F5. F16

FORBES, Allan. Taverns and stagecoaches of New England ... Ed. R. M. Eastman. Boston, State Street Trust Co., 1953 - 54.   2 v. illus., map., facsims. 23 cm. 53-2997 rev.   F5. F6

FORD times. New England journeys. Special ed. (Dearborn, Mich., Ford Motor Co., 1953)
128 p. illus. 18 cm. 54-24619.   F5. F62

FROST, John Edward. Yankee homecoming; official sketch book. (Boston? 1958)   96 p. illus. 26 cm.
58-1422.   F5. F7

GREENE, Jacob Lyman. The New England town. ... Hartford, Conn., The Case, Lockwood & Brainard co., printers, 1897.   1, 32 p. 19 cm. 3-25500.   F5. G81

GRIFFIN, Arthur. New England, full color photos; original essays by 47 famous New England writers. Ed. Robb Sagendorph. Winchester, Mass. (1962)   104 p. 44 mounted col. illus. 27 x 35 cm.
62-19441.   F5. G825

HALE, Edward Everett. New England history in ballads. Boston, Little, Brown & co., 1903.
xv, 182 p. front., 9 pl. 22 cm.   F5. H16

HOLBROOK, Stewart Hall. The Old Post Road; the story of the Boston Post Road. (1st ed.) New York, McGraw-Hill (1962)   273 p. 24 cm. (American trails series) 62-9989.   F5. H6

HUBBARD, Charles Daniel. Camping in the New England mountains. Manchester, Me., Falmouth Pub. House, 1952.   109 p. illus. 27 cm. 53-54.   F5. H8

JENKINS, Stephen. The old Boston post road. New York and London, G. P. Putnam's sons, 1913.
xxiv, 453 p. front., plates, maps (part fold.) facsims. 23 cm. Bibliography: p. 427-434. 13-25381.   F5. J52

NEW ENGLAND

JOHNSON, Clifton. New England; a human interest geographical reader. New York, The Macmillan company; London, Macmillan and co., ltd., 1917.   ix, (3) p. 371 p. incl. front., illus., map. 19½ cm. 17-8898.
F5. J69

JOHNSON, Frances Ann. New England pocket series. (Littleton? N.H., 1953 -   1 v. illus., maps. 13 cm. Contents. - Robert Rogers and his rangers. 53-36015.
F5. J693

KENT, Louise (Andrews) Village greens of New England. (1st ed.) New York, M. Barrows (1948) 280 p. illus. 24 cm. 48-3957*.
F5. K4

KITTREDGE, George Lyman. The old farmer and his almanack ... Boston, W. Ware and co., 1904. xiv, 403 p. front. (port.) illus., plates, map, facsims. 22½ cm. 4-37129.
F5. K62

— New York, B. Blom (1967)   xiv, 403 p. 21 cm. 67-13333.
F5. K62

LITERARY New England. (Portland, Me., 1905)   20 x 25 cm.
F5. L77

McKENNEY, Lewis Timothy. The New England people, builders of America. Boston, Meador publishing co., 1942.   191 p. front., plates. 20½ cm. 42-2299.
F5. M2

MANN, William Justin. Little walks on enchanted ground, by William Justin Mann. Brattleboro, Vt., Stephen Daye press (c. 1935)   277 p. front., plates, ports. 19½ cm. 35-4318.
F5. M34

MARSH, George Perkins. The Goths in New-England. A discourse delivered at the anniversary of the Philomathesian society of Middlebury college, Aug. 15, 1843. 39 p. 20 cm. 17-14597.
F5. M36

MITCHELL, Edwin Valentine. It's an old New England custom. New York, Vanguard Press (1946) 277 p. illus. 21 cm. (American customs series) 46-7197 rev.*
F5. M66

MIXER, Knowlton. Old houses of New England. New York, The Macmillan co., 1927. xx, 346 p. incl. front., illus. 22 cm. 27-23395.
F5. M68

MUSSEY, June Barrows. Old New England ... with hundreds of old engravings. New York, A. A. Wyn, inc. (1946)   127. p. incl. front., illus. (incl. ports., maps) 30½ cm. 47-127.
F5. M8

NELSON, Florence Agnes. Lest we forget; sketches of rural New England in the 19th century. 207 p. illus. 21 cm. 49-11933*.
F5. N4

NORTHEND, Mary Harrod. Historic homes of New England ... Boston, Little, Brown, and co., 1914.   xvi, 274 p. xcv pl. (incl. front.) on 48 l. 25 cm. 14-17489.
F5. N87

NORTHEND, Mary Harrod. We visit old inns. Boston, Small, Maynard & co., (c. 1925) xii, 176 p. front., plates. 24 cm. 25-10021.
F5. N88

PORTER, Noah. ... The New England meeting house. (New Haven) Yale university press, 1933 34 p. 23 cm. (Tercentenary pamphlet series xviii) 33-28139.
F5. P78

PRESSEY, Park. Have you seen this old house? or, Priscilla's quest for a family roof-tree. Hallowell, Me., L. Tebbetts (1959)   95 p. 24 cm.
F5. P82

ROGERS, Alfred Paul. Notes of a countryman. Boston, B. Humphries, inc., 1938.   53 p. front., plates. 21 cm. 38-37907.
F5. R65

SAGENDORPH, Robb Hansell, comp. That New England. (1st ed. Dublin, N.H., Yankee, Inc., 1966) 191 p. 32 cm. 66-29385.
F5. S15

SANBORN, Edwin Webster. Social changes in New England in the past fifty years. Boston, G.H. Ellis, 1901.   23 p. 23½ cm. "Repr. from the Report of the proceedings of the Amer. social science assoc. 6-34947.
F5. S19

SHERWOOD, Herbert F. Historic places of New England. Issued by General passenger dept. the

New York, New Haven and Hartford railroad. (New York, Rand McNally & co., 192-?) 1, 60 p.
illus., fold. map. 23 x 12 ½ cm. 25-1083.
                  F5. S56

SHURCLIFF, Arthur Asahel. New England journal. Boston and N.Y., Houghton Mifflin co., 1931.
ix, 94 p. illus. 21 ½ cm. 31-16345.
                  F5. S58

SHURCLIFF, Arthur Asahel. Second New England journal. Cambridge, Mass., The Riverside press, 1942. xii, 135 p. illus. 21½ cm. 42-12574.
                  F5. S582

SNOW, Edward Rowe. Legends of the New England coast. New York, Dodd, Mead, 1957.
268 p. illus. 21 cm. 57-12134.
                  F5. S7

SPOFFORD, Mrs. Harriet Elizabeth (Prescott) New-England legends. Boston, J.R. Osgood & co., 1871. 4, 40 p. illus. 24 cm. 7-35027.
                  F5. S76

STONE, Andrew Leete. The work of New England in the future of our country. Boston, Wright & Potter, 1865. 48 p. 23 cm. 17-13779. 22-16580.
                  F5. S87 or 872

STOWE, Lyman Beecher. New England - the leaven of the nation. (N.Y., 1935) 13 numb. l.
28 ½ x 22 cm. 37-7897.
                  F5. S89

STRAND, Paul. Time in New England; photos by Paul Strand, text selected and edited by Nancy Newhall. N.Y., Oxford University Press, 1950. xv, 248 p. illus. 29 cm. 50-10407.
                  F5. S9

SWEETSER, Seth. Our favored inheritance a motive to fidelity. Worcester, S.A. Howland. 1846.
24 p. 22 ½ cm. 17-20616.
                  F5. S97

TAFT, Lewis A. Profile of old New England; yankee legends, tales, and folklore. N.Y., Dodd, Mead (c. 1965) xiii, 271 p. 21 cm. 65-10462.
                  F5. T3

WEBSTER, Clarence Mertoun. Puritans at home. N.Y., Harcourt, Brace & co., (c. 1936)
5, 3-230 p. 21 cm. 36-19412.
                  F5. W43

WHITEFIELD, Edwin. The homes of our forefathers. Being a selection of the oldest and most interesting historical houses and noted places in Maine, N.H. and Vermont. From original drawings taken on the spot. Reading, Mass., E. Whitefield, 1886. 3, 36 col. pl. 25 x 19 ½ cm. 6-20077. F5. W58

— Boston, Whitefield and Crocker, 1882. 2 p., 2 l. 33 col. pl. 25 ½ x 19 ½ cm. 6-20078.
                  F5. W59

WIGGIN, Kate Douglas (Smith) A Thanksgiving retrospect; or, Simplicity of life in old New England.
Boston and N.Y., Houghton Mifflin co., 1928. 3, (3) - 37 p. illus. 17 cm. Originally pub. in the Woman's home companion, Nov. 1906 and now repr. with ... changes and corrections by Nora A. Smith. 28-24259 rev.
                  F5. W62

WORTH, Henry Barnard. The development of the New England dwelling house. Lynn, Mass., 1911.
24 p. illus. 23 cm. 11-32022.
                  F5. W93

WRIFFORD, Anson. Trait of the character, pursuits, manners, customs and habits, manifested by the inhabitants of the northeastern states, in their common pursuits of life. By Uncle Daniel (pseud.)
Portland (Me.) 1837. 68 p. 20 ½ cm. 44-37800.
                  F5. W95
                  Rare book coll.

ZOOK, Nicholas. Houses of New England open to the public. Barre, Mass., Barre publishers, 1968.
126 p. illus. 25 cm. 68-17070.
                  F5. Z6

ANTIQUITIES.

HUMPHREY, Zephine. A book of New England, (New York) Howell, Soskin (1947) 292 p. illus.
21 cm. Bibliography: p. (291) - 292. 47-4304.
                  F6. H8

SAVILLE, Marshall Howard. Archaeological specimens from New England. (New York, Museum of the American Indian Heye foundation, (1919) 10 p. illus., pl. 16 ½ cm. Bibliographical notes: p. 10. 20-2334.
F6. S27

EARLY TO 1775.

ADAMS, Amos. A concise, historical view of the perils, hardships, etc. ... which have attended the planting and progressive improvements of New-England ... Boston, 1769. 66 p. 18 cm. 23-2876.
F7. A2
Office

— London, Reprinted for E. and C. Dilly, 1770. 2, 68 p. 20 cm. 1-7568.
F7. A21

ADAMS, James Truslow. The founding of New England. Boston, The Atlantic monthly press (c.1921) xi, 482 p. front., maps, facsims. 23 cm. Bibliographical foot-notes. 21-9397.
F7. A22

ADAMS, James Truslow. Revolutionary New England, 1691 - 1776. Boston, The Atlantic monthly press (c.1923) xiv, 469 p. front., illus. (facsims.) plates, ports. 23 cm. Forms vol. 2 of the author's series "The history of New England. Bibliographical foot-notes. 23-15926.
F7. A223

ADAMS, John Quincy. The New England confederacy of MDCXLIII. Boston, C.C. Little and J. Brown, 1843. 47 p. 23 ½ cm. 1-13312.
F7. A23

ANDREWS, Charles McLean. The fathers of New England; a chronicle of the Puritan commonwealths. New Haven, Yale university press, 1919. x, 210 p. front., plates, ports., fold. map. 21 cm. Bibliographical note: p. 201 - 204. 19-3162.
F7. A 56
— 1921. ix, 210 p. col. front., fold. map. 18 cm. "Bibliographical note": p. 201-204. 22-12128.
F7. A57

AUSTIN, John Osborne. The journal of William Jefferay, gentleman. ... 1591 - 1675. (Providence, R.I.) 1899. x, 189 p. front. (col. coat of arms) pl. 20 ½ cm. 99-5663 rev.
F7. A93

BARBER, John Warner. New England scenes ... principally of a religious nature ... New Haven, L.H. Young, 1833. viii, (9) - 106 p. front., plates. 15 cm. 1-7570.
F7. B23

BARNES, Viola Florence. The Dominion of New England, a study in British colonial policy. New Haven, Yale university press, 1923. viii, 303 p. 23 cm. "Bibliographical note": p. (278) - 288. 23-17159.
F7. B26

— New York, F. Ungar Pub. Co. (1960) 303 p. 60-13979.
F7. B26

BAXTER, James Phinney. The pioneers of New France in New England ... Albany, N.Y., J. Munsell's sons, 1894. 2, 450 p. plates. 22 cm. (Munsell's historical series, no. 21) 1-13314.
F7. B35

BELL, Margaret. Women of the wilderness. N.Y., E.P. Dutton & co., inc., 1938. 384 p. 22 cm. "First edition." 38-27407.
F7. B44

BENEDICT, Erastus Cornelius. The beginning of America; a discourse delivered before the N.Y. historical society ... 1863. N.Y., 1864. 64 p. 25 cm. 2-21299.
F7. B46

BISBEE, Ernest Emerson. The New England scrap book of stories and legends of old New England. Lancaster, N.H., Bisbee Press, c.1947. (64) p. illus. 24 cm. 48-16389*.
F7. B55

BLISS, William Root. Side glimpses from the colonial meeting-house. Boston and N.Y., Houghton, Mifflin & co., 1894. 5, 256 p. 20 cm. 1-24369.
F7. B64

— Detroit, Gale Research Co., 1970. 256 p. 22 cm. 70-140410.
F7. B64

BOLTON, Charles Knowles. Terra Nova; the northeast coast of America before 1602; annals of Vinland, Markland, Estotiland, Drogeo, Baccalaos and Norumbega. Boston, F.W. Faxon company, 1935. xiii p., 194 p. incl. front., illus., maps, geneal. tab. pl. 22 cm. (Useful reference series, no. 56) 35-14829.

F7. B68

BOLTON, Charles Knowles. The real founders of New England; stories of their life along the coast, 1602 - 1628. Boston, F.W. Faxon co., 1929. xiv, 192 p. front., illus. (incl. maps, facsims.) 22 cm. (Useful reference series, no. 38) "Some authorities": p. 178-182. 29-19510 rev.

F7. B69

BOLTON, Mrs. Ethel (Stanwood) Immigrants to New England, 1700 - 1775. Salem, Mass., The Essex institute, 1931. 2, 235 p. 23½ cm. "Reprinted from the Historical collections of the Essex institute, vols. lxiii, lxiv, lxv, lxvi and lxvii." 31-9484.

F7. B 74

— Baltimore, Genealogical pub. co., 1966. 235 p. 23 cm. 66-28669.

F7. B74

BRERETON, John. A briefe and true relation of the discoverie of the north part of Virginia. Ann Arbor, University Microfilms (1966) 48 p. 22 cm. (March of America facsimile series, no. 16) 66-26301.

F7. B78

BRIEF description of the towns in New England ... 1650. With an introduction, by Samuel A. Green. Cambridge, J. Wilson and son, 1902. 8 p. 24 cm. 2-7928.

F7. B82

BRIEF review of the rise and progress ... of New England, especially the province of Massachusett's-Bay. London, Printed for J. Buckland, 1774. 32 p. 21 cm. 1-7571.

F7. B85
Office

BURKE, James, jr. Quaint old New England. Hartford, Conn., Triton syndicate, inc. (c.1936) 94 p. illus. 16 cm. 38-4828.

F7. B88

BURT, John. Earthquakes, the effects of God's wrath. A sermon ... Newport, (1755) 17 p. 16 cm. 25-11809.

F7. B9
Office

BYINGTON, Ezra Hoyt. The Puritan as a colonist and reformer. Boston, Little, Brown and co., 1899. xxvi, (3) - 375 p. pl., 2 port. (incl. front.) 22 cm. Bibliography: p. (xxiii)- xxvi. 99-4884 rev.

F7. B95

BYINGTON, Ezra Hoyt. The Puritan in England and New England. Boston, Roberts bros., 1896. xi, 406 p. front. (port.) 22 cm. "Authorities": p. (xxv) - xxix. 1-151.

F7. B96

— Boston, Little, Brown & co., 1900. xiii, 457 p. pl., 2 port. (incl. front.) 21½ cm. 0-6595 rev.

F7. B97

CARROLL, Peter N. Puritanism and the wilderness; the intellectual significance of the New England frontier, 1629 - 1700. New York, Columbia University Press, 1969. xi, 243 p. 24 cm. 78-84673.

F7. C3

CHAMPION, Judah. A brief view of the distresses, hardships and dangers ... in settling New England. ... two sermons. Hartford, 1770. 44 p. 19 x 14½ cm. 15-13268.

F7. C45
Office

Chester, Joseph Lemuel. Influence of the county of Essex on the settlement and family history of New England. (London, J. Henry & J. Parker, 1863?) 5 p. 21½ cm. Reprinted from the Gentleman's magazine, v.215, Dec. 1863. 6-40524.

F7. C52

CHITWOOD, Oliver Perry. Colonial America. (Morgantown, W.Va., 1928) 2 v. 27 cm.

F7. C53

CHOATE, Rufus. The romance of New England history. (Boston, 1900) 19 cm.

F7. C54

CLARK, Charles E. The easter frontier; the settlement of Northern New England, 1610 - 1763. (1st ed.) New York, A.A. Knopf, 1970. xxiv, 419, xvi p. 25 cm. 78-111231.

F7. C6
1970

COMPANY for propagation of the gospel in New England and the parts adjacent in America. Some correspondence between the governors and treasurers of the New England company in London and the commissioners of the United Colonies in America ... To which are added the journals of the Rev. Experience Mayhew in 1713 and 1714. London, 1896. xxxii, 127 p. 24 cm. A12-46. F7. C73 1896

— New York, B. Franklin (1970) xxxii, 127 p. 23 cm. 73-126413 MARC. F7. C73 1970

COOPER, William. The danger of people's losing the good impressions made by the late awful earthquake. Boston, 1727. 2, 23 p. 16½ cm. 15-2166. F7. C77 Office

COTTON, John. A holy fear of God, and his judgments exhorted to: ... Boston, 1727. 2, xvi, 24, 7 p. 17 cm. 20-3602. F7. C83 Office

COUNCIL for New England, Records of the. Reprinted from the proceedings of the American antiquarian society... Cambridge, 1867. 83 p. 23 cm. 1-7572. F7. C85

BRIGHAM, Clarence Saunders. ... New England's most precious book. Records of the "Council for New England" recently found. (Boston? 1912?) 1 l. 42 x 23 cm. Reprinted from the Boston transcript, Sat. Dec. 21, 1912. CA 29-725 unrev. F7. C89

CRAWFORD, Mary Caroline. Social life in old New England. Detroit, Tower Books, 1971. xiii, 515 p. illus. 19 cm. "Facsimile reprint of the 1914 ed." Includes bibliographical references. 71-102645 MARC. F7. C92 1914a

DANFORTH, John. A sermon occasioned by the late great earthquake... Boston, 1728. 2, 46, 5 p. 17½ cm. 15-9281. F7. D16 Office

DANIEL, Richard. The present state of New England (circa 1675) by Richard Daniel, gent. ... New York, J.O. Wright & co., 1899. 15 p. 16½ cm. 50 copies printed. 21-4841. F7. D18 Office

DEAN, John Ward. The story of the embarkation of Cromwell and his friends for New England. (Reprinted from the N.E. hist. and gen. register) Boston, 1866. 11 p. 25 cm. 2-28058. F7. D27

DEANE, Charles. Communication respecting the seal of the "Council for New England." (Cambridge, Mass., 1867) 4 pp. 8º. 30 copies reprinted from the Proceedings of the Mass. hist. soc., ser. 1 v. 9. 1-16228-M1. F7. D28

DEPLORABLE state of New-England, by reason of a covetous and treacherous governour, ... London, 1708. 4, 39 p. 21 cm. 6-29966. Imperfect. An arraignment of the administration of Governor Joseph Dudley. Reprinted in Mass. hist. soc. Collections. 1879. 5th ser. v. 6, p. 97* - 131*. F7. D42 Office

DEXTER, Franklin Bowditch. The influence of the English universities in the development of New England. Cambridge (Mass.) University press, 1880. 17 p. 2 fold. diagr. 24½ cm. 10-34661. F7. D52

DOUGLAS, James. New England and New France; ... N.Y. and London, G.P. Putnam's sons, 1913. x, 560 p. front., plates (part fold.) ports., maps (part fold.) plans (1 fold.) facsims. 23 cm. 13-19046. F7. D69

— N.Y., Russell & Russell (1972) 560 p. illus. 22 cm. 79-173516. F7. D69 1972

DOW, George Francis. Domestic life in the New England in the seventeenth century. Topsfield, Mass., 1925. 5, 48 p. front., plates. 24 cm. 25-23828. F7. D699

— N.Y., B. Blom, 1972. 48 p. illus. 21 cm. 72-83087. F7. D699 1972

DOW, George Francis. The pirates of the New England coast, 1630 - 1730. (New York) Argosy-
Antiquarian, 1968.   xxii, 394 p. illus. 25 cm. 68-9158.   F7.   D7
                                                                                                          1968

— Mass., Marine research society, 1923.   xxii, 394 p. front., plates, etc. 26½ cm. 23-13269.   F7. D71

DRAKE, Samuel Adams. The making of New England, 1580 - 1643. N.Y., C. Scribner's sons, 1886.
x p. 251 p. incl. front., illus. 19½ cm. 9-10375.   F7. D72

— 1900.   251 p. incl. front., illus. 19½ cm. 2-22085/3.   F7. D76

DRAKE, Samuel Gardner. Result of some researches among the British archives for information relative to the founders of New England: made in the years 1858, 1859 and 1860. Originally collected for
and published in the N.E. hist. and gen. register, and now corrected and enlarged. Boston, 1860.
143 p. front. (fold. map) ports. 24 cm. 1-7554.   F7. D77
                                                                                                          1860

— Baltimore, Genealogical Pub. Co., 1963.   130 p. 24 cm.   F7. D77
                                                                                                          1963
                                                                                                          L H & G

DUMMER, Jeremiah. A defence of the New-England charters. London, 1721.   4, 80 p. 20½ cm.
3-5891.   F7. D88

— Boston, Re-printed by B. Green ... 1745.   2, 43 p. 20½ cm. First ed. 1721. 3-5892.   F7. D89
                                                                                                     Rare book coll.

— London, Printed for J. Almon (1765)   88 p. 19½ cm. 3-5894.   F7.   D9

EARLE, Alice (Morse) Customs and fashions in old New England. New York, C. Scribner's sons,
1893.   4, 387 p. 19 cm. 1-7573 rev.   F7. E12
                                                                                                          1893

— 1894.   4, 387 p. 18½ cm. First pub. 1893. 35-30126 rev.   F7. E12
                                                                                                          1894

— Detroit, Singing Tree Press, 1968.   387 p. 22 cm. 68-17959.   F7. E12
                                                                                                          1968

— Williamstown, Mass., Corner House Publishers, 1969.   387 p. 22 cm.   F7. E12
                                                                                                          1969

EARLE, Alice (Morse) The Sabbath in Puritan New England. New York, C. Scribner's sons, 1891.
viii, 335 p. 19 cm. 4-4189/3 rev.   F7. E14

— Detroit, Singing Tree Press, 1968.   viii, 335 p. 21 cm. 68-17961.   F7. E14
                                                                                                          1968

Williamstown, Mass., Corner House Publishers, 1969.   viii, 335 p. 22 cm.   F7. E14
                                                                                                          1969

ELLIOTT, Charles Wyllys. The New England history ... to ... 1776. New York, C. Scribner,
1857.   2 v. 8°. 1-7574-M1.   F7. E46

— New York, C. Scribner; Boston, Sanborn, Carter, Bazin & co., 1857. 2 v. 23 cm. 6-27434.   F7. E461

FELT, Joseph Barlow. The customs of New England. Boston, 1853.   1, 208 p. 23½ cm. 1-7575.
                                                                                                          F7. F32

— New York, B. Franklin (1970)   208 p. 23 cm. 68-56742.   F7. F32
                                                                                                          1970

FIELD, Edward. The colonial tavern; a glimpse of New England town life in the seventeenth and eighteenth centuries. Providence, R.I., Preston and Rounds, 1897. viii, 296 p. 23 cm. 1-7576. F7. F49

FISKE, John. The beginnings of New England; or, The Puritan theocracy in its relations to civil and religious liberty. Boston and New York, Houghton, Mifflin and co., 1889. xvii, 296 p. front. (fold. map) 20½ cm. 1-7577. F7. F54

— 1892. xvii, 296 p. front. (fold. map) 20½ cm. 14-13142. F7. F55

— 1898. xxxix, 328 p. front., illus., plates (part double) ports., facsims. maps. 26 cm. 98-1508 rev. F7. F56

— 1899. xvii, 296 p. front. (fold. map) 20½ cm. 11-13687. F7. F565

— 1900. xvii, 296 p. front. (fold. map) 20½ cm. 1-7578/4. F7. F57

— (c.1902) xxiii, 376 p. incl. front. (port.) p. maps, fld. facsim. 20 cm. "Bibliographical note": p. 349-360. 38-31148. F7. F571

— (c.1917) xvii, 296 p. front. (fold. map) 20½ cm. "Bibliographical note": p. (279)-287. 22-2713. F7. F573

— 1930. vi, 328 p. incl. facsims. front., illus. fld. map. 21½ cm. "Bibliographical note": p. 312-318. 30-26400. F7. F58

FORBES, Allan. Some Indian events of New England; a collection of interesting incidents in the lives of the early settlers of this country and the Indians. Boston, 1934. viii, (2), 94 p. incl. front., illus., ports. 23½ cm. 34-22235. F7. F75

FORBES, Allan. Other Indian events of New England; ... (Boston, 1941) vii, 102 p., incl. front., illus. 23½ cm. 42-17454. F7. F755

FOSTER, Stephen. Their solitary way; the Puritan social ethic in the first century of settlement in New England. New Haven, Yale University Press, 1971. xxii, 214 p. 23 cm. Bibliography p. 191-208 76-151573 MARC. F7. F 76 1971

... FOUNDERS of New England, The. Boston, Old South meeting-house, 1894. (136) p. 18 cm. (Old South leaflets xii) 4-27946. F7. F77

FOX, George. Something in answer to a letter ... of John Leverat, Governour of Boston, to William Coddington Governour of Rode-Island, Dated, 1677. (n.p., 1678?) (Boston, 1922) facsim. 11 p. 21½ cm. (Americana series; photostats by the Mass hist. soc. no. 61) 22-7158. F7. F785 Office

FOXCRAFT, Thomas. The earthquake, a divine visitation. A sermon ... Boston, 1756. 2, 51 p. 20 cm. 15-27876. F7. F79 Office

FOXCRAFT, Thomas. Observations historical and practical on the rise and primitive state of New-England. ... Boston, 1730. 4, 46 p. 20 cm. 17-15792. F7. F795 Office

FOXCRAFT, Thomas. The voice of the Lord, ... Boston, 1727. 2, 52 p. 20 cm. 15-11547. F7. F8 Office

FRIEDERICI, Georg. ... Das puritanische Neu-England, ... Halle a. Saale, M. Niemeyer, 1924. 104 p. 24½ cm. 28-4527. F7. F9

HAYNES, Williams. Captain John Gallop, master mariner and Indian trader. Stonington, Conn., Pequot Press (c.1964) 31 p. 23 cm. 64-7606. F7. G2. H3

GARDINER, Henry. New England's vindication. London, 1660. Portland, Me., Printed for the Gorges society, 1884. 83 p. facsim. tab. 22 x 18½ cm. Gorges soc. Publications I. 3-44. F7. G22 Microfilm 19006 F

GARDNER, Grace H. Pastimes of colonial children, a juvenile illustrated by the author. New York, William-Frederick Press, 1957.   35 p. illus. 21 cm. 57-10168.   F7.G224

GARGAN, Mrs. Helena Nordhoff. ... Pilgrim, Puritan and Papist in Massachusetts. Boston, Press of T. A. Whalen & co., 1902.   33 p. 24 cm. (N. E. Catholic historical soc. Pubs. no. 4) 5-4364.   F7. G23

GORGES, Ferdinando. America painted to the life. The true history of the Spaniards proceedings in the conquests of the Indians, and of their civil wars among themselves, from Columbus his first discovery, to these later times. As also, of the original undertakings of the advancement of plantations into those parts; with a perfect relation of our English discoveries, shewing their beginning, progress and continuance, from the year 1628 to 1658. Declaring the forms of their government, policies, religions, maners, customs, military discipline, wars with the Indians, the commodities of their countries, a description of their towns and havens, the increase of their trading, with the names of their governors and magistrates. More especially, an absolute narrative of the north parts of America, and of the discoveries and plantations of our English in Virginia, New-England, and Berbadoes. Publisht by Ferdinando Gorges, esq. ... London, Printed for Nath. Brook at the Angel in Cornhil, 1658 - 59.
4 pt. in 1 v. 18½ x 14½ cm. Four works printed separately, each with separate t.-p. and pagination. Pt. (3) is merely a reprint, with new t.-p. and preface, of Edward Johnson's History of New England, and has same running title: Wonder-working Providence of Sions Saviour, in New England... Contents. - pt. I American painted to the life ... pt. 2 A breife narration of the originall undertakings of the advancement of plantations into the parts of America ... pt. 3. America painted to the life. ... pt. 4. America painted to the life. The history of the Spaniards proceedings in America ... Rc-2726 rev.

F7. G66

ARCHER, Gabriel. Bartholomeus Gosnols reys van Engeland na het norder gedeelte van Virginien, anno 1602. Layden, P. Vander Aa. 1706.   16, (2) p. double plate, fold. map. 18 cm. First pub. in English in Samuel Purchas' Pilgrimes, pt. 4, London 1625. 7-16411.

F7. G67
Office.

ARCHER, Gabriel. Gosnold's settlement at Cutty Hunk. Boston, 1901. 19 cm.   F7.G671

BRERETON, John. A briefe and true relation of the discoverie of the north part of Virginia ... reproduced in facsimile from the first edition of 1602, with an introductory note by Luther S. Livingston. New York, Dodd, Mead & co., 1903.   vii, 24 p. 23 x 18 cm. Reprinted from the Bibliographer (New York) v. 1. 5-10488.

F7.G672

GOSNOLD monument on Cuttyhunk, The; a description of the exercises held at the dedication of the monument in August, nineteen hundred and three ... New York, T. A. Hine (1903?)   2, 30 p. front. 17 x 15 cm. "Copied from the New Bedford evening standard." 6-36451.   F7.G674

HALE, Edward Everett. Gosnold at Cuttyhunk. Worcester, Mass., C. Hamilton (1902)
7 p. 26 cm. "From Proceedings of the American antiquarian society" 6-41543.   F7.G675

... Gosnold memorial, being a full account of the proceedings at the dedication of the Gosnold memorial at Cuttyhunk ... 1903 ... (New Bedford, 1903)   16 p. 26 cm. (The Old Dartmouth historical sketches, no. 4) 18-14909.   F7. G69

HALLER, William. The Puritan frontier: town-planting in New England colonial development, 1630 - 1660. New York, Columbia University Press, 1951.   119 p. 23 cm. Bibliography p. 111-116. A52-5386.   F7. H23
1951a

— New York, Ams Press (1968)   119 p. 23 cm. 78-76657.   F7. H23
1968

HANSCOM, Elizabeth Deering. The heart of the Puritan; selections from letters and journals ... New York, The Macmillan company, 1917.   xiii, 281 p. front. 21 cm. 17-29768.   F7. H24

HAVEN, Samuel Foster. History of grants under the great Council for New England ... Boston, Press of J. Wilson and son, 1869.   36 p. 24 cm. 8-33616.   F7. H38

HAWKS, Francis Lister. The history of New England, illustrated by tales, sketches, anecdotes, and

adventures ... By Lambert Lilly, schoolmaster (pseud.) Boston, W. Hyde, 1831. 184 p. incl. front., illus. 15½ cm. 1-7579 rev.
   F7. H39
   Rare book coll.

— Boston, W. D. Ticknor, 1842. 184 p. incl. front., illus. 16 cm. 1-7580 rev.   F7. H395

HERRICK, C. The early New-Englanders; what did they read? London, Alexander Moring ltd., 1918. 19 p. 24½ cm. "Reprinted from 'The Library,' Jan.,, 1918." 19-4220.   F7. H56

HIGGINSON, Francis. New-England plantation. Or, a short and true description of the commodities and discommodities of that countrey. London, Printed by T. C. and R. C. for M. Sparke, 1630. 11 l. 19 cm. First ed. Two others were pub. in the same year. 2-18514.
   F7. H63
   Office

CASTELL, William. A petition of W. C. exhibited to the high court of Parliament now assembled, for the propagating of the Gospel in America, and the West Indies; ... (London) Printed in the yeare 1641. 1, 5-19 p. (With Higginson, F. New-Englands plantation ... London, 1630) The "petition" is also prefixed to the author's "Short discoverie of the coasts and continent of America ..." London, 1644 and is appended to the reprint of the same in Osborne's "Collection of voyages and travels ..." London, 1745. 2-13739.
   F7. H63
   Office

HIGGINSON, Francis. New-Englands plantation. Amsterdam, Theatrum Orbit Terrarum; New York, De Capo Press, 1970. 24 p.
   F7. H63
   1970

— New York, B. Franklin (1971) 31 p. 23 cm. 78-154869.
   F7. H 63
   1971

— (Washington, P. Force, 1835) 14 p. 23½ cm. (In Force Tracts, v. 1 no. 12) Reprint of 1st ed. 2-13282.
   F7. H635

— (Rochester, G. P. Humphrey, 1898) 15, (2) p. 24 cm. Reprint from Force tracts. 4-15775.   F7. H64

— Salem, Mass., The Essex book and print club, 1908. 132 p. 23 cm. 9-7806.
   F7. H645
   Office

— (New York, New England society, 1930) 2 p. l., facsim. (27) p. 21½ cm. 31-24969.   F7. H647

HOAR, George Frisbie. The obligations of New England to the county of Kent. ... Worcester, Mass., C. Hamilton, 1885. 30 p. 26 cm. 4-35124.   F7. H67

HOOKE, William. Nevv Englands teares, for old Englands feares. ... a sermon ... London, Printed by T. P. for I. Rothwell and H. Overton, 1641. 2, 23 p. 18½ cm. 8-6905.
   F7. H78
   Office

HORTON, Edward Augustus. The culmination of the Puritan theocracy. Boston, J. S. Lockwood, 1900. 32 p. 24½ cm. 10-8757.   F7. H82

HOWE, Henry Forbush. Prologue to New England. New York, Toronto, Farrar & Rinehart, inc. (1943) xi, 324 p. illus. (maps, plan) pl. 22 cm. 43-2702.   F7. H85

— Port Washington, N. Y., Kennikat Press (1969 c1943) xi, 324 p. illus. 22 cm. 68-26231.
   F7. H85
   1969

HUBBARD, William. A general history of New England, ... to MDCLXXX. Pub. by the Mass. historical society. Cambridge, Hillard & Metcalf. 1815. vi, (8), (7) - 676 p. 22½ cm. 1-13316.
   F7. H87
   Office

— 2d ed. collated with the original MS.   Boston, C. C. Little and J. Brown, 1848.   1 v. (various pagings) 25 cm. F7. H87 1848

HUMBLE address of the publicans of New-England, to which king you please.   With some remarks upon it ... London ... 1691.   35 p.   19½ x 15 cm.   8-10523. F7. H91 Office

HUMPHREY, Mrs. Frances A.   How New England was made,   Boston, D. Lothrop company (c. 1890) 267 p. incl. illus., plates, ports., facsim.   21½ x 18 cm.   1-7581. F7. H92

JOSSELYN, John.   An account of two voyages to New-England, wherein you have the setting out of a ship, with the charges; the prices of all necessaries for furnishing a planter, ... etc.   A large chronological table of the most remarkable passages ... to the year 1673.   London, Printed for G. Widdows, 1674.   4, 279 (i.e. 277), (3) p.   15 cm.   4-9724. F7. J84

JOSSELYN, John.   An account of two voyages to New-England, made during the years 1638, 1663. Boston, W. Veazie, 1865.   vii, 211 p.   23 cm.   22-10201. F7. J85

JOSSELYN, John.   A description of New-England.   Published by John Seller.   (London? 1682?) (Boston, 1925)   facsim.   4 numb. l.   front. (fold. map)   52½ x 39 cm.   (Americana series; photostat by the Mass. hist. soc. no. 146) 25-25193. F7. J86 Office

KNIGHT, Sarah (Kemble)   The journals of Madam Knight and Rev. Mr. Buckingham.   From the original manuscripts, written in 1704 & 1710.   New York, Wilder & Campbell, 1825.   129 p.   19 cm. 1-13318. F7. K71 Office

KNIGHT, Mrs. Sarah (Kemble)   The private journal of a journey from Boston to New York in the year 1704.   Albany, F. H. Little, 1865.   xii, (13) - 92 p. incl. illus., facsim.   21½ x 17 cm.   L.C. copy lacks facsim. A11-2737 rev. F7. K715

— Norwich, Conn., The Academy press, 1901.   2, 7-78 p.   22½ cm.   10-3165. F7. K72 Office

— Boston, Small, Maynard & co., 1920.   xiv, 72 p.   front. (fold. map)   21 x 13 cm.   21-10698. F7. K723 Office

— New York, P. Smith, 1935.   St. Clair Shores, Mich., Scholarly Press, 1970.   xiv, 27 p.   71-131763. F7. K724 1920a

— New York, P. Smith, 1935.   xiv, 72 p.   front. (fold. map)   21 x 13 cm.   Facsim. of 1920 ed.   35-12871 Rare Book Coll. F7. K724 1935

— New York, Garrett Press, 1970.   vii, xiv, 72 p.   19 cm.   76-106751. F7. K724 1970

— Upper Saddle River, N. J., Literature House (1970)   xiv, 72 p.   22 cm.   77-115471. F7. K724 1970b

— Boston, D. R. Godine, 1972 (c. 1971)   39 p.   illus.   24 cm.   71-172647. F7. K724 1972

— With an introductory note by George Parker Winship, and a new pref. by Kenneth Silverman. F7. K724 1972b

LAUER, Paul Erasmus.   ... Church and state in New England.   Baltimore, The Johns Hopkins press, 1892.   106 p.   24½ cm.   (Johns Hopkins university studies ... 10th ser. II - III)   Bibliographical foot-notes.   4-9368. F7. L37

LAWRENCE, Robert Means.   New England colonial life.   Cambridge, Mass., The Cosmos press, inc., 1927.   5, 276 p. front. 22½ cm. 27-14243.   F7. L41

LECHFORD, Thomas. Plain dealing: or, Newes from New-England ... London, Printed by W. E. &
I. G. for N. Butter, 1642.   4, 80 p. 18½ x 14½ cm. First ed. 3-15642.   F7. L46
Office

— With a new introd. by Darrett B. Rutman.   New York, Johnson Reprint Corp., 1969.
xxiii, 211 p. facsim. 20 cm. 68-30726.   F7. L46
1969

— Ed. with introd. and notes by J. Hammond Trumbull.   With a new preface by Everett H. Emerson,
New York, Garrett Press, 1970.   vii, xl, 211 p. (The Amer. literature and culture series) 70-106752.   F7. L46
1970

LETTER from a gentleman in Boston, to Mr. George Wishart ... concerning the state of religion in
New-England.   Edinburgh (1742) (Edinburgh) ... Clarendon historical society, 1883.   16 p. 23 cm.
4-33549.   F7. L65

LEVERMORE, Charles Herbert. Forerunners and competitors of the Pilgrims and Puritans; or,
Narratives of voyages made by persons other than the Pilgrims and Puritans of the Bay colony to the
shores of New England ... 1601 - 1625 ...   Brooklyn, N.Y., 1912.   2 v. fold. map. 24½ cm. A17.511 rev.
F7. L66

MASSACHUSETTS (Colony) Court of admiralty. The trials of eight persons indited for piracy, etc.
... 1717 ... Boston, Printed by B. Green, for John Edwards ... 1718. (Boston, 1925)
facsim: 2 p. 25 numb. l. 35½ cm. (Americana series; photostats by the Mass. hist. soc. No. 132) 41-24189.   F7. M35
1718a

— The tryals of sixteen persons for piracy, etc. ... 1726 ... Boston, Printed for and sold by
Joseph Edwards, 1726. (Boston, 1939)   facsim. 24 p. 29 cm. Photostat Americana. 2d series. no. 75.   F7. M36
42-5166.   1726a
Rare book coll.

MATHER, Cotton. Magnalia Christi americana: or, The ecclesiastical history of New-England ...
1620 - 1698. London, Printed for T. Parkhurst, 1702.   7 pt. in 1 vol. double map. 32½ cm. 1-24698.
F7. M41
Office

ROBINSON, George Washington. Errata in Cotton Mather's Magnalia. Cambridge, Mass., 1943.
64 p. 19½ cm. "50 copies printed." A43-1051.   F7. M412
Rare book coll.

MATHER, Cotton. Magnalia Christi americana. 1st American ed., from the London edition of 1702.
Hartford: Silas Andrus. 1820.   2 v. 23 cm. 1-7582.   F7. M42

— Hartford, S. Andrus & son, 1853.   2 v. front. (port.) 23 cm. 1-28305-M2.   F7. M43

MATHER, Increase, supposed author. A brief relation of the state of New England ... London,
Printed for R. Baldwine, 1689.   18 p. 18½ cm. 6-19154.
F7. M433
Office

— (Reprint. In Force, Peter. Tracts ... Washington, 1836 - 46. v. 4 (1846) no. 11 17 p.)
4-27251.   F7. M435
Office

MATHER, Increase. An essay for the recording of illustrious providences ... Boston in New Eng-
land, Printed by Samuel Green for Joseph Browning ... 1684.   11, 372, (8) p. 14 cm. 18-19974.
F7. M4355
Office.

— Printed at Boston, and ... sold by George Calvert ... London, 1684. 11 p. 372, (8) p. 14 cm.
18-19975.
 F7. M4357
 Office

MATHER, Increase. A narrative of the miseries of New-England by reason of an arbitrary government erected there. (London, 1688) 8 p. 20 cm. 48-37618*.
 F7. M4359
 Rare book coll.

MATHER, Increase. Remarkable providences illustrative of the earlier days of American colonisation. With introductory preface, by George Offor. London, J. R. Smith, 1856. xix, (16), 262 p. front. (port.) 16½ cm. (Library of old authors) 18-11699. 36-3757.
 F7. M436 & F7. M437
 Office

—. London, Reeves and Turner, 1890. 3, (v) - xix p., 8 l., 262 p. front. 18 cm. (Library of old authors) 10-25258 rev.
 F7. M438

MAVERICK, Samuel. A briefe discription of New England and the severall townes therein, ... (Boston, Press of D. Clapp & son) 1885. 28 p. 22 x 18 cm. Reprint, from the N. E. hist. and geneal. register of Jan., 1855. Also printed in the Proceedings of Mass. hist. soc. vol. xxi. 2-20089.
 F7. M46

MAYHEW, Jonathan. A discourse on Rev. xv. 3d, 4th. Occasioned by the earthquakes in Nov., 1755. Boston, Printed by Edes & Gill, and R. Draper, 1755. 72 p. 20 cm. 15-4535.
 F7. M466
 Office

MAYHEW, Jonathan. The expected dissolution of all things, ... Boston, Printed by Edes & Gill, and by R. Draper, 1755. 76, 5 p. 18 cm. 15-11564.
 F7. M467
 Office

MILLER, Perry. The New England mind: from colony to province. Cambridge, Harvard University Press, 1953. xi, 513 p. front. 25 cm. "Bibliographical notes": p. (487) - 498. 53-5072. Sequel to next item.
 F7. M54

MILLER, Perry. The New England mind; the seventeenth century. New York, The Macmillan co., 1939. xi, 3 - 528 p. 24 cm. 39-22760.
 F7. M56
 1939

— Cambridge, Harvard University Press (c. 1954) xi, 528 p. 24 cm. Bibliographical refs. 54-7507.
 F7. M56
 L. H. & G. Rm. 1954

MORGAN, Edmund Sears. The Puritan family; essays on religion and domestic relations in seventeenth-century New England. Boston, Mass., The Trustees of the Public library, 1944. 118 p. incl. pl., facsims. 27½ cm. "Reprinted from the Feb., March, Apr., Sept., 1942 and Jan., May, 1943 issues of More books, the bulletin of the Boston public library." Bibliographical refs. incl. in "Notes" (p. 105 - 118) 44-7048.
 F7. M8

— New ed., rev. and enl. New York, Harper & Row (1966) x, 196 p. 21 cm. (Harper torchbooks.)
65-25695.
 F7. M8

MORISON, Samuel Eliot. The Puritan pronaos; studies in the intellectual life of New England in the seventeenth century. New York, New York university press; London, H. Milford, Oxford university press, 1936. 7, (3) - 281 p. 24 cm. 36-11726.
 F7. M82

MORISON, Samuel Eliot. The intellectual life of colonial New England. (2d ed.) New York, New York University Press, 1956. 288 p. 21 cm. First pub. in 1936 under title: The Puritan pronaos. Bibliographical footnotes. 56-8487.
 F7. M82
 1956

MORSE, Jedidiah. A compendious history of New England, designed for schools and private families. Charlestown (Mass.) Printed and sold by Samuel Etheridge, 1804. xii, (13) - 388 p. front. (fold. map) 17½ cm. 1-7583.
 F7. M88
 Rare book coll.

— London, C. Taylor, 1808.   2, (iii) - vi, (2), 207 p.   19 cm.   1-7584.   F7. M89

— 2d ed., with improvements by the authors.   Newburyport, Thomas & Whipple, 1809 .   viii, (13) - 336, ix, p.   front. (fold. map)   17½ cm.   1-7585.   F7. M895
Rare Book Coll.

— 3d. ed., enl. and improved.   Charlestown (Mass.) Printed by S. Etheridge, 1820.   xxxix, (41) - 324 p. 18 cm. 1-7586.   F7. M90

ADAMS, Hannah.   A narrative of the controversy between the Rev. Jedidiah Morse ... and the author. Boston: ... 1814.   viii, 31, 3 p. 24½ cm. 5-11355.   F7. M905

LOWELL, John.   Review of Dr. Morse's "Appeal to the publick," principally with reference to that part of it, which relates to Harvard college.   By a friend of that college.   (Boston, 1814)   42 p. 23½ cm. Bound with above item. 5-11356.   F7. M905

MORSE, Jedidiah.   An appeal to the public, on the controversy respecting the revolution in Harvard college ...   Charlestown (Mass.)   1814.   viii, 190, (2) p. 23½ cm.   Relating to the charges of plagiarism in the preparation of the Compendious history of New England.   7-9877 rev.   7-9876.   F7. M91 & F7. M92

— Boston, Printed by Samuel T. Armstrong, 1814.   33 p.   23½ cm.   17-14593.   F7. M97

MORSE, Sidney Edwards.   Remarks on the controversy between Doctor Morse and Miss Adams.   2d ed., with additions.   Boston, 1814.   35 p. 24 cm. 17-14594.   F7. M98

NEAL, Daniel.   The history of New-England containing an impartial account of the civil and ecclesiastical affairs of the county to ... 1700.   London, Printed for J. Clark, R. Ford, and R. Cruttenden, 1720.   2 v. front. (fold. map) 19½ cm. paged continuously.   3-6356.   F7. N34
Office

— London, Printed for A. Ward (etc.) 1747.   2 v. fold. map. 20½ cm. 12-26596.   F7. N36
Rare book coll.

NEW-ENGLAND a degenerate plant. ...   London, 1659.   20 p. 17½ cm. 8-6921.   F7. N51
Office

NEW ENGLAND and New York in 1676; a reproduction of the map and descriptions, as given in the John Speed atlas, London; (1676) to which is added historical notes and references.   Boston, The University company (c. 1910)   22 p. fold. map. 16 x 14 cm. Reproduced from the atlas pub. in 1676 under title: A prospect of the most famous parts of the world. 11-1895.   F7. N52
Map Div.

NEW-ENGLAND'S faction discovered; or, A brief and true account of their persecution of the Church of England; ... (London, Printed for J. Hindmarsh, 1690)   8 p. 24½ x 20 cm. 7-14882.   F7. N58

PAINE, Thomas.   The doctrine of earthquakes. Two sermons ...   Boston: Printed for D. Henchman . ... 1728.   87 p. 17 cm. 18-20074.   F7. P13

PAINE, Thomas.   The temporal safety of the Lord's people ...   Boston, Printed ... for S. Gerrish. 1732.   2, 19 p. 16½ cm. 18-20073.   F7. P14

PALFREY, John Gorham.   History of New England.   Boston, Little, Brown, 1858-90.   5 v. maps (partly double, incl. fronts. v. 1, 3, 4) 25 cm. 1-7587.   F7. P15

PALFREY, John Gorham.   History of New England during the Stuart dynasty.   Boston, Little, Brown, and company, 1865.   3 v. illus., maps (partly double, incl. front.) 24 cm. Forms v. 1-3 of above item. 7-23995.   F7. P16

PALFREY, John Gorham.   A history of New England, ... being an abridgment of his "History of New England during the Stuart dynasty."   New York, Hurd and Houghton, 1866.   2 v. 19 cm. 1-7588.
F7. P17

PALFREY, John Gorham. A compendious history of New England from the revolution of the seventeenth century to the death of King George the First.   (1689 - 1727) Boston, H. C. Shepard, 1872.
xii, 469 p. 19½ cm. "Sequel to A history of N. E. 2 v. 1866" 1-14469.
F7. P18

PALFREY, John Gorham. A compendious history of New England from the accession of King George the Second to the first general congress of the Anglo-American colonies.   (1728 - 1765) Boston, H. C. Shepard, 1873.   xii, 439 p. 19½ cm. Sequel to above item. 1-14470.
F7. P181

PALFREY, John Gorham. A compendious history of the first century of New England ... Boston, H. C. Shepard, 1872.   3 v. 12°.   The first two vols. are a re-issue of the author's History of N. E. ... 1866; v. 3 was also issued separately under title "... history of N. E. from the revolution of the 17th cent to the death of King Geo. the First." 1872. 1-14472-M1.
F7. P19

PALFREY, John Gorham. A compendious history of New England from the discovery by Europeans to the first general congress of the Anglo-American colonies.   Boston, H. C. Shepard, 1873.   4 v. 19 cm.
Reissue of above item with addition of a fourth vol. covering 1728 - 1765. Vol. 4 was also issued separately (F7.P181) 1-14471.
F7. P195

— Boston, J. R. Osgood and co., 1884.   4 v. 19½ cm. 4-17796/2*.
F7. P21

PARKER, Herbert. Courts and lawyers of New England. New York, The American historical society, inc., 1931.   4 v. fronts., plates, ports., facsims. 28 cm. Paged continuously. 31-5367.
F7. P24

PECK, Wallace. The story of the Puritans; a go-as-you-please history (part fact, part fiction) from the first leeway voyage of the Mayflower down to the close of the doughnut dynasty.   St. Johnsbury (Vt.) C. T. Walter, 1889.   90 p. front., illus., 4 pl. 19½ x 15 cm. 17-9757.
F7. P36

PERLEY, Sidney. Historic storms of New England. ... Salem, The Salem press publishing and printing co., 1891.   x, 3-341 p. 23½ cm. 3-21055.
F7. P45

PETTENGILL, Samuel Barrett. The Yankee pioneers; a saga of courage.   Rutland, Vt., C. E. Tuttle Co. (1971)   175 p. illus. 19 cm. 73-158785 MARC.
F7. P47

PORTER, Noah. A discourse on the settlement and progress of New-England. Delivered in Farmington ... 1820. Hartford, 1821.   20 p. 23 cm. 1-7589.
F7. P84

POUND. Capt. Thomas Pound. By John H. Edmonds. Cambridge, J. Wilson, 1918.   1, (2), 25 - 84 p. front. (fold. map) 25 cm. Reprinted from the Pubs. of the Colonial soc. of Mass. vol. xx) 19-10557.
F7. P87

PRINCE, Thomas. A chronological history of New-England in the form of annals ... 1602 ... to ... 1730. Boston, S. Gerrish, (1736 - 55)   2 v. in 1. 17½ cm. v. 2 appeared 20 years after v. 1 under the title "Annals of New England" in 3 numbers. The last number breaks off in the middle of a sentence. This comprises all that was ever published of the history and is very rare. (Covers only until Aug. 5, 1633) 1-14466.
F7. P94
Rare book coll.

— A new ed. (Boston) Cummings, Hilliard, and co., 1826.   xxi, (2), 25-439 p. 23½ cm. 1-14467. F7. P95
Office

— 3d ed. To which is added, a memoir of the author, etc. By Samuel G. Drake. Boston, Antiquarian bookstore, 1852.   13, (3) - 12, (iii) - xxi, (2), 25-439 p. front., illus., plates, ports., coat of arms. 23 cm. "This edition consists of but thirty copies." "We have completed the (last) sentence from Winthrop's Journal." 1-14468.
F7. P96

— Edinburgh, 1887-88.   5 v. 17½ cm. (Bibliotheca curiosa) Reprint of 1826 ed. 2-18530 rev.
F7. P97

PRINCE, Thomas. Earthquakes the works of God and tokens of His just displeasure. Two sermons ... Boston (1727)   3, 45, (3) p. 19 cm. 5-42809.
F7. P98
Office

— Boston, 1755.   23 p. 17½ cm. 24-15725.
F7. P982

PRINCE, Thomas. An improvement of the doctrine of eathquakes. 1755. 16 p. 17½ cm. 24-11480. F7. P985

RHODE ISLAND (Colony) Court of vice-admiralty. Tryals of thirty six persons for piracy (etc.) ... 1723. (Boston, 1939)   facsim. 1, 14 p. 29½ cm. (Photostat Americana. 2d series no. 79) 41-24190.
F7. R5
1723a

RIPLEY, Charles. An oration, on the colonization of New England, delivered Dec. 22, 1838, before the Pilgrim society of Louisville. Louisville, Ky, Prentice & Weissinger, 1839. 44 p. 8º. 1-16225 rev.
F7. R58

ROBBINS, Thomas. An historical view of the first planters of New-England. Hartford, Peter B. Gleason and co., 1815. x, (13) - 300 p. 17 cm. 1-7590.
F7. R63

ROBINSON, Mrs. Therese Albertine Louise (von Jacob) Geschichte der colonisation von Neu-England. Leipzig, F.A. Brockhaus, 1847. xviii, 709 p. fold. map. 22 cm. 1-7591 rev.
F7. R66

ROBINSON, Therese Albertine Louise (von Jacob) Talvi's History of the colonization of America. Ed. by William Hazlitt ... London, T.C. Newby, 1851. 2 v. 19 cm. Translated from the German. 2-19821.
F7. R67

RUTMAN, Darrett Bruce. American Puritanism; faith and practice. Philadelphia (1970) xii, 139 p. 21 cm. (Pilot books) 79-100370.
F7. R8

SAVAGE, James. A genealogical dictionary of the first settlers of New England, showing three generations of those who came before May, 1692, on the basis of Farmer's Register ... Boston, Little, Brown and company, 1860 - 62. 4 v. 24½ cm. "Genealogical notes and errata, etc... By C.H. Hall" inserted in v.1. 6-45244 rev.
F7. S26

— A genealogical cross index of the four volumes of the Genealogical dictionary of James Savage. By O.P. Dexter ... New York, O.P. Dexter, 1884. 38 p. 24 cm. 6-45244 rev.
F7. S26 Index
Cat. Div. and Geneal. Sect.

— Genealogical notes and errata to Savage's Genealogical dictionary, etc. By Mrs. Caroline Wells (Healey) Dall. Lowell, Mass., G.M. Elliott (187-?) 8 p. 22½ cm. Originally pub. in the N.E. hist. and geneal. register for April, 1873. 6-45377 rev.
F7. S26

SECOND part of the tragedy of Amboyna; or, A true relation of a most bloody, treacherous and cruel design of the Dutch in New Netherland in America, for the total ruining and murthering of the English colonies in New England. London, 1653. New York, Reprinted 1915. 4, 7 p. 21½ cm. Refers to the execution of certain Englishmen by the Dutch authorities on the island of Amboyna in 1622. 16-7868.
F7. S44

SEWALL, Joseph. The duty of a people to stand in aw of God, ... A sermon preach'd ...the evening after the earthquake. 2d ed. ... Boston, D. Henchman, 1727. 28 p. 18 cm. 18-20075.
F7. S46 Office

SMITH, Asa Dodge. The Puritan character. Montreal, 1858. 36 p. 22½ cm. 1-16224.
F7. S56

SMITH, John. Advertisements for the unexperienced planters of New-England, or anywhere. Or, The path-way to experience to erect a plantation. ... By Captaine Iohn Smith. London, 1631. 4, 40 p. fold. map. 17½ x 13½ cm. 8-5921.
F7. S61

— ... with additions and corrections as published in 1635. Boston, W. Veazie, 1865. viii, 72 p. illus. (seal and coat of arms) fold. map. 23 x 17 cm. 1-15928.
F7. S62

SMITH, John. (A description of New-England: or The observations and discoveries of Captain Iohn Smith (admirall of that country) in the north of America in the year of our Lord 1614 ... London, Printed by Humfrey Lownes, for Robert Clerke ... 1616. 9, 61 (2) p. fld. map. 17 x 13½ cm. 7-15406.
F7. S63 Office

— (Washington, P. Force, 1837) 6, 34 (2) p. 23½ cm. (From Force tracts v.2 (1838) no. 1) Reprint. Does not include the map of the New England coast, found in the original. 4-27025.
F7. S634

— With a fac-simile of the original map. Boston, W. Veazie, 1865. vii, 89 p. incl. fold. map. 26 cm. 1-15930. 1-15931.
F7. S 64 or 641

— (Rochester, G.P. Humphrey, 1898) xii, 40, (2) p. 24 cm. Reprint from Force tracts. 4-15777.
F7. S643

— Boston, 1901. 19 cm.   F7. S644

SMITH, John. Twee scheeps-togten ... gedaan na Nieuw-Engeland. De eerste in het jaar 1614. Leyden, P. vander Aa. 1707. 34 p. fold. pl., fold. map. 12°. 1-15932-M1.   F7. S65 Office

SMITH, John. New Englands trials. Declaring the successe of 80 ships employed thither these eight yeares; and the benefit of that countrey by sea and land. ... The 2d ed. London, Printed by W. Iones, 1622. (Washington, P. Force, 1837) 23 p. 23½ cm. Force tracts v.2 (1838) no.2. 4-27019.   F7. S668

— 2d ed. London, 1622 (Reprinted, Cambridge, Mass., H. O. Houghton and co., 1867) (34) p. 28 cm. "Sixty copies printed" 1-15933 rev. 6-837.   F7. S67 and S671 Office

— Amsterdam, Theatrum Orbis Terrarum; New York, Da Capo Press, 1971. (23) p. 23 cm. (The English experience ... no. 416) 70-171793 MARC.   F7. S67 1620a

— Cambridge (Mass.) Press of J. Wilson and son, 1873. 10, (16) p. fold. map. 19½ cm. 17-14368.   F7. S674 Office

— (Rochester, G. P. Humphrey, 1898) 23, (2) p. 24 cm. (American colonial tracts .. v.2, no.2) 4-27020.   F7. S68

SMITH, Josiah. The greatest sufferers not always the greatest sinners. A sermon ... occasioned by the terrible earthquake in New-England. Boston, 1730. 2, 21 p. 17 cm. 15-27850.   F7. S7 Office

STILES, Ezra. Extracts from the itineraries and other miscellanies of Ezra Stiles, ... 1755 - 1794. New Haven, Yale university press, 1916. vi, 620 p. illus. 25 cm. 16-22319.   F7. S85

SYMMES, William. A sermon ... On the public thanksgiving in Massachusetts-Bay. Salem, Samuel Hall, 1769. 24 p. 20 x 15½ cm. 18-2275.   F7. S98 Office.

THORNTON, John Wingate. The historical relation of New England to the English commonwealth. (Boston, A. Mudge & son) 1874. 105 p. 25½ cm. 1-7592.   F7. T51

TOLMAN, George. The old women, a paper read before the Concord antiquarian society. Concord, 1916. 24 p. 23½ cm. On the life of women in N.E. in colonial times. 17-3896.   F7. T65

TRUE relation concerning the estate of New-England, as it was presented to His Majesty. (Boston, D. Clapp & son) 1886. 15 p. 22 x 18 cm. Reprinted from the N.E. hist. and geneal. reg., Jan. 1886. 1-7564.   F7. T86

UNITED colonies of New England. The New England federation, 1643. Boston, 1906.   F7. U56

UNITED colonies of New England. Commissioners. Extracts from the records of the United Colonies of New England. ... Hartford (Press of Case, Lockwood and co.,) 1859. 46 p. 27 cm. 7-16685.   F7. U57

VAUGHAN, Alden T. New England frontier; Puritans and Indians, 1620 - 1675. 1st ed. Boston, Little, Brown (1965) xvii, 430 p. 22 cm. 65-20736.   F7. V 3

VAUGHAN, Alden T. The Puritan tradition in America, 1620 - 1730. New York, Harper & Row (1972) xxviii, 348 p. 21 cm. (Documentary history of the U.S. Includes bibliographical references. 78-174703. MARC.   F7. V32 1972

— Columbia, University of South Carolina Press (1972) xxviii, 348 p. 24 cm. 74-184660.   F7. V32 1972 b

WALLER, George Macgregor. Puritanism in early America. Boston, Heath (1950)   x, 115 p. 28 cm.
(Problems in American civilization ... Amherst College) Bibliography: p. (113) - 115.   51-4731 rev.   F7. W 3

WARD, Harry M. The United Colonies of New England, 1643 - 90. (1st ed.) New York, Vantage Press (1961)   434 p. 21 cm. 60-15581.   F7. W32

WEBSTER, Daniel. Speech of Mr. Webster, at the celebration of the New York New England society, December 23, 1850. Washington, Printed by Gideon and co., 1851.   13 p. 20½ cm. 1-21602.   F7. W37

WEEDEN, William Babcock. Economic and social history of New England, 1620 - 1789, by William B. Weeden ... Boston and New York, Houghton, Mifflin and company, 1890.   2 v. 21 cm. Paged continuously.
1-7565/6.   F7. W38

WEEDEN, William Babcock. Economic and social history of New England, 1620 - 1789, ... Boston and New York, Houghton, Mifflin and company, 1891.   2 v. 21 cm. Paged continuously. 8-34772.   F7. W382

WEEDEN, William Babcock. Economic and social history of New England, 1620 - 1789. New York, Hillary House Publishers, 1963.   2 v. (xvi, 964) p. 22 cm. 63-21189.   F7. W383

WEEDEN, William Babcock. Three commonwealths, Massachusetts, Connecticut and Rhode Island; their early development. ... Worcester, Mass., Press of C. Hamilton, 1903.   37 p. 24½ cm. Reprinted from the proceedings of the American antiquarian soc., Oct. 21, 1902. 6-40265.   F7. W39

WHITE, Mrs. Elizabeth (Nicholson) Mary Browne; the true life and times of the daughter of Mr. John Browne, gent., commissioner of the United Colonies of New England ... (Providence, R. I., Priv. print., 1935.   5, 3-266 p. incl. mounted front. 21½ cm. "References": p. 245-248. 36-15246.   F7. W54

WHITE, Henry. The early history of New England, illustrated by numerous interesting incidents. ... 4th ed. Concord, N.H., I. S. Boyd, 1841.   iv, (5) - 420 p. 18 cm. Bibliography included in preface. Ed. pub. in N.Y., 1859 under title: Indian battles. 1-7593.   F7. W58

— 5th ed. Concord, N.H., I. S. Boyd, 1842.   iv, (7) - 420 p. 18½ cm. 17-24902.   F7. W582

— 9th ed. Boston, Sanborn, Carter, Bazin & co. (1841)   iv, (7) - 428 p. 19½ cm. 17-12065.   F7. W586
                                                                                          Toner coll.

WHITE, Henry. Indian battles: with incidents in the early history of New England. ... New York, D. W. Evans & co. (c. 1859)   iv, (5) - 428 p. 19 cm. 2-5186.   F7. W59

WHITRIDGE, Joshua Barker. An oration delivered on the anniversary of the New England society, Charleston, S.C., Dec. 22, 1835. ... Charleston, 1836.   3, (5) - 61 p. 23½ cm. 1-10290.   F7. W62

WIGGLESWORTH, Samuel. A religious fear of God's tokens, explained and urged; ... on account of the terrible earthquake ... Boston, 1728.   2, iii, 42 p. 17½ cm. 20-3022.   F7. W65
                                                                                             Office

WILLIAMS, William. Divine warnings to be received with faith and fear, ... a discourse on ... the terrible earthquake ... Boston, Samuel Gerrish, 1728.   xii, 132 p. 13½ cm. (Imperfect) 15-13267.   F7. W 72
                                                                                          Rare book coll.

WINSHIP, George Parker. Sailors narratives of voyages along the New England coast, 1524 - 1624; ... Boston, Houghton, Mifflin & co., 1905.   5, 3-292 p. 3 maps, 3 facsim. 25 cm. 5-42412.   F7. W76
                                                                                             Office

— New York, B. Franklin (1968)   292 p. illus. 25 cm.   F7. W76
                                                                  1968

WINTHROP, John. Winthrop's conclusions for the plantation in New England. Boston, Old South meeting house, 1894.   12 p. 19 cm. (Old South leaflets, 12th series, 1894 no. 3)   F7. W78

WINTHROP papers ... 1498 - 1644. (Boston) The Massachusetts historical society, 1929 - 1947.

5 vol. col. front., plates, port., map. facsims. (part fold., 1 col.) geneal. tab. 25½ cm. 29-18409.   F7. W79

WINTHROP papers. New York, Russell & Russell (1968 -   2 v. illus. 25 cm. 68-10956.   F7. W8

WOODBRIDGE, William. An address before the Detroit young men's society, delivered by request, April, 1848. Detroit, 1849.   23 p. 22 cm. 17-22214.   F7. W88

WRIGHT, Thomas Goddard. Literary culture in early New England, 1620 - 1730. New Haven, Yale university press ... 1920.   322 p. 23 cm. Bibliography: p. 295 - 304. 21-571 rev.   F7. W95 1920

— New York, Russell & Russell, 1966.   322 p. 23 cm. 66-24771.   F7. W95 1966

DOMINION OF NEW ENGLAND, 1686 - 1689.

ANDROS tracts, The: Being a collections of pamphlets and official papers issued during the period between the overthrow of the Andros government and the establishment of the second charter of Massachusetts. Boston, The Prince society, 1868 - 74.   1 v. front. (port.) geneal. tab. 22 x 17½ cm. (Pubs. of the Prince society ... v. 5-7) 3-24558.   F7. 5. A53

— With notes and memoir of Sir Edmund Andros, by W. H. Whitmore. New York, B. Franklin (1971?) 3 v.   F7. 5. A53 1971

ANDROS. A memoir of Sir Edmund Andros ... By Wm. Henry Whitmore. Boston, 1868.   49 p. front. (port.) 28½ cm. Reprinted from the "Andros tracts" pub. by the Prince soc. 3-2747. L.C. copy replaced by microfilm.   F7. 5. A55 Microfilm 15507 F

APPEAL to the men of New England, with a short account of Mr. Randolph's papers. (Boston, 1689) 15 p. 19 cm. 2-10495.   F7. 5. A64 Office

BRODHEAD, John Romeyn. The government of Sir Edmund Andros over New England, in 1688 and 1689. Morrisania, N. Y., 1867.   2, 40 p. 23½ cm. 9-15721.   F7. 5. B86

BYFIELD, Nathaniel. An account of the late revolution in New-England. ... London, 1689. 20 p. 19½ x 15 cm. 4-20408.   F7. 5. B98 Office

— Edinburgh, Reprinted in the year 1689.   7 p. 18 x 14 cm. 4-15539.   F7. 5. B891

— Reprint from Force, Peter. Tracts ... Washington, 1836-46. v. 4 (1846) No. 10 4-27250 F7. 5. B99

— New York, Reprinted for J. Sabin, 1865.   3, (5) - 26 p. 21½ x 17½ cm. Imperfect. 1-21472.   F7. 5. B992

FURTHER queries upon the present state of the New-English affairs. By S. E. New York, Reprinted for J. Sabin, 1865.   3, 18 p. 28 cm. Relates to the period of the Andros government in N. E. 2-20078 Add.   F7. 5. F98

GT. BRITAIN. Laws, statutes, etc., 1685-1688 (James II) Commission of King James the Second to Sir Edmund Andros, June 3, 1686. (Mss.) (From Force, Peter. Tracts ... Washington, 1836 - 46. v. 4 (1846) no. 8.   Print. in colls. of the Mass. hist. soc. 3d ser. v. 7 p. 138-149. 4-27248.   F7. 5. G78

MATHER, Increase. A vindication of New England ... n. p., 1690?   1, 27 p. 17½ x 15 cm. Reprinted in Andros tracts, v. 2 p. 20 and v. 3, p. 2. 6-19152.   F7. 5. M43 Office

PALMER, John. The present state of New-England impartially considered, in a letter to the clergy. (n. p., 1689)   44 p. 19 x 14½ cm. 6-34302.   F7. 5. P17 Office

PALMER, John. An impartial account of the state of New England; or, The late government there, vindicated. ... London ... 1690. 40 p. 19½ x 15 cm. 6-34303. F7.5.P18
Office

RAWSON, Edward, supposed author. The revolution in New England justified, and the people there vindicated from the aspersions cast upon them by Mr. John Palmer, ... Boston, 1691. 3 p. 48 p. 19½ cm. 4-8392. F7.5.R26
Office

— Boston, 1773. 59 p. 18 cm. 4-8393. F7.5.R27
Office

— Reprint from Force, Peter. Tracts ... Washington, 1836-46. v. 4 (1846) no. 9. 59 p. 4-27249. F7.5.R28

1775 - 1865.

ABBOT, Jacob. New England, and her institutions. By one of her sons. Boston, J. Allan & co., 1835. 4, (2), (ix) - xi, (13) - 271 p. 19½ cm. (The American popular library) 1-13319. F8.A13
Rare Book Coll.

— Hartford, S. Andrus & son, 1847. 2, (ix) - xi, (13) - 271 p. 16½ cm. 10-15921. F8.A134

EATON, Samuel. A sermon delivered at the interment of the Hon. Jacob Abbot, ... Brunswick, Me., 1820. 20 p. 21 cm. 18-12813. F8.A135
Rare book coll.

ADAMS, Henry. Documents relating to New-England Federalism. 1800 - 1815. Boston, Little, Brown, and co., 1877. xi, 437 p. 23 cm. Documents vi - viii were separately pub. Boston, 1829 under title: Correspondence of John Quincy Adams ... and several citizens of Mass. ... 8-34790 rev. F8.A21

ADAMS, James Truslow. New England in the republic, 1776 - 1850. Boston, Little, Brown and co., 1926. xiv, 438 p. front., illus. (facsims.) plates, ports. 23 cm. v. 3 of the author's "History of New England" 26-9006. F8.A23

AYER, Mrs. Sarah Newman (Connell), Diary of. Portland, Me., Lefavor-Tower co., 1910. 2, 404 p. 25 cm. 12-12476. F8.A97

BECKETT, Sylvester Breakmore. Guide book of the Atlantic and St. Lawrence, and St. Lawrence and Atlantic rail roads ... Portland, Sanborn & Carter. 1853. vi, (2), (7) - 180 p. incl. illus., plates. pl., fold. map. 19½ cm. 1-21366. F8.B39

BERNHEIM, Marc. Growing up in old New England. Foreword by Barnes Riznik. New York, Crowell-Collier Press (c. 1971) ix, 100 p. illus. 28 cm. 75-151160. F8.B45

BLISS, Sylvester. A geography of New England: being a descriptive key, to accompany the "Outline map of New England" Boston, J. P. Jewett & co., 1847. 96 p. 16°. 1-7594-M1. F8.B64
Map div.

BLISS, Theodore. Theodore Bliss, publisher and bookseller; a study of character and life in the middle period of the xix century. Norwalk, O., American pub. co., 1911. 92 p. 23 cm. 12-7879. F8.B65

— Northampton ... for the Northampton historical society, 1941. 6, (3) - 79 p. 23½ cm. 41-9949. F8.B65
1941

BOUDINET, Elias. Journey to Boston in 1809. Ed. Milton Halsey Thomas. Princeton University Library, 1955. xii, 97 p. illus., ports. 25 cm. Bibliographical footnotes. 56-177. F8.B68

CARTER, Robert. A summer cruise on the coast of New England. Boston, Crosby and Nichols; New York, O. S. Felt, 1864. viii, 261 p. 18 cm. 1-7595. F8.C32

— With an introduction by Rossiter Johnson ... (New ed.) Boston, Cupples and Hurd, 1888.
xiv, 261 p. front. (fold. map) 19 cm. Imperfect: p. 255-258 wanting. 1-7596.   F8. C33

CHART and description of the rail-road from Boston to New York, via Worcester, Springfield, Hartford, and New Haven. ... Boston, Bradbury & Guild (1849) 84 p. illus. 20 cm. 1-21383.   F8. C48

COLTON, Joseph Hutchins. Colton's traveler and tourist's guide-book through the New-England and Middle states and the Canadas: ... New York, J. H. Colton, 1850.   1, v-vii, 94 p. 2 fold. maps (incl. front.) 16 cm. 1-23434.   F8. C72 Office

CONNECTICUT infantry. Excursion of the Putnam phalanx to Boston, Charlestown and Providence ... 1859. Hartford, Conn., The Phalanx, 1859. 107 p. front. 23 cm. 12-11176.   F8. C75

CORNELL, William Mason. Recollections of "ye olden time," with biographical sketches of eminent clergymen, statesmen, merchants ... etc., in Mass., R. I., Conn., N. H., and Pa. Boston, Lee and Shepard; N.Y., C. T. Dillingham, 1878.   viii, 436 p. 9 pl., 6 port. (incl. front.) 19 cm. 14-3400.   F8. C8

CRANE, Mrs. Bathsheba H. Life, letters, and wayside gleanings, for the folks at home. Boston, J. H. Earle (1880)   480 p. incl. front. (port.) 22½ cm. The experience of a minister's wife in various parishes, inc. Northampton, Boston, Dorchester, Woonsocket, Greenfield, North Springfield. 12-31662.   F8. C89

DISTURNELL, John, comp. The eastern tourist; being a guide through the states of Connecticut, Rhode Island, Massachusetts, Vermont, New Hampshire, and Maine. Also, a dash into Canada ... New York, J. Disturnell, 1848.   144 p. front. 15½ cm. 1-24368.   F8. D61 Office

DODGE, Nathaniel Shatswell. Sketches of New England ... By John Carver (pseud) New York, E. French, 1842.   vi, (9) - 286 p. 18½ cm. 8-7817.   F8. D64

DWIGHT, Timothy. Travels; in New-England and New-York. New-Haven, T. Dwight, 1821-22.
4 v. 2 fold. maps (incl. front., v.2) 23 cm. 1-7597.   F8. D99

— London, Printed for W. Baynes and son ... 1823.   4 v. 3 front. fold. map. 22 cm. 1-7598.   F8. D995

— Ed. Barbara Miller Solomon et al. Cambridge, Mass., Belknap Press, 1969.   4 v. 25 cm.
69-12735.   F8. D9952

DWIGHT, Theodore. Sketches of scenery and manners in the United States. By the author of the "Northern traveller." New York, A. T. Goodrich, 1829.   iv, (9) - 188 p. front., plates. 18½ cm. 1-16784.   F8. D996 Office

EASTMAN, Ralph Mason. Some famous privateers of New England ... (Boston) ... State street trust co., 1928.   vii, 87 p. incl. front., illus. (incl. ports., facsims.) 22½ cm. Bibliography: p. v. 28-15356 rev.   F8. E13

FENNELLY, Catherine. Life in an old New England country village. New York, T. Y. Crowell Co. (1969)   viii, 211 p. 27 cm. 69-18668.   F8. F43

FENNELLY, Catherine. The New England village scene: 1800. Sturbridge, Mass., Old Sturbridge Village (1955)   15 p. illus. 22 cm. (Old Sturbridge Village booklet series, 1) 55-33007.   F8. F44

GEMMING, Elizabeth. Huckleberry Hill; child life in old New England. New York, T. Y. Crowell Co. (1968)   x, 147 p. illus. 24 cm. 68-21602.   F8. G4

GORLIER, Claudio. L'universo domestico; studi sulla cultura e la societa della Nuova Inghilterra nel secolo xix. Roma, Edizioni di Storia e letteratura, 1962.   291 p. 23 cm. Includes bibliographical refs.
75-283165.   F8. G6

GUILD, William. ... New York and the White Mountains; with a complete map, etc. Boston,

Bradbury & Guild, 1852. 80 p. front. (fold. map) illus. 20 ½ cm. 1-13315.   F8. G95

HAYWOOD, Charles Fry. Minutemen and mariners; true tales of New England. New York, Dodd, Mead (1963) 269 p. 21 cm. 63-21823.   F8. H35 1963

— Rev. ed. New York, Dodd, Mead (c. 1967) 277 p. 21 cm. 67-26840.   F8. H35 1967

KENDALL, Edward Augustus. Travels through the northern parts of the United States in the year 1807 and 1808. New-York: I. Riley, 1809. 3 v. 21 ½ cm. 1-16785.   F8. K33

NEW ENGLAND tour of His Royal Highness, the Prince of Wales, (Baron Renfrew,) ... Boston, Bee printing company, 1860. 52 p. 25 cm. 7-23987.   F8. N53

— 2d ed. ... Boston, Bee printing co., 1860. 1, (7) - 56 p. 23 ½ cm. 3-28898 rev.   F8. N532

OGDEN, John Cosens. A view of the New-England Illuminati: who are indefatigably engaged in destroying the religion and government of the United States; ... Philadelphia ... 1799. 20 p. 20 ½ cm. 18-12805.   F8. O34 & O342 Rare book coll.

PEAK, John. Memoir of Elder John Peak, written by himself ... Boston, 1832. 203 p. front. (port.) 20 cm. 12-20465.   F8. P35

RAILWAY manual; containing railroad maps of the entire route from Boston north ... with ... guide to Lake Winnipiscogee and the White Mountains. Boston, G. W. Briggs, 1849. 48 p. incl. maps. 16°. 1-7599-M1.   F8. R15 Office

ROGERS, Nathaniel Peabody, A collection from the newspaper writings of ... Concord (N. H.) J. R. French, 1847. xxiv, 380 p. front. (port.) 18 ½ cm. 9-11013.   F8. R71

ROGERS, Nathaniel Peabody, A collection of the miscellaneous writings of. 2d ed. Manchester, N. H., W. H. Fisk ... 1849. xxiv, 380 p. front. (port.) 19½ cm. 9-11014.   F8. R72

ROLLINS, Mrs. Ellen Chapman (Hobbs) New England bygones. By E. H. Arr (Pseud.) Philadelphia, J. B. Lippincott & co., 1880. 214 p. 19 cm. 1-7600.   F8. R75

— New ed., enl. and illustrated. Introd. by Gail Hamilton. Philadelphia, J. B. Lippincott & co., 1883. 243 p. front., illus., plates. 25 cm. 1-7601 rev.   F8. R76

SOMERBY, Frederic Thomas. Hits and dashes: or, A medley of sketches and scraps, touching people and things. By "Cymon" (pseud.) ... Boston, Redding & co., 1852. 2, (vii) - viii, (9) - 152 p. 18 ½ cm. CA 12-1238 unrev.   F8. S69

STAUFFER, Vernon. New England and the Bavarian Illuminati ... New York, 1918. 375 p. 24 ½ cm. Bibliography: p. 361 - 374. 19-7334.   F8. S79

— New York, Russell & Russell (1967) 374 p. 22 cm. 66-27153.   F8. S79 1967

TOCQUE, Philip. A peep at Uncle Sam's farm, workshop, fisheries, etc. ... Boston, C. H. Pierce and co., 1851. xii, 229 p. front., plates. 19 ½ cm. 1-16792.   F8. T63

TRAVELLER'S guide in New England, The. New York, A. T. Goodrich, 1823. 94p. 16cm. 1-7602. F8. T77 Office

TUDOR, William. Letters on the eastern states. New York, Kirk & Mercein, 1820. 1, (v) - vi p. (5) - 356 p. 20 ½ cm. 1-7603.   F8. T91

— 2d ed.   Boston, Wells and Lilly, 1821.   viii, (9) - 423 p. 22 cm. 1-7604.   F8. T92

WACHUSETT club, Worcester, Mass.   Log of the cruise of schooner Julius Webb, which sailed from Norwich, Ct., July 23d, 1858 ...   Worcester, 1858.   40 p. 21 cm. 3-28526.   F8. W12

WHITE, Franklin.   Photographic scrap book, containing views of mountains scenery, views in Boston, New York, Greenwood cemetery, etc.   Lancaster, N.H., 1858.   48 phot. on 10 l. 25½ x 20½ cm. 2-19143-4.
F8. W58 and F8. W59
Office

WYATT, Mrs. Sophia Hayes.   The autobiography of a landlady of the old school, with personal sketches of eminent characters, places, and miscellaneous items.   Boston, 1854.   iv, 284 p. front. (port.) 19½ cm. Reminiscences of Dover, N.H., and of other places in New England. 13-33776. 13-33775.   F8. W97 or W98

1865 TO DATE.

ABBOTT, Katharine M.   Old paths and legends of New England; ...   New York and London, G. P. Putnam's sons, 1903.   xvii, 484 p. front., illus., fold. map. 21½ cm. Map in pocket. 3-19703.   F9. A 12

— 1907.   2, iii-xiv, (2), 408 p. incl. illus., map. front., plates. 22 cm. 7-40881.   F9. A13

— Detroit, Singing Tree Press, 1969 (c.1907)   xvii, 484 p. illus. 72-75227.   F9. A13
1969

AMERICAN automobile association.   Guide to New England, Maritime province, Quebec. ... Washington, D.C., ... c.1944.   148 p. illus. (maps) 23½ cm. 44-37300.   F9. A56
1944

ANGLE, Helen M. (Blondel)   The log or diary of our automobile voyage through Maine and the White Mountains, written by one of the survivors.   Stamford, Conn., R.H. Cunningham (c.1910)   91 p. illus. 16½ cm. 11-7316 rev.   F9. A58

BACON, Edwin Munroe.   Literary pilgrimages in New England to the homes of famous makers of American literature ...   New York, Boston (etc.) Silver, Burdett & co., (1902)   xiii, 532 p. incl. front. (map) illus. 20½ cm. 3-32.   F9. B14

BAKER, Louis Harrington.   ... The favorite motor ways of New England, historical and descriptive. New York, H. MacNair, 1915.   352 p. illus. (incl. maps) 18 cm. 15-13017.   F9. B16

BLANCHARD, Fessenden Seaver.   An outboard cruising guide to New England, Eastern New York State and adjacent Canadian waters.   New York, Dodd, Mead, 1958.   167 p. illus. 24 cm. 58-10428.
F9. B5

BOLLES, Frank.   Land of the lingering snow.   Chronicles of a stroller in New England ...   Boston and New York, Houghton, Mifflin and co., 1891.   2, 234 p. 18 cm. 1-7606/4.   F9. B69

BOSTON and Albany railroad.   The railway panoramic guide ... A panoramic description of ... all objects of interest along the road ...   New York, Boston and Philadelphia, The Overland pub. co. (1878)   3-62 p. illus. 4º. 1-16794-M1.   F9. B73

BOSTON and Lowell railroad corporation.   ... Summer saunterings by the B. and L. ...   Issued by Passenger dept., B. and L. railroad. (Boston, 1885)   166 p. front., illus. (incl. plans) 3 fold. maps. 20 cm.   17-22112.   F9. B738

— Ed. for 1886.   176 p. incl. front., illus. 3 fold. maps. 20½ cm. 1-16892 rev.   F9. B74

BOSTON and Maine railroad company.   Along New England shores.   (Boston) 1917.   (72) p. illus., fold. map. 20½ cm. The New England coast from Boston to Mt. Desert. 25-3681.   F9. B78

BOSTON and Maine railroad. Lakes and streams. 5th ed. Boston, 1901. 20½ x 10½ cm. F9.B784

BOSTON and Maine railroad company. ... Mountains of New England. (Boston, 1901?) 15 x 20½ cm.
F9.B786

— (Cambridge, c.1908)   1 v. 15½ x 21 cm.   F9.B7861

BOSTON and Maine railroad. New England lakes ... (Cambridge c.1908) 1 v. 15½ x 21 cm. F9.B7864

BOSTON and Maine railroad. ... Picturesque New England, historical, miscellaneous. (n.p., n.d.)
39 pl. 15½ x 20 cm. CA 26-284 unrev.   F9.B7868

— (Cambridge, c.1908)   1 v. 15½ x 21 cm.   F9.B787

BOSTON and Maine railroad company. Rivers of New England. Boston, 1901? 15 x 20½ cm. F9.B788

— (Cambridge, c.1908)   1 v. 15½ x 21 cm.   F9.B7881

BOSTON and Maine railroad. ... Seashore of New England. (Boston, 19 -) 30 pl. CA 34-1552. F9.B7889

— (Cambridge, c.1908)   1 v. 15½ x 21 cm.   F9. 789

BOSTON and Maine railroad. Outdoors in New England. Boston, (1909) (92) p. 9-23232. F9.B7893

BOSTON and Maine railroad company. Summer excursions to the White Mountains, etc. ... and the New England beaches. ... (Boston) 1891. 92 p. incl. map. 8º. 1-16221-M1.   F9. B79

BREARLEY, William Henry. Seventh season of the grand pleasure excursions ... Detroit (1883)
24½ cm.   F9. B82

BREWER, Daniel Chauncey. The conquest of New England by the immigrant ... New York & London, G. P. Putnam's sons, 1926. vi, 369 p. 19½ cm. 26-12327.   F9. B83

BRIGHAM, A. P. ... Geography of New England, Maine ... (c.1916)   F9. B85

BRUCE, Wallace. The Connecticut by daylight, from New York to the White mountains, etc. By Thursty McQuill (pseud.) New York, American news co., 1874. 108 p. illus. 17½ cm. 1-7607. F9. B88

— New York, G. Watson (1884) 74 p. illus. 18 cm. L.C. copy replaced by microfilm. 1-16891 rev. F9. B89
Microfilm 15016 F

BULLARD, Frederic Lauriston. Historic summer haunts from Newport to Portland ... Boston, Little, Brown, and co., 1912. xii, 329 p. front., plates. 22½ cm. 12-23770 rev.   F9. B96

BURT, Henry Martyn. Burt's guide through the Connecticut valley to the White mountains and the river Saguenay. Springfield, Mass., New England pub. co., 1874. 298 p. illus., fold. pl. maps (part fold.)
16½ cm. 1-7608.   F9. B97
Microfilm 15017 F

CHAMBERLAIN, Allen. Vacation tramps in New England highlands. Boston and New York, Houghton Mifflin co., 1919. xii, 164 p. front., plates, maps (part double) 18 cm. 19-8748.   F9. C44

CHAMBERLAIN, Samuel. Ever New England; photos by Samuel Chamberlain, with an introd. by Donald Moffat. New York, Hastings house (1944) 7, (274) p. of illus. 21 x 16½ cm. 44-40339. F9. C45

CHAMBERLAIN, Samuel. Six New England villages: Hancock, N.H.; Litchfield, Conn.; Little Compton, R.I.; Old Bennington, Vt.; Old Deerfield, Mass.; Wiscasset, Me. New York, Hastings House (1948) 104 p. illus. 25 cm. Chiefly illustrations. 48-7147*.   F9. C46

CONNECTICUT circle magazine. Photo record, hurricane and flood, New England's greatest disaster. ... (New York, New England historical events association, inc., c.1938) (64) p. illus. 32½ cm.
40-11216.   F9. C64

CONSOLIDATED tours of the eastern states and Canada, with descriptive guide and historical notes, 1936 ... (Chester, Vt., The National survey co.; ... 1936) (136), 3-34, 80, 55, 34, (24), 40 p. illus., maps (part fold.) 22 cm. A collection of circulats. 37-9997. F9. C66

— 1937. (108) p. incl. illus., maps. 23½ cm. 41-31877. F9. C66 1937

CRAWFORD, Mary Caroline. Little journeys in old New England ... Boston, L. C. Page & company (1906) 2, iii-viii p., 11 - 390 p. front. (port.) 15 pl. 20 cm. 7-11187. F9. C89

DAME, Lawrence. New England comes back. ... New York, Random house (c. 1940) xi, 319 p. illus., plates. 22 cm. "First printing." 40-7051. F9. D19

DANIELS, Jonathan. ... A southerner discovers New England. (New York) The Macmillan co., 1940. viii p., 398 p. 22 cm. 49-27433. F9. D23

DE COSTA, Benjamin Franklin. The Atlantic coast guide. A companion for the tourist between Newfoundland and Cape May ... Boston, A. Williams and co., 1873. 88, 136 p. 2 fold. maps. 17½ cm. Treats almost entirely of the New England coast. 1-16171 Add. F9. D29

DE LUXE hotels of New England, containing photographic views and descriptions ... Boston, Mass., C. B. Webster & co. (c. 1914) (62) p. illus. 28 cm. 14-12094. F9. D36

DERRAH, Robert H. By trolley through western New England. Boston, 1904. 4, 105, (8) p. illus., fold. maps. 17½ cm. 4-19625. F9. D43

DRAKE, Samuel Adams. Nooks and corners of the New England coast. New York, Harper & brothers (c. 1875) 459 p. incl. front., illus., plates, map. 22½ x 17 cm. 8-2681. 1-7609. F9. D75 & D.76

— 1876. 459 p. incl. front., illus. (incl. ports., facsim.) plates, maps. 22 cm. 37-18045. F9. D763

— (1903) 459 p. incl. front., illus., maps. 23 cm. 3-11684. F9. D77

— Detroit, Singing Tree Press, 1969. 459 p. illus. 23 cm. 69-19883. F9. D77 1969

EASTERN railroad company. Ramblings along the eastern shore of New England ... (Boston, 1879) 95, (14) p. incl. front., illus. 9 pl. fold. map. 18½ cm. 17-22111. F9. E12 Toner coll.

EASTERN summer resort manual; containing illustrations and descriptive matter pertaining to a great many hotels and summer resorts throughout New England ... Boston, Eastern summer resort agency, c. 1900. 76 p. illus. 23½ cm. 0-4179 rev. F9. E13

EATON, John S. Guide to the Boston and Maine railroad, the White mountains, and all principal points in the New England states ... For 1870 ... (Boston, 1870) 1, viii, 7-166 p. illus. 12° 1-7610-M1. F9. E14

EMERSON, Philip. The geography of New England. New York, The Macmillan co., 1922. 96 p. illus. (incl. maps) 25½ cm. 23-13949. F9. E48

EMERSON, Philip. ... The New England states. New York, The Macmillan co,; London, Macmillan & co.; 1901. viii, 128 p. illus., 6 maps. 19 x 15 cm. 1-23414. F9. E5

FAVORITE seaside resorts of America. v. 1, no. 1. Providence, Frazier and Whiting, 1884 40 p. illus., fold. chart. 35½ cm. No more pub? 1-14454 rev. F9. E27

FEDERAL writer's project. ... Here's New England! A guide to vacationland ... Boston, Houghton Mifflin co., 1939. vi, 122 p. maps (1 fold. in pocket) 21 cm. 39-15700. F9. F44

FEDERAL writers' project. New England hurricane, a factual, pictorial record ... Boston, Hale, Cushman & Flint (c. 1938) 220, (2) p. illus. 26 cm. 38-34970. 39-5463. F9. F45 or F453

NEW ENGLAND

FLOTOW, Edith Potter. Memories of New England. Chicago, 1923. 32 p. illus. 24-2920. F9. F64

FROST, John Edward. Fancy this; a New England sketch book. Boston, Waverly house (c. 1938) (106) p. illus. 25 ½ cm. 39-146. F9. F76

GAGE, William C. "Chicago to the sea." Eastern excursionist; a complete guide to the principal eastern summer resorts... Battle Creek, Mich., New York, 1883. 124 p. illus. 21 cm. 1-16315. F9. G13

GEOGRAPHY of New England. (New York, Cincinnati, etc.) c. 1921. 32 p. illus. 31 x 25½ cm. F9. G322

GEOGRAPHY of the New England states. New York, D. Appleton & co., 1877. xiv p. incl. illus., maps. 28 x 22 cm. 2-23706. F9. G33

GEOGRAPHY of the New England states... (Cincinnati & New York) Van Antwerp, Bragg & co., 1884. 16 p. illus., maps. fol. 1-13320-M1. F9. G34

GEOGRAPHY of the New England states. (New York) American book company, c. 1898. 32 p. illus. (incl. maps) 31 cm. 2-13010 rev. F9. G35

GRIEVE, Robert, ed. Guide book to the mountains of New Hampshire and the shores of southern New England... Providence, Journal of commerce co., 1899. xvi, 144 p. illus. obl. 16°. Aug.31, 99-41. F9. G83

GRIEVE, Robert, ed. Journal of commerce guide book to the shores of southern New England... Providence, Journal of commerce co., 1897. 176 p. illus. obl. 16°. 1-7611-M1. F9. G84

GRIEVE, Robert. ... The New England coast; its famous resorts. An illustrated guide and souvenir. Providence, J.A. & R.A. Reid, c. 1891. 104 p. illus. fol. 1-7612-M1. F9. G85

HALE, Edward Everett. A family flight around home... Boston, D. Lothrop and co. (1884) 366 p. incl. front., illus., plates. 23 cm. 1-23971. F9. H16

HALE, Edward Everett. Tarry at home travels... New York, London, The Macmillan co., 1906. xxvi, 429 p. incl. illus., plates, ports., map, plan. 6-35582. F9. H165

HALE, Mrs. Louise (Closser) We discover New England... New York, Dodd, Mead & co., 1915. 5, 314 p. front., plates, fold. map. 22 ½ cm. 15-24247. F9. H17

HALL, Joseph Davis. Twentieth century vacation; travels after my own notion at the seashore and mountains of New England, by Mrs. T. Wilberforce (Pseud.) ed. Providence, J.D. Hall & co., 1900. 96 p. illus. (incl. port.) 23 ½ cm. 0-3981 rev. F9. H18

HANDBOOK of New England; an annual publication. 1916 - (no. 1 - Boston, P.E. Sargent (1916 - v. illus. (incl. maps) 18 ½ cm. 16-15736. F9. H23

HARLOW, Louis K. The lakes of New England. Twelve etchings... Boston, S.E. Cassino (c.1892) 7 l. 6 pl. obl. 12°. Six etchings, not twelve, though apparently complete. 1-13321-M1. F9. H29

HARLOW, Louis K. The picturesque coast of New England, from twelve original water colors... Boston, S.E. Cassino, 1887. 12 pl. obl. fol. 1-7613-M1. F9. H31

HAWTHORNE, Hildegarde. Old seaport towns of New England... New York, Dodd, Mead & co., 1916. viii, 3 - 312 p. front., plates. 22 ½ cm. 16-23386 rev. F9. H39

HAYNES, George H. The great resorts of New England illustrated... New York, Moss eng. co. (c. 1890) 4 l. illus. obl. 12°. 1-7614-M1. F9. H42

HOTEL greeters of America. The greeters guide of New England;... v.1, no.1 - Apr. 1936 - (Boston) 1936 - v. illus. 19 ½ cm. 38M1218T. F9. H83

HOWE, Frances S. 14000 miles, a carriage and two women, ... (Fitchburg) 1906. 4, 287 p. front.
21 ½ cm. "Many of these informal reports ... were written for the Boston evening transcript ... " 6-43915. F9. H85

HUBBARD, Charles Daniel. An old New England village, the people, the ways, the atmosphere of the olden days; Portland, Me., Falmouth Pub. House, 1947. 107 p. illus. 32 cm. 47-11649*. F9. H9

— 1966. 107 p. 21 cm. 66-22133. F9. H9 1966

IDEAL tour, The. (New York, Press of the Kalkhoff co.) v. illus., fold. maps. 23 x 11 ½ cm. Guide for an automobile tour through New England. 14-10704 rev. F9. I19

INGERSOLL, Ernest. Down east latch strings; or, Seashore, lakes and mountains by the Boston and Maine railroad. (Boston) Boston & Maine railroad, 1887. 5, 256 p. front., illus. (incl. facsim.) maps (part fold.) 22 ½ cm. 1-7615. F9. I 47

JOHNSON, Clifton. A book of country clouds and sunshine ... Boston, Lee and Shepard, 1897.
7-213 p. incl. illus., plates. front. 24 cm. 7-32895. F9. J 62

JOHNSON, C. The farmer's boy. 1894. 1 v. F9. J 64

— New York, T. Y. Crowell & co. (1907) x, 164 p. front., illus., 16 pl. 21 cm. 7-29711. F9. J 65

JOHNSON, Clifton. Highways and byways of New England, ... New York, London, The Macmillan co., 1915. xi, 299 p. incl. front. plates. 20 cm. 15-24246. F9. J 655

JOHNSON, Clifton. The New England country. Boston, Lee and Shepard, 1893 (1892) x, 121 p. incl. front., illus., plates. 27 cm. 1-7616. F9. J 67

KEYES, George L. Keyes' hand-book of northern pleasure travel: to the White and Franconia mountains, etc. ... Boston, G. L. Keyes, 1874. 240 p. illus., maps (part fold.) 17 cm. 1-16896. F9. K435
— 1875. 288 p. illus., pl., maps. 16º. 1-16895-M1. F9. K44

LAMPTON, William James. The trolley car and the lady; a trolley trip from Manhattan to Maine ... Boston, R. G. Badger, 1908. 3, 11-85 p. front., illus. 19 cm. 8-22252. F9. L23

LAUGHLIN, Clara Elizabeth. So you're seeing New England! And if I were going with you, these are some of the places I'd suggest ... Boston, Little, Brown and co., 1940. viii, (3) - 560 p. front., plates. 17 ½ cm. "First ed." "A brief reading list": p. (517) - 522. 40-27493. F9. L35

LEONARD'S traveller's instructor; a descriptive guide of the route between New York & Boston, via Newport, Fall River and Taunton. New York, W. A. Leonard, c.18 - v. 23 cm. CA26-406 unrev. F9. L58
Toner coll.

LONGWELL, Charles Arthur. Vacation impressions ... (New York? 1902) 51 p. illus., pl. 23 cm.
3-27 rev. F9. L85

MABIE, Hamilton Wright. Our New England: her nature described. ... Boston, Roberts brothers, 1890. 3, 24 p. front., plates. 25 x 32 cm. 1-7617. F9. M11

McCAFFREY, Henry. Descriptive guide, 1000 mile excursion. Baltimore, 1878. 19 ½ cm. F9. M12

MACOWEN, Arthur H. A thousand miles with the "Queer quartette." Being an account of a trip by bicycle and boat from the city of Philadelphia to the White mountains and return, ... By Chris Wheeler (pseud.) Philadelphia, American athletic pub. co., 1891) 85 p. front. (group port.) 20 cm. 1-16782. F9. M17

MANN, Henry. Features of society in Old and in New England. Providence, S. S. Rider, 1885.
viii, 103 p. 16 ½ x 14 ½ cm. 8-20415. F9. M28

NEW ENGLAND

MARLOWE, George Francis.   Byroads of old New England; some tales of less-known persons and places along the way.   ... New York, Exposition Press (1954)   153 p. illus. 21 cm.   53-12073.   F9. M29

MARLOWE, George Francis.   Coaching roads of old New England, their inns and taverns and their stories ... New York, The Macmillan co., 1945.   xvi, 200 p. incl. front., plates. 21 cm.   45-784.   F9. M3

MITCHELL, Edwin Valentine.   The horse & buggy age in New England ...   New York, Coward-McCann, inc., 1937.   viii, 232 p. illus. 22 cm.   37-28582.   F9. M58

MURPHY, Thomas Dowler.   ... New England highways and byways from a motor car; ... Boston, L. C. Page & co., 1924.   5, 327 p. col. front., plates (part col.) fold. map. 24½ cm.   24-15989.   F9. M95

NEW ENGLAND automobile guide book.   Boston (1905)   19½ x 11½ cm.   F9. N52

NEW ENGLAND calendar for engagements.   1940 -   New York, Hastings house (c. 1939)   v. illus. 21 cm.   44-30862.   F9. N523

NEW ENGLAND directory of hotels, etc.   Boston, The N. E. summer resort and information bureau, inc., c. 1911.   1 v. 22½ cm.   11-11899.   F9. N526

NEW ENGLAND states, The.   New York, etc. American book co., c. 1896   31 cm.   F9. N53

NEW YORK to Boston and the White mountains.   A guide of the route via Norwich, etc.   New York, Taintor brothers, 1868.   2, 67, (4) p. fold. maps. 15½ cm.   1-22208.   F9. N57

PERKINS, Mrs. Lucy (Fitch)   A book of joys; the story of a New England summer ...   Chicago, A. C. McClurg & co., 1907.   212 p. col. front., 4 col. pl. 23½ cm.   7-34806.   F9. P44

PHILLIPS, John Charles.   Quick-water and smooth; a canoeist's guide to New England rivers ... Brattleboro, Stephen Daye press, 1935.   2, 7-239 p. fold. map. 17½ cm.   35-3744.   F9. P48

PICTURESQUE and architectural New England ... Descriptive, picturesque, architectural.   Boston, D. H. Hurd & co. (1899)   2 v. illus., plates. 26½ x 35 cm.   99-2146 rev.   F9. P52

PIDGEON, Daniel.   Old-world questions and New-world answers ...   London, K. Paul, Trench & co., 1884.   viii, 369 p. fold. map. 20 cm.   Investigation of industrial and social conditions in N. E.   15-7563.   F9. P55

— New York, Harper & bros. 1885.   2, 193 p. 19 cm.   8-33096.   L.C. copy replaced by microfilm.   F9. P56
Microfilm 15018 F

PRIME, William Cowper.   Along New England roads ... New York, Harper & bros., 1892.   4, 200 p. 18 cm.   1-7618.   F9. P95

PROVIDENCE and Stonington steam ship co.   Summer resorts with routes and rates.   1891.   F9. P96

RAND, McNally & co.'s handy guide to the New England states ...   Chicago and New York, Rand, McNally & co., 1897.   4, (5)-268 p. front., plates, fold. maps. 17½ cm.   1-15916 rev.   F9. R18

— 3rd ed.   1898.   268 p. illus., pl., maps. 16°.   Aug 31, 98-69.   F9. R19

— 4th ed.   1899.   3, (5) - 273 p. front., plates, fold. maps. 17 cm.   Sept. 7, 99-134 Add.   F9. R2

RAYMOND's vacation excursions ...   Boston (1882)   11½ x 14½ cm.   F9. R27

RAYMOND & Whitcomb company.   The seven states tour through New England.   New York, Boston, etc. c. 1912.   20 cm.   F9. R28

RED CROSS.   U.S.   American national Red cross.   New York - New England hurricane and floods, 1938; official report of relief operations.   Washington, D. C., (1939)   vii, (3), 106 p. incl. front., illus., tables. 23 cm.   Bibliography: p. 106.   40-26534.   F9. R295

REDWAY, Jacques Wardlaw. Geography of the New England states. (Southern section) To accompany Butler's complete geography. Philadelphia, E. H. Butler and co. (1888) 17 p. incl. illus., maps. 4°. 1-16886-M1. F9. R32

ROSE, Jack Manley, illus. Northeast from Boston ... New York, G. P. Putnams's sons, 1941. 16 p. col. front., 1 illus., 50 pl. on 27 l. 31 x 23½ cm. 41-12183. F9. R6

ROUPP, Florence J. Rebirth of a citizen. New York, Comet Press Books (1954) 249 p. 23 cm. 53-11150. F9. R63

SEATON, George Whiting. What to see and do in New England; how to get the most out of your trip ... New York, Prentice-Hall, inc., 1940. xvi, 302 p. front., illus. (maps) plates. 21 cm. 40-8761 rev. F9. S43

SLADE, Daniel Denison. Twelve days in the saddle: a journey on horseback in New England during the autumn of 1883 ... By Medicus (pseud.) Boston, Little, Brown, and co., 1884. 5, 7-73 p. 16 x 12½ cm. 1-7619. F9. S63

SLATER, George A. The hills of home; American life pictured in New England in the last half of the nineteenth century, ... Port Chester, N.Y., 1930. 28 p. incl. port. 23 cm. 30-22775. F9. S64

— New York, W. E. Rudge, 1931. 48 (2) p. front. (port.) plates. 18 cm. 31-33760. F9. S642

SMITH, Joseph Warren. Gleanings from the sea: showing the pleasures, pains and penalties of life afloat with contingencies ashore. Andover, Mass., The author, 1887. 2, (iii) - xi, (13) - 399 p. front. (port.) illus. plates. 23½ cm. 4-20142. F9. S65

SNOW'S hand-book; northern pleasure travel: the White and Franconia Mountains, etc. Boston, Noyes, Snow, 1878. 256 p. illus., fold. map. 19 cm. 54-49578. F9. S66

SWEETSER, Moses Foster. Here and there in New England and Canada ... (Boston) Boston & Maine railroad, 1889. 3 v. fronts., illus., fold. maps. 20½ cm. 1-13322. F9. S97

SWEETSER, Moses Foster. New England: a handbook for travellers. A guide to the chief cities and popular resorts of New England ... Boston, J. R. Osgood and co., 1873. xvi, 399 p. fold. front., fold. maps. fold. plans. 17 cm. 1-7620. F9. S985

— New ed. rev. and augm. Boston, J. R. Osgood and co., 1874. xvi, 431 p. 17 cm. 1-7621. F9. S99

— 8th ed., rev. and augm. Boston, J. R. Osgood & co., 1884. xvi (479) p. 1-7622. F9. S995

— 12th ed. Boston, Houghton, Mifflin & co., 1891. xvi, 453 p. 1-7623. F9. S997

— 13th ed. Boston, Houghton, Mifflin & co., 1892. xvi, 463 p. 1-21431 Rev. F9. S998

SWEETSER, Moses Foster. Picturesque New England ... Illustrated from original sketches ... (Boston) Boston & Maine railroad (c. 1892) (32) p. illus. obl. 24°. 1-7624-M1. F9. S999

TAINTOR, Charles Newhall. Connecticut River route: a guide book of the most direct route from New York to the White Mountains; with ... description of towns and villages ... New York, Taintor brothers & co., c. 1875. (v) - vi, 7-118 p. illus. (incl. plan) fold. map. 17 cm. 1-13323. F9. T13

— 1887. (138) p. illus., fold. map. 17½ cm. 5-18360. F9. T131

TAINTOR, Charles Newhall. The Newport and Fall River route between New York and Boston. A descriptive guide ... New York, Taintor brothers (1869) 7-61 p. pl., fold. map. 16½ cm. 4-28335. F9. T133

TAINTOR, Charles Newhall. The Fall River and Newport routes between New York and Boston. A descriptive guide ... New York, Taintor brothers, Merrill & co., 1884. 62 p. illus., fold. map. 16°. 1-22479-M1. F9. T135

TAINTOR, Charles Newhall. Northern New England and Canada resorts. A handbook for tourists and travelers, describing the routes from New York and Boston to the White Mountains, etc. ... New York, Taintor brothers, Merrill & co., 1877.   126 p. illus., pl., fold. map. 17 cm. 1-22210.   F9. T14

— 1887.   (214) p. illus., 3 fold. maps. 18 cm. 4-28341.   F9. T143

TAINTOR, Charles Newhall. The northern route. Boston to the White Mountains, etc. ... New York, Taintor brothers (c. 1869)   93, (4) p. illus., fold. maps. 16½ cm. 2-22451. 4-7251.   F9. T15 or T151

TAINTOR, Charles Newhall. The Shore line route. From New-York to Boston. With descriptive sketches ... New-York, Taintor brothers, 1867.   2, 43 (i.e. 44) p. illus., fold. map. 16½ cm. 1-22209 rev.   F9. T18
1867
Rare book coll.

— 1879.   2, 43 (i.e. 58) p. illus., fold. map. 17½ cm. 46-30942.   F9. T18
1879
Rare book coll.

TOWNE, Charles Hanson. Jogging around New England ... New York, London, D. Appleton-Century co., inc., 1939.   xiv, 205 p. incl. front., illus. 21½ cm. 39-14034.   F9. T68

TRAIN and trolley trips through New England. The vacation guide. Hartford, Conn., The Guyde publishing co. (c. 1921)   41, (55) p. illus., fold. map. 17½ cm. CA 21-357 unrev.   F9. T75

TRAVELERS atlas-guide to New England ... Series 2, v. 1 -   (Hartford, Conn., The Trolley press) c. 1911 -   v. maps. 20 cm. 11-16547.   F9. T77

TRIPS, trolley and steamboat ... to interesting places in Massachusetts, Rhode Island, Connecticut. Providence, R.I., c. 1905.   17 cm.   F9. T82

... TROLLEY trips through New England ... Hartford, Conn., Guyde pub. co., c. 19 -   v. fronts., illus., maps. 17½ 18 cm. 10-13164.   F9. T83

TROLLEY trips through southern New England ... (4th ed.) Hartford, Conn., White & Warner, 1902. 112 p. incl. front., illus., 9 maps. 16½ cm. 2-24147.   F9. T84

TROLLEY wayfinder, The; official publication of the New England street railway club ... Boston.   v. illus., maps. 16½ x 10½ cm. 3-21007 rev.   F9. T86

TYARKS, Frederic Ewald. ... New England; where to go, what to see. New York, Harian publications (c. 1941)   64 p. 21½ cm. (The American travel series) 41-1764 rev.   F9. T95

TYLER, Leslie H., ed. An album of pictures of the New England hurricane and floods of September, 1938 ... New Haven, Conn., c. 1938.   (64) p. illus. 23½ x 31 cm. Illustrations: p. (3) - (64) 38-37908.   F9. T97

U.S. Army. Corps of Engineers. Supplemental report on hurricane of Sept. 21, 1938 and its effect on the coastal region. Providence, R.I., U.S. Engineer Office, 1939.   105 l. 26 plates, maps (part fold.) diagrs. 27 cm. 43-51889 rev.*   F9. U65

VACATIONS. New England ed. Consolidated tours. (Chester, Vt., National Survey)   v. illus., maps. 31 cm. 49-2085*.   F9. V3

VERRILL, Alpheus Hyatt. Along New England shores ... New York, G.P. Putnam's sons, 1936.   xxi, 298 p. front., plates. 21 cm. 36-15247.   F9. V47

WAITE, Otis Frederick Reed, ed. Guide book for the eastern coast of New England. Concord, E.C. Eastman & co.; Boston, Lee & Shepard; ... 1871.   iv, (5) - 220 p. 2 fold. maps. 17 cm. 1-7625 rev.   F9. W14

WALLING, Henry Francis. New-York to Boston via Long Island sound. Steamboats and connecting railroads, with descriptive sketches ... New-York, Taintor brothers & co., 1867.   79 p. fold. maps. 16 cm. 1-22204 rev.   F9. W19

WALLING, Henry Francis. New-York to the White Mountains via Long Island sound and Connecticut river ... N.Y., Taintor bros & co., 1867. 4, 5-45 p. maps (part fold.) 16 cm. 1-7605. F9 W 21

WALLING, Henry Francis. The shore line route. (Also numbered F9.T18) F9. W23

WALLING, Henry Francis. The Springfield route. From New-York to Boston. With descriptive sketches.... New-York, Taintor brothers & co,, 1867. 46 p. maps. 24°. 1-22203-M1. F9. W24

WARREN, David M. A special geography of the New England states; prepared for the New England editions of "Warren's common school geography, etc. Philadelphia, Cowperthwait & co., 1879. 34 p. incl. illus., maps. fol. 1-13324-M1. F9. W28

WEBB'S New England railway and manufacturers' statistical gazetteer; containing an interesting sketch of every station, village and city on each railroad in New England ... Pub. by Webb brothers & co. .. Providence, 1869. 28, (33) - 568 p. illus., plates. 31½ x 24 cm. 1-7626 rev. F9. W36

WHITE Mountain route souvenir ... Brattleboro, Vt., A. E. Atwood (c.1894) (4) p. 60 pl. obl. 24°. 1-7627-M1. F9. W58

WHITESIDE, Clara Walker. Touring New England on the trail of the Yankee ... Philadelphia, The Penn publishing company, 1926. xiv, 297 p. front., illus., plates. 24½ cm. 26-14664. F9. W62

WILSON, Rufus Rockwell. New England in letters ... New York, A. Wessels co., 1904. xi, 384 p. col. front., 5 col. pl. 19½ cm. 4-15558. F9. W75

WOMEN'S city club of Boston. ... Guide to New England. Where to shop and where to stop in Boston and along New England motor trails. ... (Boston) c.1929. v. illus. (incl. maps) 20 cm. 30-29370 rev.
F9. W87

WOOD, Florence Dorothy. New England country; the Northeastern States, ... Chicago, Childrens Press (1962) 93 p. illus. 24 cm. 62-9074. (Enchantment of America series) F9.3.W 6

CONNERY, Donald S. One American town. New York, Simon and Schuster (1972) 222 p. illus. 22 cm. 70-185770. F10. C 6

REGIONS, A - Z.

ALLIS, Marguerite. Connecticut river, ... New York, G. P. Putnam's sons (c.1939) xiii, 310 p. front., plates. 22 cm. Bibliography: p. 297-299. 39-27349. F12.C7 A5

BACON, Edwin Munroe. The Connecticut River and the valley of the Connecticut ... historical and descriptive. New York and London, G.P. Putnam's sons, 1906. xx p., 487 p. 25 cm. 6-27342. F12.C7 B2

BURT, Henry Martyn. Burt's illustrated guide of the Connecticut Valley ... Northampton, New England publishing company, 1867. vi, 7-281 p. front. (fold. map) illus., plates. 19½ cm. 7-32902. F12.C7 B9

CONNECTICUT River Watershed Council. The Connecticut River guide. Greenfield, Mass., 1966 82 p. 19 cm. F12.C7C6

HARD, Walter R. The Connecticut ... New York, Toronto, Rinehart & company, inc. (1947) x, 310 p. illus. (incl. map) 21 cm. Bibliography: p. 299 - 301 47-3553. F12.C7H3

LIFE along the Connecticut river; introduction by Charles Crane ... Brattleboro, Vt., Stephen Day press, 1939. 120 p. front., illus. (incl. map) 32 x 24 cm. 39-27348. F12.C7L5

ROBERTS, George Simon. Historic towns of the Connecticut River Valley ... Schenectady, N.Y., Robson & Adee (c.1906) vii, 494 p. front., illus. 25 cm. 6-24568. F12.C7R6

STEKL, William F. The Connecticut River. ... Middletown, Conn., Wesleyan University Press (1972) 142 p. illus. 72-3727. F12.C7S8

VERRILL, Alpheus Hyatt. The heart of old New England, ... New York, Dodd, Mead & co., 1936. xx, 208 p. front., illus. (map) plates, diagr. 21 cm. 36-9544. F12.C7V4

WHITTLESEY, Charles Wilcoxson. Crossing and re-crossing the Connecticut river; a description of the river from its mouth to its source, with a history of its ferries and bridges ... (New Haven, The Tuttle, Morehouse & Taylor co.) 1938. 7, 143 p. front., illus. 22½ cm. Bibliography: p. 143. 38-17447. F12.C7W4

WIGHT, Charles Albert. Some old time meeting houses of the Connecticut Valley, ... (Chicopee Falls, Mas., The Rich print, c.1911) 5, 144 p. front., plates, ports., etc. 23 cm. 11-8578. F12.C7W6

YOUNG, Hazel. Islands of New England; ... Boston, Little, Brown (1954) 214 p. illus. 22 cm. 54-5124. F12.I8Y6

ELEMENTS IN THE POPULATION.

NEW ENGLAND Catholic historical society. Publications. (no. 1-6) Boston, 1901-06. 6 v. in 2. illus. (incl. ports.) 24½ cm. 6-10617. F15.C2N5

NEW ENGLAND Catholic historical society, ... Report of. 1st - 1900 - 24 cm. 6-10618. F15.C2N5

WALSH, Louis S. The early Irish Catholic schools of Lowell, Massachusetts, 1835 - 1852. Boston, T.A.Whalen & co., 1901. 20 p. 24½ cm. (N.E.Catholic hist. soc. Pubs, no.2) 5-6253. F15.C2N5

COLLINS, Charles W. ... The Acadians of Madawaska, Maine. Boston, T.W.Whalen & co., 1902. 66 p. 24 cm. (N.E.Catholic hisc. soc. Pubs. no.3) 5-5542. F15.C2N5

GARGAN, Mrs. Helena Nordhoff. ... Pilgrim, Puritan and Papist in Massachusetts. Boston, T.A. Whalen & co., 1902. 33 p. 24 cm. (N.E.Catholic hist. soc. Pub.s no.4) 5-4364. F15.C2N5

CONNOLLY, Arthur Theodore. ... Fr. Sebastian Rasle. Boston, Mass., New England Catholic historical society, 1906. 29 p. 24½ cm. (N.E.Catholic hist. soc. Pubs. no.5) 7-21283 rev. F15.C2N5 no.5

MEMORIAL volume of the one hundredth anniversary celebration of the dedication of the Church of the Holy Cross, Boston. (Boston) The New England Catholic historical soceity, 1904. 137 p. illus. (incl. ports.) 24½ cm. (New England Catholic hist. soc. Publications, no. 6) 5-3186 rev. F15.C2N5 no.6

LOVE, William De Loss. The fast and thanksgiving days of New England. Boston and New York, Houghton, Mifflin and company, 1895. vii, 607 p. front. (facsim.) 2 fold. facsim. 21 cm. Calendar and bibliography: p. 464 - 598. 1-7628. F15.F3L8

FORGET, Ulysse. Les Franco-Américains et le "melting pot"; et, Onomastique franco-américaine. (Fall River? Mass., 1949) 52 p. 23 cm. 49-53610*. F15.F7F6

"...CHINESE of the eastern states, The." With the complements of the Société historique franco-américaine. Boston, Manchester, L'Avenir national publishing co., 1925. 23 p. 23½ cm. 27-3887. F15.F8C5

DUCHARME, Jacques. The shadows of the trees; the story of French-Canadians in New England. New York, London, Harper & brothers (1943) ix, 258 p. illus. (map) 21 cm. "First ed." "Bibliography of Franco-American literature": p. 245 - 258. 43-5264. F15.F8D8

GOULET, Alexandre. ... Une Nouvelle-France en Nouvelle-Angleterre; préface de Émile Lauvrière ... Paris, E. Duchemin, 1934. 3, iii, (5)-158 p. incl. tabs., map. 25 cm. Bibliography p. 153-8. 41-31899. F15.F8G68

GUIDE des adresses des Canadiens-francais de la Nouvelle-Angleterre ... Fall River, Mass., Fall

River publishing co., 1899.   432 p. pl. 23½ cm.   99-4072 Rev.   F15.F8G9

GUIDE français de la Nouvelle-Angleterre.   Et de l'état de New-York.   (1) -   éd.   Contenant les noms, le genre d'affaire et l'adresse des marchands, manufacturiers, etc., etc.   Lowell, Mass., La Société de publications françaises des États-Unis (1887 - 90)   2 v. illus. 22½ cm.   8-15352.
F15.F8G92

HAMON, E.   Les Canadiens-Français de la Nouvell-Angleterre,   Québec, N.S.Hardy, 1891.
2, (vii) - xv, 483 p. 23½ cm. 5-11019.   F15.F8H2

O'BRIEN, Michael Joseph.   Pioneer Irish in New England.   New York, P.J.Kenedy & sons (c.1937)
xiv, 15-325 p. 20½ cm. 38-796.   F15.I6 O3

BROCHES, Samuel.   Jews in New England.   New York, Bloch publishing co., 1942 -   1 v. facsim.
23 cm.   Bibliography: v.1 p. 67-8.   42-17528.   F15.J5 B7

HÜHNER, Leon.   The Jews of New England (other than Rhode Island) prior to 1800. . . .   (Baltimore, Lord Baltimore press, 1903)   (75) - 99 p. 24½ cm. From the Pubs. of the American Jewish historical soc., no. 11, 1903.
4-23277.   F15.J5H8

LAKE of Old and New England, The.   (Boston? S.E.Cassin? 1891?)   12 l. 12 pl. 16 x 31½ cm.   3-22597.
F15.L2L2

EGLESTON, Melville.   The land system of the New England colonies.   (New York, Evening post print, 1880)   47 p. 26½ cm. 3-30759.   F15.L3E3

CARVALHO, Eduardo de.   Os Portugueses na Nova Ingleterra.   Rio de Janeiro, "A Leitura Colonial" (1931)   xvi, 358 p. facsims. 19 cm. 74-280152.   F15.P8C3

TAFT, Donald Reed.   Two Portuguese communities in New England.   New York, 1923.   359 p. incl. front. (map) 23 cm. Bibliography: p. 351-357. 23-17612. 23-17483.   F15.P8T3 or P8T4

— New York, AMS Press, 1967.   357 p. illus. 23 cm. Bibliography: p. 351 - 357. 75-29903 MARC.   F15.P8T3
1967

— New York, Arno Press, 1969.   359 p. 22 cm. (The American immigration collection) 69-18792.   F15.P8T3
1969

ATHERTON, Charles Humphrey.   An address delivered at Concord before the New Hampshire historical society, ... 1831.   29 p. 8°. On the tenure and transmission of real estate. 1-26415-M2.   F15.R3A8

PERRY, Arthur Latham.   Scotch-Irish in New England.   Boston, 1891.   55 p. 23½ cm. 1-7629.
F15.S4P4

— 2d ed.   New York, C.Scribner's sons, 1896.   55 p. 23½ cm. Partial list of authorities": p. 55. 45-25692.
F15.S4P4
1896

NEW ENGLAND
SUPPLEMENTARY INDEX OF PLACES

BACCALAOS. 16
BOSTON. 10, 32, 34
CAMBRIDGE. 10
CAPE COD Towns. 10
CHARLESTOWN. 32
CONCORD. 10
CONNECTICUT. 29, 32, 41
CONNECTICUT River and Valley. 42, 43
CUTTY HUNK. 20
DEERFIELD. 10
DORCHESTER. 32
DROGEO. 16
ESSEX Co. 16
ESTOTILAND. 16
FALL RIVER. 40
FRANCONIA Mountains. 38, 40
GREENFIELD. 32
HANCOCK, N.H. 35
HARTFORD. 10, 32
LAKE WINNIPISCOGEE. 33
LITCHFIELD, Conn. 35
LITTLE COMPTON, R.I. 35
MADAWASKA, Me. 43
MAINE. 32, 34
MARKLAND. 16

MASSACHUSETTS. 29, 32, 41
MOUNT DESERT. 34
NEW HAMPSHIRE. 32
NEW HAVEN. 10, 32
NEWPORT. 10, 35, 40
NORTHAMPTON. 32
NORTH SPRINGFIELD. 32
NORUMBEGA. 16
OLD BENNINGTON, Vt. 35
OLD DEERFIELD, Mass. 35
OLD STURBRIDGE. 32
PLYMOUTH. 10
PORTLAND. 10, 35
PROVIDENCE. 10, 32
RHODE ISLAND. 29, 32, 41
RUTLAND, 10
SAGUENAY RIVER. 35
SALEM. 10
SPRINGFIELD 32
VERMONT. 32
VINLAND. 16
WHITE MTNS. 33, 34, 35, 36, 38, 40, 42
WISCASSET, Me. 35
WOONSOCKET. 32
WORCESTER. 32

MAINE

SELECTED BIBLIOGRAPHIES FOR MAINE

BANGOR, Me. Public Library. Bibliography of the State of Maine. Boston, G. K. Hall, 1962.
803 p. 37 cm. Contents: Author catalog. - Dictionary catalog. 73-155965 MARC.
Z1291. B 32

NOYES, Reginald Webb. A guide to the study of Maine local history ... (Ann Arbor? Mich.) 1936.
v numb. l., 87 numb. l., 2 l. 28 cm. Supplement to Drew B. Hall's Reference list on Maine local history. Mimeographed. 37-31911.
Z1291. N 93
L H & G

WILLIAMSON, Joseph. A bibliography of the state of Maine from the earliest period to 1891 ... In two volumes ... Portland, The Thurston print, 1896. 2 v. 23 ½ cm. "Comp. under the auspices of the Maine historical society." 4-11228.
Z1291. W 73

MOUNT KATAHDIN. A bibliography for Mt. Ktaadn(?), revised. Compiled by Edward S. C. Smith... (Boston, Houghton Mifflin Co. ?) 1924. 12 p. 24 cm. Reprinted from the Appalachia number of Bulletin of Appalachian mountain club, Dec., 1924. GS 25-190 Rev.
Z1292. K2 S58

PISCATAQUIS Co. A bibliography of Piscataquis County, Maine, comp. by John Francis Sprague. Dover, Observer pub. co., 1916. 31 - 43 p. 23 cm. Reprinted from the "Piscataquis County historical society, its by-laws and membership, etc., and a bibliography of Piscataquis County," 1916. 17-8903.
Z1292. P6 S7

MAINE CLASSIFICATION F16 - F30

16	Periodicals. Societies. Collections.
.5	Museums. Exhibitions, exhibits.
17	Gazetteers. Dictionaries. Geographic names.
.3	Guidebooks.
18	Biography (Collective). Genealogy (Collective).
.2	Historiography.
	Historians, see E 175.5.
18.5	Study and teaching.
19	General works. Histories.
.3	Juvenile works.
.5	Minor works. Pamphlets, addresses, essays, etc.
.6	Anecdotes, legends, pageants, etc.
20	Historic monuments (General). Illustrative material.
21	Antiquities (Non-Indian).
	By period.
22	Early to 1620.
	Attempts at colonization: Pemaquid, Me.; Popham Colony.
23	1620–1775.
	Lygonia Colony (Plough Patent); Trelawney Plantation; etc.
	Biography: Edward Godfrey, etc.
	Cf. E 83.72, War with eastern Indians, 1722–1726.
	F 27.K3, Kennebec Patent.
	F 27.M95, Muscongus or Waldo Patent.
	F 29.B9, Pejepscot Purchase.
	F 1036–1039, Acadia.
	F 1039.B7, Boundary between French and English possessions in Acadia.
24	1775–1865.
	Separation from Massachusetts and admission as a state, March 15, 1820.
	Biography: William King, etc.
	Cf. E 263.M4, Maine in the Revolution (General); E 230.5–241, Military operations and battles.
	E 398, International boundary troubles and the Aroostook War, 1839.
	E 511, Civil War, 1861–1865 (General).
25	1865–1950.
	Biography: Harris Merrill Pleisted, etc.
	Cf. D 570.85.M2–21, World War I, 1914–1918.
	D 769.85.M2–21, World War II, 1939–1945.
26	1951–
27	Regions, counties, etc., A–Z.
	Acadia National Park, see F 27.M9.
.A5	Androscoggin Co.
	Lake Androscoggin, etc.
.A53	Androscoggin River and Valley.

Regions, counties, etc., A–Z—Continued.

.A7 Aroostook Co.
> Aroostook River and Valley, (General, and Maine), etc.
> Cf. F 1044.A7, New Brunswick.

.B7 Boundaries.
> Cf. E 398, Northeastern boundary disputes, 1783–1845.
> F 42.B7, New Hampshire boundary.
> F 1039.B7, Ancient boundary of Acadia.

.C3 Casco Bay and islands (Collectively).
> Individual islands, see F 27.C9, Cumberland Co.

.C9 Cumberland Co.
> Orr's Island, Peak Island, Sebago Lake, etc.
> Saco Bay, see F 27.Y6.
> Saco River and Valley, see F 27.S15.

.D2 Dead River and Valley.
Dochet Island, see F 27.W3.

.F8 Franklin Co.

.H3 Hancock Co.
> Mount Desert Island, see F 27.M9.

Isles of Shoals, see F 42.I8.
Kennebago Lake, see F 27.R2.

.K2 Kennebec Co.
> Lake Cobbosseecontee, etc.

.K3 Kennebec Patent. Plymouth Company (1749–1816).
.K32 Kennebec River and Valley.
.K7 Knox Co.
> Matinicus Island, see F 27.M3.

.L7 Lincoln Co.
> Monhegan Island, see F 27.M7.

.M18 Magalloway Valley.
.M3 Matinicus Island.
.M7 Monhegan Island.
.M8 Moosehead Lake region.
.M9 Mount Desert Island.
> Acadia National Park (Sieur de Monts National Monument, Lafayette National Park), etc.
> Cf. F 1038, Jesuit station, 1609.

.M95 Muscongus or Waldo Patent.
> Including greater part of Waldo and Knox and a portion of Lincoln counties.

.O9 Oxford Co.
> Parmachenee Lake, etc.

.P3 Passamaquoddy Bay, Maine.
> Cf. F 1044.P3, New Brunswick.

Pejepscot Patent (Brunswick), see F 29.B9.
.P37 Penobscot Bay region.
.P38 Penobscot Co.
.P4 Penobscot River and Valley.
.P48 Piscataqua River and Valley, Maine.
> Cf. F 42.P4, General, and New Hampshire.

.P5 Piscataquis Co.
> Debsconeag Lake region, Mount Katahdin, Chesuncook Lake, etc.

.R2 Rangeley Lakes. Kennebago Lake.
Saco Bay, see F 27.Y6.
.S15 Saco River and Valley.
.S18 Sagadahoc Co.
St. Croix (Dochet) Island, see F 27.W3.
.S2 St. Croix River and Valley (General, and Maine).
> Cf. F 1044.S17, New Brunswick.

  .S25 St. George (George's) River.
  .S3 St. John River and Valley, Maine.
      Cf. F 1044.S2, General, and New Brunswick.
  .S7 Somerset Co.
  .W16 Waldo Co.
      Waldo Patent, *see* F 27.M95.
  .W3 Washington Co.
      Narraguagus Valley, St. Croix (Dochet) Island, etc.
  .Y6 York Co.
      Saco Bay, Boon Island, etc.
      Saco River and Valley, *see* F 27.S15.

29 Cities, towns, etc., A–Z.
  e. g. .A9 Augusta.
     .B2 Bangor.
     .B3 Bar Harbor.
     .B9 Brunswick.
        Pejepscot Purchase. Pejepscot Company (Brunswick Proprietors).
     .K3 Kennebunk.
     .P9 Portland.
     .Y6 York.

30 Elements in the population.
  .A1 General works.
  .A2–Z Individual elements.
      For a list of racial, ethnic, and religious elements (with cutter numbers), *see* E 184,

MAINE

F 16 - F 30

PERIODICALS. SOCIETIES. COLLECTIONS.

BAXTER, James Phinney, ed. The Trelawny papers, ed. and illus. with historical notes and an appendix. Portland, (Me.) Hoyt, Fogg and Donham, 1884.   xxxl. 520 p. illus., fold. maps (part col.) facsims. 26 cm.   Pub. also as v. 3 of the Me. Hist. Society's Documentary History of the State of Maine.   51-48868.   F16. B3

DOOLITTLE, Duane. Only in Maine; selections from Down East Magazine. Barre, Mass., Barre Publishers, 1969.   ix. 274 p.   24 cm.   70-86910.   F16. D58

DOWN East. (Camden, Me.)   v. in   illus. 28 cm.   F16. D6

GORGES Society, Portland, Me. (Publications (v. 1-5) Portland, Me., Printed for the Gorges society, 1884 - 93)   5 v. plates (partly fold.) ports. fold. maps. plans (partly fold.) facsims. (partly fold.) fold. geneal. tables.   22 x 18½ cm.   Contents. - I. Gardiner. H. New England's vinidcation. - II. Baxter. J.P. George Cleeve of Casco Bay. 1630 - 1667. III. - Rosier. J. Rosier's Relation of Waymouths voyage to the coast of Maine. 1605.   IV. Thayer. H.O. The Sagadahoc colony.   V. Baxter. J.P. Christopher Levett, of York. the pioneer colonist in Casco Bay.   1893.   5-39197.
            F16. G66
            Microfilm 15519 F

LEE, William Storrs. Maine; a literary chronicle ... New York, Funk & Wagnalls (1968) xv, 487 p. illus. 24 cm.   68-15601.   F16. L4

MAINE. State historian. Report of. 1907/8 Waterville, 1909.   1 v. 22½ cm. Henry S. Burrage. state historian. 9-16675.   F16. M12

MAINE annual, The. v. 1 -   Freeport, Me., Bond Wheelwright (1962 -   27 cm.   F16. M13

MAINE'S natural resources, A guide to, ... Frank Downie (et al)   Freeport, Me., Bond Wheelwright Co. (1962)   68 p. 27 cm. 62-20545. (The Maine annual. v. 1)   F16. M13
            vol. 1

CLIFFORD, Harold Burton. You and your job in Maine. Freeport, Me., Bond Wheelright Co. (c. 1964)   69 p. 24 cm. (The Maine annual. v. 2)   62-52530.   F16. M13
            vol. 2

MAINE facts. Rockland, Me., Courier-Gazette, inc.   v. illus.. maps. 22 cm.   F16. M137

MAINE genealogical society, Portland, Me. By-laws of the Maine genealogical society. Portland, Me. ... 1889. Portland, 1893.   29 p. 17½ cm. 10-11238.   F16. M14

45

MAINE genealogical society. Reports. 1897, 1904. Portland, Me., 1897 - 1905. 2 v. ports. 23½ - 24½ cm. Title varies. CA 6-1100 unrev'd. F16. M15

MAINE genealogist and biographer, The. A quarterly journal. Pub. under the direction of the Maine genealogical and biographical soc. Wm. Berry Lapham, ed. v. 1-3; Sept. 1875 - June, 1878. Augusta, Me. 3 v. ports. 24 cm. No more pub. 4-14754. F16. M155

MAINE historical and genealogical recorder, The. v. 1 - 9. 1884 - 98. Portland, Me., S. M. Watson (etc.) 1884 - 98. 9 v. port., facsim., tab. 23 cm. Quarterly, 1884 - 95; monthly, 1898. None pub. for 1890 - 92, 1894, 1896 - 97. S. M. Watons, ed. 3-6341. F16. M18

BANGOR historical magazine ... Joseph W. Porter, ed. and pub. v. 1 - 6; July 1885 - June, 1891. Bangor, 1885-91. 6 v. ports. 23½ cm. monthly. Continued as the Maine historical magazine. 1-8840. F16. M21

MAINE Historical Society. List of members. Portland. 19 cm. 55-26417. F16. M28

MAINE historical society. Act of incorporation, by-laws and list of members of the Maine historical soc. Portland, Me. (S. Berry) 1902. 21 p. 23½ cm. 7-23983. F16. M31

— 1927. 29 p. 23 cm. 27-15857. F16. M316

MAINE historical society, Centennial of the, April 11, 1922. Portland, 1922. 51 p. 23 cm. 29-27710. F16. M318

MAINE historical society, Collections of the. (1st ser.) v. 1-10; 2d ser., v. 1-10; 3d ser., v. 1 - Portland, The Society, 1831 - 19 - v. fronts. (part fold.) illus., ports., maps (part fold.) plans (part fold.) facsims. 22½ - 23½ cm. Indexes: in the 1st series only v. 9 and the 1865 reprint of v. 1 have individual indexes; v. 10 is a combined index for the series. Beginning with the 2d series each vol. has its own index, and there is no general index vol. 4-11128 (rev. '17) F16. M33

MAINE historical society. Proceedings ... Nov. 16, 1899 - Portland, 1902 - v. 23½ - 24½ cm. 6-29967 rev. F16. M34

MAINE historical society. Documentary history of the state of Maine ... Published by the Maine historical society, aided by appropriations from the state. Portland, 1869 - 1916. 24 v. plates, maps (part fold.) facsims. (part fold.) 23 - 25 cm. No more pub? Contents. - I. A history of the discovery of Maine, by J. G. Kohl. II. A discourse on western planting .. by R. Hakluyt. III. The Trelawny papers. IV - VI. The Baxter manuscripts. VII - VIII. The Farnham papers. ix - xxiv. The Baxter manuscripts. 6-7665 rev. F16. M38

MAINE historical society. An address delivered ... by William Willis ... at Augusta ... 1857; containing biographical notices of the former presidents of the society. Portland ... 1857. 2, 54 p. 22½ cm. 12-11177. F16. M39

NORTHWARD-HO! Covering Maine's inland resorts, Moosehead Lake, the Rangeleys, Belgrade lakes and Poland Spring. Lewiston, Me., 1908 - 1909. 2 v. illus. 25 cm. Weekly during the season. Ed: H. L. Jillson. CA 9-6524 unrev. F16. N87

PINE cone, The, a panorama of Maine. (Portland, State of Maine Publicity Bureau) v. illus., ports. 21 cm. quarterly. 57-43900. F16. P5

SOCIETY of the sons of the state of Maine, Illinois, Proceedings at the banquet of ... 1881. Chicago, 1881. 45 p. 25½ cm. 3-11069. F16. S69

SCAMMON, Jonathan Young. An address delivered before the Society of the sons of the state of Maine in Illinois ... 1882. Chicago, 1882. 39 p. 24½ cm. 15-5263. F16. S7

SPRAGUE'S journal of Maine history, vol 1 - April 1, 1913 - (Dover, 1913 - v. illus., plates, ports., facsim. 23 cm. 14-9185. F16. S76

MAINE 3

MUSEUMS. EXHIBITIONS, EXHIBITS.

U.S. Library of Congress.   Maine: the sesquicentennial of state-hood; an exhibition in the Library of Congress, Washington, D.C., Dec. 21, 1970 - Sept. 6, 1971.   Washington, 1970.   86 p. illus. 26 cm.   72-609482.   F16.5.U5

GAZETTEERS. DICTIONARIES. GEOGRAPHIC NAMES.

ATTWOOD, Stanley Bearce.   The length and breadth of Maine.   August, Me., Kennebec journal print shop (1946)   3 - 279 p. xxiv pl. (maps) on 12 l. 26½ cm. Key and bibliography"; p.6-8. 47-465.   F17. A8
L.H. & G.

BALLARD, Edward.   ... Geographical names on the coast of Maine ...   (Washington, 1871?)   19 p. 29½ cm. United States Coast survey. 8-17148.   F17. B3

CHADBOURNE, Ava Harriet.   Maine place names and the peopling of its towns.   Portland, Me., B. Wheelwright Co. (1955)   530 p. 23 cm. 55-11060.   F17. C45
L.H. & G.

ECKSTORM, Mrs. Fanny (Hardy)   Indian place-names of the Penobscot valley and the Maine coast. Orono, Me., 1941.   xxix, 272 p. 2 fold. maps. 23 cm. Bibliography: p.242 - 254. 41-46230.   F17. E2
G. & M.

HAYWARD, John.   A gazetteer of the United States, comprising a series of gazetteers of the several states and territories.   Maine.   Portland, Me., S.H. Colesworthy; Boston, B.B. Mussey ... 1843.   92 p. 1 illus. 24½ cm. 1-8841.   F17. H42

RUTHERFORD, Phillip R.   The dictionary of Maine place-names.   Freeport, Me., Bond Wheelwright Co. (c.1970)   xx, 283 p. 16 x 24 cm. 70-132915.   F17. R8

VARNEY, George Jones.   A gazetteer of the state of Maine.   Boston, B.B. Russell, 1881.   8, (7) - 611 p. incl. front., illus. 24 cm. 1-8842.   F17. V31
Geneal. Sect. Ref.

GUIDEBOOKS.

APPALACHIAN Mountain Club.   The A.M.C. Maine mountain guide.   1st - ed.; 1961 -   Boston.   v. fold. col. maps (part in pocket) 16 cm.   F17.3.A6

MAINE Leauge of Historical Societies and Museums.   Maine; a guide 'down east'.   Dorris A. Isaacson, ed.   2nd ed.   Rockland, Me., Courier-Gazette, 1970.   xxiv, 510 p. illus. 21 cm.
F17.3.M3
1970

WEBER, Carl Jefferson.   Maine, poets' corner of America.   2d ed., rev.   Augusta, Me., Dept. of Economic Development (n.d.)   22 p. 23 cm.   F17.3.W4
1900z

U.S. Bureau of the census.   ... Heads of families at the first census of the United States taken in the year 1790 ...   Washington, Govt. print. off., 1907 - 8.   12 v. fronts. (fold. maps) 29½ cm. 7-35273.   F17.5.U58

WHO's who at Bar Harbor, Northeast Harbor, Southwest Harbor, Seal Harbor, York Harbor, York Beach, Ogunquitt, Kennebunkport, Prout's Neck, Belgrade, Poland Spring.   Salem, Mass., The Salem press co., c.19 -   v. illus. 24 cm. 20-4765.
Directories

BACON, George Fox.   Northern Maine, its points of interest, and its representative business men, embracing Houlton, Presque Isle, Caribou, Ft. Fairfield, Danforth, Lincoln, Mattawamkeag, Winn and Kingman.   Newark, N.J., Glenwood pub. co., 1891.   87 p. illus. 26½ cm. 1-8862.   F17.7.B 13

BACON, George Fox.   Rockland, Belfast and vicinity: its representative business men and its points of interest, embracing Rockland, Belfast, Camden, Rockport, Bucksport, Ellsworth, Thomaston, Waldoboro', Warren. Damariscotta, Wiscasset, Newcastle.   Newark, N.J., Glenwood pub. co., 1892.   176 p. illus. 27 cm. 1-8864.   F17.7.B 14

BUSINESS and profession manual of the principal cities and towns in the state of Maine, including Portland, Lewiston, Bangor, Bath, Waterville, Skowhegan, Gardiner, Belfast, Biddeford, Saco, Westbrook, Auburn, Augusta, Camden, Old Town, Brewer, Randolph, Hallowell, Rockland ... 1st - ed. (1903 -   Boston, The Colonial advertising co., 1903.   v. 23½ cm. 3-9601.
Directories

MAINE state directory and gazetteer ... a complete list of the business of each city and town in the state ... 1893 -   Methuen, Mass (etc.) Union publishing co., 1893 - c. 19 -   v. 24½ cm.   0-3513 rev.   Directories

WILLIS, William.   A business directory of the subscribers to the new map of Maine ...   Portland, J. Chace, jr. & co. ... 1862.   344 p. 21½ cm. 16-8186 rev.
Directories

BIOGRAPHY (COLLECTIVE). GENEALOGY (COLLECTIVE).

BEEDY, Helen Coffin.   ... Mothers of Maine.   Portland, The Thurston print, 1895.   4, (11) - 451 p. 23½ cm. 4-20166.   F18. B41

BIOGRAPHICAL encyclopaedia of Maine of the nineteenth century.   Boston, Metropolitan publishing and engraving co., 1885.   6, (9) - 441 p. 50 port. 30 cm. Ed. Henry Clay Williams. 3-18903.   F18. B61

BIOGRAPHICAL sketches of representative citizens of the state of Maine ...   Boston, New England Historical publishing co., 1903.   452 p. ports. 29 x 22 cm. 9-17544.   F18. B63

BOWLER, Ernest C.   An album of the attorneys of Maine, with a portrait and brief record of the life of each.   Bethel, Me., News publishing co., 1902.   vii, 9-316 p. illus. (ports.) 26½ x 20½ cm. 12-40322. F18. B78

BRIEF biographies, Maine; a biographical dictionary of who's who in Maine, vol. I -   Lewiston, Me., Lewiston journal co. (1926 -   v. 20 cm. "Revised and re-issued biennially." 27-888.   F18. B83

BUXTON, Henry.   Assignment down east; with sixty photos by Wayne Buxton and endpapers drawn by Andrew Wyeth.   Brattleboro, Vt., Stephen Daye press (c. 1938)   294 p. plates, ports., facsim. 22½ cm. 38-13378.   F18. B89

CHASE, Henry, ed.   Representative men of Maine.   A collection of portraits with biographical sketches ...   Portland, Me., The Lakeside press, 1893.   250, liii, (3) p. incl. ports. 28½ cm. 3-18902. F18. C48

GRIFFITH, Frank Carlos, comp.   Maine's hall of fame; Griffith's list of men and women born in Maine who have risen to distinction ...   (South Poland? Me.) c. 1905.   12 p. 28 cm. 5-26770.   F18. G85

KENISTON, Frank W.   Biographies of Dover-Foxcroft.   (Bangor? Me.) 1948.   154 p. port. 23 cm. 49-3578 *   F18. K45

KENISTON, Frank W.   Biographies of Guildford, Sangerville, Abbot, and Parkman, Maine.   (Auburn, Me., Merrill & Webber co.) 1942.   109 p. incl. port. 23 cm. 43-7270.   F18. K46

KING, Marquis Fayette, comp.   Changes in names by special acts of the Legislature of Maine, 1820 - 1895.   (Portland? Me., Priv. print.) 1901.   3 p. (3) - 67 p. 23 cm. 4-2413.   F18. K53
L. H. & G.

MAINE

LIBBY, Charles Thornton.   Genealogical dictionary of Maine & New Hampshire.   1928 - 1939.
29 - 12014.   F18. L69

LITTLE, George Thomas, ed. et al.   Genealogical and family history of the state of Maine;   New York, Lewis historical pub. co., 1909.   4 v. fronts., illus., plates, ports. 27½ cm. 9-22211.   F18. L77

MAINE writers research club.   Just Maine folks ...   (Lewiston, Me., The Journal printshop, c.1924)
6, (17) - 331 p. front., illus., ports. 19½ cm. 25-3560.   F18. M23

McINTYRE, Philip W.   Men of progress of Maine.   (pt. 1) Boston, 1896.   28 cm.   F18. M53

MEN of progress;   biographical sketches and portraits of leaders in business and professional life in and of the state of Maine;   comp. under the supervision of Richard Herndon ...   Boston, New England magazine, 1897.   2, 626 p. illus. (ports.) 29 cm. 18-16820.   F18. M54

NOYES, Sybil, et al, comp.   Genealogical dictionary of Maine and New Hampshire.   Portland, Me., The Southworth-Anthoensen press, 1928 - 1939.   7, 795 p. 24 cm. 29-12014 rev.   F18. N68
                                                                                                                   L. H. & G.

— Baltimore, Genealogical Pub. Co., 1972.   795 p. 23 cm. Reprint of 1928-39 ed. 79-88099 MARC.   F18. N68
                                                                                                                   1972

OWEN, Howard.   Biographical sketches of the members of the Senate and House of representatives of Maine ...   August? 1897 -   5 v. 25½ cm. 3-2231 rev.   F18. O97

POPE, Charles Henry.   The pioneers of Maine and New Hampshire, 1623 to 1660; a descriptive list, drawn from records of the colonies, towns, churches, courts and other contemporary sources. ... Boston, C. H. Pope, 1908.   xi, 252 p. 24½ cm. "Authorities quoted": p. vii-ix. 8-19566.   F18. P82
                                                                                                                   1908

— Baltimore, Genealogical Pub. Co., 1965.   xi, 252 p. 23 cm. 65-22477.   F18. P82
                                                                                                                   1965

PROMINENT men of Maine;   individual biographic studies with character portraits.   New York, Historical records, inc., c.1940.   1 v. front. (port.) 20 cm. 1 41-14289.   F18. P87

RIDLON, Gideon Tibbetts.   Saco Valley settlements and families.   Historical, biographical, genealogical, traditional ...   Portland, Me., 1895.   xiv, 1250 p. front., plates, ports., fold. plan. 24 cm. 1-8917.   F18.
                                                                                                                   F27. S3R5

SARGENT, William Mitchell.   Maine wills.   1640 - 1760.   Portland (Me.) Brown, Thurston & co., 1887.   xii, 953 p. 23½ cm. ... Maine historical society. 4-14749.   F18. S24

— Baltimore, Genealogical Pub. Co., 1972.   72-5681.   F18. S24
                                                                                                                   1972

STAPLES, Arthur Gray.   The inner man; or, Some contemporary portraits of prominent men of Maine ...   (Lewiston, Me., Lewiston journal co.) 1923.   6, (3) - 248 p. 25 cm. 24-447.
                                                                                                                   F18. S73

SPENCER, Wilbur Daniel.   Maine immortals, including many unique characters in early Maine history.   August, Me. (Northeastern press) 1932.   viii, (2) 316 p. 21 cm. 32-21635.   F18. S86

WILLIS, William.,   A history of the law, the courts, and the lawyers of Maine ...   Portland, Bailey & Noyes, 1863.   2, iv, (v)-viii, (9)-712 p. ports. 22 cm. 6-9315.   F18. W73

YORK CO., Me. Register of deeds.   York deeds.   (1642 -   Portland, J. T. Hull (etc.) 1887 - 1896. (Bethel, Me.) 1903 -   v. 23 cm. Vol. 1 - 11 under direction of the Maine historical soc; v. 12 - 16 under direction of the Maine genealogical society. v.17 pub. for the state by E. C. Bowler. 1-8919.   F18 W 62

GENERAL WORKS. HISTORIES.

ABBOTT, John Stevens Cabot.   The history of Maine, from the earliest discovery of the region by the Northmen until the present time; ...   Boston, B. B. Russell; Portland, J. Russell, 1875.
556 p. incl. illus., tables.   front. (port.)   23½ cm.   1-8843.   F19. A13

— rev. ... and five chapters of new matter added by Edward H. Elwell.   2d ed.   Portland, Brown Thurston co., 1892.   608 p. front. (port.) illus., plates.   24 cm.   First edition 1875.   1-8844.   F19. A14

BANKS, Ronald F.   A history of Maine. ... 1600 - 1970.   Dubuque, Iowa, Kendall/Hunt Pub. Co. (1969)   vii, 375 p. illus.   F19. B3

BEAM, Lura.   A Maine hamlet.   New York, W. Funk (1957)   236 p. 22 cm. 57-10556.   F19. B4

BESTON, Henry.   White pine and blue water, a State of Maine reader.   (New York) Farrar, Straus (1950)   xxii, 410 p. 23 cm. 50-8431.   F19. B47

BOOK for the children of Maine, for the use of families and schools.   Portland, S. Colman, 1831.
118 p. illus. 20 cm. 3-32081.   F19. B72
Rare book coll.

BRACE, Gerald Warner.   Between wind and water.   (1st ed.)   New York, W. W. Norton (c. 1966)
219 p. 22 cm. 66-12794.   F19. B77

CHADBOURNE, Ava Harriet, comp.   Readings in the history of education in Maine ...   Bangor, Me., Burr press, 1932.   104 p. 27½ cm.   Includes bibliographies.   32-4490.   F19. C42

CHAMBERLAIN, Joshua Lawrence.   Maine: her place in history.   Address delivered at the Centennial exhibition ... 1876 ...   Augusta, Sprague, Owen & Nash, 1877.   v, 129 pp. fold. map. 8vo. 1-8845-M1
F19. C44

— 1877.   2, (3) - 108 p. maps (part fold.) fold. chart. 24 cm. 1-8846.   F19. C45

CLIFFORD, Harold Burton.   Maine and her people.   Freeport, Me., Bond Wheelwright Co. (c. 1957)
330 p. illus. 24 cm. 57-14930.   F19. C55
1957

— (1958)   327 p. illus. 24 cm. Includes bibliography. 58-6497.   F19. C55
1958

— (1963)   iv, 346 p. 24 cm.   F19. C55
1963

COE, Harrie Badger.   Maine, resources, attractions, and its people; a history.   New York, The Lewis pub. co. inc., 1928.   4 v. plates, ports., maps. 27½ cm.   Vols. 3-4 contain biographies.   29-7213.   F19. C67

COOLIDGE, Austin Jacobs.   History and description of New England. Maine.   Boston, A. J. Coolidge, 1860.   iv, 406 p. front., illus., plates, fold. map. 24½ cm. 1-8847.   F19. C77
1860

DOLE, Nathan Haskell.   Maine of the sea and pines; a description of its scenic beauty ...   Boston, L. C. Page & co., (c. 1928)   x, 375 p. col. front., plates, fold. maps. 24½ cm. Bibliog. p. 348-354. 28-15182.   F19. D66

DUNNACK, Henry Ernest.   The Maine book.   August, Me., 1920.   xiii, 338 p. front., illus., col. pl., ports. 26 cm. "Author bibliography": p. 322 - 323: "Books on Maine": p. 324 - 326.   F19. D9

ELKINS, L. Whitney.   The story of Maine;   coastal Maine ...   Bangor, Me., The Hillsborough co., (c. 1924)   392 p. illus., pl. 24 cm. 24-17801.   F19. E5

FARRINGTON, Inez.   My Maine folks.   Portland, Me., B. Wheelwright Co. (1956)   96 p. 22 cm.
56-58224.   F19. F3

MAINE

GREENLEAF, Jonathan.   Sketches of the ecclesiastical history of the state of Maine ...   Portsmouth, (N.H.) H. Gray, 1821.   vi, (7) - 293, 77, (1) p.   17 ½ cm.   6-13606.   F19. G79

GREENLEAF, Moses.   A survey of the state of Maine ...   Portland, Shirley and Hyde, 1829.
viii, (9) - 468 p. incl. tables.   22 cm.   And atlas of 5 fold. maps, 2 fold. diagr.   33 ½ cm.   2-2210 rev.   F19. G81 1829

— Augusta, Maine State Museum (1970)   468 p.   "Reprint of the text of 1829 which was based on the Rutherford's A statistical view of the district of Maine, first pub. in 1816."   71-128108.   F19. G81 1970

HANDFUL of spice; a miscellany of Maine literature and history.   Ed. by Richard S. Sprague.
Orono, University of Maine Press, 1968.   v, 205 p.   illus.   F19. H34

HATCH, Louis Clinton, ed.   Maine; a history. ...   New York, The American historical society, 1919.   5 v.   fronts., plates, ports.   28 cm.   Part of v. 3 and v. (4-5) contain biographical material.   19-15873 rev. 2   F19. H36

HEBERT, Richard A.   Modern Maine; its historic background, people, and resources.   New York, Lewis Historical Pub. Co. (1951)   4 v.   illus., ports.   28 cm.   Includes bibliographies.   51-8085.   F19. H4

JONES, Herbert Granville.   I discover Maine; little-known stories about a well-known state. ...
Portland, The Machigonne press, 1937.   vii, 99 p. incl. mounted front., illus.   23 ½ cm.   38-21313 rev.   F19. J66

JONES, Herbert Granville.   The King's Highway from Portland to Kittery; stage-coach and tavern days on the old post road. ...   Portland, Me., Longfellow Press (1953)   226 p.   illus.   23 cm.   53-13415.
F19. J665

JONES, Herbert Granville.   Maine memories; little-known stories about a well-known state ...
Portland, Me., Harmon publishing co., 1940.   223 p.   illus., pl.   24 cm.   41-4387 rev.   F19. J67

KALER, James Otis.   Geography of Maine.   (Portland, The Eagle press, c. 1910)   23 p.   18 cm.
10-20282.   F19. K14

MAINE.   State library, Augusta.   Maine forts.   By Henry E. Dunnack ...   Augusta, Me., Charles E. Nash & son, 1924.   252 p. incl. front., illus., pl., ports., plans, charts.   24 cm.   24-27275.   F19. M25

MARBLE, Albert Prescott.   Maine: its geography and history. ...   Repr. from the Proceedings of the Worcester soc. of antiquity for 1883.   Worcester, 1884.   22 p.   23 ½ cm.   2-8477 rev.   F19. M31

MILLS, Hiram Francis.   Natural resources and their development. ...   Maine ...   Augusta, Stevens & Sayward, 1867.   23 p.   fold. map.   22 ½ cm.   1-8872.   F19. M65

MOULTON, Augustus Freedom.   Maine historical sketches.   (Lewiston, Me.) Printed for the state, 1929.   6, 293 p.   front., plates, port.   23 ½ cm.   30-12592.   F19. M92

RICH, Louise (Dickinson)   The coast of Maine, an informal history.   New York, Crowell (1956)
308 p.   illus.   21 cm.   56-6326.   F19.   R5 1956

— (1962)   340 p.   21 cm.   62-12804.   F19.   R5 1962

— (1970)   xiv, 385 p.   illus.   74-120995.   F19.   R5 1970

RICH, Louise (Dickinson)   State of Maine.   (1st ed.)   New York, Harper & Row, c. 1964)
xvi, 302 p.   22 cm.   64-12679.   F19.   R52

ROBERT, Kenneth Lewis.   Trending into Maine ... illustrations by N. C. Wyeth.   Boston, Little, Brown and co., 1938.   10, 3-394 p.   col. front., col. plates.   25 cm.   First ed.   38-11226.   F19.   R63
Rare Book Coll.

— Garden City, N.Y., Doubleday, Doran & co. inc., 1944   9, 3-421 p. col. front., col. plates. 22 cm.
Revised edition. 44-5282.
 F19. R63
 1944

— Reprinted Nov. 1938.   9, 3-394 p. col. front., col. plates. 22½ cm. 40-24864.
 F19. R634

SIMPSON, Dorothy. The Maine Islands, in story and legend ... (1st ed.) Philadelphia, Lippincott (1960)   256 p. 22 cm. 60-7852.
 F19. S5

SPRAGUE, John Francis. Maine one hundred years, 1820 - 1920 ... Dover, Me., 1920.
2, (3) - 88 p. illus. (incl. ports.) 23½ cm. 24-6089.
 F19. S76

STARKEY, Glenn Wendell. Maine, its history, resources and government. Boston, New York (etc.) Silver, Burdett & co. (c. 1920)   x, 249, xii p. illus. (incl. map) 20 cm. 20-16083.
 F19. S79

— (c. 1930)   x, 249, xii p. illus. (incl. map) 20 cm. 30-30334.
 F19. S79
 1930

— (c. 1938)   x, 249, xii p. illus. (incl. map) 20 cm. 38-21116.
 F19. S79
 1938

— (1947)   x, 203, xiii p. illus. (incl. map) 20 cm. 47-649.
 F19. S79
 1947

STORMS, Roger C. A history of three corners. Lee, Me., Lee Academy, 1971.   168 l. 28 cm.
 F19. S82

VARNEY, George Jones. A brief history of Maine. Portland, Me., McLellan, Mosher & co., 1888.
336 pp. front., illus., pl. 21 cm. 2-1309-M2.
 F19. V29

VARNEY, George Jones. The young people's history of Maine ... Portland, Me., Dresser, McLellan & co., 1873.   xviii, (13) - 258 p. incl. front., illus. 20 cm. 1-8848.
 F19. V31

VERRILL, Alpheus Hyatt. Romantic and historic Maine. New York, Dodd, Mead & co., 1933.
xx p., 277 p. front., illus. (incl. map) plates, ports. 21 cm. 33-5294.
 F19. V47

WHIPPLE, Joseph. The history of Acadie, Penobscot Bay and River, with a more particular geographical view of the district of Maine than has ever before been published. ... Bangor, 1816.
102 p. 22 cm. "A portion of this work originally appeared in the Bangor register." Pub. also at Bangor, 1816, under title: A geographical view of the district of Maine ... including the history of Acadie, etc. 17-1853.
 F19. W57

WILLIAMSON, William Durkee. The history of the state of Maine ... Hallowell, Glazier, Masters & co., 1832.   2 v. 23½ cm. 1-8849.
 F19. W72

— (Freeport, Me., Cumberland Press, 1966?)   2 v. 22 cm. Facsimile of 1832 ed. 66-22134.
 F19. W722
 G & M

— ... A new impression ... Hallowell, Glazier, Masters & Smith, 1839.   2 v. fronts. (v. 1 port.) 23 cm.
26-2506.
 F19. W73

JUVENILE WORKS.

BAILEY, Bernadine (Freeman) Picture book of Maine. Rev. ed. Chicago, A. Whitman, 1963.
c. 1957.   32 p. 17 x 21 cm.
 F19.3. B3
 1963

CARPENTER, John Allan. Maine. (Chicago) Childrens Press (c. 1966) 95 p. 24 cm. AC 66 - 10303.
 F19.3. C3

MAINE 9

FREEMAN, Melville Chase. The story of Maine for young readers... Freeport, Me., Wheelwright Co. (1962) 92 p. illus. 28 cm. 62-20544.   F19.3.F7

MINOR WORKS. PAMPHLETS, ADDRESSES, ESSAYS, ETC.

MAINE. Dept. of Economic Development. Facts about Maine; the offer of the Pine Tree state. Augusta, Maine, 1968. 79 p. illus. 15 cm.   F19.5.A5

HISTORIC MONUMENTS (GENERAL). ILLUSTRATIVE MATERIAL.

ABBOTT, Berenice. A portrait of Maine. Text by Chenoweth Hall. New York, Macmillan (1968) 170 p. illus. 29 cm. 68-27801.   F20. A2 1968

BOWDOIN College Museum of Art. As Maine goes; photographs by John McKee (exhibition) 1 v. (unpaged) 29 cm.   F20. B6

COFFIN, Robert Peter Tristram. Coast calendar. ... Indianapolis, Bobbs-Merrill Co. (1949) 1 v. (unpaged) illus. 33 cm. 49-10036*   F20. C64

FARNHAM, Mary Frances. Documents relating to the territorial history of Maine, 1603 - 1871. Portland, 1900 - (01?) 2 v. 24½ cm.   F20. F23

HINSDALE, Guy. The climate of Maine. New York, 1902? 20 cm.   F20. H63

KNOWLES, Katharine. Along the Maine coast. Photos by Katharine Knowles. Text by Thea Wheelwright. (Barre, Mass., Barre Publishers c. 1967) 129 p. 27 cm. 67-14592.   F20. K57

McKENNEY, Lewis Timothy. Memories of Maine... Illus. by L. Clayton McKenney... Boston, Meador pub. co., 1934. 210 p. incl. front., illus. 20½ cm. 34-18513.   F20. M165

MAINE federation of women's clubs. Maine in history and romance... Lewiston, Me., Lewiston journal co., 1915. 6, 242 p. front., plates, ports. 24½ cm. A16-1335.   F20. M2

MAINE federation of women's clubs. The trail of the Maine pioneer. Lewiston, Me., Lewiston journal co., 1916. 6, 340 p., front., illus., plates, ports., facsims. 24½ cm. A17-444.   F20. M22

MAINE historical memorials... (August?) Printed for the state, 1922. xi, 199 p. plates, ports. 23½ cm. 23-27027.   F20. M24

MAINE writers research club. Historic churches and homes of Maine; with photgraphic illus. Portland, Me., Falmouth book house, 1937. x, 289 p. incl. plates. 23 cm. 38-2646.   F20. M275

MAINE writers research club. Maine, my state... (Lewiston, Me., The Journal printshop, c. 1919) 1, 7-350 p. front., illus. (incl. ports.) 20 cm. "Good books on early Maine history": p. 345-346. 19-16306.   F20. M28

MARRINER, Ernest Cummings. Remembered Maine. Waterville, Me., Colby College Press, 1957. 149 p. 24 cm. 58-98.   F20. M32

MITCHELL, Edwin Valentine. It's an old State of Maine custom. New York, Vanguard Press (1949) 248 p. illus. 22 cm. 49-9766.   F20. M58 1949

MOORE, Jim. Maine coastal portrait, by three Maine photographers... Rockland, Me., Seth Low Press (1959) 110 p. illus. 32 cm. 59-4287.   F20. M62

NASON, Mrs. Emma (Huntington) Old colonial houses in Maine built prior to 1776. August, Me. (Kennebec journal) 1908. x, 106 p. incl. front. 22 pl. 24½ cm. 8-15274.   F20. N26

NOBLE, Ruth Verrill. Maine profile, with photos from the first three years of the Maine calendar.

Cambridge, Mass., Berkshire Pub. Co. (1954)　96 p. illus. 22 cm. Includes bibliography. 54-14824.　F20. N6

ROBERTS, Kenneth Lewis. Don't say that about Maine! Waterville, Colby College Press, 1951 (c. 1948)　31 p. front. 19 cm. "Reprinted from Sat. evening post for Nov. 6, 1948." 52-2874.　F20. R6

SWETT, Sophia Miriam. Stories of Maine. New York, Cincinnati (etc.) American book co. (c.1899)　278 p. front. (map) illus. 19 cm. 99-5752 rev.　F20. S97

TANNER, Virginia. A pageant of the state of Maine in celebration of the official dedication of the Carlton bridge, Bath, Maine ... acted ... by citizens of Bath, Brunswick, Woolwich and Wiscasset .. 1928. (August, Me., c.1928)　136 p. illus. (incl. plans) 24 cm. 30-10455.　F20. T16

WARNER, Maurice J. Civil War memorials erected in the State of Maine. (Augusta) Maine Civil War Centennial Commission, 1965.　79 p. 24 cm. 67-63055.　F20. W3

WILLARD, Benjamin J. Captain Ben's book. A record of the things which happened to Capt. Benjamin J. Willard, pilot and stevedore ... Portland, Me., Lakeside press, 1895.　204 p. incl. front. (port.) illus. pl. 23½ cm. Maritime life on the Maine coast and in Portland. 14-11460.　F20. W69

ANTIQUITIES.

MOOREHEAD, Warren King. ... A report on the archaeology of Maine ... explorations, 1912 - 1920 together with work at Lake Champlain, 1917. Andover, Mass., The Andover press, 1922.　272 p. illus., maps (part fold.) diagrs. (part fold.) 25 cm. "Selected bibliography": p. (265) - 268. 22-11367.　F21. M8

SMITH, Walter Brown. ... Indian remains of the Penobscot Valley ... Orono, Me., University press, 1926.　90 p. illus. plates. 23 cm. 27-27014.　F21. S65

SMITH, Walter Brown. ... The Jones cove shell-heap at West Gouldsboro, Maine. Bar Harbor (Sherman pub. co.) 1929.　28 p. plates. 23½ cm. (Lafayette national park musuem. Bulletin I)　F21. S66

EARLY TO 1620.

BALLARD, Edward, ed. Memorial vol. of the Popham celebration ... 1862: commemorative of the planting of the Popham colony ... 1607. Portland (Me.) Bailey & Noyes, 1863.　xiv, (9) - 369 p. fold. maps. 23 cm. 1-7928.　F22. B18

POOR, John Alfred. English colonization in America. A vindication of the claims of Sir Ferdinando Gorges, as the father of English colonization in America. New York, D. Appleton & co., 1862.　144 p. 23 cm. (With Ballard - Memorial volume of the Popham celebration ...) 1-7929.　F22. B18

BOURNE, Edward Emerson. Address on the character of the colony found by George Popham ... 1607. Portland, B. Thurston, 1864.　60 p. 23 cm. 1-8850.　F22. B77

BROWN, Lenard E. Significance of St. Sauveur Mission, estab. 1613, Mount Desert Island. Washington, Office of History and Historic Architecture ... 1970.　iv, 57 l. 8 plates (incl. maps) 27 cm. 71-612223.　F22. B85

CARTLAND, John Henry. Ancient pavings of Pemaquid. (Pemaquid Beach, Me., J. H. Cartland) 1899.　11 p. pl. 23 cm. 99-4380 rev.　F22. C32

CARTLAND, John Henry. Ten years at Pemaquid; sketches of its history and its ruins. Pemaquid, Me., 1899.　vi, 196 p. plates, plan. 24 cm. 99-4729 rev.　F22. C33

CARTLAND, John Henry. Twenty years at Pemaquid; sketches of its history and its remains ... Pemaquid Beach, Me., 1914.　224 p. plates, ports., map, fold. plan. 21½ cm. 15-25851.　F22. C34

DAVIES, James. A relation of a voyage to Sagadahoc; now first printed from the original manuscript in the Lambeth palace library; ed. ... Rev. B. F. De Costa. Cambridge (Mass.) J. Wilson and son, University press, 1880. 43 p. front. (facsim.) illus. 26 cm. 1-8851. F22. D25

DECOSTA, Benjamin Franklin. The voyage of Pierre Angibaut, known as Champdoré, ... to the coast of Maine, 1608. Albany, J. Munsell's sons; (Boston, D. Clapp & son, printers) 1891. 7 p. 25 cm. Repr. from N.E. hist. and geneal. register, April, 1891. 3-31314. F22. D29

HAVEN, Samuel Foster. Remarks on the Popham celebration of the Maine historical society. Boston, Press of J. Wilson and son, 1865. 32 p. 23½ cm. 1-8852. F22. H38

HILL, Winfield Scott. The site of Fort Saint George, erected by Captain George Popham, in 1607. Reprinted from the Kennebec journal. (August, Me., 1891?) 4 p. 23½ cm. 4-25034. F22. H65

HOUGH, Franklin Benjamin. Pemaquid in its relations to our colonial history ... (Bath? Me., 1876) cover-title, 36 p. 23½ cm. Also in Collections of the Maine historical soc., v.7. 16-2315. F22. H84

KALER, James Otis. ... The story of Pemaquid. New York, T. Y. Crowell & co. (1902) 181 p. pl., map, plan. 18½ cm. 2-7322. F22. K14

KOHL, Johann Georg. ... A history of the discovery of Maine. With an appendix on the voyages of the Cabots, by M. d'Avezac ... Portland, Bailey and Noyes, 1869. 2 p. viii p, 9 - 535 p. 22 maps (partly fold.) 23 cm. (Maine hist. soc. Documentary history of the state of Maine, v.1) 3-8373. F22. K79

LAPHAM, William Berry, comp. Popham beach as a summer resort, with a sketch of Popham colony and the ancient province of Sabino ... Augusta (Me.) Maine farmer job print, 1888. 15 p. illus. 8°. 1-8853 - M1. F22. L31

MAINE historical society. Tercentenary of the landing of the Popham colony at the mouth of the Kennebec River. Aug. 29, 1907. Portland, Maine historical society, 1907. 3, 58 p. 2 pl. (incl. front.) port., plan. 24 cm. 8-9835. F22. M22

MEMORIAL, humbly shewing the past and present state of the land lying waste and un-inhabited between Nova-Scotia, and the province of Main in New-England ... (London? 1721) (Boston, 1941) 2 p. 37 cm. (Photostate Americana. 2nd series. Photostated at the Mass. hist. soc. No. 130) 43-14225. F22. M4 1721 a Rare book coll.

PINFOLD, Charles. Doctor Pinfold's state of the case of the petitioner's, for settling His Majesties waste land, lying between Nova Scotia, and the province of Main in New-England ... (London? 1721) (Boston, 1941) 1, (3) p. 37 cm. (Photostat Americana. 2d series. Photostated at the Mass. historical society. No. 130) 43-14224. F22. M4 1721a Rare book coll.

ABSTRACT of the scheme of government so far as it related to the grantees in trust, for settling the land lying between Nova-Scotia and the province of Maine in New England ... (London? 1721) (Boston, 1941) (4) p. 37 cm. (Photostat Americana. Second series ... Photostated at the Mass. Hist. soc. No. 130) 43-14009. F22. 1721a Rare book coll.

PATTERSON, James Willis. Responsibilities of the founders of republics: an address on the peninsula of Sabino ... Boston, J. K. Wiggin, 1865. 38 p. 22½ cm. 1-8854. F22. P31

PEMAQUID monument association. Wiscasset, Me. By-laws and charter of the Pemaquid monument association. Wiscasset, 1888. 8 p. 16 cm. 8-17733. F22. P39

POOR, John Alfred. The first colonization of New-England. An address ... commemorative of the planting of the Popham colony ... New York, A. D. F. Randolph, 1863. iv, 58 p. map. 1-15961. F22. P82

POPHAM colony; a discussion of its historical claims, with a bibliography of the subject.   Boston, J.K. Wiggin and Lunt, 1866.   72 p. 25½ cm.   Bibliography p. (65) - 72.   7-16679.   F22. P83

ROSIER, James.   Rosier's Relation of Waymouth's voyage to the coast of Maine, 1605, with an introduction and notes.   By Henry S. Burrage.   Portland Me., Printed for the Gorges society, 1887. xi, 176 p. front., pl., port., 2 fold. maps. 22 x 18½ cm. (The Gorges soc.) (Publications III) 3-42.   F22. R81

SEWALL, Rufus King.   Pemaquid, its genesis, discovery, name and colonial relations to New England. n.p.   Printed by the Lincoln County historical soc., 1896.   21 p. 23 cm.   1-15795.   F22. S51

SEWALL, Rufus King.   Ancient voyages to the Western continent; three phases of history on the coast of Maine.   N.Y., Knickerbocker press (1895)   ix, 79 p. front., illus., plates, fold. map. 18½ cm. 1-8858.   New York, The   F22. S52

SHORT sketch of ancient Pemaquid, Maine.   (n.p., 1914?)   3 p. illus. 21 cm.   F22. S56

SYLVESTER, Herbert Milton.   ... Ye romance of olde Pemaquid.   Boston, Stanhope press, 1908. 431 p. incl. illus., plates, plan. front. 24½ cm. 8-8548.   F22. S98

THAYER, Henry Otis.   The Sagadohoc colony, comprising The relation of a voyage into New England; Portland, Me., Printed for the Gorges society, 1892.   xi, 276 p. front. (port.) 4 pl. 2 maps, fold. plan, facsim. 22 x 19 cm. (Gorges Soc. Publication V.)   "The literature": p. (87) - 156. "The Popham family": p. 240 - 255. 3-493.   F22. T37
Microfilm 15019 F

— New York, Research Reprints (1970)   xi, 276 p. illus. 21 cm. 76-124800.   F22. T37
1970

— (New York) B. Blom (1971)   xi, 269 p. illus. 21 cm. Bibliography: p. (87) - 156. 76-173865 MARC.   F22. T37
1971

THORNTON, John Wingate.   Colonial schemes of Popham and Gorges.   Boston, 1863.   20 p. 26½ cm. 1-8855.   F22. T51

1620 - 1775.

CHURCH, Benjamin.   The history of the eastern expeditions of 1680, 1690, 1692, 1696 and 1704 against the Indians and French.   Boston, J.K. Wiggin and W.P. Lunt, 1867.   xxxii, 203 p. front. (fold. map) 21½ x 16½ cm. 1-7545.   F23
F1. L69

GYLES, John.   Memoirs of odd adventures, strange deliverances, etc. ... in the district of Maine. Cincinnati, Spiller & Gates, printers, 1869.   v, (7) - 64 p. 24 cm. 10-32510.   F23
E87. G99

SANBORN, Victor Channing.   Stephen Bachiler and the Plough company of 1630.   Exeter (Mass.) 1903.   15, 23½ cm.   Reprinted from the Genealogist,   Apr., 1903. 37-7901.   F23
F67. B125

SMITH, Francis Ormond Jonathan.   Mr. Smith's review of the "Letter of Leonard Jarvis to his constituents of the Hancock and Washington district, in Maine."   (n.p., 1835)   15 p. 17 cm. 11-23170.
F23
E340. J3J31

BAXTER, James Phinney, ed.   ... The Baxter manuscripts ... Published by the Maine historical society, aided by appropriations from the state.   Portland, 1889 - 1916.   19 v. 23½ x 25½ cm. (Documentary history of the state of Maine, vol. IV - VI, IX - XXIV)   No more published? 6-7664 rev.   F23. B35

BAXTER, James Phinney.   George Cleeve of Casco bay, 1630 - 1667, with collateral documents ...

56

Portland, Me., Printed for the Gorges society, 1885. 339 p. plates, port., fold. map. facsims. (1 fold.) 22 x 19 cm.
(Gorges society publications II) L.C. copy replaced by microfilm. 3-43.
F23. B36
Microfilm 15010 F

BAXTER, James Phinney. ... The Trelawny papers. See F16.M38 F23. B37

BISBEE, Ernest Emerson. ... The state o' Maine scrap book of stories and legends of "Way down East," ... Lancaster, N.H., The Bisbee press, c.1940. (56) p. illus. 23½ cm. 40-12528 rev. F23. B57
1940

— c.1946. (56) p. illus. 23 cm. 47-21360. F23. B57
1946

BURRAGE, Henry Sweetser. The beginnings of colonial Maine, 1602 - 1658. (Portland, Me.) Printed for the state (Marks printing house) 1914. xv, 412 p. front., plates, maps (part fold.) 23½ cm. 14-8527. F23. B95

BURRAGE, Henry Sweetser. Gorges and the grant of the province of Maine, 1622: a tercentenary memorial. (Portland?) Printed for the state, 1923. xv, 178p. front., plates, plan. 23½ cm. 23-27338 rev. F23. B953

BURRAGE, Henry Sweetser. The Plymouth colonists in Maine. (Portland? Me., 1899?) 31 p. 24 cm.
4-18837. F23. B96

DE PEYSTER, John Watts. The Dutch at the North pole and the Dutch in Maine. New York, Printed for the New York historical society, 1857. 80 p. 23½ cm. 1-16016. F23. D41

DE PEYSTER, John Watts. Proofs considered of the early settlement of Acadie by the Dutch.
(New York, 1858) 19 p. 24½ cm. 1-15802. F23. D42

FARNHAM, Mary Frances, comp. ... The Farnham papers. See F16.M38 F23. F23

FOLSOM, George. A discourse delivered before the Maine historical society ... Portland, 1847.
80 p. 23 cm. 1-8856. F23. F67

FROST. Eliot historical soc., Eliot Me. Exercise... in commemoration of Major Chas. Frost on the 200th anniversary of his massacre by the Indians ... 1697. (n.p., 1897) 46 p. 4º. 1-568.
F23. F9

FROST. Memoir of Chas. Frost. By Usher Parsons. (Boston? 1888?) 15 p. 23 cm. Includes historical material about Maine, especially the troubles with Indians. CA 26-512 unrev. F23. F92

FULLER, Henry Morrill. Sir Ferdinando Gorges, 1566 - 1647 ... New York, Newcomen Society in North America, 1952. 24 p. illus. 23 cm. 53-243. F23. F95

GODFREY, Edward. To the Right Honourable The Parliament of the Commonwealth of England, ... The Humble Petition of Edward Godfrey, et al of the Provinces of Mayne and Liconia, in New-England.
(n. p., 1659) (Boston, 1921) facsim: broadside. 40 x 28½ cm. 23-4644. F23. G57
Office

GODFREY. Edward Godfrey; his life, letters, and public services, 1584-1664. By Charles E. Banks.
(Cambridge, The Riverside press) 1887. 1, 88 p. front. 22 x 18½ cm. 4-22368. F23. G58
Office

GORGES. Sir Ferdinando Gorges ... By J. P. Baxter. 1890. 3 v. F23. G66

GORGES. Gorges of Plymouth Fort: a life of Sir Ferdinando Gorges ... by Richard A. Preston. Toronto, University of Toronto Press, 1953. vii, 495p. illus., maps, tables. 26 cm. Bibliographical note: p. 346 - 361. Notes and references: p. 362 - 445. A55-4382. F23. G666

GORGES. Sir Ferdinando Gorges and his province of Maine. Incl. the brief relation, the brief narration, his defence, the charter granted to him, his will, and his letters. Comp. James P. Baxter.

New York, B. Franklin (1967)   3 v.   23 cm.   F23.G68.B3
                                                                                                              1967

GORGES. A proprietary experiment in early New England history: Thomas Gorges and the Province of
Maine. By Robert E. Moody. (Boston) Boston University Press, 1963.   33 p. 23 cm.   63-16336.   F23.G68.M6

HALE, Robert. ... Early days of church and state in Maine. Brunswick, Me., The College, 1910.
52 p. 20½ cm.   Bibliography: p. (51) - 52.   11-1444.   F23. H16

HOLMES, Herbert Edgar. The makers of Maine; essays and tales of early Maine history, ...
Lewiston, Me., The Haswell press, 1912.   10, (9) - 251 p. front., plates, port., map. 23½ cm. 13-10216.
                                                                                                    F23. H75

HOUGH, Franklin Benjamin. Papers relating to Pemaquid and parts adjacent ... comp. from offical
records in the office of the secretary of state at Albany, N.Y.   Albany, Weed, Parsons & co., 1856.
vii, 136 p. 25 cm.   1-23457.   F23. H83
                                                                                               or   F22. H83

MAINE (Colony) Province and court records of Maine ...   Portland, Maine historical society, 1928 -
64.   3 v. front., facsims. 25 cm.   28-13951.   F23. M22

MANCHESTER. Stephen Manchester, the slayer of the Indian chief Polin... in 1756... with his ancestry. By Nathan Goold. (Portland? Me., 1897)   18 p. 23½ cm. Repr. from Col.... of Me. hist. soc. 34-16581.   F23. M32

MANTOR, Agnes P. Our state of Maine; its story briefly told ...   (Farmington, Me., The Knowlton
& McLeary co., printers) c. 1933.   43 p. 23 cm. "Books about Maine": p. (3)   33-12120.   F23. M35

MATTHEWS, Albert. Origin of the name of Maine ...   Cambridge, J. Wilson and son, 1910. 24½ cm.
(366) - 382 p. Repr. from Pubs. of the Colonial soc. of Mass., vol. XII. 10-23177.   F23. M43

PEPPERRELL. The hero of our heroic age; a sketch of Col. William Pepperrell. By Ivory F. Frisbee.
Boston, Heintzemann press, 1900.   17 p. front., pl., port. obl. 16°. Nov.1-1900-113.   F23. P42

RIGBY. Col. Alexander Rigby: a sketch of his career and connection with Maine as proprietor of the
Plough patent and president of the province of Lygonia. By Chas. E. Banks. (Portland, Me.) 1885.
57 p. front. (port.) illus. (map, coats of arms) 23½ x 18 cm. Repr. from Me. hist. and geneal. recorder. 21-4365.   F23. R56

SAWTELLE, William Otis. Historic trails and waterways of Maine ... Augusta, Me., Maine Development commission (c. 1932)   2, 108 p. illud., 2 mspd (1 fold.) 23½ cm. 32-20640.   F23. S29

SEWALL, Rufus King. Ancient dominions of Maine, embracing the earliest facts, the recent discoveries, etc. etc. Bath, E. Clark and co.; Boston, Crosby and Nichols ... 1859.   x, (13) - 366 p. front.,
illus., plates. 21½ cm. 1-8857.   F23. S51

SMITH, Marion Jaques. A history of Maine, from wilderness fo statehood. Portland, Falmouth Pub.
House (1949)   348 p. illus., ports., maps. 22 cm. 49-6441*   F23. S6

SPENCER, Wilbur Daniel. Pioneers on Maine rivers, with lists to 1651, compiled from the original
sources. Portland, Me., 1930.   414 p. incl. illus., maps, plans. 23½ cm. 31-210.   F23. S74

SPRAGUE, John Francis. Three men from Maine: Sir William Pepperrell, Sir William Phips, James
Sullivan, and A bit of old England in New England, by Bertram E. Packard. Dover-Foxcroft, Me.,
Sprague's Journal of Maine history, 1924.   89 p. illus. (incl. ports.) 23½ cm. 24-20758.   F23. S76

STACKPOLE, Everett Schermerhorn. The first permanent settlement in Maine. (Dover-Foxcroft?
Me., 1926?)   27 p. fold. map. 23 cm. (Ex. from Sprague's journal of Maine history v. XIV no. 4) 38-17414.   F23. S85

SULLIVAN, James. The history of the district of Maine. Boston, Printed by I. Thomas and E. T.
Andrews, 1795.   vii, iv, (5) - 421 p. front. (fold. map) 21 cm. 1-8859.
— Index of names and places in Sullivan's District of Maine. Portland, Me., A.J. Huston (1914?)
(13) p. 21 cm.   F23. S95

58

MAINE 15

SULLIVAN, James.   History of the district of Maine.   August, Maine State Museum (1970)
vii, 421 p. 23 cm. (map in pocket) 75-128109.
F23. S95
1970

SYLVESTER, Herbert Milton.   ... The land of St. Castin.   Boston, W.B. Clarke co., 1909.
380 p. incl. front., illus. plates. 24½ cm. Contents. - Norumbegua. - Sainte Croix. - Pentagoet. - Sainte Famille - L'isle des Monts Déserts. 9-28145.
F23. S96

SYLVESTER, Herbert Milton.   ... The Sokoki trail.   Boston, Stanhope press, 1907.   465 p. incl.
illus., plates. 24½ cm. Contents: ... (Biddeford) - The Isle of Bacchus (Richmond Island, Cape Elizabeth - ... The Plough patent, later province of Lygonia - ... Scarborough - ... Saco River and Valley. 7-8234.
F23. S97

SYLVESTER, Herbert Milton.   Maine pioneer settlements.   Boston, W.B. Clarke co., 1909.
5 v. fronts., illus., plates, plan. 24½ cm. Contents. - Ole Cascoe - Old York - The Sokoki trail - Old Pemaquid - The land of St. Castin. 10-655.
F23. S98

VINTON, John Adams.   Thomas Gyles and his neighbors, 1669 - 1689; or The settlement of the lower Kennebec.   Boston, D. Clapp & son, printers, 1867.   13 p. 25½ cm. (N.E. hist. and gen. register v.21 (1867)
5-17854.
F23. V79

WALDO, Samuel.   A defence of the title of the late John Leverett, esq.; to a tract of land in the eastern parts of the province of the Massachusetts bay, commonly called Muscongus lands, lying upon St. George's Muscongus and Penobscott rivers.   (Boston) 1736.   41 p. 30 cm. 1-8860.
F23. W16

1775 - 1865.

ADDRESS to the people of Maine.   Washington, Davis and Force, 1820.   14 p. 21½ cm. 19-8793.
Signed by members of the House of representatives in Congress from Maine.
F24. A22
Office

ALDRICH, Peleg Emory.   Massachusetts and Maine, their union and separation.   A paper read before the American antiquarian society ... 1878.   Worcester, C. Hamilton, 1878.   24 p. 25½ cm. 12-11178.
F24. A36

APPEAL to the people of Maine on the question of separation ... (n. p., 1816)   21 p. 23½ cm. 9-20806.
F24. A64
Rare book coll.

BANKS, Ronald.   Maine becomes a state; the movement to separate Maine from Massachusetts, 1728 - 1820.   (1st. ed.)   Middletown, Conn., Pub. for the Maine Historical Society by Wesleyan University Press (c. 1970)   xx, 425 p. illus. 25 cm. 74-120262.
F24. B35

HASKINS, David Greene, jr.   Biographical sketches of Captain Ebenezer Davis, and his son, the Hon, Charles Stewart Davis, of Portland, Maine ...   Cambridge, Press of J. Wilson and son, 1873.
17 p. 2 port. (incl. front.) 25½ cm. 18-15731.
F24. D24

DAVIS, Daniel.   An address to the inhabitants of the district of Maine, upon the subject of their separation from the present government of Massachusetts.   Portland ... 1791.   54 p. 21½ cm. 1-8880.
F24. D26
Office

FAIRFIELD, John., the letters of; ... ed. ... by Arthur Staples ... Lewiston, Me., Lewiston journal company, 1922.   xxxiv, 475 p. incl. front., plates, ports. 24½ cm. 23-27007.
F24. F16

PACKARD, Bertram E.   An address made by Bertram E. Packard, before the Kennebec historical society, (1923) on John Gardiner, barrister. (n.p., 1923) 15 p. 24½ cm. 25-13336.   F24. G22

GARDINER, Robert Hallowell, Early recollections of, 1782 - 1864. Hallowell, Me., 1936.
3 p. l., 5-226 p. front., plates, ports. 23½ cm. 37-720. Contains brief notices of the Hallowell, Gardiner, Vaughan, Dumaresq and Tudor families.   F24. G25

GOULD, Edward Kalloch. British and Tory marauders on the Penobscot. Rockland, Me., 1932.
41, (5) p. illus., port. 23½ cm. Muster and pay rolls of revolutionary coast guard companies on the Penobscot river and bay: p. 33-41.
32-35028.   F24. G68

GRAHAM, Daniel McBride. The life of Clement Phinney. Dover, N.H., W. Burr, 1851. x, (13) - 190 p. front. (port.) 17 cm. 5-458.   F24. G73

SMITH, Edgar Crosby. Moses Greenleaf, Maine's first map-maker. A biography: with letters, unpublished manuscripts and a reprint of Mr. Greenleaf's rare paper on Indian place-names, also a bibliography of the maps of Maine. Bangor, Printed for the De Burians (1902. xviii, 165 p. front. (port.) pl., fold. map, facsim. 21 cm. Bibliography of the maps of Maine p. (137) - 165. Issued separately in 1903. 3-4215.   F24. G8

HISTORY of the proceedings and extraordinary measure of the Legislature of Maine for 1830 ... Portland, 1830. iv, (5) - 120 pp. 8º. 1-8881 - M1.   F24. H67

DUDLEY, Dean. ... Recollections of Gen. King, first governor of Maine. Communicated by J.F. Anderson. (From the Franklin patriot, Farmington, by Deane Dudley) Portland, 1884.
23 cm. v.1, p. (95) - 106. 4-25644.   F24. K54

ECKSTORM, Mrs. Fannie (Hardy) David Libbey, Penobscot woodman and river-driver. Boston, American Unitarian association, 1907. 3 p. 109 p. 18½ cm. 7-23501.   F24. L69

MAINE. Convention, 1816. An address to the people of Maine on the question of separation. ... Published by order of the convention. (n.p., 1816) 24 p. 22½ cm. 13-16542.
   F24. M19
   Office

MAINE (district) Constitutional convention, 1819. ... Petition of a convention of the people of the district of Maine, praying to be admitted into the Union as a separate and independent state, accompanied with a constitution for said state. Dec. 8. 1819. Washington, Printed by Gales & Seaton. 1819.
35 p. 24½ cm. (U.S. 16th Cong., 1st sess. House. Doc. 3) 6-5569 rev.   F24 M22
   Office

MASSACHUSETTS. General court. Resolves of the General court of the commonwealth of Massachusetts, respecting the sale of eastern lands ... Boston, Printed by Young and Minns, 1803.
287 p. 21½ cm. 8-33576.   F24. M39
   Rare book coll.

MASSACHUSETTS. General court. Committee for sale of easter lands. Report of the Committee for the sale of eastern lands: containing their accounts ... 1783 - 1795. (Boston, 1795) 29 p. 41 cm.
8-10493.   F24. M41
   Office

— ... 1795 - 1801. (Boston, 1801) 11 p. 44 cm. 8-10494.   F24. M42
   Office

GOODWIN, Daniel Raynes. Memoir of John Merrick, esq., prepared for the Maine historical society. (Philadelphia, H.B. Ashmead, printer) 1862. 39 p. 21½ cm. 12-26363.   F24. M56

MILLER, Frank Burton. Soldiers and sailors of the plantation of lower St. Georges, Maine, who served in the war for American independence, ... Rockland, Me., 1931. 66 p. front. (port.) 23 cm.
31-31826.   F24. M64

DAGGETT, Windsor Pratt. A down-east Yankee from the district of Maine. Portland, Me., A.J.

Huston, 1920.   3, 80 p. front., plates, ports., facsim.   24 cm.   Concerns John Neal of Portland.   20-21414.   F24. N34
                                                                                                                          Office

POOR, John Alfred.   Memorial of John A. Poor in behalf of the European & North American railway co.,
and for a state policy favorable to immigration, and the encouragement of manufactures.   Augusta,
1861.   51 p. 22½ cm.   Printed by order of the Senate (of Maine)   9-31338.   F24. P82

MEMORIAL of Hon. Toppan Robie.   Portland, Me., 1871.   1, (5) - 29 p. 24½ cm.   20-16010.   F24. R65

SMITH, Francis Osmond, Jonathan, 1806 - 1872.   The uniform record of all political parties in
Maine.   Washington, 1856.   22½ cm.   F24. S65

SPRINGER, John S.   Forest life and forest tress: comprising winter camp-life among the loggers,
and wild-wood adventure. ... Maine and New Brunswick.   New York, Harper & brothers, 1851.
xii, (13) - 259 p. incl. illus., plates.   front.   19½ cm.   24-1242.   S24. S76
                                                                                                                          1851

— 1856.   xii, (13) - 259 p. incl. illus., plates.   front.   18½ cm.   1-8861.   F24. S76
                                                                                                                          1856

U.S. Bureau of the Census.   Heads of families at the First Census ... 1790. Maine.   Washington,
Govt. Print. Off., 1908.   Spartanburg, S.C., Reprint Co., 1963)   105 p. 28 cm. 64-60351.   F24.   U5
                                                                                                                          1963

— Baltimore, Genealogical Pub. Co., 1966.   105 p. 29 cm.   F24.   U5
                                                                                                                          1966
                                                                                                    L.H. & G.

WINTHROP, Theodore.   Life in the open air, and other papers.   Boston, Ticknor and Fields, 1863.
iv, (3) - 374 p.   front. (port.) pl.   19 cm.   Concerning civil war life.   4-27260.   F24. W79

— (3d ed.) 1866.   iv, 374 p.   front. (port.) pl.   19 cm.   5-1230.   F24. W793

1865 - 1950.

ARIEL (Steam yacht)   Log of the "Ariel" in the gulf of Maine. ... New York, ... Photo-gravure co.
(1855)   50 l. pl. 8 x 28 cm.   Log of Mr. Elson's steam yacht .. by Mr. Parson.   2-1297 - M2.   F25.   A69
                                                                                                                          Microfilm 15021 F

AVERILL, Gerald.   Ridge runner; the story of a Maine woodsman.   (1st ed.)   Philadelphia, J.B.
Lippincott Co. (1948)   217 p. 20 cm.   Autobiography.   48-5365*   F25.   A8

AVERY, Myron Haliburton.   The silver aisle, the Appalachian trail in Maine.   Augusta, Me., The
Maine Appalachian trail club; Bangor, Me., The Bangor and Aroostook railroad, 1937.   31 p. illus.
(incl. map) 23½ cm. 38-239.   F25.   A83

BAILEY, Bernadine (Freeman)   Picture book of Maine.   Chicago, A. Whitman, c.1957.   unpaged.
illus. 17 x 21 cm. 57-7144.   F25.   B15

BAKER, Orville Dewey.   Addresses and memorials of, (1847 - 1908) ed. by Manley H. Pike.   Augusta,
Me., The Kennebec journal, 1909.   vii, 172 p. port. 21½ cm. 11-20499.   F25.   B16

BANGOR and Aroostook.   In pine-tree jungles; a hand-book for sportsmen and campers in the
great Maine woods.   Bangor, Me., Bangor & Aroostook railroad (1902)   174 p. illus., col. pl. 23 cm.
   Written and arranged by Fred H. Clifford.   2-12940.   F25.   B23

BANGOR and Aroostook.   Haunts of the hunted; the vacationer's guide to Maine's great north country.
Bangor, Me., Bangor & Aroostook railroad co. (1903)   184 p. front. (fold. map) illus., col. plates. 22½ cm.
   Written and arranged by Fred. H. Clifford.   3-11597.   F25.   B24

18 LOCAL HISTORIES IN THE LIBRARY OF CONGRESS

BANGOR and Aroostook railroad company. State of Maine. (Bangor, Me., 1895?) 17 cm.
F25. B29

BAXTER, Percival Proctor, governor of Maine, Addresses, 1921 - 1925. (Augusta, 1921-25)
48 pamphlets in 1 v. plates, ports. 23 cm. 25-17590.
F25. B32

BECKFORD, William Hale. Leading business men of Lewiston, Augusta and vicinity, embracing also, Auburn, Gardiner, Waterville, Oakland, Dexter, Fairfield, Skowhegan, Hallowell, Richmond, Bath, Brunswick, Freeport, Canton, Buckfield, Mechanic Falls, South Paris, Norway, Farmington and Winthrop, with an historical sketch of each place, illustrated. Boston, Mercantile pub. co., 1889.
2, (7) - 360 p. illus. 25 cm. 5-36852.
F25. B34

BISHOP, William Henry. ... Fish and men in the Maine islands. ... New York, Harper & brothers, 1885. 129 p. incl. illus. plates. 19 cm. 1-8865.
F25. B62

BODWELL. In memoriam. Hon. Joseph R. Bodwell, governor of Maine... ed. Wm. B. Lapham. Pub. by order of the governor and Council. Augusta, 1888. 64 p. front. (port.) 23½ cm. 14-4035.
F25. B66

BRADSHAW, Marion John. The Maine land; a portfolio of views taken in vacationland ... (Alliance, O., Bradshaw printing service, 1941) (176) p. illus. (maps) 148 (i.e.149) pl. (incl. front.) on 75 l. 24½ cm. 41-13257.
F25. B73

BRADSHAW, Marion John. The Maine scene; a portrait of the State of Maine. (Patron's ed. Bangor, 1947) 176 p. 176 (i.e.177) pl., maps. 25 cm. Companion vol. to B73. 47-6354 *.
F25. B735

BRADSHAW, Marion John. The nature of Maine as seen by a teacher of philosophy; 177 photographs of beautiful Maine. (Alliance, O., Bradshaw printing service, 1944) (176) p. 177 pl. (incl. fronts.) on 89 l. 24 cm. 44-9248.
F25. B74

BUNKER, Benjamin. Bunker's text book of political deviltry. A record of Maine's small bore politicians and political bosses ... Waterville, Me., ... Kennebec democrat office, 1889.
148, (2) p. illus. (incl. ports.) 21 x 16½ cm. 15-23533.
F25. B9
Microfilm 15022 F

CARLETON, Leroy T. Carleton's pathfinder and gazetteer of the hunting and fishing resorts of the state of Maine, together with a digest of the laws pertaining to inland fisheries and game. (Dover, Me., Observer pub. co., 1899) 176 pp. illus. port. 8°. Mar. 29, 1901-21.
F25. C28

CHAMBERLAIN, Joshua Lawrence. Maine. Boston, Little, Brown & co., 1882. 22 p. 19½ cm. From the Encyclopaedia britannica, 9th ed. 1-8866 rev.
F25. C44

CHAMBERLAIN, Samuel. The coast of Maine, a photographic panorama. New York, Hastings house (c. 1941) 101 p. front., illus. 21 x 15½ cm. Illustrations: p. 5 - 101. 41-13768.
F25. C45

CHASE, Mary Ellen. A goodly heritage. New York, H. Holt and company (c. 1932) 6, 3-298 p. illus., pl., facsim. 21 cm. An account, largely autobiographical, of Maine seacoast life during the 25 or 30 years preceding the great war. 32-27062.
F25. C48

— New York, (c. 1945) 2 p., 11 - 261 p. 16½ cm. 46-20984.
F25. C48
1945

CHILD, Charles. Roots in the rock. (1st ed.) Boston, Little, Brown (1964) 346 p. 22 cm. 64-10475.
F25. C5

CITRIN, Michael Mayo. The Maine sketchbook. drawings and descriptions of vacationland's most interesting spots. Portland, Me., The M. M. Citrin co., 1937. 20 l. 17 pl., map. 30½ cm. 37-8795.
F25. C58

COATSWORTH, Elizabeth Jane. Country neighborhood. New York, The Macmillan co., 1944.
4 p, 181 p. illus. 21 cm. "First printing." 44-9075.
F25. C62

MAINE

COATSWORTH, Elizabeth Jane.   Maine memories.   Brattleboro, Vt., S. Greene Press, 1968.
ix, 165 p. illus., map. 21 cm. 68-18586.   F25.C623

COATSWORTH, Elizabeth Jane.   Maine ways;   New York, Macmillan Co., 1947.   213 p. illus. 21 cm.
"1st printing." 47-5093*.   F25.C625

COBB, Irvin Shrewsbury.   Maine, ... with illustrations by John T. McCutcheon.   New York, George H. Doran co. (c.1924)   vii, 11-55 p. incl. front., plates. 19 cm. 24-9446.   F25.C64

COFFIN, Robert Peter Tristram.   Maine doings; with decorations by the author.   (1st ed.) Indianapolis, Bobbs-Merrill (1950)   266 p. illus. 23 cm. 50-5899.   F25.C66

COFFIN, Robert Peter Tristram.   Yankee coast; ...   New York, Macmillan Co., 1947.   333 p. illus. 23 cm. 47-4980*.   F25.C67

COLLIER, Sargent F.   Down East: Maine, Prince Edward Island, Nova Scotia, and the Gaspe. Boston, Houghton Mifflin, 1953.   148 p. illus. 26 cm. 53-11199.   F25.C69

DAVIS, Will R.   Village down East; sketches of village life on the northeast coast of New England, before "gas-buggies" came, by John Wallace ...   Brattleboro, Vt., Stephen Daye press (1943)   184 p. illus. (incl. map) 22 x 27 cm. 43-11396.   F25. W3
F25. D27

— Freeport, Me., Bond Wheelwright Co.   (1966?c.1943)   185 p. 22 x 26 cm. 66-23588.   F25. D27 1966

DE COSTA, Benjamin Franklin.   Sketches of the coast of Maine and Isles of Shoals, with historical notes.   By B.F. De Costa.   New York, 1869.   221 p. incl. mounted front. 22 x 17 cm. 1-8867.   F25. D29

DRAKE, Samuel Adams.   The Pine-tree coast ...   Boston, Estes & Lauriat, 1891.   393 pp. incl. illus., pl. front., pl., map. 8°. 1-8868-M1.   F25. D76

EMERSON, Walter Crane.   The latchstring to Maine woods and waters ...   Boston and N.Y., Houghton Mifflin co., 1916.   xi, 228, (2) p. front., plates (1 double) 21 cm. 16-12262.   F25. E53

EMERSON, Walter Crane.   When north winds blow ...   Lewiston, Me., Journal printshop and bindery, 1922.   6 p., 3-229 (1) p. plates, port. 21 cm. 23-1175.   F25. E56

FARRINGTON, Inez.   Maine is forever.   With photos by Ruth Nelson.   Manchester, Me., Falmouth Pub. House (1954)   164 p. illus. 21 cm. 54-7450.   F25. F3

FEDERAL writers' project.   Maine, a guide 'down east', ... sponsored by the Maine development commission ...   Boston, Houghton Mifflin co., 1937.   xxvi, 476 p. plates, maps (1 fold. in pocket) 21 cm. (American guide series) "Selected reading list" p. (454)-458. 38-30.   F25. F44

— 2d ed. rev.   Boston, Houghton Mifflin Co., 1969.   xii, 460 p. illus. 21 cm. 69-12741.   F25. F44 1969

FENN, William Henry.   The hope of Maine.   A discourse delivered Thanksgiving day ... 1868. Portland (Me.) Hoyt & Fogg, 1868.   23 p. 25½ cm. 12-11179.   F25. F47

GOODWIN, Harry Leon.   Maine woods and water folk, and stories of hunting and fishing.   Farmington, Me., The author, 1898.   139 p. incl. illus., plates (part fold.) front. 21½ cm. 1-8869.   F25. G65

GOULD, John.   And one to grow on; recollections of a Maine boyhood; with drawings by F. Wenderoth Saunders.   New York, W. Morrow, 1949.   253 p. illus. 21 cm. 49-2045*.   F25.G68 1949

GOULD, John.   Last one in; tales of New England boyhood ...   With illus. by F. Wenderoth Saunders. (1st ed.) Boston, Little, Brown (c.1966)   Autobiographical 248 p. 20 cm. 66-22675.   F25. G69

GRAHAM, Elinor (Mish)   Maine charm string.   New York, The Macmillan co., 1946.   4, 231 p. 21 cm.
"First printing."   46-4950.   F25.G74

GRAHAM, Elinor (Mish)   My window looks down East.   New York, Macmillan, 1951.   218 p. 22 cm.
"First printing."   51-4246.   F25.G745

GRAHAM, Elinor (Mish)   Our way down East.   New York, The Macmillan co., 1943.   4, 173 p. 21 cm.
"First printing."   43-14486.   F25.G 75

GREEN, Charles Warren.   Maine.   Philadelphia, J.B. Lippincott co., 1890.   7 pp.   12⁰   from Chambers's encyclopaedia.   1-8870-M1   F25. G79

GRIFFIN, Ralph H.   Letters of a New England coaster, 1868 - 1872.   284 p. 22 cm.   Dec.18,58   F25.   G8

HAMLIN, Helen.   Nine Mile Bridge; three years in the Maine woods, ... with decorations by the author.   New York, W.W.Norton & co. inc. (1945)   233 p. illus. (incl. map) 21½ cm. "First ed." 45-1913.
F25.H35

HASENFUS, Nathaniel John.   More vacation days in Maine; drawings by J.C. Ronan and Richard C. Hasenfus; photos ...   West Roxbury, Mass., Sagadahoc Pub. Co. (1949)   245 p. illus., ports., maps.
24 cm.   Sequel to H38.   "2d ed."   49-5113*.   F25.H375

HASENFUS, Nathaniel John.   We summer in Maine; drawings by J. Clifford Ronan, photos by Clarence H. White, Jr.   (1st ed.)   West Roxbury, Mass., Sagadhoc Pub. Co. (1946)   165 p. illus., ports., map.
24 cm.   Sequel: More vacation days in Maine (F25.H375)   F25.H38

HAYNES, George Henry.   The state of Maine, in 1893.   New York, The Moss engraving co., 1893.
98 p. incl. illus., port. 17 x 25 ½ cm.   2-14122.   F25. H42

HEATH, Herbert Milton.   A son of Maine: Herbert Milton Heath ... Ed. ... Gertrude E. Heath.
Augusta, C.E. Nash & son, 1916.   5, 194 p. port. 26 cm. 17-12155.   F25. H43

HUBBARD, Lucius Lee.   Woods and lakes of Maine; a trip from Moosehead Lake to New Brunswick in a birch-bark canoe ... illustrations by Will L. Taylor.   Boston, J.R. Osgood & co., 1884.
xvi, (17) - 223 p. incl. front., illus., plates. 21 ½ cm.   1-8871.   F25. H87

HUESTON, Mrs. Ethel (Powelson)   Coasting down East, with pencil drawings ... by Edward C. Caswell.   New York, Dodd, Mead & co., 1924.   4, 304 p. front., illus., plates. 23 cm. 24-24645 rev.
F25. H88

IN the Maine woods.   1900 -   (Bangor) Bangor and Aroostook Railroad.   v. illus. (part col.) maps (part fold. part col.) 21 - 27 cm.   0-1751 rev.*   F25. B21

INTERNATIONAL steamship co.   The sea coast resorts of eastern Maine.   (Buffalo, N.Y., 1891)
23 cm.   F25. I60

INTERNATION steamship co.   Toward the sunrise: a guide to the seacoast resorts of eastern Maine, New Brunswick, Nova Scotia, Prince Edward Island and Cape Breton ... Boston, International steamship co., 1895.   101 (1) p. incl. illus., tab. front., fold. maps. 23 cm.   2-14936.   F25. I61

JENNISON, Keith Warren.   The Maine idea; stories and pictures ... New York, Harcourt, Brace and co., (1943)   3, 89 p. illus. 24 x 18 ½ cm.   "First ed.   43-6916.   F25. J. 4

JENNISON, Keith Warren.   Remember Maine.   With photos by George French.   (1st ed.)   New York, Durrell Publications (1963)   88 p. 24 cm.   63-22223.   F25. J 42

GOOLD, Nathan.   Marquis Fayette King.   Boston, D. Clapp & son, 1905.   7 p. front. (port.) 25 cm.
Reprinted from N.E. hist. and geneal. register, July 1905.   5-43026.   F25. K54

KNOWLTON, William Smith.   The old schoolmaster; or, Forty-five years with the girls and boys.

MAINE   21

Augusta, Me., 1905.   269 p. front. (port.) plates. 21½ cm.   5-24236.   F25. K73

LOOMIS, Alfred Fullerton.   Ranging the Maine coast; illus. by Edward A. Wilson.   New York,
W. W. Norton & co., 1939.   274 p. incl. col. illus., maps, plates. 26 cm.   39-27868.   F25. L66

LUNT, Dudley Cammett.   The woods and the sea; wilderness and seacoast adventures in the State of
Maine.   Drawings by Henry B. Kane. (1st ed.) New York, A. A. Knopf, 1965.   ix, 304 p. 22 cm.
64-19098.   F25. L8

LYNCH, John Fairfield.   The advocate; an autobiography and series of reminiscences.   Portland,
Me., G. D. Loring, 1916.   226 p. front. (port.) 23½ cm.   A 16-1303.   F25. L97

MAINE.   Development commission.   Eastward ho! To Maine.   August, Me., (c. 1932)   (64) p. incl.
illus. (1 col.) map. 23 x 20½ cm.   32-20638.   F25. M18

MAINE.   Development commision.   Facts about Maine, the offer of the Pine Tree State.   (Augusta)
1946.   54 p. illus. 15 cm.   47-32014*.   F25. M182

MAINE central railroad company.   Maine.   Present condition of the state ...   Advantages of the state
as a summer resort.   Augusta, 1885.   40 p. front. (fold. map) 23 cm.   2-19324.   F25. M22

MAINE central railroad company.   Maine's monopoly ...   Portland, Maine.   n. d.   20½ x 10 cm.
                                                                                                        F25. M23

MAIN central, The.   A journal of travel.   The official organ of the Maine central railroad co.   Portland, Me., S. C. Manley, 18 -   9 v. in 6. illus. 34 cm.   monthly.   C A 5-925 unrev.   F25. M24

MAINE writers research club.   Maine, past & present.   Boston, N. Y. (etc.) D. C. Heath and co.,
(c. 1929)   x, 321 p. front., illus. 20½ cm.   "Compilation of ... stories of Maine towns and counties." 29-10234.   F25. M26

MARBLE, Albert P.   Geography of Maine ...   (Cincinnati, N. Y., Van Antwerp, Bragg & co. 1880)
10 pp. incl. illus., map. fol.   1-13325-M1.   F25. M31

MITCHELL, Dorothy.   Along the Maine coast, pictured by W. N. Wilson.   N. Y., London, Whittlesey
house, McGraw-Hill book co., inc. (1947)   4, 3-97 p. incl. col. front., illus. 23½ cm.   47-4106.   F25. M52

MITCHELL, Edwin Valentine.   Anchor to windward.   ... illus. by Ruth Rhoads Lepper.   N. Y.,
Coward-McCann, incl (c. 1940)   5, 3-270 p. illus. 22 cm.   "Music in the Maine coast": p. 87-101. 40-29574.   F25. M56

MITCHELL, Edwin Valentine.   Maine summer;   illus. by Ruth Lepper.   N. Y., Coward-McCann, inc.
(c. 1939)   210 p. illus. 22½ cm.   39-27601.   F25. M57

NUTTING, Wallace.   Maine beautiful, ... a pictorial record covering all the counties of Maine, with
text between.   Framingham, Mass., Old America co. (c. 1924)   2, 3-302 p. incl. illus., plates. 26 cm.
24-23162.   F25. N97

— Garden City publishing co., inc. (c. 1935)   2 p, 3-302 p. incl. illus., plates. 26 cm.   35-15265.
                                                                                                        F25. N97
                                                                                                         1935

"OPEN season" and resting retreats among the lakes, rivers, and mountains of northern Maine and
New Brunswick.   Issue by the Easter R. R., Maine Central R. R. (and others)   (Boston, Franklin press,
1880)   67 p. fold. front., illus., plates, maps. 18 cm.   1-8873.   F25. O61

PATTANGALL, William Robinson.   The Meddybemps letters, reproduced from the Machias union of
1903 - 1904; Maine's hall of fame, reproduced from the Maine democrat of 1909 - 10; Memorial
addresses. (Lewiston, Me.) Lewiston journal co., 1924.   359 p. front., ports. 24 cm.   25-17810.   F25. P32

PEABODY, Henry G.   The coast of Maine ... illus. with fifty views.   Boston, H. G. Peabody, 1889.
71 l. 50 pl., map. obl. 4°.   1-8874-M1.   F25. P35

65

22   LOCAL HISTORIES IN THE LIBRARY OF CONGRESS

PEABODY, Henry Greenwood. Seashore of New England; an illustrated lecture. (Pasadena? Cal., c. 1908)   1, 20 p. 23 cm. The shore north of Boston. 8-18061.
 F25. P353

PEPPER, Annie (Grassie) What Maine offers and why Maine is cool. (Portland, Me., Maine Central Railroad, 190-?)   7 p. map (on cover) 21 cm. 50-47922.
 F25. P42

PISCATAQUIS County historical society, Dover, Me. Joseph Bradford Peaks; addresses on his life and character ... Dover, Observer pub. co., 1915.   41 p. front. (port.) pl. 23½ cm. 15-26000.
 F25. P67

PLAISTED, Gen'l Harris M., Life and public services of. Portland, Me., The New era pub. co., 1880.   31 p. 22 cm. Portrait on cover. 17-16291.
 F25. P69
 Office

RICH, Louise (Dickinson) ... Happy the land. Phila. and N.Y., J.B. Lippincott co. (1946) 259 p. plates, ports. 21 cm. "First ed." 46-11929.
 F25. R48

RICH, Louise (Dickinson) We took to the woods; twenty-one photos. Phila., N.Y., J.B. Lippincott co. (1942)   322 p. incl. front. plates, ports. 21 cm. "First ed." 42-24308.
 F25. R5

RICH, Louise (Dickinson) Geliebte Wälder; ein Stück unbekanntes Amerika. Rüschlikon-Zch., A. Muller (1947)   215 p. illus., ports., map. 23 cm. Translation of We took to the woods. 52-17794.
 F25. R515

RICH, Louise (Dickinson) Vi drog till skogs. Stockholm, Natur och kultur (1944)   295 p. illus., map. 22 cm. 50-46417.
 F25. R516

ROBINSON, Bernice (Nelke) Our island lighthouse (by) Bernice Richmond (pseud.) N.Y., Random house (1947)   5, 3-275 p. illus. (maps) 21 cm. "First printing" 47-2855.
 F25. R58

ROBINSON, Bernice (Nelke) Winter harbor (by) Bernice Richmond (pseud.) decorations by John O'Hara Cosgrave II. N.Y., H. Holt and co. (1943)   4, 3-211 p. incl. front., illus. plates, ports. 22 cm. 43-12864 rev.
 F25. R6

ROLLINS, Albert Moore. Eastern Maine practical guide. Portland, Me., The Lakeside press co., 1905.   72 p. illus. 20½ cm. 5-10489.
 F25. R75

SHELTON, Alfred Cooper. Down to the sea in Maine; photographs and foreword by A.C. Shelton. N.Y., E.P. Dutton & co., inc., 1942.   116 p. illus. 23 x 27½ Illus. p. 33-116. "First ed." 42-12128.
 F25. S5

SMITH, Alta Lillian. As Maine goes. Portland, Falmouth Pub. House (1948)   80 p. of illus. 26 cm. "A photograph sketchbook of Maine" 48-9294*.
 F25. S64

SPERRY, Willard Learoyd. Summer yesterdays in Maine; memories of boyhood vacation days ... illus. by Charles H. Woodbury. N.Y. and London, Harper & brothers, 1941.   xi, 263 p. incl. front., illus. 21½ cm. "First ed." 41-20682.
 F25. S66

STANTON, Gerrit Smith. "Where the sportsman loves to linger." A narrative of the most popular canoe trips in Maine. N.Y., J.S. Ogilvie pub. co. (c. 1905)   123 p. front. (map) illus. 20 cm. 5-36821.
 F25. S75

STATE of Maine publicity bureau. Maine, vacation land the year round. Portland, (1924) cover-title, 3 - 51 (4) p. illus. 23 x 21 cm. 24-27186.
 F25. S78

STEELE, Thomas Sedgwick. Canoe and camera: a two hundred mile tour through the Maine forests. N.Y., O. Judd co., 1880.   139 p. incl. illus., plates, map. front., map. 21 x 14 cm. Map in pocket wanting. L.C. copy replaced by microfilm. 1-8875.
 F25. S81
 Microfilm 15520 F

STEELE, Thomas Sedgwick. Paddle and portage, from Moosehead Lake to the Aroostook River, Maine. Boston, Estes and Lauriat, 1882.   14, (15) - 148 p. incl. front., illus., plates. fold. map. 20½ cm. 1-8876.
 F25. S82

MAINE

STOKES, J. Bispham. Down the West branch. A canoeing trip in Maine, 1899. Philadelphia, Press of the Leeds & Biddle co., 1900.   48 p. 18 x 14 cm. 2-2211 - M2.   F25. S87

SUMMER resorts - Maine. Pamphlets, broadsides, clippings, and other miscellaneous matter on this subject, not separately cataloged, are classified in :   F25. S899

SWEETSER, Moses Foster. Picturesque Maine. With descriptions ...   Portland, Chisholm brothers (1880)   65 p. plates. 20 ½ cm. 1-8877.   F25. S97

TEG, William. Almuchicoitt, Land of the Little Dog. Boston, Christopher (1950)   315 p. illus., map. 21 cm. 50-1891.   F25. T 4

TRAVELLERS' guide. A complete list of the stations, distances & fares, from Portland, on the railroads and steamboats in the state of Maine ...   Portland, G. A. Jones & co., 1873.   32 l. 24º. 1-8878-M1.   F25. T77

U.S. 62d Cong., 1st sess., 1911. ... Amos L. Allen (late a representative from Maine) Memorial addresses. Delivered in the House of representatives of the U. S. ...   Washington (Govt. print. off.) 1913.   40 p. port. 26 ½ cm. 13-35502.   F25. U5

VACATIONLAND; an illustrated register of hotels and camps in Maine and New Hampshire. ... resort proprietors and ... Maine central railroad.   (N. Y.) Annually.   v. illus. (incl. maps) 20 ½ x 11 ½ cm. 15-13407.   F25. V11

VIEWS of Maine ...   Boston, Heliotype ptg. co., c. 1886.   10 l. 10 pl. 14 x 23 ½ cm. 1-8879.   F25. V67

WALDRON, Edward A. The sea coast resorts of eastern Maine, New Brunswick, Nova Scotia, Prince Edward Island, and Cape Breton. ... International steamship co. ...   (Buffalo, N. Y., Matthews, Northrup & co., 1890)   140, (4) p. front. (fold. map) illus. 24 cm. 1-20005.   F25. W16

WALDRON, Edward A. The sea coast resorts of eastern Maine. ...   1891.   23 cm.   F25. W163

— 1893.   F25. W17

1951 TO DATE.

CLAES, Frank E. Maine coast, portraits. Designed and composed by Tom I. Peers. (Camden, Me.) Camden Herald Pub. Co. (1967)   1 v. 29 cm.   F26. C55

DONOVAN, John C. Congressional campaign: Maine elects a Democrat.   (N. Y.) Holt (1958) 13 p. 28 cm. (Case studies in practical politics) 58-6328.   F26. C6 D6

LUND, Morten. Cruising the Maine coast.   N. Y., Walker (1967)   224 p. 29 cm. 67-13228.   F26. L8

PRATSON, Frederick John. The sea in their blood. Illus. with photos by the author. Boston, Houghton Mifflin Co., 1972.   xiii, 143 p. illus. 27 cm. 79-177531.   F26. P 7

WALKER, David Bradstreet. A Maine profile; some conditioners of her political system. Brunswick, Me., Bowdoin College, Bureau for Research in Municipal Govt., 1964.   55 p. 23 cm.   F26. W3

REGIONS, COUNTIES, ETC., A - Z.

ALLAGASH. The Allagash. By Lew Dietz. Illus. by George Loh. (1st ed.) N. Y., Holt, Rinehart, Winston (1968)   xxiv, 264 p. illus. 21 cm. (Rivers of America) 68-12043.   F27. A4 D5

Away from it all.   South Brunswick (i.e. Brunswick)   By Dorothy Boone Kidney.   A.S.Barnes (1969)
200 p. illus. 22 cm. 68-27204.
F27.A4K5

ANDROSCOGGIN County, Resident and business directory of,   including the cities of Auburn and Lewiston and the towns of Durham, East Livermore, Greene, Leeds, Lisbon, Livermore, Mechanic Falls, Minot, Poland, Turner, Wales and Webster ... 1900/01, 19 -   Auburn, Me., Merrill & Webber co., 1900 -   fold. map. 24 cm. Title varies Aug. 2, 1900-49 Additions.
Directories

ANDROSCOGGIN County directory, Turner's ... Auburn Me., A.R. Turner pub. co., 1894 - 98.
24 cm. 12-12822.
Directories

ANDROSCOGGIN.   Camp Sunny Crest for girls, Lake Androscoggin, Leeds Centre, Maine. ... (N.Y., c. 1918)   (24) p. illus. 12 x 16 cm. 19-1809.
F27.A5C18

ANDROSCOGGIN county, Maine, History of ... Georgia Drew Merrill, ed.   Boston, W.A. Fergusson & co., 1891.   xiv, (17) - 432, 432a - 432f, 433 - 690, 690a - 690b, 691 - 879 p. 26 cm. plates, ports. 1-8884 rev.
F27. A5M5

ANDROSCOGGIN River Valley, gateway to the White Mountains, by D.B. Wight. (1st ed.) Rutland, Vt., C.E. Tuttle Co. (1967)   561 p. 22 cm. 67-18141.
F27.A53W5

AROOSTOOK County (Maine) business and residential directory.   Newton, Mass., Newton journal pub. co., c. 1905 -   fold. map. 23½ cm. 6-41788.
Directories

AROOKSTOOK County, ... Poole & Yeaton's business directory, guide and reference book of ... Bangor, Me., 18 -   19 cm. 24-17078.
Directories

AROOKSTOOK: with some account of the excursions thither of the editors of Maine, in the years 1858 and 1878, and of the colony of Swedes, settled in the town of New Sweden.   By Edward H. Elwell ... Portland, 1878.   50 p. 23½ cm. 13-5126.
F27. A7E7

AROOSTOOK.   Pine, potatoes and people; the story of Aroostook.   By Helen Hamlin. (1st ed.) New York, W.W. Norton (1948)   238 p. maps. 22 cm. 48-6862 *.
F27. A7H3

AROOSTOOK River, Report of an exploration and survey of the territory on the ... 1838. By Ezekiel Holmes.   August, Smith & Robinson, 1839.   78 p. 21 cm. The survey was authorized by the Board of internal improvements of Maine. 1-8885.
F27. A7H7

ARROOSTOOK county, 100th anniversary of.   Houlton pioneer times ... Houlton, Me., 1939.
52 p. illus. 61 cm. v. 81 no. 26 of the Houlton pioneer times, June 29, 1939. 41M2343T.
F27.A7H74

AROOSTOOK.   In fair Aroostook, where Acadia and Scandinavia's subtle touch turned a wilderness into a land of plenty.   By Clarence Pullen.   Bangor, Mc., Bangor & Aroostook railroad company, 1902.
94 (2) p. incl. front., illus., map. 21 cm. 3-1828.
F27. A7P3

AROOSTOOK.   Extracts from address of Edward Wiggin, esq., ... 1885. Portland (Me.) 1887.
26 p. 25½ cm. 13-5127.
F27. A7W6

AROOSTOOK, History of. vol. I ... comp. and written by Hon. Edward Wiggin. (Presque Isle, Me., The Star-herald press, c. 1922)   2 pt. in 1 v. front., illus., plates, ports. 23½ cm. Part I also issued separately. Contents: ... facts, names and dates rel. to the early settlement of all the different towns and plantations of the county. Pt. 2. Sketch of the development of Aroostook ... Part 2 by George H. Collins. 22-5218 rev.
F27. A7W62 or A7W63

AROOSTOOK: our last frontier; Maine's picturesque potato empire, by Charles Morrow Wilson; illus. with 32 photos and 12 caricatures.   Brattleboro, Vt., Stephen Daye press (c. 1937)   199, (15), (201) - 240 p. illus., plates, ports. 22½ cm. "An album of Aroostook personalities..." (15) p. following p. 199. 37-22483.
F27. A7W7

BOOTHBAY Harbor.   Harbor ahoy! Rest for the weary; written by Harold H. Kynett ... (Philadelphia, Pa., E. Stern & co., inc., 1936)   2, 9 - 59 p. front. (map) illus. 24½ cm. 37-1340.
F27. B5K9

MAINE

BOUNDARIES. International boundary commission (U.S. Alaska and Canada) ... Joint report upon the survey and demarcation of the boundary between the U. S. and Canada from the source of the St. Croix river to the St. Lawrence river. ... Washington, Govt. print. off., 1925.   xv, 512 p. incl. illus., tables, diagrs. front., fold. maps. 31 cm. and atlas of 61 (i. e. 62) maps. 97 ½ x 67 cm. 25-26497 rev. 2   F27.B7 I 54

— Triangulation and precise traverse sketches to accompany report ... 1924. (Washington, Govt. print. off., 1924)   15 maps (14 fold.) 31 cm. Issued in portfolio. 25-26497 rev. 2.   F27.B7 I 542

BOUNDARIES. International boundary commission (U.S., Alaska and Canada) ... Joint report upon the survey and demarcation of the boundary between the U. S. and Canada from the source of the St. Croix river to the Atlantic ocean ... Washington, U.S. Govt. print. off., 1934.   xiv, 318 p. incl. illus., tables, diagrs. front., fold. maps. 31 cm. and atlas (18 (i. e.19) maps) 97 x 66 cm. 34-26687 rev.   F27.B7 I 56

BOUNDARIES. International Boundary Commission (U.S., Alaska, and Canada) Maintenance of the boundary between Canada and the U.S. under the provision of Article IV of the Treaty of 1925 ... Ottawa, Washington, 1955.   182 p. 27 cm.   F27.B7 I 57

BUZZARD'S BAY. The middle road. By Llewellyn Howland. Illus. by Lois Darling. South Dartmouth, Mass., Concordin Co. (1961)   134 p. 24 cm.   F27. B9H6

CASCO BAY directory, The ...   Portland, Me., Beverley, Mass., Crowley & Lunt, 19 -
v. illus., fold. maps. 24 cm. Title varies. 4-15561 rev.
                                                                                              Directories

CASCO BAY, Chronicles of.   By Daniel Clement Colesworthy.   Portland, Sanborn and Carter, 1850.
(9) - 56 p. 23 cm. "Marriages in Portland (and) "Deaths in Portland" (1804) p. 38 - 42. 1-8886.   F27. C3C6

CASCO BAY. The island and shore gems of beautiful Casco bay.   By George Henry Haynes.   Intro. by J. P. Baxter.   New York, Moss eng. co. (1892)   24 l. illus., map. obl. 24°. 1-8887-M1.   F27. C3H4

CASCO BAY, buried treasure of; a guide to locations for the modern hunter.   By Ben Kennedy. Falmouth, Me., (1963)   79 p. 23 cm.   F27. C3K4

CASCO BAY ... Ye romance of (by) Herbert Milton Sylvester.   Boston, Stanhope press, 1904.
348 p. front. (port.) illus. 24 ½ cm. Drawings by the author. 4-32754.   F27. C3S9

COBBOSSEECONTEE pilot, The; containing sailing directions, descriptions of rocks ... boats, guides etc. etc. for lake Cobbosseecontee, Kennebec county.   Boston, D. C. Robinson, 1900.   77 p. front., illus. 20 cm. 0-2317 rev.   F27. C6R6
— Chart of lake Cobbosseecontee.   Drawn and pub. by Daniel C. Robinson. Boston, Mass., 1900.
col. map. 39 x 94 ½ cm.   F27. C6R6
                                                                                              map

CUMBERLAND county, General directory of the towns in, and business directory of Portland ... 1900/01 Boston, Union pub. co.   23 ½ cm. 1-30292 rev.
                                                                                              Directories

CUMBERLAND. The Portland suburban directory.   A general directory of the towns of Cumberland, Falmouth, Freeport, Gray, New Gloucester, North Yarmouth, Scarboro and Yarmouth ... Portland, Me., Crowley & Lunt.   24 ½ cm. 15-27964.
                                                                                              Directories

CASCO BAY. The beauties of Portland and scenic gems of Casco Bay.   Portland, Me., G. W. Morris (1895)   58, 67 - 80 p. incl. illus., plates. 4 pl. 19 x 26 ½ cm. 19-7285.   F27. C9B3

CUMBERLAND County. Biographical review; this volume contains biographical sketches of leading citizens of Cumberland County.   Boston, Biographical review pub. co., 1896.   2, (9) - 706 p. incl. ports. 29 x 24 cm. 8-22372.   F27. C9B6

CUMBERLAND County, History of. , By W. Woodford Clayton.   With illustrations and biographical

69

sketches of its prominent men and pioneers ... Philadelphia, Everts & Peck, 1880. 456 p. illus., plates, fold. map. 30½ cm. 1-8888.
F27. C9C6

PEAKS ISLAND and its people, A history of. Also a short history of House Island, Portland, Maine. By Nathan Goold. Portland, Me., The Lakeside press, 1897. 84 p. front., pl., map. 19½ cm. 2-10417.
F27. C9G6

CHEBEAGUE, The stone sloops of and the men who sailed them; also some Chebeague miscellany. By Zarah William Hauk. (n.p.) 1949. 97, 11 l. illus., maps. 28 cm. Bibliography: leaf 1. 50-37487.
F27. C9H3

CASCO BAY yarns, by Williams Haynes ... illus. with photos by the author. New York, D.O. Haynes & co. (c.1916) 189 p. front., plates. 18½ cm. Reprinted in part from various periodicals. 16-15458.
F27. C9H4

CASCO BAY, The isles of, in fact & fancy. By Herbert G. Jones, with pen & ink sketches by the author. Portland, Me., Jones book shop, 1946. 6, (3) - 141 p. incl. illus. (incl. map) plates. 23½ cm. 46-21028 rev.
F27. C9J6

CUMBERLAND County. Sebago Lake Land in history, legend & romance; illustrated with photos and pen sketches. By Herbert Granville Jones. Portland, Me., (c.1949) 130 p. illus., maps. 24 cm. 50-5216.
F27. C9J62

CUMBERLAND County. Cousins and Littlejohn's island, 1645 - 1893 (by) Katherine Prescott Kaster. (Portland, Me., Loring printing co., 1942?) 1, 128 p. illus. (maps) 22½ cm. 42-24886.
F27. C9K3

CUMBERLAND County. History of Bustins Island, Casco Bay, 1660 - 1960. By George B. Richardson, Bustins Island, Me., c.1960. 84 p. 25 cm.
F27. C9R5

CUMBERLAND County. The story of Orr's Island, by Annie Haven Thwing ... Boston, Geo. H. Ellis, co., inc., 1925. 3, 18 p. plates. 19 cm. "Authorities" 3d prelim. leaf. 25-12625.
F27. C9T5

DEAD RIVER region, Sportsmen's and tourists' guide book to the ... By Arthur W. Robinson. Boston, 1885. 199 p. front., fold. map. 16°. 1-8889-M1.
F27. D2R6

DEBSCONEAG fish and game club. A word from the Maine woods. 1903? 15½ cm.
F27. D22D3

DEBSCONEAG; written and designed by Winfield M. Thompson. Boston, The Barta press (1902) 16 p. illus., fold. map. 15½ cm. 2-25698.
F27. D22T4

DOCHET (St. Croix) Island. By William Francis Ganong. Ottawa, 1902. 25 cm.
F27. D6G2

FRANKLIN County. Biographical review. See Oxford county, F27.O9B6

FRANKLIN County directory, northern part ... Strout's. Farmington, Me., F.M. Strout, 19
v. 23½ cm. 26-4617.
F27. F8A18

HANCOCK County. Old Hancock county families; containing genealogies of families resident in Hancock county in 1933, whose ancestors of their surnames settled in the town in which they live, in or before 1790 ,,, by William Macbeth Pierce. First series. Ellsworth, Me., Hancock county publishing co., 1933. 3, 133 p. 23½ cm. "A series of 35 articles ... in the Ellsworth American, in 1932-33." 34-8767.
F27. H3P6

KENNEBEC County. The frontier missionary: a memoir of the life of the Rev. Jacob Bailey, missionary at Pownalborough, Me., etc. By William Stoodley Bartlet. N.Y. Stanford & Swords, 1853. xi, 365 p. front., illus., ports., map, facsim. 22½ cm. Also pub. as v.2 of Collections of Prot. Episcopal Church Soc. 7-2013.
K27. K2B28

KENNEBEC County, Directory of, embracing cities of Augusta, Gardiner, Hallowell and Waterville ... 1899/1900, 1903/4 - 19 -   Portland, Me., Portland directory co. 24 cm. Title varies. 99-3761 (rev. 33)
Directories

MAINE 27

KENNEBEC County, Illustrated history of; 1625 - 1799 - 1892; editors: Henry D. Kingsbury, Simeon L. Deyo ... N.Y., H.W. Blake & co., 1892. 2 v. illus., plates, ports. 27½ cm. 1-13326. F27. K2K5

KENNEBEC yesterdays. By Ernest Cummings Marriner. Waterville, Me., Colby College Press, 1954. 320 p. illus. 24 cm. 54-44008. F27.K2M37

KENNEBEC County. Communication of His Excellency the governour ... relative to the removal of Sheriff Lithgow ... Printed by order of the General court, 1808. 18 p. 22½ cm. Lithgow was sheriff of Kennebec Co. at that time. 9-20802. F27. K2M4

KENNEBEC County. A northern countryside, by Rosalind Richards, illus. from photos by Bertrand H. Wentworth. N.Y., H. Holt and co., 1916. vi, (3) - 210 p. 21 cm. Sketches descriptive of Gardiner and the surrounding region. 16-9566. F27. K2R5

KENNEBEC River. A narrative of the extraordinary sufferings of Mr. Robert Forbes ... during an unfortunate journey through the wilderness, from Canada to Kennebeck River, 1784. By Arthur Bradman. Philadelphia, 1794. 16 p. 23½ cm. 4-20088. F27. K3B7
Office

KENNEBEC patent. Order of both branches of the legislature of Massachusetts, to appoint commissioners to investigate the causes of the difficulties in the county of Lincoln ... Boston, 1811 173 p. 21½ cm. With ms. notes by J. Wingate Thornton. 1-8890. F27. K3M4

KENNEBEC patent. Statement of the Kennebeck claims, by the Committee appointed by a resolve of the General court of ... 1783, on the subject of unappropriated lands in the county of Lincoln ... Boston, 1786. 29 p. 21 cm. 1-8891. F27.K3M41
Office

KENNEBEC patent. The unmasked nabob of Hancock County: or, The scales dropt from the eyes of the people. By Charles Peirce. Portsmouth, N.H., 1796. 24 p. 18 cm. A satire. 22-6283. F27.K3P37

KENNEBEC patent. A patent for Plymouth in New England. To which is annexed, Extracts from the records of that colony, etc. Boston, 1751. 1, 19 p. 20 cm. Printed by order of the Plymouth proprietors. 1-14477 rev. F27. K3P7
Office

KENNEBEC patent. A schedule of lands, etc. to be sold at publick auction, ... in Boston, by the proprietors of the Kennebeck purchase ... 1816. (Boston? 1816) 18 p. 23½ cm. 24-12355. F27.K3P73
Office

KENNEBEC patent. A strange account of the rising and breaking of a great bubble. (Boston) 1767. 22 p. 19 cm. An attack on the Plymouth company. 17-22855. F27.K3S89
Office

KENNEBEC patent. "A new Plymouth colony at Kennebeck"; ... an earnest appeal for the erection of a Pilgrim memorial monument, in Maine ... Address by Archie Lee Talbot. (Brunswick? 1930) 14 p. illus. (port.) 23 cm. 30-18801. F27.K3T13

KENNEBEC Valley. Kennebec, cradle of Americans, by Robert P. Tristram Coffin. Illus, by Maitland de Gogorza. N.Y., Toronto, Farrar & Rinehart, (c1937) x, 292 p. illus. 21 cm. 37-27396. F27.K32C6

KENNEBEC River. Land of the Kennebec; "ye great and beneficial river", 1604 - 1965, by Stanwood C. Gilman and Margaret Cook Gilman. Boston, Branden Press (c.1966) 173 p. 23 cm. 66-12293. F27.K32G5

KENNEBEC Valley. History of the lower Kennebec, 1602 - 1889. By Parker McCobb Reed ... Bath, Me. (Sentinel & times print) 1889. 72 p. 22½ cm. 1-8892. F27.K32R3

KENNEBEC River. By Louise Dickinson Rich. Illus, by Lili Rathi. (1st ed.) N.Y., Holt, Rinehart and Winston (c1967) 125 p. 23 cm. AC 66-23422. F27.K32R5

KENNEBEC Valley, The. This work is devoted to the early history of the valley; also relating many incidents and adventures of the early settlers ... (By) S. H. Whitney, 1887. Augusta, Sprague, Burleigh & Flynt, 1887.   122 p. 20 cm. 7-18018.
F27. K32W6

KNOX County, Directory of ...   Portland, Me., Portland directory co., c. 19 -   23 cm.   CA 28-9 unrev.

Directories

KNOX County, Art work of ... (Chicago?) The W. H. Parish pub. co., 1895.   1 p. 15 numb. 1. 1 illus. 53 pl. 35 x 28 ½ cm. Issued in 9 parts. "Historical sketch of Knox County. By True P. Pierce": 15 numb. 1. 13-14107.
F27. K7A7

MATINICUS and CRIEHAVEN. Gems of the ocean; arranged and comp. by R. B. F. Rockland, Me., Opinion print., 1914.   2, (3) - 38 p. illus. 19 cm. 16-2599.
F27. K7F4

LINCOLN County. Rev. Jacob Bailey, his character and works, by Charles E. Allen. (n. p.) 1895
16 p. 21 ½ cm. 7-2006.
F27. K2B27

LINCOLN County, Chronicles of, compiled by R. B. Fillmore ... Augusta, Kennebec journal print shop, 1924.   152 p. illus. 23 ½ cm. 26-1344.
F27. L7F5

LINCOLN County,, Second prospectus concerning Probate record of. Maine genealogical society, Portland, Me., 1894.   25 ½ cm.
F27. L7M2

LINCOLN County. Drogeo land. (by) Mrs. Julia Ann (Dyke) Mountfort. (Damariscotta, Me., Lincoln county news, 1936?)   18 p. illus. 23 cm. 39-21929.
F27. L7M6

LINCOLN County probate records ... comp. William Davis Patterson. Portland, Me., 1893.
F27. L7P16

LINCOLN County, The probate records of. 1760 to 1800. Comp. and ed. for the Maine genealogical society by William D. Patterson ... Portland, Me., 1895.   12, (iii) - xxi p., 368, 53 p. 22 ½ cm. 4-18973.
F27. L7P2

LINCOLN County, Memorials of the bar of, 1760 - 1900, by R. K. Sewall ... (2d ed.) Wiscasset, The Sheepscot echo print, 1900.   3, (5) - 40 p. front. (port.) illus., plates. 23 cm. 10-31045.
F27. L7S5

MAGALLOWAY, Pioneers of the, from 1820 to 1904, by Granville P. Wilson. Old Orchard, Me., 1918.
64 p. incl. front. plates, ports. 19 ½ cm. 18-14382.
F27. M18W7

MATINICUS isle; its story and its people, by Charles A. E. Long ... Lewiston journal printshop, 1926.   4, 5-235 (12) p. illus. (incl. ports., double map) 23 ½ cm. pt. I. Historical. pt. II. Genealogical. 26-16245 rev.   F27. M31L7

MONANA Island. The island shepherd. By Yolla Niclas. Photos. by the author. New York, Viking Press (1959)   90 p. illus. 26 cm. 59-16737.
F27. M68N5

MONHEGAN Island ... By Wolcott W. Ellsworth. (Hartford) 1912   18 cm.
F27. M7E4

MONHEGAN Island. The fortunate island of Monhegan; a historical monograph, by Charles Francis Jenney. (From vol. 31 of the Procs. of the Amer. antiquarian soc.) With additions. Worcester, Mass., The Davis press, 1922.   78 p. 1 illus., fold. map. 26 cm. 24-2611.
F27. M7J5

MONHEGAN, the cradle of New England, by Ida Sedgwick Proper. Portland, Me., The Southworth press, 1930.   xvii, 275 p. front., illus., plates. 21 cm. Bibliographical foot-notes. 30-20654.
F27. M7P96

MOOSEHEAD lake region, Paddle drippings in the. By Hattie B. Coe. Portland, Me., (1894)
19 ½ x 10 cm.
F27. M8C7

MOOSEHEAD Lake and vicinity, Farrar's illustrated guide book to ... the wilds of northern Maine, and the head-waters of the Kennebec, Penobscot, and St. John rivers. By Charles A. J. Farrar. Boston, Lee & Shepard; N. Y., C. T. Dillingham, 1878.   1, 19 - 174 p. front., illus. (incl. map) 17 cm. 1-8893.   F27. M8F2

MAINE

MOOSEHEAD Lake and vicinity, Summer vacations at. A practical guide-book for tourists: describing routes for the canoe-man ... Illus. with twenty views ... By Lucius L. Hubbard. Boston, A. Williams and co., 1879. xii, 145 p. plates, fold. map. 15 cm. 1-8894. F27.M8H74 1879

— 1880. xii, 145 p. front., 9 pl. 2 maps. 16 cm. 1-8895. F27.M8H74 1880

— 3d ed. rev. and enl. Hubbard's guide to Moosehead lake ... Boston, 1882. xii, 206 p. front., 1 illus., plates, maps (part fold.) 15 cm. 1-8896. F27.M8H74 1882

— 4th ed. rev. and enl. Cambridge, 1889 xii, 211 p. front., plates, maps. 15 cm. 1-8897. F27.M8H74 1889

— 4th ed. rev. and enl. Cambridge, 1893 xii, 217 p. front., plates, maps. 15½ cm. 1-8898. F27.M8H74 1893

MOOSEHEAD lake and vicinity ... Foxcroft, Me., S. S. Davis & S. J. Chase, 1891. 1 p, 12 pl. obl. 32º 1-8899-M1. F27.M8M8

MOOSEHEAD lake and vicinity, A summer at. (Boston, Chase & Wallace, 1888. 21 pp. illus. obl. 24º 1-8900-M1. F27.M8S9

MOOSEHEAD lake, and northern Maine, Guide to ... By John M. Way, jr. Boston, Bradford & Anthony, 1874. 2, (3) - 4, (7) - 87 p. fold. map (in pocket) 14 cm. 1-8901. F27.M8W3

ACADIA National Park; history basic data, by Lenard E. Brown. Washington, Office of History and Historic Architecture, Eastern Service Center, 1971. iii, 191 p. illus. 27 cm. Bibliography: p. 39-92. 75-614584 MARC. F27.M9B7

ACADIA National Park. Green grows Bar Harbor; reflections from Kebo Valley. Introd. by Cleveland Amory. Acadia National Park, island history, ... Photos. and text by Sargent F. Collier. Bar Harbor? Me., c1964 107 p. 24 cm. 63-23150. F27.M9C63

MOUNT DESERT, the most beautiful island in the world. Photos. by Sargent F. Collier, text by the photographer and Tom Horgan. Boston, Houghton Mifflin, 1952. ii, 106 p. illus., ports., map. 26 cm. 52-10372. F27.M9C64

MOUNT DESERT, Scenes in the isle of, coast of Maine. By Benjamin Franklin De Costa. N. Y., 1868. 138 p. 10 phot. 21½ x 17 cm. 8-31952. F27. M9D2

— N.Y. 1871. 138 p. 10 phot. 21½ x 17 cm. 12-11180. F27.M9D22

MOUNT DESERT, Rambles in; with sketches of travel on the New-England coast ... By Benjamin Franklin De Costa. N.Y., A. D. F. Randolph & co.; Boston, W. Williams & co., 1871. 280 p. front. First issued under title: Scenes in the isle of Mount Desert. Present ed. has additional chapters. 39-2498. F27.M9D24

MOUNT DESERT, The hand-book of ... By Benjamin Franklin De Costa. Boston, A. Williams & co.; N. Y., T. Whittaker, 1878. xiii, (7) - 161 p. front., 3 maps (1 fold.) 17 cm. Earlier edition issued under title: Scenes in the Isle of Mount Desert. Present ed. has two additional chapters. 15-9287. F27.M9D28

MOUNT DESERT island, and the Cranberry isles ... By E. H. Dodge. Ellsworth, Me., N. K. Sawyer, 1871. 64 p. 23½ cm. 1-8902. F27. M9D6

... ACADIAN forest, The. By George Bucknam Dorr. Bar Harbor, Me., The Wild gardens of Acadia (1917?) 6 p. illus., pl. 23 cm. 19-499. F27.M9D69

ACADIA National Park. By George Buckman Dorr. Bangor, Me., 1942 - 48. 2 v. illus., ports. 24 cm. 42-18516 rev. F27.M9D695

SIEUR DE MONTS national monument, The. By George B. Dorr. (Washington, 1917) 4 p. 23½ cm.
F27. M9D7

SIEUR DE MONTS ... The seacoast national park in Maine, viewed in the light of its relation to bird life and bird study, by Henry Lane Eno ... (Bar Harbor? Me., 1916?) 17 p. front. 23 cm. 19-495.
F27. M9E59

MOUNT DESERT Island. ... An Acadian plant sanctuary. By Merritt Lyndon Fernald. Bar Harbor, Me., The Wild gardens of Acadia (1917?) 11 p. illus. 23½ cm. 19-496.
F27. M9F36

MOUNT DESERT Island ... Natural bird gardens on. By Edward Howe Forbush. Bar Harbor, Me., The Wild gardens of Acadia (1917?) 11 p. illus. 23½ cm. 19-7535.
F27. M9F69

SIEUR DE MONTS national monument: address upon its opening ... 1916. (Bar Harbor? Me., 1916?) 22 p. 22½ cm. 19-494.
F27. M9L16

MOUNT DESERT Island. Bar Harbor and Mount Desert Island. By William Berry Lapham. N.Y., Press of Liberty printing co. (1886) 48 p. illus. 19½ cm. 1-8903.
F27. M9L3

MOUNT DESERT Island, Bar Harbor and ... By William Berry Lapham. 2d ed., rev. and enl. Bar Harbor, Me., 1887. 44 p. illus. 23½ cm. 1-8904.
F27. M9L4

— 3d ed. rev. and enl. Augusta, Maine farmer job print., 1888. 72 p. illus. 23½ cm. 1-8905.
F27. M9L5

LAFAYETTE national park. The morning dawn, Bar Harbor, Maine; a very comprehensive poem ... By the Rev. Leonard W. A. Luckey ... N.Y., c1923. 36 p. illus. 23 cm. 24-18925.
F27. M9L9

— 3d souvenir edition. N.Y. c1923. 1, 38 p. illus. 23½ cm. 26-9534.
F27. M9L92

MOUNT DESERT, on the coast of Maine. By Mrs. Clara Barnes Martin. Portland, B. Thurston and co., 1867. 36 p. 19½ cm. 12-11181.
F27. M9M26

— Portland, Loring, Short & Harmon, 1874. 95 p. 5 mounted phot. 2 fold. maps. 18 cm. 2-5189.
F27. M9M27

— 4th ed. Portland; Loring, Short and Harmon, 1877. 5, (9) - 95 p. 5 mounted phot. fold. map. 19 cm. 1-8906.
F27. M9M3

— 6th ed. Portland; Loring, Short & Harmon, 1885. 115 p. front., plates, fold. map. 18½ cm. 1-8907.
F27. M9M4

MOUNT DESERT Island, The story of. By Samuel Eliot Morison. (1st ed.) Boston, Little, Brown (1960) 81 p. 20 cm. 60-9352.
F27. M9M6

MOUNT DESERT Island, Scenery of. N.Y., The Albertype co. (1888) 2 p. 20 pl. obl. 24º. 1-8908-M1
F27. M9S2

SIEUR DE MONTS national monument and its historical associations ... (Bar Harbor, Me., The Wild gardens of Acadia, 1917) 29, 33 p. illus. 23 cm. Contents: Sieur de Monts national monument - The White Mountain national forest. - Notch of the White Mountains. 19-3754.
F27. M9S45

SIEUR DE MONTS publications. (Bar Harbor, etc.) 1916 - 17. v. illus.
F27. M9S46

MAINE   31

SIEUR DE MONTS Publications - Department of the Interior - (Washington, Govt. print. office)
GS 16-557 rev.   23½ cm.   F27.M9S46
   ... The Sieur de Monts national monument.   4 p. illus. (incl. map) 1916.   No. 1
   ... Addresses upon its opening.   22 pp. 1916.   19-494.   No. 2
   ... The seacoast national park in Maine, viewed in the light of its relation to bird life ...
       17 p. front. 1916.   19-495.   No. 3
   ... An Acadian plant sanctuary.   11 p. illus. 1917.   19-496.   No. 5
   ... Wild life and nature conservation in the eastern states.   9 p. illus. 1917. 19-497.   No. 6
   ... Man and nature.   15 p. illus. 1917.   19-498.   No. 7
   ... The Acadian forest.   6 p. illus. 1917.   19-499.   No. 8
   ... The Sieur de Monts national monument as commemorating Acadia and early French
       influences of race and settlement in the U.S.   15 p. illus. 1917. 18-26257.   No. 9
   ... De Monts and Acadia, an appreciation.   12 p. illus. 1917.   19-3097.   No. 11
   ... Two national monuments: the desert and the ocean front.   13 p. illus. 1917.   No. 14
   ... Natural bird gardens on Mount Desert Island.   11 p. illus. 1917. 19-7535.   No. 15
   ... The Sieur de Monts national monument and its historical association.   Sieur National
       Monument; White Mountains national forest; Notch of the White Mountains.   29, 33 p. 1917. 19-3754.   No. 17
   ... An old account of Mt. Washington.   33 p. incl. illus. 1918.   19-7538.   No. 18
   ... National parks and monuments.   11 p. illus. 1918.   19-7537.   No. 19
   ... The Sieur de Monts national monument and the Wild gardens of Acadia ...
       18 (2) p. illus. 1918.   19-7536.   No. 22

MOUNT DESERT; a history, by George E. Street.   Ed. by Samuel A. Eliot ... Boston and N.Y.,
Houghton, Mifflin and co., 1905.   xvi, 370 p. front., plates, ports., double map, plan, facsims. 21½ cm. 5-28370.   F27. M9S9

— New ed., revised by the editor.   1926.   x, 339 p. front., ports., etc. Bibliographical notes": p. (315)-328. 26-14662.
F27. M9 S9
1926

MOUNT DESERT Island, Traditions and records of Southwest Harbor and Somesville.   By Mrs. Seth
S. Thornton ... (Auburn, Me., Merrill & Webber co.) 1938.   vi, 346, (2) p. front., plates, port. 23½ cm.
38-38696.   F27. M9T5

... LAFAYETTE national park ...   Report. U.S. Congress.   House.   Committee on public lands.
(Washington, Govt. print. off., 1919)   5 p. 23 cm. 19-26103.
F27. M9U4

MOUNT DESERT National park.   Hearing before the subcommittee of the Committee on public lands,
House of representatives, 65th Congress, 2d session ... 1918.   Washington, Govt. print. off., 1918.
38 p. 23½ cm. 44-23282.   F27.M9U42

ACADIA national park.   U.S. Dept. of the interior ... National park service ... Circulars of general
information regarding Acadia and Lafayette national parks.   21-26871 rev.2.   F27.M9U48

SIEUR DE MONTS national monument ... The coastal setting, rocks, and woods of the.   U.S. National
park service.   Washington, Govt. print. off., 1917.   12 p. illus. 24 cm. 17-26496.   F27. M9U5

LAFAYETTE national park ... An anlaysis of, a report by Robert Sterling Yard ... Washington, The
National parks association, 1924.   46, (2) p. illus. 23½ cm. 24-23813.   F27. M9Y2

OXFORD County, ... Directory of.   1904, 1906, 1908, 1912, 1916/17 - 1922/23, 1925/26 -
Portland, Me., Portland directory co., c1903 -   illus. 24 cm. title varies. 4-1824 (rev.33)

Directories

OXFORD county directory, ... Turner's   1896/97   Auburn, Me., A. R. Turner pub. co., c1896
  v. 23½ cm. 33-33155.

Directories

OXFORD County.   Biographical review; this volume contains biographical sketches of leading citizens of Oxford and Franklin counties ... Boston, Biographical review publishing co., 1897. 2 p. (9) - 639 p. incl. ports. 29 x 23 cm. Atlantic states series of biographical reviews, vol. xv) 13-2609.   F27. O9B6

OXFORD County, Sketches of. By Thomas T. Stone ... Portland (Me.) Shirley and Hyde, 1830. 111 (1) p. 14½ cm. 1-8910.   F29. O9S8

OXFORD Hill, The, and other papers, by Charles E. Waterman. Auburn, Me., Press of Merrill & Webber co. (1929?) 90 p. 19½ cm. Contents. - The Oxford Hills. - Mansion and man - Androscoggin Valley paper-makers. - Gem stones of the White Mountain foot hills - Andrew Craigie. 30-29375.   F27. O9W32

PARMACHENEE. Diary of Daniel E. Heywood, a Parmachenee guide at Camp Caribou ... Bistol, N.H., 1891. 101 p. front. (port.) 22½ cm. 11-21034.   F27. P2H6

PASSAMAQUODDY. See F29. E2K4

PASSAMAQUODDY, All around the bay of, with the interpretation of its Indian names ... by Albert S. Gatschet ... Washington, Judd & Detweiler, 1897. p. 16 - 24. 25 cm. (Reprinted from the National geographic magazine, vol. VIII no. 1, 1879) 24-31380.   F27. P3G2

PASSAMAQUODDY. Souvenir of Quoddy, points of interest on our eastern boundary. Eastport, Me., C. E. Brown (1893) 1 p. 20 pl. obl. 24º. 1-13327-M1.   F27. P3S7

DEER ISLE's history, comprising that territory now the towns of Deer Isle, Stonington and Isle au Haut, by Mildred Sellers Allen ... (Rockland, Me., Courier-gazette press, 1934) 44 p. incl. plates, port., map. 23½ cm. 36-18389.   F27. P37A5

PENOBSCOT Bay. Land of enchantment; the Penobscot Bay, Mount Desert region of Maine. Text and photos. by Dan Stiles (speud) George Canterbury Haig. Concord, N.H., Sugar Ball Press, 1945. 181 p. plates, map. 24 cm. 46-70 rev. *   F27. P37H3

PENOBSCOT Bay. Island ad-vantages. Stonington, Me., 19 - v. illus. 26½ cm. weekly. Caption title. Pub. in the interest of the islands of Penobscot bay. 43-46649.   F27. P37 I 8

PENOBSCOT Bay. treasures; drawings, text and photos. by Carolyn and Margaret Olmsted. Portland, Me., Falmouth Pub. House (1950) 118 p. illus. 26 cm. 50-9963.   F27. P37O4

PENOBSCOT country, Summer Island, by Eliot Porter. Ed. David Brower. San Francisco, Sierra Club (c1966) 200 p. 35 cm. 66-20402.   F27. P37P6

— (c1968) 160 p. illus. (Abridged)   F27. P37P6
1968

PENOBSCOT County, History of, with illustrations and biographical sketches. Cleveland, Williams, Chase & co., 1882. 922 p. front., plates, ports., maps. 30½ cm. 12-25006.   F27. P38H6

PENOBSCOT: Down East paradise. By Gorham Bert Munson. With woodcuts by Carroll Thayer Berry. (1st ed.) Phila., Lippincott (1959) 399 p. illus. 22 cm. 59-7106.   F27. P4M8

KATAHDIN. A.M.C. Katahdin guide; a guide to paths on Katahdin and in the adjacent region. Appalachian Mountain club. Boston. v. fold. maps. 16 cm. Began pub. with the 5th ed. 1938. Formerly included as a chapter in the club's A.M.G. White Mountain guide, 3d - 6th eds. 1917-25. 33-12116 rev. *   F27. P5A7

KATAHDIN section of Guide to the Appalachian Trail in Maine. Reprint (2d ed.) Issued by Maine Appalachian Trail Club, inc. Washington, 1950. 1 v. (various pagings) illus. 2 fold. maps. 17 cm. 50-11773 rev.
   F27. P5A74
1950

— 3d. ed. Washington, 1952. 1 v. (various pagings) 52-39724.   F27. P5A74

— 5th ed. (Kents Hill) (1961) vi, 51-237 p. 7 p. 17 cm.   F27. P5A74
1961

MAINE 33

— (c1969)   vi, 195 p.   2 fold. maps.   17 cm.   F27.P5A74
1969

KATAHDIN. Greatest mountain: Katahdin's wilderness. Excerpts from the writings of Percival Proctor Baxter. And photos. by Constance Baxter. With a historical essay by Judith A. and John W. Hakola. (San Francisco) Scrimshaw Press, 1972.   21, (94) p. illus. 72-76270.
F27.P5B38

KATAHDIN. Donn Fendler, lost on a mountain in Maine; a brave boy's true story of his nine-day adventure alone in the Mount Katahdin wilderness ... (Wellesley, Mass., The Welles pub. co., 1939) 123 p. illus. (incl. ports.) 22 cm. "First printing, Sept. 1939" 39-33967.   F27.P5F45

KATAHDIN skylines. By Harold Walter Leavitt. Orono, University of Maine Press, 1970.
xx, 99 p. illus., maps (1 fold. col.) 23 cm.   University of Maine studies, no. 90) 73-632804.   F27. P5L4

PISCATAQUIS County, History of. By Rev. Amasa Loring ... Portland, Me., Hoyt, Fogg & Donham, 1880.   vii, (9) - 304 p. incl. front. (map) 23 cm. 1-8911.   F27. P5L8

PISCATAQUIS County historical society, Collections of. v. 1 -   (Dover, 1910 -
   v. plates, ports. 23½ cm. 11-10448.   F27. P5P5

PISCATAQUIS County, Historical collections of, consisting of papers read at meetings of Piscataquis County historical society ... Dover, Observer press, 1910.   vi, 522 p. pl. ports. 23½ cm. 11-10822.
F27. P5P5

PISCATAQUIS County historical society, its by-laws and membership, etc. and a bibliography of Piscataquis County. Dover, Observer pub. co., 1916.   43 p. front. (port.) 24 cm. Bibliography ... p. (29) - 43.
17-17539.   F27.P5P54

KATAHDIN fantasies; stories based on old Indian legends. By Marion Whitney Smith. (Millinocket? Me., 1953.   44 p. illus. 23 cm. 54-16556.   F27. P5S6

PISCATAQUIS biography and fragments. By John Francis Sprague. Bangor, C.H.Glass, 1899.
4, 102 p. 8º. Jan 25, 1900-209.   F27. P5S7

PISCATAQUIS County. Canoeing in the wilderness, by Henry D. Thoreau; ed. Clifton Johnson; illus. Will Hammell. Boston and N.Y., Houghton Mifflin co., 1916.   x, 191 p. col. front., col. plates. 20 cm.
16-11058.   "The record of the journey is the latter half of his The Maine woods."   F27.P5T42

PISCATAQUIS County. The Maine woods. By Henry D. Thoreau ... Boston, Ticknor and Fields, 1864.
3, 328 p. 19 cm. First ed. edited by Sophia Thoreau and W.E. Channing. The first of the papers was pub. in the "Union magazine", N.Y. in 1848; the second in the "Atlantic monthly" in 1858, the last is here first printed. 1-8882 rev.   F27.P5T43
Office

— arr. with notes by Dudley C. Lunt. Illus. Henry Bugbee Kane. (1st ed.) New York, Norton (1950)   340 p. illus. map. 22 cm. 50-6651.   F27.P5T43
1950

— Decorated by Clare Leighton. N.Y., Crowell (1961)   423 p. 21 cm.   F27.P5T43
1961

— Ed. Joseph J. Moldenhauer. Princeton, N.J., Princeton University Press, 1972.   485 p. 21 cm.
73 - 181875.   F27.P5T43
1972

— Boston, J.R.Osgood, 1873.   3, 328 p. 18 cm. 17-13769.   F27.P5T44

— Boston and N.Y., Houghton, Mifflin, 1892.   3, 328 p. 20 cm. 1-8883.   F27.P5T46

— with intro. by Annie Russell Marble. N.Y., T.Y.Crowell (c1906)   xv, 359 p. front. 16 cm. 6-23057.
F27.P5T5

77

— illus. by Clifton Johnson. N.Y., T.Y. Crowell & co., (c1909) xiv, 423 p. incl. front. 32 pl. 21½ cm. Title vignette (portrait) 9-22215.
F27.P5T51

PIXCATAQUIS County. A word from the Maine woods. By Henry David Thoreau. (Bangor, Me., Bangor & Aroostook railroad co., c.1907) 40 p. illus. 21 cm. "Pages 5 to 31 is an excerpt from "Ktaadin" and 'The Maine woods'". 7-30618.
F27.P5T62

KATAHDIN and Chesuncook, by Henry David Thoreau. From "The Maine woods;" abridged and ed. by Clifton Johnson. Boston, N.Y., Houghton Mifflin (c.1909) vi, 93 (2) p. front., 7 pl., map. 18½ cm. 9-9454.
F27.P5T68

KATAHDIN, The legends and yarns of, by Charles A. Watkins. (Millinocket, Me., Millinocket press) c.1942. 38 l. 20 x 28 cm. 43-2040.
F27   P5W3

KATAHDIN, Explorations west and northwest of, in the late nineteenth century. 2d ed. (Augusta) Reprinted by Maine Appalachian Trail Club, 1950. ii, 57 l. 29 cm. 50-56246.
F27. P5W5
1950

RANGELEY Lakes, Guide to the. By Samuel Farmer. Portland, Me., Loring, Short & Harmon, 1879. 62 p. front. (double map) 19½ cm. 1-8912.
F27. R2F2

RANGELEY Lakes. Farrar's illustrated guide book to the Androscoggin lakes, and the head-waters of the Connecticut, Macalloway, and Androscoggin rivers ... By Capt. Charles Alden John Farrar. Boston, Lee & Shepard; N.Y., C.T. Dillingham, 1883. 350 p. incl. front., illus. fold. map. 20 cm. "Eighth edition." 1-16791.
F27. R2F3
1883

RANGELEY, Richardson, Kennebago, Umbagog, and Parmachenee lakes, Dixville notch, and Andover, Me., and vicinity ... By Charles Alden John Farrar ... Boston, Farrar and Johnson, 1876. 127 p. illus., plates, fold. map. 16½ cm. 1-8913.
F27. R2F4
1876

— With a new and correct map ... (3d ed.) Boston, Lee & Shepard. N.Y. C.T. Dillingham, 1878. 13, 55, 133 p. front. (fold. map) illus. 15½ cm. Reissue of the first ed. 1877, to which is prefixed the new matter and t.-p. of the second rev. ed. for 1877 and the additions and t.-p. of the present (3d) ed. 1-16080.
F27. R2F4
1878

RANGELEY Lakes. "Sportsmen's paradise." Rangeley lakes, Parmachenee, Kennebago, and Seven ponds, via Boston & Maine, Maine central railroad, and Sandy river railroad. By George Henry Haynes. (Lewiston, Me., Journal press, 1887) 78 p. illus., fold. map. 21 x 17 cm. 1-8914 rev.
F27, R2H4

RANGELEY Lakes. Pioneer days of Rangeley. By Joel Sherman Hoar. Rangeley, Me., J.S. Hoar, 1928. 46 p. illus. (incl. facsims.) 18½ cm. "Founded on stories and facts gleaned from the older generation." 28-20119.
F27. R2H7

RANGELEY. By Robert Gardner McClung. (Boston, c1925) 1, 11 p. map. 19½ cm. 25-17037.
F27. R2M13

KENNEBAGO summer (by) Le Roy Nile. Farmington, Me., The Knowlton & McLeary co. (1947) 2, 7-107 (3) p. illus. 19½ cm. 47-17243.
F27. R2N5

SACO Valley settlements and families, historical, biographical, genealogical, traditional, and legendary ... by G.T. Ridlon, Sr. Rutland, Vt., C.E. Tuttle Co. (1969) xvii, 1250 p. 24 cm. 69-16174.
F27.S15R5
1969

ST. CROIX, An international community on the, 1604 - 1930. By Harold A. Davis. Orono, Me., University Press, 1950. xi, 412 p. maps (1 fold.) 23 cm. Bibliography: p. (373) - 388. 50-63326.
F27. S2D3

STE CROIX (Dochet) Island; a monograph rev. and. enl. from the author's ms. notes. By William Francis Ganong. Ed. Susan Brittain Ganong. (2d ed.) Saint John, N.B., 1945. xix, 125 p. illus., maps

MAINE 35

part fold. 25 cm. "From the Transactions of the Royal Soc. of Canada, 2d series, vol. VIII section II." 48-10734 * F27. S2G3

ST. CROIX, the sentinel river; historical sketches of its discovery, early conflicts and final occupation by English and American settlers ... By Guy Murchie. New York, Duell, Sloan and Pearce (1947)
xx, 281 p. illus., ports., maps. 22 cm. Bibliographical footnotes. 47-11847 rev. * F27. S2M8

SAINT CROIX island, 1604 - 1942, by Barrett Parker. (Cambridge, Mass., Crimson print. co., 1942)
19, (1) p. incl. front. (map) illus. (plan) 23 cm. 47-33500. F27. S2P3

ST GEORGE'S River, The. By Albert Trowbridge Gould. (Beverly Farms? Mass.) 1950.
xii, 188 p. illus., port., map. 26 cm. 50-32885. F27. S25G6

SACO Valley. Pigwacket ... By George Hill Evans ... (Conway, N. H.) 1939 - v. front. (map)
19½ cm. (Conway historical soc. Publication no. 1) "Ballads and verses relating to Lovewell's fight" ... "Bibliography of principal sources.."
pt. 1, p (127) - 135. 41-1220. F27. S3E83

SACO Valley settlements and families. Historical, biographical, genealogical, traditional, and legendary ... By G. T. Ridlon ... Portland, Me., 1895. xiv, 1250 p. front, plates, ports., fold. plan. 24 cm. 1-8917.
 F27. S3R5

SOMERSET County, business and personal directory ... 1929/30. Farmington, Me., The Knowlton & McLeary co., c1929. v. illus. (incl. ports.) 23 cm. CA 30-1036 unrev. Directories

SOUTH SOLON: the story of a meeting house. By Mildred H. Cummings. Drawings by Philip Bornarth. (Skowhegan?) South Solon Historical Soc., 1959. 54 p. F27. S7C8

WALDO County. Monterey, or The mountain city; containing a description of ... the southern part of the county of Waldo. By M. Dakin. Boston, Mead's press, 1847. 26 p. 18½ cm. 15-20680.
 F27. W16D2

WASHINGTON County. See F29. E2K4

WASHINGTON County. Calais, Eastport and vicinity, their representative business men, and points of interest, embracing Calais, Eastport, Machias, Machiasport, Milltown, Jonesport, Princeton, Millbridge, Cherryfield and Lubec. By Geo. F. Bacon. Newark N. J., Glenwood pub. co., 1892.
3, (3) - 119 p. incl. front., illus. 26½ cm. 1-8863. F27. W3B2

WASHINGTON Co. Pleasant river. By Dale R. Coman. Illus. by the author. (1st ed.) New York, W. W. Norton (1966) 169 p. 22 cm. 66-11660. F27. W3C6

WASHINGTON County. Way down east in Maine; the story of a pioneer family, as told by themselves. John Thomas Greenan, ed. Morristown, N. J., Compton Press (1958) 210 p. illus. 23 cm. 58-34732.
 F27. W3G7

WASHINGTON County. The Narraguagus Valley: some account of its early settlement and settlers. By J. A. Milliken. Machias, Me., (1886) cover-title, 24 (i. e. 25) p. 22 cm. Includes the towns of Steuben, Milbridge, Harrington and Cherryfield, in Washington County, Maine. 9-2385. F27. W3M6

WASHINGTON County railway company. Vacation days in Washington County; gazetteer of lakes, streams and points of interest, with maps and list of guides ... Boston, Rand Avery supply co. (1907)
72 p. illus., fold. maps. 20½ x 10 cm. 7-30348. F27. W3W3

YORK County. See F27. S3R5

YORK deeds. (1642 -   Portland, J. T. Hull, 1887 - 1896; (Bethel, Me.) 1903 -   See F18. Y62

YORK County. Voice of the yeomanry! Proceedings of the York County convention ... Democratic party ... 1812. Boston, 1812. 16 p. 23½ cm. 18-3918. F27. Y6
 E357. D6

YORK County. General directory of Biddeford and Saco; including a business directory of York County. Biddeford, Me., J.E. Butler (18 -   v. 16 cm. 13-24545.   Directories

YORK County. The old families of Salisbury and Amesbury, Mass., with some related families of Newbury, Haverhill, Ipswich and Hampton. By David W. Hoyt. ... Providence, R.I. (Snow & Farnham) 1897 - 1917. 3 v. 24 cm. Paged continuously. Issued in 13 parts; v. 1, pts. 1 - 5, 1897 - 1899; v.2, pts. 6 - 11, 1902 - 1905; v.3, pts. 1 - 2, 1916. 5-34047 rev. 2.
F27. Y6
F74. S16H8

—— Additions and corrections. By David W. Hoyt. Providence, R.I., Snow & Farnham, 1919. 1 p. p. 1057 - 1097. 23 cm. 5-34047 rev.
F27. Y6
F74. S16H8

YORK County, The history of, and a rambling narrative about the town of Eliot and its mother-town old Kittery ... By Ralph Sylvester Bartlett. (Boston, Jerome press) c1938. 2, 21 p. mounted port. 23 cm. 39-2781.
F27. Y6 B3

YORK County, History of. With illustrations and biographical sketches of its prominent men and pioneers ... Philadelphia, Everts & Peck, 1880. 442 (i.e. 445) p. plates, ports., map. 30½ cm. "Roster of soldiers from York County in the war of the rebellion": p. 122 - 149. 1-8918.
F27. Y6C6

BOON ISLAND. A narrative of the sufferings ... of Capt. John Dean and company ... cast away on Boon-Island ... 1710. London (1711) Tarrytown, N.Y., Reprinted, W. Abbatt, 1917. 21 p. 26½ cm. (The Magazine of history ... Extra number 59 (pt.2)) 17-24215.
F27. Y6D
E173. M24 no. 59

— now reprinted in 1722. (London? 1722) 15 p. 19½ cm.   4-30126.
F27. Y6D28
Office
F27. B7D1

— Revis'd and re-printed with additions in 1727, by John Deane, commander. (London, 1727) 3, 22 p. 18½ cm. 17-16290.
F27. Y6D29
Office

— 5th ed. (London?) 1762. 2, 28 p. 19½ cm. First pub. in 1711. 4-30127.
F27. Y6 D3
Office
F27. B7D2

— Introd. by Mason Philip Smith. (Portland, Me.) Provincial Press, c1968) 22 cm.
F27. Y6D3
1968

BOON ISLAND. A true account of the voyage of the Nottingham galley of London, John Dean commander, from the river Thames to New-England, near which place she was cast away on Boon-Island ... 1710, by the captain's obstinacy ... with an account of the fasehoods in the captain's narrative ... By Christopher Langman, mate, et al. London, 1711. 4, 36 p. 17 cm. 4-29761.
F27. Y6L2
F27. B71.2

SACO Bay, Shores of. A historical guide to Biddeford Pool, Old Orchard beach, Pine Point, Prout's Neck. By J.S. Locke. Boston, J.S. Locke and co., 1880. 105 p. fold. front., illus., plates, ports. 19½ cm. 1-8915.
F27. Y6L8

SACO BAY. Historical sketches of Old Orchard and the shores of Saco Bay; Biddeford Pool, Old Orchard Beach, Pine Point, Prout's Neck. By J.S. Locke. Enl. ed. Boston, C.H. Woodman, 1884. 103 p. col. front., illus., plates (1 fold.) ports. 19½ cm. 1-8916.
F27. Y6L82

YORK County. Witch trot land; being a bit about the mother of Maine, York county, or Yorkshire, or New Somersetshire, from which all Maine counties came ... By ... Anne Mountfort and Katherine Marshall. (Damariscotta, Me., Lincoln county news, 1937) 43 p. illus. 23 cm. 39-10256.
F27. Y6M7

MAINE

YORK County. A Maine county, rich in beauty and historic lore. By Harriet Brockman Samuels. (Princeton, N.J.) 1961.   39 p. 23 cm.   F27. Y6S3

YORK County. A time to recall: the delights of a Maine childhood. By Helen V. Taylor. Drawings by Erik Blegvad. (1st ed.) New York, W.W. Morton (1963)   224 p. 22 cm. 63-15876.
F27. Y6T3

YORK County. Legends of Cape Neddick, by Ralph H. Winn. With illus. by Edward H. Hergelroth. Freeport, Me., Bond Wheelwright Co. (c1964)   xi, 99 p. 27 cm. (The Maine that was series, 1) 64-24942.
F27. Y6W5

YORK County, Maine, marriage returns, 1771 - 1794; pub. by George Walter Chamberlain ... Malden, Mass. (1909)   14 p. 24½ cm.   "Reprinted from the N.E. Hist. and geneal. register, Apr. 1909" 10-7984.
F27. Y6Y5

YORK County, Index to the probate records of. 1901 - 1911. ... Harry B. Ayer ... (Biddeford, Me.,) Biddeford journal, 1911.   2, 3-134 p. 35 x 21½ cm. 13-1177-8.
— Supplement, (n. p., 1911?)   1, 21 p. 34½ x 20½ cm.   F27. Y6Y55

YORK institute, Saco, Act of incorporation, constitution and by-laws of. Est. 1866. Biddeford, 1867. 8 p. 22 cm. 7-41329.   or Y6Y64   F27. Y6Y6

YORK Institute publications. v. 1, no. 1-2 ... Saco, Me., 1884.   2 v. 22-23 cm. 7-41327.
F27. Y6Y7

CITIES, TOWNS, ETC., A - Z.

ACTON, The history of. By Joseph Fullonton. Dover (N.H.) 1847.   iv, (5) - 36 p. 18½ cm. 8-34785.
F29. A18F9

ACTON, Shapleigh, Parsonsfield, Newfield, Lebanon, 1907, The town register. Comp. by Mitchell and Davis. Brunswick, Me., H.E. Mitchell co., 1907.   216 p. 22 cm. 12-19886.   F29. A18M6

ALBION, on the Narrow Gauge, by Ruby Crosby Wiggin. (Clinton? Me., 1964)   282 p. 24 cm.
F29. A28W5

ALFRED, Lyman, Dayton, Hollis and Waterboro, The town register, 1905. Comp. by H.E. Mitchell et al. Brunswick, Me., 1905.   231 p. 22½ cm. 12-19511.   F29. A3M6

ALFRED, York County, A centennial history of. By Usher Parsons. Phila., Sanford, Everts, 1872.   36 p. 15½ cm. 11-13686.   F29. A3P2

ALNA. Centennial memorial services of old Alna meeting-house, Alna, Maine, Sept. 11, 1889. By Rugus King Sewall. Wiscasset, 1896.   24 p. incl. 2 pl. front., pl. 22 cm. 4-35126.   F29. A4S5

APPLETON register, 1903. By Harry C. Pease. Appleton? 1903.   17 cm.   F29. A6P3

AUBURN, Souvenir of. (N.Y., The Albertype co., 1893)   2 p., 24 pl. obl. 24º. Issued by National shoe and leather bank, Auburn, Me. 1-8920-M1.   F29. A8S7

AUGUSTA, Hallowell and Gardiner directory. (v. 1) - 1867 -   Boston, Littlefield, directory pub. co., 1867.   1 v. fold. maps. 20½ x 24 cm. 9-12799.
Directories

AUGUSTA, Gardiner and Hallowell, Directory of, embracing towns of Farmingdale, Manchester, Randolph, Richmond, West Gardiner and Winthrop ... Portland, Me., Portland directory co. 19 -   v. 23 cm. 25-19579.
Directories

AUGUSTA, Gardiner, Hallowell and Waterville, Directory of ... (1901 - 1902)   Auburn, Me., Merrill & Webber, 1901 -   1 v. 24 cm.   1-17673-M4 Sept. 5.

        Directories

AUGUSTA, Hallowell, Gardiner and Waterville, Turner's directory. v. 1 -   Auburn, A. R. Turner, pub. co. c.1897 -   1 v. 24 cm.   9-12798.

        Directories

AUGUSTA. ... Anthony's business directory, guide and manual of Augusta, Gardiner, Hallowell, Waterville, Oakland, Fairfield ... Comp. by the Anthony pub. co. (Boston) 1890.   127 p. 19 cm.   9-12797.

        Directories

AUGUSTA, Vital records of, to the year 1892 ... ed. Ethel Colby Conant ... Pub. ... Maine historical soc. (Auburn, Merrill & Webber) 1933 -   v. 23½ cm. "Alphabetical index from church records, church registers, records of clergymen, family Bibles, public records and other available sources." Contents. - 1. Births and marriages. 33-28157.

        F29. A9A78

AUGUSTA, Historical notes on.   By Joseph T. Beck.   Farmington, Knowlton & McLeary Co., 1962-63.
2 v. illus. 23 cm. Includes bibliography. 62-41760.

        F29. A9B4

AUGUSTA.   ... Maine's capitol.   Written and compiled by the Federal writers' project ... Sponsored by the Dept. of education of the state of Maine ... Augusta, Kennebec journal print shop, 1939.
60 p. illus. (incl. plans) 23 cm. (American guide series) 43-5471.

        F29. A9F4

AUGUSTA.   Report of Commission on the enlargement of the State house to the Legislature of Maine. (Augusta) 1911.   18 p. plates. 22½ cm. 11-25338.

        F29. A9M2

AUGUSTA, The history of ... including the diary of Mrs. Martha Moore Ballard, 1785 to 1812.   By Charles Elventon Nash.   vii, 612 p. 25 cm. Signatures printed in 1904, first published in 1961.

        F29. A9N3

AUGUSTA, The history of ... with biographical sketches and genealogical register.   By James W. North.   Augusta, Clapp and North, 1870.   xii, 990 p. incl. geneal. tab. fold. front., illus., plates, ports., fold. plans. 23½ cm. "A genealogical registers of some families of early settlers ... p. (801) - 966. 1-8921.

        F29. A9N8

AUGUSTA, capital city of Maine, Pocket guide of, with street map ...   19 -   (Augusta) Augusta print shop c. 19   v. fold. map. 14½ x 8 cm. 42-50706.

        F29. A9P6

AUGUSTA.   A year and a day along Bond Brook.   By Alberta Van Horn Shute.   South Windham, Me., Living Word Press (1954)   30 p. illus. 23 cm. 54-44562.

        F29. A9S5

AUGUSTA.   Oration at the centennial celebration of the erection of Fort Western ...   By Nathan Weston.   Augusta, W. H. Simpson, 1854.   23 p. 21½ cm. 1-8922.

        F29. A9W5

AUGUSTA-Hallowell on the Kennebec, compiled by workers of the Writers' program of the Work projects administration in the state of Maine ... (Augusta) Kennebec journal print shop, 1940.
123 p. plates, 3 fold. maps. 23 cm. (American guide series) Bibliography: p. (108) 41-52359.

        F29. A9W8

BALDWIN. (Certified copies of the plan and resolves relating to a grant of land to Samuel Whittemore, Amos Lawrence and others, in leiu of a township (Walpole, N. H.) lost by the running of the line between New Hampshire and Mass. in 1774) (Boston, 1815)   3, (3) - 8 p. incl. map. 24½ cm. 45-51383.

        F29. B17B3
        Rare book coll.

BANGOR directory; containing the names of the inhabitants, their occupations, etc. ...   Bangor, Me., J. Burton, jr. 1834.   24, 72 p. front. (fold. plan) 18 cm. 39-32908.

        F29. B2A18
        Office

BANGOR, Brewer and Penobscot County directory ...   1851, 1864/5, 1869/70, 1871/2, 1873/4, 1875/6, 1877/8, 1879/80, 1882, 1884, 1885, 1887/8, 1890, 1892/3.   (v. 1 - 14) Boston, Littlefield directory

MAINE 39

pub. co., 1851 - 92. 14 v. fold. maps. 19½ x 24 cm. Title varies. Another and earlier series, usually bearing title "Bangor directory," was issued, 1843 - 1867, by S.S. Smith and his successors, Smith & Hill. A later series "Directory of Bangor and Brewer," published by Cannon & co., Bangor, began in 1891. 12-37194 rev.

                                         Direcories

BANGOR and Brewer, Directory of ... (no 1 - (1891 - Bangor, Me., Cannon & co., 1891 -
11 v. fold. maps. 24 cm. Title varies. 1-20339 additions.

                                         Directories

BANGOR directory; ... Bangor, S.S. Smith, 1846. 104 p. 15½ cm. 12-10743.

                                         Directories

BANGOR directory for 1846? - 1867/68. v. (- - 6) to which is added a directory of Brewer ...
Bangor (Me.) Smith & Hill, 18   - 67. v. 15½ - 19 cm. Title varies. 12-10743 additions.

                                         Directories

BANGOR; its points of interest and its representative business men. Inc. an historical sketch of Brewer. By Geo. F. Bacon. Newark, N.J. Glenwood pub. co., 1891. 95, (1) p. illus. 26½ cm. 1-8923 rev.
                                         F29. B2B1

BANGOR, The centennial celebration of the settlement of . 1869. Bangor, B.A. Burr, 1870.
1, 182 p. front. 24 cm. 1-8924.
                                         F29. B2B2

BANGOR. Bangor Board of trade. Bangor, 1906. 14½ cm.   F29.B2B24

BANGOR, a city of progress. Bangor, C.H. Glass & co., (1912?) 32 p. illus. 23½ cm.
                                         F29.B2B243

BANGOR historical society ... Fiftieth anniversary of the; proceedings at the Bangor public library...
1914. Bangor, 1914. 88 p. front., ports. 24 cm. 14-18739.   F29.B2B245

BANGOR historical society. Proceedings. 1914/15. Bangor, 1916. v. plates. 24½ cm.
                                         F29.B2B247

BANGOR. its summer attractions and industrial advantages; issued by the Bangor Board of trade.
(Bangor, C.H. Glass & co.) 1906. 64 p. illus. (incl. ports.) 19½ cm. 6-41933.   F29. B2B25

BANGOR. Leading business men of Bangor, Rockland and vicinity; embracing Ellsworth, Bucksport, Belfast, Camden, Rockport, Thomaston, Oldtown, Orono, Brewer ... Boston, Mercantile pub. co.,
1888. 1, (5) - 260 p. illus. 25 cm. 1-8925.   F29. B2B4

BANGOR, The city of; the industries, resources, attractions and business life of Bangor and its environs ... Comp. and pub. by E.M. Blanding ... Bangor, Me., Press of Industrial journal, 1899.
256 p. illus. (incl. ports.) 19½ cm. 1-8926.   F29. B2B6

BANGOR. A sketch of Bangor, by George F. Godfrey, with illus, from photos, by the author. Boston, J.R. Osgood and co., 1882. 68 p. plates. 15½ x 24½ cm. L.C. copy replaced by microfilm. 1-8927.   F29. B2G5
                                        Microfilm 15220 F

BANGOR, League of Women Voters of. Bangor (1960) 24 p. 23 cm.   F29. B2L4

BANGOR. Comrades of all wars. Bangor - it's people and history. Memorial book, Norman N. Dow post, Veterans of foreign wars ... (Bangor) H.V. Knox, 1936. (52) p. illus. (incl. ports.) 28 cm. 37-14805.
                                         F29. B2V5

BAR HARBOR, Cranberry Isles, Ellsworth-Mount Desert, Southwest Harbor, ... Directory of.
Portland, Fred L. Tower cos., 19 - v. illus. 23½ cm. CA 28-966 unrev.   Directories

BAR HARBOR, Mt. Desert Island and adjacent resorts, Cottage directory for. For the season of 1895 - 1896. Bar Harbpr, Bar Harbor press co., 1895 and 1896.   2 v. fold. map. 17 - 20½ cm. "Issued supplementary to the Bar Harbor record." 12-37180.
  F29. B3A18
  Directories

BAR HARBOR life. Society ed. of the Bar Harbor record. Bar Harbor press co.   v. illus. 30½ cm. Weekly during the summer season. Vol. numbering irregular. CA 8-1330 unrev.
  F29. B3B2

BAR HARBOR, by F. Marion Crawford; illus. by C. S. Reinhart. New York, C. Scribner's sons, 1896. 3, 59 (1) p. incl. plates. front. 16 cm. (American summer resorts) 1-8928.
  F29. B3C8

BAR HARBOR, Directory of ... also a historical sketch and guide ... By A. J. Grant. Ellsworth, W. F. Stanwood & W. H. Perry, 1886.   (7) - 62 p. 12°. 1-8929-M1.
  F29. B3G7

BAR HARBOR, Sherman's guide, business directory and reference book. By Alick J. Grant. Bar Harbor, W. H. Sherman, 1890.   120 pp. illus., map. 12°. 1-16894-M1.
  F23. B3G8

BAR HARBOR, The story of, an informal history recording 150 years in the life of a community. By Richard Walden Hale. N. Y., I. Washburn (1949)   259 p. illus., map. 21 cm. "Sources, notes, and bibliography": p. 243-252. 49-5010*.
  F29. B3H27

BAR HARBOR, Naval visits to. By Leonard Opdycke. Bar Harbor Times Pub. Co., 1952. 31 p. illus. 21 cm. 52-40490 rev.
  F29. B3O6

BATH, Brunswick and Richmond directory ... v. 1 -   1867/8 - 1887. Boston, Mass., W. A. Greenough & co., 1867 -   7 vols. 20 - 23½ cm. Title varies. 12-37202.
  Directories

BATH city directory ... and the towns of Arrowsic, Georgetown, Phippsburg, West Bath and Woolwich ... Portland, Me., Beverly, Mass., Crowley & Lunt, 19   v. fold. map. 24 cm. 22-5453.
  Directories

BATH, Davis' city directory of ... Also a directory of the towns of Arrowsic, Phippsburg, West Bath and Woolwich. ... 1902 - 1904. Bath, Me., and Portland, Me., City directory co., 1902.   24 cm. 2-24084.
  Directories

BATH and Sagadahoc County, Directory of. Ed. 1905 - 1906. Methuen, Mass., Union pub. co., 1905 -   v. 24 cm. 5-6651.
  Directories

BATH pocket directory for 1879 - 80. Comprising a list of residents, churches, etc. (Bath, J. W. Kelly) c1879.   cover-title, 68 p. 15 cm. 12-37192.
  Directories

BATH, ... Directory of the city of, and county mailing list (1912) - Boston, Mass., Guide pub. co., c1912 -   v. fold. map. 24 cm. 12-26769.
  Directories

BATH, The Edward Clarence Plummer history of, by Henry Wilson Owen. Bath, The Times company, 1936.   547, xxviii p. front. (port.) illus., plates, maps (part fold.) 24 cm. "Military history": p. (501)-526. 37-3006.
  F29. B4O9

BATH and environs, History of, Sagadahoc County. 1607 - 1894. By Parker McCobb Reed. Portland, 1894.   526 p. incl. front., plates, ports. 22½ cm. 1-8930.
  F29. B4R3

BELFAST and Camden directory ... (1890) By A. B. Sparrow. Ayer, Mass., E. B. Butterfield, 1890. 219 p. illus. 23½ cm. 13-4020.
  Directories

BELFAST city directory 1894 - 5. Containing a general directory of the citizens, business and streets, and other useful information. Shirley Village, Mass., A. B. Sparrow, c1894.   120 p. illus. 23½ cm. 13-4021.

                                                                 Directories

BELFAST resident and business directory ... (1899 - 1900) Comp. by Henry O. Archibald ... Belfast, E. E. Pillsbury, 1899.   100 p. illus. 24 cm. 99-3463 rev.

                                                                  Directories

BELFAST, History of, to 1825. By Herman Abbott, Intro. and notes by Joseph Williamson ... Belfast, Miss G. E. Burgess, 1900.   1, 18 p. 23 cm. Reprinted from the Republican journal of 1900. 1-16589-M1.   F29. B5A2

BELFAST, Vital records of ... to 1892 ... Ed. Alfred Johnson ... (Portland?) Pub. under authority of the Maine historical soc., 1917 - 19.   2 v. 23½ cm. Alphabetical indexes to the manuscript records of the town, supplemented by information from church registers, cemetery inscriptions and other sources. Contents: I. Births - I.. Marriages and deaths. 19-778 rev.   F29. B5B5

BELFAST. Reminiscences of John Davidson, A Maine pioneer. By Alfred Johnson. Boston (F. H. Gilson co.) 1916.   16 p. 25 cm. Reprinted from N. E. hist. and geneal. register, 1916. 17-20807.   F29. B5D25

BELFAST register, 1907, The, comp. by Mitchell, Walton and Lawton. Brunswick, Me., The H. E. Mitchell co., 1907.   215 p. incl. front. 22 cm. 12-19512.   F29. B5M6

BELFAST, A history of, with introductory remarks on Acadia. By William White. Belfast (Me.) E. Fellowes, 1827.   119, (1) p. 17½ cm. 1-8931.   F29. B5W5

BELFAST, History of the city of. By Joseph Williamson ... Portland, Loring, Short, and Harmon, 1877 - 1913.   2 v. fronts., illus. (incl. maps) plates, ports., plans (part fold.) fold. facsim. 24½ cm. "Newspapers and other publications": v. 1 p. 347-362; "Bibliography, 1875 - 1900": v. 2 p. (91) - 107. ... Births, deaths and marriages, 1875 - 1900 ... v. 2 p. (328) - 581. 1-8932 rev. 2.   F29. B5W6

BELGRADE and Sidney register, comp. by Mitchell & Davis, 1904. Kent's Hill, The H. E. Mitchell pub. co., 1904.   66, xv p. 22 cm. 12-19868.   F29. B53M6

BENTON. Town of Sebasticook-Benton, 1842 - 1942, by Chester E. Basford ... (and others) 100th year historical survey committee. (Fairfield, The Galahad press, 1942)   54 p. illus., fold. map. 24 cm. 43-46420.   F29. B55B4

BENTON. The town register: Benton, Clinton, Fairfield, 1909. August, Me., The Mitchell pub. co., 1909.   3 p. l., (41) - 352 p. front. (fold. map) plates, ports. 22 cm. Maine reference manual, p. 41-160. 12-19869.   F29. B55T7

BERWICK, York County, Burial inscriptions and other data of burials in, to the year 1922. ... Wilbur D. Spencer ... Sanford, Me., The Averill press, printers, 1922.   133 p. 21½ cm. 23-6189.   F29. B6S65

BERWICK, A list of revolutionary soldiers of. Compiled from the records of the town, by W. D. Spencer. (Berwick, Me., W. D. Spencer?) 1898.   18 p. 23 cm. 1-8933.   F29. B6S7

BETHEL. East Bethel Road. By Eva Bean. Bethel, Me., Citizen Print Shop, 1959.   452 p. 24 cm.   F29. B7B4

BETHEL. Report of the centennial celebration at Bethel, ... 1874. Portland, 1874.   78 p. 23½ cm. Historical address by N. T. True: p. 10 - 49. 1-8934.   F29. B7B7

BETHEL. I was a summer boarder. By Ruth Crosby. Boston, Christopher Pub. House (1966)   142 p. 21 cm.   F29. B7C75

BETHEL. History of Bethel, formerly Sudbury, Canada, Oxford County, Maine, 1768 - 1890; with a brief sketch of Hanover and family statistics; comp. by William B. Lapham ... Augusta, Me., Press of the Maine farmer, 1891.   xv, (1), 688 p. front., 1 illus., plates, ports., plan. 24 cm. 1-8935.

F29. B7L1

BETHEL.   The town register: Greenwood, Bethel, Hanover, Woodstock, Gilead.   1911.   Brunswick, Me., The Maine map & register co., 1911.   1 p, (9) - 85, 72 p. 3 fold. maps. 22½ cm. 12-19870.   F29. B7T7

BIDDEFORD.   General directory of Biddeford and Saco; inc. a business directory of York County. 1866.   Biddeford, Me., J. E. Butler & co., (18 -   v. 16 cm. 13-24545.

Directories

BIDDEFORD, Saco and Old Orchard Beach, Manning's directory ... 1870 -   v. fold. map. 23½ x 26 cm. 7-21311.

Directories

BINGHAM sesquicentennial history.   Skowhegan, Me.   Skowhegan Press, 1962.   110 p. 23 cm.

F29. B76H5

BLUEHILL.   Dedication of Bowlders and tablets to John Roundy and James Candage, founders, and an early settler of Bluehill, Me., with memorial addresses, by R. G. F. Candage ... at Blue Hill Neck, .. 1905.   Ellsworth, Hancock County pub. co., 1905.   21 p. front. (port.) illus., plates. 23 cm. 18-15290.

F29. B78C17

BLUEHILL, Historical sketches of, by R. G. F. Candage ... Ellsworth, Hancock County pub. co., 1905. 83 p. illus. (plan) 23 cm.   Printed for the Bluehill historical society. 7-1954.   F29. B78C18

BLUEHILL.   Settlement and progress of the town of Bluehill.   An historical address, by R. G. F. Candage ... at Bluehill falls, ... 1886.   Bluehill, The Ladies' social library, 1886.   43 p. front. (port.) 23½ cm. 1-8936.   F29. B78C2

BLUEHILL; all vital statistics recorded on the town books ... 1799 to 1809, compiled by Grace Limeburner.   North Brooksville, Me. (1942?)   1, 13, 3 numb. l. 28½ x 22 cm. 42-51499.   F29. B78L5

BLUEHILL, incorporated Jan. 30, 1789 ... Compiled by Grace Limeburner ... North Brooksville, 1941.   29 numb. l. 28 cm. 43-754.   F29. B78L53

BLUE HILL, Hancock county, Souvenir of.   (Blue Hill?) E. A. Macomber (1895)   1 p. 20 pl. obl. 12°. 1-8937-M1.   F29. B78S7

BOOTHBAY region directory ... for the towns of Boothbay, Boothbay Harbor, Damariscotta, Edgecomb, Newcastle, Southport, Squirrel Island, Wiscasset ...   v. 1 -   1931/33 -   Beverly, Mass., Portland, Me., Crowley & Lunt, c1931 -   v. fold. map. 24 cm. Ca31-1100 unrev.

Directories

BOOTHBAY region, The, 1906 to 1960.   By Harold Burton Clifford.   Freeport, Me., Bond Wheelwright Co. (1961)   354 p. 23 cm. 61-14423.   F29. B79C58

BOOTHBAY.   A century in one of the early New England churches.   A sermon ... 1866.   By Leandor S. Coan ... Boston, T. R. Marvin & son, 1866.   26 p. 23 cm. 12-1182 rev.   F29. B79C6

BOOTHBAY.   History of Boothbay, Southport and Boothbay Harbor.   1623 - 1905.   With family genealogies, by Francis B. Greene ... Portland, Loring, Short & Harmon, 1906.   2, (iii) - vi, (3), 10 - 693 p. front., plates, ports., maps (partly fold.) plans. 25½ cm. 7-15314.   F29. B79G8

BOOTHBAY.   Family genealogies of the Boothbay region from ... 1730.   By Francis Byron Greene. Revisor: Vivian Powers.   Boston, Powers Studio (1969)   185 p. illus. 24 cm.   Originally pub. as part of the author's History of Boothbay, Southport, etc., 1623 - 1905.   F29. B79G82

BOOTHBAY.   The shipping days of old Boothbay from the revolution to the world war, with mention of adjacent towns, by George Wharton Rice.   Boothbay Harbor, 1938.   xv, 419 p. plates, ports., map, facsims. 23½ cm. "Notes and references": p. (375) - (380) 39-140.   F29. B79R5

MAINE   43

BOWDOIN, Vital records of, to the year 1892 ... Ed. Rachel Townsend Cox.   Pub. under authority of
the Maine historical soc. (Auburn, Merrill & Webber co.) 1944-5.   3 v. 23 cm. Contents. - I. Births. -
II. Births and deaths. - III. Marriages. 44-42679 rev.   F29.B7918C6

BOWDOINHAM, The history of the town of, 1762 - 1912, by Silas Adams ... Fairfield, Me., Fairfield
pub. co., 1912.   295 p. front., plates, ports., maps (partly fold.) plan. 24 cm. 12-18163.   F29.B792A2

BRIDGEWATER, History of. By Annie E. Rideout.   Manchester, Me., Falmouth Pub. House, 1953.
153 p. 24 cm. 54-19782 rev.   F29.B798R5

BRIDGTON, Casco, Harrison, Naples and Raymond ... Directory of ...   Portland, Me., Portland
Directory co., c19 -   v. 23 cm. CA 28 - 45 unrev.
                                                                                             Directories

BRIDGTON. Pictorial souvenir booklet of Bridgton-on-the-Lakes ... comp. by Clayton Boutilier.
Bridgton-on-the-Lakes, The Times press (c1941)   (96) p. illus. 23 cm. 41-25584.   F29.B8B68

BRIDGTON, An address, delivered ... at the dedication of the town house in ... 1852. Portland, B.
Thurston, 1852.   44 p. 8°. 1-8938-M1.   F29. B8C8

BRIDGTON. Moody Bridges, Pondicherry, and the beginnings of Bridgton.   By Blynn Edwin Davis.
Bridgton, (1959)   79 p. 23 cm.   F29. B8D3

BRIDGTON. An account of the ceremonies at the dedication of the Soldiers' monument, Bridgton,
Maine ... 1910, ... addresses ... and biographical sketches, by Philip Willis McIntyre. (Bridgton?
Me., 1910)   1, (5) - 48 p. pl., ports. 24½ cm. 17-14349.   F29.B8M15

BRIDGTON town register, The, 1905, comp. by Mitchell, Bean & Hartford.   Brunswick, Me., The
H.E. Mitchell co., 1904.   109 (i.e. 111) p. 22 cm. 12-19871.   F29. B8M6

BRISTOL. Vital records of old Bristol and Nobleboro in the county of Lincoln, including the present
towns of Bremen, Damariscotta, South Bristol, and the Plantation of Monhegan.   Ed. Christine (Huston)
Dodge. (Portland?) 1947 - 51.   2 v. map. 23 cm. "Pub. under the authority of the Maine historical soc." Contents. -
v.1. Births and deaths. - v.2. Marriages. 47-46619 rev.*   F29.B82D6

BRISTOL. A history of the towns of Bristol and Bremen ... including the Pemaquid settlement.   By
John Johnston ... Albany, N.Y., J. Munsell, 1873.   v, (3), 524 p. front., illus., ports. fold. map. 24 cm. 1-8939.
                                                                                            F29.B82J7

BROOKS. Sketches of Brooks history, compiled by Seth W. Norwood.   (Dover, N.H., J.B. Page, c1935)
8, 454 p. illus. (incl. ports.) 23½ cm. Includes short biographies and genealogies. "References": p. (422) - 423. 35-9035.
                                                                                            F29.B84N6

BROOKSVILLE, Traditions and records of, collected by the Brooksville historical society, 1935-36:
Grace Limeburner, Angie R. Baldwin, Abbie L. Tapley (and others) ... (Auburn, Me., Merrill &
Webber co.) 1936)   152 p. 23½ cm. "Our ancestors ... The first families": p. (19) - 60. "Gravestone inscriptions": p. (107) -
108, 118 - 121. "Men of Brooksville in the wars": p. (109) - 117. 37-2455.   F29.B85B8

BROOKSVILLE; all vital statistics recorded in the town books ... 1827 to 1837, compiled by Grace
Limeburner. North Brooksville, (1942?)   19, 6, 4 numb. l. 28½ x 22 cm. Reproduced from type-written copy.
42-51500.   F29.B85L5

BROWNFIELD, Reminiscences of; short sketches from the history of the town ... By Mrs. Eliza Ann
(Gibson) Stickney. E. Brownfield, Me., 1901.   3, 69 p. illus., pl. 28 cm. 9-18927.   F29.B87S8

BROWNFIELD, History of.   By William Teg.   Carbrook Press, 1966.   202 p. 24 cm.
                                                                                            F29.B87T4

BRUNSWICK. Resident and business directory of the town of Brunswick and Topsham village, with
maps. 1910. Comp. by H.E. Mitchell ... and others.   August, Me., The Mitchell pub. co. (1910)

87

153 (i.e. 157) p. fold. map. 22½ cm. 12-20997.

Directories

BRUNSWICK directory (including Topsham) The. v. 1 -   1917/18   Beverly, Mass., Portland, Me., Crowley & Lunt, c1917 -   v. front. (fold. plan) 24 cm. 17-20183.

Directories

BRUNSWICK. Celebration of the 150th anniversary of the incorporation of the town of Brunswick ... 1889. Brunswick, Me., Pejepscot hist. soc., 1889.   2, 92 p. front., plates. 24 cm. 1-3444* Cancel. F29. B9B8

BRUNSWICK; a sketch of the town, its advantages as a place of residence and its attractions as a summer resort. Brunswick, Me., Press of A.G. Tenney, 1887.   59 p. maps (part fold.) 15 cm. Prefatory note signed: E.C. Guild. 1-8943.

F29. B9G9

BRUNSWICK's golden age (by) Edward Chase Kirkland. Lewiston, Me., 1941.   45 p. 20 cm. 42-5394.

F29. B9K5

BRUNSWICK. Remarks on the plan and extracts of deed lately pub. by the proprietors of the township of Brunswick ... (Boston, 1753)   8, 4 p. 23½ x 18 cm.   Printed by order of the "Proprietors of the Kennebeck purchase from the late colony of New Plymouth" (Plymouth company) 6-36797.

F29. B9P32
Office

BRUNSWICK. An answer to the Remarks of the Plymouth company ... on the plan and extracts of deeds pub. by the proprietors of the township of Brunswick. ... Boston, 1753.   33 p. 21 cm.   Relating to a controversy over conflicting grants to territory west of the lower Kennebec River ... 2-11357 Additions.

F29. B9P34
Office

BRUNSWICK. A defence of the remarks of the Plymouth company, etc. etc. Boston, 1753.
50 p. 22½ x 18 cm.   Printed by order of the "Proprietors of the Kennebeck purchase ... 6-36796.

F29. B9P35
Office

BRUNSWICK. Collections of the Pejepscot historical society. v. 1 pt. 1 - (2)   Brunswick, Me., The Society, 1889.   2 pt. plates. 23½ - 24 cm.   No more published. 9-900.

F29. B9P4

BRUNSWICK. Celebration of the 150th anniversary of the incorporation of the town of Brunswick ... 1899. Brunswick, Me., Pejepscot hist. soc., 1889.   2, 92 p. front., plates. 24 cm. Collections. v.1, pt.2) 1-3444 Additions.

F29. B9P4

BRUNSWICK, A description of; in letters, by a gentleman from South Carolina, to a friend in that state. Brunswick, Joseph Griffin, 1820.   28 p. 24½ cm. 8-20224.

F29. B9 P9
Rare Book Coll.

BRUNSWICK. History of Brunswick, Topsham, and Harpswell, including the ancient territory known as Pejepscot. By George Augustus Wheeler and others ... Boston, A. Mudge & son, 1878.   viii, 959 p. front., illus., ports., fold. map. 23½ cm. 1-8940.

F29. B9 W5

BUCKFIELD, Oxford County, A History of, ... to the close of the year 1900, by Alfred Cole ... and others. Buckfield, Me., 1915.   758 p. incl. illus., plates, ports., plan. mounted front. 24 cm. 16-646.   F29. B92C6

BUCKSPORT, past and present. (n.p.) 1951.   54 p. illus., ports. 23 cm. 51-26000.   F29. B93B8

BUXTON. A report of the proceedings at the celebration of the first centennial ... of the town of Buxton ... 1872 ... By J.M. Marshall. Portland (Me.) Dresser, McLellan & co., 1874.   288 p. 2 phot. 23½ cm. Genealogies: p. (141) - 246. 1-8942 additions.

F29. B96B7

BUXTON. Records of the proprietors of Narraganset township, no. 1, now the town of Buxton, York County, Maine ... 1733 to ... 1811, with a documentary introduction by William F. Goodwin ... Concord, N.H., 1871.   xx, 400 p. 25 cm. 1-8941.

F29. B96B9

MAINE

BUXTON, The records of the Church of Christ in, during the pastorate of Rev. Paul Coffin. (1763 - 1817) Cambridge, Mass., 1868)   88 p. 24 cm. 8-34771.   F29.B96B94

BUXTON. Captain Daniel Lane and his wife, Molly Woodman. By Ellis Baker Usher. (Milwaukee? 1912)   (10) p. illus. 19½ cm. References: p. (9) - (10) 12-5615.   F29.B96U8

BUXTON. An address, delivered at Buxton, ... being the first centennial celebration of the settlement of this town ... 1850. By Nathaniel West Williams. Portland, Thurston & co., 1850.
34 p. 8°. 1-8944 rev.   F29.B96W7

BUXTON. A sermon by Rev. Paul Coffin, preached ... 1762 in Narraganset no. 1, now Buxton ...
2, (3) - 95 p. front., plates, ports., plans, facsim. 24 cm. ... contains Bibliography of Buxton. 10-726.   F29.B96W8

CALAIS. Manning's Calais, Eastport and Lubec directory ... v. 1 -   Portland, Me., H.A. Manning co., c1935 -   v. illus. 23½ cm. 37-33492.
Directories

CALAIS. Annals of Calais and St. Stephen, New Brunswick; including the village of Milltown, Me., and the present town of Milltown, N.B., by I.C. Knowlton. Calais, J.A. Sears, 1875.   208 p. 18 cm.
1-8945.   F29.C15K7

CAMDEN. Resident and business directory of Camden and Rockport, 1899.   North Cambridge, Mass., E.A. Jones, c1899 - 19   v. 24 cm. 99-4301 rev.
Directories

CAMDEN herald, The. vol. 28 - 39, no. 16, 1906 - 1907. Camden, Me., 1906-07.   2 v. illus.
56½ x 39½ cm. Contains "History of Camden and Rockport. By Reuel Robinson," pub. separately in 1907. 8-3797.   F29.C2C18

CAMDEN mountains, The, the Norway of America; a handbook of mountain, ocean and lake scenery on the coast of Maine. With 60 illus. by Wm. Goodrich Beal. Boston, Lee and Shepard, 1890.
56 p. front., illus. obl. 24°. 1-8916-M1.   F29.C2 C2

CAMDEN. A picture tour of Camden; where the mountains meet the sea. By Frank E. Clees.
(n.p., 1961)   unpaged. 25 cm.   F29. C6C6

CAMDEN, Sketches of the history of the town of; including incidental references to the neighboring places and adjacent waters. By John L. Locke ... Hallowell, Masters, Smith and co., 1859.
xii, (7) - 267 p., incl. plates. 20 cm. 1-8947.   F29. C2L8

CAMDEN on the coast of Maine; and its advantages for summer homes. by John R. Prescott. Providence, R.I., J.R. Prescott, 1900.   108 p. illus. sq. 8°. May 31, 1900 - 86.   F29. C2P9

CAMDEN on the coast of Maine, Glimpses of. by John R. Prescott. Newtonville, Mass., 1904.
18 x 24 cm.   F29.C2P93

— 1916.   128 p. illud. 18½ x 24 cm. 16-6613.   F29.C2P94

CAMDEN and Rockport, History of, by Reuel Robinson. (Camden, Me., Camden pub. co., c1907)
xiii, 644 p. incl front. (port.) illus. 20½ cm. 7-25046.   F29. C2R6

CAMDEN, on the coast of Maine, Tourist's guide of picturesque ... Camden, Me., Camden Herald print, 1886.   60 pp. pl. 8°. 1-8948-M1.   F29. C2S6

CANAAN. Old Canaan during the revolution, by Lillian Clayton Smith; Grandmother's grandmother, by Louise Helen Coburn. (Skowhegan, Me., Press of the Independent reporter, 1910)   (16) p. 22 cm.
11-1067.   F29.C25S6

CANTERBURY. The town register; Epsom, Canterbury ... 1909.   lv.   F29.C27T7

CANTON. The Canton and Dixfield register, 1905, comp. by Mitchell and Davis. Brunswick, Me.,

The H. E. Mitchell co., 1905.   117 p. 22 cm.   12-19873.   F29.C28M6

CAPE ELIZABETH, A history of. By William B. Jordan, Jr.   Portland, Me., House of Famouth (1965)
385 p. 24 cm.   F29.C285J6

CAPE ELIZABETH, Collections from.   Comp. written, and edited by Chris Roerden.   Bicentennial ed.
Pub. by the Town of Cape Elizabeth, 1965.   144 p. 28 cm.   F29.C285R6

CARIBOU, Early history of, 1843 - 1895, by Stella King White.   Houlton? Me., 1945.   5, 147 p. plates,
ports. 21½ cm.   A 46-4891.   F29.C29W5

CASTINE sixty years ago, a historical address delivered ... 1900, by Rev. George Moulton Adams.
Boston, S. Usher, 1900.   17 p. 23½ cm. 10-31044.   F29. C3A2

CASTINE, The centennial of ... 1896.   Pub. and sold for the benefit of the town library.   Castine,
Me., 1896.   67 p. incl. front. plates. 23½ cm. 1-210.   F29. C3C3

CASTINE, a dramatized biography of a town ... by Sydney Greenbie and Marjorie Barstow Greenbie.
(1st ed. n.p.) Traversity Press, 1948.   95 p. 23 cm. 48-3336*   F29. C3G7

CASTINE.   History of Castine, Penobscot, and Brooksville; including the ancient settlement of Pentagöet; by George Augustus Wheeler ... Bangor, Burr & Robinson, 1875.   x, (13) - 401 p. front., plates, ports.,
maps. 23½ cm. 1-8950.   F29. C3W5

CASTINE past and present; the ancient settlement of Pentagöet and the modern town, by George Augustus Wheeler ... Boston, Rockwell and Churchill press, 1896.   ix, 112 p. plates, 2 port. (incl. front.) fold.
map, plans (1 fold.) 21 cm. 1-8949.   F29. C3W6

CASTINE. Wilson Museum. Castine (1958)   unpaged. illus. 22 cm. 58-26325.   F29.C3W64

CHERRYFIELD.   Dedication of the soldiers' monument at Cherryfield ... 1874 ... Portland, Bailey &
Noyes, 1874.   47 p. 23½ cm. Address by I. Washburn. 10-11231.   F29. C4C4

CHERRYFIELD register, The, 1905, by Mitchell & Campbell.   Brunswick, Me., The H. E. Mitchell co.,
1905.   92 p. 22 cm. 12-19874.   F29. C4M6

CHESTERVILLE, History of.   By Oliver Sewall.   Farmington, Me., J. S. Swift, 1875.   96 p. 23 cm.
1-8951.   F29. C5S5
Slav Room

CLINTON, History of.   By Carleton Edward Fisher.   August, Me., K. J. Printing (c1970)   x, 409 p. illus.
71-113202.   F29. C55F5

CLINTON, Vital records of ... to 1892; births, marriages and deaths.   By Carleton Edward Fisher.
(Winthrop? Me.) 1967.   357 p. 24 cm.   F29.C55F53

CLINTON. The Clinton and Benton register, 1904; comp. by Mitchell & Daggett.   Kent's Hill, Me.,
H. E. Mitchell pub. co., 1904.   131 p. 22½ cm. 19-6611.   F29. C6M6

COLUMBIA.   Centennial historical sketch of the town of Columbia as gathered from the town records, family records and traditional history ... 1796 - 1896.   By Levi Leighton ... (Machias, Me., Press of the Republican, 1896)   31 p. 20 cm. 8-34779.   F29. C6L5

CORINNA, A brief history of, from its purchase in 1804 to 1916, by Lilla E. Wood.   Bangor, Me., J. P.
Bass pub. co., 1916.   55, (1) p. illus. (incl. ports.) 23 cm. Most of the text of chapters I - X originally appeared in the Bangor
daily commercial ... 1916.   Chapter XI includes marriage intentions, marriages and births, 1817 - 1833; chapter XII, lists of selectmen town
clerks and treasurers; chapter XIII, civil war veterans. A16-1304.   F29.C65W8

CORINTH.   Early gleanings and random recollections of the town of Corinth ... 1792 - 1883.   By
Mason S. Palmer. Bangor, B. A. Burr, 1883.   34 p. 23½ cm. 1-8952.   F29. C7P1

90

MAINE 47

CUMBERLAND. The Cumberland and No. Yarmouth register, 1904, comp. by Mitchell, Russell and Strout. Brunswick, Me., The H. E. Mitchell pub. co., 1904. 100 p. 22 cm. 12-19875. F29.C77M6

CUSHING. Chronicles of Cushing and Friendship, containing historical, statistical, and miscellaneous information of the two towns ... Rockland, Me., The Maine home journal, 1892. 80 p. illus. 18 cm. 4-8784. F29. C8C5
Microfilm 27971 F

CUSHING'S Island. An historical sketch, guide book, and prospectus of Cushing's island, Casco bay, coast of Maine, by Wm. M. Sargent ... New York, American photo-engraving co. (c1886) 100 p. incl. front., illus., pl., map. 23 x 18 cm. 1-8953. F29. C9S2

CANTON and Dixfield register, The, 1905, comp. by Mitchell and Davis. Brunswick, Me., H. E. Mitchell co., 1905. 117 p. 22 cm. 12-19873. F29.C28M6

DAMARISCOTTA. Centennial celebration at Damariscotta and Newcastle ... 1876, together with the historical address delivered by Gen. James A. Hall ... Waldboro (Me.) Miller & Atwood, 1876. 18 p. 8° 1-8954-M1. F29. D1D1

DAMARISCOTTA. The town register: Damariscott, Newcastle, Bristol, Bremen, Muscongus Island, 1906, comp. by Mitchell, Daggett, Sawyer and Lawton. Brunswick, Me., The H. E. Mitchell co., 1906. 281 p. 22 cm. p. 5 - 100, "General reference." 12-17534. F29. D1M6

DAMARISCOTTA. The story of the Great Salt Bay and Vaughn's Pond. By Harold Webber Castner. (Damariscott? Me., 1950) 34 p. illus., maps. 23 cm. Cover title. 50-4564. F29. D13C3

DAMARISCOTTA. The Blackstones and their Indian's paradise (old Damariscotta) By Edward Joshua Lincoln. (Damariscotta? Me., 1952) 52 p. illus. 22 cm. 52-40965. F29. D13L5

DARK HARBOR. Facts and fancies and repetitions about Dark Harbor, by one of the very oldest cottagers (1890 - 1932) Nrs. E. A. Daniels (Caroline T.) written for ... Edna H. Barger. (Cambridge, Mass., The Cosmos press) 1935. 3, 58 p. 18 cm. 35-14830. F29. D2D3

DEER ISLE, An historical sketch of the town of, by George Lawrence Hosmer, with notices of its settlers and early inhabitants. Boston, Stanley and Usher, 1886. 292 p. front. (port.) 20½ cm. 1-8955 rev. F29. D3H8

— Boston, The Fort Hill press, (c1905) 289 p. front. (port.) fold. map 21cm. Contains map and index not found in original edition of 1886. 5-41607 rev. F29. D3H82

DEER ISLE. A Yankee town in the Civil War: being a pioneer chronicle of the vanished town of old Deer Isle, in Maine, during the crucial years, 1861 - 1865 ... By Vernal Hutchinson. Deer Isle, Me., 1957. 58 p. 22 cm. Includes bibliography. 57-31376. F29. D3H9 1957

— Freeport, Me., Bond Wheelwright Co. (1967) Now titled: A Maine town in the Civil War; 114 p. 21 cm. 67-16827. F29. D3H9 1967

DENNYSVILLE. Memorial of the 100th anniversary of the settlement of Dennysville, 1886. Portland, Me., B. Thurston and co., 1886. 115 p. 23½ cm. Contains genealogies of principal families - Tax-payers, 1807. - List of voters, 1815. 1-8956. F29. D4D4

DEXTER, ... The early history of the town of, by Halcyon Chase. (Dexter, 1904) 32 p. illus. (incl. ports.) 29 x 23 cm. Supplement to Eastern gazette, issue of August 4, 1904. 16-14552. F29. D5C48

DEXTER, Brief history of, prepared by members of the Class of 1916, Dexter high school ... (Dexter, Me., Eastern gazette, 1916) 19, (1) p. illus. 27 x 20½ cm. 17-13508. F29. D5D5

DEXTER. The Dexter register, 1904, comp by Mitchell and Remick. Kent's Hill, Me., The H. E. Mitchell pub, co., 1904. 134 p. 22 cm. 12-19495. F29. D5M6

48 LOCAL HISTORIES IN THE LIBRARY OF CONGRESS

DEXTER, History of; prepared by Miss Ella J. Mower and the pupils of her school.   Dexter, Me.,
Gazette book and job print, 1908.   14 p. 22 ½ cm. 17-14352.   F29. D5M9

DOVER and Foxcroft register, The, 1904, comp. by Mitchell & Remick.   Kent's Hill, Me., The H. E.
Mitchell pub. co., 1904.   154 p. 22 cm. 12-19496.   F29. D7M6

DRESDEN, History of, formerly a part of the old town of Pownalborough, from its earliest settlement
to the year 1900 ... by Charles Edwin Allen. (August, Me., Kennebec journal print shop) 1931.
8 p., (3) - 894 p., incl. front., illus., ports. maps (1 fold.) facsims. (1 fold.) 24 cm. 31-11722.   F29. D8A42

DURHAM, History of, with genealogical notes.   By Everett S. Stackpole ... Lewiston, Press of Lewiston Journal co., 1899.   vii, 314 p. front., plates, ports., map, plan, facsim. 24 cm. Genealogical notes, p. 148-290; All
marriages not mentioned in foregoing genealogies, down to 1840, p. 291 - 296; All births ... to 1865, p. 297 - 299; All deaths ... to 1888, p. 299 -
300. 1-8957.
                                                                                                    F29. D9S7

EAST LIVERMORE and Livermore register, The, 1903 - 4, by Mitchell & Daggett.   Kent's Hill, Me.,
The H. E. Mitchell pub. co., 1903.   148 p. 22 ½ cm. 10-222 rev.   F29. E13M6

EASTPORT ... A directory ... of the town of.   Portland, Me., Putnam, Tower & co. (1888 -
1 v. front. (plan) 23 ½ cm. 11-2894.
                                                                                                    Directories

EASTPORT city directory, The ... tog. with a business directory of Calais ... Eastport, Me., City
directory co., c. 1901.   1 v. illus., port. 23 cm. 1-15277.
                                                                                                    Directories

EASTPORT: a maritime history, by C. Donald Brown.   (Eastport, Me., Border History Research &
Pub. Center, 1968.   15 p. illus. 26 cm. 68-58518.   F29. E2B7

EASTPORT and Passamaquoddy; a collection of historical and biographical sketches, comp. by William
Henry Kilby; with notes and additions.   Eastport, Me., E. E. Shead & co., 1888.   2, (7) - 505 p. incl.
front., illus. maps. 20 ½ cm. Contains material on early settlers of Eastport. 1-8958.   F29. E2K4

EASTPORT, and vicinity, The history of: a lecture, delivered April, 1834 ... By Jonathan D. Weston
... Boston, Marsh, Capen and Lyon, 1834.   61 p. 22 cm. 10-21668 rev.   F29. E2W5

EDDINGTON.   Memoir of Col. Jonathan Eddy of Eddington, Me: with some account of the Eddy family,
and of the early settlers on Penobscot River.   By Joseph W. Porter ... Augusta (Me.) Sprague, Owen &
Nash, printers, 1877.   72 p. 23 ½ cm. 7-31012.   F29. E21P8
                                                                                                    E275. E21

ELIOT.   The Eliot and York, Maine, York Harbor and York Beach directory ... (Candia, N. H.)
W. E. Shaw, 19 -   v. 24 ½ cm. 22-660.
                                                                                                    Directories

ELIOT.   History of the centennial of the incorporation of the town of Eliot ... 1910; ed. by Aaron B.
Cole and J. L. M. Willis.   Eliot (Me.) A. Caldwell, 1912.   1, ii, 138 p. front., plates, ports., facsims. 23 ½ cm.
13-736 rev.
                                                                                                    F29. E4C6

ELIOT miscellany.   Bits of forgotten history. (Eliot? Me., 1876?)   10 p. 27 cm. 18-5785.
                                                                                                    F29. E4E4

GREENACRE on the Piscataqua.   (By) Anna Josephine Ingersoll.   New York, The Alliance pub. co.,
(1900)   22 p. plates, ports. 19 ½ x 11 ½ cm.   Jan 24, 1901 - 94.   F29. E4I4

ELIOT.   Old Eliot; a quarterly magazine of the history and biography of the upper parish of Kittery,
now Eliot ... J. L. M. Willis ... ed. v. 1 - 9; Eliot, Me., 1897 - 1909.   9 v. in 7. illus., plates, ports.
24 cm. Monthly, 1897 - 99; quarterly, 1901 - 03, 1906 - 09. No numbers issued for 1900, 1904 - 05. No more published. 11-15741.
                                                                                                    F29. E4O4

92

MAINE 49

ELLSWORTH, History of, by Albert H. Davis.   Lewiston, Me., Lewiston journal printshop, 1927.
244 p. illus. (incl. ports.) 23½ cm. 27-19768.   F29. E5D2

EMBDEN town of yore; olden times and families there and in adjacent towns, by Ernest George Walker ... Skowhegan, Me., Independent-reporter co., 1920.   xiv, (2) 700 p. incl. front., illus., plates, ports., maps (part double) 24 cm. 29-22925.   F29. E53W17

FARMINGDALE, Vital records of, to ... 1892. Ed. Henry Sewall Webster.   Pub. under authority of the Maine historical society.   Gardiner, The Reporter Journal press, 1909. 96 p. 23½ cm. Alphabetic digest of the ms. records of the town, supplemented by private and other records. 9-25292.   F29. F19F2

FARMINGTON, Franklin County, A history of.   By Francis Gould Butler ... Farmington, Press of Knowlton, McLeary, 1885.   1, 683 p, (12) p. front., plates, ports. 23 cm. Marriages, births, deaths: 12 p. at end.
1-8959 rev.   F29. F2B9

FARMINGTON, A history of ... to 1846.   By Thomas Parker.   Farmington, Me., J. S. Swift, 1846.
136 p. 22½ cm. 1-8960.   F29. F2P2

— 2d ed. 1875.   120 p. 24 cm. First edition, 1846. 1-8961.   F29. F2P3

FARMINGTON, Wilton, Chesterville, New Sharon, The town register, 1910.   Brunswick, Me., The Maine map & register co., 1910.   205, 72 p. 6 maps (5 fold.) 22½ cm. "Maine reference manual" 12-16465. F29. F2T74

FAYETTE, History of.   By Joseph H. Underwood.   Ed. and completed by Russell C. Tuck.   Augusta, Me., C. E. Nash, 1956.   174 p. port., fold. maps, facsim. 24 cm. 58-36408.   F29. F25U5

FORT FAIRFIELD, History of and biographical sketches, by C. H. Ellis.   Fort Fairfield, Me., 1894.
10, (25) - 382 p. incl. front., plates, ports. pl. 21½ cm. 1-8962.   F29. F7E4

FOXCROFT, 1812 - 1912.   Proceedings of the centennial celebration ... 1912.   John Francis Sprague, ed.   Dover, 1917.   2, 49 - 134 p. illus. 23 cm. "Reprinted from Sprague's Journal." 10-3706. F29. F7F7

FORT FAIRFIELD, The historic pageant of and the Aroostook Valley ... 1916.   For Fairfield, Me. "Review" press, c1916)   55 p. illus. (incl. music) 20½ cm. 16-17373.   F29. F7H67

FOXCROFT.   Old Foxcroft; traditions and memories, with family records, comp. by Mary Chandler Lowell ... Concord, N. H., The Rumford press (c. 1935)   x, 262 p. 1 illus., 4 port. on 1 pl. 23½ cm. 36-1262.
                                                                                                     F29. F7L6

FORT FAIRFIELD, Views of.   Fort Fairfield, Me., 1889.   1 p., 20 pl. obl. 24°. 1-8963-M1.   F29. F7V6

FRANKFORT, History of the town of, by Erasmus Jones.   Winterport (Me.) Advertiser job print, 1897.   1, 57 p. illus., pl. 19½ cm. Includes the early history of Winterport, which was set off from Frankfort in 1860. 2-3376.
                                                                                                     F29. F8J7

FREEPORT register, The, 1904.   comp. by Mitchell and Campbell.   Brunswick, Me., The H. E. Mitchell pub. co., 1904.   108 p. 22 cm. 12-19497.   F29. F84M6

FREEPORT, Three centuries of, by Florence G. Thurston and Harmon S. Cross.   Freeport, Me., 1940.   x, (3) - 254 p. illus., plates, ports. 23½ cm. 40-12529.   F29. F84T5

FRYEBURG, an historical sketch, by John Stuart Barrows.   Fryeburg, Pequawket press, 1938.
4, 300 p. front., plates. 23½ cm. "Sources of information": p. 280 - 281. 39-1418.   F29. F9B37

FRYEBURG, The centennial celebration of the settlement of, with the historical address, by Rev. Samuel Souther ... Worcester (Mass.) Tyler & Seagrave (1864)   79 p. 23½ cm. 1-8964.
                                                                                                     F29. F9F9

FRYEBURG Webster centennial, celebrating the coming of Daniel Webster to Fryeburg, 100 years ago ... Fryburg, Me., A. F. Lewis, 1902.   83 p. incl. port. plates. 21½ cm. 2-11607.   F29. F9F94

93

FRYEBURG. The Illustrated Fryeburg Webster memorial. Fryeburg, Me., A. F. & C. W. Lewis, 1882. 39 p. plates, port. 23½ cm. 1-13328. F29. F9 I3

FRYEBURG. Festival of the Fryeburg septuagenarians, born in 1834: ... Fryeburg, A. F. Lewis, 1904. 1, 143 p. port. 23 cm. 5-36836. F29. F9L6

FRYEBURG. The town register: Fryeburg, Lovell, Sweden, Stow and Chatham, 1907, comp. by Mitchell, Davis and Daggett. Brunswick, Me., The H. E. Mitchell co., 1907. 2, (17) - 107 (i. e. 95), 64 (i.e. 66) p. 22½ cm. Introduction, p. 5-16, omitted? 12-19498. F29. F9M6

GARDINER. The Gardiner story, 1849 - 1949; historical sketches of the plantation, town, city, and noted people, written by Robert J. Erskine and others. Pub. by the city of Gardiner, 1949. (76) p. illus., ports., fold. map (laid in) 23 cm. 49-5690*. F29. G3E7

GARDINER, The centennial of ... 1903. Gardiner, Me., 1903. 79 p. front., plates, ports. 23 cm. "A brief sketch of Gardiner's early history," by J. S. Maxcy: p. 23 - 46. 5-1238. F29. G3G3

GARDINER, Vital records of, to the year 1892. Ed. Henry Sewall Webster ... Pub. under authority of the Maine historical society. Gardiner, Me., The Reporter-journal press, 1914-15. 2 v. 23½ cm. Contents. - pt. I. Births. - pt. II. Marriages and deaths. 14-31276 rev. F29. G3G35

GARDINER. The city of Gardiner. Its water power, industries, water front, picturesque avenues, attractions and surroundings ... (Gardiner, Me.) The Board of trade, 1896. 112 p. illus. (incl. port.) 19 x 26½ cm. 42-11487. F29. G3G37

GARDINER. History of Gardiner, Pittston and West Gardiner, with a sketch of the Kennebec Indians etc. ... with genealogical sketches of many families. By J. W. Hanson ... Gardiner (Me.) W. Palmer, 1852. xi, (12) - 343, (8) p. front., plates. 19 cm. L. C. copy replaced by microfilm. 1-8965. F29. G3H2
Microfilm 24350 F

GARDINER. ... Silvester Gardiner (by) Henry Sewall Webster. Gardiner, Me., The Reporter-journal press, 1913. 52 p. 23 cm. (Gardiner historical series, no. 2) 13-6968. F29. G3W3

GARLAND, History of, by Lyndon Oak. Dover, Me., The Observer pub. co., 1912. xii, 401 p. front. (port.) 23½ cm. 13-9175. F29. G35O2

GEORGETOWN, Vital records of, copied by E. M. Trafford. Boston, Research publication co., 1903. 1, 56 p. 25 cm. 3-32516. F29. G4G4

GEORGETOWN, Vital records of, to the year 1892; ed. Mary Pelham Hill ... Pub. under the authority of the Maine historical soc. (Auburn, Me., Press of Merrill & Webber co.) 1939 - 43. 3 v. 23 cm. 39-28777. F29. G4G43

GEORGETOWN. The town register: Phippsburg, Georgetown, Arrowsic, West Bath, Westport, The town register, 1906; comp. by Mitchell, Daggett, Sawyer and Lawton. Brunswick, Me., The H. E. Mitchell co., 1906. 210 p. 22 cm. p. (5) - 100, "General reference" (Maine) 12-19499. F29. G4M6

GORHAM, ... Dedication of the Soldiers' monument at ... 1866. Portland, Press of B. Thurston and co., 1866. 32 p. 23 cm. 12-24158. F29. G6G59

GORHAM, Celebration of the 150th anniversary of ... 1886. Portland, Me., B. Thurston & co., 1886. 2, 133 p. front., plates. 23½ cm. 1-8966. F29. G6G6

GORHAM. ... Publishments, marriages, births and deaths from the earlier records of Gorham. Comp. by Marquis F. King ... Portland, Maine genealogical soc., 1897. 12, (206) p. illus. 24 cm. ... from the Portland Evening express, 1895. 4-13422. F29. G6G62

GORHAM. A sketch of the life of General James Irish of Gorham, 1776 - 1863. By Lyndon Oak. Boston, Lee & Shepard, 1898. 70 p. front., ports. 24 cm. "Family records of General James Irish and his descendants": p. 59 - 70. 10-537 rev. F29. G6 I58

MAINE 51

GORHAM, Bi-centennial history of, 1736 - 1936; an account of the anniversary celebration of the town, comp. and ed. by Walter H. Johnson; illus. by Hayden L. V. Anderson. Westbrook, Me., H. S. Cobb, 1936.   171 p. illus. (incl. ports.) 23 ½ cm. 38-2887.   F29. G6J6

GORHAM, History of, by Hugh D. McLellan. Comp. and ed. by his daughter, Katharine B. Lewis. Portland, Smith & Sale, 1903.   1, 860 p. front., illus., plates, ports., plans (1 fold.) 24 cm. Genealogy: p. (383) - 843. 3-4676.   F29. G6M2

GORHAM. The centennial anniversary of the settlement of Gorham; an address ... 1836.   36 p. 23 cm. 1-8967 rev.*   F29. G6P6

GORHAM, A history of the town of. Prepared at the request of the town, by Josiah Pierce. Portland, (Me.) Foster and Cushing, 1862.   iv, (5) - 239, (1) p. 22 ½ cm. "Biographical notices" p. 153-231. 1-8968.   F29. G6P7

GOULDSBORO, Historical researches of. Gouldsboro, Me., Daughters of liberty, 1904.   108 p. map, plan. 21 ½ cm. 4-4563.   F29. G7D2

GOULDSBORO. The peninsula. By Louise (Dickinson) Rich. Drawings by Grattan Condon. (1st ed.) Philadelphia, Lippincott (1958)   281 p. illus. 22 cm. 58-11132.   F29. G7R5

GRAND LAKE Stream plantation, Hinckley Township; or, a sketch, by Minnie Atkinson. Newburyport, Mass., Newburyport herald press (c. 1920)   5, 122 p., front., plates. 25 cm. 20-22636.   F29. G75A87

GRAY. The Gray and New Gloucester register, 1905, comp. by Mitchell, Daggett, Weston and Reed. Brunswick, Me., The H. E. Mitchell pub. co., 1905.   110 p. 22 ½ cm. 12-19500.   F29. G77M6

GREENE, Androscoggin county, Sesquicentennial history of the town of, 1775 - 1900, with some matter extending to a later date, compiled by Walter Lindley Mower. (Auburn, Me., Press of Merril & Webber co.) 1938.   1, (v) - xiv, 578, (2) p. illus. (incl. ports.) mounted fodl. map, facsim. 39-4229.   F29. G8M7

GREENE & Leeds, Souvenir of. Brunswick, Me., The Maine map & register co. (1911)   43 p. incl. 2 pl., 2 maps. 27 ½ x 35 ½ cm. 12-11994.   F29. G8S7

GUILFORD centennial, 1816 - 1916 ... (John Francis Sprague, ed.)   (In Sprague's journal of Maine history ... 1916 v. 4, p. 65-190) "Vital records": p. 162-190. 17-13766.   F29. G9G9

GUILFORD and Sangerville town register, 1904, comp. by Mitchell, Remick & Bean. Kents Hill, Me., The H. E. Mitchell pub. co., 1904.   108 p. 22 cm. 12-19501.   F29. G9M6

HALLOWELL. City hall dedication and Hallowell reunion, with oration, poem, etc. Hallowell, Register press, 1899.   43, (1) p. front., plates, ports. 19 cm. 5-36577.   F29. H15H2

HALLOWELL, Vital record of, to the year 1892 ... (Auburn, Me.) Under authority of the Maine historical society, 1924.   v. 23 ½ cm. 24 - 27223.   F29. H15H26

HALLOWELL. Old Hallowell on the Kennebec, by Emma Huntington Nason ... Augusta, Me., (Burleigh & Flynt) 1909.   7, 359 p. front., plates, ports. 25 cm. 9-31504.   F29. H15N3

HALLOWELL. Historic Hallowell. Compiled by Katherine H. Snell and Vincent P. Ledew. ... 1962.   112 p. illus. 29 cm.   F29. H15S65

HARPSWELL register, The, 1904, comp. by Mitchell and Campbell. Brunswick, Me., The H. E. Mitchell pub. co., 1904.   102 p. illus. 21 ½ cm. 12-19502.   F29. H2M6

HARPSWELL. Historic Harpswell, its historic Congregation church and famous ministers. 1758 - 1903. By Rev. Charles N. Sinnett. Haverhill, Mass., C. C. Morse & son, 1903.   19 p. 23 ½ cm. 3-28366.   F29. H2S6

HARPSWELL. Souvenir, Elijah Kellogg church, Harpswell. (Franklin, Mass., 1911)   19 ½ cm.   F29. H2S71

95

HARPSWELL. Beautiful Harpswell; the Neck and its 45 island jewels, written and illustrated by Margaret and Charles Todd. (Orr's Island? Me., 1967) 58 p. 23 cm.
F29. H2T6

HARRISON, Centennial history of, containing the centennial celebration of 1905, and historical and biographical matter, comp. and ed. by Alphonso Moulton and others ... Pub. by the authority of the town. Portland, Me., Southwood printing co., 1909. xii, 727 p. front., plates, ports. 24½ cm. 11-8430.
F29. H3M8

HARRISON, Early settlers of, with an historical sketch of the settlement, progress and present condition of the town. By Rev. G. T. Ridlon. Skowhegan (Me.) Kilby & Woodbury, 1877) 4, (7) - 138 p. 22½ cm. 1-1749.
F29. H3R5

HARRISON, My first sixty years in, by Ernest E. Ward. With a few home-drawn sketches by the author. Denmark, Me., printed by Cardinal Print. Co. (1966) 85 p. 24 cm.
F29. H3W3 1966

— 1967. 92 p. 23 cm.
F29. H3W3 1967

HERMON, Penobscot County, Centennial souvenir and history of, 1814 - 1914. Carmel, Me., Carmel print (1914) 1, 33 p. illus. 18½ cm. 16-2600.
F29. H5H5

HIRAM (by) William Teg. (Cornish, Me., The Webb-Smith printing co., 1941) 107 p. 23½ cm. 41-12184.
F29. H6T4

HIRAM, History of. Sesquicentennial (i.e. rev.) ed. By William Teg. Cornish, Me., Carbrook Press (c. 1964) 137 p. 23 cm.
F29. H6T42

HOULTON directory, The. 1895, 1900. Boston, Mass. (etc.) A. B. Sparrow, c. 1895 - 19
v. 24 cm. Vol. for 1900 also issued in Houlton, Presque Isle, Fort Fairfield and Caribou directory. 32-15161.
Directories

HOULTON, Presque Isle, Fort Fairfield and Caribou directory. 1900. (Boston, A. B. Sparrow, c. 1900) 414 p. fold. map. 24 cm. Title from cover. No more pub? 1-29784 rev.
Directories

HOULTON, The story of, from the public records, and from the experiences of its founders, their descendants, and associates to the present time ... By Francis Barnes. Houlton, Me., W. H. Smith, 1889. (126) p. 20 cm. 1-8969.
F29. H8B2

HOULTON, History of the town of ... 1804 - 1883. By an old pioneer. (J. Kendall) Haverhill, Mass., C. C. Morse & son, 1884. 60 p. front. 23 cm. 1-8970.
F29. H9K3

HOULTON, The story of. By Cora M. Putnam. Portland, Me., House of Falmouth (1958) 423 p. illus. 24 cm. 59-33177.
F29. H8P8

INDUSTRY, History of. By William Allen. 2d ed., improved and enl., 1869. Skowhegan, Smith & Emery, printers, 1869. 48 p. 22½ cm. 1-8971.
F29. I4A4

INDUSTRY, Franklin County, A history of the town of ... embracing the cessions of New Sharon, New Vineyard, Anson, and Stark. ... including the history and genealogy of many of the leading families. By William Collins Hatch. Farmington, Me., Knowlton, McLeary & co., 1893. xiv, (13) - 862 p. front., plates, ports. 23½ cm. 1-8972.
F29. I4H3

ISLAND FALLS, A history of ... 1843 - 1972, and a collection of historical sketches. Compiled by Nina G. Sawyer. (Caribou, Me., c. 1972) 154 p. illus. 28 cm.
F29. I78S29

ISLESBORO sketch, An, by Joel Cook. With illustrations by Louis K. Harlow. (Boston) Boston

MAINE 53

photogravure co., 1890.   36 p. incl. front., illus. plates. 21 cm. 1-13329.   F29. I8C7

ISLESBOROUGH, History of. By John Pendleton Farrow ... Bangor, T.W. Burr, 1893. xii, 313 p. front.,
plates, ports., double map, plans. 24 cm. 1-8973.   F29. I8F2

ISLESBORO. The town register: Islesboro, Castine, Penobscot, Brooksville, 1906, comp. by Mitchell,
Daggett, Lawton and Sawyer. Brunswick, The H.E. Mitchell co., 1906.   247 p. illus. 22 cm. p. 5 - 100,
"General reference" 12 - 19503.   F29. I8M6

JACKMAN. and the Moose River region, by John Francis Sprague. Dover, (Me.) 1915. 1, 53 - 80 p.
illus. (incl. port.) 22 ½ cm. Reprinted from Sprague's journal of Maine history. 16-22717.   F29.J 13S7

JAY, Franklin County, History of, by Benjamin F. Lawrence. Boston, Griffith-Stillings press, 1912.
vi, 93 p. front., plates, ports., fold. map. 23 ½ cm. 13-10217.   F29. J3L4

JAY register, The, 1905, comp. by Mitchell and Davis. Brunswick, The H.E. Mitchell co., 1905.
88 p. 22 cm. 12-19504.   F29. J3M6

JEFFERSON, Centennial celebration of the town of, Lincoln County... 1907; comp. by Alberto A.
Bennett. Lewiston, Me., Journal printing co., 1908.   61 p. plates, port. 23 ½ cm. 8-27440.   F29. J4J4

JONESBOROUGH. The revolution. Life of Hannah Weston; with a brief record of her ancestry.
Also, a condensed history of the first settlement of Jonesborough, Machias and other neighboring towns.
By a citizen ... (George Washington Drisko) Machias, Me., C.O. Furbush & co., 1857.   163 p.
15 ½ cm. Genealogy: p. 112 - 121. 7-13471 rev.   F29. J7D7

— 2d ed. Machias, Me., G.A. Parlin, 1903.   4, (3) - 140 p. 18 ½ cm. "First ed. 1857" 37-14811.   F29.J7D72

JONESPORT register, The, 1905, comp. by Mitchell and Campbell. Brunswick, Me., The H.E. Mitchell co., 1905.   112 p. 22 cm. 12-19505.   F29. J8M6

KENNEBUNK, Chronicles of, being scenes and episodes in an old Maine village & vicinity, by Wm. E.
Barry; with illustrations by the writer, redrawn by Rockwell Kent. (New York, Redfield, etc. co.)
5, 7 - 86 p. front. (map) illus. 23 ½ x 31 cm. 25-2143.   F29. K3B26

KENNEBUNK. A stroll by a familiar river, comprising the colloquy of saunterers by its lower course,
and household words pertaining to its early history, by Wm. E. Barry. (Kennebunk, Me.) Enterprise
press, c.1911.   6 p. 2 - 90 numb. l. front., 11 pl. 2 port. 29 cm. 12-15727.   F29.K3B27

KENNEBUNK. A stroll thro' the past, accompanied by an invisible associate, and using an 18th century
stage-route and river ford, preceded by a summary of the early ownerships ... by William E. Barry.
Portland, Me., Southworth press, 1933.   vi, 93 p. front. (port.) plates, map. 26 ½ cm. 33-13072.   F29.K3B28

KENNEBUNKPORT. Leading business men of Kennebunkport, Kennebunk and Old Orchard beach, with
an historical sketch of each place, by William Hale Beckford. Boston, Mercantile pub. co., 1888.
1, (5) - 62 p. illus. 25 cm. 1-8974 rev.   F29. K3B3

KENNEBUNK port, history of ... 1602 to 1837. By Charles Bradbury. Kennebunk, Printed by J.K.
Remich, 1837.   301 p. front. 18 ½ cm. "Brief notices of the earlier settlers": p. 223 - 287. 1-8974a.   F29. K3B7
Rare Book Coll.

— Durrell Publications, 1967.   338 p. 22 cm. 67-26541.   F29. K3B7
1967

KENNEBUNKPORT. Ropes' ends; traditions, legends and sketches of old Kennebunkport and vicinity,
by Annie Peabody Brooks. Kennebunkport, Me., The author, 1901.   236 p. incl. front. plates, ports. 20 cm.
1-23745.   F29. K3B8

KENNEBUNK, District of. A list of vessels built, from 1800 - 1873. Comp. by Seth E. Bryant.
Kennebunk, 1874.   12 p. 27 ½ cm. 13 - 5128.   F29. K3B9

KENNEBUNKS, The; "Out of the past." By Kenneth Joy.   Freeport, Me., B. Wheelwright Co. (1967)
xvi, 135 p. 24 cm.   67-21208.
F29. K3J6

KENNEBUNK, Old family portraits of.   Kennebunk, Me., The Brick store museum, 1944.   (24) p. illus.
(ports.) 22 cm. Bibliography: p. (23) 45-2169.
F29. K3K38

KENNEBUNK, Old houses of; photos. by Victor Camp.   Kennebunk, Me., The Brick store museum
(1939)   (15) p. illus. 20 cm. 45-43159.
F29. K3K4

KENNEBUNK and Wells, The town register, 1905, comp. by Mitchell, Holt and Lawton.   Brunswick,
Me., The H. E. Mitchell co., 1905.   100, 130 (i.e.136) p. 22 cm. p. 5 - 100 "General reference" 12-19506.   F29. K3M6

KENNEBUNK, History of ... to 1890.   Including biographical sketches.   By Daniel Remich.   (Portland, Me., Lakeside press co., c1911)   viii, 542, xxxvi p. front. (port.) 25 cm. 11-28842.   F29. K3R3

KENNEBUNK, Military and naval history of residents of, who enlisted during the late civil war.   By
Andrew Walker.   Kennebunk (Me.) 1868.   24 p. 22 cm. 12-11183.
F29. K3W17

KENNEBUNKPORT.   Picturesque nooks on the coast of Maine, in and around Kennebunkport ... N.Y.,
H. W. Rankin (1894)   1 p. 15 pl. obl. 32° 1-8975-6-M1.   F29. K3P6
— 1895.   4 l. 4 pl. obl. 12°.   F29. K3P7

KENNEBUNKPORT, Old-time dwellings in; reprint mostly from "The turn o' the tide" by Joy Wheeler
Dow, with photos. by the author.   Kennebunk, The Star print, inc., 1926.   82 p., incl. front., illus., map.
16 cm. 26-14501.
F29. K32D7

... KINGFIELD register.   By H. E. Mitchell.   (Kingfield, 1902)   30 p. 23 cm. 12-19507.   F29. K5M6

KITTERY POINT.   Colonial village.   Kittery Point Gundalow Club (1948?)   82 p. illus. 23 cm. Bibliography:
p. (63) - 65.   A 48-8677*
F29. K6F7

KITTERY.   Perfecting or valuation lists of Kittery, 1760, contributed by Nathan Goold.   (n. p., 1899?)
18 p. 24½ cm. 6-38850.
F29. K6K6

KITTERY.   Old Kittery, 1647 - 1947; 300th anniversary.   (Kittery, 1947)   36 p. illus. 23 cm. 47-28203*
F29. K6K63

KITTERY, ancient and modern ... (Kittery booklet committee, Newburyport, Mass., c.1931)
40, (4) p. illus. (incl. map) 23 cm. Folded map mounted on inside of cover. Bibliography: p. 36. 31-19248.   F29. K6K69

KITTERY, ancient and modern ... (Kittery community service assoc., Kittery, c.1925)   40 p. illus.
(incl. map) 23 cm. Folded map mounted on inside of cover. CA 27-121 unrev.
F29. K6K7

KITTERY.   Old Kittery, land of adventure, 1647, and Captain Francis Champernowne (1614 - 1687)
New York, Newcomen Society of England, American Branch, 1947.   40 p. illus. 23 cm. 47-6445*
F29. K6P4

KITTERY.   A record of the services of the commissioned officers and enlisted men of Kittery and
Eliot, who served their country on land and sea in the American revolution, 1775 to 1783.   By Oliver
Philbrick Remick.   Boston, A. Mudge & son (1901)   2, 223 p. 23½ cm. 2-7927.
F29. K6R3

KITTERY.   Old Kittery and her families, by Everett S. Stackpole ... Lewiston, Me., Press of Lewiston
journal co., 1903.   822 p. illus. (incl. ports., maps) 24 cm. 3-20054.   F29. K6S7

LAMOINE and its attractions as a place of summer sojourning ... by John C. Winterbotham.   (Boston,
W. H. Couillard, 1888)   1, 28 p. front (port.) pl. obl. 16°. 1-8977 - M1.   F29. L2W7

LEBANON.   Soldiers of the American revolution, of Lebanon, Me.   By George Walter Chamberlain ...
Weymouth, Mass., Weymouth & Braintree, 1897.   48 p. 24 cm. 1-8978.   F29. L4C4

LEBANON, Vital records of, to the year 1892 ... ed. George W. Chamberlain ... (Boston) Under authority of the Maine historical soc., 1922 - 23.   3 v.   23½ cm.   Contents. - v.1. Births - v.2. Marriages - v.3. Deaths. 22-17061 rev.   F29. L4L4

LEBANON. Historic Lebanon; Lebanon and the grand work of its Congregational church in 138 years. B Charles N. Sinnett. Haverhill, Mass., C. C. Morse & son, 1903.   16 p. 22 cm. 4-22372.   F29. L4S6

LEE. The story of an old New England town. History of Lee, Maine. Comp. and ed. by Vinal A. Houghton ... Wilton, Me., Nelson print, 1926.   5, 248 p. plates, ports. 23½ cm. 26-11081.   F29. L48H3
                                                                                                                                                                F29. L48H8

LEEDS, History of the town of, Androscoggin county, from ... 1780; by J. C. Stinchfield, et al. (Lewiston, Me., Press of Lewiston journal, 1901)   viii, 419 p. front., pl., port. 23½ cm. 2-18376.
                                                                                                                                                                F29. L5S8

... LEWISTON and Auburn directory ... (v. 1 -   1872 -   Boston, Mass., W. A. Greenough & co., 1872 -   v.   24 cm. Title varies. 19-15071.   Directories

LEWISTON and Auburn directory ... Manning's. 19 -   v. -   Manning co., c. 19 -
    v. 23 cm. CA 31 - 126 unrev.   Directories

... LEWISTON and Auburn business directory, guide and manual ... 1890 -   Boston, Purdy & Leavitt, c. 1890.   v. 18 cm. CA 33 - 585 unrev.   Directories

LISBON town register, The, 1905, comp. by Mitchell & Campbell. Brunswick, Me. The H. E. Mitchell co., 1905.   117 p. 22 cm. 12-19508.   F29. L68M6

LISBON, Souvenir of. 1911. Brunswick, Me., The Maine map & register co. (1911)   60 p. incl. plates, maps. 26½ x 35½ cm. 12-11996.   F29. L68S7

LINCOLN, Penobscot County, History of the town of, 1822 - 1928, by Dana Willis Fellows ... Lewiston, Me., Dingley press, (c. 1929)   436, (8) p. incl. illus., pl., ports. 23½ cm. "Genealogy of town of Lincoln": p. (267) - 430. 29 - 16528.   F29. L7F3

LITCHFIELD, History of and an account of its centennial celebration, 1895. Augusta, Kennebec journal print, 1897.   548 p. plates, ports. 23½ cm. 1-1785.   F29. L7 L7

LIVERMORE, History of the town of. By I. T. Monroe. (c. 1928)   1v.   F29. L8M7

LIVERMORE, Notes, historical, descriptive, and personal, of, in Androscoggin (formerly in Oxford) county, Maine ... Portland, Bailey & Noyes, 1874.   109 p. front., mounted photos. 24½ cm. 1-8979.
                                                                                                                                                                F29. L8W3

MACHIAS, Narrative of the town of, the old and the new, the early and the late, by George W. Drisko ... Machias, Me., Press of the Republican, 1904.   5, 589 p. incl. front., plates, ports. 22½ cm. "Genealogy": p. (345) - 578. 4-21111 Rev.   F29. M1D7

MACHIAS. Memorial address on the occasion of the centennial anniversary of the formation of Centre street Congregation church, at Machias, Me. By H. F. Harding. ... Machias, C. O. Furbush, 1884. ix, 70 p. 20 cm. 8-34778.   F29. M1H2

MACHIAS, Memorial of the centennial anniversary of the settlement of. Machias, C. O. Furbush, 1863. 179, (1) p. 22 cm. "Machias genealogies": p. 151 - 179. 1-8980.   F29. M1M1

MADAWASKA and Aristook settlements in 1831, State of the. Report of John G. Deane ... to Sameul E. Smith, governor of the state of Maine.   (In New Brunswick hist. soc. colls., St. John, N.B. 1914, v.3, p. 344-484) 20-1677.
                                                                                                                                    F1041.N53 vol. 3
                                                                                                                                    F29. M

MADAWASKA, ... The Acadians of. By Charles W. Collins ... Boston, T. A. Whalen, 1902. 66 p. 24 cm. N. E. Catholic historical soc. Publications no. 3) 5-5542.   F29. M2C6

MADISON register, The, 1903, comp. by Mitchell and Randall. Kent's Hill, Me., H. E. Mitchell co., 1903.   137 p. illus. 22 cm. 12-19509. F29. M3M6

MARS HILL, typical Aroostook town. Sketches by Norma Smith Tweedie. (Presque Isle, Me., Northern Printers, 1952)   74 p. illus. 24 cm. 53-17559. F29. M35T8

MECHANIC FALLS register, The, 1904, by Mitchell and Denning. Kent's Hill, Me., The H. E. Mitchell co., 1904.   92 p. illus. 21 cm. 12-19510. F29. M4M6

MECHANIC FALLS, Historical sketch of the town of. Mechanic Falls, Me., Ledger pub. co., 1894.   55 p. incl. front. (port.) illus., pl. 8°. 1-8981 - M1. F29. M4W3

MILLBRIDGE register, The, 1905, comp. by Mitchell & Campbell. Brunswick, Me., The H. E. Mitchell co., 1905.   88 p. 22 cm. 12-19876. F29. M6M6

MONMOUTH and Wales, History of, by Harry H. Cochrane ... illus. by the author ... East Winthrop (Me.) Banner co., 1894.   2 v. front., plates, ports. fold. plans. 24 cm. "Genealogical appendix" v.2. 1-8982. F29. M7C6

MONSON. Semi-centennial address of Chas. Davison, poems, by W. S. Knowlton, etc. Monson, 1872. Portland, Hoyt, Fogg & Breed, 1872.   36 p. 8°. 1-8983 - M1. F29. M8M8

— Foxcroft, F. D. Barrows, 1892.   38 p. 19½ cm. 3-29123. F29. M8M82

MORRILL in the county of Waldo, History of the town of ... by Timothy W. Robinson. Belfast, Me., City job print, 1944 - 57.   2 v. pl., ports. 24 cm. 45-15636.   vol. I. 1794 to 1887. 1944.   Vol. II. A genealogical history of the families of Morrill, by Theoda Mears Morse and Mr. and Mrs. Charles White.   1959.

F29. M85R6

MOSCOW, Makers of. Moscow History Committee. Photo. copying by Mrs. Stanley Redmond. Skowhegan, Me., Independent-Reporter Press, 1966.   xii, 66 p. illus., maps, ports. 23 cm.

F29. M854M6

MOUNT VERNON and Readfield register, 1908. Compilers: F. A. Hunton and Clyde Childs. Augusta, Me., The Mitchell-Cony co., 1908.   48, (29) p. fold. map. 22½ cm. 12-19877. F29. M9H9

NEW GLOUCESTER centennial ... 1874, by T. H. Haskell. Portland, Hoyt, Fogg & Donham, 1875.   139, (2) p. 21½ cm. 1-8984. F29. N4N5

NEW HARBOR,, ... A brief description of Danforth Point, New Harbor, with an account of the Danforth Point trust. Exeter, N. H., The Academy press, 1924.   (8) p. illus. (incl. maps) 28½ cm. "New Harbor, Monhegan, and Pemaquid in the early days", 1400 - 1694: p. (3) - (4) CA 34 - 1365 unrev. F29. N42D2

NEW PORTLAND register, 1902, by H. E. Mitchell. (Kingfield, Me., W. P. Watson, 1902)   33 p. 22½ cm. 12-19878. F29. N46M6

NEW SWEDEN, Celebration of the decennial anniversary of the founding of, ... 1880. Andrew Wiren and others. (Portland, Me., B. Thurston) 1881.   87 p. 23 cm. 1-8985. F29. N5N5

NEW SWEDEN, The story of, as told at the Quarter centennial celebration of the founding of the Swedish colony in the woods of Maine, ... 1895. Portland (Me.) Loring, Short & Harmon, 1896.   2, (9) - 134 p. front. (port.) illus. 24 cm. 1-8986. F29. N5N6

NEW VINEYARD and Strong register, 1902. By H. E. Mitchell and E. K. Woodard. (Kingfield? 1902)   47 p. 22½ cm. 12-19879. F29. N57M6

NEWCASTLE. The history of ancient Sheepscot and Newcastle (Me.) including early Pemaquid, Damariscotta, and other contiguous places ... tog. with the genealogy of more than four hundred families; by David Quimby Cushman ... Bath, E. Upton, 1882.   xvii, 458 p. front., pl., port., map. 22½ cm. Genealogy: p. 351 - 437. 1-13330. F29. N6C9

MAINE 57

NEWCASTLE. ... Erster jahresbericht des vereins für erdkunde zu Dresden. 1865.   F29. N6E7

NEWCASTLE, Early town records of ... 1756 - 1779. Copied from the original manuscript records. Damariscotta, Me., 1914.   (50) p. 31 x 23 ½ cm. 20-1714.   F29.N6N53

NEWPORT, ... A brief history of, 1814 - 1914. By William H. Mitchell. (Newport, A.W. Lander, 1914)   55, (3) p. illus. 23 cm. 15-17148.   F29.N63M6

NOBLEBORO, Souvenir of. 1911. Brunswick, Me., The Maine map & register co. (1911) 3, 13 - 21 p. 23 - 31 numb. 1. 2 pl. 2 maps. 26 ½ x 35 ½ cm. Printed one side of leaf only. 12-11993.   F29.N68S7

NORRIDGEWOCK, The history of; comprising memorials of the aboriginal inhabitants ... biographical sketches ... By William Allen ... Norridgewock (Me.,) E.J. Peet, 1849.   252 p. plates. 18 cm. 1-8987.
    F29. N7A4

NORRIDGEWOCK. History of the old towns, Norridgewock and Canaan, comprising Norridgewock, Canaan, Starks, Skowhegan, and Bloomfield ... By J.W. Hanson ... Boston, The author, 1849. 371, (1) p. front., 1 illus., plates. 19 ½ cm. 1-8988.   F29. N7H2

NORRIDGEWOCK. What of our revolutionary heritage? Address before the Dover-Foxcroft chapter of the D.A.R. ... 1936, by Mary C. Lowell. (Dover-Foxcroft, Me., Observer pub. co., c.1937) 24 p. 23 ½ cm. 37-20446.   F29. N7L6

NORRIDGEWOCK, Early days of, by Henrietta Danforth Wood ... Skowhegan, Me., The Skowhegan press, 1941.   2, 124 p. 23 ½ cm. 42-12833.   F29. N7W6 1941

NORTH BERWICK register, 1904, comp. by Mitchell & Campbell. Kent's Hill, Me., The H. E. Mitchell pub. co., 1904.   112 p. 22 cm. 12-19380.   F29.N73M6

NORTH BRIDGTON, The story of, 1761 - 1958; a little history, a little legend, and some recollections. By Guy Maxwell Monk. (North Bridgton? Me.) 1958.   70 p. illus. 24 cm. 58-40280.   F29.N734M6

NORTHEAST HARBOR, Directory and hand book. By Mrs. Stella Louise (Jones) Hill. (Fairfield, Me.) 1912.   15 x 8 cm.   F29.N74H6

NORTHEAST HARBOR; reminiscences, by an old summer resident (William Warren Vaughan) (Hallowell, Me.) White & Horne, 1930.   86, (1) p. 20 ½ p. 30-16592.   F29.N74V37

NORTH HAVEN. Our island town, by our townspeople and friends, prepared by Lillie S. Bousfield. Bar Harbor, Me., The Bar Harbor times (1941)   2, 136 p. plates. 22 cm. 42-5916.   F29.N743B7

NORTH LOVELL. Sanctuary; a finding of life, by E.W. Paisley. New York, E.P. Dutton, 1940. 5, 9-253, (1) p. 21 cm. 40-27581.   F29.N745P3

NORTH YARMOUTH. Captain Walter Gendall, of North Yarmouth. A biographical sketch by Charles Edward Banks. Yarmouth, Me., "Old times" office, 1880.   1, 27 p. facsim. 23 cm. 4-33439.
    F29. N75G3

NORTH YARMOUTH. Old times: a magazine devoted to the preservation and publication of documents relating to the early history of North Yarmouth. Including ... Harpswell, Freeport, Pownal, Cumberland and Yarmouth. ... Also genealogical reocrds of the principal families ... v. 1 - 8; 1877 - 84. Yarmouth, Me., 1877 - 84.   8 v. in 2. pl., port., facsim. 23 cm. quarterly. No more pub. 3-3171.
    F29.N75O4

NORTH YARMOUTH, Ancient, and Yarmouth, 1636 - 1936; a history (by) William Hutchinson Rowe ... Yarmouth, Me., 1937.   xiii, 427 p. front., plates, ports., map. 23 ½ cm. 38-2245.   F29.N75R6

NORWAY and South Paris, A directory of ... 1888. Portland, Me., Putnam, Tower, c.1888.
   v. 23 ½ cm.
    Directories

101

NORWAY, Centennial history of, Oxford County, 1786 - 1886, including an account of the early grants and purchases ... with genealogical registers ... by William Berry Lapham ... Portland, Me., B. Thurston, 1886. xvi, 659 p. front., plates, ports., map. 24 cm. 1-8989.
 F29. N8L3

NORWAY register, 1903-4 (by) Mitchell. Kent's Hill? 1903) 113 p. 22½ cm. 12-19881.
 F29. N8M6

NORWAY, The history of; comprising a minute account of its first settlement, town officers, etc. etc. By David Noyes. Norway, The author, 1852. (7) - 215, (1) p. 22 cm. "Record of deaths ... 1820 - 1852 ... p. 193 - 207. 1-8909.
 F29. N8N9

NORWAY centennial poem, delivered on the occasion of the centennial celebration ... 1886. Norway, Me. (B. Thurston, 1886) 23 p. sq. 16° 1-8990-M1.
 F29. N8P6

NORWAY, A history of ... by Charles F. Whitman. Norway, Me. (Lewiston journal printshop) 1924. 581 p. incl. illus., pl. front. (port.) 23½ cm. 24-15717.
 F29. N8W6

OAKFIELD, Souvenir of. 1911. Brunswick, Me., The Maine map & register co. (1911) 31 p, incl. 2 pl. fold. map. 27½ x 35½ cm. Printed on one side of leaf only. 12-11995.
 F29. O1S7

OAKLAND register, comp. by H. E. Mitchell, 1903. Kent's Hill, The author, 1903. 115 p. 21½ cm. 12-19882.
 F29. O2M6

OCEAN PARK, The story of, an informal seventy-fifth anniversary history, 1881 - 1956. Ocean Park, Me., Ocean Park Assoc., 1956. 121 p. illus. 20 cm. Includes bibliography. 56-58057.
 F29. O3J3

OGUNQUIT Village, History of, with many interesting facts of more recent interest. By Esselyn Gilman Perkins. Portland, Me., Falmouth Pub. House (1951) 66 p. illus. 21 cm. 51-39141.
 F29. O34P4

OLD ORCHARD beach, ... directory ... (Saco, Me., Murphy Caron co.) c. 19 - v. 23 cm. CA 36-311 unrev.
 Directories

OLD ORCHARD BEACH. Pen and pencil sketches. By J. S. Locke. Boston, Graves Locke, (1879) 2, 7 - 48 p. illus., fold. col. pl., double plan. 19½ cm. 1-8991.
 F29. O4L8

OLD ORCHARD BEACH. By J. S. Locke. Portland, G. W. Morris (1900) 81 p. incl. front. illus., pl. obl. 12°. Oct. 11. 1900-71.
 F29. O4L8

OLD ORCHARD and vicinity. (Portland, L. H. Nelson Co., 1906) (32) p. of illus. 20 x 25 cm. 48-42360*
 F29. O4N4

OLD ORCHARD BEACH. Old Orchard house. (Portland, 1892) (28) p. illus. obl. 32° 1-8992-M1.
 F29. O4O4

OLDTOWN. Sketches of the town of Old Town, Penobscot County ... to 1879; with biographical sketches, by David Norton. Bangor, S. G. Robinson, 1881. 152 p. 23 cm. 1-8993.
 F29. O5N8

ORONO register, 1904, comp. by Mitchell and Remick. Brunswick, Me., The H. E. Mitchell pub. co., 1904. 97 (1) p. 22½ cm. 12-19883.
 F29. O7M6

ORONO. ... Centennial celebration, and dedication of town hall, Orono, ... 1874 ... Portland, Bailey & Noyes, 1874. 168 p. front., plates. 23½ cm. 1-8994.
 F29. O7O7

ORR'S ISLAND, Historical sketch of, with landscape descriptions. By W. H. Doughty. (Portland, Me., Six towns times print., 1899) 53 (6) p. front., illus. 11½ x 14½ cm. 99-4906 rev.
 F29. O8D7

OTISFIELD. Sketch of the life and times of Dr. David Ray. By Grinfill Blake Holden. Boston, 1881. 24 p. incl. front., illus. 18½ cm. 2-26038.
 F29. O88H7

MAINE

OTISFIELD. The town register: Otisfield, Harrison, Naples, and Sebago, 1906, comp. by Mitchell and Davis. Brunswick, Me., The H. E. Mitchell co., 1906. 169 p. 22 cm. 12-19884.
F29.O88M6

OTISFIELD, Vital records of, to the year 1892; births, marriages and deaths. Pub. under authority of the Maine Historical Soc. Portland) 1948. 348 p. 23 cm. 49-4394*.
F29.O88O8

OXFORD, ... Annals of ... 1829 to 1850. Prefaced by a brief account of the settlement of Shepardsfield plantation, now Hebron and Oxford, and supplemented with genealogical notes ... Comp. and pub. by Marquis Fayette King. Portland, Me., 1903. 2, (iii) - xii, 298 p. front. (port.) illus. (incl. plans) 25 cm. 4-2418 rev.
F29.O9K5

PALERMO, History of the town of, incorporated 1804. By Milton E. Dowe. (Palermo, 1954) 51 p. illus. 23 cm. 56-44763.
F29.P16D6

PALERMO, A history of the early settlement of, by Allen Goodwin. Belfast, Me., The Age pub. co., 1896. 34 p. 16 cm. 45-46478.
F29.P16G6

PARIS, History of ... to 1880, with a history of the grants of 1736 & 1771, together with personal sketches, a copious genealogical register and an appendix. By Wm. B. Lapham and others ... Paris, Me., 1884. 3, (3) - 816 p. front., illus., plates, ports., plan. 24½ cm. "Genealogical registers": p.491-778. 1-8895. F29.P2L3

PARIS register, 1906, comp. by Mitchell and Davis. Brunswick, Me., The H. E. Mitchell co., 1906. 154 p. fold. map. 21½ cm. 12-19885.
F29.P2M6

PARIS. Centennial of the First Baptist church in Paris, ... 1891. Paris (Me.,) Oxford democrat office, 1892. 85, (1) p. 22½ cm. 1-16577.
F29.P2P2

PARIS. A city on a hill (Paris Hill) with high lights that hit it, by Charles E. Waterman ... Auburn, Me., Press of Merrill & Webber (1931) 102 p. 19½ cm. 31-7240.
F29.P2W3

PARKMAN, History of; mainstream democracy in Parkman, 1794 - 1969, by Roger C. Storms. Freeport, Me., Dingly Press, 1969. 108 p. illus. 24 cm.
F29.P23S75

PARSONS FIELD, A history of the first century of the town of. ... 1885. Portland, Me., B. Thurston, 1888. xiv, 499, (1) p. front., 2 pl., ports., fold. plan. 23½ cm. Preface signed: J. W. Dearborn. Contains Genealogies (pt. IV) and Personal sketches (part III) 1-8996.
F29. P3D2

PEMAQUID. The story of ancient Pemaquid, metropolis of the New World. By Harold Webber Castner. (Damariscotta, Me., 1950) 23 p. illus. 24 cm. 50-3281.
F29.P39C3

PEMAQUID, A history of, with sketches of Monhegan, Popham and Castine, by Arlita Dodge Parker. Boston, MacDonald and Evans, 1925. 226 (16) p. front., illus., plates, ports., map. 24 cm. 30-12829.
F29.P39P23

PEMAQUID and Monhegan. Address of Hon, Charles Levi Woodbury ... before the Hyde Park historical society, ... 1891. (Hyde Park, Mass., 1892?) 18 p. 23 cm. Reprinted from the Hyde Park historical record for 1891 - 92. CA 34-1392 unrev.
F29.P39W7

PENOBSCOT. Death records ... (Brooksville historical soc., North Brooksville, Me., 1940?) 9, 13, 4, 2 numb. l. 29 cm. Reproduced from type-written copy. Includes "Items of interest regarding the families of those whose names are recorded in the Penobscot town records." 41-15598.
F29.P395B7

PENOBSCOT. Family records recorded on the town books prior to the year 1875, Penobscot, Maine. (Brooksville historical soc., North Brooksville, Me., 1940?) 1, 78 numb. l. 28 cm. Reproduced from type-written copy. 41-15599.
F29.P395B73

PENOBSCOT. Marriages ... (Brooksville historical soc., North Brooksville, Me., 1940?)   2, 2 - 39,
17 numb. l. 29 cm.   Reproduced from type-written copy.   41-15600.   F29. P395B74

PENOBSCOT. Vital statistics, copied from town records, Penobscot, 1787 to 1875 (by) Brooksville
historical soc., North Brooksville, Me., 1940.   3, 2 - 53 numb. l. 28½ cm.   Typed copy. 41-15601.   F29. P395B75

PENOBSCOT. A copy of all gravetone inscriptions found in the town of Penobscot, bearing date of
death prior to 1876 ... Compiled by Grace Limeburner.   North Brooksville, Me., 1941.   30 l. 29 cm.
Type-written.   "Notes relating to some of the families whose names appear in these records": l. 23 - 30. 42-18526 rev.   F29. P395L5

PERU, in the county of Oxford, The history of ... 1789 - 1911.   Residents and genealogies of their
families, also a part of Franklin plan.   By Hollis Turner.   Augusta, Me., Maine farmer (1912)
313, (1) p. plates, ports. 23 cm. 12-23454.   F29. P4T9

PHIPPSBURG on the Kennebec, 1607 - 1964.   By Stanwood C. Gilman.   Phippsburg? Me., 1964)
32 p. 28 cm.   F29. P45G5

PHIPPSBURG, Vital record of, to the year 1892.   Pub. under the authority of the Maine historical soc.
(Auburn, Me., Merrill & Webber) 1935.   431, (1) p. 23 cm. 36-27934.   F29. P45P4

PHIPPSBURG, fair to the wind.   Foreword by Robert M. York.   Phippsburg Historical Soc., Lewiston,
Me., 1964.   108, xvii p. "First printing"   F29. P45P43
                                                                                          1964

— 1965.   108 p. 24 cm.   F29. P45P43
                                                                                          1965

PITTSFIELD ... on the Sebasticook ... 1866 - 1966.   By Sangor Mills Cook.   Bangor, Me., Furbush-
Roberts, (c. 1966)   191 p. 24 cm.   F29. P47C6

PITTSFIELD register, 1904, comp. by Mitchell & Daggett.   Kent's Hill, Me., The H. E. Mitchell pub.
co., 1904.   136 p. 22 cm. 12-19887.   F29. P47M6

PITTSTON, Vital records of, to the year 1892.   Pub. under authority of the Maine historical soc.
Gardiner, Me., The Reporter-Journal press, 1911.   387 p. 23½ cm. 11-29858.   F29. P5P6

PITTSTON, ... Land titles in old, (by) Henry Sewall Webster.   Gardiner, Me., The Reporter-journal
press, 1912.   55 p. 23 cm.   By "Old Pittston" is here meant the town as it existed at the time of its incorporation.   It comprised the
territory now lying in Pittston, Randolph, Gardiner, most of West Gardiner, and part of Farmingdale." 12-37129.
                                                                                          F29. P5W3

POLAND SPRING and about there.   By Frank Carlos Griffith.   South Poland, 1903.   18½ x 23 cm.
                                                                                          F29. P7G8

POLAND SPRING. The Hill-top.   v. 1 - 13; South Poland, Me., 1894 - 1906.   13 v. in 7. illus., plates.
27 cm.   "Pub. Sunday mornings for ten weeks, during July, Aug. and Sept. ... (for) Poland Spring visitors." 6-18419.   F29. P7H6

POLAND SPRING centennial; a souvenir. (N.Y., A.H. Kellogg) 1895.   88 p. incl. front., illus. pl., coat of
arms. 17 x 22½ cm. 1-8997.   F29. P7P7

POLAND, History of ... By H.A. & G.W. Poole.   Mechanic Falls, Me., Poole brothers, 1890.
vi, 145 p. front. (fold. map) illus., plates, ports. 28 cm. 1-8998.   F29. P7P8

POLAND centennial ... 1895.   With illus., and biographical sketches by Alvan B. Ricker and others.
(N.Y., A.H. Kellogg, c. 1896)   6, 117 p. incl. front., illus., plates, ports., facsim. 23½ cm. 3-25503.   F29. P7R5

POLAND SPRING; views and a brief descitpion of the Poland Spring house ... and other points of interest.   South Poland, Me., Boston, etc. Hiram Ricker, c. 1916.   (36) p. illus. 20½ x 25½ cm. 16-25268.
                                                                                          F29. P7R53

MAINE   61

PORTER, as a portion of Maine: its settlement, etc., by Thomas Moulton.   Portland, Me., Hoyt, Fogg
& Donham, 1879.   96 p. 23 cm.   Marriages ... to 1858: p. 87 - 96. 1-8999.   F29. P8M9

PORTER, History of. By William Teg. Illus. with photos. 1st ed.   Kezar Falls, Me., Parsonsfield -
Porter Historical Soc. (1957)   315 p. illus. 24 cm. 57-58517.   F29. P8T4

PORTLAND.   Account of the great conflagration in Portland ... 1866, by John Neal; and a new business
guide, ... Portland (Me.) Starbird & Twitchell, 1866.   64, viii p. 23 ½ cm. 11-28342.   F29. P9N27
                                                                                             F29. P9A18

PORTLAND and vicinity, Directory of.   Portland, Me. The Thurston print. 1823 - 1907.   37 v. 23 ½ cm.
Title varies.   Sept. 21, 99-38 Additions.   Directories

PORTLAND directory & register; containing the names ... of the heads of families, etc.   Portland,
J. Adams, jr., 1823 - 27.   2 v. front. (fold. plan, v.2) 14 ½ cm.   Another directory of Portland for 1823 was pub. by A.W. Thayer.
4-30420 Additions.
                                                                                          Directories

PORTLAND directory;   Portland (Me.) S. Colman (1831?)   86 p. front. (fold. plan) 17 ½ cm. 4-30421.
                                                                                          Directories

PORTLAND and vicinity, Directory of.   The Thurston print, 1856 - 1909.   37 v. 8°. Sept. 21. 99-38.
                                                                                          Directories

PORTLAND. ... Davis' city of Portland directory.   Portland, Me., City directory co., 1902.
1 v. map. 28 cm. 2-10134.   Directories

PORTLAND directory, The ...   Portland, (Me.) A.W. Thayer, 1823.   104 p. 15 cm. 4-30419.
                                                                                     Directories; Office

PORTLAND blue book, The, including Augusta, Bath, Biddeford, Brunswick, Lewiston, Sanford, South
Portland and Westbrook.   New York, Dau pub. co.   v. 21 ½ cm. 11-30057.
                                                                                          Directories

PORTLAND almanac & register: 1860. By C. Augustine Dockham.   Portland (Me.) Printed by B.
Thurston, 1860.   108 (i.e. 112) p. illus. 14 ½ cm. 11-4174.
                                                                                          Directories

PORTLAND business directory and business man's guide ... By Atwell & co.   Portland, B. Thurston,
1868 -   1 v. 20 cm. 7-40117.   Directories

PORTLAND, Anthony's standard business directory and reference book of Portland and vicinity, Saco
and Biddeford, ... (1898 -   (New Bedford, Mass., Anthony pub. co., 1897 -
1 v. 23 ½ cm. 7-40727.   Directories

105

PORTLAND, South Portland and Cape Elizabeth, Street guide.　　Portland, Me., Fred. L. Tower, c. 19 -
　　　　v. 23 cm.　　41-36265.　　　　　　　　　　　　　　　　　　　　　　　　　　　　　　　　　　F29. P9A2

PORTLAND, its representative business men and its points of interest ... By George Fox Bacon.
Newark, N.J., Glenwood pub. co., 1891.　　200 p. illus. 4º. 1-9000-M1.　　　　　　　　　　　F29. P9B1

PORTLAND Jewry, its growth and development.　By Benjamin Band.　Portland, Me., Jewish Historical
Society (1955)　　117 p. 24 cm. 56-17715.　　　　　　　　　　　　　　　　　　　　　　　　　F29. P9B2

PORTLAND and vicinity, Leading business men of; embracing Saco, Biddeford, Saccarappa and
Deering.　Illus.　Boston, Mercantile pub. co., 1887.　　1, (5) - 228 p. illus. 25 cm. 1-9001.
　　　F29. P9B3

PORTLAND and vicinity, Loring, Short & Harmon's illustrated guide book for.　By 'Our young woman
about town.' (Mary S. (Deering) Caswell.　With a summary history of Portland, by Wm. Willis.
Portland (1873)　　100 p. front., pl., maps. 16º 1-9002-M1.　　　　　　　　　　　　　　　　F29. P9C3

PORTLAND.　The youthful haunts of Longfellow, by George Thornton Edwards.　Portland, Me., G.T.
Edwards, 1907.　　xxix, 205 p. incl. illus., plates, ports. front., pl. 19½ cm. 7-26432.　　　　　F29. P9E2

PORTLAND and vicinity.　By Edward H. Elwell ... Portland, Me., Loring, Short, & Harmon, and
W. S. Jones, 1876.　　142 p. front. (ports.) illus. 24½ cm. 1-9003.　　　　　　　　　　　　　F29. P9E5

... PORTLAND and vicinity, with a sketch of Old Orchard beach and other Maine resorts.　By Edward
H. Elwell ... (Rev. ed.)　Portland, Me., Loring, Short & Harmon; Providence, R.I., 1881.
142 p. front., illus., port. group. 25 cm. (2d and rev. ed.) 1-9004.　　　　　　　　　　　　　　F29. P9E6

PORTLAND and vicinity, an illustrated souvenir and all-the-year-round guide to the city of Portland,
with sketches of Old Orchard beach, Cushing's and Peak's island, and other famous resorts ...　by
Edward H. Elwell.　Rev. and ed. by Robert Grieve. (3d ed.)　Providence, R.I., J.A. & R.A. Reid;
Portland, Me., Loring, Short & Harmon (1888?)　　4, (3) - 162 p. illus. (incl. ports.) 26½ cm. 11-13688.
　　F29.P9E65

PORTLAND.　Mother Goose comes to Portland; text and illus. by Frederic W. Freeman.　Portland,
Me., Southworth print. co., 1918.　　(61) p. illus. 19 cm. 19-130.　　　　　　　　　　　　　F29.P9F79

PORTLAND, Sketches in and about, by Will Ourcadie (pseud.) (Frederic William Freeman)　Portland,
Smith & Sale, 1917.　　2 p, 14 pl. 1 illus. 20½ cm. 17-30370.　　　　　　　　　　　　　　　F29. P9F8

PORTLAND.　Samuel Freeman - his life and services.　By ... William Freeman.　(Portland? Me.,
1893)　　32 p. port. 25 cm. 22-10233.　　　　　　　　　　　　　　　　　　　　　　　　　　F29.P9F85

... PORTLAND past and present, issued under the endorsement of the Portland board of trade and city
government; comp. by C. Bancroft Gillespie ... Portland, Me., Evening express pub. co., 1899.
236 p. incl. illus., ports. 25 cm. A 17-110.　　　　　　　　　　　　　　　　　　　　　　　　F29.P9 G4

PORTLAND.　To Portland on Casco Bay (by) Clara Adelia Goold.　Portland, Smith & Sale, 1916.
16 l. front., plates. 14½ x 14½ cm.　Poem, printed on one side of leaf only. 17-675.　　　　　F29. P9G48

PORTLAND.　Falmouth Neck in the revolution, by Nathan Goold ... Portland, Me., Thurston print,
1897.　　1, 56 p. illus. 23 cm.　"This is not intended as a full history of the revolutionary period at Falmouth Neck ... but is supplementary and explanatory of ... Willis' History of Portland, Goold's Portland in the past (etc.)" 6-13959.　　　　F29. P9G5

PORTLAND.　The Wadsworth-Longfellow house; Longfellow's old home, Portland, Maine; its history
and its occupants, by Nathan Goold.　(Portland, Me.) The Maine historical society, 1905. 28 p. incl.
front., illus. 24 cm. 5-26901.　　　　　　　　　　　　　　　　　　　　　　　　　　　　　　F29. P9G6

—　(n. p.) Lakeside printing co., 1908.　　40 p. incl. front., illus. 24½ cm. 8-22973.　　　　　F29. P9G63
　　　1908

— (Rev., Portland, Me., 1960)   43 p. 22 cm. Rev. 1951 by Me. historical soc. Repr. 1965.   F29.P9G63
1960

PORTLAND in the past; with historical notes of old Falmouth, by William Goold.   Portland, Me.,
B. Thurston & co., 1886.   543 p. front., plates, ports. 23½ cm. L.C. copy replaced by microfilm.   F29.P9 G7
Microfilm 18705

PORTLAND soldiers and sailors.   A brief sketch of the part they took in the war of the rebellion.   Pub.
... by members of Bosworth post, Grand army of the republic.   Portland (Me.) B. Thurston & co.,
1884.   56 p. 23 cm. 6-19145.   F29.P9G75

PORTLAND and vicinity, Guide book for, to which is appended A summary history of Portland, by Hon.
Wm. Willis ... Portland, B. Thurston ... 1859.   104 p. incl. illus., plates. pl., maps (1 double) 16 cm. 1-9006 rev.
F29.P9 G8

PORTLAND.   Hand-book of Portland, Old Orchard, Cape Elizabeth and Casco Bay ... John T. Hull,
ed. and pub.   Portland, Southworth bros., 1888.   3, 246 p. illus., 3 maps (2 fold., incl. front.) 2 plans. 21 cm.
1-9007.   F29. P9H9

PORTLAND.   ... Report of John T. Hull ... as to the title of certain islands within the limits of the city
of Portland.   (Portland, 1884)   33 p. 22 cm. 18-13510.   F29.P9H92

PORTLAND, Centennials of.   1675, 1775, 1875 and 1975.   By Charles P. Ilsley.   Somerville, Mass.,
G.B.King, 1876.   56 p. 20 cm. In verse; with notes. 6-43084.   F29. P9 I3

PORTLAND.   In and about Portland.   (Portland, c.1908)   1 v. 20½ x 25½ cm.
F29. P9 I35

— Portland, 1912.   20 x 25½ cm.   F29. P9 I36

PORTLAND.   Old Portland town (by) Herbert G. Jones; sketches by the author.   Portland, Me., The
Machigonne press, 1938.   5, 3 - 127, (1) p. illus. 23½ cm. 39-2081 rev.   F29. P9J7

PORTLAND.   ... The story of Old Falmouth, by James Otis (pseud.) (James Otis Kaler)   127 p. front.,
pl., plans (1 double) 19 cm. (Pioneer towns of America) "That portion of the state of Maine now called Portland, Deering, Stroudwater, Westbrook, Cape Elizabeth, South Portland, Falmouth, and the islands of Casco Bay, formed one large tract of land known as Falmouth; and today we
refer to it as Old Falmouth .. " 1-10175.   F29. P9K2

PORTLAND.   ... Exercises at the unveiling of the statue of Henry Wadsworth Longfellow, Portland,
... 1888.   Portland, Brown, Thurston & co., 1888.   41 p. front. 20 cm. 0 00074.
F29. P9L7

PORTLAND.   Impressions in and about Portland, selected by Carrie Thompson Lowell.   Portland,
A.W. Lowell (c.1910)   46 p. incl. front., illus. 17½ cm. 10-17610.   F29. P9L8

PORTLAND, The historical pageant of, produced on the eastern promenade as a free civic celebration
of the 4th of July, 1913.   Author and director: Constance D'Arcy Mackay ... Portland, Southworth
print. co., c. 1913.   47, (1) p. illus. 20½ cm.   F29. P9M16

PORTLAND ... Longfellow memorial fund.   Maine historical soc. 1901.   28½ cm.   F29. P9M2

PORTLAND.   Portland by the sea; an historical treatise, by Augustus F. Moulton.   Augusta, Me.,
Katahdin pub. co., 1926.   8, (13) - 243, (9) p. front., plates, ports., double map. 20 cm. 27-1478.   F29. P9M8

PORTLAND, Account of the great conflagration in, ... 1866, by John Neal; and a new business guide
... Portland (Me.) Starbird & Twitchell, 1866.   64, viii p. 23½ cm. 11-28342.   F29. P9N27

PORTLAND illustrated.   By John Neal.   Portland (Me.) W.S. Jones, 1874.   160 p. front. (port.) illus.
21 cm. 1-9008.   F29. P9N3
Office

PORTLAND.   Report of the Committee for the relief of Portland.   New York, August, 1966.   Brooklyn, The Union steam presses, 1866.   43 p. 22½ cm. 19-15067. F29. P9N4

PORTLAND at the beginning of the 20th century ... Showing its superior advantages on account of its shipping facilities, etc.   (New York) The New York industrial recorder, 1900.   40 p. illus. 41½ cm. Special number of the New York industrial recorder. 10-23245. F29. P9N5

PORTLAND, Ballads of, by Moses Owen ... (Portland, Me.) W. S. Jones, c. 1874.   160 p. front. (port.) 15 cm. In verse. 13-5129. F29. P9O9

PORTLAND.   Some old papers recently found in the stone tower of the First parish church of Portland.   By Rev. John Carroll Perkins.   (Portland, 1894)   30 p. 23½ cm. CA 26-399 unrev. F29. P9P4

PORTLAND and gems of Casco Bay.   Portland, Me. (191 -?)   (89) p. illus. 21 x 31½ cm. F29. P9P72

PORTLAND.   Dedication of the Portland army and navy union hall.   Portland, Elwell, Pickard & co., 1867.   22, (1) p. 22 cm. 13-23477. F29. P9P74

PORTLAND.   ... Centennial celebration; an account of the municipal celebration of the 100th anniversary of the incorporation of the town of Portland ... 1886.   Portland (Me.) Owen, Strout, 1886.   379, (1) p. plates. 23½ cm. 7-6936.
1-9010.
F29. P9P78
F29. P9P79

PORTLAND, City of.   The dedication of Lincoln park ... 1909, in observance of the 100th anniversary of the birth of Abraham Lincoln.   Portland, Smith & Sale, 1909.   35, (1) p. front., plates, ports., fold. plan. 24½ cm. 10-6837. F29. P9P8

PORTLAND.   Exercises at dedication of the new City hall and memorial organ ... 1912.   Pub. by authority of the City hall building commission.   (Portland, Me., Southworth print. co.) 1912.   79 p. front., plates. 25 cm. 19-4229. F29. P9P83

PORTLAND.   Report of the Committee ... to investigate the causes and consequences of the riot ... 1855.   Portland, B. D. Peck, city printer, 1855.   50 p. 21½ cm. 1-9009. F29. P9P87

PORTLAND, and what I saw there.   Portland, Me., Chisholm brothers, c. 1909.   20 x 25½ cm.
F29. P9P92
1909

— 14th ed. improved by new plates and text.   Portland, Me., c. 1920.   (32) p. illus. 20½ x 25½ cm.
F29. P9P92
1920

— 15th ed.   c. 1923.   (32) p. illus. 20½ x 25½ cm. 23-18937.
F29. P9P92
1923

PORTLAND, The visitors' hand-book of, and its summer delights ... Portland board of trade ... (2d ed.) (Portland, Me., 1896)   1, 73 p. illus., fold. pl., fold. maps. 20 x 10½ cm. 16-21605. F29. P9P93

PORTLAND.   ,,, Baptisms and admissions from the records of First church in Falmouth, now Portland, Maine.   With appendix of historical notes.   Comp. by Marquis F. King ... Portland, Me., Maine genealogical society, 1898.   2, 219 p. front., illus. (incl. plans) pl., 2 facsim. 24 cm. Printed on one side of leaf only. Reprint from Portland evening express. 4-2417. F29. P9P95

PORTLAND.   Centennial oration, by Thomas Brackett Reed.   Portland, Me., 1876.   23 cm.
F29. P9 R3

MAINE 65

PORTLAND. Extracts from the journals kept by the Rev. Thomas Smith ... in Falmouth, in the County of York (now Cumberland ... 1720 - 1788. Portland, T. Todd, 1821. v, (9) - 164, (3), 154, (2) p. 20½ cm. 1-9011.
F29. P9S6

— (2d ed.) 1849. vi, (7) - 483, (1) p. front., illus., ports. double plan. 23½ cm. 1-9012.
F29. P9S61

PORTLAND, Tourists' hand book of. Portland, Me., Portland board of trade (c. 1910) 56 p. illus. fold. maps. 20 x 10½ cm. 10-15647.
F29. P9T7

PORTLAND, Views of. Portland, Me., Hoyt, Fogg & Donham, 1885. 18 pl. obl. 16°. 1-9014-M1.
F29. P9V6

PORTLAND, Views of. Portland, Me., 1904. 20 x 25 cm.
F29. P9V62

PORTLAND. Report of collections in Washington, D.C. in behalf of sufferers by the fire in Portland. Executive committee for relief of Portland fire sufferers. (Washington, 1867) 7 p. 22½ cm. 7-9650.
F29. P9W3

PORTLAND, The history of; with notices of the neighbouring towns, and of the changes of government in Maine ... By William Willis ... Portland, Day, Fraser & co., 1831-33. 2 v. front. (fold. map) 2 pl. (1 fold.) 2 fold. plans. 23½ cm. 1-9013.
F29. P9 W7

PORTLAND. The history of Portland ... 1632 - 1864 ... By William Willis. 2d ed. - rev. and enl. Portland, Bailey & Noyes, 1865. xiii p, (9) - 928 p. front. (fold. pl.) 2 pl, 2 fold. maps, port., facsim. 23½ cm. The first 12 chapters (through p. 308) are also found in the 1865 reprint of Collections of the Maine historical soc., vol. I, 1st series. A 14-2451.
F29. P9W72

PORTLAND. Portland city guide, compiled by workers of the Writers' program of the Work projects administration in the sate of Maine ... Sponsored by the city of Portland. (Portland) The Forest city print. co., 1940. xiv, 337 p. illus. (incl. maps) plates. 21 cm. (American guide series) "Selected reading list": p. (317) - 318. 40-30610.
F29. P9W8

POWNAL, History of the town of, written for its centennial ... 1908, by Mrs. Ettie J. Latham. (Lewiston, Me., Lewiston journal co., 1908) 40 p. 19½ cm. 8-31274.
F29. P92L3

PRESQUE ISLE register, The, 1904, comp. by Mitchell and Pettingill. Brunswick, Me., The H, E. Mitchell pub. co., 1904. 130 (i.e. 134) p. 22 cm. 12-19888.
F29. P93M6

PRESQUE ISLE, Aroostook county, Maine. Photogravures. Presque Isle, J. B. Smart (1895) 2 p. 18 pl. obl. 12°. 1-0015 - M1.
F29. P93P9

PROUTS NECK, Old, by Augustus F. Moulton ... Portland, Me., Marks printing house, 1924. 123 p. front. (port.) 7 pl. 20½ cm. 24-23167.
F29. P96M8

PROUTSNECK. Prout then and now, 1888 - 1970. Prouts Neck Association, c. 1971) 96 p. illus. 28 cm.
F29. P96P7

RANDOLPH, Vital records of, to the year 1892. Pub. under authority of the Maine historical soc. Gardiner, The Reporter-journal press, 1910. 144 p. 23½ cm. Alphabetic digest of the ms. records of the town, supplemented by private and other records. 10-33132.
F29. R3R3

RICHMOND register, 1909, comp. by Charles W. Jack. August, Me., The Mitchell-Cony co., 1909. 44, (25) p. front (map) 22 cm. (Pt. 2) Maine reference manual. 12-19889.
F29. R5J12

RICHMOND. A historical almanac, 1888, containing historical matter concerning the town of Richmond, collected from town records and other sources ... C. W. Richards ... c. 1887. (26) p. 20 cm. 18-2848.
F29. R5R5

ROCKLAND. Manning's Rockland, Camden, Thomaston, including North Haven, Owls Head, Rockport, South Thomaston, St. George, Union, Vinalhaven, Warren directory ... Springfield, Mass., H. A.

Manning co., 19 -   v. illus. 23½ cm. CA 32-132 unrev.

Directories

ROCKLAND. ... The Maine magazine. Special ed. Rockland, Camden and environs, 1907. (n. p.,) 1907?)   56 p. illus., (incl. ports.) 30 cm. Contents.- Rockland. - Thomaston. - Camden. - Rockport. - Warren. 1--31043.   F29. R6M21

ROCKLAND. The Samoset ... Ricker hotel co. 1903.   18 cm.   F29. R6 R8

ROCKPORT. The Rockport register, 1904, comp. by Mitchell, Carroll and Pressey. Kent's Hill, Me., The H. E. Mitchell pub. co., 1904.   96 p. 22 cm. 12-19890.   F29. R64M6

ROCKPORT. History of Camden and Rockport, by Reuel Robinson ... (Camden, Me., Camden pub. co., c. 1907)   xiii, 644 p. incl. front. (port.) illus. 20½ cm. 7-25046.   F29. R64R6

RUMFORD and Mexico, Directory of, no. 1 - 3. Auburn, Me., Merrill & Webber, 1903 - 8.
3 v. 24 cm. 4-1824.

Directories

RUMFORD. Manning's Rumford, Bethel, Albany, Andover, Dixfield, Hanover, Mexico, Milton Plantation, Newry, Peru and Roxbury (Maine) directory ... Portland, Me., H. A. Manning co. c. 19 -
v. 23 cm. CA 33-203 unrev.

Directories

RUMFORD, Oxford county, History of ... by William B. Lapham ... Augusta, Maine farmer, 1890.
xv, 432 p. front., 1 illus., plates, ports. 24 cm. Records of intention of marriage, 1802 - 1889: p. (263) - 284. Family records: p. (285) - 423. 1-9016.   F29. R8L3

SACO and Biddeford, The business directory of. For the year 1849. Saco, Cowan and Hanscom, 1849.   108 p. 17 cm.   Abridged history of Saco and Biddeford, p. 3-10. 12-10732.

Directories, Office

SACO. ... Colonel Thomas Cutts, Saco's most eminent citizen in the country's early days ... by George Addison Emery; read before the Maine historical soc., 1912. Saco, Me., 1917.   19 p. 3 pl. 3 port. (incl. front.) 23 cm. 18-18266.   F29. S1C9

SACO. The proprietors of Saco and a brief sketch of the years following the first settlement of the town, also a little about an old bank in Saco, Me. Saco, Me., York national bank, 1931.   59 p. incl. front. (port.) illus., plates, col. plans. 18 cm. 39-7633.   F29. S1D5

SACO. An address delivered in Saco, ... 1862. On the 100th anniversary of the organization of the First church in Saco, by Rev. Edward S. Dwight ... Saco, W. Noyes, 1862.   27 p. 23 cm. 8-15371 rev.   F29. S1D9

SACO. Sands, spindles, and steeples; (a history of Saco) By Roy P. Fairfield. Published under the auspices of the York Institute with the assistance of the Saco Tercentenary Committee. Portland, Me., House of Falmouth (1956)   xi, 461 p. illus., ports., fold. maps. 22 cm. Bibliography: p. (433) - 443. 56-44156.   F29. S1F3

SACO. History of Saco and Biddeford, with notices of other early settlements ... including the provinces of New Somersetshire and Lygonia. By George Folsom. Saco, A. C. Putnam, 1830.
v, (9) - 331 p. front., map, facsim. 18½ cm. 1-9017* Cancel. L.C. copy replaced by microfilm. Also in Rare Book Coll.   F29. S1F6
Microfilm 8784 F

SACO register, with Old Orchard, 1906; comp. by Mitchell, Daggett, Holt, Lawton and Sawyer. Brunswick, Me., The H. E. Mitchell co., 1906.   260 p. 22½ cm. 19-6616.   F29. S1M6

SACO, Old times in; a brief monograph on local events ... by Daniel E. Owen. Saco, Me. (Biddeford times print) 1891.   4, (v) - viii, 172 p. front., illus., plates, ports., maps (partly fold.) 22 cm. 9-29285.   F29. S1O9

SACO. First book of records of the town of Pepperellborough now the city of Saco; printed by vote of the City council, March 18, 1895. Portland, Me., The Thurston print, 1896.   2, (7) - 299 p. 23 cm.

MAINE 67

The record of marriages extends from 1796 to 1832; that of births is arranged by families, not chronologically; the record of deaths covers the period 1804 to 1840, including some earlier dates. 1-9018.   F29. S1S1

SACO. First book of records of the First church in Pepperrellborough (now Saco, Maine) Saco, Me., York institute, 1914.   2, 78 p. 23 cm.   Covers the period 1762 - 1798.   15-13024.   F29.S1S12

ST. GEORGE chronicles, containing an historical sketch from 1605 to 1892, together with names and ages of the inhabitants. A complete business directory and biographical sketches ... Rockland, Me., The Maine home journal, 1892.   (3) - 102 p. illus., ports. 18½ cm.   3-29508. L.C. copy replaced by microfilm.
F29.S15S2
Microfilm 10015

— compiled by Joseph T. Simmons (and) Mabelle Andrews Rose ... Augusta, Press of C. E. Nash & son, 1932.   78 p. front. 23½ cm. "The township comprises some eleven villages ... Port Clyde, Martinsville, Tenant's Harbor, Willardham, Long Cove ... St. George ... Glenmore, Elmore, Wallston, Clark Island and Spruce Head." - p.3. 33-14837.
F29.S15S22

SALEM, Our first old home day at. ... 1904. Boston, D. C. Heath, 1905.   xvi, 227 p. incl. front., illus. 20½ cm. 5-27411.   F29.S16O9

SANFORD, Alfred, Lebanon, Shapleigh, Waterborough, and Lyman, The directory of. Methuen, Mass., The Methuen transcript co.   v. 24 cm. 1-26517.
Directories

SANFORD and Springvale, Directory of, 1913.   Portland, Me., Portland directory co.   v. 23½ cm. 13-20842.
Directories

SANFORD, The history of. 1661 - 1900. By Edwin Emery. Comp., ed. and arr. by William Morrell Emery. Fall River, Mass., The compiler, 1901.   xvi, 537 p. front., ports. 24 cm. "Biographies and genealogies": p. (391) - 517. 1-9019.   F29. S2E5

SANFORD, a bicentennial history. ... Albert L. Prosser, editor. Sanford Historical Committee, 1968.   x, 504 p. illus.   F29.S2S25

SANGERVILLE, 1814 - 1914. Proceedings of the centennial celebration ... 1914. Dover, 1914. 2, (103) - 182 p. illus. 24 cm. "Reprinted from Sprague's journal of Maine history." Record of births, marriages and deaths: p. 164 - 179. 14-22866.   F29.S25S2

SCARBOROUGH becomes a town. By Dorothy Shaw Libbey. (Portland, Me.) B. Wheelwright Co. (1955)   282 p. illus. 21 cm. 55-6263.   F29. S3L5

SCARBOROUGH register, 1905, comp. by Mitchell and Campbell. Brunswick, Me., The H. E. Mitchell co., 1905.   96 p. 22 cm. 12-19891.   F29. S3M6

SCARBOROUGH, Grandfather tales of, by Augustine F. Moulton; foreword by John Clair Minot. Augusta, Me., Katahdin pub. co., 1925.   6, 3 - 209 p. front., illus. (incl. ports.) 23½ cm. 26-2332.
F29.S3M88

SCARBOROUGH, The settlement of. Charles Pine, hunter and Indian fighter, by Augustus F. Moulton. (Portland, Me., 1895)   35 p. 23½ cm. 19-7546.
F29. S3M9

SEDGWICK. All vital statistics recorded on the town books from 1799 - 1809, compiled by Grace Limeburner. North Brooksville, Me. (1942?)   1 p., 24, 5 numb. l. 28½ x 22 cm. 42-51457.   F29. S4L5

SEDGWICK, gravestone inscriptions, all gravestone inscriptions found in the cemeteries of this town bearing date of death prior to 1875. Compiled by Grace Limeburner. North Brooksville, Me., 1941. 37 l. 29 cm. Typewritten.   F29. S4L52

SEDGWICK, incorporated ... 1789, named in honor of Major Robert Sedgwick. All vital statistics recorded on town records prior to the year 1800. Compiled by Grace Limeburner ... North Brooksville, Me., 1941.   1 p., 48 numb. l. 29 cm. Type-written. "Collection no. 1." 43-29189.   F29.S4L53

SEDGWICK. Centennial of the First Baptist church, Sedgwick, June 11 - 18, 1905; two historical papers: I. Historical sketch ... by Arthur Warren Smith; II. Rev. Daniel Merrill. (n.p., 1905)
64 p. 22½ cm. 6-34774.   F29. S4S4

SHAPLEIGH, A history of. By Amasa Loring ... Portland (Me.) Printed by B. Thurston, 1854.
40 p. 21½ cm. 1-9020.   F29. S5L8

SKOWHEGAN on the Kennebec, by Louise Helen Coburn and others. (Skowhegan, 193-)   1, 81 p.
22½ cm. 39M 2442 T.   F29. S55C6

— (The Independent-reporter press) 1941.   2 v. fronts., illus. (incl. ports., plans) 24 cm. 42-2300.   F29. S55C63

SMALL POINT, "the cape of many islands", 1667 - 1965 (by) Stanwood C. and Margaret Gilman. (Phippsburg? Me., 1965)   62 p. 28 cm.   F29. S6G5

SOLON. The town register, 1903: Solon & Bingham (by) Mitchell. (Kent's Hill, Me., 1903)
110 p. 22 cm. 12-19892.   F29. S65M6

SOUTH BERWICK. Address delivered by George Lewis ... 1902, at the 200th anniversary of the founding of the Congregational church in South Berwick. South Berwick, The Independent press, 1902.
30 p. 20½ cm. 27-3867.   F29. S67L4

SOUTH BERWICK register, 1904, comp. by Mitchell & Campbell. Kent's Hill, Me., The H. E. Mitchell pub. co., 1904.   150 p. 22 cm. 12-19893.   F29. S67M6

SOUTH PARIS. Manning's South Paris (township of Paris) and Norway directory, including Buckfield, Greenwood, Hebron, Oxford, Sumner, Waterford and Woodstock ... Portland, Me., H.A. Manning co., c. 19 -   v. 23 cm. CA 33-202 unrev.
Directories

SQUIRREL ISLAND, Souvenir of, introduction and historical sketch by Rev. S. P. Merrill. Waterville (Me.) E.A. Pierce, 1895.   32 pp. front., pl. obl. 24°. 1-9021-M1   F29. S7S7

SQUIRREL ISLAND. Squirrelana. Squirrel Island, 1954.   unpaged. 20 cm. Articles from the Squid and addresses delivered on the ... 50th anniversary of the Squirrel Island Library, 1954. 54-38979.   F29. S7S72

STANDISH. The town register: Standish, Baldwin, Cornish, Limerick, Limington, 1905. Comp. by Mitchell, Daggett, Bassett and Goodyear. Brunswick, Me., The H. E. Mitchell co., 1905.
260 p. 22½ cm. p. 5 - 100, "General reference" (Maine) 12-19894.   F29. S76M6

STOCKTON SPRINGS, The story of. (Stockton Springs) Historical Committee (1955)   223 p. illus. 22 cm.
56-19269.   F29. S78E4

STOCKTON SPRINGS, Historical sketch of, written and compiled by Faustina Hichborn; ed. by Herbert C. Libby ... Waterville, Me., Press of Central Maine pub. co., 1908.   4, 133 p. plates, ports. 19 cm.
A 15-1914.   F29. S78H6

SULLIVAN and Sorrento since 1760. By Lelia Ardell (Clark) Johnson. Ellsworth, Me., Hancock County Pub. Co., 1953.   410 p. illus. 24 cm. 54-21112.   F29. S79 J 6

SUMNER, Centennial history of the town of. 1798 - 1898. West Sumner, C. E. Handy, jr., 1899.
202, xxx, (2) p. incl. front., illus., ports. 19 cm. L.C. copy replaced by microfilm.   F29. S8S8
Microfilm 15055 F.

SURRY. All vital statistics recorded on the town books ... 1813 - 1823, compiled by Grace Limeburner. North Brooksville, Me. (1942?)   1 p., 8, 6 numb. l. Reprod. from type-written copy. 42-51503.   F29. S83L5

MAINE

SUTTON'S ISLAND. John Gilley, Maine farmer and fisherman, by Charles W. Eliot. Boston, American Unitarian association, 1904. 3, 72 p. 18½ cm. "Reprinted from the Century magazine." 4-27134.
F29.S85E4

SWAN'S ISLAND, A history of. By H.W. Small. Ellsworth, Me. Hancock County pub. co., 1898. 2, (3) - 244 p. 23½ cm. 1-2204.
F29.S9S6

SWAN'S ISLAND. Biography of an island. By Perry D. Westbrook. New York, T. Yoseloff (1958) 224 p. illus. 22 cm. 57-12360.
F29.S9W4

SWEDEN. Memoir of Col. Samuel Nevers, late of Sweden ... By Wm. Nevers 3d ... Norway (Me.) Press of G.W. Millett, 1858. iv, (5) - 80 p. 13½ x 11 cm; 13-2640.
F29.S94N5

THOMASTON. History of Thomaston, Rockland, and South Thomaston, from ... 1605; with family genealogies. By Cyrus Eaton ... Hallowell (Me.) Master, Smith & co., 1865. 2 v. 20 cm. 1-9022.
F29.T4E1

THOMASTON register, 1904, compiled by Mitchell & Gastonguay. Kents Hill, Me., The H.E. Mitchell pub. co., 1904. 102 (i.e.116) p. 22 cm. 12-19895.
F29.T4M6

THOMASTON. A town that went to sea. By Aubigne Lermond Packard. Portland, Me., Falmouth Pub. House (1950) viii, 416 p. illus., ports. 22 cm. 51-550.
F29.T4P3

THOMASTON. Journals of Hezekiah Prince, jr., 1822 - 1828. Introd. by Walter Muir Whitehill. Foreword by Robert Greenhalgh Albion. N.Y., Crown Publishers (c.1965) xxii, 448 p. 24 cm. "Published for the Maine historical society." 65-24321.
F29.T4P7 1965

TOPSHAM. Resident and business directory of the town of Brunswick and Topsham villages, 1910. Comp. by H.E. Mitchell and others. August, Me., The Mitchell pub. co., (1910) 153 (i.e.157) p. fold. map. 22½ cm. 12-20997.
Directories

TOPSHAM, Vital records of, to the year 1892 ... Editor, Mary Pelham Hill ... Published under authority of the Maine historical soc. (Concord, Rumford press) 1929. v. 23 cm. Alphabetical indexes to the manuscript records of the town, supplemented by information from church registers, cemetery inscriptions and other sources. 29-27374.
F29.T67T68

TRANS ALPINE, History of, the southernmost part of the town of Lincoln, beyond the Alps. By May Murray Bailey. (Lincoln, Me., 1950) 109 p. illus., ports., map. 24 cm. "Genealogy of Trans Alpine": p. (43) - 108. 50-32392.
F29.T7B3

TURNER register, 1903 - 4, comp. by B.V. Davis. Kent's Hill, Me., The H.E. Mitchell pub. co., 1904. 109 p. 22½ cm. 12-19896.
F29.T9D2

TURNER, A history of ... to 1886, by W.R. French ... Portland, Me., Hoyt, Fogg & Donham, 1887. viii, 312 p. front. (plan) plates, ports. 23 cm. Marriages, 1785 - 1797: p. 159 - 166. 1-9023.
F29.T9F8

UNION, A history of the town of, in the county of Lincoln, to the middle of the 19th century; with a family register of the settlers before the year 1800 ... By John Langdon Sibley. Boston, B.B. Mussey, 1851. ix, 540 p. front. (port.) 20½ cm. "Family register": p. 429 - 517. 1-9024.
F29.U5S5

UNION, past and present. An illustrated history of the town of Union, ... Union, Me., The Union weekly times, 1895. 96 p. front., illus., plates, ports. 23 cm. Pages 84 - 96, blank. "Many extracts have been made from Sibley's History of Union." - Pref. 8-34777.
F29.U5U5

UNITY, History of, by James R. Taber. August, Maine farmer press, 1916. 144 p. front. (port.) 24 cm. 17-4805.
F29.U58T2

UNITY, A history of the town of. By James Berry Vickery. Manchester, Me., Falmouth Pub. House (c.1954)   254 p. illus., ports. 24 cm. An enlargement of the author's master's thesis, University of Maine, presented under title: Chapters in the history of Unity, Maine.   Bibliography: p. (211) - 215.   54-7444.   F29.U58V5

VASSALBORO register, comp. by Mitchell & Davis, 1904.   Kent's Hill, The H. E. Mitchell pub. co., 1904.   118 p. 22 cm. 12-19897.   F29. V3M6

VINALHAVEN.   Days of Uncle Dave's fish house; Vinalhaven seafarers are recalled (by) Ivan E. Calderwood.   (1st ed.) Rockland, Me., Courier-Gazette, 1969.   274 p. illus.
F29. V7C3

VINALHAVEN, A brief historical sketch of the town of Vinalhaven ...   Prepared by order of the town, on the occasion of its 100th anniversary.   Rockland, Me., The Free press office, 1889.
78 p. 24 cm. "References": p. 78. 1-9025.   F29. V7V7

VINALHAVEN, A brief historical sketch of the town of ...   Rockland, Me., Star job print., 1900.
84 p. 22½ cm. First ed. 1889. Present ed. continued to 1900 by Albra J. Vinal. 7-25104.   F29. V7V8

WALDOBORO, History of the town of, by Samuel L. Miller ... (Wiscasset, Emerson, 1910)
281 p. front. (port.) plates. 23 cm. 11-30422.   F29. W1M6

WALDOBORO.   The town register: Waldoboro, Nobleboro and Jefferson, 1906, comp. by Mitchell, Daggett, Sawyer and Lawton.   Brunswick, Me., The H. E. Mitchell co., 1906.   264 p. 22 cm. p. 5 - 100, "General reference" Maine. 12-19898.   F29. W1M7

WALDOBORO.   The German colony and Lutheran church in Maine.   An address ... 1869 ... Gettysburg, J. E. Wible, 1869.   24 p. 22½ cm. 12-11184.   F29. W26P7
F29. W1P7

WALDOBORO.   History of old Broad Bay and Waldoboro.   By Jasper J. Stahl.   Portland, Me., Bond Wheelwright Co. (1956)   2 v. illus., ports., maps. 25 cm. Bibliographical footnotes. 56-5858.
F29. W1S79

WALDOBORO, The centennial celebration of the incorporation of.   July 4, 1873.   Pub. by George Bliss, Bangor, B. A. Burr, 1873.   52 p. 20½ cm. 1-9026.   F29. W1W2

WARREN, Annals of the town of; with the early history of St. George's, Broad Bay, and the neighboring settlements on the Waldo patent.   By Cyrus Eaton.   Hallowell, Masters, Smith, 1851.   xi, 437 p. incl. port. fold. maps. 20 cm. Genealogical table: p. 375 - 437. 1-9027.   F29. W2E1

— 2d ed.   Hallowell, Masters & Livermore, 1877.   xvi, 680 p. incl. port. front., ports., fold. map, fold. plan, fold. facsim. 20½ cm. "Genealogical table": p. 498 - 651. 1-9028.   F29. W2E2

WARREN.   From Warren to the sea, 1827 - 1852; letters of the Counce and McCallum families. Intro. by William A. Baker.   Foreword by Robert G. Albion.   Middltown, N. Y. (1970)   xix, 203 p. illus. 23 cm. 70-125809.   F29. W2F7

WATERFORD, Notes on the history of, ed. by Thomas Hovey Gage, jr.   Worcester, Mass., 1913.
87 p. 20½ cm. "A partial bibliography, 'Artemus Ward' ": p. (86) - 87. 14-5804.   F29. W3G13

WATERFORD.   The town register: Waterford, Albany, Greenwood, E. Stoneham.   1906.   Comp. by Mitchell and Davis.   Brunswick, Me., The H. E. Mitchell co., 1906.   136 p. 22½ cm. 12-19899.
F29. W3M6

WATERFORD, Oxford County, The history of, comprising Historical address, by Henry P. Warren; record of families, by Wm. Warren ...   Pub. by direction of the town.   Portland, Hoyt, Fogg, & Donham, 1879.   1, (v) - vi p., (9) - 371 p. 23 cm. 1-9029.   F29. W3W2

WATERVILLE, Fairfield, Oakland, and Winslow ... Directory of, 19 -   Portland, Me.,
Portland directory co., c. 19 -   v. 23 cm. 25-7305.   Directories

MAINE 71

WATERVILLE, Military history of, including the names and record, so far as known, of all soldiers from Waterville, in the several wars of the republic; a portion of the records of the Waterville monument assoc ... by Brevet Brig. General Isaac S. Bangs. Augusta, Kennebec journal print, 1902.
75 p. front., port. 24½ cm. 3-1136. F29.W33B2

WATERVILLE. A chronology of municipal history and election statistics, Waterville, 1771 - 1908, designed for a book of reference; comp. and ed. by Clement M. Giveen. Augusta, Me., Maine farmer, 1908. 278, (4) p. front., illus., ports. 23½ cm. F29.W33G5

WEBSTER, West Gardiner, Litchfield and Monmouth register, 1909. Augusta, Me., The Mitchell pub. co., 1909. 3, 65 (24) p. front. (fold. map) 21½ cm. Pt. 1, "Maine reference manual" listed in table of contents is omitted.
12-19900. F29.W37W3

WELLS and Kennebunk, history of ... to the year 1820, at which time Kennebunk was set off, and incorporated. With biographical sketches. By Edward E. Bourne. Portland, B. Thurston, 1875.
xxiii, 797 p. illus., pl., 2 port. (incl. front.) 24 cm. 1-9030. F29. W4B7

WELLS. Historical discourse ... 1851, at the 150th anniversary of ... the First Congregational church ... in Wells, by Rev. Jas. R. Cushing. Portland, 1851. 22 p. 22 cm. 2-10422.
F29. W4C9

WEST GARDINER, Vital records of, to the year 1892. Gardiner, Me., The Reporter-journal press, 1913. 109 p. 23½ cm. Alphabetical indexes to the manuscript records of the town, supplemented by information from church registers, cemetery inscriptions and other sources. West Gardiner was formed from Gardiner in 1850. In 1852 a portion of West Gardiner was set off to form part of Farmingdale. 13-25977. F29.W47W5

WEST NEWFIELD, An historical sketch of the Congregational church, presented at the centennial anniversary, 1901, by ... Rev. Gilbert H. Bacheler. Norwich, The Bulletin, 1901. 16 p. 23½ cm.
4-1386. F29.W5 B2

WESTBROOK city directory, 1909 ... directories of the adjoining towns of Windham and Gorham ... Westbrook, Me., H.S. Cobb, c.1908 - 1 v. 24 cm. 9-3195.
Directories

WESTBROOK city directory. Boston, Union pub. co., 1900. v. 24 cm. 0-6980 rev.
Directories

WESTBROOK Gorham and Windham, Directory of ... (1915/16) - Portland, Me., Portland directory co., c.1915 - v. front. (fold. map) 23½ cm. 16-1386.
Directories

WESTBROOK. Highlights of Westbrook history, compiled by Ernest R. Rowe and others. Marion B. Rowe, ed. (Westbrook, Me.,) Westbrook Woman's Club (1952) 237 p. illus. 24 cm. 53-26520.
F29. W6 R6

WINDHAM, Sketches of the history of, 1734 - 1935; the story of a typical New England town, by Frederick Howard Dole; illus. by Raymond E. Hanson ... Westbrook, Me., H.S. Cobb, 1935.
155, (2) p. illus. 23½ cm. 35-37736. F29.W7D55

WINDHAM in the past, by Samuel Thomas Dole; ed. by Frederick Howard Dole. Auburn, Me., Merrill & Webber co., 1916. 611 p. incl. front. (port.) illus. 24 cm. "Genealogy": p. (285) - 611. 16-15606. F29. W7D6

WINDHAM, in the war of the revolution, 1775 - 1783, by Nathan Goold. Portland, Me., H.W. Bryant, 1900. 16 p. 24 cm. 6-8172. F29. W7G6

WINDHAM register, 1904, comp. by Mitchell & Russell. Kents Hill, Me., The H.E. Mitchell pub. co., 1904. 110 p. 22 cm. 12-19901. F29. W7M6

WINDHAM. A historical address ... 1839, at the centennial anniversary of the settlement of Windham; by Thomas Laurens Smith. Portland (Me.) A. Shirley, 1840. 32 p. 23½ cm. 8-15368. F29. W7S5

WINDHAM, History of town of.   Prepared at the request of the town, by Thomas Laurens Smith.
Portland (Me.) Hoyt & Fogg, 1873.   104 p. 24 cm. 1-9031.   F29. W7S6

WINSLOW register, comp. by Mitchell & Davis, 1904.   Kent's Hill, The H. E. Mitchell pub. co., 1904.
103 p. 22 cm. 12-19902.   F29. W76M6

WINSLOW, Vital records of, to the year 1892, births, marriages and deaths; Pub. under the authority
of the Maine historical soc.   (Auburn, Me., Merrill & Webber co.) 1937.   325 p. 28 cm. 37-28393.
                                                                           F29. W76W6

WINTER HARBOR.   Gouldsboro land improvement company's Grindstone inn and lands, Winter Harbor,
Maine.   (Boston, Boston photogravure co., c. 1891)   (38) p. illus. 15½ x 10½ cm. 1-9032.
                                                                           F29. W8G6

WINTER HARBOR.   Gouldsboro land improvement co.'s Grindstone inn and lands, Grindstone Neck,
Winter Harbor.   (Phila., Dreka, c. 1892)   (46) p. illus. 16 x 11 cm. 1-9033.   F29. W8G7

WINTERPORT.   An old river town, by Ada Douglas Littlefield; being a history of Winterport, (old
Frankfort), Maine, illus. from photos.   New York, Calkins and co., 1907.   xiii, 249 p. front., illus.,
plates, fold. plan. 21 cm. 8-3505.   F29. W83L7

WINTHROP register, 1903 - 4, by Mitchell & Remick.   Kent's Hill, Me., H. E. Mitchell pub. co., 1904.
99 p. 22 cm. 12-19903.   F29. W9M6

WINTHROP, History of, with genealogical notes, by Everett S. Stackpole ... Pub. by vote of the town.
Auburn, Merril & Webber (pref. 1925)   1, (11) - 741, (1) p. front. (port.) illus., fold. map. 23½ cm.   Military history:
p. 117 - 174. "Genealogical notes": p. 247 - 704. "Marriages not found in ... Genealogical notes": p. (705) - 728. 26-383.
                                                                           F29. W9S7

WINTHROP, A brief history of ... 1764 to 1855.   By David Thurston... Portland, B. Thurston, 1855.
xi, (1), (13) - 247 p. 19 cm. 1-9034.   F29. W9T5

WINTHROP.   An account of the centennial celebration at Winthrop .. 1871, ...   Augusta, Sprague,
Owen & Nash, 1871.   69 p. 23 cm. 1-9035.   F29. W9W9

WISCASSET, the home of my ancestors and the place of may birth, by Maud Fuller Briggs.   (n. p.,
194 -?)   26 p. incl. mounted pl. mounted plates. 22½ cm. 45-32501.   F29. W93B7

WISCASSET in Pownalborough; a history of the shire town and the salient historical features of the
territory between the Sheepscot and Kennebec rivers, by Fannie S. Chase.   Wiscasset, Me. ...
1941.   xv, 640 p. front., plates, ports., map, facsims. 26 cm. Includes biographies. 42-1075.   F29. W93C5

WISCASSET in early days; historical notes pertaining to the old town on the Sheepscot River, by Wm.
Davis Patterson.   Bath. Me., Times co. (c. 1929)   32 p. illus. (incl. port.) 23 cm. 29-18095.
                                                                           F29. W93P31

WISCASSET fire society.   Proceedings ... at its centennial meeting ... 1901.   lv.   F29. W93W92

WISCASSET fire society, Proceedings at its quarterly meeting ... Wiscasset, Me., 19 -   v. front.,
illus. 22 cm. CA 17-3605 unrev.   F29. W93W93

WOODSTOCK, History of, with family sketches and an appendix, by William B. Lapham.   Portland, S.
Berry, 1882.   5, (3) - 315 p. front., ports. 23 cm. 1-9036.   F29. W95L3

WOODSTOCK, Sumner and Buckfield town register, 1905.   Comp. by Mitchell and Davis.   Brunswick,
Me., The H. E. Mitchell co., 1905.   137 p. 22½ cm. 12-19904.   F29. W95M6

YARMOUTH register, 1904, comp. by Mitchell and Russell.   Kent's Hill, Me., The H. E. Mitchell
pub. co., 1904.   112 p. 22 cm. 12-19905.   F29. Y2M6

MAINE 73

YARMOUTH. Reminiscences of a Yarmouth schoolboy, by Edward Clarence Plummer ... Portland, Marks printing house, 1926.   263 p. front., plates, ports. 20 cm.   27-587.   F29. Y2P6

YARMOUTH personages, an introduction. An attempt to revive the memory of individuals whose names were once household words in old North Yarmouth and Yarmouth. (By) William Hutchinson Rowe. (Yarmouth? Me., 191 - ?)   (19) p. 20½ x 10 cm. 17-21762.   F29. Y2R87

YORK, History of, successively known as Bristol (1632), Agamenticus (1641), Gorgeana (1642), and York (1652) ... By Charles Edward Banks ... and others. Boston, Mass. (Calkins press) 1931 -
   v. front., illus., plates, ports., maps (part fold.) facsims. (1 fold.) 24½ cm.   32-7699.   F29. Y6B28

— Baltimore, Regional Pub. Co., 1967.   2 v. 24 cm.   No more pub? Reprint of the 1931-35 ed.   67-29600.
   F29. Y6B28 1967

YORK. Agamenticas, Bristol, Gorgeanna, York; an oration delivered by the Hon. James Phinney Baxter ... on the 25oth anniversary of the town, tog. with a brief history of York ... York, Me., Old York historical and improvement soc., 1904.   2, 136 p. illus., plates, ports. 24½ cm. "Historical sketch of York" (p. 34 - 82) 5-2970.   F29. Y6B3

YORK. Ancient city of Georgeanna and modern town of York ... by Geo, Alex, Emery. Boston, G. A. Amery, 1873.   xii, (13) - 192 p. incl. front. 14 cm. 1-9037.   F29. Y6E5

YORK. New England miniature, a history of York. Freeport, Me., Bond Wheelwright (1961)
284 p. 23 cm. 61-14421.   F29. Y6E7

YORK. "Nor' by east." By Elizabeth N. Little. (Newton, Mass., c.1885)   13 l. illus. 13½ x 17 cm.
18-15131.   F29. Y6 L7

YORK. Old York, proud symbol of colonial Maine, 1652 - 1952; By Edward Walker Marshall. Illus. by Cecile Newbold. N.Y., Newcomen Soc. in North America, 1952.   24 p. illus. 23 cm. "2d print. May, 1952" 52-14905.   F29. Y6M28

YORK. An address delivered at the dedication of the new Town hall in York ... 1874. By Nathaniel G. Marshall ... Portsmouth, 1874.   31 p. 22½ cm. 10-221.   F29. Y6M3

YORK. The town register: York and Kittery, 1906, comp. by Mitchell, Daggett, Holt, Lawton and Sawyer. Brunswick, Me., The H. F. Mitchell co., 1906.   237 p. 22 cm. p. 5 - 100, "General reference" (Maine)
12-19906.   F29 Y6M6

YORK, Handbook history of the town of ... by Edward C. Moody. August, Me., York pub. co., (1914)
2, (3) - 251 p. port. 23½ cm. 16-6349.   F29. Y6M8

YORK. Souvenir of York beach. (Boston, H.G. Peabody, 1888)   10 pl. obl. 24º. 1-9038-M1.
   F29. Y6S7

YORK. Souvenir of York harbor. Boston (H.G. Peabody, 1888)   10 pl. obl. 24º. 1-9039-M1.   F29. Y6S8

YORK. ... Ye romance of old York (by) Herbert Milton Sylvester. Boston, Stanhope press, 1906.
427 p. illus. 24½ cm. (His Maine coast romance (II))   6-28412.   F29. Y6S9

YORK. The silent watcher; or, York as seen from Agamenticus, by Sybil Warburton ... Boston (The Heintzemann press) 1897.   70 p. front., illus. 20 cm. 8-8582.   F29. Y6W2

YORK institute, Saco, Me., Act of incorporation, constitution, 1867.   lv.   F29. Y6Y6

— 1891.   lv.   F29. Y6Y64

— 1866. 1v.   F29.Y6Y67

YORK institute, Saco. ... Publications, v.1, no. 1-2 1884. 2 v.   F29. Y6Y7

YORK necrology. (n.p., 18 -) Copied from "A book of mortality" in possession of Mr. J.H. Moody, parish clerk... Introductory paragraph signed Marquis F. King. 10-5620.   F29. Y6Y8

ELEMENTS IN THE POPULATION.

LAWTON, R. Franco-Americans of the state of Maine, and their achievements; historical, descriptive and biographical. Lewiston, Me., H.F. Roy, 1915. 2, 9 - 211 p. front., illus. (incl. ports.) 24 cm. 19-18679.
    F30. F8L4

POHOMAN, Henry N. The German colony and Lutheran church in Maine. See F29.W26P7

WALKER, David Bradstreet. Politics and ethnocentrism; the case of the Franco-Americans. Brunswick, Me., Bowdoin College, Bureau for Research in Municipal Government, 1961. 48 p. 23 cm.
    F30. F8W3

MAINE
SUPPLEMENTARY INDEX OF PLACES

ABBOT. 48
ACADIE, ACADIA. 52, 57, 85
AGAMENTICUS. 117
ALBANY. 110, 114
ALFRED. 111
AMESBURY. 80
ANDOVER. 78, 110
ANSON. 96
ARROOSTOOK. 99
AROOSTOOK RIVER. 66
ARROWSIC. 84, 94
AUBURN. 48, 62, 68, 99
AUGUSTA. 48, 62, 70, 105
BALDWIN. 112
BANGOR. 48
BAR HARBOR. 47, 73, 74
BATH. 48, 62, 105
BELFAST. 48, 83
BELGRADE. 46, 47
BENTON. 90
BETHEL. 110
BIDDEFORD. 48, 80, 105, 106, 110
BIDDEFORD POOL. 80
BINGHAM. 112
BLOOMFIELD. 101
BREMEN. 87, 91
BREWER. 48, 83
BRISTOL. 9, 117
BROAD BAY. 114
BROOKSVILLE. 90, 97
BRUNSWICK. 62, 84, 105, 113
BUCKFIELD. 62, 112, 116
BUCKSPORT. 48, 83
BUSTIN'S ISLAND. 76
CALAIS. 79, 92
CAMDEN. 48, 83, 84, 109, 110
CANAAN. 101
CANTON. 62
CAPE ELIZABETH. 106, 107
CAPE NEDICK. 81
CARIBOU. 47, 96
CASCO BAY. 70, 87, 107
CASTINE. 97, 103
CHATHAM. 94
CHERRYFIELD. 79
CHESTERVILLE. 93

CLARK ISLAND. 111
CLINTON. 85
CORNISH. 112
COUSINS ISLAND. 70
CRANBERRY ISLES. 73, 83
CUSHING'S & PEAK'S ISLAND. 106
DAMARISCOTTA. 48, 86, 87, 100
DANFORTH (Point) 47, 100
DAYTON. 81
DEER ISLE. 76
DEERING. 106, 107
DEXTER. 62
DIXFIELD (Notch) 75, 78, 89, 91, 110
DOVER FOXCROFT. 48
DURHAM. 68
EAST LIVERMORE. 68
EAST STONEHAM. 114
EASTPORT. 79, 89
EDGECOMB. 86
ELIOT. 80, 98
ELLSWORTH. 48, 83
ELMORE. 111
FAIRFIELD. 62, 82, 85, 114
FALMOUTH. 69, 106, 107, 108
FARMINGDALE. 81, 104
FARMINGTON. 62
FORT FAIRFIELD. 47, 96
FOXCROFT. 92
FREEPORT. 62, 69, 101
FRIENDSHIP. 91
GARDINER. 48, 62, 70, 81, 82, 104
GEORGETOWN. 84, 94
GILEAD. 86
GLENMORE. 111
GORGEANNA. 117
GORHAM. 115
GRAY. 69
GREENE. 68
GREENWOOD. 86, 112, 114
HALLOWELL. 48, 62, 70, 81, 82
HAMPTON. 80
HANCOCK Co. 71
HANOVER. 69, 86, 110
HARPSWELL. 88, 101
HARRINGTON. 79
HARRISON. 87, 103

HAVERHILL. 80
HEBRON. 103, 112
HINCKLEY TOWNSHIP. 95
HOLLIS. 81
HOULTON. 47
HOUSE ISLAND. 70
IPSWICH. 80
ISLE AU HAUT. 76
ISLE OF SHOALS. 63
JEFFERSON. 114
JONESPORT. 79
KENNEBAGO. 78
KENNEBUNK. 97, 115
KENNEBUNKPORT. 47
KINGMAN. 48
KITTERY. 80, 92, 117
LEBANON. 81, 111
LEEDS. 68
LEWISTON. 48, 62, 68, 105
LIMINGTON. 112
LINCOLN. 47, 113
LISBON. 68
LITCHFIELD. 115
LITTLEJOHN'S ISLAND. 70
LIMERICK. 112
LIVERMORE. 47, 92
LONG COVE. 111
LOVELL. 94
LUBEC. 79, 89
LYGONIA. 110
LYMAN. 81, 111
MACHIAS (MACHIASPORT) 79, 97
MANCHESTER. 81
MARTINSVILLE. 111
MATTAWAMKEAG. 47
MECHANIC FALLS. 62, 68
MEXICO. 75, 110
MILLBRIDGE. 79
MILLTOWN. 79, 89
MILTON PLANTATION. 110
MINOT. 68
MONHEGAN. 87, 100, 103
MONMOUTH. 115
MOODY BRIDGES. 87
MOOSEHEAD LAKE. 46, 66
MOUNT DESERT (ISLAND) 54, 84
MUSCONGUS (ISLAND) 59, 91
NAPLES. 87, 103
NARRAGANSET. 88
NEW GLOUCESTER. 69, 95
NEW SHARON. 93, 96
NEW SOMERSETSHIRE. 110

NEW SWEDEN. 68
NEW VINEYARD. 96
NEWBURY. 80
NEWCASTLE. 48, 86, 91
NEWFIELD. 81
NEWRY. 110
NOBLEBORO. 87, 114
NORTH HAVEN. 109
NORTH YARMOUTH. 69, 91, 117
NORTHEAST HARBOR. 47
NORWAY. 62, 112
OAKLAND. 62, 69, 114
OGUNQUITT. 47
OLD ORCHARD BEACH. 80, 86, 97, 106, 107, 110
OLDTOWN. 48, 83
ORONO. 83
ORR'S ISLAND. 70
OWLS HEAD. 109
OXFORD. 112
PARKMAN. 48
PARMACHENEE LAKES. 78
PARSONSFIELD. 81
PASSAMAQUODDY. 92
PEJEPSCOT. 88
PEMAQUID. 54, 55, 56, 58, 87, 100
PENOBSCOT. 54, 90, 97
PENOBSCOT BAY & RIVER. 52
PENTAGOET. 90
PEPPERELLBOROUGH. 110, 111
PERU. 110
PHIPPSBURG. 84, 94
PINE POINT. 80
PISCATAQUIS. 66
PITTSTON. 94
POLAND. 68
POLAND SPRING. 46, 47
PONDICHERRY. 87
POPHAM. 103
POPHAM COLONY. 55
PORT CLYDE. 111
PORTLAND. 48, 54, 69
POWNAL. 101
PRESQUE ISLE. 47, 48, 96
PRINCETON. 79
PROUT'S NECK. 47, 80
RANDOLPH. 48, 81, 104
RANGELEYS (The) 46
RAYMOND. 87
READFIELD. 78
RICHARDSON. 78
RICHMOND. 62, 81, 84
ROCKLAND. 48, 83, 113

ROCKPORT. 48, 83, 89, 109, 110
ROXBURY. 110
RUMFORD. 75
SACCORAPPA. 106
SACO. 48, 80, 86, 105, 106
SACO VALLEY. 49
SAGADAHOC. 55
SAGADAHOC Co. 84
ST. GEORGE(S) 60, 109, 111, 114
ST. STEPHEN. 89
SALISBURY. 80
SANFORD. 105
SANGERVILLE. 48, 95
SCARBORO. 69
SEBAGO. 103
SEBAGO LAKE Land. 70
SEBASTICOOK-BENTON. 85
SEVEN PONDS. 78
SHAPLEIGH. 81, 111
SHEEPSCOT. 100
SIDNEY. 85
SKOWHEGAN. 48, 62, 101
SOMESVILLE. 75
SORRENTO. 112
SOUTH BRISTOL. 87
SOUTH PARIS. 62, 101
SOUTH PORTLAND. 105, 106, 107
SOUTH THOMASTON. 109, 113
SOUTHPORT. 86
SOUTHWEST HARBOR. 47, 75, 83
SPRINGVALE. 111
SPRUCE HEAD. 111
SQUIRREL ISLAND. 86
STARK(S) 96, 101
STEUBEN. 79
STONINGTON. 76
STOW. 94
STRONG. 100
STROUDWATER. 107

SUMNER. 112, 116
SWEDEN. 94
TENANT'S HARBOR. 111
THOMASTON. 48, 83, 109, 110
TOPSHAM. 87, 88
TURNER. 68
UMBAGOG. 78
UNION. 109
VINALHAVEN. 109
WALDOBORO'. 48
WALES. 68, 100
WALLSTON. 111
WARREN. 48, 109, 110
WATERBORO. 81
WATERBOROUGH. 111
WATERFORD. 112
WATERVILLE. 48, 62, 70, 82
WEBSTER. 68
WELLS. 98
WEST BATH. 84, 94
WEST GARDINER. 81, 94, 104, 115
WEST GOULDSBORO. 54
WESTBROOK. 48, 105, 107
WESTPORT. 94
WILLARDHAM. 111
WILTON. 93
WINDHAM. 115
WINN. 47
WINSLOW. 114
WINTERPORT. 93
WINTHROP. 62, 81
WISCASSET. 48, 86
WOODSTOCK. 86, 112
WOOLWICH. 84
YARMOUTH. 69, 101
YORK. 92
YORK BEACH. 47
YORK Co. 80, 86
YORK HARBOR. 47

ADDITIONS TO INDEX

SAGADAHOC VALLEY. 45, 46   SORRENTO. 112

NEW HAMPSHIRE

SELECTED BIBLIOGRAPHIES FOR NEW HAMPSHIRE

DOVER, N.H. Public library. ... A list of books and pamphlets in the Dover public library relating to New Hampshire. Dover, N.H., H. E. Hodgdon, printer, 1903.   172, iii p.   23 cm.   5-39116.
                                                                                                                        Z1311.D 65

HAMMOND, Otis Grant. Check list of New Hampshire local history ...   Concord, N.H., New Hampshire historical soc., 1925.   106 p.   22 ½ cm.   25-27289.   Z1311.H 22

DOVER. Bibliography of Dover, N.H., containing titles of (1) works on Dover; (2) works written by residents of Dover, while residents; (3) works bearing the publication imprint of Dover. Concord, N.H., I. C. Evans, printer, 1892.   Compiled by John R. Ham, M.D. 74 p. 22 ½ cm. 1-2325.   Z1312.D74 H1

DARTMOUTH COLLEGE. ... Bibliography of Dartmouth college and Hanover, N.H. ... Concord, E. N. Pearson, public printer, 1894.   Compiled by James Thayer Gerould. 69 p. 22 ½ cm. "(Reprinted from the state librarian's report)" 24th, 1892/4, p. 149 - 216; N.H. library assoc. Reports of committees on bibliographies. 1-2318* Cancel.   Z1312.H24 G3

MANCHESTER. Bibliography of Manchester, N.H. A collection of books, pamphlets, and magazines, (numbering over sixteen hundred.) From 1743 to 1885 ... Preserved by S. C. (Sylvester Clark) Gould ... Nutfield, Londonderry, Chester, Harrytown, Derryfield, Manchester. Part I. Manchester, N.H., S.C. & L.M. Gould, 1885.   52 p. 22 ½ cm. Comp. by John W. Moore. No more published. 10-18497.
                                                                                                                        Z1312.M26 G7
                                                                                                                        1885

— 2d ed. with additions. Manchester, N.H., S.C. & L.M. Gould, 1885.   60 p. 22 cm. 1-2328 Rev.
                                                                                                                        Z1312.M26 G7
                                                                                                                        1885 a

MANCHESTER. Bibliography of Manchester, N.H. 1737 to 1894. By S. C. Gould ... Concord, E. N. Pearson, printer, 1894.   115 p. 23 cm. Reprinted from state librarian's report. 1-2330.
                                                                                                                        Z1312.M26 G7
                                                                                                                        1894

WARNER. Bibliography of Warner, by Mary Bartlett Harris. (Concord, N.H., Rumford print. co., 1904)   34 p. 22 ½ cm. First pub. as appendix to New Hampshire state library report, 1902/04. 5-39115.   Z1312.W2 H2

WHITE Mountains. A bibliography of the White Mountains, by Allen H. Bent. Boston, Pub. for the Appalachian mountain club, by Houghton Mifflin co., 1911.   3, (v) - vii, 114 p. front., ports. 22 ½ cm. 11-7858.   Z1312.W5 B4

— Bent's Bibliography of the White Mountains. Ed. by E. J. Hanrahan. Somersworth, New Hampshire Pub. Co., 1971.   xi, 114 p. ports. 23 cm. 79-179457 MARC.
                                                                                                                        Z1312.W5 B4
                                                                                                                        1971

NEW HAMPSHIRE CLASSIFICATION.   F31 - F45

31		Periodicals. Societies. Collections.
.5		Museums. Exhibitions, exhibits.
32		Gazetteers. Dictionaries. Geographic names.
.3		Guidebooks.
33		Biography (Collective). Genealogy (Collective).
.2		Historiography.
		Historians, *see* E 175.5.
.5		Study and teaching.
34		General works. Histories.
.3		Juvenile works.
.5		Minor works. Pamphlets, addresses, essays, etc.
.6		Anecdotes, legends, pageants, etc.
35		Historic monuments (General). Illustrative material.
36		Antiquities (Non-Indian).
		By period.
37		Early to 1775. Mason's Grant.
		Biography: John Mason, etc.
		Cf. F 52, New Hampshire Grants.
		E 83.72, Wars with eastern Indians, 1722–1726.
		E 199, French and Indian War, 1755–1763.
38		1775–1865.
		Biography: William Henry Young Hackett, Isaac Hill, etc.
		Cf. E 263.N4, New Hampshire in the Revolution.
		E 359.5.N3, War of 1812.
		E 520, Civil War, 1861–1865 (General).
39		1865–1950.
		Biography: Harry Bingham, Charles Doe, etc.
		Cf. D 570.85.N25–26, World War I, 1914–1918.
		D 769.85.N25–26, World War II, 1939–1945.
		E 726.N3, War of 1898 (Spanish-American War).
40		1951–
41		White Mountains.
.1		Periodicals. Societies. Collections.
.2		Gazetteers. Dictionaries. Geographic names.
.3		General works.
.32		Minor works. Pamphlets, addresses, essays, etc.
.37		Historic monuments (General). Illustrative material.
		By period.
.44		Early to 1865.
.5		1865–1950.
.52		1951–
.6		Regions, places, etc., A–Z.
		e. g. .F8 Franconia Notch.
		.P9 The Profile.
		.W3 Mount Washington.
		Political divisions are classed in F 42–44.

42   Regions, counties, etc., A–Z.
- .B4   Belknap Co.
- .B7   Boundaries.
  - New York-New Hampshire dispute over New Hampshire Grants, see F 52.
- .C3   Carroll Co.
  - Mount Pequawket (Kearsarge), Ossipee Mountain Park, etc.
  - Mount Kearsarge, Merrimack Co., see F 42.M5.
- .C5   Cheshire Co.
  - Mount Monadnock, etc.
- .C65 Connecticut River and Valley, N. H.
  - Cf. F 12.C7, New England.
- .C7   Coos Co.
  - Indian Stream, etc.
- .G7   Grafton Co.
  - Newfound (Pasquaney) Lake, etc.
- .H6   Hillsboro (Hillsborough) Co.
  - Uncanoonuc Mountains, etc.
- .I8   Isles of Shoals.
- Kearsarge, Mount, Carroll Co., see F 42.C3.
- Kearsarge, Mount, Merrimack Co., see F 42.M5.
- Magalloway Valley, see F 27.M18.
- .M4   Merrimac River and Valley, N. H.
  - Cf. F 72.M6, General, and Massachusetts.
- .M5   Merrimack Co.
  - Mount Kearsarge, etc.
- .P4   Piscataqua River and Valley (General, and N. H.).
  - Cf. F 27.P48, Maine.
- .R7   Rockingham Co.
  - Lake Massabesic, etc.
  - Isles of Shoals, see F 42.I8.
- .S8   Strafford Co.
- .S87 Sullivan Co.
- .S9   Sunapee Lake.
- Waterville Valley, see F 44.W32, Waterville, N. H.
- White Mountains, see F 41.
- .W7   Lake Winnipesaukee.

44   Cities, towns, etc., A–Z.
- e. g. .C7   Concord.
-       .D7   Dover.
-       .M2   Manchester.
-       .N2   Nashua.
-       .P8   Portsmouth.
-       .W32 Waterville.
  - Waterville Valley, etc.

45   Elements in the population.
- .A1   General works.
- .A2–Z Individual elements.
  - For a list of racial, ethnic, and religious elements (with cutter numbers), see E 184,

NEW HAMPSHIRE
F 31 - F 45

PERIODICALS. SOCIETIES. COLLECTIONS.

COLLECTIONS, historical and miscellaneous, and monthly literary journal.   v. 1 - 3; Apr. 1822 - Nov./Dec. 1824.   Concord, N.H., Hill and Moore.   3 v. 24 cm. 1-7930 rev. *
           F31. C6
           Rare Book Coll.

DIRECTORY of New Hampshire historical information.   1966 -   Wolfeboro, N.H., Association of Historical Societies of New Hampshire.   v. illus. 22 cm.
           F31. D5

ECHOES from the Dartmouth-Lake Sunapee region of New Hampshire.   v. -   (New London, N.H., Dartmouth-Lake Sunapee regional association, 1939 -   v. in   illus. (incl. ports.) maps. 30 cm. monthly (irregular)   Title varies slightly. 44-45108.
           F31. E3

HASTINGS, Mrs. Susannah (Willard) Johnson, 1730 - 1810.   Mrs. Johnson's captivity.   (In Collections topographical, historical and biographical, relating ... to New-Hampshire. v.1, p.177-239) 11-25231.
           F31. F23

GRANITE monthly, The; a New Hampshire magazine devoted to history, biography, literature, and state progress.   v. 1 -   Concord, N.H., H. H. Metcalf; (etc.) 1877 - 1930.   v. in   illus., plates, ports., maps. 23 - 30 cm. Title varies. "Index of authors and subjects of first ten volumes" and "List of portraits": v. 10 p. (399) - 412. No more pub. L.C. set incomplete. 5-18238-9 (rev. '37)
           F31. G75

— Index ... v. 1 - 34 (Apr. 1877 - June 1903)   (In Bulletin of the New Hampshire pub. libraries. new ser. v.4-5, p. 29 - 135)
           Z732.N55N2

GRANITE state magazine; an illustrated monthly devoted to the history, story, scenery, industry and interest of New Hampshire.   v. 1-7, no. 4.   Manchester, N.H., Granite state pub. co. (etc.) 1906 - (14)   7 v. in 8. illus., plates, ports. 24 cm. Monthly, 1906 - 07; quarterly, 1908; monthly, 1909-14. Publication suspended from Jan. to June 1909, June, 1910 - July 1911. Jan. 1912 to Nov. 1914. No more published. 14-20008.
           F31. G76

HISTORICAL New Hampshire.   Nov. 1944 -   (Concord) New Hampshire Historical soc.   v. in   illus., ports. 24 cm. irregular. 50-21159.
           F31. H57

NEW HAMPSHIRE (Provincial and state papers)   Pub. by authority of the legislature of New Hampshire.   v. 1 -   Concord (etc.) 1867 - 19   v. illus., maps (part fold.) plans (part fold.) fold. facsims. 23½ x 25 cm.   Vol. 24 has maps in pocket. 8-12839.
           F31. N42

v. 1 - 7, Provincial papers.
v. 8, States papers.
v. 9, 11 - 13, Town papers.
v. 10, Provincial and state papers.
v. 14 - 17, Rolls and documents relating to soldiers in the revolutionary war.
v. 18, Miscellaneous provincial and state papers.
v. 19, Provincial papers.
v. 20 - 22, Early state papers.
v. 23, ... Documents in the Public Record Office in London... relating to ... New Hampshire.
v. 24 - 25, Town charters.
v. 26, The New Hampshire grants.
v. 27 - 28, Township grants.
v. 29, Documents relating to the Masonian patent.
v. 30 - ... State papers series (Misc. Revolutionary documents)
v. 31 - Probate records.
v. 40, Court records, 1640 - 1692.

NEW HAMPSHIRE. Publication of early state and province papers. Report ... Concord, N.H., Republican press association, 1890. 12 p. 23 cm. 18-17041. F31. N44

NEW HAMPSHIRE antiquarian society, Collections of the, no. 1 - 4. Contoocook, The Antiquarian society, 1874 - 79. 106 p. 23 cm. Contents. - no. 1 - Mowry, W. A. Who invented the American steamboat? no. 2. Walker, Mrs. Thomas. The Shurtleff manuscripts, no. 153. - no. 3. Secomb, D. F. A list of the centenarians of New Hampshire, who have deceased since 1705. - no. 4. Ketchum, Silas. Address at the annual meeting, July 15, 1879. 15-21020. F31. N45

NEW HAMPSHIRE historical society. Act of incorporation, constitution and by-laws ... 21 (2) p. 24½ cm. 17-15477. F31. N5

NEW HAMPSHIRE historical society, Addresses delivered at the observance of the centennial of the, Concord, The Society (1923) 71 p. 23½ cm. 24-27072. F31. N515

NEW HAMPSHIRE historical society, The. Concord, 1940. 23 p. front., plates, port. 23 cm. 41-3101. F31. N517

NEW HAMPSHIRE historical society. Proceedings v. 1 - 5. 1872/88 - 1905/12. Concord. 5 v. ports. 24 cm. Vol. 1 pt. 2 includes the "Report ... in defence of General John Sullivan" 7-18610 rev.* F31. N52

NEW HAMPSHIRE historical society. Report. (Concord) v. 23 cm. annual. Formerly included in the Society's Manual. Title varies. 59-31687. F31. N538

NEW HAMPSHIRE historical society. Collections. v. 1 - Concord (etc.) 1824 - 19 -
v. illus., port. fold. map. 22 - 25 cm. Vol. 10 has title: New Hampshire historical society. A list of documents in the Public record office in London, England, relating to the province of New Hampshire. Contents (of v. 1 - 10 may be found in Bibliography of American historical societies, by A.P.C. Griffin. 2d ed. 2907) - v. 11. The Indian Stream republic, etc. 9-13120. F31. N54

NEW HAMPSHIRE historical society, Collections of the. v. 3. Concord ... 1832; Manchester, Repr. by J. B. Clarke, 1870. 304 p. 23½ cm. 9-11751. F31. N54 vol. 3

NEW HAMPSHIRE historical society, Manual of the. (Concord) 18 - 1929. v. 13 - 23 cm. irregular. Vols. for 1923 - 1929 include the society's reports for 1922 - 1928. 21-27283 rev.* F31. N546

NEW HAMPSHIRE historical society. Reports. 1921. Concord. 31 p. 23 cm. Reports for the years 1922 - 1928 included in the society's manual, 1923 - 1929. 22-22248 rev.* F31. N55

NEW HAMPSHIRE historical society. Dedication of the building of the. Concord, 1912. 132 p. front., 1 illus., plates, ports. 30½ cm. 12-24798. F31. N58

NEW HAMPSHIRE historical society building, the unwritten history of the. (Concord) 1920. 1, 46 p. illus. 22 cm. 20-27299. F31. N65

NEW HAMPSHIRE

NEW HAMPSHIRE Old home week association ... Annual report of Old home week. (1st - 1899 - 19 -   Manchester (etc.) 1900 -   v. plates, ports. 23 cm. Title varies. 1-21486 rev.
 F31. N73

NEW HAMPSHIRE profiles. v. 1 -   Dec. 1951 -   (Portsmouth)   v. illus. (part col.) ports. 31 cm. monthly. 56-21052.
 F31. N76

REPERTORY, The. v. 1 -   (Keene, N.H., Repertory pub. co.,   v. illus. (incl. map) 26 cm. monthly. 38M4025T.
 F31. R47

SKETCH book of nature and outdoor life. A monthly magazine of outdoor inspiration from New Hampshire the picturesque. v. 1 -   June 1909 -   Manchester, N.H., A.E.Vogel, 1909 - 1 v. 18 cm. 11-10800.
 F31. S62

SONS of New Hampshire, Festival of the ... Celebrated in Boston, Nov. 7, 1849.   Boston, J. French, 1850.   178 p. 2 port. (incl. front.) 24½ cm. With this is bound Second festival ... Boston, 1854. 1-7631.
 F31. S69
 AC901. W3 vol. 58

SQUARE deal, The. v. 1 -   (Nashua, N.H., Guide pub. co., 1914 -   v. illus. 29½ cm. weekly. 38M4838T.
 F31. S78

GAZETTEERS. DICTIONARIES. GEOGRAPHIC NAMES.

FARMER, John. A gazetteer of the state of New-Hampshire.   Concord, J.B.Moore, 1823.   iv, (5) - 276 p. front. (fold. map) illus., plates. 18 cm. 1-7931.
 F32. F23

FOGG, Alonzo J. The statistics and gazetteer of New-Hampshire. Containing descriptions of all the counties, towns and villages, etc.   Concord, N.H., D.L.Guernsey, 1874.   xiv, 674 p. front., illus., plates, fold. map, tables. 23 cm. 1-7932.
 F32. F65

HAYWARD, John. A gazetteer of New Hampshire, containing descriptions of all the counties, towns, and districts, etc.   Boston, J.P.Jewett, 1849.   264 p. front., 1 illus., plates. 20 cm. 1-7933.
 F32. H42
 G & M

HUNT, Elmer Munson. New Hampshire town names and whence they came.   Peterborough, N.H., Noone House (1971, c.1970)   xxi, 282 p. 23 cm. 79-125806.
 F32. H85
 1971
 L.H. & G.

MERRILL, Eliphalet, comp. Gazetteer of the state of New-Hampshire ...   Exeter, Print. C.Norris & co. for the authors, 1817.   218, (13) p. incl. tables. 21½ cm. Contents. - (pt. I) A general view, geographical and statistical. - pt. II. Gazetteer of New-Hampshire. - pt. III. Topographical and statistical tables. 1-7934.
 F32. M56

NEW HAMPSHIRE ... Communities, settlements, and neighborhood centers in the state of New Hampshire. An inventory prepared by the State planning and development commission, Concord, New Hampshire. (Concord, 1937)   5, 45 (i.e.58) numb. l. map. 27½ cm. 37-28141.
 F32. N48
 L.H. & G.

GUIDEBOOKS

NEW HAMPSHIRE vacation guide. (Concord)   v. illus. (part col.) 21 - 27 cm. annual.
 F32.3.N48

DUNHAM'S Southern New Hampshire directory, including the towns of Amherst, Bennington, Fitzwilliam, Greenfield, Hancock, Jaffrey, Lyndboro, Merrimack, Milford, Mont Vernon, New Ipswich, Peterborough, Rindge, Temple and Wilton ... 19 Winthrop, Mass., C. H. Dunham, c 19 -
v. 24 cm.   CA 30-1072 unrev. Directories

U.S. Bureau of the census. ... Heads of families at the first census of the U. S. taken in the year 1790 ... Washington, Govt. print. off., 1907 - 8.   12 v. fronts. (fold. maps) 29½ cm. 7-35273.   F32.5.U58

NEW HAMPSHIRE business directory ... 186 -   Boston, Mass., Briggs & co., 186 -   v. 22½ cm.
33-38669. Directories

NEW HAMPSHIRE state directory and gazetteer for 1892 -   Boston, Mass., Union pub. co.,
1892 - c. 1920.   v. fold. maps. 24 cm. 99-3621 (rev. '20) Directories

BIOGRAPHY (COLLECTIVE). GENEALOGY (COLLECTIVE).

BELL, Charles Henry.   The bench and the bar of New Hampshire, including biographical notices of deceased judges of the highest court, and lawyers of the province and state, and a list of the names of those now living.   Boston ... Houghton Mifflin, 1894.   xv, 795 p. 25 cm.   "Biographical notice of the author" by Jeremiah Smith: p. (ix) - xv. 4-20172. F33. B43

BIOGRAPHICAL sketches of the governor, councilors and members of the Senate and House of representatives of the New Hampshire legislature for 1881/2 -   v. 1 -   Concord, N. H.,
A. C. Clark (etc.) 1881 - 19 -   v. 23½ cm. 7-769 rev. F33. B6

GOSS, Winifred (Lane) Colonial gravestone inscriptions in the state of New Hampshire, pub. by the Historic activities committee of the National society of the colonial dames of America ... Dover, N. H., 1942.   160 p. 23 cm. References: p. (6) 43-3390. F33. G6

HAZEN, Henry Allen.   The pastors of New Hampshire, Congregational and Presbyterian. Bristol, N. H., Print. R. W. Musgrove, 1878.   32, (2) p. 23½ cm. Pub. by request of the General association of Congregational churches ... 4-30130. F33. H42

MEN of progress; biographical sketches and portraits of leaders in business and professional life in and of the state of New Hampshire; comp. ... Richard Herndon; ed. ... the Manchester union. Boston, New England magazine, 1898.   233 p. illus. 29 cm. 98-1243 rev. F33. M53

METCALF, Henry Harrison, comp.   New Hamsphire women. A collection of portraits and biographical sketches of daughters and residents of the Granite state ... Concord, N. H., The N. H. pub. co., 1895.   249 p. illus. (ports.) 21 x 29 cm. Alternate pages blank. 45-48595. F33. M57

METCALF, Henry Harrison.   One thousand New Hampshire notables; brief biographical sketches of New Hampshire men and women, native or resident, prominent in public ... work. Concord, N. H., The Rumford print. co., 1919.   viii, 558 p. incl. illus. (ports.) port. 20 cm. 19-12406. F33. M58

MOSES, George Higgins, comp.   New Hamsphire men. A collection of biographical sketches, with portraits, of sons and residents of the state who have become known in commercial, professional and political life ...   Concord, N. H., The N. H. pub. co., 1893.   xi, 408 p. illus. (ports.) 20½ x 28 cm. 15-9305.
F33. M9

NATIONAL society of the colonial dames of America. New Hampshire. Gravestone inscriptions gathered by the Old burial grounds committee of the National society of the colonial dames of America in the state of N. H.; comp. by Mrs. Josiah Carpenter, chairman.   Cambridge .. Riverside press, 1913.   2, 63 p. 20 cm. 14-11195. F33. N27

NEW HAMPSHIRE. Probate court. Cheshire county.   (n. p., 193-?)   11 l. 28 cm. Copied by Mary Philbrook.
"Index to probate records copied from index in the office of the probate clerk at Keene, Cheshire county, and includes all records shown in that index ... 1769 to 1800."   38M3105T. F33. N34

NEW HAMPSHIRE

NEW HAMPSHIRE. Probate courts. Index to probate records in office of probate clerk, county of Rockingham, at Exeter, 1753 - 1800 ... (n.p., 193-?) 74 l.. 28 cm. 38M3104T.
F33. N38

NEW HAMPSHIRE genealogical record. v. 1 - 5. Dover, N.H., 1904 - 08. 5 v. 23 cm.
F33. N54

NEW HAMPSHIRE notables; brief biographical sketches of New Hampshire men and women, ... 216 p. incl. front., illus. (ports.) 23½ cm. "The design has been to include only living subjects ... a number ... have died since ... (the sketches were) printed, the fact of death ... being notes in the 'Addenda'." 33-22576.
F33. N57
1932

— Concord, N.H., Concord Press, 1955. 211 p. ports. 25 cm. 57-24648.
F33. N57
1955
L.H. & G.

SKETCHES of successful New Hampshire men ... Manchester, J.B. Clarke, 1882. vii, (9) - 315 p. ports. 24 cm. Each biography ... has its author's name attached. 6-5578.
F33. S62

SOUVENIR of New Hampshire legislators, 1897 - Concord, N.H., (1897 - 19 - v. 24½ x 25 cm.
F33. S72

STEARNS, Ezra Scollay, ed. Genealogical and family history of the state of New Hampshire; ... New York, Chicago, The Lewis pub. co., 1908. 4 v. fronts., plates, ports. 27½ cm. Paged continuously. 8-32968.
F33. S79

WILLEY, George Franklyn. State builders; an illustrated historical and biographical record of the state of New Hampshire at the beginning of the twentieth century, by the State builders pub. co. Manchester, N.H., The N.H. pub. corp., 1903. 5, 503 p. front., illus., plates, ports. 24½ cm. 4-14598.
F33. W71

GENERAL WORKS. HISTORIES.

COFFIN, Charles Carleton. The future of New Hampshire. An address before the New Hampshire press association. (Boston) Print. Boston stereo. foundry, 1881. cover-title, 23 p. fold. map. 20 cm. 12-10326.
F34.
HC107.N4C6

BARNES, Mary R. A brief history of New Hampshire ... (Manchester, N.H., 1923) 32 p. 23 cm.
F34. B25

BARSTOW, George. The history of New Hampshire ... 1614, to ... 1819. Concord, N.H., I.S. Boyd, 1842. iv, 456 p. front., ports. 23½ cm. 7-14158.
F34. B27

— 2d ed. 1853. iv, 456 p. 22½ cm. 1-7935.
F34. B28

BARTLETT, John Henry. A synoptic history of the Granite state ... Chicago, N.Y., Donohue & co., (c.1930) xvi, 175 p. front., pl., ports., map. 19½ cm. 39-32119.
F34. B32

BELKNAP, Jeremy. The history of New-Hampshire. Vol. I. Comprehending the events of one complete century from the discovery of the river Pascataqua. Phila. ... R. Aitken, 1784. viii, 361, lxxxiv p. 21½ cm. No more pub. of this ed. Vol. 2-3 printed Boston, 1791 - 92; v. 1 reprinted Boston 1792. 12-26595.
F34. B42
Rare Book Room

— Boston, 1791 - 2. 3 v. fold. map. 20½ cm. Imprint varies. Contents. - v.1. The events of one complete century ... v.2. The events of seventy five years, from 1715 to 1790. - v.3. A geographical description of the state; with sketches of its natural history, etc. 1-7936.
F34. B 43
Rare book room

— (Dover, N.H.) Printed for O. Crosby and J. Varney, by Mann and Remick. 1812. 3 v. fold. map. 22½ cm. Imprint varies slightly. Contents as above. 1-7937.

F34. B44

— 2d ed., with large additions and improvements, published from the author's last manuscript. Boston: Bradford and Read. 1813. 3 v. front. (fold. map) 22½ cm. Contents as above. 5-13606.

F34. B442

— From a copy of the original edition, having the author's last corrections. ... To which are added notes ... By John Farmer ... v. 1. Dover (N.H.) Stevens, Ela and Wadleigh, 1831. xvi, 512 p. front. (port.) 23 cm. No more published. 1-7938.

F34. B45

— With a new introd. by John Kirkland Wright. New York (Johnson Reprint Corp.) 1970. 2 v. 23 cm. 70-122255.

F34. B45 1970

— Dover, N.H., G. Wadleigh, 1862. 2, (iii) - xvi, 512 p. front. (port.) 26 cm. A copy of the Dover edition of 1831, with new t.-p. added. 16-23656.

F34. B46

BOWLES, Mrs. Ella (Shannon) Let me show you New Hampshire; with an introduction by Kenneth Roberts. New York, London, A.A. Knopf, 1938. 4, vii-xviii, 368, xxxiii p. front., plates, 2 fold. maps, diagrs. 22½ cm. "First edition." 38-27408.

F34. B69

BROWNE, George Waldo. The story of New Hampshire. Introd. by Ernest W. Butterfield ... illus. by Frank Holland and others. Manchester, N.H., Standard book co. inc., 1925. 276 p. incl. front., illus., pl. 20½ cm. 27-5938.

F34. B83

CHARLTON, Edwin Azro. New Hampshire as it is ... Claremont, N.H., Tracy and Sanford, 1855. 592 p. front., plates, ports. 22½ cm. Contents - pt. I. A historical sketch ... to ... 1788 - pt. II. A gazetteer ... - pt. III. A general view ... soil, productions, climate ... biographical sketches ... 1-7939.

F34. C48

COOLIDGE, Austin Jacobs. History and description of New England. New Hampshire. Boston, A.J. Coolidge, 1860. iii, (376) - 719 p. illus., plates, fold. map. 24½ cm. Reprinted from v. 1 of the author's History and description of New England. 1-27954.

F34. C77

FARMER, John. A catechism of the history of New-Hampshire ... for the use of schools and families. 2d ed. Concord, Hoag and Atwood, 1830. vi, (7) -108 p. incl. front., illus. 14½ cm. 1-7940.

F34. F23
Rare book room

FEDERAL writers' project. New Hampshire stories ... Sponsored by: Manchester city library ... Compiled by Harry E. Flanders. (n.p., 1939?) - v. plates, map. 28 cm. 39-29133 rev.

F34. F45

HILDRETH, Hosea. A book for New-Hampshire children, in familiar letters from a father. 4th ed. - rev. and cor. Exeter, F. Grant, 1834. 108 p. double front. (map) illus. 16½ cm. 15-23523.

F34. H 63
Rare book room

— 5th ed. 1839. 116 p. front. (col. map) illus. 16½ cm. 9-21148.

F34. H64
Rare book room

JOHNSON, Frances Ann. New Hampshire for young folks. Concord, N.H., The Sugar ball press, 1944. 212 (10) p. incl. illus. (incl. maps) plates, ports. front. 22½ cm. 45-157.

F34. J6

McCLINTOCK, John Norris. Colony, province, state, 1623 - 1888. History of New Hampshire. Boston, B.B. Russell, 1889. 698, xx p. front., illus., plates, ports. 23 cm. Plates printed both sides. 1-7941. F34. M12

METCALF, Henry Harrison. New Hampshire in history; or, The contribution of the Granite state to the development of the nation ... Concord, N.H. Print. W.B. Ranney co., 1922. 106 p. front., ports. 19½ cm. 23-5613.

F34. M58

NEW HAMPSHIRE

PARSHLEY, Edward J. New Hampshire: a historical sketch. 1938. Pub. by the New Hampshire State planning and development commission. Concord, N.H. (1938) 1, 17 numb. l. 28 cm. Photoprinted. 39-28150.
F34. P36

PILLSBURY, Hobart. New Hampshire; resources, attractions, and its people; a history ... New York, The Lewis historical pub. co., inc., 1927. v. fronts., plates, ports., maps, facsim. 27½ cm. Vols. 1 - 4 paged continuously. Vols. 5 -   contain biographical material. 28-11089.
F34. P64

POTTER, C.E. Military history of New Hampshire. (1866) v.
F34. P86

POTTER, Chandler Eastman. The military history of the state of New-Hampshire, from its settlement, in 1623, to the rebellion, in 1861. Concord, Print. McFarland & Jenks, 1866 (1868) 392, 401 p. 24½ cm. Reprinted from the Report of the adjutant general of New Hampshire for 1866 vol. 2 pt. 1, p. 1-394; and for 1868 pt. 2, p. 1 - 401. 8-16039.
F34. P862

— With an added index prepared by the staff of the New Hampshire Historical Society.
F34. P86
1972

SANBORN, Edwin David. History of New Hampshire ... to the year 1830; with dissertations ... to the year 1874. Manchester, N.H., J.B. Clarke, 1875. viii, (9) - 422 p. 23½ cm. 1-7943.
F34. S19

SANBORNE, Franklin Benjamin. ... New Hamsphire; an epitome of popular government. Boston, and N.Y., Houghton, Mifflin and co., 1904. x, 354 p. front. (map) 18½ cm. 4-10074.
F34. S21

SQUIRES, James Duane. The Granite State of the United States; a history of New Hampshire from 1623 to the present. New York, American Historical Co. (1956) 4 v. illus., ports. 28 cm. Includes bibliographies. Vols. 3 - 4: Family and personal history. 56-2076.
F34. S68
L.H. & G.

SQUIRES, James Duane. New Hampshire; a students' guide to localized history. New York, Teachers College Press, 1966. x, 36 p. 23 cm. 66-13065.
F34. S69

STACKPOLE, Everett Schermerhorn. History of New Hampshire ... New York, The American historical society (1916) 4 v. fronts., plates, ports., map. 25 cm. 17-5388.
F34. S77

WEBSTER, Daniel. Speeches of the Hon, Daniel Webster of Mass., ... in Boston, Nov. 7th, 1849. Boston, J. French, 1849. 23 p. 23 cm. 14-21256.
F34. W36

WEBSTER, Nathan Burnham. New Hampshire. Philadelphia, J.B. Lippincott co., 1891. 5 p. 12°. Appears as article "New Hampshire" in Chambers's encyclopaedia. 1-7944-M1.
F34. W38

WHITON, John Milton. Sketches of the history of New-Hampshire, from its settlement in 1623, to 1833. Concord (N.H.) Marsh, Capen and Lyon, 1834. vi, (7) - 222 p. 18½ cm. 1-7945.
F34. W62

JUVENILE WORKS.

BAILEY, Bernadine (Freeman) Picture book of New Hampshire. Pictures by Kurt Wiese. Chicago, A. Whitman, c.1961. 17 x 22 cm. 61-9971.
F34.3. B29

— Rev. ed. 1965. 32 p. 17 x 21 cm.
F34.3. B29
1965

BAILEY, Lillian. Up and down New Hampshire. (Oxford, N.H., Equity Pub. Corp. 1960) 127 p.
F34.3. B3

CARPENTER, John Allan. New Hampshire. Illus. by Tom Dunnington. Chicago, Childrens Press
(c. 1967)   93 p. 24 cm. 67-20097.   F34.3.C3

PIPER, Doris Delaware. Stories of old New Hampshire, 1623 - 1850. (Orford, N.H., Equity Pub.
Corp., c. 1963)   vi, 175 p. 24 cm. 63-22139.   F34.3.P5

SQUIRES, James Duane. The story of New Hampshire. Drawings by Laurence R. Webster. Princeton, N.J., Van Nostrand (c. 1964)   xiii, 187 p. 22 cm. 64-19835.   F34.3.S65

YATES, Elizabeth. New Hampshire. New York, Coward-McCann (c. 1969)   124 p. illus. 26 cm. "Publ. simultaneously in Canada by Longmans" 71-84729.
                                                                                                                                                F34.3.Y37
                                                                                                                                                1969

ANECDOTES, LEGENDS, PAGEANTS, ETC.

SPEARE, Eva Augusta (Clough. New Hampshire folk tales. Rev. Plymouth, N.H., 1964.   279 p.
19 cm. "Sixth printing" Previous ed., 1945, compiled by Mrs. Moody P. Gore and Mrs. Guy E. Speare.
                                                                                                                                                F34.6.S6
                                                                                                                                                1964

See also F35.G85; G852; G85 (1945); N55

HISTORIC MONUMENTS (GENERAL). ILLUSTRATIVE MATERIAL.

BACON, George Fox. Central New Hampshire and its leading business men; embracing Plymouth,
Laconia, Lake Village, Franklin, Franklin Falls, Tilton, Bristol, Meredith, Ashland, Wolfeboro' and
Wiers(!) Boston, Mercantile pub. co., 1890.   120 p. illus. 26½ cm. On cover: Wolfboro and its leading business men.
6-9058.   F35. B12

CLARKE, Edmund Palmer. Holiday hearsay; with decorations by Kay Hoppin. Center Ossipee, N.H.
The Independent press, 1939.   5, 144 p. illus. 23½ cm. "This second series of New Hampshire papers first appeared in the
columns of the Granite state news, of Wolfeboro Falls." 39-6007.   F35. C57

GILMAN, Arthur. My Cranford, a phase of the quiet life ... Boston and N.Y., Houghton Mifflin co.,
1909.   xv, (5), 3 - 224, (4) p. front., 15 pl. 19½ cm. "Hollis, N.H. furnishes the setting for most of the especially striking features (though
the place is not named), and the illustrations are made from excellent photographs of houses and scenes in that town."- Ill. list of spring books,
Houghton Mifflin co. 9-6273.   F35.G48

GORE, Effie (Kibbt) "Mrs. Moody P. Gore" comp. New Hampshire folk tales. (Plymouth) New
Hampshire federation of women's clubs, 1932.   xvi, 265, (1) p. front., plates. 19½ cm. 33-2385.
                                                                                                                                                F35. G85

— 1936.   xv, 287 p. front., plates. 19½ cm. 36-12636.   F35.G852

— 1945.   x, 278 p. 19 cm. "First printing, Sept., 1932 ... Fifth printing, Aug., 1945." 45-21524.   F35.G85
                                                                                                                                                1945

HAMMOND, Otis Grant. Some things about New Hampshire; an address before the Rotary Club of
Concord ... 1926. Concord, N.H., 1926.   1, 16 p. 17½ cm. CA 28-571 unrev.   F35. H22

JOHNSON, Frances Ann. Do you know New Hampshire? Artist: Claude L. Brusseau. Littleton,
N.H., Printed by Courier Print Co., 1951 -   1 v. illus. 18 cm. "A series of New Hampshire cartoons." 54-25319.
                                                                                                                                                F35. J6

NEW HAMPSHIRE Sesqui-centennial celebration. Comp. by the secretary and pub. by the commission.
Penacook, N.H., The W.B. Ranney co., (1926)   95 p. 22½ cm. 26-27356.   F35. N52

NEW HAMPSHIRE

NEW HAMPSHIRE. State Historical Commission. New Hampshire historical markers; texts and locations of historical markers erected by the State of N.H. under legislative direction, and a sketch of New Hampshire history. (Concord) 1964.   1 v. (unpaged) 23 cm.   65-63317.
F35. N53

NEW HAMPSHIRE's daughters. Folk-lore sketches and reminiscences of New Hampshire life ... pub. and arranged by the Folk-lore committee. Boston, ... (1910)   47, (1) p. incl. port. 24 cm.   11-1932.
F35. N55

NEW HAMPSHIRE - Historic houses, etc. Pamphlets, broadsides, clippings, and other miscellaneous matter on this subject, not separately cataloged, are classified in F35.Z7

EARLY TO 1775.

A short narrative of the claim, title and right of the heirs of the Honourable Samuel Allen, esq; deceased, to the province of New-Hampshire in New-England; transmitted from a gentlewoman in London to her friend in New England. (Boston, 1728) (Boston, 1939)   facsim.: 13 p. 23½ cm. (Photostat Americana. Second series ... Photostated at the Mass. historical society. no. 93)   41-16439.
F37. A7
1728a
Rare book room

BELKNAP, Jeremy. Journey to Dartmouth in 1774. Ed. Edward C. Lathem from the manuscript journal. Hanover, N.H., Dartmouth Publications (1950)   25 p. map (on lining paper) 17 cm.   50-13178.
F37. B45

BOWLES, Mrs. Ella (Shannon) New Hampshire: its history, settlement and provincial periods. Sponsored by ... Works progress administration ... New Hampshire State board of education, Concord, 1938.   1, 159, (28) p. 28 cm. Mimeographed. "Books from which you can get additional information" at end of most of the chapters. "Material consulted in writing": (12) p. at end.   39-28182.
F37. B795

CHASE, Francis. Gathered sketches from the early history of New Hampshire and Vermont ... Claremont, N.H., Tracy, Kenney & co., 1856.   215 p. front., plates. 18½ cm.   8-5937.
F37. C48

— Somersworth, New Hampshire Pub. co., 1970.   215 p. illus.   74-122102.
F37. C48
1970

CIVIL, military and ecclesiastical register of the province of New Hampshire, for the year 1772. Portsmouth, N.H., print. D. & R. Fowle ... (n.p., 19 - ?)   16 p. 14½ cm.   11-32576.
F37. C58

DANIELL, Jere R. Experiment in republicanism; New Hampshire politics and the American Revolution, 1741 - 1794. Cambridge, Mass., Harvard University Press, 1970.   xiv, 261 p. illus. 25 cm. 75-122219.
F37. D26

DAVIES, Mrs. Julia Elizabeth (Hickok) Colonial New Hampshire. Cincinnati, The Ebbert & Richardson co., 1932.   40 p. 23 cm. (On cover: ... Studies in the coloniol (!) period for use in the public schools)   32-31295.
F37. D29

FASSETT, James Hiram. Colonial life in New Hampshire. Boston, Ginn & co., 1899.   iv, 145 p. front., illus., pl., ports. 18 cm.   99-262 rev.
F37. F24

FRY, William Henry. ... New Hampshire as a royal province. New York, Columbia university, Longmans, Green & co,, ... 1908.   526 p. 25½ cm. Bibliographical foot-notes.   9-2759.
F37. F94
              320 p. 24 cm.   A10-1791.   F37. F943

— New York, Ams Press (1970)   526 p. 73-130938.   F37. F94
                                                                                                1970

GIFFEN, Daniel H.   The New Hampshire colony.   (New York) Crowell-Collier Press (c.1970)
102 p. illus. 24 cm. 76-93178.   F37. G5

BROWN, William Howard.   Colonel John Goffe, eighteenth century New Hampshire.   Manchester,
L. A. Cummings Co. (1950)   284 p. illus., map, plans. 22 cm. Bibliography: p. 275 - 284. 50-13046.
                                                                                                F37. G6B7

HAMMOND, Otis Grant.   ... The Mason title and its relations to New Hampshire and Massachusetts,
by Otis Grant Hammond ... Worcester, Mass., The Society, 1916.   21 p. map. 25 cm. Reprinted from Proceedings of American antiquarian society for October 1916. 17-15503.   F37. H22

JENNESS, John Scribner.   Notes on the first planting of New Hampshire and on the Piscataqua patents.
Portsmouth, print L. W. Brewster, 1878.   91 p. maps. 22 cm. 2-8478.   F37. J54

JENNESS, John Scriber.   Transcript of original documents in the English archives relating to the early
history of the state of New Hampshire.   New York, Priv. print., 1876.   viii, 161 p. fold. map. 27 cm.
10-14023.   F37. J55

LIVIUS, Peter.   The memorial of Peter Livius, esq. one of His Majesty's Council for the province of
New Hampshire, in New England, to the Lords commissioners for trade and plantations; ... (London)
1773.   1, 50 p. 21 cm. 8-18439.   F37. L78
                                                                                        Rare book room

McMURTRIE, Douglas Crawford.   Three printed New Hampshire documents of 1699, being facsimiles
of the printed exchanges of messages between the legislature of N. H. and Lord Bellomont ...   Chicago, The Black cat press, 1935.   5 p., facsim. (2 p., 2 l.) 31 cm. 36-6723.   F37. M24
                                                                                        Rare book room

DEAN, John Ward.   Capt. John Mason, the founder of New Hampshire.   Including his tract on Newfoundland, 1620; ... Together with a memoir by Charles Wesley Tuttle.   Boston, The Prince society,
1887.   xii, 492 p. illus. (facsims.) 2 pl. (1 fold.) fold. map, geneal. tab. 22 x 18 cm. 3-24569. (E186 p. 85 vol. 17) F37. M4

— New York, B. Franklin (1967)   xii, 492 p.   F37. M4
                                                                                                1967

NEW HAMPSHIRE (Colony)   Governor and council.   The New Hampshire grants ...   1895.
1 v.   F37. N45

NEW HAMPSHIRE (Colony) Governor and council.   ... Town charter, including grants of territory ...
1894-5.   2 v.   F37. N46

NEW HAMPSHIRE (Colony) Probate court.   Probate records of the province of New Hampshire ...
1635 - (1771) Concord, N. H., Rumford print. co., 1907 - 41.   9 v. plans (part fold.) 24 cm. (New Hampshire
State papers series, v. 31 - 39) 0-827 rev. 3.   F37. N52

PENROSE, Charles.   ... Colonial life in maritime New-Hampshire, 1756, by Charles Penrose ... A
Newcomen address, 1940.   (Princeton, The Princeton University press, c.1940)   32 p. illus. (incl.
facsims.) 23 cm. "First printing: June 1940." 40-13583.   F37. P46

PROPRIETORS of Mason's patent in New Hampshire.   ... Township grants of lands in New Hampshire
included in the Masonian patent issued subsequent to 1746 by the Masonian proprietary ... Arthur
Stillman Batchelor, ed ... Concord, E. N. Pearson, public printer, 1896.   2 v. plans (part fold.) 24 cm.
Provincial and state papers, v. 27 - 28. 15-27598.   F37. P96

SNOW, Leslie Perkins.   Historical address by.   Three-hundredth anniversary of the settlement
of New Hampshire at Portsmouth, N.H. ... 1923.   Penacook, N.H. The W. B. Ranney co., (1923?)
36 p. front. (port.) 23½ cm. 24-27022.   F37. S67

128

NEW HAMPSHIRE 11

1775 - 1865.

U.S. Bureau of the Census. Heads of families at the first census of the U.S. taken in the year 1790: New Hampshire. Washington, Govt. Print. Off., 1907. (Spartanburg, S.C., Reprint Co., 1964. 146 p. 28 cm. 64-61301.
  F38. A57
  1964

— Baltimore, Genealogical Pub. Co., 1966. 146 p. 29 cm.
  F38. A57
  1966
  L.H. & G.

BARTLETT, Josiah. A memoir of the Hon. Josiah Bartlett, of Stratham, N.H., who died April 16, 1838, aged seventy years. Gilmanton, N.H., Printed by A. Prescott, 1839. 7 p. 22½ cm. 38-11798.
  F38. B27
  Rare book room

BOSTON, Concord and Montreal railroad co. Guide to the lakes and mountains of New Hampshire, via the several routes connecting with the Boston, Concord & Montreal railroad at Concord, N.H. Concord, Printed by Tripp & Osgood, 1852. 45 p. incl. illus., pl. front. (fold. map) 20 cm. 3-28348.
  F38. B74

BRADLEY, Cyrus Parker. Biography of Isaac Hill, of New-Hampshire. With an appendix, comprising selections from his speeches, etc. Concord, N.H., J.F. Brown, 1835. 245 p. 14½ cm. 11-21035 rev.
  F38. B81

CALFE. A sermon... at the funeral of the Hon. John Calfe... 1808. By John Kelly. Concord, Print. Geo. Hough, 1808. 22 p. 22 cm. (Moore pamphlets v.28 no.12) 17-6916.
  AC901. M7 v. 28

CARTER, James Gordon. A geography of New-Hampshire, with a new map of the state, for families and schools. Portsmouth, N.H., N. March; Boston, Hilliard, Gray, Little, and Wilkins, 1831. 1, x, 246 p. map. 14½ cm. 1-10765. Map wanting.
  F38. C32
  G & M

COLE, Donald B. Jacksonian democracy in New Hampshire, 1800 - 1851. Cambridge, Mass., Harvard University Press, 1970. xi, 283 p. 22 cm. 79-127878.
  F38. C6
  1970

CRAM, Jacob. Journal of a missionary tour in 1808 through the new settlements of northern New Hampshire and Vermont... Rochester, N.Y. (The Genesee press) 1909. 37 p. 22 cm. (Half-title: Rochester reprints. XI) 9-10345.
  F38. C88

DAY, Pliny Butts. A discourse delivered at the funeral of Benj. Mark Farley, esq., in Hollis, N.H., Sept., 1865. Boston, S. Chism, 1866. 23 p. 23 cm. 17-9003.
  F38. F23

GOODWIN. Ichabod Goodwin (1794-1882) sea captain, merchant, financier, railroad president, Civil War Governor of New Hampshire. By Charles Penrose. New York, Newcomen Soc. in North America, 1956. 36 p. illus. 23 cm. 57-4155.
  F38. G66

HACKETT, Frank Warren. Memoir of William H.Y. Hackett; with selections from his writings. Priv. print. Portsmouth (Boston, Rand, Avery) 1879. 4, 156 p. front. (port.) 23½ cm. Record of descendants of William Hackett, who lived in Salisbury in 1667. 11-8210.
  F38. H2

HACKETT, Frank Warren. A sketch of the life of William H.Y. Hackett. Boston, for private distribution, 1879. 12 p. front. (port.) 25½ cm. "Reprinted from the New England hist. and geneal. register for Jan., 1879." 14-17084.
  F38. H3

HAYES, John Lord. A reminiscence of the Free-soil movement in New Hampshire, 1845. Cambridge, J. Wilson and son, 1885. 44 p. illus. 23½ cm. 4-5279.
  F38. H41

JACKSON, Charles Thomas. Views and map, illustrative of the scenery and geology of the state of New Hampshire. Boston, Thurston, Torry, and co., 1845. 20 p. plates (1 col.) fold. map. 29½ x 24 cm. Plates are the same as those in N.H. Geological survey, 2840 - 44. Final report on the geology ... of N.H. GS5-64.   F38. J13

JOURNAL of an excursion made by the corps of cadets, of the American literary, scientific and military academy, under Capt. Alden Partridge. June, 1822. Concord (N.H.) Print. Hill and Moore, 1822. 38 p. pl. 20 cm. The route of the excursion was from Norwich, Vt. to Concord, N.H. by way of Enfield and Salisbury, returning through Hopkinton, Hillsborough and Newport. 36-33538.   F38. J68

LADD, - An address to the citizens of New-Hampshire, on the approaching election of state officers. By a citizen. (n.p., 1804) 11 p. 16½ cm. Imperfect: text injured by trimming. 9-20816.   F38. L15

LANE, Samuel. A journal for the years 1739 - 1803. Concord, N.H., New Hampshire historical soc., 1937. vi, 115 p. front. (facsim.) plates, plans. 23½ cm. 37-30359.   F38. L23

MARSHALL, Gertrude Weeks. Indian Stream republic and the Indian Stream war; an authentic bit of New Hampshire history. Groveton, N.H., c.1935. 44 p. front. (fold. map) 23 cm. 35-7488.   F38. M27

PLUMER. Memoir of Wm. Plumer, senior ... By Albert Harrison Hoyt. Boston, D. Clapp, 1871. 12 p. 25 cm. "Reprinted from the N.E. historical and genealogical register for Jan., 1871." 12-11185.   F38. P73

ROBINSON, William Erigena, Speech of, in exposition of New Hampshire Democracy in its relation to Catholic emancipation ... New York, Tribune office, 1852. 15 p. 23½ cm. 21-4393.   F38. R66
Toner coll.

TUCK. Amost Tuck. By Chas. R. Corning. Exeter, N.H., The Newsletter press, 1902. 99 p. 20½ cm. 3-5243.   E415.9. T88C8

UPTON, Richard Francis. Revolutionary New Hampshire: an account of the social and political forces underlying the transition from royal province to American commonwealth. Hanover, Dartmouth college publications, 1936. x, 276 p. incl. front. (facsim.) illus. (facsims.) 22½ cm. Maps on lining-papers. Bibliography: p. (251) - 265. 36-18030.   F38. U68

— Port Washington, N.Y., Kennikat Press (1970) x, 276 p. 22 cm. 70-120896.   F38. U68 1970

— New York, Octagon Books, 1971. xvi, 276 p. 74-148460.   F38. U68 1971

WALKER, Joseph Burbeen. New Hampshire's five provincial congresses, July 21, 1774 - Jan. 5, 1776; Concord, N.H., Rumford print. co., 1905. 75 p. 24½ cm. 5-32672.   F38. W16

WALLACE, Cranmore. A geography of New Hampshire, with a sketch of its natural history, for schools. Boston, Carter and Hendee, 1829. 71 p. front. (fold. map) pl. 14½ cm. 1-7947 rev.   F38. W18

STEARNS, Ezra Scollay. A monograph: Meshech Weare. Priv. print. Concord, N.H., Republican press association, 1894. 22 p. 26½ cm. 5-25474 rev.   F38. W36

WILSON. Sketch of Gen. James Wilson of New Hampshire. By James F. Briggs. Manchester, N.H., Manchester historic association, 1902. 1, 26 p. port. 23 cm. 5-4110 rev.   F38. W74

1865 - 1950.

BARTLETT, John Henry. Sketches from my scrap books and diaries. Portsmouth, N.H., Print. S.R. Blaisdell (1948) 122 p. illus., ports. 20 cm. A 48-6999*.   F39. B3

NEW HAMPSHIRE 13

BELL. A memorial of Charles Henry Bell, Exeter, N.H. Priv. print. (n.p.) 1894. 22 p. 26½ cm.
14-14069. F39. B43

BELL. Memoir of Charles Henry Bell. By Rev. Edmund F. Slafter. ... Boston, Priv. print., 1895.
24 p. front. (port.) 27½ cm. "Reprinted from N. E. hist. and geneal. register for Jan., 1895." 14-14072. F39. B432

BATCHELLOR, Albert Stillman. Address before the Grafton and Coos counties bar association at the meeting held at Woodsville, for the presentation of memoirs of Harry Bingham ... 1900. Concord, N.H., Rumford press, 1902. 19 p. 23 cm. 2-19819. F39. B6

BINGHAM. Memorial of Hon. Harry Bingham, ... Ed. by Henry Harrison Metcalf ... Concord, N.H., Priv. print, 1910. xiv, 505 p. 3 port. 23½ cm. 10-20739. F39. B62

BOSTON and Maine railroad company ... The Monadnock region ... 2d ed. 1900. 10 x 20½ cm.
(Picturesque New England series, no. 14) F39. B87

CLAFLIN, Sumner Franklin. Claflin's red book of rambles, ... Concord (N.H.) Rumford print. co. 1906. 1, 100 p. front. (port.) illus., plates. 23½ cm. Miscellaneous articles, including New Hampshire travel sketches. 14-13136.
F39. C58

CLAFLIN, Sumner Franklin. Wayside notes of "little pitchers" gathered among New Hampshire hills, by Sumner F. Claflin ... Concord, N.H., Rumford print. co., 1907. iv, 107 p. front. (port.) plates. 23 cm.
14-13135. F39. C585

CONCORD and Montreal railroad. Summer excursions to the White and Franconia Mountains. 1892.
F39. C74

DOE. Memoir of Hon. Charles Doe, late chief justice of the Supreme court of New Hampshire. By Jeremiah Smith ... Concord (N.H.) Republican press association, 1897. 30 p. front. (port.) 23 cm.
8-4627. F39. D64

FARRAR, Charles Alden John. Through the wilds; a record of sport and adventure in the forests of New Hampshire and Maine. Boston, Estes & Lauriat (1892) xiv, 415 p. front., illus. 23½ cm. 1-8821.
F39. F23

FEDERAL writers' project. ... New Hampshire, a guide to the Granite state ... Boston, Houghton, Mifflin co., 1938. xxix, 559 p. illus., plates, maps (1 fold. in pocket) 21 cm. (American guide series) "Selected reading list": p. 539 - 540. 38-6192. F39. F43

HALE. Memorial of Samuel Whitney Hale, Keene, N.H. ... 1822 - 1891. By W. De Loss Love, jr. Hartford, Conn., The Case Lockwood & Brainard co., 1895. 27 p. front. (port.) plates. 22 cm. 11-19498.
F39. H16

HADLEY, Amos. Life of Walter Harriman, with selections from his speeches and writings, by Amos Hadley. Boston and N.Y., Houghton, Mifflin and co., 1888. vii, 385 p. front., pl., ports. 22½ cm. Harriman was colonel of the 11th N.H. infantry in the civil war and later prominent in state politics. 11-19270. F39. H29

JENNISON, Keith Warren. New Hampshire; stories and pictures arranged by Keith Jennison. New York, H. Holt and co. (1944) 2, (3) - 102 p. illus. 25 cm. 44-8180. F39. J4

JENNISON, Keith Warren. New Hampshire, stories and pictures. Peterborough, N.H., R. Smith (c. 1961) 102 p. illus. 25 cm. 61-15902. F39. J4
1961

JOHNSON, Frances Ann. New Hampshire pocket series. Exclusive editions. (Littleton? N.H., 1953-
6 v. illus., ports. 13 cm. Contents. - 1. The Old Man of the Mountains. - 2. The Cannon Mountain Aerial Tramway. - 3. The Flume. - 4. The Willey House Site. - 5. Daniel Webster, statesman. - 6. Franklin Pierce, 14th President. 53-36016. F39. J6

MURPHY. Francis Parnell Murphy, governor of New Hampshire; biography of an American, by Samuel R. Guard and Lloyd Graham. East Aurora, N.Y., The Roycroft shops (c. 1940) 6, 3 - 144 p.
front., plates, ports. 20½ cm. 40-11632. F39. M86

NEW HAMPSHIRE. Catalogue of New Hampshire farms for summer homes.   Concord, 1895.
48 p. map. 8°. 1-2749.   F39. N55

— Manchester, 1899.   31 pp. map. 8°. · 1-2750.   F39. N56

NEW HAMPSHIRE, Lakes and summer resorts in.   Issued by State board of agriculture.   Concord,
I. C. Evans, 1892.   97 p. incl. plates. 2 fold. pl. (incl. front.)   23 ½ cm.   Later issues (1893, 1897) pub. under title: Gems of the
Granite state.   1-2751.   F39. N57

NEW HAMPSHIRE farms for summer homes.   3d ed.   Issued by the State board of agriculture ...
(Concord, N. H., The Rumford print. co., 1905)   48 p. incl. front., illus. 23 x 28 ½ cm. 13-23478.
                                                                                                                     F39. N574

— 4th ed.   1906.   48 p. incl. front., illus.   23 x 28 cm.   6-39275.   F39. N575

— 5th ed.   1907.   56 p. incl. front., illus.   23 x 28 cm.   16-14551.   F39. N576

— 6th ed.   1908.   48 p. incl. front., illus.   22 ½ x 28 cm.   16-11149.   F39. N577

— 7th ed.   1909.   53, (1) p. incl. front., illus.   23 x 28 cm.   16-14550.   F39. N578

— 8th ed.   1910.   44 p. incl. front., illus. (incl. port.)   23 x 28 cm.   11-10451.   F39. N579

— 9th ed.   1911.   60 p. incl. front., illus.   23 x 28 cm.   11-22515.   F39. N58

NEW HAMPSHIRE.   Bureau of labor.   Special report of the summer boarding business and resorts in
New Hampshire (1st) - 2nd.   1899 - 1906.   Manchester, N. H., 1900 - 1906.   2 v. plates, fold. maps.
23 cm.   Earlier reports ... have title: Lakes and summer resorts ... ; Gems of the Granite state ...   1-2756 additions.   F39. N59

NEW HAMPSHIRE farm homes.   12th and 13th eds.   (Concord, The Rumford press, 1915 and 1916?)
56 p. incl. front, illus., plates. 23 x 28 cm.   16-27010; 42 p. incl. front., illus.   23 x 28 cm.   17-27310.   F39. N62
                                                                                                                     1915 & 1916

NEW HAMPSHIRE.   Disaster emergency committee, Report of, on the flood and gale of September,
1938.   (Concord, 1938)   2, 92 p. incl. illus. (maps) tables, diagr. 27 ½ cm.   Photoprinted. 39-28302.
                                                                                                                     F39. N625

NEW HAMPSHIRE.   Report of the New Hampshire Flood reconstruction council on the flood of March,
1936.   (Concord, 1936)   1, 80 p. incl. maps, tables. 28 cm.   Lithographed. 36-28358.   F39. N63

NEW HAMPSHIRE, Lakes and summer resorts in.   Manchester, J. B. Clarke, 1891.   54 p. fold. front.,
pl. 23 cm.   Later eds. issued by the N. H. Board of Agriculture.   3-15617.   F39. N65

NEW HAMPSHIRE Seacoast Regional Development Association.   The seacoast region of New Hampshire.
Portsmouth (1946)   30 p. illus. 20 cm. 47-27365*.   F39. N657

NEW HAMPSHIRE.   State planning and development commission.   This is New Hampshire.   (Concord,
Rumford press, 1946?)   32 p. of illus. (part col.) 38 x 30 ½ cm.   Map on p. (4) of cover. 46-27428.   F39. N66

NEW HAMPSHIRE troubadour, The.   v. 1 -   Apr. 1931 -   (Concord, 1931 -
     v. in   illus. 16 cm.   monthly.   Issued by the N. H. Board of publicity, Apr. 1931; by the State development commission, May, 1931 -
Feb. 1935; by the State planning and development commission, Mar. 1935 -   A special issue called World's fair edition accompanies vol. 9.
42-927 rev.   F39. N67

NUTTING, Wallace.   New Hampshire beautiful ... illus. by the author with 304 pictures ...   Framingham, Mass., Old America co. (c. 1923)   2, 3 - 302 p. incl. illus., plates. 26 cm.   23-17482.
                                                                                                                     F39. N98

— Garden City, N. Y. ... (1937)   256 p. incl. front., illus., plates. 26 cm.   "Reissue in de luxe edition ... 1937."
37-15029.   F39. N985

ORDWAY, Nehemiah George, Letter of, to the New Hampshire Republican state committee, relative to the falsehoods of George G. Fogg ... Washington, 1869.   30 p. 22 cm. 12-7865 rev.

F39. O65

POORE, Benjamin Perley. Sketches of the life and public services of Frederick Smyth ... Manchester, N.H., J.B. Clarke, print., 1885.   459 p. 2 port. (incl. front.) 7 pl. 22 ½ cm. 13-19348.

F39. P82

RAND. Hon, Edward Dean Rand; a memorial address by Albert S. Batchellor. ... 1886. Haverhill, N.H., Cohos steam press (1886)   24 p. 23 cm.. 13-6010.

F39. R18

ROLLINS, Frank West. The tourists' guide-book to the state of New Hampshire. 2d ed. Concord, N.H., The Rumford press, 1902.   365 p. front., pl., fold. maps. 16 cm. 2-24092.

F39. R75

STEARNS. Memorial of Onslow Stearns, Concord, N.H. (Concord? 1879?)   31 p. front. (port.) 22 ½ cm. 17-19190.

F39. S79

THYNG, J. Lake country sketches. Salem, Mass. (etc.) The author, 1879 - 82.   2 v. illus., pl. 4º.
Contents. - Ancient Ahquedaukenash, The weirs on Lake Winnepesaukee - Legends and pictures of New Hampshire lakes and mountains.   1-7948-M1

F39. T53

TOLMAN, Newton F. North of Monadnock. (1st ed.) Boston, Little, Brown (1961)   236 p. 21 cm. (An Atlantic Monthly press book) 61-16655.

F39. T6

TUCK. Banquet given in honor of Edward Tuck by the New Hampshire historical society, Concord, ... 1911.   3 p. 16 ½ x 23 cm.

F39. T88

WEYGANDT, Cornelius. The heart of New Hampshire; things held dear by folks of the old stocks ... New York, G.P. Putnams's sons (1944)   xvi, 3 - 210. p. front., plates, map. 21 cm. 44-5530.

F39. W46

WEYGANDT, Cornelius. New Hampshire neighbors; country folks and things in the White hills, ... New York, H. Holt and co. (c.1937)   xv, 368 p. front., plates, port., double map, facsim. 22 cm. 37-27428.

F39. W48

WEYGANDT, Cornelius. November rowen; a late harvest from the hills of New Hampshire ... New York, London, D. Appleton-Century co., 1941.   xiv p., 308 p. front., plates, ports. 22 cm. 41-8227.

F39. W483

WHITE, Mrs. Armenia Smith (Aldrich) comp. In memory of Nathaniel White: born in Lancaster, N.H., 1811; died in Concord, N.H., 1880 ... Concord, N.H. Print. Republican press assoc., 1881. 123 p. front. (port.) 21 cm. 10-13088 rev.

F39. W58

... WOLFEBORO, Laconia, the Weirs, Tilton, Franklin, Ashland and Plymouth. Central New Hampshire ed., 1908. New York, American suburbs co., c.1908.   16 p. illus. 40 ½ cm. (American suburbs illustrated. v.3, no.5) 11-30230.

F39. W85

1951 TO DATE.

SEASONS of New Hampshire, The. Ed. Daniel Ford. Introd. by Walter Peterson. Photos, by John P. Adams (and others) Somersworth, New Hampshire Pub. Co. (1969)   78 p. illus. 77-82160.

F40. S4

TOLMAN, Newton F. Our loons are always laughing. New York, I, Washburn (1963)   180 p. 21 cm. 63-19798.

F40. T6

WHITE MOUNTAINS.   PERIODICALS. SOCIETIES. COLLECTIONS.

IDLER, The; devoted to the interests of White Mountain tourists.   v. 1; June 22 - Sept. 7, 1880. North Conway, N.H., 1880.   1 v. 35½ cm.   weekly.   No more published?   20-23477.   F41.1.I19

WHITE MOUNTAIN echo and tourists' register, The.   v. 1 - 24.   Bethlehem, N.H. (etc.) 1878 - 24 v. in 11. illus. (incl. maps) 42 cm.   Weekly during the summer season.   Authorized organ of the U.S. hay fever association, 1879 - 7-34262.   F41.1.W58

WHITE MOUNTAINS.   GAZETTEERS. DICTIONARIES. GEOGRAPHIC NAMES.

KINGDON's Dictionary of the White mountains and other New-England summer resorts.   Boston, The author, 1894.   74 p. 16½ cm.   1-8798 rev.   F41.2.K52

NEW HAMPSHIRE.   State Planning and Development Commission.   The mountains of New Hampshire; a directory locating the mountains and prominent elevations, comp. by Mary Louise Hancock, research librarian.   Concord, 1949.   145 p. illus. 19 cm.   49-45202 *.   F41.2.N4 1949

... RESIDENT and business directory of the west side of the White Mountains.   See Directories p. 145

WHITE MOUNTAINS.   GENERAL WORKS.

ANDERSON, John.   The book of the White Mountains.   N.Y., Minton, Balch & co., 1930.   300 p. front. plates. 23 cm.   Bibliography: p. (289) - 293.   30-19267.   F41.3.A54

BISBEE, Ernest Emerson.   ... The White mountain scrap book of stories and legends of the Crystal hills or White mountains of New Hampshire.   Lancaster, N.H., The Bisbee press, c.1938. 49 p. illus. 23½ cm.   39-7255 rev.   F41.3.B57 1938

— c, 1939.   (52) p. illus. 23½ cm.   Map on p. (2) and text on p. (3) - (4) of cover.   39-7256 rev.   F41.3.B57 1939

— c.1945.   (56) p. illus. 24 cm.   46-12839 rev.   F41.3.B57 1945

— c.1946.   (64) p. illus. 24 cm.   47-27318*.   F41.3.B57 1946

— c.1956.   64 p. illus. 24 cm.   56-44913.   F41.3.B57 1956

EARLY, Eleanor.   Behold the White mountains.   Boston, Little, Brown & co., 1935.   xiii, 219 p. 17½ cm.   35-7065.   F41.3.E26

KILBOURNE, Frederick Wilkinson.   Chronicles of the White Mountains, ...   Boston & N.Y., Houghton Mifflin co., 1916.   xxxii, (1), 433, (1) p. front., plates, map. 21½ cm.   16-11601.   F41.3.K48

VOSE, Arthur W.   The White Mountains; heroes and hamlets.   Barre, Mass., Barre Publishers, 1968.   107 p. illus. 23 cm.   68-29797.   F41.3.V65

CONNOR, Daniel P.   "Old man Thompson," by Concubar (pseud.)   Manchester, N.H., c.1911. 15 p. 2 pl., 2 port. (incl. front.) 17½ cm.   11-29855.   F41.37.C75

NEW HAMPSHIRE 17

WHITE MOUNTAINS. EARLY TO 1865.

BIGELOW, Jacob. ... An old account of Mt. Washington. ... Bar Harbor, Me., The Wild Gardens of Acadia (1918?)   33, (1) p. incl. illus. 23 cm. (Sieur de Monts publications, xviii) 19-7538.   F27.M9S46 no.18
F41.44

BECKETT, Sylvester Breakmore. Guide book of the Atlantic and St. Lawrence, and St. Lawrence and Atlantic rail roads, inc. a full description of ... the White Mountains ... Portland, Sanborn & Carter 1853.   vi, (2), (7) - 180 p. incl. illus., plates. pl., fold. map. 19½ cm. 1-21366.   F41.44.B39

BELKNAP, Jeremy. Journal of a tour to the White Mountains in July, 1784. Boston, Mass. hist. soc., 1876.   21 p. fold. map. 25 cm. "From the 'Belknap papers,' published by the Massachusetts historical society". 1-8799.   F41.44.B43

BIGELOW, Jacob. Some account of the White mountains of New Hampshire. ... (Boston, 1816)   18 p. 22½ cm. "From the New England journal of medicine and surgery for Oct., 1816." 1-8800.   F41.44.B59

BOARDMAN, Harvey. A complete and accurate guide to and around the White mountains ... Boston, Crosby, Nichols & co., 1859.   26 p. fold. map. 15½ cm. 45-44537.   F41.44.B7

BRADLEE, John E. ... Pocket guide ... to the White Mountains and Lake Winnipisseogee ... Boston, J.E. Bradlee, 1861.   72 pp. front. (map) 16°. 1-8801-M1.   F41.44.B81

CRAWFORD, Mrs. Lucy. The history of the White Mountains, from the first settlement of Upper Coos and Pequaket. White Hills (Portland, Print. F.A. & A.F. Gerrish) 1846.   iv, (5) - 204 p. 16 cm. 1-10767.   F41.44.C88

— Portland, Me., Hoyt, Fogg & Donham, 1883.   206 p. front. (port.) illus. 19½ cm. 1-8802.   F41.44.C89

— Hanover, N.H., Dartmouth Pubs., 1966.   xxvi, 279 p. 20 cm. 66-17763.   F41.44.C893

EASTMAN, Samuel Coffin. The White Mountain guide book. Concord, (N.H.) E.C. Eastman, 1858.   2, 152 p. illus. 18 cm. 1-8815.   F41.44.E27

— 2d ed. 1859.   ix, (11) - 179 p. illus., fold. maps. 19 cm. 14-11889.   F41.44.E273

GUIDE to the White Mountains and lakes of New Hampshire: with minute & accurate descriptions of the scenery and objects of interest on the route ... Concord, N.H., Tripp & Morril, 1850.   48 p. 24°. 1-8803-4-M1.   F41.44.G94

— 2d ed. 1851.   72 p. pl., map. 24°. 1-8803-4-M1.   F41.44.G95

— 4th ed ... Boston, Redding & co., N.Y., E.H. Tripp (1853?)   3, (5) - 108 p. incl. illus. 4 pl. 3 fold. maps. 3-16107.   F41.44.G97

HALL, Frederick. A trip from Boston to Littleton, through the notch of the White Mountains. By B.K.Z. Washington, J. Gideon, jr. print., 1836.   30 p. 21½ cm. First pub. in the "Baltimore patriot." 1-8809 rev.   F41.44.H17

HALL, Frederick. Miscellaneous notices among the White Mountains, and other places, ... (N.Y., 183-?)   4 p. 24½ cm. (With his a Trip from Boston to Littleton ... 1836. Copy 2) 3-4630.   F41.44.H17 copy 2

KING, Thomas Starr. The White Hills; their legends, landscape, and poetry. With 60 illus ... Boston, Crosby, Nichols, and co., 1860.   xv, (3), 403 p. front., illus. (incl. map) 21 x 16½ cm. 1-8823.   F41.44.K55

— 1862.   xv, (3), 403 p. front., illus. (incl. map) 20½ cm. 38-17426.   F41.44.K55 1862

McLELLAN, Isaac. The avalanche of the White Hills: Aug. 28th, 1826. Boston, Jones' power press office, 1846.   (3) - 18 p. 23 cm. 16-20793 rev.   F41.44.M16

MELCHER, Edward. A sketch of the destruction of the Willey family by the White Mountain slide ... Aug. 28, 1826 ... Lancaster, N.H., J.S. Peavey, print., 1880.   1, 25 p. 17 cm.   19-8794.
    F41.44.M51

OAKES, William. Scenery of the White Mountains: with sixteen plates from the drawings of Isaac Sprague. Boston, Crosby, Nichols and co., c. 1848.   2, 4 p. 16 l. 16 pl. 44 cm. 2-5522.
    F41.44.O15

SOUTHWICK, Edward W. Tour to the White hills ... Notes of a tour ... in July, 1841.   (n.p., 1841) 11 p. 8°. 1-8805-M1.
    F41.44.S72

SPAULDING, John H. Historical relics of the White Mountains. Also, a concise White Mountain guide ... Boston, N. Noyes, 1855.   ix, 96 p. incl. front. 17 cm. 1-8806.
    F41.44.S73

— 3d ed. Mt. Washington, J.R. Hitchcock (1858)   xi, 104, (1) p. incl. front. 17 ½ cm. 17-15809.
    F41.44.S732
    Toner coll.

— 3d ed. Mt. Washington, J.H. Spaulding, 1858.   xi, 113, (1) p. incl. front. 17 ½ cm. 17-15808.
    F41.44.S74

WHITE, Franklin. Photographic views from Mount Washington and vicinity, and the Franconia range. Lancaster, N.H., 1859.   2 l. 24 photos. (partly col.) fol. 1-10768.
    F41.44.W58
    Rare Book Room
    copy 2 on shelf

— 2d series. (Lancaster? N.H., 1860)   1 p. 25 photos. 19 ½ x 17 ½ cm. Chiefly White Mountain scenes. Other series were pub. in 1859 and 1861. 11-19269.
    F41.44.W585
    Rare Book Room

WHITE, Franklin. Photographic views for 1861. (Lancaster, N.H., 1861)   12 mounted photos. 24 cm. 1-8807 rev.*
    F41.44.W59
    Rare Book Room

WHITE Mountains, The, described and illustrated ... Profusely illus. with engravings ... New York, A. Harthill and co., (1860?)   65 p. illus. 23 ½ cm. 17-18127.
    F41.44.W62
    Toner Coll.

WILLEY, Benjamin Glazier. Incidents in White Mountain history ... Boston, N. Noyes; Dover, N.H., E.J. Lane, 1856.   xii, (13) - 307 p. incl. front. plates, fold. map. 19 ½ cm. 1-8808.
    F41.44.W71

— 3d thousand. Boston, N. Noyes; N.Y., M.W. Dodd ... 1856.   xii, (13) - 321, (1) p. incl. front. 7 pl. 19 ½ cm. "Guide from New York and Boston to the White Mountains. By Nathaniel Noyes": p. (309) - (322) 17-9761.
    F41.44.W712

— 4th thousand. 1857.   xii, (13) - 324 p. incl. front. 7 pl. 19 ½ cm. 17-12066.
    F41.44.W713
    Toner coll.

— 1858.   xii, (13) - 324 p. incl. front. plates. 19 ½ cm. 31-23220.
    F41.44.W7135

— 5th ed. 1859.   xii, (13) - 324 p. incl. front. 5 pl. fold. map. 19 ½ cm. 17-12067.
    F41.44.W714
    Toner coll.

WHITE MOUNTAINS. 1865 - 1950.

DARTMOUTH college. Handbook, Dartmouth outing club, with guide to the cabins and trails, ed. Dick Goldthwait '33. Brattleboro, Vt., The Vt. print. co., 1932.   136 p. illus., maps (part fold.) 17 cm. Includes bibliographies. 33-10423.
    F41.5
    F57.G8D2

SIEUR de MONTS national monuments and its historical associations ... (Bar Harbor, Me., The Wild Gardens of Acadia, 1917)   29, 33 p. illus. 23 cm. (Sieur de Monts pubs. xvii) 19-3754.
    F27.M9S46 no. 17

NEW HAMPSHIRE   19

WEYGANDT, Cornelius.   New Hampshire neighbors.   See F39.W48

ALBUM photographs.   White Mountains, N.H.   (Boston, C. Pollock, 1883)   10 photos. obl. 32°. 1-8810-M1.
 F41.5.A34

APPALACHIAN Mountain Club.   The A.M.C. White Mountain guide; a guide to paths in the White Mountains and adjacent regions.   (1st) - Boston.   v. illus., maps (part fold., part col.) 14 - 16 cm. Title varies. 7-23955 rev.*
 F41.5.A64

ATKINSON, Justin Brooks.   Skyline promenades; a potpourri.   N.Y., A.A. Knopf, 1925. 255, (1) p. incl. map. 21½ cm. 25-8863.
 F41.5.A8

BOSTON and Maine railroad. ... Among the mountains ... 3d ed. Boston, ... 1901. 46, (1) p. incl. front., illus., 2 fold. maps. 20½ x 10½ cm. (Picturesque New England series. no. 4) CA 34-1192 unrev.
 F41.5.B73

BOSTON and Maine railroad co.   The White Mountains of New Hampshire, in the heart of the nation's playground.   Boston, Mass., c.1910. (72) p. illus. 20½ cm. 10-12416.
 F41.5.B74
 1910

— c.1915.   (72) p. illus., fold. map. 20½ cm. 15-12017.
 F41.5.B74
 1915

— 1917.   (71) p. illus., fold. map. 20½ cm. 25-3682.
 F41.5.B74
 1917

BREARLEY, William Henry.   A summer's vacation at the White Mountains.   Third season.   (Detroit, Mich., W.H. Brearly, c.1879) xv, (1), (17) - 61 p. illus., maps. 24 cm. 2-2410-M2.
 F41.5.B82

BURT, Frank H.   A tour among the mountains.   Mount Washington and surroundings.   Mount Washington, N.H. ... Among the clouds (1879) 34, (4) p. 5 l. illus. obl. 48°. 1-8811-2-M1.
 F41.5.B97

— 2d ed. 1882.   39, (2) p. illus. obl. 48°. 1-8811-2-M1.
 F41.5.B98

— 4th ed. 1884.   45, (3) p. illus., map. obl. 48°. 1-8813-M1.
 F41.5.B99

DRAKE, Samuel Adams.   The heart of the White Mountains; their legend and scenery ... With illus. by Hamilton Gibson ... N.Y., Harper & brothers, 1882 (1881) xii p., 318 p. incl. front., illus., ports., maps. 30½ cm. 1-8814.
 F41.5.D76

EASTMAN, Samuel Coffin.   The White Mountain guide book.   3d ed.   Concord, E.C. Eastman; Boston, Lee & Shepard, 1863.   xi, (13) - 222, (7) p. front. (fold. map) illus. 16½ cm. 16-11536.
 F41.5.E137

— 4th ed. 1864.   xi, 13 - 240 p. illus., 2 fold. maps. 17 cm. 1-8816.
 F41.5.E14

— 6th ed. 1866.   xi, 13 - 244 p. front. (fold. map) illus. 17 cm. 17-12055.
 F41.5.E146
 Toner coll.

— 10th ed. 1872.   xii, 13 - 248 p. illus., 2 fold. maps (incl. front.) 16½ cm. 1-8817.
 F41.5.E15

— 11th ed. 1873.   xii, 13 - 250 p. illus., 2 fold. maps (incl. front.) 16½ cm. 1-8818.
 F41.5.E16

— 13th ed. 1876.   xi, 13 - 232 p. illus., 2 fold. maps (incl. front.) 17 cm. 1-8819.
 F41.5.E17

— 15th ed. 1879.   x, 13 - 233 p. illus., golf. pl., fold. maps (incl. front.) 17 cm. 1-8820.
 F41.5.E18
 Microfilm 15221 F

GAGE, William C.   "The Switzerland of America."   A complete guide book to the scenery of New Hampshire, describing her mountains, lakes, rivers, etc. etc.   Rev. ed.   Providence, R.I., J.A. and R.A. Reid; N.Y. American news co. ... 1879.   122 p. illus., fold. map. 20 cm. 1-8822.
 F41.5.G13

GANNON, Frederic Augustus. Our friends the White Mountains of New Hampshire, ... a story of tramps over Gulfside trail, from Mount Madison to Mount Washington ... (Salem, Mass., Newcomb & Gauss, print., c.1921)   19 p. front. 19 cm. 22-4453.   F41.5.G2

GEMS of American scenery, consisting of stereoscopic views among the White Mountains, with descriptive text. Niagara Falls, N.Y., C.Bierstadt; N.Y., E.Bierstadt, 1875.   26 l. pl., map. 12°. 1-10769-M1.
                                                                                                                   F41.5.G32

— N.Y., Harroun & Bierstadt (c.1878)   4, (6)-99 p. incl. plates. double map. 20 cm. 1-10770.   F41.5.G33

HARRINGTON, Karl Pomeroy. Walks and climbs in the White Mountains, ... New Haven, Yale university press, 1926.   xiv, 123 p. incl. front., illus. 19 cm. 26-14301.   F41.5.H32

HASKELL, Ray Isaac. What I know about Mount Agassiz, Bethlehem and the White Mountains. (Lewiston, Me., Journal printshop) c.1914.   29 p. illus. 23½ cm. 14-12804.   F41.5.H34

HOBART, Arthur. A record of the perambulations of the Pemigewassett perambulators, by their scribe. Boston ,,, print. Rockwell & Rollins, 1866.   79, (1) p. front., plates. 23 x 23 cm. 9-25829.
                                                                                                                   F41.5.H68

HUNT, Richard. White mountain holidays .. illus. with photos. Portland, Me., Falmouth pub. house, 1941.   6, (3)-200 p. front., plates. 20½ cm. Map on lining papers. 41-6954.   F41.5.H8

KING, Thomas Starr. The White Hills; their legends, landscape, and poetry. Boston, Estes and Lauriat, 1887.   xi, (1) 403 p. front., illus., plates. 22½ cm. First ed. copyrighted 1859. 1-8824.   F41.5.K55
                                                                                                      Microfilm 15221 F

KNEELAND, Frederick Newton. White mountain glimpses ... (Florence, Mass., The Bryant print. co.) 1896.   56 p. incl. front., illus. 16 x 24 cm. 1-8825 rev.   F41.5.K68

LUDLUM, Stuart D. Exploring the White Mountains 100 years ago. (1st B & L 20th century ed.) Utica, N.Y., Brodock & Ludlum (1972)   68 p. illus. 28 cm. 72-77668 MARC.   F41.5.L8

MAINE Central railroad co. The White Mountains of New Hampshire and coast and woods of Maine. Supplementary to "The front door-yard of our country" (Boston, Rand Avery supply co., 1890)
   80 p. incl. front., illus. 2 fold. maps. 20 cm. CA 25-886 unrev.   F41.5.M22

O'KANE, Walter Collins. ... Trails and summits of the White Mountains ... Boston and N.Y., Houghton Mifflin co., 1925.   x, 308 p. front., illus. (maps) plates. 17 cm. (The Riverside outdoor handbooks) 25-9571.
                                                                                                                   F41.5.O42

PACKARD, Winthrop. White Mountain trails; tales of the trails to the summit of Mount Washington and other summits ... Boston, Small, Maynard and co. (c.1912)   xiv, 311 p. front., plates. 22 cm. Reprinted from the "Boston evening transcript." 12-13660.   F41.5.P11

POOLE, Ernest. The great White hills of New Hampshire ... illus. by Garth Williams. Garden City, N.Y., Doubleday, 1946.   4, 472 p. illus. 22 cm. "Source list": p. 460-464. 46-4383.   F41.5.P6

ROBERTS, Guy. ... Natural wonders of the White Mountains, the Profile, the Flume, Indian head, etc. etc. Cambridge, Mass., The Murray print. co., (c.1924)   68 p. illus. 19½ cm. (Natural curiosity series) 24-12209.   F41.5.R64

SCENES ... of the White Mountains ... (1903)   F41.5.S28

SOUVENIR view book of the White Mountains, N.H. containing the principal views of the Franconia Notch, etc. etc. (Chicago, 1923)   (24) p. of col. illus. 17½ x 21 cm. 23-10219.   F41.5.S73

STIRLING, Edmund. A descriptive reading on the White Mountains ... Philadelphia, W.H.Rau, 1890. 2, 805-815 p. 12°. The description only. Part of a projected work, never pub. in collective form. 1-16219-M1.   F41.5.S83

NEW HAMPSHIRE 21

SWETT, William B.   Adventures of a deaf-mute.   (Boston) Boston deaf-mutes' mission, 1874.
iii, 4 - 48 p. illus. (port.) 21½ cm. 1-16220. F41.5.S924

SWEETSER, Moses Foster.   Views in the White Mountains.   Portland (Me.) Chisholm bros., 1879.
2, (14) p. 12 pl. 15 cm. 1-10771. F41.5.S93

— 1879.   2, (4) p. 21 l. 21 pl. 35½ cm. 1-10773. F41.5.S94

— 1879.   3, (4) p., 12 l. 12 pl. 21½ cm. 1-10772. F41.5.S95

SWEETSER, Moses Foster.   The White Mountains: a handbook for travellers.   A guide to the peaks, passes and ravines, etc. ...   Boston, J.R. Osgood and co., 1876.   xiv, (2), 436 p. front., fold. plates, fold. maps. 17 cm. 1-10774. F41.5.S96

— Boston, Ticknor and co., 1888.   9th ed.   xiv, (2), 436 p. 6 fold. pl., 6 maps (5 fold.) 17 cm. 1-8826.
F41.5.S97

— 11th ed., rev. and enl.   Boston and N.Y., Houghton, Mifflin, 1891.   xiv, (2), 436 p. fold. plates, fold. maps. 16½ cm. 1-8827. F41.5.S98

— 12th ed.   1892.   xiv, (2), 436 p. fold. plates, fold. maps. 16½ cm. 1-8828. F41.5.S99

— Ed. and rev. by John Nelson.   Boston and N.Y., Houghton Mifflin co., 1918.   xv p., 387 (1) p. fold. plates, fold. map. 16 cm. 18-12719. F41.5.S992

SWEETSER, Moses Foster.   Chisholm's White Mountain guide-book ...   Portland, Chisholm bros., (c.1912)   172 p. incl. plates. front., 2 fold. maps. 19½ cm. 12-16843 rev. F41.5.S995

— (c.1913)   172 p. incl. plates. front., 3 fold. maps. 19½ cm. 13-16155 rev. F41.5.S996

— (c.1917)   174 p. incl. plates. front., fold. maps/ 20 cm. 17-18478. F41.5.S997

VIAL.   "Our house of Jack" by Concobar (pseud) (Daniel P. Connor)   Manchester, N.H. (Bechard & co.) c.1912.   14 p. 2 port. (incl. front.) plates. 18½ cm. 13-1058. F41.5.V61

VIEWS in the White Mountains.   Portland, Me., C.R. Chisholm and bros. (c.1878)   20 p. 12 pl.
15 x 11½ cm. 1-8829. F41.5.V66

— Portland, Me., c.1912.   (48) p. illus. 20½ x 26 cm. F41.5.V67

VIEWS of the White Mountains.   22d ed., improved by new plates and text.   Portland, Me., Chisholm brothers, c.1917.   (48) p. illus. 20½ x 25½ cm. 17-16561. F41.5.V673

— 23d ed., improved by new plates and text.   Portland, Me., Lakeside print. co., c.1920.
(32) p. illus. 20½ x 25½ cm. 20-14447. F41.5.V674

WALDRON, Holman D.   With pen and camera thro' the White Mountains;   Portland, Me., Chisholm bros., c.1896.   (48) p. illus. 24 x 32 cm. 1-8830. F41.5.W16

— c.1907.   (48) p. illus. 23 x 31½ cm. 7-20976. F41.5.W17

WARD, Julius Hammond.   The White Mountains; a guide to their interpretation. ...   N.Y., D. Appleton and co., 1890.   viii p., 258 p. front., plates, fold. map. 18 cm. 1-8831. F41.5.W26

WEYGANDT, Cornelius.   The White hills; mountain New Hampshire, Winnepesaukee to Washington, ...   N.Y., H. Holt and co. (c.1934)   x, 3 - 399 p. front., plates, 4 port. on 1 l. 22 cm. 34-13948. F41.5.W38

WILLEY, Benjamin Glazier.   History of the White Mountains.   New and rev. ed., with illus. by Frederick Thompson.   North Conway, N.H., Boston, I.N. Andrews, c.1869.   xii, (13) - 296 p. 3 pl. (incl. front.) 19½ cm. 1st ed. 1855 under title: Incidents in White mountain history. 9-10999 rev. F41.5.W55

WHITE MOUNTAINS. REGIONS, PLACES, ETC. A - Z.

CRAWFORD NOTCH. The Willey slide; its history, legend, and romance ... A narrative giving briefly the history of Crawford Notch and the Willey slide, also the Soltaire legend and the Nancy romance. By Guy Roberts. 1st ed. (Littletown, N.H., Courier print. co.) c. 1923.   42 p. illus. 16 x 8 cm.   CA 23-201 unrev.
F41.6. C8R6

— 2d ed.   c. 1924.   43, (1) p. illus. 16 cm. 24-7735.
F41.6. C8R61

DIXVILLE NOTCH. Martha Washington, a woman for the ages; a sequence of five sonnets, by Henry Davis Nadig. Errol, N.H., 1932.   (11) p. 1 illus. 21 cm. On "Martha Washington profile, Dixville notch," 32-16718.
F41.6. D6N2

FRANCONIAN NOTCH ... The Franconian gateway and region of Lost River, by G. Waldo Browne ... illus. by J. Warren Thyng, and others.   Manchester, N.H., Standard book co., inc., 1926. 155 p. incl. front., illus. 21 ½ cm. (Rivers of New England series) 27-886.
F41.6. F8B8

FRANCONIA NOTCH and the Pemigewasset valley, Guidebook to the. By Frank O. Carpenter. Boston, A. Moore, 1898.   4, 136 p. illus., fold. plates. 17 ½ cm. 1-8832 rev.
F41.6. F8C3

FRANCONIA Mountains, A Journal of an excursion to the: by a corps of cadets of the Norwich university, under Capt. Alden Partridge, July, 1837. (Northfield, Vt., 1837)   14 p. 20 ½ cm. 20-3025.
F41.6. F8J8
Rare Book Room

FRANCONIA NOTCH. A report on a study of the Franconia notch state reservation and suggested plan for future development. Made at the request of Governor Robert O. Blood. Concord, N.H., Research and planning division, the State planning and development commission, 1942.   3, 30 p. incl. tables. 25 cm. Reproduced from type-written copy. 42-37525.
F41.6. F8N4

FLUME. The Flume and all about it ... A little story telling about the flume in Franconia Notch ... By Guy Roberts. 1st ed. (Littletown, N.H., Courier print. co.) c. 1923.   folded strip (15 p.) illus. 16 x 8 cm.   CA 23-202 unrev.
F41.6. F8R6

FRANCONIA NOTCH. Indian Head; its debut and legends ... A brief sketch giving the facts and legends about Indian Head in Franconia Notch ... by Guy Roberts. 2d ed. (Littletown, N.H., Courier print. co., c. 1923.   folded strip (12 p.) illus. 16 x 8 cm. CA 23-203 unrev.
F41.6. F8R63

FRANCONIA NOTCH. Profile House, Franconia Notch, White Mountains. A summers sojourn. By Taft and Greenleaf. (N.Y., A.H. Kellogg, 1895)   39, (1) p. illus. obl. 24º. 1-10775-M1.
F41.6. F8T1

FRANCONIA NOTCH; history and guide. By Sarah N. Brooks Welch. (Littleton? N.H.) c. 1959. 32 p. illus. 23 cm. 59-34888.
F41.6. F8W4

GLEN. The Glen, White mountains. A description of this famous resort. (By) Charles R. Milliken. Boston, Robinson engraving co. (c. 1891)   72 p. incl. front., 1 illus., plates. fold. map. 19 ½ cm. 1-8833.
F41.6. G5M6

PASSACONAWAY in the White Mountains, by Charles Edward Beals, jr.; illus. from photos. Boston, R.G. Badger ... (c. 1916)   343 p. front., plates. 20 ½ cm. 16-25266.
F41.6. P28B3

PRESIDENTIAL range of the White Mountains, The trails and peaks of the, by Henry Bradford Washburn, jr. ... (Worcester, Mass., The Davis press, c. 1926)   4, 11 - 79, (1) p. illus., fold. map. 15 ½ cm. 26-6746 rev.
F41.6. P8W2

PROFILE, The. That old man and his dream. By Charles G. Chase. (Boston, The author, 1893) (26) p. front., illus. 8º. The "Profile," White Mountains. 1-8839-M1.
F41.6. P9C4

PROFILE, The. Views of the Profile Mountain and the Profile Rock, or the "Old man of the mountain," at Franconia ... Boston, S.N. Dickinson, print., 1847.   2 l. 2 pl. 42 x 32 cm. Drawings by Isaac Sprague. Also pub. in the author's Scenery of the White Mountains, Boston, 1848. 7-34834.
F41.6. P9O11

NEW HAMPSHIRE 23

PROFILE, The, and how it was saved; a brief story giving the facts about the Profile in the Franconia Notch ... by Guy Roberts. (Littleton, N.H., Courier print, co.) c.1917.   folded strip (22 p.) illus. 16 cm.
17-13531.   F41.6. P9R6

PROFILE, The. The old man of the mountains; past and present efforts to save The Great Stone Face. By Mabelle (Geddes) Russell. New Hampshire Recreation Div., c.1959.   24 p. 23 cm.
F41.6. P9R8

SANDWICH Mountains. At the north end of Bearcamp water. Chronicles of a stroller in New England from July to December, by Frank Bolles ... Boston and N.Y., Houghton, Mifflin, 1893.   2, 297 p. 18 cm.
1-8836/4.   F41.6. S1B6

— 1917.   4, 297, (1) p. front., plates, 20 cm. 17-14710.   F41.6. S1B62

WASHINGTON Mountain. Among the clouds ... The first daily newspaper printed on the summit of Mount Washington. v. 1 -   Mount Washington, N.H. (H.M. Burt) 1877 - 19 -   v. illus.
31 - 48½ cm. CA 5-846 unrev.   F41.6. W3A5

— (Special souvenir illustrated editions) Mount Washington, N.H. (1896?)   v. 32 - 48½ cm.
F41.6. W3A52

WASHINGTON, Mount. Three days on the White Mountains; being the perilous adventure of Dr. B. L. Ball on Mount Washington, during Oct. 25, 26, 27, 1855. Written by himself. Boston, N. Noyes, 1856.   72 p. 19 cm. 1-8837.   F41.6. W3B18

WASHINGTON, Mount. Panoramic view from ... By Robert Erastus Blakeslee. (Mount Washington, N.H., 1904)   13 cm.   F41.6. W3B6

WASHINGTON, Mt. The story of Mount Washington. By Frank Allen Burt. Hanover, N.H., Dartmouth Pubs., 1960.   303 p. 25 cm.   F41.6. W3B88

WASHINGTON, Mt. Mount Washington; a handbook for travelers, with illus. and panoramic view by Frank H. Burt ... Boston, G.H. Ellis co., print., 1904.   91, (1) p. front., illus., fold. plates. 19 cm. 4-18487 rev.
F41.6. W3B9

— 3d. ed. Boston, G.H. Ellis co., printers, 1906.   5, 7 - 92 p. incl. front., illus. fold. pl. 19 cm. 6-23689.
F41.6. W3B92

WASHINGTON, Mt. Ascent of Mount Washington. Carriage road. Surveys and location. Mount Washington road co. (n.p., 1855)   12 p. front. 12º. 1-16218-M1.   F41.6. W3M8

WASHINGTON, Mt. Mount Washington in winter, or the experiences of a scientific expedition upon the highest mountain in New England - 1870 - 71 ... (by C.H. Hitchcock and others. Boston, Chick and Andrews, 1871.   vii, 363 p. front. (map) plates, diagr. 19½ cm. 1-8838.   F41.6. W3M9

WASHINGTON, Mount. Bradford on Mount Washington, by Bradford Washburn; illus. with 33 photos. taken by the author and others. N.Y., London, G.P. Putnam's sons, 1928.   xi, 123 p. front., illus. (plans) plates, ports. 20½ cm. 28-23982 rev.   F41.6. W3W2

REGIONS, COUNTIES, ETC., A - Z.

BELKNAP County. The lakes region directory for Alton, Alton Bay, Center Harbor, Gilford, Melvin Village, Meredith, Moultonboro, Tuftonboro, Wolfeboro, and the Weirs. 1937 -   v. 1 - North Hampton, N.H., Crosby pub. co., inc., c.1937.   v. 23½ cm. 38-4616.   Directories

BELKNAP County. Biographical review ... containing life sketches of leading citizens of Belknap and Strafford counties, ... Boston, Biographical review pub. co., 1897.   2, (9) - 604 p. incl. ports. ports.
29 x 23½ cm. (Atlantic states series of biographical reviews vol. xxi) 21-19732.   F42. B4B6

141

BELKNAP County.   History of Merrimack and Belknap counties.   Ed. Duane Hamilton Hurd.   See
F42. M5H9   Copy 2:   F42. B4H9

BOUNDARIES.   Commission to survey the boundary between New Hampshire and Maine.   Report of
the survey between N. H. and Me. during the year 1874.   By J. H. Huntington and others.   Concord,
C. C. Pearson, state printer, 1875.   15 p. 22 cm.   7-34829.   F42. B7C7

BOUNDARIES.   The boundary line between Massachusetts and New Hampshire, from the Merrimack
River to the Connecticut.   By Samuel Abbott Green.   Lowell, Mass., Lowell courier pub, co., 1894.
30 p. 23 cm.   3-6084.   F42. B7G7

BOUNDARIES.   The northern boundary of Massachusetts in its relation to New Hampshire: a part of
the Council's report made to the American antiquarian society, at Worcester, on Oct. 21, 1890.   By
Samuel A. Green.   Cambridge, J. Wilson and son, 1890.   23 p. 24½ cm.   10-12989.   F42. B7G7

BOUNDARIES.   Report of the Commissioners appointed to ascertain and establish the true jurisdictional
line between Massachusetts and New Hampshire, ...   Manchester, J. B. Clarke, public printer,
1887 - 94.   3 v. fold. maps. 22 - 23½ cm.   1-7949 rev.   F42. B7N5

BOUNDARIES.   Report of commissioners appointed to settle the line between New-Hampshire and
Maine.   (Concord, N. H., A. M'Farland, printer, 1828)   18 p. 25 cm.   8-15818.   F42. B7N6

BOUNDARIES.   ... Report of Henry O. Kent, commissioned on the part of New Hampshire to ascertain,
survey and mark the eastern boundary of said state, from the town of Fryeburg to the Canada line.
1859.   Concord, G. G. Fogg, state printer, 1859.   24 p. 21½ cm.   10-31025.   F42. B7N7

CARROLL County, History of ... Ed. Georgia Drew Merrill.   Boston, Mass., W. A. Ferguson & co.,
1889.   xiii, 987 p. pl., ports., fold. map. 26½ cm.   1-13331.   F42. C3M5

CHESHIRE County.   Keene suburban (New Hampshire) directory for the towns of Winchester, Troy,
Swanzey, Marlboro, Hinsdale, Chesterfield.   v. 5 -   1908   Springfield, Mass., H. A.
Manning co., c. 1908.   1 v. 23 cm.   8-27365.   Directories

CHESHIRE County.   Directory and mailing list of Cheshire County, consisting of the following towns
for 1912/13 -   (v. 1) -   Alstead, Ashuelot (see Winchester), Chesterfield, Dublin, Fitzwilliam,
Gilsum, Harrisville, Hinsdale, Jaffrey, Marlow, Marlboro, Nelson, Rindge, Richmond, Spofford (see
Chesterfield), Surry, Sullivan, Swanzey, Troy, Walpole, Winchester, Westmoreland ...   Springfield,
Mass., Beaman's advertising agency, c. 1912 -   1 v. front. (fold. map) 23½ cm. 12-403.   Directories

MONADNOCK guide.   Henry I. Baldwin, ed.   Concord, N. H., Society for the Protection of New
Hampshire Forests, 1970.   128 p. illus., maps (1 fold. col. in pocket) 18 cm.   F42. C5B3

CHESHIRE County.   Biographical review ... containing life sketches of leading citizens of Cheshire
Hillsboro counties, ...   Boston, Biographical review pub. co., 1897.   2, (9) - 481 p. incl. ports. 29 x 23½ cm.
(Atlantic states series of biographical reviews vol. xxiii) 18-853. L. C. copy replaced by microfilm.   F42. C5B61
                                                                                                       Microfilm 21545 F

MONADNOCK.   The annals of the Grand Monadnock, by Allen Chamberlain ...   Concord, N. H., Society
for the protection of New Hampshire forests, 1936.   6, 195 p. plates (1 fold.) ports., fold. maps. 22½ cm. 36-16533.
                                                                                                       F42. C5C46

CHESHIRE County, ... Gazetteer of, 1736 - 1885.   Comp. and pub. by Hamilton Child ...   Syracuse,
N. Y., Print. Journal office, 1885.   2 pts. in 1 v. illus., ports., fold. map. 24 cm.   7-6444.
                                                                                                         F42. C5C5

CHESHIRE County, An index to the 1800 Federal census of.   Compiled by James V. Gill.   Danville,
Ill., Illiana Genealogical Pub. Co., c. 1967.   54 p. 28 cm.   F42. C5G5

CHESHIRE and Sullivan counties, History of.   By Duane Hamilton Hurd.   Philadelphia, J. W. Lewis &
co., 1886.   2 v. in 1. pl., port., map. 4°.   1-7950-M1.   F42. C5H9

NEW HAMPSHIRE 25

MONADNOCK. To Monadnock; the records of a mountain in New Hampshire through three centuries, gathered by Helen Cushing Nutting. (N.Y., Stratford press, c. 1925) 3, 7 - 273 p. front., plates, fold. map. 19½ cm. 25-20944.
F42. C5N9

CHESHIRE County, Historic homes of. By Marjorie Whalen Smith. (Brattleboro, Vt., Printed by Griswold Offset Print., 1968 - 71) 2 v. illus. 23 cm. "Appeared originally as a series of weekly articles in the Keene evening sentinal, starting in 1962." Bibliography: v. 1, p. (160) 68-30928 MARC.
F42. C5S6

MONADNOCK, The heart of, by Elizabeth Weston Timlow ... illus. from photos. by Herbert W. Glenson ... Boston, B. J. Brimmer co., 1922. 3, 146 p. front., plates. 16 cm. 23-7690.
F42. C5T5

COOS County. North country directory (including nine towns) ... a complete residential directory of the northern section of Coos County, including the towns of Colebrook, Columbia, Jefferson (including Riverton), Lancaster, Northumberland (including Groveton), Stark (including Crystal and Percy), Stewartstown and Stratford (including North Stratford) v. 1 - 1928/30 - Beverly, Mass., Portland, Me., Crowley & Lunt, c. 1928. v. 24 cm. CA 29-325 unrev.
Directories

INDIAN STREAM Territory, The struggle for. By Roger Hamilton Brown. Cleveland, Western Reserve University Press, 1955. (c. 1954) 104 p. illus. 23 cm. Includes bibliography. 55-8969.
F42. C7B7

COOS County, History of ... (By Mrs. Georgie Drew Merrill) ... Syracuse (N.Y.) W.A. Fergusson & co., 1888. 956 p. plates, ports., fold. map. 26 cm. Includes biographical sketches. 1-7951.
F42. C7M5

INDIAN STREAM, Report of the commissioners to. Nov. 1836. (Concord? N.H., 1836) 72 p. plan. 21 cm. Plan wanting. 8-20763.
F42. C7N5

COOS County. Spiked boots, sketches of the North Country. By Robert Everding Pike. (Eatontown, N.J., 1959) 193 p. 23 cm.
F42. C7P5

— 1961. 266 p. 24 cm.
F42. C7P5
1961

GRAFTON County. See F41.44.W71 ; F44.H45P8

GRAFTON County. Resident and business directory of the west side of the White Mountains ... including the towns of Bath, Bethlehem (including Maplewood and Beth Jct.), Franconia (including Profile), Haverhill (including Woodsville, No Haverhill, Haverhill, East Haverhill and Pike), Lisbon (including Sugar Hill), Littleton, Whitefield ... (1914/16 - v. 1 - Beverly, Mass., Littleton, N.H., Crowley & Lunt, c. 1914 - 1 v. fold. front., fold. maps. 24½ cm. 14-13664.
Directories

GRAFTON County. Book of biographies. The volume contains biographical sketches of leading citizens of Grafton County ... Buffalo, Biographical pub. co., 1897. 432 p. port. 30 x 24 cm. 3-11770.
F42. G7B7

CARDIGAN, Mt. ... To the summit of Cardigan, by the "Nomad" (Joseph Edgar Chamberlin) Read before the Chile club, Aug., 1921; reprinted from the Boston Evening transcript, Aug. 15, 1921. (Boston) The Rosemary press (c. 1922) (7) p. 23 cm. 22-20284.
F42. G7C3

GRAFTON County. ... Gazetteer of Grafton County. 1709 - 1886. Comp. and pub. by Hamilton Child ... Syracuse, N.Y., Syracuse journal co., print., 1886. 2 pts. in 1 v. plates, ports. 24 cm. Contents. - pt. I. Gazetteer of Grafton County, 1709 - 1886. - pt. II. Business directory of Grafton County, 1885'86. 1-7953.
F42. G7C5

HILLSBOROUGH County. Historical sketch of the Hillsborough County congresses, held at Amherst, 1774 & 1775; with other revolutionary records: comp. by Edward D. Boylston. Amherst, N.H., Farmers' cabinet press, 1884. 53 p. 21½ cm. 18 - 10815.
F42. H6B7

HILLSBOROUGH County record: a glimpse of the business and resources of thirty-one towns. By

J. R. Dodge. Nashua, N.H., Dodge & Noyes, 1853.   156 p. 13½ x 8 cm.   19-12964.   F42. H6D6

HILLSBOROUGH County. An index to the 1800 Federal census of Grafton and Hillsborough counties ... By Maryan R. Gill.   Danville? Ill., Maryan R. Gill, c.1972.   88 p. 29 cm.   F42. H6G5

GREEN, Samuel (Abbott) Some Indian names. n.p., 1889. 24 cm.   F42. H6G7

UNCANOONUC Mountains, The ... geology, scenery, casino, railroad, and views ... Wirtten and comp. by George V. Hamlin ... Manchester, N.H., Print. Ruemely press, 1913.   42 p. illus., 4 pl. 20½ cm. 18-14012.   F42. H6H2

HILLSBOROUGH County, History of. Comp. under the supervision of D. Hamilton Hurd ... Philadelphia, J.W. Lewis & co., 1885.   ix, 748 p. ports., double map. 28 cm. 1-7954.   F42. H6H9

ISLES OF SHOALS, off Portsmouth, Brief history of the, written by E. Victor Bigelow ... (Lowell, Mass.) Pub. by the Congregational summer conference, Star Island, 1923.   72 p. illus. 18½ cm. "Other histories of the islands": p. 2. 28-535.   F42. I8B6

ISLES OF SHOALS in summer time, The. By William Leonard Gage. Hartford, Case, Lockwood & Brainard, 1875.   24 p. 18 cm. 1-7955-M1.   F42. I8G5

ISLES OF SHOALS. An historical sketch. By John Scribner Jenness. New York, Hurd & Houghton; Cambridge, The Riverside press, 1873.   182 p. front., illus., port. fold. maps. 18 cm. 1-7956.   F42. I8J5

— 2d ed. 1875.   1, 214 p. front., illus., port. fold. maps. 18 cm. 1-7957.   F42. I8J6

— Boston, N.Y., Houghton, Mifflin, 1901.   1, 214 p. front., illus., plates, port., 3 maps. 18 cm.   1-29513 rev.
F42. I8J7

ISLES OF SHOALS, Ninety years at the, by Oscar Laighton. Boston, Mass., The Beacon press, inc., 1930.   3, 154 p. front., illus., pl., ports. 21 cm. Includes biography of Celia Thaxter ... with selections from her poems. 32-11432.
F42. I8L2

ISLES OF SHOALS. Ancient and modern Isles of Shoals. From their first discovery to the present time ... by M. Tzl. Montegeu. Boston, G.A. Emery, 1872.   5, vi - viii, 9 - 35, (1) p. 13½ cm. 1-10776.
F42. I8M7

ISLES OF SHOALS, Souvenir of the. Phot. Henry G. Peabody. (Boston, H.G. Peabody, 1888) 10 pl. obl. 24°. 1-7958-M1.   F42. I8P3

ISLES OF SHOALS. "They live on a rock in the sea!" The Isles of Shoals in colonial days. By Charles Penrose. New York, Newcomen Soc. in North America, 1957.   48 p. illus. 23 cm. 59-1381.
F42. I8P35

ISLES OF SHOALS, History of the. By Lyman V. Rutledge. Boston, Starr-King Press (1958 - 1 v. illus., ports., maps (on cover) plan. 23 cm. 58-3162.   F42. I8R8

— Barre, Mass., Barre Publishers, 1965.   xii, 210 p. 24 cm. 65-21726.   F42. I8R82

ISLES OF SHOALS, Among the. By Celia Thaxter ... Boston, J.R. Osgood, 1873.   184 p. front., plates. 15 cm. 1-7959.   F42. I8T3

— Boston, N.Y., Houghton, Mifflin, 1901.   184 p. front., 3 pl. 15½ cm. 24th impression. First ed. Boston, 1873. 1-29594/3 rev.
F42. I8T4

ISLES OF SHOALS. Dedication of a memorial to Rev. John Tucke, 1702 - 1773, Star Island, Isles of Shoals, ... 1914 ... dedicated by the N.H. historical society. (Concord? The Society, 1914) 2, (3) - 68 p. front. 25 cm. 14-22348.   F42. I8T8

KEARSARGE. Report of the majority of the committee on the name "Kearsarge." By John M. Shirley, esq.   (In N.H. hist. soc. Proceedings. Concord, 1872 - 1888. v.1, p. (136) - 181) 9-21950.   F42. K 2

KEARSARGE. As to Kearsarge mountain and the corvette named for it. Concord, N.H., Republican press assoc., 1879. 50 p. 16°. 1-7960 rev. F42.K2A7

KEARSARGE. Facts about the Carroll county Kearsarge mountain, ... Read before the Appalachian mountain club, by G.V. Fox. (n.p., 1877) 17 p. 26 cm. 1-16217 rev. F42.K3F7

MAGALLOWAY, Pioneers of the, from 1820 to 1904, by Granville P. Wilson. Old Orchard, Mer., The author, 1918. 64 p. incl. front. plates, ports. 19½ cm. 18-14382. F27.M18W7

MERRIMACK Valley, The. Boston and Maine railroad co. Boston, 1898. 20½ x 10 cm. (Picturesque New England series no. 10) F42.M4B8

MERRIMACK archaeological survey, The, a preliminary paper by Warren King Moorehead; with supplementary notes by Benjamin L. Smith on the Concord valley. Salem, Mass., Peabody museum, 1931. 79 p. illus., fold. map. 25 cm. 31-23345. F42.M4M7

MERRIMACK County. Biographical review ... containing life sketches of leading citizens of Merrimack and Sullivan counties ... Boston, Biographical review pub. co., 1897. 2, (9) - 594 p. incl. pl., ports. 29 x 24 cm. (Atlantic states series of biographical reviews: vol. xxii) 8-22371. F42.M5B6

MERRIMACK.County. History of Merrimack and Belknap counties, ... Ed. D. Hamilton Hurd. Philadelphia, J.W.Lewis & co., 1885. x, 915 (i.e. 933) p. plates, ports., double map. 28 cm. 1-7961.
F42.M5H9

KEARSARGE, Mt. ... Mount Kearsarge and Mount Pequawket ... historical notes relating to the conflicting names of, submitted to the U.S. Geographic board ... together with the decision of the Board ... Washington, Govt. print. off., 1916. 14 p. 23 cm. "The U.S. Geographic board at its meeting on Jan. 6, 1915, decided that Kearsarge was the proper name of the mountain located in Merrimack County and Pequawket of the one in Carroll County." 16-26201.
F42.M5U5

MERRIMACK County. See also F44.C7C93

NEWFOUND LAKE. A guide to Pasquaney Lake (or Newfound Lake) and the towns upon its borders. By R. W. Musgrove ... Bristol, N.H., Musgrove print. house, 1910. 3, 54 p. front., plates. 15½ cm. Contents. - Introd. - Pasquaney or Newfound Lake. - Bristol. - Hebron. - Bridgewater - Alexandria. 10-16726.
F42.N74M8

OSSIPEE Mountain Park, In. Moultonborough, N.H. Pt. I. (Boston, Boston photogravure co., c. 1890) 10 pl. 13 x 15½ cm. 2-21284. F42.O8I3

PISCATAQUA, Picturesque bits on the. By Hendricks A. Hallett. Portsmouth, N.H., Hoyt & Dow (1888) 6 pl. 8°. 1-7962-M1. F42.P4H2

PISCATAQUA Valley. The architectural heritage of the Piscataqua; houses and gardens of the Portsmouth district of Maine and New Hampshire, by John Mead Howells ... New York, Architectural book pub. co., (c.1937) 2, ix - xxvi, 217 p. incl. illus., plates, plans. front., map. 32 cm. "Books on architecture and the allied crafts used in America prior to 1830": p. xvii - xx. 38-25. F42.P4H6
NA707.H74

PISCATAQUA Valley. ... Colonial backgrounds of the Piscataqua region (by) William Safford Jones ... A Newcomen address. (Princeton, Princeton university press) 1944. 24 p. illus. 23 cm. 46-12430.
F42.P4J6

PISCATAQUA pioneers, 1623 - 1775; register of members and ancestors; John Scales, ed. Dover, N.H. (Press of C.F. Whitehouse) 1919. 212 p. illus. 23 cm. 20-14460 rev. F42. P4P4
1919

— Mrs. Wendell Burt Folsom, ed. Exeter, N.H. (Dover, Press of C.F. Whitehouse) 1942. 3, (5) - 72 p. front. (port.) 23 cm. 43-18077. F42. P4P4
1942

— register of members and ancestors 1905 - 1967. Comp. by Dallas Wylie Prugh. (Exeter? N.H.) 1967.   221 p.   23 cm.   F42. P4P4

PISCATAQUA pioneers.   ... Proceedings of the annual meeting ... (York Village, Me., 19
  v.   22 cm.   31-33669.   F42. P4P43

PISCATAQUA pioneers. Act of incorporation and by-laws of the "Piscataqua pioneers." Portsmouth, N.H., 1940.   12 p.   15½ cm.   41-15846.   F42. P4P5

PISCATAQUA, Ports of; soundings in the maritime history of the Portsmouth, N.H., customs district from the days of Queen Elizabeth and the planting of Strawberry banke to the times of Abraham Lincoln and the waning of the American clipper, by William G. Saltonstall ... Cambridge, Mass., Harvard university press, 1941.   xii, 244 p. plates, ports., 2 maps (1 double) facsim.   28 cm.   Bibliography: p. (227) - 235.   A41-4303.
F42. P4S3
1941

— New York, Russell & Russell (1968)   244 p.   25 cm.   68-10943.   F42. P4S3
1968

ROCKINGHAM County. The Manchester suburban New Hampshire directory for the towns of Auburn, Bedford, Candia, Deerfield, Goffstown, and Londonderry ... v. 1 -   1914 -   (Canaan, N.H., W.E. Shaw, c.1914 -   1 v.   23½ cm.   14-3720.   Directories

— Salem, Mass., The Henry M. Meek pub. co., c.1916 .   v.   24½ cm.   16-14787.   Directories

ROCKINGHAM County. The Southern New Hampshire directory, including the towns of Atkinson, Kingston, Newton, Pelham, Plaistow and Salem ... v. 1 -   1917/18 -   Salem, Mass., The Henry M. Meek pub. co., c.1917.   v.   24½ cm.   18-13116.   Directories

ROCKINGHAM County municipal directory and Raymond, Fremont, Hampstead, Sandown, Windham, New Hampshire, directory ...   (Candia, N.H.) W.E. Shaw, c. 19 -   v. 23½ cm.
CA 34-111 unrev.   Directories

ROCKINGHAM County. Biographical review; this volume contains biographical sketches of leading citizens of Rockingham County, ...   Boston, Biographical review pub. co., 1896.   3, (9) - 645, (1) p.
incl. 76 port.   2 pl.   29 x 22½ cm.   (Atlantic states series of biographical reviews, vol. xvii)   9-8954.
F42. R7B6

MASSABESIC, Lake, The story of. By Francis B. Eaton.   (From Manchester historic association. Collections.
v.3, p. 121 - 138.   11-13689 rev.   F42. R7E2

ROCKINGHAM County, History of, and representative citizens, by Charles A. Hazlett ... Chicago, Ill., Richmond-Arnold pub. co., 1915.   1, 5 - 1306 p. incl. plates, ports., plan. pl., ports., map.   27½ x 23½ cm.   15-19441.
F42. R7H4

ROCKINGHAM County. History of Rockingham and Strafford counties, with biographical sketches of many of its pioneers and prominent men. Comp. under the supervision of D. Hamilton Hurd ... Philadelphia, J.W. Lewis & co., 1882.   xiv, 890 p. plates, ports., double map.   28 cm.   1-7963 rev.   R7H9 copy replaced by microfilm.   18433 F.   F42. R7H9
F42. S8H9

STRAFFORD County, Index to the probate records of ... in the office of the probate clerk ... 1769 - 1800 ... By the N.H. historical society. (Concord? 193-)   19 l.   28 cm.   45-26747.
F42. S8N4

STRAFFORD County, History of, and representative citizens, by John Scales ... Chicago, Ill., Richmond-Arnold pub. co., 1914.   1, (5) - 953 p. incl. plates, ports. pl., ports., map.   28 x 23 cm.   16-14791.
F42. S8S28

NEW HAMPSHIRE   29

STRAFFORD County. Revolutionary pension declarations, Strafford County, 1820 - 1832; comprising sketches of soldiers of the revolution; comp. from the court records by Lucien Thompson ... Manchester, N.H., The Ruemely press, print., 1907.   35 p. 23 cm.   "Reprinted from the Granite state magazine for Aug., 1907." 7-38078.
F42. S8T4

SULLIVAN County. The story of a young man's tramp across three states, cooking his meals & camping along three hundred and sixty miles of road in N.H., Vt. and N.Y. ... by William Moore. N.Y., The Markey press, c.1911.   76 p. 17 cm. Across Sullivan Co., N.H., Windsor and Rutland counties, Vt., Washington Co., N.Y. to the Hudson; thence down the river to New York. 11-22352.
F42. S87
F127. H8M8

SULLIVAN County centennial celebration at Newport, July 4 and 5, 1927. Pub. by the General committee. Newport, The Argus press (1927)   84 p. front., 2 pl., ports. 22½ cm. 28-8562.
F42. S87S8

SUNAPEE, Lake. (N.Y.) c.1912. Boston and Maine railroad.   20½ cm.
F42. S9B7

SUNAPEE, Lake. Colby's Guide and souvenir of the central lake region of New Hampshire. ... describing ... over twenty N.H. towns, presenting lake Sunapee region, Kearsarge mountain and surrounding country, Kezar lake region, Mascoma lake and the Enfield Shaker settlement, Corbin's Blue Mountain park, Bradford springs, Millen and Half-moon lakes, Royal arch, etc., and embracing the adjacent towns of Enfield, Hopkinton and Henniker ... By Nat Colby. New London, N.H., Leonard & Colby (1897)   115 p. illus., fold. map. 22½ cm. 1-7964 rev.
F42. S9C6

SUNAPEE, Lake, Soo-Nipi Park lodge. (New York, 1907)   20½ x 26½ cm.
F42. S9S62

SUNAPEE, Lake, Souvenir of. Concord, N.H., J.M. Runals, 1893.   10 pl. obl. 8°. Sketches by J. F. Gilman. 1-7965-M1.
F42. S9S7

WATERVILLE Valley, The; a story of a resort in the New Hampshire mountains. By Lewis Nathaniel Goodrich. Lunenburg, Vt., North Country Press, 1952.   77 p. illus. 24 cm. 52-40138.
F42. W38G6

WILD River wilderness, The. By D.B. Wright. (Littleton, N.H., Courier Print. Co., 1971)   158 p. illus. 24 cm.
F42. W66W5

WINNIPESAUKEE, Lake. Farewell, old Mount Washington; the story of the steamboat era on Lake Winnipesaukee, by Edward H. Blackstone. Staten Island, N.Y., Steamship Historical Soc. of America (1969)   viii, 135 p. illus. 21 x 27 cm.
F42. W7B47

WINNIPESAUKEE, Lake. Three centuries on Winnipesaukee (by) Paul H. Blaisdell. Concord, N.H. (Printed by the Rumford press) 1936.   77 p. front., plates, fold. map. 24½ cm. 36-19285.
F42. W7B5

WINNEPESAUKEE and about there ... Boston, Boston and Lowell railroad, 1886.   73 p. incl. front., illus. plates. 20 cm.
F42. W7B6

WINNIPESAUKEE, Lake, in the foot hills of the White Mountains of New Hampshire. Boston, Mass., Issued by the ... Boston & Maine railroad, c.1915.   (64) p. incl. front., illus. fold. map. 21½ cm. 15-9846.
F42. W7B7

WINNIPESAUKEE; a potpourri (by) E. Palmer Clarke. (Rochester, N.H. The Record press, inc.) 1935.   152 p. front., plates, facsim. 20½ cm. 35-31919.
F42. W7C6

WINNIPISEOGEE. Notes made during an excursion to the highlands of New Hampshire and Lake Winnipiseogee. By a gentleman of Boston. (Nathan Hale) Andover, Flagg, Gould, & Newman, 1833.   184 p. 12°. 1-7966-M1.
F42. W7 H1
Copy 2 in Rare Book Room

WINNIPESAUKEE. Follow the mount (by) Bruce D. Heald. Meredith, N.H., 1968.   96 p. illus. 23 cm.
F42. W7H4

WINNIPESAUKEE.   Picturesque Lake Winnipesaukee and Alton Bay, N.H.   Alton Bay, c.1905.
15½ x 23½ cm.
F42. W7P6

WINNEPESAUKEE cleft and great prehistoric dam; the lake's various outlets, etc. (by) Edgar Harlan Wilcomb.   Worcester, Mass., 1923.   2, 28 p. illus., fold. pl., maps. 18½ cm.   23-16300.
F42. W7W6

WINNEPESAUKEE Lake country gleanings; historical sketches and stories of the early days (by) Edgar Harlan Wilcomb.   Worcester, Mass., 1923.   2, 33 p. illus. double pl. 18½ cm.   23-16299.
F42. W7W62

CITIES, TOWNS, ETC., A - Z.

ACWORTH.   Officers and committees for the centennial celebration, to be holden at Acworth ... 1868.   Claremont, N.H., Print. Claremont manufacturing co., 1868.   8 p. 19 cm.   4-35131.
F44. A1A1

ACWORTH, History of, with the proceedings of the centennial anniversary, genealogical records, and register of farms.   Ed. J. L. Merrill.   Acworth, Pub. by the town (Springfield, S. Bowles) 1869.
viii, (9) - 306 p. 58 port. (incl. front.) 23½ cm.   7-41872.
F44. A1M5

ACWORTH, Inscriptions from the ancient gravestones of.   A transcript of the records in the old cemetery ... Together with a list of revolutionary soldiers of the town.   Transcribed by Charles B. Spofford and others.   (Claremont, N.H., 1908)   23 p. 24½ cm.   9-773.
F44. A1S7

ALSTEAD, A sermon preached at, on the first Sabbath in Jan., 1826.   With historical sketches of the town.   By Seth S. Arnold ... Alstead, N.H., Newton and Tufts, 1826.   48 p. 10 - 31042.
F44. A4A7

ALSTEAD.   New Hampshire borns a town (by) Marion Nicholl Rawson, illus, by the author.   N.Y., E.P. Dutton, 1942.   319 p. incl. front., illus. 24 cm. "First ed." 42-9283.
F44. A4R3

AMHERST.   Oration of Hon. Charles H. Bartlett ... at the dedication of the Soldiers' monument at Amherst ... 1890.   Manchester (N.H.) Printed by J.B. Clarke, 1890.   19 p. 22½ cm.   5-3879.
F44. A5B2

AMHERST in the great civil conflict of 1861 - 65.   Comp. by Edward D. Boylston.   Amherst, N.H., E.D. Boylston, print., 1893 (i.e.1894)   172 p. incl. illus., ports. front., ports. 20 cm.   5-42444 rev.
F44. A5B7

AMHERST.   Fragrant memories; or, The dead of a hundred years: 1760 - 1860.   A recall of the dead of the first century of the town of Amherst, read at the centennial, May, 30, 1860, by Edward D. Boylston.   Amherst, (N.H.) The Farmers' cabinet press, 1881.   36 p. 20 cm.   A poem.   24-6801.
F44. A5B72

AMHERST, Historical discourse delivered at, on the 100th anniversary of the dedication of the Congregational meeting-house, by ... J.G. Davis.   With sketches of persons, places, and churches connected with the parish originally called Souhegan West. by A. Heald and others.   Concord, N.H., Republican press assoc., 1874.   124 p. 23 cm.   1-7633.
F44. A5D2

AMHERST.   Colonial Amherst; the early history, customs and homes; geography and geology, of Amherst, life and character of General and Lord Jeffery Amherst ... Comp. by Emma P. Boylston Locke.   (Milford, N.H., Print W.B. & A.B. Rotch) 1916.   1, (7) - 122 p. illus., fold. pl., port. 23½ cm.
16-22667.
F44. A5L8

AMHERST, Rambles about; embracing an historical and descriptive sketch of the town ... By William B. Rotch.   Amherst, N.H., Farmers' cabinet press, 1890.   67 p. front., illus., map. 21 cm.   12-11167.
F44. A5R8

NEW HAMPSHIRE   31

AMHERST, Hillsborough County, History of the town of, (first known as Narraganset township number three, and subsequently as Souhegan West) ... 1728 to 1882, with genealogies of Amherst families ... By Daniel F. Secomb. Concord, N.H., Print. Evans, Sleeper & Woodbury, 1883. vii, (1) 978 p. front. (map) illus., plates, ports., facsims. 23 cm. Genealogies and family register: p. 477-844, 928 - 936; Marriages in Amherst, not inc. in the family registers: p. 844-854. 1-7967 additions.   F44. A5 S 4

AMHERST. An historical address, delivered in the town hall, at Amherst ... 1874, on the occasion of the hundedth anniversary of the dedication of the Congregational meeting-house ... By William B. Towne. Concord, N.H., Republican press assoc., 1874. 32 p. front. (port.) 8° 1-7968-9-M1
                                                                                                          F44. A5T7

ANDOVER, History of, 1900 - 1965 (by) Ralph G. Chaffee. (Orford, N.H., Equity Pub. Corp., (c. 1966) vii, 216 p. 24 cm.. 66-29438.   F44. A6C46

ANDOVER Center, Civil and religious history of, by Lyman Clark ... Haverhill, Mass., C.C. Morse & son, 1901. 1, 18 p. 22 cm. 2-1827.   F44. A6C5

ANDOVER, History of the town of, 1751 - 1906, prepared by John R. Eastman ... Concord, N.H., Print. Rumford print. co., 1910. 2 v. in 1. plates (partly fold.) ports., fold. maps. 24 cm. Based partly on material collected by G.E. Emery before his death. Contents. - pt. I. Narrative - pt. 2. Genealogies. 10-25854.   F44. A6 E2

ANDOVER. A topographical and historical sketch of the town of Andover, in the county of Hillsborough, ... By Jacob B. Moore. Concord (N.H.) Print. Hill and Moore, 1822. 24 p. 23½ cm. 1-7970.
                                                                                                          F44. A6M8

ANTRIM. Souvenir program of the sesqui-centennial of the town of Antrim, ... 1927. Issued by the Publicity committee. (Antrim, N.H., H.W. Eldredge, print., 1927) 1, 74 p. illus. 22½ cm. 34-40373.
                                                                                                          F44. A7A7

ANTRIM. History of the town of Antrim ...to June, 1877, with a brief genealogical record of all the Antrim families. By W.R. Cochrane ... Pub. by the town. Manchester, N.H., Mirror steam print., 1880. xxiv, 791 p. front., plates, ports., double map. 24 cm. 1-7971 rev.   F44. A7C6

ANTRIM, History of the town of, for a period of one century; from 1744 to 1844. By John M. Whiton. Concord (N.H.) McFarland & Jenks (1852) xi, (13) - 95 p. 24 cm. 1-7972.   F44. A7W5

APTHORP. Table of the representation of Apthorp and Littleton in the New Hampshire provincial congress, and House of representatives 1775 - 1887 ... Littleton, N.H., E.B. Wallace, 1887. 7 p. 22½ cm. 1-7975.   F44. A8B3

ATKINSON. The ... Atkinson, Kingston, Newton, Pelham, Plaistow & Salem directory ... Boston, Mass., Hyde pub. co., c. 19 - v. 23½ cm. CA 27-235 unrev.   Directories

ATKINSON illustrated. L.C.S.A. Photos. by G.W.W. Bartlett. Lynn, Mass., Souvenir pub. co., 1895. 2 p., 13 pl. obl. 24°. 1-13332-M1.   F44. A9A9

ATKINSON, Historical discourse delivered at, on the centennial anniversary of the Congregational church ... Lawrence, Mass., G.S. Merrill & Crocker, 1875. 36 p. 8°. 1-7973 rev.
                                                                                                          F44. A9M8

AUBURN. The Manchester suburban (New Hampshire) directory, including the towns of Auburn, Bedford, Candia, Goffstown, Hooksett, Londonderry, Merrimack ... Manchester, N.H., Robinson pub. co., c. 19 - v. 23 cm. CA 33-1032 unrev.   Directories

BARNSTEAD. The Barnstead reunion, celebrated at Barnstead ... 1882. Ed. Horace N. Colbath. Concord, N.H., Printed by I.C. Evans, 1884. 132 p. ports. 23 cm. 1-7974.   F44. B2C6

BARNSTEAD, History of, from its first settlement in 1727 to 1872. By Jeremiah P. Jewett. ... rev.,

149

32　　　　　　　　　LOCAL HISTORIES IN THE LIBRARY OF CONGRESS

enl. and pub. by Robert B. Caverly ... Lowell, Mass., Marden & Rowell, print., 1872.　　viii, (9) - 264 p.
front. (mounted phot.) plates, ports.　21½cm.　1-7976.
　　　　　　　　　　　　　　　　　　　　　　　　　　　　　　　　　　　　　　　F44. B2J5

BARRINGTON, A history of.　By Morton H. Wiggin.　(n. p., 1966)　181 p. 23 cm.　　F44.B22W5

BATH.　Address delivered to the inhabitants of Bath ... 1854.　By Rev. David Sutherland.　With an
historical appendix by Rev. Thomas Boutelle.　Boston, G. C. Rand & Avery, 1855.　135 p. 19 cm. 5-37652.
　　　　　　　　　　　　　　　　　　　　　　　　　　　　　　　　　　　　　　　F44. B23S9

BEDFORD.　Centennial historical discourse of the Presbyterian church, Bedford, N.H., ... 1876, by
Rev. Ira C. Tyson ... Manchester (N. H.) J. B. Clarke, 1876.　31 p.　21½ cm.　1-7634.　　F44. B3
　　　　　　　　　　　　　　　　　　　　　　　　　　　　　　　　　　　　　　　BX9211.B29T9

BEDFORD, An address delivered at, on the 100th anniversary of the incorporation of the town, ... 1850.
45 p.　22½ cm.　1-16216.
　　　　　　　　　　　　　　　　　　　　　　　　　　　　　　　　　　　　　　　F44　B3B2

BEDFORD, History of, being statistics, comp. on the occasion of the 100th anniversary of the incorporation of the town ... 1850.　Boston, ... A. Mudge, 1851.　viii, (9) - 364 p. 1 illus. 2 maps (incl. fold. front.)
23 cm.　Genealogies of old Bedford families: p. 278 - 353.　1-13333.　　　　　　　F44　B3B3

BEDFORD, History of, from 1737, being statistics compiled on the occasion of the 150th anniversary
of the incorporation of the town ... 1900.　Pub. by the town.　Concord, N.H., The Rumford print. co.,
1903.　x, 1132 p. 22 pl. (incl. front.) 2 fold. maps.　23½ cm.　Greatly enlarged from the "History of Bedford" pub. by the town, Boston,
1851.　7-41354.　　　　　　　　　　　　　　　　　　　　　　　　　　　　　　　F44　B3B4

BEDFORD.　The diary of Matthew Patten of Bedford.　From 1754 to 1788.　Pub. by the town.　Concord, N. H., The Rumford print. co., 1903.　545 p. front. 24 cm.　4-22350.　　　　F44. B3P3

BEDFORD.　A historical sketch of Bedford, being a discourse delivered ... 1841 ... By Thomas
Savage ... Manchester, N. H., Emerson & Murray, 1841.　16 p. 22 cm.　13-14401.　　F44. B3S2

BEDFORD.　John Goffe's legacy.　By George Woodbury.　Illustrated by Arthur Conrad.　(1st ed.)
New York, W. W. Norton (1955)　272 p. illus. 22 cm.　55-14967.　　　　　　　　　F44. B3W58

BEDFORD.　John Goffe's mill; By George Woodbury.　illus. by Arthur Conrad.　(1st ed.) New York,
W. W. Norton (1948)　245 p. illus. 22 cm.　48-7546*.　　　　　　　　　　　　　　F44. B3W6

BENTON.　Some things about Coventry-Benton, New Hampshire.　By William F. Whitcher.　Woodsville, N. H., News print, 1905.　vii, 313 p. front., plates, ports., plans. 22½ cm.　8-8605.　F44.B38W5

BERLIN and Gorham, New Hampshire directory ... Schenectady, N. Y., H. A. Manning co., c. 1920 -
　　v.　23½ cm.　21-185.
　　　　　　　　　　　　　　　　　　　　　　　　　　　　　　　　　　　　　　　Directories

BETHLEHEM　The early history of the town of.　By Simeon Bolles.　Woodsville, N. H., Enterprise
print. house, 1883.　2, 108 p. 14½ cm.　1-8086.　　　　　　　　　　　　　　　　　F44. B4B6

BETHLEHEM and its surroundings.　By Elizabeth K. Churchill.　Providence (R. I.) S. S. Rider, 1876.
57 p.　24º.　1-7977-M1.　　　　　　　　　　　　　　　　　　　　　　　　　　　F44. B4C5

BETHLEHEM, Early history of the town of.　By Hattie Whitcomb Taylor.　(Bethlehem? N. H.)
48 p.　23 cm.
　　　　　　　　　　　　　　　　　　　　　　　　　　　　　　　　　　　　　　　F44. B4T3

BOSCAWEN.　One hundred and fiftieth anniversary of the settlement of Boscawen and Webster,
Merrimack Co., ... 1883.　Also births recorded on the town records from 1733 - 1850.　Concord,
N. H., Print. Republican press assoc., 1884.　2, (3) - 211 p. ports. 23½ cm.　10-12985.　F44. B7B7

BOSCAWEN, Proceedings of the centennial celebration at ... 1876.　Fisherville, N. H., Print S.G.
Noyes, 1876.　27 p. 21 cm.　12-11168.　　　　　　　　　　　　　　　　　　　　　F44. B7B8

BOSCAWEN.　The history of Boscawen and Webster ... 1733 to 1878.　Comp. by Charles Carleton

150

Coffin ... Concord, N.H., Print Republican press association, 1878.   xxix, 666 p. front., illus., plates, ports., double map. 23½ cm. Port. wanting. 1-7978*.
    F44. B7C6

BOSCAWEN. A chronological register of Boscawen, in the county of Merrimack, and state of New Hampshire ... to 1820. ... descriptive, historical & miscellaneous. Comp. by an order of the town ... By Ebenezer Price ... Concord, Print J.B. Moore, 1823.   116 p. 24 cm. 1-7979.
    F44. B7P9

BOW. Diary of Sarah Connell Ayer. Andover and Newburyport, Mass.; Concord and Bow, New Hampshire; Portland and Eastport, Maine. Portland, Me., Lefacor-Tower co., 1910.   2, 404 p. 25 cm. 12-12476.
    F44. B
    F8. A 97

BOW, The town book of; town meetings, 1767 - 1820, genealogy, 1710 - 1890, copied from the original records, by Priscilla Hammond. (Concord? N.H.) 1933.   1, 341 numb. l. 28 cm. Type-written (carbon copy) CA34-1034 unrev.
    F44. B69B6
    Rare Book Room

BRADFORD. Proceedings of the Bradford centennial celebration at Bradford, Merrimack Co., ... 1887. Bradford, N,H., A.P. Howe, 1887.   110 p. 21½ cm. A 13-2036.
    F44.B73B7

BRADFORD. Lafayette memorial exercises, 1825 - 1913. Bradford, N.H. ... 1913. (D.A.R. New Hampshire, Mercy Hathaway White chapter, Bradford)   (Warner, Independent press, 1913) cover-title, (12) p. 2 pl. 18 cm. 26-21803.
    F44.B73D2

BRISTOL and Newfound Lake district directory ... (Candia, N.H.) W.E. Shaw, c19   v. 23½ cm. 25-22458.
    Directories

BRISTOL. A guide to Bristol, Pasquaney lake and neighboring towns ... Bristol, N.H., Enterprise print. house print., 1892.   3, 59 p. front., pl. 12°. 1-7981-M1.
    F44.B76M8

BRISTOL, Historical sketches of the Methodist Episcopal church, Bristol. By R.W. Musgrove and Rev. O. Cole. Bristol, N.H., R.W. Musgrover, 1890.   24 p. illus. 8°. 1-7982-M1.
    F44.B76M9

BRISTOL. History of the town of Bristol, Grafton County, New Hampshire ... by Richard W. Musgrove. Bristol, N.H., Print, R.W. Musgrove, 1904.   2 v. fronts., plates, ports., maps (partly fold.) fold. plans. 24 cm. v. 1. Annals. - v.2. Genealogies. 4-15551.
    F44.B76M91

BROOKFIELD, Milton, Sanbornville, Wakefield, New Hampshire, and Lebanon, Me., directory. ... (Candia, N.H.) W.E. Shaw, c.19   v. 22 cm. CA 28-82 unrev.
    Directories

BROOKLINE. History of Brookline, formerly Raby, Hillsborough County, with tables of family records and genealogies, by Edward E. Parker. Pub. by the town. (Gardner, Mass., Meals print. co., 1914) 664 p. front., illus., plates, ports., maps. 24 cm. "Marriages. 1743 - 1914": p. 438 - 455. 15-12429.
    F44.B8P24

BROOKLINE. Oration delivered at the centennial celebration, in Brookline, N.H. ... 1869. By I.B. Sawtelle. Fitchburg, Mass., Print. Fitchburg reveille office, 1869.   40 p. 21 cm. 1-7980 rev.
    F44.B8 S2

CAMPTON. Chronological list of members. From 1800 - 1874 of the Congregational church in Campton. By Rev. Quincy Blakely. (n.p., 1930?)   11 numb. l. 26½ cm. Type-written (carbon copy) ... With this is bound: These gravestone inscriptions in the towns of Campton, etc. See next item. 31-8004 rev.
    F44.C13B6

CAMPTON. These gravestone inscriptions in the towns of Campton and Thornton, were collected by Mrs. Etta M. Burleigh and Mrs. Mary E. Neal Hanaford. (n.p., 1930?)   2 p. 2 - 72 numb. l., 6 l. 26½ cm. Bound with above item. Type-written. Revolutionary soldiers record: 5 leaves at end. 31-8005.
    F44.C13B6

CAMPTON, The centennial celebration of the town of, ... 1867. Concord, A.G. Jones, 1868. iv, (5) - 118 p. 12°. "The early history of Campton. By Rev. Isaac Willey": p. 10 - 60. 1-13334-M1.
    F44.C13C3

CAMPTON. A historical discourse delivered at the centennial celebration of the Congregational church in Campton ... 1874, by Rev. Quincy Blakely ... Boston, Print. A. Mudge & son, 1876.   78 p. 24 cm. 6-38848.
    F44.C13C35

CANAAN and Enfield, New Hampshire, directory 1914/15 -   ; embracing a general directory of the two towns, and the towns of Dorchester, Orange and Grafton ... v. 1 -   (Canaan, W. E. Shaw, c. 1914 -   v. 23½ cm.   15-2611.   Directories

CANAAN, The history of, by William Allen Wallace, ed. by James Burns Wallace.   Concord, N.H., The Rumford press, 1910.   ix, 748 p. front., plates (partly fold.) ports. 23½ cm. Manuscript unfinished at author's death. Old families, p. 493 - 579; Genealogy, p. 581 - 654; Marriages from the town records, p. 654 - 665. 11-3363.   F44. C15W3

CANDIA, History of; once known as Charmingfare; with notices of some of the early families.   By F. B. Eaton.   Manchester, N.H., J.O. Adams, print., 1852.   151, (1) p. front., plates, fold. map. 21½ cm. "Notices of early families": p. (49) - 106.   1-7983 Additions.   F44. C2E1

CANDIA, History of the town of.   By J. Bailey Moore.   Manchester, N.H., G.W. Browne, 1893. xvi, (17) - 528 p. front., plates, ports., fold. map. 23 cm. 1-13335.   F44. C2M8

CANDIA, Reminiscences of, by Wilson Palmer.   Cambridge (Mass.) Riverside press, 1905. 3, (v) - vi, 346 p. front., plates, ports. 20 cm. 5-27410.   F44. C2P17

CANTERBURY, History of the town of, 1727 - 1912, by James Otis Lyford ... Concord, N.H., The Rumford press, 1912.   2 v. front., plates, 2 fold. maps, plans. 24 cm. Contents. - v.1. Narrative - v.2. Genealogy and appendix. 12-24495.   F44. C23L9

CANTERBURY.   The town register: Epsom, Canterbury, Loudon, Deerfield, Northwood, Chichester, 1909.   Augusta, Me., The Mitchell-Cony co. inc., 1909.   2, (9)-115, (4), 119 p. pl. 22 cm. 12-19872.   F44. C27T7

CHARLESTOWN, History of ... 1735 to ... 1833.   By Jaazaniah Crosby ... Concord, Marsh, Capen & Lyon, 1833.   41 p. 21½ cm. Reprinted in v.4, Collections of the N.H. historical society, under title: Annals of Charlestown. Separte editions pub. under that title in 1834 and 1905. 8-34776.   F44. C4C89

— (Reprinted by The Novelty press, 1905)   (40) p. front. (port.) 12 pl. plan. 20 x 16½ cm. Repr. from v.4 Collections of the N.H. historical society. 6-23874.   F44. C4C9

CHARLESTOWN.   Second history of Charlestown, N.H., the Old Number Four; embracing a summary of the early history of the town ... 1876 to 1954.   By Martha McD. Frizzell and others.   (Littleton? N.H., 1955)   x, 446 p. illus., ports., maps (2 fold. l.) 23 cm. Bibliography: p. 430 - 433. 56-17711.   F44. C4F7

CHARLESTOWN.   Historical address at the dedication of a monument in Charlestown, N.H.   By Rev. B. Labaree ... Boston, T.R. Marvin, 1870.   28 p. 24 cm. The monument was erected to commemorate the captivity of Mrs. Susannah Johnson and other settlers of Charlestown, taken by Indians in 1754. 5-34813.   F44. C4L1

CHARLESTOWN,   History of Charlestown, N.H., the old No. 4, embracing the part borne by its inhabitants in the Indian, French and revolutionary wars ...   Also genealogies and sketches of families from its settlement to 1876.   By Rev. Henry H. Saunderson.   Claremont, N.H., The town (1876) viii, 726 p. front., plates, ports., plan. 23½ cm. 1-7984.   F44. C4S2

CHESTER, History of old, from 1719 to 1869.   By Benjamin Chase.   Auburn, N.H., The author, 1869. xvi, 702 p. front., illus., pl., ports., fold. plan. 24 cm. "A notice of the early settlers, or The genealogical and biographical history of Chester": p. (462) - 620. History of Candia and Raymond: p. 632 - 670. 1-7985.   F44. C5C4

CHESTER, History of, including Auburn.   A supplement to the History of old Chester, pub. in 1869. Comp. and pub. by John Carroll Chase.   Derry, N.H. (Haverhill, Mass., Print. Record pub. co.) 1926. xvi, 535 p. front., plates, ports., map. 25 cm. 27-16094.   F44. C5C45

CHESTER.   The dedicatory proceedings of the soldiers' monument at Chester, ... 1904; comp. and ed. by George C. Hazelton.   (N.Y., The Trow press) 1905.   4, 126 p. front., plates, ports., facsims. 24½ cm. 5-26898.   F44. C5H4

CHESTERFIELD, Cheshire County, History of ... 1736 to ... 1881; tog. with family histories and genealogies, by Oran E. Randall.   Brattleboro, Vt., D. Leonard, print., 1882.   iv, (9) - 525 p. front. (fold. chart) ports. 24 cm. 1-7986.   F44. C6R2
        Rare book room

NEW HAMPSHIRE

CHESTERFIELD. Historical sermon at the reopening of the Congregational church, Chesterfield, the 3d Sabbath of July, 1900. By Rev. Chas. N. Sinnett. Haverhill, Mass., C. C. Morse & son, 1902. 1, 14 p. 22½ cm. 6-21248*.   F44. C6S5

CHESTERFIELD, Sketch of. "Township no. one", and history of the Congregational church from 1770 to 1900. By Rev. Chas. N. Sinnett. Haverhill, Mass., C. C. Morse & son, 1902. 1, 14 p. 21½ cm. 3-4894 rev.   F44. C6S6

CLAREMONT. Manning's Claremont, Newport and Sunapee (New Hampshire) directory ... Springfield, Mass., H. A. Manning co., c. 19 -   v. 23½ cm. 38M2514T.   Directories

CLAREMONT. Dedication of a soldiers' monument, at Claremont, N. H., ... 1869. Claremont, N. H., Print, Claremont manufacturing co., 1869. 48 p. 23 cm. 18-2968.   F44. C65C65

CLAREMONT, The industries of, past and present. By Simeon Ide. Claremont, Claremont manufacturing co., 1879. 36 p. 16½ cm. 2-3890-M2.   F44. C65I2

CLAREMONT, The grantees of; reprinted from "Granite monthly." Also a chronological list of the town officers, representatives and postmaster. 1767 - 1893. Reprinted from "The National eagle." Comp. by Charles B. Spofford. (Concord? N. H., 1893) 23, 15 p. 25½ cm. 15-19108.   F44. C65S69

CLAREMONT. Grave stone records; from the ancient cemeteries in the town of Claremont. With historical and biographical notes. Comp. by Charles B. Spofford. Claremont, N. H., G. I. Putnam, 1896. 86 p. 25 cm. 4-15536 rev.   F44. C65S7

CLAREMONT war history; 1861 to 1865: with sketches of New-Hampshire regiments, and a biographical notice of each Claremont soldier, etc. By Otis F. R. Waite. Concord (N. H.) McFarland & Jenks, print., 1868. xi, (13) - 300 p. 19 cm. 1-16215.   F44. C65W2

CLAREMONT, History of the town of, for a period of 130 years from 1764 to 1894, by Otis F. R. Waite. Pub. by authority of the town. Manchester, N. H., Print. John B. Clarke co., 1895. 3, (v) - x, 540 p. front., plates, ports., 3 fold., aps. 23½ cm. 7-41869.   F44. C65W3

COLEBROOK. Even to this valley, by Ellsworth H. Bunnell. (1st ed.) Detroit, Harlo (c. 1971) 110 p. illus. 23 cm. 78-156950.   F44. C68B8

COLEBROOK; a place up back of New Hampshire, by William H. Gifford. Colebrook, N. H., The News and Sentinel (c. 1970) vi, 408 p. illus. 24 cm. 78-118756.   F44. C68B5

CONCORD. The Concord directory, containing the names of the legal voters and householders, belonging to the Centre Village and its adjacent neighborhood ... Concord, 1830. 24 p. 17½ cm.
    Directories
    Rare Book Room

CONCORD. Lothrop's Concord city directory and Merrimack county directory, 1898/99 - 1908/09, 1910 - 1913, 1915 - 1917, 1919 - 1920, 1922, 1924, 1926, 19 -   Boston, Mass., Union pub. co., 1898 - c. 19 -   v. fold. maps. 24 cm. Title varies. 22-19488 (rev. '31)   Directories

CONCORD. The Concord directory. June, 1834. Containing the names of all heads of families, males of 21 years of age, and all others doing business in Concord Centre village ... Concord, Print. Observer office (1834) 36 p. 19 cm. The second directory of Concord, the first having appeared in 1830. 10-13012.   Directories

CONCORD. A directory containing the names, occupations and residence of the inhabitants of Concord Centre village. Concord, Print. E. B. Tripp, 1850. 108 p. illus., fold. map. 16 cm. 10-13011 rev.*.   Directories

CONCORD directory, containing the names, occupations and residence of the inhabitants of Concord Centre village, with other matters of great local interest. Concord, C. L. Wheler, 1853-4. 89 p. front. (fold. map) illus. 15½ cm. 10-13019.   Directories

CONCORD. The Concord directory, containing the names and business of citizens in the compact part of the city, with a business key thereof, and also of societies, etc. to which is added a business key of Fisherville. By David Watson and others. Concord, Merriam & Merrill, 1856. 1, (11) - 96 p. front., (fold. map) 16 cm. 10-13013 rev.
Directories

CONCORD and its points of interest ... By George Fox Bacon. ... Concord, N.H., Concord commercial club, 1890. 32 p. illus. 4°. From "The leading business men of Concord ..." 1-7987 - M1. F44. C7B2

CONCORD and vicinity, The leading business men of, embracing Penacook, East and West Concord. By Geo, F. Bacon ... Boston, Mercantile pub. co., 1890. 1, 91 p. illus. 27 cm. In double columns. 3-18900.
F44. C7B23

CONCORD. Autobiography of Nathaniel Bouton, former pastor of the First Congregation church of Concord ... N.Y., A.D.F. Randolph, 1879. 87 p. 24½ cm. 7-11139. F44. C7B6

CONCORD. 1725 - Third semi-centennial of Concord - 1875. A discourse on the growth and development of Concord ... By Nathaniel Bouton. Concord (N.H.) Print, Republican press assoc., 1875. 48 p. 23 cm. 1-7988. F44. C7B7

CONCORD, The history of, from its first grant in 1725, to the organization of the city government in 1853, with a history of the ancient Penacooks. ... By Nathaniel Bouton ... Concord (N.H.) B.W. Sanborn, 1856. 2, 786 p. front., illus., plates, ports., fold. map, plans, fold. facsim. 23½ cm. 1-7989.
F44. C7B8

CONCORD. Words of William E. Chandler; address of June 8, 1915 on the 150th anniversary of the chartering of the town of Concord ... Concord, N.H., Rumford press (1915) 17 p. 25½ cm. 15-26899.
F44. C7C4

CONCORD. Reverend Enoch Coffin. Concord's first preacher, 1726 - '28. By John C. Thorne. (Concord? N.H., 19 -? 6 p. illus. 25½ cm. 3-14781. F44. C7C5

CONCORD, the city beautiful; its attractions and advantages. Issued by the Concord commercial club. Concord (Printed by Rumford press) 1909. 64 p. illus. 19½ cm. 10-5330. F44. C7C55

CONCORD town records, 1732 - 1820; printed by authority of joint resolutions passed by the City council Apr. 9, 1889, and Feb. 13, 1894. Concord, N,H., Republican press assoc., 1894. iv, 576 p. 2 maps (1 fold.) 23½ cm. 6-16520-1.
— Index to Concord town records, 1732 - 1820; pub. by the city of Concord ... Comp. by Otis G. Hammond. Concord, N.H., Rumford press, 1900. 73 p. 23½ cm. 6-16520-1.
F44. C7C6

CONCORD, History of, from the original grant in 1725 to the opening of the 20th century; prepared under the supervision of the City history commission; James O. Lyford, ed. ... (Concord, N.H., The Rumford press, 1903) 2 v. fronts., illus. 28 cm. Paged continuously. 3-22838 rev. F44. C7C7
— Commissioners' map of Concord; prepared for the History of Concord by Will B. Howe ... 1902. Boston, G.H. Walker & co. (1903) map. 85½ x 77½ cm. fold. to 28 cm. 3-22838 rev.
F44. C7C8

CONCORD, picturesque and historic ... Concord, N.H. (c. 1908) 15½ x 23 cm. F44. C7C9

CONCORD. Wayside jottings; or, Rambles around Concord (by) Howard M. Cook. (Concord? 1909) xiii, 201 p. incl. front. (port.) plates. 20 cm. Pub. originally in the Concord evening monitor and Daily patriot, 1907 - 09. 10-1167.
F44. C7C93

CONCORD. A monograph of the Rev. Israel Evans, chaplain in the American army during the entire revolutionary war, 1775 - 1783. By John Calvin Thorne. (Concord? 1902) 26 p. illus., port. 25 cm. 11-30525. F44. C7E92

CONCORD. A list of the pastors, deacons, and members of the First Congregational church, in Concord ... 1730 - 1830. Concord, Print. A. M'Farland, 1830. 21 p. 22½ cm. 10-31046. C44. C7F5

NEW HAMPSHIRE 37

CONCORD. Gravestone inscriptions, East Concord, compiled by Priscilla Hammond. Concord, N.H., 1932. 2, 68 numb. 1. 28 cm. Type-written (carbon copy) "All ... gravestone records of the ... Old fort cemetery ... and the Pine grove cemetery." 35-29245.
F44. C7H2
Rare Book Room

CONCORD. Col. William Kent, Concord, N.H. 1793 - 1886. (Concord, N.H., 1886) (3) - 13 p. 19½ cm. 11-23163.
F44. C7K3

CONCORD. Sixty years in Concord and elsewhere. Personal recollections of Henry McFarland. 1831 - 1891 ... Concord, N.H. (The Rumford press) 1899. 331 p. front. (port.) plates. 19 cm. 0-1305 rev.
F44. C7M1

CONCORD. Annals of the town of Concord, in the county of Merrimack, and state of New Hampshire, from its first settlement in the year 1726, to the year 1823. With several biographical sketches. By Jacob B. Moore ... Concord, J.B. Moore, 1824. 1, ii, (5) - 112 p. 23½ cm. 1-7990.
F44. C7M8

CONCORD. Official proceedings at the dedication of the statue of Commodore George Hamilton Perkins at Concord, N.H., on the 25th day of April, 1902. Concord (Rumford print. co., 1903) 48 p. front., 2 pl. 24½ cm. 8-13933.
F44. C7O3

CONCORD. Chronicles of an old New England farm; the house and farm of the first minister of Concord, N.H., 1726 - 1906, by Joseph B. Walker ... Concord, N.H., 1906. 2, 14, 35, 70 p. front., plates, fold. plan. 22 cm. A reprint ... of three papers. 6-37959.
F44. C7W17

CONCORD. The New Hampshire covenant of 1774; a paper read before the New Hampshire historical society, Apr. 8, 1903, and reprinted from the Granite monthly of Oct., 1903, by Joseph B. Walker. Concord, N.H., The Rumford print. co., 1903. 12 p. illus. (facsim.) 24½ cm. 4-3636.
F44. C7W2

CONCORD. Diaries of Rev. Timothy Walker, the first and only minister of Concord ... 1730 - 1782. Ed. ... by Joseph B. Walker. Concord, N.H., I.C. Evans, 1889. 80 p. 22½ cm. 1-5738.
F44. C7W25

CONCORD. At the bend in the river, Concord, New Hampshire bicentennial, 1765 - 1965. By Stephen W. Winship. 1965. 1 v. (unpaged) 24 cm.
F44. C7W5

CONWAY through the years and whither. By Ruth Burnham Horne. Conway historical soc. (c. 1963) xi, 148 p. illus., port., maps. 24 cm.
F44. C73H6

CORNISH. The Cornish, Plainfield, Meriden, Grantham, Croydon, N.H. and Weathersfield, Vt., directory. (Canaan, N.H.) W.E. Shaw, 1915. v. 23½ cm. 16-1679.
Directories

CORNISH. "Aspet" Saint-Gaudens National historic site - part II; historical data, by John W. Bond. (Washington) 1969. 37 l. illus. 72-605424.
F44. C8B6

CORNISH, History of the town of, with genealogical record, 1763 - 1910, by Wm. H. Child ... Concord, N.H. The Rumford press (1911?) 2 v. fronts., illus., plates, ports., fold. map. 24 cm. "Births, marriages and deaths in Cornish not recorded in genealogies": v. 1, p. (347) - 368. I. Narrative. - II. Genealogy. 14-13592.
F44. C8C5

CROYDEN, An historical and statistical sketch of, from its incorporation to the year 1852 ... By John Cooper. Concord (N.H.) Print. Tripp & Osgood, 1852. 52 p. 19 cm. First pub. in 1850 in Collections of the N.H. historical soc. v.6, p. 212 - 242, under name of Lemuel P. Cooper. 4-4306.
F44. C9C7

CROYDEN, 1866. Proceedings at the centennial celebration on Wed. June 13, 1866. A brief account of the leading men of the first century ... By Edmund Wheeler. Claremont, N.H., Print. Claremont manufacturing co., 1867. 173 p. front., ports. 23 cm. 1-7991.
F44. C9W5

CROYDEN. Introductory address of Hon. William P. Wheeler, of Keene, N.H. ... at the centennial celebration, at Croydon, N.H., June 13, 1866. Claremont, N.H., Print. Claremont manufacturing co., 1867. 26 p. 23 cm. 19-3121.
F44. C9W53

DANVILLE, Fremont, Hampstead, Raymond, Sandown, Windham, New Hampshire, directory ...
(Candia, N.H.) W.E.Shaw, c. 19 -   v.   23½ cm.   CA 28-313 unrev.   Directories

DEERFIELD, Tales of old (by) Joanne F. Wasson.   Concord, N.H., Evans Print. Co. (c.1964)
78 p.   24 cm.   "A collection of stories... (from) the Deerfield post, Dec. 1956 to Nov. 1962."
                                                                                 F44. D4W3

DERRY directory, The ... 19 -   (Derry, N.H.) The Derry news, c. 19 -
v.   24 cm.   CA 33-742 unrev.   Directories

DERRY and Chester (N.H.) directory, The ... 1916/17 -   v.1 -   Salem, Mass., The Henry
M. Meek pub. co., c.1916.   v.   front. (fold., ap) 24 cm.   16-15463.   Directories

DERRY and Chester, New Hampshire, directory ... v.1 -   1933 -   v. 23½ cm.   CA. 34-249 unrev.
                                                                                 Directories

DERRY.   Darkness brought to light.   A poem: revealing the mysteries of Sam, in Derry.   By the
author.   (n. p.) 1855.   20 p. 11 cm.   9-26192.   F44. D43D2
                                                                                 Rare Book Room

DERRY.   Rural doin's by C. Quincy Ives.   Philadelphia, Dorrance (c.1967)   vii, 54 p. 20 cm. 67-18548.
                                                                                 F44. D43 I9

DERRY.   Houses of the English Range and Beaver Lake Derry, N.H.; an informal story.   By Harriett
Chase Newell.   (Littleton? N.H.) 1959.   176 p. 23 cm.   F44. D43N4

DERRY.   Houses of West Derry, a pictorial story.   By Harriet Chase Newell.   (Littleton? N.H.)
1963.   384 p. 23 cm.   F44. D43N42

DERRY.   Outlying districts of Derry; a pictorial story, by Hariett Chase Newell.   (Derry? N.H.)
1965.   212 p. 23 cm.   F44. D43N43

DERRY, Glimpses of, 1719 - 1969.   250th Nutfield Anniversary Committee.   Derry, N.H., Ed Hatch
print. (1969)   63 p. illus. 28 cm.   79-17081 MARC.   F44. D43T9

DERRY.   Houses of Derry Village; an informal story.   By Harriett Chase Newell.   (Derry Village?
N.H.) 1951.   171 p. illus. 23 cm.   52-18599.   F44. D44N4

DOVER.   Norris' Dover directory, containing the names of the heads of families, and others doing
business in Dover village ... By D.L.Norris.   (18   no.   Dover (N.H.) E. Wadleigh,
18   v.   13½ cm.   16-4791.   Directories

DOVER suburban New Hampshire directory for Barrington, Lee, Madbury, Newington and Rollinsford
... 19   (Dover, N.H.) W.E.Shaw, 19   v.   22½ cm.   35-21368.   Directories

DOVER.   The leading business men of Dover, Rochester, Farmington, Great Falls and Berwick ...
Boston, Mercantile pub. co., 1890.   85, (1) p. illus. 27 cm.   Cover-title: Great Falls and its leading business men.
4-20148.   F44. D7B2

DOVER.   A bill of mortality for the Society of Friends in Dover, N.H., from 1708 to 1791.   Also a
general bill of mortality for Dover, N.H. (from 1773 to 1802) ... (Dover, N.H.) Print. J.K. Remich,
1803.   25 p. 22½ cm.   15-3559.   F44. D7B5

DOVER, The First parish in.   250th anniversary, Oct. 28, 1883.   Dover, printed for the Parish,
1884.   148 p. 24½ cm.   3-18824.   F44. D7D63

DOVER.   Collections of the Dover historical society.   Vol. 1.   Dover, Print, Scales & Quimby, 1894.
3, 305 p. 23 cm.   No more pub.   "The Publishing committee ... have gathered in this volume many of the widely separated records of marriages,
births, deaths and baptisms in Dover, N.H., down to the year 1850."   14-10431.
                                                                                 F44. D7D7
                                                                                 F44. D7D7 vol. 1

NEW HAMPSHIRE

DOVER. 89th anniversary of the national independence, July 4, 1865, at Dover. Full report of the celebration ... Dover, N.H., B. Barnes, jr., 1865.　36 p. 8°. 1-16780-M1.

F44. D7D8

DOVER, N.H., in the U.S. navy in 1861 - 1865. By John R. Ham. Dover, N.H., N.E. Stiles, print. 1892.　(11) p. 21½ cm. CA 25-560 unrev.

F44. D7H19

DOVER (N.H.) physicians, The. Read before the N.H. medical soc. ... 1879, by John Randolph Ham .. Concord, Print. Evans, Sleeper and Evans, 1879.　22 p. 23 cm. 5-34052.

F44. D7H2

DOVER. Journal of the Rev. John Pike, of Dover. Ed. with an intod. and nores by the Rev. A.H. Quint ... Cambridge (Mass.) Press of J. Wilson and son, 1876.　40 p. 23½ cm. "Reprinted from the Proceedings of the Massachusetts historical soc. v.14, p. 117-152, Sept. 1875. "Marriages recorded",1686- 1710: p. 38-40. 1-13336.

F44. D7P6

DOVER, N.H.; historical sketch of Dover's participation in the Spanish-American war, May 12, 1898 to Oct. 31, 1898; comp. by Fred E. Quimby, city clerk. (Dover? N.H., 1898?)　19 p. 23 cm. "List of those who signed the roll in Dover for a naval reserve corps": p. 10 - 11. "Muster-in-roll of Capt. Frank E. Rollins, Co. F ... First regiment of New Hampshire volunteer infantry": p. 14-18. 29-19839.

F44. D7Q6

DOVER. 100th anniversary of the national independence, July 4, 1876; its celebration by the city of Dover ... and oration by Rev. Alonzo H. Quint. Dover, N.H., Morning star steam job print., 1876.　53 p. 23½ cm. 1-16867.

F44. D7Q7

DOVER. Historical memoranda concerning old Dover. By John Scales. v. 1. Dover, N.H. 1900. 22½ cm.

F44. D7S2

DOVER. Historical sketch, views and business directory of Dover. Dedicated to the State grange P. of H. ... (Dover, G.J. Foster & co., 1926)　(40) p. illus. (incl. ports.) 23 cm. 27-3891.　F44. D7S21

DOVER. History of Dover ... (Tercentenary ed.) Containing historical, genealogical and industrial data of its early settlers, their struggles and triumphs. By John Scales. (Manchester, N.H.) Printed by authority of the City councils, 1923 -　v. front., plates, port., fold. maps. 24 cm. 24-23294.

F44. D7S22

DOVER. A discourse delivered in the First church of Dover, May 18, 1873, on the 250th anniversary of the settlement of Dover, by George B. Spalding ... Dover, N.H., Freewill Baptist print. estab., 1873. 29 p. 20 cm. 1-7992.

F44. D7S7

DOVER pulpit during the revolutionary war, The, a discourse commemorative of the distinguished service rendered by Rev. Jeremy Belknap ... preached by Rev. George B. Spalding ... 1876. Dover, N.H., Morning star steam job print., 1876.　31 p. 23½ cm. 7-6876.

F44. D7S72

DOVER. Sketch of Dover, N.H.; topographical, historical, ecclesiastical, statistical, etc., from the earliest period to the present time. By S.C. Stevens. Dover, S.C. Stevens, 1833.　24 p. 17½ cm. Originally pub. in Dover directory, March, 1833 ... 10-33447.

F44. D7S8
Rare Book Coll.

DOVER. Landmarks in ancient Dover, New Hampshire. By Mary P. Thompson. Complete ed. Durham, N.H. (Concord Republican press assoc.) 1892.　284 p. 3 maps. 25 cm. "The township of Dover originally comprised not only the present city of that name, but the townships of Durham, Lee, Madbury, Rollinsford, and Somersworth, the greater part of Newington, a portion of Newmarket and ... Greenland." 2-13485 rev.

F44. D7T4
Rare Book Room

DOVER, Landmarks in Ancient Dover, by Mary P. Thompson. (Durham, N.H.) Durham Historic Association, 1965 (c.1892)　284 p. 24 cm.

F44. D7T4
1965

DOVER. Notable events in the history of Dover, from the first settlement in 1623 to 1865, by George Wadleigh. Dover, N.H., 1913.　4, 334 p. front. 24½ cm. 13-19167.

F44. D7W12

DOVER. A compendious history of the First parish in Dover; taken from the sermons preached on

the first Sabbath in Jan., 1831, by Rev. H. Winslow ... Dover (N.H.) C.C.P. Moody, 1832.   16 p. 23½ cm.
9-30373.
F44. D7W7

DUBLIN days, old and new; New Hampshire fact and fancy.   Illus. with photos. by the author and others.
New York, Exposition Press (1952)   156 p. illus. 22 cm. 51-11828.
F44. D8A37

DUBLIN, Souvenir of; illus. by Chasmar & Co., New York, from photos. by French of Keene.   Boston, Press of Rockwell and Churchill, 1891.   27 p. illus. 14 x 21 cm. 1-7993 rev.*
F44. D8A4

DUBLIN. Early Dublin. A list of the revolutionary soldiers of Dublin. By Samuel Carroll Derby ...
Columbus, O. (Press of Spahr & Glenn) 1901.   34 p. 22½ cm.
— Additions and corrections, Oct., 1904. (Columbus? 1904)   4 p. 23 cm.
— Supplement. (Columbus, 1913)   7 p. 23 cm. 1-16011 rev.
F44. D8D5

DUBLIN, The history of, containing the address by Charles Mason, and the proceedings at the centennial celebration ... 1852; with a register of families.   Boston, Print. J. Wilson and son, 1855.   vi, (2) 433 p. front., plates, ports., fold. map. 23 cm. 1-7994 additions.
F44. D8D8

— continued and additional chapters to 1917 by Rev. Josiah L. Seward. Dublin, N.H., Pub. by the town, 1920.   xxiv p., 1018 p. front., plates, ports., facsims. 24½ cm. "Reprinted and augmented ed." 20-6641.
F44. D8D82

DUNBARTON. Record of the centennial celebration, of the incorporation of the town of Dunbarton, ... 1865. Manchester, N.H., H.A. Gage, 1866.   124 p. 22½ cm. Ed. Silvanus Hayward. 18-2206.   F44. D9D8

DUNBARTON, Sketch of. By Miss Ella Mills. Manchester, N.H., Manchester historic assoc., 1902.
1, 20 p. 23 cm. 2-20536.
F44. D3M6

DUNBARTON, Merrimack County, History of the town of, from the grant by Mason's assigns, in 1751, to the year 1860. By Caleb Stark. Concord, G.P. Lyon, 1860.   2, (vii) - viii, (9) - 272 p. 24 cm. 1-7995* cancel.
F44. D9S8

DURHAM pageant, The. 1640 - ye olden days on ye Oyster River - 1776. Durham, New Hampshire. (Manchester, N.H., Williams print. co., 1918)   (8) p. illus. 23 cm. "An out-door drama ... in celebration of the 200th anniversary of the founding of the Durham Congregational church." CA 25-1503 unrev.
F44. D96D9

DURHAM. Report from the village, by Philbrook Paine. Illus. by Larry Lurin. (1st ed.) New York, W.W. Norton (c. 1965)   191 p. 22 cm. 65-11003.
F44. D96P3

DURHAM, History of the town of (Oyster River Plantation) with genealogical notes, by Everett S. Stackpole and Lucien Thompson ... (Durham? N.H.) Pub. by vote of the town (1913)   2 v. fronts. (ports.) illus., fold. map. 23½ cm. Contents. - v.1. Narrative. - v.2. Genealogical. 14-22609.
F44. D96S7

EASY ALSTEAD. Short history of Mill Hollow; early industrial center of Easy Alstead, New Hampshire, 1753 - 1968, by Heman Chase. (Springfield, Vt. Print, E. and M. Hurd, c. 1969)   x, 115 p. illus. 23 cm.
F44. E15C45

EATON, Civil War veterans buried in. Snowville, N.H., 1962.   unpaged. 23 cm.
F44. E18H4

EATON, The early days of, by Nella and Keith Henney. For the town of Eaton. (1st ed. North Conway? N.H., 1967.   vii, 107 p. 24 cm.
F44. E18H42

ENFIELD. 100th anniversary of the organization of the Shaker church, Enfield, N.H., ... 1893. Enfield, N.H., Abbott's power print, 1893.   36 p. 19½ cm. 1-7996.
F44. E5
BX9768. E7A3

EPPING, Barrington, Lee, Madbury, Northwood, New Hampshire directory, The ... (Candia, N.H.) W.E. Shaw, c. 19 -   v. 23½ cm. CA 28-266 unrev.
Directories

NEW HAMPSHIRE

EPSOM, A topographical and historical sketch of. By Jonathan Curtis ... Pub. in 1823. (Republished by request.) Pittsfield, N.H., Analecta pub. house, 1885. 12 p. 21 cm. 2-1825. F44. E6C9

EPSOM, Church records of, 1761 - 1774, compiled by Priscilla Hammond. (Concord? N.H.) 1933. 29 numb. 1. 28 cm. Type-written (carbon copy) CA 34-1041 unrev. F44. E6E6
Rare Book Room

EXETER, Crowley & Lunt's directory for, and surrounding towns. Beverly, Mass., Crowley & Lunt. 1911. 1 v. front. (fold. map) 24 cm. 12-573. Directories

EXETER, New Market, and South Newmarket directory and history. 1872 ... Also containing sketches of business; origin and sketches of families; register of deaths in Exeter since 1840, etc. Comp. by J. L. Beckett. Boston, D. Dudley, 1872. 152 (i.e.172) p. 23½ cm. 15-27855. Directories

EXETER in 1776. Sketches of an old New Hampshire town as it was a hundred years ago. Prepared for the ladies centennial levee held in Exeter, Feb 22, 1876. Exeter (N.H.) News-letter press, 1876. 39 p. 22 cm. 1-7997. F44. E9B4

EXETER, History of the town of. By Charles H. Bell. Exeter (Press of J. E. Farwell & co., Boston) 1888. ix, 469, 88 p. front. (fold. facsim.) 2 fold. plans. 23½ cm. Genealogical, 88 p. at end. 7-11191. F44. E9B45

EXETER, Men and things of. Sketches from the history of an old New Hampshire town. By Charles Henry Bell. Exeter, Printed at The Newsletter press (1871) 2, 73 p. 25 cm. Reprinted from the Exeter News-letter. 1-7998. F44. E9B5

EXETER. The town register: Exeter, Hampton, 1908, comp. by Mitchell, Bartlett, Lawton, and others. Augusta, Me., The Mitchell-Cony co., 1908. 256 p. fold. map. 23 cm. 12-21885. F44. E9M6

EXETER, A brief record of events in, during the year 1861, tog. with the names of the soldiers of this town in the war. By Elias Nason ... Exeter, print. S. Hall, 1862. 16 p. 19½ cm. 3-21056. F44. E9N19
Rare Book Room

EXETER, A brief record of events in, during the year 1862; tog. with the names of the soldiers of this town in the war. By Elias Nason. ... Exeter, Fogg & Fellowes, 1863. 20 p. 18½ cm. 3-699. F44. E9N2

EXETER, The First church in. 1638 - 1888 - 1698 - 1898. By John Taylor Perry. Exeter (The News-letter press) 1898. 129 p. 24 cm. Jan. 12, 99-26. F44. E9P4

EXETER. The Lincolnshire origin of some Exeter settlers. By V. C. Sanborn. The daughters of Balthazar Willis. By Virginia Hall. (Boston, 1914) 19 p. 25½ cm. Reprinted from N.E. historical and genealogical register for Jan., 1914. 17-20833. F44. E9S19

FARMINGTON. The town register: Farmington, Milton, Wakefield, Middleton, Brookfield, 1907 - 8, comp. by Davis, and others. Augusta, Me., The Mitchell-Cony co., inc., 1908. 3, (9) - 267 p. 22 cm. 12-21886. F44. F3D2

FARMINGTON, Souvenir of ... By Mrs. Adelaide Cilley Waldron. (Farmington, N.H.) Farmington news print (1904) (30) p. illus., fold. pl. 15 x 24 cm. 6-22943. F44. F3W2

FITZWILLIAM, The history of, from 1752 - 1887. By John F. Norton. With a genealogical record of many Fitzwilliam families by Joel Whittemore ... New York, Burr print. house, 1888. xvi, (17) - 829 p. incl. front. (coat of arms) plates, ports., fold. maps, fold. plan. 23½ cm. 1-7999. F44. F5N8

FRANCESTOWN, History of, from its earliest settlement 1758 to 1891. With a brief genealogical record of all the Francestown families. By W. R. Cochrane ... and George K. Wood ... Nashua, N.H., J. H. Barker, printer, 1895. v, (2), 1016, xv p. front., plates, ports., fold. maps, plan. 23½ cm. Genealogies: p. (475) - 1007. 1-8000. F44. F8C6

FRANCESTOWN, Frances' town; a history of Francestown,, (by) John R. Schott. (Francestown)

Town of Francestown, 1972. xiv, 314 p. illus., fold. map. 24 cm. 72-83948.   F44. F8S3

FRANKLIN, New Hampshire, directory, 1910.   Boston, Mass., Union pub. co., 1910 -
1 v. 24½ cm. 10-23676.   Directories

FRANKLIN.   The Daniel Webster birth place celebration at Franklin, on Aug. 28, 1913; ... (Concord, N.H., Rumford press, 1913)   13, (6) p. incl. facsims. 23 cm. 13-24432.   F44. F83C4
E340. W4C4

FRANKLIN.   The spirit of Franklin, Franklin historical pageant, written to commemorate the centenary, 1928, by Mrs. Alice M. Shepard and others ... (Franklin, N.H., Towne & Robie, 1928)
32 p. front. (port.) pl. 24 cm. 28-18396.   F44. F83S5

GILMANTON, The history of, embracing the proprietary, civil, literary, ecclesiastical, biographical, genealogical, and miscellaneous history, from the first settlement to the present time; inc. what is now Gilford, to the time it was disannexed.   By Daniel Lancaster.   Gilmanton (N.H.) Printed by A. Prescott, 1845.   viii, (13) - 304 p. front. (fold. map) 22 cm. "Genealogical history": p. 255-290. 1-8002.   F44. G4L2

GILSUM, History of the town of, from 1752 to 1879 ... By Silvanus Hayward ... Manchester, N.H., Print. for the author, by J.B. Clarke, 1881.   468 p. front., plates, ports., 3 maps (2 fold.) 26 cm. "Genealogical": p. (251) - 430. 1-8001.   F44. G45H4

GOFFSTOWN, Weare, Hookset, Suncook, Pittsfield and Candia citizens directory, 1888 -
v. 1 -   Haverhill, N.H., W.E. Shaw (1888 -   v. 23 cm. 22-16706.   Directories

GOFFSTOWN.   A brief history of the Congregational church in Goffstown, being part of a sermon preached by Samuel L. Gerould ... July 9, 1876, with a few later additions.   Bristol, N.H., R.W. Musgrove, print., 1881.   19 p. 21 cm. 1-8003.   F44. G6G3

GOFFSTOWN, History of the town of, 1733 - 1920, by George Plummer Hadley ... Pub. by the town. (Concord, N.H., The Rumford press, c.1922 - 24)   2 v. front., illus., plates, ports., maps (part fold.) 23½ cm.
Contents. - v.1. Narrative - v.2. Genealogy. 24-15722.   F44. G6H2

GOFFSTOWN.   The Goffstown register, 1905, comp. by Mitchell and Weston.   Brunswick, Me., The H.E. Mitchell co., 1905.   96 p. 22 cm. 12-21880.   F44. G6M6

GOSHEN; South Conway, New Hampshire, by Nellie M. Carver.   Portland, Me., House of Falmouth (c.1971)   153 p. illus. 24 cm.   F44. G65C3

GREENLAND.   Rambles about Greenland in rhyme.   By M. O. Hall.   Boston, A. Mudge & son, print., 1900.   238 p. front., illus., pl., port., maps, plan, facsim. 24 cm. Contents. - Rambles about Greenland in rhyme. - History of the town of Greenland from 1653 to 1829. - Families and subjects of interest. 2-3375.   F44. G8H2

HAMPSTEAD.   A memorial of the town of Hampstead.   Historic and genealogic sketches.   Proceedings of the centennial celebration, 1849. ... etc.   Comp. by Harriette Eliza Noyes.   Boston, Mass., G.B. Reed, 1899 - 1903.   2 v. fronts., illus., plates, ports., facsims. 24 cm. Vol. II has title: A memorial history of Hampstead, New Hampshire ... Congregational church, 1752-1902. 0-673 rev.   F44. H2N9

HAMPSTEAD.   Address delivered July 4th, 1849 at the centennial celebration of the incorporation of the town of Hampstead.   By Isaac W. Smith. Manchester, N.H., American office - J.O. Adams, print., 1849.   84 p. 22 x 12 cm. 1-16214.   F44. H2S5

HAMPSTEAD.   History of the town of Hampstead for one hundred years.   By Isaac W. Smith.   As contained in a historical address delivered July 4, 1849.   Haverhill, Mass., 1884.   46 p. 22 cm. 1-8004.
F44. H2S6

HAMPTON.   The immensity of God.   A sermon delivered to the Congregational society in Hampton, 1797 ... by Jesse Appleton ... Newburyport: - Print. Edmund M. Blunt - 1797.   32 p. 21 cm. 25-13600.
F44. H3A7
Rare Book Room

HAMPTON. An historical address, delivered at Hampton ... 1838, in commemoration of the settlement of that town ... By Joseph Dow ... Concord, Print. A. McFarland, 1839. 44 p. 20½ cm. 1-10777.
 F44. H3D7

HAMPTON, History of the town of. From ... 1638 to ... 1892. By Joseph Dow. Ed. and pub. by his daughter ... Salem, Mass., Print. Salem press pub. and print. co., 1893. 2 v. in 1. front., plates, ports., 2 fold. maps, 2 facsim. (1 fold.) 24 cm. Paged continuously. Vol. 2 (p. 581 - 1104) genealogical and biographical. 1-10778.
 F44. H3D8

HAMPTON. The day of trouble near, the tokens of it, and a due preparation for it; in three sermons ... and an appendix, giving some account of the earthquake, as it was in Hampton ... By Nathaniel Gookin ... Boston: Printed for D. Henchman ... 1728. 4, 75 p. 17½ cm. 6-8261.
 F44. H3G6
 Rare Book Room

— Exeter, Print. Samuel Winslow, 1796. vi, (7) - 102 p. 15½ cm. 24-11502.
 F44. H3G6
 1796
 Rare Book Room

HAMPTON. Along the Hampton shore, by Harry Alden Johnson. (Haverhill, Mass., W. D. Cram co., c. 1913) 35, (1) p. illus. 18½ cm. 13-15224.
 F44. H3J6

HAMPTON, Historical sketch of, for 250 years, 1638 - 1888, and of the Congregational church in Hampton. Haverhill, Mass., C. C. Morse & son, 1901. 1, 25 p. 21½ cm. 2-4673.
 F44. H3R8

HAMPTON BEACH; the Atlantic City of New England ... (By Percy Gardner Lamson) (Manchester, N. H., c. 1922) (16) p. illus. 15 cm.
 F44. H31L2

HAMPTON FALLS, History of ... by Hon. Warren Brown. Concord, N. H., The Rumford press, 1900 - 18. 2 v. fronts., illus., plates, ports. 24 cm. 1-2211 rev.
 F44. H32B8

HANCOCK. A copy of inscriptions on the gravestones in the old cemetery, or Pine Ridge cemetery, so called, in Hancock, New Hampshire. (n. p., 1910?) 136 p. illus. (incl. plan) 23 cm. 13-5034.
 F44. H4H2

HANCOCK, The history of, 1764 - 1889. by William Willis Hayward ... Pub. by Orland Eaton, and others ... Lowell, Mass., Vox populi press: S. W. Huse & co., 1889. xvii p., 1070 p. incl. plans, facsims. front., plates, ports., fold. maps. 23 cm. pt. I. History of Hancock. - pt. II. Genealogical register. 1-13337.
 F44. H4H4

HANCOCK. New England flavor; memories of a country boyhood. By Hayden Sanborn Pearson. Illus. Leonard Vosburgh. (1st ed.) New York, W. W. Norton (1961) 249 p. 22 cm. 61-11344.
 F44. H4P4

HANOVER and Lebanon directory ... 1888 -   v. 1 -   Haverhill, N. H., W. E. Shaw (1888 -   v. 24 cm. 24-20944.
 Directories

HANOVER, New Hampshire, directory, The, including Lyme, N. H., 1916 -   v. 1 - (Canaan, N. H.) W. E. Shaw, c. 1916 -   v. 24 cm. 16-3943.
 Directories

HANOVER. A history of Dartmouth college and the town of Hanover, by Frederick Chase. Ed. by John K. Lord ... Cambridge, (Mass.) J. Wilson and son, 1891 - 1913. 2 v. fronts., illus. (incl. facsims.) plates, ports., plans (1 double) 24½ cm. 1-7635 rev.
 F44. H41C4

HANOVER, The records of the town of, 1761 - 1818 ... print. by vote of the town under the direction of Herbert Darling Foster and others. Hanover, 1905. vi, 336 p. 23½ cm. 6-9483.
 F44. H41H2

HANOVER. The gossiping guide to Dartmouth and to Hanover. By Mrs. Mary R. Hatch. (Hanover, N. H., The Dartmouth press, 1905?) 55, (1) p. front., illus., ports., fold. map. 19½ x 16 cm. 5-36840.
 F44. H41H3

HANOVER, A history of the town of, by John King Lord, with an appendix on Hanover roads by Prof.
J. W. Goldthwaite. (Hanover) Print, for the town of Hanover by the Dartmouth press, 1928.
3, 339 p. plates, ports., maps (1 fold.) 25 cm. "Lists of men entering the military service of the U.S. from Hanover, N.H., in the wars of
1861 - 1865 and 1917 - 1918": p. 194 - 217. 29-457.
F44.H41L8

HARRISVILLE. Factory under the elms; a history of Harrisville, 1774 - 1969, by John Borden Armstrong. Cambridge, Mass., Pub. for the Merrimack Valley Textile Museum by the M.I.T. Press
(c. 1969)   xx, 320 p. illus. 24 cm. 70-90748.
F44.H43A8

HAVERHILL, History of, by J.Q. Bittinger. Haverhill, N.H. (Cohos steam press) 1888.
442 p. ports., map. 23 cm. 1-8005.
F44.H45B6

HAVERHILL'S historic highlights. By Harold King Davison. (1963) 143 p. 23 cm.
F44.H45D3

HAVERHILL town affairs one hundred years ago. Woodsville, N.H., News book and job print, 1909.
48 p. 23 ½ cm. "Made up largely from the records of the Haverhill town clerk for the year 1809 ... 17-20818.
F44.H45H45

HAVERHILL. Seventy years ago. Reminiscences of Haverhill Corner, by Arthur Livermore.
Woodsville, N.H., News print, 1902.   52 p. 22 cm. 18-3440.
F44.H45L7

HAVERHILL. Historical sketches of the discovery, settlement, and progress of events in the Coos
country and vicinity, principally included between the years 1754 and 1785. By Rev. Grant Powers ...
Haverhill, N.H., J.F.C. Hayes, 1841.   vi, (9) - 240 p. 18 ½ cm. The Coos, or Cohos, county" was the region centering in
Haverhill, N.H. and Newbury, Vt., covering a considerable portion of the present counties of Grafton, N.H. and Orange, Vt. The appendix contains
two papers relating to early Hollis, N.H. 1-7952.
F44.H45P8

HAVERHILL in the war of the revolution, by William F. Whitcher. (Concord, N.H., 1912)
p. (133) - 140. 25 cm. 39M204T.
F44.H45W47

HAVERHILL. Historical address on the occasion of the one hundred and fiftieth anniversary of the
settlement of the town of Haverhill, ... 1912, by William F. Whitcher. (Haverhill? N.H.) Priv. print.,
1912.   23 p. 23 cm. 18-3687.
F44.H45W5

HAVERHILL, History of the town of, by William F. Whitcher. (Concord, N.H., The Rumford press)
1919.   ix, 781 p. front., plates, ports., fold. plan, facsim. 24 ½ cm. 21-8529.
F44.H45W52

HAVERHILL. Wells River bridge, and other Haverhill toll bridges. By William F. Whitcher.
Woodsville, N.H., News print, 1904.   23 p. 3 pl. 22 cm. 18-6580.
F44.H45W53

HENNIKER. History of the town of Henniker, Merrimack County, from the date of the Canada grant
by the province of Massachusetts, in 1735, to 1880; with a genealogical register of the families of
Henniker. By Leander W. Cogswell. Concord (N.H.) Print, Republican press assoc. 1880.
807, (1) p. front., ports., fold. facsim. 22 ½ cm. 1-8006.
F44. H5C6

HENNIKER, Bradford, Warner and Hopkinton, The town register, 1908. Augusta, Me., The Mitchell-
Cony co., inc., 1908.   212 p. 22 cm. 12-21881.
F44. H5T7

HILL. The story of Hill, by Dan Stiles (pseud.) George Canterbury Haig. Concord, N.H., Sugar
Ball Press, 1942.   72 p. plates, plan. 24 cm. 43-2437 rev.*
F44.H53H3

HILLSBOROUGH, Antrim, and Weare, New Hampshire directory, The ... also of Deering, Francestown, New Boston, Washington and Windsor, N.H., 1922 -   v. 1 -   (Candia, N.H.)
W.E. Shaw, c. 1922 -   v. 23 ½ cm. 22-9583.
Directories

HILLSBOROUGH, The history of, 1735 - 1921, by George Waldo Browne ... Manchester, N.H., John B.
Clarke cp.. print., 1921 - 22.   2 v. fronts., plates, ports., map, fold. plan. 24 cm. Contents. - v.1. History and description. -
v.2. Biography and genealogy. 28-25531.
F44.H55B8

HILLSBORO. Legends of Center folks: their homes and institutions, now and long ago, by Lisabel Gay. (Conford, N.H., The Rumford press) 1928. 2, 78 p. illus. 24½ cm. Descriptive of Hillsboro Center. 29-3154. F44.H55G3

HILLSBOROUGH. The Hillsborough register, 1905, comp. by Mitchell, Daggett and Weston. Brunswick Me., The H.E. Mitchell co., 1905. 98 p. 21½ cm. 12-21882. F44.H55M6

HILLSBOROUGH. Annals of the town of Hillsborough, Hillsborough County, N.H. From its first settlement ot the year 1841. By Charles James Smith. Sandbornton, N.H., Print. for the publisher by J. C. Wilson, 1841. 2, (3) - 72 p. 23½ cm. 7-41870. F44.H55S6

HINSDALE. The town register: Hinsdale, Walpole, Westmoreland, Winchester, Chesterfield, 1909. Augusta, Me., The Mitchell pub. co., 1909. 2, (9) - 111, (2), 150 p. 22 cm. 12-21883.
F44.H57T7

HOLDERNESS; an account of the beginnings of a New Hampshire town, by George Hodges. Boston and New York, Houghton, Mifflin and co., 1907. xvi, 102 p. front., plates, ports., maps, plans, facsim. 20 cm. 7-19786.
F44. H6H5

HOLLIS, seventy years ago. Personal recollections, by Henry Gilman Little. Grinnell, Ia., Ray & MacDonald, print., 1894. x, 11 - 235 p. front., ports. 17½ cm. "A reprint of a series of letters pub. during the years 1891 and 1892 in the Hollis times." - Pref. 1-8007. F44. H7L7

HOLLIS. An address delivered on the centennial celebration, to the people of Hollis, N.H. ... 1830. By Rev. Grant Powers ... Dunstable, N.H., Print, Thayer & Wiggin, 1830. 35 p. 22 cm. 1-8008.
F44. H7P8

HOLLIS. Peter Powers, pioneer; the story of the first settler in Hollis, New Hampshire, by Rudge Nichols and Caroline N. Poole; illus. Sears Gallagher. Print. for the 200th anniversary. (Concord, N.H., The Rumford press, c.1930) 2, (vii) - ix p., 130, (2) p., illus., plates, maps (1 double) facsims. 21 cm. Bibliography: p. (131 - 132) 30-27841. F44. H7P85

HOLLIS. Early history of Hollis, by Hon. Samuel T. Worcester ... (Nashua? N.H., 1874?) 23 p. 24 cm. "... for the N.E. hist. and gen. register for Jan., 1874." CA 31-510 unrev.
F44. H7W89

HOLLIS, History of the town of, from its first settlement to the year 1879. With many biographical sketches of its early settlers, their descendants, and other residents. Illus. with maps and engravings. By Samuel T. Worcester ... Boston, A. Williams & co., 1879. 393, (1) p. plates, ports., 2 maps (incl. front.) 23 cm. Marriages, 1743-1877: p. 343-361; Family registers 1739-1800: p. 362-393. 1-8009. F44. H7W9

HOOKSETT historical sketches 1822 - 1968 (by Charles R. Hardy. Manchester, N.H. Print. L.A. Cummings Co.) 1969. vii, 231 p. illus., map, ports. 24 cm. F44.H77H3

HOPKINTON, Life and times in ... By C.C. Lord. Concord, N.H., Republican press assoc., 1890. x, 583 p. plates, ports., maps (1 fold.) 23½ cm. Contents - pt. I. Descriptive and historical. - pt. 2. Personal and biographical - pt. 3. Statistical and documentary. 1-8010 rev. F44. H8L8

HUDSON, History of, formerly a part of Dunstable, Mass., 1673 - 1733, Nottingham, Mass., 1733 - 1741. District of Nottingham, 1741 - 1746, Nottingham West, 1746 - 1830, Hundson, 1830 - 1912, by Kimball Webster, ed. by George Waldo Browne. Manchester, N.H., Granite state pub. co., 1913. 2, 648 p. front., plates, ports., map. 23 cm. 14-638. F44.H85W3

INTERVALE. Intervale park, Intervale, N.H. Boston, Willard tract repository, 1883. 32 p. illus. (plans) plates. 13½ cm. 1-8834. F44. I6C9

INTERVALE, The ... by Winfield S. Nevins. Salem, Mass., Printed at the Salem press, 1887. 60 p. front., pl., plan. 18½ cm. 1-8835. F44. I6N4

JAFFREY. History of Jaffrey (Middle Monadnock) New Hampshire, an average country town in the

heart of New England, by Albert Annett and Alice E. E. Lehtinen, and others.   (Jaffey, N.H.) Pub. by the town, 1937, '34.   2 v. fronts., illus., plates, ports., fold. map. 23½ cm. Contents. - I. Narrative. - II. Genealogies.
37-4126.
F44.J2 A8

JAFFREY, History of the town of, from the date of Masonian charter to the present time, 1749 - 1880; with a genealogical register of the Jaffrey families, and an appendix containing the proceedings of the centennial celebration in 1873.   By Daniel B. Cutter ... Concord, N.H., Print. the Republican press assoc., 1881.   648 p. front., illus. (plan) plates, ports., fold. map. 23 cm. 1-8011.
F44. J2C9

JAFFREY.   ... Proceedings of the centennial celebration of the 100th anniversary of the incorporation of the town of Jaffrey, N.H. ... 1873 ... Winchendon (Mass.) F.W. Ward & co., 1873.   107 p. 8°.
1-8012 - M1.
F44. J2 J2

JAFFREY, An address del. at the centennial celebration in, ... 1873.   By Joel Parker.   Winchendon (Mass.) F.W. Ward & co., 1873.   1, 48 p. 8°. 1-8013-M1.
F44. J2 P2

JAFFREY.   Copy of that portion of the proprietors' records of Tyng's Township relating to the present town of Jaffrey, Comp and presented to the town of Jaffrey by the city of Manchester in recognition of the gift of the original records to the city by the town.   (Manchester? N.H.) 1896.   14 p. 24½ cm.   "Index to proprietors' records of Tyng's Township, now the city of Manchester": p. (13) - 14. 18-12656.
F44. J2T9

JEFFERSON, History of the town of, 1773 - 1927, by George C. Evans ... Manchester, N.H., Print. Granite state press, 1927.   5, (15) - 320 p. front., plates, ports., map. 19½ cm. 27-21778.
F44. J4E9

KEENE directory, The Keene directory co.   v. front. (fold. map) illus. 24 cm. 13-11334.
Directories

KEENE and vicinity, its points of interest, and its representative business men, embracing Keene, Hinsdale, Winchester, Marlboro, Walpole, Swanzey and Charlestown.   By George Fox Bacon. Newark, N.J., Mercantile pub. co., 1891.   110 p. illus. 4°. 1-8014-M1.
F44. K2B1

KEENE.   "Remember the days of old."   A semi-centennial discourse preached in the First Congregational church, Keene ... 1868, by Rev. Z.S. Barstow ... N.Y., T. Whittaker, 1873.   26, (2) p. 23 cm.
1-8017
F44. K2B3

KEENE's revolutionary soldiers and the house whence they started for Lexington.   Exercises commemorative of April 21, 1775, at Keene, held by Ashuelot chapter, D.A.R. April 21, 1897.   (Keene, Sentinel print. 1897)   20 p. front. 17½ cm. 1-24071 - M1.
F44. K2D3

KEENE, A history of the town of from 1732, when the township was granted by Massachusetts, to 1874, when it became a city.   By S.G. Griffin.   Keene, N.H., Sentinel print. co., 1904.   2, (3) - 792 p. front., illus., plates, ports., fold. maps, plans (partly fold.) 24 cm. 5-6132.
F44. K2G8

KEENE, Annals of the town of, from its first settlement, in 1734, to the year 1790 ... By Salma Hale ... Concord (N.H.) Print. J.B. Moore, 1826.   69 p. 24 cm.   First pub. in the Collections of the N.H. historical society.
1-8015.
F44. K2H18

— with corrections, additions, and a continuation, from 1790 to 1815.   Print. J.W. Prentiss, 1851.
120 p. 2 maps (1 fold.) 23½ cm.   First printed in Colls. of the N.H. hist. soc, 1827. 1-8016.
F44. K2H2

KEENE.   "Upper Ashuelot"; a history of Keene, by Keene History Committee.   (Keene, c.1968)
vi, 728 p. illus. 24 cm.
F44. K2K28

KEENE, Vital statistics of the town of, comp. from the town records, First church and family records, the original Fisher record and the newspapers, by Frank H. Whitcomb, city clerk.   ... Keene, N.H. Sentinel print. co., 1905.   268 p. 23 cm. 5-35777.
F44. K2K3

KEENE.   A sketch of Keene, the gem of the Ashuelot Valley.   Originally pub. in the Granite monthly

164

NEW HAMPSHIRE   47

for Feb., 1895, to which are added reminiscences and sketches of Keene people, originally pub. in the New Hampshire sentinel, over the signature "Ash Swamp." (By) Thomas C. Rand ... (Keene, 1895?) 44 p. front. (port.) 23 cm. 5-37648.   F44. K2R2

KEENE and Roxbury. Historical notes with keyed map of Keene and Roxbury, Cheshire county, from manuscript by Samuel Wadsworth, ed. Robert P. Hayward and others. ... Kenne, N.H. Sentinel print. co., 1932. viii, (78) p. front. (port.) 1 illus., fold. map (in pocket) 23½ cm. 32-29608.   F44. K2W2

KEENE. An historical address, delivered in Keene, on July 4, 1876. ... by William Orne White. Keene, Sentinel print. co., 1876. 34 p. 22 cm. 1-8018.   F44. K2W5

KENSINGTON. Re-told tales; or, Little stories of war times ... and the part Kensington played in them, by Harold F. Blake ... Farmington, Me., The Knowlton & McLeary co., 1917. 93 p. pl., port. 18 cm. 17-4997.   F44. K37B6

KENSINGTON, The history of, 1663 to 1945 (282 years) with a family and homestead register of the pioneer families, early settlers and permanent citizens of the town. By Roland Douglas Sawyer. Farmington, Me., Print. Knowlton & McLeary Co., 1946. 404 p. illus., ports. 24 cm. 48-14060*.
       F44. K37S3

LACONIA, Lakeport amd The Weirs (New Hampshire) directory ... 1895/96 - Springfield, Mass., H.A. Manning co., 1895 - v. fold. maps. 23½ x 24½ cm. 1-17648.   Directories

LACONIA. The illustrated Laconian. History and industries of Laconia, N.H. Comp. by Charles W. Vaughan ... (Laconia, N.H.) L.B. Martin, 1899. 248 p. illus. (incl. ports., maps) 25½ cm. 1-8019 rev.
       L44. L1V3

LAKEPORT. Lakeport's ancient homes: recollections by Major John Aldrich ... of Franconia eighty years ago and of the homes of Lakeport in 1844, with notes of their occupants then and later ... Lakeport, N.H., For the author, 1917. 86 p. front., plates, ports. 20½ cm. "The Aldrich family": p. 76 - 84. Bibliography: p. 85 - 86. 19-3709.   L44. L19A3

LANCASTER sketch book, by Persis F. Chase ... Brattleboro, Vt., F.E. Housh & co., 1887. 2, (7)-114 p. "Most of the ... articles appeared in ... the Lancaster gazette, with the exception of some ... which were published in the Portland transcript." Pref. 1-8021.   F44. L2C4

LANCESTER. The centennial celebration of the settlement of the town of Lancaster, ... 1864. Reported by J.M.W. Yerrinton. Lancaster, E. Savage, (1864) 72 p. 23 cm. 1-8020.   F44. L2L2

LANCASTER. The 150th anniversary of Lancaster, 1764 - 1914; the official report of the celebration held in Aug., 1914; ed. David M. White. (Lancaster) The Committee (1914) 4, 7 - 140, (2) p. front., plates, ports. 24½ cm. 15-84.   F44. L2L23

LANCASTER. History of Lancaster, N.H. Written and ed. by Rev. A.N. Somers. Pub. and issued by order of the town through James W. Weeks, and others. Concord, N.H., The Rumford press, 1899. x, 652 p. front., plates, ports., facsim. 23½ cm. 1-2165.   F44. L2S6

LANGDON.. History and genealogical register of the town of Langdon, Sullivan county, from the date of its severance from Walpole and Charlestown, from 1787 to 1930 ... by Frank Burnside Kingsbury ... Pub. by the author. White River Junction, Vt., Right print. co., 1932. viii, 777 p. incl. front., illus. (incl. ports.) fold. map. 24 cm. 33-8259.   F44. L24K5

LEBANON directory ... Lebanon, N.H., A.B. Freeman, 1882 - 1 v. plates. 22 cm. 13-22566.
       Directories

LEBANON. W.E. Shaw's Lebanon, New Hampshire, directory, 1915/16 - embracing ... the villages of East Lebanon (Mascoma), West Lebanon (Westboro), and farming districts ... v. 1 - (Canaan, N.H.) W.E. Shaw, c.1915 - v. 23½ cm. 16-243.   Directories

48 LOCAL HISTORIES IN THE LIBRARY OF CONGRESS

LEBANON.   July 4th, 1761: an historical discourse in commemoration of the 100th anniversary of the charter of Lebanon, delivered July 4th, 1861, by Rev. D.H. Allen ... Boston, J.E. Farwell & co., 1862.   100 p. 24 cm. 1-8022 rev.   F44. L4A4

LEBANON.   Historical recolllections. A discourse delivered at Lebanon, N.H., on Thanksgiving day, 1830, embracing the leading events in the civil and ecclesiastical history of said town to the close of the Rev. Isaiah Potter's ministry.   By Phinehas Cooke.   Concord (N.H.) A. M'Farland, 1831.   17 p. 8°. 1-8023.   F44. L4 C7

LEBANON, History of, 1761 - 1887, by Rev. Charles A. Downs.   Illus. Concord, Rumford print. co., 1908.   xiii, 459 p. front., plates, ports., fold. plan. 24 cm. 9-30353.   F44. L4D6

LEBANON.   Three ancient cemeteries in New Hampshire, near junction boundary lines of Lebanon, Plainfield and Grantham.   By Thomas Hills ... Boston, D. Clapp, 1910.   64 p. 25 cm. 11-1064.   F44. L4H6

LEBANON.   Program for the dedication of the Lebanon town hall, Oct.29, 1924.   (Lebanon? 1924?)   (8) p. 23 cm. CA 32-229 unrev.   F44. L4L35

LEBANON Historical Society.   Report. 1st -   1959 -   (Lebanon, N.H.)   v. illus. 28 cm. annual.   F44. L4L46

LEBANON.   The Lebanonian. v. 1 -   Dec. 1897 -   Lebanon, N.H., H.E. Waite & co., 1897 -   v. in illus. 31 cm. monthly. CA 15-303 unrev.   F44. L4L5

LEBANON.   Historical sketches of early Lebanon.   Comp. by Ethel Rock Millen for the Lebanon Historical Soc.   1st ed. Canaan, N.H. Reporter Press, 1965.   194 p. 24 cm.   F44. L4M5

LEBANON.   A sermon, delivered at the interment of Col. Thomas Waterman, who died suddenly, at Lebanon, ... 1838 ... By Rev. Phinehas Cooke ... (Lebanon? N.H.) T. Mann, print. (1838)   (3) - 14 p. 20 cm. 17-10774.   F44. L4W3

LEBANON.   Marking the spots; addresses delivered in commemoration of marking the spots connected with the early religious life of Lebanon. (Lebanon, N.H., Free press office, 1908)   75 p. incl. 2 pl. 22½ cm. 10-3116.   F44. L45M3

LEE.   Old home week, Lee, Aug. 23, 1916.   250th anniversary of settlement of the territory; 150th anniversary of incorporation of the town.   Address by John Scales ... (Dover, N.H., C.F. Whitehouse, print., 1916)   50 p. 23 cm. 17-3609.   F44. L47S2

LISBON's 10 score years, 1763 - 1963, by Hazel Ash Pickwick, assisted by Mable S. Jesseman. Lisbon, N.H. (1963)   ix, 95 p. 23 cm.   F44. L5P5

LITTLETON directory, The ... (1st) c.1903.   Directories

LITTLETON.   Woodland and meadow; out of door papers written on a New Hampshire farm, by W.I. Lincoln Adams ... Illus. with photos. by the author and others.   New York, The Baker and Taylor co., 1901.   122, (1) p. incl. front., illus. 26 cm. Life at Hilltop farm, Littleton. 1-25514.   F44. L7A2

LITTLETON.   The relations of the town and the state.   An historical address delivered at the centennial celebration of the incorporation of Littleton, July 4, 1884 ... with an appendix.   By Albert Stillman Batchellor.   Concord, N.H., Patriot steam job print. (1886?)   27, (5) p. 8°. 1-13338 - M1.   F44. L7B3

LITTLETON.   Third appendix to address on Relations of the town and the state, by A.S. Batchellor.   Additions and corrections, Dec. 1888.   Concord, N.H., Print. Republican press assoc., 1888.   4 p. 21 cm. 1-13339.   F44. L7B4

LITTLETON, Picturesque and progressive Littleton and the White Mountains ... St. Johnsbury, Vt.,

NEW HAMPSHIRE

C. T. Ranlet, 1898.   74 p. illus. obl. 8°. 1-8024-M1.   F44. L7C6

LITTLETON, History of ... by James Robert Jackson ... Cambridge, Mass., Pub. for the town by the University press, 1905.   3 v. fronts., plates (1 col.) ports., maps (partly fold.) plan, facsim. 24 cm. Contents. - v.1. Annals. - v.2. Topical history. - v.3. Genealogy comp. by George C. Fisher. 5-17617.
F44. L7J2

LITTLETON. Chiswick, 1764. Apthorp, 1770. Littleton, 1784. Exercises at the centennial celebration of the incorporation of the town of Littleton, 1884. Pub. by the town. Concord, N.H., N.H. Democratic press co., 1887.   328 p. incl. map. 23½ cm. 1-8025.
F44. L7L7

LITTLETON, ... An historical sketch of. Its rise and development. The men who made and are making its history ... Comp. by J.H. Walbridge. Littleton, N.H., Cooper & Sparrow, 1897.
(48) p. illus. 30 x 23 cm. (Supplement to the White Mountains republic journal, v.31 no. 16, Dec.1897) 1-8026 rev.
F44. L7W1

LONDONDERRY. Some Presbyterian U.E. loyalists. By D.W. Clendennan.   (From Ontario historical soc. Papers and records. Toronto, 1901. v. 3, p. 117-122) Mainly an account of the settlement and revolutionary history of Londonderry, with mention of some loyalists of Londonderry. 14-4713.
F44. L8C6
F1056. O58 vol. 3

LONDONDERRY. Col. John Goffe. A sketch by his great grandson, Gordon Woodbury, esq., read before the Manchester historic assoc. ... 1899.   (In Manchester historic assoc. Collections, v. 1. p. 233 - 272)
3-9536.
F44. M2M3

LONDONDERRY, Vital records of; a full and accurate transcript of the births, marriage intentions, marriages and deaths in this town from the earliest date to 1910. Comp. from the town books, church records, graveyard inscriptions and other sources, by Daniel Gage Annis. Manchester, N.H., The Granite state pub. co., 1914.   1, (7) - 320, (8) p. front. (port.) 24 cm. 15-2824.
F44. L8L8

LONDONDERRY. The Londonderry celebration. Exercises on the 150th anniversary of the settlement of old Nutfield, comprising the towns of Londonderry, Derry, Windham, and parts of Manchester, Hudson and Salem, N.H. ... 1869. Comp. by Robert C. Mack. Manchester, J.B. Clarke, 1870.
124 p. incl. illus., facsims. front., ports. 22½ cm. 1-8027.
F44. L8M2

— Another copy.   124 p. incl. illus. facsims. front., ports. 24½ cm. Only 60 printed. 38-31173.
F44. L8M22
Rare Book Room

LONDONDERRY. Houses of the Double Range and East Derry, N.H.; an informal story. By Harriet Chase Newell. (Littleton? N.H.) 1954.   145 p. illus. 23 cm. 55-27377.
F44. L8N4

LONDONDERRY. A century sermon, delivered in the East parish meeting house, Londonderry ... 1819 ... Containing a sketch of the history of the town from its earliest settlement. By Edward L. Parker ... Print. George Hough, Concord, 1819.   44 p. 25½ cm. 7-29682.
F44. L8P18

LONDONDERRY. The history of Londonderry, comprising the towns of Derry and Londonderry, N.H., by Rev. Edward L. Parker ... With a memoir of the author. Boston, Perkins and Whipple, 1851.
1v, 358 p. front., plates, ports., fold. map. 19 cm. Genealogical history: p. 254 - 312. The eastern portion of the original town was set off in 1828 and incorporated as Derry. 1-8028.
F44. L8P2

LONDONDERRY. Centennial discourse. Historical of the town of Londonderry, and its Presbyterian church and society. ... Exeter, News-letter press, 1876.   29 p. 8°. 1-8029-M1.
F44. L8P4

LONDONDERRY. Willey's book of Nutfield; a history of that part of New Hampshire comprised within the limits of the old township of Londonderry, from its settlement in 1719 to the present time ... ed. George F. Willey. Derry Depot, N.H., G.F. Willey, 1895.   367 p. incl. front., illus., ports., fold. map. 30½ x 24½ cm. Lists of names and dates from Shipley graveyard in the present town of Londonderry: p. 331 - 350. 1-8030 rev.
F44. L8W7

LYMAN, Historical sketches of, by E.B. Hoskins. Lisbon, N.H., C.P. Hibbard, 1903.   3, (9) - 149 p. 18 port. (incl. front.) 18 cm. Contents. - Historical sketches. - Biographical sketches. - Miscellaneous sketches. 4-4886.
F44. L88H8

LYNDEBOROUGH.   Historical address given at the 150th anniversary of the settlement of the town of Lyndeborough, ... 1889.   By Rev. Frank G. Clark ... Concord, N.H., Republican press assoc., 1891. 68 p. 21½ cm. 1-8031.
F44. L9C6

LYNDEBOROUGH, The history of the town of, 1735 - 1905, by Rev. D. Donovan and Jacob A. Woodward. Pub. by the town ... (Tufts College, Mass.) Tufts college press, H.W. Whittemore & co,, 1906. xvi, 932 p. incl. front. 18 pl., 45 port. on 43 pl., fold. plan. 23½ cm. p. 647-904, Genealogies. 6-34964.
F44. L9D6

MADISON.   Carroll County graveyards: Madison,, formerly part of Eaton, New Hampshire. (Compiled by Alvah and Mary Carver.   Conway, N.H.) 1961.   11 l. 28 cm.
F44. M14C3

MANCHESTER.   City of Manchester and the Amoskeag manufacturing co.   Issued under the auspices of the Manchester Chamber of commerce ... (Manchester, N.H., Print. office of Amoskeag manufacturing ci.) c. 1912.   (94) p. illus. 15½ x 20 cm. 12-23481.
HC108. M2A4

MANCHESTER, Directory for the city of, by James O. Adams.   Sept., 1846.   Manchester, N.H. Print. the American office, 1846.   148 p. 14½ cm. 7-39285.
Directories

MANCHESTER directory, The ... 1846, 1852 - 1860, 1864 - 1866, 1869, 1871 -   v. 1 - Boston, Mass,, Sampson & Murdock co. etc. etc. 1846 - 19 -   v. fronts. (fold. maps) 14½ x 24 cm. 98-1241 rev.
Directories

MANCHESTER almanac, city directory, and business index, for 1879 -   Comp and pub. by John B. Clarke.   Manchester, N.H., Mirror steam print. works, 1879 -   1 v. front. (fold. plan) 23 cm. 7-38080.
Directories

MANCHESTER.   ... Anthony's standard business directory and reference book of Manchester and Concord . . . (Manchester? N.H., Anthony pub. co.) c. 1895.   96 p. illus. (plans) 23½ cm. 7-39288.
Directories

MANCHESTER.   Pocket business directory.   no. 3.   1879.   1 v.
Directories
1879

MANCHESTER, and its leading business men, embracing also, those of Goffstown ... Boston, Mercantile pub. co., 1891.   126 p. illus. 4°. 1-7636-M1.
F44. M2B1

MANCHESTER on the Merrimack, the story of a city.   Illus. by John O'Hara Cosgrave II.   Manchester, N.H., L.A. Cummings Co. (1948)   353 p. illus. 22 cm. 48-9797*.
F44. M2B58

MANCHESTER.   Derryfield (now Manchester, N.H.) in the revolution, by George Waldo Browne. Manchester, N.H. 1902.   1, 8 p. 23½ cm. 5-3927.
F44. M2B8

MANCHESTER.   The town church of Manchester, by Thomas Chalmers ... Manchester, The Jubilee committee, 1903.   155 p. front., plates, ports. 20 cm. 4-14203.
F44. M2C4

MANCHESTER.   A brief record of its past and a picture of its present, incl. an account of its settlement and of its growth as town and city ... and sketches of its representative citizens.   By Maurice D. Clarke.   Manchester, N.H., J.B. Clarke, 1875.   463 p. plates, ports., plans. 22½ cm. 1-8032.
F44. M2C5

MANCHESTER.   Daily mirror and American.   Souvenir ed.   Manchester, N.H., Oct. 11, 1892 ... (Manchester, N.H., 1892)   64 p. illus. (partly col.) 46 cm. 8-15797.
F44. M2D13

MANCHESTER.   The Mirror's pictorial Manchester, 1846 - 1896.   (Manchester, The John B. Clarke co., 1896)   200 p. of illus. 23½ x 32 cm. 18-19023.
F44. M2D14

MANCHESTER men.   Soldiers and sailors in the civil war, 1861 - '66.   By George C. Gilmore. Concord, N.H., The Rumford press, 1898.   167 p. incl. pl. front. (port.) 25 cm. The even numbered pages after p. 20 are blank. 1-24511 Additions.
F44. M2G4

NEW HAMPSHIRE 51

MANCHESTER. L'état-civil franco-américain. Philip Henry La Ronde, ed. Manchester, N.H., De Henris Associates, c.1951 - 52. 2 v. 28 cm. 52-17792 rev. Contents. - (1) Le recueil des mariages de la paroisse Saint Antoine, 1900 - 1950. - 2. Le receuil des mariages de la paroisse Saint Jean-Baptiste, 1914 - 1951.
F44. M2L3

MANCHESTER. Ceremonies at the dedication of the monument erected by the city of Manchester, to the men who periled their lives to save the Union in the late civil war, Sept. 11, 1879 ... Manchester, N.H. Mirror print., 1880. 126 p. front., 4 pl. 26½ cm. 3-4953.
F44. M2M18

MANCHESTER. Semi-centennial of the city of Manchester, Sept. 6,7,8,9, 1896. Comp. Herbert W. Eastman ... Manchester, N.H., Print. John B. Clarke co., 1897. 204 p. incl. front., illus. (incl. ports.) 25½ cm. 1-8035.
F44. M2M2

MANCHESTER, Brief historical sketch ... Comp. and issued by the Manchester Board of trade ... (Manchester, N.H., Mirror press) 1890. 83 p. 16 cm. Cover-title" Statistics of the "Queen city" of New Hampshire. 4-27952.
F44. M2M23

MANCHESTER, Centennial celebration of, June 13, 1810 - 1910, by the Manchester historic association ... Manchester, N.H., Pub. by the authority of the city government, 1910. 44 p. front., plates, ports. 24½ cm. 18-22493.
F44. M2M24

MANCHESTER historic association, ... Collections ... Manchester, N.H. Printed by the J.B. Clarke co., 1897 - v. fronts., illus., plates, ports., fold. map. 23½ cm. Imprint varies. 12-36743.
F44. M2M3

MANCHESTER. The Historic quarterly. Manchester historic association. Collections, v. 2-3; 1900/01 - 1902/03. Manchester, N.H., Manchester historic assoc, 1901 - 03. 2 v. illus., plates, ports. 23½ cm. (Manchester historic assoc. Collections. v.2, pt. 1; v.3) The first vol. of "The Historic quarterly" is numbered on covers "vol. 2" apparently taking its volume no. from the society's "Collections" in which it appears. No more pub. 25-5894.
F44. M2M3

MASSABESIC. The story of Lake Massabesic. By Francis B. Eaton. (In Manchester historic association. Collections. Manchester, 1903. v.3, p. 121-138) 11-13689.
F44. M2M3
— Copy 2, detached.
F42. M4E1

MANCHESTER as a village. By William E. Moore. (In Manchester historic assoc. Collections. v.3, p. 211-214) 14-4714.
F44. M2M3 vol. 3
— Copy 2, detached.
F44. M2M85

MANCHESTER historic association. Early record of Londonderry, Windham, and Derry ... Ed. with introd., notes, and index, by George Waldo Browne ... Manchester, N.H., Pub. with appropriations made by Londonerry, Derry and Windham, under the auspices of the Manchester historic assoc, 1908 - v. fronts. (ports.) illus., pl. 23½ cm. (Manchester historic assoc. Collections, vol. v -   Contents. - I. Political proceedings, 1719 - 1762. - II. Homestead boundaries, 1719 - 1745. - III Vital records of Londonderry, 1710 - 1910. 9-27140.
F44. M2M3 vol. 5-7

MANCHESTER. Early records of the town of Manchester, formerly Derryfield, N.H., 1751 -   ; a complete and exact transcript of the records of the clerks ... Ed. George Waldo Browne ... Manchester ... 1905 - v. illus., plates, ports., fold. map. 24½ cm. (Manchester historic assoc. Collections. vol.s viii - 6-38092 rev.
F44. M2M3

MANCHESTER union, The. 75th anniversary number, Manchester, N.H., 1938. 1 v. illud. 58 cm. v. 75 no. 312 of the Manchester union, Mar. 29, 1938. 39M4845T.
F44. M2M37

MANCHESTER. Contributions to the history of Derryfield, ... By William E. Moore ... (Manchester, N.H.) The author (c.1896-97) 5 pt. in 1 vol. 23 cm. Paged continuously. Contents. - I. Topography and landscape ... II. Some special local features ... III. The local flora and fauna. - IV. Indians and early settlements. - v. Occupation and settlements. 1-8036.
F44. M2M8

MANCHESTER, yesterday and today (described pictorially) Art work by John Noga. New England Advertising Associates, inc. Manchester, N.H. (1946) 1 v. (unpaged) illus. 29 cm. 48-12165*.
F44. M2N4

169

MANCHESTER. The Manchester of America, the great industrial metropolis of New Hampshire, richly endowed by nature as a manufacturing and distributing center ... (New York) The New York industrial recorder, 1900.   28 p. illus. (incl. ports.) 41½ cm. 10-23244.   F44. M2N5

MANCHESTER up to date; story of the city, 1846 - 1896, by David Lane Perkins. Stories, anecdotes, and biographical sketches of prominent Manchester men ... Manchester, N.H., G. F. Willey, 1896. 2, (11) - 82, (2) p. illus., ports. 30½ cm. 18-13988.   F44. M2P4

MANCHESTER. Pocket business directory and industrial and social statistics of the city of Manchester, N.H., 1879. Manchester, Temple & Farrington, 1879.   31 p. front., illus., pl. 24°. 1-8037-M1.
F44. M2P7

— 1884. No. 4. Manchester, 1884.   14½ cm.   F44. M2P75

MANCHESTER. The history of Manchester, formerly Derryfield, in New-Hampshire; including that of ancient Amoskeag, or the middle Merrimack Valley; tog. with the address, poem, etc. ... of the centennial celebration, of the incorporation of Derryfield ... By C. E. Potter ... Manchester, C. E. Potter, 1856.   xiii, 67, 763 p. front., plates, ports., plan, facsims. (1 fold.) 23 cm. 1-8038.   F44. M2P8

MANCHESTER, Souvenir of. Photo-gravures. Brooklyn, N.Y., The Albertype co., 1900. 1 p. 16 pl. obl. 24°. Nov. 1, 1900-09.   F44. M2S7

MANCHESTER. Le guide canadien-français de Manchester, pour 1894 - 95, contenant un almanach complet des adresses, le mouvement de la population canadienne dpuis 23 ans, un aperçu historique de la ville de Manchester, des paroisses et des sociétés canadiennes ... Manchester, N.H., La Cie John B. Clarke, 1894.   300 p. plates, ports. 23 cm. 7-39287.   F44. M2T2

MANCHESTER of yesterday; a human interest story of its past, with 100 illus. Manchester, N.H., Granite state press (c. 1939)   xxv, 561 p. incl. front., illus. 23½ cm. 39-30890.   F44. M2T56

MANCHESTER. Proprietors' records of Tyng Township, 1735 - 1741, with notes and sketches by George Waldo Browne. Manchester (N.H.) Manchester historic assoc., 1901.   iv, (2), 88 p. front., illus. 22½ cm. Also pub. in the Collections of the Manchester historic assoc. v.2. 3-24757.   F44. M2T9

MANCHESTER. Willey's semi-centennial book of Manchester, 1846 - 1896, and Manchester ed. of the Book of Nutfield. Historic sketches of that part of New Hampshire comprised within the limits of the old Tyng Township, Nutfield, Harrytown, Derryfield, and Manchester ... By George Franklin (!) Willey. Biographical, genealogical, political, anecdotal; illus. with 500 engravings. Manchester, N.H., G. F. Willey, 1896.   1, 361 p. incl. illus., plates, ports. front., plates. 31 x 25 cm. 18-13987.   F44. M2W7

MARLBOROUGH. History of Marlborough, Cheshire County. With the report of its centennial celebration in 1876; also embracing genealogies and sketches of families from 1764 to 1880. By Charles A. Bemis. Boston, Press of G. H. Ellis, 1881.   ix, 726 p. front., plates, ports. 24 cm. 1-8039 rev.
F44. M3B4

MARLBORO. The town register: Marlboro, Troy, Jaffrey, Swanzey, 1908. Augusta, Me., The Mitchell-Cony co., inc., 1908.   2, (9) - 96, 120 p. fold. map. 22 cm. 12-21884.
F44. M3T7

MASON. The substance of two lectures, on the history of Mason, delivered before the Lyceum in Mason village ... By Ebenezer Hill ... Fitchburg (Mass.) W. J. Merriam, 1846.   16 p. 4°. 1-8033-M1.
F44. M4H5

MASON. Memoir of the Rev. Ebenezer Hill, pastor of the Congregational church, ... 1790 - 1854. By John B. Hill. Boston, L. A. Elliot & co.; Bangor, D. Bugbee & co., 1858.   113, (1) p. front. (port.) illus., facsim. 24½ cm. (With his History of the town of Mason, N.H. ... Boston, 1858) 1-8041.   F44. M4H6

MASON, History of the town of, from the first grant in 1749, to the year 1858. By John B. Hill. Boston and Bangor, 1858.   iv, (5) - 324 p. illus., fold. pl., ports. 24½ cm. "Record of marriages, deaths, and family registers": p. (161) - 212d. "Biographical sketches of natives and citizens of Mason": p. (266) - 312. Bound with previous book. 1-8040.   F44. M4H6

NEW HAMPSHIRE

MASON. Proceedings of the centennial celebration of the 100th anniversary of the incorporation of the town of Mason, N.H., ... 1868. Prepared ... by J.B. Hill. Boston, Elliott, Thomes & Talbot, 1870.
115 p. front., port. 8° 1-8034-M1.
F44.M4 H7

MASON. In commemoration of the two hundredth anniversary of the incorporation of the town of Mason, 1768 - 1968. Mason, N.H., 1968. 205 p. illus.
F44.M4M37

MEREDITH. Old Meredith and vicinity, Laconia, N.H., Mary Butler chapter D.A.R. (c.1926)
vii, 114 p. incl. front., illus. fold. plan. 24½ cm. 26-12264.
F44. M5D3

MEREDITH, annals and genealogies, arranged by Mary E. Neal Hanaford. (Concord, N.H., The Rumford press) 1932. 5, (3) - 760 p. 24 cm. 33-18727.
F44. M5H3

MEREDITH. The town register: Meredith, Tilton, Gilmanton, Sanbornton, Gilford, Belmont, New Hampton, 1908. Augusta, Me., The Mitchell-Cony co., inc., 1908. 3, (9) - 87, 165 p. 23 cm. 12-19907.
F44. M5T7

MERIDEN. Book of words; the pageant of Meriden, ... in celebration of the 100th anniversary of the founding of Kimball union academy. (By) William Chauncy Langdon ... (Hanover, N.H., The Dartmouth press, c.1913) 64 p. 23 cm. 13-16161.
F44. M56L2

— Second edition, July, 1913. 64 p. 23 cm. 29-18810.
F44. M56L22

MERRIMACK. Address delivered on occasion of centennial celebration of the town of Merrimack ... 1846. By Rev. Stephen T. Allen. Re-printed ... 1899. Nashua, N.H., American folding box co., printers, 1901. 60 p. 21½ cm. The appendix, p. (40) - 60, includes an account of the celebration, sketch of the town, biographical and genealogical notes. 24-11496.
F44. M58A4

MILFORD. Directory for Milford, Mont Vernon, Amherst, Lyndeboro, Wilton and Merrimack, New Hampshire. Salem, Mass., New England Directory Co. v. 24 cm. Title varies. 7-6713 rev.
Directories

MILFORD, our home town; a history of Milford for young people (by Alberta T. Hagar and Edith F. Hunter. Milford? N.H. c.1963) 61 p. illus., group port., maps. facsim. 27 cm.
F44. M6H3

MILFORD. Soldiers' memorial light and fountain ... Historical sketch of the rocks around the fountain. Arranged by Mrs. Oliver W. Lull. Milford, N.H., Cabinet book print., 1900. 58 p. front., plates, ports. 21½ cm. 16-20784.
F44. M6L95

MILFORD. Celebration of the 100th anniversary of the incorporation of Milford, ... 1894 ... Milford, Cabinet print, 1894. 89 p. front., illus., plates, ports. 24 cm. 18-2208.
F44. M6M6

MILFORD in the great war. Memorial book ... (1922) 1 v.
F44. M6M63

MILFORD, the granite town of New Hampshire. Milford Civic Club. (Milford, 1940) 32 p. illus., map. 20 cm. 49-3777*.
F44. M6M65

MILFORD, The history of, by George A. Ramsdell. Family registers by William P. Colburn. Pub. by the town. Concord, N.H., The Rumford press, 1901. xv, 1023 p. front., pl., port., fold. maps, plan. 23½ cm. 2-18430.
F44. M6R2

MILTON, Milton Mills, Wakefield, Sanbornville, Union, New Hampshire, and Lebanon, Maine, directory. (Candia, N.H.) W.E. Shaw, c. 19 - v. 23½ cm. CA 34-105 unrev.
Directories

MONROE, The history of, 1761 - 1954. By Frances Ann Johnson. (Littleton, N.H.) 1955.
638 p. 24 cm.
F44. M8J6

MONT VERNON, History of the town of. By Charles James Smith. Boston, Blanchard print. co., 1907.
viii, 245, 197 p. front., plates, ports. 24 cm. Pt.2: Genealogy. 9-16811.
F44. M9S6

MOULTONBOROUGH. Red Hill wanderings. By Thomas Francis Sheridan. (Chicago, Claflin-Hill print. co., 1912) 15 p. 16½ cm. Redhill is located in the town of Moultonborough. F44.M93S5

NASHUA. Gill's Nashua and Nashville directory. By James A. Dupee. 1843. Nashville (N.H.) C.T. Gill, 18 v. front., plates. 16½ cm. 16-4788. Directories

— for the year 1850. By Kimball & Dodge. Nashua, Printed by the publishers, 1850. 118 p. 15 cm. 9-30715. Directories

— for the year 1856. Nashua, L. Waterman, 1856. 1, 11 - 175 p. illus. 15 cm. 9-30709. Directories

— for the year 1866. Nashua, N.P. Greene, 1866. 122 p. 19½ cm. 9-30716. Directories

NASHUA. W.A. Greenough co's ... Nashua directory incl. Hudson, N.H. ... no. 1 - 1864/5 - 1874/5, 1877/8 - 1883/4, 1885, 1887/8, 1889 Boston, Mass., W.A. Greenough co. 1864 - 19 v. fold. maps. 19½ - 25½ cm. 1-31208 (rev. '32) Directories

NASHUA. Bagley's Nashua, N.H. pocket manual & business directory, of the inhabitants, institutions, business firms, etc ... 1887 - 88. Nashua, N.H., G.E. Bagley & co., c.1887. (165) p. 15½ cm. "First edition." 9-30708. F44.N2A18

NASHUA. Abstract history of the Church of Christ in Dunstable, (now the First Congregational church of Nashua,) ... address of Rev. Cyrus Richardson ... (Nashua, N.H.) Print. E.H. Spalding (1885?) 13 p. 21½ cm. "Twelve copies only printed." Printed on one side of leaf only. 16-20794. F44.N2A19
Rare Book Room

NASHUA. Leading business men of Nashua and vicinity, embracing Milford, Wilton, Greenville, Derry and Derry Depot, also East Pepperell. By Geo. F. Bacon ... Boston, Mercantile pub. co., 1890. 117 p. illus., ports. 17 cm. In double columns. 3-18901. F44.N2B12

NASHUA. Murder of Caroline H. Cutter by the Baptist ministers and Baptist churches. By Calvin Cutter. 22 p. 12°. 1-28312-M2. F44.N2C8

NASHUA. Certain grants of land made in the year 1684, now within the limits of Nashua, N.H. By Samuel Abbott Green. (Cambridge, Mass., 1894?) 5 p. 24½ cm. Reprinted from the Proceedings of the Massachusetts historical society, Nov. 8, 1894. 6-5822. F44.N2G7

NASUA. An account of the Soldiers' and sailors' monument, erected by the people of the city of Nashua, N.H. in the year 1889 ... Nashua, N.H., J.H. Barker, print., 1889. 124 p. front. 23½ cm. Comp. by F.G. Noyes. 4-11986. F44.N2N22

NASHUA. The official report of the smi-centennial celebration ... June, 1903. Comp. and pub. by the Telegraph pub. co. (1903) 215 p. incl. illus., plates. front. 17 x 25½ cm. 3-28994. F44.N2N25

NASHUA conflagration, The, 1930 ... Boston, National fire protection assoc. (1930) 19 p. illus. (incl. map) 23 cm. CA 30 - 1375 unrev. F44.N2N32

NASHUA. History of the city of Nashua, from the earliest settlement of old Dunstable to the year 1895; with biographical sketches of early settlers, their descendants and other residents. Judge Edward E. Parker, editor-in-chief. Nashua, N.H., Telegraph pub. co., 1897. 3, v - xii, 622 p. incl. front. (facsim.) illus., ports. 31 x 23½ cm. 1-8042 additions. F44.N2P2

NASHUA. An account of some of the early settlers of West Dunstable, Monson and Hollis, N.H. by Charles S. Spaulding. Nashua, N.H., The Telegraph press, 1915. 3, 3 - 251 p. 22 cm. 16-14744. F44.N2S73

NELSON. Celebration by the town of Nelson, (originally called "Monadnock no. 6" and incorporated as "Packersfield") of the 150th anniversary of its first settlement, 1767 - 1917 ... to which is added the names and records of the pioneer settlers of Packersfield, ... (New York, The Evening post job print., 1917) 2, 5 - 192 p. 3 pl. 24 cm. Bound with the next item. 19-6720. F44. N4N4

NELSON. Names and services of those, born or sometime resident in Nelson, who, as volunteers, answered the call to arms for the preservation of the Union ... 1861 - 1865. (New York, The Evening post job print., 1915?) 90 p. 2 pl. 24 cm. Bound with previous item. 19-6719.
F44. N4N4

NELSON, A history of, 1767 - 1967. Keene, N.H., Sentinel Print. Co. (1968) 298, (48) p. illus. 24 cm. "Homestead and cemetery directory, Nelson. Nelson bicentennial, 1767 - 1967" (48) p. at end.
F44. N4S79

NELSON. Homestead and cemetery directory, Nelson; Nelson Bicentennial, 1767 - 1967. (1st ed. Nelson? N.H. 1967) (48) p. (map in pocket) 21 cm. Ed. and pub. by Parke H. Struthers.
F44. N4S8

NEW BOSTON. Address delivered at the centennial celebration ... 1863, by Clark B. Cochrane. Albany, N.Y., J. Munsell, print., 1863. 41 p. 24 cm. 26-17551.
F44. N5 C5

NEW BOSTON, History of. Comp. and written by Elliott C. Cogswell ... Boston, G.S. Rand & Avery, 1864. 469 p. front., plates, ports., fold. map. 24 cm. "Biographical and genealogical sketches": p. (349) - 453. 1-8043.
F44. N5 C6

NEW DURHAM, The history of; from the first settlement to the present time, including that part of Alton which was formerly New Durham Gore. By Ellen Cloutman Jennings. New Durham, 1962. 94 p. 23 cm.
F44. N52J4

NEWBURY. Manual of Mount Sunapee, ed. by Philip W. Ayres ... Pub. for the Sunapee branch of the Soc. for the protection of N.H. forests. (New York, The Knickerbocker press, c.1915) viii, 40 p. front., plates, maps (1 fold.) 19 cm. 15-14930.
F44. N53A9

NEWCASTLE, historic and picturesque, by John Albee. Illus. by Abbott F. Graves. Bostob (Press of Rand Avery supply co,) 1884. viii, 155 p. illus. plates (1 fold.) port. 19½ cm. 1-8044.
F44. N6A3

NEWCASTLE discourse, delivered at Newcastle ... 1849, by Lucius Alden ... Portsmouth, Print. C.W. Brewster, 1849. 23 p. 22 cm. 18-2267.
F44. N6A35

NEWCASTLE. Bicentennial souvenir, 1693 - 1893: New Castle, comp. by Chester B. Curtis. (Concord, N.H., Republican press assoc., 1893) 51 p. illus. 23 cm. Part of the extracts are taken from "New Castle, historic and picturesque," by John Albee. 1-8045 rev.
F44. N6C9

NEWCASTLE. Portsmouth and Newcastle ... cemetery inscriptions. By A.H. Locke ... 1907 1912. 1 v.
F44. N6L8

NEWFIELDS, History of, 1638 - 1911, by Rev. James Hill Fitts, ed. and arranged by Rev. N.F. Carter. Concord, N.H. (The Rumford press) 1912. viii, 785 p. front., plates, ports., maps (1 fold.) facsim. 24 cm. 12-10315.
F44. N63F5

NEW HAMPTON, Reminiscences of; also a genealogical sketch of the Kelley and Simpson families, and an autobiography by Frank H. Kelley ... Worcester, Mass., Printed by C. Hamilton, 1889. 2, ix, (11) - 147 p. front., pl., port. 28 cm. 3-13313 Additions.
F44. N66K3

NEW IPSWICH. Border adventures: or, The romantic incidents of a New-England town; and other poems. By Eugene Batchelder ... Boston, Ticknor, Reed & Fields, 1851. 48 p. 18½ cm. 8-11865.
F44. N7B3

NEW IPSWICH, The history of, 1735 - 1914, with genealogical records of the principal families; comp. and written by Charles Henry Chandler ... Fitchburg, Mass., Sentinel print., 1914. xiv, 782 p. incl. illus., plan. front. (port.) plates, map. 24 cm. 15-8992.
F44. N7C45

NEW IPSWICH, The history of, from its first grant in 1736, to the present time: with genealogical notices of the principal families, and also the proceedings of the centennial celebration. Boston, Gould and Lincoln, 1852. 2, viii, (9) - 488, iv. p. front., illus., pl., ports., fold. map, plan. 25 cm. 1-8047. F44. N7K4

NEW IPSWICH. Celebration proceedings of the 150th anniversary of New Ipswich ... 1900 ... Comp. by Frederic William Jones ... New Ipswich, N.H., The Celebration committee, 1900.   91 p. 22 cm. 1-23433.
    F44. N7N7

NEW IPSWICH in the war of the rebellion; what its men and women did, by Mrs. L.A. Obear ... Worcester, Mass., L.P. Goddard (1898)   71 p. 19 cm. 16-7874 rev.
    F44.N7O12

NEW LONDON. A history of the town of New London, Merrimack County, 1779 - 1899 ... Concord, N.H., The Rumford press, 1899.   x, 774 p. 27 pl. 85 port. (incl. front.) 3 maps, plan, facsim. 24 cm. 3-21678.
    F44. N72L8

NEW LONDON. Mirror to America; a history of New London, 1900 - 1950. Appendices compiled in part by Helen Kidder Greenaway, Mildred Crockett Tunis and others.   Concord, N.H. Evans Print., 1952.   xxiv, 549 p. illus., ports., maps. 22 cm. 52-3772.
    F44.N72S68

NEWMARKET. Old Newmarket; historical sketches, by Nellie Palmer George.   Exeter, N.H., The News-letter press, 1932.   133 p. 23 cm. 35-14609.
    F44.N75G3

NEWPORT. Lothrop's Newport, New Hampshire, directory, 1896/97 - 19 -   Boston, Union Pub. co. (inc.) c. 1896 - 19   v. 24 cm. 1-23064 rev. 2.   With this directory for 18 - is bound Claremont directory.   Directories

NEWPORT. The book of old Newport; old drawings and photographs of Newport; comp. by Marcia J. and Samuel H. Edes ... Newport, Argus and Spectator, c. 1909.   (53) p. illus. 23 x 31 cm. 10-1443.
    F44.N76E2

NEWPORT, Tales from the history of. By Samuel Harcourt Edes.   (Newport, N.H., The Argus-Champion, 1963)   113 p. 22 cm.
    F44.N76E24

NEWPORT business directory and advertiser.   Newport (N.H.) The business men, 1870.   82 p. 17 cm. "A sketch of the early history of Newport": p. (17) - 25. "Sketches of churches": p. (63) - 76. 19-1146.   Directories

NEWPORT, The history of, from 1766 to 1878, with a genealogical register ... By Edmund Wheeler. Concord, N.H. the Republican press assoc., 1879.   600 p. front., 1 illus., plates, ports. 23 cm. 1-8046. L.C. copy replaced by microfilm.
    F44.N76W5
    Microfilm 22246 F

NEWTON, Kingston, Plaistow and Westville, New Hampshire, directory.   v.   Canaan, N.H., W.E. Shaw.   v. 24 cm. 16-12906.
    Directories

NORTH CONWAY. The daughter of an earl: intimate sketches of the life and accomplishment of Lady Blanche Murphy, comp. and ed. by Ellen Louise (Slade) Bigelow.   Boston, Mass., Marshall Jones Co., 1928.   x, 155 p. front., illus. (coat of arms) plates, ports., facsim. 24 cm. 28-25855.
    F44. N8
    CT275.M78A3 1928

NORTH CONWAY, Picturesque. Ten drawings from my sketch-book while rambling in the valley of the Saco ... Boston, Damrell & Upham (1889)   27 p. incl. illus., pl. 8°. 1-8048-M1.
    F44. N8W3

NORTH HAMPTON. Reminiscences of a fifty-years pastorate. A half-century discourse ... by Jonathan French ... Portsmouth, C.W. Brewster & son, print., 1852.   46 p. 22½ cm. 2-1856-M2.
    F44.N82F8

NORTH LONDONDERRY, Historical sketch of, and of the Baptist church therein for 100 years, 1799 - 1899. By Arthur Locke ... Haverhill, Mass., C.C. Morse & son, 1902.   11 p. 22 cm. 3-31545.
    F44.N84L8

NORTH WOODSTOCK. A little pathfinder to places of interest in or near North Woodstock. 4th ed. (North Woodstock, N.H.) North Woodstock improvement assoc., 1921.   32 p. 3 double maps (incl. front.) 15½ cm. 21-14066.
    F44.N85N8

NORTHFIELD. Bygones. Some things not generally known in the history of Northfield.   Read before

NEW HAMPSHIRE

the Northfield and Tilton woman's club. (By) Lucy R. H. Cross. Concord, N.H., 1900. 15 p. 25½ cm.
16-20789. F44.N87C78

NORTHFIELD, History of, 1780 - 1905. In two parts with many biographical sketches and portraits also pictures of public buildings and private residences ... by Lucy R.H.Cross. Concord, N.H. Rumford print. co., 1905. 2 v. in 1. fronts., plates, ports., 2 fold. maps. 24 cm. Pt. 2. Genealogies. 9-21694.
F44.N87C8

NOTTINGHAM. History of Nottingham, Deerfield, and Northwood, comprised within the original limits of Nottingham, Rockingham County, N.H., with records of the centennial proceedings at Northwood, and genealogical sketches ... Manchester (N.H.) J.B.Clarke, 1878. xi, 790 p. front., plates, ports. 23½ cm. 1-8049. F44. N9C6

ORFORD. Thanks to the past; the story of Orford, by Alice Doan Hodgson. Orford, N.H., Historical Fact Publications, c.1965. viii, 448 p. 21 cm. F44. O6H6

ORFORD. Centennial celebration of the town of Orford, containing the oration, etc. ... (Manchester, N.H., H.A.Gage, print., 1865) 145 p. 21½ cm. "Biographical sketches": p. (103) - 142. "Soldiers from Orford who served in the late war": p. 143 - 144. Bound at end: Strong family: (2) p.; Sawyer family: 1 l. 1-10780. F44. O6O6

OSSIPEE. The early settlers' meeting house at Leighton's corner. By Minnie Imogene Leighton. (Center Ossipee, N.H., Independent press, c.1933) 3, 32, 33 - 38 p. illus., plates, ports., plans. 20½ cm.
33-22166. F44. O8L4

PEMBROKE, History of. 1730 - 1895. by Rev. N. F. Carter and others ... Concord, N.H. Republican press assoc., 1895. 2 v. in 1. fronts., illus., plates, ports., map (1 fold.) fold. facsim. 24 cm. Contents. - I. Historical - II. Genealogical. 1-8050. F44. P3C3

PEMBROKE, History of.. By John Norris McClintock. (n.p., 1883) 208 p. 24½ cm. "This is all that was printed of a history of Pembroke, by John N. McClintock. Differences arising between him and the town, the work was stopped, and this edition was afterwards almost entirely destroyed." 15-25686. F44. P3M12
Rare Book Room

PEMBROKE, A brief history of the First Congregational church in. By Rev. Isaac Willey. Bristol, N.H., Print. R.W.Musgrove, 1876. 48 p. 22½ cm. 1-8051. F44. P3W7

PENACOOK, The history of, from its first settlement in 1734 up to 1900. Comp. by David Arthur Brown. Concord, N.H., The Rumford press, 1902. viii, 570 p. front. (port.) illus., plates (1 fold.) 24½ cm.
Includes biographical sketches. 3-8592. F44. P33B8

PENACOOK in the war for the union. By Hon. John C. Linehan ... Concord, N.H. Republican press assoc., 1889. 23 p. 24½ cm. 6-18868. F44. P33L7

PERCY. United State Circuit court ... The Percy summer club vs. Joseph C. Astle ... an examination of the evidence in support of the proposition that a natural fresh-water pond ... is public; By Albert S. Batchellor and others. Concord, N.H., Rumford print. co., 1905. 236 p. fold. map, plan. 26 cm.
6-37268. F44. P35B12

PERCY. Prelude to the argument for the defendants in Percy summer club. By A.S.Batchellor.
1 v. F44. S35B121

PETERBOROUGH, Jaffrey and Temple, New Hampshire, directory ... also ... Bennington, Greenfield and Hancock, N.H. 1922 - v. 1 - (Candia, N.H.) W.E.Shaw, c.1922 -
v. 23½ cm. 22-22726. Directories

PETERBOROUGH. The Irish pioneers and founders of Peterborough. The following response to the above toast was delivered by James F. Brennan, at the celebration of the 150th anniversary of Peterborough ... (Peterborough? N.H., 1889?) 7 p. 24 cm. 10-23176. F44. P4 B7

PETERBOROUGH, Origin of the name of the town of. By James F. Brennan ... (Peterborough? 190-?)
7 p. 23 cm. 8-15379. F44. P4B8

175

PETERBOROUGH, register, The, 1905, comp. by Mitchell and Weston. Brunswick, Me., The H. E. Mitchell co., 1905. 100 p. illus. 22 cm. 12-21876.
F44. P4M6

PETERBOROUGH, History of. By George Abbot Morison. Rindge, N.H., R.R. Smith, 1954.
2 v. illus., ports., maps (part fold.) 25 cm. Biographical references included in "Notes" (v.1, p. ii - viii) Contents. - I. Narrative. - 2. Genealogies. 54-11782.
F44. P4M7

PETERBOROUGH. An address delivered at the centennial celebration in Peterborough ... 1839. By John Hopkins Morison. Boston, Print. I. R. Butts, 1839. 99 p. 21½ cm. 1-5879.
F44. P4M8

PETERBOROUGH. The proprietors of Peterborough, with some considerations on the origin of the name, by Samuel Eliot Morison. (Peterborough, N.H. The Peterborough historical soc., 1930) 36 p. front. (port.) 24½ cm. 31-18241.
F44. P4M85

PETERBOROUGH. Inscriptions on gravestones in the two old cemeteries on the east hill in Peterborough. (Peterborough, Transcript print. co., 1908) 68 p. illus. 23 cm. 9-1974.
F44. P4P3

PETERBOROUGH. Proceedings of the sesqui-centennial celebration held at Peterborough, ... 1889. Peterboro', transcript office, 1890. 131 p. front., plates. 23½ cm. 1-8053.
F44. P4P4

PETERBOROUGH. History of the town of Peterborough, Hillsborough County, with the report of the proceedings at the centennial celebration in 1839; an appendix containing the records of the original proprietors; and a genealogical and historical register. By Albert Smith ... Boston, G. H. Ellis, 1876. 13 p., (17) - 360, 375 p. front., pl., ports., fold. map. 24 cm. Genealogy and history of Peterborough families: (pt.2) p. 1-365. 1-8054.
F44. P4S6

PETERBOROUGH, in the American revolution, by Jonathan Smith ... (Peterborough historical soc., 1913. viii, 423 p. 23½ cm. 13-16824.
F44. P4S7

PITTSFIELD. History of Pittsfield, in the great rebellion, by H. L. Robinson ... Pittsfield, N.H. (Concord, N.H. Republican press assoc.) 1893. 217 p. front., pl. ports. 19 cm. 6-21577.
F44. P6R6

PLAINFIELD. Two county cemeteries in New Hamsphire, near junction boundary lines of Enfield, Grantham, Lebanon and Plainfield. By Thomas Hills ... Boston, D. Clapp & son, 1908. 18 p. 25 cm. 8-32959.
F44. P67H6

PLAINFIELD. Historical address and other exercises on the 100th anniversary of the First Baptist church, of Plainfield (Meriden) ... 1892. Lebanon, N.H., A.B. Freeman, 1892. 20 p. 8°. 1-8055-M1
F44. P67P7

PLYMOUTH, Ashland and Meredith, New Hampshire, directory, 1919 -   (Cannan, N.H.) W. E. Shaw, c. 1919 -   v. front. 23½ cm. 20-3358.
Directories

PLYMOUTH. Historical discourse commemorative of the centennial anniversary of the Congregational church, Plymouth. Preached ... 1865, by Henry A. Hazen ... Boston, Congregational pub. soc., 1875. 38 p. 23 cm. 6-40523.
F44. P7H4

PLYMOUTH. Historical sketch, articles of faith and covenant, principles and rules, and catalogue of members, past and present, of the Congregational church, Plymouth. Boston, J. E. Farwell print., 1867. 44 p. 21½ cm. 6-15336.
F44. P7P74

PLYMOUTH. The 150th anniversary of the granting of the charter of the town of Plymouth ... 1763... (Concord, The Rumford press, 1913) 72 p. front., 15 pl., ports. 23½ cm. Plates printed on both sides. 16-18344.
F44. P7P79

PLYMOUTH, Twenty decades in: 1763 - 1963. By Eva Augusta (Clough) Speare. Plymouth, N.H., Bicentennial Commission (1963) 184 p. 23 cm.
F44. P7S6

NEW HAMPSHIRE 59

PLYMOUTH, History of; vol. I. Narrative - vol. II. Genealogies ... (by) Ezra S. Stearns ... Cambridge, Mass., Printed for the town by the University press, 1906.   2 v. fold. front., plates, fold. map, fold. plan. 24½ cm. 6-34787.
F44. P7S7

PLYMOUTH.   The town register: Ashland, Plymouth, Sandwich, Campton, Holderness, Center Harbor, Moultonboro, 1908.   August, Me., The Mitchell-Cony co., inc., 1908.   3, (9) - 109, (2), 157 p. 22 cm. 12-21877.
F44. P7T7

PORTSMOUTH.   Manning's Portsmouth, Greenland, New Castle, Rye, Durham (New Hampshire) Kittery (Maine) directory ... v.   18   Boston, Mass., H. A. Manning co.,   v. fold. maps. 24 - 25½ cm. 1-31663 rev. 2.
Directories

PORTSMOUTH directory, The ... (1850), 1856/7, 1860/61 ... Portsmouth, C. W. Brewster, 1851 - 61. 3 v. 15½ x 9 cm. Title varies. 8-10597 rev.
Directories

PORTSMOUTH register and directory ... (1834-39/40) Portsmouth, J. M. Edmonds, 1834 - 39. 2 v. 18 cm. Title varies. 10-3185 rev.
Directories
Office

PORTSMOUTH.   Edmonds' town directory ... Portsmouth, N. H., J. M. Edmonds, 1839.   vii, (8) - 216 p. map. 16 cm. Second no. of Portsmouth register and directory pub. by Edmonds. 10-3185.
Directories

PORTSMOUTH city book and directory ... (1851) - 56/7 1860/61. Portsmouth (N. H.) C. W. Brewster (1851) - 61.   3 v. 15½ cm. Title varies. 8-10597.
Directories

PORTSMOUTH directory, The ... Comp. Dean Dudley. Portsmouth (N. H.) 1867.   132 p. 48 p. 21½ cm. 8-10580.
Directories

PORTSMOUTH.   An historical discourse delivered at the celebration of the 200th anniversary of the formation of the North church ... 1871, by Rev. George M. Adams ... Portsmouth, F. W. Robinson, 1871.   72 p. incl. front. 24½ cm. 7-10439.
F44. P8A19

PORTSMOUTH, Annals of, comprising a period of 200 years... with   biographical sketches of a few of the most respectable inhabitants. By Nathaniel Adams ... Portsmouth (N. H.) The author, 1825. v, (7) - 400 p. 23 cm. 1-8056 rev.
F44. P8A2

— Name & subject index ... Work projects administration ... (Portsmouth?) 1940. 46 l. 25½ cm. Reproduced from type-written copy. 1-8056 rev.
F44. P8A2
Index

PORTSMOUTH.   An account of the several religious societies in Portsmouth, from their first establishment and of the ministers of each ... by Timothy Alden, jun. ... Boston, Munroe, Francis & Parker, print., 1808.   40 p. 22½ cm. 6-13955.
F44. P8A27

PORTSMOUTH.   An old town by the sea, by Thomas Bailey Aldrich.   Boston and N. Y., Houghton, Mifflin, 1893.   4, 128 p. 18½ cm. 1-8057/4.
F44. P8A3

— 1894.   4, 128 p. 18½ cm. "Fourth edition." 41-31878.
F44. P8A32

— (c. 1917)   6, 128 p. front., plates. 20 cm. "Visitor's edition." 17-15085.
F44. P8A35

PORTSMOUTH, Exeter, Newmarket, South Newmarket and Epping, and their leading business men, by Geo. F. Bacon ... Boston, Mercantile pub. co., 1891.   74 p. illus. 26½ cm. 4-20149.
F44. P8B2

PORTSMOUTH, Vignettes of; being representations of divers historic places in old Portsmouth, done by Helen Pearson; with descriptive text arranged by Harold Hotchkiss Bennett. Portsmouth, N. H., Helen Person and H. H. Bennett (c. 1913)   54 p. incl. plates. 21 cm. Plates printed on both sides. 13-20564.
F44. P8B47

PORTSMOUTH.   Rambles about Portsmouth.   Sketches of persons, lcoalities, and incidents of two

centuries: ... By Chas. W. Brewster ... Portsmouth, N.H. C.W.Brewster, 1859 - 69. 2 v. 23 cm.
Vol. 2 has title: Rambles about Portsmouth. Second series. 1-8058 rev. F44. P8B8

— — Name and subject index ... First series, 1859. Work projects administration ...
(Portsmouth? 1941?) 118 l. 20½ cm. Reproduced from type-written copy. 1-8058 rev. F44. P8B8
Index 1st series

— Name and subject index ... Second series, 1869 ... Work projects administration
(Portsmouth? 1941?) 101 l. 20½ cm. Reproduced from type-written copy. 1-8058 rev. F44. P8B8
index 2d series

— 2d ed. First series. Portsmouth, N.H., L.H.Brewster, 1873. 381 p. 23 cm. 3-5130.
F44. P8B81

— Another issue. Appendix (20 p. at end) Sons and daughters of Portsmouth resident abroad in 1873.
F44. P8P81
1873a

PORTSMOUTH. A discourse, delivered at Portsmouth ... 1789. On the occasion of the President of the United States honoring that capital with a visit. By Joseph Buckminster ... Portsmouth, N.H. Print. John Melcher, 1789. 21 p. 18½ cm. 16-2769. F44. P8B92

PORTSMOUTH. The celebration of the centennial anniversary of the introduction of the art of printing into New Hampshire, in the city of Portsmouth ... 1856. ... Portsmouth, E.N. Fuller, 1857.
60 p. 21 cm. With facsimile of the N.H.Gazette, Oct. 7, 1756. 1-13534. F44. P8C39
Z209. N54c

PORTSMOUTH; a camera impression, by Samuel Chamberlain. New York, Hastings house (c.1940)
73 p. front., illus. 19 cm. 69 pages of illustrations. 40-14453. F44. P8C45

PORTSMOUTH, New Hampshire, has been the homeport of many historic ships and crews. (Portsmouth?) 1920) (24) p. illus., fold. map. 9 x 15½ cm. 21-7165. F44. P8C48

PORTSMOUTH. Federal fire society of Portsmouth ... (Portsmouth, The Society, 1905) 90 p. 23 cm.
"Biographical notes of members of the ... society" ...: p. (13) - 66. 6-27437. F44. P8F3

PORTSMOUTH. The graves we decorate. Storer post, no. 1, Department of New Hampshire, Grand army of the republic, Portsmouth, N.H. Prepared ... by Joseph Foster ... With an appendix containing the list of graves and additional records prepared in 1893. Portsmouth, J.D. Randall, 1907.
20 p. 76 p. 24 cm. The appendix is: Record of the soldiers, sailors and marines, etc. See next item. 8-18427.
F44. P8F6

PORTSMOUTH. Record of the soldiers, sailors and marines who served the U.S.A. in the war of the rebellion and previous wars: buried in the city of Portsmouth and the neighboring towns of Greenland, Newcastle, Newington and Rye. ... By Joseph Foster ... Portsmouth, N.H., Print. Portsmouth journal, 1893. 76 p. 24 cm. Bound with previous item. 8-18428. F44. P8F6

PORTSMOUTH. The graves we decorate. Additional list, 1907 - 1915. "Fifty years after Appomattox." Prepared ... by Joseph Foster ... (Portsmouth, 1915) 14 p. 24 cm. 16-23272.
F44. P8F62

— Fifty-two years after Appomattox ... (Portsmouth, 1917) 74 p. 24 cm. 17-16983 rev. F44. P8F63

PORTSMOUTH. The soldiers' memorial. Portsmouth, N.H. Appendix to The graves we decorate. (Portsmouth, The Randall press, 1921) 62 p. 23½ cm. 17-16983 rev. F44. P8F64

— (Portsmouth? 1923) 32 p. 23½ cm. "Index of The graves we decorate, printed records, 1917, 1921 and 1923" p. 25 - 32.
41-31879. F44. P8F643

PORTSMOUTH. Historical monuments, bronze tablets and cannon, in Portsmouth and vicinity. Both in state of Maine and New Hampshire. By Joseph Foster ... (Portsmouth, 1914) 5 l. 27 cm.
CA 25-494 unrev. F44. P8F65

NEW HAMPSHIRE 61

PORTSMOUTH. The soldiers' memorial. Portsmouth, N.H. 1893 - 1921. Storer post, no. 1, Dept. of New Hampshire, Grand army of the republic ... Prepared by Joseph Foster ... (Portsmouth, 1921) 328 p. 23½ cm. Various pagings. Contents. - Record prepared for Memorial day, 1893. - The graves we decorate, 1907; 1915; 1917. - The soldiers' memorial, 1921. - Presentation of flags, 1890. - Presentation of portraits, 1891. 20-10400.   F44.P8F68

PORTSMOUTH. The presentation of flags to the schools of Portsmouth, N.H. ... 1890 ... Portsmouth, N.H., 1890.   36 p. 23½ cm. (With The soldiers' memorial ... 1921) 22-12445.   F44.P8F68

PORTSMOUTH ... The soldiers' memorial. Portsmouth, N.H., 1893 - 1923. Prepared by Joseph Foster ... (Portsmouth, 1923)   (362) p. 23½ cm. Various pagings. Contents. - Presentation of flags, 1890 - Presentation of Portraits, 1891. ... The graves we decorate, 1907; 1915; 1917; The soldiers' memorial, 1921; 1923. 33-33127.   F44.P8F682

PORTSMOUTH guide book: comprising a survey of the city and neighborhood, with notices of the principal buildings, sites of historical interest and public institutions ... Portsmouth (N.H.) J.H. Foster, 1876.   167 p. 24º. 1-8059-M1.   F44.P8F7

— By Sarah H. Foster ... Portsmouth (N.H.) Portsmouth journal job print., 1896.   4, (2), (5) - 148 p. 16 cm. 4-8594 rev.   F44.P8F72

    — Name and subject index ... Work projects administration. (Portsmouth? 1941?) 62 l. 16½ x 14 cm. Reproduced from type-written copy. 4-8594 rev.   F44.P8F72 Index

PORTSMOUTH. History of Fort Constitution and "Walbach tower", Portsmouth harbor, N.H. By a student of Dartmouth college. Ed. George B. Griffith. Portsmouth, C.W. Brewster & son, printers, 1865.   16 p. 22½ cm. 20-17061 rev.   F44.P8F85

PORTSMOUTH. "An old town by the sea," by W.O. Fuller. 2d ed. Portsmouth, N.H., Thomas Bailey Aldrich memorial, 1909.   16 p. illus. 15½ cm. 10-14747.   F44.P8F9

PORTSMOUTH, historic and picturesque, a volume of information; being a very complete and accurate compendium of over 200 historic places and things, from the earliest settlement, in 1623 ... (by) C.S. Gurney. Portsmouth, N.H., C.S. Gurney, 1902.   3, 225, (3) p. incl. illus., pl., maps, plan. 18 x 23½ cm. 3-24 rev.   F44.P8G9

— Name and subject index (and) names and location index of illustrations ... W.P.A. (Portsmouth? 1941?)   126 l. 17½ x 14 cm. Reproduced from type-written copy. 3-24 rev.   F44.P8G9 Index

PORTSMOUTH. Memorial address delivered May 30, 1892, at Portsmouth ... by Frank Warren Hackett. Portsmouth, M. Goodrich, 1893.   16 p. 2 port. (incl. front.) 23½ cm. 5-11241.   F44. P8H1
    E642. H12

PORTSMOUTH. Praises on tombs in the old North burial ground where sleep patriots of the revolution ... By Arthur Ilsley Harriman ... (Portsmouth, N.H., c.1932)   3 p. 38 p., illus. 18½ cm. "References": 1 leaf at end. 32-20120.   F44. P8H3

PORTSMOUTH. The four meeting houses of the North parish of Portsmouth. By Charles Albert Hazlett.   (In the Granite monthly. v.40, p. (37) - 44) 11-14934 rev.   F44. P8H4
    F31.G75 vol. 40

PORTSMOUTH. Historical sketch of the North church. ... By Edwin Holt. Portsmouth, C.W. Brewster, print., 1838.   30 p. 23 cm. 8-34782.   F44. P8H7

PORTSMOUTH. Sketches of a New-England village, in the last century. Boston, J. Munroe & co., 1838.   2, (3) - 110 p. 16½ cm. 7-12612.   F44. P8L3
    PZ3.L5115 S

PORTSMOUTH and Newcastle, cemetery inscriptions; abstracts from some two thousand of the oldest tombstones, by Arthur Locke ... Portsmouth. 1907.   44 p. front. (port) 23 cm. 7-28617 rev.   F44. P8L8

PORTSMOUTH, An historical calendar of.   Miss Frances A. Mathes and others, ed. ... Portsmouth, N.H. (Box club of the North church) The Randall press, c.1907.   3, 69 numb. l. illus. 17½ x 26 cm. 8-808.
   F44. P8M4

PORTSMOUTH.   Among old Portsmouth houses, by Ralph May.   Boston, Mass., Print Wright & Potter, (1946)   39 p. front., plates. 23½ cm. 47-19640.
   F44. P8M44

PORTSMOUTH.   Early Portsmouth history, by Ralph May.   Boston, C.E. Goodspeed & co., 1926. 5, (13) - 285 p. front., plates. 24 cm. "References": p. (271) - 285. 27-47.
   F44. P8M45

PORTSMOUTH.   The Moffatt-Ladd house, its garden and its period, 1763, Portsmouth, N.H., by Philip Dana Orcutt.   (Portsmouth) The N.H. soc. of colonial dames of America, 1935.   48 p. incl. front., plates, ports. 24½ cm. "First edition." 35-9466.
   F44. P8O73

PORTSMOUTH JUBILEE, The.   The reception of the sons of Portsmouth resident abroad ... 1853 ... A record of the proceedings ... names of visitors, etc.   Portsmouth, C.W. Brewster & son, 1853. 80 p. 22½ cm. 19-10573.
   F44. P8P7

PORTSMOUTH.   1645 - 1656.   Portsmouth records.   A transcript of the first 35 pages of the earliest town book ... with notes by Frank W. Hackett.   Portsmouth, (Washington, D.C., R.O. Polkinhorn print.,) 1886.   xii, (13) - 76 p. 24½ cm. 1-14473.
   F44. P8P73

PORTSMOUTH.   The re-union of '73.   The second reception of the sons and daughters of Portsmouth resident abroad ... 1873.   Portsmouth, N.H., C.W. Gardner (1873)   95, (1) p. 23 cm. 1-8060.
   F44. P8P75

PORTSMOUTH in the year 1824 being some interesting facts about Portsmouth since the year 1824. Portsmouth, N.H., First national bank, 1912.   (24) p. illus., 2 pl. double facsim. 19 cm. Plates printed on both sides. 12-22246.
   F44. P8 P8

PORTSMOUTH.   Records of North church, Portsmouth, compiled by Mrs. Louise H. Rainey. ... N.Y? 1940?   69 l. 28 cm. Type-written. Record of births, marriages and deaths, 1779 - 1835. 40-33306.
   F44. P8R3

PORTSMOUTH.   Glimpses of an old social capital (Portsmouth) as illus. by the life of the Rev. Arthur Browne and his circle, by Mary Cochrane Rogers.   Boston, Printed for the subscribers, 1923. xii, 92 p. front., plates, ports. 26½ cm. 23-15932.
   F44. P8R7

PORTSMOUTH, Strawberry Banke in; official guidebook and map.   (Ed. Nancy R. Beck)   Portsmouth, N.H., c.1966)   xvii, 70 p. 22 cm.
   F44. P8S7

PORTSMOUTH, A pageant of; a pageant in celebration of the tercentenary of the first settlement in New Hampshire, spring of 1623, written and produced by Virginia Tanner, for the tercentenary celebration ... 1923 ... (Concord, N.H., Rumford press, 1923)   95 p. illus. 23½ cm. 23-15606.
   F44. P8T16

PORTSMOUTH.   Strawberry Bank's bank, and the Marquis de Lafayette, 1824.   New York, Newcomen Soc. 1950.   36 p. illus. 23 cm. 50-13004.
   F44. P8T7

PORTSMOUTH.   Jonathan Warner (1726 - 1814): merchant & trader, King's councillor, mariner, jurist.   Illus. by Cecile Newbold Barnett.   New York, Newcomen Society, 1950.   40 p. illus., port. 23 cm. 50-14460.
   F44. P8W4

PORTSMOUTH.   The Macpheadris-Warner House, 1716, Portsmouth, N.H.; a registered national historic landmark, something about it and two of its early occupants, Archibald Macpheadris and Jonathan Warner, by W.G. Wendell (Rev. ed.) Portsmouth, N,H. (1966)   29 p. 23 cm.
   F44. P8 W4 1966

PORTSMOUTH.   The story of strawberry banke in Portsmouth with original source materials.   By Elaine Macmann Willoughby.   (n.p.) 1970.   44 p. illus. 22 cm.
   F44. P8W47

NEW HAMPSHIRE

PORTSMOUTH, the life of a town. By Ola Elizabeth Winslow. New York, Macmillan (c. 1966)
vii, 136 p. 22 cm. "1st printing" 66-11111. F44. P8W5

RANDOLPH old and new; its ways and its by-ways, by George N. Cross. (Randolph, N.H. (Town of Randolph (c. 1924) 7, (3) - 260 p. front., plates, ports. 20½ cm. 25-229. F44. R17C8

RAYMOND, New Hampshire, fifty years ago; an address at the "Old home week celebration" Raymond, N.H., ... 1901, by David H. Brown ... Chicago, The Lakeside press, 1901. 16 p. 21½ cm. 2-5370.
 F44. R2B8

RAYMOND, The history of. By Joseph Fullonton ... Dover, N.H. Morning star job print., 1875.
vi, (7) - 407 p. front., illus., ports. 22 cm. "Genealogy": p. 178 - 356. 1-8061. F44. R2F9

RICHMOND. History of the town of Richmond, Cheshire County, from its first settlement, to 1882. By William Bassett. Boston, C.W. Calkins & co., print., 1884. xiv, 578 p. front., illus., plates, ports., double plan. 23½ cm. "The genealogy of families": p. 255-538. "Biographical sketches": p. 539 - 554. 1-8062. F44. R47B3

RINDGE, Dedication of the Ingalls memorial library at, ... 1895. Concord, N.H., Republican press assoc., 1895. 51 p. 24½ cm. 8-24359. F44. R5
 Z733. R558

RINDGE. Historical discourse delivered on the fortieth anniversary of his pastorate in Rindge ... 1801, by Rev. A.W. Burnham ... Boston, Crosby & Nichols, 1862. 102 p. 8°. 1-8063-M1.
 F44. R5B9

RINDGE, History of the town of, from the date of the Rowley Canada or Massachusetts charter, to the present time, 1736 - 1874, with a genealogical register of the Rindge families, by Ezra S. Stearns ... Boston, Press of G.H. Ellis, 1875. 2, 788 p. illus. (incl. facsims., coats of arms) pl. ports. 23 cm. "Genealogical register": p. (419) - 775. 1-10779. F44. R5S7

RINDGE. The Snowton sleigh-ride. By Marcus Woodman (Pseud?) David Stowe supposed author. Snowton (Rindge? N.H.) The author, 1846, reprint, 1883. 15 p. 24 cm. Humorous account of a sleigh-ride from Rindge, N.H., to Fitchburg, Mass., in Jan. 1846. 19-12972. F44. R5S8

ROCHESTER, New Hampshire, Resident and business directory of ... (18   South Framingham,
Mass., W.F. Richardson & co., 18   v. 23½ cm. 22-16689.   Directories

ROCHESTER city directory, The ... 1899 -   Boston, Tolman pub. co., 1899 -
 v. 23½ cm. 99-4834 rev.   Directories

ROCHESTER, History of the town of ...1722 to 1890. By Franklin McDuffee; ed. and rev. by Silvanus Hayward ... Manchester, The J.B. Clarke co., print., 1892. 2 v. front., illus., plates, ports., fold. map, fold. plan, fold. facsim. 23½ cm. 1-8064. F44. R6M1

RYE, Dedication of town hall in ... 1873. Historical addresses. (Rye? N.H., 1873) 19 p. 8°.
1-8065-M1. F44. R9A3

RYE, History of the town of, from its discovery and settlement to Dec. 1903, by Langdon B. Parsons. Concord, N.H., Rumford print. co., 1905. vi, 675 p. front. (port.) illus., 2 fold. maps. 24 cm. "Genealogy": p. (293) - 572. 5-29137. F44. R9P2

RYE. A half century sermon ... Preached at Rye ... 1835, by H. Porter ... Portsmouth, Miller & Brewster, 1835. 24 p. 8°. 1-8066-M1. F44. R9P8

RYE on the rocks; the tale of a town: a Yankee saga told by a Yankee. By William A. Varrell. (Portsmouth? N.H., 1962) 149 p. 24 cm. F44. R9V3

SALEM, Canobie Lake district, Pelham and Atkinson directory, The. (Canaan, N.H.) W.E. Shaw.
v. 23½ cm. 16-905.   Directories

SALEM. Canobie Lake park, Salem, N.H. (Boston, c.1909) 1 v. 15½ x 21 cm.
F44.S14C3

SALEM, History of. Comp. and written by Edgar Gilbert ... Concord, N.H., Rumford print. co., 1907. xiv, 444, 139, 24 p. front., plates (1 fold.) ports., maps (1 fold.) charts. 24 cm. 7-40884.
F44.S14G4

SALISBURY, The history of, from date of settlement to the present time ... Collated by John J. Dearborn. Ed. James O. Adams and others. Manchester, N.H. Print. W.E. Moore, 1890. vi, 892 p. front., illus., pl., ports., map. 24½ cm. Genealogy and biography: p. (439)-863. 1-8067.
F44.S15D2

SANBORNTON, History of ... By Rev. M.T. Runnels ... Boston, Mass., A. Mudge, print., 1882, '81. 2 v. fronts., plates, ports., 2 fold. maps. 24 cm. Contents - I. Annals. - II. Genealogies. 1-8068.
F44.S18R9

SANDWICH. Midsummer in Whittier's country, a little study of Sandwich Center, by Ethel Armes, with sketches by the author. Birmingham, Ala., Advance press (1905?) 5, (15)-62 p. incl. front., illus., pl. 18½ cm. 10-13001 rev.
F44. S2A6

— Sewanee, Tenn., Print. University press, 1910. 73, (1) p. illus. 18½ cm. 10-7898 rev.
F44. S2A7

SANDWICH, N.H. cemeteries. Collected and arranged by Mrs. Harriet Vittum Lighton ... (Sandwich?) 1930. 4, 4-159 numb. l., 27½ cm. 32-33208.
F44. S2L5

SANDWICH. New Hampshire. Lake region inscriptions; Whiteface Intervale, Sandwich; Perkins ground. New Durham; Further memorials of Meredith. Worcester, Mass., F.P. Rice, 1900. 28 p. 4°. 50 copies printed. 1-19054.
F44. S2R4

SANDWICH Historical Society. Annual excursion. (Center Sandwich) v. illus., ports. 24 cm. Includes papers on local history and an annual summary of local news. 56-37102.
F44. S2S3

SANDWICH. Record marriages and baptisms with notes by Dr. Q.E. Marston. (n.p.1898?) 20 cm. Proof-sheets.
F44. S2T2

SHARON. Sliptown: the history of Sharon, 1738-1941, by H. Thorn King, Jr. (Rutland, Vt., C.E. Tuttle Co. (1965) 233 p. 22 cm. 64-7961.
F44. S48K5

SHELBURNE, History of, by Mrs. R.P. Peabody. Gorham, N.H., Mountaineer print., 1882. 127 p. pl. 17½ cm. "History of the Shelburne lead mine": p. 96-104. 1-8069
F44. S5P3

SOUTH HAMPTON, Marriages and baptisms at, 1743-1801. From a ms. copy of the church record. Pub. ... by G.A. Gordon. Boston, 1899. Reprinted from the N.E. hist. and geneal. register, Oct. 1898, Apr. & July, 1899. 1-16583*.
F44. S65S6

STEWARTSTOWN, The vital statistics of. From 1770 to 1888. Contains names and dates of the original grant, incorporation, settlement, marriages, births, & deaths. Comp. and pub. by C.E. Tewksbury (town clerk) (Stewartstown, N.H. C.E. Tewksbury, 1888) 52, (4) p. 19½ x 15½ cm. 1-21352.
F44. S77T3

STODDARD, Cheshire County, History of. From the time of its incorporation in 1774 to 1854 ... With some sketches from its first settlement in 1768, by Isaiah Gould. Marlboro' N.H., W.L. Metcalf print., 1897. 139 p. 21½ cm. "Persons married by Isaac Robinson," 1803-1854: p. (131)-139. 1-8070.
F44. S8G7

STRATFORD, History of the town of, 1773-1925, by Jeannette R. Thompson; pub. by vote of the town. Concord, N.H., The Rumford press, 1925. xii, 525 p. incl. front., illus., ports. fold. map. 23½ cm. 26-1342.
F44.S82T4

STRATHAM. Genealogical gleanings; church records of Stratham, N.H., 1746-1869 (i.e. 1913) compiled by Priscilla Hammond. , (Concord? N.H.) 1933. 69 numb. l. 28 cm. Type-written (carbon copy) Contents. - pt. 1. 1746-1869. - pt. 2. 1869-1913. CA 34-1062 unrev.
F44.S825S8
Rare Book Room

SULLIVAN, A history of the town of, 1777 - 1917, by Rev. Josiah Lafayette Seward ... (Keene, N.H., Sentinel print. co., c.1921) 2 v. front., illus., plates, ports., fold. map, plans. 23½cm. Contents. - v.1 (History) - v.2. Genealogies. 21-16543. F44.S83S5

SUNAPEE, The story of, by John Henry Bartlett ... Washington, D.C., Press of B.S. Adams, c.1941. 196 p. illus. (incl. ports., maps) 23½cm. 41-19931. F44.S837B3

SUNCOOK Valley, New Hampshire, directory, The: Allentown, Barnstead, Chichester, Epsom, Pittsfield, Pembroke, Suncook ... (Candia, N.H.) W.E. Shaw, c.19 v. 23 cm. CA 28-395 unrev. Directories

SURRY. History of the town of Surry, Cheshire County, New Hampshire, from date of severance from Gilsum and Westmoreland, 1769 - 1922, with a genealogical register and map of the town, by Frank Burnside Kingsbury ... Surry, N.H., Pub. by the town, 1925. viii, 3 - 1064 p. front. (fold. map) illus. (incl. ports.) 24½cm. 26-15070. F44.S86K5

SUTTON. Dedication of the Pillsbury memorial town hall in Sutton. Concord, N.H., Republican press assoc., 1893. 171 p. pl., 2 port. (incl. front.) 25 cm. 8-8583. F44.S9D2

SUTTON, Narrative history of, celebrating the 150th anniversary of the incorporation of the town ... 1934. (n.p., 1934?) 18 p. 21½cm. 43-41154.
F44.S9R9

SUTTON, The history of: consisting of the historical collections of Erastus Wadleigh, esq., and A.H. Worthen. Comp. and arr. by Mrs. Augusta Harvey Worthen ... Concord, N.H., Print. Republican press assoc., 1890. 2 v. fronts., plates, ports. 23½cm. Vol. 2, Genealogy. Paged continuously. 1-8072. F44.S9W9

SWANZEY, The history of, from 1734 to 1890. By Benjamin Read ... Salem, Mass., The Salem press pub. and print. co., 1892. xiv, 585 p. front., illus., plates, ports., fold. map, fold. plan. 24 cm. "Genealogies": p. (269) - 504; "Biographical and supplementary": p. 505 - 573. 1-8071. F44.S97R2

TAMWORTH narrative, The. Freeport, Me., B. Wheelwright Co. (1958) 336 p. illus. 21 cm. includes bibliographies. 58-11266. F44.T15H3

TAMWORTH. Memoir of the Rev. Samuel Hidden. By E.C. Cogswell. Boston, Crocker & Brewster, 1842. xiii, (17) - 332 p. front. (port.) 16½cm. 1-263. F44.T15H6

TAMWORTH. The fishbasket papers; the diaries, 1768 - 1823 of Bradbury Jewell, esq., of Tamworth, Durham and Sandwich. Ed. by Marjory Gane Harkness. Peterborough, N.H., R.R. Smith (c.1963) xii, 236 p. 23 cm. 63-17175. F44.T15J4 1963

TEMPLE, The history of. By Henry Ames Blood ... Boston, Print. G.C. Rand & Avery, 1860. v, (2), (3) - 352 p. front., plates, ports. 23 cm. "Family records": p. (201) - 279. 1-8073. F44.T2B6

TILTON, New Hampshire, directory, The ... and a resident directory of Belmont and Gilmanton, N.H. (Canaan, N.H.) W.E. Shaw, v. 24 cm. 20-16086. Directories

TILTON. An account of the 75th anniversary of the Congregational church of Northfield and Tilton ... 1897 ... Concord, N.H., Print. Republican press assoc., 1897. 43 p. 22½cm. 2-1847-M2.
F44.T5T5

TROY, An historical sketch of and her inhabitants, from the first settlement of the town, in 1764, to 1855. By A.M. Caverly ... Keene (N.H.) Printed at the N.H. sentinel office, 1859. ix, (13) - 299 p. front., ports. 19½cm. Includes genealogical sketches. 1-8075. F44.T8C3

TROY, Historical sketch of the town of, and her inhabitants from the first settlement of the territory now within the limits of the town in 1764 - 1897. By M.T. Stone. Keene, N.H. Sentinel print. co. (1897) xi, 576 p. front., illus., 2 pl. (incl. ports.) 24 cm. "Genealogical register": p. (321) - 565. 1-8074. F44.T8S8

TUFTONBORO, New Hampshire; an historical sketch, by Rev. John W. Hayely ... (Concord, N.H., The Rumford press) 1923.   v, 111 p. front. (port.) fold. plan. 23½ cm. 23-11092.
F44. T9H4

TUFTONBORO.   The castle and the club.   The Bald Peak Colony Club.   By Elizabeth Crawford Wilkin, (Boston, Nimrod Press, c.1964)   170 p. 24 cm. 64-7854.
F44. T9 W8

WAKEFIELD.   Old-time child-life.   By E.H. Arr (pseud.) ... Mrs. Ellen Chapman (Hobbs) Rollins. Philadelphia, J.B. Lippincott, 1881.   188 p. 18 cm. Sketches of New England village life in the author's birthplace, Wakefield, Carroll County, N.H. Names of places and persons are disguised. 15-7565.
F44. W14R7

WALPOLE.   Bellows Falls and vicinity, illus. ... attractions and historical facts of Bellows Falls and the surrounding villages of Saxtons River, Rockingham and Westminster, Vt., and Walpole and Charlestown, N.H., comp. and pub. by P.H. Gobie ... Bellows Falls, Vt., The P.H. Gobie press (c.1912)   (109) p. incl. front., illus. 24½ x 30½ cm. 12-11746.
F59. B39G5

WALPOLE as it was and as it is, containing the complete civil history of the town from 1749 to 1879 ... also a history of 150 families that settled in the town previous to 1820, with biographical sketches of a large number of its prominent citizens, and also, a census of the town ... 1878. By George Aldrich ... Claremont, N.H. Print. Claremont manufacturing co., 1880.   404 p. front., ports. 23½ cm.
F44. W2 A3

WALPOLE, A history of.   By Martha (McDanolds) Frizzell.   Drawings: Howard Sartwell Andros ... Walpole, Walpole Historical Soc., 1963.   2 v. illus., ports., maps (1 fold. inserted in v.1)
F44. W2F7

WARNER, The history of, for 144 years, from 1735 to 1879.   By Walter Harriman.   Concord, N.H., The Republican press assoc., 1879.   581 p. front., ports., map. 23½ cm. Includes biographical sketches. 1-8084.
F44. W21H2

WARNER.   Historical discourse delivered at the centennial celebration of the Congregational church in Warner, N.H. ... 1872, by Henry S. Huntington ... Concord (N.H.) 1872.   61 p. 21½ cm. 6-40522.
F44. W21H9

WARNER, Historical sketches of the town of, by Dr. Moses Long.   (Manchester) C.H. Bell, 1870. 1, 26 p. 25½ cm. "Originally pub. at Concord (in the Collections of the N.H. historical soc. v.3) 1832. Thirty copies only, reprinted in separate form..." 1-11991.
F44. W21L8

WARREN, Address delivered at the centennial celebration of the town of ... 1863, by William Little ... Manchester, N.H. ... C.F. Livingston, 1863.   18 p. 22 cm. 18-2260.
F44. W22L68

WARREN, The history of; a mountain hamlet, located among the White Hills of New Hampshire.   By William Little.   Manchester, N.H., W.E. Moore, printer, 1870.   xiii, (3), (17) - 592 p. front., illus. (incl. maps) photos., ports. 24 cm. 1-8085.
F44. W22L7

WARREN, History of the town of, from its early settlement to the year 1854: including a sketch of the Pemigewasset Indians.   By William Little.   Concord, N.H., McFarland & Jenks, 1854.   1, (vii) - viii, (9) - 170 p. 19½ cm. 16-8153.
F44. W22L69

WASHINGTON, History of, from the first settlement to the present time. 1768 - 1886.   Comp. by a committee ... Claremont, N.H. Claremont manufacturing co., 1886.   x, 696 p. front., plates, ports. 24 cm. 1-8077.
F44. W3W3

WATERVILLE Valley, The.   A history, description, and guide, by A.L. Goodrich.   (Salem, Mass?) 1892.   29 p. plate, fold. map. 19½ cm. 5-32148.
F44. W32G8

— Ed. 2, rev.   (n.p.) 1904.   45 p. incl. front., plates. fold. map. 17 cm. 6-15332.
F44. W32G82

— Ed. 3, rev.   (Auburndale? Mass.) 1916.   58 p. incl. front., plates. fold. map. 17 cm. Map in separate cover. "The Waterville valley ... lies almost entirely in the town of Waterville, N.H." 17-1118.
F44. W32G84

NEW HAMPSHIRE 67

WEARE, The history of, 1735 - 1888. By William Little. David Cross and others ... furnished the material. Lowell, Mass., Print S. W. Huse, 1888. x, 1064 p. front., plates, ports. 24 cm. Genealogy of families in Weare: p. (709) - 1032. 1-8078.
F44. W4L7

WEARE. Captain Samuel Philbrick house, Weare, (by) William Wallace Taylor. (Dearborn, Mich., 1933) 31 numb. l. 28½ x 22½ cm. Carbon copy. Caption title: Some account of the life of Capt. Samuel Philbrick ... together with a short history of the Philbrick family ... 33-31471.
F44. W4T3

WEIRS, The. Report of the commission for the preservation, tprotection and appropriate designation of the Endicott rock at the Weirs, in the town of Laconia, ... Concord, I. C. Evans, 1893. 22 p. front. 23 cm. 1-2761.
F44. W5N5

WEIRS, Rambles about the; nooks and corners and points of interest of an old historic locality ... (by) Edgar Harlan Wilcomb. Worcester, Mass., 1923 - v. illus. 18½ cm. (On cover: Winnipesaukee Lake country gleanings. Booklet A-1) 23-17996.
F44. W5W6

WENTWORTH, History of the town of, by George F. Plummer. Concord, N. H. The Rumford press, 1930. xix, 401 p. front., plates. 23½ cm. 30-33983.
F44. W53P53

WEST LEBANON ... An historical discourse, delivered at the twenty-fifth anniversary of the West Lebanon Congregational church... 1874. By A. B. Rich ... Concord, N. H. Print. the Republican press assoc., 1874. 29 p. 22½ cm. 24-17723.
F44. W57R4

WILMOT. Eighteen hundred and froze-to-death, a legend of 1816; an Old home day poem by Ernest Vinton Browne; ... Wilmot, N. H. ... Junius press, 1934. 6 p. 12 numb. l., illus., 4 pl. 28 cm. Printed on one side of leaf only. "First edition, 30 copies." 36-24895.
PS3503. R797E5 1934

WILTON. History of the town of Wilton, Hillsborough County, with a genealogical register by Abiel Abbot Livermore and Sewall Putnam ... Lowell, Mass., Marden & Rowell, print., 1888. xi, 575 p. plates, ports., plan. 23½ cm. 1-8079.
F44. W6L7

WILTON. The celebration of the 150th anniversary of the settlement of Wilton ... 1889. By Charles W. Marshall ... Nashua, N. H. Gazette book and job print., 1889. 115 (i.e.114) p. front. 23½ cm. 18-2203.
F44. W6M3

WILTON. An address, delivered at the centennial celebration in Wilton ... 1839. By Ephraim Peabody. Boston, B. H. Greene, 1839. 103 p. 23 cm. 1-8080.
F44. W6P3

WILTON, Historical sketches of, 1739 - 1939 ... pub. in connection with the 200th anniversary ... Compiled and ed. by Hamilton S. Putnam ... (Wilton, N. H.) The Wilton historical soc., 1939. 95 p. incl. illus. (incl. map) plates. 28 cm. 40-30611.
F44. W6P87

WINDHAM (Rockingham County) The history of. 1719 - 1883. A Scotch settlement (commonly called Scotch-Irish), embracing nearly one third of the ancient settlement and historic township of Londonderry ... By Leonard A. Morrison ... Boston, Mass., Cuples, Upham & co., 1883. x, 862 p. front., illus., plates, photos., ports., fold. map. 24 cm. "History of families in Windham": p. (297) - 835. 1-8081-2.
F44. W7M9
Microfilm 22943 F

WINDHAM. History and proceedings of the celebration of the 150th anniversary of the incorporation of the settlement of Windham ... 1892 ... Windham, N. H., The Executive committee, 1892. ix, 124 p. incl. 1 illus., facsim. ports. 23½ cm. 1-8083.
F44. W7W7

WINNIPESAUKEE. Season of 1905, Lake Winnipesaukee, New hotel Weirs, E. C. Hibbard. The Weirs, N. H. (1905) 12 x 16½ cm.
F44. W74S3

WOLFEBORO. Lake Wentworth. By Walter Parker Bowman. Wolfeboro, N. H., Lake Wentworth Assoc., 1956. 223 p. illus., ports., maps, fold. col. chart (in pocket) 28 cm. "Acknowledgements and biographical information": p. (195) - 198. 56-10358 rev.
F44. W8B6

WOLFEBORO, History of by Benjamin Franklin Parker ... Pub. by the town ... (Cambridge, Mass., Caustic & Claflin) 1901.   557 p. pl., port., plan. 24 cm. 2-18425.   F44. W8P2

WOLFEBORO.   The town register: Wolfeboro, Ossipee, Effingham, Tuftonboro, Tamworth, Freedom, 1908. Augusta, Me., The Mitchell-Cony co.inc., 1908.   2, (9) - 117, (2), 139 p. fold. map. 22 cm. 12-21878.
F44. W8T7

ELEMENTS IN THE POPULATION.

VERRETTE, Adrien.   Paroisse Saint Charles-Borromée, Dover, 1893 - 1933, publié par la Société Saint Jean-Baptiste de Dover.   (Manchester, N.H. "L'Avenir national") 1933.   3, xi - xii p., 15 - 383, (3) p. mounted col. front., plates, ports. 24½ cm. Issued in 2 parts with special covers. 33-23844.
BX4603. D6S3

WRITERS' PROGRAM.   Festal days, songs and games of the Franco-Americans of New Hampshire ... Manchester, N.H., Granite state press (194-?)   49 p. illus. 23 cm. Without music. 42-20633.
F45. F7W7

BRENNAN, James F.   ... The Irish settlers of southern New Hampshire ... (Peterborough? 1910)
11 p. 22½ cm. Reprinted from Journal of American Irish historical society, vol. IX, 1910. 12-24136.
F45. I6B8

REPORT of the attorney-general of New Hampshire, in the matter of the Swedes at Suncook.   Concord, N.H., P.B. Cogswell, 1883.   39 p. 22 cm. 8-18584.   F45. S9N5

LAMB, Fred William.   The great tornado of 1821 in New Hampshire; ... Manchester, N.H., 1908.
15 p. port. 24½ cm. Authorities: p. 14-15. 18-6166.   F45. T68L2

NEW HAMPSHIRE
SUPPLEMENTARY INDEX OF PLACES

AHQUEDAUKENASH. 133
ALEXANDRIA. 145
ALLENTOWN. 183
ALSTEAD. 142
ALTON. 141, 173
ALTON BAY. 141, 148
AMHERST. 122, 171
AMOSKEAG. 170
ANTRIM. 162
APTHORP. 167
ASHLAND. 126, 133, 176, 177
ASHUELOT. 142
ATKINSON. 146, 181
AUBURN. 146, 149, 152
BARNSTEAD. 183
BARRINGTON. 156, 158
BATH. 143
BEDFORD. 146, 149
BELKNAP Co. 145
BELMONT. 171, 183
BENNINGTON. 122
BERWICK. 156
BETH JCT. 143
BETHLEHEM. 138, 143
BRADFORD. 162
BRADFORD SPRINGS. 147
BRIDGEWATER. 145
BRISTOL. 126, 145
BROOKFIELD. 159
CAMPTON. 177
CANDIA. 146, 149, 160
CANOBIE LAKE. 181
CANTERBURY. 152
CENTER HARBOR. 141, 177
CHARLESTOWN. 164, 165, 184
CHESHIRE Co. 122
CHESTER. 156
CHESTERFIELD. 142, 163
CHICHESTER. 152, 183
CHISWICK. 167
CLAREMONT. 174
COLEBROOK. 143
COLUMBIA.
CONCORD. 130, 151, 168
CORBIN'S BLUE MOUNTAIN PARK. 147
COVENTRY-BENTON. 150
CROYDON. 155

CRYSTAL. 143
DARTMOUTH. 119, 161
DEERFIELD. 146, 152, 175
DEERING. 162
DERRY. 167, 169, 172
DERRY DEPOT. 172
DERRYFIELD. 168, 169, 170
DORCHESTER. 152
DUBLIN. 142
DUNSTABLE. 172
DURHAM. 157, 183
EAST DERRY. 167
EAST LEBANON (MASCOMA) 165
EAST PEPPERELL. 172
EFFINGHAM. 186
ENFIELD. 130, 147, 152, 176
ENFIELD (Shaker settlement) 147
EPPING. 177
EPSOM. 152, 183
EXETER. 177
FARMINGTON. 156, 159
FISHERVILLE. 154
FITZWILLIAM. 122, 142
FORT CONSTITUTION. 179
FRANCESTOWN. 162
FRANCONIA. 143, 165
FRANKLIN. 126, 133
FRANKLIN FALLS. 126
FREEDOM. 186
FREMONT. 146, 156
FRYEBURG. 142
GILFORD. 141, 160, 171
GILMANTON. 171, 183
GILSUM. 142, 183
GOFFSTOWN. 146, 149, 168
GORHAM. 150
GRAFTON. 152
GRAFTON Co. 144, 162
GRANTHAM. 155, 166, 176
GREAT FALLS. 156
GREENFIELD. 122
GREENLAND. 157, 177, 178
GREENVILLE. 172
GROVETON. 143
HAMPSTEAD. 146, 156
HAMPTON. 159
HANCOCK. 122

HARRISVILLE. 142
HARRYTOWN. 170
HAVERHILL. 143
HEBRON. 145
HILLSBOROUGH. 130
HILLSBORO Co. 142
HINSDALE. 142, 164
HOLDERNESS. 177
HOLLIS. 126, 162, 172
HOOKSETT. 149, 160
HOPKINTON. 130, 147, 162
HUDSON. 167, 172
JAFFREY. 122, 142, 170, 175
JEFFERSON. 143
KEENE. 142
KEARSARGE (Mountain) 147
KEZAR (Lake region) 147
KINGSTON. 146, 147, 174
LACONIA. 126, 133, 185
LAKE VILLAGE. 126
LAKE WENTWORTH. 185
LAKEPORT. 165
LANCASTER. 143
LEBANON. 161, 176
LEE. 156, 157, 158
LISBON. 143
LITTLETON. 135, 143, 149
LONDONDERRY. 146, 149, 169, 185
LOUDON. 152
LYME. 161
LYNDEBORO. 122, 171
MADBURY. 156, 157, 158
MANCHESTER. 164, 167
MAPLEWOOD. 143
MARLBORO. 142, 164
MARLOW. 142
MASCOMA (Lake) 147
MELVIN VILLAGE. 141
MEREDITH. 126, 141, 176, 182
MERIDEN. 155, 176
MERRIMACK. 122, 149, 171
MERRIMACK Co. 142, 153
MIDDLETON. 159
MILFORD. 122, 172
MILL HOLLOW. 158
MILLEN & HALF-MOON LAKES. 147
MILTON. 159
MILTON MILLS. 171
MONADNOCK. 133, 172
MONSON. 172
MONT VERNON. 122, 171
MOULTONBORO. 141, 177

MOULTONBOROUGH. 145
MOUNT AGASSIZ. 138
MOUNT MADISON. 138
MT. PEQUAWKET. 145
MOUNT SUNAPEE. 173
MOUNT WASHINGTON. 136, 137
NASHVILLE. 172
NELSON. 142
NEW BOSTON. 162
NEW DURHAM. 182
NEW HAMPTON. 171
NEW IPSWICH. 122
NEWCASTLE. 177, 178, 179
NEWFOUND LAKE. 151
NEWINGTON. 156, 157, 178
NEWMARKET. 157, 159, 177
NEWPORT. 130, 153
NEWTON. 146, 149
NORTHFIELD. 183
NORTHUMBERLAND. 143
NORTHWOOD. 152, 175
NUTFIELD. 167, 170
ORANGE. 152, 154
OSSIPEE. 186
PACKERSFIELD. 172
PASQUANEY LAKE. 151
PELHAM. 146, 149, 181
PEMBROKE. 183
PENACOOK. 154
PEQUAKET. 135
PERCY. 143
PETERBOROUGH. 122
PIKE. 143
PITTSFIELD. 160, 183
PLAINFIELD. 155, 166, 176
PLAISTOW. 146, 149, 174
PLYMOUTH. 126, 133
PORTSMOUTH. 128, 173
PROFILE. 143
RAYMOND. 146, 156
RICHMOND. 142
RINDGE. 122, 142
RIVERTON. 143
ROCHESTER. 156
ROLLINSFORD. 156, 157
ROXBURY. 165
ROYAL ARCH. 147
RYE. 177, 178
SALEM. 146, 149, 167
SALISBURY. 130
SANBORNTON. 171
SANBORNVILLE. 151, 171

SANDOWN. 146, 156	TYNG TOWNSHIP. 170
SANDWICH. 177, 183	UNION. 171
SLIPTOWN. 182	UPPER COOS. 135
SNOWTON. 181	WAKEFIELD. 151, 159, 171, 184
SOMERSWORTH. 157	WALPOLE. 142, 163, 164, 165
SOUTH CONWAY. 160	WARNER. 162
SOUTH NEWMARKET. 159, 177	WASHINGTON. 139, 162
SPOFFORD. 142	WEARE. 160, 162
STARK. 143	WEBSTER. 150
STEWARTSTOWN. 143	WEIRS (THE) 126, 133, 141, 165
STRAFFORD Co. 141, 146	WEST DUNSTABLE. 172
STRATFORD. 143	WEST LEBANON. (WESTBORO) 165
SUGAR HILL. 143	WESTMORELAND 142, 163, 183
SULLIVAN. 142	WESTVILLE. 174
SULLIVAN Co. 145	WHITEFIELD. 143
SUNAPEE. 153	WILTON. 122, 171, 172
SUNCOOK. 160, 183, 186	WINCHESTER. 142, 163, 164
SURRY. 142	WINDHAM. 146, 156, 167, 169
SWANZEY. 142, 164, 170	WINDSOR. 162
TAMWORTH. 183, 186	WINNEPESAUKEE. 139
TEMPLE. 122, 175	WINNEPESAUKEE (LAKE) 133, 185
THORNTON. 151	WINNIPISSEOGEE (LAKE) 135
TILTON. 126, 133, 171, 175	WOLFEBORO'. 126, 133, 141
TROY. 142, 170	WOODSVILLE. 143
TUFTONBORO. 141, 186	

ADDITIONS TO INDEX

HENNIKER. 147   LAKE SUNAPEE. 119

VERMONT

SELECTED BIBLIOGRAPHY FOR VERMONT

GILMAN, Marcus Davis. The bibliography of Vermont; or, A list of books and pamphlets relating in any way to the state. With biographical and other notes. (With additions by other hands.) Burlington, Printed by the Free press assoc., 1897. vii, 349 p. 27 cm. Over 7,000 title (including 3,452 Vermont imprints) arranged alphabetically by authors, with some form and subject headings. Appeared first in the Montpelier Argus and patriot, 1879 - 80. Ed. ... by George Grenville Benedict, who added 563 titles and 73 biographical sketches ... 3-8357* Cancel.

Z1343.G48B

VERMONT CLASSIFICATION   F46 - F60

46		Periodicals. Societies. Collections.
.5		Museums. Exhibitions, exhibits.
47		Gazetteers. Dictionaries. Geographic names.
.3		Guidebooks.
48		Biography (Collective). Genealogy (Collective).
.2		Historiography.
		Historians, *see* E 175.5.
.5		Study and teaching.
49		General works. Histories.
.3		Juvenile works.
.5		Minor works. Pamphlets, addresses, essays, etc.
.6		Anecdotes, legends, pageants, etc.
50		Historic monuments (General). Illustrative material.
51		Antiquities (Non-Indian).
		By period.
52		Early to 1791.

New Hampshire Grants; Green Mountain boys; etc.
Biography: Ira Allen, Thomas Chittenden, etc.
Cf. E 263.V5, Vermont in the Revolution (General);
   E 230.5–241, Military operations and battles.
F 37, New Hampshire colonial history.
F 122, New York colonial history.
F 127.A3, Albany County, N. Y.
F 127.W3, Charlotte (now Washington) County, N. Y.

53		1791–1865.

Admission as a state, March 4, 1791; etc.
Biography: Jacob Collamer, etc.
Cf. E 359.5.V3, War of 1812; E 355, Military operations.
   E 533, Civil War, 1861–1865 (General); E 470.95, St. Alban's Raid.

54		1865–1950.

Cf. D 570.85.V5–51, World War I, 1914–1918.
   D 769.85.V5–51, World War II, 1939–1945.
   E 726.V 5, War of 1898 (Spanish-American War).

55		1951–
57		Regions, counties, etc., A–Z.
	.A2	Addison Co.

Lake Dunmore, etc.

	.B4	Bennington Co.

Hoosic River and Valley, Vt. (Cf. F 72.B5, Massachusetts;
F 127.H73, General, and New York); etc.

	.B7	Boundaries.

Cf. F 42.B7, New Hampshire boundary.
F 72.B7, Massachusetts boundary.
F 127.B7, New York boundary.
New Hampshire-New York dispute over land in the present state of Vermont, *see* F 52.

.C2	Caledonia Co.
.C4	Lake Champlain region, Vt.

    Cf. F 57.G7, Grand Isle Co.
    F 127.C6, General, and New York.

.C5	Chittenden Co.
.C7	Connecticut River and Valley, Vt.

    Cf. F 12.C7, New England.

.E7	Essex Co.
.F8	Franklin Co.

    Missisquoi River and Valley, *see* F 57.M7.

.G7	Grand Isle Co.
.G8	Green Mountains.

    Hoosic River and Valley, Vt., *see* F 57.B4.

.L2	Lamoille Co.
.L22	Lamoille River and Valley.
.M3	Mount Mansfield.
.M5	Lake Memphremagog region, Vt.

    Cf. F 1054.M5, Quebec.

.M7	Missisquoi River and Valley, Vt.

    Cf. F 1054.B8, General, and Quebec.

.O56	Ompompanoosuc Parish.

    Cf. F 59.N9, Norwich.
    F 59.T4, Thetford.

.O6	Orange Co.
.O7	Orleans Co.

    Missisquoi River and Valley, *see* F 57.M7.

.R9	Rutland Co.

    Lake Bomoseen, etc.

.W3	Washington Co.
.W6	Windham Co.
.W7	Windsor Co.
.W73	Winooski River.

59   Cities, towns, etc., A–Z.

    e. g.
.B4	Bennington.
.B8	Brattleboro.
.B9	Burlington.
.M7	Montpelier.
.N9	Norwich.

    Ompompanoosuc Parish, *see* F 57.O56.

.T4	Thetford.

Elements in the population.

60   .A1   General works.
    .A2–Z   Individual elements.

    For a list of racial, ethnic, and religious elements (with cutter numbers), *see* E 184, p. 27–29.

VERMONT

F 46 - F 60

PERIODICALS. SOCIETIES. COLLECTIONS.

BROOKLYN Society of Vermonters, The.   Record of its organization and dinner ... 1891 ... Brooklyn, (Eagle press), 1891) 56 p. 23½ cm. 5-13237.   F46. B 87

BUFFALO society of Vermonters.   ... Roll of members ... Buffalo, 1900?)   (16) p. 19 cm. Organized 1894.   CA 19-74 unrev.   F46. B 92

DANA, John Cotton.   Vermont broadsides. Woodstock, Vt., The Elm tree press, 1912.   58 l. 29½ cm.   Consists of ... 56 broadsides of various sizes ... "poems, extracts from speeches and books. They all relate to Vermont. Many of them ... are of historic interest. 18-17120.   F46. D 16

GREATER Vermont association.   Bulletin no. -   (n. p., 1912?)   19½ cm.   F46. G 78

ILLINOIS association of sons of Vermont.   Annual reports ... (1st) - 5/6th.   Chicago, 1877 - 82.
4 v. 23 cm.   No more pub?   9-899 rev.   F46. I 29

INTER-STATE journal.   An illustrated monthly of the Connecticut Valley.   v. 1 - 10, Apr. 1900 - 1906.   White River Junction, Vt., C. R. Cummings, 1900 - 06.   10 v. in 2, illus. (incl. ports.) plates. 31 cm.
5-32187.   F46. I 61

MILLER, John Wesley.   Inter-state journal index.   Tiffin, Ohio, 1969.   48 p. 28 cm.
                                                                                                    F46. I 61
                                                                                                    Index

PACIFIC Coast association of the native sons of Vermont, The.   San Francisco, 1881.   1 pam. 22½ cm.
                                                                                                    F46. P 12

RURAL Vermonter.   v. 1 -   Fall, 1962 -   (Woodstock, etc. Vermont)   v. ports. 26 cm.
illus., maps.   Frequency varies.   Title varies.   F46. R 8

SONS of Vermont, First reunion of the, at Worcester, Mass., ... 1874.   Worcester, Print. C. Hamilton, 1874.   60 p. 24½ cm.   1-13340.   F46. S 69

VERMONT ... Index to the papers of the surveyors-general, pub. by authority of number 221, acts of 1906, by the secretary of state ... Rutland, Ct., The Tuttle co,, 1918.   170 p. front. (fold. map) 23 cm.
18-17858.   F46. V 35

VERMONT antiquarian, The   (A quarterly magazine devoted to the history and antiquities of Vermont and the Champlain and Connecticut valleys) v. 1 - 3; Burlington, Vt., The Research pub. co., (1902-05)   3 v. plates, ports. map. 24 cm. No more pub. 7-12926.   F46.V 42

VERMONT autograph and remarker. Huntington, Vt. (J. Johns, 1843)   1 no. 13½ x 10½ cm. A "miniature mimic newspaper" ... pub. at irregular intervals. Formerly called 'Huntington gazette' CA 5-849 unrev.   F46.V 43
Rare Book Room

VERMONT historical society. News and notes. Montpelier.   v. in   illus. 24 cm. monthly.
F46. V 5

VERMONT historical society. Constitution and by-laws ... Woodstock, Vt., Davis & Greene, print., 1860.   16 p. 23½ x 14 cm. Rc-3063.   F46.V 52

VERMONT historical society, Collections of the ... Montpelier, printed for the soc., 1870 - 71.
2 v. front. (v.2, port.) 23½ cm. 1-Rc-3064.   F46.V 53

VERMONT historical society. Index to the Collections of the Vermont historical society, vols. 1 - 10. Vomp. Earle Williams Newton, director. Montpelier, Vermont hist. soc., 1946.   vii, 87 p. 24 cm. Indexes v.1-2 of the society's colls., pub. 1870-71 and v.3-10, the latter being a regrouping and reissue of the addresses and papers written for the society prior to 1930 and orig. pub. in its biennial Proceedings (old series) 48-2733.   F46.V 53
Index vols. 1 -10

VERMONT life. v. 1 -   fall 1946 -   (Montpelier, Vermont Development Commission)
v. in   illus., ports., maps. 28 cm. quarterly. 51-31012.   F46.V 54

VERMONT history. - 1926/28; new ser., v. 1 -   1930 -   Montpelier (etc.) Vermont historical society.   v. in   illus., ports., maps. 24 cm. Frequency varies. Title varies. L.C. set lacks v.13. Indexes: New ser., v.1-10, 1930 - 42. 12-39720 rev. 4*   F46.V 55

VERMONT historical society. Addresses delivered before the Vermont historical society, in the representatives' hall, Montpelier, ... 1866. Montpelier, Walton's, 1866.   2, (3) - 44, (49) - 72 p.
4-3613.   F46.V 56

VERMONT quarterly gazetteer; a historical magazine, embracing a digest of the history of each town, civil, education, religious, geological and literary ... Ed. Abby Maria Hemenway ... no. 1-6; Ludlow, Vt., (1869-63)   616 p. plates, ports. 26 cm. Afterwards issued in volume form under title: The Vermont historical gazetteer ... 4-14753 rev.   F46.V 58

— 1868 - 91.   5 v. fronts., illus., plates, ports. 24½ cm. Title varies. Imprint varies. "This work ... at first issued in numbers, ... was called the Vermont quarterly gazetteer." Contents. - v.1. Addison, Bennington, Caledonia, Chittenden and Essex Counties. - v.2. Franklin, Grand Isle, Lamoille and Orange counties. Inc. also the natural history of Chittenden county and index to vol. 1 - v.3. Orleans and Rutland counties. Index to vols. 2-3. - v.4. Washington county, with histories of Swanton in Franklin county, Groton, in Caledonia county, and Hubbardton in Rutland county. - v.5. Windham county, with histories of Sutton in Caledonia county, and Bennington in Bennington county.

F46.V583

— Index to the contents of the Vermont historical gazetteer. Prepared ... George W. Wing ... Rutland, Vt., The Tuttle co., 1923.   2, (vii) - xii, 1118 p. 24½ cm.   "No two copies of the gazetteer have been ... bound alike." Rc3092 rev. 2.   F46.V583
Index

VERMONT review. v. 1-2; May/June 1926 - July/Aug. 1928. (Chelsea, E.A. Rockwood, 1926 - 28)
2 v. in 1. 30 cm. bimonthly. No more pub? 32-19220.   F46.V 63

VERMONT society of Southern California. Year book. Los Angeles, city, Cal. 19 -
v. illus. (ports.) 23 cm. CA 11-2034 unrev.   F46.V 66

VERMONTER, The. Index to the Vermont, vol. 1 - 17; pub. by the Vermont historical soc,, E. Lee Whitney, comp.   (In Vermont hist soc. Proceedings ... 1911-1912. p. (115) -162) 13-24537.   F46. V 7
F46.V55 1911-12

188

VERMONT

VERMONTER, The. The state magazine. v. 1 - Aug., 1895 - St. Albans, Vt., C. S. Forbes, 1895 - 1905; White River Junction, Vt., C. R. Cummings, 1906 - v. illus., plates, ports., maps, facsims. 25½ x 30½ cm. monthly. Subtitle varies. Absorbed the Inter-state journal in Jan. 1906. 5-32194 (rev. '21) F46. V 7

VERMONTER, Index to the, 1914 through 1939, vols. 18 - 44 ... Comp. and issued by the Free public library commission, Montpelier, Vt. (Montpelier) Vt. hist. soc. (c.1941) 108 p. 23 cn. 5-32194 x[1]
F46. V 7
Index vols. 18 - 44
1914-39

MUSEUMS. EXHIBITIONS, EXHIBITS.

BENNINGTON Museum, The, one of America's outstanding regional museums. (Bennington, Vt., (1971) 1 v. (unpaged) illus. 31 x 32 cm. 75-158129. F46.5.B45

GAZETTEERS. DICTIONARIES. GEOGRAPHIC NAMES.

DEAN, James. An alphabetical atlas, or, Gazetteer of Vermont; affording a summary description of the state, its several counties, towns, and rivers. Montpelier, Print. Samuel Goss ... 1898
43 p. 21 cm. Rc-3080. F47. D 28

— 1808. 43 p. 20½ cm. 4-7826. F47. D 29

GEORGE, Noah J. T. comp. A pocket geographical and statistical gazetteer of the state of Vermont. Haverhill, N.H., S.T. Goss, 1823. vii, (9) - 264 p. 13½ x 8 cm. 3-14605. F47. G 34
Rare Book Room

HAYWARD, John. A gazetteer of Vermont: containing descriptions of all the counties, towns, and districts in the state, ... Boston, Tappan, Whittemore and Mason, 1849. iv, (5) - 216 p. front. (map) 20 cm. Rc-3111. F47. H 42

HUDEN, John Charles. Indian place names in Vermont. (Burlington, Vt.) 1957. (Vermont University Monograph no. 1) 58-26541. F47. H 8

THOMPSON, Zadock. A gazetteer of the state of Vermont; containing a brief general view of the State, a historical and topographical description of all the counties, towns, rivers, etc. Montpelier, E. P. Walton, print., 1824. vi, (9) - 310 p. front. (fold. map) plates. 18 cm. Rc-3081.
F47. T 47

THOMPSON, Zadock. History of Vermont, natural, civil, and statistical, in three parts, with a new map of the state, and 200 engravings. Burlington, C. Goodrich, 1842. 3 pt. in 1 v. front. (fold. map) illus. 24 cm. 16-9907. F49. T483

— Burlington, 1853. 4 pt. in 1 v. front. (fold. map) illus. 24 cm. 1-21609. F49. T 49

VERMONT, the land of Green mountains ... Essex Junction, Vt., Vermont Bureau of publicity, Office of secretary of state (1913) 202, vi p. illus. 23 cm. 13-15218 rev. F47. V 45

GUIDEBOOKS.

HARD, Walter R. The Vermont guide. Brattleboro, Vt., Book Cellar, c.1958. 64 p. illus. 21 cm. 58-11709. F47.3.H3
1958

HARD, Walter R.   The new Vermont guide, by Walter Ward, Jr., and others.   Brattleboro, Vt., S. Greene, c.1964.   81 p. 21 cm.   64-17557.
F47.3.H3
1964

DIRECTORIES.

VERMONT business directory, for 1870 - 89 ... Boston, Mass., Briggs directory and pub. co., 1870 - 89.   18 v. 24 cm.   Title varies.   No. ed. for 1881.   7-38090.
Directories

VERMONT state directory and gazetteer ... 18   Methuen, Mass. Union pub. co., 18   - 19   v.   24½ cm.   Title varies.   1-31076 rev.
Directories

VERMONT directory and farmers' almanac, ... Claremont, N.H. 18   v. 15 cm.
Directories

U.S. Bureau of the census ... Heads of families at the first census of the U.S. taken in 1790.   Washington, Govt. print. off., 1907 - 08.   12 v. fronts. (fold. maps) 29½ cm. 7-35273.
F47.5.U58

VERMONT directory and commercial almanac ... no. 1 -   1855 -   Rutland, Tuttle, Gay & co.; 1854 -   v. illus., maps. 14 cm.   10-14018 rev.
F47.5.V45

BIOGRAPHY (COLLECTIVE). GENEALOGY (COLLECTIVE).

U.S. Census Office.   Heads of families at the second census of the U.S. taken in the year 1800: Vermont.   Baltimore, Genealogical Pub. Co., 1972.   233 p. 29 cm.   Reprint of 1938 ed.   71-39493 MARC.
F48.A 43
1972

— Montpelier, Vt. historical soc., 1938.   233 p. incl. tables, front. (fold. map) 29 x 24 cm. 39-28821.
F48.U 55

BARDEN, Merritt Clark.   Vermont, once no man's land. ..   Rutland, Vt., The Tuttle co., 1928.   xvi, 197 (i.e.219) p. front., illus. (incl. plans, coats of arms) plates. 26 cm.   "A genealogical summary of the families who have lived along the New York border in Vermont, and their connection with those who lived over the line in New York."   29-1204.
F48.B 24

BIOGRAPHICAL encyclopaedia of Vermont in the 19th century.   Boston, Metropolitan pub. and engr. cr., 1885.   vi, (9) - 422 p. 43 port. 30 cm.   In double columns.   3-18806.
F48.B 61

CARLETON, Hiram.   Genealogical and family history of the state of Vermont; a record of the achievements of her people in the making of a commonwealth and the founding of a nation; ...   New York, Chicago, The Lewis pub. co., 1903.   2 v. fronts., illus., plates, ports. 28 x 22½ cm.   4-7975.
F48.C 28

CROCKETT, Walter Hill, ed.   ... Vermonters; a book of biographies.   Brattleboro, Stephen Daye (c.1931)   254 p. 19½ cm.   (The Green mountains series) 31-16883.
F48.C 86

— Second edition.   (c.1932)   254 p. 19½ cm.   32-13644.
F48.C862

DEMING, Leonard.   Catalogue of the principal officers of Vermont, as connected with its political history, from 1778 to 1851, with some biographical notices, etc. by Leonard Deming ...   Middlebury (Vt.) The author, 1851.   112 p. 23½ cm.   3-28220.
F48.D 38

—   216 p. 22½ cm.   "Appendix to Deming's Catalogue of Vermont officers": p. (121) - 208.   Rc-3087.
F48.D 39

DODGE, Prentiss Cutler.   Encyclopedia, Vermont biography; a series of authentic biographical sketches of the representative men of Vermont and sons of Vermont in other states.   1912.   Burlington, Vt., Ullery pub. co., 1912.   372 p. ports. 17 cm.   13-5028.
F48.D 64

HILLS, Frederick Simon, comp.   Men of Vermont state.   Individual library ed., with biographic

studies, character portraits and autographs.   Albany, N.Y., The Albany argus art press, 1925 -
v. port. 30 cm. 27-14508.   F48.H 65

JEFFREY, William Hartley.   Successful Vermonters; a modern gazetteer of Caledonia, Essex and Orleans counties, containing an historical review of the several towns and a series of biographical sketches ... East Burke, Vt., The Historical pub. co., 1904.   1, xii, (2), (5) - 361, 158, 274 p. illus., ports. 25½ cm. 20-2619.   F48.J 46

— 1907.   3, 479, (1) p. illus., ports. 25 cm. 22-4167.   F48.J 463

KENT, Dorman Bridgman Eaton.   One thousand men.   (Montpelier) The Vermont historical society, c. 1915.   144 p. 23 cm. From Proceedings of Vermont historical soc., 1913 - 1914. Names and brief mention of one thousand prominent native Vermonters. 17-2407.   F48.K 37

KENT, Dorman Bridgman Eaton.   Vermonters.   (Montpelier) Vermont historical soc., c. 1937
187 p. 23 cm. An enlarged ed. of the author's "One thousand men" see above item. 37-10938.   F48.K372

LEE, John Parker.   Uncommon Vermont; with an introd. by John Spargo.   Rutland, Vt., The Tuttle co. (c. 1926)   4, (11) - 207 p. 1 illus. 19½ cm. "Books that have been consulted": p. 205-207. 27-3698.   F48.L 45

MEN of progress; biographical sketches and portraits of leaders in business and professional life in and of the state of Vermont; comp. under the supervision of Richard Herndon; ed. G. Grenville Benedict.   Boston, New England magazine, 1898.   312 p. illus. (ports.) 29 cm. 98-1244 rev.
F48.M 53

SPURLING, Mrs. Fannie (Smith)   Gravestone inscriptions ... Delavan, Wisconisn, 1937.   3, 39 p. 29 cm. Mimeographed. 38M4837T.   S48.S 78

ULLERY, Jacob G.   Men of Vermont: an illus. biographical history of Vermonters and sons of Vermont.   Brattleboro, Transcript pub. co., 1894.   3 pts. in 1 v. ports., facsim. 28½ cm. Contents. - pt. I. Introd. by Redfield Proctor. Historical biographies, by C.H. Davenport. Judges of the Supreme court, by Hiram A. Huse. Vermont inventors, by Levi K. Fuller. Queer characters, by Hiram A. Huse. - pt. II. Biographies of Vermonters, 1892 - 94. - pt. III. Biographies of sons of Vermont. 4-2423.
F48.U 41

VERMONT marriages ...   Burlington, Vt., Boston, Mass., Research pub. co., 1903.   1 v. 23½ cm. 12-39772.   F48.V 55

— Genealogical pub. co., 1967.   1 v. 24 cm. 67-30525.   F48.V 56
L.H. & G. Ref. coll.

GENERAL WORKS. HISTORIES.

Vermont. Dept. of Education.   Vermont and its opportunites.   Ed. Ralph E. Noble, commissioner of education.   (Montpelier?) ... 1944.   20 p. illus. 23 x 10 cm. 55-46255.   F49.A 52

BASSETT, Thomas D.   Outsiders inside Vermont: travellers' tales over 358 years.   An anthology ... Brattleboro, Vt., Greene Press (c. 1967)   viii, 136 p. 21 cm. 67-27301.   F49.B 3

BECKLEY, Hosea.   The history of Vermont; with descriptions, physical and topographical.   Brattleboro, G.H. Salisbury, 1846.   xvi, (17) - 396 p. 19½ cm. 1-Rc-3082.   F49.B 39

BISHOP, Alicia R.   My little Vermont book.   Illus. Ferris K. O'Connell.   Maps by the National Survey, Chester, Vt.   (South Londonderry? c. 1966)   72 p. 24 cm.   F49.B 55

BUTLER, James Davie.   Deficiencies in our history.   An address delivered before the Vermont historical and antiquarian soc ... 1846. Montpelier, Eastman & Danforth, 1846.   36 p. 21 cm. 2-11306.
F49.B 98

6   LOCAL HISTORIES IN THE LIBRARY OF CONGRESS

— (Woodstock, Vt., Elm tree press, 1910)   4, (5) - 43 p.   front., port.   21½ cm.   10-21787.

F49.B982

CARPENTER, William Henry. The history of Vermont, from its earliest settlement to the present time. Philadelphia, Lippincott, Grambo, 1853.   1, 260 p. front. 17 cm. 1-Rc-3083.

F49.C 29

CARTER, Robert M. Studies in Vermont history, geography and government, St. Johnsbury, Vt., Carter & co. (c. 1937)   95 p. front. (map) illus. (incl. maps) 20 cm. Includes bibliographies. 37-18225.   F49.C 34

CHIPMAN, Daniel. The life of Hon. Nathaniel Chipman, formerly member of the U.S. Senate, and chief justice of the state of Vermont. By his brother ...   Boston, C. C. Little and J. Brown, 1846. xii, (5) - 402 p. 24 cm. 7-16418.

F49.C 54

COLLINS, Edward Day. A history of Vermont ... with geological and geographical notes, bibliography, chronology, maps, and illus. Boston, Ginn & co., 1903.   x, 325 p. incl. front. (port.) illus. maps. 19 cm. 3-26357.

F49.C 71

— Rev. ed. Boston, New York, etc. Finn & co., (c. 1916)   x, 351 p. incl. front. (port.) illus. maps. 19 cm. 16-12261.

F49.C715

CONANT, Edward. Geography, history and civil government of Vermont ... Rutland, Vt., The Tuttle co., 1890.   288 p. illus. (incl. maps) 21 cm. Rc-3084.

F49.C 74

— 5th ed., rev. and enl. by Mason S. Stone ... Rutland, Vt., The Tuttle co., 1907.   445 p. front., illus., ports., maps. 21 cm. "Reference books pertaining to the history and geography of Vermont ..." p. (9) - 10. 7-27030.

F49.C744

COOLIDGE, Austin Jacobs. History and description of New England. Vermont. Boston, A. J. Coolidge, 1860.   iv, 705 - 974, 11, (8) p. front., illus., plates, fold. map. 24½ cm. Reprinted from v. 1 of the author's History and description of New England. A list of "Natives of Vermont resident in Boston and vicinity" and "Biographical notices": 11, (8) p. at end. Rc-3086 rev.

F49.C 77

CRAIG, Frank H. Vermont sketches, 1924, by Frank H. Craig ... Barre, Granite City press, 1924. 63 p. front., illus. 23½ cm. 28-28056.

F49.C 87

CRANE, Charles Edward. Let me show you Vermont; with an introd. by Dorothy Canfield Fisher. New York, London, A. A. Knopft, 1937.   xix, 347, xxiv p. front., plates, maps (1 fold.) 22½ cm. "First edition." 37-27328.

F49.C 88

CROCKETT, Walter Hill. Vermont, the Green Mountain state. New York, The Century history co., inc., 1921.   4 v. fronts., plates, ports., maps, plans, facsims. 24½ cm. 21-21207.   F49. C 9

DAVIS, Gilbert Asa. Historical address, delivered at Windsor, Vt., ... 1877, at the celebration of the 100th anniversary of the adoption of the consitution of the state of Vermont ... Rutland, Tuttle & co., print., 1879.   23 p. 24 cm. 19-3950.

F49.D 26

EASTMAN, Francis Smith. A history of Vermont, from its first settlement to the present time. With a geographical account of the country, and a view of its original inhabitants. For the use of schools. Brattleboro', Holbrook and Fessenden, 1828.   iv, (7) - 110 p. 16 cm. Rc-3088 rev.

F49.E 13
Rare Book Room

FISHER, Dorothea Frances (Canfield) Memories of Arlington, Vermont. (1st ed.) New York, Duell, Sloan and Pearce (1957)   c   214 p. 20 cm. (Memories of my home town) 57-11058.   F49.F 55

FISHER, Dorothea Frances (Canfield) Vermont tradition; the biography of an outlook on life. (1st ed.) Boston, Little, Brown (1953)   488 p. 22 cm. 53-10226.   F49.F 57

FOLSOM, William R. Vermonters in battle, and other papers. Montplier, Vermont Historical Soc.,

VERMONT

(1953)   xvi, 236 p. illus., maps. 24 cm. 54-670.   F49. F 6

FULLER, Edmund. Vermont; a history of the Green Mountain State. Montpelier (Vt.) State Board of Education (1952)   284 p. illus. 23 cm. 52-62606. rev.   F49. F 8

— Studying Vermont history; a teacher's guide. Montpelier, State Dept. of Education, 1954.
47 p. illus. 28 cm. "Represents the cooperative effort of many Vermont teachers, etc."   F49. F 8
Guide

GARDNER, Abraham Brodkins. In memoriam. (Bennington? Vt., 1881?)   30 p. 22 cm. 4-24808.
F49.G 22

GREENE, Frank Lester. Vermont, the Green Mountain state; past, present, prospective. Pub. by the Vermont Commission to the Jamestown tercentennial exposition. (St. Albans) St. Albans messenger co., print., 1907.   80 p. illus. 23 cm. 8-9823 rev.   F49.G 79

HALL, Benjamin Homer. History of eastern Vermont, from its earliest settlement to the close of the 18th century. With a biographical chapter and appendixes. New York, D. Appleton & co., 1858.
xii, 799 p. illus. (incl. ports., facsims.) 23 cm. That portion of the state east of the Green Mountains comprised in old counties of Cumberland and Gloucester (now Windham, Windsor, Orange, Washington, Caledonia, Essex and Orleans counties) 1-Rc-3089.   F49.H 17

— Albany, N.Y., J. Munsell, 1865.   2 v. front. (facsim.) illus. (incl. ports.) 27 cm. Paged continuously. First ed. 1858
(see item above for details) 10-14017.   F49.H175

HALL, Samuel Read. The child's assistant to a knowledge of the geography and history of Vermont.
2d ed. By S.R. Hall. Montpelier, Print. E.P. Walton, 1829.   vi, (7) - 90 p. 14 cm. 19-1177.
F49.H182
Rare Book Room

— 3d ed. ... Montpelier, Vt. E.P. Walton, 1833.   75 p. illus. 18 cm. 19-1178.   F49.H183
Rare Book Room

HALL, Samuel Read. The geography and history of Vermont, ... Also the Constitution of the U.S. with notes and questions. 2d ed. rev. by Pliny H. White ... Montpelier, C.W. Willard, 1868.
(7) - 270 p. illus., maps (1 fold.) 19 cm. Recommended by the Board of education of Vermont, for use in the schools of the state. 13-5131.
F49. H 2

HAZEN, Henry Allen. New Hampshire and Vermont: an historical study. (Reprinted from the Proceedings of the N.H. historical soc.) Concord, N.H., Republican press assoc.) 1894.   15 p. 25 cm.
4-33435.   F49.H 42

HEATON, John Langdon. ... The story of Vermont. Illus. by L.J. Bridgman. Boston, Lothrop co.,
(c. 1889)   319 p. incl. illus., plates. front. 21½ cm. (Half-title: The story of the states. v.4) 1-Rc-3091.   F49.H 43

HEMENWAY, Abby M. Notes by the path of the Gazetteer. 1886 -   v.   F49.H 49

HILL, Ralph Nading. Contrary county, a chronicle of Vermont; illus. by George Daly. New York, Rinehart (1950)   309 p. illus. 22 cm. Bibliography: p. 293 - 299. 50-12397.   F49.H 55

— (2d ed.) Brattleboro, Vt., Stephen Greene Press (1961)   255 p. 22 cm.   F49.H 55
1961

HILL, Ralph Nading. Yankee kingdom: Vermont and New Hampshire. Illus. by George Daly. (1st ed.) New York, Harper (1960)   338 p. 22 cm. (A Regions of America book) 60-7529.
F49.H555

HISTORICAL souvenir of Vermont, with the story of old Vermont in pictures, from drawings by R.F. Heinrich for the National life insurance co.; a summary of events leading to the formation of the state, ... historical notes on each town ... Chester, Vt., The National survey co., c. 1941.   96 p. illus.
(incl. map) 23 cm. Bibliographical references included in Foreword. 41-21320.   F49.H 57

HOSKINS, Nathan. A history of the state of Vermont, from its discovery and settlement to the close of the year 1830.   Vergennes (Vt.) J. Shedd, 1831.   316 p. 18 cm. Rc-3093. F49.H 82

KIMBALL, Miriam Irene.   Vermont for young Vermonters, ... New York, D. Appleton, 1904.
xviii, 413 p. incl. front., illus., maps, facsim. 19½ cm. 4-14167. F49.K 49

— Boston, New York (etc.) D. C. Heath & co. (c.1926)   xix, 423 p. incl. front., illus. double map. 19 cm.
26-14028. F49.K492

MAUNSELL, David.   Gazetteer of Vermont heritage; a concise account of the discovery, settlement, and progress of interesting and remarkable events in the green mountain country ... Chester, Vt., National Survey, c.1966.   95 p. 28 cm. F49. M 3

NEWTON, Earle Williams.   The Vermont story; a history of the people of the Green Mountain State, 1749 - 1949. ... Montpelier, Vt. Historical Soc., 1949.   x, 281 p. illus. (part col.) ports. (part col.) maps (part col.) 28 cm. (The American States) Bibliography: p. 272 - 274. 49-9803*. F49.N 49

PRATT, Walter Merriam.   Adventure in Vermont, wherein we buy a house and have the pleasure of restoring it with the atomosphere and gracious living of an earlier day ... 49 illus.   Cambridge, Mass., University press (1943)   xv, 182 p. incl. front., illus. plates, ports. 23½ cm. 43-14928.
F49. P 7

ROBINSON, Rowland Evans.   ... Vermont: a study of independence.   Boston and New York, Houghton, Mifflin, 1892.   vi, 370 p. front. (fold. map) 18 cm. (Half-title: American commonwealths ... v.14) Rc-3094/3.
F49.R 66

RURAL Vermont; a program for the future, by two hundred Vermonters.   Burlington, The Vermont commission on country life, 1931.   ix, 385 p. illus. (maps) pl., diagrs. 23 cm. Contains bibliographies. 31-35533.
F49.R 93

SLOCUM, Harold W.   The story of Vermont.   New York, Chicago (etc.) C. Scribner's sons (c.1926) x, 140 p. illus (incl. ports., map) 18 cm. 26-15029. F49.S 63

STONE, Arthur Fairbanks.   The Vermont of today, with its historic background, attractions and people, ... New York, Lewis historical pub. co., inc., 1929.   4 v. fronts., plates, ports., facsim. 27½ cm.
Vols. 1-2 and 3-4 paged continuously. Biographical sketches: v.3-4. 30-9716.
F49.S 87

THOMPSON, Zadock.   History of the state of Vermont, from its earliest settlement to the close of the year 1832.   Bulington (!), E. Smith, 1833.   252 p. 17½ cm. 1st ed. Rc-3095. F49.T 47

THOMPSON, Zadock.   History of Vermont, natural, civil, and statistical, in three parts, with a new map of the state, and 200 engravings.   Burlington, Pub. for the author, by C. Goodrich, 1842.
3 pts. in 1 v. illus., map. 24 cm. Map wanting. 1-Rc-3096. F49.T 48

— Burlington, C. Goodrich, 1842.   3 pt. in 1 v. front. (fold. map) illus. 24 cm. 16-9907.
F49.T483

THOMPSON, Zadock.   Index, History of Vermont, natural, civil and statistical, edition of 1842; comp. by William Arba Ellis ...   (In Vt. hist. soc. Proceedings ... 1911-12 p. (163) - 266) 13-24536.   F49.T 49
F46.V 55 1911-12

THOMPSON, Zadock.   History of Vermont, natural, civil and statistical, in three parts, with an appendix. 1853. Burlington, The author, 1853.   4 pt. in 1 v. front. (fold. map) illus. 24 cm. 1-21609.
F49.T 49

THOMPSON, Zadock.   Appendix to the History of Vermont ... , 1853.   Burlington, The author, 1853.
63 p. front. (fold. map) illus. 24 cm. Also in the the 1853 ed. of the author's History of Vermont. 18-6576. F49.T493

THOMPSON, Zadock.   History of the state of Vermont; for the use of families and schools.   Burlington

(Vt.) Smith and co., 1858.   252 p. 16 cm.   17-19934. F49.T499
Toner coll.

VERMONT.   Records of the governor and Council of the state of Vermont ... Ed. and pub. by authority of the state by E. P. Walton.   Montpelier, J. & J. M. Poland, 1873-80.   8 v. fronts., plates, ports., fold. map. 24 cm. 1-Rc-3097. F49.V 52

VERMONT life.   Green Mountain treasury; a Vermont life sampler.   Ed. by Walter Hard, Jr. and others.   New York, Harper (1961)   188 p. 28 cm. 61-6434.   F49.V 55

VERMONT life.   A treasury of Vermont life, ed. by Stephen Greene (and others)   Woodstock, Vt., Countryman Press (1956)   viii, 191 p. illus. (part col.) ports., maps. 28 cm. 56-10843. F49.V 56

WILGUS, William John.   The role of transportation in the development of Vermont, ... Montpelier, Vermont historical soc., 1945.   104 p. incl. front., maps (part fold. 1 in pocket) diagr. 28 x 22 cm. Bibliography: p. 100-102. 45-37381. F49.W 67

WILLIAMS, Samuel.   The natural and civil history of Vermont.   Pub. according to act of Congress. Print. Walpole, Newhampshire, by Isaiah Thomas and David Carlisle, jun., 1794.   xvi, (17) - 416 p. front. (fold. map) 21½ cm. 1-13341. F49.W 71
Rare Book Room

— 2d ed. cor. and much enl.   Burlington, Vt., Print. Samuel Mills ... 1809.   2 v. front. (fold. map) 20½ cm. Rc-3098. F49.W 72

WOLF, Marguerite Hurrey.   Vermont is always with you.   Drawings by George Daly.   Brattleboro, Vt., S. Greene Press, 1969.   ix, 121 p. illus. 25 cm. 76-88772. F49.W 8

JUVENILE WORKS.

BAILEY, Bernadine (Freeman)   Picture book of Vermont.   Pictures by Kurt Wiese.   Chicago, A. Whitman, c. 1961.   (unpaged) 17 x 21 cm. 61-9972. F49.3.B3

— Rev. ed.   Chicago, A. Whitman (1965)   32 p. (The United States books) F49.3.B3
1965

CARPENTER, John Allan.   Vermont.   Illus. by Phil Austin.   Chicago, Childrens Press (c. 1967) 95 p. 24 cm. (Enchantment of America) AC67-10278.   F49.3.C3

KELLEY, Shirley Whitney.   Little settlers of Vermont; a true story of the journey of a pioneer family through New England.   (Orford, N.H., Equity Pub. Corp., 1963)   105 p. 24 cm. 63-17889. F49.3.K4

O'NEIL.   Growing up in Vermont.   2d ed.   Rutland, Vt. (C. E. Tuttle Co., 1960)   89 p. 29 cm. "A complete and revised photo offset reproduction of the first ed." 60-7301.   F49.3.O6
1960

ANECDOTES, LEGENDS, PAGEANTS, ETC.

HARD, Margaret (Steel)   Footloose in Vermont.   Middlebury, Vermont Books (1969)   64 p. 23 cm. F49.6.H3

HISTORIC MONUMENTS (GENERAL). ILLUSTRATIVE MATERIAL.

VERMONT. Historic Sites Commission. Report. (Montpelier) v. illus. 23 cm. biennial. Period covered by report ends June 30. 51-62229.
F50. A 3

ALLEN, Elizabeth. Sketches of Green Mountain life; with an autobiography of the author. Lowell (Mass.) N. L. Dayton, 1846. 160 p. 15 cm. Tale dealing chiefly with life in Vermont. 5-37456.
F50. A 42

BENTON, Josiah Henry. Remarks of J. H. Benton, jr., president of the Vermont association of Boston at its annual banquet ... 1905. Boston (The University press, Cambridge, 1905) 1, 14 p. 24½ cm. 6-1111.
F50. B 47

CONANT, Edward. The Vermont primary historical reader and lessons on the geography of Vermont. ... Rutland, Vt., The Tuttle co,, 1895. 227 p. illus. (incl. maps) 20 cm. Rc-3085.
F50. C 75

CONANT, Edward. Vermont historical reader and lessons on the geography of Vermont ... 4th ed. rev. and enl. by competent authority. Rutland, Vt., The Tuttle co,, 1907. 254 p. illus. (incl. maps) plates. 20 cm. 7-37718.
F50. C 76

CONGDON, Herbert Wheaton. Old Vermont houses; the architecture of a resourceful people; illus. by the author. Brattleboro (Vt.) Stephen Daye press, 1940. 190 p. incl. front., illus. 25½ cm. "This book (is) the product of its illustrations which were originally made for the Old buildings project planned by the Robert Hull Fleming museum." - Introd. "First ed." 40-27378.
F50. C 78

CROWN Point Road Association. Historical markers on the Crown Point Road. Illus. by Peg Armitage. Maps by Carl E. Hollender. (Springfield? Vt.) c. 1955) 43 p. 22 cm.
F50. C 84

DOUGLASS, Paul Franklin. The Yankee tradition ... Burlington, (Vt.) Free press print. co., 1941. xix, (3) - 91 p. illus. 22 cm. "The substance of this little vol. was delivered as the address at the annual meeting of the Vermont historical soc. in the sesquicentennial year of Vermont's statehood." 44-10450.
F50. D 6

FISHER, Mrs. Dorothea Frances (Canfield) Vermont summer homes. (Montpelier, Vt., Vermont bureau of publicity, c. 1932) (32) p. illus. 24½ cm. 32-18702.
F50. F 63
— c. 1935. (32) p. illus. 24½ cm. 35-27695.
F50. F 63
1935

GEOGRAPHICAL and historical poem on Vermont. By a citizen of Washington County. Northfield, Vt., C. O. Kimball, 1852. 12 p. front. (fold. map) 16 cm. 5-3010.
F50. G 34

HILL, Ralph Nading. Vermont; a special world. Montpelier, Vermont Life Magazine (c. 1969) 167 p. illus. 28 cm. 68-29894.
F50. H 5

HOLMES, Kenneth B. Historic Vermont, a guide to some historic sites and roadside markers. Ed. Earle W. Newton. Montpelier, Historic Sites Commission (1949?) 43 p. illus., maps. 27 cm. 51-806.
F50. H 6

MERKLE, George. This is Vermont; life in historical Vermont from 1609 to the present ... (2d ed.) Ramsey, N. J. Model Craftsman Pub. Corp. (1965, c. 1953) 80 p. 21 cm. 65-15719.
F50. M 4
1965

MUSSEY, June Barrows. Vermont heritage, a picture story; illus. with over 170 old engravings from the Museum Society, Brattleboro, Vt. State ed., with a chapter on Vermont government, by Doris E. Robbins. New York, A. A. Wyn, 1947. 80 p. illus., ports., map. 24 cm. 47-5991*.
F50. M 8
1947

VERMONT

— another ed. 1947. 64 p. illus., ports., map. 24 cm. 47-5979*. F50. M 8
1947a

SONS of the American Revolution. Markers and tablets located in or near Vermont, which commemorate historic events and men of the Revolutionary days in Vermont. Burlington, 1956. 24 p. illus. 21 cm. 56-38461. F50. S 75

STAFFORD, Wendell Phillips. Vermont ... Middlebury, Vt., 1910. 14 l. 23½ cm. Printed on one side of leaf only. In verse. 11-10005. F50. S 77

WILLIAMS, Mrs. Harret (Langdon) Geographical and historical poem on Vermont. West Randolph, Vt., Buck's book and job press (c.1893) 24 p. 18½ cm. 17-19963. F50. W 72

EARLY TO 1791.

ALLEN, Ethan. A concise refutation of the claims of New-Hampshire and Massachusetts-Bay to the territory of Vermont; with occasional remarks on the long disputed claim of New-York to the same. Bennington, 1780. 29 p. 19 cm. Rc-3099. F52. A 42
Rare Book Room

ALLEN, Ethan. The present state of the controversy between the states of New-York and New-Hampshire on the one part, and the state of Vermont on the other. Hartford (Conn.) Print, Hudson & Goodwin, 1782. 16 p. 18 cm. Pub. anonymously. 1-Rc-3101. F52. A 43
Rare Book Room

ALDERMAN, Clifford Lindsey. Gathering storm; the story of the Green Mountain Boys. New York, J. Messner (c.1970) 189 p. 22 cm. (Milestones in history) 71-123179. F52. A432
1970

ALLEN, Ira. Miscellaneous remarks, on the proceedings of the state of New-York against the state of Vermont etc. Hartford, Print. Hannah Watson, 1777. 13 p. 21 cm. Rc-3103. F52. A 44

ALLEN, Ira. The natural and political history of the state of Vermont, one of the United States of America. ... London, Print. J. W. Myers, 1798. vii, 300 p. 21 cm. Rc-3105. F52. A 45
Rare Book Room

— Rutland, Vt., C. E. Tuttle Co. (1969) 179 p. 24 cm. 69-19611. F42. A 45
1969

ALLEN, Ira. Some miscellaneous remarks, and short arguments, on a small pamphlet, dated ... 1776 ... And some reasons given, why the district of the New-Hampshire grants had best be a state. Hartford, Print. Ebenezer Watson, 1777. 26 p. 21½ x 16½ cm. 2-9671. F52. A 46
Rare Book Room

— (Boston, 1924) facsim. 26 numb. l. 25½ cm. 24-17979. F52. A465
Rare Book Room

ALLEN, Ira. A vindication of the conduct of the General assembly of the state of Vermont, held at Windsor ... 1778, against allegations and remarks of the protesting members ... Dresden (N. H.) Print. A. Spooner (1779) 48 p. 16 cm. Regarding the annexation to Vermont of 16 towns east of the Connecticut river. 1-15919. F52. A 47
Rare Book Room

— (1936) 1 v. Photostated at the Massachusetts historical soc. no. 12) F52. A472
Rare Book Room

BEMIS, Samuel Flagg. Relations between the Vermont separatists and Great Britain, 1789 - 1791,

contributed by S. F. Bemis. (New York, 1916) p. 547 - 560. 27 cm. "Reprinted from the American historical review, vol. xxi, no. 3, April, 1916." CA 33-43 unrev.
F52. B 43

BENEDICT, George Grenville. The recovery of the Fay records. (From Vermont historical soc. Proceedings ... 1903 - 04. p. (49) - 55. 9-22113.
F52. B 46

BENTON, Reuben Clark. The Vermont settlers and the New York land speculators. Minneapolis, Housekeeper press, 1894. 188 p. 22 cm. Rc-3107.
F52. B 47

CHASE, Francis. Gathered sketches from the early history of New Hampshire and Vermont; containing vivid and interesting account of a great variety of the adventures of our forefathers, and of other incidents of olden time. Claremont, N.H., Tracy, Kenney & co., 1856. 215 p. front., plates. 18½ cm. Frontispiece wanting. 8-5937.
F52. C 48

DEAN, Leon W. The admission of Vermont into the Union, (Montpelier) Vermont historical soc., 1941. 8, 62 p. 23 cm. 41-8388.
F52. D 35

DE PUY, Henry Walter. Ethan Allen and the Green-Mountain heroes of '76. With a sketch of the early history of Vermont. Buffalo, Phinney & co., 1853. xvii, (19) - 428 p. pl., map. 19 cm. Issued later under title: The mountain hero. Ethan Allen's narrative of his captivity: p. 213 - 278. 6-45841.
F52. D 4
Rare Book Room

— Books for Libraries Press (1970) xvii, 248 p. 23 cm. 70-114874.
F52. D 4
1970

DE PUY, Henry Walter. The mountain hero (Ethan Allen) and his associates. Boston, Dayton & Wentworth, 1855. xvii, (19) - 428 p. incl. front. (port.) pl., map. 20 cm. 1st ed., Buffalo, 1853 pub. under title: Ethan Allen and the Green-Mountain heroes of '76. 1-18239.
F52. D 42
Rare Book Room

DE PUY, Henry Walter. Ethan Allen and the Green-Mountain heroes of '76. Buffalo, Phinney & co., 1859. xxvii, (19) - 428 p. pl., map. 19½ cm. Issued under title: The mountain hero (Boston, 1855) 25-13910.
F52. D 45

HALL, Hiland. The history of Vermont, from its discovery to its admission into the Union in 1791. Albany, N.Y., J. Munsell, 1868. xii, 521 p. incl. map. fold. front. 24 cm. "Biographical sketches of the principal persons mentioned in this work": p. (451) - 476. Rc-3090.
F52. H 16

HALL, Hiland. Why the early inhabitants of Vermont disclaimed the jurisdiction of New York, and established an independent government. An address delivered before the New York historical soc. ... 1860. Bennington, Vt., C. A. Pierce & co., print., 1872. 16 p. 21½ cm. 14-4041.
F52. H165

— Reprinted 1884. 14 p. 23 cm. 21-3712. Frontispiece wanting.
F52. H 17

HOUGHTON, George Frederick. Mr. Houghton's address. (Montpelier, Vt., 1848?) An outline of the controversy of the New Hampshire grants, with a sketch of the life and services of Col. Seth Warner. CA 25-378 unrev.
F52. H 8

JILLSON, Clark. Address on New Hampshire and Vermont: their unions, secessions and disunions. Delivered before the New Hampshire antiquarian soc. ... 1879. Worcester, C. Jillson, 1882. 1, 40 p. 24 cm. 2-1360.
F52. J 61

JONES, Matt Bushnell. Vermont in the making, 1750 - 1777. Cambridge, Mass., Harvard university press, 1939. xiv, 471 p. map. 22 cm. Bibliography: p. (441) - 457. 39-14447.
F52. J 76

— (Hamden, Conn.) Archon Books, 1968. xiv, 471 p. 22 cm. 68-20380.
F52. J 76
1968

O'CALLAGHAN, Edmund Bailey, ed. ... Controversy between New York and New Hampshire,

VERMONT 13

respecting the territory now the state of Vermont. (From The documentary history of the state of New York ... v. 4 (1851) p. (529) - 1034. Bibliography: p. 1025-1026. 7-36270.
 F52.O 15

GANNETT, Ezra Stiles. The useful man. A sermon delivered at the funeral of Hon, Charles Paine, at Northfield, Vt., ... 1853 ... Northfield, Print. Woodworth & Gould, 1853. (7) - 63 p. 23 cm. 15-10661.
 F52.P 14

PERKINS, Nathan. A narrative of a tour through the state of Vermont ... April to June, 1789 ... Woodstock, Vt., The Elm tree press, 1920. 31 p. incl. front. (2 port.) 22½ cm. 22-9637.
 F52.P 44

— Rutland, Vt., C. E. Tuttle Co., c. 1964. 44 p. (on double leaves) 22 cm. 64-21009.
 F52.P 44
 1964

SPARGO, John. David Redding, queen's ranger, who was hanged in Bennington, Vt. ... 1778; a study in historical reconstruction. Bennington, Vt., Bennington historical museum and art gallery, 1945. 5, 68 p. front. (port.) facsim. 23½ cm. Bibliographical references included in "Notes" (p. 67-68) Cover-title: The story of David Redding who was hanged. 46-21503.
 F52.R4S7

SARGENT. The early history of Vermont; an address delivered by the Hon. John G. Sargent, attorney general of the U.S. at the city hall, Montpelier, Vt. ... 1927, in honor of the sesqui centennial of the independence of the state ... (Montpelier, Capital city press, 1927?) 79 p. 23 cm. History from 1761 to March 1778. 29-18795.
 F52.S 24

SMITH, Philip Henry. Curiosities in American history. The Green Mountain boys: or Vermont and the New York land jobbers ... Pawling, N.Y., P.H. Smith, 1885. 130 p. 4 pl. 15½ x 12 cm. Rc-3108.
 F52.S 65

THOMPSON, Charles Miner. Independent Vermont ... Boston, Houghton Mifflin co., 1942. xv p. 574 p. front., ports. 23½ cm. Bibliography: p. (559) - 561. 42-4912.
 F52.T 46

THOMPSON, Daniel Pierce. An address pronounced in the Representatives' hall, Montpelier ... 1850, before the Vermont historical soc. ... Pub. by order of the legislature. Burlington, Free press office print., 1850. 22 p. 21 cm. An account of the Council of safety of Vermont and of the early revolutionary history of the state. 1-15972.
 F52.T 47

U.S. Bureau of the Census. Heads of families at the First Census of the U.S. taken in the year 1790. Washington, Govt. print off., 1907. (Spartanburg, S.C., Reprint Co., 1963) 95 p. 28 cm. 64-60350.
 F52. U 5

— Baltimore, Genealogical Pub. Co., 1966. 95 p. 29 cm.
 F52. U 5
 1966
 L.H. & G.

VAN DE WATER, Frederic Franklyn. The reluctant republic; Vermont, 1724 - 1791 ... New York, The John Day co. (c. 1941) 7, 3-344 p. plates, port. 22½ cm. "Sources": p. (341) - 344. 41-8390.
 F52.V 25

VERMONT. state papers; being a collection of records and documents, connected with the assumption and establishment of government by the people of Vermont; together with the journal of the Council of safety, the first constitution, the early journals of the General assembly and the laws from the year 1779 to 1786, inclusive. ... Comp. and pub. by William Slade ... Middlebury, J.W. Copeland, print., 1823. xx, (9) - 567. 22 cm. 1-6537 rev.
 F52. V 4

VERMONT. The proceedings of the convention of the respresentatives of the New-Hampshire settlers; containing their covenant-compact and resolutions; and also, twelve acts of outlawry, passed by the legislature of the province of New-York, against those settlers, and their answer to the same. Hartford: Print. Ebenezer Watson, 1775. 17 p. 34 cm. 17-22227.
 F52. V 43
 Rare Book Room

— New York city, Reprinted in facsim. for C.F. Heartman, 1917. 2, 17 p. 36½ cm. 17-14989 rev. F52.V 435

VERMONT. Proceedings of Grand committee of the legislature of the state of Vermont, at Charlestown ... 1781. Print. Exeter, 1782. New York city, Reprinted for C. F. Heartman, 1917.
4.p. 4 numb. 1. of facsims. 37½ cm. 17-22843.
F52. V 44

VERMONT. ... Charters granted by the state of Vermont, being transcripts of early charters of townships and smaller tracts of land granted by the state of Vermont, with an appendix ... also historical and bibliographical notes relative to Vermont towns, originally comp. in 1895 by Hiram A. Huse ... continued and brought up to date. Bellows Falls, P. H. Gobie press, inc., 1922. xi, 424 p. fold. map.
23½ cm. (State papers of Vermont, v. 2) 23-27365.
F52. V 47

VERMONT ... Petitions for grants of land, 1778 - 1811. Pub. by authority, by Rawson C. Myrick, secretary of state, 1939. Ed. Mary Greene Nye. (Brattleboro, The Vermont print. co., 1939)
547 p. pl. 23½ cm. (State papers of Vermont, v. 5) 40-28182.
F52. V 48

VERMONT. Celebration at Westminster ... 1927, to commemorate the 150th anniversary of the declaration of independence of Vermont ... (Bennington?) The Vermont state sesqui-centennial commission, 1927. 38 p. 23 cm. Cover-title: Declaration of the independecne of Vermont. 27-27396 rev.
F52. V 5

VERMONT. A copy of a remonstrance, of the council of the state of Vermont, against the resolutions of Congress of the 5th of December last, which interfere with their internal police. Hartford, Print. Hudson & Goodwin, 1783. 20 p. 19 cm. 7-11155.
F52. V 53

VERMONT illustrated. Supplement of the Middlebury register. Text compiled by William H. Bliss. Middlebury, Vt., Print, the Register co., (c. 1934) 159 p. plates. 27 cm. Originally issued as a quarterly, in eight numbers, 1898 - 1901 ... 35-3156.
F52. V 58

WHITNEY, Luthera. Old-time days and ways, by Luthera Whitney; with 61 homestead drawings by W. Parker Bodfish. Boston, D. Lothrop (c. 1883) (38) p. front., illus. 23½ x 18½ cm. Pioneer life in Vermont. 17-1551.
F52. W 62

WILBUR, James Benjamin. Ira Allen, founder of Vermont, 1751 - 1814 ... Boston and New York, Houghton Mifflin co., 1928. 2 v. fronts. (v. 1 col.) plates, ports., map, facsims. 24½ cm. Bibliography: v. 2, p. (527)-531. 28-15601.
F52. W 65

WILBUR, La Fayette. Early history of Vermont. By La Fayette Wilbur ... Jericho, Vt., Roscoe print. house, 1899 - 1903. 4 v. plates, port. 21½ cm. 99-3875 rev.
F52. W 66

WILLIAMS, Samuel. Vermont during the war for independence (a contemporary account) by Samuel Williams, being three chapters taken from the author's "Natural and civil history of Vermont" pub. in 1794 ... Schenectady, N. Y., B. Johnson, 1944. (2), 211 - 310 p. illus. (map) 20 cm. 45-851.
F52. W 68

WILLIAMSON, Chilton. Vermont in a quandary, 1763 - 1825. Montpelier, Vt. Historical Soc., 1949.
xiv, 318 p. ports., maps. 23 cm. (Growth of Vermont, v. 4) Issued also as thesis, Columbia U. Bibliography p. (298)-306. 49-2275
A 49-3830 rev.   Also numbered F52. W69 1949a.
F52. W69

WOODARD, Florence May. The town proprietors in Vermont: the New England town proprietorship in decline, ... New York, 1936. 2, 7 - 165 p. 22½ cm. Thesis Columbia university, 1936. 37-11281; 37-11280.
Also numbered F52. W772 and H31. C7 no. 418.
F52. W 77

1791 - 1865.

ALLEN, Ira. ... Gen. Allen's statement, respecting a large cargo of cannon and arms purchased in France, for the use of the militia of Vermont and taken by an English 74 in 1796 ... (n. p., 1804?)
15 p. 20 cm. Relates to the capture of the ship Olive Branch. 19-6748.
F53. A 39
Rare Book Room

ALLEN, Ira. A concise summary of the second volume of the Olive Branch, a book containing an

VERMONT 15

account of Governor Chittenden's giving written instructions to Gen. Ira Allen in 1795 to purchase military stores in Europe ... To which is subjoined, General Allen's circular letter, on the subject of a ship canal of commerce, and the advantage of British America in preserving peace between Great Britain and the U.S. ... Philadelphia, Printed for the author, 1807. 24 p. 22 cm. (Miscellaneous pamphlets, v. 731, no. 5) Summary of v. 2 of Ira Allen's Particulars of the capture of the ship Olive Branch, Phila., 1805. 7-6946.   F53.A 41

ALLEN, Ira. Copies of letters to the governor of Vermont ... respecting a conspiracy against the author ... with the opinion of the attorney general on the case of the Olive Branch. Philadelphia: Printed for the author, 1810. 32 p. 21 cm. 20-3317.   F53.A419
Rare Book Room

ALLEN, Ira. Copies of letters to the governor of Vermont, etc. etc. Philadelphia, (1811) 61 p. 21½ cm. 6-45838.   F53.A 42
Rare Book Room

ALLEN, Ira. Ira Allen's memorial to the government of the U.S. (Washington, 1806) 6 (i.e. 7) p. 21½ cm. Relates to the capture of the ship Olive Branch. 7-5370.   F53.A 43
Rare Book Room

ALLEN, Ira. Particulars of the capture of the ship Olive Branch laden with a cargo of arms, etc., the property of Major-General Ira Allen, destined for supplying the militia of Vermont and captured by His Britannic Majesty's ship of war, Audacious; together with the proceedings and evidence before the High Court of Admiralty of G.B. London, Print. J.W. Myers, 1798 - 1805. 2 v. 21 - 24 cm. Vol. 2 includes a résumé of v. 1 and in some respects may be considered a complete work. cf. Sabin. 7-5356 rev.*   F53.A 44
Rare Book Room
vol. 2 Jefferson Coll.

ALLEN, Ethan. A narrative of Colonel Ethan Allen's captivity, from the time of his being taken by the British, near Montreal ... 1775, to the time of his exchange ... 1778: containing his voyages and travels, with the most remarkable occurrences respecting himself, and many other continental prisoners ... Written by himself ... Philadelphia, Printed for the author, 1799 (i.e. 1779?) (In Allen, Ira. Particulars of the capture of the ship Olive Branch. Phila., 1805. v. 2. 3-9553.   F53.A 44
vol. 2

ALLEN, Ira. Address to the freemen of Vermont and legislature thereof respecting a cargo of military stores captured by the British. ... Philadelphia, 1808. 27 p. 22 cm. Includes extracts from the author's History of Vermont. 49-35392*.   F53.A448
Rare Book Room

ALLEN, Ira. Statements applicable to the cause of the Olive Branch, which was a cargo of cannon and arms, purchased by the authority of the governor of Vermont ... and captured ... by an English man of war (in 1796,) ... By Ira Allen, claimant of the cargo of the Olive Branch. Philadelphia, Printed for the author ... 1807. 16 p. 21 cm. 20-12706.   F53.A 45
Toner collection

ALLEN, Joseph Dana. A journal of an excursion, made by the corps of cadets of the A.L.S. & M. academy, Norwich, Vt., under command of Capt. A. Partridge, June, 1824. Windsor, Vt., Print, S. Ide, 1824. 48 p. 19½ cm. The route was from Norwich to Whitehall, N.Y., thence to Burlington, Vt. and Plattsburgh, N.Y., returning to Norwich by way of Vergennes, Middlebury and Royalton, Vt. 17-20829.   F53.A 47
Rare Book Room

CHIPMAN, Daniel. A memoir of Thomas Chittenden, the first governor of Vermont; with a history of the constitution during his administration. Middlebury (Vt.) Printed for the author, 1849. viii, (9) - 222 p. 18½ cm. 7-16417.   F53.C 54

CHITTENDEN. Exercises at the dedication of the monument erected by the state to Thomas Chittenden, first governor of Vermont, at Williston, Vt., ... 1896. (Burlington, Free press assoc., print., 1896) 53 p. incl. front. 2 pl. 26 cm. 7-16416.   F53.C 55

COLLAMER. Memorial address on the life and character of the Hon. Jacob Collamer, read before the

Vermont historical society ... 1868 ... Rutland, Tuttle & co., 1868. 27 p. 23½ cm. 21-8438.

F53.C 63

COLLAMER, Statue of. Addresses on the presentation of the statue of Jacob Collamer, of Vermont ...1881. By James M. Tyler. Washington, 1881. 15 p. 22 cm. 7-20554*.

F53.C 68

COLLAMER. Addresses on the death of Hon. Jacob Collamer ... 1865. Washington, Govt. print. off., 1866. 85 p. 22 cm. 7-20564 rev.

F53.C 69

GRAHAM, John Andrew. A descriptive sketch of the present state of Vermont. One of the United States of America. London, ... H. Fry, 1797. vii, 186 p. incl. front. (port.) illus. 22 cm. Rc-3110.

F53.G 74
Rare Book Room

HASWELL. Anthony Haswell, printer-patriot-ballader; a biographical study with a selection of his ballads and an annotated bibliographical list of his imprints, by John Spargo ... Rutland, Vt., The Tuttle co., 1925. xv, 293 p. 35 facsim. (incl. front.) 33cm. Bibliography: p. (241) - 293. 26-538.

F53.H
Z232.H35S7

HEMENWAY, Abby Maria. Clarke papers. Mrs. Meech and her family. Home letters, familiar incidents and narrations linked for preservation. Burlington, Vt., Pub. by Miss Hemenway (1878) 2, 312 p. 17½ cm. 1-26877.

F53. H48
CS71.C6   1878

LINSLEY. A sketch of the life and character of Charles Linsley, read before the Vermont historical society. By E.J. Phelps. Pub. by the society. Albany, N.Y., J. Munsell, 1866. 20 p. 23 cm. 20-867.

F53.L 75

LUDLUM, David McWilliams. Social ferment in Vermont, 1791 - 1850, by David M. Ludlum. New York, Columbia university press, 1939. x, (3) - 305 p. 23½ cm. "A Vermont bibliography, 1791 - 1850": p. 279 - 305. 39-22998.

F53.L 84

MARSH. Memorial address on the life and character of the Hon. Charles Marsh, LL.D., read before the Vermont historical society ... 1870, by James Barrett ... Montpelier, Journal steam print., 1871. 54 p. 23½ cm. 43-22332.

F53.M3B3

NAVIN, William E. ... Vermont in 1843, and the Rutland R.R. A centenary address by William E. Navin ... A Newcomen address, 1943. (Princeton, Princeton university press, 1943) 48 p. illus., plates. 23 cm. 44-2768.

F53.   N3

SKINNER. The life and character of the Hon. Richard Skinner; a discourse read before and at the request of the Vermont historical society ... 1863, by Winslow C. Watson. Albany, N.Y., J. Munsell, 1863. 30 p. 23 cm. 14-15954.

F53. S 6

THOMPSON, Zadock. First book of geography, for Vermont children ... Burlington, C. Goodrich, 1849. vi, (7) - 74 p. incl. front., illus., maps. 24°. 1-Rc-3112.

F53.T 47
Rare Book Room

THOMPSON, Zadock. Geography and geology of Vermont, with state and county outline maps. For the use of schools and families. Burlington, Chauncey Goodrich, print., 1848. 3, (9) - 219 p. incl. front. (map) illus. 17 cm. Rc-3113.

F53. T48
G. & M.

VIATOR, pseud. A Traveller's Observations on Vermont. Worcester, Pine Tree Press, 1961. (8) p. 16 cm. "Reprinted from the Farmer's Library" or, Vermont political and historical register, Sept. 2, 1793."

F53. V 5

WHITE. Pliny Holton White. By Dorman Bridgman Eaton Kent. (In Vermont historical soc. Proceedings ... 1915-1916. p. (87) - 92. 18-14009.

F53.W
F46.V55 1915-16

WHITE. Memorial address on the life and services of Rev. Pliny H. White, pronounced before the Vermont historical soc, ... 1869, by Henry Clark ... Montpelier, Journal print., 1869. 15 p. 22½ cm.
18-15753. F53. W 58

WILLIAMS. Obituary notices, and other testimonials of respect, on the occasion of the death of the Hon, Cha's K. Williams ... by the Hon. Isaac F. Redfield ... Rutland, G. A. Tuttle, print., 1854.
40 p. 21½ cm. 19-3122. F53. W 72

1865 - 1950.

AIKEN, George David. Speaking from Vermont ... New York, Frederick A. Stokes, 1938. xv, 233 p.
front. (port.) 21 cm. 38-27765. F54. A 55

ATWOOD, R. E. comp. Stories and pictures of the Vermont flood, Nov., 1927 ... (Burlington, Vt., c. 1927) 32 p. illus. 27 cm. 28-2683. F54. A 88

BAILEY. Horace Ward Bailey, Vermonter; a memorial by his friends, comp. and ed. by Frank L. Fish. Rutland, Vt., 1914. 339 p. front. (port.) 23½ cm. 15-288. F54. B 15

BARNARD. Hon. Daniel Barnard: a memorial address by Hon. Henry Robinson ... Delivered before the Grafton and Coos bar assoc. ... 1892. Woodsville, N.H., Cohos steam press (1892) 16 p. front. (port.) 23 cm. 20-869. F54. B 25

BATTELL, Joseph, ed. Bread loaf inn. Ripton, Vt., 1895. 42 p. illus., map. 26 cm. 2-19345.
F54. B 33

BEERS, Lorna Doone. Wild apples and north wind. Illus... Stefan Martin. (1st ed.) New York, Norton (c. 1966) 219 p. 22 cm. 66-13350. F54. B 4

BIGELOW, Walter J. Vermont, its government, 1919 - 1920. Montpelier, Vt., The Historical pub. Co., 1919. 150 p. illus. (ports.) 25 cm. 20-12887. F54. B 59

CENTRAL Vermont railway. Summer homes among the green hills of Vermont. St. Albans, 1895.
21½ cm. F54. C 39

— 1901. 22½ cm. F54. C396

— 1903. 22½ cm. F54. C398

CRANE, Charles Edward. Winter in Vermont. New York, A. A. Knopf, 1941. xiv, 304, (2), viii p. front.,
plates, fold. map. 22½ cm. "First ed." 41-20683. F54. C 7

DUNBAR, Horace. A Vermont encounter. (San Diego, Calif., Frye Smith, ltd.) 1938. 4, 11 - 94 p.
incl. illus., plates. 19 cm. 39-25461. F54. D 86

FEDERAL writers' project. ... Vermont; a guide to the Green mountain state ... Boston, Houghton Mifflin, 1937. xxi, (3) - 392 p. plates, maps (1 fold. in pocket) double diagr. 21 cm. (American guide series) Bibliography: p. (372) - 379. 37-28648. F54. F 45
1937

— Ed. Ray Bearse. 2d ed., rev. and enl. Boston, Houghton Mifflin, 1966. xix, 456 p. 21 cm.
65-11887. F54. F 45
1966
L. H. & G.

— Ed. Ray Bearse. 3d ed., rev. Boston, Houghton Mifflin, 1968. xix, 452 p. illus. 21 cm. (The new American guide series) 68-14344. F54. F 45
1968

18   LOCAL HISTORIES IN THE LIBRARY OF CONGRESS

FLINT, Winston Allen. The progressive movement in Vermont; ... Washington, D.C., American council on public affairs (c. 1941)   2, 110 p.   23½ cm.   Bibliography: p. 108 - 110.   41-20684.
                                                                                                      F54. F 55

FOLLETT, Mrs. Muriel. New England year; a journal of Vermont farm life ... wood engravings by Herbert Waters. Brattleboro, Vt., Stephen Daye press (c. 1939)   222 p. incl. front., illus.   20½ cm.   39-27981.
                                                                                                      F54. F 65

— Detroit, Gale Research Co., 1971.   222 p. illus.   73-145711.   F54. F 65
                                                                                                            1971

GRANGER, Kathleen (B.)   New York, Vanguard Press (c. 1966)   192 p. 22 cm.   66-16633.
                                                                                                            F54. G 7

GUYOT, Arnold Henry. Geography of Vermont. (New York) C. Scribner's sons, 1879.   127 p. incl. illus., map. fol.   1-13342-M1.
                                                                                                        F54. G 98

HARD, Walter R. This is Vermont; ... illus. with 32 photographs and 16 reproductions of paintings from Vermont art exhibits. Brattleboro, Vt., Stephen Daye, 1936,   8, 318 p. plates. 22½ cm.   36-16898.
                                                                                                         F54. H 36

— Third printing.   36-22482.   F54. H363

JEFFREY, William Hartley. Vermont, a souvenir of its government, 1902 - 1903. East Burke, Vt., The Historical pub. co., 1903.   135 p. front., illus. (incl. ports.)   24 x 18½ cm.   5-17835 rev.   F54. J 46

JENNISON, Keith Warren. Green Mountains and rock ribs. (1st ed.) New York, Harcourt, Brace (1954)   90 p. illus. 24 cm.   54-11325.
                                                                                                       F54. J 465

JENNISON, Keith Warren. Vermont is where you find it ... New York, Harcourt, Brace (c. 1941)   4, 118 p. illus.   24 x 18½ cm.   "First edition."   41-22540.   F54. J 47

JOHNSON, Luther B. Floodtide of 1927; a gathering of reports and pictures which tell their story graphically of the great November flood in Vermont state. Randolph, Vt., Roy L. Johnson co. (c. 1927) iv, 181 p. front. (port.) illus.   21½ cm.   28-697.   F54. J 66

JOHNSON, Luther Brunham. Vermont in floodtime. Randolph, Vt., Roy L. Johnson co. (c. 1928) iv, 209 p. front., illus. (incl. maps)   22 cm.   "First edition."   28-8901.   F54. J 67

JOHNSON, Otto T. Nineteen-six in Vermont. (Proctor? Vt.) (1944)   181 p. 19 cm.   A44-3452.
                                                                                                       F54. J 68

KINSLEY, Earle S. Recollections of Vermonters in state and national affairs, b..   Rutland, Vt., (Woodstock, Vt., The Elm tree press) 1946.   3, ix - xv, 168 p. incl. front., illus. (incl. ports., facsims.)   27 cm.   47-1254.
                                                                                                         F54. K 5

LEWIS, Oma Barnes. I love Vermont — but ...; life in the Green Mountains. (1st ed.) New York, Exposition Press (1956)   123 p. 21 cm.   56-12283.   F54. L 4

MARSHALL, Bernard. The gentleman from East Blueberry; a sketch of the Vermont legislature. State vs. Burton; a drama of the court room. (By) Bernard Marshall. Montpelier, Vt., Capital city press (c. 1909)   128 p. 19 cm.   9-23793.   F54. M 36

MARTIN. ... In memoriam, Howard Lucius Martin; died March 21, 1915. Society of Colonial wars. (Burlington? 1915)   (4) p. 22 cm.   CA 28-696 unrev.   F54. M 37

MATHER, Melissa. Rough road home. (1st ed.) Philadelphia, Lippincott (1958)   256 p. 21 cm. Autobiographical.   58-9537.   F54. M 38

NEEDHAM, Walter. A book of country things. Told by Walter Needham. Recorded by Barrows

VERMONT

Mussey. Brattleboro, Vt., S. Green Press, 1965.   viii, 166 p. 21 cm. 65-14693.
   F54. N 4

NUTTING, Wallace. Vermont beautiful ... illus. by the author with 304 photos.   Framingham and Boston, Old America co. (c.1922)   2, 3 - 302 p. incl. plates. 26 cm. 23-2379.
   F54. N 9

— in cooperation with Old America co. by the Garden City pub. co., 1936.   x, 13 - 254 p. incl. front., plates. 26 cm. (His States beautiful series) "Reissue in de luxe edition ... 1936." 36-35294.
   F54. N 93

O'NEIL, Mary J. Growing up in Vermont. Illus. by Lucy Doane. Rutland, Vt., 1950.   89 p. illus. (part col.) ports. 29 cm. Includes songs with music. 50-9244.
   F54. O 5

ORTON, Vrest. And so goes Vermont; a picture book of Vermont as it is; ... Weston, Vt., The Countryman press; N.Y., Farrar & Rinehart (1937)   3, 82 p. of illus. 28½ cm. 37-16668.
   F54. O 78

PAGE, Carroll Smalley. A Green Mountain boy born and bred. (Hyde Park? Vt., 1916)   14 p. 23 cm. 26-407.
   F54. P 16

PROCTOR, Mortimer Robinson. Vermont, the unspoiled land. (Rutland, Vt., The Tuttle co., 1915)   (5) - 93 p. illus., fold. map. 15½ x 23 cm. On cover: The Green Mountain tour, Vermont. 17-20806.
   F54. P 96

STEELE. Address on the life and services of the late Hon. Benjamin H. Steele, delivered at Derby Line, Vt. ... 1874, by Hon. George N. Dale ... Pub. in the Stanstead journal. (New Orleans, L. Graham) 1874.   21 p. 22½ cm. 20-874.
   F54.   S
   E664. S81D13

SPEAR, Victor I. Vermont, a glimpse of its scenery. Montpelier, 1893.   14½ x 23½ cm.
   F54. S 74

THOMPSON, Dorothy, Concerning Vermont. (Brattleboro, Vt.) E. L. Hildreth (c.1937)   14 p. 15 cm. "Originally appeared in the N.Y. herald tribune." 44-24404.
   F54. T 47

VERMONT's visitors' handbook to lodging and eating places. Montpelier (etc.)   v. illus. 19 - 23 cm. Title varies: Where to stop when in Vermont. - Vermont hotels, tour-homes and cabins. Issued by the Vermont Publicity Service, etc. 24-27176 rev. 2*.
   F54. V 33

VERMONT. The lake region of eastern Vermont ... Essex Junction, Vt., Vermont Bureau of publicity, Office of the secretary of state (1917)   63 p. illus. 21 cm. On cover: Lakes of eastern Vermont. 19-27057 rev.
   F54. V 41
   1917

— 1924.   62 p. incl. illus., tables. 21 cm. On cover: Lakes of eastern Vermont. 24-27175 rev.
   F54. V 41
   1924

VERMONT. The lake region of western Vermont ... Morrisville, Vt., Vermont Bureau of publicity, Office of the secretary of state (1918)   61 p. incl. front., illus. 21 cm. On cover: Lakes of western Vermont. 18-12915 rev.
   F54. V 42

VERMONT. The lakes of Vermont ... Montpelier, Vt., Vermont bureau of publicity, Office of the secretary of state (1927)   95 p. incl. front., illus. fold. plates. 21 cm. 27-22653 rev.
   F54. V425

— 1928.   72 p. incl. front., illus. 23 cm. 28-21229 rev.
   F54. V425
   1928

VERMONT. Vermont lakes and mountains. Montpelier, Vt., Vermont Bureau of publicity, Office of secretary of state, c.1932.   96 p. illus. (incl. map) 23 cm. 32-27646 rev.
   F54. V 43

VERMONT, designed by the Creator for the playground of the continent ... (Montpelier, Vt.) Bureau of publicity of the Dept. of state (1911)   80 p. plates.   22½ cm.   On cover: Vermont summer resorts.   11-25751 rev.   F54.V 44

VERMONT tours.   Development commission.   Montpelier.   v. illus. 23 cm.   Issued 1933 -   by Publicity service ...   34-2755 rev. 2*.   F54.V 46

VERMONT.   Good homes in Vermont.   A list of desirable farms for sale.   Issued by the State board of agriculture, 1893.   Montpelier, Watchman pub. co., 1893.   47 p.   map.   22½ cm.   Cover-title: A list of desirable Vermont farms at low prices.   2-24650.   F54.V 51

— 1895.   109 p. illus. 8°.   1-24712 - M1.   F54.V 52

VERMONT.   ... Report on summer travel for 1894.   Montpelier, Watchman pub. co., 1894.   8 p. 22 cm.   8-8614.   F54.V 528

VERMONT.   The resources and attractions of Vermont.   With a list of desirable homes for sale, issued by the State board of agriculature.   Montpelier, Watchman pub. co., 1891.   109 p. front. (fold. map) illus. 21 cm.   5-18340.   F54.V 53

VERMONT, its opportunities for investment in agriculture, manufacture, minerals, its attractions for summer homes ... (St. Albans, Messenger co. print, 1903)   (62) p. incl. illus. front.   22½ x 27 cm.   4-27766.   F54.V 54

VERMONT: its resources and industries.   Embracing historical and descriptive sketches of the Green Mountain state, and the principal cities and towns there in ... Glens Falls, N.Y., C.H.Possons, 1889.   2, (vii) - ix, (30) - 254, (6) p. illus. 23½ cm.   13-13705.   F54.V 55

VERMONT vacation guide.   1950 -   ed.   (Burlington, Vt. Pubs. Corp., etc.)   v. illus. 23 cm. annual.   Title varies.   50-13329 rev.   F54.V 56

VERMONTER, The, St. Albans, Vt.   ... Greater Vermont number.   1904.   25½ cm.   F54.V 58

WALTER, Charles True.   Lights and shadow of the flood of 1927; Vermont at its worst, Vermonters at their best ... illus. Zenas C. Jenks.   (St. Johnsbury, Vt., The Cowles press, inc.) c. 1928.   3, (9) - 109 p. illus.   26½ cm.   28-10386.   F54.W 25

WOODBURY.   ... In memoriam, Urban Andrain Woodbury, died ... 1915.   Society of colonial wars.   (Burlington? 1915)   (4) p. 22 cm.   CA 28-695 unrev.   F54.W 88

WRITERS' program.   Vermont, a profile of the Green mountain state   ... New York, Fleming pub. co., (c. 1941)   (57) p. front., illus. 18½ x 15½ cm.   (Amer. pictorial guide series) 41-17601.   F54.W 9

WOLFE, Marguerite Hurrey.   Anything can happen in Vermont.   Photos: Lewis A. Harlow.   (1st ed. Coral Gables, Fla.)   W.B. House, 1965)   151 p. 22 cm.   65-18407.   F55.W 6

REGIONS, COUNTIES, ETC., A - Z.

ADDISON County, Gazetteer and business directory of, for 1881-82.   Comp. and pub. by H. Child ... Syracuse, Print. Journal office, 1882.   541 (i.e. 557) p. front., illus., plates, ports., fold. map. 24 cm.   Imperfect: t.p. wanting.   L.C. Copy replaced by microfilm.   1-6538.   F57.A2C5
Microfilm 9376 F

ADDISON county.   By Abby Maria Hemenway.   Ludlow, Vt., Miss A.M. Hemenway (1860)   120 (8) p. front. (port.) 26 cm.   (Her Vermont quarterly gazetteer, no. 1, July 4, 1860) 2-11293.
F57.A 2H4

ADDISON county, History of, with illus. and biographical sketches of some of its prominent men and pioneers, ed. H.P. Smith.   Syracuse, N.H. D. Mason, 1886.   774 p. lxii p., ports., double map.   26 cm.

"Brief personals": p. (i) - lvi. "Biographical": p. 733 - 774. 1-16571 rev.
F57.A2 S7
Microfilm 21661 F

ADDISON County. Statistical and historical account of the county of Addison. Written at the request of the Historical society of Middlebury, by Samuel Swift. Middlebury, A.H. Copeland, 1859. 132 p. front. (port.) pl. 23 cm. Rc-3114.
F57.A2 S9

BENNINGTON County. Farmers' and country merchants' almanac and ready reference book. 1870. Containing historical sketches of the counties of Albany, Rensselaer, Washington, Warren, Schenectady, Saratoga, Rutland, and Bennington ... Albany, N.H., C. Van Benthuysen & sons (1870) 207 p. 23 cm. 10-5637.
F57.B
F127.A3 F2

BENNINGTON county, genealogical gleanings, transcribed and gathered by Elijah Ellsworth Brownell ... Philadelphia, Penna., 1941. 6 p. 207 numb. l. 27 ½ cm. Includes the 1810 federal census, lists of the principal civil officers of Vermont with Bennington county connections, and Bennington county officers. 42-6070.
F57.B4 B7

BENNINGTON County, Gazetteer and business directory of, 1880-81. Comp. and pub. by Hamilton Child ... Syracuse, N.Y., Printed at the Journal office, 1880. 500 p. front. (fold. map) illus., pl. 23 cm. Includes a history of the county. 20-1106.
F57.B4 C5

BENNINGTON county, ed. Abby Maria Hemenway. Ludlow, Ct., Miss A.M. Hemenway (1861) (121) - 260, 13 p. front. (port.) 25 cm. (Her Vermont quarterly gazetteer, no. II, Oct. 1861, and part of no. III, April, 1862) 2-11292.
F57.B4 H4

BOMOSEEN, Lake. An account of the celebration of the 4th of July, 1881, at Mason's point, lake Bomoseen ... Compiled by John M. Currier ... (Castleton? Vt.) Pub. under the auspices of the Rutland county historical soc. (1881) 2, (6) - 49 p. 22 cm. 4-24219 rev.
F57.B6 C9

BOMOSEEN, Lake: its early history, conveyances, fishing, hunting, resorts, islands - their names ... Poultney, (Vt.) Journal job print., 1882. 28 p. 8º. 1-Rc-3115.
F57.B6 S7

CALEDONIA and Essex counties, Gazetteer of, 1764 - 1887. Comp. and pub. by Hamilton Child ... Syracuse, N.Y., The Syracuse journal co., 1887. 2 v. in 1. illus., ports., fold. map. 24 cm. Pt. 2 has title:... Business directory of Caledonia and Essex counties ... Includes historical and biographical sketches. 3-4895.
F57.C2 C5
F57.E7 C5

CALEDONIA county. By Abby Maria Hemenway. Ludlow, Vt., Miss A.M. Hemenway (1862) 261-452 p. port. 24 ½ cm. (Her Vermont quarterly gazetteer, being part of no. III, Apr. 1862, and no. IV, Oct., 1862) 2-11294.
F57.C2 H4

CHAMPLAIN, Lake. The Lake Champlain and Lake George valleys, by Wallace E. Lamb ... New York, The American historical co., (c.1940) 3 v. fronts., illus. (9ncl. maps) ports. 27 ½ cm. Vols. 1 and 2 paged continuously. Vol. 3 consists of biographies. 40-9204.
F57.C4
F127.C6 L3

CHITTENDEN County. Look around Jericho, Underhill and Westford, by Lillian Baker Carlisle, ed. (and others) Samuel J. Hatfield, photos. Burlington, Vt., Chittenden County Historical soc. (1972) iv, 44 p. illus. 23 cm. (Heritage series pamphlet no. 2) 72-82608.
F57.C5C37

CHITTENDEN County, Gazetteer and business directory of, for 1882 - 83. Comp. and pub. by Hamilton Child ... Syracuse, N.Y., Print. Journal office, 1882. 8, 9 - 584 p. illus., front. (fold. map) plates, ports. 24 cm. 4-23263.
F57.C5 C5

CHITTENDEN county. By Abby Maria Hemenway. Ludlow, Vt., Miss A.M. Hemenway: Albany, N.Y., J. Munsell (1863) (453) - 616 p. front. (port.) 26 cm. (Her Vermont quarterly gazetteer, no. v - vi, Jan. and Aug. 1863) Incomplete. 2-11291.
F57.C5 H4

CHITTENDEN County, History of, with illustrations and biographical sketches of some of its prominent men ... Ed. W.S. Rann. Syracuse, N.Y., D. Mason, 1886. 867 p. illus., ports. 26 x 20 ½ cm. 8-12271.
F57.C5 R2

CONNECTICUT River Valley in southern Vermont and New Hampshire, The; historical sketches, by Lyman S. Hayes. Rutland, Vt., The Tuttle co., (c.1929)   2, 3-358 p. 20 cm. 29-14770.
                                                                                                                                               F57.C7 H4

DUNMORE and Silver lake. Indelible photographs ... Brandon, Va. (i.e. Vt.) J.H.Grimes, c.1891.
1 p., 16 pl. obl. 24°. 1-Rc-3116.   F57.D9 D9

CALEDONIA County. Successful Vermonters; a modern gazetteer of Caledonia, Essex and Orleans counties, containing an historical review of the several towns and a series of biographical sketches ... by William H. Jeffrey. East Burke, Vt., The Historical pub. co., 1904.   xii, (2), (5) - 361, 158, 274 p. illus., ports. 25½cm. 20-2619.   F57. E 7

ESSEX County. Memorial sketches, written of many friends by George Needham Dale (G.N.D.) Pub. in the Essex County herald from time to time through a quarter century. (Island Pond, Vt., Essex County herald press, 1903)   3, 384 p., 4 p. ports. 23½cm. Compiled by Porter Hinman Dale. 24-8608.
                                                                                                                                  F57.E7 D2

FRANKLIN County. History of Franklin and Grand Isle counties, Vermont; with illustrations and biographical sketches of some of the prominent men and pioneers. Ed. Lewis Cass Aldrich. Syracuse, N.Y.. D. Mason & co., 1891.   1, (5) - 821 p. illus., ports. 25½cm. L.C. copy replaced by microfilm. 1-27840.
                                                                                                           F57.F8 A3
                                                                                               Microfilm 27994   F

FRANKLIN County. Gazetteer and business directory of Franklin and Grand Isle counties, for 1882-83. Comp. and pub. by Hamilton Child ... Syracuse, N.Y., Print. Journal office, 1883.
612 p. illus., pl., ports. 24 cm. Includes a history of the county, with biographical sketches. 20-1107.   F57.F8 C5

FRANKLIN County. History of Franklin and Grand Isle counties; with illus. and biographical sketches of some of the prominent men and pioneers. Ed. Lewis Cass Aldrich. Syracuse, N.Y., D. Mason & co., 1891.   1, (5) - 821 p. illus., ports. 25½cm. 1-27840.   F57.F8 A3

GREEN Mountains. Handbook, Dartmouth outing club, with guide to the cabins and trails, ed. Dick Goldthwait '33. Brattleboro, Vt., The Vt. print. co., 1932.   136 p. illus., maps (part fold.) 17 cm. Includes bibliographies. 33-10423.   F57.G8 D2

GREEN Mountains. Footpath in the wilderness; the long trail in the Green mountains of Vermont. Middlebury, Vt., Middlebury college press, 1941.   vi, 102 p. incl. plates. 23½cm. 41-13258.
                                                                                                                                  F57.G8 F6

GREEN Mountain club incor. Guide book of the long trail. (1st) -   1917 -
Rutland, Vt., Print. The Tuttle co., 1917 -   v. fold. front., illus. (maps) 15½ - 23 cm.   F57.G8 G8
                                                            GS 17-335 rev.

GREEN Mountains of Vermont. By William Storrs Lee. Illus. Edward Sanborn. Photos. by the author. (1st ed.) New York, Holt (1955)   318 p. illus. 24 cm. 55-10642.   F57.G8 L4

GREEN Mountains. The Monroe sky-line trail; New Jersey man writes of his summer's work. By Will Seymour Monroe. (Burlington? Vt., 1917)   13 p. 15½cm. "Reprinted from the Burlington free press and times, March 24, 1917." CA 26-289 unrev.   F57.G8M75

GREEN Mountains. Blythe mountain, by Christopher Morley. Brattleboro, Vt., Stepehn Daye press (1931)   26 p. incl. front. 27½cm. "First appeared in "The bowling green" in the Saturday review of literature, July 19, 1930." 31-35529.   F57.G8M85

GREEN Mountains. ... Trails and summits of the Green Mountains, by Walter Collins O'Kane ... Boston and New York, Houghton Mifflin, co., 1926.   xi, 372 p. front., plates, maps (1 fold.) 17 cm. (The Riverside outdoor handbooks) 26-12990.   F57.G8O3

VERMONT 23

GREEN Mountains. The lure of Vermont's silent places: "the Green Mountains," by Roderic Marble Olzendam. Essex Junction, Vt., Issued by the Vermont Bureau of publicity, Office of secretary of state (1918?)   62 p. incl. illus., pl. 21 cm. 19-1015.
F57.G8 O4

GREEN Mountains. The Lion's claw trail, the Camel's hump region of the Green Mountains of Vermont. By Louis J. Paris. (Burlington, Vt., 1916)   15 p. 14½ cm. "Reprinted from the Burlington free press, September 1, 1916." CA 26-288 unrev.
F57.G8P23

GREEN Mountains of Vermont, The. Montpelier, Vt., Vermont Publicity bureau, Office of the secretary of state (1921)   76 p. illus. (incl. map) 21½ cm. 23-27084 rev.
F57.G8V52

— (1928)   cover-title, 64 p. illus. (incl. map) 23 cm. 28-27304 rev.
F57.G8V52
1928

LAMOILLE County. Gazetteer and business directory of Lamoille and Orleans counties, for 1883-84. Comp. and pub. by Hamilton Child ... Syracuse, N.Y., Printed at the Journal office, 1883.
658 (i.e.726) p. illus., ports., fold. map. 24½ cm. 7-28616.
F57.L2 C5

LAMOILLE Valley; Belvidere, Cambridge, Craftsbury, Eden, Elmore, Greensboro, Hardwick, Hyde Park, Johnson, Morristown, Stowe, Walden, Waterville, Wolcott, Woodbury directory ... Burlington, Vt., Florence B. Chase, c19 -   v. illus., fold. map. 24 cm. 25-15547.
Directories

MANSFIELD, Mount. Mansfield; the story of Vermont's loftiest mountain, by Robert L. Hagerman. (1st ed. Essex Junction, Vt., Essex Pub. Co., 1971)   103 p. illus. 26 cm. 70-181081 MARC.
F57.M3H3

MANSFIELD, Mount, and its environs. Views and sketches ... By H. Moore. Concord, N.H., H.P. Moore, 1861.   23 p. 6 pl. 16º. Cover-title: Moore's New England views ... 1-16213-M1.
F57.M3M7

MEMPHREMAGOG. Lake Memphremagog region ... Boston and Maine railroad. (New York, The Kalkhoff co.) c.1910.   (36) p. illus., fold. map. 20½ cm.
F57.M5 B7

MEMPHREMAGOG, Lake. Beautiful waters, devoted to the Memphremagog region in history, legend, anecdote, folklore, poetry, drama, compiled and printed by William Bryant Bullock. Newport, Vt., Memphremagog press, 1926.   208 p. front., illus. (incl. map) plates. 20 cm. 26-24125.
F57.M5 B9

MEMPHREMAGOG, Lake, A hand book for, with route list, by John Ross Dix ... Boston, Printed by Evans & co. (1860)   56 p. illus. 17½ cm. Rc-3117 rev.
F57.M5 D6

MEMPHREMAGOG, Lake, Statistics of the manufactures and commerce of, by E. Harrington. Stanstead (P.Q.) L.R. Robinson, 1864.   8 p. 21 cm. 5-3015.
F57.M5 H2

MEMPHREMAGOG. Uriah Jewett and the sea serpent of Lake Memphremagog; from notes left by the late George C. Merrill ... Newport, Vt. 1917.   22 p. front., pl. 22½ cm.
F57.M5 J5

MEMPHREMAGOG, Lake, and Newport, Vermont ... (n.p.) Davis and Livingston, 1908.   15½ x 23 cm.
F57.M5L19

MEMPHREMAGOG, Lake. Brochure of Owl's head mountain house, Lake Memphremagog ... (New York, A.H.Kellogg, c.1889)   69, (3) p. illus., map, plan. obl. 16º. 1-21374-M1.
F57.M5 O9

MISSISCO Valley, History of. By Samuel Sumner. With an introductory notice of Orleans County, by Rev. S.R. Hall. Pub. under the auspices of the Orleans County, historical soc. Irasburgh (Vt.) A.A. Earle, print., 1860.   75, (1) p. 23½ cm. 1-19707.
F57.M7 S9

OTTER CREEK in history; an address by Hon Henry W. Hill ... Originally delivered ... 1914.
(In Vt. historical soc. Proceedings ... 1913-14. p. (125) - 148) 15-22444.
F57.O
F46. V55

209

OMPOMPANOOSUC parish, The, by Emanuel C. Charlton. Bradford, Vt., The Opinion press (c1906) 2, (3) - 35 p. plates, ports. 23 cm. "The Ompompanossuc parish ... embraces about an equal part of the towns of Thetford and Norwich." 17-1122 rev.
    F57.O56C5

ORANGE County, Gazetteer of, 1762 - 1888. Comp. and pub. by Hamilton Child ... Syracuse, N.Y., The Syracuse journal co., printers, 1888. 2 v. in 1. ports. 24 cm. Includes a history of the county with biographical sketches. Part 2 has title: ... Business directory of Orange County ... 20-1104.
    F57.O6C53

ORLEANS County, Biography of the bar of. By Frederick W. Baldwin ... Montpelier, Vermont watchman and state journal press, 1886. 303 p. 22 port. (incl. front.) 25 cm. Many of the sketches contributed by other writers. 4-2424.
    F57.O7 B2

ORLEANS County historical society. Proceedings ... (Derby, Vt.) 1887 - 1908. 4 pam. 23 cm.
    F57.O7 O7

ORLEANS County. Historical address before the Orleans County historical soc., delivered at Hazen's Notch, by Hon, F.W. Baldwin ... 1903. (In Orleans County historical soc. Proceedings, 1902-3. p. i - ix) 4-35828.
    F57.O7 O7

RUTLAND County. Book of biographies; this volume contains biographical sketches of leading citizens of Rutland County ... Buffalo, N.Y., Chicago, Ill., Biographical pub. co., 1899. iv, (11) - 432 p. incl. ports. port. 30 x 24 cm. 19-1305.
    F57.R9 B7

RUTLAND County, genealogical gleanings. Transcribed and gathered by Elijah Ellsworth Brownell. Philadelphia, Pa., 1942. 6, 317 numb. 1. 27½ cm. Reproduced from type-written copy. Includes the 1810 federal census of Rutland county, lists of principal civil officers .. with Rutland county connections, and Rutland county officers and pensioners. 43-6262.
    F57.R9 B8

RUTLAND County, Gazetteer and business directory of, for 1881-82. Comp. and pub. by Hamilton Child ... Syracuse, N.Y. Printed at the Journal office, 1881. 256, (257) - 643 p. front. (fold. map) illus., plates. 24½ cm. Includes a history of the county, with biographical sketches. 19-2227.
    Directories

RUTLAND County. How Neshobe came up into the Green Mountains; also the discovery of Lake Bombazon by Samuel de Champlain; comp. by John MacNab Currier. Newport, Vt., 1914. 34 p. front., plates. 23½ cm. "On Oct. 20, 1761, the town of Brandon was chartered by Capt. Josiah Powers ... by the name of Neshobe." 24-162.
    F57.R9 C9

RUTLAND County, The history of. Civil, ecclesiastical, biographical and military. By Abby Maria Hemenway. White River Junction, Vt., White River paper co., 1882. 4, (403) - 1245 p. 25 cm. ... extracted from The Vermont historical gazetteer ... Vol. III. L.C. copy replaced by microfilm. 8-18453.
    F57.R9 C9
    Microfilm 22922 F

RUTLAND County historical society, Castleton, Ct. Proceedings. v. 1 - 2. (Rutland? 1882) 2 v. 8°.
    F57.R9 R9

RUTLAND County historical society. 1781. Rutland County. 1881. Centennial celebration of the organization of Rutland County ... Comp. and pub. by Lyman Williams Redington ... Montpelier, Argus and patriot book print, 1882. 194 (i.e. 196) p. 23½ cm. (Its Proceedings v. 1) 3-17738.
    F57.R9 R9
    vol. 1

RUTLAND County, History of, with illustrations and biographical sketches of some of its prominent men and pioneers. Ed. H. P. Smith and W. S. Rann. Syracuse, N.Y., D. Mason & co., 1886. 1, 9 - 959 p. illus., pl., ports. 26 cm. 1-19999 rev.
    F57.R9 S6

RUTLAND County, Statistics of the Rutland County bar, with biographical notices of the most distinguished of its deceased members: also, a list of the county officers from 1781 to 1847. Comp. and prepared by Charles L. Williams ... Brandon, Print. J. F. M'Collam, 1847. 31 p. 22 cm. 12-11169.
    F57.R9 W7

RUTLAND County. Nature studies in the Rutland valley. Photos. by L. F. Brehmer. Rutland, Vt.,

VERMONT

Brehmer bros., 1899.   (29) p. illus. obl. 8° May 4, 99-13.   F57.R92B8

WASHINGTON County. Montpelier and Barre suburban directory for the towns of Northfield, Waterbury, Moretown, Middlesex, Waitsfield, Berlin, East Montpelier, Calais, Plainfield, Marshfield, Williamstown, Topsham, Washington, Orange, 1910 -   (no. 1 -   Springfield, Mass., H. A. Manning co., c. 1909 -   v. 23 cm. 10-2669.   Directories

WASHINGTON County ... Gazetteer of, 1783 - 1889. Ed. William Adams. Comp. and pub. by Hamilton Child. Syracuse, N.Y., The Syracuse journal comp., print., 1889.   2 v. in 1. illus., ports. 24 cm. Part 2 has title: ... Business directory of Washington County. 20-1103.   F57.W3 C5

WASHINGTON County. The history of the towns of Plainfield, Roxbury and Fayston ... with Marshfield or Middlesex papers in fifty copies ... Montpelier, Vt., A. M. Hemenway, 1882.   p. 713 - 768, 177 - 248. pl. 25½ cm. "From vol. iv of the Vermont historical gazetteer" 16-19538.   F57.W3H28

WASHINGTON County, The history of, in the Vermont historical gazetteer: incl. a county chapter, and the local histories of the towns of Montpelier, East Montpelier, Barre, Berlin, Cabot, Calais, Fayston, Marshfield, Middlesex, Moretown, Northfield, Plainfield, Roxbury, Waitsfield, Warren, Waterbury, Woodbury and Worcester, by native and resident historians. Collated and pub. by Abby Maria Hemenway. Montpelier, Vt., Vermont watchman and state journal press, 1882.   2, 932 p. front., illus., ports. 25 cm. "Bibliography of Montpelier. By M. D. Gillman": p. 313 - 324. Rc-3118.   F57.W3 H4

WINDHAM County, Gazetteer and business directory of, 1724 - 1884. Comp. and pub. by Hamilton Child ... Syracuse, N.Y., Print. at the Journal office, 1884.   304, 304^1 - 304^{104}, (305) - 624 p. illus., ports., fold. map. 24 cm. Includes a history of the county, with biographical sketches. 15-9306.   F57.W7 C5

WINDHAM County's famous covered bridges. By Victor Morse. Rev. with an introd. by Richard Sanders Allen. Brattleboro, Vt., Book Cellar, 1960.   43 p. 22 cm. 60-15872.   F57.W6 M6
1960

WINDHAM County. Cemetery inscriptions from the towns of Wardsboro, Stratton, Jamaica and Dover, all in Windham County; copied by J. I. Wyer, jr. and others. Albany, N.Y. state library, 1918. 108 numb. l. double map. 25½ x 20½ cm. Autographed from type-written copy. 1 original and 3 carbons made. 19-17767.   F57.W6 W9

WINOOSKI River. The Winooski, heartway of Vermont; By Ralph Nading Hill. illus. George Daly. New York, Rinehart (1949)   xii, 304 p. illus., fold. map. 21 cm. (Rivers of America) Bibliography: p. 283 - 293. 49-8844*.   F57.W63H55

WINDSOR County. The Woodstock, Vt., directory, Ottauquechee district ... with the residents of Barnard, Bridgewater, Hartland, Pomfret, Reading, Sharon ... 19   (Woodstock) W. E. Shaw, c. 19   v. 23½ cm. 19-1996.   Directories

WINDSOR County, History of, with illustrations and biographical sketches of some of its prominent men and pioneers; ed. Lewis Cass Aldrich and others. Syracuse, N.Y., D. Mason & co., 1891. (3) - 1005 p. illus., port. 25½ x 20 cm. 3-7938.   F57.W7 A3

WINDSOR County, Gazetteer and business directory of, for 1883-84. Comp. and pub. by Hamilton Child ... Syracuse, N.Y., Print. at the Journal office, 1884.   288, 288$^{1-20}$, (289) - 666 p. illus., port., fold. map. 24½ cm. Includes a history of the county with biographical sketches. 19-2226.   F57.W7 C5

CITIES, TOWNS, ETC., A - Z.

ANDOVER, The local history of. The general history of the town, by Hiland H. Gutterson ... biographical sketches by Rev. Wm. A. Balch ... and others. Abby Maria Hemenway, ed. ... Chicago, 1886.   1, (17) - 94 p. front., pl., ports. 26 cm. Rc-3119.   F59.A5 H4

ANDOVER, The local history of, by Hiland H. Gutterson and others; Abby Maria Hemenway, ed. Perth Amboy, N.J. (C. F. Heartman) 1922.   5, (17) - 94 p. 1 illus., pl., 3 port. 26 cm. 22-6327.
F59.A5 H5

ATHENS, History of, with genealogies, 1799 - 1960. By Lora W. M. Wyman. Ann Arbor, Mich., Litho. Edwards Bros. (c. 1963)   xiii, 196 p. 23 cm. 63-23350.
F59.A8 W9

BALTIMORE, The history of the town of. By Annie Maydora (Olney) Pollard. Montpelier, Vt. Historical Society (c. 1954)   208 p. illus. 24 cm. 55-19000.
F59.B13P6

BARNARD, History of, with family genealogies, 1761 - 1927 ... by William Monroe Newton ... (Montpelier) The Vermont historical soc (c. 1928)   2 v. plates, ports., maps (2 fold.) plans. 24½ cm. Includes lists of Barnard men who fought in the revolution, war of 1812 and civil war. I. Historical. - II. Genealogical. 30-2912.
F59.B15N5

BARNET, History of, from the outbreak of the French and Indian war to present time; with genealogical records of many families, by Frederic Palmer Wells ... illus. by Rev. C.B. Bliss and others. Burlington, Vt., Free press print. co., 1923.   xiv, 689, (2) p. front., plates, ports., maps (1 fold.) 25 cm. 23-8831.
F59.B16W4

BARRE.   Manning's Barre and Montpelier (Vermont) directory; including Barre Town, Berlin, East Montpelier, Middlesex, Northfield, Plainfield and Williamstown ... (v. 1) -   Springfield, Mass., H. A. Manning co., c. 1890 - 19   v. fold. maps. 23½ - 24 cm. Title varies. imprint varies. 99-3459 rev.
Directories

BARRE in the great flood of 1927; a history of tragic events and of great loss sustained in Vermont city, Nov. 3 - 4, by Dean H. Perry ... (Barre, Vt., c. 1928)   4 - 117 p. front., illus. (incl. ports) 23½ cm. 28-5751.
F59.B17P4

BARTON LANDING, history of. An address read before the Orleans County historical soc. ... 1892. By Hon, B. F. D. Carpenter ... Newport (Vt.) The Society, 1893.   20 p. 23½ cm. 4-23276.
F59.B2 C2

BARTON directory, The. Newport, Vt., D. C. Davis.   v. 22½ cm. Includes the Orleans, Vt., directory. Contains also the Newport and West Derby, Vt. directory, inverted, with separate t.-p. 17-16867.
Directories

BELLOWS FALLS, township of Rockingham, Vermont, and village of North Walpole, New Hampshire, directory; including Athens, Chester and Westminster, Vt., Alstead, Charlestown and Walpole, N.H.   v. fold. maps. 23½ cm. 7-4176 rev.
Directories

BELLOWS FALLS and vicinity, illus. ... attractions and historical facts of Bellows Falls and the surrounding villages of Saxtons River, Rockingham and Westminster, Vermont, and Walpole and Charlestown, New Hampshire, comp. and pub. by P.H. Gobie, ed. L.S. Hayes ... Bellows Falls, Vt., The P.H. Gobie press (c. 1912)   (109) p. incl. front., illus. 24½ x 30½ cm. 12-11746.
F59.B39G5

BENNINGTON.   Pathfinder to Greylock Mountain, the Berkshire Hills and historic Bennington ... Maps showing roads, street railways and Greylock summit (by) W. H. Phillips ... (Amherst? Mass.) 1910.   139 (2) p. illus. (incl. port.) fold. maps. 20½ cm. 10-14106.
F59.B4
F72.B5P5

BENNINGTON, Vermont, 1777 - 1927. A record of the celebration, held at Bennington, ... 1927, in honor of the 150th anniversary of the battle of Bennington and the 150th year of the separate existence of the state of Vermont.   1927. ... (Burlington, The Lane press, inc., 1927)   120 p. 23 cm. 28-27030.
F59.B4
E241.B4V4

BENNINGTON.   Humorous tales of Bennington-on-the-hill, collected and written for her sons and daughters by one who was born near the site of the old continental store house. Richard Seymour Bayhan. Cleveland, O. (Central pub. house, c. 1918)   68 p. front., plates, ports. 15 cm. 18-16002.
F59.B4B35

VERMONT 27

BENNINGTON, Souvenir program historical pageant of. Given by the people of the town in honor of the 150th anniversary of its settlement ... 1911 ... (Troy, N.Y., Troy Times art press, 1911)
36 p. illus. 23½ cm. 12-1247.   F59.B4B46

BENNINGTON. Historical Museum and Art Gallery. Publications. no. 1 -   (Bennington) 1930 -
no. illus. 24 cm. 55-52916.   F59.B4 B6
— No. 1. The true story of Capt. David Mathews and his State line house ... by John Spargo. 1930.   12 p. 2 pl. 23½ cm. 30-17697.
— No. 2. ... Iron mining and smelting in Bennington, 1786 - 1842 ... by John Spargo. 1938.   30 p. 23 cm. Four letters reprinted from the Bennington evening banner. 42-44782.
— No. 3. The A.B.C. of Bennington pottery wares ... By John Spargo. (c. 1938)
3, 38 p. incl. illus., pl. 23½ cm. 39-16103.

BENNINGTON. The Hill of Bennington; a battle-poem for the sesqui-centennial celebration of the battle of Bennington ... 1927, with seven associated lyrics and ballads, by Daniel L. Cady ... Rutland, Vt., The Tuttle co. (c. 1927)   2, 3 - 24 p. pl., port. 23 cm. 27-18330.
F59.B4C13

BENNINGTON's book, being the complete chronicle of a New England village, with various digressions and disertations (!) on life ... by Alexander B.R. Drysdale. (Troy, N.Y., Troy times art press, c. 1927)   4, (7) - 93 p. 23 cm. 27-18327.   F59.B4 D8

BENNINGTON. Historical sketch of buildings now or once located in the village on the hill at Bennington, formerly known as Bennington Center, and now called Old Bennington; original list comp. Hiram Harwood in 1837, rev. and enl. by Deacon Samuel Chandler in 1870; added to by others.   Cleveland, O., Central pub. house (c. 1930)   3 - 50 p. front., illus. (incl. ports., map) 23 cm. 30-32745.
F59.B4H34

BENNINGTON, The local history of, 1860 - 1883. The military history of the county ... with Bennington villages ... and their industries. Abby Maria Hemenway, ed. Chicago (1887?)   108 p. incl. front., plates, port. 24 cm. 1-8087.   F59.B4 H5

BENNINGTON. Memorials of a century. Embracing a record of individuals and events, chiefly in the early history of Bennington, and its First church. By Isaac Jennings ... Boston, Gould and Lincoln, 1869.   xviii, (19) - 408 p. front. (plan) pl. 20½ cm. 1-Rc-3120.   F59.B4 J 5

BENNINGTON. The one hundred year old meetinghouse of the church of Christ in Bennington: being a record of the centennial of the same held ... 1906. Prepared by Rev. Isaac Jennings ... Cambridge, Mass., The Riverside press, 1907.   xii, 185 p. front., plates. 20½ cm. 7-33564.   F59.B4 J 6

BENNINGTON. Gleanings from old Bennington, by William Justin Mann. (Boston? c. 1924)   (25) p. 2 pl. 18½ cm. "These Gleanings first appeared ... somewhat abbreviated, as 'Little walks about Boston', in the Boston post ..." 24-28078.
F59.B4 M3

BENNINGTON. Sketches of historic Bennington, by John V. d. S. and Caroline R. Merrill. Cambridge, Print. the Riverside press, 1898.   4, 99 p. 10 pl. (incl. front.) 19½ cm. Chapters 1 - 2 (p.1-28) reprinted under title "Old Bennington and the Bennington battle, by Caroline R. Merrill," Cambridge, 1909. C-253 rev.   F59.B4 M5

— 1907.   4, 99 p. front., plates, port. 20 cm. 1st ed. Cambridge, 1898. 14-11886.   F59.B4M55

BENNINGTON and its surroundings. By Andrew J. Nutting. (Bennington? c. 1866)   16 p. front. 23 cm.
1-16212 rev.   F59.B4 N9

BENNINGTON, Souvenir calendar of. (Bennington, M.E. Watson, 1897)   1 p. 12 pl. obl. 12°.
1-Rc-3122.   F59.B4S68

BENNINGTON, Souvenir of. Photographs in black ... E.S. Gokay, photog ... New York, The Albertype co. (c. 1889)   1, 18 p. obl. 32°. 1-Rc-3121.   F59.B4 S7

BENNINGTON, A pageant at, in celebration of the 150th anniversary of the battle of Bennington, 1777 -

213

1927, written and prod. by Virginia Tanner; acted and sung and danced by the citizens of Bennington ... (Concord, N.H., Rumford press, c.1927)   92 p. illus. 23½ cm. 27-17921.   F59.B4 T2

BERLIN, Early history of, 1763 - 1820. By Mary Greene Nye. Montpelier, Vt., Towne and Dodge; agent: Vermont hist. soc., 1951 (i.e. 1954)   98 p. illus. 21 cm. 55-25899.   F59.B45N9

BRADFORD. Long ago in Bradford; or, Christopher's adventures. By Marguerite E. Grow. Barre, Vt., Printed by Modern Print. Co. (1960)   289 p. 24 cm.   F57.B7 G7

BRADFORD, A history of, containing some account of the places of its first settlement in 1765, and the principal improvements made, and events which have occurrred down to 1874 ... With various genealogical records, and biographical sketches of families ... By Rev. Silas McKeen. Montpelier, Vt., J.D. Clark & son, 1875.   459, (2) p. 2 port. (incl. front.) 22 cm. 1-Rc-3126.   F59.B7 M1

BRAINTREE, The history of, including a memorial of families that have resided in town, by H. Royce Bass ... Rutland, Vt., Tuttle & co., state printers, 1883.   208 p. front. (fold. map) 23 cm. A 12-1464.   F59.B73B3

BRANDON; a history of the town dedicated to its citizens, 1761 - 1961. (1961 (c.1962)   294 p. 24 cm.   F59.B78A52

BRANDON. A pilgrimage to the monuments of the early settlers of Brandon; an address commemorating the 150th anniversary of the granting of the town patent, by Rev. William Van Derveer Berg. ... (Brandon, Vt., A.G. Farr, 1911)   (35) p. 25 cm. 19-2106.   F59.B8 B4

BRATTLEBORO, Proceedings in the celebration at, ... 1892, of the 400th anniversary of the discovery of America by Christopher Columbus. Brattleboro, The Phoenix job print., 1892.   64 p. plates. 23½ cm. 11-15749.   F59.B E119.48.B82

BRATTLEBORO directory ... 1874. Brattleboro? Vt.) R.S. Dillon & co. (1874 -   v. 25 cm. 15-2164.   Directories

BRATTLEBORO directory. 1901 ... also directory of Chesterfield, N.H., Dummerston, Guilford, Marlboro, Newfane, Putney and Vernon, Vt. ... Boston, Mass., Union pub. co.   v. 24 cm. 1-26538.   Directories

BRATTLEBORO. Manning's Brattleboro and Putney (Vermont) and Chesterfield and Hinsdale (New Hampshire) directory ... Springfield, Mass., H.A. Manning co. 19 -   v. fold. maps. 23½ cm. Title varies. 7-26443 rev. 2.   Directories

BRATTLEBORO, Beck's professional and business gazetteer and directory of. Comp. Fernando C. Beck. Worcester, Mass., G.G. Davis, 1899.   24 p. illus. fol.   Mar 23, 99-10.   F59.B8 B3

BRATTLEBORO, Windham County, Vermont; early history, with biographical sketches of some of its citizens, by Henry Burnham. Brattleboro, D. Leonard, 1880.   2, (17) - 191 p. 24½ cm. Reissued in 1891 in Vermont historical gazetteer ... vol. v. Collated by Abby Maria Hemenway. 1-Rc-3127.   F59.B8 B9

BRATTLEBORO, The attractions of. Glimpses of the past and present. By Henry M. Burt ... Brattleboro, Vt., D.B. Stedman, printer, 1866.   108 p. front., pl. 19½ cm. Rc-3128 Rev.   F59.B8B91

BRATTLEBORO, Annals of, 1681 - 1895, comp. and ed. by Mary R. Cabot ... Brattleboro, Vt., Press of E.L. Hildreth & co., 1921 - 22.   2 v. fronts., illus. (incl. plans) plates, ports., maps. facsims. 26 cm. Vols. 1 - 2 include biographical material. 21-22323 rev.   F59.B8C12

BRATTLEBORO. Grout's miscellanea: or, A selection of pamphlets from the later writings of the Rev. Lewis Grout ... Brattleboro, Vt., The phoenix job print., 1900.   16 v. in 1. front., ports., plan. 22 cm. 11-30229.   F59.B8 G8

VERMONT 29

BRATTLEBORO. Picturesque Brattleboro with over 200 illus.   Ed. Frank T. Pomeroy.   Northampton, Mass., Picturesque pub. co. (c. 1894)   96 p. incl. front., illus. (incl. ports., facsims.)   30 ½ cm.   Rc-3129.
F59.B8 P7

BRISTOL, History of (1762 - 1940) comp. by Carrie K. Harvey and Clara M. Kellogg for the Outlook club of Bristol. (Omaha, Neb., W. Gail, 1941)   115 p. incl. front., plates, group port.   25 cm.   42-12835.
F59.B85H3

BROOKLINE, The local history of. The general history of the town, by Charles P. Stickney. The history of the Baptist church, by John B. Stebbins ... Written for vol. v of the Vermont historical gazetteer ... Abby Maria Hemenway, ed.   Chicago, 1886.   48 p. incl. port. ports. 26 ½ cm. Rc-3130 rev.
F59.B87S8

BURLINGTON city directory and business advertiser.   Burlington, Free press assoc., 1889
   v. fronts. (fold. maps) 18 ½ cm. 18-5794.
Directories

BURLINGTON city and Winooski directory for 1889/90 - 19   (Burlington, Vt.) L. P. Waite & co., c. 1889 - c. 1913   25 v. fold. maps.   24 cm. Title varies. 1-13965 (rev. '15)
Directories

BURLINGTON, Vermont and Lake Champlain: photo-gravures.   Brooklyn, N. Y., The Albertype co., 1900.   1 p. 15 pl. obl. 24°. Dec 27, 1900-1.
F59.B9 A5

BURLINGTON. We Americans; a study of cleavage in an American city, by Elin L. Anderson. New York, Russell & Russell (1967, c. 1937)   xii, 286 p. 22 cm. 66-27035.
F59.B9 A9 1967

BURLINGTON. Picturesque Burlington; a handbook of Burlington, Vermont, and Lake Champlain, by Joseph Auld. 143 illus. Burlington, Vt., Free press assoc., 1893.   (vii) - xiii, 180 p. front., illus., plates, map. 22 ½ cm. Rc-3131.
F59.B9 A9

— 2d ed. 164 illus. Burlington, Vt., Free press assoc., 1894.   1, xi-xiv, 190 p. front., illus., plates, map. 22 ½ cm. Rc-3132.
F59.B9A91

BURLINGTON. Beautiful Burlington, by Hon. G. G. Benedict of Burlington. Practical Burlington, by Nath'l C. Fowler jr. of New York. (Burlington, Vt., Free press print, 1907)   1, 17 p. front., illus. 24 cm. 9-23289.
F59.B9 B4

BURLINGTON. Facts about Burlington, Vt: the "Queen city" and its institutions; its drives, rambles, views, places of interest, and its resources.   Glen Falls, N. Y., C. H. Possons, 1888.   24 p. illus. 14 ½ x 11 ½ cm. 11-30228.
F59.B9F14

BURLINGTON. Round about Burlington. By Charles Sumner Lord.   Winooski, Vt., Vermont illus, co., 1900.   (183) p. illus. (incl. ports.) 20 ½ x 28 ½ cm. 4-19874.
F59.B9 L8

BURLINGTON. Look around Burlington, by Lilian Baker Carlisle and others.   Burlington, Vt., Chittenden County Historical Soc. (1972)   28 p. illus. 23 cm. (Heritage series pamphlet no. 1) 78-189231 MARC.
F59.B9 M8

BURLINGTON, Vt. as a manufacturing, business and commercial center. With brief sketches of its history, attractions, leading industries, and institution ... By Charles H. Possons. (Glen's Falls, N. Y.) For the Burlington board of trade, 1889.   108 p. front., illus. 8°. 1-Rc-3133.
F59.B9 P8

BURLINGTON. Exercises attending the dedication of a memorial tower erected in honor of General Ethan Allen upon Indian Rock, in Burlington, by the Vermont soc. of Sons of the American revolution ... 1905. ... Burlington, Free press print. co., 1906.   50 p. 7 pl. port. 23 ½ cm. 6-38543.
F59.B9 S6

BURLINGTON. Proceedings of the Vermont antiquarian society, Burlington, 1897 to 1900.   ... (Burlington, Vt., 1900)   2, (3) - 96 p. 24 ½ cm. No more pub. 7-12924.
F59.B9 V5

CALAIS. A treatise by Reuben D. Waters, on the town of Calais and vicinity, with some sketches of Jewish, pagan, Mahometan, and other religions; character of Bonaparte, Columbus, and notaries. (Calais? Vt.) Pub. for the author, 1852. 31 p. 21 cm. 17-16957. F59.C14W3

CASTLETON. Epitaphs of Castleton church yard. Comp. John McNab Currier. (Castleton, 1887?) 48 p. 24½ cm. Also issued with the addition of nine epitaphs in the Proceedings of the Rutland County historical society, 1887, p. 95 - 143. Rc-3134 rev. F59.C3C9

CAVENDISH, History of. By Lois Wheeler. Proctorsville, Vt., 1952. 70 p. illus. 24 cm. Includes bibliography. 53-18475. F59.C33W4

CHESTER's mystery man (by) Walter R. Hard, Jr. and Stephen Greene. Brattleboro, Vt., Pub. Stephen Greene Press for the Chester Art Guild, Chester, Vt., c.1966) 16 p. 23 cm. F59.C5A63

CORINTH, History of, 1764 - 1964. Comp. and ed. by Town of Corinth history Committee. (1st ed.) Corinth (c.1964) xxxi, A-K, 508 p. 24 cm. F59.C7 C6

CORNWALL. Retrospection; a poem recited by the author at a celebration commemorating the 150th anniversary of the settlement of Cornwall, 1911. (Burlington, Vt., Free press print. co., c.1911) (6) p. 25½ x 15½ cm. 12-2976. F59.C8 G8

CORNWALL, History of the town of, by Rev. Lyman Matthews ... Middlebury, Mead and Fuller ... 1862. xii, (13) - 356 p. 1 illus., pl. 7 port. (incl. front.) 23 cm. "Record of families settled previously to 1800": p. 283 - 290. Rc-3135. F59.C8 M4

CORNWALL. The dedication of the Samson memorial, Cornwall, Vermont. Mary Baker Allen chapter D.A.R., ... 1915. (Cornwall? Vt., 1915?) 27 p. 22 cm. 19-4217. F59.C8 S2

CORNWALL. Two centuries of Cornwall life. By Beulah M. Sanford. Rutland, Vt., Print. Sharp Printing, 1962. 111 p. illus., ports., map. 24 cm. F59.C8S25

COVENTRY, Orleans county, A history of. By Pliny H. White ... Irasburgh, A.A. Earle, 1859. 61, vii p. 22½ cm. Rc-3136. F59.C9 W5

COVENTRY. An account of the erection and exercises at the dedication of the monument erected and presented to the town of Coventry, Vt., by Riley E. Wright, in honor of the soldiers of Coventry in the civil war ... 1912. (Newport, Vt., Express and Standard, print., 1912) 51, (2) p. pl., ports. 23½ cm. 12-25797. F59.C9W9

CRAFTSBURY. Dedication, soldiers' memorial ... (Craftsbury, 1922) 6 p. 26 cm. F59.C93C8

CRAFTSBURY. Soldiers' record, town of Craftsbury, 1861 - 1865, by George F. Sprague. (Craftsbury?) 1914. 85, (3) p. 1 illus. (port.) 21½ cm. 18-11583. F59.C8 S7

DANBY, The history and map of, by J.C. Williams. Rutland, Vt., Printed by McLean & Robbins, 1869. 393 p. fold. front. (map) 22½ cm. Rc-3137. F59.D2 W7

DERBY, History of, by Cecile B. Hay and Mildred B. Hay. Littleton, N.H., Print. Courier Print., 1967. 240 p. illus. 24 cm. F59.D4 H3

DORSET, The story of, by Zephine Humphrey, and others; with occasional drawings by Katherine Field White. Rutland, Vt., The Tuttle co. (c.1924) 288 p. incl. illus., plates. front. 19 cm. 24-19653. F59.D7 H8

DOVER, History of; 200 years in a hill town. By Nell M. Kull. Brattleboro, Vt., Book Cellar, 1961. viii, 200 p. 23 cm. 61-17648. F59.D75K8

DUMMERSTON, The history of the town of, by D.L. Mansfield. (From vol. v of the Vermont historical gazetteer) Ludlow, Vt., Miss A.M. Hemenway, 1884. 1, 216 p. front., port. 8°. 1-Rc-3138. F59.D8 M2

VERMONT   31

ESSEX. The memorial record of.   Prepared by L. C. Butler.   Burlington, R. S. Styles, printer, 1866
59, (2) p.   20 cm.   Rc-3139 rev.
                                                                                                F59. E7 B8

ESSEX centennial.   The one hundredth anniversary of the settlement of Essex ... 1883.   Montpelier,
Vt., Argus and patriot book and job print,, 1883.   64 p. 23 cm. 20-891.
                                                                                                F59. E7 E7

FAIR HAVEN.   Rutland suburban directory including Fair Haven, Poultney, Castleton, Hampton, N. Y.,
P. O., Hubbardton, Pittsford, Chittenden, Brandon, Wallingford, Clarendon, 1911,   Springfield,
Mass., H. A. Manning co., c. 1910 -   1 v. 23 ½ cm.   10-27314.   Directories

FAIR HAVEN, A history of the town of.   In three parts.   By Andrew N. Adams.   Fair Haven, Leonard
& Phelps, printers, 1870.   vi, (9) - 516 p. front. (fold. map) fold. plan. 21 cm. Biographical and family notices: p. (281) -
510. 1-Rc-3140.   F59. F1 A2

FAIRFIELD, Some early records of, selected and ed. by Gilbert Harry Doane.   Pub. in commemoration of the 150th anniversary of the first settlement of the town ... Burlington, Vt., Free press interstate print. corp., 1938.   3, 3 - 56 p. 23 ½ cm. 39-4020.   F59. F3 D6

FAIRLEE.   The town under the cliff; a history of Fairlee, by Philip G. Boston.   Fairlee (1957)
187 p. illus. 24 cm. 58-15935.   F59. F4 R6

GEORIGA.   Eighty-three years a servant; or, The life of Rev. Alvah Sabin, by Alvah S. Hobart.
Cincinnati, O., Print for the author by the Review print. co., 1885.   174 p. 2 port. (incl. front.) 21 cm.
12-12554.   F59. G3 H6

GRAFTON, History of the town of.   By Francis A. Palmer.   Brattleboro, Shaw Press, 1954.
120 p. illus. 24 cm. 55-20154.   F59. G7 P3

GRAFTON, History of, 1754 - 1971, and sidelights on Grafton history, by Helen M. Pettengill for the
Grafton Historical Soc.   (Grafton, Vt., c. 1971)   80 p. illus.   F59. G7 P4

GREENSBORO.   The memorial record of the soldiers who enlisted from Greensboro, to aid in subduing
the great rebellion of 1861-5, accompanied by a brief history of each regiment that left the state.
Prepared by E. E. Rollins.   Montpelier, Print. at the Freeman print. house, 1868.   77 p. 17 ½ cm.
7-23982.   F59. G8 R7

GUILDHALL, A history of, containing some account of the place - of its first settlement in 1764, ...
With various genealogical records, and biographical sketches of families and individuals, ... Together
with a brief sketch of Essex County, Vermont.   By Everett Chamberlin Benton ... Waverley, Mass.,
E. C. Benton, 1886.   4, (17) - 270 p. incl. illus., plates, ports. 22 ½ cm. Rc-3141.   F59. G9 B4

GUILFORD, Official history of, 1678 - 1961.   With genealogies and biographical sketches.   (Guilford)
Pub. by the town ... 1961.   xi, 580 p. 24 cm.   F59. G9 P3

GUILFORD, The local history of, 1754 - 1888, by Gen. J. W. Phelps, and others.   For vol. v of the
Vermont historical gazetteer.   Abby Maria Hemenway, pub. ... Chicago, 1888.   80 p. 27 ½ cm.
15-19113.   F59. G9P53

HARDWICK: town records to 1860.   (Hardwick, 1928)   1 p. 115 l. 28 cm. Mimeographed. Compiled for Miss
Alison B. Hitchcock, by the town clerk, Sept. 1928. CA 33-466 unrev.   F59. H2 H3

HARTFORD, White River Junction and Windsor, Vermont, directory, The; embracing ... White River
Junction, Wilder, Hartford, Dewey's Mills, West Hartford, Quechee, Vt., West Lebanon, N. H. ...
Complete classified business directory of Hartford, Windsor and Woodstock, Vt.   (Canaan, N. H.) W. E.
Shaw,   1 v. 23 ½ cm. 16-904.   Directories

HARTFORD.   The Old and the new; an occasional magazine devoted to the institutions and history of
the town of Hartford, ... no. 1 - 3   Dec. 15, 1899 - Jan. 1910.   White River Junction, Vt. (1899);
Hartford, Vt., 1901 -   5 v. illus., plates, map. 22 ½ cm. 11-10801.   F59. H3 O4

217

HARTFORD, An album of the town of, 1761 - 1969, by John W. St. Croix. (White River Junction, Vt., Print. Right Print. co., c.1969.   ix, 148 p. illus. 79-82316.   F59.H3S29

HARTFORD, Pictorial history of the town of, 1761 - 1963. By John W. St. Croix. Hartford, 1963.   xv, 186 p. 24 cm. 63-22342.   F59.H3 S3

HARTFORD, History of, 1761 - 1889. The first town on the New Hampshire grants chartered after the close of the French war. By William Howard Tucker ... Burlington, Vt., The Free press assoc., 1889.   xv, 488 p. 1 illus., 3 port. (incl. front.) 24 cm. "Genealogies": p. (406) - 476. 1-Rc-3142.   F59.H3 T8

HARTLAND in the revolutionary war: her soldiers; their homes, lives and burial places; the muster rolls of Captain Elias Weld's, etc. companies; also, Hartland in the war of 1812 and in the Mexican war. Comp. by Dennis Flower, 2d ed. ... Hartland, Vt., Solitarian press (1914?)   49, (1) p. 21 x 17 cm. 17-3094.   F59.H33F6

HARTLAND. Report of the celebration of the 150th anniversary of Vermont's independence; celebrated at Hartland, Oct. 6, 1927, under the auspices of the Hartland historical society. (Hartland, Vt., 1927)   36 p. front. 23 cm. Cover-title: The Vermont sesqui-centennial celebration. "... The names of the heads of families" in Hartland, April 5, 1771: p. 16. 29-16530.   F59.H33H35

HINESBURG. Ann account of the centennial celebration of the First Congregational church of Christ in Hinesburgh ... 1890. Burlington, Vt., Free press assoc., 1890.   78 p. 26 cm. "Comp. from the Free press, Vermont chronicle, and other papers." - p.7. 21-17515.   F59.H56H5

HUBBARDTON, Sketches of the history of the town of, with remarks on the ancient customs and practices of the people, and some miscellaneous articles. By an old man (Amos Churchill) ... Rutland (Vt.) Press of G. A. Tuttle and co., 1855.   2, (3) - 64 p. 18 cm. "First pub. in the Rutland herald and Brandon post, in the winter of 1855." 18-11582.   F59.H75C5

IRA, History of, by S. L. Peck, town clerk for over forty years ...   Rutland, Vt., The Tuttle Co., 1926.   83 p. illus. (incl. ports.) 23 ½ cm. 27-14535.   F59.I6 P3

JAMAICA. Historical notes: Jamaica, Windham county, Vermont, compiled and ed. by Warren E. Booker. (Brattleboro, Vt., E. L. Hildreth) 1940.   viii, 244 p. front. (double map) illus., plates, facsims. 23 ½ cm. Bibliography inc. in "Introduction" p. (iii) "Genealogy": p. (173) - 214. 41-2775.   F59.J3 B6

JERICHO, The history of; ed. by Chauncey H. Hayden, and others. Burlington? Vt., The Free press print., 1916 - 63.   vol. 2 ed. by Elinor I. Merle. 17-13630.   F59. J5 H3

JERICHO, The soldiers' record of. Prepared by E. H. Lane. Burlington, Vt., R. S. Styles, 1868.   iv, 5 - 47 p. 20 cm. 1-21604.   F59. J5 L2

JOHNSON, Vermont ... copyrighted ... by William Lamkie ... Johnson, Vt., The Green mountain year book ass'n., c.1931.   (132) p. illus. (incl. maps) plates, ports. 22 ½ cm. Running title: Green mountains year book. Various pagings. "Suggestive reading list of Vermont books": p. 34. 31-5319.   F59.J7L22

JOHNSON, History of the town of, 1784 - 1907. Comp. and pub. under the direction of the Oread literary club for the benefit of the Johnson Public library fund. 1907. Burlington, Free press print. co., 1907.   83 p. front., illus., plates, ports. 21 ½ cm. 7-39014.   F59. J7 O6

LONDONDERRY, The history with genealogical sketches of, by Addison E. Cudworth. Montpelier, Vt., The Vermont historical soc., 1936.   228 p. front. (port.) 23 ½ cm. 36-2359.   F59.L6 C8

LOWER WATERFORD. A Vermont village, by Dr. C. E. Harris. (Yarmouth Port,, Mass., The Register press, 1941)   4, 105 p. 3 pl. 23 ½ cm. 42-11296.   F59.L7 H3

LUDLOW, History of. Charlestown, N. H., I. H. Harding (and) A. F. Harding, c. 1949.   239 p. illus., ports., maps. 24 cm. 49-51312*.   F59.L9 H3

LUDLOW and her neighbors, being a special sourvenir edition of the Vermont tribune, illus. and de-

voted to the interests of the villages of Ludlow, Proctorsville, Cavendish and Chester, all in Windsor County. Ludlow, Vt., Printed at the Vermont tribune office, 1899.   63 p. illus. (incl. ports.) 30 x 23 cm.
Cover title: Special souvenir ed. & supplement of the Vermont tribune.   20-7260.   F59.L9 V5

LUDLOW, Record of deaths in the town of, from 1790 to 1901, inclusive. Comp. by Rufus S. Warner. Ludlow, Vt., R. S. Warner, print., 1902.   2, 72 (2) p. 19 cm. 18-19962.   F59.L9 W2

MANCHESTER, 1761 - 1961; a pleasant land among the mountains (by) Edwin L. Bigelow and Nancy H. Otis. Manchester, 1961.   317 p. illus. 24 cm.   F59.M2 B5

MANCHESTER, The early history of. An address delivered in Music Hall, Manchester ... 1875. By Loveland Munson ... Manchester, Vt., Journal print., 1876.   iv, (5) - 63 p. 24 cm. Rc-3143.
F59.M 2M9

MARLBOROUGH. The history of the town of Marlborough, Windham County, Vermont, by the Rev. Ephraim H. Newton, with an introd. by John Clement. Montpelier, Vt. historical soc., 1930.
4, 330 p. plates, ports. 23½ cm. "Genealogical and biographical notes": p. 127-278. 30-12281.   F59.M4N56

MARSHFIELD, History of, by Ozias C. Pitkin and Fred E. Pitkin. (North Andover, Mass.) 1941.
1 v. plates, maps, diagrs. 29½ cm. Loose-leaf; reproduced from type-written copy. "Revised" "Family histories of settlers and residents of Marshfield": p. 95 - 308. 41-24875.   F59.M43P57

MIDDLEBURY, Statistical account of the town of. Part first. By Frederick Hall ... Boston, Print. S. Phelps, 1821.   38 p. 22 cm. Pub. also in Mass. historical soc. Collections, ser. 2 v.9, p. 123-158. 8-31708.   F59.M6H17

MIDDLEBURY. Oration by Prof. Brainerd Kellogg, and poem by Mrs. J. C. R. Dorr, delivered at the pioneer centennial celebration, Middlebury ... 1866. Middlebury, Register book and job print., 1866.
35 p. 23 cm. Oration on John Chipman, the first settler of Middlebury. 12-3255.   F59.M6 K2

MIDDLEBURY. Stagecoach north, being an account of the first generation in the state of Vermont by W. Storrs Lee ... New York, The Macmillan company, 1941.   xi p., 2 l., 210 p. illus. 21 cm. "First printing." "Sources": p. 203 - 210. 41-10889.   F59.M6 L4

MIDDLEBURY. Town father, a biography of Gamaliel Painter; by William Storrs Lee. With chapter decorations by Edward Sanborn. New York, Hastings House (1952)   242 p. illus. 21 cm. 52-11810.
F59.M6L42

MIDDLEBURY. Semicentennial sermon, containing a history of Middlebury, delivered 1840 ... By Thomas A. Merrill ... Middlebury, Print. E. Maxham, 1841.   92 p. 21 cm. Manuscript addenda, 1 p.
16-6785 rev.   F59.M6 M2

MIDDLEBURY historical society. Papers and proceedings. 1885.   8°. v. 1 pt. 2.
F59.M6 M3

MIDDLEBURY historical society. The marble border of western New England. Its geology and marble development in the present century ... (Middlebury, Vt.) Pub. by the society, 1885.
2, vi, (7) - 68 p. col. chart. 23 cm. (Its Papers and proceedings, vol. I pt. II) GS6-523.   F59.M6 M3

MIDDLEBURY register. (Centennial supplement. 1836 - 1936) Middlebury, Vt., 1936.   1 v. illus.
58 cm. With the regular news section, forms v. 101, no. 1 of the Middlebury register, issued May 22, 1936. 39M4964T.
F59.M6M36

MIDDLEBURY. History of the town of, in the county of Addison, Vermont: to which is prefixed a statistical and historical account of the county, written at the request of the historical society of Middlebury, by Samuel Swift. Middlebury, A. H. Copeland, 1859.   132, 7, (141) - 444 p. front., plates, ports. 23½ cm.
The work comprises the "Statistical and historical account of the county of Addison", p. 1 - 132 (also issued separately) and "History of the town of Middlebury", with special t.-p., pref. and table of contents. 7 p., p. 141 - 444. Rc-3144 Rev.   F59.M6 S9

MIDDLETON, The history of, in three discourses, delivered before the citizens of that town ... 1867 by the Hon. Barnes Frisbie ... Rutland, Vt., Tuttle & co,, 1867.   130 p. 22½ cm. Rc-3145.   F59.M62F9

MIDDLETOWN SPRINGS. History of the Hoadley monument and unveiling ceremonies, ed. by La Roy Southworth. Middletown Springs, Vt., 1904. 46 p. incl. front., illus. (port.) pl. 15½ x 23½ cm. Cover-title: Memorial day souvenir May 30, 1904 ... 21-17519. F.59.M62S7

MONTPELIER (Vermont) directory ... Springfield, Mass., H. A. Manning co., 1908 - 1 v. fold. map. 23 cm. 9-1234. Directories

MONTPELIER city directory ... 1897/8 - Newburgh, N.Y.. L. P. Waite & co., c.1897 - v. 24½ cm. CA 33-477 unrev. Directories

MONTPELIER. The flood, Nov. 3 & 4, 1927, Montpelier, Vt. By Joseph G. Abair. (Montpelier, Print. Capital city press, c.1928) (32) p. illus. 14 x 20 cm. 42-11297. F59.M7A25

MONTPELIER, History of: a discourse delivered in the Brick church, Montpelier, Vt. ... 1842. By Rev. John Gridley ... Montpelier, E. P. Walton and sons, 1843. 48 p. 21½ cm. Rc-3146.
F59.M7 G8

MONTPELIER, The history of the town of, inc. that of the town of East Montpelier, for the first one hundred and two years ... Montpelier, Vt., Miss A. M. Hemenway, 1882. vii, 251 - 592 p. front., illus., plates, ports. 25 cm. From vol. iv of the Vermont historical gazetteer. Rc-3147. F59.M7 H4

MONTPELIER. Services at the dedication of Green Mount cemetery, Montpelier ... 1855, with the rules and regulations. Montpelier, E. P. Walton, jr., printer, 1855. 40 p. 23½ cm. 21-11143.
F59.M7 M7

MONTPELIER, History of the town of ... 1781 to 1860. Together with biographical sketches of its most noted deceased citizens. By D. P. Thompson. Montpelier, E. P. Walton, print., 1860.
viii, (9) - 312 p. front. (port.) 22½ cm. 1-Rc-3148. F59.M7 T4

MORRISTOWN, History of, by Anna L. Mower. (Morrisville, Vt., Messenger-sentinel co.) 1935.
5, 324 p. fold. front., plates, ports. 24 cm. 36-432. F59.M9 M6

NEWBURY. 150th anniversary of the settlement of Newbury, Vt. Old home week, ... 1912. Groton, Vt., The Groton times print, 1912. 49, 6 p. plates, ports., plan. 26 cm. 14-5181. F59.N4N45

NEWBURY, History of, from the discovery of the Coos country to present time. With genealogical records of many families. By Frederic P. Wells, in behalf of the town. St. Johnsbury, Vt., The Caledonian co., 1902. xiv, 779 p. front., plates (part fold.) ports., fold. maps. 25 cm. Bibliography of Newbury: p. 247-250. 2-7319. F59.N4 W4

NEWFANE ... Centennial proceedings and other historical facts and incidents relating to Newfane, the county seat of Windham County, Vermont. Brattleboro, D. Leonard, print., 1877. v, (9) - 256 p. ports. 23½ cm. "Biographical sketches": p. (34) - 97. "Family genealogies": p. 155 - 176. Rc-3149.
F59.N5 N5

NEWFANE. Dedication of soldiers' monument at Newfane ... 1916. Soldiers' monument assoc. (Rutland, Vt., The Tuttle co., 1916) 51 p. front. 23 cm. 19-492. F59.N5S6

NEW HAVEN. The torrent; or An account of a deluge occasioned by an unparalleled rise of the New Haven River, in which nineteen persons were swept away ... 1830. By Lemuel B. Eldridge ... Middlebury (Vt.) Print. Free press, by E. D. Barber. vi, (7) - 61 p. 15½ cm. 8-25402. F59.N3 E3

NEW HAVEN., a rural historical town of Vermont; oration by Hon. J. B. Grinnell and addresses ... Burlington (Vt.) Free press assoc., 1887. 32 p. 22½ cm. 18-13990. F59.N5 G8

NEWPORT and West Derby directory Newport, Vt., D. C. Davis, v. fold. map. 22½ cm. 16-22064. Directories

NEWPORT. Illustrated history of the old log-bridge across Lake Memphremagog at "The Narrows", by John MacNab Currier ... Newport, Vt., 1917. 22 p. front. 23½ cm. 22-19774. F59.N55C9

NORTH BENNINGTON, The history and development of. Haviland hamlet - 1761 to 1776; Sage's city - 1776 to 1828; North Bennington - 1828 to date. By Herbert Stebbins Walbridge. (Rutland? Vt.) 1937. 2, 71 p. port., map. 20 ½ cm. A 41-530.   F59.N75W3

NORTHFIELD. ... Centennial proceedings and historical incidents of the early settlers of Northfield, Vt., with biographical sketches of prominent business men who have been and are now residents of the town. By Hon. John Gregory. Montplier, Vt., Argus and patriot book and job print., 1878. vi, (9) - 319 p. front., illus., plates, ports. 23 ½ cm. "Biographic sketches": p. (55) - 231. Rc-3150.   F59.N8 G8

NORTHFIELD. The town slate, Northfield, Vermont. Early settlement, history, resources, development, and progress. A series of comprehensive sketches ... Ed. by John H. Walbridge ... East Burke, Vt., W.H. Jeffrey (1903?) 53 p. illus. (incl. ports.) 23 ½ cm. 19-7862.   F59.N8 W2

NORWICH. The Ompompanoosuc Valley ... ed. by F.L. Belanger. Union Village, Vt., The Methodist church soc. (c. 1911) (88) p. incl. illus., plates. maps. 25 cm. The Ompompanoosuc flows through the towns of Strafford, Thetford and Norwich, Vt. This pamphlet describes Pompanoosuc, Union Village and other villages in these towns. 11-9251.
     F59.N9 B2

NORWICH, A history of (Pub. by the authority of the town) ... (by) M.E. Goddard, Henry V. Partridge. Hanover, N.H., The Dartmouth press, 1905. 4, (3) - 276 p. plates, ports. 22 ½ cm. 6-3621.
     F59.N9 G5

NORWICH. "Know your town"; the 1940 survey of Norwich, produced through community cooperation. (Norwich) The Norwich woman's club, 1942. 103 p. front. (maps) plates, diagrs. 27 cm. 43-6263.
     F59.N9N6

NORWICH. The charter of Norwich, and names of the original proprietors: with brief historical notes. By the Rev. Edmund F. Slafter ... Boston, D. Clapp & son, printers, 1869. 8 p. 22 ½ cm. "Reprinted from the N.E. hist. and geneal. register for Jan., 1869." 1-13343.   F59.N9 S6

PLAINFIELD. The history of the towns of Plainfield, Roxbury and Fayston ... with Marshfield or Middlesex papers in fifty copies ... ed. Abby Maria Hemenway. Montpelier, Vt., A.M. Hemenway, 1882. p. 713 - 768, 177 - 248. pl. 25 ½ cm. "From vol. iv of the Vermont historical gazetteer ... " 16-19538. Imperfect: p. 197 - 200 wanting.   F57.W3H28

PAWLET for one hundred years. By Hiel Hollister ... Albany, Print. J. Munsell, 1867. 272 p. 19 cm. "Family sketches": p. 155-267. Rc-3151. L.C. copy replaced by microfilm.   F59.P3 H7
Microfilm 21480 F

PEACHAM, the story of a Vermont hill town. By Ernest Ludlow Bogart. Montpelier, Vermont hist. soc., 1948. 494 p. illus., ports., maps. facsims. 25 cm. Bibliography: p. (479) - 482. 48-10227*.   F59.P35B6

PEACHAM, Decoration day, ... 1905. Exercises at the dedication of markers, Sons of the American revolution, at the graves of eleven revolutionary soldiers in the cemetery and old grave-yard. By Jane Elisabeth Cowles ... (Peacham, Vt., 1906) (12) p. 16 x 8 cm. 6-14319.
     F59.P35C8

PEACHAM, People of, by Jennie Chamberlain Watts and Elise A. Choate. Ed. Richard G. Wood with assistance from the Peacham Historical Assoc. Montpelier, 1965. vii, 458 p. 25 cm. Fold. map (in pocket) 65-22720.   F59.P35V4

PERU. Reunion celebration together with an historical sketch of Peru, Bennington County, Vermont, and its inhabitants from the first settlement of the town. By Ira K. Batchelder. Brattleboro, Phoenix job print., 1891. vii, 144 p. front., ports. 23 ½ cm. 2-2224 rev.   F59.P4 B3

PITTSFORD, History of the town of, with biographical sketches and family records. By A.M. Caverly ... Rutland, Tuttle & co., print. 1872. viii, 751 p. front., ports., fold. plan. 24 cm. Rc-3152.
     F59.P6 C3

PITTSFORD. Evergreen Cemetery, Pittsford, Vermont. St. Alphonsus Cemetery, Pittsford, Vermont.

Bump Cemetery, North Chittenden, Vermont. Records from Town Clerk's Office. Comp. Fannie (Smith) Spurling. (Delavan, Wis., 1946) 58 p. 28 cm. 48-14059*. F59.P6 S6

PLYMOUTH. Genealogical records of the founders and early settlers of Plymouth, Vermont. Compiled by Blanche Brown Bryant and Gertrude Elaine Baker. DeLand, Fla., E.O. Painter Print. Co., 1967. xvi, 422 p. 26 cm. F59.P7 B7

PLYMOUTH. Vermont explained by a typical Vermont village, which is to say Plymouth, by John Cotton Dana. Woodstock, Vt., The Elm tree press (c. 1925) (52) p. front., illus. (incl. maps) ports. 19½ cm. 25-27749. F59.P7D16

PLYMOUTH, Vermont, birthplace of President Coolidge; photo-gravures ... Rutland, Vt., G.E. Chalmers (1925) 1 p. 20 pl. (incl. ports.) 15½ x 21 cm. 25-17546. F59.P7P76

POMFRET. A biographical sketch of the Rev. Aaron Hutchinson of Pomfret, by Rush C. Hawkins. New York (Gilliss bros & Turnure Art age press) 1888. 35 p. 24 cm. 3-27035. F59.P75H3

POMFRET, Vermont (by) Henry Hobart Vail ... Emma Chandler White, ed. (Boston, Cockayne, 1930) 2 v. fronts., illus., plates, ports., facsims., fold. maps. 24½ cm. Vol. I includes "A list of the ... grantees or proprietors of the township of Pomfret", "The pioneer settlers", "Pomfret men - soldiers and sailors in the civil war". Vol. II includes genealogical records. 30-8621.
F59.P75V2

POULTNEY, A history of the town of, from its settlement to the year 1875, with family and biographical sketches and incidents. Pub. by J. Joslin, and others. Poultney, Journal print office, 1875. viii, (9) - 368 p. 22½ cm. "Family and biographical": p. 197-365. 1-Rc-3153. F59.P8 J 8

POULTNEY; a chronicle of yesterday. By Alison Rees Latham. Illus. Gilbert Myers. 1st ed. Poultney, Vt., 1961. 79 p. illus. 23 cm. 61-17465. F59.P8 L3

POWNAL, ... Marriages in, to 1850, from books *1 and *2 of the town records, copied and arranged by Elmer I. Shepard ... Williamstown, Mass., 1941. 2 p. 51 numb. l. 27½ cm. (Berkshire genealogical (!) notes no 3) Reproduced from type-written copy. 42-18525. F59.P85S5

PUTNEY, The history of, 1753 - 1953; ed. Edith De Wolfe and others. Putney, Fortnightly club of Putney, Vermont, 1953. 221 p. illus. 22 cm. Includes bibliography. 54-20076. F59.P9 D4

PUTNEY, The history of the town of, by Rev. Amos Foster ... Ludlow, Vt., Miss A.M. Hemenway, 1884. 1, (217) - 272 p. 2 port. (incl. front.) 27 cm. From vol. v of the Vermont historical gazetteer. "Biographical": p. 239 - 248. Rc-3154. F59.P9 F7

RANDOLPH, Views of. (Randolph, Buck print. co., 1906?) 24 p. illus. 20½ x 24 cm.
F59.R18V6

READING. Centennial celebration, tog. with an historical sketch of Reading, Windsor County, Vermont, and its inhabitants from the first settlement of the town to 1874. By Gilbert A. Davis. Bellows Falls, Press of A.N. Swain, 1874. 2, (iii) - v, (7) - 169 p. incl. ports. 22½ cm. "Personal and family recollections": p. (117) - 169. Rc-3155. F59.R2 D2

READING. History of Reading, Windsor County, Vermont. Vol. II. By Gilbert A. Davis. (Windsor? Vt., 1903) 3, (5) - 375, (12) p. front., illus., plates, ports. 20½ cm. Supplementary to the author's "Centennial celebration, tog. with an historical sketch of Reading, etc." See above item. 22-7139. F59.R2D22

READING. A rural poem, written for the centennial celebration of the settlement of the town of Reading, held at Felchville ... 1872. By Honestus Stearns. Springfield, Vt., E.D. Wright, print., 1873. 19 p. 15½ cm. 19-4964. F59.R2 S7

ROCHESTER, History of the town of. Pub. by order of the town. By Wendall Wales Williams. Montpelier, Vt., E. Ballou, print., 1869. 3, (iii) - iv, 92 p. 18 cm. Rc-3156 rev. F59.R6W7

ROCKINGHAM, History of the town of, incl. the villages of Bellows Falls, Saxtons River, Rockingham,

Cambridgeport and Bartonsville, 1753 - 1907, with family genealogies, by Lyman Simpson Hayes. Bellows Falls, Vt., The town, 1907. xvi, 850 p. front., illus., plates (part fold.) ports., fold. map, plans (part fold.) facsims. 24 cm. "A few books pub. in Bellows Falls" (1829 - 1854): p. 434-437. 7-35636. F59.R7 H12

ROCKINGHAM. The old Rockingham meeting house, erected 1787 and the first church in Rockingham, 1773 - 1840, by Lyman S. Hayes ... and William D. Hayes ... Bellows Falls, Vt. (The P.H. Gobie press) 1915. 102 p. front., plates, plans, facsim. 25 cm. Bibliography: P. (95) 15-9584. F59.R7H23

ROCKINGHAM, History of the town of: incl. the villages of Bellows Falls, Saxtons River, Rockingham, Cambridgeport, and Bartonsville, 1907 - 1957, with family genealogies, by Frances Stockwell Lovell and Leverett C. Lovell. Bellows Falls, Vt., Pub. by the town, 1958. 553 p. illus. 24 cm. 59-21556. F59.R7 L6

ROCKINGHAM. Records of the First church of Rockingham, Vermont, from its organization ... 1773, to ... 1839. Copied by Thomas Bellows Peck, with an historical introduction ... Boston, Press of D. Clapp, 1902. xi, 60 p. front., illus. (plan, facsims.) pl. 24½ cm. Reprinted from the N.E. historical and genealogical register. v.54-56, 1900-1902. 2-28520. F59.R7 R7
— Copy 2. (With Rockingham, Vital records ... Boston, 1908) 2-28520. F59.R7 R6

ROYALTON, Burning of, by Indians; a careful research of all that pertains to the subject, incl. a reprint of Zadock Steele's narrative ... by Ivah Dunklee ... Boston, G.H. Ellis co., printers, 1906. 3, (5) - 88 p. plates, ports. (incl. front.) 25 cm. 6-28226. F59.R74D9

ROYALTON, History of, with family genealogies, 1769 - 1911, by Evelyn M. Wood Lovejoy. Pub. by the town and the Royalton woman's club. Burlington, Vt., Free press print., 1911. xxi, 1146 p. plates, ports., 3 fold. maps, facsims. 24½ cm. 12-146. F59.R74L8

ROYALTON. The church of baptised bretherin, Royalton; a record of its meetings, conferences and councils for the years 1790 to 1806 ... Woodstock, Vt., The Elm tree press, 1919. 1, 71 p. 24 cm. 21-17516. F59.R74R68

ROYALTON. Commemorative exercises at the 100th anniversary of the organization of the Congregational church, Royalton, Vermont. (Royalton? Vt., 1877) 41 p. 21½ cm. 1-13633.
F59.R74R7

RUPERT. The gravestone inscriptions of Rupert, Bennington County, Vermont; copied and verified 1911 - 12, by Levi Henry Elwell ... Amherts, Mass., Composition and presswork, 1913. 4, 79 p. 21 cm. 14-22090. F59.R8 E5

RUPERT. A glimpse of the early history of Rupert (by) Naomi Sheldon Guibord. West Rupert, Vt. (n.d.) 20 p. 22½ cm. 43-13808. F59.R8 G8

RUPERT, Vt.; historical and descriptive, 1761 - 1898. By George Hibbard. Rutland, Vt., The Tuttle co. (1899) 211 p. 24 cm. 1-16568 Additions. F59.R8 H6

RUPERT. Out of the saltbox; the savour of old Vermont. By Simpson Ruth Basey. Illus. by Kathleen Voute. Chicago, Rand McNally (1962) 256 p. 22 cm. 62-19547.
F59.R8 S5

RUTLAND. The art book of Rutland. By Louis F. Brehmer. Rutland, Vt. (1903) 23 x 29 cm.
F59.R9 B8

RUTLAND, The churches of, with illus. and historical sketches. Portraits by C.A. Moore. Rutland, Vt., Brehmer bros,, 1900. (20) p. illus., pl. 8°. Aug. 16, 1900-39. F59.R9 C5

RUTLAND. Historical Rutland; an illus. history of Rutland, from the granting of the charter in 1761 to 1911. By Frank Everett Davison. Reproductions and orig. photos. by Louis F. Brehmer; Rutland, Vt., P.H. Brehmer (c.1911) 2, 3 - 69 p. incl. illus., plates, map. 26½ cm. 11-22397. F59.R9 D2

RUTLAND. Official military and naval records of Rutland, in the war of the rebellion, 1861 - 1866.

Men credited to town; residents since the war or buried in cemeteries within the limits of the original town.   Compiled by ... J.H.Goulding. 1889-90-91. Rutland, The Tuttle co., print., 1891.
100 p. 23 cm. 1-26426 rev.
F59.R9 G6

RUTLAND, The gateway of the Green mountains ... Rutland, Vt., L.F.Brehmer, c.1909.
(4) p. plates (partly fold.) 19 x 26 cm.
F59.R9R92

RUTLAND.   Old Rutland; side lights on her honorable and notable story during one hundred and sixty years.   1761 - 1922, by Edward Lowe Temple ... (Rutland, Vt., A.J.Novak print. co., c.1923)
53 p. illus. 23½ cm. 23-13947.
F59.R9 T2

RUTLAND ... Centennial celebration of the settlement of, ... 1870, incl. the addresses, etc.   Comp. by Chauncey K. Williams.   Rutland, Tuttle & co., print., 1870.   viii, 122 p. 24 cm. Rc-3157 rev.
F59.R9 W7

ST. ALBANS and Swanton (Vermont) directory ... 1886/87   Springfield, Mass., H.A.Manning co., 1886 - c19   v. maps (part fold., part double) 23½ cm. 1-24580 rev.
Directories

ST. ALBANS.   ... Standard directory of St. Albans city (census as of Aug. 1936) (v.1) - 1936 -   St. Albans, Vt., A.M.Hall, c.1936.   v. 23½ cm. 37-33520.
Directories

ST. ALBANS, A centennial history of.   Organized July 28, 1788.   By Henry K. Adams.   St. Albans, Vt., Wallace print. co., 1889.   vii, 149 p. 18½ cm. 1-16738 rev.
F59.S1 A2

ST. ALBANS and vicinity as a summer resort.   By Albert Clarke.   St. Albans, Messenger job print. house, 1872.   40 p. front., plates. 22 cm. Rc-3158 Rev.
F59.S1 C5

ST. ALBANS.   Sketches of early life in St. Albans, Vt., written by members of Bellevue chapter, D.A.R.   (St. Albans) c.1925.   75 p. 19 cm. 25-16091.
F59.S1 D2

ST. ALBANS, The history of, civil, religious, biographical and statistical.   By L.L.Dutcher.   With valuable contributions from Hon. James Davis, and others ... And the history of Sheldon, Vt., by H.R.Whitney and others.   St. Albans, Vt., S.E.Royce, 1872.   1, (289) - 382, (1) p. front. (port.) 25 cm.
"Pub. from ... Miss Hemenway's Vermont historical gazetteer, vol. II." Rc-3159.
F59.S1 H4

ST. ALBANS.   Advantages, resources and attractions of St. Albans, Vt.   Its location, railroad facilities, churches, chools, literary and social life; industries and institutions; and general features. (Glens Falls, N.Y.) Pub. for the Board of trade, 1889.   104 p. incl. front.,illus. 23 cm. Compiled by C.H. Possons. Rc-3160 Rev.
F59.S1 S1

ST. ALBANS.   History of the St. Albans raid.   Annual address before the Vermont historical society delivered at Montpelier, Vt. ... 1876. By Hon, Edward A. Sowles. St. Albans, Messenger print. works, 1876.   48 p. 22½ cm. (Vermont historical soc. Proceedings, 1876) Rc-3077 rev.
F59.S1 S7

ST. JOHNSBURY.   Manning's St. Johnsbury and Lyndonville including Lyndon township, Barnet, Concord, Danville, Kirby, and Waterford (Vermont) directory ... 1897, 19   v. fold. map. 23½ cm.
1-30534 rev.
Directories

ST. JOHNSBURY.   Soldiers record of the town of St. Johnsbury, in the war of the rebellion, 1861 - 5. Comp. by Hon, Albert G. Chadwick.   St. Johnsbury, Vt., C.M.Stone & co., printers, 1883.
iv, (5) - 215 p. 22½ cm. 13-18451.
F59.S12C4

ST. JOHNSBURY, The town of; a review of 125 years to the anniversary pageant 1912, by Edward T. Fairbanks ... St. Johnsbury, The Cowles press, 1914.   592 p. front., pl., ports. 24 cm. "Prepared under the auspices of the St. John de Crevecoeur chapter of the D.A.R." 15-1640.
F59.S12F16

ST. JOHNSBURY.   Book of words; the pageant of St. Johnsbury, in celebration of the 125th anniversary of the founding of the town (by) William Chauncy Langdon, master of the pageant ... 1912. (St. Johnsbury, Vt., Caledonian press c.1911)   86 p. 23 cm. 12-28476.
F59.S12L2

VERMONT

ST. JOHNSBURY, and an important industrial beginnings, 1830 (by) Colonel Robert H. Morse ... New York, The Newcomen soc. of England, American branch, 1945.   16 p. incl. front., illus. 23 cm. 46-6796.
F59.S12M6

ST. JOHNSBURY illustrated. A review of the town's business, social, literary, and educational facilities, with glimpses of picturesque surroundings. Comp. by Arthur F. Stone ... St. Johnsburgy, Vt., C. M. Stone & co., 1891.   1, 100 p. front., illus. (incl. ports.) 23½ x 31 cm. 4-3643.
F59.S12S8

SALEM, Annals of. By Pliny H. White. (n.p., 1865?)   4 p. 24 cm. 1-16211.
F59.S14W5

SALISBURY ... Dedication of the monument to Ann Story ... Salisbury, Vermont, ... 1905. (Salisbury, Vt., The Vermont society of colonial dames, 1905)   47 p. 2 pl. 2 port. 23½ cm. 13-23468.
F59.S16N2

SALISBURY, History of. By John M. Weeks, with a memoir of the author ... Middlebury, Ct., A.H. Copeland, 1860.   xii, (9) - 362 p. front., ports. 19 cm. Rc-3161 Additions.
F59.S16W3

SHAFTSBURY. The gravestone records of Shaftsbury, Bennington County, Vermont, copied and verified 1908 - 10, by Levi Henry Elwell ... Amherst, Mass., 1911.   vi, (2), 76 p. 21 cm. 13-1334.
F59.S48E5

SHAFTSBURY, The story of; with an account of Jacob Howard, who wrote the resolutions on which the Republican Party was founded. (1st ed.) Shaftsbury, 1954.   50 p. illus. 23 cm. Includes bibliography. 54-37210.
F59.S48R4

SHELBURNE Museum, A pictorial history of the (by) Richard Lawrence Greene and Kenneth Edward Wheeling. Shelburne, Vt., Shelburne Museum, 1972.   127 p. illus. (part col.) 31 cm.
F59.S49G7

SHELBURNE, The history of. By Marie Harding and Charlotte Tracy. Printed in co-operation with the Shelburne Museum by the Excelsior Press, 1963.   76 p. 22 cm.
F59.S49H3

"SHELBURNE Museum," a treasury of early American life in a Vermont community! By Ralph Nading Hill. Illus. by Richard F. Bartlett. New York, Newcomen Soc. in North America, 1955.   32 p. illus. 23 cm. 56-58026.
F59.S49H49

SHELBURNE Museum, The story of, by Ralph Nading Hill and Lilian Baker Carlistle. Shelburne, Vt., Shelburne Museum, 1955.   55 p. illus. 29 cm. 55-12962 rev.
F59.S49H5
Book not in L. of C.

— 2d ed. 1960.   113 p. illus. 29 cm.
F59.S49H5
1960

SHELBURNE Museum. Museum pamphlet series. no. 1 -   Shelburne (1956 -
no. illus. 23 cm. 56-58949.
F59.S49S47

— The carriages at Shelburne Museum. By Lilian Baker Carlisle. 1956.
v, 71 p. 23 cm. (Museum pamphlet no. 1) Bibliography p. 64. 56-58914.

— Pieced work and applique quilts at Shelburne Museum. By Lilian Baker Carlisle. 1957.
95 p. illus. 23 cm. (Museum pamphlet no. 2) 57-14118.

— Woodworking tools at Shelburne Museum. By Frank H. Wildung. 1957.   79 p. illus. 23 cm. (Museum pamphlet no. 3) 57-14121.

— Hat boxes and bandboxes at Shelburne Museum. By Lilian Baker Carlisle. 1957.
xiii, 195 p. 23 cm. (Museum pamphlet no. 4) 59-15284.

— Blacksmiths' and farriers' tools at Shelburne Museum; a history of their development from forge to factory, by H. R. Bradley Smith. 1966.   271 p. 24 cm. (Museum pamphlet no. 7)

SHERBURNE, An informal history of the Town of, by Madeline C. Fleming. (Sherburne, Vt.) 1967.
153 p. 29 cm.
F59.S492F5

SHOREHAM, History of the town of, from date of its charter, ... 1761, to the present time, by Rev.

Joseph F. Goodhue. Middlebury, A.H. Copeland, 1861. vi, (2), 198 p. front., plates, port. 23½ cm. Written by request of the Middlebury historical soc. Rc-3163 Rev.
 F59.S5 G6

SOUTH HERO, in the garden spot of Vermont, by Wilbur Le Roy Wood. Providence, R.I., Print, Rollinson & Hey, 1923. 46 p. illus., fold. map. 24½ cm. 23-12530.
 F59.S6 W8

SOUTH WOODSTOCK. ... The valley of the Kedron; the story of the South parish, Woodstock; by Mrs. Mary Grace Canfield. drawings by Muriel A. Thomas. South Woodstock, Vt., Kedron associates (c.1940) xiv, 3-323 p. illus., plates, ports., facsims. (1 fold.) 21 cm. 40-33546.
 F59.S65C3

SPRINGFIELD (Vermont) directory including Charlestown, N.H. ... Springfield, Mass., H.A. Manning co., 1909 - 1 v. 23½ cm. 9-24937.
 Directories

SPRINGFIELD, Folklore of, by Mary Eva Baker, illus. by Russell W. Porter and others. Springfield, Vt. (The Altrurian club of Springfield) 1922. 8, 177, (7) p. incl. front. (5 port.) illus. 23 cm. 22-21957.
 F59.S7 B2

SPRINGFIELD, The history of, 1885 - 1961, with an introductory chapter to 1885. Springfield, Vt., William L. Bryant Foundation, 1972. ix, 726 p. illus. 24 cm. 75-188646.
 F59.S7B37

SPRINGFIELD. Eureka, the first village in Springfield, Vermont. By Mary W. Ellis. (Springfield?) Historical Committee of Miller Art Center, 1959. 28 p. 23 cm.
 F59.S7 E4

SPRINGFIELD, History of the town of, with a genealogical record, by C. Horace Hubbard and Justus Dartt. 1752 - 1895. Boston, G.H. Walker & co., 1895. xi, 618 p. front., illus., plates, ports. 23½ cm. "Genealogical record": p. 198 - 516: "Early marriages": p. 531 - 552. 1-Rc-3162.
 F59.S7 H8

STOWE. History of Stowe (from 1763 to 1934) by Walter J. Bigelow. (Hartford) 1934. xiv, 251 p. front. (port.) plates, 2 maps on fold. l. 24½ cm. 34-21827.
 F59.S8 B5

STOWE: ski capital of the east, 1763 - 1963, by Edwin L. Bigelow. Stowe Historical Soc. (c.1964) xvii, 216 p. 25 cm. 64-15446.
 F59.S8B52

STOWE. The memorial record of the soldiers from Stowe, Vermont, who fought for our government, during the rebellion of 1861 - 5. Prepared by R.A. Savage. Montpelier (Vt.) Printed Freeman steam print., 1867. 104 p. 18½ cm. 6-20085.
 F59.S8 S2

THETFORD. Book of words; the pageant of Thetford, in celebration of the 150th anniversary of the granting of the charter. (By) William Chauncy Langdon, master of the pageant. (White River Junction, The Vermonter press, 1911) 64 p. 22 cm. Cover-title: The pageant of Thetford. 11-22120.
 F59.T4 L2

THETFORD of the grants (by) Mrs. William Slade ... (Thetford? Vt., 1941) 9 p. 1 illus. 22½ cm. "Reprinted from Annual report of the town officers of the town of Thetford for the year ending Feb. 1, 1941." 43-4303.
 F59.T4 S6

TOPSHAM, Sketches of the town of, Orange County, 1929. By Frank H. Craig. Bradford, Vt., The Green Mountain press (1929) 2, 9 - 198 p. illus., port. 23½ cm. 30-15019.
 F59.T67C88

VERSHIRE. The town of Ely. Argument of the Hon. Luke P. Poland before the special committees of the legislature upon the subject, against the bill to re-change the name of the town of Ely to Vershire ... 1880. (Montpelier? 1880) 24 p. 22½ cm. 11-34829.
 F59.V48P7

VERNON, The history of the town of, by A.H. Washburn and his wife Lucinda W.B. Washburn. (From vol. v. of the Vermont historical gazetteer) Ludlow, Vt., Miss A.M. Hemenway, 1885. 1, (273) - 352 p. front., port. 4°. 1-Rc-3164.
 F59.V5 W3

WAITSFIELD. The memorial record of. Prepared by Rev. A.B. Dascomb. Montpelier, Print. Freeman steam print., 1867. 30 p. 18 cm. 9-1962.
 F59.W1 D2

WAITSFIELD, An address delivered at, ... 1906, at the unveiling of a tablet erected in memory of soldiers of the American revolution buried in that town. By Matt Bushnell Jones. St. Johnsbury, Vt., The Caledonian press, 1906.   1, 23 p. front., port. 22 cm. 7-11173.   F59.W1 J7

WAITSFIELD, History of the town of, 1782 - 1908, with family genealogies, by Matt Bushnell Jones. Boston, Mass., G. E. Littlefield, 1909.   viii, 524 p. front., plates, fold. map, plans (1 fold.) 25½ cm. 9-12866.   F59.W1 J8

WALLINGFORD, People of, a compilation, by Birney C. Batcheller. Brattleboro, Vt., Stephen Daye press (c. 1937)   328 p. front., pla;tes, ports., maps (part fold.) 2 facsim. (1 fold.) 24½ cm. 38-21310.   F59.W18B3

WALLINGFORD, History of, by Walter Thorpe ... Rutland, Vt., The Tuttle co. (c. 1911)   222, (2) p. incl. front., illus. 24 cm. 12-139.   F59.W18T5

WARDSBORO, by John P. Warren ... Chicago, 1886.   32 p. 27 cm. Reprinted from Abby M. Hemenway's "The Vermont historical gazetteer..." Rc-3166 Rev.   F59.W2 W2

WATERBURY, History of, 1763 - 1915, ed. and comp. by Theodore Graham Lewis; pub. by Harry C. Whitehill. Waterbury, Vt., The Record print (c. 1915)   viii, 286 p. plates, 5 port. on 1 pl., facsim. 23½ cm. 16-667.   F59.W32L6

WATERBURY. When the water came to Waterbury; a tragedy in three acts depicting scenes of the great flood of November, 1927, as they occurred on the panoramic stage of Vermont's most devastated valley, comp. from Marion's work shop ... ed. by Lloyd E. Squier. Waterbury, Vt., The Record print, c. 1928.   80 p. illus. 27 cm. 28-21428.   F59.W32S7

WELLS, History of, for the first century after its settlement; by Hiland Paul, with biographical sketches by Robert Parks, esq. Rutland, Tuttle & co., print. 1869.   154 p. 19 cm. Rc-3167.   F59.W4 P2

WELLS, A history of the town of, from its settlement, with family and biographical sketches and incidents. By Grace Esther Pember Wood. (Wells, Vt.) 1955.   150 p. illus. 24 cm. Includes bibliography. 55-28221.   F59.W4 W6

WEST BRATTLEBORO ... A discourse on the early history of the Congregational church in, delivered ... 1876. By the Rev. Lewis Grout ... Brattleboro, D. Leonard, print. (1877 ?)   32 p. 22½ cm. 11-32023.   F59.W49G8

WESTMINSTER. On historic ground; the site of the old court house at Westminster marked by the D. A. R. ... 1902 ... historic address of Alfred S. Hall ... Brattleboro, E. L. Hildreth & co., 1902.   21, (2) p. illus. 23 cm. 3-20611.   F59.W5 D2

WESTMINSTER, The double history of. The history of the east parish, by F. J. Fairbanks. The history of the west parish by A. Stevens. From vol. v of the Vermont historical gazetteer ... Chicago, Jameson & Morse, 1885.   112 p. port. 4°. 1-Rc-3168.   F59.W5 F1

WESTMINSTER, History of. By Mary Elizabeth Minard. Vermont sesquicentennial souvenir of Westminster, 1791 - 1941. (Westminster, c. 1941)   xiv, 174 p. incl. illus., plates, ports. 23½ cm. "Pub. by the town of Westminster": "First ed." "Biographies": p. (33) - (70) 41-14726.   F59.W5 M5

WESTON. An address, delivered at a re-union of the sons of Weston, ... 1853. By Rev. Asa D. Smith. With a sketch of the accompanying exercises. Boston, Press of T. R. Marvin, 1853.   45 p. 24 cm. Rc-3169.   F59.W51S6

WHEELOCK, Town of; Vermont's gift to Dartmouth College. By Eleanor Jones Hutchinson. (Rochester, Vt., Emerson Pub. Co., 1961)   217 p. 28 cm.   F59.W56H8

WHITING. The story of the old white meeting house, in Whiting, Vermont. By Edwin Sawyer Walker. Chicago, Oliphant print., 1899.   22 p. pl. 8°. Jan 25, 1900-225.   F59.W58W18

WHITINGHAM, History of from its organization to the present time. By Leonard Brown. Brattleboro, Vt., F. E. Housh, 1886.   235 p. 23 cm. Rc-3170 rev.*
    F59.W59B8

WHITINGHAM, Green leaves from: a history of the town. By Clark Jillson. Worcester, Mass.,
Private press of the author, 1894.   224 p. front. (port.) illus. (incl. facsim.) 24 cm. Rc-3171.
    F59.W59J6

WHITINGHAM.   Annual report of the auditors ... Brattleboro (Vt.) 1867.   24 p. 21 cm.
    F59.W59W6

WILLISTON story, The, by F. Kennon Moody and Floyd D. Putnam. Essex Junction, Vt., Roscoe print.
house, 1961.   96 p. 23 cm.
    F59.W593M6

WILMINGTON.   Attractions of Wilmington and vicinity ... by O. Jones. Jacksonville, Vt., F. L.
Stetson, 1887.   23 p. front., illus. sq. 16º. 1-Rc-3172.
    F59.W6 J7

WILMINGTON reunions, 1890 - 1970, by Barbara H. Look, and family genealogies by Margaret C.
Greene. Bennington, Vt., Print. Broad Brook Press (c.1970)   79 p. illus. 23 cm.
    F59.W6 L6

WILMINGTON. (Reunion ed.) By John Hill Walbridge. Wilmington, Vt., The Times press, 1900.
67 p. illus. (incl. ports.) 31 cm. On cover: Supplement to the Deerfield Valley times ... 10-31047 rev.
    F59.W6 W1

WILMINGTON.   Reunion of the sons and daughters of the town of Wilmington held at Wilmington ...
1890. Containing a brief account of the measures which resulted in the reunion. ... to which are
added historical and chronological notes. (Wilmington, Vt.) ... supervised by C. M. Russell, 1890.
214 p. 23½ cm. 5-36870.
    F59.W6 W6

WINDSOR. History of the First Congregational church of Windsor, from 1768 to 1898, by Ezra Hoyt
Byington ... With statistics comp. by Gilbert A. Davis ... Windsor, Vt., Printed by the Journal co.,
1898.   109 p. incl. front., illus., ports. 23 cm. 21-17513.
    F59.W7 B9

WINDSOR register, 1905, The, comp. by Mitchell & Carr. Brunswick, Me., The H. E. Mitchell co.,
1905.   75 p. 23½ cm. 12-21879.
    F59.W7 M6

WINDSOR. The birthplace of Vermont; a history of Windsor to 1781, by Henry Steele Wardner. New
York, Priv. print. by C. Scribner's sons, 1927.   xii, 562 p. front., plates, ports. 24½ cm. Bibliographical foot-notes.
27-14536.
    F59.W7 W2

WINDSOR. The centennial at Windsor, ... 1876. Being a record of the proceedings at the celebration; and containing the address and poem then delivered; also a veiw of Windsor as it now is.
Windsor, The Journal co., 1876.   80 p. 20 cm. Rc-3173.
    F59.W7 W7

WOLCOTT. A narrative of the sufferings of Seth Hubbell & family, in his beginning a settlement in
the town of Wolcott, in the state of Vermont. Danville, Vt., E. & W. Eaton, print., 1826.
24 p. 18½ cm. Third ed. 2-18517.
    F59.W75H9
    Rare Book Room

   — A narrative of the captivity & sufferings of Ebenezer Fletcher of New-Ipswich ... 1813.
bound with above book.   22 p. 19 cm. 2-18511.

WOODSTOCK directory, The, Ottauquechee district ... with the residents of Barnard, Bridgewater,
Hartland, Pomfret, Reading, Sharon, ... 19   (Woodstock) W. E. Shaw, c 19
    v. 23½ cm. 19-1996.
    Directories

WOODSTOCK. By Henry Boynton. (n.p. 189 -?   27 cm.
    F59.W8 B7

WOODSTOCK, History of, by Henry Swan Dana ... Boston and New York, Houghton, Mifflin, 1889.
vi, (vii) - xv, 641 p. front., plates, ports., double map. 24½ cm. Genealogies: p. (589) - 623. 1-Rc-3174.
    F59.W8 D3

VERMONT 43

WOODSTOCK. "My grandmothers" and other tales of Old Woodstock, by Margaret L. Johnson. Woodstock Historical Society, 1957.   64 p. 23 cm.
F59.W8 J6

WOODSTOCK, then & now; Woodstock, Vermont, as seen by the camera from 1854 until the present. Designed by Frank Lieberman. (Woodstock) Print. the Woodstock Chamber of Commerce by the Elm Tree Press, 1957.   48 p. illus. 28 cm. 57-12970.
F59.W8 T4

WORCESTER. A record of births, marriages and deaths, in Worcester, Vermont, from Oct., 1813 to June 18, 1858. Alphabetically arranged. By Simon C. Abbott. Montpelier, E.P. Walton, print., 1858.   31 p. 15½ cm. 19-4157.
F59.W9 A2

ELEMENTS IN THE POPULATION.

Vermont. Committee to Study Equal Opportunity. Equal opportunity in Vermont. Report of the committee to study proposal no. 31. (Montpelier) Legislative Council of the State of Vermont, 1968.   16 l. 28 cm. 74-633516.
F60.N3A43

VERMONT
SUPPLEMENTARY INDEX OF PLACES

ADDISON Co. 188, 219
ALBANY Co. 207
ARLINGTON. 192
ATHENS. 212
BARNARD. 211, 228
BARNET. 224
BARRE. 211
BARTONSVILLE. 223
BELLOWS FALLS. 222, 223
BELVIDERE. 209
BENNINGTON. 188
BENNINGTON Co. 188
BERKSHIRE HILLS. 212
BERLIN. 211, 212
BRANDON. 210, 217
BRIDGEWATER. 211, 228
CABOT. 211
CALAIS. 211
CALEDONIA Co. 188, 191, 193
CAMBRIDGE. 209
CAMBRIDGEPORT. 223
CASTLETON. 217
CAVENDISH. 219
CHESTER. 212, 219
CHITTENDEN Co. 188, 217
CLARENDON. 217
CONCORD. 224
CRAFTSBURY. 209
CUMBERLAND Co. 193
DANVILLE. 224
DEWEY'S MILLS. 217
DOVER. 211
DUMMERSTON. 214
EAST MONTPELIER. 211, 212
EDEN. 209
ELMORE. 209
ELY. 226
ESSEX Co. 188, 191, 193, 207, 208, 217
FAIR HAVEN. 217
FAYSTON. 211, 221
GLOUCESTER Co. 193
GRANDE ISLE Co. 188, 208
GREENSBORO. 209
GREYLOCK MTN. 212
GROTON. 188
GUILFORD. 214
HARDWICK. 209

HARTFORD. 217
HARTLAND. 211, 228
HAVILAND HAMLET. 221
HAZEN'S NOTCH. 210
HUBBARDTON. 188, 217
HYDE PARK. 209
JAMAICA. 211
JERICHO. 207
JOHNSON. 209
KIRBY. 224
LAKE BOMBAZON. 210
LAKE CHAMPLAIN. 215
LAKE MEMPHREMOGOG. 220
LAMOILLE Co. 188
LYNDONVILLE. 224
MARLBORO. 214
MARSHFIELD. 211, 221
MIDDLESEX. 211, 212, 221
MONTPELIER. 211, 212
MORETOWN. 211
MORRISTOWN. 209
NESHOBE. 210
NEWFANE. 214
NEWPORT. 212
NORTH CHITTENDEN. 222
NORTHFIELD. 211, 212
NORWICH. 210, 221
ORANGE. 211
ORANGE Co. 188, 193
ORLEANS. 212
ORLEANS Co. 188, 191, 193, 208, 209
PITTSFORD. 217
PLAINFIELD. 211, 212
POMFRET. 211, 228
POMPANOOSUC. 221
POULTNEY. 217
PROCTORSVILLE. 219
PUTNEY. 214
QUECHEE. 217
READING. 211, 228
RENSSELAER Co. 207
ROCKINGHAM. 212, 223
ROXBURY. 211, 221
RUTLAND. 217
RUTLAND Co. 188, 207
SAGE'S CITY. 221
SARATOGA Co. 207

SAXTONS RIVER. 212, 223	WASHINGTON. 211
SCHENECTADY Co. 207	WASHINGTON Co. 188, 193, 207
SHARON. 211, 228	WATERBURY. 211
SHELDON. 224	WATERFORD. 224
STOWE. 209	WATERVILLE. 209
STRAFFORD. 221	WEST DERBY. 212, 220
STRATTON. 211	WEST HARTFORD. 217
SUTTON. 188	WESTFORD. 207
SWANTON. 188, 224	WESTMINSTER. 212
THETFORD. 210, 221	WHITE RIVER JUNCTION. 217
TOPSHAM. 211	WILDER. 217
UNDERHILL. 207	WILLIAMSTOWN. 211, 212
UNION VILLAGE. 221	WINDHAM Co. 188, 193
VERNON. 214	WINDSOR. 217
WAITSFIELD. 211	WINDSOR Co. 193
WALDEN. 209	WINOOSKI. 215
WALLINGFORD. 217	WOLCOTT. 209
WARDSBORO. 211	WOODBURY. 209, 211
WARREN. 211	WOODSTOCK. 211, 217
WARREN Co. 207	WORCESTER. 211

ADDITIONS TO INDEX

FRANKLIN Co. 188

MASSACHUSETTS

SELECTED BIBLIOGRAPHIES FOR MASSACHUSETTS

FLAGG, Charles Allcott. A guide to Massachusetts local history; being a bibliographic index to the literature of the towns, cities and counties of the state, including books, pamphlets, articles in periodicals and collected works, books in preparation, etc., etc. ... Salem, Mass., The Salem press co. (1907)   ix, 256 p.   maps.   25 cm.   7-35115.
F1295. F 65

MASSACHUSETTS historical society. Catalogue of the library ... Boston, Printed for the Society, 1859 - 60   2 v.   23 cm.   Third catalogue of the library (1st issued 1796; 2d, 1811)   3-16692.
F1295. M 39
1859

MASSACHUSETTS historical soc. ... Handbook of the publications and photostats, 1792 - 1933 ... Boston, Mass., 1937.   2, 144 p.   23 ½ cm.   "Second ed., rev. and corr."   38-12705.
Z1295. M41H
1937

SANFORD, Edwin G. The Pilgrim Fathers and Plymouth Colony: a bibliographical survey of books and articles published during the past fifty years. ... (Boston) Boston Public Library, 1970.
29 p.   23 cm.   Intended to supplement The Pilgrims, issued by the Boston Public Library in 1920.   74-160696.
Z1295. S 25

BOSTON. ... The Massachusetts bay colony and Boston; a selected list of works in the Public library of the city of Boston. Boston, The Trustees, 1930.   2, (3) - 165 p.   19 ½ cm.   (Brief reading lists.   no. 43.   May, 1930)   Compiled by Mr. L. E. Taylor.   31-7212.
Z1296. B7 B 88

BOSTON. The Boston metropolitan district; its physical growth and governmental development; a bibliography compiled by Katherine McNamara with the assistance of Caroline Shillaber ... Cambridge, Bureau for research in municipal government, Harvard graduate school of public administration and Dept. of regional planning, Harvard graduate school of design, 1946.   2, 197 p.   front. (map)   28 ½ x 22 cm.   Publication.   (New ser. no. 14)   A 47-729.
Z1296. B7 M2

BROOKLINE. Some works relating to Brookline, Mass., from its settlement to the year 1900. With notes and corrections. By Charles Knowles Bolton ... Brookline, The Riverdale press: C. A. W. Spencer, 1900.   91 - 179 p.   21 ½ cm.   Reprinted from the publications of the Brookline historical publication society.   Pub. nos. 19 - 20.   Printed on one side of leaf only.   4-16384.
Z1296. B8 B 6

CHARLESTOWN. Bibliography of Charlestown, Mass., and Bunker Hill ... By James F. Hunnewell. Boston, J. R. Osgood, 1880.   vii, 100 p.   double plan, 2 facsim. (incl. front.)   23 ½ cm.   1-11295-6.   Also in his A century of town life.   Boston, 1888.   24 ½ cm.   p. (261) - 300)   1-11295-6.
Z1296. C 47 H

GROTON. ... Bibliography of Groton, 1673 to 1888. (By Samuel Abbott Green) Maps, plans, etc. Groton, Mass., 1888.   (173) - 226 p.   2 facsim.   24 cm.   (Groton historical series.   vol. II, no. VII)   Arranged chronologically.   4-21043.
Z1296. G8 G7

MELROSE. Bibliography of Melrose. By Elbridge H. Goss. Printed in the Melrose journal ... May ... (to) ... Dec. ... 1888. Melrose (Mass.) L. F. Williams, printer, 1889.   (36) p.   22 cm.   Interleaved.   With biographical notices.   9-24388.
Z1296. M6 G6

NANTUCKET. The history of Nantucket Island; a bibliography of source material with index and inventory. Compiler: Marie M. Coffin. Nantucket Island, Mass. (Nantucket Historical Trust, 1970)
viii, 63 p.   illus., maps.   27 cm.   75-116579 MARC.
Z1296. N3 C63

WORCESTER. Bibliography of Worcester. A list of books, pamphlets, newspapers and broadsides, printed in the towns of Worcester, Mass., from 1775 to 1848. With historical and explanatory notes. By Charles Lemuel Nichols. Worcester, Priv. print. (press of Franklin P. Rice) 1899.   xi, 216 p.   front. (port.) facsim.   23 cm.   "In a measure intended as a memorial of (Isaih Thomas's) work in Worcester."   4-11521.
Z1296. W9 N6
Rare Book Coll.

— 2d ed. Worcester, Priv. print. ... 1918.   xi, 244 p.   front. (port.) facsims.   23 cm.   75 copies printed.
"Corrections and additions have been gathered together in the Addenda (p. (193) - 225) ..."   40-17770.
Z1296. W9 N6
1918

MASSACHUSETTS CLASSIFICATION F61 - F75

61	Periodicals. Societies. Collections.
.5	Museums. Exhibitions, exhibits.
62	Gazetteers. Dictionaries. Geographic names.
.3	Guidebooks.
63	Biography (Collective). Genealogy (Collective).
.2	Historiography.
	Historians, *see* E 175.5.
.5	Study and teaching.
64	General works. Histories.
.3	Juvenile works.
.5	Minor works. Pamphlets, addresses, essays, etc.
.6	Anecdotes, legends, pageants, etc.
65	Historic monuments (General). Illustrative material. Antiquities (Non-Indian).

By period.

67   Early to 1775.

        Dorchester Company; Massachusetts Bay Company; persecution of Quakers; Province of Massachusetts; Puritans; etc.

        Biography: Roger Conant, Thomas Dudley, John Endecott, Daniel Gookin, Anne (Marbury) Hutchinson, Thomas Hutchinson, Cotton Mather, Increase Mather, Peter Oliver, Thomas Pownall, John Read, Timothy Ruggles, Samuel Sewall, John Winthrop (1588–1649), etc.

        Cf. BF 1575–1576, Witchcraft delusion.
           E 83.67, King Philip's War, 1675–1676.
           E 83.72, War with the eastern Indians, 1722–1726.
           E 196, King William's War, 1689–1697.
           E 197, Queen Anne's War, 1702–1713.
           E 198, King George's War, 1744–1748.
           E 199, French and Indian War, 1755–1763.
           F 7.5, Andros and his province of New England, 1688–1689.

68   New Plymouth Colony.

        Pilgrims; annexation to Massachusetts, 1691 (forming the counties of Barnstable, Bristol, and Plymouth); etc. Pilgrim Society, Plymouth; Society of Mayflower Descendants; etc. Old Colony Historical Society, Taunton, *see* F 74.T2.

        Biography: Isaac Allerton, William Bradford, William Brewster, Myles Standish, etc.

69 1775–1865.

   Shays' Rebellion, 1786–1787, etc.

   Biography: James Bowdoin, Christopher Gore, David Henshaw, Samuel Howe, Amos Lawrence, Theophilus Parsons, Samuel Phillips, William Phillips, Paul Revere, Caleb Strong, etc.

   Cf. E 263.M4, Massachusetts and the Revolution; E 211–216, Preliminaries; E 230.5–241, Military operations and battles.
    E 309, F 483, Cession of western lands.
    E 359.5.M3, War of 1812.
    E 513, Civil War, 1861–1865 (General).
    F 127.G2, .H7, .T6, Lands in western New York.
    F 273, Trouble with South Carolina over Negro citizens, 1845.

70 1865–1950.

   Biography: James Michael Curley, Frederic Thomas Greenhalge, Samuel Hoar, Roger Wolcott, etc.

   Cf. D 570.85.M4–41, World War I, 1914–1918.
    D 769.85.M4–41, World War II, 1939–1945.
    E 726.M4, War of 1898 (Spanish-American War).

71 1951–

72 Regions, counties, etc., A–Z.

   Barnstable Co., *see* F 72.C3.
 .B5 Berkshire Co.
   Berkshire Hills, Greylock Mountain, Hoosic River and Valley, Mass. (Cf. F 57.B4, Vermont; F 127.H73, General, and New York), Mohawk Trail (Cf. F 127.M55, New York), Mount Everett, etc.

   "Boston Ten Townships," N. Y., *see* F 127.T6.
 .B7 Boundaries.
   Cf. F 42.B7, New Hampshire boundary.
    F 1039.B7, Ancient boundary of Acadia.
   Massachusetts territorial claims to western New York, *see* F 127.G2.

 .B8 Bristol Co.
 .B9 Buzzards Bay region.
 .C3 Cape Cod. Barnstable Co.
   Cape Cod Bay, Sparrow-hawk (Ship) wreck (1626), etc.

 .C46 Charles River.
 .C7 Connecticut River and Valley, Mass.
   Cf. F 12.C7, New England.

   Dukes Co., *see* F 72.M5.
 .E5 Elizabeth Islands.
   Cuttyhunk, Nashawena, Naushon, Nonamesset, Pasque, and Penikese Islands.

 .E7 Essex Co.
   Cape Ann, Ipswich (Agawam) River, North Shore, Saugus River, etc.

 .F8 Franklin Co.
   Deerfield River, Pocumtuck Valley, etc.

 .H2 Hampden Co.
 .H3 Hampshire Co.
   Mill River, Mount Holyoke, Mount Tom, etc.

 .H7 Housatonic River and Valley, Mass.
   Cf. F 102.H7, General, and Connecticut.

 .M5 Martha's Vineyard. Dukes Co.
   "Massachusetts Ten Townships," N. Y., *see* F 127.T6.

.M6	Merrimac River and Valley (General, and Mass.)
	Cf. F 42.M4, New Hampshire.
.M7	Middlesex Co.
	Concord River, etc.
.N2	Nantucket Co.
	Nantucket, Muskeget, and Tuckernuck Islands.
.N6	No Mans Land (Island).
.N8	Norfolk Co.
.P6	Plum Island.
.P7	Plymouth Co.
	North River, South Shore, etc.
.S9	Suffolk Co.
	Cf. F 73, Boston.
.S94	Swift River Valley. Quabbin Reservoir. Ware River Valley.
.W9	Worcester Co.
	Wachusett Mountain, etc.

73	Boston. Table IV.[1]
.1	Periodicals. Societies. Collections.
.15	Museums. Exhibitions, exhibits.
	Foreign Exhibition, 1883, see T 460.
.18	Guidebooks.
.25	Biography (Collective). Genealogy (Collective).
	Including vital records, epitaphs.
.27	Historiography.
.29	Study and teaching.
.3	General works. Histories.
.33	Juvenile works.
.35	Minor works. Pamphlets, addresses, essays, etc.
.36	Anecdotes, legends, pageants, etc.
.37	Historic monuments. Illustrative material.
.39	Antiquities (Non-Indian).
	By period.
.4	Early to 1775.
	The fires of 1711, 1737, 1760, etc.
	Biography: William Blackstone, etc.
	Cf. E 215.4–8, Events just prior to Revolution.
.44	1775–1865.
	Cf. E 450, Fugitive slave riots.
.5	1865–1950.
	Fire of 1872, etc.
.52	1951–
	Sections. Localities. Districts, etc.
.6	General works.
.61	Cemeteries.
	Copp's Hill Burial Ground, Granary Burial Ground, King's Chapel Burial Ground, Mount Hope Cemetery, etc.
.62	Churches.
	Prefer NA for architecture, BX for religious aspects.
.625	Hotels, taverns, etc.

	.627	Places of amusement.
	.63	Harbor.
	.64	Monuments. Statues.
	.65	Parks. Squares. Circles.

                Boston Common, Franklin Park, etc.

   .67   Streets. Bridges. Railroads, etc.

           e. g. .A1   General works.
                  .P3   Park Street.
                  .S7   State Street.
                  .T7   Tremont Street.
                  .W3 Washington Street.

   .68   Suburbs. Sections of the city. Rivers.

           .B4   Beacon Hill.
                Brighton, *see* F 74.B73.
           .C3   Castle Island.
                Charlestown, *see* F 74.C4.
                Dorchester, *see* F 74.D5.
           .E2   East Boston.
           .R2   Rainsford Island.
                Roxbury, *see* F 74.R9.
           .S7   South Boston.
                West Roxbury, *see* F 74.W59.

   .69   Wards.

          Buildings.

   .7   Collective.
   .8   Individual, A–Z.

           e. g. .C9   Crown Coffee House.
                  .F2   Faneuil Hall Market.
                  .O4   Old State House.
                  .P3   Parker House.
                  .S8   State House.

   .9   Elements in the population.

           .A1   General works.
           .A2–Z Individual elements.

                For a list of racial, ethnic, and religious elements (with cutter numbers), *see* E 184, p. 27-29.

74   Other cities, towns, etc., A–Z.

           e. g. .B73 Brighton.
                  .C1   Cambridge.
                  .C4   Charlestown.
                  .C8   Concord.
                  .D5   Dorchester.
                  .G9   Groton.
                  .P8   Plymouth.
                  .P96 Provincetown.
                  .R9   Roxbury.
                  .S1   Salem.
                  .S8   Springfield.
                  .T2   Taunton.
                          Old Colony Historical Society, etc.
                  .W59 West Roxbury.
                  .W9 Worcester.

75   Elements in the population.

           .A1   General works.
           .A2–Z Individual elements.

                For a list of racial, ethnic, and religious elements (with cutter numbers), *see* E 184, p. 27-29.

MASSACHUSETTS

F 61 - F 75

PERIODICALS. SOCIETIES. COLLECTIONS.

BAY State historical league. ... Publications (I) - IV. (Somerville, Mass., 1903 - 1909.
4 vols. 16½ x 24½ cm. Appeared at irregular intervals. 11-10432.   F61. B35

CAIN, George L. The crime and scandal of 1923 - 1924; dedicated to the shock troops of the hell hound brigade of the Massachusetts society of Washington, D.C. (Washington? 1926?)
194 p. 22½ cm. 34-11008.   F63. C 25

COLONIAL Society of Massachusetts. Publications. v. 1 -   Boston, The Society, 1895 - 19 -
   v. fronts., illus., plates (part col.) ports., maps. plans. facsims., diagrs. 25 cm. Some vols. called Transactions or Collections.
1-280.   F61. C 71

— Indexes. Index to vols. i - xxv, 1892 - 1924. Boston, The Society, 1932.
3, (ix) - xvi, 203 p. 25 cm. 1-280 x^1.   F61. C 71
   Index

COLONIAL Society of Massachusetts, Boston. Annual meeting, 1910. p. 146-181. 24½ cm.   F61. C714

— An appeal to members by the Council, 1908. 10 p. 24½ cm. 18-15845.   F61. C716

— By-laws with the certificate of incorporation, etc. 1898. v, (9) - 17 p. 24½ cm. 25-7731.   F61. C718

— Same. 1903. v, (4), (11) - 19 p. illus. 24½ cm. 5-41577.   F61. C 72

— Same. 1936. 13 p. 24 cm. 36-29798.   F61. C 72
   1936

— List of members. 1923. 29 p. 25 cm. 23-18573.   F61. C724

— Handbook, 1892 - 1952. Boston, 1953. 98 p. 24 cm. 54-27662.   F61. C728

— The events of the year 1935; being an address lately delivered before the members of the Colonial society of Mass. ... 1935. By Dr. Samuel Eliot Morison ... Boston, ... 1936   1, 5 p. 18½ x 14 cm.
37-9454.   F61. C745
   Rare Book Coll.

231

EDMONDS, John Henry. ... The Massachusetts archives. ... Worcester, Mass., The Society, 1922. 45 p. 24½ cm. "Repr. from the Proceedings of the Amer. antiquarian soc. for April, 1921" 24-18924. F61.E 24

GOVERNOR and company of Massachusetts bay in New England. Publications. (1929 - No. I - F61.G 78

— Miscelleaneous printed matter published by this body is classified in F61.G79

LIBERTY's advocate. No. 5. Oct. 21, 1843. Amesbury & Salisbury, Mass., Pettengill & Colby, 1843 - 1 no. 40 cm. (in binder 53 cm.) No. 5 includes letter by John S. Whittier. F61.L 52
Rare Book Coll.

MAKERS of Boston, The. Boston, Old South meeting house, 1884. (71) p. 18 cm. (Old South leaflets II. 1824) 4-15754. F61.M 19

MASSACHUSETTTS historical society. Act of incorporation and by-laws. (Cambridge ... 1853) 12 p. 25½ cm. 2-12078. F61.M 25

— with a list of officers, etc. 1873. 21 p. 23½ cm. 2-12079. F61.M 26

— 1882. 23 p. 22 cm. 2-12080. F61.M 27

— 1897. 27 p. 24½ cm. 1-12002. F61.M 28

— 19? F61.M284

MASSACHUSETTS historical society. Annual report of the treasurer. 1859-96, 98, 99 - 1904, 05 - (Boston, 1859 - 1909) 52 v. 23½ cm. CA 9-156 unrev. F61.M 29

— Constitution. 1792. 20½ cm. F61.M 32

— List of officers and members, 1897. 22 p. 24½ cm. 1-12003. F61.M 33

— Laws and regulations. 1833. 8 p. 23½ cm. 6-45828. F61.M 34

MASSACHUSETTS historical society. Proceedings. v. 1 - 20; 1791/1835 - 1882/83. 2d ser., v. 1 - 20; 1884/85 - 1906/07. 3d ser., v. (41) - Boston, The Society, 1859 - 19 v. fronts., illus., plates (part col.) ports., maps, facsims. 23 - 25 cm. Indexes: v. 1 - 20, 1791/1835 - 1882/83. 2d ser., v.1-20, 1884/85 - 1906/7; 3d ser. v. 41-60. 1907/08 - Oct. 1926/June 1927. 9-885 (rev. '42) F61.M 38

— Index to the third series of the Proceedings of the Mass. historical soc., vols. 41 - 60, 1907 - 1926. Boston, 1941. 454 p.

MASSACHUSETTS historical society. Proceedings ... (at the annual general meeting) 1855, 1857, 1900, 1904. Boston, 1855 - 1904. 4 pam. 8°. F61.M382

MASSACHUSETTS historical society. ... Collections, v. 1 - (Cambridge, Mass., The Mass. hist. soc., etc. 1794 - 1941. v. fronts., illus., plates, ports., maps, plan. facsims. 21 - 25½ cm. Vols. 1 - 70 comprise 1 - 7th series (10 vols. in each series) Beginning with v. 71 the series numbering is discontinued. Second series, v. 5-6 paged continuously. "All the volumes of the first and second series and col. I of the third have been reprinted." (In the Lib. of Congress set vols. 2, 5 and 2d ser. vol. 3 are reprints. For the statement above quoted, also for full bibliographical information ... and for the contents of the volumes (1st ser.) v.1 - 7yj ser. v.5, cf. Griffin, Bibliography of American historical society. 2d ed. 1907, p. 346 - 360. Vol. 10 of each series contains general table of contents and index for the series. 9-889 (rev. '28) F61.M41
vols. 1-8 in Rare Book coll.

MASSACHUSETTS historical society. Handbook, 1791 - 1948. Boston, 1949. 182 p. illus., ports. 25 cm. 49-2273*. F61.M425

... Handbook of the publications and photostats, 1792 - 1933 ... 1934. F61.M426
1934

MASSACHUSETTS

— 1792 - 1935. Boston, 1937.   2, 144 p. 23½ cm. ... Indexes the Collections, Proceedings and special publications.
38-12705.
F61.M426
1937
Z1295.M41H

MASSACHUSETTTS historical society. Here we have lived: the houses of the Mass. historical soc.
Boston, 1967.   (31) p. illus., map., plan. 25 cm. (A Mass. hist. soc. picture book)
F61.M427
F61.M428

MASSACHUSETTS historical society, A short account of, by Charles C. Smith ... Boston, 1908.
63 p. 26 cm. 14-21193.
F61.M 43

— 1918.   3. 99 p. front. 25 cm. 19-7397.
F61.M433

MASSACHUSETTTS historical society. Other minor works numbered F61.M447, M448, M45, M451, M452, M456, M65, W79

MASSACHUSETTS magazine, The, devoted to Massachusetts history, genealogy, biography. v. 1 - 10, v. 11, no. 1: Jan. 1908 - Jan. 1918. Salem, Mass., The Salem press co. (1908 - 18)   11 v. in 10.
illus., plates, ports., fold. geneal. tabl. 25 cm. quarterly. 9-25075 rev.
F61.M 48

MASSACHUSETTTS. Secretary of the commonwealth. (A statement and schedule of the "public records and documents, belonging to the commonwealth" in the secretary's office ... (n. p., 1821?)
19 p. 23 cm.
F61.M 72

QUABOAG historical society; a sketch of its organizationa and work 1894 - 99 ... Spencer, Mass., E. E. Dickerman, print., 1900.   35 p. incl. illus., port. 25 cm. 25-7732.
F61.Q 35

STORY of Massachusetts. Boston, Old South meeting house (The Directors of the Old South work) 1905.   (172) p. 18½ cm. (Old South leaflets. xxiii. 1905) 6-43116.
F61.S 88

MUSEUMS. EXHIBITIONS, EXHIBITS.

RUBIN, Jerome. A guide to Massachusetts museums, historic houses, points of interest. (Newton, Mass., Emporium Pubs., 1972)   119 p. 23 x 11 cm. 72-81231.
F61.5.R8

GAZETTEERS. DICTIONARIES. GEOGRAPHIC NAMES.

GANNETT, Henry. ... A geographic dictionary of Massachusetts. Washington, Gov't print. off., 1894.   126 p. 24 cm. (Bulletin of the U. S. Geological survey no. 116) 2-4309.
F62.G 19
G & M R R

HAYWARD, John. A gazetteer of Massachusetts, containing descriptions of all the counties, towns and districts ... also, of its principal mountains, rivers, etc. ... Boston, J. Hayward, 1846.
444 p. incl. 1 illus., tables. front., plates. 20 cm. 45-45652.
F62.H 42
1846

— 1849. 452 p. incl. tables. front., plates. 20 cm. 1-12004.
F68.H 42
1849
G & M

MASSACHUSETTS localities. A finding list of Massachusetts cities and towns; and of villages, certain lesser localities, railroad stations, etc. etc. Compiled by Mass. geodetic survey ... (Boston) 1938.   3, 78 p. maps (1 folded) 21 cm. Mimeographed. "Mass. WPA project no. 16565" 39-28221.
F62.M37

NASON, Elias.   A gazetteer of the state of Massachusetts; with numerous illustrations on wood and steel.   Boston, B.B. Russell, 1874.   576 p. front., illus., pl., ports. fold. map. 23½ cm. 1-12005.   F62.N 26

— 1890.   724 p. front., illus., pl. 23½ cm. 1-12006.   F62.N 27
G & M

SPOFFORD, Jeremiah.   A gazetteer of Massachusetts; containing a general view of the state, with an historical sketch of the principal events from its settlement to the present time, and notices of several towns, alphabetically arranged.   Newburyport, C.Whipple, 1828.   348 p. front. (fold. map) 18 cm. 1-12007.
F62.S 76
G & M

— 2d ed. - rev. cor., and a large part re-written.   Haverhill, E.G. Frothingham, 1860.
iv, (9) - 372 p. front. (fold. map) 18 cm. 1-12008.   F62.S 77

WHITMORE, William Henry.   An essay on the origin of the names of towns in Massachusetts, settled prior to 1775.   To which is prefixed an essay on the name of the town of Lexington.   Boston, J. Wilson and son, 1873.   2, (3) - 37 p. 23½ cm.   Repr. from the Proccedings of the Mass. hist. soc. 1872-3.   17-25227.   F62.W 6

WRITERS' program.   The origin of Massachusetts place names of the state, counties, cities, and towns, compiled by workers of the Writers' project of the W.P.A. in Mass.   New York, Harian pubs., 1941.   vi, 55 p. 21½ cm. Bibliography: p. 54-55. 41-52742.   F62.W 8
L.H.& G.

DIRECTORIES.

U.S. Bureau of the census. ... Heads of families at the first census of the U.S. taken in the year 1790. ... Washington, Govt. print. off., 1907 - 08.   12 v. fronts. (fold. maps) 29½ cm. 7-35273.   F62.5.U58

SOUTH shore social register and who's who on Cape Cod ... 1903.   v. illus., plates, fold. maps. 24 cm.
3-18659 rev.   Directories

DIRECTORY of stopping places in Massachusetts for tourists and vacationists.   Mass. Industrial commission ... (Boston, 1931)   70 p. illus. (incl. maps) 20½ x 10½ cm. 31-27889 rev.   F62.7.M25

— 1932.   89 p. illus. (incl. maps) 20½ x 10½ cm. 38-20401.   F62.7.M25
1932

BIOGRAPHY (COLLECTIVE). GENEALOGY (COLLECTIVE).

LIST of persons whose names have been changed in Massachusetts.   1780 - 1892.   Collated and pub. by the Secretary of the Commonwealth ...   Baltimore, Genealogical Pub. Co., 1972.
522 p. 22 cm. 75-39364.   Original 1885 ed. numbered F63.M402.   F63. A 5
1972

BAILEY, Frederic William.   Early Massachusetts marriages prior to 1800 ... New Haven, Conn., Bureau of American ancestry (1897 - 1914)   3 v. 23 cm. Contents - 1st book. Worcester County. - 2d book. Plymouth County. - 3d book. Middlesex, Hampshire, Berkshire and Bristol counties.   0-7103 rev.   F63.B 15

— Baltimore, Genealogical Pub. Co., 1968.   3 v. in 1. 23 cm. Reprint of the 1897 - 1914 ed. with a reprint of the 1900 ed. of Plymouth County marriages, 1692 - 1746 (54 p. at end) 68-28249.   F63.B 16
L.H.& G.

BIOGRAPHICAL encyclopaedia of Mass. of the nineteenth century.   1879 - 83.   2 v.   F63.B 61
R.R.

BIOGRAPHICAL sketches of representative citizens of the commonwealth of Massachusetts ... Boston, Graves & Steinbarger, 1901.   2, (9) - 1092 p. incl. ports. 4 port. 29 x 22 cm. (American series of popular biographies: Massachusetts ed.) 10-199.   F63.B 64

MASSACHUSETTS

BOSTON Press club. Men of Massachusetts. Specimen pages. Boston, 1902. F63.B 74

BROWN, John Howard. Men of mark in Massachusetts ... Boston, Mass., Johnson-Wynne co., 1904. 22½ cm. F63.B 87

COMLEY, William J. Comley's history of Massachusetts. With portraits and biographies of some of the old settlers, and many of her most prominent manufacturers, professional and business men ... Boston, Comley brothers, 1879. vi, 9 - 45, iv, 203 - 462 p. incl. plates, ports. 24 x 20½ cm. Many numbers omitted in pagination. 6-21573. F63.C 73

CRAWFORD, Mary Caroline. Famous families of Massachusetts, ... Boston, Little, Brown, and co., 1930 2 v. fronts., ports. 24½ cm. 30-32010. F63.C 89

CUTTER, William Richard. Genealogical and personal memoirs relating to the families of Boston and eastern Massachusetts. New York, Lewis historical pub. co., 1908. 4 v. fronts., illus., plates, ports. 27½ cm. Paged continuously. 9-11679. F63.C 99

— 1910. 4 v. fronts., plates, ports. 27 cm. 10-9807. F63.C993

DAVIS, William Thomas. Bench and bar of the commonwealth of Massachusetts ... (Boston) The Boston history co., 1895. 2 v. fronts., ports. 26½ cm. 6-20083. F63.D 26

ENCYCLOPEDIA of Massachusetts, biographical - genealogical; comp. with the assistance of ... William Richard Cutter and others. New York, Boston (etc.) The American historical soc. (inc.) 1916. 5 v. fronts., plates, ports. 28 cm. 17-13992. F63.E 56

FLAGG, Charles Allcott. An index of pioneers from Massachusetts to the West, especially the state of Michigan ... Salem, Mass., The Salem press co,, 1915. 1, iii, 86 p. 23½ cm. x 17½ cm. "Originally pub. in the Mass. magazine, Salem, Mass." 24-15733. F63.F 53

FORBES, Abner. The rich men of Massachusetts: containing a statement of the reputed wealth of about fifteen hundred persons, with brief sketches of more than one thousand characters. Boston, Fetridge and co., 1851. viii, (9) - 208 p. 22½ cm. 5-3871. F63.F 69

— Boston, Print. for Redding & co., 1852. viii, (9) - 224 p. 21½ cm. 16-10382. F63. F 7

HURD, Charles Edwin. ... Genealogy and history of representative citizens of the commonwealth of Massachusetts, ... Boston, New England historical pub. co., 1902. 3, (9) - 835 p. incl. ports. 29 cm. (New England library of genealogy and personal history) 9-8955. F63.H 96

KINGMAN, Bradford. (Manuscript records of marriages, deaths, etc. of the first settlers in the towns of Plymouth, Scituate, Taunton, Eastham, Barnstable, Rehoboth, Swansey and Sandwich) 189-? (188) p. 23 cm. Includes blank leaves. F63.K 56

KNAPP, S. L. Biographical sketches ... 1821. 1 v. F63.K 61

KNAPP, Samuel Lorenzo. Biographical sketches of eminent lawyers, statesmen, and men of letters ... Boston, Richardson and Lord, 1821. iv, (5) - 360 p. 22 cm. 5-37658. F63.K 62

MARDEN, George Augustus. 1880. Government of the commonwealth of Massachusetts. A souvenir. Historical, descriptive, and biographical sketches by various authors ... Boston, J. R. Osgood & co., 1880. 2 v. fronts., plates, ports. 35 cm. 3-19136. F63.M 32

LIST of persons whose names have been changed in Massachusetts. 1780 - 1883. (Collated and pub. by the secretary of the commonwealth ...) Boston, Wright and Potter print., 1885. 1, (5) - 426 p. 25 cm. 7-31288. F63.M402

— 1893. 522 p. 25 cm. 2-3871. F63.M 41

MEN of Massachusetts; a collection of portraits of representative men in business and professional life in the commonwealth of Massachusetts. Pub. under the editorial auspices and direction of the Boston press club. Boston (Rockwell and Churchill press) 1903. xxiv, 386 p. of ports. 24 cm. The portraits occupy p. 1 - 386. 17-7714.
F63. M 53

MEN of progress; one thousand biographical sketches and portraits of leaders in business and professional life in the commonwealth of Massachusetts; Comp. under the supervision of Richard Herndon; ed. Edwin M. Bacon. Boston, New England magazine, 1896. 1, (9) - 1027 p. illus. (ports.) 28½ x 22 cm. 3-2349 rev.
F63. M533

MORSE, Abner. The genealogy of the descendants of several ancient Puritans ... Boston, 1857 - 61. v. 1 - 3. 24½ cm.
F63. M 88

POPE, Charles Henry. The pioneers of Massachusetts, a descriptive list, drawn from records of the colonies, towns and churches and other contemporaneous documents. Boston, C.H. Pope, 1900. 549, (1) p. 27½ cm. 0-3744 rev.
F63. P 87
Geneal. Sect. Ref.

— Supplement. (Boston, 1901) xv, (1) p. 27 cm. 0-3744 rev.
F63. P821
Rare Book Coll.

— Facsimile, positive.
F63. P821a

— Facsimile, negative.
F63. P821b

— Baltimore, Genealogical Pub. Co., 1965. 549 p. 24 cm. "Originally pub.... 1900" 65-22478.
F63. P822

PROMINENT men of Massachusetts; individual biographic studies with character portraits. Library ed. New York, Historical records, inc., c.1940 - 1 v. front. (port.) 29 cm. Contents. - (v.1) Edward Willard Burt. 41-14727.
F63. P835

PUTNAM, Eben. The printed vital records of Massachusetts, under the act of 1902. (Boston, 1905) 1, 10 p. 23 cm. "From the Genealogical magazine, April, 1905." 5-18249.
F63. P 85

RAND, John Clark. One of a thousand, a series of biographical sketches of one thousand representative men resident in the commonwealth of Massachusetts, 1888 - 89. Boston, First national print co., 1890. 4. 707 p. illus. (incl. ports., facsim.) 28½ cm. 3-19135. rev.
F63. R 18

REPRESENTATIVE men and old families of southeastern Massachusetts, containing historical sketches of prominent and representative citizens and genealogical records of many of the old families ... Chicago, J.H. Beers, 1912. 3 v. ports. 28 x 21½ cm. Paged continuously. Includes Bristol, Plymouth and Barnstable counties. 16-11302.
F63. R 4

REPRESENTATIVE men of Massachusetts, 1890 - 1900. The leaders in official, business and professional life of the commonwealth. (anon) Everett, Mass., Mass. pub. co., 1898. 491 p. port. 4°. 26.
F63. R 42

SONS of the Puritans; a group of brief biographies. Boston, American Unitarian assoc. (c.1908) 8, 244 p. ports. 20 cm. "The sketches ... are reprinted from the Harvard graduates' magazine." 8-30957.
F63. S 69

TOOMEY, Daniel P. Massachusetts of today; a memorial of the state, historical and biographical, issued for the World's Columbian exposition at Chicago. Boston, Columbia pub. co., 1892. 619 p. incl. front., illus., ports. 31 cm. 1-12126.
F63. T 67

TOWNSEND, Charles Delmar. Border town cemeteries of Massachusetts. West Hartford, Conn., Chedwato Service (1953) 88 p. 21 cm. 54-25311.
F63. T 7

U.S. Bureau of the Census. Heads of families at the First Census of the U.S. ... 1790: Massachusetts. Washington, Govt. print. off., 1908. (Spartanburg, S.C.) 1964. 363 p. 28 cm. 64-62657.
F63. U 5

WHO'S who in Massachusetts; a volume containing a biographical history of every important living

MASSACHUSETTS

person in the commonwealth ... v. 1 -   Boston, Larkin, Roosevelt & Larkin, 1940 -
v. 23½ cm. 40-4249.   F63.W 59

WHO'S who in state politics, 1907. Boston, Practical politics, c.1907 - 1910.   3 v. illus. (ports.)
15½ x 9½ cm. 7-15568.   F63.W 62

MASSACHUSETTS biography. Pamphlets, broadsides, clippings, and other miscellaneous matter on this subject, not separately cataloged, are classified in F63.Z9

GENERAL WORKS. HISTORIES.

ADAMS, Charles Francis.   Massachusetts; its historians and its history.   An object lesson.
Boston and New York, Houghton Mifflin co., 1893.   2, 110 p. 20½ cm. 1-12009.   F64.A 21

— Freeport, N.Y., Books for Libraries Press (1971)   110 p. 23 cm. 73-146849.   F64.A 63
                                                                                                                             1971

AUSTIN, George Lowell.   The history of Massachusetts, from the landing of the Pilgrims to the present time, etc. etc.   Boston, B.B. Russell (etc.) 1876.   xix, 578 p. incl. front. ports. 23½ cm. 1-12011.
                                                                                                                             F64.A 93

— 1884.   xx, 598 p. incl. front. plates, ports. 23 cm. 1-12012.   F64.A 94

BARBER, John Warner.   Historical collections, being a general collection of interesting facts, traditions, biographical sketches, anecdotes, etc. relating to the history and antiquities of every town in Mass., with geographical descriptions.   Illus. by 200 engravings.   Worcester, Dorr, Howland & co., 1839.   viii, (9) - 624 p. front., illus., plates, fold. map. 23 cm. L.C. copy replaced by microfilm. 1-12013 Mi.   F64.B 23
                                                                                                                             Microfilm 8785 F
                                                                                                                             Toner Coll.

— Worcester, W. Lazell, 1844.   viii, (9) - 624 p. front., illus., plates, fold. map. 22½ cm. 1-12014.   F64.B 24

BARRY, John Stetson.   The history of Massachusetts ...   Boston, Phillips, Sampson and co., 1855 - 57,   3 v. 23 cm. Contents. - v.1. The colonial period to 1692 - v.2. The provincial period (1692 - 1775) - v.3. The commonwealth period (1775 - 1820) 1-14478.   F64.B 27

— 4th ed.   Boston, The author, (c.1856 - 57)   3 v. 24 cm. 17-11281.   F64.B275
                                                                                                                             Toner coll.

— Boston, Phillips, Sampson, & co., 1857.   3 v. 24 cm. Bibliographical foot-notes. 1-14479.
                                                                                                                             F64.B 28

BAY state historical league.   Little journeys, geographical and historical, Bay State historical league ... (Framingham, Mass.) c.1941 -   v. fold. map, fold. facsim. 22½ cm. Contents. - Journey no. 1. Boston bay to the south shore and cape Cod, by Channing Howard. 42-928.   F64. B 3

BOSTON herald, The.   Scenes and characters of the Massachusetts Bay colony ... (1930)   1 v.
                                                                                                                             F64.B 75

BRADFORD, Alden.   History of Massachusetts ... Boston, Richardson and Lord (etc.) 1822-29.
3 v. 22 cm. Contents. - v.1. 1764 tp 1775. - v.2. 1775 - 1789. - v.3. 1790 - 1820. 1-12015.
                                                                                                                             F64.B 79

— New York, Research Reprint (1970)   3 v. 21 cm. 71-124779.   F64.B 79
                                                                                                                             1970

BRADFORD, Alden.   History of Massachusetts, for 200 years ... 1620 to 1820 ... Boston, Hilliard, Gray, and co., 1835.   xii, (13) - 480 p. front. (fold. map) 25½ cm. Map wanting. A 12-42.   F64. B 8

BROWNE, George Waldo.   The story of the old Bay state; a young people's history of Mass.   Manchester, N.H., Standard book co., 1929.   2, 9 - 326 p. front., illus. (incl. ports.) 20 cm. 30-2361.

 F64.B 87

BULLOCK, Alexander Hamilton.   Addresses delivered on several occasions.   With a memoir by George F. Hoar.   Boston, Little, Brown and co., 1883.   1, (v) - xlv p., 365 p. 23 cm. 15-815.

 F64. B 9

BURLINGHAME, Anson.   Defence of Massachusetts.   Speech of Hon. Anson Burlinghame, in the U.S. House of representatives ... 1856.   Cambridge (Mass.) Printed for private distribution, 1856.
33 p. front. (port.) 22½ cm. 5-42308.   F64.B 92

— (Washington, D.C., Buell & Blanchard, print. 1856)   7 p. 22½ cm. 18-5815.   F64.B921

CARPENTER, William Henry.   The history of Massachusetts, from its earliest settlement to the present time.   Philadelphia, Lippincott, Grambo & co., 1853.   3, (5) - 330 p. front. (port.) 17½ cm. 1-12016.

 F64.C 29

CHADWICK, Mrs. Mara Louise Pratt.   ... Stories of Massachusetts.   Boston, Educational pub. co., 1892.   2, 3-348 p. illus. 18 cm. (Young folk's library of American history) 1-12023 Add. F64.C 43

CHASE Manhattan Bank.   Massachusetts, the Bay State.   New York (1936)   70 p. 14 cm. (The Manhattan library, v.9-S) Pub. by the bank under its earlier name: Bank of the Manhattan Co. 36-32616 rev*.

 F64.C 45

CLARK, Mary.   Conversations on the history of Massachusetts, from its settlement to the present period; for the use of schools and families.   By a friend of youth.   Boston, Munroe & Francis, 1831.
180 p. illus. 24º. 1-12017-M1.   F64.C 59

CLARK, Mary.   A concise history of Massachusetts, from its first settlement ... New York, D. & G.F. Cooledge; Boston, Munroe and Francis, 1837.   iv, (5) - 180 p. front., illus. 16º. 1-12018-M1.

 F64.C 60

CLARK, William Horace.   The story of Massachusetts, ... New York, The American historical soc., (c.1938)   4 v. fronts., illus. (incl. facsims.) plates, ports. 27½ cm. Vol. 4 biographical. 38-23198. F64.C 63

DAVIS, Garrett.   Speech of Hon, Garrett Davis, of Kentucky, in Committee of the whole; in which he gives a sketch of the political history of Mass.   Washington, Towers & co., print., 1864.
39 p. 25 cm. 18-2970. 11-20205. F64.D 26 or D262

GREEN, Samuel Abbott.   Remarks on the Boston magazine, the Geographical gazetteer of Mass., and John Norman, engraver.   Cambridge, J. Wilson and son, 1904.   7 p. 24 cm. 11-25753.

 F64.G 79

GREENLEAF, Thomas.   Geographical gazetteer of the towns in the commonwealth of Mass.   (Boston, Greenleaf and Freeman, 1784 - 85)   98 p. fold. plan. 20½ cm. Issued in parts appended to the monthly numbers of the Boston magazine, Oct. 1784 - Dec. 1785.   Includes only Suffolk County and part of Middlesex County.   All pub. 8-18220.

 F64.G 81

GRIFFIS, William Elliot.   Massachusetts: a typical American commonwealth.   Cambridge, J. Wilson and son, 1893.   3, (5) - 38 p. illus. 22½ x 18 cm. Apparently prepared for distribution at the World's Columbian exposition, Chicago.
1-13345.   F64.G 85

HALE, Edward Everett.   ... The story of Massachusetts.   Boston, D. Lothrop (c.1891)   359 p. front., plates, port., fold. map. 21½ cm. 1-12019.   F64.H 16

HART, Albert Bushnell.   Commonwealth history of Mass., colony, province and state;   ... New York, The States history co., 1927 - 30.   5 v. fronts., plates, ports., maps, facsims. 24½ cm. Maps on lining papers.
"Select bibliography" at end of each chapter.   Contents. - v.1. 1605 - 1689. - v.2. 1689 - 1775. - v.3. 1775 - 1820. - v.4. 1820 - 1889.
v.5. 1889 - 1930. 27-18867 rev.   F64.H 32

MASSACHUSETTS

— New York, Russell & Russell, 1966.   5 v. 22 cm. 66-27095.   F64.H322

HILDRETH, Hosea. A book for Massachusetts children, in familiar letters from a father, for the use of families and schools. Boston, Hilliard, Gray, Little & Wilkins, 1829.   iv, 132 p. front. (fold. map) illus. 18½ cm. 1-12020.   F64.H 64

— 2d ed. Boston, Hilliard, Gray, Little and Wilkins, 1831.   iv, 142 p. front. (fold. map) 9-23612.   F64.H645

— Rev. and enl. ed. Boston, J. P. Jewett and co., 1857.   164 p. front. (map) illus. 16°. 1-12021-M1.   F64.H 68

HISTORICAL records survey. Proclamations of Massachusetts issued by governors and other authorities, 1620 - 1936 ... W. P. A. Boston, Mass., 1937.   2 v. 27½ cm. Mimeographed. Bibliography: vol. I. p. 1 - 4. Contents. - v.1. 1620 - 1775. - v.II. 1776 - 1936. 38-26714.   F64.H 67

HOLLAND, Josiah Gilbert. History of western Massachusetts. The counties of Hampden, Hampshire, Franklin, and Berkshire. Embracing an outline, or general history ... and separate histories of its one hundred towns ... Springfield, S. Bowles and co., 1855.   3 pts. in 2 v. map. 12°. 1-12022-M1.   F64.H 73

HOWE, Henry Forbush. Massachusetts; there she is, behold her. Illus. and maps by John O'Hara Cosgrave II. (1st ed.) New York, Harper (1960)   290 p. (A Regions of America book) 60-13447.   F64.H 75

HOWE, Henry Forbush. Salt rivers of the Massachusetts shore; illus. by John O'Hara Cosgrave II. New York, Rinehart (1951)   xiv, 370 p. illus., map. 21 cm. (Rivers of America) Bibliography: p. 351-358. 51-14004.   F64.H 76

LITT, Edgar. The political cultures of Massachusetts. Cambridge, Mass., M. I. T. press (1965) xiv, 224 p. 21 cm. 65-26663.   F64.L 58

LOCKWOOD, John Hoyt. Western Massachusetts; a history, 1636 - 1925. New York and Chicago, Lewis historical pub. co., inc., 1926.   4 v. fronts., plates, ports., facsims., coats of arms. 27½ cm. Vols. 3-4 contain biographical material. 27-6655.   F64.L76

MARLOWE, George Francis. The old bay paths, their villages and byways and their stories ... illus. with photos. by Samuel Chamberlain. New York, Hastings house (1942)   126 p. incl. plates. 21 cm. "References": p. 125 - 126. 42-23537.   F64. M 3

MASSACHUSETTS. Tables of bearings, distances, latitudes, longitudes, etc. ascertained by the Astronomical and trigonometrical survey ... Boston, Dutton and Wentworth, 1846.   2, xxxviii, 73 p. 27½ cm. 1-16210 rev.   F64.M 43   Map div.

MASSACHUSETTS. ... Historical data relating to counties, cities and towns in Mass. Prepared by the secretary of the commonwealth, Div. of public records. Boston, Wright & Potter print. co., 1920. 73 p. 23½ cm. 20-27342.   F64.M5   L. H. & G.

REID, William James. Massachusetts; a students' guide to localized history. New York, Bureau of Publications, Teachers College, Columbia University, 1965.   x, 29 p. 23 cm. (Localized history series) 64-7874.   F64.R 38

REID, William James. Massachusetts, history and government of the Bay State. New York, Oxford Book Co., 1956.   300 p. illus. 20 cm. Includes bibliography. 56-1714.   F64. R 4

SANDROF. Ivan. Massachusetts towns; an 1840 view. Barre, Mass., Barre Publishers, 1963) 116 p. 21 cm. (illus. with wood engravings of fifty-eight Massachusetts towns, drawn in 1840 by J. W. Barber. Special foreword by Mrs. Endicott Peabody.) 63-18871.   F64.S 34

— ... and a special foreword by Mrs. Endicott Peabody. (Barre, Mass., Barre publishers, 1965) 102 p. 21 cm.   F64.S 35

WINSLOW, Douglas Kenelm.   Mayflower heritage; a family record of the growth of Anglo-American partnership.   New York, Funk & Wagnalls (1957)   200 p. illus. 21 cm. Includes bibliography. 57-4154.

F64.W 75

WINTHROP, Robert Charles.   Introductory lecture to the course on the early history of Mass., by members of the Mass. historical society ...   Boston, Press of J. Wilson and son, 1869.   27 p. 23 cm. 1-12024.

F64.W 79

WRIGHT, Harry Andrew.   The story of western Massachusetts.   New York, Lewis Historical Pub. Co. (c. 1949)   4 v. illus., ports., maps. 28 cm. Vols. 3-4: Personal and family history. 50-6039.

F64.W 85

JUVENILE WORKS.

BAILEY, Bernadine (Freeman)   Picture book of Massachusetts, ... Pictures by Kurt Weise.   Rev. ed. Chicago, A. Whitman, 1965.   32 p. 17 x 21 cm. (The United States books)

F64.3.B3 1965

CARPENTER, John Allan.   Massachusetts from its glorious past to the present.   Illus. by Phil Austin.   Chicago, Childrens Press (1965)   95 p. 24 cm. (Enchantment of America) 65-20880.

F64.3.C3

COIT, Margaret L.   Massachusetts.   New York, Coward-McCann (1967)   126 p. 25 cm. (States of the nation, 6) 67-24216.

F64.3.C6

DEXTER, Lincoln A.   Bay State briefs; a social studies primer of the Commonwealth of Massachusetts. Rev. ed.   Wilbraham? Mass., c. 1963)   134 p. 23 cm.

F64.3.D4 1963

MINOR WORKS. PAMPHLETS, ADDRESSES, ESSAYS, ETC.

MACONI, Carole J.   Massachusetts, birthplace of a Nation.   Yankee Colour photos. by Roger W. Maconi and others.   Southborough, Mass., Yankee Colour Corp., c. 1966)   26 p. 16 x 24 cm. (A Historama booklet) 67-20420.

F64.5.M3

MASSACHUSETTS Bar Association.   Our Massachusetts heritage.   (Boston?) 1954.   (12) p. illus. 22 x 28 cm. 55-25572.

F64.5.M37

HISTORIC MONUMENTS (GENERAL). ILLUSTRATIVE MATERIAL.

BACHELLER, Edward Franklin.   Colonial landmarks of the old Bay state.   Lynn, Mass., Souvenir pub. co., 1896.   (28) p. plates. 16½ x 20 cm. 1-12026 rev.   or 14-20030 rev.

F65.B 12 or B 13

BACON, Edwin Munroe.   Historic pilgrimages in New England; among landmarks of Pilgrim and Puritan days and of the provincial and revolutionary periods ...   New York, Boston (etc.) Silver, Burdett & co., (c. 1898)   xiv, 475 p. incl. front., illus. (incl. ports., maps) 19½ cm. 98-1784/5

F65.B 14

BROOKS, Elbridge Streeter.   Stories of the old Bay state.   New York, Cincinnati (etc.) American book co., 1899.   284 p. incl. front., illus. 19 cm. 99-891 rev.

F65.B 86

CHASE, Levi Badger.   The Bay path and along the way.   (Norwood, Mass.) Print. for the author, 1919.   xxii, 246 p. front. (port.) illus. (maps) plates. 20½ cm. 20-3360.

F65.C 48

COMER, William Russell.   Landmarks "in the Old Bay state.   (Wellesley, Mass.) The author, 1911.   x, 350 p. incl. front., illus. 20 cm. 11-30048.

F65.C 73

MASSACHUSETTS

FEDERAL Writers' project. A report of progress, June 15, 1939. Boston (1939) 2 p, 2 - 19 numb. l. 28 cm. 40-26610.
F65. F 45

FOWLE, William Bentley. An elementary geography for Massachusetts children. Boston, Fowle and Capen (1845) 224 p. illus. (incl. maps) 16 x 13 cm. 3-20622.
F65. F 75

GREEN, Samuel Abbott. Early mile-stones leading from Boston; and mile-stones at Groton. Cambridge, J. Wilson & son, University press, 1909. 27 p. illus. 24½ cm. Repr. from the Proceedings of the Mass. hist. soc. for Jan. 1909. 9-12807.
F65. G 79

HALLETT, Benjamin Franklin. Oration before the Democratic citizens of Worcester County ... 1839 Worcester, E. W. Bartlett, 1839. 48 p. 22 cm. 2-6422.
F65. H 18

HAWTHORNE, Nathaniel. Grandfather's chair: a history for youth. Boston, E. P. Peabody; N. Y., Wiley & Putnam, 1841. vii, (9) - 140p. 13 cm. First edition. Continued by his Famous old people, and Liberty tree, both pub. in Boston the same year. The three were afterward issued together under title: The whole history of grandfather's chair. 6-39286.
F65. H 34
Rare Book Coll.

— 2d ed. Boston, Tappan and Dennet, 1842. vii, (9) - 139 p. incl. front. 15½ cm. 17-14336.
F65. H3403
Rare Book Coll.

HAWTHORNE, Nathaniel. Famous old people: being the second epoch of Grandfather's chair. Boston, E. P. Peabody, 1841. vii, (9) - 158 p. 12½ cm. First ed. 6-39288.
F65. H3405
Rare Book Coll.

HAWTHORNE, Nathaniel. Liberty tree, with the last words of Grandfather's chair. Boston, E. P. Peabody, 1841. 160 p. 13 cm. 48-32615*.
F65. H3408
Rare Book Coll.

— Boston, Tappan and Dennet, 1842. viii, (9) - 156 p. incl. front. 16 cm. 6-39287.
F65. H341
Rare Book Coll.

HAWTHORNE, Nathaniel. True stories from history and biography. Boston, Ticknor, Reed and Fields, 1851. v, 335 p. 4 pl. (incl. front.) 17½ cm. 6-39285. Contents. - The whole history of grandfather's chair. - Biographical stories: Benjamin West. Sir Isaac Newton. Samuel Johnson. Oliver Cromwell. Benjamin Franklin. Queen Christina.
F65. H 35
Rare Book Coll.

— 1866. 352 p. front., 3 pl. 17½ cm. 6-40414.
F65. H 36

— 1879. (v) - vi, (9) - 290 p. 15 cm. 6-40773.
F65. H 37

HAWTHORNE, Nathaniel. ... True stories from New England history. Boston, N. Y., Houghton, Mifflin, 1883. 3 v. 18 cm. (Riverside literature series no. 7-9) 6-42202.
F65. H372

HAWTHORNE, Nathaniel. Grandfather's chair; a history for youth. N. Y., J. W. Lovell (1884) 225 p. 18½ cm. (Lovell's library ... v. 7, no. 376) 4-22953.
F65. H 38

— 1885. N. Y., J. B. Alden. 225 p. 19½ cm. 22-16581.
F65. H382

— N. Y., Maynard, Merrill, 1896. 1, 85 p. 16½ cm. (Maynard's English classic series no. 184) 14-1626.
F65. H385

— Rev. and enl. ed. Boston & New York, Houghton, Mifflin, 1896. xxvi, 226 p. illus., plates, 2 port. (incl. front.) facsim. 18 cm. (Riverside literature series nos. 7, 8, 9) 4-36347.
F65. H386

— Boston, N. Y., Chicago, Houghton, Mifflin. 190? xxvi, 307 p. incl. map. front., illus., plates, ports., facsim. 19½ cm. (The Riverside school library) 4-18087/5.
F65. H387

— N. Y., Boston, Thomas Y. Crowell (1898) iv, 245 p. col. front., plates. 17½ cm. 98-20 rev.
F65. H392

— Philadelphia, H. Altemus, 1898. 282 p. incl. illus (etc.) (Altemus' young peoples' lib. 98-1025 rev.
F65. H394

— N. Y., Boston, University pub. co., 1901. viii, 183 p. incl. front., illus., ports. 18½ cm. (Standard lit. ser. no. 46) 1-30593 rev.
F65. H398

HAWTHORNE, Nathaniel. True stories from N. England history, 1620-1803. N.Y. ... The Macmillan co., 1904. xxxii, 336 p. incl. front. 15 cm. (Macmillan's pocket Amer. & English classics) 4-26866. F65. H 4

HISTORIC American Buildings survey. Massachusetts catalog; list of measured drawings, photographs and written documentation in the Survey 1964. John C. Poppeliers, ed. (Boston, Mass. Hist. Commission) 1965. 69 p. 23 cm. 66-63291. F65. H 64

HITCHCOCK, Edward. Sketch of the scenery of Massachusetts ... Northampton, J.H. Butler, 1842. 75 p. illus., 14 pl. (incl. front.) 29 x 22 ½ cm. Extracted from his Final report on the geology of Mass. Amherst and Northampton, 1841. 6-40542. F65. H 67

HOLTON, Edith Austin. Yankees were like this. New York and London, Harper & bros., (1944) 5, 268 p. illus. 22 cm. "First edition." 44-8012. F65. H 74

KEIR, Robert Malcolm. ... Some influences of environment in Mass ... Lancaster, Pa., New era print., 1917. 25 p. front., illus. (maps, diagrs.) plates. 25 cm. Reprinted from the Bulletin of the Geographical soc. of Philadelphia, vol. xv, no. 3 and vol. xv, no. 4. 18-2749. F65. K 27

MASSACHUSETTS. General court. House of representatives. ... Report on the removal of the seat of government. (Boston, 1839) 16 p. 25 cm. 21-12503.
F65. M 4

MASSACHUSETTS Historical Commission. Massachusetts historic landmarks. (2d ed.) Boston, 1966. (24) p. 21 cm. 68-65386. F65. M 44 1966

MASSACHUSETTS. Special commission on the celebration of the tercentenary of the founding of the Mass. bay colony. Historical markers erected by Mass. bay colony tercentenary commission; ... Boston ... 1930. 39 (13) p. front., 1 illus., plates. 26 cm. 30-32739. F65. M 51

MASSACHUSETTS on the sea, 1630 - 1930, pub. by the commonwealth of Massachusetts ... Compiled by the Marine committee, appointed by Mass. Bay colony tercentenary commission. (Boston) 1930. 2, 32 p. plates. 26 ½ cm. 30-19269. F65. M 52

MASSACHUSETTS. Pathways of the Puritans, comp. by Mrs. N.S. Bell for the Massachusetts bay colony tercentenary commission. Framingham, Mass., Old America co. (c. 1930) xx, 212 p. front., plates, ports. 25 ½ cm. 30-30106 rev. F65. M 54

MUNROE, James Phinney. The New England conscience, with typical examples, ... Boston, R.G. Badger (c. 1915) 219 p. front., pl., ports. 19 ½ cm. 16-237. F65. M 96

SHANKLE, George Earlie. Massachusetts, state name, flag, seal, song, bird, flower, and other symbols ... and descriptive comments on the capitol building, etc. N.Y., H.W. Wilson co., 1933. 16 p. col. front., pl. 22 ½ cm. "A list of outstanding state histories": p. 14-15. 33-17975. F65. S 43

SIMMONS, James Raymond. The historic trees of Massachusetts. Boston, Marshall Jones co., 1919. xxi, 139 p. front., plates. 24 ½ cm. 19-17189. F65. S 59

TODD, Charles Burr. In olde Massachusetts; sketches of old times and places during the early days of the commonwealth. N.Y., The Grafton press (c. 1907) viii, 253 p. front., 13 pl. 20 cm. 7-23474. F65. T 63

U.S. General Accounting Office. Audit of Boston National Historic Sites Commission, April, 1961. Washington, 1961. 6 l. 27 cm. 61-61914. F65. U 6

WHITEFIELD, Edwin. The homes of our forefathers; being a collection of the oldest and most interesting buildings in Mass. Boston, A. Williams, 1879. 3 p. 22 col. pl. 18 ½ x 23 ½ cm. 6-20075. F65. W 57

— 3d ed. Boston, A. Williams, 1880. 3 p. 32 col. pl. 25 x 19 ½ cm. 6-20074. F65. W 58

MASSACHUSETTS

— New ed. Dedham, Mass., E. Whitefield, 1892.   2 p. 39 l. 39 mounted col. pl. 25 cm. 6-20073.   F65.W 59

— Boston, A. Williams co., 1879; c.1906.   3 p. 35 col. pl. 18½ x 25 cm. 15-14708.   F65.W593

WILLIAMS, Wilbur Herschel. Young people's story of Mass., by Herschel Williams ... illus. by E. F. Ward. N. Y., Dodd, Mead (c.1916)   viii p, 287 p. front., plates. 20½ cm. 16-20261.   F65.W 72

ANTIQUITIES.

MOOREHEAD, Warren King. The Merrimack archaeological survey ... with supplementary notes by Benjamin L. Smith on the Concord valley. Salem, Mass., Peabody museum, 1931.   79 p. illus., fold. map. 25 cm. 31-23345.   F66
F42.M4M7

NICHOLS, Arthur Howard. Bells of Paul and Joseph W. Revere. Boston, 1911.   40 p. front., plates. 25½ cm. Repr. from the Hist. colls. of the Essex institute, Salem, Mass. 12-7704.   F66
F69.R435

BULLEN, Ripley P. Excavations in northeastern Mass. Andover, Phillips Academy, 1949. xii, 152 p. illus., maps. 25 cm. (Papers of the Peabody Foundation for Archaeology) Bibliography p. 147-152. 49-48491*.   F66.B 84
E51.P56 vol. 1 no. 3

JOHNSON, Frederick. Grassy Island; archaeological and botanical investigations of an Indian site in the Taunton River. Andover, Mass., Phillips Academy, 1947.   viii, 68 p. illus., maps. 25 cm. (Papers of the Robert S. Peabody Foundation for Archaeology) Bibliography: p. (65) - 68. 48-265*.   F66.J6
E51.P56 vol. 1 no. 2

MASSACHUSETTS Archaeological Society. Bulletin. v. 1 - Attleboro (etc.) Mass. v. in illus., plates. 20 cm. quarterly. Began publication in 1939. Indexes: Vols. 1 - 17, 1939 - July 1956. 1 v. 44-31718 rev.*   F66.M368

MASSACHUSETTS archaeological society. Contributuions. Cambridge, Mass., 1941 - v. illus., plates. 24 cm. 41-11226.   F66.M 37

MASSACHUSETTS archaeological society. Miscellaneous printed matter published by this body is classififed in F66.M379

EARLY TO 1775.

ADAMS, Brooks. The emancipation of Massachusetts. Boston and N. Y., Houghton, Mifflin, 1887. vi, 382 p. 20 cm. 1-12027.   F67.A 21

— 2d ed. 1887.   vi, 382 p. 20 cm. 14-13154.   F67.A212

— Rev. and enl. ed. 1919.   vi, (3) - 534 p. 21½ cm. First ed. Boston, 1887. 19-14787.   F67.A 22

— With a new introduction by Perry Miller. Boston, Houghton, Mifflin, 1962.   534 p. 21 cm. (Sentry edition)   F67.A 22
1962

ADAMS, C. F. Antinomianism in the colony of Massachusetts Bay. 1636 - 1638 ... 1894. 4, (11) - 415 p. 22½ x 18 cm. Pubs. of the Prince society v. 21 3-24575.   F67.A225
Microfilm 8658 F

— N. Y., B. Franklin (1966)   415 p. 23 cm.   F67.A225
1966

ADAMS, Charles Francis. Three episodes of Massachusetts history: the settlement of Boston bay;

the Antinomian controversy; a study of church and town government.   Boston & N.Y., Houghton, Mifflin, 1892.   2 v. 2 fold. maps (incl. front.) 20½ cm. Paged continuously. 1-12010.   F67.A 23

— 1893.   2 v. 2 fold. maps (incl. front.) 20 cm. Paged continuously. v.1 532 p. v.2. (533) - 1067 p. 8-34787.   F67.A 24

— Rev.   New York, Russell & Russell, 1965 (c1892)   2 v. (1067 p.) 23 cm. 65-18782.
F67.A242

ADAMS, Herbert Baxter. ... Village communities of Cape Anne and Salem, from the historical collections of the Essex institute.   Baltimore, Johns Hopkins university, 1883.   2, 81 p. 23½ cm. (Johns Hopkins university studies in historical and political science ... (1st ser.) ix-x)   "The ... six papers have appeared in separate form, during the past two years, in the Historical collections of the Essex institute." 4-8532.   F67.A 25

ALLEN, Rowland Hussey.   The New-England tragedies in prose.   I. The coming of the Quakers. II. The witchcraft delusion.   Boston, Nichols and Noyes, 1869.   156 p. 19 cm. 1-7569* Cancel.
F67.A 42

AMERICAN antiquarian society.   Antiquarian papers.   Memorial of Gov. John Endecott, etc.   Worcester, C. Hamilton, 1879.   2, (3) - 78 p. front., port. 25 cm. From the Proceedings of the Amer. antiquarian soc., Oct. 21, 1873, and Oct. 21, 1878. 17-18146.   F67.A 5

AMERICAN legion.   National historian.   Report ... (1930)   v.   F67.A 54

ANDREWS, Henry Franklin.   List of freemen, Massachusetts Bay colony 1630 - 1691 ... (Exira, Ia.) Exira print., 1906.   (33) p. 26 cm. 7-41871.   F67.A 57

APPLETON, William Sumner.   The loyal petitions of 1666.   Remarks read before the Mass. hist. soc .. 1891.   Cambridge (Mass.) J. Wilson & son, 1891.   10 p. 24 cm.   8-14400.
F67.A 65

ATHERTON.   Hope Atherton and his times; a paper read by Arthur Holmes Tucker ... 1926. (Deerfield? 1926?)   4, 72 p. 25½ cm. 39-14766.   F67.A 85

BACHILER, Stephen, an unforgiven Puritan.   (By) Victor C. Sanborn.   Concord, N.H., N.H. hist. soc., 1917.   36 p. 23 cm. 18-11585.   F67.B 11

BACHILER, Rev. Stephen.   By Charles E. Batchelder.   (Boston, 1892)   23 p. 24½ cm. "Reprinted from the N.E. historical and genealogical register for Jan. 1892" 4-24805.   F67.B 12

BACHILER, Stephen and the Plough company of 1630.   By V.C. Sanborn ... Exeter (Mass.) W. Pollard & co. ltd., 1903.   15 p. 23½ cm. Reprinted from the Genealogist, vol. xix, April, 1903. 37-7901.   F67.B125

BANKS, Charles Edward.   The planters of the commonwealth; a study of the emigrants and emigration in colonial times: to which are added lists of passengers to Boston and to the Bay colony, etc. etc. Boston, Houghton Mifflin, 1930.   xiii, (3) - 231 p. front. (port.) maps, facsims. 25 cm. 31-211.
F67.B 19
Geneal. Section Ref.

— Baltimore, Genealogical pub. co., 1967.   xiii, 231 p. 24 cm. 67-30794.   F67.B 19
1967

BANKS, Charles Edward.   The Winthrop flett of 1630; an account of the vessels, the voyage, the passengers and their English homes ... Boston, Houghton, Mifflin, 1930.   4, (vii) - ix p., (3) - 118 p. front., plates, ports., 2 maps (1 fold.) facsims. 25 cm. 30-17289.   F67.B 21
Rare Book Coll.

— Baltimore, Genealogical Pub. Co., 1968.   ix, 118 p. illus. 23 cm. 68-57951.
F67.B 21
1968

MASSACHUSETTS 15

BARRINGTON, William Wildman Barrington. The Barrington-Bernard correspondence and illustrative matter, 1760 - 1770, drawn from the "Papers of Sir Francis Bernard" (sometime governor of Mass. - Bay) Cambridge, Harvard university ... 1912. xxiii, 306 p. 22 ½ cm. (Harvard historical studies vol. xvii) 13-1061.
F67.B 27

BAXTER, Joseph. The duty of a people to pray to, and bless God for their rulers ... A sermon ... Boston, Print. B. Green, 1727. 2, 36 p. 18 cm. 25-20015.
F67.B 35
Rare Book Coll.

BEAL, Boylston A. ... Speech, delivered at the Central reference library ... 1920. London, J. R. Want (1920) 8 p. 21cm. Borough of Southwark. Mayflower tercentenary celebration. A study of the "educational, literary, and artistic side of the Puritan movement in America". CA 26-835 unrev.
F67.B 37

BELCHER. Christ abolishing death and bringing life and immortality to light in the gospel. A sermon occasioned by the death of the Honourable Mary Belcher late consort of His Excellency our present governour. By Thomas Price. Boston, Print. J. Draper ... 1736. 41 p. 22 x 17 cm. 4-31968. F67.B 42
Rare Book Coll.

BIRCKHEAD. The Puritan's contribution to to-day ... (New York? 1910?) 14 p. 21 cm. 11-10450.
F67.B 61

BONAZZI, Tiziano. Il sacro esperimento. Teologia e politica nell'America puritana. Bologna, Il mulino, 1970. 515 p. 21 ½ cm.
F67. B 7

BOSTON. Citizens. To the King's most Excellent Majesty. The Humble Address of divers of the Gentry, Merchants and others ... Inhabiting in Boston, Charlestown and Places adjacent ... London, Print. Henry Hills, 1691. (Boston, 1928) facsim. 8 p. 25 cm. Photostat reproductions by the Mass. hist. soc. no. 212) CA 29-430 unrev.
F67.B 74
Rare Book Coll.

BOSTON herald. Scenes and characters of the Massachusetts Bay colony, 1630 - 1700. Souvenir ed. (Boston, Old colony distributing co., 1930) (18) p. col. illus. (incl. ports.) 23 x 30 ½ cm. 30-16385.
F67.B 75

BOURNE, Richard, missionary to the Mashpee Indians. By Mary Farwell Ayer. Boston, D. Clapp, 1908. 7 p. front. 25 cm. Repr. from the N.E. hist. and geneal. register for April, 1908. 16-21623.
F67.B 77

BRADFORD. The surrender of the Bradford manuscript. By Justin Winsor ... Cambridge (Mass.) J. Wilson and son, 1897. 8 p. 24 ½ cm. Repr. from the Proceedings of the Mass. hist. soc., Apr. 1897. 44-19682.
F67.B8W5

BRIEF state of the services and expences of the province of the Massachusett's Bay, in the common cause. London, J. Wilkie, 1765. 24 p. 21 cm. 9-6142.
F67.B 85
Rare Book Coll.

BROWN, Robert Eldon. Middle-class democracy and the Revolution in Mass., 1691 - 1780. Ithaca, Pub. for the Amer. Hist. Soc. by Cornell University Press (1955) ix, 458 p. 24 cm. Bibliography: p. 409-438. 56-13503.
F67.B 86

— New York, Russell & Russell (1968) ix, 458 p. 68-10906.
F67.B 86
1968

BRUCE, James F. ... Life and opinion in Mass. from 1630 - 1649. Sydney, W.A. Gullick, govt. printer, 1912. 35 p. 24 ½ cm. (New South Wales, the Teachers' college, Sydney. Records of the Education soc. no. 13) 12-23449.
F67.B 88

BULKELEY, Peter and his times, by Elizabeth Lowell Everett. Leominster, Mass., Goodhue print. (1935) 44 p. 21 cm. 38-24840.
F67.B 92

BURNET, William. Civil rulers raised up by God to feed his people. A sermon ... by Thomas

Prince ... Boston, Printed for Samuel Gerrish, 1728.   2, 24 p. 18 cm.   17-6690.   F67.B 96
                                                                                                 Rare Book Coll.

SABIN's reprints, quarto series (nos. 1 - 10.   N.Y., Reprinted for J. Sabin, 1865) 10 v. fold. map.
29½ x 23 cm. No more pub. 7-14884.   Contents. no. I. Byfield, N. An account of the late revolution in New-England. F67.B988.
no. II. A relation of Maryland. F184.R271.   no. III. Whitfield, H.A. A farther discovery of the present state of the Indians in New England.
E78.M4E4.   no. IV. Certain inducements to well minded people. F2016.C41.   no. V. Corporation for the promoting and propogating the gospel
of Jesus Christ in New England, London. Strength out of weakness. E78.M4E44.   no. VI. Corporation for the promoting and propogating the gospel
of Jesus Christ in New England, London.   A further manifestation of the progress of the gospel, among the Indians in New England. E78.M4E48.
VII. New England's first fruits. E78M4E32. no. VIII. E.S. Further queries upon the present state of the New-English affairs. F7.E. no.IX. (Wilson,
J.) supposed author.   The day breaking if not the sun rising of the gospel with the Indians in New England. E78.M4E34. no. X. Shepard, T. The
clear sunshine of the gospel breaking forth upon the Indians in New-England.   E78.M4E36.   F67.B988

COTTON, John, The life of.   By A.W. M'Clure ... Boston, Mass. Sabbath school soc., 1846.
xii, (13) - 300 p. 19½ cm.   (Lives of the chief fathers of New England ... vol. I) 5-39205.   F67.C
                                                                                                       F3.L68 v. 1

CAWEIN, Madison J.   An ode read .. 1907, at the dedication of the monument erected at Gloucester,
in commemoration of the founding of the Mass. Bay colony ... 1623.   Louisville, Ky., J.P. Morton,
1908.   25 p. 19½ cm.   "On old Cape Ann": p. (17) - 25.   20-2627.   F67.C 38

CENTINEL, Vincent, pseud.   Massachusetts in agony: or, Important hints to the inhabitants of the
province ... Boston, D. Fowle, 1750.   19 p. 22½ cm.   2-13748.   F67.C 39
                                                                                                        Rare Book Coll.

CHECKLEY, John; or, The evolution of religious tolerance in Massachusetts bay.   ... by the Rev.
Edmund F. Slafter ... Boston, The Prince soc., 1897.   2 v. front., facsim. 22 x 18 cm. Publications of the Prince
Soc. v. 22-23. 3-24560.rev.   F67.C 48
                                                                                                        E186.P85 vol. 22-23

CHILD, John.   New-England's Jonas cast up at London: or, A relation of the proceedings of the court
of Boston ... against divers honest and godly persons, for petitioning for government in the commonwealth ...   London, T.R. and E.M., 1647.   (22) p. 18 x 14 cm. 6-3824.   Reprint in Force, Peter .. Tracts ...
Washington D.C. v. 4 (1846) no. 3 E187.F69 vol. 4   F67.C 52
                                                                                                        Rare Book Coll.

— With an introd. and notes by W.T.R. Marvin.   Boston, W.P. Lund, 1869.   lii, 40 p. 20½ x 16½ cm.
1-19982.   F67.C 53

CHILD, Doctor Robert, the remonstrant, by George Lyman Kittredge ... Cambridge, J. Wilson, 1919.
        146 p. 25 cm.   Repr. from the Pubs. of the Colonial soc. of Massachusetts vol. xxi. 20-1091. F67.C 54

CINCINNATUS, L. Quincius, pseud.   A letter to the freeholders and other inhabitants of the Massachusetts-Bay, relating to their approaching election of representatives ... Boston, Rogers & Fowle
(1749?)   8 p. 19½ cm. 9-20815.   F67.C 57
                                                                                                        Rare Book Coll.

CLARKE, Herman Frederick.   John Hull, a builder of the Bay colony ... Portland, Me., 1940.
331 p. 26 cm.   F67.C 58

CLARKE, John.   Ill newes from New-England: or A narrative of New-Englands persecution.   Wherin
is declared that while old England is becoming new, New-England is becoming old.   London, Print.
H. Hills, 1652.   10 p. 76 p. 19 cm. 4-9695.   F67.C 59
                                                                                                        Rare Book Coll.

CONANT, Roger, and the early settlements on the north shore of Massachusetts, by Frances Rose-
Troup ... (n.p.) Print. Roger Conant family assoc., 1926.   18 p. 23½ cm. 35-30122.
                                                                                                        F67.C 72

CONANT, Roger, in America as governor and citizen; an historical address delivered at the Conant
family reuinion ... 1901, by Mrs. Sarah S. Bartlet. (Roxbury, Mass., 1901)   12 p. 1-20243.   F67.C 74

MASSACHUSETTS 17

CONANT, Roger, a founder of Massachusetts, by Clifford K. Shipton.   Cambridge, Mass., Harvard university press, 1944.   xii, 3-171 p. front., illus. (maps) plates (1 fold.) 22½ cm. A45-733 rev.
— Family edition supplement. (n. p., 1944)   175-197 p. pl. 23 cm.
F67.C755

COOK, Arthur Malcolm.   Lincolnshire links with the U. S. A.   With an introd. by the Earl of Ancaster Lincoln (Eng.) The Subdeanery, 1956.   90 p. illus. 19 cm. 56-46841.
F67.C757
L. H. & G.

COOKE, Elisha.   Mr. Cooke's just and seasonable vindication: respecting some affairs transacted in the late General Assembly at Boston, 1720.   (Boston, 1720)   20 p. 17 cm. 52-49958.
F67.C 76
Rare Book Coll.

CORNWELL, Sir George.   ... A dialogue between Sir George Cornwell, a gentleman lately arrived from England ... and Mr. Flint ... descended from a good family of the first settlers of New-England. ... Printed in London, and re-printed in Boston, 1769.   14 p. 19 cm. A satirical description of the leading Tories of Boston, 1769. 13-22246.
F67.C 8
Rare Book Coll.

COTTON, John.   Gods promise to His plantation.   London, Print, W. Jones for J. Bellamy. ... 1630.   20 p. 18 cm. L.C. copy imperfect. 49-56418*.
F67.C 83
Rare Book Coll.

— Boston, 1894.   19 cm.
F67.C 84

— Boston, 1894.   16 p. 19 cm. (Old South leaflets. 12th series. 1894. no. 6)
F67.C 85

COTTON.   A letter to a friend in the country, etc. (on the Memorial of Mr. Roland Cotton) (Boston, 1740)   11 p. 20½ cm. 21-4838 rev.
F67.C 86
Rare Book Coll.

CRADOCK, Sir Mathew, Historical discourse on the life, deeds and character of.   By David Roberts. Salem, Mass.. Ives and Pease, print., 1856.   16 p. 23 cm. 7-20547.
F67.C 88

CUSING, Abel.   Historical letters on the first charter of Massachusetts government.   Boston, J. N. Bang, print., 1839.   (11) - 204 p. 15 cm. 1-12028*.
F67.C 98

DAWES, Mrs. Sarah Elizabeth.   Colonial Massachusetts; stories of the Old Bay state.   New York, Boston, etc. Silver, Burdett,, 1899.   187 p. illus. 20 cm. 99-2515 rev.
F67.D 27

DEANE, Charles.   The forms in issuing letter-patent by the crown of England, with some remarks on the Massachusetts charter ... by Charles Deane ... Cambridge, J. Wilson, 1870.   24 p. 24½ cm. 1-12029.
F67.D 29

DENISON, Major-General Daniel.   (Boston? 1869)   24 p. 25½ cm. N.E. hist. and geneal. register, July, 1869, by Daniel Denison Slade. 12-11170.
F67.D 39

DIKE, Norman Staunton.   Narrative of Anthony Dike; ... (Cambridge, Mass., Shea bros. print., 1942.   44 p. 23 cm. 42-24196.
F67.D 56

DOW, George Francis.   Every day life in the Massachusetts bay colony.   Boston, The Society for the preservation of New England antiquities, 1935.   xii, 293 p. front., illus., plates, ports., facsims. 26 cm. 36-1841.
F67.D 68

— New York, B. Blom (1967)   viii, 290 p. 90 plates. 24 cm. 67-13326.
F67.D 68
1967

DOWNING, Emanuel.   By Frederick Johnson Simmons.   (Montclair, N. J.) 1958.   93 p.
F67.D69S5

DUDLEY. Ossa Josephi. Or, The bones of Joseph. ... preached ... after the funeral of the very Honourable and excellent Joseph Dudley, esq; late governor of His Majesty's provinces of the Massachusetts-Bay ... By Benjamin Colman. Boston, print. B. Green, for Benj. Eliot, 1720. 2 p., iv, 44, (3) p. 18½ cm. 19-15062. F67. D 79 Rare Book Coll.

DUDLEY, Joseph, The public life of; a study of the colonial policy of the Stuarts in New England, 1660-1715, by Everett Kimball ... New York, etc. Longmans, Green, 1911. viii, 239 p. 23 cm. Harvard historical studies ... vol. xv. 11-16293. F67. D 8

DUDLEY, Thomas. Gov. Thomas Dudley's letter to the Countess of Lincoln, March, 1631. With explanatory notes, by Dr. John Farmer ... Washington, P. Force, 1838. 19 p. 23½ cm. (Force Tracts v. 2 no. 4) 4-27027*. F67. D 83

— (Rochester, G. P. Humphrey, 1898) 3, 17 p. 24 cm. American colonial tracts monthly v. 2 no. 4. 4-27022*. F67. D 84

DUDLEY, Thomas, The life and work of, the second governor of Massachusetts, by Augustine Jones ... Boston and N.Y., Houghton, Mifflin, 1899. xi, 484 p. front., plates, facsims. 22½ cm. 99-2120 rev. F67. D 85

DUDLEY, Thomas - 1576 - 1653, governor of Massachusetts Bay colony ... by George Ellsworth Koues. (New York, 1912) 11 p. 23 cm. (Society of colonial wars in the state of New York. Pub. no. 20) 14-12717. F67. D853

DUDLEY, Thomas, The life of, several times governor of the colony of Massachusetts. Written, as is supposed, by Cotton Mather. Ed. Charles Deane. Cambridge (Mass.) Press of J. Wilson, 1870. 20 p. 24½ cm. 100 copies reprinted from Proceedings of the Mass. historical soc. 7-31018. F67. D856

DUMMER. The vanity of every man at his best estate. A funeral sermon on the Hon. William Dummer ... By Mather Byles. Print. Green & Russell, Boston, 1761. 224, 3 p. 19½ x 15 cm. 7-31019. F67. D882

DUNSTER papers. By John T. Hassam. Cambridge, J. Wilson, 1895. 10 p. 24 cm. 7-6957 rev. F67. D 92

DUNTON, John. Letters written from New England, by John Dunton. (New York, B. Franklin (1966) xxiv, 340 p. 23 cm. (American classics in history and social science, 2; Franklin Research and source works series, 131) F67. D 94 1966

DYER, David. A discourse, on the characteristics of the Puritans ... Boston, Press of T. R. Marvin, 1846. 24 p. 23½ cm. 17-12088. F67. D 97

DYER. Mary Dyer, Quaker; two letters of William Dyer of Rhode Island, 1659 - 1660. (Cambridge, Mass., Print. for W. C. Ford by the University Press, n. d.) (13) p. (in portfolio) 37 cm. Each letter reproduced in facsimile and accompanied by a transcription. 48-37617*. F67. D987

DYER, Mary, of Rhode Island, the Quaker martyr that was hanged on Boston common, June 1, 1660; by Horatio Rogers ... Providence, Preston and Rounds, 1896. (v) - vi, 115 p. 19½ cm. 7-32951. F67. D 99

DYER, William, a Somerset royalist in New England. By Louis Dyer. (Sherborne? 1899?) 7, 4, 4 p. 21 cm. Reprinted from Notes and queries for Somerset and Dorset vol. vi p. 269-73, 303-06, 353-56. 9-30675. F67. D994

EARLY Massachusetts history. Boston, Old South meeting house, 1883. (Old South leaflets. I) 4-15753. F67. E 13

ECLIPSE, The. (Boston) 1754. 8 p. 20 cm. A tract published in opposition to a proposed excise measure in Massachusetts. 8-3839. F67. E 19 Rare Book Coll.

ELLIS, George Edward. I. The aims and purposes of the founders of Massachusetts. II. Their treatment of intruders and dissentients. Two lectures ... By George E. Ellis. Boston, J. Wilson, 1869. 100 p. 24½ cm. 16-10388. F67.E 44

ELLIS, George Edward. The Puritan age and rule in the colony of the Massachusetts Bay, 1629-1685. Boston & N.Y., Houghton, Mifflin, 1888. xix, 576 p. 2 maps. 23½ cm. L.C. Copy replaced by microfilm. 1-12036.
F67.E 47
Microfilm 8786 F

— New York, B. Franklin, (1970) xix, 576 p. 23 cm. 75-122838. F67.E 47 1970

ENDICOTT, Charles Moses. Memoir of John Endicott, first governor of the colony of Massachusetts Bay ... Salem, Print. Observer office, 1847. 116 p. front. (port.) 30 x 24 cm. 7-31287.
F67.E 54

ENDICOTT, John. Address at the commemoration of the landing of John Endicott ... By William C. Endicott. Salem, Print, the Salem press, 1879. 38 p. 23 cm. 19-10562. F67.E 55

ENDECOTT. John Endecott and John Winthrop; address by William C. Endicott ... Boston, Mass. (Thomas Tood co.) 1930. 32 p. front., pl., ports. 24 cm. 31-3121. F67.E553

ENDECOTT, John; a biography, by Lawrence Shaw Mayo ... Cambridge, Mass., Harvard university press, 1936. 6, (3) - 301 p. front. (port.) plates, map, 2 facsims. 26 cm. 36-37511.
F67.E557

— St. Clair Shore, Mich., Scholarly Press, 1971. 301 p. 22 cm. 78-145171. F67.E557 1971

ENDECOTT wills, inventories, and matters connected with the estate of Governor John Endecott ... By Robert Samuel Rantoul. Salem, Mass., Salem press, 1889. 23 p. 25 cm. Reprinted from Historical colls. Essex institute, vol. xxv, 1888. 3-3178. F67.E 56

ENDECOTT. ... A note on the authenticity of the portraits of Gov. Endecott. By Robert S. Rantoul. (Salem? Mass., 1883?) 19 p. 24½ cm. From Historical colls. of the Essex institute, v.20 p. 1-18.
F67.E564

ENDECOTT. A memorial of Governor John Endecott. Read before the American antiquarian soc. ... By Stephen Salisbury ... Worcester, Mass., Print C. Hamilton, 1874. 44 p. 25½ cm. 7-31316.
F67.E568

ENGLISH advice to the freeholders, etc. of the province of the Massachusetts-Bay. Boston, Print. James Franklin in Queen-street. 1722. 6 p. 17½ cm. Signed "Brutus" - "Cato." 2-19351.
F67.E 58
Rare Book Coll.

ESSEX institute. The fifth half century of the arrival of John Winthrop, at Salem, Mass. Commemorative exercise by the Essex institute, June 22, 1880. Salem, 1880. 64 p. 25 cm. 4-29767.
F67.E 78

EVERETT, Edward. An address delivered ... 1830 ... the anniversary of the arrival of Governor Winthrop at Charlestown. Charlestown, W. W. Wheildon; Boston, Carter and Hendee, 1830. 51 p. 24 cm. 7-23554. F67.E 93

EVERETT, Elizabeth Lowell. Ye governour and companie of Massachusetts bay. Philadelphia, Dorrance & co., (c. 1931) 187 p. 21½ cm. Bibliography: p. 185-187. 31-35530. F67.E 95

FETL, Joseph Barlow. Who was the first governor of Massachusetts? Boston, Press of T. R. Marvin, 1853. 17 p. 23 cm. 1-12031. F67.F32

FISHER, Herbert Albert Laurens. The Bay colony; a tercentenary address, Boston and N.Y.,

Houghton, Mifflin, 1930. viii, 52 p. 22½ cm. 30-19746. F67.F 52

FOSTER. The character and blessedness of a diligent and faithful servant: a sermon delivered at Brookfield, 1779, at the funeral of the Honourable Jedediah Foster ... By Nathan Fiske. Providence, Print. Bennett Wheeler (1779) 30, (7) p. 21½ cm. Imperfect. 9-13134. F67.F54
Rare Book Coll.

FOXCROFT. A funeral-discourse preached after the death of the honourable Francis Foxcroft ... By Nathaniel Appleton. Boston, Print. for S. Gerrish, 1728. 31 p. 17 cm.
F67.F6A67
Rare Book Coll.

FRANKLAND, Agnes (Surriage) lady. The barefoot maid at the Fountain inn, by Charles Edward Cheney. (Chicago) Chicago literary club, 1912. 2, 7-40 p. 19 cm. 12-17467.
F67.F 83

FRANKLAND, Sir Charles Henry, baronet; or Boston in the colonial times. By Elias Nason ... Albany, J. Munsell, 1865. (7)-129 p. 22 cm. (Munsell's series of local American history, no. 2) 3-11690.
F67.F 84

GOODELL, Abner Cheney. An address delivered in the Old South meeting house in Boston,, Nov. 27, 1895 ... in commemoration of the 600th anniversary of the first summoning of citizens and burgesses to the Parliament of England ... Boston, The Rockwell and Churchill press, 1897. 36 p. 23½ cm. 10-223. F67.G 64

GOOKIN, Frederick William. Daniel Gookin, 1612 - 1687, assistant and major general of the Massachusetts Bay Colony; his life and letters and some account of his ancestry ... Chicago, priv. print. (R.R. Donnelley) 1912. xvi, 207 p. incl. front., illus., plates, facsims. (1 fold.) coats of arms. 26½ cm. 13-3081. F67.G 65
Rare Book Coll.

GREAT Britain. Privy council. The report of the Lords of the committee upon Governour Shute's memorial, with His Majesty's order in council thereupon. (London? 1725) 10 p. 8°. Title-page and p. 1-2 supplied in ms. 1-21434-M1. F67.G 78
Rare Book Coll.

GREEN, Samuel Abbott. Ten fac-simile reproductions relating to New England, by Samuel Abbott Green. Boston, Mass., 1902. 4, 54 p. illus., facsim. 37 x 27½ cm. Contents. - Stephen Daye, the earliest printer in this country - Map of Mass., 1637. - Benjamin Thompson, the earliest American poet. - The names of streets, etc. in Boston, 1708. - Blodget's plan of the battle near Lake George, 1755. - The stamp act, 1765. - The seat of war, near Boston, 1775. - Gen. Rufus Putnam's plan of towns in Worcester County, 1785. - Dr. Prescott's plan of Groton, Mass., 1794. - State street, Boston, 1801. 2-28280. F67.G 81
Rare Book Coll.

— Boston, Mass., 1903. 4, 36 p. 23 facsim. 37 x 27½ cm. 3-31448. Contents. - Some engraved portraits of the Mather family. - The south and north batteries. - An early Boston imprint, 1681. - The Boston news-letter, 1704. - Reprints of early Boston newspapers. - Panorama of Boston, 1775. - The midnight ride of Paul Revere. - The battle of Bunker Hill. - The crossed swords. - Lawrence Academy, Groton, Mass.
F67.G 82

GREENOUGH, Chester Noyes. John Dunton's Letters from New England, ... Cambridge, J. Wilson, 1912. (213)-257 p. facsim. 25½ cm. Repr. from the Pubs. of the Colonial soc. of Mass. vol. xiv. 13-16009. F67.G 85

GRIDLEY, Jeremy. paper read before the society, ... 1902, by R.G.F. Candage. Brookline, Mass., The Society, 1903. 32 p. front. 25 cm. (Pubs. of the Brookline historical soc. no. 1) 7-15396. F67.G 86

GRIFFITH, Roy Brady. Skilled labor, the Puritan heritage. Cambrige, Mass., The Perry-Estabrook press, 1924. 2, 3-14 p. front. 27½ cm. 24-23945 rev. F67.G863

GROSVENOR, William Mercer. The Puritan remnant ... The twelfth annual sermon of the New England society in the city of New York ... (New York, 1911) 11 p. 21 cm. 18-18941.
F67.G 87

MASSACHUSETTS

HALL, George D., company. Official chronicle and tribute book; containing a record of the establishment of the Massachusetts Bay colony in New England by the Puritans, and the setting up of independent government in America ... (Boston) 1930.   448 p. incl. front. (map) illus., ports. 30 cm. 30-19747.
    F67.H 16

HALLOWELL, Richard Price. The Quaker invasion of Massachusetts. Boston, Houghton, Mifflin, 1883.   vi, 227 p. 18½ cm. 7-32914.
    F67.H 18

— 3d ed. Boston, 1884.   vi, 227 p. 18½ cm. 7-32936.
    F67.H 19

HARVARD. John Harvard's life in America; or, Social and political life in New England in 1637-1638, by Andrew McFarland Davis ... Cambridge, J. Wilson, 1908.   45 p. 24½ cm. "Reprinted from the Pubs. of the Colonial society of Mass. vol. xii. 8-20366.
    F67.H 33

HARVARD, John, and his times, by Henry C. Shelley ... with illus. from photos. Boston, Little, Brown, 1907.   xiv, 331 p. front., plates, ports., plan, facsim. 21½ cm. 7-34809.
    F67.H 34

HAVEN, Samuel Foster. A brief passage at arms in relation to a small point of history. (Worcester, Mass., Press of C. Hamilton, 1877)   29 p. 25½ cm. A discussion of the question whether Endecott and his company embarked in a single ship. Papers pub. in the Boston daily advertiser in 1850. 2-19316.
    F67.H 38

HIGGINSON, Rev. Francis, Memoir of. By Joseph B. Felt ... Boston, T. Prince, print., 1852.   1, 23 p. 23½ cm. 11-22514.
    F67.H 63

HIGGINSON, T. W., Life of. ... (1891)   1 v.
    F67.H633

HILLS, Joseph, and the Massachusetts laws of 1648. Reprinted from the History of Malden, Mass. 1633 - 1785. By Deloraine P. Corey. Boston, W. S. Hills, 1899.   1, (165) - 185 p. 23 cm. 11-24441.
    F67.H 65

HISTORICAL digest of the provinical press; being a collation of all items of personal and historic reference relating to American affairs printed in the newspapers of the provincial period beginning with the appearance of The present state of the New-English affairs, 1689 ... and ending with the close of the revolution, 1783 ... Massachusetts series, vol. one. Comp. and ed. under direction of Lyman H. Weeks and others. Boston, The Society for americana, inc., 1911.   xiii, 564 p. front., plates, ports., facsims. (part double) 24½ cm. "List of authorities": p. 11 - 18. No. more pub. Contents. - 1689 - 1707. 11-13734 rev.
    F67.H 67
    E187.H67

HOWE, Daniel Wait. The Puritan republic of the Massachusetts Bay in New England. ... Indianapolis, The Bowen-Merrill co. (1899)   xxxviii, 422 p. 23½ cm. "Table of citations": p. xxxiii - xxxviii. 99-5081 rev.
    F67.H 85

HUTCHINSON, Mrs. Anne (Marbury) Scarlet Anne, by Theda Kenyon. New York, Doubleday, Doran, 1939.   4, 312 p. 20 cm. A narrative poem. "First edition." Bibliography: p. 308. 39-3794.
    F67.H 9
    PS3521.E62S3 1939

HUMFREY, John, Massachusetts magistrate; did he marry the daughter of the third Earl of Lincoln? By Elroy McKendree Avery. Cleveland, 1912.   22 p. 23 cm. An answer to the New York times. 12-19128.
    F67.H 9

HUTCHINSON, Anne. An American Jezebel; the life of Anne Hutchinson, by Helen Augur. New York, Brentano's (c. 1930)   5, 3-320 p. incl. facsim. front., ports. 22 cm. Bibliography: p. 305-313. 30-6384.
    F67.H906

HUTCHINSON, Anne. Saints and sectaries; Anne Hutchinson and the Antinomian controversy in the Massachusetts Bay colony. Williamsburg, Va., Pub. for the Institute of Early Amer. Hist. and Culture, by the University of N. C. Press. (1962)   379 p. 24 cm.
    F67.H907

HUTCHINSON, Anne. A woman misunderstood; Anne, wife of William Hutchinson, by Reginald Pelham Bolton ... New York (Print. for the author by the Schoen print. co.) 1931. ix, 137 p. 23½ cm.
"Bibliographic memoranda": p. 135-137. 31-4305.
  F67.H908

HUTCHINSON, Mrs. Anne; a paper read before the N. E. historic genealogical soc. ... 1901, by Prof. Henry Leland Chapman, of Bowdoin college. (Boston? 1901) 27 p. 24½ cm. 12-11171.
  F67.H 91

HUTCHINSON, Anne; a biography, by Edith Curtis, with an introduction by M. A. De Wolfe Howe. Cambridge, Washburn & Thomas, 1930. xi, 122 p. 20 cm. 30-10230 rev.
  F67.H914

HUTCHINSON, Anne. A colony leader; Anne Hutchinson, by Doris Faber. Illus. by Frank Vaughn. Champaign, Ill., Garrard Pub. Co. (1970) 64 p. illus. 24 cm. (Colony leaders) 75-111907.
  F67.H92 F3

HUTCHINSON, Anne. The Antinomian controversy. 1636 - 1638; a documentary history. Ed. with introd. and notes, by David D. Hall. (1st ed.) Middletown, Conn., Wesleyan University Press (c. 1968) viii, 447 p. 24 cm. First ed. 68-17148.
  F67.H92H3

HUTCHINSON, Anne. Unafraid; a life of Anne Hutchinson, by Winnifred King Rugg. Freeport, N.Y., Books for Libraries Press (1970) xii, 263 p. port. 23 cm. 73-114891.
  F67.H92R8
  1970

HUTCHINSON, Ann, in Mass. By T. Hutchinson. ... 1907. v.
  F67.H 93

HUTCHINSON, Anne. Unafraid; a life of Anne Hutchinson, by Winnifred King Rugg. Boston and New York, Houghton Mifflin, 1930. xiii, 263 p. front. 22½ cm. "Works consulted": p. (255) - 257. 30-4549.
  F67.H932

HUTCHINSON, Thomas. The life of Thomas Hutchinson, royal governor of the province of Massachusetts Bay, by James K. Hosmer ... Boston and N.Y., Houghton, Mifflin, 1896. xxviii, 453 p. front. (port.) pl., fold. facsim. 23 cm. 4-17030/4. L.C. copy replaced by microfilm.
  F67.H935
  Microfilm 18510 F

HUTCHINSON, Thomas. ... Copy of letters sent to Great Britain, by His Excellency Thomas Hutchinson, the Hon. Andrew Oliver, and several other persons, ... Boston, print. Edes and Gill, 1773. (In Hosmer, James K. The life of Thomas Hutchinson. Boston, 1896. p. 429 - 442) L.C. copy replaced by microfilm. 12-8923.
  F67.H935
  Microfilm 18510 F

HUTCHINSON, Thomas. The diary and letters of His Excellency Thomas Hutchinson ... captain-general and governor-in-chief of ... Massachusetts Bay ... Comp. ... By Peter Orlando Hutchinson ... London, S. Low, Marston, Searle & Rivington, 1883-86. 2 v. fronts., illus., col. pl., facsim. 23 cm. L.C. copy replaced by microfilm. "Pedigree of Hutchinson of Lincolnshire": v.2, p. 456-478. 4-31132.
  F67.H 94
  Microfilm 8659 F

— New York, B. Franklin (1971) 2 v. 73-132679.
  F67.H 94
  1971

HUTCHINSON, Thomas. A collection of original papers relative to the History of the colony of Massachusetts-bay. Boston, Print. Thomas and John Fleet, 1769. 1, ii, 576 p. 20½ cm. 1-12032.
  F67.H 95
  Rare Book Coll.

HUTCHINSON, Thomas. The history of ... Massachusetts Bay ... Boston, Print. Thos. & John Fleet, 1764-1828. 3 v. 20 - 22½ cm. Vol. 2 contains index to v.1-2 1-13583.
  F67.H 96
  Rare Book Coll.

MASSACHUSETTS 23

— 2d ed.   London, M. Richardson, 1765 - 1828.   3 v. 20 - 21 cm.   1-13584 add.   F67.H 97

— Ed. from the author's ms., by ... John Hutchinson.   London, J. Murray, 1828.   xx, 551 p. 20 cm.
(His History of ... Mass. Bay. 2d ed. 1765-1828 v. 3) 1-12528.   F67.H 97 v.3

— 3d ed.   With additional notes and corrections.   Salem (Mass.) Print. Thomas C. Cushing, for Thomas and Andrews, Boston, 1795-1828.   3 v. 22½ cm. 1-13585 rev.
F67.H 98
Rare Book Coll.

HUTCHINSON, Thomas.   Additions to Thomas Hutchinson's History of Massachusetts Bay, ed. Catherine Barton Mayo.   Worcester, The Society, 1949.   (11) - 74 p. 25 cm. "Reprinted from the Proceedings of the American Antiquarian Soc. for April 1949." 50-14268.   F67.H9803
1949

HUTCHINSON, Thomas, royal governor of the province of Massachusetts Bay.   By James Kendall Hosmer.   New York, Da Capo Press, 1972 (c.1896)   xxviii, 453 p. illus. 22 cm. (The American scene: comments and commentators) 70-124926.   F67.H9806
1972

HUTCHINSON, Thomas.   The faithful man abounding with blessings.   A funeral discourse upon the death of the Honourable Thomas Hutchinson, esq ... 1739. By Samuel Mather ... Boston: Print. J. Draper, for N. Proctor, 1740.   1, 32 p. 19 cm. 46-41030.   F67.H9807
Rare Book Coll.

HUTCHINSON, Thomas.   Index of persons and places mentioned in Hutchinson's Massachusetts (last ed. of vol. I and II., Boston, 1795, and only ed. of vol. III, London, 1828) Made by J. Wingate Thornton ...   N.Y., 1879.   15 p. 24 cm. 1-12033.   F67.H981

HUTCHINSON, Thpmas.   The history of the colony and province of Massachusetts-bay.   Ed. from the author's own copies of vols. I & II and his manuscript of vol. III, with a memoir and additional notes, by Lawrence Shaw Mayo.   Cambridge, Mass., Harvard university press, 1936.   3 v. 24½ cm.
36-12398.   F67.H985

JEFFERSON, Charles Edward.   "The Puritan vision of God" ... The sixth annual sermon preached before the New England society in the city of New York ... 1905, by the Rev. Charles E. Jefferson ... (N.Y.) Print. by order of the Society (1905?)   21 p. 21 cm. 18-15732.   F67.J 45

JOHNSON, Edward.   A history of New-England.   From the English plantation in the yeere 1628 until the yeere 1652. ... With the names of all their governors, magistrates, and eminent ministers ... London, Print. for N. Brooke, 1654.   2, 239 (i.e.236) p. 18½ cm. Paging irregular. Rc-2724 rev.   F67.J 66
Rare Book Coll.

JOHNSON, Edward.   Wonder-working providence of Sions Saviour in New England.   London, 1654. With an historical introduction and an index by William Frederick Poole ... Andover (Mass.) W.F. Draper, 1867.   4, cliv, (2), 265 p. front. (facsim.) 23½ cm. Reprint of original ed. 1-Rc-2725.   F67.J 67

JOHNSON, Edward.   ... Johnson's Wonder-working providence, 1628 - 1651; ed. J. Franklin Jameson ... with a map and two facsims.   N.Y., C. Scribner's sons, 1910.   viii, 3-285 p. fold. map, 2 facsim. (incl. front.) 22½ cm. (Half-title: Original narratives of early American history) 10-9809.   F67.J675

KILBY, Christopher; a memoir prepared for the New-England historical and genealogical register for Jan. 1872, by Charles W. Tuttle.   Boston, Print, D. Clapp, 1872.   11 p. 24½ cm. 3-27043.
F67.K 48

KING, Henry Melville.   Early Baptists defended.   A review of Dr. Henry M. Dexter's account of the visit to William Witter, in "As to Roger Williams."   Boston, H. Gannett, 1880.   49 p. 18½ x 15½ cm.
An enlarged edition pub. Providence, 1896, under title: A summer visit of three Rhode Islanders to the Massachusetts Bay in 1651. 6-16528.
F67.K 51

KING, Henry Melville. A summer visit of three Rhode Islanders to the Massachusetts Bay in 1651. ... Providence, Preston and Rounds, 1896.   vi, (7) - 115 p. 19½ cm. First ed., Boston, 1880, pub. under title: Early Baptists defended ... 1-12034.
    F67.K 52

LAWRENCE, Henry Wells. The not-quite Puritans; some genial follies and peculiar frailties of our reverend New England ancestors ... Boston, Little, Brown, 1928.   x, (3) - 228 p. front., plates, facsims. 21 cm. "Authorities": p. (225) - 228. 28-23640.
    F67.L 42

LECHFORD, Thomas. Note-book kept by Thomas Lechford ... in Boston ... 1638 - 1641. Cambridge, W. Wilson, 1885.   2, xxviii, 460 p. 25 cm. Archaeologia Americana. Transactions and collections of the American antiquarian soc. vol. vii) 6-34789.
    F67.L 45

LEE, Samuel. Letters of Samuel Lee and Samuel Sewall relating to New England and the Indians, ed. George Lyman Kittredge ... Cambridge, J. Wilson, 1912.   1, (142) - 186 p. 24½ cm. "Reprinted from the Pubs. of the Colonial society of Mass., vol. xiv" 25-14368.
    F67.L 47

LETTER to a gentleman chosen to be a member of the honourable House of representatives, to be assembled at Boston on Feb. 10, 1731. (Boston, 1731)   16 p. 18 cm. 1-12035 rev.
    F67.L 65
    Rare Book Coll.

LETTER to the freeholders, and qualified voters, relating to the ensuing election ... Boston, Print. Rogers and Fowle, 1749.   12 p. 20 x 15½ cm. 7-23954.
    F67.L 66
    Rare Book Coll.

LEVERETT. — Report of (the New England Historic Genealogical Society's) Heraldic Committee on the question Was John Leverett a knight?. Boston, D. Clapp, 1881.   vi, 22 p. 24 cm. "Reprint from the New-England historical and genealogical register for July and Oct., 1881." 34-36152.
    F67.L6615

LEVERET, John, A sermon preached upon ... the death of. By Samuel Willard. Boston, Print. John Foster, 1679.   13 p. 19½ cm. 18-14589.
    F67.L662
    Rare Book Coll.

LINCOLN, Waldo. The province snow, "Prince of Orange." From Proceedings of the Amer. antiquarian soc. ... 1901. Worcester, Mass., Press of C. Hamilton, 1901.   57 p. 24½ cm. 2-2987-M2.
    F67.L 73

LYNDE, Benjamin. The diaries of Benjamin Lynde and of Benjamin Lynde, jr,; with an appendix. Boston, Priv. print. (Cambridge, Riverside press) 1880.   xvi, 251 p. front., ports., facsim., geneal. tab. 22 cm. "Family of Lynde" p. (iii) -(xvi). Pedigree of Browne and Lynde. 3-4167.
    F67.L 98

MAULE, Thomas. An abstract of a letter to Cotton Mather. (N.Y., Print. William Bradford, 1701. (Boston, 1936)   facsim. 19 p. 23 cm. (Photostat Americana. 2d series, no. 10) 37-15956.
    F67.M
    BX7730.M35
    Rare Book Coll.

McSPADDEN, Joseph Walker. Massachusetts; a romantic story for young people. illus. Howard L. Hastings. New York, J.H. Sears (c. 1926)   128 p. incl. illus., plates, col. front. 21 cm. (Romantic stories of the states) Maps on lining papers. 26-15382.
    F67.M 18

MASSACHUSETTS (Colony) A journall or daye book. (1907)
    F67.M 28

MASSACHUSETTS (Colony) Records of the governor and Company of the Massachusetts Bay. 1853 - 54.   5 v. in 6. fol.
    F67.M 32

MASSACHUSETTS (Colony) Council. Letters of the Right Honorable Earl of Hillsborough. 1769. 1 v.
    F67.M325

MASSACHUSETTS (Colony) Council. Letters to the Right Honorable the Earl of Hillsborough ...

MASSACHUSETTS

(1769?) 165 p. 21½ cm.
 F67.M327
 Rare Book Coll.

MASSACHUSETTS (Colony) Records of the Court of assistants of the colony of the Massachusetts Bay, 1630 - 1692 ... Boston, Pub. by the county of Suffolk, 1901-28. 3 v. front., illus., facsims. (1 double) 25½ cm. Contents. - v.1. 1673 - 1692. v.2, pt. 1. 1630 - 1641. - pt. 2. 1641 - 1644. - v.3. Restored fragments of records from 1642 to 1673. 10-5835 rev.
 F67.M33

MASSACHUSETTS (Colony) A Declaration of the General Court of the Massachusetts ... 1659. Concerning the execution of two Quakers. Printed by their order in New-England. Reprinted in London, 1659. (Boston, 1927) facsim. broadside. 33½ x 25 cm. fold. to 19 x 12½ cm. (American series; photostats by the Mass. hist. soc. no. 194) CA 28-251 unrev.
 F67.M334
 Rare Book Coll.

MASSACHUSETTS (Colony) A true Relation of the Proceedings against certain Quakers, at the generall Court of the Massachusetts ... 1659. London, print by A.W. 1660. (Boston, 1927) facsim. broadside. 33 x 25 cm. fold. to 19 x 12½ cm. (Americana series; photostats by the Mass. hist. soc. no. 194) CA 28-252 unrev.
 F67.M334
 Rare Book Coll.

MASSACHUSETTS (Colony) The humble petition and address of the General court sitting at Boston ... unto the high and mighty prince Charles the Second. ... 1660. 8 p. 18½ x 14½ cm. 18-3700.
 F67.M335
 Rare Book Coll.

MASSACHUSETTS (Colony) Gov. John Endecot's humble petition ... (1916)
 F67.M336

MASSACHUSETTS (Colony) Copy of the complaint ... against Sir Francis Bernard ... (n. p. 1770?) 15 p. 22½ cm.
 F67.M339 or M34
 Rare Book Coll.

MASSACHUSETTS (Colony) The proceedings of the Council, and the House of representatives of the province of the Massachusetts-Bay, relative to the convening, holding and keeping the General assembly at Harvard-college in Cambridge: ... Boston, Print. Edes and Gill ... 1770. 83 p. 22 cm. 3-32075 rev.
 F67.M342
 Rare Book Coll.

MASSACHUSETTS (Colony) A continuation of the proceedings ... relative to the convening, holding and keeping the General assembly at Harvard-college, in Cambridge. Boston, Edes and Gill, print., 1770. 66 p. 20 cm. Bound with the above, copy 2. 20-11365.
 F67.M342
 Rare Book Coll.

MASSACHUSETTS (Colony) The humble request ... (1905)
 F67.M35

MASSACHUSETTS (Colony) The Puritans farewell to England ... the humble request ... 1912.
 F67.M36

MASSACHUSETTS (Colony) The explanatory charter granted by H.M. King George to the province of the Massachusetts-Bay in New-England. (Boston, 1725) (Boston, 1940) facsim. 8 p. 21 cm. (Photostat Americana. Second series, no. 116. Photostated at the Mass. hist. soc.) 41-27489.
 F67.M368
 1725a
 Rare Book Coll.

MASSACHUSETTS (Colony) His Excellency, The Earl of Bellomont's speech to the Hon. the Council and House of Representatives, ... 1699. (Boston, Bart. Green and John Allen, print., 1699. Boston, 1923) facsim. 3 numb. l. 29 cm. (Americana series no. 84. photostats by the Mass. hist. soc. 25-11803 rev.
 F67.M372
 Rare Book Coll.

MASSACHUSETTS (Colony) The Address of the Hon. the Lieut. Governour Stoughton ... June 2, 1699.

Boston, Print. Barth. Green & John Allen, 1699.   Boston, 1923)   facsim: 4 numb. l. 29 cm.   (Americana series:
photostats by the Mass. hist. soc.   no. 84.   25-11086 rev.
                                                  F67. M372
                                                  Rare Book Coll.

MASSACHUSETTS (Colony)   The Answer of the House of Representatives to His Excellency the Earl of Bellomont's speech ... 6 June, 1699.   Boston, Barth. Green and John Allen, Print., 1699.   Boston, 1923.   facsim. 2 l. 20 cm.   Americana series: photostats by the Mass. hist. soc.   no. 84.   25-11804 rev.   F67. M372
                                                  Rare Book Coll.

MASSACHUSETTS (Colony)   A Congratulatory Address of the House of Representatives of His Majesties Province of the Massachusetts-Bay... 6 June, 1699.   Boston, Barth. Green and John Allen, Print., 1699. Boston, 1923.   facsim. 2 numb. l. 29 cm. (Americana series; photostats by the Mass. hist. soc. no. 84) 25-11805 rev.   F67. M372
                                                  Rare Book Coll.

MASSACHUSETTS (Colony)   Letters to the ministry from Governor Bernard, General Gage, and Commodore Hood.   etc. etc.   Boston, Edes & Gill, 1769.   108 p. 19 cm.   8-14867.
                                                  F67. M374
                                                  Rare Book Coll.

MASSACHUSETTS.   Dept. of education.   ... The Massachusetts bay colony and the General court. The observance of the tercentenary of the Mass. bay colony ... and 150th anniversary of the adoption of the constitution of the commonwealth of Mass. ...   Washington, U.S.Govt. print. off., 1930. iii, 35 p. 23 cm.   Bibliographies p. 24 - 31.   30-26675.
                                                  F67. M38

MASSACHUSETTS.   Dept. of education.   ... Material suggested for use in ... the tercentenary of Massachusetts bay colony ... (1903)   F67. M383

MASSACHUSETTS.   ... Report of the Special commission on the celebration of the tercentenary of the founding of the Mass. Bay colony ...   Boston, Wright & Potter print., 1929.   33 p. 23 cm.   29-27033.
                                                 F67. M386

MASSACHUSETTS Bay tercentenary, inc.   ... Bulletin.   19   F67. M388

MASSACHUSETTS Bay tercentenary in 1930, Historical background for the, by Samuel Eliot Morison ... Boston, 1928.   12 p. fold. front. (map) 25 cm. (Mass. Bay tercentenary inc. Bulletin no. 10) 30-9205.   F67. M388 No. 10

MASSACHUSETTS; or, the first planters of New-England, the end and manner of their coming thither, and abode there ...   Boston, Green and Allen ... 1696.   1, 56 p. 15 cm.   Bound with next item. 4-1123.
                                                 F67. M39
                                                Rare Book Coll.

MASSACHUSETTS.   David serving his generation; or, A sermon ... occasioned by the death, of the Rev. Mr. John Baily ... 1698.   39 p. 15 cm.   Bound with above.   32-4052.
                                                 F67. M 39
                                                Rare Book Coll.

MASSACHUSETTS historical soc.   Lecture delivered ... before the Lowell institute.   1869.
                                                 F67.   M4

MASSACHUSETTS.   The first charter and the early religious legislation of Mass.   By Joel Parker. (In Mass. hist. soc. Lecutres .. on .. the early history of Mass.   Boston, 1869.   p. 355-439) 1-12048.   F67.   M4

MASSACHUSETTS and its early history.   Introductory lecture by Robert Charles Wintrhop. (In Mass hist. soc., Boston. Lecutres ... on ... the early history of Mass.   Boston, 1869.   p. 1-27) 1-12025.   F67.   M4

MATHER.   The Mathers weighed in the balances, by Delano A. Goddard, and found wanting.   Boston, Daily advertiser; London, H. Stevens, 1870.   32 p. 16 x 13 cm.   12-23840.   F67. M 41
                                                 Rare Book Coll.

MATHER.   ... Diary of Cotton Mather, 1681 - 1724.   Boston, The Society, 1911 - 12.   2 v. fronts.

facsim. 24½ cm. (Half-title: Collections of the Mass. hist. soc. ser. 7, v. 7-8) Contents. - pt. 1. 1681 - 1708. - pt. 2. 1709 - 1724.
11-14733 rev.
F67.M42

MATHER, Cotton, Diary of. New York, F. Ungar (1957?)   2 v. fold. map. 25 cm.) (American classics)
Contents. - v.1. 1681 - 1709 (i.e. 1708) - v. 2. 1700 - 1724. 57-8651.
F67.M4213

MATHER, Cotton, The diary of, for the year 1712. Ed. with introd. and notes by Wm. E. Manierre, II. Charlottesville, University Press of Va. (1964)   xxvii, 143 p. 24 cm. 64-13720.
F67.M4214

MATHER, Cotton, Selected letters of. Comp. with commentary by Kenneth Silverman. Baton Rouge, La. State University Press (1971)   xxvi, 446 p. port. 24 cm. 78-142338 MARC.
F67.M4215

MATHER, Cotton. Did James F. Skunk forge the Cotton Mather letter? The answer is: Definitely no. By David Rankin Barbee. (n.p., 1946)   26 p. 23 cm. "Reprinted from Tyler's quarterly historical and genealogical magazine, Jan. 1946." 47-7791*.
F67.M4217

MATHER, Cotton, first significant figure in American medicine, by Otho T. Beall, Jr., and Richard H. Shryock. Baltimore, John Hopkins Press (1954)   ix, 241 p. port., facsim. 24 cm. (Publications of the Institute of the History of Medicine. 1st ser.: Monographs, v. 5) "Reprinted from vol. 63 of the Proceedings of the American Antiquarian Society." Bibliographical footnotes. 54-8009 rev.
F67.M4218

MATHER, Cotton, keeper of the Puritan conscience, by Ralph and Louise Boas ... N.Y. and London, Harper & bros., 1928.   ix, 271 p. front. (port.) 1 illus., plates, map, facsims. 22½ cm. 28-27598.
F67.M422

— Hamden, Conn., Archon Books, 1964 (c. 1928)   ix, 271 p. 21 cm. (Archon books) 64-15910.
F67.M422
1964

MATHER, Cotton. The holy walk and glorious translation of blessed Enoch. A sermon preached ... two days after the death of ... Cotton Mather ... 1728. By Benj. Coleman. Boston, Print. for J. Phillips & T. Hancock, 1728.   2, 31 (3) p. 17½ x 10 cm. 3-3446.
F67.M4225
Rare Book Coll.

MATHER, Cotton. A modest enquiry into the grounds and occasions of a late pamphlet, intitled, A memorial of the present deplorable state of New-England ... London, 1707.   30 p. 22 cm. 6-20508.
F67.M4227
1707
Rare Book Coll.

MATHER, Cotton, and the Jews. By Lee M. Friedman ... (Baltimore, 1918)   p. 201 - 210. 23 cm. Reprinted from the Publications of the American Jewish historical soc., no. 26, 1918. 20-17483.
F67.M423

MATHER, Cotton. Israel's mourning for Aaron's death. A sermon preached ... after the death of ... Cotton Mather ... 1727,8. Boston, Print. for S. Gerrish, 1728.   34 p.
F67.M4235
Rare Book Coll.

MATHER, Cotton. A letter said to have been written by Cotton Mather, shown to be a miserable forgery. By Samuel Abbott Green. (Cambridge? Mass., 1908?)   3 p. 24 cm. Letter giving details of a scheme to capture and sell into slavery William Penn and his company. 11-25754.
F67.M424

MATHER, Cotton. Cotton Mather's election into the Royal society, by George Lyman Kittredge; repr. from the Pubs. of the Colonial Soc. of Mass., vol. xiv. Cambridge, J. Wilson, 1912. p. (81) - 114. 25½ cm. 12-5145.
F67.M4215
Copy 2 in Rare Book Coll.

COTTON MATHER, The life and times of; or, A Boston minister of two centuries ago; 1663 - 1728. By Rev. Abijah P. Marvin. Boston and Chicago, (1892)   v, 582 p. pl., 2 port. (incl. front.) 21½ cm. 12-23836.
F67.M426

— 1972. F67.M426 1972

MATHER, Cotton. An abridgement of the Life of the late Rev. ... Dr. Cotton Mather ... Taken from the account of him pub. by his son, the Rev. Mr. Samuel Mather ... By David Jennings. London, Print. for J. Oswald and J. Brackstone, 1744. xii, (4), 143 p. 16 cm. 12-23841.
F67.M427
Rare Book Coll.

— A new ed. Edinburgh, Waugh and Innes, 1822. 2, xii, (13) - 242 p. 15 cm. 12-23839. F67.M428

MATHER, Cotton, The life of. By Samuel Mather. Philadelphia, Amer. Sunday school union, 1829. iv, (5) - 107 p. 14 cm. 12-23838.
F67.M429
Rare Book Coll.

MATHER, Cotton, The life of. By Samuel Mather ... Boston, Print. for Samuel Gerrish, 1729. 2, iv, 6, 10, 186 p. 19½ cm. "A catalogue of the books published by Dr. Mather": p. 161-179. 12-23837.
F67.M43
Rare Book Coll.

MATHER, Cotton. The departure of Elijah lamented; a sermon occasioned by the ... decease of ... Cotton Mather ... by Thomas Prince. Boston, Print. for D. Henchman, 1728. 26 p. 21 cm. 59-56909.
F67.M44
Rare Book Coll.

MATHER, Cotton, the Puritan priest, by Barrett Wendell. N.Y., Dodd Mead, (1891) vi, 321 p. front. (ports.) 18 cm. ("Makers of America") 4-16976/2.
F67.M45

— Cambridge, Harvard university press, 1926. viii p., 321 p. front. (port.) 20½ cm. "Authorities": p. (309) - 310. 26-10867.
F67.M452

— With a new introd. by Alan Heimert. N.Y., Harcourt Brace (1963) 248 p. 21 cm. (A Harbinger book) 63-12740.
F67.M452 1963

MATHER, Cotton. The admirable Cotton Mather. By James Playsted Wood. New York, Seabury Press (c.1971) ix, 164 p. 22 cm. 76-129212.
F67.M455

MATHER, Increase, Diary of, March, 1675 - Dec. 1676. Tog. with extracts from another diary by him, 1674 - 1687. With an introd. and notes, by Samuel A. Green. Cambridge, J. Wilson, 1900. 54 p. 24 cm. 5-25477.
F67.M463
Rare Book Coll.

MATHER, Increase. Reasons for the confirmation of the charter belonging to the Mass. colony in New England ... (1691) (1936) (Photostat americana. 2d series, no. 8. Photostated at the Mass. hist. soc.)
F67.M466
Rare Book Coll.

MATHER, Increase. Remarks on an original portrait of the Rev. Increase Mather, and on some of the engravings taken from it. By Samuel A. Green ... Cambridge, J. Wilson, 1893. 10 p. 24½ cm. Reprinted from the Proceedings of the Mass. historical soc. for March, 1893. 27-744.
F67.M473

MATHER, Increase. Memoirs of the life of the late Rev. Increase Mather, who died ... 1723. With a preface by the Rev. Edmund Calamy. London, J. Clarke & R. Hett, 1725. 4, 88 p. front. (port.) 20 cm. An abridged edition of Cotton Mather's "Parentator," said to be by Samuel Mather, son of Increase Mather. 10-25319.
F67.M474
Rare Book Coll.

MATHER, Increase. Parentator. Memoirs of remarkables in the life and the death of the ever-memorable Dr. Increase Mather ... Boston, Print. B. Green for Nat. Belknap., 1724.

1, x, xiv, 239, (5) p. 17½ cm. 1-20756.   F67.M476
                                                                                     Rare Book Coll.

MATHER, Increase, the foremost American Puritan, by Kenneth Ballard Murdock ... Cambridge,
Harvard university press, 1925.   xv, 442 p. front., plates, ports., double map, facsims. 25 cm. "Appendix c. List of
books referred to": p. (407) - 415. "Appendix D. Checklist of Mather's writings": p. (416) - 422. 25-21276.   F67.M477
                                                                                     Copy 2 in Rare Book Coll.

— New York, Russell & Russell, 1966.   xv, 442 p. 22 cm. 66-24736.   F67.M477
                                                                                     1966

MATHER, Increase, The portraits of, with some notes on Thomas Johnson, an English mezzotinter,
by Kenneth Murdock. Cleveland, For private distributuion by W.G. Mather, 1924.   x, 70 p. x port.
(incl. col. front.) 26 cm. 25-842.   F67.M478
                                                                                     Rare Book Coll.

MATHER, Increase, the agent of Massachusetts colony in England for the concession of a charter. By
William Henry Whitmore ... Boston, Print. T.R. Marvin, 1869.   24 p. 21½ x 17 cm. Reprinted from the Andros
tracts, pub. by the Prince soc. of Boston. 3-6348.   F67. M48

MATHER, Increase. A representative Massachusetts Puritan, Increase Mather ... By George
Parker Winship. A portion of an introductory essay to a bibliography of the published writings of
Increase Mather compiled by Thomas J. Holmes ... Cambridge, Harvard University press, 1931.
xi p. 19½ cm. 32-12858.   F67.M484

MATHER. The Mathers; three generations of Puritan intellectuals, 1596 - 1728. By Robert Middle-
kauff. New York, Oxford University Press, 1971.   xii, 440 p. 24 cm. 79-140912.
                                                                                     F67.M4865

MATHEWS, Albert. Notes on the Massachusetts royal commission, 1681 - 1775 ... Cambridge, J.
Wilson, 1913.   119 p. 24½ cm. "Reprinted from the Pubs. of the Colonial soc. of Mass., vol. xvii." 13-33601.
                                                                                     F67. M49

MAUDUIT, Israel. A short view of the history of the colony of Massachusetts Bay ... London, J. Wilkie,
1769.   2, 71 p. 20½ cm. 1-12039.   F67. M 5
                                                                                     Rare Book Coll.

— 3d ed. to which is now added the original charter ... London, J. Wilkie, 1774.   1, 5 - 93 p. 21½ cm.
1-12040.   F67.M512

— 4th ed. London, J. Wilkie, 1776.   71 (i.e. 61), 95 - 100, 3-31 p. 21 cm. 8-3803 rev.   F67.M513

MAUDUIT, Jasper, agent in London for the province of the Massachusetts-Bay, 1762-1765. The Charles
Grenfill Washburn collection of letters and papers. Boston, The Mass. hist. soc., 1918.   xxxvii,
194 p. 25 cm. (Mass. hist. soc. collections, v.74) 18-17859.   F67. M 52

MAYHEW, Thomas, patriarch to the Indians (1593-1682) The life of the worshipful governor and
chief magistrate of the island of Martha's vineyard ... By Lloyd C.M. Hare ... New York, London,
D. Appleton and co., 1932.   xii, 231 p. front. (geneal. table) plates, maps. 29 cm. Short bibliography included in the preface.
32-10945.   F67.M526

— New York, AMS Press (1969)   xii, 231 p. illus. 76-104347.   F67.M527
                                                                                     1969

— N.Y. D. Appleton, St. Clair Shore, Mich., Scholarly Press, 1971.   76-145070.
                                                                                     F67.M526
                                                                                     1971

MEAD, Edwin Doak. The Massachusetts tercentenary ... (Boston, Print. Thomas Todd co., 1930)
16 p. 23½ x 12 cm. "Re-printed, revised, from the Boston transcript." CA 30-1242 unrev.   F67. M54

MERRILL, William Pierson.   Our better portion ... The thirteenth annual sermon of the New England society in the city of New York.   (New York? 1912)   17 p. 21 cm. 26-20983.   F67. M56

MERRIMAN, Titus Mooney.   The Pilgrims, Puritans, and Roger Williams, vindicated ... Boston, Bradley & Woodruff, 1892.   xii, 312 p. 20 x 15 cm. 1-12041 rev.   F67. M57

MERRIMAN, Titus Mooney.   "Welcome, Englishmen": or, Pilgrims, Puritans and Roger Williams vindicated.   2d ed.   Boston, Arena pub. co., 1896.   xii, 320 p. 20 x 15½ cm. 1-12042 rev.
F67. M 58

MINOT, George Richards.   Continuation of the history of the province of Massachusetts Bay ... 1748 (to 1765)   With an introductory sketch of events from its original settlement.   Boston, Print. Manning & Loring, 1798-1803.   2 v. 22½ cm. Continuation of Thomas Hutchinson's History of Massachusetts-Bay. 1-13586.
F67. M66
Rare Book Coll.

MITCHELL, Stewart.   The founding of Massachusetts, a selection from the sources of the history of the settlement, 1628 - 1631.   Boston, The Mass. hist. soc., 1930.   211 p. plates, ports., facsims. (part fold.) charts. 24½ cm. "From the Proceedings of the Mass. hist. soc. vol. lxii." 30-22785 rev.   F67. M67

MOORE, George Henry.   Notes on the tithing men and the ballot in Mass.   Worcester, Mass., Press of C. Hamilton, 1884.   14 p. 25½ cm. From the Proceedings of the American antiquarian soc. 7-2494.   F67. M 8

MOORE, Jacob Bailey.   Lives of the governors of New Plymouth, and Massachusetts Bay; from the landing of the Pilgrims at Plymouth in 1620, to the union of the two colonies in 1692.   Boston, C. D. Strong, 1851.   iv, (2), (9) - 439 p. front. (port.) 22½ cm. First pub. under title: Memoirs of Amer.governors. 3-27739.   F67. M82

MOORE, Jacob Bailey.   Memoirs of American governors.   v. I.   New York, Gates and Stedman, 1846.
iv, (2), (9) - 430 p. 4 port. (incl. front.) 23½ cm. No morepub. 3-27738. 18-22800.   F67. M825
Toner coll. F67. M826

MORGAN, Edmund Sears, ed.   The founding of Massachusetts; historians and the sources.   Indianapolis, Bobbs-Merrill Co. c. 1964.   xii, 479 p. 21 cm. 63-12192.   F67. M855

MORISON, S. E.   Historical background for the Massachusetts bay tercentenary ... 1928.
F67. M856

MORISON, Samuel Eliot.   Massachusettensis de conditoribus; or, The builders of the Bay colony, reporting, by means of eleven short and succinct discourses respecting the lives, characters, and remarkable deeds of several of the most eminent and worthy persons ... among the first generation of planters in New England ... Boston, Houghton, Mifflin, 1930.   xiii, 365 p. col. front., plates, ports., map, facsims. 25 cm. Contains biographies of Richard Hakluyt, John Smith, Thomas Morton, John White, John Winthrop, Thomas Shepard, John Hull, Henry Dunster, Nathaniel Ward, Robert Child, John Winthrop, jr., John Eliot & Anne Bradstreet. Bibliography p. (347)-355. 30-14520.   F67. M86

MORTON, Thomas.   New English Canaan or New Canaan.   Containing an abstract of New England, composed in three bookes. ...   Amsterdam, Print. J. F. Stam, 1637.   188 (3) p. 18 cm. 1-12043.
F67. M88
Rare Book Coll.

— Printed by C. Green, 1632 (!)   (Washington, P. Force, 1838)   125, (2) p. 23½ cm. (From Force, Peter. Tracts. v.2 (1838) no. 5)   F67. M89

— 1637.   F67. M895

— New York, Da Capo Press, 1969.   188 p. 23 cm.   F67. M895
1637a

— With introductory matter and notes by Charles Francis Adams, Jr.   New York, B. Franklin (1967) vi, 381 p. 23 cm.   F67. M895
1967

MASSACHUSETTS

NEWHALL, James Robinson. Y^e great and general courte in collonie times. By Obadiah Oldpath. (James R. Newhall) Pub. by Israel Augustus Newhall and Howard Mudge Newhall. Lynn, Mass., The Nichols press - T. P. Nichols, 1897.   viii, 9 - 504 p. 20 cm. 1-12044.   F67.N 54

NORTHEND, William Dummer. The Bay colony; a civil, religious and social history of the Massachusetts colony and its settlements from the landing at Cape Ann in 1624 to the death of Governor Winthrop in 1650 ... Boston, Estes and Lauriat (c. 1896)   1, viii, 349 p. 2 port. (incl. front.) 20 cm. 1-12045.
F67.N 87

OATH of a free-man ... The ... With a historical study by Lawrence C. Wroth and A note on the Stephen Daye press by Melbert B. Cary, jr. New York, 1939.   (18) p. 22 cm. 39-7070.
F67.O127

OLIVER. The faithful servant approv'd at death ... A sermon ... Occasion'd by the much lamented death of the Hon, Daniel Oliver. By Thomas Prince. Boston: Print. S. Kneeland, 1732.   3, 35 p. 19 ½ cm. 3-10510.
F67.O 14
Rare Book Coll.

OLIVER, Peter. The Puritan commonwealth. An historical review of the Puritan government in Mass. in its civil and ecclesiastical realtions from its rise to the abrogation of the first charter ... Boston, Little, Brown, 1856.   xii, 502 p. 23 ½ cm. 1-12046.   F67.O 48

OLIVER, Peter, the last chief justice of the Superior court of judicature of the province of Massachusetts Bay. A sketch by Thomas Weston ... Boston, Cupples, Upham, 1886.   36 p. front. (port.) 23 cm. 12-12839.
F67.O 49

OTIS, James. A vindication of the conduct of the House of representatives of the province of the Massachusetts Bay ... Boston: Print. Edes & Gill, 1762.   iv, (5) - 53 p. 20 ½ cm. 9-20801.
F67.O 88
Rare Book Coll.

PARKER, Joel. The first charter and the early religious legislation of Massachusetts. A lecture ... Boston, Press of J. Wilson, 1869.   85 p. 23 ½ cm. 1-12047.   F67.P 23

PENDLETON, Everett Hall. Brian Pendleton and his Massachusetts, 1634 - 1681. (South Orange? N.J., 1951)   xi, 259 p. illus., facsims. 24 cm. Bibliographical footnotes. 51-26593.   F67.P4P4

PHILLIPS, Mary Schuyler. Colonial Massachusetts ... (Cincinnati, The Ebbert & Richardson co., c. 1916)   44 p. 23 cm. The Colonial damesoof America in the state of Ohio. Studies in the colonial period for use in the public schools) 16-16105.
F67.P 55

PHIPS. A funeral-sermon occasion'd by the death of the Hon, Spencer Phips ... By Nathaniel Appleton Boston, Print. J. Draper, 1770.   43 p. 20 cm.   F67.P565

PHIPS. Stormy knight: the life of Sir William Phips. By Clifford Lindsey Alderman. (1st ed., Philadelphia, Chilton Books (c. 1964)   171 p. 21 cm. 64-14290.   F67.P566

PHIPS, William, and the treasure ship. By Harold W. Felton. Drawings by Alvin Smith. New York, Dodd, Mead (c. 1965)   156 p. 24 cm. 65-19216.   F67.P5664

PHIPS, Sir William, treasure fisherman and governor of the Massachusetts bay colony, by Alice Lounsberry. New York, C. Scribner's sons, 1941.   xii, 323 p. 2 port. (incl. front.) illus. (facsims., coat of arms) pl. 22 cm. Bibliography: p. (311) - 317. 41-8228.
F67.P567

PHIPS. Pietas in patriam: the life of his excellency Sir William Phips, knt. Late captain general, and governour in chief of the province of the Massachuset-Bay ... By (Cotton Mather) London, Print. S. Bridge for N. Hiller, 1697.   6, 110, (6) p. 26 cm. Reprinted in 1699, and also included in Mather's "Magnalia Christi americana ... " London, 1702 and later editions. 2-18527.
F67.P 57
Rare Book Coll.

PHIPS, Sir William, The life of.   By Cotton Mather.   Ed. with a pref. by Mark Van Doren.   New York, AMS Press (1971)   xi, 208 p.   19 cm.   75-137260.   F67.P 57 1971

— New York, Covici-Friede, 1929.   xi, 208 p.   front. (port.)   21 cm.   Pub. in 1697 under title: Pietas in patriam: the life of His Excellency Sir Wm. Phips.   30-2356.   F67.P573

PHIPS.   The Knight of the Golden Fleece.   By Virginia Perkins.   Illus. by Howard Simon.   (1st ed.) Boston, Little, Brown (1959)   219 p.   illus.   21 cm.   59-5290.   F67.P 58

PIKE, Robert.   The new Puritan;   New England two hundred years ago; some account of the life of Robert Pike, the Puritan who defended the Quakers, etc.   By James S. Pike.   New York, Harper & bros., 1879.   237 p.   19 cm.   3-18837.   F67.P 63

PLUMSTEAD, A., comp.   The wall and the garden; selected Massachusetts election sermons 1670 - 1775.   Minneapolis, University of Minnesota Press (1968)   viii, 390 p.   facsims.   24 cm.   68-19742.   F67.P 65 1968

POEM presented to His Excellency William Burnet, on his arrival at Boston ... Paterson? N.J. (1897)   5 p.   23 cm.   3-30668.   F67.P 74

POWNALL, Thomas, governor of Massachusetts Bay, author of the letters of Junius; ... by Charles A.W. Pownall ... London, H. Stevens, son & Stiles; (Binghamton, N.Y., Print Binghamton book mfg. co.)   c.1908.   1, 488 p.   24 cm.   8-36378.   F67.P 88

— London, H. Stevens, son & Stiles (c.1908).   ix, 470, 56, 25 p.   front., illus., plates, ports., maps, facsim. (part fold.) fold. diagr.   25½ cm.   "The works pub. by Thomas Pownall" p. Appendix p. 3-6. Genealogy Appendix p.19-25.   9-9266.   F67. P 89

POWNALL, Thomas, British defender of American liberty; a study of Anglo-American relations in the eighteenth century.   By John A. Schutz.   Glendale, Calif., A.H. Clark Co., 1951.   340 p.   illus., port., map, facsim.   25 cm.   (Old Northwest historical series, 5)   Bibliography: p. (291) - 309.   51-5674.   F67.P893

PRATT, Phinehas.   A declaration of the affairs of the English people that first inhabited New England. Ed., with notes, by Richard Frothingham, jr.   Boston, Press of T.R. Marvin & son, 1858.   20 p.   23 cm.   "Prepared for publication in the 4th vol. of the 4th series of the Mass. hist. soc's Collections.   1-20006.   F67.P 91

PRINCE, Samuel.   The grave and death destroyed ... a sermon ... after the decease & funeral of Samuel Prince.   By Thomas Prince.   Boston, S. Gerrish, 1728.   23 p.   21 cm.   F67.P94P7

QUINCY, Edmund.   The instability of humane greatness ... a funeral discourse upon the ... death of the Hon. Edmund Quincy ... By John Hancock ... Boston, Print. S. Kneeland, and T. Green, 1738.   3, 31 p.   20½ cm.   12-26141 rev.   F67.Q 73 Rare Book Coll.

QUINCY, John, master of Mount Wollaston; provincial statesman; colonel of the Suffolk regiment ... an address ... by Daniel Munro Wilson.   Boston, G.H. Ellis print., 1909.   84 p.   front., plates, ports., facsim.   21½ x 18 cm.   9-21152.   F67.Q 75

RANDOLPH, Edward; including his letters and official papers from the New England, middle, and southern colonies in America, ... 1676 - 1703.   By Robert Noxon Toppan ... Boston, Prince soc., 1898 - 1909.   7 v.   front. (port. v.6) 22 x 18½ cm.   Pubs. of the Prince soc. v.24-28, 30-31.   98-1272 rev.   F67.R 19

— New York, B. Franklin (1967)   7 v.   22 cm.   F67.R 19 1967

READ, John.   Sketch of the life of the Hon. John Read, 1680 - 1749; also of Chief-Justice Charles Morris, 1711 - 1781.   Prepared by Charles J. McIntire ...   Cambridge (Mass.) 1898.   16 p.   23 cm.   13-5272.   F67.R 29

READ, John. Sketch of the life of the Hon. John Read, of Boston, 1722 - 1749. By George B. Reed. Boston, Priv. print. (T. Todd) 1879.   18, iv p. 23 cm.   13-5273.   F67. R 3

— Boston, 1903.   26 p. front. (facsim) 25½ cm. "Repr. from the Procs. of the Bostonian soc. for 1903" 6-25799.   F67. R 32

REPORT of a French Protestant refugee, in Boston, 1687: trans. from the French by E. T. Fisher. Brooklyn, N. Y. (Albany, J. Munsell, print.) 1868.   v, (7) - 42 p. 22 x 18½ cm.   1-12049.
F67. R 42

ROSE-TROUP, Frances (James) The Massachusetts bay company and its predecessors ... New York, The Grafton press (c. 1930)   xi, 176 p. 22 cm.   The new Grafton historical series. Bibliography: p. 163-164. 30-15560 rev.
F67. R79

RUGGLES, General Timothy, 1711-1795. By Henry Stoddard Ruggles ... (Wakefield? Mass.) Priv. print., 1897.   40 p. front. (coat of arms) 24½ cm.   12-30961.   F67. R 93

RUSSELL, James. The character and reward of a good and faithful servant illus. in a sermon, ... following the death ... of the Hon. James Russell ... By Jedidiah Morse. Print. Samuel Hall, Boston. 21 p. 21½ cm. 9-27488.   F67. R 96
Rare Book Coll.

SEWALL. Judge Sewall's gifts in the Narragansett country, by Caroline Hazard ... (Providence, Roger Williams press, 1936)   23 p. 24½ cm. 37-9450.   F67. S
F82. H 39

SAUNDERSON, Henry Hallam. Puritan principles and American ideals. Boston, Chicago, The Pilgrim press (1930)   xi, 255 p. 19½ cm. 30-12287.   F67. S 25

SAWYER, Joseph Dillaway. History of the Pilgrims and Puritans, their ancestry and descendants; basis of Americanization, ... N. Y., The Century history co. (1922)   3 v. front., illus. (incl. ports., maps, facsims.) 26 cm. 22-19063.   F67. S 27

SECOND letter from one in the country, to his friend in Boston. (Boston, 1729)   4 p. 25½ cm. In reference to a proposal to provide a fixed salary for the governor of Mass. 8-18422.   F67. S 44

SEWALL, Samuel. ... Samuel Sewall's diary, ed. by Mark Van Doren. (New York) Macy-Masius, 1927.   272 p. 19½ cm. (An American bookshelf. 1)   first pub. in 3 vols. by the Mass. historical soc. (1878-1882) 27-23367.
F67. S515

— N. Y., Russell & Russell, 1963.   272 p. 23 cm. 62-16693.   F67. S515
1963

SEWALL, Samuel, The diary of. Ed. and abridged, with an introd. by Harvey Wish. N. Y., G. P. Putnam's Sons (1967)   189 p. 21 cm. 66-20302.   F67. S5162

SEWALL, Samuel. The selling of Joseph, a memorial ...   (Photostat Americana. 2d series ... Photostated at the Mass. hist. soc. no. 4)   F67. S517
Rare Book Coll.

— Ed., with notes and commentary, by Sidney Kaplan. (Amherst) University of Mass. Press, 1969. 66 p. 22 cm. 74-87832.   F67. S517
1969

SEWALL, Samuel, and the world he lived in. By Nathan Henry Chamberlain. Boston, De Wolfe, Fiske, 1897.   xv, 319 p. plates, ports. 20 cm. Based on the "Diary of Samuel Sewall" 3-4904/5.   F67. S 52

— 2d ed. New York, Russell & Russell (1967)   319 p. 22 cm. 66-24679.
F67. S 52
1967

SEWALL, Samuel. An address on the life and character of Chief-Justice Samuel Sewall. By George
E. Ellis. Boston, 1885. 1, 28 p. front. (port.) 25 cm. 14-14071. F67.S525

SEWALL, Samuel, The vocabulary of from 1673 to 1699, by Robert David Highfill. Chicago, 1927.
xii, 393 l. 29 cm. Typescript (carbon copy) Thesis - University of Chicago. F67.S528

SEWALL, Samuel. A difference of opinion concerning the reasons why Katharine Winthrop refused to
marry Chief Justice Sewall. By Robert Charles Winthrop, jr. Boston, Priv. print., 1885.
25 p. 24½ cm. 11-13690. F67.S 53

SEWALL, Mrs. Hannah. The valley of Baca. ... A sermon preached on the death of Mrs. Hannah
Sewall ... By Cotton Mather ... Boston: Print. B. Green. 1717. 1, 4, 28 p. 15 cm. 37-20755.
F67.S535
Rare Book Coll.

SEWALL, Joseph. Nineveh's repentance and deliverance. A sermon ... By Joseph Sewall ... Boston,
Print. J. Draper for D. Henchman, 1740. 3, 33 p. 20½ cm. 15-11546. F67.S 54
Rare Book Coll.

SEWALL, Samuel. A sermon ... Upon the death of the Hon. Samuel Sewall ... By Thomas Prince ...
Boston, Print. B. Green, 1730. 2, 36, 4 p. 22 cm. 42-48682. F67.S545
Rare Book Coll.

SEWALL, Samuel; a Puritan portrait, by T.B. Strandness. (East Lansing?) Michigan State University
Press, 1967. xiv, 234 p. 67-28876. F67.S546

SEWALL, Samuel, of Boston. New York, Macmillan (1964) vii, 235 p. 22 cm. 63-16140.
F67.S547

SEWALL, Samuel, A discourse occasioned by the death of ... By Jonathan Mayhew. Boston ... 1760.
66 p. 21 cm. 36-11415. F67.S 55
Rare Book Coll.

SHRIMPTON, Samuel, The case of. By Worthington Chauncey Ford ... Cambridge, J. Wilson, 1905.
16 p. 24½ cm. Reprinted from the Proceedings of the Mass. hist. soc. Jan. 1905. 5-24705. F67.S 56

SKELTON, Edward Oliver. The story of New England, illus., being a narrative of the principal
events from the arrival of the Pilgrims in 1620 and of the Puritans in 1624 to the present time ...
Boston, E.O. Skelton, 1910. 140 p. incl. front., illus., facsims. 18 cm. 10-7899. F67.S 62

SLICER, Thomas Roberts. The seventh annual sermon on Forefathers' day ... 1906. N.Y., Print.
by order of the Society (N. E. soc. in the city of New York) 1906? 19 p. 20½ cm. 18-15733.
F67.S 63

SMITH, Robert. The Massachusetts coony. (N.Y.) Crowell-Collier Press (1969) 152 p. illus. 23 cm.
(A Forge of freedom book) 69-19575. F67.S 66

SOME observations relating to the present circumstances of the province of the Massachusetts-bay;
humbly offered to the consideration of the General assembly ... Boston, Print. D. Fowle, 1750.
20 p. 19 x 15½ cm. 11-4660. F67.S 69
Rare Book Coll.

SOUTHWICK, Henry Lawrence. ... The policy of the early colonists of Massachusetts toward
Quakers and others whom they regarded as intruders. 1881. Boston, Old South meeting house,
1885. viii, 21 p. 23 cm. (Old South prize essays) 3-31518 rev. F67.S 72

STIFLER, Susan Reed. Church and state in Massachusetts, 1691 - 1740. Urbana, Ill., 1914.
203 p. 24½ cm. Thesis - University of Illinois. Pub. also as University of Illinois studies in the social sciences vol. III no. 4. Bibliography:
p. 195-202. 15-27243. F67.S 84
1914

MASSACHUSETTS 35

STODDARD, John. A strong rod broken and withered. A sermon ... on the death of the Hon. John Stoddard ... By Jonathan Edwards. Boston, ... 1748. 29 p. 18½ cm. 5-20517.
  F67.S 86
  Rare Book Coll.

SULLIVAN, William. An address to the members of the bar of Suffolk, Mass., 1824. Boston, North American review, I. R. Butts, print., 1825. 63 p. 21½ cm. 10-31052.
  F67.S 95

TAILOR, William. Man humbled by being compar'd to a work. A sermon preached ... after the funeral of the Hon. William Tailer ... By William Cooper. Boston, B. Green, 1732. 2, ii, 25 p. 21 cm. 15-11528.
  F67.T125
  Rare Book Coll.

TAILER, Gov. Wm., Chair given to by Queen Anne, and the petition of Christopher Talbot. (Boston 1907) 3 p. 24 cm.
  F67.T 13

TERCENTENARY conference of city and town committees, inc.) Celebrating a 300th anniversary; a report of the Massachusetts bay tercentenary of 1930 ... (Boston, 1931) 6, (11) - 131 p. incl. illus., plates, ports. 26 cm. "Publications": p. 104 - 109. 31-19244.
  F67.T 38

THIRD extraordinary budget of epistles and memorials between Sir Francis Bernard of Nettleham, baronet, some natives of Boston, and the present ministry ... (Boston? Edes & Gill? 1769) 8 p. 18 cm. Correspondence relating to the refusal of the people of Boston to pay import duties ... 20-5374.
  T67.T 44
  Rare Book Coll.

THORNTON, John Wingate. The landing at Cape Anne; or, The charter of the first permanent colony on the territory of the Massachusetts company. ... Boston, Gould and Lincoln; N.Y. Sheldon, Lamport, and Blakeman, 1854. xii, 84 p. front. (fold. facsim.) map. 22 cm. 1-12050.
  F67.T 51

THUMB, Thomas. The monster of monsters: a true and faithful narrative of a most remarkable phenomenon lately seen in this metropolis ... (Boston) Print Z. Fowle, 1754. 24 p. 17 cm. A satirical account of the debate on the Excise bill. 9-34987.
  F67.T 53
  Rare Book Coll.

 — Extract from the Journal of the House of representatives ... Relating to the imprisonment of Daniel Fowle and Royall Tyler. (Boston, 1755) 14 p. 17 cm. Bound with the above. 9-34984.
 — An appendix to the late Total eclipse of liberty ... Boston, 1756. 24 p. Bound with the above.
 — A total eclipse of liberty: being a true and faithful account of the arraignment, and examination of Daniel Fowle ... barely on suspicion of his being concern'd in printing and publishing a pamphlet entitled, The monster of monsters ... Boston, 1755. 1, 32 p. 17 cm. Bound with above. 9-34985-6.
  F67.T 53
  Rare Book Coll.

TUCKER, John. Remarks on a discourse of the Rev. Jonathan Parsons ... entitled, Freedom from civil and ecclesiastical slavery ... Boston, Mills and Hicks, 1774. 36 p. 21 cm. 17-23102.
  F67.T 89

TUTTLE, Julius Herbert. Massachusetts and her Royal charter granted March 4, 1628-29 ... Boston, Massachusetts soc. of the Order of the founders and patriots of America, 1924. 1, 16 p. illus. (ports.) 18½ cm. 24-19540. 29-11980.
  F67.T 95
  F67.T952

UNDERHILL, John, captain of New England and New Netherland, by Henry C. Shelley ... New York, London, D. Appleton, 1932. xii, 473 p. front., plates, ports., facsims., coat of arms. 24½ cm. 32-11428.
  F67.U
  F122.U68

UPSALL, Nicholas. By Augustine Jones ... Reprinted from the N.E. hist. and geneal. register for Jan., 1880. Boston, D. Clapp, 1880. 12 p. front. 26 cm. 19-13178.
  F67.U 68

VANE, Sir Henry, jr., governor of Mass. and friend of Roger Williams and Rhode Island, by Henry Melville King ... Providence, R.I., Preston & Rounds, 1909. vii, (2), 10 - 207 p. 20 cm. 9-25201.
  F67.V 24

WHITE, John. New England and New college, Oxford; a link in Anglo-American relations, by David Ogg ... Oxford, The Clarendon press, 1937.   24 p. front., plates. 21½ cm.   Concerns William of Wykeham and John White. 38-13867.
    F67.W
    LF655.O45

WALL, Robert Emmet. Massachusetts Bay; the crucial decade, 1640 - 1650. New Haven, Yale University Press, 1972.   x, 292 p. map. 23 cm. 72-75210.
    F67.W 17

WALLEY, John. A true servant of his generation characterized ... A sermon preached on the death of the Hon, John Walley ... By Ebenezer Pemberton ... Boston, Print. B. Green, 1712.   1, 32 p. 18 cm. 15-10662.
    F67.W 19
    Rare Book Coll.

WARD, Mrs. May (Alden) Old colony days. ... Boston, Roberts bros., 1896.   280 p. 19 cm. 1-23423.
    F67.W 25

WARD, Nathaniel (ca. 1578 - 1652) By Jean Beranger. Bordeaux, Société bordelaise de diffusion de travaux des lettres et sciences humaines, 1969.   290 p. 25 cm.
    F67.W26B4

WARE, Horace Everett. The charter and the men. Oct. 1901. Society of colonial wars in the commonwealth of Mass. (n.p., 1901)   31 p. 23½ cm. 2-14726.
    F67.W 27

WARE, Horace Everett. The transfer to Mass. of its charter government, 1630. Read before the Milton historical soc. Cambridge, J. Wilson, 1912.   23 p. fold. map. 24½ cm. 12-18475.
    F67.W 28

WASHBURN, Emory. Sketches of the judicial history of Mass. from 1630 to the revolution in 1775. Boston, Little and Brown, 1840.   407 p. 22 cm. 6-9297.
    F67.W 31

WERTENBAKER, Thomas Jefferson. The Puritan oligarchy; the founding of American civilization. N.Y., C. Scribner's Sons, 1947.   xiv, 359 p. illus., ports. 24 cm. 47-30879*.
    F67. W 4

— 1970.   xiv, 359 p. illus. 71-100352.
    F67. W 4
    1970

WHARTON, Richard, a seventeenth century New England colonial, by Viola F. Barnes ... Cambridge, J. Wilson, 1926.   2, 239 - 270 p. 25 cm. Repr. from the Pubs. of the Colonial soc. of Mass. v.26. Bibliographical foot-notes. CA 28-568 unrev.
    F67. W 52

WHEELOCK, Mr. Ralph, Puritan; a paper read before the Connecticut hist. soc. ... by Lewis W. Hicks ... (Hartford) Case, Lockwood & Brainard co., 1899.   iv, (5) - 51 p. front. (coat of arms) 24½ cm. 21-2808.
    F67. W 54

WHEELWRIGHT, John. His writings, including his Fast-day sermon, 1637. ... Boston, Print. for the Prince soc., 1876.   1, viii, 253 p. front., 3 facsims. 22½ x 18 cm. Pubs. of the Prince soc. v.9) Bibliography: p. (149) - 151. p. (149) - 151. 3-24559.
    F67.W547

— Freeport, N.Y., Books for Libraries Press (1970)   viii, 251 p. 23 cm. 70-128897.
    F67.W547
    1970

— N.Y., B. Franklin (1971)   viii, 253 p. 23 cm.
    F67.W547
    1971

WHEELWRIGHT, John, Memoirs of. By Charles Henry Bell. Cambridge, Print. J. Wilson, 1876.   148 p. facsims. 23 cm. 48-38523*.
    F67.W548

WHEELWRIGHT, John, 1592 - 1679, by John Heard, jr. ... Boston, and N.Y., Houghton, Mifflin, 1930.   6, (3) - 137 p. front., plates, ports. 21½ cm. 30-32003.
    F67.W 55

WHITE, John. The planters plea. Or The grounds of plantations examined, and usuall objections

MASSACHUSETTS

answered. London, Print. William Jones, 1630. 2, 84 p. 18 cm. 7-12045. "The work... contains facts relating to the earliest attempts at settlement in Massachusetts Bay, which can be found nowhere else, and these facts furnished by the persons who were themselves engaged as adventurers in these attempts."
F67.W 57
Rare Book Coll.

— N.Y., Da Capo Press, 1968. 84 p. 21 cm. (The English experience no. 60) 68-54669.
F67.W 57
1968

— (Washington, P. Force, 1837) 2, 47 p. 23½ cm. (In Force Tracts... v.2 (1838) no. 3) 4-27026 rev.
F67.W576
E187.F69

— (Rochester, G.P. Humphrey, 1898) 1, vi, 49, (2) p. 24 cm. Amer. colonial tracts monthly. (v.2) no. 3, July 1898) 4-27021.
F67.W 58

— printed in facsimile with an introd. by Marshall H. Saville. Rockport, Mass., The Sandy bay historical soc. and museum, 1930. 7 p., facsim.: 2, 84 p. 25 cm. (Sandy bay historical soc. and museum publications. v.1) 31-24981.
F67.W584

WHITE, John. The planting of colonies in New England. Boston, 1905.
F67.W 59

WHITE, John, the patriarch of Dorchester (Dorset) and the founder of Massachusetts, 1575 - 1648, with an account of the early settlements in Mass., 1620 - 1630, by Frances Rose-Troup... N.Y., London, G.P. Putnam's sons, 1930. xii, 483 p. 2 pl. incl. front. facsim. 24 cm. Bibliography: p. 467 - 469. "John White's pedigree": p. 403 - 417. "John White's works": p. 418 - 446. 31-3916.
F67.W595

WHITMORE, William Henry. The Massachusetts civil list for the colonial and provincial periods, 1630 - 1774. Being a list of names and dates of appointment of all the civil officers... Albany, J. Munsell, 1870. 172 p. 24 cm. Includes civil list for Plymouth colony: p. 35 - 40. 12-12549.
F67.W 61

— Baltimore, Genealogical Pub. Co., 1969. 172 p. 68-57949.
F67.W 61
1969

WILLARD, Josiah. The character of Caleb. In a sermon delivered... after the funeral of the Hon. Josiah Willard... By Thomas Prince... Boston, Print. S. Kneeland, 1756. 2, 30 p. 19 cm. 15-13270.
F67.W 69
Rare Book Coll.

SEWALL, Joseph. A tender heart pleasing to God... A sermon preached... after the death of the Hon. Josiah Willard... By Joseph Sewall...Boston, Print. S. Kneeland, 1756. 2, 22 p. 19 cm. 15-13271.
F67.W695
Rare Book Room

WINTRHOP, John. A declaration of former passages and proceedings betwixt the English and the Narrowgansets... (1926) (Photostat americana. Second series. Photostated at the Mass. hist. soc. no. 2)
F67.W 75

WINTHROP, John, Journal of; ship Arbella, Isle of Wight to Cape Ann in New England 1630, with A partial list of passengers. Lincoln, Mass., Sawtells of Somerset, 1969. 35, xviii p. 22 cm. 75-83773.
F67.W758
1969

WINTHROP, John. A journal of the transactions and occurrences in the settlement of Mass. and the other New-England colonies... 1630 to 1644: written by John Winthrop, esq., first governor of Mass. and now first pub. from a correct copy of the original manuscript... Hartford, Print. Elisha Babcock, 1790. 3, 364, (4) p. 21 cm. 1-13346.
F67.W 76
Jefferson coll.

WINTHROP, John. The history of New England from 1630 - 1649... From his original manuscripts. With notes... By James Savage... Boston, Print. Phelps and Farnham, 1825-6. 2 v. front. (port.) fold. facsim. 23 cm. First ed. pub. under title: A journal of the transactions and occurences in the settlement of Mass... 1-12051.
F67.W 78

— Boston, Little, Brown, 1853. 2 v. front. (port.) fold. facsim. 22½ cm. 1-12052. F67.W783

WINTHROP, John. Winthrop's journal, "History of New England," 1630 - 1649; ed. by James Kendall Hosmer ... New York, C. Scribner's sons, 1908. 2 v. front., fold. map, facsims. (partly fold.) 23 cm. (Half-title Original narratives of early American history ...) 8-17771. F67.W785

WINTHROP. A review of Winthrop's journal, as ed. and pub. by Hon. James Savage, under the title "The History of New England 1630 - 1649. Pub. in the N. E. hist. and geneal. reg. Oct. 1853 and Jan. 1854. Boston, Dutton & Wentworth, print., 1854. 23 p. front., ports. 24 cm. 1-12400. F67.W791

WINTHROP, John. Some old Puritan love-letters - John and Margaret Winthrop - 1618 - 1638; ed. by Joseph Hopkins Twichell. N.Y., Dodd, Mead, 1893. xviii, (19) - 187 p. incl. front. (port.) 2 fold. facsim. 20½ cm. 16-9743. F67.W7954

— 1894. xviii, 187 p. incl. front. (port.) 2 fold. facsim. 23 cm. 4-17365/4. F67.W7955

WINTHROP. Puritans and Yankees; the Winthrop dynasty of New England, 1630 - 1717. Princeton, N.J., Princeton University Press, 1962. xi, 379 p. 25 cm. 62-7400. F67.W7957

WINTHROP. The Puritan dilemma; the story of John Winthrop. By Edmund Sears Morgan. Ed. Oscar Handlin. (1st ed.) Boston, Little, Brown (1958) 224 p. 21 cm. (The Library of American biography) Includes bibliography. 58-6029. F67.W798

WINTHROP, John, governor of the Company of Massachusetts Bay in New England. By Robert George Raymer. (1st ed.) New York, Vantage Press (c1963) 182 p.
F67.W799

WINTHROP, John. Reading for children. History. John Winthrop. By Mrs. Nina Moore Tiffany. Cambridge, (Mass.) J. Wilson and son, 1886. 1, 32 p. 17 cm. 14-20920.
F67. W 8

WINTHROP, John and the great colony; or, Sketches of the settlement of Boston and of the more prominent persons connected with the Mass. colony. By Charles K. True ... New York, Nelson & Philips; Cincinnati, Hitchcock & Walden (1875) 207 p. incl. front., pl. 17 cm. Based on the author's Shawmut: or, The settlement of Boston by the Puritan Pilgrims, Boston, 1846. 15-27869. F67. W 81

— 1877. 207 p. incl. front., pl. 17 cm. 29-25253. F67.W812

WINTHROP, John, first governor of the Massachusetts colony, by Joseph Hopkins Twichell. New York, Dodd, Mead, 1891. xv, 245 p. front. (port.) 18 cm. (Makers of America) 13-33768. F67.W813

WINTHROP, John . .. A sketch of the life of John Winthrop, the younger, founder of Ipswich, Mass. in 1633, by Thomas Franklin Waters. 2d ed. (Cambridge) Print. for the Society, 1900. vi, 78 p. front. (port.) 6 facsim. 26 cm. (Pubs. of the Ipswich historical soc. vii) 13-7173. F67.W815

WINTHROP. Life and letters of John Winthrop, governor of the Massachusetts-Bay company at their emigration to New England, 1630. By Robert C. Winthrop. Boston, Ticknor and Fields, 1864 - 67. 2 v. pl., 3 port. (incl. fronts.) 4 facsim. (1 fold.) 23½ cm. 4-17081. F67.W817

WINTHROP, John, Life and letters of. By Robert Charles Winthrop. New York, Da Capo Press, 1971. 2 v. 24 cm. 72-152833. F67.W8172

WINTHROP. Presentation of statues of John Winthrop and Samuel Adams. By George F. Hoar. Washington, 1876. 21½ cm. F67. W 82

WINTHROP. ... Report of the Commission to procure memorial statues for the national Statuary hall at Washington. 1876. Boston, A.J. Wright, 1877. 61 p. 3 pl. (1 double) 23 cm. Appendix contains: Proceedings in the Congress of the U.S. on the presentation of the memorial statues of John Winthrop and Samuel Adams ... 8-14849. F67. W 83

MASSACHUSETTS

WINTHROP, Margaret, by Alice Morse Earle ... New York, C. Scribner's sons, 1895. xiii, 341 p.
fold. facsim. 18 cm. (Women of colonial and revolutionary times. v.1) 12-31988 rev.
F67.W 84

— (Spartanburg, S.C. Reprint Co., 1968) xiii, 341 p. 22 cm. Massachusetts heritage series, no. 2) 67-30156.
F67.W 84
1968

WINTHROP, Wait. The character and blessedness of the upright. A sermon occasion'd by the death of the Hon. Wait Winthrop ... By Joseph Sewall. Boston, Print. T. Crump, 1717. 1, 48 p. 14 cm.
5-19176.
F67.W 87
Rare Book Coll.

WOOD, James Playstead. Colonial Massachusetts. (Camden, N.J.) T. Nelson (1969) 176 p. illus.
23 cm. 71-82917.
F67.W874

WOOD, William. New Englands prospect; a true, lively and experimentall description of that part of America commonly called New England ... London, Print. T. Cotes for I. Bellamie, 1634.
98, (5) p. fold. map. 21 cm. L.C. copy imperfect. 49-52342 *.
F67.W877
Rare Book Coll.

— Boston, John Wilson, 1865. New York, B. Franklin, 1967. xxxi, 131 p. 23 cm. (B. Franklin: Research and source works series, 131) (American classics in history and social science, 2)
F67.W877
1967

— New York, Da Capo Press, 1968. 98, (5) p. 21 cm. (The English experience mo. 68) 68-54670.
F67.W877
1968

— London, Tho. Coates, for John Bellamie, 1635. 4, 83, (5) p. fold. map. 18 x 13 cm. 2d ed. 1st ed. pub. in 1634. 3-935.
F67.W 88

— Boston, Printed for the Society, 1865. xxxi p. 4 l., 131 p. map. 21½ x 17½ cm. (Prince soc., Boston. Pubs. v.1) 3-937.
F67.W 89

— (Boston? Reprinted for E.M. Boynton, 1898?) x, 103, (6) p. front. (double map) 22 x 17½ cm. 5-36908. F67. W 9

WOODBURY, Charles Levi. An old planter in New England. John Woodbury. (Boston, 1885)
103 p. 2 pl. 27½ cm. 3-20266.
F67. W95

YOUNG, Alexander. Chronicles of the first planters of the colony of Massachusetts Bay, from 1623 to 1636. ... Boston, C.C. Little and J. Brown, 1846. viii, 571 p. front. (port.) map. 22½ cm. Bound with this is Francis Higginson's New-England's plantation. 1-12053-M1. 2-18516 rev.
F67.Y 68

— New York, Da Capo Press, 1970. viii, 571 p. 24 cm. 71-87668.
F67.W 68
1970

NEW PLYMOUTH COLONY.

ABBOT, Abiel. A discourse delivered ... at Plymouth, Dec. 22, 1809, at the celebration of the 188th anniversary of the landing of our forefathers in that place. Boston, Print. Greenough and Stebbins, 1810. 28 p. 23½ cm. 25-3660.
F68.A 12

ADAMS, J.Q. An oration ... Plymouth, Dec. 22, 1802.
F68. A 2

ADDISON, Albert Christopher. The romantic story of the Mayflower pilgrims, and its place in the life of to-day ... with numerous original illus. Boston, L.C. Page, 1911. 3, v-xiv, 192 p. incl. plates, ports. front. 24½ cm. 11-26979.
F68.A 22

— New ed. with explanatory notes. Boston, The Page co., 1918. xxii, 192 p. incl. plates, ports. front. 24½ cm. 18-23549.
F68.A 23

ALBRO, John Adams. The fathers of New England. A discourse delivered at Cambridge .. 1844. Boston, C. C. Little and J. Brown, 1845.   40 p. 22½ cm. 15-2154.   F68. A 34

ALFONSO, Jose Antonio. ... Los peregrinos del Mayflower i su influencia americana; ... Santiago de Chile, Imprenta universitaria, 1921.   16 p. 18½ cm. 43-34722.   F68. A348

ALLERTON, Isaac, first assistant of Plymouth colony. E. B. Patten, compiler. 1908. Minneapolis, Press of Imperial print. (1908)   18 p. 22½ cm. 10-2008.   F68. A 44

AMES, Azel. The May-flower and her log, July 15, 1620 - May 6, 1621, chiefly from original sources. Boston and N. Y., Houghton, Mifflin, 1901.   xxii, 375 p. front., pl., port., maps, facsim. 28 cm. Bibliography: p. 345 - 357. 1-10743.   F68. A 51
Rare Book Coll.

ARBER, Edward. The story of the Pilgrim fathers, 1606 - 1623; as told by themselves, their friends, and their enemies. London, Ward and Downey; Boston, (etc.) Houghton, Mifflin, 1897.   x, 634 p. front. (port.) map. 19 cm. 1-12054. (Contains: Winslow, Edward. Good news from New England p. 509-600) 8-22380.
F68. A 66

ARCHER, Gleason Leonard. Mayflower heroes. illus. by Henry C. Pitz. N. Y. and London, The Century co. (1931)   xv, 346 p. incl. front., plates, maps. 21 cm. 31-33609.   F68. A 68

ARCHER, Gleason Leonard. With axe and musket at Plymouth. New York, The Amer. hist. soc., 1936.   305 p. front., plates. 27½ cm. 36-16532.   F68. A687

ATWOOD, William Franklin. The Pilgrim story, being largely a compilation from the documents of Governor Bradford and Governor Winslow ... together with a list of Mayflower passengers. ... illus. by Leo Schreiber. Plymouth, The Memorial press (1940)   74, (2) p. illus. 19½ cm. Bibliography included in the preface. 40-35097.   F68. A 78

BACON, Leonard. An address before the New England society of the city of New York on forefathers' day, Dec. 22, 1838. New York, E. Collier, 1839.   46 p. 24 cm. 17-14585.
F68. B118

BACON, Leonard. The genesis of the New England churches. ... New York, Harper & bros., 1874. xiv, (2), (17) - 485 p. incl. front., illus. 7 pl., 2 port., 2 maps. 21 cm. 8-29774.   F68. B 12

— New York, Arno Press, 1972.   485 p. illus. 23 cm. (Religion in America, series II) 74-38435.   F68. B 12
1972

BAILEY, Richard Briggs. Pilgrim possessions as told by their wills and inventories. (Weston? Mass.) 1951.   150 l. illus. 30 cm. Bibliography: leaves (148) - 150. 51-24630.   F68. B 13

BAKER, George Pierce. The Pilgrim spirit; a pageant in celebration of the tercentenary of the landing of the Pilgrims at Plymouth ... Boston, Marshall Jones co., (1921)   3, 5 - 136 p. 19 cm. Verse by Robert Frost, Hermann Hagedorn; Josephine Preston Peabody, and Edwin Arlington Robinson." 21-12352.   F68. B 14

BAKER, George Pierce. "The Pilgrim spirit"; Plymouth tercentenary pageant. (Boston, The Southgate press, c.1921)   (32) p. 25½ cm. 21-16544.   F68. B 15

BAKER, Henry Moore. The pilgrim Puritans. A lecture ... Washington, Gibson bros., print., 1890.   16 p. 22½ cm. 4-36302.   F68. B 16

BANKS, Charles Edward. The English ancestry and homes of the Pilgrim fathers, who came to Plymouth on the "Mayflower" in 1620, the "Fortune" in 1621 and the "Anne" and the "Little James" in 1623. New York, The Grafton press (c1929)   xi, 187 p. fold. map, facsim. 25 cm. 29-10699.
F68. B 19
Rare Book Coll.
shelf & L. H. & G.

MASSACHUSETTS 41

— Southern Book Company, 1962. F68. B19

BANVARD, Joseph. Plymouth and the Pilgrims; or, Incidents of adventure in the history of the first settlers. Boston, Gould and Lincoln, 1851. 2, (3) - 288 p. incl. illus., map. front., 2 pl. port. 17½ cm. 15-13279 rev. F68. B 2

— 1853. 2, (3) - 288 p. incl. illus., map. front., plates, port. 16½ cm. 1-12055. F68.B 21

— New ed., rev. and enl. Chicago, Interstate pub. co. (1886) 303 p. front., illus., plates, port., map. 18½ cm. 1-12056. F68.B 22

BARTLETT, Robert Merrill. The pilgrim way. Philadelphia, Pilgrim Press (1971) xi, 371 p. illus. 26 cm. Includes bibliographical refs. 70-172790 MARC. F68.B 27

BARTLETT, William Henry. The Pilgrim fathers; or, The founders of New England in the reign of James the First. London, A. Hall, Virtue & co., 1853. 3, (v) - xii, (13) - 240 p. front., illus., plates. 24½ cm. 1-12057. F68.B 29

— London, T. Nelson, 1863. x, (13) - 230 p. front., illus., plates. 22 cm. 25-13911. F68.B295

— De Pelgrim-vaders... Leiden, P. H. van den Heuvell, 1859. x, 306 p. front. 8°. 1-12058-M1. F68.B 30

BATES, Esther Willard. A pageant of Pilgrims. ... A pageant setting forth the historical story of the Pilgrims ... Boston, Chicago, The Pilgrim press (c. 1920) 1, v-xii, 42 p. front., plates. 19½ cm. 20-14455. F68.B 32

— Boston and Los Angeles, (Walter H. Baker co., 1936) 69 p. 19 cm. CA 36-313 unrev. F68.B 322

BAYLIES, Francis. An historical memoir of the colony of New Plymouth ... Boston, Hilliard, Gray, Little and Wilkins, 1830. 4 pt. in 2 v. 22½ cm. Contents. - v.1. 1620 - 1641. v.2. 1641 - 1692. 1-12059. F68.B 35

— With some corrections, additions, and a copious index ... Boston, Wiggin & Lunt, 1866. 2 v. fronts., ports., fold. maps, fold. geneal. tab. 25 cm. 1-12060. F68.B 36

BEALS, Frank Lee. Real adventure with the Pilgrim settlers; William Bradford, Miles Standish, Squanto. Ed. Lowell C. Ballard, illus. John Masters and J. H. Cheek. (Eureka Springs? Ark., 1951) 44 p. illus. 22 cm. (American heroes series) 52-21267. F68.B367

— San Francisco, H. Wagner Pub. Co. (1954) 41 p. illus. 22 cm. 54-10430. F68.B367

BEARDSLEY, Frank Grenville. The builders of a nation, a history of the Pilgrim fathers ... Boston, R. G. Badger (1921) 356 p. 21½ cm. 21-14220. F68.B 37

BECK, Barbara L. The Pilgrims of Plymouth. New York, F. Watts, 1972. 89 p. illus. 22 cm. 79-187970. F68.B 38

BEECHER, Lyman. The memory of our fathers. A sermon delivered at Plymouth ... 1827. Boston, T. R. Marvin, print., 1828. 39 p. 23½ cm. 15-12394. F68. B 4

BITTINGER, Frederick William. The story of the Pilgrim tercentenary celebration at Plymouth in the year 1921. Plymouth (The Memorial press) 1923. 155 p. incl. front., illus. 24 cm. 24-333. F68.B 55

BLACK, Frank Swett. Address of Honorable Frank S. Black before the New England soc., New York ... 1908. 7 p. 23 cm. 14-5964. F68.B 62

BLANCHARD, Jonathan. Christ purifying His temple ... A sermon preached ... 1865 ... Boston, Congregational board of pubs., 1866.   29 p. 24 cm. 15-2155.   F68.B 63

BLAXLAND, George Cuthbert. "Mayflower" essays on the story of the Pilgrim fathers as told in Governor Bradford's ms. History of the Plimoth plantation ... London, Ward & Downey, 1896. vi, 146 p. fold. map. 20 cm. 1-12061.   F68.B 64

— Freeport, N.Y., Books for Libraries Press (1972)   vi, 146 p. 23 cm. (Essay index reprint series) 78-89713.
F68.B 64
1972

BLOOMINGTON, Harry. Plymouth tercentenary, illus. with a brief history of the life and struggles of the Pilgrim fathers, incl. original program of the "Pilgrim spirit", etc. ... New Bedford, Mass., (Commercial pub. co.) 1921.   (98) p. incl. front. (port.) illus. 2 fold. pl. 25 cm. 22-7403.
F68.B 66

BOAST, Mary. The 'Mayflower' and Pilgrim story: chapters from Rotherhithe and Southwark; illus. David Burch and others, 1970.   3-56 p. (2 fold.) illus. facsims., maps. 22 cm. Bibliography: p. 54-56.
F68.B 69

BORRESON, Mary Jo. Let's go to Plymouth with the pilgrims. Illus. by Gerald McCann. N.Y., G.P. Putnam (1963)   48 p. 22 cm. (Let's go history series) 63-15566.   F68.B 72

BOSTON. A memorial of the Pilgrims; the presentation to the city of Boston ... of an ancient railing from the city of Boston in Lincolnshire. Boston, Mass., Print. the Boston public library ... 1919.
3, 14 p. incl. facsim. 2 pl. (incl. front.) 31½ cm. 19-12798.   F68.B 74

BOWMAN, George Ernest. The Mayflower compact and its signers, with facsimiles and a list of the Mayflower passengers, 1620 - 1920. ... Boston, Mass. soc. of Mayflower descendants, 1920.
19 p. illus. (facsims.) 23½ cm. 21-11772.   F68.B745

BOYNTON, Charles Brandon. Oration delivered before the New England society of Cincinnati, on the anniversary of the landing of the Pilgrims ... 1847. Cincinnati, Collins & Van Wagner, print., 1848.
32 p. 20½ cm. 44-45395.   F68.B747

BRADFORD, William. The Mayflower pilgrims, being a condensation in the original wording and spelling of the story written by Gov. Wm. Bradford ... Comp. by John T. Wheelwright in the year of the tercentenary. Boston, Print. McGrath-Sherrill, 1921.   6, 47 p. 10 l. front., illus. (incl. port., maps) 23½ x 17½ cm. 22-3087.   F68.B748

BRADFORD, Alden. A sermon delivered at Plymouth, ... 1804 ... Boston, Print. Gilbert and Dean, 1805.   24 p. 23 cm. 15-4515.   F68.B 75

BRADFORD, William. History of the Plimoth plantation containing an account of the voyage of the 'Mayflower' ... Now reproduced in facsimile ... with an introd. by John A. Doyle ... London, Ward and Downey; Boston, Houghton, Mifflin, 1896.   2, 17 p. facsim. (535 p.) 36½ cm. The evenly numbered pages are generally blank. 1-16539.
F68.B 78
Rare Book Coll.

— ... Now first printed from the original manuscript, for the Massachusetts historical society. Pub. at the charge of the Appleton fund. Boston, Little, Brown, 1856.   xix, 476 p. 25 cm. Covers years 1608 - 1646. Reissue of the greater part of v. 3 of the 4th series of Collections of the Mass. hist. soc. 1-12062. L.C. copy replaced by microfilm.
F68.B 79
Microfilm 8660 F

— ... Arranged and annotated for schools. N.Y., E. Maynard (1890)   4 p. illus. (incl. 2 maps) 18½ cm. 1-12063.
F68.B794

BRADFORD Manuscript, The. Account of the part taken by the American antiquarian soc. in the return of the Bradford ms. to America. Worcester, C. Hamilton, 1898.   108 p. 5 port. (incl. front.) 25 cm. 3-30872.
F68.B799

BRADFORD, William. Bradford's history "Of Plimoth plantation." From the original manuscript. With a report of the proceedings incident to the return of the manuscript to Mass. Printed under the direction of the secretary of the commonwealth ... Boston, Wright & Potter, 1898. lxxvii, 555 p. front., ports., facsims. 25 cm. 1-12064.
F68.B8

— 1899. lxxvii, 555 p. front., ports., facsims. 23 cm. 13-22179.
F68.B801

BRADFORD, William. ... Bradford's history of Plymouth plantation, 1606 - 1646; ed. William T. Davis ... with a map and three facsims. N.Y., C. Scribner's sons, 1908. xv, 3-437 p. fold. map, 3 facsim. (incl. front.) 22½ cm. 8-7375.
F68.B802

— Rendered into modern English, by Valerian Paget. N.Y., The John McBride co., 1909. xxvi, 349 p. 19½ cm. 9-28567.
F68.B803

— Pub. for the Mass. historical soc. by Houghton Mifflin, 1912. 2 v. fronts. (v.2 col. port.) illus., plates (1 double) maps (part fold.) fold plan., facsims. (part fold.) 25 cm. Fold. map in pocket at end of each vol. 12-29493.
F68.B805

— N.Y. Russell & Russell (1968) (c1912) 2 v. illus. 25 cm. 68-10904.
F68.B805 1968

— rendered into modern English by Harold Paget. N.Y., E.P. Dutton, (1920) xxviii, 353 p. 22 cm. 20-21983.
F68.B806

BRADFORD, William. The history of Plymouth Colony, a modern English version (by Harold Paget) with an introd. by George F. Willison. N.Y., Pub. for the Classic Club by W.J. Black (1948) xxvii, 428 p. maps, facsims. 20 cm. 48-3459*.
F68.B807

BRADFORD, William. Of Plymouth Plantation, 1620 - 1647; the complete text, with notes and introd. by Samuel Eliot Morison. New ed. N.Y., Knopf, 1952. xliii, 448, xv p. maps. 25 cm. First ed. pub. in 1856 under title: History of Plymouth Plantation. 51-13222.
F68.B8073

— N.Y., Modern Library, (1967) xii, 448, xv p. 19 cm. (Modern library of the world's best books 379)
F68.B8073 1967

BRADFORD, William ... Extracts from Bradford's History of Plymouth Plantation. New York, A. Lovell & co., 1896. 32 p. 18 cm. 8-16246.
F68.B808

BRADFORD, William. Pilgrim courage ... Selected episodes from his original history of Plimoth Plantation and passages from the journals of Wm. Bradford and Edward Winslow. Adapted and ed. by E. Brooks Smith and others. (1st ed.) Boston, Little, Brown (1962) 108 p. 24 cm. 62-8314.
F68.B8085

BRADFORD, William. Of Plymouth Plantation. Selected and ed., with an introd. by Harvey Wish. New York, Capricorn Books (1962) 227 p. 21 cm. 62-8170.
F68.B8086

BRADFORD, William. The voyage of the Mayflower from William Bradford's Of Plymouth Plantation 1620 - 1647. Boston, Old South Assoc. (1966, c.1952) 32 p. 20 cm. (Old South leaflets, nos. 232-233) 66-19788.
F68.B8088 1966

BRADFORD, William. A letter of Wm. Bradford and Isaac Allerton, 1623. 27 cm.
F68.B81

BRADFORD. Who identified Bradford's manuscript? By John Ward Dean. (Boston, 1883) 24½ cm.
F68.B82

BRADFORD, William. The voyage of the Mayflower. Boston, 1905.
F68.B823

BRADFORD, William, A colony leader; by Charles P. Graves.   Illus. Marvin Besunder.   Champaign, Ill., Garrard Pub. Co. (1969)   64 p. illus. 24 cm. 69-10371.   F68.B8235

BRADFORD.   Rebel Pilgrim; a biography of Governor William Bradford.   By Wilma Pitchford Hays. Philadelphia, Westminster Press (1969)   96 p. 69-10387.   F68.B824

BRADFORD, William, of Plymouth, by Albert H. Plumb.   Boston, R.G. Badger (1920)   112 p. front. 21 cm. 21-2836.   F68.B825

BRADFORD of Plymouth.   By Bradford Smith.   (1st ed.)   Philadelphia, Lippincott (1951)   338 p. 22 cm. "Notes and sources": p. 322 - 330. 51-11198.   F68.B827

BRECK, Samuel.   Discourse before the Soc. of the sons of New England of ... Philadelphia, on the history of the early settlement of their country ...   Philadelphia, J.C. Clark, print., 1845.   44 p. 23 cm. 3-24761.   F68.B829

BREWSTER.   Chief of the Pilgrims; or, The life and time of William Brewster, ruling elder of the Pilgrim co. that founded New Plymouth ...   By the Rev. Ashbel Steele ... Illus. with 5 steel engravings.   Philadelphia, J.B. Lippincott, 1857.   xxviii p. (33) - 416 p. illus., 8 pl. (incl. front.) 22 cm. 7-12024.   F68.B 84

— Freeport, N.Y., Books for Libraries Press (1970)   xxviii, 416 p. illus. 72-133535.   F68.B 84 1970

BREWSTER, William, of the Mayflower; portrait of a pilgrim, by Dorothy Brewster.   N.Y., N.Y. University Press, 1970.   xiii, 116 p. illus. 73-133014.   F68.B84B7

BREWSTER.   Elder William Brewster, of the "Mayflower": his books and autographs, with other notes.   By Justin Winsor.   Cambridge (Mass.) J. Wilson, 1887.   17 p. 24½ cm. Reprinted from the Proceedings of the Mass. hist. soc. March, 1887. 7-12026.   F68.B842

BRIEF sketch of the character and sufferings of the Pilgrims who settled at Plymouth, Dec. 1620. Boston, Print. J.H.A. Frost, 1820.   8 p. 23½ cm. 5-5128.   F68.B 85

BRIGHAM, William.   The colony of New Plymouth, and its relations to Massachusetts: a lecture of a course by members of the Mass. hist. soc., Boston, J. Wilson and son, 1869.   27 p. 23½ cm. Pub. also in Mass. hist. soc. Lectures before the Lowell institute. 1869. p. 163-189. 10-3088.   F68.B 86

BROOKS, Dexter M.   Of Plymouth Plantation.   Plymouth, Mass., Leyden Pub. Co., 1949.   unpaged. illus. 21 cm. 57-55490.   F68.B866

BROWN, Hugh Stowell.   The Pilgrim fathers: a lecture illustrative of the government prize picture, The departure of the Pilgrim fathers.   Manchester, T. Agnew (1854)   46 p. fold. pl. 21 x 16½ cm. 17-14587.   F68.B868

BROWN, John.   The Pilgrim fathers of New England and their Puritan successors ... New York, Chicago (etc.) F.H. Revell co. (1895)   1, (5) - 368 p. incl. plates. port. front. 23 cm. American edition. 1-12065.   F68.B 87

— 3d Amer. ed.   N.Y., Chicago, etc. F.H. Revell co. (1896)   vii, (5) - 368 p. incl. front., illus., 9 pl., port. 22½ cm. 16-9742.   F68.B874

— 4th ed.   London, The Religious tract soc., 1920.   352 p. incl. front., illus., plates, port. 19 cm. 20-16197.   F68.B 88

BULFINCH, Stephen Greenleaf.   A discourse suggested by Weir's picture of the embarkation of the Pilgrims ... Washington, Print. Gales and Seaton, 1844.   13 p. 21½ cm. 18-7521.   F68.B 916

BUCKINGHAM, Samuel Giles.   A memorial of the Pilgrim fathers. ... Springfield, S. Bowles, 1867. 52 p. 21 cm. 1-12066.   F68. B 92

MASSACHUSETTS 45

BURBANK, Alfred Stevens. A brief history of the Pilgrims, comp. from the writings of Governor Bradford and Governor Winslow ... With alphabetical list of Mayflower passengers. Plymouth, Mass., A.S. Burbank (1920?)   v, 57 p. 18 cm. 21-4840.   F68.B 94

BUREAU of military and civic achievement. The Mayflower passengers, their children and grandchildren ... (Washington, D.C., 1921)   30 p. 26 x 10 ½ cm. CA 21-475 unrev.   F68.B 95

BUREAU of military and civic achievement. Mayflower descendants and their marriages for two generations after the landing ... Washington, D.C., (1922)   39, (3) p. 23 x 10 cm. Pub. 1921 under title of F68.B95 above. 22-10635.   F68.B951

— 2d ed. Washington, D.C., 1922.   40 p. 22 x 10 cm. 22-4454.   F68.B952

BUSHNELL, Horace. The fathers of New England. An oration ... New-York, G.P. Putnam, 1850. 44 p. 18 cm. 1-12067.   F68.B 97

CARPENTER, Edmund Janes. The Mayflower Pilgrims ... New York, Cincinnati, The Abingdon press (1918)   255 p. front. (port.) plates. 21 cm. 18-9770.   F68.C 29

CARVER, John, the first governor of Plymouth colony ... An earnest plea for a statue in Plymouth ... Address by Archie Lee Talbot ... (Plymouth? 1927)   9 p. illus. (port.) 22 ½ cm. 27-27533.   F68.C 32

CARVER, John. National memorial, a bronze statue of John Carver the great leader of the Pilgrims, their first governor ... Address ... (Augusta? Me.) c. 1932.   19 p. incl. port. 22 ½ cm. 35M1870.   F68.C324

CASS, Lewis. Address delivered before the New England society of Michigan. Detroit, F.P. Markham, 1849.   47 p. 24 ½ cm. 17-23198.   F68.C 34
     Toner Coll.

CAVANAGH, William Henry. Colonial expansion, including the rise and fall of historic settlements (by) William Henry Cavanagh. Boston, R.G. Badger (1924)   263 p. 22 cm. 24-12011.   F68.C 37

CHANDLER, Joseph Ripley. "The pilgrims of the rock." An oration, delivered ... before the Society of the sons of New England of Philadelphia ... Philadelphia, J.C. Clark, 1846.   31 p. 8°. 2-11377.   F68.C 44

CHAPIN, Stephen. The duty of living for the good of posterity. A sermon ... Portland (Me.) Print. T. Todd, 1821.   48 p. 22 cm. 1-12068.   F68.C 46

CHESTER, John. A sermon in commemoration of the landing of the New-England Pilgrims. Albany, Print. E. and E. Hosford, 1820.   31 p. 24 cm. 15-4512.   F68.C 52

CLARK, Mary. Biographical sketches of the fathers of New England, intended to acquaint youth with the lives, characters, etc. of those who founded our civil and religious institutions. Concord (N.H.) Marsh, Capen and Lyon, 1836.   v, (7) - 180 p. 14 ½ cm. Contents. - John Robinson. - John Carver. - Edward Winslow. - William Brewster. - William Bradford. - Robert Cushman. - Myles Standish. - John Winthrop. - Roger Williams. 4-22945.   F68.C 55

COBB, Alvan. God's culture of his vineyard. A sermon ... Taunton, E. Anthony, 1832. 24 p. 22 cm. 15-11531.   F68.C585

COCKSHOTT, Winnifred. The Pilgrim fathers; their church and colony ... London, Methuen & co. (1909)   xv, 348 p. front. (port.) plates, map. 23 cm. "Chief authorities": p. xiii-xv. 10-2297.   F68.C 6

CODMAN, John. The faith of the pilgrims; a sermon ... Boston, Perkins and Marvin, 1832. 28 p. 22 cm. Bound with Francis, Convers. A discourse delivered at Plymouth, Mass ... 1832 and Worcester, New England's glory and crown. 56 p. 22 cm.   F68.C 63

COHEN STUART, Martinus. The Pilgrim fathers' first meeting for public worship in North America. A brief historical sketch, illustrative of a picture by J. Geo. Schwartze... Trans. from the Dutch. Utrecht, Kemink and son, 1860.   35 p. 23½ cm. 1-16208 rev.   F68.C 67

— 2d ed.   Amsterdam, W.H. Kirberger, 1866.   35 p. front. 20½ cm. 16-9494 rev.
F68.C673

COLEMAN, William Macon. The history of the primitive Yankees; or, The Pilgrim fathers in New England and Holland... Washington, Columbia pub. co., 1881.   v, (7) - 62 p. 22½ cm. 1-16282.
F68.C 69

CONANT, Sylvanus. An anniversary sermon preached at Plymouth... Boston, Print. Thomas & John Fleet, 1777.   31 p. 20½ cm. 15-2165.   F68. C 7
Rare Book Coll.

CONGREGATION club. In remembrance of the ceremonial unveiling of the Pilgrim-fathers' bronze-tablet presented by the Boston Congregation club to the Delfshaven Reformed church... Rotterdam, J.M. Bredée (1906)   43 p. incl. cover-title. 4 pl. 26 x 18½ cm. English and Dutch. 9-21185.   F68.C 73

CONNECTICUT... Celebration as authorized by the Connecticut legislature of 1919 in commemoration of the 300th anniversary of the landing of the Pilgrims at Plymouth Rock, 1620... Hartford, Conn., 1920.   8 p. 23½ cm. 21-19755.   F68.C 74

CONNECTICUT. The proceedings by the state of Connecticut in commemoration of the tercentenary anniversary of the landing of the Pilgrims... 1620 - 1920. (Hartford? 1921?)   35, (4) p. 21 cm. 21-27160.   F68.C 75

CONNECTICUT. A public letter from the state of Connecticut to the children in her schools. Tercentenary anniversary of the landing of the Pilgrims... 1620-1920. (Hartford? 1921)   4 p. 21½ cm. 21-19751.   F68.C 76

COPP, Joseph A. "The old ways" - or the Pilgrims and their principles. A discourse on the anniversary of the landing of the Pilgrims... Boston, T.R. Marvin, 1857.   24 p. 23½ cm. 15-2168.
F68.C 78

CORDNER, John. The vision of the Pilgrim fathers. An oration, spoken before the New England soc. of Montreal... Montreal, H. Rose, 1857.   54 p. 22 cm. 1-12069.
F68.C 79

COUNCIL for New England. The first Plymouth patent: granted June 1, 1621. Ed. Charles Deane. Cambridge, Priv. print., 1854.   viii, (9) - 16 p. illus. (facsim.) 24½ x 21 cm. From Mass. hist. soc. Collections, 4th ser. v.2. 1-12070.   F68.C 85

COWIE, Leonard W. The Pilgrim Fathers. London, Wayland Ltd., 1970.   128 p. illus., facsims., maps, ports. 24 cm. index. (The Wayland documentary history series) Bibliography p. 121.   F68.C 86

— (1st Amer. ed.) N.Y., Putnam (1972)   128 p. illus. 24 cm. (The Putnam documentary history series) 78-171586.
F68.C 86
1972

CRAFTS, William. Address delivered before the New-England society of South-Carolina... Being the 200th anniversary of the landing at Plymouth of the ancestors of N.E. Charleston... print. T.B. Stephens, 1820.   16 p. 23½ cm. 14-7364.   F68.C 88

CRANDON, Edwin Sanford. ... Old Plymouth days and ways; 18th century celebrations of the landing of the Pilgrims... (Boston) Rosemary press, for the use of the members of the Chile club (1921) 26 p. front., illus. 23½ cm. 22-1049.   F68.C885

CRAWFORD, Mary Caroline. In the days of the Pilgrim fathers... Boston, Little, Brown, 1920. xiv, 331 p. front., plates, ports., maps, facsims. 21½ cm. 20-9735.   F68. C 9

MASSACHUSETTS   47

— Detroit, Singing Tree Press, 1970.   xiv, 331 p. illus. 23 cm. 74-129572.   F68. C 9 1921a

CUSHMAN, Robert Woodward. Plymouth's Rock: "the rock whence we were hewn" A discourse ... on the 230th anniversary of the embarkation of the Pilgrims. Boston, J. M. Hewes, print., 1855. 31 p. 23½ cm. 6-38066.   F68. C 98

DAVIS, John. A discourse before the Mass. historical soc. ... At their anniversary commemoration of the first landing of our ancestors ... Boston, John Eliot, 1814.   31 p. 24 cm. 1-12071.   F68. D 26

DEXTER, Henry Martyn. The England and Holland of the Pilgrims ... Boston and N. Y., Houghton, Mifflin, 1905.   xii, (5), 4-673 p. front., illus., 5 pl. map. 22½ cm. "Index of publications": p. 655-662. Bibliographical footnotes. 5-33037.   F68. D 5

DEXTER, Henry Martyn. Pilgrim memoranda. Boston, Todd, 1870.   39 p. 8°. Ed. of 25 copies. 1-12075-M1.   F68. D 52

DEXTER, Henry Martyn. Memoranda, historical, chronological etc. prepared with the hope to aid those whose interest in Pilgrim memorials, and history, is freshened by this jubilee year ... Boston, Print. for the use of Congregational ministers, 1870.   39 p. 23½ cm. 5-5561.   F68. D 53

DEXTER, Morton. The story of the Pilgrims. Boston and Chicago, Congregational Sunday-school and pub. soc. (1894)   ix, 11-363 p. front., plates. 18½ cm. 17-3663.   F68. D 54

DILLINGHAM, William Henry. An oration delivered before the Soc. of the sons of New England of Philadelphia ... Philadelphia, J. C. Clark, print, 1847.   38 p. 24½ cm. 15-4510.   F68. D 57

DONOVAN, Frank Robert. The Mayflower compact. Illus. Hedda Johnson. N. Y., Crosset & Dunlap (1968)   175 p. illus. 21 cm. 68-29981.   F68. D 65

DRAKE, Samuel Adams. On Plymouth rock ... Boston, Lee & Shepard, 1897.   173 p. incl. front., illus. 18 cm. 1-12076/3.   F68. D 76

DRAPER, Andrew Sloan. ... An address at Forefathers; convocation ... The Pilgrim and his share in American life. Champaign, Ill., Gazette print. (1896)   23 p. 16 cm. 1-4201.   F68. D 77

DUNKIN, Benjamin Faneuil. Address, delivered before the members of the New-England society in Charleston (S. C.) Charleston, Print. Courier office, 1820.   8 p. 19 cm. 16-23666.   F68. D 9

DUTTON, Samuel William Southmayd. The fathers of New England - Religion their ruling motive in their emigration. New Haven, A. H. Maltby, 1851.   17 p. 23 cm. 15-4514.   F68. D 97

ECKHOF, Albert. Three unknown documents concerning the Pilgrim fathers in Holland ... With 6 facsims. The Hague, M. Nijhoff, 1920.   2, 35 p. illus., 5 facsim. on 3 pl. 22 cm. 20-20511 rev.   F68. E 26

ELDRIDGE, Azariah. An address delivered before the New England society, in Ann Arbor, Mich ... Ann Arbor, E. B. Pond, print., 1861.   15 p. 20½ cm. 45-47206.   F68. E 35

EMMONS, Nathaniel. A sermon ... Dedham (Mass.) Print H. & W. H. Mann, 1821.   24, 4 p. illus. (music) 23½ cm. 17-15509.   F68. E 54

EVERETT, Albert. Early franchise rights in Massachusetts and other New England colonies. Hornell, N. Y., Wilsons' assoc., print. (1936)   61 p. 22 cm. 39-5677.   F68. E 92

EVERETT, Charles Carroll. A sermon ... Bangor, print. B. A. Burr, 1865.   10 p. 24 cm. 15-10664.   F68. E 93

EVERETT, Edward. An oration ... Boston, Cummings, Hilliard & co., 1825.   46 p. 21 cm.
19-3252.
                                                                                                                                     F68. E 94

—   73 p. 22 ½ cm. 1-12078.   F68. E 95

EVERETT, Edward. Remarks at the Plymouth festival ... in commemoration of the embarkation of the Pilgrims. Boston, Crosby, Nichols, 1853.   18 p. 24 cm. 44-24406.
                                                                                                                                         F68. E 96
                                                                                                                               Rare Book Coll.

FLEMING, Thomas J. One small candle; the pilgrims' first year in America. (1st ed.) New York, W. W. Norton, (1964)   222 p. 22 cm. 64-17513.   F68. F 55

FORD, Worthington Chauncey. Address made at the general court of the Society of colonial wars in the state of Rhode Island and Providence plantations ... (Providence, 1921?)   5 - 14 p. 23 ½ cm. 21-19752.
                                                                                                                             F68. F 7

FOUNTAIN, David Guy. The 'Mayflower' pilgrims and their pastor. Worthing, Walter, 1970.
80 p. illus. 19 cm.   F68. F 73

FRANCIS, May E. History of the Pilgrims, ...(Waterloo, Ia., W. B. Howell, print.) 1915.   31 p. 16 cm.
17-13319.   F68. F 8

FROST, John Edward. Immortal voyage ... and pilgrim parallels: problems, protests, patriotism, 1620 - 1970. North Scituate, Mass., Hawthorne Press (1970)   x, 110 p. illus. 20 x 25 cm.
                                                                                                                                         F68. F 86

FRUITS of the Mayflower; or, Conversations respecting the Pilgrim fathers. New York, M. W. Dodd, 1849.   108 p. 16 cm. 6-20069.   F68. F 94

FULLER, Dr. Samuel, of the Mayflower (1620), the pioneer physician. By Thomas F. Harrington ... (Baltimore, The Friedenwald co., 1903)   21 p. 23 ½ cm. From the Johns Hopkins hospital bulletin vol. xiv, no. 151, Oct., 1903. 11-19271.   F68. F 96

FURNESS, William Henry. The spirit of the Pilgrims. An oration delivered before the Soc. of the sons of N. E. of Philadelphia ... Philadelphia, Print. J. C. Clark, 1846.   22 p. 23 ½ cm. 5-3873.
                                                                                                                             F68. F 98

GALE, Nahum. The Pilgrims' first year in New England. Boston, Mass. Sabbath school soc. (1857)
viii, (7) - 336, (4) p. front., plates, maps. 16 cm. 1-12079.   F68. G 15

GERSON, Noel Bertram. Rock of freedom; the story of the Plymouth Colony ... Drawings by Barry Martin. N. Y., J. Messner (1964)   190 p. 22 cm. 64-20155.   F68. G 4

GILL, Crispin. Mayflower remembered; a history of the Plymouth pilgrims. New York, Taplinger Pub. Co. (1970)   206 p. illus. 23 cm. 75-106909.   F68. G53
                                                                                                                                          1970

— Newton Abbot, David & Charles, 1970.   206 p. plates. illus., maps. 23 cm. index. Bibliography: p. 195-197.
                                                                                                                                               F68. G 53
                                                                                                                                          1970b

GOODWIN, Henry Martyn. The Pilgrim fathers. A glance at their history, character and principles, in two memorial discourses, ... Rockford, Ill., Bird, Conick, & Flint, print., 1870.   36 p. 23 cm.
18-3921.   F68. G 64

GOODWIN, John Abbot. The Pilgrim fathers. Oration delivered before the City council and citizens of Lowell ... Lowell, Mass., Penhallow print., 1877.   50 p. 24 cm. 1-12080 rev.
                                                                                                                                            F68. G 65

MASSACHUSETTS

GOODWIN, John Abbot. The Pilgrim republic; an historical review of the colony of New Plymouth, with sketches of the rise of other New England settlements ...   Boston, Ticknor and co., 1888.   xli, 662 p. incl. front., illus., map. pl. 24½ cm. "The chief sources of information": p. xii-xviii. 1-12081 rev.   F68.G 66

GOODWIN, John Abbot. The Puritan conspiracy against the Pilgrim fathers and the Congregational church, 1624.   Boston, Mass., Cupple, Upham & co., 1883.   20 p. 25½ cm. 17-23205.   F68.G664

GOODWIN, John Abbott. "What new doctrine is this?"   Lowell, Mass., 1881.   25 cm.   F68.G 67

GORDON, George Angier. The genius of the Pilgrim.   New York, Boston, (etc.) The Pilgrim press (1913)   2, (7) - 31 p. 18½ cm. 13-5027.   F68.G 69

GREAT BRITAIN. Notes regarding the guns of the Mayflower, prepared for the information of the Plymouth Plantation Foundation ... London, O.B. Press, 1950.   7 p. illus. 33 cm. 55-32220.   F68.G 72

GREENE, Evarts Boutell. The place of the Pilgrims in American history, etc. etc.   (Urbana) University of Illinois press, 1921.   42, (6) p. 20½ cm. 21-15846.   F68.G 75

GREENE, Richard Henry. List of passengers who came to Plymouth in the "Mayflower" on her first trip in 1620.   New York, 1896.   19 cm. 1-12082-M1.   F68.G 79   Rare Book Coll.

GREEN, Samuel. A discourse ... on the 208th anniversary of the landing of the Pilgrim fathers.   Boston, Pierce & Williams, 1829.   36 p. 23½ cm. 15-8352.   F68.G792

GREGG, Frank Moody. The founding of a nation; the story of the Pilgrim fathers, their voyage on the Mayflower, their early struggles, etc. as told in the journals of Francis Beaumont, cavalier. ...   Cleveland, The Arthur H. Clarke co., 1915.   2 v. col. fronts., plates, maps (1 double) 24½ cm. Bibliography: v.2, p. (343) - 346. 15-13572.   F68.G 81

— New York, George H. Doran co. (1915)   3, 9 - 481 p. 21 cm. 20-20570.   F68.G 812

GRIFFIS, William Elliot. The influence of the Netherlands in the making of the English commonwealth and the American republic ... A paper read before the Boston Congregation club ...   Boston, DeWolfe, Fiske, (1891)   40 p. 21 cm. 3-24640.   F68.G 84

GRIFFIS, William Elliot. The Pilgrims in their three homes, England, Holland, America ...   Boston and New York, Houghton, Mifflin, 1898.   2, (iii) - vi, 296 p. front., plates, ports., map, facsims. 18½ cm. 1-12083/3   F68.G 85

— 1900.   2, (iii) - vi, 295, (1) p. 6 pl. (incl. front.) 2 port., 3 maps on 1 plate, 3 facsim. 18½ cm. 8-16275.   F68.G 86

— Rev. ed. ... Boston and N.Y., Houghton, Mifflin, 1914.   vii, 312 p. front., plates, ports., map, facsims. 18½ cm. 14-20790.   F68.G862

GRIFFIS, William Elliot. Young people's history of the Pilgrims ...   Boston, and New York, Houghton, Mifflin, 1920.   xi, 353 p. front., plates. 21½ cm. 20-10074.   F68.G 87

GROH, Lynn. The Pilgrims, brave settlers of Plymouth. Illus. Frank Vaughn.   Champaign, Ill., Garrard Pub. Co. (1968)   95 p. 24 cm. 68-10094.   F68.G 88

HALL, Elvajean. Pilgrim neighbors; more true pilgrim stories. Illus. Jon Nielson.   Chicago, Rand McNally (1964)   175 p. 21 cm. 64-16833.   F68.H 14

HALL, Elvajean. Pilgrim stories. Rev. and expanded. Illus. John Nielson.   Chicago, Rand McNally (1962)   176 p. 21 cm. 62-8046.   F68.H15 1962

HALL, Jonathan Prescott. A discourse delivered before the New England soc. in the city of New York ... N.Y., G.F.Nesbitt, print., 1848. 77 p. 22 cm. 1-16227. F68.H 17

HALL-QUEST, Olga (Wilbourne) How the Pilgrims came to Plymouth, illus. James MacDonald. New York, E.P. Dutton, 1946. 115 p. front. (map) illus. 21 cm. "First ed." Bibliography: p. (117) 46-4157. F68.H175

HALLEY, Robert. Lecture on the Pilgrim fathers ... illustrative of the government prize picture. Manchester (Eng.) T. Agnew and sons (1854) 1, (5) - 35 p. fold. pl. 19½ x 16 cm. 1-12084.
F68.H18

HANKS, Charles Stedman. Our Plymouth forefathers, the real founders of our republic. Boston, D. Estes (1908) 5, 339 p. front., illus. 20½ cm. 9-9526. F68.H 24

HANNAH, Samuel D. Plymouth corporation, a trading company, located at Plymouth, a proprietory plantation ... 1928. (Library of Cape Cod history and genealogy no. 3) F68.H246

HARRIS, James Rendel. The finding of the "Mayflower" London, N.Y., Longmans, Green, 1920. v, 58 p. plates, facsim. 24 cm. 22-2386. F68.H258
L.H. & G.

HARRIS, James Rendel. The last of the "Mayflower," by Rendel Harris. Manchester, The University press: London, N.Y., Longmans Green, 1920. 4, 122 p. 24 cm. "Pub. for the John Rylands library." 20-14551.
F68.H 26
L.H. & G.

HARISS, James Rendel. The return of the "Mayflower," an interlude. Manchester, The University press; London, N.Y., Longmans Green, 1919. vi, 35, (3) p. illus. (music) 2 pl. (incl. front.) 23½ cm. 19-12979.
F68.H 27

HARRIS, James Rendel. Souvenirs of the "Mayflower" tercentenary. no. 1 - Manchester, The University press; London, New York (etc.) Longmans, Green, 1920 - no. facsims. (part fold.) 23½ cm. 21-1835. F68.H275

HAWES, Joel. "One soweth and another reapeth." Or, New England's indebtedness to the Pilgrim fathers. A discourse ... Hartford, Hutchinson & Bullard, 1859. 23 p. 23 cm. 24-28080.
F68.H 28

HAXTUN, Mrs. Annie Arnoux. Signers of the Mayflower compact. New York, Repr. from the Mail and express, 1896-99. 3 pt. in 1 v. illus. 29 x 23 cm. 5-34158.
F68.H 29 or H291

— Baltimore, Genealogical Pub. Co., 1968. 3 pts. in 1 vol. (128) p. illus., coats of arms, geneal. tables. 29 cm. 67-28609.
F68.H292
L.H.& G.

HEARNSHAW, Fossey John Cobb. The story of the Pilgrim fathers, expecially showing their connection with Southampton. ... Southampton, W.H. Smith (1910) 2, 3-32 p. front., plates. 24½ cm. A series of 10 articles reprinted from Southampton times, May, June and July, 1909. 10-15655. F68.H 43

HILLARD, George Stillman. A discourse delivered before the New England soc. in the city of New-York, ... N.Y., G.F.Nesbitt, print., 1852. 31 p. 21½ cm. 1-15960 rev.
F68.H 64

HILLS, Leon Clark. ... History and genealogy of the Mayflower planters and first comers to ye olde colonie ... Washington, D.C., Hills pub. co., (1936-41) 2 v. illus. (maps, plan) 23½ cm. (Cape Cod series) 36-36463 rev. F68.H648

HISTORY of the Pilgrims; or, A grandfather's story of the first settlers of New England ... Boston, Print. J.R. Marvin for the Mass. Sabbath school union, 1831. 142 p. incl. front. 15 cm. 1-12085.
F68.H 67

MASSACHUSETTS

HITCHCOCK, Gad. A sermon preached at Plymouth ... 1774 ... in commemoration of the first landing of our New-England ancestors ... Boston, Print. Edes and Gill, 1775. 44 p. 21 cm. 15-13260.
F68.H675
Rare Book Coll.

HOAR, George Frisbie. Oration delivered at Plymouth ... 1895, at the celebration of the 275th anniversary of the landing of the Pilgrims. Washington, 1895. 18 p. 23½ cm. In double columns. 4-37274.
F68.H679

HOAR, George Frisbie, Speech of, ... 1898, at the banquet of the New England society, of Charleston, South Carolina. Washington, D.C., The Saxton print., 1899. 16 p. 23½ cm. 7-18214.
F68.H6795

HOAR, George Frisbie, Speech of, at the banquet of the New England society of Pennsylvania. Washington, Saxton print., 1903. 12 p. 23½ cm. 11-32024.
F68.H 68

HOLMES, Abiel. Two discourses, on the completion of the second century from the landing of the forefathers of Newengland ... Cambridge, Print. Hilliard and Metcalf, 1821. 28 p. 24 cm. 15-19137.
F68.H 75

HOLMES, John Milton. The Pilgrim temple-builders; ... New York, Tibbals & Whiting, 1866. 38 p. 23 cm. 15-13258.
F68.H 76

HOLMES, Knowlton B. The Mayflower and her master's table, comp. from the writings of Governor Bradford and Governor Winslow, and the old records of Plymouth Colony, town and church. (Plymouth, Rogers Print, 1952) 39 p. illus. 20 cm. 54-36610.
F68.H762

HOLMES, Oliver Wendell. Oration delivered before the New England society, in the city of New York ... (n.p., 1856?) 46 p. 23½ cm. 1-16226.
F68.H763
Rare Book Coll.

HOOG, Aletta. Geen goud, maar God, ... geillustreerd door P. van Looy. Nijkerk, G.F. Callenbach (1920?) (5) - 61 p. illus. 19 cm. 20-23610.
F68.H 77

HOPKINS, Mark. The central principle. An oration delivered before the New-England society of New-York ... New York, E. French, 1854. 36 p. 23½ cm. 19-3255.
F68.H 79
Toner Coll.

HOWE, Paul Sturtevant. The religious and legal constitution of the Pilgrim state; the facts of early Pilgrim history ... (Cape May, N.J., A.R. Hand, 1923) 3, 9-129 p. front. (port.) plates. 23½ cm. Bibliography: p.) (114) 24-25772.
F68.H 85

HUNT, Timothy Dwight. Address delivered before the New England society of San Francisco ... San Francisco, Cooke, Kenny, 1853. 20 p. 23 cm. 19-12959.
F68.H 93

HUNTER, Joseph. Collections concerning the early history of the founders of New Plymouth, the first colonists of New England. London, J.R. Smith, 1849. 70 p. 20 cm.. Reprinted in abridged form in the Collections of the Mass. historical society, 4th series, v.1 p. (52) - 85. 2-26723 rev.
F68.H 94

HUNTER, Joseph. Collections concerning the church or congregation of Protestant Separatists formed at Scrooby in north Nottinghamshire, in the time of King James I: the founders of New-Plymouth, the parent-colony of New-England. London, J.R. Smith, 1854. vii-xiv p. 205 p. 22½ cm. 1-12086.
F68.H 95

HUNTINGTON, William Reed. The Puritan strain ... a sermon preached ... before the New England society in the city of New York ... N.Y., A.G. Sherwood, 1901. 19 p. 19½ cm. A plea for the return to Puritan ideals in modern social life. 23-1896.
F68.H 97

JAMES, Sydney V., ed. Three visitors to early Plymouth; letters about the pilgrim settlement in N.E. during its first seven years. (Plimoth Plantation" 1963. xii, 84 p. 24 cm.
F68.J 27

JAMESON, John Franklin. The arrival of the Pilgrims ... a lecture ... (Providence, Print. by the University (Brown) 1920. (5) - 40 p. 19 ½ cm. 21-8530 Rev. F68. J 3

JILLSON, Willard Rouse. The Mayflower compact; bright torch of liberty and freedom. Frankfort, Ky., Roberts Print., 1966. 21 p. 23 cm. F68. J 5

DeGERING, Etta. Christopher Jones, captain of the Mayflower. Illus. William Ferguson. New York, D. McKay (1965) xii, 112 p. 21 cm. 65-22963. F68.J6D4

KALER, James Otis. Mary of Plymouth; a story of the Pilgrim settlement. New York, Cincinnati (etc.) American book co., 1910. 156 p. illus. 19 cm. 10-7074. F68.K 14

KEIGWIN, Albert Edwin. Return of the Pilgrim fathers; historical pageant commemorating the 300th anniversary of the landing of the Pilgrims. New York, ... Presbyterian church (1920) 24 p. illus. (plans) 23 cm. 20-17669. F68.K 27

KENILWORTH, Ill. How the Pilgrim spirit came to Illinois: a pageant ... New Trier township high school in commemoration of the tercentenary of the landing of the Pilgrims. (Kenilworth? 1921) 36 p. illus. 28 cm. 21-19756. F68.K 3

KIMBALL, Rosamond. The coming of the Mayflower; a pilgrim pageant ... (Boston, Perry Mason co., c. 1920) 22 p. 20 ½ cm. 21-14723. F68.K 5

— 34 p. 23 cm. 21-14724. F68.K 52

KUYPER, Henriette Sophia Suzanna. De Pilgrimfathers in Nederland, 1608 - 1620. Kampen, J. H. Kok, 1920. 57 p. 21 ½ cm. 21-11141. F68.K 97

LABAREE, John Codman. The Plymouth pilgrims. A sermon ... Randolph, Mass., Print Mrs. S. P. Brown, 1871. 20 p. 22 ½ cm. 18-4491. F68. L 12

LALLY, Albert V. The story of the Pilgrim fathers ... (Boston, The Vincent co., 1930) 3, 11 - 55 p. illus. 18 ½ cm. 30-7972. F68. L 21

LANGDON, George D. Pilgrim colony; a history of New Plymouth, 1620 - 1691. New Haven, Yale University Press, 1966. xi, 257 p. 24 cm. 66-21526. F68. L 25

LANGDON, William Chauncy. The Pilgrim tercentenary pageant of Marietta, Ohio ... (Marietta? 1920) 48 p. 24 cm. 20-15382. F68. L 27

LANGDON-DAVIES, John. The Mayflower & the Pilgrim fathers. 1st Amer. ed. New York, Putnam, (1966) 24 p. 35 cm. Issued in portfolio. (Jackdaw no. 4) (A coll. of contemporary documents) F68. L 3

LEE, E. Rosalind. The Pilgrim fathers, their trials and adventures; with illus. by Alice M. Odgers. London, The Sunday school assoc., 1920. 83 p. front., plates, map. 16 cm. Bibliog.: p. 83. 21-16028. F68. L 47

LEWIS, Benjamin Roland. Pageantry and the Pilgrim tercentenary celebration ... with suggestions for programs, bibliographies, etc. Salt Lake City, University of Utah (1920) 64 p. 23 cm. Bibliography: p. (62) - 64. 23-27140. F68. L 65

LEYDEN. Leyden documents relating to the Pilgrim fathers, permission to reside at Leyden and betrothal records ... Facsimile, transcript, translation and annotations by Dr. D. Plooij of Leyden and others. Leyden, E. J. Brill, ltd., 1920. xii, (2) p. ii numb. l., (2) p. ii-lxix numb. l. (2) p. lxx-lxxiv numb. l., (3) p. incl. facsims. 39 ½ cm. 20-16196. F68. L 68
Rare Book Coll.

LEYDEN pilgrim messenger, The; an international journal ed. by the Leyden pilgrim fathers society and by the trustees of the William the Silent fund. no. 1; May 1922. Leyden, E. J. Brill, (1922) 96 p. facsim. 25 cm. No more pub? 26-387. F68.L685

MASSACHUSETTS

LIBBY, Charles Thornton. Mary Chilton's title to celebrity, investigated in behalf of a descendant of John Haward, minimus. Boston, The Fort Hill press, 1926.   27 p. front. (facsim.) 25½ cm. "... Mary Chilton is said to have been the first female who set foot on the Plymouth shore, 1620": p. (5) 27-25099.   F68. L 7

LODGE, H. C. The pilgrims of Plymouth. 1921.   F68.L 82

LORD, Arthur. ... Plymouth and the Pilgrims. Boston and N. Y., Houghton Mifflin, 1920.   4, 177 p. 20 cm. 20-19250.   F68.L 86

LOVE, William De Loss. Obedience to rulers - the duty and its limitations. A discourse ... New Haven, Storer & Stone, print., 1851.   16 p. 23 cm. 15-23169.   F68.L 89

LOWITZ, Sadyebeth. The pilgrims' party; a really truly story ... with illus. by Anson Lowitz. New York, Stein and Day, 1964.   unpaged (73) p. 19 x 23 cm.   F68. L9 1964

McGOVERN, Ann. ... if you sailed on the Mayflower. Illus. J. B. Handlesman. N.Y. Four Winds Press, 1969.   80 p. illus. 16 x 22 cm. 74-124182.   F68. M 12

McINTYRE, Ruth A. Debts hopeful and desperate; financing the Plymouth Colony. (Plymouth, Mass., Plimoth Plantation (1963)   86 p. 24 cm.   F68. M14

MACKAYE, Percy. The Pilgrim and the Book. New York, American Bible soc.(1920)   xvii, 83 p. 24 cm. 21-6229 Rev.   F68.M145

— N. Y. and Los Angeles, S. French, 1932.   xxi, 83 p. 23½ cm. 31-33122.   F68.M145 1932

MACKENNAL, Alexander. Homes and haunts of the Pilgrim fathers ... (Illus.) Charles Whymper. London, The Religious tract soc; Philadelphia, J. B. Lippincott, 1899.   8, 13-200 p. incl. illus., plates, plan. col. front. 30 cm. 1-12087 rev.   F68. M15

— London, The Religious tract soc., 1920.   xii, 13-143 p. illus. 29 x 23 cm. 21-222.   F68. M152

— Philadelphia, G. W. Jacobs, 1920.   xii, 13-143 p. col. front., illus. 29 x 23½ cm. 21-2443.   F68.M153

MANN, Joel. A discourse delivered in Bristol ... on the anniversary of the landing of our ancestors at Plymouth. Warren (R. I.) Print. by S. Randall, 1821.   19 p. 20½ cm. 17-14598.   F68.M 27

MANSFIELD, Mrs. Blanche (McManus) The voyage of the Mayflower. N. Y., E. R. Herrick (1897) 6, 3-72 p. illus. 23 cm. 1-12088 rev.   F68.M 28

MARBLE, Mrs. Annie (Russell) The women who came in the Mayflower. Boston, Chicago, The Pilgrim Press (1920)   vi, 3-110 p. 19½ cm. Bibliographical foot-notes. 20-8510.   F68. M 3

MARSH. Remarks on an address delivered before the New England society of the city of New York ... by George P. Marsh. Boston, C. Stimpson, 1845.   23 p. 18 cm. 19-7378.   F68.M 36

MARTYN, Carlos. The Pilgrim fathers of New England: a history. N. Y., American tract soc. (1867)   432 p. 22½ cm. 17-5263 Rev.   F68.M 38

MASON, Thomas W. New light on the Pilgrim story ... London, Congregational union of England and Wales, inc. (1920)   xviii, 176 p. col. front., 29 pl., map. 22½ cm. 21-3491.   F68.M 39

MASSACHUSETTS. ... Exercises on the 300th anniversary of the landing of the Pilgrims ... (Boston, 1921?)   64 p. 24 cm. 21-11769.   F68.M397

MASSACHUSETTS. List of plays, pageants, tableaux, etc. suitable for the celebration of the Pilgrim tercentenary. From Wm. Carroll Hill, secretary, the Pilgrim tercentenary commission ... Boston, (1920)   9 numb. l. 28 cm. Autographed from type-written copy. CA 21-332 unrev.   F68.M398

MASSACHUSETTS.   Report of the Pilgrim tercentenary commission ...   Boston, Wright & Potter print., 1917.   61 p. 9 pl. (part fold.) 23½ cm. 17-27457.   F68. M 4

MATHEWS, Basil Joseph.   The Argonauts of faith; the adventures of the "Mayflower" Pilgrims ... with a foreword by Viscount Bryce ... illus. by Ernest Prater.   London, Hodder and Stoughton (1920)
xiii, 192 p. col. front., illus. (maps) col. plates. 19 cm. Pub. also with title: The quest of liberty. 20-8509.   F68. M 42

— New York, George H. Doran (1920)   xi, (2), 17-185 p. maps. 19½ cm. 20-10629.   F68. M422

— (1921)   xiii, 17-185 p. col. front., illus. (maps) col. plates. 19½ cm. 21-3292.   F68. M423

MATHEWS, Basil Joseph.   The quest of liberty; the adventures of the "Mayflower" pilgrims ... illus. Ernest Prater.   N.Y. George H. Doran (1920)   xiii, (2), 17-185 p. col. front., illus. (maps) col. plates. 19½ cm. "Originally pub. with title "The Argonauts of faith"." 23-13406.   F68. M425

MATTHEWS, Albert.   The term Pilgrim fathers.   Cambridge, J. Wilson, 1915.   (293) - 391 p. 24½ cm. "Reprinted from the Pubs. of the Colonial soc. of Massachusetts, vol. xviii. Bibliog. of Plymouth discourses p. 384-91. 16-7129.   F68. M 43

MAYFLOWER compact, 1620.   Chicago, D.V. Welsh, 1954.   6 p.
F68. M 45

— Worcester, Mass., A.J. St. Onge, 1970.   43 p. 75 m.   F68. M452

MAYFLOWER descendant, The; a quarterly magazine of Pilgrim genealogy and history. v. 1 - Jan. 1899 -   Boston, The Mass. soc. of Mayflower descendants, 1899 -   v. plates, facsims. 24½ cm. Title varies. 5-32185 Rev.   F68. M 46

MIDDLEBURY historical soc.   Forefathers' day.   272d anniversary and semi-centennial observance ... Middlebury, The Middlebury hist. soc., 1892.   5 p. 22½ cm. 3-23009.
F68. M 62

MOLLOY, Anne Stearns.   The years before the Mayflower; the Pilgrim in Holland.   Illus. with maps, old prints and drawings by Richard Cuffari.   N.Y., Hastings House (1972)   159 p. illus. 22 cm. Bibliography: p. 153-154. 74-150014 MARC.   F68. M 73
1972

MONK, Lillian Hoag.   Old Pilgrim days ... Los Angeles, H.A. Miller, 1920.   188 p. front., plates. 19½ cm. 20-15381.   F68. M 74

MOORE, David.   A pageant of the Mayflower and the Pilgrim fathers.   ...   (Cambridge, Eng., G.E. Bigg, 1920)   24 p. 22 cm. 25-21854.   F68. M 76

MORISON, Samuel Eliot.   The Pilgrim fathers, their significance in history; an address at the unveiling of a tablet to the Mayflower Pilgrims in the state house at Concord, N.H. ...   Concord, Print. for the soc. of Mayflower descendants in the state of N.H. (Boston, The Merrymount press) 1937.
2, 27 p. 23 cm. 37-15425.   F68. M 87

MORISON, Samuel Eliot.   The story of the "Old Colony" of New Plymouth, 1620 - 1692.   Illus. by Charles H. Overly.   (1st ed.) N.Y., Knopf, 1956.   296 p. illus. 22 cm. 56-8893.
F68. M873

MORTON, Nathaniel.   New-Englands memoriall: or, A brief relation of the most memorable and remarkable passages of the providence of God ... Cambridge, Print. S.G. and M.J. for John Usher of Boston, 1669.   6, 198, (10) p. 17½ x 14½ cm. 1-12090.   F68. M 88
Rare Book Coll.

— with an introduction by Arthur Lord.   Boston, The Club of odd volumes, 1903.   1, 21, (12), 198, (10) p. 23½ x 19 cm. Facsimile ed. of the original ed. Cambridge, 1669. 3-17519.   F68. M882
Rare Book Coll.

MASSACHUSETTS

— ed. by Howard J. Hall ... N.Y., 1937. 1, ix p., facsim. (5, 198 (10) p.) 19½ cm. (Scholars' facsims. and reprints)
"Facsimile reproduction of the copy in the N.Y. Public Library. 38-10717. F68.M883

— Boston, Reprinted for Daniel Henchman, 1721. 5, 348 p. 16 cm. 1-12091. F68.M885
Rare Book Coll.

— Boston: printed. Newport, Reprinted ... 1771. viii, 208, (8) p. 18½ cm. With this is bound: Church, Benjamin.
The entertaining history of King Philip's war ... Newport, Repr. 1772. 1-12092 & 2-13753 F68.M 89
Rare Book Coll.

— Plymouth, Mass. Reprinted by A. Danforth, 1826. xii, (13) - 204 p. 18 cm. 1-12093 Rev. F68.M 90

— Containing besides the original work, and the supplement annexed to the 2d ed., large additions in marginal notes, and an appendix; with a ... copy of an ancient map. By John Davis ... Boston, Print Crocker and Brewster, 1826. vi, (7) - 481 p. front. (fold. map) 21½ cm. 1-12094. F68.M 91

— 6th ed. Also Governor Bradford's History of Plymouth colony; portions of Prince's Chronology; Governor Bradford's Dialogue; Governor Winslow's visit to Massasoit ... etc. Boston, Congregational board of publication, 1855. xxii, 515 p. front., port. 23½ cm. 1-12095. F68.M 92

MORTON. Samuel Gorton's letter to Nathaniel Morton. Warwick, June 30, 1669 (Mss) (From Force Tracts v.4 (1846) no. 7. 17 p) 4-27247. F68.M925

MOURT's relation. A relation or Journall of the beginning and proceedings of the English plantation setled at Plimoth in New England, by certaine English adventurers both merchants and others. ... As also a relation of foure severall discoveries since made ... London, Printed for John Bellamie ... 1622. 6. 72 p. 18½ cm. The main part of the narrative was probably written by William Bradford and Edward Winslow. G. Mourt (George Morton?) by whose name the relation is commonly known, seems to have had no other connection with it than that of writing the preface and giving the book to the press. 7-15407. F68.M928
Rare Book Coll.

— with an intorduction and notes by Henry Martyn Dexter. Boston, J.K. Wiggin, 1865. xlvii, 176 p.
2 fld. maps. 21½ x 17 cm. 3-8746. F68.M928
F1.L69 no.1

— Ann, Arbor, University Microfilms (1966) 72 p. 22 cm. (March of America facsimile series, no. 21) 66-26306.
F68.M928
1622a

— With an introd. and notes by Henry Martyn Dexter and a new pref. by Everett H. Emerson. N.Y., Garrett Press, 1969. xlvii, 176 p. 23 cm. 74-106748. F68.M928
1969

— With an introd. and notes by Henry M. Dexter and a new pref. by Everett H. Emerson.
F68.M928
1972

— With historical and local illustrations of providences, principles, and persons: by George B. Cheever. N.Y., J. Wiley, 1848. ix, (5) - 369 p. 19½ cm. 40-24866. F68.M9287

— With Historical and local illustrations of principals, providences, and persons. By George B. Cheever ... Glasgow and London, T.W. Collins (1849) 309 p. front. 19½ cm. A14-1559.
F68.M929

— .... by George B. Cheever. 2d ed. N.Y., J. Wiley, 1849. ix, (5) - 369 p. 19½ cm. 1-12096.
F68.M 93

— Selections. The Cape Cod journal of the Pilgrim fathers, reprinted from Mourt's relation, with introd. and notes by Lyon Sharman. Provincetown, The Advocate gift shop (1920) xvi, 52 p.
14½ x 8½ cm. 20-20890. F68.M932

— Homes in the wilderness; a pilgrim's journal of Plymouth plantation in 1620, by William Bradford and others of the Mayflower company. Illus. with drawings by Mary Wilson Stewart. New York, W. R. Scott, (1939) 2, 74, (2) p. illus. (incl. maps) 22½ x 19 cm. 40-27095.
 F68.M935

— The Pilgrim fathers; a journal of their coming in the Mayflower to New England and their life and adventures there: ed. with preface and notes by Theodore Besterman ... (London) Reprinted from the rare 1622 ed. at the Golden cockerel press, 1939. 87, (1) p. incl. front. illus. 25½ cm. 40-6431.
 F68.M936
 Rare Book Coll.

— Ed. from the original printing of 1622, with introd. and notes, by Dwight B. Heath. N.Y., Corinth Books (1963) xxiii, 96 p. 21 cm. 62-17660.
 F68.M9363

MUDGE, Zachariah Atwell. Views from Plymouth rock; a sketch of the early history of the Plymouth colony. Designed for young people. N.Y., Cincinnati, (1869) 451 p. incl. front., illus. 4 pl., map. 18 cm. 1-12097.
 F68.M 94

MURPHY, Ethel Allen. The watcher for the dawn; a masque of heritage ... (Louisville, Ky., Mayes print. 1920) 20 p. 22½ cm. 21-780.
 F68.M 97

NATIONAL council of the Congregational churches of the U.S. Proceedings at the unveiling of the John Robinson memorial tablet in Leyden, Holland, ... 1891.... Boston, T. Todd, print.1891. 36 p. front., pl., mounted phot. 24½ cm. 13-5275 Rev.
 F68.N 36

NELSON, Loveday A. Our Pilgrim forefathers; Thanksgiving studies ... Chicago, N.Y., A. Flanagan (1904) 31 p. illus. 18 cm. 12-37099. 35-19938.
 F68.N 42 or N422

NEW HAMPSHIRE. Report of the Committee on celebration of tercentenary centennial of landing of the Pilgrims ... (Concord, 1919) 6 p. 23 cm. 20-7972.
 F68.N 52

NEW PLYMOUTH colony. A declaration of the warrantable grounds and proceedings of the first associates of the government of New-Plymouth; in their laying the first foundations of this government, and in their making laws, and disposing of the lands within the same. ... Boston, Greenleaf's printing-office, 1773. 24 p. 19 cm. 6-36153.
 F68.N 54
 Rare Book Coll.

NEW PLYMOUTH colony. Records of the colony of New Plymouth... Printed by order of the legislature of the commonwealth of Mass. Ed. by Nathaniel B. Shurtleff and another. Boston, W.White, 1855-61. 12 v. in 10. 30½ cm. Contents. - v.1-6. Court orders. - v.7. Judicial acts ... 1636-1692. - v.8. Miscellaneous records (including births, marriages, deaths and burials, etc. - v.9-10. Acts of the Commissioners of the United Colonies of New England, 1643-1679. - v.11. Laws, 1623-1682. - v.12. Deed, etc. 1620-1651. 1-12098.
 F68.N 55

NEW PLYMOUTH colony. The book of the general laws of the inhabitants of the jurisdiction of New-Plimouth; collected out of the records of the General court and lately revised ... Cambridge, Print Samuel Green 1672. (Boston, 1942) facsim.: 2, 47, (8) p. 34 cm. (Photostat Americana. 2d series. Photostated at the Mass. hist. soc. No. 169) 43-5370.
 F68.N 57
 1671a
 Rare Book Coll.

NEW YORK public library ... The Pilgrim tercentenary exhibition in ... N.Y. 1920. (4) p. 25½ cm. 21-11140.
 F68.N 58

NICKERSON, Warren Sears. Land ho! - 1620; a seaman's story of the Mayflower; her construction, her navigation and her fist landfall, ... Boston and N.Y., Houghton Mifflin, 1931. xix, 155 p. front., pl., maps (1 fold., mounted) plans. 23½ cm. "Some of the sources of information... p. (153)-155. 31-33758.
 F68.N 65

NOBLE, Frederick Alphonso. The Pilgrims ... Boston, N.Y. (etc.) The Pilgrim press, 1907. xvi, (3), 4-483 p. front., 7 pl. 25 cm. 7-39538.
 F68.N 74

MASSACHUSETTS 57

NOYES, Ethel J. The women of Plymouth colony; a paper written for and read at a meeting of the Society of Mayflower descendants in the District of Columbia. (Washington, B.S. Adams, 1915) 2, 7-22 p. 18 cm. 15-14088.   F68.N 95

NOYES, Ethel Jane Russell Chesebrough. The women of the Mayflower and women of Plymouth colony. Plymouth, Mass. (Memorial press) 1921. 197 p. front., illus. 20 cm. 21-8526.   F68.N952

— Ann Arbor, Mich., Gryphon Books, 1971. 197 p. illus. 22 cm. 75-145709.   F68.N952 1971

OCCASIONAL papers in Old Colony studies. no. 1 - (Plymouth, Mass.) Plimoth Plantation, 1969 - 28 cm.   F68. O 3

PARRY, Hugh. The historical pageant of the "Mayflower," 1620 - 1920 ... with a foreword, council chamber scene and epilogue by Dr. J. Rendel Harris. London, National council of the Evangelical Free churches (1920?) vi, 57 p. 21½ cm. 21-5358.   F68.P 26

PATH of the Pilgrim church, from its origin in England to its establishment in New England. An historical sketch. Written for the Massachusetts Sabbath school soc., (1862) 267 p. 3 pl. (incl. front.) map. 15½ cm. 17-9758.   F68.P 29

PAYNE, Elizabeth Ann. Meet the pilgrim fathers. Illus. by H.B. Vestal. New York, Random House (1966) 86 p. 22 cm. AC 66-10438.   F68.P 32

PEABODY, Oliver William Bourn. A discourse ... Burlington (Vt.) University press, 1846. 22 p. 23½ cm. 21-17518.   F68.P 35

PEIRCE, Ebenezer Weaver. Peirce's colonial lists. Civil, military and professional lists of Plymouth and Rhode Island colonies ... 1621 - 1700. Boston, A. Williams, 1881. viii, 156 p. 24 cm. 1-12100.   F68.P 37

— Baltimore, Genealogical Pub. Co., 1968. viii, 156 p. 24 cm. 68-24684.   F68.P37 1968 L.H. & G.

PIERPONT, John. The Pilgrims of Plymouth: a poem delivered before the New England society in the city of New York ... Boston, Crosby, Nichols and co., 1856. 30 p. 24 cm. 3-29000.   F68.P 45

PILGRIM FATHERS. Pamphlets, broadsides, clippings and other miscellaneous matter on the subject not separately cataloged are classified in F68. P 5

PILGRIM FATHERS genootschap te Leiden. Statuut en huishoudelijk reglement van het Pilgrim fathers genootschap te Leiden (Leyden Pilgrim fathers soc. ... Leiden, 1921) 13 (i.e.25) p. 19½ cm. Text in Dutch and English. 21-19746.   F68.P 53

PILGRIM FATHERS, The, or The lives of some of the first settlers of New England. Designed for Sabbath school libraries. Portland, Shirley, Hyde, 1830. vi, (7) - 123 p. 15 cm. 16-3752.   F68.P 55

PILGRIM notes and queries; pub. by the Massachusetts society of Mayflower descendants. v. 1 - Mar. 1913 - Boston, Mass., 1913 - v. 24½ cm. monthly ... 16-23262.   F68.P 61

PILGRIM society. An account of the Pilgrim celebration at Plymouth ... Boston, Crosby, Nichols, 1853. 182 p. 22½ cm. 7-13574.   F68.P 62

PILGRIM society. Catalogue of the historical collection and pictures in Pilgrim hall, Plymouth. (Plymouth, Mass., The Memorial press) 1913. 66, (2) p. illus. (incl. port., facsim.) 19½ cm. 40-19850.   F68.P622 1913

— (n. p., 1916) 76 p. illus. 19 cm. 19-19556. F68.P622
1916

— comp. and arr. by Rose T. Briggs. Plymouth, 1941. 79 p. plates, ports. 23 cm. 49-35037*. F68.P622
1941

PILGRIM memorial, Illustrated. Boston (18 -) 78½ x 53 cm. fold. to 26½ x 18 cm. F68.P623

PILGRIM society. The illustrated Pilgrim memorial ... (1860) - Boston, Office of the national monument to the forefathers (1859) v. illus. 24 cm. 2-20086. F68.P624

PILGRIM society. The proceedings at the celebration by the Pilgrim society at Plymouth ... of the 250th anniversary of the landing of the Pilgrims. Cambridge (Mass.) J. Wilson, 1871. 208 p. 24½ cm. 7-13573. F68.P627

PILGRIM society. The proceedings at the celebration by the Pilgrim society ... of the completion of the national monument to the Pilgrims. Plymouth, Avery & Doten, print. 1889. 176 p. front., 5 pl. 23 cm. 9-11008. F68.P6272

PILGRIM society. The proceedings at the celebration by the Pilgrim society ... of the 275th anniversary of the landing of the Pilgrims. Plymouth, Avery & Doten, 1896. 76 p. front., ports. 23 cm. 7-13571. F68.P628

PILGRIM society. Report on the expediency of celebrating in future the landing of the Pilgrims on the 21st of Dec. Boston, The Society, 1850. 12 p. 23½ cm. 1-12101. F68.P 63

PLOOIJ, Daniël. The Pilgrim fathers from a Dutch point of view ... N.Y., The N.Y. university press, 1932. xi, 154 p. plates, 2 port. (incl. front.) facsims. 23½ cm. "Select bibliography": p. (135)-140. 32-16644. F68.P675

— N.Y., AMS Press (1969) xi, 154 p. 23 cm. 71-100509. F68.P675
1969

— St. Clair Shores, Mich., Scholarly Press, 1970. x, 154 p. illus. 21 cm. 79-131801. F68.P675
1970

PLYMOUTH cordage co. Pilgrim tercentenary; observances at Plymouth ... (Plymouth? 1920) 15 p. illus. 15½ cm. "Plymouth and Pilgrim bibliography": p. 12-15. CA 27-498 unrev. F68.P 71

PLYMOUTH society of Keokuk, Ia., The officers and members of ... Keokuk, Daily Gate City office print, 1858. 31 p. 22½ cm. 4-31154. F68.P 73

POPE, Charles Henry. The Plymouth scrap book; the oldest original documents extant in Plymouth archives ... Boston, C.E. Goodspeed, 1918. ix, 149 p. front., facsims. 28½ cm. 19-2022. F68.P 8

PORY, John. John Pory's lost description of Plymouth colony in the earliest days of the Pilgrim fathers, together with contemporary accounts of the English colonization elsewhere in New England ... ed. with introd. and notes, by Champlin Burrage ... Boston, N.Y., Houghton Mifflin, 1918. xxiv, 65 p. pl., fold. maps., facsims. 26½ cm. 18-11188. F68.P 82

POST, Truman Marcellus. The Pilgrim fathers. A discourse in commemoration of the Pilgrim fathers, ... St. Louis, Print at the Union job office, 1849. iv, (5) - 47 p. 23½ cm. 17-16972. F68.P 85

POWELL, Walter A. The Pilgrims and their religious, intellectual and civic life. Wilmington, Del., Mercantile print. co., 1923. 266 p. plates 21½ cm. Bibliography: p. 265-266. 24-331. F68.P 88

PRATT, Walter Merriam. The Mayflower Society House, being the story of the Edward Winslow house, the Mayflower Society (and) the Pilgrims. 2d ed. Cambridge, Mass., Priv. print., University Press, 1950. 32 p. illus., ports. 26 cm. 52-23863. F68. P 9 1950

PUTNAM, Eben. Two early passenger lists, 1635 - 1637. (Repr. from the N. E. historical and genealogical register for July 1921) Boston, 1921. 12 p. 23½ cm. 21-21528. F68.P 98 L.H. & G.

— Baltimore, Genealogical Pub. Co., 1964. 13 p. 23 cm. F68.P 98 1964

REYNOLDS, Florence. ... Paul Revere, an original radio play with a radio play manual for teachers and directors. Cleveland, O., The Harter pub. co., 1938. xvi, (2) p. 3-27 numb. l., 28-38 p. illus. 27 cm. 40-37470. F69. R PN6120. R2A17 no. 1

RICHARDS, Norman. The story of the Mayflower Compact. Illus. Darrell Wiskur. Chicago, Childrens Press (1967) 30 p. 25 cm. 67-22901. F68.R 5

ROBBINS, Chandler. Sermon preached at Plymouth, Dec. 22, 1793; being the anniversary of the landing of our ancestors. Boston, Stockbridge; Re-printed by Loring Andrews, 1796. 46 p. 17½ cm. Imperfect: Half-title? wanting. 3-30958. F68.R 58 Rare Book Coll.

ROBINSON, John. The pastor of the Pilgrims, a biography of John Robinson by Walter H. Burgess. N.Y., Harcourt Brace & Howe; London, Williams and Norgate, 1920. xii, 426 p. front., plates, map, plan, facsims. 22½ cm. 20-20311. F68.R 62

ROBINSON, John, ... New facts concerning, by Champlin Burrage ... Oxford, Print. H. Hart at the University press; London, H. Frowde, 1910. 35 p. front. (facsim.) 22½ cm. 11-1066 Rev. F68.R 63

ROBINSON, John, the Pilgrim pastor (by) Ozora S. Davis ... Boston, N.Y., etc. The Pilgrim press (1903) xiii, 366 p. front., plates, facsim. 18½ cm. 4-4261. F68.R 64

ROBINSON, John, The memory of ... By Alvan Lamson. Boston, Crosby, Nichols, 1852. 40 p. 23½ cm. 18-4490. F68.R 65

JOHNSON, John. ... An answer to John Robinson of Leyden by a Puritan friend, now first published from a manuscript of 1609. Ed. by Champlin Burrage ... Cambridge, Harvard university press ... 1920. xiii, 94 p. facsim. 23½ cm. 20-12134. F68.R 67

ROBINSON, Frederick James. John Robinson (1575? - 1625), by the Rev. F.J. Powicke ... London, Hodder and Stoughton, (1920) xii, 132 p. 19 cm. "Authorities": p. ix-x. 21-7267. F68.R675

ROMEYN, John Brodhead. The duty and reward of honouring God. A sermon ... the anniversary of the landing of the Pilgrims of New-England. N.Y., F. & R. Lockwood, 1822. 30 p. 22½ cm. 24-20929. F68.R 76

ROOSEVELT, Theodore, Address of, on the occasion of the laying of the corner stone of the Pilgrim memorial monument. Provincetown, Mass., ... 1907. Washington, Govt. print. off., 1907. 64 p. 21 cm. 29-2695. F68.R 79

ROWLAND, William Frederick. A sermon, delivered ... the 2d centennial anniversary of the landing of the Pilgrims of New-England. Exeter (N.H.) Print. J.J. Williams, 1821. 19 p. 22 cm. 15-27873. F68.R 88

ROYAL, Henry Wasson. The Pilgrims & early Plymouth, an address. Plymouth, Mass., Pilgrim Soc. (19 -) 12 p. 20 cm. 49-38598*. F68.R 9

RUSSELL, William Shaw. Guide to Plymouth, and recollections of the Pilgrims. Boston, G. Coolidge, 1846.   xii, 306, vi, 76, xx p. front., plates, fold. map, facsims. 16 ½ cm. 1-12102.   F68.R 96

SANFORD, Enoch. Sketch of the Pilgrims who founded the church of Christ in New England. Boston, Perkins and Marvin, 1831.   71 p. 15 cm. 6-42188.   F68.S 22
Rare Book Coll.

SAWYER, Joseph Dillaway. "The Pilgrim spirit", shown in the Pilgrim pageant staged at Plymouth ... N.Y., The Century history co. (1921)   2, 7-54 p. illus. (incl. ports., facsims.) 31 x 23 cm. 22-120.
F68.S 27

SCOTT, Benjamin. Lays of the Pilgrim fathers; comp. in aid of the fund for completing the Memorial church of the Pilgrim fathers, in Southwark. London, Longman, Green, Longman, and Roberts, 1861.   71 p. incl. front. 2 pl. 19 cm. 18-17056.   F68. S 4

SCOTT, Benjamin. The Pilgrim fathers neither Puritans nor persecutors. A lecture delivered at the Friends' institute ... London, A.W. Bennett, 1866.   39 p. 22 ½ cm. 17-14569.   F68.S 42

— 2d ed. London, A.W. Bennett, 1869.   39 p. 21 cm. 17-5273.   F68.S 43

SEWARD, William Henry. Oration ... Dec., 1855. (Washington, 1856)   22 ½ cm.   F68.S 51

— Dec., 1856. Albany, 1856.   23 cm.   F68.S 52

SHAW, Hubert Kinney. Families of the Pilgrims, comp. for the Massachusetts Society of Mayflower Descendants. Boston, Mass. Soc. of Mayflower Descendants, 1956.   178 p. 24 cm. Bibliography: p. 172. 56-4135.   F68.S 55

SHULER, Marjorie. Mapping family history ... (Boston, The Christian science pub. soc., 1936)   1 l. illus. (map) 39 ½ cm. 38M4520T.   F68.S 58

SMITH, Bradford. Our debt to the Pilgrims. Plymouth, Choir Alley Press, 1957.   20 p. illus. 23 cm. 57-34197.   F68.S59

SMITH, E. Brooks. The coming of the Pilgrims, told from Governor Bradford's firsthand account. Illus. by Leonard E. Fisher. (1st ed.) Boston, Little, Brown (1964)   60 p. 20 x 26 cm. 64-10182.
F68.S597

SMITH, Edward Leodore. Rev. Ralph Smith, first settled minister of Plymouth, 1629-1636 ... Boston, 1921.   3, 16, 18 p. 23 cm. 21-11929.   F68. S 6

SMITH, Henry Justin. The master of the Mayflower. Chicago, N.Y., Willett, Clark & co. 1936.   6, 241 p. 20 ½ cm. "Note on the sources": p. 241. 36-13992.   F68.S 63

SOCIETY of Mayflower descendants. The Mayflower quarterly. v. 1 -   Oct. 15, 1935 -
"Pub. by the General society of Mayflower descendants." 42-44035.   F68.S 64

SOCIETY of Mayflower descendants, General society of, organized at Plymouth, Mass., Jan. 12, 1897. (Plymouth? 1897?)   28 p. 14 cm. 40M820T.   F68.S 65

SOCIETY of Mayflower descendants, The General society of; meetings, officers and members arr. in state societies, ancestors and their descendants. (N.Y., The De Vinne press) 1901.   vi, (4), 3-447 p. front. (port.) illus., plates. 25 cm. 1-11934 Rev.   F68.S 66

SOCIETY of Mayflower descendants. Mayflower index, compiled and ed. for the General soc. of Mayflower descendants by William Alexander McAusland, historian general ... (Boston) 1932.   2 v. 25 cm. Paged continuously. 32-16837.   F68.S6614

— Rev. by Lewis E. Neff. (Tulsa, Okla.) 1960.   3 v. in 2. 24 cm. Vols. 1-2, rev. ed.   F68.S6614
of the first ed.   1960
L.H. & G.

MASSACHUSETTS 61

— Corrections (Plymouth? Mass. 1964.   (8) p.   24 cm.   F68.S6614
                                                                                        1960
                                                                                        Corrections

SOCIETY of Mayflower descendants. ... Order of exercises, dedication of the Cole's Hill memorial
... (Plymouth? Mass., 1921?)   31 p. pl. 23½ cm. CA 29-727 unrev.   F68.S662

SOCIETY of Mayflower descendants. Report of the secretary general. Proceedings of the ... triennial congress ... (Plymouth? Mass., 1909)   1 v. 21 cm. CA 10-3 unrev.   F68.S663

SOCIETY of Mayflower descendants. California. Bulletin no. 89. 1917.   1 v. 20 cm. F68.S665

SOCIETY of Mayflower descendants. California. Membership, 1915.   F68.S6654

SOCIETY of Mayflower descendants, Register of, in the state of California ... San Francisco, 1917.
    v. front., plates, facsims. 24½ cm. 17-27950.   F68.S666

SOCIETY of Mayflower descendants. Constitution, by-laws, etc. in the state of Colorado ... Denver,
1911.   7-44 p. front., illus., pl. 23 cm. 14-13134.   F68.S667

— Connecticut. Register. (Hartford)   v. 12 - 18 cm. 57-34192.   F68.S669

— Connecticut, 10th anniversary of the organization of the Society ... in. (Hartford, Plimpton
press, 1906)   28 p. 2 pl. 3 port. 17cm. 6-45827.   F68. S67

— District of Columbia. Annual. (19   (Washington, 19   v. 22½ cm. 24-13563.   F68.S 68

— District of Columbia ... Constitution and by-laws, etc. Washington, D. C., 1906. 39 p. front.
illus. 24 cm. 6-24808.   F68.S682

— District of Columbia. ... Officers and members, etc. Washington, D. C., 1899. 15 p. 23½ cm.
1-23288.   F68.S683

— District of Columbia, Register of the Society ... in. (Washington, 1970)   596 p. 24 cm.
79-84641.   F68.S6837

— District of Columbia, The Society ... in ... Washington, D. C., 1920. 58 p. 2 pl. (incl. front.)
23½ cm. 20-11924.   F68.S684

— District of Columbia. Miscellaneous printed matter pub. by this body is classified in F68.S689

— Illinois. Publication no. 1 - 3. Chicago (Oliphant print.) 1900 -   v. fronts., plates (part col.)
ports., fold. maps, facsims. 25 cm. CA 6-1736 unrev.   F68.S 74

— Illinois. Officers and members, 1907. Chicago 1907.   20 cm.   F68.S742

— Indiana. 25th anniversary ... (Indianapolis?) 1940.   69 p. illus. (ports.) 23 cm. 41-19145. F68.S745

— Iowa. Lineage record of the members of the Society ... (Ames? Ia., 1933)   188 l. 16 x 24½ cm.
34-23210.   F68.S747

— Maine, The by-laws and membership roll of the Socciety ... in. Portland, Lefavor-Tower co.,
1904.   43 p. pl. 17½ x 13½ cm. 5-17857.   F68.S 75

— Maine. ... By-laws and regulations with membership roll ... Portland, 1908.   (7) - 91 p.
plates, facsim. 24 cm. 8-34783.   F68.S752

— Maine. ... Membership roll ... Portland, 1913.   5-30 p. 23½ cm.   F68.S753

— Massachusetts. ... Officers, committees, etc. etc. Boston, (1906) 25 p. 24½ cm. 6-22944. F68.S755

— Massachusetts. ... Officers & committees, etc. Boston, (1916)   42 p. 24½ cm. 18-9420.
 F68.S756

— Michigan, Society ... in the State of. (Yearbook) (n.p.)   v. 19 cm. 56-21047.   F68.S757

— New Jersey. A record of the names of the passengers on the good ship "Mayflower" ... 1620, from whom descent has been proved ... Compiled by the late Herbert Folger ... (New York? 192-)
12 p. 20 cm. 24-15724.   F68.S7584

— New York. Bulletin of the Society ... no. 1-6. N.Y., 1904-17.   v. plates. 25½ cm. 9-26430.
 F68.S762

— New York. Constitution and by-laws ... (N.Y., 1894)   20 p. 13½ cm.   F68.S7625
 1894

— New York. Constitution and by-laws. (N.Y., 1898)   55 p. 12½ cm.   F68.S7625
 1898

— New York. Constitution and by-laws. (N.Y. 1901)   56 p. 12½ cm.   F68.S7625
 1901

— New York. Constitution and by-laws ... (N.Y., 1905)   40 p. 18 cm. 6-10829.   F68.S7625
 1905

— New York. Constitution and by-laws ... Hartford, 1907. 126 p. front., pl. 23½ cm. 14-7611.   F68.S7625
 1907

— New York. Constitution and by-laws ... (Brooklyn, 1910)   47 p. 15½ cm. 10-31048.   F68.S7625
 1910

— New York. ... Record book. 1st -   New York, 1896 - 19 -   v. fronts., plates (part col.) ports. 24½ cm. 1-16081 Rev.   F68.S763

— New York. Miscellaneous printed matter pub. by this body is classified in   F68.S764

— Ohio. Society .... in the State of Ohio. (n.p.) 1942.   93 p. 19 cm. 50-40186.   F68.S7649

— Ohio. ... (Register) Cincinnati, 1913.   141 p. front. 24½ cm. 13-21080.   F68.S765

— Oklahoma. Lineage of the Society of ... in the State of Oklahoma.   174 p. 24 cm. 59-14782.
 F68.S7653

— Pennsylvania. Historical sketch, 1896 - 1956. Philadelphia (1956 or 7)   94 p. illus. 19 cm.
58-16336.   F68.S7655

— Rhode Island. The first record-book of the Society ... Providence, 1904.   39 p. incl. front.
(facsim.) 17½ x 14 cm. 7-762.   F68.S766

— Rhode Island. The second record-book of the Society ... Providence, 1908.   154 p. front.
24½ cm. 9-4602.   F68.S767

— Rhode Island. The third record-book ... Providence, 1911.   226 p. front. 24½ cm. 11-20383.
 F68.S768

— Rhode Island. Lineages of the Society ... (Providence, 1966)   xlii, 397 p. 24 cm. 66-18221.
 F68.S7683

— Rhode Island. —— Supplement. (Providence, 1968)   407-452 p. 23 cm.   F68.S7683
 Suppl.

MASSACHUSETTS

— Texas, Mayflower descendants in the State of ... San Antonio, (1967-71)   2 v. 22 cm. Bibliographies: v. 1, p. 397-404. 66-28869.   F68.S76862H3

SPRING, Gardiner. A tribute to New-England: a sermon ... New-York, L. & F. Lockwood, 1821. 44 p. 20½ cm. 1-12106.   F68.S 77

STANDISH, Miles, the Puritan captain. By John S. C. Abbott ... New York, Dodd & Mead, 1872. 3, vii, (8) - 372 p. front., illus. (map) plates. 19 cm. 4-14727.   F68.S 78

STANDISH, Miles, captain of the pilgrims, by John S. C. Abbott. New York, Dodd, Mead, 1898. 2, vi, (2), (9) - 372 p. incl. map. front. 19 cm. 0-3611 Rev.   F68.S 79

STANDISH, Myles, with an account of the exercises of consecration of the monument on Captain's hill, Duxbury ... Prepared by Stephen M. Allen ... Boston, A. Mudge, print., 1871. 76 p. plates. 25 cm. 13-19377.   F68. S 8

STANDISH, Miles, Footprints of. By the Rev. B. F. De Costa. Charlestown, Re-printed from the church monthly for private distribution, 1864. 24 p. 19½ cm. 1-12074.   F68.S 82

STANDISH, Captain Myles, by Tudor Jenks ... New York, The Century co., 1905. viii, 250 p. incl. illus., plates, ports. front. 20 cm. 5-28371.   F68.S 83

STANDISH, Myles, The exploits of, by Henry Johnson (Muirhead Robertson) ... New York, D. Appleton, 1897. xii p. 278 p. front. (port.) plates. 20½ cm. Bibliography: p. (277) - 278. 13-19378.   F68.S 84

STANDISH, Myles, "the captain of Plymouth." By Edward McKnight ... Chorley, W. J. Sandiford, 1901. 2, 16 p. front. (port.) 20½ x 17 cm. Repr. from the Chorley library journal. Bibliography: p. 14-16. 2-17690.   F68.S 86

STANDISH, Captain Myles: his lost lands and Lancashire connections. A new investigation. By the Rev. Thomas Cruddas Porteus ... Manchester, The University press; London, New York (etc.) Longmans, Green, 1920. 5, 115 p. front. (port.) illus. (incl. map) 5 pl. 19 cm. (Pubs. of the University of Manchester. Historical series. No. xxxviii) Bibliography: 4th preliminary leaf. 20-23000.   F68.S 87

STANDISH, Myles; notes, comments and genealogy. Ed. annotated and pub. by Thomas Carpenter Read. Charleston, S. C., (1961)   29 p. illus. port. 22 cm.   F68.S 88

STEPHENSON, Walter, ed. Norwich and the Pilgrim fathers, the Mayflower tercentenary, ... Norwich (Eng.) Jarrold & sons, (1920)   80 p. incl. front., illus. 18½ cm. 21-12134.   F68.S 89

STODDARD, Francis Russell. The truth about the Pilgrims. New York, Soc. of Mayflower Descendants in the State of N. Y. (1952)   206 p. illus. 20 cm. 52-25972.   F68.S 92

SULLIVAN, William. A discourse delivered before the Pilgrim society ... Boston, Carter and Hendee, 1830.   60 p. 24 cm. 3-6069.   F68.S 95

THOMSON, Jay Earle. The land of the Pilgrims, silent reading, and the poem, The courtship of Miles Standish, by Jay Earle Thomson ... New York, Boston (etc.) D. C. Heath, (1925)   vii, 291 p. illus. 19½ cm. 25-24987.   F68.T 52

TIFFANY, Mrs. Nin (Moore) Pilgrims and Puritans: the story of the planting of Plymouth and Boston. Boston, Ginn & co., 1888.   3, 197 p. incl. illus., plates, ports., maps. front., maps. 18 cm. 1-12089.   F68.T 56

TOON, Peter. The Pilgrims' faith; historical research, by the author. Callington (Cornwall) Gospel Communication (1970)   2-79 p. illus., 2 facsims., maps. 20 cm.   F68.T 66

TOWNE, Edward Cornelius. Studies in Pilgrim story; the Pilgrims and Holland ... (Boston, The Barta press, 1905)   64 p. front. (port.) 2 pl. 25½ cm. 6-3551 Rev.   F68.T 74

TUNNELL, Mrs. Edith. History of the Pilgrims of the Mayflower as portrayed on the map of England and Holland. (Yonkers, c1936)   2 l. 33 cm. and map. 33½ x 50½ cm. 38M5285T.   F68.T 88 and 882

TUNNICLIFF, Harry George.   The story of the Pilgrim fathers, retold for young people ...   illus. by Harold Copping.   New York, Chicago (etc.) F. H. Revell co. (1920)   3, 5-157 p. front., plates. 20 cm.
20-17014.
F68.T 92

U. S. Congress. House. Plymouth-Provincetown Celebration Commission. Hearings ... Washington. U. S. Govt. Print Off., 1970.   ii, 21 p. 78-609036.
F68.U 56

U. S. Congress. ... Pilgrim tercentenary celebration ... Report ... (Washington, Govt. print. off., 1920)   10 p. 23 cm. 20-26281.
F68.U 58

U. S. Congress. ... Tercentenary of the landing of the Pilgrims.   Report of the Joint committee ... Washington, Govt. print. off., 1920.   12 p. 23 cm. 20-26288.
F68.U 59

U. S. President, (Harding) ... The achievement of the centuries. Address of the President ... at the tercentenary celebration of the landing of the Pilgrims ... Washington, Govt. print. off., 1921.
8 p. 23 cm. 21-26704.
F68.U 6

UPHAM, Charles Wentworth.   An oration delivered before the New England society in the city of New York ...   By Charles W. Upham.   2d ed.   Boston, J. Munroe, 1847.   64 p. 22½ cm. 17-19935.
F68.U 67
Toner coll.

USHER, Ellis B.   Puritan principles and influence.   An address delivered ... at the annual dinner of the Congregational club of Milwaukee ...   (La Crosse, Wis? 1901?)   (4) p. 27½ cm. 2-7167.
F68.U 85

USHER, Roland Greene.   The Pilgrims and their history.   ... New York, The Macmillan co., 1918.
x, 310 p. front., pl., ports., maps, facsim. 19½ cm. Contains "Bibliographical notes." 18-19815.
F68.U 86

USHER, Roland Greene.   The story of the Pilgrims for children.   ... New York, The Macmillan co., 1918.   xiii, 142 p. front., illus., plates. 20 cm. 18-18125.
F68.U 87

— 1930.   xiii p, 142 p. incl. front., illus. 16½ cm. 30-26386.
F68.U 87
1930

VANCURA, Zdenek.   The Pilgrim Fathers and the beginnings of American literature.   Praha, Universita Karlova, 1965.   90 p. 24 cm. Summary in English.
F68. V 3

WADDINGTON, John.   ... Track of the hidden church; or, The springs of the Pilgrim movement, by John Waddington ... With an introduction by Rev. E. N. Kirk.   Boston, Congregational board of publication (1863)   xxviii, 308 p. 20 cm. 17-20633.
F68.W 14

WARENSTAM, Eric.   Mayflower och pilgrimerna.   Stockholm, Forlaget Filadelfia (1957)
232 p. illus. 21 cm. Includes bibliography. 58-28644.
F68.W 16

WALSH, John E.   The Mayflower compact ... the first democratic document in America,   New York, F. Watts (c1971)   55 p. illus. facsim., port. 23 cm. 73-134369.
F68. W 2

WASHBURN, Robert Collyer.   Prayer for profit: being the colorful story of our Pilgrim fathers ... New York, Sears pub. co., 1930.   305 p. 21 cm. 30-9235.
F68.W 31

WEBSTER, Daniel.   ... The American spirit as expressed in the First settlement of New England and selections from other orations ... ed. for school use, by Sarah Elder ... Chicago, New York, Scott, Foresman (1920)   2, 7-97 p. 18 cm. "Bibliographies": p. 29-32. 20-22226.
F68.W 36

WEBSTER, Daniel.   A discourse ... In commemoration of the first settlement of New-England. Boston, Wells and Lilly, 1821.   104 p. 24 cm. 1-12107.
F68.W 37

— 2d ed.   55 p. 20½ cm. 1-12108.
F68.W 38

MASSACHUSETTS

— 3d ed. 1825. 75 p. 24½ cm. 9-27148. F68.W 39

— 4th ed. 1826. 60 p. 22 cm. 17-9018. F68.W393
Toner coll.

— Wehlitz, Lou Rogers. The first Thanksgiving. Illus. by Michael Lowenbein. Chicago, Follett Pub. Co. (1962) 29 p. 62-8711. F68. W 4

WEIR, Robert Walter. The picture of the embarcation of the Pilgrims from Delft-Haven, in Holland; painted by Robt. W. Weir... N.Y., Piercy & Reed, print., 1843. 13 p. incl. pl. 22½ cm. 3-21031.
F68.W 42

WEISGARD, Leonard. The Plymouth Thanksgiving. 1st ed. Garden City, N.Y., Doubleday, (1967)
1 v. (unpaged) 27 cm. 67-15379. F68.W 44

WEST, Samuel. An anniversary sermon... In grateful memory of the first landing of our pious New-England ancesters... Boston, Printed Draper and Folsom, 1778. 79 p. 18½ cm. 15-28193.
F68.W 52

WHITTEMORE, Henry. The signers of the Mayflower compact, and their descendants,... New York, Mayflower pub. co. (1899) 48 p. front., illus. (coats of arms) pl. 30 cm. "Grinnell and allied families": p. 33-48.
4-12563. F68.W 62
Microfilm 8661 F

WILLISON, George Findlay. The Pilgrim reader; the story of the Pilgrims as told by themselves & their contemporaries, friendly & unfriendly. (1st ed.) Garden City, N.Y., Doubleday, 1953.
xvii, 585 p. maps. 22 cm. Bibliography: p. (567) - 570. 53-5045. F68.W 74

WILLISON, George Findlay. ... Saints and strangers, being the lives of the Pilgrim fathers & their families, with their friends & foes; & an account of their posthumous wanderings in limbo, their final resurrection & rise to glory, & the strange pilgrimages of Plymouth rock. New York, Reynal & Hitchcock (1945) ix, 513 p. front. (port.) 21 cm. "Selective bibliography": p. 487-494. 45-6745.
F68.W 75

— London, Toronto, W. Heinemann (1946) x, 446 p. front. (port.) 20 cm. "Selective bibliography": p. (424) - 430. 47-17020. F68.W 75
1946

— New York, Ballantine Books (1965) 380 p. 18 cm. F68.W 75
1965

— (Revised ed.) London, Heinemann, 1966. xii, 307 p. maps, tables. 22½ cm. Bibliog.: p. 291-297. F68.W 75
1966
MRR alc.

WINSLOW, Edward By W. Sterry-Cooper. Birmingham, Eng., Reliance Print., 1953. 67 p. illus.
23 cm. 54-29636. F68.W55S8

WINSLOW, Edward (o.v. 1610-11) King's scholar and printer. By George Gregerson Wolkins. King's scholar and printer. Worcester, Mass., The Society, 1951. 238-266 p. 25 cm. "Reprinted from the Proceedings of the American Antiquarian Soc. for Oct. 1950." Bibliographical footnotes. 52-3324 rev. F68.W76W6

WINSLOW, William Copley. The Pilgrim fathers in Holland; their condition, and their relation to and treatment by the authorities and the people, with special reference to the proposed monument at Delfshaven... Boston and Chicago, Congregational Sunday-school and pub. soc. (1891) 24 p. 23½ cm.
17-25226. F68.W 77

WINTHROP, Robert Charles. An address, delivered before the New England society, in the city of New York. Boston, New York, 1840. 60 p. 24 cm. 1-16222. F68.W 78

WINTHROP, Robert Charles. Oration on the 250th anniversary of the landing of the Pilgrim fathers at Plymouth ... Boston, J. Wilson, 1871.   93 p. 23½ cm. 1-12109*. L.C. copy replaced by microfilm.

          F68.W 79
    Microfilm 15222 F

—   87 p. 24 cm.   10-1517.   F68.W791

WISNER, Benjamin Blydenburg. Influence of religion on liberty. A discourse in commemoration of the landing of the Pilgrims ... Boston, Perkins & Marvin, 1831.   36 p. 21 cm. 1-16207.

    F68.W 81

WOOD, Herbert George. Ventures for the kingdom; study in the history of the Pilgrim fathers ... London, Hodder and Stoughton, (1920)   xiv, 254 p. 19 cm. 22-4457.   F68.W 87

WOOD, John Sumner. Cupid's Path in ancient Plymouth; the last Pilgrim houses. (Germantown? Md., 1957)   112 p. illus. 23 cm. 59-30587.   F68.W873

WOODBRIDGE, John. The jubilee of New England. A sermon ... in commemoration of the landing of our fathers at Plymouth ... Northampton, Print. T.W. Shepard, 1821.   28 p. 22½ cm. 15-28198.

    F68.W 88

WOODBRIDGE, William. An address delivered before the New England society of Michigan ... Detroit, Print. Harsha & Willcox, 1849.   24 p. 23 cm. 25-1058.   F68.W89

WRIGHT, Charles Baker. Gleanings from Forefathers', a memorial souvenir. Middlebury, Vt., Middlebury historical soc., 1926.   xvi, 96 p. front. 18½ cm. 28-3336.

    F68.W 94

YEADON, Richard, Speech of ... at the Pilgrim celebration ... N.Y., G. Trehern, 1853.   8 p. 8°. 2-5503.   F68. Y37

YOUNG, Alexander. Chronicles of the Pilgrim fathers of the colony of Plymouth, from 1602 - 1625. Boston, C.C. Little and J. Brown, 1841.   xvi, 504 p. front. (port.) illus., maps. 23 cm. Contents. - Gov. Bradford's History of Plymouth colony. - Bradford's and Winslow's journal (i.e. Mourt's relation) - Cushman's Discourse. - Winslow's Relation. - Winslow's brief narration. - Gov. Bradford's Dialogue. - Gov. Bradford's Memoir of Elder Brewster. - Letters. 1-12110.   F68.Y 68
    R.R. A1

— New York, Da Capo Press, 1971.   xvi, 504 p. 24 cm. 78-87667.   F68.Y 69
    1971

— 2d ed. 1844.   xvi, 502 p. front. (port.) illus. maps. 23 cm. 25-12682.   F68.Y682

ZINER, Feenie. The pilgrims and Plymouth Colony. New York, American Heritage Pub. Co. (1961) 153 p. 26 cm. (American Heritage junior library) 61-14735.   F68. Z 5
    1962

1775 - 1865.

ADDRESS to the citizens of Massachusetts, on the approaching state elections. (n.p., 1810) 8 p. 13½ cm. Advocates the election of Elbridge Gerry and William Gray ... 17-23218.   F69. A 2

ADDRESS to the independent citizens of Massachusetts, on the subject of the approaching election. Worcester, Pub. at the Spy office, 1810.   23 p. 22½ cm. Selected principally from "The New England patriot" (by John Lowell) Recommending the re-election of Christopher Gore as governor of Mass., etc. 21-7157.   F69.A215

ADDRESS of the Whig members of the Senate and House of representatives of Mass. to their constituents ... Boston, Press of T.R. Marvin, 1843.   16 p. 24½ cm. 10-5621.   F69.A 23

MASSACHUSETTS

1775 - 1865.

AMERICAN Antiquarian Society. Index of deaths in Massachusetts centinel and Columbian centinel, 1784-1840. (Worcester) 1952. 12 v. 26 cm. Typescript (carbon copy) 52-40178. F69. A 5

AMORY, Katharine (Green) "Mrs. John Amory" The journal of Mrs. John Amory ... 1775 - 1777, with letters from her father, Rufus Greene, 1759-1777 ... Boston, Priv. print., 1923. x, 101 p. plates, ports., facsims. 27 cm. 23-17792. F69. A 52

AWFUL calamities; or, The shipwrecks of Dec., 1839, being a full account of the dreadful hurricanes of Dec. 15, 21 & 27, on the coast of Mass. ... 5th ed. Boston, Press of J. Howe, 1840. 24 p. 1 illus. 21 cm. 1-12112. F69. A 96

BIDWELL, Barnabas. An address to the people of Massachusetts. (n.p., 1804) 22 p. 21½ cm. Recommending James Sullivan for governor. 9-20798. F69. B 57

— (n.p.) 1805. 24 p. 21 cm. Second recommendation of James Sullivan for governor. 9-20799. F69. B 58

BIGELOW, George Tyler, Memoir of, sometime chief justice of Mass. By George B. Chase ... Boston, J. Wilson, 1890. 38 p. front. (port.) 24½ cm. Repr. from Proceedings of the Mass. hist. soc. 18-8241. F69. B 59

BIRD, Francis William; a biographical sketch. Boston, Priv. print., 1897. 2, 168 p. 2 port. (incl. front.) 21 cm. 5-5121. F69. B 6

BOSTON. Proceedings of a great Whig meeting of citizens of Boston, ... 1838. Boston, Print. Perkins & Marvin, 1838. 19 p. 23½ cm. 10-34662. F69. B 74

BOWDOIN, James. Address of the Hon. Robert C. Winthrop ... Bowdoin college. Boston, Redding & co., 1849. 15 p. 21 cm. 7-11145. F69. B AC901. W3 vol. 45

BOWDOIN, James. Extract from a discourse by the Rev. J. S. Buckminster ... after the interment of Hon. James Bowdoin. Albany, Print,, J. Munsell, 1848. 8 p. 25 cm. 16-23667. F69. B 77

BOWDOIN, James. An eulogy, illustrative of the life ... of the late Hon. James Bowdoin ... with notices of his family; ... By William Jenks ... Boston, Print. John Eliot, 1812. 40 p. 26 x 21 cm. 7-11143. F69. B 78 Jefferson coll.

BOWDOIN, James. An eulogy, on the Honourable James Bowdoin, late president of the American academy of arts and sciences ... Boston, Print. Thomas and Andrews, 1791. 24 p. 23 cm. 45-43957. With this is bound the next item. F69. B7815 Rare Book Coll.

BOWDOIN, James. A philosophical discourse ... Boston, Print, Adams and Nourse, 1786. 71 p. fold. pl. 26½ cm. Bound with above item. 45-43958. F69. B7815 Rare Book Coll.

BOWDOIN, James. A sermon ... occasioned by the death of the Hon. James Bowdoin. By Peter Thacher ... Boston, Print, Thomas and Andrews, 1791. 27 p. 20 x 15½ cm. 7-11150. F69. B783 Rare Book Coll.

BOWDOIN, James. Governor Bowdoin and his family; a guide to an exhibition and a catalogue, by Robert L. Volz. Brunswick, Me., Bowdoin College, 1969. xi, 86 p. 23 cm. F69.B784

— Boston, Ticknor, Redd and Fields, 1849. 68 p. 24 cm. 7-11146. F69.B785

BRAGG, Arial. Memoirs of Col. Arial Bragg. Written by himself ... Milford, G. W. Stacy, print., 1846. iv, (5) - 86 p. 16 cm. 1-13613. F69. B 8

BRAUER, Kinley J.   Cotton versus conscience; Massachusetts Whig politics and southwestern expansion, 1843-1848.   Lexington, University of Kentucky Press (1967)   vi, 272 p. 23 cm. 66-26692.
F69.B 83

BOWDOIN, Madam Elizabeth, A sermon ... after the interment of, relict of the late Hon. James Bowdoin. By William Emerson.   Boston, Print. D. Carlisle, 1803.   20 p. 22½ cm. 15-27871.
F69.B 84

BRIGGS, George N.   Great in goodness; a memoir of George N. Briggs ...   By Wm. C. Richards ...   Boston, Gould and Lincoln; N.Y., Sheldon, 1866.   iv, 5-451 p. incl. 5 pl. front. (port.) pl. 20½ cm. 14-3397.
F69.B 85

— 1867.   iv, 5-451 p. incl. plates. front. (port.) pl. 20½ cm. 33-6840.
F69.B 85
1867

BROOKS, Gov. John, Memoir of.   By Charles Brooks.   Boston, 1865.   7 p. port. 25½ cm. Printed also in the N. E. hist. and geneal. register, July, 1865. 12-11172.
F69.B 87

BROOKS, Peter C.   God with the aged: a sermon preached ... after the death of Hon. Peter C. Brooks.   By N. L. Frothingham ...   Boston, Print. J. Wilson, 1849.   15 p. 23½ cm. 17-9445.
F69.B875

CARTER, James Gordon.   A geography of Massachusetts: for families and schools.   Boston, Hilliard, Gray, etc., 1830.   x, 224 p. front. (fold. map) 15 cm. 1-12113.
F69.C 32
G. & M.

CLARKE, James Freeman.   The duties of Massachusetts.   A sermon ...   Boston, Wright & Potter, 1868.   46 p. 23½ cm. Printed by order of the Mass. House of representatives. 8-6896.
F69.C 59

CLIFFORD, John H., Memoir of.   By Robert C. Winthrop ...   Boston, Print, J. Wilson, 1877.   30 p. front. (port.) 24 cm. "Reprinted from Proceedings of the Mass. hist. soc., Oct. 1877." "1877." 18-8234.
F69.C 63

COBB, David, Some remarks on the life of.   By Francis Baylies.   1864.   1 v.
F69.C652

— Albany, J. Munsell, 1864.   18 p. front. 24½ cm. From the New England hist. and geneal. register. "Cobb genealogy": p. 17-18. 10-30919.
F69.C653

COBB, General David.   A brief memoir of General David Cobb, of the revolutionary army.   (Boston) Priv. print, (1873)   8 p. front. (port.) 26 x 21 cm. "Repr. from 'Memorials of the Soc. of the Cincinnati of Mass.' 1873." 16-27479.
F69.C654

COBB, Elijah, 1768-1848; a Cape Cod skipper, with a foreword by Ralph D. Paine.   New Haven, Yale university press; 1925.   5, 111 p. front. (port.) pl., facsims. 21 cm. 25-23063.
F69.C 67

COOMBS, William.   A sermon occasioned by the death of Mrs. William Coombs.   By Daniel Dana.   Newburyport, Edward Little, 1814.   27 p. 20½ cm. 17-12087.
F69.C 76

COOPER, Samuel.   A sermon preached before His Excellency John Hancock, esq. ...   (Boston) Print, T. & J. Fleet, and J. Gill (1780)   2, 55 p. 20 cm. 15-11527.
F69.C 77

CRANCH, Richard.   A discourse ... at the interment of the Hon. Richard Cranch.   By Peter Whitney ...   Boston, Press of John Eliot, 1811.   19 p. 23 cm. 17-19619.
F69.C 89

CURRIER, Festus Curtis.   ... Reminiscences and observations of the nineteenth century ...   Fitchburg, Sentinel print., 1902.   106 p. 20 cm. Fitchburg historical soc. 20-6168.
F69.C 95

CURRIER, Festus C., born at Holliston, Mass. ... 1825, Reminiscences of.   Fitchburg, Mass., 1900.   106 p. front. (port.) 20 cm. Repub. from Fitchburg sentinel. 17-30114.
F69.C 96

CURTIS, Benjamin Robbins.   Address to the people of Massachusetts.   (Boston, 1851?)   16 p. 23 cm.   On the coalition of 1851 between the Democratic and Free-soil parties in Mass. 10-21797.
F69.C 97

MASSACHUSETTS

DARLING, Arthur Burr. Political changes in Massachusetts, 1824-1848; a study of liberal movements in politics ... New Haven, Yale university press, 1925. xii, 392 p. front., ports. 22½ cm. "Bibliographical note": p. (363) - 369. 25-23065.
F69.D 22

— Cos Cob, Conn., J. E. Edwards, 1968. xii, 392 p. 23 cm.
F69.D 22 1968

DAVIS, Andrew McFarland. ... The Shays rebellion a political aftermath ... Worcester, Mass., The Society, 1911. 25 p. 25 cm. Repr. from the Procs. of the Amer. antiquarian soc., 1911. 11-32560.
F69.D 25

DAVIS, Samuel. Journal of a tour to Connecticut. - Autumn of 1789. (From Mass. hist. soc. Proceedings. Boston, 1871. 23½ cm. v. 11, p. 9-32) 8-36494.
F69.D 26

DEAN, John Ward. History of the gerrymander. Boston, Priv. print., 1892. 11 p. illus. (incl. map) 25 cm. Reprinted from the New-England hist. and geneal. register for Oct., 1892. 3-30959.
F69.D 29

DEARBORN, Henry. ... An address ... on the life and character of the late Henry A. S. Dearborn. By George Putnam. Roxbury, Norfolk county journal press, 1851. 32 p. 23 cm. Printed by order of the city council. 5-19375.
F69.D 3

DEMOCRATIC party. Proceedings and address of the Massachusetts Democratic state convention, ... 1838, with names of the delegates. (Worcester? 1838) 12 p. 25 cm. 10-31026.
F69.D 38

DENNY, Col. Thomas, A sermon, delivered at ... the funeral of. By John Nelson ... Leicester (Mass.) Print. Hori Brown, 1815. 16 p. 22 cm. 19-10876.
F69.D 41
Toner coll.

DICKINSON, Rodolphus. A geographical and statistical view of Massachusetts proper. Greenfield, Print. Denio and Phelps, 1813. 80 p. 22½ cm. 1-12115.
F69.D 54
Rare Book Coll.

DIX, John. Local loiterings, and visits in the vicinity of Boston. By a looker-on. Boston, Redding & co., 1845. 147 p. 19 cm. 1-12116 Rev.
F69.D 61

EDMONDS, John Henry. ... How Massachusetts received the Declaration of independence ... Worcester, Mass., The Society, 1926. 28 p. 25 cm. Reprinted from Proceedings of the Amer. antiquarian soc. for Oct., 1925. 26-18386.
F69.E 24

ENDICOTT. A discourse delivered ... after the funeral of Hon. John Endicott. By Alvan Lamson ... Boston, Crosby, Nichols, 1857. 24p. 24 cm. 10-6476.
F69.E 56

EUSTIS. A sermon ... on the death of His Excellency William Eustis ... By James Barnaby ... Newburyport, W. & J. Gilman, 1825. 20 p. 23 cm. 10-7618.
F69.E 7

EUSTIS. A sermon on the death of His Excellency, William Eustis ... By Thomas Gray ... Boston, Office of the Christian register ... 1825. 26 p. 23½ cm. 15-23534.
F69.E 85

EUSTIS. A sermon, prached at the funeral of His Excellency William Eustis ... By Daniel Sharp ... Boston, Print. ... True and Greene ... 1825. 22 p. 24½ cm. 5-30329.
F69.E 9

FISHER. A sermon, ... after the interment of the Hon. Jabez Fisher ... By Nathanael Emmons ... Providence, Print. D. Heaton, 1807. 24 p. 19½ cm. 14-17083.
F69.F 53

GILL, Rebecca. A sermon ... occasioned by the death of Madame Rebecca Gill ... By Joseph Russell. Boston, Print, Rhoades & Laughton, 1798. 26 p. 19½ x 15 cm. 16-21611.
F69.G 47
Rare Book Coll.

GILL, Rebecca. A sermon occasioned by the death of Madam Rebecca Gill ... By Peter Thacher ... Boston, Print. Rhoades and Laughton, 1798. 23 p. 19½ cm. 17-6707.
F69.G474

GORDON, George Wm., The record of. The slave trade at Rio de Janeiro, seizure of slave vessels, conviction of slave dealers, personal liberation of slaves, etc. Boston, The American headquarters, 1856. 15 p. 23 cm. 5-16549. F69.G 64

GORE. Funeral sermon on the late Hon. Christopher Gore ... By F.W.P.Greenwood ... Boston, Wells and Lilly, 1827. 19 p. 21½ cm. 17-13797. F69.G654

GORE. Memoir of the late Hon. Christopher Gore, of Waltham, Mass. By Samuel Ripley. (Cambridge, E.W. Metcalf, 1833?) 17 (i.e. 21) p. 22 cm. Reprinted from the Mass. hist. soc. collections, 3d series, v. 3, p.191-209. 11-4707. F69.G 66

GRAY, William, of Salem, merchant; a biographical sketch, by Edward Gray ... Boston and N.Y., Houghton Mifflin, 1914. vii, 124 p. front., plates, ports., facsim. 26½ cm. 14-14162. F69.G 76

GREEN, Samuel Abbott. Remarks ... relating to the importation of foreign goods ... (Boston? 1894) 24 cm. F69.G 79

GREENLEAF. The Christian standard of honor. A discourse ... following the death of Hon. Thomas Greenleaf. By William P. Lunt ... Boston, Little Brown, 1854. 34 p. 23½ cm. Appendix: Genealogy of the Greenleaf family: p. 23-34. 16-11125. F69. G 8

GRIFFIN, John Quincy Adams. A series of letters, written by Amaziah Bumpus (pseud.) and addressed to Gov. John Davis ... Rev. by the author. Dedham (Mass.) Norfolk Democrat press, 1842. 40 p. 25½ cm. "Originally pub. in the Norfolk Democrat." 15-10650. F69.G 85

HALL, Van Beck. Politics without parties: Massachusetts, 1780-1791. (Pittsburgh) University of Pittsburgh Press (1972) xvii, 375 p. 24 cm. Includes bibliographical references. 78-158186 MARC. F69. H 3

HAWTHORNE, Nathaniel, Passages from the American note-books of ... Boston, Ticknor and Fields, 1868. 2 v. 18½ cm. 1-22521. F69.H 39
Rare Book Coll.

HAYNES, G.H. A know nothing legislature. (1897) 1 v. F69.H 41

HAYWARD, John. The Massachusetts directory; being the first part of the New-England directory. Boston, J. Hayward, 1835. iv, (5)-198 p. 15½ cm. 1-14482. F69.H 42

HENSHAW. A refutation, by his friends, of the calumnies against David Henshaw, in relation to the failure of the Commonwealth bank, and the transfer of South Boston lands to the United States. Boston, Beals & Greene, 1844. 60 p. 25 cm. 11-24440. F69.H 52

HIGGINSON, Thomas Wentworth. Cheerful yesterdays ... Boston and New York, Houghton, Mifflin, 1898. 5, 374 p. 19½ cm. Originally contributed to the Atlantic monthly. 11-21033. F69.H 62

HIGGINSON, Thomas Wentworth. Life and times of Stephen Higginson, member of the Continental congress (1783) and author of the "Laco" letters, relating to John Hancock (1789) ... Boston and N.Y., Houghton, Mifflin, 1907. vii, 305 p. front., plates, ports., facsims. 20½ cm. 7-30144. F69.H 63

HOLTEN. A discourse delivered ... at the interment of the Hon. Samuel Holten ... By Benjamin Wadsworth ... Andover, Print. Flagg & Gould, 1816. 31 p. 24½ cm. 10-6472. F69.H 75

HOMER, James Lloyd. Notes on the sea-shore; or, Random sketches. In relation to the ancient town of Hull, its settlement, its inhabitants, etc. ... by the "Shade of Alden." Boston, Redding & co., 1848. vii, (9)-54 p. front. 8°. 1-12117-M1. F68.H 76

HOMER, James Lloyd. Nahant, and other places on the north-shore; being a continuation of Notes on the sea-shore, by the Shade of Alden ... Boston, Printed by W. Chadwick, 1848. vii, (9)-48 p. 23 cm. Imperfect. p. 17-24 duplicated; p. 33-40 omitted. 1-12118. F69.H 77

HOWE. Address of Chief Justice Parker to the bar of the county of Suffolk at a meeting held for the purpose of testifying their respect for the memory of the Hon. Samuel Howe ... Boston, Nathan Hale, 1828. 14 p. 23 cm. 5-14700.   F69.H 85

HOWE. A sketch of the character of the late Hon. Samuel Howe ... By John M. Williams ... Worcester, Griffin and Morrill, print., 1828. 16 p. 22½ cm. 19-4147.   F69.H853

HUNTINGTON, Samuel. By Susan D. Huntington. (In The Connecticut magazine. Hartford, Conn. 1900. v. 6, p. 247-253) 12-6386.   F69.H 95

KING. Two discourses, occasioned by the decease of the Hon. Daniel P. King. ... by F. P. Appleton. Boston, Print. G. R. Carlton (1850) 16 p. 24 cm. 11-22528.   F69.K 54

KNAPP, Samuel Lorenzo. Extracts from the journal of Marshal Soult (pseud.) ... Newburyport, W. B. Allen, 1817. 143 p. 19 cm. 10-8719.   F69.K 67
Rare Book Coll.

KOSSUTH, L. First speech in Faneuil Hall. 1852. 1 v.   F69.K 86

LAWRENCE. Extracts from the diary and correspondence of the late Amos Lawrence ... Ed. by his son, William R. Lawrence. Boston, Print. J. Wilson, 1855. xii, 307 p. front., pl., ports. 24 cm. 11-26707. L. C. copy replaced by microfilm.   F69.L 38
Microfilm 19392 F

— Boston and N. Y. ... 1855. viii, (3), (ix) - xiv, 15-369 p. pl., 2 port. (incl. front.) 25 cm.   F69.L382

— Boston and Dover, (1855) 3, (v) - xiv, 15-369 p. front. (port.) pl. 19½ cm. 29-25238.   F69.L383

— Boston and New York, 1856. viii, (3), (ix) - xiv, 15-369 p. front., pl., ports. 21 cm. 11-26863.   F69.L384

— Boston and New York, 1858. xiv, 15-369 p. incl. facsim. pl., 2 port. (incl. front.) 19½ cm. 32-12849.   F69.L386

LAWRENCE, Amos, ... Sketch of, by C. Adams. N. Y., Phillips & Hunt; Cincinnati, Walden & Stowe, 1883. 16 p. 19 cm. (Home college series, no. 90) 11-26709.   F69.L 41

LAWRENCE. Extract frm a sermon ... following the interment of the late Amos Lawrence. By Rev. F. T. Gray. Boston, J. Wilson, 1853. 16 p. 16½ cm. 5-14704.   L69.L415

LAWRENCE, Amos, A discourse commemorative of. By Mark Hopkins ... Boston, Press of T. R. Marvin, 1853. 36 p. 22½ cm. 11-26708.   F69.L 42

LAWRENCE. The moral power of character. A sermon preached ... after the funeral of Amos Lawrence. By S. K. Lothrop. Boston, Eastburn's press, 1853. 26 p. 23 cm. 5-11376.   F69.L428

LAWRENCE. The poor boy and the merchant prince; or, Elements of success drawn from the life and character of the late Amos Lawrence. A book for youth. By William M. Thayer ... Boston, Gould and Lincoln; New York, Sheldon, Blakeman, 1857. (v) - xviii, (19) - 349 p. 17½ cm. 11-26706.   F69.L 43

— 1860. (v) - xviii, (19) - 349 p. 17½ cm. 37-38772.   F69.L 43
1860

LEE, Colonel Henry, Memoir of; with selections from his writings and speeches; prepared by John T. Morse, jr. Boston, Little, Brown, 1905. viii, (3) - 441 p. 7 pl., 2 port. (incl. front.) 22 cm. 5-39581.   F69.L 47

LELAND, John. The Yankee spy, calculated for the religious meridian of Massachusetts ... by Jack Nips (pseud.) Boston, Print. for John Asplund (1794) 20 p. 20 cm. L. C. copy lacks t.-p. Mainly a criticism of religious discrimination in the constitution and laws of Mass. 9-20795 Rev. 2.   F69.L 54

MASSACHUSETTS. An address from the General court, to the people of the commonwealth of Massachusetts. Boston, Adams & Nourse, 1786. 40 p. 21½ cm. 9-20814.

F69.M405
Rare Book Coll.

MASSACHUSETTS. The patriotick proceedings of the legislature of Massachusetts, during their session from Jan. 26 to March 4, 1809. Boston, Print. J. Cushing, 1809. 2. 130 p. 22½ cm. 8-9311.

F69.M 41

MASSACHUSETTS. Patriotism and piety. The speeches of His Excellency Caleb Strong, esq., to the Senate and House ... of Massachusetts ... 1800 to 1807. Newburyport, Print. Edmund M. Blunt, 1808.
xii, 13-202 p. front. (port.) 18½ cm. 16-2762.

F69.M412

MASSACHUSETTS. (Decision of the Supreme judicial court held at Great Barrington, Berkshire County, March, 1787, in the case of Peter Wilcox and Nathaniel Austin ... Boston? 190-?) (4) p. 23½ cm.
CA 12-1236 Unrev.

F69.M414

MASSACHUSETTS. Address to the free and independent people of Massachusetts. (Boston, 1812)
8 p. 20 cm. Recommending the nomination of Caleb Strong for governor, etc. 21-7158.

F69.M416

MASSACHUSETTS. "Our houses and our castles." A review of the proceedings of the nunnery committee, of the Massachusetts legislature; ... By Charles Hale. Boston, C. Hale, 1855.
62 p. 24 cm. 11-4705.

F69.M 42

MASSACHUSETTS. Answer of the Whig members of the legislature of Massachusetts ... to the Address of His Excellency Marcus Morton ... Boston, Printed Perkins & Marvin, 1840. 36 p. 24 cm.
9-27171.

F69.M453

MORTON. A refutation of the charge of abolitionism, brought by David Henshaw, and his partizans, against the Hon. Marcus Morton. Boston, Felch's press, 1845. 32 p. 22½ cm. 10-1541.

F69.M455

MINOT, George Richards. The history of the insurrections, in Massachusetts, in the year 1786, and the rebellion consequent thereon. Worcester, Mass., Print, Isaiah Thomas, 1788. iv, (5) - 192 p.
21 cm. 1-13347 rev.

F69.M 65
Jefferson coll.

— 2d ed. Freeport, N.Y., Books for Libraries Press (1970) 192 p. 23 cm. 70-107823.

F69.M 65
1970

— New York, Da Capo Press, 1971. iv, 192 p. 23 cm. 76-148912.

F69.M 65
1971

— 2d ed. Boston, Pub, James W. Burditt ... 1810. iv, (5) - 192 p. 23 cm. 1-12119.

F69.M 66
Rare Book Coll.

MINOT. Sketch of the life of the Hon. G. R. Minot ... Boston, D. Clapp, 1873. 11 p. 23½ cm. Reprinted from the 'Polyanthos,' March, 1806." 12-26590.

F69.M 67

MOULTON, Horace. The young pastor's wife. Memoir of Elizabeth Ann Moulton: containing her biography, diary, letters, etc. Boston, Waite, Peirce and co., 1845. ix, (5) - 275 p. 15½ cm. 13-2725.

F69.M 92

NEW ENGLAND historic genealogical society. ... Proceedings ... commemorative of the organization of the government of Mass ... Boston, The Society's house, 1880. 67 p. incl. front. 23½ cm.
3-32509.

F69.N 54

NEW ENGLAND society of Brooklyn, N.Y. Proceedings at the dedication of a tablet at Petersham, Mass., to mark the surprise and capture in that town of the insurgents under Daniel Shays ... 1787. (Brooklyn, Eagle press, 1927) 21 p. 2 l. pl. 22½ cm. 27-19574.

F69.N 56

MASSACHUSETTS

NOBLE, John. A few notes on the Shays rebellion. Reprinted from the Proceedings of the American antiquarian soc. Worcester, Mass., Press of C. Hamilton, 1903. 35 p. 25½ cm. 4-18872.
F69.N 74

ORNE. A sermon, ... occasioned by the death of the Hon. Azor Orne ... By Ebenezer Hubbard ... Printed at Salem, by Thomas C. Cushing, 1796. 31 p. 22 cm. 14-15960.
F69.O 72
Rare Book Coll.

ORNE, Henry. Reply of Colonel Orne to the attacks of Mr. Nathaniel Greene, and David Henshaw, and others, in the Boston statesman. Boston, Putnam & Hunt, 1829. 48 p. 24½ cm. 12-12840.
F69.O 74

PALFREY, John Gorham. Letter to a Whig neighbor, on the approaching state election, by an old conservative. 2d ed. Boston, Crosby, Nichols, & co., 1855. 27 p. 23½ cm. 11-4706.
F69.P 14

PALFREY, John Gorham. ... To the Free soil members of the General court of Massachusetts for the year 1851. (Boston, 1851) 4 p. 23½ cm. Opposing the proposed alliance of Democrats and Free-soilers ... 10-25132.
F69.P 15

PARKER. A sermon preached ... after the decease of the Hon. Isaac Parker ... by John G. Palfrey ... Boston, N. Hale and Gray & Bowen, 1830. 32 p. 21½ cm. 16-11117.
F69.P 22

PARSONS. A sketch of the character of the late Chief Justice Parsons, exhibited in an address to the Grand jury ... By Isaac Parker ... Boston, Print. John Eliot, 1813. iv, (5) - 32 p. 21½ cm. 20-20875.
F69.P 25
Toner coll.

PERKINS, Thomas Handasyd, Memoir of; containing extracts from his diaries and letters. By Thomas G. Cary. Boston, Little, Brown, 1856. 2, 304 p. front. (port.) 24½ cm. 12-16490.
F69.P 46

— New York, B. Franklin (1971) 304 p. port. 23 cm. Reprint of the 1856 ed. 77-164040 MARC.
F69.P 46
1971

PHILLIPS. A sermon preached ... after the interment of the late Hon. John Phillips. By John G. Palfrey ... Boston, Print. Munroe and Francis, 1823. 24 p. 23 cm. 13-2726.
F69.P 53

PHILLIPS. A sermon, preached ... on the day of the interment of His Honor Samuel Phillips ... By Thomas Baldwin ... Boston, Print. Young and Minns, 1802. 21 p. 21½ cm. 5-26578.
F69.P 56
Rare Book Coll.

PHILLIPS. A memoir of His Honor Samuel Phillips. By John L. Taylor ... Boston, Congregational board of publication, 1856. xi, 391 p. 2 pl. 3 port. (incl. front.) fold. facsim. 24 cm. 9-887.
F69.P 57

PHILLIPS. A sermon occasioned by the death of the Hon. William Phillips ... By Benjamin B. Wisner ... Boston, Hilliard, Gray, Little, and Wilkins, 1827. 52 p. 22 cm. 1-19526 Rev.
F69.P 58

PHINNEY. Biographical sketch, personal and descriptive, of Sylvanus B. Phinney, of Barnstable, Mass. Boston, Rand Avery co., print., 1888. 96 p. front. (port.) pl. 23½ cm. Principally a collection of Phinney's writings. 19-4154.
F69.P592

PHILLIPS, Samuel. A discourse ... at the funeral of His Honor Samuel Phillips ... By David Tappan. Boston, Print. Young and Minns, 1802. 27 p. 20 cm. 18-12648.
F69.P 63
Rare Book Coll.

PICTORIAL views of Massachusetts for the young. Worcester, E. Dorr (1846) 88 p. 15 cm. (Juvenile books)
F69.P 65

PRESCOTT. The stay and the staff taken away. A discourse occasioned by the death of the Hon.

William Prescott ... By Alexander Young. Boston, C. C. Little and J. Brown, 1844. 34 p. 22 cm.
5-11423. F69.P 92

RANTOUL. Second speech of Mr. Rantoul, of Massachusetts, on the coalition in Massachusetts ... (Washington, Print. the Congressional globe office, 1852) 8 p. 24½ cm. 18-14880.
F69. R 2

REVERE, Paul. Boston and some noted émigrés; a collection of facts and incidents ... relating to some well-known citizens of France who found homes in Boston and New England, with which are included accounts of several visits made by one of the authors to La Rochelle and to the homes of the ancestors of Paul Revere. By Allan Forbes and Paul F. Cadman. Issued by the State street trust co. of Boston ... (Boston, Walton advertising & print. co.) 1938. 98 p. front., illus. (incl. ports.) 23½ cm.
38-18373. F69.R
F73.9.F7F7

REVERE, Paul. ... Paul Revere's own account of his midnight ride, April 18-19, 1775. With a short account of his life, by S. E. Morison. (Boston, Old South assoc., 1922?) 12 p. 19½ cm. (Old South leaflets. General series v. 9 no. 222) Bibliography p. 12. 22-17954.
F69.R412

REVERE, Paul. Paul Revere's own story; an account of his ride as told in a letter to a friend, together with a brief sketch of his versatile career, comp. by Harriet E. O'Brien. (Boston) Priv. print., P. Walton, 1929. 2, ix-xiv, 47 p. front. (port.) 1 illus., plates, facsims. 28½ cm. Bibliography: p. 46-7. 29-9413.
F69.R413

REVERE, Paul. Paul Revere's three accounts of his famous ride. With an introd. by Edmund S. Morgan. Boston (Mass. hist. soc.) 1961. (36) p. 28 cm. (A Mass. Hist. Soc. picture book)
F69.R414
1961

— 1967. (38) p. 67-65228. F69.R414
1967

— (2d ed. 1968) (36) p. 28 cm. F69.R414
1968

REVERE, Paul, The spirit of - a glorious heritage for American industry, by C. Donald Dallas ... A Newcomen address. (Princeton, Print, Princeton university press) 1944. 52 p. incl. mounted col. front. (port.) illus. (incl. 1 mounted; facsim.) 23 cm. 44-6557.
F69.R415

REVERE, Paul and his famous ride, by Charles C. Farrington. Bedford, Mass., The Bedford print shop, 1923. 6, 5-89 p. front. (port.) plates. 20½ cm. 23-12060.
F69.R417

— 1929. P 7, 5-96 p. front. (port.) 1 plates. 21 cm. 29-18092. F69.R417
1929

REVERE, Paul. Two if by sea. Written and illus. by Leonard Everett Fisher. New York, Random House (1970) 64 p. illus. 27 cm. 76-105683.
F69.R4172

REVERE, Paul. America's Paul Revere, written by Esther Forbes; pictures by Lynd Ward. Boston, Houghton Mifflin, 1946. 1, 46 p. illus. (part col.) 28½ x 23½ cm. 46-11949.
F69.R4174

REVERE, Paul, and the world be lived in (by) Esther Forbes, Boston, Houghton Mifflin, 1942. xiii, 510 p. col. front., illus., plates, ports., facsims. 23½ cm. Bibliography: p. (491) - 496. 42-36229.
F69.R4175

REVERE, Paul, The life of, by Elbridge Henry Goss ... With portraits, etc. Boston, J.G. Cupples, 1891. 2 v. fronts., illus., plates, ports., facsims. 20½ cm. 13-6009.
F69.R 42

— Freeport, N.Y., Books for Libraries Press (1971) 2 v. 23 cm. 78-157339. F69.R 42
1971

MASSACHUSETTS

— 1972.   F69.R 42 1972

REVERE, Paul, rider for liberty, by Charles P. Graves. Illus. Vance Locke. Champaign, Ill., Garrard Pub. Co. (1964)   80 p. 23 cm. (A Discovery book) 64-10938.   F69.R4217

REVERE, Paul; the man behind the legend. By Margaret Green. New York, J. Messner (1964) 191 p. 22 cm. 64-12775.   F69.R422

REVERE. Paul Revere's first ride. By Charles Henry Hart ... (Boston? 1907)   4 p. 24½ cm. Reprinted from the Proceedings of the Mass. historical soc., Feb., 1907. 7-19554.   F69.R423

REVERE, Paul: colonial craftsman. By Regina Kelly. Illus. Harvey Kidder. Boston, Houghton Mifflin (1963)   188 p. (Piper books) 63-15655.   F69.R426

REVERE, Paul, the torch bearer of the revolution, by Belle Moses ... New York (etc.) D. Appleton, 1916.   viii, 3-269 p. front., plates, ports. 19½ cm. 16-22316.   F69.R 43

REVERE, Paul, a picture book. New York, Metropolitan museum of art, 1944.   (32) p. illus. 25½ cm.   F69.R434

REVERE, Paul. Bells of Paul and Joseph Revere, by Arthur H. Nihcols. Boston, Mass., 1911. 40 p. front., plates. 25½ cm. 12-7704.   F69.R435

REVERE, Paul, Early bells of. By Arthur Howard Nichols. Boston, 1904.   9 p. illus. 24 cm. Reprinted from New England historical and genealogical register, for April, 1904. 18-12641.   F69.R437

REVERE, Paul. Early American; the story of Paul Revere, by Mildred Mastin Pace, illus. Henry S. Gillette. New York, C. Scribner's sons, 1940.   5, 140 p. illus. 21½ cm. 40-34254.   F69.R438

REVERE, Paul (by) Gladys R. Saxon. Illus. Jo Kotula. Chicago, Follett Pub. Co. (1965) 31 p. 21 cm. (Follett beginning-to-read books) 65-14474.   F69.R439

REVERE, Paul. The Paul Revere album, by Howard W. Spurr; containing a complete description of Goss' "Life of Col. Paul Revere," and more than twenty engravings ... Boston, H. W. Spurr coffee co., 1897.   43 p. illus. (incl. ports.) 22 cm. 13-5276.   F69.R 44

REVERE, Paul. The silver punch bowl made by Paul Revere to commemorate a vote of the honorable House of representatives of the Massachusetts Bay in 1768. By Benjamin Franklin Stevens. (Reproduced from the "Boston Sunday herald" of Jan. 20, 1895) Boston, N. Sawyer, print., 1895. 22 p. 2 front. 24½ cm. 3-8709.   F69.R442

— (Providence, Livermore & Knight, 1903)   (26) p. illus. 21 x 16 cm. 6-23875.   F69.R443

REVERE, Paul, by Emerson Taylor ... (New York) E. V. Mitchell and Dodd, Mead, 1930.   ix, 237 p. front., plates, ports. 22½ cm. 30-27935.   F69.R446

REVERE, Paul, An outline of the life and works of Col.; with a partial catalogue of silverware bearing his name. Newburyport, Mass., Towle mfg. co. (1901)   35, (59), 63 p. front., illus. 27½ cm. 5-2988.   F69.R448

REVERE. Let's go with Paul Revere. By Louis Wolfe. Illus, by Charles Dougherty. New York, G. P. Putnam's Sons. (1964)   47 p. 21 cm. (Let's go history series) 64-18031.   F69.R449

ROBINSON, William Stevens. "Warrington" pen-portraits: a collection of personal and political reminiscences from 1848 to 1876, from the writings of William S. Robinson. With memoir, and extracts from diary ... Boston, Ed. and pub. by Mrs. W. S. Robinson, 1877.   xvii, (2), 587 p. front. (port.) 21 cm. 8-12294.   F69.R 65

— Boston, Lee and Shepard, 1877.   xvii, 587 p. port. 21 cm. 55-55800.   F69.R 66
Rare Book Coll.

RUSSELL.   Eulogy on the Hon. Benjamin Russell, ...   By Brother Francis Baylies.   Boston, Print. at the office of the Freemasons' magazine, 1845.   66 p. 22 cm. 5-13760.   F69.R 96

RUSSELL.   The duty of resignation under afflictions ...   a sermon ... occasioned by the death of the Hon. Thomas Russell ...   By Jedidiah Morse.   Boston, Print, Samuel Hall, 1796.   31 p. 19½ cm. 13-6008.   F69.R 97
Rare Book Coll.

RUSSELL.   A sermon preached to the society in Brattle-street, Boston ... occasioned by the death of the Hon. Thomas Russell.   By Peter Thacher ...   Boston, Print. Benjamin Sweetser, 1796.   32 p. 18 x 15½ cm. 13-6007.   F69.R975
Rare Book Coll.

RUSSELL.   An eulogy on the Hon. Thomas Russell ...   By John Warren.   Boston, Print. Benjamin Sweetser, 1796.   31, 3 p. 22½ x 18 cm. 1-8334.   F69.R978
Rare Book Coll.

SAVAGE, James.   Letters of James Savage to his family ... Boston, 1906.   iv, 288 p. front. (port.) 18½ cm. 16-17966.   F69.S 26

SILSBEE portrait, ... The.   Report of proceedings on the occasion of the reception of the portrait of Nathaniel Silsbee by the Senate of Mass.   Boston, Wright & Potter print., 1882.   18 p. 23½ cm. (Senate doc. 296) CA 25-509 unrev.   F69.S 58

STARKEY, Marion Lena.   A little rebellion.   (1st ed.)   New York, Knopf, 1955.   258 p. 22 cm. 55-9292.   F69.S 85

STEARNS, Monroe.   Shay's rebellion, 1786 - 7, Americans take up arms against unjust laws.   New York, F. Watts, (1968)   66 p. illus. 23 cm. (A Focus book) 68-17705.   F69.S 87

STRONG.   An address to the people of this commonwealth.   (Boston, 1807)   20 p. 21 cm. Issued by the Federalist members of the General court, regarding the attempt ... to displace Gov. Strong. 9-20800.   F69.S922

STRONG.   An appeal to the old Whigs of Massachusetts.   (Boston?) 1806.   20 p. 21½ cm. A campaign document, urging the election of Caleb Strong. 6-12186 Rev.   F69.S923

STRONG.   A memoir of Caleb Strong, U.S. senator and governor of Mass.   By Henry Cabot Lodge. Cambridge, Press of J. Wilson, 1879.   29 p. 23½ cm. Reprinted from the early Proceedings of the Mass. hist. soc. 12-11173.   F69.S925

STRONG.   Gov. Strong's calumniator reproved, in a review of a Democratic pamphlet entitle, Remarks on the governor's speech ... By No bel-espirt (pseud. John Lowell) Boston: From the office of the Repertory and daily advertiser.   W.W. Clapp, print., 1814.   21 p. 23½ cm. 9-20797.   F69.S926

STRONG.   An answer to the questions, Why are you a Federalist? and Why shall you vote for Gov. Strong?)   (Boston?) 1805.   22 p. 24½ cm. Published anonymously. 6-20945.   F69.S928

STRONG.   A report of the trial of Andrew Wright, printer of the "Republican spy", on an indictment for libels against Governor Strong ...   Northampton, Pub. by Andrew Wright, 1806.   32 p. 24½ cm. 6-14332.   F69.S929

STURGIS.   Memoir of the Hon. William Sturgis. ...   By Charles G. Loring.   Boston, Press of J. Wilson and son, 1864.   64 p. 25 cm. Also pub. in Mass. hist. soc. Proceedings, v.7, 1863-64. 15-3556 rev.   F69.S935

SULLIVAN.   Life of James Sullivan: with selections from his writings.   By Thomas C. Amory ... Boston, Phillips, Sampson and co., 1859.   2 v. front. (port.) 23 cm. 13-19851.   F69.S 94

MASSACHUSETTS

SULLIVAN. A sermon preached at the church in Brattle street, Boston ... after the publick funeral of His Excellency James Sullivan ... By Joseph Buckminster ... Boston, J. Belcher, print., 1809.
41 p. 23 cm. 13-24915.
F69.S945

SULLIVAN. Firmness and gentleness united in the Christian character: a sermon ... succeeding the death of Hon. Richard Sullivan. By Rev. S.K. Lothrop ... Boston, Print. J. Wilson, 1862.
19 p. 24 cm. 18-8946.
F69.S 95

SULLIVAN. Memoir of Hon. William Sullivan ... By Thomas C. Amory. Cambridge, University press, 1879.   13 p. 24½ cm. Reprinted from Mass. hist. soc. Proceedings, v.2, p. 150-160. 9-22134.
F69.S955

SUMNER. Memorial record. In memory of Hon. Increase Sumner. A funeral discourse by Rev. Evarts Scudder. ,,, Bridgeport, Conn., Gould & Stiles, 1871.   74 p. front. (port.) 22 cm. 14-15501.
F69.S 96

SUMNER. A sermon, preached at Cambridge ... after the interment of His Excellency Increase Sumner ... By Abiel Holmes ... Boston, Print. Manning & Loring (1799?)   24 p. 23½ cm. 13-19571.
F69.S 97
Rare Book Coll.

SUMNER. A sermon ... occasioned by the death of His Excellency Increase Sumner ... By Eliphalet Porter ... Boston, Print. Young & Minns, 1799.   27 p. 21½ cm. 15-27851.
F69.S977
Rare Book Coll.

SUMNER. A sermon preached ... at the interment of His Excellency Increase Sumner ... By Peter Thacher. Boston, Print. Young & Minns, (1799)   xviii p. 21 cm. 5-20018.
F69.S 98

THOMAS, Isaiah, Memoir of, by his grandson Benjamin Franklin Thomas. Boston (Albany, Munsell, printer) 1874.   73 p. front. (port.) 24½ cm. 12-11174.
F69.T 45

TRASK, William Blake. Memoir of Samuel Blake. (Communicated to the N.E. historical and genealogical register for July, 1867) (Boston? 1867?)   3 p. 25½ cm. 34-21945.
F69.T 82
Toner Coll.

U.S. Bureau of the Census. Heads of families at the first census of the U.S. taken in the year 1790: Massachusetts. Baltimore, Genealogical Pub. Co., 1966.   363 p. 29 cm.
F69.U 52
1966
L.H.& G.

UPHAM, Charles Wentworth, Memoir of. By George E. Ellis. Cambridge (Mass.) Press of J. Wilson, 1877.   43 p. front. (port.) 24½ cm. Reprinted from the Proceedings of the Mass. hist. soc. Dec., 1876. 1-10275.
F69.U 67

WARREN, Joseph Parker. The Confederation and the Shay's rebellion, (New York? 1905)
42-67 p. 27 cm. Reprinted from the American historical review, vol. xi, no. 1, Oct. 1905. 6-1318.
F69.W 26

WENTWORTH, Ruth Starbuck. Older America ... Los Angeles, Calif. (1921)   folder (8 p.)
22 x 35½ cm. fold. to 22 x 9 cm.
F69.W 47

WHO shall be governor? The contrast, containing sketches of the characters and public services of the two candidates for the office of chief magistrate of the commonwealth of Mass. Worcester: Pub. at the Spy office, 1809.   11 p. 19 cm. On the candidacy of Christopher Gore and Levi Lincoln. 22-9835.
F69.W 62
Rare Book Coll.

WILLARD, Joseph, Memoir of. By Mrs. Susanna Hickling (Lewis) Willard. From the "Proceedings of the Mass. historical soc" for 1866-1867. Cambridge, Press of J. Wilson, 1867.   25 p. 24 cm.
11-22527.
F69.W 69

WILLARD, Joseph Augustus. Half a century with judges and lawyers ... Boston and New York, Houghton, Mifflin, 1895.   iv, 371 p. front. (port.) 18 cm. 12-40459.
F69.W 7

WILLISTON.   A discourse commemorative of Hon, Samuel Williston ... By W.S.Tyler ... Springfield, Mass., C.W.Bryan, 1874.   85 p. front. (port.) 23 cm. 2-19799.   F69.W 73

WILSON.   Mr. Hallett's reply to Mr. Wilson's "personal explanation"   "The question of veracity" evaded by Senator Wilson and again settled against him.   (n.p., 1856)   8 p. 23½ cm. 11-4708.
F69.W 75

WOOD, Isaiah. The Massachusetts compendium; stating the boundaries of Massachusetts proper; of the district of Maine; of the several counties therein, and of each of the several towns, etc. etc. Hallowell (Me.) Print. Goodale & Burton ... 1814.   iv, (5) - 72, (2) p. 14½ cm. 1-12120.   F69.W 87
Rare Book Coll.

WORLD which Emerson knew, ... The.   Boston (The Directors of the Old South work) 1903.
(192) p. 18½ cm. (Old South leaflets. xxi. 1903) 7-13457.   F69.W 92

1865 TO DATE.

ABBOTT, Katharine Mixer.   South shore trolley trips. ... (Boston, The Heintzemann press) 1898.
108, (4) p. illus., fold. map. 11 x 15 cm. 1-12121 Rev.   F70.A 13

ABBOTT, Katharine M.   Twentieth century trolley trips; Boston, the blue hills of Milton and Plymouth. Lexington, Concord, Medford, Lowell, Marblehead. Gloucester, Newburyport. Hampton Beach, Dover, Rochester, N.H. ... Boston, C.B.Webster & co., 1901.   128 p. illus., map. obl. 32°.
1-17537-M1 Sept. 5.   F70.A 14

ABRAMS, Richard M.   Conservatism in a progressive era; Massachusetts politics, 1900 - 1912. Cambridge, Mass., Harvard University Press, 1964.   xiv, 327 p. 22 cm. 64-21236.
F70.A 18

AMERICAN library association, Handbook of the 24th annual conference of, Boston and Magnolia ... 1902. (Cambridge, Caustic & Claflin, print., 1902)   77, 22 p., front., illus., pl., map, facsim. 19 cm.
Early printing in Boston, and the ms sources of Mass. history, p. 72-77. 2-20837.   F70.A 51

BACON, Gaspar Griswold.   Individual rights and the public welfare; addresses by the Hon. Gaspar G. Bacon ... Boston, Priv. print., 1935.   x, 318 p. 21½ cm. 36-1259.   F70.B 24

BAILEY, Bernadine (Freeman)   Picture book of Massachusetts; pictures by Kurt Wiese. Chicago, A. Whitman, 1949.   (28) p. illus. (part col.) map. 17 x 21 cm. 49-9300*.   F70.B 27
1949

BLODGETT, Geoffrey.   The gentle reformers: Massachusetts Democrats in the Cleveland era. Cambridge, Mass., Harvard University Press, 1966.   xiii, 342 p. 22 cm. 66-13178.   F70. B 6
1966

"BOSTON 1907"   (Portland, Me., Nelson's international series of souvenir books, 1904)   (32) p. illus.
20 x 25 cm.   F70.B 73

BOSTON and Maine R.R.   Charles River to the Hudson.   (1908)   1 v.   F70.B 74

BRIDGMAN, Arthur Milnor.   A souvenir of Massachusetts legislators ... Stoughton, Mass., A.M. Bridgman (1892-19   v. illus. (incl. facsim.) plates (1 col.) ports. 23½ cm. annual. 1-25816 Rev.   F70.B 83

BRIDGMAN, Raymond Landon.   The independents of Massachusetts in 1884.   Boston, Cupples, Upham & co., 1885.   65 p. 20 cm. 12-20466.   F70.B 84

BRIDGMAN, Raymond Landon.   Ten years of Massachusetts.   Boston, D.C.Heath, 1888.   127 p.
18½ cm. 1878 - 1887. 1-12122.   F70.B 85

MASSACHUSETTS

BUTLER. The record of Benjamin F. Butler since his election as governor of Massachusetts. Boston, 1883.   45 p. 21 cm. 3-27047.   F70.B 98

COOLIDGE, Calvin, Pres. U.S. Have faith in Massachusetts; a collection of speeches and messages. 2d ed. enl. Boston, Houghton Mifflin, 1919.   x, 275 p. 20 cm.   F70.C 77 1919a
Rare Book Coll.

— Boston and New York, Houghton Mifflin, 1919.   ix, 224 p. front. (port.) 20 cm. 19-15762.   F70.C77

CURLEY, James Michael. I'd do it again, a record of all my uproarious years. Englewood Cliffs, N.J., Prentice-Hall (1957)   372 p. illus. 23 cm. 57-8558.   F70.C 83

CURLEY. The purple shamrock; the Hon. James Michael Curley of Boston. By Joseph Francis Dinneen. (1st ed.) N.Y., W.W. Norton (1949)   331 p. illus., ports. 22 cm. 49-10270*.   F70.C847

CURLEY. That man Curley, being an interesting and instructive journey around, with and about Dr. James Michael Curley, the enigmatic political figure of Massachusetts. Boston, E.L. Donnelly Co., 1947.   119 p. ports. 19 cm. 47-5312*.   F70.C 85

CURLEY. ... The reign of James the First; a historical record of the administration of James M. Curley as governor of Mass., by Wendell D. Howie ... (Cambridge, Mass., Warren pubs., 1936.   108 p. pl. 22 cm. 36-12634.   F70.C 87

DERRAH, Robert H. Street railway guide for eastern Massachusetts. Comp. ... by Robert H. Derrah. Boston, R.H. Derrah (1896)   21 p. front. (fold. map) 18 cm. 4-28333.   F70.D417

— Boston, Keeden press, 1898.   178 p. front. (fold. map) illus. 18½ cm. 4-5235.   F70.D 42

— for eastern Massachusetts and Rhode Island ... 4th ed. Boston, The Lufkin press, 1899.   210 p. front. (fold. map) illus. 17½ cm. 99-3259 Rev.   F70.D 43

— for eastern New England ... 7th ed. Boston, The J.K. Waters co., 1903.   256 p. front. (fold. map) illus. 17½ cm. 3-14877.   F70.D 44

DERRAH, Robert H. By trolley through eastern New England ... Boston, Mass., 1904.   2, 154 (6) p. illus., fold. maps. 17½ cm. 4-19624.   F70.D445

DRAPER. Leiutenant Governor Eben D. Draper. By John N. McClintock. (Boston, 1908)   30 cm.   F70.D 76

EATON, Asa B. Executive and legislative departments of the state of Massachusetts. 1868. Photographed by A.B. Eaton ... Lowell, Stone & Huse, print., 1868.   35 p. 280 photos. 22 cm. 44-12723.   F70.E 3

ELIOT, Samuel Atkins. Biographical history of Massachusetts; biographies and autobiographies of the leading men in the state; Samuel Atkins Eliot ... editor-in-chief. Boston, Mass., Massachusetts biographical society, 1909 -   v. front., ports. 25 cm. 9-3042 Rev.   F70.E 42

— 1911 -   v. fronts., ports. 24½ cm. 12-26028.   F70.E 43

EXCURSIONS in the bay. Boston to Cape Ann and Provincetown. Boston, Hall & Whiting (1881)   42 p. illus. obl. 32°. 1-16206-M1.   F70.E 96

FALL River Line. The tip end of Yankee Land. Issued by the Fall River and Newport Lines and Old Colony Railroad Co. (n.p.) 1885.   64 p. illus., fold. maps. 21 cm. 1-12409*.   F70.F 19

FEDERAL writers' project. ... Massachusetts; a guide to its places and people, written and compiled by the Federal writers project of the W.P.A. for the state of Mass. ... Boston, Houghton, Mifflin, 1937.   xxxvi, 675 p. plates, maps (1 fold. in pocket) 21 cm. "Fifty books about Mass." p.(637)-8. 37-28502.   F70.F295
L.H.& G.

—   xxxvi, 675 p., plates, maps (1 fold. in pocket) 21 cm.   40M3052T.   F70. F295
   1937a

FELLOWS, Henry Parker.   Boating trips on New England rivers ... illus. by Willis H. Beals.   Boston, Cupples, Upham and co., 1884.   xiv, (15) - 176 p. incl. front. (map) illus.   20 cm.   Concerns the Sudbury, Concord, Merrimac, Housatonic and Nashua rivers.   11-10282.   F70. F 32

GIFFORD.   Complimentary dinner to Stephen N. Gifford ... clerk of the Massachusetts senate ... Boston, Press of G. H. Ellis, 1883.   46 p.   23 ½ cm.   5-14697.   F70. G 45

GIFFORD.   A memorial of Stephen Nye Gifford, clerk of the Massachusetts Senate ... Boston (Wright and Potter print.) 1886.   56 p. front. (port.)   24 cm.   4-5211.   F70. G 46

GIRAUDOUX, Jean.   ...   America.   Paris, B. Grasset (1938)   2, (7) - 216 p. 19 cm.   First pub. 1918.   38-22945.   F70. G482

GLADDEN, Washington.   From the Hub to the Hudson: with sketches of nature, history and industry in north-western Massachusetts.   Boston, New England news co., 1869.   iv, (5) - 149 p., plates. 17 cm.   1-12123.   F70. G 54

GREENHALGE.   In commemoration of the life and public services of Frederic T. Greenhalge, late governor of the commonwealth.   (Boston) Printed by order of the General court (1896)   65 p. front. (port.)   23 cm.   17-13771.   F70. G 78

GREENHALGE.   The life and work of Frederic Thomas Greenhalge, governor of Massachusetts, by James Ernest Nesmith.   Boston, Roberts brothers, 1897.   viii, (3) - 456 p. 2 port. (incl. front.) 23 cm. Includes a selection from the writings of Greenhalge.   14-9162.   F70. G 8

GREENHALGE.   A personal tribute to Governor Frederic T. Greenhalge, by his private secretary, Henry A. Thomas ... Boston, Wright & Potter print., 1896.   22 p. front. (port.) 23 ½ cm.   18-8232.   F70. G 85

GUIDE to Concord, Mass., and other historic places.   Concord, Lexington, Sudbury, Bedford, Acton, Boston.   (Hudson, Mass., Wood pub. co., 19 - ?)   80 p. illus. (incl. ports.) 23 ½ cm.   7-27734.   F70. G 94

GUYOT, Arnold Henry.   Geography of Massachusetts.   (New York) Scribner, Armstrong & co., 1876. (107) - 115 p. incl. illus., maps.   30 ½ x 24 ½ cm.   3-26063.   F70. G 97
                                                                                                                                                                    Map div.

GUYOT, Arnold Henry.   New England states; special geography of Massachusetts and Vermont; designed to accompany Guyot's new intermediate geography.   (New York) Ivison, Blakeman, Taylor & co., 1884.   16 p. incl. illus., maps. 4°.   1-13348-M1.   F70. G 98
                                                                                                                                                                    Map div.

HAILE.   In memoriam; William Henry Haile, born Sept. 23, 1833; died Feb. 13, 1901.   (Springfield? Mass., 1901?)   iv, 84 p. incl. facsims. front. (port.) 23 ½ cm.   1-16048.   F70. H 15

HENDERSON, Helen Weston.   A loiterer in New England.   New York, George H. Doran, 1919. xviii p, 21-445 p. front., plates, ports., map. 22 ½ cm.   Limited to localities in Mass.   19-17082.   F70. H 49

HENNESSY, Michael Edmund.   Four decades of Massachusetts politics, 1890-1935.   (Norwood, Mass.) The Norwood press, 1935.   xii, 562 p. front., ports. 20 ½ cm.   35-8546.   F70. H496

—   Freeport, N.Y., Books for Libraries Press (1971)   xii, 562 p. illus. 23 cm.   76-150187.   F70. H496
                                                                                                                                                              1971

HENNESSY, Michael Edmund.   Twenty five years of Massachusetts politics, 1890 - 1915.   Boston, Mass., Practical politics, inc., 1917.   7 p. 398 p. plates, ports. 24 cm.   17-6903.   F70. H 5

HILL, Henry B.   Jottings from memory, from 1823 to 1901.   (n. p., 1910)   128 p. port. 21 ½ cm. 19-5251.   F70. H 63

MASSACHUSETTS

HOAR, George Frisbie, Speech of, at the ratification meeting in Music hall, Boston ... 1889. (Boston? 1889?) (4) p. 24½ cm. "Issued by the Republican state committee." 21-10659. F70.H 64

HOAR, Samuel, Memoir of ... read ... by Woodward Hudson. (Cambridge, Mass. The Riverside press)1905. 51 p. 19 cm. 6-1364. F70.H 66

HOAR. Tributes of the bar and of the Circuit court of the United States to the memory of Sherman Hoar. Boston, G.H. Ellis, print., 1899. 61 p. 23 cm. 11-21019. F70.H 67

HUTHMACHER, J. Massachusetts people and politics, 1919-1933. Cambridge, Belknap Press of Harvard University Press, 1959. 328 p. illus. 22 cm. Includes bibliography. 59-9276. F70. H 8

IN and about historic Boston. (Portland, Me., 1904) 20 x 25 cm. F70. I 35

— (1908) 1 v. 20½ x 25½ cm. F70. I 36

KNOWLTON, Marcus Perrin, late chief justice of the Supreme judicial court of the commonwealth of Mass.; a memorial. (Boston) Priv. print., 1919. 3, v-(vi), 55 p. port. 25 cm. 19-16560. F70.K 73

KOCH, Felix John. A little journey to historic and picturesque shrines of central New England, for home and school, intermediate and upper grades, ... Chicago, A. Flanagan co. (1907) 181 p. illus. 19½ cm. 7-10605. F70.K 76

LAWSON, Thomas William. Murder of McCall by big boodle. (n.p., 1918) 15 p. 25 cm. 19-10565. F70. L 4

LEACH, James Edward. The log of the yacht Pilgrim, summer of 1883. Boston, F. Wood, print., 1884. 23 p. front., port. 25½ cm. 2-2226-M2. F70.L 41

LEADING manufacturers and merchants of central and western Massachusetts. Historical and descriptive review of the industrial enterprises of Worcester, Hampden, Hampshire, Berkshire, and Franklin counties. Illus. New York (etc.) International pub. co. (1886) 4, v-xi, (33) - 349 p. illus. 25 cm. 9-29283. F70. L42

LEAGUE of American wheelmen. ... Road book of Massachusetts, containing also some of the principal through routes of other states and Canada. 13th ed. ... (Boston, 1898) (298) p. illus. 18 cm. 1-12124. F70.L 43

LEAVITT, Robert Keith. The chip on grandma's shoulder. (1st ed.) Philadelphia, Lippincott (1954) 255 p. 21 cm. 54-5593. F70.L 44

MARBLE, Albert P. Geography of Massachusetts; a supplement to the Eclectic series of geographies ... (Cincinnati, New York) Van Antwerp, Bragg & co., 1878. 16 p. incl. illus., map. fol. 1-13349-M1. F70.M 31

MASON. Proceedings of the Suffolk bar and Superior court in memory of Albert Mason, chief justice of the Superior court, June 16, 1905. Boston, G.H. Ellis print., 1905. 44 p. front. (port.) 23½ cm. 5-40586. F70.M 39

MASSACHUSETTS. ... Valedictory address of His Excellency Alexander H. Bullock ... Boston, Wright & Potter, 1869. 60 p. 23 cm. 11-32025. F70. M 4

MASSACHUSETTS. ... Report of the commissioners on the Topographical survey and map of Mass. Boston (1885 - v. in plates. 23 cm. Title varies slightly. 1-16082. F70.M 41

MASSACHUSETTS: a guide to the Pilgrim State. Ed. Ray Bearse. 2d ed. rev. and enl. Boston, Houghton Mifflin, 1971. xiv, 525 p. illus. 21 cm. (The New American guide series) 68-16270. F70.M425 1971

MASSACHUSETTS. Guide to the Berkshires to the capes bridle trail, four hundred and fifty miles of bridle trail located and marked under the direction of the association. 1934. Boston, Mass. forest and park association (1934)   101, (3) p. maps (1 fold.) 15½ x 9 cm. CA 36-759 Unrev.   F70. M 43

NEW YORK, New Haven and Hartford R. R. co. ... Manual of Old Colony summer resorts. Boston, 1895.   20 cm.   F70. N 53

NUTTING, Wallace. Massachusetts beautiful ... illus. by the author with 304 pictures covering all the counties in Mass. Framingham, Old America co. (1923)   2, 3-301 p. incl. illus., plates. 26 cm. 23-10216.
F70. N 98

— Garden City, N.Y., Pub. in cooperation with Old America co. by the Garden City pub. co., 1935.
254 p. incl. front., illus., plates. 26 cm. 35-18401.   F70. N 98
1935

OLD Colony railroad. The Old Colony; or, Pilgrim land, past and present. (Boston) Fall River line and Old colony railroad, 1886.   84, (6) p. front., illus., maps. 8°. 1-12125-M1.   F70. O 44

Old Colony railroad co. Southeastern Massachusetts: its shores and islands, woodlands and lakes, and how to reach them. With information for the sportsman and tourist ... Boston, Old Colony railroad, 1878.   42, (6) p. front. (fold. map) illus. 19 cm. 35M3158.   F70. O 45
Toner Coll.

OLD Colony railroad co. Southeastern Massachusetts; its shores and islands, woodlands and lakes, and how to reach them, etc. Boston, Old Colony railroad, 1879.   49, (7) p. front. (fold. map) illus. 19 cm. 35M3157.   F70. O 45
1879
Toner coll.

— Boston, press of G. H. Ellis, 1880.   49, (8) p. illus., fold. map. 18½ cm. 1-16205.   F70. O 45
1880

OLIVER, Henry Kemble. By Jesse Henry Jones. (Boston, 1886)   47 p. front. (port.) 1 illus. (music)
25½ cm. From the 17th annual report of the Mass. bur. of statistics of labor: 1886. 2-22618 Rev.   F70. O 48

PARKER. Memoir of Francis Jewett Parker, by William Carver Bates. Boston, D. Clapp, 1909.
6 p. front. (port.) 22½ cm. Reprinted from the New England historical and genealogical register for July, 1909. 18-11586.   F70. P 23

PHILLIPS, Wendell. The people coming to power! Speech of Wendell Phillips, esq., at the Salisbury Beach gathering ... Boston, Lee & Shepard, 1871.   24 p. 19½ cm. Speech in favor of the candidacy of Gen. Butler for governor. 12-8209.   F70. P 55

PIERCE. Memoir of Henry Lillie Pierce. By James M. Bugbee ... Cambridge, J. Wilson, 1897.
27 p. front. (port.) 25 cm. Reprinted from the Proceedings of the Mass. hist. soc. May, 1897. 12-26343.   F70. P 61

PORTER. Memoir of Edward Griffin Porter, by Samuel Swett Green. Reprinted from the Publications of the Colonial society of Massachusetts, vol. vi. Cambridge (Mass.) J. Wilson and son, 1901.
10 p. front. (port.) 24½ cm. 1-26935.   F70. P 84

RAYMOND. With furled sail; reminiscences (by) Robert L. Raymond. (Dedham, Mass., The Transcript press, 1946)   2, 162 p. 21 cm. 46-5008.   F70. R 3

RICE, Alexander Hamilton. Massachusetts, and how she is governed. Address of His Excellency Alexander H. Rice, delivered at the ratification meeting in Faneuil hall. Boston, Republican state committee, 1878.   23 p. 19½ cm. 18-2966.   F70. R 49

RICHARDSON, Mrs. Mary J. Memorial letters to my grandchildren. Boston, Beacon press, 1893.
220 p. front., illus., plates, ports. 22½ cm. 11-10281.   F70. R 52

ROBINSON. ... An address commemorative of the life and services of George D. Robinson, governor

MASSACHUSETTS

of the commonwealth, 1884-86, by Henry Cabot Lodge.   Boston, G. H. Ellis, print., 1896.
28 p.   24 ½ cm.   13-23475. F70. R 66

RUSSELL.   Speeches and addresses of William E. Russell.   Selected and ed. by Charles Theodore Russell, jr.   Boston, Little, Brown, 1894.   4, (vii) - xvi, 469 p. front. (port.) 21 ½ cm.   15-850.
F70. R 96

RUSSELL.   Governor Russell and his canvass of Cape Cod.   By Lloyd McKim Garrison.   November 7th, 1892 ...   New York, The Republic press, 1893.   19 p.   24 cm.   10-208. F70. R 97

SHERMAN, Edgar Jay.   Some recollections of a long life.   Boston, Priv. print., 1908.   322 p. front., plates, ports.   24 cm.   8-30379. F70. S 55

SMITH, Matthew Hale.   The Old Colony railroad: its connections, popular resorts, and fashionable watering-places.   By Burleigh (pseud.)   Boston, Press of Rand, Avery, 1874.   23 p. illus., fold. map. 19 cm.   7-34352. F70. S 64

— Boston, 1875.   The   31 p. front. (fold. map) illus., fold. tab. 19 cm.   1-13350. F70. S 65

STEVENS.   A brief sketch of the life of General Hazard Stevens.   Boston, G. H. Ellis co., print., 1908. 19 p. 23 cm.   CA 25-258 Unrev. F70. S 84

TAYLOR, Frank Hamilton.   Old places & new people, or Our pilgrimage, and what we saw.   (Boston, Print. Rand Avery supply co., 1883)   38, (16) p. illus., 2 fold. maps (incl. front.) 21 cm.   1-16779 Rev. F70. T 3

TALBOT, Thomas.   A memorial.   (n. p.) Priv. print., 1886.   40 p. front. (port.) 23 cm. 16-17947. F70. T 45

TODD, Charles Burr.   In olde Massachusetts; sketches of old times and places during the early days of the Commonwealth.   New York, Grafton Press.   Ann Arbor, Mich., Grypton Books, 1971.
viii, 253 p. illus. 22 cm.   77-99060. F70. T 65
1971

TOURIST'S guide to southern Massachusetts.   Camp meeting ed.   New Bedford, Taber bros., 1868.
14 p. fold. map. 24°.   1-16204-M1. F70. T 72

TRUMBULL.   ... Recollections of James Russell Trumbull ... by his niece   Anna Elizabeth Miller. Northampton, Mass., Dept. of history of Smith college (1922)   (143) - 214. 23 cm.   22-22732.
F70. T 86

WADLIN, Horace G.   Massachusetts.   Philadelphia, J. B. Lippincott, 1891.   8 p. 12°.   Appears as article "Massachusetts" in Chambers's encyclopaedia.   1-12127-M1. F70. W 12

WAYMAN, Dorothy (Godfrey)   David I. Walsh, citizen-patriot.   Milwaukee, Bruce Pub. Co. (1952)
366 p. illus. 23 cm.   52-12759. F70. W2W39

WARNER, Frances Lester.   Pilgrim trails; a Plymouth-to-Provincetown sketchbook, by Frances Lester Warner; with drawings by E. Scott White.   Boston, The Atlantic monthly press (1921)
4, 47 p. front., plates. 24 cm.   21-11176. F70. W 28

WINSOR, Justin.   Massachusetts.   Boston, Little, Brown, 1882.   29 p. 20 cm.   1-12128. F70. W 77

WOLCOTT, Roger, by William Lawrence.   Boston and New York, Houghton, Mifflin, 1902.
v, 238 p. front., pl., port. 19 ½ cm.   2-29032. F70. W 85

WOLCOTT.   Public services in memory of Roger Wolcott, Symphony hall, Boston, 1901.   Printed by order of the General court.   (n. p., 1902?)   62 p. front. (port.) 25 cm.   5-13613. F70. W 86

MASSACHUSETTS   Dept. of Commerce.   Your Massachusetts facts package.   (Boston, 1962)
18 pieces (in portfolio) 30 cm.   63-62718. F71. A 53

FARMER, Gene. Massachusetts: the anatomy of quality. Color photography (by) Ted Polumbaum. (Boston? 1967)   128 p. 29 cm. 68-16743.   F71. F 3

JENNISON, Keith Warren. To Massachusetts with love; commentary and pictures arranged by Keith Jennison. Brattleboro, Vt., Durrell Pubs. (1970)   96 p. illus. 24 cm. 72-106943.   F71. J 45

LEVIN, Murray Burton. The compleat politician; political strategy in Massachusetts. With George Blackwood. (1st ed.) Indianapolis, Bobbs-Merrill (1962)   334 p. 24 cm. 62-18204.

F71. L 4

LEVIN, Murray Burton. Kennedy campaigning; the system and the style as practiced by Senator Edward Kennedy, by Murray B. Levin. Boston, Beacon Press (1966)   xix, 313 p. 21 cm. 66-23780.

F71. L 44

REGIONS, COUNTIES, ETC., A - Z.

INLAND Massachusetts illustrated. A concise résumé of the natural features and past history of the counties of Hampden, Hampshire, Franklin, and Berkshire, their towns, villages, and cities, etc, etc. Springfield, Mass., The Elstner pub. co., 1890.   272 p. illus. 23 cm. 2-2199.   F72. A15 I55

— 1891.   292 p. illus. (incl. ports.) 22 ½ cm. 1-16598.   F72. A15 I56

BARNSTABLE County. ... Hyannis, Harwich, Harwichport, East and West Harwich, Cotuit, Osterville, Dennis, Dennisport, East and West Dennis, Yarmouthport, South Yarmouth and Chatham. Barnstable County ed., 1908. New York, American suburbs co., 1908.   16 p. illus. 40 ½ cm. (American suburbs illustrated. v. 3, no. 4) 11-30227.   F72. B2 H9

BERKSHIRE County directory for 1875, The. Boston, Briggs & co.   v. 22 ½ cm. A business directory. 13-21570.   Directories

BERKSHIRE County. ... Resident and business directory of southern Berkshire County, inc. the towns of Great Barrington, Sheffield, Stockbridge, Alford, Egremont, Monterey, New Marlborough and West Stockbridge,   Great Barrington and Beverly, Mass., Crowley & Lunt, 1907-1910. 2 v. 23 cm. 7-40030.   Directories

BERKSHIRE County. The South Berkshire directory ... a general directory of the towns of Alford, Egremont (North and South), Great Barrington (incl. Housatonic), Monterey, Mount Washington, New Marlboro (incl. Clayton, Hartsville, Mill River and Southfield), North Canaan, Conn. ... Sheffield (incl. Ashley Falls), Stockbridge (incl. Interlaken and Glendale), West Stockbridge (incl. State Line) ... 1907/08, -   Great Barrington, Beverly, Mass., Crowley & Lunt, 1907 -
v. fold. maps. 22 ½ x 24 cm. 7-40030 (rev. '30)   Directories

BERKSHIRE County. An address to the inhabitants of the county of Berkshire. Respecting their present opposton to civil government. Hartford: Printed by Watson and Goodwin (1778?) 28 p. 19 ½ cm. 5-4578.   F72. B5 A3
Rare Book Coll.

BERKSHIRE Hills, Among the. (Pittsfield, Mass., The Kennedy-MacInnes co., 1909)   1 v. 20 x 25 ½ cm.
F72. B5 A5

BERKSHIRE County. Odes and hymns, written and designed for the Berkshire jubilee. By Ezekiel Bacon. Utica, N.Y., 1844.   12 p. 19 cm. 18-18212.   F72. B5 B2

BERKSHIRE County ... (Pittsfield? Mass., 1904)   23 cm.   F72. B5 B36

BERKSHIRE Hills, The, a historic quarterly. v. 1-4, Sept. 1900 - Aug. 1904; (new ser.) v. 1-2, Oct. 1904 - July 1906. Pittsfield, Mass., 1900-06.   6 v. in 3. illus. 30 ½ x 32 cm. 7-30470.
F72. B5 B4

MASSACHUSETTS 85

BERKSHIRE historical and scientific society. Berkshire book: by its historical and scientific society. vol. I. Pittsfield, Mass., The Sun print., 1892. 3, (3) - 319, (iii) - vii p. 23 cm. A reissue in a bound volume of the four pamphlets issued in 1886, 1889, 1890 and 1891 ... nos. 1-4 of the series later known as Collections. 1-12129 Rev.   F72. B5 B5

— Collections. (Pittsfield) The Society, 1886-1913. 3 v. illus., port. 22 ½ cm. No more pub? Title varies. Issued also in a bound volume (F72. B5B5) 10-22920 rev.   F72. B5 B6

BERKSHIRE history. v. 1 - spring 1971 - Pittsfield, Mass., Berkshire County Historical Soc. v. illus. 23 cm. semiannual. 73-617075.   F72.B5 B63

BERKSHIRE jubillee, celebrated at Pittsfield, Mass., ... 1844. Albany, W. C. Little; Pittsfield, E. P. Little, 1845. 244 p. incl. front., plates. 23 ½ cm. 1-12407.   F72.B5 B65

BERKSHIRE life insurance co. Drives and walks, Pittsfield and vicinity. Pittsfield, Mass., The Berkshire life insurance co. (n. d.) 74 p. 16 ½ cm. 6-33814.   F72. B5B68

BERKSHIRE county, Biographical review ... containing life sketches of leading citizens of ... Boston, Biographical review pub. co., 1899. 2, (9) - 596 p. incl. pl., ports. ports. 29 x 24 cm. (Atlantic states series of biographical reviews) vol. xxxi) 13-5712.   F72. B5 B7
   Microfilm 14524 F

BERKSHIRE County: a cultural history. By Richard Davenport Birdsall. New Haven, Yale University Press, 1959. 401 p. illus. 22 cm. Includes bibliography. 59-6792.   F72.B5 B72

MOHAWK Trail, The; its history and course, with map and illus. together with an account of Fort Massachusetts and of the early turnpikes over Hoosac Mountain, by William B. Browne ... Pittsfield, Mass., Sun print., 1920. 40 p. illus., fold. map. 23 cm. "Authorities": p. 40. 21-1680.   F72.B5 B78

BERKSHIRE, The book of, describing and illustrating its hills and homes ... By Clark W. Bryan. Great Barrington, Mass., New York, etc., C. W. Bryan (1886) 292 p. incl. front., illus. fold. map. 18 x 14 cm. 1-12130.   F72. B5 B8

BERKSHIRE, A new book of, which gives the history of the past, and forecasts the bright and glowing future of Berkshire's hills and homes, etc. Springfield, Mass., C. W. Bryan (1890) 324 p. incl. front., illus. 17 ½ x 13 ½ cm. 1-12131.   F72. B5 B9

BERKSHIRES, The. By Samuel Chamberlain. New York, Hastings House (1956) 103 p. (chiefly illus.) 24 cm. 56-10273.   F72.B5 C38

BERKSHIRE county, ... Gazetteer of, 1725 - 1885. Comp. and pub. by Hamilton Child ... Syracuse, N. Y., Print. at the Journal office, 1885. 2 v. in 1. illus., pl., port., fold. map. 24 cm. Map wanting. 2-501 Rev.   F72. B5 C5

BERKSHIRE County, Historic homes and institutions and genealogical and personal memoirs of. Ed. Rollin Hillyer Cooke ... New York, Chicago, The Lewis pub. co., 1906. 2 v. fronts., illus., plates, ports. 27 ½ cm. 9-2380.   F72.B 5 C7

BERKSHIRE hills, ... The, comp. and written by members of the Federal writers' project of the W. P. A. New York and London, Funk & Wagnalls co., 1939. xiv p. 368 p. front., plates, maps (1 fold.) 21 ½ cm. "First ed." 39-27644.   F72.B5 F37

BERKSHIRE hills, ... Winter sports and recreation in the, compiled by workers of the Federal writers' project of the W. P. A. (Pittsfield, Mass.) 1937. (24) p. illus., fold. map. 27 ½ cm. 40-12942.   F72.B5F376

BERKSHIRE, A history of the county of; in two parts. ... By gentlemen in the county ... (David Dudley Field, ed. Pittsfield, Print. S. W. Bush, 1829. iv, (7) - 468 p. front. (fold. map) plates (1 fold.) ports. fold. col. chart. 19 x 10 ½ cm. 1-12132.   F72. B5 F4

BERKSHIRES, The real tour to the. By Carey Stillman Hayward. Pittsfield, Mass., Print, Eagle print.

315

and bind. co., 1913. 48 p. illus., fold. map. 20½ x 11 cm. 13-12336. F72. B5 H4

BERKSHIRES, The real tour to ... By Carey Stillman Hayward. Pittsfield, Mass., Print. by Eagle print. and bind. co., 1914. 80 p. illus., fold. map. 20½ x 11 cm. 14-11503. F72. B5 H42

BERKSHIRE County, History of, with biographical sketches of its prominent men ... New York, J.B. Beers & co., 1885. 2 v. in 1. illus., plates, ports., maps (1 fold.) plans. 28 cm. 1-12133. F72. B5 H6

BERKSHIRE hills, Ye olde, prepared by the Housatonic railroad. (New York, Press of American bank note. co., 1891. 105 p. incl. front., illus. 2 fold. maps. 23½ cm. CA 33-189 Unrev. F72. B5 H8

BERKSHIRE County. Stories from our hills, by Jean Jarvie ... (North Adams, Mass., Excelsior print. co., (1926) 7, (17) - 143 p. illus. (incl. maps) plates, port. 23 cm. 26-3519. F72. B5 J 3

GREYLOCK reservation commission ... Annual report of the (1901) - 1924. Boston, Wright & Potter print. co., 1902 - (25) 24 v. in 1. plates, fold. maps, diagr. 23½ cm. No more pub. 10-33109 Rev. F72. B5 M4

MOHAWK trail, The. (North Adams, Excelsior print., 1914) (48) p. 8 pl. 21½ cm. "Official program ... of the Pageant of the Mohawk trail, presented at North Adams ... 1914" p.(13 - 48) 22-10743. F72. B5 M67

MOHAWK trail, The; photo-gravures. North Adams, Mass., Frank Martin (1917) 2 p., 12 pl. 21 x 24½ cm. 17-24993. F72. B5 M69

BERKSHIRES, The, through the camera of Arthur Palme. Biographical sketch (by) Walter Prichard Eaton ... (Pittsfield, Mass., Palme-Grove Pub. Co., 1951) 1 v. (chiefly illus., port., map) 21 cm. 51-6276. F72. B5 P18

BERKSHIRE County. Its past history and achievements. By Charles J. Palmer. (n.p., 19 -?) 24 p. 23 cm. "Origin of the names of the towns and villages of Berkshire Co." p. 11-24. 7-758 Rev. F72. B5 P2

BERKSHIRE, The: the purple hills. Roderick Peattie, ed. New York, Vanguard Press (1948) 414 p. illus., maps. 24 cm. (American mountain series) 48-2653*. F72. B5 P3 1948

GREYLOCK Mountain, the Berkshire Hills and historic Bennington, Pathfinder to ... Maps showing roads, street railways and Greylock summit (by) W. H. Phillips ... (Amherst? Mass.) 1910. 139, (2) p. illus. (incl. port.) fold. maps. 20½ cm. 10-14106. F72. B 5 P5

BERKSHIRE Hills, Historical scenes in the, from Connecticut to Vermont and over the Mohawk trail, by Joseph E. Peirson; comp. by W. S. Weld. (Pittsfield, Mass., Berkshire life insurance co., 1919) (26) p. illus. 15½ x 21 cm. 19-17754. F72. B5 P6

GREYLOCK, The glory of, written as a souvenir of an excursion ... by Francis W. Rockwell. Boston, Mass. (Seaver-Howland press) 1921. 4, 56 p. front., plates. 23½ cm. 21-21359. F72. B5 R67

GREYLOCK. Guide to the Greylock state reservation, by Francis Williams Rockwell, jr. ... Ed. of 1917. (Pittsfield, Mass., Sun print.) 1916. 37 p. illus., fold. map, fold. plan. 17½ cm. 17-2029. F72. B5 R68

BERKSHIRE Hills, Among the; an unconventional trio, by one of them, Elizabeth Alvena Harding Sleeper. (n. p.) 1894. 40 p. 18 cm. 1-12134 rev.* F72. B5 S6

BERKSHIRE County. Taghconic; or Letters and legends about our summer home. By Godfrey Greylock (pseud.) Joseph Edward Adams Smith. Boston, Redding and co., 1852. vi, (9)-228 p. 19 cm. 8-16851. F72. B5 S7

— Boston, Lee & Shepard, 1879. 381 p. 19 cm. A 13-1072. F72. B5 S73

BERKSHIRE, two hundred years in pictures, 1761 - 1961. Compiled, designed and ed. by William H. Tague and Robert B. Kimball. Text by Richard V. Happel. (Pittsfield, Mass., Berkshire Eagle, 1961)

MASSACHUSETTS 87

113 p. 28 cm. 61-13809. F72. B5 T3

BERKSHIRE County. Autumn loiterers, by Charles Hanson Towne ... with drawings by Thomas Fogarty. New York, George H. Doran (1917) viii, 15-129 p. front., illus., plates. 19½ cm. 17-29815.
F72. B5 T74

MOHAWK trail. The trail of the Mohawk, miles of magnificent mountain scenes, unrivaled on the Atlantic Coast. North Adams, Mass., C. R. Canedy (1916) (48) p. illus. (incl. map) 16 x 22½ cm. 16-16925.
F72. B5 T76

BERKSHIRE County. Picturesque Berkshire ... Complete in two parts, with 1200 illus. By Charles Forbes Warner. Northampton and Springfield, (1893) 2 v. fronts., illus. (incl. ports.) 33½ x 27 cm. 1-12135 Rev.
F72. B5 W2

BOUNDARIES. The northern boundary of Massachusetts in its relation to New Hampshire: a part of the Council's report made to the American antiquarian soc. ... By Samuel A. Green. Cambridge, J. Wilson, 1890. 23 p. 24½ cm. 10-12989. F72. B7 G6

— Worcester, Mass., Press of C. Hamilton, 1891. 24 p. 24½ cm. 4-27637. F72. B7 G7

BOUNDARIES. The case of the provinces of Massachusetts-Bay and New-York, respecting the boundary lines between the two provinces. Boston, Print. Green & Russell ... 1764. xxx p. 32 cm. (In Journal of the hon. House of representatives of H. M. province of the Mass. Bay ... Boston, 1763. Appendix) 8-14402.
F72. B7 H9
Rare Book Coll.

BOUNDARIES. A Rhode Island imprint of 1731, by Douglas C. McMurtrie. Providence, R.I., 1936.
9 p. 22½ cm. Extract from the Rhode Island historical society collections for Jan. 1936. 39-2534.
F72. B7 J5

BOUNDARIES. A conference between the Commissaries of Massachusets-Bay, and the Commissaries of New-York ... 1767. Boston, Print. Richard Draper ... 1768. 26 p. 9 p. 24½ x 19½ cm. 6-21559 rev.
F72. B7 M3
Rare Book Coll.

BOUNDARIES. Report of the Massachusetts commissioners on the New Hampshire and Vermont boundaries. (Boston? 1895?) 22 p. fold. map. 23 cm. 2-19157.
F72. B7 M34

BOUNDARIES. (Report of) the committee to whom was referred so much of the governor's message as relates to the boundary line between this commonwealth, and the state of Connecticut. (Boston, 1826) 6 p. 21½ cm. Relates to the gore of land in Southwick, Mass., projecting south of the general division line between the two states. 12-30221.
F72. B7 M45
Rare Book Coll.

BOUNDARIES. (Report) (Boston, Dutton and Wentworth, 1848) 140 p. 22½ cm. 1-13582. F72. B7 M5

BOUNDARIES. Topographical survey comm. Report on the Mass. and N.Y. boundary. (1900)
1 v. F72. B7 M6

BOUNDARIES. ... Report of the commissioners on the topographical survey, relative to the boundary line between the commonwealth of Mass. and the state of Rhode Island and Providence Plantations. (Boston, 1899) 53 p. fold. map. 23 cm. (House. No. 1230) 8-31949. F72. B7 M62

BOUNDARIES. The western boundary of Massachusetts: a study of Indian and colonial history. By Franklin Leonard Pope ... Pittsfield, Mass., Priv. print., 1886. 61 p. front. (fold. map) 23½ cm. Bibliographical foot-notes. 1-12136. F72. B7 P8

BOUNDARIES. The first official frontier of the Massachusetts Bay, by Frederick Jackson Turner ... Cambridge, J. Wilson, 1914. (250) - 271 p. 25½ cm. Repr. from the Pubs. of the Colonial soc. of Mass. CA 25-999 Unrev.
F72. B7 T9

317

BOUNDARIES. Report of the Commissioners appointed by the government to establish boundary line monuments between Vermont and Massachusetts and at the south-west corner of New Hampshire and the south-east corner of Vermont. New York and Albany, Wynkoop Hallenbeck Crawford co., 1900. 21 p. fold. map. 23 cm. 8-14411.   F72. B7 V5

BRISTOL county directory, The ... 1867/68 -   Boston, Mass., The Briggs directory and pub. co., 1867 -   v. 23½ cm. 14-3709.   Directories

BRISTOL County business directory for 1903.   1 v.   Directories

BRISTOL County, History of, with biographical sketches of many of its pioneers and prominent men. Comp. under the supervision of D. Hamilton Hurd ... Philadelphia, J.W. Lewis, 1883.   xii, 922 p. illus., pl., ports., maps (2 double) 28 cm. 1-12138.   F72. B8 H9

BRISTOL County, A history of, editor-in-chief, Frank Walcott Hutt ... N.Y. and Chicago, Lewis historical pub. co., 1924.   3 v. fronts., plates, ports., coats of arms. 28 cm. Biographical sketches comprise last part of v. 2 and all of v. 3. 24-14601.   F72. B8 H93

BRISTOL County. Our county and its people; a descriptive and biographical record of Bristol County, prepared and pub. under the auspices of the Fall River news and the Taunton gazette, with the assistance of Hon, Alanson Borden ... (Boston) The Boston history co., 1899.   xii, 799, 418 p. illus., plates, ports., maps. 26 cm. 5-16864.   F72. B8 O9

BUZZARD'S BAY, Colonial times on, by William Root Bliss ... Boston and New York, Houghton, Mifflin, 1888.   ix p. 185 p. front. (map) plates. 20½ cm. The northern and western shores of the Bay; originally the town of Rochester, now Wareham, Marion and Mattapoisett. 1-12139.   F72. B9 B6

— 1900.   252 p. incl. map. 20 cm. 0-4159 Rev.   F72. B9 B7

BUZZARD'S BAY and vicinity. Photo-gravures. Harwichport, Mass., W. L. Kelley, 1896. 16 pl. 13 x 18½ cm. 1-12140.   F72. B9 B9

BUZZARD'S BAY. At Gray Gables and walks along the shore of Buzzard's Bay. With illus. from watercolors & sketches by L.K. Harlow and with an historical and descriptive sketch of Buzzard's Bay and poems by well known writers illustrative of the scenery. New York, R. Tuck, 1895.   15 p. front., illus., col. pl. obl. 12°. 1-12141-M1.   F72. B9 H2

BUZZARD'S BAY. Sou'west and by west of Cape Cod. By Llewellyn Howland. Cambridge, Harvard Univ. Press, 1947.   xi, 229 p. illus. 21 cm. 47-5293*   F72. B9 H6

BUZZARD'S Bay. New York, New Haven and Hartford railroad co. (New York, 1911)   22 x 10½ cm.   F72. B9 N5

BUZZARD'S BAY. Cape Cod and Buzzards Bay; reminders, memories, contacts. New York, Newcomen Society of England, American Branch, 1948.   32 p. illus. 23 cm. 48-23447*.   F72. B9T7

CAPE COD. Dunham's Cape Cod directory ... for the towns of Barnstable, Bourne, Brewster, Chatham, Dennis, Eastham, Falmouth, Harwich, Mashpee, Orleans, Provincetown, Sandwich, Truro, Wellfleet, Yarmouth (incl. 143 villages) ... v. 1 -   Winthrop, Mass., and West Barrington, R. I., C. H. Dunham, 1929.   1 v. 24 cm. CA 30-609 Unrev.   Directories

CAPE COD. About Cape Cod ... (Boston, Thomas Todd co. print. 1936)   128 p. illus. (incl. ports., map) 20½ cm. "Books worth reading, a selected list": p. 96, 98. 36-6656.   F72. C3 A26

CAPE COD. This quiet place; a Cape Cod chronicle, by Everett S. Allen. Drawings by Michael McCurdy. (1st ed.) Boston, Little, Brown (1971)   280 p. illus. 24 cm. 78-154948.   F72. C3 A65

CAPE COD. Old Cape Cod; the land, the men, the sea, by Mary Rogers Bangs. Boston and New York, Houghton Mifflin co., 1920.   5, 298 p. front., plates. 21½ cm. 20-19426.   F72. C3 B2

— 1931.   5, 309 p. front., plates. 21½ cm. 31-26968.   F72. C3 B2 1931

MASSACHUSETTS

CAPE COD. Cape Cod color; being a pot-pourri of promiscuous paragraphs concerning fish, flesh, and fowl, with a few stray observations upon flowers, fruits, and institutions on the Cape, by Arthur W. Bell; Boston and N.Y., Houghton Mifflin, 1931. x, 170 p., front. 20 cm. 31-14969.
F72. C3 B37

CAPE COD (by) William Berchen and Monica Dickens. New York, Viking Press (1972) 94 p. illus. 23 x 25 cm. (A Sudio book) 72-185985.
F72. C3 B38 1972

CAPE COD pilot; Federal writers' project, W.P.A. for the state of Mass., by Jeremiah Digges (pseud.) Josef Berger. Provincetown, Mass., Modern pilgrim press, 1937. 4. 403 p. plates. 22 ½ cm. Bibliography: p. 390-391. 37-12550.
F72. C3 B39

— Cambridge, Mass., M.I,T. Press (1969) xii, 401 p. 21 cm. 69-20266.
F72. C3 B39 1969

CAPE COD, A modern pilgrim's guide to, by Jeremiah Digges (Josef Berger) and others. (Rev. ed.) Provincetown, Mass., Modern Pilgrim Press (1947) 78 p. illus. 21 cm. "Material formerly appearing in three booklets, the Oceanside guide, the Bayshore guide, and the Guide to Provincetown, has been revised and brought tog." 47-28587*.
F72. C3B397

— (1936) 32 p. front. (map) illus. 21 ½ cm. 36-17254 Rev.
F72. C3 B4

CAPE COD. The outermost house; a year of life on the great beach of cape Cod, by Henry Beston, illus ... by Wm. A. Bradford and others. Garden City, N.Y., Doubleday, Doran, 1928. xv, (2), 222 p. front., illus. (map) plates. 21 ½ cm. 28-23978.
F72. C3 B42

— New York, Rinehart (1949) ix, 222 p. map. 20 cm. 49-8958*.
F72. C3 B42 1949

CAPE COD. Your Cape Cod; photographs by Gustav H. Seelig and Randall W. Abbott, text by Marillis Bittinger, comp. and ed. by Paul W. Bittinger. Plymouth, Mass., Memorial Press (1947) 80 p. illus. 23 cm. 47-5923*.
F72. C3 B5

CAPE COD. The Dolphin guide to Cape Cod, Martha's Vineyard and Nantucket. Garden City, N.Y., Doubleday (1964) x, 188 p. 18 cm. 64-11737.
F72. C3 B55

CAPE COD and the Old colony, by Albert Perry Brigham ... with 35 illus. and maps. New York and London, G.P. Putnam's sons, 1920. xi, 284 p. front., plates, 2 maps (1 fold.) diagr. 21 cm. 20-14826.
F72. C3 B8

CAPE COD and the Old colony, by Albert Perry Brigham ... With 35 illus. and maps. New York and London, G.P. Putnam's sons (1920) xi, 284 p. front., plates, 2 maps (1 fold.) diagr. 21 cm. "Third impression." 41M397T.
F72. C3 B83

CAPE COD and all the Pilgrim land. Sandwich, and Hyannis, The Cape Cod pub. co., 19 - v. illus. 30 ½ cm. monthly. Title varies. CA 26-239 Unrev.
F72. C3 C26

CAPE COD association in Boston, Constitution of the, with an account of the celebration of its first anniversary at Boston. Boston, Eastburn's press, 1852. 80 p. 24 cm. 1-16203.
F72. C3 C3

CAPE COD beacon, The. (Yarmouthport, Mass., C.W. Swift, 1937 - v. illus. 20 cm. monthly (June-Aug. semimonthly) "Formerly the Provincetown beacon ..." 41M524T.
F72. C3C318

CAPE COD. "Ships logs and captains' diaries of old Cape Cod": copyright ... (by) Cape Cod Chamber of commerce, Hyannis, Mass., Harry V. Lawrence, chairman ... (Boston, The Berkeley press) 1937. 36 p. illus. 35 ½ x 21 ½ cm. Bibliography: p. (30) 37-12548.
F72. C3C33

CAPE COD compass. (Falmouth, Mass.) v. illus. 31 cm. annual. 52-65313.
F72. C3C332

CAPE COD information guide (and) directory. (Centerville, Mass., Scrimshaw Press, 1965) 80 p. 22 cm. 65-27437.
F72. C3C335

CAPE COD sea reminiscences, G.V.C. Yarmouthport, Mass., C.W.Swift, 1913. 8 p. 25 cm.
(Library of Cape Cod history and genealogy, no. 69) 17-20839.
F72.C3 C34

CAPE COD. Pictorial tales of, compiled and ed. by Louis Cataldo and Dorothy Worrell. (1st ed.)
Hyannis, Mass., Tales of Cape Cod, inc. (1956) unpaged. illus. 31 cm. 56-58055.
F72.C3 C38

CAPE COD, a photographic sketchbook. By Samuel Chamberlain. New York, Hastings House (1953)
71 p. (chiefly illus.) 25 cm. 53-6150.
F72.C3 C49

CAPE COD in the sun; photographs and comment, by Samuel Chamberlain. New York, Hastings house
(1937) 95 p. incl. front., illus. 32 cm. 37-27427.
F72.C3 C5

CAPE COD'S way, an informal history. By Scott Corbett. New York, Crowell (1955) 310 p. illus.
21 cm. 55-7325.
F72.C3 C58

CAPE COD. We chose Cape Cod. By Scott Corbett. New York, Crowell (1953) 307 p. 21 cm.
52-13127.
F72.C3 C6

CAPE COD. Old shipmasters ... By Aurin B. Crocker. 1924. (Library of Cape Cod history and genealogy no. 16)
F72.C3 C67

CAPE COD. Blue-water men and other cape Codders, by Katharine Crosby. New York, The Macmillan co., 1946. 6, 288 p. front., plates. 21 cm. "First printing." 46-5174.
F72.C3 C69

CAPE COD. byways ... By Joshua F. Crowell. (Library of Cape Cod history and genealogy no. 1)
F72. C3 C7

CAPE COD. Collector's luck; a thousand years at Lewis Bay, Cape Cod, by Betty Bugbee Cussack.
(1st ed. Stoneham, Mass.) G.R.Barnstead print. 1967. xxiv, 238 p. 23 cm. 67-22345.
F72. C3 C8

CAPE COD. Cabo de Baxos; or, the place of Cape Cod in the old cartology, with notes on the neighboring coasts ... By B.F. De Costa. New York, T. Whitaker, 1881. 13 p. front. (map) 25½ cm. Revised
from the N.E. historical and genealogical register, Jan. 1881. 1-12145.
F72. C3 D2
Map Div.

BARNSTABLE County, History of. 1620 - 1637 - 1686 - 1890. Ed. Simeon L. Deyo ... New York,
H.W.Blake, 1890. xii, 1010 p. plates, ports. 28 cm. "Limited ed." A 17-1142.
F72.C3 D29
Microfilm 8787 F

CAPE COD. Exploring old Cape Cod. By Doris Doane. Drawings by Richard Fish. Chatham,
Mass., Chatham Press (1968) 40 p. illus. 16 x 23 cm.
F72.C3 D56

CAPE COD. Down the Cape; the complete guide to Cape Cod, by Katharine Smith and Edith Shay ...
New York, Dodge pub. co. (1936) xi, 222 p. plates, fold. map. 19½ cm. "First ed." 36-27299 rev.
F72. C3 D6
1936

— (New York) R.M.McBride (1947) ix, 230 p. illus., map. 25 cm. 47-5922*.
F72. C3 D6
1947

CAPE COD. Cape-scapes, by George Hibbert Driver. Boston, Mass., The Chapple pub. co., 1930.
62 p. front., plates. 18½ cm. 30-18547.
F72.C3 D78

CAPE COD. And this is Cape Cod! By Eleanor Early. Boston and New York, Houghton Mifflin,
1936. 4, 223 p. front. 17½ cm. 36-9277.
F72.C3E135

CAPE COD summer. By Eleanor Early. Boston, Houghton Mifflin, 1949. xx, 306 p. 21 cm. Originally
pub. in 1936 under title: And this is Cape Cod!
F72.C3E135
1949

MASSACHUSETTS

CAPE COD, a plain tale of the lure of the old colony country for many men of many minds - or, The joys of a vacation between Buzzards Bay and Provincetown. By Walter Prichard Eaton. (New York) The New York, New Haven and Hartford railroad co., (1923) (42) p. illus., plates, fold. map. 20½ cm. 24-18945.
F72. C3 E14

CAPE COD, The history of: the annals of Barnstable County, including the district of Mashpee. By Frederick Freeman ... Boston, Printed for the author, by Geo. C. Rand & Avery, 1858-62.
2 v. ports. 25 cm. 1-12146.
F72. C3 F7

— Yarmouth Port, Mass., Parnassus Imprints, 1965. 2 v. 24 cm. 65-28358. F72. C3 F72

CAPE COD. A description of the eastern coast of the county of Barnstable, from Cape Cod, or Race-Point ... to Cape Malebarre ... By a member of the Humane society. (James Freeman) Boston: Print. Hosea Sprague, 1802. 15 p. 22 cm. Reprinted from the Mass. hist. soc. coll. 1st ser. v. 8, p. 110-119. 1-12147.
F72. C3 F8

CAPE COD sketch book (a Fancy this book) by Jack Frost. New York, Coward-McCann, (1939)
(96) p. illus. 25½ cm. 39-32210.
F72. C3 F85

CAPE COD and Cape Cod national seashore. By Paul Giambarba. (Centerville) Mass., Scrimshaw Press (1968) 64 p. illus. 22 cm. 68-25354.
F72. C3 G48

CAPE COD, The picture story of, from Iyanough to John F. Kennedy (written by Paul Giambarba. 1st ed.) Centerville, Mass., Scrimshaw Press (1965) 63 p. 22 cm. 65-27438.
F72. C3 G5

CAPE COD land titles ... 1927. By Samuel D. Hannah. (Library of Cape Cod history and genealogy, no. 6)
F72. C3 H3

CAPE COD. ..."Cast-up" lands ... By Samuel D. Hannah. 1927. (Library of Cape Cod history and genealogy no. 8)
F72. C3 H33

CAPE COD. ... Permissive uses of the common lands of proprietary plantations ... By Samuel D. Hannah. 1927. (Library of Cape Cod history and genealogy, no. 7)
F72. C3 H36

CAPE COD (by) Hans W. Hannau. (Munich, W. Andermann) Distributed by Doubleday (1967)
60 p. 17 cm. (Panorama books) 67-14921.
F72. C3 H38

CAPE COD. Homeward bound for lower Cape Cod ... By Rudolph Newton Merritt Hopkins. ... Plymouth, Mass., The Memorial press, 1933. 42 p. incl. illus., port. 20 cm. 33-29188.
F72. C3 H6

CAPE COD, Stories of, by Jack Johnson ... A "discovery book," romantic facts of all the cape Cod towns. (Plymouth, Mass., print. the Memorial press, 1944) 2, 87 p. 19½ cm. 44-47431.
F72. C3 J6

CAPE COD; its people and their history, by Henry C. Kittredge ... Boston and New York, Houghton Mifflin co., 1930. 4, (vvi)-xii, 330 p. front., plates, ports., etc. 22½ cm. Bibliog. p. (313)-316. 30-5060. F72. C3 K62

CAPE COD; its people and their history, by Henry C. Kittredge. 2d ed. with a post-epilogue, 1930 - 1968 by John Hay. Boston, H. Mifflin Co., 1968. xii, 344 p. illus. 22 cm. 68-21055.
F72. C3 K62
1968

CAPE COD, Mooncussers of, by Henry C. Kittredge ... Boston and New York, Houghton Mifflin, 1937.
vi, 226 p. front., plates. 21½ cm. 37-2896.
F72. C3K625

— (Hamden, Conn.) Archon Books, 1971 (1937) vi, 226 p. 23 cm. 70-143889. F72. C3K625
1971

CAPE COD, Shipmaster of, by Henry C. Kittredge ... Boston and New York, Houghton Mifflin co., 1935. 5, 3-319 p. front., plates, ports. 21 cm. "Acknowledgments" p. 295-(300); Bibliography p. 301-(306) 35-5097. F72. C3 K63

— (Hamden, Conn.) Archon Books, 1971. (1935)   319 p. illus. 23 cm. 74-143890.
    F72. C3 K63
    1971

CAPE COD journey. By Katharine Knowles. Photos. by   Barre, Mass., Barre Publishers, 1966. 93 p. 26 cm. 66-05050.
    F72. C3 K66

CAPE COD, The pageant of (by) William Chauncy Langdon, master of the pageant. ... (Boston, Blanchard print. 1914)   2, 7-66 p. 23 cm. 14-16584.
    F72. C3 L3

CAPE COD. Where land meets sea; the tide line of Cape Cod, written and engraved by Clare Leighton. New York, Rinehart (1954)   202 p. illus. 26 cm. 54-7922.
    F72. C3 L4

CAPE COD. Sailing directions, to accompany Major J. D. Graham's chart of Cape Cod harbor. With extracts from his report on the tides, soundings, currents, etc. Boston, Boston marine insurance offices, 1841.   16 p. 8°. 1-16202-M1.
    F72. C3 L6

CAPE COD yesterdays, by Joseph C. Lincoln; paintings and drawings by Harold Brett. Boston, Little, Brown, 1935.   3, (v) - xv p., (3) - 286 p. front., illus., port. 25 cm. 35-12168.
    F72. C3 L67
    Rare Book Coll.

—   xv, (3) - 286 p. col. front., illus., plates, port. 23 cm. "Reprinted Oct., 1935." A35-1814.
    F72. C3L672

CAPE COD. The ancient wreck. Loss of the Sparrow-hawk in 1626. Remarkable preservation and recent discovery of the wreck. By Charles W. Livermore. Print. A. Mudge, 1865.   38 p. illus. (incl. map) 19 cm. 1-12150.
    F72. C3 L7

— Y^e antient wrecke.   38 p. illus., map. 19 cm. Identical to above except for title. 2-26827.
    F72. C3 L71

—   44 p. illus. (incl. map) 19 ½ cm. 4-12564.
    F72. C3 L72

CAPE COD. Romantic Cape Cod, written and compiled by James Westaway McCue. Harwick, Cape Cod, Goss print, 1941.   (72) p. illus. 28 ½ cm. 41-15373.
    F72. C3 M2

CAPE COD. Block prints of old Cape Cod buildings, by William A. Miller, jr. 1st ed. (Yarmouth Port, Mass.) The artist (1935)   47 p. incl. front., plates. 19 ½ cm. Descriptive letterpress on versos facing the plates. 35-14528.
    F72. C3 M65

CAPE COD. It's an old Cape Cod custom. By Edwin Valentine Mitchell. New York, Vanguard Press (1949)   242 p. illus. 22 cm. (American customs series) 49-9162*.
    F72. C3 M68
    1949

CAPE COD. Quaint Cape Cod and its summer delights. N.Y., New Haven and Hartford railroad co., (New Haven) 1911.   21 ½ x 10 ½ cm.
    F72. C3 N5

CAPE COD. An account of the discovery of an ancient ship on the eastern shore of Cape Cod. (Communicated by Amos Otis ...)   (In New England hist. and geneal. register, v. 18, p. 37-44) 1-12148.
    F72. C3 O8

—   10 p. front. (map) pl. 24 ½ cm. From New England hist. and geneal. register.
    F72. C3 O81

CAPE COD. A discourse pronounced at Barnstable ... at the celebration of the second centennial anniversary of the settlement of Cape Cod. By John Gorham Palfrey. Boston, F. Andrews, 1840. 50 p. 23 cm. 1-12152.
    F72. C3 P1

—   71 p. 22 cm. 16-12310.
    F72. C3 P13

CAPE COD, A trip around: our summer land and memories of my childhood; written by E. G. Perry ... (Boston, Press of the C. S. Binner co., 1895?)   188 p. illus. (incl. ports.) 24½ x 19 cm. 1-12153.
    F72. C3 P4

MASSACHUSETTS

CAPE COD, new and old, by Agnes Edwards (pseud.) Agnes Edwards Rothery, with illus. by Louis H. Ruyl.   Boston and New York, Houghton Mifflin, 1918.   xvi, 239 p. front., illus., plates. 21½ cm. 18-11843.
F72. C3 R8

CAPE CODDITIES, by Dennis and Marion Chatham (pseud. for Roger Livingston Scaife) with illus. by Harold Cue.   Boston and N.Y., Houghton Mifflin, 1920.   3, 164, (2) p. front., illus. 20 cm. Reprinted from various periodicals. 20-10073 Rev.
F72. C3 S27

CAPE COD, Rambling 'round, comp. and ed. by Ethel P. Shaw and William P. Shaw.   Text by E. P. Shaw, photos, by W. P. Shaw.   (Worcester, Mass., 1948)   64 p. illus. (part col.) map (on lining-papers) 23 cm. 48-3956*.
F72. C3 S46

CAPE COD.   Sand in their shoes; a Cape Cod reader, ed. by Edith Shay and Frank Shay.   Boston, Houghton Mifflin, 1951.   xvi, 364 p. 22 cm. 51-10627.
F72. C3 S47

CAPE COD.   Souvenir; a letter from Cape Cod ... Orleans, Mass., 1913.   5-39 p. front., plates. 20 cm. Signed: Bradford Sherman. 14-12425.
F72. C3 S5

CAPE COD legends.   Ed. Elisabeth Shoemaker.   (Boston, The Berkeley press, 1935)   43 p. illus. 19½ cm. 35-21892.
F72. C3 S55

CAPE COD, A pilgrim returns to, by Edward Rowe Snow ... Boston, Mass., The Yankee pub. co., (1946)   413 p. incl. col. front., plates, ports. 24 cm. Folded map. Bibliography: p. (400) - 401. 46-7923.
F72. C3 S74

CAPE COD.   Souvenir of quaint cape Cod.   (Boston, Tichnor brothers, inc., 194 -?)   (48) p. of illus. 25½ cm. 45-33126.
F72. C3 S76

CAPE COD, the right arm of Massachusetts.   An historical narrative, by Charles F. Swift ... Yarmouth, Register pub. co., 1897.   4, 391 p. illus., ports., map. 23½ cm. 1-12154 Rev.
F72. C3 S9

CAPE COD.   My own Cape Cod, by Gladys Taber.   (1st ed.) Philadelphia, J. B. Lippincott Co. (1971) 251 p. illus. 22 cm. 75-151491.
F72. C3T18

CAPE COD ahoy! A travel book for the summer visitor, by Arthur Wilson Tarbell.   Boston, R.G. Badger (1932)   347 p. front., plates. 19½ cm. 32-30369.
F72. C3 T25

— Boston, Little, Brown, 1934.   xiii, (3) - 367 p. front., plates. 19½ cm. 34-39883.
F72. C3 T25 1934

— Boston, Little, Brown, 1937.   xiii p. (3) - 379 p. front., plates. 19½ cm. 37-19334.
F72. C3 T25 1937

CAPE COD.   I retire to cape Cod, by Arthur W. Tarbell.   New York, S. Daye inc. (1944) xiv, 143 p. incl. front., illus. 21 cm. 44-40167.
F72. C3 T26

CAPE COD and the offshore islands, by Walter Teller.   Englewood Cliffs, N.J., Prentice-Hall (1970) x, 256 p. illus. 24 cm. 73-97739.
F72. C3 T3

CAPE COD.   By Henry David Thoreau ... Boston, Ticknor and Fields, 1865.   3, 252 p. 18 cm. First edition, ed. Sophia E. Thoreau and William Ellery Channing.   The first four chapters were published in Putnam's magazine in 1855; the 5th and 8th appeared in the Atlantic monthly in Oct. and Dec., 1864. 3-21052.
F72. C3 T37
Rare Book Coll.

— 1866.   2, 252 p. 17½ cm. 16-9905.
F72. C3 T38

— Boston, J. R. Osgood, 1875.   2, 252 p. 18½ cm. 17-21232.
F72. C3 T39

— with illus. from sketches in colors by Amelia M. Watson ... Boston and New York, Houghton, Mifflin, 1896.   2 v. fronts., illus. 19½ cm. 3-21051.
F72. C3 T4

— With an introd. by Joseph Wood Krutch and illus. by R.J. Holden.   Portland, Me., Print. at the Anthoensen Press for the members of the Limited Editions Club, 1968.   xiv, 215 p. illus. 27 cm.
F72. C3 T4 1968

— Thoreau's Cape Cod, with the early photographs of Herbert W. Gleason.   Ed. with an introd. by Thea Wheelwright.   Barre, Mass., Barre Pub., 1971.   xxviii, 102 p. illus. 22 cm. 79-163877 MARC.
F72. C3T4i13

— ... with an introd. by Annie Russell Marble.   New York, T.Y. Croweel & co. (1907)   2, iii-xiii, 263 p. front. 19 cm. (The Astor prose series) 7-37720.
F72. C3 T42

— ... illus. by Clifton Johnson.   New York, T.Y. Crowell & co. (1908)   xii, 319 p. incl. front. 32 pl. 21½ cm. 8-22336.
F72. C3 T43

— with introd. and illus. from photographs, by Charles S. Olcott.   Boston and New York, Houghton Mifflin, 1914.   xi, 336 p. front., plates. 20 cm. "Visitor's edition." 14-14155.
F72. C3T433

— arranged with notes by Dudley C. Lunt.   Introd. by Henry Beston.   Illus. by Henry Bugbee Kane. (1st ed.)   New York, Norton (1951)   300 p. illus., map. 22 cm. 51-10937.
F72. C3T434

— Decorated by Clare Leighton.   New York, Crowell (1961)   319 p. 21 cm. 61-66082.
F72. C3 T434 1961

— Inledning och overs. av Gustav Sandgren. (Ny uppl.) Stockholm, Tiden (1967)   105 (2) p. 18 cm.
F72. C3T4359 1967

CAPE COD, Guide to.   Based on Cape Cod, by Henry David Thoreau.   Ed. and illus. by Alexander B. Adams.   With a biographical sketch of Thoreau by Ralph Waldo Emerson.   New York, Devin-Adair Co. (1962)   x, 148 p. illus., map. 24 cm. 62-20031.
F72. C3 T437

CAPE COD.   Little pilgrim's guide, by Jonathan Tree; with picutres by Inez Hogan.   Provincetown, Mass., The Modern pilgrim press (1936)   23 p. illus. (incl. map; part col.) 21 cm. 36-13039.
F72. C3 T7

CAPE COD.   Earning a living on olde Cape Cod.   By Marion Vuilleumier.   Illus. by Louis Edward Vuilleumier.   Craigville, Mass., Craigville Press, 1968.   80 p. 23 cm. Reprinted from Cape Cod Standard-Times.
F72. C3 V8

CAPE COD.   Sketches of old Cape Cod.   By Marion Vuilleumier.   Illus. by Louis Edward Vuilleumier. Taunton, Mass., W.S. Sullwold Pub. (1972)   96 p. illus. 23 cm.
F72. C3 V82

CAPE COD in picture and story.   By Wainwright Johnson. Wainwright.   Cotuit, Mass., Picture Book Press (1954)   64 p. illus. 22 cm. 54-3894.
F72. C3 W3

CAPE COD.   Wellfleet, Truro, and Cape Cod.   Frederick S. Rich, editor-in-chief.   (Wellfleet, Mass.) Rich Family Association (introd. 1969-   29 cm. 78-94418.
F72. C3 W4

CAPE COD; where to go, what to do, how to do it, by Julius M. Wilensky.   Ed. Frank G. Valenti. Stamford, Conn., Wescott Cove Pub. Co., 1969.   172 p. illus. 29 cm. 70-83970.
F72. C3 W48

CAPE COD.   ... Old Cape Cod windmills ... by Daniel Wing.   1925.   (Library of Cape Cod history and genealogy. no. 14)
F72. C3 W5

CHARLES RIVER.   The defences of Norumbega and a review of the reconnaissances of Col. T.W. Higginson, and others; a letter to Judge Daly ... by Eben Norton Horsford.   Boston and New York, Houghton, Mifflin, 1891.   iv, 84 p. front., plates, maps (partly fold.) 25½ x 33½ cm. 1-25297.
F72. C46

MASSACHUSETTS

CHARLES RIVER. A poem. By Thomas C. Amory ... Cambridge, J. Wilson and son, 1888.
3, 185 p. 20 cm. 18-19897. F72.C46 A

CHARLES RIVER, Pageant of... 1914... By Mrs. Isabella (Fiske) Conant. (Wellesley, Mass., Maugus print., 1914) (8) p. 23 x 12½ cm. In verse. 15-885. F72.C46 C7

CHARLES RIVER. The poetry of the Charles and its poets, by Louis Kinney Harlow, illus. by Louis K. Harlow. Boston, L. Prang & co., 1893. 8 col. pl. (incl. front.) 3 port. 18 x 27 cm. 17-5270.
F72.C46 H2

CHARLES RIVER. The Charles, by Arthur Bernon Tourtellot, illus. by Ernest J. Donnelly. New York, Toronto, Farrar & Rinehart, inc. (1941) x, 356 p. illus. 21 cm. (The Rivers of America) Bibliography: p. 343-348. 41-52052. F72.C46 T7

CONCORD RIVER. A week on the Concord and Merrimack rivers. By Henry David Thoreau. Boston and Cambridge, J. Munroe; New York, G. P. Putnam, 1849. 413 p. 19½ cm. First ed. 8-14408.
F72. C5 T2

— Boston, Ticknor and Fields, 1862. 413 p. 20 cm. 14-1318. F72.C5 T45
Rare Book Coll.

— New and rev. ed. Boston, Ticknor and Fields, 1868. 415 p. 18½ cm. 8-14409. F72. C5 T5

— with an introd. by Nathan H. Dole. New York, T. T. Crowell & co. (1900) 4, vii-xxiv, 399 p. front., plates. 19 cm. 0-4240 Rev. F72.C5 T52

— illus. by Clifton Johnson. New York, Thomas Y. Crowell (1911) 4, v-xxii, 492 p. front., plates. 21½ cm. 11-20622. F72.C5 T53

— New York, Hurst (1912) 355 p. 20 cm. 49-32791*. F72.C5 T54

— ed. with an introd. by Odell Shepard ... New York, Chicago (etc.) C. Scribner's sons (1912)
4, vii-xxviii, 292 p. 17½ cm. (The modern student's library) 21-9999. F72.C5 T56

— With wood-engravings by the editor. New York, E. P. Dutton (1932) vii, 360, (2) p. incl. front.
19½ cm. (Open-air library,) "Printed in Great Britain." 32-27284. F72.C5 T57

CONNECTICUT VALLEY. Suburban directory and mailing list of central and western Massachusetts for 1911/12 -   consisting of the following towns: Ashfield, Blandford, Chester, Chesterfield, Charlemont, Colrain, Conway, Cummington, Deerfield, Granby, Granville, Goshen, Hadley, Hatfield, Hawley, Leyden, Leverett, Montague, including Turners Falls and Millers Falls, Pelham, So. Hadley, Sunderland, Southampton, Southwick, Russell, Plainfield, Westhampton, Worthington, Whately, Woronoco, Montgomery. Springfield, Mass., Beaman's advertising agency, c. 1911.
1 v. fold. map. 24 cm. 11-3269. Directories

CONNECTICUT VALLEY. Valley of the Connecticut and Northern Vermont. Boston and Maine railroad. Boston, 1901. 20 x 10½ cm. F72, C7 B7

CONNECTICUT River, The. Importance of opening it to navigation from Hartford, Conn., to Holyoke, Mass. with report of Smith S. Leach, major U.S. Engineer corps. Survey of the river, with methods and probably cost of improvements. Prepared by the Ways and means committee of the Connecticut River navigation assoc. Springfield, Mass., Springfield print. and bind. co., 1898. 36 p. 2 fold. maps.
23 cm. 3-26281. F72.C7 C64

CONNECTICUT VALLEY historical society ... a maintenance fund of 100,000 dollars to be established by members and friends of the society. (Springfield, 1912) (17) p. 9 pl. (incl. front.) 24 x 18 cm. 12-9164.
F72.C7 C68

CONNECTICUT VALLEY historical society, Papers and proceedings of the. 1876 - 19 - Springfield, Mass., The Society, 1881-19 - v. fronts., plates, ports. 24½ - 25½ cm. 1-12151. F72.C7 C7

CONNECTICUT VALLEY in Massachusetts, History of, with illus. and biographical sketches of some of its prominent men and pioneers ... Philadelphia, L. H. Everts, 1879.   2 v. fronts., illus. (incl. facsims.) plates, ports., maps. 31 x 21 ½ cm. Paged continuoulsy.   v. 1. History of the Connecticut Valley and of Hampshire County. - v. 2. History of Franklin County and of Hampden County. 1-12155.
F72. C7 H6

CONNECTICUT VALLEY.   River gods, their story in Pioneer valley, by Elizabeth Shoemaker.   (Boston, Printed at the Berkeley press, 1941)   16 p. illus. (incl. ports.) 30 ½ cm. 41-14728.
F72. C7 S5

CONNECTICUT VALLEY, Early days in the, by Alice M. Walker, illus. and cover design by Miss Martha Genung.   Amherst, Mass., 1901.   51 p. illus. 18 ½ cm. 6-8175.
F72. C7 W2

CONNECTICUT VALLEY.   Through the old-time haunts of the Norwottuck and Pocumtuck Indians, by Frances J. White.   Springfield, Mass. (Print. F. A. Bassette co.) 1903.   42 p. incl. front., illus., map. 19 cm. 3-26279.
F72. C7 W5

CONNECTICUT VALLEY.   Indian deeds of Hampden County, being copies of all land transfers from the Indians recorded in the county of Hampden ...   Ed. by Harry Andrew Wright.   Springfield, Mass., 1905.   2, (7) - 194 p. 24 cm. Includes also records of the counties of Hampshire, Worcester, Berkshire and Franklin.   5-36823.
F72. C7 W8

CUTTYHUNK, The story of.   By Louise Taylor Haskell.   (New Bedford, Mass., Reynolds Print., 1953) 53 p. 24 cm. Includes bibliography. 53-25014.
F72. C88 H38

NAUSHON Island, Early history of, by Amelia Forbes Emerson.   (Boston) Priv. print. (Thomas Todd co., printers) 1935.   xi, 502 p. front., plates, ports., maps, facsims. 25 ½ cm. "Sources": p. (485)-487. 35-13975.
F72. E5 E6

NAUSHON data.   By Amelia (Forbes) Emerson.   Concord, Mass., 1963.   235 p. 27 cm. 63-12994.
F72. E5 E63

THREE ISLANDS: Pasque, Nashawena, and Penikese.   By Alice Forbes Howland.   (Boston?) 1964. xvi, 127 p. 25 cm.
F72. E5 H6

ESSEX COUNTY.   Declaration of the county of Essex ... by its delegates ... 1812.   Salem, Print. T. C. Cushing, 1812.   16 p. 19 cm. 3-28997* Cancel.
F72. E
E357.6.I65

ESSEX resolutions.   (Newburyport, E. W. Allen, printer, 1808)   14 p. 22 cm. 9-20387.
F72. E
E336.5.T67

ESSEX COUNTY.   A handbook of conservation, with special reference to the landscape features in Essex county; ... Salem, Mass., Society for the preservation of the landscape features of Essex county, Mass., and the Peabody museum (1936)   9, 3-84 p. illus., plates, fold. map, diagrs. 24 cm. 37-9696.
F72. E7
QH75. S6

ESSEX COUNTY directory, The ... 1866, 1869/70 - 71, 1873-81, 1883/4 - 1889.   Boston, Mass., The Briggs directory and pub. co., 1866 - 1889.   14 v. 10-10291.
Directories

ESSEX - County history and directory ... Boston, C. A. & J. F. Wood, 1870.   (621) p. 24 cm. 22-16686.
Directories

ESSEX COUNTY.   North Essex directory of Georgetown, Merrimac, Newbury, Rowley, Salisbury, West Newbury, Massachusetts ... Boston, Mass., G. Richardson, 1907-09.   2 v. 24 cm. 7-22405.
Directories

ESSEX COUNTY.   The North shore blue book and social register; containing lists of the summer residents of the principal resorts along the North shore (Massachusetts) from Nahant to Newburyport inclusive ... 1896. Cambridge, Mass., Hyde Pub. corp. (1896 - 19   v. illus., fold. maps. 20 ½ x 24 cm. 1-18534 Rev.
Directories

MASSACHUSETTS

ESSEX COUNTY. Who's who along the north shore of Massachusetts Bay ...   Salem, Mass., The
Salem press co., 1907 - 1910.   3 v. front., illus. 23½ cm. 7-25649.   Directories

ESSEX COUNTY. Trolley trips on a Bay state triangle for sixty sunny days. By Katharine M. Abbott
... (Lowell, Print. Thompson & Hill) 1897.   86, (2) p. incl. illus., 2 maps. 10½ x 15 cm. 6-42973 Rev.
                                                                                                  F72. E7 A22

ESSEX COUNTY, Along the coast of. A guidebook with an introd. by Richard W. Hale, Jr. (Boston,
Junior League of Boston (1970)   xvi, 206 p. illus. 24 cm.   F72. E7 A4

ESSEX COUNTY. Along the old North Shore with President Taft ... (Portland, Me., 1910)
20 x 25½ cm.   F72. E7 A45

CAPE ANN, Along the old roads of. Gloucester, Mass., Print. F. S. & A. H. McKenzie, 1923.
3, (9) - 106 p. 19½ cm. 23-10766.   F72. E7 A46

CAPE ANN. Know Cape Ann; the garden spot of the Atlantic. By Edward Vassar Ambler. (n. p.)
North Shore Press, 1931.   88 p. 23 cm.   F72. E7 A52

ESSEX COUNTY, Municipal history of. Tercentenary ed. A classified work, devoted to the county's
remarkable growth in all lines of human endeavor... Benj. F. Arrington, ed.-in-chief ... New York,
Lewis historical pub. co., 1922.   4 v. fronts. (v. 1-3) plates, ports., map. 27½ cm. Vols. iii-iv contain biographical
material. 23-2813.   F72. E7 A7

CAPE ANN; a tourist guide, by Roger W. Babson and Foster H. Saville. Rockport, Mass., Cape Ann
old book shop, 1936.   118, (3) p. illus. (incl. doubles maps) 19 cm. "Books relating to Cape Ann": p. 116-118. 36-17934.
                                                                                          F72. E7 B 24

CAPE ANN, tourist's guide. (Latest rev. ed.) By Roger W. Babson and Foster H. Saville. Gloucester, Mass., Cape Ann community league, inc., 1946.   127 (4) p. illus. (incl. maps) diagr. 18½ cm. "Books relating to Cape Ann": p. 116-117. 47-2558.   F72. E7 B23
                                                                                              1946

ESSEX COUNTY, Trades and tradesmen of, chiefly of the seventeenth century, by Henry Wyckoff Belknap. Salem, Mass., The Essex institute, 1929.   2; 96 p. front. (port.) plates. 24½ cm. 29-3626. F72. E7 B43

ESSEX COUNTY. Biographical review ... containing life sketches of leading citizens of Essex County
... Boston, Biographical review pub. co., 1898.   3, (9) - 618 p. incl. ports. 29 cm. (Atlantic states series of biographical reviews vol. xxviii) 10-14293.   F72. E7 B5

ESSEX COUNTY. Views along shore ... Boston and Portsmouth steamship co. (Boston, T. H. Brackett,
1891)   (36) p. illus., fold. map. obl. 24º. 1-12156-M1.   F72. E7 B6

CAPE ANN, Bits of life on ... By Ada Chastina? Bowles. (illustrations from original photos.) Boston,
Allen, print., 1892.   (19) p. illus. obl. 24º. 1-14484-M1.   F72. E7 B7

ESSEX COUNTY. Seaboard towns; or, Traveller's guide book from Boston to Portland: containing a
description of the cities, towns and villages .... Incl. historical sketches, legends, etc. ... By
Joseph H. Bragdon, Newburyport, Moulton & Clark; Boston, A. Williams & co. 1857.   2, 204 p. illus.
16½ cm. 10-8761.   F72. E7 B8

CAPE ANN summer directory ... c. 1911.   1 v.   Directories

ESSEX COUNTY, A geography of; for young children; ... By J. G. Carter and W. H. Brooks ... Boston,
Carter & Hendee, 1830.   viii, (9) - 118 p. 24º. 1-12157-M1.   F72. E7 C3

CAPE ANN through the seasons, a photographic sketchbook. By Samuel Chamberlain. New York,
Hastings House (1953)   36 p. (chiefly illus.) 25 cm. 53-6149.   F72. E7 C48

ESSEX COUNTY, The wheelman's hand-book of. Containing brief sketches of the various cities and

towns of the county, with a list of their objects of interest ...   Also, the history of the League of Essex county wheelmen.   By G. Chinn and F. E. Smith.   Marblehead (etc.) G. Chinn (etc.) 1884.
35 p. 8°.   1-12158-M1. F72. E7 C5

— 3d ed.   Beverly, Mass. (Citizen steam press) 1886.   59 p. 21 cm.   4-33635. F72. E7 C6

CAPE ANN, The Saga of (by) Melvin T. Copeland & Elliott C. Rogers.   Freeport, Me., Bond Wheelwright Co. (1960)   254 p. illus. 22 cm.   60-10075. F72. E7 C7

DODGE, Laurence G.   Puritan paths from Naumkeag to Piscataqua; an excursion from Rum Corner to Trundle Bed Lane, by the Dodges.   (Newburyport, Mass.) Newburyport Press, 1963.   219 p. 24 cm.
F72. E7 D6

ESSEX COUNTY.   Old wood engravings, views and buildings in the county of Essex.   By George Francis Dow.   Salem, Mass., 1908.   14 l. illus. 26 cm.   76 copies printed.   9-12000. F72. E7 D7

IPSWICH RIVER.   The river Agawam, an Essex County waterway, by George Francis Day.   Topsfield, Mass., 1926.   3, 16 p. front., plates, port. 24 cm. (The Essex tracts, no. vii)   Agawam, the Indian name for Ipswich River. 27-3056. F72. E7 D717

ESSEX COUNTY, Two centuries of travel in, a collection of narratives and observations made by travelers, 1605-1799; coll. and annotated by George Francis Dow.   Topsfield, Mass., The Topsfield historical soc., 1921.   xvi, 189 p. front. (map) 6 pl. 24 cm.   21-13997. F72. E7 D72

ESSEX COUNTY.   The Essex antiquarian; a quarterly magazine devoted to the biography, genealogy, history and antiquities of Essex County ... v. 1-13.   Salem, Mass., The Essex antiquarian, 1897 - 1909.   13 v. illus., plates, ports., maps. 24-25 cm.   No more pub.   The genealogical dictionary of Essex County families, carried from Abbe to Brown in these vols. is continued in the "Massachusetts magazine." 5-32200 Add. E72. E7 E4

ESSEX-County historical and genealogical register ... v. 1, v. 2, nos 1-7.   Ipswich, Mass., M. Van B. Perley, 1894 - (95)   2 v. in 1. illus., plates, ports. 26½ cm.   No more pub.   L.C. copy replaced by microfilm.   3-11710.
E72. E7 E5
Microfilm 8662 F

ESSEX historical society.   Incorporated June 11, 1821.   (Salem, 1821)   8 p. 21½ cm.   In 1848 the "Essex county natural history society" and the "Essex historical soc." united to form the Essex institute.   1-12165 Rev. F72. E7 E67

ESSEX historical society, An address in commemoration of the 75th anniversary of the founding of the.   Salem, The Salem press, 1897.   99-132 p. illus. 24½ cm. (From the Historical collections of the Essex institute, vol. xxxii, 1896) 3-29503. F72. E7 E676

ESSEX institute, Act of incorporation, constitution and by-laws of the.   Salem, W. Ives and G. W. Pease, print., 1855.   24 p. 24 cm.   1-12159. F72. E7 E68

ESSEX institute, By-laws of the.   (Salem) 1876.   8 p. 23½ cm.   1-12160. F72. E7 E69

— Charter and by-laws.   Salem, 1889.   25 p. 24½ cm.   2-658-M2. F72. E7 E692

— Charter and by-laws, 1899.   14 p. 19½ cm.   8-32759. F72. E7 E695

— Annual report.   1898/99 - 10 Salem, Mass., The Institute, 1899 -   v. plates, ports., plans, facsim. 23½ cm.   10-22921 (rev. '33) F72. E7 E75

— Proceedings.   v. 1-6, 1848-1868.   Salem, Mass., 1856-70.   6 v. illus., plates, fold. tab. 23½ cm.
An index is included in "A rough subject index to the pubs. of the Essex institute" (F72. E7E811)   1-23964. F72. E7 E76

— Report of the horticultural exhibition, held in Salem ... 1850.   (Salem, 1850?)   18 p. 24½ cm.
(With its Proceedings.   Salem, 1856) 1-12163. F72. E7 E76

— The Naturalists' directory.   pt. I - II.   North America and the West Indies.   Salem, Pub. by the

MASSACHUSETTS

Essex institute, 1865.   20 ½ cm.   4-2774-5.

F72.E7 E76

— Bulletin of the Essex institute.   v. 1-30.   Salem, Mass., 1870 - 98.   30 v. in 29. illus., plates (partly col.) 24 cm. No more pub. 7-15634.

F72.E7 E77

— Historical collections. v. 1 -   Apr. 1859 -   Salem.   illus., plates, ports., maps, facsims., geneal. tables. 22-25 cm. Indexes: Vols.1-40, 1859-1904. 1 v. Subject index. Vols. 1-67, 1859-1931. 1 v... 6-18417 rev 2*.   F72.E7 E81

— A rough subject index to the publications of the Essex institute: Proceedings, v.1-6; Bulletin, v.1-22; Historical collections, v.1-27. By Gardner M. Jones. (From the Historical collections of the Essex institute, vol. xxvii) (Salem, Mass., 1890?)   29 p. 25 cm. 2-14845.

F72.E7E811
Microfilm 8763 F

— Catalogue of negatives in the Essex institute collections.   Salem, Mass., 1925.   (121) p. 28 ½ cm. 25-19999.

F72.E7 E82

— Catalogue of portraits in the Essex institute, Salem, Mass., covering three centuries; with an introd. by Henry Wilder Foote.   Salem, Mass., The Essex institute, 1936.   2, iii-xii p., 306 p. front., ports. 24 cm. Includes biographical sketch on the subject of each portrait. 37-1852.

F72.E7E825
G. R. & B.

— Commemoration of the semi-centennial anniversary of the historical department of the Essex institute ...   (Salem) Salem press (1871)   4 p. 8°. Programme. 1-12161-M1.

F72.E7 E83

— An historical notice of the Essex institute.   Act of incorporation, constitution and by-laws ... Salem, Print. by the Institute, 1865.   44 p. 25 ½ cm. 1-12162.

F72.E7 E85

— The Essex institute, treasure house of American beginnings.   Salem, Mass., 1929.   29, (3) p. illus. (incl. ports., facsims.) 25 cm. 43-49257.

F72.E7 E85
1929

— The first half century of the Essex institute, commemorated at Salem ... 1898 ... Salem, Mass., The Salem press, 1898.   100 p. front., illus. 22 ½ cm. 8-27438.

F72.E7 E89

— Miscellaneous matter published by the Essex Institute is classified in:

F72.E7E899

ESSEX COUNTY, The story of, editor-in-chief, Claude M. Fuess ... compiled by Scott H. Paradise ... New York, American historical society, inc. (1935)   4 v. fronts., illus., pl., ports. 27 cm. Vols. 1-2 include bibliographies; v.3-4 contain biographical material. 36-644.

F72.E7 F83

ESSEX COUNTY. ... Family genealogies; Lucie Marion Gardner, A.B., editor ... (Browning-Buffington. Salem, Mass., 1909) -   1 no. 26 ½ cm. A continuation of the Genealogical dictionary of Essex County families, ... in the Essex antiquarian. Reprinted from the Mass. magazine, Oct. 1909.

F72.E7 G15

ESSEX COUNTY.   Romance & reality of the Puritan coast; with many little picturings authentic or fanciful, by Edmund H. Garrett.   Boston, Little, Brown, 1897.   221 p. incl. front., illus., plates. 19 ½ cm. 1-12169.

F72.E7 G2

ESSEX COUNTY. ... The north shore of Massachusetts, by Robert Grant; illus. by W.T.Smedley. New York, C. Scribner's son, 1896.   4, 63 p. incl. front., illus., plates, map. 18 ½ cm. (American summer resorts) 1-12170.

F72.E7 G7

SAUGUS RIVER.   Semi-historical rambles among the eighteenth-century places along Saugus River. By Nathan M. Hawkes.   Salem, Mass., Salem press pub., 1889.   35 p. 24 ½ cm. 2-29747.

F72.E7 H3

ESSEX COUNTY.   The north shore of Massachusetts bay.   A guide and history of Marblehead, Salem neck and Juniper point, Beverly, and Cape Ann.   By Benjamin D. Hill and Winfield S. Nevins.   Salem,

Mass., Print. at the Salem press, 1879.   (72) p. illus. 16½ cm. 1-12166.   F72. E7 H6

— An illustrated guide to Marblehead, Salem, Peabody, Beverly, Machester=by-the-sea, Magnolia, Gloucester, Rockport. and Ipswich.   4th ed. Salem, Mass., 1881.   144 p. illus., fold. map. 20 x 11 ½ cm. 1-12167.   F72. E7 H64

— Salem, Mass., Salem press ... 1890.   103 p. front. (fold. map) illus. 18½ cm. 1-12168.   F72. E7 H66

ESSEX COUNTY, History of, with biographical sketches of many of its pioneers and prominent men. Comp. under the supervision of D. Hamilton Hurd ... Philadelphia, J.W. Lewis, 1888.   2 v. illus., plates. ports., double map. 27½ cm. 1-12171.   F72. E7 H9

CAPE ANN: Cape America, by Herbert A. Kenny.   With line drawings by Tom O'Hara.   (1st ed.) Philadelphia, Lippincott (1971)   viii, 294 p. illus. map. 70-141904.   F72. E7 K4

CAPE ANN.   Pigeon Cove and vicinity.   By Henry C. Leonard.   Boston, F.A. Searle, 1873. viii, 193 p. incl. front., illus. 18 cm. 1-12142.   F72. E7 L5

ESSEX COUNTY.   ... The North Shore review; "Old colonial days" number ... (Marblehead, Mass.) Pub. in the interest of the Marblehead his. soc., 1915.   (84) p. illus. 31 cm. 16-3944.
F72. E7 M3

ESSEX COUNTY ... records.   Massachusetts (Colony) Probate court.   24½ cm.   F72. E7 M4

ESSEX COUNTY, The probate records of, 1635 -   Salem, Mass., The Essex institute, 1916 -
   v. 23½ cm. 17-25753.   F72. E7 M42

ESSEX COUNTY, Records and files of the quarterly courts of.   Salem, Mass., Essex institute, 1911 - 1921.   8 v. 23½ cm. Another transcript of the earlier part of this material was printed in the Essex antiquarian, v. 3-13.   12-951 Rev. 2
F72. E7 M44

ESSEX COUNTY.   Mount Everett reservation commission.   ... Annual report.   1908 - 1910. Boston, 1910 -   1 v. 23 cm. 10-33192.   F72. E7 M55

ESSEX Institute.   New England treasure of American beginnings: Essex Institute.   By Walter McIntosh Merrill.   New York, Newcomen Soc. in North America, 1957.   28 p. illus. 23 cm. 58-3993.
F72. E7 M6

ESSEX memorial, The, for 1836: embracing a register of the county.   By James R. Newhall.   Salem (Mass.) H. Whipple, 1836.   vii, (9) - 281 p. front. (fold. map) 17½ cm. 1-12172.   F72. E7 N5

ESSEX COUNTY.   The North shore.   (Portland, Me., 1903)   20 x 25 cm.   F72. E7 N8

ESSEX COUNTY, Partial list of revolutionary soldiers in ...   (n.p.) 1898.   23 cm.
F72. E7 P3

ESSEX COUNTY, The Indian land titles of.   By Sidney Perley.   Salem, Mass., Essex book and print club, 1912.   6, 3-144 p. front. (double map) 3 pl. port., 10 facsim. 22½ cm. 13-1821.   F72. E7 P4

ESSEX COUNTY.   Whittier-land; a handbook of North Essex, containing many anecdotes of and poems by John Greenleaf Whittier never before collected, by Samuel T. Pickard ... Boston and New York, Houghton, Mifflin, 1904.   xi, 160 p. front., illus., double pl., double map. 19 cm. 4-10894.   F72. E7 P6

CAPE ANN, Pleasure drives around.   Gloucester, Mass., Procter brothers (1896)   95, (5) p. front., illus., plates. 19½ cm. 19-4145.   F72. E7 P7

ESSEX COUNTY, The part taken by in the organization and settlement of the Northwest territory.   Reprinted from Historical collections, Essex Institute, vol. xxv, 1888.   Salem, Mass., Salem press, 1889.   72 p. illus. 24½ cm. A coll. of extracts from letters, speeches, and other sources. 3-20626 Additions.   F72. E7 R2

MASSACHUSETTS

CAPE ANN. Tragabigzanda; or, Cape Ann, an informer; the romance, legend, and history of Cape Ann, past and present, written and illus. by F. J. G. Robinson. (Boston, The Progressive print) 1935. 32 p. illus. 21 ½ cm. 35-15261.   F72. E7 R6

ESSEX COUNTY. The romantic shore, by Agnes Edwards (pseud. for Agnes Edwards Rothery) Salem, Mass., The Salem press co., 1915. vii, 202 p. illus. 20 cm. 16-1741 Rev.   F72. E7 R8

CAPE ANN. ... Champlain and his landings at cape Ann, 1605, 1606, by Marshall H. Saville ... Worcester, Mass., The Society, 1934. 25 p. 24 ½ cm. Reprinted from the Proceedings of the American antiquarian society, Oct. 1933. 35-23538.   F72. E7 S3

ESSEX institute. To-day: a paper printed during the fair of the Essex institute and Oratorio society, at Salem, Mass. ... 1870. 40 p. 29 cm. 4-2745.   F72. E7 T6

ESSEX COUNTY, Standard history of, embracing a history of the county from its first settlement to the present time .... The most historic county of America. By Cyrus Mason Tracy. Boston, C. F. Jewett, 1878. 424 p. front., port., map. fol. Ed. by H. Wheatland. 1-12173-M1.   E72. E7 T7

ESSEX COUNTY. Views of the north shore. A collection of 25 photogravure views of gems of the north Massachusetts coast. Boston, C. B. Webster, 1889. 4 p. 25 pl. 17 ½ x 24 cm. 1-12174.   E72. E7 V6

IPSWICH RIVER, its bridges, wharves and industries, by Thomas Franklin Waters. (Salem, Mass.) Print. for the Society, 1923. 40 p. 4 pl. 24 ½ cm. (Publications of the Ipswich historical society, xxiv) 24-24854.   F72. E7 W25

ESSEX institute. The Weal-reaf. A record of the Essex institute fair, held at Salem ... 1860. 8 nos. illus. 8°. 1-5855.   F72. E7 W3
    Rare Book Coll.

CAPE ANN. In and around Cape Ann: a hand-book of Gloucester, Mass., and its immediate vicinity. For the wheelman tourist and the summer visitor, by John S. Webber, jr. ... Gloucester, Mass., Print. Cape Ann advertiser, 1885. (5) - 97 p. front., plates. 17 ½ x 14 cm. 1-12143.   F72. E7 W4

ESSEX institute. Henry Wheatland; ... founder of the Essex institute ... (A memorial. Salem, 1893) 77 p. front. (port.) 23 cm. 10-30403.   F72. E7 W5

FRANKLIN, Hampden and Hampshire counties business directory ... 19 Worcester, Mass., F. S. Blanchard, 19 - v. maps. 19 ½ cm. 34-15334.   Directories

FRANKLIN COUNTY. Suburban directory and mailing list of the following towns for 1912/13 - Buckland, Bernardston, Erving, Gill, Heath, Leyden, Millers Falls, Northfield, Shelburne, Wendell, Mass. (and many towns in Vermont and New Hampshire. (Springfield, Mass., Beaman's advertising agency) 1912. v. fold. map. 23 ½ cm. 12-4613.   Directories

FRANKLIN COUNTY suburban (Mass.) directory 1913 - for the towns of Ashfield, Bernardston, Buckland, Charlemont, Chesterfield, Colrain, Conway, Cummington, Deerfield, Erving, Gill, Goshen, Hawley, Heath, Leyden, Millers Falls, Monroe, Montague City, Montague Center, New Salem, Shelburne, Shelburne Falls, Northfield, Rowe, Sunderland, Turners Falls, Warwick, Wendell, Whatley ... Springfield, Mass., H. A. Manning co., 1913 - 1 v. 23 ½ cm. 13-7513.   Directories

FRANKLIN COUNTY. Catalogue of the relics and curiosities in Memorial hall, Deerfield, Mass., collected by the Pocomtuck Valley memorial assoc. Deerfield (Mass.) The Association, 1886. 108 p. 23 cm. 1-12403.   F72. F8 P6

— 2d ed. Deerfield, The Association, 1908. 152 p. 22 ½ cm. 9-12004.   F72. F8 P65

POCUMTUCK VALLEY memorial association, History and proceedings of the. Deerfield, Pub. by the Association, 1890-1905. 4 v. 8°. 1-12404-M1.   F72. F8 P8

POCUMTUCK VALLEY memorial association, History and proceedings ... 1890 - 1898 ... Deerfield, Mass., 1901.   22½ cm.   specimen page.   F72. F8 P82

POCUMTUCK VALLEY memorial association, A guide to the museum of the. By George Sheldon. With original illus. by Frances S. and Mary E. Allen.   Deerfield (Greenfield, Mass., T. Morey & son, print.) 1908.   3-61 p. incl. front., illus., plates, port., facsims. 19½ cm. 37-20763.   F72. F8 P87

FRANKLIN COUNTY. Picturesque Franklin (Mass.) 1891.   Ed. Charles Forbes Warner.   (Northampton, Wade, Warner, 1891)   123 p. incl. front., illus. 34 x 28 cm. 1-12175 Rev.   F72. F8 W2

HAMPDEN County.   ... Atlas of the boundaries of the city of Holyoke and towns of Agawam, Blandford, Chester, Granville, Montgomery, Russell, Southwick, Tolland, Westfield, West Springfield, Hampden County; city of Northampton and towns of Chesterfield, Easthampton, Goshen, Hatfield, Huntington, Southampton, Westhampton, Williamsburg, Worthington, Hampshire County; Whately, Franklin County ... (Boston?) 1914.   78 p. incl. maps. 52½ x 43 cm. 16-4328.   F72. H 2

HAMPDEN County. The Springfield suburban directory for the towns of Agawam, East Longmeadow, Hampden, Longmeadow, Ludlow, Southwick, Wilbraham ... no. 1 -   Springfield, Mass., The Price & Lee co., 1896 - 19 -   v. 24 cm. 1-31060.   Directories

HAMPDEN County directory, The ... a complete index to the mercantile, manufacturing and professional interests of the county ... 18 -   Boston, Briggs & co., 18   v. 23 cm.
CA 33-854 unrev.   Directories

HAMPSHIRE County. An address, delivered in the new court house, in Springfield, Hampden County, at the dedication of the same ... 1874, containing sketches of the early history of the old county of Hampshire, etc. By William G. Bates. Springfield, Mass., C. W. Bryan, print., 1874.   96 p. front., 2 pl. 24 cm. 1-12176 Rev.   F72. H2 B2

HAMPDEN County. Biographical review. This volume contains biographical sketches of the leading citizens of Hampden County ... Boston, Biographical review pub. co., 1895.   9-1138 p. incl. ports. plates (ports.) 29 cm. 1-2491.   F72. H2 B4

HAMPDEN County. "Our county and its people;" a history of Hampden County; ed: Alfred Minot Copeland ... (Boston) The Century memorial pub. co., 1902.   3 v. illus. 26 cm. 2-25938* Cancel.   F72. H2 C7

HAMPDEN County, 1636 - 1936, by Clifton Johnson ... New York, The American historical soc., inc., 1936.   3 v. fronts., illus. (incl. map) pl., ports. 27½ cm. Vols. 1-2 paged continuously. Vol. 3, biographical.   37-8791.
F72. H2 J 6

HAMPDEN County. Picturesque Hampden. 1500 illustrations. By Charles Forbes Warner. Northampton, Mass., Picturesque pub. co. (1891)   2 v. fronts., illus. (incl. ports.) 33½ cm. Contents. - pt. I. Springfield and the eastern half of the county. - pt. II, Holyoke and the western half of the county. 1-12177 Rev. 2   F72. H2 W2

HAMPSHIRE County.   ... Atlas of the boundaries of the cities of Chicopee and Springfield and towns of Brimfield, East Longmeadow, Hampden, Holland, Longmeadow, Ludlow, Monson, Palmer, Wales, Wilbraham, Hampden County; Belchertown, Granby, South Hadley, Ware, Hampshire County; Brookfield, North Brookfield, Southbridge, Sturbridge, Warren, West Brookfield, Worcester County ... 1912. (Boston? 1912)   (73) p. incl. tables. maps. 52½ cm. 12-33440.   F72. H 3

HAMPSHIRE County. Northampton suburban Massachusetts directory for the towns of Hatfield, Hadley, Williamsburg, Haydenville, Conway, Chesterfield, Cummington, Goshen, Sunderland, Leverett, Southampton, Westhampton, Whately, Deerfield, South Deerfield ... Springfield, Mass., H. A. Manning co.,   v. fold. map. 24 cm. 12-24184.   Directories

HAMPSHIRE County. Biographical review; this volume contains biographical sketches of the leading citizens of Hampshire County ... Boston, Biographical review pub. co., 1896.   (9) - 580 p. incl. ports. ports. 29 x 23½ cm. (Atlantic states series of biographical reviews. vol. xi) 13-5711.   F72. H3 B6

MASSACHUSETTS

HAMPSHIRE COUNTY. Things that I remember at ninety-five, by Mrs. Olive Cleaveland Clarke. (n.p.) 1881. 14 p. 19½ cm. Reminiscences of life in Hampshire County. 23-6161. F72. H3 C6

MT. HOLYOKE hand-book, The, and tourists' guide for Northampton, and its vicinity ... Northampton, Mass., Hopkins, Bridgman & co., 1851. 72 p. 24° 1-12178-M1. F72. H 3 E2

MILL RIVER. A full and graphic account of the terrible Mill River disaster, caused by the breaking of a reservoir in Hampshire County, May 16, 1874. ... Springfield, Mass., Weaver Shipman, print., 1874. 48 p. incl. 2 port. 3 pl. 22½ cm. 3-19166. F72. H3 F9

HAMPSHIRE County, ... Gazetteer of, 1654-1887. Comp. and ed. by W.B. Gay ... Syracuse, N.Y., W.B. Gay (1886) 2 v. in 1. front., illus., ports. 24 cm. Includes biographical and genealogical sketches. 1-13352 Rev. F72. H3 G2

HAMPSHIRE history, The, celebrating 300 years of Hampshire County. Comp. by the Tercentenary Editorial Committee: Lawrence E. Wickander and others. Northampton, Hampshire County Commission, 1964. xiv, 364 p. F72. H3 H35

MOUNT HOLYOKE and vicinity. Historical and descriptive ... By Clifford C. Johnson. Northampton, Mass., Gazette print., 1887. 32 p. front., illus. sq. 12°. 1-12179-M1. F72. H3 J7

HAMPSHIRE County. Historic Hampshire in the Connecticut valley; happenings in a charming old New England county from the time of the dinosaur down to about 1900, by Clifton Johnson ... 200 illus. Springfield, Mass., Milton Bradley (1932) 4, 406 p. col. front., illus. (incl. map) 21½ cm. 32-26878. F72.H3 J 73

MOUNT TOM. Views on and about Mt. Tom and of Mt. Tom railroad. By L. D. Pelissier. Holyoke, Mass., 1912. 24½ cm. F72. H3 P3

HAMPSHIRE County. Picturesque Hampshire; a supplement to the quarter-centennial (edition of the Hampshire County) journal. By Charles Forbes Warner. Northampton, Mass. (Wade, Warner & co.) 1890. 112 p. incl. front., illus. 33½ x 28 cm. 3-26852 Rev. F72. H3 W2

MARTHA'S VINEYARD. ... Two sites on Martha's vineyard, by Douglas S. Byers and Frederick Johnson. Andover, Mass., Phillips academy, The Foundation, 1940. viii, 104 p. illus., plates. 25 cm. Bibliography: p. 103-104. 40-30738. F72. M5
E78. M4 B9

MARTHA'S VINEYARD. Thomas Mayhew, patriarch to the Indians (1593-1682) The life of the worshipful governor and chief magistrate of the island of Martha's Vineyard; ... By Lloyd C. M. Hare ... New York, London, D. Appleton, 1932. xii, 231 p. front. (geneal. tab.) plates, maps. 29 cm. Short bibliography included in the preface. 32-10945. F72. M5
F67. M 526

MARTHA'S VINEYARD. A brief narrative of the success which the Gospel hath had, among the Indians, of Martha's Vineyard ... With some remarkable curiosities, concerning the numbers, the customs, and the present circumstances of the Indians on that island. ... Boston, Print. Bartholomew Green, 1694. (Boston, 1940) facsim: 55 p. 21 cm. (Photostat Americana. Second series ... no. 119) Photostated at the Mass. historical society. 41-9479. F72. M5
E78. M4 M73

MARTHA'S VINEYARD. From off island; the story of my grandmother, by Dionis Coffin Riggs, in collaboration with Sidney Noyes Riggs. New York, London, McGraw-Hill (1940) xvi, 347 p. incl. front. plates, ports. 21 cm. Bibliography: p. 345-347. 40-7967. F72. M5
CT275. C6416R5

MARTHA'S VINEYARD. Richardson's blue book and directory of cottagers of Oak Bluffs, Martha's Vineyard. Newark, N.J., Mercantile pub. co., 19 v. 22½ cm. 22-2384.
Directories

333

MARTHA'S VINEYARD. Tales and trails of Martha's Vineyard, by Joseph C. Allen ... Boston, Little, Brown, 1938.   5, (3) - 234 p. front., plates. 19½ cm. 38-27382.   F72. M5 A6

MARTHA's VINEYARD, The history of ... By Charles Edward Banks ... Boston, G.H. Dean, 1911 - 25. 3 v. fronts., illus., plates, ports., maps, facsims. 25 cm. Contents. - v.1. General history. - v.2. Town annals. - v.3. Family genealogies, 1641-1800. 12-25264 Rev.   F72. M5 B21

— Edgartown, Dukes County Historical Society, 1966.   3 v. facsims. 25 cm.   F72. M5 B22

MARTHA'S VINEYARD, a camera impression, by Samuel Chamberlain. New York, Hastings house (1941)   73 p. front., illus. 19 x 16 cm. 67 p. of illus. 41-13769.   F72. M5 C5

MARTHA'S VINEYARD. It began with a whale; memories of Cedar Tree Neck, (by) John Tobey Daggett. (Marblehead? Mass., 1963.   113 p. 24 cm.

F72. M5D3

MARTHA'S VINEYARD, Sketches of, and other reminiscences of travel at home, etc. By an inexperienced clergyman. (Samuel Adams Devens) Boston, J. Munroe, 1838.   viii, 207 p. 18 cm.   Re-printed in part from the Christian register, 1836-37. 1-12180.   F72. M5 D4

MARTHA'S VINEYARD hurricane, 1944; photographed by Clara F. Dinsmore. (Edgartown, Mass., 1944)   (48) p. illus. 18 x 23 cm. 44-51980.   F72. M5 D5

MARTHA'S VINEYARD, a pleasant island in a summer sea, a land of old towns, new cottages, high cliffs, white sails, etc. By Walter Prichard Eaton, pub. by the New York, New Haven and Hartford railroad co., etc. (New York, Press of the Kalkhoff co., 1923)   (48) p. illus., fold. col. map. 20½ cm. 24-178.   F72. M5E14

MARTHA'S VINEYARD. Photos. by Alfred Eisendstaedt. Text by Henry Beetle Hough. New York, Viking Press (1970)   70 p. illus. 23 x 25 cm. (A studio book) 71-100971.   F72. M5 E22

MARTHA'S VINEYARD: its history and advantages as a health and summer resort. By G.W. Eldrige ... Providence, R.I., E. L. Freeman, print., 1889.   60 p. front., plates, maps. 24½ cm. 1-12181.

F72. M5 E3

MARTHA'S VINEYARD, Fifty glimpses of ... Chicago and N.Y. (1827)   16½ x 22½ cm.

F72. M5 F4

MARTHA'S VINEYARD, Fishing and vacation guide to. 1948 -   (Boston) Salt Water Sportsman.
  v. illus. 29 cm. 49-53675*.   F72. M5 F5

MARTHA'S VINEYARD. Capawack, alias Martha's Vineyard. By Warner Foote Gookin. Edgartown (Mass.) Dukes County Historical Soc., 1947.   58 p. 24 cm. Appeared first in the Vineyard Gazette in 1946. Bibliography and notes: p. 46-58. 48-14457*.   F72. M5 G55

MARTHA'S VINEYARD, A greeting from. Indelible photographs. Woonsocket, R. I., J. N. Chamberlain, 1894.   15 pl. (1 double) 13 x 18½ cm. 1-12182.   F72. M5 G6

— Cottage city, Mass., J. N. Chamberlian, 1896.   15 pl. (1 fold.) 13 x 18 cm. 1-12183.   F72. M5 G7

MARTHA'S VINEYARD, The history of Cedar Neck (Martha's Vineyard) set to words by C.G. Hine. (n.p.) Priv. print., 1907.   viii, 104 p. 21 x 17½ cm. 15-28183.

F72. M5 H59

MARTHA'S VINEYARD, The story of, from the lips of its inhabitants, newspaper files and those who have visited its shores ... collected and arranged by C.G. Hine and illus. C.G. and Thos. A. Hine. New York, Hine bros. (1908)   v, 224 p. front., illus., double map. 19½ x 16 cm. 8-17711.   F72. M5 H6

MARTHA'S VINEYARD. Singing in the morning, and other essays about Martha's Vineyard. By Henry Beetle Hough. Illus. Will Huntington. New York, Simon and Schuster, 1951.   xii, 242 p. illus. 24 cm. 51-5144.   F72. M5 H67

MASSACHUSETTS 105

MARTHA'S VINEYARD. A funeral sermon delivered in the meeting house at Holmes's Harbour, Martha's Vineyard, Nov. 1, 1795. Occasioned by the death of Mr. John Holmes ... By David Leonard. Boston: Print. Manning and Loring. 1795. 23 p. 21½ cm. 19-8792.
F72. M5 H7
Rare Book Coll.

MARTHA'S VINEYARD, summer resort, 1835-1935, by Henry Beetle Hough ... Rutland, Vt., The Tuttle pub. co., (1936) 276 p. front., plates, plans. 24 cm. 36-16899. F72. M5 H74

MARTHA'S VINEYARD, An introduction to, and a guided tour of the island. By Gale Huntington. (Oak Bluffs) Martha's Vineyard print., 1969. vii, 133 p. illus. 23 cm. 78-87904. F72. M5 H8

MARTHA'S VINEYARD. The Mayhew Manor of Tisbury; address ... by Ida M. Wightman under the supervision of Charles Edward Banks. Baltimore, 1921. 36 p. illus., ports. 24 cm. (Order of Colonial Lords of Manors in America. Publications, no. 10) Bibliographical footnotes. 54-49293. F72. M5 M3

MARTHA'S VINEYARD and its attractions ... New York, G. W. Richardson (1914?) 40 p. illus. 34½ x 27 cm. 15-16225. F72. M5 M5

MARTHA'S VINEYARD, historical, legendary, scenic, by Henry Franklin Norton. (Hartford, Conn., H. F. Norton, R. E. Pyne, 1923) (7) - 94 p. illus. (incl. map) 25½ cm. 23-13530. F72. M5 N8

MARTHA'S VINEYARD and Nantucket, A guide to. By Richard Luce Pease. With a directory of the Cottage City. Boston, Rockwell & Churchill, print., 1876. 82 p. front. (fold. map) illus., mounted phot. 13½ x 17 cm. 1-12184 Rev. F72. M5 P3

MARTHA'S VINEYARD. An island summer. By Walter Magnes Teller. Illus. Donald McKay. (1st ed.) New York, Knopf, 1951. 221 p. illus. 22 cm. 51-3316. F72. M5 T4

MARTHA'S VINEYARD, Visitor's guide to. ... Vineyard Grove, Mass., Packard, Stedman, 1876. 14 p. map. 16°. 1-12185-M1. F72. M5 V8

MERRIMAC River. Up and down the Merrimac. A vacation trip. By Pliny Steele Boyd. Boston, D. Lothrop (1879) vi, 7-185 p. front., plates. 18 cm. (Idle hour series) 1-12186. F72. M6 B8

MERRIMAC River. The poetry of the Merrimac and the coast, by Louis Kinney Harlow. Illus. Louis K. Harlow. Boston, L. Prang, 1893. 7 col. pl., 3 port. 18 x 27 cm. 18-6169.
F72. M6 H2

MERRIMAC Valley. The Historical and genealogical researches and recorder of passing events of Merrimack Valley. Being a repository of antiquities relating to the history, biography, genealogy, heraldry, etc. etc. of the Merrimack Valley ... v. 1, no. 1-2. Haverhill, A. Poor (1857-58) (9) - 300 p. illus., pl., ports. 38½ cm. No more pub. 1-12188 Additions. F72.
F72. M6 H5

MERRIMACK, The. By Raymond Peckham Holden. Illus. Aaron Kessler. New York, Rinehart, (1958) 306 p. illus. 21 cm. (Rivers of America) Includes bibliography. 58-10701. F72. M6 H6
L. H. & G.

MERRIMACK River, ... The exploration of, 1638, by order of the General court of Massachusetts, with a plan of the same. Communicated by J. Kimball. (Salem, Mass., 1878) 153-171 p. map. * 8°. From Essex institute. Historical collections, v. 14, no. 3. 1-21397-M1. F72. M6 K4

MERRIMACK River, The; its source and its tributaries. Embracing a history of manufactures, and of the towns along its course ... By J. W. Meader. Boston, B. B. Russell, 1869. viii, 9-307 p. front. (fold. map) 23½ cm. 1-12187. F72. M6 M4

MERRIMACK Valley, "The People's guide" of the. (1930) 1 v. F72. M6 P41

335

MERRIMACK River, Report on the alterations in the channel of. By William Prescott. (Concord, N.H., 1863)   10 p. fold. map. 8°. 2-5696.   F72. M6 P9

MIDDLESEX County. Biographical review ... Containing life sketches of leading citizens of Middlesex County ... Boston, Biographical review pub. co., 1898.   2, (9) - 838 p. incl. ports. 29 x 24 cm. (Atlantic states series of biographical reviews) vol. xxviii. 8-9829 Revised.   F72. M7 B6

MIDDLESEX County. Beneath old roof trees, by Abram English Brown ... Boston, Lee and Shepard, 1896.   2, vii-xiii, 343 p. front., illus., plates. 19 cm. (Footprints of the patriots) 1-16074.   F72. M7 B67

MIDDLESEX County. ... Beside old hearth-stones, by Abram English Brown ... Boston, Lee and Shepard, 1897.   xvii, 367 p. incl. front., illus. plates, facsims. (1 fold.) 19 cm. 1-16075.   F72. M7 B7

MIDDLESEX County. An historic tour; a pilgrimage to the birthplace of American liberty, and the homes of our foremost authors. By John J. Busch. Pub. ... for Busch's auto tours. Boston, Hudson print., (1913)   38, (2) p. illus. 18½ cm. 13-17087.   F72. M7 B9

MIDDLESEX County, A geography of, for young children ... By J.G. Carter and W.H. Brooks. Cambridge (Mass.) Hilliard and Brown, 1830.   106 p. front., pl., maps. 24°. 1-12189-M1.   F72. M7 C3

MIDDLESEX County and its people; a history, by Edwin P. Conklin ... New York, Lewis historical pub. co., 1927.   4 v. fronts., plates, ports. 27½ cm. Vols. 3-4 contain biographical material. 28-11086.   F72. M7 C7

MIDDLESEX County. Historic homes and places and genealogical and personal memoirs relating to the families of Middlesex County ... prepared under the editorial supervision of William Richard Cutter ... New York, Lewis historical pub. co., 1908.   4 v. fronts., illus., plates, ports. 26 cm. 8-27628.   F72. M7 C9

MIDDLESEX County, History of, containing carefully prepared histories of every city and town in the county, by well-known writers .... By Samuel Adams Drake ... Boston, Estes and Lauriat, 1880.   2 v. fronts., illus. (incl. plans) plates, ports., double map. 29½ cm. 1-12190.   F72. M7 D6
    Microfilm 21863 F

MIDDLESEX, Historic fields and mansions of. By Samuel Adams Drake ... Boston, J.R. Osgood, 1874.   xiv, 442 p. front., illus., plates, fold. map. 20½ cm. 1-15956.   F72. M7 D7

MIDDLESEX County. Historic mansions and highways around Boston, by Samuel Adams Drake. Rev. ed. Rutland, Vt., C.E. Tuttle (1971)   xx, 440 p. illus. 18 cm. (Tut books) 73-157256.   F72. M7 D7 1971

MIDDLESEX, Old landmarks and historic fields of. By Samuel Adams Drake ... Boston, Roberts bros., 1876.   xiv, 442 p. front. (fold. map) illus. 21 cm. Previously pub. under title: Historic fields and mansions of Middlesex. 1-15957 Revised.   F72. M7 D8

— (3d ed.) Boston, Roberts bros., 1895.   xiv, 442 p. front., illus. 18½ cm. 20-23597.   F72. M7 D83

MIDDLESEX County. Historic mansions and highways around Boston. Being a new and rev. ed. of "Old landmarks and historic fields of Middlesex." By Samuel Adams Drake ... Boston, Little, Brown, 1899.   xvi, 440 p. front., illus., plates, fold. map. 20 cm. 99-5063 Rev.   F72. M7 D9

MIDDLESEX County. Ancient Middlesex with brief biographical sketches of the men who have served the country officially since its settlement. By Levi S. Gould. (Somerville, Mass.) Somerville journal print, 1905.   3, (5) - 336 p. incl. illus., ports., facsims. 25½ cm. 5-32125.   F72. M7 G8

MIDDLESEX County, History of, with biographical sketches of many of its pioneers and prominent men. ... By Duane Hamilton Hurd. Philadelphia, J.W. Lewis, 1890.   3 v. pl., port., map, facsim. 4°. 1-12191-M1.   F72. M7 H9

MIDDLESEX County. Boy scouts hikes in Greater Boston; a dozen of each, a preliminary manual of

MASSACHUSETTS 107

walks, covering field, historical and industrial features, particularly adapted to the needs of Boy scouts of the Greater Boston federation ... Boston, The Hikes manual committee, 1919. 48 p. fold. front., maps. 16½ cm. 19-14294. F72. M7 M4

MIDDLESEX County. Index to the Probate records of the county of Middlesex ... Cambridge, Mass., 1914, '12. 3 v. in 2. 37 x 30 cm. Contents: vol. I, A to K; vol. II, L to Z. Covers period 1684 to 1910. 15-23618 Revised. F72. M7 M55

MIDDLESEX County. Dedicatory exercises at the new Registry of deeds and probate building, Cambridge, Mass. ... 1900. (Cambridge, Mass., 1900) 31 numb. l. incl. pl. 23 cm. 7-34356. F72. M7 M68

MIDDLESEX County manual. Lowell, Mass. Penhallow print., 1878. (7) - 92, (95) - 110, (117) - 144 p. 20 cm. 7-21487. F72. M7 M7

CONCORD River, by Laurence Eaton Richardson. With photos. of Katharine Knowles. Barre, Mass., Barre Publishers, 1964. 73 p. 23 cm. 64-14908. F72. M7 R5

CONCORD River. A week on the Concord and Merrimack Rivers. By Henry David Thoreau. Boston, Houghton, Mifflin, 1961. xli, 435 p. 21 cm. (Sentry edition, 1) F72. M7 T5 1961

— Decorated by Clare Leighton. New York, Crowell (1961) 492 p. 21 cm. F72. M7 T5 1961a

— Ed. with introd. and notes by Walter Harding. New York, Holt, Rinehart (1963) xxiii, 340 p. 63-7886. F72. M7 T5 1963

CONCORD and the Merrimack, The; excerpts from A week on the Concord and Merrimack Rivers. Arranged with notes by Dudley C. Lunt; illus. by Henry Bugbee Kane. (1st ed.) Boston, Little, Brown (1954) xiv, 268 p. illus., maps. 22 cm. 54-11126. F72. M7 T52

CONCORD and Merrimack Rivers. A word-index to A week on the Concord and Merrimack rivers. By James Karabatsos. Hartford, (Conn.) Transcendental Books (1971) 99 l. illus. 29 cm. 79-31438 MARC. F72. M7T534 1971

MIDDLESEX County. Interim report of the Boston National Historic Sites Commission pertaining to the Lexington-Concord Battle Road. Washington, U.S. Govt. Print. Off., 1959. x, 151 p. illus., maps, plans. 24 cm. (86th Cong., 1st sess. House Doc. no. 57) Includes bibliography. 59-60798. F72. M7 U5

NANTUCKET. Briefe eines amerikanischen landmanns an den ritter W. S. in den jahren 1770 bis 1781. ... By Michel Guillaume St. Jean de Crèvecoeur, called Saint John de Crèvecoeur. Leipzig, S. L. Crusius, 1788-89. 3 v. fold. pl. 19 cm. Orig. pub. in London, 1782 with title: Letters from an American farmer. 12-1826. F72. N F163. C 994

NANTUCKET. Letters from an American farmer, describing certain provincial situations, manners, customs, etc. Written to a friend in England by J. Hector St. John ... (Michel Guillaume St. Jean de Crèvecoeur) Philadelphia, press of Mathew Carey, 1793. viii, (9) - 240 p. 17 cm. First ed. London, 1782. 2-6755. F72. N E163. C95

— Lettres d'un cultivateur américain ... Paris, Cuchet, 1787. 3 v. fronts. etc. 20 cm. Greatly enlarged from the edition of 1784. 2-6752 Additions. F72. N E163. C99

— Lettres d'un cultivateur américain ... Paris, Cuchet, 1784. 2 v. 20 cm. A free translation, by the author, of "Letters from an American farmer," with large additions. 2-6753. F72. N E163. C97

337

NANTUCKET.   A nest of love disturbed; or, The farmer's dialogue, for Nantucket, 1811.   Boston, Print. J. Belcher, 1811.   15 p.   22 cm.   18-18276.   F72. N2
AC 901. B3 vol. 56

NANTUCKET.   The resident and business directory of Nantucket ... and map of Nantucket.   1909 - (v. 1 -   Boston, Boston suburban book co., 1909 -   1 v. fold. map. 24½ cm. 9-23774.
Directories

NANTUCKET directory, The ... Boston, Union pub. co.   v. 24 cm. 19-16556.   Directories

NANTUCKET.   Lothrop's Nantucket blue book and directory 1927.   1 v.   F72. N2 A18
1927

NANTUCKET scraps: being the experiences of an off-islander, in season and out of season, among a passing people, by Jane G. Austin.   Boston, J. R. Osgood and co., 1883.   vi, 354 p. 17½ cm. 12-30466.
F72. N2 A9

NANTUCKET landfall; By Dorothy C. Blanchard.   illus. William Barss.   New York, Dodd, Mead, 1956.   241 p. illus. 21 cm. Includes bibliography. 56-6648.   F72. N2 B55

NANTUCKET.   Quaint Nantucket ... By William Root Bliss ... Boston and New York, Houghton, Mifflin, 1896.   vi, 225 p. 8° 1-12192-M1.   F72. N2 B6

NANTUCKET.   September days on Nantucket, by William Root Bliss.   Boston and New York, Houghton, Mifflin, 1902.   5, 145 p. 20 cm. 2-16101.   F72. N2 B7

NANTUCKET.   ... Island Nantucket, by C. F. Brooks ... (New York, 1917)   197-207. illus. (map, tables, diagrs.) 25½ cm. Reprinted from the Geographical review, vol. iv, no. 3, Sept. 1917. 18-2261.   F72. N2 B87

NANTUCKET, a camera impression, by Samuel Chamberlain.   New York, Hastings house (1939)
73 p. front., illus. 19 x 15½ cm. 69 p. of illustrations. 39-24399.   F72. N2 C45

NANTUCKET Island, The old house on.   In two parts.   By Ida Gardner Coffin.   ... New York, C. Francis press, 1905.   xii, (13) - 128 p. front., 6 pl. 2 port. 20 cm. 5-27065.   F72. N2 C6

NANTUCKET.   Historical notes of the island of Nantucket, and tourist's guide.   By R. Cook.   Nantucket, 1871.   23 p. 24°. 1-12193-M1.   F72. N2 C7

NANTUCKET.   Books and baskets, signs and silver of old-time Nantucket (by) Everett U. Crosby. (Nantucket, Mass., Print. by the Inquirer and mirror press, 1940)   2, (7) - 72 p. illus. (incl. facsims.) 23½ cm. 40-32706.   F72. N2 C76

NANTUCKET in print (by) Everett U. Crosby.   (Nantucket, Mass., Tetaukimmo press, 1946)
225 p. incl. facsims. pl., fold. maps. 23½ cm. Check lists of writings about Nantucket: p. 159 - 212. 46-6881.   F72. N2 C79

NANTUCKET.   Ninety five per cent perfect.   Nantucket's changing prosperity, future probabilities. The spoon primer.   Silversmiths of old-time Nantucket.   Nantucket's underground moon.   By Everett Uberto Crosby.   (Nantucket, Mass., Tetaukimmo Press, 1953)   214 p. illus. 24 cm. 53-31334.
F72. N2C798

NANTUCKET.   "95% perfect"; the older residences at Nantucket, viewed and analyzed by Everett U. Crosby.   (Nantucket, Mass., Print. by the Inquirer and mirror press, 1937)   75 p. incl. front., illus. (map) plates. 23½ cm. 37-16670.   F72. N2 C8

NANTUCKET; a history, by R. A. Douglas-Lithgow .... with illus. and a map.   New York and London, G. P. Putnam's sons, 1914.   xiii, 389 p. front., plates, ports., fold. map. 23½ cm. Bibliography p. xi-xii. 14-12350.
F72. N2 D73

NANTUCKET, Churches and pastors of, from the first settlement to the present time.   1659 - 1902. By Rev. Myron Samuel Dudley ... Boston, D. Clapp, 1902.   21 p. front. 24 cm. 2-23880.   F72. N2 D8

MASSACHUSETTS 109

NANTUCKET centennial celebration, 1695, 1795, 1895; historic sites and historic buildings. Comp. by Myron Samuel Dudley. Nantucket, R.B. Hussey, print., 1895. 23 p. 25 cm. 4-7004.
F72.N2 D84

NANTUCKET. An island patchwork, by Eleanor Early, illus. Virginia Grilley. Boston, Houghton, Mifflin, 1941. vii, 289 p. illus. 21 cm. 41-8389.
F72. N2 E3

NANTUCKET. Brief historical data and memories of my boyhood days in Nantucket, by Joseph E.C. Farnham. (Providence, Snow & Farnham co., 1915.) xvi, 242 p. front., illus., plates, ports., map, fold. facsim. 24 cm. "Family record": p. (240) - 242. 19-3485.
F72. N2 F2

NANTUCKET. Fifty glimpses of Nantucket island from recent photographs. Boston, J.F. Murphy (1897) 46 p. illus. obl. 16°. 1-12194-M1.
F72. N2 F4

NANTUCKET. The glacier's gift, with fourteen illustrations, by Eva C. G. Folger. New Haven, Conn., The Tuttle, Morehouse & Taylor co., 1911. 5, 145 p. front., plates, port. 21½ cm. 11-19626.
F72.N2 F56

NANTUCKET, Handbook of, containing a brief historical sketch of the island, with notes of interest to summer visitors. By Isaac H. Folger. Nantucket, "Island review" office, 1874. 91 p. map. 15 cm. 1-12195.
F72. N2 F6

— 1875. 97 p. front. (map) 15 cm. 1-12196.
F72. N2 F7

NANTUCKET. Early Nantucket and its whale houses, by Henry Chandlee Foreman. Drawings and photos. by the author where noted. New York, Hastings House (1966) ix, 291 p. 26 cm. 66-18350.
F72.N2 F75

NANTUCKET. A grandfather for Benjamin Franklin; the true story of a Nantucket pioneer and his mates, by Florence Bennett Anderson. Boston, Meador pub. co., 1940. 462 p. front., illus., plates, maps (1 fold.) 20½ cm. Bibliography: p. 457-460. 40-30612.
F72. N2 F8

NANTUCKET. A Nantucket ghost walks again - over the teacups. By Edward G. Freehafer. New York, The New York public library, 1940. 20 p. 25½ cm. A 41-664.
F72.N2 F83

NANTUCKET. A list of the wrecks around Nantucket since the settlement of the island, and the incidents connected therewith, embracing over 500 vessels. Comp. by Arthur H. Gardner. Nantucket, A.H. Gardner, 1877. 63 p. front. (map) 23 cm. 9-30372.
F72. N2 G2

NANTUCKET. Wrecks around Nantucket since the settlement of the island, and the incidents connected therewith, embracing over 700 vessels. Comp. by Arthur H. Gardner. Nantucket, The Inquirer and mirror press (1915) 149 p. incl. front. plates, fold. map. 23 cm. Rev. ed. of F72.N2G2. 15-14086.
F72.N2 G22

NANTUCKET. The triumphant Captain John, and Gardners and Gardiners; twelve colonial founders of families. By William Edwards Gardner. Nantucket, Whaling Museum Pubs. (1958) 104 p. illus. 22 cm. Includes bibliography. 58-40201.
F72.N2 G23

NANTUCKET. Innside Nantucket. By Frank Bunker Gilbreth. Illus, Donald McKay. New York, Crowell (1954) 231 p. illus. 21 cm. 54-9159.
F72. N2 G4

NANTUCKET. Of whales and women; one man's view of Nantucket history. By Frank Bunker Gilbreth. New York, Crowell (1956) 242 p. illus. 21 cm. Includes bibliography. 56-10602.
F72.N2 G43

NANTUCKET, The island of, what it was and what it is; being a complete index and guide to this noted resort ... Comp. by Edward K. Godfrey. Boston, Lee and Shepard; New York, C.T. Dillingham, 1882. vi, 365 p. 2 fold. maps (incl. front.) 17 cm. 1-12197.
F72. N2 G5

NANTUCKET odyssey; a journey into the history of Nantucket. By Emil Frederick Guba. Waltham, Mass., 1951. 157 p. illus. 22 cm. 55-40217.
F72. N2 G8

— 2d ed. rev. and enl. Waltham, Mass., 1965. ix, 438 p. illus. 23 cm. F72. N2 G8 1965

NANTUCKET. The heart of Siasconset. By Rev. Phebe A. Hanaford ... New Haven, Conn., Press of Hoggson & Robinson, 1890. viii, (9) - 180 p. incl. front. (map) illus. 18 x 14½ cm. 16-9469 Rev. F72.N2 H23

NANTUCKET, Early settlers of; their associates and descendants; comp. by Lydia S. Hinchman. Philadelphia, Print. J. B. Lippincott, 1896. 158 p. 21 cm. 1-12198 Rev. F72. N2 H6

— 2d and enl. ed.) Philadelphia, Ferris & Leach, 1901. 8, 347 p. front., illus., plates, ports., fold. plan, geneal. tab., facsim. 24½ cm. 2-1765 Rev. F72.N2 H61

— illus. with photographs and drawings by Margaretta S. Hinchman. Philadelphia, W. A. Henry press, 1926. 8, 330 p. front., illus., plates, ports., etc., geneal. tables. 24 cm. Third edition. 35-9784. F72.N2 H63

— Philadelphia, Wellington print., 1934. 8, 330 p. front., illus., plates, ports., fold. plan, geneal. tables. facsim. 24 cm. Fourth edition. 35-9788. F72.N2 H64
Rare Book Coll.

NANTUCKET. Historic Nantucket. v. 1 - Nantucket, Mass., Nantucket Historical Assoc. v. in illus., ports. 23 cm. semiannual. 56-35099. F72.N2 H68

NANTUCKET. "The sanctuary of our fathers." A centennial discourse, preached ... By Rev. S. D. Hosmer ... Nantucket, Hussey & Robinson, print., 1865. 16 p. 23 cm. 12-11194.
F72.N2 H78

NANTUCKET, Papers relating to the island of, with documents relating to the original settlement of that island, Martha's Vineyard and other islands adjacent ... By Franklin B. Hough ... Albany, (J. Munsell) 1856. xviii, 162 p. incl. facsims., coat of arms. fold. map. 22 x 17 cm. Papers dated 1641-1692. Dukes county was set off from N. Y. to Mass. 1695 and Nantucket was detached from Dukes County the same year to form a separate county. 1-12199. F72. N2 H8
Rare Book Coll.

NANTUCKET. Talks about old Nantucket, by Christopher Coffin Hussey. (n.p., 1901) 70 p. 4 pl. 2 port. (incl. front.) 18 x 15 cm. 13-22170. F72.N2 H97

NANTUCKET. The Inquirier and mirror. Centennial number. Nantucket, Mass., 1921.
(84) p. illus. 36 cm. Issued as a supplement to the regular edition of June 25, 1921. 21-15116. F72. N2 I58

NANTUCKET. William Rotch of Nantucket, by Augustine Jones. Philadelphia, The American Friend pub. co., 1901. 30 p. incl. front., ports. 16½ cm. From the American Friend, 1901. 4-3235. F72. N2 J 6

NANTUCKET. Miniatures, Nantucket, Mass. By Thomas Wallace Jones. (Cincinnati, Ohio, 1905) 8 x 10½ cm. F72. N2 J 7

NANTUCKET brevities; a glimpse of the environment. By Harold H. Kynett, (Philadelphia) 1966. 128 p. 26 cm. F72.N2 K85

NANTUCKET. On-islanders and off-islanders; both look at Nantucket, by Harold H. Kynett. (Philadelphia, Print. E. Stern Majestic Press) 1971. 200 p. illus. 26 cm. 77-31274 MARC.
F72.N2K855

NANTUCKET. The pervasive spirit; an off-islander views Nantucket. By Harold H. Kynett with photographic aid from Charles Sayles. (Philadelphia, Print. E. Stern Majestic Press) 1968. 161 p. illus. 26 cm. F72.N2 K86

NANTUCKET. Quaker heritage; niceties of Nantucket, by Harold H. Kynett with camera shots by the author plus photographic help from Charlie Sayle ... (Philadelphia) Priv. print. (by) the Kynetts, 1967. 168 p. 26 cm. F72.N2 K87

NANTUCKET. Unforgettable intimacies; memories for comfort. By Harold H. Kynett with help from

MASSACHUSETTS

the photos. of Charlie Sayle. (Philadelphia) 1965. 158 p. 26 cm. F72. N2 K9

NANTUCKET. Why Nantucket? questions and suggestions. Written by Harold H. Kynett. (Philadelphia) 1970. 192 p. illus. ports. F72.N2 K92

NANTUCKET, Aerial views of. By Henry Lang. (Nantucket, 1926) 16 photos. 21 x 27 ½ cm. Map laid in. CA 27-281 unrev. F72. N2 L2

NANTUCKET scrap basket, The; being a collection of characteristic stories and saying of the people of the town and island of Nantucket. Comp. and ed. and arranged by William F. Macy and Roland B. Hussey. Nantucket, The Inquirer and mirror press, 1916. 3, ix-xii, 183 p. front., plates, ports. 19 cm. 16-14477. F72.N2M217

NANTUCKET, The history of; being a compendious account of the first settlement of the island by the English, tog. with the rise and progress of the whale fishery ... By Obed Macy ... Boston, Hilliard, Gray and co., 1835. xi, 300 p. front. (map) pl. 18cm. 1-12200. F72. N2 M1

— 2d ed. Mansfield, Macy & Pratt, 1880. xiv, (17) - 313 p. front. (map) pl. 21 cm. 9-30099. F72. N2 M2

— Boston, Hilliard, Gray, 1835. New York, Research Reprints (1970) xi, 300 p. 77-124803. F72. N2 M2 1970

— 2d ed. Clifton (N.J.) A.M.Kelley, 1972 (1880) xiv, 313 p. 22 cm. 72-140546 MARC. F72. N2 M2 1972

— 2d ed. rev., expanded, and re-arranged by William F. Macy. Boston and New York, Houghton, Mifflin, 1930. x, 163 p. 17½ cm. 30-17083. F72.N2M217 1930

NANTUCKET'S oldest house (1686) "The Jethro Coffin house", "The Horseshoe house", written and compiled for the Nantucket historical association by William F. Macy ... Nantucket, The Inquirer and mirror press, 1929. 35 p. front., plates. 20½ cm. 29-16009. F72.N2M218

NANTUCKET, The story of old; a brief history of the island and its people from its discovery down to the present day, by William F. Macy. Nantucket, The Inquirer and mirror press, 1915. vii, 108 p. front. (map) plates. 19½ cm. 15-14548. F72.N2 M22

NANTUCKET. The story of old Nantucket; a brief history of the island and its people from its discovery down to the present day, by William F. Macy ... 2d ed., rev. and enl. ... Boston and New York, Houghton Mifflin co., 1928. xi p. 2 l. 190 p. front., plates. 17 cm. 28-12814. F72.N2 M22 1928

NANTUCKET. Magnificent island; a Nantucket pictorial essay. Photos by Louis S. Davidson (and others) Ed. James F. Crowley. (n.p., 1968, c.1966) 1 v. (chiefly illus.) 31 cm. 68-3049. F72.N2 M24 1968

NANTUCKET, Vital records of, to the year 1850 ... Boston, The New England historic genealogical soc ... 1925-28. 5 v. 23½ cm. (New England historic genealogical soc. Vital records of the towns of Mass. Alphabetical indexes to the records of the town, supplemented by ... church registers, cemetery inscriptions, etc. 25-27172. F72.N2N126

NANTUCKET, The. ... Nantucket, 1885. 14 x 16 cm. F72. N2 N15

NANTUCKET Historical Association. Proceedings. 1st - annual meeting; 1895 - Nantucket, Mass. v. in illus. 24 cm. Indexes: vols. 51-55, 1945-49. 1 v, 7-40922 rev.* F72. N2 N16

— ... Bulletin. Nantucket, 1896 - 2 v. and 1 no. F72. N2 N2

— Quakerism on Nantucket since 1800, by Henry Barnard Worth. 1896. 38 p. 23 cm. (Nantucket historical assoc. Bulletin v.1, no. 1. 4-18873.

— ... Timothy White papers, 1725 - 1755. Introd. by Myron Samuel Dudley. 1898. 96 p. Bulletin v.1 no. 2. 1-12405.

— ... Nantucket lands and landowners, by Henry Barnard Worth. 1901-13. 335, xxiv, (337) - 419, xiv p. Bulletin, v.2 no. 1-7. 4-17892 rev.

— ... A century of Free masonry in Nantucket, by Alexander Starbuck. 1903. 44 p. Bulletin vol. 3, no. 1. 10-14025.

— The Nantucket Whaling Museum. 1959. 42 p. Bulletin no. 2, vol. 4.

NANTUCKET historical association, Centennial catalogue of the. Nantucket, Inquirer and mirror press, 1895. 27 p. 24 cm. 40-16147. F72.N2N236

NANTUCKET historical association, Constitution and by-laws of the. (Inquirer and mirror print) 1894. 19 p. 15½ cm. 24-7453. F72. N2 N24

NANTUCKET historical association. The 1800 house; an exhibit. (Nantucket, 1968) 23 p. illus. 23 cm. F72.N2 N25

NANTUCKET, illustrated. Copyright ... by A. Wittemann ... New York, The Albertype co., 1888. 15 pl. 12 x 17 cm. 1-12201 Rev. F72. N2 N3

NANTUCKET. 'Sconset cottage life: a summer on Nantucket Island. By A. Judd Northrup. New York, Baker, Pratt & co., 1881. vii, (9) - 160 p. 17½ cm. 1-11627. F72. N2 N7

— 2d ed. Syracuse, N.Y., C.W. Bardeen, 1901. ix, 11-160 p. illus. (map) plates. 17½ cm. 1-23743. F72. N2 N8

NANTUCKET. Through the hawse-hole; the true story of a Nantucket whaling captain (by) Florence Bennett Anderson. New York, The Macmillan co., 1932. ix, 276 p. front., plates, ports., facsims. 22½ cm. 32-19470 Rev. F72. N2 P7

NANTUCKET, Guide to ... By John Henry Robinson. (Washington, D.C.) 1905. 22 x 18 cm.
F72. N2 R6 1905

— 2d ed. (n.p.) 1910. 40 p. illus., fold. map. "Books relating to Nantucket" p. 40. 21½ cm.
F72. N2 R6 1910

— 3d ed. (Washington, National capital press) 1918. 64 p. illus., fold. map. 21½ cm. 18-13474.
F72. N2 R6 1918

— 5th ed. (Washington, D.C., National capital press) 1928. 63 p. illus., maps. 21½ cm. Books relating to Nantucket: p. 63. 28-30242. F72. N2 R6

— 7th ed. (Nantucket?) 1948. 71 p. illus., fold. col. maps. 22 cm. 49-13189*. F72. N2 R6 1948

NANTUCKET, 106 views of. By John Henry Robinson. (Washington, D.C.) 1911. 18 x 24 cm.
F72.N2 R65

NANTUCKET. Memorandum written by William Rotch in the 80th year of his age. Boston and New York, Houghton Mifflin, 1916. xi, 88 p. front., plates, ports. 21 cm. 16-14478.
F72.N2 R84

NANTUCKET. The old Nantucket gaol; an exhibit of the Nantucket Historical Association (by Edouard A. Stackpole. Nantucket, 1968. 15 p. 23 cm. F72.N2 S68

MASSACHUSETTS 113

NANTUCKET. The history of Nantucket, county, island and town, including genealogies of first settlers, by Alexander Starbuck ... Boston, C. E. Goodspeed, 1924. 871 p. incl. front., illus., tables. 4 fold. maps. 23½ cm. Genealogy: p. 653-832. 25-12525. F72. N2 S7

— Rutland, Vt., C. E. Tuttle (1969) viii, 871 p. illus. 24 cm. 69-13507. F72. N2 S7 1969

NANTUCKET. Three Bricks and Three Brothers; the story of the Nantucket whale-oil merchant, Joseph Starbuck, by Will Gardner. Cambridge, (Mass.) Print. at the Riverside press, 1945. xi, 113 p. illus. (incl. facsims.) plates, ports. 21 cm. (Whaling museum. Publications) 46-1801. F72.N2S734

NANTUCKET. My house and I; a chronicle of Nantucket, by Mary Eliza Starbuck ... Boston and New York, Houghton Mifflin, 1929. 1 4 p. 293 p. front., plates, ports., facsim. 21½ cm. 29-17671. F72. N2 S75

NANTUCKET, the far-away island, by William Oliver Stevens; illus. by the author. New York, Dodd, Mead, 1936. xi, 313 p. col. front., illus. 22½ cm. Maps. 36-9547. F72.N2 S77

NANTUCKET. The first Nantucket tea party; illus., decorated and illuminated by Walter Tittle. New York, Doubleday, Page & co. (1907) (82) p. col. front., col. illus. 15 col. plates. 26 cm. 7-38632. F72. N2 T6

NANTUCKET. The tourist's guide to Nantucket and Martha's Vineyard. A sketch of these famous watering places; their attractions, drives and places of amusement ... (Boston) J. F. Murphy (1902) 153 p. illus., fold. maps. 15 cm. 24-14336. F72. N2 T7

NANTUCKET. Argument settlers; what has happened on and around Nantucket. A compilation of facts and events connected with the history of Nantucket from its discovery to the present day. (Nantucket, The Inquirer and mirror press, 1917) 61 p. 16 cm. 17-20182 Rev. "Copyright by Harry B. Turner." F72. N2 T8

— (2d ed.) 1920. (5) - 76 p. 15½ cm. 20-9731 Rev. F72.N2 T82

— (5th ed.) 1936. 120 p. 18½ cm. 37-12558. F72.N2T825

NANTUCKET."argument settlers"; a complete history of Nantucket in condensed form. Who? When? What? Where? (Nantucket, The Inquirer and mirror press, 1944) 115 p. plates. 21 cm. 6th ed. 44-32303. F72.N2T825 1944

NANTUCKET: old and new. By Henry Sherman Wyer. Centennial ed. Nantucket, H. S. Wyer, 1895. 4 l. 16 pl. 14½ x 21 cm. 20-2086. F72.N2 W89

NANTUCKET, picturesque and historic. Nantucket, H. S. Wyer, 1901. (14) p. 53 pl. obl. 8°. 1-23948-M1 Oct. 31. F72. N2 W9

NANTUCKET. Sea-girt Nantucket; a hand-book of historical and contemporaneous information for visitors ... Comp. and pub. by Henry S. Wyer. Nantucket, H. S. Wyer, 1902. 204 p. front., illus. pl., fold. map. 17 cm. 2-17872. F72.N2 W93

— 2d ed. Nantucket, H. S. Wyer, 1906. 207 p. front., illus., plates, fold. map. 17 cm. 6-34284. F72.N2 W94

NANTUCKET. Spun-yarn from old Nantucket; consisting mainly of extracts from books now out of print, with a few additions. Ed. and pub. by H. S. Wyer. Nantucket, The Inquirer and mirror press, 1914. 311 p. front., illus., plates, group of ports. 20 cm. 14-10890 Rev. F72. N2 W95

NOMAN'S LAND; isle of romance, by Annie M. Wood. New Bedford, Mass., Reynolds print., 1931. 166, (2) p. incl. front., illus. plates, ports., map. 23½ cm. 32-2324. F72. N6 W8

NORFOLK County. ... Anthony's standard business directory and reference book of Attleboro,

No. Attleboro, Wrentham, Franklin, Medway, Millis, Dedham, Medfield, Foxboro, Sharon, Canton, Stoughton, Easton, Avon, Holbrook, Randolph, Massachusetts ... (1900-01) (Attleboro, Mass.) F. A. Folsom, 1900.   168 p. 23½ cm. Nov. 8, 1900-07 Additions.   Directories

NORFOLK and Plymouth counties business directory ... 190   Worcester, Mass., F. S. Blanchard, 190   v. maps. 20 cm. CA 33-721 Unrev.   Directories

NORFOLK County. Biographical review ... containing life sketches of leading citizens of Norfolk County ... Boston, Biographical review pub. co., 1898.   2, (9) - 710 p. incl. ports. port. 29 x 23½ cm. (Atlantic states series of biographical reviews vol. xxv) 8-16772.   F72. N8 B6

NORFOLK County, History of, 1622 - 1918. Louis A. Cook, supervising ed. ... New York, Chicago, The S. J. Clarke pub. co., 1918.   2 v. plates, ports. 28 cm. Vol. 2 contains biographical sketches. 20-6642.   F72. N8 C7

NORFOLK County manual, and year book for 1876. Comp., prepared and pub. by Henry O. Hildreth. Dedham, Mass., 1877.   2, 156 p. 23 cm. 9-33913.   F72. N8 H6

NORFOLK County, History of, with biographical sketches of many of its pioneers and prominent men. Comp. under the supervision of D. Hamilton Hurd. Philadelphia, J. W. Lewis, 1884.   xii, 1001 p., plates, ports., double map, facsims. 28 cm. 1-12202.   F72. N8 H9

NORFOLK Couny, Probate index, 1793 - 1900. Dedham, Mass., Transcript press, 1910. 2 v. 25 cm. 10-24499 Rev.   F72. N8 M45

NORFOLK County. The Court house investigation. Comments of the County commissioners and portions of the arguments of Messrs, T. E. Grover, and R. M. Morse; with the report of the account ... Dedham, Mass., Transcript steam job print., 1896.   85 p. 22½ cm. 10-5398.   F72. N8 N8

PLUM ISLAND. By T. F. Waters. Ipswich, Mass., 1918.   1 v.   F72. P6 W2

PLYMOUTH and Bristol counties register, The ... Boston, Union pub. co., 18   v. 24 cm. Title varies. 99-2026 Rev.   Directories

PLYMOUTH and Barnstable counties, General business directory of ... Boston, Dean Dudley 1879 - 1 v. 23½ cm.   Directories

PLYMOUTH County. Biographical review ... containing life sketches of leading citizens of Plymouth County ... Boston, Biographical review pub. co., 1897.   638 p. incl. ports. 29 x 23½ cm. (Atlantic states series of biographical reviews vol. xviii) 16-13907.   F72. P7 B6

PLYMOUTH County. History of shipbuilding on North River, Plymouth County, with genealogies of the shipbuilders, and accounts of the industries upon its tributaries. 1640 to 1872. By L. Vernon Briggs ... Boston, Coburn bros., print., 1889.   xv, 420 p. incl. illus., facsims. front., plates, ports., maps. 24 cm. 1-12203.   F72. P7 B8

— New York, Research Reprints (1970)   xv, 420 p. illus. 74-124805.   F72. P7 B8 1970

PLYMOUTH and Barnstable counties ... Directory and history of, for 1873-4. Containing a history and register, and alphabetical list of the professions, etc. Boston, D. Dudley, 1873.   xx, 206(i. e. 248) p. illus., fold. map. 24 cm. 17-3098.   F72. P7D77

PLYMOUTH and Barnstable counties, Historical sketches of towns in. Boston, D. Dudley & co., 1873. p. (77) - 150, 150a - 150z, 150aa - 150pp. incl. facsims. 23 cm. Reprinted from his "Directory and history of Plymouth and Barnstable counties ..." 1873. 13-5116.   F72. P7 D8

PLYMOUTH County. The variety book containing life sketches and reminiscences, by Lewis Ford. Boston, "Washington press": ... 1892.   243 p. 23½ cm. 9-9710.   F72. P7 F
   HN57. F8

MASSACHUSETTS

PLYMOUTH County. The Pilgrim shore, by Edmund H. Garrett ... Boston, Little, Brown, 1900. 234 p. incl. col. front., illus., plates. 19½ cm. Contents. - Preface. - Dorchester. - Neponset. - Quincy. - Weymouth. - Hingham. - Hull. - Cohasset. - Scituate. - Marshfield. - Duxbury. - Kingston. - Plymouth. 0-6779 Rev.
F72. P7 G3

PLYMOUTH County, History of, with biographical sketches of many of its pioneers and prominent men. Comp. under the supervision of D. Hamilton Hurd ... Philadelphia, J.W. Lewis, 1884. viii, 1199 p. plates, ports., map. facsim. 28 cm. L.C. copy replaced by microfilm. 1-12204.
F72. P7 H9
Microfilm 8876 F

PLYMOUTH County. Indian names of places in Plymouth, Middleborough, Lakeville and Carver, with interpretations of some of them, by Lincoln Newton Kinnicutt. Worcester, Mass. (The Commonwealth press) 1909. 64 p. 24 cm. 10-25100.
F72. P7 K6

PLYMOUTH, An address to the citizens of the county of. (n.p., 1812) 8 p. 23½ cm. Opposing the war with Great Britain. 5-4362* Cancel.
F72. P7 P
E357.6. P73

PLYMOUTH County. Historic sketches of Hanson, Lakeville, Mattapoisett, Middleboro', Pembroke, Plympton, Rochester, Wareham, and West Bridgewater. By Ebenezer Weaver Peirce ... Boston, Mass., The author, 1873. 2, 75 p. illus. 24½ cm. 16-23650.
F72. P7 P37

PLYMOUTH County directory, and historical register of the Old Colony, containing an historical sketch of the county, and of each town in the county ... an alphabetical list of the voters, etc. Middleboro, Mass., S.B. Pratt, 1867. 9-160, 148, 92 p. front. (fold. map) illus., plates. 24 cm. 17-20622.
F72. P7 P76
or Directories

PLYMOUTH County marriages, 1692 - 1746, literally transcribed ... reprinted from vols. 1 and 2 of "The Genealogical advertiser," 1898-1899. Cambridge, Mass., L.H. Greenlaw, 1900. 48 p. 25 cm. In the Genealogical advertiser, 1900 v. 3, p. 49-54, is pub. a continuation of the records here repr. from the earlier vol. 8-29769.
F72. P7 P78

PLYMOUTH County. The old Coast road from Boston to Plymouth, by Agnes Edwards (pseud. for Agnes Edwards Rothery) with illus. by Louis H. Ruyl. Boston and N.Y., Houghton Mifflin, 1920. xxix, 203 p. incl. front., illus. plates. 21 cm. 20-26574.
F72. P7 R84

PLYMOUTH County. South Shore light. (Scituate, Mass.) v. in illus., ports. 31 cm. irreg. 49-32284*.
F72. P7 S6

PLYMOUTH County. History of Plymouth, Norfolk and Barnstable counties; author, Elroy S. Thompson ... New York, Lewis historical pub. co., 1928. 3 v. fronts., plates, ports., facsims. 27½ cm. Vol. 3 contains biographical material. 29-7212.
F72. P7 T5

PLYMOUTH Harbor, Early explorers of, 1525 - 1619, by Henry F. Howe. Plymouth, Plimoth Plantation, 1953. 30 p. 21 cm.
F72. P73 H68

SUFFOLK County. Early recorders and registers of deeds for the county of Suffolk. 1639 - 1735. By John T. Hassam. Cambridge, W. Wilson, 1898. 52 p. illus. (facsims.) 24½ cm. Reprinted from the Proceedings of the Mass. historical soc. for May, 1898. 1-12205.
F72. S9 H3

SUFFOLK County. Registers of deeds for the county of Suffolk. 1735 - 1900. By John T. Hassam. Cambridge, J. Wilson, 1900. 75 p. 24½ cm. Continuation of the author's Early recorders and registers of deeds for the county of Suffolk. Reprinted from the Proceedings of the Mass. hist. soc. for March, 1900. 2-22064.
F72. S9 H31

SUFFOLK County. Registers of probate for the county of Suffolk. 1639 - 1799. By John T. Hassam. Cambridge, J. Wilson, 1902. 107 p. 24½ cm. Reprinted from the Proceedings of the Mass. historical soc. for March 1902. 2-27755.
F72. S9 H35

SUFFOLK wills, Index to ... 1881. 24½ cm.
F72. S9 I 3

SUFFOLK, Index to the Probate records of the county of. ... 1636 to ... 1893. Prepared under the supervision of Elijah George ... Boston, Rockwell and Churchill, print., 1895. 3 v. 35½ x 28 cm. The original Suffolk County of 1643 was of vast extent. Norfolk County and parts of Plymouth and Worcester counties were formerly in Suffolk. 10-31054 Rev. 2
F72. S9 M45

SUFFOLK, Essex and Middlesex Counties. Where to go. How to get there. A guide book to places historic and beautiful, in Suffolk, Essex and Middlesex counties ... By W. T. Preston. Lynn, Mass., T. P. Nichols, 1894.   116 p. 16º 1-12206-M1.   F72. S9 P8

SUFFOLK County, Professional and industrial history of. ...(Boston) The Boston history company, 1894.   3 v. 225 port. (incl. fronts.) 26 cm. 4-1373.   F72. S9 P9

SUFFOLK County ... The book of possessions. (2d ed.) (Boston, Rockwell and Churchill, print., 1881)   xi, 137 p. incl. plans. fold. plan. 23½ cm. (In Boston, Registry dept. Records relating to the early history of Boston ... 2d ed. v. 2 pt. II) A descriptive list of real estate in Boston, 1645-1648 under names of owners ... 1-13878. Add.   F72. S9 S8

SUFFOLK County. Suffolk deeds. liber I -   (1629 -   Boston, 1880 - 19   v. facsims. 24 cm. 14-11888.   F72. S9 S9

SWIFT River Valley. Quabbin reservoir; memories of conditions that existed in the Swift and Ware river valleys while Quabbin reservoir was being developed, by Walter E. Clark. New York, N. Y., The Hobson book press, 1946.   2, vii-viii p., 272 p. plates. 21½ cm. Reproduced from type-written copy. 46-5099.   F72. S94 C5

SWIFT River Valley. Ghost towns 'neath Quabbin reservoir, by Evelina Gustafson. Boston, Norwood, Amity press, 1940.   5, 13-125 p. incl. front., illus., plates. pl. 20½ cm. 40-13301.   F72. S94 G8

SWIFT River Valley. Quabbin, the lost valley; By Donald W. Howe. ed. by Roger Nye Lincoln. Sketches by Elizabeth Howe Lincoln. Ware, Mass., Quabbin Book House, 1951.   xviii, 631 p. illus., ports. 26 cm. 51-14976.   F72. S94 H6

WACHUSETT, Mount. Annual report. Wachusett Mountain state reservation commission. Boston, v. 23½ cm. 10-33197.   F72. W12 M4

WENHAM great pond, by John C. Phillips. Salem, Peabody museum, 1938.   xii, 108, (2) p. illus. (incl. map) plates. 26 cm. 38-36017.   F72. W5 P5

WORCESTER County. Proceedings of a convention of delegates from forty one towns, in the county of Worcester ... 1812. Print. at Worcester, by Isaac Sturtevant, 1812.   21 p. 22½ cm. 18-14430.
   F72. W9
   E257. 6. F29

WORCESTER County. The great powwow; the story of the Nashaway valley in King Philip's war, by Clara Endicott Sears ... Boston and New York, Houghton Mifflin, 1934.   x, 288 p. front., illus., plates, port. 19½ cm. 34-5940.
   F72. W9
   E83. 67. S42

WORCESTER County. Addresses before the members of the bar, of Worcester County, Mass. ... Worcester, Press of C. Hamilton, 1879.   ix, (9) - 250 p. 3 port. (incl. front.) 25 cm. 6-14428.
   F72. W9
   Law

WORCESTER County. ... Anthony's standard business directory. (1902 - 1903) Representing the progressive up-to-date business firms, of selected towns in Worcester and Middlesex counties, who want your trade ... (Natick, Mass.) Anthony pub. co., 1902 -   23½ cm.   Directories

WORCESTER County business directory for 1903 -   Worcester, Mass., F. S. Blanchard, 1 v. illus. (map) 19½ cm. 8-27419.   Directories

WORCESTER County directory, The for (1866, 1868, 1870, 1872, 1874, 1876, 1878, 1880, 1881, 1883, 1885, 1887, 1888 ... Boston, Briggs & co. (1866) - 88.   13 v. 23½ cm. 8-14403.   Directories

WORCESTER County register, The ... 1890/91 -   Boston, Union pub. co., 1890 - v. 24½ cm. 99-1233 Rev.   Directories

MASSACHUSETTS

WORCESTER suburban directory, The for the towns of Auburn, Boylston, Grafton, Holden, Leicester, Millbury, Paxton, Shrewsbury and West Boylston ... v. 1 -   Worcester, Mass., New England directory co., 1896 -   v. illus. 23½ cm. 0-2485 Rev.   Directories

WORCESTER County. Suburban directory and mailing list of Hampden, Franklin and Worcester counties, for 1912/13 -   including ... Barre, Belchertown, Brimfield, Enfield, Erving, Greenwich, Hardwick, Leverett, Ludlow, Monson, New Braintree, New Salem, No. Dana, Pelham, Petersham, Philipston, Prescott, Richmond, N.H., Royalston, Shutesbury, Templeton (including Brooks Village, Baldwinville, East Templeton, Otter River), Wales, Warren, Warwick, Wendell, West Brookfield, West Warren, Wilbraham ... Springfield, Mass., Beaman's advertising agency, 1912 -   v. front. (fold. map) 24 cm. 12-15730.   Directories

WORCESTER County. The Fitchburg suburban directory, embracing the towns of Ashburnham, Ashby, Hubbardston, Lunenberg, Princeton, Sterling, Templeton, Westminster ...   Boston, The A.E. Foss co., 1918.   v. 24 cm. 18-20404.   Directories

WORCESTER County. Greater Worcester directory; Auburn, Berlin, Boylston. 1919. Salem, Mass., The Salem press co.   v. 23½ cm. 19-10819.   Directories

WORCESTER County. Reminiscences of the Rev. George Allen, of Worcester. With a biographical sketch and notes by Franklin P. Rice. Worcester, Mass., Putnam and Davis, 1883.   127 p. front. (port.) 23½ cm. 6-45837.   F72. W9 A4

WORCESTER County. Historical collections. By Holmes Ammidown ... New York, Pub. by the author, 1874.   2 v. fronts., ports., fold. maps, fold. plan. 25 cm. 1-12001* Cancel.   F72. W9 A5

— 2d ed. New York, 1877.   2 v. ports., fold. maps. 25 cm. 56-48295.   F72. W9 A5 1877

WORCESTER County. Biographical review ... containing life sketches of leading citizens of Worcester County ... Boston, Biographical review pub. co., 1899.   2, (9) - 1229 p. incl. plates, ports. 28½ x 24½ cm. (Atlantic states series of biographical reviews vol. xxx) 11-32575.   F72. W9 B5

WORCESTER County ... warnings, 1737 - 1788. With an introduction by Francis E. Blake, and an index of surnames. Worcester, Mass., F.P. Rice, 1899.   101 p. 25½ cm. (Systematic history fund publications no. 1) Lists of those "warned" under act of 1692-3. 1-13353.   F72. W9 B6

WORCESTER County, A geography of; for young children. By James G. Carter and William H. Brooks. Lancaster, Carter, Andrews, 1830.   vii, 61 p. front., plates. 15 cm. Imperfect: map wanting. 1-12207.   F72. W9 C3

WORCESTER County. Central Massachusetts Regional Planning Commission. Historical Highlights. (Worcester) 1969.   1 v. (various pagings) 29 cm.   F72. W9 C4

WORCESTER County, Argument for the division of, on the petition of O.L. Huntley and others ... By Rufus Choate. Boston, W. White, 1854.   67 p. nar. 8°. 1-12208-M1.   F72. W9 C5

WORCESTER County. Historic homes and institutions and genealogical and personal memoirs of Worcester County, with a history of Worcester society of antiquity; prepared under the editorial supervision of Ellery Bicknell Crane ... New York, Chicago, The Lewis pub. co., 1907.   4 v. fronts., illus., plates, ports. 27½ cm. 7-38070.   F72. W9 C8

WORCESTER County, History of, supervising editor-in-chief, Ellery Bicknell Crane ...   New York and Chicago, Lewis historical pub. co., 1924.   3 v. fronts., plates, ports., coat of arms. 28 cm. Biographical sketches comprise last part of v. 2 and all of v. 3. 24-20539.   F72. W9 C83

WORCESTER County. Master minds at the commonwealth's heart, by Percy H. Epler ... Worcester, Mass., F.S. Blanchard, 1909.   6, (9) - 317 p. illus., plates, ports. 20½ cm. Contents. - Artemas Ward. - Eli Whitney. - Elias Howe. - Wm. Morton. - Dorothy Dix. - Clara Barton. - Geo. Bancroft. - John Gough. - Geo. Hoar. - Luther Burbank. 9-32377.   F72. W9 E6

WORCESTER County, Pleasure resorts in, and how to reach them. Containing descriptive sketch of Lake Quinsigamond and its environs, with other popular places for the summer excursionist. By Edward Rice Fiske. Worcester, E. R. Fiske, 1877.   62 p. illus. 17 cm. 1-12209.

F72. W9 F5

WORCESTER County, History of, embracing a comprehensive history of the county from its first settlement to the present time ... Boston, C. F. Jewett, 1879.   2 v. fronts., plates, map. 26½ cm. 1-12408.

F72. W9 H6

WORCESTER County, History of, with biographicl sketches of many of its pioneers and prominent men. Comp. under the supervision of D. Hamilton Hurd ... Philadelphia, J. W. Lewis, 1889.   2 v. illus., pl., ports., double map. 28 cm. 1-12210.

F72. W9 H9

WORCESTER County. Picturesque Worcester ... Complete in three parts, with 2500 illus; by Elbridge Kingsley and Frederick Knab. Pt. 1 - 2. Springfield, Mass., The W. F. Adams co., 1895.   2 v. fronts. (1 col.) illus. 33 x 28 cm. (Picturesque series) No. more pub. 6-13742 Rev.

F72. W9 K5

WORCESTER County, Indian names of places in, with interpretations of some of them, by Lincoln N. Kinnicutt. Worcester, Mass. (The Commonwealth press) 1905.   59 p. 24 cm. 6-36889 Rev.

F72. W9 K6

WORCESTER County. Proceedings of the senate and House of representative upon the petition of George R. M. Withington and others, praying that Hames G. Carter be removed from his office of justice of the peace for the county of Worcester ... Boston, G. C. Rand, print., 1849.   74 p. 22½ cm. 10-31050.

F72. W9 M4

WORCESTER County, Index to the probate records of the county of Worcester ... 1731 to 1920. Prepared under the supervision of George H. Harlow ... Worcester, Mass., O. B. Wood, 1898-1920.   5 v. 27½ cm. 27-11109.

F72. W9 M45

WACHUSETT Mountain state reservation commission. Annual report. 1st, 1901 - 9th, 1909. Boston, 1901 - 1908.   9 v. 23½ cm. 10-33197.

F72. W9 M5

WORCESTER County; a narrative history, by John Nelson ... New York, The American historical society, 1934.   3 v. fronts. (v. 1, 3) plates, ports. 27½ cm. Vols. 1-2 paged continuously. V. 3 biographical. 34-30691.

F72. W9 N4

WORCESTER district in Congress, The, from 1789 to 1857: a paper read before the Worcester society of antiquity. By Franklin P. Rice. 2d ed. Worcester, Mass., 1890.   21 p. 24½ cm. 42-40351.

F72. W9 R5

WORCESTER County. Address at the social festival of the bar of Worcester County. By Hon. Emory Washburn. Worcester, Print. H. J. Howland (1856)   2, (3) - 37 p. 22½ cm. 10-31051.

F72. W9 W2

WORCESTER County. Substance of the remarks of Mr. Washburn before a committee of the legislature, upon the petition of Gilman Day and others for a division of Worcester county. Worcester, Print. E. R. Fiske, 1855.   76 p. 23½ x 14 cm. 1-12211.

F72. W9 W3

WORCESTER, The history of the county of ... with a particular account of every town from its first settlement to the present time ... By Peter Whitney ... Printed at Worcester, Mass., by Isaiah Thomas ... 1793.   vi, 7-339 p. front. (fold. map) 21½ cm. 1-12212.

F72. W9 W6
Rare Book Coll.

WORCESTER County. Peter Whitney and his History of Worcester County. By John C. Crane. Worcester, Mass., F. P. Rice, 1889.   25 p. front. (port.) 24½ cm. Reprint from Proceedings of Worcester society of antiquity, 1888. 15-5293.

F72. W9 W62

WORCESTER County. An address to the members of the bar of Worcester County. By Joseph Willard. Lancaster, Carter, Andrews, print., 1830.   144 p. 23½ x 14½ cm. 1-16019.

F72. W9 W7

BOSTON   119

WORCESTER County statistical record, and military roll of hone ... the names in full of all the volunteers from Worcester County, in the service of the U. S.   Worcester, E. R. Fiske, 1862.
166 p. fold. plan. 15 cm. 4-9986.   F72.W9 W91

WORCESTER magazine and historical journal, The. v.1-2; Worcester, Mass., Rogers and Griffin print., 1826.   2 v. port. 25 cm. Semi-monthly. No more pub. 1-13354.   F72.W9 W94

WORCESTER historical society. (Circular, May 20, 1911. Worcester, 1911) (3) p. 28 x 21½ cm.
11-25755.   F72.W9 W96

WORCESTER south chronicles. A brief history of the Congregational churches of the Worcester south conference, of Mass. 1670 - 1876. Ed. by a committee of the conference. Worcester, Print. L. P. Goddard, 1877.   66 p. 23 cm. 7-34839.   F72.W9 W98

BOSTON

BOSTON. PERIODICALS. SOCIETIES. COLLECTIONS.

... RECORDS relating to the early history of Boston ...   v.1 -   1876 -
Boston, Rockwell and Churchill, city printers (etc.) 1876 -   v. plates, fold. maps, facsims. 22½ x 24 cm.
Contents include: Boston tax lists, Boston town records, Charlestown land records, Dorchester town records, Roxbury land and church records, Boston births, baptisms, marriages, deaths, Boston directory, 1789, Records of Boston selectmen, Dorchester births, marriages, and deaths, etc. 1-13355.

— 2d ed. Boston, Rockwell and Churchill, 1881 -   1-13355.   F73.1. B74

— 3d ed. Boston, Rockwell and Churchwill, 1896 -   1-13355.   F73.1. B74

... BOSTON town records ... (1631) - 1822. Boston, Municipal printing office, 1877 - 1906.
11 vols. (In records relating to the early history of Boston v. 2, 7, 8, 12, 14, 16, 18, 26, 31, 35, 37) 1-12214.   F73.1. B74

BOWDITCH, Nathaniel Ingersoll. ("Gleaner" articles) Boston, Rockwell and Churchill, print., 1887.
A series of articles relating to the history of estates lying on or around Beacon Hill, Boston; reprinted from the Boston daily transcript of 1855.
1-13870.   F73.1. B74

BOSTON year book. Boston, 1924 -   v. illus., ports., tables, diagrs. 26 cm. Issued by Statistics dept., 1924 -
25-9899.   F73.1. B75

... BOSTON history in the Boston poets. Boston, Old South meeting house (The Directors of the Old South work) 1907.   (156) p. 19 cm. (Old South leaflets. xxv. 1907) 10-25858.   F73.1. B76

BOSTON life.   F73.1.B765

BOSTON weekly-magazine, The, no. 1-3. Mar. 2-16. 1743. (1937)   1 v. (Photostat Americana. 2d series.
no. 25)   F73.1. B78

BOSTONIAN. v.1 -   1971 -   (Boston, Unitrust Pub. Co.)   v. illus., ports. 28 cm. monthly.
                                                                                                    F73.1.B 79

BOSTONIAN society. Collections of the Bostonian society. vol. 1, nos. 1-3. Boston, Old State house, 1886 - 88.   3 pts. illus., plates, ports. 25½ cm. No more pub. 5-34631.   F73.1.B 80

BOSTONIAN society, Proceedings of the, at the annual meeting ... v. 1 -   Boston, By order of the society, (1882) - 19 -   v. fronts. (part col.) illus., plates (part col.) ports., maps, facsims. 23½ x 24½ cm. 10-26200.
                                                                                                    F73.1.B 86

BOSTONIAN society ... Publications. v.1-12; 2d ser. v.1 -   v. fronts. illus., plates, ports., maps (part fold.) plans, facsims. 24½ cm. 7-18607 Rev.   F73.1.B 88

349

BOSTONIAN society. Catalogue of the collections of the Bostonian society in the memorial halls of the Old state house, Boston. Prepared by Samuel Arthur Bent, clerk of the soc. ... Boston, 1893. 91 p. 24½ cm. 3-5039.
F73.1.B89

— 2d enl. ed. Boston, 1895. 109 p. 24½ cm. 18-13581.
F73.1.B895

HISTORICAL festival Boston news-letter. v.1, no. 1 - Boston, 1897 - 1 v. facsim. 36 cm. daily (except Sunday) 38M1165T.
F73.1.H 57

MAKERS of Boston, The. Boston, Old South meeting house, 1884. (71) p. 18 cm. (Old South leaflets. II) 4-15754.
F73.1
F61.M19

NEW BOSTON; a chronicle of progress in developing a greater and finer city - under the auspices of the Boston-1915 movement. v.1-2. Boston, Boston 1915, inc., 1910-11. 2 v. in 3. illus. 25½ cm. monthly. 26-12088.
F73.1.N 52

SATURDAY club, The early years of the, 1855-1870, by Edward Waldo Emerson ... Boston and New York, Houghton Mifflin, 1918. xii, (2), 515 p. front., pl., ports. 24½ cm. 19-1503.
F73.1.S 25

— Freeport, N.Y., Books for Libraries Press (1967) xii, 515 p. 22 cm. (Essay index reprint series) 67-23211.
F73.1.S 25
1967

SATURDAY club, The; a century completed, 1920 - 1956. Ed. by Edward W. Forbes and John H. Finley, Jr. Boston, Houghton Mifflin, 1958. xix, 410 p. ports., table. 25 cm. Consists chiefly of biographical sketches. 57-13110.
F73.1.S253

SATURDAY club, Later years of the, 1870 - 1920, ed M.A. De Wolfe Howe ... Boston and New York, Houghton Mifflin, 1927. xvii, 427 p. front., ports. 24½ x 18½ cm. This volume is a successor to The early years of the Saturday club - F73.1.S25. 27-24546.
F73.1.S254

— Freeport, N.Y., Books for Libraries Press (1968) xvii, 427 p. 22 cm. (Essay index reprint series) 68-29217.
F73.1.S265
1968

SATURDAY club, the early years of the, by Thomas Lynn Johnson. Cleveland, The Rowfant club, 1921. 69 p. front. (port.) 19½ cm. (Rowfantia, an occasional publication of the Rowfant club. no. ix) 22-3522 Rev.
F73.1.S 26

VERMONT association of Boston. Report of the proceedings of the Association for ... including the annual meeting and officers for ... Boston, The Association. v. ports. 22½ cm. 24-180.
F73.1.V 52

BOSTON. GUIDEBOOKS.

AMERICAN Federation of Arts. The cultural resources of Boston. New York (1965) 134 p. 23 cm. 65-16641.
F73.18.A 4

BOSTON passport (by) Robert E. Lockwood. Cambridge, Mass., Owl Pub., 1970. 122 p.
F73.18.B67

CHESLER, Bernice. In and out of Boston with children. Barre, Mass., Barre Publishers (1966) 140 p. 23 cm. 66-14858.
F73.18.C 5

— (New enl. ed.) Barre, Mass., Barre Publishers (1969) xiv, 282 p. illus. 23 cm. 69-14581.
F73.18.C 5
1969

BOSTON

HALL, Jeanne D.   The complete guide to Boston & Cambridge.   Photos. by George M. Hall.   Ed. by Dan Langdale (and others)   Boston, Burdette (1967)   189 p. 15 cm. 67-24033.
F73.18. H3

MULTILINGUAL Travel Services.   Discover Boston.   Boston, (1971)   5 v. 18 cm.
F73.18. M 8

RUBIN, Jerome.   Comprehensive guide to Boston; a comprehensive reference to Boston's sights, pleasures and services,   (Newton, Mass., Emporium Publications, 1972.   457 p. illus. 23 cm. 72-81232.
F73.18. R 8

ULRICH, Laurel.   A beginner's Boston.   Illus. mostly by Carolyn Peters.   (Cambridge, Mass., Cambridge Ward Relief Soc? 1970)   233 p. illus. 24 cm.   "A new enlarged ed. of 'Boston's First guide book' ".
F73.18. U 4
1970

BOSTON. DIRECTORIES.

BOSTON directory, The ... including all localities within the city limits, as Allston, Brighton, Charlestown, Dorchester, Hyde Park, Roslindale, Roxbury, West Roxbury ... 1789, 1796, 1798, 1800, 1803, 1807, 1809 -   1816, 1818, 1820,   1825-19-   Boston, Sampson & Murdock co.,
1789 - 19   v. fold. maps. 15 - 28 cm. 99-4369 rev. 2.   Directories

BOSTON blue book, The ... containing ... Boston, Brookline, Cambridge, Chestnut Hill and Milton ...
(1878) - 19   Boston, Sampson and Murdock co.   v. fold. maps. 17 cm. 1-28117 (rev. 31)   Directories

CLARK's West-end blue-book.   Boston, E. E. Clark, 1872 -   v. 15 cm. CA 33-476 unrev.   Directories

"RED BOOK, The"   Or directory of the élite of Boston.   Private address and carriage directory. Ladies visiting and shopping guide (1879)   (Boston) E. E. Clark.   1 v. 17½ cm. Running title: Boston blue book.
Directories

RED BOOK, The: or, A list of addresses in the west end of Boston ... 1886 -   Boston, Cupples, Upham, and co., 1886 -   v. 16½ x 12½ cm. CA 33-578 unrev.   Directories

SOCIAL register, Boston.   New York city, Social register assoc. (18   - 19   v. 17 cm.
0-970 Rev.   Directories

PROVIDENCE and surrounding territory general classified business directory ... New York, General pub. co. of New York, 19 -   v. 23 cm. CA 36-459 unrev.   F73.24
F89. P9A184
Directories?

REFERENCE register, The; a compendium for general business reference, comprising the financial, commercial, industrial and legal interests of the cities of New York, Philadelphia, Baltimore, Boston and Newark, N.J.   New York city, White Orr & co.   v. 26 cm. 19-871 Rev.   Directories

BOSTON register and business directory ... v. 1-89; 1836 - 1926. Boston, Sampson & Murdock co., (1836) - 1926.   89 v. illus., fold. maps. 13 - 24 cm. No morepub. 10-1791 Rev.   Directories

A.B.C. shopping guide ... in Boston ...   2d ed.   Spring 1887 -   (Boston) 1887 -
v. 11½ cm.   Directories

BOSTON and surrounding territory general classified business directory ... New York, General pub. co. of New York, 19 -   v. 23 cm. 37-18226.   Directories

351

BOSTON business directory, The ... 18 -   Boston, Mass., Littlefield directory pub. co., 18
   v. fold. maps. 23½ cm. 14-3708.   Directories

BOSTON business by streets ... listing places of business in numerical order upon their respective streets ... v. 1 -   Boston, Sampson & Murdock co., 1929 -   v. 28 cm. CA 30-1107.   Directories

BOSTON business - street directory. no. 1   Boston, G. Coolidge, 1867.   v. illus. 14 cm.
   contains also, Boston and its environs, an illustrated guide. CA 33-490 unrev.   Directories

BUYERS' blue book ...   New York, The Buyer's blue book co., inc. (19 -   v. 23½ cm.
23-10769.   Directories

GREATER Boston business directory ... including Arlington, Braintree, Brookline, Cambridge, Chelsea, Dedham, Everett, Lexington, Malden, Medford, Melrose, Milton, Newton, Quincy, Revere, Somerville, Waltham, Watertown, Weymouth, Winchester, Winthrop ...   Boston, Mass., Griffith-Stillings press.   v. fold. map. 23½ cm. 14-14317.   Directories

COMPLETE business directory of Boston ... Commercial ed.   1857 -   v. 1 -   (Boston, 1857 -
   v. 23 cm.   Directories

BOSTON business directory ... New York, Puritan pub. co.   v. 18 cm. 7-26440.   Directories

BOSTON business directory, metropolitan directory ... of Boston and vicinity ... (1862/63 -
Boston, D. Dudley & co., 1862 -   v. fold. maps. 16½ x 24 cm. 20-12173.   Directories

CITY business directory (of Boston) ... 1894 -   Boston, Mass., The City business directory pub. co., (1894)   v. 24 cm.   Directories

GREATER Boston business directory ... 1914.   1 v.   Directories

DIRECTORY of the cities and towns on the line of the Boston and Providence, Taunton and New Bedford and Providence and Worcester railroads, comprising complete business directories of over 20 different cities and town, including Boston, Providence, Worcester, Taunton, New Bedford, Pawtucket, Woonsocket, Milford and many other places.   Boston, Greenough, Jones & co., 1871.   (7) - 458 p. 24 cm.
11-16717.   Directories

MERCANTILE business directory of Boston.   no. 1 -   1859 -   Boston, 1859 -
v. 13½ cm.   Directories

OFFICE building directory, Boston, 1908.   1 v.   Directories

SHARPE'S Boston business directory ... 1893 -   Boston, 18-   v. 23½ cm.   Directories

SKETCHES and business directory of Boston and its vicinity.   For 1860 and 1861.   Boston, Damrell & Moore and G. Coolidge (1860)   xiii, (9) - 522 p. front. (fold. map) illus. 27 x 21 cm. 19-7287.   Directories

TEL-U-WHERE direcionary ... Boston ed.   Spring, 1923 -   Boston, Tel-u-where co, of America (1923)   v. illus. 23 cm. 24-339.   Directories

WOMEN'S city club of Boston.   Guide to shops and service ... (Boston) Women's city club of Boston (1922 -   v. front. (map) 20½ cm. 22-24996.
                                                                                               Directories

WRIGHT, A. E.   A. E. Wright's Boston, New York, Philadelphia & Baltimore, commercial directory ...
New York & Phila., 1840 -   v. 24 cm.   Directories

BOSTON. BIOGRAPHY (COLLECTIVE). GENEALOGY (COLLECTIVE).

See also: F73.1.B74; F73.62.O4B7; F73.61.C3C6; F73.61.G7C6; F63.C99; F73.1.S25; F73.3.L27

... BOSTON births from 1700 to 1800. Boston, Rockwell & Churchill, 1894. iv, 379 p. 23½ cm.
(24th report of the Record commissioners ...) A record of Births for the period 1630 - 1699 is included in the 9th report, 1883. 1-13869 Rev.
F73.25.B74
L.H. & G.

... BOSTON births, baptisms, marriages, and deaths, 1630-1699. Boston, Rockwell and Churchill, 1883. (Record commissioners. 9th Report.) Includes also bap. records of the First church. 1-13867.
F73.25.B75
L.H. & G.

... BOSTON marriages from 1700 to 1809. Boston, Municipal printing office, 1898-1903.
2 v. 23½ cm. (Report of the Record commissioners, v.28, 30) L.C. copy replaced by microfilm. 1-13868 Additions.
F73.25.B76
Microfilm 8663 F

BOSTON, (Lists of tax-payers in the town of, 1674 - 1695) (In Records relating to the early history of Boston.) Boston, 1876. (Appendix B to the First report of the Record commissioners, 1876) 5-18364.
F73.25.B762
L.H. & G.

—— 2d ed. 1881. 5-18365.
F73.25.B763
L.H. & G.

BOSTON. At a legal meeting of the freeholders and other inhabitants of the town of Boston ... a correct list - stating the amount of real and personal estate, etc. Boston, Print. True and Greene, 1822. 9-206 p. 27½ cm. 8-23503.
F73.25.B765

BOSTONIANS as seen by Boston newspaper cartoonists. Boston, 1906. 2 p. 36 mounted pl. 29½ x 35½ cm.
14-4874.
F73.25.B78

CODMAN, Ogden. Index of obituaries in Boston newspapers 1704-1800. Boston Athenaeum. Boston, G.K. Hall, 1968. 3 v. 27 cm.
F73.25.C 6
L.H. & G.

FOXCROFT, Thomas. ... Marriages of Rev. Thomas Foxcroft. Boston, 1717-1769. Transcribed by Rev. Anson Titus ... (Boston, Print. D. Clapp, 1888) 7 p. 24½ cm. Reprinted from the N.E. hist. and genealogical register for April and July, 1888. 5-3003.
F73.25.F79

FREEMAN, James. Funeral sermons preached at Kingschapel, Boston. Boston, Print. Sewell Phelps, 1820. 68 p. 22½ cm. Concerns Mrs. Susan Bulfinch, Rev. Samuel Cary and Joseph Coolidge. 24-30206.
F73.25.F84

GLADDEN, Sanford Charles. An index to the vital records of Boston, 1630 - 1690. Boulder, Color., Print. Empire Repro. and print. Co., 1969. ii, 188 p. 27 cm.
F73.25.G55
L.H. & G.

LORING, James Spear. The hundred Boston orators appointed by the minicipal authorities and other public bodies, 1770 - 1852 .... Boston, J.P. Jewett; Cleveland, Jewett, Proctor & Worthington, 1852.
viii, 694 p. 23 cm. 5-37663.
F73.25.L74

—— 1853. viii, 720 p. 24½ cm. 19-17576.
F73.25.L74
1853

—— 1855. viii, 727, (1) 728-730 p. 24 cm. 37-31885.
F73.25.L74
1855

MEN of Boston and New England. (Boston) The Boston American, 1913. 186 p. of ports. (incl. illus.) 27½ cm.
14-15055.
F73.25.M53

MOODY, Robert Earle. Boston men and the winning of American independence; the story of America shown in the lives of some of the most illustrious men of Boston ... and illus. by portraits .... Boston, 1948. iv, 23 p. ports. 16 cm. 48-19004*. F73.25.M 7

"OUR first men": a calendar of wealth, fashion and gentility; containing a list of those persons taxed in the city of Boston, credibly reported to be worth one hundred thousand dollars, with biographical notices of the principal persons ... Boston, Pub. by all the booksellers, 1846. 48 p. 22 cm. 23-767.
F73.25.O92
Rare Book Coll.

— Rev. ed. 1846. 48 p. 22 cm. 4-29772. F73.25.O93

STATE street trust co. Forty of Boston's immortals; showing illustrations and giving a brief sketch of forty men of the past whose work would entitle them to a niche in a Boston hall of fame. Boston, Print. for the State street trust co., (1910) (44) p. illus. (ports.) 22 cm. 11-1898. F73.25.S79

STATE street trust company. Mayors of Boston; an illustrated epitome of who the mayors have been and what they have done. Boston, Print. for the State street trust co. (1914) 48 p. illus. (ports.) 23½ cm. 14-6293. F73.25.S 8

U.S. Treasury dept. Particular of sub-division list of all lands, lots, buildings and wharves, being within the town of Boston, in the assessment district no. one in the fourth division ... owned, possessed or occupied ... 1798. (In Records relating to the early history of Boston. v.22) 1-12216.
F73.25.U58

WHO'S who in Boston. Boston, (1931) 3 p., 36 numb. l. 28 cm. "Comp. by D. Pittler. 43-30544. F73.25.W67

WILSON, Thomas L. The aristocracy of Boston; who they are and what they were; being a history of the busines and business men of Boston, for the last forty years. By one who knows them. Boston, The author, 1848. 32 p. 22 cm. 6-9507. F73.25.W75

BOSTON. GENERAL WORKS. HISTORIES.

KYLE, George Alexander. The eighteen fifties; being a brief account of School street, the Province house and the Boston five cents savings bank, Boston, The Boston five cents savings bank, 1926. 5, (3) - 106 p. illus. (incl. ports., plans, facsims.) 23½ cm. 27-4397 Rev.
F73.3
HG2613.B74B65

BEEBE, Lucius Morris. Boston and the Boston legend, illus. by E.H. Suydam. New York, London, D. Appleton-Century co., 1935. xv, 372 p. col. front., illus., plates. 24 cm. 35-18402. F73.3.B44

BOSTON and its story, 1630 - 1915; a relation prepared by Edward M. Hartwell ... and others. Boston, Printing dept., 1916. 200 p. front., plates, ports., fold. map, facsim., fold. tab. 18½ cm. 17-16560.
F73.3.B 76

BOSTON town records ... (1631) - 1822. Boston, Municipal print. office, 1877-1906. 11 v. 23½ cm. (Records relating to the early history of Boston vols. 2, 7, 8, 12, 14, 16, 18, 26. 31, 35, 37) 1-12214. F73.3.B 81

BOSTON. Chamber of Commerce. Metropolitan Boston; a collection of three publications on the history and present characteristics of the region. (Boston, 1947) 36, 12, (4) p. maps. 28 cm. 48-873*.
F73.3.B812

BOSTON. City planning board. From Trimountaine to Boston. 1630. 1930. A brief history of the city of Boston, together with a statement of its commercial and industrial opportunites; its points of special interest... Comp. and ed. by Elisabeth M. Herlihy .... Boston, Print. dept., 1930. 76 p. incl. front., illus., maps. fold. pl. 18 cm. 31-19466. F73.3.B814

BOSTON. Tercentenary committee. Fifty years of Boston; a memorial volume issued in commemora-

BOSTON

tion of the tercentenary of 1930; compiled by the Subcommittee on memorial history ... (Boston, 1932) xx, 799 p. incl. front., illus., ports., maps. 28 cm. 33-726.   F73.3.B818

BOSTON. Selectmen. Selectmen's minutes, 1701 - 1822. Boston, Rockwell and Churchill, 1884 - 12 vols. (Report of the Record commissioners ... vols. 11, 13, 15, 17, 19, 20, 23, 25, 27, 33, 38, 39) 1-12215 Additions.   F73.3.B 82

BOSTON, 1630 - 1880. Boston, Rand, Avery & co., 1880. 8 p. illus. (incl. maps, facsims.) 58½ x 40 cm. Extracts from "King's Hand-book of Boston", from the "Town record, II" and from the "Boston journal". 24-30829.   F73.3.B 87

BUTTERWORTH, Hezekiah. Young folks' history of Boston. Boston, Estes and Lauriat, 1881. xii, (15) - 480 p. incl. front., illus., plates, ports., maps. double plan. 19 cm. 1-12223.   F73.3.B 98

BUTTERWORTH, Hezekiah. Popular history of Boston ... Boston, Estes and Lauriat (1894) xii, (15) - 480 p. incl. front., illus., plates, ports., maps, plan. (18½ cm. 1st pub. under previous title. 1-12224.   F73.3.B 99

CARVER, Robin. Stories about Boston, and its neighborhood. Boston, Lilly, Wait and L.C. Bowles, 1833. 3, (5) - 184 p. front., illus. 14 x 11 cm. 1-12225.   F73.3.C 33
Rare Book Coll.

CARVER, Robin. History of Boston. Boston, Lilly, Wait, Colman, and Holden, 1834. viii, (9) - 160 p. incl. illus., plates. front. 15 x 13 cm. 1-12226.   F73.3.C 34
Rare Book Coll.

CRAWFORD, Mary Caroline. Romantic days in old Boston; the story of the city and of its people during the nineteenth century ... with numerous illus. Boston, Little, Brown, 1910. xix, 411 p. front., plates, ports. 21 cm. 10-24173.   F73.3.C 89

— 1922. xxi, 441 p. front., plates, ports. 21½ cm. 22-22280.   F73.3. C 9

DEARBORN, Nathaniel. Boston notions; being an authentic and concise account of "that village," from 1630 to 1847. Boston, Print. N. Dearborn, 1848. xx, (7) - 426 p. front., illus., plates (partffold.) ports., maps (part fold.) fold. plans, facsims. (part fold.) 16 cm. 1-12227.   F73.3.D 28

DEARBORN, Nathaniel. Dearborn's reminiscences of Boston, and guide through the city and environs. Boston, Print. N. Dearborn (1851) xii, (13) - 180 p. front., illus., plates, port., map, plans (1 fold.) fold. facsim. 15½ cm. 1-12228.   F73.3.D 29

DRAKE, Samuel Adams. Around the Hub. A boy's book about Boston. Boston, Roberts brothers, 1881. 267 p. front., illus. 20 cm. 1-12229.   F73.3.D 75

EGAN, Joseph Burke. Citizenship in Boston, plan and text (by) Joseph B. Egan ... revision and photos. (by) Leonard M. Patton ... biographical sketches etc.... Philadelphia, Chicago, The John C. Winston co. (1925) xxii, 423 p. front., illus. (incl. ports.) diagrs. 19 cm. Bibliography: p. 421-423. 25-7013.   F73.3.E 28

ELLIS, George Edward. Sketch of the cities of Boston and Cambridge ... Boston, Little, Brown, 1875. 28 p. 12º. 1-12232-M1.   F73.3.E 47

FROST, John Edward. Boston, America's home port; a sketch book. (Boston, Hawthorne Press, 1955) 92 p. illus. 26 cm. 56-17889.   F73.3. F 7

GILMAN, Arthur. ... The story of Boston. A study of independency, ... New York & London, G.P. Putnam's sons, 1889. viii, 507 p. front., illus. (incl. ports.) fold. pl., 3 fold. maps. 20 cm. (Great cities of the republic v. 3) 1-12233.   F73.3.G 48

GREEN, Martin Burgess. The problem of Boston; some readings in cultural history. (1st ed.) New York, W.W. Norton (1966) 234 p. 22 cm. 65-18019.   F73.3. G 7

— London, Longmans, 1966. 234 p. 22½ cm. Bibliography: p. 217-221.   F73.3. G 7
1966a

GREGG. Fortieth anniversary of the election of Washington Parker Gregg as clerk of the Common council of the city of Boston .... Boston, Print. by order of the City council, 1882. 82 p. front. (port.) 26½ cm. 2-22617.
F73.3. G 8

GUINDON, Frederick A. Boston and her story ... Boston, New York, D. C. Heath (1921) iv, 145 p. front., illus. (incl. ports., maps, facsims.) 19 cm. 21-9896.
F73.3. G 9

HEPBURN, Andrew. Biography of a city, Boston; the story of a great American city and its contribution to our national heritage. New York, scholastic Book Services (1966) 158 p. 20 cm.
F73.3. H 4

HISTORICAL sketch of Boston, containing a brief account of its settlement, rise and progress, with a glance at its present and prospective prosperity. Boston, Print. E. L. Mitchell, 1861. 96 p. front., illus. 19 cm. 2-23884.
F73.3. H 67

HOMANS, Isaac Smith. Sketches of Boston, past and present, and of some few places in its vicinity ... With 120 engravings and three maps. Boston, Phillips, Sampson; Crosby and Nichols, 1851. 3, (v) - viii, 246, 112 p. front., illus., 3 fold. maps. 17½ cm. 17-18119.
F73.3.H758
Toner Coll.

— 1851. 3, (v) - viii, 246, 112 p. front., illus., plates. 15½ cm. 1-12234.
F73.3. H 76

— Boston, F. C. Moore, 1856. xi, (v) - vi, (xiii) - xv, 246 p. illus., plates. 15 cm. 1-12235.
F73.3. H 77

HOWE, Mark Antony De Wolfe. Boston, the place and the people. illus. Louis A. Holman. New York, The Macmillan co.; London, Macmillan & co., 1903. xv, 397 p. incl. illus., plates, ports., facsims. front. 21 cm. 3-26974/2 Revised.
F73.3. H 85

— New York and London, Macmillan, 1924. xv, 397 p. incl. illus., plates, ports., maps, facsims. front. 19½ cm. 24-29288.
F73.3. H 85
1924

KOREN, John. ... Boston, 1822 to 1922. The story of its government and principal activities during one hundred years. (Boston) City of Boston print. dept., 1922. 255 p. front., plates, ports. 23½ cm. 24-3050.
F73.3. K 84

— 1923. 214 p. front., plates, ports. 23½ cm. 36-33557.
F73.3. K842

LANGTRY, Albert Perkins. Metropolitan Boston; a modern history; New York, Lewis hist. pub. co., 1929. 5 v. fronts. (vol. i - iv) plates, ports., col. coats of arms. 27½ cm. Contents. - i-iii. History. - iv-v. Biography. 29-29713.
F73.3. L 27

LODGE, Henry Cabot. ... Boston ... London and New York, Longmans, Green, 1891. xi, 242 p. 2 fold. maps (incl. front.) 19 cm. (Historic towns) 1-12236.
F73.3. L 82

PICTORIAL history of Boston. 250th anniversary. 1630. 1880. Boston, Photo-electrotype co. (1880) p6 p. illus. fol. 1-12242-M1.
F73.3. P 61

QUINCY, Josiah. A municipal history of the town and city of Boston, during two centuries. 1630 - 1830. Boston, C. C. Little and J. Brown, 1852. xi, 444 p. front., plan. 23½ cm. 1-12243.
F73.3. Q 75

SAVAGE, Edward Hartwell. Boston events. A brief mention and the date of more than 5,000 events that transpired in Boston from 1630 to 1880 .... Boston, Tolman & White, print., 1884. 218 p. 20½ cm. Appendix contains: Boston topography, 1630. - Boston old highways, 1660-1708. - Boston nomenclature of streets. - Boston wharves, 1820. 1-12237.
F73.3. S 26

SCUDDER, Horace Elisha. Boston town. ... Boston, Houghton, Mifflin, 1881. viii, (9) - 243 p. incl. illus., plates, plan. 21 cm. 1-12238.
F73.3. S 43

SEABURG, Carl. Boston observed. Boston, Beacon Press (1971) 328 p. illus. 26 cm. Includes bibliographical references. 78-156453 MARC.
F73.3. S 44
1971

SHAW, Charles. A topographical and historical description of Boston, from the first settlement of the town to the present period ... Boston: Oliver Spear, 1817.   311 p. front., plates, fold. facsim. 18 cm. 1-12239.   F73.3.S 53

SHURTLEFF, Nathaniel Bradstreet. A topographical and historical description of Boston. Boston, Print. by request of the City council, 1871.   2, (iii) - ix, 720 p. fold. maps. 27 cm. 1-12240.   F73.3.S 56

— 3d ed. Pub. by order of the Common council, 1891.   lvi, 720 p. front. (port.) 1 illus., plates, fold. maps. 27 cm. 24-15019.   F73.3.S564

— 3d ed. 4th impression. 1891.   lvi, 720 p. front. (port.) pl., maps, plans. 27 cm. 3-5066.   F73.3.S 57

SNOW, Caleb Hopkins. A history of Boston, the metropolis of Massachusetts, from its origin to the present period. Boston, A. Bowen, 1825.   iv, (4), (9) - 400 p. front., illus., plates, maps, 3 plans (1 fold.) 23½ cm. 1-12241.   F73.3.S 68

— 2d ed. Boston, A. Bowen, 1828.   iv, (4), (9) - 427 p. illus., 18 pl., 3 maps (incl. front.) 23½ cm. 17-12051.   F73.3.S685   Toner Coll.

SPRAGUE, Charles. An ode: pronounced before the inhabitants of Boston ... 1830, at the centennial celebration of the settlement of the city. Boston, J. H. Eastburn, city printer, 1830.   22 p. 22½ cm. 17-23219.   F73.3.S 75

STATE street trust co. Boston, England, and Boston, New England, 1630 - 1930; reproductions of rare prints with a commentary of historic notes ... in commemoration of the 300th anniversary of the naming of Boston. Boston ... 1930.   vii, 45 p. incl. front., illus., plates. plates. 23 cm. 30-22388.   F73.3.S785

BOSTON'S growth; a bird's-eye view of Boston's increase in territory and population from its beginning to the present. Boston, Mass.... State street trust co., (1910)   45 p. illus. (incl. maps) 23 cm. 11-698.   F73.3.S 79

STATE street trust co. Boston, one hundred years a city; a collection of views made from rare and old prints and old photos. showing the changes which have occurred in Boston during the 100 years of its existence as a city, 1822 - 1922. (Boston, 1922)   xii, 49 p. incl. front., illus., maps. 23½ cm. 22-7404.   F73.3. S 8

SULLIVAN, Thomas Russell. Boston, new and old, by T. R. Sullivan; drawings by Lester G. Hornby ... Boston and New York, Houghton Mifflin, 1912.   viii, 108 p., col. front., illus., plates. 26 cm. 12-27607.   F73.3.S 95

TAYLOR, Alice. Boston. (Prepared with the cooperation of the American Geographical Society) Garden City, N.Y., Doubleday (1957)   63 p. illus. 21 cm. 58-142.   F73.3. T 3

— (1962)   63 p. 21 cm. (Know your America program)   F73.3. T 3 1962

— (1967)   64 p. 21 cm. (Know your America program)   F73.3. T 3 1967

THWING, Annie Haven. The crooked & narrow streets of the town of Boston 1630 - 1822. Boston, Marshall Jones, 1920.   xi, 282 p. front., plates, fold, plans. 24½ cm. 20-19769.   F73.3.T 54

— Detroit, Singing Tree Press, 1970.   xi, 282 p. illus. map. 23 cm. 74-129974.   F73.3.T 54 1920a

U.S. Information Agency. Boston, city of tradition. (Washington, 1961?)   35 p. (Cities of America) 62-60352.   F73.3.U 54

WESTON, George F.   Boston ways: high, by, and folk.   Boston, Beacon Press (1957)   261 p. illus.
24 cm.   57-11303.
F73.3. W 5

WHITEHILL, Walter Muir.   Boston, a topographical history.   Cambridge, Mass., Belknap Press of Harvard University Press, 1959.   xxix, 244 p. illus., maps. 25 cm.   Bibliographical references included in "Notes" (p.207 - 233)   59-12978.
F73.3.W 57

WHITEHILL, Walter Muir.   Boston; a topographical history.   2d ed., enl.   Cambridge, Mass., Belknap Press of Harvard University Press, 1968.   xl, 299 p. illus. 25 cm.
F73.3.W 57
1968

WHITMORE, William Henry.   An historical summary of fires in Boston.   (Boston, 1872.)   (3) - 12 p.
24½ cm.   1-12245.
F73.3.W 61

WINSOR, Justin.   The memorial history of Boston, incl. Suffok County.   1630 - 1880.   Boston, J.R. Osgood and co. 1880 - 81.   4 v. fronts., illus., plates, ports., maps, plans, facsims. 27½ cm.   1-12246 Rev.
F73.3. W 76
Microfilm 21708 F

— Boston, J.R. Osgood, 1881 - 83.   4 v. fronts., illus., plates, ports., maps, plans, facsims. 28½ cm.   14-13147.
F73.3.W 77

WOOD, James Playsted.   Boston, Illus. Robert Frankenberg.   New York, Seabury Press (1967)
143 p. 22 cm. 67-24461.
F73.3. W 8

BOSTON.   JUVENILE WORKS.

CURREN, Polly.   Hear ye of Boston.   Pictures by Kurt Werth.   New York, Lothrop, Lee & Shepard (1964)   39 p. 27 x 28 cm.   64-21193.
F73.33.C 8

EPSTEIN, Samuel.   Young Paul Revere's Boston.   Illus. Cary.   Champaign, Ill., Garrard Pub. Co. (1966)   93 p. 24 cm.   66-13279.
F73.33.E 6

WESTON, George F.   The key to Boston.   Philadelphia, Lippincott (1961)   128 p. 21 cm.   (Keys to the cities series) 61-7980.
F73.33.W 4

WILLIAMS, Barbara.   Boston, Seat of American history.   New York, McGraw-Hill (1969)
64 p. illus. 24 cm.   (Big cities of America) 72-91688.
F73.33. W 5

BOSTON.   HISTORIC MONUMENTS (GENERAL). ILLUSTRATIVE MATERIAL.

See also: F73.67.C52G79;   F73.8.P3S7

ELLIOTT, Mrs. Maud (Howe)   Three generations ....   Boston, Little, Brown, 1923.   6, (3) - 418 p.
front., ports. 21½ cm. 23-15949.
F73.37
PS1588.A3   1923

AMORY, Cleveland.   The Proper Bostonians.   (1st ed.)   New York, E.P. Dutton, 1947.   381 p. port., map. 23 cm. (American society series, v.1) "Acknowledgments and bibliography": p. 361-367.   47-11061*.   (Numerous printings. Eleventh printing, April 1948.
F73.37.A 5

ANNIVERSARY record.   A programme of the celebration of the 250th anniversary of the settlement of Boston, 1880.   Boston, H.A.M'Glenen, 1880.   8 p. illus. fol. 1-12221-M1.
F73.37.A54

BOSTON 129

BAXTER, James Phinney. ... A New England pantheon, trust created under the will of James Phinney Baxter, late of Portland, Maine .... (August, Me., 1924)   3, 9, 2-14 numb. l. 29 x 22½ cm. Autographed from type-written copy. 24-13764.
F73.37.B 35

BAXTER, James Phinney. A New England pantheon, to commemorate the principles and achievements of the pioneers whose ideals were the seed of free government. How can it be made worthy of the people of New England. Portland, Stephen Berry co., print., 1917.   8 p. 23 cm. (With above item) 24-13765.
F73.37.B 35

BAXTER, James Phinney. A New England temple of honor ... Boston (Spartan press inc.) 1920.   8 p. 23½ cm. (With item F73.37.B35) "Reprinted from the New England historical and genealogical register for April, 1920." 24-13766.
F73.37.B 35

BOSTON. Celebration of the 250th anniversary of the settlement of Boston ... 1880. Boston, Print. by order of the City council, 1880.   172 p. front. (fold. plan) plates, ports., facsim. 27 cm. 1-12222.
F73.37.B 44

BOSTON. Report of the Commission on marking historical sites of the city of Boston, 1924-1937. (Boston, 1937?)   151 p. incl. front., illus. (incl. port.) plates.. 26 cm. 39-22357.
F73.37.B495

BOSTON. Tercentenary of the founding of Boston. An account of the celebration .... Compiled by direction of His Honor James M. Curley .... (Boston, Printing dept., 1930)   xii, 392 p. incl. front., illus., ports., tabl. form. 26 cm. 32-14280.
F73.37.B 53

BOSTON. Record commissioners. ... Miscellaneous papers. Boston, Rockwell and Churchill, 1886.   3, 302 (i.e. 314) p. 2 fold. plans. 24 cm. (A report (10th) of the record commissioners) 1-13876.
F73.37.B 75

BOSTON common, The; or, Rural walks in cities. By a friend of improvement ... Boston, G.W. Light, 1838.   (5) - 64 p. front. 19½ cm. 1-21605.
F73.37.B 77
Rare Book Coll.

BOWDITCH, Nathaniel Ingersoll. "Gleaner" articles. Boston, Rockwell and Churchill, 1880.   1, 187 p. 24 cm. (Fifth report of the Record commissioners of Boston, 1880) 6-7046.
F73.37.B775

— 1887.   x, 232 p. 24 cm. (Fifth report of the Record commissioners, Rev. ed.) 1-13870.
F73.37 B78

BROWN, John Perkins. The Thomas Creese house, Boston, being the description of a typical town-house of the early eighteenth century and containing a history of the site thereof from the time of Anne Hutchinson to the present day. Boston, 1940.   4, 43 p. front., plates, double map, plans. 24½ cm. "This house ... was familiarly known to the last two generations as 'The Old corner bookstore'." 40-5231.
F73.37.B 86

BUSHEE, Frederick Alexander. ... Ethnic factors in the population of Boston. ,,, New York, Pub. for the American economic assoc. by the Macmillan co., London, S. Sonnenschein, 1903.   vi, 171 p. 24½ cm. (American economic association. Publications. 3d series, v.4, no.2) 3-14875.
F73.37.B 97

CARTER'S ink company. Little known Boston; a collection of landmarks from drawings by Francis Hight, made with a Carter fountain pen and Carter fountain pen ink. Boston, Mass., The Carter's ink co. (1927)   3, 9-45 p. illus. 19½ cm. 27-20831.
F73.37.C 32

DOWST, Henry Payson. Random notes of Boston. drawing by John Albert Seaford. Boston, H.B. Humphrey co., 1913.   4, 11 - 91, (3) p. incl. front., illus., plates. 26 cm. 13-21335.
F73.37.D 75

DRAKE, Samuel Adams. Old landmarks and historic personages of Boston. Boston, J.R. Osgood, 1873.   xvii, 484 p. incl. front., illus. 19½ cm. 1-12230.
F73.37.D 76

— 1874.   xvii, 484 p. incl. front., illus. 19½ cm. 7-26243.
F73.37.D763

— (5th ed.) 1876.   xv, 484 p. front., illus. 18½ cm. 1-12231.
F73.37.D 77

— New and rev. ed.   Boston, Little, Brown, 1900.   xviii, 484 p. front., illus., plates (incl. ports.) 21 cm.
0-6385 Rev.   F73.37.D 78

— Detroit, Singing Tree Press, 1970.   xviii, 484 p. illus. 76-99068.   F73.37.D 79

— Rutland, Vt., C. E. Tuttle (1971)   xxi, 484 p. illus. 19 cm. (Tut books.H.) 70-157258 MARC.   F73.37.D792

ELIOT, Samuel. The functions of a city. An oration before the city authorities of Boston ... 1868.
Boston, A. Mudge, 1868.   31 p. 23 cm. 1-26427.   F73.37.E 42

ERNST, Carl Wilhelm. Constitutional history of Boston, An essay ... (Boston, 1894)
(9) - 173 p. 27 cm. Extracted from Professional and industrial history of Suffolk County ... 1894, v.3. 3-26839 Rev.   F73.37.E 71

FAGAN, James Ocatvius. ... The New England squeak and other stories, being the strange adventure
of Heroic yet primitive people, ... (Boston, Press of Geo. H. Ellis, 1931)   3, 88 p. front., illus., plates,
ports. 18 cm. Principally stories about Boston. 31-19628.   F73.37.F 16

FEDERAL writers' project. An almanack for Bostonians, 1939 -   Being a truly amazing and
edifying compendium of fact and fancy ...   New York, M. Barrows (1938 -   1v. illus. 21½ cm.
39-9237.   F73.37.F 45
                                                                                                    Rare Book Coll.

GREEN, Samuel Abbott. Ten fac-simile reproductions relating to old Boston and neighborhood.
Boston, (Cambridge, print. J. Wilson) 1901.   4, 44 p. facsim. 37½ cm. 2-5-M2.   F73.37.G 79

GULLIVER, Frederic Putnam. The geographical development of Boston. ... Chicago, Print. Rand,
McNally (1903)   323-329 p. incl. 5 maps. 24½ cm. "Reprinted from the Journal of geography, vol. ii no. 6, June 1903."
5-40536.   F73.37.S 93

HALE, Edward Everett. ... Historic Boston and its neighborhood; an historical pilgrimage personally
conducted by Edward E. Hale; arranged for seven days ... New York, D. Appleton, 1898.
xv, 186 p. front., ports., plan, facsim. 18½ cm. (Appletons' home reading books ...) 98-1968/4 Rev.   F73.37.H 16

HALL, George D., company. Official program of the city of Boston tercentenary celebration ...
Boston, 1930.   208 p. incl. front., illus., ports. 28 cm. 31-6282.   F73.37.H 18

HASSAN, Frederick F. Liberty tree, Liberty hall. 1775. Lafayette and loyalty! (Boston, 1891)
16 p. 18 cm. 4-14755* Cancel.   F73.37.H 35

HOLMES, Oliver Wendell. Dr. Holmes's Boston, ed. Caroline Ticknor ... Boston and N. Y., Houghton
Mifflin, 1915.   xiv, 213, (3) p. front., plates (1 double) 25½ cm. 15-20976.   F73.37.H 52

HORSFORD, Eben Norton. The Indian names of Boston, and their meaning. By Eben Norton Horsford
... Cambridge, J. Wilson, 1886.   26 p. 4 maps. 31½ x 28 cm. 8-15375.   F73.37.H 81

HOWE, Mark Antony De Wolfe. Boston landmarks, with photos, by Samuel Chamberlain and reproductions of old prints. New York, Hastings house (1946)   6, 3-133 p. incl. plates (1 double) 21 cm. 47-1111.
                                                                                                    F73.37.H 84

HOWE, Mark Anthony De Wolfe. I'm from Boston; scenes from the living past, illus. by picture and
story. Boston, The Atlantic monthly press (1920)   (19) p. illus. 15½ x 13½ cm. 21-701 Rev.
                                                                                                    F73.37.H 86

LAWLOR, David F. A Boston image; 100 photos. by Dave Lawlor. (Boston, 1962)   (unpaged) 28 cm.
                                                                                                    F73.37. L 3

LINSCOTT, Robert Newton. State of mind; a Boston reader. (New York) Farra, Straus (1948)
xiv, 428 p. 22 cm. (City and country readers series) 48-7771*.   F73.37. L 5

— 1972.   F73.37. L 5
                                                                                                    1972

BOSTON

MANN, Albert William. ... Walks and talks about historic Boston ... Boston, The Mann pub. co., (1917)   3, 586 p. illus., pl., ports. 25½ cm. 17-25471.
F73.37.M28

ORDWAY, Warren. Carols and candles on Christmas eve. (Boston, Lincoln & Smith press, 1930)
(10) p. illus. 19½ cm. 31-640.
F73.37.O65

PALMER, Robert M. Palmer's views of Boston, past and present. New York? 1910.   18½ x 26 cm.
F73.37.P17

PEABODY, Henry Greenwood. Colonial and revolutionary landmarks of Boston; an illustrated lecture by Henry G. Peabody. (Pasadena, Cal., H.G. Peabody, 1913)   21 p. 23 cm. 14-3283.
F73.37.P35

POTTER, Joseph S. The past, present and future of Boston. Speech ... on the subject of uniting certain cities and towns with the city of Boston .... Boston, Wright & Potter, print., 1873.
84 p. 23½ cm. 1-12247.
F73.37.P84

RICHMOND, James Cook. A midsummer's day-dream; libellous; or, A little book of the vision of Shawmut. By Admonish Crime (pseud) ... Libell I. Milwaukee, Daily news book and job steam print., 1859.   36 p. 16 cm. Satire on Boston. 22-13253.
F73.37.R 5

SCUDDER, Winthrop Saltonstall, ed. A history of the Gardiner Greene estate on Cotton hill, now Pemberton square, Boston. Boston, T.R. Marvin, print., 1916.   28 p. front., pl., ports., plans. 24½ cm.
"Reprinted from the Publications of the Bostonian society." 34-32603.
F73.37.S36

SIRKIS, Nancy. Boston. Introd. by Edward M. Kennedy. New York, Viking Press (1966)
154 p. 29 cm. (A Studio book) 66-16069.
F73.37.S55

SOUVENIR programme. Two hundred and fiftieth anniversary of the settlement of Boston. 1630 - 1880. (Boston) C.W. Calkins (1880)   15 p. 8º 1-12256-M1.
F73.37.S65

STARK, James Henry. Antique views of ye towne of Boston. Boston, Mass., Photo-electrotype engraving co. (1882)   378 p. incl. illus., plates (partly fold.) ports., maps, fold. plans, facsims. 28½ cm. 1-12257.
F73.37.S 7

— Boston, Morse Purce co. (1907)   378 p. incl. illus., plates (partly fold.) ports., fold. maps, facsims., fold. plates.
28½ cm. First pub. 1882. 7-27166.
F73.37.S73

STATE street trust company. Boston's story in inscriptions; being reproductions of the markings that are or have been on historic sites. Boston, (1908)   (37) p. illus. 23 cm. 8-12230.
F73.37.S79

STATE street trust company. Forty of Boston's historic houses; a brief illustrated description of the residences of historic characters of Boston ... Boston, (1912)   (44) p. illus. 23 cm. 12-1944.
F73.37.S795

STATE street trust company. Some interesting Boston events. Boston, (1916)   78 p. illus. 23 cm.
"Authorities": p. 78. 16-5326.
F73.37.S 8

STATE street trust company. Some events orf Boston and its neighbors. Boston, 1917.   v, 62 p. illus.
(incl. ports.) 23½ cm. "Authorities consulted": p. iv. 17-6237.
F73.37.S82

SWIFT, Lindsay. Literary landmarks of Boston; a visitor's guide to points of literary interst in and about Boston ... Boston and New York, Houghton, Mifflin, 1903.   58 p. illus. 17½ cm. 3-16252.
F73.37.S97

— (1922)   vi, 58 p. illus. 17½ cm. Revised by Caroline Ticknor. 22-12901.
F73.37.S972

THACHER, Peter. A sermon preached to the church and society in Brattle-street ... Boston, Print.
Young and Minns, 1800.   18 p. 22 cm. Impercet. 1-16548.
F73.37.T36
Rare Book Coll.

TOLMAN, George R. 12 sketches of old Boston buildings. Boston, The Heliotpye print., 1882.
xii pl. 41 x 34 cm. 11-34048.
                                    F73.37.T 65
                             Div. of Fine Arts. E.A.A.

ANSWER to a pamphlet, entitle, "Considerations on the public expeidency of a bridge from one part of Boston to the other". Boston, Print. E. Lincoln, 1806. 31, 8 p. 23½ cm. 1-26375.
                                    F73.37.T 92

U.S. Final report of the Boston National Historic Sites Commission ... Washington, U.S. Govt. Print. off., 1961. 61-61952.
                                    F73.37. U 5

WARNER, Frances Lester. Merry Christmas from Boston, by Frances Lester Warner. Boston, The Atlantic monthly press (1921) (20) p. illus. 13½ cm. 22-433.
                                    F73.37. W 3

WHEILDON, William Wilder. Curiosities of history: Boston ... 1630 - 1880. Boston, Lee and Shepard; New York, C.T. Dillingham, 1880. x, 13-141 p. map, fold. facsim. 19 cm. 1-12244. F73.37. W 56

— 1880. x, 11-141 p. incl. map. facsim. 19½ cm. 3-28494.   F73.37 W 57

WHITEFIELD, Edwin. Homes of our forefathers in Boston, Old England, and Boston, New England. From original drawings by Edwin Whitefield. Boston, E. Whitefield, 1889. 84 p. col. front., col. pl. 25½ cm. 2-12683.
                                    F73.37. W 59

— 1889. 3, 3-138 p., 64 col. mounted pl. 30 cm. 1-12261.   F73.37. W 6

WHITEHILL, Walter Muir. Boston: portrait of a city. Barre, Mass., Barre Publishers, 1964. 112 p. 23 cm. 64-14908.
                                    F73.37. W 63

WHITEHILL, Walter Muir. Destroyed Boston building. (Massachusetts Hist. Soc., 1965. 31 p. 22 cm. (Mass. Historical Society Picture book no. 12)
                                    F73.37. W 64

BOSTON. ANTIQUITIES.

JOHNSON, Frederick. ... The Boylston street fishweir, a study of the archaeology, biology, and geology of a site on Boylston street in the Back Bay district of Boston ... Andover, Mass., Phillips academy, The Foundation, 1942. xii, 212 p. incl. illus., tbales, diagrs. xiv pl. on 9 l., maps (1 fold. 25 cm. Bibliography: p. 200-212. 42-16076.
                                    F73.39 J 6

BOSTON. EARLY TO 1775.

ADAMS, Samuel. An appeal to the world; or, A vindication of the town of Boston, from many false and malicious aspersions contain'd in certain letters and memorials, written by Governor Bernard and others .... Pub. by order of the town. Boston, Edes and Gill, 1769. 37 p. 12° Anon. 1-12248-M1.
                                    F73.4. A 21

ADDISON, Albert Christopher. The romantic story of the Puritan fathers and their founding of new Boston and the Massachusetts Bay colony ... Boston, L.C. Page, 1912. xiv, 243 p. front., plates, ports., facsims. 24½ cm. 12-22800.
                                    F73.4. A 22

ADDRESS to the inhabitants of the province of the Massachusetts-Bay in New England; more especially to the inhabitants of Boston; occasioned by the late illegal and unwarrantable attack upon their liberties .... Boston, Print. Rogers and Fowle (1747) 8 p. 22 cm. 2-9075.
                                    F73.4. A 25

ASPINWALL, William. A volume relating to the early history of Boston, containing the Aspinwall notarial records from 1644 to 1651. Boston, Municipal printing office, 1903. 1, x, 455 p. 2 pl. (incl. front.) 23½ cm. (Records relating to the early history of Boston. v. 32) 5-7754.
                                    F73.4. A 84

BOSTON

BLACKSTONE. An address delivered at the formation of the Blackstone monument association, tog. with the preliminaries ... 1855. (By Sylvanus Chace Newman. Pawtucket, R.I., Print. Pearce & Estey, 1855. 39 p. 1 illus. 23½ cm. 37-14205.
F73.4.B
E286.P337

BAENSCH, Emil. A Boston boy, the first martyr to American liberty .... Manitowoc, Wis., The author (1924) 44 p. incl. pl. 15½ cm. 24-9696.
F73.4. B 13

BENTON, Josiah Henry. The story of the old Boston town house, 1658 - 1711 ... with portraits and illus. Boston (The Merrymount press) 1908. xi, 212 p., 2 l. 3*- 60* p. front., pl., ports., plan, facsims. 26 cm. "Authorities consulted": p. 21*- 26*. 9-1233.
F73.4. B 47

BLACKSTONE, William, Boston's first inhabitant. By Thomas Coffin Amory. (Boston, Rockwell & Churchill, print., 1877.) 36 p. 19 cm. Published anonymously. 7-8590.
F73.4. B 63

— 2d ed. 1877, 38 p. 19½ cm. Published anonymously. 7-8591.
F73.4.B 631

BLAXTON, William. Read by Thomas Coffin Amory ... 1880. Boston, Old state house, 1886. 2, (3) - 25 p. 25½ cm. (Collections of the Bostonian soc. vol. I no. 1) 3-28521.
F73.4.B 632

BLACKSTONE, Rev. William, the pioneer of Boston. By John C. Crane ... Worcester, Mass., C.R. Stobbs, print., 1896. 14 p. front. 23 cm. 2-28233.
F73.4.B 638

BLACKSTONE, William, in his relation to Massachusetts and Rhode Island ... By the Rev. B.F. De Costa. New York, M.H. Mallory, 1880. 24 p. 21 cm. Reprinted from the Churchman of Sept. 25th and Oct. 2, 1880. 7-8642.
F73.4. B 64

BLACKSTONE, William. Reading for children. History. By Mrs. Nina (Moore) Tiffany. Cambridge (Mass.) J. Wilson, 1884. 14 p. 17 cm. Published anonymously. 7-8578.
F73.4. B 65

BLANEY, Henry Robertson. Old Boston, reproductions of etchings in half tone; ... Boston, Lee and Shepard, 1896 (1895) 135 p. 2 l. incl. front., plates. 26 cm. Printed on one side of leaf only. 1-12250 Add.
F73.4. B 66

BOSTON. An appeal to the world. See F73.4.A21. 1-12248.
F73.4.B 711

— London, Reprinted for J. Almon, 1770. 2, 3-58 p. 21 cm. 1-12249 Additions.
F73.4.B 712

BOSTON in the revolution illustrated; a souvenir for patriotic Americans. Boston, Rand Avery co. (1888) 15 p. illus. (incl. map, facsims.) 39½ cm. Caopyright, 1888, by Moses King. 4-35810.
F73.4. B 74

BOSTON. A volume of records relating to the early history of Boston .... Boston, Municipal printing office, 1900. 2, (iii) - vi, 389 p. 2 pl. 23½ cm. (Records rel. to the early history of Boston v.29) 5-10021.
F73.4. B 78

BOSTON two hundred years ago, or The romantic story of Miss Ann Carter (daughter of one of the first settlers,) and the celebrated Indian chief, Thundersquall; with may humorous reminiscences and events of olden time. Boston, 1830. 16 p. incl. front. 30 cm. 19-14390.
F73.4. B 79

BRIDGE, Thomas. Jethro's advice recommended to the inhabitants of Boston ... to chuse well-qualified men ... for town officers. Boston, Print, John Allen ... 1710. 32 p. 15½ cm. 7-41469.
F73.4. B 85
Rare Book Coll.

— 2d ed. Boston, Print. S. Kneeland and T. Green, 1733. 3, 24 p. 17 cm. 9-20809.
F73.4. B 86
Rare Book Coll.

BROWN, Richard D. Revolutionary politics in Massachusetts; the Boston committee of correspondence and the town, 1772 - 1774. Cambridge, Mass., Harvard University Press, 1970. xiv, 282 p. illus. 24 cm. 71-119072.
F73.4. B 89

CHECKLEY, Samuel.   Diary of Rev. Samuel Checkly 1735, ed. Henry Winchester Cunningham ... Cambridge, J. Wilson, 1909.   2, 271 - 306 p. front. (facsim.) 24½ cm.   Reprinted from the Publications of the Colonial soc. of Massachusetts, vol. xii.   Written on the blank leaves of an interleaved copy of "The New England diary, 1735" 9-23000.   F73.4.C 51

COLMAN, Benjamin.   It is of the Lord's mercies that we are not consumed.   A sermon preach'd ... after a most merciful and wonderful preservation of the town from being consumed by fire ....   Boston, Print. J. Draper ... 1737.   20 p. 20½ cm. 20-3023.   F73.4.C 69
Rare Book Coll.

CRAWFORD, Mary Caroline.   St. Botolph's town; an account of old Boston in colonial days ... Boston, L. C. Page, 1908.   xii, 365 p. front., plates, ports., fold. map. 20 cm. 8-28847.   F73.4.C 89

DICKERSON, Oliver Morton.   Boston under military rule (1768 - 1769) as revealed in a Journal of the times ...   Boston, Chapman & Grimes (1936)   xiii, 137 p. 27 cm.   A daily journal of happenings.   It was widely reprinted in American newspapers and in some publications in England.   The authors have not been identified. 37-12256.   F73.4.D 53

— New York, Da Capo Press, 1970.   xiii, 137 p. 27 cm. 70-118029 MARC.   F73.4.D 53
1970

— Westport, Conn., Greenwood Press (1971)   xiii, 137 p. illus. 70-114511.   F73.4.D 53
1971

DRAKE, Samuel Gardner.   The history and antiquities of Boston ... from its settlement in 1630, to the year 1770. ...   Boston, L. Stevens, 1856.   x, 840 p. front., illus., plates (partly fold.) ports., facsim. 26 cm.   Originally pub. in 16 parts. 1-13356.   F73.4.D 77

EDMONDS, John Henry.   The Burgis views of New York and Boston.   A paper read before the Bostonian society ...   (Boston, 1915)   22 p. fold. front. 25 cm.   Reprinted from Proceedings of the annual meeting of the Bostonian soc. 1915. 17-2423.   F73.4.E 25

GOODWIN, Daniel.   Provincial pictures by brush and pen: an address delivered before the Bostonian soc. ...   Chicago, Fergus print., 1886.   84 p. 23½ cm.   Sketches of various members of the Pitts and Bowdoin families and of their connection with the colonial history of Boston and Mass. 5-6276.   F73.4.G 65

GRIFFIN, William Robinson.   Illustrated guide to colonial Boston - 1630, and the midnight ride of Paul Revere to every Middlesex village and farm.   Lowell, Mass., 1948.   41 p. illus. 22 cm. 48-2632*.   F73.4. G 7

JENNINGS, John Edward.   Boston, cradle of liberty, 1630 - 1776.   Garden City, N.Y., Doubleday, (1947)   x p. 3 l., 335 p. plates, 23½ cm.   "First edition." 47-30197.   F73.4. J 4

JOHNSON, Edward.   ... The founding of Boston.   From Captain Edward Johnson's "Wonder-working Providence," pub. in London in 1654.   (Boston, Directors of the Old South work, 1907)   20 p. 20 cm. (Old South leaflets. General series v. 8 no. 176) 20-20844.   F73.4. J 66

KALER, James Otis.   Ruth of Boston; a story of the Massachusetts Bay colony, by James Otis (pseud.) New York, Cincinnati (etc.) American book co. (1910)   160 p. illus. 19 cm. 10-7900.   F73.4.K 14

GREEN, Samuel Abbott.   Note-book kept by Capt. Robert Keayne, an early settler of Boston.   Remarks made before the Mass. historical soc. ...   Cambridge (Mass.) J. Wilson, 1889.   7 p. 24 cm.   Relates chiefly to the ecclesiastical trials of Richard Wait and Mrs. Ann Hibbens of the First church. 11-22526.   F73.4.K 26

KENT, Mrs. Louise (Andrews)   In good old colony times; a historical picture book, with text by Louise Andrews Kent and Elisabth Kent Tarshis.   Boston, Houghton Mifflin, 1941.   xii, 99 p. col. front., col. plates. 22 cm.   "Some books about Boston": p. 100. 41-12185.   F73.4. K 4

KILBY, Christopher; a memoir prepared for the New England historical and genealogical register for Jan., 1872, by Charles W. Tuttle.   Boston, Print. D. Clapp, 1872.   11 p. 24½ cm. 3-27043.   F73.4.K 48

BOSTON 135

LAMB, George. Series of plans of Boston showing existing ways and owners of property, 1630 - 1635 - 1640 - 1645. Comp. ... from town records, Book of possession, Mass. Bay records, Savage's Winthrop, Lechford's Diary, Aspinwall's notarial records and Suffolk County deeds. Scale, about 600 ft. to an inch. Boston, Municipal print., 1905.   17 p. 4 fold. plans. 23 cm. 7-26247.
 F73.4.L 21
 Map div.

MATHER, Increase. Burnings bewailed: in a sermon, occasioned by the lamentable fire which was in Boston, 1711. Boston print., 1711.   2, 36 p. 16 cm. 18-19977.
 F73.4.M 42
 Rare Book Coll.

MAYHEW, Jonathan. God's hand and providence to be religiously acknowledged in public calamities. A sermon occasioned by the great fire in Boston .... Boston ... 1760.   38 p. 21 cm. 6-19804.
 F73.4.M 46
 Rare Book Coll.

PIERCE, Edward Lillie. The diary of John Rowe, a Boston merchant, 1764 - 1779. A paper read ... before the Mass. historical society ... Cambridge, J. Wilson, 1895.   (11) - 108 p. 24½ cm. 13-6006.
 F73.4.P 61

PORTER, Edward Griffin. Rambles in old Boston .... Illus. by George R. Tolman. Boston, Cupples, Upham, 1887 (1886)   xviii p., 5 l., (9) - 439 p. incl. illus., plates, plan, map, etc. 25 cm. 1-12254.
 F73.4.P 84

QUINCY, Josiah. An address to the citizens of Boston ... 1830, the close of the second century from the first settlement of the city. Boston, J.H. Eastburn, print., 1830.   68 p. 22 cm. 1-12255.
 F73.4.Q 75

ROSS, Marjorie Drake. The book of Boston, the Colonial period, 1630 to 1775. With photos. by Samuel Chamberlain. New York, Hastings House Pub. (1960)   127 p. 60-9122.
 F73.4. R 6

RUTMAN, Darrett Bruce. Winthrop's Boston; portrait of a puritan town, 1630 - 1649. Chapel Hill, Pub. University of North Carolina Press for the Institute of Early Amer. hist. and culture at Williamsburg, Va. (1965)   x, 324 p. 24 cm. 65-13667.
 F73.4. R 8

— New York, W.W. Norton (1972)   x, 324 p. 20 cm. (The Norton library, N 627) 70-39159.
 F73.4. R 8
 1972

SEYBOLT, Robert Francis. The town officials of colonial Boston, 1634 - 1775 ... Cambridge, Mass., Harvard university press, 1939.   xiii p., 2 l., (3) - 416 p. 24½ cm. 39-13854.
 F73.4.S 49

TRUE, Charles Kittredge. Shawmut: or, The settlement of Boston by the Puritan pilgrims ... Boston, Waite, Pierce, 1845.   136 p. incl. col. front. 15½ cm. Also pub. under title: Tri-Mountain; or, The early history of Boston. 22-7155.
 F73.4.T 85
 Rare Book Coll.

TRUE, Charles Kittredge. Tri-Mountain; or, The early history of Boston ... Boston, Heath & Graves (1845)   136 p. front., pl. 15½ cm. See previous item. 12-26589.
 F73.4.T858
 Rare Book Coll.

— Shawmut, etc. Boston, Waite, Peirce, 1846.   136 p. incl. front. 16 cm. 1-12259.
 F73.4.T 86
 Rare Book Coll.

— Boston, C. Waite, 1847.   136 p. incl. front. 16 cm. 1-12260.
 F73.4.T 87

— Boston, Strong & Brodhead, 1848.   136 p. incl. front. 16 cm. 17-17334.
 F73.4.T873
 Toner coll.

— Tri-Mountain, etc. Philadelphia, American Baptist pub. soc. (1855)   108 p. front., plates. 15 cm. 1-12258.
 F73.4.T883

VALENTINE, John, progenitor of the Valentine family in New England and a man of mark in Boston, by William Valentine Alexander.   (Rutland, Vt., Tuttle pub. co., 1937)   65 p. front., illus., plates, plan, facsim.   22½ cm.   37-2556.

F73.4.V 29

WARDEN, Gerard.   Boston, 1689 - 1776.   (1st ed.)   Boston, Little, Brown (1970)   404 p. 24 cm.
70-100577.

F73.4.W 37

WINSHIP, George Parker.   Boston in 1682 and 1699; A trip to New-England, by Edward Ward, and A letter from New England, by J. W.   Providence, R.I. (Club for colonial reprints) 1905.
xxviii, (5), 34-95 p. 22½ cm. (Club for colonial reprints of Providence, R.I. 2d publication.) 5-42409.

F73.4.W 77
Rare Book Coll.

— Reprinted, with an introd. and notes by George Parker Winship.   New York, B. Franklin (1970)
xxviii, 95 p. 68-57126.   23 cm.

F73.4.W 77
1970

WINSLOW, Anna Green.   Diary of Anna Greene Winslow, a Boston school girl of 1771, ed. by Alice Morse Earle.   Boston and New York, Houghton, Mifflin, 1894.   2, (iii) - xx p. 121 p. 2 pl. 4 port. (incl. front.) facsim.   20 cm.   4-16943/3.

F73.4.W 78

— Detroit, Singing Tree Press, 1970.   xx, 121 p. illus. 23 cm.   "Facsimile reprint of the 1894 edition."   71-124586.

F73.4.W 78
1894a

BOSTON. 1775 - 1865.

ANDREWS, John.   Letters of John Andrews, esq. of Boston, 1772-1776.   Compiled and ed. from the original ms., with an introd. by Winthrop Sargent ...   Cambridge, Press of J. Wilson, 1866.   23 cm.
100 p.   Reprinted from the Proceedings of the Mass. historical soc., 1866, v. 8, p. 316-412.   3-5680 rev.

F73.44.A56

BALTIMORE.   Citizens.   Proceedings of the great meeting of the friends of civil and religious liberty, ... for the purpose of giving an expression of public opinion upon recent outrages committed at Boston upon the constitutional rights of adopted fellow citizens.   (Baltimore) Bull & Tuttle, print. (1837)
8 p. 21½ cm.   Signed by Samuel Moore, president, and ten others. 9-27173.

F73.44.B18

BOSTON.   Report on the petition of Isaac P. Davis.   (Boston, 1813)   22 cm.

F73.44.B73
Rare Book Coll.

BOSTON.   Two plans for forming the town of Boston into an incorporated city.   Pub. by order of the .... (Boston, 1784)   8 p. 19 cm. 1-12251.

F73.44.B735
Rare Book Coll.

BOSTON.   Report of the town Convention.   (Boston, Gilbert and Dean, print., 1804)   8 p. 23 cm.
Report on proposed alterations in the county and town government.   8-9187.

F73.44.B75
Rare Book Coll.

BOSTON castigator ... v. 1, no. 1-19; Aug. 7 - Dec. 11, 1822.   Boston, L.T. Hall, 1822.
(76) p. 28½ cm. weekly.   Ed. by Lucius Sarcastic, jr., pseud. 8-10488.

F73.44.B76

BOWEN, Abel.   Bowen's new guide to the city of Boston and vicinity ...   Boston, J. Munroe (1849)
36 p. front., pl., fold. map. 16°   1-12262-M1.

F78.44.B 78

BOWEN, Abel.   Bowen's picture of Boston, or The citizen's and stranger's guide to the metropolis of Massachusetts, and its environs ...   Boston, A. Bowen, 1829.   252 p. front., illus., plates, fold. map, fold. plan.
17½ cm. 39-21905.

F73.44.B798
Rare Book Coll.

— 2d ed. enl. and impr.   Boston, Lilly, Wait, 1833.   7, (9)-316p., illus., etc. 15 cm. 1-12263.

F73.44.B81

BOSTON

— 3d ed. Boston, Otis, Broaders, 1838. 5, (9) - 304 p. front., illus., plates, fold. maps, fold. plan. 15½ cm. 1-12264.
F73.44.B 82

BOWEN'S Boston news-letter, and city record ... Jerome V.C. Smith, ed. ... v.1-2; Nov. 5, 1825 - Dec. 30, 1826. Boston, A. Bowen, 1826. 2 v. illus. 24½ cm. weekly. 6-12278.
F73.44.B 83

BOYLSTON, Thomas. The will of Thomas Boylston., late of London. (Boston? 181-) 16 p. 24 cm. 5-12652.
F73.44.B 84

BRISCOT de Warville, Jean Pierre. Boston in 1788. (Boston, 1902) 19½ cm.
F73.44.B 85

CLAPP, Otis. A letter to the Hon. Abbott Lawrence and the Hon. Robert G. Shaw on the present condition and future growth of Boston. Boston, Print. J. Wilson, 1853. 16 p. 13½ cm. On the railroad facilities of Boston. 13-21563.
F73.44.C 58

CRAWFORD, Mary Caroline. Old Boston days & ways from the dawn of the revolution until the town became a city. Boston, Little, Brown, 1909. xv, 463 p. front., illus., plates, ports., map, facsim. 21 cm. Continuation of the author's "St. Botolph's town." 9-28413.
F73.44.C 89

— Boston, Little, Brown, 1924. 2, (iii) - xv, 463 p. front., illus., plates, ports., map, facsim. 22½ cm. 24-25114.
F73.44.C 89 1924

DERBY, Elias Hasket. Boston: a commercial metropolis in 1850. Her growth, population, wealth and prospects. As originally pub. in Hunt's merchants' magazine for November, 1850. Boston, Redding & co., 1850. 16 p. 22½ cm. 8-30444.
F73.44.D 42

DWIGHT, Timothy. Boston at the beginning of the 19th century. (Boston, 1903) 19½ cm.
F73.44.D 99

GREEN, Samuel Abbott. Refutation of the alleged ill-treatment of Captain Fenton's wife and daughter. Boston, 1894) 23½ cm.
F73.44.G 79

GUIDE-BOOK for strangers visiting the cupola of the State house, in Boston ... Boston, A.J. Wright's steam-press print., 1848. 24 p. front. (fold. map) illus. 15½ cm. 1-12252.
F73.44.G 94

— Boston, Wright & Hasty, print., 1851. 23 p. front. (map) 24°. 1-21775-M1.
F73.44.G 95

HALE, Edward Everett. A New England boyhood ... New York, Cassell pub. co. (1893) xxv, 267 p. front., illus., plates. 19½ cm. 4-16961/4.
F73.44.H 15

— Boston, Little, Brown, 1900. xxvi, 500 p. front. 20 cm. 0-1715 Rev.
F73.44.H152

HALE, James W. Old Boston Town, early in this century; by an 1801-er ... New York, Print. G.F. Nesbitt (1883?) 56 p. 18½ cm. Eleven letters ... signed: Oxygenairian. 4-14731 rev.
F73.44.H156

HALES, John Groves. A survey of Boston and its vicinity; shewing the distance from the Old state house ... to all the towns and villages not exceeding fifteen miles therefrom ... together with a short topographical sketch of the country ... Boston, Print. E. Lincoln, 1821. 156 p. front., fold. map. 18½ cm. 1-12265 Rev.
F73.44.H 16

HILDRETH, Richard. My connection with the Atlas newspaper; including a sketch of the history of the Amory hall party of 1838 .... Boston, Whipple and Damrell, 1839. 24 p. 18½ cm. 9-27172.
F73.44.H 64

KIRKER, Harold. Bulfinch's Boston, 1787 - 1817. New York, Oxford University Press, 1964. ix, 305 p. 24 cm. 64-24862.
F73.H4 K 5

KNAPP, Samuel Lorenzo. Extracts from a journal of travels in North America, consisting of an account of Boston and its vicinity. By Ali Bey (pseud.) Translated from the original manuscript ... Boston: Print. Thomas Badger, Jun. 1818. 124 p. 19 cm. 1-12266. F73.44.K 67

LIDSTONE, James Torrington Spencer. The Bostoniad: giving a full description of the principal establishments, together with the most honorable and substantial business men, in the Athens of America. Boston, Pub. under universal patronage (Hollis & Gunn prs.) 1853. (5) - 62 p. 18½ cm. In verse. 6-4454.
F73.44.L 71

LIFE in town, or the Boston spy. Being a series of sketches illustrative of whims and women in the 'Athens of America.' By an Athenian ... Boston, Redding and co.; New York, Burgess & Stringer ... 1844. 24 p. front. 27 cm. 10-31049. F73.44.L 72
Rare Book Coll.

MALLORY, Richard P. A panoramic view from Bunker Hill monument. Engraved by James Smillie from a drawing by R. P. Mallory. Boston, Redding & co., 1848. 16 p. illus., 2 pl. (1 fold.) 23 cm. 1-12267 Rev. F73.44.M 25

MAY, Samuel. Memoir of Col. Joseph May, 1760 - 1841. By Samuel May, of Leicester ... Boston, D. Clapp, 1873. 12 p. front. (port.) 23½ cm. Repr. from the N.E. Hist. and geneal. reg., 1873. 12-23857. F73.44.M 43

MICHIGAN central railroad company. Boston, Mass. Fort Dearborn, Ill., 1903. 20½ cm.
F73.44.M 59

MIDGLEY, R.L. Sights in Boston and suburbs; or, Guide to the stranger. Illus. by Billings, Hill, Barry, and John Andrew. Boston, J.P.Jewett; Cleveland, O., Proctor & Worthington, 1856. 2, 2, 5, 225 p. front., illus., 2 maps (1 fold.) fold. plan. 17 cm. Later ed. under title: Boston sights ... 1-12268. F73.44.M 62

MIDGLEY, R.L. Boston sights; or, Hand-book for visitors. ... Boston, A. William, 1865. 1, 2, 5, 214 p. illus., 2 fold. maps. 17½ cm. First ed. under title: Sights in Boston ... 1856. 9-11764. F73.44.M625

OTIS, Mrs. Eliza Henderson (Bordman) "Mrs. Harrison Gray Otis" ... Report of Mrs. Harrison Gray Otis on donations for soldiers. 1864. (Boston, J.E.Farwell, print., 1864) 6 p. 23 cm. 17-15485.
F73.44.O 88

PARKER, Theodore. A sermon of the moral condition of Boston, preached at the Melodeon, ... Boston, Crosby and Nichols, 1849. 74 p. 19 cm. 19-17971.
F73.44.P 24

PEABODY, Mary J. Old Boston for young eyes ... (Cambridge, Mass.) Priv. print, for the Fair for the Mass. soc. for the prevention of cruelty to children. J. Wilson, 1880. 27 p. illus., 3 pl. (incl. front.) map. 22½ cm. 20-6426. F73.44.P 35

QUINCY, Josiah. An address commemorative of the organization of city government in Boston. ... Boston, Municipal print., 1897. 72 p. front., ports. 26½ cm. 1-12269. F73.44.Q 75

QUINCY, Josiah. Farewell address as mayor of Boston, 1829. 20 p. (Old South leaflets, v.8, no,. 182. Boston, 1907) F73.44.Q 76

ROSS, Marjorie Drake. The book of Boston; the Federal period 1775 - 1837. With photos, by Samuel Chamberlain. New York, Hastings House (1961) 176 p. 24 cm. 61-14214.
F73.44.R 82

— New York, Hastings House Publishers (1964) 166 p. 24 cm. 64-19070. F73.44.R823

ROSSITER, William Sidney. Days and ways in old Boston; drawings by Malcolm Fraser and Jacques Reich ... Boston, R.H.Stearns, 1915. 144 p. front., illus. (incl. ports.) plates, maps, facsims. 23 cm. 14-21591.
F73.44.R 83

ROWE, John. Letters and diary of John Rowe, Boston merchant, 1759-1762, 1764 - 1779; ed. by Anne Rowe Cunningham ... Boston, W.B.Clarke, 1903. 4; 453 p. 9 pl. 22½ cm. 3-18489 Rev. F73.44.R 87

BOSTON

— (New York) New York Times (1969)   453 p. illus. 23 cm. (Eyewitness accounts of the American Revolution.)
76-76564.   F73.44.R 87
                                                                                                   1969

RUSSELL, Benjamin B.   Russell's horse railroad guide for Boston and vicinity ... (Boston) B.B. Russell
(1862)   18 p. 32°. 1-16201-M1.   F73.44.R 96

SALISBURY, Samuel, a Boston merchant in the revolution, by Charles L. Nichols ... Worcester, Mass.,
The Society, 1926.   20 p. 25 cm.   Reprinted from the Proceedings of the American antiquarian society for April, 1925.   28-4032.
                                                                                                   F73.44.S 16

SHOCKING calamity! Particulars of the tragical death of Mrs. Ann Taylor, her son William Francis
Taylor, Mrs. Elizabeth Brewer ... who fell victims to the awful conflagration in Broad street, Boston.
Comp. by a gentleman who was an eye-witness to the distressing scene.   Boston, For N. Coverly
(1821)   24 p. incl. front. 12°. 1-12270-M1.   F73.44.S 55

SNOW, Caleb Hopkins.   A geography of Boston, county of Suffolk and the adjacent towns.   With historical notes.   For the younger class of readers.   Boston, Carter and Hendee, 1830.   iv, (5) - 162 p. front.,
illus., fold. map, fold. plan. 14½ cm. 1-12271.   F73.44.S 67
                                                                                                   Rare Book Coll.

SONS of the American revolution.   Boston in the revolution; a souvenir of the 17th congress, national
soc. of the Sons of the Amer. revolution ... Boston, Mass. soc. S.A.R., 1906.   48 p. illus. (incl. facsims.)
23½ cm. 8-9208.   F73.44.S 69

STATE street trust company.   A collection of interesting and historic prints; being a brief presentation of some of the originals and reproductions in the possession of the State street trust co.   Boston,
Print. fot the State street trust co., (1909)   (46) p. illus. 23 cm. 9-25403.   F73.44.S 79

STRANGER's guide in the city of Boston, Reprint of.   Pocket ed. for the anniversaries.   Containing a
safe and clear directory of some of the most reputable business houses in the city ... 1849.   (2d ed.)
Boston, Andrews and co., 1849.   63 p. 12½ cm. 3-20625.   F73.44.S 89

WHITING, Lilian.   Boston days, the city of beautiful ideals; Concord and its famous authors; the
golden age of genius; dawn of the 20th century ...   Boston, Little, Brown, 1902.   xii, 485 p. front., pl.,
port., facsim. 20½ cm. 2-29910.   F73.44.W 59

— Boston, Little, Brown, 1911.   xii, 543 p. front., plates, ports., facsims. 21½ cm. 11-12844.   F73.44. W 6

WINES, Enoch Cobb.   A trip to Boston, in a series of letters to the editor of the United States gazette.
By the author of 'Two years and a half in the navy.' Boston, C.C. Little and J. Brown, 1838.
xii, (13) - 224 p. 17 cm. 1-12273.   F73.44.W 76

BOSTON. 1865 - 1950.

BOSTON ....   Report of the commissioners on the annexation of Dorchester ... (Boston, 1869)
20 p. 23 cm. (City doc. no 28) 12-6962.   F73.5
                                                                                                   F74. D5B74

HUMPHREYS, Mrs. Eliza M.J.(Gollan)   America - through English eyes; by "Rita"   ... London,
S. Paul, (1910)   246 p. front. (port.) 19½ cm. 11-24691.   F73.5
                                                                                                   E168.H927

PAYNE, Edward F.   Dickens days in Boston; a record of daily events, ... Boston and New York,
Houghton Mifflin, 1927.   xv, 274 p. front., plates, ports., facsims. 24½ cm. Bibliog.: p.(ix)-xi. 27-23560.   F73.5
                                                                                                   PR 4582.P3

PILOT, The ... Centenary edition.   Commemorating the 100th anniversary of the Pilot and the 300th

anniversary of the founding of Boston. (Boston, 1930) (145) p. illus. 60 x 47 ½ cm. 41M2476T.
F73.5
BX1418.B7P5

SHANNON, Martha A. Boston days of William Morris Hunt. Boston, Marshall Jones, 1923.
x p. 3 l. 3-165 p. front., plates, ports. 24½ cm. 24-2709.
F73.5
ND237.H9S5

SKETCHES and business directory of Boston and vicinity. For 1860 and 1861. Boston, Damrell & Moore and G. Coolidge (1860) xiii, (9) - 522 p. front. (fold. map) illus. 27 x 21 cm. 19-7287.
F73.5
F73.24.S 62

ALBUM photographs. Historical Boston. Boston, C. Pollock (1883) 1 p., 10 pl. obl. 32°. 1-12274-M1.
F73.5.A 33

ALBUM photographs. Modern Boston ... Boston, C. Pollock, 1883. 1 p., 10 pl. obl. 32°. 1-12275-M1.
F73.5.A 34

AMERICAN association for the advancement of science. A handbook of the principal scientific institutions of Boston and vicinity. With a brief account of the more important public works, of the geology and geography, and of places of historical interest. Boston, Rockwell and Churchill press, 1898.
118 p. plates. 18½ cm. 18-4008.
F73.5. A 5

AMERICAN bankers' association. Points of interest in Boston and envirions. (Boston, 1937)
106 p. front., illus., plates. 19 cm. 37-23648.
F73.5. A 58

ATHEARN, Clarence Royalty. Boston in seven days ... with ten maps. New York, R.M. McBride, 1926. 3, 155 p. front., maps. 18½ cm. 26-14562.
F73.5.A 86

ATKINS, Arthur L. Cyclist's road book of Boston and vicinity. (2d ed.) Boston, Print. for the author, 1886. 43 p. 16½ cm. 1-20007.
F73.5.A 87

AUTHENTIC and comprehensive guide and history of Boston ... Mechanics' fair ed. Boston, Shepard, Norwell (1878) 96 p. illus. 16° 1-12276-M1.
F73.5.A 93

BACON, Edwin Munroe. Bacon's dictionary of Boston; with an historical introduction by George E. Ellis ... Boston and New York, Houghton, Mifflin, 1886. xiv, 469 p. 19½ cm. 1-12278.
F73.5.B 12

BACON, Edwin Munroe. Boston; a guide book. Prepared for the Convention of the National educational association .... Boston, Ginn & co., 1903. x, 190 p. illus., maps, plans. 17½ cm. 3-16253.
F73.5.B 13

— Rev. ed., 1908. Boston, Ginn & co., (1909) x, 190 p. front., illus. (incl. plans) maps. 17½ cm. 33-7578.
F73.5.B132

BACON, Edwin Munroe. A guide book of Boston, adopted by the New England hardware dealers' association for the joint convention .... (Boston, The Woodberry press, 1916) 40, x, 191, (41) - 88 p. illus., pl., col. maps, col. plans. 17½ cm. 16-15548.
F73.5.B134

BACON, Edwin Munroe. Boston; a guide book to the city and vicinity ... rev. by Le Roy Phillips. Boston, New York, Ginn and co. (1922) v-viii, 136, (8) p. front., illus. (incl. maps) 17½ cm. 22-13202.
F73.5.B135

— (1928) ix, 157 p. incl. front., illus. plates, plans. 17½ cm. 28-6101.
F73.5.B135
1928

BACON, Edwin Munroe. Rambles around old Boston; with drawings by Lester G. Hornby. Boston, Little, Brown, 1914. viii, 205 p. incl. illus., plates. front., pl. 24½ cm. 14-20365.
F73.5.B 14

BOSTON

BANKETTE company, inc. The tercentenary art book of Boston. Boston, Mass., The Bankette co., (1930)   54 p. illus. (incl. port.) 27½ cm. 30-20100.   F73.5.B 21

BARBER, Harold F.   Smith ... (Hyde Park, 1911)   16½ cm.   F73.5.B 23

BAXTON, Charles. Boston and the Back Bay. Boston, Mass., Reed & Lincoln (1884)   93 p. 14 x 11 cm. 1-12279.   F73.5.B 36

BENZAQUIN, Paul. Holocaust! (1st ed.) New York, Holt (1959)   248 p. 22 cm. 59-14396.   F73.5. B 4

BENSAQUIN, Paul. Fire in Boston's Cocoanut Grove; holocaust! Boston, Branden Press (1967)   248 p. 23 cm. First ed. pub. in 1959 under title: Holocaust. 67-28548.   F73.5. B 4 1967

BOSTON. (Portland, Me., L.H. Nelson co., 1907)   (48) p. illus. 20½ x 25 cm.   F73.5.B 69

— 1908.   20½ x 25½ cm.   F73.5.B 71

— 1910.   20 x 25 cm.   F73.5.B712

— 1912.   20 x 25½ cm.   F73.5.B713

BOSTON and its suburbs. A guide book. Boston, Stanley & Usher, 1888.   xx, (3) - 204 p. plates, fold. plan. 17½ cm. Copyrighted by Edward O. Stanley. 1-12280.   F73.5.B 73

BOSTON book, The; containing matter relating to the second International Congregational council, at Boston ... 1899. Boston, The Congregationalist, 1899.   232 p. incl. front., illus. fold. map. 19 cm. 99-5178 Rev.   F73.5.B733

BOSTON fire, The, Nov. 9, 1872 ... (Boston) Boston chamber of commerce ... (1922)   32 p. illus. 22½ cm. CA 23-204 unrev.   F73.5.B 74

BOSTON; a great modern manufacturing and commercial community built on historic ground around America's national shrines. (Boston) Convention bureau, Boston chamber of commerce (1931)   4, 95 p. illus. 35½ cm. 31-11888.   F73.5.B7403

BOSTON. Reception and entertainment of the Chinese embassy, by the city of Boston, 1868. Boston, A. Mudge, print., 1868.   77 p. 24½ cm. 9-28969.   F73.5.B741

BOSTON. Reception of the President of the United States by the City council of Boston. Boston, A. Mudge, print., 1867.   25 p. 24 cm. 9-7794.   F73.5.B742

BOSTON. Report of the Commissioners appointed to investigate the cause and management of the great fire in Boston. Boston, Rockwell & Churchill, print., 1873.   xxiv, 662 p. incl. plan. 24 cm. 1-12281.   F73.5.B743

BOSTON globe. Boston, the gateway to New England ... (Boston) The Boston globe, 1922.   48 p. illus. (incl. port., map) diagrs. 32½ cm. 22-5217.   F73.5.B745

BOSTON herald, The. The Sunday herald, diamond jubilee number, Aug. 28, 1921 ... (Taunton, Mass., 1921)   (88) p. illus. (part col.) 63 cm. Photostat copy. 22-14856.   F73.5.B7456

BOSTON historic and picturesque; a calendar for 1905. New York, 1904.   35 x 27½ cm.   F73.5.B746

BOSTON in half tone. Lynn, Mass., Souvenir pub. co. (1892)   23 pl. obl. 24° 1-12288-M1.   F73.5.B 82

BOSTON in your vest pocket ... A most convenient guide ... (Boston, 1886) 76 (12) p. illus., pl., fold. map. 9 cm. Compiled by Otto Schumm. 1-15981.
F73.5.B821

BOSTON old and new ... Boston, Mass., 1904. 17 x 23 ½ cm.
F73.5.B 83

BOSTON. Photo-gravures. Boston, C. Pollock, 1891. 18 l. 16 pl. 14 x 20 ½ cm. 1-12289.
F73.5.B 85

BOSTON picture book, The; over one hundred historic and characteristic views in and around Boston, Boston, I. P. Fox, 1895. 2 p., 34 pl. obl. 16°. 1-12290-M1.
F73.5.B 87

BOSTON road book, The ... Boston, G. H. Walker, 1898. 72 p. illus., fold. map. 16°. 1-12291-M1.
F73.5.B 89

BOSTON and vicinity, Souvenir of ... (Boston, Mass., Boston souvenir view book co., 1905) (48) p. illus. 17 x 25 cm.
F73.5.B895

BOSTON street railway guide ... containing a full description of all horse car lines entering Boston. ... Boston, Moore & co. (1880) 136 p. 17 cm. 1-12292.
F73.5. B 9

BOSTON, what to see and how to see it; a serviceable and trustworthy guide. Cambridge, Mass., M. King (1883) 126 p. illus. 24°. 1-12293-M1.
F73.5.B 93

— Boston, Rand Avery co (1886) 126 p. illus., fold. map. 24°. 1-16200-M1.
F73.5.B931

BOSTON yesterday and today. (Boston, Court square press, 1939) 31 p. illus. 20 ½ cm. 40-852.
F73.5.B934

BRADFORD, Gamaliel. The government of the city of Boston. Address of Gamaliel Bradford, at the Lyceum hall, Dorchester, March 14, 1884. (Boston? 1884?) 12 p. 22 ½ cm. 47-33349.
F73.5.B937

BOSTON, How to see: a trustworthy guide book. Special ed. National encampment of the Grand army of the republic; issued only be Macullar, Parker & co. ... (Boston) M. King corp., 1890. 138 p. illus., fold. map. 24°. 1-12294-M1.
F73.5.B 94

BOSTON. King's How to see Boston. A trustworthy guide book ... Ed. and pub. by Moses King ... (Boston, M. King, 1895) 288 p. illus. (incl. plans) 16 ½ x 12 ½ cm. 1-12295.
F73.5.B 95

— 1895. 288 p. illus., pl., maps. 16 cm. 2-15497.
F73.5.B952

BOSTON, Stranger's guide around Boston, and how to leave it. (Boston) Allen, print. (1885) folder (6 p.) 48°. 1-16199-M1.
F73.5.B 97

BOSTON. Brown's new guide-book and map for Boston ... Boston, H. A. Brown, 1872. 96 p. map. 24°. 1-12296-M1.
F73.5.B 98

BOSTON. A guide-book of Boston for physicians, prepared for the 57th annual session of the American medical assoc. ... 1906; ed. Dr. Walter L. Burrage. Boston, The Merrymount press, 1906. xi, 234 p. illus., plates, maps, plans. 20 cm. 6-22876.
F73.5.B985

— for the 72d annual session of the Amer. medical assoc. ... 1921. Cambridge, The University press, 1921. 2, 190 p. front. (fold. map) illus., plan. 20 cm. 21-9998.
F73.5.B987

BUSHEE, Frederick Alexander. Ethnic factors in the population of Boston. New York, Arno Press, 1970. (c. 1903) vi, 171 p. 23 cm. (The American immigration collection, series 2) 76-129393.
F73.5.B989 1970

CASWELL, Gilbert Frank. Boston: today. Boston, Beacon Hill Press (1952) 400 p. illus. 17 cm. (A Bean pot book, BP 101) 52-3570.
F73.5.C328

BOSTON

CHAMBERLAIN, Samuel. Historic Boston in four seasons; a camera impression. N.Y., Hastings House (1938)   73 p. front., illus. 19 cm. Includes 60 p. of illustrations. 38-27767.   F73.5.C 39

CHANDLER & co.'s full account of the great fire in Boston! and the ruins. Over 30 illus. Boston, W.H. Chandler, 1872.   62 p. illus. 23 cm. 1-12297.   F73.5.C 43

— 1872.   62 p. illus. 24 cm. 2d (?) ed. including later news of the fire. 7-38283.   F73.5.C432

CHANDLER'S visitor's guide in and around Boston. Directing strangers about the city and suburbs, to all places of note. With calendar for 1871. Boston, W.H. Chandler, 1870.   127 p. illus. 16º. 1-12298-M1.
F73.5.C 45

COFFIN, Charles Carleton. The story of the great fire. Boston, Nov. 9-10, 1872, by "Carleton" (pseud.) an eye-witness. Illus. by Billings, from sketches taken on the spot. Boston, Shepard and Gill, 1872.   32 p. incl. illus., map. front. 19½ cm. 20-3307.   F73.5.C 67

COLONIAL sight-seeing auto co. Colonial sight seeing auto tours, map of Boston, the Gray line, seven distinct tours ... (Boston, 1921)   (16) p. illus. (incl. map) 21½ x 20½ cm. CA 21-476 unrev.   F73.5.C675

COMMERCIAL bulletin, Boston: Saturday, June 11, 1892. Commercial, industrial and financial development of Boston. Boston, 1892.   (24) p. illus. (incl. plans) 60½ x 46½ cm. 8-2698.
F73.5.C 68

COMPANION, The. A pocket directory and general guide to Boston and vicinity ... (v.1 Sept/Oct. 1883. Boston, The Companion pub. co., 1883 -   v. illus. 23 cm. monthly. Contains floor plans of Boston theatres. 33-36342.   F73.5.C685

CONGREGATIONALIST and herald of gospel liberty. Official Boston book of the International council of Congregational churches ... council program, roll of delegates, guide and map of Boston... Boston, The Pilgrim press (1920)   38 p. illus. 19 cm. 20-13600 Rev.   F73.5.C 72

CONNECTICUT River lumber co. Boston: its commerce, finance and literature ... 1892. New York, The A.F. Parsons pub. co., 1892.   x, (25) - 285 p. illus. 26½ x 20½ cm. 1-295.   F73.5.C 74

CONWELL, Russell Herman. History of the great fire in Boston ... 1872. Boston, B.B. Russell; Philadelphia, Quaker-City pub. house ... 1873.   312 p. front. (ports.) illus., plates, plan. 19 cm. 1-12299.
F73.5.C 76

COPELAND, Robert Morris. The most beautiful city in America. Essay and plan for the improvement of the city of Boston. Boston, Lee & Shepard, 1872.   46 p. fold. plan. 23 cm. Folded plan wanting. 1-16198.   F73.5.C 78

CURTIS, George Carroll. ... A description of the topographical model of metropolitan Boston. G.C. Curtis, sculptor ... Pub. by the board of Paris expostion managers of the commonwealth of Mass. Boston, Wright & Potter, print., 1900.   37 p. fold. front., illus., fold. map. 25½ cm. 0-6193 Rev.
F73.5.C 97

DELEGATES' guide to Boston and vicinity, containing general information regarding the city and its vicinity and the 14th International Christian endeavor convention ... Comp. by F.W. Walsh. (Boston, Miller & Whalen, 1895)   (50) p. illus., fold. plan. 8º. 1-12300-M1.   F73.5.D 34

EARLY, Eleanor. And this is Boston! (and seashore and country too) Boston and New York, Houghton Mifflin, 1930.   x, 256 p. incl. front. 17 cm. 30-17698.   F73.5.E 13

— 1930.   x, 256 p. incl. front. 17 cm.   F73.5.E132

— 2d ed. 1938.   xxiv, 256 p. incl. front. 17 cm. 38-19106.   F73.5.E133

FITZGERALD, John Francis. Letters and speeches of the Hon. John F. Fitzgerald, mayor of Boston, 1906-07, 1910-13. Boston, Print. dept., 1914.   xiii, 166 p. front. (port.) 23½ cm. 24-16072.   F73.5.F 55
Rare Book Coll.

FITZGERALD. "Honey Fitz"; three steps to the White House: the life and times of John F. (Honey Fitz) Fitzgerald. Indianapolis, Bobbs-Merrill (1962) 335 p. 24 cm. 62-10012.
 F73.5.F55C8

FIVE cent Boston guide, The. Boston, 1904. 16 cm. F73.5.F 56

FORBES, Esther. The Boston book. Photographs by Arthur Griffin. Boston, Houghton, Mifflin, 1947. 122 p. illus., col. plates. 25 cm. 47-4979*.
 F73.5. F 6

FROST, John Edward. "The old home town," by Jack Frost. An overseas sketch folio of Boston for New England youths in service ... (Boston, The Hawthorne press, 1945) (16) p. illus. 23 cm. 45-7077.
 F73.5. F 8

FROTHINGHAM, Frank E. The Boston fire, November 9 and 10, 1872. Its history, together with the losses in detail of both real and personal estate. ... Boston; Lee, Shepard & Dillingham, 1873. 115 p. fold. plan. 19 cm. 8-10495.
 F73.5. F 94

GETCHELL, Everett Lamont. Field lessons in the geography and history of the Boston Basin; a handbook for teachers. Boston, Little, Brown, 1910. 3, (v) - xiii, 186 p. fold. map. 18½ cm. 10-27725.
 F73.5.G 39

GREEN. Citizens' candidate for mayor, Samuel A. Green. City election, Dec. 12, 1882 ... (Boston, 1882) 12 p. 19 cm. 11-25756.
 F73.5.G 79

GRIEVE, Robert. Picturesque Boston. An illustrated guide to the city as it appears to-day ... Providence, R.Y., J.A. & R.A. Reid, 1889. 120 p. incl. illus., pl. 4°. 1-12301-M1.
 F73.5.G 84

GUIDE to metropolitan Boston ... Boston, G.H. Walker, 1899. 136 p. incl. front., illus. fold. maps. 17½ cm. CA 31-115 unrev.
 F73.5.G 93

— (3d ed.) Boston, Mass., G.H. Walker, 1901. 141 (i.e. 144) p. 18 cm. 1-16631.
 F73.5.G 95

— (4th ed.) 1902. 142, (2) p. incl. front., illus. fold. maps. 18 cm. 2-19409.
 F73.5.G951

— 5th ed. 1903. 142 p. incl. front., illus. 2 fold. maps. 18 cm. 3-18487.
 F73.5.G952

HAWES, Harriet B. Ready-guide: Boston, Cambridge, Brookline ... 1936. 1 v. F73.5.H 38

HELIOTYPE pictures of the great fire in Boston, giving views of the burnt district. 2d series. Boston, J.R. Osgood (1872) 6 pl. 24°. 1-12302-M1.
 F73.5.H 47

HERNDON, Richard. Boston of to-day; a glance at its history and characteristics. With biographical sketches and portraits of many of its professional and business men. ... Boston, Post pub. co., 1892. vi, 461 p. illus., plates, ports. 28½ cm. 1-12303.
 F73.5.H 55

HISTORY of the great conflagration; or, Boston and its destruction. Embracing a brief history of its early settlement and progress to dae: together with a full and graphic account of its destruction by fire ... 1872. ... Philadelphia, Pa., Cincinnati, O., W. Flint, 1872. iii, 5-7, 19-142 p. incl. plates. front., double map. 21 cm. 1-12304 Rev.
 F73.5.H 67

HOWE, Helen Huntington. The gentle Americans, 1864 - 1960; biography of a breed. New York, Harper & Row, 1965. xix, 458 p. 22 cm. 65-20431.
 F73.5.H 84

HOWE, Mark Antony De Wolfe. Memories of a hostess; a chronicle of eminent friendships drawn chiefly from the diaries of Mrs. James T. Fields ... Boston, The Atlantic monthly press (1922) 5, (3) - 312 p. front., plates, ports., facsims. 21 cm. 22-19693.
 F73.5.H 85

HUMPHREY, Grace. Father takes us to Boston. Philadelphia, The Penn pub. co. (1928) 239 p. col. front., illus., plates. 19½ cm. 28-19022.
 F73.5.H 92

BOSTON

ILLUSTRATED Boston, the metropolis of New England. New York, American pub. and engraving co. (1889)   xiii, (33) - 305 p. illus. (incl. ports.) 27 cm. 1-16613.
F73.5. I 29

ILLUSTRATED guide to Boston and the country around Boston, J. F. Murphy, 1907.   3, (7) - 184, (4) p. front., illus., plates, fold. map, plan. 17 ½ cm. 7-26433.
F73.5. I 31

INTERNATIONAL congress of navigation. Boston, twelfth International congress of navigation. (Boston, New York, The Barta press, 1912)   55 p. illus. 16 x 23 ½ cm. 13-11849.
F73.5. I 61

INTERNATIONAL congress of zoology. ... Points of interest in and about Boston. (Medford? Mass., The Tufts college press, 1907)   32 p. 20 cm. 20-20155.
F73.5. I 65

JONES, Thomas Wallace. Miniatures of Boston. (Cincinnati, O., 1904)   8 x 10 ½ cm.
F73.5. J 79

KING, Moses. The Back-Bay district and the Vendome. (Boston) 1880.   31 p. illus. 23 ½ cm. 1-12306.
F73.5. K 52

KING, Moses. Boston: a series of 75 selected photographic views. Boston, M. King (1898)
38 pl. on 19 l. 14 ½ x 20 ½ cm. Text (1 p.) by E. M. Bacon. 1-12307 Rev.
F75.5. K 33

KING, Moses. Macullar, Parker company's selected views of Boston. (Boston) M. King, 1898.
16 pl. obl. 24°. 1-12308-M1.
F73.5. K 54

KING, Moses. ... King's Boston views ... Boston, M. King, 1895.   24 p. of illus. 38 cm. 1-12305 Rev.
F73.5. K 55

KING, Moses. King's hand-book of Boston ... Cambridge, Mass., M. King, 1878.   294 p. illus., plates, double plan. 20 ½ cm. 1-15797 Rev.
F73.5. K 56

— 1879.   304 p. illus., plates. 20 ½ cm. 1-15798 Rev.
F73.5. K 57 or 58

— 1883.   360 (i.e. 363) p. illus., plates. 20 ½ cm. 1-15800 Rev.
F73.5. K 59

— 1885.   387 p. front., illus., plates, fold. plan. 20 ½ cm. 1-15801 Rev.
F73.5. K 6

LANE, Thomas Wakeman. A descriptive reading on Boston ... Philadelphia, W. H. Rau, 1890.
2, 299 - 311 p. 12°. 2-10029.
F73.5. L 26

... LETTERS written by a gentleman in Boston to his friend in Paris describing the great fire, with introductory chapters and notes by Harold Murdock. Boston and New York, Houghton Mifflin, 1909.
4, vii-viii, 3-160 p. front., illus., plates, facsims. 25 ½ cm. 9-23233.
F73.5. L 65
Rare Book Coll.

LOMASNEY, Martin Michael. Boston mahatma. By Leslie G. Ainley. (Boston?) W. M. Prendible, 1949.   x, 246 p. port. 24 cm. 49-51315*.
F73.5. L68A6

LYONS, Agnes Claire. Invitation to Boston, a merry guide to her past, present, and future ... Photos. by Samuel Chamberlain, maps by Chadbourne & Wilcox. (1st ed.) New York, M. Barrows (1947)   xiii, 258 p. illus., maps. 22 cm. "A Village Green Press book." 47-11134*.
F73.5. L 9

McCORD, David Thompson Watson. About Boston; sight, sound, flavor & inflection. With drawings by the author. (1st ed.) Garden City, N. Y., Doubleday, 1948.   192 p. illus. 20 cm. 48-8942*
F73.5. M 17

McDUFFEE, Alice Louise. Nutshell Boston guide; a unique handbook for tourist, student and citizen. 3d ed. 1910. Cambridge, Mass., The University press, 1910.   2, 85, (2) p. front., illus., fold. map. 18 ½ cm. 10-18010.
F73.5. M 19

— 1911. 18 cm. F73.5.M191

— 1912. 2, 85, (2) p. front., illus., fold. map. 18 cm. 12-22022. F73.5.M192

MASSACHUSETTS library association. Condensed guide to certain historic places in Boston and vicinity, for the use of the members of the American library assoc. during the conference. Boston, Wright & Potter print., 1921. 52 p. front., fold. map. 17 cm. "A few helpful guides and readable books about Boston and eastern New England": p. 52. 37-15413. F73.5.M 27

MORISON, Samuel Eliot. One boy's Boston, 1887 - 1901. Boston, Houghton Mifflin, 1962. 81 p. 23 cm. "Memories and impressions" 62-16645. F73.5.M 6

NATIONAL association of power engineers. Official souvenir programme, 21st annual convention ... (Boston? 1902) 80 p. illus. (incl. ports., plan) 12½ x 18 cm. 2-24093 Rev. F73.5.N 27

NEW pocket guide through Boston and vicinity. A complete handbook, directing visitors where, when, and how to go through the city and suburbs ... Boston, J.R.Osgood, 1875. 80 p. fold. map. 16°. 1-12309-M1. F73.5.N 53

NORCROSS, Otis. In memoriam. Boston, Priv. print. (Press of T.R.Martin) 1883. 94 p. front. (port.) 27½ cm. 1-9336. F73.5.N 82

O'BRIEN, Edward Joseph Harrington. Walks and talks about Boston, ... 1916 convention, National wholesale grocers assoc. Boston, Mass., Ball pub. co., 1916. 2, vii-xiii, 175 p. incl. front., illus., plates, maps, diagrs. 19½ cm. 16-14140. F73.5.O 14

OLD colony trust company. Public service rate book. Boston, New York, The Barta press, 1912. 184 (1) p. front., illus. 24½ cm. 12-13046. F73.5.O 44

ONE hundred and fifty glimpses of Boston, Cambridge, Lexington, Concord, reproduced from the latest photos. Boston, J.F.Murphy, 1903. 3-80 p. of illus. 16½ x 23½ cm. 3-13065. F73.5.O 58 1903

— 1904. 78 p. of illus. 16 x 23½ cm. CA 26-509 unrev. F73.5.O 58 1904

PARKS, Edward Luther. Dr. Parks, his book ... (Boston) Pub. for private circulation (Print. Thomas Todd co.) 1911. 32 numb. l. pl., ports. 23 cm. Printed on one side of leaf only. 11-20627. F73.5.P 28

PARLEY, Peter (pseud.) "Round the hub" Boston, 1895. 10½ cm. F73.5.P 29

PEARSON, George Francis. Olde Boston towne ... Lexington, Mass., 1930. 19 p. illus. 18½ cm. On cover: The Gray line tercentenary number, 1930. 30-20104. F73.5.P 36

— Boston? 1953. 45 p. illus. 23 cm. Verse and prose. 53-37773. F73.5.P 36 1953

PERKINS, Augustus Thorndike. Losses to literature and the fine arts by the great fire in Boston. Prepared for the New-England Historic Genealogical Society. Boston, Press of D. Clapp, 1873. 10 p. 24 cm. "Reprinted from the N.E. historical and genealogical register for Oct., 1873." 58-52714. F73.5. P 4 Rare Book Coll.

PICTORIAL guide to Boston and the country around ... Boston, The G.W.Armstrong dining room and news co., 1902. 203 p. incl. illus., pl. front., fold. map. 17 cm. 2-15635. F73.5.P 61

— 1903. 2, 203 p. front., illus., plates, fold. map. 17½ cm. 3-13608. F73.5.P 62

PIERCE, Henry Gill. Boston on Massachusetts Bay; a short sketch of the old city, with a trip to Marblehead and the Program of the thirty-second annual convention of the Heating and piping contractors national association. (Worcester and Boston, The Commonwealth press, 1921) 2, 7-61 p. illus. (incl. maps, facsim.) 20½ cm. 21-9894. F73.5.P 65

BOSTON

PRINDLE, Mrs. Frances Weston (Carruth) Fictional rambles in & about Boston. ... New York, McClure, Phillips, 1902.   xxiii, 380 p. incl. front., illus., plates. 21 cm. 2-27221 Rev.   F73.5. P 8

PROSPECT union association. Recreation in and about Boston; a handbook of opportunities ... Boston and New York, Houghton Mifflin, 1930.   xix, 220 p. front., plates. 17 cm. Includes bibliographies. 30-17292.
F73.5. P 96

PULSIFER, David. Guide to Boston and vicinity, with maps and engravings. Boston, A. Williams, 1866.   viii, 293 p. front., illus., fold. maps, fold. facsim. 18 cm. 1-12310.   F73.5. P 98

— 1867.   viii, 293 p. front., illus., fold. maps, fold. facsim. 18 cm. 1-12311.   F73.5. P 99

RAND, McNally and co. Fifty glimpses of Boston; reproduced from recent photos. ...Chicago and New York, Rand, McNally, 1895.   48 p. illus. 17 x 23 cm. 1-12314 Rev.   F73.5. R 2

— 1898.   54 p. illus. 16 x 22 cm. 1-12315 Rev.   F73.5. R 22

— 1900.   63 p. illus. 16½ x 22½ cm. July 26, 1900-155.   F73.5. R 23

RAND, McNally & co.'s handy guide to Boston and environs ... Chicago and N.Y., Rand, McNally, 1895.   154 p. front., plates, fold. map. 18 cm. Pub. also under title A souvenir guide to Boston ... 1-12312.   F73.5. R234 1895

— 1897.   154 p. front., plates, fold. map. 17½ cm. 1-12313.   F73.5. R234 1897

— 1898.   154 p. front., plates, fold. map. 17 cm. 35-29239.   F73.5. R234 1898

— Editions also of 1899 (3d); 1900 (4th); 1905 (9th); 1905 (10th); 1906 (10th)

RAND, McNally Boston guide to the city and environs, with maps and illus. ... New York, Chicago, Rand, McNally, 19 -   v. illus., plans, maps. 19½ cm. 22-659.   F73.5. R 24

ROAD book of Boston and vicinity for bicyclers, riders and drivers. Ed. Charles A. Underwood ... 7th ed. Boston, The Sparrell print, 1893.   96 p. front. (fold. map) illus. 16°. 1-12316 Rev.
F73.5. R 61

— 8th ed. Boston, Sparrell print, 1895.   84 p. illus. 16°. 1-12317 Rev.   F73.5. R 62

RUSSELL, Francis. The great interlude; neglected events and persons from the First World War to the depression. (1st ed.) New York, McGraw-Hill (1964)   212 p. 21 cm. 63-22157.
F73.5. R 8

SHACKLETON, Robert. The book of Boston, ... illus. by R.L. Boyer. Philadelphia, The Penn pub. co., 1916.   4, 332 p. col. front., illus., plates. 20½ cm. 16-22764.   F73.5. S 52

SIGHTS from the towers of Boston, an illustrated guide ... (Boston, Press of G.H. Ellis, 1890?) 81 p. illus., fold. maps. 19½ cm. "11th edition, revised and corrected to date."   F73.5. S 55

SMITH, Chalres Frost. Notes and pictures of Boston ... Photographs by the Maynards, Waban, Mass. Boston, C.F. Smith, 1923.   (31) p. illus. 31 cm. 23-4708.   F73.5. S 63

— 1928.   (40) p. illus. 31 cm. "Revised edition." 28-15600.   F73.5. S 63 1928

SMITH, Dexter. Cyclopedia of Boston and vicinity ... Boston, Cashin & Smith, 1886.   276 p. fold. map, fold. plan. 19½ cm. 1-12318.   F73.5. S 64

— (2d ed.) 1887.   iv, 5-276 p. fold. plan. 19½ cm. 1-12319.   F73.5. S 65

— (4th ed._ Boston, C. M. Cashin, 1889.   223 p. fold. map. 12°. 1-12320-M1.   F73.5.S 66

SOUVENIR guide to Boston and environs.   Boston, G. W. Armstrong (1895)   154 p. front., pl., fold. map. 12°. Same as Rand, McNally & co.'s handy guide to Boston and environs. 1-12321-M1.   F73.5.S 70

SOUVENIR of the (Hub)   Boston, C. E. Brown (1895)   6 p., 50 pl. 14 x 21 cm. Picture of the hub of a wheel on t.-p., in place of the word. 1-12272*.   F73.5.S 71

SOUVENIR of Boston.   Boston, 1879-80.   11 x 16½ cm.   F73.5.S 72

STANWOOD, Edward. Boston illustrated. Boston, J. R. Osgood (1872)   122, (2) p. illus. (incl. map, plan) 20½ cm. 1-12282 Rev.   F73.5.S 79
1872

— Editions of 1875; 1878; 1883 (new and revised); 1886; 1893 (illus. by Charles H. Woodbury ... Ed. Edwin M. Bacon); also 1893a.

STRANGER'S guide: or, Explanations of the locations, objects, etc. as seen from the Bunker Hill monument.   Charlestown (Mass.) J. B. Goodnow (1886)   16 p. 32°. 1-21417-M1.
F73.5.S 87

STRANGER'S illustrated guide to Boston and its suburbs ... Boston, Photo-electrotype co. (1881) 3, 234 p. illus., fold. maps. 12°. Comp. by James Henry Stark. 1-12322-M1.   F73.5.S 88

STRANGER'S new guide through Boston and vicinity.   Being a complete handbook, directing visitors where to go, when to go, and how to go ... Boston, C. Thatcher (1865)   84 p. fold. map. 16°. 1-12323-M1.   F73.5.S 89

— Boston, A. Williams, 1869.   81 p. fold. map. 15½ cm. 17-24917.   F73.5.S 9

— Boston, J. R. Osgood, 1872.   64 p. fold. map. 24°. 1-16197-M1.   F73.5.S 92

THIS week in Boston.   v. 1 - 6, 8; July 30, 1905 - 09.   (Boston) The Innovation pub. co., 1905-09. 7 vols. illus. (maps) 21 cm. 6-18421.   F73.5.T 44

TWO hundred and twenty-five glimpses of Boston and historical surroundings, reproduced from latest photographs.   Boston, The Union news co., 1912.   80 p. illus. 17½ x 25 cm. 12-28673.
F73.5.T 97

UP-TO-DATE guide book of Boston and surroundings.   Boston, Mass., The New England news co., (1913)   128 p. illus., fold. map. 16½ cm. 13-12338.   F73.5.U 71

VIEWS of Boston and Harvard university.   (Portland, Me., 1904)   20½ x 25 cm.   F73.5.V 67

— (1906)   48 p. illus. 20 x 25 cm.   F73.5.V 68

WAINWRIGHT, Wainwright Johnson.   Boston in picture and story.   Cotuit, Mass., Picture Book Press (1954)   64 p. illus. 22 cm. 54-3893.   F73.5. W 3

WHERE can I get a car?   A street car directory of the city of Boston and surroundings ... comp ... by T. W. Preston.   Lynn, Mass., Nichols press (1894)   51 p. 16°. 1-12324-M1.   F73.5.W 56

WHITEHILL, Walter Muir.   A brief guide to institutions and sites of historic interest in Boston, prepared for the visit of military representatives of the North Atlantic Treaty Organization to the Bostonian Society on 24 March 1957.   Boston, Bostonian Society, 1957.   22 p. illus. 22 cm. 57-2412.
F73.5.W 58
L. H. & G.

WILSON'S annual reference book ... of greater Boston ... (Boston?) 1904-07.   2 vols. illus., plans. 20 cm. 8-822.   F73.5.W 75

BOSTON

WINN, Robert Mullin. "A guide at a glance" of historic Boston. (Wollaston, Mass.) 1947.
48 p. illus., maps. 23 cm. 47-7799*.
F73.5.W 78

— (Wollaston? Mass., 1954) 48 p. illus. 23 cm. 54-42426.
F73.5.W 78 1954

WOODS, Robert Archey. Americans in process; a settlement study. New York, Arno Press, 1970.
ix, 389 p. 23 cm. (The American immigration collection series 2) 78-129419.
F73.5.W 85 1970

BOSTON. 1951 TO DATE.

CHIANG, Yee. The silent traveller in Boston. Written and illus. by Chiang Yee. (1st ed.) New York, W.W.Norton (1959) xii, 275 p. illus. (part col.) 22 cm. Includes Chinese poems by the author with English translations. 59-10935.
F73.52.C48

LEVIN, Murray Burton. The alienated voter, politics in Boston. New York, Holt Rinehart and Winston (1960) 84 p. 24 cm. 60-12202.
F73.52.L 4

SOUTH END Historical Society. A picture of South End; or, The citizens and strangers guide to the metropolis of Massachusetts and its southerly environs with curious addenda. (Boston, 1968)
44 p. illus. 22 cm.
F73.52.S 6

WHITEHILL, Walter Muir. Boston in the age of John Fitzgerald Kennedy. (1st ed.) Norman, University of Oklahoma Press (1966) xv, 208 p. 19 cm. (The centers of civilization series) 66-10289.
F73.52.W 5

BOSTON. CEMETERIES.

BOSTON Cemetery department. Annual report. Boston, 1901-08. 8 v. in 7. 8°. (Contains historical sketch and matters appertaining the the Copp's Hill burial-ground (1900-01) and Historical sketch of the first burying place in Dorchester (Dorchester north ground) incl. town records, record of all tombs, etc. etc. (1904/05)
F73.61.A 2

GREEN, Samuel Abbott. Inscriptions on the bronze tablets recently placed on the gates of the older burial grounds in Boston. Cambridge J. Wilson, 1883. 8 p. 23½ cm. Reprinted from the Proceedings of the Mass. historicl soc. May, 1883. 1-12325.
F73.61.A5G7

MERRIAM, John McKinstry. Historic burial-places of Boston and vicinity ... Worcester, Mass., Press of C. Hamilton, 1892. 39 p. 26 cm. From Proceedings of the American antiquarian soc. ... 1891. 18-6883.
F73.61.A5M5

ROWLANDS, Walter. Curious old gravestones in and about Boston, selected by Walter Rowlands ... photographed by Howland Shaw Chandler ... Boston, 1924. 4, p. 50 pl. 31 cm. In portfolio. 24-18656.
F73.61.A5R6

CENTRAL burying ground, Gravestone inscriptions and records of tomb burials in the, Boston Common, and inscriptions in the South burying ground, Boston. Salem, Mass., The Essex institute, 1917.
167 p. 23½ cm. 17-8380.
F73.61.C3C6

COPP'S HILL burial ground, Historical sketch and matters appertaining to the. Pub. by the cemetery department of the city of Boston ... Boston, Municipal print. office, 1901. 26 p. plates. 24 cm.
2-5507.
F73.61.C7B7

COPP'S HILL burial ground, Epitaphs from. With notes. By Thomas Bridgman ... Boston and Cambridge, J. Munroe, 1851. xxiii, 252, 8 p. front., illus. 20 cm. Repub. in 1852 under title "Memorials of the dead in Boston.
... 1-12219.
F73.61.C7B8

COPP'S HILL burying ground. Memorials of the dead in Boston; containing an exact transcript from inscriptions, epitaphs and records on the monuments and tombstones in Copp's Hill burying ground ... Illus. by copious historical and biographical notices of the early settlers of the metropolis of New England. By Thomas Bridgman. Boston, Munroe and Francis, 1852. xxiii, 252, (4), 15 p. front., illus. 19½ cm. Also appeared under title: Epitaphs from Copp's Hill burial ground ... 1851. The preface to "The graveyards of Boston ... by Wm. H. Whitmore", 1878 states: "Mr. Bridgman's transcript was not exact and was very far from exhaustive. Out of the 2000 inscriptions here copied, about 800 are not to be found in Mr. Bridgman's book." 10-3090.   F73.61.C7B83

COPP'S HILL and burial ground, Old; with historical sketches, by E. McDonald ... Jan. 1, 1879. Boston, W. F. Brown (1879)   28, (1) p. 2 pl. 23½ cm. First ed. 3-24090.   F73.61.C7M13

— Boston, Printed by B. Parks, 1882.   47, (2) p. illus. 23 cm. 1st ed., Boston, 1879. 3-24097.   F73.61.C7M133

— (5th ed.) Boston, Print. B. Parks, 1885.   53, (3) p. illus. 24 cm. 3-24096.   F73.61.C7M136

— (15th ed.) Boston, Industrial school press, 1895.   57, (5) p. illus. 23½ cm. 2-24095. F73.61.C7M139

COPP'S HILL burying ground, Historical sketch of, with inscriptions and quaint epitaphs ... 17th ed. By John Norton. (Boston) 1921.   32 p. front., plates. 23 cm. 22-13534.   F73.61.C7N8

COPP'S HILL. The graveyards of Boston. First volume, Copp's Hill epitaphs. Prepared for publication by William H. Whitmore. Albany (N. Y.) J. Munsell, 1878.   xxiii, 116 p. illus. 25½ x 16 cm. No more pub. 6-35835.   F73.61.C7W6

EVERGREEN cemetery, An address delivered at the consecration of, Brighton ... 1850. By Frederic A. Whitney ... With an appendix. Boston, Print. J. Wilson, 1850.   24 p. 23½ cm. 7-16666.
F73.61.E9W6

FOREST HILLS cemetery; its establishment, progress, scenery, monuments, etc. ... By William Augustus Crafts. Roxbury, J. Backup, 1855.   2, (iii)-iv p. 237 p. front., plates. 19½ cm. 12-9111.
F73.61.F7C8

FOREST HILLS. An address delivered before the city government and citizens of Roxbury, at the consecration of the cemetery at Forest Hills, 1848. By George Putnam ... Printed by order of the city council. Roxbury, J.G. Torrey, city printer, 1848.   28 p. 23½ cm. 15-2709.
F73.61.F7P9

GRANARY burial ground, Historical sketch and matters appertaining to the. Pub. by the Cemetery dept. of the city of Boston ... Boston, Municipal print. office, 1902.   37 p. plates, fold. plan. 23½ cm. 3-52.   F73.61.G7B7

GRANARY burial-ground, ... A sketch of the origin and history of the. (Boston, 1879)   21 p. 22½ cm. (City of Boston. Doc. 47-1879) 3-18638.   Bound with this are also: Doc. 96-1879. Report of the joint special committee on intramural interments and Doc. 110-1879. Communications relating to intramural interments.   F73.61.G7B75

GRANARY burial ground. The Pilgrims of Boston and their descendants: with an introduction by Hon. Edward Everett; also, inscriptions from the monuments in the Granary burial ground, Tremont street. By Thomas Bridgman ... New York, D. Appleton; Boston, Phillips, Sampson, 1856. xvi, 406 p. front., illus., plates, ports., fold. geneal. tab. 23 cm. 1-12220.   F73.61.G7B8

GRANARY burying ground, Gravestone inscriptions and records of tomb burials in. By Ogden Codman. Salem, Mass., The Essex institute, 1918.   255 p. 23½ cm. Based upon a compilation made by Thomas B. Wyman, jr. for William H. Whitmore about 1878. 19-3757.   F73.61.G7C6

KING'S CHAPEL burying ground, Historical sketch and matters appertaining to the ... Pub. by the Cemetery department of the city of Boston ... Boston, Municipal print. office, 1903.   52 p. plates, plans. 23½ cm. 3-31443.   F73.61.K5 B7

KING'S CHAPEL Burial-Gound. Boston. City Council. Special Committee on Interments. (Boston, 1879)   4 p. 24 cm. Consists mainly of excerpts from reports of the Board of Health. 10-31057 rev.*   F73.61.K5B79

BOSTON 151

KINGS'S CHAPEL. Memorials of the dead in Boston; containing exact transcripts of inscriptions on the sepulchral monuments in the King's Chapel burial ground. With copious historical and biographical notices of the early settlers of the metropolis of New England. By Thomas Bridgman. Boston, B. B. Mussey, 1853.   3, (5) - 339, (4), 17 p. front. (double plan) illus. 20 cm. 1-12218.   F73.61.K5B8

KING'S CHAPEL? Remarks by the president (of the Mass. historical soc. ... on the preservation of the graveyard adjoining their premises. Boston, 1880)   126 - 133 p. 8°. Reprinted from the Proceedings of the Massachusetts historical society, Sept., 1879. 1-12326-M1.   F73.61.K5W7

MOUNT HOPE cemetery in Dorchester and West Roxbury: with exercises at the consecration, ... 1852. Boston, Crosby, Nichols, 1852.   40 p. 23 cm. 6-39417 Rev.   F73.61.M9.M9

BOSTON. CHURCHES.

GRAFF, Myrtle S. Guide book to Trinity church in the city of Boston. (Boston) Council of the Church service league, 1924.   57 p. incl. front., illus., plan. 18½ cm. 24-12635.   F73.62
BX5980.B7T9

LEAHY, William Augustine. The Catholic churches of Boston and its vicinity and St. John's seminary, Brighton. A folio of photogravures with notes and historical information ... Ed. de luxe. Boston and New York, McClellan, Hearn, 1892.   43 l. plates. 26 x 39 cm. 1-12338.   F73.62.A1 L2

PIKE, James, ed. History of the churches of Boston, giving a full account, in denominational divisions, of all the church, organizations of the city, from their formation to the present time, with dates and complete statistics ... Boston, Ecclesia pub. co., 1883.   v. illus. 25 cm. Contents. - Div. 1. Baptist and Presbyterian. 1-16805.   F73.62.A1P5

BOSTON church and musical directory of Boston, Cambridge, Brookline and other adjacent suburbs ... with portraits of the leading artists and phots. of churches in Boston ... Boston, W.G. James,
  v. illus. (incl. ports.) 20 cm.   7-3108.   F73.62.A18B7

BRATTLE Square. The Manifesto church. Records of the church in Brattle square, Boston, with lists of communicants, baptisms, marriages, and funerals, 1799-1872. Boston, The Benevolent fraternity of churches, 1902.   xvi, 448 p. 4 pl. (incl. front.) 8 port., 4 facsim. 25 cm. 3-987.   F73.62.B8B7

BRATTLE street, A history of the church in. By its pastor, Samuel Kirkland Lothrop. Boston, W. Crosby and H. P. Nichols, 1851.   vi, 217 p. 18½ cm. Six sermons. 17-28143.   F73.62.B8L75

BRATTLE square, Memorial of the church in. A discourse preached in the church in Brattle square on the last Sunday of its use for public worship ... By Samuel K. Lothrop ... Boston, Press of J. Wilson, 1871.   56 p. 23½ cm. 5-26563.   F73.62.B8L8

BRATTLE square, A sermon preached in the church in ... By John G. Palfrey ... Boston, Print. for O.C. Greenleaf, by Phelps & Farnham, 1825.   81 p. 22 cm. 17-25217.   F73.62.B8P15

CHRIST church. The alarm on the night of April 18, 1775. By Richard Frothingham. (Boston, 1877) 12 p. 24 cm. A discussion of the disputed question as to the church in which Paul Revere's signal lanterns were displayed. The writer contends that it was not Christ church, but the building known as the Old North church ... 2-2959 Rev.   F73.62.C
E216.F97

CHRIST church. The King's gift to Christ church, Boston, 1733, by Percival Merritt ... Cambridge, John Wilson, 1917.   (299) - 331 p. 24½ cm. Repr. from the pubs. of the Colonial Soc. of Mass. 18-19966.   F73.62.C5M5

FIRST church. Observations historical and practical on the rise and primitive state of New-England. With a special reference to the old or first gather'd church in Boston. A sermon ... By Thomas Foxcroft ... Boston, Print. S. Kneeland and T. Green, for S. Gerrish, 1730.   4, 46 p. 20 cm. 17-15792.
F73.62.F5
F7.F795

381

FIRST church. The commemoration by the First church in Boston of the completion of 250 years since its foundation. ... Printed by order of the society. Boston, Hall & Whiting, 1881. 3, (v) - xx, 218 p. front., plates, ports. 23½ cm. Historical sermons by Rev. Rufus Ellis. 6-40429. F73.62.F5B7

FIRST church. An address in recognition of six tablets erected to do honor to Governor Henry Vane, Mistress Anne Hutchinson, Governor John Leverett, Governor Simon Bradstreet, Mistress Anne Bradstreet, Governor John Endecott ... by James Eells. (Boston, Geo. H. Ellis co.print., 1904?) 32 p. 18 cm. 7-27749. F73.62.F5E27

FIRST church in Boston, History of the. By Arthur Blake Ellis. Boston, 1880. 22½ cm. F73.62.F5E47

FIRST church in Boston, History of the, 1630 - 1880. By Arthur B. Ellis. With an introd. by George E. Ellis ... Boston, Hall & Whiting, 1881. lxxxviii, 356 p. front., plates, ports., facsims. 24 cm. 6-40430. F73.62.F5E471

FIRST church, The last sermon preached in ... By Rufus Ellis, pastor ... Boston, Press of J. Wilson, 1868. 32 p. front., pl. 22½ cm. 19-20272. F73.62.F5E474

FIRST church in Boston, An historical sketch of the, from its formation to the present period. To which are added two sermons ... By the late Rev. William Emerson ... Boston, Munroe & Francis, 1812. 2, (9) - 256 p. 23½ x 14 cm. 6-15329. F73.62.F5E5

FIRST church. The shade of the past. For the celebration of the close of the second century since the establishment of the Thursday lecture. By N. L. Frothingham ... Boston, Russell, Odiorne, and Metcalf, 1833. 15 p. 21½ cm. 17-2870. F73.62.F5F9

FIRST Baptist church. An address delivered on the 100th anniversary of the organization of the First Baptist church, Boston, June 7, 1865, by Rollin Heber Neale ... Boston, Gould and Lincoln, 1865. 80 p. 24 cm. 6-37093. F73.62.F5N3

FIRST church. Five sermons ... With a preface giving some account of the fire, Oct. 2, 1711. By Benjamin Wadsworth. Boston, Print. by J. Allen for Benj. Eliot, 1714. xi, 168 p. 13 x 7½ cm. Imperfect: p. v-viii wanting. 18-20077. F73.62.F5W2

KING'S chapel. The commemoration by King's chapel, of the completion of 200 years since its foundation ... Also three historical sermons (by H. W. Foote) Boston, Little, Brown, 1887. vi p., 2 l., (3) - 200 p. front., illus., plates, ports., facsims. 24½ cm. 17-28147. F73.62.K5B7

KING'S chapel, A brief sketch of the history of. (Boston, 1898) (8) p. illus., pl. 24 cm. 7-30336. F73.62.K5B8

KING'S chapel, Annals of, from the Puritan age of New England to the present day, by Henry Wilder Foote ... Boston, Little, Brown, 1882 - 1940. 3 v. fronts., illus., plates, ports., plans., facsims. 24 cm. 17-28124 Rev. 2. F73.62.K5F5

KING'S chapel and the evacuation of Boston. A discourse by Henry Wilder Foote ... Boston, G.H. Ellis, 1876. 23 p. 23½ cm. 17-15772. F73.62.K5F6

KING'S chapel, A history of, the first Episcopal church in New England; comprising notices of the introduction of Episcopacy into the northern colonies. By F. W. P. Greenwood ... Boston, Carter, Hendee, 1833. xii, 215 p. front., illus. 17½ cm. 17-30834. F73.62.K5G8

KING'S chapel. Pamphlets, broadsides, clippings, and other miscellaneous matter on this subject, not separately cataloged, are classified in F73.62K5Z9.

NORTH church. Enquiring of the fathers, or Seeking wisdom from the past. Discourses preached in the New North church ... By Francis Parkman ... Boston, Print. S.N. Dickinson, 1839. 40 p. 24½ cm. 6-37500. F73.62.N5P24

BOSTON 153

NORTH church. A visit to the "Old North church," Boston. By Charles Downer. (Boston) 1893.
20 p. illus. (incl. ports., facsim.) 24 cm. 17-30829.
 F73.62.O3D7

OLD SOUTH church. The South meeting-house, Boston. (1669 - 1729) By Mary Farwell Ayer.
Boston, Press of D. Clapp, 1905.   6 p. front. (map) plates. 24 cm. Reprinted from the New-England historical and genealogical register, July, 1905. 6-1921.
 F73.62.O4A9

OLD SOUTH church. Exercises at a consecration of the flag of the Union, by the Old South society in Boston, May 1st, 1861. Boston, Print. A. Mudge, 1861.   16 p. 23½ cm. 6-40432.
 F73.62.O4B6

OLD SOUTH church. ... An historical catalogue of the Old south church (Third church) Boston. Boston, Print. for private distributuion, 1883.   x, 370 p. 3 port., 3 facsim. (incl. front.) 24½ cm. Imperfect, portraits wanting. 3-4879 Rev. 2.
 F73.62.O4B7

OLD SOUTH church (Third church) Boston. Memorial addresses ... Boston, Cupples, Upham, 1885.
131 p. 24½ cm. 2-6301.
 F73.62.O4B8

OLD SOUTH church. Our heritage, Old South church, 1669 - 1919. (Norwood, Mass.) Imprinted for the Old South society by the Plimpton press (1919)   94 p. pl. 19 cm. 20-7053. F73.62.O4B82

OLD SOUTH church. The 250th anniversary of the founding of the Old South church (Third church, 1669) in Boston. (Norwood, Mass.) Imprinted for the Old South society by the Plimpton press (1919)
ix, 138 p. 23 cm. "The historical discourse," by Rev. G.A. Gordon: p. (25) - 84. 20-2280. F73.62.O4B83
ix, 138 p. 23 cm.

OLD SOUTH meeting house in Boston, History of the. By Everett W. Burdett. Boston, B.B. Russell, 1877.   3, (3) - 106 p. front., illus. 23½ cm. 1-12342.
 F73.62.O4B9

OLD SOUTH Meeting-house. Report of a meeting of the inhabitants of Cambridge, in Memorial hall, Harvard college ... Boston, Press of G.H. Ellis, 1877.   29 p. 22½ cm. 10-31634. F75.62.O4C1

OLD SOUTH church. The A B C of American independence, a concise history of the Old South church ... By William Peter Cherrington. Boston, Hooper, Lewis (1901)   17 p. illus. 15½ cm. Dedication signed: W.P.C. compiler. 3-11501.
 F72.62.O4C5

OLD SOUTH church. The Dial of the Old South clock ... no. 1-10; Dec. 5-15, 1877. Boston (H.P. Chandler) 1877.   (126) p. daily except Sunday. 7-12703 Additions.
 F73.62.O4D5

OLD SOUTH meeting-house, ... Speech of President Eliot for aid in the preservation of the. Boston, A. Mudge, print., 1878.   14 p. 23½ cm. 18-4042.
 F73.62.O4E4

OLD SOUTH, The; or, The romance of early New England history, by James O. Fagan. Boston, Press of Geo. H. Ellis co., 1923.   2, 3-141 p. front. (fold. plan) illus. (part col.) plates, ports. 19 cm. 23-9776.
 F73.62.O4F2

OLD SOUTH church. 1669 - 1882. An historical catalogue of the Old south church (Third church) Boston. By Hamilton Andrews Hill. Boston, Print. for private distribution, 1883.   x, 370 p. front., port., facsim. 24½ cm. 3-4879.
 F73.62.O4H57

OLD SOUTH church. History of the Old South church (Third church) Boston, 1669 - 1884, by Hamilton Andrews Hill ... Boston and New York, Houghton Mifflin, 1890.   2 v. fronts., illus. (incl. plans) ports., facsims. (partly fold.) 24½ cm. Bibliography, by A.P.C. Griffin: v.2, p. (581)-655. 6-40400.
 F73.62.O4H6

OLD SOUTH meeting-house, ... Arguments in behalf of petitions for aid in the preservation of the. Boston, A. Mudge, print., 1878.   48 p. 23½ cm. 2-19330.
 F73.62.O4M4

OLD SOUTH association in Boston, The; list of officers, members, committees, etc. Boston, Print. for the use of the Corporation, 1912.   51 p. 23 cm. 12-20350.
 F73.62.O4O4

— 1912. 58 p. 22½ cm. 19-3272. F73.62.O4O42

— 1929. 61 p. 22 cm. 29-27704. F73.62.O4O45

OLD SOUTH church, Oration delivered in the, by Wendell Phillips. (Boston, R. Hildreth, 1876)
11 p. 23 cm. 6-37686. F73.62.O4P5

OLD SOUTH meeting house, The. 16 p. (Old South leaflets, v. 8, no. 183.) Boston, 1907. F73.62.O4P51

OLD SOUTH meeting house, Oration delivered in the, by Wendell Phillips. (Rev. by himself) Boston, Sold at the Old South, 1884. 12 p. 23½ cm. 6-37685. F73.62.O4P52

OLD SOUTH meeting house. ... Speech of Hon. Wendell Phillips for aid in the preservation of the Old South meeting house. Boston, A. Mudge, print., 1878. 14 p. 23 cm. 18-4783.
F73.62.O4P53

OLD SOUTH church. Tax-exemption no excuse for spoliation: considerations in opposition to the petition, now before the Massachusetts legislature, to permit the sale of the Old South church. By Josiah Phillips Quincy ... Boston, Proprietors of "Old and New," 1874. 12 p. 23 cm. 20-2074.
F73.62.O4Q7

OLD SOUTH church of Boston, History of the ... Pub. for the benefit of the Old South fund. (Boston, Print. R. Hildreth) 1876. 2, 73 p. 24 cm. 17-30822. F73.62.O4S6

OLD SOUTH church of Boston ... Pub. for the benefit of the Old South fund. By Elizabeth Putnam Sohier. (Boston) 1929. 71 p. 22½ cm. First pub. 1876. 31-3139. F73.62.O4S6
1929

OLD SOUTH church in Boston, The history of, in four sermons ... By Benjamin B. Wisner ... Boston, Crocker & Brewster, 1830. 122 p. fold. plan. 23½ cm. 19-10894. F73.62.O4W8

SECOND church. The story of the Second Church in Boston, the original Old North, including the Old North Church mystery. Boston (1959) 92 p. 22 cm. F73.62.S4B6

SECOND church in Boston, The; commemorative services held on the completion of 250 years since its foundation, 1649 - 1899. Boston, The Society, 1900. xv, 206 p. front., illus., plates, facsim. 24½ cm.
8-34784. F73.62.S4B7

SECOND church in Boston, The historical and other records belonging to the. (Boston, 1888)
12 p. 19 cm. Signed Francis H. Brown. 10-3143. F73.62.S4B8

SECOND church in Boston, Historical sketch of the. Comp. by George H. Eager. Boston, Press of Robinson print. co., 1894. 43 p. incl. illus., pl. front. (port.) 18½ cm. 17-24897. F73.62.S4E12

SECOND Church. Two discourses containing the history of the Old North and New brick churches, united as the Second church in Boston ... By Henry Ware ... Boston, Pub. by J. W. Burditt; S. Phelps print., 1821. 61 p. 21½ cm. 17-20606. F73.62.S4W2

SECOND church. A history of the Second church, or Old North, in Boston. To which is added a History of the New Brick church ... By Chandler Robbins ... Boston, Print. J. Wilson, 1852.
viii p. 320 p. 5 port. (incl. front.) 24½ cm. "Admissions and baptisms": p. 226-291. 17-28148. F73.62.S4R6

BOSTON. HARBOR.

ABORN, Peleg. A descriptive and historical sketch of Boston harbor and surroundings ... Boston, W. M. Tenney, 1885. 86 p. front. (fold. map) illus., pl. 12°. Ed. P. Aborn. 1-16306-M1. F73.63.A 15

— (1885) (4) - 5, (2), 7 - 83 p. front. (fold. map) illus. 16½ cm. 40M1831T. F73.63.A152

BOSTON

ASSOCIATED banks, trust companies and bankers of Boston. The port book of Boston; prepared under the supervision of the Publicity committee, 39th annual convention of the American bankers assoc. Boston, 1913.   2, 9-34 p. front., illus., plans (1 fold.) 19½ cm. 13-21525.   F73.63.A 84

BALLOON view of Boston harbor. Boston, J.H. Daniels (1879)   fold. plan. 16°. 1-12327-M1.
F73.63.B 19

CALLENDAR, George. Nautical remarks and observations for the chart of the harbour of Boston. Composed from different surveys; but principally from that taken in 1769, by Mr. George Callendar ... London, For the author, 1775.   11 p. 8°. 1-12328-M1.   F73.63.C 15

CONNELLY, Patrick Joseph. Islands of Boston harbor, 1630-1932, "green isles of romance", compiled by Patrick J. Connelly ... introd. by Joe Mitchell Chapple ... Dorchester, Mass., Chapple pub. co., 1932.   47 p. illus. (incl. map) 23½ cm. 32-29216.   F73.63. C 8

"Down the harbor." A pictorial guide of Boston harbor, showing all the principal objects of interest, to travelers and pleasure seekers. (Boston, P. Driscoll, 1873)   fold. plan. 12°. 1-12329-M1.
F73.63.D 78

...MESSAGE (of George S. Boutwell, governor of Mass., transmitting first report of the Commissioners, appointed under the Resolves concerning Boston harbor and Back Bay, approved May 3d, 1850) (Boston, 1851)   20 p. 2 fold. maps. 25 cm. (General court 1851. House Doc. 106)   CA 25-510 Unrev.   F73.63. M 4

SNOW, Edward Rowe. The islands of Boston harbor, their history and romance, 1626 - 1935, by Edward Rowe Snow. Andover, Mass., The Andover press (1935)   367 p. front., plates, ports., maps (1 fold. in pocket) facsim. 23½ cm. Maps on lining-papers. "First ed." 36-520.   F73.63.S 66

SNOW, Edward Rowe. The islands of Boston harbor, 1630-1971. New York, Dodd, Mead (1971)
xiv, 274 p. illus. 22 cm. 71-169730 MARC.   F73.63.S 66
1971

SNOW, Edward Rose. The romance of Boston bay ... Boston, Mass., The Yankee pub. co., (1944)
7, (19) - 319 p. incl. 1 illus., plates, ports. col. front., fold. map. 24 cm. 44-47898. "1st ed. Dec. 1944"   F73.63.S678

SNOW, Edward Rose. Sailing down Boston bay ... Boston, Mass., The Yankee pub. co., (1941)
9-57 p. illus. (incl. ports.) 2 fold. maps. 23 cm. 43-3505.   F73.63.S 68

STARK, James Henry. Illustrated history of Boston harbor. Comp. from the most authentic sources, giving a complete and reliable history of every island and headland in the harbor, from the earliest date to the present time ... Boston, Photo-electrotype co., 1879.   2, (3) - 167 p. front., illus., plates, ports. 17 cm. 1-12330.   F73.63.S 79

— 1880.   vii, 99 p. front., illus., plates, fold. map. 17 cm. 1-12331.   F73.63.S 80

TILESTON, Edward G. Tileston's off-hand sketches in Boston harbor ... Pen and ink drawings. Centennial 1876. E.G.T. (Boston) 1876.   79 p. incl. front. (map) pl. obl. 24°. 1-16305-M1.
F73.63.T 57

WHARF RAT, The. T. Wharf; notes and sketches collected during a quarter century of living on Boston's waterfront, presented by the Wharf rate, a magazine of limited circulation and doubtful value pub. now and then since 1928. Comp. Z. William Hauk. Boston, Alden-Hauk, 1952.
185 p. illus. 29 cm. 53-3906.   F73.63.W 53

WHELAN, M. Hand-book of the Boston and Hingham steamboat company ... A complete guide to the great watering places of Boston ... Boston, A. Mudge, 1880.   48 p. illus., fold. map. nar. 16°.
1-12332-M1.   F73.63.W 56

WRITERS' program. ... Boston looks seaward, the story of the port, 1630 - 1940, compiled by workers of the Writers' program of the W.P.A. Boston, B. Humphries, inc., 1941.   14 p. 15-316 p. incl. maps. front., plates. 22½ cm. (American guide series) 42-9007.   F73.63. W 8

BOSTON. MONUMENTS. STATUES.

WHITEHILL, Walter Muir.   Boston statues.   With photos, by Katharine Knowles.   Barre, Mass.,
Barre Publishers, 1970.   120 p. illus. 27 cm. 72-128387.   F73.64.A1W45

BOSTON.   Dedication of the monument on Boston Common erected to the memory of the men of Boston
who died in the civil war.   Boston, Print. by order of the City council, 1877.   144 p. front., 9 pl.
27 cm. Binder's title Army and navy monument memorial. 3-9013.   F73.64.A5B6

DEVENS, Charles.   An oration delivered in Boston, at the dedication of the soldiers and sailors'
monument, on Boston common.   Boston, (Press of Rockwell & Churchill, 1877)   16 p.   28 cm.   35-30103.
                                                                                F73.64.A5D4

BEACON HILL.   Sentry, or Beacon Hill; the beacon and the monument of 1635 and 1790.   By William W.
Wheildon.   Concord, Mass., Author's private print. office, 1877.   2, vii, (9) - 116 p. front., illus., plates, plans.
24½ cm. 1-12260a.   F73.64.B36W5

COLLINS, Patrick A., A memorial to; history of its inception, establishment and dedication ... Pub.
by the Collins memorial committee.   Boston, G.H. Ellis co., 1909.   31p. 2 port. (incl. front.) 24½ cm.
9-13913.   F73.64.C72C7

EMANCIPATION.   Bronze group commemorating emancipation.   A gift to the city of Boston from Hon.
Moses Kimball.   Dedicated Dec. 6, 1879 ... (Boston) Printed by order of the City council, 1879.
75 p. front. (phot.) 24 cm. (City document no. 26) 7-18232.   F73.64.E5B7

FORBES, Allan.   Other statues of Boston; reproductions of other statues of Boston as a sequel to our
brochure of 1946 entitled "Some statues of Boston,"   Boston, State Street Trust Co. (1947)
93 p. illus. 23 cm. 48-118*.   F73.64. F 57

FORBES, Allan.   Some statues of Boston; reproductions of some of the statues for which Boston is
famous, with information concerning the personalities and events so memorialized.   Boston, State
street trust co. (1946)   75 p. illus. 23 cm. 47-15509 rev.   F73.64. F 6

FRANKLIN.   Memorial of the inauguration of the statue of Franklin.   Boston, Prepared and printed
by authority of the City council, 1857.   412 p. 4 pl. (incl. front.) 23½ cm. 14-5645.   F73.64.F8S5
                                                                                Toner Coll.

HOOKER.   The equestrian statue of Major General Joseph Hooker erected and dedicated by the
commonwealth of Massachusetts.   Print. by order of the governor and Council.   Boston, Wright &
Potter print. co., 1903.   202 p. front., plates, ports. 26½ cm. 5-16599.   F73.64.H6M3
                                                                                1903

— 1903.   129 p. 26 cm.   F73.64.H6M3
                                                                                1903a
                                                                                Rare Book Coll.

PHILLIPS.   Exercises at the dedication of the statue of Wendell Phillips, July 5, 1915.   City of Boston,
Printing dept., 1916.   61 p. front., plates, ports. 27 cm. Prepared by order of the City council. 17-1518.   F73.64.P56B7

SHAW.   Exercises at the dedication of the monument to Colonel Robert Gould Shaw and the 54th regiment of Massachusetts infantry, May 31, 1897 ... Boston, Municipal print. office, 1897.
71 p. front. 26 cm. Pub. by order of the City council. 12-24138.   F73.64.S53E9

SOLDIERS' and SAILORS' monument, Erection and dedication of the, in the army and navy lot, in
Mount Hope cemetery, belonging to the city of Boston ... Boston, Print. by order of the City council,
1867.   46 p. 2 front. 22½ cm. (City doc. no. 80) 3-5232.   F73.64.S68B7

— 1867.   46 p. front. (plan) pl. 22 cm. 13-24901.   F73.64.S68B72

WARREN.   Monument to Joseph Warren, its origin, history and dedication, 1898 - 1904.   Boston,

Municipal print. office, 1905. 110 p. 6 pl. (incl. front.) port. 25 cm. 5-36838.
F73.64.W28B7

WASHINGTON. ... An account of the erection ... statue of Washington. (1869) 1 v.
F73.64.W31B7

WASHINGTON. An address delivered at the Music hall, Boston, in aid of the fund for Ball's equestrian statue of Washington ... by Robert C. Winthrop. Boston, Little, Brown, 1859. 60 p. 22 cm. 17-5809.
F73.64.W31W7

BOSTON. PARKS. SQUARES. CIRCLES.

BAXTER, Sylvester. Boston park guide including the municipal and metropolitan systems of Greater Boston. Prepared with the use of official illustrations and maps, by special permission of the Boston and Metropolitan park commissions. Boston, The author, 1895. 2, 69 p. front., illus., plates, maps (Partly fold.) 23½ cm. 12-16776.
F73.65.A18B3

BOSTON COMMON in colonial and provincial days, by Mary Farwell Ayer. Boston, Privately printed (D. D. Updike) 1903. 5, 47 p. front., 2 pl., 4 plans. 23 cm. 3-32787.
F73.65.C7A89
Map div.

BOSTON COMMON, Early days on, by Mary Farwell Ayer, with many illustrations after old prints. Boston, Priv. print., 1910. vii, 78 p. front., plates, map, plans. 27 cm. 10-12417.
F73.65.C7A9

BOSTON COMMON; a diary of notable events, incidents, and neighboring occurrences, by Samuel Barber ... Boston, Christopher pub. house (1914) 5, (9) - 288 p. 20½ cm. 15-2609.
F73.65.C7B2

BOSTON COMMON; a diary of notable events, incidents, and neighboring occurrences, by Samuel Barber ... 2d ed. Boston, Christopher pub. house (1916) 5, (9) - 288, xlvii p. 20½ cm. 16-10316.
F73.65.C7B22

BOSTON COMMON, The public rights in. Being the report of a committee of citizens. Boston, Press of Rockwell and Churchill, 1877. xv, 64 p. 23½ cm. 20-5500.
F73.65.C7B7

BOSTON COMMON in the seventeenth century. ... Boston (Industrial school for cippled and deformed children, 1903) (9) p. pl. 15 cm. 31-14898.
F73.65.C7B75

BOSTON COMMON. Life of Campestris ulm, the oldest inhabitant of Boston common, by Joseph Henry Curtis; with maps and illustrations. Boston, W. B. Clarke co., 1910. 88 p. front., plates, ports., maps. 26½ cm. Aged elm tree standing on the Beacon street front of the common. Authories cited: p. 87-88. 10-30093.
F73.65.C7C9

BOSTON COMMON; scenes from four centuries, by M. A. De Wolfe Howe. Cambridge, Print. at the Riverside press, 1910. x, 87 p. front., plates, plans, facsim. 28½ cm. "Sources of information": p. (80) - 82. 10-30097.
F73.65.C7H8

— Boston and New York, Houghton Mifflin, 1921. 5, 89 p. front., plates. 23½ cm. 21-26890. F73.65.C7H82
Rare Book Coll.

BOSTON COMMON. By Jeremiah Mason. Boston, J. H. Eastburn, print., 1843. 19 p. 21 cm.
Opinions on the question of the right of the city to sell certain lands claimed to be originally part of the common. 16-21592. F73.65.C7M3

BOSTON COMMON, The great tree on. By J. C. Warren ... Boston, Print. J. Wilson, 1855.
20 p. front., double plan. 24½ cm. 3-13314. F73.65.C7W3

FRANKLIN Park. ... History of the West Roxbury park: how obtained. Disregard of private rights. Absolute injustice. Arbitary laws. Right of eminent domain. 1873 to 1887 ... Gloucester (Mass.) Cape Ann breeze print, 1887. 103 p. 28½ cm. 12-17088 Rev. 2.
F73.65.F83S2

HAYMARKET (by) Wendy Snyder.   Cambridge, Mass., MIT Press (1970)   1 v. (unpaged) illus.
20 x 26 cm.   75-113727.   F73.65.H3S6

PUBLIC GARDEN, ... Report of the Joint committee on public lands in relation to the, July, 1850.
Boston, J.H. Eastburn, city printer, 1850.   52 p. fold. plan. 24 cm. (City doc. no. 18) 9-786.   F73.65.P9B7

BOSTON.   STREETS. BRIDGES. RAILROADS, ETC.

BOSTON street directory, a complete pocket guide to the streets, avenues ...   (1876 - 1885) Boston,
Sampson, Murdock, & co., 1876-85)   2 v. 14 - 16 cm.   F73.67.A1A2

EVERYWHERE in Boston and how to get there.   Rev. ed. ... Boston, Chase-Myrick, trustee, 1907.
260 p. 15½ x 8 cm. Includes a street directory of Brookline, Cambridge, Chelsea, Everett, Malden, Medford, Melrose and Somerville. 7-37721.
                                                                                                          F73.67.A1A2
                                                                                                          1907

HYDE'S street list of Boston, locating by district ...   (1903 - 1904, 1906) Boston, G.M. Hyde.
3 v.   18 cm.   F73.67.A1A2

EVERYWHERE in Boston and how to get there.   Rev. ed ... Boston, The Boston co-press, print.,
1903.   321 p. 15½ x 7½ cm.   7-37722.
                                                                                                          F73.67.A1A2
                                                                                                          1903

— Also editions of 1930 (Revised edition); 1935; 1943.

BOSTON arrow street guide ... (Boston, R.I. Polk, 19 -   v. 16½ cm.   39-21904.
                                                                                                          F73.67.A1B7

BOSTON house numbers by census tracts.   Boston, Boston council of social agencies, 1935.
2, viii, 65 numb. l. 28 cm. Reproduced from type-written copy.   41-27142.   F73.67.A1B73

— Boston, Printing dept., 1941.   2, 54, vii p. front. (fold. map) 28 cm.   41-27143.   F73.67.A1B73
                                                                                                          1941

COMPLETE street guide to Boston ... (1941 -   New York, "Geographia" map co., 19 -
    v.   2 maps on fold. l. 15½ x 8 cm. 42-28683.   F73.67.A1C6

OFFICIAL street directory of the city of Boston, giving cross streets and numbers at intersections;
theatre diagrams, office buildings, etc. etc. ... Boston, Sampson & Murdock, 1920.   168 p. fold.
map, diagrs. 17½ cm.   21-1199.   F73.67.A1O3

STREET list of Boston ,,. 1903.   F73.67.A1S9

ATLANTIC avenue: its relation to the mercantile and economical interests of the city. Remarks
addressed to the street commissioners on behalf of petitioners for its extension and widenting. By
Josiah Quincy. Boston, Wright & Potter, 1873.   11 p. 8°. 1-12334-M1.   F73.67.A8Q7

CHESTNUT street. While on the hill, a stroll down Chestnut street, by Charlotte Greene. Boston,
The Four seas company, 1930.   31 p. incl. front. (ports.) illus. 20 cm. Bibliography: p.31. 30-29652. F73.67.C52G79

DEVONSHIRE street; a collection of facts and incidents together with reproductions of illustrations
pertaining to an old Boston street, by Perry Walton. Boston, Printed for the Second national bank ...
1912.   2, (7) - 47 p. illus. (incl. map) 24½ cm. 15-25375.   F73.67.D49W2

EASTERN avenue. ... Report of Joint special committee on the Eastern avenue ... (Boston, J.E. Farwell, city printers, 1861)   15 p. 2 fold. plans (incl. front.) 2 fold. diagr. 23½ cm. (City document no. 58) 8-20774.
                                                                                                          F73.67.E2B7

BOSTON

PARK street. Old Park street and its vicinity, by Robert Means Lawrence ... Boston and New York, Houghton Mifflin, 1922.   ix, 172 p. col. front., plates. 21½ cm.   22-12548.   F73.67.P3L4

STATE street: a brief account of a Boston way. Boston, Printed for the State street trust co., (1906) 2, 42 p. illus. (incl. facsims.) 23 cm.   7-29672.   F73.67.S7S7

STATE street events; a brief account of divers notable persons & sundry stirring events having to do with the history of this ancient street. (Boston) Imprinted for the State street trust co. of Boston, 1916.   51 p. front., illus. (incl. facsims.) 23½ cm.   "Authorities": 1 p. at end.   16-13770.   F73.67.S7S72

TREMONT street. The site of Saint Paul's cathedral, Boston, and its neighborhood, by Robert Means Lawrence. Boston, R.G. Badger, 1916.   299 p. front., plates. 24 cm. ... "some information regarding the owners and occupiers of the land in that vicinity." Sources of information: p. 283-284.   16-18626.   F73.67.T7L4

TREMONT street, Views of. (Boston, 1894)   265-268 p. plates (partly fold.) 28 cm. From the Bulletin of the Boston public library, Oct. 1894.   6-27428.   F73.67.T7V6

WASHINGTON street, old and new; a history in narrative form of the changes which this ancient street has undergone since the settlement of Boston. By Edwin Munroe Bacon. (Boston, C.B. Webster, print. 1913)   (46) p. illus. (incl. plan) 23½ cm.   13-9168.   F73.67.W3B12

WASHINGTON street. Some old sites on an old thoroughfare and an account of some early residences thereon. Boston, Print for Macullar Parker co. (1918)   30 p. incl. illus., ports., facsims. front. 23 cm. 18-11844.   F73.67.W3M17

BOSTON. SUBURBS. SECTIONS OF THE CITY. RIVERS.

SUBURBAN blue book containing lists of the residents of Brookline, Cambridge, Malden, Melrose, Roxbury and Winchester. 1892 -   Boston, E.A. Jones, 1891 -   v/ fold. maps. 21 x 16 cm.   CA 33-618 Unrev.   Directories

BACON, Edwin Munroe. Walks and rides in the country round about Boston; covering 36 cities and towns, parks and public reservations, within a radius of twelve miles from the State house. Boston and New York, Pub. for the Appalachian mountain club by Houghton, Mifflin, 1897.   vi, 419 p. illus., 4 fold. maps. 16½ cm.   1-12277.   F73.68.A1B2

CHAMBERLAIN, A.C. Allen. By broomstick train. Little journeys about Boston's suburbs on the electric cars. (Boston, The Boston transcript co.) 1895.   45 p. front., illus., pl. 8°. Reprinted from the Boston evening transcript. 1-12335-M1.   F73.68.A1C4

LEADING business men of Back Bay, South End, Boston Highlands, Jamaica Plain and Dorchester ... Boston, Mercantile pub. co., 1888.   3, (9) - 224 p. illus. 25 cm.   20-2089.   F73.68.A1L4

OLD colony railroad company. Suburban homes on the "Old colony" ... Boston, 1889.   20½ cm.
       F73.68.A1O4

SUBURBAN Boston street directory   De luxe ed. Newton Centre, Mass., The Bellman pub. co. (1934 -   v. 17½ cm.   36-1061.   F73.68.A1S8

BEACON HILL, The lights of; a Christmas message, by Abbie Farwell Brown ... Boston and New York, Houghton Mifflin, 1922.   15 p. illus. 15 cm.   22-21328.   F73.68.B4B8

BEACON HILL, its ancient pastures and early mansion, by Allen Chamberlain ... Boston and New York, Houghton Mifflin, 1925.   xiv, 309 p. front., plates, ports., plans, diagr. 25½ cm. 25-18269.
       F73.68.B4C4

BEACON HILL and the carol singers. By John R. Shultz. (Illus. were drawn and engr. on wood by Thacher Nelson. 1st ed.) Boston, Wood, Clarke Press, 1923.   20 p. illus. 22 cm.   55-52014.   F73.68.B4S5

BEACON HILL, The little streets of, by Emilie Blackmore Stapp; with etchings by Jeannette A. Stewart. Cambridge, Mass., J. F. Olsson, 1928.   3, 5-16 p. plates. 19 cm. In verse. 29-3770.   F73.68.B4S8

CASTLE ISLAND. Historic Fort Independence and Castle Island. By A. F. Gregory.   Cambridge (1908)   16½ cm.   F73.68.C3G8

CASTLE ISLAND, its 300 years of history and romance, by Edward Rowe Snow. Andover, Mass., Print. Andover press (1935)   45 p. 1 illus., plates, ports. 23 cm. Pub. also as a chapter in the author's "The islands of Boston harbor".   36-763.   F73.68.C3S6

EAST BOSTON directory, The: containing the names, occupations, places of business, and residences of the inhabitants ... By George Adams ... 184-   Boston, 'Boston directory' office, 184 -
   v. illus. 14½ cm.   19-1016.   Directories

EAST BOSTON, A history of; with biographical sketches of its early proprietors, and an appendix. By William H. Sumner ... Boston, J. E. Tilton, 1858.   viii, 801 p. front., plates, ports., fold. plans, fold. geneal. tab. 23 cm.   1-15950.   F73.68.E2S9

RAINSFORD Island. ... (Boston, 1847)   24 cm. (City document no. 37, City of Boston)   F73.68.R2B7

SOUTH STREET. Collection of facts and couments relative to the project of a bridge from South street to Dorchester Neck, and the annexation of that peninsula to the town of Boston ... Boston: Print. E. Lincoln, 1805.   62 p. 21½ cm. (Bailey pamphlets, v. 65, no. 1)   18-18233.   F73.68.S7
   AC901.B3 vol. 65

SOUTH BOSTON directory: containing the names and business of the citizens, with a variety of other information. Vol. I. By George Adams ... South Boston, 1852.   96 p. 15½ cm. 17-20634.
   F73.68.S7A2

SOUTH BAY. Address of His Excellency, Alexander H. Bullock, to the Council, upon the question of improving the flats in South Bay: and accompanying documents. Boston, Wright & Potter, state printers, 1868.   34 p. 23½ cm. 8-18085.   F73.68.S7B7

SOUTH BOSTON, Illustrated history of, issued in conjunction with and under the auspices of the South Boston citizens' assoc; comprising an historic record and pictorial description of the district, past and present, compiled by C. Bancroft Gillespie ... South Boston, Inquirer pub. co., 1900.
   2, (3)-258, (2) p. illus. (incl. ports., maps) 23½ cm. Includes biographical sketches. 1-7128.   F73.68.S7G4

SOUTH BOSTON, History of; formerly Dorchester Neck, now ward xii, of the city of Boston. By Thomas C. Simonds. Boston, D. Clapp, 1857.   331 p. illus., plates, 2 port. (incl. front.) plans. 19½ cm. Detached from Dorchester and added to Boston 1804.   1-11632.   F73.68.S9S5

SOUTH BOSTON. An oration, delivered before the inhabitants of South Boston, 1835, the 59th anniversary of American independence. By J. V. C. Smith. Boston, Russell, Odiorne, 1835.
56 p. 22½ cm.   6-37687.   F73.68.S7S6

SOUTH BOSTON, History of, (its past and present) and prospects for the future, with sketches of prominent men, by John J. Toomey and Edward P. B. Rankin. Illus. Boston, The authors, 1901.
   xii, 570, (xiii)-xxxii p. front., illus. (incl. ports., map) 23½ cm. "Representative men..." p. (481-570) 9-30101.   F73.68.S7T6

THOMPSON. The four Thompsons of Boston Harbor, 1621 - 1965 with an appendix (by) Raymond W. Stanley. (1st ed.) Boston, 1966.   78 p. 23 cm.   66-17323.   F73.68.T5S7

BOSTON. BUILDINGS. COLLECTIVE.

BANKETTE company, inc. The tercentenary art book of Boston. Boston, (1930)   54, (2) p. illus. (incl. port.) 27½ cm.   30-20100.   F73.7
   F73.5.B 21

BOSTON 161

CAHILL, Thomas H. The auditorium, containing the plan of seats in all the theatres and public halls in Boston. Carefully cor. and rev. to the present time ... Boston, T. H. Cahill (1875) 46 p. 24°. 1-12336-M1.
F73.7.C 12

CAHILL, Thomas H. The pocket auditorium. Containing plans of seats of all the theatres and halls of Boston ... Boston, New England news co., 1878. 24 p. 14 cm. 1-12337*
F73.7.C 14
Rare Book Coll.

CITY HALL, Boston, The. Corner stone laid ... 1862. Dedicated ... 1865. Boston, Print. by authority of the City council, 1866. vii, 130 p. front., plates (partly fold.) plans. 24½ cm. 10-31139.
F73.7.C 73

DAMRELL, Charles Stanhope. A half century of Boston's building. The construction of buildings, the enactment of building laws and ordinances, etc. ... a chapter of Boston's big fire, fire losses, etc. Boston, L. P. Hager, 1895. 2, (17) - 524 p. illus. (incl. ports.) plates, fold. diagr. 29 cm. 1-15955 rev. F73.7.D 16

DRAKE, Samuel Adams. The old Boston taverns and tavern clubs ... Boston, Cupples, Upham, 1886. 70 p. illus. 19 cm. 2-9916.
F73.7.D 76

— New illustrated ed. with an account of "Cole's inn," "The Bakers' arms," and "Golden ball," by Walter K. Watkins; also a list of taverns, giving the names of the various owners, etc. ... Boston, W. A. Butterfield, 1917. 8, 9-124 p. front., illus., plates, ports. maps (1 fold.) facsims. 21 cm. First ed. Boston, 1886. 17-31890.
F73.7.D 77

POPE, Frederick. Some prominent buildings in the newer Boston ... Boston? (1903) 15½ x 9 cm.
F73.7.P 82

SEVEN landmarks of Boston. East Boston, Mass., Beacon print. co., 1891. 8 l. pl. obl. 24° 1-12339-M1.
F73.7.S 49

WESTMAN, Barbara. The bean and the scene; drawings of Boston and Cambridge. Introd. by Herbert A. Kenny, Barre, Mass., Barre Publishers, 1969. 34 p. col. illus. 23 x 28 cm. 74-87004.
F73.7. W 4

WHITING, John Eaton. A schedule of the buildings and their occupancy, on the principal streets and wharves in the city of Boston. Surveyed and pub. expressly for the use of insurance companies ... Boston, Press of W. L. Deland (1877) 211 p. 22 x 28 cm. On cover: Whiting's buildings and their occupancy in Boston. 24-22326 Rev.
F73.7.W 58

BOSTON. BUILDINGS, INDIVIDUAL.

BOSTON EXCHANGE. Remarks made by Hon. T. H. Perkins at the laying of the corner stone of the Boston exchange ... 1841. Boston, Print. S. N. Dickinson, 1841. 24 p. 21½ cm. 20-22904.
F73.8.B7P4

CITY HALL, Proceedings at the dedication of the, Sept. 18, 1865. Boston, Pub. by order of the City council, 1865. 36 p. 23½ cm. 2-17401.
F73.8.C5B7

COURT STREET. No 47 Court street, Boston. By John Tyler Hassam. Boston, 1903. 24½ cm.
F73.8.C8H3

CROWN COFFEE HOUSE, Ye; a story of old Boston, by Walter K. Watkins. Boston, Henderson & Ross, 1916. 55 p. incl. front., illus., pl., ports., plan. 23 cm. 16-6923.
F73.8.C9W3

FANEUIL. A funeral oration deliver'd at the opening of the annual meeting of the town, March 14, 1742. In Faneuil-hall in Boston: occasion'ed by the death of the founder, Peter Faneuil ... by John Lovell. Boston, Print. Green, Bushnell, and Allen, for S. Kneeland and T. Green, 1743. 14 p. 25½ x 20½ cm. 26-19567.
F73.8.F.
F73.4.F 23

FANEUIL HALL MARKET, (Report) of the committee of both branches of the City council, on the extension of. (Boston, 1826)   36, (2) p. 24½ cm.   CA 21-314 Unrev.   F73.8.F2B7

FANEUIL HALL and Faneuil hall market; or, Peter Faneuil and his gift, by Abram English Brown ... Boston, Lee and Shepard, 1900.   x, 218, (3) - 671 p. incl. illus., ports. front., plates, ports. 24½ cm. Pt. II: The merchants of Faneuil hall market.   0-2503 Rev.   F73.8.F2B8

FANEUIL HALL; cradle of liberty, by Norma R. Fryatt. New York, World Pub. Co. (1970) 125 p. illus. 26 cm.   70-101854.   F73.8.F2F78

FANEUIL HALL MARKET, Remarks on the constitutionality of the memorial of the City council, for an extension of. By Josiah Quincy. (Boston, Phelps and Farnham, print., 1826)   12 p. 23½ cm. 26-23349.   F73.8.F2Q6

HANCOCK HOUSE, The influence of the, in the colonies, by R. T. H. Halsey ... (New York? 1924?) (8) p. illus. 23 cm.   CA 25-1495 Unrev.   F73.8.H3H2

... LEVERETT street jail. (Boston, 1841)   11 p. 25 cm.   (City document no. 25) 9-27468.   F73.8.L6B7

OLD STATE HOUSE, Re-dedication of the, Boston, July 11, 1882. Boston, By order of the City council, 1882.   77 p. 4°.   1-12340-M1.   F73.8.O4B74

OLD STATE HOUSE, Re-dedication of the, Boston, July 11, 1882. Boston, Print. by order of the City council, 1882.   77 p. 26 cm.   Address of William H. Whitmore: p. 9-71.   1-12341.   F73.8.O4B75

— 2d ed. Boston, Print. by order of the City council, 1883.   179 p. front., illus., plates, ports., plan, facsim., diagrs. 27½ cm.   9-30377.   F73.8.O4B76

— 3d ed. Boston, Print. by order of the City council, 1885.   216 p. front., illus., plates, ports., plans, facsims., diagrs. 27½ cm.   9-30378.   F73.8.O4B77

— 4th ed. Boston, Printed by order of the City council, 1887.   236 p. front., illus., plates, ports., plans, facsim., diagrs. 27½ cm.   9-30379.   F73.8.O4B78

— 5th ed. Boston, Printed by order of the Ctiy council, 1889.   236 p. front., illus., plates, ports., plans, facsim., diagrs. 27½ cm.   9-30380.   F73.8.O4B79

— 6th ed. Boston, Print. by order of the City council, 1893.   236 p. front., illus., plates, ports., plans, facsim., diagrs. 27½ cm.   9-30100.   F73.8.O4B81

OLD STATE HOUSE. The Massachusetts building, Hampton Roads, Virginia. Jamestown ter-centennial exposition, 1607 - 1907. The Old state house in Boston, reproduced. (n.p., 1907) 31 p. illus. 18 cm.   10-5332.   F73.8.O4M3

OLD STATE HOUSE. Report of hearing before the Committee on cities, March 8, 1907 on the bill ... to preserve the Old state house an an historic and patriotic memorial ... Boston, The Rockwell & Churchill press, 1907.   22 p. pl. 23½ cm.   7-17342.   F73.8.O4M4

OLD STATE HOUSE. Prytaneum bostoniense. Notes on the history of the Old state house, formerly known as the Town house in Boston - the Court house in Boston - the Province court house - the State house - and the City hall; by George H. Moore ... Boston, Cupples, Upham, 1885-86.   2 v. 24½ cm. 1-12343.   F73.8.O4M82

— 2d ed., with additions. Boston, Cupples, Upham, 1887.   39 p. 25 cm.   1-12344.   F73.8.O4M84

OLD TOWN-HOUSE of Boston, The ... Boston, 1883. (Boston, 1887)   11 p. 1 illus. 15½ cm.   Second ed. 1-12345.   F73.8.O4O4

OLD STATE HOUSE. An address to the members of the City council, on the removal of the municipal government. 1830.   F73.8.O4O8

OLD STATE HOUSE. The vanity of zeal for fasts, without true judgement, mercy and compassions. A sermon ... after the destruction of the Province court-house by fire. By Thomas Prentice ... Boston, Print. Rogers and Fowle, 1748.   27 p. 19½ cm.   16-21913.   F73.8.O4P9
Rare Book Coll.

OLD STATE-HOUSE, The, defended from unfounded attacks upon its integrity. Being a reply to Dr. G. H. Moore's second paper ... By William H. Whitmore. Boston, 1886.   8 p. 23½ cm. 4-35834.   F73.8.O4W6

(PARK SQUARE STATION.) A blight on Boston. How shall it be removed? ... By John Albree. Boston, The Berkeley press, 1906.   16 p. front., illus. 23½ cm.   Comments on the abandonment of land formerly used for railroad purposes ...   7-8231.   F73.8.P2A3

PARKER HOUSE, Boston and the; a chronicle of those who have lived on that historic spot where the new Parker house now stands in Boston, by James W. Spring ... Boston, Priv. print., J. W. Whipple, 1927.   xiii, 230 p. incl. illus., facsims. front., plates, ports., fold. map. 21 cm.   28-7786.   F73.8.P3S7

STATE HOUSE, The ... By Ellen Mudge Burrill. Printed under the direction of the secretary of the commonwealth ... Boston, Wright & Potter print., 1901.   66 p. front. 16 cm.   6-37978.   F73.8.S8B9
1901

— (3d ed.) 1907.   111 p. pl. 18½ cm.   7-29677.   F73.8.S8B9
1907

— (5th ed.) 1914.   119 p. v p. plates. 18½ cm.   14-31278.   F73.8.S8B9
1914

— (7th ed.) 1921.   150 p., vii p. front., plates. 18½ cm.   21-11178.   F73.8.S8B9
1921

— (6th ed.) 1917.   133 p., vi p. front., plates. 18½ cm.   17-28806.   F73.8.S8B9
1917

— (8th ed.) 1924.   166, viii p. front., plates. 19 cm.   24-15277.   F73.8.S8B9
1924

— 9th ed. 1927.   190, x p. front., plates. 19 cm.   27-25385.   F73.8.S8B9
1927

— 9th ed. 1933.   167, 167a-b, 168-190, x p. front., plates, port. 19 cm. "Fourth printing." 33-20420.   F73.8.S8B9
1933

STATE HOUSE. A new guide to the Massachusetts State House, by Sinclair H. Hitchings and Catherine H. Farlow. Prepared as a public service to the Commonwealth of Mass. by the John Hancock Mutual Life Insurance Co. (Boston, 1964)   108 p. 23 cm.   F73.8.S8H5

STATE HOUSE. Centennial of the Bulfinch State house. Exercises before the Massachusetts legislature. Boston, Wright & Potter print., 1898.   74 p. front., plates, ports. 25 cm.   1-12346.   F73.8.S8M41

STATE HOUSE. (Report of Committee appointed to procure plans and estimates for a fire-proof building in rear of State house. Boston, 1853)   22 p. fold. front. 23½ cm.   (General court, 1853. Senate Doc. 59) CA 21-330 Unrev.   F73.8.S8M415

STATE HOUSE. A history of the emblem of the codfish in the hall of the House of representatives, comp. by a committee of the House ... Boston, Wright & Potter print., 1895.   62 p. plat;es, ports. 25 cm. 1-12347.   F73.8.S8M42

STATE HOUSE. Report of the State house commission to the Massachusetts legislature on additions to the State house. Authorized by chapter 150, Resolves of 1912. Boston, Wright & Potter print., 1913.
22 p. 23 cm.   15-27228.
F73.8.S8M5

STATE HOUSE. The Massachusetts State House. Massachusetts. State Library. Boston, 1953.
155 p. illus. 20 cm.   53-62835.
F73.8.S8M6

STATE HOUSE. Our state capitol illustrated. Boston, A. M. Bridgman, 1894.   2, 70 pl. 17½ x 22½ cm.
1-12348.
F73.8.S8O9

STATE HOUSE, in Boston, The ... By David Pulsifer. Boston, Wright and Potter, print., 1865.
24 p. front., illus., fold. plan.   19½ cm.   1-16196.
F73.8.S8P89

— Boston, Rand, Avery, 1881.   24 p. front., illus. 20 cm.   1-12349 Rev.
F73.8.S8P9

STATE HOUSE. The old Representatives' Hall, 1798 - 1895. An address delivered before the Mass. House of representatives ... By Alfred Sellye Roe ... Boston, Wright and Potter print., 1895.
72 p. front., plates, ports. 25 cm.   5-32493.
F73.8.S8R7

STATE HOUSE. Our State house, illustrated, historical, and biographical ... Boston. Tappan pub. co., 1900.   130 p. illus. obl. 16°. March 14, 1901-22.
F73.8.S8T2

VASSALL HOUSE. A home of the olden time. By Thomas C. Amory. Boston, Print. D. Clapp, 1872.
(5) - 27 p. 25½ cm. Description of the house on Summer street, erected about 1730 by Leonard Vassall, with accounts of the families which occupied it.   8-10577.
F73.8.V3A5

BOSTON. ELEMENTS IN THE POPULATION.

HANDLIN, Oscar. Boston's immigrants, 1790 - 1865; a study in acculturation ... Cambridge, Harvard university press; London, H. Milford, Oxford university press, 1941.   xviii, 287 p. incl. illus. (incl. maps, plans) tables, diagrs. 22½ cm.   Note on sources: p. (251) - 268.   A41-4664.
F73.9.A1H3

— 1959.   382 p. illus. 22 cm.   59-7653.
F73.9.A1H3 1959

FORBES, Allen. Boston and some noted émigrés; a collection of facts and incidents, with appropriate illustrations, relating to some well-known citizens of France who found homes in Boston and New England ...   Issued by the State street trust co ...   (Boston, Walton advertising & print. co.) 1938.
98 p. front., illus. (incl. ports.)   23½ cm.   38-18373.
F73.9.F7 F7

CULLEN, James Bernard. The story of the Irish in Boston: tog. with biographical sketches of representative men and noted women ... Boston, J.B. Cullen & co., 1889.   v, 443 p. front., illus., ports. 22½ cm.   Contains biographical sketches.   1-12351.
F73.9.I7 C9

— Rev. ed. Boston, H.A.Plimpton, 1893.   v, 630, xiii p. incl. illus., ports. front. 33 x 28 cm. 18-20080.
F73.9.I7C92

GUIDA degli italiani in Boston. Boston, Mass., Radford-Magee directory co., 1909 -
v. 24 cm.   9-31824.
F73.9.I8G9

ROSEN, Benjamin. The trend of Jewish population in Boston; a study to determine the location of a Jewish communal building, ... (Boston, 1921)   3, (9) - 28 p. tables (1 fold.) 27 cm.   21-6791.
F73.9.J4P5

EHRENFRIED, Albert. A chronicle of Boston Jewry; from the Colonial settlement to 1900. (Boston? 1963)   viii, 771 p. 21 cm.
F73.9.J5 E5

WIEDER, Arnold A. The early Jewish community of Boston's North End; a sociologically oriented study of an Eastern European Jewish immigrant community in an American big city neighborhood between 1870 and 1900. With an introd. by Jerome Himelhoch. (Waltham, Mass.) Brandeis University, 1962. 100 p. 24 cm.   F73.9.J5W5

DANIELS, John. In freedom's birthplace; a study of the Boston negroes, ... Boston and New York, Houghton Mifflin, 1914. xiii, 496 p. incl. tables. 20 cm. 14-3718.   F73.9.N4D2

— New York, Negro Universities Press (1968) xiii, 496 p. 22 cm. 68-55880.   F73.9.N4D2 1968

— New York, Arno Press, 1969. ix, xiii, 496 p. 22 cm. (The American Negro, his history and literature) 69-18575.   F73.9.N4D2 1969

SILK, Leonard Solomon. What kind of neighbors? A survey of attitudes toward non-segregation in Boston's South End and Roxbury districts,... (Boston, Division of Social Studies of Simmons College) 1950. 32 p. illus., map. 22 cm. 50-58323.   F73.9.N4S5

BLACK and White in Boston; a report based on the Community Research Project. (By) Donald D. Dollin and others. (Boston, Research Dept., United Community Services of Metropolitan Boston) 1968. vi, 44 p. 29 cm.   F73.9.N4U5

WRETLIND, Eric. Svensk kalender i Boston, utgifven af Eric Wretland. Boston, Utgifvarens förlag, 1881. 88 p. 20 cm. Contains more then 2,000 names, addresses, etc. of Swedes in Boston. 17-19876.   F73.9.S28W9

OTHER CITIES, TOWNS, ETC. A - Z.

ABINGTON. Celebration of the 150th anniversary of the incorporation of Abington ... 1862 ... Boston, Wright & Potter, print., 1862. 114 p. front. (plan) 23½ cm. 1-11204.   F74.A1A13

ABINGTON. ... Official program of the commemorative exercises of the 200th anniversary of the incorporation of the town of Abington ... participated in by the towns of Abington, Rockland and Whitman ... Rockland, A.I. Randall, print., 1912. 72, (24) p. illus. (incl. ports.) 23½ cm. 12-12938.   F74.A1 A14

ABINGTON, Vital record of, to the year 1850 ... Boston, N.E. hist. geneal. soc., ... 1912. 2 v. 23 cm. v.I. Births. v.2. Marriages and deaths. 13-2538.   F74.A1 A2

ABINGTON. Old Abington's 250th anniversary: development of the town. Abington, Historical society of Old Abington, 1962. 81 l. 29 cm.   F74.A1 H44

— 1962. 27 l. 29 cm.   F74.A1 H45

ABINGTON, Plymouth County, An historical sketch of. With an appendix. By Aaron Hobart. Boston, Print. S.N. Dickinson, 1839. (5)-176 p. 23½ cm. 7-11190.   F74.A1 H5

ABINGTON, Plymouth County, History of the town of, from its first settlement. By Benjamin Hobart. Boston, T.H. Carter, 1866. xix, 453 p. front. (port.) plates. 20½ cm. Memorials of families in Abington: p. 343-453. 1-11205.   F74.A1 H6

ABINGTON'S part in the building of a great commonwealth and a powerful nation (by) Charles Francis Meserve, Squirrel island, Me. (n.p.) 1930. 20 p. 23 cm. Bibliography: p.20. 31-8001.   F74.A1 M5

ACTON, Vital records of, to the year 1850. Boston, Mass., The New England hist. and geneal. soc., 1923. 311 p. 23 cm. 24-27188.   F74.A17A17

ACTON, An address delivered at, being the first centennial anniversary of the organization of that town ....   By Josiah Adams ... Boston, Print. J. T. Buckingham, 1835.   48 p. pl., fold. map. 21 cm.
7-39295 Rev.
F74. A
AC901. W3 vol. 28 no. 4

ACTON.   Crosby's Acton and Maynard directory ... 1926 -   Boston, Crosby pub. co., 1926 -
v. 24 cm.   26-6372.
Directories

ACTON.   Memorial stones dedicated by the town of Acton ... 1895.   (Reprinted from the Proceedings of the Mass. hist. soc.) Cambridge, J. Wilson, 1895.   7 p. 24½ cm. 3-21686.   F74. A17 P8

ACTON.   ... Souvenir of the celebration of the 120th anniversary of the Concord fight.   (Acton, F. P. Wood, 1895)   24, (2) p. illus. (incl. ports.) 24 cm.   8-25408.   F74. A17 S7

ACUSHNET, Dartmouth and Westport, ... Directory of ...   v. 1 -   1927 -   Salem, Mass., Crosby pub. co., 1927.   v.   24 cm.   CA 27-96 Unrev.   F74. A22 A18

ACUSHNET cemetery.   Memorial record of the dead of families of the early settlers interred in the old colonial burying ground ... in the old township of Dartmouth, now Acushnet.   New York, C. Hyllested, print., 1881.   21 p. 24 cm.   13-5132.   F74. A22 A2

ACUSHNET Centennial ... 1860 "Land of the Cushenas" 1960. (Acushnet, Mass., 1960)   52 p. 28 cm.
F74. A22 A6

ACUSHNET, Bristol County, A history of the town of.   By Franklyn Howland ... New Bedford, Mass., The author, 1907.   8, (7) - 398 p. illus., ports. 26 cm.   8-10854.   F74. A22 H8

ADAMS directory, 1887.   Pittsfield, Mass., Press of Eagle print.   v. fold. maps. 24 cm.
Directories

ADAMS directory, 1886 - 96.   4 v.   Directories

ADAMS directory, including ... Cheshire, 1899 - 1903.   3 v.   Directories

ADAMS, Cheshire and Williamstown directories 1910.   1 v.   Directories

ADAMS, ... First records of the town of.   Worcester, Massachusetts record soc., 1892.
11 p. 24 cm. 25-3661.   F74. A25 A25

ADAMS.   Historic Adams; the past and present of the town and a bank.   Issued by the Greylock national bank in commemoration of its fiftieth anniversary.   (Boston) Print, Walton ad. & print., 1941.
27 p. incl. front., illus., ports. 19½ cm.   41-10451.   F74. A25 G7

ADAMS.   Unveiling the McKinley statue, Adams, Mass.   (New York, The Knickerbock press, 1903)
44 p. front., plates, ports. 23½ cm.   6-23881.   F74. A25 U6

ALFORD.   Vital records of Alford, to the year 1850 ...   Boston, 1902.   32 p. 23½ cm. (New-England historic genealogical soc.)   3-5251.   F74. A3 A3

AMESBURY, Vital records of, to the end of the year 1849.   Topsfield, Mass., Topsfield hist. soc., 1913.   600 p. 23½ cm. 13-21492.   F74. A4 A4

AMESBURY improvement association.   Transactions of the Amesbury historical society.   v. 1 - (Amesbury?) 1901 -   1 v. 23½ cm.   6-1320.   F74. A4 A5

AMESBURY.   The history of a house (built by Squire Bagley, in Amesbury) its founder, family and guests, by Mary Beecher Longyear.   Illus. by Photos. of the house and the original furniture and objects found in the house in 1922.   Brooklin, Mass., The Zion research foundation, 1925.   4, 69 p. plates, ports., facsim. 19½ cm.   25-6830.   F74. A4 B2

MASSACHUSETTS

— 2d ed. rev. Brookline, Mass., Longyear Foundation, 1947 (i.e. 1948) vii, 70 p. illus., ports. 20 cm.
48-15611*.
F74. A4 B2
1948

AMESBURY, History of, including the first seventeen years of Salisbury, to the separation in 1654; and Merrimac, from its incorporation in 1876; by Joseph Merrill. Haverhill (Mass.) Press of F. P. Stiles, 1880. xxiii, 451 p. front., illus., ports., fold. map. 23½ cm. 1-11206. F74. A4 M5

AMESBURY, History of. Beginning with the arrival of the Winthrop Fleet 1630 at Salem and Boston through 1967. Amesbury, Mass., Whittier Press, 1968. 239 p. illus.
F74. A4 R4

AMESBURY. ... A chronological record of the principal events that have occurred in Amesbury, from the organization of the township of Merrimac in 1638 to 1900; by Emily B. Smith. Amesbury, J. E. Brierly, 1901. 38 p. 22 cm. Cover-title: Amesbury records. 1638. 1-25840. F74. A4 S6

AMHERST directory ... 1884/5 -   New Haven, Conn., Price, Lee, 1884 -   23½ cm.
12-11041.
Directories

AMHERST directory including Hadley and Belchertown ...   Springfield, Mass., H. A. Manning co., 1895 - 1912. 7 v. fold. maps. 23 - 23½ cm. 9-1235 Additions.
Directories

AMHERST, Street list of the town of, 1926, 1927. (Amherst? 1926-7) 2 v. 23 x 12½ cm.
F74. A5 A2

AMHERST. Around a village green; sketches of life in Amherst, by Mary Adele Allen. Northampton, Mass., The Kraushar press (1939) 94 p. front., plates, ports. 22 cm. 39-30831.
F74. A5 A45

AMHERST. Records of the town of from 1735 to 1788. Reprinted from the Amherst record of 1883-4. Ed. J. F. Jameson. Amherst, Mass., Press of J. E. Williams, 1884. iv, (5) - 100 p. 22½ cm. 1-11207.
F74. A5 A5

AMHERST. An historical review. 150th anniversary of the First church of Christ in Amherst. Amherst, Mass. Press of the Amherst record, 1890. 121, (2) p. 3 pl. (incl. front.) 2 port. 23 cm. 8-17397.
F74. A5 A6

AMHERST. Manual of the Second Congregational church, Amherst, containing historic documents, list of pastors, by-laws of the incorporated church and a list of members received and dismissed from the date of organization, 1782. (Amherst, Press of Carpenter & Morehouse) 1924. 3, (3) - 70 p. plates, facsim. 19½ cm. 26-3099.
F74. A5 A65

AMHERST, ... The history of the town of. Pub. in two parts. Part I - General history of the town. Part II - Town meeting records. Comp. and pub. by Carpenter & Morehouse. Amherst, Mass., Press of Carpenter & Morehouse, 1896. xxiii p, 640, (2) p., 263 p. front., plates, ports., map. 24 cm. 1-13358.
F74. A5 C3

AMHERST. Historical address delivered at the centennial celebration, in Amherst ... By M. F. Dickinson, jr. Amherst, Mass., McCloud & William, print., 1878. viii, (9) - 44 p. 23 cm. 1-11208.
F74. A5 D5

AMHERST as poetry, by Maxwell H. Goldberg. Amherst, Mass., The Newell press (1941)
32 p. 22 cm. 41-6155.
F74. A5 G6

AMHERST, The handbook of. Prepared and published by Frederick H. Hitchcock. Seventy illus. Amherst, Mass., 1891. vi, 197 p. incl. illus., plates, port., map. 21 cm. 1-11209 Rev.
F74. A5 H6

AMHERST, Mass., The handbook of. Rev. ed. Amherst, Mass., F. H. Hitchcock. 1894.
v, 188 p. incl. illus., plates, port., map. 20½ cm. 1-11210 Rev.
F74. A5 H7

AMHERST. Mary Mattoon and her hero of the revolution (General Ebenezer Mattoon) by Alice M. Walker. Amherst, Mass. (Press of Carpenter & Morehouse) 1902. 83 p. front., plates, ports. 18 cm. 3-5965. F74.A5 M44

AMHERST. The village of Amherst, a landmark of light. By Frank Prentice Rand. Amherst, Mass., Amherst Historical Soc., 1958. 337 p. illus. 24 cm. Includes bibliography. 58-49300. F74. A5 R3

AMHERST. Some useful information concerning the places of interest in Amherst. Amherst, Mass., M. McCloud, 1875. 31 p. illus. 14 cm. 21-18368. F74. A5 S7

AMHERST. Y^e Amherst girl of ye olden tyme, by Alice M. Walker. Cover design by Miss Martha Genung. Amherst, Mass., 1901. 31 p. 19 cm. 6-7667. F74.A5 W17

AMHERST, Historic homes of, by Alice M. Walker. Pub. under the auspices of the Amherst historical society. Amherst, Mass. (Press of Carpenter & Morehouse) 1905. 4, 100 p. front., plates, ports. 19½ cm. 5-14822. F74.A5 W18

AMHERST. Through Turkey Pass to Amherst and beyond, by Alice M. Walker. Amherst, Mass., 1903. 52 p. front., illus. 19½ cm. 3-11295. F74. A5 W2

ANDOVER. The Andover and North Andover directory ... 1916 - v. front. (fold. map) 24½ cm. 16-3488. Directories

ANDOVER. Diary of Sarah Connell Ayer. Andover and Newburyport, Mass; Concord and Bow, N.H. Portland and Eastport, Me. Portland, Me., Lefavor-Tower co., 1910. 404 p. 25 cm. 12-12476.
F74.A
F8.A97

ANDOVER, The Townsman directory of ... Andover, Mass., The Andover press, 19 - v. fold. map. 24½ cm. 24-17758. Directories

ANDOVER, Resident and business directory of ... Newton, Mass., Newton journal pub. co., 1891 - v. fold. map. 24 cm. 12-14297. Directories

ANDOVER and North Andover directory, Crosby's ... Wollaston, Mass., Crosby pub. co., 19 - v. 24 cm. CA 28-79 Unrev. Directories

ANDOVER, History of, from its settlement to 1829. By Abiel Abbot. Andover (Mass.) Flagg and Gould, 1829. 204 p. 19 cm. 1-16883. F74. A6 A2

ANDOVER. ... Certain peculiar earthworks near Andover ... by Warren K. Moorehead ... Andover, Mass., The Andover press, 1912. 7-55 p. illus., fold. plans. 23½ cm. 13-23635.
F74.A
E51.P55 no. 5

ANDOVER. Historical sketch of the Memorial hall, Andover. With the rules and regulations. Lawrence, Mass., G.S. Merrill & Crocker, 1873. 19 p. 8°. 1-11211-M1. F74. A6 A6

ANDOVER, Mass. Proceedings at the celebration of the 250th anniversary of the incorporation of the town ... Andover, Mass., The Andover press, 1897. 3, (13)-173 p. ports., facsims. 27½ cm. 1-11212.
F74. A6 A7

ANDOVER, Vital records of, to the end of the year 1849. ... Topsfield, Mass., Topsfield historical soc., 1912 (i.e. 1911-1912) 2 v. 23½ cm. v.1. Births. - v.2. Marr. and deaths. 11-7322 Add. F74.A6 A75
L. H. & G.

ANDOVER. Historical manual of the South church in Andover, Mass. Andover, Print. W. F. Draper, 1859. 200 p. front. (port.) pl. 20 cm. 6-40434 Add. F74. A6 A86

ANDOVER. Supplementary manual of the South church, Andover, Mass. Andover, Print. W. F. Draper,

1882. 35 p. 20½ cm. Supplementing the "Historical manual" of 1859. 11-34735. F74.A6 A87

ANDOVER, Historical sketches of, (comprising the present towns of North Andover and Andover). By Sarah Loring Bailey ... Boston, Houghton, Mifflin, 1880. xxiv, 626 p. front., plates, ports., maps, facsim. 24 cm. 1-11213. F74.A6 B25

ANDOVER. An address delivered ... at the dedication of the Memorial hall, Andover ... by Rev. Phillips Brooks. Andover, Trustees of the Memorial hall; (Lawrence, Mass., Geo. S. Merrill & Crocker, print.) 1873. 33 p. 24½ cm. 1-11214. F74.A6 B8

ANDOVER: symbol of New England; the evolution of a town. By Claude Moore Fuess. (Andover) Andover Hist. Soc., 1959. 480 p. 25 cm. F74.A6 F8

ANDOVER. Four generations; population, land, and family in Colonial Andover (by) Philip J. Greven, Jr. Ithaca, N.Y., Cornell University Press, 1970. xvi, 329 p. 23 cm. 76-87018. F74.A6 G7

ANDOVER. ... The record of Andover during the rebellion. Comp. by Samuel Raymond. Andover, (Mass.) W.F. Draper, print., 1875. viii, 232 p. 24 cm. 1-16195. F74.A6 R2

ANDOVER. Old Andover days; memories of a Puritan childhood, by Sarah Stuart Robbins. Boston, New York (etc.) The Pilgrim press, 1908. xi, 188 p. front., 4 pl. 19 cm. 8-30581. F74.A6 R6

ARLINGTON directory. 1894. Directories

ARLINGTON, Resident and business directory of, 1902-3, (v.5) ... N. Cambridge, E.A. Jones, 1902. fold. map, diagr. 23½ cm. 2-24081. Directories

ARLINGTON, Vital records of, to the year 1850. Boston, ... 1904. 162 p. 23½ cm. New England historic genealogical society. Vital records of the towns of Mass. 4-18520. F74.A7 A7

ARLINGTON. How Arlington won the flag on the town house. By Edward H. Bartlett. Arlington? The Stedman press (1905?) 8 p. 20½ cm. 10-13004. F74.A7 B2

ARLINGTON, History of the town of. Formerly the second precinct in Cambridge or district of Menotomy, afterward the town of West Cambridge. 1635 - 1879. With a genealogical register of the inhabitants of the precinct. By Benjamin and William R. Cutter. Boston, D. Clapp, 1880. iv, 368 p. front. (fold. plan) illus., plates, port. 24 cm. Genealogical register: p. (181) - 335. 1-11215 Rev. F74.A7 C9

ARLINGTON pageant to commemorate the dedication of the New Town hall, The, written and planned by Mrs. Cyrus Edwin Dallin ... Arlington, (Boston, Print. the Stetson press) 1913. 28 p. illus. 23 cm. 13-13757. F74.A7 D14

ARLINGTON, Town of, past and present; a narrative of larger events and important changes in the village precinct and town from 1637 to 1907, by Charles S. Parker. Arlington, C.S. Parker, 1907. 331 p. illus., fold. plan. 23½ cm. 7-19585. F74.A7 P2

ARLINGTON. Memorial address at the dedication of monument to the memory of Capt. Solomon Peirce, a soldier of the revolution, by Arthur W. Peirce; Old cemetery, Arlington, Mass. ... 1903. (Tufts college, Mass., The Tufts college press, 1904) 29 p. front. 20 cm. 8-32769. F74.A7 P3

ARLINGTON. West Cambridge on the 19th April, 1775. An address delivered in behalf of the Ladies' soldiers' aid soc. of West Cambridge, by Samuel Abbot Smith. Boston, A. Mudge, print., 1864. 66 p. 20 cm. 1-11216. F74.A7 S6

ASHBURNHAM directory ... no. 1 - 1881. (New York, New York pub. co., 1881) 56 p. 17½ cm. 12-17414. Directories

ASHBURNHAM. The Fitchburg suburban directory, 1910. v. IV. Embracing the towns of Ashburnham, Ashby, Hubbardston, Lunenburg, Princeton, Sterling, Templeton and Westminster ... Boston, W. E. Shaw.   1 v.   24½ cm.   11-754.   Directories

ASHBURNHAM, ... Vital records of, to the end of the year 1849. Worcester, F. P. Rice, 1909.
215 p. 23½ cm. 9-7126.   F74. A8 A8

ASHBURNHAM. An half century sermon, delivered at Ashburnham ... 1818. By John Cushing ... Worcester: Print. William Manning, 1818.   23 p. 22 cm. 25-3659.   F74. A8 C9

ASHBURNHAM, 1885 - 1965, to commemorate the 200th anniversary of the incorporation of the town (by) Raymond P. Holden and Barbara B. Holden. (Ashburnham, Stevens Pub. Library) 1970.
222 p. illus. 25 cm. 73-131001.   F74. A8 H6

ASHBURNHAM, History of, from the grant of Dorchester Canada to the present time, 1734 - 1886; with a genealogical register of Ashburnham families. By Ezra S. Stearns ... Ashburnham, Pub. by the town, 1887.   1022 p. front., illus., plates, ports. 23 cm. Genealogical register: p. (575) - 1007. 1-11218.   F74. A8 S7

ASHBY. Gravestone records from the old yard, Ashby, Mass., compiled by Richard J. Fowle. Thetford, Vermont, 1937.   2 p., 2-12 numb. l. 28 cm. Typewritten. 39M2926T.   F74. A83 F6

ASHFIELD bicentennial; Ashfield, Mass., 1765 - 1965. (Ashfield, 1965)   48 p. illus. 23 cm.
F74. A85A77

ASHFIELD, Vital records of, to the year 1850. Boston, Mass. The New England historic geneal. soc., 1942.   273 p. 23 cm. 42-20628.   F74. A85 A8

ASHFIELD. Historical sketches of the times and men in Ashfield, Mass., during the revolutionary war, by Barnabas Howes ... North Adams, Mass., Mrs. E. B. Walden, book and job print. (1884)
22 p. 19 cm. 1-11217.   F74. A85 H8

ASHFIELD, History of the town of, from its settlement in 1742 - 1910, by Frederick G. Howes. Also a historical sketch of the town written by Rev. Thomas Shepard in 1834. (Ashfield, Mass.) Pub. by the town (1910?)   2 v. 24 cm. 13-9659.   F74. A85H85

ASHLAND, Hopkinton and Upton, Resident and business directory of ... Hopkinton, Mass., A. E. Foss, 190 -   v. 24 cm. 7-21313.   Directories

ASHLAND, History of the town of, prepared by the Historical records survey ... W. P. A. Framingham, Mass. Print. Lakeview press, 1942.   4, 7-141 p. fold. map. 23½ cm. Bibliography: p. 212-122.
42-24814.   F74. A86 H5

ASHLAND. Historical facts relating to the Cutler Mills school district of Ashland, nos. 6 and 5, formerly no. 13 of Framingham. Including references to the Parks Corner (no. 3) district of Framingham, of which no. 13 was formerly a part. By Wellington Evarts Parkhurst. Clinton (Mass.) Press of W. J. Coulter, 1897.   35 p. illus. (incl. port.) 23 cm. "The Parkhurst family": p. (29) - 35. Other biographical and genealogical notices included. 22-10763.   F74. A86 P2

ATHOL directory ... 1893 -   New Haven, Conn., The Price & Lee co. (1893 - 19-
v. fronts. (fold. maps) 23½ cm. 1-26038.   Directories

ATHOL. A centennial discourse delivered Sept. 9, 1950 before the First church and society in Athol, at the celebration of the 100th anniversary of the organization of said church. By Samuel F. Clarke. Boston, W. Crosby & H. P. Nichols, 1851.   95 p. 23 cm. 10-5632.   F94. A
AC901. W3 v. 123

ATHOL. Orange directory ... 18 -   New Haven, Conn., The Price & Lee co.   v. fold. maps.
23½ cm. 99-2679 Rev.   Directories

ATHOL directory (1893) - 1895, 1897 - 1906/7. (v.1) - 3, 5 - 11. New Haven, Conn., The Price &

MASSACHUSETTS   171

Lee co. (1893) - 1906.   10 v. fronts., fold. plans. 24 cm.   1-26038 Additions.   Directories

ATHOL, ... Vital records of, to the end of the year 1849.   Worcester, Mass., F. P. Rice, 1910.
230 p. 23½ cm.   10-8873.   F74.A87 A7

ATHOL, past and present, by Lilley B. Caswell ... Athol, Mass., The author, 1899.   vii, 448 p. front.,
illus., plates, ports. 24½ cm.   Includes biographical sketches.   1-2212 Rev.   F74.87 C3

ATHOL. The home of the ancient dead restored. An address delivered at Athol, Mass ... by Rev.
John F. Norton, at the reconsecration of the ancient cemetery of Athol ... Athol depot, R. Putnam,
1859.   24 p. 22 cm.   1-16767 Rev.   F74.A87 N8

— 2d ed.   1859.   24 p. 22 cm.   31-8006.   F74.A87N82

ATHOL. The record of Athol in suppressing the great rebellion. Prepared for publication by a
committee of the town. Boston, G. C. Rand & Avery, 1866.   264 p. 19½ cm.   Prepared mainly by John F.
Norton. 1-15996.   F74.A87 N9

ATHOL. A story of a New England town; address by Henry H. Sprague given at Athol, Old home week,
... 1903. Boston, Little, Brown, 1904.   3, 48 p. fold. facsim. 24 cm. (Bibliography) p. (49) 6-20093.
                                                                                           F74.A87. S7

ATTLEBORO, North Attleboro, and Plainville, directory ...   Providence and Boston, Sampson, Murdock, 18 -   v. fronts. (maps) 24 cm.   Nov. 30, 98-5.   Directories

ATTLEBORO. Court records filed at the town Clerks Office, 1801 - 1836, Attleboro, and copied by
Marion Pearce Carter, 1935 - 1942. (Attleboro? 1942 or 3)   100 l. 28 cm.   Typescript (carbon copy)
55-46257.   F74.A89 A5

ATTLEBORO, Vital records of, to the end of the year 1849.   Salem, Mass., The Essex institute,
1934.   745 p. 23 cm.   34-23632 Rev.   F74.A89A65

ATTLEBORO.   1899.   1 v.   F74.A89 A7

ATTLEBOROUGH. A brief history of the town from its settlement to the present time ... (Attleboro,
Mass., 1876)   The brief history occupies 19 col. of the Centennial number, July 4, 1876, of the Attleboro chronicle. 1-11219-M1.
                                                                                           F74.A89 A8

ATTLEBORO. Baptizms (!) marriages, deaths, admitted to communion, Old town church, Attleboro.
First church, 1740 - 1856. ' Copied by Elizabeth J. Wilmarth ... pub. by Marion Pearce Carter ...
(Attleboro) 1928.   2 p., 2-22 numb. l., 4 l. 28 cm.   Mimeographed. 33-6843.
                                                                                           F74.A89A83

ATTLEBORO. Membership and vital records of the Second Congregational church of Attleboro, copied
from the original records by Marion Williams Peirce Carter; ... Washington, D. C., C. Shepard II,
1924.   48 numb. l. 28 cm. (Shepard genealogical series, no. 16) Autographed from type-written copy. 24-23157.   F74.A89A85

ATTLEBORO Sun, The. Fiftieth anniversary edition 1889 ... 1939. Attleboro, Mass., 1939.
1 v. illus. 58 cm.   42-48445.   F74.A89 A9

ATTLEBORO. Cemetery records, Attleboro - Rehoboth. Burial hill and Conant burying ground, alias
Briggs corner cemetery, alias Oak Knoll cemetery ... copied, compiled and privately pub. by
Marion Pearce Carter ... (Attleboro) 1928.   2 p., 2-3, 11 numb. l. 28 cm. Autographed from type-written copy.
29-15887.   F74.A89 C3

ATTLEBORO. Records of six cemeteries in Attleboro ... copied, compiled and privately pub. by
Marion Pearce Carter ... Attleboro, Mass., 1928.   2 p, 3, (1), 4, (1), (1) numb. l. 28 cm. Mimeographed.
Covers Old Hatch grave yard, Old Peck grave yard, Burial yard at Attleboro Falls, Island cemetery, Follett family burying ground, Thayer family
burying ground, Dodgeville cemetery.   33-5244.   F74.A89C32

ATTLEBORO. Tomb stone records of Old Kirk cemetery, Attleboro, copied, compiled and privately pub. by Marion Pearce Carter ... (Attleboro) 1928. 2 p., 34 numb. l. 28 cm. Mimeographed. 32-34867.

F74.A89C33

ATTLEBORO. A historical sketch of the Second Congregational church in Attleborough: ... By Jonathan Crane, pastor of the church. Boston, Damrell & Moore, print., 1849. 44 p. 21½ cm. 8-20242.

F74.A89 C8

ATTLEBORO, Sketch of the history of, from its settlement to the present time. By John Daggett. Dedham (Mass.) H. Mann, print., 1834. 136 p. 22½ cm. 1-11220.

F74.A89D17

ATTLEBOROUGH, A sketch of the history of ... By John Daggett. Ed. and completed by his daughter. Boston, Press of S. Usher, 1894. 788 p. front. (port.) plates. 24 cm. 1-11221.

F74.A89 D2

AUBURN, ... Vital records of the town of (formerly Ward), to the end of ... 1850. With the inscriptions from the old burial grounds, collected and arranged by Franklin P. Rice. Worcester, Mass., F. P. Rice, 1900. xiii, 142 p. 25 cm. 1-11222 Rev.

F74. A9 A9

AUBURN, A historical sketch of, from the earliest period to the present day with brief accounts of early settlers and prominent citizens. Sponsored by the Auburn centennial committee. Written and compiled by the Federal writers' project of the W. P. A. (Worcester, Mass., Chas. D. Cady print.) 1937. 63 p. illus. (incl. map) 24 cm. 39-7543.

F74. A9 F5

AUBURNDALE; views of its beauty places, mention of its facilities. (Auburndale?) Auburndale village improvement soc. (1910) (32) p. illus. 13½ x 17½ cm.

F74.A95 A8

AUBURN DALE, Early days in; a village chronicle of two centuries, 1665 - 1870, containing reminiscences of early settlers, illustrations and maps. (Auburndale, Mass.) Pub. under the auspices of the Education committee of the Auburndale woman's club, 1917. 116 p. incl. illus., map, facsims. front., fold. map. 18½ cm. Foreword signed: Louise Peloubet, Clara A. Winslow. 17-19711.

F74.A95 P4

AYER, Littleton, Groton and Harvard directory ... v. 1 -   Boston, W. E. Shaw, 1907 -
1 v. 23½ cm. 8-2223.

Directories

AYER. Historical discourse relative to the South Groton Christian union, 1855 - 1864, and the First Unitarian parish of Ayer, 1864 - 1885, by Lyman Clark ... Ayer, Mass., J. H. Turner, prin. (1886)
20 p. 22 cm. 1-11223 Rev.

F74.A97 C6

AYER. Reminiscences of James C. Ayer and the town of Ayer ... By Charles Cowley ... 2d ed. Lowell, Mass., Printed by the Penhallow print. (1879) 2, (7) - 156 p. 22½ cm. 16-11540.

F74.A97C78

— 3d ed. (1880) 2, (7) - 156 p. 23 cm. 7-1978.

F74. A97 C8

BARNSTABLE, Yarmouth and Dennis, The ... resident directory of. 1895 -   Quincy, Mass., The J. H. Hogan co., 1895 -   v. 24 cm. 12-37173.

Directories

BARNSTABLE and Yarmouth, Resident and business directory of, 1901 - ... Hopkinton, Mass., A. E. Foss, (1901 -   1 v. 23½ cm. 1-12863.

Directories

BARNSTABLE, Bourne, Falmouth, Sandwich and Mashpee, directory ... v. 1 -   Salem, Mass., The New England directory and blue book co., 1926 -   v. 24 cm. 26-14305.

Directories

BARNSTABLE town records. Yarmouthport, Mass., C. W. Swift, 1910. 60 p. 26½ cm. (Library of Cape Cod history and genealogy, no. 105) Between 1649 and 1779. 12-39435.

F74.B14B17

BARNSTABLE. The Cape Cod centennial celebration at Barnstable, ... 1839, of the incorporation of the town ... 1639. Correctly reported and rev. Barnstable, S. B. Phinney, 1840. 92 p. 24 cm. 1-12144.

F74. B14 B2

MASSACHUSETTS

BARNSTABLE. Report of proceedings of the tercentenary anniversary of the town of Barnstable. Hyannis, Mass., The Barnstable tercentenary committee, 1940. xv, 215 p. incl. front., illus. 23½ cm. .... by Donald G. Trayser. 40-31937.   F74.B14 B3

BARNSTABLE. Records of the West parish of Barnstable, 1668 - 1807. Boston, Mass. historical soc., 1924. 160 l. of facsims. 38½ x 26½ cm. "... 14 copies reproduced." 24-7323.   F74.B14B37

BARNSTABLE. Sketch of Third Barnstable Baptist church and meeting house, with membership enrollment. By Mrs. Lizzie S. Crocker. (n.p.) 1927. 2, 9-28 p. pl. 24½ cm. 28-12472.   F74.B14 C9

BARNSTABLE. Horse and buggy days on old Cape Cod (by) Hattie Blossom Fritze. (1st ed.) Barnstable, Mass., Great Marshes Press (1966) x, 197 p. 22 cm.   F74.B14F7

BARNSTABLE, The Congregational church in the east precinct, Barnstable, 1646 - 1899. Comp. from the parish records by Miss D. E. Hinckley ... Barnstable, F.B. & F.P. Goss, 1899. 24 p. 3 pl., 2 plans. 19½ cm. Cover-title: Barnstable, Mass., Unitarian church. Illustrated sketch. 1646-1899. Sept. 21, 99-64.   F74.B14 H6

BARNSTABLE, Address delivered at, by Henry Crocker Kittredge at the dedication of a tablet in honor of the soldiers of Barnstable, July 4, 1925. Barnstable, Priv. print., 1925. 8 p. 21 cm. 27-752.   F74.B14 K5

BARNSTABLE families, Genealogical notes of, being a reprint of the Amos Otis papers, originally pub. in the Barnstable patriot. Rev. by C. F. Swift, largely from notes made by the author ... Barnstable, Mass., F.B. & F.P. Goss, 1888 - 90. 2 v. in ;. 22½ cm. 4-11457.   F74.B14 O8

BARNSTABLE. The romance of a Barnstable bell ... 1922. (Library of Cape Cod history and genealogy no. 25)   F74.B14 R6

BARNSTABLE and Yarmouth sea captains and ship owners, by Francis William Sprague. List of sailings from New England to San Francisco, 1849 - 1856, by Leavitt Sprague. (Boston, Mass.) Priv. print. (T. R. Marvin, print.) 1913. 52 p. 2 port. (incl. front.) plates. 25 cm. 14-1433.   F74.B14 S7

BARNSTABLE sea captains, by F. W. Sprague. Yarmouthport, Mass., C. W. Swift, 1913. 5 p. 25½ cm. (Library of Cape Cod history and genealogy, no. 68) 17-20837.   F74.B14S75

BARNSTABLE; three centuries of a Cape Cod town, by Donald G. Trayser, with articles by Phyllis Bearse, Sarah H. Boult and others ... Maps by James F. McLaughlin, sketches by Vernon Coleman ... Hyannis, Mass., F.B. and F.P. Goss, 1939. xiv, 500 p. illus., plates. 23½ cm. 39-23552 Rev.   F74.B14T73

BARRE. A memorial of the 100th anniversary of the incorporation of the town of Barre ... 1874. Containing the Historical discourse by Rev. James W. Thompson ... etc. Pub. by the town. Cambridge, Press of J. Wilson, 1875. 2, 281 p. fold. map. 24 cm. 2-10423.   F74.B15 B2

BARRE, ... Vital records of, to the end of the year 1849. Worcester, F. P. Rice, 1903. 276 p. 23½ cm. 3-23035.   F74.B15B24

BECKET, Dalton, Hancock, Hinsdale, Lanesboro, Lee, Lenox, Otis, Richmond, Sandisfield, Stockbridge, Tyringham, Washington, West Stockbridge, Directory of. Pittsfield, Mass., Berkshire directory co., 19 - v. 24½ cm. CA 26-642 Unrev.   Directories

BECKET sons in a Massachusetts settlement of New Connecticut. New Haven, 1953 (i.e. 1954) 58 p. 23 cm. 54-22954.   F74.B18 A7

BECKET, Vital records of, to the year 1850. Boston, Pub. by the New-England historic geneal. soc. ... 1903. 98 p. 23½ cm. 3-20945.   F74.B18 B2

BECKET, The town of.   By Samuel Abbott Green.   (Cambridge? 1890?)   2 p. 24 cm.   11-25757.
F74.B18 G7

BECKET, A bicentennial history of, incorporated June 21, 1765; by Cathaline Alford Archer and others. Compiled by Esther Turner Moulthrop for the Becket Historical Society.   (Pittsfield, 1965)
215 p.   24 cm.   65-19574.
F74.B18 M6

BEDFORD, Vital records of, to the year 1850.   Boston, Pub. by the New England historic genealogical soc ... 1903.   142 p. 23½ cm.   4-4888.
F74.B 2 B2

BEDFORD.   Genealogy of Bedford old families, with biographical notes.   By Abram English Brown ... Bedford (Mass.) The author, 1892.   48, (4) p. illus. 27½ cm.   In double columns.   4-11989.
F74.B2 B76

BEDFORD.   Governor Winthrop's farm.   A chapter of old Bedford history.   By Abram English Brown. Boston, 1892.   From New England magazine.
F74.B2 B78

BEDFORD, History of the town of, from its earliest settlement to the year ... 1891 ... with a genealogical register of old families.   By Abram English Brown ... Bedford, Pub. by the author, 1891.
2, 110, 48, (4) p. incl. illus., facsim. front., pl., port., plans, facsim. 28 cm.   3-2749.
F74. B2 B8

BEDFORD.   Wilderness town; the story of Bedford, by Louise K. Brown.   (Bedford? Mass., 1968)
218 p. 24 cm.
F74. B2B82

BEDFORD sesqui-centennial celebration, ... 1879.   Historical discourse, by Jonathan F. Stearns ... Also, a sketch of the celebration.   Boston, A. Mudge, print., 1879.   84 p. 24 cm.   1-11224.
F74. B2 S7

BELCHERTOWN.   Historical sketch of the Congregational church in Belchertown, from its organization, 114 years, with notices of the pastors and officers, and list of communicants chronologically arranged, tracing genealogies, intermarriages and family relatives.   ...   By Hon. Mark Doolittle ... Northampton, Mass., Hopkins, Bridgman & co., 1852.   xii, (13) - 282 p. 19 cm.   6-18420.
F74.B207D7

BELCHERTOWN.   150th anniversary of the incorporation of the town of Belchertown, ... 1911; a sketch of the celebration and the Historical address, by Rev. Payson W. Lyman.   Belchertown, Mass., Press of L. H. Blackmer, 1912.   23 p. front. (port.) 23½ cm.   A14-1671.
F74.B207L9

BELCHERTOWN in the 18th century, History of.   By William E. Shaw.   Ed. William A. Doubleday. Amherst, Mass., Newell Press, 1968.   xvi, 116 p. illus. 24 cm.
F74.B207S5
1968

BELLINGHAM.   Confessions of boyhood (by) John Albee.   Boston, R.G. Badger, 1910.   267 p. 19½ cm.
A narrative of life in Bellingham and Worcester, Mass., and in Norwich, Conn.   10-13158.
F74.B21 A3

BELLINGHAM.   Vital records of Bellingham, to the year 1850.   Boston, Pub, by the New-England historic genealogical soc ... 1904.   222 p. 23½ cm.   4-36134.
F74.B21 B2

BELLINGHAM, History of the town of, 1719 - 1919, by George F. Partridge.   (Bellingham) Pub. by the town, 1919.   3, 221 p. front. (map) plates, ports. 22½ cm.   19-17757.
F74.B21 P3

BELMONT, Resident and business directory of. ...   Boston, Boston suburban book co., 1896 - 1910.
3 v.   23½ cm.   7-5688 Add.
Directories

BELMONT directory ... 1907.
Directories

BELMONT.   Argument of Ivers J. Austin, counsel for the remonstrants from Watertown, against the peition for the incorporation of the town of Belmont ... Boston, Print. A. Mudge, 1857.   58 p. fold. map. 24 cm.   2-21652.
F74.B22 A9

MASSACHUSETTS

BELMONT. Cambridge against Belmont. Argument of Hon. W. W. Warren against annexation. Boston, 1880. 24 p. 23½ cm. 19-4222. F74.B22 W2

BELVIDERE. Prospectus for a manufacturing establishment at Belvidere, on Merrimack river. With a topographical account of the place, and incidental remarks. (Belvidere, Mass., 1822)? 24 p. 8°. 1-11225-M1. F74.B23 P9

BERKLEY, History of the town of, including sketches of the lives of the two first minsters, Rev. Samuel Tobey and Rev. Thomas Andros ... By Rev. Enoch Sanford ... New York, K. Tompkins, print., 1872. 60 p. 23 cm. 1-11226. F74.B27 S1

BERLIN, Memorial record of the soldiers of, in the great rebellion, with the exercises at the dedication of the tablets of the deceased ... Clinton, Print. W.J. Coulter, 1870. 46 p. 23 cm. 12-24159. F74. B3 B3

BERLIN, Vital records of, to the end of the year 1899; coll. and compiled by Frances L. Eaton; ed. Martha L. Duren. Marlboro, Mass., Frances L. Eaton, 1935. 380 p. 23 cm. 36-10807. F74. B3B34

BERLIN, History of the parish and town of. By A. Carter. Worcester, Mass., 1878. 40 p. 18½ cm. 1-11227. F74. B3 C3

BERLIN, History of the town of, from 1784 to 1895. By William A. Houghton. Worcester, Mass., F.S. Blanchard, print., 1895. viii, 584 p. front., illus., plates, ports., 2 maps (1 double) plan. 24 cm. "Genealogical": p. 246-544. "Biographical": p. (547)-562. 1-11228. F74. B3 H8

BERNARDSTON, History of the town of. With genealogies. By Lucy Cutler Kellogg. Greenfield, Mass., Press of E. A. Hall, 1902 - 1962. 2 v. 24 cm. 3-6506. F74.B32 K3

BEVERLY city directory and North Shore map. vol. I - Beverly, Mass., Crowley & Lunt, 1903 - 1913. 6 v. fold. maps. 24 - 24½ cm. 3-17576 Rev. Directories

BEVERLY directory, The ... Salem, Mass., The Henry M. Meek pub. co., 1895 - 1911. 4 v. fold. maps. 24 cm. 13-22561. Directories

BEVERLY, Danvers, Marblehead, Peabody, Essex and Manchester, The suburban directory for ... Salem, Mass., H. M. Meek, 1888 - 1899. 3 v. 24 cm. 0-5590 Rev. Directories

BEVERLY city directory, The. 1903 - 04. 2 v. Directories

BEVERLY, Manchester and Magnolia, Blue book of, for 1893. Boston, E. A. Jones, 1893 - v. fold. map. 20½ x 16 cm. CA 33-485 Unrev. Directories

BEVERY, Early records of the town of. Vol. I - Copied by Augustus A. Galloupe. Boston, E. Putnam, 1907. 1 v. 24 cm. Reprinted from the Genealogical magazine, v. 1 - An exact copy of the ms. records, differing from the publication "Vital records of Beverly". 9-6058. F74.B35B28

BEVERLY citizen, The. Special illustrated semi-centennial ed. Beautiful Beverly ... (Beverly, Mass., 1900) 16 p. illus. (incl. ports.) 35 cm. Four columns to the page. 4-27591. F74.B35 B3

BEVERLY, Vital records of, to the end of the year 1849 ... Topsfield, Mass., Topsfield historical soc., 1906-7. 2 v. 23½ cm. v. I. Births. - II. Marriages and deaths. 6-13928 Additions. F74.B35B36

BEVERLY. Historic Beverly; being an account of the growth of the city of Beverly from the earliest times to the present, with short sketches of the men and women who contributed so much to the upbuilding ... in the early days; text by Beverly historical soc; illus. Alice Bolam Preston. Beverly chamber of commerce, 1937.   38 p. illus. (incl. ports., map, facsims.) 27½ cm.   "First ed."   37-19333.

F74.B35 B5

BEVERLY real estate recorder.   Containing a list of real estate, both houses and land, now being offered for sale ... classified by streets alphabetically arranged ... Beverley, Mass., E. M. Bates, 1896.   1 v.   port.   22½ cm.   1-11229-M1 Cancel.   F74.B35 B6

BEVERLY Farms, Old days at, by Mary Larcom Dow.   Beverly, Mass., North shore print., 1921.
81 p. incl. front. ports. 21 cm.   21-19418.   F74.B35 D7

BEVERLY, Records of the First church in, 1667 - 1772, copied by William P. Upham, the baptismal records annotated by Augustus A. Galloupe ... Salem, Mass., Printed for the Essex institute, 1905.
2 p. 270 p. 25 cm.   Reprinted from the Essex institute Historical collections.   23-763.   F74.B35F52

BEVERLY, The register of baptisms of the First church in, 1667 - 1710, with annotations by Augustus A. Galloupe.   Boston, Research pub. co., 1903.   50 p.   24½ cm.   3-31532.   F74.B35F54

BEVERLY Tercentenary, 1668 - 1968, historical highlights ... by Chester E. Frost and Laurance S. Hovey.   (Beverly? Mass., 1968)   44 p. illus. 23 cm.   F74.B35F68

BEVERLY'S diverse (by Chester E. Frost. 1969)   1 v. (unpaged) illus. 23 cm.   F74.B35 F7

BEVERLY, The old planters of, and the thousand acre grant of 1635, by Alice Gertrude Lapham ... Cambridge, Printed at the Riverside press for the Beverly historical soc. and the Conant family assoc., 1930.   vi, 133 p. front., plates, maps (1 fold.) facsim. 22½ cm.   Foreword contains bibliography. 30-15938.   F74.B35L31

BEVERLY, History of, civil and ecclesiastical, from its settlement in 1630 to 1842.   By Edwin M. Stone.   Boston, J. Munroe, 1843.   iv, 324 p. front., illus. 19½ cm.   1-11230.   F74.B35 S8

BEVERLY.   An address delivered in the First parish, Beverly, ... 1867, on the 200th anniversary of its formation.   By Christopher T. Thayer ... Boston, Nichols and Noyes, 1868.   79 p. 23 cm.
1-11231.   F74.B35 T3

BEVERLY Farms.   Argument of Fred H. Williams, before the legislative Committee on towns, Feb. 27, 1889, in favor of the incorporation of the town of Beverly Farms.   Boston, D. Gunn, prs., 1889.
40 p. 23 cm. 1-11232 Rev.   F74.B35 W7

BILLERICA.   Argument of Hon. Josiah G. Abbott, in behalf of the petitioners before the Joint special committee of the legislature of Massachusetts, on the petition of C. P. Talbot and others, praying for the repeal of the act of 1860 for the removal of the dam across Concord River, at Billerica ... 1862. Boston, Wright & Potter, print., 1862.   60 p.   23½ cm.   It was claimed that the raising of the water ... at Billerica, had injured certain tracts of land in the towns of Wayland and Sudbury.   7-41858.   F74.B4 A13

BILLERICA, Chelmsford, Dracut, Tewksbury, Tyngsboro and Westford, The Lowell suburban directory for ...   no. 1 -   Salem, Mass., Henry M. Meek pub. (1896 - 19 -   v. 24 cm.   1-29758 Rev.
F74.B4 A18

BILLERICA, Vital records of, to the year 1850.   Boston, Mass., Pub. by the New England historic genealogical soc. ... 1908.   405 p. 23 cm.   8-6065.   F74. B4 B6

BILLERICA, Celebration of the 200th anniversary of the incorporation of ... 1855; inc. the proceedings of the committee, address, poem, etc.   Lowell, S. J. Varney, 1855.   152 p. 23 cm.   1-11233.
F74. B4 B7

BILLERICA, Records of, from 1658 to 1676.   (Washington? D.C., 1934)   374 numb. l. 28 x 21½ cm.
37M667T.   F74. B4 B8
Rare Book Coll.

BILLERICA. v. 1 -   June 1912 -   Billerica, 1912 -   v. illus. (incl. maps) 25 cm.
monthly. 41M2184T.   F74. B4 B88

406

MASSACHUSETTS

BILLERICA, An half-century discourse, addressed to the people of Billerica, ... 1813. By their reverend pastor, Henry Cummings. Cambridge, Mass., Print Hilliard and Metcalf ... 1813. 31 p. 21½ cm. 2-1836 Rev.
F74. B4 C9

BILLERICA, An historical memoir of. Containing notices of the principal events in the civil and ecclesiastical affairs of the town, from its first settlement to 1816 ... Amherst, N.H., R. Boylston, 1816. 36 p. 8°. 1-11234-M1.
F74. B4 F2
Rare Book Coll.

BELLINGHAM. Century sermons. Two discourses, delivered at Bellingham in the year 1822. The first giving the ... history of the town ... the second, the memoirs of the three ministers who died in the town ... By Abial Fisher, jun. ... Worcester, Print, W. Manning, 1822. 28 p. 23½ cm. 18-23767.
F74. B4 F5
Rare Book Coll.

BILLERICA, History of, with a Genealogical register, by the Rev. Henry A. Hazen ... Boston, A. Williams, 1883. viii, 319, 183, (2), 506-509 p. front., plates, ports., fold. plan. 24½ cm. 1-11235* Cancel.
F74. B4 H4

BILLERICA. A centennial oration, by the Rev. Elias Nason ... Lowell, Print. Marden and Rowell, 1876. 25 p. 24 cm. 1-16868.
F74. B4 N2

BILLERICA. Old families of the First parish. By Mrs. M. H. Sage ... (Boston) Print, for private distribution by J. B. Holden, 1898. 19 p. front. 26 cm. 5-40503.
F74. B4 S2

BLANDFORD. ... Blandford's bicentennial official souvenir, pub. in connection with the 200th anniversary of the founding of the town ... ed. and pub. by Edgar Holmes Plummer ... (Blandford, 1935) (36) p. illus. (incl. ports., map) 28 cm. "Sketches of Blandford folks" p. (31) - (36) 35-12853.
F74.B45 B3

BLANDFORD monthly, The. Blandford, Mass., 1901 - 1903. 24 nos. 26½ cm.
F74.B45 B4

BLANDFORD. Address delivered before the Literary association, Blandford ... upon the history of that town. By William H. Gibbs ... Springfield, G. W. Wilson, print., 1850. 76 p. fold. geneal. tab. 18½ cm. 1-11236.
F74.B45 G4

BLANDFORD, A discourse delivered at. Giving some account of the early settlement of the town and the history of the church. By Rev. John Keep ... Ware, Mass., 1886. 23 p. 23½ cm. 10-31056.
F74.B45 K2

BLANDFORD, Soldiers and sailors of the revolution from, compiled by Sumner Gilbert Wood ... West Medway, Mass. (1933) 52 p. 23½ cm. 33-11645.
F74.B45W78

BLANDFORD, The taverns and turnpikes of, 1733 - 1833, by Sumner Gilbert Wood ... (Blandford) The author, 1908. 5, 329 (23) p. front., plates, ports., fold. map. 21½ cm. 9-837.
F74.B45 W8

BOLTON, Vital records of, to the end of the year 1849. Worcester, Mass., F. P. Rice, 1910. 232 p. 23½ cm. 10-8872.
F74. B5 B5

BOLTON. Address delivered in the First parish church in Bolton ... 1876, at the centennial celebration of the anniversary of American independence; and also in observance of the 138th anniversary of the incorporation of the town: by Richard S. Edes. Clinton (Mass.) Print. W. J. Coulter, 1877. iv, 57 p. 23½ cm. 1-11237.
F74. B5 E2

BOLTON. Argument of Hon. Geo. F. Hoar, of Worcester ... on petition ... to be annexed to the town of Hudson ... Boston, J. E. Farwell, print., 1867. 47 p. 23½ cm. 24-12354.
F74. B5 H5

BOLTON. An oration, delivered at Bolton, ... 1866, at the dedication of the tablets ... to commemorate the deceased volunteers of the town in the war of the great rebellion ... Clinton (Mass.) Printed at the office of the Clinton courant, 1867.   43 p.   8°.   1-21432-M1.

F74. B5 L8

BOURNE, Falmouth and Sandwich, Resident and business directory of ... 1900   Hopkinton, Mass.,
A. E. Foss, 1900 -   v.   23½ cm.   0-6954 Rev.
Directories

BOURNE, History of, from 1622 to 1937, by Betsey D. Keene ... Yarmouthport, Mass., C. W. Swift, 1937.   vi, 221, xiv p.   front., 1 illus., plates, map.   21 cm.   37-15576.

F74. B52 K4

BOXBOROUGH, Vital records of, to the year 1850.   Comp. by Thomas W. Baldwin ... Boston, Mass. (Wright & Potter print.) 1915.   78 p.   23½ cm.   15-24546.

F74. B53 B5

BOXBOROUGH: a New England town and its people.   Comp. for the Middlesex County history.   With sketches and illustrations, additional, by Lucie Caroline Hager ... Philadelphia, J. W. Lewis, 1891.
218 p.   front., plates, ports.   22½ cm.   Reprinted with additions from "History of Middlesex County ... 1890"   1-11238.   F74. B53 H1

BOXFORD town records, 1685 - 1706, copied by Sidney Perley.   (From the Historical collections of the Essex institute, vol. xxxvi)   (Salem, 1900)   41-103 p.   22 cm.   2-7161.

F74. B54 B5

BOXFORD, Vital records of, to the end of the year 1849.   Topsfield, Mass., Topsfield historical soc., 1905.   274 p.   23½ cm.   5-15534 Rev.

F74. B54 B6

BOXFORD, The dwellings of.   By Sidney Perley ... Salem, Mass., The Essex institute, 1893.
2, 275 p.   illus.   23 cm.   Also pub. in Historical collections of the Essex insitute, v. 26-29, 1889-1892.   14-18737.   F74. B54P38

BOXFORD, The history of, from the earliest settlement known to the present time: a period of about 230 years.   By Sidney Perley ... Boxford, Mass., The author, 1880.   vii, 9-418 p.   front., plates, port.
23½ cm.   1-11239.   F74. B54 P4

BOYLSTON and West Boylston directory ... 1905.   1 v.   Directories

BOYLSTON.   A brief history of the First Congregation church, Boylston, Mass.   Being a sermon preached by the pastor, Rev. Israel Ainsworth ... 1886 ... Worcester, Mass., Press of Sanford and Davis, 1887.   15 p.   23½ cm.   "Printed in the Worcester daily spy, Aug. 16, 1886"   7-27739.   F74. B56A29

BOYLSON ... Centennial celebration of the incorporation of the town of Boylston ... 1886.   Worcester, Mass., Press of Sanford & Davis, 1887.   140 p.   (4) p. (music)   front.   24 cm.   1-11240.

F74. B56 B8

BOYLSTON.   ... Vital records of the town of Boylston, to the end of the year 1850.   Collected and arranged by Franklin P. Rice.   Worcester, F. P. Rice, 1900.   124 p.   25½ cm.   edition of 120 copies.
3-20624.   F74. B56B85

BOYLSTON, A brief historical sketch of the town of ...   By Matthew Davenport.   Lancaster (Mass.) Print, by Carter, Andrews, 1831.   (5) - 28 p.   22½ cm.   1-11241.   F74. B56 D2

BOYLSTON.   The years of many generations considered: two sermons, preached in Boylston ... giving a history of the Congregational church ...   By William H. Sanford ... Worcester, C. B. Webb, print. 1853.   71 p.   24 cm.   17-17353.   F74. B56S22

BRADFORD.   Celebration of the 100th anniversary of the Declaration of independence of the U. S. held at Bradford, July 4, 1876.   Haverhill, Gazette print., 1877.   44 p.   23 cm.   1-16893.

F74. B58 B5

BRADFORD, Vital records of, to the end of the year 1849.   Topsfield, Mass., Topsfield historical soc., 1907.   373 p.   23 cm.   7-15573 Rev.   F74. B58 B6

BRADFORD, Memorial history of, from the earliest period to the close of 1882.   By J. D. Kingsbury.

MASSACHUSETTS

Haverhill, Mass., C. C. Morse, print., 1883.   144 p. 25 cm.   Church membership roll, 1682 - 1882: p. 34 - 62.
1-11242.   F74.B58 K5

BRADFORD. A discourse, delivered in the East parish in Bradford, 1820; two hundred years after the first settlement in New-England. Containing a history of the town. By Gardner B. Perry ... Haverhill, Print. Burrill and Hersey, 1821.   72 p.   22 cm.   8-12860.   F74.B58 P3

BRADFORD, History of, from the earliest period to the close of 1820, by Gardner B. Perry. Haverhill, Mass., C. C. Morse, print., 1872.   69 p.   25 cm.   Reprint of F74.B58P3.   1-11243.
F74.B58 P4

BRADFORD, Mass., An historical sketch of, in the revolution. (Including East Bradford, now Groveland) By Louis A. Woodbury ... Groveland, Mass. (Ambrose and co., print.) 1895.   viii, 112 p. front., illus. (port.) plates. 16 x 12 ½ cm.   1-11244.   F74.B58 W8

BRAINTREE directory, The ...   v. 1 - 2.   Boston, Boston suburban book co., 1907 - 1910.
2 v. fold. maps. 24 cm.   7-14826 Additions.   Directories

BRAINTREE, Resident and business directory of, 1907.   1 v.   Directories

BRAINTREE. An address on the occasion of opening the new town hall, in Braintree ... 1858. By Charles Francis Adams. Boston, W. White, print., 1858.   86 p. 23 ½ cm.   24-13547.
F74. B6 A2

BRAINTREE, The ancient iron works at. (The first in America) By Samuel A. Bates.   ... South Braintree, F. A. Bates, 1898.   29 p.   20 ½ cm.   1-11245.   F74. B6 B3

BATES. Biography of Samuel Austin Bates of Braintree. By Frank A. Bates. (Reprint from "Genealogy of the descendants of Elder Edward Bates of Weymouth, Mass.") ... South Braintree, Mass., F. A. Bates, 1900.   11 p. front. (port.) 21 ½ cm.   Edition of 150 copies.   18-12649.   F74.B6 B32

BRAINTREE. Centennial celebration at Braintree, Mass. ... 1876. Boston, A. Mudge, print., 1877.   95 p.   24 cm.   1-11246-M1.   F74. B6 B9

BRAINTREE, Records of the town of. 1640 to 1793. Ed. Samuel A. Bates. Randolph, Mass., D. H. Huxford, print., 1886.   2, 939 p.   24 cm.   1-11247.   F74.B6 B97

BRAINTREE, A brief history of the town of. ...   compiled and written for the Tercentenary committee Marion Sophia Arnold, ed. (Boston, Press of Thomas Todd co., 1940)   64 p. front., plates. 23 cm.
40-10871 Rev.   F74.B6 B98

BRAINTREE estates. no. 1 - 2. (South Braintree? Mass., 1904 -   2 nos. 21 cm.   "An attempt to furnish descriptions of some of the homestead properties of this ancient town ... 6-19695.   F74.B6 B99

BRAINTREE. ... Bowditch mill privilege. (South Braintree? Mass., 1904)   7 p. 21 cm. (Braintree estates. no. 1 March, 1904)   5-42435.   F74.B6 B99

BRAINTREE. Thomas farm. (South Braintree? Mass., 1904)   (9) - 17 p. 21 cm. (Braintree estates. no. 2 Oct., 1904)   5-42436.   F74.B6 B99

BRAINTREE. John Adams' town; a child's history of old Braintree as told to Peter by Mary. Written and illus. by Maryrose Larkin. (n.p. 1968)   vii, 39 p. illus. 21 cm.
F74. B6 L3

BRAINTREE. Extracts from John Marshall's diary, Jan. 1689 - Dec. 1711. With an introd. by Samuel A. Green. Cambridge, J. Wilson, 1900.   24 p.   24 ½ cm.   11-25758.
F74. B6 M3

BRAINTREE and Quincy, A history of old, with a sketch of Randolph and Holbrook, by William S. Pattee, Quincy (Mass.) Green & Prescott, 1878.   xiv, 660 p. incl. front. plates, ports. 23 ½ cm.   1-11248.   F74. B6 P3

BRAINTREE soldiers' memorial, The: a record of the services in the war of the rebellion of the men of Braintree, Mass. ... with appendices containing a list of Braintree volunteers in the Union army and navy from 1861 to 1865, etc.   Boston, A. Mudge, print., 1877.   52 p. 24 cm.   1-16194.

                                                           F74. B6 T3

BREWSTER, Vital records of the town of, to the end of the year 1849; literally transcribed under the direction of George Ernest Bowman ... Boston, Mass., Mass. soc. of Mayflower descendants at the charge of the Cape Cod town record fund, 1904.   xi, 281 p. 23½ cm.   4-33236.   F74.B64 B6

BREWSTER.   Records of the Brewster Congregational church, Brewster, Mass., 1700 - 1792. (Boston, Merrymount press) Priv. print., 1911.   3, 169 p. 22½ cm. 25 copies.   Another transcript of the same records is in the Mayflower descendant.   11-27877.
                                                           F74.B64B65
                                                           Rare Book Coll.

BREWSTER.   Our village, by Joseph C. Lincoln ... New York, D. Appleton, 1909.   7, 3-182 p. front., 3 pl. 20 cm.   Reprinted from various periodicals.   9-11524.   F74.B64 L7

BREWSTER.   Mortuary record from the gravestones in the old burial ground in Brewster, with biographical and genealogical notes.   Comp. and ed. by Charles E. Mayo.   Yarmouth, Mass., Register pub. co., 1898.   79, (3) p. pl. 23 cm.   4-11458 Rev.   F74.B64 M4

BREWSTER, ... Vital records of the town of.   By Eben Putnam.   (Boston, 1905)   3 p. 23 cm.   From the Genealogical quarterly, Jan. 1905.   5-18250.   F74.B64 P9

BREWSTER ship masters, by J. Henry Sears.   With foreword by Joseph C. Lincoln ... tog. with a chapter in reminiscence by Joseph H. Sears.   Yarmouthport, Mass., C. W. Swift, 1906.   4, 80 p. front., plates, ports. 22½ cm.   6-33644.   F74.B64 S4

BRIDGEWATER.   Shoe and leather trade of the last hundred years, by Seth Bryant.   Boston, Mass., S. Bryant, 1891.   136 p. front. (port.)   20 cm.   8-14224.   F74.B7
                                                           HD9787.U45 B8

BRIDGEWATERS, The, W. A. Greenough co.'s Bridgewater, East Bridgewater and West Bridgewater directory, 19 -   Boston, W. A. Greenough co., 19   v. 24 cm.   CA 31-326 Unrev.   Directories

BRIDGEWATER.   Records of John Cary, the first town clerk of Bridgewater, Mass., from 1656 to 1681.   Pub. by Loring W. Puffer, Brockton, Mass.   Brockton, W. L. Puffer, 1889.   2, 14 p. 22 cm.   10-8644.   F74. B7 B8

BRIDGEWATER, Vital records of, to the year 1850 ...   Boston, Mass., Pub. by the New England historic genealogical soc. ... 1916.   2 v. 23½ cm.   v. I. Births. v. II. Marriages and deaths.   16-27376.
                                                           F74. B7 B85

BRIDGEWATER.   Celebration of the 200th anniversary of the incorporation of Bridgewater ... 1856 ...   Boston, Print, J. Wilson, 1856.   viii, (9) - 167 p. front., port. 24½ cm.   1-11249.   F74. B7 B9

BRIDGEWATER.   Proceedings of the 250th anniversary of old Bridgewater at West Bridgewater ... 1906.   Bridgewater, Mass., A. H. Willis, print., 1907.   149 p. incl. illus., 2 pl. pl., ports. 23½ cm. 8-29798.
                                                          F74.B7 B92

BRIDGEWATER book, The ... Boston, G. H. Ellis, print., 1899.   40 p. illus., 12 pl. (incl. front.) 29 cm.   5-16863.   F74.B7 B93

BRIDGEWATER.   A semi-centennial discourse before the First Congregation society in Bridgewater ... 1871.   By Richard Manning Hodges ... With historical notes.   Cambridge (Mass.) Press of J. Wilson, 1871.   59 p.   23 cm.   1-21440.   F74. B7 H6

BRIDGEWATER in the rebellion, A history of.   By Arthur Hooper, late member of the Third and Fifty-eighth regiments, Mass. volunteers. Boston, F. W. Barry, print. 1880.   85, (3) p. 24½ cm. Including the records of the Bridgewater men who served in the war.   1-11250.   F74. B7 H7

MASSACHUSETTS

BRIDGEWATER. Old Bridgewater, Mass., a classic town whose early learned ministers were moulders of New England character; an address delivered by Rev. George A. Jackson ... 1904. (Bridgewater? Mass.) E. Alden, 1905.   (10) p. 22½ cm.   6-9499.   F74. B7 J2

BRIDGEWATER, Epitaphs in old. By Williams Latham. Illus. with plans and views. Bridgewater, 1882.   viii, 253 p. front., plates, port., plans. 23½ cm.   "A complete list of all epitaphs in all old public grave-yards commenced before 1800, with plans and with some account of the old grave yards of three towns of West Bridgewater, Bridgewater and East Bridgewater ... and also most of the epitaphs in private ... yards."   9-30381.   F74. B7 L3

BRIDGEWATER, History of the early settlement of, including an extensive Family register. By Nahum Mitchell. Boston, Print. for the author by Kidder & Wright, 1840.   400 p. 23½ cm.   1-11251.   F74. B7 M6

— Bridgewater, Mass., Reprinted by H. T. Pratt, 1897.   vi, 424p. front. (port.) pl. 24 cm.   1-11252.   F74. B7 M7

BRIGHTON day. Celebration of the 100th anniversary of the incorporation of the town of Brighton, 1907. Boston, Municipal print. office, 1908.   63 p. front., ports., double pl. 27 cm.   Brighton was annexed to Boston in 1874.   9-19170.   F74.B73 B3

BRIGHTON Evangelical Congregational church, 1827 - 1927. By George E. Brock. (Brighton, Mass., Print. at the Item press, 1927?)   36 p. incl. illus., pl. 25 cm.   Editor, J.M. Ayer.   29-27709.   F74. B73 B8

BRIGHTON. An oration delivered at the dedication of the soldiers' monument, in Evergreen cemetery, Brighton ... 1866, by Rev. Frederic Augustus Whitney. With an appendix, containing the other exercises, and notices of the deceased soldiers. Boston, S. Chism, Franklin print, house, 1866.   61 p. incl. pl.   24 cm.   1-5796.   F74.B75 W5

BRIGHTON. Historical Brighton. v. 1 - 2; an illus. history of Brighton and its citizens, by J. P. C. Winship. Boston, G. A. Warren, 1899 - 1902.   2 v.   illus. (incl. ports.) plates.   28 cm.   Oct. 5, 99-210.   F74.B73 W7

BRIMFIELD, Historical celebration of the town of.   ... 1876. With the historical address of Rev. Charles M. Hyde, etc. Springfield, Mass., The C. W. Bryan co., print., 1879.   vi, 487 p. front., plates, ports., fold. map., facsim. 24 cm.   Genealogy: p. (366) - 476.   1-11253.   F74.B75B72

BRIMFIELD, Vital records of, to the year 1850. Boston, Mass., New England historic genealogical soc., 1931.   336 p. 23 cm.   31-20861.   F74.B75B78

BRIMFIELD, Annals of the church in. By the pastor of the church ... Springfield (Mass.) S. Bowles, print., 1856.   83 p. front. (fold. map)   22½ cm.   Appendixes showing the origin of the churches in Holland, Wales and Monson. Names of church members, 1724 - 1856, p. 49 - 72.   10-8758.   F74.B75 M8

BRIMFIELD, Stage days in, a century of mail and coach (by) Mary Anna Tarbell. (Springfield, Mass., The F. A. Bassette co., print., 1909.   32, (2) p. incl. front., illus. 23½ cm.   9-29350.   F74.B75 T2

BROCKTON. History of the Brockton relief fund in aid of sufferers from the R. B. Grover factory fire, Brockton, Mass. ... 1905. Prepared by Rev. Albert F. Pierce ... Boston, Fort Hill press, S. Usher (1907)   117 p. front. (port.)   5 pl.   24 cm.   8-10085.   F74. B8 HV 620 1905

BROCKTON. Manning's Brockton directory ... v. 187-   Boston, H. A. Manning co., 187 -   v. fold. maps.   23½ x 26 cm.   99-2072 Rev.   Directories

BROCKTON, Vital records of, to the year 1850. Boston, New England historic genealogical soc., 1911.   371 p. 23 cm.   13-2539.   F74. B8 B8

BROCKTON'S honor roll of her sons who made the supreme sacrifice in the world war. (Brockton) Brockton world war victory assoc., 1919.   108 p. illus. (ports.) 24 cm.   20-12069.   F74.B8 B85

BROCKTON. A genealogy of the families who have settled in the North parish of Bridgewater. To which is added an historical sketch of North-Bridgewater. By Moses Cary. Boston, Print. Bannister and Marvin, 1824. 48 p. 21 cm. 1-11254.
F74. B8 C2
Rare Book Coll.

BROCKTON, The book of the pageant of, written by Suzanne Cary Gruver. Produced in connection with the centennial celebration of the incorporation of the town of North Bridgewater, now Brockton ... 1921. (Brockton, Mass., Newsom & Toner, print., 1921) (3) - 42 p. front. 23 cm. 22-8322.
F74. B8 G9

BROCKTON. History of North Bridgewater ... from its first settlement to the present time, with family registers. By Bradford Kingman ... Boston, The author, 1866. 3, v-xii, 696 p. front., plates, ports., double map. 23½ cm. Name of town changed in 1874 to Brockton. 1-11255.
F74. B8 K5

BROCKTON, History of, 1656 - 1894. Syracuse, N.Y., D. Mason, 1895. 814, 122 p. 27 cm. "List of publications by the people of Brockton": p. 789 - 794. 5-9974 rev.*
F74. B8 K6

— A genealogist's index; compiled by Elizabeth Hayward. West Hartford, Conn., Chedwato Service, 1957. 15 p. 27 cm.
F74. B8 K6
Index.

BROCKTON and its centennial, chief events as town and city, 1821 - 1921 ... Warren P. Landers, ed. Brockton, Mass., Pub. by the city of Brockton, 1921. 5, 13 - 200 p. front., illus. (incl. ports., facsims.) fold. plates. 23½ cm. 22-2109.
F74. B8 L25

BROCKTON, a city of enterprise. By Hamilton Lowe. (Boston, 1911) (14) p. illus. (incl. ports.) pl. 25 cm. "By courtesy of the New England magazine, September, 1911." CA 28-806 Unrev.
F74. B8 L9

BROCKTON women ... Copyright, 1892 by Bethia Hayward Thayer ... New York, The Albertype co., 1892. (25) p. 18 pl. (incl. ports.) 18 x 14 cm. 6-7692.
F74. B8 T3

BROCKTON, Views of. (Portland, Me., L. H. Nelson co., 19 -?) 20½ x 25 cm.
F74. B8 V5

— Portland, Me., 1905. 20 x 25 cm.
F74. B8 V6

BROOKFIELD. An exposition of difficulties in West Brookfield, connected with anti-slavery operations, together with a reply to some statements in a pamphlet put forth by "Moses Chase" ... By the Board of managers of the W. B. anti-slavery society. West Brookfield, Mass., The Anti-slavery society, 1844. 59 p. 24 cm. Signed: John M. Fisk. 11-12569.
F74. B85
E449.W 51

BROOKFIELD. Quabaug, 1660 - 1910: an account of the 250th anniversary celebration held at West Brookfield, Mass. ... 1910; comp. and ed. by Charles J. Adams ... under the direction of the Committee on publication of ... the towns of Brookfield, West Brookfield, North Brookfield and New Braintree. Worcester, Mass., Davis press, 1915. 127 p. front., plates, ports. 23 cm. 15-23614 Rev.
F74. B85 A2

BROOKFIELD, A story of old, by Frances Bartlett, of Boston, read at the annual meeting of the Quaboag historical society ... 1902 ... (Columbia, S.C., The R. L. Bryan co., 1902) 13 p. 17 cm. 10-31027.
F74. B85 B2

BROOKFIELD, ... Vital records of, to the end of the year 1849. Worcester, Mass., F. P. Rice, 1909. 549 p. 23½ cm. 9-15729.
F74. B85 B7

BROOKFIELD. Anniversary exercises commemorating the 187th anniversary of the church, and the 150th of the precinct, held in the First parish church ... 1904. (Spencer, Mass., W. J. Heffernan-Leader print. 1905) 42 p. incl. 2 pl., port. 19½ cm. 7-27737.
F74. B85 B8

BROOKFIELD, An address on the early history of old, delivered at West Brookfield ... by the Rev. L. T. Chamberlain ... (Brooklyn, N.Y., Press of Larkin & co., 1895?) 36 p. 22½ cm. 11-6057.
F74. B85 C4

MASSACHUSETTS

BROOKFIELD. Colonial Quaboag ... By Elizabeth (Carlton) Coes. Brookfield, Mass., Podunk Pedlar Press, 1960. 35 p. 23 cm. F74.B85 C6

BROOKFIELD. An historical discourse delivered at West Brookfield, on occasion of the 150th anniversary of the First church in Brookfield ... 1867. By Samuel Dunham. Springfield, Mass., S. Bowles & co., print., 1867. 123 p. front. (port.) 23 cm. 1-11256. F74.B85 D9

BROOKFIELD. Remarkable providences to be gratefully recollected, religiously improved, and carefully transmitted to posterity. A sermon .... Together with some marginal notes etc. giving an account of the first settling of the town in the year 1660, etc. By Nathan Fiske ... Boston, Print. Thomas and John Fleet, 1776. 31, v. p. 18 cm. 1-11257. F74.B85 F5
Rare Book Coll.

— (West Brookfield, Mass., Print. T. Morey, 1860) 25, iv p. 22 cm. 3-2325. F74.B85 F53
Rare Book Coll.

BROOKFIELD, An historical discourse, delivered at ... 1828. By Joseph I. Foot ... Brookfield, Print. by E. and G. Merriam, 1829. 64 p. 24 cm. 17-2409.
F74.B85 F68

— With Capt. Thomas Wheeler's narrative, now annexed, and additional notices of occurrences in the town, since the first publication ... West Brookfield, Merriam & Cooke, 1843. 96 p. 20 cm. 1-11677 Rev. F74.B85 F7

BROOKFIELD. The sovereignty of God in determining the boundaries of human life. A sermon, preached at Brookfield ... 1784, at the funeral of Josiah Hobbs, jun., ... who was killed by lightning ... By Nathan Fiske ... Print. at Worcester, by I. Thomas, 1784. 24 p. 24 x 14½ cm. 21-8428.
F74.B85 H68
Rare Book Coll.

BROOKFIELD, Memorials of. A poem, delivered ... 1867, the 150th anniversary of the Congregational church. By Rev. Francis Horton ... Springfield, Mass., S. Bowles, print., 1868. 20 p. 23 cm. 11-32026. F74.B85 H8

BROOKFIELD. Quaboag plantation alias Brookfield; a seventeenth century Massachusetts town, by Louis E. Roy. (Brookfield, Mass., 1965) 308 p. 24 cm. F74.B85 R6

BROOKFIELD. Reminiscences of a half-century pastorate. A discourse, delivered by Micah Stone, senior pastor of the Evangelical church in Brookfield ... 1851 ... West Brookfield (Mass.,) O. S. Cooke, 1851. 72 p. 23½ cm. 1-11258 Rev. F74.B85 S8

BROOKFIELD. ... A bi-centennial oration made in West Brookfield, ... 1860. At the celebration of the 200th anniversary of the settlement of the town of Brookfield. By Lyman Whiting ... West Brookfield (Mass.) Print. T. Morey, 1869. 2, (3) - 92 p. 23 cm. 7-27742. F74.B85 W6

BROOKLINE directory ... v. 1 -   Boston, W. A. Greenough, 1868 - 19 -
v. fold. maps. 24 - 26½ cm. 20-15299. Directories

BROOKLINE. Spencer's Brookline directory ... (v. 1 -   Brookline, Mass., C. A. W. Spencer, 1894-
v. 23½ cm. 20-5359. Directories

BROOKLINE; the history of a favored town, by Charles Knowles Bolton ... Brookline, Mass. C. A. W. Spencer, 1897. 2, (3) - 213 p. plates, ports., fold. map. 18½ cm. 1-16331. F74. B9 B6

BROOKLINE. What the small town may do for itself, by Charles Knowles Bolton ... (Boston, 1896) 3 p. 24 cm. "Reprinted from the New England magazine, March, 1896." 8-3835. F74.B9 B64

BROOKLINE. Muddy River and Brookline records. 1634 - 1838. By the inhabitants of Brookline ... (Boston, J. E. Farwell, print., 1875. 703 p. 23 cm. The hamlet of Muddy River (a part of Boston) was incorporated as the town of Brookline in 1705. 1-11259. F74. B9 B7

BROOKLINE, Town records of ... (Brookline, etc.) Pub. by vote of the town, 1888 - 82 (v.3, '88)
3 v.   24½ cm.   1-11260.
F74.B9 B72

BROOKLINE, Vital records of, to the end of the year 1849.   Salem, Mass., The Essex institute, 1929.
244 p.   23 cm.   29-13363.
F74.B9 B74

BROOKLINE.   Proceedings at the dedication of the Town hall, Brookline, ... 1873.   Brookline, Prepared and print. by authority of the town; (Cambridge, J. Wilson, print.) 1873.   64 p.   24½ cm.   1-11261.
F74.B9 B76

BROOKLINE.   A guide to the local history of Brookline, prepared by the History committee of the Brookline education soc., 1897.   (Brookline, The Riverdale press, C. A. W. Spencer) 1897.
24 p.   front., plates.   21½ cm.   "General references": p. 23.   Bibliography: p. 24.   25-12811.
F74.B9 B78

BROOKLINE historical publication society, Publications of the.   1st - ed series; no. 1 - 20 ...
Brookline, The Riverdale press: C. A. W. Spencer, 1897 - 1900.   2 v. in 1. illus., plates, port., maps. 21 cm.
5-37452.   Contents. - 1. Letter from Rebecca Boylston. - 2. The Sharp papers in the Brookline Public Library. - 3. Brookline in the revolution. - 4. Papers of the White family of Brookline, 1650-1807. - 5. Roxbury church records relating to Brookline. - 6. Early notices of local events. - 7. Letter from Brigadier-General Edward A. Wild to the Brookline war committee. - 8. First parish church records of baptisms, marriages and deaths for 100 years. - 9. History of the lyceum movement in Brookline. - 10. Brookline in the civil war. - 11. Three glimpses of Brookline in 1700, 1800 and 1900. - 12. Major Thompson's deposition. - 13. The Brookline town meeting. - 14. The Devotion family of Brookline. - 15. Extracts from the account book of John Goddard of Brookline. - 16. More early notices of local events. - 17. Town papers. - 18. Brookline in the anti-slavery movement.   19-20. Some works relating to Brookline.

F74. B9 B8

BROOKLINE historical society, Proceedings of the at the annual meeting ... 1902 - 1910.   Brookline, Mass., 1902 - 1910.   9 v. in 8.   plates, ports.   24½ cm.   10-20864.
F74.B9 B83

BROOKLINE historical society, Publications of the (no. 1 - 3)   Brookline, Mass., 1903 - 04.
3 v.   plates, ports., map, geneal. tab.   24½ cm.   10-20870.
F74.B9 B85
— Jeremey Gridley ... by R. G. F. Candage.   (no. 1)   32 p.   7-15396.
— In memoriam, John Emory Hoar, by R. G. F. Candage.   (no. 2)   10-27801.
— Elhanan Winchester, preacher and traveller, by John Emory Hoar.   (no. 2)   10-27800.
— Recollections of Brookline, by Mrs. Mary W. Poor ...   (no. 2)   10-27799.
— Brookline village, 1865 to 1902, from notes of Martin Kingman ...   (no. 2)   10-27798.
— John White of Muddy River ...   (no. 3)   5-33687.
— The centennial of Blue Hill academy.   (no. 3)   5-33686.
— Land ownership in Brookline ... by Theodore F. Jones ... with genealogical additions, by Charles F. White.   (no. 5)   44 p.   24-873.

BROOKLINE ... Boston, The Edison electric illuminating co., 1909.   23 cm.
F74.B9B905

BROOKLINE.   The Chronicle souvenir of the bicentennial.   Brookline, Mass., C. A. W. Spencer, 1905.
64 p.   illus. (incl. ports.)   35½ x 28 cm.   6-40531.
F74. B9 C5

BROOKLINE.   Burials and inscriptions in the Walnut street cemetery of Brookline, with historical sketches of some of the persons buried there; comp. by Harriet Alma Cummings.   Brookline, The Riverdale press, print., 1920.   135 p.   front., illus.   23½ cm.   20-22567.
F74.B9 C86

BROOKLINE, History of the town of, by John Gould Curtis; a memorial to Edward W. Baker; prepared under the direction of the Brookline historical soc.   Boston and New York, Houghton Mifflin, 1933.
xxiii, 349 p.   front., plates, ports., fold. map.   22½ cm.   33-30716.
F74.B9 C88

BROOKLINE.   A discourse, occasioned by the death of the Rev. Mr. Joseph Jackson ... delivered at his interment ... 1796.   By Jacob Cushing ... Boston, Print. S. Hall, 1797.   (5) - 23 p.   23 cm.
11-21032.
F74. B9 C9
Rare Book Coll.

BROOKLINE, ... A history of, from the first settlement of Muddy River until the present time; 1630 - 1906; commemorating the 200th anniversary of the town ... By John William Denehy.   Brookline,

MASSACHUSETTS

The Brookline press co., 1906. 255 p. front., illus. (incl. ports.) 30 ½ cm. 7-21722. F74. B9 D3

BROOKLINE, Recollections of. Being an account of the houses, the families, and the roads, in Brookline, in the years 1800 to 1810, by Samuel Aspinwall Goddard. Birmingham, Eng., Print. E. C. Osborne (1873) 16 p. 21 ½ cm. First pub. in the Brookline transcript ... 1873. 7-27754. F74.B9 G57

BROOKLINE, Sketch of the history and government of. Boston, 1940. 74 p. map. 28 cm. "Reprinted from the inventory of the town and city archives of Mass., no. 11, vol. iv" List of sources: p. (50) - 54. 50-42607. F74. B9 H5

BROOKLINE trunk, The. By Louise (Andrews) Kent. Illus. by Barbara Cooney. Boston, Houghton Mifflin, 1955. 306 p. illus. 22 cm. 55-9954. F74. B9 K4

BROOKLINE. Some old Brookline houses built in this Massachusetts town before 1825 and still standing in 1948; a compilation of existing data, to which has been added architectural and biographical notes, constructional details, photographs and floor plans. (Brookline) Brookline Historical Society, 1949. 160 p. illus., map. 24 cm. Includes "References." 49-4449*. F74.B9 L58

BROOKLINE. An address at the opening of the Town hall, in Brookline, ... 1845. By John Pierce ... Boston, White & Potter, print., 1846. 52 p. 22 cm. Appendix contains biographical and historical sketches. 1-11262. F74. B9 P6

BROOKLINE. Reminiscences of forty years, delivered ... 1837 ... by John Pierce ... Boston, M. Pratt, print., 1837. 35 p. 23 cm. 12-40121. F74.B9 P65

BROOKLINE. John Fitzgerald Kennedy National Historic Site, Massachusetts. Washington, U.S. Office of History and Historic Architecture, Eastern Service Center, 1971. vii, 74 p. illus. 27 cm. Bibliography: p. 71-74. 79-614830 MARC. F74. B9 T6

BROOKLINE. U.S. Congress. Senate. Committee on Interior and Insular Affairs. John Fitzgerald Kennedy national historic site; report, to accompany S. 1161. (Washington, U.S. Govt. Print. Off., 1967) 4 p. 24 cm. 67-61270. F74. B9 U5

— report to accompany H. R. 6424. (Washington, U.S. Govt. Print. Off.) 1967. 4 p. 24 cm. 67-61441. F74.B9U515

— Hearing, Ninetieth Congress, first session on S. 1161. March 20, 1967. Washington, U.S. Govt, Print. Off., 1967. iii, 9 p. 24 cm. 67-61454. F74.B9 U52

BROOKLINE. Address at the dedication of the new town hall of Brookline, on the 22d of Feb., 1873, by Hon. Robert C. Winthrop. Cambridge, Press of J. Wilson, 1873. 42 p. 23 cm. 3-8386. F74. B9 W7

BROOKLINE, Historical sketches of. By Harriet F. Woods. Boston, Pub. for the author, by R. S. Davis and co., 1874. vii, (9) - 430 p. 21 cm. 1-11263. F74. B9 W8

BUCKLAND centennial, ... 1879. Addresses, poems, songs, etc. (Northampton, Metcalf & co., print., 1879?) 40 p. 22 ½ cm. 1-11264. F74.B97 B9

BUCKLAND. Vital records of Buckland, to the end of the year 1849. Salem, Mass., The Essex institute, 1934. 214 p. 23 cm. 34-9005. With this are issued, Vital records of Colrain and Vital records of Montague. F74.B97B94

BUCKLAND, The history of, 1779 - 1935, by Fannie Shaw Kendrick, with genealogies by Lucy Cutler Kellogg. Pub. by the town of Buckland ... Buckland, Mass. (Rutland, Vt., Print. by the Tuttle pub. co.) 1937. ix, 799 p. front., plates, ports., maps (1 fold.) 23 ½ cm. "First ed." 38-4829. F74.B97 K4

BUCKLAND. Official souvenir program for Buckland's and Shelburne's welcome to her soldier and sailor boys, given in honor of the return of the boys who served in the world war, 1917-1918 ... (Shelburne Falls? Mass., 1919) (8) p. 16 ½ cm. 24-24420. F74.B97 O3

BURLINGTON, Vital records of, to the year 1850.   Comp. by Thomas W. Baldwin ... Boston, (Wright & Potter print.) 1915.   100 p.   23½ cm.   15-24547 Rev.   F74.B98 B9

BYFIELD, The story of, a New England parish, by John Louis Ewell ... Boston, G. E. Littlefield, 1904.   xv, 344 p. front., plates, ports., maps (2 fold.) plans, facsims. (2 fold.) 25 cm.   4-2505 Rev.   F74.B99 E9

BYFIELD parish, A contribution to the history of. (An outside view) By William Little. (Newburyport, Mass., C. B. Huse, pr., 1893)   12 p. 23½ cm. Prepared for the West Newbury natural history club in 1891. 10-17555.   F74.B99 L7

CAMBRIDGE.   Harvard and Cambridge; a sketch book by Jack Frost.   John Edward Frost.   New York, Coward-McCann, (1940)   vi, 89 p. illus. (incl. ports.) 25½ cm. 40-34144.   F74.C LD2157. F7

CAMBRIDGE.   The Soldier's field (by) Henry Lee Higginson, major, First Massachusetts cavalry ... (Boston? 1890?)   4, (3) - 12 p. 24 cm. 10-17781.   F74.C E541.H2 H6

CAMBRIDGE.   Cambridge sketches, by Frank Preston Stearns ... Philadelphia & London, J.B. Lippincott, 1905.   374 p. incl. front. 6 port. 20 cm. 5-11051.   F74.C1 E415.8.S79

CAMBRIDGE directory ...   (v.1 -   Boston, W. A. Greenough, 184 -   - 19-
v. fronts. (fold. maps) 15 - 26 cm. 8-10603 (rev. '17)   Directories

CAMBRIDGE directory and almanac for (1848, 1850-54) (1st, 3d-5th, 7th eds.)   Cambridge, J. Ford (1848) - 54.   5 v. fold. plans. 14½ cm. First Cambridge directory pub. 1847. 8-10603.   Directories

CAMBRIDGE directory for 1860 ... Cambridge (Mass.) Thurston, Miles & Pritchett, 1860.
252 p. front. (fold. plan) illus. 17½ cm. 8-10602.   Directories

CAMBRIDGE directory, for 1863/4: containing ... a complete list of Cambridge soldiers.   Cambridgeport (Mass.) G. Fisher (1863)   xxxi, 231 p. front. (fold. plan) 17½ cm. 8-10601.   Directories

CAMBRIDGE, Blue book of (188 -   Boston, Boston suburban book co., 188 - 19 -
v. illus. (incl. ports.) fold. plans. 18½ x 21½ cm. 1-30563 Rev.   Directories

CAMBRIDGE.   Old Cambridge and new.   By Thomas C. Amory ... Boston, J. R. Osgood, 1871.
45 p. 23½ cm. "Reprinted from the New-England hist. and geneal. register, July, 1871. With additions. 1-11265.   F74. C1 A5

CAMBRIDGE.   Burgoyne and his officers in Cambridge, 1777 - 1778, by Samuel F. Batchelder. (Cambridge? Mass.) 1926.   17 - 80 p. fold. map., fold facsim. 24 cm. Reprinted from the Proceedings of the Cambridge Hist. soc., 1918. 26-17568.   E281. B 32

CAMBRIDGE and vicinity.   Its representative business men and its points of interest ... By George Fox Bacon.   Newark, N.J., Mercantile pub. co., 1892.   150, (2) p. illus. 4°. 1-11266-M1.   F74.C1 B13

CAMBRIDGE, The beginnings of the First church in, by Hollis R. Bailey.   Cambridge, Mass., Priv. print., 1932.   36 p. front. (port.) 2pl. 23 cm. Bibliography: p. (37) 34-5033.   F74.C1 B24

CAMBRIDGE.   Bits of Cambridge history, by Samuel Francis Batchelder.   Cambridge, Harvard university press, 1930.   5, (3) - 349 p. front., plates, ports., fold. map, facsims. (1 fold) 22½ cm. 30-28489.   F74.C1 B29

CAMBRIDGE.   The Washington elm tradition, "Under this tree Washington first took command of the American army".   Is it true? The evidence collected and considered by Samuel F. Batchelder ... (Cambridge, Mass.) 1925.   36 p. 20 cm. "Reprinted from the Cambridge tribune, 1925." 26-411.   F74. C1 B3

CAMBRIDGE.   ... Acceptance and unveiling of the statue of John Bridge, the Puritan, presented to the

MASSACHUSETTS

city of Cambridge ... by Samuel James Bridge. Cambridge, Tribune pub. co., 1883. 22 p. front. 24 cm. 7-12011. F74. C1 C2

CAMBRIDGE fifty years a city, 1846 - 1896; an account of the celebration of the 50th anniversary of the incorporation of the city of Cambridge ... ed. Walter Gee Davis ... Cambridge, The Riverside press, 1897. 3, (3) - 191 p. front., plates, ports. 25 cm. 1-11267. F74. C1C21

CAMBRIDGE in the "centennial." Proceedings ... in celebration of the centennial anniversary of Washington's taking command of the Continental army, on Cambridge common. Cambridge, Print. by order of the City council, 1875. 125, (2) p. front., pl. 25½ cm. 1-11268. F74. C1 C23

CAMBRIDGE 75 years a city, 1846 - 1921. A brief account of the interesting events in connection with the celebration of the 75th anniversary of the city of Cambridge ... (Boston, E. L. Grimes, print.) 2, 7-128 p. fronts., plates, ports. 23½ cm. 23-4066. F74. C1 C24

CAMBRIDGE. Exercises in celebrating the 250th anniversary of the settlement of Cambridge ... Cambridge, C. W. Sever, 1881. iv, (7) - 163 p. illus., plates, ports. 25½ cm. 1-11269. F74. C1 C25

CAMBRIDGE. Memorial to the men of Cambridge who fell in the first battle of the revolutionary war. Services of dedication ... Cambridge, Press of J. Wilson, 1870. 40 p. 24½ cm. 1-11270.
F74. C1 C31

CAMBRIDGE. The register book of the lands and houses in the "New Towne" and the town of Cambridge, with the records of the proprietors of the common lands, being the records generally called "the proprietors' records" (1634 - 1829) Cambridge, (J. Wilson) 1896. vii, 409 p. facsim. 25 cm. Being vol. I of the printed records of the town. 1-11271 Additions. F74. C1 C36

CAMBRIDGE. The records of the town of Cambridge (formerly Newtowne) 1630 - 1703. The records of the town meetings, and of the selectmen, comprising all of the first volume of records, and being vol. II of the printed records of the town. Cambridge, 1901. vi, 397 p. front. (map) facsim. 24½ cm. 1-26732-M2. F74. C1 C37

CAMBRIDGE. The soldiers' monument in Cambridge. Proceedings in relation to the building and dedication of the monument erected in the years 1869 - 70, by the city government of Cambridge, in honor of those of her soldiers and sailors who died in defence of the union of the states, in the war of the rebellion. Cambridge, Press of J. Wilson, 1870. 104 p. front. 24½ cm. "Prepared and pub. by order of the City council." 1-16193. F74. C1C375

CAMBRIDGE. Trustees of the subscription fund for Cambridge volunteers, Report of. Cambridge, Press of J. Ford, 1863. 10 p. 24 cm. 10-14258. F74. C1 C38

CAMBRIDGE, Vital records of, to the year 1850 ... Comp. by Thomas W. Baldwin ... Boston, (Wright & Potter print.) 1914-15. 2 v. 23½ cm. v.1. Births. - v.2. Marr. and deaths. 14-3960 Rev. F74. C1 C4

CAMBRIDGE. Records of the Church of Christ at Cambridge ... 1632 - 1830, comprising ... baptisms, marriages, deaths, etc. etc. copied and ed. by Stephen Paschall Sharpes ... Boston, E. Putnam, 1906. viii p., 579 p. facsim. 23 cm. 6-35823 rev.
F74. C1C466

CAMBRIDGE. Services at the celebration of the 250th anniversary of the organization of the First church in Cambridge ... Cambridge, J. Wilson, 1886. 2, (7) - 174 p. 24 cm. 8-16845.
F74. C1C467

CAMBRIDGE historical society. Publications. 1 - 3. Cambridge, Mass., The Society, 1906 - 1908. 3 v. 24 cm. 7-12705. F74. C1C469

CAMBRIDGE chronicle. Semi-centennial souvenir of Cambridge. '46 - '96. Cambridge, Mass., Cambridge chronicle (1896) 138 p. illus. (incl. ports.) 41 cm. 1-167 Rev. F74. C1C473

CAMBRIDGE. The Harvard bridge. A souvenir. 1630, 1890. The university city ... (Cambridge,

F. S. Hill) 1890.   32 p. incl. illus., pl., port. 52 cm.   1-16551.   F74.C1 C48

CAMBRIDGE tribune.   Tercentenary souvenir.   1636 - 1936.   (Cambridge, Mass., 1936)
1 v.   illus.   57 cm.   Forms p. (9) - 24 of the issue for Sept. 11, 1936.   Followed by the regular issue and the issue for Sept. 18 containing the "Tercentenary news extra"   41M2200T.   F74.C1C485

CAMBRIDGE.   Historic Cambridge in four seasons; a camera impression by Samuel Chamberlain. New York, Hastings house (1942)   73 p. front., illus.   19 x 16 cm.   Illustrations: p. 5-73.   42-50704.
F74.C1 C54

CAMBRIDGE, An historic guide to, comp. by members of the Hannah Winthrop chapter, National soc., D.A.R. ...   Cambridge, Mass., 1907.   4, 207 p. front., illus., plates, maps. 24 cm.   7-8509.
F74.C 1 D 2

CAMBRIDGE.   Address at the celebration of the 175th anniversary of the founding of Cambridge ... by Charles William Eliot ... (Cambridge, The Society, 1905)   P. (41) - 42.   24½ cm.   Reprinted from the Proceedings of the Cambridge historical soc. I.   10-23099.   F74. C1 E4

CAMBRIDGE, A history of, (1630 - 1913) by Samuel Atkins Eliot ... together with biographies of Cambridge people.   Cambridge, Mass., The Cambridge tribune, 1913.   3, (9) - 308 p. front., illus., plates, ports. 29 cm.   14-635.   F74.C1 E42

CAMBRIDGE.   Historic Cambridge common, by Charles C. Farrington.   Bedford, Mass. (The Bedford print shop) 1918.   32 p.   plates.   15 cm.   19-1808.   F74.C1 F24

CAMBRIDGE.   The sightseer in Cambridge; a guide for visitors, compiled and print. for the Tory row bookshop ... By Henry Wilder Foote.   (Brandon, Vt., The Otter Valley press, 1936)
41 (i.e. 43) p. illus. (map)   19 cm.   41-24876.   F74. C1 F7

CAMBRIDGE.   Historic houses and spots in Cambridge and near-by towns; by J. W. Freese ... Boston and London, Ginn & co., 1897.   viii, 144 p. illus. 19 cm.   1-11272.   F74. C1 F8

CAMBRIDGE of 1896, The.   A picture of the city and its industries fifty years after its incorporation. Done by divers hands and ed. by Arthur Gilman ... under the direction of a committee of the city government and citizens ... Cambridge, Riverside press, 1896.   xx p. 424 p.   front., plates, ports. 25 cm.
1-11273.   F74. C1 G5

CAMBRIDGE.   Theatrum majorum.   The Cambridge of 1776; wherein is set forth an account of the town, and of the events it witnesses: with which is incorporated the diary of Dorothy Dudley ... tog. with an historical sketch ... ed. for the Ladies centennial committee by A.G. (Arthur Gilman)   (2d ed.)   Cambridge, Printed; Boston, Lockwood, Brooks, and co., 1876.   v, (2), (2), (3) - 123 p. front., illus. (incl. map) 22 cm.   1-11981.   F74.G1 G53

— Port Washington, N.Y.   (1970)   79-120869.   F74.C1 G53
1970

— (New York) New York Times (1971)   v. 123 p. illus.   23 cm.   73-140861.   F74.C1 G53
1971

CAMBRIDGE.   Address on the seal of the Society ... by Mary Isabella Gozzaldi ... (Cambridge, The Society, 1908)   p. (5) - 19.   pl.   24½ cm.   Repr. from the Proceedings of the Cambridge hist. soc.   10-23097.   F74. C1 G6

CAMBRIDGE.   The Craigie house, Cambridge, during its occupancy by Andrew Craigie and his widow ... From Proceedings of the American antiquarian soc. ... Worcester, Mass., C. Hamilton, 1900.
43 p.   26 cm.   Bibliography: p. 41 - 43.   1-23984-M1.   F74. C1 G7

CAMBRIDGE.   A hand-book for passengers over the Cambridge railroad, with a description of Mount Auburn cemetery.   Boston, W. V. Spencer, 1858.   68 p. front. (double plan) illsu., pl.   15½ cm.   1-11274.
F74. C1 H23

MASSACHUSETTS 189

— 1858. 70 p. front. (double plan) illus., pl. 15½ cm. 1-11275. F74.C1 H24

CAMBRIDGE. Guide through Mount Auburn. A hand-book for passengers over the Cambridge railroad. 5th ed. Boston, Bricher & Russell, 1864. 78 p. front., illus., plan. 15½ cm. Another edition of above item. 37-31891. F74.C1 H25

CAMBRIDGE. Epitaphs from the old burying ground in Cambridge. With notes, by William Thaddeus Harris ... Cambridge, J. Owen, 1845. vii, 192 p. illus. 21½ cm. 6-5886.
F74. C1 H3

CAMBRIDGE. America's unknown city, Cambridge, Mass., 1630 - 1936. The Harvard trust co. presents a part of the history of Cambridge heretofore little emphasized ... (Cambridge? 1936) 27 p. illus. 23 cm. 36-24722. F74.C1 H35

CAMBRIDGE. Address at the celebration of the 275th anniversary of the founding of Cambridge ... by Thomas Wentworth Higginson ... (Cambridge, The Society, 1905) p. (48) - 53. 24½ cm. Reprinted from Proceedings of the Cambridge hist. soc. I. 10-23095. F74. C1 H5

CAMBRIDGE. Old Cambridge, by Thomas Wentworth Higginson ... New York (etc.) The Macmillan co., 1899. v. 203 p. 18 cm. (National studies in American letters) 99-2108 Rev. F74. C1 H6

CAMBRIDGE. Historical facts; an outline of the salient events in the history of Cambridge, for the boys and girls of our beloved city, by a graduate of the Cambridge high school. Boston, Mass., Newetowne pub. co., 1914. 16 p. 20 cm. 14-14753. F74.C1 H67

CAMBRIDGE, The history of. By Abiel Holmes ... Print, Samuel Hall, Boston, 1801. 67 p. 22 cm. 1-11276. F74. C1 H7

CAMBRIDGE. A sermon, preached at Cambridge ... the first Lord's day in the nineteenth century. By Abiel Holmes ... Cambridge, Print, William Hilliard. 1801. 27 p. 22 cm. 6-13952.
F74.C1 H75

CAMBRIDGE. Lucius Robinson Paige. 1802 - 1896. A memorial sketch ... Worcester, Mass. (Press of C. Hamilton) 1897. 11 p. 22½ cm. Reprinted from the Proceedings of the American antiquarian soc. 1896. 7-6956. F74. C1 H8

CAMBRIDGE. ... Cambridge vest-pocket guide. By Moses King. Cambridge (Mass.) M. King, 1883. 122 p. 9½ cm. 34-25068. F74. C1 K6
Miniature Coll.

CAMBRIDGE in 1775. By Rupert Ballou Lillie. (Wenham? Mass., 1949) 42 p. illus., fold. map. 24 cm. Bibliographical footnotes. 49-26077*. F74.C1 L55

CAMBRIDGE. ... Report of the finance committee. Cambridge, W. H. Wheeler, print., 1883. 20 p. 21½ cm. 25-5889. F74.C1 L75

CAMBRIDGE. The Longfellow memorial association, 1882 - 1922, an historical sketch, by Winthrop S. Scudder. Cambridge, Mass., Print. by the Association, 1922. 21 p. front. (port.) plates. 18½ cm. First printed in the Boston Sunday herald of Sept. 3, 1922. 23-9309. F74. C1 L8

CAMBRIDGE. Address at the celebration of the 275th anniversary of the founding of Cambridge ... by Alexander McKenzie ... (Cambridge, The Society, 1905) p. (35) - 40. 24½ cm. Reprinted from Proceedings of the Cambridge historical society I. 10-23101. F74. C1 M2

CAMBRIDGE. Address on some Cambridge men I have known ... by Alexander McKenzie ... (Cambridge, The Society, 1908) p. (19)-36. 24½ cm. Repr. from Procs. of the Cambridge hist. soc. III. 10-23096. F74.C1 M25

CAMBRIDGE. The Dunvegan and the Montrose; being a description of the apartment hotels just erected on the corner of Massachusetts ave. and Shepard st., Cambridge ... Cambridge, For the owner, by W. Bradley, 1899. (23) p. illus., pl. 16°. June 29, 99-77. F74. C1 M3

419

CAMBRIDGE sketches by Cambridge authors, ed. by Estelle M. H. Merrill, "Jean Kincaid," with preface by Dr. Alexander McKenzie. (Cambridge, Mass.) Cambridge Young women's Christian assoc. (1896) 2, (vii) - xiii, 264 p. incl. front., plates. 21 cm. 1-11278. F74. Cl M5

CAMBRIDGE, 1890. Contains a correct map of the city, suggestive hints to buyers ... by Arthur Metcalf Morse. ... Cambridge, A. M. Morse (1890) 40 p. map. 24°. 1-11279-M1. F74. Cl M8

CAMBRIDGE. The story of Kendall square, a bit of history concerning the new location of Murray and Emery company. Cambridge, Mass. (Murray and Emery co.) 1916. 16 p. col. front., illus., plates. 18½ x 16 cm. 16-1683. F74. Cl M98

CAMBRIDGE. A discourse on the Cambridge church-gathering in 1636; delivered in the First church ... 1846. By William Newell ... Boston, J. Munroe, 1846. 65 p. 23½ cm. 6-37977. F74. Cl N5

CAMBRIDGE. Two discourses delivered before the First parish in Cambridge; one, upon leaving the old meeting house, and the other, at the dedication of the new. By William Newell, pastor ... Cambridge, J. Munroe, 1834. 56 p. 22½ cm. 18-448. F74. Cl N6

CAMBRIDGE. Reminiscences of Old Cambridge, by Charles Eliot Norton ... (Cambridge, Mass., The Society, 1905) p. (11) - 23. 24½ cm. Repr. from Proceedings of the Cambridge hist. soc. 10-23090. F74. Cl N8

CAMBRIDGE: candids and comments. Candids by Tom O'Hara; Comments grave and gay by Newell Keyes. Watertown, Mass., N. Keyes (1966) 100 p. 21 cm. F74. Cl O4

CAMBRIDGE. Souvenir guide book of Harvard college and its historical vicinity ... By Frederick A. Olsson. Cambridge, Mass., F. A. Olsson (1895) 26 p., front., pl. 12°. 1-11282-M1. F74. Cl O5

CAMBRIDGE, History of. 1630 - 1877. With a genealogical register. By Lucius R. Paige. Boston, H. O. Houghton; New York, Hurd and Houghton, 1877. xvi, 731 p. front. (port.) plans. 24 cm. Genealogical register: p. (477) - 731. 1-11283. F74. Cl P125

— Supplement and index, comprising a biographical and genealogical record of the early settlers and their descendants; with references to their wills and the administration of their estates in the Middlesex county registry of probate. By Mrs. Mary Isabella Gozzaldi. Cambridge, The Cambridge historical society, 1930. iv, 800 p. 24½ cm. 31-2232. F74. Cl P126

CAMBRIDGE. Address at the celebration of the 275th anniversary of the founding of Cambridge ... By Herbert Parker ... (Cambridge, The Society, 1905) p. (27) - 31. 24½ cm. Reprinted from Proceedings of the Cambridge historical society, I. 10-23098. F74. Cl P2

CAMBRIDGE, U.S.A; hub of a new world. By Christopher Rand. New York, Oxford University Press, 1964. 195 p. 21 cm. 64-24865. F74. Cl R3

— in Russian. 1968. 198 p. 20 cm. F74. Cl R313

CAMBRIDGE. The Ruggles mansion, Cambridge. Contributed by Henry Stoddard Ruggles ... (In The N.Y. geneal. and biographical record. 1925. v.56 no. 2, p. 102) CA 30-182 unrev. F74. Cl R9

CAMBRIDGE. Two hundred years ago; or, A brief history of Cambridge. By S. S. S(impson). 1859 1 v. 24°. F74. Cl S5

CAMBRIDGE. Poem at the celebration of the 275th anniversary of the founding of Cambridge ... by William Roscoe Thayer ... (Cambridge, The Society, 1905) p. (43) - 47. 24½ cm. Reprinted from Proceedings of the Cambridge historical society, I. 10-23100. F74. Cl T3

CAMBRIDGE. Notes on Colonel Henry Vassall (1721 - 1769) his wife, Penelope Royall, his house at Cambridge, and his slaves Tony & Darby ... By Samuel Francis Batchelder. Cambridge, Mass., 1917. (5)-85 p. 5 pl. 2 port., etc. 23½ cm. Repr. from Proceedings of the Cambridge hist. soc. v.x. 18-3386. F74. Cl V3

MASSACHUSETTS 191

CAMBRIDGE. The beard and the braid; drawings of Cambridge, by Barbara Westman, with her own observations. Barre, Mass., Barre Publishers (1970) 35 p. illus. 23 x 28 cm. 76-128388.
F74.C1 W47

CAMBRIDGE, Weston's guide-book and souvenir of. By Louis F. Weston. (Cambridge, Mass., L. F. Weston, 1896) 88 p. port. 24°. 1-11285-M1.
F74. C1 W5

CAMBRIDGE. Text by Walter Muir Whitehill. Photos. by Katherine Knowles. (Barre, Mass., Barre Publishers, (1965) 1 v. (unpaged) 23 cm. 65-16657.
F74.C1 W55

CANTON, Easton, Sharon and Stoughton, Brockton suburban directory of ... 1939 -   v. 1 -
   v. 24 cm. 39-32911.   Directories

CANTON directory, The. Providence, R. I., C. D. White co., 1911 -   1 v. 24 cm. 11-20875.
Directories

CANTON, Easton, Sharon, The Brockton suburban directory for ... 1917/18 -   v. 1 -
Salem, Mass., The Henry M. Meek pub. co., 1917 -   v. front. (fold. map) 24 cm. 17-6001. Directories

CANTON. History of the Redman farm, so called, and of the title thereto, situate in Canton, Now mostly owned by Henry L. Pierce, esq., of Boston. Compiled by Ellis Ames ... Boston, Print. W. Bense, 1870. 32 p. fold. plan. 24 cm. Contains some Redman family history. 1-11286.
F74. C2 A5

CANTON. The record of births, marriages and deaths and intentions of marriage, in the town of Stoughton, 1727 - 1800, and in the town of Canton 1797 - 1845, preceded by the records of the South precinct of Dorchester 1715 - 1727. Ed. Frederic Endicott ... Canton, Mass., Print. W. Bense, 1896.
vii, 317 p. 24 cm. 1-11287.
CANTON. Report of the Committee on town seal, and report of the Committee on naming the streets of Canton. Canton, Print. W. Bense, 1881. 35 p. 23½ cm. 11-6058.
F74.C2 C25

CANTON ... Boston, The Edison electric illuminating co., c.1909. 23 cm.   F74.C2 C34

CANTON. ... Centennial celebration at Canton. Historical address, by Hon. Charles Endicott. Boston, W. Bense, print., 1876. 47 p. 23 cm. 1-11288 Rev.
F74. C2 E5

CANTON, History of the town of. By Daniel T. V. Huntoon. Pub. by the town. Cambridge, J. Wilson, 1893. xiv, 666 p. incl. front., illus., plates, ports., 3 fold. plans. 23 cm. 3-9965.
F74. C8 H9

CARLISLE, History of the town of, 1754 - 1920; with biographical sketches of prominent persons, by Sidney A. Bull. Cambridge, Mass., The Murray print. co., 1920. xi, 365 p. front., plates, ports. 22 cm.
20-23478.
F74.C23 B9

CARLISLE, Vital records of, to the end of the year 1849. Salem, Mass., The Essex institute, 1918.
100 p. 23½ cm. 18-27314.
F74.C23 C2

CARLISLE. A discourse upon the history of the establishment of the first parish in Carlisle. Delivered ... 1879 by Rev. James J. Twiss. Lowell (Mass.) Stone, Bacheller & Livingston, print., 1879.
21 p. 24 cm. 1-16734.
F74.C23 T9

CARVER, Vital records of, to the year 1850. Boston, New England historic genealogical soc ... 1911.
179 p. 23 cm. 13-3033.
F74.C28 C3

CARVER, History of the town of. Historical review, 1637 - 1910. Henry S. Griffith. New Bedford, Mass., E. Anthony print., 1913. xiii p., 366 p. front., plates, ports. 24 cm. 13-18208.
F74.C28 G8

CENTERVILLE. Old home week celebration, ... 1904. Historical notes. Centerville ... Boston, The Sparrell print., 1905. 148 p. front., illus. (incl. ports.) 24 cm. 20-3834.
F74.C29 C3

421

CHARLEMONT, frontier village and hill town, by Allan Healy.   (Charlemont, Mass., Pub. by the Town of Charlemont) 1965.   xi, 222 p.   27 cm.   66-5150.   F74. C3 H4

CHARLEMONT, Vital records of, to the year 1850.   Boston, Pub. by the New England historic genealogical soc., 1917.   166 p.   23 ½ cm.   18-27122.   F74. C3 V8

CHARLEMONT as a plantation.   An historical discourse at the centennial anniversary of the death of Moses Rice, the first settler of the town ... .   By Joseph White.   Boston, Press of T. R. Marvin, 1858.   48 p.   23 cm.   1-11289.   F74. C3 W5

CHARLESTOWN.   Register of the Charlestown schools, 1847 - 1873 - pupils - by James Edward Stone.   Boston, Old Charlestown school boys assoc., 1917.   iv, (91) p.   23 ½ cm.   17-12044.
F74. C
LA306. C5S6

CHARLESTOWN.   An account of the conflagration of the Ursuline convent.   At the request of several gentlemen, the author was induced to publish the following statement of facts, in relation to the Ursuline convent, which was destroyed by fire ... 1834.   By a friend of religious toleration ... Boston, Printed for the publisher, 1834.   35 p.   19 cm.   18-8951.   F74. C4 A17

CHARLESTOWN directory, The ... 18   - 1874.   Boston, Sampson, Davenport, 18   -73.
v. fronts. (fold. maps) 15 ½ - 22 ½ cm.   9-16493 Rev.   Directories

CHARLESTOWN, An historical sketch of ... read to an assembly of citizens at the opening of Washington hall ... 1813.   By Josiah Bartlett.   Boston, John Eliot, 1814.   (Lowell, Reprinted for G. M. Elliott, 1881)   24 p.   25 ½ cm.   4-7504 Rev.   F74. C4 B2

CHARLESTOWN.   Report of the committee, realting to the destruction of the Ursuline convent ... 1834.   Boston, J. H. Eastburn, city printer, 1834.   16 p.   23 cm.   1-11290 Rev.   F74. C4 B7

CHARLESTOWN.   The history of the First church, Charlestown, in nine lectures, with notes.   By William I. Budington ... Boston, C. Tappan, 1845.   258 p. front. (port.)   23 ½ cm.   6-15338.
F74. C4 B9

CHARLESTOWN.   Our Puritan fathers, our glory: a sermon preached in commemoration of the 220th anniversary of the founding of the First church in Charlestown ... 1852.   By William I. Budington ... Charlestown, McKim & Cutter, 1852.   32 p.   23 cm.   10-6929.   F74. C4 B95

CHARLESTOWN.   The closing argument on behalf of the Bunker Hill monument association at the public hearing before the mayor and aldermen of Charlestown, in favor of the new avenue to the monument.   By G. Washington Warren ...   Boston, Bunker Hill monument assoc., 1869.   55 p.   front.
27 ½ cm.   16-21927.   F74. C4 B97

CHARLESTOWN land records (1638 - 1802)   (Boston, Rockwell and Churchill, 1878)   vii, 273 p.
22 ½ cm.   (3d report of the Record commissioners of the city of Boston)   3-20630.   F74. C4 C2

CHARLESTOWN land records, 1638 - 1802.   (2d ed.)   (In Record commissioners 3d report)   1-13872.
F74. C4 C3

CHARLESTOWN.   List of persons assessed a state, town and county tax, in the town of Charlestown, for the year 1844.   Pub. by order of the town.   Charlestown, Aurora power press, 1845.
56 p.   24 ½ cm.   15-18150.   F74. C4 C35

CHARLESTOWN.   Proceedings at the dedication of the soldiers' and sailors' monument by the City council of Charlestown ... 1872.   Charlestown, Print. at the Chronicle office, 1872.   29 p.   23 ½ cm.
10-23167.   F74. C4 C4

CHARLESTOWN.   The commemoration of the 250th anniversary of the First church, Charlestown ... 1882.   (Cambridge, Print. J. Wilson) 1882.   60 p.   24 ½ cm.   2-1657-M2.   F74. C4 C58

MASSACHUSETTS

CHARLESTOWN, Records of the First church in 1632 - 1789. Boston, Print. for J. F. Hunnewell, by D. Clapp, 1880.   4, 168, xxvii p. 6 facsim. (incl. front.) 31 cm. "Sixty-two copies) 1-11292.   F74. C4 C6

CHARLESTOWN convent, The: its destruction by a mob, on the night of August 11, 1834. With a history of the excitement before the burning ... Also, the trials of the rioters ... and a contemporary appendix. ... Boston, P. Donahoe, 1870. 5-98 p. 23½ cm. 1-11291.   F74. C4 C69

CHARLESTOWN. Hannah Corcoran, the missing girl of Charlestown. The mysterious disappearance unraveled. The convent and the confessor. Attempt at abduction foiled! A full and complete report of the riot in Charlestown ... Boston, Palfrey & co., 1853. (3) - 16 p. 22½ cm. Port. on t.-p. 11-79.
F74. C4 C7
Rare Book Coll.

CHARLESTOWN. In memoriam. Sister Sainte Claire, order of St. Ursula ... Charlestown (Mass.) Advertiser press, 1876. 3, 5-25 p. pl., fold. geneal. tab. 20½ cm. 12-11826.   F74. C4 D19

CHARLESTOWN. The story of Mt. Benedict, by B. F. De Costa ... (Somerville, Mass.) Citizen press, 1893. 14 p. 21 cm. Originally print. in the Somerville Citizens beginning Apr., 1893. 11-78.   F74. C4 D2

CHARLESTOWN. Documents relating to the Ursuline convent in Charlestown. Boston, Reprinted by S. N. Dickinson, 1842. v, (7) - 32 p. 22½ cm. 1-21617.   F74. C4 D6
Rare Book Coll.

CHARLESTOWN, The history of. By Richard Frothingham, jr. ... Charlestown, C. P. Emmons; Boston, C. C. Little and J. Brown, 1845 - 49. 368 p. illus., plates, port., maps, facsims. 23 cm. Pub. in 7 parts. 1-11293 Additions.   F74. C4 F9

CHARLESTOWN. A candid review of the project of annexation, by a Charlestown man. Charlestown (Mass.) De Costa & William, print., 1854. 12 p. 23 cm. 16-27476 Rev.   F74. C4 G85

CHARLESTOWN. Diary kept by Capt. Lawrence Hammond, of Charlestown, Mass., 1677 - 1694. With notes and an introduction, by Samuel A. Green. Cambridge (Mass.) Wilson and son, 1892. 31 p. 24½ cm. Orig. pub. in the Proceedings of the Mass. hist. soc. 2d ser. v. 7, p. 144-172. 11-16630.   F74. C4 H2

CHARLESTOWN. A century of town life: a history of Charlestown, 1775 - 1887. With surveys, records and 28 pages of plans and views. By James F. Hunnewell ... Boston, Little, Brown, 1888. xiv, 316 p. front., plates, plans, facsim. 24½ cm. Records of the First church: p. 193-260. Bibliography of Charlestown and Bunker Hill (supplementing the author's Bibliography of Charlestown, etc. Boston, 1880): p. (261) - 300. 1-11294.   F74. C4 H9

CHARLESTOWN. Memorial of James Frothingham Hunnewell, read before the Bostonian society ... 1911, by Harold Murdock. Boston, Priv. print., 1911. 14 p. front. (port.) 22 cm. 11-12850.   F74. C4 H93

CHARLESTOWN and Somerville, Annexation of to Boston. A condensed report of the argument of Hon. Ellis W. Morton, before the committee of the legislature on towns, in behalf of the petitioners for an act authorizing the union of Charlestown and Somerville with Boston ... 1871. Boston, A. Mudge, print., 1871. 34 p. 24 cm. 1-11297 Rev.   F74. C4 M8

CHARLESTOWN. Considerations respectfully submitted to the citizens of Boston and Charlestown, on the proposed annexation of these two cities. By Josiah Quincy, sen. Boston, Print. J. Wilson, 1854. 11 p. 23½ cm. 6-16523.   F74. C4 Q7

CHARLESTOWN. Six months in a convent, or, The narrative of Rebecca Theresa Reed, who was under the influence of the Roman Catholics about two years, and an inmate of the Ursuline convent on Mount Benedict, Charlestown, nearly six months in the years 1831-2. Boston, Russell, Odiorne & Metcalf; New York, Leavitt, Lord and co., 1835. 192 p. 14 cm. 13-5277.   F74. C4 R32

CHARLESTOWN. Supplement to "Six months in a convent," confirming the narrative of Rebecca Theresa Reed, by the testimony of more than 100 witnesses, ... containing a minute account of the elopement of Miss Harrison ... and an exposition of the system of cloister education, by the Committee

of publication. ... Boston, Russell, Odioren; New York, Leavitt, Lord, 1835.   vi, (7) - 264 p.
14 cm.   (With above item)   13-5274.   Also separate F74. C4R324.
F74. C4 R32

CHARLESTOWN.   Six months in a convent ...   (another copy)   192 p.   15½ cm.   36-6712.
F74. C4R322
Toner Coll.

CHARLESTOWN.   An answer to Six months in a convent, exposing its falsehoods and manifold absurdities.   By the lady superior.   With some preliminary remarks.   Boston, J. H. Eastburn, 1835.
xxxvii, 66 p.   24 cm.   13-7172 Rev.
F74. C4 R33

— 2d ed.   1835.   xxxvii, 67 (i. e. 66) p.   23½ cm.   12-11825 Rev.
F74. C4 R34

— 3d ed.   1835.   xxxvii, 66 p.   23½ cm.   13-7171 Rev.
F74. C4 R35

CHARLESTOWN.   A review of the Lady Superior's reply to "Six months in a convent", being a vindication of Miss Reed.   Boston, W. Peirce, 1835.   51 p.   23 cm.   24-15749.
F74. C4 R36

CHARLESTOWN.   Old Charlestown; historical, biographical, reminiscent, by Timothy T. Sawyer.
Boston, J. H. West co., 1902.   527 p.   front. (port.)   20½ cm.   First pub. in the Charlestown enterprise, 1888-1902.
2-20016 Rev.
F74. C4 S2

CHARLESTOWN.   A schedule of the ancient colored inhabitants, of Charlestown, on record prior to 1800 ... (Charlestown? 1870?)   (4) p.   25½ cm.   Reprinted from the Charlestown chronicle of Jan. 1, 1870.   43-27435.
F74. C4 S3

CHARLESTOWN.   Souvenir of the 50th anniversary of the dedication of Bunker Hill Monument, 1843 - 1893.   Charlestown, Mass., Bunker Hill Times (1893)   86 p.   31 cm.
F74. C4 S6

CHARLESTOWN.   The founding of Charlestown by the Spragues, a glimpse of the beginning of the Massachusetts Bay settlement, by Henry H. Sprague.   Boston, W. B. Clarke, 1910.   39 p.   fold. facsim.
24½ cm.   11-4218.
F74. C4 S7

CHARLESTOWN.   Register of the Charlestown men in the service during the civil war, 1861 - 1865, by James Edward Stone.   Boston, Old Charlestown school boys association, 1919.   iv, (210) p.   fold. pl.
23½ cm.   Various pagings.   19-6573.
F74. C4 S87

CHARLESTOWN, A short history of, for the past 44 years, and other subjects, by Joseph Thompson.
Charlestown, De Costa & Homans, print., 1848.   71 p.   22½ cm.   10-11228.
F74. C4 T4

CHARLESTOWN.   The burning of the Ursuline convent: a paper read before the Worcester society of antiquity ... 1889.   By Ephraim Tucker.   Worcester, Mass., 1890.   24 p.   20½ cm.   8-15802.
F74. C4 T8

CHARLESTOWN.   The burning of the convent.   A narrative of the destruction, by a mob, of the Ursuline school on Mount Benedict, Charlestown, as remembered by one of the pupils.   Boston, J. R. Osgood, 1877.   vi, 198 p.   15½ cm.   6-42560.
F74. C4 W6

CHARLESTOWN.   The burning of the convent, by Louise (Goddard) Whitney.   New York, Arno Press, 1969.   148 p.   23 cm.   (Mass violence in America)   70-90196.
F74. C4 W6
1969

CHARLESTOWN.   The genealogies and estates of Charlestown, 1629 - 1818.   By Thomas Bellows Wyman ... Boston, D. Clapp, 1879.   2v.   fronts.   25½ cm.   Paged continuoulsy; v.1: xii, (2), 566 p.; v.2: (567) - 1178.
4-12561.
F74. C4 W9

CHARLTON.   Address at the dedication of the Dexter memorial town hall, Charlton, by Hon. Charles J. McIntire.   Private copy.   (n. p., 1906)   84 p.   2 pl. (incl. front.)   6 port.   23 cm.   7-23794.   F74. C42C38

MASSACHUSETTS

CHARLTON. Addresses at the unveiling of the portrait of General Salem Towne, presented to the town of Charlton by Judge Stephen P. Twiss ... in Dexter memorial hall ... 1909. (Charlton? 1909) 32 p. front., pl., ports. 23½ cm. 15-14731.   F74.C42C39

CHARLTON, Vital records of, to the end of the year 1849. Worcester, Mass., F. P. Rice, 1905. 268 p. 23½ cm. 5-13952.   F74.C42 C4

CHARLTON. Historical address, delivered in Charlton ... 1876, by Rev. John Haven. Pub. by request. Southbridge, Mass., Journal print., 1876. 17 p. 22½ cm. 1-16777.   F74.C42 H2

CHARLTON historical sketches, by Rev. Anson Titus, jr. ... Southbridge, Print. G. M. Whitaker, 1877. 28 p. 22 cm. Reprinted from Southbridge journal. 13-18449.   F74.C42 T6

CHATHAM. ... The 200th anniversary of the incorpoation of the town of Chatham; a memorial or report of the celebration ... 1912 ... Pub. by authority of the Town celebration committee, 1913. 119 p. plates. 23 cm. 14-20607.   F74.C43 C4

CHATHAM. Historical address delivered by James W. Hawes ... 1912, on the occasion of the celebration of the 100th anniversary of the incorporation of Chatham, confined chiefly to the preiod before 1860. Yarmouthport, Mass., C. W. Swift, 1912. 38 p. 25 cm. (Library of Cape Cod history and genealogy, no. 78) 12-25272.   F74.C43 H3

CHATHAM. Monomoy and its shoals. From Annual report of Mass. Board of harbor and land commissioners for the year 1886. Boston, Wright & Potter, print., 1887. 14 p. 23 cm. 10-31141.   F74.C43 M6

CHATHAM. ... Early Chatham settlers, by William C. Smith ... Yarmouthport, Mass., C. W. Swift, 1915. 38 p. 25½ cm. (Library of Cape Cod history and genealogy, no. 36) 15-21637.   F74.C43S47

CHATHAM, Congregational church in, 1720 - 1920. Historical address on the 200th anniversary of the organization of the church. By William C. Smith. (Chatham, Mass.) Chatham monitor print, 1920. 31 p. illus. 22½ cm. 21-12487.   F74.C43S46

CHATHAM. A history of Chatham, formerly the constablewick or village of Monomoit. With maps and illustrations and numerous genealogical notes. By William C. Smith. Hyannis, Mass., F.B. & F.P.Goss, 1909 - 1917. 3 v. front., illus., plates, maps (1 fold.) facsim. 25 cm. 9-21020.   F74.C43 S5

CHATHAM. The scallop shanty; a Chatham play, by Carol Wight; cuts by Alice Wight; written for the Chatham branch of the American Red cross ... (Wareham, Mass., Courier print., 1918) 63 p. illus. 24 cm. 18-19822.   F74.C43 W6

CHELMSFORD, The history of, from its origin in 1653, to the year 1820 - together with an historical sketch of the church, and biographical notices of the four first pastors. To which is added a memoir of the Pawtuckett tribe of Indians. With a large appendix. By Wilkes Allen ... Haverhill: Print. P. N. Green, 1820. 192 p. 23 cm. 1-11298.   F74.C45 A4

CHELMSFORD; proceedings at the celebration of the 250th anniversary of the incorporation of the town ... 1905; report of the committee of arrangements. (N.p., 1905) 83 p. front. (port.) 3 pl. 26 cm. Ed. Wilson Waters. 8-26500.   F74.C45 C4

CHELMSFORD, Vital records of, to the end of the year 1849. Salem, Mass., The Essex institute, 1914. 460 p. 23½ cm. 14-11766.   F74.C45C45

CHELMSFORD. A wintersnight tale. By Charles Henry Dalton. Boston (D. B. Updike) 1904. 3, 21 p. 23½ cm x 14½ cm. Reminiscences of Chelmsford. 18-7664.   F74.C45D52

CHELMSFORD. Extracts from the note-book of the Rev. John Fiske, 1637 - 1675. With an introduction by Samuel A. Green. Cambridge, J. Wilson, 1898. 24 p. 23½ cm. The first 25 p. were printed in the Historical colls. of the Essex Institute v.1. The present work is a reprint from the Procs. of the Mass. hist. soc. 2d ser. v.12. 9-884.   F74.C45 F5

CHELMSFORD, History of, by the Rev. Wilson Waters ... Lowell, Mass., Print. Courier-citizen co., 1917. xiv, (2), 893 p. front., plates, ports., maps (part double) plans (part double) facsims. 25 cm. List of interments in Forefather's burying ground: p. 721 - 753. 17-20746.
F74. C45 W3

CHELSEA. Lothrop's Chelsea city directory ... 1847/48, 1850, 18 - co., 1847 - v. front. illus., fold. maps. 13½ - 24½ cm. 25-8056 Rev.
Boston, Union pub.
Directories

CHELSEA, A documentary history of, including the Boston precincts of Winnisimmet, Rumney Marsh, and Pullen Point, 1624 - 1824; collected and arranged, with notes, by Mellen Chamberlain ... Boston, Print, for the Massachusetts hist. soc., 1908. 2 v. 8 pl., 4 ports. on 3 pl. (incl. front.) 5 fold. maps. 25 cm. 8-17378.
F74. C5 C4

CHELSEA. Chelsea's roll of honor. (Chelsea, Mass., 1863) p. (83) - 120. 24 cm.
F74. C5 C 49

CHELSEA. Roll of honor of the city of Chelsea. A list of the soldiers and sailors who served on the quota of Chelsea, in the great civil war for the preservation of the Union from 1861 to 1865, with a partial record of each man ... Also an appendix including the names of Chelsea men who served to the credit of other states, cities and towns. Chelsea, H. Mason, print., 1880. 213 p. 13 cm. Pub. by authority of the City council. 1-11299.
F74. C5 C5

CHELSEA, Vital records of, to the year 1850. Comp. by Thomas W. Baldwin ... Boston, Mass. (Wright & Potter print.) 1916. 558 p. 23½ cm. 16-3491.
F74. C5 C55

CHELSEA ... Boston, The Edison electric illuminating co., 1909. 23 cm.
F74. C5 C64

CHELSEA evening record ... Fiftieth anniversary souvenir edition ... Chelsea, Mass., 1940. 8, 8, 8, 8, 8, 8, 8, 8 p. illus. 57½ cm. Forms v. 49, no. 255, issued Oct. 21, 1940. 42M99T.
F74. C5 C67

CHELSEA. ... The city of Chelsea ... Her history, her achievements, her opportunites. Chelsea, Mass., Chelsea gazette, 1898. 203 p. illus. 8°. Souvenir ed. of the Chelsea gazette. 1-11300-M1.
F74. C5 G5

CHELSEA. The Newdigate fine, by W. T. R. Marvin. (Boston, T. R. Marvin, print., 1914) 22 p. 2 facsim. (incl. front.) 24½ cm. Repr. from Pubs. of the Bostonian society. 14-7091.
F74. C5 M3

CHELSEA, The burning of, by Walter Merriam Pratt; with numerous illustrations from original photos. Boston, Sampson pub. co., 1908. 149 p. front., plates, map. 21 cm. 8-19884.
F74. C5 P9

CHELSEA. Seven generations; a story of Prattville and Chelsea, by Walter Merriam Pratt. (Norwood, Mass.) Priv. print., 1930. xiii, 419 p. front., illus. (incl. facsims.) plates, ports. 23½ cm. Maps on lining papers. 30-15232.
F74. C5 P96

CHELSEA. Souvenir book of the great Chelsea fire, ... 1908 ... (Boston?) 1908. 1v. 10½ x 15½ cm.
F74. C5 S7

CHELSEA. ... Report no. 118 on the Chelsea conflagration of ... 1908 ... Underwriters' bureau of New England. Boston and South Framingham, 1908. 1 v. 24½ cm.
F74. C5 U5

CHESHIRE, History of the town of. By Mrs. Ellen M. Raynor and Mrs. Emma L. Petitclerc. Introd. chapter by Judge James M. Barker. Holyoke, Mass. and New York city, C. W. Bryan, print., 1885. 214, (5) p. 22½ cm. 1-11301.
F74. C55 R2

CHESTER, Vital records of, to the year 1850. Boston, Mass., The New England historic genealogical soc. ... 1911. 256 p. 23½ cm. 11-7321.
F74. C56 C5

CHESTER. A history of the town of Murrayfield, earlier known as township no. 9 and comprising the present towns of Chester and Huntington, the northern part of Montgomery, and the southeast corner of Middlefield. 1760 - 1763. By Alfred M. Copeland ... Springfield, Mass., C. W. Bryan, print., 1892. 175 p. incl. illus., plan. fold. plan. 23 cm. 1-11302*. Cancel.
F74. C56 C8

MASSACHUSETTS

CHESTERFIELD. History and genealogy of the families of Chesterfield, 1762 - 1962. Bicentennial Genealogy Committee. (Chesterfield) Town of Chesterfield (1963?) 427 p. 24 cm.
F74. C57 A5

CHICOPEE. Annals of Chicopee street; records and reminiscences of an old New England parish for a period of 200 years, by Clara Skeele Palmer. Springfield, Mass., H. R. Johnson, 1899. 87 p. front., plates. 22 cm. 99-4001 Rev. 2.
F74. C58 P2

CHILMARK, Vital records of, to the year 1850. Boston, Pub. by the New-England historic genealogical soc. ... 1904. 96 p. 24 cm. 4-22349.
F74. C583 C5

CLARKSBURG, then and now, 1749 - 1962. By Ethel Mae Marsden. (Clarksburg? Mass.) 112 p. illus., ports. 23 cm.
F74. C587 M3

CLINTON, Lancaster directory ... 18   - 1885/6, 188/9, 1890/91, 1891, 1891/2, 1893/94, 1894 - 1918, 1920, 1922, 1924-25, 1927, 1929 -   v. - 6, 8 -   New Haven, Conn., The Price and Lee co., 18 -   v. fold. maps. 23½ cm. 99-691 Rev.
Directories

CLINTON. List of persons above the age of twenty in the town of Clinton ... Jan. 1, 1939 - v. in 23 cm. 46-44886.
F74. C59 A3

CLINTON. centennial volume, 1850 - 1950: the story of Clinton, incorporated ... 1850, and the Clinton centennial celebration. (Clinton, 1951) 223 p. illus. 28 cm. 52-1889.
F74. C59 A53

CLINTON. Semi-centennial celebration of the incorporation of the town of Clinton ... 1850; June, 1900. (Clinton, Print. W. J. Coulter, 1900) 176 p. illus. (incl. maps, facsim.) plates, ports., fold. plan. 28 cm. Ed. Andrew E. Ford. 2-6988.
F74. C59 C5

CLINTON. Historical papers read at meetings of the Clinton historical society ... Clinton, Mass., Clinton historical soc. (1912 -   v. 23½ cm. Vol. 1 -   ed. W. E. Parkhurst. 12-13051.
F74. C59 C6

CLINTON. History of the origin of the town of Clinton, 1653 - 1865, by Andrew E. Ford. Clinton, Press of W. J. Coulter, Courant office, 1896. viii, 696 p. plates, ports., maps (part fold.) 23 cm. 1-16570.
F74. C59 F7

COHASSET, A narrative history of the town of. (Cohasset) Committee on Town History, 1898 - 1956. 2 v. illus., ports., maps (4 fold. 1 in pocket) facsims. 22 cm. Vol. 2 by Burtram J. Pratt. 99-361 rev.*
F74. C6 B5

COHASSET. Addresses at the unveiling of a memorial, July 4, 1914, commemorating the discovery of Cohasset in 1614 by Captain John Smith. Cohasset, Mass., The Town, 1914. 19 p. incl. front. 23½ cm. 14-17883.
F74. C6 C5

COHASSET, Centennial anniversary of the town of ... 1870. Oration by Hon. Thomas Russell. Speeches by Gov. Claflin and others. Boston, Wright & Potter, print., 1870. 69 p. 23½ cm. 1-11303.
F74. C6 C6

COHASSET. Commemoration of the 150th anniversary of the independent government of the town of Cohasset ... 1921. Cohasset, Mass., Pageant committee, 1922. 48 p. illus. 23 cm. 31-18487.
F74. C6 C63

COHASSET, Vital records of, to the year 1850. Comp. by Thomas W. Baldwin ... Boston, Mass. (Wright & Potter, print.) 1916. 237 p. 23½ cm. 17-11235.
F74. C6 C66

COHASSET, The genealogies of the families of, comp. ... by George Lyman Davenport and others ... supplementary to the narrative history of Cohasset, by Rev. E. Victor Bigelow, pub. in 1898. (Cohasset, Mass.) Pub. under the auspices of the Committee on town history, 1909. 2, iii-xii p. 631 p. front., plates, ports. 24 cm. 9-32686.
F74. C6 D3

COHASSET. Two discourses, containing the history of the church and society in Cohasset .... With a geographical sketch of Cohasset. By Jacob Flint ... Boston, Print. Munroe and Francis, 1822. 28 p. 23½ cm. 8-12858.
F74. C6 F6

COHASSET. Spindrift from a house by the sea. By John J. Rowlands. Illus. by Henry B. Kane. (1st ed.) New York, W. W. Norton (1960)   232 p.   22 cm.   60-7585.   F74. C6 R6

COLRAIN, Vital records of, to the end of the year 1849. Salem, Mass., The Essex institute, 1934.
209 p.   23 cm.   34-9006.   F74. C7
                                         F74. B97B94

COLRAIN, The searly settlers of; or, Some account of ye early settlement of "Boston township no. 2, alias Colrain, adjoyning on ye north sid of Deerfield." An address ... by Charles H. McClellan. Greenfield, Mass., W. S. Carson, print., 1885.   86 p.   24 cm.   1-11304.
                                         F74. C7 M2

CONCORD. Men of Concord and some others as portrayed in the Journal of Henry David Thoreau, ed. Francis H. Allen, with illus. by N. C. Wyeth. Boston, Houghton Mifflin, 1936.   xi, 255 p., col. front., illus., col. plates.   24½ cm.   36-35971.
                                         F74. C
                                         PS3053. A25
                                         1936

CONCORD. Town of Concord, directory ... Boston, H. Howard, 1921 -   v. fold. map. 24 cm.
21-3969.   Directories

ALBUM of Concord views ... Concord, Mass., H. J. Walcott, jr., 1895.   10 pl. obl. 24⁰. 1-11305-M1.
                                         F74. C8 A3

CONCORD guide book, The. Ed. by George B. Bartlett. Illus. by Miss L. B. Pumphrey and Robert Lewis. Boston, D. Lothrop (1880)   157 p. incl. front., illus., plates, ports. 20 cm. 1-11306.
                                         F74. C8 B2

CONCORD: historic, literary and picturesque. 15th ed., rev., by George B. Bartlett. With map and illus. and a full index. Boston, Lothrop pub. co., 1895.   200 p. incl. front., illus., plates, port., double map. plates, port.   17½ x 13½ cm.   First ed. pub. 1880 under title: "The Concord guide book."   1-11307.   F74. C8 B3

CONCORD, Memories of, by Mary Hosmer Brown; illus. from photos. and from paintings by J. Randoph Brown. Boston, The Four seas co. (1926)   111 p. front., plates. 19½ cm. 27-8156.
                                         F74. C8 B8

— 1972.   F74. C8 B8
                                         1972

CONCORD. Celebration of the 250th anniversary of the incorporation of Concord, ... 1885. 1635 - 1885. Concord, Mass., Pub. by the town (1885)   95 p. 23½ cm. Prepared and ed. by J. S. Keyes and others. 1-11308.
                                         F74. C8 C7

CONCORD. Ceremonies at the dedication of the Soldiers' monument, in Concord, Mass. Concord, Print. B. Tolman, 1867.   75 p. front. (mounted phot.) 18½ cm. List of 32 soldiers from Concord. 33-16478. F74. C8 C74

CONCORD. Births, marriages, and deaths, 1635 - 1850. Printed by the town. (Boston, T. Todd, print., 1895.   vii, 496 p. 24½ cm. By George Tolman and others. 1-11309.
                                         F74. C8 C8
                                         L. H. & G.

CONCORD. Tercentenary, 1635 - 1935, Concord, ... 1935. (Boston, Thomas Todd co., print., 1935.
35 p. illus. (incl. port.) 23½ cm. Pencil drawings by Lester G. Hornby. 36-4907.
                                         F74. C8C813

CONCORD, a few of the things to be seen there. Concord, Mass., The Patriot press, 1902.
15 p. front., plates, ports., double map. 18 cm. 34-29274.
                                         F74. C8C815
                                         Houdini Coll.

CONCORD and Lexington; the best collection of views of these historic towns ever published in book form, from original photos. by E. F. Worcester. Boston, Hudson print., 1916.   (40) p. of illus. front. (fold. plan) 18 x 23½ cm. 16-20265.
                                         F74. C8C818

CONCORD. Celebration of the 269th birthday of Concord by the Antiquarian soc. of that town ... 1904. ... with address by Mr. P. K. Walcott, tog. with a list of members of the society. (Boston) Printed for the society, Beacon press (1904)   30 p.   23 cm.   6-1112.   F74. C8 C82

CONCORD antiquarian society, Publications of the, no. 1 - 11.   (Concord, 1902-3)   11 v. in 1. plates, port. fold. map. 22½ cm. 6-6168.   F74. C8 C83
- — Preliminaries of Concord fight, by George Tolman.   28 p.   4-7838.
- — The Concord minute men, by George Tolman.   27 p.   4-7837.
- — Wright's tavern, by George Tolman.   26 p.   front.   23 cm.   4-7836.
- — Concord and the telegraph. By Alfred Munroe.   22 p.   4-7834.
- — Story of an old house, by John S. Keyes.   17 p.   4-7833.
- — John Jack, the slave, and Daniel Bliss, the Tory, by George Tolman.   21 p.   4-7835.
- — The plantation at Musketequid; by Albert E. Wood.   26 p.   4-7832.
- — Events of April 19th, by George Tolman.   36 p.   4-7831.
- — How our great-grandfathers lived, by Albert E. Wood.   25 p.   4-7830.
- — Indian relics in Concord, by Adams Tolman.   26 p.   4-7829.
- — "Graves and worms and epitaphs;" by George Tolman.   30 p.   4-7828.

CONCORD. Colonial Concord, a study in pen and ink. By James Hugh Dee. Concord, Mass., 1951. unpaged. illus. 28 cm. 51-34676.   F74. C8 D4

CONCORD. Some reminiscences of old Concord. By Priscilla Rice Edes. (Gouverneur, N. Y., C. A. Livingston, print. (1903)   (35) p. port. 16½ x 13 cm. 3-2859.   F74. C8 E2

CONCORD. A historical discourse, delivered ... on the second centennial anniversary of the incorporation of the town. By Ralph Waldo Emerson ... Concord, G. F. Bemis, print., 1835.   52 p. 24½ cm. 17-5247.   F74. C8 E53
Rare Book Coll.

CONCORD. Tales of old Concord, by Mary R. Fenn. Illus. by Mimi Aloian. Concord, Mass., Privately print. for the Women's Parish Assoc., 1965.   40 p. 23 cm.   F74. C8 F4

CONCORD, The drama of; a pageant of three centuries, by Allen French; a part of the tercentenary celebration of the incorporation of Concord ... 1935. Concord (Mass.) The Production committee, 1935.   xv, 101 p. 19 cm. 36-1263.   F74. C8 F86

CONCORD. Historic Concord, a handbook of its story and its memorials, with the story of the Lexington fight, by Allen French. Concord, Mass. (Cambridge, The Riverside press) 1942. vi, 102 p. 2 front. (incl. maps) illus. 17½ cm. "Reading list": p. (97) - 100. 42-17323.   F74. C2F865

CONCORD. Old Concord, by Allen French; with drawings by Lester G. Hornby. Boston, Little, Brown, 1915.   xii, 186 p. incl. front., illus., plates. 24½ cm. 15-21157.   F74. C8 F87

CONCORD. Historic Concord and Lexington ... (1903)   F74. C8 H6

CONCORD, The history of. v. 1 -   ... By Alfred Sereno Hudson ... Concord, Mass., The Erudite press, 1904 -   1 v. front., plates, ports., fold. map, facsims. 24 cm. 5-27143.   F74. C8 H88

CONCORD. Supposed decay of families in New England disproved by the experience of the people of Concord, by Edward Jarvis ... Reprinted from the N. E. historical and genealogical register for Oct., 1884. Boston, Press of D. Clapp, 1884.   12 p. 24½ cm. 9-28882.   F74. C8 J 3

CONCORD. Old Concord, her highways and byways, by Margaret Sidney (pseud. for Mrs. Harriet Mulford (Stone) Lothrop) ... Boston, D. Lothrop (1888)   3, 9 - 114 p. incl. front., illus. plates. 23 cm. 1-11310.   F74. C8 L8

— Illus. by Miss Mary Wheeler and others.   (1892)   178 p. incl. illus., plates. 23 cm. 1-11311.   F74. C8 L9

CONCORD. Old Concord, seen through western spectacles, by Samuel Merwin. Boston and New York, Houghton Mifflin, 1926.   32 p. illus. 16½ cm. 26-20773.   F74. C8 M3

CONCORD. Genealogies of some old families of Concord, and their descendants in part to the present generation ... Ed. Charles Edward Potter. Vol. I. Boston, A. Mudge, print., 1887.   3, 5-143 p. pl., 14 port. (incl. front.)   35 x 28 cm.   No more pub?   7-18033.

F74. C8 P8

CONCORD. A collection of historical and other papers, by Rev. Grindall Reynolds, to which are added seven of his sermons. Concord, Mass., The editor, 1895.   xv, 499 p. front. (port.)   22 cm.   Ed. Alice Reynolds Keyes.   4-5275.

F74. C8 R38

CONCORD. The story of a Concord farm and its owners. (By) Grindall Reynolds ... 1883. A lecture delivered before the Concord lyceum. (Concord? Mass., 1883?)   29 p.   23 cm.   An account of the farm known as Lee's Hill.   6-42567.

F74. C8 R4

CONCORD. Half century discourse, delivered ... 1828 ... By Ezra Ripley ... Concord, Print. H. Atwill, 1829.   47 p.   22½ cm.   1-11312.

F74. C8 R5

CONCORD. The story of the Minute man ... by Roland Wells Robbins. Stoneham, Mass., G. R. Barnstead (1945)   30 p.   illus. (incl. ports.)   18½ cm.   45-9385.

F74. C8 R6

CONCORD: American town (by) Townsend Scudder. Boston, Little, Brown, 1947.   5, (3) - 421 p. 23 cm.   "First edition."   "Bibliographical notes and acknowledgements": p. 391-395.   47-2755.

F74. C8 S35

CONCORD, A history of the town of; from its earliest settlement to 1832; and the adjoining towns, Bedford, Acton, Lincoln, and Carlisle; containing various notices of county and state history not before published. By Lemuel Shattuck ... Boston, Russell, Odiorne; Concord, J. Stacy, 1835. viii, 392 p.   22 cm.   1-11313.

F74. C8 S5

CONCORD. Memoirs of members of the Social circle in Concord. 2d ser., from 1795 to 1840 ... Cambridge, Priv. print., The Riverside press, 1888.   xiii, 386 p.   266 p.   22½ cm.   6-5580.

F74. C8 S56

— Third series, from 1840 to 1895 ... Cambridge, Priv. print., The Riverside press, 1907. xiii, 260 p.   ports.   23 cm.   Introd. signed: John S. Keyes and others.   7-7449.

F74. C8 S57

— Fourth series, from 1895 to 1909 ... Cambridge, Priv. print., The Riverside press, 1909. xiii, 343 p.   ports.   23 cm.   Introd. signed: John S. Keyes and others.   10-9806.

F74. C8 S58

CONCORD. Souvenir and guide to historic Concord and Lexington. 1903.

F74. C8 S6

CONCORD. Sketches from Concord and Appledore. Concord thirty years ago; Nathaniel Hawthorne; Louisa M. Alcott; Ralph Waldo Emerson; Matthew Arnold; David A. Wasson; Wendell Phillips; Appledore and its visitors; John Greenleaf Whittier. By Frank Preston Stearns ... New York, G. P. Putnam's sons, 1895.   xii, 276 p. front., plates, ports., facsims. 20 cm.   1-11314.

F74. C8 S7

CONCORD, The story of, told by Concord writers; ed. by Josephine Latham Swayne. Boston, The E. F. Worcester press, 1906.   5, (7) - 314, viii p. front., plates, ports., fold. plan. 20½ cm.   7-10585.

F74. C8 S9

— 2d rev. ed. Boston, Meador pub. co., 1939.   428 p. incl. front., poates, ports., fold. map. 20½ cm. 39-30832.

F74. S8 S9
1939

CONCORD. Classic Concord, as portrayed by Emerson, Hawthorne, Thoreau and the Alcotts, ed. with biographical sketches, by Caroline Ticknor; illus. with drawings by May Alcott. Boston and New York, Houghton Mifflin, 1926.   ix p., 2 l., 3-271 p. front., plates. 24½ cm.   26-8876.

F74. C8 T4

CONCORD minute men; by George Tolman ... (Concord, Mass.) The Society (1902?)   27 p. front. 23½ cm.   7-23980.

F74. C8 T5

— CONCORD. The Concord minute men, Wright's tavern, Preliminaries of Concord fight; three pamphlets. (n. p.) Society for the Preservation of Colonial Culture (1968)   28, 27, 26 p.   22 cm.

MASSACHUSETTS 201

Cover title. Reprint of the 1901 edition. F74. C8 T5 1968

CONCORD: some of the things to be seen there ... by George Tolman. Concord, Mass., 1903. 19 cm. F74. C8 T6

CONCORD. Early town records; a paper read before the Concord antiquarian society in April, 1896, by George Tolman. Concord, Mass., Priv. print., 1915. 20 p. 23 cm. 17-4803. F74. C8 T7

CONCORD, Indian relics in. By G. Tolman. (1902?) 1 v. F74. C8 T75

CONCORD. The Wayside; Minute Man National Historical Park. Washington, Office of History and Historic Architecture, Eastern Service Center, 1970. viii, 165, (73) p. illus. 26 cm. (Historic grounds report) Bibliography: p. 156 - 159. 72-614263 MARC. F74. C8 T76

CONCORD. Captain Brown's house; historic data; Minute Man Historical Park, by Ricardo Torres-Reyes. (Washington) U. S. Division of History, Office of Archaeology and Historic Preservation, 1969. ii, 39 l. illus., facsim. 27 cm. 70-605429. F74. C8 T77

CONCORD in the colonial period; being a history of the town of Concord, from the earliest settlement to the overthrow of the Andros government, 1635 - 1689, by Charles H. Walcott ... Boston, Estes and Lauriat, 1884. xiv, 172 p. double map. 22½ cm. "List of authorities cited": p. (xi)-xii. 1-11315. F74. C8 W2

CONCORD; a pilgrimage to the historic and literary center of America; illustrated by reproductions of photographs which show the natural beauty of Concord and its historic landmarks, together with a brief history of the town and an account of the incidents and people that have made it famous. Boston, P. Walton, 1922. 26, (11) p. incl. front., illus., map. 27 cm. 22-13915. F74. C8 W3

— ... 3d ed. Boston, P. Walton, 1930. 27, (12) p. incl. front., illus., plates, etc. 30-22747. F74. C8 W3 1930

CONCORD: climate for freedom, by Ruth R. Wheeler. Concord, Mass., Concord Antiquarian Soc., 1967. xv, 253 p. illus. 23 cm. 67-31527. F74. C8 W49

CONCORD. The plantation at Musketequid; read before the Concord antiquarian society, by Albert E. Wood. (Concord) The Concord antiquarian soc. (1902?) 26 p. front. (fold. map) 23 cm. (Concord antiquarian soc. Publication no. 7) 4-7832. F74. C8 W8

CONCORD. The people of Concord, by James Playsted Wood. Drawings by Richard Cuffari. New York, Seabury Press (1970) 152 p. illus. 22 cm. 71-97035. F74. C8 W84

CONWAY. Celebration of the 100th anniversary of the incorporation of Conway ... 1867; including a historical address by Rev. Charles B. Rice, etc. Northampton, Bridgman & Childs, 1867. 137 (i.e. 136) p. 25½ cm. 1-11316. F74. C84 C8

CONWAY, Vital records of, to the year 1850. Boston, The New England historic genealogical soc., 1943. 276 p. 23 cm. 43-17547. F74. C84 C83

CONWAY, 1767 - 1967. Ed. by Deane Lee. (Conway, Mass.) Pub. by The Town, 1967. 260 p. illus. 25 cm. F74. C84 L4

CONWAY, History of, 1767 - 1917, by the people of Conway; Rev. Charles Stanley Pease, ed. Springfield, Mass., Springfield print., 1917. 345 p. incl. front., illus., plates, port. 23½ cm. "Family genealogies": p. (241) - 345. 17-25789. F74. C84 P3

COTTAGE CITY, Martha's Vineyard, Directory of ... 1883 - Providence, H. P. Porter, 1883 - v. illus. (map) 19 cm. CA 33-615 unrev. Directories

COTTAGE CITY. Webb's Cottage City (Martha's Vineyard) directory ... No. 1 - 1885 - New York, W.S. Webb, 1885 - v. fold. map. 24 cm. CA 33-616 unrev. Directories

431

COTTAGE CITY illustrated. 1888 ... Woonsocket, R. I.   J. N. Chamberlain, 1888.   18 pl. obl. 16°.
1-11317-M1.
                                         F74. C85 C8

COTTAGE CITY, Martha's Vineyard, Portfolio of views of. Boston, B. Coolidge & A. N. Houghton
(1886) 2 p. 10 pl. obl. 12°.   1-11318-M1.   F74. C85 P8

COTTAGE CITY. Edgartown division. Argument of Hon. C. R. Train before the Committee on towns, in behalf of the petitioners, for an act to incorporate the northern part of Edgartown (Oak Bluffs, Vineyard Grove, etc.) as a new town, to be called Cottage City, Boston, Feb. 14, 1879. Boston, Rand, Avery, print., 1879. 20 p. 8°. 1-23709-M1.   F74. C85 T7

CUMMINGTON. Sketches and directory of the town of Cummington. West Cummington, Mass., The author, 1881. 2, 46 p. incl. pl. 8°. 1-11319-M1.   F74. C3 M6

DALTON, Vital records of, to the year 1850. Boston, Pub. by the New England historic genealogical soc., 1906. 82 p. 23½ cm. 6-13933.   F74. D13 D2

DANA. Address at the 100th anniversary of the town of Dana, by Richard H. Dana. (n. p.) 1901.
18 p. 23 cm. 6-13730.   F74. D15 D2

DANA centennial, The; report of the addresses and proceedings at the celebration on Dana common on the twenty-second day of August, 1901. Barre, Mass., Mrs. J. C. Spooner, print. (1901?)
2, 103 p. 21 cm. 7-40031.   F74. D15 D3

DANA, Vital records of, to the year 1850, compiled by Thomas W. Baldwin ... Boston, Mass. (Bangor, Me., Burr print.) 1925. 66 p. 23 cm. 26-5306.   F74. D15 D4

DANVERS, Marblehead, Peabody, Beverly, Manchester, Essex, Wenham, Topsfield ... Directory of.
v. 2. Boston, D. Dudley, 1875. 1 v. map. 24 cm. 10-10292.   Directories

DANVERS. Account of the centennial celebration in Danvers ... 1852, together with the proceedings of the town in relation to the donation of George Peabody ... (Boston, Print. Dutton and Wentworth) 1852. 3, (3) - 208 p. front., plates, ports. 23½ cm. 1-11320 Rev.   F74. D2 D2

DANVERS. The celebration of the 150th anniversary of the establishment of the town of Danvers, as a separate municipality. June, 1902. Print. by vote of the town, 1907. Boston, S. Usher (1907)
222 p. front., plates, ports. 25 cm. 8-4357.   F74. D2D206

DANVERS. Centennial celebration at Danvers ... 1852. ... Boston, Print. Dutton and Wentworth, 1852. 63 p. front. (port.) 24 cm. 1-11321.   F74. D2 D21

— Boston, 1852. 208 p. port. 23 cm. 10-31552.   F74. D2 D22

DANVERS. Proceedings at the reception and dinner in honor of George Peabody .... To which is appended an historical sketch of the Peabody institute ... Boston, H. W. Dutton, print., 1856.
vi, 195 p. 2 port. (incl. front.) plates. 23½ cm. 1-11322.   F74. D2 D3

DANVERS. Report of the committee appointed to revise the soldiers' record. Danvers (Mass.) The town, 1895. vii, 165 (i.e. 169) p. front., pl. 24 cm. 1-21362.   F74. D2 D32

DANVERS, Vital records of, to the end of the year 1849. ... Salem, Mass., The Essex institute, 1909 - 10. 2 v. 23½ cm. 9-7127.   F74. D2 D33

DANVERS. Baptisms at church in Salem village, now North parish, Danvers. Communicated by Henry Wheatland. (From the Essex historical collections, vol. xvi) Salem, Print. at the Salem press, 1880. 47 p. 24½ cm. 2-10428.   F74. D2 D38

DANVERS. Proceedings at the celebration of the 200th anniversary of the first parish at Salem village, now Danvers ... 1872; with an historical address by Charles B. Rice ... Boston, Congregational pub. soc., 1874. 272 p. front. (port.) illus., plates, facsim. 24 cm. 1-16752 Rev. F74. D2 D39

MASSACHUSETTS

DANVERS. Old anti-slavery days. Proceedings of the commemorative meeting, held by the Danvers historical society, at the Town hall, Danvers ... 1893 .... Danvers, Danvers mirror print, 1893.
xxvii p.   151 p.   port. group.   23 ½ cm.   1-11323.   F74. D2 D4

DANVERS historical society. The historical collections. v. 1 -   Danvers, Mass., The Society, 1913 -   v. fronts., illus., plates, ports., maps, plans, facsims. 23 ½ cm.   Includes "Necrology".   13-17320 Rev.   F74. D2 D42
— Index to the Historical collections of the Danvers hist. soc., vols. i-v.   Danvers, Mass., The Society, 1919.   68 p.   23 cm.   F74. D2 D42 Index
— ... Index to vols. vi - xx; under direction of the Committee on publication.   Danvers, Mass., The Society, 1933.   135 p.   22 ½ cm.   (colls. of the Danvers hist. soc. vol. 21)   13-17320.   F74. D2 D42 vol. 21

DANVERS. Souvenir. Danvers, Mass. illustrated.   (Danvers) Danvers mirror (1896)
(28) p.   illus.   fol.   1-11324-M1.   F74. D2 D45

DANVERS, History of the town of, from its early settlement to the year 1848. By J. W. Hanson ... Danvers, The author, 1848.   vii, (9)-304 p.   illus. (incl. coat of arms)   19 ½ cm.   1-11325.   F74. D2 H2

DANVERS. Historic Danvers. Photographed, pub. and print. by Frank E. Moynahan.   Danvers, Mass., 1894.   (47) p.   plates, map.   15 ½ x 22 ½ cm.   1 (Author's preface signed: Ezra D. Hines.   1-11326 Rev.   F74. D2 H6

DANVERS. Some Danvers acres and associations connected therewith, by Ezra D. Hines.   1897. Salem, Mass., Newcomb & Gauss, print., 1930.   2, (3) - 22 p.   front., plates.   25 cm.   30-15225.
F74. D2 H65

DANVERS. Eulogy, at the funeral of General Gideon Foster, delivered in the Unitarian church, in Danvers ... 1845, by Daniel P. King, with notes.   Danvers (Mass.) G. R. Carlton- Courier press, 1846.   32 p.   22 ½ cm.   7-38313.   F74. D2 K5

DANVERS. A resume of her past history and progress, tog. with a condensed summary of her industrial advantages and development. Biographies of prominent Danvers men and a series of comprehensive sketches of her representative manufacturing and commercial enterprises. Copyrighted ... by F. E. Moynahan. Danvers, Mass., The Danvers mirror, 1899.   3. 202 p.   illus. (incl. ports.)   24 cm.
99-4274 Rev.   F74. D2 M9

DANVERS. Historical sketch, of school district number thirteen, North Danvers: or, as it is known abroad, Danvers plains: or, by its ancient name, Porter's plains, to distinguish it from Shillaber's plains, South Danvers.   Salem (Mass.) Print. the Gazette office, 1855.   32 p.   23 cm.   9-16277.
F74. D8 O8

DANVERS. From Muddy Boo to Blind Hole, by Charles Sutherland Tapley.   Danvers, Mass., Priv. print., 1940.   24 p.   front.   23½ cm.   42-15273.   F74. D2 T16

DANVERS. Chronicles of Danvers (old Salem village) 1632 - 1923, by Harriet Silvester Tapley ... Danvers, Mass., The Danvers historical soc., 1923.   xii, 283 p.   front., plates, ports., facsims.   25 cm.   23-9783.
F74. D2 T17

DARTMOUTH. The New Bedford suburban directory for Dartmouth, Acushnet and Westport ... v. 1 - Salem, Mass., The Henry M. Meek pub. co., 1917 -   v.   24 ½ cm.   18-12722.   Directories

DARTMOUTH. A sketch of Elder Daniel Hix, with the history of the First Christian church in Dartmouth, for 100 years.   By S. M. Andrews.   New Bedford (Mass.) E. Anthony, print., 1880.
vi, 204 p.   18 cm.   Lists of church members and marriages included.   11-21031.   F74. D25 A5

DARTMOUTH. ... The villages of Dartmouth in the British raid of 1778.   Comp. by Henry Howland Crapo in 1839-40 ... (New Bedford, 1909)   29 p. incl. illus., port.   26 cm.   (Old Dartmouth historical sketches, no. 23)
16-27477.   F74. D25C89

DARTMOUTH, Vital records of, to the year 1850 ... Boston, Mass., The New England historic genealogical soc., 1929-30.   3 v.   23 cm.   30-27213.   F74. D25D23

DARTMOUTH. The field notes of Benjamin Crane, Benjamin Hammond and Samuel Smith. Reproduced in facsimile from the original notes of survey of lands of the proprietors of Dartmouth, including what is now the city of New Bedford, and the towns of Dartmouth, Westport, Fairhaven, and Accushnet. New Bedford, Mass., The New Bedford Free pub. library, 1910. xvi, viii p., 2 l., 767 p. illus. (incl. facsims.) 39½ x 27 cm. Reproduction in facsimile and transcription in parallel columns. 11-14780. F74. D25 D3

DARTMOUTH. Centennial celebration. Proceedings in connection with the celebration at New Bedford ... 1864, of the 200th anniversary of the incorporation of the town of Dartmouth. Print. by order of the City council of New Bedford. New Bedford, Mass., E. Anthony, print., 1865. 129 p. 23½ cm. 1-11327. F74. D25 N5

DARTMOUTH. Old Dartmouth historical sketches no. 1 - (New Bedford? Mass., 1903 -
v. illus., plates, ports., fold. map, plan. fold. facsim. 26½ cm. Nos. 1 - 44; 46 - 51 include the old Dartmouth hist. soc. proceedings. 1903- 1921. 5-31619 (rev. '29) F74. D25 O4

DARTMOUTH. Five Johns of old Dartmouth, by William Arthur Wing. (n. p., 1909) (4) p. 26 cm.
Biographical sketches of John Smith, Jonathan Russell, John Howland, John Akin, John Shepherd. 10-3153. F74. D25 W7

DEDHAM. The Norfolk repository. Devoted to news, politics, morals, and polite literature ... By H. Mann. v. 1 - Dedham, Mass., H. Mann, 1806 - v. 29 - 31 cm. weekly. No numbers issued from Sept. 18, 1805 to Mar. 24, 1806 inclusive. 42-32259. F74. D
AP2. A2 N7

DEDHAM. The resident and business directory of Dedham. Dedham, The Standard pub. co., 18 -
v. plates, fold. map. 23 cm. Directories

DEDHAM. Resident and business directory of Dedham and Westwood ... 1899 - 19
Directories

DEDHAM and Westwood directory ... 19 - Directories

DEDHAM. Polk's Dedham and Westwood directory ... 1899, 1902, 1905, 1907/8, 1911, 19
Boston, New York city, R. L. Polk, 1899 - v. fold. maps. 23½ cm. 26-11312 Rev. Directories

DEDHAM and Westwood directory ... 1939 - v. 1 - North Hampton, N. H., 1939 -
v. 23½ cm. 39-32918. Directories

DEDHAM tavern, Tale of a; history of the Norfolk hotel, Dedham, Mass., by Walter Austin. Cambridge, Priv. print. at the Riverside press, 1912. 5, 195 p. front., 1 illus., plates, ports., facsims. 19½ cm. 12-25269. F74. D3 A9

DEDHAM. An alphabetical abstract of the record of births, in the town of Dedham, 1844 - 1890. Comp. by Don Gleason Hill, town clerk. Dedham, Mass., The Dedham transcript, 1894.
xviii, 206 p. 25 cm. Supplementing "The record of births, marriages and deaths ... 1886." 1-11332. F74. D3 D31

— 1895. ix, 217 p. 25 cm. 1-11333. F74. D3 D32

DEDHAM. An alphabetical abstract of the record of marriages, in the town of Dedham, 1844 - 1890. Arranged under the names of the grooms, with an index of the names of brides. Comp. by Don Gleason Hill, town clerk. Dedham, Mass., The Dedham transcript, 1896. iv, 165 p. 25 cm.
1-11334. F74. D3 D33

DEDHAM. Dedication of the Memorial hall, in Dedham, ... 1868. With an appendix. Dedham, Mass., Printed by J. Cox, jr., 1869. 91 p. 24 cm. 7-27743. F74. D3 D36

DEDHAM, The early records of the town ... Dedham, Mass., Dedham transcript press, 1886 - 1936.
6 v. illus. (incl. facsims.) port. 25 cm. v. 1 & 2. Records of births, marriages and deaths, etc. v. 3. General records of the town,1636 - 1659. - v. 4. 1659 - 1673. - v. 5. 1672 - 1706. 1-11335 Additions. F74. D3 D 4

DEDHAM. List of persons assessed for a poll tax in Dedham, 1893. Compiled and print. as provided

by chapter 305, Acts of 1890 ... Dedham, Mass., Transcript steam job print, 1893. 25 p. 23 cm.
35-29236. F74. D3 D46

— Dedham, Mass., 18 -   v. 23½ cm. 1-11331 Rev. F74. D3 D47

DEDHAM. Proceedings at the celebration of the 250th anniversary of the incorporation of the town of Dedham ... 1886. Cambridge, J. Wilson, University press, 1887. vii, (9) - 214 p. front. (facsim.) 24½ cm. Contains music. 1-11330. F74. D3 D5

DEDHAM. Proceedings at the dedication of the Avery school building, Dedham ... 1895. With an appendix. Dedham, 1896. ix, (11) - 51 p. front., plates, 26 cm. 1-11329. F74. D3 D52

DEDHAM. The record of the town meetings, and abstract of births, marriages, and deaths in the town of Dedham. 1887 - 1896. ... index by Don Gleason Hill ... Dedham, Mass., Transcript steam job print, 1896. (780) p. plates, fold. plans. 24½ cm. 2-1924 rev. F74. D3 D55

DEDHAM. Official commemoration and chronicle issued in honor of the 300th anniversary of the historic town of Dedham, 1636 - 1936 .... Dedham, Mass., Pub. by the Transcript press, under the direction of the Dedham Tercentenary committee (1936) 204 p. front., illus. (incl. ports.) maps. 30½ cm.
42-9008. F74. D3 D6

DEDHAM. "Old Dedham days and ways"; an historical festival under the auspices of the Men's club of the First Congregational church ... (Boston, The Metcalf press) 1904. 24 p. illus., port.
26 x 20½ cm. 5-36487. F74. D3 D776

DEDHAM. ... Commemorative services at the 250th anniversary of the gathering of the First church in Dedham ... Observed ... 1888. Dedham, Pub. by the Joint committee of the two churches, 1888.
114 p. 24 cm. 2-6203 Rev. F74. D3 D78

DEDHAM historical register, The. v. 1-14; 1890 - 1903. Dedham, Mass., The Society, 1890 - 1903.
14 v. fronts., illus., plates, ports., maps (part fold.) facsims. 24 cm. quarterly. No more pub? 5-32203 Rev. F74. D3 D8

DEDHAM historical society. Annual reports ... 1889 - 92. Dedham, Mass. 24½ cm.
F74. D3 D86

DEDHAM. A list of revolutionary soldiers who served Dedham in the revolution, 1775 - 1783. This list is based upon the Massachusetts soldiers and sailors of the revolutionary war, pub. by the commonwealth and supplemented by the town and parish records of Dedham. (Dedham) Dedham hist. soc., 1917. 13 p. 23 cm. 17-24432. F74. D3 D88

DEDHAM. A plan of Dedham village, 1636 - 1876. With descriptions of the grants of lots to the original owners, transcribed from the town records; the plan showing approx. the situation of the original grants with relation to the present village. (Dedham) The Dedham hist. soc., 1833.
15 p. fold. plan. 26 cm. 1-11337. F74. D3 D9

DEDHAM. Our fathers God, the hope of posterity. Some serious thoughts on the foundation, rise and growth of the settlements in New England. ... A discourse delivered at Dedham ... 1738 ... By Samuel Dexter ... Boston: Print. S. Kneeland ... 1738. 2, 51 p. 18 cm. 8-34769.
F74. D3 D95
Rare Book Coll.

— 2d ed. Boston, Repr. by Thos, Fleet, jun. ... 1796. 51 p. 20 cm. 8-34770. F74. D3 D96
Rare Book Coll.

DEDHAM. An historical address delivered before the citizens of the town of Dedham ... 1836, being the 2d centennial anniversary of the incorporation of the town. By Samuel F. Haven. Dedham, Print. H. Mann, 1837. 79 p. 23 cm. 1-11338° Cancel. F74. D3 H3

DEDHAM. A history of the First church and parish in Dedham, in three discourses ... 1838. By Alvan Lamson ... Dedham, Print. H. Mann, 1839. 104 p. 22½ cm. 4-7011. F74. D3 L2

DEDHAM. Other men have labored: a sermon preached ... 1879, by Rev. Calvin S. Locke ... Pub. by request. Dedham, Mass., Print. H. H. McQuillen, 1880.   29 p.   23 cm.   7-27751.   F74. D3 L8

DEDHAM. A New England town: the first 100 years, Dedham, 1636 - 1736 (by) Kenneth A. Lockridge. (1st ed.) New York, W. W. Norton (1970)   xv, 208 p. maps.   21 cm.   (The Norton essays in American history) 69-14703.   F74. D3 L8 1970

DEDHAM, Historical annals of, from its settlement in 1635, to 1847. By Herman Mann. Dedham, Mass., H. Mann, 1847.   viii, (9) - 136 p.   23 cm.   1-11339.   F74. D3 M2

DEDHAM's ancient landmarks and their national significance. By Edward Huntting Rudd ... Dedham, Mass., The Dedham transcript print. and pub. co., (1908)   7, 57 p. incl. pl. front., 5 pl. 26½ cm. 9-545.   F74. D3 R9

DEDHAM in picture and story, pt. 4 - 6, by Frank Smith. (Dedham, Mass., 1927-29)   3 pts. 20½ x 22 cm.   F74. D3 S5

DEDHAM, A history of, by Frank Smith ... Dedham, Mass., The Transcript press, inc., 1936. 6, (3) - 543, (7) p. front., plates, maps (1 fold.) facsims. 23½ cm. Roster of officers and men from Dedham in the revolutionary war, the civil war and the first world war. 36-23569.   F74. D3 S6

DEDHAM. Contentment and community spirit; address delivered at the tercentenary of the town of Dedham on Sept. 20, 1936, by Charles Warren. (Dedham, Mass., 1936)   27 p.   23½ cm.   Re-print from the Official commemoration and record book of the 300th anniversary of the town. 37-18065.   F74. D3 W3 Rare Book Coll.

DEDHAM, The history of, from the beginning of its settlement ... 1635, to May, 1827. By Erastus Worthington ... Boston, Dutton and Wentworth, print., 1827.   146 p.   23 cm.   1-11340.   F74. D3 W9

DEERFIELD, Memories of old, by Gertrude Porter Ashley ... Deerfield, Mass., The author, 1934. 4, 7 - 45 p. front., plates. 19½ cm. 34-18514.   F74. D4 A7

DEERFIELD, Epitaphs in the old burying-ground at, copied by C. Alice Baker and Emma L. Coleman. Deerfield, Mass., The Pocumtuck Valley memorial assoc., 1924.   2, 49 p. front., plates. 24 cm. 25-13749.   F74. D4 B3

DEERFIELD. Frontier of freedom; the soul and substance of America portrayed in one extraordinary village, Old Deerfield, by Samuel Chamberlain and Henry N. Flynt. Illus. by Samuel Chamberlain. New York, Hastings House (1952)   154 p. illus. 24 cm.   52-9645.   F74. D4 C47

— (Rev. and enl. ed.) New York, Hastings House (1957)   170 p. (chiefly illus.)   24 cm.   58-16337.   F74. D4 C47 1957

DEERFIELD. Historic Deerfield: houses and interiors, by Samuel Chamberlain and Henry N. Flynt. Illus. by Samuel Chamberlain. (Rev. and enl. ed.) New York, Hastings house (1965)   182 p. 26 cm. Rev. and enl. edition of the 'Frontier of freedom'. 65-17610.   F74. D4 C47 1965

— 1972.   F74. D4 C47 1972

DEERFIELD. A historic and present day guide to old Deerfield, by Emma Lewis Coleman. Boston, 1907.   5, 116 p. front., 16 pl., 3 port. 19 cm. Some books about Deerfield: p. 113-116. 7-40883.   F74. D4 C6

DEERFIELD, Vital records of, to the year 1850. Comp. by Thomas W. Baldwin ... Boston, (Wright & Potter, print.) 1920.   328 p. 23½ cm. 21-2051.   F74. D4 D3

DEERFIELD. A description of Deerfield, intended as an exhibition of the plan of a contemplated gazetteer of Massachusetts proper. By Roldolphus Dickinson. Deerfield, Mass., Pub. by the author. G. J. Newcomb, print. 1817.   8 p.   21½ cm.   18-2846.   F74. D4 D5

DEERFIELD. A white bird flying. By Rufus Chester Field. (1st ed.) New York, Pageant Press (1963)   41 p.   21 cm.   F74. D4 F5

DEERFIELD. An old custom, the liberty pole of Deerfield, 1774 (by Helen and Henry Flynt. Greenwich? Conn.) Priv. print., 1946.   (7) p.   24 cm.   52-40844.   F74. D4 F55

DEERFIELD, The story of, by Mary Williams Fuller. Brattleboro, The Vermont print., 1930. 48 p.   front., plates, maps (1 fold.) plan.   16 cm.   30-18546.   F74. D4 F96

DEERFIELD. A brief sketch of the first settlement of Deerfield. Together with a few of the events which took place there in early times. By one of the descendants of the first settlers of the town (Elihu Hoyt) Greenfield (Mass.) J. P. Fogg, print., 1833.   iv, (5) - 48 p.   front.   15 x 11½ cm.   Preface signed: E.H.   18-23783.   F74. D4 H5
                                                                                                                    Rare Book Coll.

— (n. p., 188-?)   iv, (5)-48 p.   16½ cm.   Facsim. reprint supposed to have been made by G. M. Elliott.   1-16807 Rev.   F74. D4 H6

DEERFIELD. Indian house memorial. Old Deerfield, Mass. (Deerfield, 1945)   39 p.   illus. 23 cm.   Signed: Marion Pendleton Drew, cutodian (and) Kelsey Flower.   46-397.   F74. D4 I 5

DEERFIELD. An address delivered at South Deerfield ... 1838, on the completion of the Bloody Brook monument, erected in memory of Capt. Lothrop and his associates, who fell at that spot ... 1675. By Luther B. Lincoln ... Greenfield (Mass.) Kneeland & Eastman, 1838.   16 p.   22½ cm. 1-11341 Rev.   F74. D4 L7

DEERFIELD. The Rev. Jonathan Ashley house, Deerfield.   (Deefield) Heritage Foundation (1962) xiv, 153 p. illus., maps, geneal. tables.   26 cm.   F74. D4 M5

DEERFIELD. Old Deerfield, containing an appreciation of early New England as evidenced by the now standing 17th century houses of Deerfield; illus. with reproductions of pencil sketches made from the houses themselves. Boston, Pinkham press (1927)   24 l. incl. plates.   22 cm.   28-21233.
                                                                                                                    F74. D4 P6
                                                                                                                    Rare Book Coll.

DEERFIELD. Boyhood memories of old Deerfield, by Frank Wright Pratt. (Portland, Me.) Priv. print. (The Southworth-Anthoensen press) 1936.   6, 3-308 p.   front.   22 cm.   36-37512.
                                                                                                                    F74. D4P73

DEERFIELD. Forty years of frontier life in the Pocumtuck valley. By George Sheldon. (Boston? 1886)   236 - 249 p.   4°.   From the New England magazine, March, 1886.   1-16793-M1.   F74. D4 S4

DEERFIELD, History of. By George Sheldon. (Deerfield? Mass., 189-?)   2 v.   19½ x 27 cm.
                                                                                                                    F74. D4 S45

DEERFIELD, ... A history of: the times when and the people by whom it was settled, unsettled and re-settled: with a special study of the Indian wars in the Connecticut Valley. With genealogies. By George Sheldon. Deerfield, Mass. (Greenfield, Mass., Press of E. A. Hall) 1895-96.   2 v.   front. (port.)   24 cm.   1-12352.   L.C. copy replaced by microfilm.   F74. D4 S5
                                                                                                                    Microfilm 16898 F

DEERFIELD. The little brown house on the Albany road, by George Sheldon ... (Boston?) 1898. 19 p.   illus.   24 cm.   "Reprinted from the New England magazine, Sept. 1898"   1-16562.   F74. D4 S6

— Deerfield, The author, 1915.   3, 51 p.   front., illus.   23 cm.   15-21980.   F74. D4 S61

DEERFIELD. The Rev. John Williams house, by George Sheldon and J. M. Arms Sheldon. Deerfield,

208   LOCAL HISTORIES IN THE LIBRARY OF CONGRESS

(Mass.) 1918.   32 p.   plates.   23½ cm.   24-163.   F74.D4S614

DEERFIELD.   The evolutionary history of a New England homestead; the Colonel Joseph Stebbins homestead in Deerfield, by J. M. Arms Sheldon, illus. by Frances S. and Mary E. Allen and others. Deerfield, Mass., 1925.   50 p.   plates, plans, facsims.   24 cm.   25-27637.   F74.D4S618

DEERFIELD.   John Sheldon and the Old Indian house homestead, by J. Arms Sheldon; a paper read before the Pocumtuck Valley memorial assoc ... 1911.   Greenfield, Mass., Print. T. Morey, (1911) 21 p.   23 cm.   13-1336.   F74.D4 S62

DEERFIELD.   "The story of Godfrey Nims," as read to the Nims family association, at Deerfield ... 1914, by Francis Nims Thompson.   (Greenfield, Mass., Print. E. A. Hall, 1914)   7, 8-19 numb. l. 23 cm.   14-14311.   F74. D4 T4

DEERFIELD.   Story of the old Willard house of Deerfield.   Written for and read at the 18th annual meeting of the Pocumtuck Valley memorial assoc. ... 1887, by Catharine B. Yale.   Boston and New York, Houghton, Mifflin, 1887.   3, 24 p.   illus.   6 pl.   33 x 26 cm.   13-33612.   F74. D4 Y2

DEERFIELD.   Negro slavery in old Deerfield.   By George Sheldon.   (Boston? 1893)   p. (49) - 60. 23 ½ cm.   Reprint from New England magazine of March, 1893.   11-2765.   F74.D4
                                                                                                                                                                                              E445.M4 S5

DENNIS.   Master mariners of Dennis.   By Neva O'Neil.   Drawings by Hope Smith.   (Dennis, Mass., Dennis Historical Soc., 1965.   48 p.   23 cm.   F74.D43 O6

DIGHTON.   Tri-city directory of Dighton, Rehoboth, Seekonk, Somerset and Swansea ...   Northampton, N. H.,, Crosby pub. co., 19 -   v.   23½ cm.   41-13013.   Directories

DIGHTON rock; a study of the written rocks of New England, by Edmund Burke Delabarre ... with 108 illus. from rare prints, photographs, drawings, charts, and maps.   New York, W. Neale, 1928. xv, 369 p.   front., illus., plates (1 double) maps, facsims. (1 double)   24½ cm.   "Bibliographies": p. 315-351.   28-22706.   F74.D45D28

DIGHTON.   Recent history of Dighton rock, by Edmund Burke Delabarre ...   Cambridge (Mass.) J. Wilson, 1919.   (285) - 462.   illus., pl. xxxii - xlvii (incl. fold. front.)   25 cm.   Reprinted from the Publications of the Colonial society of Massachusetts, vol. xx.   "Bibliography of Dighton rock": p. 438 - 461.   26-385.   F74. D45 D3

DIGHTON.   Town records, book one -   Dighton, Mass.   Copied ... under the direction of Elizabeth Janet MacCormick and others.   (Jackson Heights, N. Y., 1939 - 1940)   2v.   29 cm.   40M1991T.
                                                                                                                                                                                              F74.D45D45

DIGHTON rock.   Pamphlets, broadsides, clippings, and other miscellaneous matter on this subject, not separately cataloged, are classified in F74.D45D49

DIGHTON rock.   ... Pedra de Dighton; o professor Delabarre desvenda o mistério das inscrições da pedra de Dighton ...   New York (New Bedford, Mass., Union print.) 1930.   45 p. incl. front., illus., ports., map, facsims., coat of arms. port. 23½ cm. 31-8015.   F74.D45 M3

DIGHTON.   Explication de la pierre de Taunston (!) dans, l'Amérique Septentrionale.   (Paris, 1839) 28 p.   2 fold. pl.   23 cm.   Auto-lithographic copy of manuscript.   1-15998 Rev.   F74.D45 M8

DIGHTON.   Town of Dighton bi-centennial, 1712 - 1912.   (Taunton, Mass., C. A. Hack, 1912) 169 p.   illus. (incl. ports., facsims.)   23 cm.   13-10091.   F74.D45 T7

DIGHTON.   Miguel Corte-Real and the Dighton Writing-Rock (by) George F. W. Young.   Taunton (Mass.) Old Colony Historical Soc., 1970.   146 p. illus.   23 cm.   Bibliography: p. 130 - 138.   70-30661 MARC.
                                                                                                                                                                                             F74.D45 Y6

DORCHESTER, Blue book of.   1885 - 86.   Containing all the streets, alphabetically arranged, and giving the names of the householders, and the intersecting streets, in their order ...   Boston, Mass., Sampson, Murdock, & co., 1885.   203 p.   19 x 14½ cm.   11-22237.   Directories

438

MASSACHUSETTS

DORCHESTER, Blue book of ... 1894 -   (v.1 -   Boston, Boston suburban book co., 1893.
9 v.   fold. maps, plans.   21 cm.   biennial.   0-2787 (rev. '15)   Directories

DORCHESTER and Milton business directory, containing town officers, schools, churches, societies, etc. ... By George Adams ... Boston, Print. David Clapp, 1850.   55 p.   15 cm.   10-11994.   Directories

DORCHESTER.   Historical sketch of the Dorchester First parish, from the writings of Daniel Weld Baker, with illus. from his photographs. Albany (Press of F. H. Evory, 1916.   4, 13-77 p.   front., plates.
21½ cm.   24-29282.   F74. D5 B2

DORCHESTER Neck.   (Now South Boston)   The raid of British troops, ... 1776.   Reprinted from the New-England historical and genealogical register ... 1899. With an account of the first settlements at the Neck, and various miscellaneous notes.   By Francis E. Blake.   Boston, Press of D. Clapp, 1899.   3, (3) - 60 p.   illus. (incl. maps, plans)   24½ cm.   10-17779.   F74. D5 B6

DORCHESTER.   ... Report of the commissioners on the annexation of Dorchester ... (Boston, 1869)
20 p.   23 cm.   (City doc. no. 28)   12-6962.   F74. D5 B74

DORCHESTER.   Memoirs of Captain Roger Clap.   Relating some of God's remarkable providences to him in bringing him into New-England; and some of the straits and afflictions, the good people he met with here in their beginnings. ...   Boston, Print., 1731; reprinted by R. & S. Draper, 1766.
33, 2-11 p.   17 cm.   A33-1140.   F74. D5 C43
                                                                                                              Rare Book Coll.

— Pittsfield (Mass.) Re-printed by P. Allen, 1824.   36 p.   22½ cm.   7-15641.
                                                                                                              F74. D5 C48

— Freeport, N.Y., Books for Libraries Press (1971)   xiv, 62 p.   23 cm.   (Collections of the Dorchester
Antiquarian and Historical Society, no. 1)   73-150176.   F74. D5C4815
                                                                                                              1971

DORCHESTER.   Roger Clap's memoirs, with account of voyage of the "Mary and John" 1630.   Ed. by Sydney Strong.   (Seattle, Pigott-Washington print. co., 1929?)   3, (5) - 57 p.   21 cm.   29-22531.
                                                                                                              F74. D5 C482

DORCHESTER.   The ancient proprietors of Jones's Hill, Dorchester, incl. brief sketches of the Jones, Stoughton, Tailer, Wiswall, Moseley, Capen and Holden families, the location and boundaries of their estates etc.   Comp. by David Clapp.   Boston, Print. for private distribution, 1883.   vi, 68 p.   24½ cm.
"... Much of the contents ... has been printed ... in the ... Dorchester news-gatherer." 9-15705.   F74. D5 C6

DORCHESTER.   The old Morton and Taylor estates in Dorchester.   By David Clapp.   Boston, Press of D. Clapp, 1892.   8 p.   24½ cm.   Repr. from the N.E. hist. and geneal. register, 1892.   3-27194.   F74. D5 C62

DORCHESTER.   The sexton's monitor, and Dorchester cemetery memorial ... By Daniel Davenport. Roxbury, Mass., Print. T.S. Watts, 1826.   x, 38 p.   18 cm.   15-27870.   F74. D5 D15

— 3d ed.   Boston, Print. A. Mudge, 1845.   86 (i.e. 36) p.   18½ cm.   10-8762.   F74. D5 D2

DORCHESTER.   Dedication of the soldiers' monument at Dorchester ... 1867.   Boston, T. Groom, 1868.   35, (3) p.   mounted phot.   24 cm.   F74. D5 D4

DORCHESTER births, marriages, and deaths to the end of 1825.   Boston, Rockwell and Churchill, print., 1890.   iv, 392 p.   24 cm.   21st report of the record commissioners of ... Boston.   6-7049.   F74. D5 D43

— (2d impression) Boston, 1891.   iv, 392 p.   23½ cm.   1-13875.   F74. D5D4301

DORCHESTER town records.   (In Boston. Record commissioners. Report. Boston, 1880. 4th)
1-13873-M4.   F74. D5D432

— 3d ed.   Boston, 1896.   329 p.   23½ cm.   5-18367.   F74. D5D433

439

LOCAL HISTORIES IN THE LIBRARY OF CONGRESS

DORCHESTER, The early records of the town of ... Boston, 1867. 25½ cm. F74.D5 D44

DORCHESTER. Grantees of meadow lands in Dorchester ... 1881. 22½ cm. F74.D5 D45

DORCHESTER, Vital records of the town of, from 1826 to 1849. Boston, Municipal print., 1905.
5, (3) - 288 p. 23½ cm. 6-21399.
F74.D5 D48

DORCHESTER antiquarian and historical society, Collections of the. no. 1 - 3. Boston, D. Clapp, 1844 - 50. 3 v. double front. 18½ x 19 cm. No more pub. Contents. - no. 1. Memoirs of Roger Clap. 1630. - no.2. Annals of the town of Dorchester. By James Blake. 1750. - no. 3. Journal of Richard Mather. 1635. His life and death. 1670. 1-23968. F74. D5 D5

DORCHESTER, History of the town of. By a committee of the Dorchester antiquarian and historical society ... Boston, E. Clapp, 1859. xii, 672 p. 23 cm. For full statement of authorship see New England historical and genealogical register v. 44, p. 399. 1-11345 Rev. F74. D5 D6

DORCHESTER book, The ... Dorchester, Mass. Christ church pub. Boston, G.H. Ellis print., 1899.
viii, 58 p. front., illus., plates. 29 cm. 10-17502.
F74.D5 D62

DORCHESTER. Proceedings of the 250th anniversary of the gathering in England, departure for America, and final settlement in New England, of the First church and parish of Dorchester, Mass., coincident with the settlement of the town. Boston, G. H. Ellis, 1880. 176 p. 23 cm. 6-40431.
F74.D5 D63

DORCHESTER, Records of the First church at ... 1636 - 1734. Boston, Mass., G. H. Ellis, 1891.
2, (iii) - xxvi, 270 p. 23½ cm. 2-8983.
F74.D5 D64

DORCHESTER historical society. ... Catalogue of the Stark collection of antiquities and curiosities Old Blake house, Columbia road, Dorchester, Mass. ... 1907. (Dorchester? 1907) 10 p. 19 cm.
7-30349.
F74.D5D655

DORCHESTER historical society.. Dorchester day; celebration of the 277th anniversary of the settlement of Dorchester ... 1907, including also a brief description of the origin of Dorchester day and the three preceding celebrations, by James H. Stark ... Boston, Municipal print., 1907.
117 p. front., plates, ports. 27 cm. 2d edition. 8-17388.
F74.D5 D66

— 279th anniversary ... 1909. Boston, Printing dept., 1909. 116 p. front., illus., plates, ports., fold. plan. 27 cm. 10-17633.
F74.D5D662

— 281st anniversary ... also, the rededication of the statue of Edward Everett, opposite to his birthplaces. (Dorchester, 1911) 11 p. illus. 22 cm. Souvenir program. 11-27954.
F74.D5D664

DORCHESTER. ... Places in Dorchester to visit during Old-home week, ... 1907. Comp. by James H. Stark ... (Boston, Keenan, print.1907) 15 p. illus. 19½ cm. Issued by the Dorchester hist. soc. 8-37655. F74.D5 D68

DORCHESTER historical society. Souvenir program, celebration ... June 6, 1908. (Dorchester, Mass., 1908) 18 cm.
F74. D5 D7

DORCHESTER, 1630 - old and new - 1903, in the old Bay colony; historic and pictorial record commemorating the three hundredth anniversary of the founding of Dorchester .... Dorchester, Mass., Print. for the tercentenary committee, Chapple pub. co., 1930. 78 p. illus., pl., fold. mounted map. 24 cm.
"Sources of historical information": p. 59. 32-24272.
F74.D5 D76

DORCHESTER. Recovery of some materials for the early history of Dorchester, general and particular. Prepared for the New England historic-genealogical register. By Samuel G. Drake. Boston, Office of the New England historic-genealogical register, 1851. 20 p. 23½ cm. Contains sketches of early settlers. Reprinted from the New England hist. and geneal. register for Oct. 1951, v.5. 9-30375.
F74. D5 D8

DORCHESTER in 1630, 1776, and 1855. An oration delivered ... 1855, by Edward Everett. Boston, D. Clapp, 1855. viii, (5) - 158 p. 23½ cm. 1-16824.
F74. D5 E9

440

MASSACHUSETTS

DORCHESTER. A discourse, delivered at Dorchester, ... 1813, at the funeral of Moses Everett. By Rev. Thaddeus Mason Harris ... Boston: Pub. by Joshua Belcher. 1813. 18 p. 24 cm. 1-23756.
F74. D5 E95

DORCHESTER. ... Catalogue of civil war relics, 1862 - 1863 - 1864, Old Blake house, Columbia road, Dorchester, Mass. ... October, 1906. (Dorchester? Mass., 1906) 11 p. 19 cm. Dorchester historical society. 7-30350 Rev.
F74. D5 F7

DORCHESTER. ... Paper on the old Dorchester burying ground, read ... 1901, by John A. Fowle. 2d ed. Dorchester, Mass., Pub. by the Society at "ye old Blake house", 1907. 22 p. illus., pl. 19 cm. Dorchester historical society. 7-22433 rev.
F74. D5 F74

DORCHESTER, An index to the vital records of Dorchester through 1825. By Sanford Charles Gladden. (Boulder) 1970. iii, 148 p. 27 cm.
F74. D5 G55

DORCHESTER, Debt of Massachusetts to. Town meeting and free school. Address by J. Evarts Greene, in Pilgrim church, Dorchester ... 1894. Worcester, Mas., Press of C. Hamilton, 1894. 9 p. 25½ cm. 41-38727.
F74. D5 G7

DORCHESTER. A sermon preached in the meeting-house of the First church, Dorchester ... 1870, being the 240th anniversary of the first assembling of the church for divine service after its landing in America. By Nathaniel Hall ... Boston, E. Clapp, 1870. 27 p. 24 cm. 4-20077.
F74. D5 H18

DORCHESTER. The annexation question. Closing argument of B. W. Harris, for the remonstrants against the annexation of Dorchester to Boston ... 1869. Boston, Rockwell and Rollins, print., 1869. 51 p. 23 cm. 10-13005.
F74. D5 H3

DORCHESTER. Historical sketch of the first burying place in Dorchester (Dorchester north ground) including town records, record of all tombs, all epitaphs now in ground and of many stones now missing, etc. (In Boston. Cemetery dept. Annual report ... 1904/5) 17-3657.
F74. D5 M3

DORCHESTER, past and present. A sermon preached in the Second church, Dorchester ... 1869. By Rev. James H. Means. Boston, M. H. Sargent, 1870. 24 p. 23½ cm. 1-11346.
F74. D5 M4

DORCHESTER. Good old Dorchester. A narrative history of the town. 1630 - 1893. By William Dana Orcutt ... Cambridge (Mass.) The author, J. Wilson, University press, 1893. xv p., (19) - 496 p. incl. front., illus., plates, ports., double facsim. 24 cm. 1-11347.
F74. D5 O6

DORCHESTER. A discourse delivered at Dorchester ... 1830, to commemorate the completion of the second century from its settlement by our Pilgrim fathers. By John Pierce ... Boston, From the office of the Daily advertiser, W. L. Lewis, print, 1830. 36 p. 24 cm. 10-12988.
F74. D5 P6

DORCHESTER. ... History of the old Blake house, and a brief sketch of the Dorchester historical society by James H. Stark ... (Dorchester? Mass.) 1907. 13 p. illus. 18½ cm. Dorchester historical society. 7-13472.
F74. D5 S72

DORCHESTER. Early matters relating to the town and First church of Dorchester. By William Blake Trask. Boston, Print. D. Clapp, 1886. 12 p. 24½ cm. Reprinted from the New England historical and genealogical register for July, 1886. 4-387.
F74. D5 T7

DORCHESTER. Epitaphs from the old burying ground in Dorchester. By Harlow Elliott Woodward. Boston Highlands, 1869. 21 p. 24½ x 15½ cm. 6-13061.
F74. D5 W9

DOUGLAS, Vital records of, to the end of the year 1849. Worcester, Mass., F. P. Rice, 1906. 192 p. 23½ cm. 6-13931.
F74. D6 D6

DOUGLAS, History of the town of, from the earliest period to the close of 1878. By Wm. A. Emerson. Boston, F. W. Bird, 1879. 2, 359 p. front., illus., fold. map. 24 cm. "Biographical and genealogical department": p. (142)-242. 1-11348.
F74. D6 E5

DOUGLAS, The town of; a pictorial presentation of the charm and industry of the community ... (by) Thos. B. Frank. (New York, Print. Barnett and Schulman co., 1934. 51, (2) p. illus. 21 cm. "First edition." 34-42835.
F74. D6 F7

DOVER, Vital records of, to the year 1850. Boston, Pub. by the New England historic genealogical soc., 1908. 107 p. 23 cm. 8-10311.
F74. D7 D6

DOVER. Dedication of the Sawin memorial building, Dover ... 1907. (Dover, Mass.) Print. by the Dover historical and natural history soc., 1908. 40 p. front., pl., ports. 23 cm. 8-27437.
F74. D7 D67

DOVER. Old home day in the town of Dover ... 1903. Dover historical and natural history soc. Natick, Mass., Press of Natick bulletin, 1903. 55 p. 23½ cm. 5-33188.
F74. D7 D7

DOVER. Old home day; proceedings of the 125th anniversary of the incorporation of the town of Dover ... 1909 ... (Dover? Mass.) Print. by the Dover historical and natural history soc., 1910. 2, (7) - 73 p. 23½ cm. 10-8052.
D74. D7 D72

DOVER. The proceedings of the dedication of the Soldiers' monument ... 1910, etc. etc. (Dover) Printed by the Dover historical and natural history soc., 1912. 83 p. 5 pl. (incl. front.) 23 cm. 12-9008.
F74. D7 D73

DOVER. In Dover on the Charles; a contribution to New England folk-lore, by Alice J. Jones ... Newport, R. I., The Milne printery, 1906. 114 p. front. 17 x 13 cm. 6-20858.
F74. D7 J 7

DOVER. Biographical sketch of the residents of that part of Dedham, which is now Dover, who took part in King Philip's war, the last French and Indian war, and the revolution ... the war of 1812; the war with Mexico; the civil war; and the war with Spain. By Frank Smith ... Dover, Mass., Print. by the Town, 1909. 88, iv p. incl. front. (map) 22 cm. 9-19167.
F74. D7 S47

DOVER. Biographical sketches of the residents of Dover, who during the first century of the town's corporate existence, 1748 - 1848, graduated from college, by Frank Smith. (Dover? Mass., 189-?) 12 p. 23 cm. 5-26490.
F74. D7 S48

DOVER. The deeds of our fathers. A Memorial day address delivered in the town house, Dover ... 1904, by Frank Smith. (Dover?) Print. by the Memorial day committee, 1904. 19 p. 22½ cm. 5-26499.
F74. D7 S 5

DOVER farms; in which is traced the development of the territory from the first settlement in 1640 to 1900, by Frank Smith ... Dover, Mass., The Historical and natural history soc., 1914. viii, 152 p. front. (port.) plates, fold. map. 23 cm. 14-21777.
F74. D7 S53

DOVER fifty years ago, by Frank Smith ... (Dover? Mass., 1930) 14 p. 21 cm. CA 30-743 Unrev.
F74. D7 S54

DOVER. The founders of the First parish, Dover, with descriptions of all the houses now standing which were built before the revolution. By Frank Smith ... (Dover?) Printed by the First parish, 1908. 24 p. front. (port.) 2 pl., map. 23½ cm. 8-24729.
F74. D7 S55

DOVER. The genealogical history of Dover, tracing all families previous to 1850, and many families that have lived in the town since, with an account of the habits and customs of the people, by Frank Smith ... Dover, Mass., The Historical and natural history soc., 1917. 3, (3) - 268 p. front. (fold. diagrs.) plates. 23 cm. 18-859.
F74. D7 S56

DOVER. Narrative history. A history of Dover, Mass., as a precinct, parish, district, and town; by Frank Smith. Dover, Mass., The town, 1897. xv, 354 p. front., plates, fold. maps. 21 cm. 1-11349.
F74. D7 S6

DOVER. Ralph Sanger ... (A paper read before the Dover historical soc. ... 1909) By Frank Smith. (Dover, Mass., 1909) 7 p. 26 cm. 9-14744.
F74. D7 S65

MASSACHUSETTS

DOVER. The Williams tavern, Dover. A paper read before the Dover historical soc ... 1908, by Frank Smith. (Dover, 1908) 7 p. 26 cm. 9-4246. F74. D7 S7

DRACUT directory, The ... Boston, Sampson, Murdock, 1900 - v. 24 cm. "Pamphlet ed."
1-29686 Rev. Directories

DRACUT. History of Dracut, called by the Indians Augumtoocooke and before incorporation, the wildernesse north of the Merrimac. First permanent settlement in 1669 and incorporated as a town in 1701, by Silas R. Coburn ... Lowell, Mass., Press of the Courier-Citizen co., 1922. xii, 433 p. front. plates, ports., maps (1 fold.) 23 cm. 22-5376. F74. D75 C6

DRACUT. Vital records of Dracut, to the year 1850. Boston, Pub. by the New England historic genealogical soc. ... 1907. 302 p. 23½ cm. 7-16397. F74. D75 D7

DRACUT. In memoriam. Citizen soldiers of Dracut, who served in the war of the American revolution, 1775 - 1783. By Old Middlesex chapter, Sons of the American revolution. (Lowell? 1905?) (12) p. pl., 3 port., fold. tab. 23½ cm. 5-29120. F74. D75 S7

DUDLEY. An anniversary discourse, delivered at Dudley, Mass. ... 1853. With topographical and historical notices of the town. By Joshua Bates. Boston, Press of T. R. Marvin, 1853. 58 p. 23½ cm.
1-11350. F74. D8 B3

DUDLEY. A souvenir of the Conant memorial church, its inception, construction, and dedication ... Printed for Hezekiah Conant. Boston, Forbes lithograph manufacturing co., 1893. viii, 130 p. 14 pl. 5 port. (incl. front.) plan. 24½ cm. Records of the Conant family: p. (115) - 126. 6-39282. F74. D8 C7

DUDLEY. Historical notice of the Congregational church in Dudley, with the articles of faith, covenant, etc. Worcester, Print. H. J. Howland, 1845. 16 p. 18 cm. 10-31058. F74. D8 C74

DUDLEY, Town records of ... Pawtucket, R. I., The Adam Sutcliffe co., 1893 - 94. 2 v. in 1. 23½ cm.
v. 1. 1732 - 1754. - v. 2. 1754 - 1794. 1-11351 Additions. F74. D8 D8

DUDLEY, ... Vital records of, to the end of the year 1849. Worcester, Mass., F. P. Rice, trustee of the fund, 1908. 288 p. 23½ cm. 8-13334. F74. D8 D85
Geneal. Sect. Ref.

DUNSTABLE, Vital record of, to the end of the year 1849. Salem, Mass., Essex institute, 1913.
238 p. 23 cm. 13-4351. F74. D9 D9

DUNSTABLE. History of the old township of Dunstable: including Nashua, Nashville, Hollis, Hudson, Litchfield, and Merrimac, N.H.; Dunstable and Tyngsborough, Mass. By Charles J. Fox. Nashua, C. T. Gill, 1846. xiv, 278 p. front., plates, map. 20 cm. 1-11352. F74. D9 F7

DUNSTABLE, ... Historical sketches of. Bi-centennial oration of Hon. George B. Loring. , ... 1873.
Lowell, Mass., G. M. Elliott, 1873. 19 p. 23 cm. 1-11353 Rev. F74. D9 L8

DUNSTABLE, A history of the town of, from its earliest settlement to the year ... 1873. By the Rev. Elias Nason ... Boston, A. Mudge, print., 1877. 316 p. front. (port.) illus. 24 cm. Inscriptions from the various cemeteries: p. 228 - 268. Lists of deaths and births: p. 268 - 277. 1-11354. F74. D9 N2

DUNSTABLE, Bi-centennial of old Dunstable. Address by Hon. S. T. Worcester ... 1873. Also Colonel Bancroft's personal narrative of the battle of Bunker Hill, and some notices of persons and families of the early times of Dunstable, including Welds, Tyngs, Lovewells, Farwells, Fletchers, Bancrofts, Joneses and Cutlers. By J. B. Hill. Nashua, N.H., E. H. Spalding, 1878. 2, (3) - 189 p.
23 cm. The old town of Dunstable included the modern towns of Dunstable and Tyngsborough, Mass. and parts of Hollis, Hudson, Litchfield, Merrimac, Nashua and Nashville, New Hampshire. 1-11356. F74. D9 S 7

DUNSTABLE. Reminiscences of old Dunstable. With sketches of events and persons of the early times ... (In Spalding, Bi-centennial of old Dunstable, 1878) 1-11355 Rev. F74. D9 S 7

DUNSTABLE. Early generations of the founders of old Dunstable, thirty families; by Ezra S. Stearns ... Boston, G. E. Littlefield, 1911.   vi, 103 p. 24 cm. 11-21843.   F74. D9 S8

DUXBURY and Kingston, Resident and business directory of, 1915 -   (no. 1) -   Boston, Mass., Union pub. co., 1915 -   v. 24 cm. 15-13022.   Directories

DUXBURY. Pictorial souvenir: John Alden, 1904.   13½ x 18½ cm.   F74. D95 A3

DUXBURY. The story of the John Alden house, built 1653, Duxbury. By Charles LaForestt Alden. Duxbury, Mass., C. L. Alden (1938) 26 p. illus. 20 cm. 39-17553.   F74. D95A325

DUXBURY. Alden homestead, Duxbury, shrine of millions of descendants of John Alden and his wife, Priscilla Mullens, by Edward S. Alden; owned by Alden kindred of America, inc ... (Holyoke, Mass., Alden press) 1932.   64 p. illus. 25 cm. 32-18011.   F74. D95A33

DUXBURY. Standish monument on Captain's Hill, Duxbury. Charter, organization, and breaking ground, laying cornerstone ... 1872 .... Prepared by Stephen M. Allen, corresponding secretary of the Standish monument association. Boston, A. Mudge, print., 1873.   61 p. illus. 23½ cm. 14-4034.
F74. D95 A4

DUXBURY. Historic Duxbury in Plymouth County, Mass., by Gershom Bradford ... Boston, 1920. 44 p. front., plates. 20 cm. 20-15384.   F74. D95B78

DUXBURY. Historic Duxbury in Plymouth county, Mass., by Laurence Bradford ... Boston, The Fish print., 1900.   vi, (11) - 128 p. front., illus., plates. 20½ cm. 0-4010 Rev.   F74. D95 B8

— 3d ed. Boston, N. Sawyer, print., 1910.   3, (11)-160 p. front., illus., plates. 20½ cm. 10-25572.   F74. D95B83

DUXBURY. Copy of the old records of the town of Duxbury. From 1642 to 1770. Made in the year 1892. Plymouth, Avery & Doten, book and job print., 1893.   348 p. 23 cm.   Copied by George Etheridge from various ms. volumes. Records of births, marriages and deaths not included. The bounds of Duxbury originally included what is now within the limits of Duxbury, Marshfield, Pembroke, Hanson, the Bridgewaters, and Brockton. 1-16584.   F74. D95 D9

DUXBURY. The 250th anniversary of the settlement of Duxbury ... 1887. Plymouth, Avery & Doten, 1887.   96 p. front., plates. 23½ cm. 6-1402.   F74. D95D92

DUXBURY, Vital records of, to the year 1850. Boston, Pub. by the New England historic genealogical soc. ... 1911.   446 p. 23½ cm. 13-33066.   F74. D95D95

DUXBURY, ancient and modern; a sketch, with map and key, by Henry A. Fish ... (Binghamton, N.Y., 1924)   17 p. fold. map. 23 cm. 24-15991.   F74. D93F 5

DUXBURY. The graves of Myles Standish and other pilgrims. By Rev. E. J. Huiginn. Boonville, N.Y., Herald and tourist steam print., 1892.   35 p. incl. map. 23 cm. 2-13196.   F74. D95 H8

— rev. and enl., by E. J. V. Huiginn. Beverly, Mass., The author, 1914.   4, (13) - 218 p. illus. (map) plates, port. 20½ cm.   Enlarged from a pamphlet having the same title, pub. in 1892. 15-1844.   F74. D95H82

DUXBURY. The story of Duxbury, 1637 - 1937, ed. E. Waldo Long. Duxbury, Mass., The Duxbury tercentenary committee (1937)   xiv, 237 p. incl. front., plates, ports., maps, facsims. 23½ cm. 37-20743.
F74. D95 L7

DUXBURY. The pilgrim town of Duxbury. Plymouth, Mass., A. S. Burbank (1900)   24 p. illus. obl. 12º. Nov. 1, 1900-232.   F74. D95 P6

DUXBURY. Pilgrim John Alden's progress; archeological excavations in Duxbury (by) Roland Wells Robbins with Evan Jones. Plymouth, Mass., Pilgrim Society, 1969.   63 p. illus. 23 cm.
F74. D95 R6

DUXBURY, History of the town of, with genealogical registers. By Justin Winsor ... Boston, Crosby

MASSACHUSETTS 215

& Nichols, 1849.   viii, (9) - 360 p. front. (port.) 23½ cm.   Genealogical register: p. 211-347. 1-11357.   F74. D95 W7

— Boston, Reprinted by Goodspeed's Book Shop, 1970.   F74. D95 W7 1970

DUXBURY. The Mayflower town. An address delivered at the 250th anniversary of the incorporation of the town of Duxbury ... 1887. By Justin Winsor. Cambridge, (Mass.) J. Wilson, 1887. 35 p. 24½ cm. 2-19338.   F74. D95W73

EAST ATTLEBOROUGH. Remarks and documents concerning the location of the Boston and Providence rail-road through the burying ground in East Attleborough. To which are added, the statutes for the protection of the sepulchres of the dead .... By a freeman of Massachusetts. (John Daggett) Boston, Print. Light and Horton, 1834. 28 p. 24 cm. 15-2157.   F74. E16 D2

EAST BRIDGEWATER. The Mitchell, Bryant and Orr families, and sketches of the last two hundred and seventy-four years; by Seth Bryant. Boston, 1894. 32 p. front. (port.) 18½ cm. 3-17340.
   F74. E18 B9

EAST BRIDGEWATER. Old and new Joppa, and other historical sketches. By Seth Bryant. Lynn, Mass., L. C. Parker, print., 1895. 24 p. front. (port.) 18½ cm. Joppa, or Jaffa, in Syria, and the village of Elmwood, formerly called Joppa, in the town of East Bridgewater. 9-253.   F74. E18B92

EAST BRIDGEWATER, Vital records of, to the year 1850. Boston, Pub. by the New England historic genealogical soc., 1917. 406 p. 23½ cm. 17-25002.   E74. E18E18

EASTHAM. ... "Hoppy" Mayo; a hero of Old Eastham, by Michael Fitzgerald. Yarmouthport, Mass., C. W. Swift, 1911. 2 l. 25½ cm. (Library of Cape Cod history & genealogy no. 94) 12-39461.
   E74. E18 F5

EAST BRIDGEWATER, The history of. By Paul John Rich. East Bridgewater, Mass., A. Baggia Press (19 -) 28 p. illus. 22 cm. Includes bibliographical references. 72-181679 MARC.   F74. E18 R5

EAST CARVER. The Well Sweep. By Betsy Thankful Moore. Silver Lake P. O., Mass., J. W. McCue, 1950. 95 p. illus. 20 cm. 50-9280.   F74. E19 M7

EASTHAM, Historical sketch of the town of. By Heman Doane. Presented to the town July 4th, 1876 ... (Copy of an original manuscript ... in the Library of Congress...) (Photostat)   F74. E2 D7 or 71

EASTHAM. Nauset on Cape Cod; a history of Eastham. Compiled by Alice A. Lowe. (Falmouth, Mass., Print. Rendall Print. Co., 1968) 155 p. illus. 24 cm.   F74. E2 L6

EASTHAM and Orleans historical papers, by Josiah Paine ... Yarmouthport, Mass., C. W. Swift, 1914. 29 p. 28 cm. (Library of Cape Cod history & genealogy, no. 55) 17-6650.   F74. E2 P14

EASTHAM. ... Founders' day edition, Aug. 26, 1916, of the early settlers of Eastham, containing sketches of all early settlers of Eastham, by Josiah Paine ... Yarmouthport, Mass., C. W. Swift, 1916. 2 v. 24½ cm. (Library of Cape Cod history & genealogy. no. 32-33) 17-20836.   F74. E2 P15

EASTHAM. A comprehensive history, ecclesiastical and civil, of Eastham, Wellfleet and Orleans, county of Barnstable, from 1644 to 1844. By Rev. Enoch Pratt ... Yarmouth, W. S. Fisher, 1844. viii, 180 p. 22½ cm. The North parish of Eastham was incorporated as the town of Wellfleet in 1763, and the South parish as Orleans in 1797. 1-11358.   F74. E2 P9

EASTHAM, 1651 - 1951: Eastham's three centuries (by) Donald G. Trayser. Nauset on Cape Cod (by) Alice Alberta Lowe. Introd. (by) Henry Beston. Eastham, Eastham Tercentenary Committee, 1951. xii, 183 p. illus., ports., maps. 24 cm. Bibliography: p. 107 - 108. 51-8084.   F74. E2 T7

EASTHAMPTON. Report of the centennial celebration at Easthampton, ... 1885. Easthampton, L. E. Torrey, 1885. 2, 138 p. front., illus. 23 cm. 10-3142.   F74. E22E13

EASTHAMPTON. Historical address delivered at the centennial celebration, in Easthampton, Mass., ... 1876. By Rev. Payson W. Lyman. Springfield, Mass., C. W. Bryan, print., 1877. viii, 85 p. 24 cm. 1-11359.
F74.E22 L9

EASTHAMPTON, History of; its settlement and growth; its material, educational, and religious interests, tog. with a genealogical record of its original families. By Payson W. Lyman. Northampton (Mass.) Trumbull & Gere, 1866. 1 , iv, (5) - 192, 2 p. 19½ cm. "Genealogical register": p. (141) - 192. 1-11360.
F74.E22L95

EASTHAMPTON, Historical sketch of ... By Luther Wright ... Northampton, Print. the Gazette office, 1852. 32 p. 23 cm. 12-14303.
F74.E22 W9

EASTON directory, The; includes the villages of Easton, Easton Centre, Eastondale, Furnace Village, North Easton and South Easton ... Providence, R. I., C. DeWitt White co. v. map. 24 cm. 11-19416.
Directories

EASTON, History of the town of. By William L. Chaffin. Cambridge, J. Wilson, 1886. xviii, 838 p. front., plates, ports., 4 maps (1 fold.) 24 cm. 1-11361.
F74. E3 C4

EASTON. Exercises held at the dedication of the soldiers' monument, Memorial day, 1882. 1 v.
F74. E3 E14

EDGARTOWN, Vital records of, to the year 1850. Boston, Pub. by the New England historic genealogical soc., 1906. 276 p. 23½ cm. 6-6460.
F74. E4 E4

EDGARTOWN. An historical discourse delivered in the Congregational meeting-house ... 1878, by Rev. John G. Hall. Boston, Beacon press, T. Todd, print., 1878. 19 p. 19½ cm. Cover title: The Mayhew church. 8-6915.
F74. E4 H2

ENFIELD. Quabbin; the story of a small town with outlooks upon Puritan life, by Francis H. Underwood ... Boston, Lee and Shepard, 1893. 2, vii - viii, 375 p. front. (port.) plates. 20 cm. 8-32684 Rev.
F74. E5 U5

ESSEX directory, The ... v.1 - 1931/32 - Beverly, Mass., Crowley & Lunt, 1931 - v. fold. maps. 24½ cm. 32-15142.
Directories

ESSEX. History of the town of Essex from 1634 to 1700. By Robert Crowell ... Boston, C. C. P. Moody, print., 1853. 166, 3 p. front., illus., fold. map. 19½ cm. 1-11362.
F74. E7 C9

ESSEX. History of the town of Essex, from 1634 to 1868, by the late Rev. Robert Crowell ... With sketches of the soldiers in the war of the rebellion, by Hon. David Choate. Essex, Pub. by the town; Springfield, Mass., Press of S. Bowles, 1868. xx, (21) - 488 p. 24 cm. The Second or Chebacco parish of Ipswich, incorporated as the town of Essex, 1819. Records of marriages and deaths 1790 - 1832: p. (454) - 474. 1-11363.
F74. E7 C91

ESSEX, Vital records of, to the end of the year 1849. Salem, Mass., The Essex institute, 1908. 86 p. 23 cm. 8-13333.
F74. E7 E6

ESSEX. Two centuries of church history; celebration of the 200th anniversary of the organization of the Congregational church & parish in Essex ... 1883. Salem, J. H. Choates, print., 1884. 214 p. front. 22½ cm. 6-38873.
F74. E7 E7

ESSEX. 150 years a town; a running account of life in the town of Essex since incorporation in 1819. Compiled and written by Leslie Harris at the request of the Essex Sesquicentennial Committee. (Manchester, Mass., Print. the Cricket Press) 1969. 94 p. 24 cm.
F74. E 7 H 3

ESSEX. Frame-up: The story of Essex, its shipyards and its people. By Dana A. Story. Barre, Mass., Barre Pub., 1964. xiii, 128 p. 24 cm. 64-14907.
F74. E7 S8

EVERETT directory, The, (1899) - 1908 (v. 19) - 24. The Henry M. Meek pub. co. (1899) - 1910. 5 v. fold. plans. 24cm. Apr. 13, 99-45.
Directories

MASSACHUSETTS 217

EVERETT. Polk's Everett city directory ...   Salem, Mass., R. L. Polk, 18 -   - 19 -
v. fold. maps.   24 cm.   99-1113 Rev.   Directories

EVERETT souvenir. 1870 - 1893. (Everett, Mass.) Everett souvenir co. (1893)   136 p. illus. (incl.
ports., plans, facsims.)   33½ x 25½ cm.   1-16732.   F74. E9 E9

FAIRHAVEN improvement association. ... Historical sketch, 1882-1903; by-laws & officers.
Fairhaven, Mass. (Printed at the Star office) 1903.   (10) p. front., plates. 17½ x 10 cm. 8-31945.   F74. F1 F2

FAIRHAVEN old home week association. A brief history of the town of Fairhaven, prepared in connection with the celebration of old home week, ... 1903, by James L. Gillingham and others. (New Bedford, Mass., Standard print, 1903)   100 p.   front., plates.   23 cm.   7-41342.   F74. F1 F3

... FAIRHAVEN. Compiled and written by members of the Federal writers' project of the Works progress administration in Massachusetts. Sponsored by the Board of selectmen of Fairhaven. (Fairhaven? Mass.) 1939.   3; 60 p.   illus. (map) plates, port.   19½ cm.   (American guide series)   39-29348.
F74. F1 F45

FAIRHAVEN. Old-time Fairhaven, erstwhile Eastern New Bedford. New Bedford, Mass., Reynolds Print., 1947-54.   3 v.   illus.   24 cm.   48-12056 rev.*   F74. F1 H3

FAIRHAVEN; a descriptive and historical sketch ... Illus. by Morton M. Snow. Boston, Franklin engr. co., 1896.   53, (8) p.   illus.   obl. 16°.   1-11364-M1.   F74. F1 J9

FAIRHAVEN. Dedication of the memorial monument to Henry Huttleston Rogers, ... 1912 ....
Fairhaven, Mass., The Millicent library (1912)   20 p.   front., pl.   21½ cm.   17-19195.   F74. F1 M6

FAIRHAVEN. The presentation of a Samurai sword, the gift of Doctor Tolchiro Nakahama, of Tokio, Japan, to the town of Fairhaven, by Viscount Kikujiro Ishii, Japanese ambassador to the U. S. ... 1918. Fairhaven, Mass., The Millicent library, 1918.   47 p. incl. front. illus. (ports.) pl. 22 cm.   The sword was presented to the town by Dr. Nakahama in commemoration of the rescue of his father ... by Capt. Wm. H. Whitfield of Fairhaven. 18-22468.
F74. F1 P9

FAIRHAVEN. ... Fifty years on the Fairhaven school board, by Job C. Tripp. The town of Fairhaven in four wars, by George H. Tripp ... (New Bedford, 1904?)   15 p. 26 cm. (Old Dartmouth historical sketches no. 6)   17-16967.   F74. F1 T83

FAIRHAVEN. ... The old men of Fairhaven (by) Job C. Tripp ... (New Bedford, 1909?)   10 p. incl. port.   26 cm.   (Old Dartmouth historical sketches, no. 27)   17-16968.   F74. F1 T85

FALL RIVER directory ... 1853 - 19   No. 1 -   Boston, Mass., Sampson & Murdock co.,
1853 - 19   v.   fronts. (fold. maps) 15½ x 24 cm.   99-128 Rev.   Directories

— Fall River directory supplement, containing business directory ... (1904) (Boston) Sampson & Murdock, 1904.   p. 1001 - 1096.   24 cm.   99-128 Rev.   Directories

FALL RIVER directory ... 1853 - 19   No. 1 -   Boston, Mass., Sampson & Murdock co.,
1853 - 19 -   v.   fronts. (fold. maps) 15½ x 24 cm.   99-128 Rev.   Directories

FALL RIVER. Les Canadiens français de Fall River. Notes historiques par H. A. Dubuque ...
Fall River, H. Boisseau, 1883.   21 p.   21 cm.   2-24897.   F74. F2 D8

FALL RIVER Indian reservation. By Hugo A. Dubuque ... Fall River, Mass., 1907.   iii, (3) - 100 p.
pl.   27 cm.   7-17106.   F74. F2 D9

FALL RIVER. Le guide canadien-francais (ou, Almanach des addresses) de Fall River, et notes historiques sur les Canadiens de Fall River. Par H. A. Dubuque. 1. ed. .... Fall River, Mass., E. U., E. F. Lamoureux, 1888.   (5) - 263 p.   20 cm.   8-16036.   F74. F2 D92

FALL RIVER, A centennial history of: comprising a record of its corporate progress from 1656 to

447

1876, with sketches of its manufacturing industries, local and general characteristics, etc., etc. Prepared under the direction of a committee of the city government, by Henry H. Earl. New York, Atlantic pub. and engr. co., 1877.   4, 252 p.   front., plates, ports., fold. map. col. plan.   30 ½ cm.   1-11365.

F74. F2 E11

FALL RIVER and its industries: an historical and statistical record of village, town, and city, from the date of the original charter of the freemen's purchase in 1656 to the present time. With valuable statistical tables, family genealogies, etc., illus. by views and portraits on steel. By Frederick Peck and others. New York, Atlantic pub. and engr. co.; Fall River, Mass., B. Earl, 1877.   4; 280 p. incl. geneal. tables.   front., plates, ports., fold. map, col. plan.   30 cm.   The same as Earl's Centennial history of Fall River. except that "Genealogies of the Anthony, Borden, Chase, Davol and Durfee families" are here substituted for p. 220-248 of that work. 1-12353* Cancel.

F74. F2E112

FALL RIVER: its rise and progress. 1803 - 1873. With valuable statistical tables, from official sources. By Henry Hilliard Earl. Fall River, Mass., B. Earl, 1873.   25, (4), 26-32 p.   13 cm.   1-11366 Rev.

F74. F2 E12

— 2d ed.   Rev. and enl.   Fall River, Mass., B. Earl, 1874.   48 p.   13 cm.   1-11367 Rev.

F74. F2 E13

— 3d ed.   Rev. and enl.   Fall River, Mass., B. Earl, 1875.   60 p.   13 cm.   1-11368 Rev.

F74. F2 E14

— 4th ed.   Rev. and enl.   Fall River, Mass., B. Earl, 1876.   64 p.   13 cm.   1-11369 Rev.   F74. F2 E15

— 5th ed.   Rev. and enl.   Fall River, Mass., B. Earl, 1878.   48 p.   13 cm.   1-11370.   F74. F2 E16

— 6th ed.   Rev. and enl.   Fall River, Mass., B. Earl, 1879.   40 p.   13 cm.   1-11371.   F74. F2 E17

— 7th ed.   Carefully revised.   Fall River, Mass., B. Earl, 1880.   40 p.   24º.   1-11372 Rev.

F74. F2 E18

— 8th ed.   Carefully revised.   Fall River, Mass., B. Earl, 1882.   48 p.   13 ½ cm.   1-11373 Rev.

F74. F2 E19

— 9th ed.   Carefully revised.   Fall River, Mass., B. Earl, 1884.   48 p.   13 ½ cm.   1-11374 Rev.

F74. F2 E20

— 10th ed.   Carefully revised.   Fall River, Mass., Earl & Bamford, 1886.   48 p.   13 ½ cm.   Imperfect: p. 3-46 wanting.   1-11375 Rev.

F74. F2 E21

— 11th ed.   Carefully revised.   Fall River, Mass., Earl & Bamford, 1888.   56 p.   13 ½ cm.   1-11376.

F74. F2 E22

— 12th ed.   Carefully revised.   Fall River, Mass., G. E. Bamford, 1890.   56 p.   14 ½ cm.   1-11377.

F74. F2 E23

— 13th ed.   Carefully revised.   Fall River, Mass. G.E. Bamford, 1892.   56 p.   16º.   1-11378-M1.

F74. F2 E24

— 15th ed.   Carefully revised.   Fall River, Mass., G. E. Bamford, 1896.   59 p.   15 x 9 cm. 1-11379 Rev.

F74. F2 E26

FALL RIVER in history, a brief presentation, in word and picture, of some of the historical objects and places in and about Fall River. Compiled by the Tercentenary committee .... Fall River, Mass., The Munroe press, 1930.   27 p. illus.   19 ½ cm.   "Some books about Fall River:: p. 2.   CA30-1373 Unrev.

F74. F2 F16

FALL RIVER historical society, ... Proceedings of the ... 1921/26 -   Fall River, Mass., The Society, 1927 -   v. front., pl.   22 ½ cm.   31-13291.

F74. F2 F18

MASSACHUSETTS

FALL RIVER, a publication of personal points pertaining to a city of opportunity. (Fall River) Fall River trade and industry assoc. (1911?)   164 p. illus. 19 cm. 20-9605.   F74. F2 F19

FALL RIVER, an historical sketch of her industry, progress, and improvement, comp. from authentic and official sources. Fall River, Mass., W. W. Armstrong, 1870.   144 p. front. (pl.) 16° 1-11280-M1.   F74. F2 F2

FALL RIVER, History of; prepared under the direction of a committee of prominent citizens ... by Henry M. Fenner and others ... New York, F. T. Smiley pub. co., 1906.   3; 264 p. front., illus., ports. 28 cm. 6-38538.   F74. F2 F3

FALL RIVER, History of, comp. for the Cotton centennial by Henry M. Fenner ... (Fall River merchants assoc., 1911.   2; 106 p. front., illus. (map) 23½ cm. 11-16292.   F74. F2 F32

FALL RIVER, History of, with notices of Freetown and Tiverton, as pub. in 1841, by Rev. Orin Fowler, tog. with a sketch of the life of Rev. Orin Fowler, etc. etc. Fall River, Almy & Milne, print., 1862.   100 p. fold. geneal. tab. 22½ cm. 1-11381.   F74. F2 F7

FALL RIVER. Massachusetts tercentenary 1630 - 1930. The pageant of Quequechan, by Ethel K. Fuller ... 1930. (Fall River, Dover press, 1930)   48 p. 23 cm. Quequechan is the Indian name for Fall River.   CA 30-1374 Unrev.   F74. F2 F96

FALL RIVER. The Fall River conflagration, ... 1928 ... Boston, Mass., National fire protection assoc. (1928)   39 p. illus. 23 cm. 29-6054.   F74. F2 N3

FALL RIVER, an authentic narrative. By the author of "Tales, national, revolutionary," etc. ... (Mrs. Catherine R. (Arnold) Williams) Boston, Lilly, Wait & co.; Providence, Marshall, Brown & co., 1833.   198 p. front. 16½ cm. An account of the circumstances leading to the trial of the Rev. Ephraim K. Avery. for the murder of Sarah M. Cornell in Fall River in Dec., 1832. 6-2163.   F74. F2W69

— 1834.   viii, (9) - 198 p. incl. front. 16 cm. 1-19742.   F74. F2 W7

FALMOUTH. The celebration of the 200th anniversary of the incorporation of the town of Falmouth, Mass. ... 1886. Falmouth, Per order of the town, 1887.   vi, (7) - 153 p. 21½ cm. 10-6774.   F74. F3 F2

FALMOUTH. ... Old burying ground records. Falmouth, Falmouth enterprise, 1903-4.   19 l. 28½ x 23 cm. Falmouth historical society. 7-3210.   F74. F3 F3

FALMOUTH. The hurricane in pictures, 1944, Falmouth, cape Cod. (Falmouth, Mass., 1944)   (48) p. 15 x 23 cm. "Photographs by Edwin Gray and Earl C. Holley." 45-152.   F74. F3 G7

FALMOUTH. Three lectures on the early history of ... Falmouth, covering the time from its settlement to 1812. ... by Charles W. Henkins ... Falmouth, Mass., L. F. Clarke, print., 1889.   3, 113, (11) p. 20½ cm. "Preface" signed: Edward H. Jenkins. 1-1789.   F74. F3 J5

FALMOUTH. Address of Hon. Daniel Needham, at the dedication of the town hall at Falmouth ... 1881. ... Ayer, Mass., Office of the Public spirit (1881)   24 p. 12°. 1-16192-M1.   F74. F3 N3

FALMOUTH on Cape Cod, picturesque, romantic, historic, by the Walton staff. Boston, Mass., P. Walton, 1925.   47 p. incl. front., illus. 29 cm. "First edition." 25-11881.   F74. F3 W2

FALMOUTH. Suckanesset; wherein may be read a history of Falmouth, by Theodate Geoffrey (pseud. for Dorothy (Godfrey) Wayman) (Falmouth, Print. Falmouth pub. co., 1930)   5, 168 p. front., illus., plates, ports. 23 cm. 30-15937 Rev.   F74. F3 W3

FITCHBURG almanac, directory & advertiser, for 1848. (v.   Fitchburg, S. & C. Shepley, 18 -   v. 13½ cm. 16-25387.   Directories

449

FITCHBURG directory ... including Leominster ... (no. 1) -   (1871 -   (New Haven) The Price
& Lee co. (1871) - 1908.   31 v.   fold. plans.   24 cm.   1-30576 Rev.   Directories

FITCHBURG.   Polk's Fitchburg suburban Massachusetts directory for the towns of Ashburnham, Ashby,
Hubbardston, Lunenburg, Princeton, Sterling, Templeton, Westminster ... 1926/27 -   Boston,
and New York, R. L. Polk, 1926 -   v.   23½ cm.   26-10809.   Directories

FITCHBURG.   ... Anthony's standard business directory, guide and reference book for Fitchburg,
Leominster and vicinity ... Meriden, Conn., Anthony pub. co., 1892.   104 p.   22 cm.   8-11875.
                                                                                      Directories

FITCHBURG.   Leading business men of Fitchburg and vicinity; embracing also Clinton, Ayer, Gardner, Leominster, Winchendon, Ashburnham, and Baldwinville ... By George Fox Bacon ...   Boston,
Mercantile pub. co., 1890.   159 p.   illus.   25 cm.   4-20147.   F74. F5 B2

FITCHBURG.   Boutwell's ready reference book and pocket memoranda for Fitchburg.   Leominster,
Boutwell & co., 1888.   56 p.   24°.   1-16191-M1.   F74. F5 B7

FITCHBURG.   Fireside legends.   Incidents, anecdotes, reminiscences, etc. connected with the early
history of Fitchburg and vicinity.   By William Andrew Emerson.   (Fitchburg, W. A. Emerson, 1890)
207 p.   front., illus.   13 x 18½ cm.   1-11383.   F74. F5 E5

FITCHBURG, past and present, by William A. Emerson ... Fitchburg, Press of Blanchard & Brown,
1887.   (xi) - xiv, (15) - 312 p.   front., illus., plates, ports.   23 cm.   "Biographical": p.(280)-289.   1-11384.   F74. F5 E6

FITCHBURG.   The old records of the town of Fitchburgh ... Compiled by Walter A. Davis, city clerk.
Fitchburg (Sentinel print.) 1898 - 1913.   8 v.   fronts (v.1, 3-5) ports., facsims.   24½ cm.   No more pub?   1-2606 Rev.

                                                                              F74. F5 F5

FITCHBURG daily sentinel ... 20th century souvenir number.   Illustrated for the Sentinel print. co.
by Gillespie & Donlan.   Fitchburg, Mass., 1892.   49 p.   illus.   44 cm.   3-9294.   F74. F5 F54

FITCHBURG.   Report of the Soldiers' monument committee, of the city of Fitchburg.   Fitchburg,
Print, at the office of H. F. Piper, 1874.   36 p.   23 cm.   1-28311.   F74. F5 F57

FITCHBURG.   Proceedings of the Fitchburg historical soc. and papers relating to the history of the
town, read by some of the members.   v. 1 - 4.   Fitchburg, Mass., The Historical society, 1895 -
1908.   4 v.   ports., map.   23½ cm.   7-18608.   F74. F5 F6

FITCHBURG soldiers of the revolution.   A paper read at a meeting of the society ....   By James F.
D. Garfield.   Fitchburg (Mass.) Sentinel print., print., 1908.   63 p.   22½ cm.   Fitchburg historical society.
Pub. also in Proceedings and papers of the society, vol. iv, p. (172) - 232.   10-2134.   F74. F5 G2

FITCHBURG'S response to the Lexington alarm ... 1775.   By J. F. D. Garfield.   Fitchburg, Sentinel
print., 1895.   24 p.   23½ cm.   Repr. from Proceedings of Fitchburg historical soc. v.1.   18-3915.   F74. F5 G3

FITCHBURG.   ... History of the meeting house in Fitchburg commonly known as "the Lord's barn" by
Rev. G. H Hardy ... Fitchburg, Sentinel print., 1910.   17 p.   19 cm.   Fitchburg historical soc.   15-23304.
                                                                              F74. F5 H26

FITCHBURG.   The city and the river.   Photos. by W. Frederick Lucas.   Drawings by Carolyn C.
Winslow.   (Fitchburg, Mass.) Fitchburg Historical Soc. 1971 -   v.   illus.   28 cm.   Bibliography:
v. 1, p. 429 - 440.   75-31689 MARC.   F74. F5 K5

FITCHBURG.   Address, at the centennial celebration, of the town of Fitchburg ... 1864.   By Charles
H. B. Snow.   Fitchburg, Print. at the office of Piper & Boutelle, 1876.   36; 55 p.   22 cm.   7-27735.
                                                                              F74. F5 S6

MASSACHUSETTS

FITCHBURG, History of the town of. Comprising also a history of Lunenburg, from its first settlement to the year, 1764 ... by Rufus C. Torrey. Fitchburg (J. Garfield, print.) 1836.   iv, (5) - 111 p. 24 cm.   10-8760.   F74. F5 T5

— Fitchburg, The Fitchburg centennial committee, 1865.   iv, (5) - 128 p.   24 cm.   1-11382.   F74. F5 T6

FITCHBURG. Town talk ... v. 1   Fitchburg, 1890 -   v. illus. 30 cm.   weekly.   F74. F5 T7
"Edited by the 'Sidewalk sifter'."   CA 28-189 unrev.

FITCHBURG in the war of the rebellion. By Henry A. Willis ... Fitchburg (Mass.) S. Shepley, 1866. 282 p. incl. tables. 24 cm.   1-16190 Additions.   F74. F5 W7

FLORENCE. Memorial. Alfred Theodore Lilly. Biographical sketch. Funeral service. Obituary notices. Dedication of the Lilly library building ... Florence, Mass., Bryant & brother, print., 1890. 126p.   front. (port.)   4 pl.   25½ cm.   11-34219.   F74. F6 M5

FLORENCE, The history of. Including a complete account of the Northampton association of education and industry ... Ed. by Charles A. Sheffield. Florence, Mass., The editor, 1895.   2, (3) - 250 p. illus. (incl. ports., maps, facsims.)   25½ cm.   Part 2 includes misc. articles and biographical sketches. 1-11385 Rev.   F74. F6 S5

FOXBOROUGH'S official centennial record, ... 1878. Pub. by authority of the town centennial committee. (Boston, Press of Rockwell & Churchill) 1879.   248, (4) p. plates, port. 24 cm.   1-11386 Additions.   F74. F7 F7

FOXBOROUGH, Vital record of, to the year 1850. Boston, The New England historic genealogical society ... 1911.   249 p.   23½ cm.   11-7320.   F74. F7 F8

FOXBOROUGH. This was Foxborough! by Mr. and Mrs. Clifford W. Lane. Foxborough, Mass., REA-Craft Press, 1966.   viii, 277 p.   illus.   F74. F7 L3

FRAMINGHAM to Framlingham; a greeting across the seas in memory of Nicholas Danforth and his descendants, by John M. Merriam. Boston, Mass., Priv. print, for the author, 1931.   2; 24 p. front., illus. (incl. facsims.) ports. 23½ cm.   31-17041.   F74. F8 M
    CS71. D18 1931

FRAMINGHAM, Resident and business directory of. South Framingham, Mass., Lakeview press, 1911   1 v.   23½ cm.   11-1874.   Directories

FRAMINGHAM, Resident and business directory of, 1912 -   (v.1 -   Boston, Union pub. co., 1912 -   v. diagrs. 24 cm.   12-17532.   Directories

FRAMINGHAM directory ... containing also the towns of Ashland, Holliston, Hopkinton, Sherborn, Southborough, Sudbury and the village of Cochituate ... Burlington, Vt., Florence B. Chase, 19   v.   23½ cm.   CA 26-767 Unrev.   Directories

FRAMINGHAM, A sketch of the history of, supposed to have been written by ? (William Ballard) while in prison, aided in the obtaining of documents, by his brothers Nemo and Aucun; authors of A residence in the South; and, A tour through the West ... Boston, Printed for the publisher, 1827. iv, (5) - 70 p.   21 cm.   10-31031.   F74. F8 B1

FRAMINGHAM, A history of, including the Plantation, from 1640 to the present time, with an appendix, containing a notice of the inhabitants of Framingham before 1800, with genealogical sketches: by William Barry ... Boston, J. Munroe, 1847.   iv, 456 p. 22½ cm.   "Genealogical register": p. (165) - 454. 1-11387.   F74. F8 B2

FRAMINGHAM, ... Town of, past and present, progress and prosperity; souvenir, 1906. J. H. Burgess, ed. ... (Framingham) Lakeview press (1906)   32 p. illus. 30½ cm. x 23 cm. At head of title: South Framingham, Framingham Centre, Saxonville. 19-10893.   F74. F8 B9

LOCAL HISTORIES IN THE LIBRARY OF CONGRESS

FRAMINGHAM. Memorial of the bi-centennial celebration of the incorporation of the town of Framingham ... 1900 ... South Framingham, Mass., Printery of G. L. Clapp (1900?) xvi, 252 p. plates, ports., fold. map, facsims. 25½ cm. 10-17778. F74. F8 F8

FRAMINGHAM, Vital records of, to the year 1850. Comp. by Thomas W. Baldwin ... Boston, (Wright & Potter print.) 1911. 474 p. 23 cm. L. of C. copy replaced by microfilm. 13-5095. F74. F8 F82
Microfilm 19805 F

FRAMINGHAM centre illustrated. Fourteen views. New York, Lithotype print (18 -)
3 pt. in 1 v. 38 phot. 18 x 27 cm. Includes also South Framingham and Saxonville. 19-10724. F74. F8 F9

FRAMINGHAM. Five Framingham heroes of the American revolution; a paper read upon invitation of the Framingham chapter of the D. A. R. ... by John M. Merriam ... 1925. Framingham, Mass., Lakeview press, 1925. 22 p. illus., pl., port., fold. facsim. 23½ cm. Includes biographical sketches of Micajah Gleason, Jonathan Maynard, Thomas Nixon, Peter Salem and John Nixon. 28-18691. F74. F8 M5

FRAMINGHAM, Sketches of ... By John McKinstry Merriam. Boston, Bellman Pub. Co., 1950.
132 p. illus., fold. map. 23 cm. 51-21479. F74. F8 M56

FRAMINGHAM. 1700 - 1900. The story of a church for two centuries; a sermon at the First parish church ... 1900, by Calvin Stebbins. (Pub. by request) South Framingham, Mass., G. L. Clapp, print., 1900. 30 p. front. 23½ cm. 4-383. F74. F8 S8

FRAMINGHAM, History of, early known as Danforth's Farms, 1640 - 1880; with a genealogical register. By J. H. Temple ... Framingham, Pub. by the town, 1887. vii, 794 p. front., ports. 24 cm.
1-11388. F74. F8 T2

FRANKLIN, A history of the town of; from its settlement to the completion of its first century ... 1878; with genealogical notices of its earliest families, sketches of its professional men, and a report of the centennial celebration. By Mortimer Blake ... Franklin, Mass., Pub. by the committee of the town, 1879. 289 p. front., illus., plates, ports., map. 24 cm. 1-11389. F74. F9 B6

FRANKLIN. The record of births, marriages and deaths in the town of Franklin, from 1778 to 1872. Ed. by Orestes R. Doe, town clerk. Franklin, Mass., Print. at the office of the Franklin sentinel, 1898. vii, (9) - 232 p. 26 cm. 2-6244. F74. F9 F9
L. H. 7 G.

FRANKLIN and Wrentham, by Dr. J. C. Gallison ... Reprinted, 1904, with slight revision and additional pictures from an article in the New England magazine, Nov. 1899. Franklin (Mass.) Sentinel press, 1904. 28 p. illus. (incl. ports.) 25½ cm. In double columns. 4-33453. F74. F9 G16

FREETOWN marriage records (Bristol county) 1686 - 1844; compiled from the original records by Mrs. Mary Phillips Herbert ... Glendale, Calif., Privately pub. by Margaret P. Creer, 1934.
63 numb. l. 28 cm. Mimeographed. 35-32246. F74. F95 H45

FREETOWN, A history of the town of, with an account of the old home festival ,,. 1902. Fall River, Press of J. H. Franklin, 1902. 287 p. illus. (incl. ports., map) 25 cm. Made up of sketches by various local writers.
4-5281. F74. F95 H6

FREETOWN. Brief sketches of Freetown, Fall River, and Fairhaven. By Ebenezer Weaver Peirce ... Boston, Print. for the author, by D. Dudley, 1872. 25 p. front., port. 23½ cm. 1-11390. F74. F95 P3

GARDNER directory ... (v. 1. New Haven, Conn., The Price & Lee co., 1885 - 19
v. fold. maps. 24 cm. Volume numbers irregular. 1-25727 Rev. Directories

GARDNER. Favorite drives around Gardner ... Illustrated. From original photographs. From papers read before the Monday club and Gardner institue. By Charles D. Burrage. The original drawings by Charles H. Stratton. (Gardner, Mass.) Press of the Gardner news co. (1896)
2, 51 p. front., illus., fold. maps. sq 8°. 1-11391-M1. F74. G2 B8

MASSACHUSETTS

— (Gardner, Mass.) Press of the Gardner news co. (1897) vi, 65 p. front., illus., etc. 1-11392-M1 F74. G2 B9

GARDNER, ... Vital records of, to the end of the year 1849. Worcester, Mass., F. P. Rice, 1907.
136 p. 23½ cm. 7-16393. F74. G2 G2

GARDNER. The early Irish settlers in the town of Gardner, by Marie M. Gearan ... (Fitchburg, Mass., 1932) 73 p. front., illus. (facsim.) pl. 23½ cm. The paper entitled "Gardner's pioneer immigrant: the Irishman", ... is here published with added data. "References": p. (4) 32-35507. F74. G2 G4

GARDNER, History of, from its earliest settlement to 1860. By Lewis Glazier. Worcester, Print. C. Hamilton, 1860. vii, (9) - 163 p. 19½ cm. 1-11393. F74. G2 G5

GARDNER, History of the town of, from the incorporation ... 1785, to the present time. By Rev. Wm. D. Herrick ... Gardner, Mass., The Committee, 1878. xv, 535 p. front., plates, ports., fold. maps. 23½ cm. 1-11394. F74. G2 H5

GARDNER, History of, 1785 - 1967, by Esther Gilman Moore, assisted by Barbara H. Smith and others, (Gardner, Mass., Print. Hatton Print., 1967) 334 p. 24 cm. F74. G2 M6

GAY HEAD. (n. p., 18 -) 1 leaf. F74.G25 G2

GAY HEAD. Report of the commissioner appointed to complete the examination and determination of all questions of title to land, and of all boundary lines between the individual owners, at Gay Head, on the island of Martha's Vineyard .... Boston, Wright & Potter, state printers, 1871. 60 p. 23 cm.
Appendix: Census of inhabitants of Gay Head. 10-3163. F74.G25 M4

GEORGETOWN, A brief history of, 1638 - 1963. (Georgetown, Georgetown Historical Society) 1963.
38 p. 22 cm. F74. G3 F5

GEORGETOWN, Vital records of, to the end of the year 1849. Salem, Mass., The Essex institute, 1928. 90 p. 23 cm. 29-11474. F74.G3 G32

GEORGETOWN, Report of the fantastical celebration in, 1857. Haverhill, Printed at the Essex banner office, 1857. 14 p. 23½ cm. 10-5396. F74. G3 R4

GEORGETOWN. Souvenir of Old home week, Georgetown, Mass., July 25-28, 1909. Boston, Press of J. G. Allen, 1909. 31 p. illus. 21 cm. "The Spofford family": p. (5) - 10. 17-24562. F74. G3 S7

GILL, Vital records of, to the year 1850. Boston, Pub. by the New-England historic genealogical soc., 1904. 97 p. 23½ cm. 4-9200. F74. G4 G4

GLOUCESTER. Radford's Gloucester, Rockport and Essex directory for 1898 ... Boston, F. H. Radford (1898) 428 p. 24 cm. "A roll of honor. Gloucester's contribution to the U.S. navy during the Spanish-American war": p. (335) - 344. 98-1358 Rev. Directories

GLOUCESTER directory, The ... comprising also the town of Rockport ... 1869, 1870/71, 1873-1879, 1880/81 -   1896/97, 1899/1900, 1902, 1903 - 1919/20, 1922/23, 1925/26 - no. 1 -
Boston, Sampson & Murdock, 1868 - 19 - v. fold. maps. 24 cm. 2-724 (rev. '28) Directories

GLOUCESTER. Program for the dedication of the Legion memorial hall and the monument to the heroes of Gloucester, Captain Lester S. Wass post no. 3, American legion, Gloucester, Mass., July 4, 1921. (Gloucester? 1921) 28 p. illus. (incl. ports.) 28½ cm. 21-20783. F74. G5 A5

GLOUCESTER, History of the town of, including the town of Rockport. By John J. Babson. Gloucester (Mass.) Procter bros., 1860. xi, 610 p. illus., plates, fold. map. 23½ cm. "Early settlers": p. 46 - 186; "New settlers": p. 239 - 247. L.C. copy replaced by microfilm. F74.G5 B18
Microfilm 8874 F

— Notes and additions ... Part first: Early settlers. Gloucester, Mass., M.V.B. Perley, 1876.
2; 94 p. 24 cm. 1-11395 Rev. 2 F74. G5 B2

— Notes and additions ... Second series. By John J. Babson. With an appendix containing indexes to parts I and II. (Salem, Mass.) Salem press pub. and print. co., 1891. 187 p. 25 cm. Including reprint of two pamphlets forming parts II and III of "Notes and additions." 1-11395 Rev. 2.
 F74. G5 B3

GLOUCESTER and Cape Ann, a camera impression, by Samuel Chamberlain. New York, Hastings house (1938)   73 p. front., illus. 19 x 16 cm. 69 pages of illustrations. 38-17338.   F74. G5 C5

GLOUCESTER, The port of, by James B. Connolly, with etchings by Max Kuehne. New York, Doubleday, Doran, 1940.   ix p. 333 p. plates. 23½ cm. "First edition." 40-30613.   F74. G5 C7

GLOUCESTER sketch-book and souvenir, by Louis C. Elson. Gloucester, Mass., The Proctor bros. co., (1904)   3; 22 p. 25 pl. 15½ x 24 cm. 4-14393.   F74. G5 E4

GLOUCESTER. Along the Gloucester waterfront, compiled by Charles Woodbury Fifield, Jr. Photos. by C. W. Fifield, Jr. (Melrose? Mass., 1955)   69 p. illus. 26 cm. 55-30090.   F74. G5 F46

GLOUCESTER. The fishermen's own book, comprising the list of men and vessels lost from the port of Gloucester, Mass., from 1874 to ... 1882, and a table of losses from 1830, together with ... other interesting facts and incidents connected with this branch of maritime industry. Gloucester, Procter bros. (1882)   2, (iii) - iv, (5) - 274 p. illus., map. 23 cm. 8-8584.   F74. G5 F5

GLOUCESTER. The diary of the Rev. Daniel Fuller with his account of his family & other matters. Written at Gloucester ... ca. 1775 & ed. by his grandson, Daniel Fuller Appleton. New-York, Imprinted for private distribution at the De Vinne press, 1894.   49 p. front. (port.) pl. 25½ x 21 cm. 20-6189.   F74. G5 F9

GLOUCESTER. Eastern Point; a nautical, rustical, and social chronicle of Gloucester's outer shield and inner sanctum, 1606 - 1850, by Joseph E. Garland. Peterborough, N.H., Noone House (1971) xiv, 424 p. illus. 27 cm. Bibliography: p. 395 - 398. 70-153378 MARC.   F74. G5 G3

GLOUCESTER. Memorial of the celebration of the 250th anniversary of the incorporation of the town of Gloucester, Mass. Aug., 1892 ... Boston, Print. A. Mudge, 1901.   x, (3) - 369 p. front., plates, ports., facsims. 25 cm. 2-3377.   F74. G5 G4

GLOUCESTER. Official souvenir, 250th anniversary; 1642 - 1892. (Gloucester, Jeffery, print., 1892)   3 l. 6 pl., map. 12°. 1-11396-M1.   F74. G5 G5

GLOUCESTER, Vital records of, to the end of the year 1849 ... Topsfield, Mass., The Topsfield historical society, 1917 - 24.   3 v. 23½ cm. 17-21764 Rev. I. Births. - II. Marriages. - III. Deaths.   F74. G5 G58
 L. H. & G.

GLOUCESTER. (Gloucester Board of trade. Gloucester, 1909)   (48) p. illus., fold. pl. 17½ x 25½ cm. 9-27670.   F74. G5 G6

GLOUCESTER, by land and sea; the story of a New England seacoast town, by Charles Boardman Hawes, with drawings by Lester G. Hornby. Boston, Little, Brown, 1923.   xiv, 226 p. col. front., illus., plates. 23 cm. 23-10850.   F74. G5 H4

GLOUCESTER. An address, delivered ... 1807: before the field officers of the regiment, etc. etc. By the Rev. Thomas Jones. Salem: Print, Pool and Palfray, 1807.   8 p. 19 cm. 1-21395.
 F74. G5 J7
 Rare Book Coll.

GLOUCESTER. In the heart of Cape Ann; or, The story of Dogtown, by Charles E. Mann. With illus. by Catherine M. Follansbee. Gloucester, Mass., Procter bros, (1896)   71 p. illus., pl., map. 17½ x 12½ cm. Dogtown is the bame of a now deserted village in the town of Gloucester. 1-11397 Rev.   F74. G5 M2

— (1906?)   77, (1) 31 p. illus., pl., map. 17½ cm. 18-23433.   F74. G5 M22

GLOUCESTER. Beginnings of Dogtown; data from days before the village was deserted, by Charles E.

MASSACHUSETTS

Mann. Gloucester, Mass., The Procter bros., 1906. 31 p. front. (map) 17½ cm. (In his In the heart of Cape Ann, or, The story of Dogtown ... 1906?) 18-23432.
F74.G5 M22

GLOUCESTER. History of the town and city of Gloucester, Cape Ann. By James R. Pringle ... Gloucester, Mass., The author, 1892. 340 p. front., illus., plates, ports. 23½ cm. 5-1314.
F74. G5 P7

GLOUCESTER. The fishermen's memorial and record book, by George H. Procter. containing a list of vessels and their crews, lost from the port of Gloucester from the year 1830 to ... 1873 .... and other matters of interest to these toilers of the sea. Gloucester (Mass.) Procter bros., 1873. iv, 172 p. illus. 23½ cm. 9-10386.
F74. G5 P9

GLOUCESTER. The ocean; a sermon preached on Thanksgiving day, ... 1851, occasioned by the sad calamity which befel the American fishing fleet on the northern shore of Prince Edward's Island .... By Rev. Miles Sanford ... Boston, J. M. Hewes, print., 1851. 22 p. 24 cm. 24-13761.
F74. G5 S2

GLOUCESTER. Souvenir: Gloucester and vicinity. Gloucester, Mass., Procter bros., 1892. 20 pl. obl. 24º 1-11398-M1.
F74. G5 S7

GLOUCESTER, The story of, permanently settled 1623; an address prepared by Frederick W. Tibbetts ... 1916. (Gloucester, Clark the printer, 1917) 52 p. illus. 23 cm. 17-13926.
F74.G5 T55

GLOUCESTER. Trial of Marshall and Ross for barn-burning. A brief exposure of a systematic attempt to mislead the public mind, and create a false sympathy in behalf of convicted incendiaries. By "A looker-on in Vienna." (Gloucester? Mass.) 1859. 20 p. 22½ cm. 11-32559.
F74. G5 T8

GOSHEN, History of the town of, from its first settlement in 1761 to 1881. With family sketches. By Hiram Barrus. Boston, The author, 1881. 262 p. front., plates, ports. 22½ cm. 1-11399.
F74. G6 B2

GOSHEN. Centennial anniversary of the incorporation of the town of Goshen ... 1881. Including addresses, poems, letters, and other matters relating to the occasion. Reading (Mass.) Chronicle job print, 1881. 64 p. 21 cm. 1-11400.
F74. G6 G6

GRAFTON. An address delivered before the inhabitants of Grafton, on the first centennial anniversary of that town ... 1835. By William Brigham. Boston, Light & Horton, 1835. 40 p. 22½ cm. 1-11401 Rev.
F74. G7 B8

GRAFTON. Address delivered at the celebration of the 150th anniversary of the incorporation of the town of Grafton ... 1885. By Frank P. Goulding. Worcester, Press of C. Hamilton, 1886. 42 p. 24 cm. 4-6487.
F74. G7 G6

GRAFTON, ... Vital records of, to the end of the year 1849. Worcester, Mass., F. P. Rice, 1906. 377 p. 23½ cm. 6-22873.
F74. G7 G7

GRAFTON. Historical oration delivered by Rev. E. Frank Howe, at the centennial celebration held at Grafton ... 1876. Worcester, Press of C. Hamilton, 1878. 46 p. 25 x 15 cm. 1-11402.
F74. G7 H8

GRAFTON, History of, from its early settlement by the Indians in 1647 to the present time, 1879. Including the genealogies of seventy-nine of the older families. By Frederick Clifton Pierce ... Pub. by the author. Worcester, Press of C. Hamilton, 1879. xiv, (15)-623 p. front., illus., plates, ports., fold. map. 24 cm. 1-11403 Cancel.
F74. G7 P6

GRANBY bicentennial, 1768 - 1968; incorporated June 11, 1768. Granby, Mass., Pub. by the town, 1968. 283 p. illus. 24 cm.
F74.G74 G7

GRANVILLE, Vital records of, to the year 1850. Boston, Pub. by the New England historic genealogical soc. ... 1914. 236 p. 23½ cm. 14-9912.
F74.G75 G6
L. H. & G.

226　　　　　　　　　　　LOCAL HISTORIES IN THE LIBRARY OF CONGRESS

GRANVILLE jubilee. The, celebrated at Granville ... 1845.　Springfield, Print. H. S. Taylor, 1845.
139 p.　front. (port.)　16 cm.　1-11404.　"Historical discourse. By Rev. Doct. Cooley": p. (26) - 92.　　　F74.G75 G7

GRANVILLE, History of.　By Albion Benjamin Wilson.　(Hartford) 1954.　xiv, 381 p., port., fold. map,
facsim.　24 cm.　54-22956.　　　F74.G75 W5

GREAT BARRINGTON directory, 18 -　　New Haven, Conn., The Price & Lee co., (18 -
　v.　24 cm.　39M4090T.　　　Directories

GREAT BARRINGTON directory ... including the town of Sheffield.　Pittsfield, Mass., Press of Gorman & Daly co.　v.　24½ cm.　1-30586 Rev.　　　Directories

GREAT BARRINGTON.　Advantages of retrospection.　A commemorative discourse .... By Rev. Calvin Durfee ... Boston, Press of T. R. Marvin, 1866.　48 p.　23½ cm.　　　F74. G8 D9

GREAT BARRINGTON.　Town diary, 1676 - 1999, and souvenir program ... Pub. on the 150th anniversary of the incorporation of the town.　Great Barrington, Berkshire courier print (1911)
(54) p.　illus.　15 x 23 cm.　12-2270.　　　F74.G8 G63

GREAT BARRINGTON, Vital records of, to the year 1850.　Boston, Pub. by the New-England historic genealogical
soc ... 1904.　　　89 p.　23½ cm.　4-9199.　　　F74.G8 G65
　　　　　　　　　　　　　　　　　　　　　　　　　　　　L.H. & G.

GREAT BARRINGTON.　St. James' church records.　Great Barrington, L. Hasbruck von Sahler.
(Great Barrington, 1903)　(70) p.　23½ cm.　4-27576.
　　　　　　　　　　　　　　　　　　　　　　　　　　　　F74.G8 G75

GREAT BARRINGTON.　Glimpses of the gem of the Berkshire hills.　Great Barrington, A. Collins
(1892)　16 p.　illus.　obl. 24º.　1-11405-M1.　　　F74. G8 G8

GREAT BARRINGTON, History of, by Charles J. Taylor ... Great Barrington, Mass., C. W. Bryan,
1882.　xiv, 516 p.　fold. map.　20 cm.　1-11406.　　　F74. G8 T2

GREAT BARRINGTON, ... History of, by Charles J. Taylor, 1676 - 1882, annotated by Ralph Wainwright Pope and others.　Part II, extension, 1882 - 1922, by George Edwin MacLean ... (Great Barrington) Pub. by the town, 1928.　xvii, (2), 620 p. incl. front. (ports.) illus. (map) plates.　23½ cm.　Contains rolls
of soldiers of Great Barrington who served in the war of the rebellion and the world war.　29-2674.　　　F74.G8 T22

GREENFIELD directory, including Montague and Deerfield ... v. 6-10.　Springfield, Mass., H.A. Manning.
1904 - 1910.　5 v. fold. maps.　23½ cm.　7-4177.　　　Directories

GREENFIELD.　Manning's Greenfield and Turners Falls (including Montague City) directory ... 18 -
Springfield, Mass., H.A. Manning, 1899 -　v. fold. maps.　23½ cm.　7-4177 (rev. '29)　　　Directories

GREENFIELD suburban directory for the towns of Shelburne Falls, Shelburne, Buckland, Deerfield,
Montague City, Millers Falls, Montague Center, Northfield, Gil Bernardston ... v. 1 -
Springfield, Mass., H. A. Manning, 1909 -　v. fold. map.　23 cm.　CA31-1059 Unrev.　Directories

GREENFIELD.　A history of the Mansion house corner, Greenfield, by Elizabeth L. Adams.　New
York, Priv. print. by the American historical society, inc., 1928.　32 p.　front., pl., port.　28½ cm.
28-30239.　　　F74.G85 A2

GREENFIELD.　Leading business men of Greenfield and vicinity; embracing also Turners Falls,
Orange, and Athol ... By George Fox Bacon.　Boston, Mercantile pub. co., 1889.　72 p. illus. 4º.
1-11407-M1.　　　F74.G85 B1

GREENFIELD gazette.　Centennial ed.　Greenfield, Mass., 1892.　172 p.　front., illus. (incl. ports.,
plans)　34½ x 28½ cm.　6-37997.　　　F74.G85 G3

GREENFIELD.　Official souvenir program, Greenfield sesqui-centennial, 1903 ... (Greenfield, Press

456

MASSACHUSETTS

of E. A. Hall, 1903) (80) p. illus. (incl. ports.) 17½ x 22½ cm. 7-41335. F74.G85G82

GREENFIELD, Vital records of, to the year 1850. Boston, Pub. by the New England historic genealogical soc. ... 1915. 299 p. 23 cm. 15-27502. F74.G85G826

GREENFIELD, One hundred years of, 1822 - 1922, issued to commemorate a century of banking, the First national bank. Greenfield, Mass. (1922) 47 p. incl. front., illus., ports. 20 cm. 22-13918. F74.G85G83

GREENFIELD, 150 years old, 1753 - 1903. Greenfield, Mass., C. M. Moody, 1903. (10) p. 59 pl. 15½ x 23 cm. 3-14253. F74.G85G84

GREENFIELD. Sesquicentennial edition, Greenfield record-gazette ... Greenfield, Mass., 1942. 1 v. illus. (incl. map) 58 cm. 42-24932. F74.G85G85

GREENFIELD. Address delivered at the opening of court in the new Court house in Greenfield ... 1873, by Hon. Whiting Griswold. Greenfield, Mass., E. D. Merriam, 1873. 51 p. 22 cm. 20-17475. F74.G85G87

GREENFIELD. In and about Greenfield. Greenfield, Mass., C. M. Moody, 1889. 1 p., 10 pl. 16½ x 23½ cm. 1-11408. F74.G85 I 3

GREENFIELD. Hearth stone tales; a condensed history of Greenfield, (by) Lucy Cutler Kellogg. Greenfield, Mass. (Hartford, Conn., Print. Case Lockwood & Brainard) 1936. viii, 125 p. front. 23½ cm. Bibliography: p. 112 - 115. 36-10786. F74.G85K46

GREENFIELD. Address of Hon. Henry Cabot Lodge, delivered at Greenfield, 1903, on the 150th anniversary of the incorporation of the town. (Greenfield, Mass., 1904?) 21 p. 23½ cm. Also pub. in Francis M. Thompson's History of Greenfield, 1904. 7-41352. F74.G85 L8

GREENFIELD. 150th anniversary of the organization of the town of Greenfield. 1903. Letter from Hon. John E. Russell. (Greenfield, 1904?) 6 p. 23½ cm. Also pub. in Francis M. Thompson's History of Greenfield, 1904. F74.G85 R9

GREENFIELD, ... History of, shire town of Franklin county, by Francis M. Thompson ... (1682 - 1929) Greenfield, Mass. (Press of T. Morey) 1904 - 31. 3 v. port., double plans. 24 cm. Paged continuously. 4-9952 Rev. F74.G85 T4

GREENFIELD. Willard's history of Greenfield ... By David Willard. Greenfield (Mass.) Kneeland & Eastman, 1838. iv, (2) p., (9) - 180 p. 16½ cm. 1-11409. F74.G85 W7

GROTON. From the hills of Shawfieldmont. By William Amos Bancroft. Groton, Mass., 1903. broadside. 25½ cm. F74. G9 B2

GROTON, Massachusetts. By William Amos Bancroft. (Groton, Mass., 1904) 22 cm. F74. G9 B3

GROTON. Old highways and landmarks of Groton, by Francis Marion Boutwell. Groton, 1884. 20 p. 23 cm. 1-2200. F74. G9 B7

GROTON, Old homesteads of. By Francis Marion Boutwell. Groton, 1883. 11 p. 23 cm. 1-1478. F74. G9 B8

GROTON. People and their homes in Groton, in olden time. By Francis Marion Boutwell. Groton, 1890. 18 p. 22½ cm. 2-12575. F74.G9 B82

GROTON. History of the town of Groton, including Pepperell and Shirley, from the first grant of Groton plantation in 1655. With appendices, containing family registers, town and state officers, population, and other statistics. By Caleb Butler ... Boston, Press of T. R. Marvin, 1848. xx, (9) - 499 p. front., pl., 2 maps (1 fold.) fold. plan, facsim. 22½ cm. 1-11411. F74. G9 B9

GROTON. Grand Army of the republic. Dept. of Massachusetts. E. D. Clark post no. 115. Memorial day ... Ayer, Mass. (1908) Broadside. 23½ cm. F74. G9 G6

GROTON. Biographical sketch. Dr. Samuel Abbott Green. (Reprint from Physicians and surgeons of America.) Boston? 189-?) (4) p. incl. port. 20½ cm. 11-25763. F74.G9 G69

GROTON. An account of the early land-grants of Groton, Mass. ... By Samuel Abbott Green. Groton, 1879. 58, (1) p. 8°. 1-11412-M1. F74. G9 G7

GROTON. An account of the lawyers of Groton, including natives who have practised elsewhere, and those also who have studied law in the town. With an appendix. By Samuel A. Green. Groton (Cambridge, J. Wilson and son) 1892. 158 p. 24 cm. 8-16818. F74.G9G704

GROTON. An account of the physicians and dentists of Groton; incl. those who, born there, have practised their progession elsewhere. By Samuel A. Green. Groton, 1890. 3; 90 p. 24 cm. 100 copies printed. 8-32776. F74.G9G706

GROTON. A brief account of some of the early settlers of Groton. Being the appendix to "Groton epitaphs". By Samuel A. Green. Groton, 1878. 28 p. 28 cm. Thirty copies printed in this form. 1-11413. F74.G9 G71

GROTON. The boundary lines of old Groton. By Samuel A. Green ... Groton, Mass., 1885. 3, (9) - 105 p. 3 maps (incl. front.) 23½ cm. 4-33612. F74.G9G712

GROTON. Colonel William Prescott and Groton soldiers in the battle of Bunker Hill, by Samuel Abbott Green. Cambridge, J. Wilson, University press, 1909. 10 p. 25 cm. From the Proceedings of the Mass. historical soc. for Nov. 1909. 10-3157. F74.G9G716

GROTON. Early church records of Groton, 1706 - 1830. With a register of births, deaths, and marriages, 1664 - 1830. From the church books and the Middlesex County records. With notes by Samuel A. Green. Groton, 1896. 42, 194, 64 p. 25 cm. Made up of 3 numbers of the author's Groton historical series: v.1, no. 10, v.4., no.1 and v.1, no. 13. 1-11414. F74.G9 G72

GROTON. An ecclesiastical council held at Groton ... 1712. By Samuel Abbott Green. (Cambridge? 1899?) 4 p. 24½ cm. 11-25759. F74.G9 G73

GROTON. Epitaphs from the old burying ground in Groton, Mass. With notes and an appendix. By Samuel A. Green ... Boston, Little, Brown, 1878. xix, 271 p. front., plates. 23½ cm. The epitaphs were copied by A. B. Coburn. Notes on early families: p. (235) - 259. 1-11415. F74.G9 G74

GROTON. Facts relating to the history of Groton, by Samuel Abbott Green ... Groton (Cambridge, J. Wilson) 1912 - 14. 2 v. illus. 25 cm. 12-24783 Rev. F74.G9 G743

GROTON, The geography of. Prepared for the use of the members of the Appalachian club, on a proposed visit to that town ... 1886. By Samuel A. Green. Groton (Cambridge, J. Wilson) 1886. 20 p. 24 cm. 3-6086. F74.G9G747

GROTON as a shire town. - Destructive tornado. - Two Groton conventions. - The soapstone quarry. Groton, Mass., 1884. 20 p. 24½ cm. (Groton historical series. vol. I no. iv) 6-4468. F74.G9 G76 vol. I
F74.G9G748

GROTON during the Indian wars. By Samuel A. Green. Groton, Mass., 1883. 214 p. 23½ cm. 6-36792. F74.G9G749

GROTON during the revolution, with an appendix, by Samuel Abbott Green ... Groton, Mass. (Cambridge, Mass., University press) 1900. 4; 343 p. incl. illus., pl. front. 23½ cm. 1-879. F74.G9 G75

GROTON historical series. A collection of papers relating to the history of the town of Groton. By Samuel Abbott Green ... Groton, 1887-99. 4 v. 25 cm. Originally pub. in separate numbers; issued irregularly from 1884 - 1898. 1-11416. F74.G9 G76

MASSACHUSETTS

GROTON, ... Bibliography of, 1673 to 1888. Maps, plans, etc. Groton, Mass., 1888.
(173) - 226 p. 2 facsim. 24 cm. (Groton historical series, vol. II no. vii) Arranged chronologically. 4-21043.
F74.G9 G76

GROTON in the witchcraft times. By Samuel A. Green. Groton, Mass. (J. Wilson, Cambridge) 1883.
29 p. 23 cm. 5-6247.
F74.G9G765

GROTON. An historical address, bi-centennial and centennial, ... 1876 .... By Samuel Abbott Green ... Groton, 1876. 86, (5) p. 26 cm. 1-11417.
F74.G9 G77

— 2d ed. Groton, 1876. 89 p. 25 cm. 1-11418.
F74.G9 G78

GROTON. An historical address delivered at Groton ... 1880 ... at the dedication of three monuments erected by the town. By Samuel Abbott Green ... Groton, 1880. 56 p. 24½ cm. Monuments erected near the site of the first meeting house 1666-76, at the residence of Wm. and Deliverance Longley and near the birthplace of Col. Wm. Prescott. 1-11419.
F74.G9 G79

GROTON. An historical address delivered at Groton ... 1905 ... on the celebration of the 250th anniversary of the settlement of the town. By Samuel Abbott Green ... Groton, 1905.
52 p. illus. 24½ cm. 5-34082.
F74.G9G792

GROTON. An historical sketch of Groton, 1655 - 1890. By Samuel A. Green. Groton, 1894.
3; 263 p. pl. 20½ cm. Repr. from "The history of Middlesex County," ed. D.H. Hurd. 1890. 1-16567.
F74.G9G793

GROTON. Letter to Michael Sheedy, jr., giving a printed design for a town seal of Groton. By Samuel Abbott Green. Boston, 1898. 1 leaf. 23 cm.
F74.G9G797

GROTON. The population of Groton at different times, with some notes on the provincial census of 1765. By Samuel Abbott Green. Cambridge, J. Wilson, 1888. 8 p. 24½ cm. 3-2340.
F74.G9G799

GROTON. Remarks on Nonacoicus, the Indian names of Major Willard's farm at Groton ... (by) Dr. Samuel A. Green ... (Cambridge, Mass., 1893?) 4 p. 24½ cm. 3-3821.
F74.G9 G81

GROTON. Roll of honor, Groton, Mass. By Samuel A. Green. (Groton, Mass., J. Wilson, print. 1897) 7 p. 24 cm. Repr. from Groton historical series, vol. iv no. v. 1-21601.
F74.G9 G82

GROTON. Three historical addresses. 1908. By S. A. Green. 1 v.
F74.G9 G83

GROTON. Three military diaries kept by Groton soldiers in different wars; with introductions by Samuel A. Green. Groton, Mass. (Cambridge, University press, J. Wilson) 1901. viii, 133 p. 23½ cm. 1-16575.
F74.G9G835

GROTON. Two chapters in the early history of Groton. By Samuel Abbott Green. Boston, Press of D. Clapp, 1882. 19 p. incl. facsims. 25½ cm. Repr. from the N. E. hist. and geneal. register, 1882. 3-31531.
F74.G9 G84

GROTON. Addresses delivered at Groton ... 1905 ... on the celebration of the 250th anniversary of its settlement. Groton, 1905. 100 p. 23 cm. 6-13403.
F74.G9 G87

GROTON, The early records of. 1662 - 1707. Ed. by Samuel A. Green. Groton, 1880. 200 p. facsims. 23½ cm. 1-11420.
F74.G9 G88

GROTON. Proceedings of the centennial celebration at Groton ... 1876, in commemoration of the destruction of the town, 1676 and the Declaration of independence ... 1776. With an oration by Samuel Abbott Green. Groton, 1876. xi, (3), (7) - 89 p. 24½ cm. 10-3159.
F74.G9 G89

GROTON, Vital records of, to the end of the year 1849. Salem, Mass., The Essex institue, 1926-7
2 v. 23 cm. 26-23121.
F74.G9 G92

GROTON historical soc. Officers and by-laws. Ayer (1904) 16 cm.
F74.G9 G94

GROTON historical society. Report of the historian for the year 19   (Ayer, Mass., H. S. Turner, print) 19   v.   24 cm.   CA 25-480 Unrev.
F74.G9 G96

GROTON. The Community, Groton; the story of a neighborhood, by Edward Adams Richardson ... 1911, Ayer, Mass. (Ayer, Mass., H. S. Turner, print., 1911)   15 p. plates. 23 cm. 12-893.
F74.G9 R52

GROTON. Moors school at old district no. 2, Groton; the story of a district school, by Edward Adams Richardson. Ayer, Mass. (H. S. Turner, print.) 1911.   32 p. front., plates, ports. 23½ cm. 12-890.
F74.G9 R53

GROVELAND. A sermon preached in the Parish meeting house, Groveland ... 1865, on the return of the soldiers from the war. By Rev. Martin S. Howard ... New Bedford, (Mass.) E. Anthony, print., 1865.   16, 11, (1), 6, 3, 3 p. 22½ cm. 18-4303.
F74.G95.H8

GROVELAND. Inscriptions from the old cemetery in Groveland (formerly East Bradford) Copied and published by Louis A. Woodbury. Groveland, Mass., 1895.   2; 105, vii p. 2 pl. (incl. front.) 25 cm. 14-14664.
F74.G95 W8

HADLEY. Genealogies of Hadley families, embracing the early settlers of the towns of Hatfield, South Hadley, Amherst and Granby. By Lucius Manlius Boltwood. Northampton, Metcalf & co., print. 1862.   2, (7) - 168 p. 23 cm. 9-17086.
F74. H1 B6

HADLEY. Celebration of the 200th anniversary of the settlement of Haldey, at Hadley ... 1859; incl. the address by Rev. Prof. F. D. Huntington, etc. Northampton, Bridgman & Childs, 1859.   98 p. 24 cm. 1-11421.
F74. H1 H1

HADLEY; the regicides, Indian and general history: a souvenir in honor of Major-General Joseph Hooker, and in anticipation of the memorial exercises at his birthplace ... 1895. Northampton, Mass., Picturesque Pub. Co. (1895)   (38) p. 28 cm. Imperfect: p. 37-38 wanting.
F74. H1 H3
Rare Book Coll.

HADLEY. Under a colonial roof-tree; fireside chronicles of early New England, by Arria S. Huntington ... Boston and New York, Houghton, Mifflin, 1891.   2; 133 p. front., plates. 22½ cm. 1-11422.
F74. H1 H9

HADLEY. Forty Acres; the story of the Bishop Huntington House; photos. by Samuel Chamberlain. New York, Hastings House (1949)   68 p. illus., ports., map. 25 cm. 49-4066*.
F74. H1 H92

HADLEY, History of, including the early history of Hatfield, South Hadley, Amherst and Granby, by Sylvester Judd, with family genealogies, by Lucius M. Boltwood. Northampton, Print. Metcalf & co., 1863.   636 p. 24 cm. 1-11423.
F74. H1 J9

— (New ed.) Springfield, Mass., H. R. Hunting, 1905.   2, iii-xliii, 504, 205 p. front. (port.) 7 pl. (1 col.) 24 cm. 5-28027.
F74. H1 J91

HADLEY. The traditionary story of the attack on Hadley ... 1675, and the alleged appearance of General Goffe, the regicide. By George Sheldon. Boston, D. Clapp, print., 1874.   15 p. 25 cm. "Reprinted from the Historical and genealogical register for Oct., 1874. 1-11424.
F74. H1 S5

HADLEY. Historical Hadley; a story of the making of a famous Massachusetts town, by Alice Morehouse Walker ... New York, The Grafton press (1906)   xii, 2; 130 p. front., 6 pl. 20 cm. (The Grafton historical series) 6-30490.
F74. H1 W2

HALIFAX, Vital records of the town of, to the end of the year 1849; literally transcribed under the direction of George Ernest Bowman ... Boston, Mass., Mass. Soc. of Mayflower descendants ... 1905. xi, 211 p. 23½ cm. 6-2517.
F74. H16 H2

HAMILTON, Middleton, Topsfield, Wenham directory ... 19   v.   Salem, Mass., The H. M. Meek pub. co., 19   v.   22½ cm. 22-15621.
Directories

MASSACHUSETTS

HAMILTON, Vital records of, to the end of the year 1849. Salem, Mass., The Essex institute, 1908. 112 p. 23 cm. 8013332. F74.H17 H2

HAMPDEN. Historical address delivered by Rev. Edward A. Chase at the centennial celebration of the Congregational church ... 1885. Hartford, Conn., Case Lockwood & Brainard, 1898. 69 p. 22½ cm. 6-38877. F74.H18 C4

HANOVER, A historical sketch of the town of, with family genealogies. By John S. Barry ... Boston, Pub. for the author by S. G. Drake, 1853. v, (6) - 448 p. front., illus. (incl. port., map, coat of arms) plates, facsims. 22½ cm. 1-11425. F74. H2 B2

HANOVER. History and records of St. Andrew's Protestant Episcopal church, of Scituate, Mass., 1725 - 1811, of Hanover, Mass., 1811 - 1903, and other items of historical interest, being vol. II of the church and cemetery records of Hanover, by Vernon Briggs ... (Boston, Press of W. Spooner) 1904. 3, (v) - ix, 188 p. front. 24 cm. 5-32488. F74.H2 B81

HANOVER, History of the town of, with family genealogies, by Jedediah Dwelley and John F. Simmons. (Hanover, Mass.) Pub. by the town, 1910. 291, 474 p. illus., plates, 2 port. (incl. front.) 25½ cm. "Genealogical work": 474 p. 11-5628. F74. H2 D9

HANOVER. A copy of the records of births, marriages and deaths and of intention of marriage of the town of Hanover. 1727 - 1857. As recorded by the several town clerks for the said town of Hanover. Rockland (Mass.) Press of the Rockland standard, 1898. vi, 319 p. 24 cm. 4-11465. F74. H2 H2

HANOVER. The record of the procession and of the exercises at the dedication of the monument ... (1878) ... in grateful memory of the soldiers and sailors of that town who died in the war for the preservation of the union. Boston, A. William, 1878. 103 p. 23 cm. L.C. copy replaced by microfilm. 5-4397.
F74. H2 H3
Microfilm 19398 F

HANOVER. History and records of the First Congregational church ... 1727 - 1865, and inscriptions from the headstones and tombs in the cemetery at Centre Hanover, 1727 - 1894. Being vol. I of the church and cemetery records of Hanover. By L. Vernon Briggs ... Boston, W. Spooner, print., 1895. vi, (2), 316 p. front., plates, ports., maps. 24 cm. 1-11426 Rev. F74. H2 H4

HANSON, Vital records of, to the year 1850. Boston, The New England historic genealogical society ... 1911. 110 p. 23½ cm. 11-7319. F74.H25 H3

HARDWICK, Vital records of, to the year 1850. Comp. by Thomas W. Baldwin ... Boston, (Wright & Potter print.) 1917. 336 p. 23½ cm. 18-2509. F74. H3 H2

HARDWICK. An address at the centennial celebration ... 1838. By Lucius R. Paige ... Cambridge, Metcalf, Torry, and Ballou, 1838. iv, (5) - 76 p. 22½ cm. 1-11427. F74. H3 P1

HARDWICK, History of. With a genealogical register. By Lucius R. Paige. Boston, New York, Houghton, Mifflin, 1883. xii, 555 p. front. (port.) 23½ cm. "Genealogical register": p. (321)-545. 1-11428. F74. H3 P2

HARVARD. An historical discourse delivered before the First Congregational society in Harvard ... 1882, by Seth Chandler. With an appendix by Samuel A. Green. Boston, G. E. Littlefield, 1884. 28 p. 23 cm. Appendix is a sketch of the early history of Harvard. 2-1900-M2. F74. H4 C4

HARVARD. Old manuscripts relating to Harvard, communicated to the Mass. historical society by Samuel A. Green. Boston, 1913. 24 p. 24½ cm. The documents include an orderly book of the American army at Cambridge ... 1775, three lists of Harvard soldiers, 1758 - 1760 and other papers. 14-4168. F74. H4 G7

HARVARD, Vital records of, to the year 1850. Comp. by Thomas W. Baldwin ... Boston, (Wright & Potter print.) 1917. 326 p. 23½ cm. 18-7634. F74.H4 H33

HARVARD, History of the town of. 1732 - 1893. By Henry S. Nourse. Harvard, W. Hapgood, 1894. ix, (11) - 605 p. front. (port.) plates, double map. 23½ cm. Contains epitaphs in Harvard burial grounds prior to 1800; Marriages, deaths and births, 1732-1800. 1-11429. F74. H4 N9

HARVARD. Lost Utopias; a brief description of three quests for happiness, Alcott's Fruitlands, old Shaker house, and American Indian museum, rescued from oblivion, recorded and preserved by Clara Endicott Sears on Prospect Hill in the old township of Harvard, by Harriet E. O'Brien. Boston, Mass., P. Walton, 1929. 62 p. incl. front., illus., port. 27 cm. 30-1914. F74.H4 O13

— 3d ed. (Brookline, Mass.) 1947. 70 p. illus., port. 28 cm. 47-6863*. F74.H4 O13 1947

HARVARD. Memoirs of old Harvard days, from 1863 to 1924, also the men and women and their descendants who made old Harvard what it is today; pub. by the author, F. S. Savage, sr. Still River, Mass., 1924. 77 p. front. (port.) plates. 24½ cm. 24-10199. F74.H4 S2

HARWICH. Resident and business directory of Harwich, Dennis and Chatham, Mass. 1901 ... Hopkinton, Mass., A. E. Foss, 1901. (2)-160 (i.e. 159) p. 24 cm. No more pub? 1-31129 Rev.

Directories

HARWICH. Our village. Vol. I. By Sidney Brooks. (n.d.) 1 v. and portfolio. illus. 28 cm. Photocopy (positive) of typescript. 55-47232. F74.H42 B7

HARWICH and Chatham, genealogical. Compiled by Vernon R. Nickerson. (Ed. Frank E. Hendricks. Taunton, Mass., 1969) 102 l. 30 cm. F74.H42 N5

HARWICH, A history of ... 1620 - 1800; including the early history of that part now Brewster; with some account of its Indian inhabitants, by Josiah Paine. Rutland, Vt., The Tuttle pub. co., 1937. 2, iii-iv, (3), 503 p. front. (port.) plates, fold. maps, plan. 23½ cm. 37-34603. F74.H42 P3

HATFIELD. 212th anniversary of the Indian attack on Hatfield, and field-day of the Pocumtuck valley memorial association ... 1889. Northampton, Mass., Gazette print. 1890. 95 p. 23 cm. Preface signed by C.M. Barton and D.W. Wells. "Genealogy": p. 60-72. 1-21429. F74.H45 B3

HATFIELD, 1670 - 1970. Compiled by the Tercentenary History Committee ... (Northampton, Mass., Print. Gazette Print. Co., 1970) xi, 92 p. 24 cm. F74.H45 H3

HATFIELD. A sermon preached at Hatfield ... 1807. At the opening of Hatfield bridge. By Joseph Lyman ,.. Northampton, Print. Wm. Butler, 1807. 16 p. 23½ cm. 24-6784. F74.H45 L9

HATFIELD, ... A history of, in three parts: I. ... social and industrial life ... II. The houses and homes of Hatfield ... III. Genealogies of the families of the first settlers. By Daniel White Wells and Reuben Field Wells. Springfield, Mass., Pub. under the direction of F. C. H. Gibbons (1910) 536 p. front., illus. (incl. ports., facsims.) 24 cm. 10-14748. F74.H45 W4

HATFIELD book, The, by Charles A. Wight ... (Springfield, Mass., The F. A. Bassette co,, print. 1908) 3, 59 p. front., plates, ports. 24 cm. 8-33298. F74.H45 W6

HAVERHILL city ... directory ... Haverhill, Mass., C. A. Richmond, 19 -
v. maps. 23½ cm. 20-4467. Issue for 1920 contains Haverhill war record. Directories

HAVERHILL and Bradford directory for 1867 - 1869/70. Boston, Mass., Langford and Chase, 1867 - 1869/70. 2 v. 18½ cm. 8-7793. Directories

HAVERHILL and Groveland directory... no. (4) 6-14, 16-18, 20-25, 27-31. W. A. Greenough, compilers, printers and publishers. Boston, (1872) - 1909. 24 v. plans (partly fold.) 25½ cm. Oct. 26, 98-24 Add.

Directories

HAVERHILL suburban directory for Georgetown, Groveland, Merrimac and West Newbury, Mass. and Plaistow, N.H. ... v.1 - Springfield, Mass., Crosby pub. co. (1933 -
v. 23½ cm. 41-26041. Directories

HAVERHILL. W. A. Greenough & co.'s Haverhill business directory supplement, April, 1882, containing a list of the ... business men who were burned out Feb. 17 and 18, 1882, together with their

MASSACHUSETTS

present address and location. W. A. Greenough, compilers and publishers ... Haverhill (Mass.) J. A. Hale, 1882. 2; 7-99, 24 p. 22½ cm. 8-3863. Directories

HAVERHILL and Groveland street directory and guide, including a vast amount of useful and instructive information ... Haverhill, Mass., The Peoples guide pub. co., 19 - v. illus. 15 x 8 cm. CA 28-7 Unrev. Directories

HAVERHILL, an historical address by the Hon. Albert Leroy Bartlett ... given at the exercises commemorative of the 275th anniversary of the settlement of the city ... 1915. Haverhill (The Record print.) 1915. 63 p. front. (port.) 22½ cm. 16-3318. F74. H5 B27

HAVERHILL. Some memories of old Haverhill in Mass., by Albert Le Roy Bartlett ... Haverhill, Mass., 1915. 105 p. incl. front. (port.) 21 cm. 15-24245. F74. H5 B28

HAVERHILL, The history of, from its first settlement, in 1640, to the year 1860 ... Haverhill, The author, 1861. xvi, (17) - 663, xx p. front. pl., port., map, facsim. 8°. 1-11430-M1. F74. H5 C4

HAVERHILL. The first era in the history of Haverhill. Comprising the period from the settlement of the plantation of Pentucket (1640) to the conclusion of permanent peace with the Indians (1715) By John B. Corliss. Haverhill, Mass., C. C. Morse, 1885. 40 p. 24½ cm. 1-11431. F74. H5 C7

HAVERHILL. Red Sunday: the Saltonstalls, the Dunstons and the Fighting Ayers; Merimack Valley history, by Francis W. Cronan. (1965) 260 p. 24 cm. F74. H5 C83

HAVERHILL. The colonial and revolutionary history of Haverhill. A centennial oration, delivered before the city government and the citizens of Haverhill, July 4, 1876 ... Haverhill, Gazette print, 1877. 38 p. 12°. 1-11432-M1. F74. H5 C9

HAVERHILL. A sermon, delivered in Haverhill ... 1820, being the second centesimal anniversary of the landing of New-England fathers, at Plymouth. By Joshua Dodge ... Haverhill (Mass.) Print. Burrill & Hersey, 1821. 28 p. 22 x 14 cm. 6-13951. F74. H5 D6

HAVERHILL. An oration delivered at the commemoration of the 250th anniversary of the settlement of Haverhill ... 1890. By Rev. Samuel White Duncan. Boston, J. G. Cupples, print., 1891. (127) - 197 p. illus. (port.) 21½ x 18½ cm. Extracted from "The story of a New England town ... 1891. 16-7873. F74. H5 D9

HAVERHILL. Historical sketch of First parish, Haverhill. By the pastor, Rev. F. A. Gilmore ... Haverhill, Mass., C. C. Morse, print. (1895) 28 p. 12°. 1-23711-M1. F74. H5 G5

HAVERHILL. ... The story of a New England town ... commemoration ... 250th anniversary ... Haverhill ... 1891. 2 v. F74. H5 H52

HAVERHILL, Vital records of, to the end of the year 1849 ... Topsfield, Mass., Topsfield historical soc., 1910 - 11. 2 v. 23½ cm. v. 1 Births. - v.2. Marriages and deaths. 10-8489 Additions. F74. H5 H54 Geneal.Section Ref.

HAVERHILL; an industrial and commercial center. Pub. by the Board of trade. Haverhill, Mass., Chase brothers, 1889. 260 p. front. (port.) illus. 25 cm. 1-11433. F74. H5 H56

HAVERHILL. History of the city of Haverhill, showing its industrial and commercial interests and opportunities; the commercial centre of a population of over 125,000, and the first shoe city in the world. Pub. by authority of the Haverhill Board of trade. (Haverhill) 1905. 118 p. front., illus. (incl. ports.) 19½ cm. 17-30117. F74. H5 H562

HAVERHILL. Centennial discourse delivered on the 100th anniversary of the organization of the Baptist church, Haverhill. With an account of the centennial celebration, and historical notes. Boston, Gould & Lincoln, 1865. iv, (5) - 96 p. 8°. 1-11447-M1. F74. H5H564

HAVERHILL. Exercises commemorative of the 150th anniversary of the West Congregational church,

Haverhill. Including historical addresses, poem, etc. Haverhill, Mass., C. C. Morse, book and job print., 1886.   59 p.   24½ cm.   7-14890.
F74.H5H565

HAVERHILL. Foundation facts concerning its settlement, growth, industries, and societies, etc. etc. Haverhill, Mass., Bridgman & Gay, 1879.   39 p.   22½ cm.   1-11434.
F74.H5 H57

HAVERHILL evening gazette ... Tercentenary edition ... Haverhill, Mass., 1940.   18, 18, 12, 12, 12, 12 p. illus.   55½ cm.   Froms v.141 no. 302, issued June 22, 1940.   42M142T.
F74.H5H573

HAVERHILL strangers' directory; what to see and where to go to see it, with complete map of the city to June 1, 1922. (Haverhill, Mass., Telegram press, 1922)   (20) p.   fold. map.   23 cm.   22-16376.
F74.H5 H62

HAVERHILL. Under the X-ray, by Ray L. Horsch. My scrapbook. 1st ed. (Haverhill, Mass., Print. Record pub. co., 1939)   3, 9-103 p.   plates, ports.   23½ cm.   The articles have appeared in the columns of the Haverhill Sunday record.   40-3513.
F74.H5 H78

HAVERHILL. The danger ahead! What may be expected in the U.S.A. if hyphenated Americans get control. The thrilling story of lawlessness, mobocracy and sectarian bigotry at Haverhill, when an American citizen was mobbed for daring to speak upon the question: "Shall public funds be given to sectarian schools", the speaker, Rev. Thomas E. Leyden ... (Somerville, Mass., Evangelist Leyden pub. co., 1921)   (32) p.   19½ cm.   CA 21-273 Unrev.
F74. H5 L6

HAVERHILL, The history of. By B. L. Mirick ... Haverhill, A. W. Thayer, 1832,   227 p. fold. front. 21 cm.   Probably written in large part by J. G. Whittier, who turned his ms. over to Mirick.   1-12354.
F74. H5 M6
Rare Book Coll.

HAVERHILL, A historical sketch of ..., with biographical notices ... by Leverett Saltonstall. Boston, print. John Eliot, 1816.   1; 56 p.   20½ cm.   From the Mass. historical colls. vol. iv, 2d ser.   1-11435.
F74. H5 S2
Rare Book Coll.

HAVERHILL. 250th anniversary of ye anciente towne of Haverhill; 1640 - 1890. By Walter K. Watkins. Worcester, Mass., F. S. Blanchard, 1890.   20 p. illus., port., facsim. fol.   1-11436-M1.
F74. H5 W3

HAWLEY. History of the town of Hawley ... from its first settlement in 1771 to 1887. With family records and biographical sketches. By William Giles Atkins ... West Cummington, Mass., The author, 1887.   3, (5) - 130, (2) p. front. (port.) 23 cm.   Contains marriages and deaths.   1-11203.
F74.H55 A8

HEATH, a historic hill town, by Edward P. Guild. Boston? 19 -)   (219) - 225 numb. l. illus.   30 cm.   Proof sheets for the Mass. magazine.
F74.H57 G9

HEATH. ... Centennial anniversary of the town of Heath ... 1885. Addresses, speeches, letters, statistics, etc., etc. Ed. by Edward P. Guild. (Boston) Pub. for the Committee (1885)   vii, 148 p. pl.   23½ cm.   1-11437 Rev.
F74.H57 H5

HEATH, Vital record of, to the year 1850. Boston, Mass., Pub. by the New England historic genealogical soc. ... 1915.   142 p.   23½ cm.   15-27051.
F74.H57 H6

HEATH. A historical discourse: delivered by Rev. Moses Miller, former pastor of the First Congregational church in Heath ... 1852 ... Shelburne Falls (Mass.) Print. G. W. Mirick, 1853.   80 p.   19 cm.   8-13335.
F74.H57 M6

HINGHAM. Directory of Hingham and Hull. 1894 ... Comp., copyrighted and pub. by The J. H. Hogan co., Quincy, Mass. Plymouth, Avery & Doten, book and job print., 1894.   199 p.   illus.   23½ cm. 8-25420.
Directories

HINGHAM. W. F. Shaw's Hingham, Cohasset and Hull directory, South shore, 1898/99 -   Boston, W. E. Shaw, 1898 -   v.   fold. map.   23½ cm.   24-17748.
Directories

MASSACHUSETTS 235

HINGHAM. Resident and business directory of Hingham and Cohasset ... Boston, Boston suburban book co., 1908 - 1 v. fold. map. 23½ cm. 8-22976. Directories

HINGHAM. The town of Hingham in the late civil war, with sketches of its soldiers and sailors. Also the address and other exercises at the dedication of the soldiers' and sailors' monument. Prepared by Fearing Burr and George Lincoln. Pub. by order of the town. (Boston, Rand, Avery & co., printers) 1876. 455 p. front., ports. 24 cm. 1-11438. F74. H6 B9

HINGHAM, The pageant of; in celebration of the 300th anniversary of the settlement and incorporation of the town of Hingham, written and directed by Percy Jewett Burrell. Presented by the people of the town ... 1935. (Boston, Buck print. co.) 1935. 47 p. illus. (music) 29 cm. 35-10628.
F74. H6 B93

HINGHAM. South Shore town. By Elizabeth Jane Coatsworth. New York, Macmillan, 1948. xii, 201 p. 21 cm. Bibliography: p. 201. 48-10806*. F74. H6 C7

HINGHAM, The settlement of, by Louis C. Cornish. Boston, The Rockwell & Churchill press, 1911. 23 p. plates. 22 cm. 12-9005. F74. H6 C8

HINGHAM; a story of its early settlement and life, its ancient landmarks, its historic sites and buildings ... (Hingham? Mass.) Old colony chapter, D. A. R., 1911. 123 p. front., illus., plates, 2 port. on 1 l. 22½ cm. 11-20623. F74. H6 D3

HINGHAM. Our old burial grounds ... By Sydney Howard Gay ... Hingham, Pub. for the Cemetery fair, 1842. 24 p. fold. front. (plan) 19 cm. 12-16464 Rev. F74. H6 G37

HINGHAM. The celebration of the 250th anniversary of the settlement of the town of Hingham ... 1885. Hingham, The Committee of arrangements, 1885. vi, (9) - 134 p. 24 cm. Prepared for publication by Francis H. Lincoln. 6-18335. F74. H6 H5
Microfilm 18539 F

HINGHAM, History of the town of ... (Hingham) Pub. by the town, 1893. 3 v. in 4. illus., plates, ports., maps (partly fold.) 25 cm. v. 1. Natural history; ancient landmarks; early settlers; military history. - v. 2, part 2. Public institutions, etc. - v. 2-3. Hingham genealogies. 1-11439. F74. H6 H6

HINGHAM. Names of the tax payers of Hingham, 1711, from the original manuscript in the possession of Frank D. Andrews. Vineland, N.J., Priv. print., 1913. 2; 3-10 p. 23½ cm. 13-24435.
F74. H6 H63

HINGHAM. The commemorative services of the First parish in Hingham on the 200th anniversary of the building of its meeting-house. 1881. Hingham, Pub. by the parish, 1882. vi p., 2 l. (3) - 169 p. front., port. 24 cm. 6-40408 Rev. F74. H6 H7

HINGHAM. The 225th anniversary of the opening of the old meeting house in Hingham ... 1907. 1682 - 1907. Boston, Geo. H. Ellis, print., 1907. 44 p. front. 20 cm. 8-2429. F74. H6 H72

HINGHAM old and new. (Hingham, Mass.) Pub. by the Hingham tercentenary committee for the town of Hingham, 1935. 5, (3) - 96 p. 3 l. incl. illus. (maps) plates. 21½ cm. 35-641. F74. H6 H75

HINGHAM. Discourse delivered to the First parish in Hingham on the 200th anniversary of the opening of its meeting house for public worship. By Rev. Edward Augustus Horton. With an appendix. Hingham (Mass.) Pub. by the Parish, 1882. 57 p. 24 cm. 6-40774. F74. H6 H8

HINGHAM. Aspects of a New England town (Hingham, Mass.) from the horse and buggy days to the event of world war I, with a treatise on "Life in the army, world war II." By H. Leavitt Horton ... (Philadelphia, Print. H. L. Raum) 1945. 35 p. illus. (incl. ports.) 21½ cm. 47-15505 Rev. F74. H6 H83

HINGHAM. A discourse delivered to the First parish in Hingham, 1869, on re-opening their meeting-house ... By Calvin Lincoln ... With an appendix. Hingham, The parish, 1873. 79 p. front. (port.) pl., 2 double plans. 23½ cm. 1-13359. F74. H6 L6

HINGHAM. An address delivered before the citizens of the town of Hingham ... 1835, being the 200th anniversary of the settlement of the town. By Solomon Lincoln. Hingham (Mass.) J. Farmer, 1835. 63 p. 23½ cm. 1-11440.
F74. H6 L7

HINGHAM, History of the town of. By Solomon Lincoln, jr. Hingham, C. Gill, jr., and Farmer and Brown, 1827. iv. (5) - 183 p. 19½ cm. 7-41868.
F74. H6 L74

HINGHAM. The Old Ship Meeting House of Hingham; by Gladys Teele Detwyler Stark; illus. by Edgar T. P. Walker. Boston, Beacon Press, 1951. 32 p. illus. 23 cm. 51-8279.
F74. H6 S7

HINSDALE, Vital records of, to the year 1850 ... Boston, 1902. 98 p. 23½ cm. (New-England historic genealogical soc. Ed. Henry Ernest Woods. 3-5254.
F74. H63 H6

HOLDEN and Paxton directory, The. Worcester, Mass., The Drew Allis co., 190 -
v. 23 cm. CA 33-684 Unrev.
Directories

HOLDEN, The history of, 1667 - 1841. By Samuel C. Damon. (Worcester, Mass., Wallace and Ripley, print.) 1841. viii, 154 p. incl. front. 22 cm. 7-13935.
F74. H7 D2

HOLDEN, The history of. 1684 - 1894. By David Foster Estes. Pub. by the town. Worcester, Press of C. F. Lawrence, 1894. x, 446 p. front., plates, ports., fold. map. 24 cm. Damon's History of Holden, 1667-1841 reprinted p. (5) - 41. Personal notices: p. (210) - 333. 1-11441.
F74. H7 E7

HOLDEN, ... Vital record of, to the end of the year 1849. Worcester, F. P. Rice, 1904.
236 p. 23½ cm. 4-9196.
F74. H7 H7
Geneal. Section. Ref.

HOLDEN, History of the town of, 1667 - 1941. By Florence Newell Prouty. Pub. by the 200th anniversary committee for the town of Holden. Worcester, Mass., The Stobbs press, 1941 -
370 p. 23½ cm.
F74. H7 P7

HOLLAND, History of the town of, by Rev. Martin Lovering. Rutland, Vt., The Tuttle co,, 1915.
2, (7) - 749 p. front. (port.) illus., plates, ports., fold. map. 24 cm. "Intentions and marriages, births, deaths": p. (260) - 294. Biographical: p. (382) - 419. "Genealogies": p. (421) - 746. 15-24750.
F74. H705L9

HOLLISTON. A history of the towns of Holliston, Medway, and Milford, incl. the counties of Worcester, Middlesex, and Norfolk, which join in this area, from 1667 to 1950. By Ernest Atherton Bragg. (n. p., 1958) 27 p. 19 cm. 58-38372.
F74. H71 B7

HOLLISTON. Centennial address delivered in Holliston, ... 1876, by Rev. E. Dowse. Pub. by the town. So. Framingham, Mass., J. C. Clark, print., 1877. 32 p. 23 cm. 7-41856.
F74. H71 D7

HOLLISTON, Vital records of, to the year 1850. Boston, Pub. by the New England historic genealogical society ... 1908. 358 p. 23 cm. 8-15351.
F74. H71 H7

HOLYOKE, ... Local and business directory of, for 1869. 1 v. front. (fold. plan) 20½ cm. 8-32979.
Directories

HOLYOKE, South Hadley, Chicopee directory ... Springfield, Mass. (etc.) The Price & Lee co., 18 - v. fold. maps. 23½ cm. 1-30486 Rev.
Directories

HOLYOKE. Blue book and social directory of Holyoke. 1889 - Springfield, Holyoke, Index pub. co., 1889 - v. 20½ cm. x 15½ cm. CA 33-688 Unrev.
Directories

HOLYOKE, ... The founding of, 1848, by Dr. Ralph H. Gabriel ... a Newcomen address, 1936. (Princeton, Princeton university press, 1936) 23 p. 23½ cm. 37-11274.
F74. H73 G3

MASSACHUSETTS

HOLYOKE'S Negro families; report to the Great Holyoke Council of Churches of a survey, made by the Christian Life and Work Department, Betty A. Mitman, chairman. Prepared by Bulkeley Smith, Jr., director of Research. (Holyoke, Mass.) 1962.   17 l.   28 cm.   F74.H73G68

HOLYOKE; a case history of the industrial revolution in America, by Constance McLaughlin Green ... New Haven, Yale university press; London, H. Milford, Oxford university press, 1939.   ix, 425 p. front., illus. (plan, facsim.) fold. map, diagrs. 23 cm. (Yale historical pubs. Miscellany, xxxiv) Bibliography: p. (393) - 401. 39-15355.
F74.H73 G7

— Archon books, 1968.   ix, 425 p. illus. 22 cm.   68-8021.   F74.H73 G7 1968

HOLYOKE, The story of, in painting and in prose: mural painting by Sante Graziana attained by the bequest of the late Joseph Allen Skinner to the Holyoke Public Library; interpretive essays by Arthur Ryan (and others. Holyoke, 1954)   32 p.   illus.   28 cm.   55-18999.   F74.H73 H6

HOLYOKE. Views of Holyoke and Northampton. (Portland, Me., 1905)   20½ x 25½ cm.   F74.H73 V6

HOLYOKE in the great war ... By Charles S. Zack. Including the towns of South Hadley, Willimansett, Belchertown, Fairview and Granby. Holyoke, Mass., Transcript pub. co. (1919)   475, (4) p. illus. (incl. ports.) 23½ cm.   19-9672.   F74.H73 Z16

HOPEDALE. Dedication of the Adin Ballou memorial, including the unveiling of the statue, a historical statement, etc. at Hopedale ... 1900. Cambridge, Print. at the Riverside press, 1901.
77 p.   front.   22 cm.   "Appendix, A biographical sketch of William Tebb"   26-3104.   F74.H74 B2

HOPKINTON, Vital records of, to the year 1850. Boston, New England historic genealogical soc. ... 1911.   462 p.   23 cm.   13-3035.   F74.H75H68

HOPKINTON. A century sermon delivered in Hopkinton ... 1815. By Rev. Nathanael Howe ... Andover, Print. Flagg and Gould, 1816.   31 p.   21½ cm.   11-19499.   F74.H75 H7

— 2d ed. 1817.   31 p.   22 cm.   6-13736 Rev.   F74.H75 H8

— 4th ed. With a memoir of the author and explanatory notes by Elias Nason. Boston, J. P. Jewett, 1851.   56 p.   24 x 14½ cm.   6-13735   F74.H75H82

HOPKINTON. Resident and business directory of Hopkinton and Holliston, for 1899 ... Needham, Mass., A. E. Foss, 1899.   2-130, (A) - p, (131) - 132 p.   24 cm.   No more pub?   0-1494 Rev.   Directories

HUBBARDSTON. An address, in commemoration of the 100th anniversary of the incorporation of the town of Hubbardston ... by Rev. John M. Stowe, of Sullivan, N.H. ... Worcester, Print. C. Hamilton, 1867.   109 p.   24 cm.   1-11442.   F74. H8 H8

HUBBARDSTON, ... Vital records of, to the end of the year 1849. Worcester, Mass., F. P. Rice, 1907.   226 p.   23½ cm.   7-16394.   F74. H8 H9
Geneal. section. Ref.

HUBBARDSTON, History of the town of, from the time its territory was purchased of the Indians in 1686, to the present. With the genealogy of present and former resident families. By Rev. J. M. Stowe. Hubbardston, Mass., Pub. by the Committee, 1881.   xix, 383 p. front., plates, ports. 24 cm.
1-12355 Rev.   F74. H8 S8

HUDSON, Bolton, Berlin, Stow, Gleasondale and Sudbury directory ... v.6   Boston, W. E. Shaw, 1909   1 v.   front., fold. map.   24 cm.   9-5871.   Directories

HUDSON, Abstract of the history of, from its first settlement to the centennial anniversary of the declaration of our national independence, July 4, 1876. By Charles Hudson. With the action of the town, and the proceedings at the celebration. (Boston) Pub. by vote of the town, 1877.   78 p. plates. 23½ cm.   10-31030.   F74. H85 H8

HUDSON, past and present. By Edward F. Worcester. (Hudson, Mass., Enterprise print.) 1899.
(92) p. illus. obl. 16°. Jan. 25, 1900-238.   F74.H85 W9

HUDSON, yesterday and today, by E. F. Worcester; a rev. ed. of Hudson, past and present. By Edward F. Worcester. (Hudson, Mass., Hudson print., 1914)   (80) p. illus. 16 x 23 cm. 15-5693.
F74.H85W92

HULL. Town of Hull directory. Boston, Mass., H. Howard. 1917.   1 v. front. (fold. map) 23½ cm.
17-24059.   Directories

HULL, Vital records of, to the year 1850. Comp. by Thomas W. Baldwin ... Boston, (Wright & Potter print.) 1911.   75 p. 23 cm. 13-5035.   F74.H89 H9

HULL. Sketch of Nantasket: (now called Hull,) in the county of Plymouth. First pub. in the Hingham gazette. By Solomon Lincoln. Hingham (Mass.) Gazette press, 1830.   16 p. 17 cm. 16-25920.
F74.H89L73
Rare Book Coll.

HULL, The naming of. By Albert Matthews. Boston, Press of D. Clapp, 1905.   12 p. 25½ cm. Reprinted from New-England historical and genealogical register for April, 1905. 26-4251.   F74.H89 M3

HUNTINGTON, History of the town of, from its first settlement to the year 1876. By Rev. J. H. Bisbee. Springfield, Mass., C. W. Bryan, print., 1876.   40 p. 24 cm. Prepared and pub. by authority of the town. 1-11443.
F74. H9 B6

HYDE PARK. Directory and register of Hyde Park and Dedham and directory of Canton ... (18 - Boston, D. Dudley & co., 18 -   v. 23½ cm. 31-2249.   Directories

HYDE PARK, Dedham, and Norwood directory ... 18   Boston, C. W. Calkins, 18 -
   v. 23 cm. 31-4348.   Directories

HYDE PARK directory, The ...   Boston, W. E. Kendall, 18   v. 23½ cm. 24-17751.   Directories

HYDE PARK directory ... 1901 - 19   (v.1 -   Boston, Guide pub. co., 1900 -
   v. fold. maps. 24 cm. 3-9124 Rev.   Directories

HYDE PARK. The first hundred years, 1868 - 1968. Hyde Park Centennial Committee. (Hyde Park, Mass., 1968)   64 p. illus., maps (on cover) ports. 39 cm. 73-296509 MARC.   F74.H98H88

HYDE PARK. ... Memorial sketch of Hyde Park, for the first 20 years of its corporate existence (1868 - 1888); also its industries, statistics, and organizations, tog. with the anniversary addresses ... Comp. by Jos. King Knight and others. Boston, L. Barta, print., 1888.   96 p. front. (ports.)
illus., plates. 24½ cm. 1-11444.   F74.H98 H9

HYDE PARK historical record. v. 1 - 6. Apr. 1891 - 1908. Hyde Park, Mass., The Hyde Park historical soc., 1892 - 1908.   6 v. in 4. illus., plates, ports. 23½ cm. Issued quarterly from Apr. 1891 to Jan. 1893, when publication was suspended; resumed in Apr. 1903 as a year book. 6-43114.   F74.H98H95

IPSWICH, Boxford, Byfield, Georgetown, Newbury, Rowley, Salisbury, Salisbury Beach, Topsfield, West Newbury, directory ... of the towns of northern Essex county ... v. 1 -   1932/34 - Beverly, Mass., Portland, Me., Crowley & Lunt, 1932.   v. fold. map. 24 cm. CA 33-127 unrev.
Directories

IPSWICH. The Agawam manual and directory ...   Ipswich, Mass., M. V. B. Perley.
   v. fronts. (ports.) illus., plates, maps. 23 cm. 12-14311.   F74. I6 A25

IPSWICH. Antiquarian papers. v. 1-4; Oct. 1879 - Apr. 1858. Ipswich, Mass., 1879 - 85.
4 v. in 1. illus. (incl. ports.) 22½ cm. monthly (irregular) No more pub. 5-35743 Add.   F74. I6 A 6

IPSWICH. Denison memorial: Ipswich, 1882, 200th anniversary of the death of Major-General Daniel

MASSACHUSETTS

Denison. Biographical sketch, by Prof. D. D. Slade. Historical sketch, by Augustine Caldwell. (Ipswich) Print. by the request of the Denison memorial committee (1882) 52 p. 24½ x 15½ cm. 1-11448.
F74. I 6 D3

IPSWICH. History of Ipswich, Essex, and Hamilton. By Joseph B. Felt. ... Cambridge (Mass.) Print. C. Folsom, 1834. xv, 304 p. 23 cm. The Third or Hamlet parish of Ipswich was incorporated as the town of Hamilton in 1793, and the Second or Chebacco parish as Essex in 1819. 1-11449.
F74. I 6 F3

— Cambridge (Mass.) Print. C. Folsom, 1834. xv, 377 p. front. (port.) 23 cm. Appendix, index of names, and index of subjects added. Sept. 1859 (p. 305 - 377) 12-11186.
F74. I 6 F32

IPSWICH. Thirtieth anniversary discourse, delivered in Ipswich, ... 1856. By Rev. Daniel Fitz, pastor of the South church. Boston, W. White, 1856. 23 p. 8°. 1-11450-M1.
F74. I 6 F5

IPSWICH. The Hammatt papers. nos. 1 - 7. (Printed from the ms. in the Public library) The early inhabitants of Ipswich, Mass. 1633 - 1700. By Abraham Hammatt. 1854. (Ipswich) Press of Ipswich antiquarian papers, A. Caldwell, A. W. Dow, 1880 - 99. (4) - 423 p. front. (port.) illus. 24 cm. 1-13357.
F74. I 6 H2

IPSWICH. A narrative of the life, experience and work of an American citizen, by George Haskell ... Ipswich, Mass., Chronicle pub. co., 1896. viii, 156 p. 23 cm. 11-19266.
F74. I 6 H3

IPSWICH. Augustine Heard and his friends, by Thomas Franklin Waters. (Salem, Mass., Newcomb & Gauss, print.) 1916. 108 p. pl., 3 port. (incl. front.) 24½ cm. Pub. also in Ipswich historical soc. Publications, v. 21. 17-12315.
F74.I 6 H43

IPSWICH. The ancient records of the town of Ipswich, vol. I - from 1634 to 1650. Ed. and pub. by George A. Schofield ... Ipswich, Mass., Chronicle motor press, 1899. (135) p. 21 cm. Reprinted from the "Ipswich chronicle," beginning Sept. 1898. No more published. 1-16581 Additions. L. C. copy replaced by microfilm.
F74. I 6 I5
Microfilm 10076 F

IPSWICH. The celebration of the 250th anniversary of the incorporation of the town of Ipswich ... 1884. Boston, Little, Brown and co., 1884. vi, (2) p. (3) - 149 p. 1 illus., plates (1 fold.) ports. 24½ cm. 1-11451.
F74. I 6 I 6

IPSWICH, Vital records of Ipswich, to the end of the year 1849 ... Salem, Mass., The Essex institute, 1910 - 1919. 3 v. 23½ cm. 11-8158 Rev. v.1. Births. - v.2. Marr. & deaths. - v.3. Bap. marr. and deaths. 11-8158 Rev.
F74. I 6 I63

IPSWICH. Guide to Ipswich, birthplace of American independence. (Ipswich, Mass.) 1922. 20 p. 22½ cm. Bibliography: p. 2. 22-13390.
F74.I 6 I 76

IPSWICH historical society, Publications of the, 1 -   Salem, Mass. (etc.) 1894 -
 v. illus., plates, ports., maps, facsims. 21 - 26½ cm. Imprint varies. 8-18355. v.1. The oration by Rev. Washington Choate. - v.2. The president's address. - v.3. Exercises at the unveiling of the memorial tablets at the South common. - v.4. Annual meeting, 1896. - v.5. The early homes of the Puritans. - v.6. ... dedication of the ancient house now occupied by the society. - v.7. A sketch of the life of John Winthrop. - v.8. The development of our town government. - v.9. A history of the old Argilla road. - v.10. The Hotel Cluny of a New England village. - v.11. The meeting house green. - v.12. Thomas Dudley and Simon and Ann Bradstreet. - v.13. Fine thread, lace and hosiery in Ipswich. - v.14. The simple cobler of Aggawam. - v.15. The old Bay road ... and a genealogy of the Ipswich descendants of Samuel Appleton. - v.16.-17. Candlewood, an ancient neighborhood in Ipswich. - v.18. Jeffrey's Neck. - v.19. Ipswich village and the old Rowley road. - v.20. The John Whipple house. - v.21 Augustine Heard and his friends. - v.22. Plum Island. - v.23. Ipswich in the world war. - v.24. Ipswich River, its bridges wharves and industries. - v.25. Glimpses of everyday life in old Ipswich. - v.26. Two Ipswich patriots. - v.27. Puritan homes.
F74. I 6 I 8

IPSWICH. The last sermon preached in the ancient meeting house of the first parish in Ipswich ... 1846. By David T. Kimball ... Boston, Temperance standard press, 1846. 32 p. 23 cm. 2-17398.
F74. I 6 K4

IPSWICH. A sketch of the ecclesiastical history of Ipswich. The substance of a discourse ... by David T. Kimball ... Haverhill, Mass., Print. at the Gazette and patriot office, 1823. 44 p. 21 cm. 8-12859.
F74. I 6 K5

IPSWICH. Old Ipswich; a magazine of local genealogy and history ... v.1, no. 1-4/5. Ipswich, The Independent press, 1899. 72 p. illus., plates. 23 cm. monthly. No more pub. 6-18649.
F74. I 6 O4

IPSWICH. Pictorial Ipswich; with complete historical annotations. Portsmouth, N.H., M.V.B. Perley, 1900. 72 l. incl. illus., pl., port., maps, plans, facsim. 8º. Nov. 1, 1900-230. F74. I6 P6

IPSWICH. Chronicle report of the 250th anniversary exercises of Ipswich ... 1884, together with a few sketches about town ... Ipswich, Chronicle press, 1884. 74 p. illus., fold. pl. 20½ cm. Reprinted from the Ipswich chronicle. 8-8588. F74. I6 P8

IPSWICH. Rambles about old Ipswich. Text by T. Frank Waters. Photographs by G. G. Dexter. Arranged by Lewis R. Hovey. Ipswich, Mass., The Independent press, 1898. (63) p. illus. obl. 16º. Pub. under the auspices of the Ipswich historical society. 1-11452-M1. F74. I6 R1

IPSWICH in the Massachusetts Bay Colony ... by Thomas Franklin Waters ... Ipswich, Mass., The Ipswich historical soc., 1905 - 17. 2 v. front., plates, ports., maps, fold. plan., facsims., diagrs. 25 cm. 5-29118 Rev. F74. I6 W3

JAMAICA PLAIN. Address at dedication of the town-house at Jamaica Plain, West Roxbury, by Arthur W. Austin. Boston, A. Mudge, print., 1868. 39 p. 23 cm. 1-16189. F74. J3 A9

JAMAICA PLAIN, Annals and reminiscences of, by Harriet Manning Whitcomb. Cambridge (Mass.) Printed at the Riverside press, 1897. 64 p. front., pl. 22½ cm. 1-11453. F74. J3 W5

KINGSTON. The ancient estate of Governor William Bradford, by Thomas Bradford Drew. (Boston, T. P. Smith printing co.) 1897. 43 p. 23 cm. "The ancient estate of Governor William Bradford at Jones River in the north part of Plymouth, now the town of Kingston, Mass." 12-24128. F74. K5 D6

KINGSTON. Death records from the ancient burial ground at Kingston; transcribed by Theodore S. Lazell from a manuscript copy, made in 1859 by the late Dr. Thomas Bradford Drew, now in the possession of George C. Burgess, of Boston ... Boston, Massachusetts soc. of Mayflower descendants, 1905. 31 p. 24½ cm. Reprinted from volume vii of the Mayflower descendant. 6-7662. F74. K5 D7

KINGSTON. ... Report of the proceedings and exercises at the 150th anniversary of the incorporation of the town of Kingston ... 1876. Boston, E. B. Stillings, print., 1876. 151 p. pl., maps (part fold.) 25 cm. 1-11454. F74. K5 K5

KINGSTON, Vital records of, to the year 1850. Boston, New England historic genealogical soc. ... 1911. 396 p. 23 cm. 13-3034. F74.K5 K52
Geneal. section, Ref.

LAKEVILLE, Freetown and Berkley directory. Providence, R. I., C. De Witt White co.
v. 24 cm. 11-31806. Directories

LAKEVILLE, Freetown and Berkely, directory, The ... 1924/25 - no. 1 - Providence, R. I., Boston, Sampson & Murdock co., 1924 - v. 24 cm. 24-29838. Directories

LAKEVILLE, History of the town of, 1852 - 1952; 100th anniversary of the town of Lakeville. (Lakeville, 1952) 247 p. illus. 23 cm. 53-15951. F74. L19 V8

LANCASTER. Notable historic spots in Lancaster, compiled by J. C. L. Clark; issued by the Committee on commemorating the 275th anniversary of the incorporation of Lancaster. (Lancaster) South Lancaster print., 1928. (8) p. 18 cm. 31-4356. F74. L2 C59

LANCASTER on the Nashua, picturesque and historical; prepared by W. A. Emerson, assisted by J. C. L. Clark. Leominster, Mass., M. A. Tolman, 1904. 96 p. incl. front., illus. 17½ x 22½ cm. 5-11059. F74. L2 E5

LANCASTER. An oration, delivered at Lancaster ... 1826. In commemoration of the 150th anniversary of the destruction of that town by the Indians. By Isaac Goodwin. Worcester, Rogers & Griffin, print., 1826. 15 p. 24 cm. 8-20244. F74. L2 G6

LANCASTER. A century-sermon preached at the First-parish in Lancaster ... 1753. By Timothy

MASSACHUSETTS

Harrington ... Boston, Print. S. Kneeland, 1753. 2; 29 p.   22 cm.   15-10663.   F74. L2 H3
Rare Book Coll.

— Leominster (Mass.): Print, S. & J. Wilder, for Mr. Joshua Fletcher, of Lancaster, 1806.
25 p.   22 cm.   19-16832.   F74. L2 H32

LANCASTER.   The birth, marriage, and death register, church records and epitaphs of Lancaster. 1643 - 1850.   Ed. Henry S. Nourse.   Lancaster (Clinton, Print. W. J. Coulter) 1890.   508 p.   facsim.
24 cm.   1-11455.   F74. L2 L2
L. H. & G.

LANCASTER.   Commemoration of the 250th anniversary of the incorporation of Lancaster ... 1903. Lancaster (Clinton, Mass., Press of W. J. Coulter) 1904.   43 p.   25 cm.   4-31136.   F74. L2 L22

LANCASTER.   Commemoration of thet 275th anniversary of the incorporation of Lancaster ... 1928. (Lancaster? 1928)   (4) p.   18 cm.   F74. L2 L23

LANCASTER, The early records of.   1643 - 1725.   Ed. by Henry S. Nourse ... Lancaster (Clinton, Print. W. J. Coulter) 1884.   364 p.   maps, facsim.   24½ cm.   1-11456.
F74. L2 L3

LANCASTER.   History of the town of Lancaster: from the first settlement to the present time, 1643 - 1879.   By Rev. Abijah P. Marvin ... Lancaster, The town, 1879.   798 p.   front., plates, maps (1 fold.) plan.
24 cm.   List of Lancaster authors and their publications: p. 625 - 632.   1-11457.   F74. L2 M3

LANCASTER, The military annals of.   1740 - 1865.   Including lists of soldiers serving in the colonial and revolutionary wars, for the Lancastrian towns: Berlin, Bolton, Harvard, Leominster, and Sterling. By Henry S. Nourse ... Lancaster (Clinton, Mass., W. J. Coulter, print.) 1889.   402 p.   front., ports.
23½ cm.   1-12356.   F74. L2 N9

LANCASTER.   Lancastriana. I. A supplement to the Early records and Military annals of Lancaster. By Henry S. Nourse.   Lancaster (Clinton, Mass., Press of W. J. Coulter) 1900.   45 p.   front. (map)
23½ cm.   13-1179.   F74. L2 N91

LANCASTER.   The story of colonial Lancaster by Marion Fuller Safford ... Rutland, Vt., The Tuttle pub. co., 1937.   4, 190 p.   front. (facsim.) plates, map.   23½ cm.   38-1838.   F74. L2 S3

LANCASTER.   Address delivered at the dedication of Memorial hall, Lancaster, 1868. By Christopher T. Thayer; and Ode, by H. F. Buswell.   With an appendix.   Boston, Nichols and Noyes, 1868.
(9) - 71 p.   23 cm.   1-12357.   F74. L2 T3

LANCASTER.   The Lancastrian towns.   By Mildred McClary Tymeson.   Photos. by Katherine Knowles.   Barre, Mass., Barre Publishers, 1967.   94 p.   23 cm.   67-14591.   F74. L2 T9

LANCASTER.   Address delivered, 1876 at Lancaster, by request of the citizens.   By John D. Washburn ... Lancaster (Worcester, Press of C. Hamilton) 1876.   58 p.   26 cm.   2-6541.
F74. L2 W3

LANCASTER.   An address in commemoration of the 200th anniversary of the incorporation of Lancaster.   By Joseph Willard.   Boston, Print. J. Wilson, 1853.   vi, 230 p.   23½ cm.   1-11458.
F74. L2 W6

LANCASTER.   Topographical and historical sketches of the town of Lancaster, in the commonwealth of Massachusetts: furnished for the Worcester magazine and historical journal.   By Joseph Willard. Worcester, Print. C. Griffin, 1826.   90 p.   23 cm.   1-11459.   F74. L2 W7

LANESBOROUGH.   Cemetery inscriptions from Lanesboro.   Copied by Josephine C. Frost.   July, 1910.   (93) type-written sheets.   27½ cm.   Various pagings.   CA 12-671 Unrev.   F74. L3 F9

LANESBOROUGH; the story of a wilderness settlement,   1765 - 1965,   by Frances S. Martin.   (Bi-centennial ed.) Lanesborough, 1965.   110 p.   24 cm.   65-21069.   F74. L3 M3

LANESBOROUGH, History of town of, 1741 - 1905 ... (pt. 1)   (n. p., 1905? -
1 v. plates, ports. 23 cm.   6-8883.   F74. L3 P2

LANESVILLE, ... The Finns in, by Helen Babson.   Los Angeles, Calif., Southern California sociological soc., University of Southern California (1920)   12 p.   22½ cm. (Studies in sociology: sociological monograph no. 13. vol. iv, no. 1. Oct. 1919) 20-11936.   F74. L32 B2

LANESVILLE.   The role of the Finnish immigrant in the history of Lanesville, 1870 - 1957.   By David F. Hayes.   (Cambridge) 1958.   34, (11) l. illus., port., maps. 28 cm.   Bibliog. l.(40)-(45) 58-49335.   F74. L32 H3
1958

LAWRENCE, The directory of the town of, June 1848.   Pub. by William Filmer.   Lawrence, Hayes, printer, 1848.   76 p.   16½ cm.   F74. L4 A18
1848
Rare Book Coll.

LAWRENCE almanac, directory, and business advertiser for 1851 ... (Lawrence, pref. 1850)
122 p.   16 cm.   F74. L4A18
1851
Rare Book Coll.

LAWRENCE directory ...   Boston, Mass., Sampson & Murdock, 1857 - 19 -
v. fold. maps.   13 - 25 cm.   1-25796 rev.   Directories

LAWRENCE.   ... Anthony's standard business directory and reference book of Lawrence and vicinity ... 1895/96   (New Bedford, Mass., Anthony pub. co.) 1895 -
v.   23½ cm.   CA 33-581 Unrev.   Directories

LAWRENCE.   An authentic history of the Lawrence calamity, embracing a description of the Pemberton mill, a detailed account of the catastrophe, a chapter of thrilling incidents, list of contributions to the relief fund, names of killed and wounded, etc.   Boston, J. J. Dyer, 1860.   96 p.   24½ cm.
5-5127.   F74. L4 A9

LAWRENCE.   Immigrant city: Lawrence, 1845 - 1921.   By Donald B. Cole.   Chapel Hill, University of North Carolina Press (1963)   ix, 248 p. illus., maps. 24 cm.   F74. L4 C6

LAWRENCE yesterday and today (1845 - 1918) a concise history of Lawrence, - her industries and institutions; municipal statistics, etc., by Maurice B. Dorgan.   Lawrence (Press of Dick & Trumpold) 1918.   263 p.   illus.   23½ cm.   19-15847.   F74. L4 D69

LAWRENCE, History of, with war records, by Maurice B. Dorgan ... (Lawrence) The author, 1924.
ix, 267 p.   front. (map) plates.   24 cm.   Rev. and greatly enlarged ed. of F74. L4D69. 25-5094.   F74. L4D692

LAWRENCE, History of the city of.   By Jonathan F. C. Hayes.   Lawrence, Mass., E. D. Green, 1868.
168 p.   24 cm.   1-11460 Rev.   F74. L4 H4

LAWRENCE.   A letter to the inhabitants of Andover and North Andover.   By Nathan W. Hazen.   Boston, Fetridge and co., 1856.   39 p.   23 cm.   In relation to the purchase of land for the new city. 11-22523.   F74. L4 H42

LAWRENCE, Vital records of, to the end of the year 1849.   Salem, Mass., The Essex institute, 1926.
125 p.   23 cm.   26-20953.   F74. L4 L35

LAWRENCE.   Committee of relief for the sufferers by the fall of the Pemberton mill.   Report of the treasurer ... 1860.   Lawrence, 1860.   51 p.   23½ cm.   10-31028.   F74. L4 L4

LAWRENCE.   Sanitary survey of the town of Lawrence, by the chairman of the commissioners ... relating to a sanitary survey of the state.   Reprinted from the report of the commission.   Boston, Print. Dutton & Wentworth, 1850.   23 p.   front. (fold. map) 5 plans. 23 cm.   10-12999.   F74. L4 M4

MASSACHUSETTS

LAWRENCE. The Lawrence gazetteer, containing a record of the important events in Lawrence and vicinity from 1845 to 1894, also, a history of the corporations, etc. etc. Lawrence, C. G. Merrill, 1894. 5, (3) - 165 p. illus. 23 ½ cm. 9-30074. F74. L4 M5

LAWRENCE. Quarter-centennial history of Lawrence, with portraits and biographical sketches ... Comp. by H. A. Wadsworth. (Lawrence, Mass.) H. Reed, 1878. v, (6) - 179, (2), (lxxxiii) - lxxxiv p. front. (phot.) illus., ports. 20 ½ cm. 8-7108. F74. L4W18

LAWRENCE, History of, with portraits and biographical sketches of ex-mayors up to 1880 and other distinguished citizens ... Comp. by H. A. Wadsworth. Lawrence, Print. H. Reed, 1880. v, (7) - 179, (2), (lxxxiii) - lxxxiv p. front., illus. (incl. plan) ports. 20 ½ cm. First issued under title of F74.L4 W18. 1-11461 Rev. F74. L4 W2

LAWRENCE. A descriptive poem of the calamity at Lawrence ... 1860. Also, Lines to the memory of John Brown. By Peter Wait. (Danvers? Mass., 1860) 16 p. 19 cm. 19-3280. F74. L4W22

LAWRENCE. A descriptive poem of the sad calamity at Lawrence ... 1860. By an eye witness. Boston, Print. C. C. P. Moody, 1860. 20 p. 19 cm. 19-19562. F74. L4 W23

LEE, Lenox, Stockbridge, Dalton, Hinsdale, directory, 1903 - 1904 ... Pittsfield, Mass., J. B. Goussett, 1902. v. 24 cm. 3-5171. Directories

LEE. The centennial celebration, and centennial history of the town of Lee. Comp. by Rev. C. M. Hyde and Alexander Hyde. Pub. by vote of the town. Springfield, Mass., C. Q. Bryan, print., 1878. iv, 352 p. front., plates, ports. 24 cm. 1-11462. F74. L5 H9

LEE. Inscriptions from the cemeteries. (n. p., n. d.) 14 cm. F74. L5 I 5

LEE, Records of the town of, from its incorporation to 1801; all the extant records of the town clerks, town treasurers, Hopland school district and Congregational church for that period; also inscriptions from the cemeteries. With an appendix containing ... matters relating to the early history of the town. Lee, Mass. Press of the Valley gleaner, 1900. 2, (3) - 374 p. incl. plates, facsims. plates, port., map, facsims. 24 cm. 1-2164. F74. L5 L5

LEE, Vital records of, to the year 1850. Boston, Pub. by the New-England historic genealogical soc. ... 1903. 239 p. 23½ cm. 3-20947. F74. L5 L53

LEE, Vital records of, 1777 - 1801, from the records of the town, Congregational church and inscriptions in the early burial grounds; all the family birth records, etc. etc. Lee, Mass., The Valley gleaner, 1899. vii, 108 p. plates, facsim. 23 ½ cm. 1-16582. F74. L5 L6

LEE. Gravestone inscriptions, Lee. Including all extant of the quarter century, 1801 - 1825. Carefully reproduced. Lee, Mass., Press of the Valley gleaner, 1901. By Dorvil M. Wilcox. 36 p. incl. 4 pl. 24 ½ cm. For inscriptions before 1801 see F74.L5L5 and for 1826-1850 see F74.L5W65. 3-26277 Additions. F74. L5 W6

LEE. Gravestone inscriptions, Lee, including all extant of the quarter century, 1826 - 1850, carefully reproduced. Lee, Mass., Press of the Berkshire gleaner, 1910. By Dorvil M. Wilcox. 95 p. incl. plates. 25 ½ cm. 11-1134. (See above item) F74. L5 W65

LEE. Soldiers buried in Lee. List of six wars in the three cemeteries, comp. by D. M. Wilcox ... (Lee, Mass., The Gleaner print, 1910) 4 p. 21 cm. Mere alphabetical list of names. 11-10279. F74. L5 W66

LEICESTER directory, The, containing an alphabetical list of the inhabitants, a classified business directory, street directory ... Worcester, Mass., The Drew Allis co., 19 v. 22 ½ cm. CA 33-584 Unrev. Directories

LEICESTER. The religious history of the First Congregational church in Leicester. A sermon by Rev. A. H. Coolidge ... 1887. Worcester, Mass., Print. C. Hamilton, 1887. 32 p. 24 ½ cm. 7-27738. F74. L55 C7

LEICESTER. Celebration of the centennial anniversary of American independence, at Leicester: 1876. Worcester (Mass.) Print. C. Hamilton, 1876. 36 p. 24 cm. 1-24363.
    F74. L55 L5

— Worcester, Mass., Press of Harrigan bros. (1876?) 18 p. 24½ cm. 37-18047. F74. L55L52
    Rare Book Coll.

LEICESTER. Celebration of the 150th anniversary of the organization of the town of Leicester ... 1871. Cambridge (Mass.) Press of J. Wilson, 1871. 77 p. 24 cm. 1-16865. F74. L55L55

LEICESTER, ... Vital records of, to the end of the year 1849. Worcester, F. P. Rice, 1903. 284 p. 23½ cm. 3-20946. F74. L55 L6

LEICESTER. Oration delivered in the town hall, Leicester, by Mr. John E. Russell, 1876. Worcester, Print. C. Hamilton, 1876. 18 p. 24 cm. 7-27745. F74. L55 R9

LEICESTER. An address commemorative of the part taken by the inhabitants of the original town of Leicester, in the events of the revolution: delivered at Leicester, 1849. By Emory Washburn. Boston, Print. C. C. P. Moody, 1849. 48 p. 23½ cm. 1-11464. F74. L55 W5

LEICESTER. Topographical and historical sketches of the town of Leicester, ... By Emory Washington. Worcester, Print. Rogers & Griffin, for the publishers of the Magazine and journal, 1826. 66 p. 24½ cm. Reprinted from Worcester magazine, June 1826, v.2, p. 65-128. 7-29652. F74. L55 W39

LEICESTER, Historical sketches of the town of, during the first century from its settlement. By Emory Washburn. Boston, J. Wilson, 1860. 2; 467 p. front., pl., ports., fold. plan. 22½ cm. Genealogies: p. 342 - 415. 1-11463. F74. L55 W4

LENOX, by George A. Hibbard. Illus. by W. S. Vanderbilt Allen. New York, Charles Scribner's sons, 1896. 4; 54 p. incl. front., plates. 18 cm. (American summer resorts) 1-11465. F74. L57 H6

LENOX. July 4, 1876! Centennial celebration at Lenox. Historical address by J. Rockwell. Pittsfield, Chickering & Axtell, print., 1876. 41 p. 8°. 1-16869-M1. F74. L57 L5

LENOX and the Berkshire highlands, by R. De Witt Mallary ... New York and London, G. P. Putnam's sons, 1902. xiii, 363 p. front., plates, ports. 21½ cm. 2-16757. F74. L57 M2

LENOX. History of Lenox and Richmond, by Charles J. Palmer. Pittsfield, Mass., Press of the Sun print., 1904. 48 p. plates. 23 cm. 4-36283 Rev. F74. L57 P2

LENOX. All things earthly, changing and transitory. A sermon preached in Lenox ... 1845 ... by Samuel Shepard. ... Lenox (Mass.) J. G. Stanley, 1845. 32 p. 23 cm. 1-11466. F74. L57 S5

LENOX; Massachusetts shire town, by David H. Wood. Drawings by Vaughn Gray. (Lenox, Mass., Pub. by the town, 1969. xiv, 219 p. illus. 70-76380. F74. L57 W6

LEOMINSTER directory, v. 1-2. 1883 - Directories

LEOMINSTER, historical and picturesque, by William A. Emerson ... Gardner, Mass., The Lithotype pub. co., 1888. (xi) - xv, (17) - 320 p. front., illus., plates, ports. 23 cm. 1-12358. F74. L6 E5

LEOMINSTER book, The, illustrated; ... 1901. William A. Emerson. (Fitchburg, Mass., Sentinel printing co., 1901) 303, (7) p. incl. front., illus. 16½ x 23½ cm. 10-5395. F74. L6 E6

LEOMINSTER, ... Vital records of, to the end of the year 1849. Worcester, Mass., F. P. Rice, 1911. 369 p. 23½ cm. 11-7324. F74. L6 L5

LEOMINSTER historical soc. ... Exercises at the unveiling of the boulder marking the site of the first house erected in Leominster, 1725. (Leominster? 1910) 24 p. 24½ cm. 22-17207.
    F74. L6 L55

MASSACHUSETTS

LEOMINSTER of to-day; over 200 choice photographic views of its churches, public buildings ... and other scenes of interest ... Leominster, Mass., K. E. Nichols, 1900. front. 361 p. incl. 177 pl. obl. 8°. Sept. 20, 1900-70.
F74. L6 L6

LEOMINSTER. A centennial discourse delivered to the First Congregational church and society in Leominster ... 1843 ... By Rufus P. Stebbins ... Boston, C. C. Little & J. Brown, 1843. 2; 112 p. 22½ cm. 4-20168.
F74. L6 S8

LEOMINSTER, The history of, or the northern half of the Lancaster new or additional grant, from June 26, 1701, the date of the deed from George Tahanto, Indian sagamore, to July 4, 1852. By David Wilder. Fitchburg, Print. at the Reveille office, 1853. 263 p. 19 cm. 1-11467* Cancel.
F74. L6 W6

LEXINGTON, Resident and business directory of, 1894 - Boston, Mass., Union pub. co., 1894 - 19 v. fold. maps. 24 cm. 99-3842 (rev. '20)
Directories

LEXINGTON ... directory ... Lexington, Mass., The Hadley press, inc., 19 v. fold. map. 23½ cm. CA 24-780 Unrev.
Directories

LEXINGTON epitaphs. A copy of epitaphs in the old burying-grounds of Lexington, by Francis H. Brown. (Lexington) The Lexington historical soc. (Spatula press, Boston) 1905. 169 p. 2 plans. 22 x 18 cm. 7-12900.
F74. L67 B8

LEXINGTON and Concord, a camera impression, by Samuel Chamberlain. New York, Hastings house (1939) 73 p. front., illus. 19 x 15½ cm. 69 p. of illus. 39-24398.
F74. L67 C5

LEXINGTON and Concord in color. With an introductory text and notes on the illus. by Stewart Beach. A collection of color photos. by Samuel Chamberlain. New York, Hastings House (1970) 94 p. illus. 25 cm. (Profiles of America) Pub. simult. in Canada by Don Mills. 78-119796.
F74. L69C32 1970

LEXINGTON, and Concord, its literary and historic shrines ... Boston, Mass., The Colonial gray line sight-seeing tours, 1921. 43 p. incl. illus., pl. 18½ cm. 21-14878.
F74. L67 C7

LEXINGTON. The Jonathan Harrington house, by Helen Clark Fernald. (Lexington, Mass., Adams press, inc., 1937. ix, 61 p. front., pl. 20½ cm. 37-31239.
F74. L67 F4

LEXINGTON. Historic Lexington and Concord; what to see and how to see it ... Lexington, Mass., O. G. Seeley (1903) (4), 7-46 (i.e. 47) p. illus. (incl. ports., plans) 18 x 26 cm. 3-26272.
F74. L57 H6

LEXINGTON. Three villages, by W. D. Howells ... Boston, J. R. Osgood, 1884. 4, (11) - 198 p. 15 cm. Contents. - Lexington, Mass. - Shirley, Mass. - Gnadenhütten, Ohio. 1-16186.
F74. L67 H7

LEXINGTON. Abstract of the history of Lexington from its first settlement to the centennial anniversary of the declaration of our national independence... 1876. By Charles Hudson. Boston, Press of T. R. Marvin, 1876. 28 p. plates. 24 cm. 1-11468.
F74. L67 H8

LEXINGTON. Genealogical register of Lexington families, from the first settlement of the town. By Charles Hudson ... Boston, Wiggin & Lunt, 1868. 296 p. front., illus., plates, ports. 24 cm. A separate publication of his "History of the town of Lexington ..." 7-14895.
F74. L6 H85

LEXINGTON, History of the town of ... from its first settlement to 1868, with a Genealogical register of Lexington families. By Charles Hudson ... Boston, Wiggin & Lunt, 1868. xv, (16) - 449, 296 p. front., plates, ports., plan. 24 cm. 1-11469* Cancel.
F74. L67 H9

— ... rev. and continued to 1912 by the Lexington historical society ... (Bi-centenary ed.) Boston and New York, Houghton Mifflin, 1913. 2 v. fronts., illus. (incl. map, plan) plates, ports., facsims. 24½ cm. I. History. - II. Genealogies. 13-11709 rev.
F74. L67H91

— Corrections and additions. (Boston? 1918) 8 p. 24 cm. (With his History of the town of Lexington, v. 2)

LEXINGTON town meetings from 1765 to 1775. Boston, 1905.   F74.L67H95

LEXINGTON. An oration delivered at Lexington on the dedication of the Town and memorial hall ... 1871, being the 96th anniversary of the battle of Lexington. By Dr. George B. Loring. Boston, Press of T. R. Marvin, 1871.   76 p.   24½ cm.   1-11470.   F74.L67 L5

LEXINGTON. ... Proceedings and addresses commemorative of the 100th anniversary of the incorporation of the town of Lexington. Pub. by vote of the town ... 1914. (Cambridge, The Riverside press, 1914)   36, (2) p. 21 cm.   15-217.   F74.L67L55

LEXINGTON. ... Record of births, marriages, and deaths to Jan. 1, 1898 ... Boston, Wright & Potter print., 1898.   ix, 484 p. 23 cm.   1-12359.   F74.L67 L6

LEXINGTON, your town, your home; pictorial report, 1946. (Lexington, 1947)   38 p. illus., maps. 28 cm.   48-12968*.   F74.L67L62

LEXINGTON. A handbook of its points of interest, historical and picturesque. Pub. under the direction of the Lexington historical society. Boston, W. B. Clarke, 1891.   75 p. illus., maps. 20 x 16 cm. 1-11471.   F74.L67 L7

LEXINGTON. Proceedings of the Lexington historical society and papers relating to the history of the town ... v. 1 - 3. Lexington, Mass., The Society, 1890 - 1905.   3 v. illus., plates, port. 22 cm. CA 10-4474 Unrev.   F74.L67L77

LEXINGTON, A memento of. (Lexington, Mass.) 1887.   12 pl.   obl. 24°.   Copyright by Albert S. Parsons and Edwin G. Champney.   1-11472-M1.   F74.L67 M5

LEXINGTON the birthplace of American liberty; a handbook containing an account of the battle of Lexington - Paul Revere's narrative of his famous ride - a sketch of the town and the places of historic interest - inscriptions on all historic tablets - directory - map and numerous illustrations, by Fred S. Piper ... Lexington, Lexington pub. co., 1902.   31, (3) p. incl. front., illus., plan. 18½ x 15 cm. 2-12942.   F74.L67 P6

— 3d ed. Lexington, Lexington hist. soc., 1910.   7-42, (2) p. front., illus., map. 22 cm. 10-15646.   F74.L67 P7

— 4th ed. Lexington, Lexington his. soc., 1915.   7-42, (2) p. front., illus. (incl. ports.) fold. map. 21½ cm. 15-15995.   F74.L67P72

— 6th ed. Lexington, Lexington hist. soc., 1920.   7-44 p. front., illus. (incl. ports., facsim.) fold. map. 21½ cm. 21-643.   F74.L67 P74

— 7th ed. Lexington (Mass.) Lexington hist. soc., 1923.   62 p. illus. (incl. ports., facsims.) fold. map. 20½ cm. 23-13526.   F74.L67P741

— 9th ed. Lexington (Mass.) Lexington hist. soc., 1934.   62 p. illus. (incl. ports., facsims.) double map. 21½ cm. 34-20401.   F74.L67P741

LEXINGTON; the birthplace of American liberty; a handbook containing a brief summary of the events leading up to the outbreak of the American Revolution ... 11th ed. Lexington, Lexington hist. soc., 1963.   60 p.   21 cm.   F74.L67P741

LEXINGTON. An address by Rev. Carlton A. Staples, in commemoration of the ordination and settlement of John Hancock ... 1698, over Cambridge Farms parish, (now Lexington) in the First parish church, (Unitarian) Lexington. ... 1898. Arlington, C. S. Parker, print., 1900.   19 p. 22 cm. 6-1129.   F74.L67 S7

LEXINGTON, A discourse delivered at, 1813, the day which completed a century from the incorporation of the town. By Avery Williams ... Boston, Print. S. T. Armstrong, 1813.   34 p.   22 cm. Title-page wanting. 1-11473.   F74.L67 W7

MASSACHUSETTS

LEXINGTON. A brief history of the Lexington historical society in observance of its 75th anniversary, 1886 - 1961. By Edwin B. Worthen. Lexington, Mass., (1962) 35 p. 23 cm. F74.L67W76

LEYDEN, History of, 1676 - 1959. By William Tyler Arms. With the collaboration of Masha E. Arms. Orange, Mass., Enterprise and Journal, 1959. 220 p. 24 cm. F74. L68 A7

LINCOLN. An account of the celebration by the town of Lincoln ... 1904, of the 150th anniversary of the incorporation, 1754 - 1904. Lincoln, Mass., Print. for the town, 1905. v p., 3 l., (2), 239 p. front. 18 pl. (1 fold.) 23 cm. 6-30903. F74. L7 L6

LINCOLN. Dedication of the new town house in Lincoln ... 1892 ... Boston, Press of T. R. Marvin, 1893. 90 p. front., plates. 24 cm. "Address by William Everett": p. (22) - 68. 1-11474 Rev. F74. L7 L7

LINCOLN, Vital records of, to the year 1850. Boston, Pub. by the New-England historic genealogical soc. ... 1908. 179 p. 23 cm. 8-10310. F74. L7 L8

LINCOLN. A sermon commemorative of 150 years of the First church in Lincoln ... 1898, containing biographical sketches of the pastors and some of the citizens of the town; by Rev. Edward G. Porter. (Reprinted from the Proceedings) Cambridge, The University press, 1899. 48 p. front., 3 pl., 9 port., plan, 2 facsim. 23 cm. 4-1387 Rev. F74. L7 P8

LITTLETON. The works of God declared by one generation to another. A sermon .... On the completion of a century from the incorporation of that town. By Edmund Foster ... Concord, Mass., Print. Joseph T. Peters (1815) 2; 28 p. 21 cm. 1-11475. F74.L77 F7

LITTLETON, Records of. Print. by order of the town. First installment. Births and deaths from the earliest records ... 1715 ... Littleton, Mass. (Patriot press, Concord, Mass.) 1900. 4, (5) - 542, 178 p. 23 cm. Comp. by J. A. Harwood. Genealogical notes of Saml. Smith: p. 398 - 534. A10-1747 rev. F74. L77 L7

LITTLETON historical society, Proceedings. no. 1 - 3; 1894/5 - 1908. Littleton, Mass., 1896 - 1908. 3 v. in 2. 24 cm. No more published. 44-31899. F74.L77L87

LITTLETON. Petitions, remonstrances, and acts relating to Littleton and Roxborough, 1782 to 1869. By George Augustus Sanderson. (Boston, G. E. Crosby, 1890) 16 p. 26 cm. 1-11476.
F74. L77 S2

LONGMEADOW'S sesquicentennial official souvenir; pub. in connection with the 150th anniversary of the founding of the town of Longmeadow, under the supervision of the executive committee of the celebration and Mr. Frank S. Burt, chairman, souvenir program committee. Ed. and pub. by Edgar Holmes Plummer. (Longmeadow) Longmeadow 150th anniversary assoc. (1933) (66) p. illus. (incl. ports.) 28½ x 22 cm. 33-34836. F74. L8 L7

LONGMEADOW. Proceedings at the centennial celebration of the incorporation of the town of Longmeadow ... 1883, with numerous historical appendices and a town genealogy ... (Longmeadow) Pub. by the secretary of the Centennial committee, under authority of the town, 1884. 321, 97 p. front., plates, ports. 25 cm. Contains Genealogical record book, by Jabez Colton ... 97 p. at end. 1-11477 Add. F74. L8 L8

LONGMEADOW. Pamphlets, broadsides, clippings, and other miscellaneous matter on this subject, not separately cataloged, are classified in F74.L8Z9.

LOWELL directory, The ... 183 - Boston, Mass., Sampson & Murdock, 183 - 19 -
  v. fold. maps. 14 - 24 cm. 99-1709 Rev. Directories

LOWELL street guide ... Boston, Mass., Sampson & Murdock, 19 - v. 16½ cm. On cover: Arrow street guide. 38-16143. F74. L9 A2

LOWELL: past, present and prospective. By James Bayles. (Lowell, Mass., Citizen newspaper co.) 1891. 74 p. illus., fold. map. 25½ cm. 1-11479. F74. L9 B3

LOWELL, Chelmsford, Graniteville, Forge Village, Dracut, Collinsville, of to-day. Their commerce, trade, and industries, descriptive and historical.   By James Bayles.   (Lowell, Mass.) Lowell daily citizen, 1893.   122, (2) p.   front., illus., port.   fol.   Rev. and enl. ed.   1-11480-M1.   F74. L9 B33

LOWELL on the Merrimack; an art souvenir.   Containing ... views of the principal public buildings, private residences, parks, and streets of the city of Lowell ...   By Elwin S. Bigelow.   Lowell, Mass., E. S. Bigelow, 1892.   54 pl.   obl. 12°.   1-11481-M1.   F74. L9 B5

LOWELL.   Les Canadiens-français de Lowell, Mass.   Récensement.   Valeur commerciale, valeur immobilière, condition religieuse, civile, et politique, noms et adresses, suivis de la constitution et des reglements de l'Union franco-américaine.   Avila Bourbonnière, ed.   Lowell, Mass., 1896.   192 p.   illus., port.   8°.   1-11482-M1.   F74. L 9 B 7

LOWELL and its people, History of, by Frederick W. Coburn ...   New York city, Lewis historical pub. co., 1920.   3 v.   fronts., plates, ports.   27½ cm.   Bibliography: v.2, p. (463) - 470.   20-2722.   F74. L9 C65

LOWELL, A hand book of business in, with a history of the city.   By Charles Cowley ...   Lowell, E. D. Green, 1856.   168 p.   illus.   23½ cm.   Rev. and enl. ed. pub. 1868 under title: History of Lowell.   1-11483.   F74. L9 C77

LOWELL.   Hand-book of the New England agricultural fair, of 1871, with Charles Cowley's History of Lowell.   Lowell, A. Colby, 1871.   x, (13) - 238 p.   front., illus., plates, ports.   18½ cm.   A reprint of the author's History of Lowell. 2d rev. ed. 1868.   9-30090.   F74. L9 C79

LOWELL, Illustrated history of.   Rev. ed.   By Charles Cowley.   Boston, Lee & Shepard; Lowell, B. C. Sargeant and J. Merrill, 1868.   (ix) - x, (2), (13)-235 p.   illus., 9 pl. (incl. front.) 12 ports., fold. map. 19½ cm.   A revised and much enl. ed. of the author's Handbook of business...1856.   17-6163.   F74. L9 C8

LOWELL, A history of.   2d rev. ed.   By Charles Cowley.   Boston, Lee & Shepard; Lowell, B. C. Sargeant and J. Merrill, 1868.   (ix) - x, (13) - 235 p.   front., illus., port., plates. 19½ cm. 1-11484.   F74. L9 C81

LOWELL.   Memories of the Indians and pioneers of the region of Lowell (Mass.)   By Charles Cowley ...   Lowell, Stone & Huse, print., 1862.   24 p.   24 cm.   4-35450.   F74. L9 C82

LOWELL.   Quaint bits of Lowell history; a few interesting stories of earlier days.   By Sara Swan Griffin ...   Lowell, Butterfield print. co., 1913.   3, 9-112 p.   4 pl., port.   24 cm.   14-9260.   F74. L9 G85

LOWELL illustrated; a chronological record of events and historical sketches of the large manufacturing corporations; comp. and ed. by Frank P. Hill; photographic designs by N. C. Sanborn ... albertype plates by the Forbes co., Boston; letterpress by Huse, Goodwin, Lowell, Mass., 1884.   92 numb. 1.   31 pl.   28 x 36½ cm.   8-16767.   F74. L9 H6

LOWELL.   Illustrated history of Lowell and vicinity; done by divers hands; ...   Lowell, Mass., Courier-Citizen co., 1897.   4, (5) - 881 p. incl. illus., ports.   31½ cm.   Illustrations incl. maps and facsims.   "Bibliography of the local history of Lowell": p. 869 - 872.   2-3878.   F74. L9 I 3

LOWELL.   In and about Lowell.   (Lowell) Mass., (1908)   1 v.   20½ x 25½ cm.   F74. L9 I 6

LOWEL magazine, ... The.   Devoted to the civic and commercial interests of Lowell.   v.1, no. 1-11; Mar. 1909 - June 1910.   Lowell, Mass., J. A. McKenna, 1910-11.   (240) p. illus. (incl. ports.) col. pl.   27 cm.   monthly (irregular)   No more published.   11-24447.   F74. L9 L8

LOWELL.   Exercises of the fiftieth anniversary commemorative of the incorporation of the city of Lowell ...   1886.   Lowell, Mass., Vox populi press, S. W. Huse, 1886.   107 p.   23½ cm.   1-12360.   F74. L9 L9

LOWELL.   (Lowell, Mass., Courier-citizen co., 189-)   16 p.   22½ cm.   Specimen pages.   F74. L9 L92

LOWELL.   Proceedings in the city of Lowell at the semi-centennial celebration of the incorporation of the town of Lowell ...   1876.   Lowell, Mass., Penhallow print., 1876.   151, 11, (2) p.   front., fold. maps.   23½ cm.   1-12361.   F74. L9 L95

MASSACHUSETTS

LOWELL, Vital records of, to the end of the year 1849 ... Salem, Mass., The Essex institute. 1930 -
4 v.   23 cm.   30-17085.
F74.L9L951

LOWELL book, The.   Boston, G. H. Ellis, 1899.   52, (4) p. front., illus., plates, ports.   28 cm.   A collection of articles by various writers descriptive of the city of Lowell.   8-16819.
F74.L9L952

LOWELL courier-citizen.   Centennial ed.   1836 - 1936.   (Lowell, 1936)   1 v. illus. 58 cm. Issued June 30, 1936.   39M4778T.
F74.L9L953

LOWELL courier-citizen.   Centennial ed., 1840 - 1940.   Lowell, Mass., 1940.   (116) p. illus. 58 cm. Forms v. 98, new ser. no. 259 of the Lowell courier-citizen, issued Oct. 31, 1940.   42M175T.
F74.L9L954

LOWELL HISTORICAL SOCIETY ... By-laws.   (Lowell, Mass., 1902)   15 p.   13½ cm.   6-35830.
F74.L9L956

LOWELL historical society, Contributions of the ... v.1, no. 1 -   Lowell, Mass., 1907 -
1 no.   pl.   23 cm.   8-2376.
F74.L9L957

LOWELL cemetery.   Annual report ... 1850 -
F74.L9 L96

LOWELL.   The parish register of St. Anne's church, Lowell.   Rev. Theodore Edson, the first and only rector ... 1824 - 1883.   Lowell, Morning mail print, 1885.   155 p.   23½ cm.   10-3141.
F74.L9L965

LOWELL, a city of spindles; pub. the Trades and labor council of Lowell.   Being a series of illustrated historical articles pertaining to the social and industrial growth of Lowell ... (Lowell, Lawler & co., print., 1900)   456 p. incl. front., illus.   23 cm.   12-2454.
F74.L9L967

LOWELL illustrated; a souvenir of the textile metropolis of industrial New England.   Lowell, 1907.
20½ x 25½ cm.
F74.L9L972

LOWELL sun, The.   (Centennial souvenir edition)   Lowell, Mass., 1936.   1 v.   illus.   55 cm.
Forms v. 58, no. 150 of the Lowell sun, issued June 27, 1936.   39M4779T.
F74.L9L976

LOWELL'S tribute to her returned soldiers of the Spanish-American war, 1898.   Co. M, 9th regiment, Co.'s C and G, 6th regiment M.V.M. at the Armory, Nov. 30, 1898.   (Lowell, 1898)
80 p.   col. front., illus. (incl. ports.)   25 cm.   18-17100.
F74.L9L978

LOWELL, an early American industrial community.   (Selections) prepared for an introductory course in the humanities and social sciences at Massachusetts Institute of Technology.   (Cambridge) Technology Press (1950)   306 p.   illus., ports., maps.   26 cm.   Bibliography: p. 305 - 306.   51-1886.
F74. L9 M3

LOWELL.   Dedicatory exercises at the new court house, Lowell, Mass ... 1898.   (Lowell? 1898)
21 numb. l.   23½ cm.   1-11485 Rev.
F74. L9 M5

LOWELL, as it was, and as it is.   By Rev. Henry A. Miles ... Lowell (Mass.) Powers and Bagley, 1845.   234 p.   front. (fold. plan) fold. pl.   16½ cm.   1-11486.
F74. L9 M6

— 2d ed.   Lowell, N. L. Dayton (etc.) 1847.   234 p.   front. (fold. plan)   16 cm.   25-2321.
F74. L9 M6
1847

— 1972.
F74. L9 M6
1972

LOWELL.   A sermon delivered at the South Congregational church in Lowell, ... following the funeral of the Hon. Luther Lawrence, who died April 17, 1839.   By Henry A. Miles.   Lowell, L. Huntress, print., 1839.   14 p.   22½ cm.   11-26705.
F74. L9 M61

LOWELL.   Irish Catholic genesis of Lowell, by George F. O'Dwyer.   Lowell, Mass., Printed by

Sullivan brothers, 1920.   3, (18) p.   23 cm.   26-20216.   F74. L9 O2

LOWELL. Old residents' historical association of Lowell. Contributions of the Old residents' v. 1-6; Jan. 1874-Jan. 1904 ... Lowell, Mass., The association, 1873-1904. 6 v. illus., plates, ports. 23½ cm. Vol. 1 - 4, 6 each composed of 4 numbers; v. 5 of 2 numbers. No more pub. 5-35752.   F74. L9 O4

LOWELL. Picturesque Lowell. Photo-gravures. Lowell, Mass., T. H. Lawler, 1896. 1 p. 16 pl. obl. 24°. Photos. by R. E. Westcott. 1-11487-M1.   F74. L9 P6

LOWELL. The Franco-Americans of Lowell. By Richard Santerre. Lowell, Mass., Franco-American Day Committee, 1972. (27) p. illus. 23 cm.   F74. L9 S2

LOWELL. Views of Lowell and vicinity. (Lowell, Mass., 1904) 20 x 25 cm.   F74. L9 V6

— (1905)   20 x 25 cm.   F74. L9 V7

LUDLOW. Christmas souvenir from - illustrating Ludlow. One of the most attractive manufacturing villages in America. (Ludlow, Mass? 1906) 13 x 17½ cm.   F74. L94 C5

LUDLOW: a century and a centennial, comprising a sketch of the history of the town of Ludlow, ... together with an account of the celebration by the town of its centennial anniversary ... 1874. Comp. by Alfred Noon ... Printed by vote of the town. Springfield, Mass., C. W. Bryan, print., 1875. xviii, 208 p. front., ports. 23½ cm. Genealogies: p. 184 - 192. 1-11488.   F74. L95 N8

LUDLOW, The history of, with biographical sketches of leading citizens, reminiscences, genealogies, farm histories, and an account of the centennial celebration ... 1874 ... Comp. by Alfred Noon ... 2d ed. rev. and enl. Springfield, Mass., Springfield, print., 1912. xiv, (19) - 592 p. incl. front., illus., plates, ports. pl. 25½ cm. Genealogies: p. (337) - 473. 13-10222.   F74. L94N81

LUNENBERG, The early records of the town of, including that part which is now Fitchburg; 1719 - 1764. A complete transcript of the town meetings and selectmen's records contained in the first two books of the general records of the town; also a copy of all the vital statistics of the town previous to the year 1764. Comp. by Walter A. Davis ... Fitchburg, Pub. by authority of the City council, 1896. vi, (7) - 384 p. front., facsims. 24 cm. 1-11489.   F74. L96 L9

LUNENBURG. The Proprietors' records of the town of, including Fitchburg and a portion of Ashby. 1729 - 1833. ... Comp. by Walter A. Davis ... Fitchburg, Pub. by authority of the City council, 1897.   x, 374 p. front., facsims. 24 cm. The town of Fitchburg ... was set off from Lunenburg in 1764 and a part of Fitchburg was incorporated in the new town of Ashby 1767. The Proprietor's lands lay in all three towns after division. 1-11490.   F74. L96L95

LYNN street directory. (Boston) The R. S. Bauer co.   90 p. 12 cm. 20-14828.   F74. L98 A2

LYNN. A century of Puritanism, and a century of its opposite; with results contrasted to enforce Puritan principles, and to trace what is peculiar in the people of Lynn to what is peculiar in its history. By Parsons Cooke ... Boston, S. K. Whipple, 1855. 444 p. 18½ cm. 10-5394.   F74. L98 C7

LYNN. Address of greeting from the Essex institute to the Lynn historical society on the occasion of its tenth anniversary celebration, ... 1906; delivered by Abner C. Goodell. (Salem? Mass., 1906?) 7 p. 23 cm. 7-36587.   F74. L98 G6

LYNN. Greater Lynn. (Lynn, Mass. Lynn chamber of commerce) 19   v. illus. 31 cm. monthly. 38M899T.   F74. L98 G7

LYNN. Hearths and homes of old Lynn, with studies in local history, by Nathan Mortimer Hawkes ... Lynn, Mass., T. P. Nichols, 1907. xvi, 350 p. front., illus., plates, ports., etc. 21 cm. 7-12499.   F74. L98H25

LYNN. In Lynn woods, with pen and camera, by Nathan Mortimer Hawkes ... Lynn, Mass., T. B. Nichols, 1893.   vi, 104 p. front., plates (1 double) 23½ cm. 1-11491.   F74. L98 H3

LYNN and surroundings, by Clarence W. Hobbs ... Lynn, Mass., Lewis & Winship, 1886. 161 p. illus. (incl. ports., map, plans) 25 cm. 1-11492.   F74. L98 H8

MASSACHUSETTS

LYNN pictures, by James Jeffrey; with designs and engravings by the author.   Lynn (Mass.) Jeffrey & Law, printers, 1880.   29 l.   front., illus., plates.   19 x 17 cm.   1-11493 Rev.   F74.L98 J4

LYNN, Sketches of; or, The changes of fifty years, by David N. Johnson ... Lynn (Mass.) T. P. Nichols, printer, 1880.   vii, 490 p.   front., plates.   20 cm.   1-11494 Additions.   F74.L98 J6

— Westport, Conn., Greenwood Press (1970)   vii, 490 p.   illus.   23 cm.   79-88510.   F74.L98 J6 1970

LYNN, The history of.   By Alonzo Lewis ... Boston, Press of J. H. Eastburn, 1829.   260 p. front., plates.   22 cm.   In the form of annals, 1629 - 1829, followed by "Description of Lynn." p. (235) - 256.   1-12362.   F74.L98 L5 Toner coll.

LYNN.   Waterman pamphlets, 73 no. 1.   AC901.W3 vol. 73 no. 1 (Rare Book Coll.) or   F74.L98 L5

LYNN.   The history of Lynn, including Nahant.   By Alonzo Lewis, — the Lynn bard ... 2d ed. Boston, Print. S. N. Dickinson, 1844.   278 p. illus., 2 pl. (incl. front.)   23½ cm.   Nahant formed part of Lynn until 1853. 1-12363.   F74.L98L51

LYNN, History of: including Lynnfield, Saugus, Swampscot, and Nahant.   By Alonzo Lewis and James R. Newhall.   Boston, J. L. Shorey, 1865.   viii, 9 - 620 p.   front., illus., plates, facsim. 24 cm.   A revision and continuation of Lewis's History of Lynn, first pub. 1829.   12-11195.   F74.L98L55

— Lynn, G. C. Herbert (1890) - 97.   2 v. illus., plates, maps, facsims. 24 cm.   A revision and continuation of Lewis's History of Lynn, first pub. 1829. Earlier ed. of v. 2 also pub. separately.   1-12364.   F74.L98 L6

LYNN.   The ways of a worker of a century ago as shown by the diary of Joseph Lye, shoemaker, by Fred A. Gannon ... Salem, Mass., Print. Newcomb & Gauss (1918)   25 p.   illus. 15 cm.   18-21664.   F74.L98 L8

LYNN: its representative business men and points of interest.   New York, Mercantile illus. co., 1893.   iii, (1) p. illus. 4º.   1-11495-M1.   F74.L98 L9

LYNN, Centennial memorial of.   Embracing an historical sketch, 1629 - 1876, by James R. Newhall, and notices of the mayors, with portraits.   Lynn, Pub. by order of the City council, 1876. viii, (9) - 204 p.   front., plates, ports.   25 cm.   1-11496.   F74.L98L92

LYNN.   The City hall of Lynn; being a history of events leading to its erection, and an account of the ceremonies at the dedication of the building ... 1867.   Pub. by order of the City council.   Lynn, T. P. Nichols, print., 1869.   xviii, 132 p.   front., illus. 23 cm.   10-5392.   F74.L98L925

LYNN.   City of Lynn, semi-centennial of incorporation.   Events and exercises of the 50th anniversary celebration ... 1900.   Lynn, Mass. (Whitten & Cass, print.) 1900.   xvi, 292 p.   front., illus., plates, ports., facsims.   24½ cm.   Ed. Walter L. Ramsdell.   1-2625.   F74.L98L93

LYNN.   Proceedings in Lynn ... being the 250th anniversary of the settlement.   Embracing the oration, by Cyrus M. Tracy, etc. and a second part, by James R. Newhall.   Lynn, Pub. by order of the City council, 1880.   vi, (7) - 224 p.   illus. 24½ cm.   Includes biographical sketches.   1-11497.   F74.L98L97

LYNN, Vital records of, to the end of the year 1849 ... Salem, Mass., The Essex institute, 1905-06. 2 v.   23½ cm.   v. 1. Births. - v. 2. Marriages and deaths.   6-13930 Additions.   F74.L98L976

LYNN.   Lynn ... Chamber of commerce (1916)   96 p.   23 x 30½ cm.   F74.L98L9765

LYNN.   (Lynn) Lynn chamber of commerce (1916)   (96) p. illus.   23 x 31 cm.   17-12851.   F74.L98L9766

LYNN.   Celebration of the 275th anniversary of the First church of Christ.   Lynn, Press of T. P. Nichols, 1907.   2, (13) - 153 p. 7 pl. (incl. front.)   23 cm.   8-4358.   F74.L98L977

LYNN.   The register of the Lynn historical society.   (no. 1) -   for the year(s) 1897 -   Ed. by the

Committee on publication. Lynn, Mass., 1898 -   v. in   fronts., illus., plates, ports., fold. map.
23½ cm.   "Index of the Register." 1897 - 1908: no. 12, p. 149-161.   6-7471.   F74.L98L98

LYNN.   Dedication of the tablet in commemoration of the Old tunnel, by the Lynn historical society.
Placed on the meeting-house of the First Congregational church ... 1909.   (Lynn, T. P. Nichols, 1909)
(8) p.   illus.   25 cm.   9-23291.   F74.L98L982

LYNN manual and Essex County road book, The ... Lynn (Mass.) E. F. Bacheller, 1888.
viii, 48 p. fold. map, fold. plan.   14½ x 11½ cm.   8-31701.   F74.L98L983

LYNN review, The.   A monthly epitome of Lynn affairs.   1st - 11th year; Nov. 1898 - 1909.   Lynn,
E. W. Ingalls, 1898 - 1909.   11 v.   illus. (ports.)   22½ cm.   6-43113.   F74.L98L986

LYNN, History of: including Lynnfield, Saugus, Swampscott, and Nahant.   1883 volume.   By James
Newhall.   Lynn, The author, 1883.   viii, 9-322 p. 4 front. (incl. ports.) illus. (incl. facsims.) plates. 23½ cm.   A
continuation of "The history of Lynn," by Alonzo Lewis and James R. Newhall, first pub. 1865. 1-12365 Rev.   F74.L98 N4

— 1864 - 1890.   Lynn, G. C. Herbert (1890)   vii, 9-352 p. 4 front. (incl. ports.) illus. (incl. facsims.) plates.   23 cm.
A reprint of the 1883 ed. with a supplement continuing the annals to 1890.   1-12366 Rev.   F74.L98N45

LYNN.   Liñ: or Jewels of the Third plantation ... By Obediah Oldpath (pseud. for James Robinson
Newhall)   Lynn (Mass.) T. Herbert and J. M. Munroe, 1862.   viii, 9-400 p. 19½ cm.   1-12367. F74.L98N47

— 2d ed. enl.   Boston, D. C. Colesworthy; Lynn, S. A. Barton, 1880.   viii, 9-500 p. front. (map) illus.,
plates.   24 cm.   1-12368.   F74.L98N48

— A new ed.   Lynn, G. C. Herbert (1890)   viii, 9-500 p. front. (map) illus., plates. 24 cm. 23-2875.
                                                                                                  F74.L98N49

LYNN in the revolution; comp. from notes gathered by Howard Kendall Sanderson ... Boston, W. B.
Clarke, 1909.   2 v. front., illus., plates, ports., maps (partly fold.) facsims. 25½ cm. Paged continuously. The Hallowell
journal: p. 149 - 183.   9-32378.   F74.L98 S2

LYNN.   Souvenir: Lynn, Swampscott, Marblehead, Nahant.   Lynn, Mass., Souvenir pub. co. (1891)
1 p. 25 pl.   obl. 24°.   1-11498-M1.   F74.L98 S7

LYNN.   A sermon, preached at Lynn ... 1795, at the interment of eight seamen.   By Thomas Cushing
Thacher ....   Print. Samuel Hall, 1795.   vii, (9) - 22 p. 18½ cm.   The seamen were members of the crew of the brig
"Peggy", cast away on Lynn beach, Dec. 9, 1795. 11-30526.   F74.L98 T3
                                                                                                  Rare Book Coll.

LYNN.   Views of Lynn and vicinity.   (Portland, Me., 19 -)   (32) p.   20 x 25 cm.   F74.L98 V6

— (Portland, Me., L. H. Nelson, 1910)   (32) p. illus.   20 x 25 cm.   F74.L98V62

LYNN.   Historic priorities in Lynn, an address given at the dedication of the society house, Lynn
historical society, ... by C. J. H. Woodbury ... Lynn, Mass., 1913.   37 p.   23½ cm. "Reprinted from the
Register of the society, vol. xvii."   14-13124.   F74.L98 W8

LYNNFIELD, Vital records of, to the end of the year 1849.   Salem, Mass., The Essex institute, 1907.
98 p. 23½ cm. 8-10309.   F74.L99 L8

LYNNFIELD.   First book of records of the First church in Lynnfield; continued from Historical
collections, Essex institute, vol. v, p. 228 ... By Eben. Parsons.   Salem, Mass., The Salem Press,
1898.   117 - 193 p.   23 cm.   Contains records for 1733 - 1824. (From Historical colls. of the Essex institute, vol. xxxiv) 5-4361.
                                                                                                  F74.L99 L9

LYNNFIELD, History of the town of, 1635 - 1895, by Thomas B. Wellman ... Boston, The Blanchard &
Watts engr. co.(1895)   xv, 268 p. front., illus., pl., port.   20½ cm.   3-4941.   F74.L99 W4

MAGNOLIA leaves ... Magnolia, Mass., 1881 - 82.   4 v. in 1.   22 cm.   F74. M1 M2

482

MASSACHUSETTS

MAGNOLIA souvenir. By H. Spaulding. Boston, F. Wood, 1886. 52 p. illus. 8° 1-11499-M1.
F74. M1 S7

MALDEN. City of Malden directory ... (v.1) -   For (1882) - 87. By Charles E. Bruce. Boston, Press of G. E. Crosby, (1882) - 87. 2 v. fronts. (v.1: port.) illus. 24 cm. 8-10578.
Directories

MALDEN directory, The. (no.1) -   1870/71 -   Boston, Sampson & Murdock co. (1870) - 19 v. fold. plans. 23½ cm. 98-911.
Directories

MALDEN, Blue book of. (1892) -   (v.1) - 3, 5 - 7. Boston, E. A. Jones (1891) - 1905.
6 v. plans (partly fold.) 21 cm. 2-710.
Directories

MALDEN, The history of, 1633 - 1785, by Deloraine Pendre Corey ... Malden, The author, 1899.
xvii, 870 p. front., illus. (incl. facsims.) 2 fold. plans. 25 cm. 98-2246 Rev.
F74. M2 C7

MALDEN. The Woodlawn cemetery in North Chelsea and Malden. ... By Henry Weld Fuller. Boston, Higgins and Bradley, 1856. viii, (9) - 125 p. front., illus., plates. 22 cm. "Proprietors of lots": p. 112-124.
11-19262.
F74. M2 F9

MALDEN. An oration delivered at Malden, on the 200th anniversary of the incorporation of the town .. 1849. By James D. Green. Boston, Print. G. C. Rand, 1850. 53 p. 23 cm. 3-28201.
F74. M2 G7

MALDEN, The bi-centennial book of. Containing the oration and poem ... with other proceedings ... and matters pertaining to the history of the place ... Pub. for the citizens of Malden. Boston, Print. G. C. Rand, 1850. 251 p. illus. 19 cm. "Old Malden families": p. 230-251. 1-11500.
F74. M2 M2

MALDEN. Births, marriages and deaths in the town of Malden, 1649 - 1850; comp. by Deloraine P. Corey. Cambridge, Print. at the University press for the city of Malden, 1903. xiv p. 393 p. 23½ cm.
Uniform in binding with the two series of vital records of Massachusetts ... 3-23027.
F74. M2M22

MALDEN. Memorial of the celebration of the 250th anniversary of the incorporation of the town of Malden ... 1899 ... Cambridge, Printed at the University press, 1900. xii, 340 p. front., plates, ports. 25 cm. 1-11501.
F74. M2M25

MALDEN. Oration, poem, speeches, chronicles, etc. at the dedication of the Malden town hall ... 1857. Malden (Mass.) C. C. P. Moody, 1857. 52 p. 8°. 1-11502-M1.
F74. M2M26

MALDEN. Proceedings of the 275th anniversary of Malden. Malden auditorium ... 1924 ... (Malden) The Malden historical soc., 1925. 44 p. front. (2 port.) illus. (facsim.) plates. 25 cm. "Malden settlers before 1665 (compiled by G. W. Chamberlain)": p. 5-6. 25-15880.
F74. M2M263

MALDEN. The 275th anniversary of Malden ... 1924. (Malden? The Dunbar-Kerr co.) 1924.
7 p. illus. 21½ x 18 cm. "Malden settlers before 1665" p. 3. 24-20928.
F74. M2 M3

MALDEN historical society, The register of. no. 1 -   1910/11 -   Lynn, Mass., 1910 -
v. plates, ports. 23 cm. 12-1313.
F74. M2 M6

MALDEN, Views of. n.p. 1806. 13½ x 20½ cm.
F74. M2 V6

MANCHESTER. The Gloucester suburban directory ... Manchester and Essex ... v. 1 - 1916 - 1 v.
F74. M26A18

MANCHESTER, Art work of. Chicago, The W. H. Parish pub. co., 1892. 19 l. illus., 72 pl. 35½ x 28 cm. 22-13933.
F74. M26A27

MANCHESTER. History of the town of Manchester, 1645 - 1895; by Rev. D. F. Lamson ... (Manchester) The town (1895) xii, 425, xiv p. incl. illus., facsim. plates, ports., plan, map. 23½ cm. 1-11503.
F74. M26 L2

MANCHESTER Town records. Salem, 1889-91. 2 v. 8°.
F74. M26M2

MANCHESTER, Vital records of, to the end of the year 1849.   Salem, The Essex institute, 1903.
296 p.   23½ cm.   4-9195 Rev.
F74. M26M3

MANSFIELD.   Polk's Mansfield, Foxboro, Norton and Raynham city directory ... Boston, Mass., and New York, R. L. Polk, 19 -   v.   24 cm.   CA 26-736 Unrev.
Directories

MANSFIELD.   Resident and business directory of Mansfield and Foxborough ... Hopkinton, Mass., A. E. Foss, 1898 - 1909.   5 v.   24 cm.   9-27450.
Directories

MANSFIELD, Vital records of, to the end of the year 1849.   Salem, Mass., The Essex institute, 1933.
230 p.   23 cm.   34-9003.
F74. M28M26

MANSFIELD.   Right and wrong, in Mansfield, Mass.   Or, an account of the pro-slavery mob of Oct. 10th, 1836: when an anti-slavery lecturer (Charles C. Burleigh) was silenced by the beat of drums, with some reasoning in favor of emancipation.   By Isaac Stearns.   Appendix, containing a list of officers and members of the Mansfield anti-slavery society.   Pawtucket, Mass., R. Sherman, print., 1837.   61 p.   22 cm.   10-34788.
F74. M28 S7

MARBLEHEAD Neck directory ... 1935 -   (Marblehead, Mass.) Marblehead Neck improvement association, 1935 -   v. double map.   19½ cm.   35-19919.
Directories

MARBLEHEAD sketches, by Anne Ashby Agge and Mary Mason Brooks ... Boston, Houghton, Mifflin (1885)   1 p.   10 pl.   38 cm.   Poetical quotations from Whittier, Emerson, Longfellow, and others.   1-12371.
F74. M3 A2

MARBLEHEAD.   A gentleman from Indiana looks at Marblehead.   By Hartley Alley.   Freeport, Me., B. Wheelwright Co. (1963)   96 p.   illus.   29 cm.   64-12189.
F74. M3 A5

MARBLEHEAD.   Old Marblehead; a camera impression, by Samuel Chamberlain.   New York, Hastings house (1940)   72, (1) p.   front., illus.   19 x 15½ cm.   69 p. of illus.   40-13104.
F74. M3 C5

MARBLEHEAD.   A discourse, on the history of the first Christian church and society in Marblehead; delivered to his people Jan. 1816, by Samuel Dana ... Boston: Print. Samuel T. Armstrong, 1816.
31 p.   22½ cm.   6-15313 Rev.
F74. M3 D17

MARBLEHEAD.   Glimpses of old Marblehead ... Marblehead, Mass., M. H. Graves (1896)
31 p.   illus.   16 x 23 cm.   1-11504 Rev.
F74. M3 G5

MARBLEHEAD.   Rev. John Barnard, of Marblehead.   By Samuel Abbott Green.   (Cambridge? 1896?)
4 p.   24 cm.   11-25760.
F74. M3 G7

MARBLEHEAD.   An artist's sketch book of old Marblehead, by Lester G. Hornby; with tex by Sylvester Baxter.   Boston, A. W. Elson, 1906.   40 numb. l. incl. illus., 18 pl.   col. front.   24½ x 33 cm.   6-46780.
F74. M3 H8

MARBLEHEAD Neck ... By Moses King.   New York, 1904.   13 x 19 cm.
F74. M3 K5

MARBLEHEAD, the historic landmarks and points of interest and how to see them, by John Kennedy Lacock ... Medford, Mass., Press of J. C. Miller, 1929.   16 p.   illus.   16½ cm.   CA 30-1250 Unrev.
F74. M3 L14

MARBLEHEAD.   Historical sermon, preached by the Rev. John W. Leek ... 1872 ... Peabody (Mass.) Printed at "The Peabody press office," 1873.   25 p.   23 cm.   18-4495.
F74. M3 L4

MARBLEHEAD; the spirit of '76 lives here (by) Priscilla Sawyer Lord (and) Virginia Clegg Gamage. Illus. with line drawings by Marion Martin Brown.   (1st ed.) Philadelphia, Chilton Book Co. (1971, c1972)   xii, 395 p.   illus.   24 cm.   Bibliography: p. (372) - 379.   73-169586 MARC.
F74. M3 L6

MARBLEHEAD, Vital records of, to the end of the year 1849 ... Salem, Mass., The Essex institute, 1903-08.   3 v.   23½ cm.   5-14241.
F74. M3 M4

MASSACHUSETTS 255

MARBLEHEAD. Manual and historical sketch of the First Congregational church, Marblehead. 1684 - 1901. (Marblehead, Mass., N. A. Lindsey, print. 1901) 107 p. 2 pl. (incl. front.) 17½ cm. 7-40106.
F74. M3M41

MARBLEHEAD, Historical society of ... 1899. (List of officers, history and by-laws) Marblehead, N. A. Lindsey, print., 1899. 9 p. 14 cm. 6-38490.
F74. M3 M43

— 1905. 13 p. 14 cm. 7-2003.
F74. M3M436

MARBLEHEAD. Old Marblehead sea captains and the ships in which they sailed ... comp. and pub. for the benefit of the Marblehead historical society by Benjamin J. Lindsey, treasurer. (Marblehead, Mass.) 1915. 137 p. illus. (incl. ports., facsims.) col. plates. 26 cm. 16-6470.
F74. M3M437

MARBLEHEAD. ... Ye old colonial days celebration. In connection with the exercises ... 1913, commemorative of Marblehead's place in colonial history, this souvenir book is issued by the Marblehead historical society ... (Marblehead, Marblehead hist. soc., 1913) (52) p. illus. 31 cm. 16-4108.
F74. M3 M44

MARBLEHEAD. (Marblehead, M. H. Graves, 1902) 27 mounted phot. 18½ x 23½ cm. 45-53855. F74. M3 M46

MARBLEHEAD, A guide to. By Samuel Roads, Jr. ... Marblehead, Mass., C. H. Litchman, 1881. 64 p. illus. 21½ cm. 1-11505.
F74. M3 R6

MARBLEHEAD. The history and traditions of Marblehead. By Samuel Roads ... Boston, Houghton, Osgood, 1880. xviii, 423 p. front., plates, ports. 22½ cm. 1-11506.
F74. M3 R7

MARBLEHEAD, The history and traditions of. By Samuel Roads, jr. ... (3d ed.) Marblehead, Press of Lindsey & co., 1897. xxiv, 595 p. front., illus. (incl. facsim.) plates, ports. 23 cm. 1-11507. F74. M3 R73

MARBLEHEAD manual, The ... Comp. by Samuel Roads, jr. Marblehead, Mass., Statesman pub. co., 1883. 96 p. 24º. 14½ cm. 1-12372-M1.
F74. M3 R8

MARBLEHEAD, The story of, by Joseph S. Robinson; sketches by Curtis Smith Hamilton especially for this history. (Lynn, Mass., 1936) 4; 91 p. illus., plates (1 col.) 23½ cm. "A century of yachting at Marblehead, by Wm. U. Swan": p. 83-91. 37-1028.
F74. M3 R83

MARBLEHEAD. The Fountain inn, Agnes Surriage and Sir Harry Frankland; a paper read before the Marblehead historical soc ... by Nathan P. Sanborn ... (Marblehead, Mass.) Pub. by the society, 1905. 43 p. front. 18 cm. 6-39296.
F74. M3 S19

MARBLEHEAD. Gen. John Glover and his Marblehead regiment in the revolutionary war; a paper read before the Marblehead historical society ... by Nathan P. Sanborn ... (Marblehead, Mass.) The Society, 1903. 56 p. front. (port.) 18 cm. 4-18846.
F74. M3 S2

MARBLEHEAD great neck, by Richard Whiting Searle. Salem, Mass. (Newcomb & Gauss print.) 1937. 37 p. front., plates, maps (part fold.) facsim. 25 cm. "Reprinted from the Historical colls. of the Essex institute vol. lxxiii. 38-34426.
F74. M3 S4

MARBLEHEAD, A souvenir of. (Marblehead, Mass.) Observer book and job print (1895?) 40 p. illus. fol. Ed. J. F. Brown. 1-16614-M1.
F74. M3 S7

MARBLEHEAD. The Lee mansion, what it was and what it is. Miss Hannah Tutt, historian, of the Marblehead historical society ... Boston, Print. C. B. Webster, 1911. 16 p. illus. 23½ cm. 18-6582.
F74. M3 T96

MARBLEHEAD. ... Scenes in Marblehead ... By Charles A. Walker. (Boston) W. Kimball (1886) 6 etchings. obl. 24º. 1-12373-M1.
F74. M3 W1

MARBLEHEAD. A discourse, occasioned by the loss of a number of vessels, with their mariners, belonging to the town of Marblehead ... By William Whitwell, pastor of the First church in said town.

485

Salem, Print. Samuel Hall, 1770.   21 p.   19½ cm.   8-25611.   F74. M3 W6
                                                                                                  Rare Book Coll.

MARION.   Lands of Sippican, on Buzzards bay, by Alice Austin Ryder.   New Bedford, Mass., Reynolds print., 1934.   3, ix-xi p. xii-xvi, 368 p. front., illus. (map) plates, ports. 23½ cm.   "First ed. Limited to 100 copies,"
Sippican is now Marion.   Bibliography: p. xiii.   34-34778.   F74. M313 R8

MARLBORO.   Directory for Marlboro, Westboro, Northboro, Southboro, Hudson, Berlin, Bolton, Stow and Sudbury, 1899   Salem, Mass., New England directory co.   v. fold. plan. 24 cm. 9-4480 Add.
                                                                                                  Directories

MARLBORO.   Leading business men of Marlboro, Hudson, S. Framingham, Natick, and vicinity; embracing also Saxonville and Cochituate.   Boston, Mercantile pub. co., 1890.   86 p. illus. 25½ cm.
In double columns.   4-20151.   F74. M32 B2

MARLBOROUGH.   Historical reminiscences of the early times in Marlborough, and prominent events from 1860 to 1910, including ... an account of the celebration of the 250 anniversary of the incorporation of the town.   By Ella A. Bigelow.   Marlborough, Mass., Times pub. co., 1910.   xvii, 488 p. incl.
front., illus., plates, ports.   24 cm.   10-20281.   F74. M32 B5

MARLBOROUGH.   A record of upwards of 600 events, with the dates of their occurrence in Marlborough and neighboring towns ... No. 2.   By Cyrus Felton ... Marlborough, Mass., The Times pub. co., print., 1880.   43 p.   23 cm.   No. 1 'A record of 450 events in Marlborough and vicinity' was pub. in 1879.   5-13205.
                                                                                                  F74. M32 F3

MARLBOROUGH.   An historical sketch of the First Congregational church in Marlborough, with the exercises at the celebration of the 50th anniversary of Rev. Sylvester F. Bucklin's ordination ...   By Levi A. Field ... Worcester, H. J. Howland, print., 1859.   iv, (5) - 82 p.   19½ cm.   Bound with following item.
6-40775.   F74. M32 F4

MARLBOROUGH.   A sermon, preached in Marlborough ... 1858, by Rev. Sylvester F. Bucklin ... Worcester, H. J. Howland, print., 1859.   52 p. 19½ cm.   Bound with above item. 6-40776.   F74. M32 F4

MARLBOROUGH.   The story of the John Brown bell, by direction of John A. Rawlins post 43, Grand Army of the Republic ... (Marlborough? Mass., 1910)   19 p. illus. (incl. ports.) 20½ cm. 10-15882.
                                                                                                  F74. M32 G6

MARLBOROUGH.   Note-book kept by the Rev. William Brinsmead, the first minister of Marlborough. Remarks made before the Mass. historical soc. ... By Samuel Abbott Green.   Cambridge, J. Wilson, 1889.   7 p.   24 cm.   3-6085.   F74. M32 G7

MARLBOROUGH.   History of the town of Marlborough ... from its first settlement in 1657 to 1861; with a brief sketch of the town of Northborough, a genealogy of the families in Marlborough to 1800, and an account of the celebration of the 100th anniversary of the incorporation of the town.   By Charles Hudson ... Boston, Press of T. T. Marvin, 1862.   xvi, (13) - 544 p. front., plates, ports., plan. 23½ cm.
"Historical sketch of Northborough. By Rev. Joseph Allen": p. (293) - 302; "Genealogical sketch of the early families in Marlborough": p. (303) - 490.   1-12374.   F74. M32 H8

MARLBOROUGH, ... First records of.   Worcester, F. P. Rice, trustee of the fund, 1909.   2; 47 p.
23½ cm.   10-1713.   F74. M32 M2

MARLBOROUGH, Vital records of, to the end of the year 1849.   Worcester, Mass., F. P. Rice, trustee of the fund, 1908.   404 p.   23 cm.   8-6063.   F74. M32 M3

MARLBOROUGH, Notes on the history of, comp. by J. A. Pitman ... Marlborough, Mass., Times pub. co., 1905.   12 (i.e. 22) p.   23 cm.   7-41340.   F74. M32 P6

MARLBOROUGH, burial ground inscriptions: Old Common, Spring Hill, and Brigham cemeteries. Worcester, Mass., F. P. Rice, trustee of the fund, 1908.   2, (3) - 6, (2) p, (9) - 218 p. front., plates. 25½ cm.
8-17408.   F74. M32 R6

MASSACHUSETTS

MARSHFIELD. ... Historical sketch of the First church in Marshfield. ... Boston, C. C. P. Moody, print., (1854)   33, (3) p.   15 cm.   (Document of the Pilgrim conference of churches no. 4)   12-24129.   F74. M4 A3

MARSHFIELD. Holly Hill and Bayberry Beach. By Edwin Welles Dwight. (Boston, 1920) 18 p.   illus. (incl. maps)   plates.   23½ cm.   F74. M4 D9

MARSHFIELD sixty years ago. A lecture delivered in Marshfield ... by Rev. George Leonard. Boston, Print. J. F. Farmer, 1872.   25 p.   22½ cm.   13-24916.   F74. M4 L5

MARSHFIELD, 70° - 40' W: 42° - 5' N; the autobiography of a Pilgrim town; being an account of 300 years of a New England town; founded by the Pilgrims; lived in and developed by the Royalists; adopted by Daniel Webster; beloved by many of the ancestors of those who today make it their home. 1640 - 1940. Marshfield, Mass., Marshfield tercentenary committee, 1940.   xix, 334 p. incl. front., illus., plates, ports., maps (part double) facsims.   24 cm.   40-13105.   F74. M4 M3

MARSHFIELD, History of, by Lysander Salmon Richards ... Plymouth, The Memorial press, 1901-05. 2 v.   front. (ports.)   24 cm.   1-28080 Additions.   F74. .M4 R5

MARSHFIELD, Vital records of, to the year 1850. Compiled by Robert M. Sherman and Ruth Wilder Sherman. (Providence?) Soc. of Mayflower descendants in the State of Rhode Island, 1970 (c1969) x, 491 p.   24 cm.   73-85851.   F74. M4 S4

MARSHFIELD. Thunder & lightning; and deaths at Marshfield in 1658 & 1666. By Nathaniel Bradstreet Shurtleff. Boston, Privately printed, 1850.   2, iii, (5) - 55 p.   19½ cm.   100 copies for private use. 1-12375.   F74. M4 S5

MARSHFIELD. Memorials of Marshfield and guide book to its localities at Green Harbor. By Marcia A. Thomas ... Boston, Print. Dutton and Wentworth, 1854.   108 p.   3pl. (incl. front.)   port.   18½ cm.   "Family sketches": p. 13 - 89.   "Burying Hill. Inscriptions and memorials of interments": p. 92 - 108.   1-11508 Rev.   F74. M4 T4

MATTAPOISETT. An account of the celebration of the 50th anniversary of the incorporation of the town of Mattapoisett ... 1907. New Bedford, Mass., E. Anthony, print., 1908.   74 p. front., plates, ports.   21 cm.   Preface signed: Irving N. Tilden and others.   9-1237.   F74. M43 M35

MATTAPOISETT and Old Rochester; being a history of these towns and also in part of Marion and a portion of Wareham. Prepared under the direction of a committee of the town of Mattapoisett. New York, The Grafton press (1907)   6, (xi) - xii p., 424 p.   front. (map) plates, port., fold. plan.   19½ cm.   (The Grafton historical series, ed. by H. R. Stiles)   7-26622.   F74. M43 M4

MAYNARD, A brief history of the town of (by) William H. Gutteridge. Maynard, Pub. by the town, 1921.   115 p. incl. front., illus. fold. map.   19½ cm.   Reference, p. (5)   21-6952.   F74. M46 G9

MAYNARD, History of, 1871 - 1971. (Maynard, Mass., Historical Committee (1971)   234 p.   illus. 23 cm.   F74. M46 M3

MEDFIELD, Millis & Medway directory, The, 1914/15. Needham, Mass., A. J. Gordon. 1 v.   24 cm.   14-14619.   Directories

MEDFIELD. Exercises at the bi-centennial commemoration of the burning of Medfield by Indians in King Philip's war, ... 1876. Medfield, Print. G. H. Ellis, 1876.   56 p.   24 cm.   1-11509.   F74. M48 M4

MEDFIELD: proceedings at the celebration of the 250th anniversary of the incorporation of the town, 1901. Boston, G. H. Ellis co., print., 1902.   112 p.   front., pl., facsim.   28½ cm.   3-8380.   F74. M48 M46

MEDFIELD. Proceedings at the dedication of the town hall, Medfied, ... 1872: with supplement containing an account of the exercises at the re-dedication ... 1874; brief sketches of the churches of the town, etc. and a record of the soldiers furnished by the town in the late war of the rebellion. Medfield, 1875.   39 p., 2 l., (43) - 63, (2) p.   front., pl.   23½ cm.   1-11510.   F74. M48 M5

MEDFIELD, Vital records of, to the year 1850.   Boston, Pub. by the New-England historic genealogical soc. ... 1903.   243 p.   23½ cm.   3-11779.   F74. M48 M54

MEDFIELD, History of the town of.   1650.   1886; with genealogies of the families that held real estate or made any considerable stay in the town during the first two centuries.   Ed. William S. Tilden.   Illus. with portraits and with engravings after drawings by John A. S. Monks.   Boston, G. H. Ellis, 1887.   (9)-556 p. illus. (incl. ports.) 24 cm.   "Genealogies": p. (279)-525.   1-11511 Rev.   F74. M48 T5

MEDFORD.   Statement of facts, relating to a private and town way in the town of Medford.   By Robert Bacon.   (Medford, Mass., 1841?)   10 p.   8°.   1-16185-M1.   F74. M5 B2

MEDFORD.   A review of the proceedings to change a private way into a town way, in the town of Medford.   With the deeds and documents relating thereto.   By Robert Bacon.   (Medford, Mass., 1842?)   32 p.   8°.   1-16184-M1.   F74. M5 B21

MEDFORD.   Address delivered in Oak-Grove cemetery, Medford, ... 1866, at the consecration of the monument erected in honor of the Medford volunteers.   By Charles Brooks.   Boston, Press of J. Wilson, 1866.   14 p.   8°.   1-16188-M1.   F74. M5 B75

MEDFORD, History of the town of, from its first settlement, in 1630, to the present time, 1855.   By Charles Brooks ... Boston, J. M. Usher, 1855.   viii, 576 p. front., illus., plates, ports. 23½ cm.   Register of families, by William H. Whitmore: p. 499-(572)   1-12376.   F74. M5 B8

— Rev., enl., and brought down to 1885, by James M. Usher.   Boston, Rand, Avery, 1886.
592 p. front., illus., plates, ports., facsims.   24 cm.   Register of families, by W. H. Whitmore: p. 519-587.   1-11512.   F74. M5 B9

MEDFORD.   The tornado of 1851, in Medford, West Cambridge and Waltham.   Being a report by Rev. Charles Brooks, and reports by other committees.   Boston, J. M. Usher, 1852.   72 p.   15½ cm.
4-15519.   F74. M5 B92

MEDFORD.   Proceedings of the celebration of the 275th anniversary of the settlement of Medford ... 1905.   Prefaced by a brief history of the town and city from the day of settlement, by John H. Hooper ... (Medford, Mass.) The Executive committee (1906)   3 p, (v)-xii, 261 p. front., plates, ports., maps.   25½ cm.
6-22868.   F74. M5 M3

MEDFORD, Vital record of, to the year 1850.   Boston, Mass., Pub. by the New England historic genealogical soc. ... 1907.   469 p.   23½ cm.   7-16398.   F74. M5 M32

MEDFORD historical register, The.   v. 1-10; Jan. 1898 -   Medford, Mass., The Medford historical society (1898-1907)   10 v. in 5. illus., plates, ports., etc.   24-25 cm.   quarterly.   5-32184.   F74. M5 M35

MEDFORD historical society, The.   Medford? Mass., 1904.   16 cm.   F74. M5 M36

MEDFORD.   "On the banks of the Mystic:" an historic festival under the auspices of the Medford historical soc. and the personal direction of Miss Margaret McLaren Eager ... Medford opera house ... 1896 ... (Boston, Pinkham press, 1896?)   (24) p. illus., port.   23½ cm.   2-24658.   F74. M5 M5

MEDFORD past and present; 275th anniversary of Medford ... 1905; issued with the approval of the printing committee of the 275th anniversary celebration.   (Medford, Mass.) Medford mercury, 1905.
170 p. illus. (incl. ports.) fold. pl.   29 x 23½ cm.   In triple columns.   5-27064.   F74. M5 M55

MEDFORD.   Two discourses preached before the first Congregational soc. in Medford ... By Caleb Stetson, minister of the soc.   Boston, Print. by I. R. Butts, 1840.   59, (1) p.   23 cm.   24-13558.
                                                                                                                                          F74. M5 S8

MEDFORD.   Register of families settled at the town of Medford.   Comp. by W. H. Whitmore ... Boston, Print. by J. Wilson, 1855.   96 p. front., plates, ports.   23 cm.   1-11513.   F74. M5 W6

MEDFORD in the revolution.   Military history of Medford. 1765-1783.   Also list of soldiers and civil officers, with genealogical and biographical notes.   By Helen Tilden Wild.   Medford, J. C. Miller, print., 1903.   67 p. front. (port.)   22½ cm.   3-3214.   F74 M5 W7

MASSACHUSETTS

MEDWAY. The biographical sketches of prominent persons, and the genealogical records of many early and other families in Medway, Mass. 1713 - 1886 ... By E. O. Jameson ... Millis, Mass. (Providence, R. I., J.A. and R.A. Reid, printers) 1886. 3, 208 p. front., illus., ports. 26 cm. Reprint, with an index added, of p. 333-529 of the author's History of Medway. 1-11514.   F74.M55 J1

MEDWYA, The history of. 1713 to 1885, ed. by Rev. E. O. Jameson. Illus. by G. J. La Croix. Pub. by the town. (Providence, R.I., J.A. & R.A. Reid, printers, 1886) 4, 7-534; 6 p. illus., pl., ports., double maps. 25½ cm. "The biographies": p. (333) - 442; "The genealogies": p. (443) - 529. 1-12377.   F74.M55 J 2

MEDWAY. Historical discourse preached on the 162nd anniversary of the First church of Christ, Medway. ... By Rev. E. O. Jameson ... Pub. by the church. Boston, A. Mudge, printers, 1877. 86 p. 23½ cm. 6-18853.   F74.M55J24

MEDWAY. The military history of Medway. 1745 - 1885. Containing the names of the inhabitant soldiers in the French and Indian wars, the Continental soldiers and Minute-men in the war of the revolution, a mention of the war of 1812, the doings of the town in the support of the war for the union, a record with biographical sketches of the Union soldiers, and portraits of Washington, Lincoln, and Grant, with other illustrations. By Ephraim Orcutt Jameson. (Providence, R. I., J.A. & R.A. Reid, printers, 1886. 3; 110 p. illus., ports. 26 cm. Reprint of p. 211-320 of the author's History of Medway. 1-11515.   F74.M55 J 3

MEDWAY. ... The handbook of Medway history. A condensed history of the town of Medway, by Orion T. Mason ... (Medway, Mass.) G. M. Billings, printer, 1913. 116 p. illus. 23 cm. 15-15363.   F74.M55 M4

MEDWAY, Vital records of, to the year 1850. Boston, Pub. by the New-England historic genealogical soc ... 1905. 345 p. 23½ cm. 5-14825.   F74.M55 M5

MEDWAY. Proceedings at the celebration of Old home day ... 1904, together with an account of the dedication of the Rev. Jacob Ide memorial in connection therewith. (Medway, Mass.) The Medway historical soc. (1904) 49 p. plates, ports. 26 cm. "Ed. Rufus G. Fairbanks." 6-29096.   F74.M55 M6

MEDWAY. A sermon, delivered at Medway ... 1813, on the close of a century, since the incorporation of the town. By Luther Wright ... Dedham: Printed at the Gazette office, 1814. 32 p. 22 cm. 24-13787.   F74.M55 W9

MELROSE directory, ... The ... v. 15. 1896. Boston, Mass., Littlefield directory pub. co., 18 1 v. front. (fold. plan) 24 cm. 8-3859.   Directories

MELROSE. Resident and business directory of Melrose, 1893 - 19 -   Boston, Mass., Union pub. co., 1892 - 19 v. fold. maps. 21 - 24 cm. 8-3821 (rev. '16)   Directories

MELROSE. The centennial Fourth. Historical address delivered in town hall, Melrose ... 1876. By Elbridge H. Goss. Also, the proceedings of the day. Melrose, Priv. print., 1876. 46 p. 24 cm. 1-12378 Rev.   F74.M57 G6

MELROSE, The history of, by Elbridge Henry Goss. Melrose, The city, 1902. xviii, 508 p. front., illus. (incl. port., facsim.) pl. 24½ cm. 3-11847.   F74.M57G62

MELROSE. Ancient Melrose and some information about its old homesteads, families and furnishings, comp. and annotated by Levi S. Gould and Franklin P. Shumway. (Melrose) Melrose historical soc., 1915. 72 p. illus. (incl. plans) 25½ cm. Repr. from Goss's "History of Melrose." 15-19629.   F74.M57G63

MELROSE memorial, The. The annals of Melrose, county of Middlesex, in the great rebellion of 1861 - '65, by Elbridge H. Goss. (Boston, A. Mudge) Priv. print. by subscription, 1868. xxix, 292 p. 22½ x 17½ cm. 1-16182.   F74.M57 G7

MELROSE, 1900 - 1950; commemorating the 100th anniversary of the founding of the town of Melrose and the 50th anniversary of the incorporation of the city of Melrose. (Melrose) Fifteith Anniversary Committee, 1950 (c1949) 183 p. illus., tables. 25 cm. Supplement to The history of Melrose, by E. H. Goss, pub. in 1902. 51-4728.   F74.M57 K4

MENDON. A poem delivered at the celebration of the 200th anniversary of the incorporation of the town of Mendon ... 1867. By Hon. Henry Chapin ... Milford, G. W. Stacy, printer, 1867.   16 p.   21 cm.   1-11516.
F74.M59 C4

MENDON. An address, by Rev. Carlton A. Staples, of Milwaukee, Wis. ... and other proceedings in commemoration of the 200th anniversary of the incorporation of Mendon. Worcester, Print. C. Hamilton, 1868.   2, (3) - 89 (i. e. 95) p., 3 l.   24½ cm.   Paging irregular.   1-11517 Rev.
F74.M59 M5

MENDON. The Proprietor's records of the town of Mendon. Incorporated May 15, 1667. Boston, Rockwell and Churchill press, 1899.   1211 p.   fold. map.   24½ cm.   "Pub. jointly by the present towns of Mendon, Uxbridge, Northbridge, Milford, Blackstone, and Hopedale, towns made wholly or largely from the territory of the original town of Mendon."   2-3877 Rev.
F74.M59 M54

MENDON, Vital records of, to the year 1850. Comp. by Thomas W. Baldwin ... Boston, Mass. (Wright & Potter print.) 1920.   518 p.   23½ cm.   21-2052.
F74.M59M55

MENDON. Proceedings of the first meeting of the Mendon historical society in Town hall, Mendon ... 1896, with constitution, addresses, and hymn. Milford, Mass., G. M. Billings, printer, 1897.   38 p.   23 cm.   9-14766.
F74.M69M56

MENDON, Annals of the town of, from 1659 to 1880. Comp. by John G. Metcalf ... Providence, R. I., E. L. Freeman, printers to the state, 1880.   vii, 723 p.   front. (port.)   illus.   23½ cm.   Made up largely of extracts from the official records of the town.   1-11518.
F74.M59 M6

MENDON. An address at Mendon before the Worcester County Unitarian conference, at the autumnal session, 1873, on the history of the First church in that town. By Rev. Carlton A. Staples ... Printed by vote of the Conference. Milford (Mass.) Print. G. W. Stacy, 1873.   24 p.   23½ cm.   7-27756.
F74.M59 S79

MENDON. A poem, by Col. Putnam W. Taft, delivered in Mendon, on the 200th anniversary of the incorporation of the town ... 1867. Worcester, Priv. print., 1876.   (5) - 22 p.   20 cm.   7-27740.
F74.M59T12

MENDON. Founders' park, dedicated by Mendon historical society. (Whitinsville, Mass., 1906)   25½ cm.
F74.M59 U9

METHUEN directory ... Methuen, Mass., Union pub. co., 1909.   1 v.   24½ cm.   9-11682.   Directories

METHUEN directory ... v. 1 -   1932 -   Palmer, Mass., Crosby pub. co., 1932 -
   v. 24 cm.   CA 32-747 Unrev.   Directories

METHUEN, The growth of. A paper read before the Methuen historical soc. by Joseph S. Howe. (Methuen, Mass., 1898)   15 p.   19 x 10½ cm.   (Methuen historical soc. Publication)   4-31148.   F74. M6 H7

METHUEN. Historical sketch of the town of Methuen, from its settlement to the year 1876. By Jos. S. Howe. Methuen, Mass., E. L. Houghton, printers, 1876.   48 p.   23 cm.   1-11519 Rev.
F74. M6 H8

METHUEN, Vital records of, to the end of the year 1849. Topsfield, Mass., Topsfield historical soc., 1909.   345 p.   23½ cm.   9-7128.
F74. M6 M6

METHUEN historical society Publications. (Methuen, 1896)   nos. 1 - 2.   21½ cm.   F74. M6 M64

METHUEN. ... The Merrimack Valley. An address delivered ... 1896, before the Methuen historical society, by Robert H. Tewksbury. (Methuen, Mass., 1896)   25 p.   21½ cm.   (Methuen historical soc. publication. No. 2)   4-31149.
F74. M6 M64

METHUEN. Ye catalog of epitaphs from ye old burying ground on Meeting-house hill in Methuen. Pub. by the Methuen historical soc. (Methuen, Press of the Methuen transcript co.) 1897.   116 p.   19 cm.   Ed. Charles W. Mann.   1-12379 Rev.
F74. M6 M65

MASSACHUSETTS

METHUEN. West Methuen of long ago; chronicles by Mable F. Noyes and Minna B. Noyes ... (Bedford, Mass., The Bedford print shop, 1929)   72 p. illus., fold. plan.   23½ cm.   29-8762.

F74.M6 N9

METHUEN, Early manufacturers in. A paper read before the Methuen historical society by Daniel W. Tenney. (Methuen, Mass., 1900?)   12 p.   18½ x 10½ cm.   (Methuen historical soc. Publication)   4-31147.

F74. M6 T2

MIDDLEBORO. Crosby's Middleboro directory ... v. 1 -   1928/9 -   Wollaston, Mass., Crosby pub. co., 1928 -   c. 24 cm.   CA 28-304 Unrev.   Directories

MIDDLEBORO. Resident and business directory of Middleboro ... 1897, 1899, 1901.   Boston, Mass., Union pub. co., 1897 - 19   v. fold. maps. 24 cm.   99-4979 Rev.   Directories

MIDDLEBOROUGH. Celebration of the 200th anniversary of the incorporation of Middleborough ... 1869. ... Pub. by request of the Committee of arrangements. Middleborough, Gazette off., 1870.   51 p. front. 23 cm. 1-11520 Rev.

F74.M62 M6

MIDDLEBOROUGH. Book of the First church of Christ, in Middleborough. With notices of other churches in that town. Boston, C. C. P. Moody, printer, 1852 (i.e. 1854)   2, (3) - 124, 53 p. 24 cm.   3-5262.

F74.M62 M7

MIDDLEBORO. 200th anniversary of the First Congregational church in Middleboro. Historical discourse by George Warren Stearns; oration by Thomas Weston ... Middleboro, The Church, 1895.   136 p. front., ports. 23 cm. 16-9256 Rev.

F74.M62M74

MIDDLEBORO. Two discourses on the divine faithfulness, as illustrated in the history of the First church in Middleborough, during the period of 150 years. By Israel W. Putnam. Boston, C. C. P. Moody, printer, 1852.   53 p. tab. 24 cm.   12-24130.

F74.M62 P9

MIDDLEBORO. Historical address delivered on the occasion of the 250th anniversary of the town of Middleborough ... by Albert H. Washburn. (New York, Appeal print. 1919)   30 p. 23½ cm. 33-33134.

F74.M62 W3

MIDDLEBORO, History of the town of, by Thomas Weston ... Boston and New York, Houghton, Mifflin, 1906 - 69.   2 v. illus. (incl. ports.) maps (part fold.) double facsims. 25 cm. L.C. copy imperfect: p. (i) - (ii) wanting.   6-23056.

F74.M62 W5

MIDDLEBORO, Record of deaths. By Alfred Wood. Boston, General Society of Mayflower Descendants, 1947.   250 p.   28 cm.

F74.M62 W6
L.H. & G.

MIDDLEFIELD. A memorial of the 100th anniversary of the incorporation of the town of Middlefield ... 1883, containing the historical discourse by Prof. Edward P. Smith of Worcester; with the addresses and letters. Middlefield, By the town, 1883.   96 p.   illus. (map) 23 cm. 9-32152.

F74.M626M4

MIDDLEFIELD, Vital records of, to the year 1850. Boston, Mass., Pub. by the New England historic genealogical society ... 1907.   vi, 9-138 p. 23½ cm. 8-6064.

F74.M626M6

MIDDLEFIELD, A history of the town of, by Edward Church Smith and Philip Mack Smith with the assistance of Theodore Clarke Smith. (Menasha, Wis.) Priv. print., 1924.   xxv, 662 p. front., illus. (incl. ports.) maps (part fold.) diagr. 23½ cm. Bibliography: p. (397) - 398. "Notes and genealogies of pioneer families": p. (399) - 653.   25-1232.

F74.M626S6

MIDDLETON, Vital records of, to the end of the year 1849. Topsfield, Mass., Topsfield historical soc., 1904.   143 p.   23½ cm.   4-18522.

F74. M63 M6
L H & G

MIDDLETON; a cultural history. By Lura (Woodside) Watkins. Salem, Mass., Essex Institute, 1970.   341 p. illus., maps, ports. 25 cm.

F74.M63 W3

262　　　　　　　　　　LOCAL HISTORIES IN THE LIBRARY OF CONGRESS

MILFORD.　Bass & company's Milford directory ... Containing a general directory of ... Milford and Hopedale ... Boston, Mass., Bass & company, 1869 - 1911.　　13 v.　map (v. 2)　24 cm.　　7-36202.
Directories

MILFORD.　Rochfort's Milford and Hopedale directory, 1900.　　1 v.　　　　　　　Directories

MILFORD.　Leading business men of Milford, Hopkinton, and vicinity; embracing also Ashland, Holliston and Hopedale ... Boston, Mercantile pub. co., 1890.　　64 p.　illus.　25 cm.　4-20150.
F74. M64B13

MILFORD.　History of the town of Milford ... from its first settlement to 1881. In two parts. Part I. - Strictly historical. Part II. - Biographico-genealogical register. By Adin Ballou. Pub. by the town. Boston, Rand, Avery, & co., 1882.　　xiv, (2), (xv) - xviii, 1154 p.　front., plates, ports., fold. map.　23½ cm.　1-11521.
F74. M64B18

MILFORD.　Exercises at unveiling of equestrian statue in memory of General William Franklin Draper, presented to the town of Milford by his wife ... 1912.　(Milford? 1912)　　(8) p.　front. (port.) pl.　23½ cm.　25-12841.
F74. M64M55

MILFORD, Vital records of, to the year 1850.　Comp. by Thomas W. Baldwin ... Boston, Mass. (Wright & Potter print.) 1917.　　378 p.　23½ cm.　18-5072.
F74. M64 M6

MILFORD and its environs ... Milford, Mass., 1908.　　15½ x 23 cm.　　　　　G74. M64M64

MILLBURY.　Centennial history of the town of Millbury ... including vital statistics, 1850 - 1899. Pub. under the direction of a committee appointed by the town.　Millbury, 1915.　　814 p.　front., plates, ports.　24 cm.　Literary material pertaining to the industries, institutions and individuals ... became the nucleus for the present volume.　16-3490.
F74. M65M58

MILLBURY, Vital records of, to the end of the year 1849.　Worcester, F. P. Rice, 1903.　　158 p. 23½ cm.　4-4889.
F74. M65 M6

MILTON, Resident and business directory of ... (1894/5) - 1910.　v. 1 - 8.　Boston, Boston suburban book co. (1894) - 1910.　　8 vols.　illus., fold. plans.　23½ cm.　8-4619.
Directories

MILTON directory ... Boston, Mass., Union pub. co. (inc.) 19　　v.　fold. map.　24 cm.　CA 24-781 Unrev.
Directories

MILTON.　A discourse occasioned by the 200th anniversary of the formation of the First Congregational society of Milton, delivered by Frederick Frothingham .... (Boston, Print. T. W. Ripley, 1878) 39 p.　22 cm.　10-31029.
F74. M66 F9

MILTON, A history of.　By Edward Pierce Hamilton.　Milton, Mass., Milton Historical Society, 1957.　　xv, 275 p.　illus., ports., maps, facsims.　26 cm.　"Suggested further reading": p. 264.　58-31576.
F74. M66 H3

MILTON.　Exercises at the 250th anniversary of the incorporation of the town of Milton.　Comp. by the committee in charge ... Boston, Poole print. (1912)　　46 p.　23½ cm.　"Bibliography and notes": p. 20 - 27. 13-21495.
F74. M66M35

MILTON records.　Births, marriages and deaths, 1662 - 1843, alphabetically and chronologically arranged.　Boston, A. Mudge & son, printers, 1900.　　4; 258 p.　front. (facsim.)　24 cm.　1-16580.
F74. M66M37

MILTON town records, 1662 - 1729, issued in observance of the tercentenary of the founding of the Massachusetts bay colony.　Milton, Mass. (Boston, The Sherril press) 1930.　　xii, 385 p.　front. (facsim.)　31½ cm.　31-7248.
F74. M66M38

MILTON ... Boston, The Edison electric illuminating co., 1909.　　23 cm.　　　F74. M66 M4

MILTON cemetery.　A catalogue of the proprietors of lots, together with a record of ancient inscrip-

492

MASSACHUSETTS 263

tions on all tablets in the cemetery prior to and including 1800. 1687 - 1800. Boston, D. Clapp, printers, 1883. 73 p. 24 cm. 16-27459.
F74.M66M43

(MILTON church records, 1681 - 1754) (Milton, Mass., Milton historical soc., 1916) 134 l. of facsim. 24 cm. 17-20819.
F74.M66M454

MILTON church records - 1678 - 1754. (Boston, Print. D. Clapp, 1870) 41 p. 26 cm. Reprinted from New England historical and genealogical register, July 1868 - Jan. 1870. 17-5238.
F74.M66M46

MILTON historical society. Annual report. 1st - 3d. (Milton? 1906 - 08. 3 v. 23 cm. 9-4683.
F74.M66 M5

MILTON catechism, The; an outline of the history of Milton, Mass., illustrated. (Milton, Mass.) Milton historical soc., 1910. 88 p. incl. front., plates. 23 cm. "General references": p. 87-88. 10-31145.
F74.M66M57

MILTON historical society, President's address and 10th anniversary reports of; a record of the society's first ten years. (Milton) Printed by vote of the Society, 1915. 28 p. 23 cm. 18-4791.
F74.M66M575

MILTON. By-laws of Milton historical society adopted 21 Jan., 1905, amended 6 June, 1905 and 4 June, 1913. (Milton? 1913) (3) p. 23 cm. CA 25-566 Unrev.
F74.M66 M6

MILTON. John Hopkins Morison, a memoir. By George Shattuck Morison. Boston and New York, Houghton, Mifflin, 1897. v, 298 p. 2 port. (incl. front.) 20½ cm. List of pub. writings of John H. Morison": p. (291) - 293. 13-2730.
F74.M66M78

MILTON. Two sermons preached in the First Congregational church in Milton ... 1862 and suggested by the centennial celebration. By John H. Morison. Boston, J. G. Torrey, printer, 1862. 55 p. 23½ cm. 11-110.
F74.M66 M8

MILTON. Address delivered before the inhabitants of the town of Milton, on the 200th anniversary of the incorporation of the town ... 1862. By James M. Robbins. Boston, D. Clapp, printer, 1862. vi, (7) - 76 p. 23½ cm. 5-1308.
F74.M66 R8

MILTON, The history of, 1640 - 1887. Ed. by Albert K. Teele. (Boston, Press of Rockwell and Churchill, 1887) xiv, 668 p. illus., plates, ports., maps (partly fold.) 2 plans (1 fold.) 24 cm. Contains record of ancient inscriptions on all tablets in Milton cemetery prior to ... 1800: p. 478-498. Early families: p. 554 - 591. 1-12380.
F74.M66 T2

MILTON. Register of marriages in Milton. From the diary of Rev. Peter Thacher. 1686 - 1727. Reprinted from the New England historical and genealogical register. Boston, D. Clapp, printer, 1883. 2; 7 p. 25 cm. 1-11522.
F74.M66 T3

MILTON. The first four meeting houses of Milton, covering a period ot two and a half centuries. (By) John A. Tucker. (Milton? Mass.) 1908. 5 p. 4 plans. 31½ cm. 8-27422.
F74.M66 T8

MILTON. Tax rates of Milton 1674 - 1800, by John A. Tucker ... (Milton) The Milton record, 1908. (15) p. incl. 2 maps. 22 cm. 9-14745.
F74.M66T85

MILTON. Robert Vose and his times, comp. by Ellen F. Vose and Mary H. Hinckley ... (n.p.) 1910. (21) p. illus., pl. 22 cm. Reprinted from the Milton record, Nov. - Dec., 1910. 11-10437 rev.
F74.M66 V9

MONSON; illustrated with pen and camera, by Charles W. Eddy ... (Ware, Mass.) 1884. 16 l. 16 pl. 20 x 25 cm. 10-8647.
F74.M68 E2

MONSON. A sermon, delivered at Monson ... 1820; the second centurial anniversary of the landing of the fathers of New-England, at Plymouth ... Hartford, Goodwin & sons, 1821. 27 p. 12°. 1-12077 - M1.
F74.M68 E5

493

MONSON, History of.   Monson historical society (Monson) 1960.   171 p.   29 cm.   F74.M68M6

MONTAGUE, Vital records of, to the end of the year 1849.   Salem, The Essex institute, 1934.
167 p.   23 cm.   With Buckland Vital records.   34-9007.
F74.M69
F74.B97B94

MONTAGUE, History of; a typical Puritan town ... by Edward Pearson Pressey.   Introductory by Robert P. Clapp; incl. short hand notes of conversations with the oldest inhabitants, 1895, by Mr. Clapp & a History of the Gunn family by Mrs. Lyman O. Gunn.   Montague, Mass., The New Clairvaux press, 1910.   264 p.   illus., pl., maps.   21 cm.   A16-1156.   F74.M69 P9

MONTGOMERY, Vital records of, to the year 1850 ... Boston, 1902.   66 p.   23½ cm.   (New England historic genealogical society)   3-5252.   F74. M7 M7

MOUNT AUBURN.   A history of the cemetery of Mount Auburn.   By Jacob Bigelow ... Boston and Cambridge, J. Monroe, 1860.   xii p., 2 l., 263 p.   front., plates, 2 fold. plans.   18 cm.   11-19267.
F74. M9 B5

MOUNT AUBURN.   A concise history of, and guide through Mount Auburn, with a catalogue of lots laid out in that cemetery; a map of the grounds, and terms of subscription, regulations concerning visitors, interments, etc. etc.   Boston, N. Dearborn, 1843.   74 p.   illus.   15 cm.   12-9112.
F74.M9 D17

MOUNT AUBURN.   ... Guide through Mount Auburn, 2d ed., and improved ... with an engraved plan of the cemetery.   By Nathaniel Dearborn ... Boston, Printed at his engraving and printing estab. (1848)   28 p.   illus., pl., fold. plan.   20½ cm.   12-9113.   F74.M9 D19

— 3d ed. with 46 monumental engravings ... By Nathaniel Dearborn ... Boston, Printed ... (1849)
32 p.   illus., pl., fold. plan.   21 cm.   12-9114.   F74.M9D191

— with 64 engravings of the monuments.   Boston, 1851.   44 p.   illus., fold. plan.   19½ cm.   2-12062.
F74. M9 D2

— 4th ed.   Boston, Bricher & Russell, 1860.   78 p.   front., illus., double plan.   15½ cm.   17-12064.   F74. M9 D24
Toner Coll.

MOUNT AUBURN: its scenes, its beauties, and its lessons.   By Wilson Flagg ... Boston and Cambridge, J. Munroe, 1861.   xii, 371 p.   front., plates.   20 cm.   11-19268.   F74. M9 F5

MOUNT AUBURN.   A catalogue of proprietors in the cemetery of Mount Auburn together with an appendix containing the charter, regulations ...   Boston and Cambridge, J. Munroe, 1855.
viii, (9) - 108 p.   fold. plan.   23½ cm.   1-11280-M1.   F74. M9 M9

MOUNT AUBURN.   Catalogue of the lots in Mount Auburn cemetery, with the names of the proprietors, etc.   Boston, Press of G. C. Rand & Avery, 1857.   ix, 159 p.   fold. plan, fold. tab.   20 cm.   1-11281.
F74.M9 M91

MOUNT AUBURN cemetery.   (New York, Wittemann brothers, 1884)   25 views on strip fold. to 8½ x 13 cm.
12-9115.   F74.M9 M92

MOUNT AUBURN memorial, The.. v.1 - June 15, 1859 -   Mount Auburn (Mass.) T. H. & D. F. Safford, 1860-   v.   33½ cm.   weekly.   CA 17-29 Unrev.   F74.M9 M95

MOUNT AUBURN cemetery, Notes on, ed. by an officer of the coporation; (Henry Parker)   Together with a full catalogue, ...   Boston, J. Munroe, (1849)   90 p.   fold. plan.   16 cm.   12-9116.
F74.M9 P24

MOUNT AUBURN.   The picturesque pocket companion, and visitor's guide, through Mount Auburn: illus. with upwards of 60 engravings on wood ... Boston, Otis, Broader, 1839.   252 p. incl. illus., plates. front.   16 cm.   11-22525.   F74. M9 P6

MASSACHUSETTS

MOUNT AUBURN biographies; a biographical listing of distinguished persons interred in Mount Auburn Cemetery, Cambridge, Mass., 1831 - 1952. (Cambridge? 1953) 216 p. 25 cm. 54-16598.
F74. M9 R8
Reference alcove

MOUNT AUBURN. An address delivered on the dedication of the cemetery at Mount Auburn ... 1831. By Joseph Story. To which is added an appendix, containing a historical notice and description of the place, with a list of the present subscribers. Boston, J. T. & E. Buckingham, 1831. 32 p. 24 cm. 5-14684.
F74. M9 S92

MOUNT AUBURN, Plan of the cemetery of. By Alex. Wadsworth. Boston, F. F. Oakley's lith., 1857. plan. 70 x 58 ½ cm. fold. to 18 ½ cm. 12-9108.
F74. M9 W12

MOUNT AUBURN illustrated. In highly finished line engraving, from drawings taken on the spot, by James Smillie. With descriptive notices by Cornelia W. Walter. New York, Martin and Johnson (1848) 3, (5) - 119 p. front. (map) plates. 28 x 21 ½ cm. (The rural cemeteries of America) 11-30527.
F74. M9 W2

NAHANT, The picture of. By Alonzo Lewis ... Lynn, T. Herbert, 1855. 32 p. front., plates, maps. 14 cm. 1-11523.
F74. N13 L6

NAHANT. An historical address delivered at the celebration of the 50th anniversary of the incorporation of the town of Nahant ... 1903, by Henry Cabot Lodge. (Nahant) 1904. 2; 22 p. map. 24 cm. 4-16785.
F74. N13 L8

NAHANT. Official programme of the celebration of the 50th anniversary of the incorporation of the town of Nahant ... 1903. Nahant, Mass. 1903. (20) p. front., 2 pl., map. 24 ½ cm. 3-31543.
F74. N13 N2

NAHANT. A sermon preached in commemoration of the founders of the Nahant church, at the dedication of a tablet erected to their memory ... 1877. By Andrew P. Peabody. Cambridge, J. Wilson, 1877. 34 p. 23 cm. "List of clergymen ... 1832-1877" p. 26-34. 24-15014.
F74. N13 P3

NAHANT, Picturesque studies at. By Frederick M. Smith) (Lynn? 1881?) 25 photos. 38 ½ cm.
F74. N13 S6

NAHANT. Letters from Nahant, historical, descriptive and miscellaneous. By William Willder Wheildon. (Charlestown) Press of the Bunker-hill aurora, 1842. 48 p. illus. 18 x 10 ½ cm. 1-12381.
F74. N13 W5

NAHANT. Some annals of Nahant, by Fred A. Wilson ... Boston, Old corner book store, 1928. xiii, 412 p. front., plates, ports., maps, geneal. tables, diagr. 24 cm. 28-18806.
F74. N13 W6

NANTASKET. Old Nantasket, by William M. Bergan. (Boston, Printed by Spaulding-Moss, 1968) 152 p. illus. 21 cm.
F74. N15 B4

— (Rev. ed.) North Quincy, Mass., Christopher Pub. House (1969) 154 p. illus. 25 cm.
F74. N15 B4 1969

— (Rev. ed.) North Quincy, Mass., Christopher Pub. House (1972) 154 p. 24 cm. 72-184508 MARC.
F74. N15 B4 1972

NANTASKET beach. A pleasure guide to Nantasket beach, and Boston harbor. Giving a complete description of the islands and fortifications of Boston harbor, and the attractions of Nantasket beach ... Boston, Deland & Barta, 1884. 63 p. illus., fold. map. 16°. 1-16181-M1.
F74. N15 F3

NANTASKET views; wreckage of the great storm, Nov. 27, 1898. Thirty views, covering coast from Pemberton to Cohasset. Dorchester, Mass., B. W. Putnam, 1899. 30 mounted phot. 18 ½ x 27 cm. 99-970 Rev.
F74. N15 N2

NANTUCKET, a photographic sketchbook.   By Samuel Chamberlain.   New York, Hastings House (1955)   71 p. (chiefly illus.)   25 cm.   55-7902.   F74.N17 C4

NATICK, Ridley's directory of.   (v.1 -   Worcester, Mass., J. Ridley, 1873 -   1 v. 22 cm.
8-34537.   Directories

NATICK directory, The ... for 1882 - 3.   Boston, W. A. Greenough, 1882.   1 v.   23½ cm.   8-34295.
Directories

NATICK directory, The ... Boston, Mass., W. E. Shaw, 1908 -   1 v. fold. map.   24½ cm.   8-34133.
Directories

NATICK, Resident and business directory of, 1911   South Framingham, Mass., Lakeview press
v.   23½ cm.   11-15207.   Directories

NATICK and Sherborn, Resident and business directory of.   (Boston, Union pub. co.)   1913.
1 v.   diagrs.   24 cm.   13-10929.   Directories

NATICK.   Town of Natick directory.   Boston, H. Howard, 1920 -   v. 24 cm.   20-20304.   Directories

NATICK, A history of, from its first settlement in 1651 to the present time; with notices of the first white families, and also an account of the centennial celebration... By Oliver N. Bacon ... Boston, Damrell & Moore, printers, 1856.   2, (3) - 261 p. front., plates, ports.   24½ cm.   1-11524.
F74. N2 B1

NATICK, History of the town of, from the days of the apostolic Eliot, 1650, to the present time, 1830. By William Biglow.   Boston, Marsh, Capen, & Lyon, 1830.   87 p.   23½ cm.   1-11525.
F74. N2 B5

NATICK.   Boutwell's ready reference book and pocket memoranda for Natick.   Leominster, Boutwell & co., 1888.   64 p.   24°.   1-16180-M1.   F74. N2 B7

NATICK.   Its advantages for residence, and as a place of business.   Prepared under the direction of the Board of selectmen, by Amos P. Cheney.   Natick, Mass., Bulletin steam print, 1889.
32 p.   13½ cm.   2-25649.   F74. N2 C5

NATICK.   Book of minutes of Col. John Jones of Dedham; with explanatory notes by his grandson, Amos Perry, of Providence, R.I. ... Boston, G. E. Littlefield; Providence, Preston & Rounds, 1894.
42 p. incl. front., illus., port., facsim.   24 cm.   2-22439.   F74. N2 J7

NATICK.   A sermon, delivered at Natick ... 1817, containing a history of said town, from 1651 to the day of delivery.   By Martin Moore ... Cambridge: Print. by Hilliard and Metcalf, 1817.
27 p.   22½ cm.   1-11526.   F74. N2 M8

NATICK, Vital records of, to the year 1850.   Comp. by Thomas W. Baldwin ... Boston, (Stanhope press, F. H. Gilson) 1910.   249 p.   23½ cm.   10-8745.   F74. N2 N4

NAUSHON ISLAND.   Letters and recollections of John Murray Forbes; ed. by his daughter Sarah Forbes Hughes ... Boston and New York, Houghton, Mifflin, 1899.   2 v. fronts., pl., ports., map, fold. facsim.
22½ cm.   0-1012 Rev.   F47.N.
E415.7.F69

NEEDHAM.   Towns of Needham and Dover directory.   Boston, H. Howard, 19   v. 24½ cm.   Directories

NEEDHAM, History of, 1711 - 1911; including West Needham, now the town of Wellesley, to its separation from Needham in 1881, with some references to its affairs to 1911, by George Kuhn Clarke ... (Cambridge) Priv. print. at the University press (1912)   3, iii, (9) - 746 p. front., plates, ports.   24½ cm.
12-9694.   F74. N3 C6

MASSACHUSETTS

NEEDHAM. Epitaphs from graveyards in Wellesley (formerly West Needham), North Natick and Saint Mary's churchyard in Newton Lower Falls, Mass; with genealogical and biographical notes, by George Kuhn Clarke. Boston, Priv. print. (T. R. Marvin & son) 1900. vii, (9) - 236 p. 25 cm.
Wellesley and North Natick were formerly part of Needham. In the case of St. Mary's churchyard, Newton Lower Falls, only those inscriptions are copied which relate to persons connected with Needham. 0-2215 Rev.
F74. N3 C7

NEEDHAM. Epitaphs from the old burying ground, Needham, Mass. With notes. By Charles Curtis Greenwood ... Dedham, Mass. (H. H. McQuillen, printer) 1898. 70 p. 25 x 16 cm. Reprinted from Dedham historical register. 6-13062.
F74. N3 G8

NEEDHAM, History and directory of, for 1888/89. Containing a complete resident, street and business directory ... also a history of the town from the first settlement to the present time. Needham, A. E. Foss, 1888. 2 - 157, (2) p. 23 cm. 19-7392.
F74. N3 H6

NEEDHAM today, a pictorial directory. By Winthrop W. McIntosh. (Needham, Mass., McIntosh Press, 1956) 48 p. illus. 23 cm. 57-18537.
F74. N3 M3

NEEDHAM'S bicentennial celebration; a record of the exercises and a memorial of the celebration at Needham, on the 200th anniversary of its incorporation. Pub. by the Celebration committee; comp. by Thomas Sutton. Needham, Print. by G. W. and W. M. Southworth, 1913. 232 p. front., plates, ports. 24½ cm. 15-12837.
F74.N3 N25

NEEDHAM. Your home town, Needham; a pictorial directory. Chamber of Commerce. (Needham? McIntosh Press, 1956) 48 p. illus. 23 cm. 57-17604.
F74.N3 N26

NEEDHAM. Report of a Special committee of the town of Needham, upon the subject of a division of the town, made December 6, 1859. Boston, Wright & Potter, printers, 1859. 8 p. 23½ cm. 8-31724.
F74. N3 N3

NEEDHAM. A sermon, delivered in Needham, 1811, on the termination of a century, since the incorporation of the town. By Stephen Palmer ... Dedham (Mass.) Printed by Herman Mann, 1811. 44 p. 22 cm. 16-13248.
F74. N3 P17

NEW ASHFORD, Vital records of, to the year 1850. Boston, Pub. by the New England historic genealogical society, ... 1916. 43 p. 23½ cm. 16-27395.
F74.N47 N5

NEW BEDFORD ... directory. v. 1 - 1836 - Boston, W. A. Greenough, 1836 - 1909. 33 v. 18 - 25½ cm. Oct. 5, 99-143 Additions.
Directories

NEW BEDFORD. Life in New Bedford a hundred years ago; a chronicle of the social, religious and commercial history of the period as recorded in a diary kept by Joseph R. Anthony; ed. by Zephaniah W. Pease. (New Bedford) Pub. under the auspices of the Old Dartmouth historical society by G. H. Reynolds (1922) 91 p. incl. illus. (facsim.) plates, ports. front. 25 cm. 23-6123.
F74. N5 A6

NEW BEDFORD. City of New Bedford, 1914; descriptive and pictorial; commemorative of the 250th anniversary of when Dartmouth became a town, 1664, New Bedford being a part thereof. Also a description of the city's beautiful suburb, Fairhaven. J. H. Burgess, writer and publisher. (New Bedford, 1914) 62 p. illus. 30½ cm. 15-14934.
F74. N5 B9

NEW BEDFORD. Illustrated New Bedford, Martha's Vineyard and Nantucket. Sketches of discoveries, aborigines, settlers, wars, incidents, towns, hamlets, scenes, camp meetings, cottages and interesting localities ... By Rev. Frederic Denison ... Providence, J. A. & R. A. Reid, printers, 1879. 9, (17) - 70 p. illus. (incl. maps) 24½ cm. 1-11527.
F74. N5 D3

NEW BEDFORD. Le directoire français de New Bedford, ... (New Bedford, Barthéleme Noël, 1896 - 1 v. 20 cm. 10-8001.
F74. N5 D5

NEW BEDFORD. History of New Bedford and its vicinity, 1602 - 1892. By Leonard Bolles Ellis. Syracuse, N. Y., D. Mason, 1892. 2, (7) - 731 p. 175 p. illus., ports., plans. 25 cm. 13-2639. L.C. copy replaced by microfilm. 13-2639.
F74. N5 E4
Microfilm 21696 F

497

NEW BEDFORD'S story, for New Bedford's children, ed. and pub. by Emma L. Gartland. New Bedford, Mass. (Printed by Reynolds print., 1930) 32 p. illus. 23 cm. "References": p. 32. 34-21921.
F74. N5 G2

NEW BEDFORD, Glimpses of. ... New Bedford, Mass., 1904. 14½ x 22 cm.
F74. N5 G5

NEW BEDFORD semi-centennial souvenir, containing a review of the history of the city, together with accounts of the whale fishery, the early industries, the great growth in the cotton manufacture and the social and economic changes. ... Ed. by Robert Grieve ... Providence, R.I., Journal of commerce co., 1897. 90 p. illus. (incl. ports.) 31½ cm. 1-16329 Rev.
F74. N5 G8

NEW BEDFORD. ... The story of Water street (New Bedford, by) Elmore P. Haskins ... (New Bedford, 1906?) 14 p. fold. map. 26 cm. (Old Dartmouth historical sketches, no. 15) 18-4808.
F74. N5 H 3

NEW BEDFORD. ... John Hawes, by Rebecca Williams Hawes ... (New Bedford, 1908?) 14 p. incl. port. 27 cm. (Old Dartmouth historical sketches, no. 22) 18-4298.
F74. N5 H38

NEW BEDFORD'S history. By Reginald B. Hegarty. 1959. 24 p.
F74. N5 H4

NEW BEDFORD. Diary of Rev. Moses How, pastor of the Middle street Christian church ... 1819 - 1826 and 1837 - 1844. ... (New Bedford, Mass., Reynolds printing, 1932) 29, (3) p. illus. (incl. ports.) 24 cm. (Sketches of New Bedford's early history, no. 59) Excerpts reprinted from the Morning mercury in 1931. Complete diary in New Bedford public library. 32-20371.
F74. N5 H8

"NEW BEDFORD in 1810." From a painting by William A. Wall ... By Henry S. Hutchinson. New Bedford, Mass., H. S. Hutchinson, 1897. front., port. 16º. 1-11528-M1.
F74. N5 H91

NEW BEDFORD, Centennial in. Historical address by Hon. William W. Crapo, delivered on the occasion of the celebration in New Bedford of the 4th July, 1876 .... Pub. by order of the City council. New Bedford, E. Anthony, printers to the city, 1876. 2, (3) - 175 p. 23 cm. Appendix of historical documents, etc.: p. (57) - 175. 1-11529.
F74. N5 N43

NEW BEDFORD, Vital records of, to the year 1850 ... Boston, Mass., New England historic genealogical soc. ... 1932 - 41. 3 v. 23 cm. 32-17124.
F74. N5 N45

NEW BEDFORD. (Views) New Bedford, Mass., H. S. Hutchinson (1896) 25 pl. obl. 8º. 1-11530-M1.
F74. N5 N47

NEW BEDFORD and Fairhaven. Providence, R. I., Dart & Bigelow, 1901. 40 pl. 13 x 21 cm. 2-1118-M2.
F74. N5 N48

NEW BEDFORD and Fairhaven. ... 1903.
F74. N5 N482

NEW BEDFORD; its history, industries, institutions and attractions. Pub. by order of the Board of trade ... Writers - Zeph. W. Pease, George A. Hough. Ed. - William L. Sayer. (New Bedford) Mercury pub. co., printers, 1889. 318, (2) p. incl. front., illus., plates. ports. 25 cm. 1-11531.
F74. N5 N52

NEW BEDFORD. Commemorative exercises, City hall, New Bedford, ... 1908. (New Bedford, Free public library, 1908) 20 p. front. 23 cm. 8-29109.
F74. N5 N536

NEW BEDFORD. ... Some facts about New Bedford. (New Bedford, Mass.) Free public library, 1906. 15½ cm.
F74. N5 N54

NEW BEDFORD mercury, The. 100th anniversary supplement. Aug. 7, 1907. New Bedford, Mass., 1907. 80 p. illus. (incl. ports.) 40 cm. 8-18210.
F74. N5 N6

NEW BEDFORD, History of, under the editorial direction of Zephaniah W. Pease ... New York, The Lewis historical pub. co., 1918. 3 v. fronts., plates, ports. 28 cm. Vols. 2-3 (paged continuously) include biographical sketches. 18-16263.
F74. N5 P36

MASSACHUSETTS

NEW BEDFORD, The history of: including a history of the old township of Dartmouth and the present townships of Westport, Dartmouth, and Fairhaven, from their settlement to the present time. By Daniel Ricketson. New Bedford, Pub. by the author, 1858.   xii, (13)-412 p. 19 cm. 1-11532.   F74. N5 R5

NEW BEDFORD of the past, by Daniel Ricketson; ed. by his daughter and son, Anna and Walton Ricketson. Boston and New York, Houghton, Mifflin, 1903. xiii, 196 p. front. (port.) 22½ cm.   Written in 1875 for the New Bedford "Evening Standard."   3-29639.   F74. N5 R53

NEW BEDFORD. A voice from the prison, being articles addressed to the editor of the New-Bedford Mercury; and a letter to G. B. Weston, and other directors of the Duxbury bank. To which are added leaves from a journal. By B. Rodman ... New-Bedford, Printed by B. Lindsey, 1840.   iv, (5) - 63 p. 23 cm. 10-4852.   F74. N5 R6

NEW BEDFORD in 1827 as told in Samuel Rodman's diary; ed. by Bradford Swan. (New Bedford, Mass.) Reynolds printing, 1935.   (32) p.   26½ cm.   Reprinted from the Morning mercury, 1934. Completes the diary, which was reprinted from the Morning mercury in 1927 in book of 350 p. by Reynolds printing the same year. 36-11398.   F74. N5 R64

NEW BEDFORD, ... Views of. New Bedford, Mass., H. S. Hutchinson (1900)   1 p. 29 pl. 17½ x 23 cm. New and enlarged edition.   1-29403 Rev.   F74. N5 V5

NEW BEDFORD and vicinity, Views of.   1903.   15½ x 24 cm.   F74. N5 V52

NEW BRAINTREE. Recollections and anticipations. A half-century and dedicatory discourse, delivered in New-Braintree, Mass ... 1846. By John Fiske, pastor of the church. Greenfield, Merriam and Mirick, printers, 1846.   34 p.   22½ cm.   1-16549.   F74. N52 F5

NEW BRAINTREE, Vital records of, to the year 1850. Boston, Pub. by The New-England historic genealogical society ... 1904.   163 p.   23½ cm.   4-9198.   F74. N52 N5

(NEW SALEM pictures) This booklet, with the exception of the last four sketches, contains brief descriptions of a number of the residents of New Salem. They were originally published in the Athol transcript, Athol, Mass., 1911 - 1912, and are here reproduced without alteration, by Rev. Haig Adadourian ... Athol, Mass., The Athol transcript co., 1913.   (2) p.   23 l.   (2) p.   23 cm.   13-16434.
F74. N524A2

NEW SALEM sesqui-centennial, The; report of the addresses and proceedings of the celebration of the 150th anniversary of the incorporation of the town of New Salem, at New Salem ... 1903. Athol, Mass., Transcript book and job print, 1904.   2, (3) - 77 p. illus. 22½ cm.   5-23365.   F74. N524N5

NEW SALEM, Vital records of, to the end of the year 1849. Salem, Mass., The Essex institute, 1927. 283 p.   23 cm.   27-18955.   F74. N524N6

NEWBURY, A sketch of the history of Newbury, Newburyport, and West Newbury, from 1635 to 1845. By Joshua Coffin ... Boston, S. G. Drake, 1845.   viii, (9) - 416 p. front., illus. (incl. plan) ports. 24 cm.   In the form of chronological annals, 1635-1844. with appendix.   1-11533.   F74. N53 C8

NEWBURY, History of, 1635 - 1902, by John J. Currier ... Boston, Damrell & Upham, 1902. 755 p. front., illus. (incl. ports., maps, facsims.) 24 cm. Additions and corrections, in author's "History of Newburyport, 1909" vol. 2 p. 562-9. 2-30402.   F74. N53C87

"OULD NEWBURY": historical and biographical sketches. By John J. Currier ... Boston, Damrell and Upham, 1896.   729 p. front., illus. (incl. ports., maps) 24 cm.   Additions and corrections in the author's History of Newburyport. 1909, v.2, p. 570 - 591.   1-11534 Rev.   F74. N53C9

NEWBURY. Old Newbury tales, an historical reader for children ... Federal writers' project. (Newburyport, Pub. for Historical society of old Newbury) 1937.   3; 69 p. illus., pl. 22 cm.   Compiled and written by workers of the W.P.A.   37-38045.   F74. N53 F4

NEWBURY. Celebration of the 250th anniversary of the settlement of Newbury ... 1885. Newburyport, Printed by order of the Historical soc. of Old Newbury, 1885.   150 p.   17½ cm. 2-3879 Rev.   F74. N53 H6

NEWBURY, Vital records of, to the end of the year 1849 ... Salem, Mass., The Essex institute, 1911.
2 v.   23 cm.   12-33095.
  F74.N53 N5
  L.H.& G.

NEWBURY.   Sons and daughters of the first settlers of Newbury, Publications of the.   no. 1 - Newbury, Mass., The Society, 1935 -   v. front., plates, ports. 24½ cm.   37-5925.   F74.N53 S6

NEWBURY.   Sketches of a few distinguished men of Newbury and Newburyport.   By Samuel Swett ... Boston, Printed by S. N. Dickinson, 1846.   23 p.   19½ cm.   Contents. - no. 1. Capt. Moses Brown, of the U.S. navy.
No more pub?   1-10223 Rev.   F74.N53 S9

NEWBURY.   250th anniversary of the settlement of Newbury; brief biographical sketches by Robert Noxon Toppan ...   Newburyport, The Society, 1885.   134 p.   18 cm.   12-11535.   F74.N53 T6

NEWBURY: a pattern of flatware made in sterling silver by the Towle mfg. co; with some history of Newbury: Massachusetts and its progenitor Newbury: England.   Newburyport, Mass., Chicago, Ill. (etc., 1907)   67 p. incl. illus., plates.   28 cm.   (In (Towle manufacturing co's. pubs. pt. 5)   Compiled ... chiefly from The history of Newbury, England, by Walter Money, and the history of Newbury, Mass., by John J. Currier ...   9-3731.   F74.N53 T7

NEWBURY.   A sermon for the 200th anniversary of the standing of the First church in Newbury, on its present site.   By Rev. Leonard Withington ...   Newburyport, E. Hale, printer, 1846.   18 p.   23½ cm.
10-31037.   F74.N53 W8

NEWBURYPORT.   Diary of Sarah Connell Ayer.   Andover and Newburyport, Mass; Concord and Bow, N.H; Portland and Eastport, Me.   Portland, Me., Lefavor-Tower co., 1910.   2; 404 p.   25 cm.   12-12476.
                                                                                                                                                                           F74.N
                                                                                                                                                                           F8.A97

NEWBURYPORT.   200th anniversary, St. Paul's parish.   Commemorative services with historical addresses.   Newburyport, Mass., printed for St. Paul's church (1912)   64 (6) p. incl. front., illus., plates, facsims.   24 cm.   12-10831.   F74.N

NEWBURYPORT.   An outline of the life and works of Col. Paul Revere; with a partial catalogue of silverware bearing his name.   Newburyport, Mass., Towle mfg. co. (1901)   35, (59), 63 p.   front., illus. 27½ cm.   Contains also "The colonial book ... Newburyport and vicinity" and "Georgian" of the Towle mfg. co.   5-2988.   F74.N55
                                                                                                                                                                                              F69.R448

NEWBURYPORT.   An account of the great fire, which destroyed about 250 buildings in Newburyport, on the night of the 31st May, 1811.   Taken principally from the statements which have appeared in the public newspapers.   2d ed., improved.   Newburyport, Print. W. & J. Gilman, 1811.   23 p.   17½ cm.
1-12382.   F74.N55 A1

NEWBURYPORT.   Life in a New England town: 1787, 1788.   Diary of John Quincy Adams, while a student in the office of Theophilus Parsons at Newburyport.   Boston, Little, Brown, 1903.
204 p.   front. (port.)   24 cm.   Reprinted from the proceedings of the Mass. historical soc.   3-21393.   F74.N55 A2

NEWBURYPORT.   History of the Marine society of Newburyport, from its incorporation in 1772 to the year 1906: together with a complete roster and a narrative of important events in the lives of its members.   Comp. by Captain William H. Bayley and others.   (Newburyport? Press of the Daily news) 1906.   4, (5) - 506 p.   plates, ports., facsims.   26½ cm.   6-30902.   F74.N55 B3

NEWBURYPORT, History of; from the earliest settlement of the country to the present time.   With a biographical appendix.   By Mrs. E. Vale Smith.   Newburyport (Boston, Press of Damrell and Moore) 1854.   414 p.   illus., pl., ports.   23½ cm.   1-12383 Additions.   F74.N55 B58

NEWBURYPORT.   The Washiad: or Siege of Washington.   An epic poem, in three cantos.   Being scenes from the experience of an office seeker, and containing some account of the conspiracy of the "Outsiders," to secure appointments to the U.S. government offices in the custom house, and post office in Newburyport.   By an eminent conservative ...   Canto first.   (Newburyport? Mass.) 1858.
26 p.   17½ cm.   The author was Edwin Blood, son of the collector of the port.   No more pub.   6-17629.   F74.N55 B6

500

MASSACHUSETTS

NEWBURYPORT. Places of historical interest within the limits of "Ould Newbury." Newburyport, Printed for the City improvement society, 1897.   10 p.   20½ cm.   4-36281.   F74.N55 C5

NEWBURYPORT. A genealogical address, giving a brief history of the parishioners and founders of the Federal street church, from 1745-6 to 1862, with the names of their descendants, now parishioners, delivered before the Ladies' and gentlemen's association of the parish, May 19, 1862. By Moody D. Cook ... Newburyport, W. H. Huse, printers, 1862.   35 p.   22½ cm.   7-35038.   F74.N77C73

NEWBURYPORT. The city of Newburyport in the civil war from 1861 to 1865 with the individual records of the soldiers and sailors who served to its credit, also the war records of many natives and residents of the city, credited to other places, by George W. Creasey ... Boston, Griffith-Stillings press, 1903.   539 p. front. (port.)   24 cm.   6-26017.   F74.N55C75

NEWBURYPORT, History of, 1764 - 1905; by John J. Currier ... Newburyport, Mass., The author, 1906 - 09.   2 v. fronts., illus. (incl. ports., maps)   24 cm.   6-5687 Add.   F74.N55 C8

NEWBURYPORT. The history and present state of the town of Newburyport, by Caleb Cushing ... Newburyport, Printed by E. W. Allen, 1826.   vii, 120 p.   18½ cm.   1-11535.   F74.N55 C9

NEWBURYPORT. Expose of Newburyport eccentricities, witches and witchcraft. The murdered boy, and apparition of the Charles-st. school-house. By H. P. Davis. (n.p., 1873)   24 p. illus.   23 cm.
1-10144.   F74.N55 D2

NEWBURYPORT. A pickle for the knowing ones; or, Plain truths in a homespun dress, by the late Lord Timothy Dexter, with an introductory essay. Reprint of edition of 1838. Boston, S. A. Tucker, 1881.   36 p. fold. front.   14½ cm.   13-12613.   F74.N55D47
Rare Book Coll.

NEWBURYPORT. Life of Timothy Dexter; embracing sketches of the eccentric characters that composed his associates. By Samuel Knapp ... Boston, G. N. Thomson, 1838.   viii, (9) - 108 p. incl. front., illus.   15½ cm.   13-18455.   F74.N55 D48
Rare Book Coll.

— including "Dexter's pickle for the knowing ones." Newburyport, J. G. Tilton; Boston, W. J. Reynolds, 1848.   viii, (9)-107p. 36 p. incl. front., illus.   16 cm.   4-20032.   F74.N55D482

NEWBURYPORT. Lord Timothy Dexter of Newburyport, first in the East, first in the West, and the greatest philosopher in the western world, by J. P. Marquand ... New York, Minton, Balch, 1925.
vi, 378 p. incl. front.   21 cm.   "A pickle for the knowing ones ... (Reprint of 1838 ed.) p. (327) - 378.   25-19573.   F74.N55D484

NEWBURYPORT. Timothy Dexter revisited. By John Phillips Marquand. Illustrated by Philip Kappel. (1st ed.) Boston, Little, Brown (1960)   306 p.   22 cm.   60-9335.   F74.N55D4843

NEWBURYPORT. Something new: or Memoirs of that truly eccentric character, the late Timothy Dexter, together with his last will and testament. Montpelier, Vt., From Parks' press, 1808.
23 p.   14 cm.   17-7725.   F74.N55D485
Rare Book Coll.

NEWBURYPORT. Timothy Dexter, known as "Lord Timothy Dexter," of Newburyport. An inquiry into his life and true character. By William Cleaves Todd ... Boston, Press of D. Clapp, 1886.
13 p.   25 cm.   Reprinted from the N. E. historical and genealogical register for Oct. 1886.   2-26036.   F74.N55D486

NEWBURYPORT. Reminiscences of a nonagenarian. Ed. and illus. by Sarah Anna Emery ... Newburyport (Mass.) W. H. Huse, printers, 1879.   336 p. illus., 5 pl.   24½ cm.   Relates principally to Newbury and Newburyport.   7-37073.   F74.N55 E5

NEWBURYPORT. Old Newburyport houses, comp. by Albert Hale. Boston, W. B. Clarke co. (1912)
4 p., 68 numb. l. illus.   28 x 23½ cm.   13-1238.   F74.N55H16

NEWBURYPORT. "The house of God": historical discourse on the sesqui-centennial of the Old South meeting-house of Newburyport, by the pastor Horace Carter Hovey. (Newburyport, Mass., Herald Press, 1906)   3, 3-27 p.   2 pl., 2 port.   23 cm.   7-7456.   F74.N55 H8

NEWBURYPORT.   Patriots and partisans; the merchants of Newburyport, 1764 - 1815.   By Benjamin Woods Labaree.   Cambridge, Mass., Harvard University Press, 1962.   242 p. 22 cm. (Harvard historical studies v. 73)   62-19217.   F74.N55 L3

NEWBURYPORT.   Old New England traits, edited by George Lunt ... New York, Hurd and Houghton, 1873.   v, 244 p.   18½ cm.   Reminiscences of old Newburyport.   1-11536.   F74.N55 L9

NEWBURYPORT.   Federalist Newburyport; or, Can historical fiction remove a fly from amber? By John Phillips Marquand.   New York, Newcomen Soc. in North America, 1952.   24 p. illus. 23 cm.   53-26786.   F74.N55 M3

NEWBURYPORT.   The Old South pilgrimage to Newburyport.   By Edwin Doak Mead.   (Boston, 1900)   14 p.   8°.   Reprinted from the New England magazine, July, 1900.   1-11537-M1.   F74.N55 M4

NEWBURYPORT.   The Christian mechanic.   A sketch of Charles Morse, of Newburyport.   Written for the Massachusettts Sabbath school society, and approved by the Committee of publication.   Boston, Mass. Sabbath school soc. (1859)   2 p., 5-252 p. 15½ cm.   13-2729.   F74.N55 M8

NEWBURYPORT.   Celebration of the 50th anniversary of the city charter of Newburyport.   1901. (Newburyport, News pub. co., printers, 1901?)   146 p.   4 port. (incl. front.)   25 cm.   6-24803.
F74.N55N46

NEWBURYPORT.   A program of the celebration of the 50th anniversary of the incorporation of the city of Newburyport.   1851 - 1901.   (Newburyport, Newburyport daily news press, 1901)   96 p. incl. illus., plates, ports.   22 cm.   7-26248.   F74.N55N47

NEWBURYPORT.   A report of the proceedings on the occasion of the reception of the sons of Newburyport resident abroad, July 4th, 1854 ...   Compiled and reported by Joseph H. Bragdon.   Pub. by order of the city government.   Newburyport, M. H. Sargent, 1854.   116 p.   23½ cm.   1-16863.
F74.N55N472

NEWBURYPORT, Vital records of, to the end of the year 1849 ... Salem, Mass., The Essex institute, 1911.   2 v.   23½ cm.   11-7325 Rev.   F74.N55N48

NEWBURYPORT.   Presentation of the statue of Washington to the city of Newburyport.   (Newburyport, Mass.) Printed by order of the City council (William H. Huse, printers) 1879.   3, (5) - 74 p. front., plates, port.   27 cm.   1-9330.   F74.N55N485

NEWBURYPORT.   Celebration of the 100th anniversary of the meeting house of the First religious society in Newburyport.   1901.   Newburyport, Printed by order of the Society, 1902.   61 p. 23 cm.   24-12319.   F74.N55N49

NEWBURYPORT.   The 150th anniversary of the foundation of the First religious society of Newburyport, originally the Third parish of Newbury.   Newburyport, W. H. Huse, printers, 1876.   72 p. 22½ cm.   Genealogy of the Lowell family: p. 70 - 72.   10-6786.   F74.N55N493

NEWBURYPORT and city government; an address delivered at the celebration of the 50th anniversary of the incorporation of Newburyport as a city ... by Albert E. Pillsbury.   (Newburyport, Mass., 1901)   32 p.   27 cm.   4-25035.   F74.N55 P6

NEWBURYPORT.   Articles and regulations of the Relief fire-society.   In Newburyport; formed the 21st March, 1775.   (n. p., 1809)   8 p.   16 cm.   CA 27-561 Unrev.   F74.N55 R4
Rare Book Coll.

NEWBURYPORT.   A historical discourse commemorative of the organization of the First Presbyterian church in Newburyport, delivered at the first centennial celebration .... By Jonathan F. Stearns, pastor.   Newburyport, J. G. Tilton, 1846.   64 p.   front. (port.)   23 cm.   10-31036.   F74.N55 S7

MASSACHUSETTS 273

NEWBURYPORT. The colonial book of the Towle mfg. co. Which is intended to delineate and describe some quaint and historic places in Newburyport and vicinity and show the origin and beauty of the colonial pattern of silverware. (Cambridge, Printed by W. Bradley) 1898. (40) p. illus. (incl. double map) 23½ cm. 160th thousand. Compiled by George P. Tilton. 18-8801. F74.N55T63

— The 5th ed. (Springfield, Mass., Press of Springfield printing and binding co., 1908) 74 p. front. (map) illus. 28 cm. Comp. and arr. by George P. Tilton from various sources. 8-18727. F74.N55T65

NEWBURYPORT. A discourse delivered at Newburyport ... 1856. On occasion of the 100th anniversary of the building of the First Presbyterian church, by the pastor, Rev. Ashbel G. Vermilye. Newburyport, Moulton & Clark, 1856. 74 p. 23½ cm. 4-31152. F74.N55 V4

NEWTON. ... Description and history of Newton. By the Rev. Jonathan Homer. (Boston, 1816) 28 p. 21½ cm. Extracted from the Collections of the Mass. historical soc. 1st ser., v. 5. 19-20264. F74. N 56

NEWTON directory, The ... vol. (I) - 1868, 1871 - 1919/20, 1921 - 19 Boston, Sampson & Murdock co., 1868 - 19 v. fold. maps. 22 - 24½ cm. 1-31210 (rev. '33) Directories

NEWTON house directory and family address book, The. 1913 - Worcester, Mass., Drew Allis co. v. front. (fold. map) 23½ cm. 13-6965. Directories

NEWTON, Blue book of. 1887 - v. F74.N56A182

NEWTON. Glimpses of Newton's past told in history and drama, by Agnes Beryl Curtis. Boston, Press of Geo. H. Ellis co., 1918. 4 p., 80 p. 20½ cm. 18-19317. F74.N56 C9

NEWTON. Life of the Rev. Joseph Grafton, late pastor of the First Baptist church, Newton, with an appendix embracing historical, statistical, and ecclesiastical information pertaining to the town of Newton. By Samuel F. Smith. Boston, J. Putnam, 1849. x, (13) - 213 p. 20 cm. 11-4704.
F74.N56 G7

NEWTON. A history of the early settlement of Newton, from 1639 to 1800. With a genealogical register of its inhabitants, prior to 1800. By Francis Jackson ... Boston, Printed by Stacy and Richardson, 1854. iv, 5-555 p. front. (port.) fold. map. 19 cm. 1-11538. F74.N56J11

NEWTON. History of the early settlement of Newton, from 1639 to 1800 ... Boston, Print. Stacy and Richardson, 1854. (Newton, 1909) iv, 5-555 p. front. (port.) fold. map. 20 cm. Photographic reproduction. 9-8771. F74.N56J12

NEWTON. The mirror of Newton, past and present. (Newton, Mass.) The Newton federation of women's clubs (1907) 169 p. illus., ports. 26 cm. 7-19059. F74.N56 M6

NEWTON. A brief notice of the settlement of the town of Newton, prepared by a committee who were charged with the duty of erecting a monument to the memory of its first settlers ... 1852. Boston, Printed by C. C. P. Moody, 1852. 38, (4) p. illus. 22½ cm. 1-11539 Rev. F74.N56 N5

NEWTON. Celebration of the 200th anniversary of the incorporation of the town of Newton ... 1888. Pub. by order of the City council ... Boston, Printed by A. L. Rand, 1891. 70 p. 24 cm. 3-32507.
F74.N56N56

NEWTON. ... The centennial celebrations of the city of Newton, Newton, By order of the city council, 1876. 167 p. front., plates, port., fold. facsim. 25½ cm. 1-16786 Rev. F74.N56 N6

NEWTON. Ceremonies at the dedication of the soldiers' monument in Newton. Boston, S. Chism, Franklin printing house, 1864. 48 p. incl. front. 19½ cm. 10-12998. F74.N56N62

NEWTON. Eliot anniversary, 1646 - 1896. City of Newton, memorial exercises ... 1896. Newton, By order of the City council, 1896. 4, (7) - 102, (4) p. incl. illus., pl., port., facsim. 22½ cm. 5-36576.
F74.N56N625

NEWTON, Vital records of, to the year 1850.   Boston, Pub. by the New-England historic genealogical soc ... 1905.   521 p. 23½ cm. 5-16895.
F74.N56N63
Geneal. section ref.

NEWTON.   The commemorative services of the First church in Newton, on the occasion of the 225th anniversary of its foundation ... 1889.   Boston, The Society, Press of Rockwell and Churchill, 1890.   271 p. 24 cm. 9-30089.
F74.N56N64

NEWTON.   The commemorative services of the First church in Newton, on the occasion of the 250th anniversary of its foundation ... 1914.   (Newton) The Church (Concord, N.H., Rumford press) 1915.   207 p. front., 2 pl. (1 fold. and col) ports. 23½ cm. 16-1940.
F74.N56 N66

NEWTON ...   Boston, The Edison electric illuminating co., 1909.   23 cm.
F74.N56N75

NEWTON, The story of, its natural beauty, attractive homes and historical associations, by John R. Prescott ... (Newton, Mass., Printed by the Garden City press, 1936)   68 p. incl. front., illus. fold. map.   10½ cm.   Enlarged from a short historical sketch first pub. as part of the Mass. "Chronicle and tribute book".   Pub. under the auspices of the Newtonville library association, inc."   36-18387.
F74.N56 P7

— (Newton? 1939)   80 p. incl. front., illus., pl. fold. map. 19½ cm. 46-41897.
F74.N56 P7
1939

NEWTON.   Tercentenary history of Newton, 1630 - 1930, by Henry K. Rowe.   (Newton, Mass.) Pub. by city of Newton, 1930.   vii, 534 p. front., plates. 24 cm. 30-30681.
F74.N56R87

NEWTON, History of.   Town and city, from its earliest settlement to the present time.   1630 - 1880. By S. F. Smith.   Boston, The American logotype co., 1880.   xi, 13-851 p. front., plates, ports., fold. map, facsim. 23½ cm. 1-11540.
F74.N56 S6

NEWTON.   King's handbook of Newton, by M. F. Sweetser ... Two hundred illustrations.   Boston, Moses King corporation, 1889.   2 p., 326 p. illus. (incl. maps) plates. 20½ cm. 1-12384.
F74.N56 S9

NEWTON.   The Town crier v. 1 - 5; v.6, no. 1 - 3;   new ser. v. -   1898 -   v.
F74.N56 T7

NEWTON.   The Town crier, v. 1, no, 1 - 20.   1903.   1 v.
F74.N56T72

NEWTON CENTER.   Centennial anniversary of the Baptist church at Newton Centre ... 1800. Boston, Print. G.J. Stiles, 1881. 105 p. front. (port.) 23½ cm. 29-14715.
F74.N562N5

NEWTON CENTER.   A print shop fifty years in Newton Centre, 1897 - 1947.   Newton Centre, 1947.   31 p. 22 cm. 48-12555*.
F74.N562T4

NEWTONVILLE.   Some Newtonville homes.   Newtonville, Mass., J. R. Prescott, under the auspices of the Newtonville improvement assoc., 1913.   65, (4) p. illus., fold. map. 14½ x 19½ cm. 14-1376.
F74.N566P9

NORTH ADAMS.   Business directory, and mercantile register of Albany, Troy, Schenectady, Kingston, Poughkeepsie, Cohoes, Amsterdam, Saratoga, Hudson, Gloversville, Pittsfield, Mass., North Adams, Mass., Glens Falls, Rensselaer, Catskill, Johnstown, and intermediate towns ... (1st) -   Troy, N.Y., 1902 -   v. 24 cm. 17-28126.
Directories

NORTH ADAMS general city directory, including Blackinton, Greylock and Braytonville ...   North Adams, Mass., J. T. Larkin,   v. fold. maps. 23 cm. Vols. for 1895-7 include Briggsville.
1-19477 Rev.
Directories

NORTH ADAMS.   H. A. Manning co.'s North Adams directory ... (v. 1 -   Springfield, Mass., H. A. Manning co., 1910 -   1 v. 24½ cm. 10-15493.
Directories

NORTH ADAMS.   City of North Adams poll tax and military list ... 1903.   Arranged in wards by the assessors, John F. Bowes and others ... North Adams, Mass., Walden & Crawley, print, 1903.   7-138 p. 7 pl. 24½ cm. 10-211.
F74. N8 B7

MASSACHUSETTS

NORTH ADAMS. Annual record of North Adams and its people showing their particular and social history and the most interesting events during the year ... including Braytonville, Greylock ... etc. Comp. F. H. Greylock. v.1. North Adams, F. H. Fleming (1886)   1 v.   12°.   1-23706-M1.
         F74. N8 F5

NORTHAMPTON. First parish. (1878)   1 v.   F74. N8 N8

NORTH ADAMS and vicinity illustrated. An illustrated book of North Adams, Adams and Williamstown, their industries, past and present ... Ed. by H. G. Rowe and C. T. Fairfield. North Adams, The Transcript pub. co., 1898.   2, (11) - 140 p.   illus., fold. pl.   35 x 26 cm.   Supplement to the North Adams transcript, Jan. 20, 1898.   10-212.
         F74. N8 R8

NORTH ADAMS, History of. 1749 - 1885. Reminiscences of early settlers. Extracts from old town records. Its public institutions, industries and prominent citizens, together with a roster of commissioned offices in the war of the rebellion. By W. F. Spear. North Adams, Mass., Hoosac valley news printing house, 1885.   2 p. 116 p.   23 ½ cm.   1-16546 Rev.
         F74. N8 S7

NORTH ANDOVER directory ... 1896/7 -   Canton, Mass., C. K. Gurney, 1896 -
     v.   24 cm.   CA 33-478 Unrev.
         Directories

NORTH ANDOVER directory, 1914 - Boston, W. E. Shaw.   1 v. fold. map. 23½ cm. 14-17276.
         Directories

NORTH BROOKFIELD. Incidents and appalling trials and treatment of Elizabeth R. Hill, from the plotting citizen confederacies in Worcester County, Mass. (New York? 1877)   199 p. fold. plan. 23 cm. 11-21028.
         F74. N81 H6

NORTH BROOKFIELD. A historical record of the soldiers and sailors of North Brookfield, and of others who counted upon the quota of the town, in the war for the preservation of the union, against the rebellion, 1861 - 1865. Regimental histories, etc. North Brrokfield, Pub. by the town, 1886.   71 p.   26 cm.   3-29027.
         F74.N81N93

NORTH BROOKFIELD, Prospectus of the History of. Testimonials of the value of the work, and some speciments from its pages. North Brookfield, 1888.   52 p. plates, map. 23 cm.   1-11549 rev.*
         F74. N81N94

NORTH BROOKFIELD, History of. Preceded by an account of old Quabaug, Indian and English occupation, 1647 - 1676; Brookfield records, 1686 - 1783 ... With a genealogical register. By Josiah Howard Temple   North Brookfield, Pub. by the town (Boston printed) 1887.   824 p. front., illus., pl., port., maps, facsim.   8°.   1-11550-M1.
         F74. N81 T2

NORTH BROOKFIELD. An oration delivered by Gen'l Francis A. Walker, at the Soldiers' monument dedication in North Brookfield, ... 1870. Also, the addresses of His Excellency Wm. Claflin, Gen. Chas. Devens and others, with a brief account of the celebration. Worcester, Goddard & Nye, print., 1870.   50 p.   front.   23 ½ cm.   7-29683.
         F74. N81 W2

NORTH MIDDLEBOROUGH, The history of the church of. In six discourses ... by ... S. Hopkins Emery ... Pub. by request of the church and congregation. Middleborough, Harlow & Thatcher, printers, 1876.   106 p.   19 cm.   6-42561.
         F74.N83 E5

NORTHAMPTON and Easthampton directory, 1882/3 -   (v.1 -   Northampton (Mass.) The Price & Lee co., 1882 - 19   v.   fold. plans.   23 ½ cm.   0-1325 Rev.
         Directories

NORTHAMPTON. The Northampton book; chapters from 300 years in the life of a New England town, 1654 - 1954. Compiled and edited by the Tercentenary Committee: Lawrence E. Wikander and others. Northampton, Mass., Tercentenary Committee, 1954.   xiii, 246 p. illus., ports. 24 cm.   55-148.
         F74. N86 A4

NORTHAMPTON. An address ... 1854, in commemoration of the close of the second century since the settlement of the town. By William Allen ... Northampton, Hopkins, Bridgman, 1855.   56 p.   23 cm.   1-11541.
         F74. A86 A5

NORTHAMPTON. Inscriptions on the grave stones in the grave-yards of Northampton, and of other towns in the valley of the Connecticut, as Springfield, Amherst, Hadley, Hatfield, Deerfield, etc., with brief annals of Northampton ... Transcribed by Thomas Bridgman. Northampton, Mass., Hopkins, Bridgman & co., 1850.   xii, (13) - 227 p. front., port. 18½ cm. 1-11542.   F74.N86 B8

NORTHAMPTON; évolution urbaine (par) Gilbert Cestre. Paris, Société d'édition d'enseignement supérieur, 1963.   376 p. 27 cm.   F74.N86C35

NORTHAMPTON, The attractions of, with sketches and descriptions of the various objects of interest in its vicinity ... by Charles Henry Chandler. Springfield, Mass., S. Bowles, 1871. 7 - 28 p. illus. 12º. 1-11543-M1.   F74.N86 C4

NORTHAMPTON.   Antiquities, historicals and graduates of Northampton. By Rev. Solomon Clark ... Northampton, Mass., Steam press of Gazette printing co., 1882. xii, (13) - 374, (2) p. front., plates. 23 cm. 1-12385.   F74.N86 C5

NORTHAMPTON. Historical catalogue of the Northampton First church, 1661 - 1891. By Rev. Solomon Clark ... Northampton, Mass., Gazette print., 1891. 239 p. front., pl., ports. 18½ cm. 11-26704.   F74.N86C51

NORTHAMPTON.   Early Northampton ... Northampton, Mass., Betty Allen chapter, D.A.R., 1914. 229, (3) p. front., illus., plates, ports. 24 cm. 15-8.   F74.N85D23

NORTHAMPTON.   Reminscences of old Northampton, sketches of the town as it appeared from 1840 to 1850, by Henry S. Gere ... (Northampton, Gazette printing co.) 1902. 151 p. incl. illus., ports., plan. front. 23½ cm. Most of these sketches appeared originally in the Hampshire gazette, 1902. 3-32080 Rev.   F74.N86 G3

NORTHAMPTON Quarter centennial ... Oct., 1887. Northampton, Wade, Warner & co., 1887. 66 p. illus. (incl. ports.) 40 cm. Hampshire county journal. Quarter centennial edition.   F74.N86 H3

NORTHAMPTON.   Old Northampton, by Charles Downer Hazen ... an address delivered before the faculty and students of Smith college ... 1904, on the occasion of the 250th anniversary of the founding of Northampton. Cambridge, The University press, 1904.   34 p. 19 cm. 4-29209.
F74.N86 H4

NORTHAMPTON.   Historical register and general directory of Northampton: containing a map of the town, historical sketch of the Northampotn, churches, pastors, schools, courts, canal, railroads ... etc., tog. with sketches of the public institutions ... Northampton, Gazette print., 1875-6. vi, (9) - 220 p. illus., pl., map. 19½ cm. Imperfect: map wanting. 2-8548.   F74.N86 H6

NORTHAMPTON.   Drives in Northampton and vicinity ... by Frederick Newton Kneeland. Northampton, Mass., Gazette print., 1888.   iv, 5 - 61 p. illus., maps. 8º. 1-11544-M1.   F74.N86 K6

NORTHAMPTON, the meadow city; over 250 illustrations. By Frederick Newton Kneeland. Northampton, Mass., F. N. Kneeland and L. P. Bryant (1894)   107 p. incl. front., illus. 31½ x 24 cm. 1-11545.
F74.N86 K7

NORTHAMPTON.   This is Northampton. Leage of Women Voters of Northampton. (Northampton) 1962. 72 p. 23 cm.   F74.N86 L4

NORTHAMPTON. Historical localitites in Northampton. Comp. by the Committee on historical localities for the celebration of the 250th anniversary of the settlement of the town ... 1904. (Northampton, Gazette printing co., 1904)   40 p. incl. front., illus. 22½ cm. 16-14555.   F74.N86 N7

NORTHAMPTON. The Meadow city's quarter-millenial book. A memorial of the celebration of the 250th anniversary of the settlement of the town. ... 1904 ... Prepared and pub. by direction of the city. (Springfield, Mass., Press of the F. A. Bassette co., 1904?)   xv, 531 p. incl. front., illus., ports., facsims. 23½ cm. 6-7412.   F74.N86 N8

NORTHAMPTON business directory and general advertiser. 1860 - 1861. Containing historical

MASSACHUSETTS

sketches of the principal business firms ... Northampton, Trumbull & Gere, 1860. 154, (2) p. 16 cm.
17-20803. F74.N86N85

NORTHAMPTON, History of, from its settlement in 1654; by James Russell Trumbull ... Northampton (Press of Gazette print.) 1898 - 1902. 2 v. fronts. (ports.) fold. maps, fold. plans, facsims. 24½ cm. 98-2318.
F74.N86 T8

NORTHAMPTON. ... Northampton of today; depicted by pen and camera, Frederick Knab, artist. By Charles Forbes Warner. Northampton, Mass., Picturesque pub. co., 1902. 96 p. incl. front., illus. 30½ cm. 3-847 Rev.
F74.N85 W2

NORTHAMPTON. Representative families of Northampton; a demonstration of what high character, good ancestry and heredity have accomplished in a New England town ... By Charles Forbes Warner. Northampton, Picturesque pub. co., 1917. v. front., plates, ports. 25 cm. 17-22877 Rev. F74.N86W24

NORTHAMPTON. A sermon, preached at Northampton ... 1808. at the opening of Northampton bridge ... By Samuel Willard ... Northampton, Bull & Butler, 1808. 19 p. 21 cm. 1-5806.
F74.N86 W6

NORTHAMPTON, Historical sketch of, from its first settlement; in a sermon ... 1815. By Rev. Solomon Williams. Pub. at the request of the town. Northampton: Printed at the Hampshire gazette office, W. W. Clapp, 1815. 24 p. front. 21½ cm. 1-11546. F74.N86 W7

NORTHBOROUGH. The day of small things. A centennial discourse, ... 1846, in commemoration of the organization of the First Congregational church in that place, and the ordination of their first minister, 100 years ago. By Joseph Allen ... Boston, W. Crosby, and H. P. Nichols, 1846.
64 p. 24 cm. 8-25417 Rev. F74.N9 A28

NORTHBOROUGH. Topographical and historical sketches of the town of Northborough, with the early history of Marlborough, in the commonwealth of Mass., furnished for the Worcester magazine. By Rev. Joseph Allen ... Worcester, W. Lincoln & C. C. Baldwin, 1826. 66 p. 23 cm. 1-11547.
F74. N9 A3

NORTHBOROUGH, Historical sketch of. By Rev. Joseph Allen. (Boston, 1862?) 10 p. 24 cm. Pub.
also in History of the town of Marlborough ... by Charles Hudson. Boston, 1862. 10-31038. F74.N9 A34

NORTHBOROUGH history, by Josiah Coleman Kent, with an introduction by Dr. Josiah M. Stanley. Newton, Mass., Garden City press, inc., printers, 1921. vi p., 3 l., 529 p. front., plates, ports. 23½ cm.
22-7632. F74. N9 K3

NORTHBOROUGH, The centennial celebration of the town of ... 1866. (Northborough) Printed for the Committee, 1866. 47 p. 23 cm. 1-11548. F74. N9 N9

NORTHBOROUGH, ... Vital record of, to the end of the year 1850. The larger part from the copy made by Gilman B. Howe ... Worcester, F. P. Rice, 1901. 153 p. 25½ cm. 3-20610.
F74. N9 N94
L. H. & G.

NORTHBRIDGE and Uxbridge directory "Blackstone Valley": a complete resident directory of Whitinsville, Uxbridge, Northbridge, No. Uxbridge, Rockdale, Linwood and farming districts 1911 - vol. ... Boston, Mass., W. E. Shaw, 1911 - 1 v. 23 cm. 11-22126. Directories

NORTHBRIDGE, Vital records of, to the year 1850. Comp. by Thomas W. Baldwin ... Boston, Mass., (Wright & Potter print.) 1916. 202 p. 23½ cm. 17-11236. F74.N92N92

NORTH BROOKFIELD. False imprisonment of Elizabeth R. Hill by Rev. Gabriel H. De Bevoise, and the selectmen of North Brookfield, Mass., and incidents resulting therefrom to Feb. 15, 1881. (New York? 1881) 83 p. 23 cm. 11-22522. F74.N94 H6

NORTHFIELD. Grandfather's captivity and escape. By Mrs. L. G. Benton. (Reprinted from the

Northwestern Congregationalist) (Minneapolis? 18 -) 6 p. 22 cm. Relates to Daniel Howe, who was taken captive by Indians ... 12-3271.
 F74.N96
 E87.H87

NORTHFIELD. (Sketch of the history of the Trinitarian Congregational church, Northfield, Mass.) Written by Mrs. A. M. D. Alexander. Northfield, Mass., 1902. 10 numb. l. 28 cm. Typewritten sheets. CA 8-921 Unrev.
 F74.N96A3

NORTHFIELD. All about Northfield; a brief history and guide, by Arthur Percy Fitt ... Northfield, Mass., Northfield press (1910) 166 p. incl. front. (facsim.) illus. (incl. maps) 19½ cm. 10-14753.
 F74.N96 F5

NORTHFIELD, Illustrated guide to. By I. H. Hull. 1903.
 F74.N96 H9

NORTHFIELD. Reminiscences of men and things in Northfield as I knew them from 1812 to 1825. by Joel Munsell. (Albany, J. Munsell, 1876) 26 p. illus. (incl. diagrs.) 23½ cm. 1-16593.
 F74.N96 M9

NORTHFIELD. Official program of the 250th anniversary celebration of the town of Northfield ... 1923. Northfield, Mass., Northfield press (1923) 35 p. plates. 23½ cm 32-12885.
 F74.N96 N7

NORTHFIELD. 250th anniversary celebration of the town of Northfield ... 1923. (Northfield?) 1923. 118 p. incl. front., illus. 23½ cm. 24-9633.
 F74.N96 N8

NORTHFIELD. A Puritan outpost, a history of the town and people of Northfield, by Herbert Collins Parsons. New York, The Macmillan company, 1937. xii, 546 p. front., plates, ports., maps (1 fold.) 24½ cm. 37-10640.
 F74.N96 P3

NORTHFIELD, Souvenir of. (East Northfield, Mass., H. R. Crowell, 1894) 15 pl. obl. 12°. 1-11551-M1
 F74.N96 S7

NORTHFIELD. A history of the town of Northfield, for 150 years, with an account of the prior occupation of the territory by the Squakheags: and with family genealogies. By J. H. Temple and George Sheldon. Albany, N.Y., J. Munsell, 1875. vi, (2), 636 p. front., illus., plates, port. 23½ cm. Inscriptions upon the tombstones in the old cemetery, copied by Mary T. Stratton: p. 575-592. 1-12386° Cancel.
 F74.N96 T2

NORTON. A history of the town of Norton, Bristol County ... 1669 - 1859. By George Faber Clark ... Boston, Crosby, Nichols, and author at Norton, 1859. xxv, 550 p. front., illus. (plan) pl., ports., map. 22½ cm. 1-11552.
 F74.N97 C5

NORTON, Vital records of, to the year 1850. Boston, Pub. by the New England historic genealogical soc ... 1906. 405 p. 23½ cm. 6-6459.
 F74.N97 N8

NORWELL. ... Historia; a magazine of local history. v. 1, no. 1-6; Nov. 1898 - Oct. 1899. Norwell, Mass., G. C. Turner, 1898-99. 48 p. 23½ cm. bi-monthly. Mimeographed. 7-23336.
 F74.N98 H7

NORWELL. A narrative history of South Scituate-Norwell. By Joseph Foster Merritt. Rockland, Mass., Printed by Rockland Standard Pub. Co., 1938. 203 p. 24 cm.
 F74.N98 M4

NORWOOD and Walpole, Resident and business directory of ... 18 - Boston, 18 -
 v. fold. maps. 24 cm. 0-3937 (rev. '17)
 Directories

OAKHAM. Biography of Deacon James Allen, by Hiram Knight, with genealogical register and testimonials. Worcester, Print. C. Hamilton, 1889. vi, (7)-67 p. front.(port.) 24½ cm. 4-24955.
 F74. O1 K7

MASSACHUSETTS

OAKHAM, ... Vital records of, to the end of the year 1849. Worcester, Mass., F. P. Rice, 1905. 133 p. 23½ cm. 5-16894. F74. O1 O1

OAKHAM. Independence day in 1797 in Oakham, by Henry P. Wright. (Oakham) Oakham historical society, 1911. 17 p. 23½ cm. 12-10469. F74.O1 W 9

OAKHAM. The settlement and story of Oakham, by H. B. Wright and F. D. Harvey. (New Haven? 1947) 2 v. (x, 1204 p.) illus., ports., maps (10 fold. in pocket, v.1) 24 cm. "Genealogical history of Oakham families, compiled by H. B. Wright ... and others": p. (349) - 1204. 48-1602*. F74.O1W915

OAKHAM, Soldiers of, in the revolutionary war, the war of 1812 and the civil war, by Henry Parks Wright. New Haven, Conn., The Tuttle, morehouse & Taylor press, 1914. 3 p., (v) - x, 325 p. front. (plan) plates, ports. 24 cm. Lists of authorities preceded several of the chapters. 15-732. F74. O1 W92

OTIS. Vital records of Otis, to the year 1850. Boston, Mass., Pub. by the New England historic genealogical society at the charge of the Eddy town-record fund, 1941. 150 p. 22½ cm. 41-46132. F74. O8 O8

OXFORD. The Huguenots in the Nipmuck country or Oxford prior to 1713, by George F. Daniels; with an introduction by Oliver Wendell Holmes... Boston, Estes & Lauriat, 1880. xiv, (17) - 168 p. front. (double map) 20 cm. 16-27458. F74. O9 D18

OXFORD, history of the town of, with genealogies and notes on persons and estates, by George F. Daniels. Oxford, Pub. by the author with the cooperation of the town, 1892. vi, (2), 856 p. front., illus., 12 pl., 2 plans, facsim., 2 diagr. 24½ cm. 3-4179. F74. O9 D2

OXFORD, The records of; including chapters of Nipmuck, Huguenot and English history from the earliest date, 1630. With manners and fashions of the time. By Mary de Witt Freeland. Albany, N.Y., J. Munsell's sons, 1894. 2 p., 429 p. 21 x 18 cm. (Munsell's historical series, no. 22) 1-11553. F74. O9 F8

— Illustrated with steel engravings. Albany, N.Y., J. Musell's Sons, 1894. iv, 613 p. ports. 23 cm. 60-55007. F74. O9 F8 1894

OXFORD. Champions of freedom. Huguenot Memorial Society of Oxford. (Oxford, Mass., 1958) 96 p. illus., ports., maps, facsims. 23 cm. Bibliography: p. (3) of cover. Bibliographical footnotes. 59-34892. F74. O9 H8

OXFORD. Historical address. Delivered at the dedication of Memorial hall, Oxford ... 1873. By Peter Butler Olney. Worcester, Press of C. Jillson, 1884. 2 p., 37 p. 23 cm. "Fifty copies. Privately printed." 43-19196. F74. O9 O4

OXFORD, ... Vital record of, to the end of the year 1849. Worcester, Mass., F. P. Rice, 1905. 315 p. 23½ cm. 5-13522. F74. O9 O8

PALMER directory, 1892. Containing a general directory of the citizens, a business and street directory, etc. A.B. Sparrow, comp. Ayer, Mass., E. B. Butterfield, 1892. 99 p. illus. 23½ cm. 13-25478. Directories

PALMER directory and mailing list, 1913. Springfield, Mass., The Beaman-Wood co. v. 24 cm. Contains also Ware directory. 13-21756. Directories

PALMER. Inscriptions from the two ancient cemeteries of Palmer. Copied and arranged by Orrin Peer Allen ... (Palmer, Mass.) Cemetery commissioners, 1902. 67 plates. 23½ cm. Covers the period 1729 - 1901. 2-23197. F74.P17 A4

PALMER, Vital records of, to the year 1850. Boston, Pub. by the New-England historic genealogical society ... 1905. 242 p. 23½ cm. 5-13520. F74.P17 P2

PALMER, History of the town of, early known as the Elbow tract: including records of the plantation, district and town. 1716 - 1889. By J. H. Temple ... With a genealogical register. (Springfield) Pub. by the town of Palmer, 1889. 602 p. front., plates, ports., fold. maps, fold. facsim. 23½ cm. "Genealogies and records": p. (407) - 572. L. C. copy replaced by microfilm. 1-11554.

F74. P17 T2
Microfilm 8764 F

PALMER. An historical address delivered at Palmer ... 1852, in commemoration of the centennial anniversary of the incorporation of the town. By Thomas Wilson, first pastor of the Second Congregational church ... Lowell, S. J. Varney, printer, 1855. 60 p. 21 cm. 10-3144.   F74. P17 W7

PAXTON, The history of. By Ledyard Bill ... Worcester, Putnam, Davis & co., 1889. iv, 3-121 p. 19 cm. "Supplement. The genealogy of some of the first settlers of the town and their descendants": p.(97)-121. 1-11555.   F74. P3 B5

PAXTON. Landmarks and memories of Paxton, by Roxa Howard Bush. Paxton, Mass., 1923. 2 p., 7 - 61 p. front., plates. 24½ cm. 23-4709.   F74. P3 B9

PAXTON. Centenary memorial of Paxton; or, The exercises of the hnudredth anniversary of the incorporation of the town; including a historical address, etc. etc. The celebration occurred June 14, 1865. Worcester, Print, E. R. Fiske, 1868. 78 p. 21½ cm. 10-7988.   F74. P3 P3

PAXTON burial ground inscriptions, to the end of the year 1849. Comp. Franklin Pierce Rice. Worcester, Mass., F. P. Rice, 1906. 32 p. front. 26 x 15½ cm. 100 copies printed. 6-34285.

F74. P3 R5

PEABODY directory, The ... Salem, The H. M. Meek pub.co., v. 24 cm. 22-16683.   Directories

PEABODY. Massachusetts Bay Tercentenary, 1630, 1930. Peabody's celebration; a brief history, some historic sites marked and a list of events ... (Peabody, Mass., Page & Goodwin, 1930) 11 p. 21½ x 10½ cm.   F74. P35 P32

PEABODY historical society. Annual report. (1st) - 12th. (1896/97) - 1909. (Peabody, 1897-1909. 12 v. plates, ports. 23 cm. 9-13122.   F74. P35 P4

— (Officers and committees) 1900 - 1901. (Peabody? Mass., 1900) (4) p. 13 cm.

F74. P35 P5

— Calendar. 1909/10. (Peabody, Mass? 1909-10. 1 sheet. 12½ x 26 cm. folded to 12½ x 10 cm.

F74. P35 P6

PEABODY. Some places of historic interest within the limits of Peabody. (Peabody, Mass., 19 -) 18 x 15½ cm.   F74. P35 S6

PEABODY. House of John Proctor, witchcraft martyr, 1692. By Wm. P. Upham. Peabody, Press of C. H. Shepard, 1904. 17, (2) p. map. 23½ cm. 6-29097.   F74. P35 U6

PELHAM. The attempted suicide of a Massachusetts town. By George H. Haynes ... Worcester, Mass., The Hamilton press, 1904. 14 p. 26 cm. Reprinted from the Proceedings of the American antiquarian soc., April, 1904." 6-41947.   F74. P4 H3

PELHAM, History of, from 1738 to 1898, including the early history of Prescott ... By C. O. Parmenter. Amherst, Mass., Press of Carpenter & Morehouse, 1898. vi, 531 p. front., plates, ports., facsims. 24½ cm. Marriages, 1746 - 1822: p. 454 - 468. 1-11556.   F74. P4 P2

PELHAM, Vital records of, to the year 1850 ... Boston, 1902. 177 p. 23½ cm. (New-England historic genealogical soc.) 3-5253.   F74. P4 P4

PEMBROKE. ... Historic Pembroke, 1712 - 1912; a special issue (of the Bryantville news) pub. on the 200th anniversary of the incorporation of the town ... 1912 ... (Bryantville, Mass.) G. E. Lewis (1912) (5) - 44 p. illus. (incl. ports.) fold. map. 39 cm. 13-14786.   F74. P41 B9

MASSACHUSETTS 281

PEMBROKE, Ancient landmarks of, by Henry Wheatland Litchfield ... Pembroke, G. E. Lewis, 1909.
188 p.   front., plates, ports.   22½ cm.   10-31021.
F74. P41 L7

PEMBROKE. The First church in Pembroke 1708 - 1908, by H. W. Litchfield ... Pembroke (Mass.) Printed for the Parish by G. E. Lewis, 1908.   3, (21) p.   front.   18½ cm.   9-16255.
F74. P41 L72

PEMBROKE, Vital records of, to the year 1850.   Boston, Mass., New England historic genealogical soc. ... 1911.   465 p.   23½ cm.   11-8159.
F74. P41 P4

PEMBROKE, Muster rolls of, during the revolution, taken from the state archives; followed by an alphabetical list of soldiers; arranged by Susan A. Smith. (n.p., 1912)   38 p.   21 cm.   13-9240.
F74. P41 S5

PEPPERELL. A thanksgiving sermon, preached at Pepperell ... 1760. ... By Joseph Emerson ... Boston: Printed and sold by S. Kneeland, 1760.   25 p.   19 cm.   19-10563.
F74. P4
E199. E56

PEPPERELL. Crosby's Pepperell, Shirley, Townsend and Dunstable directory ... South Boston, Mass., Crosby pub. co., 19 -   v.   24 cm.   CA 26-657 Unrev.
Directories

PEPPERELL. The claims of Congregational churches. A centennial address: being a plea in vindication of the rights of the First church of Christ in Pepperell.   Delivered ... 1847.   By Charles Babbidge ... Boston, W. Crosby and H. P. Nichols, 1847.   44 p.   22½ cm.   6-15340.
F74. P43 B2

PEPPERELL. Diary kept by the Rev. Joseph Emerson of Pepperell ... 1748-49, with notes and an introduction by Samuel A. Green.   Cambridge, J. Wilson, 1911.   23 p.   24½ cm.   From the proceedings of the Mass. hist. soc. for Dec. 1910.   11-3365.
F74. P43 E5

PEPPERELL. ... Address delivered on the 150th birthday of the First church of Christ in Pepperell ... 1897, by Emeline Harrington ... The Pepperell print., 1897.   18 p.   24 cm.   37-9455.
F74. P43 H3

PEPPERELL, Military record of. Historical address given in Prescott hall ... 1877, by C. P. Shattuck. Nashua, N.H., H. R. Wheeler, printer, 1877.   38 p.   22½ cm.   10-1505.
F74. P43 S5

PERU, Vital records of, to the year 1850 ... Boston, 1902.   112 p.   23½ cm.   New-England historic genealogical soc.   3-5255.
F74. P45 P5

PETERSHAM. Planning one town: Petersham, a hill town in Massachusetts, by John D. Black and Ayers Brinser.   Cambridge, Harvard University Press, 1952.   x, 75 p.   maps, tables.   24 cm.   52-10750.
F74. P5 B5

PETERSHAM. The history of Petersham, incorporated April 20, 1754. Volunteerstown or Voluntown, 1730 - 1733, Nichewaug, 1733 - 1754. By Mabel Cook Coolidge for the Petersham Historical Soc. inc. (Petersham? 1948)   408 p.   illus., ports., 4 fold. maps (in envelope)   23 cm.   48-25754*.
F74. P5 C6

PETERSHAM, ... Vital record of, to the end of the year 1849.   Worcester, Mass., F. P. Rice, 1904.
193 p.   23½ cm.   4-18419.
F74. P5 P6
L. H. & G.

PETERSHAM. 1754 - 1904. 150th anniversary of the incorporation of the town of Petersham ... 1904. (Boston, Print. Everett press co., 1904)   60 p.   front.   22½ cm.   12-14975.
F74. P5 P61

PETERSHAM. An address delivered in Petersham ... 1854 in commemoration of the 100th anniversary of the incorporation of that town. By Edmund B. Willson.   Boston, Crosby, Nichols, 1855.
iv, (5) - 133 p.   23 cm.   1-11557.
F74. P5 W7

PETERSHAM. Address delivered ... 1929, on the 175th anniversary of the incorporation of the town ... by the Hon. John Munro Woolsey ... (New York, Pandick press, 1929)   2 p. (3) - 55 p.   front. (map)
26 cm.   30-6894.
F74. P5W91

511

LOCAL HISTORIES IN THE LIBRARY OF CONGRESS

PHILLIPSTON, ... Vital records of, to the end of the year 1849. Worcester, Mass., F. P. Rice, 1906. 121 p. 23½ cm. 6-13932.
F74. P56 P5

PIGEON COVE, its early settlers & their farms, 1702 - 1840. By Allen Chamberlain. (Boston, Printed by Thomas Todd co., 1940) 93 p. front., fold. map. 23½ cm. 40-14870.
F74. P57 C5

PITTSFIELD. The history of Pittsfield, from the year 1876 to the year 1916, by Edward Boltwood. (Pittsfield) The City of Pittsfield (1916) 3 p., 387 p. plates, ports., fold. map. 25 cm. 17-18812.
F74. P6 B6

PITTSFIELD. Septuagenarian dinner. Report of the speeches, poem and other proceedings at a dinner given ... by the citizens of Pittsfield to their townsmen who had reached the age of 70 years. Official report. Albany, N.Y., J. Munsell, 1870. 48 p. 23 cm. 10-31039.
F74. P6 C5

PITTSFIELD, A history of the town of, By Rev. David D. Field ... Hartford, Press of Case, Tiffany and Burnham, 1844. 80 p. front. (fold. map) 23 cm. 1-11558.
F74. P6 F4

PITTSFIELD. The gem city of the Berkshires. (Pittsfield, Mass., 1900?) 18½ cm.
F74. P6 G3

— By Sears Chester Lyon. Pittsfield, Mass. (1905) 20 cm.
F74. P6 L9

PITTSFIELD. The proceedings at the dedication of the Soldiers' monument, at Pittsfield ... 1872 ... Pittsfield, Mass., Chickering & Axtell, printers, 1872. 72 p. front. (phot.) 23½ cm. 1-11560. L. C. copy replaced by microfilm.
F74. P6 P6
Microfilm 27599 F

PITTSFIELD. Proceedings in commemoration of the organization in Pittsfield ... 1764 of the First church of Christ. Pittsfield, Mass., Press of the Sun printing co., 1889. 135 p. front., illus. (facsims.) plates, port. 24 cm. 2-5498.
F74. P6 P7

PITTSFIELD. An address by Rev. Henry Neill, and a poem by Oliver Wendell Holmes, delivered at the dedication of the Pittsfield (rural) cemetery ... 1850, with other matter, and a map of the grounds. By the committee of publication. Pittsfield, Mass., Axtel, Bull and Marsh, print., 1850. 64 p. front. (fold. pl.) fold. map. 23½ cm. 12-9117.
F74. P6 P73

PITTSFIELD, The history of ... Comp. and written, under the general direction of a committee, by J. E. A. Smtih. By authority of the town. Boston, Lee and Shepart, 1869 - 76. 2 v. fronts., illus., plates, ports., fold. map, facsim. 24½ cm. 1-11561.
F74. P6 S6

PITTSFIELD, Souvenir views of, amid the Berkshire Hills. (Pittsfield, Mass., England brothers, 1908) 1 v. 20½ x 25½ cm.
F74. P6 S74

PITTSFIELD, The history of, 1916 - 1955. By George Findlay Willison. (Pittsfield) Pub. by the city of Pittsfield, 1957. 519 p. illus., port., fold. map. 24 cm. 57-45318.
F74. P6 W5

PLAINFIELD, History of the town of, from its settlement to 1891, including a genealogical history of 23 of the original settlers and their descendants, with anecdotes and sketches. By Charles N. Dyer. Northampton, Mass., Press of Gazette print., 1891. 187 p. front., illus., ports. 22½ cm. "Genealogical history": p. 127 - 187. 1-11562 Rev.
F74. P7 D9

PLAINFIELD. Plain tales from Plainfield; or, The way things used to be. By Clara Elizabeth Hudson. Northampton (Mass.) 1962. 54 p. 24 cm. 63-14517.
F74. P7 H8

PLAINFIELD. Topographical description and historical sketch of Plainfield ... By Jacob Porter ... Greenfield, Print. by Prince and Rogers, 1834. 44 p. 22 cm. 1-11563.
F74. P7 P8

— 44 p. 24 cm. 1-11564.
F74. P7 P9

MASSACHUSETTS

PLYMOUTH, Directory and history of ... (1887)   South Framingham, Mass., W. F. Richardson & co., 1887 -   v. illus.   24 cm.   33-33128.   Directories

PLYMOUTH.   Lothrop's Plymouth directory ... including the section of Kingston served by North Plymouth post office ... 1899 - 19   Boston, Mass., Union pub. co., 1899 -
v. fold. maps.   24½ cm.   1-15323 (rev. '33)   Directories

PLYMOUTH directory, The ... 1890   Shirley, Mass., A. B. Sparrow, 1890 -
v. illus.   23½ cm.   33-33129.   Directories

PLYMOUTH, Resident and business directory of, 1899 - 19   Boston, Union pub. co., 1899 - 19
v. fold. maps.   24½ cm.   1-15323 Rev.   Directories

PLYMOUTH.   "Dying, and, behold, we live."   Or, Obituaries of some Manomet people who entered into their rest between Nov. 1897, and Jan. 1899.   By Rev. Haig Adadourian ... Printed for private distribution.   (Plymouth, Mass., The Memorial press) 1899.   50 p.   front. (port.)   23½ cm.   4-15549.
F74. P8 A19

PLYMOUTH.   Manometiana number four; or, A collection of the epitaphs of the "old Burial Hill," Plymouth, Manomet, Mass.   Comp. by Rev. Haig Adadourian ... Plymouth, Mass., 1899.
38 p.   21½ x 13 cm.   The compiler had previously issued 3 pamphlets dealing with the village of Manomet.   6-13025.   F74. P8 A2

PLYMOUTH, Pilgrim guide book to, with a brief outline of the Pilgrim migration and settlement at Plymouth, by William Franklin Atwood ... Plymouth, Mass. (The Memorial press) 1940.
77 p.   illus.   17½ cm.   (Pilgrim book series)   40-33547.   F74. P8 A7

PLYMOUTH.   Pilgrim Plymouth guide to objects of special historic interest ... together with a brief historical outline of the Pilgrim migration from the inception of the congregation at Scrooby, England, to the permanent settlement of Plymouth.   (Boston, Mass., Blanchard print.) 1921.   85, (7) p. illus. (incl. ports.)   17½ cm.   21-11930.   F74. P8 A8

PLYMOUTH.   The Pilgrim picture book of historic Plymouth, with guide map, 125 illustrations.   Plymouth, Mass., The Memorial press, 1940.   (28) p.   illus.   31 cm.   (Pilgrim book series)   40-33548.
F74. P8 B5

PLYMOUTH in my father's time (by) Ellis W. Brewster.   Plymouth, Mass., Pilgrim Society (1968)
98 p.   illus.   21 cm.   F74. P8 B68

PLYMOUTH.   A guide to Plymouth and its history, compiled from inscriptions on tablets, monuments and statues erected in honor of its founders, the Pilgrims ... by Helen T. Briggs and Rose R. Briggs; illus. by Raymond C. Dreher.   (Plymouth, Mass.) The Pilgrim soc. and The Plymouth antiquarian soc. (1938)   54, (3) p.   illus.   19 cm.   "Authorities": p. (3) at end.   39-3583.   F74. P8 B7

PLYMOUTH Rock; history and significance (by) Rose R. Briggs.   (Plymouth, Mass., Pilgrim soc., 1968)   20 p.   illus.   23 cm.   (Pilgrim Society Booklet series)   F74. P8 B73

PLYMOUTH.   Guide to historic Plymouth.   By Alfred Stevens Burbank.   Localities and objects of interest ... Plymouth, Mass., A. S. Burbank (1896)   96 p. incl. illus., pl.   18 cm.   1-11565.   F74. P8 B96

— Plymouth, Mass., A. S. Burbank (1900)   96 p. incl. front., illus.   17½ cm.   0-4674 Rev.   F74. P8 B96 1900

— Plymouth, Mass., A. S. Burbank, (1908)   96 p. incl. illus., pl.   19 cm.   8-30718.   F74. P8 B96 1908

— Plymouth, Mass., A. S. Burbank (1910)   96 p. incl. illus., pl.   20 cm.   10-22438.   F74. P8 B96 1910

— Plymouth, Mass., A. S. Burbank (1913)   96 p. illus.   19½ cm.   13-26111.   F74. P8 B96 1913

— Plymouth, Mass., A. S. Burbank (1916)   96 p. illus. 19½ cm. 16-15178.   F74. P8 B96 1916

— Plymouth, Mass., A. S. Burbank (1917)   96 p. illus. 19½ cm. 17-25453.   F74. P8 B96 1917

— Plymouth, Mass., A. S. Burbank (1919)   96 p. illus. 19 cm. 20-1908.   F74. P8 B96 1919

— Plymouth, Mass., A. S. Burbank (1921)   96 p. illus. 19½ cm. 21-12351.   F74. P8 B96 1921

— Plymouth, Mass., A. S. Burbank (1928)   95, (1) p. illus. 19½ cm. 28-20564.   F74. P8 B96 1928

PLYMOUTH. Plimoth plantation; then and now, by Jean Poindexter Colby. Photos by Plimoth Plantation, The Plymouth Area Chamber or Commerce, and Corinthia Morss. New York, Hastings House (1970)   128 p. illus. 24 cm. (Famous museum series) 70-130046.   F74. P8 C58

PLYMOUTH. Brief guide to Plymouth, for automobilists, for pedestrians; giving the history and the location of the principal places of interest: Plymouth Rock, the monument, Pilgrim hall, Burial hill, old houses, harbors, etc. By Kenneth Cole. (Haverhill, Mass., W. D. Cram, printer) 1913. 16 p. illus. (incl. plans) 19 cm. 13-16158.   F74. P8 C6

PLYMOUTH. A brief history of the First church in Plymouth, from 1606 to 1901, by John Cuckson ... Boston, G. H. Ellis co., 1902.   xvi, 118 p. 21 cm. 3-24229.   F74. P8 C9

PLYMOUTH. Ancient landmarks of Plymouth. Part I. Historical sketch and titles of estates. Part II. Genealogical register of Plymouth families. By William T. Davis ... Boston, A. William, 1883. viii, 350; 312 p. 3 plans (2 fold.) 24½ cm. L. C. copy replaced by microfilm. 1-12073.   F74.P8 D165
Microfilm 14351 F

— 2d ed.   Boston, Damrell & Upham, 1899.   viii p., 3 l., 350, 383 p. 24½ cm. 7-21642.   F74.P8 D17

PLYMOUTH, History of the town of, with a sketch of the origin and growth of Separatism. Illustrated. By William R. Davis ... Philadelphia, J. W. Lewis, 1885.   3, 5-188 p. front., plates, facsims. 28 cm. This was originally written as a contribution to "History of Plymouth County, Mass. ... 1884." 1-12072.   F74.P8 D18

PLYMOUTH memories of an octogenarian, by William T. Davis ... Plymouth, Mass., Printed by the Memorial press (1906)   542 p. front. (port.) 24 cm. 7-1951.   F74. P8 D2

PLYMOUTH. Burial Hill, Plymouth: its monuments and gravestones numbered and briefly described, and the inscriptions and epitaphs thereon carefully copied. By Benjamin Drew ... Plymouth, Mass., D. W. Andrews (1894)   2, viii, (3) - 177 p. 19 cm. 1-11566.   F74. P8 D7

PLYMOUTH, Old houses in. Pen and ink sketches by H. C. Dunham. Plymouth, A. S. Burbank, 1893. 1 p., 6 pl. obl. 4°. 1-11567-M1.   F74. P8 D9

PLYMOUTH, written by Walter Prichard Eaton; illustrations by Cameron Wright. (New York) The New York, New Haven and Hartford railroad co., 1928.   46, (2) p. incl. front., illus., double facsim. (map) 27½ cm. 28-19179.   F74. P8 E2

PLYMOUTH. Fifty photographic views of Plymouth. Boston, J. F. Murphy, 1898.   32 p. illus. 17 x 23 cm. Pages 3 - 32 are illustrations. 1-11568 Rev.   F74. P8 F4

PLYMOUTH. Masonic ceremonies ... at Plymouth ... 1859. (Plymouth? 1859)   23½ cm.   F74. P8 F8

PLYMOUTH. Glimpses of pilgrim Plymouth. Plymouth, A. S. Burbank, 1888.   2 p., 19 pl. obl. 32°. 1-11569-M1.   F74. P8 G5

MASSACHUSETTS 285

— Plymouth, A. S. Burbank, 1890.   22 l. 15 pl. obl. 24º. 1-11570-M1.   F74. P8 G6

PLYMOUTH.   May-flower memories of old Plymouth, by Louis K. Harlow.   Boston, L. Prang, 1889.
10 col. pl. 19 ½ x 25 ½ cm. 19-10858.   F74. P8 H2

PLYMOUTH.   Historic Plymouth ... Plymouth, Mass. (1895)   20 ½ x 11 cm.   F74. P8 H6

PLYMOUTH.   Pilgrims path; the story of Plymouth in words and photos.   By Desider Holisher.   New York, Stephen-Paul (1947)   109 p. illus. 24 cm. 47-11130*.   F74. P8 H65

PLYMOUTH.   Miniatures of Plymouth.   By Thomas Wallace Jones.   (Cincinnati, O., 1904)
8 x 10 ½ cm.   F74. P8 J 7

PLYMOUTH.   Epitaphs from Burial Hill, Plymouth from 1657 to 1892.   With biographical and historical notes ... By Bradford Kingman ... Brookline, Mass., New England illustrated historical pub. co., 1892.   xv, 330 p. front., illus., pl., map, double plan. 23 cm. 6-13063.   F74. P8 K5

PLYMOUTH.   Historic Plymouth from pen drawings: Plymouth Rock, Pilgrim hall, Site of first house, National monument, Old Howland house, Gov. Bradford's grave, Harlow house, Old powder house, copyright ... by A. E. Morton, jr. ...   New Bedford, Mass., The Taber press (1921)   1 p., 8 pl.
15 x 21 ½ cm. 21-12002.   F74. P8 M8

PLYMOUTH.   Records of the Old Colony club, 1769 - 1773.   (Boston? 1887?)   p. (381) - 444. facsim.
24 ½ cm. From the Proceedings of the Mass. historical soc. for Oct. 13, 1887. 11-10438.   F74. P8 O4

PLYMOUTH.   Handbook of old Burial Hill, Plymouth.   Its history, its famous dead, and its quaint epitaphs.   By Frank H. Perkins.   Plymouth, Mass., A. S. Burbank (1896)   49 p. incl. illus., pl. 18 ½ cm.
6-12304.   F74. P8 P38

— Plymouth, Mass., A. S. Burbank, (1902)   72 p. incl. illus., pl. 18 ½ cm. 2-18019.   F74. P8 P4

PLYMOUTH.   ... Pilgrim memorial marine park and strandway association ... (Melrose, Mass.)
1917.   1 sheet. 22 ½ x 30 ½ cm.   F74. P8 P63

PLYMOUTH.   Pilgrim Plymouth. (Plymouth, Mass. A. S. Burbank, 1890)   Illus. sheet fold. in 12. sq. 16º.
1-23712 - M1.   F74. P8 P64

PLYMOUTH.   Pilgrim Plymouth illustrated.   Plymouth, Mass., A. S. Burbank (1900)   32 p. illus.
obl. 12º Oct. 4, 1900-130.   F74. P8 P642

PLYMOUTH.   Pilgrim Plymouth.   (Philadelphia, 1905)   9 ½ x 14 cm.   F74. P8 P65

— Plymouth, Mass., A. S. Burbank 1913.   12 mounted pl. 26 ½ x 32 ½ cm. 13-16159.   F74. P8 P66

PLYMOUTH.   Pilgrim Plymouth; the official souvenir book, authorized by the Plymouth tercentenary committee.   (Plymouth, Mass., A. S. Burbank, 1921)   12 pl. 21 x 25 cm. 21-12276.   F74. P8 P67

PLYMOUTH, Records of the town of; pub. by order of the town ... Plymouth, Avery & Doten, book and job printers, 1889 - 1903.   3 v. 23 ½ cm. v. 1 1636 - 1705. - v.2. 1705 - 1743. - v.3. 1743 - 1783. 1-12387 Add.
F74. P8 P82

PLYMOUTH.   Pilgrim Plymouth; information for the tourist ... Issued for the Plymouth chamber of commerce.   Plymouth, Mass. (The Memorial press, 1935)   (26) p. illus. (incl. port.) pl. 23 cm. 36-25765.
F74. P8 P828

PLYMOUTH, an illustrated description of the points of civic, natural and historical interest in the town made famous by the landing of the Pilgrims.   (Boston) Pub. for the Plymouth chamber of commerce, 1926.   27 p. front., illus. 24 ½ cm. 26-13324.   F74. P8 P83

PLYMOUTH, First church.   Pamphlets, broadsides, clippings, and other miscellaneous matter on this subject, not separately cataloged, are classified in F74.P8P846.

PLYMOUTH. Old Plymouth days and ways; handbook of the historic festival in Plymouth ... 1897, Margaret M. Eager, director. Plymouth, Mass. (Boston, Printed by the T. P. Smith printing co.) 1897.   72 p.   illus.   24 x 18 ½ cm.   12-11175.   F74. P8 P85

PLYMOUTH. Proceedings of the 160th anniversary of the Second Congregational church in Plymouth (Manomet) Mass., held on Nov. 9, 1898 ... Comp. by Rev. Haig Adadourian. Plymouth, Mass., 1899.   67 p.   pl., ports., map.   22 ½ cm.   1-5102 Rev.   F74. P8 P87

PLYMOUTH Antiquarian Society, A history of the. Plymouth, Mass., 1959.   unpaged.   23 cm.   F74. P8 P875

PLYMOUTH rock. Photo-gravures. Plymouth, A. S. Burbank, 1896.   2 p.   16 pl.   obl. 24º.   1-11571-M1.   F74. P8 P89

PLYMOUTH. Pilgrim memorials, and guide for visitors to Plymouth village: with a lithographic map, and seven copperplate engravings. By Wm. S. Russell ... Boston, Printed for the author by C. C. P. Moody, 1851.   viii, 148 p.   front. (fold. plan) plates, facsim.   19 cm.   1-12103.   F74. P8 R88

— (2d ed.) Boston, Crosby, Nichols and co., 1855.   203 p.   front. (fold. plan) plates, facsims.   20 cm.   1-12104 Additions.   F74. P8 R89

— (3d ed.) Boston, Crosby, Nichols, Lee and co., 1860.   229 p.   front. (fold. plan) illus., plates, facsims.   20 cm.   1-12105 Additions.   F74. P8 R 9

— 3d ed. Boston, Crosby and Nichols, 1864.   228 p.   front. (fold. plan)   plates, facsims.   19 cm.   12-23315.   F74. P8 R91

PLYMOUTH, Husbandmen of: farms and villages in the Old Colony, 1629 - 1692 (by) Darrett B. Rutman. Boston, Pub. for Plimoth Plantation by Beacon Press (1967)   xi, 100 p.   24 cm.   67-25868.   F74. P8R93

PLYMOUTH. A souvenir of Plymouth parks; containing a brief history of their acquisition by the town, views of some of the most attractive localities and a map of Morton park. Plymouth, Mass., A. S. Burbank, 1901.   31 l.   front. (port.)   42 illus., map.   18 x 23 cm.   1-25547-M3.   F74. P 8 S 7

PLYMOUTH. Clark's in Plymouth Harbor; the Pilgrim Fathers' island, 1620 - 1690. Chronicled by Sarah Wingate Taylor. (Peterborough, N.H., Pub. for Cedarfield by R. R. Smith, 1965)   37 p.   23 cm.   F74. P8 T25

PLYMOUTH, History of the town of; from its first settlement in 1620, to the year 1832. By James Thacher ... Boston, Marsh, Capen & Lyon, 1832.   xi, (13) - 382 p.   front., fold. map.   19 ½ cm.   1-11572.   F74. P8 T3

PLYMPTON, Vital records of, to the year 1850. Boston, Mass., The New England historic genealogical soc ... 1923.   540 p.   23 ½ cm.   24-4015.   F74. P84 P8

— 2d ed. enl. and cor. Boston, Marsh, Capen & Lyon, 1835.   iv, (5) - 15, (13) - 401 p.   1-11573.   F74. P8 T4

PLYMPTON. Historical address read at the 200th anniversary of the town of Plympton ... 1907, by John Sherman. (Plymouth, Mass., Print. Bittinger bros., 1907)   14 p.   23 cm.   10-25102.   F74. P84 S5

PRINCETON, History of the town of ... 1759 - 1915, by Francis Everett Blake ... Princeton, Pub. by the town, 1915.   2 v.   front., 1 illus., plates, ports., plans, facsims.   23 ½ cm.   "Bibliography of Princeton, Mass.": v.1, p. 396 - 402.   v.I. Narrative - v.II. Genealogies.   15-21985.   F74. P9 B6

PRINCETON. The Goodnow memorial builidng, Princeton, Mass. ... Worcester, 1885.   21 cm.   F74. P9 G6

PRINCETON. History of Princeton; civil and ecclesiastical; from its first settlement in 1739 to

MASSACHUSETTS

to 1852. By Jeremiah Lyford Hanaford ... Worcester, C. B. Webb, printer, 1852. viii, (9) - 204 p. 19 cm. 1-11574.   F74. P9 H2

PRINCETON. Lucy Keyes, the lost child of Wachusett Mountain. By Francis E. Blake. Boston, Press of D. Clapp, 1893. 23 p. front., illus., pl. 23½ cm. An account of the disappearance of Lucy Keyes, of the town of Princeton, who wandered away from home... 1755, and was never seen again by her family. 19-6631. F74. P9 K4

PRINCETON. Celebration of the 100th anniversary of the incorporation of the town of Princeton, 1859, including the address of Hon. Charles Theodore Russell, the poem of Prof. Erastus Everett and other exercises ... Worcester, W. R. Hooper, printer, 1860. 119 p. 23 cm. 1-11575. F74. P9 P92

PRINCETON. The dedication of Goodnow memorial building and Bagg hall ... 1887. Worcester, L. P. Goddard, 1887. 108 p. front. (port.) pl. 23½ cm. 7-27744. F74. P9 P924

PRINCETON. Soldiers of the revolution, Princeton, Mass. (Princeton? 1897?) 8 p. 24 cm. Reprinted from the Town report of Princeton for 1897. 4-30121. F74. P9 P93

PRINCETON, ... Vital records of, to the end of the year 1849. Worcester, Mass., F. P. Rice, 1902. 195 p. 23½ cm. 3-5656. F74. P9 P94
L H & G

PRINCETON, The history of, from its first settlement; with a sketch of the present religious controversy in that place. Designed for the use of the inhabitants. By Charles Theodore Russell ... Boston, Printed by H. P. Lewis, 1838. viii, 130 p. 23 cm. 3-28364. F74. P9 R9

PROVINCETOWN, Resident directory of, (18 -   Boston, Press of G. H. Ware, 18
v. 23 cm. CA 26-302 Unrev. Directories

PROVINCETOWN. The Pilgrims and their monument, by Edmund J. Carpenter ... New York, D. Appleton, 1911. x, 309 p. front., plates, ports. 23 cm. 11-3981. F74. P96 C18

PROVINCETOWN, the tip of the cape. By Edmund J. Carpenter. (Boston, The Barta press) 1900. 2 p. 18 pl. obl. 8°. Oct. 11. 1900-20. F74. P96 C2

PROVINCETOWN profiles and others on Cape Cod. Barre, Mass., Barre Gazette, 1958. 146 p. 24 cm. 58-12084. F74. P96 C7

PROVINCETOWN. Official program of the dedicatory exercises attendant upon the laying of the cornerstone of the Pilgrim monument at Provincetown, Mass., 1907. By Cora Gray West Fuller. (Provincetown, Mass., Provincetown beacon press, 1907) 61 (3) p. illus. (incl. ports.) 27 cm. 7-34354.
F74. P96 F9

PROVINCETOWN. The Pilgrim monument, marking the fist landing place of the Pilgrim fathers at Provincetown, Mass., 1620 ... By Edwin Atkins Grozier. (Provincetown? 1920) 7 p. illus. 34 x 27½ cm. 27-17272. F74. P96 G8

PROVINCETOWN. The log of Provincetown and Truro on Cape Cod, by Mellen C. M. Hatch. Provincetown, Mass., 1939. 78 p. illus. 20½ cm. Bibliography: p. 78. 39-21846. F74. P96 H3

— (1951) 86 p. illus. 21 cm. Includes bibliography. 51-7029. F74. P96 H3
1951

PROVINCETOWN; or, Odds and ends from the tip end. A brief historical description of Provincetown, past and present ... By Herman Atwell Jennings. (Yarmouthport, Mass., F. Hallett, printer) 1890. 212 p. incl. front., illus., port. pl. 18½ cm. 1-11576 Additions. F74. P96 J 5

PROVINCETOWN book, The, by Nancy W. Paine Smith. Brockton, Mass., Tolman print, inc. (1922) (7) - 260 p. front., illus. 20½ cm. "List of books": p. (252) - 254. 22-11366. F74. P96 S6

PROVINCETOWN, A modern pilgrim's guide to, with planned tour for motorists. By Paul Smith. (Provincetown, Mass., 1951) 28 p. illus. 22 cm. 51-39140. F74. P96 S64

PROVINCETOWN.   By Henry Harlow Sylvester.   (Provincetown, H. H. Sylvester, 1881)   24 p. 24º.
1-11577-M1.   F74. P96 S9

PROVINCETOWN.   ... Report of the Trustees of public reservations, on the subject of the province lands.   Feb., 1893.   (Boston, 1893)   55 p.   vii pl., fold. map.   23½ cm.   (Massachusetts. General court. 1893. House. Doc. no. 339)   10-5365 rev.   F74. P96 T7

PROVINCETOWN.   Time and the town, a Provincetown chronicle, by Mary Heaton Vorse.   New York, The Dial press, 1942.   vii, 9-372 p.   21½ cm.   42-18815.   F74. P96 V6

PROVINCETOWN, in picture and story.   By Wainwright Johnson Wainwright.   Cotuit, Mass., Picture Book Co. (1953)   95 p.   illus.   22 cm.   53-32934.   F74. P96 W3

QUINCY.   Memoir of the life of Eliza S. M. Quincy.   Boston (Printed by J. Wilson) 1861.   3, (5) - 267 p.
23½ cm.   12-24385.   F74. Q
E302.6. Q7Q74

QUINCY.   Directory and history of Quincy ... Made by J. H. Hogan ... Plymouth, Avery & Doten, book and job printers, 1888.   329 p.   illus.   23½ cm.   8-19761.   Directories

QUINCY.   Manning's Greenough Quincy directory ... (v. 1 -   Boston, Mass., H. A. Manning co., 1894 - 19 -   v.   maps (part fold.)   23½ - 25½ cm.   0-6062 Rev. 2.   Directories

QUINCY directory for (1882 - 3) - 84.   (v. 1 - 2)   Quincy (Mass.) Green & Prescott (1882) - 84.
2 v.   23 cm.   8-19760.   Directories

QUINCY, Weymouth and Braintree directory, The (v. 4 - 6)   (1876) - 1880/81.   Boston, C. W. Calkins (1876) - 1880.   3 v.   fold. maps.   24 cm.   8-19759.   Directories

QUINCY directory, The (1891) - 93.   Ayer, Mass., E. B. Butterfield (1891) - 93   2 v.   23½ cm.
8-19762.   Directories

QUINCY.   Address of Charles Francis Adams, jr., and proceedings at the dedication of the Crane memorial hall, at Quincy, Mass., May 30, 1882 ... Cambridge, J. Wilson, 1883.   5, (3) - 48 p.
front., 3 pl., port.   23½ cm.   1-12388.   F74. Q7 A4

QUINCY.   The centennial milestone.   An address in commemoration of the 100th anniversary of the incorporation of Quincy, Mass.   By Charles Francis Adams.   Cambridge, J. Wilson, 1892.
59 p. incl. front. pl.   23 cm.   1-12391.   F74. Q7 A43

QUINCY.   History of Braintree (1639 - 1708) the north precinct of Braintree (1708 - 1792) and the town of Quincy (1792 - 1889) by Charles Francis Adams.   Cambridge, Printed at the Riverside press, 1891.   3, 365 p. 24 cm.   1-12389.   F74. Q7 A45
Rare Book Coll.

QUINCY.   Some phases of sexual morality and church discipline in colonial New England ... (Reprinted from the Proceedings of the Mass. historical soc., June 1891)   Cambridge, J. Wilson, 1891.
43 p.   8º.   (With his history of Braintree, 1891)   1-12390-M1.   F74. Q7 A45
Rare Book Coll.

QUINCY.   The Adams mansion, the home of John Adams and John Quincy Adams, presidents of the U.S., by Henry Adams, 2d ... Quincy, Mass., Printed for the Adams memorial soc., 1935.
2, 42 p. incl. illus., plates, ports. front., plates, plans.   24½ cm.   2d ed.   38-11582.   F74. Q7 A5

QUINCY.   The birthplaces of Presidents John and John Quincy Adams in Quincy, Mass., by Henry Adams ... Quincy, Mass., Printed for the Adams memorial soc., 1936.   2, 21 p.   front., illus. (incl. ports., map) 25 cm.   38-10715.   F74. Q7 A6

QUINCY.   Ancient and modern Germantown.   By Martha Maude Bartlett.   (Miami? Fla., 1949)
(20) p.   illus.   23 cm.   50-23950.   F74. Q7 B3

MASSACHUSETTS

QUINCY. New beginnings: Quincy and Norfolk County, Massachusetts (by) James R. Cameron. Quincy, Mass., Quincy Historical Soc., 1966. 27 p. 23 cm. F74. Q7 C3

QUINCY. Commemorative booklet of the third centennial anniversary exercises of the incorporation of the ancient town of Braintree; with appendix and the history of Quincy, "The north precinct of the ancient town of Braintree." By William Churchill Edwards (and) Frederick Ames Coates. (Quincy, Mass., Golden print, 1940) (66) p. front. (port.) illus. (incl. map) 21½ cm. 41-15847. F74. Q7 E3

QUINCY. Historic Quincy ... by William Churchill Edwards. Pub. by the city of Quincy in commemoration of the 100th anniversary of the Town house, 1844 - 1944. (Quincy, Franklin printing service, 1946) 111 p. incl. front., illus. (incl. maps) 9 port. on 1 l. 23½ cm. Bibliography: p. 108-111. 46-6795.
F74.Q7 E34

— (Rev. ed. Quincy) City of Quincy, 1954. 334 p. illus., ports., maps. 22 cm. Bibliography: p. 284 - 288. 54-37069. F74.Q7 E34 1954

— (3d ed. Quincy) City of Quincy, 1957. 415 p. illus., ports. 22 cm. Bibliography: p. 341 - 346. 58-25483.
F74.Q7 E34 1957

QUINCY. A brief record of the physicians of Quincy, from the earliest times, comp. and pub. by Annie E. Faxon, for the benefit of the hospital fund ... 1890. (Boston, Press of Rockwell and Churchill) 1890. 31 p. 18 cm. 5-272. F74. Q7 F2

QUINCY. A memorial of God's goodness. Being the substance of two sermons, preach'd in the First church of Christ in Braintree ... 1739. ... By John Hancock ... Boston, Printed and sold by S. Kneeland & T. Green, 1739. 2, ii, 37 p. 19 cm. 16-5367 Rev. F74. Q7 H2
Rare Book Coll.

QUINCY. Two discourses, delivered ... 1839, on the occasion of the 200th anniversary of the gathering of the First Congregational church, Quincy ... By William P. Lunt. Boston, J. Munroe, 1840. 147 p. illus. 23 cm. 1-11578 Rev. F74. Q7 L9

QJINCY. The "Chappel of ease" and church of statesmen. Commemorative services at the completion of 250 years since the gathering of the First church of Christ in Quincy ... (Quincy, Mass.) Printed for the Society, 1890. viii, 159 p. front., illus., plates, ports., facsim. 24 cm. 1-13637.
F74. Q7 Q7

QUINCY historical guide and map, published by the Quincy tercentenary committee. (Quincy, Mass.) Quincy historical soc., 1925. 48 p. illus., fold. map. 15½ cm. Bibliography: p. (47) 25-10429. F74.Q7 Q76

QUINCY. The President John Adams and President John Quincy Adams birthplaces, and changes down to the present time. Prepared for the Quincy Historical Society by Waldo Chamberlain Sprague, historian. (Quincy) 1959. unpaged. ills. 22 cm. 59-29177. F74.Q7 Q78

QUINCY; historical information, with route map ... (Quincy) Quincy historical society, 1921. 30 p. fold. map. 15½ cm. 21-18196. F74. Q7 Q8

QUINCY. A pageant of Quincy, a pageant in celebration of the tercentenary of the first settlement in Quincy, 1625 - 1925, written and produced by Virginia Tanner for the tercentenary celebration of Quincy ... (Concord, N.H., Rumford press, 1925) 123 p. illus. (incl. port., facsims.) 24 cm. 39-7660.
F74. Q7 T3

QUINCY. An historical sketch of the old church, Quincy. By Rev. Frederick A. Whitney. From the New England historical and genealogical register. Albany, J. Munsell, 1864. 17 p. front., 1 illus. (plan) 24½ cm. 1-11579. F74. Q7 W5

QUINCY. A commemorative discourse pronounced at Quincy, 1840, on the second centennial anniversary of the ancient incorporation of the town. With an appendix. By George Whitney. Boston,

J. Munroe, 1840.   4, 71 p.   24 cm.   1-11580. F74. Q7 W6

QUINCY.   Some account of the early history and present state of the town of Quincy, in the commonwealth of Massachusetts.   By George Whitney.   (Boston) Christian register office, S. B. Manning, printer (1827)   64 p.   front.   25 cm.   1-11581 Rev. F74. Q7 W7

QUINCY, old Braintree, and Merry-Mount; an illustrated sketch, by Daniel Munro Wilson.   Boston, Press of G. H. Ellis, 1906.   64 p.   illus.   26½ x 20½ cm.   6-35585. F74. W7 W73

QUINCY, Three hundred years of, 1625 - 1925, historical retrospect of Mount Wollaston, Braintree and Quincy, by Daniel Munro Wilson; Chronicle of the tercentenary celebration ... 1925, by Timothy J. Collins.   Pub. by authority of the City government of Quincy, Mass.   (Boston, Wright & Potter) 1926.   xiv, 455 p. front., illus., plates, ports.   24 cm.   27-9286 Rev. F74. Q7 W74

QUINCY.   Where American independence began; Quincy, its famous group of patriots; their deeds, homes, and descendants, by Daniel Munro Wilson ... Boston and New York, Houghton, Mifflin, 1902.
xiii, 289 p.   front., pl., port.   21 cm.   2-29426. F74. Q7 W75

RANDOLPH.   Resident and business directory of Randolph, Holbrook and Avon ... v. 1.   1908. Boston, Mass., Boston suburban book co., 1908. -   1 v.   fold. map, plans.   24 cm.   8-19882.
Directories

RANDOLPH, Holbrook and Avon directory, The.   ... Providence, R. I., C. De Witt White co., 1911.
1 v.   24 cm.   11-9545.
Directories

RANDOLPH, Holbrook and Avon, Directory of the towns of.   Boston, Mass., Bay State directory co., 1914 -   1 v.   24 cm.   14-7089.
Directories

RANDOLPH, Avon and Holbrook directory.   1940 -   v. 1 -   Comp. and pub. by H. D. Whitaker.   North Hampton, N. H., 1940 -   v. 23½ cm.   41-13014.
Directories

RANDOLPH.   Historical sketches of the town of Randolph before 1800 with genealogical notices of early families by Dr. Ebenezer Alden, from the Randolph transcript, 1857 - 1858.   (Randolph? Mass., 1923?)   2 p, 62 numb. l., 63 - 135 numb. l. 28½ cm.   Type-written copy.   23-14448. F74. R17A35

RANDOLPH.   Proceedings at the 150th anniversary of the organization of the First Congregational church, Randolph ... 1881.   Boston, T. Todd, printer, 1881.   150 p.   front., plates, fold. facsim.   24 cm.
6-42195. F74. R17 R2

RAYNHAM, History of, from the first settlement to the present time.   By Rev. Enoch Sanford ... Providence, Hammond, Angell, printers, 1870.   51 p.   24½ x 15 cm.   1-11583. F74. R2 S2

READING.   Historical address and poem, delivered at the bi-centennial celebration of the incorporation of the old town of Reading, 1844.   Boston, Print. S. N. Dickinson, 1844.   131 p.   19½ cm.   1-11582.
F74. R2 R2

READING.   Anthony's standard business directory ... of Reading, N. Reading ... 1899 -
Directories

READING.   Genealogical history of the town of Reading, including the present towns of Wakefield, Reading, and North Reading, with chronological and historical sketches, from 1639 to 1874.   By Hon. Lilley Eaton ... Boston, A. Mudge, printers, 1874.   xxviii, 815 p.   front., illus., plates, ports.   23½ cm.
1-11584. F74. R28 E1

READING.   Ancient Redding in Massachusetts bay colony; its planting as a Puritan village and sketches of its early settlers from 1639 to 1652, by Loea Parker Howard.   (Boston, Thomas Todd co., printers, 1944)   2, vii - viii p., 56 p.   21 cm.   43-16582. F74. R28H48
Rare Book Coll.

READING.   The beginning of Reading and Lynnfield (by) Loea Parker Howard.   (Reading, Mass.,

MASSACHUSETTS

Reading chronicle press, inc.) 1937.   5 - 33 p.   20 cm.   37-14683.   F74.R28 H5

READING. The Parker tavern; being an account of a most interesting house built by Abraham Bryant in 1694, together with some facts about early owners. By Loea Parker Howard. Reading, Mass., Priv. print., Reading antiquarian soc. (1930)   31 p. incl. front., illus.   19 cm.   35-12860.
F74.R28H57

READING men in the early colonial wars, by Loea Parker Howard. (Reading, Mass., Printed by the Reading chronicle press, inc. pref. 1934)   (v) - xii, 35 p.   20 cm.   34-36142.   F74.R28 H6

READING, Vital records of, to the year 1850. Comp. by Thomas W. Baldwin ... Boston, Mass. (Wright & Potter print.) 1912.   586 p. 23 cm.   13-4760.   F74.R28 R3
L.H. & G.

REHOBOTH, Vital record of, 1642 - 1896. Marriages, intentions, births, deaths. With supplement containing the record of 1896, colonial returns, lists of the early settlers, etc. By James N. Arnold ... Providence, R.I., Narragansett historical pub. co., 1897.   xxvii, 926 p. 29 cm. 4-12742.   L.C. copy replaced by microfilm.
F74. R3 A6
Microfilm 8765 F

REHOBOTH, The history of; comprising a history of the present towns of Rehoboth, Seekonk, and Pawtucket, from their settlement to the present time; together with sketches of Attleborough, Cumberland, and a part of Swansey and Barrington, to the time that they were severally separated from the original town. By Leonard Bliss ... Boston, Otis, Broaders, 1836.   v, 294 p.   23½ cm.   1-11585.
F74. R3 B6

REHOBOTH in the past. An historical oration delivered on the 4th of July, 1860, by Sylvanus Chace Newman ... Also an account of the proceedings in Seekonk .... Pawtucket, Printed by R. Sherman, 1860.   112 p.   22 cm.   1-12392.   F74. R3 N5

REHOBOTH. Anawan rock pageant; or, The atonement of Anawan; a tercentenary drama from the Indian point of view, written and produced by Henry E. Oxnard ... Rehoboth, Mass., The author; Boston and Chicago, The Pilgrim press, 1921.   54 p. front., plates.   23 cm.   22-5215.
F74. R3 O98

REHOBOTH. Historic Rehoboth: record of the dedication of Goff memorial hall ... 1886 ... By Edgar Perry. (Attleborough, Mass., Perry & Barnes, printers, 1886.   130 p. illus., plates, ports.   22 cm. 1-11586.
F74. R3 P4

REHOBOTH. Historical addresses, poem, and other exercises at the celebration of the 250th anniversary of the settlement of Rehoboth, held Oct. 3, 1894. Ed. by Thomas W. Bicknell ... (n. p., 1894?)   157, (2) p. front., ports.   21 cm.   21-10635.   F74. R3 R3

REHOBOTH. A history of Rehoboth; its history for 275 years, 1643 - 1918, in which is incorporated the vital parts of the original history of the town, pub. in 1836, and written by Leonard Bliss, jr. By Rev. George H. Tilton ... Boston, Mass., The author, 1918.   x, 417 p. front., illus., plates, ports., maps (1 fold.) facsims. 24 cm. 18-12914.
F74. R3 T58

REHOBOTH. Early Rehoboth, documented historical studies of families and events in this Plymouth colony township, by Richard Le Baron Bowen ... Rehoboth, Mass., Priv. print. (by the Rumford press, Concord, N.H.) 1945 - 50.   4 v. front., plates, fold. map, facsims.   23½ cm.   45-19846.   F74. R33 B6

REVERE, Business and resident directory of. Boston, Mass., Union pub. co.   v.   24½ cm.   11-32201.
Directories

REVERE. ... City of Revere directory. Boston, H. Howard, 1916 -   1 v.   24 cm.   16-23102.
Directories

REVERE city directory .. of the inhabitants, business, town, government, societies, streets, etc. ... v.1 -   1940 -   North Hampton, N.H., Crosby pub. co., 1940 -   v. 23½ cm. 40-24868.   Directories

REVERE. The history of the town of Revere as compiled by Benjamin Shurtleff, 1937. (Boston, Beckler press, inc., 1938) 618 p. plates, maps. 23½ cm. Includes short genealogies. "Authorities": p. 515 - 592. 38-8237.
F74. R4 S5

RICHMOND; the story of a Berkshire town and its people, 1765 - 1965, by Katharine Huntington Annin. (Richmond, Mass.) Richmond Civic Assoc., 1964. xiii, 214 p. 24 cm. 64-25261.
F74. R53 A6

RICHMOND, Vital records of, to the year 1850. Boston, Pub. by the New England historic genealogical society ... 1913. 113 p. 23½ cm. 14-9911.
F74. R53 R5

ROCHESTER. Mattapoisett and Old Rochester; being a history of these towns and also in part of Marion and a portion of Wareham. Prepared under the direction of a committee of the town of Mattapoisett. New York, The Grafton press (1907) 6, (xi) - xii p., 424 p. front. (map) plates, port., fold. plan. 19½ cm. (The Grafton historical series) 7-26622.
F74. R6 M4

ROCHESTER'S official bi-centennial record. Containing the historical address of Rev. N. W. Everett; the responses by Lieut. Gov. Long, Hon. W. W. Crapo, Judge Thos. Russell, and others. Also, a full account of the proceedings of the day. New Bedford, Mercury pub. co., printers, 1879. 2, (3) - 125 p. 2 port. (incl. front.) 22 cm. 1-11587.
F74. R6 R6

ROCHESTER, Vital record of, to the year 1850 ... Boston, Pub. by the New England historic genealogical soc. ... 1914. 2 v. 23½ cm. 15-4637.
F74. R6 R7

ROCKLAND and Abington directory, The ... 1898, 1900, 1902, 1904, 1907, 1909, 1911/12, 1916, 1919, 1922 Boston, (etc.) The A. E. Foss co., 1989 - 19 - v. fold. map. 23½ cm. 0-3751.
Directories

ROCKLAND and Abington directory The. ... New York city, Boston, Mass., R. L. Polk, 19 - 24 cm. CA 26-783 Unrev.
Directories

ROCKLAND. Division of Abington. Closing argument of Hon, Ellis W. Morton ... in behalf of the petitioners for an act to incorporate that part of Abington called East Abington, as a new town, to be called Rockland ... 1874. Boston, A. Mudge, printers, 1874. iii p., (7) - 50 p. front. (fold. map) 23½ cm. 10-31040.
F74. R6 M8

ROCKPORT, a town of the sea, by Arthur P. Morley ... Cambridge, The Murray printing co. (1924) 2, 3-52 p. illus. 20½ cm. 24-29761.
F74. R68 M8

ROCKPORT, Vital records of, to the end of the year 1849. Salem, Mass., The Essex institute, 1924. 120 p. 23 cm. 24-27283.
F74. R68 R64

ROCKPORT. Alluring Rockport, an unspoiled New England town on Cape Ann ... By George Willis Solley; illus. by H. Boylston Dummer ... (Rockport, Mass., G. Butman, 1925) 122 p. front., illus., plates. 22 cm. Includes sketches of Pigeon Cove and Dogtown. 25-2353.
F74. R68 S6

ROCKPORT. A masque of Rockport in five scenes, based on the history of the town from 1614 - 1914 ... written by Virginia Tanner and presented ... under the auspices of the women's auxiliary to Leander M. Haskins hospital ... (Rockport) Rockport review printery (1914) (8) p. 24 cm.
F74. R68 T2

ROWLEY. ... Copy of the record of deaths of the First church in Rowley. Communicated by Geo. B. Blodgette. (Salem, Mass., 1878?) 42 p. 24 cm. From the Historical collections of the Essex institute, vol. xiv. 4-12739.
F74. R88 B6

ROWLEY, Early settlers of; a genealogical record of the families who settled in Rowley before 1700, with several generations of their descendants, compiled by George Brainard Blodgette; revised, ed.

MASSACHUSETTS

and pub. by Amos Everett Jewett. Rowley, Mass., 1933. xiii, 472 p. front. (double map) plates (1 double) ports., facsim. 24½ cm. Pub. in part in the Essex institute Historical collections, 1882 - 1887. 33-2230. F74. R88B612

ROWLEY. Inscriptions from the old cemetery in Rowley, Mass., copied by Geo. B. Blodgette. Salem, Mass., Salem press, 1893. 78 p. 25 cm. A13-1001. F74. R88B614

ROWLEY. ... Record of deaths from gravestones in Rowley, including all before the year 1800 ... Communicated by Geo. B. Blodgette. (Salem, Mass., Salem press, 1879) 43 - 63 p. 24½ cm. 4-27757. F74. R88B62

ROWLEY. An address, delivered at Rowley, Mass., 1839, at the celebration of the second centennial anniversary of the settlement of the town, embracing its ecclesiastical history from the beginning. By James Bradford ... Boston, F. Andrews, 1840. 54 p. 19 cm. 22-10765. F74. R88 B7

ROWLEY. The history of Rowley, anciently including Bradford, Boxford, and Georgetown, from the year 1639 to the present time. By Thomas Gage. With an address, delivered at the celebration of the second centennial anniversary of its settlement. By Rev. James Bradford. Boston, F. Andrews, 1840. xx, 483 p. front., illus., plan. 20 cm. 1-11588. F74. R88 G1

ROWLEY, "Mr. Ezechi Rogers plantation," 1639 - 1850, by Amos Everett Jewett and Emily Mable Adams Jewett. Rowley, Jewett Family of America, 1946. x, 350 p. illus., ports., maps, facsims. 25 cm. Bibliography: p. 322 - 323. 47-22536 *. F74. R88 J 4

ROWLEY. The autobiography of an octogenarian, containing the genealogy of his ancestors, sketches of their history, and of various events that have occurred during his protracted life ... By D. N. Prime ... Newburyport, W. H. Huse, printers, 1873. x, (11) - 293 p. front. (port.) 18½ cm. 9-20753. F74. R88 P9

ROWLEY. Early records of Rowley. First record of the First church, copied and communicated to the Essex institute by George B. Blodgette ... Salem, Mass., The Salem press co., 1898. 77 - 116, 103 - 128, 243 - 256, 273 - 303 p. 22 cm. Admissions and baptisms. 1665 - 1783. From the Historical collections of the Essex institute. vol. xxiv ... (xxxv) 1-11589 rev. F74. R88R86

ROWLEY. The early records of the town of Rowley. 1639 - 1672. Being vol. 1 of the printed records of the town. Rowley, Mass., 1894. xv, 255 p. 24 cm. Sketches of early settlers, p. v - xv. No more pub. 1-13361. F74. R88R87

ROWLEY, Vital records of, to the end of the year 1849. Salem, Mass., The Essex institute, 1928-31. 2 v. 23 cm. 28-23038 rev. F74. R88R89

ROWLEY. ... The tercentenary celebration of the town of Rowley ... 1939. (Rowley, 1942) 5 - 206 p. illus., fold. map. 24 cm. 44-26995. F74. R88 R9

ROWLEY historical society. Publications. no. (1) - Rowley, Mass., The Society ... 1921 - v. illus., plates. 21½ x 24½ cm. 31-19462. F74. R88R95

ROXBURY directory, The ... 1848/49 - (v. 1 - Roxbury, J. Backup 1848 - v. fold. map. 14½ - 22½ cm. 16-5372. Directories

ROXBURY, Blue book of ... 1897 - 1915. Boston, Mass., Boston suburban book co., 1897 - 8 v. fold. maps. 21 cm. biennial. 5-7582 (rev. '15) Directories

ROXBURY and Dorchester, Blue book of. Boston, Mass., Boston suburban book co., 1913 v. fold. map, plans. 21 cm. 15-16221. Directories

ROXBURY. The Rev. Amos Adams (1728 - 1775) patriot minister of Roxbury, and his American ancestry, by Robert Means Lawrence ... Boston, (S. Ward co., printers) 1912. 17 p. incl. 1 pl. 24½ cm. 13-2133. F74. R9 A2

ROXBURY. Memorial sermons in recognition of the 250th anniversary of the founding of the First religious soc. in Roxbury. By Rev. John G. Brooks. Boston ... 1882. 60 p. 25½ cm. 6-38872. F74. R9 B8

ROXBURY. Argument on the question of the annexation of Roxbury to Boston, before the legislative committee ... 1865. By Hon. John H. Clifford. Reported by J. M. W. Terrinton. Boston, Wright & Potter, 1867.   20 p.   8°.   1-16179-M1.   F74. R9 C6

ROXBURY, Glimpses of, comp. by the "Mary Warren" chapter, D.A.R. in the commonwealth of Massachusetts. 1905. Boston, Print. the Merrymount press (1905)   30 p.   20 x 11 ½ cm.   17-12316.   F74. R9 D23

ROXBURY. An address delivered on the 8 October, 1830, the second centennial anniversary of the settlement of Roxbury. By H. A. S. Dearborn ... Roxbury, Mass., C. P. Emmons, 1830.   40 p.   21 ½ cm.   17-19938.   F74. R9 D28
Toner Coll.

ROXBURY, The town of: its memorable persons and places, its history and antiquities, with numerous illustrations of its old landmarks and noted personages. By Francis S. Drake. Roxbury, Pub. by the author, 1878.   vi, (2), 475 p.   front., illus., plates, ports., fold. map.   22 cm.   1-11590.   F74. R9 D7

— Boston, Municipal printing office, 1905.   2 p. (iii) - vi, (2), 475 p.   illus., 2 pl. (incl. front.) 2 port., fold. map.   24 cm.   (Records relating to the early history of Boston, v. 34)   Reprinted from ed. of 1878.   6-21398.   F74. R9D 72

ROXBURY. The history of Roxbury town. By Charles M. Ellis. Boston, S. G. Drake, 1847.   3, (5) - 146 p.   24 cm.   Pt. II, which was to complete the work, was never published.   1-11591.   F74. R9 E4

ROXBURY. Change: a poem pronounced at Roxbury ... 1830. By Thomas Gray, jr. Roxbury, (Mass.) C. P. Emmons, 1830.   25 p.   21 cm.   19-10335.   F74. R9 G7
Toner Coll.

ROXBURY centennial. An account of the celebration in Roxbury, 1876. With the oration of Gen. Horace Binney Sargent, speeches at the dinner and other matters. Boston, Press of Rockwell and Churchill, 1877.   104 p.   23 ½ cm.   1-11592.   F74. R9 R9

ROXBURY land records.   (In Boston. Record commissioners. A report ... (6th) containing the Roxbury land and church records.   Boston, 1881.   23 ½ cm.   (v. 6) p. 1-70)   1-13874. 19-12132.   F74. R9 R91 or 92

(ROXBURY church records, 1632 - 1775)   (In Boston. Record commissioners. A report ... (6th) containing the Roxbury land and church records.   Boston, 1881.   23 cm.   p. 71-212)   1-13879. 19-12133.   F74. R9 R91 or 92

ROXBURY, Vital records of, to the end of the year 1849. Salem, Mass., The Essex institute, 1925 -   v.   23 cm.   26-1145.   F74. R9R925

ROXBURY Magazine, The, pub. by the Branch alliance of the All Souls Unitarian church, Roxbury. Boston, G. H. Ellis, printer, 1899.   48 p.   front., illus., plates, ports.   28 x 21 cm.   12-24154.   F74. R9 R93

ROXBURY. Memorial of the Reverend George Putnam, late pastor of the First religious society in Roxbury. Boston, Pub. for the Society, 1878.   59, (1) p.   front. (port.) pl.   26 cm.   1-20533 Rev.
F74. R9R935

ROXBURY. History of the First church in Roxbury, 1630 - 1904, by Walter Eliot Thwing, with an introduction by Rev. James De Normandie ... Boston, W. A. Butterfield, 1908.   xxi, 428 p.   8 plates (incl. front.) 3 plans, 3 facsim.   23 ½ cm.   "Authorities": p. xxi.   8-13662.   F74. R9R936

ROXBURY historical society, organized as the Roxbury military historical soc ... 1891, reorganized as the Roxbury historical society ... 1901, etc. Charter, by-laws and list of officers and members, 1903. Boston, Rockwell and Churchill press, 1903.   15 p.   22 cm.   4-1131.   F74. R3 R34

ROXBURY historical society. Year-book. Roxbury, The Society, 19 -   v.   20 ½ cm.   20-10883.
F74. R9 R95

ROXBURY. Argument in opposition to the project of annexing Boston and Roxbury. By Nathaniel F. Safford. (Boston? 1867?)   38 p.   23 cm.   10-8781.   F74. R9 S12

MASSACHUSETTS 295

ROXBURY. Shuman's varieties ... Ed. and pub. at Shuman's clothing bazaar ... Roxbury, Nov. 5, 1865 ... Roxbury (Mass.) 1865.　28 p.　illus.　18½ cm.　18-16106.　　F74. R9 S5

ROXBURY. Lives of Isaac Heath. and John Bowles, elders of the church, and principal founders of the grammar school in Roxbury: and of Rev. John Eliot, jr., preacher to the Indians, and first pastor of the church in Newton. By J. Wingate Thornton ... (Roxbury) 1850.　216 p.　19 cm.　50 copies printed for private distribution.　Includes genealogical material.　3-5672.　　F74. R9 T5

ROYALSTON. A historical discourse delivered Oct. 14, 1866, in commemoration of the 100th anniversary of the First Congregational church in Royalston, by E. W. Bullard. Worcester, A. B. Adams, printer, 1866.　40 p.　23 cm.　10-31035.　　F74. R92 B8

ROYALSTON. A commemorative address, at Royalston ... the hundredth anniversary of its incorporation. By Hon. A. H. Bullock .... Winchendon (Mass.) Printed by F. W. Ward, 1865. iv, (5) - 207 p.　21½ cm.　1-11593.　　F74. R92 B9

ROYALSTON. ... The history of the town of Royalston, by Lilley B. Caswell; including Royalston's soldier record, written and comp. by Hon. Fred W. Cross. (Athol, Mass.) The Town of Royalston, 1917.　xv, 566 p. xii, xxi p.　front., illus., plates, ports., map.　24 cm.　19-6950.　　F74. R92 C3

ROYALSTON, ... Vital records of, to the end of the year 1849. Worcester, Mass., F. P. Rice, 1906. 196 p.　23½ cm.　6-6461.　　F74. R92 R9

RUSSELL, Tombstone inscriptions of the town of. Compiled by Mrs. Max Lederer and others. (Westfield? Mass.) 1962.　67 l.　31 cm.　Typescript (carbon copy)　　F74. R95 L4

RUTLAND. A brief chronicle of Rufus Putnam and his Rutland home, by Eben Francis Thompson. (Worcester, Mass.) Priv. print. (The Commonwealth press) 1930.　23 p. incl. front. (port.) illus. 23½ cm. 30-27813.　　F74. R97
　　F483. P99

RUTLAND - "The cradle of Ohio." A little journey to the home of Rufus Putnam. (By) E. O. Randall. (In Ohio archaeological and historical quarterly, v.18 p. 54 - 78)　18-8594.　　F74. R97
　　F486. O51 vol. 18

RUTLAND and the Indian troubles of 1723-30. By Francis E. Blake. Worcester, Mass., F. P. Rice, 1886.　53 p.　pl., plan.　24½ x 14½ cm.　Also in Proceedings of the Worcester soc. of antiquity v.7.　1-21405.　F74. R97 B6

RUTLAND home of Major General Rufus Putnam, The; by Stephen C. Earle, with illustrations from photos. by the author. Worcester, Mass., Press of G. G. Davis, 1901.　4, (7) - 20 p. 11 pl., 2 port. (incl. front.)　24½ cm.　2-1452.　　F74. R97E13

RUTLAND, History of, 1713 - 1968, by Timothy C. Murphy. (1st ed. Rutland, Mass., Rutland Historical Soc., 1970)　xiii, 201 p.　illus.　24 cm.　　F74. R97 M8

RUTLAND. Monumental inscriptions in the old cemetery at Rutland "laid out" 1717 ... ed. by David Everett Phillips ... Columbus O., The "Old Northwest" genealogical soc., 1902.　36 p.　front.　23½ cm. 3-6512.　　F74. R97 P7

RUTLAND. Colonial life in Rutland. Address of Burton W. Potter, in the Congregational church in Rutland ... 1894. Summer lecture course. Worcester, Press of L. P. Goddard, 1894. 16 p.　23½ cm.　1-16587.　　F74. R97P74

RUTLAND. Rufus Putnam memorial association. ... Charter. By-laws, list of officers and members. Worcester, Mass., 1908.　1 v.　20 cm.　CA 11-193 Unrev.　　F74. R97 P9

RUTLAND, A history of; from its original settlement, with a biography of its first settlers. By Jonas Reed ... Worcester, Mirick & Bartlett, printers, 1836. (Worcester, Reprinted by Tyler & Seagrove, 1879)　viii, (9) - 195 p. fold. plan.　19½ cm.　Reprinted from the ed. of 1836.　Supplement to Reed's History of Rutland, from 1836 to 1879. By Daniel Bartlett. p. (169) - (196)　1-8088.　　F74. R97 R3

525

RUTLAND, ... Vital records of, to the end of the year 1849.   Worcester, Mass., F. P. Rice, 1905.
255 p.   23½ cm.   5-13521.   F74. R97 R8

RUTLAND.   Picturesque Rutland.   Containing views of buildings and localities, and brief historical sketches of the town of Rutland.   Pub. by Rutland Fire department.   Worcester, E. H. Tripp, printer (1904?)   64 p. incl. illus., plans.   23½ cm. x 27 cm.   24-20918.   F74. R97R85

SALEM.   Old-time ships of Salem.   Salem, Mass., Essex institute, 1917.   70 p. incl. illus., col. plates.   28½ cm.   The illus. are reproductions of old water colors ... the text is by Robert S. Rantoul and Wm. O. Chapman.   18-15609.   F74. S1
HE767. S3E7

SALEM.   Travellers and outlaws; episodes in American history, by Thomas Wentworth Higginson ... Boston, Lee and Shepard; New York, C. T. Dillingham, 1889.   5, 11 - 340 p.   18 cm.   "Appendix of authorities" p. 327 - 336.   3-18840.   F74. S1
E19. H63

SALEM.   Seeing Salem with Ralph Jester; a book of pictures and a few remarks on the manners and modes of the Puritans ... (Hollywood, Calif.) Paramount pictures, inc., 1937.   24 numb. 1. illus.   28½ cm.   In portfolio.   "A book of pictures giving a glimpse of the life and times of the early New England settlers.   The reproductions are stills from the motion picture, Maid of Salem."   "List of references": leaf at end.   37-11802.   F74. S1
PN1997. M255J4

SALEM.   Salem 1626, Roger Conant, the leader of the old planters   By Frank A. Gardner.   Salem, Mass., Roger Conant co-operative bank, 1926.   16 p. incl. front. (port.) illus.   19½ cm.   26-4278.   F74. S1
F67. C745

SALEM.   Portraits of shipmasters and merchants in the Peabody museum of Salem, with an introduction by Walter Muir Whitehill.   Salem, Peabody museum, 1939.   xii, 185 p. front., ports. 25½ cm.   "Key to the abbreviated references": p. 165.   40-204.   F74. S1
N7593. P4

SALEM vessels and their voyages; a history of the "Astrea", (and other ships) with some account of their masters ... by George Granville Putnam.   Salem, Mass., The Essex institute, 1925.   iv, 164 p.   front., plates, ports., facsim.   25 cm.   Reprinted from the Essex institute hist. colls. v. lx and lxi.   25-27897.   F74. S1
HF3163. S33P8 Ser. III

SALEM vessels and their voyages; a history of the "George" (and other ships)   By George Granville Putnam.   Salem, Mass., The Essex institute, 1924.   iv, 166 p. front., plates, ports., facsims.   25 cm.   Series II.   Reprinted from the Essex institute Historical collections, v. lix and lx.   24-13257.   F74. S1
HF3163. S33P8 ser. II

SALEM.   A copy of the Church-Covenants which have been used in the Church of Salem ...   Boston, ... J. F. 1680.   (Boston, 1928)   facsim.   8 p.   17 cm.   (Americana series; photostat reproductions by the Mass. historical soc. no. 214)   CA 29-426 Unrev.   F74. S1
BX7235. S33 1680a
Rare Book Coll.

SALEM.   The story of New England, illustrated ... by Edward Oliver Skelton ... Boston, E. O. Skelton, 1910.   140 p. incl. front., illus., facsims.   18 cm.   10-7899.   F74. S1
F67. S62

SALEM almanac & year book, The.   1879 -   F. W. Putnam, pub.   Salem, Printed at the Salem press, 1879 -   1 v.   21 cm.   7-36559.   Directories

SALEM directory, The ... also directories for the towns of Beverly, Peabody, Danvers, and Marblehead ... 1837, 1842, 1846, 1850-51, 1853, 1855, 1857, 1859, 1861, 1864, 1866, 1869, 1872, 1874, 1876, 1878-1897, 1881-2, 1884, 1886;   v. (1) - 22.   Boston, Sampson, Murdock, etc.   1837 - 1886.
22 v.   fronts., (maps, part fold.)   15½ - 23½ cm.   7-38354 Rev.   Directories

SALEM.   Crosby's Salem, Peabody, Danvers and Marblehead directory ... v. 1 -   Wollaston,

MASSACHUSETTS 297

Mass., Crosby pub. co., 1929 - v. fold. map. 24 cm. CA 29-611 Unrev. Directories

SALEM directory, The ... 18   Salem, Mass., The Henry M. Meek pub. co. 18   - 19
 v. fold. maps. 24½ cm. 1-25712 Rev. Directories

SALEM. The Naumkeag directory for Salem, Beverly, Danvers, Marblehead, Peabody, Hamilton, Manchester, Middleton, Topsfield, Wenham ... Salem, Mass., The H. N. Meek pub. co., 1882 - 1910. 16 v. 24 cm. Sept. 14, 99-103. Directories

SALEM with a guide, by George Arvedson. Salem, Mass., 1926. 47 (7) p. illus. (incl. port.) 18 cm.
26-12261. F74. S1 A7

SALEM. Old Salem. By Eleanor Putnam (pseud. for Mrs. Harriet Leonora (Vose) Bates. Ed. by Arlo Bates. Boston and New York, Houghton, Mifflin, 1886. 120 p. 12°. 1-11594-M1.
 F74. S1 B42

SALEM. Historic Salem, points of interest; by Henry W. Belknap. (Salem, Essex institute, 1920?)
(8) p. illus. 23 cm. 20-20902. F74. S1 B43

SALEM. The diary of William Bentley, pastor of the East church, Salem, Mass. ... Salem, Mass., The Essex institute, 1905-14. 4 v. front., plates, ports., facsims. 24 cm. v. 1. 1784-1792. - v. 2. 1793 - 1802. - v. 3. 1803 - 1810. - v. 4. 1811 - 1819. 6-10941 Rev. F74. S1 B46

— Gloucester, Mass., P. Smith, 1962. 4 v. 21 cm. F74. S1 B462

SALEM. Record of the parish list of deaths. 1785 - 1819. By Rev. William Bentley, pastor of the East church, Salem ... Salem, Printed for the Essex institute, 1882. 2, 177 p. 25 x 16 cm. From the Historical collections of the Essex institute. 1-11595. F74. S1 B47

SALEM. John Bertram of Salem; his own account of incidents in his life. Santa Barbara? Calif., 1964. 30, 65 p. 27 cm. Reproduced from the author's manuscript journal. F74. S1 B5

SALEM pilgrim, The: his book. By John Wright Buckham. Salem, Mass., D. Low, 1903.
22 p. illus. 18½ cm. 5-19638. F74. S1 B9

SALEM. The young mariners; a history of maritime Salem (by) Robert Carse. (1st ed.) New York, W. W. Norton (1966) 191 p. 21 cm. 66-16767. F74. S1 C3

SALEM. Historic Salem in four season; a camera impression by Samuel Chamberlain. New York, Hastings house (1938) 73 p. front., illus. 19 cm. 38-17837. F74. S1 C5

SALEM. A stroll through historic Salem, by Samuel Chamberlain. New York, Hastings House (1969) 122 p. illus. 24 cm. 78-79738. F74. S1 C52

SALEM. An inventory of the contents of the shop and house of Captain George Corwin of Salem, who died Jan. 3, 1684-5. With a short introductory note by George Francis Dow. 1st ed. Salem, Printed for G. F. Dow and his friends at the press in City Hall alley, 1910. 19 p. front. (port.) 25 cm. (The Essex tracts, no. iv) Ed. of 100 copies. 11-979. F74. S1 C8

SALEM. Homes and hearths of Salem. By George F. Davenport. Salem, Mass., The Salem observer press, 1891. 3, (5) - 112 p. 20 cm. Originally pub. in the weekly issues of the Salem observer. 1-11596. F74. S1 D2

SALEM. What to see in Salem. By Albert W. Dennis. 1903. F74. S1 D3

— (4th ed.) (Salem, Mass., The Salem press, 1915) (16) p. illus. (incl. map) mounted port. 23 x 19 cm. 15-17951.
 F74. S1 D32

SALEM. The life and times of Richard Derby, merchant of Salem, 1712 to 1783, by James Duncan Phillips. Cambridge, The Riverside press, 1929. 116 p. plates, 2 port. (incl. front.) 25½ cm. "Derby wills and land title": p. (51) - 116. "Works consulted": p. 48 - 50. 29-17470. F74. S1 D36

SALEM. Facts connected with the inquisition, recently held in Salem. By Charles U. Devereux. Salem, Mass., 1863. 22 cm. F74. S1 D4

SALEM. The Holyoke diaries, 1709 - 1856; ... with an introduction and annotations by George Francis Dow. Salem, Mass., The Essex institute, 1911. xviii, 215 p. front., plates, ports. 24½ cm. Genealogy of the Holyoke family: p. xii-xviii. 12-13239. F74. S1 D7

SALEM. Anniversary sermon. A sermon delivered in the South church, Salem ... by Brown Emerson. Salem, Chapman and Palfray, printers, 1843. 31 p. 22½ cm. 25-1082. F74. S1 E4

SALEM. The chronicles of three old houses, by Caroline O. Emmerton. (Boston, Thomas Todd co., printers) 1935. 2, 3-57 p. incl. illus. (incl. plans) geneal. tab. plates. 20 cm. 36-5786. F74. S1 E46

SALEM. Eighteenth century baptisms in Salem, hitherto unpub. Copied from the original records and alphabetically arranged by James A. Emmerton ... (Salem) Salem press, 1886. 126 p. 23½ cm. Reprinted from the Historical collections of the Essex institute. 2-14658. F74. S1 E5

SALEM. The fifth half century of the landing of John Endicott at Salem. Commemorative exercises by the Essex institute ... 1878. From the Historical collections of the Essex institute. Salem, Printed for the Essex institute, 1879. vii, 229 p. front. (port.) 24½ cm. F74. S1 E7

SALEM. Report of the committee of the Essex institute on the first Church of the Pilgrims. (Salem, 1865) 8 p. 1-12164-M1. F74. S1 E77

SALEM. First church in Salem, 1634. Salem, The Essex institute, 1871. 32 p. 15 cm. 1-11597 Rev. F74. S1 E8

SALEM. An account of the First church built in Salem, 1634. 5th ed. Salem, The Essex institute, 1890. 26 p. 15 cm. 11-13693. F74. S1 E85

SALEM. Memoir of the Rev. Francis Higginson. By Joseph B. Felt ... Boston, T. Prince, printer, 1852. 23 p. 23½ cm. 11-22514. F74. S1F
F67. H63

SALEM, The annals of, from its first settlement. By Joseph B. Felt ... Salem, W. & S. B. Ives, 1827. 611 p. 22½ cm. Issued in 5 numbers, with Appendix and Index. Arranged chronologically 1626 - 1783. 1-11598. F74. S1 F3
Rare Book Coll.

— 2d ed. Salem, W. & S. B. Ives; Boston, J. Munroe, 1845-49. 2 v. fronts. (ports.) illus., plates, plans. 19 cm. "First settlers": v. 1, p. 167 - 176. 1-11599. F74. S1 F4

SALEM. Did the First church of Salem originally have a confession of faith distinct from their covenant? By Joseph B. Felt ... Boston, Press of E. L. Balch, 1856. 28 p. 23 cm. 1-13622. F74. S1 F46

SALEM. Two discourses, delivered on taking leave of the old church of the East society in Salem ... 1845. By James Flint ... Salem (Mass.) Printed at the Observer office, 1846. 48 p. 22½ cm. 6-15328 Rev. F74. S1 F6

SALEM. A story of the Arbella, of pioneer Village, and of Lincoln's address. By Frederic Augustus Gannon. Salem, Mass., Cassino Press (1945) 11 p. 15 cm. F74. S1 G3
Rare Book Coll.

SALEM. Rev. John Higginson, of Salem. By Samuel Abbott Green. (Cambridge? 1896?) 4 p. 24 cm. 11-25761. F74. S1 G7

SALEM. Harmony Grove cemetery, Salem. Salem, G. M. Whipple and A. A. Smith, 1866. 80 p. front., plates, fold. plan. 17½ cm. "List of proprietors": p. 33 - 78. 11-22524. F74. S1 H24

SALEM. Main-street, by Nathaniel Hawthorne, with a preface, by Julian Hawthorne. Canton, Pa.,

MASSACHUSETTS 299

The Kirgate press, 1901.   61 p.   front.   20 cm.   2-177 rev.   F74. S1 H25
Rare Book Coll.

SALEM. ... The Custom house, and Main street, by Nathaniel Hawthorne; with an introduction and notes. Boston, New York (etc.) Houghton, Mifflin (1899)   v, 94 p.   17½ cm.   (The Riverside literature series no. 38)   Apr. 12, 1900-31.   F74. S1 H3

SALEM, Visitors' guide to. By Thomas Franklin Hunt. Salem, Mass., H. P. Ives, 1880.   54, xxxii p. illus., 11 pl.   19 cm.   Later eds. with changes and additions, issued in 1883 and 1885 under title : Pocket guide to Salem.   3-23036.
                            F74. S1 H89

—— Salem, Mass., H. P. Ives, 1880.   54, xxxii p. illus., 10 pl., facsim.   19½ cm.   1-12393.   F74. S1 H90

SALEM. ... Pocket guide to Salem. 1883. By Thomas Franklin Hunt. Salem, H. P. Ives (1883) 104 p.   10½ cm.   1-12395 Rev.   F74. S1 H91

— (Salem) H. P. Ives (1885)   78 p.   sq. 24°.   1-12396-M1.   F74. S1 H92

SALEM, Visitors' guide to. By Thomas Franklin Hunt. Salem, E. Putnam. 1894.   viii, 185 p. front., plates.   17 cm.   Bibliography: p. 174 - 175.   4-37300.   F74. S1 H925

— 35th thousand. Salem, Mass., The Essex institute, 1895.   vi, 215 p. 21 pl. (incl. front.)   17 x 14 cm. 1-12394.   F74. S1 H93

— 54th thousand ... Salem, Mass., The Essex institute, 1916.   4, viii, 218 p. incl. illus. (incl. ports., map) plates. front.   17 cm.   30-4279.   F74. S1 H932

— 69th thousand. Salem, Mass., The Essex institute, 1937.   2, iii-vi, 271 p. front., illus. (incl. ports.) map. 17 cm.   37-16672.   F74. S1 H934

SALEM, Patriots of. Roll of honor of the officers and enlisted men, during the late civil war, from Salem ... Comp. with great care from the best authorities, by T. J. Hutchinson and Ralph Childs. Salem, The Salem pub. co., 1877.   vi, (9) - 126 p.   23 cm.   6-18875.   F74. S1 H96

SALEM. The Salem fire, by Arthur B. Jones ... illus. with photos. Boston, The Gorham press, 1914.   137 p. front. (port.) illus. (map) plates.   20½ cm.   14-17631.   F74. S1 J 7

SALEM. When I lived in Salem, 1822 - 1866, by Caroline Howard King; with a preface by Louisa L. Dresel. Brattleboro, Vt., Stephen Daye press, 1937.   222 p. plates, 2 port. (incl. front.) 20½ cm.   37-31241.
                            F74. S1 K5

SALEM. Mackintire's photographic glimpses of Salem (Mass.) By Albert C. Mackintire. (Salem, A. N. Webb, 1896)   27 pl. obl. 24°.   1-11600-M1.   F74. S1 M1

SALEM. Memorial services at the centennial anniversary of Leslie's expedition to Salem ... 1775 ... by the city authorities of Salem. Salem (Printed at the Salem observer steam print.,) 1875. 91 p.   illus.   25 cm.   71-269150 MARC.   F74. S1 M26

SALEM. A pageant drama of Salem, written at request of Post 23, American legion ... by Nellie S. Messer ... (Salem, Mass., Printed by Newcomb & Gauss, 1926.   48 p.   20 cm.   26-17692.   F74. S1 M3

SALEM. Streets and homes in old Salem, describing many points of interest and a motor route through the city, prepared by N. S. Messer ... Revised ... 1941. (Beverly, Mass., The Quality press, 1941)   18 (2) p.   illus. (incl. map)   17½ cm.   42-51497.   F74. S1 M33

SALEM. Memories of old Salem, drawn from the letters of a great-grandmother, by Mary Harrod Northend. New York, Moffatt, Yard, 1917.   7, 13 - 341 p. incl. illus., plates, ports. front., pl. 24½ cm. 17-27755.   F74. S1 N86

SALEM. A new history of old Salem, and the towns adjacent - viz: Danvers, Beverly, Marblehead,

and Lynn. By Ralph Noter ... (no. 1) Salem, Pub. at the bookstore of J. P. Jewett, 1842.
18 p. front.   24 cm.   In satirical style.   'No. 1 includes only a portion of the early history of Salem.   8-20769.   F74. S1 N9

SALEM. Old houses of Salem ... Salem, Pub. at the office of "To-day," 1870.   15 p. illus.   23 cm.
10-31034.   F74. S1 O4

SALEM, Historical sketch of. 1626. 1879. By Chas. S. Osgood and H. M. Batchelder. Salem, Essex institute, 1879.   viii, 280 p. front., plates, ports.   25 cm.   1-11601.   F74. S1 O8

SALEM. The ships and sailors of old Salem; the record of a brilliant era of American achievement, by Ralph D. Paine ... New York, The Outing pub. co., 1909.   xv, 693 p. front., plates, ports., chart, facsims.   24½ cm.
First pub. as a serial in Outing, Jan. 1908 - Apr. 1909, under title Old Salem ships and sailors.   9-16435* Cancel.   F74. S1 P2

— ... New ed. ... Chicago, A. C. McClurg, 1912.   xv, 515 p. front., plates, etc.   22 cm.   12-22018.   F74. S1 P21

— Revised with a new preface by the author and with a new and complete index. Boston, Charles E. Lauriat, 1923.   xvii, 471 p. col. front., plates, ports., map, facsims.   21½ cm.   24-17971.   F74. S1 P22

SALEM. An account of the life, character, etc. of the Rev. Samuel Parris, of Salem village, and of his connection with the witchcraft delusion of 1692. Read before the Essex institute ... 1856. By Samuel P. Fowler. Salem (Mass.) W. Ives and G. W. Pease, printers, 1857.   20 p.   23 cm.   36-33563.
F74. S1 P3
Toner coll.

SALEM, The history of, by Sidney Perley ... 1626 - (1716) Salem, Mass., S. Perley, 1924-28.
3 v. fronts., illus., plates, ports., etc. 24 cm. v.1. 1626-1637. - v.2. 1638-1670. - v.3. 1671-1716. 24-19373 Rev.   F74. S1 P4

SALEM. Chestnut street 40 years ago and the people who lived in and around it; written by one of them. James Duncan Phillips. (Boston, Thomas Todd co., 1938)   5, 30 p. 22½ cm.   41-2776.
F74. S1 P455

SALEM. Famous Salem entertainments of the nineties ... by the author of "Salem in the nineties". James Duncan Phillips. (Boston, Thomas Todd co., 1939)   5, 17 p. 22½ cm.   39-33663 Rev.
F74. S1 P457

SALEM in the seventeenth century, by James Duncan Phillips. Boston and New York, Houghton Mifflin co., 1933.   xxi, 426 p. plates, ports. (incl. front.) fold. map (in pocket) facsims. 25 cm. "List of works consulted": p. (337) - 343.
33-30801.   F74. S1 P46
Rare Book Coll.

SALEM in the eighteenth century, by James Duncan Phillips ... Boston and New York, Houghton Mifflin co., 1937.   xix, (2), 533 p. front., plates, ports. etc. 21½ cm. "List of works consulted": p. (455) - 461. 37-36381.   F74. S1 P47

SALEM in the nineties and some of the people who lived there; written by one of them. James Duncan Phillips. (Boston, Thomas Todd co., 1937)   4, 33 p. 22½ cm.   39-1904 Rev.   F74. S1 P475

SALEM. Town house square in the nineties, and some of the people who crossed it, written by one of them. James Duncan Phillips. (Boston, Thomas Todd co., 1940)   5, 19 p. 22½ cm.   41-2192.
F74. S1 P48

SALEM. Ryal Side from early days of Salem colony, by Calvin P. Pierce ... Cambridge, Printed at the Riverside press for the Beverly historical soc., 1931.   xiv, 174 p. plates, ports., 2 fold. maps (incl. front.)
22½ cm. Concerning the settlement and early ownership of the lands at Ryal Side which was part of the town of Salem until 1753 when it became annexed to Beverly. In 1857 the western portion was annexed to Danvers. 31-21508.   F74. S1 P5

SALEM. Inscriptions from the burying-grounds in Salem. By David Pulsifer. Boston, Press of J. Loring, 1837.   28 p. 24 cm. Introductory note signed: Old Mortality. 20-10899.   F74. S1 P7

SALEM. An inquiry into the authenticity of the so-called first meeting house at Salem, Mass. ... Danvers, Mass., E. Putnam, 1899.   p. 207 - 223. fold. facsim. 24 cm. (In Putnam's historical magazine n.s. v.7, no. 8)
11-6048.   F74. S1 P8

530

MASSACHUSETTS

SALEM. The first meeting house in Salem; a reply to certain strictures made by Robert S. Rantoul, president of the Essex institute, in his "Powerful defence of the old Salem relic" ... by Abner Cheney Goodell ... (Read at a meeting of the directors, 1900) (n.p., 1900?) 68 p. 25 cm. Bound with above item. 11-6052. F74. S1 P8

SALEM. A letter to Mr. Thomas Carroll, of Peabody, concerning the first meeting-house in Salem, by Gilbert L. Streeter. Salem, Mass., Newcomb & Gauss, printers, 1900. 13 p. 22½ cm. Bound with above items. 11-6053. F74. S1 P8

SALEM vessels and their voyages; a history of the European, African, Australian and South Pacific Islands trade as carried on by Salem merchants, particularly the firm of N. L. Rogers & brothers, by George Granville Putnam. Salem, Mass., The Essex institute, 1930. 8, 175 p. front., plates, ports. 25 cm. Reprinted from the Essex institute Historical collections, vols. lxv and lxvi. 30-13531. F74. S1 P9

SALEM. The diary of William Pynchon of Salem. A picture of Salem life, social and political, a century ago. Ed. by Fitch Edward Oliver ... Boston and New York, Houghton, Mifflin, etc., 1890. ix, 349 p. 22½ cm. The diary extends from 1776 to 1789. 12-24368. F74. S1 P95

SALEM. ... Some claims of Salem on the notice of the country ... By Robert Samuel Rantoul. 1896. 24½ cm. F74. S1 R2

SALEM. Chronicles of old Salem; a history in miniature. By Frances Diane Robotti. With a foreword by Russell Leigh Jackson; illus. from the collections of the Essex Institute. Salem, Mass., 1948. xi, 129 p. illus., ports., facsims. 24 cm. Bibliography: p. 119-120. 49-7257*. F74. S1 R6

SALEM. The first centenary of the North church and society, in Salem. Commemorated July 19, 1872. Salem, Printed for the Society, 1873. vii, 222 p. front., illus., ports. 23½ cm. "Proprietors and occupants of pews in the first meeting house": p. 197-222. 41-35250. F74.S1 S
BX9861. S3N58

SALEM. Celebration at North Bridge, Salem ... 1862. Oration by Dr. George B. Loring. Boston, J. E. Farwell, printers to the city, 1862. 30 p. 23½ cm. 15-18140. F74. S1 S12

SALEM. Publishments of the intentions of marriage of the town of Salem. vol. I. 1708-1760. Salem, Mass., The Salem press pub. and print. co., 1891. 46 p. 24½ cm. From the Salem press historical and genealogical record, July, 1890 - Apr. 1891. No more pub. 7-23948. F74. S1 S13

SALEM, Town records of. (v.1) - 1634 - Salem, Mass., The Essex institute, 1868 - v. 23½ cm. Vol. 1 is Historical collections of the Essex institute 2d ser. v.1 pt. 1. 15-2612. F74. S1 S135

SALEM, Vital records of, to the end of the year 1849 ... Salem, Mass., The Essex institute, 1916-25. 6 v. 23½ cm. 17-10371. F74. S1 S136
Geneal. Sect. Ref.

SALEM. The colonial village built at Salem, to commemorate the 300th anniversary of the arrival of the Winthrop fleet ... 1630. Board of park commissioners, city of Salem. (Salem) 1930. 1 p. 8 numb. l. 28 cm. Autographed from type-written copy on one side of leaf only. 31-7253. F74.S1 S1365

SALEM. Massachusetts Bay tercentenary. Guide to Salem, 1630, Forest River park, Salem, Mass. ... 1930. (Salem, Board of park commissioners, 1930) 32 p. incl. front., illus., ports. 21 cm. 30-19271. F74. S1 S 137

SALEM. A reference guide to Salem, 1630, Forest river park, Salem. Rev. ed., enl. 1935. Salem, Mass., Board of park commissioners (1935) 52 p. incl. front., illus. (part col. incl. ports.) 21 cm. Pub. in 1930 under title: Massachusetts Bay tercentenary. Guide to Salem, 1630. 35-24880. F74. S1 S138

SALEM. Address of Henry L. Williams, mayor of Salem, on the occasion of the dedication of the City hall extension ... 1876, with the proceedings of the City council. Salem, Printed at the office of the Salem gazette, 1876. 27 p. 23½ cm. 10-31033. F74. S1 S14

SALEM. Proceedings upon the dedication of Plummer hall, at Salem ... 1857: including Mr. Hoppin's address and Judge White's memoir of the Plummer family.   Salem, Printed by W. Ives and G. W. Pease, 1858.   97 p.   front.   24 cm.   1-11602 Rev.   F74.S1 S146

SALEM.   The records of the Salem Commoners, 1713 - 1739, copied by George Francis Dow.   Salem, Mass., Printed for the Essex institute, 1903.   180 p.   22 ½ cm.   4-17876.
F74.S1 S15

SALEM.   Exercises in commemoration of the 300th anniversary of the gathering of the First church in Salem ... 1929.   (Cambridge, Mass.) Priv. print. (Riverside press) 1930.   xxiii, 122, (2) p.   front., pl. (ports.)   22 ½ cm.   30-9708.   F74.S1 S167

SALEM.   Notes and extracts from the "Records of the first church of Salem, 1629 to 1736."   Communicated by J. A. Emmerton.   (Salem, Mass., 1877?)   28 p.   8°.   1-11604-M1.   F74.S1 S17

SALEM.   Notes and extracts from the "Records of the First church in Salem, 1629 to 1736."   Communicated by James A. Emmerton ...   Salem, Printed at the Salem press, 1879.   28 p.   24 ½ cm.   From the Historical collections of the Essex institute, vol. xv, p. 71.   36-33540.   F74.S1 S172
Toner Coll.

SALEM.   ... Dedication of memorial windows and lectern, May 26, 1925.   Harmony Grove cemetery. Blake memorial chapel.   (n. p., 1925)   (22) p.   22 ½ cm.   CA 31-34 Unrev.   F74.S1S 175

SALEM.   The claims of the Tabernacle church, to be considered the Third church in Salem; or, the Church of 1735 ... (Salem, Mass.) Salem observer press, 1847.   56 p.   24 cm.   10-3158.
F74.S1 S18

SALEM.   (Portland, Me., 1904)   20 ½ x 25 cm.   F74.S1 S23

SALEM, Beverly, Danvers and Peabody: their representative business men and points of interest. New York, Mercantile illustrating co., 1893.   164 p.   illus.   4°.   1-11603-M1.   F74.S1 S26

SALEM, past and present.   Salem, Mass., Albany, Bigelow & Washburn, 1891.   5 l.   16 pl.   obl. 24°. 1-11605-M1.   F74.S1 S31

— 1896.   8 l.   24 pl.   obl. 24°.   1-11606-M1.   F74.S1 S32

SALEM.   A short story of three centuries of Salem, 1626 - 1926, by Joseph B. Saunders.   (Salem, Mass., Deschamps bros., printers) 1926.   109 p.   plates, ports.   23 ½ cm.   26-12770.   F74.S1 S37

SALEM.   A half century in Salem, by M. C. D. Silsbee.   Boston and New York, Houghton, Mifflin, 1887.   3, 120 p.   18 ½ cm.   1-11607.   F74. S1 S5

SALEM.   ... Salem historical calendar.   For the year 1892.   By Alexander A. Stewart.   Salem, Mass., A. A. Stewart, 1891.   (12) p.   obl. 16°.   1-12397-M1.   F74. S1 S8

SALEM.   Reminiscences of a New England church and people, by Sarah Eden Smith.   Salem, Mass., The Salem press co., 1907.   2, 27 p.   front., illus. (incl. ports.)   pl.   20 ½ x 16 cm.   7-37247.   F74. S1 S65

SALEM.   A discourse pronounced at the request of the Essex historical soc. ... 1828, in commemoration of the first settlement of Salem, in the state of Mass.   By Joseph Story.   Boston, Hilliard, Gray, Little, and Wilkins, 1828.   90 p.   24 cm.   1-11608.   F74. S1 S9

SALEM.   Memoir of Capt. William Traske, of Salem, 1628 - 1666.   By William Blake Trask.   Boston (Press of D. Clapp) 1899.   18 p.   2 facsim.   24 cm.   Reprinted from the New-England historical and genealogical register for Jan. 1899, for private distribution.   6-16059.   F74. S1 T7

SALEM.   The old shipmasters of Salem, with mention of eminent merchants, by Charles E. Trow ... New York and London, G. P. Putnam's sons, 1905.   xxvii, 337 p.   front., plates, ports.   21 cm.   5-6126.
F74. S1 T8

MASSACHUSETTS 303

SALEM. Address at the re-dedication of the fourth meeting-house of the First church in Salem ... 1867. By Charles W. Upham ... Salem, Printed at the office of the Salem gazette, 1867.   74 p. 23 cm.
15-10370.   F74.S1 U67

SALEM; an epic of New England, by Benjamin Collins Woodbury, written in commemoration of the tercentenary of the founding of Salem; pub. with the authority of the Old planters soc. Boston, Press of Geo. H. Ellis co., 1926.   ix, 65 p. 22 cm. 26-13927.   F74.S1W
PS3545.O56S3 1926

SALEM. Old Naumkeag: an historical sketch of the city of Salem, and the towns of Marblehead, Peabody, Beverly, Danvers, Wenham, Manchester, Topsfield, and Middleton, by C. H. Webber and W. S. Nevins. Illustrated. Introd. by Henry L. Williams. Salem, A. A. Smith; Boston, Lee & Shepard, 1877.   x, (2), 312 p. incl. front., illus. 19½ cm. 1-11609 Additions.   F74. S1 W3

SALEM. An address, delivered at the consecration of the Harmony Grove cemetery, in Salem ... 1840. By Daniel Appleton White. Salem, Printed at the Gazette press, 1840.   33, xviii p. 23½ cm.
15-11552.   F74.S1 W48

SALEM. A brief sketch of a lecture delivered before the Essex instiute ... 1856, respecting the founders of Salem and the First church. By Daniel Appleton White. Salem, W. Ives and G. W. Pease, printers, 1856,   14 p. 23½ cm. 4-20074.   F74.S1 W52

SALEM. Old houses of Salem. (By) Geo. Merwanjee White. (Ed. limited) (Salem, Salem gazette press, n. d.)   2 p., 9 l., 10 mounted pl. in portfolio. 37 x 29 cm. 10-14259.   F74.S1 W55

SALEM. Puritan city; the story of Salem, by Frances Winwar ... New York, R. M. McBride (1938)
x, 307 p. front., plates, ports., facsims. 21 cm. "First ed." 38-27728 Rev.   F74.S1 W57

SALEM. Baker's island, now and then, by DeWitt D. Wise. Salem, Mass., Pub. by the authority of the Baker's island association, 1940.   x, 174 p. illus. (incl. ports., facsims.) 23½ cm. 41-21369.
F74.S1 W59

SALEM. Now, then Baker's Island, by DeWitt D. Wise. Salem, Mass. Baker's Island Assoc., 1964.
199 p. 24 cm.   F74. S1 W6

SALEM. A memorial of the old and new Tabernacle, Salem, 1854-5. By Samuel M. Worcester ... Boston, Crocker and Brewster; Salem, H. Whipple, 1855.   84 p. front., pl. 19 cm. 5-26564.
F74. S1 W9

SALISBURY. ... Directory of Salisbury, Hampton, Seabrook & Plum Island beaches, with map of Salisbury Beach. (Haverhill? Mass.   v. double map. 18 - 19 cm. 11-19629.   Directories

SALISBURY'S earliest settlers, by John Q. Evans. A paper read at a meeting of the Town improvement soc. held at Salisbury ... 1896. Re-published from the Amesbury news. Amesbury (Mass.) C. S. Morse, printer, 1896.   12 p. 24 cm. 17-5251.   F74.S16 E9

SALISBURY. The old families of Salisbury and Amesbury, with some related families of Newbury, Haverhill, Ipswich and Hampton. By David W. Hoyt ... Providence, R. I. (Snow & Farnham, printers) 1897-1917.   3 v. 24 cm. Paged continuously. Issued in 13 parts. 5-34047 Rev. 2.   F74.S16 H8

— Additions and corrections for the old families of Salisbury and Amesbury, supplemental to those ending on p. 1037, vol. III By David W. Hoyt. Providence, R.I. (Snow & Farnham co., printers) 1919.   p. 1057 - 1097. 23 cm. 5-34047 Rev.   F74.S16 H8

SALISBURY Beach reservation commission. ... First annual report ... Boston, Wright & Potter printing co., 1913.   8 p. incl. tabl 23 cm.   F74.S16 M3

SALISBURY. Vital records of, to the end of the year 1849. Topsfield, Mass., Topsfield historical soc., 1915.   636 p. 23½ cm. 15-17748.   F74.S16 S2

SALISBURY. Records of First church, at Salisbury, Mass., 1687 - 1754. Communicated by William

533

P. Upham ... Salem, Printed for the Essex institute, 1879.   47 p. 25 cm. From the Historical collections of the Essex institute, vol. xvi.   17-22192.
 F74.S16 S4

SALISBURY. The West parish church, Salisbury, Mass. 100th anniversary ... 1885. Boston, The Gunn Curtis co., printers, 1885.   43 p. front. 24 cm. 22-7840.
 F74.S16 S46

SANDISFIELD, Vital records of, to the year 1850. Sandisfield revolutionary soldiers. Compiled and ed. by Capt. Elizur Yale Smith ... Rutland, Vt., The Tuttle pub. co. 1936.   111 p. 23½ cm. "Sandisfield soldiers in the American revolution ..." p. 111.   37-13372.
 F74.S165 S7

SANDWICH Historical Society, The. By Robert Paul Ashley. (1st ed. Plymouth, Mass., Leyden Press, 1967)   25 p. illus. 23 cm. (The Acorn series, no. 1)   70-32123 MARC.
 F74.A17 A9

SANDWICH, the town that glass built. By Harriot Buxton Barbour. Illus. with drawings by Robert Hallock and with photos. Boston, Houghton Mifflin, 1948.   viii, 318 p. illus. 22 cm. "Selected bibliography": p. 307-310.   48-7492*.
 F74.S17 B3

— Clifton (N.J.) A. M. Kelley, 1972 (1948)   viii, 318 p. illus. 22 cm. (Houghton Mifflin reprint editions) Bibliography: p. 307-310.   72-153175 MARC.
 F74.S17 B3 1972

SANDWICH. Three old timers: Sandwich, Barnstable, Yarmouth, 1639-1939, by Edward Darling and William A. Miller, jr. South Yarmouth, Cape Cod, The Wayside studio (1939)   2, 47, (10) p. incl. plates. front. 20 cm. 39-24718.
 F74.S17 D26

SANDWICH. The Nye house at Sandwich ... by Bernard Peterson. 1925.   (Library of Cape Cod history and genealogy no. 12)
 F74.S17 P5

SANDWICH and Bourne, colony and town records. Yarmouthport, Mass., C. W. Swift, 1910. (36) p. 25½ cm. (Library of Cape Cod history & genealogy no. 104)   The town of Bourne was not set off from Sandwich till 1884. 12-39468.
 F74.S17 S15

SANDWICH. 250th anniversary celebration of Sandwich and Bourne, at Sandwich ... 1889, by Ambrose E. Pratt ... Official proceedings. Falmouth, Mass., Local pub. and print. co., 1890.   131 p. 21½ cm. 5-1123.
 F74.S17 S17

SANDWICH. Addresses by E. T. Tucker ... and John H. Dillingham. (1907?)   1 v.
 F74.S17 T8

SANDWICH. A brief account of the sufferings and services of Christopher Holder for the faith of Friends. By William Arthur Wing. (Sandwich? Mass., 1908)   (4) p. 17½ x 7½ cm. 11-32027.
 F74.S17 W7

SAUGUS. Polk's Lynn suburban (Massachusetts) directory ... including Saugus, Swampscott, Nahant and Lynnfield ... Salem, Mass., New York, R. L. Polk, 1932.   v. 23½ cm. CA 32-391 Unrev.
 Directories

SAUGUS. The first iron works restoration. (n.p., 1953)   30 p. illus. 23 cm. 57-21477.
 F74.S18 F48

SAUGUS. First iron works gazette. v. 1 - Mar. 1951 -   Saugus, Mass. (First Iron Works Assoc.)   v. in illus., ports. 24 cm. quarterly. 57-17205.
 F74.S18 F5

SAUGUS, cradle of American industry, by Paul A. Haley. (Saugus, Mass., Printed by Saugus pub. co., 1938)   55 p. illus. (incl. facsim.) 20½ cm. 43-35093.
 F74.S18 H3

SAUGUS. Inscriptions from the old burying ground at Saugus Centre. Copied by John T. Moulton. (From the historical collections of the Essex institute, vol. xxv) Salem? 1888? 24 p. 24½ cm. 2-19833.
 F74.S18 M8

SAUGUS, Vital records of, to the end of the year 1849. Salem, Mass., The Essex institute, 1907. 81 p. 23½ cm. 8-9790.
 F74.S18 S2

MASSACHUSETTS

SAVOY, History of the town of ... By H. Miller. West Cummington, Mass., H. E. Miller, 1879.
24 p. sq. 16°. 1-11610-M1. F74. S2 M6

SCITUATE and Marshfield, Resident and business directory of. Boston, H. Howard, 1 v. 24 cm.
15-19459. Directories

SCITUATE. Old Scituate. (Scituate, Mass.) Chief Justice Cushing chapter, D. A. R., 1921.
4, 292 p. illus. (incl. ports., facsim.) 22½ cm. 21-13419. F74. S3 D18

SCITUATE, History of, from its first settlement to 1831. By Samuel Deane. Boston, J. Loring, 1831.
2, 406, (2) p. 22 cm. Family sketches: p. 211 - 394. 1-11611. F74. S3 D2
Rare Book Coll.

— (North Scituate, Mass., Reprinted by Bates & Vinal, 1899) iv, 406, (2) p. 23 cm. "Family sketches":
p. 211 - 394. 16-7869. F74. S3 D25
Microfilm 24674 F

SCITUATE, 1636 - 1936; an illustrated historical account of an old New England town wherein history and literature have gone hand in hand and where an old oaken bucket has played a famous part, by Will Irwin ... in commemoration of the 300th anniversary of the incorporation of the town. (Scituate, Mass.) Scituate tercentenary committee, 1936) 45, (3) p. incl. front., illus. fold. map. 24 cm. 39-18331.
F74. S3 I 7

SCITUATE, The early planters of; a history of the town of Scituate, from its establishment to the end of the revolutionary war, by Harvey Hunter Pratt. (Scituate, Mass.) The Scituate historical soc., 1929.
7, 386, (10) p. front. (port.) plates, maps. 23½ cm. "Biographical sketches": p. (210) - 386. 29-21292. F74. S3 P91

SCITUATE, Vital records of, to the year 1850 ... Boston, Pub. by the New England historic genealogical soc., at the charge of the Eddy town-record fund, 1909. 2 v. 23½ cm. 9-7325.
F74. S3 S5

SCITUATE: Second church records (in abstract) 1645 - 1850 ... Boston, W. J. Litchfield, 1909.
111 p. 23 cm. Reprinted from the New England historical and geneal. register, Jan. 1903 - Oct. 1907. 9-31976. F74. S3 S6

SHARON. Origin and early history of the first parish, Sharon, Mass. A sermon, preached on the occasion of the 150th anniversary of the formation of the church ... 1890, by George Willis Cooke ... Boston, H. M. Hight, printer, 1903. 27 p. 23½ cm. 3-14436. F74. S4 C7

SHARON. Annals of Sharon, by Jeremiah Gould, 1830. (From Publications of the Sharon historical soc. Boston, 1904.
no. 1 p. (3) - 21) 24½ cm. 7-23702. F74. S4 G6

SHARON. Old home week, 1906, Sharon souvenir program ... (Malden, Mass., G. E. Dunbar, printer, 1906) (12) p. illus. 23½ cm. 7-41842. F74. S4 S38

SHARON, Vital records of, to the year 1850. Comp. by Thomas W. Baldwin ... Boston (Stanhope press, F. H. Gilson co.) 1909. 193 p. 23½ cm. 9-7324. F74. S4 S39

SHARON Historical Society, Publications of the. April, 1904 - 1910. 19 - 24 cm. 10-20871.
F74. S4 S4

— Annals of Sharon, by Jeremiah Gould, 1830. no. 1, p. (3) - 21. 7-23702.
— An address delivered ... at the Federal Street Theatre, Boston ... by Deborah Gannet ... who served three years with reputation (undiscovered as a female) in the late American army.
no. 2, p. (3) - 32. 7-23999.
— ... The church records of Rev. Philip Curtis of Sharon, 1742 - 1797, John G. Phillips, ed.
64 p. no. 5. 8-18612.
— ... A memorial of Eugene Tappan, esq., late corresponding secretary ... 70 p. no. 6.
10-6096.
SHARON ... Boston, The Edison electric illuminating co., 1909. 12 p. illus. 23 cm. F74. S4 S56

SHARON. The healthiest town in New England ... By William B. Wickes. Canton, Printed at the

535

office of the Canton journal, 1882.   28 p.   illus.   8°.   1-11612-3-M1.   F74 S4 W 6

— Sharon, Printed at the office of the "Sharon advocate," 1884.   27 p.   illus.   8°.   1-11612-3-M1.
F74.S4 W61

— Sharon, Printed at the office of the "Sharon advocate," 1885.   32 p.   illus.   8°.   1-11614-5-M1.
F74.S4 W62

— 1886.   32 p.   8°.   1-11614-5-M1.   F74.S4 W63

— 1887.   32 p.   8°.   1-11616-M1.   F74.S4 W64

SHARON.   The best town to live in: Sharon, the healthiest town in the state ... By William B. Wickes. (Sharon, 1889)   48 p.   nar. 24°.   1-11617-M1.   F74.S4 W65

SHARON, the healthiest town in New England ... By William B. Wickes.   Sharon, Printed at the office of the Sharon advocate, 1890.   50 p.   nar. 24°.   1-11618-9-M1.   F74.S4 W66

— 1891.   55 p.   24°.   1-11618-9-M1.   F74.S4 W67

— 1892.   50 p.   nar. 24°.   1-14476-M1.   F74.S4 W68

SHARON, the healthiest town in New England, Wickes hand book of ...   Sharon, Printed at the office of the Advocate, 1896.   60 p.   nar. 24°.   1-11620-M1.   F74.S4 W69

SHEFFIELD.   Historical address at the Sheffield centennial commemoration ... 1876.   By General J. G. Barnard.   Sheffield, 1876.   29 p.   23½ cm.   3-15618.   F74. S5 B2

SHEFFIELD.   A mother's peace offering to American houses; or, The martyr of the nineteenth century.   By Mrs. L. J. Little.   New-York, J. A. Gray, printer, 1861.   109 p.   23½ cm.   11-19500 .
F74. S5 L7

SHEFFIELD, Centennial celebration of the town of ... 1876.   By the secretaries of the committee appointed by the town.   Sheffield, 1876.   103 p.   23½ cm.   1-11621.   F74. S5 S5

SHEFFIELD (and) Mt. Washington in the Berkshires.   (Rowan and Barbara Wakefield, editors.   Sheffield, 1948)   31 p.   illus. (part col.) col. map.   27 cm.   (Their seeing New England, v.1)   48-10077*.   F74. S5 W3

SHELBURNE, Vital records of, to the end of the year 1849.   Salem, Mass., The Essex institute, 1931.
190 p.   23 cm.   31-30067.   F74.S52 S5
L. H. & G.

SHELBURNE, History and tradition of, compiled by Mrs. Walter E. Burnham (and others.   Shelburne) 1958.   222 p.   illus.   29 cm.   59-21414.   F74.S52 S52

SHERBURNE, History of, from its incorporation, 1674, to the end of the year 1830; including that of Framingham and Holliston, so far as they were constituent parts of that town.   By William Biglow ... Milford, Mass., Print. and pub. by Ballou & Stacy, 1830.   80 p.   22½ cm.   1-11622.
F74. S55 B5

SHERBORN.   A genealogical register of the inhabitants and history of the towns of Sherborn and Holliston, by Rev. Abner Morse ... Boston, Press of Damrell & Moore, 1856.   4, 340 (i. e. 347) p.   8 ports. (incl. front.) plan.   24 cm.   4-13423.   F74.S55 M8

SHERBORN, Vital records of, to the year 1850.   Comp. by Thomas W. Baldwin ... Boston, Mass. (Stanhope press, F. H. Gilson co.) 1911.   229 p.   23 cm.   13-5096.   F74.S55 S5

SHIRLEY.   Farm life a century ago: a paper read upon several occasions by Ethel Stanwood Bolton. (n. p.) Priv. print., 1909.   24 p.   23 cm.   9-14002.   F74. S5 B6

MASSACHUSETTS

SHIRLEY. Inscriptions from the cemetery at Shirley Centre, Mass. By Mrs. Ethel (Stanwood) Bolton. Shirley Centre, Mass... (Boston, 1903) 28 cm. F74. S6 B6

SHIRLEY uplands and intervales; annals of a border town of old Middlesex, with some genealogical sketches, by Ehtel Stanwood Bolton. Boston, G. E. Littlefield, 1914. x, 394 p. front., illus., plates, ports., fold. map. 22½ cm. 15-1504. F74. S6 B62

SHIRLEY. Historical address, delivered in Shirley ... 1876. By Seth Chandler. (Copy of an original manuscript ... in the Library of Congress ...) (1938) (Photostat; positive) 1 v. F74. S6 C381

SHIRLEY, History of the town of, from its early settlement to 1882. By Seth Chandler ... Shirley, Mass., The author, 1883. vi, (9) - 744 p. front., illus., plates, ports., map. 23½ cm. Genealogical register: p. (337) - 693. 1-11623. F74. S6 C4

SHIRLEY. Leominster, Shirley and Ayer street railway. Business guide ... (with a sketch of the town of Shirley) by E. S. Bolton. (Ayer) 1904. 18 x 23½ cm. F74. S6 L5

SHIRLEY, Vital records of, to the year 1850. Boston, Mass., Pub. by the New England historic genealogical soc. ... 1918. 18 - 14523. F74. S6 S 5

SHREWSBURY, ... Vital records of, to the ened of the year 1849. Worcester, Mass., F. P. Rice, 1904. 282 p. 23½ cm. 4-18518. F74. S63 S6

SHREWSBURY. Manual of the Congregational church in Shrewsbury, with list of members, 1879. Worcester, Press of C. Hamilton, 1879. 40 p. 19½ cm. 7-27750. F74. S63 S62

SHREWSBURY, The town of, its location, advantages and attractions as a place of residence and for business. Shrewsbury, Mass., Pub. by the Railroad committee, 1890. 32, 16 p. illus., 4 pl. (incl. front.)' 23½ cm. 7-27746. F74. S63 S64

SHREWSBURY. A sermon delivered at Shrewsbury, by Joseph Sumner ... 1812. Print. at Worcester, by Isaac Sturtevant, 1812. 30 p. 23 cm. 24-15719. F74. S63 S9 1812

— 2d ed. Print. at Worcester, by William Manning, 1819. 26 p. 24 cm. 24-16083. F74. S63 S9 1819

SHREWSBURY. Family register of the inhabitants of the town of Shrewsbury, from its settlement in 1717 to 1829, and of some of them to a later period. By Andrew H. Ward ... Boston, S. G. Drake, 1847. iv, (3) - 294 p. front. (port.) 23 cm. This publication is a portion of a work ... entitled a 'History of the town of Shrewsbury ... 1717 to 1829 ... including an extensive family register.' " 10-17512. F74. S63W12

SHREWSBURY, A history of the town of, furnished for the Worcester magazine and historical journal. By Andrew H. Ward. Worcester (Mass.) Printed by Rogers & Griffin, 1826. iv, 36 p. 24½ cm. Reprinted from the Worcester magazine for May, 1826, v.2, p. 1-36. 7-29653. F74. S63W16

SHREWSBURY, History of the town of, from its settlement in 1717 to 1829, with other matter relating thereto not before pub. including an extensive family register. By Andrew H. Ward ... Boston, S. G. Drake, 1847. 508 p. front. (port.) 21½ cm. A portion of this work was issued separately under title: Family register of the inhabitants of the town of Shrewsbury ... 1847. (F74. S63W12) 1-11624. F74. S63 W2

SHREWSBURY, Old times in. Gleanings from history and tradition. By Elizabeth Ward. (New York, The McGeorge printing co.) 1892. 187 p. incl. illus., plates, port., facsims. front. 20 cm. 1-11625. F74. S63W5

SIASCONSET. A pictyure booke of ye pachworke vyllage Sconsett by ye sea .... New York, E. T. Underhill, 1885. (23) p. illus. 8°. 1-11626-M1. F74. S65 G4

SIASCONSET, The evolution of. By Roland B. Hussey. (Nantucket? Mass., 1954) 50 p. illus. 16 x 19 cm. 54-43951. F74. S65 H8

SIASCONSET. The credible chronicles of the patchwork village, 'Sconset by the sea. By Edward Fitch Underhill. New York, E. T. Underhill, 1886. 148, (2) p. front., illus., map. 16 cm. 1-11628.
F74.S65 U5

SIASCONSET. The old houses on 'Sconset Bank, the first history of Siasconset, Nantucket Island, America's most unique village. Ed. illus. and with a pref. by Henry Chandlee Forman. Nantucket, Myacomet Press, 1961. 37 p. 24 cm.
F74.S65 U55

SIASCONSET. By Edward Fitch Underhill. Boston, 1887. 29½ cm.
F74.S65 U58

SOMERSET. Resident and business directory of Somerset, Dighton and Swansea, 1904, 1908. Hopkinton, Mass., A. E. Foss & co., 2 v. 24 cm. 8-23908.
Directories

SOMERSET, History of the town of; Shawomet purchase 1677, incorporated 1790. By William A. Hart. Pub. by the town of Somerset. (Fall River, Mass., Printed by C. J. Leary) 1940. 4, 247 p. illus. (incl. ports., facsim.) 2 fold. plans. 24 cm. 41-10612.
F74.S69 H3

SOMERVILLE. W. A. Greenough co.'s Somerville directory ... (no. 1 - 1869/70 - 1871/2, 1873 - 1874, 1875/76 - 1879/80, 1881, 1883 - 1885, 1887, 1889 - 1890, 1892 - 1920, 1924 - 1925, 1927, 1929/30 Boston, 1869-19 - 23½ - 25½ cm. 1-31234.
Directories

SOMERVILLE, Centennial history of ... 1842 - 1942. (Somerville, The City press, 1942?) 176 p. incl. illus. (incl. ports., maps) col. pl. 28½ x 22½ cm. Compiled for Somerville post no. 19 American legion, by William J. Donovan and ed. by John D. Kelley. 43-47296.
F74. S7 A5

SOMERVILLE'S history. By Charles D. Elliot. Somerville, Mass., 1896. 66 p. 24½ cm. Printed from the 'Illustrated souvenir of the city of Somerville' ... 1-16739.
F74. S7 E4

SOMERVILLE. Historical address delivered by Ex-Mayor Wm. H. Furber, in the High school building ... 1876. Boston, J. E. Farwell, printer, 1876. 24 p. 24 cm. 1-11629-M1.
F74. S7 F9

SOMERVILLE, The story of, by M. A. Haley. Boston, The Writer pub. co., 1903. vi, 157 p. incl. front. plates. 19 cm. "References": p. 156-157. 3-33026.
F74. S7 H1

SOMERVILLE. Historic leaves, pub. by the Somerville historical soc., Somerville, Mass. v.1 - Apr. 1902 - (Somerville, 1902 - v. illus., pl., ports. 24 cm. quarterly. 18-8394.
F74. S7 H6

SOMERVILLE fifty years ago, boyhood memories of the early 'eighties, by William Preble Jones. Somerville, Mass., 1933. 70 p. plates. 23 cm. 33-19368.
F74. S7 J 67

SOMERVILLE, past and present; an illustrated historical souvenir commemorative of the 25th anniversary of the establishment of the city government of Somerville, ed. by Edward A. Samuels ... Boston, Samuels and Kimball, 1897. 7, 17 - 671 p. incl. front., illus., plates, ports., maps. 25 cm. 98-403 Rev.
F74. S7 S19

SOMERVILLE, past and present ... (Prospectus) Ed. E. A. Samuels. 1897.
F74. S7 S2

SOMERVILLE, Fiftieth anniversary of the city of ... 1922. (Somerville, Somerville Journal print) 1922. 60 p. port., groups. 23½ cm. 25-6694.
F74. S7 S7

SOMERVILLE. Boston, The Edison electric illuminating co., 1909. 23 cm.
F74.S7 S716

SOMERVILLE; the beautiful city of seven hills, its history and oportunities ... Issued under the direction of the Somerville Board of trade. Somerville, Mass., A. Martin, 1912. 200 p. incl. illus., plates, ports. 23½ cm. 12-20144.
F74.S7 S72

SOMERVILLE historical society. Publication no. 1. (Somerville, Mass., 1901) 1 v. 24 cm.
F74.S7 S73

MASSACHUSETTS

SOMERVILLE. Ye olden times at the foot of Prospect Hill: handbook of the historic festival in Somerville. ... 1898. Somerville, Mass. (Somerville journal) 1898. 7-96 p. front., illus., 3 pl. 24½ cm. 4-12540. F74.S7 S735

SOMERVILLE: its representative business men and its points of interest. New York, Mercantile pub. co., 1892. 80 p. illus. 4°. 1-16330-M1. F74.S7 S74

SOMERVILLE journal souvenir of the semi-centennial. 1842-1892. Somerville (Mass.) The Somerville journal co., 1892. 44 p. illus. fol. 1-11630-M1. F74.S7 S75

SOMERVILLE, ... Representative men of, from the incorporation of the city in 1872 to 1898. Containing the last Board of selectmen, etc. etc. Comp. and pub. by Walter Frye Turner. (Boston, Robinson press) 1898. 103 p. incl. front., ports. 26½ x 21 cm. 8-1147. F74.S7 T9

SOUTHAMPTON. Address delivered at Southampton, Mass., at the centennial celebration of the incorporation of that town ... 1841. By B. B. Edwards ... Andover, Printed by Allen, Morrill and Wardwell, 1841. 54 p. 22 cm. 3-32070. F74.S71 E2

SOUTHAMPTON, The pageant of ... 1930. By Mira Poler. (Westfield, Mass., W. F. Leitch, printers 1930) (12) p. 24 cm. "... Celebrating the 200th anniversary of the settling of ... Southampton. CA 30-1371. F74.S71 P76

SOUTH ATTLEBORO, Inscriptions on the grave stones in cemetery at ... copied and privately pub. by Marion Pearce Carter ... Attleboro, Mass., 1930. 15 numb. l. 28 cm. Autographic reproduction of typewritten copy. CA 31-407 Unrev. F74.S715C23

SOUTHBORO. Historical sketches concerning the town of Southboro, and other papers, written by Dea. Peter Fay ... Marlboro, Mass., Pratt bros., 1889. 75 p. front. (port.) 22½ cm. 7-40703. F74.S72 F2

SOUTHBOROUGH. A sermon delivered at Southborough ... 1827, the day which completed a century from the incorporation of the town ... Boston, J. Marsh, 1827. 39 p. 8°. 1-11631-M1. F74.S72 P2

SOUTHBOROUGH, ... Vital records of, to the end of the year 1849. Worcester, F. P. Rice, 1903. 187 p. 23½ cm. 3-23029. F74.S72 S7 L H & G

SOUTHBOROUGH. A record of the soldiers of Southborough, during the rebellion, from 1861 to 1866, together with extracts from public documents, etc. Marlboro', Mirror steam job press, 1867. 127 p. 1 pl. 23½ cm. 4-7003. F74.S72 S73

SOUTHBRIDGE, History of, by Moses Plimpton. Delivered before the Southbridge lyceum, or literary association ... 1836. Southbridge, Journal steam book print, 1882. 48 p. front. (port.) 23½ cm. 10-3161. F74.S73 P7

SOUTHBRIDGE. Quinabaug historical society, Southbridge, Annual calendar, 6th. Southbridge, 1904-5. 1 v. 16½ cm. F74.S73 Q49

SOUTHBRIDGE. Leaflets of the Quinabang historical society, as pub. by the Society; devoted to the local history of Southbridge, Sturbridge, Dudley and Charlton. v.1 - 1899 - Southbridge, (1902 - v. plates, ports., maps. 20 cm. 9-17532. F74.S73 Q5

SOUTHBRIDGE and Sturbridge directory ... 1928 - Springfield, Mass., H. A. Manning co., 1928 - v. illus. 23 cm. CA 29-142 Unrev. Directories

SOUTHBRIDGE, Sturbridge, Brimfield, and Charlton resident directory, The ... v.6, 1907. Boston, W. E. Shaw, 1907. 1 v. 24 cm. 8-825. Directories

SOUTHBRIDGE and Sturbridge directory ... 19 - Salem, Mass., The H. M. Meek pub. co., 19 - v. 24 cm. 22-15622. Directories

SOUTHBRIDGE. Histoire des Franco-Americains de Southbridge, par Felix Gatineau ... Framingham, Mass., Lakeview press, 1919. 253 p. plates, ports. 22½ cm. 41-20873. F74.S73 G3

SOUTH HADLEY. In old South Hadley, by Sophie E. Eastman ... Chicago, The Blakely print. (1912) 5, 221, (2) p. front., plates, ports. 25½ cm. 12-16320. F74.S735 E2

SOUTH NATICK. John Eliot's village of praying Indians. South Natick, Mass., Mrs. Stowe's "Oldtown." By Leverett Richmond Daniels. (South Natick? 1930) (18) p. illus., plates. 15 x 23½ cm. CA 31-429 Unrev. F74.S74 D18

SOUTH NATICK. Proceedings at the reunion of the descendants of John Eliot, "the apostle to the Indians," at Guilford, Conn., 1875. Second meeting at South Natick, Mass., 1901; and the 250th anniversary of the founding of South Natick ... (South Natick, Mass. The Historical, natural history, and library society of South Natick, 1901) 114 p. 4 pl. (1 fold.) 23½ cm. 4-7813. F74.S74 H55

SOUTH NATICK. The historical collections of the Historical, natural history and library society of South Natick. v. 1 - South Natick, Mass., The Society, 1909 - 1 v. illus., plates. 22 cm. 9-29058. F74.S74 H56

SOUTH NATICK. A review of the first fourteen years of the Historical, natural history and library society of South Natick, with the field-day proceedings of 1881 - 1882 - 1883. South Natick, Mass., The Society, 1884. 126 p. 24 cm. 1-11633. F74.S74 H6

SOUTH WELLFLEET, History and lore of, written for the South Wellfleet neighborhood assoc. by Margaret T. Dooley. (Boston, Print. Angel guardian press) 1938. (28) p. illus. 23 cm. 38-9610. F74.S75 D6

SOUTH WORTHINGTON parish, The, by the Rev. George Reed Moody, pastor of the Methodist Episcopal church ... 1899 - 1905. (South Worthington, Mass., 1905) 2, 7-103 p. illus. (incl. ports.) 24 x 31 cm. 26-393. F74.S758M7

SOUTH YARMOUTH. Yesterday's tide, by Florence W. Baker, with articles by Helen M. Berry and others. (Clinton, Mass., The Colonial press, 1941) x, 309 p. plates, ports. 20½ cm. "A collection of sketches descriptive of earlier scenes and activities in ... South Yarmouth." 41-9950. F74.S76 B3

SOUTH YARMOUTH. Old Quaker Village, South Yarmouth, Mass. ... reminiscences gathered and ed. by E. Lawrence Jenkins. (Yarmouthport, Mass., C. W. Swift) 1915. 51 p. 25½ cm. (Library of Cape Cod history and genealogy, no. 38) 15-11016. F74. S65 J5

SPENCER. Polk's Spencer, Warren, Brookfield directory ... New York city, Boston (etc.) R. L.Polk 19 - v. 23½ cm. CA 28-81 Unrev. Directories

SPENCER, History of, from its earliest settlement to the year 1841, including a brief sketch of Leicester, to the year 1753. By James Draper ... Worcester (Mass.) Spooner and Howland, printers, 1841. viii, (9) - 159 p. front. (plan) 22½ cm. 45-47761. F74.S77 D7 1841

— 2d ed., enlarged and improved ... Worcester, Print. H. J. Howland (1860) viii, (9) - 276 p. front., ports., plan. 23 cm. "Genealogies, etc." p. 159 - 272. 1-11634. F74.S77 D7 1860

SPENCER. Leading business men of Spencer, Brookfield and vicinity; embracing Spencer, North Brookfield, Brookfield, East Brookfield, West Brookfield, Warren and West Warren. Illustrated. Boston, Mercantile pub. co., 1889. 66, (2) p. illus. 25 cm. 1-16564. F74.S77 L4

SPENCER, ... Vital records of, to the end of the year 1849. Worcester, Mass., F. P. Rice, 1909. 276 p. 23½ cm. 9-23235. F74.S77 S7

SPENCER, Historical sketches relating to, by Henry M. Tower ... Spencer, Mass., W. J. Heffernan - Spencer leader print, 1901 - 09. 4 v. illus., ports., map, facsim. 23½ cm. 7-23949 Add. F74.S77 T7

MASSACHUSETTS

SPRINGFIELD suburban directory for Agawam Center, Feeding Hills, East Longmeadow, Hampden, Ludlow, Wilbraham (Mass.) Suffield (Conn.) ... v. 1 -   Springfield, Mass., H. A. Manning co., 1926. -   v. maps. 23 cm. CA 27-287 Unrev.   Directories

SPRINGFIELD, West Springfield, Longmeadow, Chicopee directory ... (v. 1 -   Springfield, Mass., The Price & Lee co., 1851 - 19   v. fold. maps. 14½ - 24 cm. 1-12868 Rev.   Directories

SPRINGFIELD house directory. 1909. ... Springfield, Mass., The Price and Lee co., 1909.
1 v. 23½ cm. 10-654.   Directories

SPRINGFIELD. Social index and blue book of Springfield, 1st -   Springfield, Mass., Index pub. co., 1889 -   v. 20½ cm. CA 31-110 Unrev.   Directories

SPRINGFIELD. Dau's blue book for Springfield, Holyoke, Northampton and Chicopee, Longmeadow, Monson, Palmer, Westfield, Mass., and Thompsonville, Conn. (v. 1 -   1899/1900 - New York city, Dau pub. co., 1899 -   2 v. 18 - 21½ cm. Nov. 9, 99-61 Add.   Directories

SPRINGFIELD. Newcomb's Springfield directory for 1858 - 1859. Containing every kind of information valuable for reference to strangers and citizens. From May, 1858, to May, 1859 ... Springfield, (Mass.) J. M. Newcomb, 1858.   159, lxviii p. map. 15 cm. 9-23613.   Directories

SPRINGFIELD. The Pynchons of Springfield; founders and colonizers, 1636 - 1702, by Frances Armytage and Juliette Tomlinson. Springfield, Mass., Connecticut Valley Historical Museum, 1969.
54 p. illus. 24 cm.   F74. S8 A18

SPRINGFIELD. Arrow street guide of Springfield, West Springfield, Longmeadow and Chicopee ...
19   New Haven, Conn., The Price & Lee co., 19 -   v. fold. map. 17 cm. 32-24500.
F74. S8 A2

SPRINGFIELD. "Springfield old and new." Tercentenary souvenir, 1636 - 1936. History and photos by Ernest Newton Bagg; aerial photos by Phoenix engraving co. ... Springfield, Mass., The historical souvenir pub. co., 1936.   (108) p. illus. (incl. ports., facsim.) 28 cm. 36-13683.   F74. S8 B15

SPRINGFIELD. Brief history of the Day house, prepared by Winthrop S. Bagg, 1905. (West Springfield, Mass.) Ramapogue historical soc. (1905)   16 p. illus. 12½ x 16 cm. 13-11848.
F74. S8 B16

SPRINGFIELD. An historical address delivered before the citizens of Springfield at the public celebration of the 275th anniversary of the settlement ... By Charles H. Barrows. Springfield, Mass., Connecticut Valley historical soc., 1916.   2, 3 - 100 p. illus. 23½ cm. 16-15737.
F74. S8 B29

SPRINGFIELD, The history of, for the young; being also in some part the history of other towns and cities in the county of Hampden, by Charles H. Harrows. Springfield, Mass., The Connecticut Valley hist. Soc., 1909.   4 p., 3-166 p. illus. 20 x 16 cm. 9-9528.   F74. S8 B3

— 1921.   5, 3 - 194 p. illus. (incl. ports., maps, facsims.) "Pilgrim edition." 21-10694.   F74. S8 B32

SPRINGFIELD. An address, delivered at the opening of the town-hall in Springfield ... 1828. Containing sketches of the early history of that town, and those in its vicinity. By George Bliss ... Springfield, Tannatt & co., 1828.   68 p. 23 cm. 11-3991 Rev.   F74. S8 B6
Rare Book Coll.

SPRINGFIELD. Historical memoir of the Springfield cemetery, read to the proprietors at their meeting ... 1857. By George Bliss ... Accompanied by an address delivered at the consecration of the cemetery ... 1841, by Rev. Wm. B. O. Peabody. Springfield, Mass., S. Bowles, printers, 1857.
23 p. 23 cm. 3-18531.   F74. S8 B63

SPRINGFIELD. Past dispensations of Providence called to mind. In a sermon delivered in the First parish in Springfield, on the 16th Oct., 1775. Just one hundred years from the burning of the town

by the Indians. By Robert Breck ... Hartford, Print. Barlow & Babcock, 1784.   28 p.   19 cm.   Half-title wanting.   1-3273.
                                                   F74. S8 B8
                                                   Rare Book Coll.

SPRINGFIELD. Sketches of the old inhabitants and other citizens of old Springfield of the present century, and its historic mansions of "ye olden tyme," with 124 illustrations and sixty autographs. By Charles Wells Chapin ... Springfield, Mass., Press of Springfield print, and bind co., 1893.
xi, 420 p. incl. illus., port., facsim.   23½ cm.   1-11635* Cancel.   F74. S8 C4

SPRINGFIELD. The city of New England is Springfield, Mass. ... (n.p., 1910)   29 p. incl. plates. 29½ cm.   F74.S8 C58

SPRINGFIELD. Sociological survey of the Negro population of Springfield, ed. William N. DeBerry. Springfield, Mass., The Dunbar community league (1940?)   15 p.   20½ cm.   43-30914.
                                                   F74. S8 D8

SPRINGFIELD. Forest park ... Springfield, Mass., M. D. Fletcher, 1895.   4 l., 11 pl.   obl. 16°. 1-11636-M1.   F74. S8 F6

SPRINGFIELD. Town into city; Springfield, and the meaning of community, 1840 - 1880 (by) Michael H. Frisch. Cambridge, Mass., Harvard University Press, 1972.   ix, 301 p. illus. 24 cm.   (Harvard studies in urban history) Originated from the author's thesis, Princeton. Includes bibliographical references.   72-178075 MARC.   F74. S8 F7
                                                      1972

SPRINGFIELD. 1895. By M. D. Fletcher. (Springfield, M. D. Fletcher, 1895)   19 pl. obl. 12°. 1-11637-M1.   F74. S8 F8

SPRINGFIELD illustrated; 100 pages containing over 130 phototype views of this up-to-date city, comp. ... by George S. Graves. (Springfield, Mass.) G. S. Graves, 1911.   13½ x 20 cm.
                                                    F74.S8 G65

SPRINGFIELD. Picturesque Springfield and West Springfield ... comp. by Geo. S. Graves. Springfield, Mass., Hotel Worthy (1912)   (31) p. illus. 24 cm.   12-7169.   F74.S8 G66

— (1912)   24 cm.   F74.S8 G67

SPRINGFIELD. Progressive Springfield. By George Storrs Graves. (Springfield, Mass., G. S. Graves, 1913)   (32) p. illus. 21 cm.   13-8106.   F74.S8 G761

SPRINGFIELD. The picturesque city, Springfield; a series of forty views showing the picturesque side of this "city of homes" ... By George Storrs Graves. Springfield, Mass., G. S. Graves, 1913. (40) p. illus.   11½ x 15½ cm.   F74.S8 G672

SPRINGFIELD memories. Odds and ends of anecdote and early doings, gathered from manuscripts, pamphlets, and aged residents. By Mason A. Green. Springfield, Mass., Whitney & Adams, 1876. 110 p. incl. map. front.   22 cm.   1-11638.   F74. S8 G7

SPRINGFIELD, 1636 - 1886; history of town and city, including an account of the quarter-millenial celebration at Springfield ... 1886, by Mason A. Green ... (Springfield) C. A. Nichols, 1888. 11, 645 p. incl. illus., plan, facsims. front., plates, ports., fold. map.   24½ cm.   1-11639.   F74. S8 G8

SPRINGFIELD. Highland Community, Springfield; facts of interest concerning its early and more recent history, its phenomenal growth and development, its residential and commercial advantages, and its educational, religious & industrial institutions. A city within a city. Springfield, Mass., Highland co-operative bank, 1921.   64 p. illus. (incl. portd., plan) 23 cm.   21-7824.   F74. S8 H63

SPRINGFIELD. Picturesque Springfield and West Springfield; pub. by Hotel Worthy. A picture-conducted tour of 70 views ... Comp. by George S. Graves ... 2d ed. (Springfield) 1912. (32) p. illus.   24 cm.   F74. S8 H8

MASSACHUSETTS

SPRINGFIELD. Her picturesque beauty and commercial enterprise ... By Stanley Johnson. (Springfield) Springfield print., 1889. 29 p. 12°. 1-16178-M1.
F74. S8 J 6

SPRINGFIELD, Miniatures of. By Thomas Wallace Jones. (Cincinnati, 1904) 8 ½ x 11 ½ cm.
F74. S8 J 7

SPRINGFIELD. King's handbook of Springfield; a series of monographs, historical and descriptive, ed. by Moses King. 150 views and portraits. Springfield, Mass., J. D. Gill, 1884. 394 p. incl. front., illus. plates, ports., fold. map. 22 cm. "Bibliography of Springfield": p. 371 - 374. 1-11640.
F74. S8 K5

SPRINGFIELD, A discourse delivered at ... 1805. On occasion of the completion and opening of the great bridge over Connecticut River, between the towns of Springfield and West-Springfield. By Joseph Lathrop ... 2d ed. Springfield, Mass. (H. Brewer, printer 1805) 16 p. 21 ½ cm. 17-6691.
F74. S8 L35

SPRINGFIELD. Baptisms, marriages, and deaths, 1736 - 1809, First church, Springfield, Mass. Copied by Ella May Lewis. Springfield, Mass., 1938. 2 p., 103 numb. l. front. 28 cm. Mimeographed. 39-31442.
F74. S8 L5

SPRINGFIELD. William Pynchon; merchant and colonizer, 1590 - 1662. Springfield, Mass., Conn. Valley Historical Museum, 1961. 44 p. 26 cm.
F74. S8 M3

SPRINGFIELD. 1636 - 1675. Early history of Springfield. An address delivered ... 1875, on the 200th anniversary of the burning of the town by the Indians. By Henry Morris. Springfield, Mass., F. W. Morris, 1876. vi, (7) - 85 p. front. (port.) pl. 21 cm. 1-11641.
F74. S8 M8

SPRINGFIELD. History of the First church in Springfield. An address delivered ... 1875. By Henry Morris ... Springfield, Mass., Whitney & Adams, 1875. 60 p. front., pl., port. 21 cm. 3-4956.
F74. S8 M83

SPRINGFIELD; the city of homes; showing its advantages as a desirable place of residence as well as a manufacturing and distributing center ... Comp. and pub. by the New York industrial recorder, assisted by the Springfield board of trade. (New York) New York industrial recorder, 1898. 40 p. illus. 42 cm. Special number of the New York industrial recorder. 1-1761 Rev.
F74. S8 N5

SPRINGFIELD. Public spirit and mobs. Two sermons delivered at Springfield ... 1851, after the Thompson riot. By George F. Simmons ... Springfield, Merriam, Chapin & co.; Boston, W. Crosby and H. P. Nichols, 1851. 31 p. 20 ½ cm. Relates to the disturbances in Springfield occasioned by the presence of George Thompson, the English abolitionist. 17-19468 Rev.
F74. S8 S5

SPRINGFIELD. The first century of the history of Springfield; the official records from 1636 to 1736, with an historical review and biographical mention of the founders, by Henry M. Burt ... Springfield, Mass., H. M. Burt, 1898 - 99. 2 v. illus., maps (partly folded) facsims. (partly fold.) 24 cm. v. 1 contains lists of early settlers, etc. v. 2 contains biographical and genealogical section. 1-24100 Add.
F74. S8 S6

SPRINGFIELD. Programme, 1636, 1911; 275th anniversary of the founding of Springfield. (Springfield, Mass., Press of Loring-Axtell co., 1911) (12) p. illus., port. 23 ½ cm. 40-19851.
F74. S8 S66

SPRINGFIELD. The First church, Springfield, 1637 - 1915; milestones through 27 decades ... Springfield, Mass. (The F. A. Bassette co., printers) 1915. 32 p. illus. 19 cm. 15-16227.
F74. S8 S72

SPRINGFIELD. Views and facts of Springfield. (Springfield, Mass., Third national bank, 1910)
F74. S8 S76

SPRINGFIELD, for 275 years; from the Springfield homestead, issues of May 22, 24, 27, 1911, anniversary week of the founding of our city. Springfield, Mass., Springfield homestead newspaper co. (1911) 88 p. illus. 39 ½ cm. 12-11541.
F74. S8 S82

SPRINGFIELD musket, The. no. 1 - 4; Dec. 20 - 23, 1864.   Springfield, Mass., S. Bowles, printers, 1864.   1 v.   32 cm.   Pub. at the fair for the Soldiers' rest.   No more pub.   5-27457.   F74. S8 S86

SPRINGFIELD, Ten famous houses of.   By Juliette Tomlinson.   Springfield, Mass., Connecticut Valley Historical Museum (1952)   unpaged.   illus.   25 cm.   52-32406.   F74. S8 T65

SPRINGFIELD present and prospective ....   Text by Eugene C. Gardner and others; drawings by James Hall and others.   Ed. James E. Tower.   Springfield, Mass., Pond & Campbell, 1905.   xviii, 214 p. incl. front., illus. plates, ports.   24 cm.   6-4951.   F74. S8 T7

SPRINGFIELD, View book of.   (Springfield, Mass., 1010)   20½ cm.   F74. S8 V6

SPRINGFIELD in the Spanish-American war, by Walter W. Ward ...   Easthampton, Mass., Press of Enterprise printing co., 1899.   187 p. front., plates, ports.   22 cm.   9-17105.   F74. S8 W1

SPRINGFIELD.   A chronicle of ancient Chestnut street.   By Mrs. Charlotte (Edwards) Warner.   (Springfield, Mass., Press of C. W. Bryan co., 1897?)   41 p. 10 pl.   21 cm.   8-8585.   F74. S8 W2

SPRINGFIELD, The genesis of; the development of the town (by) Harry Andrew Wright.   Springfield, Mass., Johnson's bookstore, 1936.   47 p. illus. (incl. maps, facsim.)   23 cm.   36-11014.   F74. S8 W97

SPRINGFIELD; compiled by workers of the ... W. P. A. in the state of Massachusetts ...   Springfield (Mass.) 1941.   84 p. illus.   27½ cm.   (American guide series)   41-8764.   F74. S8W975

STERLING, ...   A brief history of, from its earliest days to the present, 1931.   (Sterling, 1931)   68 p. incl. illus. (incl. map) port.   24 cm.   "To commemorate the 150th anniversary of the incorporation of the town ..."   31-23216.   F74. S84 B8

STERLING.   One hundred fiftieth anniversary of the incoporation of the town of Sterling; exercises in the First parish church ....   (Sterling? Prv. print. by Mary E. Butterick, 1931?)   60 p. incl. front.   18½ cm.   32-16990.   F74. S84 S8

STOCKBRIDGE.   Memoirs of Col. William Edwards, formerly of Stockbridge and Northampton ...   written by himself ... with notes and additions by his son ... and by his grandson ....   (Washington, D.C., Press of W. F. Roberts, 1897)   iv, 123 (6) p.   23 cm.   Printed, not published.   3-4168.   F74. S83 E2

STOCKBRIDGE.   An historical sketch, Congregational, of the church in Stockbridge; by Rev. David D. Field ...   New York, J. A. Gray, printer, 1853.   30 p.   22½ cm.
— Addenda to church history. (New York, 1968?)   (31) - 32, (3) - 13 p.   22½ cm.   3-31519 Add.   F74. S86 F4

STOCKBRIDGE childhood.   By Elizabeth Campbell Field.   (Asheville, N.C., Priv. print. at the Stephens Press) 1947.   93 p.   20 cm.   48-14987*.   F74. S86 F44

STOCKBRIDGE, past and present; or, Records of an old mission station.   By Miss Electa F. Jones.   Springfield (Mass.) S. Bowles, 1854.   275 p.   20 cm.   "Biographical sketches": p. 255 - 267.   1-11642.   F74. S86 J7

STOCKBRIDGE.   Address at the dedication of the soldiers' monument in Stockbridge ....   New York, Baker & Godwin, printers, 1867.   20 p.   8º.   1-21430-M1.   F74. S86 S4

STOCKBRIDGE, 1739 - 1939; a chronicle, by Sarah Cabot Sedgwick and Christina Sedgwick Marquand; foreword by Rachel Field.   (Great Barrington, Mass., Printed by the Berkshire courier) 1939.   xix p. 306 p. front., plates, ports.   22½ cm.   Bibliography: p. (293) - 300.   39-25736.   F74. S86 S43

STONEHAM.   A brief history of the town of Stoneham, from its first settlement to the present time: with an account of the murder of Jacob Gould ....   By Silas Dean ...   Boston, Printed at S. R. Hart's,

MASSACHUSETTS 315

1843.   36 p.   19 cm.   1-11643.   F74.S88 D2

STONEHAM, History of.   By William B. Stevens, esq., with biographical sketches of many of its pioneers and prominent men.   ... Stoneham, Mass., F. L. & W. E. Whittier, 1891.   (3) - 352 p. incl. illus., port.   3 port.   23 ½ cm.   Biographical sketches: p. (108) - 142, 192 - 346.   3-5812.   F74.S88 S8

STONEHAM, Vital records of, to the end of the year 1849.   Salem, Mass., The Essex institute, 1918.   191 p.   23 ½ cm.   18-27123.   F74.S88 S85

STONEHAM.   Two hundredth anniversary of the town of Stoneham, 1725 - 1925.   (Stoneham? 1925?)   35 p.   illus.   23 ½ cm.   36-25747.   F74.S88 S89

STOUGHTON.   Polk's Stoughton directory 1930/31 -   Boston, Mass., New York, N. Y., R. L. Polk, 1930 -   v.   23 ½ cm.   CA-30-515 Unrev.   Directories

STOUGHTON, Resident and business directory of ...   Boston, Boston suburban book co., 1907.   v.   24 cm.   7-8277.   Directories

STOUGHTON directory, The, 1897/8 -   (Newton? Mass.) Newton journal pub. co. ... 1897 -   v.   24 cm.   2-24427 (rev. '28)   Directories

STOUGHTON.   200th anniversary in commemoration of the incorporation of the town of Stoughton ....   (Stoughton, Tolman-Davidson advertsing press, inc., 1926)   (40) p.   illus.   28 cm.   27-12496.   F74.S886 E95

STOUGHTON.   In memoriam.   Proceedings of A. St. John Chambre post, no. 72, Grand army of the republic, Department of Mass. on Memorial day.   Boston, Printed by J. S. Spooner (1872)   16 p.   24 ½ cm.   11-25903.   F74.S886 G7

STOUGHTON.   Through the years to seventy.   By Frank Wesley Reynolds.   (n. p., 1957)   284, (128) p.   illus., ports., maps (part fold.)   29 cm.   58-16333.   F74.S886 R4

STOW, Vital records of, to the year 1850.   Boston, New England historic genealogical society ... 1911.   270 p.   23 cm.   13-3036.   F74.S89 S82
Geneal. Section Ref.

STOW, 1633 - 1933, compiled in honor of the 250th anniversary of the town.   By Olivia Stockton (Murray) Crowell.   Stow, Mass., Rev. and Mrs. R. R. Crowell (1933)   ix, 111 p.   front., plates, ports., map, facsim. (7 l.)   26 ½ cm.   33-38014.   F74.S89 C87

STOW.   1702 - 1902.   The 200th anniversary of the First Parish church of Stow.   Sermons by Rev. J. Sidney Moulton, pastor, and Samuel Collins Beane.   (Stow? Mass.) 1902.   28 p. incl. pl.   3-28372.   F74.S89 S86

STURBRIDGE.   A tour of Old Sturbridge Village.   By Samuel Chamberlain.   New York, Hastings House (1955).   72 p. (chiefly illus.)   21 cm.   55-9058.   F74.S93 C46

—   (Rev. ed.)   New York, Hastings House (1957)   72 p.   21 cm.   F74.S93 C46 1957

—   (Rev. ed.)   New York, Hastings House (1961)   72 p.   21 cm.   F74.S93 C46 1961

—   (Rev. ed.)   New York, Hastings House (1965)   72 p.   21 cm.   F74.S93 C46 1965

—   (Rev. ed.)   New York, Hastings House (1969)   72 p.   21 cm.   F74.S93 C46 1969

—   1972.   F74.S93 C46 1972

STURBRIDGE, An historical sketch of, from its settlement to the present time. By Joseph S. Clark ... Brookfield, E. and L. Merriam, printers, 1838.   48 p.   23 cm.   1-11644.   F74.S93 C5

STURBRIDGE. A historical sketch of Sturbridge and Southbridge. By George Davis. West Brookfield, Mass., Press of O. S. Cooke and co., 1856.   v, (7) - 233 p. 22 cm.   1-11645.   F74.S93 D2

STURBRIDGE. Historical sketch of the First Congregational church, Sturbridge, by George H. Haynes. Worcester, The Davis press, 1910.   68 p. front., illus. (plan) pl. 22½ cm. 11-6015.
F74.S93 H4

STURBRIDGE. Old Sturbridge Village. An accounting of the year. (Hartford)   v. illus. 22 cm. 59-33206.   F74.S93 O45

STURBRIDGE. Old Sturbridge Village, a guidebook. Sturbridge (1957)   45 p. illus. 22 cm. (Old Sturbridge Village booklet series, 6) 57-3873.   F74.S93 O5

— (3d ed: rev.) Sturbridge (1960)   64 p. 22 cm.   F74.S93 O5 1960

— (4th ed.) (1961)   70 p. 22 cm.   F74.S93 O5 1961

— (5th ed.) (1966)   77 p. 22 cm.   F74.S93 O5 1966

STURBRIDGE. Record of births, marriages, and deaths, of the town of Sturbridge, from the settlement of the town to 1816 ... Southbridge, Mass., G. M. Whitaker, 1879.   109 p. 21½ cm. 1-11646.
F74.S93 S9

STURBRIDGE, Vital records of, to the year 1850. Boston, Pub. by the New England historic genealogical soc. ... 1906.   393 p. 23½ cm. 6-22874.   F74.S93 S92

STURBRIDGE. Manual for the use of the members of the Congregational church, in Sturbridge. West Brookfield, Merriam & Cooke, printers, 1843.   46 p. 18½ cm. 7-27748.   F74.S93 S93

STURBRIDGE. The story of Old Sturbridge Village. By Charles Van Ravenswaay. New York, Newcomen Society in North America, 1965.   24 p. 23 cm. 1st printing: Nov. 1965.   F74.S93 V3

SUDBURY. The Wayside inn. Its history and literature. An address delivered before the Society of colonial wars at the Wayside inn, Sudbury, Mass. ... by Samuel Arthur Bent ... Boston, 1897. 27 p. front. 23 cm. 1-11647.   F74.S94 B4

SUDBURY. Longfellow's Wayside inn, a camera impression, by Samuel Chamberlain. New York, Hastings house (1938)   72 p. front., illus. 19 x 16 cm. 38-23201.   F74.S94 C5

SUDBURY. A brief history of the towne of Sudbury ... together with the programme of the exercises enacted in commemoration of its 300th anniversary, 1639 - 1939. Text compiled and written by members of the ... W. P. A. administration in Mass. (Sudbury? 1939)   64, (2) p. front., illus.) (map) plates. 23 cm. 41-15602.   F74.S94 F4

— Newly rev. and reprinted. (Sudbury) Mass., 1968.   64 p. illus. 23 cm.
F74.S94 F4 1968

SUDBURY. Inscriptions from the old cemetery at Sudbury. Copied by Lucy Hall Greenlaw ... Boston, Press of D. Clapp, 1906.   21 p. 25 cm. Reprinted from the New England historical and genealogical register, v. 61. 7-6645.   F74.S94 G8

SUDBURY. The annals of Sudbury, Wayland, and Maynard. By Alfred Sereno Hudson ... (Ayer, Mass., A. S. Hudson) 1891.   14 p., 214 p., 40, vi p., front., plates, port., maps. 28 cm. Mainly reprinted from articles on the three towns contributed to D.H. Hurd's History of Middlesex Co., 1890.   1-11648.   F74.S94 H8

MASSACHUSETTS 317

SUDBURY, The history of. 1638 - 1889. By Alfred Sereno Hudson ... (Boston, Printed by R. H. Blodgett) 1889. xii, 660 p. front., plates, ports., maps (partly double) 23½ cm. 1-11649. F74.S94 H9

SUDBURY. Old Sudbury; the second in a series of portrayals of old New England towns; illus, with reproductions of pencil sketches from the original domiciles built in the 17th and 18th centuries. Boston, Mass., Pinkham press (1929) 48 p. incl. front., illus. 22 cm. 30-5231. F74.S94 P65

SUDBURY. Puritan village, the formation of a New England town. By Sumner Chilton Powell. (1st ed.) Middletown Conn., Wesleyan University Press (1963) xx, 215 p. 29 cm. 63-8862.
F74.S94 P74

SUDBURY. Bi-centennial celebration at Sudbury, Mass .... Full report of exercises, including the oration by Prof. Edward J. Young ... (Sudbury, Mass.) Trustees of the Goodnow library; (Lowell, Mass., Print. Marden and Rowell) 1876. 44 p. illus. 25 x 15 cm. 1-11650.
F74.S94 S9

SUDBURY, Vital record of, to the year 1850. Boston, Pub. by the New-England historic genealogical soc ... 1903. 332 p. 23½ cm. 3-23028. F74.S94 S93

SUNDERLAND. A record of Sunderland in the civil war of 1861 to 1865. Comp. by Jesse L. Delano, in 1881. According to vote of the town. Amherst, Mass., J. E. William, printer, 1882.
43, (3) p. 23½ cm. 7-21597. F74.S96 D3

SUNDERLAND. 1673. 1899. History of the town of Sunderland, which originally embraced within its limits the present towns of Montague and Leverett; by John Montague Smith. With genealogies prepared by Henry W. Taft and Abbie T. Montague. Greenfield, Mass., Press of E. A. Hall, 1899.
xii, 244 p., 245 - 656, (2) p., 2 l., 659 - 684 p. incl. map. front., plates, ports., map, facsims. 23½ cm. 1-1787. F74.S96 S6

SUTTON, History of the town of, from 1704 to 1876; including Grafton until 1735; Millbury until 1813; and parts of Northbridge, Upton and Auburn. Comp. by Rev. William A. Benedict and Rev. Hiram A. Tracy. Worcester, Pub. for the town by Sanford and co., 1878. 837 p. incl. illus., plates. plates, 2 port. (incl. front.) plan. 24 cm. 1-11651. F74.S98 B4

SUTTON. Inscriptions in the cemeteries of Sutton, by Reuben Rawson Dodge. Worcester, Mass., Press of C. Hamilton, 1898. 32 p. 19½ cm. 7-28534. F74.S98 D6

SUTTON. List of teachers in school districts nos. 9 and 10, Sutton, from 1790 to 1897. By Reuben Rawson Dodge. Worcester, Press of C. Hamilton, 1897. 24 p. 15½ cm. 7-29675.
F74.S98 D62

SUTTON. ... Bi-centennial of the town of Sutton ... official programme ... (Sutton? 1904)
8 p. 19½ cm. 7-29232. F74.S98 S88
Geneal. Section Ref.

SUTTON, ... Vital records of, to the end of the year 1849. Worcester, Mass., F. P. Rice, 1907.
478 p. 23½ cm. 7-16395. F74.S98 S9

SUTTON. Manual of the First Congregational church, in Sutton, containing a history of its formation, etc. Worcester, Goddard & Nye, steam print., 1871. 40 p. 19 cm. F74.S98 S92
— Supplement. Worcester, Mass., Print. C. Hamilton, 1891. 12 p. 19 cm. 7-29651.
F74.S98 S93

SWAMPSCOTT: historical sketches of the town. By Waldo Thompson ... Lynn, Press of T. P. Nichols, 1885. xi, 241 p. illus., plates. 20 cm. 1-11652. F74.S99 T4

SWAMPSCOTT. The Lynn suburban directory of Swampscott, Saugus and Nahant ... 1895/96 - 19 - Salem, Mass., H. M. Meek pub. co., 1895 - v. fronts. (fold. maps) 23 - 24 cm. 1-25731. Directories

SWAMPSCOTT, Saugus, Nahant and Lynnfield directory, 1931 - v.1 - Palmer, Mass., Crosby pub. co., 1930 - v. 23½ cm. CA 31-16 Unrev. Directories

547

318   LOCAL HISTORIES IN THE LIBRARY OF CONGRESS

SWAMPSCOTT historical society. ... Report. (Swampscott, The Society, 19
   v. fold. pl., plan.   22 ½ cm.   28-1877.   F74.S99 S9

SWANSEA.   North Swansea cemetery records; a reprint with some additions from three small yards,
i.e. "Slade burying ground", "Col. Peleg Slade private cemetery" and "the Bleachery grave yard" in
the town of Swansea and locality in Massachusetts ... compiled and privately pub. by Marion Pearce
Carter ... Attleboro, Mass., 1927. Reprint, 1930.   19 numb. 1.   28 cm.   Autographic reproduction of type-
written copy.   CA 31-406 Unrev.   F74.S993C32

SWANSEA.   A copy of the index of Swansea vital records, book B. & a few records of book D., 1702 -
1800 ... copied and pub. 1930 by Marion Pearce Carter ... Attleboro, Mass. (1930)   2, 115 p.
21 ½ x 28 cm.   Autographic reproduction of type-written copy.   CA 31-408 Unrev.   F74.S993S92

SWANSEA.   John Myles and religious toleration in Massachusetts, by Thomas W. Bicknell.   Boston,
1892.   2, 30 p.   22 ½ cm.   From the Magazine of New England history, v.2, no. 4, 1892, p. (213) - 242.   5-16842.
                                                                                F74.S995 B6

SWANSEA.   Book A, records of the town of Swansea.   1662 to 1705.   Ed. by Alverdo Hayward Mason.
East Braintree, Mass., A. H. Mason, 1900.   (82) p.   26 cm.   8-8987.   F74.S995 S8

SWANSEA.   Proceedings and addresss at the dedication of the town hall, in Swansea ...   Fall River,
Mass., Almy & Milne, printers, 1892.   80 p., incl. 2 pl. front., port.   21 ½ cm.   7-26256.   F74.S995S86

SWANSEA, History of, 1667 - 1917; comp. and ed. by Otis Olney Wright. (Swansea) The Town, 1917.
7, (3) - 248 p.   plates, ports., map.   24 cm.   "Family records": p. (137) - 189.   "Personal sketches": p. (191)-232.   18-5074.
                                                                                F74.S995W95

TAUNTON directory, The ...   1850, 1855, 1857, 1859, 1861, 1864, 1866, 1869, 1870/71, 1872, 1874,
1876, 1878, 1880, 1881/82   1885/86, 1887/88, 1189 - 19   Providence, R. I.,
Sampson & Murdock co., 1850 - 19   v. fold. maps. 14 - 25 cm.   1-30643 (rev. '32)   Directories

TAUNTON.   Reminiscences of Taunton.   In ye auld lang syne.   By Charles R. Atwood.   Taunton
(Mass.) Printed at the Republican steam print., 1880.   266 p.   front. (port.)   18 cm.   1-11653.
                                                                                F74. T2 A8

TAUNTON.   Pageant of patriotism ... Sabbatia Lake, Taunton ... 1911.   By Ralph Davol. (Taunton,
Mass., Davol press, 1911)   16 p.   23 ½ cm.   11-19415.   F74. T2 D2

TAUNTON, History of, from its settlement to the present time, by Samuel Hopkins Emery.   With an
introductory notice by Hon. Edmund Hatch Bennett ... Syracuse, N.Y., D. Mason, 1893.   2, (9) - 768,
110 p.   illus. (incl. facsims.) plates, ports., double maps.   25 cm.   L.C. copy replaced by microfilm.   1-11654-5.
    — Supplement.   1894.   13 p.   25 cm.   F74. T2 E5
                                                                         Microfilm 22264   F

TAUNTON, The ministry of, with incidental notices of other professions.   By Samuel Hopkins Emery
... With an introductory notice by Hon. Francis Baylies ... Boston, J. P. Jewett; Cleveland, O., Jewett,
Proctor & Worthington ... 1853.   2 v.   fronts., ports.   19 cm.   6-27419.
                                                                                F74. T2 E6

TAUNTON.   Thomas Coram in Boston and Taunton; a paper read before the American antiquarian soc.,
... by Hamilton Andrews Hill.   Worcester, Mass., Press of C. Hamilton, 1892.   18 p.   25 ½ cm.
5-1228.   F74. T2 H6

TAUNTON and the Machinists' national bank; high lights in the history of the city and a record of the
bank ... pub. in commemoration of over 80 years in banking, 1928. (Boston, Mass., Walton advertising and printing co., 1928)   2, 33 p. front., illus. (incl. ports., facsims.)   24 cm.   28-15975.
                                                                                F74. T2 M15

TAUNTON.   Old Colony historical society (Proceedings)   Taunton, (1893?)- 1909   2 v.
                                                                                F74. T2 O37

548

MASSACHUSETTS

TAUNTON. Collections of the Old colony historical society. no. 1 -   1878 -   Taunton, Mass., The Society, 1879 - 99.   6 v. front. (no. 1) illus., plates, ports.   23½ cm.   1-12099.
F74. T2 O4

TAUNTON. A catalogue of the portraits and other objects of historic value belonging to the Old colony historical society ....   Arranged by the librarian of the Society.   (Taunton, Gorham printer, 1907)   21 p. incl. front.   22½ cm.   7-25105.
F74. T2 O5

TAUNTON. Celebration of the semi-centennial anniversary of the founding of the Old Colony historical soc.   Commemorative oration ... by John Ordronaux ... Taunton, Mass., The Old Colony historical soc., 1903.   44 p.   23 cm.   7-36582.
F74. T2 O57

TAUNTON illustrated. Taunton, Mass., Hunter bros., 1889.   15 pl.   obl. 32°.   1-11656-M1.
F74. T2 T1

TAUNTON. 150th anniversary of the signing of the Declaration of Independence ... 1926. Robert Treat Paine, signer.   (Taunton, 1926)   20 p.   23 cm.   26-23331.
F74. T2 T17

TAUNTON. Quarter millennial celebration ....   Taunton, City government, 1889.   426 p. front., pl. 8°.   1-11657-M1.
F74. T2 T2

TAUNTON. 250th anniversary of ye anciente towne of Taunton ... 1889. Worcester, Mass., F. S. Blanchard, 1889.   32 p.   illus., port., facsim.   fol.   1-11658-M1.
F74. T2 T3

TAUNTON, Vital records of, to the year 1850 ... Boston, The New England historic genealogical soc. ... 1928 - 29.   3 v.   23 cm.   29-14028.
F74. T2 T35

TAUNTON celebration of the Massachusetts bay tercentenary, 1630, 1930.   (Taunton) Taunton tercentenary committee, 1930.   64 p. incl. front., illus.   23 cm.   31-2227.
F74. T2 T37

TEMPLETON. An historical discourse in commemoration of the one hundredth anniversary of the formation of the First Congregational church in Templeton. With an appendix, embracing a survey of the municipal affairs of the town. By Edwin G. Adams ... Boston, Crosby, Nichols, 1857.   vi, 175 p.   23½ cm.   6-15335.
F74. T27 A2

TEMPLETON, Vital record of, to the end of the year 1849. Worcester, Mass., F. P. Rice, 1907.   212 p.   23½ cm.   7-16396.
F74. T27 T2

TEWKSBURY directory, The ... no.   Boston, Mass., Sampson, Murdock,   v. 23½ cm.
"Pamphlet edition." Pub. also as part of the Lowell suburban directory. 1-29835 Rev.
Directories

TEWKSBURY; a short history, by Edward W. Pride. Issued under the auspices of the Tewksbury village improvement assoc. Cambridge, Mass., Riverside press, 1888.   3, 73 p.   18½ cm.   1-11659.
F74. T3 P9

TEWKSBURY, Vital records of, to the end of the year 1849. Salem, Mass., Essex institute, 1912.   246 p.   23 cm.   13-5097.
F74. T3 T3

TISBURY, Records of the town of ... 1669 - 1864. Arranged and copied by Wm. S. Swift ... and Jennie W. Cleveland ... Boston, Wright & Potter print., 1903.   xii, 841 p.   24½ cm.   Preface signed Charles E. Banks.   4-5232.
F74. T5 T5

TISBURY, Vital record of, to the year 1850. Boston, Pub. by the New England historic genealogical soc. ... 1910.   244 p.   23½ cm.   10-8542.
F74. T5 T6
L. H. & G.

TOPSFIELD. An address, delivered at Topsfield ... 1850; the 200th anniversary of the incorporation of the town. By Nehemiah Cleaveland ... New-York, Pudney & Russell, printers, 1851.   74, xxxix p.   front., ports.   23½ cm.   1-11660.
F74. T6 C6

549

TOPSFIELD, History of, by George Francis Dow. Topsfield, Mass., The Topsfield historical soc., 1940.   6, 517 p. plates, 2 port. (incl. front.)   24 cm.   "Printing and bibliography": p. 451 - 474.   41-10613.   F74. T6 D68

TOPSFIELD deaths from 1658 - 1800, compiled from town, church and county court records. By Geo. Frs. Dow ... Salem, Mass., The Salem press, 1897.   129 - 181 p.   23 cm.   From the historical collections of the Essex institute, vol. 33, 1897.   2-22144.   F74. T6 D7

TOPSFIELD. Early records of the church in Topsfield. Communicated by John H. Gould ... (Salem, Mass., 1888?)   27 p.   23½ cm.   "From the historical collections of the Essex institute, v. xxiv, p. 181." "Baptisms", 1688 - 1725: p. 6 - 27.   1-11661.   F74. T6 G6

TOPSFIELD. The celebration of the 250th anniversary of the incorporation of the town of Topsfield ... 1900. (Topsfield, Mass., The Society, 1900)   vi, 156 p. front., plates, ports. 23 cm. The historical collections of the Topsfield historical society. vol. vi. 1900)   6-2135.   F74. T6 T46

TOPSFIELD, Town records of ... 1659 - 1778. Topsfield, Mass., The Topsfield historical soc., 1917 - 20.   2 v.   24 cm.   18-5075 Revised.   F74. T6 T49

TOPSFIELD, Vital records of ... Topsfield, Topsfield historical soc., 1903 - 16.   2 v.   23½ cm.   3-19755 Rev. 2.   F74. T6 T5

TOPFIELD, Historical manual of the Congregational church of. 1663 - 1907. Topsfield, Mass., Pub. by the church, 1907.   4, 5 - 60 p.   front., 2 pl., 13 port., plan.   23 cm.   8-10487.   F74. T6 T56

TOPSFIELD. The historical collections of the Topsfield historical society. v. 1 - 12. 1895 - 1906, 1908. Topsfield, Mass., The Society, 1895 - 1908.   13 vols. illus., plates, ports., map, facsim.   22½ -23 cm. Vol. 1 is 2d ed. Index to vols. i - x: v. 10, p. 145 - 152.   7-18609.   F74. T6 T6

TOWNSEND. Remarks on the names of Townsend Harbor, Massachusetts, and of Mason Harbor and Dunstable Harbor, New Hampshire ... (by) Dr. Samuel A. Green ... (Cambridge, Mass., 1896?)   3 p.   24½ cm.   3-3822.   F74. T7 G6

TOWNSEND. A number of villages near Groton, formerly known as "Harbors," by Samuel A. Green. Groton, Mass., 1917.   7 p.   24 cm.   (Groton historical tract. no. 1) Reprinted from Proceedings of the Mass. historical society for Feb. 1896. Issued separately, 1896, with title: Remarks on the names of Townsend Harbor (etc.)   19-13694.   F74. T7 G7

TOWNSEND. Historical discourse, preached on the ... 136th anniversary of the organization of the Orthodox Congregational church of Christ, in Townsend. By G. H. Morss ... Boston, Printed by A. B. Morse, 1870.   32 p.   23 cm.   8-17395.   F74. T7 M8

TOWNSEND, History of, from the grant of Hathorn's farm, 1676 - 1878. By Ithamar B. Sawtelle ... Fitchburg, The author, 1878.   455 p. ports., map. 23½ cm.   1-11662.   F74. T7 S2

TRURO. Deaths in Truro, Cape Cod, 1786 - 1826. Taken from the diary of Rev. Jude Damon. By John Harvey Treat. (Salem, Mass.) Salem press pub. and print., 1891.   26 p.   24½ cm.   3-31530.   F74. T9 D2

TRURO - Cape Cod; or, Land marks and sea marks, by Shebnah Rich ... 77 illustrations. Boston, D. Lothrop (1883)   7, 5-580 p. incl. front., illus., plates, ports., map.   23½ cm.   1-11663.   F74. T9 R4

— 2d ed., rev. and cor. Boston, D. Lothrop, 1884.   580 p. incl. front., illus., plates, ports., map.   23 cm. A18-1931.   F74. T9 R4 1884

TRURO baptisms: 1711 - 1800. By John Harvey Treat. Lawrence (Mass.) J. Ward, Jr., 1886. 66 p.   24 cm.   58-51497.   F74. T9 T72

TRURO, Vital records of the town of, to the end of the year 1849, literally transcribed ... Boston, Massachusetts soc. of Mayflower descendants, 1933.   xiii, 480 p.   23½ cm.   33-17573.   F74. T9 T8 L. H. & G.

MASSACHUSETTS 321

TYNGSBORO, Vital records of, to the end of the year 1849.   Salem, Mass., Essex institute, 1912.
119 p.   23 cm.   13-5098.   F74.T97T88

TYNGSBORO centennial record, pub. by the Young people's league, Tyngsboro, Mass.   1876 ...
Lowell, Printed at the office of the Weekly journal, 1876.   24, (2) p.   23 cm.   3-5230.   F74.T97 T9

TYRINGHAM.   A hinterland settlement: Tyringham, Mass. and bordering lands.   (2d ed. Pittsfield, Mass., Printed by Eagle Print. and Binding Co., between 1962 and 1965)   95 p. illus., facsim., maps, plan, ports.   24 cm.   72-288888.   F74.T98 M9 1962

TYRINGHAM: old and new, by John A. Scott ... (Pittsfield, Sun print., 1905?)   43 p.   15 cm.   10-13003.   F74.T98 S4

TYRINGHAM, Vital records of, to the year 1850.   Boston, Pub. by the New England historic genealogical soc. ... 1903.   108 p.   23½ cm.   3-23026.   F74.T98 T9 L.H.& G.

UPTON.   By William George Poor.   This book sponsored by descendants of four friends in the town's second century.   Upton, Mass. (Milford, Mass., The Charlescraft press) 1935.   5, (9) - 194 p. incl. front., illus. plates, ports., maps, double facsim.   23½ cm.   1st printing, June 1935; 2d printing, Aug. 1935.   36-12586.   F74.U7 P62

UPTON'S first story years, by Rev. William G. Poor.   (Upton? Mass., 1935)   25 p. illus. (map) 23 cm.   36-29772.   F74.U6 P63

UPTON, ... Vital records of, to the end of the year 1849.   Worcester, F. P. Rice, 1904.
190 p.   23½ cm.   4-22348.   F74. U7 U7 L.H.& G.

UXBRIDGE.   Resident and business directory of Uxbridge and Northbridge ... 1898/9 ...
Needham, Mass., A. E. Foss, 1898 -   v.   22 cm.   99-415 Rev.   Directories

UXBRIDGE.   Address delivered at the Unitarian church, in Uxbridge, in 1864, with further statements ....   By Henry Chapin.   Worcester, Press of C. Hamilton, 1881.   xvi, (17) - 214 p. front. (port.) 24 cm.   2-22086.   F74. U9 C4

UXBRIDGE.   A sketch of the history of the First Congregational society of Uxbridge.   By Rev. Cyrus A. Roys.   (n.p., 1904)   16 p. front., pl., port.   24½ cm.   6-4476.   F74. U9 R8

UXBRIDGE year by year, 1727 - 1927, compiled by Beatrice Putnam Sprague, photographed by Ralph Henry Alton.   In commemoration of the 200th anniversary of the incorporation of Uxbridge.   Woonsocket, R. I., E. L. Freeman co., 1927.   126 p. front., plates. 24 cm.   27-18003.
F74. U9 S7

UXBRIDGE bi-centennial ... 1927.   (Woonsocket, R.I., E. L. Freeman co., printers, 1927)
24 p.   illus.   28 cm.   27-17270.   F74.U9 U94

UXBRIDGE, Vital records of, to the year 1850.   Comp. by Thomas W. Baldwin ... Boston, Mass,, (Wright & Potter print.) 1916.   420 p.   23½ cm.   17-11814.   F74.U9 U95 L.H.& G.

UXBRIDGE.   Old home week souvenir of Uxbridge.   Issued by the Old home week committee.   Comp. and ed. by Arthur E. Seagrave and Edward T. McShane ... 1908.   Uxbridge, Printed by Uxbridge and Whitinsville transcript pub. co. (1908)   (144) p. illus. (incl. ports.) 16 x 25 cm.   10-8690.   F74.U9 U97

VINEYARD HAVEN.   Sketches of old homes in our village, by Mrs. Howes Norris.   Vineyard Haven, Mass., Sea Coast defence chapter, D.A.R. (1921)   22 p.   20½ cm.   21-16649.   F74. V8 N8

WABAN, early days, 1681 - 1918.   Waban, Mass. (Newton Centre, Mass., The Modern press) 1944.
xv, 294 p. incl. front., illus. (incl. ports.) 23 cm.   "General bibliography": p. 294.   45-1295.   F74. W03 M3

551

WAKEFIELD, Stoneham, Reading, North Reading and Lynnfield directory ... 1869, (1874, 1882) 1884/5 -   19   v. (1) -   Salem, Mass., The H. M. Meek pub. co. ...
1869 -   v. fronts. (fold. maps)   24 cm.   0-5613 (rev. '27)   Directories

WAKEFIELD Congregational church; a commemorative sketch. 1644 - 1877. By Rev. Charles R. Bliss, pastor of the church ... Wakefield, W. H. Twombly, printer, 1877.   90 p.   24 cm.   7-36569.
F74. W1 B6

WAKEFIELD, Hand-book of. A strangers' guide and residents' manual ... Wakefield, Mass., The Citizen and banner press, 1885.   vi, (9) - 116 p.   front., illus., pl. 16°.   1-11664-M1.
F74. W1 E15

WAKEFIELD. Inaugural exercises in Wakefield, including the historical address and poem, delivered on the occasion of the assumption of its new name, by the town formerly known as South Reading ... 1868. Boston, Printed by W. Richardson, 1872.   100 p.   front.   23½ cm.   1-5733.   F74. W1 W13

WAKEFIELD, Vital records of, to the year 1850. Comp. by Thomas W. Baldwin ... Boston, Mass. (Wright & Potter, print.) 1912.   341 p.   23 cm.   13-5032.   F74. W1 W17

WAKEFIELD souvenir of the celebration of the 250th anniversary of ancient Reading ... 1894. ... Containing the official program of the exercises in both towns ... Wakefield, C. W. Eaton and W. E. Eaton (1894)   (106) p.   illus.   4°.   1-16545-M1.   F74. W1 W18

WAKEFIELD, History of, compiled by William E. Eaton and History committee. (Wakefield) 1944.
263 p.   illus. (incl. ports., facsims.)   maps (2 fold.)   23½ cm.   Wakefield tercentenary.   44-8990.   F74. W1 W2

WALES. An address delivered in Wales ... 1862; being the centennial anniversary of the municipal organization of the town; with additions ... to Jan 1, 1866 .... By Absalom Gardner ... Springfield (Mass.) S. Bowles, printers, 1866.   44 p.   22½ cm.   1-11665.   F74. W17 G2

WALPOLE, The story of, 1724 - 1924; a narrative history prepared under authority of the town and direction of the Historical committee of bi-centennial, by Willard De Lue. Norwood, Mass., Ambrose press, inc., 1925.   vii, 303 p.   304* - 304* p., 307 - 374 p.   illus., plates, ports., facsims.   22 cm.   Bibliography: p. 345 - 353.
26-1619   F74. W19 D2

WALPOLE. Addresses on Sir Robert Walpole and Rev. Phillips Payson, men prominent in the early history of Walpole. ... by Isaac Newton Lewis. (Walpole) First historical society of Walpole, Mass., 1905.   6, & - (21) p., 23 - 55 p.   front., plates, ports.   21 x 16 cm.   6-30487.   F74. W19L55

WALPOLE, A history of, from earliest times ... by Isaac Newton Lewis ... (Walpole, Mass.) First historical society of Walpole, Mass., 1905.   ix, 217 p. incl. front. plates. ports., facsim.   23½ cm.   6-4954.
F74. W19 L6

WALPOLE. The minute men and other patriots of Walpole, Mass., in our long struggle for national independence, 1775 - 1783, by Isaac Newton Lewis ... (Walpole, Mass.) The First Walpole historical soc., 1913.   59 p.   front., 1 illus.   21 cm.   14-12351.   F74.W19L62

WALPOLE. The dedication of a monument to the memory of the men of Walpole and vicinity who served in the French and Indian war; presented to the town of Walpole by George A. Plimpton ... (New York? 1901?)   23 p. incl. maps.   21 x 16 cm.   4-28476.   F74. W19 P7

WALPOLE, Vital records of, to the year 1850 ... Boston, 1902.   216 p.   23½ cm.   (New England historic genealogical society)   3-5256.   F74. W19 W2
L. H. & G.

WALPOLE ... Boston, The Edison electric illuminating co. 1909.   23 cm.
F74.W19W27

WALTHAM directory ... no. 18   Boston, Mass., W. A. Greenough.
v.   fold. maps.   24 cm.   99-3872 Rev.   Directories

MASSACHUSETTS

WALTHAM directory, The, containing a general directory of the citizens, numerical house directory, business directory, city and county register ... 1923 -   vol. no. 1 -   Boston, Sampson & Murdock, 1923 -   v. front. (fold. map) 24 cm. 23-11093.   Directories

WALTHAM. Polk's Waltham suburban diectory ... including Weston, Wayland and Lincoln ... Salem, Mass., New York, R. K. Polk (19   v. 24 cm. CA 31-1079 Unrev.   Directories

WALTHAM, Souvenir of ... By Charles H. Leighton. 1903.   F74. W2 L5

WALTHAM, past and present; and its industries. With an historical sketch of Watertown from its settlement in 1630 to the incorporation of Waltham ... 1738. By Charles A. Nelson ... 55 photographic illustrations. Cambridge (Mass.) T. Lewis, 1879.   152 p. front., photos. (incl. 2 port.) 20 x 14½ cm. 1-11666.
F74. W2 N4

WALTHAM. Historical address delivered before the citizens of Waltham ... 1876, by Josiah Rutter. With an account of the celebration of the day. (Waltham, Mass., Waltham free press office) 1877. 29 p. pl. 25½ cm. 1-16778.   F74. W2 R9

WALTHAM. Proceedings at the celebration of the sesqui-centennial of the town of Waltham, held in Music hall ... 1888. Waltham, Press of E. L. Barry, 1893.   104 p. illus., port. 24½ cm. 3-19778.
F74. W2 W2

WALTHAM, Vital records of, to the year 1850. Boston, Pub. by the New-England historic genealogical soc ... 1904.   298 p. 23½ cm. 4-18521.   F74. W2 W3
L. H. & G.

WALTHAM ... Boston, The Edison electric illuminating co., 1909.   23 cm.   F74. W2W39

WALTHAM. Report of the committee of the Waltham Union league, organized in 1863. Boston, Printed by J. Wilson, 1863.   28 p. 23 cm. 10-23093.   F74. W2 W5

WALTHAM. Publication no. 1 -   Waltham historical soc. Waltham, Mass., Waltham pub. co. printers, (1919) -   v. illus. 23 cm. 19-8776. v. 5 contains Waltham families p. (83) - 153.   F74. W2 W6

WARE. Manning's Ware, Palmer ... Three Rivers, Thorndike, Bondsville, and Tenneyville, Monson, Mass. and Stafford, Willington, Conn. directory ... (vol. 1) -   Springfield, Mass., H. A. Manning co., 1903 -   v. 24 cm. 13-24934 (rev. '37)   Directories

WARE, history of, by Arthur Chase. Cambridge, The University press, 1911.   viii p., 4 l., (3) - 294 p. front., plates (1 double) group of ports., fold. map, plans (partly double) 25 cm. 11-22314.   F74. W27 C4

WARE, History of, 1911 - 1960, by John Houghton Conkey and Dorothy Dunham Conkey. Pub. for the Bicentennial of the town of Ware. (Ware?) 1961.   xix, 353 p. 24 cm. 61-10999.
F74. W27 C6

WARE. Early grants and incorporation of the town of Ware. By Edward H. Gilbert. New York, Printed for the author, Fords, Howard and Hulbert, 1891.   iv, 5 - 58 p. illus., 4 fold. maps. 23 cm. 3-2491 Additions.   F74. W27 G4

WARE. An address, delivered at the opening of the new Town-hall, Ware ... 1847. Containing sketches of the early history of that town, and its first settlers. By William Hyde ... Brookfield, Mass., Merriam and Cooke, printers, 1847.   56 p. 24½ cm. 1-11667 Rev.   F74. W27 H9

WARE. The Manor of peace, Ware, Mass. Reverend Grindall Rawson and his ministry, by Alfred Baylies Page ... (Boston?) Priv. print., 1907.   13 p. 24½ cm. 8-15812.   F74.W27P13

WARE. Historical sermon delivered at Ware First parish ... 1830, by Augustus B. Reed .... (Ware? Mass., Printed for J. H. G. Gilbert) 1889.   21 p. 22½ cm. 50 copies printed. 18-12654.
F74. W27 R3

324 LOCAL HISTORIES IN THE LIBRARY OF CONGRESS

WAREHAM, Mattapoisett, Marion and Rochester, Mass., directory.   Boston, A. E. Foss co.,
v.   24½ cm.   4-8574 (rev. '15)   Directories

WAREHAM.   Dunham's Wareham, Mattapoisett, Marion and Rochester, Mass., directory ... 1924/25 - v. 1 -   Salem, Mass., C. H. Dunham, 1924 -   v.   24 cm.   25-233.
                                                                                                                    Directories

WAREHAM - sixty years since.   A discourse delivered at Wareham, Mass. ... 1861, by E. Burgess. Boston, Press of R. R. Marvin, 1861.   24 p.   23½ cm.   9-30713.   F74.W28 B9

WAREHAM.   Glimpses of early Wareham, by Daisy Washburn Lovell.   Illus. by Mary E. Clarke. Taunton, Mass., Wareham Historical Soc. (1970)   139 (8) p.   illus.   24 cm.   79-130942.   F74.W28 L6

WARREN, History of.   By Olney I. Darling.   West Brookfield, T. Morey, printer, 1874.   24 p.
19½ cm.   1-11668 Rev.   F74.W29 D2

WARREN.   Historic Fort Warren, by Edward Rowe Snow.   Boston, Mass., The Yankee pub. co. (1941)   5 - 87 p.   illus. (incl. ports.)   fold. map.   22½ cm.   41-12186.   F74.W29 S6

WARREN.   Western 1741 - 1834.   Warren 1834 - 1891.   An account of the 150th anniversary of the incorporation of the town of Warren ... 1891 ... by Hon, Solomon B. Stebbins ... Boston, Press of N. Sawyer, 1891.   72 p.   front., fold. map.   25 cm.   10-3162.   F74.W29 S8

WARREN, ... Vital records of Warren (formerly Western), to the end of the year 1849.   Worcester, Mass., F. P. Rice, 1910.   196 p.   23½ cm.   10-8543.   F74.W29 W4
                                                                                                               L. H. & G.

WARWICK, History of the town of, from its first settlement to 1854.   By Hon, Jonathan Blake. Brought down to the present time by others.   With an appendix.   Boston, Noyes, Holmes, and co., 1873.   240 p.   front. (port.)   double plan.   19 cm.   Record of marriages ... 1806 - 1844, and Record of deaths ... 1807 - 1872 ... p. 206 - 226.   1-11669.   F74. W3 B6

WARWICK.   Twenty-five years in old Warwick.   An address delivered on Memorial day ... 1904 ... by Rev. A. D. Mayo ... City of Washington, R. Beresford, printer, 1905.   35 p.   23½ cm.   6-36450.
                                                                                                                F74. W3 M3

WARWICK; biography of a town, 1763 - 1963.   By Charles A. Morse.   Cambridge, Mass., Dresser, Chapman & Grimes (1963)   279 p.   21 cm.   63-12108.   F74. W3 M6

WASHINGTON.   A poem delivered on the 4th of July, 1859, at Washington village, Needham, by Josiah L. Fairbanks, of Boston.   Boston, C. W. Calkins, printer, 1859.   12 p.   19½ cm.   10-30654.
                                                                                                                F74.W31 F16

WASHINGTON, Vital records of, to the year 1850.   Boston, Pub. by the New-England historic genea- logical soc ... 1904.   57 p.   23½ cm.   4-9197.   F74.W31 W3
                                                                                                               L. H. & G.

WATERTOWN.   Crosby's Watertown directory ...   Boston, Mass., Crosby pub co., 19 -
v.   front. (fold. map)   24 cm.   CA 26-655 Unrev.   Directories

WATERTOWN directory ... (no. 10), 17, 19.   W. A. Greenough, compilers, printers and publishers. Boston, (1889) - 1909.   3 v.   23½ cm.   8-1545.   Directories

WATERTOWN.   Genealogies of the families and descendants of the early settlers of Watertown, in- cluding Waltham and Weston; to which is appended the early history of the town ... By Henry Bond ... 2d ed.   ... Boston, The N. E. Historic-genealogical soc. ... 1860.   2 v. in 1.   illus., plates, ports., 2 maps (1 fold.)   facsims.   25 cm.   10-17787.   1st edition 1855.   See F74. W33 B8   F74.W33 B7

WATERTOWN.   Family memorials.   Genealogies of the families and descendants of the early settlers of Watertown, incl. Waltham and Weston; to which is appended the early history of the town ... By

554

MASSACHUSETTS

Henry Bond ... Boston, Little, Brown; New York, J. Wiley ... 1855. 2 v. in 1. front., illus., plates, ports., 2 maps (1 fold.) 23 cm. Paged continuously. 1-11671. F74.W33 B8

WATERTOWN, An historical sketch of, from the first settlement of the town to the close of its second century. By Convers Francis ... Cambridge, E. W. Metcalf, 1830. 151 p. 22½ cm. 1-11672. F74.W33 F8

WATERTOWN. A record of the First parish in Watertown. Comp. by Arthur B. Fuller ... Watertown (Mount Auburn, Printed at the Memorial office) 1861. 16 p. 18½ cm. 17-16958. F74.W33 F9

WATERTOWN. Three discourses preached before the Congregational society in Watertown; two, upon leaving the old meeting-house; and one, at the dedication of the new. By Convers Francis, pastor ... Cambridge, Folsom, Wells, and Thurston, 1836. 79 p. 22 cm. (With his An historical sketch of Watertown. Cambridge, 1830. copy 3) 19-3277. F74.W33 F8 Copy 3. Toner.

WATERTOWN. Epitaphs from the old burying ground in Watertown. Collected by William Thaddeus Harris ... With notes by Edward Doubleday Harris. Boston, 1869. 2, iii, 70 p. 25 cm. 3-3512. F74.W33 H3

WATERTOWN. By-laws of the Historical society of Watertown. With a list of past and present officers and members ... Watertown, Press of F. G. Barker, 1893. 15 p. 16½ cm. 3-5041. F74.W33H73

WATERTOWN. Historical society, Watertown, Mass. Rev., 1908. Boston, Press of D. Clapp, 1908. 30 p. 17 cm. 8-31936. F74.W33H74

WATERTOWN. Address of Wm. H. Ingraham, esq., and oration by Rev. J. F. Lovering, at the centennial celebration, White's hill grove, Watertown, Mass. ... 1876. (Watertown, 1876) 35 p. 22½ cm. 1-16827 Rev. F74.W33 I4

WATERTOWN, A glimpse at. By a "native" (Francis Leathe) ... (2d ed.) Boston, 1851. iv, (5) - 42 p. 17½ cm. In verse. 18-13212. F74.W33 L4

WATERTOWN soldiers in the colonial wars and the American revolution, compiled by G. Frederick Robinson and Albert Harrison Hall. Watertown, Mass., The Historical soc. of Watertown, 1939. 75 p. 1 illus., plates (1 double) facsims. 24½ cm. Ed. of 100 copies. 40-1956. F74.W33R63 Rare Book Coll.

WATERTOWN. Great little Watertown; a tercentenary history, by G. Frederick Robinson and Ruth Robinson Wheeler. (Watertown, Mass.) Pub. at the request of the Watertown historical soc., 1930. 6, (3) - 150 p. front., plates, ports., maps (1 fold.) facsim. 23½ cm. Bibliography at end of part of the chapters. Founders of Watertown: p. (112) - 136. 30-15346. F74.W33R66

WATERTOWN. Record of the West precinct of Watertown, 1720 to 1737-38. Waltham, Mass., Pub. by order of the Board of aldermen, 1913. 2, (7) - 135 p. 23½ cm. The West precinct of Watertown was incorporated in 1738 as a separate town under the name of Waltham. 16-2787. F74.W33W28

WATERTOWN records ... Prepared for publication by the Historical society. Watertown, Mass. ... 1894 - 1928. 6 v. in 5. front., illus., fold. maps, fold. plan, facsims. 25 cm. Contents. - v.1. The 1st and 2d books of town proceedings, with the land grants and possessions, and the 1st book and supplement of births, deaths, and marriages. - v.2. The 3d book of town proceedings and the 2d book of births, marriages and deaths to the end of 1737 ... - v. 3. The 4th book of town proceedings, and the second book of births, marriages and deaths from 1738 to 1822. - v.4. East Congregational and precinct affairs, 1697 to 1737 ... - v. 5. The 5th book of town proceedings, 1745/6 to 1769 and the 6th book of town proceedings, 1769 to 1792, incl. notes of Watertown lands; grants and possessions ... - v. 6. The sixth book of town proceedings, 1769 - 1792. 1-11670 Rev. F74.W33 W3

WATERTOWN'S military history. Authorized by a vote of the inhabitants of the town of Watertown. Pub. in 1907, under the direction of a committee representing the Sons of the American revolution, and Isaac B. Patten post 81, Grand army of the republic. Boston, D. Clapp, printers, 1907. xvii, 281 p. 16 pl., 4 port., plan, 7 facsim. 24 cm. 8-16240. F74.W33 W4

WATERTOWN. ... The Watertown record ... Historical sketches of ancient Watertown, which once comprised Watertown, Waltham, Weston, and part of Lincoln and Belmont. (v. 1, no. 1 - 2; May - June 1861) (Mount Auburn? Mass., 1861)   2 no.   23½ cm.   Supplement to the Mt. Auburn memorial.   Paged continuously. No more pub.   17-27561.
F74.W33W45

WATERTOWN. Historical sketch of the town of Watertown, commemorating the 275th anniversary of its settlement as an English colony, embracing a detailed account of the limits of the town and the history of the old mill and the great bridge. By Solon Franklin Whitney. Boston, Mass., Press of Murray and Emery co., 1906.   24 p.   map.   24 cm.   6-15333.
F74.W33 W6

WAYLAND. Proceedings at the dedication of the town hall, Wayland ... 1878; with brief historical sketches of public buildings and libraries. Wayland, Prepared and pub. by authority of the town, 1879. 79 p.   23½ cm.   3-9545.
F74.W35 W3

WAYLAND. The town of Wayland in the civil war of 1861 - 1865, as represented in the army and navy of the American union ... Prepared and pub. by order of the town of Wayland. Wayland (Mass.) 1871. 452 p.   22½ cm.   3-27742.
F74.W35 W4

WAYLAND, Vital records of, to the year 1850. Boston, Mass., Pub. by the New England historic genealogical soc. ... 1910.   160 p.   23½ cm.   10-8874.
F74.W35 W5

WEBSTER. Hanks' Webster and Southbridge directory (1887/8   ... Comp. and pub. by Wilbur F. Hanks ... Poughkeepsie, Haight & Dudley, printers (1887 -   1 v.   23½ cm.   7-35040.   Directories

WEBSTER and Dudley, Mass., directory ... The.   19 -   Salem, Mass., The H. M. Meek pub. co., 19   v.   24 cm.   22-15623.   Directories

WEBSTER (including that part of Dudley Township lying near to Webster) and Oxford (Mass.) including Grosvenordale, Mechanicsville, Wilsonville, North Grosvenordale (Conn.) directory ... 1928 - Springfield, Mass., H. A. Manning co., 1928 -   v.   23 cm.   CA 29 - 161 Unrev.   Directories

WEBSTER, Dudley, Southbridge and Sturbridge diectory ... no. 1   1896/7 -   Salem, Mass., H. M. Meek, 1896 -   v.   23½ cm.   99-5772 Rev.   Directories

WEBSTER, Dudley, Southbridge and Sturbridge directory. (v. 1 -   1902 -   New Haven, Conn., The Price & Lea co. (1902 -   v.   24 cm.   2-7106 Rev.   Directories

WEBSTER, Dudley and Oxford, Mass., resident directory ... v. 6.   Boston, Mass., W. E. Shaw, 1907.   1 v.   24 cm.   8-823.   Directories

WEBSTER. Leading business men of Webster, Southbridge, Putnam, and vicinity; embracing also Danielsonville, East Douglass and Oxford ... Boston, Mercantile pub. co., 1890.   78 p.   illus.   25 cm. In double columns.   Cover-title: Leading business men of Danielsonville.   4-25659.
F74.W36B13

WELLESLEY. Town of Wellesley, Mass., directory ... Boston, H. Howard, 19 - v.   24 cm.   CA 24-779 Unrev.
Directories

WELLESLEY and Needham directory, The. Needham, Mass., A. J. Gordon, 1911 1 v.   23 cm.   11-15206.
Directories

WELLESLEY. Guide to Ridge Hill farms, Wellesley, Mass. and social science reform. September, 1877. By William Emerson Baker. Boston, Getchell brothers, 1877.   152, (1) p.   map.   16°. 1-11673-M1.
F74.W38 B1

— 1877.   16½ cm.
F74.W38B15

WELLESLEY, History of the town of, by the late Hon. Joseph E. Fiske, ed. and enl. by Ellen Ware Fiske. Boston, Chicago, The Pilgrim press (1917)   xiii, 92 p.   front. (facsim.) plates.   24½ cm.   "Genealogies of some of the older residents of the town": p. 68 - 77.   17-25470.
F74.W38F54

MASSACHUSETTS

WELLESLEY, Glimpses of.   (Boston, The Barta press, 1904)   1 p., l., 26 pl.   15½ x 23 cm.
F74.W38G55

WELLESLEY.   Life, letters and diary of Horatio Hollis Hunnewell (1810 - 1902); with a short history of the Hunnewell and Welles families, and an account of the Wellesley and Natick estates, by ... Hollis Horatio Hunnewell.   Boston, Priv. print. (New York, The De Vinne press) 1906.   3 v. fronts. plates (1 col.) ports., fold. maps, plans (1 fold.) facsims.   27 cm.   53 copies printed.   6-42360.
F74.W38 H9

WELLESLEY.   (Reasons for presenting a petition to the legislature of 1881, asking that a part of the town of Needham be set off and incorporated as a new town by the name of Wellesley)   (Wellesley? Mass., 1881?)   4 p.   fold. map.   24 cm.   CA 30-1011 Unrev.
F74.W38W37

WELLESLEY.   Our town.   A monthly magazine devoted to the interests of the town of Wellesley. v. 1 - 6; Jan. 1898 - Dec. 1903.   (Wellesley Hills, Mass., C. M. Eaton, etc.) 1898 - 1903.   6 v. in 3. plates, ports.   23 - 26 cm.   No more pub.   9-16249.
F74. W4 O9

WELLFLEET.   Historical address, delivered before the town of Wellfleet, by A. W. Holbrook ... 1876.   Pub. by order of the town authorities.   Provincetown (Mass.) Advocate printing establishment, 1876.   13 p.   8°.   1-16866-M1.
F74.W33 H7

WELLFLEET, History of, from early days to present time; comp. by Everett I. Nye.   (Hyannis, Mass., F. B. & F. P. Goss, printers) 1920.   48 p.   5 pl., port.   22 cm.   21-7141.
F74.W39N99

WENHAM, The history of, civil and ecclesiastical, from its settlement in 1639, to 1860.   By Myron O. Allen.   Boston, Printed by Bazin & Chandler, 1860.   vi, (13) - 220 p.   19½ cm.   1-11674.
F74. W4 A4

WENHAM.   Two sermons, delivered on the second centennial anniversary of the organization of the first church, and the settlement of the first minister in Wenham.   By Daniel Mansfield ...   Andover, Print. Allen, Morrill and Wardwell, 1845.   72 p.   23½ cm.   2-17337.
F74. W4 M3

WENHAM.   Inscriptions from gravestones in the old burying ground in Wenham.   Copied by Wellington Pool, August, 1882.   (Salem? 1887?)   28 p.   illus.   24½ cm.   From the Essex institute Historical collections, v. 20 - 24, 1883 - 87.   3-2801.
F74. W4 P8

WENHAM, Vital records of, to the end of the year 1849.   Salem, Mass., The Essex institute, 1904. 227 p.   23½ cm.   6-13929 Rev.
F74. W4 W4

WENHAM town records, 1642 - 1706 ...   (Wenham, Mass.) Wenham historical soc., 1930. 210 p.   23½ cm.   A "copy of the 1st book of records of Wenham", copied by Wm. P. Upham, in 1871.   30-21005.
F74. W4 W42

WENHAM.   Town of Wenham ... 1908 ... order of exercises in connection with the unveiling of the memorial tablet ... in commemoration of the first preaching of the gospel in Wenham, by the Rev. Hugh Peters, pastor of the church in Salem, 1636 - 1641.   (Beverly, Mass., Enterprise print., 1908) 36 p.   illus., pl.   23 cm.   9-16513.
F74. W4 W45

WEST BOYLSTON.   Historical address delivered at the re-dedication of the Brick meeting house, West Boylston ... 1890, by James H. Fitts.   Exeter, N.H., Printed by J. Templeton, 1890. 26 p.   22½ cm.   9-30087.
F74. W44 F5

WEST BOYLSTON.   Manual of the Congregational church in West Boylston, Mass. ...   Prepared by James H. Fitts, pastor.   Clinton (Mass.) Print. W. J. Coulter, Courant office, 1870.   64, 9 p.   19½ cm. 7-26258.
F74. W44 F6

WEST BOYLSTON.   Historical memorandum and genealogical register of the town of West Boylston, from its early settlement to 1858; tog. with miscellaneous items and incidents.   By Benjamin F. Keyes.   Worcester, Spy printing house, 1861.   4, (5) - 84 p.   20 cm.   1-11676 Rev.
F74. W44 K4

WEST BOYLSTON. Sesquicentennial celebration, town of West Boylston, 1808 - 1958, illus. and produced by the Art Committee ...   West Boylston, 1958)   unpaged. illus. 25 cm.   58-25434.
F74.W44W38

WEST BOYLSTON, ... Vital records of, to the end of the year 1849.   Worcester, Mass., F. P. Rice, 1911.   153 p.   23½ cm.   11-7323.
F74.W44 W4

WEST BRIDGEWATER, Vital records of, to the year 1850.   Boston, New England historic genealogical soc. ...   1911.   222 p. 23 cm.   13-3037.
F74.W46 W5

WEST DENNIS.   The Baker zone in West Dennis ... by Sylvanus C. Evans.   1928.   (Library of Cape Cod history and genealogy, no. 5)
F74.W47 E9

WEST DENNIS.   The white spire; history of the West Dennis church and village, 1835 - 1885.   West Dennis, Cape Cod, Mass., West Dennis Community Church, 1967.   44 p. 23 cm.
F74.W47 P4

WESTFIELD.   Western Massachusetts history; the Westfield area (by) Stephen J. Pitoniak, Sr.   Westfield, Mass., 1970.   87 p. illus. 23 cm.
F74.W49 P5

WESTFIELD.   Mundale, the West parish of Westfield, Mass., in the olden days. Written and compiled by Eloise Fowler Salmond.   Springfield, Mass., The Pond-Ekberg co. press, 1934.   3, 9 - 93 p. incl. fold. mounted map.   plates, port.   24½ cm.   34-19481.
F74.W49 S2

WESTFIELD.   See also F74.W68

WEST MEDWAY.   Epitaphs from the old burying ground, West Medway ...   By Herbert N. Hixon.   Dedham, Mass., 1900.   29 p.   25 cm.   "Reprinted from the Dedham historical register."   1-16585.
F74.W54 H5

WEST NEWBURY.   An invoice and valuation of the rateable polls and estates, within the town of West Newbury, as taken by the assessors, on the first day of May, 1851, and the first days of May, 1852.   West Newbury, Printed by a vote of the town, Indian Hill press, 1852.   34 p. 23½ cm.   19-1012.
F74.W56 W5

WEST NEWBURY, Vital records of, to the end of the year 1849.   Salem, Mass., The Essex institute, 1918.   122 p.   23½ cm.   18-27315.
F74.W56W64

WEST NEWTON half a century ago, by Lucy Ellis Allen.   (Newton, The Graphic press, 1917)   2, 32 p.   19 cm.   18-3531.
F74.W57 A4

WEST ROXBURY magazine, pub. by a committee for the First parish, West Roxbury ... Hudson, Mass., The E. F. Worcester press, printers, 1900.   56 p. front., illus., plates, facsim. 29 cm.   10-14260.
F74.W59 W6

WEST SPRINGFIELD.   Steadfastness in religion, explained and recommended in a sermon ... by Joseph Lathrop ... 1796.   West-Springfield (Mass.): Printed by Edward Gray, 1797.   34 p. 18½ cm.   19-7399.
F74. W6 L3
Rare Book Coll.

WEST SPRINGFIELD.   An address delivered at West Springfield ... 1856 ....   By William B. Sprague ... Albany, Van Benthuysen, printer, 1856.   55 p.   21 cm.   27-755.
F74.W6 L39

WEST SPRINGFIELD.   An address delivered at West Springfield ... 1856 ....   By William B. Sprague ... With an appendix.   Springfield, Mass., S. Bowles, printers, 1856.   102 p. 22½ cm. 11-26703.
F74. W6 L4

WEST SPRINGFIELD.   An historical discourse, delivered at West Springfield ... 1824 ....   By William B. Sprague ...   Hartford, Printed by Goodwin & co., 1825.   91 p. 23 cm. 16-8165.
F74. W6 S76

WEST SPRINGFIELD, a town history (by) Esther M. Swift.   (West Springfield, West Springfield Heritage Assoc., 1969.   xii, 344 p. illus. 27 cm. 77-96767.
F74. W6 S95

MASSACHUSETTS

WEST SPRINGFIELD, Account of the centennial celebration of the town of, ... 1874, with the historical address of Thomas E. Vermilye ... Comp. by J. N. Bragg. (Springfield, Mass., C. W. Bryant, printers) 1874.   144 p. plates, 2 port. (incl. front.) 24 cm. Genealogies: p. (109) - 124. 1-11690.   F74.W6 W5

WEST SPRINGFIELD, Vital records of, to the year 1850. Boston, The New England historic genealogical soc., 1944 - 45.   2 v. 22½ cm. A 45-3509 Rev.   F74.W6 W56
Geneal. Sect. Ref.

WEST STOCKBRIDGE, Vital records of, to the year 1850. Boston, Mass., Pub. by the New England historic genealogical soc ... 1907.   115 p. 23½ cm. 7-16399.   F74.W62 W5

WESTON. Reception of the returned soldiers of Weston, and memorial service in honor of the fallen. 1865. Waltham (Mass.) Hastings's Sentinel office, 1865.   23 p. 22½ cm. 13-5133.   F74.W64 W55

WESTBOROUGH. Twenty years of the Westborough historical society; an address by the president, Rev. S. I. Briant ... 1909. Westborough, Mass., Chronotype printing co., 1909.   11 p. 23 cm. 10-13759.   F74.W65 B8

WESTBOROUGH, The history of. Part I. The early history. By Hemen Packard De Forest. Part II. The later history. By Edward Craig Bates. Westborough, The town, 1891.   2, (iii) - xvi p. 504 p. front., plates (1 fold.) ports., fold. map, plans. 23½ cm. 1-11675.   F74.W65 D3

WESTBOROUGH. The hundredth town. Glimpses of life in Westborough. 1717 - 1817. By Harriette Merrifield Forbes. Boston, Press of Rockwell and Churchill, 1889.   209 p. incl. front., illus. 19 x 15½ cm. 4-21116.   F74.W65 F6

WESTBOROUGH. The diary of Rev. Ebenezer Parkman, of Westborough, Mass. ...1737, 1778, 1779 and 1780 ... Ed. by Harriette M. Forbes. (Westborough, Mass.) The Westborough historical soc., 1899.   viii, 9 - 327 p. front., illus., plates, ports. 20 x 16½ cm. For location of other ms. diaries of Parkman see American antiquarian soc. Proceedings, Oct. 1907. 0-16 Rev.   F74.W65 P2

WESTBOROUGH, ... Vital records of, to the end of the year 1849. Worcester, Mass., F. P. Rice, 1903.   258 p. 23½ cm. 3-14598 Rev.   F74.W65 W4

WESTBOROUGH. More old houses in Westborough, and vicinity, with their occupants. (Westborough) The Westborough historical soc., 1908.   58 p. plates. 23 cm. 19-18687 Rev.   F74.W65W49

WESTBOROUGH. Some old houses in Westborough, and their occupants; with an account of the Parkman diaries. (Westborough) The Westborough historical soc., 1906.   2, 3 - 70 p. plates. 23 cm. 19-18688 Rev.   F74.W65W493

WEYMOUTH, Quincy and Braintree directory for 1870/71 - 73. Boston, D. Dudley, 1870 - 73.   2 v. fronts. (fold. maps) 24 cm. 7-39274.   Directories

WEYMOUTH directory, The, 1891 ... Made by A. B. Sparrow and D. C. Parsons; E. B. Butterfield, pub., Ayer, Mass. Fitchburg, Sentinel printing co. print, 1891.   (2) - 177 p. 23 cm. 7-39271.   Directories

WEYMOUTH and Braintree, Resident directory of, 1896, containing also a business, street, and social directory of each town ... Comp., copyrighted and pub. by the J. H. Hogan co., Quincy, Mass. Hyannis, Mass., F. B. & F. P. Goss, printers, 1896.   409 p. 23½ cm. 7-38084.   Directories

WESTFIELD directory ... including Blandford, Chester, Granville, Granville Center, West Granville, Huntington, Montgomery, Russell, Southwick and Woronoco, Mass. ... 18 -   Springfield, Mass., The Price & Lee co.; ... 18 -   v. fold. maps. 24 cm. 9-26169 Rev.   Directories

WESTFIELD, History of. A sermon, by Rev. John Alden ... 1851, at the remodelling of their house of worship ... Springfield (Mass.) G. W. Wilson, printer, 1851.   20 p. 23 cm. 1-11678 Rev.   F74.W68 A3

WESTFIELD, A historical sketch of. By Emerson Davis ... Westfield (Mass.) J. Root, 1826.   36 p. 21½ cm. 1-11679.   F74.W68 D2

WESTFIELD. The history of the celebration of the 250th anniversary of the incorporation of the town of Westfield ... 1919, and appendix with reminiscences of the last half-century. (Concord, N.H., Printed by the Rumford press, 1919) xiv, 239 p. incl. front. plates, ports., facsims. 24 cm. 21-13613.
F74. W68 G7

WESTFIELD, 1669 - 1969; the first 300 years. Ed. by Edward C. Janes & Roscoe S. Scott. Westfield, Mass., Westfield Tri-Centennial Assoc. (1968) viii, 476 p. illus., maps. 24 cm. 68-59386.
F74. W68 J 3

WESTFIELD. A sermon commemorative of the 200th anniversary of the First Congregational church of Westfield ... by ... Rev. John H. Lockwood ... 1879 ... Westfield, Mass., Clark & Story, printers, 1879. 55 p. 24 cm. 6-38847.
F74. W68 L8

WESTFIELD and its historic influences, 1669 - 1919; the life of an early town, with a survey of events in New England and bordering regions to which it was related in colonial and revolutionary times, by Rev. John H. Lockwood ... (Westfield, Mass.) Printed and sold by the author (1922) 2 v. fronts., plates, ports., maps (1 fold.) 22½ cm. 22-25234.
F74.W68L82

WESTFIELD'S quarter millennial anniversary official souvenir ... Pub. in connection with the 250th anniversary of the founding of the town of Westfield .... Ed. by Edgar Holmes Plummer ... Westfield, Mass., Westfield's 250th anniversary assoc. (1919) 144 p. illus., ports. 20 x 27½ cm. 19-14111.
F74.W68P73

WESTFIELD. A history of the town of Westfield; comp. for the public schools from Greenough's History of Westfield in the Annals of Hampden County and other sources, by Chester D. Stiles ... Westfield, Mass., J. D. Cadle, 1919. 50 p. 23½ cm. 20-14143.
F74. W68 S8

WESTFIELD historical calendar, 1669 - 1920. (Westfield, Mass., Westfield times co, print, 1919) 57 l. illus. 18 x 24 cm. Text parallel with back of cover. Printed on side of leaf only. 20-1305.
F74. W68 W4

WESTFIELD jubilee, The: a report of the celebration at Westfield, on the 200th anniversary of the incorporation of the town ... 1869, with the historical address of the Hon. William G. Bates, etc. Westfield, Mass., Clark & Story, 1870. viii, (9) - 226 p. 23½ cm. 1-11680.
F74. W68 W5

WESTFIELD and the world war. United States declared war Aptil 6, 1917; armistice signed Nov. 11, 1918. (Westfield, Westfield times co, print., 1919) 55 p. illus. (incl. ports.) 23 cm. 20-6360.
F74.W68W53

WESTFIELD. See also F74.W49

WESTFORD, souvenir of the dedication of the J. V. Fletcher library, June 4th, 1896. (Lowell) Lowell mail print (1896) 93 p. illus. (incl. ports.) 24 cm. 10-21069.
F74. W69
Z733. W53

WESTFORD. An address delivered by request before the Ornamental tree assoc., Westford, 1876. By Edwin R, Hodgman ... Lowell, Mass., Stone, Huse & co., printers, 1876. 17 p. 24½ cm. 6-45231.
F74. W69 H7

WESTFORD, History of the town of, 1659 - 1883. By Rev. Edwin R. Hodgman ... Lowell, Mass., Morning mail co., printers, 1883. viii, 494 p. front., plates, ports., fold, map. 24½ cm. Records of marriages, 1728 - 1844 ... deaths, 1704 - 1848, p. 372 - 434. Genealogy of early families, p. (435) - 486. 1-11681.
F74. W69 H8

WESTFORD. Patriotism in Westford in 1775. By Edwin Ruthven Hodgman. (n.p., 1879?) 4 p. 24 cm. 1-11682.
F74. W69 H9

WESTFORD, Vital record of, to the end of the year 1849. Salem, Mass., The Essex institute, 1915. 325 p. 23½ cm. 5-12430.
F74. W69 W5

WESTHAMPTON. "Saying the catechism" seventy-five years ago, and the historical results. An address delivered before the New England historic-genealogical soc., 1878. By Dorus Clarke ... Boston, Lee & Shepard; New York, C. T. Dillingham, 1879. 46 p. 16 cm. A sketch of Westhampton. 1-15804.
F74. W7 C6

MASSACHUSETTS

WESTHAMPTON. Memorial of the reunion of the natives of Westhampton ... 1866. Waltham, Office of the Free press, 1866.   85 p.   23 cm.   1-11683.   F74. W7 W6

WESTHAMPTON sesquicentennial ... 1928. Church sesquicentennial ... 1929. (Northampton, Mass., Press of F. M. Crittenden, 1929?)   101 p.   22 cm.   33-31502.   F74.W7 W65

WESTMINSTER. The history of Redemption Rock (Westminster, Mass.) ... By S. Hathaway. Worcester, Mass., F. S. Blanchard, printers, 1898.   14 p.   front.   23½ cm.   An account of the capture by the Indians ... of Mrs. Mary Towlandson, of Lancaster, Mass. in 1676, with some notes on the Hoar family.   4-7257.   F74. W62 H3

WESTMINSTER, History of (first named Narragansett no. 2) from the date of the original grant of the township to the present time, 1728 - 1893; with a biographic-genealogical register of its principal families, by William Sweetzer Heywood ... Lowell, Mass., S. W. Huse, 1893.   xvi, 963 p.   front., plates, ports., fold. map, double plan.   24 cm.   1-11684.   F74. W72 H6

WESTMINSTER. A poem, delivered at the celebration of the 100th anniversary of the incorporation of Westminster. By William S. Haywood. Boston, Press of R. R. Marvin, 1860.   24 p.   24 cm.   Reprinted from Celebration of the 100th anniversary of the incorporation of Westminster ... 1859.   16-21929.   F74.W72H63

WESTMINSTER. A history of the town of Westminster, from its first settlement to the present time. By Charles Hudson. Mendon, Mass., G. W. Stacy, printer, 1832.   42 p.   25 cm.   6-8171.   F74. W72 H8

WESTMINSTER. Historical poem, to be read at the dedication of the Soldiers' monument, in Westminster ... 1868. By Robert Peckham ... Fitchburg (Mass.) Printed at the Fitchburg sentinel office, 1868.   26 p.   22 cm.   4-33443.   F74. W72 P3

WESTMINSTER. Historical discourse delivered on occasion of the 125th anniversary of the Congregational church, and the 50th anniversary of the Sunday school, in Westminster ... 1868 ... by A. Judson Rich ... Springfield, Mass., S. Bowles, printers, 1869.   98 p.   24 cm.   1-11685.   F74. W72 R5

WESTMINSTER. Celebration of the 100th anniversary of the incorporation of Westminster, containing an address, by Hon. Charles Hudson ... etc. Boston, Press of T. R. Marvin, 1859.   127 p.   23 cm.   1-11686.   F74. W72 W6

WESTMINSTER, ... Vital records of, to the end of the year 1849. Worcester, Mass., F. P. Rice, trustee of the fund, 1908.   258 p.   23 cm.   8-10308.   F74. W72 W7

WESTMINSTER, A history of, 1893 - 1958. Ed. by Newton R. Tolman. Peterborough, N. H., R. R. Smith (1961)   xi, 347 p.   25 cm.   61-17914.   F74. W72W72

WESTMINSTER. An account of the exercises connected with the 150th anniversary celebration of the town of Westminster, 1909; together with historical and legendary reminiscences connected with the town. By Wilbur F. Whitney. Gardner (Mass.) Meals printing co. (191-)   200, (2) p. incl. front., illus., ports.   20½ cm.   13-5031.   F74.W72W73

WESTON, Wayland and Lincoln, Mass, ... Directory of. Boston, Mass., Hyde pub. co., 19   v.   24 cm.   CA 29-367 Unrev.   Directories

WESTON. Waltham suburban directory, containing general directories of ... Weston, Wayland, Cochituate, and Lincoln, Mass., and a ... directory of Waltham, with a street map of Weston and a township map of Middlesex County ... v. 4 - 5, 1906/7, 1909. Boston, G. Richardson,   2 v.   23 cm.   6-14221.   Directories

WESTON. Once upon a pung. By Brenton H. Dickson. (Boston? 1963)   84 p.   22 cm.   F74. W74 D5

WESTON. Oration delivered before the inhabitants of Weston, at the town-hall ... 1876, by Charles H. Fiske. Weston (Mass.) ... 1876.   38 p.   24½ cm.   1-11687.   F74. W74 F5

WESTON. A sermon, delivered at Weston ... 1813, on the termination of a century since the incorporation of the town. By Samuel Kendal ... Cambridge: Printed by Hilliard and Metcalf, 1813.
60 p. 24½ cm. 8-7815.
F74.W74 K4

WESTON, History of the town of, 1630 - 1890, by Col. Daniel S. Lamson. Boston, Press of Geo. H. Ellis co., 1913. vii, 214 p. front. (port.) 12 pl. 24 cm. 16-22668.
F74.W74 L2

WESTON, a Puritan town, by Emma F. Ripley. Illus. by Margaret F. Kronenberg. Weston, Mass., Benevolent-Alliance of the First Parish, 1961. 270 p. 25 cm.
F74.W74 R5

WESTON. Town of Weston. Births, deaths and marriages, 1707 - 1850. 1703 - Gravestones - 1900. Church records, 1709 - 1825. Appendix and addenda, Cent society, gleanings from the town files, bits of genealogy, errors, indexes, etc. Boston, McIndoe bros,, printers, 1901. vi, 649 p. 23½ cm.
Ed. by Mary Frances Peirce. 3-20341.
F74.W74W57
L.H. & G.

WESTON. Town of Weston. Records of the First precinct, 1746 - 1754, and of the town, 1754 - 1803. Boston, A. Mudge, printers, 1893. iv, 558 p. 23½ cm. Comp. by Mary Frances Peirce. The West precinct of Watertown was incorporated as the town of Weston in 1713. The Second precinct ... was incorporated 1754 as the town of Lincoln. 1-11688.
F74.W74 W6

WESTON. Town of Weston. Records of the town clerk, 1804 - 1826. Boston, A. Mudge, printers, 1894. iv, 437 p. 24 cm. Preface signed: Mary Frances Peirce. 17-9546.
F74.W74W602

WESTON. Town of Weston. The tax lists 1757 - 1827. Boston, A. Mudge, printers, 1897.
v, 438 p. fold. plan. 13½ cm. Preface signed: Mary Frances Peirce. 1-11689.
F74.W74W62

WESTON. An account of the celebration by the First parish of Weston, of its 200th anniversary ... 1898 ... Weston, Mass., Printed for the Parish, 1900. 251 p. front., plates, ports. 23½ cm. 29-2671.
F74.W74W72

WESTON. See also F74.W64W55

WESTPORT. Description and map of a superb seaside resort. Westport point and Horseneck beach (Bristol co., Mass.) By Henry Alvin Brown. (n. p.) 1885. folder (8 l. incl. map) 32°. 1-16611-M1.
F74.W75 B8

WESTPORT. The hurricane at Westport harbor ... 1938; personal observations by Richard K. Hawes Fall River, Mass., Printed by the Dover press (1938) 2, 18 p. incl. front. (map) pl. 23 cm. 38-34758.
F74.W75H38

WESTPORT, Vital records of, to the year 1850. Boston, Pub. by the New England historic genealogical soc ... 1918. 296 p. 23½ cm. 18-27355.
F74.W75 W5

WESTWOOD. A history of the Clapboard Trees or Third parish, Dedham, now the Unitarian parish, West Dedham, 1736 - 1886, by George Willis Cooke ... Boston, G. H. Ellis, 1887. 139 p. illus. (incl. port., map, facsims.) 24 cm. 1-11328.
F74.W757C7

WEYMOUTH, Directory of, which includes North Weymouth, Weymouth Heights, Weymouth Center, East Weymouth, Weymouth Landing and South Weymouth. Boston, Mass., The A. E. Foss co., 19
v. 23½ cm. 22-2514.
Directories

WEYMOUTH, Directory and history of ... Made by J. H. Hogan ... Plymouth, Avery & Doty, book and job print., 1888. 307 p. illus. 24 cm. 7-38083.
Directories

WEYMOUTH, Resident and business directory of ... Boston, Mass., Boston suburban book co., 1907
- v. fold. map. 24 cm. 7-37245.
Directories

WEYMOUTH. W. E. Shaw's Weymouth directory ... 1899 - v. 1 - Boston, Mass., W. E. Shaw, 1899 - v. fold. map. 24 cm. 24-17757.
Directories

WEYMOUTH. A discourse delivered in the North church, Weymouth ... 1851. By Joshua Emery, jr. ... Boston, Press of T. R. Marvin, 1851. 18 p. 23 cm. 9-30714.
F74.W77 E5

MASSACHUSETTS 333

WEYMOUTH ways and Weymouth people. Reminiscences by Edmund Soper Hunt. Boston, Priv. print., 1907. 307 p. front. (port.) 24½ cm. "Hunt ancestry": p. 309 - 316. 7-7464. F74.W77 H9

WEYMOUTH. An oration delivered at the dedication of the soldiers' monument in North Weymouth ... 1968, by Hon. George B. Loring. With an appendix, containing other exercises and record of the deceased soldiers. Weymouth, C. G. Easterbrook, Weymouth weekly gazette press, 1869. 44 p. incl. pl. 23½ cm. 10-23094. F74.W77 L8

WEYMOUTH. Proceedings on the 250th anniversary of the permanent settlement of Weymouth, with an historical address by Charles Francis Adams, jr., July 4th, 1874. Boston, Wright & Potter, 1874. 107 p. 23½ cm. 1-11691. F74.W77 W6

WEYMOUTH, Vital records of, to the year 1850 ... Boston, Pub. by the New England historic genealogical soc. ... 1910. 2 v. 23½ cm. 10-8875. F74.W77W67

WEYMOUTH, History of ... Pub. by the Weymouth historical soc., Howard H. Joy, president. Under direction of the town. (Boston, Wright & Potter print.) 1923. 4 v. illus., plates, fold. map. 23½ cm. "Genealogy of Weymouth families, by George Walter Chamberlain": v. 3 - 4. 29-22565. F74.W77W69

WEYMOUTH historical society (Publications) nos. 1 - 3. (Weymouth; Boston, Printed) The Weymouth historical soc., 1881 - 1905. 3 v. plates, map. 26½ cm. 6-15413. F74.W77 W7

— No. 1. ... The original journal of General Solomon Lovell ... by Gilbert Nash. 1881. 127 p. 2 pl., map. 25 cm. "Robert Lovell genealogy": p. (109) - 116. 6-2146.
— No. 2. ... Historical sketch of the town of Weymouth, 1622 to 1884. Comp. by Gilbert Nash. 1885. x, 346 p. 26½ cm. 6-2147.
— No. 3. ... Wessagusset and Weymouth, an historical address by Charles Francis Adams, jr. (and other papers) 1905. 163 p. 26½ cm. 6-15414.
— No. 6. The shoe industry of Weymouth, compiled by Bates Torrey ... 1933. 126 p. illus., plates, ports., facsim. 23½ cm. 33-4956.
— No. 7. Weymouth town government, its beginning and development, by Clarence W. Fearing ... (South Weymouth) 1941. 36 p. 23½ cm. 41-8391.

WEYMOUTH. The book of records of the Second church of Christ in Weymouth. Baptisms and marriages. By John J. Loud ... Boston (Press of Somerset print.) 1900. 36 p. 24½ cm. The records extend from 1722 to 1818. 6-9489. F74.W77W76

WEYMOUTH. See also p. 559

WHATELY, 1771 - 1971; a New England portrait, by Ena M. Cane. Family records compiled by Paul F. Field. Introd. by Alice Scott Ross. Photos. by Gordon Daniels and Morris Dwight. Line drawings by Morris Dwight, Jr. Northampton, Mass., Printed for the Town of Whately (by) Gazette Print. Co., 1972. xi, 356 p. illus. 24 cm. Bibliography: p. 162 - 163. 72-183501 MARC. F74.W78.C3

WHATELY, History of the town of, including a narrative of leading events from the first planting of Hatfield: 1661 - 1899, as revised and enl. by James M. Crafts, with family genealogies. Orange, Mass., Printed for the town by D. L. Crandall, 1899. 628, (8) p. front., plates, ports. 23½ cm. Rev. and enl. from J. H. Temple's "History of the town of Whately ... 1660-1871". 2-28279. F74.W78 C8

WHATELY, History of the town of, including a narrative of leading events from the first planting of Hatfield: 1660 - 1871. By J. H. Temple ... With family genealogies. Boston, Printed for the town, by T. R. Marvin, 1872. 332 p. front., facsims. 24 cm. 1-11692. F74.W78 T2

WHITMAN. Town of Whitman directory ... 1895. Boston, H. Howard, 1895 - 19 v. fold. maps. 24 cm. 17-13696 Rev. Directories

WILBRAHAM, History of, 1763 - 1963. Bicentennial ed. General editor: Charles L. Merrick. Wilbraham? Mass., 1964. ix, 309 p. 26 cm. 64-8640. F74. W8 M4

WILBRAHAM, The history of; prepared in connection with the celebration of the 150th anniversary of the incorporation of the town ... 1913, by Chauncey E. Peck. (Wilbraham? Mass., pref. 1914) x, (2), 469 p. incl. illus., pl. port. 24 cm. 15-16768. F74. W8 P36

334   LOCAL HISTORIES IN THE LIBRARY OF CONGRESS

WILBRAHAM. An historical address, delivered at the centennial celebration of the incorporation of the town of Wilbraham ... 1863. By Rufus P. Stebbins. With an appendix. Boston, G. C. Rand & Avery, 1864.   3, 5 - 317 p. front., plates. 23½ cm.   p. (173) - 313, Appendix ... including Marriages of early settlers, Births and deaths which took place before the incorporation of the town and Genealogies of the families of some of the first settlers.   1-11693.

F74. W8 S8

WILLIAMSBURG, A history of, compiled by Phyllis Baker Deming. 175th anniversary. Northampton, Mass., The Hampshire bookshop, 1946.   xvi, 416 p. front., plates, ports. 23½ cm. 46-18564.

F74.W815D4

WILLIAMSTOWN, the first two hundred years, 1753 - 1953. Ed. Robert Romano Ravi Brooks and others. Authors: Helen H. Allen (and others) Williamstown (Mass.) McClelland Press, 1953.   xv, 458 p. illus., ports. 23 cm. Bibliography: p. 437 - 438. 53-3716.

F74. W82 B7

WILLIAMSTOWN. Boyhood reminiscences; pictures of New England life in the olden times in Williamstown. By Judge Keyes Danforth. New York, Gazlay brothers, 1895.   6, 9 - 177 p. front. (port.) 15½ cm. A number of the articles were previously pub. in the North Adams transcript. 7-21156.

F74.W82D18

WILLIAMSTOWN and Williams college, by N. H. Egleston. Williamstown, Mass., 1884.   3, 3 - 76 p. illus., pl., port. 23½ cm. 1-11694.

F74. W82 E3

WILLIAMSTOWN, the "Berkshire hills" and thereabout ... Fitchburg railroad co., "Hoosac tunnel route". (Glens Falls, N.Y., C. H. Possons) 1890.   60 p. front., illus. 17½ cm. 1-16783 Rev.

F74. W82 F8

WILLIAMSTOWN. Centennial discourse, delivered in Williamstown, Mass. ... 1865, by Mason Noble. North Adams, Mass., J. T. Robinson, printers, 1865.   60 p. 22½ cm. 1-11695.

F74. W82 N7

WILLIAMSTOWN, Origins in, by Arthur Latham Perry ... 2d ed. New York, C. Scribner's sons, 1896.   viii, 650 p. illus., port. 24½ cm. 1-11696.

F74. W82 P4

WILLIAMSTOWN and Williams college, by Arthur Latham Perry ... New York, C. Scribner's sons, 1899.   viii p., 2 l., 847 p. front., illus., ports. 24 cm. 44-26264.

F74.W82P43

WILLIAMSTOWN. ... Identification of "unidentified wives" in "Williamstown vital records to 1850." Marriages in New Lebanon, N.Y., of persons from Williamstown. By Elmer Irwin Shepard. (Williamstown, Mass.) 1940 - 42.   11 numb. l., 2 l. 22 cm. (Berkshire genealogical notes. No. 1) Reproduced from type-written copy; additions and corrections in manuscript. 44-12020.

F74.W82S54

WILLIAMSTOWN. A day in Williamstown; guide for visitors (by) M. E. Sherman. Williamstown, Mass., The Forget-me-not shop, 1915.   63 p. illus. 16 cm. 15-13401.

F74.W82S55

WILLIAMSTOWN, Souvenir of. Photo-gravures. Brooklyn, N.Y., The Albertype co., 1900. 16 pl. 13½ x 18½ cm. 0-5308 Rev.

F74.W82S68

WILLIAMSTOWN, Souvenir of. Williamstown? Mass., 1903.   14 x 19 cm.

F74.W82 S7

WILLIAMSTOWN, Souvenir of. (Williamstown? Mass) 1904.   14 x 18 cm.

F74.W82S72

WILLIAMSTOWN. "The Berkshire hills," Greylock hall ... Williamstown, Mass. Streeter & Swift. Troy, N.Y., Times print. (1872)   14 p. incl. illus., pl. 24°. 1-15958-M1.

F74. W82 S9

WILLIAMSTOWN, Vital records of, to the year 1850. Boston, Pub. by the New England historic genealogical soc., 1907.   vi, 9 - 173 p. 23½ cm. 7-16400.

F74. W82 W7
L H & G

WILMINGTON. Souvenir and guide-book to points of interest in Wilmington, Mass. By Arthur Thomas Bond. 1904.   20½ cm.

F74. W88 B7

WILMINGTON, 1730 - 1880; historical addresses delivered in the meeting-house of the Church of

564

MASSACHUSETTS

Christ in Wilmington ... 1880, upon the 150th anniversary of the incorporation of the town. By Daniel P. Noyes. Boston, Press of Cochrane & Sampson, 1881. 55 p. 24 cm. 51-49571. F74.W83 N6

WILMINGTON records of births, marriages and deaths, from 1730 - 1898. Alphabetically and chronologically arranged by James E. Kelley. Edward M. Nichols, town clerk. Lowell, Mass., Printed by Thompson & Hill, 1898. 255 p. 24 cm. 4-18513. F74.W74 W7

WINCHENDON and Ashburnham directory (1885/6) - 1890/91 - New Haven, Conn., Price, Lee & co. (1885) - 89. 2 v. 23½ cm. 8-10582. Directories

WINCHENDON, directory, The ... v.3, 1907/8. Boston, W. E. Shaw, 1907 - 1 v. fold. map. 23½ cm. 8-824. Directories

WINCHENDON, History of the town of, from the grant of the township by the legislature of Mass. in 1735, to the present time. By Ezra Hyde. Worcester, Print. H. J. Howland (1849) viii, (9) - 136 p. 18 cm. 1-11697. F74.W84 H9

WINCHENDON, History of the town of, from the grant of Ipswich Canada, in 1735, to the present time. By Rev. A. P. Marvin ... Winchendon, The author, 1868. 528 p. front., illus., plates, ports., fold. plans, fold. tables. 24 cm. "Genealogy and personal history": p. 444-480. 1-11698. F74.W84 M3

WINCHENDON, ... Vital records of, to the end of the year 1849. Worcester, F. P. Rice, 1909. 223 p. 23½ cm. 9-7387. F74.W84 W7

WINCHESTER directory ... no. Boston, Mass., W. A. Greenough v. 24 cm. 1-6333 Rev. Directories

WINCHESTER, Blue book of (1895) - (v. 1 - v. illus., fold. maps. 20½ x 23 cm. 12-9000. Directories

WINCHESTER society blue book ... 190 Boston, F. H. Radford, 190 - v. fold. map. 23 cm. CA 6-757 Unrev. Directories

WINCHESTER, History of, by Henry Smith Chapman; drawings by W. H. W. Bicknell ... (Winchester, Mass.) Pub. by the town, 1936. x, 396 p. col. front., illus., plates, ports., fold. maps. 24 cm. 36-19413. F74.W85 C5

WINCHESTER. July 4th, 1890. 250th anniversary of the first white settlement within the territory of Winchester ... (Boston, The Barta press, 1890) 32 p. illus. 26 x 20½ cm. 1-16735. F74.W85 W7

WINCHESTER record, The, Printed for the members of the Winchester historical and genealogical soc. (1886) 2 v. plates, ports., maps, facsim. 23 cm. CA 9-6471 Unrev. F74.W85 W9

WINDSOR, Vital records of, to the year 1850. Boston, Pub. by the New England historic genealogical soc. ... 1917. 153 p. 23½ cm. 18-5071. F74.W86 W7

WINTHROP. Crosby's Winthrop directory 1929/30 - v. 1 - Wollaston, Mass., Crosby pub. co., 1929 - v. 23½ cm. CA 29-160 Unrev. Directories

WINTHROP directory ... Boston, Mass., W. A. Greenough, 1911 - 1 v. front. (fold. map) 23½ cm. 11-23047. Directories

WINTHROP directory, The, 1916/17 - v. 1 - new house guide and rev. map. Salem, Mass., The Henry M. Meek pub. co., 1916 - v. front. (fold. map) 24 cm. 17-6002. Directories

WINTHROP. Ocean spray souvenir ... containing a list of the summer and permanent residents of that part of Winthrop known as Cottage Hill, Ocean Spray and Winthrop Highlands, together with a list of cottages ... 18 Ocean Spray, (Mass.) G. E. B. Putnam (18 v. fold. map. 19½ x 15 cm. CA 34-977 Unrev. Directories

WINTHROP days ... By Mary Priscilla Griffin. Winthrop (Mass.) 1905. 17 x 27½ cm. F74.W88 G8

WINTHROP. Historic Winthrop, 1630 - 1902; a concise history of Winthrop, comp. by Charles W. Hall; photographs by Rev. Albert L. Squiers and W. E. R. Wells. Boston, Winthrop pub. co., 1902. 43, (5) p. incl. illus., pl. 18 x 28½ cm. 2-20017. F74.W88 H2

WINTHROP. History of the Deane Winthrop house, Winthrop, Mass. ... By Channing Howard. (Winthrop) Winthrop improvement and historical assoc. (1942?) 12 p. illus. 17 cm. 45-15548.
F74.W88 H6

WINTHROP. Descriptive history and real estate guide of the town of Winthrop (Mass.) Containing full and accurate descriptions of over six hundred building lots and beach privileges, beside may desirable country seats and residences, now offered for sale. By S. Ingalls. (Boston) C. W. Hall, 1877. 16 p. 16°. 1-11699-M1. F74.W88 I 4

WINTHROP. Photo-glimpses in and around Winthrop. By J. H. White. (Boston, 1893) 19 pl. obl. 12°. 1-11700-M1. F74.W88 W5

WOBURN. Manning's Woburn and Winchester directory ... 1868 - Boston, Mass., H. A. Manning company, 1868 - 19 - v. fronts., illus., plates, fold. maps. 22½ - 25½ cm. 2-1169 Rev. Directories

WOBURN. 1642 - 1892. Legends of Woburn, now first written and preserved in collected form ... to which is added a chrono-indexical history of Woburn by Parker Lindall Converse ... Woburn, Mass., Printed for subscribers only, 1892 - 96. 2 v. fronts., illus., plates. 21½ cm. 1-11701. F74.W89C76

WOBURN. Transcript of epitaphs in Woburn First and Second burial-grounds. Chronologically arranged, with brief illustrative notes. By William R. Cutter and Edward F. Johnson ... Woburn, Andrews, Cutler & co., printers, 1890. 160 p. 24 cm. (In Woburn records ... F74.W89W82)
F74.W89 C9

WOBURN. John Lakin's deed, 1653. Communicated by the Hon, Samuel A. Green ... (Boston, 1891) 3 p. 23 cm. Reprinted from the N.E. historical and genealogical register for Jan. 1891. 12-18988. F74.W89L19

WOBURN.men in the Indian and other wars previous to the year 1754. By Arthur G. Loring and Wm. R. Cutter. Supplementary to the names in Diary of Lieut. Samuel Thompson ... Boston, D. Clapp, printers, 1897. 16 p. 24 cm. The "Diary of Lieut. Samuel Thompson, a soldier in the French war, during the year 1758" was pub. in Sewall's Hist. of Woburn, 1868, and repub. with notes by W.R. Cutter, Boston, 1896. 8-16847. F74.W89 L8

WOBURN. Abstract of early Woburn deeds recorded at Middlesex County registry 1649 - 1700, by Edward F. Johnson. With some explanatory notes. (Woburn, Mass., The News print, pref. 1895) 2, (3) - 78, xii p. map. 23 cm. Edition of 50 copies. First appeared in 'The News' of Woburn. They are believed to include all Woburn deeds bearing date in the 17th century and now on record at Cambridge. 16-20037. F74.W89 M6
Rare Book Coll.

WOBURN. Rumford historical association, Woburn. Incorporated 1877. Boston, A. Mudge, printers, 1892. 16 p. incl. illus., ports. 23½ cm. 9-23193. F74.W89R93

WOBURN. Rumford historical association, 1903. (Woburn? 1903) 24 p. incl. pl. 15 x 11½ cm. 11-26702. F74.W89R94

WOBURN, The history of, from the grant of its territory to Charlestown, in 1640, to the year 1860. By Samuel Sewall ... With a memorial sketch of the author, by Rev. Charles Sewall. Boston, Wiggin and Lunt, 1868. 2, iv, (iii) - vi, (7) - 657 p. front. (port.) 24 cm. "Genealogical notices of the earliest inhabitants of Woburn and their families": p. (591) - 657. 1-11702. F74.W89 S5

— 1868. 2, iv, (iii) - x, (7) - 677 p. front. (port.) 24½ cm. Probably a copy of the original edition of 1868, with an index by George M. Champney (p. 659 - 677) added in 1881. 15-10658. F74.W89S52

WOBURN. Proceedings ... 1892, at the 250th anniversary of the incorporation of the town of Woburn. Woburn, Printed for the city; (The New print) 1893. 233 p. front., plates, ports., facsims. 23 cm. 1-11703.
F74.W87 W8

MASSACHUSETTS 337

WOBURN records of births, deaths, and marriages ... Alphabetically and chronologically arranged by Edward F. Johnson. Woburn, Mass., Andrews, Cutler & co., printers ... 1890 - 19
   v. facsims. 24 - 22 cm. Contents. - pt. 1. Births, 1640 - 1873. Extracts from a bibliography of Woburn. By W.R. Cutter. Genealogy. - pt. 2. Deaths, 1640-1873. Epitaphs in Woburn first and second burial grounds ... pt. 3. Marriages, 1640-1873. Notes on the family of Dea. Edward Convers. - pt. 4. Births, 1873-1890 ... Contributions to a bibliography of the local history of Woburn ... - pt. 5. Deaths, 1873 - 1890. Additional material for a bibliography of the local history of Woburn. - pt. 6. Marriages, 1873-1890. The proprietors' book of record. 1739-1765. pt. 7. Births, 1891-1900. - pt. 8. Deaths, 1891-1900. - pt. 9. Marriages, 1891-1900. 1-11704.
   F74.W89W82

WOBURN. Transcript of epitaphs in Woburn First and Second burial-grounds. Chronologically arranged, with brief illustrative notes. By William R. Cutter and Edward F. Johnson ... Woburn, Andrews, Cutler & co., printers, 1890. 160 p. 24 cm. (In Woburn records F74.W89W82) 6-42363.
   F74.W89W82

WOBURN. ... Boston, The Edison electric illuminating co., 1909. 24 p. illus. 23 cm.   F74.W89W925

WOODS HOLE index. no. 1 - 2; July 1 - Aug. 1, 1926. Woods Hole, Mass.) The Dolphin press (1926) 24, 24 p. illus. 25 cm. monthly. No more pub? 27-14519 Rev.
   F74.W895W8

WORCESTER. Le Worcester canadien ... directoire des Canadiens-français de Worcester, guide historique, commercial et industriel. v. 18 Worcester, Mass., J. E. Rochette, 18 -
   v. illus., ports. 19½ - 23 cm. 1-31086 Rev.
   Directories

WORCESTER village directory, The, containing the names of the inhabitants, their dwelling houses and places of business, arranged according to the streets and squares, to accompany a map of the village of Worcester. Worcester, C. Harris, 1829. 12 p. 15 cm. 19-13189.   Directories
   Rare Book Coll.

WORCESTER. Le Guide français de Worcester, Mass. pour 1916, contenant l'almanach des adresses ... Worcester, Mass., La Compagnie de publication Belisle, v. 23 cm. 16-14768.   Directories

WORCESTER house directory and family address book, The; a supplement to the Worcester directory. no. (1) - 1888 - 19 Worcester, Sampson & Murdoch co. (1888) - 19
   v. 23½ cm. biennial. 8-14415 (rev. '33)
   Directories

WORCESTER and suburban society blue book, The ... 1899/1900   1st   ed. New York city, The Blue books company (etc.) 1899 - 19 v. 17½ - 21½ cm. 99-4781 Rev.   Directories

WORCESTER society blue book ... with a supplementary list of first families of Springfield and Holyoke, Mass. 1899/00, 1910. New York. Dau pub. co., 1899 - 1910. Nov. 2, 99-66.   Directories

WORCESTER railroad and express guide, and business directory, 1871. Worcester, 1871.
   12½ cm.
   Directories

WORCESTER. Business directory of the city of Worcester, for 1871/2. By Henry J. Howland. Worcester, L. H. Bigelow, 1871. 8, (13) - 143 p. 16½ cm. 8-14883 Additions.   Directories

WORCESTER business directory and manual, 1894/5, containing a classified list of all the business firms and a complete street directory, with a new Worcester County gazetteer ... Lynn, Mass., H. Clark, 1894. 159 p. 19½ cm. 8-14882.   Directories

WORCESTER, Fitchburg, Gardner, Greenfield, Leominster, Milford, Southbridge, Clinton, Webster, Athol, Winchendon and surrounding territory ... classified business directory, "buyers' blue book". 1935/36 - Mass., The New England directory co., inc. (1935 - v. 22 cm. CA 36-45 Unrev.
   Directories

WORCESTER manufacturer ... The, containing a list of the manufacturers, with statistics of consumption and production, capital invested, hands employed, wages paid, and much other information of the city of Worcester, Mass., no. (Worcester, Mass.) F.S. Blanchard, 1882 -
   1 v. 24½ cm. 8-29134.
   Directories

WORCESTER business directory and manual, 1894/5, containing a classified list of all the business firms and a complete street directory, with a new Worcester County gazetteer ... Lynn, Mass., H. Clark & co., 1894. 159 p. 19½ cm. 8-14882.   Directories

WORCESTER city guide and street directory. Worcester, Sampson & Murdock. v. 16½ cm.   Directories

WORCESTER, Album souvenir of. (Worcester, 1889) 12½ x 16½ cm.   F74. W9 A34

WORCESTER. Historical remarks concerning the Mechanic street burial ground, in the city of Worcester, offered to the joint committee of the legislature of Mass. ... 1878. By Rev. George Allen ... Worcester, Print. Tyler & Seagrave, 1878. 17 p. 24 cm. 7-27752.   F74. W9 A43

WORCESTER. Art work of Worcester ... Chicago, The W. H. Parish pub. co., 1894. 19 l. illus., 71 pl. 35 cm. Pub. in 12 parts. 7-30330.   F74. W9 A7

WORCESTER. A historical discourse delivered at Worcester, in the Old south meeting house ... 1863; the 100th anniversary of its erection. By Leonard Bacon ... With introductory remarks by Hon. Ira M. Barton ... And an appendix. Worcester, Print. E. R. Fiske, 1863. 106 p. front. 23½ cm. 6-15314.   F74. W9 B2

WORCESTER. Epitaphs from the cemetery on Worcester common, with occasional notes, references, and an index. By W. S. Barton. Worcester, Printed by H. J. Howland (1848) 36 p. 23 x 14½ cm. 6-13734.   F74. W9 B3

WORCESTER. Livre d'or des Franco-Américains de Worcester, par Alexandre Belisle. Worcester, Mass., Imprimé par La Compagnie de publication Belisle (Pref. 1920) 363 p. 24 cm.   F74. W9 B4

WORCESTER. A report on politics in Worcester. Cambridge, Joint Center for Urban Studies of the Mass. Institute of Technology and Harvard University, 1960. 1 v. 28 cm.   F74. W9 B5

WORCESTER. Incidents of the first and second settlements of Worcester. By Francis E. Blake. Worcester, Mass., F. P. Rice, 1884. 33 p. 25 cm. Repr. from Procs. of the Worcester soc. of antiquity. 1-11705.   F74. W9 B6

WORCESTER. Some Worcester matters, 1689 - 1743. By Francis E. Blake. Worcester, Mass., F. P. Rice, 1885. 17 p. 25 cm. Repr. from Procs. of the Worcester soc. of antiquity for 1885. 7-26262.   F74. W9 B64

WORCESTER Main street sixty-three years ago. By Henry H. Chamberlin. Worcester, Mass., F. P. Rice, 1886. 24 p. 25 cm. Repr. from the Procs. of the Worcester soc. of antiquity for 1885. 7-26261.   F74. W9 C4

WORCESTER. Notre-Dame-des-Canadiens et les Canadiens aux États-Unis, par l'abbé T. A. Chandonnet ... Montreal, Imprimé par G. E. Desbrats, 1872. 2, vii-xvi, 171 p. 21½ cm. 12-11191.   F74. W9 C42

WORCESTER. John Chandler of Worcester, his will, by Charles A. Chase. Paper read before the Worcester society of antiquity ... 1905. Worcester, Mass., The Blanchard press (1907?) 15 p. 25 cm. 8-12261.   F74. W9 C43

WORCESTER'S north end. The Nathan Patch house. The Henchman farm. Two papers read before the Worcester society of antiquity ... 1902. By Charles A. Chase. Worcester, Mass., Press of C. Hamilton, 1903. 23 p. front. 25½ cm. Repr. from the Society's Proceedings v. 18. 7-26260.   F74. W9 C45

WORCESTER. The school history of Worcester. By Caroline Van Dusen Chenoweth. Worcester, Mass., O. B. Wood, 1899 (c.1898) 167 p. illus. 19 cm. Mar. 2, 99-7.   F74. W9 C5

WORCESTER. The citizen's and stranger's guide in the city of Worcester: containing a ... map of the city ... together with a safe directory to the best business establishments in the city. Worcester (Mass.) H. J. Howland (1848) 26 p. fold. map. 24°. 1-16177-M1.   F74. W9 C6

MASSACHUSETTS 339

WORCESTER. The executors of the will of the late A. Swan Brown ... present for sale ... the Hermitage and Wildwood Park, at Worcester, Mass. ...   J. E. Conant & co.   (Lowell, Mass., 1904)
20 ½ x 28 ½ cm.   F74. W9 C7

WORCESTER. Historical notes, on the early settlements of Worcester, with notices of the settlers, from the year 1665 to 1704, by Ellery B. Crane ... Worcester, Mass., Printed by C. Hamilton, 1885.
27 p.   front. (facsim.)   2 maps.   25 ½ cm.   7-26259.   F74. W9 C86

WORCESTER. Leading business men of Worcester and vicinity; embracing Millbury, Grafton, Westboro, Upton, Uxbridge, Leicester, Whitinsville. By C. H. Cummings. Illustrated. Boston, Mercantile pub. co., 1889.   (5)-304 p.   illus.   25 cm.   1-11706.   F74. W9 C9

WORCESTER. Jottings from Worcester's history, by U. Waldo Cutler. Worcester, Mass., Worcester historical soc., 1932.   viii, 11-142 p.   23 cm.   Originally printed in the periodical, "This week in Worcester."
32-12289.   F74. W9 C95

WORCESTER. Report of the Committee on historical research and marking local sites, of the Colonel Timothy Bigelow chapter, D. A. R.   Worcester (The Commonwealth press) 1903.   19 p. incl. plan.   18 cm.
3-29020.   Cover title: The first school house in Worcester.   F74. W9 D18

WORCESTER. The first school house in Worcester. Dedicatory exercises at the unveiling of the tablet ... 1903, upon the site of the school house where John Adams, second president of the U.S. taught from 1755 - 1758.   Taoblet placed and this record pub. by the Col. Timothy Bigelow chapter, D. A. R.   Worcester, Mass., Printed by the Commonwealth press (1903)   39 p. incl. front., pl.   18 ½ cm.
10-3140.   F74. W9 D19

WORCESTER. An address delivered at the dedication of the town hall, in Worcester on the second day of May, 1825. By John Davis.   Worcester, Print. W. Manning (1825)   36 p.   24 cm.   3-29026.
F74. W3 D2

WORCESTER. A list of the soldiers in the war of the revolution, from Worcester, Mass., with a record of their death and place of burial. Comp. and arranged by Mary Cochran Dodge.   Worcester, Mass., Col. Timothy Bigelow chapter, D. A. R. (1902)   28 p.   23 ½ cm.   3-32196.   F74. W9 D6

WORCESTER legends; incidents, anecdotes, reminiscences, etc., connected with the early history of Worcester and vicinity. Comp. by William A. Emerson, corrected by Franklin P. Rice ... (Worcester) Denholm & McKay co., 1905.   (61) p.   front., illus.   13 ½ x 19 ½ cm.   6-19691.   F74. W9 E5

WORCESTER. Exercises at the placing of a memorial stone and tablet near birthplace of George Bancroft, Salisbury street, Worcester, on the centennial of his birth ... 1900. (Worcester) Press of F. S. Blanchard (1900)   (8) p.   illus.   24 cm.   10-7223.   F74. W9 E9

WORCESTER, The story of (by) Albert Farnsworth ... (and) George B. O'Flynn ... Worcester (Mass.) The Davis press, inc., 1934.   4, (11)-214 p.   illus., diagrs.   19 ½ cm.   34-4839.   F74. W9 F24

WORCESTER. Fifty glimpses of Worcester and Lake Quinsigamond. An up-to-date booklet for the visitor, the resident, and for transmission to show something of Worcester, the most rapidly growing city in New England.   Worcester, Mass., The Denholm & McKay co., 1902.   (7) p. 29 l., (14) p. illus.
15 x 22 ½ cm.   12-32336.   F74. W9 F4

WORCESTER. Notes on the life and character of Dr. William Paine. By George E. Francis ... Worcester, Mass., Press of C. Hamilton, 1900.   17 p.   24 ½ cm.   From Proceedings of the Amer. antiquarian soc., 1900.
6-41001.   F74. W9 F8

WORCESTER. Dedication of the statue of the Hon. George Frisbie Hoar, Worcester ... 1908. (Worcester, Belisle print. & pub. co, 1908)   62 p.   pl., port.   25 cm.   10-3611.   F74. W9 G3

WORCESTER. Gleanings from the sources of the history of the Second parish, Worcester; by Samuel S. Green ... Worcester, Press of C. Hamilton, 1883.   22 p.   front. (port.)   2 pl.   25 ½ cm.   From Proceedings of the Amer. antiquarian soc., 1883.   1-11707.   F74. W9 G7

WORCESTER, England, and Worcester, Mass. by Samuel Swett Green ... Worcester, Mass., Press of F. S. Blanchard, 1908.   40 p.   4 pl. (incl. front.) 2 port. 25½ cm.   9-3124.   F74. W9 G9

WORCESTER. History of the Worcester guards and the Worcester city guards from 1840 to 1896. By Lieutenant S. Hathaway, Old guards of 1840. Worcester, Mass., F. S. Blanchard, printers, 1896. 67 p.   plates, ports.   23 cm.   8-36509.   F74. W9 H26

WORCESTER. A sketch of historical reality with the blendings of the romance of ideality. By Samuel Hathaway. Worcester, Mass., F. S. Blanchard, printers, 1897.   38 p. front. (port.) 23 cm.   Cover-title: Old Worcester.   7-26257.   F74. W9 H3

WORCESTER. Address delivered before the city government and citizens, on the 200th anniversary of Worcester ... 1884, by George F. Hoard. Worcester, Mass., Press of C. Hamilton, 1885. 43 p.   26½ cm.   1-11708.   F74. W9 H6

WORCESTER. The heart of the commonwealth: or, Worcester as it is; being a correct guide to all the public buildings and instituteion, and to some of the principal manufactories and shops ... With many engravings, and a new map of the city. Worcester, Mass., H. J. Howland, 1856. viii, (9) - 131 p.   illus., fold. plan.   22½ x 18½ cm.   1-11709 Additions.   F74. W9 H8

WORCESTER. Minatures of Worcester. By Thomas Wallace Jones. (Cincinnati, O., 1904) 8 x 10 cm.   F74. W9 J7

WORCESTER. ... Historical notes relating to the second settlement of Worcester, by Lincoln N. Kinnicutt ... Worcester, Mass., The Society, 1916.   19 p.   pl. (2 plans)   25 cm.   Reprinted from Proceedings of American antiquarian soc, 1916.   17-15504.   F74. W9 K5

WORCESTER. Carl's tour in Main street ... By John Stocker Coffin Knowlton. (4th ed.) Worcester, Mass., Sanford and Davis, 1889.   2; 246 p.   front.   19½ cm.   By J. S. C. Knowlton and Clarendon Wheelock. First pub. in the Worcester palladium in 1855 and reprinted in that paper, 1857-1858 and again in 1874.   14-10177.   F74. W9 K7

WORCESTER. Light. (A journal of social Worcester and her neighbors) v. 1 - 4; Mar. 1, 1890 - Feb. 27, 1892. Worcester, Mass. (F. E. Kennedy, etc.) 1890 - 92.   4 v. illus. (incl. ports.) plates. 31 cm.   weekly.   No more pub?   15-15658.   F74. W9 L4

WORCESTER. An address delivered on the consecration of the Worcester rural cemetery ... 1838. By Levi Lincoln. Boston, Dutton and Wentworth, printers, 1838.   36 p.   24 cm.   2-19346.   F74. W9 L45

WORCESTER. History of Worcester from its earliest settlement to Sept., 1836: with various notices relating to the history of Worcester county. By William Lincoln ... Worcester, M. D. Phillips, 1837. viii, 383 p.   23 cm.   1-11710.   F74. W9 L5

— Worcester, C. Hersey, 1862.   2 v. in 1.   fronts., 1 illus., ports. Paged continuously. 1-11711.   F74. W9 L6

WORCESTER, History of. From 1836 to 1861. With interesting reminiscences of the public men of Worcester. By Charles Hersey ... Worcester, H. J. Howland, 1860.   (In F74. W9L6 p. (313) - 448) A continuation of Lincoln's history.   1-11712.   F74. W9 L6

WORCESTER in the war of the revolution; embracing the acts of the town from 1765 to 1783 inclusive. With an appendix. By Albert A. Lovell. Worcester, Mass., Printed by Tyler & Seagrave, 1876. 128 p.   front., fold. plan.   25½ x 15 cm.   1-11713.   F74. W9 L9

WORCESTER, History of, in the war of the rebellion. By Abijah P. Marvin ... Worcester (Mass.) The author, 1870.   582 p.   front., ports., plan.   23½ cm.   1-16816.   F74. W9 M2

— New ed., with additions and corrections. Worcester (Mass.) The author, 1880.   iv, (3) - 606 p. front., pl., ports., plan.   23½ cm.   6-18864.   F74. W9 M22

WORCESTER. Svenskarne i Worcester, 1868 - 1898. Strödda anteckningar, historiker och biografier

MASSACHUSETTS

om svenskarne, deras lif och verksamhet i staden Worcester under de senaste 30 åren ... Worcester, Mass., Skandinavias bok-och tidningstryckeri, 1898.   2, 181 p. illus. 8°. Dec. 14, 98-91.

F74. W9 N7

WORCESTER. History of Worcester and its people, by Charles Nutt ... New York city, Lewis historical pub. co., 1919.   4 v. fronts., illus., plates (part col.) ports. 26 cm. Vols. 3-4 contain biographical matter. "Early settlers, their ancestry and descendants v. 1, p. (43) - 270. "Lists of Revolutionary soldiers..." v. 1 p. 557-564. 24-10997.   F74. W9 N9

WORCESTER, The story of (by) Thomas F. O'Flynn ... Boston, Little, Brown, 1910.   vii, 159 p. front. (port.) plates, maps. 19½ cm. 10-21352.

F74. W9 O3

WORCESTER, Random recollections of, 1839 - 1843. Being remarks made at a meeting of the Worcester society of antiquity held June 3, 1884. By Nathaniel Paine.   Worcester, Private press of F. P. Rice, 1885.   46 p. illus., 9 pl. (incl. front.) 2 plans. 27½ cm. 7-27755.

F74. W9 P14

WORCESTER. Societies, associations and clubs of Worcester. By Mr. Nathaniel Paine ... (Philadelphia? 1889?)   20 p. 28½ cm. Reprinted from the History of Worcester County. 8-10492.

F74. W9 P15

WORCESTER'S old common; remarks made at the annual banquet of the Worcester board of trade ... 1901, by Nathaniel Paine. Worcester, Priv. print. (Press of F. S. Blanchard) 1901.   (21) p. illus. 26 cm. 25 copies printed. 42-40085.

F74. W9 P16

WORCESTER. Five hundred past and present citizens of Worcester. Photographed by Claflin, Worcester, and Black, Boston. (Worcester?) G. R. Peckham, 1870.   504 port. on 56 mounted phot. 19 x 16 cm. 7-29670.

F74. W9 P3

WORCESTER. The physical geography of Worcester. By Joseph H. Perry ... with illustrations by J. Chauncey Lyford. Worcester, Mass., Worcester natural history soc., 1898.   40 p. plates. 24 cm. 1-16590.

F74. W9 P4

WORCESTER. Men of Worcester in caricature; drawings by L. C. Phifer. Worcester, Mass., L. C. Phifer, 1917.   2, 281, (3) p. illus. 26½ cm. 17-19710.

F74. W9 P54

WORCESTER. Proceedings at the semi-centennial anniversary of the connection of Caleb Arnold Wall, (of the Worcester spy.) with the Worcester County press ... 1887. Worcester, Mass., Press of D. Seagrave, 1887.   33 p. 24 cm. 3-29111.

F74. W9 P9

WORCESTER. Dictionary of Worcester and its vicinity. With maps of the city and of Worcester county. 1st issue. Worcester, F. S. Blanchard, 1889.   103, (4) p. fold. maps (incl. front.) 18½ cm. 1-11714.

F74. W9 R4

— 2d issue. Reprinted from the Worcester commercial. Worcester, F. S. Blanchard, 1893.   135 p. 20½ cm. 1-11715.

F74. W9 R5

WORCESTER. A souvenir of ye Old south meetin' house. 1719. By Franklin Pierce Rice. Worcester, Mass. 1887. (Worcester, F. S. Blanchard, 1887)   24 p. illus, (incl. facsims.) 29½ cm. Published anonymously. 4-33411.

F74. W9 R6

WORCESTER. A summary military history of Worcester. By Franklin P. Rice ... Worcester, Mass., Putnam, Davis, 1895.   12 p. 24 cm. 45-46476.

F74. W9 R62

WORCESTER. The Worcester book: a diary of noteworthy events in Worcester, from 1657 to 1883. By Franklin P. Rice ... Worcester, Putnam, Davis, 1884.   159 p. front., plates, plan. 26 x 15 cm. In calendar from. 1-11716.

F74. W9 R7

WORCESTER. The Worcester of 1898. Fifty years a city. A graphic presentation of its institutions, industries and leaders. Ed. Franklin P. Rice. Worcester, Mass., F. S. Blanchard, 1899.   809 p. incl. front., illus. (incl. ports.) 27 cm. 99-3659 Rev.

F74. W9 R8

WORCESTER. Public libraries (of Worcester) By Samuel Swett Green ...   p. (199) - 219 of above title.

WORCESTER. "Catholicity and its growth in Worcester." By John J. Riordan ... (Boston, 1897?)
(22) p. illus. (incl. ports.) 23½ cm. From Donahoe's magazine, Dec., 1897. 8-4636.
F74. W9 R84

WORCESTER. An address delivered at the opening of the new court house in Worcester ... 1845, by the Hon. Lemuel Shaw ... Worcester, Printed by H. J. Howland, 1845. 14 p. 22 cm. 13-23474.
F74. W9 S3

WORCESTER. Skandinavisk adresskalender öfver Worcester, Mass. ... Worcester, Mass., T. Hanson (1907) - 1910. 2 v. 24 cm. 10-11223.
F74. W9 S4

WORCESTER. The city of Worcester; its public buildings and its business. By Henry M. Smith. (Worcester) Sanford & Davis, 1886. 63 p. illus. 18 cm. 1-11717 rev.*
F74. W9 S6

WORCESTER. Old landmarks and historic spots of Worcester, by John Pearl Spears ... Worcester, Mass., Commonwealth press, 1931. 6, 164 p. front., plates. 24 cm. 31-10066.
F74. W9 S65

WORCESTER. Ecclesiastical history of the city of Worcester, by Charles Emery Stevens ... (Philadelphia, 1889) 41 p. 28½ cm. Repr. from Hurd's History of Worcester County v.2. 9-30376.
F74. W9 S7

WORCESTER. Old Worcester, about 1840. Fourth paper in continuation ... By Mrs. E. O. P. Sturgis. Worcester, Mass., 1902. 25½ cm.
F74. W9 S8

WORCESTER. The city of Worcester and vicinity and their resouces ... comp. ... by J. H. Sutherland. Worcester, Mass., The Worcester spy, 1901. 124 p. incl. pl., port. pl. 28 x 36½ cm. 3-8594.
F74. W9 S9

WORCESTER. The theatre and public halls of Worcester. Worcester, Mass., Putnam & Davis, 1880. 12 p. 16°. 1-21603-M1.
F74. W9 T35

— 3d ed. with latest revision. Worcester, Mass., 1883) 16 p. 16°. 1-11718-9-M1.
F74. W9 T37

— 4th ed. Worcester, Putnam, Davis, (1888) 20 p. 16°. 1-11718-9-M1.
F74. W9 T38

WORCESTER. This week in Worcester and county. (Worcester, Mass., This week in Worcester county, inc., etc., 19 - v. illus. (incl. ports.) 27½ cm. 42-31534 Rev.
F74. W9 T39

WORCESTER. The diary of Isaiah Thomas. 1805 - 1828. 1909. 2 v.
F74. W9 T4

WORCESTER, city of prosperity. 16th annual convention National metal trades association, the Bancroft, Worcester ... 1914. By Donald Tulloch ... Worcester, Mass. (The Commonwealth press) 1914. 324 p. illus. (incl. ports., plans) diagrs. 23 cm. 14-18940.
F74. W9 T9

WORCESTER centennial, 1848 - 1948; historical sketches of the settlement, the town and the city. Worcester of 1948. Comp. and written by Midlred McClary Tymeson ... Worcester, Mass., Worcester Centennial, 1948. 83 p. illus., port., maps. 28 cm. 48-4460*.
F74. W9 T96

WORCESTER. An ancient instance of municipal ownership. By Samuel Utley. (In American antiquarian soc. Proceedings, v.17, 1907) 12-6379.
F74. W9 U9

WORCESTER, Views of ... (Portland, Me., 1905) 20½ x 25 cm.
F74. W9 V6

WORCESTER. North Worcester: its first settlers and old farms. An historical address, delivered before the Chamberlain district farmers' club, at the residence of A. S. Lowell, North Worcester ... 1889. By Caleb A. Wall ... Worcester, The author, 1890. 21 p. 23½ cm. 1-11720 Rev.
F74. W9 W1

WORCESTER. Eastern Worcester: its first settlers and their locations. Historical and genealogical. In three chapters. By Caleb A. Wall ... Worcester, Pub. by the author, 1891. 52 p. 23 cm. 7-26255.
F74. W9 W16

WORCESTER, Reminiscences of, from the earliest period, historical and genealogical, with notices of

MASSACHUSETTS

early settlers and prominent citizens. and descriptions of old landmarks and ancient dwellings ... By Caleb A. Wall. Worcester, Mass., Printed by Tyler Seagrave, 1877.   viii, (9) - 392 p. front., plates, port., fold. map, fold. plan.   24 cm.   1-11721.
F74. W9 W2

WORCESTER, Tornado in; an exploratory study of individual and community behavior in an extreme situation.   By Anthony F. Wallace.   Washington, National Academy of Sciences, National Research Council, 1956.   xi, 165 p. illus., maps. 28 cm. (National Research Council. Disaster study no. 3) Publication no. 392. Bibliography: p. 161 - 163.   56-60015.
F74. W9 W25

WORCESTER.   Address upon the celebration of the 200th anniversary of the adoption by the General court of a resolve vesting the inhabitants of Worcester with the powers and privilages of other towns within the Province.   (By) Charles G. Washburn.   Worcester, Mass., The Davis press, 1922.   35 p.   23 cm.   24-17109.
F74. W9 W27

WORCESTER.   Manufacturing and mechanical industries of Worcester ... by Charles G. Washburn. Philadelphia, J. W. Lewis, 1889.   68 p.   4°.   Reprinted from the History of Worcester co.   1-11722-M1.
F74. W9 W3

WORCESTER.   Smith's barn; "a child's history" of the West side, Worcester, 1880 - 1923, by R. M. Washburn ... Worcester, Printed by the Commonwealth press ... 1923.   147 p. front. (port.)   21 cm. Lettered on cover: Profiles of pertinent people.   23-9053.
F74. W9 W35

WORCESTER.   Early roads and the dwellers thereon in the northern portion of Worcester.   A paper prepared by Henry M. Wheeler, for the Worcester soc. of antiquity ... Worcester, 1904.   58 p.   25½ cm.   Reprinted from v. 20 of the Proceedings of the Society.   7-26254.
F74. W9 W52

WORCESTER.   Recollections of two New England houses.   Built by Rev. Joseph Wheeler, of Worcester.   A paper read before the Worcester soc. of antiquity ... 1903.   By Henry M. Wheeler ... Worcester, Mass., The Hamilton press, 1904.   39 p.   2 pl.   25½ cm.   Reprinted from v. 19 of the Proceedings of the Society.   7-26253.
F74. W9 W55

WORCESTER.   Celebration by the inhabitants of Worcester, Mass., of the centennial anniversary of the Declaration of independence.   July 4, 1876.   To which are added historical and chronological notes. Worcester, Printed by order of the City council, 1876.   146 p.   pl., facsims. (2 fold.)   23½ cm.   1-16781.
F74. W9 W65

WORCESTER.   Celebration by the inhabitants of Worcester, of the centennial anniversary of the Declaration of independence ... 1876.   To which are added historical and chronological notes.   Worcester, Printed by order of the City council, 1876.   146 p. pl., facsim. 29 cm. 10-31032.
F74.W9W651

WORCESTER.   1684.   1884.   Celebration of the 200th anniversary of the naming of Worcester ... 1884.   Worcester, Mass., Printed by order of the City council, 1885.   176 p. front. (facsim.) plans.   23½ cm.   Bibliography (by N. Paine): p. (167) - 174.   1-11724.
F74. W9 W67

—   29 cm.   1-11725.
F74.W9W671

WORCESTER.   Ceremonies at the laying of the corner-stone of the new City hall in Worcester ... 1896, and at the dedication of the building ... 1898, with an account of the semi-centennial celebration of the incorporation of Worcester as a city ... 1898.   Worcester, Mass., Pub. by order of the City council, 1898.   86 p.   26 cm.   1-11726.
F74. W9 W69

WORCESTER births, marriages and deaths.   Comp. by Franklin P. Rice ... Worcester, Mass., Worcester society of antiquity, 1894.   527 p.   25 cm. (Collections of the Worcester soc. of antiquity, v.xii (no. 42-44)   1-21330 Rev.
F74. W9 W71
L. H. & G.

WORCESTER semi-centennial ... 1898.   (Worcester, Sanford-Sawtelle co., stationers & engravers, 1898)   (4) p. illus. (incl. ports.)   21 x 17 cm.   7-29233.
F74. W9 W72

WORCESTER town records ... (1722 - 1848) ed. by Franklin P. Rice.   Worcester, Mass., The Worcester soc. of antiquity, 1879 - 95.   7 v. in 6. plans (1 double) 25 cm. (Worcester soc. of antiqutity Collections. vol 2, no. 6, 8; 4, no. 14-16; 8, no. 28-30; 9, no. 32-34; 11, no. 36-38; 15, no. 48-51)   3-9539.
F74.W9W725

WORCESTER. The new city hall in Worcester; a testimonial to the City hall commission from the City council. Worcester (Press of F. S. Blanchard) 1899. (7)-146 p. 10 pl. (incl. front.) 6 ports., 2 plans. 7-26263. F74.W9 W73

WORCESTER. Dedication of the soldiers' monument at Worcester ... 1874 ... Worcester, Printed by order ot the Monument committee, 1875. 90 p. front. 27½ cm. 9-11009. F74.W9 W74

WORCESTER. (Worcester, Mass. 1909) 1 v. 20½ x 25 cm. F74.W9 W75

WORCESTER and its points of interest; with illustrations from original photographs. New York, Mercantile illustrating co., 1895. 120 (3) p. illus. 20½ x 27½ cm. Sketches of the business firms of Worcester. 7-27741. F74.W9W753

WORCESTER. Forty immortals of Worcester & its county. A brief account of those natives or residents who have accomplished something for their community or for the nation. (Worcester, Mass.) Issued by the Worcester bank and trust co., 1920. 72 p. incl. front., ports. 24½ cm. A22-573. F74.W9W754

WORCESTER. Historic events of Worcester; a brief account of some of the most interesting events which have occurred in Worcester during the past 200 years, issued by the Worcester bank and trust co. in commemoration of the 200th anniversary of the incorporation of the town of Worcester. (Worcester, Mass.) 1922. vii, 63 p. incl. front., illus. 23½ cm. 22-5375. F74.W9W7542

WORCESTER. Some historic houses of Worcester; a brief account of the houses and taverns that fill a prominent part in the history of Worcester, together with interesting reminiscences of their occupants. Illus. with rare prints and photos. (Worcester) Print. for Worcester bank & trust co., 1919. vii, (1), 71 p. incl. front., illus. 23½ cm. "Authorities consulted": p. 71. 20-2719. F74.W9W7545

WORCESTER bi-centennial. (2d ed.) Worcester, Mass., F. S. Blanchard, 1884. 12 p. illus. (incl. facsims.) 58 cm. (With Worcester bi-centennial., 1884) 10-11237. F74.W9W755

WORCESTER bi-centennial. Worcester, Mass., F. S. Blanchard, 1884. 12 p. illus. (incl. facsims.) 57½ cm. 4-35811. F74.W9W7552

WORCESTER, the city of varied industries. An old New England municipality rendered pre-eminent by inventive genius ... 1658 to 1909. Worcester, The Blanchard press (1909) (22) p. illus. 22 cm. 10-8689. F74.W9 W76

WORCESTER, heart of the commonwealth of Massachusetts ... Chamber of commerce. (Worcester, The Davis press, 1921?) 11 p. illus. 23 x 10 cm. CA 26-162 Unrev. F74.W9 W77

WORCESTER city guide and street directory ... with map. Worcester, Drew Allis co., v. fold. map. 16½ cm. 11-16288. F74.W9W775

WORCESTER. Dedication of the equestrian statue of Major-General Charles Devens and of the monument to the soldiers of Worcester County in the war for the union ... 1906. Worcester, Mass. (The Commonwealth press) 1907. (38) p. front. (port.) 4 pl. 23½ cm. 7-23559. F74.W9W78

WORCESTER daily spy. Industrial ed. June 1770 - June, 1896, 126th anniversary ... (Worcester, Mass., 1896) (16) p. illus. (incl. port.) 60 cm. Seven columns to the page. 4-27590. F74.W9 W79

WORCESTER Fire Society. Reminiscences and biographical notices of past members. (1st) - ser. Worcester, 1870 - 19 v. in 26 cm. 7-18598 rev.* F74.W9 W8

WORCESTER. Sketches of fifteen members of Worcester fire society, by Isaac Davis. Worcester, Printed by C. Hamilton, 1874. 17 p. 25 cm. 7-27753. F74.W9 W82

WORCESTER. The history, articles of faith, covenant, and standing rules, of the First church in Worcester, with a catalogue of its officers and members. April 1, 1864. Worcester, Adams & Brown, printers (1864) 41 p. 19 cm. 9-30371. F74.W9 W83

MASSACHUSETTS 345

WORCESTER. Manual and catalogue of the (First church) Old south, Worcester ... 1877. Organized ... 1716. Worcester, Noyes, Snow, printers, 1877. 44 p. front. 19½ cm. 8-4632. F74.W9W834

WORCESTER historical society. ... Bulletin. (Worcester, 19 - v. 23 cm. 42-47409. F74.W9 W84

WORCESTER society of antiquity, Collections of the. v. 1 - 16. Worcester, Mass., The Society, 1881 - 99. 16 v. in 17. illus., plates, ports., plans, facsim., tables, diagrs. 25 cm. Issued in parts numbered 1-54 in order of publication, but not always consecutive in the volumes. Includes the following: Proceedings ... 1875-99 (in v. 1, 2, 5-7, 9, 13, 14, 16) Worcester town records, 1722-1848 (in v. 2, 4, 8, 10, 11, 15) Inscriptions from the old burial grounds ... 1727 to 1859: with biographical and historical notes (in v. 1) Records of the proprietors ... (in v. 3) Records of the court of general sessions of the peace ... 1731-1737 (in v. 5) The abolitionists vindicated ... (in v. 7) Worcester births, marriages and deaths (in v. 12) Superseded by Proceedings of the Worcester society of antiquity, which continues the volume numbering of the Collections, i.e. v. 17, etc. 4-20343-5 Rev. F74. W9 W85

— A list of historical, biographical, genealogical and other papers; burial ground inscriptions; proprietary, town and court records; births, marriages and deaths, contained in the first fifteen volumes of Collections of the Worcester soc. of antiquity. Prepared by Franklin P. Rice ... 1897. (Worcester, Press of F. S. Blanchard, 1898?) 4 p. (With its Collections. v.15) 4-20343-5 Rev. F74. W9 W85

WORCESTER society of antiqutity, Proceedings of the ... 1875 - 1911. Worcester, Mass., The Society, 1881 - 1914. 25 v. in 26. illus., plates, ports., maps, facsims., tables, diagrs. 25 cm. The Proceedings for 1875 to 1899, inclusive, form part of the society's Collections; beginning with 1900, the Proceedings replace the Collections and continue their volume numbering v. 17 - 25. Continued as: Publications ... new series. 3-9540 Rev. F74. W9 W85

WORCESTER society of antiquity, Constitution and by-laws of the ... Worcester, Mass., The Society, 1879. 11 p. 25½ cm. 4-378 Rev. F74.W9W853

WORCESTER historical society ... Officers, committees, list of members, etc. (Worceser, 19 v. 16 cm. 24-10987. F74.W9W8575

WORCESTER historical society ... Publications ... new series, no. 1 - April, 1928 - Worcester, Mass., The Worcester historical soc. (1928 - v. 22½ cm. 29-7557. F74.W9W858

WORCESTER historical society ... 25th anniversary. (menu) (1900) 1 v. F74.W9W859

WORCESTER historical society. Report of committee charged with placing the memorial to mark the birthplace of George Bancroft, America's foremost historian ... With brief account of the formal exercises. 1900 ... Worcester (1900) 24 p. front., pl., ports. 23½ cm. Reprinted from Proceedings of the Worcester soc. of antiquity, Oct. 1900. 10-3156 Rev. F74.W9W8595

WORCESTER illustrated. 1875. Worcester, Mass., J. A. Ambler (1875) 56 p. illus. 23½ cm. 1-11729. F74. W9 W86

WORCESTER in 1850. Worcester (Mass.) H. J. Howland (1850) 64 p. illus., 2 fold. maps (incl. front.) 16 cm. The greater part of the material for this sketch is taken from Lincoln's History of Worcester. 1-11730. F74.W9W861

WORCESTER: its past and present. A brief historical review of 200 years, with an exhibit of the industries and resources of the city at the commencement of the third century of her existence ... with a descriptions of points of interest, etc., biographical sketches and portraits ... Worcester, Mass., O. B. Wood, 1888. 247 p. front., illus., 19 port. 32½ x 27½ cm. 3-18808. F74.W9W863

WORCESTER magazine, The; devoted to good citizenship and municipal development. v. 1 - 13; Jan. 1901 - Dec., 1910. Worcester, Mass., Press of F. S. Blanchard, (1901 - 10) 13 v. illus., plates, ports., maps. 25 cm. monthly. Pub. by the Board of trade. 5-35731. F74.W9W865

WORCESTER records, The. Proceedings at a dinner given at the Lincoln House in Worcester ... 1897, to Franklin P. Rice in recognition of work accomplished in the development of systematic history. (Worcester? Mass., 1897?) 34 p. 25 x 15 cm. 1-11723. F74. W9 W87

WORCESTER, the heart of the commonwealth. (Philadelphia, 1905) 20 x 25 cm. F74. W9W 92

WORCESTER vest pocket guide.   Cambridge, Mass., M. King (1882)   96 p.   9 cm.   7-26250.   F74.W9 W93

WORCESTER historical society.   Circular, May 20, 1911 ...   F74.W9 W95

WORCESTER'S 200th anniversary, 1684 - 1884.   Worcester, Mass., H. R. Cummings, 1884.
(8) p.   43 cm.   Bound with: Worcester bi-centennial (2d ed.) Copy 2.   F74.W9 W97

WORCESTER bi-centennial (2d ed.)   Worcester, Mass., F. S. Blanchard, 1884.   12 p. 58 cm.
F74.W9W755

WORTHINGTON.   Secular and ecclesiastical history of the town of Worthington, from its first settlement to the present time.   By James Clay Rice.   Albany, N.Y., Weed, Parsons & co., printers, 1853.   72 p.   23 cm.   1-11731.   F74.W93 R5

WORTHINGTON, Vital records of, to the year 1850.   Boston, New England historic genealogical soc., ... 1911.   159 p.   23 ½ cm.   12-40168.   F74.W93 W9

WRENTHAM.   A sermon delivered at Wrentham ... 1773, on compleating the first century since the town was incorporated.   By Joseph Bean ...   Boston, Printed by John Boyle, 1774.   36 p. 20 cm.
15-2153.
F74.W95 B3
Rare Book Coll.

WRENTHAM.   History and directory of Wrentham and Norfolk for 1890.   Containing a complete resident, street and business directory, etc.   History of the towns, from the first settlement to the present time, by Samuel Warner.   Comp. and pub. by A. E. Foss, Needham.   Boston, Press of Brown bros., 1890.   141 p.   23 ½ cm.   The historical sketches are taken from the History of Norfolk County by D. H. Hurd, 1884.
10-31055.   F74.W95 W2

WRENTHAM, Vital records of, to the year 1850 ...   Comp. by Thomas W. Baldwin ...   Boston, Mass. (Stanhope press, F. H. Gilson co.) 1910.   2 v.   23 ½ cm.   10-33151 Additions.   F74.W95 W8
Geneal. Section Ref.

YARMOUTH.   Gravestone records in the Ancient cemetery and the Woodside cemetery, Yarmouth, ... comp. by George Ernest Bowman ...   Boston, Mass., Massachusetts Society of Mayflower descendants ... 1906.   47 p.   25 cm.   6-5688.   F74. Y2 B7

YARMOUTH.   Early days of Yarmouth in Plymouth colony; written specially for the Yarmouth centenary, by Ella W. Bray.   South Yarmouth, Cape Cod, The Wayside studio (1939)   16 p.   20 cm.   39-19039.
F74.Y 2 B 8

YARMOUTH.   A history of the First Congregational church, Yarmouth, in a discourse delivered ... 1873, by John W. Ddoge.   Yarmouth Port, Mass., Register steam job print., 1873.   59 p.   24 cm.
6-15330.   F74. Y2 D6

YARMOUTH.   The glory of the church.   A sermon preached at the dedication of the new edifice of the First Congregational church, Yarmouth ... 1870, by ... Rev. J. W. Dodge.   Yarmouth Port, Register job print., 1871.   22 p.   21 ½ cm.   (Bound with above item) 6-15331.   F74. Y2 D6

YARMOUTH.   ... Captain William Hedge of Yarmouth, by James W. Hawes.   Yarmouthport, Mass., C. W. Swift, 1914.   4 p. 25 ½ cm. (Library of Cape Cod history & genealogy no. 44) 14-21054.   F74.Y2 H39

YARMOUTH.   ... Ancient houses, by Capt. Thomas Prince Howes.   Yarmouthport, Mass., C. W. Swift, 1911.   (6) p.   25 ½ cm.   (Library of Cape Cod history & genealogy, no. 96) 12-39469.   F74. Y2 H8

YARMOUTH.   Summer street - Hawes lane, Yarmouthport...   By Ellen H. Shields.   1928.
(Library of Cape Cod history and genealogy no. 4)   F74. Y2 S5

YARMOUTH.   History of old Yarmouth.   Comprising the present towns of Yarmouth and Dennis. From the settlement to the division in 1794 with the history of both towns to these times.   By Charles F. Swift.   Yarmouth Port, The author, 1884.   281, (2) p.   ports., map, etc. 22 ½ cm.   1-15954.   F74. Y2 S9

MASSACHUSETTS

YARMOUTH. A discourse delivered 150 years ago. By George Weekes, of Harwich, Mass. With a preface by Sidney Brooks, a descendant. Cambridge (Mass.) Press of J. Wilson, 1876. xvi, 5 - 30, 24 p. 19½ cm. 13-18892 Rev.
F74. Y2 W3

YARMOUTH. ... West Yarmouth's houses 75 years ago from Parker's River westward, by Daniel Wing. Yarmouthport, Mass., C. W. Swift, 1915. 21 p. 25½ cm. (Library of Cape Cod history & genealogy. no. 39) 17-20838.
F74. Y2 W7

YARMOUTH. The celebration of the 250th anniversary of the founding of old Yarmouth, including the present towns of Yarmouth and Dennis. ... 1889. Yarmouth, Pub. by the Committee, 1889. 147 p. incl. front., plates. pl. 23½ cm. 8-9207.
F74. Y2 Y2

ELEMENTS IN THE POPULATION.

ALBANIANS. The Albanian struggle in the old world and new, compiled and written by members of the Federal writers' project of the W.P.A. Boston, The Writer, inc., 1939. ix, 3 - 168 p. plates, facsim. 20½ cm. Bibliography: p. 162 - 163. 39-27485.
F75. A
DR701. S5F4

ACADIANS. ... Des Acadiens déportés à Boston, en 1755. (Un épisode du grand dérangement.) Par Pascal Poirier. Ottawa, Impr. pour la Société royale du Canada, 1909. 125 - 180 p. 24 cm. (Des Mémoires de la Société royale du Canada vol. II, section I) 9-29266.
F75. A
F1038. P75

ARMENIANS. Historical review, contributions to civilization: of the Armenians, French, Germans, Greeks, Italians, Letts, Lithuanians, Poles, Russians, Swedes, Syrians, Ukrainians. Issued by the Committee on racial groups of the Mass. bay tercentenary, inc., 1630: 1930. (Boston? 1930?) (98) p. 23 cm. Twelve different articles by different authors. 32-34841.
F75. A1 M25

ARMENIANS. ... The Armenians in Massachusetts, written and compiled by the Federal writer's project of the W.P.A. for the state of Massachusetts. The Armenian historical soc., cooperating sponsor ... Boston, The Armenian historical soc., 1937. 148, (5) p. incl. plates (incl. music) ports., facsims. 20½ cm. (American guide series) Bibliography: p. (147) - 148. 38-4823.
F75. A7 F4

CHINESE. "... The Chinese of the eastern states." With the compliments of the Société historique franco-américaine, Boston, Mass. Manchester, N.H., L'Avenir national pub. co., 1925. 23 p. 23½ cm. Reprinted from L'Avenir national, Nov. 19, 1924. 27-3887.
F75. F8
F15. F8 C5

FRIENDS. ...Wenlock Christison, and the early Friends in Talbot County, Maryland ... By Samuel A. Harrison. Baltimore (Print. J. Murphy) 1878. 2, vii-viii, 5 - 76 p. 24½ cm. (Maryland historical soc. Fund publication, no. 12) Relates largely to the persecution of the Quakers in Massachusetts. 1-Rc-3368.
F75. F9
F176. M 37

FRIENDS. A Declaration of the General Court of the Massachusetts ... 1659. Concerning the execution of two Quakers. Printed by their order in New-England. Reprinted in London, 1659. (Boston, 1927) facsim.: broadside. 33½ x 25 cm. fold. to 19 x 12½ cm. photostat by the Mass. hist. soc. no. 194) CA28-251 unrev. With this is bound: A true relation of the Proceedings against certain Quakers, etc. ... 1659.
F75. F9
F67. M334

FRIENDS. Early history of the Puritans, Quakers and Indians, with a biography of the Quaker martyr Lawrence Southwick, emigrant founder of the Southwick family in America, etc. (Lynn, 1931) 20 p. illus. 23 cm. Signed: Walter H. Southwick. 31-22364.
F75. F9 S7

GREEKS. Immigrant races in Massachusetts. The Greeks. Written tor the Mass. Bureau of immigration by William I. Cole ... (Boston? 1919?) (6) p. 24 cm. 21-27176.
F75. G7 C6

IRISH. Charitable Irish society, founded 1737; its constitution and by-laws, with a list of officers and members, etc. etc. Boston, Mass., The Society, 1917. 124 p. fold. tab. 15 cm. CA24-314 Unrev.
F75. I 6 C4

IRISH.   The pre-revolutionary Irish in Massachusetts, 1620 - 1775, by George Francis Donovan ...
(Menasha, Wis., George Banta pub. co., 1932)   4; 158 p.   23 cm.   Thesis - St. Louis university, 1931.   Bibliography:
p. (140) - 153.   33-1538.   F75. I 6 D 8

IRISH.   The constitution and by-laws, of the Hibernian relief society, instituted ... 1827.   To which
is added, sundry resolutions, etc.   Boston, J. G. Scobie, printer, 1827.   24 p.   16 cm.   11-22429.
                                                                                                                                  F75. I 6 H 6

ITALIANS.   Leading Americans of Italian descent in Massachusetts, by Joseph William Carlevale ...
Foreword by Daniel L. Marsh ... Plymouth, Mass., Print. the Memorial press (1946)   861 p.   20 cm.
"Companion volume to .. (the author's) Who's who among Americans of Italian descent in Connecticut." 46-7410.   F75. I 8 C 3

JEWISH.   Early Jewish residents in Massachusetts.   By Lee M. Friedman ... (Baltimore, 1915)
79 - 90 p.   25 cm.   Reprinted from Publications of the Amer. Jewish historical soc., no. 23, 1915.   18-6566.   F75. J 5 F 8

MASSACHUSETTS
SUPPLEMENTARY INDEX OF PLACES

ABINGTON. 395, 522
ACCUSHNET. 433, 434
ACTON. 430
ADAMS. 505
AGAWAM. 332
AGAWAM CENTER. 541
ALFORD. 314
ALLSTON. 351
AMESBURY. 533
AMHERST. 460, 506
ARLINGTON. 352
ASHBURNHAM. 450, 565
ASHBY. 400, 450
ASHFORD. 325, 331
ASHLAND. 400, 451, 492
ASHLEY FALLS. 314
ATHOL. 456, 567
ATTLEBOROUGH. 521
AUBURN. 347, 547
AVON. 344, 520
AYER. 450, 537
BAKER'S ISLAND. 533
BALDWINVILLE. 347, 450
BARNSTABLE. 318, 322, 534
BARNSTABLE Co. 236, 321
BARRE. 347
BARRINGTON. 521
BAYBERRY BEACH. 487
BEDFORD. 430
BELCHERTOWN. 332, 347
BELMONT. 556
BERLIN. 467, 471
BERNARDSTON. 331
BEVERLY. 329, 526, 527, 532, 533
BLACKSTONE. 490
BLANDFORD. 325, 332, 559
BOLTON. 467, 471
BONDSVILLE. 553
BOSTON. 242 - 268, 309, 524
BOURNE. 318, 402, 534
BOXFORD. 468, 523
BOYLESTON. 347
BRADFORD. 462, 523
BRAINTREE. 352, 518, 520, 559
BREWSTER. 318, 462
BRIDGEWATER. 412
BRIGHTON. 351
BRIMFIELD. 347, 539

BRISTOL Co. 236
BROCKTON. 421
BROOKFIELD. 332, 505, 540
BROOKS VILLAGE. 347
BUCKLAND. 331, 456
BUZZARD'S BAY. 486
BYFIELD. 468
CAMBRIDGE. 351, 352, 376, 399, 405
CANTON. 344, 468
CAPE ANNE. 244, 309, 329, 454
CAPE COD. 313, 318
CARLISLE. 430
CARVER. 345
CEDAR NECK. 334
CHARLEMONT. 325, 331
CHARLESTOWN. 349, 351, 566
CHARLTON. 539
CHATHAM. 314, 318, 462
CHELMSFORD. 406, 477
CHELSEA. 352
CHESHIRE. 396
CHESTER. 325, 332, 559
CHESTERFIELD. 325, 331 332
CHESTNUT HILL. 351
CHICOPEE. 332, 541
CLAYTON. 314
CLINTON. 450, 567
COCHITUATE. 451, 486, 561
COHASSET. 464, 465, 495
COLLINSVILLE. 477
COLRAIN. 325, 331
CONCORD. 308, 369, 376, 475
CONWAY. 325, 331, 332
COTUIT. 314.
COTTAGE HILL. 565
CUMBERLAND. 521
CUMMINGTON. 325, 331, 332
DALTON. 403, 473
DANIELSVILLE. 556
DANVERS. 405, 526, 527, 532, 533
DARTMOUTH. 396, 499
DEDHAM. 344, 352, 468
DEERFIELD. 325, 331, 332, 456, 506
DENNIS. 314, 318, 402, 462, 576, 577
DENNISPORT. 314
DIGHTON. 538
DOGTOWN. 454
DORCHESTER. 349, 369, 381, 421, 523

DORCHESTER NECK. 390
DOVER. 496
DRACUT. 406, 477
DUDLEY. 539, 556
DUNSTABLE. 511
EAST BROOKFIELD. 540
EAST & WEST DENNIS. 314
EAST DOUGLASS. 586
EAST & WEST HARWICH. 314
EAST LONGMEADOW. 332, 541
EAST TEMPLETON. 347
EAST WEYMOUTH. 562
EASTHAM. 318
EASTHAMPTON. 332
EASTON. 344, 421
EGREMONT. 314
ENFIELD. 347
ERVING. 331, 347
ESSEX. 405, 453, 469
ESSEX Co. 346, 482
EVERETT. 352
FAIRHAVEN. 434, 452
FALL RIVER. 452
FALMOUTH. 318, 402, 408
FEEDING HILLS. 541
FITCHBURG. 347, 400, 480, 567
FORGE VILLAGE. 477
FOXBORO. 344, 484
FRAMINGHAM. 400, 536
FRAMINGHAM CENTRE. 451
FRANKLIN. 344
FRANKLIN County. 332, 347
FREETOWN. 449
GARDNER. 450, 567
GEORGETOWN. 326, 462, 468, 523
GIL BERNARDSTON. 456
GILL. 331
GLEASONDALE. 467
GLENDALE. 314
GLOUCESTER. 331, 483
GOSHEN. 325, 331, 332
GRAFTON. 347, 547, 569
GRANBY. 325, 332, 460
GRANITEVILLE. 477
GRANVILLE. 325, 332, 559
GRANVILLE CENTER. 559
GRASSY ISLAND. 243
GREAT BARRINGTON. 314
GREEN HARBOR. 487
GREENFIELD. 567
GREENWICH. 347
GROSVENORDALE. 556

GROTON. 402
GROVELAND. 462, 463
HADLEY. 325, 397, 506
HAMILTON. 469, 527
HAMPDEN. 332, 347, 541
HAMPDEN Co. 326, 331, 541.
HAMPSHIRE. 331
HAMPSHIRE Co. 332
HAMPTON. 533
HANCOCK. 403
HANSON. 345
HARDWICK. 347
HARTSVILLE. 314
HARWICH. 314, 318
HARWICHPORT. 314
HATFIELD. 325, 332, 460, 506, 563
HAWARD. 402, 471
HAWLEY. 325 331
HAYDENVILLE. 332
HEATH. 331
HIGHLAND COMMUNITY. 542
HINSDALE. 403, 473
HOLBROOK. 344, 409, 520
HOLDEN. 347
HOLLIS. 443
HOLLISTON. 451, 492, 536
HOLLY HILL. 487
HOLYOKE. 332, 541, 567
HOPEDALE. 490, 492
HOPKINTON. 451, 492
HOUSATONIC. 314
HUBBARDSTON. 400, 450
HUDSON. 443, 486
HULL. 464
HUNTINGTON. 332, 426, 559
HYANNIS. 314, 319
HYDE PARK. 351
INTERLAKEN. 314
JUNIPER POINT. 329
KINGSTON. 444, 513
LAKE QUINSIGAMOND. 569
LAKEVILLE. 345
LANESBORO. 403
LEE. 403
LEICESTER. 347, 569
LENOX. 403, 473
LEOMINSTER. 450, 471, 537, 567
LEVERETT. 325, 332, 347, 547
LEWIS BAY. 320
LEXINGTON. 308, 352, 376
LEYDEN. 325, 331
LINCOLN. 430, 553, 556, 561

LINWOOD. 507
LITCHFIELD. 443
LITTLETON. 402
LONGMEADOW. 332
LOWELL. 308, 406
LUDLOW. 332, 347, 541
LUNENBURG. 400, 450, 451
LYNN. 534, 547
LYNNFIELD. 481, 482, 520, 547, 534, 552
MAGNOLIA. 405
MALDEN. 352, 389
MANCHESTER. 405, 527, 533
MARBLEHEAD. 308, 329, 405, 482, 526, 527, 533
MARTHA'S VINEYARD. 319, 340, 343, 497
MARION. 487, 554
MASHPEE. 318, 321, 402
MATTAPOISETT. 345, 522, 554
MECHANICSVILLE. 556
MEDFIELD. 344
MEDFORD. 308, 352
MEDWAY. 344, 466
MELROSE. 352, 389
MENOTOMY. 399
MERRIMAC. 326, 397, 443, 462
MERRIMACK. 243
MERRIMACK RIVER. 325, 337
MIDDLEBORO'. 345
MIDDLEBOROUGH. 345
MIDDLEFIELD. 426
MIDDLESEX Co. 346, 466, 561
MIDDLETON. 460, 527, 533
MILFORD. 466, 490, 567
MILL RIVER. 314
MILLBURY. 347, 546, 547, 569
MILLER FALLS. 325, 331
MILLIS. 344
MILTON. 308, 351, 352
MONOMOIT. 425
MONROE. 331
MONSON. 347, 541, 553
MONTAGUE. 325, 331, 456, 547
MONTAGUE CENTER. 331, 456
MONTEREY. 314
MONTGOMERY. 325, 332, 426, 559
MOUNT WASHINGTON. 314, 536
MOUNT WOLLASTON. 520
MUDDY RIVER. 413
MUNDALE. 558
MURRAYFIELD. 426
NAHANT. 300, 326, 481, 482, 534, 547
NANTUCKET. 319, 335, 497
NARRAGANSETT #2. 561

NASHAWENA. 326
NATICK. 486
NEW BEDFORD. 352, 434
NEW BRAINTREE. 347, 412
NEW MARLBORO'. 314
NEW MARLBOROUGH. 314
NEW SALEM. 331, 347
NEWBURY. 326, 468
NEWBURYPORT. 326, 398, 499
NEWTON. 352
NEWTON LOWER FALLS. 497
NORFOLK. 576
NORFOLK Co. 466, 519
NORTH ANDOVER. 398, 399
NORTH ATTLEBORO. 344, 401
NORTH BRIDGEWATER. 412
NORTH BROOKFIELD. 332, 540
NORTH CHELSEA. 483
NORTH DANA. 347
NORTH NATICK. 497
NORTH PLYMOUTH. 513
NORTH READING. 520, 552
NORTH SHORE. 326, 327, 329, 330, 435
NORTH UXBRIDGE. 507
NORTH WEYMOUTH. 562
NORTHAMPTON. 332, 467, 541, 544
NORTHBRIDGE. 490, 547, 551
NORTHFIELD. 331, 456
NORTON. 484
NORWOOD. 468
OAK BLUFFS. 333
OCEAN SPRAY. 565
OLD ROCHESTER. 487
ORANGE. 400, 456
ORLEANS. 318, 445
OSTERVILLE. 314
OTIS. 403
OTTER RIVER. 347
OXFORD. 556
PALMER. 541, 553
PASQUE. 326
PAWTUCKET. 521
PAXTON. 347
PEABODY. 405, 526, 527, 532, 533
PELHAM. 325, 347
PEMBERTON. 495
PEMBROKE. 345
PENIKESE. 326
PEPPERELL. 457
PETERSHAM. 302, 347
PHILIPSTON. 347
PITTSFIELD. 315, 504

PLAINFIELD. 325
PLAINVILLE. 401
PLUM ISLAND. 533
PLYMOUTH. 289, 296, 308
PLYMOUTH-PROINCETOWN. 294
PLYMPTON. 345
PRESCOTT. 347
PRINCETON. 400, 450
PROVINCETOWN. 309, 318
PULLEN POINT. 426
PUTNAM. 556
QUINCY. 352, 559
RANDOLPH. 344, 409, 520
RAYNHAM. 484
READING. 552
REHOBOTH. 401, 438
REVERE. 352
RICHMOND. 403, 474
ROCHESTER. 345, 554
ROCKDALE. 507
ROCKLAND. 395
ROCKPORT. 453
ROSLINDALE. 351
ROWE. 331
ROWLEY. 326, 468
ROXBURY. 349, 351, 380, 389
ROYALSTON. 347
RUMNEY MARSH. 426
RUSSELL. 325, 559
SALEM. 244
SALEM NECK. 329
SALISBURY. 326, 397, 468
SALISBURY BEACH. 468
SANDISFIELD. 403
SANDWICH. 318, 319, 402, 408
SAUGUS. 481, 482, 547
SAXONVILLE. 451, 486
SEABROOK. 533
SEEKONK. 438, 521
SHARON. 344, 421
SHAWFIELDMONT. 457
SHAWOMET PURCHASE. 538
SHEFFIELD. 314, 456
SHELBURNE. 331, 456
SHELBURNE FALLS. 331, 456
SHERBORN. 451, 496
SHIRLEY. 457, 511
SHUTESBURY. 347
SHREWSBURY. 347
SIPPICAN. 486
SOMERSET. 438
SOMERVILLE. 352

S. FRAMINGHAM. 451, 486
SOUTH SCITUATE. 508
SOUTH WEYMOUTH. 562
S. YARMOUTH. 314
SOUTHAMPTON. 325, 332
SOUTHBOROUGH. 451
SOUTHBRIDGE. 332, 546, 556, 567
SOUTHFIELD. 314
SOUTHWICK. 325, 332, 559
SPRINGFIELD. 332, 506, 567
STERLING. 400, 450, 471
STOCKBRIDGE. 314, 403, 473
STONEHAM. 552
STOUGHTON. 344, 421
STOW. 467
STURBRIDGE. 332, 539, 556
SUDBURY. 451, 467
SUNDERLAND. 325, 331, 332
SWAMPSCOT(T). 481, 482, 534
SWANSEA. 438, 538
SWANSEY. 521
TAUNTON. 352
TEMPLETON. 347, 400, 450
TENNEYVILLE. 553
TEWKSBURY. 406
THORNDIKE. 553
THREE RIVERS. 553
TIVERTON. 449
TOLLAND. 332
TOPSFIELD. 460, 468, 527, 533
TOWNSEND. 511
TRURO. 318, 517
TURKEY PASS. 398
TURNER'S FALLS. 325, 331, 456
TYNGSBORO. 406
TYNGSBOROUGH. 443
TYRINGHAM. 403
UPTON. 547, 569
UXBRIDGE. 490, 507, 569
WAKEFIELD. 520
WALES. 347
WALTHAM. 352, 488, 554, 556
WARE. 332
WAREHAM. 345, 487
WARREN. 332, 347, 540
WARWICK. 331, 347
WASHINGTON. 403
WATERTOWN. 352, 404
WAYLAND. 546, 553, 561
WEBSTER. 567
WELLESLEY. 496, 497
WELLFLEET. 318, 445

WENDELL. 331, 347
WENHAM. 460, 527, 533
WESSAGUSSET. 563
WEST BOYLSTON. 347
WEST BRIDGEWATER. 345
WEST BROOKFIELD. 347, 413, 540
WEST CAMBRIDGE. 399, 488
WEST GRANVILLE. 559
WEST NEEDHAM. 496
WEST NEWBURY. 326, 462, 468, 499
WEST ROXBURY. 351, 381, 470
WEST SPRINGFIELD. 332, 541, 542, 543
WEST STOCKBRIDGE. 314, 403
WEST WARREN. 347, 540
WESTBORO. 569
WESTERN NEW BEDFORD. 447
WESTFIELD. 332, 541
WESTFORD. 406
WESTHAMPTON. 325, 332
WESTMINSTER. 400, 450
WESTON. 553, 554, 561
WESTPORT. 396, 433, 434
WESTWOOD. 434

WEYMOUTH. 352, 518
WEYMOUTH CENTER. 562
WEYMOUTH HEIGHTS. 562
WEYMOUTH LANDING. 562
WHATELEY. 325, 331, 332, 507
WHITINSVILLE. 569
WHITMAN. 395
WILBRAHAM. 332, 347
WILLIAMSBURG. 332
WILLIAMSTOWN. 396, 505
WILSONVILLE. 556
WINCHENDON. 450, 567
WINCHESTER. 352, 389
WINNISIMMET. 426
WINTHROP. 352
WINTHROP HIGHLANDS. 565
WORCESTER. 352
WORCESTER Co. 466
WORONOCO. 325, 559
WORTHINGTON. 325, 332
WRENTHAM. 344
YARMOUTH. 318, 402, 534
YARMOUTHPORT. 314

ADDITIONS TO INDEX

BROOKLINE. 351, 352, 389
DANFORTH'S FARMS. 452

MARSHFIELD. 535
SOUTH HADLEY. 325, 332, 460

RHODE ISLAND

SELECTED BIBLIOGRAPHIES FOR RHODE ISLAND

BARTLETT, John Russell. Bibliography of Rhode Island. A catalogue of books and other publications relating to the state of Rhode Island, with notes, historical, biographical and critical. Printed by order of the General assembly. Providence, A. Anthony, Printed to the state, 1864.   iv, (5) - 287 p. 25 cm.   4-10780.
Z1331. B 29

BRIGHAM, Clarence Saunders. Bibliography of Rhode Island history ... (Boston and Syracuse, The Mason pub. co.) 1902.   (651) - 681 p.   25 cm.   "Reprinted from Field's 'Rhode Island and Providence Plantations,' vol. 3, p. 653 - 681." 4-8960.
Z1331. B 85

BRIGHAM, Clarence Saunders. ... List of books upon Rhode Island history ... (Providence) Dept. of education, state of Rhode Island, 1908.   8 p. 23 cm. (Rhode Island educational circulars. Historical series - I)
Z1331. B 852

CHAPIN, Howard Millar. Bibliography of Rhode Island bibliography ... Providence (Preston & Rounds) 1914.   (9) p.   23 ½ cm.   (Half-title: Contributions to Rhode Island bibliography, no. I) 14-21328.
Z1331. C4 No. 1

NEWPORT. A contribution to the bibliography and literature of Newport, R. I.; comprising a list of books, published or printed, in Newport, with notes and additions, by Charles E. Hammett, jun. Newport, R. I., Hammett, jun., 1887.   185 p. front. 26 x 21 cm. 4-10837.
Z1332. N5 H2

RHODE ISLAND CLASSIFICATION F 76 - F 90

76	Periodicals. Societies. Collections.
.5	Museums. Exhibitions, exhibits.
77	Gazetteers. Dictionaries. Geographic names.
.3	Guidebooks.
78	Biography (Collective). Genealogy (Collective).
.2	Historiography.
	Historians, *see* E 175.5.
.5	Study and teaching.
79	General works. Histories.
.3	Juvenile works.
.5	Minor works. Pamphlets, addresses, essays, etc.
.6	Anecdotes, legends, pageants, etc.
80	Historic monuments (General). Illustrative material.
81	Antiquities (Non-Indian).
	By period.
82	Early to 1775.

      First Rhode Island Charter, 1663; the Narragansett country; union of plantations at Newport, Portsmouth, Providence, and Warwick, 1636–1643; etc.

      Biography: John Clarke, Samuel Gorton, Roger Williams, etc.

      Cf. E 83.67, King Philip's War, 1675–1676.

83	1775–1865.

      Cf. E 215.6, Gaspee affair.
        E 263.R4, Rhode Island in the Revolution (General);
          E 230.5–241, Military operations and battles.
        E 528, Civil War, 1861–1865 (General).

.4	Dorr Rebellion, 1842.

      Biography: Thomas Wilson Dorr, etc.

84	1865–1950.

      Cf. D 570.85.R4–41, World War I, 1914–1918.
        D 769.85.R4–41, World War II, 1939–1945.
        E 726.R4, War of 1898 (Spanish-American War).

85	1951–
87	Regions, counties, etc., A–Z.
.B6	Block Island (Manisees).
.B7	Boundaries.

      Cf. F 72.B7, Massachusetts boundary.
        F82, Massachusetts claims to Narragansett country.
        F 102.B7, Connecticut boundary.

.B86	Bristol Co.
.K3	Kent Co.
.N2	Narragansett Bay region.
.N5	Newport Co.

      Block Island, *see* F 87.B6.
      Rhode Island (Island), *see* F 87.R4.

        .P3   Pawtuxet River and Valley.
        .P5   Pettaquamscutt Purchase.
        .P9   Providence Co.
        .R4   Rhode Island (Island) (Aquidneck).
        .W3   Washington Co.

89   Cities, towns, etc., A–Z.
        e. g. .N5   Newport.
               .P9   Providence.

90   Elements in the population.
        .A1   General works.
        .A2–Z Individual elements.
                  For a list of racial, ethnic, and religious elements (with cutter numbers), *see* E 184, p. 27–29.

RHODE ISLAND

F76 - F90

PERIODICALS. SOCIETIES. COLLECTIONS.

BOOK NOTES, consisting of literary gossip, criticisms of books and local historical matters connected with Rhode Island. Providence, S. S. Rider, 1884 - 1916. v. 1-33; Apr. 14, 1883 - Dec. 16, 1916. 33 v. in 17 illus., ports. 23 cm. biweekly. Publication suspended Apr. - Dec. 1887. No more pub.   17-26988.
                        F76
                        Z1219.B775

CHARTERS and legislative documents, illustrative of Rhode-Island history; showing that the people of Rhode Island, from the foundation of the state, until their constitution of 1842, possessed and exercised the rights of self-government ... Providence, Knowles & Vose, printers, 1844. 68 (2) p.
25 ½ cm. 17-18305.
                        F76
                        JK3205. C5

GAZETTE françoise; an account of the French newspaper printed on the press of the French fleet at Newport, Rhode Island, 1780 and 1781. Providence, R. I. historical soc., 1916. 11 p. incl. front., illus. (facsim.) 23 cm. 26-16188.
                        F76
                        PN4899.N344G3

NARRAGANSETT club. (Circular regarding its publications) (Providence) 1865 - 72.   21 ½ cm.
                        F76. N 205
                        Rare Book Coll.

NARRAGANSETT club, Publications of the. (First series) v. 1 - 6. Providence (Providence press co., printers) 1866 - 74.   6 v. 22 ½ x 13 ½ cm. Chiefly reprints, incl. reproductions of the title-pages, of the original editions of the works of Roger Williams. No more pub. 3-20323.
                        F76. N 21
                        Rare Book Coll.

NARRAGANSETTS historical register, The, a magazine devoted to the antiquities, genealogy and historical matter illustrating the history of the state of Rhode Island and Providence Plantations ... James N. Arnold, ed. v. 1 - 8, v.9, no. 1 - 2; July 1882 - Apr. 1891. Providence, The Narragansett historical pub. co., 1882 - 91.   9 v. illus., pl., ports. 23 ½ cm. quarterly. No more pub. Rc-2942.
                        F76. N 23

RHODE ISLAND (Colony) Records of the colony of Rhode Island and Providence Plantations, in New England. Print. by order of the General assembly. Ed. John Russell Bartlett. Providence, A. C. Greene, 1856-65.   10 v. ports. 23 cm. Contents. - v.1. 1636 - 1663. - v.2. 1664 - 1677. - v.3. 1678 - 1706. - v.4. 1707 -

1740. - v. 5. 1741-1756. - v. 6. 1757-1769. - v. 7. 1770-1776. - v. 8. 1776-1779. - v. 9. 1780-1783. - v. 10. 1784-1792. 1-Rc-2981.
F76. R29

— New York, Ams Press (1968)   10 v. ports. 23 cm. 68-56849.   F76.R292

RHODE ISLAND. Office of commissioner of education. Rhode Island educational circulars. Historical series. 1 -   (Providence) 1908 -   v. 23½ cm. 9-2372 Rev.   F76. R32

— ... List of books upon Rhode Island history, prepared by Clarence S. Brigham ... 1908.
8 p. 23 cm. (No. 1)   9-2373.

— ... Roger Williams, the founder of Providence - the pioneer of religious liberty, by Amasa M. Eaton ... 1908.   19 p. 23 cm. (no. 2) E8-862.

— ... The destruction of the Gaspee, by Horatio B. Knox ... 1908.   15 p. (No. 3)

— ... The influence of physical features upon the history of Rhode Island, by David W. Hoyt ... 1910.   20 p. 6 pl. (No. 4)   10-33407.

— ... Points of historical interest in the state of Rhode Island ... 1911. 84 p. illus. (No. 5)
11-23186 Rev.

— Oliver Hazard Perry and the battle of Lake Erie, by George Bancroft. 1912.   55 p.
(No. 6) 13-33141.

RHODE ISLAND. State bureau of information. Historical publication, no. 1 -   Providence,
1928 -   v. front., illus., fold. map, plan. 23½ cm. 28-29667.   F76. R334

— The battle of Rhode Island ... by Howard Willis Preston .... 1928.   56 p. incl. front.,
illus., plan, fold. map. (No. 1) 28-27317.

— Address of His Excellency Norman S. Case, governor of Rhode Island .... 1929.
20 p. front. (port.) (No. 2) 34-38730.

— Rhode Island's historic background, by Howard Willis Preston. 1930.   48 p. incl. front.,
illus., ports., maps. diagr. (No. 3) 30-27603.

— 2d ed. 1933.   48 p. etc. 34-8759.

— Rhode Island and the sea, by Howard Willis Preston. 1932.   140 p. illus. (map) diagr.
(No. 4) 32-27391.

— Washington's visits to Rhode Island, gathered from contemporary accounts, by Howard W. Preston .... 1932.   38 p. incl. front. (map) illus. (No. 5) 32-27379.

— Autograph letters and documents of George Washington now in Rhode Island collections.
1932.   171 p. front. (port.) illus. (facsims) (No. 6) 32-27483.

RHODE ISLAND historical magazine, The.   v. 1 - 7; July 1880 - Apr. 1887. Newport, R. I., The
Newport historical pub. co. (1880 - 87)   7 v. pl., ports., map. 23½ - 25 cm. quarterly. No more pub. 9-11769.
F76. R35

RHODE ISLAND historical society, The charter, constitution, and circular of the. Inc. June, 1822.
Providence, Print. Jones & Wheeler (1822)   8 p. 24 cm. 12-11575.   F76. R 41

— Constitution, adopted Dec. 10, 1870. Providence, Providence press co. print. 1871.
11 p. 17 cm. 4-10000.   F76. R414

— Charter, adopted April 2, 1878. Providence, Angell, Hammett, printers, 1878.   12 p. 19½ cm.
2-21283.   F76. R42

— Charter and by-laws. Rev. 1892. Providence, Print. Snow & Farnham, 1892.   19 p. 23½ cm.
4-10001.   F76. R423

— Charter and by laws ... 1914. Providence (Standard print. co.) 1914.   13 p. 23½ cm. 18-11620.
F76. R426

— Annual report of the board of trustees ... 1836 (and ... 1839) (Providence, 1836-39)
2 v. 22 - 23½ cm. No more pub. 1-22659 Additions.   F76. R 43

RHODE ISLAND historical society. Collections. v. 1 - 34; (1827) - Oct. 1941. Providence.
34 v. in 19. illus., plates, ports., maps, facsims. 22 - 26 cm. Irregular, 1827 - 1902; quarterly, 1918 - 41. Superseded by Rhode Island history. Rc 2945 rev.*   F76. R47

580

RHODE ISLAND

— A key into the language of America ... By Roger Williams. 1643. Repr. 1827. (17) - 163, (2) p. (v. 1) Rc-2948 Rev.

— Simplicity's defence against seven-headed policy. By Samuel Gorton ... 1835. (7) - 278 p. (vol. 2) 1-Rc-2946.

— The early history of Narragansett ... By Elisha R. Potter, jr. 1835. xix, 315 p. (vol. 3) 1-Rc-2950.

— An historical discourse, on the civil and religious affairs of the colony of Rhode-Island. By John Callender. (2d ed.) 1838. 270 (2) p. (vol. 4) Rc-2943.

— Annals of the town of Providence. By William R. Staples. 1843. 5, (iii) - vi, (9) - 670 p. (vol. 5) 1-Rc-2947.

— The invasion of Canada in 1775: including the Journal of Captain Simeon Thayer ... By Edwin Martin Stone. 1867. xxiv (i.e. xxvi) 104 (i.e. 116) p. plan. (v. 6 pt. 1) Rc-3061.

— Revolutionary correspondence from 1775 to 1782 ... Printed from the manuscript collections of the R.I. historical soc. (v. 6 p. (105) - 300 and app. (4) p., p. (371) - 377) 1-Rc-2949 Additions.

— Materials for a history of the Baptists in Rhode Island. By Rev. Morgan Edwards. (In v. 6 p. (301) - 370, 378 - 380) Reprint of part of the author's "Materials towards a history of the Baptists in Jersey," 1792, which forms the 2d vol. and last on pub. of a projected history of American Baptists in 12 vols. 1-10217.

— Early attempts at Rhode Island history. Ed. ... by William E. Foster. (v. 7 p. (7) - 134) 6-3804.

— The Narragansetts. By Henry C. Dorr. (In v. 7 p. (135) - 237) 6-3802.

— Early votaries of natural science in Rhode Island. By Charles W. Parsons. (In v. 7 p. (239) - 263) 6-3801.

— The first commencement of Rhode Island college (1769) .... By Reuben A. Guild. (in v. 7, p. (265) - 298.) 6-3800.

— The British fleet in Rhode Island. By George C. Mason. (In v. 7 p. (299) - 325) 6-3799.

— Nicholas Easton vs. the city of Newport. By George C. Mason. (In v. 7, p. (327) - 344) 6-3798.

— ... The diary of John Comer. Ed. with notes by C. Edwin Barrows. 132 p. (vol. 8) 3-20943.

— The proprietors of Providence, and their controversies with the freeholders. By Henry C. Dorr. 1897. 4, 141 p. (vol. 9) 6-3803.

— Harris papers, with an introd. by Irving B. Richman ... 1902. 410 p. fold. map. (vol. 10) 5-9975.

RHODE ISLAND history. v. 1 - Jan. 1942 - Providence. 23 cm. F76.R472

RHODE ISLAND historical society. A half century memorial. An address ... by Henry C. Whitaker. Providence, Providence press co., 1873. 48 p. 26 cm. 1-10268. F76.R48

RHODE ISLAND historical society. Necrology. 19 - Providence, 19 - v. 23½ cm. 16-22085. F76.R487

RHODE ISLAND historical society, Proceedings of the. 1872 - 1891/92; 1900/01 - 1913/14. Providence ... 1872-92; 1902-14. 34 v. in 26. port., facsim. 23½ cm. No more pub. 7-34261 Rev. F76.R49

RHODE ISLAND historical society. Report ... on the reconstruction of the west wing of the society's building ... Providence, 1914. (11) p. illus. 23½ cm. 18-8233. F76.R4915

RHODE ISLAND historical society. Reports of the treasurer ... v. 23½ cm. 18-6561. F76.R4917

RHODE ISLAND historical society. ... Sketch of its history, with list of papers read at its stated meetings. Providence, 1890. 37 p. 23 cm. 9-22105. F76.R492

RHODE ISLAND historical society, incorporated, 1822. (n.p., 1910?) 14 p. 14½ cm. Historical sketch. 11-13694. F76.R493

RHODE ISLAND historical society ... News sheet. no. 1 - 52; Feb. 1, 1902 - Apr. 1, 1916. (Providence, 1902-16) 52 no. 23 cm. quarterly. No more pub. 19-7531. F76.R495

RHODE ISLAND historical society, Publications of the.   New ser., v. 1 - 8; April 1893 - Jan. 1901. Providence, The Society, 1893-1900.   8 v. pl., port., facsim. 24 cm. (quarterly) 3-21033.

F76. R51

— The town records of Rhode Island; a report, by Amos Perry ...   1893.   (In v. 1 p. 99 - 182)   9-19164.

— Plea of the Petuxet purchasers, and a history of the first deed, etc. before the king's commissioners 1677. 1893.   (In v. 1 p. 183 - 213)   7-38322.

— Indian slaves of King Philip's war.   (In v. 1 p. 234 - 238)   9-21949 Rev.

— Note on the transaction of Roger Williams and others, in selling Indians into slavery. By James G. Vose.   (In v. 1 p. 239 - 240)   9-21948.

— Studies in colonial history ...   (In v. 1 p. 241 - 291)   3-20339.

— Know-nothingism in Rhode Island.   By Charles Stickney)   (In v. 1 p. 243 - 257)   3-20332 Rev.

— The development of the nominating convention in Rhode Island.   By Neil Andrews, jr. (In v. 1 p. 258 - 269)   3-20336.

— Early history of the colonial post office.   By Mary Emma Woolley.   (in v.1 p. 270-291) 3-20333.

— Glimpses of ancient Sowams.   By Virginia Baker.   (In v. 2 p. 196-202)   7-39278.

— The proprietors of Providence, and their controversies with the freeholders. (v. 3 p. 143 - 158, 199 - 230; v. 4 p. 75 - 106, 139 - 170. 203 - 226)   Repub. 1897 as v. 9.   1-1539 Rev.

— The papers of Major-Gen. Nathanael Greene.   By John Franklin Jameson. v. 3 p. 159 - 167)   9-22112.

— Fac-simile of the signatures of the settlers of the town of Warwick ...   By Henry Lehré Greene.   (v. 4 p. 107 - 123)   7-38301.

— One branch of the Greene family ...   By Simon Henry Greene.   (v. 4 p. 171 - 184)   CA 17-150.

— Rhode Island revolutionary debt.   By Amos Perry.   (v. 4 p. 234 - 243)   9-22114.

— The war of 1812.   By William Cory Snow.   (v. 5 p. 143-183)   7-38336.

— The Havana expedition of 1762 in the war with Spain.   By Asa Bird Gardiner ... v. 6 p. 167 - 189)   7-38300.

RHODE ISLAND historical society.   Miscellaneous printed matter published by this body is classified in F76. R513

RHODE ISLAND historical society.   ... Museum illustrating the history of the state ... (Catalogue) Providence (Standard print.) 1916.   32 p. front., plat;s. 23 cm. 16-18057.   F76. R514

RHODE ISLAND historical society ...   Address by William Gammell.   Providence, B. Cranston, 1844. 30 p. 23 cm. 1-22538.   F76. R515

RHODE ISLAND historical society.   A discourse ....   By George Washington Greene ...   Providence, Gladding and Proud, 1849.   22 p. 23½ cm. 1-22539.   F76. R516

RHODE ISLAND historical society.   Greene - Staples - Parsons.   An address ... by Samuel G. Arnold.   Providence, Hammond, Angell, print., 1869.   22 p. 24½ cm. 4-9707.   F76. R518

RHODE ISLAND historical society.   The library and cabinet, etc.   By Amos Perry.   Providence, Snow & Farnham, 1892.   24 p. 23½ cm. 3-31517.   F76. R519

RHODE ISLAND historical tracts. (1st series) no. 1 - 20; 2d series no. 1 - 5.   Providence, S. S. Rider, 1877 - 96.   25 v. in 26. ports., maps, etc. 21 x 16 cm. - 21½ x 17 cm. 6-4456.   F76. R52

— The capture of General Richard Prescott by Lt.-Col. William Barton.   1877.   65 p. (port.) double map, facsim. (1st ser. no. 1)   Rc-2971.

— Visits of the Northmen to Rhode Island.   By Alexander Farnum.   1877.   41 p. (no.2) Rc-2966.

— History of the Wanton family of Newport.   By John Russell Bartlett.   1878.   152 p. (no. 3) Rc-2965.

— William Coddington in Rhode Island colonial affairs, by Dr. Henry E. Turner.   1878. 60 p. (1st ser. no. 4)   Rc-2964.

— Memoir concerning the French settlements and French settlers in the colony of Rhode Island.   1879.   138 p. (in. 1st ser. no. 5)   1-Rc-2963.

— The centennial celebration of the battle of Rhode Island ...   1878.   118 p. (1st ser. no. 6)

— The journal of a brigade chaplain in the campaign of 1779 against the Six Nations ...   By the Rev. William Rogers.   1879.   136 p. (1st ser. no. 7)   1-13362.

RHODE ISLAND

— Some account of the bills of credit or paper money of Rhode Island ... 1710 ... 1786. By Elisha R. Potter. 1880.   xii, 229 p. facsims. (1st ser. no. 8) 1-Rc-2956.

— A true representation of the plan formed at Albany, in 1754, for uniting all the British northern colonies ... By Stephen Hopkins. 1880.   xxxi, 65 p. (1st ser. no. 9) Rc-2961.

— A short reply to Mr. Stephen Hopkins's vindication ... By Philolethes. 1755.   (1st ser. no. 9 p. 47 - 65) 12-39431.

— An historical inquiry concerning the attempt to raise a regiment of slaves by Rhode Island during the war of the revolution. By Sidney S. Rider. 1880.   xii, 86 p. incl. tables. (1st ser. no. 10) 1-Rc-2957.

— Bibliographical memoirs of three Rhode Island authors: Joseph K. Angell, Frances H. (Whipple) McDougall, Catharine R. Williams; by Sidney Rider. 1880.   vi, 92 p. (1st ser. no. 11) 1-Rc-2953.

— The medical school formerly existing in Brown university, its professors and graduates. By Charles W. Parsons ... 1881.   3, 59 p. (1st ser. no. 12) Rc-2958.

— The diary of Thomas Vernon, a loyalist .... With notes by Sidney S. Rider.   viii, 150 p. (1st ser. no. 13) Rc-2954.

— Roger Williams's "Christenings make not Christians," Ed. by Henry Martyn Dexter. 1881.   4, 62 p. (1st ser. no. 14) Rc-2955.

— The planting and growth of Providence ... by Henry C. Dorr. 1882.   267 p. (1st ser. no. 15)

— A looking glass for the times ... By Peter Folger. Providence, S. S. Rider, 1883. (7) - 12, 24 p. (1st ser. no. 16) Rc-2970.

— A defence of Samuel Gorton and the settlers of Shawomet. By George A. Brayton ... 1883.   8, 120 p. (1st ser. no. 17) Rc-2969 Rev.

— Gleanings from the judicial history of Rhode Island. By Thomas Durfee ... 1883. 164 p. (1st ser. no. 18) 1-Rc-2960.

— Stephen Hopkins, a Rhode Island statesman. By William E. Foster ... 1884. 2 v. facsim., geneal. tab. (1st ser. no. 19) Rc-2967.

— Additions and corrections to the first series of Rhode Island historical tracts, with an index to the same. 1895.   84 p. (1st ser. no. 20) Rc-2968 Rev.

— An inquiry concerning the origin of the clause in the laws of Rhode Island (1719 - 1783) disfranchising Roman Catholics. By Sidney S. Rider. 1889.   72 p. (2d ser. no. 1) Rc-2972.

— An inquiry concerning the authenticity of an alleged portrait of Roger Williams, by Sidney S. Rider. 1891.   31 p. incl. 3 port. (2d ser. no. 2) Rc-2973.

— A century of lotteries in Rhode Island. 1744 - 1844. By John H. Stiness ... 1896. xi, 123 p. illus., facsims. (1 fold.) (2d ser. no. 3) Rc-2974.

— The forgeries connected with the deed given by the sachems Canonicus and Miantinomi to Roger Williams of the land on which the town of Providence was planted. By Sidney S. Rider. 1896. vi, 128 p. fold, plan, fold, facsim. (2d ser. no. 4) Rc-2975.

— Soul liberty. Rhode Island's gift to the nation. By Sidney Smith Rider. 1897. viii, 86 p. (2d ser. no. 5) 3-20619.

RHODE ISLAND year book. (Providence)   v. illus. 28 cm.

F76. R55

SONS of Rhode Island. An oration on the annals of Rhode Island and Providence Plantations, by the Rev. Francis Vintom, and A rhyme of Rhode Island and the times, by George William Curtis. New York, Printed for the assoc. by C. A. Alvord, 1863.   80 p. 22½ cm. Rc-2976.

F76. S 69

GAZETTEERS. DICTIONARIES. GEOGRAPHIC NAMES.

PARSONS, Usher. Indian names of places in Rhode-Island: collected by Usher Parsons for the R. I. historical soc. Providence (R.I.) Knowles, Anthony, printers, 1861.   iv, (5) - 32 p. front. (port.) 23½ cm. 4-20403.

F77. P 27

PEASE, John Chauncey. A gazetteer of the states of Connecticut and Rhode-Island.   Hartford: Print. and pub. William S. Marsh, 1819.   vii, 389 p. 2 port. (incl. front.) 2 fold. maps. 21½ cm. Rc-3197.

F77. P 36

U.S. Geographic board.   Official gazetteer of Rhode Island.   Compiled by the Rhode Island

Geographic board in cooperation with the U.S. Geographic board.   Washington, U.S. Govt. print. off., 1932.   iii, 95 p.   23 cm.   32-28197.   F77.U 58

DIRECTORIES.

AGRICULTURAL directory of the state of Rhode Island, and the towns of Attleboro, Bellingham, Blackstone, Douglas, No. Attleboro, Rehoboth (etc.) ... in Massachusetts, and the towns of Groton, Killingly, North Stonington, Plainfield (etc.) ... in Connecticut; containing the names and post-office addresses, and in most cases, the acreages of 10,500 persons engaged in agricultural pursuits or owners of farm lands, etc. etc.   (1st -   issue)   1894 -   Providence, R.I., Sampson, Murdock, 1894.   v. front. (fold. map)   24 cm.   40M1847T-2.   Directories

U.S. ... Heads of families at the first census of the U.S. taken in the year 1790 ... Washington, Govt. print. off., 1907 - 8.   12 v.   fronts. (fold. maps)   29½ cm.   7-35273.   F77.5.U58

BIOGRAPHY (COLLECTIVE). GENEALOGY (COLLECTIVE).

RHODE ISLAND.   Graves Registration Committee.   Report.   (Providence?)   v.   23 cm.   annual. Began publication with 1950/51 issue.   53-63033.   F78.A 52

RHODE ISLAND (Colony) General Assembly.   Census of the inhabitants of the Colony of Rhode Island and Providence plantations, 1774.   Arranged by John R. Bartlett.   Baltimore, Geneal. Pub. Co., 1969.   v. 238, 120 p.   69-17130.   F78.A 59
1969

ARNOLD, James Newell.   Vital records of Rhode Island.   1636 - 1850.   First series.   Births, marriages and deaths.   A family register for the people.   Providence, R.I., Narragansett historical pub. co., 1891 -   v.   29½ cm.   2-3733.   v.1. Kent County. - v.2-3. Providence County. - v.4. Newport County. v.5. Washington County. - v.6. Bristol County. - v.7. Friends and minister. - v.8. Episcopal and Congregational. - v.9. Seekonk (incl. East Providence), Pawtucket and Newman Congregational church - v.10. Town and church. - v.11. Church records. - v.12. Revolutionary rolls and newspapers. - v.13. Deaths, Providence journal S to Z. Providence gazette, A to J, 1762 - 1830. - v.14. Providence gazette - Deaths K to Z. Marriages, A, B, C, 1762-1825. - v.15. Providence gazette - Marriages D to Z. U.S. chronicle - Deaths, A to Z - v.16, U.S. chronicle - Marriages; American journal, Impartial observer, and Providence journal - Marriages and deaths; Providence semiweekly journal - Marriages - v. 17. Providence Phenix , Providence patriot, and Columbian Phenix - Marriages - A to R. - v.18. Providence Phenix, Providence patriot, and Columbian Phenix - Marriages: S to Z; deaths: A to M. - v.19. Providence Phenix, Providence patriot, and Columbian Phenix - Deaths: N to Z; Rhode Island American - Marriages: A to G - v. 20. Rhode Island American: Marriages: H to Z. Deaths: A and B.   F78.A 75

AUSTIN, John Osborne.   The ancestral dictionary.   Central Falls, R.I., E.L. Freeman (1891)
4 p., 74 numb. l. front. (port.)   22½ cm.   8-22433.   F78.A 92

AUSTIN, John Osborne.   Ancestry of thirty-three Rhode Islanders (born in the 18th century); also twenty-seven charts of Roger Williams' descendants to the fifth generation, and an account of Lewis Latham, falconer to King Charles I; with a chart of his American descendants to the fourth generation and a list of 280 existing portraits of Rhode Island governors, chief justices, etc.   Albany, N.Y., J. Munsell's sons, 1889.   2, 139 (i.e. 141) p.   35 cm.   8-18608.   F78.A 93

AUSTIN, John Osborne.   The genealogical dictionary of Rhode Island; comprising three generations of settlers who came before 1690.   (With many families carried to the fourth generation.)   Albany, N.Y., Print. J. Munsell's sons, 1887.   viii, 440 p. (6) p.   36½ x 27½ cm.   9-15740.   F78.A935

— Another copy.   Albany, J. Munsell's sons, 1887 (1885)   viii, 443 p.   37 cm.   F78.A935
1887a
Rare Book Coll.

— With additions and corrections by John Osborne Austin and additions and corrections by G. Andrews Moriarty.   An a new foreword by Albert T. Klyberg.   Baltimore, Genealogical Pub. Co., 1969.
viii, 496 p. 36 cm. Reprint of the 1887 ed.   68-56072.   F78.A935
1969
L.H. & G.

RHODE ISLAND 7

AUSTIN, John Osborne. One hundred and sixty allied families. (Salem, Mass., Print at the Salem press, 1893) xviii, 288 p. 4 double geneal. tab. 30 x 24 cm. 8-18609. F78.A 94

BARTLETT, John Russell. Memoirs of Rhode Island officers who were engaged in the service of their country during the great rebellion of the South. Illus, with 34 portraits. Providence, S. S. Rider, 1867. viii, (9) - 152 p. pl., 34 ports. 35 cm. 3-19138. F78.B 28
Rare Book Coll.

— Providence, S.S. Rider, 1867. viii, (9) - 452 p. pl., 34 port. 26½ x 22½ cm. 33-36308. F78.B 281

BIOGRAPHICAL cyclopedia of representative men of Rhode Island. Providence, National biographical pub. co., 1881. 589 p. 132 port. 28½ cm. In double columns. 3-18891. F78.B 61

HALL, Joseph Davis. Biographical history of the manufacturers and business men of Rhode Island, at the opening of the 20th century. Providence, R. I., J. D. Hall, 1901. 336 p. illus. 27½ cm. 2-3946-M2. F78.H 17

JACKSON, Ronald V. Rhode Island 1800 census. (Salt Lake City, Utah) Accelerated Indexing Systems, 1972. 31, 222 p. illus. 29 cm. F78.J 3

MEN of progress; biographical sketches and portraits of leaders in business and professional life in the state of Rhode Island and Providence plantations, compiled under the supervision of Richard Herndon; Ed. Alfred M. Williams and Wm. F. Blanding. Boston, New England magazine, 1896. 282 p. ports. 28½ cm. 3-18892 Rev. F78.M 64

REPRESENTATIVE men and old families of Rhode Island; genealogical records and historical sketches of prominent and representative citizens and of many of the old families ... Chicago, J. H. Beers, 1908. 3 v. ports. 29 cm. Paged continuously. 11-12771. F78.R 42

SMITH, Joseph Jencks. Civil and military list of Rhode Island. 1647 - 1800. A list of all officers elected by the General assembly .... Providence, R. I., Preston and Rounds, 1900. vii, 659 p. 28 cm. Imperfect: p. i - vii, 1 - 4 wanting, supplied by photostat. Supplemented by "Civil and military list of Rhode Island. 1800 - 1850. 1901. Each vol. contains its own index, but a much more complete and satisfactory one is F78. S 67. 1-29578. F78.S 65
Geneal. Section Ref.

SMITH, Joseph Jencks. Civil and military list of Rhode Island. 1800 - 1850. A list of all officers elected by the General assembly .... Also, all officers in revolutionary war, etc. etc. Providence, R. I., Preston and Rounds, 1901. vi, 799 p. 28 cm. Supplement to above item 1-26556 Rev.

F78.S 66

SMITH, Joseph Jencks. New index to the Civil and military lists of Rhode Island. Providence, R.I., J. J. Smith, 1907. 182 p. 28 cm. The two vols. were pub. 1900-1901. See F78.S 65. 7-19058. F78.S 67
Geneal. Section Ref.

UPDIKE, Wilkins. Memoirs of the Rhode Island bar. Boston, T. H. Webb, 1842. xii, (13) - 311 p. 20½ cm. 6-8250. F78.U 66

VOLKEL, Lowell M. An Index to the 1800 federal census of Rhode Island. (n.p., 1970) 74 p. 28 cm. F78.V 6

GENERAL WORKS. HISTORIES.

ARNOLD, Samuel Greene. History of the state of Rhode Island and Providence plantations. New York, London, D. Appleton, 1859 - 60. 2 v. pl., fold. maps. 24 cm. 2-18842. F79.A 76

— Photo-offset. Spartanburg, S.C., Reprint Co., 1970. 23 cm. (Rhode Island heritage series no. 2)
F79.A76
1970

585

BATES, Frank Greene. Rhode Island and the formation of the Union. ... New York, 1898.
(v) - ix, 11 - 221 p.   24 cm.   Thesis (PH. D.) - Columbia university, 1899. Repr. from vol. x no. 2 of Studies in history, economics and public law, Columbia university. Bibliography: p. 217 - 220.   4-9717.
F79. B 32

BICKNELL, Thomas Williams.   The history of the state of Rhode Island and Providence Plantations ... New York, The American historical soc., 1920.   5 v. fronts., plates, ports., maps. 27½ cm. Vols. 1 - 3 paged continuously. Vols. 4 - 5 unnumbered, are biographical. 20-9789 Rev.
F79. B 58

CARROLL, Charles.   Rhode Island; three centuries of democracy ... New York, Lewis historical pub. co., 1932.   4 v. fronts., plates (1 col.) ports. 27½ cm. Vols. 3 - 4 contain biographies. 32-6330.
F79. C 26

CLAUSON, James Earl. These plantations, with a foreword by Sevellon Brown and illus. by Milton Halladay and Paule Loring.   Providence, R. I., Print. the Roger Williams press, E. A. Johnson co. (1937)   6, 3-119 p. front. (port.) illus. 24½ cm. ... "chosen from a much larger number written for, and published in, the Evening bulletin of Providence under the heading, 'These plantations'." 37-38850.
F79. C 56

CORBETT, Scott. Rhode Island. New York, Coward-McCann (1969)   124 p. illus. 26 cm. (States of the Nation, 13)   69-19507.
F79. C 65

DURFEE, Job. A discourse, delivered before the Rhode-Island historical soc. ... 1847. Providence, C. Burnette, 1847.   32 p.   21½ cm.   1-16307.
F79. D 95

— Providence, C. Burnett, 1847.   42, 5 p. 22½ cm. 1-16308.
F79. D 96

FEDERAL writers' project. ... Rhode Island, a guide to the smallest state ... Boston, Houghton, Mifflin co., 1937.   xxvi, 500 p. plates, ports., maps (1 fold. in pocket) 21 cm. (American guide series) Bibliography: p. (475) - 479. 37-28463.
F79. F 38
Geneal. Section Ref.

FIELD, Edward. State of Rhode Island and Providence plantations at the end of the century: a history ... Boston & Syracuse, The Mason pub. co., 1902.   3 v. illus., port., plans, facsim. 25 cm.   2-13122.
F79. F 45

GLEESON, Paul F. Rhode Island; the development of a democracy. Providence, R. I. State Board of Education, 1957.   xx, 332 p. illus., ports., maps. 24 cm. Includes bibliographies. 58-62844.
F79. G 55

GREENE, Frank B.   Rhode Island. Philadelphia, J. B. Lippincott, 1891.   5 p. 19 cm. Appears as article "Rhode Island" in Chambers's encyclopedia. Rc-2977.
F79. G 78

GREENE, George Washington. A short history of Rhode Island ... Providence, J. A. & R. A. Reid, 1877.   xxvi, 356 p. front., map. 20½ cm. Rc-2978.
F79. G 79

LIPPINCOTT, Bertram. Indians, privateers, and high society. A Rhode Island sampler. (1st ed.) Philadelphia, Lippincott (1961)   301 p. 22 cm. 61-8663.
F79. L 5

MINER, Lillian Burleigh. Our state: Rhode Island. Providence, R.I., Printed at the Oxford press (1925)   4, 248 p. front., illus. 20 cm. "Good reading for Rhode Islanders": p. 235 - 236. 25-9570.
F79. M 65

MONAHON, Clifford Philip. Rhode Island; a students' guide to localized history. New York, Teachers College Press, Teachers College, Columbia University, 1965.   x, 36 p. 23 cm. (Localized history series) 65-15072.
F79. M 7

MUNRO, Wilfred Harold. ... Picturesque Rhode Island. Pen and pencil sketches of the scenery and history of its cities, towns and hamlets, and of men who have made them famous. Providence, J. A. and R. A. Reid, 1881.   304 p. illus., maps (partly fold.) 25½ cm. 1 map wanting. 1-Rc-2979.
F79. M 96

POTTER, Elisha Reynolds. An address delivered before the Rhode Island historical soc. ... 1851. Providence, G. H. Whitney, 1851.   27 p.   23½ cm. Rc-3059.
F79. P 86

RHODE ISLAND

PRESTON, H. W. Rhode Island's historic background ... 1930. (Rhode Island. state bureau of information. Historical publication no. 3)
F79.P 92

PRESTON, Howard Willis. Rhode Island's historic background. State of Rhode Island and Providence Plantations, Rhode Island tercentenary commission. (Providence, Remington press) 1936.
62 p. incl. front., illus. (incl. ports., maps) diagr. 25 cm. 36-27936.
F79.P 93

PROVIDENCE. Official chronicle and tribute book of Rhode Island and Providence Plantations; this volume contains a chronicle of three hundred years of outstanding events, its industrial and commercial development, etc. Compiled by Lucia Hammond Wheeler ... (Providence) Pub. by G. D. Hall, inc. for Official chronicle committee, The Providence tercentenary committee, 1936. 159 p. illus. 28 cm. 38-528.
F79.P956

PROVIDENCE institution for savings. "The Old stone bank" history of Rhode Island, presented by Providence institution for savings... Providence, R.I., 1929 - 44. 4 v. front., illus., plates. 24 cm. 30-13826.
F79.P 97

RHODE ISLAND Dept. of education. Rhode Island education circulars. 1924. 1 v.
F79.R 48

RHODE ISLAND. The book of Rhode Island, an illustrated description of the advantages and opportunities of the state of Rhode Island and the progress that has been achieved, etc. ... Distributed by Rhode Island State bureau of information, in cooperation with Rhode Island conference of business associations, compilers and publishers. (Providence, Remington press) 1930. 299 p. incl. front. (port.) illus. 28½ cm. 30-27514.
F79.R 49

RICHMAN, Irving Berdine. ... Rhode Island, a study in separatism, by Irving Berdine Richman ... Boston and New York, Houghton, Mifflin, 1905. x, (3) - 395 p. front. (fold. map) 18½ cm. (American commonwealths) Bibliography: p. (353) - 385. 5-34187.
F79.R 53

— Boston and New York, Houghton, Mifflin, 1905. x 23 cm. 5-36822.
F79.R532

ROSS, Arthur Amasa. A discourse, embracing the civil and religious history of Rhode-Island. Providence, H. H. Brown, 1838. iv, (5) - 161 p. 19 cm. Rc-2982 Rev.
F79.R 82

TANNER, Earl C. Rhode Island; a brief history. (Providence) Rhode Island State Board of Education, 1954. xxi, 172 p. illus. 23 cm. Bibliography: p. 167 - 168. 54-63141.
F79.T 35

WILLIAMS, Thomas. A sermon, on the conclusion of the second century from the settlement of the state of Rhode-Island and Providence Plantations. Providence, Print. Vose, 1837. Print, Knowles, Vose, 1837. 32 p. 23½ cm. 17-30104.
F79.W 72

JUVENILE WORKS.

BAILEY, Bernadine (Freeman) Picture book of Rhode Island. Pictures by Kurt Wiese. Chicago, A. Whitman, 1958. unpaged. illus. 17 x 21 cm. (Her The United States books) 58-12320.
F79.3.B3

— 1966. 32 p. 17 x 21 cm. 58-12320.
F79.3.B3 1966

CARPENTER, John Allan. Rhode Island. Illus. by Roger Herrington. Chicago, Childrens Press (1968) 95 p. 24 cm. (Enchantment of America) 68-12824.
F79.3.C3

HISTORIC MONUMENTS (GENERAL). ILLUSTRATIVE MATERIAL.

Rhode Island's tercentenary miscellanies ... (By) Arthur W. Brown. Volume I ... Providence, R.I.,

LOCAL HISTORIES IN THE LIBRARY OF CONGRESS

The Wm. R. Brown print. (1937)   viii, 224 p. illus. (incl. ports., facsims.) fold. map. 23 cm. Prose and verse. No. more pub?   A 40-3386.
F80. B 7
1937

DOWNING, Antoinette Forrester. Early homes of Rhode Island; drawings by Helen Mason Grose, photos by Arthur L. LeBoeuf. Richmond, Va., Garrett and Massie, 1937.   xviii p. 480 p. incl. front., illus., plates.   25 cm.   Bibliography: p. 467 - 470.   37-25285.
F80. D 69

FOSTER, William Eaton. Some Rhode Island contributions to the intellectual life of the last century, by William E. Foster. From Proceedings of the Amer. antiquarian soc., 1892. Worcester, Mass., Press of C. Hamilton, 1892.   32 p.   24½ cm.   10-11998.
F80. F 75

HOYT, David Webster. ... The influence of physical features upon the history of Rhode Island ... (Providence) Dept. of education, state of R. I., 1910.   20 p. 6 pl. 23½ cm. (R.I. education circulars. Historical series - iv)   10-33407.
F80. H 86

JACKSON, Henry. An account of the churches in Rhode-Island. ... Providence, G. H. Whitney, 1854.   134 p.   front.   23 cm.   10-3160.
F80. J 14

KIMBALL, Gertrude Selwyn. Pictures of Rhode Island in the past, 1642 - 1833, by travellers and observers. Providence, R. I., Preston & Rounds co., 1900.   xiii, 175 p.   23½ cm.   Extracts from traveller's narratives, etc.   0-153 Rev.
F80. K 49

LASWELL, George D. "Corners and characters of Rhode Island", ... Providence, R. I., The Oxford press, 1924.   v.   front. (port.)   illus.   31 cm.   25-227.
F80. L 34

NATIONAL society of the colonial dames of America. Old houses in the south county of Rhode Island ... Providence, Print. for the Society (Boston, D. B. Updike) 1932.   v. illus. (incl. plan) map. 27½ cm.   33-5291.
F80. N 26

PROVIDENCE. Dept. of public schools. Handbook of historical sites in Rhode Island; pub. in connection with the tercentenary celebration of the founding of Providence. Providence, R.I., Dept. of public schools, 1936.   96 p. illus., fold. map.   23 cm.   Bibliography: p. 88 - 89.   36-1260.
F80. P 93

PROVIDENCE. Old home week committee. The official program of the Old home week ... 1907, including handy guide to Providence ... (Providence, Remington print., 1907)   (16) p. illus. (map) 24 cm.
F80. P 95

— Official souvenir and program. Issued by the Publicity department. (Providence, Remington printing co.) 1907.   112 p. illus. (incl. ports., maps, facsims.)
F80. P 96

PYLE, Katharine. Once upon a time in Rhode Island ... illus. by Helen B. Mason. (Garden City, N.Y., Doubleday, Page, 1914)   5, 204 (2) p. incl. plates. illus.   19½ cm.   Pub. by the Soc. of colonial dames in Rhode Island.   15-4678 Rev.
F80. P 98

RHODE ISLAND, ... Points of historical interest in the state of, prepared with the cooperation of the Rhode Island historical soc.   (Providence?) R.I., Department of education, 1911.   84 p. illus. 23 cm. (R.I. education circulars. Historical series - v)   11-23186 Rev.
F80. R 47

RHODE ISLAND historical society ... Report of Committee on marking historical sites in Rhode Island ... Providence, R. I., E. L. Freeman, print. 1914.   183 p. front., plates. 23½ cm.   14-31830.
F80. R 49

FOSTER, William Eaton. Address before the R. I. society of the Sons of the American revolution ... 1891. New York, The Republic press, 1892.   16 p.   23 cm.   18-20452.
F81. F 75

RHODE ISLAND

EARLY TO 1775.

ADAMS, James Truslow. Rhode Island's part in making America. An address ... (Providence) State of Rhode Island public education service, 1923. 12 p. 23 cm. (Rhode Island. Dept. of public instruction. R. I. education circulars) E 24-5.
F82. A 14

ADLAM, Samuel. Origin of the institutions of Rhode Island. A lecture ... before the Newport historical society. Providence, J. F. Greene, print. 1871. 25 p. 23 cm. 3-5045.
F82. A 23

ARNOLD, James N., ... Report of, ... to inquire into the present condition of the Governor Benedict Arnold burial place, and the title thereto. Providence, E.L. Freeman, 1901. 47 p. 23 cm. 2-3363.
F82. A 74

ALDERMAN, Clifford Lindsey. The Rhode Island Colony. (New York) Crowell-Collier Press (1969) 134 p. illus. 23 cm. "First printing" 69-10461.
F82. A748

ARNOLD, James Newell. A statement of the case of the Narragansett tribe of Indians, as shown in the manuscript collection of Sir William Johnson ... To which are added a few other important papers illustrating the said case. Newport, R.I., Mercury pub. co., 1896. 70 p. 3 fold. maps. 24 cm. 10-8685.
F82. A 75

ARNOLD, Samuel Greene. The spirit of Rhode Island history. A discourse, delivered before the R. I. historical soc ... Providence, G. H. Whitney, 1853. 32 p. 23 cm. Rc-2983.
F82. A 76

ASPINWALL, Thomas. Remarks on the Narraganset patent. Read before the Mass. historical soc. ... 2d ed. Providence, S. S. Rider, 1865. 40 p. 25½ x 15 cm. Rc-2984.
F82. A 84

BEALS, Carleton. Colonial Rhode Island. (Camden, N.J.) T. Nelson (1970) 160 p. illus. 22 cm. (Colonial histories) 73-99437.
F82. B 4

BOWEN, Richard Le Baron. The Providence oath of allegiance and its signers, 1651-2; contributed by Frederick S. Peck ... Providence (Concord, N.H., The Rumford press) 1943. x, 92 p. front. (facsim.) illus. (facsims.) plans (1 fold.) 23½ cm. "First edition." 44-1763.
F82. B 67

BROWN, James. The letter book of James Browne of Providence, merchant, 1735 - 1738, from the original manuscript in the library of the R. I. historical soc, with an introd. by George P. Krapp ... Providence, Print. for the R.I. hist. soc., 1929. xiv, 15 - 66 p. incl. facsim. 23½ cm. 29-22595.
F82. B 87

— Freeport, N.Y., Books for Libraries Press (1971) 66 p. illus. 23 cm. Reprint of the 1929 ed. Includes biographical references. 75-164613 MARC.
F82. B 87
1971

CALLENDER, John. An historical discourse on the civil and religious affairs of the colony of Rhode-Island and Providence Plantations .... 1638, to the end of the first century. Boston, Print. S. Kneeland and T. Green, 1739. 14, 120 p. 19 cm. 8-18217.
F82. C136
Rare Book Coll.

— with a memoir of the author, etc. ... and annotations and original documents .... By Romeo Elton. Providence, Knowles, Vose, 1838. 270, (2) p. 22½ cm. (Collections of the R.I. historical soc. vol. iv) Rc-2943.
F82. C 14 or 142

— 3d ed. Boston, T. H. Webb; N.Y., Bartlett & Welford; 1843. viii, (9) - 270 p. facsim. 22 cm. Rc-2944.
F82. C 15

— 3d. ed. Freeport, N.Y., Books for Libraries Press (1971) viii, 270 p. 23 cm. 79-150172.
F82. C 15
1971

CHAPIN, Howard Millar. Documentary history of Rhode Island. v. 1 - 2. Providence, Preston and Rounds, 1916 - 19.   2 v. illus., plates, fold. maps, plans, facsims. (part fold.) 23 cm. v.1. History of the towns of Providence and Warwick to 1649 and of the colony to 1647. - v.2. History of the towns of Portsmouth and Newport to 1647 and the court records of Aquidneck. 16-17375 Rev.
                                                      F82. C 46

CHAPIN, Howard Millar. Rhode Island in the colonial wars. A list of Rhode Island soldiers & sailors in King George's war, 1740 - 1748. Providence, Print. for the (R. I. historical) Soc., 1920.   38 p.   23½ cm.   20-20569.   F82. C 48

CHAPIN, Howard Millar. Rhode Island privateers in King George's war, 1739 - 1748 ... Providence, R. I. historical soc., 1926.   4, 5 - 225 p. front., plates, ports., facsims.   23½ cm.   27-2643.   F82. C483

CHAPIN, Howard Millar. The Tartar, the armed sloop of the colony of Rhode Island in King George's war ... Providence, 1922.   2, 67, viii p. plates (1 fold.) facsims.   23½ cm.   23-10113.
                                                      F82. C 49

CHAPIN, Howard Millar. The trading post of Roger Williams with those of John Wilcox and Richard Smith ... Providence, Printed for the Society (of colonial wars) by E. L. Freeman co. (1933)   2, 7 - 26 p. illus. (map) 23 cm.   34-16117 Rev.   F82. C495

CHILD, Mrs. Anne P. Whatcheer, a story of olden times. One of sister Rhody's collection of historical facts for the amusement and instruction of young people. ... Providence, Knowles, Anthony, printers, 1857.   ix, 104 p.   16 cm.   3-27743.   F82. C 53

BICKNELL, Thomas Williams. ... Story of Dr. John Clarke, the founder of the first free commonwealth of the world on the basis of "full liberty in religious concernments," 1st ed. Providence, R. I., The atuhor (1915)   212, (4) p. front., plates, ports., map, facsims. 28 cm.   15-24807.
                                                  F82. C 59

CLARKE. The hero of Aquidneck, a life of Dr. John Clarke, by Wilbur Nelson ... New York, etc., Fleming H. Revell co. (1938)   95 p. front.   19½ cm.   38-13784.   F82. C596

CODDINGTON. William Coddington of Rhode Island, a sketch by Emily Coddington Williams. Newport, R. I., Priv. print. (Boston, The Merrymount press) 1941.   vi, 80 p.   25 cm.   Bibliographical footnotes. 42-2301.   F82. C65W5

GLEESON, Alice Collins. Colonial Rhode Island ... Pawtucket, R. I., The Automobile journal pub. co. (1926)   5, 260 p. illus. (incl. ports., facsims.) 21 cm.   26-16921.   F82. G 56

GORTON. A defence of Samuel Gorton and the settlers of Shawomet ... by George Arnold Brayton. Providence, S. S. Rider, 1883.   8, 120 p. sq 8°. (Rhode Island historical tracts. 1st. ser. no. 17) 1-Rc-2909.
                                                  F82. G 64

GORTON. Some notices of Samuel Gorton, one of the first settlers of Warwick, R. I., during his residence at Plymouth, Portsmouth, and Providence ... Boston, Print. Coolidge and Wiley, 1850.   41 p.   24 cm.   25 copies reprinted from the N. E. hist. and genealogical register for July, 1850. 25-12681.   F82. G 65

GORTON. Samuel Gorton's letter to Lord Hyde in behalf of the Narragansett sachems. (Providence) Print. for the Society (of colonial wars) by E. L. Freeman co., 1930.   20 p.   23½ cm.   "From the original in the John Carter Brown library." 32-14428.   F82. G 66

GORTON, Samuel. Simplicities defence against seven-headed policy. Or innocency vindicated, being unjustly accused, and sorely censured, by that seven-headed church-government united in New England ... London, Print. J. Macock, 1646.   8 p. 111 p. illus.   18 x 13½ cm.   Reissued in 1647 with differences in secondary title. 1-22530.
                                                F82. G 67
                                               Rare Book Coll.

— with notes explanatory of the text, etc. By William R. Staples ... Providence, Marshall, Brown, 1835.   (7) - 278 p. 22 cm. (In R. I. historical soc. Collections. Providence, 1835. vol. 11) 1-Rc-2946.
                                                F82. G 68

RHODE ISLAND

— Reprint from Force Tracts ... v. 4 (1846) no. 6. 116 p. 4-27246.

F82.G 69

GORTON. The life and times of Samuel Gorton; the founders and the founding of the republic ... and a history of the colony of Providence and Rhode Island plantations ... comp. ... by Adelos Gorton ... Philadelphia (G. S. Ferguson, print.) 1907. x, 11 - 154 p. illus. 24½ cm. 7-32381.

F82.G 71

GORTON, Samuell: a forgotten founder of our liberties; first settler of Warwick. By Lewis G. Janes ... Providence, Preston and Rounds, 1896. vi, (7) - 141 p. (The Rhode Island series ... 3) 11-4714.

F82.G 73

GORTON, Samuell. Massachusetts' war with Samuell Gorton. The settlement of Warwick, R.I. (1642-3) etc. etc. (By) William Greene Roelker ... (Warwick?) Rhode Island Pendulum, 1942. 8, vii p. 23 cm. 44-1270.

F82.G 76

HARRIS papers, with an introd. by Irving B. Richman ... (Providence, 1902) 410 p. fold. map. 24 cm. (Collections of the R. I. historical soc. vol. x) Rel. to the career of Wm. Harris, one of the founders of R.I. 5-9975.

F82.H 31

HAZARD, Caroline. Judge Sewall's gifts in the Narragansett country, ... (Providence, Roger Williams press, 1936) 23 p. 24½ cm. From R.I. Hist. soc.'s quarterly in 1898. 37-9450.

F82.H 39

HAZARD, Thomas, son of Robt. call'd College Tom. A study of life in Narragansett in the 18th century, by his grandson's granddaughter, Caroline Hazard. Boston and N.Y., Houghton, Mifflin, 1893. viii, 324 p. front. (map) facsims. 22½ cm. 11-21030.

F82. H 4

KOOPMAN, Harry Lyman. The Narragansett country; glimpses of the past ... Providence, 1927. 55 p. 19½ cm. 27-1872.

F82.K 75

— Providence, Print. for the Society (of colonial wars) by E. L. Freeman co. (1927) 55 p. 19½ cm. 29-14692.

F82.K752

LOPEZ of Newport; colonial American merchant prince, by Stanley F. Chyet. Detroit, Wayne State University Press, 1970. 246 p. 24 cm. 78-93898.

F82.L66C5
1970

LOVEJOY, David Sherman. Rhode Island politics and the American Revolution, 1760 - 1776. Providence, Brown University Press, 1958. 256 p. fold. map. 24 cm. (Brown University studies, v. 23) Bibliographical references included in "Notes" (p. 196 - 220) 58-10478.

F82.L 68
L.H. & G.

MACSPARRAN, James. A letter book and abstract of out services, written during the year 1743-1751 Ed. ... by Rev. Daniel Goodwin ... with portraits. Boston, D. B. Updike, 1899. 4, vii - xliv p. 197 p. ports. 22½ cm. 0-162 Rev.

F82.M 17

MILLER, Charles T. Settlement of Rhode Island. Illus. by Walter F. Brown. New York, The Graphic co., 1874. 15 l. of illus. 25½ x 29 cm. Cartoons and verses. 8-20210.

F82.M 64

MILLER, William Davis. Early houses of the King's province in the Narragansett country, with drawings by Norman Morrison Isham. Wakefield, R.I., 1941. 3, 33 p. illus. 19 cm. 41-10340.

F82.M 66

PAINE, George Taylor. A denial of the charges of forgery in connection with the sachems' deed to Roger Williams. (Providence, Standard print., 1896) 71 p. facsim. 21½ x 17 cm. 2-14218.

F82.P 14

PARRINGTON, Vernon Louis. ... Roger Williams, seeker. (New York, Harcourt, Brace, 1927?) (62) - 75 p. 21½ cm. Reprinted from vol. 1 of Vernon L. Parrington's 'Main currents in American thought' Bibliographical foot-notes. CA 28-380 Unrev.

F82.P 26

PHILLIPS, Mary Schuyler.   Colonial Rhode Island ... (Cincinnati, The Ebbert & Richardson co., 1916)   36 p. 23 cm.   The Colonial dames of America in the state of Ohio. Studies in the colonial period for use in the public schools) 18-15160.
 F82. P 56

PITMAN, John.   A discourse delivered at Providence ... 1836, in commemoration of the first settlement of Rhode-Island and Providence Plantations.   Being the second centennial anniversary ...   Providence, B. Cranston, 1836.   72 p. 22 cm. Rc-2985.
 F82. P 68

POTTER, Elisha Reynolds.   The early history of Narragansett; with an appendix of original documents ...   Providence, Marshall, Brown, 1835.   xix, 315 p. 22 cm.   (In R.I. historical soc. Collections. vol. iii) 1-Rc-2950.
 F82. P 86

POTTER, Elisha Reynolds.   Several purchases of the lands west of Wickford sold by the committee of the colony for the sale of the vacant lands in 1709 ...   Providence, Printed for the society (of colonial wars) by E. L. Freeman co. (1937?)   10 p. illus. (map) 23 cm. 37-31865.
 F82. P 87

PRESTON, Howard Willis.   Rhode Island and the sea, ...   Providence (E. L. Freeman co.) 1932.
140 p. illus. (map) diagr. 23½ cm. (State bureau of information. Historical pub. no. 4) Authorities p. 89-90. 32-27391.
 F82. P 89

PROPRIETORS of lands in the Narragansett country, The records of the, otherwise called the Fones record ...   By James N. Arnold ... Providence, R. I., Narragansett historical pub. co., 1894.
ix, 199 p. 23½ cm. (Rhode Island colonial gleanings, vol. 1) 1-10218.
 F82. P 96

RHODE ISLAND (Colony)   Rhode Island court records; records of the Court of trials of the colony of Providence Plantations, 1647 - 1670.   Providence, 1920 - 22.   2 v. 23½ cm. 22-2732 Rev.
 F82. R 4

RHODE ISLAND (colony)   ... Records of the Vice-admiralty court of Rhode Island, 1716 - 1752, ed. Dorothy S. Towle, with an introd. by Charles M. Andrews.   Washington, D.C., The American historical assoc., 1936.   3 p. 595 p. 25½ cm. (American legal records - v. 3) 37-7861.
 F82. P415

RHODE ISLAND (Colony)   The correspondence of the colonial governors of Rhode Island, 1723 - 1775; pub. by the National soc. of the colonial dames of America ...   ed. Gertrude Selwyn Kimball ... Boston and N.Y., Houghton, Mifflin, 1902-3.   2 v. fronts., plates, ports. 23 cm. 3-846.
 F82. R 44

— N.Y., Books for Libraries Press (1969)   2 v. illus. 22 cm. (Select bibliographies reprint series)   70-95070.
 F82. R442

RHODE ISLAND (Colony)   A vindication of the Governour and Government of H. M. Colony of Rhode Island, etc.   From the unjust Aspersions and Calumnies of John Menzies ... Relating to the Proceedings ... in the Affair of several Slaves, and other Goods ... from a ship lately lying at Tarpawlin-Cove, etc.   (n. p., 1727?) (Boston, 1927)   12 p. 25½ cm. (Americana series; photostat by the Mass. hist. soc. no. 198) CA 29 - 424 Unrev.
 F82. R 46
 Rare Book Coll.

RHODE ISLAND tercentenary, 1636 - 1936.   A report by the Rhode Island Tercentenary commission of the celebration of the 300th anniversary of the settlement of the state of R. I. and Providence Plantations in 1636 by Roger Williams. (Providence) 1937.   158 p. incl. front. plates. 23½ cm. 37-27774.
 F82. R 48

RHODE ISLAND land evidences, vol. I, 1648 - 1696, abstracts.   Providence (R.I. hist. soc.) 1921.
246, xxv p. front. (fold. map) 23½ cm.   Abstracts made by Dorothy Worthington from vol. i of four ancient volumes now in the office of the secretary of state. 21-18384.
 F82. R 5

— With pref. to the reprint ed. by Albert T. Klyberg.   Baltimore, Genealogical Pub. Co., 1970.
246, xxv p. 23 cm. 79-77882.
 F82. R 5
 1970

RICHMAN, Irving Berdine.   Rhode Island; its making and its meaning; a survey of the annals of the

RHODE ISLAND

commonwealth from its settlement to the death of Roger Williams, 1636 - 1683 ... with an introd. by James Bryce ... New York and London, G. P. Putnam's sons, 1902. 2 v. fold. maps. 22½ cm. 2-26760/3.
F82.R 52

RIDER, Sidney Smith. An inquiry concerning the origin of the clause in the laws of Rhode Island (1719 - 1783) disfranchising Roman Catholics. Providence (S. S. Rider) 1889. 72 p. 21½ x 16½ cm. (Rhode Island historical tracts. 2d ser. no. 1) Rc-2972.
F82.R528

RIDER, Sidney Smith. The lands of Rhode Island as they were known to Caunounicus and Miantunnomu when Roger Williams came in 1636. An Indian map of the principal locations known to the Nahigansets. ... Providence, R. I., The author, 1904. 4, 297 p. front., illus., plates, etc. 24 cm. 4-25120.
F82.R 53

RIDER, Sidney Smith. A retrospect from the round tower of the Pomham club, ... Providence, Priv. print. club copy, 1889. 19 p. illus. 15½ cm. Rc-2986 Rev.
F82.R 54 or 541

SANFORD, Peleg. The letter book of Peleg Sanford of Newport, merchant (later governour of Rhode Island) 1666 - 1668. Transcribed ... by Howard W. Preston ... Providence, Printef for the Rhode Island historical soc., 1928. vi, 7 - 84 p. front., plates, facsim. 23½ cm. 29-14771.
F82.S 22

SOCIETY of colonial wars. A map of Acquidnesset or North purchase of the Atherton partners. Providence, Printed for the Society by E. L. Freeman co. (1932) 2, 11 - 13 p. map. 23½ cm. 33-3885.
F82.S 66
Rare Book Coll.

SOCIETY of colonial wars. The Narragansett mortgage; the documents concerning the alien purchases in southern Rhode Island. Providence, Printed for the Society by E. L. Freeman co. (1926) 2, 9 - 45 p. 23 cm. 30-6909.
F82.S 67

SWAN, Bradford Fuller. The case of Richard Chasmore alias Long Dick ... Providence, Print. for the Society (of colonial wars) by the Roger Williams press (1944) 2, vii - viii, 26 p. 23½ cm. (Publication no. 36) A 46-859.
F82.S 9

TURNER, Henry Edward. Settlers of Aquidneck, and liberty of conscience. The Newport, R.I. historical pub. co., 1880. 54 p. 24½ cm. Rc-2987.
F82.T 94

UPDIKE, Daniel Berkeley. Richard Smith, first English settler of the Narragansett country, R.I., with a series of letters writen by his son, Richard Smith, jr., to members of the Winthrop family ... with illus. from drawings by Edmund Hort New. Boston, The Merrymouth press, 1937. xix, 118 p. plates. 24½ cm. 38-112.
F82.U 73

WHITE, Mrs. Elizabeth (Nicholson) The true story of Frances, the falconer's daughter, wife of William Dungan (and others) ... Providence (Roger Williams press, priv. print.) 1932. 4, 3 -176 p. incl. front., illus. fold. map. 21½ cm. 32-32239.
F82. V19

WEBB, Robert N. The colony of Rhode Island ... Illus. with contemporary prints and maps. New York, Watts, 1972. 89 p. illus. 22 cm. (A First book) 70-189517.
F82.W 37

WEEDON, William Babcock. Early Rhode Island; a social history of the people. New York, The Grafton press (1910) x, 381 p. front., plates, facsims. 19½ cm. (Grafton hist. series) 10-30090.
F82.W 39

WHITE, Elizabeth (Nicholson) Anne of Kings Towne. Illus. by Mary Elmore. (East Providence? R.I., 1955) 51 p. illus. 21 cm. 55-32217.
F82.W5W4

WILLIAMS, Roger. An answer to a letter sent from Mr. Coddington of Rode Island, to Governour Leveret of Boston in what concerns R. W. of Providence. (n.p., 1678) (Boston, 1922) facsim.: 10 p., 2 l. 24½ cm. (Americana series; photostat by The Mass. hist. soc. no. 66) 23-4655.
F82.W 62
Rare Book Coll.

— Providence, Print. for the Society (of colonial wars) by the Roger Williams press (1946) 5 p. facsim. 9 p. 23½ cm. (Publication no. 38) 47-20702.
F82.W6213

— (Providence, 1876) 9 (1) p. 23 cm. Detached from R. I. historical soc. Proceedings, 1875/6. F82.W622

WILLIAMS, Roger. An answer to a scandalous paper which came to my hand from the Massachusets clamouring against the purchase and slandering the purchasers of Qunnunnagut iland. Providence, The Roger Williams press, 1945. (19) p. 2 illus. (facsim.) 23½ cm. (Soc. of colonial wars. Rhode Island. Publication no. 37) 47-20701. F82.W 63

WILLIAMS, Roger, Letters and papers of, 1629 - 1682. Boston, Mass. historical soc., 1924. 294 l. of facsims. 38½ x 27½ cm. "eighteen copies have been reproduced." 24-7324.
F82. W 65
MSS R. R.

WILLIAMS, Roger. The Roger Williams calendar. (Central Falls, R.I., E. L. Freeman, printers, 1897) vi, 370 p. 20½ cm. 16-3047. F82. W 69

WILLIAMS, Roger. Master Roger Williams, a biography. By Ola Elizabeth Winslow. New York, Macmillan, 1957. 328 p. illus. 22 cm. Includes bibliography. "First printing." 57-10016. F82.W692

WILLIAMS, Roger, Memorial of. By Zachariah Allen. Providence, Cooke & Danielson, printers (1860) 12 p. 14½ cm. 15-11542. F82. W 7

— 1860. 10 p. 17 cm. 14-1336. F82. W 71

WILLIAMS, Roger, celebration (re-dedication of statue of religious liberty) under auspices of B'nai B'rith ... (n. p., 1936) 29 numb. l. pl. 27½ cm. Reproduced from type-written copy. 38-4422 Rev.
F82.W717

WILLIAMS, Roger. The irrepressible democrat, Roger Williams, by Samuel Hugh Brockunier ... New York, The Ronald press co. (1940) xii, 305 p. facsim. 24 cm. (Ronald series in history) Bibliographical foot-notes. 40-31938. F82.W718

WILLIAMS, Roger; a study of the life, times and character of a political pioneer, by Edmund J. Carpenter ... New York, The Grafton press (1909) xxxiv, 253 p. front., 3 pl. 20 cm. (The Grafton historical series) 9-31830. F82. W 72

— Freeport, N.Y., Books for Libraries Press (1972) xxxiv, 246 p. illus. 23 cm. 72-000013.
F82. W 72
1972

WILLIAMS, Roger. ... Report upon the burial place of Roger Williams, by Howard M. Chapin. Providence, 1918. 30 p. front., illus. (maps, diagrs.) map. 27 cm. Rhode Island historical society. 19-1988.
F82.W725

WILLIAMS, Roger, and the King's colors; the documentary evidence (by) Howard Millar Chapin. Providence, Print. for the Society (of colonial wars) by E. L. Freeman co. (1928) 7 - 26 p. 2 col. pl. 23 cm. 29-8908. F82.W726

WILLIAMS, Roger, by Henry Chupack. New York, Twayne Publishers (1969) 168 p. 21 cm. (Twayne's United States authors series.) 68-24306. F82.W7264

WILLIAMS, Roger. The gentle radical; a biography of Roger Williams, by Cyclone Covey. New York, Macmillan Co. (1966) viii, 273 p. 21 cm. "First printing." 66-19094. F82.W727

WILLIAMS, Roger. The discovery of American liberty. By Rev. P. S. Davies ... (Appleton, Wis., The Post pub. co., printers, 1904) (8) p. 21½ cm. A tribute to Roger Williams. 15-2152. F82.W728

WILLIAMS, Roger. As to Roger Williams, and his 'banishment' from the Massachusetts Plantation; with a few further words concerning the Baptists, the Quakers, and religious liberty ... by Henry Martyn Dexter ... Boston, Congregational pub. soc., 1876. vi, 146 p. 26 cm. 15-821.
F82. W 73

RHODE ISLAND

WILLIAMS, Roger, prophet and pioneer, by Emily Easton. Boston and New York, Houghton Mifflin 1930. ix, 399 p. front. (port.) 22½ cm. "List of sources": p. (379) - 380. 30-13850. F82.W737

— Freeport, N.Y., Books for Libraries Press (1969) ix, 399 p. 23 cm. (Select bibliographies reprint series) 71-102235. F82.W737 1969

— New York, AMS Press. (1969) ix, 399 p. port. 22 cm. "Reprint of 1930 ed." 76-101266. F82.W737 1969 b

— 1972. F82.W737 1972

WILLIAMS, Roger. ... Roger Williams, the founder of Providence - the pioneer of religious liberty, by Amasa M. Eaton ... Dept. of education, state of R. I. (Providence, R.I., E.L. Freeman co., 1908) 19 p. 23 cm. (Rhode Island educational circulats. Historical series II) E8-862. F82.W 74

WILLIAMS, Roger. Lone journey; the life of Roger Williams, by Jeanette Eaton, illus. by Woodi Ishmael. New York, Harcourt, Brace, (1944) 4 p, 3-266 p. incl. illus. (incl. facsims.) plates, map. 22½ cm. 44-8239. F82.W742

WILLIAMS, Roger. Life of Roger Williams, the earliest legislator and true champion for a full and absolute liberty of conscience. By Romeo Elton ... London, A. Cockshaw (1852) viii, 173 p. 16½ cm. 14-3689. F82. W75

— London, A. Cockshaw; New York, G. P. Putnam (1852) vii, 173 p. 17½ cm. 14-3690. F82.W752

— Providence, G. H. Whitney, 1853. viii, 173 p. 17½ cm. 14-3691. F82.W753

WILLIAMS, Roger; das Abenteuer der Freiheit. (von) Karl Dietrich Erdmann. Kiel, F. Hirt, 1967. 27 p. 23 cm. F82.W755

WILLIAMS, Roger, New England firebrand, by James Ernst. New York, The Macmillan co., 1932. xiv, 538 p. front. 23 cm. 32-22812. F82.W757

— New York, AMS Press (1969) xiv, 538 p. illus. 23 cm. 76-90097. F82.W757 1969

WILLIAMS, Roger. Life of Roger Williams, founder of the state of Rhode Island. By William Gammell ... Boston, Gould, Kendall & Lincoln, 1846. 4, (v) - ix, (5) - 221 p. front. (port.) facsim. 19½ cm. 14-3681. F82. W 77

— Boston, Gould and Lincoln, 1854. 4, (v) - ix p., (5) - 221 p. front. (port.) facsim. 18½ cm. Imperfect: frontispiece and facsimile wanting. 16-21622. F82.W773

WILLIAMS, Roger, witness beyond Christendom, 1603 - 1683 (by) John Garrett. (New York) MacMillan Co. (1970) x, 306 p. 21 cm. "1st printing." 76-109449. F82.W7732

WILLIAMS, Roger and the Massachusetts magistrates. Ed. with an introd. by Theodore P. Greene. Boston, D. C. Heath, 1964. xi, 125 p. 34 cm. (Problems in American civilization) readings selected by the Dept. of American Studies, Amherst College) F82.W7733

WILLIAMS, Roger, Footprints of. By Reuben Aldridge Guild. Providence, Tibbitts & Preston, 1886. 48 p. 25 cm. "Reprinted from the Providence journal." 48-33345*. F82.W7735

WILLIAMS, Roger, by May Emery Hall ... Boston, Chicago, The Pilgrim press (1917) xviii, 212 p. front., plates. 19½ cm. "Authorities": p. (v) - vi. 17-24423. F82.W776

WILLIAMS, Roger, Notes concerning. By Almon D. Hodges, jr. ... Boston, Priv. print., 1899. 60 - 64 p. 24 cm. 24-12316. F82.W777

WILLIAMS, Roger, The spirit of, with a portrait of one of his descendants ... By Lorenzo D. Johnson. Boston, Pub. for the author, by Cassady and March, 1839.   vi, (7) - 94 p. front. (port.) 16½ cm.
14-3688 Rev.
F82.W 78

WILLIAMS, Roger.   Memoir of Roger Williams, the founder of the state of Rhode-Island.   By James D. Knowles ... Boston, Lincoln, Edmands, 1834.   xx, (21) - 437 p. front. (facsim.) 19 cm. 13-33610.
F82.W785

WILLIAMS, Roger. ... The story of Roger Williams and the founding of Rhode Island, by Etta V. Leighton.   Dansville, N.Y., F.A.Owen pub. co., 1912.   32 p. illus. 18½ cm. (Instructor literature series No. 198) 43-29987.
F82.W786

WILLIAMS, Roger, his life, work, and ideals, by Charles Smull Longacre ... illus. by Robert M. Eldridge.   Takoma Park, Washington, D.C., Review and herald pub. assoc. (1939)   191 p. incl. front. (port.) illus. 20½ cm. 40-2910.
F82.W787

WILLIAMS, Roger; his contribution to the American tradition.   By Perry Miller.   (1st ed.)   Indianapolis, Bobbs-Merrill (1953)   273 p. 23 cm. (Makers of the American tradition series) 53-8874.
F82.W788

WILLIAMS, Roger; the church and the state (by) Edmund S. Morgan.   (1st ed.)   New York, Harcourt, Brace & World (1967)   170 p. 21 cm. 67-25999.
F82.W789

WILLIAMS, Roger, Foot-prints of; a biography, with sketches of important events in early New England history, with which he was connected.   By Rev. Z. A. Mudge ... New York, Carlton & Lanahan; San Francisco, E. Thomas; (1871)   285 p. incl. front., 4 pl. 18 cm. 13-33609.
F82.W 79

WILLIAMS, Roger; a colony leader.   By Helen Stone Peterson.   Illus. by Ray Burns.   Champaign, Ill., Garrard Pub. Co. (1968)   64 p. illus. 24 cm. (Colony leaders) 68-11351.
F82.W7914

WILLIAMS, Roger.   Roger Williams, John Cotton, and religious freedom; a controversy in new and old England (by) Irwin H. Polishook.   Englewood Cliffs, N.J., Prentice-Hall (1967)   vi, 122 p. 21 cm. (American historical sources series: research and interpretation) 67-20229.
F82.W792

WILLIAMS, Roger.   Ceremonies at the unveiling of the monument to Roger Williams, erected by the city of Providence, with the address by J. Lewis Diman ... 1877.   Providence, Angell, Hammett, 1877.   52 p. 2 mounted phot. (incl. front.) 25½ cm. (City doc. no. 31) 13-33786.
F82.W793

WILLIAMS, Roger.   Historical sketch of the progress of the Roger Williams monument assoc., with an appeal to the public in behalf thereof.   Providence, A. C. Greene, printer, 1867.   16 p. 18½ cm.
14-4709.
F82.W795

WILLIAMS, Roger, and the fight for religious freedom, by Clifford Smyth ... New York and London, Funk & Wagnalls co., 1931.   171 p. 18½ cm. (His Builders of America, v. 6) 31-35719.
F82.W7956

WILLIAMS, Roger; earliest of the fathers of American democracy.   With appendix showing fourteen generations of descent from Roger Williams to Roderick Davis Stitt.   By Edward W. Stitt.   (New Rochelle? N.Y., 1958)   23 l. 28 cm. 59-37358.
F82.W7958

WILLIAMS, Roger, the prophetic legislator, a paper read before the R. I. historical soc.   By Thomas T. Stone ... Providence, A. C. Greene, 1872.   16 p. 13 cm. 14-14048.
F82.W796

WILLIAMS, Roger, the pioneer of religious liberty, by Oscar S. Straus ... New York, The Century co., 1894.   xvii, 257 p. incl. front. (facsim.) 20 cm. 4-16973/3.
F82.W797

— ... with an interpretation by R. E. E. Harkness, etc. etc.   New York, London, Pub. for the Oscar S. Strauss memorial assoc. by D. Appleton-Century co., 1936.   ix, 257 p. front. (facsim.) 20½ cm.
37-721.
F82.W797
1936

RHODE ISLAND

— Freeport, N.Y., Books for Libraries Press (1970)   lx, 257 p.   23 cm.   76-137385.
F82.W797 1970

WILLIAMS, Roger, prophet and pioneer of soul-liberty, by Arthur B. Strickland.   Boston, Chicago (etc.) The Judson press (1919)   xx, 152 p. incl. front., illus., plates, ports., facsims.   24 cm.   "A selected bibliography" p. 149 - 150.   19-14786 rev. 2.
F82. W 8

WINSLOW, Edward.   Hypocrisie unmasked: by a true relation of the proceedings of the governour and company of the Massachusets against Samuel Gorton (and his accomplices) a notorious disturber of the peace and quiet of the severall governments wherein he lived....   London, Printed by R. Cotes for J. Bellamy, 1646.   4 p. 103 p.   18½ x 15 cm.   4-3630.
F82. W 85
Rare Book Coll.

— with an introd. by Howard Millar Chapin.   New York, B. Franklin (1968)   xiv, 103 p.   24 cm.   68-57130.
F82. W 85 1968

— Reprinted from the original ed. issued at London in 1646; with an introd. by Howard Millar Chapin.   Providence, The Club for colonial reprints, 1916.   xiv, (12) 103 p.   22½ cm.   100 copies printed.   17-1005.
W82.W852

WOODWARD, Carl Raymond.   Plantation in Yankeeland; the story of Cocumscussoc, mirror of colonial Rhode Island..   Chester, Conn., Pequot Press (1971)   ix, 198 p. illus.   24 cm.   A publication of the Cocumscussoc Association, Wickford, R.I.   Bibliography: p. (185) - 188.   77-175811 MARC.
F82. W 86

WROTH, Lawrence Counselman.   ... Roger Williams; Marshall Woods lecture, in Sayles hall, 1936 ....   Providence, R.I., Brown university, 1937.   2, 3 - 41 p. incl. front. (facsim.)   23½ cm.   (Brown university papers. xiv)   "A note on the sources": p. 39 - 41.   38-2145.
F82. W 87

1775 - 1865.

ALLEN.   Memorial of Zachariah Allen.   1795 - 1882. By Amos Perry.   Cambridge, J. Wilson, 1883.   108 p. 5 l incl. facsims. front. (port.)   23½ cm.   5-14209.
F83. A 43

ANTHONY, Henry Bowen.   A complete report of the American-Republican legislation caucus in Newport.   From the Providence daily post, July 29, 1857.   Providence, S. S. Rider, 1885.   36 p.   21 cm.   "A burlesque political squib."   10-5388.
F83. A 62

ARNOLD, James Newell.   The Rhode Island declaration of independence.   The Arnold family of Smithfield, Rhode Island.   (Providence? 1907?)   20a, 118 p.   22½ cm.   38-11799.
F83. A 68

BRENNAN, Joseph, brother.   ... Social conditions in industrial Rhode Island: 1820 - 1860 ...   Washington, D.C., The Catholic university of America, 1940.   ix, 181 p.   23 cm.   Bibliography: p. 179-181.   41-3102.
F83. B 7 1940

BROWN, Moses. Let freedom ring! A biography of Moses Brown. By Robert M. Hazelton.   New York, New Voices Pub. Co. (1957)   262 p.   illus.   23 cm.   57-49143.
F83. B 86

BROWN, Moses: his life and services.   A sketch, read before the R.I. historical soc. ... By Augustine Jones ... Providence, The Rhode Island print. co., 1892.   47 p.   24½ cm.   8-6296.
F83. B 87

BROWN, Moses, reluctant reformer.   By Mack Thompson.   Chapel Hill, Pub. for the Institute of Early Amer. History and Culture at Williamsburg, Va. by the U. of N.C. Press (1962)   316 p.   22 cm.
F83. B875

BROWN, William Waterman, Memorial of.   Rhode Island infantry.   (Providence, 1887?)
52 p.   front. (port.)   pl.   23 cm.   21-12601.   F83.B 88

BURGES, Tristram.   Address to the landholders and farmers of Newport county,. d. 1829.   Providence, Printed at the office of the Daily advertiser.   1829.   22 p.   21 cm.   37M906T.   F83.B 94
                                                                                                                                        Toner Coll.

— 2d ed.   1829.   22 p.   25 x 14 ½ cm.   21-4864.   F83.B 95

COLEMAN, Peter J.   The transformation of Rhode Island, 1790 - 1860.   Providence, Brown University Press, 1963.   xiv, 314 p.   24 cm.   63-14420.   F83. C 6

DEMOCRATIC party.   At the general Republican convention of delegates from all the towns in this state ... the following prox, or list of general officers, was unanimously recommended ... (Newport: From the press of the Rhode-Island Republican.   William Simmons, printer, 1812)   48 p.   19 ½ x 14 ½ cm.
These documents, the correspondence of a British agent sent to New England in 1809 to report upon the political feeling in that section, were purchased by the U.S. government and pub. at Washington in March, 1812.   20-6181.   F83.D 38
                                                                                                                                        Rare Book Coll.

DURFEE, Job.   A discourse delivered before the Rhode-Island historical soc ... on the character and writings of Chief Justice Durfee.   By Rowland G. Hazard ... Providence, C. Burnett, jr., 1848.
45 p.   24 cm.   1-1060.   F83.D 95

FENNER, James, Letters to, in 1811 and 1831.   (Providence, 1831?)   16 p.   20 cm.   Two open letters signed "A Republican" and "Another Republican," respectively.   6-12361.   F83. F 33

FRIEZE, J.   A concise history ... suffrage ... Rhode Island.   1842.   1 v.   F83. F 91

HAZARD, Thomas Benjamin.   Nailer Thom's diary; otherwise, The journal of Thomas B. Hazard of Kingstown, R.I., 1778 to 1840, which includes observations on the weather, records of births, marriages and deaths, etc. etc.   Print. as written and introd. by Caroline Hazard ... Boston, The Merrymount press, 1930.   xxiv, 808 p.   28 ½ cm.   30-25828.   F83.H 42
                                                                                                                                        Rare Book Coll.

HAZARD, Caroline.   Introduction to "Nailer Tom's diary ...   (Boston, E. B. Updike, The Merrymount press, 1930)   (vii) - xxiv p.   "Twenty-five copies printed."   F83.H422

HINTS to the farmers of Rhode-Island.   By a freeman.   Providence, R. I., Office of the Republican herald, J. S. Greene, printer, 1829.   18 p.   14 cm.   9-27472.   F83.H 66

HOWLAND, John.   A discourse delivered before the R. I. historical soc. ... on the life and times of John Howland, late president of the society.   By Edward B. Hall.   Providence, G. H. Whitney, 1855.
36 p.   23 cm.   11-21021.   F83.H 86

HOWLAND, John.   The life and recollections of John Howland ... By Edwin M. Stone.   Providence, G. H. Whitney, 1857.   348 p.   front. (port.) pl., facsim.   20 cm.   Genealogy of the Howland family: p. 342 - 343.   11-21029.
                                                                                                                                        F83.H865
                                                                                                                                        Microfilm 18706 F

LETTER to the Hon, James F. Simmons.   By a Rhode-Island conservative.   (Providence, 1845)
8 p.   23 ½ cm.   Condemning Simmons for supporting the candidacy of Charles Jackson as governor of R.I.   21-13619.   F83. L 65

NATIONAL Republica party.   Examination of certain charges against Lemuel H. Arnold, the National Republican candidate for governor ...   Providence, 1831.   28 p.   24 cm.   17-15478.   F83.N 27

POLISHOOK, Irwin H.   Rhode Island and the union, 1774 - 1795.   Evanston, Northwestern University Press, 1969.   x, 268 p.   24 cm.   (Northwestern University studies in history, no. 5)   69-18021.   F83.P 63

POTTER, Elisha Reynolds.   An address, to the freemen of Rhode-Island.   By a landholder.   Providence, Print. the Herald office, 1831.   16 p.   21 cm.   Advocating the re-election of Gov. Fenner.   9-27471.   F83.P 86

RHODE ISLAND

PRESTON, Howard Willis. Rhode Island and the loyalists ... (Providence, 1928-29)
2 v. 23 cm. Reprinted from the R. I. historical soc. Collections, Oct. 1928, Jan. 1929. CA 30-1262 Unrev.
F83. P 9

ROGERS, Horatio. Discourse before the Rhode Island historical society at its centennial celebration of Rhode Island's adoption of the federal constitution ... Pub. by the society. (Providence, R.I.) The Providence press, 1890. 44 p. 23 cm. 4-386.
F83. R73

U.S. Bureau of the Census. Heads of families at the First Census of the U.S. taken in the year 1790. Rhode Island. Washington, Govt. Print. Off., 1908. (Spartanburg, S.C., Reprint Co., 1963)
71 p. 28 cm. 64-60349.
F83. U 5
L.H.& G.

— Baltimore, Genealogical Pub. Co., 1966. 71 p. 29 cm.
F83. U 5
1966

UPDIKE. Facts relative to the political and moral claims of Wilkins Updike, for the support of the Whig electors of the western district. By John Wilkes Richmond. Providence, 1847. 16 p. 23½ cm. 21-3731.
F83. U 65

UPDIKE, Wilkins. An address to the people of Rhode Island, upon the claims of Wilkins Updike to a seat in the Congress of the U.S. (n.p., 1847) 8 p. 24½ cm. Signed: A true whig. 21-3730 Rev.
F83. U 66

WEST, George M. William West of Scituate, R.I., farmer, soldier, statesman ... St. Andrews, Fla., Panama city pub. co., 1919. 4 p. 32 numb. 1. incl. 4 pl. 27 cm. Edition limited to 50 copies. 20-2097.
F83. W 51

DORR REBELLION, 1842.

ANTHONY, Henry Bowen. The Dorriad: or, The hero of two flights ... Boston, J. Jones, 1842.
12 p. 19 cm. In verse. Not the same as the next title 17-7722.
F83. 4. A59
Rare Book Coll.

ANTHONY, Henry Brown. The Dorriad, and The great Slocum dinner; with introductory remarks and annotations. Providence, S.S. Rider, 1870. 53 p. 20 cm. 12-16489.
F83. 4. A62

BOWEN, Francis. The recent contest in Rhode Island: an article from the North American review, for April, 1844. Boston, Otis, Broaders, 1844. (5) - 69 p. 22 cm. Rc-2988.
F83. 4. B78

CURTIS, George Ticknor. The merits of Thomas W. Dorr and George Bancroft, as they are politically connected. By a citizen of Massachusetts. 2d ed. Boston, Print. J.H. Eastburn, 1844.
41 p. 23 cm. 10-1523.
F83. 4 C97

DORR, Thomas Wilson. Report of the trial of Thomas Wilson Dorr, for treason against the state of Rhode Island, containing the arguments of counsel, and the charge of Chief Justice Durfee. By Josiah S. Pitman ... Boston, Tappan & Dennet, 1844. 131 p. 24 cm. 11-13692.
F83. 4. D71

EVENTFUL day in the Rhode-Island rebellion, The: a poem. By a looker on. Providence, H.H. Brown, 1842. 12 p. 19½ cm. Rc-2989.
F83. 4. E93

FACTS involved in the Rhode Island controversy, with some views upon the rights of both parties. Boston, B.B. Mussey, 1842. 43 p. 21 cm. 17-2871.
F83. 4. F14

GODDARD, William Giles. An address to the people of Rhode-Island, delivered in Newport, ... 1843 ... on the occasion of the change in the civil government of Rhode Island, by the adoption of the constitution ... Providence, Knowles and Vose, print., 1843. 80 p. 23 cm. 6-38827.
F83. 4. G57

GOODELL, William. ... The rights and the wrongs of Rhode Island: comprising views of liberty and law, of religion and rights, as exhibited in the recent and existing difficulties in that state. Whitesboro, N.Y., Press of the Oneida institue, 1842. 120 p. 21½ cm. (Christian investigator - no. 8)
10-1544.
F83.4.G64

JEWETT, Charles Coffin. The close of the late rebellion, in Rhode Island. An extract from a letter by a Massachusetts man resident in Providence. Providence, B. Cranston, 1842. 16 p. 22½ cm.
17-6934.
F83.4.J4
1842
Toner Coll.

— 16 p. 23 cm. 3-28208.
F83.4.J4
1842a

KENYON, Archibald. The object and principles of civil government, and the duty of Christians thereto. Being a discourse ... Providence, Print. B.T. Albro, 1842. 11 p. 23 cm. 15-13259.
F83.4.K37

KING, Dan. The life and times of Thomas Wilson Dorr, with outlines of the political history of Rhode Island. Boston, The author, 1859. 368 p. incl. front. (port.) 18½ cm. 7-23807.
F83.4.K52

— Freeport, N.Y., Books for Libraries Press (1969) 368 p. 23 cm. (Select bibliographies reprint series)
74-95071.
F83.4.K52
1969

McDOUGALL, Mrs. Frances Harriet (Whipple) Greene) Might and right; by a Rhode Islander ... Providence, A.H. Stillwell, 1844. xii, (13) - 324 p. front. (port.) 19 cm. A history of the Dorr rebellion. 10-12247.
F83.4.M14

— 1844. xii p, (15) - 345 p. front. (port.) 19½ cm. Appendix to the second edition. A sketch of the life and character of Thomas Wilson Dorr: p. (325) - 345. 17-10103 rev.
F83.4.M143

MOWRY, Arthur M. ... The constitutional controversy in Rhode Island in 1841. ... Washington, Govt. print. off., 1896. p. 361 - 370. 24 cm. From the Annual report of the American historical association for 1894. 28-18689.
F83.4.M92

MOWRY, Arthur May. The Dorr war; or, The constitutional struggle in Rhode Island ... with an introd. by Albert Bushnell Hart ... Providence, R.I., Preston & Rounds, 1901. xvi, 420 p. front. (port.) illus., pl., map. 26½ cm. Bibliography: p. 400 - 406. 1-27894a-M2.
F83.4.M93

POTTER, Elisha Reynolds. Speech of Mr. Potter, of Rhode Island, on the memorial of the Democratic members of the legislature of Rhode Island. Washington, Print. at the Globe office, 1844.
13 p. 22 cm. 10-1542.
F83.4.P86

RANDALL, Dexter. Democracy vindicated and Dorrism unveiled. Providence, Print. H.H. Brown, 1846. 100 p. 22½ cm. 10-15727.
F83.4.R18

RHODE ISLAND. ... Protest and declaration of the state of Rhode-Island and Providence Plantations against any interference by the Congress ... with the internal government and the constitution of said state. (Providence? 1844) (3) p. 25 x 19½ cm. 10-1543.
F83.4.R47
Rare Book Coll.

RIDER, Sidney S., & brother. Ballads of the Dorr war; collected from the papers of the day, to which is added an epigram never before printed. Providence, S.S. Rider & Bro., 1869.
37 p. 20½ cm. Printed on one side of leaf only. Only 25 copies printed. 13-5134.
F83.4.R54
Rare Book Coll.

SIEGE at Chepachet. (Providence, 1842) 8 p. 23½ cm. In verse. 17-7716.
F83.4.S57
Rare Book Coll.

RHODE ISLAND. Charge of the Hon. Chief Justice Durfee, delivered to the Grand jury, at the March term of the Supreme judicial court, at Bristol, Rhode Island, 1842. (Bristol? 1842) 16 p. 23½ cm.
18-14915. F83.4.S95

TREADWELL, Francis C. The conspiracy to defeat the liberation of Gov. Dorr; or, The Hunkers and Algerines identified, and their policy unveiled .... New-York, J. Windt, 1845. 47 p. 23 cm.
7-24332. F83.4.T78

TUCKER, Mark. A discourse preached on Thanksgiving day ... Providence, B. F. Moore, printer, 1842. 16 p. 24 cm. 17-18140. F83.4.T89

U.S. Congress. House. Select committee on Rhode Island. Rhode Island - Interference of the executive in the affairs of. June 7, 1844. ... (Washington) Blair & Rives, print. (1844?)
1070 p. 23 cm. (28th Cong. 1st sess. House Rep. 546) Rc-2990 Rev. F83.4.U58

— (Washington) Blair & Rives, printers (1845) 1075 p. 23 cm. 19-13195.
F83.4.U59
Toner Coll.

U.S. President (Tyler) ... United States troops in Rhode Island, etc. Message from the President of the U.S., in answer to a resolution of the House of representatives relative to the employment of U.S. troops in R.I. ... (Washington) Blair & Rives, printers (1844) 179 p. 22½ cm. (28th Cong. 1st sess. House) Ed. doc. 225) 13-24899. F83.4.U 7

WAYLAND, Francis. The affairs of Rhode Island. A discourse delivered in the meeting-house of the First Baptist church, Providence ... 1842. Boston, W. D. Ticknor, 1842. 32 p. 22½ cm.
19-12958. F83.4.W34
Toner Coll.

— 3d ed. Providence, B. Cranston and H. H. Brown, 1842. 32 p. 21 cm. Rc-2992.
— 2d ed. Providence, Print. H. H. Brown, 1842. 31 p. 23 cm. 15-13257. F83.4.W35

WAYLAND. "The affairs of Rhode Island," being a review of President Wayland's "discourse;" a vindication of the sovereignty of the people, and a refutation of the doctrines of doctors of despotism. By a member of the Boston bar (John Augustus Bolles) ... Boston, B.B. Mussey, 1842. 30 p. 24 cm.
4-20075. F83.4.W353

WEBSTER, Daniel. The Rhode Island question. Mr. Webster's argument in the Supreme court of the U.S., in the case of Martin Luther vs. Luther M. Borden and others ... 1848. Washington, Print. J. & G. S. Gideon, 1848. 20 p. 22½ cm. 10-5633. F83.4.W38

1865 - 1950.

THE STATE; for a better and greater Rhode Island. v. 1 - 2, v.3 no. 1 - 6; June 17, 1905 - June, 1907. Providence, R.I. (The State printing & pub. co.) 1905 - 07. 3 v. in 1. illus. 39½ cm. Weekly, June 17, 1905 - Nov. 3, 1906; monthly, Dec. 1906 - June, 1907. No more pub. 8-31531.
F84
HN51.S8

AMERICAN historical company, inc. Richard William Jennings, a biographical memorial, ... New York, 1931. 45 p. port. 33 cm. Alternate pages blank. 31-18485 Rev. 2. F84.A 53
Rare Book Coll.

BOYLE, Thomas M. Album of fifty-five original serial photographs of the devastation in Rhode Island created by the hurricane and tidal wave of Sept. 21, 1938. Photographed by Thomas M. J. Boyle, comp. by John E. Middleton, jr. Providence, 1938. 55 mounted photos., 3 l. 30 x 24½ cm. 44-23446.
F84.B67

DENISON, Frederic. The past and the present. Narragansett sea and shore. An illus. guide to

Providence, Newport, Narragansett Pier, Block island, Watch Hill, Rocky Point, Silver Spring, and all the famous sea-side resorts of Rhode Island, with a map of Narragansett bay. ... Providence, J. A. & R. A. Reid, 1879.   88 p. front., illus. (incl. double map) 24½ cm. Rc-3002.   F84. D 46

EVENING tribune, The. Rhode Island in 1913. (Providence, 1913)   48 p. illus. 43 cm. Supplement to the Evening tribune, Jan. 1, 1913. 13-10192.   F84. E 93

KNOW Rhode Island. (1st) -   (Providence) 1927 -   v. illus. 21 - 23 cm. 28-27111 rev.*   F84. K 5

LEADING manufacturers and merchants of Rhode Island; historical and descriptive review of the industrial enterprises of the city of Providence, Pawtucket, Central Falls, Woonsocket, Westerly and Newport. New York, Boston (etc.) International pub. co., 1886.   viii, 33-213 p. illus. 25½ cm. 5-35756.   F84. L 32

NORTON, Vernon C. A common man for the common people; the life of Thomas P. McCoy, 1883 - 1945. (n. p., 1945?)   78 p. ports. 23 cm. 47-6169*.   F84.M3N6

POTTER. Historical research and educational labor illustrated in the work of Elisha Reynolds Potter, late judge of the Supreme court of Rhode Island.   An address ....   By Sidney S. Rider. Providence, The Frankin press co., 1901.   19 p. 20½ cm. 23-1728 Rev.   F84. P 67

PROVIDENCE. Chamber of commerce. Rhode Island industries catalogued. (Providence, Standard print. co., 1904)   88, (32) p. incl. illus., ports. 19½ x 27½ cm. 6-1115.   F84. P 76

PROVIDENCE journal co. The great hurricane and tidal wave, Rhode Island ... 1938 ...   (Providence journal co. (1938)   128 p. illus. (incl. map) 28 cm. Includes 118 pages of illustrations. 38-34759.   F84. P 78

PROVIDENCE Journal Co. Hurricane Carol lashes Rhode Island ... 1954. (Providence, 1954)   80 p. illus. 28 cm. 54-14432.   F84. P 8

RHODE ISLAND. Pleasures and pleasure spots in Rhode Island. State of Rhode Island and Providence Plantations. Office of the Secretary of state. State bureau of information. Providence (Remington press) 1930.   56 p. incl. front. illus. 25 cm. (Annual bulletin no. 3) 30-27602.   F84. R 49

TALLMAN, Mrs. Mariana M (Bisbee) Pleasant places in Rhode Island, and how to reach them.   ... Providence, The Providence journal co., 1893.   205 p. front. (map) illus. 20 x 15 cm. 1-Rc-2993.   F84. T 14

— 1894.   321 p. illus. (incl. map) 21 cm. 1-Rc-2994.   F84. T 15

SYMPOSIUM on Rhode Island in the Year 1975. Providence, College, R. I. in the year 1975, 1969. Proceedings. Kingston, Bureau of Govt. Research, University of R. I., 1970.   88 p. 23 cm. 75-633255.   F85. S 95 1969

REGIONS, COUNTIES, ETC., A - Z.

BLOCK ISLAND, an illustrated guide, by Beatrice Ball. Block Island, R. I., Pub. for C. C. Ball (1909)   6, 76 p. illus., fold. map. 18½ cm. 9-21597.   F87. B6 B2

BLOCK ISLAND; hotels, residences and places of interest. Providence, R. I., D. Rubin, 1900.   23 pl. obl. 24°. Nov. 1. 1900-34.   F87. B6 B6

BLOCK ISLAND, illustrated (views) New York, A. Wittemann (1888)   2 p, 18 pl. obl. 32°. 1-Rc-2995.   F87. B6 B7

BLOCK ISLAND. Picturesque Block Island. With maps of the island and harbor village, and epitome of history of Block Island ... By C. H. Hadley. (Palmer, Mass., C. B. Fisk, 1888) (22) p. illus., maps. obl. 24°. 1-Rc-2996. F87. B6 H1

BLOCK ISLAND: a hand-book, with map, for the guidance of summer visitors ... By "Ben Mush" (pseud. for James Hall) ... Norwich, Conn., J. Hall, 1877. 50 p. front. (fold. map) 15 x 12 cm. Rc-2997 Revised. F87. B6 H2

BLOCK ISLAND. A copy of the old epitaphs in the burying ground of Block-Island. By Edw. Doubleday Harris ... Cambridge (Mass.) Press of J. Wilson, 1883. 3, (3) - 66 p. 20 ½ cm. Edition of 100 copies. 1-6540. F87. B6 H3

BLOCK ISLAND. I. A map and guide. II. A history (abridged). By Rev. Samuel T. Livermore. Hartford, Conn., Press of the Case, Lockwood and Brainard co., 1882. 125 p. incl. fold. map. plates. 20 cm. Much is taken from the author's "History of Block Island" pub. in 1877. Rc-2998. F87. B6 L7

BLOCK ISLAND; an illus. history, map and guide, by Rev. Samuel T. Livermore. Revised and brought down to date, 1901. A large number of illus. and a considerable amount of new reading matter ... have been added; ed. Chas. E. Perry. Providence, R. I., For C. C. Ball by Snow & Farnham, print. (1901) 45, 46 - 156 p. illus., plates, port. 18 ½ cm. 1-26548. F87.B6 L71

BLOCK ISLAND, A history of, from its discovery, in 1514, to the present time, 1876, by Rev. Samuel T. Livermore ... Hartford, Conn., The Case, Lockwood & Brainard co., 1877. 371 p. 19 ½ cm. 1-Rc-2999. F87.B6 L8

— Reproduced and enhanced by the Block Island Committee of Republication for the Block Island Tercentenary Anniversary. (Greenfield? Mass.) 1961. 371, (17) p. 21 cm. 61-17173.
F87. B6 L8 1961

BLOCK ISLAND illustrated: with a descriptive sketch and outline of history ... By Edward E. Pettee. Boston, Deland & Barta, 1884. 122, vi p. front. (fold. map) illus. 8°. 1-Rc-3000.
F87. B6 P4

BLOCK ISLAND lore and legends. By Ethel Colt Ritchie. Block Island, R.I., F. Norman Associates (1955) 93 p. illus. 20 cm. Includes bibliography. 55-30535. F87. B6 R5

— (1956) 98 p. illus. 20 cm. Includes bibliography. 56-30885.
F87. B6 R5 1956

BLOCK ISLAND scrapbook, by Maizie (pseud. for Mary H. Rose) 1st ed. New York, Pageant Press (1957) 345 p. illus. 24 cm. 57-6776. F87. B6 R6

BLOCK ISLAND, A historical sketch of, by William P. Sheffield. Newport, J. P. Sanborn & co., print. 1876. 2, (3) - 62 p. 23 cm. Rc-3001. F87. B6 S5

BLOCK ISLAND. Depositions of officers of the Palatine ship "Princess Augusta" wrecked on Block Island 27th Dec., 1738 and which was apparently the "Palatine" of Whittier's poem. Issued at the General Court of the Society of Colonial Wars in the State of R.I., etc. (Providence, 1939) 11 p. 24 cm. 48-31389*. F87. B6 S6

BOUNDARIES. Rhode Island boundaries, 1636 - 1936. By John Hutchins Cady. (Providence) State of Rhode Island and Providence Plantations, State Planning Board, 1936. 24 p. maps. 28 cm. (Special report no. 7) 50-45058.
F87. B7 C3 1936

— (Providence) Rhode Island tercentenary commission, 1936. 31 p. incl. maps. 28 ½ cm. 37-27504.
F87. B7 C3 1936 b

BRISTOL County (records of births, marriages and deaths) By James Newell Arnold. Providence, R.I., Narragansett historical pub. co., 1894.   3 pt. in 1 vol. 20 ½ cm. (His Vital record of Rhode Island, 1636-1850. 1st ser. ... v. 6) 16-6861.
  F87.B86 A7

BRISTOL County. ... Episcopal and Congregational (church records of births, marriages and deaths) By James Newell Arnold. Providence, R. I., Narragansett hist. pub. co., 1896.   xlv, 631 p. (His Vital record of R. I., 1636-1850, 1st ser. vol. viii) 16-6863.
  F87.B86A72

KENT County (records of births, marriages and deaths) By James Newell Arnold. Providence, R.I., Narragansett hist. pub. co., 1891.   4 pt. in 1 v. (His Vital record of Rhode Island. 1636 - 1850. 1st ser .. v.1) 16-6866.
  F87. K3 A7

NARRAGANSETT Bay, its historic and romantic association and picturesque setting, by Edgar Mayhew Bacon ... illus. with fifty drawings by the author and with numerous photos. New York and London, G. P. Putnam's sons, 1904.   xii, 377 p. incl. front., illus., plates. fold. map. 25 cm. 4-24551.
  F87. N2 B2

NARRAGANSETT Bay. A guide to Providence River and Narragansett Bay; from Providence to Newport: in which all the towns, villages, islands and important objects on both sides are named in order, with an account of the prominent historic incidents connected with them. By Joseph Banvard. Providence, Coggeshall & Stewart, 1858.   vi, (7) - 66 p. 15 ½ cm. 16-9500.
  F87.N2 B23

NARRAGANSETT. South county studies of some 18th century persons, places & conditions in that portion of Rhode Island called Narragansett, by Esther Bernon Carpenter; with an introd. by Caroline Hazard, compiled largely from letters now first pub. by Oliver Wendell Holmes. Boston, Print. for the subscribers, 1924.   xv, 296 p. front. 23 ½ cm. 24-20759.
  F87. N2 C3

— Freeport, N. Y., Books for Libraries Press (1971)   xv, 296 p. 75-160961.
  F87. N2 C3
  1971

NARRAGANSETT Bay. Collected papers on The inscribed rocks of Narragansett Bay, by Edmund B. Delabarre ... Providence, R. I., Preston and Rounds co., 1925.   3, 149 p. illus. (incl. map) plates, charts. 22 ½ cm. Reprinted from R. I. historical collections vols. xiii, 1920 to xviii, 1925. Bibliography: p. 27-28. 25-24216.
  F87, N2 D2

NARRAGANSETT and Mount Hope bays. Picturesque Narragansett; an illustrated guide to the cities, towns and famous resorts of Rhode Island. With a sketch of the city of Fall River, Mass. 3d ed. By Robert Grieve. Providence, R. I., J. A. & R. A. Reid (1888?)   192 p. illus. (incl. ports.) fold. pl., fold. map. 26 cm. Rc-3003.
  F87. N2 G8

NARRAGANSETT Bay, A guide to: Newport, Narragansett Pier, Block Island, Watch Hill, Rocky Point, Silver Spring, and all the famous resorts along shore, with a sketch of the city of Providence. A new map of Narragansett Bay. Providence, J. A. & R. A. Reid, 1878.   94 p. front. (fold. map) 18 ½ cm. 11-13695.
  F87. N2 G9

NARRAGANSETT. Anchors of tradition; a presentment of some little known facts and persons in a small corner of colonial New England called Narragansett, to which are added certain weavings of fancy from the thread of life upon the loom of time, by Caroline Hazard ... New Haven, Yale university press, 1924.   viii, 242 p. 22 ½ cm. 25-1476.
  F87. N2 H4

NARRAGANSETT. Ancient paths to Pequot, by William Davis Miller, with a map by Norman Morrison Isham. Issued on the occasion of the meeting in Rhode Island of the General assembly of the Society of colonial wars ... Providence, Print. for the Soc. by E. L. Freeman co. (1936)   16 p. illus. (map) 23 cm. 36-35304.
  F87. N2 M5

NARRAGANSETT. A brief account of the William Withington plat of Boston Neck with a description of the shares of the proprietors (by) William Davis Miller. Issued at the annual court of the Society

RHODE ISLAND

of colonial wars in the state of Rhode Island ... Providence, Printed for the Society by E. L. Freeman (1925)   2, 9 - 29 p.   4 maps.   23 cm.   25-3619.   F87.N2 M6

NARRAGANSETT Bay. Newport and the resorts of Narragansett Bay, 1878, containing maps of Newport and Narragansett Bay, yacht lists, tide tables, list of Newport summer residents, etc., etc. (Newport) W. P. Clarke (1878?)   90 p.   maps (1 fold.)   19 cm.   54-49577.   F87. N2 N4

NARRAGANSETT Bay, Souvenir of ... Providence, R.I., Prov. heliograph co. (1896)   22 pl.   obl. 24°.
1-Rc-3004.   F87. N2 S7

NARRAGANSETT Bay. Hand-book of the Continental steamboat co., By M. M. Whelan. A complete guide to the great sea-shore resorts on Narragansett bay ... Corrected time-table and rates of fare ... (Boston, Duffy, Cashman co., printers, 1882)   56 p.   illus., fold. map.   16 cm.   44-49261.
F87. N2 W5
Rare Book Coll.

NEWPORT County (records of births, marriages and deaths) By James Newell Arnold. Providence, R.I., Narragansett historical pub. co., 1893.   7 pt. in 1 v.   front. (map)   29½ cm.   (His Vital record of Rhode Island. 1636 - 1850. 1st ser ... v. 4)   16-6865.   F87. N5 A7

NEWPORT County, History of. From the year 1638 to the year 1887, including the settlement of its towns, and their subsequent progress ... Edited by Richard M. Bayles ... New York, L. E. Preston, 1888.   x, 1060 p.   illus., plates, ports., map.   27 cm.   3-11695.   F87. N5 B3

PAWTUXET. The Pawtuxet valley directory, Rhode Island ... the villages of Anthony, Arctic, Arkwright, Bakersville, Centreville, Clyde, Crompton, Fiskeville, Harris, Jackson, Lippitt, Natick, Phenix, Pontiac, Quidnick, River Point, Washington, Westcott ... Providence, R.I., C. De Witt White, 1908.   v.   24 cm.   9-833.   F87. P3 A18

PETTAQUAMSETT, The story of (by) Mary Kenyon Huling ... (Providence, R.I., The Reynolds press, 1936)   25, (2) p.   illus. (map)   22 cm.   "First ed., May, 1936."   39-7390.   F87. P5 H8

PROVIDENCE County (records of births, marriages and deaths) By James Newell Arnold. Providence, R.I., Narragansett historical pub. co., 1892.   2 v.   front. (ma0)   29½ cm.   (His Vital record of Rhode Island. 1636 - 1850. 1st ser. ... v. 2-3)   16-6862.
F87. P9 A7

PROVIDENCE County, History of. Ed. Richard Mather Bayles, assisted by a corps of writers ... New York, W. W. Preston, 1891.   2 v.   plates, ports., map.   27 cm.   Includes biographical sketches.   2-4129 Rev.
F87. P9 B3

RHODE ISLAND (Island) The Yankee tar. An authentic narrative of the voyages and hardships of of John Hoxse, and the cruises of the U.S. frigate Constellation ... Written by himself. With an extract from the writings of Rev. John Flavel. Northampton (Mass.) Print. J. Metcalf, 1840.   200 p.   incl. front.   16½ cm.   11-22245.   F87.R
E323. H 87

RHODE ISLAND (Island) History of Rhode Island. By Rev. Edward Peterson ... New-York, J. S. Taylor, 1853.   xvi, (17) - 379 p.   front., plates, facsims.   22 cm.   Relates to the island of Rhode Island or Aquidneck only.
1-Rc-2980.   F87. R4 P3

WASHINTON County. (records of births, marriages and deaths) By James Newell Arnold. Providence, R.I., Narragansett hist. pub. co., 1894.   7 pt. in 1 v.   front. (map)   29½ cm.   (His Vital record of Rhode Island. 1636 - 1850. 1st ser. ... v.5)   16-6864.   F87. W3 A7

WASHINGTON and Kent counties, incl. their early settlement and progress to the present time; a description of their historic and interesting localities; sketches of their towns and villages; portraits of some of their prominent men, and biographies of many of their representative citizens. By J. R. Cole ... New York, W. W. Preston, 1889.   xiv, 1344 p.   plates, ports., map.   27½ x 19½ cm.   9-21918.
F87. W3 C6

CITIES, TOWNS, ETC., A - Z.

BARRINGTON. Armstrong's Bristol, Warren and Barrington directory, 1937/38 -   including Hampden Meadows, Nayatt, West Barrington ... v.1 -   Cranston, R.I., J.H. Armstrong co., 1937 -   v.   24 cm.   38-4615.
           Directories

BARRINGTON. Dunham's Barrington, Bristol and Warren directory ... 19   West Barrington, R.I., Winthrop, Mass., C.H. Dunham, 1930 -   v.   23½ cm.   CA 30-710 Unrev.
           Directories

BARRINGTON. An historical address and poem, delivered at the centennial celebration of the incorporation of the town of Barrington ... 1870. With an historical appendix. Ed. Thomas W. Bicknell, Providence, Print. Providence press co., 1870.   3, (5) - 192 p.   front., plates, ports., fold. plan.   21 cm.
Rc-3006.   F89. B2 B5

BARRINGTON, A history of, by Thomas Williams Bicknell ... Providence, Snow & Farnham, printers, 1898.   viii, 620 p.   front., illus., plates, etc.   23½ cm.   "Biographies of leading citizens": p. (566)-602.   98-2232 Rev.   F89. B2 B6

BARRINGTON. Sowams; with ancient records of Sowams and parts adjacent - illus. by Thomas W. Bicknell. New Haven, Conn., Associated publishers of American records, 1908.   vi, 195, (9) p. incl. port. front., plates, ports., maps (1 fold.) facsims.   25 cm.   8-19182.   F89. B2 B64

BARRINGTON. Rev. John Myles and the founding of the first Baptist church in Massachusetts; an historical address delivered at the dedication of a monument in Barrington ... by Henry Melville King ... Providence, R.I., Preston & Rounds, 1905.   vii, 112 p.   19½ cm.   Bibliography: p. (99) - 103.   6-625.
           F89. B2 K5

BARRINGTON on the Narragansett as a place of residence. (Barrington, R.I.) Rural improvement soc. of Barrington, R.I., 1890.   (26) p. front., illus.   22½ x 31 cm.   Rc-3005 Rev.   F89. B2 R8

BRISTOL, Warren and Barrington directory ... 1876/77,   19 -   Boston, Union pub. co., 1876 - 19   v.   fold. maps.   24cm.   6-33497 Rev.
           Directories

BRISTOL. The D'Wolf inn, Bristol. (Bristol, R.I., 19 -?)   18½ cm.   F89. B8 D5

BRISTOL. Mount Hope; a New England chronicle. By George Locke Howe. New York, Viking Press, 1959.   312 p. illus.   22 cm.   59-5643.   F89. B8 H84

BRISTOL, a town biography, by Mark Antony De Wolfe Howe ... Cambridge, Mass., Harvard university press, 1930.   4, 3-172, (2) p. front., plates, ports., facsim.   19 cm.   "Special ed. limited to 25 copies."
"Sources of information": p. 161 - (164)   30-20103.   F89. B8 H85
           Rare Book Coll.

BRISTOL. "Songs of September", for the 250th anniversary of the town of Bristol; "Founders' day", Sept. 24, 1930, By M. A. De Wolfe Howe ... (Bristol, R.I., 1930)   (7) p. 19½ cm.   Poem.   "Reprinted from the Bristol Phoenix."   30-30508.   F89. B8 H86
           Rare Book Coll.

BRISTOL. Historical sketches of the First Congregational church, Bristol, 1689 - 1872. By J. P. Lane, pastor. Providence, Providence press co., printers, 1872.   126 p.   19½ cm.   6-20088 Add.
           F89. B8 L2

BRISTOL. Manual of the First Congregational church, Bristol, 1687 - 1872. Containing forms, principles and rules adopted by the church; the distinctive features of Congregationalism ... a history of the church, with biographical notes of the early members, etc. ... 1680 to 1872. Comp. by J. P. Lane, pastor. Providence, Providence press co. print., 1873.   vi, (13) - 233 p.   19½ cm.
6-40520* Cancel.   F89. B8 L3

BRISTOL. Celebration of the 200th anniversary of the settlement of the town of Bristol ... 1880 ... By Wm. J. Miller. (Providence, Print. Providence press co., 1881)   (v) - viii, 194 p. 24 cm.   Rc-3007 Rev.
           F89. B8 M6

RHODE ISLAND

BRISTOL. The history of Bristol, R.I. The story of the Mount Hope lands, from the visit of the Northmen to the present time. Containing accounts of the Indian wars, the character and lives of the early settlers, etc. By Wilfred H. Munro ... Providence, J.A. & R.A. Reid, 1880. 396 p. front., illus., pl., ports. 23½ cm. Rc-3008 Rev.
F89. B8 M9

BRISTOL. Tales of an old sea port; a general sketch of the history of Bristol, including ... an account of the voyages of the Norsemen ... and personal narratives of some notable voyages accomplished by sailors from the Mount Hope lands ... Princteon, Princeton unversity press, 1917. 2 p., 292 p. plates. 21½ cm. 18-33.
F89. B8 M94

BRISTOL. Two discourses, by Thomas Shepard, pastor of the Catholic Congregational church, in Bristol. Providence, Sayles, Miller & Simons, steam printers, 1857. 55 p. front. 21 cm. 12-11577.
F89. B8 S5

BRISTOL. Souvenir views of Bristol. (Bristol?) K. H. De Wolf, 1902. 3 p., 50 pl. 20½ x 25½ cm. 2-3454-M2.
F89. B8 S7

BRISTOL. Sketches of old Bristol, written and ed. by Charles O. F. Thompson. Providence, R.I., Printed by the Roger Williams press, 1942. 3, ix-xiii, 418 p. 23½ cm. 43-4004.
F89. B8 T5

BRISTOL. The book of Bristol. Pub. as an official souvenir of the celebration of the 275th anniversary of the settlement of the town. Bristol, R.I., Franklin Print. Co., 1955. unpaged. illus. 31 cm. 55-57457.
F89. B8 T7

BRISTOL. The way of the world, or, A short sketch of the modern customs of mankind, delineated, in a variety of methods ... Comp. and written, in prose and verse. By Joseph Wardwell, alias Joseph, the dreamer. (n.p.) Printed for the author. 1813. vii, 8 - 24 p. 19 cm. 24-6800.
F89. B8 W25
Rare Book Coll.

BURRILLVILLE and North Smithfield directory, Providence, R.I., White Gordon co., v. 24 cm. 10-16729.
Directories

BURRILLVILLE; as it was, and as it is, by Horace A. Keach. Providence, Knowles, Anthony, printers, 1856. x, 170 p. 18½ cm. Rc-3009.
F89. B9 K2

CENTERDALE. Annals of Centerdale in the town of North Providence, its past and present, 1636 - 1909, by Frank C. Angell ... (Central Falls, R.I., Press of E. L. Freeman co,, 1909) 2, (xi) - xv, 196 p. incl. illus., map. front. (port.) pl. 24 cm. 9-17204.
F89. C3 A4

CHARLESTON. Historical sketch of the town of Charlestown, from 1636 to 1876. Transcribed and written by William Franklin Tucker ... By order of the Town council. Westerly, R.I., G.B. & J.H. Utter, printers, 1877. 88 p. 23½ cm. Rc-30-10.
F89. C4 T8

COVENTRY. The home of Gen. Nathanael Greene at Coventry. (Coventry? R.I.) The General Nathanael Greene homestead ass'n. inc., 1925. 61 p. incl. front. plates, port. 23½ cm. 26-2176.
F79. C7 G3

CRANSTON: a historical sketch, by J. Earl Clauson, pub. by order of the 150th anniversary committee. Providence, R.I., T. S. Hammond, 1904. 52 p. front., plates, group of ports. 21½ cm. 10-25099.
P89. C8 C6

CRANSTON bicentennial, 1754 - 1954 ... celebrating 200 years of progress. Official souvenir book. (Cranston, 1954) 76 p. illus. 29 cm. 57-43907.
F89. C8 C7

CRANSTON directory, The. Providence, Boston, Sampson & Murdock co. v. 24 cm. 13-19960.
Directories

CUMBERLAND and Lincoln directory ... Providence, R.I., C. De Witt White, 1909 - 1 v. 24 cm. 9-17127.
Directories

CUMBERLAND.   Armstrong's Cumberland and Lincoln, directory, 1937 -   v. 1 -
Cranston, R.I., J. H. Armstrong co., 1937.   v.   24 cm.   37-33527.   Directories

CUMBERLAND.   Three holes in the chimney, or, A scattered family, by Didama (pseud. for Mrs.
Betsey Ann White)   Newton (Mass.) B. A. White, 1886.   3, (ix) - xvii, (19) - 297 p.   front., plates.   18½ cm.
The family of Benjamin May, in Cumberland and Smithfield, and other places.   8-6372.   F89. C9 W5

EAST GREENWICH.   History of the town of East Greenwich and adjacent territory, from 1677 to
1877.   By D. H. Greene.   Providence, J. A. & R. A. Reid, 1877.   263 p. front., 2 pl. 19½ cm. 3-32077 Rev.
F89. E15 G7

EAST GREENWICH, The history of, 1677 - 1960; with related genealogy.   By Martha E. McPortland.
Illus. by S. Jerome Hoxie.   East Greenwich, R.I., East Greenwich Free Lib. Assoc., 1960.
300 p.   24 cm.   F87. E15 M2

EAST GREENWICH.   Notes and queries concerning the early bounds and divisions of the township of
East Greenwich, as set forth in William Hall's plat, 1716.   By William Davis Miller.   Issued at the
annual court of the Society of Colonial Wars in the State of Rhode Island and Providence Plantations.
Providence, 1937.   19 p.   maps.   24 cm.   47-42173*.   F89. E15 M5

EAST GREENWICH.   Charles MacCarthy, a Rhode Island pioneer, 1677.   By Thomas Hamilton
Murray ... (Somerset, O., 1901)   15 p.   23½ cm.   "Reprinted from the Rosary magazine of Nov. 1901, Somerset, Ohio."
2-19455 Rev.   F89. E15 M9

EAST PROVIDENCE directory, The, 18 -   Providence, R.I., Sampson & Murdock co., 1890 - 1916.
11 v.   fold. maps.   21½ x 24 cm.   1-25704 Rev.   Directories

EAST PROVIDENCE.   ... Seekonk (including East Providence), Pawtucket and Newman Congregational
church (records of births, marriages and deaths)   Providence, R.I., Narragansett hist. pub. co.,
1897.   xxxviii, 596 p.   front. (map)   29½ cm.   (His Vital record of R.I. 1636-1850. 1st. ser. v. ix) 16-6860.   F89. E18 A7

EAST PROVIDENCE.   An historical sketch of the town of East Providence (r.I.) delivered before the
town authorities and citizens of East Providence ... 1876, by George N. Bliss.   Providence, J. F.
Greene, printer, 1876.   52 p.   19 cm.   Rc-3011 Rev.   F89. E18 B6

EAST PROVIDENCE.   The old Rehoboth cemetery, "the ring of the town", at East Providence, near
Newman's church ... copied, compiled and pub., 1932, by Marion Pearce Carter ... Attleboro,
Mass. (1932)   2 p., 58 numb. l.   28 cm.   Mimeographed.   CA 33-849 Unrev.   F89. E18C26

GLOCESTER.   A brief history of the town of Glocester, preceded by a sketch of the territory while a
part of Providence.   By Elizabeth A. Perry.   Providence, Providence press co., printers, 1886.
136 p.   23 cm.   Rc-3012.   F89. G5 P4

GREENE.   A history of Greene and vicinity, 1845 - 1929, by Squire G. Wood.   Providence, R.I.,
Priv. print., 1936.   101 p.   front. (port.)   illus. (map)   geneal. tables.   23½ cm.   "History of the 'South farm' now part of
the 'Arnold farms': the Nichols family, the Wood family, 1929": p. (71) - 101.   37-13805.   F89. G7 W6

HOPKINTON.   The Hopkinton and Charlestown directory.   (Westerly, R.I.) H. P. Everett,
v.   24 cm.   17-14551.   Directories

HOPKINTON.   ... Historical sketch of the town of Hopkinton from 1757 to 1876, comprising a period
of 119 years.   Prepared by Rev. S. S. Griswold, and delivered ... 1876.   Hope Valley, R.I., L. W. A.
Cole, job printer, 1877.   94, (2) p.   18½ cm.   Rc-3014.   F89. H7 G8

HOPKINTON.   First Hopkinton cemetery association. ... Dedication of Ministers' monument...
1899.   Plainfield, N. J., Printed for the Assoc. by the American Sabbath tract soc., 1899.
26 p.   front., 2 pl.   22 cm.   Rc-3013.   F89. H7 H6

HOPE VALLEY.   Tercentenary map and description of early Hope Valley (Carpenter's; or Middle iron
works) and Wyoming (Brand's iron works) ... Pub. by the Hopkinton tercentenary committee ...

RHODE ISLAND

(Westerly, R.I., The Utter co., printers, 1936)   13, (1) p. illus. (map) 23 cm. 38-12578.

F89. H7 H8

JAMESTOWN and New Shoreham directory ... also names of the summer residents and in most cases their winter address. Providence, R.I., C. De Witt White co.   v. 23½ cm. 12-20145.

Directories

JAMESTOWN and New Shoreham directory ... v. 1 -   1926/27 -   Providence, R.I., Sampson & Murdock co., 1926.   v. 24 cm. CA 26-751 Unrev.   Directories

JAMESTOWN historical society. Bulletin. (19 - v.   F89. J3 J4

JAMESTOWN windmill, The, by Maud Lyman Stevens. Newport, R.I., R. Ward, printer, 1916.
26 p. pl. 14½ cm. 35-30115.   F89. J3 S7

JAMESTOWN. History of Jamestown on Conanicut Island in the State of Rhode Island. By Walter Leon Watson. (Providence? 1949)   107 p. illus., maps (1 fold. inserted) 24 cm. Bibliography: p. 106. 50-180.

F89. J3 W4

LINCOLN. Historical sketch of the town of Lincoln. Comp. and written by Welcome A. Greene, under the direction and advice of Charles Moles and others, a committee appointed by the Town council ... Central Falls, R.I., E.L. Freeman, printers, 1876.   26 p. 23 cm. Rc-3015 Rev.

F89. L7 G8

LINCOLN. Once in a hundred years; a pictorial history. (Lincoln, R.I.) Centennial publication of the Town of Lincoln, R.I., 1971.   168 p. illus. (part col.) 25 cm. 72-181497 MARC.   F89. L7 O5

LITTLE COMPTON. Fragmentary sketches and incidents, in Little Compton & Tiverton, during the revolution, and the war of 1812. By P. F. Little, esq. Never before published. Little Compton, R.I., 1880.   32 p. 18½ cm. 3-30955.   F89. L8 L7

LITTLE COMPTON. The 200th anniversary of the organization of the United Congregational Church, Little Compton ... 1904. Little Compton, R.I., The United Congregation soc. (1906)
120 p. front., plates, ports., facsims. 24½ cm. 19-16932.   F89. L8 L72

LITTLE COMPTON families, from records compiled by Benjamin Franklin Wilbur. (1st ed.) Little Compton, R.I., Little Compton Historical Soc., 1967.   xvii, 817 p. 24 cm.

F89. L8 W5

MIDDLETOWN. An historical sketch of Middletown, from its organization, in 1743, to the centennial year, 1876. By Hon. Samuel Greene Arnold. Newport (R.I.) J. P. Sanborn, Mercury steam print. 1876.   48, xiv p. 22½ cm. Rc-3016.   F89. M6 A7

MIDDLETOWN. Taylor-Chase-Smythe House: John Taylor, a founder of Middletown, 1702 - 1740. By Arlene Murray Ringer Lattu. (1st ed.) Newport? R.I., 1954.   unpaged. illus. 28 cm. Includes bibliography. 59-35715.   F89. M6 L3

NARRAGANSETT. Inscriptions on the grave-stones in the old churchuard of St. Paul's, Narragansett, North Kingstown, Rhode Island, with a records of the inscriptions in the graveyard of the old church at Wickford, comp. by James N. Arnold. Boston, Priv. print., The Merrymount press (1909?)
vii, 36 p. 22 cm. 20-8774.   F89. N2 A7

NARRAGANSETT Pier Illustrated. Pub. by the Hotel men's association. (N.Y., Press of the Moss eng. co., 1891)   (69) p. illus. obl. 8°. 1-Rc-3017.   F89. N2 N2

NARRAGANSETT Pier. Street scenes, hotels, residences and places of interest. Providence, R.I., D. Rubin, 1900.   33 pl. 13½ x 19½ cm. 0-5496 Rev.   F89. N2 N3

NARRAGANSETT blue book: a summer souvenir and guide for the principal resorts and cities on and

609

about Narragansett bay ... Comp. James Allan Reid. Providence, R.I., The American book exchange, 1896. 7 - 125 p. illus. 14 ½ cm. 4-14748 Rev.
F89. N2 R3

NARRAGANSETT Pier, Views of. (Providence, R.I.) Tibbitts & Preston, 1884. 24 pl. obl. 16°. 1-Rc-3018.
F89. N2 V6

NEWPORT. Boyd's Newport city directory ... 1856/57, (etc.) 1856 —   v. 15 - 22 cm. 10-256. Newport, R.I., A. J. Ward
Directories

— An historical discourse on the civil and religious affairs of the colony of Rhode Island and Providence Plantations. By John Callender ... Boston, Print. S. Kneeland, 1739. (85) p. 15 ½ cm. (In Boyd's Newport city directory ... 1856-'57) 7-18198.

NEWPORT, City directory of. Newport, R.I., Eastern pub. co., 19   v. front. (fold. map) 24 ½ cm. 38-31180.
Directories

NEWPORT directory ... 18   19   Boston, Mass., Providence, R.I., Sampson & Murdock co.   v. fold. maps. 23 ½ - 25 ½ cm. 1-17636 Rev.
Directories

NEWPORT blue book. Cottage owners. Those who summer at the city by the sea. Hotels ... Boston, H. L. Yarrington, 1884. 62 p. 20 cm. 9-27162.
Directories

NEWPORT. Social register, Newport, 1887. New York, The Social register assoc. (1887) 64 p. 18 cm. 9-27161.
Directories

NEWPORT. Who's who at Newport and Bar Harbor, 1915 —   Salem, Mass., The Salem press co., 1915 —   1 v. illus. 23 ½ cm. 15-18908.
Directories

NEWPORT. Polk's classified buyers' guide, reprinted from Polk's Newport city directory for 19 - and Polk's Newport tax list ... Boston, Mass., R. L. Polk, 19   v. 23 cm. 41-23729.
Directories

NEWPORT. The ruined mill, or round church of the Norsemen, at Newport, compared with the round church at Cambridge, and others in Europe, by F. J. Allen ... (Cambridge, Eng.) 1921. p. (91) - 107. illus. (incl. plans) pl. vi - x. 21 ½ cm. "From the Cambridge antiquarian society's communications, vol. xxii." Bibliography: p. 106-107. 22-8247.
F89. N5 A4

NEWPORT. A gentleman from Indiana looks at Newport & the Narragansett Bay Area. Phot. by Hartley Alley. With text by Jean Alley. And a foreword by Claiborne Pell. Freeport, Me., Bond Wheelwright Co. (1967) 126 p. 29 cm. 67-16833.
F89. N5 A8

NEWPORT. History of the First Baptist church in Newport; a discourse delivered on Thanksgiving day ... 1876. By C. E. Barrows ... Newport, J. P. Sanborn, printers, 1876. 64 p. 22 cm. 1-13363 Rev.
F89. N5 B3

NEWPORT. "The city by the sea," Newport. Its approaches by sea and land; objects and points of interest ... By James H. Bowditch. Providence (R.I.) J. A. & R. A. Reid, 1884. 120 p. illus., fold. map. 25 cm. Rc-3019.
F89. N5 B7

NEWPORT. The Old Stone Mill. By Herbert Olin Brigham. Newport, R.I., Franklin Print. House, 1948. 32 p. 21 cm. 55-24852.
F89. N5 B75

— 2d ed. Newport, R.I., Franklin Print House, 1955. 32 p. illus. 23 cm. 55-44909.
F89. N5 B75
1955

NEWPORT. The controversy touching the old stone mill, in the town of Newport. With remarks, introductory and conclusive. By Charles Timothy Brooks. Newport, C. E. Hammett, jr., 1851. 91 p. incl. 1 illus., pl. front. 18 cm. Rc-3020.
F89. N5 B8

RHODE ISLAND 33

NEWPORT, by W. C. Brownell; illus. by W. S. Vanderbilt Allen. New York, C. Scribner's sons, 1896. 3, 85 p. incl. plates, plan. front. 18 cm. (American summer resorts) 1-Rc-3021.   F89. N5 B9

NEWPORT. Visit to grand-papa; or, A week at Newport. By Sarah S. Cahoone. New-York, Taylor and Dodd, 1840. 213 p. 4 pl. (incl. front.) 19 cm. Also pub. N. Y., 1842, under title: Sketches of Newport and its vicinity. 17-13790.   F89.N5 C12 Toner Coll.

NEWPORT. Sketches of Newport and its vicinity; with notices respecting the history, settlement and georgraphy of Rhode Island. By Sarah S. Cahoone. Illus. with engravings. New-York, J. S. Taylor, 1842. 213 p. front., plates. 19½ cm. A narrative for children in story form. See above item. Rc-3022.   F89.N5C123

NEWPORT. Early recollections of Newport, from the year 1793 to 1811. By George G. Channing. Newport, R.I., A. J. Ward, C. E. Hammett; Boston, Mass., Nichols and Noyes, 1868. xiv, (17) - 284 p. 19 cm. 1-Rc-3023.   F89. N5 C4

NEWPORT, Block island and Narragansett pier ... A brief history, and tourists' guide ... Boston, The Botolph press, 1895. 111 p. illus., fold. maps. 16½ cm. Rc-3024.   F89. N5 C5

NEWPORT. The city and scenery of Newport. Illustrations, drawn on stone by John Collins ... Burlington, N.J., 1857. 8 p. 13 col. pl., map. 30 x 44 cm. Rc-3025.   F89. N5 C7

NEWPORT, A hand-book of. By the author of "Pen and ink sketches," etc. (John Dix) Newport, R.I., C. E. Hammett, jr., 1852. xii, (13) - 170 p. incl. front., illus. 17 cm. Rc-3026 Rev. 2.   F89. N5 D6

NEWPORT Historical Society, a survey, June-July, 1958. By Gilbert Harry Doane. (Newport? R.I., 1958) 35 p. 24 cm. 59-40475.   F89.N5 D65

NEWPORT: the city by the sea. Four epochs in her history. An age of shadowy tradition. An era of commercial success and social splendor. A generation of decadence. A half century of unparalleled development. By Chas. H. Dow. Newport, J. P. Sanborn, 1880. 120 p. 17 cm. 2-5496.   F89. N5 D7

NEWPORT story, The. By James Gibson Edward. (Newport? R.I., 1952) 71 p. illus. 22 cm. 53-17554.   F89. N5 E3

NEWPORT. This was my Newport, by Maud Howe Elliott. Cambridge, Mass., The Mythology co., A. M. Jones, 1944. xxiv, 279 p. front., illus. (facsims.) plates, ports. 24 cm. 44-9074.   F89. N5 E4

NEWPORT. Gazette françoise. A facsimile reprint of a newspaper, printed at Newport on the printing press of the French fleet in American waters during the revolutionary war, with an introd. by Howard M. Chapin. New York, The Grolier club, 1926. 12 p., facsim.: (30) p. 32½ cm. Reprint of the only known file of the Gazette (no. 1-7 and suppl., 17 nov., 1780 - 2 janvier, 1781) 27-3338.   F89. N5 G2

NEWPORT. Gazette françoise. No. 1 (-7) Du Vendredi 17 Nov., 1780 (- Samedi 30 Décembre 1780. Supplement a la Gazette dur 30 Décembre 1780. Du Mardi 2 Janvier 1781) (Colophon: A Newport, De l'Imprimerie Royale de l'Escadre, Rue de la Pointe, No. 641 (1780-81) (Boston, 1927) facsim.: 8 no. in 1 v. (30 l.) 38 cm. (Americana series; photostat by the Mass. hist. soc. no. 186) 27-17086.   F89.N5 G22 Rare Book Coll.

NEWPORT. The city by the sea, Newport ... By Robert Grieve. Providence, J.A. & R.A. Reid, 1889.   F89.N5 G84

NEWPORT. The story of the Jews in Newport; two and a half centuries of Judaism, 1658 - 1908, by Morris A. Gutstein ... Introd. by David De Sola Pool ... New York, Block pub. co., 1936. 5, 9-393 p. front., plates, ports., plans, facsims. 25 cm. "Selected bibliography": p. 383 - 384. 37-1024.   F89. N5 G9

NEWPORT. History of the re-union of the sons and daughters of Newport, July 4th, 1884, by Frank

G. Harris. Newport, Davis & Pitman, printers, 1885. 171 p. front., illus., plates. 24 cm.

F89. N5 H3

NEWPORT. Oldport days. By Thomas Wentworth Higginson. With ten heliotype illustrations, from views taken in Newport, R. I., expressly for this work. Boston, J. R. Osgood, 1873. 4, (11) - 268 p. front., plates. 19½ cm. 1-1122.

F89. N5 H6

NEWPORT. Historic Newport. (Newport, R. I., Newport Chamber of commerce, 1933) (59) p. illus., plates. 24½ cm. 33-22018.

F89. N5 H67

NEWPORT. The Jews of Newport, by Leon Hühner ... Address delivered on the occasion of unveiling the memorial tablet in the old Jewish synagogue at Newport, R. I., Sept. 7, 1908. (n. p., 1908) 11 p. 16½ x 14 cm. 8-32236.

F89. N5 H8

NEWPORT. Samuel Hubbard, of Newport. 1610 - 1689. By Ray Greene Huling. (Providence? 188-?) 39 p. 23½ cm. "Reprinted from Narragansett historical register." 24-17742.

F89. N5 H83

NEWPORT. Lee's guide to Newport, the ocean city ... by Henry Lee. New York, H. Lee (1884) 129 p. 16°. 1-16176-M1.

F89. N5 L4

NEWPORT. A reminiscence of Newport before and during the revolutionary war. By E. B. Lyman. Newport, R. I., The Milne printery, 1906. 40 p. 16½ cm. 6-21395.

F89. H5 L9

NEWPORT. The Newport Tower ... a special interim report made to the Council of the city of Newport ... 1955, by Arlington H. Mallery, and others. (Newport? R. I., 1955) 1 v. illus., map, plans. 22 x 36 cm. Includes the Preliminary report (4 l. at end) 57-20306.

F89. N5 M22

NEWPORT. Merchants and mansions of bygone days; an authentic account of the early settlers of Newport, by Elton Merritt Manuel ... Newport, R. I., R. Ward, 1939. 5 - 32, vi p. 23½ cm. 40-3981.

F89. N5 M24

NEWPORT illustrated, in a series of pen & pencil sketches. By the editor of the Newport Mercury (George Champlin Mason) ... New York, D. Appleton (1854) 110 p. front., illus., plates. 18½ cm. Rc-3027.

F89. N5 M3

— Engravings by Whitney, Jocelyn & Annin, N. Y. Newport, R. I., C. E. Hammett, jr. (1875) 135 p. front., illus., plates, fold. map, facsim. 19½ cm. Map wanting. Rc-3028.

F89. N5 M4

— (Rev. and continued by C. E. Hammett, jr.) Newport, R. I., C. E. Hammett, jr. (1891) 76 p. front. (fold. map) illus., pl., port., facsim. 12°. 1-Rc-3029.

F89. N5 M5

NEWPORT. Reminiscences of Newport, by George Champlin Mason ... Newport, R. I., C. E. Hammett, jr., 1884. 407 p. front., illus., pl., port., facsim. 23 cm. 2-13570.

F89. N5 M6

NEWPORT. Re-union of the sons and daughters of Newport, Aug. 23, 1859. By George C. Mason. Comp. and printed by order of the general committee of arrangements. Newport, R. I., F. A. Pratt, 1859. vi, (7) - 297 p. illus. 20 cm. 1-Rc-3030.

F89. N5 M7

NEWPORT towner (by) Philip Ainsworth Means. New York, H. Holt (1942) xxi, 344 p. front., plates, plans, facsims. 24 cm. Bibliography: p. 305 - 332. 42-14829.

F89. N5 M73

NEWPORT villa owners' summer visitors' and residents' guide to the reliable business interest of the city, for 1883. Together with a list of all the cottage rentals, etc., 1883. Boston, W. G. Morrison (1883) 72 p. fold. map. 24 cm. 10-5625.

F89. N5 M8

NEWPORT. This is Newport, a book of photographs. By Beth Murray. Providence, Plantations Press, 1948. (55) p. of illus. 21 cm. 48-7931*.

F89. N5 M9

NEWPORT. (Portland, Me., 1912) 20 x 25 cm.

F89. N5 N4

RHODE ISLAND 35

NEWPORT. Portland, Me., L.H. Nelson co., 1907. (48) p. illus. 20 x 25 cm. CA 17-134 Unrev.
F89.N5 N42

NEWPORT; a sketch ... (Newport) Newport progress committee, 1904. (46) p. front., illus.
16½ x 25 cm. 9-26066.
F89.N5 N44

NEWPORT, and how to see it, with list of summer residents. Newport, R.I., Davis & Pitman (1871)
58 (2) p. incl. illus., 7 pl. front., 2 pl. 17 cm. 17-18122.
F89.N5 N46
Toner Coll.

NEWPORT casino. ... Official bulletin and program (1909) (New York, 1909) (1) v. illus. 25 cm.
F89.N5 N49

NEWPORT Historical Society. Report. Newport, R.I. 23 cm. annual. F89.N5 N6

NEWPORT Historical Society. Bulletin. Jan. 1912 - Newport, R.I. v. 23½ cm.
12-6620.
F89.N5N615

— Newport County lotteries ... by Mr. Hamilton B. Tompkins. (no. 1 - 2) 1912. 13-12755.
— The battle of Rhode Island ... by Lloyd M. Mayer. (In no. 4.) 1912. 13-12754.
— ... Governor William Coddington ... by Mrs. Sarah K. Birckhead. (In no. 5) 1913. 13-12753.
— ... The visit of General Washington to Newport in 1781. ... by Mrs. French E. Chadwick. In no. 6) 1913. 13-15255.
— ... Early inhabitants of Rhode Island ... By Miss Maud Lyman Stevens. (In no. 7) 1913. 13-12786.
— ... Election day in Newport; a recollection of childhood, by Miss M. E. Powel. (In no. 8) 1913. 14-8880.
— ... On the so-called portrait of Governor Wm. Coddington in the City hall at Newport; ... by Hamilton B. Tompkins. (In no. 9) 1913. 19-8802.
— Perry centennial observance in Newport, by Alvah H. Sanborn. (In no. 9) 1913. 19-8801.
— Newport cemeteries; by Hon. Robert S. Franklin. (In no. 10) 1913. 14-19999.
— ... The old State house at Newport ... Prof. William McDonald. (In no. 11) 1914. 14-8533.
— ... The Newport historical soc. in its earlier days, by Edith May Tilley. (In no. 12) 1914. 14-20026.
— Newport newspapers in the 18th century; ... by George Parker Winship. (In no. 14) 1914. 17-6004.
— ... The story of election day ... by Miss M. E. Powel. (In no. 15) 1915. 17-6005.
— ... Some of our founders; sixty years ago; ... by Miss M. E. Powel. (In no. 16) 1915. 17-6006.
— ... The battle of Rhode Island, by ex-Governor Charles Warren Lippitt; (In no. 18) 1915. 17-6007.
— ... The scope and purpose of an historical society in Newport, by the Hon. Wm. Paine Sheffield. (In no. 20) 1916. 18-4186.
— ... More light on the old mill at Newport ... by F. H. Shelton. (In no. 61) 1927.
— ... The first European visitors to Narragansett Bay ... by Rev. Roderick Terry. (In no. 22) 1917. 18-4187
— ... The romance of Newport ... by Miss Maud Lyman Stevens. (In no. 24) 1918. 18-4468.
— ... The Coddington portrait ... by Judge Darius Baker ... (In no. 25) 1918. 18-12312.
— Measures of defence in old Newport ... by Maud Lyman Stevens. (In no. 26) 1918. 19-4161.
— ... The history of the Liberty tree of Newport ... by Rev. Roderick Terry. (In no. 27) 1918. 19-4208.
— Recollections of Jacob Chase ... by Lloyd M. Mayer. (In no. 28) 1919. 19-19144.
— ... Benedict Arnold, first governor of Rhode Island ... by Hamilton B. Tompkins. (In no. 30) 1919. 19-16898.
— ... Miss Jane Stuart, 1812 - 1888, her grandparents and parents ... by Miss Mary E. Powel. (In no. 31) 1920. 20-12619.
— ... An old Newport loyalist, by Katharine Johnstone Wharton. (In no. 32) 1920. 20-12621.
— The old Hazard house, by Maud Lyman Stevens; (In no. 33) 1920. 21-4380.
— ... The early relations between the colonies of New Plymouth and Rhode Island ... by the president (Roderick Terry) (In no. 34) 1920. 21-19205.
— ... Some recollections of Newport artists;.. by Mrs. Maud H. Elliott. (In no. 35) 21-2424.

613

NEWPORT Historical Society. Bulletin. Continued.   F89.N5M615

— ... Some old Newport houses; ... by Mrs. Marie J. Gale.   (In no. 36) 1921.   21-13296.
— ... A few French officers to whom we owe much ... by Miss M. E. Powel.   (In no. 38) 1921.   21-19204.
— ... Some old Rhode Island grist mills ... by Mr. Charles P. Coggeshall.   (In no. 39) 1922.   22-7815.
— ... The old house on Franklin street ... by Hon. Darius Baker.   (In no. 40) 1922.   22-7816.
— ... The Robinson family and their correspondence with the Vicomte and Vicomtesse de Noailles ... by Anna Wharton Wood.   (In no. 42) 1922.   23-788.
— ... The Newport Banisters ... by ... the Hon. Darius Baker.   (In no. 41) 1923.   23-2841.
— ... The commission of Governor Coddington and the early charters of Rhode Island.   (In no. 44) 1923.   28-11583.
— The log of the Lawrence ... Ed. (Lloyd M. Mayer)   (In no. 44) 1923.   28-12169.
— Presidential visits to Newport ... by Miss Mary E. Powel.   (In no. 45) 1923.   24-3341.
— ... The romance of the two Hannahs ... by Anna Wharton Morris.   (In no. 46) 1923. 23-18582.
— ... Butts Hill fort celebration ... by H. W. H. Powel.   (In no. 47) 1923.   23-18103.
— ... Historic types of Newport houses; ... by Mrs. William W. Covell.   (In no. 48) 24-3891.
— ... Colonel Higginson and his friends in Newport ... by Maud L. Stevens.   (In no. 49) 1924.   24-10982.
— ... The reception by the Newport historical soc. of Green End revolutionary fort ... by Lloyd M. Mayer.   (In no. 51) 1924.   24-31500.
— ... "Jamestown" ... by A. O'D. Taylor.   (In no. 52) 1925.   25-844.
— ... A decade of Newport as seen by two wandering sons ... by Miss Anna F. Hunter.   (In no. 53) 1925.   25-12665.
— ... A few words about some old buildings in Newport ... by Mary Edith Powel.   (In no. 55) 1925.   26-4230.
— ... Memories of the long ago, 1839 - 1925 ... by George B. Smith.   (In no. 56) 1926.   26-4231.
— Formation and service of the First regiment Rhode Island detached militia ... by Geo. B. Smith.   (In no. 58) 26-15732.
— Some old Newport letters belonging to and read by the president of the society.   (In no. 59) 1926.   26-18006.
— ... David Melville and his early experiments with gas in Newport ... by Edith May Tilley.   (In no. 60) 1926.   27-3212.
— ... A Newport romance of 1804 ... by Miss Anna F. Hunter.   (In no. 61) 1927.   27-8391.
— "Some old papers relating to the Newport slave trade." (By Roderick Terry)   (In no. 62) 1927.   27-16413.
— ... History of the old Colony house at Newport ... by (Roderick Terry)   (In no. 63) 28-528.
— ... The old Easton farm ... by Miss M. E. Powel.   (In no. 64) 1928.   28-1720.
— ... The Newport mercury ... by Mrs. Alvah H. Sanborn.   (In no. 65) 1928.   28-12478.
— ... Dedication of the monument in King park ... in commemoration of the landing of the French ... 1780.   (In no. 66) 1928.   28-30610.
— ... Newport streets ... by Miss Maud Lyman Stevens.   (In no. 67) 1928.   29-1780.
— ... Sea coasts, their influence on history ... by Mrs. William W. Covell.   (In no. 68) 1929.   29-1595.
— ... Items of Newport interest in early Boston newspapers ... by Miss Edith May Tilley.   (In no. 69) 1929.   29-16926.
— ... Recollections of my uncle Edward King ... by Mrs. Wm. H. Birckhead.   (In no. 71) 1929.   30-4292.
— ... Story of "Oldport days", by Miss Ethel K. Simes-Nowell.   (In no. 71) 1929.   30-4291.
— ... Exercises at the unveiling of the bronze table to the memory of the founders of the society ... (By Theophilus Topham Pitman)   (In no. 72) 1929.   29-30541.
— ... The Seventh day Baptist meeting house ... by Mrs. R. Sherman Elliott.   (In no. 73) 1930.   30-4293.
— The why of a Newport marine museum, by (Roderick Terry)   (In no. 73) 1930.   30-4294.
— ... "More items of Newport interest in old Boston newspapers" ... by Miss Edith May Tilley.   (In no. 74) 1930.   30-11217.
— "The colonial theatre in New England" ... by Prof. B. W. Brown.   (In no. 76) 1930.   30-28434.

RHODE ISLAND 37

NEWPORT Historical Society. Bulletin. Continued.   F89.N5M615

— ... Trinity church and some of its members, by Miss Maud L. Stevens. (In no. 77)) 1930. 30-30506.
— ... A Newporter's wanderings in genealogical by-paths ... by Miss Edith May Tilley. (In no. 78) 1931. 31-7250.
— ... Excerpts from the European diary of the Rev. Doctor Thayer. ... by Thatcher Thayer. (In no. 79) 1931 31-9952.
— ... The Bull family of Newport ... by Henry Bull .. (In no. 81) 1931. 32-11072.
— ... The third coming of the French, by (Lloyd Minturn Mayer) (In no. 82) 1932. 32-11061.
— ... Kay street during my life, by Miss Anna F. Hunter. (In no. 83) 1932. 32-11073.

NEWPORT Historical Society. Handbook. v. 23 cm. 42-30844.   F89.N5N617

NEWPORT historical society. Indian and prehistoric exhibition and lawn fete ... 1914. (Newport, Ward, printer, 1914) (12) p. 22 cm. 14-22105.   F89.N5N618

NEWPORT historical society. Loan exhibition of antiques and heirlooms ... 1911. Newport, R.I., Mercury pub. co. (1911) 21 p. front., plates. 22½ cm. 11-32028.   F89.N5 N62 1911

— (1912) 28 p. front., plates. 22½ cm. 12-29596. (Title: relics and heirlooms)   F89.N5N62 1912

— (1913) 30 p. front., plates, facsim. 23 cm. 13-18334. (Title: relics and heirlooms)   F89.N5N62 1913

NEWPORT historical society. ... (A new building for library purposes)   F89.N5N624

NEWPORT historical society. Newport historical soc., Newport, R.I. (Newport, 1894) 10 p. 23 cm. 7-32878.   F89.N5 N63

NEWPORT historical society. Miscellaneous printed matter pub. by this body is classified in   F89.N5N639

NEWPORT household directory. Containing a complete street directory, giving the location of each street ... also a complete list of builings, etc. Providence, Sanford pub. co., Newport, C.E. Hammett, 1887. 122 p. front. (fold. map) 16½ cm. 10-5397.   F89.N5 N64

NEWPORT pathfinder ... Newport, R.I., B. G. Oman, 1 v. illus. 17 x 13½ cm. 9-18171.   F89.N5 N67

NEWPORT service society. The book of Newport ... 2d ed. (Newport, R.I., Press of R. Ward) 1930. 107 p. incl. front., illus. (incl. map) 24½ cm. 31-35662.   F89. N5 N7

NEWPORT Tower. By Kathleen Merrick O'Loughlin. St. Catherines, Ont., 1948. 20 p. 23 cm. 50-56243.   F89. N5 O4

NEWPORT. Washington-Rochambeau celebration, 1780 - 1955, Newport. Preservation Society of Newport County. (Official souvenir program) Newport (1955) 40 p. illus. 30 cm. 59-35707.   F89. N5 P7

NEWPORT; a tour guide. Text by A. L. Randall. Photos by Robert P. Foley. Maps by R. H. Baker. Newport, R.I., Catboat Press, 1970. 120 p. illus. 14 x 22 cm. 76-128562.   F89. N5 R3

NEWPORT. Gazette francois; an account of the French newspaper printed on the press of the French fleet at Newport, 1780 and 1781. Providence, R.I. historical soc., 1926. 11 p. incl. front., illus. (facsim.) 23 cm. 26-16188.   F89. N5 R4

NEWPORT, Scenic views of.   Fall River, Mass., E. P. Charlton (190 -?)   (24) p. illus. 16 x 21 cm.
F89.N5 S28

NEWPORT.   Seventy-five photographic views of Newport ... 1903.   F89.N5 S46

NEWPORT.   The story of colonial Newport. By Margaret M. Shea. (Newport, R.I.) 1962.
28 p.   24 cm.   F89.N5 S48

NEWPORT.   An address delivered by William P. Sheffield ... 1882. With notes. Newport, R.I., J. P. Sanborn, printer, 1883.   67 p.   23½ cm.   Cover-title: Privateersmen of Newport.   1-16175.
F89. N5 S49

NEWPORT.   Historical address ... 1876. With an appendix. By William P. Sheffield. Pub. by order of the City council.   Newport, J. P. Sanborn, printers, 1876.   68, xv p.   22½ cm.   Rc-3031.
F89. N5 S5

NEWPORT pleasures and palaces. By Nancy Sirkis. Introd. by Louis Auchincloss. New York, Viking Press (1963)   158 p.   30 cm.   (A Studio book)   63-9512.   F89.N5 S56

NEWPORT.   In and around Newport. 1891. A guide to the place, showing where and how to see the most, in a short ime ... By Clarence Stanhope. (Providence, Press of the Ryder & Dearth co., 1891)   102, (2) p.   illus.   28½ cm.   Rc-3032.   F89. N5 S7

— 1892. (Newport, Daily news job print, 1892)   133 p.   illus.   28 cm.   Rc-3033.   F89.N5 S71

NEWPORT.   A history of the Vernon house in Newport, by Maud Lyman Stevens. Newport, The Charity organization soc., 1915.   58 p.   front., plates.   23 cm.   15-13404.   F89.N5 S84

NEWPORT.   Town and country.   1896 -   F89. N5 T7

NEWPORT. When Rochambeau stepped ashore; a reconstruction of life in Newport in 1780. By Arthur Tuckerman. Newport, R.I., Preservation Society of Newport County (1955)   24 p.   illus. 24 cm.   Includes bibliography.   56-899.   F89. N5 T8

NEWPORT: our social capital, by Mrs. John King Van Rensselaer ... with frontispiece in color by Henry Hutt, may illustrations ... by Edward Stratton Holloway. Philadelphia and London, J. B. Lippincott, 1905.   17, 17-401 p.   col. front., illus., 52 pl., 4 maps.   29½ cm.   5-39584.   F89. N5 V2
Rare Book Coll.

NEWPORT, Views of. (Newport, R.I., 1905)   19½ x 25 cm.   F89. N5 V6

NEWPORT historic guide, illustrated. By Earl Washburn. Drawings by Ruth Rhoades Lepper. (Newport, R.I., The Franklin printing house, 1946)   101 p.   illus.   21½ cm.   46-21165.
F89.N5 W18

— photos by John R. Hopf.   Rev. (Newport? R.I., D. Washburn, 1958)   103 p. illus. 23 cm. 58-47832.
F89.N5 W18
1958

— 3d rev. ed.   compiled by Delphine Washburn. (Newport? R.I., D. Washburn, 1963)
63 p.   23 cm.   F89.N5 W15
1963

NEWPORT.   Haut ton Newport, per se ... A complete encyclopaedia and guide to all the principal points of interest ... From the pen of "Fair Harvard." (William Tucker Washburn) Providence, Frazier & Whiting, 1884.   80 p.   illus., pl., fold. map.   15 x 24 cm.   1-16174.   F89. N5 W2

NEWPORT.   Ideal Newport in the 18th century, by William B. Weedon ... Worcester, Mass., The Davis press, 1907.   14 p.   23½ cm.   7-26272.   F89. N5 W4

RHODE ISLAND

NEWPORT. A guide to Newport. By Gabriel Weis. Newport, New York, G. Weis (1916) 24 p. 18 cm. 16-15655. F89.N5 W45

NEWPORT. Did the Norsemen erect the Newport round tower (by) Barthinius L. Wick. (Cedar Rapids, Iowa, The Torch press, 1911) 26 p. 2 pl. 23½ cm. 11-30420. F89.N5 W5

NORTH KINGSTOWN, An historical sketch of, delivered at Wickford ... 1876, by David Sherman Baker, jr. Providence, E. A. Johnson, printers, 1876. 26 p. 23 cm. Rc-3034. F89. N8 B1

NORTH KINGSTOWN, Facts and fancies concerning, by Pettaquamscutt chapter, Daughters of the American revolution. North Kingstown, R.I., 1941. 2. 143 p. front., illus. 24 cm. "First ed." 41-23312. F89. N8 D3

NORTH PROVIDENCE and Johnston directory. Providence, R.I., White, Gordon co., 1910. 1 v. 24 cm. 10-16748. Directories

NORTH PROVIDENCE. Armstrong's North Providence, Johnston and Smithfield directory, 1937 - including Allendale, Centredale, Esmond ... (etc.) containing a house, business and street directory ... v. 1 - Cranston, R.I., J. H. Armstrong co., 1936 - v. 24 cm. 37-38787. Directories

NORTH PROVIDENCE centennial. A report of the celebration at Pawtucket, North Providence, of the 100th anniversary of the incorporation of the town ... 1865. Pawtucket, R. Sherman, printer, 1865. 91 p. 24½ cm. Rc-3035. F89. N9 N9

NORTH PROVIDENCE. Report of the centennial celebration ... 1865, at Pawtucket, of the incorporation of the town of North Providence. Providence (Knowles, Anthony, printers) 1865. 118 p. 30½ x 25 cm. 3-26840 Rev. F89.N9 N91

PASCOAG herald, June, 1894. Souvenir historical number. (Pascoag, R.I., Herald printing co., (1894) 8, 28 p. illus. 55 cm. 8-9295. F89.P28 P2

PAWTUCKET. The Pawtucket and Woonsocket directory ... together with a business directory, town record, village record, government of town officers, and a variety of general information. 1857. By William Henry Boyd. New York, W. H. Boyd, (pref. 1856) 204 p. 15½ cm. 11-12623. Directories

PAWTUCKET and Central Falls directory. no. 1875 Providence, Boston, Sampson & Murdock co. 18 - 19 v. fold. maps. 23½ cm. 0-4765 Rev. Directories

PAWTUCKET. Historical sketch of the town of Pawtucket. Prepared by Rev. Massena Goodrich, per vote of the town council. Pawtucket (R.I.) Nickerson, Sibley, 1876. 189 p. 24 cm. Rc-3037. F89. P3 G6

PAWTUCKET. The lower Blackstone river valley; the story of Pawtucket, Central Falls, Lincoln, and Cumberland, Rhode Island; an historical narrative, by John Williams Haley, assisted by Hon. Roscoe Morton Dexter and others. Pub. by Lower Blackstone river valley district committee of the Rhode Island and Providence Plantations tercentenary committee, inc. Pawtucket, R.I., E. L. Freeman co., 1936. 169 p. front., plates, ports. 23½ cm. 37-15414. F89. P3 H3

PAWTUCKET. A hive of diversified industries, Pawtucket. By Robert A. Kenyon. (Pawtucket, R.I., 1910) 15 p. 3 pl. (2 fold.) port. 18½ cm. F89. P3 K3

PAWTUCKET ... Reproductions by Providence heliograph co. Providence, R.I., Dart & Bigelow, 1897. 48 pl. 14 x 20½ cm. 2-12067. F89. P3 P3

PAWTUCKET, past and present; being a brief account of the beginning and progress of its industries and a resume of the early history of the city. Pawtucket, R.I., Slater trust co., 1917. vi, 55 p. incl. front., illus. pl. 23½ cm. 17-3765. F89. P3 S63

PAWTUCKET. A guide to historic Pawtuxet. By Hazel Wade Kennedy. Providence, R.I., Print. by Oxford Press (1972)   31 p. illus. 23 cm.   72-181588 MARC.   F89.P32 K4

PORTSMOUTH. The early records of the town of Portsmouth; ed., in accordance with a resolution of the general assembly, by the librarian of the R.I. historical soc. Providence, R.I., E. L. Freeman, state printers, 1901.   xii, 462 p. front. (facsims.) 24 cm. 2-22462.   F89. P7 P7

PORTSMOUTH, History of, 1638 - 1936. (By Edward Homer West) (Providence, J. Green, 1936) (61) p. plates. 23½ cm. 37-38768.   F89. P7 W5

PROVIDENCE and Rhode Island register and business directory 1880 -   vol. 1 - Providence, R.I., Sampson, Murdock (1879) - 1901.   16 v. fold. maps. 14 - 20½ cm. 99-88 Rev.
Directories

PROVIDENCE directory and Rhode Island business directory   no. (1 -   1824 - Providence, R.I., Sampson & Murdock, 1824 - 19 -   v. fold. maps. 18 - 24 cm.   Directories

PROVIDENCE house directory and family address book ... containing a complete list of names of householders and business places arranged by street numbers ... 1892,   Providence, R.I., Sampson & Murdock co., 1892 - 19   v. 21 - 24 cm. 99-2592 Rev.   Directories

PROVIDENCE. Guide to business men of Providence. Pocket annual ... Jan., 1900 - Providence, R.I., Universal guide pub. co., 1900 -   v. 20½ x 8½ cm. 0-2906 Rev.
Directories

PROVIDENCE and Rhode Island and southern Massachusetts classified business directory ... "buyers blue book". 1935/36 -   Boston, Mass., The New England directory co. (1935 - v. 22 cm. CA 36-46 Unrev.   Directories

PROVIDENCE and surrounding territory general classified business directory ... New York, General pub. co. of New York, 19   v. 23 cm. CA 36-459 Unrev.   Directories

PROVIDENCE household directory ... also, a complete street directory ... 188   Providence, R.I., W. F. Sanford, 188   v. 16½ cm. CA 33-720 Unrev.   Directories

PROVIDENCE street directory, also a complete list of streets in Cranston, East Providence, Pawtucket and Central Falls ... 1901,   (Providence) Sampson, Murdock, 1901 - v. maps (part fold.) 12½ - 16½ cm. 1-20319. Rev.   Directories

PROVIDENCE. An account of the English homes of three early "proprietors" of Providence, William Arnold, Stukeley Westcott and William Carpenter, by Fred A. Arnold ... Providence (Press of E. A. Johnson) 1921.   43 p. incl. illus., map. 25½ cm. 50 copies privately printed. 21-14638.   F89.P9 A85

PROVIDENCE. Unusual and artistic illustrations of Providence; twelve pencil drawings by Whitman Bailey ... (Providence, Standard printing co., 1913)   12 l. illus. 27½ x 35½ cm. Calendar for 1914. 14-3068.   F89. P9 B 16

PROVIDENCE, old and new. Views of the city in the past and present made from original photos. by L. Baker ... Providence, R.I., Providence photogravure engr. co. (1897)   1 p. 54 pl. obl. 16º. 1-Rc-3039.   F89. P9 B18

PROVIDENCE, illustrated. Providence, L. Baker (1896)   1 p. 40 pl. obl. 24º. 1-Rc-3040.
F89. P9 B19

PROVIDENCE. views of the city made from original photos. By Leander Baker. Providence, R.I., L. Baker (1903?)   (32) p. of illus. 14 x 20½ cm. 3-12321.   F89. P9 B2

PROVIDENCE, the southern gateway of New England, proud of its honorable history, happy in its present prosperity ... By Henry Ames Barker. (Providence, Remington print. co., 1910) 63 p. incl. illus., col. pl., facsims., map. 22½ cm. 10-20279 Rev.   F89.Pl B27

RHODE ISLAND

PROVIDENCE, the southern gateway of New England, commemorating the 150th anniversary of the independence of the state of Rhode Island ... 1926. By Henry Ames Barker. (Providence) Historical pub. co. (1926)   264 p. incl. illus., port.   31 cm.   A29-810.   F89. P9B274

PROVIDENCE. Seventeenth century place-names of Providence plantations, 1639 - 1700; comp. by Clarence S. Brigham ... Providence, 1903.   28 p.   fold. map.   25 cm.   Repr. from the Collections of the R.I. historical soc. v. 10.   4-9705.   F89. P9 B8

PROVIDENCE. The civic and architectural development of Providence, 1636 - 1950. By John Hutchins Cady.   Providence, Book Shop, 1957.   320 p.   illus., maps.   29 cm.   Bibliographical footnotes.   57-59339.   F89. P9 C143

PROVIDENCE. Highroads and byroads of Providence; by John Hutchins Cady; drawings by Helen Mason Gross.   Providence, Akerman-Standard Press, 1948.   69 p.   19 cm.   F89. P9 C145

PROVIDENCE. Walks around Providence, by John Hutchins Cady. (Providence, The Akerman-standard press) 1942.   43 p.   illus. (map)   18 cm.   43-315.   F89. P9 C15

PROVIDENCE. Names of the owners or occupants of buildings in the town of Providence from 1749 to 1771. (By Kingsley Carpenter) Providence, S. S. Rider, 1870.   25 p.   20½ cm.   "Privately printed and only 100 copies."   1-13364 Rev.   F89. P9 C2

PROVIDENCE. Owners and occupants of the lots, houses and shops in the town of Providence, in 1798 ... also owners or occupants of houses in the compact part of Providence in 1759 ... by Henry R. Chace ... (Providence, R. I. and New York, Print. Livermore & Knight, 1914)   28 p. xviii (i.e.19) plans on 10 l.   30 cm.   14-10885.   F89. P9 C4

PROVIDENCE. Ancient documents relative to the old grist-mill, with some remarks on the opinions of Messrs. Hunter and Greene, counsel employed by the town to examine the same. (By Benjamin Cowell) (Providence) Herald office, 1829.   32 p.   23½ cm.   20-9593.   F89. P9 C8

PROVIDENCE. The planting and growth of Providence illustrated in the gradual accumulation of the materials for domestic comfort, the means of internal communication and the development of local industries, by Henry C. Dorr.   Providence, R. I., S. S. Rider, 1882.   3 p., 267 p.   21 x 16½ cm. (R.I. historical tracts. 1st ser. no. 15)   Rc-2959 Rev.   F89. P9 D7

PROVIDENCE. The proprietors of Providence, and their controversies with the freeholders. (In R.I. historical soc. 1895-96, v.3, no. 3, p. 143 - 158, no. 4, p. 199 - 230; v.4, no. 2, p. 75 - 106, no. 3, p. 139 - 170, no. 4, p. 203 - 226)   1-6539-M1.   F89. P9 D74

PROVIDENCE. The proprietors of Providence, and their controversies with the freeholders. By Henry C. Dorr. (Providence, R. I., 1897)   4 p, 141 p.   25 cm.   (Collections of the R.I. historical soc. vol. ix) Issued also in the Publications of the society. v. 3 - 4, 1895 - 1897.   6-3803.   F89. P9 D742

PROVIDENCE. Memorial of Thomas Arthur Doyle, mayor of the city of Providence ... Providence, R. I., Prepared and print. by authority of the City counci, 1887.   86 p.   front. (port.)   27½ cm.   17-1537.   F89. P9 D76

PROVIDENCE. A historical discourse delivered on the 250th anniversary of the planting of Providence. By Thomas Durfee. Providence, S.S. Rider, 1887.   69 p.   23½ cm.   8-8579.   F89. P9 D86

PROVIDENCE. Oration delivered at the dedication of the Providence County Court house ... 1877, by the Hon. Thomas Durfee ... Providence, E. L. Freeman, printers, 1879.   38 p.   1 illus.   21½ cm. Rc-3038.   F89. P9 D9

PROVIDENCE. Tax lists of the town of Providence during the administration of Sir Edmund Andros ... 1686 - 1689, etc. Comp. by Edward Field ... Providence, H. W. Preston, 1895.   63 p.   24 cm. Rc-3041.   F89. P9 F4

PROVIDENCE. A little guide to Providence. By Jessie Barker Gardner. Providence, 1907.
24 x 11 cm. F89. P9 G2

PROVIDENCE. Jewish Americans; three generations in a Jewish community (by) Sidney Goldstein (and) Calvin Goldscheider. Englewood Cliffs, N.J., Prentice-Hall (1968) xvii, 274 p. 24 cm. (Ethnic groups in American life series) 68-24185. F89.P9 G64

PROVIDENCE. One hundred years; an address by Theodore Francis Green, delivered at the centennial celebration of Providence the city, at Roger Williams park, June 4, 1932. (Providence? 1932)
15 p. 20 cm. 32-30532. F89.P9 G75

PROVIDENCE. The legal opinion of Richard W. Greene, on the question of the town's interest in the ancient grist mill. Providence, H. H. Brown, printer, 1830. 14 p. 23½ cm. 20-9594.
F89.P9 G79

PROVIDENCE. The Providence Plantations for 250 years. An historical review of the foundation, rise and progress of the city of Providence ... also, sketches of the cities of Newport and Pawtucket ... together with an account of the celebration of the 250th anniversary of the settlement of Providence, ... by Welcome Arnold Greene, and a large corps of writers. Providence, R.I., J.A. & R.A. Reid, 1886. 3, (11) - 468, (2) p. incl. front., illus. 37 cm. Rc-3042 Rev. F89. P9 G8

PROVIDENCE. An historical discourse delivered at the celebration of the second centennial anniversary of the First Baptist church in Providence ... 1839. By William Hague ... Providence, B. Cranston; Boston, Gould, Kendall and Lincoln, 1839. 192 p. 19 cm. 6-20089. F89. P9 H2

PROVIDENCE illustrated guide; a handbook for residents and visitors, by John Williams Haley ... Providence, R.I., Haley & Sykes, 1931. 143 p. incl. front., illus. 17 cm. 32-9344. F89. P9H26

PROVIDENCE. Plea of the Petuxet purchasers, and a history of the first deed, etc. before the king's commissioners 1677. (By William Harris) Providence, Printed for the Society, 1893.
(31) p. 24½ cm. (From R.I. hist. soc. Publications, new ser. v.1) 7-38322. F89.P9 H31

PROVIDENCE. Almon Danforth Hodges and his neighbors. An autobiographical sketch of a typical old New England. Edd. Almon D. Hodges, jr. Boston, Priv. print. (T. R. Marvin, printers) 1909.
4, (7) - 353 p. front., illus., plates, ports., facsims. 25 cm. One hundred copies printed. 10-1448. F89. P9 H6

PROVIDENCE. The home lots of the early settlers of the Providence Plantations, with notes and plats. By Charles Wyman Hopkins. Providence, R.I. (Providence press co.) 1886. vii, 78 p. pl., 4 double plans, 3 facsim. (1 double) 30½ x 26 cm. L.C. copy replaced by microfilm. Rc-3043. F89. P9 H7
Microfilm 8767 F

PROVIDENCE. The legal opinion of the Hon. William Hunter, on the question of the town's interest in the ancient grist mill. (Providence) Printed at the Patriot office, 1829. 15 p. 23½ cm. 20-9595.
F89.P9 H94

PROVIDENCE. Illustrated hand-book of the city of Providence, ... (Providence? 1876?)
136 p. illus. (incl. port., map) 24 cm. 11-10436. F89. P9 I 2

PROVIDENCE. The meeting house of the First Baptist church in Providence; a history of the fabric, by Norman M. Isham ... Issued ... on the 150th anniversary of the dedication of the house ... 1775. Providence (Print. the Akerman-Standard co.) 1925. xiii, 33 p. incl. front. illus., plates, plans. 23½ cm.
26-16567. F89. P9 I 7

PROVIDENCE in colonial times, by Gertrude Selwyn Kimball, with an introd. by J. Franklin Jameson ... Boston & New York, Houghton Mifflin, 1912. xxi, 392 p. front., plates, ports., 2 maps (1 fold.) facsims.
25 cm. 12-3639. F89.P9 K49

— New York, Da Capo Press, 1972 (1912) xxi, 392 p. illus. 22 cm. (The American scene) 76-87452.
F89. P9 K49
1972

PROVIDENCE. King's pocket-book of Providence. (Ed. by) Moses King. Subscription ed. Providence, R. I. Tibbitts & Shaw (1882)   124 p.   21 cm.   13-5135.   F89.P9 K54

PROVIDENCE. A modern city: Providence, and its activities, ed. by William Kirk ... Chicago, The University of Chicago press, 1909.   ix, 363 p. front., 8 pl., map.   23 cm.   9-26166.   F89.P9 K59

PROVIDENCE. Old Providence; a collection of facts and traditions relating to various buildings and sites of historic interest in Providence ... Providence, R. I., Printed for the Merchants national bank of Providence, 1918.   xi, 65 p. incl. front. (port.) illus.   22 cm.   Bibliography: p. 64-65.   18-12113.   F89.P9 M55

PROVIDENCE. The story of the old Market-house, 1771 - 1927, by Katharine A. Milan.   Providence, The Akerman-standard co. (1927)   (16) p.   22½ cm.   Printed to accompany the reproduction of 'Market Square' painted for their calendar for 1928.   28-24315.   F89.P9 M6

PROVIDENCE. Angell's Lane; the history of a little street in Providence. By George Leland Miner. Providence, Akerman-Standard Press, 1948.   198, xxxvi p. illus., maps, facsims.   25 cm.   "A list of Rhode Island painters and sculptors ... " p. iii-xxi.   Bibliographical footnotes.   48-3084*.   F89.P9 M64

PROVIDENCE. Third annual convention New England typographical union ... 1912. Providence, The Visitor printing co. (1912)   (40) p.   illus. (incl. ports.)   31 cm.   F89.P9 N3

PROVIDENCE. The News-tribune. Tercentenary edition. Providence, R. I., 1936.   1 vol. illus.   55 cm.   With the regular news section, forms v.34, no. 147 of the News-tribune, June 20, 1936.   40M35T.   F89.P9 N48

PROVIDENCE. Reminiscences of Rhode Island and ye Providence Plantations. (By Isaac Pitman Noyes) (Washington, 1905)   47 p.   22 cm.   5-34627-8 Rev.   F89.P9 N6
— (Supplement) ... (Washington? 1905)   16 p.   22 cm.   F89.P9 N61
— (2d supplement) ... (Washington, 1905)   24 p.   21 cm.   5-34627-8 Rev.   F89.P9 N62
— (3d supplement) ... (Washington, 1905)   34 p.   20½ cm.   F89.P9 N63
— (4th supplement) ... (Washington, 1905)   37 p.   21 cm.   5-34627-8 Rev.   F89.P9 N64
— (5th supplement) ... (Washington, 1906)   7 p.   21 cm.   F89.P9 N65

— (Washington, 1905)   47 p.   Second ed.   25-19993.   F89.P9 N7

PROVIDENCE. The defenders of Providence during King Philips war, by Howard W. Preston ... (Providence? 1928)   8 p. incl. pl.   23 cm.   Repr. from the R.I. historical soc. Colls. Apr. 1928.   Ca 30-1261.   F89.P9 P67

PROVIDENCE. Notes on old Providence. The old County house in Providence, by Howard W. Preston. Providence, Preston & Rounds, 1918.   8 p.   24 cm.   "The building was known by various names, 'the County house,' 'the County court house,' 'the Colony house,' 'the Court house.'"   18-12887.   F89.P9 P7

PROVIDENCE. The City hall, Providence. Corner-stone laid ... 1875. Dedicated ... 1878. Providence, R. I., Prepared and printed by authority of the City council, 1881.   viii, 108 p. front., 5 plans.   27 cm.   11-10431.   F89.P9 P79

PROVIDENCE. ... The progress of Providence. A centennial address to the citizens of Providence by Hon. Samuel Greene Arnold. Providence, Providence press co., 1876.   55 p.   26 cm.   Rc-3046.   F89.P9 P795

PROVIDENCE. 250th anniversary of the settlement of Providence ... 1886. Providence, Printed by authority of the City council, 1887.   viii, 236 p. front., pl.   31 x 25 cm.   Contains music.   Rc-3045.   F89.P9 P8

PROVIDENCE. Report of the exercises at the dedication of the statue of Ebenezer Knight Dexter, presented to the City of Providence by Henry C. Clark ... 1894. (Providence) The Providence press, Snow & Farnham, 1894.   44 p.   front. (port.) pl.   23½ cm.   11-10435.   F89.P9 P82

PROVIDENCE. Alphabetical index of the births, marriages and deaths, recorded in Providence ... Providence, S. S. Rider, 1879 - 19   v.   26½ cm.   55 copies of v. 17, 46 of v. 18 and 50 of v. 19. 12-31286 Rev.   F89.P8 P86

PROVIDENCE. Alphabetical index of the births, marriages and deaths recorded in Providence. Vol. I. Births. From 1636 to 1850 inclusive. Reprinted with some additions. Providence, 1928.
2 p., 147 p.   24 cm.
                                               F89. P9 P862

PROVIDENCE. ... Alphabetical lists of the names of persons deceased, born, and married, in the city of Providence (no. 1-3) 1866 (-1868) Prepared by Edwin M. Snow, city registrar. Providence, Hammond, Angell (etc.) printers, 1867 - 70.   3 v.   23 cm.   8-16742.
                                               F89. P9 P87

PROVIDENCE. Report of the Commissioners of the cove lands, made pursuant to resolutions of the Board of aldermen of the city of Providence. Providence, Angell, Burlingame, printers, 1877.
2, 19, vi, 180 p.   plans (partly fold.)   23½ cm.   11-13696.
                                               F89. P9 P875

PROVIDENCE. History of the Providence riots, from Sept. 21 to Sept. 24, 1831. Providence, H. H. Brown, 1831.   3, (v) - vi, (7) - 20 p.   22 cm.   A 38-1825 Rev.
                                              F89. P9 P876
                                              Rare Book Coll.

PROVIDENCE. Index to the probate records of the Municipal court of the city of Providence. From 1646 to and including the year 1899. Prepared under the direction of Edward Field ... (Providence) The Providence press, Snow & Farnham, printers, 1902.   iv, 333 p.   36 cm.   12-2437.
                                               F89. P9 P88

PROVIDENCE. The early records of the town of Providence, v. I - XXI ... Printed under authority of the City council ... by ... (the) Record commissioners ... Providence, Snow & Farnham, city printers, 1892 - 1915.   21 v.   fronts. (ports.) illus., plates, plans (part fold.) facsims. (part fold.) 23½ x 19 cm. Publication suspended with v. 21.   6-21252 rev. 2.
                                               F89. P9 P9

— Index, containing also a summary of the contents of the volumes and an appendix of documented research data to date on Providence and other early 17th century Rhode Island families, by Richard Le Baron Bowen. Providence, R.I. historical soc., 1949.   xii, 97 p.   23½ x 19 cm.
                                               F89. P9 P9
                                               Index

PROVIDENCE. First (- fifth) report of the Record commissioners relative to the early town records ... (Providence) Show & Farnham (etc.) city printers, 1892 - 97.   5 v. fold. map, 2 fold. facsim. 23½ x 18½ cm. Contains indexes to the Providence town papers, Index to plats of streets, and Maps and plans of Providence.   6-21253.
                                               F89. P9 P91

PROVIDENCE. Historical catalogue of the members of the First Baptist church in Providence. Comp. and ed. by Henry Melville King, pastor emeritus; with the valuable aid of Charles Field Wilcox ... 1908. Providence, F. H. Townsend, 1908.   189 p. front., 4 pl., 15 port.   26 cm.   9-7022.
                                               F89. P9 P93

PROVIDENCE. Mechanics' festival. An account of the 71st anniversary of the Providence assoc. of mechanics and manufacturers ... 1860, together with a sketch of the early history of the association .... Prepared by Edwin M. Stone, under the direction of the select committee of the assoc. Providence, Knowles, Anthony, printers, 1860.   119, 18 p.   front.   24 cm.   4-14738.
                                               F89. P9 P94

PROVIDENCE. Illustrated. Pub. in twelve parts. (Chicago?) H. R. Page, 1891.   23 l.   71 pl. 35 x 29 cm.   16-11517.
                                               F89. P9 P95

PROVIDENCE (views) Providence, R.I., Dart Bigelow (1896)   47 pl.   obl. 24°.   1-Rc-3044.
                                               F89.P9 P956

PROVIDENCE. ... Objections to the majority report of the Commission on railroad terminal facilities, presented to the City council ... 1883. Providence, The Public park assoc., 1884.
13 p.   24 cm.   12-30218.
                                               F89. P9 P94

PROVIDENCE. Westminster street, Providence, as it was about 1824, from drawings made by

Francis Read and lately presented by his daughter, Mrs. Marinus W. Gardiner, to the R. I. historical soc. Providence, Printed for the Society, 1917.   1 p., 7 pl. (4 fold.)   27½ x 15 cm.   17-23200.
F89.P9 R28

PROVIDENCE.   Renumbering of Broad and Canal streets.   Providence, Sampson, Murdock & co. (1888)   8 p.   8°.   2-5495.
F89.P9 R35

PROVIDENCE County court house.   Report of the Commissioners on decorations and improvements, and proceedings on the legislative visit ... 1885.   Pub. by order of the General assembly of Rhode Island.   Providence, E. L. Freeman, printers, 1885.   85, (2) p.   front., illus.   23 cm.   3-21060.
F89. P9 R4

PROVIDENCE.   Proceedings at the dedication of the Soldiers' and sailors' monument, in Providence, to which is appended a list of the deceased soldiers and sailors whose names are scupltured upon the monument.   Providence (R. I.) A. C. Greene, printer, 1871.   67 p.   23 cm.   3-28354 Rev.   F89. P9 R44

— 67 p.   30½ x 26 cm.   3-12486.
F89.P9 R45

PROVIDENCE.   Reports relating to the title of the state to certain lands in the Woonasquatucket Valley, and establishing boundary line between the city of Providence and the town of North Providence. Providence, The Public park assoc., 1884.   44 p.   23½ cm.   11-13691.
F89.P9 R46

PROVIDENCE.   Annual report.   Rhode Island.   State house commissioners.   Providence, 1898 - 99.
2 v.   23 cm.   11-4733.
F89.P9 R47

— 2d, 1905; 5th, 1907; 6th, 1908.   Providence, 1906 - 1908.   3 v.   23½ cm.   CA 7-180.
F89.P9 R48

PROVIDENCE.   The forgeries connected with the deed given by the sachems Canonicus and Miantinomi to Roger Williams of the land on which the town of Providence was planted.   By Sidney S. Rider. Providence, S. S. Rider, 1896.   vi, 128 p.   fold. plan, fold. facsim.   21½ x 16½ cm.   (R. I. historical tracts. 2d ser. no. 4)   Rc-2975.
F89.P9 R54

PROVIDENCE.   Oration, by Horatio Rogers, delivered at the laying of the corner stone of the new City hall ... 1875.   Providence, Priv. print. (Press of Angell Burlingame) 1875.   20 p.   plates, ports., facsim.   29½ cm.   Extra illustrated.   "Only 10 copies of this ed. printed..."   1-6541.
F89.P9 R69
Rare Book Coll.

— (From Providence. City council. The City hall ... Providence, 1881. p. 29-39)   11-10430.
F89. P9 R7

PROVIDENCE.   The Providence world war memorial, by Henry T. Samson.   Providence, The Akerman-Standard co. (1929)   16 p.   22 cm.   30-17014.
F89. P9 S3

PROVIDENCE, A souvenir of (views)   New York, A. Wittemann (1888)   (2) p. 20 pl. obl. 32°.
1-Rc-3047.
F89. P9 S7

PROVIDENCE.   Annals of the town of Providence, from its first settlement, to the organization of the city government ... 1832.   By William R. Staples.   Providence, Print. Knowles and Vose, 1843.
vi, (9) - 670 p.   23 cm.   Rc-3048.
F89. P9 S8

PROVIDENCE.   The pageant of Benefit street down through the years, by Margaret Bingham Stillwell, illus. by the author.   Providence, R. I., The Akerman-Standard press, 1945.   7, 17-143 p. illus.
22½ cm.   45-10328.
F89. P9 S82

PROVIDENCE.   While Benefit street was young, by Margaret Bingham Stillwell.   Providence, R. I., The Akerman-standard press, 1943.   6, (15) - 37 p.   illus.   19½ cm.   43-44078.
F89. P9 S83

PROVIDENCE.   The Colony house, by Frank H. Swan.   Providence, The Ackerman-Standard co. (1931)   18 p.   pl.   22 cm.   32-15863.
F89. P9 S9

LOCAL HISTORIES IN THE LIBRARY OF CONGRESS

PROVIDENCE, Views of. (Portland, 19 -)   20 x 25 cm.   F89. P9 V6

PROVIDENCE. Angell's apple orchard, 1774 - 1929, by Professor Arthur E. Watson. Providence, The Akerman-Standard co. (1929)   22 p.   22½ cm.   A historical sketch of the First Baptist church, Providence. 29-15906.   F89. P9 W2

RICHMOND. Historical sketch of the town of Richmond from 1747 to 1876 ... Prepared by James R. Irish ... Hope Valley, R.I., L.W.A.Cole, printer, 1877.   iv, (5) - 96 p.   18½ cm.   Rc-3050.
                                                                                                            F89. R4 I6

SCITUATE. An historical address, delivered in Scituate ... 1876 ... by C. C. Beaman. Phenix (R.I.) Capron & Campbell, printers, 1877.   59, 8 p.   23 cm.   Rc-3051.   F89. S4 B3

SEKONNET. Three sides to the sea; memories of a S'cunnet childhood. By David Patten. New York, Rinehart (1956)   243 p.   illus.   21 cm.   56-8876.   F89. S45 P3

SMITHFIELD, History of the town of, from its organization, in 1730-1, to its division, in 1871, comp. in accordance with the votes of the towns of Smithfield, North Smithfield, Lincoln and Woonsocket, by Thomas Steere. Providence, R.I., E. L. Freeman, printers, 1881.   8p., 230 p.   23 cm. Rc-3052.   F89. S6 S8

SOUTH KINGSTOWN and Narragansett directory, 1910. Providence, R.I., White, Gordon co., 1910.   1 v.   24 cm.   10-23515.   Directories

SOUTH-KINGSTOWN, A history of, by Charles Comstock. Reprinted with a foreword by William Davis Miller. Kingston, R.I., 1934.   5 p., (5) - 41 p.   illus.   22½ cm.   A satirical narrative.   A35-323.
                                                                                                                    F89. S7 C6

SOUTH KINGSTOWN. Dr. Joseph Torrey and his record book of marriages (by) William Davis Miller. Providence, R.I. historical soc., 1925.   24 p.   2 facsim. (incl. front.)   23 cm.   Covers years 1736-1783.   25-17347.
                                                                                                                    F89. S7 M5

TIVERTON. Armstrong's Tiverton, Portsmouth, Middletown, and Little Compton directory. 1937 - including Adamsville, Island Park, Sakonnet, Bristol Ferry, North Tiverton, Tiverton, Four Corners ... v. 1 -   Cranston, R.I., J.H.Armstrong co., 1937 -   v.   24 cm.   37-15338.
                                                                                                                   Directories

TIVERTON, Portsmouth, Middletown and Little Compton directory ... v. 1 -   1921/22 - Salem, C. H. Dunham, 1921 -   v.   24 cm.   23-5681.   Directories

TIVERTON heights: Tiverton. Its historic surroundings, and its beautiful scenery. (Fall River, Mass., The Daily evening news print., 1884)   19 p.   16°.   1-Rc-3053.   F89. T6 K5

TOWER HILL. A preliminary report on the excavations at the house of Jireh Bull on Tower Hill. Issued at the General court of the Soc. of colonial wars in the state of R.I. ... Providence, Printed for the Soc. by E. A. Johnson & co. (1917?)   3 - 16 p.   illus. (plans)   2 pl. (incl. front.)   24½ cm.   18-7670.
                                                                                                                   F89.T73 R4

WALLUM Pond. The Wallum Pond estates, by Harry Lee Barnes. (Providence?) 1922. 80, v p.   illus., plates, ports.   23½ cm.   Reprinted from the R.I. hist. soc. Collections, with additions.   24-17724.   F89.W15 B3

WARREN and Barrington directory ... 1897. Boston, Sampson, Murdock, 1897 -   v.   fold. map.   23½ cm.   CA 33-719 Unrev.   Directories

WARREN. The history of Warren in the war of the revolution, 1776 - 1783. By Virginia Baker. Warren, R.I., The author, 1901.   68 p.   front.   19½ cm.   1-15045.   F89.W19 B2

WARREN. 200th anniversary of Warren; historical sketch, 1747-1947 (and program) By Henry Jarvis Peck. (Warren, 1947)   111 p.   illus.   24 cm.   "Sources of information for this history": p. (5)   48-2545*.
                                                                                                                   F89.W19 P4

RHODE ISLAND

WARREN. The centennial discourse on the 100th anniversary of the First Baptist church, Warren ... 1864, by A. F. Spalding, pastor of the church. With an appendix containing the proceedings connected with the occasion, etc. Providence, Knowles, Anthony, printers, 1865.   2, 76 p.   24 cm.
12-11817 Rev.   F89.W19 S7

WARREN. A discourse delivered at the dedication of the new church edifice of the Baptist church and society in Warren ... 1845. By Josiah P. Tustin ... Providence, H. H. Brown, 1845.
viii, (9) - 193, vi, (5) - 125 p.   15 cm.   Supplement: The history of Warren .. By G. M. Fessenden.   6-21541 Rev.   F89.W19 T9

WARREN. The history of Warren, from the earliest times; with particular notices of Massasoit and his family. By Guy M. Fessenden. Providence, H. H. Brown, 1845.   vi, (5) - 125 p.   15 cm.   (In above item)   6-21540 Rev.   F89.W19 T9

WICKFORD. The Apponaug, East Greenwich, and Wickford directory, 1907 containing a ... directory of ... North Kingstown and East Greenwich, also the villages in Warwick of Norwood, Lincoln Park, Jefferson Park, Hills Grove, Greenwood, Apponaug, Cowesett, Chepiwanoxet ... Providence, R. I., C. D'W. White, 1907 -   v.   24 cm.   7-29597.   Directories

WARWICK. Armstrong's Warwick and East Greenwich directory, 1936 -   Cranston, R. I., J. H. Armstrong co., 1936 -   v.   24 cm.   CA 36-264 Unrev.   Directories

WARWICK, East Greenwich and North Kingstown directory. Providence, R. I., Boston, Mass., Union pub. co., 1914.   1 v.   24 cm.   14-14617.   Directories

WARWICK. Report on the settlement of Warwick, 1642: and the seal of the R. I, historical soc. By William D. Ely, chairman. Reprinted from Proceedings of the society. (Providence, J. A. & R. A. Reid, printers, 1887?)   38 p.   21 cm.   3-21707.   F89. W2 E5

WARWICK. The history of Warwick, from its settlement in 1642 to the present time ... By Oliver Payson Fuller ... Providence, Angell, Burlingame, printers, 1875.   vi, 380 p. front. (port.) illus., plates, map.   21 ½ cm.   Rc-3054.   F89. W2 F9

WARWICK. Historical sketches of the churches of Warwick, by Oliver P. Fuller. To which is added a record of persons joined in marriage in that town by Elder John Gorton. From 1754 to 1792. Providence, S. S. Rider, 1880.   106 p.   22 ½ cm.   The "Historical sketches" are reprinted from the author's History of Warwick, 1875, appendix.   1-13365 Rev.   F89. W2 F92

WARWICK. Fac-simile of the signatures of the settlers of the town of Warwick, with historical sketches appertaining thereto. By Henry Lehré Greene.   (From R. I. historical soc. Publications. 1896. new series v. 4.   7-38301.   F89. W2 G7

WARWICK. Episodes in Warwick history, by Ernest L. Lockwood ... (Warwick, R.I.) City of Warwick historical committee of the R. I. tercentenary celebration, 1937.   5, (7) - 40 p. illus. (map) plates. 19 ½ cm.   Bibliography included in foreword.   37-4578.   F89. W2 L6

WARWICK. The early records of the town of Warwick, edited in accordance with a resolution of the General assembly, by the librarian of the R. I. historical soc. Providence, R. I., E. A. Johnson co., 1926.   vi, 361 p. double front. (facsims.)   24 cm.   27-27338.   F89.W2 W18

WARWICK. Town records. Warwick, R. I. (n. p., 1912)   v.   28 cm.   CA 13-1541 Unrev.   F89. W2 W2

WATCH HILL. The stolen bride; or, A tale of old Watch Hill (poem) by Annie M. Burdick. New York, The Middlemore press (1903)   31 p. front., illus. 21 cm. "A brief history of Watch Hill": p. 21-31. 3-17960.   F89. W3 B9

WATCH HILL. Views of Watch Hill, and the neighboring shore of Little Narragansett Bay. From recent negatives by W. B. Davidson. Westerly, R. I., O. Stillman, 1891.   1 p., 12 pl.   21 x 25 ½ cm. Rc-3055.   F89. W3 D2

WATCH HILL.   The Larkin house, Watch Hill.   (New York, The Sanitary engineer press, 1887)
22 p.   illus.   sq. 16°.   1-22608-M1.   F89. W3 L3

WATCH HILL.   Early land holders of Watch Hill ... by Reginald E. Peck.   (Westerly, R.I., The
Utter co., printers, 1936)   27, (5) p. front., illus. (2 maps) 23½ cm.   36-12638.   F89. W3 P4

WATCH HILL.   Souvenir of Watch Hill.   Photo-gravures.   Brooklyn, N.Y., The Albertype co.,
1900.   1 p., 15 pl.   obl. 24°.   Nov. 1, 1900-11.   F89. W3 S7

WEEKAPAUG.   At the end of the pond.   By Dorothy Snowden Rose.   Illus. by James D. Platt.   (New
York?) 1963.   iii, 67 p.   19 cm.   F89. W36 R6

WEEKAPAUG.   At the end of the pond; historical reminiscences of Weekapaug.   By Dorothy Snowden
Rowe   (1st trade ed.   Stonington, Conn. Pequot Press 1964 (1963)   iii, 64 p.   19 cm.   64-16452.
                                                                                           F89. W36 R6
                                                                                           1964

WEST WARWICK.   Armstrong's West Warwick and Pawtuxet valley directory ... including Anthony,
Arctic, Arkwright, Bakersville, Centreville, Clyde, Crompton, Fiskeville, Harris, Hope, Jackson,
Lippitt, Natick, Phenix, Quidnick, River Point, Washington, Westcott ...   v. 1 -   Cranston,
R.I., J.H. Armstrong co., 1936 -   v. illus. (map)   24 cm.   CA 36-385 Unrev.   Directories

WESTERLY and Pawcatuck directory.   Providence, R.I., Boston, Mass., Sampson & Murdock co.,
18   - 19   v. fold. maps.   24 cm.   99-5018 Rev.   Directories

WESTERLY.   Leading business men of Westerly, Stonington, and vicinity; embracing Mystic River,
Mystic Bridge, Noank and Ashaway ... Boston, Mercantile pub. co., 1889.   78 p. illus.   8°.
1-Rc-3956.   F89. W5 B3

WESTERLY.   The town that saved a state, Westerly; written during the Rhode Island tercentenary in
1936 for the Westerly Rhode Island committee, by Mary Agnes Best ... Westerly, R.I., The Utter co.,
1943.   283 p.   24½ cm.   44-6630.   F89. W5 B37

WESTERLY., The hurricane, Sept. 21, 1938, Westerly, Rhode Island, and vicinity, historical and
pictorial ... (By William A. Cawley)   (Westerly, R.I., Printed by the Utter co., 1938)
(56) p.   illus.   30 cm.   "First printing Oct. 1938 ... Second printing, Nov. 1938.   40-4553.   F89. W5 C3

—   (56) p.   illus.   30½ cm.   42-6786.   F89. W5 C3
                                                                                           1938a

WESTERLY'S oldest witness; how Westerly and the Washington Trust Co. have progressed together
for 150 years.   By Ralph Bolton Cooney.   Westerly, R.I., Washington Trust Co., 1950.
ix, 84 p.   illus., group port.   22 cm.   50-13262.   F89. W5 C6

WESTERLY and its witnesses, for two hundred and fifty years.   1626 - 1876.   Including Charlestown,
Hopkinton, and Richmond, until their separate organization, with the principal points of their subsequent history.   By Rev. Frederic Denison ... Providence, J. A. & R. A. Reid, 1878.   314 p. front.,
plates, ports., map.   25 cm.   Rc-3057.   F89. W5 D3

WESTERLY.   Constitution, by-laws, officers, committees and members of Westerly historical soc.,
1913 - 1914 ... Westerly, R.I., The Utter co. print. (1914?)   6, (2) p. 23 cm.   19-4211.   F89. W5 W52

WESTERLY.   Records and papers, the Westerly historical soc. ... 1913/15 - 19   Westerly,
R.I., 1915 -   v.   23 cm.   16-7057 Rev.   F89. W5 W53

WESTERLY.   Official program, 250th anniversary of the founding of Westerly ... 1669 - 1919.
(Esterly, The Utter co., printers, 1919)   3 - 29, (2) p.   illus., 7 port. on 1 pl.   21½ cm.   20-6415.
                                                                                           F89. W5 W55

WESTERLY.   Old Westerly, now constituting the towns of Charlestown, Hopkinton, Richmond and

RHODE ISLAND

Westerly. Rhode Island's jubilee year, 1636 - 1936. Westerly chamber of commerce. Western Washington county tercentenary committee. (Westerly, R.I., The Utter co., printers, 1936) 23 p. illus. 15½ x 12 cm. 36-32819.   F89. W5 W6

WESTERLY. Old "Westerle," now constituting the towns of ... etc. Text by George B. Utter, drawings by Milo R. Clarke. (Westerly, R.I., The Utter co., printers, 1936) 2, 7 - 55 p., 2 l. illus., maps (1 fold.) 16½ cm. 38-9294.   F89. W5 W62

WICKFORD. Old Wickford "the Venice of America." By Mrs. F. Burge Griswold ... Milwaukee, The Young churchman co., 1900. 240 p. front., illus., plates, ports. 19½ cm. 1-15036.   F89. W6 G8

WICKFORD. Wickford and its old houses; a report to the Main street association of Wickford, based on the records of the town of North Kingstown, by Hunter C. White. Pub. by the Main street assoc. of Wickford, R.I. ... (Providence, R.I., The Reynolds press) 1936. 35 p. incl. illus., maps. fold. map. 24 cm. 37-15341.   F89. W6 W5

WOONSOCKET, R.I. and Blackstone, Mass., directory ... 187   - 19   ; Providence, Boston, Sampson & Murdock co., 187   v. fold. maps. 24 cm. 99-458 Rev.   Directories

WOONSOCKET directory ... v.   187 -   Providence, Boston, Sampson & Murdock, 187 -   v. fold. maps. 25 cm. 1-30657 Rev.   Directories

WOONSOCKET. Débuts de la colonie franco-américaine de Woonsocket, Rhode Island, par Mlle. Marie Louise Bonier. Framingham, Mass., Lakeview press, 1920. 342, iv (i.e. vi) p. plates, ports., plan. 24 cm. 20-18585.   F89. W9 B7

WOONSOCKET. A picture of Woonsocket; or, The truth in its nudity; to which are added translations from the best French, Spanish and Italian writers. By Thomas Man ... (n.p.) Printed for the author, 1835. 108 p. front., pl. 19 cm. 22-1579.   F89. W9 M26

WOONSOCKET. A numbering of the inhabitants: together with statistical and other information, relative to Woonsocket ... By S. C. Newman. Woonsocket, Print. by S. S. Foss, 1846. 55 p. 19 cm. 8-20249.   F89. W9 N5

WOONSOCKET, History of. By E. Richardson. Woonsocket, S. S. Foss, printer, 1876. 264 p. 22 cm. "Appendix A. Genealogy": p. 187 - 255. Rc-3058.   F89. W9 R5

ELEMENTS IN THE POPULATION.

BOUVIER, Leon F. An ethnic profile of the state of Rhode Island. (Kingston) University of Rhode Island (1968) 34 l. maps. 28 cm. (Occasional papers in political science N-8) 68-65273.   F90. A1 B68

ISHAM, Norman Morrison. Early Rhode Island houses: an historical and architectural study. By Norman M. Isham ... (and) Albert F. Brown ... Providence, R.I., Preston & Rounds, 1895. 3, (5) - 100 p. front., plates, fold. map, plans, diagrs. 26 cm. Fold. map in pocket. Rc-3060.   F90. A6 I 7

FRENCH. France and Rhode Island, 1686 - 1800, by Mary Ellen Loughrey ... New York, King's Crown press, 1944. vii, 186 p. 23 cm. Bibliography: p. (161) - 174. A 45-1429. Thesis (PH.D.) Columbia university, 1943.   F90. F7 L6 1944

—   vii, 186 p. 23 cm. Bibliography: p. (161) - 174. A 45-1872.   F90. F7 L6 1944a

GERMAN. Rhode Island German directory 1900 - 1901. Deutsches adressbuch fuer Rhode Island, 1900 - 1901 ... (Providence, 1902) 76 p. 23 cm. 10-5627.   F90. G3 R4

HUGUENOTS. The star of La Rochelle; being the true story of the life of Esther Le Roy, wife of

Gabriel Bernon, 1652 - 1710, by Elizabeth Nicholson White. Providence (Press of E. A. Johnson co.) 1930. 2, vii-ix, 130 p. incl. col. front., illus., pl. 21½ cm. 30-28724. F90.H9 B52

— 2d edition, June, 1930. 32-17491. F90.H9 B53

HUGUENOTS. Memoir concerning the French settlements and French settlers in the colony of Rhode Island. By Elisha R. Potter ... Providence, S. S. Rider, 1879. 138 p. plans. 21 x 16 cm. (R. I. historical tracts. 1st ser. no. 5) A settlement of Huguenots made in 1686 at a place called Frenchtown (In modern North Kingston and East Greenwich) and soon dispersed. Genealogical notes of certain families: p. (85) - (136) Rc-2963. F90. H9 P6

— Baltimore, Genealogical Pub. Co., 1968. 138 p. 24 cm. 68-27007. F90. H9 P6 1968

IRISH. The Irish vanguard of Rhode Island. By Thomas Hamilton Murray ... Boston, 1904. 27 p. 23½ cm. Reprinted from vol. iv Journal of the American-Irish historical society. 5-35980. F90. I 6 M 9

ITALIANS. Italo-Americans of Rhode Island; an historical and biographical survey of the origin, rise and progress of Rhode Islanders of Italian birth or descent, by Ubaldo U. M. Pesaturo. 2d ed. (Providence, R.I., Visitor print.) 1940. 193 p. illus. (incl. ports.) 23½ cm. 41-1765.
F90. I8 P47

JEWS. Rhode Island and consanguineous Jewish marriages. By Benjamin H. Hartogensis. (Baltimore, 1911) p. 137 - 146. 25 cm. Repr. from pubs. of the Amer-Jewish hist. soc., 1911. 12-25520. F90.J
HQ1019.U7R4

JEWS. The story of the Jews of Newport; two and a half centuries of Judaism, 1658 - 1908, by Morris A. Gutstein ... Introd. by David De Sola Pool ... New York, Block pub. co., 1936. 5, 9 - 393 p. front., plates, ports., plans, facsims. 25 cm. "Selected bibliography": p. 383 - 384. 37-1024.
F90.J 5
F89. N5 G9

JEWS. The Greater Providence Jewish community; a population survey. Providence, Sponsored by the General Jewish Committee of Providence. By Sidney Goldstein. 1964. xix, 256 p. 28 cm.
F90. J 5 G6

JEWS. Rhode Island Jewish historical notes. v. 1 - Providence, Rhode Island Jewish Historical Assoc. v. in illus., ports., facsims. 24 cm. semiannual (irregular) Indexes: Vols. 1 - 2, 1954 - Apr. 1958. v.2 no. 4. 59-31695. F90. J 5 R5

RHODE ISLAND
SUPPLEMENTARY INDEX OF PLACES

ADAMSVILLE.   624
ALLENDALE.   617
ANTHONY.   605, 626
APPONAUG.   625
AQUIDNECK.   593
ARCTIC.   605, 626
ARKWRIGHT.   605, 626
ASHAWAY.   626
BAKERSVILLE.   605, 626
BARRINGTON.   624
BLACK ISLAND.   602, 604, 611
BRISTOL FERRY.   624
CENTRAL FALLS.   602, 617, 618
CENTREDALE.   617
CENTREVILLE.   605, 626
CHARLESTOWN.   608
CHEPIWANOXET.   625
CLYDE.   605, 626
CONANICUT ISLAND.   609
COWESETT.   625
CRANSTON.   618
CROMPTON.   605, 626
CUMBERLAND.   617
E. GREENWICH.   625
E. PROVIDENCE.   618
ESMON.   617
FISHERVILLE.   605, 626
FOUR CORNERS.   624
GREENWOOD.   625
HAMPDEN MEADOWS.   606
HARRIS.   605, 626
HELLS GROVE.   625
HOPE.   626
IDLAND PARK.   624
JACKSON.   605, 626
JEFFERSON PARK.   625
JOHNSTON.   617
KENT COUNTY.   605
LINCOLN.   607, 608, 617, 624
LINCOLN PARK.   625
LIPPITT.   605, 626
LITTLE COMPTON.   624
LITTLE NARRAGANSETT BAY.   625

MIDDLETOWN.   624
MOUNT HOPE BAY.   604
MYSTIC BRIDGE.   626
MYSTIC RIVER.   626
NARRAGANSETT.   581, 624
NARRAGANSETT BAY.   613
NARAGANSETT PIER.   611
NARRAGANSETT Sea and Shore.   602, 604
NATICK.   605, 626
NAYATT.   606
NEWPORT.   602, 604, 605, 628
NEW SHOREHAM.   609
NOANK.   626
NORTH KINGSTOWN.   609, 625, 627
NORTH PROVIDENCE.   607, 623
NORTH SMITHFIELD.   607
NORTH TIVERTON.   624
PAWTUCKET.   602, 608, 617, 618, 626
PHENIX.   605, 626
PONTIAC.   605
PORTSMOUTH.   624
PROVIDENCE.   581, 583, 590, 602, 604
QUIDNICK.   605, 626
RIVER POINT.   605, 626
ROCKY POINT.   602, 604
SAKONNET.   624
SEEKONK.   608
SILVER SPRING.   602, 604
SMITHFIELD.   617, 624
SOWAMS.   606
STONINGTON.   626
TIVERTON.   609
WARREN.   606
WARWICK.   590, 591, 625
WASHINGTON.   605, 626
WATCH HILL.   602, 604
WEST BARRINGTON.   606
WESTCOTT.   605, 626
WESTERLY.   602
WICKFORD.   617, 625
WOONASQUATUCKET VALLEY.   623
WOONSOCKET.   602, 617, 624
WYOMING.   608

CONNECTICUT

SELECTED BIBLIOGRAPHIES FOR CONNECTICUT

FLAGG, Charles Allcott.   ... Reference list on Connecticut local history ...   Albany, University of the state of New York, 1900.   (175) - 283 p.   24 ½ cm.   (New York state library. Bulletin 53, Dec. 1900. Bibliography (v. 2) 23)   3-20016.

Z1265. F 5

WETHERSFIELD.   Wethersfield history; a bibliography.   By Frances Stremlau.   Ed. 170 Children's literature, fall 1964 - 65.   (Wethersfield? Conn.) 1965.   26 l.   29 cm.   72-223880 MARC.

Z1266. W46 S7

CONNECTICUT CLASSIFICATION F 91 - F 105

91	Periodicals. Societies. Collections.
.5	Museums. Exhibitions, exhibits.
92	Gazetteers. Dictionaries. Geographic names.
.3	Guidebooks.
93	Biography (Collective). Genealogy (Collective).
.2	Historiography.
	Historians, *see* E 175.5.
.5	Study and teaching.
94	General works. Histories.
.3	Juvenile works.
.5	Minor works. Pamphlets, addresses, essays, etc.
.6	Anecdotes, legends, pageants, etc.
95	Historic monuments (General). Illustrative material.
96	Antiquities (Non-Indian).

By period.

97	Early to 1775.

Early grants by the Council for New England; Dutch posts; etc.
Biography: John Winthrop, 1606–1676; etc.

Cf. E 83.63, Pequot War, 1636–1638.
E 83.67, King Philip's War, 1675–1676.
E 199, French and Indian War, 1755–1763.
F 7.5, Government of Andros, 1688–1689.
F 157.W 9, Claims to Wyoming Valley, Susquehanna Company.

98	New Haven Colony.

Cf. F 102.N5, New Haven County.
F 104.N6, New Haven.

99	1775–1865.

Cf. E 263.C5, Connecticut in the Revolution (General);
  E 230.5–241, Military operations and battles.
E 309, F 483,497.W5, Cession of western lands.
E 357.7, Hartford Convention, 1814.
E 359.5.C7, War of 1812.
E 409.5.C6, War with Mexico, 1845–1848.
E 499, Civil War, 1861–1865 (General).
F 157.W9, Susquehanna claims.

100	1865–1950.

Cf. D 570.85.C8–81, World War I, 1914–1918.
D 769.85.C8–81, World War II, 1939–1945.
E 726.C7, War of 1898 (Spanish-American War).

101	1951–
102	Regions, counties, etc., A–Z.
.B7	Boundaries.

Cf. F 72.B7, Massachusetts boundary.
F 127.B7, New York boundary.
F 157.W9, Pennsylvania-Connecticut boundary dispute ("Connecticut Gore," Susquehanna Company).

.C2 Lake Candlewood.
.C7 Connecticut River and Valley, Conn.
   Cf. F 12.C7, New England.
.F2 Fairfield Co.
    Firelands, *see* F 497.W5.
    Fishers Island, *see* F 127.F5.
.H3 Hartford Co.
.H7 Housatonic River and Valley (General, and Conn.).
   Cf. F 72.H7, Massachusetts.
.L6 Litchfield Co.
    Highland Lake, Litchfield Hills, etc.
    Berkshire Hills, *see* F 72.B5.

    Long Island, *see* F 127.L8.
.M6 Middlesex Co.
.N2 Naugatuck River and Valley.
.N5 New Haven Co.
   Cf. F 98, New Haven Colony.
.N7 New London Co.
.T6 Tolland Co.
    Western Reserve, *see* F 497.W5.
    Westmoreland (township, 1774; county, 1775),
      see F 157.W9, Wyoming Valley, Pa.
.W7 Windham Co.

104   Cities, towns, etc. A–Z.
       e. g. .H3   Hartford.
              .L7   Litchfield.
              .N6   New Haven.
              .N7   New London.
              .N93 Norwich.
              .S8   Stamford.

105   Elements in the population.
       .A1   General works.
       .A2–Z   Individual elements.
                For a list of racial, ethnic, and religious elements (with cutter numbers), *see* E 184, p. 27–29.

CONNECTICUT

F 91 - F 105

PERIODICALS. SOCIETIES. COLLECTIONS.

CONNECTICUT. (Stratford) Vol. 34 no. 2 -   Oct/Nov. 1971 -   v.   illus.   29 cm.
72-620015.   F91. C26

CONNECTICUT resources bulletin, no. 1 -   (Hartford, 1941 -   v. illus.   28 cm.
41-46154.   F91.C285

CONNECTICUT. ... Connecticut town records, June 30, 1930; compiled under the direction of Lucius B. Barbour, examiner of public records.   Hartford, Conn., The Library, 1930.   53 p.   23 cm.
(Bulletin of the Conn. state library, no. 15)   31-27536.   F91.C 29

CONNECTICUT association, Festival of the, at the Revere house, Boston, Jan. 14, 1857. With the consitution, officers, and members of the association.   Boston, Press of R. R. Marvin, 1857.
52 p.   23 cm.   3-11070.   F91.C 31

CONNECTICUT historical society, The act of incorporation, and the constitution of the, with an address to the public.   Hartford, C. Babcock, printer, 1825.   14 p.   22 ½ cm.   3-5040.
F91.C 61

CONNECTICUT historical soc, The charter of the incorporation and by-laws of the, together with a list of the officers, etc.   Hartford, Print. by Case, Tiffany, 1839.   11 p.   22 ½ cm.   1-22554.
F91.C 62

CONNECTICUT historical society.   Annual report ... 1890 - 19   Hartford, The Society,
1890 - 19   v.   23 ½ cm.   Title varies.   6-13597.   F91.C 65

CONNECTICUT historical society, Bulletin of the.   no. 1 -   Nov. 1934 -   Hartford, 1934 -
23 cm.   quarterly.   35-28089.   F91.C 67

CONNECTICUT historical society, Collections of the.   v. 1 -   Hartford, The Society, 1860 -
   v. facsims.   23 ½ - 25 cm.   9-898.   Partly analyzed as follows: F91. C 7
— The Talcott papers.   vol. 4 - 5.   1892-6
— Hartford town votes ... 1635 - 1716.   vol. 6.   1897.
— Orderly book and journals kept by Connecticut men while taking part in the American revolution.   1775 - 1778.   vol. 7.   1899.
— Rolls and lists of Connecticut men in the revolution.   1775 - 1783.   vol. 8.   1901.
— Rolls of Connecticut men in the French and Indian war, 1755 - 1762.   vol. 9-10.   1903-5.

— The Law papers. vols. 11, 13, 15. 1907 - 14.
— Lists and returns of Connecticut men in the revolution. 1775 - 1783. vol. 12. 1909.
— Original distribution of the lands in Hartford among the settlers, 1639. vol. 14. 1912.
— The Wolcott papers. vol. 16. 1916.
— The Fitch papers. vols. 17, 18. 1918 - 20.
— The Pitkin papers. vol. 19. 1921.
— Huntington papers. vol. 20. 1923.
— The Wyllys papers. vol. 21. 1924.
— Records of the Particular court of Connecticut, 1639 - 1663. 1928.
— Deane papers. The. vol. 23. 1930.
— Hoadly memorial. Early letters and documents relating to Connecticut, 1643 - 1709 ... vol. 24. 1932.
— John Cotton Smith papers. vols. 25, 26, 27 - 29. 1948 - 54.

CONNECTICUT historical society. Historical documents and notes. Genesis and development of the Connecticut historical soc. and associated institution in the Wadsworth Athenaeum. Hartford, Conn., The Society, 1889.   114 p.   23½ cm.   3-28507.   F91.C715

CONNECTICUT historical society. A regular monthly meeting ... Oct. 1906.   17½ cm.   F91.C 72

CONNECTICUT historical society. Miscellaneous printed matter pub. by this body is classified in
F91.C748

CONNECTICUT historical society, An open letter of the president and members of the. By James Terry. Dec., 1906. (Hartford? 1906)   14 p.   22½ cm.   8-20365.   F91.C 76

CONNECTICUT holiday. v. 1 -   1957 -   (Hartford, Connecticut Holiday Publishers)
v.   illus. (part col.)   29 cm.   annual.   57-37894.   F91. C78

CONNECTICUT magazine, The. Devoted to Connecticut in its various phases of history, literature, scenic beauty, art, science, industry. v. 1 - 11; v. 12, no. 1 - 3; Jan. 1895 - 1908. Hartford, Conn., The Connecticut quarterly co. 1895 - 1908.   12 v. in 10.   illus., plates, ports., facsims.   25 - 27½ cm.
Quarterly, 1895-98; monthly, 1899-Feb. 1900; bimonthly Mar.-Dec. 1900; irreg. 1901-05; quarterly 1906-08. No more pub.   5-11243 Rev. 2
F91. C8

NEW HAVEN Colony Historical Society, New Haven. Journal. v. 1 -   Mar. 1952 -
New Haven, Conn.   24 cm.   quarterly.   illus., ports.   F91. N 4

SILHOUETTES; the Connecticut magazine. v. 1, v. 2, no 1 - 6; May 1927 - Feb. 1929. (Hartford, Sherwood press, 1927 - 19)   2 v. in 1.   illus.   29½ cm.   monthly.   Subtitle varies.   No more pub?   37-18044.
F91. S 56

GAZETTEERS. DICTIONARIES. GEOGRAPHIC NAMES.

GANNETT, Henry. ... A geographic dictionary of Connecticut. Washington, Govt. print. off., 1894.   67 p. (Dept. of the interior. Bulletin of the U.S. Geological survey. no. 117)   2-4310.   F92. G19

PEASE, John Chauncey. A gazetteer of the states of Connecticut and Rhode Island. With an accurate and improved map of each state. Hartford, Print. and pub. by William S. Marsh, 1819.   vii, 389 p.
2 port. (incl. front.) 2 fold. maps.   21½ cm.   1-Rc-3197.   F92. P 36

RAND McNALLY gazetteer and map of Connecticut and Rhode Island ... Chicago, New York (etc.) (1923)   12 p.   28 cm.   F92. R 18

SELLERS, Helen Earle. Connecticut town origins. Stonington, Conn., Pequot Press (1964?)
96 p.   23 cm.   (Connecticut booklet no. 10)   Reprinted from the Connecticut register and manuel, 1942 edition."   64-20862.
F92. S 4
L. H. & G.

CONNECTICUT

TRUMBULL, James Hammond. Indian names of places, etc., in and on the borders of Connecticut: with interpretations of some of them. Hartford (Press of the Case, Lockwood & Brainard co.) 1881.
xi, 93 p.　24½ cm.　9-21150.
F92.T 86

GUIDEBOOKS.

CULLEN, Mrs. R. Connecticut trips; what, when, where, Waterbury, Conn., Heminway Corp. (1971)　iv, 130 p.　illus.　27 cm.　77-147410.
F92.3.C8

KEYARTS, Eugene. 42 more short walks in Connecticut, Chester, Conn., Pequote Press (1972)
viii, 87 p.　maps.　18 cm.　74-187173.
F92.3.K4

U.S. ... Heads of families at the first census of the U.S. taken in the year 1790 ... Washington, Govt. print. off., 1907 - 08.　12 v.　fronts. (fold. maps)　29½ cm.　7-35273.
F92.5.U58

DIRECTORIES.

Connecticut business directory and gazetteer ... 18　- 19　Boston, Mass., Union pub. co.
v.　24½ cm.　2-2083 Rev.
Directories

BIOGRAPHY (COLLECTIVE). GENEALOGY (COLLECTIVE).

BAILEY, Frederick William, ed. Early Connecticut marriages as found on ancient church records prior to 1800. ... New Haven, Conn., Bureau of American ancestry (1896 - 1906)　7 v. 23 cm.
From records of Congregational churches, with a few Episocpal church records in book 7. 99-4863 Rev.
F93.B 15

— Baltimore, Genealogical Pub. Co., 1968.　7 v. in 1.　23 cm.　Reprinted ... With additions, corrections, and introduction by Donald Lines Jacobus, and with integrated errata." 68-18785.
F93.B16
L.H. & G.

BIOGRAPHICAL encyclopaedia of Connecticut and Rhode Island of the nineteenth century. New York, Metropolitan pub. and engr. co., 1881.　iv, (5) - 376 p. 48 port. 30 cm. Ed. Henry Clay Williams. L.C. copy replaced by microfilm.　3-18890.
F93.B 61
Microfilm 8768 F

BROWN, Leonard B. Biographical sketches of the state officers ... Connecticut. v. 1. Hartford, 1885.　24 cm.
F93.B 87

CHADWICK, Earl Leslie. The conservative advocate; a book of biographies of Connecticut's successful men, with essays on conservatism by well known writers. (Hartford, Conn.) E. L. Chadwick, 1909.　(122) p.　illus. (ports.)　23½ cm.　10-1958.
F93.C 43

CUTTER, William Richard, and others. Genealogical and family history of the state of Connecticut; a record of the achievements of her people in the making of a commonwealth and the founding of a nation. New York, Lewis historical pub. co., 1911.　4 v. fronts., plates, ports.　28 cm. Paged continuously.　11-24384.
F93.C 99

DAUGHTERS of founders and patriots of America. Connecticut chapter. Family records (Heretofore unpublished) collected in commemoration of the 300th anniversary of the settlement of Connecticut. (Derby, Conn.) ... 1935.　305 p.　23½ cm.　"Editor, Mrs. John Laidlaw Buel." 35-15774.
F93.D 27
Geneal. Sect. Ref.

EARDELEY, William Applebie Daniel. Connecticut cemeteries ... 1673 - 1910 ... Brooklyn, N.Y., 1914 - 17.　8 v.　illus.　28½ cm.　Type-written copy.　CA 25-1532 Unrev.
F93.E 14

ENCYCLOPEDIA of Connecticut biography, genealogical-memorial; representative citizens; compiled with the assistance of ... Samuel Hart and others.   Boston, N.Y. (etc.) The American historical soc., 1917 - (23)   10 v.   fronts., plates, ports.   27½ cm.   18-12314 Rev.

F93. E 56

GOODWIN, Nathaniel.   Genealogical notes, or Contributions to the family history of some of the first settlers of Connecticut and Massachusetts.   Hartford, F. A. Brown, 1856.   xx, 362 p.   23 cm.   4-13420.

F93. G 65
Geneal. Sect. Ref.

— Baltimore, Genealogical Pub. Co., 1969.   xx, 362 p.   23 cm.   75-76817.

F93. G 65
1969
L. H. & G.

HINMAN, Royal Ralph.   A catalogue of the names of the first Puritan settlers of the colony of Connecticut; with the time of their arrival in the colony ...   Hartford, Print. E. Gleason, 1846.   367 p. front. (port.) 22½ cm.   Five numbers and index in one vol. with continuous paging.   1-1128.

F93. H 65
Microfilm 24763 F

— Baltimore, Genealogical Pub. Co., 1968.   "Repr. of 1846 ed."   336 p.   23 cm.   67-28617.

F93. H 65
1968

HINMAN, Royal Ralph.   A catalogue of the names of the early Puritan settlers of the colony of Connecticut; with the time of their arrival in the country and colony, etc.   Hartford, Press of Case, Tiffany, 1852 - 56.   884 p.   front., pl., ports. 23½ cm.   Issued in 6 numbers; no. 5 terminates with "Danielson; in 1856 the 6th number was pub. relating to the E. Hinman family only.   1-1129 Additions.

F93. H 66

HINMAN, Royal Ralph.   A family record of the descendants of Sergt. Edward Hinman, who first appeared at Stratford in Connecticut about 1650. ...   (In his Catalogue of the names of the first Puritan settlers of the Colony of Conn.   1-1130.

F93. H 66

JACOBUS, Donald Lines.   List of officials, civil, military, and ecclesiastical of Connecticut colony. ... 1636 ... - 1677, and of New Haven colony throughout its separate existence; also soldiers in the Pequot war who then or subsequently resided within the present bounds of Connecticut.   Connecticut tercentenary publication of the Connecticut society of the Order of the founders and patriots of America.   New Haven, R. M. Hooker, for the Publication committee, 1935.   v, 65 p.   23½ cm. 36-2196.

F93. J 23
L. H. & G.

LOOMIS, Dwight.   The judicial and civil history of Connecticut.   Ed. by Hon. Dwight Loomis ... Boston, The Boston history co., 1895.   vi, 639 p.   60 port.   26½ cm.   5-10323.

F93. L 86

MANWARING, Charles William.   A digest of the early Connecticut probate records. ...   Hartford, Conn., R. S. Peck, printers, 1904 - 06.   3 v.   front. (port., v. 3)   25 cm.   (v. 2-3: 26 cm.)   Contents: Hartford district. v. 1. 1635-1700. - v. 2. 1700-1729. - v. 3. 1729-1750.   4-14168.

F93. M 29

MEN of progress; biographical sketches and portraits of leaders in business and professional life in and of the state of Connecticut; comp. under the supervision of Richard Herndon; ed. by Richard Burton.   Boston, New England magazine, 1898.   480 p.   illus. (ports.)   29 cm.   19-14526.

F93. M 53

NASH, Frederick H.   Ye names & ages of all ye old folks in every hamlet, city and town in ye state of Connecticut, now living, with ye sketches of 20 living centenarians   ...   New Haven, Print. Price, Lee, 1884.   52 p.   22½ cm.   Includes names of more than 6,000 people 80 years of age and over.   3-15619.

F93. N 24

NORTON, Frederick Calvin.   The governors of Connecticut; biographies of the chief executives of the commonwealth... Patron's ed.   Hartford, Conn, The Connecticut magazine co., 1905.   10 p.   385 p. 44 port.   25½ cm.   6-3618.

F93. N 88

CONNECTICUT

OSBORN, Norris Galpin. Men of mark in Connecticut; ideals of American life told in biographies and autobiographies of eminent living Americans, ed. by Colonel N. G. Osborn ... Hartford, Conn., W. R. Goodspeed, 1906 - 10.   5 v.   front., ports.   24 cm.   8-12559 Rev. 2.   F93.O 81

PERRY, Charles Edward, ed. Founders and leaders of Connecticut, 1633 - 1783, ed. by Charles Edward Perry ... Boston, New York (etc.) D. C. Heath (1934)   xi, 319 p. front., illus. (incl. ports.) 20½ cm.
"Selected bibliography": p. 311 - 312.   34-19997.   F93.P 38

PERRY, Charles Edward, ed. Founders and leaders of Connecticut, 1633 - 1783. Freeport, N.Y., Books for Libraries Press (1971)   ix, 319 p. illus. 23 cm. (Essay index reprint series) Reprint of the 1934 ed.
Bibliography: p. 311 - 312.   78-177965 MARC.   F93.P 38
1971

PROMINENT men of Connecticut; individual biographic studies with character portraits.   Library ed. New York, Historical records, inc., 1940 -   4 v. front. (ports.) coat of arms.   20 cm.   Contents. - v.1. John J. Mettler. - v.2. Achille Francois Migeon. - v.3. Anson W. H. Taylor. - v.4. Joseph Ralph Ensign. 41-14493.   F93.P 76

REPRESENTATIVE men of Connecticut, 1861 - 1894.   Everett, Mass., Massachusetts pub. co., 1894.
iv, 5 - 460 p.   82 port.   30½ cm.   3-18889.   F93.R 42

SPALDING, John A. Illustrated popular biography of Connecticut. Hartford, Conn., Press of the Case, Lockwood & Brainard co., 1891.   374 p. incl. po., ports.   26 cm.   6-5577.   F93. S73

STEVENSON, Elias Robert. Connecticut history makers, containing sketches and portraits of men who have contributed to the progress of the state in manufacturing, finance, business, literature, the professions, arts and other fields of activity ... Waterbury, Conn., American-Republican, inc., 1929 -   v.   ports.   25 cm.   30-125.   F93.S 84

U.S. Bureau of the Census. Heads of families at the First Census of the U. S. taken in the year 1790: Connecticut. Washington, Govt. Print. Off., 1908. (Spartanburg, S.C., 1964)   308 p.   28 cm.
64-62655.   F93. U 5

VOLKEL, Lowell M. An index to the 1800 federal census of Fairfield and Hartford Counties, State of Conn. (Danville, Ill. 1968)   (89) p.   28 cm.   F93.V 65

VOLKEL, Lowell M. An index to the 1800 Federal census of Litchfield, New Haven, Tolland, and Windham Counties, State of Conn. (Danville? Ill., 1969)   1 v. (unpaged) 28 cm.
F93.V653

WHO'S who in Connecticut ... 1933 -   New York city, Lewis historical pub. co., inc.
(1933 -   v.   front., ports.   20½ cm.   33-9417.   F93.W 57

GENERAL WORKS. HISTORIES.

ACORN Club of Connecticut. Report of Connecticut towns. Hartford, Connecticut Historical Soc., 1949.   (10) p; 23 cm.   A prospectus ...   49-4856*   F94 A 6

BARBER, John Warner. Connecticut historical collections, containing a general collection of interesting facts, traditions, biographical sketches, anecdotes, etc. relating to the history and antiquities of every town in Connecticut, with geographical descriptions. Illus. by 180 engravings. New Haven, J. W. Barber; Hartford, A. Willard, 1836.   viii, (9) - 560 p. front., illus., plates, fold. map. 23 cm.   Map mutilated.   17-10119.   F94.B 23
Toner Coll.

— 2d. ed. New Haven, Durrie & Peck and J. W. Barber (pref. 1837)   viii, (9) - 560 p. front., illus., plates, fold. map.   23½ cm.   1-13366.   F94.B 24

— New Haven, Durrie & Peck, etc. (1846)   viii, (9) - 576 p. etc.   1-13367.   F94.B 25

LOCAL HISTORIES IN THE LIBRARY OF CONGRESS

BRETT, John Alden, ed. ... Connecticut yesterday and today, celebrating 300 years of progress in the Constitution state; ... Hartford, The John Brett co. (1935?)   284 p. illus. (incl. ports., maps, facsims.) 28½ x 22 cm. 36-5176.
F94. B 74

BURPEE, Charles Winslow. Burpee's The story of Connecticut, by Charles W. Burpee ... New York, The American historical co., 1939.   4 v. fronts., illus. (incl. maps, facsim.) plates, ports., col. coats of arms. 27½ cm. Vols. 1-2 paged continuously; v. 3-4 (also paged continuously) contain "Personal and family records". 39-32703.
F94. B 87

BUSHNELL, Horace. Speech for Connecticut. Being an historical estimate of the state, delivered before the Legislature ... 1851. Print. by order of the Legislature. Hartford, Boswell and Faxon, 1851.   43 p.   24 cm.   Rc-3176.
F94. B 9

CARPENTER, William Henry, ed. The history of Connecticut, from its earliest settlement to the present time. Philadelphia, Lippincott, Grambo, 1854.   287 p. front. (port.) 16º. (Lippincott's histories of the states)   1-Rc-3177.
F94. C 2

CHAPMAN, Edward Mortimer. New England village life. Ann Arbor, Mich., Gryphon Books, 1971. vi, 232 p.   22 cm.   Facsimile reprint of 1937 ed.   72-143643.
F94. C38 1937a

CHASE Manhattan Bank. Connecticut, the Nutmeg State. New York (1935)   85 p. 14 cm. (The Manhattan library, v. 2 - 8) Pub. by the bank under its earlier name: Bank of the Manhattan Co.   36-13997 rev.*.
F94. C 4

CLARK, George Larkin. A history of Connecticut, its people and institutions ... with 100 illus. and maps. New York and London, G. P. Putnam's sons, 1914.   xx, 609 p. front., plates, ports., fold. maps, facsims.   23½ cm.   "Authorities consulted": p. 561 - 563.   14-10888.
F94. C 59

CONNECTICUT ... The colony of Connecticut and its beginning, growth, and characteristics, to the observance of its tercentenary celebration in 1935 ... Washington, U. S. Govt. print off., 1935. viii, 35 p. fold. map.   23½ cm.   (U. S. 74th Cong., 1st sess. Senate Doc. 53)   Bibliographies interspersed.   35-26439.
F94. C 66

CONNECTICUT. Facts about Connecticut, compiled and pub. by the Connecticut chamber of commerce, inc. Hartford (1929)   4 p. 196, (10) p., 2 l.   21½ cm.   30-1255.
F94. C 75

CONNECTICUT, The Tercentenary of, 1635 - 1935. The Connecticut ode. The Tercentenary in review. Connecticut celebrates. Connecticut and her founders. The evolution of the government of Connecticut. (New Haven?) The Tercentenary commission of the state of Connecticu (1936) (5) - 55 p.   23 cm.   36-27713.
F94. C 8

CONNECTICUT. Tercentenary commission. Committee on education in the schools. The story of Connecticut to help its school teachers and pupils enliven its history ... State Board of education. (New Haven, Printed at the printing-office of the Yale university press) 1933.   50 p. fold. map. 23 cm. Bibliography: p. 48 - 50.   33-27957.
F94. C 82

CONNECTICUT. Tercentenary commission. Committee on historical publications. ... Instruction to contributors. (New Haven? 1932)   3 p.   23 cm.   33-28234.
F94. C 85

CROFUT, Florence S. Marcy. Guide to the history and the historic sites of Connecticut, ... pub. under the auspices of the Tercentenary commission of the state of Conn. for the Conn. D. A. R ... New Haven, Yale university press; London, H. Milford, Oxford university press, 1937. 2 v. fronts., illus. (incl. ports.) maps (part fold.) 27 cm. Paged continuously. Includes "References"; Bibliography: p. (877) - 913. 37-30355.
F94. C 88

DELANEY, Edmund T. The Connecticut shore, Photos. by Katharine Knowles. Barre, Mass., Barre Publishers, 1969.   120 p. illus. 25 cm. 69-12345.
F94. D 4

(DUTCHER, George Matthew) ... Connecticut's tercentenary, a retrospect of three centuries of self-government and steady habits. (New Haven) Pub. for the Tercentenary commission by the Yale university press, 1934.   29, (3) p.   23 cm.   34-27652 Rev.
F94. D 76

CONNECTICUT

DWIGHT, Theodore, jr. The history of Connecticut, from the first settlement to the present time. New York, Harper & brothers (1840) (v) - xiv, (15) - 450 p. 15 ½ cm. 7-23345.
F94. D 88

— New York, Harper & bros., 1872. (v) - xvii, (ix) - xiv, (15) - 450 p. 16 cm. (The family library) 9-3130. L. C. copy replaced by microfilm.
F94. D 95
Microfilm 8769 F

FOX (G) and Company, Hartford. A century in Connecticut, written and pub. by G. Fox and Co. commemorating the 100th anniversary of its founding in Hartford, Conn. 1847 - 1947. (Hartford, 1948) 64 p. illus. 36 cm. Bibliography: p. 57 - 64. 49-905*.
F94. F 69

GOODRICH, Charles Augustus. Stories on the history of Connecticut; designed for the instruction and amusement of young persons ... Hartford, D. F. Robinson, 1829. 203 p. illus. 14 ½ cm. Rc-3180.
F94. G 6
Rare Book Coll.

HISTORICAL, statistical and industrial review of the state of Connecticut. Part 1 ... This issue is complete in itself and is a portion of a large volume now in progress, representing the industries of Connecticut. New York, W. S. Webb, 1883. 2, (9) - 15, (65) - 268 p. front. (port.) illus. 26 cm. Prospectus. 4-26198.
F94. H 67

HOLCOMB, Robert N. Story of Connecticut ... pictures and text by Robert N. Holcomb. Hartford, Conn., The Hartford times (1935 - v. illus. 27 cm. 35-21895.
F94. H686

HOLLISTER, Gideon Hiram. The history of Connecticut, from the first settlement of the colony to the adoption of the present constitution ... New Haven, Durrie and Peck, 1855. 2 v. front., illus., pl., port. 8°. 1-Rc-3181.
F94. H 7

JOHNSTON, Alexander. ... Connecticut; a study of a commonwealth-democrary, ... Boston and New York, Houghton, Mifflin, 1887. xiv, 409 p. front. (fold. map) 18 cm. (American commonwealths. Ed. by H. E. Scudder. v. 10) Rc-3178.
F94. J 7

— 1891. xiv, 409 p. 18 ½ cm. Bibliography: p. (397) - 400. 13-5301.
F94. J 71

— 1898. xiv, 409 p. Rc-3179.
F94. J 72

— ... with a supplementary chapter by Clive Day ... (New ed.) 1903. 4 p. (vii) - xiv, (2), 428 p. front. (fold. map) 18 ½ cm. Bibliography: p. (415) - 418. 3-27976/3.
F94. J 73

LEE, William Storrs. The Yankees of Connecticut. Illus. by Ralph Lee. (1st ed.) New York, Holt (1957) 301 p. illus. 25 cm. 57-10422.
F94. L 4

MILLS, Lewis Sprague. The story of Connecticut ... New York, Chicago (etc.) Scribner's sons (1932) xviii, 414 p. illus. 18 ½ cm. "Useful references": p. 409 - 410. 33-2227.
F94. M 62

— (1935) xviii, 416 p. illus. 18 ½ cm. "Useful references": p. 411 - 412. 35-19386.
F94. M 62
1935

— (1943) xv, 496 p. incl. front., illus. (incl. ports., maps) 18 ½ cm. "Useful references: p. 491. 43-4852.
F94. M 62
1943

— 4th ed., rev. and enl. New York, Exposition Press (1953) 496 p. illus. 19 cm. Includes bibliography. 52-5704.
F94. M 62
1953

— 5th ed., rev. and enl. West Rindge, N.H., R. R. Smith (1948) 497 p. illus. 19 cm. 57-12427.
F94. M 62
1958

MIX, Irene Howe, comp. ... Connecticut's activities in the wars of this country; a summary.

Washington, U. S. Govt. print. off., 1932.   67 p. incl. tab.   23 ½ cm.   (U.S. 72d. Cong., 1st sess. Senate Doc. 14)
Bibliography: p. 65 - 67.   32-36320.
F94. M 68

MORGAN, Forrest, ed.   Connecticut as a colony and as a state; or, One of the original thirteen; ...
Hartford, The Pub. soc. of Connecticut, 1904.   4 v. fronts., plates, ports., 2 maps.   24 cm.   4-9654 Additions.
F94. M 84

OSBORN, Norris Galpin.   History of Connecticut in monographic form ... New York, The States
history co., 1925.   5 v. fronts., plates, ports., map, facsims. (1 double) diagr.   24 ½ cm.   Contains bibliographies.   25-14641.
F94. O 82

SANFORD, Elias Benjamin.   A history of Connecticut.   ... Hartford, S. S. Scranton, 1887.
x, 11 - 381 p. incl. front. (map) illus.   20 cm.   Rc-3182.
F94. S 2

— Rev. ed. 1922.   x, 11 - 450 p. incl. front. (map) illus.   plates.   20 cm.   23-1762.
F94. S 21

SHEPARD, Odell.   Connecticut, past and present.   New York, London, A. A. Knopf, 1939.
xix, 316, xi p. front., plates.   22 ½ cm.   "First edition."   39-27511.
F94. S 48

VAN DUSEN, Albert Edward.   Connecticut.   New York, Random House (1961)   x, 470 p. 29 cm. 61-6263.
F94. V 3

JUVENILE WORKS.

BAILEY, Bernadine (Freeman)   Picture book of Connecticut.   Pictures by Kurt Wiese.   Chicago, A.
Whitman, 1955.   unpaged.   illus.   17 x 21 cm.   (Her The United States books)   55-8827.
F94. 3. B3

— Rev. ed.   Chicago, A. Whitman, 1962.   (32) p.   17 x 21 cm.   55-8827.
F94. 3. B3
1962

— Chicago, A. Whitman, Rev. ed. (1966)   32 p.   17 x 21 cm.
F94. 3. B3
1966

CARPENTER, John Allan.   Connecticut.   Illus. by Phil Austin.   Chicago, Childrens Press (1966)
95 p.   24 cm.   (Enchantment of America)   66-10300.
F94. 3. C3

HOYT, Joseph Bixby.   The Connecticut story.   Elliott H. Kone, ed.   (New Haven) Readers Press
(1961)   339 p.   29 cm.   61-18424.
F94. 3. H6

HAMPHREVILLE, Frances T.   This is Connecticut.   Color photos by Florence Huck and Frances T.
Humphreville.   Syracuse, L. W. Singer (1963)   310 p.   illus. (part col.) ports. (part col.) coat of arms, facsims.
24 cm.   64-2405.   Not in L. of C.
F94. 3. H8

HISTORIC MONUMENTS (GENERAL). ILLUSTRATIVE MATERIAL.

BALDWIN, Simon Eben.   The New Haven convention of 1778 ... New Haven, 1882.   23 ½ cm.
F95. B 18

BURRELL, Percy Jewett.   ... America's making in Connecticut; a pageant of the races ...   Presented ... in Hartford, Oct. 8, 9, 10, 1935 ... (Hartford? 1935)   (12) p.   25 cm.   37M951T.
F95. B 87

CONNECTICUT emigrant, The.   A dialogue, between Henry - an intended emigrant ... his wife ...
his father ... his mother ... his son.   ... By a descendant of the Connecticut pilgrims.   Hartford,
Printed for the purchasers, 1822.   12 p.   18 cm.   In verse.   21-16571.
F95. C 72
Rare Book Coll.

CONNECTICUT Historical Commission.   Historic conservation: progress and prospects.   Hartford,
1969.   52 l.   illus., maps.   28 cm.   74-629602.
F95. C725

CONNECTICUT

CONNECTICUT homes. 1943 - (Hartford, H. F. Morse Associates) v. in illus. 31 cm. irregular. 49-40021*.
F95.C 73

CONNECTICUT real estate register, The. Hartford, Conn., 1868, no. 1. 1 v. 8°. semi-annual. 1-22962-M4.
F35.C 75

DEXTER, Franklin Bowditch. The history of Connecticut, as illus. by the names of her towns. ... Worcester, Mass., Press of C. Hamilton, 1885. 30 p. 24½ cm. Reprinted from the Proceedings of the American antiquarian soc. for April, 1885. 7-23986.
F95.D 52

GUERNSEY, Jessie E. ... Connecticut history series. 1904. 1 v. (Connecticut. Board of Education. Connecticut document ... no. 246)
F95.G 93

HAIG, George Canterbury. The face of Connecticut, by Dan Stiles (pseud.) Sketches by Charles R. De Carlo. Woodcuts by Joel Anderson. Canterbury, N.H., Sugar Ball Press (1962) 107 p. 23 cm.
F95. H 3

LITCHFIELD Associates. A guide to historic sites in Connecticut. Text by Eric Hatch. Photos. taken especially for this guide by Jerrems C. Hart and Guido Organschi. Middleton, Conn., Pub. for the Connecticut Historical Commission by Wesleyan University Press, 1963. unpaged. 63-11945.
F95.L 57

MASON, H. F. Randolph. Historic houses of Connecticut open to the public. Introd. by Robert J. Craig. Stonington, Conn., Pequot Press, 1963. 64 p. 23 cm. (Connecticut booklet, no. 5) 63-16432.
F95.M 26

— 2d ed. Stonington, Conn., Pequote Press (1966) 59 p. 23 cm. 66-24973.
F95. M26 1966

MATTHIES, Katharine, comp. Trees of note in Connecticut, compiled ... for the Connecticut D.A.R. (New Haven, The printing office of the Yale university press) 1934. 34 p. incl. front., illus. fold. map. 24 cm. 35-476.
F95.M 28

NATIONAL pageant and dramatic events in the history of Connecticut, ... The. Testimonial to Mrs. Harriet Beecher Stowe. Opera house, Hartford, Conn ... 1889 ... Hartford, Clark & Smith, print. (1889) 8 p. 30 x 24 cm. CA 25-497 Unrev.
F95.N 26

NATIONAL society of the colonial dames of America. Connecticut houses; a list of manuscript histories of early Connecticut homes, presented to the Conn. state library by the Conn. soc. of Colonial dames of America. Comp. by Mrs. Elford Parry Trowbridge. Hartford, Conn state lib., 1916. 33 p. 23 cm. (Bulletins of the Conn. state library, no. 7) 16-14829.
F95.N 27

— Hartford, Conn., The State, 1924. 27 p. 23 cm. (Bulletin of the Conn. state library, no. 10) 25-27094.
F95.N272

— Hartford, Conn., The State, 1931. 39 p. 23 cm. (Bulletin of the Conn. state lib. no.16) "A list of 655 manuscript histories ... arranged alphabetically by towns in which the houses are located." 32-27310.
F95.N2722

NATIONAL soc. of the colonial dames of America. Old houses of Connecticut, from material coll. by the Committee on old houses of the Conn. soc. of the Colonial dames of America, ed. by Bertha Chadwick Trowbridge ... New Haven, Yale university press ... 1923. xxvii, 519 p. col. front., illus. (incl. plans) 29½ cm. 23-17387.
F95.N273

NATIONAL society of the colonial dames of America. Old inns of Connecticut; ed. by Marian Dickinson Terry from material collected by the Committee on historic buildings of the National soc. of the colonial dames of America ... Hartford, Conn., The Prospect press, 1937. 253 p. incl. illus., plates. facsims. front. 29½ cm. Bibliographical note: p. 253. 38-17265.
F95.N 28

NEWTON, Caroline Clifford. Once upon a time in Connecticut. Boston, New York (etc.) Houghton, Mifflin (1916) vii, 140 p. plates, ports. 19½ cm. Pub. under the auspices of the Colonial dames of Conn. "References" at end of each story. 16-8366.
F95.N 55

PRENDERGAST, William J. Exploring Connecticut. Stonington, Conn., Pequot Press (1965)
1 v. (unpaged)   23 cm.   (Connecticut booklet, no. 9)   Some stories first appeared in the New Haven register's feature, Know your state.
65-20563.
  F95. P 7

(ROSENBERRY, Mrs. Lois (Kimball) Mathews) ... Migrations from Connecticut prior to 1800. (New Haven) Pub. for the Tercentenary commission by the Yale university press, 1934.   36 p.   23 cm.
"The material from which this pamphlet was prepared is taken entirley from the author's book 'The expansion of New England'." - Bibliographical note, p. 36.   34-27658 Rev.
  F95. R 78

STERRY, Iveagh Hunt. They found a way: Connecticut's restless people.   Brattleboro, Vt., Stephen Daye press, 1938.   376 p.   22½ cm.   38-32220.
  F95. S 75

TODD, Charles Burr. In olde Connecticut; being a record of quaint, curious and romantic happenings there in colonie times and later ....   New York, The Grafton press (1906)   x, 244 p.   20 cm.   (The Grafton historical series; ed. H. R. Stiles)   6-19924.
  F95. T 63

— Detroit, Singing Tree Press, 1968.   244 p.   20 cm.   68-26612.
  F95. T 63
  1968

UNITED committees on historical landmarks of Connecticut. Historical landmarks of Connecticut. New Haven, 1897.   23 cm.
  F95. U 75

WILLARD, Lawrence F. Pictorial Connecticut. New Haven, College and University Press (1962)   254 p.   illus.   28 cm.   62-22026.
  F95. W 5

ANTIQUITIES.

Archaeological Society of Connecticut. Bulletin. New Haven.   no. in   v.   illus.   28 cm.   Two no. a year, 19 - 46; annual, 1947 -   52-24607.
  F96. A732

BULL, Norris Langdon. ... Connecticut archaeological appraisal. Hartford, Conn., 1931 -
 v.   plates.   24½ cm.   32-1656.
  F96. B 94

EARLY TO 1775.

ALLIS, Marguerite. Connecticut trilogy; with drawings by the author. New York, G. P. Putnam's sons (1934)   xvi, 318 p. incl. front., illus.   22 cm.   A story of the first three Connecticut settlements - Hartford, Saybrook and New Haven.   Bibliography: p. 303 - 305.   34-27075.
  F97. A 96

ALLIS, Marguerite. Historic Connecticut (originally pub. under the title of "Connecticut trilogy") with photographs by Samuel Chamberlain and drawings by the author. New York, Grosset & Dunlap (1938)   xvi, 343 p.   front., illus., plates.   26 cm.   Bibliography: p. 327 - 329.   38-29576.
  F97. A463

(ANDREWS, Charles McLean) ... The beginnings of Connecticut, 1632 - 1662. (New Haven) Pub. for the Tercentenary commission by the Yale university press, 1934.   81 p.   23 cm.   35-27637 Rev.
  F97. A536

(ANDREWS, Charles McLean) ... Connecticut and the British government. (New Haven) Pub. for the Tercentenary commission by the Yale university press, 1933.   35 p.   23 cm.   Reprinted from Fane's Reports on the laws of Connecticut. Acorn club publications, 1915.".   33-28122 Rev.
  F97. A 54

ANDREWS, Charles McLean. Connecticut's place in colonial history; and address delivered before the Conn. soc. of colonial wars ... 1923 ... New Haven, Pub. for the Conn. soc. of colonial wars by the Yale university press, 1924.   2, 49 p.   21 cm.   24-7527.
  F97. A 55

CONNECTICUT

ANDREWS, Charles McLean. ... The river towns of Connecticut: a study of Wethersfield, Hartford, and Windsor ... Baltimore, Publication agency of the Johns Hopkins university, 1889.   126 p.   plan.   24½ cm.   (Johns Hopkins university studies in historical and political science ... 7th ser., vii-ix)   4-7961.
F97.A 56
G & M

ANDREWS, Frank De Witte.   Connecticut soldiers in the French and Indian war; bills, receipts and documents printed from the original manuscripts, with an introduction by Frank D. Andrews ... Vineland, N.J., Priv. print., 1925.   41 p.   23½ cm.   "57 copies only."   25-18649.
F97.A 58

BAILEY, Edith Anna. ... Influences toward radicalism in Connecticut, 1754 - 1775.   Northampton, Mass., Dept. of history and government of Smith college (1920)   (179) - 252 p.   23 cm.   (Smith college studies in history, vol. v, no. 4)   20-23473.
F97.B 15

BATES, Albert Carlos.   "Charter oak," by Albert C. Bates ... (Hartford, Conn., The Case, Lockwood & Brainard co.) 1907.   9 p.   19 cm.   7-34817.
F97.B 32

BATES, Albert Carlos.   The charter of Connecticut; a study, ... Hartford, Conn. hist. soc., 1932.   72 p.   24½ cm.   32-27526.
F97.B 33

BEERS, William A.   Major Nathan Gold, of the old town of Fairfield, Conn.   A summary of his important public services in the colony of Connecticut. ... (Bridgeport, Conn., Hunt & Baxter, printers) 1882.   (5) - 23 p.   19½ cm.   13-12785.
F97.B 41

BENTON, Josiah Henry.   Andrew Benton, 1620 - 1683; a sketch.   Boston, The Merrymount press, 1900.   30 p.   illus. (incl. plans)   pl.   25 cm.   0-3409 Rev.
F97.B 46

BINGHAM, Charles E.   Thomas Bingham, Connecticut pioneer: a story of very early colonial times, 1658 - 1730.   Essex, Conn., Pequot Press (1968)   ix, 101 p.   illus.   24 cm.   68-58870.
F97. B 5

BOLLES, John Rogers.   The Rogerenes; some hitherto unpublished annals belonging to the colonial history of Connecticut, pt. I.   A vindication, by John R. Bolles, pt. II.   History of the Rogerenes, by Anna B. Williams, appendix of Rogerene writings ... Boston, Stanhope press, F. H. Gilson (1904)   396 p.   25½ cm.   The Rogerenes were a religious sect founded by John Rogers.   4-22000.
F97.B 69

BOWEN, Clarence Winthrop.   The charter of Connecticut.   (In American hist. soc. Annual report ... 1912.   14-21901.
F97.B 78

BOYSE, Joanna, a saint of the Puritan calendar, by Lillian E. Prudden.   Boston, Priv. print., 1936.   4, 23 p.   front.   22½ cm.   "To a large degree the story can be traced in 'Peter Prudden and some of his descendants' by the same author, pub. in 1901."   37-831.
F97.B 79

BULKELEY, Gershom.   The people's right to election or alteration of government in Connecticott, argued in a letter; etc., etc.   Philadelphia, Printed by assignes of William Bradford, anno 1689.   (Boston, 1937)   facsim.   18 p.   (Photostat Americana. 2d series ... Photostated at the Mass. hist. soc. no. 26)   37-13758.
F97.B 86
Rare Book Coll.

BULKELEY, Gershom.   Some seasonable considerations for the good people of Connecticut.   (New York, Printed by William Bradford, 1694) (Boston, 1941)   facsim.   62 p.   23½ cm.   (Photostat Americana. 2d series ... Photostated at the Mass. hist. soc. No. 132)   41-14494.
F97.B 87
Rare Book Coll.

BUSHMAN, Richard L.   From Puritan to Yankee; character and the social order in Connecticut, 1690 - 1765 (by) Richard L. Bushman.   Cambridge, Mass., Harvard University Press, 1967.   xiv, 343 p.   22 cm.   (A publication of the Center for the Study of the History of Liberty in America, Harvard University)   67-17304.
F97.B 89

COLEMAN, Roy V.   The Old patent of Connecticut ... Westport, Conn., 1936.   54 p.   maps.   21½ cm.   36-24377.
F97.C 65

CONNECTICUT (Colony)   The public records of the colony of Connecticut (1636 - 1776) ...   transcribed and published ...   Hartford, Press of the Case, Lockwood & Brainard co. 1850-90.
15 v. fold. map, facsims. 23½ cm.   Imprint varies.   A continuation, pub. uniformly with the above, has title: The public records of the state of Connecticut.   Rc-3188 Rev.   Contents. - v.1. Records of the General and particular courts, Apr. 1636 - Dec. 1649. Records of the General court, Feb. 1650 - May 1665. Record of wills and inventories, 1640 - 1649. Code of laws, established by the General court, May 1650. Appendix. - v.2. The charter of Connecticut. Records of the General court, May 1665 - Oct. 1677. Journal and correspondence of the Council, 1675 - 1677. Appendix. - v.3. Records of the colony of Connecticut, May 1678 - June 1689. Appendix. Extracts from the records and files of the Commissioners of the United Colonies (of New England) 1652 - 1684. - v.4. Aug. 1689 - May 1706. Council journal, May 1696 - May 1698 - v.5. Oct. 1706 - Oct. 1716. Council journal, Oct. 1710 - Feb. 1717. - v.6. May 1717 - Oct. 1725. Council journal, May 1717 - Apr. 1726. - v.7. May 1726 - May 1735. Council journal, May 1726 - Feb. 1727/8 - v.8. Oct. 1735 - Oct. 1743. - v.9. May 1744 - Nov. 1750. - v.10. May 1751 - Feb. 1757. - v.11. May 1757 - Mar. 1762. - v.12. May 1762 - Oct. 1767. Reasons why the British colonies in America, should not be charged with internal taxes, by authority of Parliament (by Thomas Fitch) - v.13. May 1768 - May 1772. Council journal, May 1770 - May 1772. - v. 14. Oct. 1772 - Apr. 1775. The Susquehannah case (1774) Report of the commissioners appointed by the General assembly of this colony, to treat with the Proprietaries of Pennsylvania, respecting the boundaries of this colony and that province.   Norwich, 1774.   An account of the number of inhabitants, in the colony of Connecticut, Jan 1, 1774. Hartford, 1774. Heads of inquiry relative to the present state and condition of His Majesty's colony of Connecticut. New-London, 1775 - v.15. May 1775 - June, 1776. Journal of the Council of safety, June 7, 1775 - Oct. 2, 1776. Appendix containing some Council proceedings, 1663 - 1710.
F97. C 7

CONNECTICUT (Colony)... The Fundamental orders of Connecticut.   (New Haven) Pub. for the Tercentenary commission by the Yale university press, 1934.   9 p. facsims. 23 cm.   (Tercentenary pamphlet series xx)   34-27651 Rev. 2.
F97. C 71

CONNECTICUT (Colony)   The Law papers; correspondence and documents during Jonathan Law's governorship ... 1741 - 1750 ... Hartford, Conn. hist. soc., 1907 - 14.   3 v. 25 cm. Collections of the Conn. hist. soc. vol. xi, xii, xv)   7-38344 Rev. 2.
F97. C 72

CONNECTICUT (Colony)   The Wolcott papers.   1916.   1 v.   (1750 - 1754)
F97. C 73

CONNECTICUT (Colony)   The Fitch papers; correspondence and documents during Thomas Fitch's governorship ... 1754 - 1766 ... Hartford, Conn. hist. soc., 1918 - 20.   2 v. (Collections of the Connecticut historical soc. vol. xvii - xviii)   19-27187 Rev.
F97. C 74

CONNECTICUT.   ... Preliminary program of the celebration of the 300th anniversary of the settlement of Connecticut, 1635 - 1935.   (New Haven, Yale university press) 1935.   23 p. 25½ cm.
"Pamphlet pub. of the Tercentenary commission of the State of Connecticut"   35-28821.
F97. C 77

CONNECTICUT.   ... Report of the Tercentenary commission to the General assembly, Jan. 27, 1931. (Hartford, 1931)   9 p. 22½ cm.   31-27640.
F97. C 78

CONNECTICUT.   ... Report to the governor, 30 June, 1936. (Hartford, 1936)   69 p. incl. tables. 23 cm.   Tercentenary commission of the state of Conn.   36-28068.
F97. C784

CONNECTICUT historical society.   Birthday of the state of Connecticut.   Celebration of the 250th anniversary of the adoption of the first constitution of the state of Connecticut, by the Connecticut historical soc. and the towns of Windsor, Hartford, and Wethersfield ... 1889.   Hartford, Conn. hist. soc., 1889.   98 p. 23 cm.   1-Rc-3189.
F97. C 8

DAVIES, Mrs. Julia Elizabeth (Hickok)   Colonial Connecticut ... (Cincinnati, The Ebbert & Richardson co., 1917)   22 p. 23 cm.   (The Colonial dames of America in the state of Ohio ... Studies in the colonial period for use in the public schools)   17-25600 Rev.
F97. D 18

(DEMING, Dorothy)   ... The settlement of the Connecticut towns ... (New Haven) Pub. for the Tercentenary commission by the Yale university press, 1933.   75 p. fold. map. 23 cm.   (Tercentenary pamphlet series vi)   33-28128.
F97. D 36

DENISON.   Captain George Denison, a biography.   By Eleanor E. Fuller.   Mystic, Conn., The George and Ann Borodell Denison soc., 1941.   33 p. 23 cm. Bibliography: p. 32-33. 42-20139.
F97. D4F8

DENISON.   Captain George & Lady Ann; the Denisons of Pequotsepos Manor. (Stonington, Conn., Pequot Press, 1963)   31 p. 23 cm. (Connecticut booklet, no. 6) 63-16433.
F97. D4H3

CONNECTICUT 13

DORR, Edward. A discourse, occasioned by the much lamented death, of the Honorable Daniel Edwards, esq; of Hartford ... 1765. Delivered soon after his decease. ... Hartford: Printed by Thomas Green (1765)   23 p.   18 x 14 ½ cm.   22-14865.
F97.E 26
Rare Book Coll.

EDWARDS, Richard, (sheriff's deputy) of Hartford colony of Connecticut, his account book from Sept. 1, 1753, to May 9, 1754, with an introd. and ancestral record, by Frank D. Andrews ... Vineland, N.J., Priv. print., 1924.   3, 26, (2) p.   23 ½ cm.   Edition of 46 copies.   25-21343.
F97.E 28

ELIOT. Jared Eliot, minister, doctor, scientist, and his Connecticut. By Herbert Thomas. (Hamden, Conn.) Shoe String Press, 1967.   xii, 156 p.   21 cm.   67-12392.
F97.E4T47

FENWICK. Re-interment of the remains of Lady Alice Apsley Boteler, wife of George Fenwick, esq., ... 1870. Hartford, 1870.   24 p.   17 cm.   Historical address by J. H. Trumbull.   12-21888.
F97.F 34

DICKINSON, Moses. A sermon, delivered at the funeral, of the Honorable Thomas Fitch, esq; late governor of the colony of Connecticut .... New-Haven, Printed by T. and S. Green, 1774.   24 p.   20 cm.   15-6408.
F97.F 54
Rare Book Coll.

— (New York, Reprinted, 1872)   35 p.   22 ½ cm.   15-3833.
F97.F 55

(FLETCHER, William Isaac) The story of the Charter oak to accompany the picture by Charles D'Wolf Brownell; comp. under the direction of the late Marshall Jewell. Hartford, Conn., The Case, Lockwood & Brainard co., 1883.   57 p.   front. (port.)   4 pl.   20 ½ cm.   17-22862.
F97. F 6

GALE. Remarks on Dr. Gale's letter to J. W., esq. (By Eliphalet Dyer) (Hartford) 1769.   27 p.   17 cm.   7-25409.
F97.G 15
Rare Book Coll.

GALE, Benjamin. Observations on a pamphlet, entitled Remarks on Dr. Gale's letter to J. W., esq; .... Shewing ... that such an imputation is highly injurious to the character of that worthy patriot. ... Hartford, Printed by Green & Watson (1770)   40 p.   17 cm.   7-25407.
F97.G158
Rare Book Coll.

GOCHER, William Henry. Wadsworth; or, The charter oak, ... Hartford, Conn., W. H. Gocher, 1904.   399 p. incl. front., plates, ports., facsims.   20 cm.   4-27367.
F97.G 57

HALL. The regards due to such as have been eminent & useful. A discourse occasioned by the death of John Hall .... By Samuel Whittelsey ... Boston: Printed for S. Gerrish, 1730.   34 p.   17 ½ cm.   11-21107.
F97.H 17

HINMAN, Royal Ralph, comp. Letters from the English kings and queens Charles II, James II, William and Mary, Anne, George II, etc. to the governors of the colony of Connecticut, together with the answers thereto, from 1635 to 1749, etc. etc. Hartford, J. B. Eldredge, printer, 1836.   vii, 10 - 372 p.   port., 2 facsim. (incl. front.)   19 cm.   1-Rc-3190.
F97.H 64

HOADLY, Charles Jeremy. The hiding of the charter. ... (Hartford, The Case, Lockwood & Brainard co.) 1900.   32 p.   24 cm.   (Acorn club, Conn. Publication no. 2)   100 printed.   0-4449.
F97.H 66

HOADLY, Charles Jeremy, comp. Hoadly memorial. Early letters and documents relating to Connecticut, 1643 - 1709 ... Hartford, Connecticut hist. soc., 1932.   xv, 210 p.   25 cm.   (Collections of the Conn. historical soc. vol. xxiv)   32-30534.
F97.H663

HOADLY, Charles Jeremy. The Warwick patent. (Hartford, The Case, Lockwood & Brainard co.) 1902.   51 p.   24 x 15 ½ cm.   (Acorn club, Conn. 7th publication.   102 copies printed.   2-19107.
F97.H 67

(HOOKER, Roland Mather) ... The Spanish ship case, a troublesome episode for Connecticut, 1752 - 1758. (New Haven) Pub. for the Tercentenary commission by the Yale university press, 1934. 34, (2) p. 23 cm. (Tercentenary pamphlet series xxv) 34-27655 Rev.
 F97.H 72

HOOKER, ... Thomas. (By Warren Seymour Archibald) (New Haven) Pub. for the Tercentenary commission by the Yale university press, 1933.   19 p.   23 cm.   (Tercentenary pamphlet series iv)   33-28124 Rev.
 F97.H 75

HOOKER, Thomas, the first American Democrat; an address by Walter Seth Logan ... (New York, 1904)   28 p.   23 cm.   (Order of Founders and patriots of America. N.Y. soc. Publications. no. 6)   4-33480.
 F97.H 77

HOOKER, Thomas. Piscator evangelicus. Or, The life of Mr. Thomas Hooker, the renowned, pastor of Hartford-church ... Essay'd by Cotton Mather ... (Boston) Printed (for Michael Perry) ... 1695.   45 p.   15 cm.   37-20777.
 F97.H772
 Rare Book Coll.

HOOKER, Thomas, and his relation to American constitutional history. An address delivered by Epaphroditus Peck ... 1904. (n.p., 1904)   12 p.   23½ cm.   5-42451.
 F97.H773

HOOKER, Thomas. By Alice Porter.   (In Conn. magazine. v. 6)   12-6384.
 F97.H775

HOOKER, ... Thomas; preacher, founder, democrat, by George Leon Walker. New York, Dodd, Mead, and co. (1891)   vi, 203 p. incl. front. (port.) 18 cm.   "Makers of America."   9-7801.
 F97.H 78

— 1972.
 F97.H 78
 1972

HOOKER, Thomas; bibliography (complete as known to date) together with a brief sketch of his life, by Harry Clark Woolley. (Hartford) 1932.   32 p.   24 cm.   (Center Church monographs, no. 1)
 F97. H 8

HUNTINGTON. Civil rulers, directed of God .... A funeral sermon for the Honorable Hezekiah Huntington ... 1773. ... By Benjamin Lord ... Norwich, Printed by Green & Spooner, 1773. 31 p.   18½ cm.   16-21896.
 F97. H 9

JOHNSTON, Alexander. ... The genesis of a New England state (Connecticut) Read before the Historical and political science assoc. ... 1883. Baltimore, Johns Hopkins university, 1883. 29 p.   23½ cm.   (Johns Hopkins university studies in historical and political science ... 1st ser. xi)   4-8534.
 F97. J 73

JOHNSTON, Johanna. The Connecticut colony. (New York) Crowell-Collier Press (1969) 136 p. illus. 23 cm. (A Forge of Freedom book)   69-19576.
 F97. J 74

JONES, Mary Jeanne Anderson. Congregational Commonwealth Connecticut, 1636 - 1662. (1st ed.) Middletown, Conn., Wesleyan University Press (1968)   xiii, 233 p.   68-27543.
 F97. J 75

LUDLOW. Mr. Ludlow goes for old England, by R. V. Coleman ... Westport, Conn., 1935. 30 p.   21½ cm.   35-3746.
 F97.L916

LUDLOW. Roger Ludlow in chancery, by R. V. Coleman. Westport, Conn., 1934.   41 p.   21½ cm. 34-5439.
 F97.L 92

LUDLOW. Roger Ludlowe; an historical sketch prepared by John H. Perry ... (Bridgeport, Conn.) Fairfield historical soc. (1914)   22 p.   23 cm.   15-1685.
 F97.L 93

LUDLOW. Roger Ludlow, the colonial lawmaker, by John M. Taylor ... New York & London, G. P. Putnam's sons, 1900.   v - ix, 166 p. front. (facsim.) 22 cm. Bibliographical notes: p. 163 - 166.   0-6110 Rev.
 F97.L 94

CONNECTICUT

MASON, Louis Bond. The life and times of Major John Mason of Connecticut: 1600 - 1672 ... New York, London, G. P. Putnam's sons, 1935.   xi, 15 - 350 p.   front., illus. (facsim.) plates, plan.   22 cm. Bibliography: p. 337 - 338.   35-22339.
F97. M 38

MEAD, Nelson Prentiss. Connecticut as a corporate colony ... Lancaster, Pa., The New era printing co., 1906.   x, 119 p.   23½ cm.   Thesis (PH.D.) - Columbia university.   6-13405.
F97. M 48

MOE, William Collins Hainsworth. Pioneers of Connecticut; an account of the discoveries and earliest settlements ... (Guilford? Conn., 193-)   8 p.   23½ cm.   38-34429.
F97. M 64

MOQUIN, Elizabeth. The story of the Charter oak of Harford. Illus. by Clarence Hansen. Hartford, Conn., Albert Lepper print., 1945.   15 p.   illus.   23 cm.   45-5852.
F97. M653

MORRIS, Mrs. Elisabeth (Woodbridge) Episodes from colonial Connecticut. (Hartford, 1935) 2, 74 p.   plates (music)   23 cm.   39-28526.
F97. M655

MORROW, Rising Lake. ... Connecticut influences in western Massachusetts and Vermont. (New Haven) Pub. for the Tercentenary commission by the Yale university press, 1936.   22 p.   23 cm. (Tercentenary pamphlet series) lviii) "Biographical note": p. 22.   36-27830.
F97. M 67

(MUNSON, Myron Andrews) ... Historical address of the first Munson family reunion held in the city of New Haven ... 1887. New Haven, Tuttle, Morehouse & Taylor, print., 1887.   (13) - 56 p.   23½ cm. Also pub. in Proceedings of the first Munson family reunion ... New Haven, 1887.   17-19083.
F97. M 96

(PETERS, Samuel) A general history of Connecticut, from its first settlement under George Fenwick, esq. to its latest period of amity with Great Britain; including a description of the country, etc. By a gentleman of the province ... London, Printed for the author; 1781.   2, 2*, 3 - 436 p.   21½ cm. 5-17831.
F97. P 29
Rare Book Coll.

— Upper Saddle River, N.J., Literature House (1970) (c. 1877)   285 p.   23 cm.   77-104540.
F97. P 29
1970

— London, 1781. To which is added a supplement, verifying many important statements made by the author. Illus. with eight engravings. New-Haven, Repub. by D. Clark and co,, Baldwin and Threadway, printers, 1829.   405 p.   front., plates.   17½ x 10½ cm.   Rc-3191.
F97. P 3

— To which are added, additions to appendix, notes, and extracts from letters, etc. By Samuel Jarvis McCormick. New York, D. Appleton, 1877.   285 p.   20½ cm.   Rc-3192 Rev.
F97. P 4
Rare Book Coll.

PETERS, Samuel. The works of Samuel Peters of Hebron, Connecticut, New-England historian, satirist, folklorist, anti-patriot, and anglican clergyman, 1735 - 1826, with historical indexes. Ed. by Kenneth Walter Cameron. Hartford, (Conn.) Transcendental Books (1967)   184 l.   29 cm.   Comprised of facsimile reproductions of the author's works, including original title pages.
F97. P 42
1967

PETERS. The Rev. Samuel Peters, his defenders and apologist, with a reply to the Churchman's review of "The trueblue laws of Connecticut," etc. By J. Hammond Trumbull ... Hartford, 1877. 26 p.   20½ cm.   Reprinted from the Hartford daily Courant.   Chiefly a review of Samuel J. McCormick's edition of Rev. Samuel Peters' General history of Connecticut.   21-4857.
F97. P 45

PITKIN. The ruler's duty and honor, in serving his generation ... a sermon, occasioned by the much lamented death of the Honorable William Pitkin ... By Eliphalet Williams ... Hartford, Printed by Green & Watson, 1770.   2, (3) - 33 p.   17 cm.   17-1098.
F97. P 6
Rare Book Coll.

SHURTLETT, William S. Minnetona; or, The Indian gift. A historical poem .... Springfield, Mass, Springfield print. co., 1881.   37 p.   24½ cm.   20-20182.
F97. S 56

STILES, Ezra. Oratio funebris pro exequiis celebrandis viri perillustris Jonathan Law ... Novi-Londini, excudebat atque vendebat Timotheus Green, 1751.   12, (3) p.   18 cm.   21-11147.
F97. S 85
Rare Book Coll.

STOUGHTON, John Alden. A corner stone of colonial commerce. ... Boston, Little, Brown, 1911. viii, 91 p. plates, facsims. 21 cm. 11-26222 Rev.
F97. S 88

THEIR Majesties colony of Connecticut in New-England vindicated, from the abuses of a pamphlet, licensed and printed at New-York, 1694. Boston, Printed by B. Green, 1694.   43 p.   18½ x 14½ cm. Imperfect: t.-p. and p. 37-43 wanting.   Rc-3193 Rev.
F97. T 3
Rare Book Coll.

TREAT. Robert Treat, founder, farmer, soldier, statesman, governor; paper read before the New Haven colony historical soc., by General George Hare Ford. (New Haven, Conn., Print. Tuttle, Morehouse & Taylor, 1914)   163 - 180 p. 25 cm.   Reprint from vol. viii, New Haven colony hist. soc., April, 1914. 14-12547.
F97. T 78

TREAT. Robert Treat, 1622 - 1710. By Charles Alison Scully. Philadelphia, 1959.   133 l.   29 cm. Includes bibliography.   59-3465.
F97. T78S3

TRUMBULL, Benjamin. A complete history of Connecticut, civil and ecclesiastical, from the emigration of its first planters from England, in MDCXXX to MDCCXIII. Vol. I. Hartford, Hudson & Goodwin, 1797.   xix, 587 p.   3 port., fold. map.   22 cm.   A 31-1201 x Rev.
F97. T 79
Rare Book Coll.

— With an appendix, containing the original patent of New-England, never before published in America. New-Haven, Maltby, Goldsmith, 1818.   2 v. front. (port.) 22½ cm. 1-Rc-3194.
F97. T 8

WELLES, Edwin Stanley. The origin of the Fundamental orders, 1639. Hartford, Conn., Priv. print., Wayside Press, Topsfield, Mass., 1936. 20 p. 23½ cm. "75 copies on mozo vellum" 36-12573.
F97. W 46

WELLES, Edwin Stanley. The life and public services of Thomas Welles, fourth governor of Conn. Wethersfield, Conn., The Welles family assoc., 1940.   18 p. fold. facsim. 23½ cm. 41-19932 Rev.
F97. W47W4

WHITE, John. Last will of Elder John White, one of the first settlers of Hartford, Conn; also a narrative of his life as a colonist. Collingwood, N.J., Print. W. Washburn (1933)   63 p.   6½ x 3½ cm. Ed. of 64 copies. 34-8461.
F97. W 64
Rare Book Coll.

WINTHROP, John. (Winthrop papers. Boston, 1890)   25 cm.
F97. W 79

WINTHROP. The younger John Winthrop, by Robert C. Black III. New York, Columbia University Press, 1966.   459 p. maps, port. 24 cm. Bibliography: p. (435) - 445. 66-20493.
F97. W8B55

WOLCOTT. The character of Moses illustrated and improved: in a discourse, occasioned by the death of the Hon. Roger Wolcott ... By Joseph Perry ... Hartford, Print. Thomas Green (1767) 28 p. 22 cm. 15-23535.
F97. W 85

WYLLYS, George. The Wyllys papers; correspondence and documents chiefly of descendants of Gov. George Wyllys of Connecticut, 1590 - 1796. Hartford, Conn, hist. soc., 1924.   xl, 567 p. illus. (facsim.) 23 cm. (Collections of the Conn. historical soc. vol. xxi) 25-27064.
F97. W 98

ZEICHNER, Oscar. Connecticut's years of controversy, 1750 - 1776. (Chapel Hill) Pub. for the Institute of Early American History and Culture at Williamsburg, Va., by the Univ. of N.C. Press (1949)   xiv, 404 p. illus., ports., maps. 25 cm. "Bibliographical essay": p. 359-382. 49-10020*.
F97. Z 4
1949

CONNECTICUT

ZEICHNER, Oscar. Connecticut's years of controversy, 1750 - 1776. Chapel Hill, University of N.C. Press (1949) xiv, 404 p. illus., ports., maps. 24 cm. Thesis - Columbia University. "Bibliographical essay": p. 359 - 382. A50-960.
F97. Z 4 1949a

— (Hamden, Conn.) Archon Books, 1970. xiv, 404 p. 24 cm. 78-122398.
F97. Z 4 1970

NEW HAVEN COLONY.

ANDREWS, Charles McLean. , ... The rise and fall of the New Haven colony. (New Haven) Pub. for the Tercentenary commission by the Yale university press, 1936. 56 p. 23 cm. (Tercentenary pamphlet series xlviii) 36-27820.
F98. A 35

ATWATER, Edward Elias. History of the colony of New Haven to its absorption into Connecticut. New Haven, Print. for the author, 1881. ix, 611 p. illus., ports., 2 fold. maps (incl. front.) 22½ cm. 1-Rc-3183.
F98. A 8

— with supplementary history and personnel of the towns of Branford, Guilford, Milford, Stratford, Norwalk, Southold, etc. Meriden, Conn., The Journal pub. co., 1902. xii, 767 (i.e. 773) p. illus. (incl. ports.) 5 fold. plans (incl. front.) 22½ cm. L.C. copy replaced by microfilm.
F98. A 81
Microfilm 24523 F

CALDER, Isabel MacBeath. The New Haven colony ... New Haven, Yale university press; London, H. Milford, Oxford university press, 1934. vi p. 301 p. front. (port.) fold. map. 23½ cm. (Yale historical publications. Miscellany xxviii) Bibliographical note: p. (264) - 273. 34-42834.
F98. C 26

— (Hamden, Conn.) Archon Books, 1970 (c. 1962) vi, 301 p. illus. 22 cm. 71-95022.
F98. C 26 1970

KINGSLEY, William Lathrop. An address on the occasion of the 250th anniversary of the settlement of New Haven .... By William L. Kingsley. New Haven, 1888. (3) - 66 p. 23½ cm. 3-31801.
F98. K 55

LAMBERT, Edward Rodolphus. History of the colony of New Haven, before and after the union with Connecticut. Containing a particular description of the towns which composed that government, viz., New Haven, Milford, Guilford, Branford, Stamford, & Southold, L.I., etc. New Haven, Hitchcock & Stafford, 1838. 216 p. front. (map) illus., plates, plans. 19 cm. "A genealogical sketch of the Lambert family of Milford, Conn.": p. (205) - 216. 1-Rc-3184.
F98. L 2

NEW HAVEN colony historical society, Papers of the. v. 1 - 1865 - v. illus., plates, ports., facsims. 23½ cm. 7-6743. New Haven, Printed for the Soc.,
F98. N 5

NEW HAVEN colony historical society, Catalogue of the objects of interest belonging to the. (New Haven) L. S. Punderson, printer, 1885. 57 p. 22½ cm. 3-6529.
F98. N 56

NEW HAVEN colony historical society, Collections of the ... New Haven, Pub. by the Society, 1907. 78 p. front., illus., plates, port. 24 cm. 7-13560.
F98. N 6

NEW HAVEN colony historical society, The constitution and by-laws of the. (New Haven, 1886) 10 p. 18½ cm. 39-32932.
F98. N 63

NEW HAVEN colony historical society building, Proceedings at the public opening of the. (New Haven 1893) 91 p. front., plates, 2 port. 26 cm. Rc-3185 Rev.
F98. N 75

NEW HAVEN colony historical society, ... Reports presented at the annual meetings ... also a list

of officers and members ... 1901 -   New Haven, The Society, 1902 -   v. plates. 22 ½ cm.
9-897 Rev.
F98.N 76

NEW HAVEN (Colony) Records of the colony and plantation of New Haven, from 1638 to 1649. Transcribed and ed. ... By Charles J. Hoadly ... Hartford, Printed by Case, Tiffany and company, 1857.
vii, 10 - 547 p.   22 cm.   Rc-3186 Rev.
F98. N 8

NEW HAVEN (Colony) Records of the colony or jurisdiction of New Haven, from May, 1653, to the union. Together with the New Haven code of 1656. Transcribed and ed. ... By C. J. Hoadly ... Hartford, Print. Case, Lockwood, 1858.   iv, 626 p. 22 cm. 1-Rc-3187.
F98.N 81

SEYMOUR, George Dudley. ... Memorials of Theophilus Eaton, first governor of the New Haven colony; New Haven, Conn., Priv. print., The Tuttle, Morehouse & Taylor co., 1938.   4, 46 p. illus., pl., port. 26 cm. 38-15113.
F98.S 48

WINTHROP, John. Winthrop-Davenport papers.   (From New York Public Library Bulletin. 1899. Vol. iii, no. 10)
9-21959.
F98. W 7

WINTHROP trust company. John Winthrop, the younger. (New London) 1922.   (11) p. illus. (incl. facsims.) 24 cm. 22-7152.
F98.W 73

1775 - 1865.

AS you were! A word of advice to straight-haired folks: addressed to the freemen of Connecticut, by one of their number. (T. G. Woodward, print. New-Haven, 1816)   16 p. 22 cm. 9-20794.
F99.A 79

BALDWIN, Alice Mary. ... The clergy of Connecticut in revolutionary days. (New Haven) Pub. for the Tercentenary commission by the Yale university press, 1936.   31 p. 23 cm. (Tercentenary pamphlet series lvi) "Bibliographical note": p. 31. 36-27828.
F99.B 26

CONNECTICUT. The public records of the state of Connecticut ... with the journal of the Council of safety ... and an appendix. ... by Charles J. Hoadly ... Hartford, Press of the Case, Lockwood & Brainard co., 1894 - 1967.   11 v. 25 cm. Rc-3195 Rev. 2.
F99. C 7

COWLES, Julia. The diaries of Julia Cowles; a Connecticut record, 1797 - 1803. Ed. from the original manuscripts ... by Laura Haldey Moseley. New Haven, Yale university press; London, H. Milford, Oxford university press, 1931.   xiii, 94 p. front., plates. 21 ½ cm. 31-14823.
F99.C 78

DAGGETT, David. Count the cost. An address to the people of Connecticut, on sundry political subjects, and particularly on the proposition for a new constitution. By Jonathan Steadfast (pseud.) Hartford: Print. Hudson and Goodwin, 1804.   21 p. 21 cm. 9-21211 Rev.
F99.D 14
Rare Book Coll.

DAGGETT, David. Steady habits vindicated: or, A serious remonstrance to the people of Connecticut against changing their government. By a friend to the public welfare. Hartford: Print, by Hudson and Goodwin, 1805.   20 p. 22 cm. 9-20792 Rev.
F99.D 15
Rare Book Coll.

DAY, Horace. Geography of the state of Connecticut, designed for schools, and intended to accompany Mitchell's New intermediate geography; with a new map of the state ... By Horace Day ... Philadelphia, E. H. Butler, 1865.   (6) p. illus. (incl. map) 30 ½ x 24 ½ cm. 20-11557.
F99.D 27

FEDERAL party. An address to the freemen of Connecticut. Hartford: Print. Hudson & Goodwin, 1803.   7 p. 22 cm. 9-20808.
F99. F 29
Rare Book Coll.

CONNECTICUT

GENERAL committee of the Republicans of Connecticut. Republican address to the freemen of Connecticut. (n.p., 1803) 16 p. 20½ cm. 25-13361.
F99.G 34
Rare Book Coll.

GOODRICH. A sermon ... at the funeral of the Hon, Chauncey Goodrich ... By Nathan Strong ... Hartford: Printed by Peter B. Gleason and co., 1815. 15 p. 21½ cm. 24-11503.
F99.G 65

GRISWOLD. A sermon, delivered at the funeral of His Excellency Matthew Griswold .... By Lathrop Rockwell ... New-London, Print. S. Green, 1802. 18 p. 22½ cm. 16-13900.
F99.G 87
Rare Book Coll.

GRISWOLD. An eulogium, commemorative of ... Roger Griswold .... By David Daggett ... New-Haven, Print. Walter & Steele, 1812. 24 p. 20 cm. 11-4710.
F99.G 88
Rare Book Coll.

HILLARD, Isaac. The Federal pye. In May, 1803, the Federal members of the General assembly of Connecticut held a grand caucus at Hartford; and pub. an address to the freemen of this state: that, and their doings in said caucus versified. Danbury, Printed for the author, 1804. 16 p. 21½ cm. 16-21926.
F99.H 64
Rare Book Coll.

(HILLIARD, Isaac) To the Honorable the General assembly of the state of Connecticut ... The memorial of Harry, Cuff, and Cato, black men, now in slavery in Connecticut, in behalf of ourselves and the poor black people of our nation in like circumstances ... (n.p., 1797?) 12 p. 21 cm. 24-15746.
F99.H646
Rare Book Coll.

HOLD-FAST, Simon (pseud.) Facts are stubborn things, or, Nine plain questions to the people of Connecticut, with a brief reply to each. Hartford, Print. Hudson and Goodwin, 1803. 23 p. 20½ cm. CA 6-2643 Unrev.
F99.H 72
Rare Book Coll.

HOLLEY. Memorial of Alexander Hamilton Holley. 1804 - 1887 ... (Hartford, The Case, Lockwood & Brainard co., 1888) 58 p. front. (port.) 22 x 17 cm. 43-47414.
F99.H75M4

(HOWARD, Mark) Despotic doctrines declared by the U.S. Senate exposed; and Senator Dixon unmasked. Hartford, Press of Case, Lockwood, 1863. 24 p. 21½ cm. 1-13368.
F99.H 85

HUNTINGTON. A sermon, delivered at the funeral of His Excellency Samuel Huntington .... By Joseph Strong. Hartford: Print. by Hudson and Goodwin, 1796. 19 p. 23½ cm. 11-19321.
F99.H 95
Rare Book Coll.

IVES, Franklin Titus. Yankee jumbles; or, Chimney corner tales of 19th century events, comprising subjects of fact, fun and fiction. New York, Broadway pub. co. (1903) v, 390 p. front. (port.) 19½ cm. 4-1661.
F99. I 95

JONES, A. D. comp. The illustrated commercial, mechanical, progessional and statistical gazetteer and business-book of Connecticut, for 1857-8. Vol. I. New Haven. T. J. Stafford, printer, 1857. 304 p. front., illus. (incl. ports.) 23½ cm. No more pub? Rc-3196 Rev.
F99 J 7

JOURNAL of an excursion, performed by a detachment of cadets, belonging to the A.L.S. & M. academy, under the command of Captain Alden Partridge. Middletown, (Conn.) Print. E. & H. Clark, 1826. 22 p. 21 cm. The route of the excursion was from Middletown overland to Poughkeepsie, thence to West Point and New York city, returning to Middletown by water. 20-3024.
F99. J 86
Rare Book Coll.

JUDD (pseud.) Judd vs. Trumbull; or, Plain truths. Addressed to the real friends of the state of Connecticut, or every sect, denomination, and party, whatever. New Haven - Print. by J. Barber, 1820. 20 p. 24 cm. In reply to a pamphlet pub., Hartford, 1819, with title: The mischiefs of legislative caucuses, exposed in an address to the people of Connecticut. By Trumbull. 20-3299.   F99. J 92

LANE, Jarlath Robert, brother. ... A political history of Connecticut during the civil war ... Washington, D. C., The Catholic university of America press, 1941. x, 320 p. 23 cm. Thesis (PH. D.) - Catholic university of America, 1941. "Bibliographical essay": p. 307 - 312. A 41-4464.   F99. L 25

LE DUC, Thomas Harold Andre. ... Connecticut and the first ten amendments to the federal Constitution. An article entitled "Connecticut and the first ten amendments to the federal Constitution," Washington, U. S. Govt, print. off., 1937. 6 p. 23½ cm. (U.S. 75th Cong., 1st sess. Senate. Doc. 96) 37-26910 Rev.   F99. L 43

MIDDLEBROOK, Louis Frank. History of maritime Connecticut during the American revolution, 1775 - 1783 ... Salem, Mass., The Essex institute, 1925. 2 v. fronts., plates, ports., maps, facsims. 23½ cm. 25-12440.   F99. M 63

MORSE, Jarvis Means. A neglected period of Connecticut's history, 1818 - 1850 ... New Haven, Yale university press; London, H. Milford, Oxford, university press, 1933. 4; 359 p. 22½ cm. (Yale historical publications. Miscellany, xxv) "Bibliographical note": p. (336) - 343. 33-14376.   F99. M 78

(MORSE, Jarvis Means) ... The rise of liberalism in Connecticut, 1828 - 1850 ... (New Haven) Pub. for the Tercentenary commission by the Yale university press, 1933. 45 p. 23 cm. (Tercentenary pamphlet series xvi) "Bibliographical note": p. 45. 33-28137 Rev.   F99. M 82

(PECK, Epaphroditus) ... The loyalists of Connecticut. (New Haven) Pub. for the Tercentenary commission by the Yale university press, 1934. 31 p. 23 cm. (Tercentenary pamphlet series xxxi) "Bibliographical note": p. 31. 35-27639 Rev.   F99. P 34

PECK, Esther Alice. A conservative generation's amusements, a phase of Connecticut's social history. Bangor, Me., Jordan-Frost print. co., 1938. xi, 119 p. 23 cm. (University of Maine studies. Second series, no. 44) Bibliography: p. 107 - 113. 38-28309.   F99. P 35

PRENTICE. In memory. Amos Wylie Prentice. (Hartford, The Case, Lockwood & Brainard co., 1894?) 32 p. port. 21 x 16½ cm. 19-13179.   F99. P 9

PURCELL, Richard Joseph. Connecticut in transition, 1775 - 1818. Washington, American historical assoc. ... 1918. x, 471 p. fold. maps. 21 cm. Bibliography: p. 421 - 455. 19-3751.   F99. P 98

— New ed., with a foreword by S. Hugh Brockunier. Middleton, Conn., Wesleyan University Press (1963) xvii, 305 p. 25 cm. 63-11058.   F99. P 98
  1963

ROSENBERRY, Mrs. Lois (Kimball) Mathews. ... Migrations from Connecticut after 1800. (New Haven) Pub. for the Tercentenary commission by the Yale university press, 1936. 29 p. 23 cm. (Tercentenary pamphlet series) liv) "Bibliographical note": p. 29. 36-27826.   F99. R 77

(SIGOURNEY, Lydia Howard (Huntley) "Mrs. C. Sigourney") Sketch of Connecticut, forty years since ... Hartford, O. D. Cooke, 1824. 278 p. 19 cm. Rc-3198 Rev.   F99. S 5

SIXTH of August; or, The Litchfield festival. An address to the people of Connecticut ... (Hartford, Printed by Hudson & Goodwin, 1806) 16 p. 21½ cm. Relating in part of the meeting of Republicans at Litchfield, Aug. 6, 1806, and the address of Joseph L. Smith there delivered. 9-20793.   F99. S 62

SHERMAN. Death disarmed of its sting. A tribute to the memory of the Hon. Roger Minott Sherman, being the discourse preached at his funeral ... By Lyman H. Atwater ... New Haven, Print. B. L. Hamlen, 1845. 20 p. 23 cm. 15-3861.   F99. S 63

CONNECTICUT 21

SKETCH of the life and character of the late Hon. Roger Minott Sherman. Extracted from the New Englander, vol. iv. New Haven, Printed by B. L. Hamlen, 1846. 21 p. front. (port.) 23 cm. 13-16546.
 F99. S 64

SMITH, John Cotton. The correspondence and miscellanies of the Hon. John Cotton Smith ... With an eulogy pronounced before the Conn. historical soc. at New Haven, May 27th, 1846. By Rev. Wm. W. Andrews. New York, Harper & brothers, 1847. xi, (13) - 328 p. 19½ cm. 15-14746.
 F99. S 75

SMITH. John Cotton Smith papers; papers of John Cotton Smith while Lieut. Governor, Acting Governor, and Governor of the State of Connecticut. Hartford, Conn. Hist. Soc., 1948 -
 v. 26 cm. (Collections of the Conn. Hist. Soc., v. 25 - 50-2726.
 F99. S76

(TRACY, Uriah) To the freemen of Connecticut. (Litchfield? 1803) 16 p. 21 cm. Address in defence of the Federal party. 7-25743.
 F99. T 76
 Rare Book Coll.

TRUMBULL. Biographical sketch of the character of Governor Trumbull. (Hartford, Print. Hudson & Goodwin, 1809) 13 p. 23 cm. Pub. also in Ely's funeral discourse. 11-30226.
 F99. T 78
 Rare Book Coll.

TRUMBULL. A discourse, occasioned by the death of His Excellency Jonathan Trumbull, esq., ... By Timothy Dwight ... New-Haven, Print. Oliver Steele ... 1809. 28 p. 22 cm. 14-1333.
 F99. T785
 Rare Book Coll.

TRUMBULL. The peaceful end of the perfect man. A discourse, delivered in Lebanon, at the funeral of His Excellency Jonathan Trumbull .... By Zebulon Ely ... Hartford, Print. Hudson and Goodwin, 1809. 16, 11 p. 20 cm. 13-33780 Rev.
 F99. T 79
 Rare Book Coll.

TRUMBULL (pseud.) The mischiefs of legislative caucuses ... 1819. 1 v.
 F99. T795

TRUMBULL, Jonathan. An address of His Excellency Governor Trumbull, to the General assembly and the freemen of the state of Connecticut; declining any further election to public office. ....
New London: Print. Timothy Green ... 1783. 10 p. 26½ cm. Rc-3200.
 F99. T 8
 Rare Book Coll.

U. S. Bureau of the Census. Heads of families at the first census of the U. S. taken in the year 1790: Connecticut. Baltimore, Genealogical Pub. Co., 1966. 227 p. 29 cm.
 F99. U 5
 1966
 L H & G

1865 - 1950.

ADDRESSES at the dedication of the statue of Hon. Richard D. Hubbard on the Capitol Grounds at Hartford, June 9, 1890. (Hartford) The Hubbard Escort, 1891. 54 p. 23 cm.
 F100. A 3

BALDWIN, Raymond E.: Connecticut statesman, by Curtis S. Johnson. Chester, Conn., Pequot Press (1972) x, 297 p. illus. 27 cm. 71-183874.
 F100. B3 J6

BURR, Henry Turner. Geography of Connecticut ... New York, etc.) 1921. p. (65) - 84. illus. (incl. map)
 F100. B 9

CENTENNIAL Senate of Connecticut, 1876. (n. p.) 1876. 32 port. 31 x 26 cm. 18-2257.
 F100. C 39

649

LOCAL HISTORIES IN THE LIBRARY OF CONGRESS

(CENTRAL New England railroad) Summer homes among the mountains. Hartford, Conn., 1894.
20 ½ cm.   F100. C 41

(CENTRAL New England railway company) Summer homes among the mountains. (Hartford, 1896)
20 ½ cm.   F100. C 43

— 1897.   20 ½ cm.   F100. C 44

— 1898.   20 ½ cm.   F100. C 45

— 1900.   20 ½ cm.   F100. C 47

— 1901.   20 cm.   F100. C 48

CHAPMAN, Edward Mortimer. New England village life. New York, B. Blom, 1971.   vi, 232 p.
21 cm.   Reprint of the 1937 ed.   73-174367 MARC.   F100. C 5
                                                                                                                           1971

COGGSWELL, John H. Fifty miles around Bridgeport: a road book for wheelmen. Embracing the territory in Fairfield and New Haven counties, tog. with a portion of Long Island from Riverhead to Bayshore along Great South bay ... Bridgeport, Conn., J. H. Coggswell, 1896.   35 p.   fold. map.
48°.   1-Rc-3199.   F100. C 6

CONNECTICUT. The Connecticut guide; what to see and where to find it. Compiled by Edgar L. Heermance. Pub. by the Emergency relief commission, Hartford, Conn., 1935. (Meriden, Print. by Curitss-Way co., 1935.   xxix, 320 p. incl. illus., maps. 21 ½ cm.   "Some books about Connecticut": p. (301) - 303.
35-28003.   F100. C 66

CONVENIENT Connecticut ... (New Haven, H. F. Morse associates, inc., 19   v. illus. 20 ½ cm.
Distributed by the Connecticut Development commission.   43-49220.   F100. C 7

CROSS, Wilbur Lucius. Connecticut Yankee; an autobiography (by) Wilbur L. Cross. New Haven, Yale university press, 1943.   viii, 428 p. front., illus., plates, ports.   24 cm.   A43-2896.   F100.C7A3

DAKIN, Wilson Sheldon. Geography of Connecticut ... Boston, New York (etc.) Ginn and co. (1926)
xiv, 162 p. incl. front., illus. maps (1 fold.) 21 ½ cm.   26-12773 Rev.   F100. D 15

(DE YOUNG, E. F.) The New Haven line of steamers ... (New York, New York engraving and print. co., 1893)   20 l.   illus.   12°.   1-21390-M1.   F100. D 52

EVENING post annual, 18 -   Biographical sketches (with portraits) of the state officers, representatives in Congress, governor's staff, and senators and members of the General ssembly of the state of Conn. Pub. annually. Hartford, Conn., Evening post association, 18   v. illus.,
ports.   30 cm.   16-8185.   F100. E 93

FEDERAL writers' project. ... Connecticut; a guide to its roads, lore, and people, written by workers of the Federal writers' project of the W. P. A. Boston, Houghton Mifflin, 1938.   xxiii, 593 p.
plates, maps (1 fold. in pocket) diagr. 21 cm. (American guide series) "Selected reading list": p. (562) - 565. 38-27339.   F100. F 45
                                                                                                                           Geneal. Sect. Ref.

GOODSELL, Daniel Ayres. Nature and character at Granite Bay. By Daniel A. Goodwell. New York, Eaton & Mains; Cincinnati, Jennings & Pye, 1901.   xv, 219 p. front., plates. 21 cm. Reminiscenes of
vacation days in a secluded hamlet on the Conn. shore of Long Island Sound. The names of localities are fictitious. 1-25379   F100. G 65

HICKS, Ratcliffe. Speeches and public correspondence of Ratcliffe Hicks ... Cambridge, The University press, 1896.   vii, 349 p. incl. front. (port.) 20 cm.   Comp. by Cornelius Gardiner.   5-3854.
                                                                                                                           F100. H 63

HOADLY. Charles Jeremy Hoadly. A memoir, by W. N. Chattin Carlton. (Hartford? Conn.) 1902.
54 p. 2 port. 24 cm. (Acorn club of Conn. 8th publication) Bibliography: p. (45) - 54. 2-21605.   F100. H67

CONNECTICUT

HUBBARD, Richard Dudley; a memorial. 1818 - 1884. (Hartford, The Case, Lockwood & Brainard co. print. 1884)   172 p.   front. (port.)   24 cm.   25-18634.   F100. H 85

HURLEY, Robert Augustine, Selected papers & address (of) (New York) The Fine editions press, 1942.   122 p.   front. (port.)   illus. (facsim.)   23 cm.   42-22761.   F100. H 9

HARTFORD. Court of common council. Proceedings... death Hon. Marshall Jewell. (1883) 1 v.   F100. J 58

JEWELL. Address on the life and character of Hon. Marshall Jewell, by Senator Orville H. Platt... 1883. Washington, D.C., R. O. Polkinhorn, print., 1883.   14 p.   23½ cm.   18-8209.   F100. J 59
Toner Coll.

LILLEY. George Leavens Lilley... Memorial proceedings of the Senate and House of representatives... Hartford (The Case, Lockwood & Brainard co.) 1909.   24 p.   front. (port.)   23 cm.   11-30522.   F100. L 72

MATTATUCK historical society. A tourists guide to Connecticut, containing lists of old and historical houses. Historical sites, and other things of interest in the state... Waterbury, Conn., The Mattatuck historical soc., 1923 -   v.   illus.   23 cm.   25-19985.   F100. M 43

(MONTEITH, James) Special geography of Connecticut; a supplement to Monteith's Comprehensive geography. New York, Chicago (etc.) A. S. Barnes, 1878.   7 p.   incl. illus., fold. map.   fol.   1-13369-M1.   F100. M 77

(NATIONAL union committee) Appeal to the electors of Connecticut, on the political issues of the present campaign. (New Haven? 1867?)   8 p.   23 cm.   43-46650.   F100. N 3

NUTTING, Wallace. Connecticut beautiful... Illustrated by the author with 304 pictures covering all the counties in Connecticut. Framingham, Mass., Old America co. (1923)   3 - 301 p. incl. illus., plates.   26 cm.   (His States beautiful series) 23-13527.   F100. N98

— Garden City, N.Y., Pub. in cooperation with Old America co. by the Garden City pub. co. (1935) 256 p. incl. front., illus., plates.   26 cm.   35-15257.   F100. N 98
1935

OSBORN, Russell Wight. A Californian through Connecticut and the Berkshires,... (Berkeley, Cal., Priv. pub.) 1916.   48 p.   23 cm.   17-3892.   F100. O 18

REILLY, Louis J. Thos. L. Reilly, public official, newspaperman, sportsman. Bridgeport, Conn., Thomas L. Reilly sons (1925)   32 p.   33 - 60 p.   port.   18 cm.   25-17587.   F100. R 36

1951 TO DATE.

BAILEY. The power broker; a biography of John M. Bailey, modern political boss (by) Joseph I. Lieberman. Boston, Houghton Mifflin, 1966.   x, 365 p.   22 cm.   66-11223.   F101. B3L5

KEYARTS, Eugene. Short walks in Connecticut. Stonington, Conn., Pequot Press (1968) ix; 85 p.   illus.   18 cm.   (Pequot handbook no. 4)   68-24038.   F101. K 4

LYFORD, Joseph P. Candidate. (New York) Holt (1969)   20 p.   28 cm.   (Case studies in practical politics)
The author's experiences in Connecticut politics in 1958.   59-12378.   F101. L 9

LOCAL HISTORIES IN THE LIBRARY OF CONGRESS

REGIONS, COUNTIES, ETC., A - Z.

HARWOOD, Pliny Le Roy. History of eastern Connecticut embracing the counties of Tolland, Windham, Middlesex and New London ... Chicago, New Haven, The Pioneer historical pub. co., 1931-32 (v.3, '31)   3 v. front., plates, ports., map, facsim. 27½ cm.   Vol. 3: Biographical. Bibliography: v.2, p. 822 - 823. 33-2922.
F102. A15H3

BOUNDARIES. The boundary disputes of Connecticut, by Clarence Winthrop Bowen ... Boston, J.R. Osgood and co., 1882.   vi, (9) - 90 p. front. (port.) illus., maps (partly fold.) facsims. 31 cm. 1-Rc-3201.   F102. B7B7

BOUNDARIES. ... Boundaries of Connecticut. (By Roland Mather Hooker) (New Haven) Pub. for the Tercentenary commission by the Yale university press, 1933.   38 p. maps (1 fold.) 23 cm.   (Tercentenary pamphlet series xi)   33-28132 Rev.
F102. B7H78

CANDLEWOOD comment; a ... digest of lake news ... v.1 -   June 1937 -   (Danbury, Conn., The Danbury printing co., 1937 -   v. illus. 19½ cm.   Monthly, June-Sept. 41-21804   F102. C2C3

CONNECTICUT River Valley (south of Middletown) directory, 1913/14 -   (v.1 -   containing ... Centerbrook, Chester, Clinton, Cobalt, Deep River, East Haddam, East Hampton, East River, Essex, Guilford, Haddam, Higganum, Ivoryton, Madison, Middlefield, Middle Haddam, Moodus, Saybrook, Shailerville, Westbrook ... Providence, R.I., C. De Witt White co., 1914 -
v.   24 cm.   14-4285.
Directories

CONNECTICUT Valley. Valley towns of Connecticut. By Martha Krug Genthe ... (New York, 1907) 32 p.   illus. (maps)   24 cm.   Reprinted from Bulletin of the American geographical soc. v.39, 1907.   8-24737.   F102. C7 G3

FAIRFIELD County. Boyd's Fairfield County directory, containing a general directory of Norwalk, South Norwalk, East Norwalk, etc. for the year 1881/2 - 1882/4, 1887/8 -   With a business directory of Fairfield County ... Comp. and pub. by W. Andrew Boyd ...   Poughkeepsie, Haight & Dudley, printers (1883-87)   3 v. 24 cm. 7-41322.   Directories

SHEFFIELD Island, Norwalk, History of. By Virginia Queen Adams. Stamford, Connecticut, 1968. 23 l.   28 cm.
F102. F2 A3

FAIRFIELD County, Leading business men of and a historical review of the principal cities ... Boston, Mercantile pub. co., 1887.   186 p. illus. 4°. 1-Rc-3202.   F102. F2 B3

FAIRFIELD County, Commemorative biographical record of, containing biographical sketches of prominent and representative citizens, and of many of the early settled families ... Chicago, J. H, Beers, 1899.   1348 p. ports. 29½ cm. 2-19057.   F102. F2 C7

FAIRFIELD County historical society. Reports and papers. ... 1882 - 1896/7. Bridgeport, 1882-97.   9 v. in 1.   7-23978.
F102. F2 F3
Microfilm 8771   F

FAIRFIELD County. The Handle, of Connecticut. v. 1 -   Apr. 21, 1933 -
(Norwalk, Conn., Henry Davis Nadig co., 1933 -   v. illus. 30 cm.   weekly. "Magazine of Fairfield county."   38M1025T.
F102. F2 H3

FAIRFIELD County. A complete copy of the inscriptions found on the monuments, headstones, etc., in the oldest cemetery in Norwalk, Bridgeport, Conn., The Standard assoc., printers, 1895. (In Fairfield County historical soc. Reports ...)   10-6838 Rev.
F102. F2   F3

FAIRFIELD County, History of, with illustrations and biographical sketches of its prominent men and pioneers. Comp. under the supervision of D. Hamilton Hurd. Philadelphia, J. W. Lewis, 1881. 13, 9 - 878 p.   illus., plates, ports., maps.   28 cm. 9-30364.
F102. F2 H8

FAIRFIELD County, Scenes in. Chicago, The W. H. Parish pub. co., 1893.   16 l. 1 illus. 70 pl. 35½ x 30 cm.   Issued in 12 parts.   13-14106.
F102. F2 S2

CONNECTICUT

FAIRFIELD County. Stamford Genealogical Society, inc. Genealogical resources of south-western Fairfield County, in the towns and cities of Darien, Greenwich, New Canaan, Norwalk, Stamford, Wilton. Stamford, Conn., Ferguson Library, 1959. 42 l. 30 cm. F102. F2 S8

FAIRFIELD County, Historic churches of, by Charles J. Stokes. Photography by Dave Nadig. (Westport, Conn.) County Books (1969) 95 p. illus. 28 cm. F102. F2 S84

HARTFORD suburban directory for Bloomfield, East Windsor, Farmington, Glastonbury, Newington, South Windsor, West Hartford, Wethersfield, Windsor and Windsor Locks ... Boston, Mass. (etc.) Union pub. co. 19 - 3 v. 24 - 24 ½ cm. 5-15555 Rev. Directories

HARTFORD County, History of, 1633 - 1928; being a study of the makers of the first constitution and the story of their lives, of their descendants, and of all who have come. By Charles Winslow Burpee. Chicago, S. J. Clarke Pub. Co., 1928. 3 v. illus., ports., maps, facsims. 28 cm. Vol. 3: Biographical. Bibliography: v.2, p. 1361. 55-46553. F102. H3 B8

HARTFORD County, Commemorative biographical record of, containing biographical sketches of prominent and representative citizens, and of many of the early settled families ... Chicago, J. H. Beers, 1901. 1591 p. port. 29 ½ cm. 2-19053. F102. H3 C7

HARTFORD County. Trips by trolley and a-wheel around Hartford. Illustrations from photos. by H. O. Warner. Hartford, E. M. White, 1898. 84 p. illus., fold. map 11 x 16 cm. Rc-3204 Rev.* F102. H3 T7

— 1901. 88 p. incl. front., illus. 16°. 1-20246-M1 Oct. 3. F102. H3 T73

HARTFORD County, The memorial history of, 1633 - 1884; ed. by J. Hammond Trumbull ... Projected by Clarence F. Jewett. Boston, E. L. Osgood, 1886. 2 v. illus., pl., port., maps, facsim. 28 cm. 1-Rc-3205* Cancel. F102. H3 T8

HIGHLAND Lake. A day's outing by rail and water. Issued by the Highland transportation co., season 1890. (New York, Thomson & co., 1890) 20 l. illus. obl. 12°. 1-21452-M1. F102. H6 H6

HOUSATONIC, Puritan river, The, by Chard Powers Smith. Illus. by Armin Landeck. New York, Toronto, Rinehart (1946) x, 532 p. incl. illus., map. 21 cm. Bibliography: p. 515 - 522. 46-4413. (Rivers of America) F102. H7 S5

LITCHFIELD County. Sketches of the early lights of the Litchfield bar. By Hon, David S. Boardman. Litchfield, Conn., J. Humphrey, jr., 1860. 38 p. 22 ½ cm. 12-11578. F102. L6 B6

LITCHFIELD County sketches, by Newell Meeker Calhoun. (Norfolk, Conn.) Litchfield County university club, 1906. 177 p. illus., map. 21 cm. 7-2086. F102. L6 C2

LITCHFIELD County revolutionary soldiers, Honor roll of. Josephine Ellis Richard, editor-in-chief. Litchfield, Conn., Mary Floyd Tallmadge chapter, D. A. R., 1912. 233 p. 24 cm. Arranged by towns. 12-18540. F102. L6 D2

LITCHFIELD County, ... Settlement of. (By Dorothy Deming) (New Haven) Pub. for the Tercenteneary commission by the Yale university press, 1933. 16 p. 23 cm. (Tercentenary pamphlet series vii) 33-28127 Rev. F102. L6 D46

LITCHFIELD County, History of, with illustrations and biographical sketches of its prominent men and pioneers. Philadelphia, J. W. Lewis, 1881. xiii, 13-730 p., plates, ports., map. 28 ½ cm. 5-4380. L. C. copy replaced by microfilm. F102. L6 H6
Microfilm 18434 F

LITCHFIELD County and the Berkshires, The pleasure book of. By Stewart Hoskins. (Lakeville, Conn., Lakeville Journal, 1947) 49 p. illus., fold. map. 21 cm. 47-28583*. F102. L6 H65

— 6th ed. 1951. 49 p. illus. 22 cm. 51-33921. F102. L6 H65 1951

— 7th ed. 1952. 57 p. illus. 22 cm. 52-39912. Title: Litchfield Hills and the Berkshires. F102.L6 H65 1952

— 8th ed. 1953. 57 p. illus. 22 cm. 53-34074. F102.L6 H65

— 9th ed. 1954. 49 p. illus., fold. map. 22 cm. 54-31339. F102.L6 H65

LITCHFIELD County. The bench and bar of Litchfield County, 1709 - 1909; biographical sketches of members, history and catalogue of the Litchfield law school, historical notes. By Dwight C. Kilbourn ... Litchfield, Conn., The author, 1909. (ix) - xv p., (3) - 344 p., x p. front., illus., plates, ports., facsims. 24 cm. 9-17999. F102. L6 K3

LITCHFIELD County; historical address delivered at Litchfield on the occasion of the centennial celebration. 1851, by Samuel Church, chief justice of the state. (In above item. p. 1 - 38) 9-17101.
F102. L6 K3

LITCHFIELD County. Sketches of the early lights of the Litchfield bar, by Hon. David S. Boardman, 1860. (In above item p. (39) - 67) 9-17102. F102. L6 K3

LITCHFIELD County. Fifty years at the Litchfield County bar; a lecture delivered before the Litchfield County bar, by Charles F. Sedgwick, esq., 1870. (In above item p. (69) - 98) 9-17103.
F102. L6 K3

LITCHFIELD County. Reminiscences of the Litchfield County bar delivered at the Centennial banquet, Nov. 18, 1899, by Hon. Donald J. Warner. (In above item p. (99) - 118) 9-17104.
F102. L6 K3

LITCHFIELD County. A biographical history of the county of Litchfield; comprising biographical sketches of distinguished natives and residents of the county, etc., etc. By Payne Kenyon Kilbourne. New York, Clark, Austin & co., 1851. viii, (9) - 413 p. front. ports. 22 cm. Rc-3206.
F102. L6 K4

LITCHFIELD County centennial celebration ... 1851. Hartford, E. Hunt, 1851. iv, (7)- 212 p. front. 22 ½ cm. 1-Rc-3207. F102. L6 L6

LITCHFIELD County. In Litchfield hills. An illustrated work of Litchfield County, in which the picturesque features of each town in the county are set forth. Pub. and edited by George Alson Marvin. Hartford, Conn., R. S. Peck, printers, 1897. 140 p. incl. illus., pl. 25 cm. Rc-3208.
F102. L6 M3

LITCHFIELD County. A statistical account of several towns in the county of Litchfield: by James Morris, esq. (New-Haven? 1815) (85) - 124 p. 24 cm. (A statistical account of the towns and parishes in the state of Connecticut. Pub. by the Connecticut academy of arts and sciences. vol. 1 no. 2) 7-23577. F102. L6 M8

LITCHFIELD County. The Berkshire and Litchfield Hills. (New York: New York, New Haven and Hartford railroad co., 1912) F102. L6 N5

LITCHFIELD County, Rural life in, by Charles Shepherd Phelps. Norfolk, Conn., Pub. under the auspices of the Litchfield County university club, 1917. 6, 3-137 p. 21 cm. Forms part of a series pub. under the auspices of the Litchfield university club. 17-14192. F102.L6 P53

LITCHFIELD County. The White memorial foundation, inc., Litchfield, 1913 - 1928. Hartford, Pub. for the trustees by the Prospect press, 1938. 102 p. incl. illus., plates. front. 28 cm. Introd. signed Samuel H. Fisher. 39-717. F102. L6 W5

MIDDLESEX County. A statistical account of the county of Middlesex. By David D. Field. Pub. by the Connecticut academy of arts and sciences. Middletown, Conn., Print. Clark & Lyman, 1819. 154 p. 20 ½ cm. (Pub. by the Connecticut academy of arts and sciences. vol. 2) 1-Rc-3209. F102. M6 F4

CONNECTICUT 27

— Name index. Compiled by Dorothy Ransom. (Orchard Lake, Mich., D. & R. Ransom,
1971) 12 p. 29 cm.
F102. M6 F4
1892
Suppl.

MIDDLESEX County, History of, with biographical sketches of its prominent men. New York,
J. B. Beers, 1884. 2, iii, 579 p. illus., plates, ports., fold. map, plan. 30 ½ cm. Mostly prepared under the supervision of
Henry Whittemore. 6-13954.
F102. M6 H6

MIDDLESEX County historical society ... Pamphlets. (no. 1) - 1901 - Middletown,
Conn., 1901 - v. front. (no. 9) 20 cm. Contain reports, list of officers and members, etc., and usually the annual
address of the president. CA 6-2037 Unrev.
F102. M6 M6

MIDDLESEX County historical society. Charter, by-laws, of officers, 1901. Middletown, Conn.,
The Society, 1901. 13 p. 20 ½ cm. (Its Pamphlets, no. 1) 6-34765 Rev.
F102. M6 M6

MIDDLESEX County historical society ... Address of the president, the Rev. Azel Hazen, on the first
decade of the society ... Middletown, Conn., Pelton & King, print., 1911. 43 p. front. 20 ½ cm.
(Its pamphlets no. 9) 11-15618.
F102. M6 M6
No. 9

MIDDLESEX County historical society. List of officers and members (Middletown, Conn., 1904)
20 cm.
F102. M6 M62

MIDDLESEX mutual assurance company. Centennial, 1836 - 1936. A brief account of the more significant events in the history of the county of Middlesex and of the growth of the Middlesex mutual
assurance co. Middletown, Conn., 1936. 6, 72 p. illus., plates, 2 port. (incl. front.) facsims. 23 cm. Foreword
signed: N. E. Davis, president. 36-14313.
F102. M6 M69

MIDDLESEX County. An index to the 1800 Federal census of Middlesex and New London counties.
Compiled by Lowell M. Volkel. (n. p.) 58 p. 28 cm.
F102. M6 V6

NAUGATUCK Valley. ... The New York industrial recorder ... Special number descriptive of and
illustrating the Naugatuck Valley, the industrial hive of Connecticut, showing the present facilities and
future possibilities of a community ... rapidly becoming one of the leading marts of trade and industry in the U.S. (New York, The N.Y. industrial recorder) 1899. 40 p. illus. 41 ½ cm. 10-23117 Rev.
F102. N 2 N5

NEW HAVEN County. Revolutionary characters of New Haven; the subject of addresses and papers
delivered before the General David Humphreys branch, no. 1. Connecticut society, Sons of the American revolution; also list of men so far as they are known from the territory embraced in the town of
New Haven, who served in the Continental army, etc. etc. New Haven ... (1911) 124 p. plates, ports.,
map, facsim. 24 ½ cm. 11-18995 Rev.
F102. N
E263. C3S 64

NEW HAVEN County, Leading business men of, and a historical review of the principal cities ... (By
William H. Beckford) Boston, Mercantile pub. co., 1887. 270 p. illus. 8°. 1-Rc-3210.
F102. N5 B3

NEW HAVEN County, Commemorative biographicl record of, containing biographicl sketches of
prominent and representative citizens and of may of the early settled families ... Chicago, J. H. Beers,
1902. 2 v. plates, ports. 30 x 21 ½ cm. 10-8756 Rev.
F102. N5 C7

NEW HAVEN County. On the four rocks of the New Haven region, East rock, West rock, Pine rock
and Mill rock, in illustration of the features of non-volcanic igneous ejections. With a guide to walks
and drives about New Haven. By James D. Dana. New Haven, Tuttle, Morehouse & Taylor, print.,
1891. vi, 120 p. illus., 7 pl. (part fold., incl. maps, plans) 23 ½ cm. Rc-3211.
F102. N5 D2

NEW HAVEN County. Walks and rides in central Connecticut and Massachusetts, by Chester R.

655

Longwell ... and Edward S. Dana ... New Haven, Conn., 1932. 2, (iii) - x, 229 p. incl. front., illus. maps (2 fold.) 20 cm. A revision and extension of 'The four rocks ...' (see above) Includes bibliographies. 32-22960. F102. N5 D22

— (Hamden, Conn., Shoe String Press (1961) xiv, 229 p. 20 cm. F102. N5 L6 1961

NEW HAVEN County. Sons of the American revolution. Roster of graves of, or monuments to, patriots of 1775 - 1783, and of soldiers of colonial wars, in and adjacent to New Haven County. (1st) - 4th; 1931 - 34. (New Haven, 1931 - 34) 4 v. in 3. 28½ cm. annual. Reproduced from type-written copy. No more pub. Title varies slightly. J. S. Hedden, compiler. 33-7585.

F102. N5 S6

NEW LONDON County. Biographical review ... containing life sketches of leading citizens of New London County ... Boston, Biographical review pub. co., 1898. (9) - 477 p. incl. ports. 29 x 23½ cm. (Atlantic states series of biographical reviews vol. xxvi) 17-28682. F102. N7 B6

NEW LONDON County, Genealogical and biographical record of, containing biographicl sketches of prominent and representative citizens and genealogical records of many of the early settled families ... Chicago, J. H. Beers, 1905. xi, 957 p. ports. 30 x 23 cm. 16-11134. F102. N7 G3

NEW LONDON County, History of, with biographical sketches of many of its pioneers and prominent men. Comp. under the supervision of D. Hamilton Hurd ... Philadelphia, J. W. Lewis, 1882. 768 p. illus., plates (partly double) ports., double map. L.C. copy replaced by microfilm. 5-13594.

F102. N7 H9
Microfilm 18540   F

NEW LONDON County, A modern history of; editor-in-chief, Benjamin Tinkham Marshall ... New York city, Lewis historical pub. co., 1922. 3 v. fronts., plates, ports., col. coat of arms, facsim. 27½ cm. Biographical sketches comprise second half of v. 2 and all of v. 3. "References" at end of chapter xiii. 25-14226. F102. N7 M3

NEW LONDON County historical society, Records and papers of the ... v. 1 - 2 1890/94 - 1912. New London, The Society (1890) - 1912. 3 v. in 4. illus., plates, ports. 23½ cm. No more pub. 7-3681 Rev.

F102. N7 N7

NEW LONDON County historical society, Collections of the, v. 1 -   New London, Conn., The New London County hist. soc., 1901 -   v. front., facsim. 24½ cm. 5-40528.   F102. N7 N8

— ... Diary of Joshua Hempstead of New London ... (vol. 1) xii, 750 p. 2-26527.
— ... Connecticut's Naval office at New London during the war of the American revolution. By Ernest E. Rogers. (vol. 2) 1933. 358 p. front., plates, ports., maps, facsims. 33-36984.

NEW LONDON County. The Norwich suburban directory containing a ... directory for ... Baltic, Canterbury, Central Village, Colchester, Fitchville, Gales Ferry, Glasgo, Griswold, Hallville, Hanover, Jewett City, Lebanon, Montville, Moosup, North Stonington, Palmertown, Pequot, Plainfield, Poquetanuck Scotland, Sterling, Uncasville, Versailles, Voluntown, Wauregan ... Providence, R. I., C. De W. White.   v. 24 cm. 12-14110.   Directories

THIMBLE ISLANDS. A brief history of the Thimble Islands in Branford, by Archibald Hanna. (Branford, Conn.) Pub. by Archon Books for the Branford Hist. Soc. (1970) 95 p. illus. 23 cm. 77-126840.

F102. T4 H3

TOLLAND County, History of, including its early settlement and progress to the present time; a descriptions of its historic and interesting localities; sketches of its towns and villages; portraits of some of its prominent men, and biographies of many of its representative citizens. By J. R. Cole ... New York, W. W. Preston, 1888. xi, 992 (i.e. 1000) p. plates, ports., map. 27 cm. 1-16755 Rev. F102. T6 C6

TOLLAND and Windham Counties, Commemorative biographical record of, containing biographical sketches of prominent and representative citizens and of many of the early settled families ... Chicago, J. H. Beers, 1903. xiii, 1358 p. ports. 30 x 23½ cm. 17-7693. L.C. copy replaced by microfilm. F102. T6 C73
Microfilm 18242 F

CONNECTICUT

WINDHAM County, History of ... Ed. by Richard M. Bayles ... New York, W. W. Preston, 1889.
xvi, 1204 p. plates, ports., map. 27 cm. 5-4381. F102. W7 B3

WINDHAM County, Historic gleanings in, by Ellen D. Larned ... Providence, R.I., Preston and Rounds, 1899. 3; 254 p. 20½ cm. 99-3377 Rev. F102. W7 L3

WINDHAM County, History of. By Ellen D. Larned ... Pub. by the author ... Worcester, Mass., Print. C. Hamilton, 1874 - 80. 2 v. fronts., ports., fold, map, fold, plan. 24 cm. 1-Rc-3212.
F102. W7 L5

WINDHAM County. Godfrey Malbone's Connecticut investment, by Howard W. Preston. (Providence?) 1923. 6 p. 2 pl. 23 cm. Reprinted from R.I. historical soc. collections, Oct., 1923. Malbone purchased land in Windham County, Conn. in 1740. 24-30830. F102. W7 P8

WINDHAM County business directory. Containing the names, business and location of all the business men in the county, agricultural, manufacturing, and other statistics. With a history of each town. West Killingly, Print. Windham County transcript office, 1861. (7) - 134 p. 20½ cm. 16-4790.
F102. W7 W7

CITIES, TOWNS, ETC., A - Z.

ANSONIA, Derby, Shelton, and Seymour directory v.6-13, 15-17, 19-25, New Haven, Conn., The Price & Lee co., 1888 - 1909. 20 v. fold. map. 24 cm. Sept. 7, 98-4 Additions. Directories

ASHFORD ... Records of the Ashford Congregational church ... pt. I - (Hartford, Conn., 1906 -) 1 v. 24½ cm. F104. A8 A8

AVON and East Granby, Directory for the towns of ... including a list of farmers and rural free delivery routes ... West Lynn, Mass. and Hartford, Conn., Clark-Delano co., 1913 -
1 v. 24 cm. 13-25298. Directories

BANTAM almanac, fact and folklore ... (Warren McArthur corporation) (New York, Bantam, Conn., 1942) 2, (3) - 22 p. illus. (maps) 21½ x 17 cm. "A short history of Bantam told in the simple style of the Old farmers almanac." Bibliography: leaf at end. 43-682. F104. B18 W3

BARKHAMSTED and New Harford, Directory for the towns of ... including a list of farmers and rural free delivery ... West Lynn, Mass. and Hartford, Conn., Clark-Delano co., 1914. v. 24 cm.
14-19368. Directories

BARKHAMSTED. Poem, by Mrs. Emma Carter Lee, and address, by Walter S. Carter, delivered at the centennial celebration at Barkhamsted ... 1879. (New York, S. B. Leverich, print., 1879?)
(20) p. 17 x 13½ cm. 17-10629. F104. B2 L37

BARKHAMSTED and its centennial 1879. To which is added, a historical appendix, containing copies of old letters, antiquarian, names of soldiers of the revolution, 1812, 1846 and 1861, etc., etc. Meriden, Republican steam print, 1881. 2; 178 p. front. (port.) illus. 23 cm. Preface signed: Wallace Lee. "Historical appendix" prepared by Henry R. Jones. Rc-3213. F104. B2 L4

BARKHAMSTED. A catalogue of Barkhamsted men, who served in the various wars, 1775 to 1865. Compiled, arranged and pub. by Wm. Wallace Lee. Meriden, Conn., Republican pub. co., 1897.
100 p. illus. 23½ cm. Rc-3214. F104. B2 L5

BARKHAMSTED. Historical address at the dedication of the Soldiers' monument in Barkhamsted ... 1897 ... By William Wallace Lee. Meriden, Conn., Republican pub. co., 1899. 8 p. front. (port.)
8°. 1-7733-M1. F104. B2 L54

BERLIN and Cromwell, Directory for the towns of ... incl. a list of farmers and rural free delivery routes, 1914 - West Lynn, Mass. and Hartford, Conn., Clark-Delano co. v. 24 cm. 14-9394.
Directories

BERLIN, Cromwell and Rocky Hill directory ... 19   Winthrop, Mass., C. H. Dunham, 19
   v.   23½ cm.   CA 30-690 Unrev.   Directories

BERLIN, The early history of; an historical paper delivered before the Emma Hart Willard chapter,
D. A. R. by Emily S. Brandegee. (Berlin? Conn., 1913)   14 p.   22½ cm.   15-2021.   F104. B4 B8

BERLIN, History of, by Catharine M. North, rearranged and ed. with foreword by Adolph Burnette
Benson ... New Haven, The Tuttle, Morehouse & Taylor co., 1916.   xiii, 294 p. front., plates, ports.
25 cm.   Includes several chapters relating to family history.   16-23069.   F104. B4 N86

BETHANY. ... Proctor & Way's Bethany and Woodbridge, Conn., directory ... New Haven, Conn.,
Proctor & Way, 19   v. fold. map. 23½ cm. CA 28-43 Unrev.   Directories

BETHANY and its hills; glimpses of the town of Bethany as it was before the railroads and the fire fiend
robbed it of its glory, by Mrs. Eliza J. Lines ... New Haven, The Tuttle, Morehouse and Taylor co.,
1905.   viii, 65 p. front., illus., plates, ports. 24 cm. Includes genealogical sketches. 16-23105.   F104.B45L75

BETHANY sketches and records.   Comp. and pub. by William C. Sharpe ... Seymour (Conn.) Record
print, 1908 - 13.   2 v. illus. 23 cm. Births, marriages and deaths: (pt. 1) p. 49 - 98. 8-31252 Rev.
   F014. B45 S 5

BETHEL directory, 18 -   New Haven, Conn., The Price & Lee co. (18   v. 24 cm.
31-3118.   Directories

BETHLEM, 1812, and Watertown, 1801. (Hartford) Acorn Club of Conn., 1961)   32 p. 24 cm.
   F104. B17 B4

BLACK ROCK, History of, 1644 - 1955, compiled by Ivan O. Justinius for Black Rock Civic and Business
Men's Club, inc., Bridgeport, Conn. Bridgeport, Conn., Antoniak Print. Service (1955)   171 p.
illus. 27 cm. 55-31926.   F104. B52 J8

BLACK ROCK, seaport of old Fairfield, 1644 - 1870; pages of history gathered by Cornelia Penfield
Lathrop ... icnl. the Journal of Wm. Wheeler ... with maps, illus. & genealogies, fully indexed.
New Haven, Conn., The Tuttle, Morehouse & Taylor co., 1930.   xi, 214 p. front., illus. (incl. facsim.)
plates, maps. 24½ cm. 30-18188 Rev. Includes bibliographies.   F104. B52 L35

BOLTON, A historical sketch of, for the Bolton bicentennial celebration, 1920 ... By Samuel Morgan
Alvord. (Manchester, Conn., The Herald print., 1920)   5 - 29 p. 4 pl. 22 cm. 20-18483.
   F104. B55 A47

BOLTON. Vital records of Bolton to 1854 and Vernon to 1852. Hartford, Conn. historical soc., 1909.
xxii, 291 p. 24 cm. (Vital records of Connecticut. Series I, Towns I) The town of Vernon was set off from the town of Bolton in 1808)
10-6048.   F104. B55 B5
   L H & G

BOLTON'S heritage; historical sketches of Bolton. Ed. Bruce G. Ronson for the Bolton Historians.
Essex, Conn., Pequot Press 1970.   viii, 220 p. illus. 24 cm.   F104.B55 R6

BOZRAH. An impartial relation of the hail-storm on the 15th of July and the tornado on the 2d of
August 1799. Which appeared in the towns of Bozrah, Lebanon, and Franklin, To which is annexed
an estimate of the damages done by the storm, made by a committee from said towns. Norwich, Print.
J. Trumbull, 1799.   30 p. 20½ cm. Preface signed: Elijah Hyde (and others) 11-3993.   F104. B6 I 3
   Rare Book Coll.

BRANFORD directory ... 1895. New Haven, Conn., The Price & Lee co., 1895 - 19   v. fold. maps.
23½ cm. 10-11224 Rev.   Directories

BRANFORD. Baptisms ... copied from Branford church records ... commencing 1688. (b. p., 1925?)
61 numb. l. 28 x 21½ cm. Autographed from type-written copy. Covers the years 1688 to 1786. 25-25165.   F104.B63 B7

CONNECTICUT

BRANFORD. Old Branford, compiled by John C. Carr from material furnished by the Historical research committee for the Branford tercentenary ... (Branford, Conn., The Branford printing co., 1935) 48 p. plan, fold. map. 23 cm. 35-20346. F104.B63 C3

BRANFORD. The past and the present, in the secular and religious history of the Congregational church and society of Branford. A semi-centennial discourse ... by the Rev. Timothy P. Gillett. New Haven, Morehouse & Taylor, printers, 1858. 32 p. front. (port.) 23½ cm. 34-21947. F104.B63 G5

BRANFORD. A history of the First church and society of Branford, 1644-1919, by J. Rupert Simonds. New Haven, Conn., The Tuttle, Morehouse & Taylor co. (1919) viii, 191 p. front., plates, ports. 20 cm. 19-17803. F104.B63 S5

BRIDGEPORT city directory, incl. Stratford, Fairfield and Southport, 18   (Bridgeport) The Price and Lee co., 1865 - 19   v. fold. maps. 19½ - 24 cm. 1-13964 Rev. Directories

BRIDGEPORT. American directory & publishing co.'s Standard city directory of Bridgeport, incl. Milford, Stratford, Fairfield, Southport, and Long Hill. 1895 -   (v. 1) - (Bridgeport) American directory and pub. co., 1895 -   v. fold. map. 24 cm. 18-10880. Directories

BRIDGEPORT. ... Proctor & Way's Bridgeport, Conn., suburban directory: Easton, Monroe, Trumbull, Weston ... 1927/28 -   New Haven, Conn., Proctor & Way, 1927 - v. fold. map. 23½ cm. CA 28-44 Unrev. Directories

BRIDGEPORT city, business and street directory ... 189-   Bridgeport, Conn., American directory & pub. co., 189-   v. fold. map. 23 cm. CA 33-743 Unrev. Directories

BRIDGEPORT, (EAST) The Creaton pub. company's East Bridgeport directory and buyers guide ... Bridgeport, Conn., The Creaton pub. co. (19 -   v. illus. 23 cm. CA 35-813 Unrev. Directories

BRIDGEPORT. Glimpses of Bridgeport. Introd. by Zalmon Goodsell, under the authority of the Board of trade ... Bridgeport, Conn., Press of the Marigold print. co., 1898. (64) p. illus. (incl. ports.) 15 x 23½ cm. Rc-3216. F104. B7 B7

BRIDGEPORT. Year book of the Bridgeport Board of trade ... 1905. (Bridgeport, Conn.) 1905. 25½ cm. F104. B7 B73

BRIDGEPORT. The bi-centennial celebration of the First Congregational church and society of Bridgeport ... 1895. New Haven, The Tuttle, Morehouse & Taylor press, 1895. 234 p. front. (port.) plates. 26 cm. Ed. by C. R. Palmer. 10-14403. F104. B7 B74

BRIDGEPORT. The Polish-Americans of Bridgeport, a social survey, by Ilona Aszody (and others) The sociology colloquium in cooperation with Dept. of Sociology, University of Bridgeport. (Bridgeport, Conn.) 1960. 47 p. F104.B7 B745

BRIDGEPORT. 25th anniversary ed. of the Bridgeport post. 1883 - 1908. (Bridgeport, 1908) 80 p. illus. 55 cm. 9-11767. F104. B7 B75

BRIDGEPORT. The Bridgeport telegram fifteenth anniversary and prosperity edition. Supplement ... (Bridgeport, Conn., 1910) 64 p. illus. 43 cm. 13-9651. F104. B7 B77

BRIDGEPORT. The story of Bridgeport, by Elsie Nicholas Danenberg; illus. by Jess Benton. (Bridgeport, Conn.) The Bridgeport centennial, inc. (1936) 4, 11-176 p. illus. (incl. ports., maps) 31 cm. Bibliography: p. 149. 36-20856 Rev. F104. B7 D3

BRIDGEPORT, 1836, originally Pequonnock, 1639. Prepared by the Mary Silliman chapter, D.A.R., for the Bridgeport tercentenary committee. (Bridgeport, Conn., Bridgeport life press, 1935) (8) p. double map. 22½ cm. 38-4582. F104.B7 D36

BRIDGEPORT, Guide to the city of ... Pub. quarterly by C. H. R. Miller ... New Haven, C. H. R. Miller, 1885.   v.   32° 1-Rc-3217.   F104. B7 G9

BRIDGEPORT.   Pioneers and patriots of Pequannock, 1636 - 1799, by William Willard Roberts, as a genealogical guide and souvenir of Connecticut's tercentenary ... Bridgeport, Conn. (Priv. print.) 1935.   (16) p. illus. (double map) 22 cm. 36-3265.   F104.B7 R63

BRIDGEPORT and vicinity, Views of.   (Portland, Me., L. H. Nelson co., 1906)   (32) p. illus. 20 ½ x 25 cm.   F104. B7 V6

BRIDGEPORT.   The Standard's history of Bridgeport.   The institutions of the city - its growth from small beginnings - the contrasts of the present with the past - the promise of the future ... comp. George Curtis Waldo.   (Bridgeport) The Standard assoc., 1897.   (v) - viii, 203 p. front., illus. (incl. maps) plates, ports. 30 ½ x 23 cm. Rc-3218.   F104. B7 W2

BRIDGEPORT and vicinity, History of, ed. by George C. Waldo, jr. ... New York, Chicago, The S. J. Clarke pub. co., 1917.   2 v. front., plates, ports. 27 ½ cm. Vol. 2 contains biographical sketches. Includes one chapter each on the towns of Stratford and Fairfield. 18-21395.   F104.B7 W24

BRIDGEPORT.   Rambles about Bridgeport and vicinity.   Drives, views, parks, attractions, places of interest, prominent manufactories, business houses, etc.   Presented by the Board of trade.   Ed. of 1875.   Bridgeport, Conn., J. A. Chickering (1875)   32 p. 24° 1-Rc-3219.
F104. B7 W5

BRISTOL, Plainville and Terryville directory, 1882 -   (v. 1 -   New Haven, Conn,, The Price & Lee co., 1882 - 19   v. fold. maps. 24 cm. 0-1773-Rev.   Directories

BRISTOL.   Our Yankee heritage: the making of Bristol.   By Carleton Beals.   (Bristol, Conn.) Bristol Pub. Library Assoc., 1954.   331 p. illus. 24 cm. Includes bibliography. 54-39492.   F104. B8 B4

BRISTOL.   Programme and addresses delivered at the 150th anniversary of the First Congregational church, Bristol, Oct. 12th, 1897 ... (Bristol, Conn., Press print, 1897)   75 p. illus. 22 cm. 6-40427.   F104. B8 B8

BRISTOL ("In the olden time New Cambridge") which includes Forestville.   Hartford, Conn., City print. co., 1907.   711 p. incl. front., illus., plates. col. pl. 24 cm. Pub. by Eddy N. Smith (and others) 9-12872.
F104. B8 B82

BRISTOL.   Centennial celebration of the incorporation of the town of Bristol, 1885.   Comp. by John J. Jennings.   Hartford, Conn., Press of the Case, Lockwood & Brainard co., 1885.   109 p. 1 illus., fold. plan. 23 cm. Rc-3220.   F104. B8 J 5

BRISTOL.   Four half-centuries in Bristol: 1735 - 1785, 1785 - 1835, 1835 - 1885, 1885 - 1935.   An address delivered by Epaphroditus Peck, at the celebration of the 150th anniversary of the incorporation of the town of Bristol... 1935.   (Bristol, 1935)   16 p. 23 cm. 35-12868.
F104.B 8 P28

BRISTOL.   A history of Bristol, by Apaphroditus Peck.   Hartford, Conn., The Lewis street bookshop, 1932.   xiv, 362 p. front., illus. (incl. map) plates. 21 ½ cm. 32-28954.   F104. B8 P29

BRISTOL.   Historical sketch of the Congregational society and church in Bristol.   With the articles of faith, covenant, and standing rules of the church.   Together with a catalogue of members since its gathering ...   (By Tracy Peck) Hartford, Print. D. B. Moseley, 1852.   91 p. 19 ½ cm. 6-15337.
F104. B8 P3

BRISTOL.   The Tories of Chippeny Hill; a brief account of the Loyalists of Bristol, Plymouth and Harwinton, who founded St. Matthew's church in East Plymouth in 1791, by E. Le Roy Pond.   New York, The Grafton press, 1909.   5, (9) - 92 p. front., plates, port., map. 19 ½ cm. At the time of the revolution, this region belonged to Farmington and Waterbury, Conn. Bibliography: p. (91) - 92. 10-1163.   F104. B8 P7

CONNECTICUT

BRISTOL. Souvenir history of the town of Bristol. Facts relative to its health, wealth and prosperity, together with statements showing its remarkable growth within the past few years and its present importance in the mercantile world ... Meriden, Conn., Journal pub. co., 1897. 79, (4) p. incl. illus., ports. 35 cm. 6-8179. F104. B8 S7

BROOKFIELD, Annals of, written and pub. by Emily C. Hawley ... Brookfield, Conn., 1929. xiv, 656 p. front., plates, map. 26 cm. 30-13. F104.B85 H4

BROOKLYN. A history of the equestrian statue of Israel Putnam, at Brooklyn, Conn. Reported to the General assembly, 1889. Hartford, Conn., Press of Case, Lockwood & Brainard co., 1888. 64 p. 2 pl., port. 23 cm. 3-28349. F104.B9 P99

BURLINGTON; historical address delivered by Epaphroditus Peck at the centennial celebration on June 16, 1906. Bristol, Conn., Bristol press pub. co. (1906) 36, (2) p. illus. 23½ cm. 6-34778. F104.B96 P3

CANTERBURY. Records of the Congregational church in Canterbury, 1711 - 1844, pub. jointly by the Conn. historical soc. and the Soc. of Mayflower descendants in the state of Conn. Hartford (Press of Finlay brothers) 1932. xii. 217 p. front.(port.) 24½ cm. Introd. signed Albert C. Bates. 33-27870. F104.C18 C2

CANTON CENTER. Historical sketch of the Congregational church and parish of Canton Center, formerly West Simsbury. Organized 1750. Comp. by Rev. Frederick Alvord and Miss Ida R. Gridley. Hartford, Conn., Press of the Case, Lockwood & Brainard co., 1886. 96 p. 23 cm. 17-24558. F104. C2 A4

CANTON. Reminiscences, by Sylvester Barbour, a native of Canton. Fifty years a lawyer, and appendix, containing a list of the officers and members, and a copy of the by-laws of the Phoebe Humphrey chapter, D.A.R. of Collinsville, Conn. Hartford, The Case, Lockwood & Brainard co., 1908. vi, (11) - 166 p. plates, ports. 23½ cm. Previously pub. in the Hartford times. 8-23893. F104. C2 B2

CANTON. Genealogical history, with short sketches and family records of the early settlers of West Simsbury, now Canton, Conn., by Abiel Brown, with an introductory and commendatory notice by Rev. J. Burt. Hartford, Press of Case, Tiffany and co., 1856. 151 p. 23½ cm. 10-22036. F104. C2 B7

— New York, re-printed, 1899. 151 p. 24 cm. 1-5426. F104. C2 B8

CANTON. ... Celebration at Collinsville, by the inhabitants of the town of Canton, of the 100th anniversary of the independence of the U. S. of America, July 4th, 1876 ... (Hartford, Print. Fowler, Miller, 1877) 3, (9) - 24 p. 21½ cm. 1-16818. F104. C2 C2

CHESHIRE, History of, from 1694 to 1840, including Prospect, which, as Columbia parish, was a part of Cheshire until 1829; comp. and written by Joseph Perkins Beach. Cheshire, Conn., Lady Fenwick chapter, D.A.R., 1912. 574 p. front. (port.) illus. 24 cm. 12-22245. F104. C5 B3

CHESHIRE. Old historic homes of Cheshire, with an account of the early settlement of the town, descriptions of its churches, academy and old town cemetery, places of interest - Roaring brook, Scott's rock, barytes and copper mines, ancient trees, etc. Comp. by Edwin R. Brown. Illus. by John R. Paddock. (New Haven, Conn., Press of C. H. Ryder) 1895. 138 p. incl. plates, ports. 21 x 27 cm. Rc-3221 Rev. F104.C5 B8

CHESHIRE. The history of Cheshire Street and vicinity, as compiled by Edmond and Alice R. Brodeur during 1969 - 71. (Cheshire, Conn., 1971) 51 p. illus. 28 cm. F104. C5 H5

CHESTER. Old homes of Chester; researches, photography and description of the homes, by Theodore Foster; historic sketch and editing by Gertrude C. Lowe. (West Haven, Conn.) O. K. Walker, 1936. (92) p. illus. (incl. coat of arms) fold. map. 23½ cm. 37-19338. F104.C53 F6

CLINTON. Hommonossit Plantation; a history of Clinton, by Susan Reischmann Balestracci. Illus. by Mable L. K. Stevens. (1st ed.) Guildford, Conn., Quarters Press, 1967. 172, (4) p. 24 cm. F104.C55 B3

CLINTON. Two hundredth anniversary of the Clinton Congregational church, held in Clinton ... 1867. New Haven, Tuttle, Morehouse & Taylor, steam printers, 1868.   54 p.   front., 2 pl.   23½ cm.   9-14001.
   F104.C55 C6

COLCHESTER. Extracts from the records of Colchester, with some transcripts from the recording of Michaell Taintor ... Transcribed by Charles M. Taintor. Hartford, Press of Case, Lockwood, 1864.   156 p.   18 cm.   2-5181 Rev.
   F104. C6 C6

— An index to Taintor's Colchester records, with genealogical matter alphabetically arranged for easy reference. Comp. by James Knox Blish. Kewanee, Ill., Kewanee verdict steam print, 1901.   42 p.   18 cm.   2-5181 Rev.
   F104.C6 C65
   L H & G

COLCHESTER. An historical address delivered at the celebration of the 200th anniversary of the First church of Christ, in Colchester ... 1903, by Edward M. Day ... Hartford, Conn., Becher & Eitel, printers and bookbinders (1903)   36 p.   23 cm.   7-34812.
   F104. C6 D2

COLEBROOK, The history of, by Irving E. Manchester, and other papers. (Winsted, Conn., The Citizen printing co.) 1935.   208 p.   plates, map.   23½ cm.   Bibliography: p. 141.   35-22997.
   F104.C62 M3

COLUMBIA. The 150th anniversary of the organization of the Congregational church in Columbia ... 1866. Historical papers, addresses, with appendix. Hartford, Print, Case, Lockwood, 1867.   iv, (5) - 96 p.   illus. (facsim.)   22½ cm.   5-1313.
   F104.C65 C6

COLUMBIA, the story of. Congregational Shurch. Women's Guild. Columbia (1954)   80 p.   illus.   24 cm.   Includes bibliography.   54-34195.
   F104.C65C63

CORNWALL. A true state of the rise and progress of the controversy in Cornwall: which has been misrepresented by Major John Sedgwick, in a late publication, called An impartial narrative of the proceedings of nine ministers, in the town of Cornwall, etc. By Hezekiah Gold ... Hartford, Print. Hudson and Goodwin, 1783.   24 p.   19 cm.   21-18628.
   F104. C7
   BX7260.G56A3

CORNWALL, Historical records of the town of. Coll. and arranged by Theodore S. Gold. Hartford, Press of the Case, Lockwood & Brainard co., 1877.   339 p.   front., illus., plates, ports. (part mounted) 23 cm.   Rc-3223.
   F104. C7 G6
   Rare Book Coll.

— 2d ed.   1904.   (5)-489 p.   front. plates, ports.   23 cm.   L. C. copy replaced by microfilm.   5-18322.
   F104. C7 G61
   Microfilm 8868 F

CORNWALL. Memorial day exercises in memory of Gen. John Sedgwick, Cornwall. May 30, 1892. Hartford, Conn., Press of the Case, Lockwood & Brainard co., 1892.   35 p.   pl., port.   23 cm. (With Historical Records, 1904, above)   5-18324.
   F104.G7 G61
   Microfilm 8868 F

CORNWALL. Funeral services of Gen. John Sedgwick, Cornwall, May 15th, 1864. Utica, N. Y., Utica state hospital press, 1893.   23 p.   23 cm. (With historical records, 1904, above) 5-18325.
   F104.G7 G61
   Microfilm 8868 F

CORNWALL, A history of, a typical New England town, by Edward C. Starr. (New Haven, Conn., The Tuttle, Morehouse & Taylor co.) 1926.   547 p.   plates, ports.   26 cm.   "Biographical": p. (249) - 390; 525-526. "Genealogical": p. (421) - 523.   26-23697.
   F104. C7 S8

COVENTRY. Births, marriages, baptisms and deaths, from the records of the town and churches in Coventry, 1711 - 1844; copies from the records by Susan Whitney Dimock. Print. for private distribution. New York, The Baker & Taylor co., 1897.   vii, 301 p.   24½ cm.   4-20153.
   F104.C75 D5
   L H & G

CONNECTICUT

COVENTRY, Historic sketch of, prepared by Maude Gridely Peterson on the occasion of the 200th anniversary of the incorporation of the town and of the organization of the First Congregational church. Bicentennial poem, by Ruth Amelia Higgins. Official program, Old home week bicentennial celebration ... 1912. (Coventry? Conn., 1912) 50 p. front. (fold. facsim.) illus. (incl. ports.) 21½ cm. 13-5136.
F104. C75 P4

CROMWELL. Middletown Upper Houses; a history of the north society of Middletown ... 1650 to 1800, with genealogical and biographical chapters on early families and a full genealogy of the Ranney family, by Charles Collard Adams ... New York, The Grafton press, 1908. xxv, 847 p. front., illus., plates, ports., facsims. 24 cm. 8-16493.
F104. C8 A2

CROMWELL, History of, a sketch by Rev. M. S. Dudley ... Middletown, Constitution office, 1880. 36 p. 22½ cm. Rc-3224 Rev.
F104. C8 D8

CROMWELL. History of the First church in Cromwell, 1715 - 1915; ed. by the Rev. Homer Wesley Hildreth, minister. (Middletown, Conn., Press of J. D. Young, 1915) iii, 65 p. front. 23½ cm. 22-6281.
F104. C8 H6

CROMWELL. Founders, fathers and patriots of Middletown Upper Houses; since 1851, Cromwell, & Conn. Pub. by the Ranney memorial and historical assoc. Cromwell, Conn. Middletown, Conn., The Stewart print., 1903. (24) p. illus., ports. 23 cm. 5-37642.
F104. C8 R2

CROMWELL. ... Friday, 17 June, 1904, Bunker Hill day. Ranney memorial and historical assoc., Cromwell. Middletown, Conn., 1904. 24½ cm.
F104. C8 R24

CROMWELL. Society of Middletown Upper Houses, inc. ... Reunion ... and dedication of memorial. (Cromwell, Conn., 1905) 23½ cm.
F104. C8 S67

CROMWELL. Society of Middletown Upper Houses, inc. (Letter to members of the society, asking for contributions) Cromwell, Conn., 1906. 24 cm.
F104. C8 S674

CROMWELL. Middletown Upper Houses. (Prospectus 1906) By C. C. Adams. 1 v.
F104. C8 S68

DANBURY. Crofutt's Danbury city directory, 1886/7 - Danbury, Conn., F. B. Crofutt, 1886 - v. 24½ cm. 10-29581 Rev.
Directories

DANBURY and Bethel directory, 1912 - 1913. (vol. 1-2) New Haven, Conn., The Price & Lee co., 1912 - . 2 v. fold. maps. 24 cm. 12-23780 Rev.
Directories

DANBURY. ... Danbury, Fairfield County, Connecticut. (By George Ancestry) (Brooklyn, 1912 - v. 19 cm. (Ancestry's genealogical series. Series B. Town records, no. 1, pt. 1 -) CA 26-412 Unrev.
F104. D2 A5

DANBURY, History of, 1684 - 1896, from notes and manuscript left by James Montgomery Bailey; comp. with additions by Susan Benedict Hill. New York, Burr print. 1896. xxii, 583 p. front., plates, ports., facsims. 27 cm. 1-Rc-3225.
F104. D2 B1

DANBURY. The Connecticut tercentenary, 1635 - 1935, and the 250th anniversary of the settlement of the town of Danbury which included the Society of Bethel, 1635-1935. A short historical sketch of the early days of both towns and program of events for the tercentennial celebration. (Danbury) Tercentenary committee (1935) 28 p. illus. (incl. port.) 23 cm. 36-28421.
F104. D2 C6

DANBURY. Landscape views of New-England. Ed. by Geo. C. Morgan. No. 1. New York, Morgan & Waterhouse, 1847. viii, (9) - 24 p. front., pl. 24½ cm. Contains two views of Danbury, and accompanying descriptive poems. 11-13697.
F104. D2 M8

DANIELSON. The Danielson directory containing ... the village of Attawaugan, Brooklyn Center, Ballouville, Dayville, Killingly, East Brooklyn, East Killingly, Elmville, Pineville, River View, etc. ... Providence, R.I., C. DeWitt White co. v. 24 cm. 13-10088.
Directories

DANIELSON directory, and surrounding villages, 1923/4 ... Attawaugan, Ballouville, Brooklyn Center, Connecticut Mills, Danielson, Dayville, East Brooklyn, East Killingly, Elmville, Goodyear, Pineville, River View, and Wauregan. no. 1 - Providence, R. I., Boston, Mass. (etc.) Samson & Murdock co., 1923 -   v.   24 cm.   23-13735.   Directories

DARIEN, Noroton and Noroton Heights directory. Providence, R. I., C. De Witt White co.
   v.   24 cm.   19-8008.   Directories

DARIEN, Town of, founded 1641, incorporated 1820, written by Henry Jay Case ... as a contribution to the Connecticut tercentenary. (Darien, Conn.) The Darien community assoc. (1935)   2, 98 p. front., plates, ports.   24 cm.   35-29168.   F104. D27C35

DARIEN Historical Society. Annual. Darien, Conn.   v.   illus.   22 cm.   56-37106.
                                                                                                                                    F104. D27 D3

DARIEN, 1641 - 1820 - 1970; historical sketches. Darien, Conn., Darien Historical Soc., (1970) viii, 123 p.   illus.   24 cm.   74-124470.   F104. D27D32

DARIEN. The story of Flatt Ridge, Darien. By Vera Colton Halstead. (New Canaan, Conn., 1949) 35 l.   illus., maps, geneal. tables.   29 cm.   Bibliography: leaf (36)   52-35580.   F104. D27 H3

DARIEN. Book of words; the pageant of Darien. The pageant of a residential community (by) William Chauncy Langdon .... (New York, The Clover press, 1913)   74 p.   23 cm.   "A study in dramatic form of the history ... of a small town within the home radius of a great metropolitan centre."   14-3989.   F104. D27 L2

DARIEN, our town; a handbook for citizens. By the League of Women Voters of Darien. Illus. by George Shellhase; map by C. Ralph Fletcher. Darien, Conn., 1949.   64 p.   illus., fold. map.   23 cm. 49-3411*.   F104. D27 L4

— (2d ed., extensively rev. Darien, Conn.) 1954.   75 p.   illus.   23 cm.   54-29255.
                                                                                                                                    F104. D27 L4
                                                                                                                                    1954

— (3d ed. extensively rev.) Darien, Conn., 1958.   84 p.   illus.   23 cm.   58-38377.
                                                                                                                                    F104. D27 L4
                                                                                                                                    1958

DARIEN. Abstract of church records of the town of Darien, from the earliest records extant to 1850. By Spencer P. Mead ... (n. p.) 1920.   2 - 135 numb. l.   27½ cm.   Type-written.   21-17537.
                                                                                                                                    F104.D27M47

DEEP RIVER; the illustrated story of a Connecticut river town, by Daniel J. Connors. Stonington, Conn., Pequot Press (1966)   vii, 70 p.   24 cm.   6-23382.   F104. D3 C6

DEEP RIVER. Saybrook's quadrimillenial. Commemoration of the 250th anniversary of the settlement of Saybrook. Hartford (Conn.) Press of Clark & Smith, 1886.   69 p.   front. (map)   23 cm. 6-34786 rev.   F104. D3 D4
                                                                                                                                    1885

DEEP RIVER. Vital records of Saybrook, 1647 - 1834. Hartford, The Connecticut Historical Society and the Conn. Society of the Order of the Founders and Patriots of America, 1952 (1948) 197 p.   25 cm.   (Vital records of Connecticut. Series I: Towns, v. 9. 7th town)   53-1795.   F104. D3 D42
                                                                                                                                    L H & G

DEEP RIVER. In the land of the patentees, Saybrook in Connecticut. Pub. by the Saybrook tercentenary committee. 2d ed. enl. (Old Saybrook, Conn.) The Acton library, 1935.   85 p.   front.   24 cm. 36-4811 rev.   F104. D3 D43
                                                                                                                                    1935

DEEP RIVER. Saybrook at the mouth of the Connecticut; the first one hundred years, by Gilman

CONNECTICUT

C. Gates. (Orange and New Haven, Press of the Wilson H. Lee co.) 1935. xii, 246 p. illus. (maps) plates.
24 cm. 35-10991. F104. D3 G33

DEEP RIVER. "Old Deep River" (town of Saybrook, Conn.) An address delivered there by Frank J. Mather.... Printed for the benefit of the Deep River public library. (Deep River, The New era press, 1914) 34 p. incl. front. (port.) 21 ½ cm. 16-10380 Rev. F104. D3 M42

DERBY, Town records of, 1655 - 1710; copied and compared with the original by Nancy O. Phillips. Derby, Sarah Riggs Humphreys chapter, D.A.R., 1901. (3) - 497 p. front. (facsim.) 26 ½ cm. 14-18942.
F104. D4 D4
L H & G

DERBY. Souvenir history of Derby and Shelton. Issued by the Evening transcript, Jan., 1896. Showing the progress of a rapidly growing community, and containing statement relative to its charming scenic attractions .... Illus. and comp. by C. B. Gillespie. Derby, Conn., The Transcript co., 1896. 71 p. illus. (incl. ports.) 34 ½ x 25 cm. 9-17545. F104. D4 G5

DERBY. The history of the old town of Derby, 1642 - 1880. With biographies and genealogies. By Samuel Orcutt ... and Ambrose Beardsley. Springfield, Mass., Press of Springfield print., 1880.
(iii) - xcvii, 844 p. front., illus., plates, ports. x 25 cm. 1-Rc-3226. F104. D4 O1

DURHAM. History of Durham, from the first grant of land in 1662 to 1866. By William Chauncy Fowler ... Pub. by the town. Hartford, Press of Wiley, Waterman & Eaton, 1866. 460 p. 23 cm.
Records of births, marriages, deaths, etc.: p. 229 - 444. Rc-3227. F104. D9 F7

EAST GRANBY. Historical sketch of Turkey Hills and East Granby. By Albert Carlos Bates. Hartford, 1949. 46 p. 26 cm. 49-4139*. F104. E1 B38

EAST GRANBY. Report of the Committee appointed by the legislature of Conn., to inspect the condition of New-Gate prison ... Hartford, C. Babcock, printer, 1825. 18 p. 24 cm. CA 16-356 Unrev.
F104. E1 C7

— Submitted, May session, 1826 ... New Haven, Print. J. Barber, 1826. 35 p. 23 cm.
CA 16-355 Unrev. F104. E1 C72

EAST GRANBY. Records of the Congregational church in Turkey Hills, now the town of East Granby, 1776 - 1858; pub. by Albert Carlos Bates ... Hartford, 1907. 158 p. 24 ½ cm. (Turkey Hills series, no. 3)
100 copies printed. 8-12259. F104. E1 E13

EAST GRANBY. A history of the copper mines and Newgate prison, at Granby. Also, of the captivity of Daniel Hayes, of Granby, by the Indians, in 1707. By Noah A. Phelps. Hartford, Case, Tiffany & Burnham, 1845. 34 p. 22 ½ cm. 1-7734. F104. E1 P4

EAST GRANBY. Newgate of Connecticut: a history of the prison, its insurrections, massacres, etc., imprisonment of the Tories, in the revolution. The ancient and recent working of its mines, etc. to which is appended a description of the state prison, at Wethersfield. By Richard H. Phelps ... Hartford, Press of E. Geer, 1844. 24 p. 22 ½ cm. 11-4715. F104. E1 P47

— 3d ed. Hartford, Press of E. Geer, 1844. 33 p. 22 cm. 11-4716. F104. E1 P48

— Albany, N.Y., J. Munsell, 1860. iv (5)-151 p. front. (port.) illus. 22 ½ x 17 ½ cm. 1-Rc-3228. F104. E1 P 5

EAST GRANBY. A history of Newgate of Connecticut (by) Richard H. Phelps. New York, Arno Press, 1969. 151 p. 23 cm. (Mass violence in America) Reprint of the 1860 ed. with a new introduction by editors of the series. 74-90189.
F104. E1 P5
1969

EAST GRANBY. Newgate of Connecticut; its origin and early history Being a full description of the famous and wonderful Simsbury mines and caverns, and the prison built over them. ... Also. An illustrated description of the state prison at Wethersfield. By Richard H. Phelps. Hartford, Conn., American pub. co., 1876. 13 - 117 p. front., illus., plates. 22 ½ cm. 11-4717. F104. E1 P52

EAST GRANBY.   Souvenir of Newgate prison, Copper hill, Conn.   (n. p., 1893)   16 pl. (incl. facsims.)
13 x 17 cm.   Rc-3229.   F104. E1 S5

— (Meriden, Conn., The Meriden gravure co., 1893)   (32) p.   illus.   12 x 16 cm.   Rc-3230.
F104. E1 S6

EAST GRANBY.   Newgate of Connecticut and other antiquities of America.   (Copper Hill, Conn.,
S. D. Viets, 1895.)   21 pl.   13 x 18½ cm.   Rc-3231 Rev.   F104. E1 S7

EAST GRANBY.   Records of the society or parish of Turkey Hills, now the town of East Granby, 1737-
1791.   Pub. by Albert Carlos Bates ...   Hartford, 1901.   78 p.   24½ cm.   (Turkey Hill series, no. 1)   100 copies
printed.   2-2719 Rev.   F104. E1 T8

EAST GRANBY.   Records of the Second school society in Granby, now the town of East Granby, 1796 -
1855; pub. by Albert Carlos Bates ...   Hartford, 1903.   47 p.   24½ cm.   (Turkey Hills series, no. 2)   100 copies
printed.   8-12260.   F104. G65 G6

EAST HADDAM.   List and record of civil war veterans.   Those who enlisted from, now reside in, or
are buried in the town of East Haddam.   The draft and other interesting incidents.   Moodus, Conn.,
The Connecticut Valley advertiser print, 1899.   35 p.   22 cm.   L.C. copy replaced by microfilm.   14-5631.
F104. E15 C4
Microfilm 2119 F

EAST HADDAM.   The story of the meeting house of the First church of Christ in East Haddam, Conn.
1794 - 1934.   (East Haddam, 1934)   (8) p.   illus.   23½ cm.   34-40380.   F104. E15E25

EAST HADDAM.   200th anniversary of the incorporation of the town of East Haddam, 1734 - 1934 ...
(East Haddam, 1934)   (4) p.   23 cm.   38M134T.   F104. E15 E3

EAST HADDAM.   The old chimney stacks of East Haddam ... by Hosford B. Niles ... New York,
Lowe & co., book and job printers, 1887.   vii, (9) - 146 p.   17½ cm.   10-21781 Rev.   F104. E15 N6

EAST HADDAM.   The Nathan Hale school house in East Haddam.   By Francis Hubert Parker.
(From the Conn. magazine.   Hartford, Conn., 1900.   v. 6, p. 243-246)   12-6387.   F104. E15 P2

EAST HAMPTON.   Early records of baptisms, marriages, deaths, and membership of the Congregational church, East Hampton (Chatham) Conn.   Middletown, Conn., Pelton & King, printers, 1900.
77 - 150 p.   23 cm.   1-16550 Rev.   F104. E17E24

EAST HAMPTON.   An historical sermon of the First church, East Hampton, preached by Rev. Joel
S. Ives ... 1876 ...   Middletown, Conn., Pelton & King, steam printers, 1876.   18 p.   23 cm.   7-12038.
F104. E17 I 9

EAST HAMPTON.   Yankee township (by) Carl F. Price.   East Hampton, Conn., Citizens' welfare club,
(1941)   xi, 212 p.   front., plates, ports.   21 cm.   Bibliography of East Hampton: p. 211-212.   41-26548.   F104. E17 P7

EAST HARTFORD.   The First Congregational church, East Hartford, Conn,, 1702 - 1902.   William
Bodle Tuthill, pastor.   (Hartford, Press of the Hartford printing co., 1902)   117 p.   front., illus.,
plates, ports., facsims.   24 cm.   23-16228.   F104. E18E18

EAST HARTFORD: its history and traditions.   By Joseph O. Goodwin.   Hartford, Press of the Case,
Lockwood & Brainard co., 1879.   xv, (17) - 249 p.   23 cm.   44-24405.   F104. E18 G6

EAST HARTLAND.   (By E. P. Jones)   (1923)   1 v,   F104. E19 J 7

EAST HAVEN directory and year book for   (East Haven, Conn.) The East Haven press.
v.   20½ cm.   15-6664.   Directories

EAST HAVEN.   ... Proctor & Way's East Haven town directory ...   New Haven, Conn., Proctor &
Way, 19   v.   illus., fold. map.   23½ cm.   CA 27-132 Unrev.   Directories

666

CONNECTICUT

EAST HAVEN. The East-Haven register: in three parts. Part I. Containing a history of the town ... 1644, to ... 1800 ... Part II. Containing an account of the names marriages, and births, of the families which first settled, or which have resided in East-Haven, from its settlement in 1644, to the year 1800. Part III. Containing an account of the deaths in the families named in the second part, from the year 1647 to the end of the year 1823. Comp. by Stephen Dodd ... New-Haven, Pub. for the author, and sold by A. H. Maltby & co., 1824. 200 p. 18½ cm. Rc-3232. F104. E2 D6

EAST HAVEN. A confession of faith, covenant, constitution and rules of practice; adopted by the Congregational church in East Haven. To which is added a catalogue of the officers and members of the church, 1775 - 1833. New Haven, Print. H. Howe, 1833. 24 p. 18½ cm. (With The East Haven register, above. 17-21044. F104. E2 D6

EAST HAVEN. Historical discourse delivered at the centennial celebration of the dedication of the Stone meeting house ... 1874. By D. William Havens. New Haven, Print. Punderson & Crisand, 1876. 88 p. front. 22½ cm. 27-11121. F104. E2 H2

EAST HAVEN. East Haven register, containing an account of the names, marriages, and births of the families which settled, or which have resided in East Haven, from its settlement in 1644 to the year 1800. By Rev. Stephen Dodd. Being an appendix to the History of East Haven, comp. by Sarah E. Hughes. New Haven, Conn., The Tuttle Morehouse & Taylor press, 1910. 168 p. front. (port.) map. 23½ cm. (With History of East Haven, below) Reprint, containing pts. 2-3 only of the original edition (New Haven, 1824) Part of the chapters of pt. 1 of that edition are reprinted in The History of East Haven, by Sarah E. Hughes, 1908 (below) A 18-904 Rev. F104. E2 H8

EAST HAVEN. History of East Haven, by Sarah E. Hughes. Initial drawings by Margery E. Thompson. New Haven, Conn., The Tuttle, Morehouse & Taylor press, 1908. (xiv) 324 p. front. (port.) 17 pl. 23½ cm. "The present work is merely a revision of Mr. Dodd's East Haven register with some chapters eliminated. ... in their place, events of local interest since 1824 have been added. Bound with above. A 18-905 Rev. F104. E2 H8

EAST LYME. The Thomas Lee house, East Lyme; a history and description, by Celeste E. Bush and Norman Morrison Isham. With an introd. and postscript by William F. Sears. (Stonington, Conn., Pequote Press (1963) (15) p. 23 cm. (Connecticut booklet no. 7) 63-11126. F104. E23 B8

EAST WINDSOR, through the years, by Michael C. DeVito. Warehouse Point, Conn., East Windsor Historical Soc. (1968) v, 148, A15 p. illus. 29 cm. F104. E3 D4

EAST WINDSOR in 1806. By David McClure. (New Haven) Acorn Club of Connecticut, 1949. 26 p. 24 cm. (Acorn club of Connecticut. 19th publication. Connecticut towns) 49-4854*. F104. E3 M3

EAST WINDSOR. History of the First ecclesiastical society in East Windsor, from its formation in 1752, to the death of its second pastor, Rev. Shubael Bartlett, in 1854 .... Hartford, Press of Case, Tiffany and co., 1857. 136 p. 20 cm. Published anonymously. (Azel Stevens Roe) 6-43556. F104. E3 R6

EAST WINDSOR. "Windsor Farmes." A glimpse of an old parish, together with the deciphered inscriptions from a few foundation stones of a much abused theology, by John A. Stoughton. Hartford (Conn.) Clark & Smith, printers, 1883. x, (9) - 150 p. front., fold. map, facsims. 27 cm. Windsor Farms was the early name of the present town of East Windsor, Conn. "Edwards family": p. (146) - 148. Rc-3325 Rev. F104. E3 S9

ELLSWORTH. A gossip about a country parish of the hills and its people, ed. by its pastor, G. F. Goodenough, a century after its birth, Ellsworth. (Amenia, N.Y., Times press) 1900. 129 p. front., plates. 23½ cm. "Family records": p. (71) - 129. 15-18151. F104. E37 G6

ENFIELD, Thompsonville, Hazardville, Suffield and Somers, directory (1901) - Springfield, Mass., H. A. Manning co. (1901) - v. fold. maps. 23½ cm. 8-12124 Add. (v. 1) - Directories

ENFIELD-Suffield directory ... Springfield, Mass., H. A. Manning, 1906 - 1909. 2 v. front. (fold. map) 23½ cm. 7-4178. Directories

ENFIELD. The history of Enfield ... Compiled from all the public records of the town known to exist, covering from the beginning to 1850 ... with the graveyard inscriptions and those Hartford, Northampton and Springfield records which refer to the people of Enfield. Ed. and pub. by Francis

Olcott Allen ... Lancaster, Pa., The Wickersham print., 1900.   3 v.   pl., fold. plan, 3 facsim. (1 fold.) 26 cm.
Paged continuously: v. 1: x, 11 - 912, lviii p;   v.2: 913 - 1904, cxxv p.;   v.3: 1905 - 2653, lxxxix p.   1-3311 Add.

F104. E4 A4

ENFIELD.   Official program of the 250th anniversary celebration of the town of Enfield ... 1930.
(Thompsonville, Conn., Press of H. C. Brainard, 1930)   40 p.   plates, ports.   24 cm.   31-9465.

F104. E4 E41

ENFIELD.   Studies in the history of Enfield (by) Henry F. Fletcher.   Litchfield, Conn., Print. the
Enquirer press (1934)   3 - 26 numb. l.   28 cm.   Includes "References".   "A sketch of the history of East Wallop": leaves 18-26.
34-35127.

F104. E4 F5

ENFIELD.   Historical sketch of the town of Enfield, compiled under the direction of the committee of
arrangements for celebrating the centennial anniversary of our independence ... 1876.   By A. Johnson
and others.   Hartford, The Case, Lockwood & Brainard co., printers, 1876.   26 p.   23 cm.   Rc-3233.

F104. E4 J 6

ESSEX.   Portrait of Essex.   Photos. by Joseph C. Farber.   Text by Marie Moore.   Barre, Mass.,
Barre Publishers, 1969.   94 p.   illus.   69-12343.

F104. E8 F3

FAIR HAVEN.   Historical sketch of old Fair Haven with additional notes ... (By Curtis Clark Bushnell)
New Haven, Press of J. T. Hathaway, 1916.   24 p.   20 ½ cm.   16-17943.

F104. F18 B9

FAIRFIELD.   The completion of two centuries; a discourse preached in Fairfield ... 1839.   By
Lyman H. Atwater, pastor of the First church in Fairfield.   Bridgeport, Conn., Standard office, 1839.
15 p.   23 cm.   11-34830.

F104. F2 A8

FAIRFIELD.   Early recollections of Fairfield life, by William Burr.   (Fairfield? Conn., 1913?)
(11) p.   23 ½ x 13 ½ cm.   20-7034.

F104. F2 B89

FAIRFIELD.   ... Fairfield, ancient and modern; a brief account, historic and descriptive, of a
famous Connecticut town, prepared in commemoration of the 270th anniversary of the town's settlement, by Frank Samuel Child ... (Farifield, Conn.) Fairfield historical soc., 1909.   75 p.   front.,
30 pl.   20 ½ cm.   Bibliography: p. 71 - 73.   9-9263.

F104. F2 C46

FAIRFIELD.   An historic mansion, being an account of the Thaddeus Burr homestead, Fairfield,
Conn., 1654 - 1915, by Frank S. Child.   (n. p., 1915)   27 p.   6 pl.   20 cm.   15-19439.

F104. F2 C48

FAIRFIELD.   An old New England town; sketches of life, scenery, character, by Frank Samuel
Child ... New York, C. Scribner's sons, 1895.   xvi, 230 p.   front. (port.) plates.   19 ½ cm.   2-10407.

F104. F2 C5

FAIRFIELD.   A country parish; ancient parsons and modern incidents, by Frank Samuel Child ...
New York, Boston (etc.) The Pilgrim Press (1911)   4, vii-ix, 251 p.   front., plates.   19 cm.   12-882.

F104. F2 C52

FAIRFIELD.   ... Fairfield, Connecticut tercentenary, 1639 - 1939; compiled by Historical publications committee, Elizabeth L. Child, chairman.   Fairfield, Conn., Fairfield tercentenary committee,
1940.   viii, 78 p.   front., illus. (incl. maps, plans) plates, ports.   23 cm.   40-34255.

F104. F2 F3

FAIRFIELD.   History and genealogy of the families of old Fairfield ... Comp. D. L. Jacobus ...
1930.   v.

F104. F2J 17

FAIRFIELD.   This is Fairfield 1639 - 1940; pages from 301 years of the town's brilliant history.
By Elizabeth Banks MacRury.   (1st ed., Fairfield? Conn., 1960)   270 p.   60-43305.

F104. F2 M34

FAIRFIELD. The old burying ground of Fairfield. A memorial of many of the early settlers in Fairfield, and an exhaustive and faithful transcript of the inscriptions and epitaphs on the 583 tombstones found in the oldest burying ground now within the limits of Fairfield ... By Kate E. Perry, also an account of the "rebuilding of the tombs," ... by Wm. A. Beers. Hartford, Conn., American pub. co., 1882.   241 p.   plates.   22 cm.   Rc-3234.   F104. F2 P4

FAIRFIELD. The history of Fairfield ... from the settlement of the town in 1639 to 1818, by Mrs. Elizabeth Hubbell Schenck ... New York, The author, 1889 - 1905.   2 v.   map.   24½ cm.   No more pub. 1-Rc-3235 Add.   F104. F2 S3

FARMINGTON. ... Farmington, one of the mother towns of Connecticut. (By Quincy Blakely) (New Haven) Pub. for the Tercentenary commission by the Yale university press, 1935.   29, (3) p. plates. 23 cm.   (Tercentenary pamphlet series xxviii)   "Bibliographical note": p. 29.   35-28347 Rev.   F104. F4 B6

FARMINGTON. Farmington, the village of beautiful homes. Photographic reproductions, illustrating every home in the town. Prominent people past and present, all of the school children, local antiques, Farmington, Conn. (A. L. Brandegee and E. N. Smith) 1906.   212 p. incl. front. (facsim.) illus., pl. 32 cm. A collection of articles by various writers.   7-13937.   F104. F4 B8

FARMINGTON. The Tories of Chippeny Hill; a brief account of the Loyalists of Bristol, Plymouth and Harwinton, who founded St. Matthew's church in East Plymouth in 1791, by E. Le Roy Pond. New York, The Grafton press, 1909.   (9) - 92 p.   front., plates, port., map.   19½ cm.   At the time of the revolution, this region belonged to Farmington and Waterbury, Conn.   Bibliography: P. (91) - 92.   10-1163.   F104. B8 P7

FARMINGTON. Sketches of the early settlements of the Plymouth colony. Historical, biographical and anecdotical. By Egbert Cowles. New Britain, Conn., Press of Adkins print., 1880.   51 p. 22 cm. 12-2903.   F104. F4 C8

FARMINGTON. The Farmington magazine.   v. 1-2; Nov. 1900 - Oct. 1902. Farmington, Conn., 1900 - 02.   2 v. in 1.   illus., pl., port.   25½ cm.   Monthly, 1900 - Oct. 1901; quarterly, Dec. 1901-1902.   No more pub. 3-3531.   F104. F4 F4

FARMINGTON. An historical address delivered at the opening of the village library of Farmington ... 1890, by Julius Gay. Hartford, Conn., The Case, Lockwood & Brainard co., printers, 1890. 19 p. 2 pl. 22½ cm.   (His historical addresses no. 1)   18-15756.   F104. F4G25 or 287

FARMINGTON. Farmington in the war of the revolution; an historical address delivered at the annual meeting of the Village library company ... by Julius Gay. Hartford, Conn., Press of the Case, Lockwood & Brainard co., 1893.   28 p.   22½ cm.   1-13370 Rev.   F104. F4G27 or 287

FARMINGTON. Farmington papers (by) Julius Gay. (Hartford) Priv. print. (The Case, Lockwood & Brainard co.) 1929.   5 - 338 p.   front., illus., plates, port., facsims.   21½ cm.   29-16006.   F104. F4G276

FARMINGTON. Farmington soldiers in the colonial wars; an historical address delivered at the annual meeting of the Village library co. ... by Julius Gay. Hartford, Conn., Press of the Case, Lockwood & Brainard co., 1897.   22 p.   22½ cm.   1-13371.   F104. F4 G28

FARMINGTON. Farmington 200 years ago; an historical address .... By Julius Gay. (Hartford, Conn.) The Case, Lockwood & Brainard co., 1904.   20p.   22½ cm.   5-32121 Rev.   F104. F4G285

FARMINGTON. Farmington 200 years ago; a paper read at a meeting of the Colonial dames of Conn ... by Julius Gay. (Hartford, Conn.) Hartford press: The Case, Lockwood & Brainard co., 1906. 14 p.   23 cm.   9-21190.   F104. F4G286

FARMINGTON. (Historical addresses delivered at the annual meeting of the Village library co. ... Hartford, Conn., 1890 - 19   v. in   2 facsim.   22½ cm.   F104. F4G287

— Schools and schoolmasters in Farmington in the olden time.   1892.   24 p. 22½ cm. 16-7106.
— An historical address delivered at the opening of the village library.   1890.   19 p. 2 pl. 22½ cm.   18-15756.

669

— The early industries of Farmington. 1898. 20 p. 22½ cm. 16-7105.
— Farmington local history - the canal. 1899. 20 p. 16-7109.
— Farmington soldiers in the colonial wars. 1897. 22 p. 1-13371.
— Farmington 200 years ago. 1904. 20 p. 5-32121 Rev.
— The library of a Farmington village blacksmith, 1712. 1900. 18 p. 16-9248.
— The swarming of the hive. 1903. 24 p. 16-7107.
— The Tunxis Indians. 1901. 21 p. 16-7108.

FARMINGTON. Old houses in Farmington; an historical address delivered at the annual meeting of the Village library ... by Julius Gay. Hartford, Conn., The Case, Lockwood & Brainard co., 1895. 20 p. 8°. 1-13372-M1.
F104. F4 G29

FARMINGTON. A short history of Farmington, by Lydia Hewes. (Farmington, Conn.) Farmington committee of the Connecticut tercentenary, 1935. 31 p. incl. front. fold. map. 21 cm. 35-9674.
F104. F4 H49

FARMINGTON. Farmington town clerks and their times (1645 - 1940) by Mable S. Hurlburt. (Hartford, Press of Finlay brothers, 1943) xxi, 404 p. incl. fold. front. (facsim.) plates, ports., maps (1 fold.) 24 cm. 44-37795.
F104. F4 H8

FARMINGTON. An historical discourse delivered at the celebration of the 100th anniversary of the erection of the Congregational church in Farmington. By Noah Porter ... Hartford, Case Lockwood & Brainard, print. 1873. 75 p. 22½ cm. 2-1826-M2.
F104. F4 P7

FARMINGTON. A historical discourse, delivered ... in commemoration of the original settlement of the ancient town, in 1640. By Noah Porter, jr. Hartford, L. Skinner, printer, 1841. 99 p. 22 cm. Contains biographical sketches. Rc-3236.
F104. F4 P8

FENWICK. The Western Neck, the story of Fenwick (by) Mabel Cassine Holman. (Hartford, Conn., Priv. print., The Case, Lockwood & Brainard co., 1930) 46 p. front. illus. (facsims.) 20 cm. Includes the early history of Saybrook. 30-20659.
F104. F5 H74

FRANKLIN. The celebration of the 150th anniversary of the primitive organization of the Congregational church and society, in Franklin. New Haven, Tuttle, Morehouse & Taylor, printers, 1869. 151 p. front. (fold. map) ports. 23½ cm. 2-7755.
F104. F8 F8

FRANKLIN. Records of the Congregational church, Franklin, 1718 - 1860, and a record of deaths in Norwich eighth society, 1763, 1778, 1782, 1784-1802. Pub. jointly by the Soc. of Mayflower descendants in the state of Conn., and the Soc. of the founders of Norwich, Conn. Hartford, Conn., 1938. 128 p. front. (fold. map) pl. 23½ cm. A 42-900.
F104. F8 F82

FRANKLIN. Franklin in 1800. By Samuel Nott. (New Haven) Acorn Club of Connecticut, 1949. 12 p. 24 cm. (Acorn club of Conn. 20th publication. Connecticut towns) 49-4893°.
F104. F8 N6

GLASTONBURY. Glastenbury for 200 years: a centennial discourse. With an appendix, containing historical and statistical papers of interest. By Rev. Alonzo B. Chapin, 1853. 252 p. front. (map) 23 cm. Genealogical accounts of families: p. 159 - 200. Rc-3237.
F104. G5 C4

GLASTONBURY. Glastonbury: from settlement to suburb, by Marjorie Grant McNulty. Illus. by Inez M. Hemlock and Flavia A. O'Rourke. (Glastonbury, Conn.) Woman's Club of Glastonbury, 1970. 144 p. illus. 23 cm.
F104. G5 M3

GOSHEN. History of the town of Goshen, with genealogies and biographies based upon the records of Deacon Lewis Mills Norton, by Rev. Augustine G. Hibbard ... 1897. Hartford, Conn., Press of the Case, Lockwood & Brainard co., 1897. 602 p. front., illus. (incl. facsims.) plates, ports., coat of arms. 24 cm. Genealogies of early Goshen families, p. 407-572; marriages, (1740-1786), (1820-1896) p. (573)-592. 1-Rc-3238 Add,.
F104. G6 H6

GOSHEN. Goshen in 1812. By Lewis Mills Norton. (New Haven) Acorn Club of Connecticut, 1949. 27 p. 24 cm. (Acorn Club of Conn. 21st publication. Connecticut towns) 49-4896*.
F104. G6 N6

CONNECTICUT

GOSHEN. An address delivered to the people of Goshen, at their first centennial celebration ... By Rev. Grant Powers ... Hartford, Print. E. Geer, 1839.   68 p. 20½ cm. 4-385.   F104. G6 P8

GRANBY. Records of the Second school society in Granby, now the town of East Granby, 1796 - 1855; pub. by Albert Carlos Bates ... Hartford, 1903.   47 p. 24½ cm. (Turkey Hills series, no. 2) 8-12260.
F104.G65 G6

GRANBY. The heritage of Granby, 1786 - 1965; its founding and history. (Granby, Conn., Salmon Brook Historical Soc., 1967)   ix, 180 p. 23 cm.   F104.G65 H4

GREENFIELD HILL. Celebration of Greenfield Hill. Address of welcome by Deacon N. B. Hill, reply by Rev. George W. Banks. Historical discourse delivered at the 150th anniversary of the formation of Greenfield church ... Southport, Conn., Chronicle print, 1876.   73 p. 23½ cm. 5-5131.
F104. G7 G8

GREENFIELD HILL. Ye church and parish of Greenfield; the story of an historic church in an historic town. 1725 - 1913. By George H. Merwin ... (New Haven, The Tuttle, Morehouse & Taylor press, pref. 1913)   107 p. front., plates, ports., map. facsim. 21 cm. 20-6184.   F104. G7 M5

GREENS FARMS. A sermon delivered ... by Thomas F. Davies: and pub. by request of the Congregational soc. in Green's Farms. New Haven, Print. B. L. Hamlen, 1839.   31 p. 24 cm. 23-6182.
F104.G75D25

GREENS FARMS. Greens Farms, the old West parish of Fairfield ... historical sketches and reminiscences, by George Penfield Jennings ... (Greens Farms, Conn.) The Congregational soc. of Greens Farms, 1933.   152 p. front., plates, ports., facsims. 24 cm. 33-18283.   F104.G75 J 3

GREENS FARMS. Greens Farms, the old West parish of Fairfield ... where the white man following the cattle trails "sits down and inhabits"; historical sketches and reminiscences by George Penfield Jennings. Greens Farms, Conn., Modern Books and Crafts (1971?)   152 p. illus. 24 cm.
F104.G75 J 3
1971

GREENWICH. Polk's Greenwich directory ... including Cos Cob, Glenville, Riverside, Sound Beach, Byram, Mianus and East Port Chester ...   New York, Chicago, (etc.) R. L. Polk & co., 19
v. illus. 24 cm. CA 28-1045 Unrev.   Directories

GREENWICH. An historical discourse delivered in the First Congregational church of Greenwich ....
Old Greenwich, Conn., 1879.   21 p. 24 cm. 6-38878.   F104. G8 C5

GREENWICH. Union cemetery, Greenwich. (Inscriptions) copied by Mr. William A. Eardeley ...
(Brooklyn, 1912)   36 numb. l. 27½ x 21 cm. Autographed from type-written copy. 13-5137 Rev.   F104. G8 E2

GREENWICH. Exercises at the celebration of the 150th anniversary of the Second Congregational church at Greenwich .... Including an historical discourse, by Rev. J. H. Linsley. And historical sketches and addresses from others. New York, Clark & Maynard, 1867.   vi, (7) - 108 p. front., plates.
23½ cm. 7-14891.   F104. G8 G8

GREENWICH. The old church tells her story; being the pageant, the anniversary addresses, and the historical papers of the 225th anniversary. Ed. ... Rev. Oliver Huckel. (Greenwich, Conn.) Second Congregational church, 1930.   188 p. incl. front. illus., plates, ports. 22½ cm. 31-25538.   F104. G8 G83

GREENWICH. Greenwich in 1940; being a brief historical sketch of the town with views of the principal buildings and homes in the community and including Who's who in Greenwich. Greenwich, Conn., The Greenwich press (1940)   vii, 140 p. incl. plates. 28½ x 22 cm. 41-3362.   F104. G8 G84

GREENWICH. Greenwich time. Tercentenary number. Greenwich, Conn., 1940.   24, (30) p. illus.
57½ cm. Forms v. 3, no. 209, issued June 20, 1940. 42M138T.   F104. G8 G78

GREENWICH. Greenwich old and new; a history, illus. with photos, of Greenwich, from colonial days to the present, by Lydia Holland and Margaret Leaf. Greenwich (Conn.) The Greenwich press, 1935. 6, (3) - 164, (9) p. incl. plates. 24½ cm. 35-34878. F104.G8 H65

GREENWICH. Other days in Greenwich; or, Tales and reminiscences of an old New England town, by Frederick A. Hubbard. New York, J. F. Tapley co., 1913. xviii, 346 p. incl. front., illus., plates, ports. 24 cm. 13-11328. F104. G8 H8

GREENWICH. Indian Harbor hotel. New York? 189- 14 cm. F104. G8 I 3

GREENWICH. Muskets and mansion; the Greenwich story, by Daniel Knapp. Greenwich, Conn., Fairview Printers, 1966. 239 p. 24 cm. 66-28837. F104.G8 K57

GREENWICH. A history of the town of Greenwich, with many important statistics. By Daniel M. Mead ... New York, Baker & Godwin, printers, 1857. 318 p. 19½ cm. Genealogies of several families: p. 277-318. 1-Rc-3239. F104. G8 M4

GREENWICH. Abstracts of records and tombstones of the town of Greenwich, by Spencer P. Mead ... (n. p.) 1913. 2 v. 27 x 21 cm. Type-written copy. 13-23469. F104.G8 M47
L H & G

GREENWICH. Abstract of church records of the town of Greenwich, by Spencer P. Mead ... (n. p.) 1913. 2 p. 2-188 numb. 1. 27 cm. Autographed from type-written copy. 14-4612. F104. G8 M475

GREENWICH. Ye historie of ye town of Greenwich, with genealogical notes ... by Spencer P. Mead ... being a revision, amplification and continuation of the History of the town of Greenwich, 1857, by Daniel M. Mead ... New York, The Knickerbocker press, 1911. xii, 768 p. front., plates, ports., fold. map. 25½ cm. "Genealogies": p. 489-687. 12-400. F104. G8 M5

GREENWICH. Pioneers and patriots of Greenwich in the colonies of New Netherlands, New Haven and Connecticut, 1640 - 1780, by W. Willard Roberts ... Bridgeport, Conn., 1936. (23) p. 22 cm. 36-17933. F104. G8 R6

GRISWOLD. Griswold - a history; being a history of the town of Griswold, from the earliest times to the entrance of our country into the world war in 1917, by Daniel L. Phillips. (New Haven -The Tuttle, Morehouse & Taylor co., 1929. xvi, 456 p. incl. front. plates (1 double) ports., maps (1 fold.) facsims. 23½ cm. 29-8155. F104.G82 P4

GRISWOLD. The revolutionary martyrs of ancient Pachaug. An historical paper prepared by Daniel L. Phillips ... Griswold? Conn., 1903) 15 p. 20½ cm. 3-13907. F104.G82 P5

GROTON. Historical Groton; comprising historic and descriptive sketches pertaining to Groton Heights, Center Groton, Poquonnoc Bridge, Noank, Mystic and Old Mystic, by local writers ... Charles F. Burgess, editor ... Moosup, Conn., F. F. Burgess (1909) 101 p. front., illus. 28 cm. 9-19869. F104.G84 B9

GROTON. New London County hist soc. Occasional publications. Free academy press, 1903 -
v. plates, maps. 23 cm. Contents. - v. 1. Caulkins, F.M. The stone records of Groton. 1903. 5-34606. F104.G84 C3

GROTON. The Groton story, by Carol W. Kimball. Stonington, Conn., Pequot Press (1965)
58 p. illus., map, ports. 23 cm. (Pequot town histories series, no. 1) Bibliography: p. 58. 65-20562. F104.G84 K5

GROTON, 1705 - 1905, by Charles R. Stark ... Stonington, Conn., Printed for the author by the Palmer press, 1922. viii, 444 p. front., plates, port. 23½ cm. 23-408. F104.G84 S7
Rare Book Coll.

GUILFORD. The Henry Whitfield house, Guilford. 2d ed. (By William Given Andrews) Guilford, Conn. (Shore line times print, 1909?) 12 p. illus. 20½ cm. 10-31665. F104. G9 A5

GUILFORD. Historical papers rel. to the Henry Whitfield house. Reprinted ... (New Haven, The Tuttle, Morehouse & Taylor press, 1911) 59 p. front., pl., plan. 23½ cm. 11-25762. F104. G9 C7

CONNECTICUT

GUILFORD. A discourse .... By John Elliott ... Middletown, Printed by T. & J. B. Dunning, 1802. 35, (3) p. 21 cm. With an appendix containing historical material relating to the church and town. 12-14294. F104. G9 E4

GUILFORD. Yester-years of Guilford, by Mary Hoadley Griswold. Guilford, Conn., The Shore line times pub. co. (1938) 165 p. double front., plates. 23½ cm. 38-24932. F104. G9 G7

GUILFORD. ... Proceedings at the celebration of the 250th anniversary of the settlement of Guilford. New Haven, Conn., The Stafford print., 1889. 288 p. 1 illus. 23½ cm. Rc-3240. F104. G9 G9

GUILFORD. (Guilford, The Board of trade, 1930) 25 p. illus., fold. map. 24 cm. 30-31138. F104. G9 G92

GUILFORD. Manual of the First Congregational church, Guilford, Conn. New Haven, Print. Tuttle, Morehouse & Taylor, 1875. 82p. 19 cm. 10-206. F104. G9 G94

GUILFORD. Old Guilford, including the land now constituting the towns of Guildford and Madison; drawings, text and hand lettering by Charles D. Hubbard. (Guilford, Conn., The Tercentenary committee of Guilford, 1939) 51 p. front., illus. (incl. map) 25½ cm. 39-12681. F104. G9 H83

GUILFORD. The Henry Whitfield house, 1639; the journal of the restoration of the old stone house, Guilford, by J. Frederick Kelly ... Guilford, Conn., The Henry Whitfield state historical museum, 1939. xxii, 60 p. incl. front., illus. 24½ cm. Pub. ... by the Prospect press, Hartford. 39-12680. F104. G9 K35

GUILFORD. Our heritage; an account of the coming, settlement and purposes of our forefathers; historical sermon delivered at the assembly of the Descendants of pioneers and early settlers ... 1935, by Rev. William C. H. Moe ... (Guilford, Conn., 1935) (8) p. 23½ cm. 38-34432. F104. G9 M6

GUILFORD. Guilford portraits; memorial epitaphs of Alderbrook and Westside with introductory elegies and essay, by Henry Pynchon Robinson ... 1815 - 1907. New Haven, Conn., The Pease-Lewis co., 1907. xxii, 249 p. ports. 18½ x 14 cm. In verse. 8-16241. F104. G9 R6

GUILFORD. The history of Guilford from its first settlement in 1639. From the manuscripts of Hon. Ralph D. Smith. Albany, J. Munsell, printer, 1877. (5) - 210 p. front., plans. 23 cm. 1-Rc-3241. F104. G9 S6

GUILFORD. A history of the plantation of Menunkatuck and of the original town of Guilford, comprising the present towns of Guilford and Madison, written largely from the manuscripts of the Hon. Ralph Dunning Smyth, by Bernard Christian Steiner. Baltimore, The author, 1897. 538 p. 23½ cm. The eastern part of Guilford was incorporated as Madison, 1826. 1-Rc-3242. F104. G9 S7

GUILFORD. Henry Whitfield, father of Guilford pioneers; historical address delivered in the First Congregational church, Guilford, ... 1934, by the Rev. William C. H. Moe. (Guilford, 1934) 12 p. 22 cm. 38-34431. F104. G9 W5

HADDAM. "Life flows along like a river;" a history of Haddam Neck. By Lillian Kruger Brooks. (1st ed. East Hampton? Conn.) Haddam Neck Genealogical Group, 1972. viii, 132 p. illus. 23 cm. Bibliography: p. (131) - 132. 72-189661 MARC. F104. H14 B7

HADDAM. Haddam in 1808. By Levi Hubbard Clark. (New Haven) Acorn Club of Connecticut, 1949. 10 p. 24 cm. (Acorn Club of Connecticut. 22d publication. Connecticut towns) 49-24790*. F104. H16 C6

HADDAM. A history of the towns of Haddam and East-Haddam. By David D. Field ... Middletown: Printed by Loomis and Richards, 1814. New York, C. L. Woodward, 1892. 48 p. 22 cm. Genealogies of the families in Haddam and East-Haddam: p. (43) - 48. Rc-3243. F104. H14 F5

HADDAM. The 200th anniversary of the First Congregational church of Haddam ... 1900. Church organized, 1696. Pastor installed, 1700. Haddam, 1902. xx, 360 p. front. 21½ cm. "From the church records": p. (189) - 360. 3-26285. F104. H14 H3

HADDAM. East. ... The 150th anniversary of the organization of the Third church of Christ, of Hadlyme society, (East Haddam, Conn.) ... 1895. Hartford, Conn., E. Geer's sons, printers, 1896.
40 p.   pl.   23½ cm.   18-4811.   F104. H16H16

HAMDEN.   ... Proctor & Way's Hamden and North Haven directory ... (v.1) -   1927/28 -
New Haven, Conn., Proctor & Way, 1927 -   v. fold. maps.   23½ cm.   CA 27-322 Unrev.
                                                                                Directories

HAMDEN. 1786. Centenary of Hamden. 1886. History of the town of Hamden, with an account of the centennial celebration ... 1886. ... under the editorial supervision of William P. Blake ... New Haven, Price, Lee, 1888.   viii, 350 p.   front. (port.)   pl.   23½ cm.   "Family history notices": p. 227 - 312.   Rc-3244 Rev.
                                                                                F104. H2 B6

HAMDEN.   The story of Hamden land of the Sleeping Giant.   By Rachel M. Hartley.   Hamden, Conn., Shoe String Press, 1962.   103 p.   illus.   22 cm.   62-21770.   F104. H2 H29

— Rev. ed.   Hamden, Conn., Shoe String Press, 1966.   xiv, 98 p.   23 cm.   62-21770.
                                                                                F104. H2 H29
                                                                                1966

HAMDEN.   The history of Hamden, 1786 - 1936 ... (By) Rachel M. Hartley.   Hamden, Conn. (New Haven, Quinnipiack press) 1943.   7, (3) - 497 p.   plates, ports., facsim.   24 cm.   Bibliography: p. (457) - 460.
43-16258.   F104. H2 H3

HAMDEN.   The history of Hamden, 1786 - 1959.   By Rachel M. Hartley.   Hamden, Conn., Shoe String Press, 1959.   506 p.   24 cm.   F104. H2 H3
                                                                                1959

HARTFORD.   Directory for the city of Hartford for the year 1799, containing the names of the business men and other residents, their occupation and location, when known, to the number of nearly 800.   Comp. by Frank D. Andrews ... Vineland, N.J., Priv. print., 1910.   34 p.   20½ cm.   10-31961 Rev.
                                                                                Directories

HARTFORD.   ... Geer's Hartford directory incl. West Hartford and East Hartford ... 1838, v. 1 -
Hartford, Conn., The Hartford print., 1838 - 19   v. illus., pl., port., fold. maps.
14½ - 25 cm.   C-233 Rev.   The 1828 directory of Hartford (the first published) is reprinted in no. 36. 1873/4, and a still earlier (1825) business directory, in no. 39, 1876/7.   Directories

HARTFORD.   Geer's Hartford city directory ... Connecticut geographical directory ... also, a directory of the town of East Hartford ... (v.1) -   (1838) - 1909.   Hartford, Conn., The Hartford print. (1838) -   66 v.   illus., pl., port., maps.   15 - 25 cm.   233 Additions.   Directories

HARTFORD, little suburban directory for the towns of Canton, Granby, Rocky Hill and Simsbury ... incl. a list of farmers and rural free delivery routes ... ed. for 1913.   Lynn, Mass., and Hartford, Conn., Clark-Delano co.   v.   24 cm.   13-11335.   Directories

HARTFORD.   Directory, and guide book, for the city of Hartford.   1844.   With a map of the city ... Comp. and pub. by Isaac N. Bolles.   (Hartford) Print. at the Republican courier office, 1844.
9 - 136 p.   front., map.   17½ cm.   9-16480 Rev.   Directories

HARTFORD.   Well's city and business directory.   (Hartford, Conn. v.1) -   Hartford,
J. Gaylord Wells, 1850 -   1 v.   illus., plates, fold. maps.   20 cm.   9-16479.   Directories

HARTFORD.   The Hartford city guide for 1871-72 ... also, a classified directory of many of the business firms ... Hartford, Coburn & Jenison, steam print, 1871-72.   276, 104 p.   front. (fold. map)
20 cm.   9-16478.   Directories

HARTFORD.   ... Hartford's dollar directory; a directory of Hartford, East Hartford and West Hartford ... (1905 -   no. 1 -   )   Hartford, Conn., Hartford directory and pub. co.,
1905 -   1 v.   fold. map.   25 cm.   5-22350.   Directories

CONNECTICUT 47

HARTFORD suburban directory for Avon, Bloomfield, Farmington, Glastonbury, Newington, South Windsor, Wethersfield, Windsor ... 19   Springfield, Mass., H. A. Manning co., 19
    v. maps. 23 cm.   CA 28 - 78 Unrev.   Directories

HARTFORD. Dau's blue book for Hartford, including Bristol, Danielson, Enfield, Farmington, Glastonbury, Litchfield, Manchester, Meriden, Middletown, New Britain, Putnam, Rockville, Southington, South Manchester, South Windsor, Windsor and Winsted 1911 -   (v. 8) - New York city, Dau pub. co.   1 v.   21½ cm.   11-15208.   Directories

HARTFORD blue-book ... v. 1 -   1897 -   Hartford, Conn. (The Blue book pub. co.)
1897 -   v. 18½ x 14 cm.   CA 33-689 Unrev.   Directories

HARTFORD. The Social register of Hartford. 1931/32 -   New Haven, Conn., Mack & Noel, 1931 -   v. 21½ cm.   CA 32-555 Unrev.   Directories

HARTFORD. Proceedings at the dedication of Charter Oak hall upon the south meadow grounds of Col. Samuel Colt. With the addresses on the occasion by Messrs, Hamersley, Stuart, and Denning. Ed. by J. Deane Alden. Hartford, Press of Case, Tiffany and co., 1856.   45 p. fold. front., pl., 3 plans (2 fold.) 23½ cm. 2-23883.   F104. H3 A3

HARTFORD. Business men of the city of Hartford in the year 1799, printed from the original manuscript with notes by Frank D. Andrews. Vineland, N.J., 1909.   24 p. 20 cm. Notes: p. 15-24. 10-25097 Rev.   F104. H3 A5

HARTFORD. A Quaker's visit to Hartford in the year 1676; ed. by Frank D. Andrews.   Vineland, N.J., Priv. print., 1914.   13 p. 23½ cm. An account, partly in his own words of the visit of the Quaker, William Edmundson, to Hartford. 14-9903.   F104. H3 A56

HARTFORD backgrounds, by Howard Bradstreet ... (Hartford, The Pyne-Davidson co.) 1930 -
    v. 23 cm.   30-28493.   F104. H3 B81

HARTFORD. The Hartford State House of 1796, by Newton C. Brainard.   (1st ed. Hartford) Conn. Historical Society (1964?)   x, 68 p. 24 cm.   F104. H3 B83

HARTFORD. Hartford's romance in state, national and world-wide affairs, 1635 - 1927, by Wolcott Haynes (pseud. for Charles Winslow Burpee) ... (Hartford) The Automobile club of Hartford, 1927. 71 p. illus., fold. map. 23 cm. In binder. 37-31898 Rev.   F104. H3 B9

HARTFORD. Governor Talcott's mansion and the city of Hartford's claim.   By John R. Campbell. (In Connecticut magazine. 1900. v. 6) 19-10710.   F104. H3 C2

HARTFORD. Restoration of the Ancient burying-ground of Hartford and the widening of Gold street; with lists of contributors to the general fund and of descendants who contributed for the preservation of family monuments; by the Ruth Wyllys chapter, D. A. R. Hartford, Conn., printed, 1904.
79 p. illus. 26½ cm. 7-21654.   F104. H3 D18

HARTFORD. A historical discourse, delivered before the Conn. historical soc. and the citizens of Hartford ... 1843. By Thomas Day ... (Hartford, 1844)   36 p. 24½ cm. 1-22555.
                                                                                                                                F104. H3 D2

HARTFORD. The great flood of 1936; a pictorial review of flood conditions in Hartford and East Hartford. Photographed and edited by Burton Deford Dechert, jr. (Hartford) 1936.   (76) p. of illus. 23½ x 31 cm. 36-17333.   F104. H3 D4

HARTFORD. The necessity of a constant readiness for death. A discourse, preached at Hartford North-Meeting house, 1766, occasioned by that alarming providence, the sudden demolition of the school-house, by gun-powder; whereby about 30 persons were wounded, six of whom are since dead. By the Rev. John Devotion ... Hartford: Print. Thomas Green ... (1766)   24 p. 16½ cm. 25-1074.   F104. H3 D5
                                                                                                                              Rare Book Coll.

HARTFORD. Extension view card ... Hartford. ... Portland, Me., 1908. 1 v. 15½ x 21 cm.
F104. H3 E95

HARTFORD. Tales of Centinel Hill. By (G.) Fox and Co. (Hartford, 1947) (29) p. col. illus.
33 cm. 48-15083*. F104. H3 F6

HARTFORD. Elihu Geer's guide to the location and numbers of streets and avenues, to which is added the ... location of each street ... in the city of Hartford. (Hartford, E. Geer) 1874.
20½ cm. F104 H3 G2

HARTFORD. The Globe. Souvenir of Hartford, Conn. (Hartford) 1892. (20) p. illus. (incl. ports.)
55 cm. 9-10353. F104. H3 G5

HARTFORD. Greater Hartford Coordinating Council for the Arts. A guide book to Greater Hartford. (Compiled by Marion H. Grant. Hartford, 1966) 3 v. 23 cm. Contents. - (1) Tours and tales. - (2) Calendars and Keys.
F104. H3 G7

HARTFORD. Souvenir and programme. Dedication of soldier's and sailor's memorial arch, ... 1886, Hartford. (Hartford?) E. S. Young (1886) 26 p. illus. 34½ x 27 cm. CA 25-561 Unrev.
F104. H3 H2

HARTFORD town votes ... 1635 - 1716. v. 1. (Hartford, Conn. historical soc., 1897)
ix, 410 p. facsim. 25 cm. (Collections of the Conn. historical soc. vol. vi) 9-29286. F104. H3 H25

HARTFORD. The Hartford handbook for new citizens and old. 1635. Tercentenary ed. (7th) 1935 ... Issued by the Board of education, Bureau of adult education at Hartford, Conn. Prepared by Howard Bradstreet, director. (Hartford) 1935. 73 p. illus. (incl. port., maps) 23 cm. E37-75 rev.
F104. H3H255
1935

HARTFORD, Conn., as a manufacturing, business and commercial center; with brief sketches of its history, attractions, leading industries, and institutions ... Hartford, Board of trade, 1889.
220 p. incl. front., illus. 23½ cm. 5-22091 F104. H3 H26

HARTFORD. Commemorative exercises of the First church of Christ in Hartford, on the 100th anniversary of the dedication of the meeting-house and the 275th anniversary of the founding of the church; 1907. Hartford, Conn., The Church, 1908. 81 p. 24½ cm. 9-8961. F104. H3 H27

HARTFORD. Commemorative exercises of the First church of Christ in Hartford, at its 250th anniversary ... 1883. Hartford, Conn., Press of the Case, Lockwood & Brainard co., 1883.
215 p. front., plates, ports., fold. map. 24½ cm. 6-40405. F104. H3 H28

HARTFORD. The First church of Christ in Hartford, anniversary exercises ... 1907; meeting house built, 1807, church founded, 1632. (Hartford, 1907) (8) p. 18 cm. 12-11579.
F104. H3H285

HARTFORD. The First church of Christ in Hartford. The ministers, the meeting houses, the memorial gifts. (Hartford) Printed by the Church, 1915. 11 p. 15 cm. 18-4810.
F104. H3H287

HARTFORD. Historical catatlogue of the First church in Hartford. 1633 - 1885 ... (Hartford) Pub. by the church, 1885. (iii) - xx, 274 p. 20½ cm. L. C. copy replaced by microfilm. 7-12505. F104. H3 H29
Microfilm 8869 F

HARTFORD. First church of Christ. Pamphlets, broadsides, clippings, and other miscellaneous matter on this subject, not separately cataloged, are classified in - F104. H3H299

HARTFORD. Original distribution of the lands in Hartford among the settlers, 1639. Hartford, Conn. historical society, 1912. xviii, (3) - 716 p. fold. map. 25 cm. (Collections of the Conn. historical society, vol. xiv)
Introd. signed: Albert C. Bates ... editor. "Early Hartford vital recores" (1644-1728): p. (573) - 625. 13-5099. F104. H3 H32

CONNECTICUT

HARTFORD. (Portland, Me., L. H. Nelson co. (1910)   20 x 25½ cm.   F104.H3 H34

HARTFORD monthly, v.1, no. 1-7; June - Dec. 1906.   1 v.   F104.H3 H35

HARTFORD. An address delivered at the request of the citizens of Hartford, ... 1835. The close of the second century, from the first settlement of the city. By Joel Hawes ... Hartford, Belknap & Hamersley, 1835.   80 p.   19½ cm.   Rc-3245.   F104.H3 H38

HARTFORD. Historical sketches of the First church in Hartford. A centennial discourse delivered in the First church, 1836. By Joel Hawes. Hartford, Hudson and Skinner, printers, 1836.   35 p. illus. (plan)   21 cm.   18-4309.   F104.H3 H39

HARTFORD. Miniatures of Hartford. (By Thomas Wallace Jones) (Cincinnati, 1904)   8½ x 11 cm.   F104.H3 J7

HARTFORD. The colonial history of Hartford, gathered from the original records ... by Rev. Wm. De Loss Love. Hartford, Conn., The author, 1914.   xviii, 369 p. plates, 2 port. (incl. front.) plans (part fold.)   24½ cm.   14-17632.   F104.H3 L9

HARTFORD. ... History of the Second church of Christ in Hartford, by Edwin Pond Parker. Hartford, Conn., Belknap & Warfield, 1892.   435 p. front., ports., fold. maps, plan, facsim.   25 cm.   8-19466.   F104.H3 P2

HARTFORD. The Friendly club and other portraits, by Francis Parsons ... Hartford, Conn., E. V. Mitchell, 1922.   223 p. front., illus., plates, port., facsim.   21 cm.   23-5680.   F104.H3 P3

HARTFORD. As they looked to the children (by) Francis Parsons. Hartford, Conn., Priv. pub., The Prospect press, 1939.   ix, 82 p.   22 cm.   Some of these sketches appeared in a book entitled The Friendly club ... (above)   39-2782.   F104.H3 P34

HARTFORD. Pictorial Hartford. (Portland, Me., 1909)   1 v.   20½ x 25½ cm.   F104.H3 P6

HARTFORD. Pocket book guide to the city of Hartford ... 1885. Advertising ed. Pub. quarterly by C. H. R. Miller ... Hartford, C. H. R. Miller, 1885.   (26) p. fold. map, fold. plan.   11 cm.   CA 25-481 Unrev.   F104.H3 P7

HARTFORD. ... Historical notices of Connecticut; pub. under the patronage of the Connecticut historical society ... By William Smith Porter. Hartford, E. Greer's press, 1842.   2 v. in 1.   21 x 12½ cm.   no. 1. 24. 12 p.; no. 2. p. 13-48.   1. Hartford in 1640. 2. Hartford and W. Hartford. Rc-3316 Rev.   F104.H3 P8

HARTFORD. Contributions to the history of Christ church, Hartford ... (By Gurdon Wadsworth Russell) Hartford, Belknap & Warfield, 1895 - 1908.   2 v. fronts., illus., plates, ports., plan, facsims. (1 fold)   24½ cm.   Contains records of baptisms, marriages, burials, etc.   9-5462 Rev.   F104.H3 R7

HARTFORD. "Up Neck" in 1825, by Gurdon W. Russell. By Gurdon Wadsworth Russell. Hartford, 1890.   145 p. front. (fold. plan) illus. (incl. map, facsims.)   23½ cm.   "The greater part was pub. in the (Hartford) Times."   Rc-3246 Rev.   F104.H3 R8

HARTFORD Jews, 1659 - 1970, by Morris Silverman. Hartford, Connecticut Historical Society (1970)   xii, 448 p. illus.   29 cm.   72-132408.   F104.H3 S5

HARTFORD. Souvenir book of the Municipal building dedication; program of exercises, pictorial review of the Municipal building and a down-to-date review of the captiol city. Hartford, Conn. (W. J. Martin) 1915.   112, 152 p. incl. front., illus., ports.   26 cm.   152 p. at end, Advertising section. 15-24538.   F104.H3 S7

HARTFORD. Souvenir of Hartford. (Portland, Me., 1908)   1 v.   20½ x 25½ cm.   F104.H3 S76

HARTFORD in the olden time; its first thirty years. By Scaeva (pseud. for Isaac William Stuart)

Ed. by W. M. B. Hartley ... Hartford, F. A. Brown, 1853.   315 p.   front., plates, fold. plan.   24½ cm.
Originally pub. in the Hartford daily courant.   7-11193.
F104.H3 S88

HARTFORD. Sunlight pictures, Hartford. Artotypes by E. Bierstadt, N.Y. From original negatives by R. S. de Lamater.   Hartford, Conn., J. H. Eckhardt (1892)   35 pl.   obl. 12°.   1-Rc-3247.
F104. H3 S9

HARTFORD.in history. A series of papers by resident authors. Ed. Willis I. Twitchell. (Hartford, The Plimpton mfg. co., 1899)   268 p.   pl.   map.   12°.   Mar 30, 99-133.
F104. H3 T9

HARTFORD. ... Diary of Rev. Daniel Wadsworth, 7th pastor of the First church of Christ in Hartford ... Hartford, Conn., Press of the Case, Lockwood & Brainard co., 1894.   149 p.   24½ cm.
Diary covers the years 1737 - 1747.   13-22912.
F104.H3 W12

HARTFORD. Address at the 250th anniversary of the First church of Christ, Hartford ... 1883, by Geo. Leon Walker.   Hartford, Conn., Press of the Case, Lockwood & Brainard co., 1883.
65 p.   22½ cm.   Also pub. in "Commemorative exercises of the First church of Christ in Hartford," 6-40406.
F104.H3 W2

HARTFORD. Crossing the Connecticut; an account of the various public crossings of the Connecticut River at Hartford since the earliest times, together with a full description of Hartford bridge ... by George E. Wright.   Hartford, Conn., The Smith-Linsley co., 1908.   xv, 159 p. col. front., illus. (incl. ports.) col. plates.   26½ cm.   8-27367.
F104. H3 W8

HARTFORD. Wright's street list and rapid transit guide to Hartford.   ... By George E. Wright. (Hartford, Conn., 1902)   15½ x 9 cm.
F104. H3 W9

HARTLAND patriotic celebration and unveiling bronze tablet on millstone used in the colonial and revolutionary wars for grinding grain for soldiers, East Hartland. Bunker hill day ... 1930 ... (Winsted, H. S. Case, printer, 1930?)   18 p.   23 cm.   Includes a list of Hartland men who fought in the French and Indian war, the revolution, war of 1812, civil war, and world war.   CA 31-507 Unrev.
F104.H33H34

HARTLAND. History of Hartland; the 69th town in the Colony of Connecticut. By Stanley Austin Ransom.   189 p.   24 cm.
F104.H33 R3

HARWINTON. Tombstone inscriptions in the old burying ground at Harwinton, with a historical sketch, by Frank D. Andrews ... Vineland, N.J., Priv. print., 1913.   (2)-21 p.   22 cm.   13-5622.
F104. H4 A5

HARWINTON. History of Harwinton, from the time it was settled through the mid 1960s., by Raymond George Bentley.   (1st ed. Winsted, Conn., Printed by Dowd Print. Co. 1970)   166 p.   illus.   24 cm.
F104. H4 B4

HARWINTON. The history of Harwinton. By R. Manning Chipman. Hartford, Press of Williams, Wiley & Turner, 1860.   152 p.   23 cm.   Rc-3248.
F104. H4 C5

HEBRON. Hebron, Connecticut. Bicentennial ... 1908. An account of the celebration of the 200th anniversary of the incorporation of the town.   1708.   1908.   Hebron, Conn., Bicentennial committee, 1910.   77 p. incl. front. (fold. map) plates, groups of ports.   24½ cm.   11-12845.
F104.H45 H4

HUNTINGTON. The salt-box house; 18th century life in a New England hill town, by Jane de Forest Shelton.   New York, The Baker & Taylor co. (1900)   302 p.   19½ cm.   Old Shelton homestead in Ripton parish, Stratford, Connecticut (town of Huntington after 1789)   0-4305 Rev.
F104. H9S 5

JEWETT CITY. Historical discourse delivered in the Congregational church, Jewett City, April 25th, 1875. By Rev. Thomas Leffingwell Shipman.   Norwich, Bulletin office print, 1875.   17 p.   22½ cm.
11-34831.
F104. J59 S5

KENSINGTON ... 200th anniversary, Kensington Congregational church. (Kensington, 1912)
123 p.   front., plates, ports.   24½ cm.   17-28677.
F104.K28K28

CONNECTICUT 51

KENSINGTON. Souvenir, Kensington, Conn. (By Edward James Lawrence) New Britain, Conn., The Lawrence studio, 1913.   (16) p.   illus.   11½ x 15½ cm.   F104.K28 L4

KENSINGTON. Historical sketch of (Kensington,) Berlin, Conn., during the last one hundred years. An address, delivered by request at the Congregational church, in that place, July 4, 1876. By Edward W. Robbins. First pub., by request, in the "Kensington church record, vol. I, 1885-6." New Britain, Conn., Press of W. A. House, 1886.   (5) - 52 p.   23½ cm.   Rc-3215 Rev.
F104.K28 R6

KENT. History of Kent, Connecticut. Including biographical sketches of many of its present or former inhabitants. 1897. (By) Francis Atwater. Meriden, Conn., Printed by the Journal pub. co., 1897.   176 p.   illus. (incl. ports.)   26 cm.   1-Rc-3249.   F104. K3 A8

KENT. Democracy in the Connecticut frontier town of Kent. By Charles S. Grant. New York, Columbia University Press, 1961.   xii, 227 p.   illus.   24 cm.   (Columbia studies in the social sciences, no. 601)
Bibliography: p. (216) - 220.   61-7713.   F104. K3 G7

— New York, Ams Press (1970)   xii, 227 p.   23 cm.   77-120201.   F104. K3 C7
1970

— With an introd. by Kenneth A. Lockridge. New York, Norton (1972)   xii, 227 p.   20 cm.   (The Norton library, N 639)   Bibliography: p. (216) - 220.   70-39175 MARC.   F104. K3 G7
1972

LAKEVILLE. The home country, Lakeville & Salisbury; a brief description of the twin towns lying at the gateway to the Berkshires. Pub. under the auspices of the Lakeville business men's association. (Cambridge, Mass., The University press) 1915.   16 p.   illus. (incl. map)   23 cm.   15-14928.
F104. L19 L2

LEBANON. An American community in action. (Lebanon, Connecticut. Washington, Distributed by the U. S. Information Service, 1950?)   20 p.   illus., ports.   20 cm.   51-60372 rev.   F104. L4 A53

LEBANON. Historic Lebanon; highlights of an historic town. By Robert Grenville Armstrong. Lebanon, Conn., First Congregational Church (1950)   79 p.   illus., ports.   24 cm.   50-11246.
F104. L4 A7

LEBANON. Address by Rev. Dr. Samuel G. Buckingham, of Springfield, Mass. ... Hartford, Conn., Press of the Case, Lockwood & Brainard co., 1891.   11 p.   23½ cm.   Cover-title: Tribute to Old Lebanon.
Reprinted from "The Lebanon war office."   10-23092.   F104. L4 B9

LEBANON. Early Lebanon. An historical address delivered in Lebanon, by request, on the national centennial ... 1876. By Rev. Orlo D. Hine ... With an appendix oc historical notes, by Nathaniel H. Morgan ... Hartford, Conn., Press of the Case, Lockwood & Brainard co., 1880.   176 p. incl. front. (port.)   illus.   19 cm.   Rc-3250 Rev.   F104. L4 H6
Microfilm 8870 F

LENANON. A historical sermon, delivered on the occasion of the 150th anniversary of the First Congregational church, Lebanon, by Rev. John C. Nichols, pastor. Haverhill, Mass., C. C. Morse, printers, 1895.   26 p.   24½ cm.   5-2276.   F104. L4 N6

LEBANON. The Lebanon war office. The history of the building, and report of the celebration at Lebanon, Flag day ... 1891 ... Pub. by the Connecticut society of Sons of the American revolution ... Ed. by Jonathan Trumbull. Hartford, Conn., Press of the Case, Lockwood & Brainard co., 1891.
96 p.   front. (port.) plates, fold. facsims.   23½ cm.   2-6624.   F104. L4 S6

LEDYARD. History of the town of Ledyard, 1650 - 1900. By Rev. John Avery. Norwich, Conn., Noyes & Davis, 1901.   334 p.   illus., 2 pl. (incl. front.) ports.   23½ cm.   Catalogue of deaths - 1713 - 1854: p. 277 - 323.
1-16633.   F104. L5 A9

LEDYARD. A catalogue of the deaths in the Second society of Groton, from the year 1770, to 1815 ... Windham (Conn.): Print. and pub. by Ansil Brown, May, 1815.   48 p.   15½ cm.   The Second society of Groton is now the Congregational church of Ledyard, Conn.   19-15437.
F104. L5 C3
Rare Book Coll.

LISBON. Historical sketch of Lisbon, From 1786 to 1900, by Henry F. Bishop.   New York, H. F. Bishop (1903)   84 p. incl. front. (port.) illus.   23½ cm.   3-26360.
F104. L6 B6

LITCHFIELD. The Litchfield book of days; a collation of the historical, biographical, and literary reminiscences of the town of Litchfield, edited by George C. Boswell ... Litchfield, A. B. Shumway, 1899.   221 p.   6 l.   front., plates, ports.   19 cm.   99-3002 Rev.
F104. L7 B7

LITCHFIELD. Historical address on St. Michael's parish, Litchfield, by the Rev. William J. Brewster, rector.   (Litchfield? Conn., 1919?)   (7) p.   21½ cm.   24-8629.
F104. L7 B8

LITCHFIELD. Historic Litchfield, 1721 - 1907; being a short account of the history of the old houses of Litchfield; comp. from Kilbourn's History of Litchfield, Geo. C. Woodruff's History of the town of Litchfield, Kilbourn's history of Litchfield tradition, the Litchfield County centennial celebration, the Litchfield book of days, and Chronicles of a pioneer school, by Alice T. Bulkeley.   Illus. from original photos. by the compiler.   (2d ed.)   (Hartford, Conn.) Hartford press; The Case, Lockwood & Brainard co., 1907.   vii, (9) - 37 p.   front.   27 pl.   25½ cm.   7-29605.
F104. L7 B9

LITCHFIELD.   ... Litchfield Hill.   (By John Denison Champlin)   (New York, 1877)   26 cm.
F104. L7 C5

LITCHFIELD. Hotel Berkshire, Litchfield.   By H. Clinton.   1908.   1 v.
F104. L7 C6

LITCHFIELD. Hotel Berkshire and the Bantam Lake house ...   By Harry Clinton.   (Litchfield? Conn.)   1908.   1 v.   15½ x 24 cm.
F104. L7 C64

LITCHFIELD. If a house could talk; being a history of a flood of released recollections, the resurrection of old letters and photos. pertaining to Litchfield and the Vaill homestead covering a past dating from 1867 to 1876 ... an unabridged past dating from 1876 to 1915 ....   New York, Priv. print. by Rogers & co., inc., 1917.   93 p.   front., plates, ports.   23½ cm.   17-28463.
F104. L7 G6

LITCHFIELD. Sketches and chronicles of the town of Litchfield, historical, biographical, and statistical; together with a complete official register of the town.   By Payne Kenyon Kilbourne ... Hartford, Press of Case, Lockwood, 1859.   vii, (17) - 264 p.   front., plates, ports., fold. map.   23½ cm.   Rc-3251.
F104. L7 K4

LITCHFIELD centennial celebration ... 1876.   Historical address by G. C. Woodruff.   Hartford, The press of the Case, Lockwood & Brainard co., 1876.   44 p.   22½ cm.   Rc-3252 Rev.
F104. L7 L7

LITCHFIELD. The bi-centennial celebration of the settlement of Litchfield ... 1920.   Comp. for the Litchfield historical soc. by Alain C. White.   Litchfield, Conn., Enquirier print, 1920.   xv, 147 p. incl. front.   plates.   23½ cm.   21-19663.
F104. L7 L74

LITCHFIELD Historical Society.   Catalogue.   Ed. by Mary B. Brewster.   Litchfield, Conn., 1930.   xiii, 159 p.   24 cm.
F104. L7L7418

LITCHFIELD. Catalogue of the Litchfield historical society ...   (New York, The Brewer press, 1905)   106 p.   22½ cm.   Several pages blank.   14-20028.
F104. L7L742

LITCHFIELD historical society.   Constitution and by-laws.   Litchfield, Conn., 1914.   10 p.   17½ cm.   18-8753.
F104. L7L743

LITCHFIELD historical society.   List of members ...   (Litchfield, 1914)   8 p.   22½ cm.   18-8936.
F104. L7 L75

CONNECTICUT

LITCHFIELD historical society. Reports of officers and committees ... (Litchfield, Conn.)
v. 24 cm. 13-16540.   F104. L7 L78

LITCHFIELD historical society. Semi-centennial of the Litchfield historical and antiquarian society; addresses at the opening of the new building, etc. Litchfield (The Tuttle, Morehouse & Taylor co., 1908) iv, 59 p. 2 pl. (incl. front.) 20½ cm. 14-20027.   F104. L7 L785

LITCHFIELD. The skeptic, and other poems. By Payne Kenyon Kilbourne. Hartford, Case Tiffany and Burnham, 1843. ix, (13) - 180 p. 19 cm. Binder's title: Harp of the vale. 28-1979.
F104. L7 K4
PS2169. K3 S5

LITCHFIELD and Morris inscriptions; a record of inscriptions upon the tombstones in the towns of Litchfield and Morris. Transcribed by Charles Thomas Payne. Litchfield, Conn., D. C. Kilbourn, 1905. 304 p. front., 12 pl. 26 cm. 5-16608.   F104. L7 P3

LITCHFIELD. Historic Litchfield; address delivered at the bi-centennial celebration of the town of Litchfield ... 1920, by Hon. Morris W. Seymour ... (Litchfield? Conn., Priv. print., 1920) 13 p. 24 cm. 20-23470.   F104. L7 S5

LITCHFIELD. The history of the town of Litchfield, 1720 - 1920. Comp. for the Litchfield historical society by Alain C. White. Litchfield, Conn., Enquirer print, 1920. (vii) - xvi, 360 p. front. (double plan) plates, ports. 23½ cm. 20-21982.   F104. L7 W58

LITCHFIELD. A genealogical register of the inhabitants of the town of Litchfield, from the settlement of the town, 1720, to the year 1800, whereby one knowing his father's name, may perhaps ascertain who were some of his antecedent progenitors. Collected from the records ... by George C. Woodruff, 1845 ... (Hartford, Conn.) The Case, Lockwood & Brainard co., 1900. 267 p. 24 cm. 1-1788.
F104. L7 W6

LITCHFIELD. History of the town of Litchfield. By George C. Woodruff. Litchfield, C. Adams, 1845. 64 p. front. (fold. plan) 22 cm. Rc-3253 Rev.   F104. L7 W7

MADISON. Madison's Heritage. Ed. by Philip S. Platt. Madison, Conn., Madison Historical Soc., 1964. x, 296 p. 22 cm. Some of these papers were first presented at meetings of the Madison hist. soc.   F104. M14 P55

MADISON. A brief history of Madison. By Kathleen Hulser Hyerson. Drawings by Gilbert Etheridge. (1st ed.) New York, Pageant Press (1960) 75 p. 24 cm.
F104. M14 R9

MADISON. From New Haven to Madison in the sixties, and other Madison sketches, by Jane Bushnell Shepherd ... New Haven, Conn., The Tuttle, Morehouse & Taylor co., 1931. 4; 130 p. front. 20½ cm. Reminiscences. 31-34607.   F104. M14 S5

MANCHESTER. Bower's Manchester directory ... 1888, 1891, 1892/3, 1894, 1896/7 - 19 Manchester, Conn., A. E. Bowers, 1888 - 19 v. fold. maps. 23½ cm. 0-6584 Rev.
Directories

MANCHESTER. Directory of the town of Manchester. Manchester, Conn., The Herald print. (19 - v. fold. map. 23½ cm. 23-9083.
Directories

MANCHESTER. ... The 100th anniversary of the organization of the First church of Christ in Manchester. Historical addresses by Rev. S. W. Robbins and Dea. R. R. Dimock, etc., etc. Hartford, Conn., The Case, Lockwood & Brainard co. print., 1880. 78 p. 23 cm. 7-7601.
F104. M18 M2

MANCHESTER. History of Manchester, by Mathias Spiess ... and Percy W. Bidwell ... (South Manchester, Conn.) Centennial committee of the town of Manchester, 1924. xvi, 306 p. incl. front. illus. 23½ cm. 28-13412.   F104. M18 S7

54 LOCAL HISTORIES IN THE LIBRARY OF CONGRESS

MANSFIELD. Births, baptisms, marriages and deaths, from the records of the town and churches in Mansfield, 1703 - 1850. Copied from the records by Susan W. Dimock. New York, The Baker & Taylor co., 1898. vi, 475 p. 24 cm. 4-20154. F104. M2 D5
L H & G

MANSFIELD CENTRE. A centennial discourse delivered in the First Congregational church, Mansfield Centre, July, 1876, by Rev. K. B. Glidden, incl. a history of the First Congregational church and a sketch of the early settlement, etc. Willimantic, Conn., Enterprise print. (1876) 43 p. 22 cm. 6-40521. F104. M2 G5

MANSFIELD CENTRE. Present Mansfield ("Centre"); a passing sketch of the village, with occasional jottings of its former history, present aspect and prospective greatnesss. From 1685 to 1879. By a way side traveler. Willimantic, Conn., Journal steam job print, 1880. (48) l. 23 ½ cm. A photograph of a ms. plan of "Mansfield street in 1879" and "1685" is attached to verso of cover. 9-17106. F104. M2 P9

MARLBOROUGH. Report of the celebration of the centennial of the incorporation of the town of Marlborough ... 1903. Comp. and pub. by Mary Hall. (Hartford, Conn.) Hartford press, The Case, Lockwood & Brainard co., 1904. 96 p. plates, ports., fold. plans, facsims., diagr. 24 cm. 4-17689.
F104. M3 H17

MATTEBESECK. Indian proprietors of Mattebeseck ... by Joseph Barratt. (Middletown, Conn., 1850) 23 ½ cm. F104. M4 B2

MERIDEN. Directory of the city of Meriden ... 1872. New Haven, Conn., 18   v. 22 ½ cm.
Directories

MERIDEN city directory ... together with a classified business directory. Also Meriden town directory ... 1873/74 -   Hartford, 18 -   v. 22 ½ cm.   Directories

MERIDEN directory. 1875/6 -   v. 1 -   New Haven, Conn., The Price & Lee co., 1875 -   19   v. fold. maps. 24 cm. 1-17639 (rev. '15)   Directories

MERIDEN. Memoirs of Francis Atwater, half century of recollections of an unusually active life. Considerable space devoted to the progress of the city of Meriden and its people. Enterprises organized in many places, covering varied lines of business ... (Meriden, Conn., Horton print., 1922) 313 p. incl. illus., ports. 21 cm. 47-37117. F104. M5 A8

MERIDEN. Recollections of a New England town, by "Faith" (Mrs. Frances A. Breckenridge) Meriden, Conn., The Journal pub. co., 1899. (3) - 222 p. 20 ½ cm. Originally printed in the Meriden daily journal. 7-22168. F104. M5 B8

MERIDEN. An historic record and pictorial description of the town of Meriden and men who have made it. From earliest settlement to close of its first century of incorporation. A century of Meriden "The silver city." Issued as the official souvenir history by authority of the general committee at the centennial celebration ... 1906. Comp. by C. Bancroft Gillespie. Early history by George Munson Curtis ... Meriden, Conn., Journal pub. co., 1906. (5) - 434, 608, 184 p. illus., fold. pl., ports., fold. maps. 25 cm. 6-30492. F104. M5 G4

MERIDEN. Centennial sermons on the history of the Center Congregational church, of Meriden, preached ... by Edward Hungerford. Hartford, Press of the Case, Lockwood & Brainard co., 1877. 75 p. 19 cm. 8-20385. F104. M5 H9

MERIDEN. Centennial of Meriden ... 1906; report of the proceedings, with a full description of the many events of its successful celebration. Old home week. Meriden, Conn., the "Silver city." Pub. under the auspices of the general centennial committee. (Meriden) The Journal pub. co., 1906. 400 p. illus. (incl. ports.) 23 ½ cm. Compiled by Francis Atwater. 7-25131. F104. M5 M48

MERIDEN. The people of Meriden extend a cordial invitation to attend the centennial celebration and Old home week ... 1906 ... (Meriden? Conn., 1906) Program. 21½ cm. F104. M5 M5

CONNECTICUT 55

MERIDEN. The Meriden daily journal. Fiftieth anniversary number ... April 17, 1936 ... (1936) 1 v. F104. M5 M6

MERIDEN. Historical sketches of Meriden. By G. W. Perkins. West Meriden, F. E. Hinman, 1849. (iv) - v, (6) - 117 p. front. (fold. map) 19½ cm. Rc-3254 Rev. F104. M5 P4

MERIDEN. The Silver city. Meriden, Conn. (Meriden, E. A. Horton, 1893) (140) p. illus. (incl. ports.) 18½ x 26 cm. Rc-3255 Rev. F104. M5 S5

MERIDEN. Souvenir of Meriden (Meriden, Conn., 1909) 1 v. 20 x 25 - cm. F104. M5 S7

MIDDLEFIELD. History of Middlefield and Long Hill. By Thomas Atkins. Hartford, Conn., Press of the Case, Lockwood & Brainard co., 1883. 175 p. 20 cm. 8-3799. F104. M58 A8

MIDDLETOWN and Portland directory, 1885/6 - 19 - (v. 1 - New Haven, Conn., The Price & Lee co., 1885 - 19 v. fold. maps. 24 cm. Imprint varies slightly. Vols. for 1889/90 - 1891/92 include lists of marriages and deaths in Middletown. 0-4753 Rev. Directories

MIDDLETOWN city directory, 1876/77. Middletown, Conn. (18 v. 23 cm. Directories

MIDDLETOWN. Centennial address, by David D. Field. With historical sketches of Cromwell, Portland, Chatham, Middle-Haddam, Middletown and its parishes. Middletown, Conn., W. B. Casey, 1853. iv p. (7) - 295 p. 19½ cm. 1-Rc-3256. F104. M6 F4

MIDDLETOWN. The leading business men of Middletown, Portland, Durham and Middlefield ... Boston, Mercantile pub. co., 1890. 47 p. illus. 27 cm. 5-35736. F104. M6 H2

MIDDLETOWN. A pamphlet containing two articles on Middletown and the Connecticut River, written by Frank K. Hallock and James L. McConaughy, respectively, and pub. at the time of the tercentenary clebration of the founding of Middletown. (Middletown, River Activities Committee of the General Tercentenary Committee of Middletown, Conn.) 1950. 27 p. 23 cm. 51-30193. F104. M6 H23

MIDDLETOWN. The addresses, delivered at the dedication of the Indian Hill cemetery: with the articles of association, by-laws, etc., etc. Middletown, C. H. Pelton, printer, 1850. 48, 3-4 p. front. (fold. plan) 22½ cm. 17-25225. F104. M6 I 6

MIDDLETOWN. An address, delivered at the dedication of the Indian Hill cemetery. By Rev. Frederick J. Goodwin ... Middletown, C. H. Pelton, print., 1850. 16 p. 22 cm. 22-13929. F104. M6 I65

MIDDLETOWN. 1650 - 1900. Mattabeseck. Middletown. A description of the exercises connected with the 250th anniversary ... 1900. Middletown, Conn., The Tribune co. (1900) 107 p. illus. 23½ cm. 12-5146. F104. M6 M6

MIDDLETOWN. The Middletown press. (Middletown-Portland bridge edition) Middletown, Conn., 1938. 1 v. illus. 58 cm. Forms issue of Aug. 6, 1938, of the Middletown press. 39M4965T. F104. M6 M67

MIDDLETOWN. Middletown and the American Revolution. By Albert Edward Van Dusen. (Middletown, Conn., Rockfall Corp. of Middletown) 1950. 35 p. map. 23 cm. Bibliographical footnotes. 51-26011. F104. M6 V3

MILFORD directory ... 1909. New Haven, Conn., The Price & Lee co., 1909 - x 1 v. 24 cm. 9-28569. Directories

MILFORD. A leaf of Milford history. A Thanksgiving sermon, preached in the First church, Milford, Conn., 1858. By Jonathan Brace ... New Haven, Print. E. Hayes, 1858. 24 p. 23 cm. 32-8229. F104. M7 B8

MILFORD. History of Milford, 1639 - 1939, compiled and written by the Federal writers' project of the Works project (i.e. progress) administration for the state of Conn. (Bridgeport, Conn., Press of Braunworth & co., 1939) xii, 204, (6) p. front., plates, maps (part fold.) 23½ cm. Bibliography: p. 193 - 196. 39-19296.
F104. M7 F4

MILFORD. Historical sketches of the town of Milford. Comp. (George Hare Ford) ... New Haven, Conn., Press of the Tuttle, Morehouse and Taylor co., 1914. 80 p. illus., plates, plans (inco. fold. front.) facsims. 25 cm. 14-14944.
F104. M7 F6

MILFORD. "A leaf of Milford history": a Thanksgiving sermon preached at the First church, Milford ... 1858, by Jonathan Brace ... (In Historical sketches, above, p. (47) - 62) 14-14945.
F104. M7 F6

MILFORD. ... Milford, Connecticut; the early development of a town as shown in its land records. (New Haven) Pub. for the Tercentenary commission by the Yale university press, 1933. 29 p. illus. (maps) 23 cm. (Tercentenary pamphlet series xiii) By Leonard W. Labaree. 33-28134 Rev.
F104. M7 L2

MILFORD. ... Proceedings at the celebration of the 250th anniversary of the First church of Christ, in Milford ... 1889. Ansonia (Conn.) Press of Evening sentinel, 1890. 189 p. front. (port.) plates, plan. 20 cm. 24-3035.
F104. M7 M75

MILFORD. Inscriptions on tombstones in Milford, erecected prior to 1800, together with a few of aged persons who died after that date. Transcribed and annotated by Nathan G. Pond. (From advance sheets of vol. v, Papers of the New Haven colony historical society) New Haven, Printed for the Soc., 1889. 69 p. pl. 24½ cm. 3-3027.
F104. M7 P6

MILFORD. The story of the memorial in honor of the founders of the town of Milford, erected by their descendants and the citizens of Milford. Dedicated Aug. 28, 1889. 20 p. front. 23 cm. 4-11973.
F104. M7 P7

MILFORD. Sixty years' recollections of Milford, and its chronology from 1637 up to and including 1916, by Nathan Stowe; the whole ed. and rev. by Newton Harrison ... Milford, Conn., 1917. 95 p. incl. front. (port.) fold. maps. 23½ cm. 17-28807.
F104. M7 S8

MONTVILLE. History of Montville, formerly the North parish of New London from 1640 to 1896, comp. and arranged by Henry A. Baker. Hartford, Conn., Press of the Case, Lockwood & Brainard co., 1895. viii, 727 p. front., plates, ports. 23½ cm. "Genealogies of the early settlers": p. (100) - 602. Rc-3257.
F104. M8 B2

MORRIS. Litchfield and Morris inscriptions ... By C. T. Payne. 1905 1 v.
F104. M87 P3

MOUNT CARMEL. The old Mount Carmel parish, origins & outgrowths, by George Sherwood Dickerman. New Haven, Pub. for New Haven colony historical soc. by Yale university press; (etc., etc.) 1925. x, 220 p. fold. front., plates, maps, facsim., diagr. 24 cm. 25-16828.
F104. M92 D4

MOUNT CARMEL. Colonial history of the parish of Mount Carmel as read in its geologic formations, records and traditions, by John H. Dickerman ... New Haven, Conn., Press of Ryder's printing house, 1904. 109 p. incl. front., illus. 26 cm. 7-21279.
F104. M92 D5

MYSTIC. The Mystic and Stonington directory containing ... directory ... of Groton, (Groton village excepted) and ... Stonington, (Pawcatuck excepted) ... Providence, R.I., C. De Witt White co., v. 24 cm. 12-2973.
Directories

MYSTIC. Maritime Mystic. By Virginia B. Anderson. Mystic, Conn., Marine Historical Assoc., 1962. viii, 88 p. 26 cm. (Marine Historical Assoc. Publication no. 39)
F104.M99A64

MYSTIC. Mystic Seaport: a camera impression. By Samuel Chamberlain. New York, Hastings House (1959) 71 p. (chiefly illus.) 21 cm. 59-10845.
F104.M99C48

CONNECTICUT 57

— (Rev. ed.) New York, Hastings House (1961) 71 p. 21 cm.   F104.M99C48
1961

MYSTIC. Mystic seaport: the age of sail, by Jean Poindexter Colby. Photos. by Louis S. Martel. Artwork and maps by Joshua Tolford. New York, Hastings House (1970) 96 p. illus. 24 cm. (Famous museum series) 69-15055.   F104.M99C58
1970

MYSTIC. A history of the statue erected to commemorate the heroic achievement of Maj. John Mason and his comrades, with an account of the unveiling ceremonies. Comp. by Thomas S. Collier ... (New London? Conn.) The Commission, 1889. 62 p. front. 23½ cm. 4-33561 Rev.   F104.M99 C6

MYSTIC, the story of a small New England seaport, by Carl C. Cutler. (Mystic, Conn., 1945) 137-177 p. illus. (incl. ports.) 25½ cm. (Publication of the Marine historical assoc. inc., vol. II no. 4. Dec. 15, 1945. 47-4273.   F104.M99 C8

MYSTIC. The three founders: Dr. Charles Kirtland Stillman, Carl C. Cutler and Edward Eugene Bradley. By Marion Dickerman. With a foreword by Philip R. Mallory. (Mystic Conn.) Marine Historical Assoc., 1965. 42 p. 23 cm.   F104.M99 D5

MYSTIC. The Log of Mystic seaport. v. 1 -   Oct.1948 -   Mystic, Conn.
  v. in   illus., ports. 23 cm. quarterly. Pub. by the Marine Historical Assoc. 58-37267.   F104.M99 L6

MYSTIC. Mystic Seaport and the origins of freedom! By Philip R. Mallory. New York, Newcomen Soc. in North America, 1954. 32 p. illus. 23 cm. "2d printing: Sept. 1954" 55-2743.   F104.M99 M3

MYSTIC. Mystic Seaport guide, including a brief history of the Marine Historical Association and description of the buildings, ships, small craft, and other exhibits. (Mystic, Conn., Marine Hist. Assoc., 1967) 62 p. 19 cm.   F104.M99M37

NAUGATUCK directory, 1911 -   New Haven, Conn., The Price & Lee co., 1911 -
1 v. front. (fold. map) 24 cm. 1911 - also bound with Waterbury, Naugatuck and Watertown directory. 11-16286.   Directories

NAUGATUCK. Fulling Mill brook; a study in industrial evolution, 1707 - 1937 (by) Fred Engelhardt ... Brattleboro, Vt., Stephen Daye press (1937) 55 p. front., illus., plates, map. 21 cm. 38-16631.   F104. N2 E6

NAUGATUCK. History of Naugatuck. By Constance (McLaughlin) Green. Naugatuck, 1948.
xii, 331 p. illus., ports., maps. 24 cm. "Bibliographicl note": p. 304-307. 49-801*.   F104. N2 G7

— New Haven, Yale Univ. Press (1949) vii, 283 p. illus., maps. 24 cm. "Bibliographicl note": p. 256-259. "2d printing, June 1949" 49-5691*.   F104. N2 G7
1949

NAUGATUCK stories and legends, by William F. Leuchars. (1st ed.) Naugatuck, Conn., Naugatuck Historical Soc. (1969) 110 p. illus. 23 cm. 77-81782.   F104. N2 L4

NEW BRITAIN directory, 18   - 19   (v.   New Britain, Conn., The Price & Lee co.
(18   - 19   v. fold. maps. 24 cm. 99-3996 Rev.   Directories

NEW BRITAIN. Memorial. Genealogy, and ecclesiastical history (of First church, New Britain) To which is added an appendix, with explanatory notes, and a full index ... By Alfred Andrews ... Chicago, Ill., A. H. Andrews, 1867. vii, (9) - 538 p. front. (port.) 23½ cm. The town of New Britain was not incorporated until 1850, but the New Britain parish, with substantially the same limits, had been established in 1754, from parts of Farmington and Wethersfield. This parish formed part of the town of Berlin, from the latter's incorporation in 1785 down to 1850. 1-Rc-3258.   F104. N5 A5

NEW BRITAIN. Names of the residents of New Britain, in the year 1799, who paid taxes ... pub. Frank D. Andrews. Vineland, N.J., 1910. 11 p. 20 cm. 11-8285.   F104.N5 A55

685

NEW BRITAIN. History of New Britain, with sketches of Farmington and Berlin. 1640 - 1889. By David N. Camp. New Britain, W. B. Thomson, 1889. 538 p. front., illus., ports. 23½ cm. 1-Rc-3259.
F104. N5 C2

NEW BRITAIN. A history of New Britain. By Herbert E. Fowler. (New Britain, Conn.) New Britain Historical Soc., 1960. 294 p. 24 cm.
F104. N5 F6

NEW BRITAIN. In and about New Britain. (New Britain) Lewis & Atwell (1892) (138) p. illus., port. obl. 12°. 1-Rc-3260.
F104. N5 I 3

NEW BRITAIN. Svenskarna i New Britain; historiska anteckningar, af John E. Klingberg. New Britain, Conn., 1911. 116 p. illus. (incl. ports.) 19½ cm. 14-8757 Rev.
F104. N5 K65

NEW BRITAIN. 1758 - 1908; 150th anniversary First church of Christ, New Britain, comp. by Deacon Charles Elliott Mitchell; 1908. (New Britain, Conn., Adkins print., 1911) 125 p. front., plates, ports., fold. map. 25 cm. 12-3430.
F104. N5 N5

NEW BRITAIN. Pocket guide of New Britain, Conn. ... and a chronology of local events from the founding of the town ... (no. 1 (Sept. 1893 (New Britain) Press of the New Britain bee (1893 - v. 11½ cm. monthly. Compiler: Sept. 1893 - T.S. Sneath. 33-38657.
F104. N5 P7

NEW BRITAIN. Official souvenir and program of the dedication of the Soldiers' monument, New Britain ... 1900. Comp. and pub. by James W. Ringrose. New Britain, Record print (1900) 88 p. illus. (incl. ports.) 23 cm. 4-18543.
F104. N5 R5

NEW BRITAIN. The story of New Britain, written by Lillian Hart Tryon, from historical sketches by Mortimer Warren. (New Britain) Esther Stanley chapter, D.A.R., 1925. vii - xi, 132 p. incl. double map. front., plates, ports. 22 cm. Bibliography: p. (131) - 132. 25-13187.
F104. N5 T7

NEW CANAAN directory ... New Cannan, Conn., A. E. MacLaughlin, 1908 - 1 v. illus. 22½ cm. 8-19135.
Directories

NEW CANAAN. The making of main street (by) Mary Louise King. With illus. from the 19th century and recent photos. by John King. (New Canaan, Conn.) New Canaan Historical Soc., 1971. 32 p. illus. 24 cm.
F104. N53 K5

NEW CANAAN. Historical account of the celebration of the 150th anniversary of the organization of the Congregational church of New Canaan ... 1883. With an appendix ... Ed. by Rev. Joseph Greenleaf and others. (Stamford, Conn., Gillespie brothers, printers, 1883) 141 p. front., pl. 24 cm. 6-38845.
F104. N53 N5

NEW CANAAN. New Canaan Congregational church records, 1733 - 1850 ... (copied by) William Applebie Daniel Eardeley ... Brooklyn, N.Y., 1923. 2 v. 28½ x 22 cm. Type-written copy. Includes baptisms, marriages, deaths, etc. 23-16210.
F104. N53N53

NEW CANAAN. Landmarks of New Canaan. New Canaan, Conn., New Canaan Historical Society, 1951. 505 p. illus. 28 cm. "One hundred and fifty-one articles which have appeared singly on the editorial page of the New Canaan advertiser." 52-18612.
F104. N53N54

NEW CANAAN historical society. Annual. v. 1 - June, 1943 - New Canaan, Conn. (1943 - 1 v. mounted illus. 23½ cm. 43-22896.
F104. N53N55

NEW CANAAN Historical Society. Readings in New Canaan history. (1st ed.) New Canaan, 1949. 290 p. illus., maps, facsims. 25 cm. 49-11104*.
F104. N53N56

NEW CANAAN. Historical address, delivered in the Congregational church, of New Canaan ... 1876. By Prof. Samuel St. John. With an appendix ... Also a list of soldiers who served in the war for the Union, and an obituary of Prof. St. John, etc. New Canaan, Conn., 1876. 64 p. front. (port.) pl. 26½ cm. Rc-3261.
F104. N53 S2

CONNECTICUT

NEW HARTFORD. Sketches of the people and places of New Hartford in the past and present.   (By Henry Roger Jones)   Section 1   New Hartford, Conn., Pub. at the office of the Tribune, 1883.   1 v.   22 cm.   Previously published in the Tribune of New Hartford.   8-29236.
    F104.N55 J 7

NEW HAVEN directory, including West Haven, 18   no.   (New Haven) The Price & Lee co., 18   - 19   v. fold. maps.   18 - 24 cm.   0-5499 rev.
    Directories

NEW HAVEN.   The New Haven list.   (1886) -   New Haven, Conn., Tuttle, Morehouse & Taylor, printers, 1886 -   v. 15½ cm.   "Society people in New Haven."   CA 33-577 Unrev.
    Directories

NEW HAVEN.   Dau's blue book for New Haven, Bridgeport, Waterbury (Connecticut) including Ansonia, Branford, Derby, Milford, Naugatuck, Norwalk, Stamford, Seymour, Stonington, Stratford, Thomaston, Wallingford, Watertown, and Westport ...   New York city, Dau pub. co., 1911-13.
2 v.   21½ cm.   11-16552 Rev.
    Directories

NEW HAVEN, Bridgeport and Waterbury society blue book ... 19   New York city, The Blue book co. (etc.) 19   v. 21½ cm.   11-16552 Rev. 2.
    Directories

NEW HAVEN.   The Social register of New Haven, 1927/28 -   New Haven, Conn., Mack & Noel, 1927.   v.   22 cm.   CA 28-53 Unrev.
    Directories

NEW HAVEN.   Addresses delivered at the laying of corner stone of the Federal building, in New Haven ... 1914.   (New Haven? 1914)   20 p.   illus. (incl. plans)   23 cm.   18-7512.
    F104. N6 A3

NEW HAVEN.   The American genealogist and New Haven genealogical magazine.   v. (1) - July 1922 -   New Haven, Conn. (etc.) D. L. Jacobus (1922 -   v.   23 - 24½ cm.   Each volume consists of 4 issues (v. 6 -   quarterly)   The first 8 vols., pub. under title New Haven genealogical magazine, are devoted almost entirely to families of the original township of New Haven.   The vols. are paged continuously, and preceded by title-pages with title: Families of ancient New Haven.   With v. 9, no. 1 (July 1932) the title became the American genealogist and New Haven genealogical magazine.   Editor: July 1922 -   D. L. Jacobus.   36-19457.
    F104. N6 A6

NEW HAVEN.   Cross-index to New Haven genealogical magazine volumes I-VIII, inclusive, Families of ancient New Haven, by Donald Lines Jacobus, compiled by Helen Love Scranton.   (New Haven) 1939.   301 p.   23 cm.   Photolithographed.   40-7052.
    F104. N6 A6
    Index vol. 1-8

NEW HAVEN.   Index to genealogical periodicals.   By Donald Lines Jacobus.   v. 1 -   New Haven, 1932 -   v.   27 cm.   32-18229 rev.*
    Z5313. U5 J2

— (Supplement) 1932 -   (In The American genealogist. v. 9 -   1933 -   )
    F104. N 6 A6
    vol. 9 - 13

NEW HAVEN.   History of the city of New Haven to the present time.   By an association of writers. Ed. by Edward E. Atwater ...   With biographies, portraits and illustrations.   New York, W. W. Munsell, 1887.   702 p.   front., illus., plates, ports., maps, plans.   29½ cm.   1-16754.
    F104. N6 A8

NEW HAVEN.   A Puritan church and its relation to community, state, and nation; addresses delivered in preparation for the three hundredth anniversary of the settlement of New Haven, by Oscar Edward Maurer ...   New Haven, Pub. for the First church of Christ in New Haven by Yale university press; London, H. Milford, Oxford university press, 1938.   iv, 208 p.   front.   21 cm.   38-16639.
    F104.N6 B12

NEW HAVEN.   Thirteen historical discourses, on the completion of 200 years, from the beginning of the First church in New Haven, with an appendix.   By Leonard Bacon ...   New Haven, Durrie & Peck; New York, Gould, Newman & Saxton, 1839.   viii, 400 p.   front. (port.)   23½ cm.   6-14317.
    F104.N6 B12

NEW HAVEN.   Stories of old New Haven ... by Ernest H. Baldwin ...   New York, London (etc.) The

Abbey press (1902)   4, (7) - 82, (3), 83 - 204 p.   plates, port., plan. facsim.   20 ½ cm.   3-4214.

F104.N6 B15

NEW HAVEN.   Stories of old New Haven (illustrated) by Ernest H. Baldwin ... Taunton, Mass., C. A. Hack (1907)   4, (7) - 203 p.   11 pl., port., plan.   20 cm.   7-41777.   F104.N6 B16

NEW HAVEN.   A brief memorial of Philip Marett.   Read by Simeon E. Baldwin, before the New Haven colony historical society ... 1890.   New Haven, Tuttle, Morehouse & Taylor, printers, 1890. 19 p.   front. (port.)   31 x 25 cm.   14-15507.   F104.N6 B18

NEW HAVEN.   History and antiquities of New Haven, from its earliest settlement to the present time. Collected and comp. from the most authentic sources.   By J. W. Barber.   Illus. with engravings. New Haven, J. W. Barber, 1831-(32)   120 p.   illus., col. plates, col. plan.   19 cm.   1-Rc-3262.   F104. N6 B 2

NEW HAVEN.   Street time, by Richard Balzer.   Text based on conversations with Fred Harris. New York, Grossman Publishers, 1972.   128 p.   illus.   27 cm.   76-184473.

F104.N6 B22
1972

NEW HAVEN.   History and antiquities of New Haven, from its earliest settlement to the present time. With biographical sketches and statistical information of the public institutions, etc., etc.   By John W. Barber ... and Lemuel S. Punderson.   (2d ed.)   New Haven, L. S. Punderson and J. W. Barber, 1856. 4, iv, (9) - 180 p.   front. (map) illus., plates (part col.)   20 cm.   10-8539.   F104. N6 B3

—— 3d ed. rev. and enl.   New Haven, Conn., J. W. Barber and L. S. Punderson, 1870. 4, iv, (9) - 216 p.   front. (map) illus. (incl. plans, facsims.) plates (1 col.)   18 ½ cm.   Rc-3263.   F104. N6 B4

NEW HAVEN.   Views in New Haven and its vicinity: with a particular description to each view. Drawn and engraved by John W. Barber.   New Haven, J. W. Barber (etc.) 1825.   11 p.   6 col. pl.   16°. 1-Rc-3264.   F104. N6 B5

NEW HAVEN.   Historical sketches of New Haven, by Ellen Strong Bartlett.   New Haven, Print. Tuttle, Morehouse & Taylor, 1897.   98 p.   illus. (incl. ports., facsim.)   28 ½ cm.   "These papers have appeared ... in the Connecticut quarterly and the New England magazine."   Rc-3265.   F104. N6 B6

NEW HAVEN.   Chronicles of New Haven green from 1638 to 1862; a series of papers read before the New Haven colony historical society, by Henry T. Blake.   New Haven, The Tuttle, Morehouse press, 1898.   280 p.   front., plates, maps, facsims.   24 ½ cm.   9-21186.   F104.N6 B65

NEW HAVEN.   Italian or American? The second generation in conflict.   By Irvin L. Child ... New Haven, Pub. for the Institute of human relations by Yale university press; London, H. Milford, Oxford university press, 1943.   5; 208 p.   24 ½ cm.   "References": p. (201) - 202.   A43-2535.

F104. N6 C5

—— With an introd. by Francesco Cordasco.   New York, Russell & Russell (1970)   206 p.   23 cm. 70-121999.

F104. N6 C5
1970

NEW HAVEN.   Hillhouse avenue from 1809 to 1900.   (By Mrs. Henrietta Frances (Silliman) Dana) (New Haven, The Tuttle, Morehouse & Taylor co,, 1907)   16 p.   illus.   20 cm.   Privately printed in 1900 and now reprinted in memory of the author.   8-8591.   F104.N6 D16

NEW HAVEN.   Historical catalogue of the members of the First church of Christ in New Haven (Center church) 1639 - 1914; comp. by Franklin Bowditch Dexter.   New Haven, 1914.   2; 469 p.   24 ½ cm. 14-12462.   F104.N6 D45

NEW HAVEN.   ... Inscriptions on tombstones in New Haven, erected prior to 1800.   (Ed. Franklin Bowditch Dexter)   (New Haven, 1882)   (471) - 614 p.   23 ½ cm.   "From the Papers of the N. H. colony hist. soc., vol. III, 1882."   19-7865.   F104. N6 D47

CONNECTICUT 61

— (Additions and corrections) 1914.   1 v.   F104.N6D472

NEW HAVEN.   New Haven in 1784.   A paper read before the New Haven colony historical soc. ... 1884, by Franklin Bowditch Dexter.   (From The 100th anniversary of the city of New Haven ... 1885.)   7-34359.
F104. N6 D5

NEW HAVEN.   The New Haven of two hundred years ago.   By Franklin B. Dexter...   (In New Haven colony historical society. Papers. v. 8. 1914)   20-17052.   F104. N6 D6

NEW HAVEN.   The history of the North church in New Haven, from its formation in May, 1742 ... to ... 1842.   In three sermons.   By Samuel W. S. Dutton ... New Haven, A. H. Maltby, 1842.   128 p.   23 cm.   10-3151.   F104. N6 D8

NEW HAVEN.   A statistical account of the city of New-Haven.   By Timothy Dwight ... (New-Haven, Printed and sold by Walter and Steele, 1811)   xi, 83 p.   22 cm.   (Connecticut academy of arts and sciences. A statistical account of the towns and parishes in ... Connecticut.   v.1, no. 1)   2-17405.   F104. N6D89

— (New Haven? 1874?)   60 p.   front. (fold. map)   22½ cm.   2-17404.   F104. N6 D9

NEW HAVEN.   East Rock park, New Haven.   Indelible photographs ... New York, A. Wittemann, 1891.   (2) p.   16 phot.   obl. 24°.   1-Rc-3266.   F104. N6 E1

NEW HAVEN.   The attractions of New Haven; a guide to the city ... By Samuel H. Elliot ... New York, N. Tibbals, 1869.   2, 141 p. double front., plates, fold, map.   15½ cm.   Rc-3267.   F104. N6 E4

NEW HAVEN.   ... Program of exercises at the dedication of a soldiers monument erected by the First Connecticut light battery, etc. ... 1905 ....   (New Haven, Conn., Press of the Price, Lee & Adkins co., 1905)   45, (3) p. front., pl., ports.   23½ cm.   6-37662.   F104. N6 F5

NEW HAVEN.   Colonial houses of New Haven.   By Susan Charlotte Gover.   Photos and descriptions by Susan C. Gower.   (New Haven) 1894.   19 l.   16 pl.   21 x 25 cm.   Fifty copies printed.   Rc-3268 Rev.
F104. N6 G7
Rare Book Coll.

NEW HAVEN.   Memorial poem delivered at Music hall ... 1868, at the memorial services, by Rev. S. Dryden Phelps, with a corrected list of soldiers' graves, etc.   New Haven, Printed by Hoggson & Robinson, 1868.   vii, (9) - 23 p.   19 cm.   12-26121.   F104.N6 G75

NEW HAVEN.   Guide to the city of New Haven, spring of 1885 ... Pub. quarterly by C. H. R. Miller ... New Haven, C. H. R. Miller (1885)   (32) p.   map.   32°.   1-Rc-3269.
F104. N6 G9

NEW HAVEN.   The east side of New Haven harbor; Morris cove (Solitary cove), the Annex (the Indian reservation), South end & Waterside, 1644 to 1868, by Marjorie F. Hayward; ... New Haven, New Haven colony historical society, 1938.   viii, 86 p. front., illus. (maps) 24 cm.   Bibliography: p. 82.   38-38247.
F104. N6 H37

NEW HAVEN.   Colonial wars of America, a synopsis of the military and civil records of some of the New Haven men originally buried on New Haven green, whose grave stones were later either installed in the crypt of Center church or removed to Grove street cemetery, compiled by James Spencer Hedden ... New Haven, Conn., 1944.   21 numb. l.   28 x 22 cm.   Reproduced from type-written copy.   Corrections and additions in manuscript.   "Authorities": leaf 1.   44-30314.   F104. N6 H4

NEW HAVEN.   Nineteenth-century historians of New Haven.   By Richard Hegel.   (Hamden, Conn., Archon Books, 1972.   x, 105 p.   illus.   23 cm.   Bibliography: p. (99) - 105.   70-181318 MARC.   F104.N6 H43

NEW HAVEN.   A modern history of New Haven and eastern New Haven County, by Everett G. Hill ... New York, Chicago, The S. J. Clarke pub. co., 1918.   2 v. plates, ports.   27½ cm.   Vol. 2 contains biographical sketches.   19-5250.   F104. N6 H5

NEW HAVEN.   An outline history of New Haven (interspersed with reminiscences) By Henry Howe. Centennial of the city ... 1884.   (New Haven, O. A. Dorman, 1884)   32 p.   20 x 12 cm.   Rc-3270*.
F104. N6 H8

NEW HAVEN.   Slogan "old elms, new ideas, New Haven."   (By Charles F. Julin)   New York, New Haven, 1912.   40 p.   illus., map.   19 cm.
F104. N6 J9

NEW HAVEN.   A historical discourse, delivered by request before the citizens of New Haven ... 1838, the 200th anniversary of the first settlement of the town and colony.   By James L. Kingsley.   New Haven, B. & W. Noyes, 1838.   115 p.   21½ cm.   Rc-3271.
F104. N6 K5

NEW HAVEN.   The trust company corner; a history from earliest times, 1638 - 1928, by Dean B. Lyman, jr.   New Haven, The Union & New Haven trust co., 1928.   5, 63 p.   front., plates.   24 cm. 28-24468.
F104. N6 L9

NEW HAVEN.   Men of New Haven in cartoon.   (New Haven?) 1906.   (54) l.   illus. (ports.)   32½ x 21½ cm. 17-30113.
F104. N6 M45

NEW HAVEN.   Dedication souvenir.   Official programme, New Haven ... 1887.   Soldiers' monument.   By Charles H. Miller.   Springfield, Mass., C. H. R. Miller, (1888)   29 p.   illus.   14 x 10½ cm. 9-11005.
F104. N6 M5

NEW HAVEN.   The fifteenth ward and the great society; an encounter with a modern city, by William Lee Miller.   Boston, Houghton Mifflin, 1966.   xxvi, 278 p.   22 cm.   66-12072.
F104. N6 M54

NEW HAVEN.   Pictures of Edgewood; in a series of photographs, by Rockwood, and illustrative text, by the author of "My farm of Edgewood".   (Donald G. Mitchell)   New York, C. Scribner, 1869. 62 p.   2 l.   front. (port.) plans (1 double) photos.   33 x 25 cm.   Rc-3272.
F104. N6 M6

NEW HAVEN.   (The differential time factor in assimilation.   By Jerome Keeley Myers.   n. p., 1951. 2 pts.   tables.   24 cm.   Thesis - Yale.   A study of the assimilation of Italians in New Haven.   Reprinted from American sociological review, v. 15, no. 3, June 1950; and from Sociology and social research, v. 35, no. 3, Jan.-Feb., 1951.   A51-4006.
F104. N6 M8

NEW HAVEN.   The hundredth anniversary of the city of New Haven, with the oration by Thomas Rutherford Bacon ... 1884.   Also a paper on New Haven in 1784, by Franklin Bowditch Dexter.   (New Haven) Pub. under the direction of N. G. Osborn and B. Mansfield, of the general committee on the centennial celebration, 1885.   97, (3) p.   23½ cm.   7-12015.
F104. N6 N58

NEW HAVEN.   ... New Haven town records, 1649 -   ed. by Franklin Bowditch Dexter.   New Haven, Printed for the Society, 1917 -   v.   24 cm.   (New Haven colony historical soc.   Ancient town records. v. 1 -   The records of the town of New Haven prior to 1650, were pub. in Records of the colony and plantation of New Haven, from 1638 to 1649, ed. C. J. Hoadly.   17-16435.
F104. N6 N59

NEW HAVEN.   Proceedings in commemoration of the settlement of the town of New Haven, 1888. (New Haven, Press of Tuttle, Morehouse & Taylor, 1888)   68, (2) p.   illus. (plan)   24½ cm.   Rc-3273.
F104. N6 N6

NEW HAVEN.   Proceedings of the city of New Haven, in the removal of monuments from its ancient burying-ground, and in the opening of a new ground for burial.   New-Haven, (Conn.) Gray & Hewit, 1822.   32 p.   fold. plan.   22½ cm.   7-14889.
F104. N6 N64

NEW HAVEN.   Vital records of New Haven, 1649 - 1850.   Hartford, The Connecticut society of the Order of the founders and patriots of America, 1917.   v.   24½ cm.   (Vital records of Connecticut.   Series I, Towns iv, pt. 1 -   17-30131.
F104. N6 N66

NEW HAVEN.   Center church.   Pamphlets, boradsides, clippings, and other miscellaneous matter on this subject, not separately cataloged, are classified in: F104. N6N694

NEW HAVEN.   Las industrias de New Haven y su vecindad, estado de Connecticut, E. U. A.   New

CONNECTICUT

Haven, Publicado baja la direccion de la Camara de comercio, 1897. 90 p. front., illus. 28½ cm.
Rc-3274. F104. N6 N7

NEW HAVEN. Confession of faith, covenant, and articles of practice, adopted by the First church in New Haven. (New Haven, Sidney's press, 1810) 16 p. 22½ cm. 21-12142.
F104. N6N715
Rare Book Coll.

NEW HAVEN. ... Manual of the First church in New Haven, for the years 1866 and 1867; containing the profession of faith, covenant, rules and arrangements, catalogues of the present members, etc. New Haven, Print. E. Hayes, 1867. 71 p. 20 cm. 19-4943. F104. N6 N72

NEW HAVEN. Report of the committee, appointed to inquire into the condition of the New Haven burying ground, and to propose a plan for its improvement. New Haven, Printed by B. L. Hamlen, 1839. 28 p. front. (fold. plan) 22½ cm. 7-16691. F104. N6 N74

NEW HAVEN. Official program of exercises incident to the dedication of the Soldiers; and sailors' monument, at East Rock park ... 1887. ... New Haven, J. B. Judson (1887) 48 p. 21 cm.
13-24900. F104. N6 N75

NEW HAVEN, 1638 - 1938, a book for students in the senior and junior high schools of New Haven, edited by Marie Campbell Gallivan ... (New Haven) Senior and junior high school curriculum subcommittee of the Superintendent's committee for school tercentenary plans (1942) iii-xii, 110 p. 24 cm. "Reference material": p. 107-110. 42-20510. F104. N6 N76

NEW HAVEN in a nut shell. (New Haven? 1904) 9½ x 12½ cm. F104. N6 N77

NEWHAVEN. A glance backward; editorial reminiscences by Norris G. Osborn ... New Haven, The Tuttle, Morehouse & Taylor co., 1905. (5) - 162 p. 17½ cm. 5-36301. F104. N6 O8

NEW HAVEN. Three centuries of New Haven, 1638 - 1938. By Rollin Gustav Osterweis. New Haven, Yale University Press, 1958. xv, 541 p. illus., ports., maps. 24 cm. 52-12064.
F104. N6 O83

NEW HAVEN. Guide to New Haven and Yale university, comp. by E. Oviatt ... New Haven, The Price & Lee co., 1901. (9) - 120 p. front., fold. map. 17½ cm. p. 111-120 advertising matter. 5-36303. F104. N6 O9

NEW HAVEN. Pardee's old Morris house, public museum and civic center at Morris Cove, New Haven, Conn. Gift of William Scranton Pardee; plans and notes by Walter Stone Pardee ... (Chicago, Ill., 1923) 15 numb. l. plates, plans, maps. 29½ cm. Photostat of type-written copy. Text parallel with back of cover. Includes "A Pardee genealogy". 24-1232. F104. N6 P2

NEW HAVEN. The New Haven state house with some account of the Green; and various matters of historical and local interest, gathered from many sources ... (By Henry Peck) New Haven, Conn., H. Peck & G. H. Coe, 1889. 282 p. illus. (incl. plans) 20½ x 15½ cm. Rc-3275. F104. N6 P3

NEW HAVEN. Saturday chronicle. 19- v. F104. N6 S2

NEW HAVEN, a book recording the varied activities of the author in his efforts over many years to promote the welfare of the city of his adoption since 1883, together with some researches into its storied past and many illustrations, by George Dudley Seymour ... New Haven, Priv. print. for the author (The Tuttle, Morehouse & Taylor co.) 1942. xxvi, 805 p. front., illus. (incl. ports., plans, facsims.) 24½ cm. 42-15625. F104. N6 S37

NEW HAVEN. Panthermania; the clash of Black against Black in one American city (by) Gail Sheehy. (1st ed.) New York, Harper & Row (1971) xv, 125 p. 22 cm. 79-158619.
F104. N6 S39

NEW HAVEN. My old New Haven and other memories briefly told, by Jane Bushnell Shepherd ... New Haven, Conn., The Tuttle, Morehouse & Taylor co., 1932. 98 p. front. 20½ cm. 32-34109. F104. N6 S4

NEW HAVEN.   Sons of the American Revolution.   ... Fourteenth annual congress.   New Haven, Conn., 1903.   21 cm.   F104. N6 S5

NEW HAVEN.   Souvenir views of New Haven and Yale university.   (New Haven, Conn., The Edw. Malley co., 1906)   (32) p. illus.   20 ½ x 25 cm.   CA 17-143 Unrev.   F104.N6 S66

NEW HAVEN.   Souvenir views of New Haven and Yale university.   (Portland, Me., L. H. Nelson co., 1910)   (32) p. illus.   20 x 25 ½ cm.   F104. N6 S7

— (1911)   20 x 25 cm.   F104.N6 S72

— (Portland, Me., L. H. Nelson co., 1915)   (24) p. of illus.   19 ½ x 25 ½ cm.   15-15324.   F104.N6 S723

NEW HAVEN.   The mayor's game; Richard Lee of New Haven and the politics of change, by Allan R. Talbot.   (1st ed.)   New York, Harper & Row (1967)   xii, 270 p.   22 cm.   67-11346.
F104. N6 T3

— New York, Praeger (1970)   xxiii, 274 p.   21 cm.   (Praeger university series, U-697)   70-110626.
F104. N6 T3 1970

NEW HAVEN.   The Thrilling panorama of New Haven history, 1638 - 1938.   New Haven, Conn., 1938.   36 p.   46 cm.   New Haven Sunday register tercentenary magazine, v. 61, no. 22.   F104.N6 T47

NEW HAVEN.   A pictorial history of "Raynham" and its vicinity ... by Charles Hervey Townshend ... (New Haven, The Tuttle, Morehouse & Taylor co.) 1900.   2, 50 p.   illus., plates, port., map.   32 x 24 ½ cm. 43-22734.   F104. N6 T6

NEW HAVEN.   The Grove Street Cemetery; a paper read before the New Haven Colony Historical Society ... 1947.   By Henry Hotchkiss Townshend.   (New Haven) The Society, 1948.   26 p.   23 cm. 48-22429*.   F104. N6 T7

NEW HAVEN.   Enjoying New Haven; a guide to the area.   By Trio Publications.   Rev. ed.   (New Haven, 1965)   124 p.   21 cm.   F104.N6 T75 1965

NEW HAVEN.   ... Deutscher tag und Schillerfeier, arrangirt von den Vereinigten deutschen gesell- schaften von New Haven, Connecticut, am 30. und 31. juli 1905.   (New Haven, 1905)   80 p.   illus. (ports.)   26 ½ cm.   10-22016.   F104. N6 V4

NEW HAVEN.   Views of New Haven and Yale university.   (New Haven, Conn., The Howe & Stetson co. 1904)   (32) p. of illus.   19 x 25 cm.   F104. N6 V6

NEW HAVEN.   New Haven Negroes, a social history, by Robert Austin Warner ... New Haven, Pub. for the Institute of human relations by Yale university press; London, H. Milford, Oxford university press, 1940.   xiv, 309 p.   front., plates, port., etc.   23 ½ cm.   Bibliographical foot-notes.   41-651.   F104.N6 W27

— New York, Arno Press, 1969.   xiv, 309 p.   24 cm.   (The American Negro, his history and literature)   78-94138.
F104.N6 W27 1969

NEW HAVEN.   Letters from the United States.   By the Rev. S. Wood ... (London, Printed by G. Smallfield, 1837)   11 p.   22 cm.   "From the Christian reformer, for Dec., 1837."   CA 28-723 Unrev.
F104. N6 W8

NEW HAVEN.   Early New Haven, by Sarah Day Woodward ... New Haven, Conn., Press of the Price, Lee & Adkins co., 1912.   119 p.   19 cm.   "Authorities": 1 p. at end.   12-880.   F104. N6 W9

NEWINGTON.   The centennial history of Newington, 1971.   Comp. and ed. by Elizabeth Sweetser

CONNECTICUT 65

Baxter. Introd. by Roger W. Eddy. (Newington) Lucy Robbins Welles Library Inc. (1971)
xvii, 316 p. illus., maps. 24 cm. F104.N62 B39

NEWINGTON. Half-century discourse. History of the church in Newington: its doctrine, its ministers, its experience: presented in the discourse delivered ... 1855 ... by J. Brace. Pub. by the Ecclesiastical society. Hartford, Press of Case, Tiffany and co., 1855. 75 p. front. (port.) 22½ cm.
19-4226. F104.N62 B7

NEWINGTON. Early days in Newington, 1833 - 1836, by Henry G. Little, 1813 - 1900. Newington, Conn., Priv. print., 1937. 122 p. port. 24 cm. "One hundred copies printed" 38-2746. F104.N62 L5

NEW LONDON. ... Connecticut's Naval office at New London during the war of the American revolution, including the mercantile letter book of Nathaniel Shaw, jr., by Ernest E. Rogers ... New London, Conn., 1933. xvii, 358 p. front., plates, ports., maps, facsims. 24½ cm. (Collections ... the New London county historical society. vol. II) Bibliography: p. (338) 33-36984. F104.N7
F102.N2N8 vol. 2

NEW LONDON. A century of banking in New London, pub. in commemoration of the 100th anniversary of the Savings bank of New London. New London, Conn. (1927) 3, 7-57 p. front., illus. (incl. ports., facsim.) 27 x 21 cm. 27-21338. F104.N7
HG2613.N384 S3

NEW LONDON city directory, for 1865-66, with a business directory, list of New London volunteers ... New London, C. Prince, 1865. 191 p. illus., fold. map. 16 cm. 9-29268. Directories

NEW LONDON. Boyd's New London directory ... with business directory of Norwich, Danielsonville, etc., 1870/71, 1876/7. (v.1 - 4) New London, Ct., E. A. Boyd, 1870 - 1875. 4 v. 19 cm.
10-257 Directories

NEW LONDON directory including Groton. (vol. 1 - 1890 - 19 New London, Conn., The Price & Lee co., 1890 - 19 v. fold. maps. 24 cm. 1-11791 Rev. Directories

NEW LONDON. God sometimes answers his people, by terrible things in righteousness. A discourse occasioned by that awful thunder-clap which struck the meeting-house in N. London ... 1735. .... By Eliphalet Adams ... N. London, Printed & sold by T. Green, 1735. 2, vi, 46 p. 15½ cm.
22-7148. F104. N7 A2
Rare Book Coll.

NEW LONDON. Leading business men of New London and vicinity, embracing Groton and Niantic ... (By William Hale Beckford. Boston, Mercantile pub. co., 1890. 83 p. illus. 27 cm. 4-20171.
F104. N7 B3

NEW LONDON. The early history of the First church of Christ, New London, Conn., by Rev. S. Leroy Blake ... New London, Press of the Day pub. co., 1897. 327 p. pl., port. 20½ cm. Rc-3276.
F104. N7 B6

NEW LONDON, a seaport for the North and West, and outport of New York; its great commercial advantages, convenient, ample and cheap wharf room, etc. By John R. Bolles ... New London (Conn.) Press of G. C. Starr, 1877. 24 p. 2 fold. maps. 22 cm. 4-25040. F104. N7 B7

NEW LONDON. History of New London. From the first survey of the coast in 1612, to 1852. By Frances Manwaring Caulkins ... New London, The author (Hartford, Ct., Press of Case, Tiffany and co.) 1852. xi, (13) - 679 p. illus. 23½ cm. "Obituaries of the early settlers": p. (267) - 374. 7-14874. F104.N7 C28

— 2d ed. Continued to 1860. New London, The author (Hartford, Ct., Press of Case, Lockwood and co.) 1860. xi, (13)-692, (673) - 679 p. illus. 24 cm. 26-23774. F104.N9 C29

— With memoir of the author. New London, H. D. Utley, 1895. xviii, 696 p. illus., port., maps. 24 cm.
Rc-3277 rev.* F104. N7 C3

— Index. (Cecelia Griswold, compiler. New London, 1950) 134 p. 23 cm. F104. N7 C3
Index

693

NEW LONDON whaling captains.   By B. L. Colby.   1936.   1 v. (Publication of the Marine historical assoc.)
F104. N7 C6

NEW LONDON.   The Day.   Sixth of May souvenir, 250th anniversary, New London.   Special ed.
New London, Conn., 1896.   8 p.   illus. (incl. ports.)   46 cm.   CA 25-1505 Unrev.   F104. N7 D27

NEW LONDON.   ... Diary of Joshua Hempstead of New London, covering a period of 47 years, from Sept., 1711, to Nov., 1758; containing valuable genealogical date relating to many New London families, references to the colonial wars, etc.... with an account of a journey made by the writer from New London to Maryland.   New London, Conn., The New London County historical soc., 1901.
xii, 750 p.   front., facsim.   24 cm.   (Collections of the New London County hist. soc. v. 1)   2-26527.   F104. N7 H49

NEW LONDON.   A study of the social and economic conditions of the Negro population of New London, conducted for the New London Council of Social Agencies by the National Urban League, as part of its Community Relations Project, Dept. of Research, New York City.   New York, 1944.   89 l.   29 cm.
47-29252*.   F104. N7 N3

NEW LONDON.   ... New London. Pettypaug point.   Brooklyn, N.Y., Priv. print., 1881.   6 numb. l.
map.   28 x 21 ½ cm.   Publication of the Historical printing club.   Ed. limited to 50 copies.   A 16-842 Rev.
F104. N7 N45

NEW LONDON.   A list of all those who are known to have been members of the First church of Christ, in New London, from the beginning to Jan. 1, 1901.   New London, Clarke & Keach, printers, 1900.   51 p.   21 cm.   10-5626.   F104. N7 N5

NEW LONDON.   A discourse delivered on the 200th anniversary of the First church of Christ, in New London ... 1870, by Thomas P. Field, with the other addresses on that occasion, and some account of the celebration ... New London, Starr & Farnham, book and job printers, 1870.
56 p.   23 cm.   6-40426.   F104. N7 N7

NEW LONDON.   History and dedication of the monument to Governor John Winthrop the younger, erected in the city which he founded, 1646, by the state of Connecticut, New London, May 6, 1905.
(In New London County historical soc. Records and papers.   1906. v. 3, pt. 1)   8-31267.   F104. N7 N75

NEW LONDON & Groton directory of streets & information.   (Everett, Mass., Interstate Pub. Co.)
v.   15 cm.   54-26903.   F104. N7 N78

NEW LONDON.   Picturesque New London.   May, 1891.   Containing views, time tables and other matters of interest ... (New London) C. J. Viets, 1891.   44 p.   illus.   8°.   1-Rc-3278.
F104. N7 P5 or P6

NEW LONDON.   Ye antient buriall place of New London.   . (By Edward Prentis)   New London, The Day pub. co., 1899.   40 p.   plates (1 fold.)   22 x 26 cm.   0-181 Rev.   F104. N7 P9

NEW LONDON.   ... New London'a participation in Connecticut's tercentenary, 1935.   Comp. and ed. by Ernest E. Rogers ... New London, Conn., The New London county historical soc., 1935.
x, 121 p.   front., illus. (incl. map) 23 cm.   (The New London county hist. soc.   Occasional pubs. v. III)   36-3787.   F104. N7 R6

NEW LONDON.   A centennial historical sketch of the town of New London, by W. H. Starr ... New London, Press of G. E. Starr, 1876.   96 p.   23 cm.   Rc-3280.   F104. N7 S7

NEW LONDON.   Views of New London.   (New London, Conn., (1908)   1 v.   20 ½ x 25 ½ cm.
F104. N7 V6

NEW MILFORD.   A memorial discourse, ... By James B. Bonar.   Pub. by the Society (Congregational) New Milford, Ct., M. L. Delavan, printer, 1876.   20 p.   19 cm.   25-3684.   F104. N73 B7

NEW MILFORD.   The 200th anniversary of the settlement of the town of New Milford ... 1907.
Address delivered by Daniel Davenport ... Bridgeport, Conn., Press of the Buckingham, Brewer & Platt co. (1907)   20 p.   23 ½ cm.   7-30340.   F104. N73 D2

CONNECTICUT 67

NEW MILFORD. Two centuries of New Milford; an account of the bi-centennial celebration of the founding of the town held June, 1907, with a number of historical articles and reminiscences; prepared under the direction of the Historical committee by various citizens of New Milford and by the editorial department of the Grafton press. New York, The Grafton press (1907) xii. 307 p. front., plates ports. 24 cm. 7-37008.
F104.N73 N7

NEW MILFORD. History of the towns of New Milford and Bridgewater, 1703 - 1882, by Samuel Orcutt. Hartford, Conn., Press of the Case, Lockwood and Brainard co., 1882. viii, 909 p. front., illus., plates, ports., plan. 23 cm. Includes a record of inscriptions in several cemeteries of New Milford and Bridgewater. "Biographical sketches": p. (563) - 635. "Genealogies": p. (637) - 813. 1-2210.
F104.N73 O6
Microfilm 8875 F

NEW MILFORD. The Weantinaug inn, New Milford. Season 1890. (New York, Gillis brothers, 1890) 16 p. incl. pl. obl. 16°. 2-6534.
F104.N73 W3

NEWINGTON. Two hundredth anniversary of the Church of Christ, Congregational, Newington ... 1922. Printed by vote of the Standing committee of the church. (Newington? Conn., 1922) (40) p. front. 23 cm. 24-11499.
F104.N75N75

NEWINGTON. Early annals of Newington, comprising the first records of the Newington ecclesiastical society, and of the Congregational church connected therewith; with documents and papers relating to the early history of the parish. Transcribed and ed. by Roger Welles ... Hartford, Press of the Case, Lockwood & Brainard co., 1874. 204 p. 23½ cm. Rc-3281.
F104.N75 W4

NEWINGTON. Centennial celebration. Historical address by Roger Welles, esq. and poem by Miss Mary K. Atwood ... July 4, 1876. Hartford, The Allen and Sherwood co., printers, 1876. 50 p. 22½ cm. 1-16826.
F104.N75 W5

NEWINGTON. A census of Newington, taken according to households in 1776, by Josiah Willard, together with some documents relating to the early history of the parish, ed. by Edwin Stanley Welles ... Hartford, F. B. Hartranft, 1909. (5) - 41 p. 26 cm. The Newington parish of old Wethersfield, which was incorporated as a town in 1871. 10-1080.
F104.M75 W6

NEWTOWN. Newtown: 1708 - 1758; historical notes and maps. By John Neville Boyle. (Limited ed.) Newtown, Conn., Bee Pub. Co. (1945?) iv-xv, 83 p. 2 fold. maps (in pocket) 24 cm. 47-29253*.
F104.N78 B6

NEWTOWN. Newtown's history and historian, Ezra Levan Johnson, with additional material, prepared by Jane Eliza Johnson ... Newtown, Conn., 1917. 284, 7, 12, 4, (2), 149, (2), 2 p. plates, ports., facsims. 23½ cm. "Genealogical section": 149 p. 21-11166.
F104.N78 J 6

NEWTOWN, past and present. By the League of Women Voters of Newtown. Cover design and 12 illus. by Newtown artists. 1st ed. (Newtown, 1955) 107 p. illus. 24 cm. Includes bibliography. 55-42639.
F104.N78 L4

NEWTOWN. The 250th anniversary of Newtown, 1705 - 1955. Ed. James A. Toby and others. (Newtown? Conn.) 1955. 56 p. illus. 23 cm. 56-23803.
F104.N78 T6

NOANK; from the papers of Claude M. Chester. Pub. in cooperation with the Noank Historical Soc. Essex, Conn., Pequot Press (1970) viii, 76 p. illus. 23 cm. 70-129504.
F104.N79 C5 1970

NORFOLK. ... History of Norfolk, Opening chapters by Rev. Joseph Eldridge. Comp. by Theron Wilmot Crissey. Everett, Mass., Mass. pub. co., 1900. viii, 648 p. front., plates, ports. 24 cm. "Norfolk's necrology." 1762 - 1899: p. 603-614. 1-2738.
F104. N8 C9

NORFOLK. The Norfolk village green, by Frederic S. Dennis; illus. from photographs. (New York) Priv. print. (Burr pub. co., 1917) 7, 3-137 p. front., plates. 24½ cm. 17-22076.
F104. N8 D4

NORFOLK.   Glimpses of Norfolk.   Photo-gravures.   Norfolk, Conn., M. H. Kendall, 1900.
1 p., 36 pl.   obl. 12°.   Feb. 21, 1901-81.
 F104. N8 G5

NORFOLK, the first two hundred years, 1758 - 1958: the Isabella Club papers.   Norfolk, Conn., Bi-centennial Committee (1958) 97 p. 23 cm. 74-285700.
 F104. N8 I 8

NORFOLK.   Baptisms, marriages, burials and list of members taken from church records of the Rev. Ammi Ruhamah Robbins, first minister of Norfolk, 1761 - 1813, in commemoration of the 150th anniversary of the organization of the church ... 1760.   (Norfolk, Conn.) Printed for C. and E. B. Stoeckel, 1910. 5, 3-141 p.   front. (port.) pl.   24½ cm.   11-982.
 F104. N8 N8

NORFOLK.   Robbins Battell.   Prepared for the 150th anniversary of the Church of Christ, Norfolk, 1910.   (New York, The De Vinne press, 1910?) 12 p.   26½ x 21 cm.   11-22317.
 F104. N8 R7

NORFOLK.   A brief history of the town of Norfolk (Conn) from 1738 to 1844 ... collected from the public records of the town, etc.   To which is added a description of the town, etc.   By Auren Roys ... New-York, Print. H. Ludwig, 1847. 89 p.   22½ cm.   Rc-3282.
 F104. N8 R8

NORTH HAVEN.   By the League of Women Voters of North Haven.   (North Haven, 1964) 48 p. map (in pocket) 23 cm.
 F104. N83 L4

NORTH HAVEN.   Catalogue of loan exhibition in connection with centennial of North Haven ... 1886. (North Haven? 1886) (24) p.   21 cm.   18-8748.
 F104. N83 N8

NORTH HAVEN in the nineteenth century.   A memorial.   Pub. by the Twentieth century committee. Comp. by Sheldon B. Thorpe ... (New Haven, The Price, Lee & Adkins co., printers) 1901.
207 p.   front. (port.)   illus.   24 cm.   15-20692.
 F104. N83N83

NORTH HAVEN.   A century sermon; or, Sketches of the history of the 18th century, Interspersed and closed with serious practical remarks.   Delivered ... 1801.   By Benjamin Trumbull ... New-Haven, Print. Read and Morse, 1801.   (New Haven, 1901) (In above. p. (185) - 201.   15-20693.
 F104. N83N83

NORTH HAVEN annals.   A history of the town from its settlement 1680, to its first centennial 1886. By Sheldon B. Thorpe.   New Haven, Conn., Press of the Price, Lee & Adkins co., 1892. 422 p.   front., illus., ports.   23½ cm.   1-16569 Rev.
 F104. N83 T5

NORTH HAVEN.   Dedication of the soldiers' monument, North Haven.   Comp. by the Veteran soldiers' association.   (New Haven, The New Haven printing co.) 1905. iv, (7) - 48 p.   illus. (incl. ports.) pl.   23½ cm.   Includes portraits of many of the North Haven soldiers of the civil war. 9-2378.
 F104. N83 V5

NORTH STAMFORD.   1782 - 1882.   Centennial celebrations ... Ed. by A. B. Davenport.   (Stamford, Conn.) The Stamford advocate office, 1882. 2 v. in 1.   22 cm.   Paged continuously.   1-20237.
 F104. N86 D2

NORWALK.   F. Killenberger's Norwalk and South Norwalk directory, including East Norwalk, West Norwalk, Broad River, Winnipauk, Silver Mine and Five Mile River.   18 - ... Comp. and pub. by F. Killenberger.   New Haven, Conn., 1883 1 v.   24 cm.   7-40729. Directories

NORWALK.   Carter & co.'s 1st - annual directory of Norwalk and South Norwalk for the years 1886/7 - ... Carter & co., pub. ... New York.   Peekskill, N.Y., Printed at the Blade office (1886 - 1 v.   23½ cm.   7-40728. Directories

NORWALK.   Directory of the town of Norwalk for (1889/90) - 1891.   (v. 1 - Philadelphia, Press of G. F. Lasher (1889) - 2 v.   24 cm.   8-2694. Directories

NORWALK directory.   v. 1 - 1891/92 - New Haven, Conn., Bridgeport, Conn., The Price & Lee co. (1891) - 19 v. fold. maps.   24 cm.   1-23066 Rev. Directories

CONNECTICUT 69

NORWALK directory ... New Haven, Conn., The Price & Lee co., 1891 - 1908.   16 v.   8°.   1-23066.
Directories

NORWALK.   An historical discourse in commemoration of the 200th anniversary of the settlement of Norwalk, in 1651; delivered in the First Congregational church in Norwalk ... 1851.   By Rev. Nathaniel Bouton ... New York, S. W. Benedict, 1851.   80 p.   23 cm.   Rc-3283.   F104. N9 B7

NORWALK.   The romance of Norwalk, by Elsie Nicholas Danenberg ... New York city, The States history co. (1929)   vi, 514 p.   front., plates, maps,   20½ cm.   (Sectional history series)   Bibliography: p. 482 - 484.
30-2910 Rev.   F104. N9 D17

NORWALK.   The ancient historical records of Norwalk: with a plan of the ancient settlement, and of the town in 1847.   Comp. by Edwin Hall ... Norwalk, J. Mallory; New York, Baker & Scribner, 1847.
320 p.   front. (fold. map) fold. plates.   19 cm.   "Town records": p. 41 - 145.   "The genealogical register": p. 181-320.   Rc-3284.
F104. N9 H2

— Norwalk, A. Selleck; New York, Ivison, Phinney, Blakeman, 1865.   320 p.   front. (fold. map) fold. plates.   19½ cm.   "Genealogical register": p. 181-320.   10-22037.   F104. N9 H3

NORWALK (v. 1 and supplement) By the Rev. Charles M. Selleck.   Norwalk, Conn., The author, 1896.   482, xliii p.   illus. (incl. plan, facsim.) pl., ports.   30 x 23 cm.   The greater part of v. 1 is devoted to genealogical sketches of the 34 original lot owners of 1650; the Supplement gives genealogy of ancient non-original home-lot households.   1-30383 Rev.
F104. N9 S4

NORWALK.   A complete copy of the inscriptions found on the monuments, headstones, &c., in the oldest cemetery in Norwalk. ... by David H. Van Hoosear ... Bridgeport, Conn., The Standard assoc., printers, 1895.   (From Fairfield County hist. soc. Reports ... 1893-5)   10-6838 Rev.   F104. N9 V2

NORWALK after 250 years, an account of the celebration of the 250th anniversary of the charter of the town, 1651 ... including historical sketches of churches, schools, old homes ... records of soldiers and sailors enlisted in Norwalk from 1676 to 1898. ...   Pub. under the auspices of the Norwalk historical and memorial library association.   South Norwalk, Conn., C. A. Freeman (1902)
3-387 p.   plates, port.   23½ cm.   Compiled by Samuel R. Weed.   13-25502.

NORWICH.   ... Stedman's directory of the city and town of Norwich ... (no. 6-7, 15-22, 25-26, 28-29, 31-45, 47, 49-53.   1866-67, 1875-1882, 1885-86, 1888-89, 1897-1905, 1907, 1909-1913) Norwich, (Conn.) Price & Lee co., 1866 - 1913.   35 v.   fold. maps.   19 - 24 cm.   1-12869 Rev.
Directories

NORWICH the rose of New England.   (By Leonard Woolsey Bacon)   (Norwich, Cranston & co., 1896)
16 p.   24 pl.   obl. 16°.   1-Rc-3285.   F104. N93 B1

— (2d ed. 1903)   18½ x 22 cm.   F104. N93 B13

NORWICH.   The leading business men of Norwich and vicinity, embracing Greeneville and Preston ... Boston, Mercantile pub. co., 1890.   (By William Hale Beckford)   80 p.   illus.   26 cm.   4-20170.
F104. N93 B3

NORWICH.   A historical discourse, delivered at the 100th anniversary of the organization of the Second Congregational church ... 1860, Norwich.   By Alvan Bond.   With an appendix.   Norwich, Manning, Platt & co., printers, 1860.   64 p.   fold. plan.   23 cm.   6-15334.
F104. N93 B7

NORWICH, History of, from its settlement in 1660, to Jan. 1845.   By Miss F. M. Caulkins ... Norwich, T. Robinson, 1845.   viii, (9) - 359 p.   front., plates.   20 cm.   Rc-3286.   F104. N93 C3

NORWICH.   History of Norwich: from its possession by the Indians, to the year 1866.   By Frances Manwaring Caulkins.   (Hartford) The author, 1866.   xi, (17) - 704 p.   front., illus., ports.   23½ cm.   Rc-3287.
F104. N93 C4

— Also a brief sketch of the life of the author, to which is added an appendix containing notes and sketches continuing the history to the close of the year 1873. (New London?) Pub. by friends of the author, 1874.   xi, 714, xi p. illus., ports. 24 cm.   49-39666*.   F104.N93 C4 1874

NORWICH.   The Norwich memorial; the annals of Norwich, in the great rebellion of 1861 - 65, by Malcolm McG. Dana ... Norwich, Conn., J. H. Jewett, 1873.   xi, (13) - 394 (i.e. 390) p. incl. illus., tables. front., pl., ports. 24 cm.   1-Rc-3288 Add.   F104.H93 D2

NORWICH.   Our brave boys. A memorial discourse, delivered in the Second Congregational church, Norwich ... 1865, by Malcolm McGregor Dana ... Pub. by request. Norwich, Bulletin job print., 1866.   2, (3) - 58 p. 20 ½ cm.   6-19135.   F104.N93D22

NORWICH.   A historical discourse delivered in Norwich ... 1859, at the bi-centennial celebration of the settlement of the town. By Daniel Coit Gilman ... 2d ed., with additional notes. Boston, G. C. Rand and Avery, city printers, 1859.   128 p. 23 cm.   Rc-3289.   F104.N93 G4

NORWICH.   The celebration of the 250th anniversary of the settlement of the town of Norwich, and of the incorporation of the city, the 125th ... 1909; by William C. Gilman. Norwich, 1912.   244 p. front., plates, ports. 24 ½ cm.   13-9178.   F104.N93G42

NORWICH.   Samuel Huntington and his family, by Albert E. Waugh. Stonington, Conn., Pequot Press (1968)   43 p. illus. 23 cm.   F104.N93H98

NORWICH.   Taxpayers of Norwich, and political hand book; comp. by Daniel Lee. 1884. New London, Print. by the Day co. (1884)   107 p. 24 cm.   Advertisments: p. 75-107.   4-6489.   F104.N93 L4

NORWICH.   A sketch of Norwich: including notes of a survey of the town: by Wm. Lester, jr., 1833. Norwich, Print. J. Dunham, 1833.   30 p. 18 ½ cm.   14-7351.   F104.N93 L6

NORWICH.   Vital records of Norwich, 1659 - 1848. Hartford, Society of colonial wars in the state of Conn., 1913.   2 v. 24 cm.   (Vital records of Conn. Series I. Towns II, pt. I - II) 13-9844 Rev.   F104.N93N68

NORWICH board of trade quarterly ... v. III, no. 1   (Norwich, Board of trade, 1909) 1 v. illus., pl., port. 25 cm.   9-18172.   F104.N93 N7

NORWICH.   Norwich, Connecticut: its importance as a business and manufacturing centre and as a place of residence. A brief review of its past and present. Issued by the Norwich board of trade, Jan., 1888. Norwich, Press of the Bulletin co., 1888.   111 p. front., plates, 2 fold. plans. 24 ½ cm. p. (77) - 111, advertising matter.   6-14313.   F104.N93 N8

NORWICH in a nutshell ... A ready-reference book of useful information for pocket, desk and household use. (Norwich) L. W. Pratt, 1892.   112 p. illus. sq. 16°.   1-Rc-3290.   F104.N93 N9

NORWICH historic homes and families. Researched and written by Marian K. O'Keefe and Catharine S. Doroshevich. Consulatant editor: Philip A. Johnson. Photography by Marian K. O'Keefe. Stonington, Conn., Pequot Press (1967)   viii, 112 p. 24 cm.   66-30461.   F104.N93D37

NORWICH.   Memorial of Col. Hugh Henry Osgood of Norwich, Conn. (Norwich, Record job print, 1899?)   59 p. front. (port.) pl. 20 ½ x 16 ½ cm.   20-11334.   F104.N93 O8

NORWICH.   Old families of Norwich, 1660 - 1800, comp. by Mary E. Perkins. Genealogies. vol. I, pt. 1 ... Norwich, Conn., 1900.   50 p. 26 ½ cm.   No more pub? Contents. - Adgate; Backus; Baldwin; Bingham. 1-31660 Rev.   F104.N93 P3

NORWICH.   Old houses of the antient town of Norwich, 1660 - 1800, with maps, illustrations, portraits and genealogies, by Mary E. Perkins. Norwich, Conn. (Press of the Bulletin co.) 1895.   (iii) - xviii, 402 p, 407 - 621 p. front., illus., plates, ports., plans. 24 x 19 cm. Pt. II. Genealogies. 1-Rc-3291.

        F104.N93 P4
        Microfilm 22017 F

CONNECTICUT

NORWICH. The Norwich jubilee. A report of the celebration at Norwich on the 200th anniversary of the settlement of the town ... 1859. With an appendix, containing historical documents of local interest. Comp., print. and pub. by John W. Stedman ... Norwich, Conn., 1859. viii p. (11) - 304 p. front. (fold. map) 1 illus., col. plates, facsims. 22½ cm. Contains music. Rc-3292.
F104.N93 S8

NORWICH: early homes and history. A paper written and delivered by Sarah Lester Tyler, at the meeting of Faith Trumbull chapter, D. A. R ... 1905. Norwich, Conn., Pub. by the Faith Trumbull chapter, D.A.R., 1906. 19 p. 24 cm. 6-42441.
F104.N93 T9

NORWICH. Views of Norwich ... Norwich, Conn. (1905) 13½ x 18½ cm.
F104.N93 V6

NORWICH. Pamphlets, broadsides, clippings, and other miscellaneous matter on this subject, not separately catalogued, are classified in:
F104.N93 Z9

NORWICHTOWN. Inscriptions from gravestones in the old burying ground, Norwich Town (by) George S. Porter ... Pub. by the Society of the founders of Norwich. Norwich, Conn., The Bulletin press, 1933. 3; 177 p. front., plates. 28½ x 22½ cm. 34-18208.
F104.N932 P7

OLD SILLTOWN; something of its history and people, being principally a brief account of the early generations of the Sill family ... By Sarah Sill (Welles) Burt. (n. p.) 1912. 148 p. illus. 25 cm.
F104.O36 B8

OLD LYME. Landmarks of Old Lyme; historic buildings, monuments and heirlooms, together with a short record of the town since 1635. (Old Lyme?) The Tercentenary committee of Old Lyme, 1935. 32 p. 23 cm. 39-32934.
F104.O36 O5

OLD SAYBROOK. ... The First church of Christ, (Congregational,) Old Saybrook. The celebration of the 250th anniversary ... 1896. Historical review and addresses. Middletown, Conn., J. S. Stewart, printer, 1896. xiv, 132 p. incl. front., illus. 23½ cm. 6-38863.
F104. O4 O4

OLD LYME. Discourse delivered on the 200th anniversary of the organization of the Old Lyme Congregational church, 1693 - 1893. By the pastor, Rev. Arthur Shirley. Lyme, Conn., G. A. Smith, steam print, 1893. 17 p. 23 cm. 18-11619.
F104.O4 S55

ORANGE. History of Orange, North Milford, Conn., 1639 - 1949. By Mary Rebecca Woodruff. (Orange?) 1949. vii, 177 p. illus., fold. map. 24 cm. 50-388.
F104. O7 W6

OXFORD. History of the town of Oxford, by Norman Litchfield and Sabina Connolly Hoyt. (n. p. 1960) 328 p. 24 cm.
F104. O9 L5

OXFORD. History of Oxford ... By W. C. Sharpe ... Seymour, Conn., Record print, 1885 - 1910. 2 v. illus., port. 22½ cm. Paged continuously. Contents. - pt. 1. Church records, births, marriages, deaths, etc. - pt. 2. (Sketches and additional vital records) 1-14483 Add.
F104. O9 S5

PLYMOUTH. History of the town of Plymouth, with an account of the centennial celebration ... 1895. Also a sketch of Plymouth, Ohio, settled by local families. Comp. by Francis Atwater. Meriden, Conn., Journal pub. co., 1895. 441, vi p. illus. (incl. ports., facsim.) 25 cm. The territory now Plymouth was originally a part of Waterbury; organized as the parish of Northbury, 1739, and in 1780 incorporated with the Westbury parish of Waterbury in the new town of Watertown. In 1795 the old Northbury parish was set off as the town of Plymouth. 1-Rc-3293.
F104. P7 A8

PONSETT. By gone days in Ponsett-Haddam; a story of Rev. William C. Knowles ... New York, Priv. print., 1914. 3, 3-65 p. 2 fold. maps (incl. front.) 23½ cm. 15-19301.
F104.P78 K7

POMFRET. Early homesteads of Pomfret and Hampton. By Susan (Jewett) Griggs. (Abington? Conn., 1950) 161, 118 p. illus., fold. maps. 24 cm. Cover title: Folklore and firesides in Pomfret, Hampton, and vicinity. 53-22389.
F104. P8 G75

POMFRET. History of Pomfret. A discourse delivered on the day of annual thanksgiving ... 1840. By D. Hunt ... Hartford, J. Holbrook, printer, 1841. 35 p. 22 cm. Rc-3294.
F104. P8 H9

POMFRET. A record of those who served in the civil war, 1861 - 1865, from the town of Pomfret. (Pomfret, 1916)   4 - 32 p.   col. pl.   23 cm.   Introd. signed: Ralph J. Sabin.   20-2098.
F104. P8 P7

POMFRET. The 150th anniversary of the organization of the First church of Christ in Pomfret ... 1865. Sermon, historical papers, etc. Danielsonville (Conn.) Transcript print, 1866.   96 p.   23 cm.
7-12506.
F104. P8 P8

PORTLAND. History of Portland, by Frances Solomon Murphy. Illus. by Sue Hall. Middletown, Conn., Stewart Press, 1969.   180 p.   illus.   24 cm.
F104. P86 M8

PORTLAND. The Portland burying ground association and its cemetery. Portland, Conn., Middlesex County printery, 1897.   77 p.   23½ cm.   Introd. note signed: F. G. (i. e. Ferdinand Gildersleeve?)   20-1746.
F104. P86 P7

PRESTON. Inscriptions from the Long society burying ground, Preston. By George S. Porter. Boston, Press of D. Clapp, 1906.   6 p.   22 cm.   "Reprinted from the New-England hist. and genealogical register, Apr., 1906."   17-30081.
F104. P9 P 8

PRESTON. The bi-centennial celebration. First Congregational church of Preston, 1698 - 1898. Together with statistics of the church taken from the church records. (Preston) The Society, 1900. viii, 201 p.   23½ cm.   Preface signed: R. H. G.   (admissions, baptisms, marriages, etc.) p. 127-199.   10-210.
F104. P9 P93

PRESTON, 1801, and Lisbon (Hanover) 1800, and Lisbon (Newent) 1801. (Hartford) 1961. 32 p.   24 cm.   (Acorn Club of Conn. Publication 29)
F104. P9 P94

PUTNAM. Directory of Putnam and Danielson. 1900 -   (v. 1 -   Putnam, Conn. (1900) - v.   24½ cm.
Directories

PUTNAM directory ... (1882) -   (Spencer? Mass.) L. M. French & co., 1882 - v.   16½ cm.   34-15329.
Directories

REDDING. The revolutionary soldiers of Redding, and the record of their services; with mention of others who rendered service or suffered loss at the hands of the enemy during the struggle for independence, 1775 - 1783; together with some account of the loyalists of the town and vicinity ... By William Edgar Grumman. (Hartford, Conn.) Hartford press: The Case, Lockwood & Brainard co., 1904.   208 p.   front., plates, ports.   23½ cm.   4-37126.
F104. R3 G8

REDDING. The history of Redding, from its first settlement to the present time. With notes on the Adams, Banks ... Stow families. By Charles Burr Todd ... New York, The J. A. Gray press, 1880. vi, (2), 248 p.   front. (port.)   24 cm.   1-Rc-3295.
F104. R3 T6

— with notes on the Adams, Banks, Barlow ... and Strong families, ... (2d ed.) New York, The Grafton press (1906)   v, (2), 303 p.   front., plates, ports.   26½ cm.   7-4521.
F104. R3 T7

RIDGEFIELD in review. By Silvio A. Bedini. With a foreword by Allan Nevins. (1st ed.) Ridgefield, Conn., Ridgefield 250th Anniversary Committee, 1958.   xiv, 396 p.   illus., ports., maps (1 fold.) facsims.   24 cm.   Bibliography: p. 373 - 376.   58-44421.
F104. R5 B4

RIDGEFIELD in 1800. By Samuel Goodrich. (Hartford) Acorn Club of Conn., 1954)   21 p.   24 cm. (Acorn Club of Connecticut. 25th publication. Connecticut towns)   54-3097.
F104. R5 G6

RIDGEFIELD. Glimpses of Ridgefield. By Mrs. Marie (Hartig) Kendall. Photo-gravures. Norfolk, Conn., M. H. Kendall, 1900.   36 pl.   18 x 23 cm.   1-30297 Rev.
F104. R5 K3

RIDGEFIELD. 1708 - Ridgefield - 1908. Bi-centennial celebration ... 1908; report of the proceedings ... Pub. by the Bi-centennial committee, Hartford, Conn., The Case, Lockwood & Brainard co., 1908.   96 p.   plates, ports.   25 cm.   16-19534.
F104. R5 R6

RIDGEFIELD. The history of Ridgefield, by George L. Rockwell. Ridgefield, Conn., Priv. print.

by the author, 1927.   583 p.   front., illus. (incl. maps) plates, ports., facsims.   24 cm.   Contains records of soldiers in the revolution and the world war.   Bibliography: p. 555.   27-23547.

F104. R5 R8

RIDGEFIELD.   The history of Ridgefield.   From its first settlement to the present time.   By Daniel W. Teller ... Danbury, T. Donovan, 1878.   4, 251 p.   front., plates.   19½ cm.   Rc-3296 Rev.

F104. R5 T2

ROCK RIDGE.   Rambles in Rock Ridge; being an account of the search of a man for the site of an agreeable home and how he found it in Greenwich.   (New York, Redfield bros., 1900)   32 p.   illus. map.   obl. 16°.   Mar. 8, 1900-59.

F104. R6 S5

ROCKVILLE, Vernon, Tolland, Ellington directory ... (v. 1 - 1916/17, 1920, 1922, 1924, 1925, 1927, 1929, 1930, 1932   Lee co. (1889) - 19   v.   fold. maps.   23½ cm.   0-5262 (rev. '32)   1889/90 - 1891/92, 1894 New Haven, Conn., The Price & Directories

ROCKVILLE.   ... The city of Rockville.   By B. Lewellyn Burr.   (In The Connecticut magazine. 1900. v. 6) p. 61-74)   12-6385

F104. R7 B9

ROCKVILLE.   History of Rockville, from 1823 to 1871.   Including also a brief sketch of facts which ante-date the incorporation of Vernon, and bring dates up to the time when this history begins.   By Wm. T. Cogswell ... Rockville (Conn.) Printed at the Journal office, 1872.   48 p.   mounted phot.   21½ cm.   Rc-3297 Rev.

F104. R7 C6

SALEM.   Chronicles of a Connecticut farm, 1769 - 1905, comp. by Mary E. Perkins ... for Mr. and Mrs. Alfred Mitchell, the present proprietors of the Mumford and Woodbridge homesteads ... Boston, Priv. print., 1905.   298 p., 2 pl., 16 port., 7 maps (partly fold) 3 fold. geneal. tab.   25½ cm.   Edition limited to 50 copies. 6-3622.

F104. S18 P4

SALISBURY.   A historical address, delivered at the commemoration of the 100th anniversary of the first annual town meeting of the town of Salisbury ... 1841.   By Samuel Church.   New Haven, Hitchcock & Stafford, printers, 1842.   96 p.   23 cm.   16-5375.

F104. S2 C56

SALISBURY.   A new-year's discourse, delivered at Salisbury, Jan. 2, 1803: containing the ancient history of the town.   By Joseph W. Crossman ... Hartford: Printed by Hudson & Goodwin, 1803. 28 p.   20½ cm.   18-22479.

F104. S2 C9

SALISBURY.   The changing landscape; Salisbury.   By Christopher Rand.   New York, Oxford University Press, 1968.   192 p.   21 cm.   68-17619.

F104. S2 R28

SALISBURY.   A historical address, before the Congregational church, in Salisbury, at their first centennial celebration ... 1844.   By Adam Reid, pastor of the church.   Hartford, Press of E. Geer, 1845.   63 p.   22½ cm.   1-16588.

F104. S2 R3

SALISBURY.   An historical sketch of Salisbury.   By Malcolm Day Rudd, and an explanatory note on Indian names, by Irvin W. Sanford.   Supplementary to Sanford's maps of Salisbury.   New York, 1899. 23 p.   23 cm.   1-13373.

F104. S2 R9

SALISBURY.   Inscriptions at Salisbury Center, Lime Rock, etc.   Comp. by Malcolm Day Rudd. Boston, D. Clapp, printers, 1898.   16 p.   14½ cm.   1-7735.

F104. S2 R94

SALISBURY.   Historical collections relating to the town of Salisbury.   vol. I -   Arr. and pub. by the Salisbury assoc. inc.   (New Haven, Conn., The Tuttle, Morehouse & Taylor co.) 1913 - 2 v.   23½ cm.   14-31026.

F104. S2 S 14

SALISBURY.   Vital records of Salisbury Town, circa 1730 -   Cemetery records.   (In Salisbury assoc. Historical collections.   1913.   v. 1, p. (23) - 123.   14-5292.

F104. S2 S 14 vol. 1

SALISBURY.   A brief military history of Salisbury; an address, delivered by Malcolm D. Rudd ... 1911.   (In Salisbury assoc. Historical collections. 1913. v. 1, p. (125) - 154)   14-5291.

F104. S2 S 14 vol. 1

SALISBURY. Historical addresses delivered by Hon. Samuel Church ... 1841, and ex-Gov. A. H. Holley ... 1876, tog. with a record of proceedings at the centennial celebration in Salisbury. Pittsfield, Mass., Chickering & Axtell, printers, 1876. 59, (3), 55 p. 22½ cm. 11-6056.

F104. S2 S18

SALISBURY. ... The 150th anniversary of the Congregational church in Salisbury. Hartford, Conn., Press of the Case, Lockwood & Brainard co., 1895. 82 p. front., plates, ports. 24½ cm. 9-251.

F104. S2 S2

SASQUA HILLS, overlooking Long Island Sound, described with pictures; (by Edward Everett Winchell) illustrations made by C. B. Tubbs. New York, F. R. Wood, W. H. Dolson co., 1916. (16) p. incl. illus., plates (4 fold.) 22 cm. 16-8816.

F104. S25 W7

SAYBROOK. Peace flag day at old Saybrook ... Aug. 16, 1861. Comp. by Edward P. Blague ... (Springfield, Mass., 1896) 22 p. illus. 19½ x 26½ cm. 22-9824.

F104. S3 B6

SAYBROOK. Glimpses of Saybrook in colonial days ... from 1636 ... - 1776. By Mrs. Chesebrough. A true copy made by Anna D. Sheffield. Old Saybrook, Conn. (1933) 68 p. 69 - 227 p. fold. plan. 27½ cm. Manuscript. "Mrs. Chesebrough wrote the history of Saybrook in 1894" 39M2364.

F104. S3 C5
Rare Book Coll.

SEYMOUR. ... The town of Seymour. By Frank G. Bassett. (In The Connecticut magazine. 1900. v. 6, p. 311 -334) 12-6383.

F104. S5 B3

SEYMOUR. Old landmarks of Seymour. By Hollis A. Campbell. (In The Connecticut magazine. v.6, p.491 - 513) 12-6382.

F104. S5 C19

SEYMOUR, past and present, by Rev. Hollis A. Campbell and others. Seymour, Conn., W. C. Sharpe, 1902. 613 p. incl. illus., map. front., port. 24 cm. 2-11715* Cancel.

F104. S5 C2

SEYMOUR. Seymour and vicinity. Historical collections, by W. C. Sharpe. Seymour, Conn., Record print, 1878. 148 p. illus., mounted photos. 22 cm. Rc-3298 Rev.

F104. S5 S4

SEYMOUR. History of Seymour, with biographies and genealogies. By W. C. Sharpe. Seymour, Conn., Record print, 1879. 244 p. front., illus., pl., 7 port. 23 cm. Rc-3299 Rev.

F104. S5 S5

SEYMOUR. Vital statistics of Seymour. Comp. by William C. Sharpe. Seymour, Conn., "Record" print, 1883 - 1911. 4 v. 22 - 23 cm. A part of the town of Derby was incorporated as Seymour in 1850. when the town records begin. Parish registers, however, begin in 1817 and cemetery inscriptions several years earlier. The final volume brings the records to the close of the year 1910. 7-32893.

F104. S5 S55
L H & G

SHARON. Poconnuck historical society's collections no. 1 - (Lakeville, Conn.) Lakeville journal, 1912 - v. port. 23½ cm. 14-8418.

F104. S5 P7

SHARON. ... Indians of the Webutuck Valley, by Myron B. Benton. (Lakeville, Conn.) Lakeville journal, 1912. 22 p. port. 23½ cm. (Poconnuck historical soc.'s collections, no. 2) 14-8420.

F104. S5 P7

SHARON. Gnadensee, the lake of grace; a Moravian picture in a Connecticut frame, by Edward O. Dyer ... Boston, Chicago, The Pilgrim press (1903) 291 p., front., plates. 21 cm. 3-14876.

F104. S53 D9

SHARON. A history of the town of Sharon, from its first settlement. By Charles F. Sedgwick. Hartford, Print, Case, Tiffany & co., 1842. 124 p. 16 cm. 7-12039.

F104. S53 S4

— 3d ed. Amenia, N.Y., C. Walsh, 1898. (7) - 204 p. front. (port.) plates. 22½ cm. 1st ed. above. 2d ed. pub. in 1877. 10-3106.

F104. S53 S42

SHARON. The original home lots of the town of Sharon; a history of the sale and settlement of Sharon together with a map.   Edited and prepared by the Publications Committee, Sharon Historical Soc. (1963)   43 p.   map (in pocket)   24 cm.   F104. S53 S5

SHARON.   Born, married and died, in Sharon.   A record of births, marriages and deaths, in the town of Sharon, from 1721 to 1879. ... (By) Lawrence Van Alstyne ... Sharon, Conn. (Press of Pawling chronicle) 1897.   143 p.   23½ cm.   Rc-3300.   F104. S53 V2

SHARON.   Burying grounds of Sharon, Amenia and North East, New York; being an abstract of inscriptions from thirty places of burial in the above named towns.   (By Lawrence Van Alstyne) Amenia, N.Y., Walsh, Griffen & Hoysradt, printer, 1903.   246, (2) p.   25½ cm.   14-3395.
F104. S53 V22

SHARON.   Picturesque and historic Sharon (by) Rev. Ulysses Grant Warren.   (New York, Blumenberg press, 1904)   141 p.   illus.   17 x 25 cm.   4-27136.   F104. S53 W2

SHELTON.   The White Hills of Shelton.   White Hills Civic Club History Committee.   Essex, Conn., Pequot Press (1968)   vi, 63 p.   illus., fold. chart.   24 cm.   68-57462.   F104. S54 W5

SHERMAN.   Historical landmarks in the town of Sherman, by Ruth Rogers ... Quaker Hill, N.Y., Pub. by the Quaker Hill conference assoc., 1907.   26 p.   19 cm.   (Quaker Hill (local history) series xvii) 8-1146.
F104. S55 R7

SILVER LANE.   Exercises at the unveiling of a tablet to commemorate the camping of the French army under Count de Rochambeau on Silver Lane in 1781 and in 1782 ... Col. Jeremiah Wadsworth branch, Conn. soc., Sons of the American revolution, Hartford.   (Hartford, 1928)   (4) p.   illus.
25½ x 20½ cm.   31-11356.   F104. S58 S7

SIMSBURY.   A record and documentary history of Simsbury, by Lucius I. Barber, 1643 - 1888.   Simsbury, Conn., The Abigail Phelps chapter, D. A. R., 1931.   6, 429 p.   front. (mounted port.)   fold. facsim.
24½ cm.   32-19469.   F104. S6 B3
Rare Book Coll.

SIMSBURY; being a brief historical sketch of ancient and modern Simsbury, 1642 - 1935, by John E. Ellsworth ... (Simsbury, Conn.) Simsbury committee for the tercentenary, 1935.   xiv, 190 p.   front., plates, ports., fold. maps.   23½ cm.   "Bibliography pertaining to Simsbury history": p. 181 - 190.   36-28120.
F104. S6 E46

SIMSBURY.   History of Simsbury, Granby and Canton, from 1642 to 1845.   By Noah A. Phelps.   Hartford, Press of Case, Tiffany and Burnham, 1845.   (9) - 176 p.   23 cm.   "Simsbury originally embraced nearly the whole territory included within the present limits of Simsbury, Granby and Canton.   Granby was set off ... in 1786, and Canton ... in 1806." - p. 9.
Register of marriages, births and deaths, in the families of the first settlers of Simsbury: p. 168-175.   1-Rc-3301.   F104. S6 P4

SIMSBURY, 1670 - 1970.   Chamber of Commerce.   (Simsbury, 1970)   92 p.   illus.   23 cm.
F104. S6 S55

SIMSBURY.   Rev. Dudley Woodbridge, his church record at Simsbury in Conn., 1697 - 1710.   Pub. with prefatory notes by Albert C. Bates ... Hartford (Press of the Case, Lockwood & Brainard co.) 1894.   32 p.   25½ cm.   100 copies printed.   8-12262.   F104. S6 S58

SIMSBURY births, marriages and deaths, transcribed from the town records, and pub. by Albert C. Bates ... Hartford (The Case, Lockwood & Brainard co.) 1898.   345 p.   facsim.   25 cm.   3-14606.
F104. S6 S6

SIMSBURY'S part in the war of the American revolution, by the Rev. Chas. E. Stowe.   Hartford, Conn., Press of the Case, Lockwood & Brainard co., 1896.   23 p.   24½ cm.   16-10383.
F104. S6 S9

SIMSBURY.   Three centuries of Simsbury, 1670 - 1970, by William M. Vibert.   (Simsbury, Conn., 1970)   272 p.   illus.   23 cm.   F104. S6 V57

SIMSBURY.   Records of Rev. Roger Viets, rector of St. Andrews, Simsbury, and missionary from the Society for the propagation of the gospel in foreign parts, 1763 - 1800.   By Albert C. Bates ... Hartford (Press of the Case, Lockwood & Brainard co.) 1893.   84 p.   25½ cm.   100 copies printed.   The original parish of St. Andrews is now included within the limits of the town of Bloomfield.   4-7258.
F104. S6 V6

SIMSBURY.   Records of Rev. Ransom Warner, 1823 - 1854, rector of St. Andrew's, Simsbury and Bloomfield, St. Peter's, Granby, St. John's, East Windsor, Conn.   Also additional records, 1777-1778, of Rev. Roger Viets, rector of St. Andrew's, Simsbury.   By Albert C. Bates ... Hartford, 1923.   42 p.   23 cm.   100 copies printed.   23-14451.
F104. S6 W3

SOMERS.   A sermon, delivered ... 1828, soon after the 100th anniversary of the organization of the church in Somers ...   By William L. Strong ... Hartford, Print. P. B. Gleason, 1828.   24 p.   23½ cm.   18-2289.
F104. S68 S9

SOUND BEACH.   The Sound Beach and Riverside directory ...   Providence, R. I., C. De Witt White co., 19   v.   23 cm.   20-18060.
Directories

SOUTH BRITAIN sketches and records.   By W. C. Sharpe.   Seymour, Conn., Record print, 1898.   167 p.   front., illus., ports.   22½ cm.   98-1160 Rev.
F104. S7 S5

SOUTHINGTON directory ... 1882, 1883.   New Haven, Conn., The Price & Lee co., 1882 - 19   v.   fold. maps.   23½ cm.   1-30395 Rev.
Directories

SOUTHINGTON.   Compounce, 1846 - 1902, by Alice J. Norton.   Bristol, Conn., 1902.   37 p. incl. front., illus., facsim.   18½ x 24 cm.   2-18613.
F104. S73 N8

SOUTHINGTON.   ... The Doctor Henry Skilton house, Southington, Hartford county, Conn... (By John Davis Skilton)   (Hartford? 1930?)   3, 6 - 10 numb. l., 3 l., a - p leaves.   illus., plates, plans, facsims.   28 x 21½ cm.   (Old houses of Connecticut ... collected and compiled by the Conn. society of colonial dames of America)   This is one of fifty reproductions ... from the original copy of the book in the Conn. state library at Hartford.   30-29408.
F104. S73 S62

SOUTHINGTON news and the Cheshire times.   Anniversary edition.   Southington, Conn., (J. M. Peterson) 1940.   8, 4, 8, 8, 8, 4 p.   illus.   57 cm.   Forms v. 79, no. 19, issued Aug. 9, 1940.   "Commemorates the 75th anniversary of the Southington news and the 300th anniversary of the town of Farmington."   42M233T.
F104. S73 S7

SOUTHINGTON.   Ecclesiastical and other sketches of Southington.   By Rev. Heman R. Timlow ... Hartford, Press of the Case, Lockwood and Brainard co.,   1875.   8, (2), 570 p. cclxxv p.   front., ports.   23½ cm.   Southington genealogies: p. i - cclxxv.   1-19750.
F104. S73 T5

SOUTH KILLINGLY.   History of the Congregational church in South Killingly, Conn., with a record of doings at its 150th anniversary.   Danielson, Conn., Transcript print (1896)   39 p.   illus.   23 cm.   16-19533.
F104. S74 S7

SOUTHPORT.   Annals of an old parish; historical sketches of Trinity church, Southport, 1725 to 1898, by Rev. Edmund Guilbert.   New York, T. Whittaker, 1898.   xiv, (2), 291 p.   front., illus., plates, ports., fold. plan.   23 cm.   99-178 Rev.
F104. S75 G9

SOUTHPORT.   An historical story of Southport.   Compiled by Charlotte Alvord Lacey.   Greens Farms, Conn., Modern Book and Crafts (1971?)   69 p.   illus.   24 cm.
F104. S75 L3

SOUTHPORT.   The Southport Congregational church, Southport ... 1843 - 1915; an historical sketch, etc.   New York, Priv. print. (by the Gilliss press) 1915.   6, 3-178 p.   23 cm.   Ed. Rev. William H. Holman.   16-13905.
F104. S75 S75

STAFFORD.   The history of the town of Stafford; pub. by the Stafford library association, in connection with the celebration of the Connecticut tercentenary.   Stafford Springs, Conn., 1935.   88 p.   24 cm.   36-19415.
F104. S78 S67

STAFFORD SPRINGS, including views from villages in the town of Stafford.   In photo-gravure.   From

CONNECTICUT

photos. taken by H. C. Thresher ... Stafford Springs, Conn., N. M. Whiton, 1895.   16 pl. obl. 24⁰.
1-Rc-3302.   F104. S78 S7

STAMFORD directory, 1897 - 19   (v. 1 -   New Haven, Conn (etc.) The Price & Lee
co., 1897 - 19   v. fold. maps. 24 cm. 1-23084 (rev. '26)   Directories

STAMFORD.   The Stamford borough directory 1881/2 ... Comp. by W. S. Webb ... Stamford, Conn.,
W. W. Gillespie, 1881.   110 p.   23 cm.   8-7791.   Directories

STAMFORD.   The Stamford directory (1883) -   ... Comp. and pub. by Gillespie brothers ...
Stamford, Conn., Gillespie bros., printers and bookinders (1883) - 75.   5 v. fold. plans. 23 cm.
7-41346.   Directories

STAMFORD directory ...   Stamford, Conn., The Price & Lee co., 1897 - 1908.   Oct. 5, 99-187.
    Directories

STAMFORD, Port Chester, and Mt. Vernon business and street directory.   18   Also containing the town governments and classified business, church and society directory of New Canaan, Sound Beach, Riverside, Cos Cob, Greenwich, Rye, Harrison, Mamaroneck, Larchmont Manor, New Rochelle and Pelhamville ... Bridgeport, Conn., American directory & Pub. co., 1892 -
1 v.   23 cm.   8-29791.   Directories

STAMFORD.   Historical address, delivered in the First Congregational church in Stamford, at the celebration of the second centennial anniversary of the first settlement of the town.   By Rev. J. W. Alvord.   New York, S. Davenport, 1842.   40 p. 22 ½ cm. Rc-3303 Rev. 2.   F104. S8 A4

STAMFORD.   Pictures of Stamford and environs ... By George Bennett.   Stamford, Conn., 1904.
13 x 21 cm.   F104. S8 B4

STAMFORD.   Davenport Ridge, Stamford, Conn.   Historical sketch.   Printed for private use.
Brooklyn, N. Y., A. B. Davenport, 1892.   16 p. pl., port. 8⁰. 1-Rc-3304.   F104. S8 D2

STAMFORD.   ... Picturesque Stamford.   A souvenir of the 250th anniversary of the settlement of the town of Stamford, containing an historical sketch, covering salient points of Stamford's history from 1641 to 1892 ... Stamford, Gillespie bros., 1892.   316 p. fold. front., illus., port. 4⁰. 1-Rc-3305.
    F104. S8 G4

STAMFORD.   History of Stamford, from its settlement in 1641, to the present time, including Darien, which was one of its parishes until 1820; by Rev. E. B. Huntington.   Stamford, The author, 1868.
4; 492 p. front., plates, ports., map. 22 cm. Births, marriages and deaths 1640 - 1700, p. (155)-167. 1-Rc-3306.   F104. S8 H9

STAMFORD soldiers' memorial, by Rev. E. B. Huntington ... Stamford, Conn., The author, 1869.
165 p.   22 cm.   1-24371.   F104. S8 H92

STAMFORD.   Stamford revolutionary war damage claims.   By Ronald Marcus.   (Stamford, Conn., Stamford historical soc., 1968)   viii, 75 l. 29 cm.   F104. S8 M3

— Essex, Conn., Pequot Press (1969)   xii, 83 p. 23 cm.   F104. S8 M3
    1969

STAMFORD.   ... Stamford - 1641 - 1900.   By Julie Adams Powell.   (From The Connecticut magazine. 1900.
v. 6, p. 209-223) 12-6381.   F104. S8 P8

STAMFORD.   The history of Stamford.   By Arlene Roth Seligman.   (N.p., 1969)   90 l.   28 cm.
    F104. S8 S4

STAMFORD.   The story of Stamford, by Herbert F. Sherwood ... New York city, The States history co. (1930)   x, 379 p. front., plate,s, ports., maps, facsims. 20 ½ cm. (Sectional history series) Biographies: p. 333-351.
Bibliography: p. 366.   30-14514.   F104. S8 S55

STAMFORD. Silver and gold, by Louise Willis Snead, with illustrations from the author's sketch book. Stamford, Conn. (Stamford trust co.) 1916.   4, 13 - 58 p. front., illus. (incl. plan) plates. 22½ cm.
Bibliography on verso of 3d prelim. leaf.   17-2332.
                F104. S 8 S67

STAMFORD registration of births, marriages and deaths, incl. every name, relationship, and date now found in the Stamford registers, from the first record down to the year 1825. By Rev. E. B. Huntington. Stamford, Conn., W. W. Gillespie, printers, 1874.   3, (5) - 139 p. 22 cm. 24-3062 Rev.
                F104. S8 S73
                L H & G

STAMFORD. City of Stamford. ... Pub. under the auspices of the Stamford board of trade ... Stamford (1915)   94, (2) p. illus. (incl. map) 17 x 25½ cm. CA 25-1016 Unrev.
                F104. S8 S75

STAMFORD. ... Stamford, records of the Congregational church ... (1746 - 1846) William Applebie Daniel Eardeley ... Brooklyn, N. Y., 1914.   6 v. 27½ cm. Type-written copy. Partial contents. - v. 1-2 Baptisms. - v. 3. Marriages. - v. 4. Marriages and deaths. - v. 5. Deaths. - v. 6. Deaths, covenant catalogue, etc. 23-14452.
                F104. S8 S76

STAMFORD. Abstracts of probate records for the district of Stamford, county of Fairfield and state of Conn., by Spencer P. Mead ... (n. p.) 1919.   3 p., 2-425 numb. 1. 27½ cm. Autographed from type-written copy. "... includes the towns of Greenwich, Ridgefield and Stamford. Stamford included during part of the period the town of Darien and part of the town of New Canaan. In 1744 a probate court for the towns of Danbury Newton and New Fairfield was created and Ridgefield was added in 1746. Prior to the creation of the above probate courts the probate records for the entire county of Fairfield are at the Probate court at Fairfield. 20-4904.
                F104. S8 S78

STAMFORD. Abstract of probate records for the district of Stamford, county of Fairfield, and state of Connecticut, 1803 - 1848. By Spencer P. Mead ... (n. p.) 1924.   3p., 2-503 numb. 1. 27 cm. Autographed from type-written copy. 25-15910.
                F104. S8 S782

STAMFORD historical sketches, by Alfred Grant Walton. (Stamford, Conn., Cunningham press, 1922)   100 p. incl. front., illus. 21 cm. 22-21329.
                F104. S8 W83

STAMFORD. Woodland cemetery. Proceedings at the dedication ... 1861.   1 v.   F104. S8 W9

STONINGTON. In the village (by) Anthony Bailey. (1st ed.) New York, A. A. Knopf, 1971.
225 p. 22 cm. 77-136478.
                F104. S85 B3

STONINGTON. The fine old town of Stonington; a historical tribute to the founders and their descendants. By Katharine B. Crandall. (Stonington? Conn., 1949)   151 p. illus. 21 cm. 50-57558.
                F104. S85 C7

— (Label: Watch Hill, R. I., Book & Tackle Shop, 1962)   151 p. 21 cm. 62-19723.
                F104. S85 C7
                1962

STONINGTON. Recollections of old Stonington (by) Anne Atwood Dodge. Stonington, Con., Pequot Press (1966)   vii, 45 p. 19 cm. 66-22117.
                F104. S85 D6

STONINGTON chronology, 1649 - 1949; being a year-by-year record of the American way of life in a Connecticut town. By Williams Haynes. Stonington, Pequot Press (1949)   151 p. illus., ports., facsims. 28 cm. 49-10159*.
                F104. S85 H3

STONINGTON. The diary of Manasseh Minor, Stonington, 1696 - 1720. Pub. by Frank Denison Miner with the assistance of Miss Hannah Miner. (n. p.) 1915.   196 p. illus., plates, facsims. (part fold.) 22 cm. 16-5988.
                F104. S85M52
                Rare Book Coll.

STONINGTON. The diary of Thomas Minor, Stonington, 1653 - 1684. Prepared for publication by Sidney H. Miner and George D. Stanton, jr. (New London, Conn., Press of the Day pub. co.) 1899.
221 p. pl., facsim. 24½ cm. 1-1465. L. C. copy replaced by microfilm.
                F104. S85 M6
                Microfilm 18707 F

CONNECTICUT 79

STONINGTON by the sea, by Henry Robinson Palmer ... Stonington, Conn., Palmer press, 1913.
112 p. front., illus. (incl. map) plates. 22 cm. 13-2458.   F104. S85 P2

— (2d ed.) Stonington, Conn., Palmer Press, 1957.   95 p. illus. 24 cm. 57-38867.
F104. S85 P2
1957

STONINGTON. The homes of our ancestors in Stonington, by Grace Denison Wheeler. Salem, Mass., Newcomb & Gauss, printers, 1903.   4; 286 p. front., illus. 24 cm. 3-22839.
F104. S85W35

STONINGTON. History of the First Congregational church, Stonington, 1674 - 1874. With the report of bi-centennial proceedings ... 1874. ... By Richard A. Wheeler ... Norwich, Conn., T. H. Davis, 1875.   x, 300 p. front. 24 cm. 2-23886.   F104. S85 W4

STONINGTON. History of the town of Stonington ... from its first settlement in 1649 to 1900, with a genealogical register of Stonington families. By Richard Anson Wheeler ... New London, Conn., Press of the Day pub. co., 1900.   4; 754 p. front. (port.) 24 cm. 0-4939 Rev.
F104. S85 W5

— Mystic, Conn., L. Verry, 1966.   754 p. port. 24 cm. 67-2773.   F104. S85 W5
1966

STONINGTON. Old Stonington in Connecticut, 1649 - 1949, and the Fannings, the Winthrops, Captain Kidd, Captain Palmer, and others. By Laurence Frederick Whittemore. New York, Newcomen Soc. in North America, 1949.   24 p. illus. 23 cm. "2d printing Dec. 1949." 50-2359.
F104. S85W53

STONY CREEK. A brief history of Stony Creek, chronicling persons and events both ancient and modern, by Gertrude Farnham McKenzie. New Haven, Press of Van Dyck & co., (1933)
26 p. 23 cm. 33-32577.   F104. S853M2

STRATFIELD in 1800. By Philo Shelton. (New Haven) Acorn Club of Connecticut, 1949.
9 p. 24 cm. (Acorn club of Conn. 23rd publication. Connecticut towns) 49-4894.   F104. S86 S5

STRATFORD. A history of the old town of Stratford and the city of Bridgeport. By Rev. Samuel Orcutt ... Pub. under the auspices of the Fairfield County historical soc. (New Haven, Conn., Press of Tuttle, Morehouse & Taylor) 1886.   2 v. illus., plates, ports., fold. maps. 25½ cm. Paged continuously; v.1: viii, 692 p; v.2: (693) - 1393 p. Vol. 2 contains also histories of Huntington, Trumbull and Monroe, towns incorporated from old Stratford. Epitaphs from the various cemeteries are included. Genealogies: v.2, p. 1113-1358. 1-Rc-3307.   F104. S87 O6

STRATFORD. ... "Who's who", a directory of Stratford ... (1st -   1937 -
Stratford, Conn., Samuel Johnson chapter, Christ church, 1937 -   v. illus., fold. map. 23 cm.
37-20020.   Directories

STRATFORD. Commemoration of the 200th anniversary of Christ church, Stratford ... 1907. (New Haven, 1907)   21½ cm.   F104. S87 S8

STRATFORD. ... The quarto-millennial anniversary of the Congregational church of Stratford. The historical address by the pastor, and a full report of all the exercises ... 1889. Bridgeport, Conn., The Standard association, printers, 1889.   115 p. incl. front., illus., 2 pl. 23 cm. 16-8154.
F104. S87 S84

STRATFORD. History of Stratford, 1639 - 1939, by Wm. Howard Wilcoxson. Stratford, Conn., Pub. under the auspices of the Stratford tercentenary commission, 1939.   xvi, 783, (43) p. incl. front. (port.) illus. (incl. maps, facsims.) 23½ cm. Includes biographical sketches. 40-5895.   F104. S87 W5

SUFFIELD. Documentary history of Suffield, in the colony and province of the Massachusetts Bay, in New England, 1660 - 1749. Collected, transcribed and pub. by Hezekiah Spencer Sheldon ... Spring-

field, Mass., Printed by the Clark W. Bryan co., 1879 - 88.   3 pt. in 1 v.   2 plans.   24 cm.   Paged continuously.
Imperfect: p. 213 - 220 wanting.   1-13374.
F104. S9 S5

SUFFIELD.   Celebration of the bi-centennial anniversary of the town of Suffield, Conn. ... 1870.
Hartford, Wiley, Waterman & Eaton, 1871.   113, (2) p.   front., plates, ports.   23½ cm.   Rc-3308.
F104. S9 S9

SUFFIELD.   Celebration of the 250th anniversary of the settlement of Suffield ... 1920, with sketches from its past and some record of its last half century and of its present.   Suffield, By authority of the General executive committee, 1921.   204 p.   front., plates, ports.   24½ cm.   23-2816.
F104. S9 S91

SUFFIELD; 250th anniversary of the founding of the town ... 1920.   Official program.   (Suffield? 1920)   64 p.   23 cm.   CA 22-244 Unrev.
F104. S9 S92

SUFFIELD.   Proceedings at Suffield ... 1858, on the occasion of the 150th anniversary of the decease of the Rev. Benjamin Ruggles, first pastor of the First Congregational church.   Springfield, Mass., S. Bowles, printers, 1859.   118 p.   front., pl.   23½ cm.   13-6004.
F104. S9 S95

SUFFIELD.   Records of the Congregational church in Suffield (except church votes) 1710 - 1836.   Hartford, Connecticut historical soc., 1941.   224 p.   24 cm.   (Vital records of Connecticut.   Ser. II - Churches, v. 7.   Fifth town)   41-26042.
F104. S9 S955

THOMPSON.   Congregational church.   Manual ... 1901.   1 v.
F104. T4 T4

TOLLAND.   Life in Tolland during the 1880's.   By Edgar Marvin Hawkins.   (Hingham? Mass.) 1960.
25, 16 l.   29 cm.
F104. T6 H3

TOLLAND.   The early history of Tolland.   An address delivered before the Tolland County historical soc ... 1861.   By Loren P. Waldo ... Hartford, Press of Case, Lockwood, 1861.   iv, (3) - 148 p.
23 cm.   Includes sketches of family history.   Rc-3309 Rev.
F104. T6 W2

TOLLAND: the history of an old Connecticut Post Road town.   Compiled by Harold Weigold for the Tolland Historical Society.   Chester, Conn., Pequot Press, 1971.   ix, 245 p.   illus.   24 cm.   Bibliography: p. (246)   79-180543 MARC.
F104. T6 W4

TORRINGFORD: in connection with the centennial of the settlement of the first pastor, Rev. Samuel J. Mills.   (By William Henry Moore)   Hartford, Case, Lockwood & Brainard, printers, 1870.
107 p.   22½ cm.   7-16667.
F104. T68 M8

TORRINGTON directory (1892/3) - 1902/3, 1909/10   New Haven, Conn., The Price & Lee co. (1892 - 19   4 v.   fold. plans.   24 cm.   (With Winsted directory)   1-27303.
Directories

TORRINGTON, Winsted, Litchfield, Norfolk, Goshen directory ... (v. 42 -   1928 -
New Haven, Conn., The Price & Lee co., 1928 -   v.   fold. maps.   24 cm.   33-14372.
Directories

TORRINGTON.   Memories of Walter Holcomb of Torrington; with a few departures in genealogy, public records, customs, etc.   (Torrington? Conn.) 1935.   2, 9-47 p.   pl., ports.   23½ cm.   35-32764.
F104. T7 H5

TORRINGTON.   History of Torrington, from its first settlement in 1737, with biographies and genealogies.   By Rev. Samuel Orcutt ... Albany, J. Munsell, printer, 1878.   vii, 817 p.   front., illus., plates, ports.   23½ cm.   1-Rc-3310.
F104. T7 O6

TORRINGTON.   A history of Torrington ... (by) John H. Thompson.   Torrington, Conn., The Torrington printing co., 1934.   36 p.   illus.   23 cm.   On cover: Compiled for use in the public schools.   34-12544.   F104. T7 T4

TRUMBULL.   They face the rising sun; a comprehensive story with genealogical material and com-

CONNECTICUT

plete charting of Unity Burial Ground - oldest cemetery in Trumbull, 1730 - 1971, by E. Merrill Beach. 1st ed. (Chester, Conn., Pequot Press) 1971. vii, 60 p. illus. 24 cm. Includes bibliographical references.
73-178157 MARC.
F104. T75 B39

TRUMBULL: church and town; a history of the colonial town of Trumbull and of its church which was the Church of Christ in Unity, the Church of Christ in North Stratford, and is now the Church of Christ in Trumbull, 1730 - 1955. (Trumbull, Conn., Historical Committee) 1955. 165 p. illus. 24 cm.
56-17888.
F104. T75 B4

TRUMBULL churches and people. By Lora M. (Freer) Wachenheim. Ed. 1: (Trumbull? Conn., Brewer-Borg Corp.) 1960. viii, 149 p. 24 cm.
F104. T15 W3

TRUMBULL people and friends, by Lora M. Freer Wachenheim. Ed. 1. Trumbull? 1965.
xiii, 324 p. 24 cm.
F104.T75W32

UNION. The history of Union, founded on material gathered by Rev. Charles Hammond ... Comp. by Rev. Harvey M. Lawson ... with assistance from many others. New Haven, Press of Price, Lee & Adkins co., 1893. viii, 508 p. ports. (incl. front.) fold. map. 22 ½ cm. "Genealogies of the families": p. (252) - 500.
Rc-3311.
F104. U5 H2

UNION in 1803. By Solomon Wales. (Hartford?) Acorn Club of Connecticut, 1954. 12 p. 24 cm.
(Acorn Club of Conn. 24th publication. Connecticut towns) 54-34194.
F104. U5 W3

VERNON. Centennial of Vernon (Rockville) ... 1908. Souvenir program containing history of the town, with events for the week, half tones of members of committees and prominent citizens, etc. Rockville, Conn., T. F. Rady, printing (1908) 120 p. illus. 27 cm. 16-20039.
F104.V5 V53

VERNON. A century of Vernon, 1808 - 1908; summary of Vernon's history, early and modern. Literary exercises at historic Congregational church at Vernon Center ... Report of the proceedings and program for the week's centennial celebration ... 1908. Pub. under the auspices of special historical committee. Rockville, Conn., Press of T. F. Rady, 1911. 159 p. plates, ports., facsim. 24 cm.
Ed. and comp. by Harry Conklin Smith. 15-17338.
F104.V5 V54

WALLINGFORD. Hank's Wallingford directory, 1887/8 - 1889/90 ... Comp. and pub. by Wilbur F. Hanks ... New Haven, Conn., The Price, Lee & Adkins co., printers, 1887 - 89. 2 v. 24 cm.
7-41326.
Directories

WALLINGFORD directory v. 1 -   New Haven, Conn., The Price & Lee co., 1893 - 1969.
9 v. 8°. Nov. 16, 99-158.
Directories

WALLINGFORD. F. Killenberger's Wallingford borough directory. 1883 - 1885/6. Willimantic, Conn., Windham pub. and print. co., 1883 - 85. 2 v. 23 cm. 8-27847.
Directories

WALLINGFORD directory ... 1887/88 - 18   New Haven, Conn., The Price & Lee co.,
1887 - 19   v. fold. maps. 23 ½ cm. 7-41326 Rev.
Directories

WALLINGFORD. A century discourse, delivered at the anniversary meeting of the freemen of the town of Wallingford ... 1770 ... By James Dana. New-Haven, T. & S. Green (1770?) 51 p. 12°.
Rc-3312.
F104. W2 D2
Rare Book Coll.

WALLINGFORD. History of Wallingford, from its settlement in 1670 to the present time, including Meriden, which was one of its parishes until 1806, and Cheshire, which was incorporated in 1780. By Charles Henry Stanley Davis ... Meriden, The author, 1870. vii, 956 p. front., illus., plates, ports., fold. plan. 24 cm. 1-Rc-3313.
F104. W2 D4

WALLINGFORD. Tales of old Wallingford (by) Clarence E. Hale. Chester, Conn., Pequot Press, 1971. vi, 154 p. illus. 21 cm. 70-175812 MARC.
F104. W2 H3

WALLINGFORD. History of the Wallingford disaster. By John B. Kendrick ... Hartford, The Case,

Lockwood & Brainard co., printers, 1878.   76 p. front., 7 pl. 23½ cm. 3-19147.

F104. W2 K3

WALLINGFORD. Wallingford in 1811 - 12. By George Washington Stanley. Acorn Club of Conn., 1961.   25 p. 24 cm. (Acorn Club of Conn. Publication 26. Connecticut towns. 65-33782.

F104. W2 S8

WALLINGFORD. ... Two hundred and fiftieth birthday anniversary of Wallingford; official program. (Wallingford? Conn., 1920)   31 p. illus. 25½ cm. 20-20524.

F104. W2 W2

WALLINGFORD historical soc. inc. ... Constitution and by-laws. Wallingford, Conn., 1920. 15 p. 14½ cm. 22-25791.

F104. W2 W3

WALLINGFORD. The master of the Gunnery; a memorial of Frederick William Gunn, by his pupils ... New York, The Gunn memorial assoc., 1887.   2, (iii) - xv, 179 p. incl. illus., port. front. (port.) 31 cm. Ed. William Hamilton Gibson. 8-31733.

F104. W22 G4

WASHINGTON. Our home in the countryside. By Adrian Van Sinderen. New York, 1957. 135 p. illus. (part col.) ports. 26 cm. 58-16334.

F104. W22 V3

WATERBURY, Naugatuck, Watertown directory ... 18   New Haven, Conn., The Price & Lee co., 18   - 19   v. fold. maps. 24 cm. 1-10033 Rev. 2.

Directories

WATERBURY. The churches of Mattatuck: a record of a bi-centennial celebration at Waterbury ... 1891. Ed. by Joseph Anderson ... New Haven, Press of the Price, Lee & Adkins co., 1892. xii, 279 p. 20 cm. 6-37683.

F104. W3 A4

WATERBURY. History of the soldiers' monument in Waterbury, by Joseph Anderson ... To which is added a list of the soldiers and sialors who went from Waterbury to fight in the war for the union ... (Hartford, Conn., Press of the Case, Lockwood & Brainard co.) Printed for the Monument committee, 1886.   viii, 170 p. 6 pl. (incl. front.) 24 cm. 9-11011.

F104. W3 A45

WATERBURY. The town and city of Waterbury, from the aboriginal period to the year 1895. Ed. by Joseph Anderson ... New Haven, The Price & Lee co., 1896.   3 v. 2 front., illus., plates, ports. 25 cm. "Family records": v. 1, appendix, p. (1 ap) - 166 ap. 98-206 Rev.

F104. W3 A5

WATERBURY. Hearings before the Connecticut Commission on Human Rights and Opportunities; an interim report. Hearings held in Waterbury, June 10, 1968 to Oct. 22, 1968. (Hartford, 1969) 84 p. 28 cm. 75-627276.

F104. W3 A53

WATERFORD. An illustrated history of the town of Waterford, by Robert L. Bachman. With William Breadheft, photographer of the contemporary scenes. Waterford, Conn., Morningside Press, 1967. v, 114 p. 28 cm. 66-30563.

F104. W3 B3

WATERBURY. The history of Waterbury; the original township embracing present Watertown and Plymouth, and parts of Oxford, Wolcott, Middlebury, Prospect and Naugatuck. With an appendix of biography, genealogy and statistics. By Henry Bronson. Waterbury, Bronson brothers, 1858. viii p., (2), 582 p. front., plates, ports., 2 maps (1 double) double facsim. 22½ cm. "Genealogy": p. (458) - 552. 1-Rc-3314.

F104. W3 B8

WATERBURY. The military history of Waterbury from the founding of the settlement in 1678 to 1891, together with a list of the commissioned officers and the records of the wars; containing also an outline of all the changes in the military organization of the state. By Charles W. Burpee ... New Haven, Conn., The Price, Lee & Adkins co., printers, 1891.   98 p. 24 cm. Rc-3315 Rev.

F104. W3 B9

WATERBURY. Mattatuck historical society. Handbook no. 1 -   1877 - 19 (Waterbury) The Society, 1914 -   v. 21½ cm. 14-7315.

F104. W3 M34

WATERBURY. Mattatuck historical society. Publications. v. 1 -   1911 -

CONNECTICUT   83

(Waterbury) Mattatuck historical society, 1911 -   v.   24½ cm.   14-5941.   F104. W3 M38

WATERBURY. Proprietors' records of the town of Waterbury, 1677 - 1761, transcribed and ed. by
Katharine A. Prichard ... (Waterbury) The Mattatuck historical soc., 1911.   xv, 260 p.   2 double facsim.
(incl. front.)   24½ cm.   (Publications of the Mattatuck hist. soc. vol. 1)   13-23486.   F104. W3M38 v. 1
                                                                                                    F104. W3 W25

WATERBURY. Ancient burying grounds of the town of Waterbury, together with other records of
church and town, comp. and ed. by Katharine A. Prichard. (Waterbury) The Mattatuck historical soc.,
1917.   338 p.   24½ cm.   (Publications of the Mattatuck hist. soc. v.2)   18-18522.   F104. W3M38 v. 2
                                                                                                    F104. W3 P8

WATERBURY. Mattatuck historical society ... The president's address at the annual meeting ... 1911
(Waterbury, The Society, 1912 -   v.   21½ cm.   13-24928.   F104. W3 M4

WATERBURY. History of Waterbury and the Naugatuck valley, by Wm. J. Pape ... Chicago, New
York, The S. J. Clarke pub. co., 1918.   3 v.   fronts., plates, ports.   27½ cm.   Vols. 2-3 contain biographical sketches.
18-21396 Rev.   F104. W3 P2

WATERBURY and her industries. Fifty attractive and carefully selected views, by the photogravure
process, as photographed from nature, of the many leading manufacturing establishments, public
buildings, churches, etc. of Waterbury, tog. with a Historical sketch of the city and its various industries, by Homer F. Bassett ...   Gardner, Mass., Lithotype printing and pub. co. (1889?)
36 p., 50 pl.   18 x 25½ cm.   2-7754.   F104. W3 W26

WATERBURY and vicinity.   (Portland, Me., 1908)   1 v.   20½ x 25½ cm.   F104. W3 W28

WATERBURY illustrated. Waterbury, Adt & brother, 1889.   (6), 32 p.   13 x 18½ cm.   Rc-3317.
                                                                                                    F104. W3 W3

WATERFORD.   See F104. W3 B3

WATERTOWN. The Old burying ground of ancient Westbury and present Watertown. Pub. by Sarah
Whitman Trumbull chapter, D. A. R. Watertown, Conn., 1938.   145 p.   illus. (incl. plan)   23½ cm.
40-19852.   F104. W33 D3

WATERTOWN. Historical sketch of Watertown from its original settlement; with the record of its
mortality, from March, 1741, to Jan., 1845, and to May, 1858 ... By N. S. Richardson ... Rev. and
enl. by Frederick Dayton. Waterbury, Print. E. B. Cooke, 1858.   72 p.   19 cm.   With this is bound
the following item. L. C. copy replaced by microfilm. Rc-3319.   F104. W33 R5
                                                                                                    Microfilm 18708 F

WATERTOWN. Third series of the historical sketch of Watertown; with the record of its mortality,
from 1858 to 1871. Prepared for publication by the late Frederick Dayton. Waterbury, Conn., Press
of Cooke, Mattoon & Robbins, 1871.   29 (4) p.   19 cm.   (Bound with above) A continuation of the above. Rc-3318.
L. C. copy replaced by microfilm.   F104. W33 R5
                                                                                                    Microfilm 18708 F

WEST HARTFORD. The West Hartford story, by Richard N. Boulton and Bice Clemow. Illus. by
Matt Klim. (West Hartford, Conn., West Hartford Pub. Co., 1954)   111 p.   illus. 27 cm.   "Special
supplement of the June 3, 1954 centennial souvenir issue of the West Hartford news, vol. xxii, no. 32." Includes bibliography. 54-32604.
                                                                                                    F104. W36 B6

WEST HARTFORD. Three centuries of a Yankee town; an address for the centennial of the town of
West Hartford, delivered in the meeting house of the First Church of Christ in West Hartford on the
evening of June 6, 1954. (Washington, 1954)   16 p.   22 cm.   55-17192.   F104. W36 B8

WEST HARTFORD. By William Hutchins Hall.   (West Hartford?) 1930.   267 p.   illus., ports., maps.
24 cm. 51-51252.   F104. W36 H3

WEST HARTFORD. Two discourses delivered ... 1863, on the completion of a century and a half
from the organization of the Congregational church in West Hartford, Conn. By Myron N. Morris.

West Hartford, Printed by W. Storer, 1863.   39 p.   23 cm.   11-34832.   F104.W36 M8

WEST HAVEN.   History of West Haven, compiled by workers of the Writers' program of the W.P.A. (West Haven, Conn., Church press) 1940.   5, 93 p.   front., plates.   26½ cm.   41-53205.
F104.W37 W7

WESTPORT, Saugatuck and Greens Farms directory.   (v.1) -   1917/18 -   Providence, R.I., C. De Witt White co., 1917 -   v.   24 cm.   17-24062.   Directories

WESTPORT, the making of a Yankee township, by Edward Coley Birge, with a postscript by Mary Coley Gage.   New York, The Writers pub. co., 1926.   x, 113 p. incl. front.   19½ cm.   26-15194.
F104.W39 B5

WESTPORT in Connecticut's history, 1835 - 1935.   ed. (Wakefield Dort) (Bridgeport, Conn., Print. by the Warner bros. co., 1935)   (5) - 126 p. incl. illus., plates, etc.   23½ cm.   36-647.   F104.W39 D67

WETHERSFIELD.   Historic sketch of the First church of Christ in Wethersfield, given from the pulpit ... 1876, by Aaron C. Adams.   Hartford, Conn., The Allen & Sherwood co., printers, 1877.   24 p.   22½ cm.   11-34833.   F104.W4 A22

WETHERSFIELD.   Some old Wethersfield houses and gardens ... By Henry Sherman Adams.   (Wethersfield, 1909)   1 v.   23½ cm.   F104.W4 A24

WETHERSFIELD.   The history of ancient Wethersfield; comprising the present towns of Wethersfield, Rocky Hill, and Newington; and of Glastonbury prior to its incorporation in 1693, from date of earliest settlement until the present time ... By Sherman Wolcott Adams.   New York, The Grafton press, 1904.
2 v.   fronts., illus., plates, ports., maps (1 fold.) facsims.   28 cm.   Contents. - v.1. History ... ed. H. R. Stiles. - v.2. Genealogies and biographies, by H. R. Stiles.   5-310.   F104.W4 A26

WETHERSFIELD.   The Connecticut tercentenary, 1634 - 1935; places of interest and historical memorials in Wethersfield.   Compiled by Frances Wells Fox.   Pub. by the Wethersfield committee of the State tercentenary committee.   (Hartford, Conn., Printed by the Bronson & Robinson co., 1935?)
(8) p.   23 cm.   35-23564.   F104.W4 F6

WETHERSFIELD.   ... Statement of the town of Glastonbury concerning their petition vs. the town of Wethersfield to make the Connecticut River the boundary line between said towns.   Hartford, Case, Lockwood & Brainard, printers, 1873.   8 p.   22½ cm.   8-25680.
F104.W4 G5

WETHERSFIELD.   The leaves of the tree; a pageant in celebration of the tercentenary of the settlement of Wethersfield ... 1934 ... written and directed by Doris Campbell Holsworth ...   (Windsor, Conn., 1934)   52 p.   front.   21½ cm.   34-17360.   F104.W4 H6

WETHERSFIELD.   History of the Webb house, by Mrs. William H. H. Smith.   Read at the Webb house before the Society of colonial dames ... 1919 ... (Hartford? Conn., 1919?)   16 p.   20½ cm.   26-9525.
F104.W4 S6

WETHERSFIELD inscriptions; a complete record of the inscriptions in the five burial places in the ancient town of Wethersfield, including the towns of Rocky Hill, Newington, and Beckley Quarter (in Berlin), also a portion of the inscriptions in the oldest cemetery in Glastonbury, comp. by Edward Sweetser Tillotson.   Hartford, Conn., W. F. J. Boardman, 1899.   372 p.   front., plates.   25½ cm.
0-1197 Rev.   L. C. copy replaced by microfilm.   F104. W4 T5
Microfilm 8873 F
L H & G

WETHERSFIELD.   Official program Wethersfield tercentenary, 1634 - 1934: Wethersfield, Glastonbury, Rocky Hill, Newington; held at Wethersfield ... 1934. (Hartford, Conn., Printed by the Case, Lockwood and Brainard co., 1934)   32 p.   front. (ports.)   23½ cm.   35-20343.   F104.W4 W24

WETHERSFIELD and her daughters: Glastonbury, Rocky Hill, Newington, from 1634 to 1934 ...

(Hartford, Conn., Printed by the Case, Lockwood & Brainard co., 1934)   123 p.   plates, ports.   23½ cm.
By Frances Wells Fox and others.   34-30172.   F104. W4 W4

WETHERSFIELD.   The Wethersfield story, by Lois M. Wieder.   Stonington, Conn., Pequot Press
(1966)   vi, 57 p.   23 cm.   (Pequot town histories no. 2)   66-28742.   F104. W4 W5

WILLIMANTIC.   The Willimantic directory, including the villages of Windham, North Windham and
South Windham ...   Price & Andrew, publishers.   New Haven, Printed by H. Bradley, 1873 -
1 v.   22½ cm.   7-40132.   Directories

WILLIMANTIC.   Killenberger's Willimantic directory.   1885 - 86 ...   With an appendix including
the towns of Colchester, Coventry, Mansfield, Windham, Lebanon, Scotland, Hebron, Columbia,
Hampton, Chaplin, Ashford, Eastford & Sprague.   Willimantic, Conn., W. H. H. Bingham (1884-85)
2 v.   23 cm.   7-40110.   Directories

WILLIMANTIC.   R. S. Dillon & co's Willimantic directory including the borough of Willimantic, Windham, North Windham, South Windham, and South Coventry, for 1888 and 1889.   6th ed.   Willimantic,
R. S. Dillon, 1888 -   1 v.   23 cm.   7-40111.   Directories

WILLIMANTIC.   Hanks/ directory of Willimantic, Colchester, and the towns of Andover, Ashford,
Chaplin, Columbia, Coventry, Eastford, Hampton, Hebron, Lebanon, Mansfield, Scotland, Sprague
and Windham.   1890 -   Meriden, Conn., Hanks & co. (1890 -   1 v.   24 cm.   7-40112.
                                                                                                            Directories

WILLIMANTIC, Windham, Coventry directory ... (v. 1 -   1891 - 1893, 1895 - 1900, 1902
1919/20, 1921, 1923/24, 1926 - 1927, 1928/29, 1930, 1932.   New Haven, Conn., The Price & Lee co.,
1891 - 19   v.   illus., fold. maps.   24 cm.   0-1370 (rev. '32)   Directories

WILLIMANTIC directory, v. 1 - 11, 13 - 17, including Windham and Coventry ...   New Haven, Conn.,
The Price & Lee co., 1891 - 09.   16 v.   Mar 30, 99-147.   Directories

WILLIMANTIC.   The leading business men of Willimantic and Colchester ... (By George Fox Bacon)
Boston, Mercantile pub. co., 1890.   (5) - 47 p.   illus.   27 cm.   In double columns.   4-25658.   F104. W46B13

WILLIMANTIC.   The Willimantic journal.   Souvenir edition.   Comp. by H. F. Donlan.   (Willimantic,
Conn.) 1894.   52 p.   illus. (incl. ports., map)   39 cm.   Four columns to a page.   4-33409.   F104. W46 W4

WILSONVILLE.   Inscriptions in the cemetery at Wilsonville, copied by Avis G. Clarke.   Oxford,
Mass., 1931.   136 numb. l.   22 cm.   "Five copies typed"   37M1349T.   F104. W48 C5
                                                                                                        Rare Book Coll.

WILTON parish, 1726 - 1800; a historical sketch ...   By Marian Olmstead.   Wilton, Conn., 1900.
44 p. incl. illus., pl.   8°.   Dec. 27, 1900-88.   F104. W5 O5

WILTON.   ... An account of the observance of the 150th anniversary of the organization of the Congregational church, Wilton ... 1876, including a historical address, by Samuel G. Willard, and a
poem, by John G. Davenport.   New York, R. J. Johnston, printer, 1876.   112 p.   23 cm.   13-21564.
                                                                                                        F104. W5 W5

WINCHESTER.   Winchester-Winsted in 1813.   By Eliphaz Alvord   (Hartford), (Acorn Club of Conn.)
1961.   16 p.   24 cm.   F104. W6 A7

WINCHESTER.   Annals and family records of Winchester, with exercises of the centennial celebration, ... 1871.   By John Boyd.   Hartford, Press of Case, Lockwood & Brainard, 1873.   xi, (9)-631 p.
front., ports.   23½ cm.   Rc-3320.   F104. W6 B7

WINCHESTER.   Official program.   1771.   1921.   150th anniversary celebration ...   (Winchester?
1921?)   32 p.   illus.   14 x 23 cm.   F104. W6 W6

WINDHAM.   How a town grew in New England: Windham, 1692 - 1778.   By Lydia Gross.   Boston,

Christopher Pub. House, 1964.   70 p.   21 cm.   64-12892.   F104.W65 G7

WINDHAM.   Bacchus of Windham, and The frog fight (by) Lillian Marsh Higbee.   Willimantic, Conn., Quality print shop, 1930.   25 p.   illus.   22½ cm.   ... narrates the history of a wooden image of Bacchus, carved by British prisoners at Windham, in 1776.   30-30036.   F104.W65H63

WINDHAM.   The story of Bacchus, and Centennial souvenir.   By Brigham Payne ... Hartford, Conn., A. E. Brooks, 1876.   4, (7) - 111 p.   front., illus., plates.   20½ cm.   14-11895.   F104.W65 P3

WINDHAM.   Historical discourse, delivered before the First church and soc. of Windham ... 1850. Being the 150th anniversary of the formation of the church.   By John E. Tyler.   Hartford, Press of Case, Tiffany, 1851.   35 p.   23 cm.   17-16955.   F104.W65 T9

WINDHAM.   A century sermon, preached before the First church in Windham ... 1800.   In commemoration of its institution ... 1700.   Containing historical facts, relative to its settlement and progress.   By Elijah Waterman ... Windham (Conn.) Print. John Byrne.   1801.   42 p.   20 x 12 cm.   6-14318.   F104. W65 W2
Rare Book Coll.

WINDHAM.   The battle of the frogs, at Windham, 1758, with various accounts and three of the most popular ballads on the subject, with an introd. by William L. Weaver.   Willimantic, Conn., J. Walden, 1857.   31 p.   22½ cm.   1-5776 Rev.   F104. W65 W3

WINDHAM.   History of ancient Windham.   Genealogy.   Containing a genealogical record of all the early families of ancient Windham, embracing the present towns of Windham, Mansfield, Hampton, Chaplin and Scotland.   Part I.   A-Bil.   By William L. Weaver ... Willimantic, Weaver & Curtiss, 1864.   viii, (9) - 112 p.   23 cm.   "Most of the genealogies herewith published appeared in the Willimantic journal in 1862 and 1863. The have been re-arranged, carefully revised and corrected, and contain much additional matter."   3-6522 Rev.   F104. W65 W4

WINDHAM.   Records of the Congregational church in Windham (except church votes) 1700 - 1851. Hartford, Conn. historical soc. and the Soc. of Mayflower descendants in the state of Conn., 1943. v-vi, 153 p.   24 cm.   (Connecticut vital records. 8)   Foreword signed: Thompson R. Harlow.   44-53704.
F104. W65 W5

WINDHAM.   A memorial volume of the bi-centennial celebration of the town of Windham.   Containing the historical addresses, poems, and a description of events connected with the observance of the 200th anniversary of the incorporation of the town, as held in the year 1892.   Pub. by the committee. Hartford, Conn., New England home printing co., 1893.   166 p.   plates.   22½ cm.   Imperfect: t. - p. wanting. Rc-3322.   F104. W65 W6

WINDHAM.   Windham, 1800, Tolland, 1804, Willington, 1805, & Pomfret, 1800.   (Hartford) Acorn Club of Connecticut, 1961.   21 p.   24 cm.   (Publication 30)
F104.W65W62

WINDSOR.   Some early records and documents of and relating to the town of Windsor, 1639 - 1703. Hartford, Connecticut historical soc., 1930.   iv, 227 p.   21 x 17½ cm.   30-27553 Rev.
F104. W7 C75

WINDSOR.   Ancient and modern Windsor ...   (By George Ellery Crosby)   Windsor, Conn., Windsor business men's association (1913)   23 p.   illus.   14 x 21 cm.   F104. W7 C9

WINDSOR.   Cemetery inscriptions in Windsor, copied under the direction of Abigail Wolcott Ellsworth chapter, D. A. R.; appendix containing Filley records.   Windsor, Conn., Pub. by the Chapter, 1929. 178, (4) p.   front.   22½ cm.   29-19877.   F104. W7 D23

WINDSOR.   Glimpses of ancient Windsor, from 1633 to 1933, by Daniel Howard and others.   (Windsor, Conn.) Windsor tercentenary committee, 1933.   104 p.   illus. (incl. port.) 23½ cm.   34-19824.
F104. W7 H78

CONNECTICUT

WINDSOR. A new history of old Windsor (by) Daniel Howard. (Windsor Locks, Conn., The Journal press) 1935.   2, (7) - 428 p. illus. (incl. ports., map) 23½ cm. "Persons of note": p. (249)-298. 35-17587.   F104. W7 H79

WINDSOR. The history of ancient Windsor, including East Windsor, South Windsor, and Ellington, prior to 1768, the date of their separation from the old town; and Windsor, Bloomfield and Windsor Locks, to the present time. Also the genealogies and genealogical notes of those families which settled within the limits of ancient Windsor, prior to 1800. By Henry R. Stiles ... New York, C. B. Norton, 1859.   xii, (2) - 922 p. front., illus., port., maps. 23 cm. Rc-3323 Rev.   F104. W7 S7

— A supplement to The history and genealogies of ancient Windsor, containing corrections and additions which have accrued since the publication of that work. By Henry R. Stiles ... Albany, J. Munsell, 1863.   134 p. 23½ cm. Rc-3323 Rev.   F104. W7 S7

WINDSOR. The history and genealogies of ancient Windsor; including East Windsor, South Windsor, Bloomfield, Windsor Locks, and Ellington. 1635 - 1891. By Henry R. Stiles ... (Rev. ed.) Hartford, Conn., Press of the Case, Lockwood & Brainard co., 1891 - 92.   2 v. fronts., plates, ports., plans, maps, facsims. 27 cm. First ed. F 104.W757 above. Contents. - v.1. History. - v.2. Genealogies and biographies. 1-Rc-3324.   F104. W7 S8

WINDSOR. Births, marriages and deaths returned from Hartford, Windsor and Fairfield and entered in the early land records of the colony of Connecticut. Volumes I and II of land records and no. D of colonial deeds. Transcribed and ed. by Edwin Stanley Welles ... Hartford, Conn. (The Case, Lockwood & Brainard co.) 1898.   73 p. 25½ cm. 4-18956.   F104. W7 W4

WINDSOR. Official program of the tercentenary celebration of the settlement of Windsor ... 1933. (Windsor, 1933)   (74) p. illus. (incl. ports.) 23 cm. 34-19823.   F104. W7 W67

WINDSOR. Report of the centennial celebration of the anniversary of our independence, at Windsor, Conn. ... 1876. By authority of the committee of arrangements. Hartford, Press of the Case, Lockwood & Brainard co., 1876.   48 p. 22½ cm. Rc-3326.   F104. W7 W7

WINDSOR. A record of the services held at the Congregational church of Windsor, in celebration of its 250th anniversary ... 1880. (Hartford, Conn.) Pub. by the church (The Case, Lockwood & Brainard co., printers) 1880.   103 p. front., illus. 23½ cm. 6-38875.   F104. W7 W8

WINDSOR historical society. ... Annual report ... 1st - 1922 -   (Windsor, 1922 -   v. pl. 23 cm. 24-6107.   F104. W7 W85

WINSTED directory ... (v. 1 - 1883/84 -   New Haven, Conn., The Price & Lee co., 1883 - 1927.   v. fold. maps. 24 cm. 1-27311 Rev.   Directories

WOLCOTT. New Connecticut. An autobiographical poem. By A. Bronson Alcott.... Boston, Priv. print., 1881.   4, (7) - 158 p. 18 cm. As used by the author. "New Connecticut" refers to Wolcott. 9-30107.   F104. W8 A2

— Ed. by F. B. Sanborn. Boston, Roberts bros., 1887.   3, (v)-xxvi, 247 p. 18 cm. 9-30106.   F104. W8 A22

— Philadelphia, A. Saifer, 1970.   158 p. 18 cm.   F104. W8 A64 1970

WOLCOTT. History of the town of Wolcott from 1731 to 1874, with an account of the centenary meeting ... 1873; and with genealogies of the families of the town. By Rev. Samuel Orcutt. Waterbury, Conn., Press of the American printing co., 1874.   xxii, 608 p. 23 cm. "Genealogies": p. 423 - 608. 1-Rc-3327.   F104. W8 O6

WOODBRIDGE. ... Records of the parish of Amity (now Woodbridge), pt. I, A-D. Arranged by Louise Tracy ... (Hartford, 1906)   (24) p. 24 cm. (Original sources of American genealogical data (reprinted from the Connecticut magazine)) No more pub. 19-15438.   F104. W86 W8

WOODBURY. Barnes' mortality record of the town of Woodbury, from the settlement of the town of

Woodbury in 1672, to the present day. Comp. by Leon M. Barnes. Index ed. Woodbury, Conn.,
L. M. Barnes, 1898.   213 p.   18½ cm.   Rc-3328.   F104.W88 B2

WOODBURY. History of ancient Woodbury, from the first Indian deed in 1659 ... including the present towns of Washington, Southbury, Bethlem, Roxbury, and a part of Oxford and Middlebury. By William Cothren ... Waterbury, Conn., Bronson brothers, 1854 - 79.   3 v. fronts. (v. 1-2: ports.) illus., plates, map, coats of arms.   22½ cm.   Title varies slightly.   Vols. 2-3 have imprint: Woodbury, Conn., W. Cothren, 1872-79. Paged continuously. Histories of the various towns set off from Woodbury, v.1, p. 218-283; v.2, p. 1400-1421. Genealogical history, v.1, p. 481 - 765; v.2, p. 1469 - 1577. Vital records of Woodbury and her daughter towns, including also Stratford, v.3. Rc-3329 Rev.

                                                                                                                                         F104.W88 C6

WOODBURY. A report of the bi-centennial jubilee of the First Congregational church, in Woodbury, Conn. ... 1870. By William Cothren. New Haven, J. H. Bentham, printers, 1870.   iv, (5) - 64 p. 23 cm.   6-15339.   F104.W88 C7

WOODBURY. Second centennial celebration of the exploration of ancient Woodbury, and the reception of the first Indian deed, held at Woodbury ... 1859. Ed. by William Cothren. Woodbury, The General committee, 1859.   105, 18, 125 - 223 p.   23 cm.   Rc-3330.   F104.W88 C8

WOODBURY. Town of Woodbury. Text and photos by Dan Stiles (pseud. for George Canterbury Haig) 1st ed.   Concord, N.H., Sugar Ball Press (1959)   112 p.   26 cm.   59-13676.

                                                                                                                            F104.W88 H3

WOODBURY. Old Woodbury Historical Society. Committee for Old Homes. Homes of Old Woodbury; tercentenary celebration of old Woodbury, Connecticut. (Woodbury? 1959)   264 p.   23 cm.

                                                                                                                                   F104.W88 O4

WOODBURY. The town and people; a chronological compilation of contributed writings from present and past residents of the town of Woodbury; ed. by Julia Minor Strong. Woodbury, Conn., Mattatuck press (Waterbury) 1901.   359 (5) p.   front., illus.   21½ cm.   2-7110.   F104.W88 S9

WOODSTOCK. The history of Woodstock, by Clarence Winthrop Bowen ... Norwood, Mass., Priv. print. by the Plimpton press, 1926 - 43.   8 v. fronts. (v. 1-6) illus., plates, ports, maps (part fold.) fold. plan, facsims.   27½ cm.   Vols. 2-8 have subtitle: Genealogies of Woodstock families.   Bibliography in v. 1 - 6.   27-2642 Rev.

                                                                                                                          F104.W9 B67

WOODSTOCK, an historical sketch, by Clarence Winthrop Bowen. Read at Roseland park, Woodstock, at the bi-centennial celebration of the town ... 1886. New York & London, G. P. Putnam's sons, 1886. 64 p.   23 cm.   1-Rc-3331.   F104. W9 B7

WOODSTOCK. ... Samuel Dexter of Woodstock, by Clarence Winthrop Bowen ... Worcester, Mass., The Society, 1926.   7 p.   25 cm.   Repr. from the Procs. of the Amer. antiquarian soc. for Apr. 1925.   26-9524.   F104. W9 D3

WOODSTOCK. Winds of change, from "Woodstock now and then." By Margaret Thompson McClellan. Pen drawings by George Holt. Putnam, Conn., Observer Co. (1950)   95 p.   illus.   23 cm.   "Taken from articles ... in the Windham County observer.   Bibliography: p. 95.   50-13992.   F104. W9 M2

WOODSTOCK ... By A. Mathewson. (Putnam, Conn. 18?)   24½ cm.   F104. W9 M4

WOODSTOCK. Vital records of Woodstock, 1686 - 1854. Hartford, The Case, Lockwood & Brainard co., 1914.   2, ix-xiii, 622 p.   24 cm.   (Vital records of Conn. Series I, Towns III)   15-5839.   F104. W9 W9
                                                                                                                                 L H & G

ELEMENTS IN THE POPULATION.

CONNECTICUT. Inter-racial commission. Report. 1943/44 -   (Hartford, 1944 - v.   23 cm.   44-41984.   F105. A1 A3

CONNECTICUT

KOENIG, Samuel. Immigrant settlements in Connecticut: their growth and characteristics. W.P.A. Federal writers' project for the state of Conn. Hartford, Conn. state dept. of education, 1938.
viii. (9) - 67 p. incl. tables, diagrs. 21½ cm. "Selected bibliography": p. 58 - 67. 38-26933.
F105. A1 K6

— Photo-offset. (San Francisco, R. and E. Research Associates, 1970) viii. 68 l. 22 cm.
F105. A1 K6 1970

— Das Volksgruppengemisch in den Vereinigten Staaten am Beispiel von Connecticut. (Stuttgart) Publikationsstelle Stuttgart-Hamburg, 1944. 48 p. 21 cm. 48-15689*.
F105. A1K625

ISHAM, Norman Morrison. Early Connecticut houses; an historical and architectural study, ... Providence, R. I., The Preston and Rounds co., 1900. 3, (v)-xiv, 303 p. illus. (incl. map, plans) 26½ cm.
0-3215 Rev.
F105. A6 I7

ITALIANS. Who's who among Americans of Italian descent in Connecticut ... (1942 - New Haven, Conn., Carlevale pub. co. (1942 - v. 21 cm. 43-2861.
F105. I8 W5

MORAVIANS. A memorial of the dedication of monuments erected by the Moravian historical society, to mark the sites of ancient missionary stations in New York and Connecticut. New York, C. B. Richardson; Philadelphia, J. B. Lippincott, 1860. viii, (5) - 184 p. illus. (incl. plan, music) 4 pl. 24 cm. 18-8820.
F105. M
E99. M9 M8

NEGROES. The historical status of the negro in Connecticut. A paper read before the New Haven colony historical soc, by William C. Fowler. copied from the Historical magazine and notes and queries concerning the antiquities, history and biography of America. Vols. xxiii - xxiv, 1874 - 1875 ... Published in Year book of city of Charleston for 1900. Charleston, S.C., Walker, Evans & Cogswell co., 1901. 81 p. 24½ cm. 1-21436 Rev.
F105. N3 F7

CONNECTICUT
SUPPLEMENTARY INDEX OF PLACES

ALDERBROOK. 673
ANDOVER. 713
ANSONIA. 687
ASHFORD. 713
ATTAWAUGAN. 663, 664
AVON. 675
BALLOUVILLE. 663, 664
BALTIC. 656
BECKLEY QUARTER (in Berlin) 712
BERLIN. 679, 685, 686
BETHEL. 663
BETHLEHEM. 716
BLOOMFIELD. 653, 675, 704, 715
BRANFORD. 645, 656, 687
BRIDGEPORT. 650, 687, 695, 707
BRISTOL. 660
BROAD RIVER. 696
BROOKLYN. 661
BROOKLYN CENTER. 663, 664
BYRAM. 671
CANTERBURY. 656
CANTON. 674, 703
CENTER GROTON. 672
CENTERBROOK. 652
CENTRAL VILLAGE. 656
CHAPLIN. 713, 714
CHATHAM. 683
CHESHIRE. 709
CHESTER. 652
CHIPPENY HILL. 660
CLINTON. 652
COBALT. 652
COLCHESTER. 656, 713
COLLINSVILLE. 661
COLUMBIA. 661, 713
COS COB. 671, 705
COVENTRY. 713
CROMWELL. 657, 658, 683
DANBURY. 706
DANIELSON. 675, 700
DANIELSONVILLE. 693
DARIEN. 653, 705, 706
DAYVILLE. 663, 664
DEEP RIVER. 652
DERBY. 657, 687, 702
DURHAM. 683
EAST BROOKLYN. 663, 664
EAST GRANBY. 657, 671

EAST HADDAM. 652, 673
EAST HAMPTON. 652
EAST HARTFORD. 674
EAST HARTLAND. 678
EAST KILLINGLY. 663, 664
EAST NORWALK. 652, 696
EAST PLYMOUTH. 660
EAST PORT CHESTER. 671
EAST RIVER. 652
EAST WALLOP. 668
EAST WINDSOR. 653, 704, 715
EASTFORD. 713
EASTON. 659
ELLINGTON. 701, 715
ELMVILLE. 663, 664
ENFIELD. 675
ESSEX. 652
FAIRFIELD. 639, 658, 659, 660, 671
FAIRFIELD Co. 650
FARMINGTON. 653, 660, 675, 685, 686, 704
FITCHVILLE. 656
FIVE MILE RIVER. 696
FLATT RIDGE. 664
FORESTVILLE. 660
FRANKLIN. 658
FULLING MILL BROOK. 685
GALES FERRY. 656
GLASGO. 656
GLASTONBURY. 653, 675, 712
GLENVILLE. 671
GNADENSEE LAKE. 702
GOODYEAR. 664
GOSHEN. 708
GRANBY. 665, 674, 703, 704
GREENVILLE. 697
GREENS FARMS. 712
GREENWICH. 653, 701, 705, 706
GRISWOLD. 656
GROTON. 684, 693
GROTON HEIGHTS. 672
GUILFORD. 645, 652
HADDAM. 682
HALLVILLE. 656
HAMPTON. 699, 713, 714
HANOVER. 656
HARTFORD. 638, 639, 640, 644, 647, 649, 667, 675
HARWINTON. 660, 669
HAZARDVILLE. 667

HEBRON. 643, 713
HIGGANUM. 652
HUNTINGTON. 678, 707
IVORYTON. 652
JEWETT CITY. 656
KILLINGLY. 663, 664
LEBANON. 649, 656, 658, 713
LIME ROCK. 701
LISBON. 700
LITCHFIELD. 648, 675, 684, 708
LITCHFIELD Co. 633
LONG HILL. 659, 683
MADISON. 652, 673
MANCHESTER. 675
MATTABESECK. 683
MATTATUCK. 710
MERIDEN. 675, 709
MIANUS. 671
MIDDLE HADDAM. 652, 683
MIDDLEFIELD. 652
MIDDLESEX. 652
MIDDLETOWN. 647, 663, 675
MILFORD. 645, 659, 687
MONROE. 659, 707
MONTVILLE. 656
MOODUS. 652
MOOSUP. 656
MORRIS. 681
MYSTIC. 672
NAUGATUCK. 687, 710
NEW BRITAIN. 675
NEW CANAAN. 653, 705, 706
NEW FAIRFIELD. 706
NEW HARTFORD. 657
NEW HAVEN. 638, 645, 655, 681
NEW HAVEN Co. 633, 650
NEW LONDON. 640, 652, 684
NEW LONDON Co. 655
NEWGATE. 665
NEWINGTON. 653, 675, 712
NEWTON. 706
NIANTIC. 693
NOANK. 672
NORFOLK. 708
NOROTON. 664
NOROTON HEIGHTS. 664
NORTH HAVEN. 674
NORTH STONINGTON. 656
NORTH WINDHAM. 713
NORTHBURY. 699
NORWALK. 645, 652, 653, 687
NORWICH. 640, 693

OXFORD. 710, 716
PACHAUG. 672
PALMERTOWN. 656
PEQUONNOCK. 659
PEQUOT. 656
PETTYPAUGPOINT. 694
PINEVILLE. 663, 664
PLAINFIELD. 656
PLAINVILLE. 660
PLYMOUTH. 660, 669, 710
POMFRET. 714
POQUETANUCK. 656
PORTLAND. 683
PRESTON. 697
PROSPECT. 661, 710
PUTNAM. 675
RAYNHAM. 692
ROCKVILLE. 675, 709
ROCKY HILL. 658, 674, 712
RIDGEFIELD. 706
RIVER VIEW. 663, 664
RIVERSIDE. 671, 704, 705
ROXBURY. 716
SALISBURY. 679
SALISBURY CENTER. 701
SAUGATUCK. 712
SAYBROOK. 638, 652, 664, 670
SCOTLAND. 656, 713 714
SEYMOUR. 657, 687
SHAILERVILLE. 652
SHELTON. 657, 665
SIMSBURY. 665, 674, 696
SOMERS. 667
SOUND BEACH. 671
SOUTH COVENTRY. 713
SOUTH MANCHESTER. 675
SOUTH NORWALK. 652, 696
SOUTH WINDHAM. 713
SOUTH WINDSOR. 653, 675, 715
SOUTHBURY. 716
SOUTHINGTON. 675
SOUTHOLD. 645
SOUTHPORT. 659
SPRAGUE. 713
STAMFORD. 645, 653, 687, 706
STERLING. 656
STONINGTON. 684, 687
STRATFORD. 645, 659, 660, 678, 687, 716
SUFFIELD. 667
TERRYVILLE. 660
THOMASTON. 687
THOMPSONVILLE. 667

TOLLAND.   701, 714
TOLLAND Co.   612, 633
TRUMBULL.   659, 707
TURKEY HILLS.   665, 666
UNCASVILLE.   656
VERNON.   658, 701
VERSAILLES.   656
VOLUNTOWN.   656
WALLINGFORD.   687
WASHINGTON.   716
WATERBURY.   660, 687, 699, 685
WATERTOWN.   658, 685, 687, 699, 710
WAUREGAN.   656, 664
WEBUTUCK VALLEY.   702
WEST HARTFORD.   653, 674
WEST HAVEN.   687

WEST SIMSBURY.   661
WESTBROOK.   652
WESTBURY.   699, 711
WESTPORT.   687
WESTSIDE.   673
WESTON.   659
WETHERSFIELD.   639, 640, 653, 665, 675, 685, 695
WILLINGTON.   714
WILTON.   653
WINDHAM.   713
WINDHAM Co.   633, 652, 656
WINDSOR.   639, 640, 653, 675
WINDSOR LOCKS.   653, 715
WINNIPAUK.   696
WINSTED.   675, 708, 713
WOLCOTT.   710
WOODBRIDGE.   658

ADDITIONS TO INDEX

COMPOUNCE.   704

MIDDLEBURY.   710, 716

MIDDLE ATLANTIC STATES

106   Atlantic States (Maine to Florida); Middle States; Appalachian Mountains (General).

Descriptive and historic works after 1825; earlier works are classed in E 162–165, 186–375.

Cf. F 157.D4, Delaware River and Valley.
  F 157.S8, Susquehanna River and Valley.
  F 172.D3, Delaware Bay and region.
  F 187.C5, Chesapeake Bay and region.
  F 187.P8, Potomac River and Valley.
  F 1035.8, Atlantic coast of Canada.

ATLANTIC COAST OF NORTH AMERICA. MIDDLE ATLANTIC STATES.

F 106

ACHENBACH, Herman. . Tagebuch meiner reise nach den Nordamerikanischen freistaaten, oder: Das neue Kanaan ... Dusseldorf, Gedruckt auf kosten des verfassers, bei J. Wolf, 1835. 2 v. front., fold. map. 22 cm. Vol. 1 wanting. 1-26179.   106.A 17

ADAMS, Joey. The Borscht Belt. New York, Bobbs-Merrill (1966)   224 p. 22 cm. "1st printing." 66-18594.   F106. A 3

ALLEN, Richard Sanders. Covered bridges of the Middle Atlantic States. Brattleboro, Vt., Stephen Greene Press, 1959.   120 p. illus. 28 cm. Includes bibliography. 59-14038.   F106.A 46

ALVES DE LIMA José Custodio. Cartas americanas. Rio de Janeiro, Imprensa nacional, 1914. xi, 64 p. pl. 25 cm. Includes articles pub. in the "Journal do commercio." 15-20354.   F106.A 47

AMERICAN Automobile Association. Mideastern tour book. Washington.   v. illus., maps. 24 cm.   F106. A 5

AMERICAN Express Company. Travellers guide: highways and places in the Mid-Atlantic States. 1967 -   (New York?) Meredith Press.   v. maps (part col.) 22 cm. 67-20704.   F106.A5113

AMERICAN summer resort and country board directory ... Ocean, mountain, and farm. New York, Allen & co. (1882)   3; 61 p. map. 8º. 1-16172-M1.   F106.A512

AMERICAN summer resort directory ... A complete guide and directory of summer hotels and boarding houses. Ocean, mountain and farm. New York, Hankins & co. (1883)   96 p. illus., map. 8º. Comp. by George D. Hankins. 1-16173-M1.   F106.A513

AMERICAN summer resorts ... New York, 1898.   14½ x 23½ cm.   F106.A 53

APPALACHIAN Trail Conference. Publication no. 1 -   Washington, 193   no. illus., maps (part fold.) 16 - 23 cm. Some numbers issued in revised eds.; some accompanied by supplements. 50-28692.   F106.A 62
    — An annotated bibliography of Katahdin, comp. Edward S. C. Smith ... 1936. 78 p. (Pub. no. 6) photoprinted. 37-9518 Rev.
    — Plans for an Appalachian trail lean-to ...   28 p. illus. 23 cm. (Pub. no. 12) 47-21707.
    — The Appalachian trail; a footpath through the wilderness for 2,050 miles ... sheet. illus. (incl. map) 44 x 54½ cm. fold. to 22 x 13½ cm. (Pub. no. 17) 47-21936.
    — Guide to the Appalachian Trail in Tennessee and N. C., etc.   x, 353, 13 p. (Pub. no. 24)
72-200261 MARC.

APPALACHIAN Trailway news. v. 1 -   Jan. 1939 -   Washington, D.C., The Appalachian
trail conference, inc. (1939 -   v. in   27½ cm.   Semiannual, 1939; 3 nos. a year, 1940- 44-37993.   F106. A623

APPALACHIAN trail conference.   Miscellaneous printed matter published by this body is classified in
F106. A629

APPLETON'S hand-book of American travel.   Northern and eastern tour.   Including New York, New
Jersey, Pennsylvania, Connecticut, Rhode Island, Massachusetts, Maine, New Hampshire, Vermont,
and the British dominions ... New York, D. Appleton; London, S. Low, son, and Marston, 1872.
viii. 284 p.   front., fold. maps.   18½ cm.   11-27436.   F106. A 66

— Revised for summer of 1873, with appendix.   New York, D. Appleton (etc.) 1873.   x, 294 p. front.
(fold. map) fold. plans.   19½ cm.   2-6381.   F106. A 67

AUTOMOBILE tours from New York.   N.Y. 1907.   18 cm.   F106. A 93

B, R.H.   Three weeks in America.   1877.   By R. H. B.   (n.p.) 1878.   19 p.   21½ cm.   "These notes were
first pub. in the form of letters to an Aberdeen newspaper."   2-1881-M2.   F106. B 114

BAILEY, Anthony.   The inside passage.   New York, Macmillan (1965)   xii, 209 p.   24 cm.   "First printing."
65-11576.   F106. B 15

BAILEY, Anthony.   Through the great city.   New York, Macmillan Co. (1967)   276 p.   21 cm.   "1st
printing"   67-13585.   F106. B 16

BALTIMORE and Ohio railroad co.   Book of the Royal blue.   (Pub. monthly by the Passenger dept. of
the Baltimore & Ohio railroad) v.1 -14; Oct. 1897 - Apr. 1911.   Baltimore, 1897 - 1911.
14 v.   illus., ports., maps.   26 cm.   No more pub.   5-32208 Rev.   F106. B17

   — ... The Baltimore & Ohio railroad and the civil war.   In v. 2 no. 10, p. 1-7.   10-8103.
   — The battle of Gettysburg.   By Thos. E. Jenkins.   In vol. 2, no. 10, p. (8) - 18.   10-8102.
   — John Brown's papers clear up mists of history.   In v.5, p. (15) - 20.   10-8104.
   — Bladensburg, an old Maryland town.   By F. J. Young.   In v.9, no. 4 p. (11) - 17.   8-5320.

BALTIMORE and Ohio railroad Reasons why.   (Chicago, 1901)   20 cm.   F106. B187

BALTIMORE and Ohio railroad company.   Baltimore and Ohio resorts and springs, summer 1905.
(Baltimore, 1905)   20½ x 20½ cm. fold. to 20½ x 10½ cm.   F106. B188

BALTIMORE and Ohio railroad co.   Routes and rates for summer tours via picturesque B. & O.   1892.
Baltimore, Md., Passenger dept., B. & O. railroad (1892)   xvii, 376 p.   front., illus., fold. maps, fold. plan.
20½ x 12 cm.   1-24678 Rev.   F106. B19

   — Baltimore (1895)   20½ cm.   F106. B193

   — Baltimore? 1905.   22 x 10½ cm.   F106. B194

   — (Baltimore) 1906.   (i) - viii, 101 p.   22 cm.   F106. B195

   — (Baltimore) 1909.   174 p.   22½ cm.   F106. B197

   — (Baltimore) 1910.   204 p.   23 cm.   F106. B198

   — (Baltimore) 1911.   204 p.   illus.   23 cm.   11-14862.   F106. B 21

BALTIMORE and Ohio railroad co.   Between Baltimore and Pittsburg on trains nos. 5 and 6 "New York
and Chicago limited"...   Baltimore, 1901.   15½ cm.   F106. B25

BELL, John H.   Western skies, a narrative of American travel in 1868.   (n.p.) Printed for private
circulation, 1870.   (379) p.   16½ cm.   Various paging.   13-5138.   F106. B 4

MIDDLE ATLANTIC STATES

BELL, Mrs. Margaret Van Horn (Dwight) A journey to Ohio in 1810 as recorded in the journal of Margaret Van Horn Dwight, ed. with an introd. by Max Farrand. New Haven, Yale university press, 1912. vi, 64 p. 21½ cm. (Yale historical manuscripts... I) 12-25270. F106.B 43

— New Haven, Yale university press, 1914. vi, 64 p. 21½ cm. Fourth impression? A journey, by wagon, from New Haven, Conn. to Warren, O. 25-15909. F106.B 434

BERKENHOFF, Hans Albert. Amerika, hast du es besser? Göttingen, Schwartz (1966) 107 p. 21 cm. F106. B46

BIGELOW, Timothy. Diary of a visit to Newport, New York and Philadelphia during the summer of 1815. Ed. by a grandson... Boston, Printed for private distribution (Cambridge, Mass., University press) 1880. 29 p. 23 cm. 1-21382. F106. B 59

BISHOP, Nathaniel Holmes. Voyage of the paper canoe: a geographical journey of 2500 miles, from Quebec to the Gulf of Mexico, during the year 1874-5. By Nathaniel H. Bishop... Boston, Lee and Shepard; New York, C. T. Dillingham, 1878. xv, 351 p. front., illus., plates, maps. 21½ cm. 1-16170. F106. B 62

— 1882. xv, 351 p. illus., 7 pl. (incl. front.) 10 maps. 21 cm. 8-2673. F106.B 622

BLOOMFIELD, Howard Van Leu. Sailing to the sun; illust. from photos taken by the author. New York, Dodd, Mead, 1942. ix, 267 p. illus., ports. 23 cm. An account of a trip by inland waterway from Long island to Florida. 42-24073. F106. B 65

— 1946. 231 p. plates, ports. 21 cm. "Revised and brought up to date." 46-4386. F106. B 65 1946

BOPP, Léon. Impressions d'Amérique. Paris, Gallimard (1959) 318 p. 21 cm. Deuxième édition. F106. B 68

BOWDITCH, Josiah Browne. ... The New England coast, Long island and the Jersey shore, Providence, R.I., The Continental printing co., 1895. 120 p. illus. (incl. port.) 27½ cm. Boston harbor edition. 41-36266. F106. B 7

BOWEN, Ezra. The Middle Atlantic states; Delaware, Maryland, Pennsylvania, by Ezra Bowen and the editors of Time-Life Books. New York, Time-Life Books (1968) 192 p. illus. 28 cm. (Time-Life Library of America) 68-18048. F106. B 72

— (1970) 192 p. illus. 28 cm. 68-18048. F106. B 72 1970

(BRAMHALL, Frank James) In summer days. To Niagara falls, Mackinac island, the St. Lawrence, the White mountains, the Hudson, the Adirondacks and the sea, via the Michigan central... (Chicago, Poole bros., 1886) 56 p. incl. front. (map) col. illus. 19 cm. Issued by the Michigan central railroad co. 1-24072 Rev. F106. B 87

(BRAMHALL, Frank J.) A summer note-book... (Chicago, Rand, McNally printers) 1895. 96 p. front., illus., fold. map. 8º. Issued by the Michigan central railroad co. 1-16169-M1. F106. B 89

BRANDT, Francis Burke. The majestic Delaware, the nation's foremost historic river. With over 150 illustrations from engravings, etc. ... Philadelphia, The Brandt and Gummere co. (1929) 192 p. incl. front., illus. 26½ cm. 29-29706. F106.B 893

BRIGHAM, Albert Perry. The Appalachian valley... (Edinburgh, 1924 p. (218)-230/ "Reprinted from the Scottish geographical magazine, vol. xl, July, 1924." F106.B 894

BRIGHAM, Albert Perry. From trail to railway through the Appalachians... Boston, New York (etc.) Ginn & co. (1907) viii, 188 p. illus., 5 maps (incl. front.) 19 cm. 7-8511. F106.B 895

721

— Port Washington, Kennikat Press (reprint 1970) viii, 188 p. illus. 21 cm. (Kennikat series on man and his environment) 78-113279.
F106.B895
1970

BROOKLYN eagle. Resort and travel directory. (Brooklyn) v. illus. 27 - 32 cm. annual. 58-52327.
F106.B899

BROWN, Ralph Hall. Mirror for Americans; likeness of the eastern seaboard, 1810 ... New York, American geographical soc., 1943. xxxii, (5) - 312 p. front., illus. (incl. ports., maps) 26 x 20 cm. American geographical society. Special publication no. 27, ed. by Elizabeth T. Platt) An account of the period told as if written by Thomas Pownall Keystone, a fictitious character, presenting ... the contemporary scene. Bibliography: p. (248)-259. Bibliographical references included in "Notes," (p. (260) - 298) 43-9759.
F106. B 9

— New York, Da Capo Press, 1968. xxxii, 312 p. illus. 27 cm. 67-27449.
F106. B 9
1968

(BRYANT, William Cullen) The American landscape, no. 1. Containing the following views: Weehawken, Catskill mountains, Fort Putnam, Delaware water-gap, falls of the Sawkill, Winnipiseogee lake. ... New York, E. Bliss, 1830. 16 p. 6 pl. 32 cm. L. C. copy imperfect: p. 11 - 16 wanting. Apparently no more pub. 2-21225 rev.
F106. B 91
Rare Book Coll.

BULLINGER, Edwin W. Season of 1895. Outing trips and tours, a guide to summer pleasure trips and excursion routes and resorts. Pub. as a supplement to Bullinger's monitor guide, v. 28, no. 26, June 24 to June 30, 1895. New York, E. W. Bullinger (1895) 120 p. illus., map. 4°. 1-16168-M1.
F106. B 93

CARTER, Annette. Exploring from Chesapeake Bay to the Poconos. Photos by Judson Laird. (1st ed.) Philadelphia, J. B. Lippincott (1971) xix, 255 p. illus. 21 cm. (A Philadelphia bulletin book) 73-134929.
F106. C 33

CAMERON, William. A month in the United States and Canada in the autumn of 1873 ... Greenock, D. L. Pollock and J. M'Cunn ... 1874. x, 295 p. 19 cm. 15-5271.
F106. C 44

(CHAPMAN, Edwin O.) New York to Washington: a complete guide book of the route from New York to Washington; describing all stations on the route, and containing a full description of the three cities of Philadelphia, Baltimore, and Washington ... New York, Taintor bros. 1876. 96 (i. e. 106) p. illus., fold. maps. 17½ cm. (Taintor's route and city guides. No. 2) 1-21361 Rev.
F106. C 46

— (1887) 107 p. illus., fold. map. 17½ cm. 4-6479.
F106. C 47

CHILDE, Cromwell. Water exploring, a guide to pleasant steamboat trips everywhere ... (2d ed.) Brooklyn, Brooklyn daily eagle, 1902. 112 p. illus. 15 cm. (Brooklyn eagle library, v. 17, no. 10, serial no. 69) 12-31309.
F106. C 52

CLEWITS, Hendrik. Amerika. "The land of the free": van noord naar zuid langs Amerika's oostkust. (door) H. C. van Dockum (pseud.) Assen, De Torenlaan (1958) 400 p. illus. 20 cm. 59-37362.
F106. C 55

CONNELLY, Thomas Lawrence. Discovering the Appalachians; what to look for from the past and in the present along America's eastern frontier. Introd. by Ralph R. Widner. Harrisburg, Pa., Stackpole Books (1968) 223 p. illus. 28 cm. 68-29596.
F106. C 76

COOPER, Morley. Cruising to Florida via the intracoastal waterway. New York, London, Whittlesey house, McGraw-Hill book co. (1946) vii, 201 p. plates, fold. tab. 23½ cm. 46-8562.
F106. C 77

CORNELL, E. Tales of Martha's Vineyard, Cape Cod, and all along shore. Eighty years ashore and afloat, or The thrilling adventures of Uncle Jethro. Boston, A. F. Graves (1873) 253 p. incl. front. (port.) plates. 19½ cm. Experience of Jethro Ripley, mainly in the Atlantic coast trade, but including an account of a whaling voyage around Cape Horn. The narrative is in the first person. 14-18162.
F106. C 8

MIDDLE ATLANTIC STATES

CROWELL, Suzanne. Appalachian people's history book. (Louisville, Ky.) Mountain Education Associates (1971)   vii, 129 p.   illus.   28 cm.   F106.C85

DARE, Charles P.   Philadelphia, Wilmington and Baltimore railroad guide: containing a description of the scenery, rivers, towns, villages, and objects of interest along the line of road; including historical sketches, legends, etc. ... Philadelphia, Fitzgibbon & Van Ness (1856)   142 p. illus., maps. 12°. 1-Rc-2410.   F106.D 21

DAVISON, Gideon Miner.   The fashionable tour: or, A trip to the Springs, Niagara, Quebeck, and Boston, in the summer of 1821. Saratoga Springs, G. N. Davison, 1822.   165 p.   15 x 9 cm. 1st ed.
Later editions issued under title: The traveler's guide through the middle and northern states ...   1-16142 Rev.   F106.D 26
Rare Book Coll.

— 1825.   (xiii) - xvii, (9) - 169 p.   14 cm.   40-24869.   F106.D261
Rare Book Coll

— 1828.   (ix) - xviii, (19) - 306 p.   front. (fold. map)   14½ cm.   16-13250 Rev.   F106.D262
Toner coll.

— 1830.   xvi, (17) - 434 p. incl. front. plates.   15 cm.   1-26794 Rev.   F106.D263

DAVISON, Gideon Miner.   The traveller's guide: through the middle and northern states, and the provinces of Canada. 5th ed. - enl. and impr. Saratoga Springs, G. M. Davison; New-York, G. & C. & H. Carvill, 1833.   (v) - xvi, (2), (19) - 448 p.   15½ cm.   6-13732 Rev.   F106.D265

— 1834.   xviii, (19) - 452 p. incl. front. 3 pl.   15½ cm.   1-16167 Rev.   F106.D266

— 1837.   xvi, (19) - 465 p.   14½ cm.   19-2233.   F106.D267

— 1840.   xiv, (19) - 395 p.   front. (fold. map)   15½ cm.   1-16166 Rev.   F106.D268

(DAVISON, Gideon Miner)   Tournée à la mode dans les États-Unis, our, Voyage de Charleston à Québec et d'Albany à Boston, par la route de Philadelphie, New-York, Saratoga, Ballston-Spa, Mont-Réal, et autres villes ou lieux remarquables ...   Tr. de l'anglais, avec notes et additions, par M. Bourgeois ... Paris, A. Bertrand, 1829.   viii, 199 p.   fold. map.   22 cm.   Translated from G. M. Davison's "The fashionable tour." ... prob. from edition of 1825.   1-16141 Rev.   F106.D 27

— 1834.   viii, 199 p.   fold. map.   21½ cm.   A reissue, with new title "Voyage aux Etats-Unis d'Amerique."   1-16140 Rev.   F106.D275

(DISTURNELL, John)   A guide between New York, Philadelphia, Baltimore and Washington. Containing a description of the principal places on the route, and tables of distances ... New York, J. Disturnell, 1837.   16 p.   front., fold. map.   13 cm.   1-23443 Rev.   F106.D 57

(DISTURNELL, John)   A guide between Washington, Baltimore, Philadelphia, New York and Boston ... New York, J. Disturnell, 1846.   62 p.   14 cm.   1-22127.   F106.D 58

— 1846.   80 p.   24°.   1-22128-M1.   F106.D 59

DISTURNELL, (John) comp.   Disturnell's guide through the middle, northern, and eastern states; containing a description of the principal places; canal, railroad, and steamboat routes; tables of distances, etc. New York, J. Disturnell, 1847.   80 p.   fold. map.   24°.   1-22496-M1.   F106.D 60

— 1848.   79 p.   maps.   16°.   1-22497-M1.   F106.D 61

DRAKE, Richard B.   An Appalachian reader.   (n. p.)   1970.   2 v. (212 p.) 28 cm.   F106. D 7

DUNLOP, Agnes Mary Robertson.   Oh say, can you see? by Elizabeth Kyle (pseud.)   London, P. Davies (1959)   222 p.   21 cm.   "First publ. ... 1959"   F106.D 93
1959

DUTTENHOFER, A. Bereisung der Vereinigten Staaten von Nordamerika, mit besonderer hinsicht auf den Erie-canal. ... Stuttgart, C. W. Löflund, 1835.   vi, (2), 134 p. incl. fold. front. plates (part fold.) fold. maps. 21½ cm. 1-27955.
F106. D 97

(DWIGHT, Theodore) The northern traveller; containing the routes to Niagara, Quebec, and the Springs; with descriptions of the principal scenes, and useful hints to strangers ... New York, Wilder & Campbell, 1825.   iv, (5) - 213 p. front., plates, maps. 15½ cm. 1-16145.
F106. D 98

— 2d ed. improved & extended. New-York, A. T. Goodrich, 1826.   iv, (2), 382, (4) p. front., plates, maps. 15 cm. 1-16144.
F106. D982

— 3d ed. rev. and extended. New-York, G. & C. Carvill, 1828.   vi, (7) - 403 p. front., plates, maps (1 double) 15 cm. The "Northern tour" by H. D. Gilpin. 16-9909.
F106. D983

— 4th ed., rev. and extended. New-York, Printed by J. & J. Harper, 1830.   viii, (9) - 444 p. front., plates, maps (1 double) 15½ cm. 16-9908.
F106. D984

— New York, Goodrich & Wiley, 1834.   432 p. plates, maps (partly fold.) 16 cm. 12-14300.
F106. D985

— 6th ed., with eighteen maps, and nine landscapes. New-York, J. P. Haven (1841)   iv, (7) - 50 (i.e. 250) p. front., plates, maps (1 double) 16 cm. Imperfect: 1 plate wanting. 1-16143.
F106. D986

ELLICOTT, Andrew, his life and letters, by Catharine Van Cortlandt Mathews ... New York, The Grafton press (1908)   x, 256 p. front., plates, ports., maps (1 fold.) plans, facsims. 23 cm. 8-13374.
F106. E 46

FARIS, John Thomson. Roaming the eastern mountains ... New York, Farrar & Rinehart (1932) xvi, 327 p. front., plates. 21½ cm. Bibliography: p. (321) 32-9861.
F106. F 22

FARIS, John Thomson. Seeing the eastern states ... Philadelphia and London, J. B. Lippincott, 1922. 3, 5-244 p. col. front., plates. 22½ cm. 22-17767.
F106. F 23

FEDERAL writers' project. ... The ocean highway; New Brunswick, New Jersey to Jacksonville, Florida ... New York, Modern age books, inc. (1938)   xxix, 244 p. front., plates, fold. map. 20½ cm. (American guide series) 38-12399.
F106. F 44

FEDERAL writers' project. ... U.S. one, Maine to Florida. New York, Modern age books, inc. (1938)   xxvii, 344 p. plates, fold. map. 20½ cm. (American guide series) 38-27179 Rev.
F106. F 45

FISHER, Ronald M. The Appalachian trail. Photographed by Dick Durrance, II. Foreword by Benton MacKaye. Washington, Special Publications Division, National Geographic Soc. (1972) 199 p. illus. 27 cm. 72-75380.
F106. F 5

FODOR, Eugene, ed. Mid-Atlantic: Washington, D.C., Maryland, Delaware, Pennsylvania, Virginia, North Carolina, West Virginia, Kentucky. (Litchfield, Conn.) Fodor's Modern Guides (1966) 464 p. 21 cm. (Fodor Shell travel guides U.S.A. v. 3) 66-18974.
F106. F 6

— 2d rev. ed. (1967)   464 p. 20 cm. 67-20079.
F106. F 6
1967

FÜNF wochen im osten der Vereinigten Staaten und Kanadas; ... Bern, A. Francke, 1913. 124 p. illus. 23 cm. 15-7329.
F106. F 95

GARBER, John Palmer. The valley of the Delaware and its place in American history ... Philadelphia, Chicago (etc.) The John C. Winston co. (1934)   x, 418 p. front., plates, ports., facsims. 23 cm. 34-22231.
F106. G 27

GARVEY, Edward B. Appalachian hiker; adventure of a lifetime. Oakton, Va., Appalachian Books (1971)   xiii, 397 p. illus. 19 cm. 76-173289.
F106. G 29

GARZÓN Jiménez, Rafael.　America y Europa en el espejo argentino, relatos de un viajero.　Cordoba R(epública) A(rgentiña) 1969.　295 p.　23 cm.　　　　　F106. G 3

GILMOR, Robert.　... Memorandums made in a tour to the eastern states in the year 1797.　By Robert Gilmor, a gentleman of Baltimore.　Reprinted from a manuscript in the Boston Public library. With views from pen-sketches by the author.　In Boston Public Library Bulletin, 1892. v. 11 (New ser., v.3) p. 72-92. plates)　1-4214 Rev.　　　　　F106. G 48

— Boston, The Trustees, 1892.　23 p.　19 pl.　27½ cm.　(Boston Public Library.　Historical manuscripts and reprints. no. 2)　Reprinted from the Bulletin.　16-11506.　　　　　F106.G487

(GILPIN, Henry Dilworth)　A northern tour: being a guide to Saratoga, Lake George, Niagara, Canada, Boston, etc., through the states of Pennsylvania, New-Jersey, New-York, Vermont, New-Hampshire, Massachusetts, Rhode-Island, and Connecticut ....　Philadelphia, H. C. Carey & I. Lea, 1825. 2, (iii) - iv p., 279 p.　fold. map.　15 cm.　1-26808 Rev.　　　　　F106. G 5

GODLEY, John Robert.　Letters from America.　London, J. Murray, 1844.　2 v.　19½ cm.　1-26809.
F106. G 58

GORDON, Jan.　On wandering wheels, through roadside camps from Maine to Georgia in an old sedan car... illus. by Jan Gordon.　New York, Dodd, Mead, 1928.　vii, 336 p.　col. front., illus.　22½ cm. 28-29806.　　　　　F106. G 66

GOSSE, Sir Edmund William.　America; the diary of a visit, winter 1884 - 1885.　Ed. with notes and an introd. by Robert L. Peters and David G. Halliburton.　1st ed.　Lafayette, Ind., English Literature in Transition: 1880 - 1920. English Dept., Purdue University, 1966.　v, 30 p.　28 cm.　(Special series no. 2) 67-63304.　　　　　F106. G 7
　　　　　1966

HALL, Edward Hepple.　The summer tourist's pocket guide to American watering-places.　With map and tables of distances.　... New York, Cathcart & Hall; London, Sampson, Low, son & Marston, 1869.　4, xxx, (5) - 156 p. incl. tables.　front. (fold. map)　14½ x 11½ cm.　1-16165.　　F106. H 17

HALL, Lorenzo T.　The American directory, and traveller's companion: containing a list of inn-keepers, on the principal mail stage roads, from Darien (Geo.) to Boston (Mass.) showing the distance from each; and also, from Washington city.　Boston, Printed by True and Greene, 1822.
36 p.　24º.　1-22564-M1.　　　　　F166.H 19

HAMLIN, Talbot Faulkner.　We took to cruising; from Maine to Florida afloat.　Drawings and photos by the skipper.　New York, Sheridan House (1951)　320 p.　illus. plans.　22 cm.　51-10478.　F166.H 22

HARTOG, Jan de.　Waters of the New World; Houston to Nantucket.　Drawings by Jo Spier.　New York, Atheneum, 1961.　276 p.　22 cm.　61-13559.　　　　　F106.H 25

— London, H. Hamilton, 1961 (i.e. 1962)　276 p.　illus.　23 cm.　　　　　F106.H 25
　　　　　1962

HAVIGHURST, Walter.　Life in America: the Northeast.　Picture maps by Janet Croninger and Robert Poterack.　Grand Rapids, Fideler Co. (1952)　128 p.　illus.　28 cm.　("Life in America" books)
F106. H 3

— Unit of teaching pictures.　(Grand Rapids, Informative Classroom Picture Publishers, 1952)　23 l., 48 pl. (in portfolio)　30 cm.　(Informative classroom picture series. Life in America library)　52-5953 rev.　F106. H3P

— (1955)　128 p.　illus.　28 cm.　56-1745.　　　　　F106. H 3
　　　　　1955
　　　　　Suppl.

— Classroom pictures.　28 l.　48 plates (in portfolio)

— (1958)　128 p.　illus.　28 cm.　58-3938.　　　　　F106. H 3
　　　　　1958
　　　　　Suppl.

— Classroom pictures.　41 p.　31 cm.　In portfolio.

— (1960)   128 p.   28 cm.   59-14776.   F106. H 3 1960

— (1964)   164 p.   28 cm.   (Title: The Northeast)   63-14055.   F106. H 3 1964 Suppl.

    — Classroom pictures.   65 p.   48 pl. (in portfolio)

— (1967)   164 p.   28 cm.   67-13386.   F106. H 3 1967

— (1970)   164 p.   illus.   28 cm.   68-56440.   F106. H 3 1970

HEPBURN, Andrew.   Rand McNally guide to the Mid-Atlantic.   Chicago, Rand McNally (1970)   207 p.   illus.   23 cm.   (Rand McNally guides)   71-115424.   F106. H 4

HINES, Duncan.   Guide to the Middle Atlantic States: New York, Pennsylvania, New Jersey, Maryland, Delaware, and the District of Columbia; where to go and what to see in the Middle Atlantic States and a guide to the best restaurants, etc.   1st ed.   Ithaca, N. Y., Duncan Hines Institute (1959)   262 p.   illus.   19 cm.   (A Duncan Hines travel guide)   59-2679.   F106. H 5

HUMPHREYS, Mrs. Phebe Westcott.   The automobile tourist; motor car journeys from Philadelphia, with historical and descriptive notes.   Philadelphia, Ferris & Leach (1905)   313, (6) p.   front., illus., 7 pl.   20 ½ cm.   5-21573.   F106. H 92

HUNTER, Will Bogert.   Ghost of the glacier and other tales.   (Chicago, 1900)   19 cm.   F106. H 96

IREDALE, Andrew.   An autumn tour in the United States and Canada.   Torquay (Eng.) G. H. Iredale, 1901.   164 p.   19 ½ cm.   2-9856.   F106. I 65

JAMES, Henry.   The American scene.   London, Chapman and Hall, 1907.   vi, 465 p.   22 ½ cm.   23-1904.   F106. J 26 Rare Book Coll.

— introd. and notes by Leon Edel.   London, Hart-Davis, 1968.   xxvi, 486 p.   21 cm.   F106. J 26 1968 b

— Same.   Bloomington, Indiana Univ. Press, 1968.   68-14605   F106. J 26 1968

— New York and London, Harper & brothers, 1907.   vi, 442 p.   21 ½ cm.   7-5704.   F106. J 27

— tog. with three essays from "Portraits of places", ed. with introd. by W. H. Auden.   New York, C. Scribner's sons, 1946.   xxx, 501 p.   plates, ports.   22 cm.   46-25289.   F106. J 273

— Introd. by Irving Howe.   New York, Horizon Press (1967)   xviii, 465 p.   24 cm.   67-27907.   F106. J 273 1967

JENNINGS, Jerry E.   The Northeast.   Grand Rapids, Fideler Co. (1967)   384 p.   28 cm.   (United States geography)   66-18377.   F106. J 4

— (1968)   384 p.   illus.   28 cm.   68-28431.   F106. J 4 1968

— (1970)   384 p.   illus.   28 cm.   74-121590.   F106. J 4 1970

JOHNSON, Clifton.   Highways and byways from the St. Lawrence to Virginia.   New York, The Mac-

MIDDLE ATLANTIC STATES

millan company (etc.) 1913.   xi, 340 p. incl. front. plates. 29½ cm. (His American highways and byways. vi)
13-20336.   F106. J 64

JOHNSON, Clifton. New England and its neighbors. New York, The Macmillan co. (etc.) 1902.
xv, 335 p. incl. front., illus. plates. 20½ cm. 2-23603/6.   F106. J 66

JOURNAL of the voyage of the sloop Mary, from Quebeck, together with an account of her wreck off
Montauk Point, L. I., anno 1701. Albany, N. Y., J. Munsell, 1866.   xvii, 50 p. 21 cm. (New York colonial
tracts. no. 1) 100 copies. "..Found in the chest of John Maher, the mate, by whom it was probably written." 1-22105 Rev.   F106. J 86
                                                                                                also in Toner Coll.

KEMBLE, Frances Anne, Journal by Frances Anne Butler ... London, J. Murray, 1835.   2 v. 22 cm.
Journal extends from Aug. 1, 1832, to July 17, 1833, during a tour of the Atlantic states. 16-14553.   F106. K 29

— New York, B. Blom (1970) 2 v. in 1 18 cm. 79-91530.   F106. K 29
                                                                                                         1970

— ... Philadelphia, Carey, Lea & Blanchard, 1835. 2 v. 19½ cm. Vol. 2 imperfect. 1-26843. Rev.
                                                                                                         F106. K 3

CUTLER, Fanny Thimble (pseud.) My conscience! Fanny Thimble Cutler's Journal of a residence
in America, whilst performing a profitable theatrical engagement: beating the nonsensical Fanny
Kemble Journal all hollow ... Philadelphia, 1835. 36 p. front. 15½ cm. 11-17598.   F106. K 32

KEMBLE. Fanny Kemble in America: or, The journal of an actress reviewed. With remarks on the
state of society in America and England. By an English lady, four years resident in the United States.
Boston, Light & Horton, 1835. 48 p. 21½ cm. 1-26844-M2.   F106. K 33

KEMBLE. Outlines illustrative of the Journal of F****** A*** K*****. Drawn and etched by Mr. —
... Boston, D. C. Johnston, 1835. 8 pl. 23½ cm. Satire on Journal of Frances Anne Kemble. 10-17615.
                                                                                                         F106. K336

KING, John T. ... Guide to Baltimore and Ohio railroad. ... (Baltimore, 1873?) 68 p. illus. 18½ cm.
4-6472.   F106. K 53

— (Baltimore, 1874?) 100 p. illus., plates, 1 port. 19 cm. 4-6471.   F106. K 54

KING, John T. Guide to Pennsylvania railroad. n. p. 1879. 19 cm.   F106. K 58

KUYPER, Henriette Sophia Suzanna. Een half jaar in Amerika. Rotterdam, D. A. Daamen (1907)
4 p. 450 p. 20 cm. 8-29219.   F106. K 97

(LAMBERTON, John P.) Appalachians. Philadelphia, J. B. Lippincott co., 1888. 6 p. 12º.
1-Rc-2408.   F106. L 22

LEACH, Douglas Edward. The Northern colonial frontier, 1607 - 1763. New York, Holt, Rinehart
and Winston (1966) xviii, 266 p. 24 cm. (Histories of the American frontier) 66-10083.   F106. L 4

LEAGUE of American wheelmen. District of Columbia division. Road book 1897. 10½ x 19½ cm.
                                                                                                         F106. L 43

LEHIGH Valley railroad company. On the Lehigh Valley. New York, 1901. 10½ x 19½ cm.
                                                                                                         F106. L 51

LUCAS, Clinton William. A trolley honeymoon from Delaware to Maine; fully illus. ... New York,
The M. W. Hazen co. (1904) 125 p. illus. 19½ cm. 4-32399.   F106. L 93

LUND, Morten. Eastward on five sounds; cruising from New York to Nantucket. New York, Walker
(1971) liii, 170 p. illus. 24 cm. 74-142834.   F106. L 95
                                                                                                         1971

MARK, John. Diary of my trip to America and Havana. Printed for private circulation. (Manchester, Eng., A. Ireland & co., printers, 1885)   vi, 105 p.   18½ cm.   5-14590.
F106.M35

— 2d ed.   Manchester (Eng.) J. E. Cornish; (etc.) 1885)   vi, 105 p.   18½ cm.   45-45286.
F106.M35 1885a

MARTIN, William Dickinson. Journal; a journey from South Carolina to Connecticut in the year 1809. Prepared by Anna D. Elmore. Charlotte (N.C.) Heritage House (1959)   ix, 53 p.   illus., port., facsim.   23 cm.   59-10867.
F106.M38

MATTHIAS, Benjamin. Hand-book for travelers. The traveler's guide between Philadelphia and Baltimore, by steam-boat and rail-road... Philadelphia, Burgess & Zieber, 1843.   47 p.   16°.   1-Rc-2413.
F106.M44

MATTHIAS, Benjamin. The traveler's guide from New York to Philadelphia, and from Philadelphia to New York, by steam boat and rail road... Philadelphia, Godey & McMichael, 1843.   96 p.   16°.   1-Rc-2414.
F106.M45

MERCHANTS and miners transportation co. Tales of the coast; stories of life and high adventure in old days along the Atlantic seaboard. Baltimore, Merchants and miners transportation co. (1926)   2, 34 p.   col. front., illus., fold. map.   19½ cm.   26-16625.
F106.M55

— and A brief history of the Merchants & miners transportation co., 1852 - seventy fifth anniversary - 1927. (Baltimore, The Read-Taylor press, 1927)   3, 63 p.   col. front., illus., fold. map.   19½ cm.   27-13915.
F106.M552

MIDDLE States, The. (New York, etc.) 1896.   32½ cm.
F106.M62

MILBERT, Jacques Gérard. Itinéraire pittoresque de fleuve Hudson et des parties latérales de l'Amérique du Nord... Paris, H. Gaugain et cie, 1828 - 29.   2 v. in 1.   34½ cm.   and atlas of 53 pl., fold. map.   51½ cm.   1-7736.
F106.M63
Rare Book Coll.

MILLER, Betty J. By George! (1st ed.) New York, Pageant Press (1957)   232 p.   illus.   21 cm.
An account of the author's cruise from New York to Florida on her yacht.   58-2923.
F106.M64

MOBIL travel guide: Middle Atlantic States; good food, lodging and slightseeing. 1962-63 --- New York, Simon and Schuster   v.   maps.   21 cm.   "1st printing."   62-12970.
F106.M67

MOORE, S. S. The traveller's directory, or A pocket companion: shewing the course of the main road from Philadelphia to New York, and from Philadelphia to Washington... Philadelphia: Printed for, and pub. by, Mathew Carey, 1802.   3, 52 p.   38 maps on 22 pl.   21½ cm.   1-23725.
F106.M81
Map div.

— 2d ed.   Philadelphia: Print. for Mathew Carey, 1804.   2, 37, 19 p.   22 maps.   22 cm.   1-23726.
F106.M82
Map div.

MYERS, Albert Cook. ... Narratives of early Pennsylvania, West New Jersey and Delaware, 1630 - 1707, ... New York, C. Scribner's sons, 1912.   xiv, 3-476 p.   fold. map, fold. plan, facsim.   23 cm.   (Original narratives of early American history... general editor, J. F. Jameson)   12-4611.
F106.M98

MYERS, J. C. Sketches on a tour through the northern and eastern states, the Canadas & Nova Scotia ... Harrisonburg (Va.) J. H. Wartmann and brothers, prs., 1849.   xvii, (19) - 475 p.   16½ cm.   14-14660.
F106.M99
Rare Book Coll.

MIDDLE ATLANTIC STATES

NEILSON, Peter. Recollections of a six years' residence in the United States of America, interspersed with original anecdotes, illustrating the manners of the inhabitants of the great western republic. By Peter Neilson. Glasgow, D. Robertson (etc.) 1830. viii, 358 (4) p. 20 cm. 4-7819.
F106.N 41
also Microfilm 01291 reel 191 no. 3

NEW YORK - New Jersey trail conference. Publication(s) 2 v. 14 cm. F106.N 48

NORTON, Charles Ledyard. ... American seaside resorts; a hand-book for health and pleasure seekers. New York, Taintor bros., 1817. 190 p. 3 pl. (incl. front.) fold. map. 16½ cm. (American summer resorts) 1-16164. F106.N 88

— ... New York, Taintor bros., Merrill & co., 1877. 121 p. illus., fold. map. 17 cm. 1-21359.
F106.N 89

— 1887. 131 p. illus., maps. 16°. 1-21360-M1. F106. N 9

OGBURN, Charlton. The winter beach. New York, W. Morrow, 1966. 321 p. 25 cm. 66-23350.
F106.O 32

OGDEN, Robert Curtis. Boston to Washington: a complete pocket guide to the great eastern cities and the Centennial exhibition ... New York, Hurd and Houghton, 1876. xii, (13) - 246 p. incl. front., illus. maps (part fold.) 16½ cm. Imperfect: folded map in pocket wanting. 1-16163 Rev. F106.O 34

(OGDEN, Robert C.) Boston à Washington; guide de poche complet pour les grandes villes de l'Est et l'Exposition du centennial ... New York, Hurd et Houghton, 1876. xi, (12) - 246 p. incl. front., illus. maps (partly fold.) 16°. Fold. map in pocket wanting. 1-16069-M1. F106.O342

(OGDEN, Robert Curtis) Boston nach Washington; ein vollständiger taschen-wegweiser fur die grossen oestlichen städte und die Säcular-ausstellung ... New York, Hurd und Houghton, 1876. xi, (12) - 232 p. incl. front., illus. fold. maps. 16½ cm. Imperfect: folded map in pocket, wanting. 1-16070 Rev. F106.O344

(OGDEN, Robert Curtis) Boston á Washington; una guia completa portátil á las ciudades grandes de la costa del mar Atlántico y á la Exhibitión centenaria ... Nueva York, Hurd y Houghton, 1876. xi, (12) - 239 p. incl. front., illus. fold. maps. 16½ cm. Folded map in pocket wanting. 1-16071 Rev. F106.O 35

(OGDEN, Robert C.) Zur weltausstellung! Ein treuer fuhrer für alle diejenigen, welche die weltausstellung zu Philadelphia, etc., etc. New York, S. Zickel (1876) xi, (12) - 261 p. incl. front., illus. map. 16°. 1-21442-M1. F106.O 38

OUR summer retreats. A handbook to all the chief waterfalls, springs ... and other places of interest in the United States ... New York, T. Nelson, 1858. iv, (5) - 64 p. front., pl. 24°. 1-16162-M1.
F106.O 93

PANGBORN, Joseph Gladding. Mountain and valley resorts on picturesque B. & O. Illus. by Thomas Moran and others. Chicago, Knight & Leonard, 1884. 32 p. col. illus. 22½ cm. Issued by the passenger dept. of the Baltimore and Ohio railroad co. 1-16156. F106.P175

PANGBORN, Joseph Gladding. Picturesque B. and O. Historical and descriptive. Chicago, Knight and Leonard, 1882. 2, (7) - 152 p. illus. 25 cm. Issued by the Passenger dept. of the Baltimore and Ohio railroad co. 1-16154.
F106. P 18

— 1883. 288 p. incl. illus., port. 31 x 25 cm. 1-16155. F106. P 19

— 1884. 4, 11 - 54 p. incl. front., illus. 22 x 18 cm. 1-16153. F106. P195

PEARSALL, Marion. Little Smoky Ridge; the natural history of a southern Appalachian neighborhood. (University) University of Alabama Press, 1959. 205 p. 21 cm. Includes bibliography. 58-59926.
F106. P 36

PECSTEEN, Yves. A la recherche d'une autre Amerique. Bruxelles, A. Goemaere, imprimeur du roi, 1954.   110 p.   18 cm.
 F106. P 37

PENNSYLVANIA railroad company. Personally conducted tours. 1899 - 1900 ... Philadelphia, 1899.   14 cm.
 F106. P 39

— to the battlefield of Gettysburg ... Philadelphia, 1900.   14 cm.
 F106. P 391

— Pleasure tours to Old Point Comfort ... (Philadelphia, 1899)   17½ cm.
 F106. P 396

PENNSYLVANIA railroad company. Summer excursion book, season of 18   (Philadelphia, 18 - 19   v. fronts., illus., fold. maps. 25 cm. 99-2586 rev.
 F106. P 43

PENNSYLVANIA railroad company. Forty beaches, highland and water resorts. (Philadelphia? 1915) 3 - 38 p. illus. (incl. map) 23 x 22 cm. (fold. to 23 x 11 cm.) CA 28-886 Unrev.
 F106. P 45

PLUMMER, Henry Merrihew. The boy, me and the cat; cruise of the Mascot, 1912-1913. (Sharon, Mass., The author, 1914) 103 p. illus., plates, maps. 28½ cm. Cruise from New Bedford, Mass., to southern Florida, and return. Autographed from typewritten copy. 14-4487.
 F106. P 73

— Rye, N.H., C. Chandler Co. (1961)   142 p.   24 cm.
 F106. P 73
 1961

PORTER, Eliot. Appalachian wilderness; the Great Smoky Mountains (by) Eliot Porter. Natural and human history by Edward Abbey. Epilogue by Harry M. Caudill. (1st ed.) New York, E. P. Dutton, 1970.   123 p.   illus.   37 cm.   79-95485.
 F106. P 86
 1970

POWELL, Lyman Pierson. ... Historic towns of the middle states. ... New York & London, G. P. Putnam's sons, 1899.   xxix, 439 p. front., illus. (incl. ports.) map. 22 cm. (American historic towns) 99-5724/4 Rev.
 F106. P 88

PUBLIC ledger resort directory. Philadelphia, Public ledger co., 1910 -   1 v.   illus. (incl. maps) 23 cm.   illus t-p.
 F106. P 97

QUICK, Tom, early American, by Frederick W. Crumb; end papers and decorations by Helen E. Banks. Narrowsburg, N.Y., The Delaware valley press, 1936.   2, iv, 85 p. front. (port.) plates. 20 cm. "Reference material and items of Americana which contain references to Tom Quick": 1 leaf at end. 36-14560.
 F106. Q 75

RAYMOND'S vacation excursions. Boston, 1882.   11½ x 14½ cm.
 F106. R 27

RECREATION travel guide: Northeastern States. 1962 -   New York, Recreation Associates.
 v. maps. 23 cm. annual. 62-5443.
 F106. R 4

RIVER and the sound, The. An account of a steamboat excursion by a party of ladies and gentlemen from Worcester, Mass., in the summer of 1869. Worcester, Print, C. Hamilton (1869) vi, (2), (9) - 72 p.   19½ cm.   19-1984.
 F106. R 62

ROBERTS, Bruce. Where time stood still, a portrait of Appalachia. Crowell-Collier Press (1970) ix, 114 p. illus. 27 cm. 77-96452.
 F106. R 73

ROOME, Henry Clay. Southward in Roamer; being a description of the inside route from New York to Florida ... New York and London, The Rudder pub. co., 1907.   95, (5) p. 15½ x 12½ cm. "Reprinted from the Rudder." 7-18573 Rev.
 F106. R 77

ROTHROCK, Joseph Trimble. Vacation cruising in Chesapeake and Delaware bays. ... Philadelphia, J. B. Lippincott, 1884.   262 p. front., illus., plates. 19 cm. 1-16161.
 F106. R 84

SCHOOLS committee on Penn memorials. On the natural history of William Penn's Delaware valley

MIDDLE ATLANTIC STATES 13

and ours ... (Philadelphia) 1932.   48 p. illus. (incl. map) 23 cm.   Part II of the committee's report.   Part I published under title: William Penn and the Delaware Indians.   32-22816.   F106. S 25

SHEPARD, Birse.   Lore of the wreckers.   Cartography by Russell H. Lenz.   Boston, Beacon Press (1961)   278 p. 24 cm. 61-6221.   F106. S 5

SHOSTECK, Robert.   Weekender's guide; places of historic, scenic, and recreational interest within 200 miles of the Washington-Baltimore area.   Washingtpn, Potomac Books (1969)   403 p. maps. 19 cm. 71-85813.   F106. S 53

SIGOURNEY, Lydia Howard (Huntley)   "Mrs, C. Sigourney."   Scenes in my native land.   Boston, J. Munroe, 1845.   iv, 319 p. front. 18½ cm.   Prose and verse.   2-388.   F106. S 56

— London, T. Allman, 1848.   iv, 256 p. front. 13 cm.   Verse and prose.   2-1829 Rev.   F106. S 57

SILLIMAN, Augustus Ely.   A gallop among American scenery; or, Sketches of American scenes and military adventure.   New-York, D. Appleton, 1843.   4; 267 p. illus. 18 cm. 2-389 Rev.   F106. S 59

— Freeport, N.Y., Books for Libraries Press (1970)   267 p. 23 cm. 70-126257.   F106. S 59 1970

— New York, A. S. Barnes, 1881.   vi, 337 p. front., illus. 21½ cm. 1-27529 a.   F106.S 595

SMITH, Elizabeth A.   A wanderer's journal.   New York, Privately printed, 1889.   107 p. 19 cm.   F106. S 64

SNOW, Edward Rowe.   Mysteries and adventures along the Atlantic coast.   New York, Dodd, Mead, 1948.   xii, 352 p. illus., ports., map (on lining papers) 22 cm. 48-9386*.   F106. S 67

— Freeport, N.Y., Books for Libraries Press (1969)   xii, 352 p. illus. 23 cm.   (Essay index reprint series) 72-80398.   F106. S 67 1969

SNOW, Edward Rowe.   Secrets of the North Atlantic islands.   New York, Dodd, Mead, 1950.
xii, 339 p. illus., ports., maps. 21 cm. 50-10687.   F106.S 675

SHOW, Edward Rowe.   Strange tales from Nova Scotia to Cape Hatteras.   New York, Dodd, Mead (1949)   xiv, 322 p. illus., ports., map (on lining papers) 22 cm. 49-11938*.   F106. S 68

SOUTHWARD by the inside route; being a description of the passage between New York and Florida by way of the canals, bays, sounds and thoroughfares ... New York and London, The Rudder pub. co., 1902.   92 p. illus., 2 fold. maps. 15½ cm.   "Reprinted from The Rudder."   7-26429.   F106., S 72

STORK'S 1700 mile summer tours ... Baltimore, (1879)   22½ cm.   F106. S 88

STRICKLAND, William Peter.   The life of Jacob Gruber.   Fifth thousand.   New York, Carlton & Porter, 1860.   384 p. front. (port.) 18½ cm. 11-19501.   F106. S 91

SUTTON, Ann.   The Appalachian Trail; wilderness on the doorstep.   With a foreword by Stewart L. Udall.   (1st ed.) Philadelphia, Lippincott Co. (1967)   xii, 180 p. 22 cm.   F106. S 94

(SWEETSER, Moses Foster)   The middle states: a handbook for travellers.   A guide to the chief cities and popular resorts of the middle states, and to their scenery and historic attractions ... Boston, J. R. Osgood, 1874.   xvi, 469 p. fold. front., maps (partly fold.) plans (partly fold.) 17 cm. 1-Rc-2415.   F106. S 97

— 1876.   xvi, 469 (i. e. 475) p. fold. front., maps (partly fold.) plans (partly fold.) 17 cm. 1-Rc-2416.   F106. S 98

TABLELAND trails. v. 1 - spring 1953 - (Oakland, Md.) v. illus.
23 cm. irregular. F106.T 12

TANNER, Henry Schenck. A geographical, historical and statistical view of the central or middle United States; containing accounts of their early settlement; natural features, etc. etc. Philadelphia, H. Tanner, jr.; New York, T. R. Tanner, 1841. v. (3) - 524 p. 4 fold. maps. 15½ cm. Includes Pennsylvania, New Jersey, Delaware, Maryland, District of Columbia and Virginia. 2-393 Rev. F106.T 16

— 2d ed. 1841. v. (3) - 524 p. fold. maps. 15½ cm. 2-394 Rev. F106.T 17
G & M

THOMPSON, Daniel Garrison Brinton. Gateway to a nation; the Middle Atlantic States and their influence on the development of the Nation. Rindge, N.H., R. R. Smith, 1956. 274 p. illus. 23 cm. Includes bibliography. 55-11153. F106.T 42

(THOMPSON, William Tappan) Major Jones's sketches of travel, comprising the scenes, incidents, and adventures in his tour from Georgia to Canada. ... Philadelphia, Carey & Hart, 1848.
192 p. 7 pl. (incl. front.) 19½ cm. (Carey & Hart's library of humorous American works) 7-40719. F106.T 46
Rare Book Coll.

Philadelphia, T. B. Peterson; New York, Johnson Reprint Corp., 1971. 192 p. illus. 23 cm.
71-174747 MARC. F106.T 46
1971

— Philadelphia, T. B. Peterson & brothers (1880) 17 - 206 p. front., plates. 17½ cm. 2-11303 Add.
F106.T 47

THORNEYCROFT, Thomas. A trip to America. Wolverhampton, Steen and Blacket, steam printing works (1869) 59 p. front. (ports.) 22 pl., map. 21 cm. In verse. 16-8173. F106.T 52
Rare Book Coll.

TOONE, Betty L. Appalachia; the mountains, the place, and the people. (1972) Illus. with photos.
F106.T 57

TORRES-REYES, Ricardo. Davis Tavern site; location study, Cumberland Gap National Historical Park, Kentucky-Tennessee-Virginia. (Washington) Division of History, Office of Archeology and Historic Preservation, 1969. iii, 38 l. 26 cm. 79-608520. F106. T 6

TRANSPORTATION. (New York) v. illus., ports. 26 cm. Quarterly. Pub. by the Passenger Dept., Lehigh Valley Railroad. 55-50390. F106.T 79

TROLLEY exploring; the pioneer electric railway guide originated by Cromwell Childe ... trips about New York and to Chicago, Boston, Philadelphia, Washington, routes in New Jersey, Connecticut and New York states. 7th ed. 1903. 15th ed., 1910. (Brooklyn) Brooklyn daily eagle, 1903-10.
2 v. illus. 15½ cm. (Brooklyn eagle library, no. 65) 3-12326 Additions. F106.T 84

TROLLEY tourist, The, a book of trolley routes in eastern Pennsylvania, New Jersey and Delaware ... giving distances, rates of fare, running time and points of interest of all trunk lines running out of Philadelphia, with connections and side trips on line out of ... Wilmington, Trenton and other cities.
19   Philadelphia, Walther printing house (19   v. illus. (incl. maps) 17 x 9 cm. 18-20455.
F106.T842

ULYAT, William Clarke. Life at the sea shore. Where to go, how to get there, and how to enjoy. Public resorts on the New England, New York and New Jersey coasts ... By Wm. C. Ulyat. Princeton, N.J., McGinness and Runyan (1880) iv, (2), (7) - 168 p. illus. 19½ cm. 7-29224 Rev. F106.U 47

VACATIONS. Mid-Atlantic ed. Consolidated tours. (Chester, Vt., National Survey)
v. illus., maps. 31 cm. 49-2182*. F106. V 3

VIGNERON, Lucien. ... De Montreal a Washington (Amerique du Nord) Paris, E. Plon, Nourrit et cie, 1887. 3, 288 p. 18½ cm. 5-37467. F106.V 53

WAINER, Nora Roberts. Waterway journey, the voyage of Nora's ark. New York, Funk & Wagnalls (1968) 247 p. illus. 22 cm. 68-16744. F106.W 22

(WALLACE, William A.) The Great Eastern's log. Containing her first transatlantic voyage, and all particulars of her American visit. By an executive officer. London, Bradbury & Evans, 1860. 91 p. 18½ cm. 4-35432. F106.W 23

WATKINS, N. J. ed. The pine and the palm greetings; or, The trip of the northern editors to the South in 1871, and the return visit of the southern editors in 1872, under the leadership of Maj. N. H. Hotchkiss ... Ed. and comp. by N. J. Watkins. Baltimore, J. D. Ehlers & co.'s engraving and printing house, 1873. 144 p. front. (port.) fold. maps. 23 cm. 2-3799. F106.W 33

(WEED, Samuel Richards) Journey of the Common council of the city of St. Louis to Pittsburgh, Philadelphia, New York, Boston, and Manchester, N. H. St. Louis, Missouri democrat print, 1865. 111 p. 25½ cm. 1-16160 Rev. F106.W 39

WERTENBAKER, Thomas Jefferson, 1879 - 1966. The founding of American civilization: the middle colonies. Illustrated. New York, Cooper Square Publishers, 1963. xiii, 364 p. 24 cm. 63-17541.
F106.W 48

WESTBROOK, Henrietta Payne. The West-brook drives; illus. by Marianna Sloan. New York, P. Eckler, 1902. vi, iv, 7-393 p. front. (port.) 16 pl. 20½ cm. An account of carriage-drives and other trips in Pennsylvania, New Jersey, New York and New England. 2-5567. F106.W 52

WESTON, Edward Payson. "The pedestrian"; being a correct journal of "incidents" on a walk from the state house, Boston, Mass., to the U. S. capitol, at Washington, D. C. ... 1861 ... New York, E. P. Weston, 1862. 48 p. 21 cm. 1-16159. F106.W 53

WHITE, Richard Dunning. The narrative of a journey from Quebec to Niagara. Through the states of New York, New England, to Halifax, Nova Scotia, "fifty-six years ago." By R. D. White ... Exeter, W. Pol;ard, printers, 1896. 36 p. 18½ cm. 16-10406. F106.W 58

WILDES, Harry Emerson. The Delaware; illus. by Irwin D. Hoffman. New York, Toronto, Farrar & Rinehart, inc. (1940) x, 3-398 p. illus. 21 cm. (The rivers of America) "Acknowledgements and bibliography": p. 369 - 381. 40-14246. F106.W 65

WILLIS, Nathaniel Parker. Mountain, lake, and river. A series of twenty-five steel line engravings from designs by W. H. Bartlett and others. The descriptive text by N. P. Willis and others. Boston, Estes and Lauriat, 1884. 96 p. front., plates. 32½ x 26 cm. Plate listing to face p. 69 wanting. Selections from the author's American scenery, London, 1840. 1-16158. F106.W733

WILLSON, Marcius. The geography, industries and resources of the several United States and territories, forming part of a series of supplementary readers. Vol. I. The six New England states, the five middle states, and the five southern Atlantic states. (n.p., 1886) 143 p. 25 cm. "Specimen selections from an unpublished work." Includes only the six New England states and New York. 2-3796 Rev. F106.W 74

WILSON, Everett Broomall. America East; its architecture and decoration. New York, A. S. Barnes (1965) 322 p. 26 cm. 65-11419. F106.W 75
1965

WILSON, Everett Broomall. Fifty early American towns. South Brunswick (N.J.) A. S. Barnes (1966) 353 p. 26 cm. 66-13843. F106.W753

WILSON'S railroad guide from New-York to Washington; with maps of New-York, Philadelphia, and Baltimore; and sectional maps of the routes. New-York, H. Wilson, 1849. 53, 27 p. illus., maps. 24°. 1-21358-M1. F106.W 76

WOOD, Florence Dorothy. Hills and harbors, the Middle Atlantic States; Delaware, Maryland, New Jersey, New York, Pennsylvania, West Virginia, District of Columbia. Illus. by Vernon McKissack. Chicago, Childrens Press (1962) 93 p. illus. 24 cm. (Enchantment of America series) 62-9073. F106.W 79

16   LOCAL HISTORIES IN THE LIBRARY OF CONGRESS

YOUNG'S Research Service, inc. New York.   Let's take a ride, describing over 100 scenic, historic
and unusual points of interest within a few hours' drive of metropolitan New York.   (2d ed.)   New
York (1960)   79 p.   22 cm.   F106. Y 6
                                                                                                                                     1960

ATLANTIC coast - Description and travel.   Pamphlets, broadsides, clippings, and other miscellaneous
matter on this subject, not separately cataloged, are classified in   F106. Z 5

NEW YORK

SELECTED BIBLIOGRAPHIES FOR NEW YORK

NEW YORK (State) Division of Archives and History. Annual listing, state and local historical research in progress. 1st -   1950 -   Albany.   v.   28 cm.   59-32659.   Z1317. A 3

NEW YORK (State) Office of State History. Research and publications in New York State history, 1969 - 1970. Albany, 1970.   v, 25 p.   28 cm.   73-63550 MARC.   Z1317. A 67

CLUM, Audna T. Hudson-Champlain reading list. Albany, Bureau of Secondary Curriculum Development, State Education Dept. (1959?)   21 p.   22 cm.   A 59-9212.   Z1317. C 55

FLAGG, Charles Allcott. ... Bibliography of New York colonial history ...   Albany, University of the state of New York, 1901.   p. (289) - 558.   24½ cm.   (New York state library. Bulletin 56, Feb. 1901. Bibliography (v. 2) 24)   3-20017.   Z1317. F 57

HISTORICAL materials relating to northern New York; a union catalog, compiled by a committee of the North Country Reference and Research Resources Council.   Ed. by G. Glyndon Cole.   (Plattsburgh? N.Y.) ... 1968.   307 p.   28 cm.   68-3051.   Z1317. H 66

NESTLER, Harold. A bibliography of New York State communities, counties, towns, villages. Port Washington, N.Y., I.J. Friedman (1968)   1 v. (unpaged) 26 cm.   (Empire State historical publications series, 51) 68-18353.   Z1317. N 45

ADIRONDACKS. Adirondack bibliography; a list of books, pamphlets and periodical articles pub. through the year 1955. Compiled by the Bibliography Committee of the Adirondack Mountain Club. (1st ed.) Gabriels, N.Y., 1958.   xviii, 354 p.   map.   25 cm.   58-6822.   Z1318. A2 A3

— Supplement. vol. 1, 1956 - 1965. vol. 2, 1966 - 1968. Blue Mountain Lake, N.Y., Adirondack Museum, 1970 -   v.   25 cm.   Z1318. A2 A3 Suppl.

BRONX. See WESTCHESTER.

CHAMPLAIN Valley. A selective bibliography of publications on the Champlain Valley. (Plattsburgh? N.Y., 1959)   viii, 144 p.   22 cm.   59-8358.   Z1318. C45 C6

LONG ISLAND. Long island bibliography, by Richard B. Sealock ... Baltimore, Md. (Ann Arbor, Mich., Edwards bros.) 1940.   xxii, 338 p.   28 x 22 cm.   Reproduced from type-written copy.   "A subject list covering the entire history of Long Island through the year 1939."   41-4320.   Z1318. L8 S 4

ORANGE County. Orange County, New York; a reader's guide and bibliography, by Matilda A. Gocek. Monroe, N.Y., Library Research Associates, 1973.   35 p.   23 cm.   73-77313 MARC.   Z1318. O7 G6

ROCHESTER. Annotated bibliography of periodical references on Rochester, New York, Jan., 1925 - Sept., 1936, by Ruth B. Goodman. Rochester, N.Y., Dept. of sociology, University of Rochester, 1937.   3 p. 49 numb. l.   27½ x 21½ cm.   Classified, with subject and author indexes. Mimeographed.   38-2720.   Z1318. R67 G6

SYRACUSE. Where to find it; bibliography of Syracuse history by Franklin H. Chase ... Pub. by the Onondaga historical assoc. ... Syracuse, N.Y., The Dehler press, 1920.   219 p.   25 cm.   Publications of Onondaga historical assoc.: p. 152 - 158.   21-674 Rev.   Z1318. S9 C 4

UTICA. A bibliography of the history and life of Utica; a centennial contribution, compiled by Utica public library from its resources. Utica, N.Y., Printed by Goodenow print. co., 1932.   4. 237 p.   illus. (incl. facsim.) 23 cm.   Classified.   "Printers of Utica and their work": p. (137) - 216.   32-22585.   Z1318. U8 U9

WESTCHESTER. ... A check list of books, maps, pictures, and other printed matter relating to the counties of Westchester and Bronx, by Otto Hufeland ... White Plains, N.Y., Pub. for Westchester County by the Westchester County historical soc., 1929.   xvi, 320 p.   23½ cm.   (Publications of the Westchester County historical society, vol. vi)   Arranged under geographical and a few topical subjects, with an author index.   29-15863.

Z1318. W5 H8
L H & G

NEW YORK CLASSIFICATION F 116 - F 130

116		Periodicals. Societies. Collections.
		Subarrangement for the New York Historical Society. Collections.
	.N62	First and second series, 1811–1859.
	.N63	Publication fund series, 1868–
	.N638	Quarterly bulletin, 1917–
	.N64	Proceedings, 1843–1849.
	.N65	Annual report of the Executive Committee.
	.N66	Charter, constitution, etc. Editions by date.
	.N67	Lists of members. Editions by date.
	.N68	Anniversary address. By date.
	.N69	Inaugural address of President. By date.
	.N7–76	Other official publications. Alphabetically by title.
	.N77A–Z	Publications about the society or its officers. By author or name of officer.
.5		Museums. Exhibitions, exhibits.
117		Gazetteers. Dictionaries. Geographic names.
.3		Guidebooks.
118		Biography (Collective). Genealogy (Collective).
.2		Historiography.
		Historians, *see* E 175.5.
.5		Study and teaching.
119		General works. Histories.
.3		Juvenile works.
.5		Minor works. Pamphlets, addresses, essays, etc.
.6		Anecdotes, legends, pageants, etc.
120		Historic monuments. Illustrative material.
121		Antiquities (Non-Indian).
		By period.
122		Early to 1775.

        English province, 1664–1774; Dutch reconquest, 1673–1674; Leisler's Rebellion, 1689; Agrarian conflicts, 1711–1715 (Cf. HD 196.N7); etc.

        Biography: Nicholas Bayard; William Burnet; Cadwallader Colden; Thomas Dongan, earl of Limerick; Caleb Heathcote; Jacob Leisler; etc.

        Cf. E 101–135, Early voyages to America.

            E 196, King William's War, 1689–1697.

            E 199, French and Indian War, 1755–1763.

            F 7.5, Andros and his government, 1688–1689.

            F 52, New Hampshire Grants.

            F 1030–1030.8, French explorations, invasions, and missionaries in western New York.

.1 New Netherlands. Dutch Colony, 1610–1664.
Biography: Arent van Curler, Adriaen van der Donck, Jonas Michaelius, Peter Minuit, Peter Stuyvesant, etc.
Cf. E 83.655, Indian uprising of 1655.
E 83.663, Esopus Indian War, 1663–1664.
F 127.R32, Rensselaerswyck.
F 167, Subjugation of the Swedes on the Delaware, 1655.

123 1775–1865.
Biography: John Watts DePeyster, James Kent, John Alsop King, Elias Warner Leavenworth, Henry Cruse Murphy, Daniel D. Tompkins, Stephen Van Rensselaer, etc.
Cf. E 263.N6, New York in the Revolution (General); E 230.5–241, Military operations and battles.
E 359.5.N6, War of 1812 (General); E 355, Military operations and battles.
E 409.5.N6, War with Mexico, 1845–1848 (General).
E 523, Civil War, 1861–1865 (General).
F 1032, Burning of the "Caroline"; the McLeod case.
HD 199, Antirent movement, 1835–1846.
HS 525–527, Antimasonic Controversy, 1827–1845.
TC 625.E6, Erie Canal.

124 1865–1950.
Biography: John Alden Dix, Daniel Drew, Roswell Pettibone Flower, Herbert Henry Lehman, Patrick Henry McCarren, James Aloysius O'Gorman, John Boyd Thacher, etc.
Cf. D 570.85.N4–5, World War I, 1914–1918.
D 769.85.N4–5, World War II, 1939–1945.
E 726.N5, War of 1898 (Spanish-American War).

125 1951–

127 Regions, counties, etc., A–Z.
.A2 Adirondack Mountains.
.A3 Albany Co.
Cf. F 52, New Hampshire Grants.
F 127.R32, Rensselaerswyck.
.A4 Allegany Co.
.A43 Allegany State Park.
.A45 Allegheny River and Valley, N. Y.
Cf. F 157.A5, General, and Pennsylvania.
Au Sable River and Valley, see F 127.E8.
.B48 Black River.
"Boston Ten Townships," see F 127.T6.
.B7 Boundaries.
Cf. F 72.B7, Massachusetts boundary.
F 142.B7, New Jersey boundary.
Massachusetts territorial claims to western New York, see F 127.G2.
New Hampshire–New York dispute over New Hampshire Grants, see F 52.
Bronx Co., see F 128.68.B8, Borough of the Bronx.
.B8 Broome Co.
Cf. F 127.G2, Genesee region.
F 127.T6, "Massachusetts (or Boston) Ten Townships."
.C3 Catskill Mountains.
Kaaterskill Park, Rip Van Winkle Trail, etc.
.C4 Cattaraugus Co.
.C5 Cayuga Co.
.C52 Cayuga Lake.

.C6   Lake Champlain region (General, and N. Y.).
             Champlain Valley; Lake Champlain Tercentenary, 1909; etc.
             Cf. F 57.C4, Vermont.
                F 57.G7, Grand Isle Co., Vt.
        Charlotte Co. (1772), see F 127.W3.

.C7   Chautauqua Co.
             Lake Chautauqua, Portage Trail, etc.

.C72   Chemung Co.
.C73   Chemung River and Valley (General, and N. Y.).
             Cf. F 157.C37, Pennsylvania.

.C76   Chenango Co.
.C77   Clinton Co.
.C8   Columbia Co.
             Livingston Manor, etc.

.C83   Constitution Island.
        Cornwall Co. (1664–1686), see F 23.

.C85   Cortland Co.
        Cumberland Co. (1768), see F 52.

.D3   Delaware Co.
.D4   Delaware River and Valley, N. Y.
             Cf. F 142.D4, New Jersey.
                F 157.D4, General, and Pennsylvania.
                F 172.D4, Delaware.

.D8   Dutchess Co.
             Little (or Upper) Nine Partners Patent, etc.

.E6   Erie Co.
.E65   Lake Erie region, N. Y.
             Cf. F 555, Lake Erie (General).

.E8   Essex Co.
             Au Sable River and Valley, Au Sable Chasm, etc.

.F4   Finger Lakes region.
             Cf. F 127.C52, Cayuga Lake, etc.

.F5   Fishers Island.
             Cf. F 129.S74, Southold.

.F8   Franklin Co.
             Mount Seward, Saranac Lakes, etc.

.F9   Fulton Co.
        Gardiner's Island, see F 129.E13.

.G19   Genesee Co.
.G2   Genesee region.   Genesee River and Valley.
             Phelps-Gorham Purchase (1788), etc.
             Cf. F 127.H7, Holland Purchase.
                F 127.T6, "Massachusetts (or Boston) Ten Townships."

.G3   Lake George.
        Gloucester Co. (1770), see F 52.
        Grand Island, see F 129.G68.

.G7   Greene Co.
             Catskill Mountains, see F 127.C3.

.H2   Hamilton Co.
             Blue Mountain Lake, Long Lake, Raquette Lake, etc.

.H5   Herkimer Co.
             West Canada Creek, etc.

.H7   Holland Purchase.   Treaty of Big Tree, 1797.
.H73   Hoosic River and Valley (General, and N. Y.).
             Cf. F 57.B4, Vermont.
                F 72.B5, Massachusetts.

.H8   Hudson River and Valley (General, and N. Y.).
             Highlands; Hudson-Fulton Celebration, 1909; Palisades; etc.
             Cf. F 142.B4, New Jersey Palisades.
                F 142.H83, New Jersey.

.J4   Jefferson Co.
.K4   Keuka Lake.
.K5   Kings Co.
> Cf. F 129.B7, Borough of Brooklyn.

.L6   Lewis Co.
.L7   Livingston Co.
> Hemlock Lake, etc.

.L8   Long Island.
> Fishers Island, *see* F 127.F5.
> Shelter Island, *see* F 127.S54.
> Cf. F 127.K5, Kings Co.; .N2, Nassau Co.; .Q3, Queens Co.; .S9, Suffolk Co.

.M2   Madison Co.

"Massachusetts (or Boston) Ten Townships," *see* F 127.T6.

.M5   Minisink region.
> Minisink Patent (1704), *see* F 142.B7.

.M55   Mohawk River and Valley.
> Mohawk Trail, N. Y., etc.
> Mohawk Trail, Mass., *see* F 72.B5.

.M4   Military tract (set off from Tryon Co., 1782).
.M6   Monroe Co.
.M7   Montgomery Co.
> Tryon Co. (1772-1784).

.N2   Nassau Co.

New Hampshire Grants, *see* F 52.
New York Co., *see* F 128.

.N5   Niagara Co.
.N6   Niagara River region (General, and N. Y.).
> Niagara frontier, Niagara River and Valley, etc.
> Cf. F 1059.N5, Niagara Peninsula, Ontario.

.N8   Niagara Falls.
> State Reservation, Goat Island, etc.
> Cf. F 1059.Q3, Queen Victoria Niagara Falls Park, Ontario.

.O5   Oneida Co.
.O52   Oneida Lake.
.O6   Onondaga Co.
> Onondaga Lake, etc.

.O7   Ontario Co.
> Cf. F 127.G2, Genesee region.
>   F 127.H7, Holland Purchase.

.O72   Lake Ontario region, N. Y.
> Cf. F 556, Lake Ontario (General).

.O8   Orange Co.
> Newburgh Bay, etc.
> Highlands, *see* F 127.H8.
> Minisink region, *see* F 127.M5.
> Wawayanda Patent (1703), *see* F 142.B7.

.O9   Orleans Co.
.O91   Oswego Co.
.O93   Otsego Co.

Palisades of the Hudson, *see* F 127.H8.
Phelps-Gorham Purchase (1788), *see* F 127.G2.

.P9   Putnam Co.
.Q3   Queens Co.
> Cf. F 128.68.Q4, Borough of Queens.

.R3   Rensselaer Co.
> Taconic Mountains, etc.

.R32   Rensselaerswyck. The Van Rensselaer Manor.
> Cf. HD 199, Antirent movement, 1835-1846.

	Richmond Co., *see* F 127.S7.
.R6	Rockland Co.
.S2	St. Lawrence Co.
	Black Lake, etc.
.S23	St. Lawrence River and Valley, N. Y.
	Cf. F 127.T5, Thousand Islands.
	F 1050, General, and Canada.
.S26	Saratoga Co.
	Mount McGregor, etc.
.S27	Schenectady Co.
.S3	Schoharie Co.
.S34	Schuyler Co.
	Watkins Glen, etc.
.S4	Seneca Co.
.S43	Seneca Lake.
.S54	Shelter Island.
.S7	Staten Island. Richmond Co. Borough of Richmond.
.S8	Steuben Co.
	Canisteo River, etc.
.S9	Suffolk Co.
	Fire Island State Park, etc.
	Fishers Island, *see* F 127.F5.
.S91	Sullivan Co.
	Minisink region, *see* F 127.M5.
.S96	Susquehanna River and Valley, N. Y.
	Cf. F 157.S8, General, and Pennsylvania.
	F 187.S8, Maryland.
.T5	Thousand Islands.
	Carleton Island, Grenell Island, etc.
.T6	Tioga Co. "Massachusetts (or Boston) Ten Townships."
	Cf. F 127.G2, Genesee region.
.T7	Tompkins Co.
	Tryon Co. (1772–1784), *see* F 127.M7.
.U4	Ulster Co.
	Lake Minnewaska, Mohonk Lake, Mount Meenahga, Shawangunk Mountains, etc.
	Catskill Mountains, *see* F 127.C3.
	Minisink region, *see* F 127.M5.
.U54	Unadilla River and Valley.
.W2	Warren Co.
	Luzerne Lake, etc.
	Cf. F 127.G3, Lake George.
.W3	Washington Co.
	Charlotte County (1772).
	Cf. F 52, New Hampshire Grants.
	F 127.G3, Lake George.
	Wawayanda Patent (1703), *see* F 142.B7.
.W4	Wayne Co.
.W5	Westchester Co.
	Fordham Manor, Philipsburg Manor, Van Cortlandt Manor, etc.
	Cf. F 128.68.B8, Borough of the Bronx.
.W9	Wyoming Co.
.Y3	Yates Co.
128	New York (City). New York (County). Table IV.[1]
.1	Periodicals. Societies. Collections.
.15	Museums. Exhibitions, exhibits.
	World's Fair, 1939–1940, *see* T 785.

.18	Guidebooks.	
.25	Biography (Collective). Genealogy (Collective).	
.27	Historiography.	
.29	Study and teaching.	
.3	General works. Histories.	
.33	Juvenile works.	
.35	Minor works. Pamphlets, addresses, essays, etc.	
.36	Anecdotes, legends, pageants, etc.	
.37	Historic monuments. Illustrative material.	
.39	Antiquities (Non-Indian).	
	By period.	
.4	Early to 1775.	

                New Amsterdam; Negro plot, 1741; etc.
                Biography: Annetje Jane Bogardus, etc.
                Cf. F 122, 122.1, New York (State).

.44   1775–1865.

                Fire, 1835; Draft riot, 1863; etc.
                Biography: Michael Floy, Philip Hone, Fernando Wood, etc.
                Cf. E 263.N6, New York in the Revolution; E 230.5–241, Military operations and battles.

.47   1865–1900.

                Riot, 1871; Blizzard, 1888; etc.
                Biography: Richard Croker, Andrew Haswell Green, John Kelly, Abram Stevens Hewitt, William Marcy Tweed, etc.

.5   1901–1950.   Greater New York.

                "General Slocum" disaster, 1904; etc.
                Biography: Edward Joseph Flynn, William Jay Gaynor, Seth Low, James John Walker, etc.
                Cf. F 127.Q3, Queens County.
                    F 127.S7, Staten Island, Richmond County.
                    F 129.B7, Brooklyn.

.52   1951–

        Sections.   Localities.   Districts, etc.

.6   General works.
.61   Cemeteries.

            e. g. .A1 General works.
                   .W8 Woodlawn Cemetery.

.62   Churches.

            Prefer NA for architecture; BX for religious aspects.

.625   Hotels, taverns, etc.
.627   Places of amusement.
.63   Harbor.
.64   Monuments.   Statues.

            e. g. .A1 General works.
                   .G7 Grant Monument (Grant's tomb).
                   .L6 Statue of Liberty.

.65   Parks.   Squares.   Circles.

            e. g. .A1 General works.
                 .B3 Battery.
                 .B8 Bronx Parkway.
                 .C3 Central Park.

		.C5	City Hall Park.
		.R5	Riverside Park.
		.Z6	Zoological Park.

.67   Streets. Bridges. Railroads.

         e. g.   .A1   General works.
                 .B6   Bowery.
                 .B7   Broadway.
                 .F4   Fifth Avenue.
                 .F7   Forty-second Street.
                 .P3   Park Avenue.
                 .R6   Riverside Drive.
                 .W2   Wall Street.

.68   Suburbs. Sections of the city. Rivers.

         e. g.   .A1   General works.
                 .B6   Bloomingdale.
                 .B8   Bronx (Borough).
                         Morrisania Manor, Pelham Manor, etc.
                         Cf. F 127.W5, Westchester Co.
                      Brooklyn (Borough), see F 129.B7.
                 .C5   City Island.
                      Coney Island, see F 129.C75.
                 .G7   Governor's Island.
                 .G8   Greenwich Village.
                 .H3   Harlem.
                 .H4   Harlem River.
                      Long Island City, see F 129.L78.
                 .Q4   Queens (Borough).
                         Cf. F 127.Q3, Queens County.
                      Richmond (Borough), see F 127.S7.
                      Rockaway Beach, see F 129.R8.
                      Staten Island, see F 127.S7.
                 .S9   Stuyvesant Village.
                 .W2   Washington Heights.

.69   Wards.

        Buildings.

.7   General works. Collective.

.8   Individual, A–Z.

         e. g.   .M8   Morris Mansion (Jumel Mansion).
                 .P4   Pennsylvania Station.
                 .R7   Rockefeller Center.
                 .V2   Van Cortlandt Mansion.
                 .W82   Woolworth Building.

.9   Elements in the population.

        .A1   General works.
        .A2–Z   Individual elements.
                    For a list of racial, ethnic, and religious
                    elements (with cutter numbers), see
                    E 184, p. 27–29.

129   Other cities, towns, etc., A–Z.

         e. g.   .A1   General works.
                 .A3   Albany.
                 .B7   Brooklyn.
                        A borough of New York (City).
                 .B8   Buffalo.
                 .C75   Coney Island.
                 .E13   East Hampton.
                        Gardiner's Island, Gardiner Manor, etc.
                 .G68   Grand Island.

.L78 Long Island City.
.H99 Hyde Park.
.O98 Oyster Bay.
Sagamore Hill, etc.
.R7 Rochester.
.R8 Rockaway Beach.
.S3 Saratoga Springs.
.S74 Southold.
Cf. F 127.F5, Fishers Island.

130 Elements in the population.
.A1 General works.
.A2–Z Individual elements.
For a list of racial, ethnic, and religious elements (with cutter numbers), *see* E 184, p. 27–29.

NEW YORK
F 116 - F 130

PERIODICALS. SOCIETIES. COLLECTIONS.

... REMARQUES. (The home journal of Central New York) (Syracuse, N.Y., The Remarques company) 18 v. illus. 41½ cm. semimonthly. CA 10-593 Unrev. F116 AP 2 R 33

VIELE, Sheldon Thompson. A glimpse of Holland in 1888. A journal-narrative of the visit of the Holland society to the Netherlands. New York, The De Vinne press, 1890. (9) - 123 p. 28½ cm. 33-31371. F116 DJ 38. V 8

ADVENTURES in Western New York history. Until bound and cataloged, issues will be found in the Periodicals Reading Room. F116.A 45
— Old Fort Niagara. By Ann Kelleran. (Buffalo Historical Soc. 1960) 16 p. 25 cm. (v. 1 no. 1)
— The Pan-American Exposition. By Isabel Vaughan James. (Buffalo and Erie County Historical Soc. 1961) 16 p. 25 cm. (v. 6)
— Prehistoric people of Western New York by Richard L. McCarthy. (Buffalo and Erie County Historical Soc. 1961) 16 p. 25 cm. (v. 7)
— The Holland Land Company in Western New York. By Robert W. Silsby. (Buffalo and Erie County Historical Soc. 1961) 16 p. 25 cm. (v. 8)
— The war of 1812 on the frontier. By Lura Lincoln Cook. (Buffalo and Erie County Historical Soc. 1961) 16 p. 25 cm. (v. 9)
— The Grand Canal: New York's first thruway (by) Eric Brunger. (Buffalo and Erie County Historical Soc. (1964) 20 p. 25 cm. (v. 12)
— People of our city and county, by Stephen Credel. (Rev. ed. Buffalo and Erie County Historical Soc. (1971) 16 p. illus. 26 cm. (v.13)
— Glass; Lancaster and Lockport, New York, by Jean W. Dunn. Buffalo and Erie County Historical Soc. (1971) 20 p. illus. 25 cm. (v.17)

HOLLAND society of New York. ... Annual banquet. (New York,) v. 26½ cm. F116.H735

HOLLAND society of New York. ... Constitution, by-laws, officers and members. 1891. New York, 1891. 73 p. 19½ cm. 3-29030. F116.H737

— New York (The De Vinne press) 1894. 73 p. 20 cm. 1-13375. F116.H 74

— New York (The Knickerbocker press) 1903. ix, 50 p. 23 cm. 8-5939. F116.H745

HOLLAND society of New York. Collections ... (New York, Printed for the Society, 1891 - 19
   v. fronts. 25 - 29 cm. Contents. - v. 1 - (2) Records of the Reformed Dutch churches of Hackensack and Schraalenburgh, N.J., pts. 1-2. 1891. - v. 3. Records of the Reformed Dutch church of New Paltz, N.Y. 1896. - v. 4. Records of the Reformed Dutch church of Bergen, N.J. now Jersey City. (1915) 5-39196 Rev.
F116.H 76

HOLLAND society of New York. Year book. (New York, 1886 - 19   v. fronts., illus., plates (part fold., part col.) ports., maps, plans (part fold.) facsims. 28½ cm. Year books for 1904-1908, 1922/23, include the records of the Reformed Dutch church of Albany, 1683-1779. For 1913-15 include the records of the Reformed Protestant Dutch church of Bergen (now Jersey City), New Jersey For 1916 includes the records of Dominie Henricus Selyns, minister of the Reformed Dutch church at Nieuw Amsterdam. 0-5976 (rev. '25)
F116.H 77

HOLLAND society of New York. Officers, committees and members. New York. v. 15 cm.
58-38238.
F116.H 78

LONG ISLAND historical society. Quarterly. v. 1 - 4, no. 1; Jan. 1939 - Jan. 1942. Brooklyn, N.Y.   4 v. in 2. illus., ports. 24 cm. 42-20785 rev.
F116.L875

LONG ISLAND historical society. Proceedings. Brooklyn, N.Y.   11 v. in 2. 24 cm. annual.
F116.L 88

LONG ISLAND historical society. List of members, etc. Brooklyn, 1875. 27 p. 25 cm. 8-15795.
F116.L884

LONG ISLAND historical society. Proceedings ... in memory of Hon. James Carson Brevoort and others. Brooklyn, 1888. 15 p. 25 cm. 3-5060.
F116.L886

LONG ISLAND historical society. Report of the building committee ... (Brooklyn? 1871)
(3) p. 8°. 1-22656-M1.
F116.L 89

LONG ISLAND historical society. History and its sources: and address ... by James Carson Brevoort ... Brooklyn, 1868. 23 p. 28½ cm. "Extracted from the Report for 1867-8" 4-9843.
F116.L895

LONG ISLAND historical society. The certificate of incorporation, etc. Brooklyn, 1863.
21 p. 23 cm. 1-13378-M1.
F116.L 9

LONG ISLAND historical society. The by-laws and certificate of incorporation, etc. 22 p. 23½ cm.
1-13377.
F116.L 9
1863 a

LONG ISLAND historical society, (Brooklyn, N.Y.)   v. pl. Some vols. include the society's report.
7-761 Additions.
F116.L919

LONG ISLAND historical society. The century book. Ed. by Walton H. Rawls. (New York, 1964)
viii, 206 p. 26 cm. 64-17238.
F116.L952

LONG ISLAND historical society, 1863 - 1938, a record: in commemoration of the 75th anniversary of the foundation of the soc. in 1863. Brooklyn, N.Y., 1938. 3 - 76 p. front. (port.) plates. 23½ cm.
38-37224.
F116.L953

LONG ISLAND historical society. Memoirs. Brooklyn, N.Y., 1867 - 89.   4 v. illus., plates (part fold.) ports., maps (part fold.) 25 cm. 5-39195.
F116.L954
   — Journal of a voyage to New York ... 1679 - 80, by Jaspar Dankers, etc. 1867. viii, xlvii, 440 p. xii col. pl. (vol. 1) 1-13379 Rev.
   — The battle of Long island ... by Thomas W. Field. 1869. xiii, ix, 549 p. v pl., 2 fold. plans. 24½ cm. (vol. ii) 1-13380.
   — The campaign of 1776 around New York and Brooklyn .... By Henry P. Johnston. 1878. viii, ix, (13) - 300 p., (5) - 209 p. (vol. iii) 2-10427.
   — George Washington and Mount Vernon; a collection of Washington's unpublished agricultural and personal letters ... 1889. xcii, 352 p. (vol. 4) 1-13381.

NEW NETHERLAND register, The.   v. 1 (no. 1 - 8):   Jan. 1911 - (1913)   New York, D. Versteeg
(1911 - 1913)   136 p.   23 cm.   No more pub?   26-20214.   F116.N 23

NEW YORK (State) Division of Archives and History.   Historical societies of New York State.
Albany, 1954 -   v.   28 cm.   55-62050 rev.   F116.N237

NEW YORK (State) Division of archives and history.   ... Handbook of historical and patriotic societies
in New York state, including list of local historians.   Albany, The University of the state of New
York press, 1926.   (3) - 63 p.   23 cm.   27-27038 rev. 2.   F116.N 24

NEW YORK (State)   State historian.   Annual report.   (1st) - 3d.   (1895/96) - 1897.   Albany and New
York, Wynkoop, Hallenbeck Crawford co., 1896-98.   3 v. col. front., plates (part fold.) ports., maps (part fold.)
plans (part fold.) 23½ cm.   The 2d and 3d reports contain papers relating to the part taken by military organizations of the state during the civil
war, colonial records, 1664 - 1675, and muster rolls, 1664 - 1775. "Appendix N" of the 3d annual report was issued separately, 1899-1904, as
v. 1-7 of the "Public papers of George Clinton ... issued in 10 vols., New York, 1899-1914.   19-4302.   F116.N 26

NEW YORK (State)   State historian.   ... Special report of Victor Hugo Paltsits ...   (Albany, 1911)
3 p.   22½ cm.   19-4162.   F116.N 27

NEW YORK (State) University.   The New York State Historian and the Division of Archives and History;
a Committee report to the New York State Commissioner of Education.   Albany ... 1964.
iii, 19 p.   23 cm.   66-7010.   F116.N275

NEW YORK genealogical and biographical record, The.   Devoted to the interests of American genealogy and biography.   v. 1 -   Jan. 1870 -   New York, New York Genea-
logical and Biographical Society.   v.   illus., ports., maps.   25 - 27 cm.   quarterly.   Supersedes the society's Bulletin.
Subject index. Vols. 1-24, 1870-93. 1 v. Vols. 1-38, 1870-1907. 1 v. Vols. 39-76, 1908-45. 1 v.   5-37675 rev.*   F116.N 28

NEW YORK genealogical and biographical society.   By laws, certificate of incorporation, etc.   New
York, G. F. Nesbitt, print., 1869.   16 p.   23½ cm.   2-22062.   F116.N 31

NEW YORK genealogical and biographical society.   Reports of officers; list of members, etc.   1898.
34 p.   front.   27 cm.   6-13947.   F116.N315

—   5 vols.   fronts.   20 cm.   F116.N 32

—   1900.   15½ cm.   F116.N321

—   1910.   40 p.   illus.   19½ cm.   F116.N324

NEW YORK genealogical and biographical society.   ... Twenty-fifth anniversary ... 1894.   New
York, 1895.   xi, 81 p.   3 pl. (incl. front.) 6 port.   27½ cm.   8-10505.   F116.N 33

NEW YORK genealogical and biographical society.   Bulletin.   v. 1, no. 1;   Dec. 1869.   (New York,
1869?)   8 p.   22½ cm.   Superseded by the N. Y. genealogical and biographical record. 4-4305.   F116.N 35

—   Photostat of above.   1939.   facsim.   8 numb. l.   41-38728.   F116.N352

NEW YORK genealogical and biographical society, Collections of the.   v. 1 -   New York,
Printed for the Society, 1890 - 19   v.   fronts., ports., facsims., co., coats of arms.   28 - 29 cm.   100 copies.
5-40505 Rev.   F116.N 36
                                                                                          Geneal. Sect. Ref.
    —   Records of the Reformed Dutch church in New Amsterdam and New York: marriages
from 11 Dec. 1639, to 26 Aug. 1801 ...   1890.   4, xii, 9-351 p. port., facsim. (v.1) 4-5040.
    —   Records of the Reformed Dutch church in New Amsterdam and New York: baptisms ...
N.Y., 1901-2.   2 v.   fronts. (v.2-3)   4-5039.
    —   Records of the Dutch reformed church of Port Richmond, S.I. baps. from 1696 to 1772;
United Brethren congregation ... S.I. births and baps. 1749 to 1853, marriages: 1764 to 1863, deaths
and burials: 1758 to 1828; St. Andrew's church, Richmond, S.I. births and baps. from 1752 to 1795,
marriages from 1754 to 1808. Ed. Tobias A. Wright. N.Y., 1909.   4, xi, (2), 10-335 p. (v. iv) 9-22999.

— Minisink valley Reformed Dutch church records. 1913.   4, xxx, 349 p. front. (port.) pl. facsim. (vol. v) 14-10142.

— ... Register of pedigrees ... v. I - II. Ed. John Reynolds Totten ... 1913 - 29. 2 v. ports., col. coats of arms. (vol. vi) 13-16029.

— ... Wawarsing Reformed Dutch church records, ed. by Royden Woodward Vosburgh ... 1922.   3, 146, 31 p. front., facsims. (vol. vii)   22-12453.

— Records of the Presbyterian church. Newtown (now Elmhurst) Queens County, L.I. (In v. 8, p. 1-83)   28-13977.

— Records of the Reformed Dutch church and of the Presbyterian church at Smithfield, Pennsylvania.   (In v. 8 p. (85) - 125)   28-13978.

— Records of the Clove Dutch Reformed church of Clove Valley, Wantage, Sussex County, New Jersey.   (In vol. 8 p. (127) - 157)   28-13979.

NEW YORK genealogical and biographical society. ... Statement of treasurer for fiscal year ... v.   20 - 21½ cm.   CA 34-1055 Unrev.   F116.N 37

NEW YORK heritage series. no. (1) -   (Spartanburg, S.C., Reprint Co.) 1964 - no. illus. 22 - 28 cm.   F116.N 42

— History of New Netherland; or, New York under the Dutch, by Edmund B. O'Callaghan. 1846 - 48.   2 v. 24 cm. (no. 2 - 3)   66-25099.

— Catherine Schuyler. By Mary Gay Humphreys. New York, Scribner, 1897. xi, 251 p. illus. (no. 4)

— The Empire State; a compendious history of the Commonwealth of New York, by Benson J. Lossing. Illus. by ... H. Ross. Hartford, American Pub. Co., 1888.   xix, 618 p. illus. (no. 5) 68-57492.

NEW YORK historical soc., Collections of the. v. 1-4, 4-5, 1809-30; 2d ser. v. 1-4. N.Y.. 1811-59. 10 v. pl., ports., maps, facsims.   22 - 25½ cm.   2d ser. v. 3 pt. 2 never published.   F116.N 62

— The constitution of the New-York historical soc. 1809. (v.1, p. 1-16)   11-21769.

— A discourse, designed to commemorate the discovery of New-York by Henry Hudson. (v.1 p. 17-45)   11-21767.

— ... The relation of John de Verrazzano ... 1524.   (v. 1 p. 45-60)   11-21766.

— ... Divers voyages and northern discoveries of ... Henry Hudson.   (v. 1, p. 61-81) 11-21765.

— ... A second voyage or employment of Master Henry Hudson.   (v. 1, p. 81-102)   11-21764.

— ... The third voyage of Master Henry Hudson.   (v. 1, p. 102-146)   11-21763.

— ... An abstract of the journall of Master Henry Hudson.   (v.1, p. 146-150)   11-21762.

— ... A larger discourse of the same voyage.   (v.1, p. 150-188)   11-21761.

— (Documents extracted from the second volume of Hazard's "Historical collections") (v.1, p. 189-303)   11-22430.

— ... East-Hampton book of laws. June 24th, 1665.   (v. 1, p. 305-428)   11-21760.

— Memorial to the Legislature of New-York.   (v.2, p. v-x)   1-15830.

— Catalogue of the books, etc. in the library of the N.Y. historical soc.   vii, 139 p. (v.2) 8-25103.

— A discourse on the benefits of civil history ... By Hugh Williamson.   (v.2, p. 23-36)   11-22513.

— A discourse ... by the Hon. De Witt Clinton ...   (v.2, p. 37-116)   2-21304.

— A discourse ... By the Hon. Gouverneur Morris ...   (v.2, p. 117-148)   11-22512.

— A discourse ... of the writings which illustrated the botanical history of North and South America. By Samuel L. Mitchill ...   (v.2, p. 149-215)   11-22511.

— An account of M. de La Salle's last expedition and discoveries in North America (v.2, p. 217-341)   6-9508.

— An extract of a translation of the History of New Sweed Land, in America ... by Thomas C. Holm ... 1702.   (v. 2, p. 343-358)   11-22510.

— An inaugural discourse ... by the Hon. Gouverneur Morris.   (v.3, p. 25-40)   1-16512.

— An anniversary discourse ... By Gulian C. Verplanck ...   (v.3, p. 41-124)   11-22509.

— A biographical memoir of Hugh Williamson ...   (v.3, p. 125-179)   11-22508.

— A discourse on the religion of the Indian tribes of North America ... By Samuel Farmar Jarvis ...   (v.3, p. 181-268)   11-22506.

NEW YORK

— An inaugural address ... By David Hosack ...   (v. 3, p. 269 - 280)   1-13399.
— An anniversary discourse ... By Henry Wheaton.   (v. 3 p. 281-320)   11-22505.
— Communications from the late Hon. Samuel Jones ...   (v. 3, p. 321-367)   15-6385.
— New-Netherlands ... An extract from the records in the Council chamber ... Annapolis ... Md., relative to the dispute between the government of New-Netherlands ... and the Lord Proprietary of Maryland ...   (v. 3, p. 368-386)   15-6384.
— Description of some of the medals, struck in relation to important events in North America.   (v. 3, p. 387-404)   11-22504.
— Continuation of the history of New-York. (By William Smith)   4, 308 p. (vol. 4) A continuation to 1762 of the author's History of the province of New York ... London, 1757. The complete work was reprinted in 1829 as v. 4-5 of the Collections of the N. Y. hist. soc. with the result that 2 different vols. of the Collections are numbered 4.   1-15846.
— The history of the late province of New-York ... to 1762. By the Hon. William Smith ... 2 v. (vols. iv - v) (See note above)   1-15848* Cancel.
— An anniversary discourse ... by Hon. James Kent.   (2d ser. v. 1, p. 9-36)   11-22414.
— ... The voyage of John de Verazzano ... 1524.   (2d ser. v. 1, p. 37-67)   11-22413.
— ... Indian tradition of the first arrival of the Dutch, at Manhattan Island. (2d ser. v. 1) p. 69-74)   11-22412.
— ... A history of the New Netherlands, by Sir N. C. Lambrechtsen ...   (2d ser. v. 1)   1-22110.
— Description of the New Netherlands, by Adriaen van der Donck.   (2d ser. v. 1)   1-15857.
— ... Extracts from the voyages of David Pieterszen de Vries.   (2d ser. v. 1, p. 243-280)   11-22411.
— ... Extracts from the New world ... By John de Laet ...   (2d ser. v. 1, p. 281-316)   11-22409.
— ... Extract from the journal of the voyage of the Half-Moon ... By Robert Juet.   (2d ser. v. 1, p. 317-332)   11-22268.
— ... Expedition of Capt. Samuel Argall ... 1613.   (2d ser. v. 1, p. 333-342)   11-22273.
— ... Letter of Thomas Dermer, describing his passage from Maine to Virginia, 1619.   (2d ser. v. 1, p. 343-354)   11-22272.
— ... Correspondence between the colonies of New Netherlands and New-Plymouth, 1627.   (2d ser. v. 1, p. 355-368)   11-22267.
— ... The charter of liberties granted to patroons and colonies, 1629.   (2d ser. v. 1)   11-22271.
— ... A catalogue of the members of the Dutch church ... 1686.   (2d ser. v. 1, p. 389-400)   11-22266.
— New Sweden, or the Swedish settlements on the Delaware.   (2d ser. v. 1, p. 401-448)   2-11094.
— ... A few particulars concerning the directors general or governors, of New Netherlands.   (2d ser. v. 1, p. 449-456)   11-22270.
— Outline of the constitutional history of New York ... By Benjamin Franklin Butler.   (2d ser. v. 2, p. 9-75)   9-34868.
— ... Memoir ... of the state of New York ... 1816. By Egbert Benson. (2d ser. v. 2)   11-22443.
— ... Narrative of the expedition of the Marquis de Nonville... 1687.   (2d ser. v. 2.   11-22442.
— ... Correspondence between Lieut. Governor Cadwallader Colden, and William Smith, jun....   (2d ser. v. 2, p. 193-214)   11-22441.
— ... Letter from Edmund Burke, to the Committee of correspondence for the General assembly of New York ...   (2d ser. v. 2, p. 215-226)   11-22440.
— ... Remarks upon the British expedition to Danbury, Conn. in 1777. By Elisha D. Whittlesey.   (2d ser. v. 2, p. 227-240)   11-22439 Rev.
— ... New York in 1692. Letter from Charles Lodwick ...   (2d ser. v. 2, p. 241-250)   11-22438 Rev.
— ... The representation of New Netherland ... (By Adriaen van der Donck)   (2d ser. v. 2, p. 251-338)   1-15861.
— ... New Netherland in 1627. Letter from Isaack de Rasieres to Samuel Blommaert ...   (2d ser. v. 2, p. 339-354.   11-22437.
— ... Memoir on the early colonization of New Netherland. By John Romeyn Brodhead.   (2d ser. v. 2, p. 355-366)   11-22436.
— ... Hudson's voyage in 1609.   (2d ser. v. 2, p. 367-370)   11-22435.
— ... Extracts from de Laet and Aitzema, relating to New Netherland.   (2d ser. v. 2, p. 371-380)   11-22434.
— ... History of the New York Chamber of commerce ... By Charles King.   (2d ser. v. 2, p. 381-446)   11-22433.
— ... Table of the killed and wounded in the war of 1812. Comp. by William Jay.   (2d ser. v. 2, p. 447-466)   11-22432.
— ... Memoir of Theophilus Eaton. By Jacob Bailey Moore.   (2d ser. v. 2, p. 467-493)   11-22431.
— ... Voyages from Holland to America, 1632 to 1644. By David Peterson de Vries.   (2d ser. v. 3, p. 1-136)   11-21759.

LOCAL HISTORIES IN THE LIBRARY OF CONGRESS

— ... A short sketch of the Mohawk Indians in New Netherland, by Johannes Megapolensis, jun. (2d ser. v. 3, p. 137-160) 11-21758.
— ... The Jogues papers, tr. and arr. ... by John Gilmary Shea. (2d ser. v. 3, p. 161-229) 2-16851.
— Extract from Castell's "Discoverie" of America, 1644. (2d ser. v. 3, p. 231-236) 2-13745.
— Broad advice to the United Netherland provinces. Tr. by Henry C. Murphy. (2d ser. v. 3, p. 237-283) 1-22222 Rev.
— ... Extract from Wagenaar's "Beschryving van Amsterdam," (2d ser. v. 3, p. 285-292) 11-22445.
— ... The seven articles from the church of Leyden, 1617 ... by George Bancroft. (2d ser. v. 3, p. 293-302) 11-22447.
— Journal of an embassy from Canada to the United Colonies of New England in 1650. By Father Gabriel Druillettes. (2d ser. v. 3, p. 303-328) 10-10361.
— ... Proceedings of the first assembly of Virginia, 1619. (2d ser. v. 3, p. 329-358) 11-22446.
— Catalogue of printed books in the library of the New York historical soc. (2d ser. v. 4) 1-13535 Rev. 2.

NEW YORK HISTORICAL SOCIETY, Collections of the. (v.1) -   1868 -   The John Watts de Peyster publication fund series. New York, Printed for the Society, 1868 - 75 vols. plates, ports., maps, facsims. 25 cm. 1-16508.   F116.N 63

— Political annals of the present United Colonies ... to ... 1763. By George Chalmers. (v. 1, p. 1-176) 6-6511.
— ... Letters on Smith's History of New York, by Cadwallader Colden. (v. 1, p. 177-235; v. 2, p. 203-212) 6-6510.
— ... Documents relating to the administration of Jacob Leisler. (v.1, p. 237-426) 6-6509.
— Loyalty vindicated ; being an answer to a late false, seditious and scandalous pamphlet, entitled, "A letter from a gent., etc." (v.1, p. 365-394) 6-6508.
— ... The Clarendon papers. (v. 2, p. 1-162) 6-6507.
— The destruction of Schenectady. (v. 2, p. 165-176) 6-6506.
— Arguments offer'd to the Right Honourable the Lords commissioners for trade & plantations relating to some acts of Assembly. (v. 2 p. 177-200) 6-6505.
— (Documents concerning) Plowden's New Albion. (v.2, p. 213-222) 6-6498.
— ... Gardiner's East Hampton, etc. (v. 2, p. 223-276) 6-6504.
— Collections of evidence in vindication of the territorial rights and jurisdiction of the state of New York ... (v. 2, p. 277-528) 6-6503.
— State of the evidence and argument in support of the territorial rights and jurisdiction of New York ... (v. 3, p. 1-144) 6-6501.
— ... Old New York and Trinity church. (v. 3, p. 145-408) 6-6500.
— Some remarks on the Memorial and remonstrance of the corporation of Trinity church; (v. 3, p. 341-372) 6-6502.
— A good conversation. A sermon ... By Francis Makemie. (v. 3, p. 409-453) 6-6499.
— The Lee papers ... 1754 - 1811. 4 v. (vols. 4 - 8) 1-13394.
— Strictures on a pamphlet, entitled, a "Friendly address to all reasonable Americans, on the subject of our political confusions." (v. 4, p. 151-166) 8-3867 Rev.
— Proceedings of a general court martial ... for the trial of Major General Lee ... 1778. (v. 6, p. 1-208) 7-9636 Add.
— ... Memoir of Major General Lee, by Edward Langworthy. (v. 7, p. 117-167) 8-3868.
— Life of Charles Lee ... by Jared Sparks ... (v. 7, p. 197-334) 8-3869.
— ... The treason of Charles Lee. (v. 7, p. 335-427) 8-3870.
— Official letters of Major General James Pattison ... (v. 8, p. 1-430) 1-13389.
— Letters to General Lewis Morris. (v. 8, p. 431-512) 1-13387 Rev.
— The conduct of Cadwallader Colden ... (vols. 9 - 10) 17-3674 rev.
— Revolutionary papers ... 3 v. (Vols. 11-13) 1-16507.
— The Thomson papers. 1765 - 1816. (v. 11, p. 1-286) 6-6528.
— ... Letters of Col. Armand (marquis de la Rouerie) 1777-1791. (v. 11, p. 287-396) 6-6527.
— (Letters to Robert Morris) By Thomas Paine. (v. 11, p. 470-488) 4-15875.
— Proceedings of a general court martial ... for the trial of Major General Schuyler. (v.12, p. 1-211) 6-6515.
— Transactions as commissary for embarking foreign troops in the English service from Germany. ... 1776 - 1777. (v. 12, p. 313-543) 6-6517.

NEW YORK

— Proceedings of a general court martial ... for the trial of Major General St. Clair ... 1778. (v.13. p. 1 - 172) 6-6525 Add.

— ... Journal of the most remarkable occurrences in Quebec ...1775 to ... 1776. (v.13, p. 173-236) Also found in Wm. Smith's History of Canada, v.2, 1815) 6-6524.

— The case of William Atwood. (v.13 p. 237-319) 6-6523.

— A sermon preached in Trinity church in New York ... 1709 ... By William Vesey. (v.13, p. 321-338) 6-6522.

— ... Rev. John Sharpe's proposals, etc. ... 1713. (v.13, p. 339-363) 6-6521.

— The first minister of the Reformed Protestant Dutch church in North America. (v.13, p. 365-387) 6-6519 Rev.

— ... Court of lieutenancy (records) 1686 - 1696. (v.13, p.389-438) 6-6518.

— The Montresor journals ... xiv, 578 p. (vol. 14) 1-13392 Add.

— Journal of Lt. John Charles Philip von Krafft, 1776 - 1784. (v.15, p.1-202) 1-13391.

— ... Letter-book of Capt. Alexander McDonald ... 1775 - 1779. (v.15, p.203-498) 1-13393*

— The Kemble papers. 2 v. (vols. 16 - 17) 1-13388.

— The burghers of New Amsterdam and the freemen of New York. 1675 - 1866. xiii, 678 p. (vol. 18) 1-13385.

— The Deane papers ... 1774 - (1790) 5 v. (vols. 19 - 23) 1-13395.

— Muster rolls of New York provincial troops. 1755 - 1764. xii, 621 p. (v.24) 1-13386 Add.

— Abstracts of wills on file in the Surrogate's office, city of New York. 17 vols. (v.25-41) Contents. - i. 1665 - 1707. - ii. 1708 - 1728. - iii. 1730 - 1744. - iv. 1744-1753. - v. 1754 - 1760. - vi. 1760 - 1766. - vii, 1766 - 1771. viii. 1771 - 1776. - ix. 1777 - 1783. - x. 1780 - 1782. - xi. Abstracts of unrecorded wills prior to 1790 (i.e. 1800) - xii. 1782 - 1784. - xiii. 1784 - 1786. - xiv. 1786 - 1796. - xv. 1796 - 1801. - xvi-xvii. Corrections (of) Abstracts of wills, vol. 1-ix, xi. 1-13396 Rev.

— Ledger number I, Chamberlain's office, corporation of the city of New York ... 1691 to ... 1699. (v.42. p. 1-110) 13-9032.

— Indentures of apprentices, 1718 to ... 1727. (v.42, p.111-199) 13-9031.

— Tax lists of the city of New York, 1695 - 1699. (v.43. p. 1-208; v.44, p.209-315) 14-19867.

— Assessment of the real and personal property of the East ward of the city of New York ... 1791. (v.44. p. 317-407) 14-19866.

— Proceedings of the General court of assizes held in the city of New York ... 1680 to ... 1682. (v.45, p.3-38) 14-21459.

— Minutes of the Supreme court of Judicature ... 1693 to ... 1701. (v.45, p. 39-233) 14-21460.

— Original book of New York deeds ... 1672/3 to ... 1675. v.46, p. 3-62. 14-21920.

— Miscellaneous documents relating to the city of New York and Long Island, 1642 - 1696. (v.46, p.63-93) 14-21918.

— Melyn papers, 1640 - 1699. (v. 46, p. 95-138) 14-21919.

— Muster and pay rolls of the war of the revolution, 1775 - 1783. 2 v. (v.47-48) 16-17941.

— Proceedings of a Board of general officers of the British army at New York, 1781. 6, 283 p. (v.49) 16-17940.

— The letters and papers of Cadwallader Colden ... 1711 - (1775) 9 v. (vols. 50-56, 67-68) 19-15059 Rev. 2

— Minutes of the Committee and of the first Commission for detecting and defeating conspiracies in the state of New York ... 1776 - ... 1778. 2 v. (vols. 57-58) 25-4703.

— Minutes of the Council of appointment ... 1778 - ... 1779. (v.58. 97 p) 25-4704.

— Papers of the Lloyd family of the manor of Queens Village, Lloyd's Neck, Long Island, New York, 1654 - 1826. 2 v. (vols. 59-60) 28-6973.

— Letter book of John Watts ... 1762 - ... 1765. xvi, 448 p. (vol. 61) 28-27799.

— Diary of William Dunlap (1766 - 1839) 3 v. (vols. 62 - 64) 31-9489.

— Letter-books and order-book of George, lord Rodney ... 1780 - 1782. 2 v. (vols. 65-66) 33-306.

— The arts and crafts in New York; advertisements and news items from N.Y. City newspapers. 3 v. (vols. 69, 81, 82) 38-18579 rev.*

— Letters from John Pintard to his daughter, Eliza Noel Pintard Davidson, 1816 - 1833. 4 v. (vols. 70-73) 40-30954 Rev.

— National academy of design exhibition record, 1826 - 1860 ... 2 v. (vols. 74 - 75) 44-7673.

-- American Academy of Fine Arts and American Art Union, 1816 - 1852. (vol. 76) 57-23841.

— Supreme Court of Judicature of the Province of New York, 1691 - 1704.   3 v. (vols. 78 - 80. 54-2292.

NEW YORK Historical Society.   Quarterly.   v. 1 -   Apr. 1917 -   New York.
v. in   illus.   24 cm.   20-2281 rev *. F116.N638

NEW YORK historical society.   Proceedings ... 1843 - 1849.   New York, Press of the Historical society, 1844 - 49.   7 v. plates, fold. map. 22½ cm.   No more pub. 1-14492. F116.N 64

— (The progress of ethnology) By John Russell Bartlett.   (1843, p. 64-88) 0-7121 rev.
— An address ... by John Romey Brodhead.   107 p. (v.2) 1-13383.
— Observations on the progress of geography and ethnology ... by John Russell Bartlett. (1846, p. 149-210) 0-7122.
— Incentives to the study of the ancient period of American history ... By Henry R. Schoolcraft.   38 p.   22½ cm.   2-12699.

NEW YORK historical society.   The charter and by-laws. 1846.   47 p. 23½ cm. 1-14488.   F116.N 64
1848

— Annual report, by-laws and list of members. 1848 - 19-   v. fronts., plates, plans. 22½-23½ cm.
F116.N 65

— ... Report of the Executive committee, 1902.   21, (3) p. 2 pl., 4 plans. 23½ cm. 8-31721.   F116.N 65
1902

NEW YORK historical society.   The constitution and by-laws, or charter and by-laws, for the following years: 1829; 1839; 1844; 1845; 1846a (2d ed. with amendments to Jan. 1853); 1862; 1873; 1875; 1881; 1902; 1904; 1909; 1914.   F116.N 66

NEW YORK historical society.   Resident members, March, 1866.   16 p. 8-20388.   F116.N 67
1866

— List of members, 1903.   15 p. 23 cm. 8-31335.   F116.N 67
1903

NEW YORK historical society.   Anniversary addresses: F116.N 68

— By Joseph Blunt, 1828.   52 p. 22 cm. 2-5338.
— By John W. Francis, 1857.   (5) - 232 p. 24½ cm. 1-14356.
— By Frederic de Peyster, 1865.   76 p. 24 cm. 1-22106.
— By Rev. Samuel Osgood, 1867.   127 p. incl. tables. 25 cm. 1-14378.
— By Frederic de Peyster, 1874.   36 p. front. (port.) 27½ cm. 2-24367.
— By Frederic de Peyster, 1876.   44 p. 11 port. 26½ cm. 2-24366.
— By Frederic de Peyster, 1879.   59, xvii p. 3 port., fold. facsim. 26½ cm. 4-22928.
— By John Jay, 1884.   239 p. map. 24 cm. 2-3393.
— By Hon. John Alsop King, 1888.   40 p. 26 cm. 4-767.
— By Hon, Seth Low, 1892.   32 p. 24½ cm. 1-14695.
— By Justin Winsor, 1896.   38 p. 24½ cm. 3-21058.
By Rev. Marvin R. Vincent, 1900.   45 p. 24½ cm. 4-134.

NEW YORK historical society.   Inaugural addresses: F116.N 69

— By Hon. Gouverneur Morris, 1816.   24 p. 21 cm. 2-29466 Rev.
— By David Hosack, 1820.   14 p. 22 cm. 1-13398.
— By Hon, Albert Gallatin, 1843.   21 p. 23½ cm. 1-22577 Rev.

NEW YORK historical society.   Other official publications:

— ... Annual report, 1862.   8 p. 24 cm. No more pub. 19-10870.   F116. N 7
— ... Circular to members, 1864.   2, 11 p. 23½ cm. 1-13384.   F116.N 72

NEW YORK

— (Memorial to the Legislature of the state asking an appropriation for the relief of the Society, 1827. 32 p. 23½ cm. 1-22658. F116.N 74

— Proceedings and addresses, reception tendered to Mr. Isaac Newton Phelps Stokes, 1926 32 p. illus. 23½ cm. 27-16410. F116.N746

— Procès verbal of the ceremony of installation of president, 1820. (Reprinted 1864) 13 p. 26½ cm. 35 copies. 5-33371. F116.N748

— Report of the special committee, 1917. (18) p. CA 29-729 Unrev. F116.N749

— Rules of the Executive committee. 1864. 7 p. 24½ cm. 1-13382. F116.N 75

— Semi-centennial celebration. 1854. 96 p. 24 cm. 1-13397. F116.N755

— The story of the New York historical society. 1939. 33 p. 21 cm. 39-15147. F116.N758

— The New York historical society, 1804 - 1904, by Robert Hendre Kelby. 1905. 4, 160 p. pl., 30 port. on 4 pl., facsim. 24½ cm. Bibliography: p. 133-160. 6-1098. F116.N765

— Knickerbocker birthday; a sesqui-centennial history of the New-York Historical Society, 1804-1954. xix, 547 p. illus., ports., maps, facsims. 24 cm. Includes bibliographies. 54-14828. F116.N768

NEW YORK historical society. Publications about the society or its officers:

— In memoriam. Frederic de Peyster ... 1882. 52 p. front. (port.) 27 cm. 14-14651. F116.N77D4

— Memoir of Robert Hendre Kelby. 1928. 16 p. incl. illus., port. 24½ cm. Reprinted from the Quarterly bulletin for Jan., 1928. 28-6850. F116.N77K18

— A memoir of William Kelby. 1898. 39 p. 24½ cm. 11-23141. F116.N77 K2

— George Henry Moore, a memoir. 3, 8 p. port. 27 cm. 9-14881. F116.N77 M8

— Entre nous, an intimate portrait of Alexander J. Wall. xii, 267 p. illus., ports. 25 cm. 50-4060. F116.N77 W3

NEW YORK historical society. An address ... by Daniel Webster ... 1852. 57 p. 22½ cm. 2-5303. F116.N 83

NEW YORK State American Revolution Bicentennial Commission. Annual report. (Albany) v. illus. 23 cm. Began with report for 1969/70. 71-615284. F116.N8335

NEW YORK (State) Historic Trust. (Albany, New York State Conservation Dept., 1967 or 8) 27 p. illus. 21 cm. 68-65175. F116.N8348

NEW YORK State Historical Association. The Yorker. v. in illus. 31 cm. bimonthly (Sept. - June) F116.N835

NEW YORK State historical association, Bulletin of the. v. (1) - Oct. 1932 - Ticonderoga (1932 - v. in 21½ cm. quarterly. A 40-3292 (rev. '42) F116.N838

NEW YORK state historical association. Dedication, headquarters building, Ticonderoga ... 1926. 19 p. illus. 15 cm. CA 28-65 Unrev. F116.N 84

NEW YORK state historical association. Post-war project proposals ... prepared by Clifford L. Lord, director. Cooperstown, N.Y., 1943. 2, 3-31 numb. l. incl. 2 mounted phot. 28½ x 22½ cm. Reproduced from typewritten copy. 43-4988. F116.N857

NEW YORK state historical association, Proceedings of the, with the Quarterly journal. 2d - 21st annual meeting with a list of new members. v. 1 - 19. (Albany, etc.) New York state hist. assoc., 1901 - 21. 19 v. fronts., illus., plates, ports., maps, facsims. 24 cm. 2-20054 rev. 2. F116.N 86

— Footprints of the red men. Indian geographical names in the valley of Hudson's river, the valley of the Mohawk, and on the Delaware ... 241 p. plates, maps. 24 cm. 1906. 7-9870.

— The Dutch records of Kingston, Ulster County (Esopus, Wildwyck, Swanenburgh, Kingston) 1658 - 1684 ... (vol. xi) Also issued separately. 13-33600.

NEW YORK state historical association. Eleventh annual meeting ... 2d ed. (Sandy Hill, N.Y., 1909?) (4) p. 23 x 15½ cm. F116.N863

NEW YORK state historical association. New York history ... v.1 -   Oct. 1919 -
(Albany) New York state hist. assoc., 1920 -   v. plates, ports., maps (part fold.) facsims. (part fold.) 23 cm.
Volume for 1925 includes: Index to Proceedings, v. 1-23 (and) Quarterly journal, v. 1-6.   21-27150 Rev.
F116.N865

NEW YORK state historical association. The Headquarters house ... Ticonderoga, N.Y., by Clifford
L. Lord, director ... Ticonderoga, N.Y., 1943.   23 p. incl. illus., 2 pl. (incl. port.) 22½ cm. 44-5862.
F116.N8655

NEW YORK state historical association. The museum and art gallery ... by Clifford L. Lord.
Cooperstown, N.Y. (Print. the Freeman's journal co., 1942)   127 p. incl. front., illus. (incl. ports.)
21½ cm. 43-6261.
F116.N866

NEW YORK state historical association and its museums; an informal guide. Cooperstown, N.Y.
(1968)   96 p. illus. 26 cm.
F116.N8667

NEW YORK state historical association. Miscellaneous printed matter published by this body is
classified in:
F116.N869

NEW YORK state library. Bulletin. History, no. 3. ... Annotated list of the principal manuscripts
in the New York State library ... Albany, University of the State of N.Y., 1899.   (209) - 237 p. 3-7519.
F116.N 88

NEW YORK state historian. The function of state historian of New York, by Victor Hugo Paltsits ...
Albany (J. B. Lyon co., printers) 1909.   14 p. 24 cm. 9-8959.
F116.N 89

NORTH country life; a digest for northern New Yorkers. v. 1 -   fall 1946 -
(Ogdensburg, N.Y., G. G. Cole)   v. illus. 19 cm. quarterly. 48-11166*.
F116.N 93

PIONEERS' association of central New York. 7th annual address ... Sept. 16, 1876. Albany, 1876.
23½ cm.
F117.P 66

SOCIETY of daughters of Holland dames, descendants of the ancient and honorable families of New
Netherland, First record book of ...   (New York; Pub. by order of the Society (The Grafton press)
1907.   129 (5) p. front., plates. 24½ cm. 100 copies. 7-31428 Rev.
F116.S 67

— Second record book ... New York, Pub. by the authority of the Board of directors, 1913.
66, (6) p. 24½ cm. 14-8530.
F116.S 672

— Third record book ... New York, Pub. by the authority of the Board of directors, 1933.
72 p. front., pl. 24 cm. 33-12858.
F116.S 673

UP-STATER, The. v. 1-2, v.3, no. 1-2; Jan. 1929 - May 1931. Watertown, N.Y., New York
development assoc., inc. (1929-31)   3 v. in 1. illus. 30 cm. bimonthly. No more pub. 32-33196.
F116.U 68

WESTCHESTER magazine. v. 1 -   Mar. 1929 -   Pleasantville, N.Y. (W. A. Johnson,
1929 -   v. illus. (incl. maps) 25½ cm. monthly. Official magazine of the Westchester county conservation association.
32-6809.
F116.W 37

GAZETTEERS. DICTIONARIES. GEOGRAPHIC NAMES.

BEAUCHAMP, William Martin. ... Aboriginal place names of New York ... Albany, New York
state education dept., 1907.   (5) - 333 p. 23 cm. (New York state museum ... Bulletin 108. Archeology 12) "List of
authorities": p. 271-278. 7-29110.
F117.B 37

BEAUCHAMP, William Martin. Indian names in New-York, with a selection from other states, etc.
Fayetteville, N.Y., Print, H. C. Beauchamp, 1893.   3, 148 p. 21½ cm. 1-16064 Rev.
F117.B 38

NEW YORK 11

BENSON, Egbert. Memoir, read before the Historical soc. of the state of New-York ... 1816. New York, Print. William A. Mercein, 1817. 72 p. 21½ cm. On the names of places in New York state. 46-39249.
    F117. B 46
    Rare Book Coll.

— 2d ed. - with notes. Jamaica (N.Y.) H. C. Sleight, printer, 1825. 127 p. 20 cm. 1-16030.
    F117. B 47

— New York, Bartlett & Welford, 1848. 72 p. 23½ cm. (Re-printed from a copy, with the author's last corrections) 1-16031.
    F117. B 48

CARPENTER, Warwick Stevens. The summer paradise in history; a compilation of fact and tradition covering Lake George, Lake Champlain, the Adirondack Mountains, and other sections reached by the rail and steamer lines of the Delaware and Hudson co. Albany, General passenger dept., the Delaware and Hudson co. (1914) 128 p. front. (port.) illus. (incl. plans) plates, fold. map. 20 cm. "This volume is the direct outgrowth of the 'Literay and historic notebook,' covering the same territory, written for the Passenger department of the Delaware and Hudson co. by Mr. Henry P. Phelps, and pub. in 1907." Bibliography: p. 125-128. 14-7090.
    F117. C 29

(DISTURNELL, John) comp. A gazetteer of the state of New-York; comprising its topography, geology, mineralogical resources, civil divisions, canals, railroads and public institutions, etc. etc. Albany, J. Disturnell, 1842. iv, (5(- 475 p. front., fold. map. 20½ cm. 1-15806.
    F117. D 59

— Albany, J. Disturnell, 1842. iv, (5) - 479 p. front., fold. map. 20½ cm. 32-6808.
    F117. D 6

— 2d ed. with additions and corrections. Albany, Printed by C. Van Benthuysen, 1843. iv, (5) - 479 p. pl. 20½ cm. 7-23979.
    F117. D 61

FORD'S travelers' and shippers' guide book "A" of New York state. Syracuse, N.Y., H. M. Ford, 1910. 124 p. 16 cm. 10-11904.
    F117. F 71

FRENCH, John Homer. Gazetteer of the State of New York: embracing a comprehensive view of the geography, geology, and general history of the State, and a complete history and description of every county, city, town, village, and locality. Syracuse, N.Y., R. P. Smith, 1860. 739 p. illus. 26 cm. 1-15805 rev.*
    F117. F 75
    1860

— Index of personal names. Compiled by Frank Place II. Cortland, N.Y., Cortland County Historical Soc., 1962. 145 p. 22 cm. (Publication no. 8)
    F117. F 75
    Index

— Supplementary index to places. Albany, University of the State of New York, State Education Dept. (1966) 37 p. 28 cm.
    F117. F 75
    Suppl. index

FRENCH, John Homer. Gazetteer of the State of New York, etc. etc. 7th ed. (Syracues, N.Y., R. P. Smith) 1860. 752 p. illus. 26 cm. 44-10783 rev.*
    F117. F 75
    1860f

— 8th ed. 44-10783 rev.*
    F117. F 75
    1860g

— Port Washington, N.Y., I. J. Friedman (1969) 739 p. illus. 25 cm. (Empire State historical publications series, no. 72) 70-101018.
    F117. F 75
    1969

GORDON, Thomas Francis. Gazetteer of the state of New York: comprehending its colonial history; general geography, geology, and internal improvements; its political state; a minute description of its several counties, towns, and villages .... Philadelphia, Printed for the author, 1836. xii, 102, 801 p. front. (fold. map) illus. (maps, plans) 22 cm. 1-15875 Rev. 2
    F117. G 7

HOUGH, Franklin Benjamin. Gazetteer of the state of New York, embracing a comprehensive account of the history and statistics of the state. With geological and topographical descriptions, and recent statistical tables ... Albany, N.Y., A. Boyd, 1872. viii, 745 (i.e. 752) p. front., plates, fold. map. 25½ cm. Starred pages 146* - 152* inserted. 1-15807.
F117.H 83

RAND McNally gazetteer and map of New York ... Chicago, New York (etc.) (1923) 28 p. 28 cm.
F117.R 18

SPAFFORD, Horatio Gates, ed. A gazetteer of the state of New-York; carefully written from original and authentic materials, arranged on a new plan, in three parts ... Albany, print. and pub. by H. C. Southwick, 1813. 334 p. front. (fold. map) 22 cm. 1-15808.
F117. S 73

— ... with an appendix ... Albany, B. D. Packard; Troy, The author, 1824. 620 p. front. (fold. map) 21½ cm. 1-15809.
F117. S 74
G & M

WESTERN New York gazetteer and business directory ... 1880/81 Cincinnati, Buffalo, A. N. Marquis & co., 1880. 1 v. 24 cm.
F117.W 47

WRIGHT, Albert Hazen. Simeon DeWitt and military tract township names. Ithaca, N.Y., Pub. by the Author for DeWitt Historical Soc. of Tompkins County, 1961. 17 p. 26 cm. (His Studies in history, no. 25)
F117. W 7

GUIDEBOOKS.

FODOR, Eugene, ed. and others. New-York - New Jersey. ((Litchfield, Conn.) Fodor's Modern Guides (1966) 398 p. (Fodor Shell travel guides U.S.A., v. 2) 66-18973.
F117.3. F6

— 2d rev. ed. (1967) 431 p. 21 cm. 67-20078.
F117.3. F6
1967

DIRECTORIES.

BREED publishing company's directory of the Delaware and Hudson company's railroad from Albany to Binghamton, also the Cherry Valley branch ... Newburgh, N.Y., Breed pub. co. v. 24½ cm. 0-6587 Rev.
Directories

BREED publishing company's directory of the New York, Ontario & western railroad, from Cornwall to Sidney, embracing ... Middletown, Meadowbrook, Little Britain (etc.) ... Newburgh, N.Y., Breed pub. co. v. 24½ cm. No vol. pub. for 1906. 0-3415 Rev.
Directories

DIRECTORY of the New York, Ontario and western railway ... from Norwich to Oswego, and Utica branch ... Newburgh, N.Y., Breed pub. co. v. 24½ cm. 1-29290 Rev.
Directories

U.S. Bureau of the census. ... Heads of families at the first census of the U. S. taken in the year 1790 ... Washington, Govt. print. off., 1907-08. 12 v. fronts. (fold. maps) 29½ cm. 7-35273.
F117.5.U58

WAITE, L. P. & co., pub. The northern New York business directory for 1890 - '91. Containing the names, business and post-office address of merchants, manufacturers and other business men in the cities and villages situated on the line of Rome, Watertown and Ogdensburg railroad, etc, etc. Newburgh, N.Y., L. P. Waite (1890) 276 p. 2 fold. maps. 24 cm. 11-3999.
Directories

BOYD'S business directory of over one hundred cities and villages in New York state ... 1869/70 Albany, N.Y., C. Van Benthuysen, 1869 - v. 24 cm. 33-31476.
Directories

NEW YORK central business gazetteer of cities and towns on the N.Y.C.R.R., containing sketches of the principal places ... 1871.   Rochester, N.Y., Carters & Flynn, 1871 -
    v. 24 cm. CA 33-1172 Unrev.
Directories

NEW YORK, Ontario and western railway classified business directory between Oswego at lake Ontario and Cornwall-on-the-Hudson ... 1886.   Newburgh, N.Y., Crum & Fowler, 1885 -
    v. double map. 23½ cm. CA 33-1176 Unrev.
Directories

NEW YORK state business directory and gazetteer ... 1859 -   Boston, Albany, 1859 -
    v. fold. maps. 24 cm. 17-28139.
Directories

PHILLIPS' standard buyer and business directory of the principal cities of New York state ... New York city, N.Y., Phillips' standard buyer, inc. (19   v. 24 cm. 25-13188.
Directories

BIOGRAPHY (COLLECTIVE). GENEALOGY (COLLECTIVE).

BIOGRAPHICAL directory of the state of New York, 1900.   Pub. by Biographical directory company (inc.) New York city, 1900.   2, 567 p. 28½ cm. 0-6875.
F118. B 61

BRYAN, George J.   Biographies of Attorney-General George P. Barker, John C. Lord, Mrs. John C. Lord, and William G. Bryan, also a lecture on journalism.   Buffalo, The Courier company, printers, 1886.   vi, (7) - 231 p. 2 port. (incl. mounted front.) 23½ cm. 32-15168.
F118. B 88

BUNGAY, George Washington.   Pen and ink portraits of the senators, assemblymen, and state officers, of the state of New York.   Albany, J. Munsell, printer, 1857.   83 p. 22½ cm. 4-20441 Rev.
F118. B 94

CALKINS, Hiram.   Biographical sketches of John T. Hoffman and Allen C. Beach, the Democratic nominees for governor and lieutenant-governor of the state of New York.   Also, a record of the events in the lives of Oliver Bascom, David B. McNeil, and Edwin O. Perrin, etc.   New York, The New York printing co., 1868.   2, (3) - 111 p. 23½ cm. 4-22943.
F118. C 15

CUTTER, William Richard.   Genealogical and family history of central New York; a record of the achievements of her people in the making of a commonwealth and the building of a nation.   New York, Lewis historical pub. co., 1912.   3 v. illus., ports. 27½ cm. 12-13659.
F118. C 98

— New York, Lewis historical pub. co., 1910.   3 v. fronts., illus., pl., ports. 27 cm. Paged continuously.
Chiefly Jefferson, Lewis, St. Lawrence, Franklin, Clinton, and Essex counties. 10-26181.
F118. C 99

— New York, Lewis historical pub. co., 1912.   3 v. illus., pl., ports., coat of arms. 27½ cm. Paged continuously. 12-12477.
F118. C992

— New York, Lewis historical pub. co., 1913.   3 v. front., plates, ports. 27½ cm. Paged continuously.
18-12348.
F118. C993

DAUGHTERS of the American Revolution. New York.   Master index, New York State DAR; genealogical records.   Mrs. George U. Baylies, State regent.   (Buffalo?) 1972.   371 p. 28 cm.
72-77240 MARC.
F118. D 3

EARLY settlers of New York state, their ancestors and descendants ... v. 1 -   July 1934 - Akron, N.Y., T. J. Foley (1934 -   v. illus. 23 cm. monthly. 38-16529.
F118. E 24
— Index (to) volumes I, II, and III; names of New York state pioneers, whose births, marriages, deaths, residences, were pub. from July, 1934 to June 30, 1937 in the above.   (102) p. 23 cm. 38-16529.
F118. E 24 Index

— Index, volumes IV, V and VI. (Akron, N.Y., T. J. Foley, 1940?) (93) p. 22 cm.
38-16529 x¹.
F118.E 24
Index vols. 4-6

EMINENT members of the bench and bar of New York, 1943 -   San Francisco, C. W. Taylor, jr.
(1943 -   v. illus. (ports.) 26 cm. 43-8085.
F118.E 53

EMPIRE state notables, 1914. New York, N.Y., H. Stafford (1914)   (5) - 701 p. illus. (ports.) 23 cm.
A collection of portraits with brief biographical inscriptions. Ed. by Hartwell Stafford. 14-18447.
F118.E 55

(FARGO, Francis F.) Personal sketches of the members of Assembly in the Legislature of New York for the year 1873, by an officer of the House. Buffalo, Express steam printing house, 1873.
32 p. 23 cm. Originally pub. in the Buffalo Daily express. 5-1340.
F118.F 22

FERNOW, Berthold. Calendar of wills on file and recorded in the offices of the clerk of the Court of appeals, of the county clerk at Albany, and of the secretary of state, 1826 - 1836 ... New York (The Knickerbocker press) 1896.   xv, 657 p. 26 cm. 1-15810.
F118.F 36
— copy 2 on microfilm.
Microfilm 18263 F

— Baltimore, Genealogical Pub. Co., 1967.   xv, 657 p. 24 cm. 67-28621.
F118.F 36
1967
L H & G

FISKE, Stephen. Off-hand portraits of prominent New Yorkers.   ... New York, G. R. Lockwood, 1884.   vii, (5) - 357 p. 20 cm. Originally pub. in the Knickerbocker. 5-1337.
F118.F 53

FITCH, Charles Elliott. Encyclopedia of biography of New York, a life record of men and women whose sterling character and energy and industry have made them preëminent in their own and many other states ... Boston, New York (etc.) The American historical society, inc., 1916 -
v. fronts., plates, etc. 28 cm. Vols. 1-3 also pub. under title: Memorial encyclopedia of the state of N.Y. 17-27880 Rev.
F118.F539

FITCH, Charles Elliott. Memorial encyclopedia of the state of New York, a life record of men and women of the past, etc., etc. Boston, New York (etc.) The American historical society, 1916.
3 v. fronts., plates (1 col.) ports. 28 cm. The same text was also pub. as v. 1 - 3 of the author's Encyclopedia of biography of New York.
17-29770 Rev.
F118.F 54

HAMM, Margherita Arlina. Famous families of New York; historical and biographical sketches of families which in successive generations have been identified with the development of the nation ...
New York (etc.) G. P. Putnam's sons (1902)   2 v. fronts., plates, ports., facsims., coats of arms. 29 cm. This work is based on a series of articles which originally appeared in the New York evening post. 2-25937.
F118.H 22

HARLOW, Samuel R. Life sketches of the state officers, senators, and members of the Assembly, of the state of New York, in 1868. By S. R. Harlow and S. C. Hutchins. Albany, Weed, Parsons, printers, 1868.   402 p. front. (port.) 21½ cm. 5-34795.
F118.H 28

HARRISON, Mitchell Charles. New York state's prominent and progressive men; an encyclopedia of contemporaneous biography ... (New York) New York tribune, 1900 - 02. 3 v. ports. 29 cm.
0-4712 Rev.
F118.H 32

HATCH, Alden. The Wadsworths of the Genesee. New York, Coward-McCann (1959)
315 p. illus. 22 cm. 58-13322.
F118.H 34
M R R Ref. Desk

HISTORY of the bench and bar of New York; ed. by Honorable David McAdam ... (and others) (New York) New York history co., 1897 - 99.   2 v. fronts., illus., ports. 27 cm. 1-7147.
F118.H 63

INTERNATIONAL press syndicate. ... The book of the bench and the bar ...   296 p. illus. (ports.)
21 x 29 cm.
F118. I 61

JENKINS, John Stilwell. Lives of the governors of the state of New York. ... Auburn (N.Y.) Derby and Miller, 1851.   xxiv, (25) - 826 p. front., ports. 23½ cm. 6-43460.
F118.J 52

748

NEW YORK

McELROY, William Henry, ed. Life sketches of executive officers and members of the Legislature of the state of New York for 1873. Albany, Weed, Parsons, printers, 1873. 366 p. front. (port.) plates, facsim. 21 cm. 5-39221.
F118.M 15 1873

McELROY, William Henry, ed. Life sketches of government officers and members of the Legislature of the state of New York for 1874. Albany, Weed, Parsons, printers, 1874. 343 p. front., ports. facsim. 21 cm. 5-39222.
F118.M151

— 1875. 333 p. front., ports. 21 cm. 19-2105.
F118.M152

MacWETHY, Lou D. The book of names especially relating to the early Palatines and the first settlers in the Mohawk valley... St. Johnsville, N.Y., The Enterprise and news, 1933. 3, 209 p. illus. (incl. ports., maps) 23½ cm. "Authorities consulted": Verso of 2d prelim. leaf. 33-9854.
F118.M 19

— Baltimore, Genealogical Pub. Co., 1969. 209 p. illus., ports., maps. 23 cm. 69-17132.
F118.M 19 1969 L H & G

MANNING, James Hilton. New York state men. Individual library ed., with biographic studies, character portraits and autographs. Albany, N.Y., The Albany argus art press, 1911 - pt. in v. plates, ports. (incl. fronts.) 30 cm. 14-6448 Rev. 2.
F118.M 28

MANNING, James Hilton, ed. New York state women. Individual library ed., with biographic studies, character portraits and autographs. Albany, N.Y., The Albany argus art press, 1914 - v. fronts. (ports.) 30 cm. 14-14641.
F118.M 29

MEN of New York, The: a collection of biographies and portraits of citizens of the Empire state prominent in business, professional, social, and political life during the last decade of the nineteenth century... Buffalo, N.Y., G.E. Matthews & co., 1898. 2 v. ports. 32½ cm. In double columns. 3-19130.
F118.M 53

MEN of New York series. Editorial compilation by the American historical company, inc. New York, 1941 - v. front. (port.) 32 cm. 42-5167.
F118.M535

MEYERS, Carol M. Early New York State census records, Hollywood, Calif. 1 v. (unpaged) 28 cm. "ed. and rearranged... in phonetic alphabetic sequence from the Documentary history of New York State, vol. 1... 1850."
F118.M 6

— (2d ed. Gardena, Calif., RAM Publishers, 1965. iv, 178 (66) p. 28 cm.
F118.M 6 1965 L H & G

MOWBRAY, Jay Henry, ed. Representative men of New York; a record of their achievements... New York city, The New York press, 1898. 3 v. fronts., ports. 29 cm. 98-512 Rev.
F118.M 93

MURPHY, William D. Biographical sketches of the state officers and members of the Legislature of the state of New York, in 1858. Albany, J. Munsell, 1858. 244 (2) p. 17 cm. 5-41683.
F118.M 97

MURPHY, William D. Biographical sketches of the state officers and members of the Legislature of the state of New York, in 1859... Albany, Printed by C. Van Benthuysen, 1859. 257 p. fronts. (port.) 18½ cm. 5-41682.
F118.M971

NASH, Mrs. Rosalyn S. Genealogical information from tables of contents of the Vosburgh collections at the Library of Congress, indexed by (1) Counties (2) Towns and villages (3) Towns and churches. Washington, D.C., 1933. 75 numb. l., 76 - 79 numb. l., 80-88 numb. l. 28½ cm. in ms.
F118.N 28 Geneal. Sect. Ref.

—   54 numb. l., 7 numb. l., 6 numb. l., 11 numb. l.   26½ cm.   Typewritten.   39M5087T.

F118.N282

NEW YORK (Colony)   Names of persons for whom marriage licenses were issued by the secretary of the province of New York, previous to 1784.   Printed by order of Gideon J. Tucker, secretary of state. Albany, Weed, Parsons, 1860.   ix, 480 p.   23½ cm.   Other licenses for the period were discovered later, and issued under title "Supplementary list of marriage licenses" as State lib. bulletin: history, no. 1.   1-15811 Add.

F118.N 48
L H & G

NEW YORK (Colony) ,... Supplementary list of marriage licenses.   Albany, University of the state of New York, 1898.   (5) - 48 p. 25 cm. State library bulletin. History no. 1)   From v. 41 of the series of manuscript marriage bonds in N. Y. state library and from other sources.   5-17846.

F118.N482

NEW YORK (Colony)   New York marriage licenses; originals in the archives of the New York historical society; contributed by Robert H. Kelby ...   (New York, 1916?)   44 p.   27 cm.   100 copies.   Reprinted from the N. Y. genealogical and biographical record, beginning July, 1915.   Additions and corrections to F118. N48.   17-13453.

F118.N483

NEW YORK (Colony)   New York marriages previous to 1784.   Baltimore, Genealogical Pub. Co., 1968. ix, 618 p.   23 cm.   Reprint of F118. N48.   67-30757.

F118.N485

NEW YORK (State)   Military minutes of the Council of appointment of the state of New York, 1783-1821. Comp. and ed. by Hugh Hastings, state historian.   Pub. by the state ... Albany, J. B. Lyon, state printer, 1901-02.   4 v. front., 3 pl. 23 cm.   Paged continuously.   vol. I. iv. 948 p.; vol. II, (949) - 1840 p; vol. III, (1841) - 2445 p.; vol. IV, (2447)- 3038 p.   Vol IV contains the index of names and general index.   3-14053.

F118.N 53

NOTABLE men of central New York; Syracuse and vicinity, Utica and vicinity, Auburn, Oswego, Watertown, Fulton, Rome, Oneida, Little Falls.   xix and xx centuries.   (Syracuse, N.Y.) D. J. Stoddard, 1903.   428 p. incl. front., ports.   24 cm.   A collection of portraits with brief biographical inscriptions.   3-31007.

F118.N 89

PELLETREAU, William Smith.   Historic homes and institutions and genealogical and family history of New York ...   New York, Chicago, The Lewis pub. co., 1907.   4 v. fronts. (v.1-3) illus., plates, ports., map, facsims.   26½ cm.   8-32777.

F118. P 38

PROCTOR, Lucien Brock.   The bench and bar of New-York.   Containing biographical sketches of eminent judges, and lawyers of the New-York bar, incidents of the important trials in which they were engaged, etc.   New-York, Diossy & co., 1870.   viii, 779 p.   2 port. (incl. front.)   23 cm.   6-2150 Rev.

F118. P 96

PROMINENT men and women of New York; individual biographic studies with character portraits. Library ed.   New York, Historical records, inc., 1940 -   5 v. fronts., plates, ports., geneal. tab., coats of arms.   29 cm.   Contents. - v.1 The Achellis family in America. - v.2. Claus Doscher. - v.3. Wolcott and allied families. - v.4. The Haynes and De Forest families in America. - v.5. Van Brunt family in America.   41-14423.

F118.P977

—   1944 -   1 v. ports., geneal. tab., coats of arms.   29 x 22½ cm.   Contents. - v.1. The Achellis family in America.   44-8756.

F118.P9772

PROMINENT men of New York; individual biographic studies with character portraits.   Library ed. New York, Historical records, inc., 1940-45.   25 v. fronts., pl., ports., coats of arms.   29 cm.   Contents. - v.1. Col. Abraham A. Anderson. - v.2. William W. Bachman. - v.3. Spotswood D. Bowers. - v.4. Dr. Harlow Brooks. - v.5. Chas. P. Caldwell. - v.6. Arthur B. Claflin. - v.7. William Forger. - v.8. Robert O. Hayt. - v.9. David C. Howard. - v.10. John Lynn. - v.11. James C. McDonald.- v.12. Percy A. Parker. - v.13. Dr. John S. Roberts. - v.14. Ulysses G. Williams. - v.15. Solomon W. de Jonge. - v.16. Judge Isaiah Fellows, jr. - v.17. Evins F. Glore. - v.18 Henry Pfeiffer. - v.19. Joshua Rosett. - v.20. Scarff-Mather.   41-14290.

F118. P 98

—   Family ed.   New York, Historical records, inc., 1941 -   2 v. ports., coats of arms.   29 cm. Contents. - v.1. Wendell T. Bush. - v.2. Scarff-Mather.   41-14291.

F118.P983

PROMINENT men of New York and New Jersey; individual biographic studies with character portraits.

NEW YORK

Library ed. New York, Historical records, inc., 1940 - 1 v. front. (port.) 29 cm. Contents. - v.1.
Ridley Watts. 41-14292.
F118. P985

PROMINENT women of New York; individual biographic studies with character portraits. Library ed.
New York, Historical records, inc., 1941 - v. front. (port.) 29 cm. Contents. - v.1. Jane Peterson. 41-14729.
F118. P987

REYNOLDS, Cuyler. Genealogical and family history of southern New York and the Hudson River Valley; a record of the achievements of her people in the making of a commonwealth and the building of a nation ... New York, Lewis historical pub. co., 1914. 3 v. fronts., illus., plates, ports. 27½ cm.
Paged continuously. 14-20396.
F118. R 45

REYNOLDS, Cuyler. Hudson-Mohawk genealogical and family memoirs; a record of achievements of the people of the Hudson and Mohawk valleys in New York state, included within the present counties of Albany, Rensselaer, Washington, Saratoga, Montgomery, Fulton, Schenectady, Columbia and Greene. ... New York, Lewis historical pub. co., 1911. 4 v. fronts., ports. 27½ cm. 11-11569.
F118. R 46

SKINNER, Charles Rufus. Governors of New York from 1777 to 1920. Albany, J. B. Lyon co., printers, 1919. 13 p. 23 cm. 20-730.
F118. S 62

SPENCER, Alfred. Spencer's Roster of native sons (and daughters) For each locality of upstate New York a roster of its eminent sons and daughters, from earliest settlement to the present time ... Bath, N.Y., The Courier press, 1941. ii, 287 p. 23½ cm. 42-4913.
F118. S 75

STILLWELL, John Edwin. Historical and genealogical miscellany; data relating to the settlement and settlers of New York and New Jersey (compiled by) John E. Stillwell ... New York, 1903 - 32.
5 v. 26½ x 23½ cm. 6-3127 Rev.
F118. S 85

— Baltimore, Genealogical Pub. Co., 1970. 5 v. 24 cm. Vols. 3-5 have subtitle: Early settlers of New Jersey and their descendants. 72-86805.
F118. S 852

TALCOTT, Sebastian Visscher. Genealogical notes of New York and New England families. ...
Albany, Weed, Parsons, 1883. xii, 747, xxxix p. 23½ cm. Imperfect: p. i-ii, v-xii, xxxix p. photostated. 4-15526.
F118. T 14

U. S. BUREAU of the Census. Heads of families at the first Census of the U.S. taken in the year 1790: New York. Washington, Govt. Print Off., 1908. (Spartanburg, 1964) 308 p. 28 cm. 64-62656.
F118. U 5

WHO'S who in New York; a biographical dictionary of prominent citizens of New York city and state ...
1st - ed., 1904 - 19 New York city, Who's who publications, inc. (1904 -
v. 20½ - 27 cm. 11-7854 (rev. '20)
F118. W 62
J. R. ref.

HISTORIOGRAPHY

HAMILTON, Milton Wheaton. The Historical Publication Program of the State of New York. Albany, University of the State of New York, State Education Dept., Division of Archives and History, 1965.
13 p. 22 cm. A65-7929.
F118. 2. H3

NEW YORK (State) Division of Archives and History. A quiz for local historians. Albany, 1961.
ii, 21 p. 28 cm.
F118. 2. N4

Study and teaching

NEW YORK (State) Office of State History. Sights and sounds of New York State history. Compiled and annotated by W. K. McNeil. Albany (1968)   iii, 52 p. 28 cm. 77-625033.
    F118.5.A56

General works. Histories.

ADAMS, Spencer Lionel. The long house of the Iroquois ... Illus. with 125 photos taken by the author. Skaneateles, N.Y. (Chicago, The Lakeside press, R. R. Donnelley) 1944.   xi, 175 p. incl. front., illus. 20½ cm. 44-9010.
    F119.A 25

ALEXANDER, De Alva Stanwood. Four famous New Yorkers; the political careers of Cleveland, Platt, Hill and Roosevelt, forming vol. 4 of The political history of the State of New York, 1882-1905. Port Washington, L.I., N.Y., I. J. Friedman (1969) (c.1923)   xvii, 488 p. 23 cm. (Empire State historical publications series, no. 69) 72-87731.
    F119.A 36 1969

ALEXANDER, De Alva Stanwood. A political history of the state of New York ... New York, H. Holt and co., 1906 - 09.   3 v. 22½ cm. 6-21392 Add.
    F119.A 37

— Port Washington, N.Y., I. J. Friedman (1969)   3 v. 23 cm. (Empire State historical publication series, no. 69) 72-87731.
    F119.A 37 1969

ALEXANDER, De Alva Stanwood. Four famous New Yorkers; the political careers of Cleveland, Plat, Hill and Roosevelt; forming vol. 4 of "The political history of the state of N.Y." 1882 - 1905 ... New York, H. Holt & co., 1923.   xviii, 488 p. 23 cm. 23-9922.
    F119.A371

AMERICAN association for the advancement of science. Communication from the governor, transmitting a memorial of the committee ... on the subject of a geographical survey of the state. Transmitted to the Legislature ... 1852. Albany, C. Van Benthuysen, printer, 1852.   24 p. 23 cm. 2-16126.
    F119.A 51

ANDERSON, John Jacob. A short history of the state of New York ... New York, Maynard, Merrill, (1901)   viii, 407 p. incl. illus., maps. 19½ cm. 2-12290.
    F119.A 54

BARBER, John Warner. Historical collections of the state of New York; containing a general collection of the most interesting facts, traditions, biographical sketches ... with geographical descriptions of every township in the state. Illus. by 230 engravings. New York, Pub. for the authors by S. Tuttle, 1841.   608 p. incl. pl. front. (ports.) illus., plates. fold. map. 24 cm. 1-15812.
    F119. B 23

— New York, Pub. for the authors by S. Tuttle, 1842.   608 p. incl. pl. front. (ports.) etc. 1-15813.
    F119. B 24

— New York, Pub. for the authors by S. Tuttle, 1846.   616 p. front. (5 port.) illus., plates. 22½ cm. 1-15814.
    F119. B 25

— New York, Pub. for the author, by Clark, Austin, 1851.   iv, (5) - 409, (8) p. illus., plates. 22½ cm. p. 233-234 mutilated. 7-24923.
    F119. B 26

— Port Washington, N.Y., Kennikat Press (1970)   608 p. illus. 78-118780.
    F119. B262

BENNETT, Clarence E. New York and her neighbors, by decades. (Schenectady, N.Y.) 1941. 89, (3) p. illus. 17½ cm. "Keyed references": p. (3) at end. 42-2474.
    F119. B 45

NEW YORK

BINGHAM, Robert Warwick. Niagara, highway of heroes; a narrative history of western New York state ... rewritten for the elementary schools by Ralph E. Theobald ... Buffalo, N. Y., Foster & Stewart pub. corp. (1943)　　3, 150 p. incl. illus. (incl. plans) ports. fronts., plates. 23½ cm.　44-2060.
　　　　　　　　　　　　　　　　　　　　　　　　　　　　　　　　　　　　　　F119. B 55

BONNEY, Mrs. Catharina Visscher (Van Rensselaer) A legacy of historical gleanings ... With illustrations and autographs ... Albany, N. Y., J. Munsell, 1875.　　2 v. fronts., illus., plates, ports. 23½ cm.　7-10452.
　　　　　　　　　　　　　　　　　　　　　　　　　　　　　　　　　　　　　　F119. B 71

— 2d ed.　Albany, N. Y., J. Munsell, 1875.　　2 v. fronts., illus., 2 pl., ports. 23½ cm.　14-20934.
　　　　　　　　　　　　　　　　　　　　　　　　　　　　　　　　　　　　　　F119. B 72

BROOKS, Elbridge Streeter. ... The story of New York. Illus. by L. J. Bridgman.　Boston, D. Lothrop (1888)　　282 p. 283-311 p. incl. illus., plates. front., fold. map. 22 cm. (The story of the states v. 1) "A selection of books touching the general story of the state of New York": p. 307-308.　1-15815.
　　　　　　　　　　　　　　　　　　　　　　　　　　　　　　　　　　　　　　F119. B 87

BRUCE, Dwight Hall. The Empire state in three centuries ... A narrative of events by Daniel Van Pelt. New York, The Century history co. (1898)　　3 v. fronts., illus. (incl. maps) ports. 27 cm. L. of C. has v. 1 and 2 only. 4-33634 Rev.
　　　　　　　　　　　　　　　　　　　　　　　　　　　　　　　　　　　　　　F119. B 89

CARMER, Carl Lamson. Dark trees to the wind; a cycle of York State years; decorations by John O'Hara Cosgrave II. New York, W. Sloane Associates (1949)　　xiv, 370 p. illus. 22 cm. "Sources consulted": p. 365 - 370.　49-11791*.
　　　　　　　　　　　　　　　　　　　　　　　　　　　　　　　　　　　　　　F119. C 27

CARMER, Carl Lamson. My kind of country; favorite writings about New York. New York, McKay (1966)　　xvi, 272 p. 22 cm.　66-24424.
　　　　　　　　　　　　　　　　　　　　　　　　　　　　　　　　　　　　　　F119. C 28

CARPENTER, William Henry. The history of New York from its earliest settlement to the present time. Philadelphia, Lippincott, Grambo, 1853.　　336 p. front. (port.) 17 cm. (Lippincott's cabinet histories) 1-15816.
　　　　　　　　　　　　　　　　　　　　　　　　　　　　　　　　　　　　　　F119. C 29

CHASE Manhattan Bank. New York, the Empire State. New York (1937)　　86 p. 14 cm. (The Manhattan library, v. 11-S) Pub. by the bank under its earlier name: Bank of the Manhattan Company. 37-12556 rev.*
　　　　　　　　　　　　　　　　　　　　　　　　　　　　　　　　　　　　　　F119. C 4

COMLEY, William J. Comley's History of the state of New York, embracing a general review of her agricultural and mineralogical resources, her manufacturing, industries, etc., together with a description of her great metropolis, from its settlement by the Dutch, in 1609. Also, an encyclopedia of biography of some of the old settlers, etc. New York, Comley brothers, 1877.　　(25) - 124, (327) - 656 p. invl. pl., port. 24 x 20 cm.　3-11790.
　　　　　　　　　　　　　　　　　　　　　　　　　　　　　　　　　　　　　　F119. C 73

CORBETT, John. The lake country. An annal of olden days in central New York. The land of gold. Rochester, N. Y., Democrat and chronicle print, 1898.　　161 p. illus. 17 cm.　98-854 Rev.
　　　　　　　　　　　　　　　　　　　　　　　　　　　　　　　　　　　　　　F119. C 78

DOTY, William Joseph, ed. The historic annals of southwestern New York. ... New York, N. Y., Lewis historical pub. co. (1940)　　3 v. fronts., illus. (incl. maps, facsims.) ports. 27½ cm. Vols. 1 and 2 paged continuously; v. 3 consists of biographies.　40-29944.
　　　　　　　　　　　　　　　　　　　　　　　　　　　　　　　　　　　　　　F119. D 68

DUNLAP, William. History of the New Netherlands, province of New York, and state of New York, to the adoption of the federal constitution ... New York, Printed for the author by Carter & Thorp, 1839 - 40.　　2 v. fronts., 2 maps (1 fold.) 23 cm.　1-15817.
　　　　　　　　　　　　　　　　　　　　　　　　　　　　　　　　　　　　　　F119. D 91

— New York, B. Franklin (1970)　　2 v. 23 cm. (Burt Franklin Research & source works series. 538. American classics in history and social science. 144)　70-130594.
　　　　　　　　　　　　　　　　　　　　　　　　　　　　　　　　　　　　　　F119. D 92

DUNLAP, William. A history of New York, for schools. By William Dunlap ... New York, Collins, Keese, 1837.　　2 v. illus., 4 pl. (incl. fronts.) 15½ cm.　1-15818.
　　　　　　　　　　　　　　　　　　　　　　　　　　　　　　　　　　　　　　F119. D 93

— New York, Harper & Bros., 1855.　　2 v. illus. 16½ cm.　9-10318.
　　　　　　　　　　　　　　　　　　　　　　　　　　　　　　　　　　　　　　F119. D 94

EASTMAN, Francis Smith. A history of the state of New York, from the first discovery of the country to the present time. Designed for the use of schools and for families. New York, E. Bliss, 1828. viii, 279 p. 18½ cm. 1-15820 Rev.   F119. E 13

EASTMAN, Francis Smith. A history of the state of New York, from the first discovery of the country to the present time: with a geographical account of the country, and a view of its original inhabitants. New York, A. K. White, 1831. 3, (5) - 456 p. 2 pl.. 3 port. (incl. front.) 19½ cm. "Catalogue of authors used and consulted ...": p. (7) - 8. 17-12054.   F119. E135 Toner Coll.

— A new ed. New York, A. K. White, 1832. 3, (5) - 455 p. front., plates, ports. 19½ cm. 8-24734.   F119. E136

— A new ed. New York, A. K. White, 1833. 3, (5) - 455 p. front., plates, ports. 19 cm. 1-15821 Rev.   F119. E 14

ELDRIDGE, Paul. Crown of empire; the story of New York State. New York, T. Yoseloff (1957) 248 p. illus. 22 cm. Includes bibliography. 57-6893.   F119. E 4

ELLIS, David Maldwyn. New York: the Empire State. Englewood Cliffs, N.J., Prentice-Hall (1961) 500 p. 26 cm. 61-13528.   F119. E 45

— 2d ed. Englewood Cliffs, N.Y., Prentic-Hall, 1964. 500 p. 26 cm. 64-7693.   F119. E 45 1964

ELLIS, David Maldwyn. A short history of New York State. Ithaca, N.Y., Pub. in co-operation with the New York State Hist. Assoc., by Cornell University Press (1957) 705 p. illus. 25 cm. Includes bibliography. 57-4153.   F119. E 46

— A history of New York state. (1967) xx, 732 p. 24 cm. 67-20587.   F119. E 46

FREDERICKSON, Alice S. The story of New York State, for student-readers of the New York herald tribune. (New York, N.Y. Herald Tribune, 1950) 61 p. illus., ports. 20 cm. Bibliography: p. 62. 50-11313.   F119. F 7

FREEDGOOD, Seymour. The gateway states: New Jersey, New York. New York, Time, inc., 1967. 192 p. 28 cm. (Time-life library of America) 67-17761.   F119. F 75

— (1970) 192 p. illus. 28 cm. 67-17761.   F119. F 75 1970

GLASSMAN, Michael. New York State, its history and its government. Brooklyn, Barron's Educational Series, 1949. x, 126 p. illus. 21 cm. 50-1 rev.   F119. G 6

— Supplement revision, 1957. Great Neck, N.Y., Barron's Educational Series, 1957. vi, 50 p. 18 cm.   F119. G 6 Suppl.

GLASSMAN, Michael. New York State (and New York City) geography, history, government. Great Neck, N.Y., Barron's Educational Series (1964) xv, 285 p. 21 cm. 64-18384.   F119. G 6 1964

— Rev. ed. (1965) xv, 295 p. 20 cm. 65-25680.   F119. G 6 1965

HALSEY, Francis Whiting. The old New York frontier; its wars with Indians and Tories; its missionary schools, pioneers and land titles, 1614 - 1800 ... New York, C. Scribner's sons, 1901. xiii, 432 p. front., plates, ports. 2 fold. maps. 21½ cm. Bibliography: p. (401) - 411. 1-31627/5 Rev.   F119. H 19

NEW YORK 21

— Fort Washington, N. Y., I. J. Friedman (1963) 432 p. 22 cm. (Empire State historical publication 21) 63-12955.
F119.H 19
1963

HENDRICK, Welland. A brief history of the Empire state ... Syracuse, N. Y., C. W. Bardeen, 1890.
vii, 9-203 p. incl. front., illus., ports., maps, facsims. 18½ cm. (School bulletin publications) 5-32176.
F119.H 46

— 4th ed. with revisions. Syracuse, N. Y., C. W. Bardeen, 1896. vii, 9-206 p. incl. front., illus., ports., maps, facsims. 18 x 14½ cm. "Books on New York state history": p. 205 - 206. 4-395.
F119.H 49

HISTORICAL recreations in the history of the empire state, by L. A. Toepp, designed to accompany Hendrick's "Brief history of the empire state." ... Honeoye, N. Y., F. B. Short, 1894. 16 p. 12º.
1-15074-M1.
F119.H491

HIGGINS, Ruth Loving. Expansion in New York, with especial reference to the eighteenth century ... Columbus, The Ohio state university, 1931. xi, 209 p. 3 fold. maps. 22½ cm. (Ohio state university studies ... Contributions in history and political science. no. 14) Bibliography: p. 163 - 188. 32-27654.
F119.H 54

— (Columbus) The Ohio state university, 1931. xi, 209 p. 3 fold. maps. 23 cm. Thesis (PH. D.) - Ohio state university 1926. Bibliography: p. 163-188. 32-32244.
F119.H542

HOLT, Solomon. The Empire State. Reviewed by Eleanor R. Hughes. New York, College Entrance Book Co. (1955) 110 p. illus. 19 cm. 55-30289.
F119.H 64

HORNE, Charles Frances. History of the state of New York ... with introd. by James Austin Holden ... Boston, New York (etc.) D. C. Heath (1916) xiii, 434 p. front. (fold. map) illus. (incl. ports.) 19 cm.
16-8818.
F119. H 8

HORTON, John Theodore. History of northwestern New York; Erie, Niagara, Wyoming, Genesee and Orleans Counties. New York, Lewis Historical Pub. Co. (1947) 3 v. illus., ports., maps. 28 cm. Vol. 3: Personal and family history. "Notes and authorities": v. 1 p. (445) - 489. 47-6239*.
F119.H 85

JOHNSON, Blanche Headley. Topical review of New York State; Auburn, N. Y., Topical Review Book Co. (1950) 77 p. illus. 20 cm. 50-3760 rev.
F119. J 6

KENT, James. An anniversary discourse,. delivered before the New-York historical soc. ... 1828. New York, G. & C. Carvill, 1829. 40 p. 22 cm. 3-28229.
F119.K 37

KIMBALL, Francis Paton. The capital region of New York state, crossroads of empire ... New York, Lewis historical pub. co., (1942) 3 v. fronts., illus., plates, ports. 27½ cm. "Comprising Albany, Rensselaer, Greene, Montgomery, Herkimer, Columbia, Schenectady, Schoharie, Fulton, Otsego counties and environs." Vol. 3: Biographical. "Reference works": v. 2, p. (555) - 559. 42-19573.
F119. K 5

LAMB, Wallace Emerson. New York state and its communities ... New York, Cincinnati (etc.) American book co. (1942) viii, 485 p. incl. front., illus. 20½ cm. 42-9284.
F119.L 25

LANDON, Harry Fay. An elementary history of northern New York. Watertown, N. Y., The Watertown daily times, 1932. 76 p. illus. (incl. ports., map) 23 cm. "Supplementary reading for the teacher" at the end of most chapters. 32-21092.
F119.L 27

LANDON, Harry Fay. The north country; a history, embracing Jefferson, St. Lawrence, Oswego, Lewis and Franklin counties, New York ... Indianapolis, Ind., Historical pub. co., 1932.
3 v. plates, ports., map. 27½ cm. Paged continuously. Vols. 2 and 3 contain biographical material. 32-10390.
F119.L 28

LOSSING, Benson John. The Empire State: a compendious history of the commonwealth of New York. Illus. by fac-similes of 335 pen-and-ink drawings by H. Rosa. New York, Funk & Wagnalls, 1887.
xix, 618 p. front., illus. (incl. ports., maps, facsims.) 25½ cm. 1-15822.
F119.L 87

LOVERING, Anna Temple. ... Stories of New York. Boston, New York (etc.) Educational publishing company (1896) 224 p. incl. illus., pl., ports., maps. 18 cm. (Young folk's library of Amer. history) 1-15823. F119.L 91

MACAULEY, James. The natural, statistical and civil history of the state of New-York ... New-York, Gould & Banks; Albany, W. Gould, 1829. 3 v. tab. 22 cm. The historical narrative extends only to 1800. 1-22107. F119.M 11

MANNELLO, George. Life in New York. (New York) Holt, Rinehart & Winston (1962) 486 p. illus. 24 cm. F119.M 33

MARTIN, Elma G. Stories of New York, for supplementary reading. Syracuse, N.Y., C. W. Bardeen, 1900. 7-122 p. incl. illus. (ports.) maps. front. 18 cm. May 30, 1901-85. F119.M 37

MAU, Clayton C. The development of central and western New York, from the arrival of the white man to the eve of the civil war, as portrayed chronologically in contemporary accounts ... Rochester, N.Y., The Du Bois press (1944) ix, 444 (i.e. 448) p. illus., plates, maps (part fold.) facsims. 22½ cm. Bibliographical foot-notes. 44-6066. F119.M 38

— Rev. ed. (Dansville? N.Y., 1958) 466 p. illus. 24 cm. 58-42538. F119.M 38 1958

MERRIAM, Hilda Doyle. North of the Mohawk; some of the fascinating history of northern New York. (Chicago?) 1950. xiii, 139 p. illus., map. 24 cm. Bibliography: p. 138-140. 50-4430. F119.M 47

NEW YORK (State) Dept. of Commerce. This is New York State. Rev. Albany, 1954. 64 p. illus. 22 cm. Earlier ed. issued in 1948. 55-62047. F119.N 53 1954

— Albany (1955) 64 p. illus. 22 cm. A 56-9288. F119.N 53 1955

— Albany (1961) 80 p. 22 cm. 61-9569. F119.N 53 1961

NEW YORK (State) State survey. Report. Albany, Weed, Parsons, 1877 - 1887. 11 v. plates (partly fold.) photos. fold. maps, facsim., tables, diagrs. 23½ - 24½ cm. 1-22122 Additions. F119.N 58

NEW YORK (State) State survey. Special report of New York State survey on the preservation of the scenery of Niagara Falls, and Fourth annual report on the triangulation of the state. For the year 1879. James T. Gardner, director. Albany, C. Van Benthuysen, 1880. 4, (7) - 96 p. xi pl. (1 fold.) 5 fold. maps, facsim. 24½ cm. (Its Fourth report) 1-22121. F119.N58 4th

NEW YORK (State) Bureau of Secondary Curriculum Development. A teaching outline for the study of New York State history and constitution. (Albany) The University of the State of New York Press, 1949. 22 p. 23 cm. (New York State University. Bulletin no. 1374) "Selected bibliography": p. 22. A50-9126 rev. F119.N 62

NEW YORK state historical association. History of the state of New York ... New York, Columbia university press, 1933-37. 10 v. fronts., illus., plates, ports., maps (1 fold.) facsims. 23½ cm. "Select bibliography at end of most of the chapters. 33-11644 Rev. F119.N 65 R.R.alc.

— Port Washington, N.Y., I. J. Friedman, 1962. 10 v. in 5. illus. maps (1 fold. in pocket, v.3) 24 cm. (Empire State historical publication 18) Includes bibliographies. 62-20154. F119.N 65 1962

OPINIONS of prominent statesmen, property holders, real estate lawyers and scientific men upon the importance of the (New York) state survey. (n.p., 1877) 16 p. 24 cm. 1-15824 Rev. F119.O 61

NEW YORK

PRENTICE, William Reed. History of New York state, for the use of high schools and academies and for supplementary reading. Syracuse, N.Y., C. W. Bardeen, 1900.   xvi, 17-558 p. incl. front. (port.) illus., maps. 18 cm. Bibliography: p. viii. 1-29556 Rev.
F119. P 92

(QUACKENBOS, George Payn) Special history of New York. (New York, D. Appleton, 1878. p. (331) - 360. illus. (incl. ports.) 19 cm. 1-16077.
F119.Q 2

RANDALL, Samuel Sidwell. History of the state of New York, for the use of common schools, academies, normal and high schools, and other seminaries of instruction. ... New York, J. B. Ford, 1870. xx, (7) - 369 p. 19½ cm. SD 34-221.
F119. R2

RAPP, Marvin A. New York State; a student's guide to localized history. New York, Teachers College Press (1968)   x, 51 p. 23 cm. (Localized history series) 68-9256.
F119. R 22

REDWAY, Jacques Wardlaw. ... The making of the Empire state ... New York, Boston (etc.) Silver, Burdett (1904)   263 p. front., illus. (incl. maps) 19 cm. (Stories of the states) 4-17692.
F119. R 32

REYNOLDS, Helen W. Dutch houses in the Hudson Valley before 1776. 1929.   1 v.
F119. R 39

ROBERTS, Ellis Henry. ... New York: the planting and the growth of the Empire state ... Boston and New York, Houghton, Mifflin, 1887.   2 v. front. (fold. map) 18 cm. (American commonwealths v. 8-9) 1-15825.
F119. R 64

— (v.1) Boston and N.Y., Houghton, Mifflin, 1892.   1 v. front. (fold. map) 18 cm.
F119. R642

— with a supplementary chapter dealing with the period from 1885 to 1900 ... Boston and New York, Houghton, Mifflin, 1904.   2 v. front. (map) 18½ cm. Paged continuously. 4-3408 Rev.
F119. R 65

RUSSELL, William. Harper's New-York class-book; comprising outlines of the geography and history of New York; biographical notices of eminent individuals; sketches of scenery and natural history; accounts of public institutions, etc. Arranged as a reading-book for schools. New York, Harper & bros., 1847.   xi, (13) - 669 p. incl. illus., maps. 19½ cm. 1-15826 Rev.
F119. R 87

SCHWARZ, Jeanne Meador. New York State in story. Original sketches by Albert Sway. (Phoenix? N.Y.) 1962.   2 v. in 1. illus. 24 cm.
F119. S 4

SEYMOUR, Horatio. A lecture on the topography and history of New-York. Utica, N.Y., D. C. Grove, printer, 1856.   41 p. 23½ cm. 3-31524.
F119. S52

SKINNER, Avery Warner. History and government of New York ... a supplement to Elementary American history and government ... New York, Chicago, Longmans, Green, 1918.   64 p. illus. 20½ cm. Contains "References for additional reading." 18-19819.
F119. S 62

SMITH, Ray Burdick, ed. History of the state of New York, political and governmental ... Syracuse, N.Y., The Syracuse press, inc., 1922.   6 v. fronts., plates (part fold.) ports. 23½ cm. Contents: - I. 1776-1822. - II. 1822-1864. - III. 1865-1896. - IV. 1896-1920. - V. National party histories. - VI. National party platforms. 24-5350.
F119. S 65

SOUTHWORTH, Mrs. Gertrude (Van Duyn) The story of the Empire state; history of New York told in story form; a supplementary reading-book for grammar grades. New York, D. Appleton, 1902. x, 213 p. front., illus. 19½ cm. 2-24853.
F119. S 72

SULLIVAN, James, ed. History of New York state, 1523 - 1927 ... New York, Chicago, Lewis hist. pub. co. (1927)   6 v. fronts., plates, ports., maps, plan, facsims. 27½ cm. Vols. 1-5 paged continuously. Vol. 6 contains biographical material. Contains "Authorities". 27-24237.
F119. S 95

TAYLOR, Alice. New York. (Prepared with the cooperation of the American Geographical Society) Garden City, N.Y., Doubleday (1962)   64 p.   21 cm.
 F119. T 3

— Garden City, N.Y., Doubleday (1966)   (Know your America program)   64 p.   22 cm.
 F119. T 3
 1966

WAINGER, Bertrand Max.   Exploring New York state ...   New York, Chicago, Harcourt Brace, 1942. xii, 372 p. incl. front., illus. (incl. ports., maps) charts. diagrs.   24½ cm.   "General bibliography for pupils": p. 361 - 364.   42-21822.
 F119. W 23

— New ed.   New York, Harcourt, Brace, 1948.   xviii, 494 p.   illus., ports., maps.   25 cm.   "Bibliography for pupils": p. (477) - 480.   48-28230*.
 F119. W 23
 1948

— 3d ed.   New York, Harcourt, Brace (1956)   497 p.   illus.   25 cm.   (Title of this ed. Exploring New York) Includes bibliographies.   56-13975.
 F119. W 23
 1956

WALWORTH, Jeannette Ritchie (Hadermann)   History of New York, in words of one syllable,... Chicago, New York (etc.) Belford, Clarke (1889)   (5) - 186 p.   illus. (incl. ports.)   22 x 18 cm.   1-15828.
 F119. W 24

WHEELER, Alfred Harvey.   New York State; its history and constitution.   Ed. A. Victor Gentilini. New York, Republic Book Co. (1950)   vi, 138 p.   illus.   19 cm.   50-1229.
 F119. W 53

WHEELER, Mary Alexandria.   New York state, yesterday and today ... with an introd. by Dixon Ryan Fox ... New York, Chicago (etc.) C. Scriber's sons (1935)   xx, 432 p. incl. front., illus. (incl. maps) 18½ cm.   Bibliography: p. 407 - 418.   35-8937.
 F119. W 54

— New York, Chicago (etc.) C. Scriber's sons (1942)   xx, 444 p. incl. front., illus. (incl. maps, ports.) 18½ cm.   Bibliography: p. 419-430.   42-23241.
 F119. W 54
 1942

— New York, Scribner, (1949)   xx, 444 p.   illus., ports.   19 cm.   Bibliography: p. 419-430.   50-348.
 F119. W 54
 1949

— New York, Scribner (1952)   444 p.   illus.   19 cm.   52-4561.
 F119. W 54
 1952

WILLIAMS, Sherman.   New York's part in history ... New York and London, D. Appleton, 1915. ix, 390 p.   front., illus. (maps) plates, ports.   21½ cm.   15-18646.
 F119. W 7

WILLIAMS, Sherman.   Stories from early New York history. ... New York, C. Scribner's sons, 1906.   vii - xviii, 320 p.   front. (port.) illus.   19 cm.   "A list of works consulted": p. 289 - 291.   6-23742.
 F119. W 72

JUVENILE WORKS.

BAILEY, Bernardine (Freeman)   Picture book of New York.   Pictures by Kurt Wiese.   Chicago, Whitman, 1950.   (28) p.   illus. (part col.)   17 x 22 cm.   50-7508.
 F119.3. B3
 1950

— Rev. ed.   Chicago, A. Whitman, (1966)   32 p.   17 x 21 cm.   (Her the United States books)
 F119.3. B3
 1966

BOMPEY, Abraham.   The New York story.   New York, Noble and Noble (1965)   vii, 87 p.   28 cm.
 F119.3. B6

CARPENTER, John Allan. New York.   Illus. by Tom Dunnington.   Chicago, Childrens Press (1967)
96 p. 24 cm. (Enchantment of America) 67-10277.
F119.3.C3

DUDLEY, Bronson. The story of New York; Indian territory to Empire State. Pictures by Charles Waterhouse. New York, Grosset & Dunlap (1968) 61 p. 24 cm. (A who, when, where book) 67-16150.
F119.3.D8

FINK, William Bertrand. Getting to know New York State. Illus. by Don Almquist. New York, Coward, McCann & Geoghegan (1971) 71 p. illus., map, ports. 23 cm. 70-150588 MARC.
F119.3.F5
1971

GREGOR, Arthur S. Gateways to America. Pictures by James G. Teason; maps by William Tanis. Chicago, Benefic Press (1961) 224 p. 13 cm. (Our growing America series) 61-7677.
F119.3.G7

McCARTHY, Agnes. New York State: its land and people. Garden City, N.Y., Doubleday, Education Division, Catholic Textbook Dept. (1963) 96 p. 28 cm. (Doubleday geography series) 63-17408.
F119.3.M2

PAULINE, Lawrence J. New York State: our cultural heritage. New York, Cambridge Book Co. (1971) viii, 342 p. illus. 24 cm. 74-177408 MARC.
F119.3.P3

VROOMAN, John J. Council fire and cannon. Reg Massie, illustrator. Chicago, Follett Pub. Co. (1962) 185 p. 22 cm. 62-8372.
F119.3.V7

YATES, Raymond Francis. Under three flags; western New York State from the ice age to the atomic age. Buffalo, H. Stewart (1958) 352 p. illus. 22 cm. 58-8223.
F119.3.Y3

MINOR WORKS. PAMPHLETS, ADDRESSES, ESSAYS, ETC.

NEW YORK (State) Dept. of Commerce. New York, the Empire State. Albany (1954) (12) p. illus. 23 x 11 cm. A 55-9131.
F119.5.A53

— Albany (1959) 28 l. 28 cm.
F119.5.A53
1959

NEW YORK (State) Temporary State Commission on Historic Observances. New York State's year of history - calendar of events. 1609-1959. (Rev. and corr. as of April 30, 1959. Albany, 1959) 80 p. 28 cm. A 59-9649.
F119.5.A57
1959

NEW YORK (State) Temporary State Commission on Historic Observances. Final report, 1959 - 1960. (Albany, 1960) 171 p. 28 cm. A 60-9910.
F119.5.A58

U.S. General Accounting Office. Audit of Hudson-Champlain Celebration Commission, May 1960; report to the Congress of the U.S., by the Comptroller General of the U.S. (Washington) 1960.
8 l. 27 cm. 61-61806.
F119.5.A59

U.S. Hudson-Champlain Celebration Commission. The 350th anniversary of the explorations of Henry Hudson and Samuel de Champlain; final report of the Hudson-Champlain Celebration Commission to the President and the Congress. New York, 1960. 81 p. 26 cm.
F119.5.A6

ANECDOTES, LEGENDS, PAGEANTS, ETC.

WALTER, George William. Chips and shavings; stories of upstate New York. Sherburne, N.Y., F. E. Faulkner, 1966. 160 p. 23 cm.   F119.6.W3

HISTORIC MONUMENTS (GENERAL). ILLUSTRATIVE MATERIAL.

BAILEY, Rosalie Fellows. Pre-revolutionary Dutch houses and families in northern New Jersey and southern New York; with an introd. by Franklin D. Roosevelt; photography by Margaret De M. Brown; prepared under the auspices of the Holland society of New York. New York, W. Morrow, 1936. 10, 11-612 p. incl. front., illus., plan. 29 cm. Bibliography: p. 583-584. 36-17444.
     F120.
     F135. B 25

JENKINS, Stephen. The old Boston post road ... with 200 illus. and maps. New York and London, G. P. Putnam's sons, 1913. xxiv, 453 p. front., plates, maps (part fold.) facsims. 23 cm. Bibliography: p. 427-434. 13-25381.
     F120.
     F5. J 52

MEYER, Max Wilhelm. Eine Amerikafahrt 1492 und 1892, mit zahlreichen zusätzen und anmerkungen in bezug auf die entdeckungsgeschichte Amerikas und das moderne seewesen ... Mit drei abbildungen. Berlin, Hermann Paetel verlag g.m.b.h. (1913) 102 p. front., pl., port. 18½ cm. 31-5517.
     F120
     G550. M 3

MARSH, Horace Pierce. Rochester and its early canal days; reminiscences of the author, while engaged on the New York state waterways, the Erie, Genesee Valley, Black River, and other lateral canals. (Rochester, N.Y., Democrat and chronicle print) 1914. 62 p. illus. 23 cm. 14-19862.
     F120. M36

NEW YORK (State) Legislature. Joint Committee on Historic Site and Historic Canal Preservation. Report. (Albany, 1958) 57 p. illus. 29 cm. A 58-9724.
     F120. N 32

NEW YORK (State) Legislature. Joint Committee to Study Historic Sites. Report. 1950-53. Albany, Williams Press. 4 v. 23 cm. Issued in the series of Legislative documents. A 53-10036.
     F120. N 33

NEW YORK (State) Dept. of Commerce. Houses of history in New York State. Albany (1956?) 32 p. illus. 13 x 20 cm. A 56-9633.
     F120. N 4

— 3d ed. Albany (1957) 40 p. illus. 14 x 20 cm. A 58-9479.
     F120. N 4
     1957

NEW YORK (State) Division of Archives and History. Historic sites of New York State. (Albany, 1956) 39 p. illus. 21 cm. A 56-9446.
     F120. N 42

— (Albany, 1958) 48 p. illus. 21 cm. A 58-8939.
     F120. N 42
     1958

— (Albany, 1960) 56 p. 23 cm. A 60-9813.
     F120. N 42
     1960

NEW YORK (State) State historian. Ecclesiastical records, state of New York. Pub. by the state under the supervision of Hugh Hastings, state historian ... Albany, J. B. Lyon, state printer, 1901-16 7 v. plates (part fold.) ports., facsims. 23 cm. 6-13746 Rev.
     F120. N 45

NEW YORK (State). Office of State History. A guide to the historical markers of New York State. Albany, 1970. iii, 129 p. illus., maps. 22 x 10 cm. 79-636101 MARC.
     F120. N 5

NEW YORK

NEW YORK (State) State engineer and surveyor. Report of the state engineer and surveyor relative to map of the state. Transmitted to the Legislature Feb. 28, 1857. Albany, C. Van Benthuysen, printer, 1857. 15 p. 22 ½ cm. 1-22571.   F120. N 53

NEW YORK (State) University. Historic and scientific sites of New York State. Prepared by John J. Vrooman, supervisor of historic sites. (Albany, 1949) 32 p. illus., ports., map. 23 cm. Reprinted from the New York red book, 1949. A 50-9331.   F120. N 6

NEW YORK historical society. Memorial of the New-York historical society to the honourable the Legislature of the state of New-York. New-York, Printed by C. S. Van Winkle ... 1814. 11 p. 21 cm. Requesting financial assistance in gathering material bearing on the early history of New York. 1-15829-30.   F120. N 62 or N 67

REYNOLDS, Helen Wilkinson. Dutch houses in the Hudson Valley before 1776 ... with an introd. by Franklin D. Roosevelt, photography by Margaret De M. Brown; prepared under the auspices of the Holland society of New York. New York, Payson and Clarke, ltd., 1929. 8, 3-467 p. incl. front., plates. fold. map (in pocket) 28 ½ cm. 30-12391.   F120. R 39 Rare Book Coll.

THOMPSON, Harold William. ... Body, boots & britches. Philadelphia, New York (etc.) J. B. Lippincott co., 1940. 5, 9-530 p. 23 ½ cm. 40-2174.   F120. T 55

TODD, Charles Burr. In olde New York; sketches of old times and places in both the state and the city ... New York, The Grafton press (1907) viii, 253 p. front., 14 pl. 19 ½ cm. (The Grafton historical series) Many of these stories were pub. in 1885 in the Evening post and Lippincott's magazine. 7-36943.   F102. T 63

— Port Washington, N.Y., I. J. Friedman (1968) viii, 253 p. 22 cm. (Empire state historical publications series no. 49) 68-18359.   F120. T 63 1968

UNITED historical and patriotic societies and associations of New York. The need of a history of New York. Pub. under the auspices of the Committee of nine ... (New York, Printed by Harper & brothers) 1915. 55 p. front., pl., port., map. 24 cm. 18-14611.   F120. U 5

(VAN RENSSELAER, Sarah (Rogers)) Ancestral sketches and records of olden times ... For private circulation only. New York, A. D. F. Randolph, 1882. xiii, 375 p. 26 cm. 6-9054 Rev.   F120. V 27

WILLIAMS, Sherman. Local history ... Syracuse, N.Y., C. W. Bardeen, 1915. 47 p. 18 ½ cm. Address delivered before the Conference of academic principals of the state of New York. 15-9450.   F120. W 72

ZOOK, Nicholas. Houses of New York open to the public. Barre, Mass., Barre Publishers, 1969. 143 p. illus. 25 cm. 69-12346.   F120. Z 66

ANTIQUITIES.

CALVER, William Louis. History written with pick and shovel; military buttons, helt-plates, badges and other relics excavated from Colonial, Revolutionary, and War of 1812 camp sites by the Field Exploration Committee of the New-York Historical Society. New York, New-York Historical Society, 1950. xiii, 320 p. illus., ports., maps. 25 cm. Bibliography: p. 263. 50-10740.   F121. C 3

SMITH, Carlyle Shreeve. The archaeology of coastal New York. New York, 1950. 95 - 200 p. 27 cm. (Anthropological papers of the American Museum of Natural History, v. 43, pt. 2) 51-1000.   F121. S 55

VAN EPPS- Hartley bulletin. v. 1 - Oct. 1935 - (Schenectady, 1935 - v. 28 cm. bimonthly. 42-42672.   F121. V 3

EARLY TO 1775.

An ACCOUNT of the antient town of Gotham. And of some transactions of the so famous wise men there. Translated from an antient Greek manuscript, found in the Vatican library ... Printed in the year 1770. 32 p. 20 cm. 24-3330.
  F122.A 17
  Rare Book Coll.

ALBANY. Minutes of the court of Albany, Rensselaerswyck and Schenectady, 1668 - 1680 ... Being a continuation of the Minutes of the court of Fort Orange and Beverwyck; trans. and ed. by A. J. F. Van Laer ... Albany, The University of the state of New York, 1926-28. 2 v. 23 cm. For minutes of the earlier court cf. Beverwyck. N.Y. Kleine banck van justitie, Fort Orange. 26-27297 Rev. See F122.1.B57
  F122.A 25

ALTER, Donald Rhodes. Mid-century political alignments in the middle provinces, 1740 - 1760 ... Urbana, Ill., 1934. 13 p. 23½ cm. Abstract of thesis (PH.D.) - University of Illinois, 1934. 34-23634.
  F122.A 36

(ATWOOD, William) The case of William Atwood, esq; by the late King William ... constituted chief justice of the province of New York in America, etc., etc. London, 1703. 23 p. 33½ x 21 cm. 10-7608.
  F122.A 88
  Rare Book Coll.

BALEN, Willem Julius van. Holland aan de Hudson; een verhaal van Nieuw Nederland. 2. druk. Amsterdam, Amsterdamsche Boek - en Courantimaatschappij, 1947. 215 p. illus., ports., maps. 23 cm. A 48-9884*.
  F122.B 124
  1947

BARTRAM, John. Observations on the inhabitants, climate, soil, rivers, productions, animals, and other matters worthy of notice ... in his travels from Pensilvania to Onondago, Oswego and the Lake Ontario, in Canada. To which is annex'd, a curious account of the cataracts at Niagara. By Mr. Peter Kalm ... London, Print. for J. Whiston and B. White, 1751. vii. (9) - 94 p. front. (fold. plan) 21 cm. 1-16152.
  F122.B 129
  Rare Book Coll.

— (Geneva, N.Y., Reprinted by W. F. Humphrey, 1895) viii, (9) - 94 p. front. (plan) pl.. fold. map. 23 cm. 16-9745.
  F122.B 133

— Ann Arbor, University Microfilms (1966) 94 p. 19 cm. (March of America facsimile series. no. 41) 66-24197.
  F122.B 133
  1966

BAYARD, Nicholas. An account of the commitment, arraignment, tryal and condemnation of Nicholas Bayard esq; for high treason in endeavouring to subvert the government of the province of New York in America .... Printed at New York by order of His Excellency the Lord Cornbury, and reprinted at London, 1703. 31 p. 32½ cm. 43-43000.
  F122. B 34
  Rare Book Coll.

— ... New York, Printed and sold by William Bradford, 1702. p. 33-36, 41-42. 30 cm.
  F122. B 35
  Rare Book Coll.

BECKER, Carl Lotus. Growth of revolutionary parties and methods. New York, 1901. 27 cm.
  F122. B 39

BEEKMAN, Henry. Colonel Henry Beekman and his times. By Edward L. Merritt. A paper read at the meeting of the Ulster county historical soc ... 1933. (Kingston, 1933) 33 p. 23 cm. CA 36-1858 Unrev.
  F122. B 415

BELLOMONT. The life and administration of Richard, earl of Bellomont, governor of the provinces of New York, Massachusetts, and New Hampshire, from 1697 to 1701. ... by Frederic de Peyster ... New York, 1879. 4. 59, xvii p. 3 port. (incl. front.) fold. facsim. 26½ cm. 4-22928.
  F122. B 44

NEW YORK

BISBEE, Ernest Emerson.   ... The Empire state scrap book of stories and legends of old New York...
Lancaster, N.H., The Bisbee press, 1939.   (56) p. illus. 23½ cm. 39-15784 rev.
 F122. B 57

BONOMI, Patricia U.   A factious people; politics and society in colonial New York.   New York,
Columbia University Press, 1971.   xiii, 342 p. 23 cm. 74-156803.
 F122. B 65

BRODHEAD, John Romeyn.   An address, delivered before the New York historical society ... 1844.
N.Y., 1844.   107 p. 22 cm. 1-13383.
 F122. B 85

BRODHEAD, John Romeyn.   The final report of John Romeyn Brodhead, agent of the state of New-York,
to procure and transcribe documents in Europe, relative to the colonial history of said state.   Albany,
E. Mack, printer, 1845.   374 p. 24½ cm. (New York. Senate doc. no. 47)   The report is accompanied by three chronological
lists: 1. Calendar to the Holland documents in the office of the secretary of state at Albany. 2. Calendar to the London documents ... 3. Calendar to the Paris documents ... The 80 vols. of transcripts were pub. in O'Callaghan's Documents relating to the colonial history of the state of
New York, v. 1-11. 1856-1861.   3-6159.
 F122.B853

BRODHEAD, John Romeyn.   History of the state of New York.   ... 1st ed.   New York, Harper &
brothers, 1853-71.   2 v. front. (map) 23½ cm. No more pub. 1-15831.
 F122. B 86

BURNET.   William Burnet, governor of New-York and New-Jersey, 1720 - 1728; a sketch of his administration in New-York, by William Nelson.   New-York, 1892.   p. 151-178. illus. (incl. ports.) 27 cm.
25 copies reprinted from J. G. Wilson's Memorial history of the city of New-York. New York, 1892)   17-24793.
 F122. B 96

CAMPBELL, Douglas.   Historical fallacies regarding colonial New York, and address delivered before
the Oneida historical soc. ... 1879.   New York, F. J. Ficker, print., 1879.   32 p. 23 cm. (Oneida
historical society at Utica. Publications, no. 2)   3-5826 Rev.
 F122.C 18

CAMPBELL.   ... Lauchlin Campbell, of Campbell Hall, and his family.   By David Barclay.
(From Historical soc. of Newburgh Bay and the Highlands. Historical papers. Newburgh. N. Y., 1902. no. 9)   8-18970.
 F122.C 19

CHRISTENSEN, Gardell Dano.   Colonial New York.   Foreword by Louis Leonard Tucker.   (Camden,
N.J.) T. Nelson (1969)   160 p. illus. 23 cm. 69-15223.
 F122.C 57

CLARKE, George.   Voyage of George Clarke, esq., to America (1703) With introd. and notes by E. B.
O'Callaghan.   Albany, N.Y., J. Munsell, 1867.   lxxxi, 126 p. front. 20½ cm. Edition 100 copies.   Contains
genealogy of the Clarke family.   1-15836 Rev.
 F122.C 59

COLDEN, Cadwallader.   The letters and papers of Cadwallader Colden ... 1711 - (1775) New York,
1918-37.   9 v. fronts. 24 - 25 cm. (Collections of the New York hist. soc. The John Watts De Peyster publication fund series. 50-56,
67-68)   Contents. - v.1. 1711-1729. - v.2. 1730-1742. - v.3. 1743-1747. - v.4. 1748-1754. - v.5. 1755-1760. - v.6. 1761-1764. - v.7.
1765-1775. - v.8. Additional 1715-1748. - v.9. Additional 1749-1775 ... 19-15059 Rev. 2.
 F122.C 67

COLDEN, Cadwallader; a representative eighteenth century official, by Alice Mapelsden Keys.   New
York, The Columbia university press, The Macmillan co., agents; 1906.   3. v-xiv, 375 p. 23 cm.
6-40257.
 F122.C684

— New York (The Macmillan co.) 1906.   xiv, 375 p. 22½ cm. Thesis (PH. D.) - Columbia University. A10-2038.
 F122.C6842

— New York, AMS Press, 1967.   xiv, 375 p. 23 cm.
 F122.C684
 1967

CALDEN, Cadwallader, 1688 - 1776.   Pamphlets, broadsides, clippings, and other miscellaneous
matter on this subject, not separately cataloged, are classified in:
 F122.C689

DENTON, Daniel.   Two important gifts to the New York public library ... Columbus' letter on the discovery of America ... & Daniel Denton's description of New York in 1670 (by Victor Hugo Paltsits) New York, 1924. 14 p. 3 facsim. 25½ cm. Location of the twenty copies of the printed edition of Denton's work which can be traced: p. 12-14. 25-8675.

F122. D
Z8187.N53

DAWSON, Henry Barton. The Sons of liberty in New York. A paper read before the N.Y. historical soc. ... (Poughkeepsie, Platt & Schram, printers) 1859. 118 p. 24½ cm. 1-24068-M1.

F122. D 27

— New York, Arno Press, 1969. 118 p. 23 cm. (Mass violence in America) 71-90172.

F122. D 27
1969

DeKAY. Colonel Thomas DeKay, a pioneer of western Orange County. By David Barclay ... (From Historical soc. of Newburgh Bay and the Highlands. Historical papers. 1900. no. 6. 8-18968.

F122. D 32

DENTON, Daniel. A brief description of New-York: formerly called New-Netherlands. With the places thereunto adjoyning. Together with the manner of its scituation, fertility of the soyle, healthfulness of the climate, and the commodities thence produced. Also some directions and advice to such as shall go thither: an account of what commodities they shall take with them; the profit and pleasure that may accrew to them thereby. Likewise a brief relation of the customs of the Indians there. London, Printed for John Hancock ... 1670. 2, 21 p. 18½ cm. For an account of all known copies of this work see "Daniel Denton's Brief description of New York ... by Felix Neumann." New York, 1902. Also F122. D above. 9-15625.

F122. D 37
Rare Book Coll.

— Ann Arbor. University Microfilms (1966) 21 p. 20 cm. (March of America facsimile series. no. 26) 66-25654.

F122. D 37
1670a

— Reproduced from the original edition, with a bibliographical note, by Victor Hugo Paltsits. New York, Pub. for the Facsimile text society by Columbia university press, 1937. 5 p. facsim: 2, 21 p. 19½ cm. (The Facsimile text society. Publication no. 40) Reproduction of the original in Columbia university library) 37-5340.

F122. D372

— A new ed. with an introd. and copious historical notes. By Gabriel Furman ... New York, W. Gowans, 1845. 17, 57 p. facsim. 23½ cm. (Gowan's bibliotheca americana. 1) 2-1875-M2.

F122. D 39

— reprinted from the original edition of 1670, with a bibliographical introduction by Felix Neumann ... Cleveland, The Burrows brothers co., 1902. 63 p. incl. facsim. 23½ cm. 2-19108.

F122. D 4
Rare Book Coll.

GOWANS' bibliotheca americana ... New York, W. Gowans, 1845 - 69. 5 v. port., map. plans. 23½ - 25 cm. Contained in vol. 1 10-17549.

F122.
F184. A 46

DE LANCEY. ... Memoir of the Hon. James De Lancey, lieutenant governor the province of New York. By Edward F. De Lancey. (In The documentary history of the state of New-York ... v. 4) 7-34373.

F122. D418

DE PEYSTER, Frederic. An address delivered before the N.-Y. historical soc. on its 60th anniversary ... New York, 1865. 76 p. 24 cm. 1-22106.

F122. D 42

DILLON, Dorothy Rita. The New York triumvirate; a study of the legal and political careers of William Livingston, John Morin Scott, William Smith, Jr. New York, 1949. 217 p. 23 cm. Thesis - Columbia Univ. Bibliography: p. 205 - 214. A 49-2032*.

F122. D 55
1949 or 1949a

— New York, AMS Press (1968) 217 p. 23 cm. 68-58567 MARC.

F122. D 55
1968

NEW YORK

DISOSWAY, Gabriel Poillon. The earliest churches of New York and its vicinity. ... New York, J. G. Gregory, 1865.   416 p. plates. 22½ cm. 6-13731. L. C. copy replaced by microfilm.

F122.D 61
Microfilm 18160 F

DOCUMENTARY history of the state of New-York, The; arranged under direction of the Hon. Christopher Morgan ... By E. B. O'Callaghan ... Albany, Weed, Parsons, public printers, 1849 - 54.
4 v. fronts., plates (part fold.) ports. (2 fold.) fold. maps, plans (part fold.) 22½ cm. 1-15832.

F122.D 63

VOLUME 1

... Papers relating to the Iroquois and other Indian tribes. 1666-1763
... Papers relating to the first settlement at Onondaga.
... Papers relating to De Courcelles' and De Tracy's expeditions against the Mohawk Indians.
... Reports on the province of New York. About 1669; 1678.
... Papers relating to M. de La Barre's expedition to Hungry Bay, Jefferson Co. 1684.
... Gov. Dongan's report on the province of New-York. 1687.
... Papers relating to M. de Denonville's expedition to the Genesee country and Niagara. 1687.
... Names of the male inhabitants of Ulster County, 1689.
... Papers relating to the invasion of New-York and the burning of Schenectady by the French. 1690.
... Civil list of the province of New-York, 1693.
... Papers relating to County de Frontenac's expedition against the Onondagoes. 1696.
...New-York army list, 1700.
... Census of the counties of Orange, Dutchess & Albany, 1702, 1714, 1720.
... Cadwallader Colden on the lands of New-York. 1732.
... Papers relating to the Susquehannah River. 1683 - 1757.
... Papers relating to the early settlement at Ogdensburgh. 1749.
... Papers relating to the first settlement and capture of Fort Oswego. 1727-1756.
... Papers relating to the Oneida country and Mohawk Valley. 1756, 1757.
... Papers relating to the French seigniories on Lake Champlain.
... Boundary line between the whites and Indians. 1765.
... Papers relating to the city of New-York.
... Papers relating to Long Island.
... Statistics of the population of the province of New-York. 1647 - 1774.
... Statistics of revenue, imports, exports, etc. 1691 - 1768.
... Statistics of revenue, imports, exports, etc. 1691 - 1768.
... Papers relating to the trade and manufactures of the province of New York. 1705-1757 (i.e. 1768)
... Report of Governor William Tryon, on the state of the province of New-York. 1774.

VOLUME 2

Papers relating to the administration of Lieut. Gov. Leisler. 1689 - 1691.
A letter from a gentleman of the city of New York to another ... 1698.
... An act for reversing the attainder of Jacob Leisler and others ... 1695.
Rate lists of Long Island. 1675, 1676 & 1683.
Manuscripts of Sir William Johnson.
(Early steam navigation)
The original steam-boat supported.
Papers relating to western New-York.
Description of the country between Albany & Niagara in 1792.
The Genesee country.
Description of the settlement of the Genesee country, by Charles Williamson.
A description of the Genesee country ... To which is added an appendix ... By Robert Munro.

VOLUME 3

... Champlain's expeditions to northern and western New York, 1609-1615.
... Papers relating to the first settlement of New York by the Dutch.

... Papers relating to the restoration of New-York to the English.
... Papers relating to the state of religion in the province. 1657 - 1712.
... Papers relating to Kings County, L.I. (1698 - 1715)
... Papers relating to the churches in Queens County.
... Papers relating to Suffolk County. (1671 - 1764)
... Papers relating to the city of New-York. (1654 - 1769)
... A full & just discovery of the weak & slender foundation of a most pernicious slander raised against the French Protestant refugees inhabiting the province of New-York ...
... Papers relating to the Palatines and to the first settlement of Newburgh, Orange County ...
... Papers relating to the manor of Livingston, including the first settlement of Schoharie. 1680 - 1795.
... Census of slaves, 1755 ...
... Papers relating to Albany and adjacent places. (1674 - 1768)
... Papers relating to Westchester County. (1656 - 1782)
... Papers relating to Ulster & Dutchess counties. (1660 - 1782)
... Papers relating to Quakers and Moravians. (1679 - 1756)
... Rev. Gideon Hawley's journey to Oghquaga, (Broome Co.) 1753.
... State of the Anglo-American church, in 1776. By the Rev. Charles Inglis.
... Prices of land in the state of New York, 1791.
The report of a committee appointed to explore the western waters in the state of New York. 1792.
Rectors of St. Peter's church, Albany.
... Medals and coins.

VOLUME 4

... Journal of New Netherland. 1647. Written in the years 1641, 1642, 43, 44, 45, 46.
... A description of New Netherland, in 1644. By Father Isaac Jogues ...
... Information relative to taking up land in New Netherland. 1650.
... Journal of the second Esopus war; by Capt. Martin Kregier. 1663.
... Extracts from a work called Breeden raedt aen de Vereenighde Nederlandsche provintien. Printed in Antwerp in 1649.
... Description of New Netherland. 1671. By Arnoldus Montanus. 1671.
... Trial for witchcraft (of Ralph Hall and Mary his wife, at New York ... 1665)
... Assessment rolls of the five Dutch towns in King's County, L.I. 1675.
... State of the province of New York. 1738.
... Reasons in support of triennial elections in the province of New York ... 1738.
... Journals of Sir Wm. Johnson's scouts. 1755, 1756.
... Papers relating principally to the conversion and civilization of the Six nations of Indians ... 1642 - 1776.
... Fort Stanwix. Capt. Green's observations on a plan of a fort ordered to be built at the Oneida carrying place.
... Controversy between New York and New Hampshire, respecting the territory now the state of Vermont.
... Memoir of the Hon. James De Lancey, lieutenant governor of the province of New York.
... Memoir of the Hon. James Duane, judge of the District court of the U.S. for New York.
... Proclamation of the last of the royal governors of New-York.
... A memorial concerning the Iroquois or Five confederate nations of Indians in the province of New-York ... By Rev. Charles Inglis ...
Great seals of New Netherland and New-York.

DOCUMENTARY history of the state of New-York, The; arranged under direction of the Hon. Christopher Morgan ... By E. B. O'Callaghan ... Albany, Weed, Parsons, 1850 - 51. 4 v. fronts., plates (part fold.) ports. (2 fold.) fold. maps, plans (part fold.) 28½ x 23 cm. 1-15833.
F122.D 64

DOCUMENTS relative to the colonial history of the state of New-York ... Albany, Weed, Parsons, print., 1853 - 87. 15 v. fronts., port., fold. maps, fold. plans, facsim. 30 x 24½ cm. No more pub. Contents. - v. 1-10. Documents relating to the colonial history of the state of New-York; procured in Holland, England and France: v. 1-2, Holland. v. 3-8. London. v. 9-10. Paris. v. 11. General index to the documents. v. 12. Documents rel. to the history of the Dutch and Swedish settlements on the Delaware River. - v. 13. Documents rel. to the history and settlements of the towns along the Hudson and Mohawk rivers (with the exception of Albany) from

NEW YORK

1630-1684. - v.14. Documents rel. to the history of the early colonial settlements principally on Long Island. - v.15. New York state archives (v.1) New York in the revolution. 1-22114*-M 1 Cancel.

F122.D 66

DOCUMENTS relative to the colonial history of the state of New York ... Report of the Select committee, on so much of the governor's message as relates to the colonial history of the state ... (Albany, 1844) 11 p. 25½ cm. (Legislature. 1844. Senate. Doc. no. 42) CA 10-791 Unrev.

F122.D 67

DOCUMENTS relative to the colonial history of the state of New York ... Report of the Select committee on the colonial agency ... (Albany, 1845) 11 p. 25½ cm. (Legislature. 1844. Senate. Doc. no. 42) CA 10-791 Unrev.

F122.D672

DANAHER, Franklin Martin. An address before the Dongan club, of Albany, N.Y., ... 1889. Albany, The Dongan club, 1889. 55 p. 26½ cm. 7-21678.

F122.D 68

DONGAN, Colonel Thomas, governor of New York. By Edward Channing. (From American antiquarian soc., Worcester. Mass. Proceedings. 1907. v. 18. 12-6376.

F122.D 69

DONGAN. Colonial Governor, Thomas Dongan of New York. By Joseph G. Hopkins. Illus. by William Wilson. New York, P. J. Kenedy (1957) 184 p. illus. 22 cm. (American background books, 2) 57-5758.

F122.D694

DONGAN. ... Thomas Dongan, governor of New York (1682-1688) ... by John H. Kennedy ... Washington, D.C., 1930. ix, 131 p. 22½ cm. (The Catholic university of America. Studies in American church history, vol. ix) Thesis (PH.D.) - Catholic university of America, 1930. Bibliography: p. 121-128. 30-15558.

F122.D695

DONGAN. Thomas Dongan, colonial governor of New York, 1683 - 1688, by Rev. Thomas P. Phelan .. New York, P. J. Kenedy (1933) xv, 154 p. front. (port.) 22½ cm. Bibliography: p. 149-150. 33-36983.

F122.D697

DREYER. Andreas Dreyer (Andries Draeyer) (Grand Forks, N.D., 1924) (21) - 29. 25½ cm. Reprinted from "Scandinavia", Grand Forks, N.D. vol. I. no. 3. March. 1924. First pub. in New York genealogical and biographical record. v. 51. 24-30832.

F122.D 75

EARLE, Alice (Morse) Colonial days in old New York. New York, C. Scribner's sons, 1896. 5, 312 p. 19 cm. 1-15834 rev.

F122.E 12

— Port Washington, N.Y., I.J. Friedman, 1962. 312 p. 21 cm. (Empire State historical publications, 16) 62-20152.

F122.E 12
1962

— Detroit, Singing Tree Press, 1968. 312 p. 20 cm. 68-21767.

F122.E 12
1968

FALCKNER. Justus Falckner, mystic and scholar, devout Pietist in Germany, hermit on the Wissahickon, missionary on the Hudson .... by Julius Freidrich Sachse ... Philadelphia, Printed for the author, 1903. iii, 141 p. front., illus., pl., port., facsim. 25½ cm. 3-9358.

F122.F 17

FORSYTH, Mary Isabella. The beginnings of New York; Old Kingston, the first state capital. Boston, R. G. Badger, 1909. 67, (2) p. 18½ cm. "Old Kingston, the first state capital." reprinted from New England magazine. 9-30185.

F122.F 73

FOX, Dixon Ryan. Yankees and Yorkers ... New York, University press; London, H. Milford, Oxford university press, 1940. x, 237 p. fold. map. 24 cm. (Anson G. Pehlps lectureship on early American history, New York university) 40-13441.

F122.F 78

— Port Washington, N.Y. I.J. Friedman (1963) 237 p. 22 cm. Empire State historical publications, 25. 63-15126.

F122.F 78
1963

GHÉLIN, Edg de. Aux Wallons qui fondèrent New-York. Éphémérides pour le troisième centennaire,

2. tirage. Mons, J. Gondry, 1924.   2, (3) - 8 p. 25½ cm. 25-2939.   F122. G 4

GOEBEL, Julius. Some legal and political aspects of the manors of New York, address ... 1928.
F122.G 63

GOODNOUGH, David. The colony of New York.   F122.G647

GOODWIN, Mrs. Maud (Wilder) Dutch and English on the Hudson; a chronicle of colonial New York. New Haven, Yale university press; (etc., etc.) 1919.   x, 213 p. front., plates, ports., fold. map. 21 cm. (The chronicles of America series ... v. 7)   Bibliographical note: p. 231-233.   19-3163.
F122.G 65

— New Haven, Yale university press, 1921.   ix, 243 p. 22-12129.   F122.G 66

GRANT, Anne (Macvicar) Memoirs of an American lady; with sketches of manners and scenery in America, as they existed previous to the revolution. London, Printed for Longman, Hurst, Rees, and Orme, 1808; New York, Research Reprints (1970)   2 v. 21 cm. 76-124799.
F122. G 7
1970

— With unpublished letters and a memoir of Mrs. Grant by James Grant Wilson. Freeport, N.Y., Books for Libraries Press (1972)   xxxviii, 307, 300 p. illus. 23 cm. List of author's works: p. 287-288 (3d group) 77-38354 MARC.
F122. G 7
1972

GT. BRITAIN. Laws, statutes, etc. ... (An act for reversing the attainder of Jacob Leisler and others) London ... 1695.   4 p. 28½ cm. 10-31407.
F122.G 78
Rare Book Coll.

GREEN, Lucy Garrison. The De Forests and the Walloon founding of New Amsterdam ... (New York, The Gilliss press, 1924.)   xiv, 80 p. 23 cm. Thesis (M.A.) - University of Nebraska. 1916. Bibliography: p. vii-viii. 24-12210.
F122.G 79

(HAWKS, Francis Lister) History of the United States: no. II; or, Uncle Philip's conversations with the children about New-York ... New York, Harper & bros., 1855.   2 v. fronts., plates. 16 cm. (Boy's and girl's library xxiii-xxiv) 1-15335.
F122.H 39

HEATHCOTE. Caleb Heathcote, gentleman colonist; the story of a career in the province of New York, 1692 - 1721. By Dixon Ryan Fox. New York, C. Scribner's sons, 1926.
viii, 301 p. front. (port.) 21 cm. 26-8875.
F122.H43

— New York, Cooper Square Publishers, 1971.   viii, 301 p. port. 22 cm. Includes bibliographical references.
74-164523.
F122.H43F6
1971

HISTORICAL records survey. Transcriptions of early county records of New York state. Prepared by the New York State Historical records survey project, Division of professional and service projects, W.P.A. ... Albany, N.Y., The Historical records survey, 1939 -   v. 27½ cm. Mimeographed.
40-26220.
F122.H 57

(IZARD, Ralph) An account of a journey to Niagara, Montreal and Quebec, in 1765; or, " 'Tis eighty years since." New York, Print. W. Osborn, 1846.   30 p. 23 cm. 17-23203.
F122. I 98
Toner coll.

JARAY, Cornell, comp. Historic chronicles of New Amsterdam, Colonial New York and early Long Island. Port Washington, N.Y., Friedman (1968)   2 v. plans. 23 cm. (Empire State historical publications series. no. 35) 68-18355.
F122. J 6

JOGUES. Isaac Jogues, discoverer of Lake George, by T. J. Campbell. New York, The American press, 1911.   4, 7-55 p. front., plates, ports. 24 cm. 11-8579.
F122. J 65

NEW YORK

JOHNSON. ... Calendar of the Sir William Johnson manuscripts in the New York state library; compiled by Richard E. Day ... Albany, University of the state of New York, 1909. 683 p. 22½ cm. (Bulletin. History. no. 8) 10-200 Rev.
F122. J 69

KATZ, Stanley Nider. Newcastle's New York; Anglo-American politics, 1732 - 1753. Cambridge, Mass., Belknap Press of Harvard University Press, 1968. xi. 285 p. 25 cm. 68-14261.
F122. K 3

(KENNEDY, Archibald) supposed author. A speech said to have been delivered sometime before the close of the last sessions ... (New York) 1755. (Boston, 1938) 1 v. (Photostat Americana. 2d series no. 70)
F122. K 47
Rare Book Coll.

LANE, Arthur Willis. Military policy in colonial New York, 1691 - 1763. Washington, 1950. 144 l. 28 cm. Thesis (M.A.) - Georgetown University. Includes bibliography. 52-32558.
F122. L 3

LEDER, Lawrence H. Robert Livingston, 1654 - 1728 and the politics of colonial New York. Chapel Hill, Pub. for the Institute of Early American History and Culture at Williamsburg, Va., by the University of North Carolina Press (1961) xii. 306 p. 24 cm.
F122. L 43

LEISLER. ... Kämpfer auf fremdem boden, Jakob Leisler. By Hans Friedrich Blunck. Munchen, Zinnen-verlag (1944) 77 p. illus. (port.) 19 cm. 46-18561.
F122. L5B55

LETTER From a Gentleman in New-York, to his Friend in London. (New-York, J. P. Zenger, 1733) (Boston, 1928) facsim. 22 cm. (Americana series: photostat reproductions by the Mass. hist. soc. no. 217) CA 28-1032 Unrev.
F122. L636
Rare Book Coll.

LETTER From A Gentleman of the City of New-York To Another, Concerning the Troubles which happen'd in That Province in the Time of the late Happy Revolution. Printed and Sold by William Bradford ... Boston, 1698. (Boston, 1923) facsim. 24 numb. l. 23 cm. (Americana series; photostat by the Mass. hist. soc. no. 92. 23-18981.
F122. L 64
Rare Book Coll.

LETTER to the freemen and freeholders of the province of New-York, relating to the approaching election of their representatives ... New York, 1750. 12 p. 19½ cm. 9-20813.
F122. L 65
Rare Book Coll.

LIVINGSTON, John Henry. The minor manors of New York; address prepared for the New York branch of the Order of colonial lords of manors in America, (n. p.) 1923. 31 p. incl. illus., pl. 24 cm. (Publications. no. 12) 23-12562 Rev.
F122. L 76

LIVINGSTON, William. A brief consideration of New York with respect to its natural advantages, its superiority in several instances over some of the neighboring colonies. Reprinted from the Independent reflector, 1753; ed. by Earl Gregg Swem ... Metuchen, N.J., Print. for C. F. Heartman, 1925. 2. v, 24 p. 23 cm. (Heartman's historical series, no. 39) 41 copies printed. 25-18694.
F122. L776

(LIVINGSTON, William) A soliloquy ... 2d ed. (Philadelphia?) Printed (by J. Dunlap?) in the year 1770. 15 p. 22 cm. An anonymous satire on Lieut-Gov. Colden of N. Y. Incorrectly attributed to William Goddard. 7-21584.
F122. L 78
Rare Book Coll.

LOYALTY vindicated from the reflections of a virulent pamphlet called (A letter from a gentleman of New-York, concerning the troubles which happened in that province, etc.) ... (Boston, Printed by Bartholomew Green and John Allen, 1698. Boston, 1920) facsim. 28 numb. l. 26 cm. (Americana series; photostat by the Massachusetts hist. soc. no. 7) 20-15576.
F122. L 92

MACGREGORIE. Major Patrick MacGregorie. By Adelaide Skeel and David Barclay. (From Historical soc. of Newburgh Bay and the Highlands. Historical papers. 1900. no. 6) 8-18967.
F122. M 14

McSPADDEN, Joseph Walker. New York, a romantic story for young people ... illus. by Howard L. Hastings. New York, J. H. Sears (1926)   128 p. incl. illus., plates, col. front. 21 cm. (Romantic stories of the state)
26-13711.
                                                    F122. M 2

MAKEMIE, Francis. A narrative of a new and unusual American imprisonment of two Presbyterian ministers: and prosecution of Mr. Francis Makemie one of them, for preaching one sermon at the city of New-York. (Boston?) Printed for the publisher, 1707.   2. 47 p. 19½ x 15 cm. 6-16543.
                                          F122. M 23
                                         Rare Book Coll.

— New-York, Re-printed and sold by H. Gaine, 1755.   6. 52 p. 19½ cm. 6-16542.
                                         F122. M 24
                                        Rare Book Coll.

— (Reprint. From Force Tracts ... Washington, 1836 - 46. v. 4, no. 4)   4-27244.
                                        F122. M 25

MARK, Irving. Agrarian conflicts in colonial New York, 1711 - 1775. New York, Columbia university press; London, P. S. King, 1940.   237 p. (Studies in history, economics and public law, ed. by the Faculty of political science of Columbia university. no. 409) Bibliography: p. 207-221. 40-33047.
                                        F122. M 36

— New York, 1940.   2. 7-237 p. 22½ cm. Thesis (PH. D.) - Columbia university. 40-35492. F122.M362

— With a new introd. by Ralph Adams Brown.   2d ed.   Port Washington, N.Y., I. J. Friedman (1965)
237 p. 22 cm. (Empire State historical publication, 33) 64-8792.   F122.M363

MILLER, John. A description of the province and city of New York; with plans of the city and several forts as they existed in the year 1695. London, T. Rodd, 1843.   2. (5) - 43 p. 21 - 115 p. 6 fold. plans. 22 cm. Imperfect: p. 113- (116) wanting. 1-16073.
                                        F122. M 64

— A new ed. with an introd. and ... notes. By John Gilmary Shea ... New York, W. Gowans, 1862. 127 p. incl. plans. 25 cm. (Gowans' bibliotheca americana. 3) 1-15779 Add.   F122. M 65

MILLER, John. New York considered and improved, 1695; pub. from the original ms. in the British museum; with introd. and notes by Victor Hugo Paltsits ... Cleveland, The Burrows brothers, 1903. 135 p. 6 fold. facsim. 23½ cm. 3-22577.
                                        F122. M 66

— New York, B. Franklin (1970)   135 p. 5 facsims. (2 fold.) 23 cm. 73-114816.
                                       F122. M 66
                                        1970

MODEST and Impartial narrative Of several Grievances and Great Oppressions That the ... Inhabitants of ... New-York in America Lye Under, By the Extravagant and Arbitrary Proceedings of Jacob Leysler and his Accomplices. Printed at New-York, and Re-printed at London, 1690.   (Boston, 1927)   facsim. 26 p. 26 cm. (Americana series; photostat by the Mass. hist. soc. no. 190) CA 27-607 Unrev.
                                        F122. M 69
                                       Rare Book Coll.

MONTAGUE, John. Arguments offer'd to the Right Honourable the Lords commissioners for trade and plantations relating to some acts of Assembly past at New-York in America. (New York) Printed (by) William Bradford ... 1701.   23 p. 22 x 18½ cm. Photocopy (positive) of p. 23 inserted; original page mutilated. 46-40572.
                                        F122. M 73
                                       1701
                                      Rare Book Coll.

MONTANUS, Arnoldus. ... Description of New Netherland. 1671. Tr. from De Nieuwe en on-bekende weereld ... Amsterdam, 1671.   (From the documentary history of the state of New-York ... v. 4)
7-34369.
                                        F122. M 76

NEW YORK

MURRAY, James. Letter of James Murray of New York to Rev. Baptist Boyd of county Tyrone, Ireland, reprinted from the Pennsylvania gazette, Oct. 27, 1737. Ed. by Earl Gregg Swem ... Metuchen, N.J., Printed for C. F. Heartman, 1925.   2. ii. 7 p.   23½ cm.   (Heartman's historical series, no. 40) 41 copies printed. 25-18693.
F122. M 96

NARATIVE of the treatment of Coll. Bayard received from the time that sentence was passed against him ... (New York, 1702) (Boston, 1940)   facsim. 6 p.   38½ cm.   (Photostat American. Second series ... Photostated at the Mass. hist. soc.   No. 102) 41-23128 Rev.
F122. N 3
1702a
Rare Book Coll.

NELLIS, Milo. The Mohawk Dutch and the Palatines; their background and their influence in the development of the United States of America. St. Johnsville, N.Y. (1951)   90 p.   illus., map.   23 cm. Includes bibliographical references.   51-1034.
F122. N 36

NEW YORK (Colony) Calendar of New York colonial commissions, 1680 - 1770; abstracted by the late Edmund B. O'Callaghan ... New York, The New-York historical soc., 1929.   2. 108 p.   24½ cm. (N.Y. hist. soc. ... Jones fund series of histories and memoirs. vii) Repr. from N.Y. hist. soc. Quarterly bulletin.   30-24149.
F122. N526

NEW YORK (Colony) ... Civil list of the province of New-York, 1693. A list of all the officers employed in civill offices in the province of New-Yorke in America the 20th of Aprill 1693, and of their sallaries. (Lond. doc. ix)   (From The documentary history of the state of N.Y. v. 1)   8-27640.
F122. N528

NEW YORK (Colony) ... Colonial records. General entries, v. 1. 1664 - 65. Transcr. from mss in the State library. Albany, University of the state of New York, 1899.   (53) - 204 p.   25 cm.   State library bulletin; history, no. 2. 1899.   7-13713.
F122. N 53

NEW YORK (Colony) Minutes of the Executive council of the province of New York ... vol. I - Ed. by Victor Hugo Paltsits, state historian. Albany, State of New York, 1910 -   v.   front. (port.) facsims. (incl. fold. map)   28 cm. Fold. map in pocket at end.   11-33013.
F122. N5345

NEW YORK (Colony) ... Calendar of Council minutes 1668 - 1783 ... Albany, University of the state of New York, 1902.   720 p.   25 cm.   (... New York. State library. Bulletin 58, March. 1902. History 6 ...)   4-11579 Rev.
F122. N535

NEW YORK (Colony) To all whom these presents may concern.   Print. William Bradford ... New York, 1713.   8 p.   32½ x 19½ cm.   The case of the royal governor in his disputes with the Assembly. 6-24676 Rev.
F122. N 54
Rare Book Coll.

NEW YORK colonial tracts. Albany, N.Y., J. Munsell, 1866-72.   4 v.   col. front.   21 cm.   Vols. 1-3 edition 100 copies. Contents. - v. 1. Journal of the voyage of the sloop Mary. from Quebec. together with an account of her wreck off Montauk Point, L.I., 1701. - v. 2. Voyage of George Clarke. esq. to America ... - v. 3. Voyages of the slavers St. John and Arms of Amsterdam. 1659, 1663, together with additional papers illustrative of the slave trade under the Dutch. Tr. from the original manuscripts... - v. 4. Letters of Isaac Bobin, esq., private secretary of Hon. George Clarke. secretary of the province of New York, 1718-1730.   1-15803.
F122. N 56
Microfilm 24336 F

NEW YORK (State) Comptroller's office. List of patents of lands, etc. to be sold in Jan., 1822. For arrears of quit rent. Albany, Print, E. and E. Hosford (1820?) (Philadelphia, 1937)   facsim. (iv. (2), 35 p.) 116 l.   28½ cm.   39-2087.
F122. N565

NEW YORK (State) Division of Archives and History. Champlain and the French in New York ... Albany, University of the State of New York, 1959.   56 p.   23 cm.   A60-9220.
F122. N567

NEW YORK (State) Secretary of state. Calendar of historical manuscripts in the office of the secretary of state, Albany, N.Y. Ed. by E. B. O'Callaghan. Albany, Weed, Parsons, printers, 1865-66. 2 v.   28½ cm. Paged continuously. v. 1. Dutch mansuscripts, 1630-34. - v. 2. English manuscripts. 1664-1776.   1-15839.
F122. N 57

NEW YORK (State) State historian. Annual report. (1st) - 3d. (1895/96) - 1897. Transmitted to the Legislature March 3, 1896 - March 14, 1898. Albany and New York, Wynkoop, Hallenbeck Crawford co., 1896-98.   3 v. col. front., plates (part fold.) ports., maps (part fold.) plans (part fold.) 23½ cm. 19-4302.
F122.
F116.N 26

NEW YORK historical society. Commemoration of the conquest of New Netherland, on its 200th anniversary. New York, The Society, 1864.   87 p. front. (double map) ports. 27½ cm. 1-15840.
F122.N 63 or 64

NURENBERG, Thelma. The New York colony. (New York) Crowell-Collier Press (1969) 136 p. illus. 24 cm. "1st printing." 77-77966.
F122.N 87

PAPERS relating to an Act of the Assembly of the province of New-York, for encouragement of the Indian trade, etc. and for prohibiting the selling of Indian goods to the French. viz. of Canada. ... Pub. by authority. Print. and sold by William Bradford in the city of New-York, 1724. (Boston, 1938)   facsim: 24 p. fold. map. 35 cm. (Photostat Americana. Second series ... Photostated at the Mass. hist. soc. no. 55) 38-11232.
F122. P 36
Rare Book Coll.

PENNYPACKER, Morton. The Duke's laws: their antecendents, implications and importance ... New York, N.Y., New York university School of law, 1944.   64 p. illus. (incl. port., plan) 25½ cm. (Anglo-American legal history series. Ser. 1, no. 9) 45-7482.
F122. P 45

PHILLIPS, Mary Schuyler. Colonial New York ... (Cincinnati, The Ebbert & Richardson co., 1916) 47 p. 23 cm. (The Colonial dames of America in the state of Ohio. Studies in the colonial period for use in the public schools) 16-14694.
F122. P 55

REASONS in support of triennial elections in the province of New York: with the king's veto on the Triennial act. 1738.   From the documentary history of the state of New-York, v. 4) 7-34372.
F122. R 28

REICH, Jerome R. Leisler's Rebellion; a study of democracy in New York, 1664 - 1720. (Chicago) University of Chicago Press (1953)   ix, 194 p. 24 cm. Bibliography: p. 188-192. 53-10910.
F122. R 3

SATTERLEE, Herbert Livingston. The political history of the province of New York ... New York, J. F. Pearson, printer, 1885.   107 p. 23½ cm. "Authorities": p. (106) - 107. Thesis (PH. D.) Columbia university. 3-18626.
F122. S 25

SCHUYLER, George Washington. Colonial New York: Philip Schuyler and his family ... New York, C. Scribner's sons, 1885.   2 v. 22 cm. 3-5265.
F122. S 39

SEVERENCE, Frank Hayward. Western New York under the French; an address delivered before the Morgan Chapter in Memorial Art Gallery, University Campus, Rochester, N.Y. ... 1919. Rochester, Lewis H. Morgan Chapter, 1920.   (23) - 40 p. map. 26 cm. (Researches and transactions of the New York State Archeological Association, Lewis H. Morgan Chapter, v. 2, no. 2) 51-47807.
F122. S 45

SMITH, Richard. A tour of four great rivers: the Hudson, Mohawk, Susquehanna and Delaware in 1769; being the journal of Richard Smith of Burlington, New Jersey; ed., with a short history of the pioneer settlements, by Francis W. Halsey ... New York, C. Scribner's sons, 1906.   2, vii-x p., xiii-lxxiii, 102 p. front., illus., plates, ports., maps, facsim. 24½ cm. 6-32121.
F122. S 63

— Port Washington, N.Y., I. J. Friedman (1964)   lxxiii, 102 p. 22 cm. (Empire State historical publication 30) 63-22216.
F122. S 63
1964

SMITH, William. Historical memoirs of William Smith, historian of the Province of New York, member of the Governor's Council and last chief justice of that Province under the Crown, etc. Ed. with an introd., biography, and notes, by William H. W. Sabine, from the previously unpublished ms. in the

NEW YORK

New York Public Library. New York, 1956 - 58. 2 v. port., maps, facsims. 29 cm. Includes bibliographies.
Contents. - 1. 1763-1776. - 2. 1776 to 1778. 56-1157 rev.
 F122.S638

SMITH, William. The history of the province of New-York, from the first discovery to the year M. DCC. XXXII. To which is annexed, a description of the country, with a short account of the inhabitants, their trade, religious and political state, and the constitution of the courts of justice in that colony ... London, Printed for T. Wilcox, 1757. xii, 255 p. fold. front. 25½ x 20 cm. Original ed. 1-15842.
 F122. S 64
 Rare Book Coll.

SMITH, William. Historical memoirs ... of William Smith. Ed. by William H. W. Sabine. (New York) New York Times (1969) xvi, 300, xxviii, 457 p. 24 cm. (Eyewitness accounts of the American Revolution)
Originally pub. in 1956-58 under title: Historical memoirs of William Smith. Includes bibliographies. 70-81077 MARC.
 F122. S 64
 1969

SMITH, William. The history of the Province of New-York. Ed. by Michael Kammen. Cambridge, Mass., Belknap Press of Harvard University Press, 1972. 2 v. illus. 24 cm. (The John Harvard library)
Includes bibliographical references. 78-160028 MARC.
 F122. S 64
 1972

SMITH, William. The history of the province of New-York, from the first discovery. To which is annexed a description of the country, etc. London, Printed for J. Almon, 1776. viii, 334 p. 21½ cm.
1-15843.
 F122. S 65
 Jefferson coll.

— 2d ed. Philadelphia: From the press of Mathew Carey, M. DCC. XCII. 276 p. 20½ cm.
First ed. was London, T. Wilcox, 1757. This is really the 3d ed. as there was an ed. with imprint London, J. Almon, 1776. 1-15844.
 F122. S 66
 Rare Book Coll.

SMITH, William The loyal Whig: William Smith of New York & Quebec (by) Leslie Francis Stokes Upton. (Toronto) University of Toronto Press (1969) ix, 250 p.
 F122.S66U6

SMITH, William. History of New-York, from the first discovery to the year M. DCC. XXXII ... With a continuation, from the year 1732, to the commencement of the year 1814. Albany: Print. Ryer Schermerhorn ... 1814. xv, (17) - 511 p. 21½ cm. The continuation covers the period from 1732 to 1747, the events of 1748-1814 being merely summarized. 1-15845.
 F122. S 67

SMITH, W. The history of the late province of New York. 1829. 2 v.
 F122. S 68

— New York, Pub. under the direction of the New-York hist. soc., 1830. 2 v. 21½ cm. 1-15849.
 F122. S 69

SMITH, William. Histoire de la Nouvelle-York, depuis la découverte de cette province jusqu'a notre siécle ... Londres, 1767. 2, (vii) - xvi. 415 p. 16½ cm. 1-15850.
 F122. S 73
 Rare Book Coll.

SPENCER, Charles Worthen. Phases of royal government in New York 1691 - 1719 ... Columbus, O., Press of F. J. Heer, 1905. 156 p. 23 cm. These (PH. D.) Columbia university. "Bibliographical note": p. 156. 6-4955.
 F122. S 78

UNDERHILL. Captain John Underhill, gent., soldier of fortune, by L. Effingham De Forest ... New York, The De Forest pub. co., 1934. 2, 104 p. 30 cm. Bibliography: p. (91) - 97. 34-38346.
 F122.U676
 Rare Book Coll.

UNDERHILL. John Underhill, captain of New England and New Netherland, by Henry C. Shelley ... New York, London, D. Appleton, 1932. xii, 473 p. front., plates, ports., facsims., coat of arms. 24½ cm.
32-11428.
 F122. U 68

VAN WYCK, Frederick. Select patents of New York towns. ... Boston, A. A. Beauchamp, 1938.
xlvii, 180 p. front., plates, ports. 24 cm. Includes bibliographies. 38-6748.
F122.V314

— Boston, A. A. Beauchamp, 1938.   xlvii, 190 p.   plates, ports., etc. 39-1414.
F122.V315

— Boston, A. A. Beauchamp, 1938.   xvii, 120 p. front., ports. 24 cm. 38-3223.
F122.V 32

VOLWILER, Albert Tangeman. George Croghan and the development of central New York, 1763-1800 (by) Albert T. Volwiler. (Albany) 1923.   p. 21-40, 21½ cm. "Reprint from the Quarterly journal of the New York state historical assoc. for Jan. 1923." 24-14360.
F122.V 94

WAKEMAN, Abram. The great highway, a world's war path; synopsis of essential events occurring chiefly enroute between Albany, Lake George and Lake Champlain. (New York city, 1927)
36 p. illus. (incl. map) 24 cm. 27-24710.
F122.W 15

WATTS, J. Letter book of John Watts ... 1928.   1 v.
F122.W 35

WOLLEY, Charles. A two years journal in New York, and part of its territories in America. A new ed., with an introd. and copious historical notes by E. B. O'Callaghan ... New York, W. Gowans, 1860.
97 p. incl. facsim. 25 cm. (Gowan's bibliotheca americana. 2) 2-1872.
F122.W 86

— With an introd. and notes by Edward Gaylord Bourne ... Cleveland, The Burrows bros. co., 1902.
75 p. incl. facsim. 23½ cm. 2-23619.
F122.W 87

WRAXALL. Biographical notice of Peter Wraxall, secretary of Indian affairs for the province of New York ... By Daniel J. Pratt. (Albany, 1870)   6 p. 24½ cm. "Communicated to the Albany institute ... "
18-8366.
F122.W 94

(YOUNG, Thomas) Some reflections on the disputes between New-York, New-Hampshire, and Col. John Henry Lydius of Albany ... New Haven: Printed and sold by Benjamin Mecom. 1764.
21 p. 20½ cm. 3-19759 Rev.
F122.Y 76
Rare Book Coll.

NEW NETHERLANDS. DUTCH COLONY, 1610 - 1664.

ALGEMEN handelsblad. ... Tercentenary supplement ... (Amsterdam, 1926)   16 p. illus. 46 cm.
F122.1.A39

ALPHEN, Daniëll François van. Dissertatio historico politica de Novo Belgio, colonia quondam nostratium ... Lugduni-Batavorum, C. C. can der Hoek, 1838.   4, 37 (3) p. 21½ cm. 1-15852.
F122.1.A45

AMSTERDAM. Burgemeester. Conditien, die door de heeren burgermeesteren der stadt Amstelredam ... t'Amsterdam, By J. Banning, 1656.   (14) p. 19 x 14½ cm. For a translation of this document see O'Callaghan, History of New Netherland, 1846-48. v.2, p. 328-333. 2-9558.
F122.1.A52
Rare Book Coll.

— t'Amsterdam, By de weduwe van J. Banning, 1659.   (14) p. 20 x 15 cm. Differs from the edition of 1656 in the changes made in the conditions. cf. Asher, Bibliog. essay, 1854-67, p. 202-205. 2-9559.
F122.1.A53
Rare Book Coll.

ARNOUX, William Henry. The Dutch in America. A historical argument ... New York, Priv. print., 1890.   54 p. 28½ x 21 cm. 2-8495.
F122.1.A76

BALBIAN VERSTER, Jan Francois Leopold de. Holland-America; an historical account of shipping and and other relations between Holland and North America ... Amsterdam, B. Houthakker (1921)
3-62 p. illus. (incl. maps, ports.)   32 cm. Published by the Holland America line. Relates principally to the colony of New Netherland. Includes a short history of the Holland-America line. 22-14884 Rev.
F122.1.B15

NEW YORK

BANTA, Theodore Melvin. Passengers to New Netherland, 1654 to 1664. From the copyrighted Year book of the Holland soc. of New York, for 1902. (New York, 1902) 37 p. 28½ cm. 17-19472.
F122.1.B 2

BEEKMAN, James William. An address delivered before the Saint Nicholas soc. of the city of New York ... 1869. (Albany) Pub. by the Society, 1870) 36 p. 26½ cm. On cover: Founders of New York. 1-15853.
F122.1.B 41

BEVERWYCK, N.Y. Minutes of the court of Fort Orange and Beverwyck, 1652- 16(60) tr. and ed. by A. J. F. van Laer, archivist, Division of archives and history. Albany, University of the state of New York, 1920-23. 2 v. facsims. 22½ cm. The records of the court for the period between Dec. 30, 1660 and Sept. 3/13, 1668 ... are missing. For minutes of the court beginning Sept. 3/13, 1668 cf. F122.A36.
F122.1.B 57

BREEDEN-RAEDT aende Vereenichde Nederlandsche provintien. Gelreland. Holland. Zeeland. Wtecht. Vriesland. Over-Yssel. Groeningen. ... Tot Antwerpen, Ghedruet by Francoys van Duynen, boeckverkooper by de Beurs in Erasmus, 1649. (46) p. 19½ cm. 1-15854.
F122.1.B 82
Rare Book Coll.

EXTRACTS from a work called Breeden raedt aen de Vereenighde Nederlandsche provintien. ... Tr. from the Dutch original by Mr. C. Amsterdam, F. Muller, 1850. (From documentary history of the state of New York v. 4) 7-34836.
F122.1.B 84

BRODHEAD, John Romeyn, comp. Transcripts of documents in the royal archives at the Hague and in the stad-huys of the city of Amsterdam. Holland documents: I-XVI; 1603-1678. (Albany, Weed, Parsons, 1856-1858) 1 v. fronts. fold. maps.
F122.1.B 87

CONDON, Thomas J. New York beginnings; the commercial origins of New Netherland. New York, New York University Press, 1968. ix, 204 p. illus., maps. 24 cm. 68-28003.
F122.1.C 6

CURLER. Arendt van Curler, first superintendent of Rensselaerwick, founder of Schenectady and the Dutch policy of peace with the Iriquois (!) By Wm. Elliot Griffis. A paper read before the Albany institute ... 1884. (Albany, 1887?) 12 p. 23½ cm. Reprinted from Transactions of the Albany institue, 1887, vol. xi, p. 169-180. 4-36322.
F122.1.C97

DILLIARD, Maud Esther. An album of New Netherland. With a foreword by V. Isabelle Miller. New York, Twayne Publisher (1963) 125 p. 32 cm. 63-9904.
F122.1.D55

DONCK, Adriaen van der. Beschryvinge van Nieuw-Nederlant, (ghelijck het tegenwoordigh in staet is) begrijpende de nature, aert, gelegentheyt en vrucht-baerheyt van het selve lant .... t'Aemsteldam, By Evert Nieuwenhof, boeck-verkooper ... 1655. 4, 100 p. illus. 20 x 15½ cm. 1-15855.
F122.1.D65

— 1656. 4, 100, (12) p. fold. map. 19½ x 15 cm. 1-15856.
F122.1.D66
Rare Book Coll.

DONCK, Adriaen van der. A description of the New Netherlands. Ed. with an introd. by Thomas F. O'Donnell. (1st ed. Syracuse) Syracuse University Press (1968) xl, x, 142 p. 24 cm. A reprint of the first English translation ... pub. in the collections of the New York Historical Society. 2d ser. v. 1 (1841) p. (125) - 242. 68-29420.
F122.1.D6613
1968

(DONCK, Adriaen van der) Vertoogh van Nieu-Neder-Land, weghens de gheleghentheydt, vruchtbaerheydt, en soberen staet desselfs. In 's Graven-Hago, Ghedruckt by M. Stael, 1650. 49 p. 19½ cm. 1-22223.
F122.1.D69
Rare Book Coll.

(DONCK, Adriaen van der) Vertoogh van Nieu Nederland; and Breeden raedt aende Vereenichde Nederlandsche provintien. Two rare tracts, printed in 1649-'50. Relating to the administration of affairs in New Netherland. Trans from the Dutch by Henry C. Murphy. New York (Baker, Godwin, printers) 1854. viii, 190 p. double map. 30 x 23 cm. 1-22224.
F122.1.D70
Rare Book Coll.

(DONCK, Adriaen van der) Remonstrance of New Netherland, and the occurrences there. Addressed to the High and Mighty States general of the United Netherlands ... 1649. With Secretary Van Tienhoven's answer. Tr. from a copy of the original Dutch ms., by E. B. O'Callaghan. Albany, Weed, Parsons, 1856.   2. iii. (7) - 65 p.   29 ½ x 23 ½ cm.   1-15859.

                                      F122.1.D71

(DONCK, Adriaen van der) The representation of New Netherland, concerning its location, productiveness and poor condition. ... printed at the Hague in 1650, tr. from the Dutch for the New York historical soc., with notes, by Henry C. Murphy. New York, Bartlett & Welford, 1849.   88 p.   22 ½ cm.   1-15860.

                                      F122.1.D72

DONCK. Adriaen van der Donck. An address delivered before the Westchester Co. historical soc.... by Thomas Astley Atkins, 1888. Yonkers, N.Y., The Statesman print, 1888.   26 p.   27 cm.   7-11165.

                                      F122.1.D73

DOWNING, Sir George. A Discourse written by Sr. George Downing. The King of Great Britain's Envoyee Extraordinary to the States of the United-Provinces. Vindicating His Royal Master from the Insolencies of a Scandalous Libel, etc. London, Printed by F. M. Domini, 1664. (Boston, 1926)   facsim: 2 p. 5-21 numb. 1.   24 ½ cm.   (Americana series: photostat by the Mass. hist. soc. no. 165)   27-732.

                                      F122.1.D76
                                      Rare Book Coll.

— Whereunto is added a relation of some former and later proceedings of the Hollanders: by a meaner hand. London, Printed for John Luttone ... 1672.   31, 139, (4) p.   16 cm.   42-47998.

                                      F122.1.D76
                                      1672
                                      Rare Book Coll.

ELTING, Irving. ... Dutch village communities on the Hudson River ... Baltimore, N. Murray, 1886.   68 p.   25 cm.   (Johns Hopkins university studies in historical and political science. 4th ser. 1)   1-22103.   F122.1.E51

EVERTSEN, Cornelis. De Zeeuwsche expeditie naar de West onder Cornelis Evertsen den jonge, 1672-1674, Nieuw Nederland een jaar onder Nederlandsch bestuur; uitgegeven door C. de Waard, met 7 platen en kaarten. 's-Gravenhage, M. Nijhoff, 1928.   1xix, 237 p.   2 pl., 2 port. (incl. front.) 3 fold. maps. 25 cm. "Aangehaalde werken": p. (205) - 208.   28-30672.

                                      F122.1.E93

GRIFFIS, William Elliot. The story of New Netherland, the Dutch in America ... Boston and New York, Houghton Mifflin, 1909.   xiv, 292 p.   front., plates (1 double) ports., facsims.   19 ½ cm.   "Authorities used in preparation of this volume": p. 279-281.   9-9529.

                                      F122.1.G85

HENRY E. HUNTINGTON library and art gallery, San Marino, Calif. Documents relating to New Netherland, 1624-1626, tr. and ed. by A. J. F. van Laer. 1924.   1 v. (The Henry E. Huntington library and art gallery ... Publications. Americana: folio series. no. 1)

                                      F122.1.H55

HOES, Roswell Randall. Original letter of Dominie Johannes Megapolensis, of Albany and New York. (From Old New York. N.Y., 1890) v. 2 p. (145) - 151)   14-4715.

                                      F122.1.H68

HOFFMAN, Charles Fenno. The pioneers of New-York. An anniversary discourse delivered before the St. Nicholas society of Manhattan ... 1847... New York, Stanford and Swords, 1848.   55 p.   20 ½ cm.   1-15862.

                                      F122.1.H69

HOLLAND society of New York. Holland society reception (Beaverwyck branch) Albany ... 1893, to the commander and officers of the Netherland's warship Van Speijk ... (Albany, Van Benthuysen print., 1893)   44 p.   front. (port.)   25 ½ cm.   17-1088.

                                      F122.1.H73

HUFFMAN, Miriam. Dutch colonial life in the New Netherland ... Des Moines, Ia., Blackhurst book co. (1943)   xiii pl. (incl. maps) in portfolio. 28 x 22 cm. (Instructive visual aids. Social science series) Bibliographical references included in introduction. 44-9250.

                                      F122.1.H 8

HOWELL, George Rogers. ... The date of the settlement of the colony of New York. By George

NEW YORK

Rogers Howell ... Albany, C. Van Benthuysen, 1897. 16 p. front. (fold. map) 23½ cm. (Publications of the New York society of the order of the Founders and patriots of America, no. 1) 2-12347.
F122.1.H85

(IRVING, Washington) A history of New York, from the beginning of the world to the end of the Dutch dynasty. Containing ... the unutterable pondering of Walter the Doubter, the disastrous projects of William the Testy, and the chivalric achievements of Peter the Headstrong, the three Dutch governors of New Amsterdam ... By Diedrich Knickerbocker (pseud.) New York, Inskeep & Bradford; Philadelphia, Bradford & Inskip (etc.) 1809. 2 v. fold. front. 18½ cm. 1st ed. 4-18970.
F122.1.I 70
Rare Book Coll.

— 1812. 2 v. fold. front. 18 cm. 43-40929.
F122.1.I 702
Rare Book Coll.

— A new ed. ... London, J. Murray, 1820. (v) - xxxii, (8), (33) - 520 p. 22 cm. 6-42754.
F122.1.J 704

— New ed. Glasgow, Printed for J. Wylie by R. Chapman, 1821. xxviii, 372 p. 20½ cm. 6-25793.
F122.1.I 705

— 4th Amer. ed. New-York, Printed by C. S. Van Winkle, 1824. 2 v. in 1. 18 cm. 6-13960.
F122.1.I 71

— London, Printed for R. Tegg, 1824. xxx, 368 p. 20 cm. Copy 2, with vignette and 3 additional plates by G. Cruikshank inserted.
F122.1.I 712
Rare Book Coll.

— London, J. Bumpus (etc.) 1825. xx, 340 p. front. 15½ cm. 2-3889.
F122.1.I 72

— London, R. Thurston, 1828. xx, (i. e. xxx), 312 p. 15½ cm. 16-16827.
F122.1.I 722

— 7th American ed. (v. 2) Philadelphia, Carey & Lea, 1832. (1) v. 20 cm.
F122.1.I 723

— A new ed. Philadelphia, Carey, Lea, & Blanchard, 1836. 2 v. 18½ cm. 6-34974 Rev.
F122.1.I725

— A new ed. Philadelphia, Carey, Lea & Blanchard, 1837. 2 v. 19 cm. (On cover: ... Works, 3-4) 3-20637 Rev.
F122.1.I 73

— New ed. Philadelphia, Lea & Blanchard, 1842. 2 v. 19 cm. 18-20091.
F122.1.I 733

— With illustrations by Felix O. C. Darley, engraved by eminent artists. New York, G. P. Putnam, 1850. xvi, (13) - 454 p. front., illus., plates (1 fold.) 22½ cm. 22-8330.
F122.1.I 74

— The author's rev. ed. ... (Knickerbocker ed.) Philadelphia, J. B. Lippincott, 1871. 528 p. front., plates. 19½ cm. 4-18965.
F122.1.I 78

— Author's rev. ed. ... Philadelphia, J. B. Lippincott, 1873. 582 p. illus. 16 cm. (On cover: Irving's works) Riverside edition. 34-21948.
F122.1.I 7813

— The author's rev. ed. New York, G. P. Putnam's Sons (1880) xii, 525 p. 20 cm. The Stratford edition. 49-40020*
F122.1.I 7817

— Author's rev. ed. ... With an essay on Irving's life and work by Charles Dudley Warner. New York, G. P. Putnam's sons (1880) lxxxvi, 525 p. front., illus., 17 pl. 21 cm. Half-title: Irving's works. Geoffrey Crayon edition ... vol. I. 1-1249.
F122.1.I 782

— New York, Hurst & co. (1883?) 253 p. 19 cm. Arlington edition. 37-15402.
F122.1.I 783

— New York, J. W. Lovell, 1883. (9) - 307 p. 18 cm. (Lovell's library, v. 5, no. 236) 6-42755.
F122.1.I 784

— Chicago, New York, and San Francisco, Belford, Clarke & co. (1885?) 6, (9) - 307 p. 19 cm.
(On cover: Irving's works) With this is bound his The Alhambra. 24-17730.
F122.1.I 785

— New ed. containing unpublished corrections of the author, with illus. by Geo. H. Boughton and others ... New York, Printed for the Grolier club, 1886. 2 v. fronts., illus., plates, facsims. (1 fold.) 24 cm. (Grolier club, New York. Publications. 17-14367.
F122.1.I 786
Rare Book Coll.

— with illus. by Edward W. Kemble ... New York (etc.) G. P. Putnam's sons, 1894. 2 v. fronts., illus. 22½ cm. Van Twiller ed. 6-42201.
F122.1.I 788

— New York and London, G. P. Putnam's sons (1897) 2 v. fronts., illus. 18 cm. Knickerbocker edition. 4-21708/3
F122.1.I 79

— Embellished by eight pictures from the hand of Maxfield Parrish. New York, R. H. Russell, 1900. xxxi, 208 p. front., plates. 23½ cm. 0-6247 Rev.
F122.1.I 83

— The whole embellish'd by eight pictures from the hand of Maxfield Parrish. New York, Dodd, Mead, 1915. xxxi, 298 p. 8 pl. (incl. front.) 28½ cm. 16-26139.
F122.1.I 833

— ed. with a critical introduction by Stanley Williams and Tremaine McDowell. New York, Harcourt, Brace, (1927) lxxvii, 475 p. incl. 1 illus., facsim. 17½ cm. (American authors series, general editor, S. T. Williams) "Selected reading list": p. lxxvii. 27-2639.
F122.1.I 834

— ed. by Anne Carroll Moore; with pictorial pleasantries by James Daugherty. Garden City, N. Y., Doubleday, Doran, inc., 1928. xi, 427 p. incl. front., illus., plates. 24½ cm. "1st ed." 28-29975.
F122.1.I 835
Rare Book Coll.

— ed. by Anne Carroll Moore; with pictorial pleasantries by James Daugherty. New York, F. Ungar Pub. Co. (1959, 1956) xi, 427 p. illus. 23 cm. 59-11666.
F122.1.I 835
1959

— Edited for the modern reader by Edwin T. Bowden. New York, Twayne Publishers (1964) 352 p. 21 cm. (Twayne's United States classics series) 64-19644.
F122.1.I 835
1964

— with original lithographs by Don Freeman. New York, The Heritage press (1940) xxxviii, 351 p. incl. front. plates. 21 cm. 40-31939.
F122.1.I 837

IRVING, Washington. Histoire de New-York, depuis le commencement du monde jusqu'a la fin de la domination hollandaise ... Ouvrage traduit de l'anglais. Paris, A. Sautelet et cie, 1827. 2 v. 21½ cm. 2-27763.
F122.1.I 84

IRVING, Washington. Humoristische geschichte von New-York, von anbeginn der welt bis zur endschaft der hollandischen dynastie ... Frankfurt am Main, J. D. Sauerländer, 1829. 298, (6) p. 14 cm. p. 1-2 wanting. 10-3164.
F122.1.I 86

IRVING, Washington. A history of New York, etc. in Russian. 363 p. with illus. 22 cm.
F122.1.I 864

IRVING, Washington. Knickerbocker sketches from "A history of New York." Illus. by F. O. C. Darley. Philadelphia, J. B. Lippincott, 1886. 87 p. incl. front., plates. 21 x 16½ cm. 6-41935.
F122.1.I 87

NEW YORK

IRVING'S Knickerbocker and some of its sources. By Harry Miller Lydenberg. New York, New York Public Library, 1953. 36 p. 26 cm. Repr. from the Bulletin of the New York Public Library of Nov.-Dec. 1952. Bibliography: p. 34-36. 54-38535.
F122.1.I 88L9

JAMESON, John Franklin. ... Narratives of New Netherland, 1609 - 1664 ... with three maps and a facsim. New York, C. Scribner's sons, 1909. xx, 3-478 p. 3 maps (incl. front.) facsim. 22½ cm. (Original narratives of early American history ...) 9-24463.
F122.1.J 31

JANVIER, Thomas Allibone. The Dutch founding of New York ... New York and London, Harper & brothers, 1903. iii, 217 p. front. (port.) 8 pl., 2 double maps, double plan. 23 cm. 3-25273/2.
F122.1.J 34

JOGUES, Isaac. ... A description of New Netherland, in 1644. By Father Isaac Jogues ... (From the documentary history of the state of New-York ... v. 4) 7-34367.
F122.1.J 65

JOURNAL of New Netherland. 1647. Written in the year 1641, 1642, 1643, 1644, 1645 and 1646. (From The documentary history of the state of New-York, v. 4) 7-34377.
F122.1.J 86

KROL. Bastiaen Jansz. Krol, krankenbezoeker, kommies en kommandeur van Nieuw-Nederland (1595-1645) ... door dr. A. Eckhof. 's-Gravenhage, M. Nijhoff, 1910. vi, 60, xxxviii p. front. (map) fold facsim. 25 cm. 12-19108 Rev.
F122.1.K82

LAMBRECHTSEN, Nicolaas Cornelis. Korte beschrijving van de ontdekking en der verdere lotgevallen van Nieuw-Nederland ... Middelburg, S. van Benthem, 1818. 102 p. fold. map. 23 cm. 1-22109.
F122.1.L22

LEYDEN. Rijksmuseum van oudheden. The Pilgrim fathers. Exhibition of documents from public and private collections at Leiden, relating to the Dutch settlements in North-America. August, 1888. (Leiden, Boekdrukkerij van P. M. W. Trap, 1888) 22 p. 27½ cm. (In Holland society of New York. Yearbook. 1888/89) 18-15001.
F122.1.L68

MEGAPOLENSIS, Johannes. Reply of Rev. Johannes Megapolensis, pastor of the church of New Amsterdam to a letter of Father Simon Le Moyne, a French Jesuit missionary of Canada, 1658. New York, Printed by the Collegiate church, 1907. 22 p. 24½ cm. Latin and English. An endeavor to show the errors of the Roman Catholic church. 7-38075.
F122.1.M49

MICHAËLIUS, Jonas, eerste predikant der Nederduitsche Hervormde gemeente op Manhattans of Nieuw-Amsterdam, het latere New-York, in Noord-Amerika, medgedeeld door mr. J. T. Bodel Nijenhuis. (In Kerkhistorisch archief. Amsterdam, 1857-66. v. 1 (1857) 5-19193.
F122.1.M61

(MICHAËLIUS, Jonas) The first minister of the Dutch reformed church in the United States. The Hague, Printed by the brothers Giunta d"Albani (1858) 25 p. 8°. Autograph presentation copy from H. C. Murphy to Peter Force. 1-22522-M1.
F122.1.M62

MICHAËLIUS, Jonas. Manhatten in 1628 as described in the recently discovered autograph letter of Jonas Michaëlius written from the settlement on the 8th Aug. ... by Dingman Versteeg. New York, Dodd, Mead, 1904. xii, 203 p. incl. front., plates, ports., facsims. 26½ cm. 4-28000 Rev.
F122.1.M63
Rare Book Coll.

MICHAËLIUS, Joseph, founder of the church in New Netherland, his life and work ... By Prof. Dr. A. Eckhof ... Leyden, A. W. Sijthoff's pub. co., 1926. 2, ix, 148 p. front., plates, facsims. (1 fold.) 27½ x 20½ cm. 26-21799.
F122.1.M65

MINNEWITT. ... Ein Deutscher gründet New York, gouverneur Peter Minnewitt. By Hans Hummel. Darmstadt, L. Kichler (1940) 228, (2) p. plates, facsims. 19½ cm. 41-15385.
F122.1.M67

— (1942) 243 p. plates, map. 20 cm. 50-43703.
F122.1.M67
1942

MINUIT. Peter Minuit; geboren in Wesel, gründete die Stadte New-York und Wilmington. (Wesel, 1963) 74 p. 21 cm.
F122.1.M 7

MOULTON, Joseph White. History of the state of New-York, including its aboriginal and colonial annals. By John V. N. Yates ... and Joseph W. Moulton ... New-York, A. T. Goodrich, 1824 -26. 1 v. in 2. fold. maps. 21 - 22 cm. 1-15851 Add.
F122.1.M92

NEDERLANDSCHE West-Indische compagnie. Accords-Puncta welcher gestalt Am. 8 Septembr. st. n. 1664. Neu-Niederland an die Englander sonder einige Hegenwehr ubergangen ... (n. p., 1664) (Boston, 1924) facsim: 4 l. 23½ x 19 cm. (Americana series: photostat reproductions by the Mass. hist. soc. no. 120) 25-13896.
F122.1.N 4
Rare Book Coll.

NEDERLANDSCHE West-Indische compagnie. Documents relating to New Netherland, 1624-1626, in the Henry E. Huntington library; trans. and ed. by A. J. F. van Laer. San Marino, Calif, The Henry E. Huntington lib. and art gallery, 1924. xxvi, 276 p. incl. facsims. 36½ cm. (... Publications. Americana: folio series. no. 1) 24-24640 Rev.
F122.1.N414

NEDERLANDSCHE West-Indische compagnie. Uryheden ende Exemptien voor de Patroonen Meesters ofte Particulieren die op Nieu-Nederlandt eenighe Colonien ende Vee sullen planten geconsidereert ten dienst van de Generale West-Indische Compagnie in Nieu-Nederlandt ... t'Amstelredam, Gedruckt by Theunis Jacobsz, 1631. (Boston, 1927) facsim.: (11) p. 23 cm. (Americana series; photostat reproductions by the Mass. hist soc. no. 197) CA 28-253 Unrev.
F122.1.N42
Rare Book Coll.

NETHERLAND chamber of commerce in America, New York. 1609 - 1909. The Dtuch in New Netherland and the United States, prsented by the Netherland chamber of commerce in America on occasion of the Hudson-Fulton celebration in New York ... 1909. (New York, 1909) 73 p. 18 cm. 9-27753.
F122.1.N44

— Photo-offset San Francisco, Rand E. Research Associates, 1970.
F122.1.N44
1970

NETHERLANDS ... Staten generaal. ... Inducements offered by the States general of Holland from 1614 to 1626 to those merchants and navigators who would discover new countries; together with the charter of privileges granted to the patroons. Ed. by Marin G. Brumbaugh ... Philadelphia, C. Sower co. (1898) 19 p. 19 cm. (Liberty bell leaflets: translations and reprints of original historical documents. no. 1) 98-1754 Rev.
F122.1.N46

NEW YORK (Colony) Laws and ordinances of New Netherland, 1638 - 1674. Comp. and trans. from the original Dutch records in the office of the secretary of state, Albany, N.Y., by E. B. O'Callaghan. Albany, Weed, Parsons, printers, 1868. xxxii, 602 p. 22½ cm. 3-25028 Rev. 2.
F122.1.N 5

NEW YORK (State) Division of Archives and History. Henry Hudson and the Dutch in New York ... Albany, University of the State of New York, 1959. 61 p. 22 cm. 59-9864.
F122.1.N52

NEW YORK (State) State library. Van Rensselaer Bowier manuscripts, being the letters of Kiliaen Van Rensselaer, 1630 - 1643, and other documents relating to the colony of Rensselaerswyck. Tr. and ed. by A. J. F. van Laer, archivist. ... Albany, University of the state of New York, 1908. 909 p. facsims. 23 cm. (History bulletin. 7) 8-29380 Rev.
F122.1.N53

NEW YORK (State) ... Communication from the secretary of state, in answer to resolutions requiring information in relation to the Documentary history ... 1854. (Albany, 1854) 64 p. 25 cm. (Legislature 1854. Assembly. Doc. 136) CA 10-4786 Unrev.
F122.1.N56

NISSENSON, Samuel George. The patroon's domain ... New York, Columbia university press, 1937. ix, 416 p. 23½ cm. (N. Y. state hist. assoc. series: no. v) Bibliography: p. (389) - 397. 37-20744.
F122.1.N58

O'CALLAGHAN, Edmund Bailey. History of New Netherland; or, New York under the Dutch. ... New York, D. Appleton; Philadelphia, G. S. Appleton, 1846-48. 2 v. fronts., port., fold. maps, fold. facsims. 23½ cm. The work closes with the English conquest, 1664. 1-27967.
F122.1.O 4

— Microfilm. Ann Arbor, Mich., University Microfilms, 1963. 1 reel. 35 mm. (American culture series, 222; 7)
Microfilm 01291 reel 222, no. 7

— 2d ed. ... New-York, D. Appleton, 1855. 2 v. 2 port., 2 fold. maps, 2 fold. facsim. 24 cm. 16-8170.
F122.1.O403
G & M

O'CALLAGHAN, Edmund Bailey. Index to volumes one, two and three of translations of Dutch manuscripts, in the office of the secretary of the state of New York. Albany, Weed, Parsons, printers, 1870. 118 p. 24 cm. v. 1-3 were translated by O'Callaghan, but not printed. 11-10263.
F122.1.O41

O'CALLAGHAN, Edmund Bailey. The register of New Netherland; 1626 to 1674. Albany, N.Y., J. Munsell, 1865. xx, 198 p. 26 cm. 1-15863.
F122.1.O42

PEECK. Jan Peeck, tavern keeper, fur trader and land owner. By William Tompkins Horton. Peekskill, N.Y., Dept. of the City Historian, 1949. 110, (2) l. illus. 30 cm. Bibliography: (2) leaves at end. 49-5826*.
F122.1.P44H67

RENSSELAERSWYCK. Minutes of the court of Rensselaerswyck, 1648-1652, translated and ed. by A. J. F. van Laer ... Albany, The University of the state of New York, 1922. 5-237 p. 3 facsim. 23 cm. 23-27332.
F122.1.R
F127.R32R32

RAESLY, Ellis Lawrence. Portrait of New Netherland. New York, Columbia university press, 1945. vi, 370 p. 23½ cm. (Columbia university studies in English and comparative literature, no. 161. Bibliography: p. (345)-354. Issued also as thesis (PH.D.) Columbia university. A 45-1615.
F122.1.R15

— Port Washington, N.Y., I. J. Friedman (1965) 370 p. 22 cm. (Empire State historical publications, 34) 64-8793.
F122.1.R15
1965

— New York, Columbia university press, 1945. 370 p. 23½ cm. Thesis (PH.D.) - Columbia universtiy, 1943. A 45-3063.
F122.1.R15
1945

REES, Otto van. Geschiedenis der Nederlandsche volkplantingen in Noord-Amerika, beschouwd uit het oogpunt der koloniale politiek. ... Te Tiel, Bij H. C. A. Campagne, 1855. 2, 162 p. 23½ cm. 1-15864.
F122.1.R32

SAINT NICHOLAS society of the city of New York, An account of the banquet given by, on the occasion of the visit of the Netherlands frigate "Prins van Oranje," at New York ... 1852. (New York) Prepared and pub. by order of the Society, 1852. 3, 63 p. front., fold. map, fold. plan. 24 cm. 8-16761.
F122.1.S14

ST. NICHOLAS society of the city of New York ... Record of the dinner given in honor of the officers of H. N. M. frigate "Van Speijk," ... 1893 ... New York, The Society (1893) 60 p. 23½ cm. 14-12726.
F122.1.S143

ST. NICHOLAS society of the city of New York, Record of the semi-centennial anniversary of ... 1885. (New York, T. L. De Vinne, printers, 1885) 42 p. 23½ cm. 9-11018.
F122.1.S145

SALMON, Lucy Maynard. The Dutch West India company on the Hudson ... with six illustrations. Poughkeepsie, N.Y. (Printed by Lansing & Broas) 1915. 51 p. front., plates. 24 cm. 15-22253.
F122.1.S 27

STEENWYCK. Cornelis Steenwyck, Dutch governor of Acadie, by John Clarence Webster; a paper read at the annual meeting of the Canadian historical assoc. in Ottawa, ... 1929. (Shediac? N.B.) Priv. print., 1929.   12 p.   front. (port.)   23 cm.   CA 30-646 Unrev.
F122.1.S81

STUYVESANT. ... Peter Stuyvesant, the last Dutch governor of New Amsterdam. By John S. C. Abbott ... New York, Dodd & Mead, 1873.   ix, (13) - 362 p.   front., pl.   18½ cm.   (His American pioneers and patriots) 1-28131-M2.
F122.1. S 9

— New York, Dodd, Mead, 1898.   ix, (13) - 362 p.   front. (port.)   19 cm.   1-25378.
F122.1. S92

STUYVESANT. Peter Stuyvesant of old New York, by Anna & Russel Crouse; illus. by Jo Spier. New York, Random House (1954)   184 p.   illus.   22 cm.   (Landmark books 43)   54-5161.
F122.1.S922

STUYVESANT. Pieter Stuyvesant, an historical documentation; compiled upon request of the Provincial Government of Friesland in commemoration of the Pieter Stuyvesant Festival at Wolvega, Friesland ... 1955. Grand Rapids, Eerdmans, 1957.   78 p.   illus., ports., facsims.   25 cm.   Bibliography: 75 - 78.   57-13734.
F122.1.S923

STUYVESANT. Peter Stuyvesant, an address delivered at the annual meeting of the Order of colonial lords of manors in America ... 1930 (by) Stuyvesant Fish. Baltimore, 1930.   39 p.   front., illus. (incl. ports., facsims.)   23½ cm.   (Publications no. 22)   34-8736.
F122.1.S924

STUYVESANT. A colony leader: Peter Stuyvesant. By Adele Louise De Lesuw. Illus. by Vincent Colabella. Champaign, Ill., Garrard Pub. Co. (1970)   64 p.   illus.   24 cm.   73-90817.
F122.1.S9245

STUYVESANT. ... Peter Stuyvesant, director-general for the West Indian company in New Netherland, by Bayard Tuckerman ... New York, Dodd, Mead, 1893.   4, (7) - 193 p.   front. (port.)   18 cm.   ("Makers of America")   4-17076/3.
F122.1.S93

STUYVESANT. Life and times of Pieter Stuyvesant, by Hendrik Van Loon. New York, H. Holt (1928) xiv, 336 p. incl. front., illus., maps.   22½ cm.   28-23642.
F122.1.S935

THEOBALD, Jacob. Story history of Dutch New York, fourth year: first half. and others. Yonkers-on-Hudson, N.Y., World book co. (1931)   vi, 122 p.   col. front., illus., col. plates.   19½ cm.
F122.1.T45

TIENHOVEN, Cornelis van. ... Information relative to taking up land in New Netherland. By Cornelis van Tienhoven, secretary of the province. 1650. Tr. from the Dutch.   (In The documentary history of the state of New-York, v. 4)   7-34371.
F122.1.T56

(VAN LAER, Arnold Johan Ferdinand) ... The translation and publication of the manuscript Dutch records of New Netherland, with an account of previous attempts at translation. Albany, University of the state of New York, 1910.   (3) - 28 p.   23 cm.   (New York state library. (Bulletin) Bibliography 46)   Education department bulletin ... no. 462.   10-9096.
F122.1.V25

VAN RENSSELAER. Miliaen van Rensselaer van 1623 tot 1636, door Dr. J. Spinoza Catella Jessurun. 's-Gravenhave, M. Nijhoff, 1917.   3, 213, xxv p.   25 cm.   18-20596.
F122.1.V
F127.R32V2

VERSTEEG, Dingman. New Netherland's founding, (New York) The Holland society of New York, 1924.   13 p.   23 cm.   "Authorities": p. 12-13.   25-2954.
F122.1.V56

VRIES, David Pietersz. de. Korte historiael ende journaels aenteyckeninge van verscheyden voyagiens in de vier deelen des wereldtsronde, als Europa, Africa, Asia, ende Amerika gedaen ... 's-Gravenhage, M. Nijhoff, 1911.   xliv, (8), 302 p.   front. (port.)   11 fold. pl., 2 fold. maps.   25 cm.   (Werken uitgegeven door de Linschoten-vereeniging III ...)   Reprint;of the ed. of 1655.   12-14155.
F122.1.V
G460.V 8

NEW YORK

VRIES, David Pietersz. de. New Netherland in 1640. Boston, 1906.
F122.1.V98

WIEDER, Frederik Caspar. De stichting van New York in Juli 1625. ... 's-Gravenhage, M. Nijhoff, 1925.   xi, 242 p. incl. facsims. fold. front. (facsim.) 28 pl. 25½ cm. Aangehaalde werken": p. (227)-232. 25-21338.
F122.1.W64

ZWIERLEIN, Frederick James. Religion in New Netherland; a history of the development of the religious conditions in the province of New Netherland 1623-1664 ... Rochester, N.Y., J. P. Smith print., 1910.   x vii, 365 p. front. (fold. map) 21 cm. "A select bibliography": p. 331-351. 11-2153 Rev.
F122.1.Z98

— New York, Da Capo Press, 1971.   vii, 351 p. 23 cm. (Civil liberties in American history) 72-120851.
F122.1.Z98 1971

1775 - 1865.

AMERICAN quarterly review... The, versus, the state of New-York. (Albany, 1832)   8 p. 24½ cm.
At head of title: Daily Albany argus, state of New-York, 1832. 9-27469.
F123.A 51

BARBÉ-MARBOIS, François, marquis de. Marbois on the fur trade, 1784. (New York, 1924)
p. 725-740. 27½ cm. Reprinted from the American historical review, vol. xxix, no. 4, July, 1924. CA 31-227 Unrev.
F123.B 23

BARNARD, Daniel Dewey. Speeches and reports in the Assembly of New-York, at the annual session of 1838. Albany, O. Steele, 1838.   xi, 228 p. 19 cm. E 10-897.
F123. B 27

BAXTER, Katharine Schyler. A godchild of Washington, a picture of the past. London and New York, F. T. Neely (1897)   651 p. incl. front., illus., plates. 30 cm. Includes sketches of many notable New Yorkers of the latter part of the 18th and of the 19th centuries. 10-31666.
F123. B 35

(BEAUFOY,) Tour through parts of the United States and Canada. By A British subject. London, Longman, Rees, Orme, Brown, and Green, 1828.   viii, 141 p. 22 cm. 1-16151.
F123. B 37

BECKER, Carl (Lotus) Election of delegates from New York. New York, 1903.   27 cm.
F123. B 39

(HALL, John Taylor) Memorial of Lewis and Susan Benedict. (New York?) Printed for the family, 1870.   55 p. 2 port. (incl. front.) 25½ cm. 14-4017.
F123. B 46

BENJAMIN, Marcus. New York during the revolution ... Washington, D.C., 1928.   29 p. 23½ cm.
Read before the society of the Sons of the revolution in the District of Columbia ... 1927. 28-5856.
F123. B 48

BENSON, Lee. The concept of Jacksonian Democracy; New York as a test case. Princeton, N.J., Princeton University Press, 1961.   xl, 351 p. 25 cm. 61-6286.
F123. B 49

BIGELOW, Timothy. Journal of a tour to Niagara Falls in the year 1805. With an introd. by a grandson ... Boston, Press of J. Wilson, 1876.   xx, 121 p. 23½ cm. Across Massachusetts and New York to Niagara, and thence by way of Lake Ontario, the Saint Lawrence. Montreal, the Sorel River, Lake Champlain, across Vermont and New Hampshire. 1-15865.
F123. B 59

(BLOODGOOD, Simeon De Witt) An Englishman's sketch-book; or, Letters from New-York ... New-York, G. and C. Carvill, 1828.   (iii) - iv, (7) - 195 p. 20 cm. 1-26744.
F123. B 65

(BRAUW, J de) supposed author. Herinneringen eener reize naar Nieuwhork gedaan in de jaren 1831 en 1832. ... Te Leiden, bij C. C. van der Hoek, 1833.   2, (3) - 220 p. 22½ cm. 1-22102.
F123. B 82

(BUECHLER, Johann Ulrich) Lotgevallen van een' Zwitsersch landverhuizer, op zijne reize naar Noord-Amerika en de West-Indiën en van daar terug, in 1816, 1817 en 1818. Haarlem, We. A. Loosjes Pz., 1819.   2, (iii) - x, 221 p.   22½ cm.   (Bound with above)   1-15866.

F123.B 82

BROOKS, Erastus.   Speech of Hon. Erastus Brooks, in the Senate ... 1855, the Lemmon slave case and slavery - secret societies and oaths, etc., etc.   (Albany? 1855)   15 p.   25 cm.   11-4703.

F123. B 87

CHALMERS, Harvey.   Tales of the Mohawk; stories of old New York State from colonial times to the age of Homespun.   Illus. by Nell Perret.   Port Washington, N.Y., I. J. Friedman (1968)   2 v.   22 cm.   (Empire State Historical publications no. 57-58)   68-18354.

F123.C 48

(CHEETHAM, James) supposed author.   An impartial enquiry into certain parts of the conduct of Governor Lewis, and of a portion of the legislature, particularly in relation to the Merchants' bank. ... With an appendix ... By Politicus (pseud.) ... New-York. Printed by James Cheetham ... 1806.   iv, (5) - 116, xxxv p.   21 cm.   9-20791.

F123.C 51
Rare Book Coll.

(CLINTON, De Witt)   An account of Abimelech Coody and other celebrated writers of New-York.   In a letter from a traveller to his friend in South Carolina.   (New York) ... 1815.   16 p.   21½ cm.   A satire.   19-3281.

F123.C 63

— (New York, Priv. print., 1864)   22 p.   26½ cm.   35 copies.   Extra illustrated copy.   22-6290.

F123.C632
Rare Book Coll.

(CLINTON, De Witt)   Letters on the natural history and internal resources of the state of New-York.   By Hibernicus (pseud.)   New York, Sold by E. Bliss & E. White, 1822.   224 p.   18 cm.   1-15867.

F123.C 64

JARVIS, William C.   The Republican; or, A series of essays on the principles and policy of free states ... Pittsfield (Mass.) P. Allen, 1820.   368 p.   17½ cm.   1-15868.

F123.C 64

COCHRAN, Thomas Childs.   New York in the confederation; an economic study ... Philadelphia, University of Pennsylvania press; London, H. Milford, Oxford university press, 1932.   ix, 3-220 p.   illus. (maps)   23½ cm.   Issued also as thesis (PH. D.) University of Pennsylvania.   Bibliography: p. 195-212.   33-5634 rev.

F123.C 66

— Port Washington, N.Y., I. J. Friedman (1970)   viii, 220 p.   22 cm.   (Empire State historical publications. series no. 84)   71-118781.

F123.C 66
1970

— 1972.

F123.C 66
1972

— Philadelphia, 1932.   ix, 3-229 p.   illus. (maps)   23½ cm.   Thesis (PH. D.) U. of Pa.   33-5635 rev.   F123.C662

COLES, George.   My first seven years in America ... Ed. by D. P. Kidder.   New York, Carlton & Phillips, 1852.   314 p.   16°.   1-22108-M1.

F123.C 68

COOLEY, James Ewing.   Speech of the Hon. James E. Cooley, before the Democracy of Syracuse, in mass meeting assembled ... 1853.   New York, J. F. Trow, printer, 1853.   47 p.   23 cm.   11-4702.

F123.C 74

(COOPER, Thomas)   A ride to Niagara in 1809, by T. C.   (Rochester, N.Y., 1915)   (9) - 49 p.   front. (fold. map)   23½ cm.   16-9805 rev.

F123.C 76

COOPER, William.   A guide in the wilderness; or The history of the first settlement in the western

784

NEW YORK

counties of New York, with useful instructions to future settlers. In a series of letters addressed by Judge Cooper, of Cooperstown, to William Sampson, barrister, of New York. Dublin, Printed by Gilbert & Hodges ... (Rochester, N.Y., G. P. Humphrey, 1897) vii, 41 p. 21½ cm. 1-15869 rev.
F123.C 77

— Freeport, N.Y., Books for Libraries Press (1970) ix, 49 p. 23 cm. 79-140352.
F123.C 77 1970

CURTIS, George William. Lotus-eating: a summer book. ... Illus. by Kensett ... New York, Harper & bros., 1852. 206 p. illus. 19½ cm. Contents. - The Hudson and the Rhine. - Catskill. - Catskill Falls. - Trenton. - Niagara. - Saratoga. - Lake George. - Nahant. - Newport. 2-2402.
F123.C 94 Rare Book Coll.

— New York, Dix, Edward, 1856. 206 p. illus. 20 cm. (Curtis's works, v. 3) 2-2403.
F123.C943

— New York, Harper & bros., 1868. 206 p. 18½ cm. 7-37060.
F123.C945

— New York, Harper & bros. (190?) 206 p. illus. 19½ cm. 4-16752/4 Rev.
F123.C948

CUTTING, Francis Brockholst. "Hards" and "softs." Reply of Mr. Cutting, of New York, in the House of representatives ... 1854, to a question put to him by Mr. Smith, of Alabama, in Committee of the whole. (Washington, Printed at the Congressional globe office, 1854) 7 p. 23 cm. 11-4701.
F123.C 96

DARBY, William. A tour from the city of New-York, to Detroit, in the Michigan territory, made between the 2d of May and the 22d of September, 1818 .... New York: Pub. for the author, by Kirk & Mercein ... 1819. Printed by E. Worthington, Brooklyn. viii, (9) - 228, lxiii, (7) p. 3 fold. maps (incl. front.) 22½ cm. 1-16150.
F123.D 21 Rare Book Coll.

— Chicago, Quadrangle Books (1962) 228, lxiii p. 22 cm. (Americana classics) 62-17141.
F123.D 21 1819 a

(DAVIS, Matthew Livingston) Letters of Marcus (pseud.) addressed to De Witt Clinton, mayor of the city of New-York. (Poughkeepsie? 1806?) 16 p. 21½ cm. Attributed by Cushing to W. P. Van Ness. "Taken from the Poughkeepsie Barometer", 1805. Pub also under title: The plot discovered. Allegation that De Witt Clinton was responsible for a coalition of Clintonians and Burrites in New York politics. 10-34657 Rev.
F123.D 25 Rare Book Coll.

(DAVIS, Matthew Livingston) The plot discovered. By Marcus (pseud.) ... Poughkeepsire: Printed by Thomas Nelson, 1807. 12 p. 24 cm. See above item. 9-20790.
F123.D 26 Rare Book Coll.

(DEMOCRATIC party. New York State) Republican nomination for governor and lt. governor. With an address to the electors of the state of New-York. (Albany, 1820) 15 p. 22 cm. 9-20820.
F123.D 38 Rare Book Coll.

— An address to the independent Federal electors of the state of New York, on the subject of the election of a governor and lt. governor of the state. (Albany, 1820) 40 x 16½ cm. (With above item) 9-20810.

DEMOCRATIC party. New York (State) Convention, 1849. ... Address and proceedings of the Democratic state convention. Held at Rome ... 1849. Albany, Print. C. Van Bethuysen, 1849. 24 p. 21 cm. At head of title: Albany argus - Extra. 10-20773.
F123.D 39

DEPEW, Chauncey Mitchell. Address by Hon. Chauncey M. Depew, delivered at Kingston ... 1877, at the centennial celebration of the formation of the state government of the state of New York.   Albany, Weed, Parsons, printers, 1877.   23 p.   23 cm.   11-6046.   F123.D 41

DE PEYSTER.   John Watts de Peyster, by Frank Allaben ... New York, Frank Allaben genealogical co. (1908)   2 v.   fronts., plates, ports.   20 cm.   (Allaben biographical series) Ancestry: v.1, p. (11) - 87.   Bibliography: v.2, p. (267) - 320.   8-21542.   F123.D 42

DE PEYSTER.   Concurremt resolution, New York state Legislature, being special act authorizing the issue of commission of Brevet Major-General to Brigadier-General De Peyster ... State of New York, in Senate, April 20, 1866 ... in Assembly, April 9, 1866 ...   (New York, Priv. print., 1866) 13 p.   22 cm.   34-29292.   F123.D425
Rare Book Coll.

DE VEAUX, Samuel.   The travellers' own book, to Saratoga Springs, Niagara Falls, and Canada ... a complete guide for the valetudinarian and for the tourist ...   Buffalo, Faxon & Read, 1841. vii, (13) - 258 p. incl. pl.   front., illus., 3pl. fold. plans.   15 cm.   1-16149 Rev.   F123.D475

— 5th ed. Buffalo, Faxon & co., 1844.   viii, (9) - 251 p.   illus., 7 pl., 2 fold. maps (incl. front.)   15 cm.   17-10086.
F123.D 48
Toner Coll.

DEWEY'S railroad hand-book, from Albany to Buffalo; containing a complete list of all the regular and flag stations, etc. etc.   Cor. and rev. by gentlemen of the failroad.   Rochester, N.Y., D. M. Dewey, 1849.   vi, (2), (9) - 32 p. incl. front. (map) 16 cm.   1-15870.
F123.D 51
Rare Book Coll.

DeWITT.   Simeon De Witt; founder of Ithaca, by William Heidt.   Carol K. Kammen, Ed.   Ithaca, N.Y., DeWitt Historical Soc. of Tompkins County (1968)   viii, 75 p.   23 cm.
F123.D53H4

DISTURNELL, John.   The traveller's guide through the state of New-York, Canada, etc.   Embracing a general description of the city of New-York; the Hudson river guide, and the fashionable tour to the Springs and Niagara falls, etc.   New-York, J. Disturnell, 1836.   71 p.   front., plates, fold. maps.   13 cm. 1-16148.   F123.D 61
Rare Book Coll.

(DISTURNELL, John)   The northern traveller; containing the Hudson River guide, and tour to the Springs, Lake George and Canada, passing through Lake Champlain ... New York, J. Disturnell, 1844. 84 p.   front., illus., 2 maps.   16 cm.   1-16147.   F123.D615
Rare Book Coll.

DISTURNELL, John.   The western traveller; embracing the canal and railroad routes, from Albany and Troy, to Buffalo and Niagara Falls.   Also, the steamboat route, from Buffalo to Detroit and Chicago.   New York, J. Disturnell, 1844.   90 p.   front., plates, maps.   15½ cm.   1-16146 Rev.
F123.D618
Rare Book Coll.

DONOVAN, Herbert Darius Augustine.   The Barnburners; a study of the internal movements in the political history of New York state and of the resulting changes in political affiliation, 1830 - 1852. New York city, The New York university press, 1925.   viii, 140 p.   2 double maps.   23½ cm.   Pub. also as thesis (PH.D.) New York university, 1917.   Bibliography: p. (127) - 134.   26-15592.   F123.D 72

— viii, 140 p.   2 double maps.   23½ cm.   Theses (PH.D.) New York university, 1917.   26-15593.   F123.D722

EATON, M.   Five years on the Erie canal: an account of some of the most striking scenes and incidents, during five years' labor on the Erie canal, and other inland waters ... Utica, Bennett, Backus, & Hawley, 1845.   (9) - 11, (19) - 156 p.   16 cm.   13-12780.   F123.E 14
Rare Book Coll.

ELECTION, The, no. 1. (New York, 1822) 15 p. 24 cm. Signed: The people's friend. 9-27470.
F123. E 38

ELLICOTT. Joseph Ellicott and stories of the Holland purchase, by Clara L. T. Williams. (Batavia, N.Y.) The author (New York, Advertising typographers) 1936. 3, 11-152 p. illus., plates, 2 port. (incl. front.) 21 cm. Bibliography: 3d prelim. leaf. 36-23574.
F123. E394

ELLICOTT. Joseph Ellicott and the Holland Land Company; the opening of Western New York, by William Chazanof. (1st ed. Syracuse, N.Y.) Syracuse University Press (1970) ix, 240 p. 24 cm. 76-130979.
F123. E394C48

EXPOSITION of the late general election in New-York. By a citizen of Pennsylvania. Philadelphia, 1826. 24 p. 21½ cm. 3-20171.
F123. E 96

EYRE, John. Travels: comprising a journey from England to Ohio, two years in that state, travels in America, etc. To which are added the Foreigner's protracted journal, letters, etc. ... 4th thousand. New York (R. Craighead, printer) 1851. 360 p. 19½ cm. An enlarged ed. of his "Christian spectator." A 10-1401.
F123. E 98

FELTON, Mrs. Life in America. A narrative of two years' city & country residence in the U.S. Hull, Print. J. Hutchinson, 1838. iv, (5) - 120 p. front. (double plan) 18 cm. 1-26798.
F123. F 3
Rare Book Coll.

— 2d thousand. London, Simpkin, Marshall, 1842. iv, (5) - 120 p. front. (fold. plan) 17½ cm. Title of this ed. is American life.
F123. F 32

— 3d thousand. Bolton Percy (Eng.) The authoress, 1843. iv, (5) - 136 p. front. (fold. plan) 17½ cm. Title - American life. Descr. of New York city, a voyage up the Hudson and a residence on L.I. 16-27451.
F123. F323

FIVE predatory tribes, ... The; or, The bolters' faction analysed. (New York, 1853) 7 p. 24 cm. (Evening post documents. 2d ser., no. 4) 10-25253.
F123. F 56

FOOT, Samuel Alfred. Autobiography: collateral reminiscences, arguments in important causes, speeches, addresses, lectures, and other writings, of Samuel A. Foot ... New York (Electrotyped by Smith & McDougal) 1872. 2 v. front., ports. 23½ cm. 10-31451.
F123. F 68

FOOTE. Ebenezer Foote, the founder; being an epistolary light on his time as shed by letters from his files, selected by his great-granddaughter Katherine Adelia Foote. Delhi, N.Y., Delaware express co., 1927. 2, (5) - 224 p. front. (port.) 23½ cm. A 30-984.
F123. F7F6

FOWLER, John. Journal of a tour in the state of New York, in the year 1830; with remarks on agriculture in those parts most eligible for settlers: and return to England by the Western Islands, in consequence of shipwreck in the Robert Fulton. By John Fowler ... London, Whittaker, Treacher, and Arnot, 1831. 2, (iii) - v, (7) - 333 p. 20 cm. 1-16139.
F123. F 78

— New York, A.M. Kelley, 1970. v, 333 p. (America through European eyes.) 22 cm. 74-100125.
F123. F 78
1970

FOX, Dixon Ryan. The decline of aristocracy in the politics of New York ... New York, 1918.
xiii, 460 p. front., illus. (maps) ports. 23 cm. Thesis (PH. D.) - Columbia university, 1917. Pub. also as Studies in history, economics and public law, ..., Columbia university, vol. lxxxvi, whole no. 198. Bibliographical foot-notes. 19-16519.
F123. F 79

— New York, Harper & Row (1965) xxxv, 460 p. 21 cm. (American perspectives) Harper torchbooks, university library. TB 3064.
F123. F 79
1965

— New York, Columbia university, Longmans, Green, agents ... 1919. xiii, 460 p. front, illus., etc. 22½ cm. Pub. also as thesis (PH. D.) Columbia university, 1917. 19-18663.
F123. F792

GILES, Charles. Pioneer: a narrative of the nativity, experience, travels, and ministerial labors of Rev. Charles Giles ... With incidents, observations, and reflections. New York, G. Lane & P. P. Sandford, 1844.   333 p. front. (port.) 18½ cm. 10-31450.
 F123.G 47

(GOODENOW, Sterling) A brief topographical & statistical manual of the state of New-York: exhibiting the situation and boundaries of the several counties ... and designating the principal places and the seat of the courts ... Albany, Pub. by J. Frary, State-street, 1811.   36 p. 18 cm. 1-15871.
 F123.G 65

— 2d ed. - enl. and improved. Containing also, an account of the grand canals; the population of each town and county ... New York, E. Bliss and E. White, 1822.   72 p. 22 cm. 1-15872.
 F123.G 66

— New-York, E. Bliss and E. White, 1822.   88 p. 22½ cm. With "second supplement, containing the alterations and additions made since 1821." 1-15873.
 F123.G662

(GOODRICH, Samuel Griswold) Peter Parley's tales about the state and city of New York. Illus. by a map and many engravings. For the use of schools. New York, Pendleton and Hill, 1832.   2, (iii) - v, (11) - 160 p. front., illus., fold. map. 14½ x 11½ cm. 1-15874.
 F123.G 68
 Rare Book Coll.

(GOODWIN, Nathaniel) Memorandum of a journey from Hartford to Niagara Falls and return in 1828; also, Hartford to Mendon in 1821; printed from the original manuscript in the possession of Frank D. Andrews. Vineland, N.J., 1909.   12 p. 18½ cm. 10-31671.
 F123.G 70

GOSSELMAN, Karl August. Resa i Norra Amerika. Nykoping, 1835.   1 v. 21 cm. 1-16138*.
 F123.G 73

GREENE, Asa) Travels in America. By George Fibbleton, esq. (pseud.) ex-barber to His Majesty, the king of Great Britain. New-York, W. Pearson, P. Hill, and others, 1833.   vi. (7) - 216 p. 19½ cm. "A satire on the Rev. Isaac Fidler's 'Travels in America.'" Sabin. 4-15522 rev.
 F123.G 79

HAMELE, Ottamar. ... And they thanked God, a chronicle of pioneering in western New York. (Washington) 1944.   24 p. 23½ cm. 44-47650.
 F123.H 18

(HAMILTON, Alexander) An address, to the electors of the state of New-York. Albany: Printed by C. R. and G. Webster, (1801)   34 p. 17 cm. 9-20788.
 F123.H 21
 Rare Book Coll.

— Re-printed, April, 1801.   23 p. 21 cm. 24-11507.
 F123.H211
 Rare Book Coll.

HAMLIN, L. Belle, ed. ... Selections from the Follett papers, I - Cincinnati, O., Press of Jennings and Graham (1910) -   v. 24½ cm. (Quarterly pub. of the Hist. and philosophical soc. of Ohio, vol. 5, no. 2; vol. 9, no. 3; vol. 10, no. 1; vol. 11, no. 1, vol. 13, no. 2. 10-17765 Rev.
 F123.H213

HAMMOND, Samuel H. Country margins and rambles of a journalist. ... New York, J. C. Derby; Boston, Phillips, Sampson ... 1855.   x. (9) - 356 p. 19 cm. Sketches of life and travel in the state of New York, first pub. in the Albany state register. 7-42542.
 F123.H 22

— Microfilm. Ann Arbor, Mich. University Microfilms (1963)
 Microfilm 01291 reel 238 no. 1 E

HARPER'S New York and Erie rail-road guide book ... With 136 engravings by Lossing and Barritt, from original sketches made expressly for this work by William Macleod. New York, Harper & bros. (1851)   viii, (9) - 173 p. incl. illus., plates. 19½ cm. From Piermont on the Hudson, through the southern tier of counties to Dunkirk on Lake Erie. 1-15876.
 F123.H 29

— 7th ed. greatly enl. New York, Harper & bros., 1854.   3, (v) - viii. (9) - 176 p. incl. illus., 5 pl. front (fold. map. 19 cm. 17-19932.
 F123.H298
 Toner Coll.

NEW YORK

— 8th ed., rev., enl., and cor. to the present date. New York, Harper & brothers, 1855-6. 3, (v) - viii, (9) - 188 p. incl. illus., plates. front. (fold. map) 18½ cm. 1-15877. F123.H 30

HARRIS. Memorial of Ira Harris. Albany, J. Munsell, 1876. 69, (2) p. front. (port.) 23 cm. 2-8722. F123.H 31

HATHAWAY, Levi. The narrative of Levi Hathway, giving an account of his life, experience, call to the ministry of the gospel of the Son of God, and travels as such to the present time ... Providence, Printed for the author, by Miller & Hutchens, 1820. 140 p. 17½ cm. The author's travels and experiences as a minister of the Christian church, chiefly in New York and New England. 11-19263. F123.H 36

HOLLEY. Myron Holley; and what he did for liberty and true religion ... (By Elizur Wright) Boston, Printed for the author, 1882. 328 p. front. (port.) 19 cm. Copy 2 on microfilm. 11-21027. F123.H 73
Microfilm 8878 F

HOTCHKIN, James Harvey. A history of the purchase and settlement of western New York, and of the rise, progress, and present state of the Presbyterian church in that section. New York, Pub. by M. W. Dodd, 1848. xvi, 600 p. front. 24 cm. A 40-1696. F123.H 76

JAGGER, William. An address to the people of Suffolk, upon the public affairs of the state. (New York, R. Craighead, printer, 1842) 24 p. 22 cm. 10-1531. F123.J 24

JAY, Peter. Memorials of Peter A. Jay; compiled for his descendants by his great-grandson, John Jay ... (New York) Printed for private circulation (The De Vinne press) 1905. xii, 308 p. pl., 9 port. (incl. front.) 21½ cm. 60 copies printed. 5-41605. F123.J 42

— (Arnheim, Holland) Printed for private circulation (by G. J. Thieme) 1929. xii, 224 p. incl. front. pl., ports. 23 cm. 30-6698. F123.J 422

JOHNSON, Samuel Roosevelt. A memorial discourse on the life, character and services of General Jeremiah Johnson, of Brooklyn, the first president of the St. Nicholas soc. of Nassau Island ... Delivered before the society in Brooklyn ... 1853. Brooklyn, I. Van Anden's press, 1854. 34 p. front. (port.) 23 cm. 6-859. F123.J 67

JOURNAL of a wanderer; being a residence in India, and six weeks in North America ... London, Simpkin, Marshall, etc., 1844. xviii, 250 p. front. (port.) 17 cm. 12-11580. F123.J 86

JOURNAL of an excursion to the United States and Canada in the year 1834: with hints to emigrants; and a fair and impartial exposition of the advantages and disadvantages attending emigration. By a citizen of Edinburgh. Edinburgh, J. Anderson, jun., 1835. viii, 168 p. 16 cm. Relates chiefly to the state of New York. 5-37457. F123.J 87

JOURNEY from New York to Montreal by way of Saratoga Springs and Niagara Falls in the year 1824; printed from the original manuscript in the possession of Frank D. Andrews ... Vineland, N.J., 1912. 21 p. 21 cm. 100 copies printed. 12-13238. F123.J 875

KASS, Alvin. Politics in New York State, 1800 - 1830. (New York) Syracuse University Press, 1965. xii, 221 p. 22 cm. 65-11679. F123.K 2

KELLY, John. The union of the New York Democracy - The Kansas-Nebraska act vindicated. Speech ... Delivered in the House of representatives ... 1856. (Washington? 1856) 7 p. 23 cm. 11-6047. F123.K 29

KELLY. Memorial of Hon. William Kelly. Presented to the New York state agricultural soc ... 1873, by Marsena R. Patrick ... Pub. by the Society. Albany, J. Munsell, printer, 1873. 46 p. 23½ cm. 14-9161. F123.K 295

KENT. Chancellor Kent at Yale, 1777-1781; a paper written for the Yale law journal, by Macgrane Coxe. New York, Priv. print., 1909. 2, (3) - 53 p. port., plates, facsim. 24½ cm. 9-14198. F123.K 37

KENT. A discourse on the life, character, and public services of James Kent, late chancellor of the state of New-York; delivered by request, before the judiciary and bar of the city and state of New-York ... 1848. By John Duer ... New-York, D. Appleton; Philadelphia, G. S. Appleton, 1848. 86 p. front. (port.) 22½ cm. 11-22448. F123.K375

KENT. Addresses and proceedings at a meeting of the bar of New-York, on the occasion of the death of William Kent. (New York? 1861) 49 p. front. (port.) 22½ cm. 3-27050. F123.K 39

KING. ... Proceedings in reference to the death of Hon. John A. King ... 1867. (New York Union league) Club house, 1867. 26 p. 20½ cm. 9-28371. F123.K 52

LEAVENWORTH. Elias Warner Leavenworth. Born Dec. 20, 1803. Died Nov. 24, 1887. (n. p., 1887?) 68 p. front. (port.) 8°. 1-13610-M1. F123.L 43

LINCKLAEN, John. Travels in the years 1791 and 1792 in Pennsylvania, New York and Vermont; journals of John Lincklaen, agent of the Holland land co., with a biographical sketch and notes. New York and London, G. P. Putnam's sons, 1897. xi. 162, 4 p. ports., fold. maps, facsim. 22 cm. List of principal authorities consulted: p. ix-xi. 1-16137. F123.L 73

(M'INTYRE, Archibald) A letter to His Excellency Daniel D. Tompkins, late governor of the state of New-York. Albany, Print. E. & E. Hosford, 1820. 56, xl p. 23 cm. 12-12861. F123.M 14

MACINTYRE. A sermon, by W. B. Sprague ... on occasion of the death of Hon. Archibald MacIntyre. 1858. 1 v. F123.M 15

MACKENZIE, William Lyon. The lives and opinions of Benj'n Franklin Butler, U.S. district attorney for the southern district of New-York; and Jesse Hoyt, counsellor at Law ... with anecdotes or biographical sketches of Stephen Allen; George P. Barker (etc.) ... Boston, Cook & co., 1845. 152 p. 22½ cm. First 8 pages of a second copy prefixed. Another edition, practically identical, was issued the same year with the author's names corrected (from Mackeinzie) 4-1524. F123.M156

McMULLIN, Phillip. New York in 1800; an index to the Federal census schedules of the State of New York, with other aids to research. Pref. by Winston DeVille. Provo, Utah, Gendex Corp., 1971. xii, 272 p. illus. 29 cm. 74-172992 MARC. F123.M159

McMURRAY, William. Remarks of Mr. McMurray, of New-York, in the Assembly, in committee of the whole, Jan. 30 and Feb. 1, 1843, on the governor's message ... (Albany, 1843) 13 p. 24 cm. 10-31670. F123.M162

MATHER, Joseph H. Geography of the state of New York. Embracing its physical features, climate, geology, mineralogy, etc., etc. Hartford, J. H. Mather & co.; New York, M. H. Newman, etc., 1847. xii, (13) - 432 p. incl. front., illus. (maps) 19½ cm. Also pub. Utica, 1848 under title: A geographical history of the state of New York. 1-15878 Rev. F123.M 42
G & M

MATHER, Joseph H. A geographical history of the state of New York ... Utica, H. H. Hawley, 1848. 2, (xi) - xii, (13) - 432 p. front., illus. (incl. maps) 19 cm. See above itme. 1-15879 Rev. F123.M 43

— 9th ed. Utica, Hawley, Fuller, & co., 1851. 2, (xi) - xii, (13) - 432 p. front., illus. (maps) 19½ cm. 1-15880 Rev. F123.M 44

MERRILL, Arch. Pioneer profiles. (Rochester, N.Y., Distributed by Seneca Book Binding Co., 1957) 215 p. plates. ports. 20 cm. 58-10. F123.M 56

MERRILL, Arch. The towpath ... (Rochester, N.Y., Printed by L. Heindl & son, 1945) 2, 180 p. illus., plates, ports. 20 cm. Reprinted from the Democrat and chronicle, Rochester, N.Y. 46-16891. F123.M 57

MILLER, Douglas T. Jacksonian aristocracy; class and democracy in New York, 1830 - 1860. New York, Oxford University Press, 1967. xiii, 228 p. 22 cm. 67-15130. F123. M 6

MILLER, Morris Smith, The address of, to the electors of the county of Oneida, on the nomination of Jonas Platt, for governor of the state of New-York ... 1810. (n. p., 1814?) 28 p. 21 cm. 17-22116.
    F123.M 64
    Toner Coll.

MILLER, Morris Smith, Speech of, on the army bills. Delivered in the House of representatives of the U. S. ... 1814. Georgetown, D. C., Richards and Mallory, 1814. 31 p. 21 cm. (Bound with above item) 17-22115.
    F123.M 64
    Toner Coll.

— Georgetown, Printed by Robert Alleson, 1814. 20 p. 21½ cm. 5-3321.
    F123.M 64
    Toner Coll.

NOAH, Mordecai Manuel. Report of the trial of an action on the case, brought by Sylvanus Miller, esq., ... against Mordecai M. Noah ... for an alleged libel. By L. H. Clarke. New-York, Printed by J. W. Palmer, 1823. 72 p. 22½ cm. 21-4386.
    F123.M 65
    Toner Coll.

MINTHORNE. A reply to the resolutions and address of a meeting convened at Martlings, in the city of New-York ... 1811. Containing, the proceedings of the Committee of safety, of '76, against Mangle Minthorne. By a Whig of '76. New-York, Printed by Henry C. Southwick, 1811. 11 p. 25 cm. 16-11522.
    F123.M 66

MONAGHAN, Frank. ... The results of the revolution ... (New York) Columbia university press, 1933. (323)-362. pl. 23½ cm. Reprinted from History of the state of New York ... v. 4. "Select bibliography": p. 360-362.
    F123.M 68

MORRIS. Obituary addresses on the occasion of the death of the Hon. Robert H. Morris ... Reported by Hayes, Hincks, Carey and Kempston. New York, W. E. & J. Sibell, printers, 1855. 115 p. front. (port.) 23 cm. 13-2638.
    F123.M 87

MURPHY. Proceedings at the dinner given by the citizens of Brooklyn at the Mansion house ... 1857, to the Hon. Henry C. Murphy, previously to his departure on his mission as minister to the Netherlands. Brooklyn, I. Van Anden, printer, 1857. 90 p. 23 cm. 27-25093.
    F123.M 95

MURPHY. Memoir of Hon. Henry C. Murphy, of Brooklyn, N. Y. Reprinted from the New York genealogical and biographical record ... 1883. New York, Trow's print. and bookbind. co., 1883. 22 p. front. (port.) 8°. 1-10242-M1.
    F123.M 97

NEW YORK hards and softs; which is the true Democracy? a brief statement of facts for the consideration of the Democracy of the Union, showing the origin and cause of the continued "division of the party." By a national Democrat. New York, Printed at the Daily news office, 1856. 80 p. 24 cm. 11-4700.
    F123.N 54

NEW YORK (State) Assessors. A report on the agricultural and other resources of the state of New York. By Theodore C. Peters, state assessor. Albany, Van Benthuysen's team print., 1864. iv, (5)-152 p. 7 fold. maps (incl. front.) 24 cm. 1-15991 Rev.
    F123.N 56

NEW YORK (State) Minutes of the Committee and of the first Commission for detecting and defeating conspiracies in the state of New York ... 1776-8, with collateral documents. To which is added Minutes of the Council of appointment, state of New York ... 1778-9 ... New York, Printed for the Soc., 1924-5. 2 v. 24½ cm. (Collections of the N. Y. hist. soc ... lvii-lviii) 25-4703.
    F123.N563

NEW YORK (State) Minutes of the Council of appointment of New York, Apr. 4, 1778 - May 3, 1779, from original manuscript in possession of Franklin D. Roosevelt, with introd. by Dorothy C. Barck. Hyde Park, Priv. print., 1925. 2, 3-97 p. 23½ cm. 50 copies printed. 44-25198.
    F123.N564
    Rare Book Coll.

NEW YORK (State)   The American revolution in New York: its political, social and economic significance.   For general use as part of the program of the Executive committee on the 150th anniversary of the American revolution.   Prepared by the Division of archives and history.   Albany, The University of the state of New York, 1926.   371 p. incl. illus. (incl. ports., maps, facsims.)   front.   23 cm.   "Works relating to the American revolution in the state of New York ... " p. 287-304.   27-27037 rev. 2.
F123.N565
1926

— Introd. to 1967 ed. by Ralph Adams Brown.   Port Washington, Ira J. Friedman (1967)   371 p.   22 cm.   (Empire State historical publication series 44)   67-16258.
F123.N565
1967

NEW YORK (State)   Speech of Governor Clinton, the the Legislature of the state of New-York ... 1819.   Albany: Print. at the Register office, 1819.   16 p.   22½ cm.   25-25177.
F123.N566

NEW YROK (State)   The Speeches of the different governors, to the Legislature of the state of New-York, commencing with those of George Clinton, and continued down to the present time.   Albany, J. B. Van Steenbergh, 1825.   247 p.   22 cm.   Includes the speeches and messages of George Clinton, John Jay, Morgan Lewis, Daniel D. Tompkins, De Witt Clinton and Joseph C. Yates.   7-24547.
F123.N568

NEW YORK.   Governor Edwin D. Morgan.   Governor's message.   New York, 1862.   21½ cm.
F123.N 57

NEW YORK (State)   University.   Souvenir program.   One hundred fiftieth anniversary of the founding of the government of the state of New York.   (Albany, J. B. Lyon co., general printers, 1927)   80 p.   incl. illus., ports.   23 cm.   27-27375.
F123.N586

NEW YORK state guide, The; containing an alphabetical list of counties, towns, cities, villages, post-offices, etc.   With the census of 1840, etc. etc.   Albany, J. Disturnell, 1842.   72 p. incl. tables.   15½ cm.   3-28225.
F123.N591

— Albany, J. Disturnell, 1843.   96 p. incl. tables.   fold. map, tables.   15½ cm.   3-28226.
F123.N592

NEW YORK state tourist, The, descriptive of the scenery of the Mohawk & Hudson rivers.   Falls, lakes, mountains, springs, rail roads & canals ... New York, A. T. Goodrich, 1840.   156 p.   2 pl.   fold. maps.   15½ cm.   18-2209.
F123.N599

NEW YORK state tourist, The.   Descriptive of the scenery of the Hudson, Mohawk, & St. Lawrence rivers ... New-York, A. T. Goodrich, 1842.   234 p.   front., 1 illus., plates. fold. maps.   15½ cm.   1-15882.
F123.N 60

NEW YORK traveller, The; containing railroad, steamboat, canal packet, and stage routes, through the state of New-York.   Also, other information useful to travellers.   New York, J. Disturnell, 1845.   iv, (5) - 48 p.   15 cm.   1-15883.
F123.N 61

NOTES on a tour through the western part of the state of New York.   Philadelphia, 1829-30.   (Rochester, N.Y., Reprinted for G. P. Humphrey, 1916)   2, (7) - 55 p.   20½ cm.   17-9554.
F123.N 67

ONTARIO and St. Lawrence steamboat co.   The great northern route.   American lines. ... handbook for travelers to Niagara Falls, Montreal and Quebec, and through Lake Champlain to Saratoga Springs ... Buffalo, Jewett, Thomas, 1852.   (3) - 158 p. incl. illus., plates.   front., fold. map.   17½ cm.   3-28495.
F123.O 58

— Buffalo, Jewett, Thomas; Rochester, D. M. Dewey, 1853.   (7) - 174 p. incl. illus., plates.   front., fold. map.   17 cm.   1-16121.
F123.O 59

"OUR travels, statistical, geographical, minerological, geographical, historical, political, and quizzical": a Knickerbocker tour of New York State, 1822.   Written by myself XYZ etc.   Ed. with introd. and notes, by Louis Leonard Tucker.   Albany, New York State Lib., 1968.   vi, 133 p. col. illus., maps (on lining papers)   22 cm. and portfolio (10 plates)   25 cm.   Incl. bibliographical refs.   79-634856.
F123. O 8
Special format

NEW YORK

(PECK, Jedidiah) The political wars of Otsego: or, Downfall of Jacobinism and despotism: being a collection of pieces, lately published in the Otsego herald. To which is added, an address to the citizens of the U.S.; and extracts from Jack Tar's journals, kept on board the ship Liberty. ... By the author of the Plough-jogger. Cooperstown: Printed for the author; by E. Phinney, M, DCC, XCVI.   vii, (9) - 122, (4) p.   21½ cm.   9-20818.   F123. P 35

(PEOPLE'S party (New York) Two speeches delivered in the New-York state convention ... 1824, with the proceedings of the convention. New-York, Printed by G. F. Hopkins, 1824.   v. (7) - 88 p. 21½ cm. 9-32222.   F123. P 4

(PHELPS, Mrs. Almira (Hart) Lincoln) ... Caroline Westerley; or, The young traveller from Ohio. Containing the letters of a young lady of seventeen, written to her sister. Harper's stereotype ed. New York, J. & J. Harper, 1833.   4 (3) - 233 p. front. 15 cm. (Boy's and girl's library. xvi) 1-15884.   F123. P 58

PICTURESQUE tourist, The; being a guide through the state of New York and Upper and Lower Canada, including a Hudson River guide; giving an accurate description of cities and villages, celebrated places of resort, etc. ... New York, J. Disturnell, 1858.   ix, (10) - 298 p. front., illus., plates, 3 maps (1 fold.) 16 cm. 1-15885.   F123. P 61

— The traveler's guide to the Hudson river, Saratoga springs, lake George, falls of Niagara and Thousand islands; Montreal, Quebec, and the Saguenay river, etc. forming the fashionable northern tour throuth the U. S. and Canada ... Compiled by J. Disturnell. New York, "American news co." (1864)   ix, (10) - 324 p. front., illus., plates, fold. map. 16½ cm. First pub. in 1858 with title: The picturesque tourist ... 1-16135.   F123. P 65

PILGRIMS of hope, The: an oratorio for the Clintonian celebration of the New year. Re-published from "The American" of Jan. 1, 1820. With additional notes and an appendix, containing "The coalition," a political tract ... Albany, Re-printed by Packard & Van Benthuysen, 1820.   iv. (5) - 46, 10 p. 19½ cm.   The first part was contributed to the "American" over the signature of Ithuriel. 9-20812.   F123. P 66

REFLECTIONS on An address to the Republican members of the Legislature, by one of their colleagues, in favour of the appointment of Rufus King to the Senate of the U. S. By a Federalist. (n.p., 1818) 8 p. 21½ cm. 9-20821.   F123. R 33

RESULT of the N. Y. state election, ... The; its causes and consquences. (Albany, 1846) 22 p. 23 cm. At head of title: Albany atlas, extra - Dec. 1846.   10-15728.   F123. R 43

RIGHTS of suffrage, The ... Hudson: Printed by Ashbel Stoddard, M, DCC, XCII.   45 p. 17 cm. 8-26475.
F123. R 57
Rare Book Coll.

REPUBLICAN party, N.Y. Oneida County. Proceedings of the Republican County convention ... Utica, 1862.   21½ cm.   F123. R65

(ROSE, William L.) A narrative of the celebrated Dyde supper. By the ed. and proprietor of the New-York morning post and morning star. New York, Printed for the author, 1811.   61 p. 21½ cm. Regarding the union of the Clinton and Burr factions of the Republican party in New York. 9-20819.   F123. R 79
Rare Book Coll.

SCISCO, Louis Dow. ... Political nativism in New York state ... New York, The Columbia university press, 1901.   259 p. 22½ cm. (Studies in history, economics and public law, ed. by the Faculty of political science of Columbia university. vol. xiii, no. 2) Pub. also as the author's thesis.   "Sources": p. 255-259. 2-25100.   F123. S 41

SIMMS, Jeptha R(oot) Trappers of New York, or A biography of Nicholas Stone & Nathaniel Foster; tog. with anecdotes of other celebrated hunters, and some account of Sir William Johnson, and his style of living. ... Albany, Printed by J. Munsell, 1850.   280 p. front. (port.) pl. 19½ cm. 6-4479.
F123. S 59
Rare Book Coll.

— Albany, Printed by J. Munsell, 1851. 287 p. front. (port.) pl. 18½ cm. 6-4480.
F123. S 59
1851

— ... 2d ed. Albany, J. Munsell, 1851. 287 p. front. (port.) plates. 18½ cm. 38-34433.
F123. S 59
1851 a

— Albany, J. Munsell, 1871. 287 p. incl. pl. front. (port.) plates. 19 cm. 8-7785.
F123. S 59
1871

— a reprint with new supplementary matter. St. Johnsville, N.Y., Printed by Enterprise and news, 1935. 300 p. incl. front., 1 illus. plates, ports. 19½ cm. 35-31925.
F123. S 59
1935

SMITH, Joshua Toulmin. Journal in America, 1837 - 1838; ed. with introd. and notes by Floyd Benjamin Streeter ... Metuchen, N.J., Printed for C. F. Heartman, 1925. 54 p. 24½ cm. (Heartman's historical series. no. 41) 99 copies printed. 25-18692.
F123. S 64

SOFTS. The softs the true Democracy of the state of New-York ... May 25th, 1856. New-York, 1856. 72 p. 22½ cm. A reply to a pamphlet with title: "New York hards and softs: which is the true Democracy ... 1856. 11-4699.
F123. S 68

SPAFFORD, Horatio Gates. A pocket guide for the tourist and traveller, along the line of the canals, and the interior commerce of the state of New York. New-York, Printed by T. and J. Swords, 1824. iv, (5) - 72 p. 14½ cm. 1-15889 Rev.
F123. S 73
Rare Book Coll.

SPAFFORD, Horatio Gates. The school boy's introd. to the geography and statistics of the state of New-York: designed for the use of common schools, under the patronage of the Legislature. Troy, E. Platt, 1825. 46 p. 17½ cm. 7-17098.
F123. S 733
Rare Book Coll.

SPAULDING, Ernest Wilder. New York in the critical period, 1783 - 1789 ... New York, Columbia university press, 1932. xiii, (3) - 334 p. incl. maps. front. (port.) 23½ cm. (New York state historical association series. v. 1) Bibliography: p. (289) - 315. 33-729.
F123. S 75

— Port Washington, N.Y., I. J. Friedman, 1963. 334 p. 23 cm. (Empire State historical publication, 19) 63-12954.
F123. S 75
1963

STARR, Chandler. An address delivered at the Whig convention held at Utica ... 1834. New-York, T. Snowden, printer, 1834. 16 p. 21½ cm. 9-27174.
F123. S 79

SUMMER month, A; or, Recollections of a visit to the falls of Niagara, and the lakes ... Philadelphia, H. C. Carey and I. Lea; New-York, H. C. Carey, 1823. vii. 250 p. 18½ cm. Ascribed to a Mr. Matthews of Mathews. 1-15890 Rev.
F123. S 95

TANNER, Henry Schenck. The travellers' hand book for the state of New-York and the province of Canada ... With maps, etc. 2d ed. New-York, T. R. Tanner, 1844. iv. (5) - 166 p. maps. 15 cm. This copy without maps. 1-15891 Rev.
F123. T 16

TAYLOR, John. ... Journal of Rev. John Taylor's missionary tour through the Mohawk & Black river countries in 1802. (In Documentary history of the state of New York, v. 3) 2-5712-3.
F123. T 24

TOMPKINS. Daniel D. Tompkins, class of 1795, by John B. Pine. (New York, 1906?) 8 p. port. 25½ cm. Printed from the Columbia university quarterly, Dec. 1906. 7-40704 Rev.
F123. T 66

TRAVELLER'S directory, The: exhibiting the distances on the principal land and water thoroughfares of the state of New-York: and showing the reciprocal and relative distances of each place from the

chief towns on three routes between Albany and Buffalo.   Rochester, Marshall, Dean, 1830.
12 p.   16 cm.   Text trimmed slightly.   18-23792.
F125. T 77
Rare Book Coll.

U.S. Bureau of the Census.   Heads of families at the first census of the U.S. taken in the year 1790: New York.   Baltimore, Genealogical Pub. Co., 1966.   308 p.   29 cm.
F123. U 5
19661
L H & G

VAN BUREN, John.   ... Speech of John Van Buren, at the ratification meeting, held ... 1853.   (New York, 1853)   8 p.   24 cm.   Evening post documents. 2d series. no. 5.   11-4698.
F123.V 21

VAN DER KEMP, Francis Adrian, 1752 - 1829, an autobiography, together with extracts from his correspondence; ed. with an historical sketch, by Helen Lincklaen Fairchild ... New York and London, G. P. Putnam's sons, 1903.   xii, 230 p.   front., illus., ports., facsims.   21½ cm.   "List of the principal authorities consulted": p. 217-220.   3-17806 Rev.
F123.V 22

VAN DER KEMP.   Scholar in the wilderness:. Francis Adrian Van der Kemp.   By Harry F. Jackson. (Syracuse) Syracuse University Press, 1963.   xi, 356 p.   22 cm.   63-19192
F123.V 22J3

(VANDEWATER, Robert J.)   The tourist; or, Pocket manual for travellers on the Hudson river, the western canal, and stage road; comprising also the routes to Lebanon, Ballston, and Saratoga Springs. New York, J. & J. Harper, 1830.   59 p.   fold. map.   16°.   1-15892-M1.
F123.V 24

— 2d ed., enl. and improved.   New-York, Printed by Ludwig & Tolefree, 1831.   69 p.   front. (fold. map)   15 cm.   17-27588.
F123.V242

— 3d ed., enl. and improved.   New York, Harper & bros., 1834.   95 p.   front. (fold. map)   16 cm. 15-12383.
F123.V243

— 4th ed., enl. and improved.   New York, Harper and bros., 1835.   106 p.   front. (fold. map)   16½ cm. 1-15893.
F123.V 25

— 6th ed.   New-York, Harper & bros., 1838.   (3) - 108 p.   front. (fold. map)   16 cm.   1-16134*-M1 Cancel.
F123.V 26

— 9th ed.   New-York, Harper & bros., 1841.   108 p. incl. front. (fold. map)   16 cm.   17-12323.
F123.V264

VAN RENSSELAER.   Character and reward of a just man.   A funeral discourse, commemorative of the life, and virtues, of the late Hon. Stephen Van Rensselaer.   ... by the Rev. William Barlow ... Albany, Print. by Packard, Van Benthuysen and co., 1839.   47 p.   21½ cm.   13-33781.
F123.V 27

VAN RENSSELAER.   A discourse on the life, services and character of Stephen Van Rensselaer ... With an historical sketch of the colony and manor of Rensselaerwyck, in an appendix.   By Daniel D. Barnard.   Albany, Printed by Hoffman & White, 1839.   70 p.   22½ cm.   14-4724.
F123.V272

— 1839.   144 p.   22½ cm.   3-5654.
F123.V273

VAN RENSSELAER.   Religion and rank: a sermon addressed to the Second Presbyterian congregation in Albany ... succeeding the funeral of the Hon. Stephen Van Rensselaer.   By William B. Sprague ... Albany, Printed by Packard, Van Benthuysen and co., 1839.   33 p.   22 cm.   13-33782.
F123.V 28

VAN RENSSELAER.   A funeral discourse, occasioned by the death of the Hon. Stephen Van Rensselaer, delivered in the North Dutch church, Albany ... 1839. By Thomas E. Vermilye ... Albany, Printed by J. Munsell, 1839.   43 p.   22 cm.   14-3685.   F123.V 29

(VERPLANCK, Gulian Crommelin) The state triumvirate, a political tale: and the epistles of Brevet Major Pindar Puff (pseud.) ... New York: Printed for the author, and sold by W. B. Gilley ... J. Seymour, printer, 1819.   215 p.   15½ cm.   2-4269.   F123.V 55
       Rare Book Coll.

VERPLANCK. The essential New Yorker, Gulian Crommelin Verplanck. By Robert William July. Durham, Duke University Press, 1951.   313 p.   ports.   24 cm.   (Duke University publications) Thesis - Columbia University.   Without thesis statement.   Bibliography: p. (290) - 304.   51-11739 rev.   F123.V57 J 8

WILLIAMSON. ... Charles Williamson, Genesee promoter, friend of Anglo-American rapprochement (by) Helen I. Cowan. Ed. under the supervision of Dexter Perkins, city historian, under the authority of the Board of trustees of the Rochester pub. library, and chairman of the Publication committee under authority of the Board of managers of the Rochester hist. soc. Rochester, N.Y., The Society, 1941.   xiv, 356 p.   front., plates, ports., map, facsim.   24 cm.   (The Rochester historical soc. Publication fund series. vol. xix)   42-12694.   F123.W
       F129.R7R58

WAYSIDE sketches; narrative of a journey in 1843, now first pub. from the manuscript for the Clements Library Associates. Ann Arbor, University of Michigan, 1967.   29 p.   24 cm.   68-63696.   F123. W 3

WEED, Thurlow. A chapter from the autobiography of Mr. Thurlow Weed. Stage-coach traveling forty-six years ago. Reprinted from "The Galaxy" of April, 1870. Albany, Printing-house of C. Van Benthuysen, 1870.   31 p.   26 cm.   3-26048.   F123. W 34

WELLS. Memorial of the life and character of John Wells. With reminiscences of the judiciary and members of the New York bar ... (New York) Priv. print. (J. F. Trow, printers) 1874.   145 p.   24½ cm.   13-6129.   F123. W 45

WILLARD. Memorial of John Willard ... consisting of addresses and notices on the occasion of his death, and in illustration of his life and character. Saratoga Springs, Steam print. G. M. Davison, 1863.   47 p.   22 cm.   6-870.   F123. W 69

YOSHPE, Harry Beller. The disposition of loyalist estates in the southern district of the state of New York ... New York, 1939.   226 p. incl. front. (facsim.) diagrs. plates, maps, facsim.   22½ cm.   Thesis (PH. D.) - Columbia university.   no. 458.   "Bibliographical note": p. 210-218.   39-31744.   F123. Y 68

— New York, Columbia university press; London, P. S. King, 1939.   226 p.   plates, maps, diagrs., 2 facsim. (incl. front.)   23 cm.   (Studies in history, economics and public law ... no. 458)   39-31743.   F123. Y682

1865 - 1950.

ABELEDO, Amaranto Antonio. ... Impresiones de los Estados Unidos ... Buenos Aires, Imp. J. H. Kidd, 1913.   12 p.   25 cm.   18-18444 Rev.   F124.A 14

ALL-ROUND route guide, The. The Hudson river; Trenton Falls; Niagara; Toronto; the Thousand Islands and the river St. Lawrence; Ottawa; Montreal; Quebec; the lower St. Lawrence and the Saguenay rivers; the White Mountains; Boston; New York. Montreal, The Montreal print. & pub. co., 1868.   86 p.   16°.   1-16133-M1.   F124. A 41

ASHEY & Adams' new map and guide of the Hudson River, Adirondack and Catskill Mountains... New York (1874)   17½ cm.   F124. A 86

BARDEEN, Charles William. A brief descriptive geography of the Empire state for the use of schools;

NEW YORK

by C. W. Bardeen ... Syracuse, N.Y., C. W. Bardeen, 1895. viii. 9-126 p. front., illus. (incl. maps) 23½ cm.
(School bulletin publications) 5-10340.
F124. B 24

BEEBE, Levi N. A descriptive geography of New York state, with historical and educational notes...
Rochester, N.Y., Educational gazette co., 1887. 116 p. illus. 16° (Empire state series) 1-15894-M1.
F124. B 41

BOWEN, Edward J. Sixty years a crusader, unmuzzled and unafraid. Fighting for political and economic justice; a collection of anecdotes of great Americans, and narratives of stirring efforts in the fields of political and economic reform, leading to a plan to cure and prevent all recessions, curb inflation, and assure continued employment and national prosperity. Albany, Bowen Publications, 1951. 308 p. illus. 24 cm. 51-7717.
F124. B 6

BREWSTER, H. Brewster's New York central rail road guide book: containing the official time tables of each division with the names of all the stations, etc. Rochester, H. W. D. Brewster, 1855.
24 p. 18½ cm. 4-6465.
F124. B 84
Rare Book Coll.

BRIGHAM, Albert Perry. Geography of New York ... (New York, Cincinnati, etc.) American book co., 1921) xl p. illus. (incl. maps) 25½ cm x 20 cm.
F124. B 85

BULL AND BOWEN'S road book of western New York. Buffalo (1885) 15½ cm.
F124. B 95

(BURLING, Ellen) Is the government of the state of New York a republic or a despotism? (New York, 1868) (8) p. 24½ cm. Signed: Anti-despotism. 11-32019.
F124. B 96

— (New York? 1868) 20 p. 23½ cm. 11-32020.
F124. B961

BUTLER, B. C. From New York to Montreal ... New York, American news co., 1873.
4. 155 p. 12°. 1-16132-M1.
F124. B 98

CARMER, Carl Lamson. Listen for a lonesome drum; a York state chronicle ... with sketches by Cyrus Le Roy Baldridge. New York, Farrar & Rinehart, inc., 1936. xvii, 381 p. incl. front. (map) illus., plates. 22 cm. 36-14564.
F124. C 36

— Decorations by John O'Hara Cosgrave, II. (New York) Sloane (1950) xii, 430 p. illus. 22 cm.
50-10369.
F124. C 36
1950

CHADBOURNE, Paul Ansel, ed. ... The public service of the state of New York during the administration of Alonzo B. Cornell, governor. Historical, descriptive and biographical sketches by various authors ... Walter Burritt Moore, assoc. editor. Boston, J. R. Osgood, 1882. 3 v. fronts., plates, ports., map. diagrs. 35 cm. 3-19132 Rev.
F124. C 43

— New York, The Photo-gravure co., 1882. 3 v. fronts., plates, ports., map. diagrs. 36 cm. 3-19133.
F124. C 44

CLINTON, Henry Lauren. Speech of Henry L. Clinton ... 1878. Importance of electing a Democratic congress, and a Democratic U. S. senator ... (New York? 1878) 17 p. 21½ cm. 43-26391.
F124. C 55

CODMAN, John. Winter sketches from the saddle. By a septuagenarian. New York (etc.) G. P. Putnam's sons (1888) 2. 205 p. front. 16½ cm. 7-21503.
F124. C 67

COLT, Mrs. S. S. The tourist's guide through the Empire state. Embracing all cities, towns and watering places, by Hudson River and New York central route ... Albany, N.Y., Ed. and pub. by Mrs. S. S. Colt, 1871. iv. 239 p. front., illus., plates. 23 cm. 1-15895.
F124. C 72

(COLTON, George Woolworth) A school geography of the state of New York, to accompany Colton's

Common school geography ... New York, Sheldon & co. (1880) 15 p. incl. illus., maps. 4°. 1-16875-M1.
F124.C725

CONCERNING some features in the making and administration of our laws, of interest to the average citizen. (n. p.. 1875) 30 p. 14 cm. 12-10739.
F124.C 74

CONKLING, Roscoe. The true reform party. Speech of Hon Roscoe Conkling, at Tweddle hall, Albany, 1875. (Albany? 1875) 27 p. 22½ cm. 12-31030.
F124.C 75

COTILLO. A new American, from the life story of Salvatore A. Cotillo, Supreme court justice, state of New York, by Nat J. Ferber, introd. by Alfred E. Smith. Illus. with photos. New York, Farrar & Rinehart, inc. (1938) xvi, 321 p. 1 illus., plates, ports. 22 cm. 38-9290.
F124.C 78

CRAM, George F., co. A descriptive review of the commercial, industrial, agricultural, historical development of the state of New York ... Chicago, New York, G. F. Cram (1914) 300 p. incl. illus., maps, plans. 29½ cm. 14-9152 Rev.
F124.C 88

"CRUCIBLE"; or, Feathering a mayor's nest. A mellow drama ... New York, C. E. Sargent, 1875. 16 p. 22 cm. A satire on A. Oakey Hall, as mayor of New York. 13-19351.
F124.C 95

DELAWARE and Hudson canal co. The summer tourist; descriptive of the Delaware and Hudson canal co.'s railroads, and their summer resorts! By B. C. Butler ... Season of 1879. Issued by the General passenger dept. ... (Boston, Rand, Avery, printers, 1879-80) 2 v. illus., fold. maps. 18 cm. 1-16131 Rev.
F124.D 33

DELAWARE and Hudson co. A summer paradise; an illus. descriptive guide to the delightful and healthful resorts reached by the Delaware and Hudson co. Albany, N.Y., The passenger dept.
v. illus. (incl. maps) 19 cm. 16-5603 Rev.
F124.D335

DELAWARE and Hudson route, The. A new through line from Philadelphia to Bethlehem, Mauch Chunk, Scranton, Cooperstown, Sharon Springs, Saratoga, Lake George, the Adirondacks, and Montreal ... New York, Taintor brothers, 1872. 185 p. illus., plates, fold. map. 16½ cm. (Taintor's route and city guides. no. 21) 1-21530.
F124.D 34

DELAWARE, Lackawanna and western railroad co. Summer excursion routes and rates. Delaware, Lackawanna and western railroad co. 1893 ... (New York, Printed by Livingston Middleditch co., 1893) 192 p. illus., fold. map. 23½ cm. 1-16126.
F124.D347

— (1894) 208 p. illus., fold. map. 23½ cm. 1-16127.
F124.D348

— (1895) 188 p. illus., fold. map. 23 cm. 1-16128.
F124.D349

— (1896) 202 p. illus., fold. map. 23½ cm. 1-16129.
F124.D 35

— (1897) 22½ cm.
F124.D351

— (Elmira, N.Y., The Advertiser press) 1898. 196 p. illus. 8°. 1-16130-M1.
F124.D352

DISTURNELL, John, comp. Summer resorts and watering places. Pleasure excursions between New York, Long Branch, Sea Girt and other sea-bathing resorts situated on the New Jersey coast, within fifty miles of the city of New York; also, including Staten island and both shores of Long island, Coney island, Rockaway beach, Flushing, etc. ... New York, J. Wiley (1877) 70 p. front., pl. 15½ cm. 1-16289.
F124.D 61

DIX. John A. Dix, a citizen, delineated by Albert H. Walker. (New York, 1910) 21 p. 23 cm. 10-27315.
F124.D628

DREW. The book of Daniel Drew; a glimpse of the Fisk-Gould-Tweed régime from the inside, by

Bouck White. New York, Doubleday, Page, 1910.   x, 423 p.   20½ cm.   10-9805 Rev.

F124.D 77

— New York, George H. Doran co. (1910)   vi, 423 p.   19½ cm.   43-45990.

F124.D7712

— Garden City, N.Y., The Sun dial press, inc. (1937)   vi, 423 p.   20½ cm.   37-32157.

F124.D772

— With a new introd. by Benton W. Davis.   Larchmont, N.Y., American Research Council (1965) xvi, 423 p.   21 cm.   (The Library of stock market classics)   65-20320.

F124.D773

DREW. Daniel Drew; aus dem Tagebuch eines amerkanischen Börsenmannes.   By Bouck White. Berlin, Von Arnim (1943)   234 p.   21 cm.   A F 48-697*.

F124.D7755

ELLS, M.   Lake and glen scenery of central New York, embracing notices of lakes Seneca, Cayuga, Keuka and Canandaignua, with particular descriptions of the famous ... Watkins and Havana glens ... Elmira, N.Y., Advertiser assoc. book and job print., 1873.   32 p.   diagr.   19½ cm.   1-15896 Rev.

F124.E 44

ERIE railway co.   Erie railway tourist.   (New York? Erie railway company, 1874)   32 p.   illus. 30 x 23 cm.   5-3930 Rev.

F124.E 64

ERIE railroad co.   Homes and sports along the Erie ... New York, 1881.   20 x 11 cm.

F124.E676

ERIE.   The Erie route: a guide of the Erie railway and its branches, with sketches of the cities, villages, scenery and objects of interest along the route, and railroad, steamboat & stage connections ... New York, Taintor brothers & co. (1875)   v, (7) - 99, (2) p.   illus., plates, fold. map.   17 cm.   Attributed to John R. Arrison.   4-6469.

F124.E 70

— (1887)   87 p.   illus., fold. map.   17½ cm.   4-6468.

F124.E 71

EXTRACTS from a summer cruise on board the famous steam yacht, Annie Laurie, during the season of 1874, on the inland waters of New York state and Canadas.   By an "old salt." ... Syracuse, Printed by F. L. Dillaye, 1875.   92 p.   pl.   20 cm.   18-2374.

F124.E 96
Toner Coll.

FAXON'S illustrated hand-book of travel by the Fitchburg, Rutland and Saratoga railway line, to Saratoga, lakes George and Champlain, the Adirondacks, Niagara falls, Montreal, Quebec, the White mountains ... Boston, C. A. Faxon, 1873.   193 p.   illus., fold. maps.   17 cm.   1-21378.

F124.F 28

FAXON'S illustrated handbook of travel to Saratoga, lakes George and Champlain, the Adirondacks, etc. Rev. ed.   Boston, C. A. Faxon, 1874.   12, 210 p. incl. front., illus. fold. maps.   16½ cm.   1-21379.

F124.F281

FAXON'S illustrated hand-book of summer travel, to the lakes, springs and mountains of New England and New York.   By Edward S. Sears ... New and rev. ed.   Boston, C. A. Faxon, 1875. 3, 285 p.   front., illus., fold. maps, fold. plan.   17½ cm.   1-21391.

F124.F282

FIERO.   Proceedings of the Senate of the state of New York on the life, character and public service of William Pierson Fiero.   Albany, N.Y. (J. B. Lyon co., printers, 1915)   31 p.   port.   26½ cm. 15-27198.

F124.F 46

FITCH, Charles Elliott.   Official New York, from Cleveland to Hughes ... New York and Buffalo, Hurd pub. co., 1911.   4 v.   pl., ports.   26 cm.   12-21172.

F124.F 54

FLOWER.   The life of Roswell Pettibone Flower, compiled by Emma Flower Taylor.   Watertown, N.Y., The Hungerford-Holbrook co., 1930.   3, (11) - 74 p.   2 port. (incl. front.)   19½ cm. 36-29793.

F124.F 66

LOCAL HISTORIES IN THE LIBRARY OF CONGRESS

"FOUR-TRACK series." no. 1 - (New York, 1893 - 19 v. illus. 21 - 24 cm. Issued by New York Central and Hudson River Railroad. Some numbers in revised editions. 56-50985.
F124.F 77

— — Health and pleasure on "America's greatest railroad." Descriptive of summer resorts and excursion routes ... (Buffalo, The Matthews-Northrup co., 1893) 350, cii p. inck. front., illus., pl. fold. maps. 8°. no. 5. 1-16123-M1.

— Same. (New York, American bank note co., 1895) 504 p. incl. front., illus. pl., fold. maps. 23 ½ cm. No. 5. 1-16124.

— Same. (New York) 1896. 532 p. incl. front., illus. maps. 23 ½ cm. No. 5. 1-27676-M2.

— ... In the Adirondack mountains ... (Buffalo, N.Y., The Matthews-Northrup co.) 1895. 64 p. illus., fold. maps. 20 ½ x 10 ½ cm. No. 6. 1-16273.

— Same. 1898. 64 p. illus., fold. maps. 8°. No. 6. 1-16272-M1.

— ... Three ways to go to New York. (New York) 1901. 10 x 20 ½ cm. No. 7.

— ... Two to fifteen days' pleasure tours on the New York central & Hudson river r.r. and connections ... (Buffalo, 1895) 64 p. illus., maps (part fold.) 20 ½ x 10 cm. No. 8. 1-16277.

— Two days at Niagara Falls ... (New York, 1896) 64 p. map. 8°. No. 9. 1-14207-M1.

— ... The Thousand Islands. 1902. 64 p. illus., 2 fold. maps. 20 ½ x 10 ½ No. 10. 2-26027.

— New York as a winter resort ... New York, 1897. 10 x 20 ½ cm. No. 18.

— New York as a summer resort. 1896. 96 p. illus., fold. map. nar. 8°. No. 19. 1-14708-M1.

— A message to Garcia; (being a preachment) By Elbert Hubbard. New York, G. H. Daniels, 1899. 16 p. 21 cm. No. 25. 56-50984.

GEOGRAPHY of the state of New York ... (By S. S. Cornell) 1878. 1 v.
F124.G 37

GOSNELL, Harold Foote. Boss Platt and his New York machine; a study of the political leadership of Thomas C. Platt, Theodore Rossevelt, and others ... with an introd. by Charles E. Merriam ... Chicago, Ill., The University of Chicago press (1924) xxiv, 370 p. plates, ports. 20 ½ cm. 24-2633.
F124.G 68

— New York, Russell & Russell (1969) xxiv, 370 p. 23 cm. 74-75466.
F124.G 68
1969

— New York, AMS Press (1969) xxiv, 370 p. 23 cm. 75-95153.
F124.G 68
1969 b

— Chicago, University of Chicago Press. St. Clair Shores, Mich., Scholarly Press (1971) xxiv, 370 p. illus. 22 cm. Includes bibliographical references. 70-145047 MARC.
F124.G 68
1971

NEW YORK (State) Dept. of Commerce. Vacation variety in New York State. (Albany, 1951) 16 p. illus. 22 cm. A 51-9632.
F124.G 72

GRADY. Proceedings of the Legislature of the state of New York on the life, character and public wervice of Thomas Francis Grady, state senator. 1912. Albany, N.Y. (J. B. Lyon co., printers, 1914) 83 p. incl. port. 26 ½ cm. 15-27196 Rev.
F124.G 73

(GREENE, Frank B.) New York. Philadelphia, J. B. Lippincott, 1891. 8 p. 12°. Appears as article "New York" in Chambers's encyclopedia. New ed. London (etc.) 1891-93. 1-15898-M1.
F124.G 79

GREEN. Proceedings of the Legislature of the state of New York commemorative of the life and public services of George E. Green, ... 1917. Albany, N.Y. (J. B. Lyon co., printers, 1917) 51 p. front. (port.) 26 cm. 29-22579.
F124.G796

GROSS, Herbert. Our New York; the Empire State and its government. New York, Oxford Book Co., 1950. iv, 51, v-vii p. illus. 20 cm. 51-665.
F124.G 83

(GUYOT, Arnold Henry) ... Geography of New York. (New York) Scribner, Armstrong, 1877. 12 p. illus. (incl. maps) 29 ½ x 24 cm. Supplement to Guyot's New Intermediate geography. 1-16876 Rev.
F124.G 98

HALL, Mrs. Lizzie Gregg. West of the Cayuga, New York, Pegasus pub. co. (1940) 88 p. 21 ½ cm. "First edition." 40-8026.
F124.H 23

(HARDEN, Edward Jenkins) Notes of a short northern tour.   For private circulation only.   Savannah, Morning news press, 1869.   38 p.   22 cm.   Text in English and Latin.   3-29126.   F124.H 25

HARLOW, Samuel R.   Life sketches of the state officers, senators, and members of the Assembly of the state of New York, in 1867.   Albany, Weed, Parsons, 1867.   418 p.   front. (port.)   21½ cm.   5-34796.
F124.H 28

HIGGINS.   Proceedings of the Legislature of the state of New York commemorative of the life and public services of Frank Wayland Higgins, late governor of the state ... 1907.   Albany (J. B. Lyon co. print., 1909)   64 p.   front. (port.)   26½ cm.   12-30068.   F124.H 63

HOTCHKISS, Caroline Woodbridge.   Geography of New York state (Human geography book I) ... (Philadelphia, 1924)   45 p.   illus. (incl. maps)   25 cm.   F124.H 73

HUGHES, Charles Evans.   Addresses and papers of Charles Evans Hughes, governor of New York, 1906 - 1908; with an introd. by Jacob Gould Schurman ... New York and London, G. P. Putnam's sons, 1908.   xxxviii, 289 p.   front. (port.)   20 cm.   8-14814.   F124.H 89

HUNGERFORD, Edward.   Pathway of empire; with an introd. by Dixon Ryan Fox ... New York, R. M. McBride & co. (1935)   xv, 325 p.   front., plates.   22½ cm.   "First edition."   35-27410.   F124.H 92

HUSTED.   Address by the Hon. Chauncey M. Depew, at the memorial services by the Legislature of the state of New York in honor of General James W. Husted.   (New York, E. C. Lockwood, printer, 1893?)   24 p.   23 cm.   3-27039.   F124.H 95

HUSTED.   Proceedings of the Legislature of the state of New York, in memory of Gen. James W. Husted ...   Albany, J. B. Lyon, printer, 1893.   46 p.   front. (port.)   25½ cm.   1-13609.
F124.H 96

KING.   Memorial of the Hon. John Alsop King, 18th president of the New York historical soc. ... New York, For the Society, 1901.   27 p.   front. (port.)   8º.   1-4219.   F124.K 52

KITCHIN, William Copeman.   A wonderland of the East, comprising the lake and mountain region of New England and eastern New York; a book for those who love to wander among beautiful lakes and rivers, etc. ... with three maps and fifty-four plates ...   Boston, The Page co., 1920.   xiv, 331 p.   col. front., plates (part col.) fold. maps.   24½ cm.   (See America first" series)   20-21409.   F124.K 62

KOLLOCK, Henry.   State of New York: embracing historical, descriptive, and statistical notices of cities, towns, villages, industries, and summer resorts ...   Illus. with nearly 200 choice engravings. New York, H. Kollock (1883)   304 p. incl. illus., plates, maps.   24½ cm.   1-15899.
F124.K 81

LADD, Carl Edwin.   Growing up in the horse and buggy days.   New York, Nesterman pub. co., 1943.   263 p.   illus.   22 cm.   (Nestor house books)   "First printing."   43-560.   F124. L 2

LANSING, Abraham.   Recollections (of) Abraham Lansing.   Ed. Charles E. Fitch.   (New York, The De Vinne press) Priv. print., 1909.   6, 3-266 p.   front., plates (1 mounted col.)   ports.   23½ cm.   A 18-1907.
F124. L 3

LAWLOR.   Geography of the Empire state ... foreword by Very Rev. Msgr. Joseph V. S. McClancy .. New York, Chicago, W. H. Sadlier (1929)   3, 73 p.   illus. (incl. maps)   26 cm.   29-7216.
F124. L 42

LAWRENCE, Richard Wesley.   The New York state gubernatorial campaign of 1930.   New York city (1932)   53 p.   21 cm.   44-40326.   F124. L 44

LEGISLATIVE correspondent's red book, containing portraits and biographies of some persons more or less prominent in public life, written entirely without respect to the libel laws, in a studious effort to conceal everything but the truth ... Comp. by the Legislative correspondents' assoc. of the state of

New York. (Legislative correspondents' special ed.) Albany, J. B. Lyon co., printers, 1913.
(80) p. illus. 19 cm. L. C. copy replaced by microfilm. 13-15943.
F124. L 5
Microfilm 8879 F

LEHMAN. Herbert H. Lehman, director general, United Nations Relief and Rehabilitation Administration, 1943-1946. Tributes and other relevant documents. Stamford, Conn., Overbrook Press (1946)
75 p. port. 25 cm. 48-11167 *.
F124. L 53

LEHMAN. Herbert H. Lehman and his era. By Allan Nevins. New York, Scribner (1963)
456 p. 24 cm. Full name: Joseph Allen Nevins. 63-8464.
F124. L532

LIGHTS of the Legislature of 1874. Written by a reporter of the Assembly. Albany, N. Y., The Argus company, printers, 1874. 48 p. 19 cm. 11-30523.
F124. L 72

LOW. Proceedings of the Senate of the state of New York, on the death of Hon. Henry R. Low. Albany, The Troy press co. print., 1889. 63 p. front. (port.) 26 cm. 1-13608.
F124. L 9

McCARREN. Proceedings of the Legislature of the state of New York commemorative of the life and public services of Patrick Henry McCarren, held ... 1910. Albany, N. Y. (1910?) 41 p. front. (port.) 26 ½ cm. 12-33580.
F124. M 13

McMAHON. Proceedings of the Bench and bar of the county of New York, in memory of Hon. Martin T. McMahon, late a judge of the Court of general sessions. (New York, M. B. Brown press, 1906)
27 p. front. (port.) 26 cm. 6-38383.
F124. M 16

MARELLI, Carlos Antonio. ... La excursión de Nueva York, organizada por el Congreso de geología de Washington ... Primera contribucion a los parques estaduales de la provincia de Buenos Aires ... Buenos Aires, 1936. 92 p. illus. (incl. maps) ports. (part fold.) diagrs. 28 ½ cm. 37-8265 rev.
F124. M 39

MARTENS, Ludwig Karlovich. Testimony of Ludwig C. A. K. Martens taken before the Joint Legislative Committee of the State of New York Investigating Seditions Activities. Clayton R. Lusk, chairman. (New York? 1919?) 138 p. 23 cm. 47-33350.
F124 M 4

MAURY, Matthew Fontaine. Geography of New York. A supplement to Maury's Manual of geography. New York, University pub. co., 1885. 8 p. incl. illus., maps. 4º. 1-16881-M1.
F124. M 45

MERRITT, Edwin Atkins. Recollections, 1828 - 1911 (by) Edwin A. Merritt. Albany, J. B. Lyon co., printers, 1911. 188 p. front., ports.. facsims. 23 ½ cm. 11-30417.
F124. M 57

MILLER, Charles Henry. New York and Long island landscapes. Etched by Barry. (New York, 1879) 32 pl. 33 ½ x 28 cm. 1-15901.
F124. M 64

(MONTEITH, James) Geography of New York. (New York, A. S. Barnes, 1877) 8 p. illus. 20 ½ x 25 ½ cm. Supplement to the N. Y. ed. of Monteith's comprehensive geography. 2-22450.
F124. M 77

MOSCOW, Warren. Politics in the Empire State. (1st ed.) New York, A. A. Knopf, 1948.
238, x p. map. 22 cm. 48-7919*.
F124. M 88

MOTT, Edward Harold, ed. The Erie route: a guide of the New York, lake Erie & western railway and its branches, with sketches of the cities, villages, scenery, etc. ... New York, Taintor bros., Merrill & co., 1882. 7 - 90 (i.e. 126) p. illus., maps (1 fold.) 18 cm. (Taintor's guide books) 1-21441.
F124. M 89

NEW ALBANY, The. ... Senatorial number ... (1892) 1 v.
F124. N 25

NEW YORK (State) Progressive democracy; addresses and state papers of Alfred E. Smith, with an introd. by Henry Moskowitz. New York, Harcourt, Brace (1928) xiii, 392 p. 22 ½ cm. 28-13918.
F124. N436

NEW YORK

— Second printing, (1928) xiii, 392 p. 21½ cm Pub. May, 1928. 2d printing June, 1928. 28-23906. F124.N437

— (3d and 4th printings) (1928) F124.N438

NEW YORK (State) Inauguration of Franklin D. Roosevelt ... (Albany? 1929) 5 l. pl., port. 21 cm.
29-12029. F124.N439

NEW YORK (State) Dept. of Commerce. Division of State Publicity. This is New York State.
Albany (1948) 64 p. illus. 22 cm. A 49-10147*. F124.N4397

NEW YORK (State) Dept. of Commerce. Vacation guide to New York State. (Albany, 1947)
168 p. maps. 22 cm. A 47-4475*. F124.N 44

NEW YORK. American book co., 1896. 31 cm. F124.N 45

(NEW YORK central railroad co.) The greatest highway in the world; historical, industrial and descriptive information of the towns, cities and country passed through between New York and Chicago vie the New York central lines ... Based on the Encyclopaedia britannica. (New York? 1921)
(3) - 130 p. illus. (incl. ports.) 19 cm. 21-14813. F124.N452

NEW YORK central and Hudson River railroad co. 1500 miles over the New York central lines ...
Buffalo and New York, 1902. 22 cm. F124.N454

NEW YORK Central and Hudson river railroad co. Health and pleasure on America's greatest railroad, being a list of the summer resorts and excursion routes on the New York central & Hudson river R.R. for the season of 1890. (Buffalo, Matthews, Northrup, 1890) 276 p. incl. front., illus. fold. maps. 4°. 1-16125-M1. F124.N456

— (New York, American bank note co., 1895) 504 p. incl. front., illus. pl., fold. maps. 23½ cm. "Four-track" series," no. 5. 1-16124. F124.N457

— (New York, N.Y. Central) passenger dept., 1896. 532 p. incl. front., illus. maps. 23½ cm. (Four-track series. no. 5) 1-27676. F124.N458

NEW YORK central and Hudson river railroad. Summer homes on the Harlem and the Hudson ...
(Buffalo, 1892) 18½ cm. F124.N459

(NEW YORK central and Hudson river railroad co.) "The Vanderbilt system" for shippers and travellers between the Atlantic seaboard, and the West, Northwest and Southwest. New York, F.B. Miller, 1887. 112, (2). 21 p. illus., plates, maps (1 fold.) 22½ x 30½ cm. 1-16122 Rev. F124.N465

NEW YORK, Lake Erie and western railraod co. Picturesque Erie. Summer homes. (Philadelphia, Allen, Lane & Scott, printers) 1888. 148 p. fold. map. 17½ cm. 1-16280 Rev. F124.N466
1888

— (New York, M.B. Brown, printer) 1890. 152 p. front. (fold. map) 17½ cm. 1-16281 Rev. F124.N466
1890

NEW YORK, Lake Erie and western railroad co. Summer excursion routes through the most picturesque scenery in America. Seaside, forest, camp and watering place. Philadelphia, Sunshine pub. co., 1881. 99 p. illus. 27 cm. 1-16612 Rev. F124.N4663

NEW YORK, Lake Erie and western railroad co. Summer homes and rambles along the Erie railway.
Issued by the General passenger dept. New York, Hopcraft (1882) 64 p. illus., fold. map. 21½ cm.
1-15903 Rev. F124.N467
1882

— (New York, M.B. Brown, printer) 1883. 44 p. fold. map. 19½ cm. 1-22580 Rev. F124.N467
1883

— 1886. iv. (5) - 107 p. illus. 22 x 10½ cm. John N. Abbott compiler. 1-16279 Rev. F124.N467
1886

NEW YORK, Ontario and western railway co.   Summer homes among the mountains on the New York, Ontario and western railway ... New York (1878 - 19   v. fronts., illus. (part col.) plates (part col.)
fold. maps.   17½ x 26½ cm.   2-13120 Rev.
F124.N468

NEWCOMB, E. Kittie.   Intermediate geography of New York state with method of teaching.   By E. Kittie Newcomb.   (New York, The Mail and express) 1891.   15 p.   illus.   20 cm.   1-15902.
F124.N 53

NEW YORK (State)   Conservation dept.   ... Recreation circular.   Albany (1919) -
v. illus., fold. maps.   23 cm.   19-27378 Rev.
F124.N 55

NEW YORK (State)   Executive dept. Division of commerce.   Nearby wartime vacations in New York state.   (Albany, Wm. Boyd print., 1943?)   39 p. incl. illus. (incl. maps (1 double)   28 cm.   43-53593.
F124.N 57

NEW YORK State vacationlands.   1949 -   Albany.   v. illus. (part col.)   14 x 20-20 cm.   annual.   Pub. by New York (State) Dept. of Commerce ...   A 49-7265 rev. 2*.
F124. N 6

NIVER, Harmon Bay.   Geography of New York state.   New York city, Hinds, Hayden & Eldredge, 1917.   47 p.   illus., maps.   26½ cm. x 21 cm.   17-28466.
F124.N 73

NUTTING, Wallace.   New York beautiful ... illus. by the author with pictures of rural New York with special reference to their aesthetic features and old life.   New York, Dodd, Mead, 1927.   vi, 305 p. incl. plates.   col. front.   25½ cm.   (His States beautiful series)   28-2.
F124.N 98

— Garden City, N.Y., Pub. in coöperation with Old America co. by the Garden City pub. co. (1936)   vi, 305 p. incl. plates.   26 cm.   "Re-issued in de luxe edition ... 1936."   37-15030.
F124.N982

O'BRIEN.   Society of the friendly sons of St. Patrick in the city of New York.   Proceedings at the banquet to Hon. Morgan J. O'Brien.   (New York? Pub. by order of the Society, 1900)   38 p. pl., port.   21 cm.   3-33145 Add.
F124.O 13

O'GORMAN.   (Society of the friendly sons of St. Patrick in the city of New York)   Proceedings at the banquet to Hon. James A. O'Gorman.   Reported and pub. by order of the society   (New York, Press of W. P. Mitchell) 1903.   48 p.   port.   20½ cm.   4-24201 Add.
F124.O 14

O'CONNELL, Daniel James Sheehy.   New York state at a glance.   For teachers, students and busy people ... Buffalo, N.Y. (D. J. S. O'Connell, 1895)   8 l.   12°.   1-15904-M1.
F124.O 18

PECKHAM.   In memory of Rufus W. Peckham, a judge of the Court of appeals, who perished on the wreck of the steamer Ville du Havre, on the voyage from New York to Havre ... 1873.   Prepared by a committee of the bar of the state of New York.   (Albany, Munsell, printer) 1874.   106 p.   front. (port.)   27½ cm.   12-20468 Rev.
F124. P 36

PHELPS, Henry Pitt.   ... New York state legislative souvenir for 189   Albany, N.Y., 1893-95.   v. illus. (ports.)   21½ cm.   6-2172 Rev.
F124. P 53

(PRESBREY, Frank)   A summer paradise ... (Albany? N.Y., 1895)   23½ cm.
F124. P 92

REDWAY, Jacques Wardlaw.   A geography of New York state, physical and descriptive. ... New York, W. D. Kerr (1890)   110 p.   illus.   19 cm.   1-15905 Rev.
F124. R 32

REPUBLICAN party.   New York (State)   The Union state ticket.   Personal character and military services.   Gallantry which, under the first Napoleon, would have made French marshals.   New York, Baker & Godwin, print. 1865.   24 p.   22½ cm.   12-9118.
F124. R 42

ROME, Watertown, and Ogdensburg railroad co.   Routes and rates for summer tours ... 1888.   (New York, Giles litho. and Liberty printing co., 1888)   176 p.   front., illus., fold. maps.   26½ cm.   1-16120.
F124. R 75

— (New York, Press of the American bank note co., 1895) 236 p. front., illus., fold, maps. 24½ cm.
1-16119. F124.R 76

ROOSEVELT, Franklin Delano. Abstracts of Roosevelt utterances, 1932. Section I - II. (Washington? 1933?) 2 v. in 1. 26½ cm. 45-51373. F124.R766

ROOSEVELT, Theodore. ... William Barnes, plaintiff-appellant, against Theodore Roosevelt, defendant-respondent. Case on appeal ... Ivins, Wolff & Hoguet, attorneys for plaintiff-appellant ... Bowers & Sands, attorneys for defendant-respondent ... Walton, N.Y. (etc.) The Reporter co., 1917.
4 v. 27 cm. Paged continuously. Supreme court. Appellate division. Fourth department. 20-17044. F124.R 77

ROOSEVELT, Theodore. Governor Theodore Roosevelt, the Albany apprenticeship, 1898 - 1900, by Wallace Chessman. Cambridge, Mass., Harvard University Press, 1965. ix, 335 p. 22 cm. Based on thesis, Harvard University. F124.R77C5

ROOT, Elihu. Speech of Hon. Elihu Root, secretary of state, at Utica, New York, 1906. Washington, D.C., C. F. Sudwarth, printer, 1906. 39 p. 22 cm. Relates to the candidacy of C. E. Hughes and W.R. Hearst for the governorship of New York state. 10-5346. F124.R 78

SULLIVAN. Proceedings of the Legislature of the state of New York on the life, character and public service of Timothy D. Sullivan. Albany, N.Y. (J. B. Lyon co., printers, 1914) 38 p. port. 26½ cm.
15-27197. F124.S
E664.S95N5

(SEXTON, John L.) Letters of Uncle Jonas Lawrence upon a partial early history of southern, central, western New York, and northern and northwestern Pennsylvania ... (Elmira, N.Y., Elmira weekly advertiser, 1886) iv, (5) - 179 (i.e. 180) p. 1 illus. 25½ cm. Originally pub. in the Elmira weekly advertiser. 44-30425.
F124. S 48

SMITH, Floyd R. Geography of New York; the state - the city. New York, Cincinnati (etc.) American book co. (1904) 135 p. incl. front., illus., maps. 20 cm. 4-22903. F124. S 64

— (1917) 136 p. incl. front., illus., maps. 19 cm. 17-13929. F124.S645

SMITH, W. A. New York state. 1920. 1 v. F124. S 67

(SOCONY mobil oil co. inc.) Historic tours in Soconyland. (New York, Standard oil co. of New York, 1925) 57, (7) p. illus. (part col. incl. maps) tab. 19½ cm. A 26-7 rev. F124. S 7

STANDARD road-book of New York state, ... The. Complete road-maps, showing quality of the roads ... Book I. Boston, Mass., National pub. co. (1897) (173) p. incl. maps. 23½ x 12 cm. 1-15897 Rev.
F124.S765

STATE of New York, The. (New York, American book co., 1898) 12 p. incl. illus., map. fol. Appendix to "New York advanced geography" ... Redway & Hinman's Natural advanced geography. 1-15906-M1. F124. S 79

STEBBINS, Homer Adolph. ... A political history of the state of New York, 1865 - 1869 ... New York, Columbia university; (etc.) 1913. 447 p. 25 cm. (Studies in history, economics and public law, ed. by the Faculty of political science of Columbia university. vol. lv no. 1 (whole no. 135) "Bibliographical note": p. 414-423. 13-15791. F124. S 82

— New York, AMS Press, 1967. 447 p. 23 cm. 71-29902 MARC. F124. S 82
1967

— New York, 1913. 2, 7-448 p. 25 cm. Thesis (PH.D.) - Columbia university, 1913. 13-18331 Rev. F124. S 83

STEWART, Albert Struthers. St. Luke's garden. Boston, Sherman, French & co., 1911. 5, 124 p.
19½ cm. 11-5250. F124. S 85

(SULZER, William) (Life and speeches of William Sulzer. n. p., 1897 - 1913) 129 pamphlets in 1 v.
port. 23 cm. 16-15254. F124. S 94

— (Washington, etc., 1902-16)   44 pamphlets in 1 v. illus., port. 22½ cm. 43-49416.
F124.S942

— (n.p., 1898 - 1917)   (101) pamphlets and leaflets in 1 v. port. 22½ cm. Includes campaign documents of the American party, campaign of 1916.   CA 19-122 Unrev.
F124.S943

SULZER.   Tammany's treason, impeachment of Governor William Sulzer; the complete story written from behind the scenes, showing how Tammany plays the fame, how men are bought, sold and delivered, by Jay W. Forrest and James Malcolm.   Foreword by Chester C. Platt ... illus. by W. K. Starrett. Albany, N.Y. (The Fort Orange press) 1913.   3, (ix) - xi, (5), 9-456 p. incl. front., illus., plates, ports., facsims. 23½ cm. 14-7004.
F124. S 95

SULZER, William.   The boss, or the governor; the truth about the greatest political conspiracy in the history of America, by Samuel Bell Thomas.   New York, The Truth publishing co., 1914. 6, 456 p. front. (port.) illus. (incl. ports.) 19½ cm. 14-11504.
F124. S 96

SWEENY, Peter Barr.   The political situation, resulting from the late state election.   (Herald interview with Peter B. Sweeny.)   (New York) The Jackson assoc. (1869)   43 p. 23 cm. From the New York herald of Nov. 26, 1869. 12-9131.
F124. S 98

(TAINTOR, Charles Newhall)   The Hudson River route.   New York to Albany, Saratoga Springs, Lake George, Lake Champlain, Adirondack Mountains, and Montreal ... New York, Taintor bros. (1869)   121 p. illus. 4 pl. fold. map. 16½ cm. 4-28337.
F124. T 14

— 1869.   129 p. illus. 16 cm. 17-24570.
F124. T142
Toner Coll.

— 1880.   (234) p. illus. (incl. plans) fold. map. 18 cm. Paging irregular. 4-28338.
F124. T 15

— 1887.   (234) p. illus. (incl. plans) 4 fold. maps. 17½ cm. Paging irregular. 4-28336 Rev.
F124. T155

(TAINTOR, Charles Newhall)   The New York central and Hudson river railroad and the Rome, Watertown, and Ogdensburg railroad ... New York, Taintor brothers, 1889.   152 p. illus., fold. maps. 18 cm. 1-22211.
F124. T 16

THACHER.   The Honorable John Boyd Thacher, man of versatility.   By Victor Hugo Paltsits.   (n.p.) 1951.   (15) p. port. 24 cm. "From New York history, Jan. 1951." Bibliography: p. (15) 51-28431.
F124. T5P3
Rare Book Coll.

TO loyal democrats!   Who are the sympathizers with the rebellion?   What the rebels say.   (n.p., 1862)   7 p. 21½ cm. 1-16758.
F124. T 62

TRAVELER'S guide, and illus. description of central New York, Niagara Falls, Saratoga Springs, etc. tog. with railroad time tables.   Buffalo, Felton & brother, 1866.   2 v. in 1. front., plates, fold. map. 17 cm. 1-22101 Rev.
F124. T 77

UTICA press summer resort guide.   (3d)   1926.   (Utica, N.Y., Utica daily press, 1926)
F124. U 86

VENZMER, Gerhard.   Atlantikfahrt, die Newyorker reise der Lucia Herzogena.   Hamburg, Weltbundverlag (1924)   264 p.
F124. V 4

VIELE, Egbert Ludovickus.   The topography and physical resources of the state of New York.   An address delivered ... before the American geographical soc., 1875.   New York, E. S. Dodge (1875) 23 p. 8°. 1-15907-M1.
F124. V 65

WAGNER.   Proceedings of the Senate and Assembly of the state of New York, in relation to the death of ... Webster Wagner, senator from the 18th district.   Albany, Weed, Parsons, 1882.   105 p. front. (port.) 4°. 1-13602-M1.
F124. W 13

NEW YORK

WALLING, Henry Francis. The Erie railway and its branches. With descriptive sketches of the cities, villages, stations, and of scenery and objects of interest along the route. ... New York, Taintor bros., 1867. 60 p. illus. (maps) 16 cm. 1-22206.   F124.W 19

WALLING, Henry Francis. The Harlem railway. With descriptive sketches of scenes and objects of interest along the route. New York, Taintor bros., 1867. 32 p. illus. (maps) 16 cm. 1-16118.
F124.W 21

WALLING, Henry Francis. The New York central railway and its branches. With descriptive sketches of the cities, villages, stations, and scenes and objects of interest along the route. ... New York, Taintor brother, 1867. 54 p. illus. (maps) 16 cm. 1-15908.   F124.W215

WARD, Hamilton, jr. Life and speeches of Hamilton Ward. 1829 - 1898. Hamilton Ward, jr. Buffalo, N.Y. Press of A. H. Morey, 1902. 3. 429 p. front., port. 23½ cm. 2-19236.
F124.W 25

WARREN, David M. A geography of New York state. Prepared for the New York editions of Warren's Common school geography and Warren's Brief course in geography ... Philadelphia, Cowperthwait, & co., 1880. 16 p. illus. (incl. maps) 30½ x 26 cm. 1-16882 rev.   F124.W 28
Map div.

WATEROUS, Lettie L. Questions upon the geography of the state of New York ... Syracuse, N.Y., C. W. Bardeen, 1903. 7 - 28 p. 19½ cm. 12-40188.   F124.W 32

WEST shore railroad co. Summer homes and tours on the line of the picturesque West shore railroad ... New York (Fulton pub. co.) 1896. 280 p. front., illus., fold. maps. 4°. 1-16117-M1.   F124.W 52

WHITBECK, Ray Hughes. ... New York ... New York, The Macmillan co.; London, Macmillan & co. ltd., 1901. viii, 115 p. illus., maps (part double) 19 x 14½ cm. (Tarr and McMurry geographies. Supplementary vol.) 1-23949.   F124.W 57

WILLIAMS, Henry T., comp. Suburban homes for city business men. A description of the country, with a statement of the inducements offered on the line of the Erie railway. A guide of the eastern division and Newburgh and Warwick branches. New York, Press of the Erie railway co., 1867. 2, 59 p. illus., plates, plans. 19 cm. 1-15909.   F124.W 72

WILLIAMS, Sherman. Geography of New York state (Human geography book II) ... (Philadelphia, 1924) 63 p. illus. (incl. maps) 25 cm.   F124.W724

WISTHALER, Johanna Sara. By water to the Columbia expostion ... Schenectady, N.Y. (E. Knauer, printer) 1894. 131 p. incl. pl. front., fold. pl., fold. map. 23 cm. 1-16116 Rev.   F124.W 81

WRITERS' program. New York, a guide to the Empire state, compiled by workers of the Writers' program of the W. P. A. in the state of New York ... New York, Oxford university press (1940) xxxi, 782 p. illus., plates, maps (3 on fold. 1. in pocket) 21 cm. (American guide series) Bibliography: p. 729-739. 40-28672.
F124.W 89
Geneal. Sect. Ref.

— (1946) xxxi, 782 (i.e. 798) p. illus., plates (1 double) maps. 46-5765.   F124.W 89
1946

— 1972.   F124.W 89
1972

1951 TO DATE.

NEW YORK (State) Dept. of Commerce. Vacation variety in New York State. (Albany, 1954) 16 p. illus. 22 cm. A 55-9136.   F125.A 52

GRINNELL, Lawrnece I.   Canoeable waterways of New York State and vicinity.   (1st ed.)   New York, Pageant Press (1956)   349 p.   illus.   21 cm.   Includes bibliography.   56-8569.   F125. G 7

THOMPSON, John Henry.   Geography of New York State.   (1st ed.)   Syracuse, N. Y.) Syracuse University Press (1966)   543 p.   27 cm.   66-14602.   F125. T 5

WALLNER, Albert.   Mein Amerikabuch.   (My U. S. Note-book); win Studiosus erlebt die U. S. A. Wien, Omnis-Verlag (1960)   287 p.   20 cm.   F125. W 3

REGIONS, COUNTIES, ETC., A - Z.

GALPIN, William Freeman.   Central New York, an inland empire, comprising Oneida, Madison, Onondaga, Cayuga, Tompkins, Cortland, Chenango counties and their people ... New York, Lewis historical pub. co., (1941)   4 v.   illus., tables, ports.   27½ cm.   Vol. 4 contains biographies.   41-23129.
F127.A15 G2

LAMB, Wallace Emerson.   Sectional historical atlas of New York State.   Illus. arr. by Mary Cunningham; original sketches by Albert Sway.   Phoenix, N.Y., F. E. Richards, 1955-56.
11 v.   illus.   22 x 28 cm.   Contents. - 1. Long Island. - 2. Lower Hudson. - 3. Mid-Hudson. - 4. Capital district. - 5. Mohawk area. - 6. Syracuse area. - 7. Binghamton area. - 8. Elmira area. - 9. Rochester area. - 10. Southwest gateway and Niagara frontier. - 11. Northern New York State.   55-37774 Rev.
F127.A15 L3

MELONE, Harry R.   History of central New York, embracing Cayuga, Seneca, Wayne, Ontario, Tompkins, Cortland, Schuyler, Yates, Chemung, Steuben, and Tioga counties ... Indianapolis, Ind., Historical pub. co., 1932.   3 v.   front., plates, ports.   27½ cm.   Paged continuously.   35-14604.
F127.A15M45

NEW YORK (State)   State planning board.   Political subdividisions of the state of New York indexed according to U.S.G.S. sheets.   Prepared by Walter Muir.   Albany, N. Y., New York State planning board, 1935.   (102) p.   map.   27½ cm.   Various pagings.   Mimeographed.   35-28379.   F127.A15N24

NEW YORK, Ontario and western railway.   ... Vacation guide; resorts in Sullivan, Ulster and Orange counties, New York.   1934 -   v.   illus., double map.   22½ cm.   34-38749.
F127.A15 N3

O'CALLAGHAN, Edmund Bailey, comp.   ... Census of the counties of Orange, Dutchess & Albany. 1702, 1714, 1720.   (In the documentary history of the state of New York, v. 1)   8-27639.
F127.A15O28

—   Philadelphia, Pa., E. E. Brownell, 1941.   (11) p.   21½ cm.   42-50702 Rev.   F127.A15 O3

ZIMM, Louise Seymour (Hasbrouck)   Southeastern New York, a history of the counties of Ulster, Dutchess, Orange, Rockland and Putnam, compiled and ed. by Louise Hasbrouck Zimm and others. New York, Lewis historical publishing co. (1946)   3 v.   fronts. (v.1,2) illus. (incl. ports.)   27½ cm.   Vols. 1-2 paged continuously.   Vol. 3 contains biographical sketches.   47-2512.   F127.A15 Z5

ADIRONDACK Mountains.   Conquering the world, by Helen Bartlett Bridgman.   New York, Cloister pub. co. (1925)   xiii, (15) - 264 p.   20 cm.   26-6157.   F127.A2
G440.B 87

ADIRONDACK Mountains.   A tour to the river Saguenay, in Lower Canada,   By Charles Lanman ... Philadelphia, Carey and Hart, 1848.   231 p.   18½ cm.   1-15912.
F127.A2
F1013.L 29

ADIRONDACK Mountains.   Lost Pond, by Henry Abbott.   New York, 1915.   37 p.   15 cm.   16-241.
F127.A2 A13

NEW YORK

RAQUETTE river, by Henry Abbott.   New York, 1931.   54 p. incl. mounted illus., mounted maps.   15 cm.
32-13992.   F127.A2A136

TIRRELL Pond, by Henry Abbott.   New York, 1928.   42 p. mounted illus., fold. map. 15 cm. Tirrell Pond lies at the base of Blue Mountain, in the Adirondacks.   29-1592.   F127.A2 A14

AD-I-RON-DAC.   (Gabriels, etc., N.Y.)   Adirondack Mountain Club)   v. in 23 cm. bimonthly (irregular)
F127.A2 A17

ADIRONDACK Forty-sixers, The.   Publications Committee: Dorothy O. Haeusser (and others.   1st ed.)   Albany, Peter Print (1958)   147 p. illus. 24 cm. 58-31479.   F127.A2 A18

ADIRONDACK Forty-sixers.   The Adirondack High Peaks and the Forty-sixers.   Ed. Grace L. Rudowalski.   With drawings by Trudy B. Healy.   Albany, N.Y., Printed by the Peters Print (1970)   xvi, 357 p. illus. 24 cm. 70-112793.   F127.A2 A19

ADIRONDACK guide; vacationland in picture, story and history.   1920 -   Lake George, N.Y., Adirondack Resorts Press (etc.)   v. illus. (part col.) fold. map (inserted) 19-23 cm.   20-17012 rev. 2*.
F127. A2 A2

ADIRONDACK league club.   Incorporated June 18, 1890.   New York (P. F. McBreen, printers) 1892 - 19   v. fronts., plates (part col., part fold.) fold. maps. 20 x 15½ cm. 7-24942.   F127.A2 A25

ADIRONDACK league club.   ... (Prospectus.   New York, P. F. McBreen, printer) 1890.   12 p. fold. map. 23½ cm. 8-18980.   F127.A2A252

ADIRONDACK life.   v.1 -   winter 1970 -   (Elizabethtown, N.Y.)   v. illus. (part col.) ports.
28 cm. quarterly.   F127.A2A254

ADIRONDACK mountain club.   ... Guide to Adirondack trails ... Albany, N.Y., The Adirondack mountain club (1934 -   v. fold. maps. 15 cm. Includes bibliographies. 34-35464.   F127.A2 A26

ADIRONDACK Mountains, Lake Champlain, Lake George ... covering every part of the Adirondacks and adjacent regions.   The tourist paradise of America ...   Watertown, N.Y., Santway photo-craft co. inc. (1921)   (62) p. of illus. (incl. maps) 15½ x 23½ cm. 21-11931.   F127.A2 A27

ADIRONDACK shadows.   Summer scenes at Lake Placid, Upper and Lower Saranac lakes, St. Regis and Loon lakes, etc. ... Glens Falls, N.Y., C. H. Possons (1888)   18 pl. obl. 24°. 1-14009-M1.
F127.A2A275

ADIRONDACKS, Association for the protection of the, New York.   (Publications)   New York?)
v. illus. 23 cm. CA 10-5232 Unrev.   F127.A2 A28

— List of officers and members.   (New York, 1903 -)   1 v. 18 cm.   F127.A2 A84

— A plea for the Adirondack and Catskill parks.   An argument for the resumption, by the state of New York, of the policy of acquiring lands for the public benefit within the limits of the forest preserve.
(n.p., 1903?)   30 p. 23 cm. Agr. 13-1863.   F127.A2 A86

ADIRONDACK Mountains.   Views along the line of the Chateaugay R.R.   By G. W. Baldwin ... (Boston) Printed by Boston photogravure co., 1888.   2 p. front. (fold. map) 20 pl. 13½ x 18½ cm. 2-21307 Rev.
F127.A2 B18

ADIRONDACKS, Views of the.   By G. Baldwin.   (Boston) Boston Photogravure Co., 1888.
(2) 1., (21) plates. 15 x 19 cm. 1-14011 rev.*   F127.A2 B2

ADIRONDACKS.   Up the Old Forge way (a Central Adirondack story.)   By David Harold Beetle.   (Utica, Utica Observer-Dispatch, 1948)   183 p. illus., ports., map. 20 cm. "Reprinted from the Utica Observer-Dispatch, Utica, New York." 49-7000*.   F127. A2 B4

ADIRONDACKS, The.   Artotype views in the north woods.   By E. Bierstadt ... New York, 1889.
16 pl.   14½ x 18 cm.   1-14010.
F127. A2 B5

ADIRONDACKS.   The Raquette river of the forest, by Charles W. Bryan, Jr.   Blue Mountain Lake, N.Y., Adirondack Museum, 1964.   ix. 122 p.   22 cm.   64-22468.
F127. A2 B9

ADIRONDACKS.   Peaks and people of the Adirondacks, by Russell M. L. Carson ... Garden City, N.Y., Doubleday, Page & co., 1927.   xxii, 269 p. incl. plates. front., pl., ports. 20 cm.   "Pub. under the auspices of the Adirondack mountain club, inc."   27-27563.
F127. A2 C3

ADIRONDACKS.   Speech delivered by the Hon. Verplanck Colvin, at the annual banquet of the New York board of trade and transportation; ... in response to the toast: "The Adirondacks - the land of magnificent mountains and lovely lakes; the source of the Hudson River, the feeder of our canals." New York, G. F. Nesbit, printers, 1885.   8 p.   23½ cm.   6-1146.
F127. A2 C7

ADIRONDACKS.   First conference on the Adirondack Park, (Proceedings)   Ed. by Allen P. Splete and others.   (Canton, N.Y., St. Lawrence University, 1972)   iii, 115 p.   28 cm.   72-82986.
F127.A2 C74
1971

ADIRONDACKS.   The Adirondack region; history and adventures of early times, by Richard Coughlin. Watertown, N.Y., Santway photo-craft co. (1921)   77 p.   16½ cm.   22-1542.
F127. A2 C8

ADIRONDACKS.   The life and adventures of Nat Foster, trapper and hunter of the Adirondacks, by A. L. Byron-Curtiss.   Utica, N.Y., Press of T. J. Griffiths, 1897.   286 p.   17 pl. (incl. front.)   18½ cm. 7-38339.
F127. A2 C9

ADIRONDACKS.   The story of a pass in the Adirondacks, by A. L. Byron-Curtiss.   Boston, The Gorham press; (etc.,1917)   224 p. front., plates. 19 cm.   "This book is a sort of compound of the author's personal experiences and observations, tog. with stories and yarns picked up by the way."   18-1145 Rev.
F127.A2 C92

ADIRONDACKS.   Delaware and Hudson railroad.   A summer paradise ... 1906.   1 v.
F127. A2 D3

ADIRONDACKS, A history of the.   By Alfred Lee Donaldson.   New York, Centruy Co., 1921.
2 v. plates, ports., fold. maps, fold. charts. 25 cm.   Bibliography: v.2. p. 290-363.   21-9060 rev.*
F127.A2 D67
— An alphabetical index to the bibliography in Donaldson's History of the Adirondacks. Compiled by the Bibliography Committee of the Adirondack Mountain Club.   Poughkeepsie, N.Y., 1949
24 p.   22 cm.   21-9060 rev.*
F127.A2 D67
Index

— Port Washington, N.Y., I. J. Friedman, 1963 (1949)   2 v.   illus.   22 cm.   (Empire State historical publication, 12)   62-21744.
F127.A2 D67
1963

ADIRONDACKS.   Why the wilderness is called Adirondack, by Henry Dornburgh.   (Glens Falls, N.Y., Daily times, 1885)   14 p.   18 x 14 cm.   1-14801 rev.
F127. A2 D7

DURANT, Kenneth, ed.   Guide-boat days and ways.   With seven sketches by Frederick B. Allen. Blue Mountain Lake, N.Y., Adirondack Museum, 1963.   xv, 267 p.   23 cm.   63-18266.
F127. A2 D8

ADIRONDACK tales, by Eleanor Early; decorations by Virginia Grilley.   Boston, Little, Brown, 1939.
5. (3) - 247 p.   illus.   17½ cm.   "First edition."   39-27435.
F127.A2 E17

ADIRONDACKS.   The eastern slope of the Adirondacks.   (New York, 1901?)   23½ cm.
F127. A2 E2

ADIRONDACKS.   Cranberry Lake, 1845 - 1959; an Adirondack miscellany.   By Albert Vann Fowler.

NEW YORK

Introd. by Walter D. Edmonds.   Blue Mt. Lake, N.Y., Adirondack Museum (1959)   160 p. illus.
21 cm.   59-3809.   F127. A2 F6

ADIRONDACKS.   Cranberry Lake from wilderness to Adirondack Park.   By Albert Vann Fowler.
(1st ed.) Adirondack Museum, Syracuse. Syracuse University Press (1968)   207 p. illus. 25 cm.
68-17845.   F127.A2 F62

ADIRONDACKS.   The Central Adirondacks, a picture story.   By Jim Fynmore.   (1st ed.) Prospect,
N.Y., Prospect Books, 1955.   unpaged (chiefly illus.)   24 cm.   55-33003.   F127. A2 F9

ADIRONDACKS.   Okara, a section in Ga-wan-ka, the Adirondack playground.   (n.p., 1920)
32 p. incl. illus., col. pl.   fold. map.   23 cm.   20-21928.   F127.A2 G28

ADIRONDACKS.   Gems of scenery.   Adirondack mountains, lake George, lake Champlain.   Glens
Falls, N.Y., C.H. Possons (1896)   (98) p. incl. illus., plates.   16 x 23½ cm.   1-14012.
                                                                              F127. A2 G3

ADIRONDACKS.   The Adirondacks; Fulton Chain - Big Moose region; the story of a wilderness, by
Joseph F. Grady.   (Little Falls, N.Y., Press of the Journal & courier co., 1933)   x, 320 p. plates,
ports., facsim.   24 cm.   Running title: The story of a wilderness.   33-31649.   F127. A2 G8

ADIRONDACKS.   Hills, lakes, and forest streams; or, A tramp in the Chateaugay woods.   By S.H.
Hammond ... New York, J.C. Derby; Boston, Phillips, Sampson, etc. 1854.   xii, (13) - 340 p. front.,
2 pl.   19 cm.   Later editions have title "Hunting adventures in the northern wilds," and "In the Adirondacks."   1-14013.   F127. A2 H2

ADIRONDACKS.   Hunting adventures in the northern wilds; or, A tramp in the Chateaugay woods ...
By S. Hammond ... New York, J.C. Derby; Boston, Phillips, Sampson, etc., 1856.   3, (v) - xii, (13) -
340 p.   col. front., 2 col. pl.   19 cm.   First pub. with title of preceding item.   1-14014.
                                                                              F127. A2 H3
                                                                              Rare Book Coll.

ADIRONDACKS.   In the Adirondacks; or, Sport in the North woods ... By Samuel H. Hammond.
Philadelphia, Columbian pub. co., 1890.   xii, (13) - 340 p.   12°.   (Columbia library, no. 9) 1-14015-M1)
See F127. A2H2.   F127. A2 H4

ADIRONDACKS.   Where to go in the Adirondacks and on Lake George and Lake Champlain.   (By
George Robert Hardie)   (Canton, N.Y., G.R. Hardie, 1909)   96 p. illus. (incl. maps) 23 cm.   9-13946.
                                                                              F127.A2 H41

ADIRONDACKS.   The Sacandaga story; a valley of yesteryear.   By Larry Hart.   Schenectady, N.Y.,
Riedinger & Riedinger, 1967.   69 p.   23 cm.   F127.A2 H43

ADIRONDACKS.   On Adirondack trails, by Harry P. Hays.   Reprinted from Altoona Tribune.   Dedicated to Henry W. Shoemaker. (Altoona, Pa.) Times tribune co., 1923.   21 p. incl. pl., ports. 23 cm.
24-15730.   F127.A2 H44

ADIRONDACKS.   The Adirondack; or, Life in the woods.   By J.T. Headley ... New York, Baker
and Scribner, 1849.   6, xi, (13) - 288 p. front., plates.   19½ cm.   1-14016.   F127. A2 H6

— 1853.   6, xi, (13) - 288 p.   8 pl. (incl. front.)   19½ cm.   17-10657.   F127. A2H603
                                                                              Toner Coll.

— New and enl. ed.   New York, C. Scribner, 1869.   9, xi, (13) - 451 p. front., 7 pl.   18½ cm.   1-14017.
                                                                              F127. A2 H61

— New ed., with additional matter ... New York, Scribner, Armstrong, 1875.   8, xi, (13) - 461 p.
front., plates, fold. map.   19½ cm.   1-14018.   F127. A2 H62

ADIRONDACKS.   Letters from the backwoods and the Adirondac.   By the Rev. J.T. Headley.   New
York, J.S. Taylor, 1850.   iv, (5) - 105 p. front. (port.)   19½ cm.   1-14019.   F127.A2 H64

ADIRONDACKS. A climber's guide to the Adirondacks; rock and slide climbs in the high peak region. Ed. and illus. by Trudy Healy. 2. ed. rev. (Glens Falls, N.Y.) Adirondack Mountains Club (1971) 108 p. illus. 16 cm. Bibliography: p. 12-13. 67-22792 MARC.
                                      F127.A2H65 1971

ADIRONDACKS. High spots; the yearbook of the Adirondack mountain club. (New York, The Adirondack mountain club, 19 v. illus., plates. 23 cm. 39-31246.
                                      F127. A2 H7

ADIRONDACKS. Life and leisure in the Adirondack backwoods. By Harold K. Hochschild. Blue Mountain Lake, N.Y., Adirondack Museum, 1962. 122 p. 28 cm. "A selection of chapters with revisions, from the author's Township 34, privately printed in 1952."
                                      F127.A2 H74

ADIRONDACKS. Township 34; a history, with digressions, of an Adirondack township in Hamilton County in the State of New York. By Harold K. Hochschild. New York, 1952. xxvi, 614 p. illus., ports., maps (part fold.) 32 cm. Bibliography: p. (569)-587. 52-68596.
                                      F127.A2 H75

ADIRONDACKS. Camp chronicles, by Mildred Phelps Stokes Hooker. With introd. and notes by Paul F. Jamieson. Blue Mountain Lake, N.Y., Adirondack Museum, 1964. x, 60 p. 19 cm. 64-24123.
                                      F127. A2 H8

ADIRONDACKS. Through the Adirondacks in eighteen days. By Martin V. B. Ives. New York and Albany, Wynkoop Hallenbeck Crawford co., 1899. 119 p. plates, ports. 26 cm. Sept. 28, 99-44.
                                      F127. A2 I 9

ADIRONDACKS. The Adirondack reader; the best writings on the adventurous and contemplative life in one of America's most loved regions. Ed. and with introd. by Paul P. Jamieson. New York, Macmillan Co. (1964) xviii, 494 p. 24 cm. "First printing" 64-12535.
                                      F127. A2 J 3

ADIRONDACKS. A Jaunt in the Adirondacks. Summer scenes at Elizabethtown, Keene Valley, Ausable Lakes, etc. Glens Falls, N.Y., C. H. Possons (1888) (18) plates. 14 x 19 cm. 1-14020*.
                                      F127. A2 J 4

ADIRONDACKS. Man of the woods (by) Herbert F. Keith. With introd. and notes by Paul F. Jamieson. (1st ed.) (Syracuse, N.Y.) Syracuse University Press, 1972. xi, 164 p. illus. 24 cm. 78-38507 MARC.
                                      F127. A2 K4

ADIRONDACKS. The Adirondacks, by T. Morris Longstreth; illus. with photos and maps. New York, The Century co., 1917. 3, v-viii p, 3 l., 3-370 p. front., plates, fold. map. 21 cm. 17-25281.
                                      F127. A2 L8

ADIRONDACKS. Exploring the Adirondack Mountains 100 years ago. Comp., ed. and annotated by Stuart D. Ludlum. With illus. by T. R. Davis and others. Utica, N.Y., Brodock & Ludlum Publications (1972) 65 p. illus. 28 cm. 72-80328.
                                      F127.A2 L83

ADIRONDACKS. The high peaks of the Adirondacks, by Robert Marshall; a brief account of the climbing of the forty-two Adirondack Mountains over 4,000 feet in height ... (Albany) The Adirondack mountain club, inc. (1922) 38 p. incl. front., illus. fold. map. 18 cm. 22-21955.
                                      F127. A2 M3

ADIRONDACKS. The story of Adirondac (by) Arthur Haynesworth Maston. With introd. and notes by William K. Verner. (New ed. Syracuse) Adirondack Museum, Syracuse University Press (1968) xxxvi, 199 p. illus., ports. 24 cm. "New ed. 1968" 68-20170.
                                      F127.A2 M34 1968

ADIRONDACKS. ... The Adirondack Mountains, by William J. Miller ... Albany, The University of the state of New York, 1917. (7)-97 p. illus., 30 pl., maps (2 fold.) 23 cm. (New York state museum bulleting ... no. 193) Bibliography: p. 88-92. 17-27409.
                                      F127. A2 M6

ADIRONDACKS. Adventures in the wilderness; or, Camp-life in the Adirondacks. By William H. H.

Murray ... Boston, Fields, Osgood, 1869.   vi, (7) - 236 p. front., plates. 18 cm. 1-14021.

F127. A2 M9

— (17th thousand) Boston, Cupples and Hurd (1889)   vi, (7) - 236 p. front., illus., plates. 19½ cm. (The green paper series no. 1) 7-15664.

F127. A2 M91

— With introd. and notes by Warder H. Cadbury. (Syracuse, N. Y.) Adirondack Museum (1970) 75, 236, 77-95 p. illus., fold. map (in pocket) ports. 24 cm. 72-132972.

F127. A2,M9 1970

ADIRONDACKS. My Adirondack pipe. Memories of a pleasant month spent in the Adirondacks, by W. S. K. Printed for private circulation. (New York, Press of W. R. Jenkins, 1887)   81 p. 18 cm. 17-9543.

F127. A2 M98

ADIRONDACKS. The Adirondacks: New York's forest preserve and a proposed National Park. New York (State) Conservation Dept. (Albany, 1967?)   64 l. 28 cm. 68-65583.

F127. A2 N55

ADIRONDACKS. Report of the Adirondack committee, Assembly of 1902. Transmitted to the Legislature April 16, 1903. Albany, The Argus co., printers, 1903.   19 p. 23½ cm. (Legislature, 1903. Assembly. Doc. 46) 18-15128.

F127. A2 N58

ADIRONDACKS. Report of the Special committee of the Assembly on the Adirondacks. Transmitted to the Legislature April 13, 1904. Albany, O. A. Quayle, state legislative printer, 1904. 11 p. 23 cm. (Assembly doc. no. 60) 8-21579.

F127. A2 N6

ADIRONDACKS. The future of the Adirondacks; the reports of the Temporary Study Commission on the Future of the Adirondacks. Blue Mountain Lake, N.Y., Adirondack Museum, 1971.   2 v. illus. 28 cm. Part of illustrative matter in pocket. Reprint of the 1970 report, which was issued in 9 vols. Includes bibliographical references. 72-177367.

F127. A2 N65 1971

ADIRONDACKS. Camps and tramps in the Adirondacks, and grayling fishing in northern Michigan: a record of summer vacations in the wilderness. By A. Judd Northrup. Syracuse, N.Y., Davis, Bardeen; New York, Baker, Pratt, 1880.   viii, (9) - 302 p. 17 cm. 1-14023.

F127. A2 N8

ADIRONDACKS. ... Trails and summits of the Adirondacks, by Walter Collins O'Kane ... Boston and New York, Houghton Mifflin, 1928.   x, 330 p. front., plates, fold. map. 17 cm. (The Riverside outdoor handbooks) 28-12817.

F127. A2 O16

ADIRONDACKS. The opening of the Adirondacks. With a map and illustrations. New York, Hurd and Houghton, 1865.   vi, (9) - 82 p. front. (fold. map) 8 pl. 18 cm. 9-21149.

F127. A2 O2

ADIRONDACKS. ... Retrospect of mountains pilgrimages, by Charles Penrose ... A Newcomen address, 1941. (Princeton, Printed at The Princeton university press, 1941)   24 p. illus. 23 cm. 41-6678.

F127. A2 P 45

ADIRONDACKS. Forever wild: the Adirondacks. Photos by Eliot Porter. Captions by William Chapman White. (1st ed.) Blue Mountain Lake, N.Y., Adirondack Museum (1966)   1 v. 36 cm. 66-20768.

F127. A2 P 62

ADIRONDACKS. Summer paradise. By F. S. Presbrey. (1895)   1 v.

F127. A2 P9

ADIRONDACKS. The Adirondack letters of George Washington Sears, whose pen name was "Nessmuk." With explanatory notes and a brief biography by Dan Brenan. Blue Mountain Lake, N.Y., Adirondack Museum, 1962.   177 p. 23 cm.

F127. A2 S 4

ADIRONDACKS. The Adirondacks: American playground. By Charles Albert Sleicher. (1st ed.) New York, Exposition Press (1960)   287 p. 22 cm.

F127. A2 S 55

ADIRONDACKS. The biography and funny sayings of Paul Smith, by Geraldine Collins. Paul Smiths, N.Y., Paul Smith's College (1965) 55 p. 24 cm. F127.A2 S 58

ADIRONDACKS. The modern babes in the wood; or, Summerings in the wilderness. By H. Perry Smith. To which is added a reliable and descriptive guide to the Adirondacks. By E. R. Wallace ... Hartford (Conn.) Columbian book co.; Syracuse, N.Y., W. Gill, 1872. 444 p. front., illus., plates, double map. 21 cm. Includes music. 1-14025 Rev. F127. A2 S 6

ADIRONDACKS. Descriptive guide to the Adirondacks. (By Edwin R. Wallace) (In Smith, H.P. The modern Babes in the wood ... Hartford (Conn) Syracuse, N.Y., 1872. 21 cm. p. 239-444. plates) 1-14024. F127. A2 S 6

ADIRONDACKS. The Adirondacks as a health resort. Showing the benefit to be derived by a sojourn in the wilderness, in cases of pulmonary phthisis, acute and chronic bronchitis, asthma, "hay-fever" and various nervous affections. Ed. and compiled by Joseph W. Stickler ... New York & London, G. P. Putnam's sons, 1886. x, 198 p. 16½ cm. 1-14026. F127.A2 S 68

ADIRONDACKS. (Adirondack views. By Seneca Ray Stoddard. Glens Falls, N.Y., 1888) 40 photos. 40 x 49 cm. Wihtout t. p. 2-24593 rev.* F127.A2 S 69

ADIRONDACKS. The Adirondacks: illustrated. By Seneca Ray Stoddard. Albany, Weed, Parsons, printers, 1874. vi, 204 p. illus., ports., fold. map. 19 cm. 1-14027 rev.* F127. A2 S 7

— Glen Falls, N.Y., 1883. xiii, 232 p. illus., maps (1 fold.) 18 cm. 6-20080 rev.* F127.A2 S704

— 20th ed. Glens Falls, N.Y., 1890. xi, 266 (i.e. 272) p. illus., maps. 19 cm. 6-24807 rev.* F127.A2 S709

— 21st ed. Glens Falls, N.Y., 1891. (278) p. illus., maps. 19 cm. 1-14028 rev.* F127.A2 S 71

— 22d ed. Glens Falls, N.Y., 1892. (276) p. illus., maps. 19 cm. 1-14029 rev.* F127.A2 S 72

— 23d ed. Glens Falls, N.Y., 1893. xii, 280 p. illus., maps. 14 cm. 18-2273 rev.* F127.A2 S721

— 24th ed. Glens Falls, N.Y., 1894. xii, 280 (i.e. 292) p. illus., ports., maps. 15 cm. 42-42416 rev.* F127.A2 S725

— 25th ed. Glens Falls, N.Y., 1895. xii, 236 (i.e. 243) p. illus., etc. 14 cm. 1-14030 rev. 2*. F127.A2 S 73

ADIRONDACKS. Adirondack memories. By Seneca Ray Stoddard. (Albany, 1898) 1 v. (plates) 16 x 22 cm. 1-14031 rev.* F127.A2 S 74

ADIRONDACKS. Among the mountains of the Adirondacks. By Seneca Ray Stoddard. Troy, N.Y., Nims & Knight, 1888. 1 l., 9 pl. 25 x 30 cm. Cover title: The Adirondack Mtns. Illus. 1-14032 rev. F127.A2 S 75

ADIRONDACKS. Bits of Adirondack life. By Seneca Ray Stoddard. (Albany Engr. Co.) 1898. 1 l. 13 plates. 16 x 22 cm. 1-14033 rev. 2*. F127.A2 S 76

ADIRONDACKS. Into the lake region of the Adirondacks; the Fulton Chain, Raquette Lake, Blue Mountain Lake, Long Lake. By Seneca Ray Stoddard. Poughkeepsie, N.Y., Press of A. V. Haight, 1900. 1 v. (chiefly plates) 17 x 24 cm. 0-5586 rev.*. F127.A2 S 77

ADIRONDACKS. Old times in the Adirondacks; the narrative of a trip into the wilderness in 1873, by Seneca Ray Stoddard. Ed. and with biographical sketch by Maitland C. de Sormo. Saranac Lake, N.Y. (Adirondack Yesteryears, 1971) 152 p. illus. 24 cm. 77-182699. F127.A2 S775

ADIRONDACKS. Through the lake country of the Adirondacks. By Seneca Ray Stoddard. Troy., N.Y., Nims & Knight (1888) 1 l. 9 plates. 25 x 30 cm. 1-14034 rev.* F127.A2 S 78

ADIRONDACKS. Wild Adirondack lakes ... By Seneca Ray Stoddard ... Troy, N.Y., Nims & Knight, 1889. 1 l. 15 plates. 15 x 19 cm. 1-14035 rev.* F127.A2 S 79

NEW YORK

ADIRONDACKS. Stoddard's northern monthly. v. 1-3, v. 4, no. 1-3; May 1906 - Sept. 1908. Glens Falls, N.Y., S. R. Stoddard, 1906-08. 4 v. illus., plages (partly col.) ports. 18 - 25½ cm. No more pub. 7-40921 Add.
F127.A2 S795

ADIRONDACKS. The Indian pass. By Alfred B. Street ... New York, Hurd & Houghton; Cambridge (Mass.) Riverside press, 1869. lviii, 201 p. 18 cm. 1-14036.
F127. A2 S 8
Rare Book Coll.

ADIRONDACKS. Woods and waters: or, The Saranacs and Racket ... By Alfred B. Street. New-York, M. Doolady, 1860. xx, 345 p. incl. front. (map) illus. plates. 19½ cm. 1-14037.
F127.A2 S 81
Rare Book Coll.

ADIRONDACKS. Historical sketches of northern New York and the Adirondack wilderness; including traditions of the Indians, early explorers, pioneer settlers, hermit hunters, etc. By Nathaniel Bartlett Sylvester ... Troy, N.Y., W. H. Young, 1877. 2, (iii) - viii, (9) - 316 p. illus., 2 port. (incl. front.) 23 cm. 1-14038.
F127. A2 S 9

ADIRONDACKS. Birch bark from the Adirondacks; or, From city to trail ... (By Frank Hamilton Taylor) New York, Adirondack railway co., 1886. 70 p. front. (fold. map) illus. 12½ x 19 cm. 1-16263 Rev.
F127. A2 T2

— 3d ed. rev. and improved ... New York and Saratoga Springs, The Adirondack railway co., 1888. 76 p. fold. front., illus., fold. maps. 13½ x 20½ cm. 1-16262 Rev.
F127. A2 T3

ADIRONDACKS. Adirondack tales; a girl grows up in the Adirondacks in the 1880's (by) Edna West Teall. (Willsboro, N.Y., Adirondack Life, 1970) 191 p. illus. 23 x 27 cm. 72-145680.
F127. A2 T4

ADIRONDACKS. Folklore from the Adirondack foothills. By Howard Thomas. Sketches by John D. Mahaffy. (1st ed. Prospect, N.Y.) Prospect Books, 1958. 150 p. illus. 22 cm. 58-4590.
F127.A2 T446

ADIRONDACKS. Tales from the Adirondack foothills. By Howard Thomas. Sketches by John Mahaffy. (1st ed.) Prospect, N.Y., Prospect Books, 1956. 150 p. illus. 22 cm. 58-40067.
F127.A2 T45

ADIRONDACKS. "... In them thar hills;" folk tales of the Adirondacks. By Helen Escha Tyler. (Saranac Lake, N.Y., 1968) 87 p. illus. 16 cm.
F127.A2 T94

ADIRONDACKS. Gazetteer of the mountains of the state of New York. Compiled by Edward M. Douglas, Map information office, Board of surveys and maps. Washington, 1927. 36 numb. l. incl. tab. 27 cm. Reproduced from type-written copy. 27-25116 Rev.
F127. A2 U5

ADIRONDACKS. Descriptive guide to the Adirondacks and handbook of travel to Saratoga Springs, Schroon Lake, lakes Luzerne, George and Champlain, the Ausable Chasm, the Thousand Islands, Massena Springs and Trenton Falls. By E. R. Wallace. Rev. and cor. by the author ... New York, The American news co.; Syracuse, N.Y., Waverley pub. co., 1875. vi, (3) - 273, (27) p. front., illus., plates, 3 fold. maps. 20 cm. Folded map in pocket. 1-16270.
F127.A2 W15

— Rev. and enl. Containing numerous illus; also, maps. Syracuse, N.Y., W. Gill, 1894. xxiii, (25) - 522 p. front., plates, ports., fold. maps. 20 cm. 1-14039.
F127. A2 W2

ADIRONDACKS. Adirondack profiles. By William L. Wessels. (1st ed. Lake George, N.Y., Adirondack Resorts Press, 1961) 202 p. 23 cm.
F127.A2 W4

— (3d ed. 1961) 202 p.
F127. A2 W4
1961 b

ADIRONDACKS. Freedom in the wilds; a saga of the Adirondacks. By Harold Weston. St. Huberts, N.Y., Adirondack Trail Improvement Soc., 1971. 230 p. illus. 25 cm. 79-160118.
F127.A2 W43

ADIRONDACKS. Adirondack country; By William Chapman White; ed. by Erskine Caldwell. (1st ed.) New York, Duel, Sloan & Pearce (1954) 315 p. 22 cm. (American folkways) 52-12652.

F127. A2 W5
1954

— Introd. by L. Fred Ayvazian. Afterword by Ruth M. White. Drawings by Walter Richards. New York, A. A. Knopf, 1967. xi, 325, (3), vi p. 22 cm. 67-22222.

F127. A2 W5
1967

ADIRONDACKS. Just about everything in the Adirondacks. By William Chapman White. Introd. by Alfred S. Dashiell. Blue Mountain Lake, N.Y., Adirondack Museum (1960) 101 p. 14 x 21 cm.

F127. A2 W52

ADIRONDACKS. Friendly Adirondack peaks, by Robert S. Wickham. (Binghamton, N.Y.) Priv. pub., 1924. 192 p. front., 1 illus., plates, 2 maps. 19½ cm. Adirondack Mountain club edition. 24-22262.

F127. A2 W63

ADIRONDACKS. Cranberry Lake, New York ... By James Foster Wilcox ... (Cranberry Lake, N.Y.) 1915. 64 p. illus. (incl. ports.) 13 x 18 cm.

F127. A2 W66

ALBANY County business directory, The ... 18 Albany, N.Y., C. S. Hayne, 18 v. fold. map. 24 cm. 12-10741.

Directories

ALBANY County directory, The ... Albany, Sampson, Murdock, 18 v. fold. maps. 24 cm. 12-10742.

Directories

ALBANY-Schenectady-Troy (Capitol district) suburban directory 1916 -   ; covering to. townships and villages in Albany, Rensselaer, Schenectady and Saratoga counties, New York ... v. 1 - Schenectady, N.Y., H. A. Manning co., 1915 - v. 23½ cm. 16-1057.

Directories

ALBANY County. American agriculturist farm directory and reference book of Albany and Rensselaer counties, 1916 - including a road map of Albany and Rensselaer counties. New York, Minneapolis (etc.) Orange Judd co. v. fold. map. 23½ cm. 16-25212.

Directories

ALBANY County. ... Early records of the city and county of Albany, and colony of Rensselaerswyck ... Trans. from the original Dutch by Jonathan Pearson ... rev. and ed. by A. J. F. Van Laer ... Albany, The University of the state of New York, 1869-19 v. 26 cm. (v.1: 25 cm.) Contents. - v.1. (Deeds) 1656-1675 (i.e. 1679) - v.2. Deeds. 1678-1704. - v.3. Notarial papers 1 and 2. 1660-1696. - v.4. Mortgages I, 1658-1660, and wills 1-2, 1681-1765. 10-209 Rev. 2.

F127. A3 A3

ALBANY County. The world war. Selective service in the county of Albany ... 1917-1918. Albany, J. B. Lyon co., printers, 1922. 142 p. front. (fold. facsim.) ports., tables (2 fold.) 23 cm. 23-5272.

F127. A3 A34

ALBANY County Historical Association. Record. (Albany) v. in 28 cm. 4 no. a year. Began publication in Nov. 1941. 57-48964.

F127. A3 A6

ALBANY County. Gazetteer and business directory of Albany & Schenectady Co., for 1870-71. Comp. and pub. by Hamilton Child ... Syracuse, Print. at the Journal office, 1870. 490 p. incl. front. (fold. map) 21½ cm. 17-28116.

F127. A3 C4 or directories

ALBANY County. The heroes of Albany. A memorial of the patriot-martyrs of the city and county of Albany, who sacrificed their lives during the late war in defense of our nation, 1861-65 ... and also brief histories of the Albany regiments. By Rufus W. Clark. Albany, S. R. Gray, 1866. viii, (11) - 870 p. col. front., illus., plates, ports. 24 cm. 4-20340.

F127. A3 C5

— 1867. viii, (11) - 870 p. col. front., illus., plates, ports. 25 cm. 7-21516.

F127. A5 C52

ALBANY County. Pilgrimages to the graves of 126 revolutionary soldiers in the towns of Guilderland, New Scotland, and Bethleham, Albany county, undertaken as a jubilee project celebrating the fiftieth

NEW YORK

anniversary, National society, D.A.R., by Tawasentha chapter.   Slingerlands, New York.   (Albany, Evory press) 1940.   (28) p.   illus. (maps, facsim.)   23 cm.   42-14918.   F127. A3 D3

ALBANY County.   ... Farmers' and country merchants' almanac and ready reference book.   1870. Containing historical sketches of the counties of Albany, Rensselaer, Washington, Warren, Schenectady, Saratoga, Rutland and Bennington; tog. with farmers' names, etc. ... Albany, N.Y., C. Van Benthuysen (1870)   207 p.   23 cm.   10-5637.   F127. A3 F2

ALBANY County.   Bi-centennial history of Albany.   History of the county of Albany, N.Y., from 1609 to 1886.   With portraits, biographies and illustrations.   (By) Howell (and) Tenney.   Assisted by local writers.   New York, W. W. Munsell, 1886.   2, xxx, 997 p.   front., illus. (incl. facsim.) ports., maps.   29 cm. Bound with: History of the county of Schenectady ... 1886.   1-14041.   F127. A3 H8

ALBANY County, Landmarks of.   Ed. by Amasa J. Parker ... Syracuse, N.Y., D. Mason, 1897. vi, 557, 172, 418 p.   ports.   25 cm.   In 3 parts: pt. II: Biographical; pt. II: Family sketches.   1-2599.   F127. A3 P2

ALBANY County.   Contributions for the genealogies of the first settlers of the ancient county of Albany, from 1630 to 1800.   By Prof. Jonathan Pearson.   Albany, J. Munsell, 1872.   182 p.   2pl.   21 x 18 cm. In double columns.   4-12546.   F127. A3 P3

ALLEGANY County.   Pocket business directory of leading firms ... Scranton, Pa., 1903.
Directories

ALLEGANY County and its people.   A centennial memorial history of Allegany county ... John S. Minard, esq., county historian ... Also histories of the towns of the county.   Mrs. Georgia Drew Merrill, ed.   Alfred, N.Y., W. A. Fergusson, 1896.   941 (i.e. 951) p.   front. (map) illus., plates, ports.   25 cm. Half-title? wanting.   1-14043.   F127. A4 A4

ALLEGANY County.   Gazetteer and business directory of Allegany County, for 1875.   By Hamilton Child.   Syracuse (N.Y.) Printed at the Journal Office, 1875.   290 p.   front., fold. map.   21 cm.   57-50677.
F127. A4 C45

ALLEGANY County, ... History of.   With illus.descriptive of scenery, private residences, public buildings, fine blocks, and important manufactories ... and portraits of old pioneers and prominent residents.   New York, F. W. Beers, 1879.   392 p.   col. front., illus. (incl. map) plates (2 col., 1 double), ports. 36½ x 30 cm.   1-14044.   F127. A4 H6

ALLEGANY County.   ... Recollections of the log school house period, and sketches of life and customs in pioneer days.   By Jno. S. Minard.   Illus. by R. J. Tucker.   Cuba, N.Y., Free press print, 1905. 6, 137, (3) p.   front. (port.)   illus.   22 cm.   5-20899.   F127. A4 M6

ALLEGANY State Park, ... A popular guide to the geology and physiography of, by A. K. Lobeck ... Albany, The University of the state of New York, 1927.   5-288 p.   illus., 3 fold. maps.   19 cm.   (New York state museum.   Handbook I)   Bibliography: p. 277-281)   27-27406.   F127. A47
QE146. A4 L6

ALLEGANY state park commission.   Annual report.   Albany, 1922 -   v. illus., plates, maps (part fold.) tables.   23 cm.   First report covers period from June 1, 1921, to Dec. 31, 1921.   25-27025.   F127. A47 N5

BLACK River.   Birth of a river; an informal history of the headwaters of the Black River.   By Thomas Clay O'Donnell.   (1st ed.) Boonville, N.Y., Black River Books, 1952.   158 p. illus.   21 cm.   First volume in a trilogy, the second and third of which are the following two items.   52-13916.
F127. B48 O3

BLACK River.   The river rolls on; a history of the Black River from Port Leyden to Carthage.   By Thomas Clay O'Donnell.   (1st ed.) Prospect, N.Y., Prospect Books, 1959.   142 p.   22 cm.
F127. B48 O33

BLACK River in the North Country.   By Howard Thomas.   (1st ed.) Prospect, New York, Prospect Books, 1963.   vi, 213 p.   illus., map.   22 cm.   F127. B48 T5

BOUNDARIES. ... Letter from Edmund Burke ... respecting the effect of the Quebec bill upon the boundaries of New York.   (In N. Y. hist. soc. Collections. 2d ser. v.2, p. 215-226) 11-22440.

F127. B7
F116. N 62

BOUNDARIES.   Yankees and Yorkers (by) Dixon Ryan Fox ... New York, University press; London, H. Milford, Oxford university press, 1940.   x, 237 p. fold. map. 24 cm.   (Anson G. Phelps lectureship on early American history, New York university. 40-13441.

F116. B7
F122. F 78

BOUNDARIES.   ... Papers relating to the Susquehannah River.   1683 - 1757.   (In The documentary history of the state of New-York ... v. 1 p. 391-420.   Documents relating to attempts of the proprietors of Pennsylvania to acquire the Indian title to lands on the upper Susquehanna. 8-27638.

F127. B 7
F122. D63 v. 1

BOUNDARIES.   Report of the Commissioners on the western boundary line between Connecticut and New York, to the General assembly ... 1857.   Printed by order of the Legislature.   Hartford, Hawley & Faxon, 1857.   15 p. 23 cm. 6-40525.

F127. B7 C 7

BOUNDARIES.   To the Honourable His Majesty's commissioners for settling the partition-line, between the Colonies of New York, and New Jersey.   By John Cruger.   New York, Print. H. Gaine.
4 p. 32 cm.

F127. B7 C 8
Rare Book Coll.

BOUNDARIES.   Two reports of a committee of His Majesty's Council for the Province of New-York, relating to the controverted line between that Province and New-Jersey.   Pub. by order of His Honour the Lieutenant Governor, in Council.   New-York, Print. J. Parker, 1754.   22 p. 32 cm.

F127. B7 N18
Rare Book Coll.

BOUNDARIES.   A state of the right of the colony of New-York, with respect to it's eastern boundary on Connecticut River, so far as concerns the late encroachments under the government of New-Hampshire. And also ... so far as concerns the grants formerly made by the French government of Canada, of lands on Lake-Champlain, etc.   Agreed to and pub. by the General assembly of the colony of New-York ... Printed by H. Gaine ... 1773.   28 p. 30 ½ cm. Bound with following item. 6-45399.   F127.B7 N 21

BOUNDARIES.   A narrative of the proceedings subsequent to the royal adjudication, concerning the lands to the westward of Connecticut river, lately usurped by New-Hampshire ...   New-York: Print. John Holt ... 1773.   28, (66) p. 30 ½ cm. Bound with above item. 6-45400.

F127.B7 N 21

BOUNDARIES.   (Letters patent to Thomas Hauly, Nathan St. John, and others of "four several tracts of land ... being part of the lands lately surrendered up by the colony of Connecticut ...   New York, Print. J. P. Zenger, 1731)   8 p. 34 cm. 6-45401.

F127.B7 N 23
Rare Book Coll.

BOUNDARIES.   ... Report of the Commissioners on the boundary lines between the state of New York and the states of Pennsylvania and New Jersey, for the year ending Dec. 31, 1882.   (Albany, 1883)
73 p. 3 pl., fold. map. 23 ½ cm. (Assembly Doc. no. 161) 9-23620.

F127.B7 N 24

BOUNDARIES.   Diagrams showing the relative position of various lines referred to in the report of the Commissioners on the New York and Connecticut boundary, made to the Legislature of New York, April, 1857.   (New York? 1857?)   4 maps on 5 sheets, 1 diagr. 22 ½ cm. 2-20073.

F127.B7 N 25

BOUNDARIES.   Report of the Commissioners to ascertain and settle the boundary line between the states of New York and Connecticut.   Transmitted to the Legislature ... 1861.   Albany, C. Van Benthuysen, printer, 1861.   63 p. 2 fold. maps. 23 cm. (Senate doc. no. 36) 20-5519.

F127.B7 N 26

BOUNDARIES.   Communication from the governor, relative to the boundary line between this state and

NEW YORK

the state of New Jersey, March 11, 1831. (Albany, N.Y., 1831)   31 p. 8°. 2-6555.
F127. B7 N 3

BOUNDARIES. ... Report of the regents of the University, on the boundaries of the state of New York ... Albany, The Argus co., printers (etc.) 1874-78.   2 v. 23½ cm. (New York (State) Legislature. Senate Doc. 108, 1873; 61, 1877) 1-14048 Add.
F127.B7 N 51
— Volume II. Being a continuation of Senate document no. 108 of 1873, and Senate document no. 61 of 1877. Albany, The Argus co., printers, 1884.   4. 867 p. map. 24 cm. An enlarged ed. of v.2 of the original report. 1-14048 Add.
F127.B7 N 52

BOUNDARIES. Report of the regents of the University of the state of New York on the re-survey of the New York and Pennsylvania boundary line ... Albany, Weed, Parsons and co., 1880.   41 p. 3 fold. maps. 23½ cm. (New York (State) Legislature. Assembly. Doc. 100, 1880) 9-785.
F127.B7 N 56

BOUNDARIES. Report of the New York commissioners on the boundary lines between the state of New York and the states of Pennsylvania and New Jersey ... Albany, Weed, Parsons, 1882.
26 p. 23½ cm. (New York (State) Legislature. Senate. Doc. 20, 1882) 7-36275* Cancel.
F127.B7 N 58

BOUNDARIES. Report of the commissioners on the boundary line between the state of New York and New Jersey ... Albany, Weed, Parsons, print., 1884.   137 p. pl., fold. map, fold. diagr. 24 cm. (New York (State) Legislature. Senate. Doc. 46) 7-36274* Cancel.
F127. B7 N 6

BOUNDARIES. Report of the Regent's Boundary commission upon the New York and Pennsylvania boundary, with the final report of Maj. H. W. Clarke, surveyor for the commission. Illus. with numerous maps and sketches. Albany, Weed, Parsons, print., 1886.   3, (5) - 490 p. maps, diagrs. (part fold.) facsims. 23 cm. (New York (State) Legislature. Senate. Doc. 71, 1886) 7-11356 Rev.
F127.B7 N 62

BOUNDARIES. Report of the Pennsylvania board of the Pennsylvania and New York joint boundary commission. Submitted to Hon, William McCandless, secretary of internal affairs ... 1877 ... Harrisburg, L. S. Hart, print., 1878.   8 p. 24 cm. 10-31382.
F127. B 7 P 4

BOUNDARIES. An argument delivered on the part of New York at the hearing before His Majesty's commissioners, appointed by his royal commission under the great seal of Great Britain, bearing date the 7th Oct., 1767, to settle and determine the boundary line between the colonies of New York and New Jersey. (New York? Print. H. Gaine?) 1769.   80 p. 28 cm.
F127. B 7 S 3
Rare Book Coll.

BROOME County. The Farm journal illustrated rural directory of Broome County (with a complete road map)   Philadelphia, Wilmer Atkinson co.,   v. illus. 23½ cm. 17-13292.
Directories

BROOME County. ... Triple cities rural directory. 19   A directory of the rural routes and sections surrounding Binghamton, Johnson City, Endicott, Union, Vestal, Conklin and Kirkwood, N.Y., comp. and pub. by the Hogan directory co. Binghamton, N.Y., 19   v. 25½ cm. 42-4197.
Directories

BROOME and Chenango counties, Williams directory of ... 18   Binghamton, N.Y., J. E. Williams, 18   v. front. (port.) 23 cm. 39M262 T.
Directories

BROOME County. Biographical review; this volume contains biographical sketches of the leading citizens of Broome county ... Boston, Biographical review pub. co., 1894.   (5) - 836 p. ports. 28½ x 23 cm. (Atlantic states series of biographical reviews, v. 3) 3-18905 Rev.
F127. B 8 B 6

BROOME County, illustrated. Binghamton, N.Y., Bellflower press, 1895.   135 p. illus., port. fol. 1-14049-M1.
F127. B 8 B 8

BROOME County. Historical address, relating to the county of Broome in the state of New York. Delivered at Binghamton ... 1876, by George Burr. Pub. under the direction of the Committee of arrangements. Binghamton, Carl, Stoppard, print., 1876.   55 p. 22 cm. 1-14050.
F127. B 8 B 9

BROOME County. Genealogical records of certain families residing in central New York State, ca. 1800, including the Thompson-Manning, Seymour-Stoddard, Ford-Darcy & Cook-Whittlesey families of Killawog, Lisle and Whitney Point in northern Broome County. Chicago, 1961. 1 v. (various pagings) 26 cm. In part reproduced from ms. copy. F127. B 8 C6

BROOME County. Race relations in Broome County; a profile for 1958 by Eunice and George Grier. (Albany) State Commission for Human Rights, Research Division. 1958. 26 l. illus. 29 cm. Includes bibliography. A 58-9877. F127.B8 N 45

BROOME County. The Susquehanna flows on; a narrative of the development of the Southern Tier, by John H. VanGorden. (1st ed. 1966) 281 p. 21 cm. F127. B 8 V3

CONSTITUTION Island. Annual report and year book ... Constitution island assoc., West Point. West Point, N.Y., 19 v. front. (port.) illus., maps. 23½ cm. CA 25-1015 Unrev. F127. C2 C6

CONSTITUTION Island; comp. for the meeting of the Garden club of America by the Constitution island assoc. (inc.) (Newburgh, N.Y., Moore printing co.) 1936. 37, (3) p. illus. (incl. ports., map) 23 cm. 37-9461. F127.C2 C63

CONSTITUTION Island; written for the Historical society of Newburgh Bay and the Highlands, at Newburgh in the county of Orange, New York. By Stuyvesant Fish. (New York, 1914) 8 p. pl. 22½ cm. 14-19132. F127. C2 F5

— Albany, J. B. Lyon co., printers, 1915. p. 573-585. 2 pl. 23 cm. "Reprinted from the Twentieth annual report of the American scenic and historic preservation society." 18-4021. F127.C2 F53

CANISTEO Valley. Stories of the Kanestio Valley, by William M. Stuart (2d ed.) Canisteo, N.Y., The Canisteo times (1929) iii-viii, 146 p. 23½ cm. 30-569. F127.C24 S93

— 3d ed. (Dansville, N.Y., F. A. Owen pub. co., 1935. 261 p. 23½ cm. 35-34045.
F127. C29 S93
1935

CATSKILLS. The Eagle guide to the Catskill Mountains. By Richard S. Barrett. (Brooklyn, Brooklyn daily eagle) 1905. 83 p. front. (fold. map) illus. 15½ cm. (Brooklyn eagle library, vol. xx, no. 2, serial no. 102) 5-32117. F127. C3 B 2

CATSKILLS. Woodstock stories, poems and essays, a book of the Catskills for the people, by William Benignus. (New York, Rosswaag's Stuyvesant press, 1921) 40 p. illus. (incl. port.) 23½ cm. 21-12353. F127.C3 B 46

CATSKILLS. ... The Catskill mountains, Pine Hill and Summit mountain; by Rev. J. Z. Butler and others. Illus. by DuBois F. Hasbrouck. Rondout, N.Y., Print. by ye Kingston Freeman co., 1883. 13 p. illus. 21½ x 16½ cm. 1-16269 Rev. F127. C3 B 9

CATSKILLS. The Catskill Mountain breeze and tourist's guide. v. 2-3. Catskill and New York (Summer resort pub. co.) 1884-85. 2 v. in 1. illus. 42½ cm. Weekly during the summer season. CA 7-6340 Unrev. F127. C3C28

CATSKILL mountain guide, with maps; showing where to walk and where to ride. Catskill, N.Y., Van Loan & Van Gorden (1876) 3, 1-24, 37-59 p. illus., maps. 8°. 1-22573-M1. F127. C3 C3

CATSKILL mountain summer resorts ... containing selected list of hotels, boarding houses and farm houses where summer guests are entertained. New York, American resort assoc., 1902. 112 p. incl. illus., map. 20 x 10½ cm. 2-19007. F127. C3 C37

CATSKILLS. A catskill souvenir; scenes on the line of the Ulster and Delaware Railroad; a historical sketch of the Ulster and Delaware Railroad, by William F. Helmer. Cornwallville, N.Y., Hope Farm Press, 1969. (25) p. 24 cm. F127.C3 C43

820

NEW YORK

CATSKILLS. The Catskill Mountains, devoted to a description of this famous summer resort region ... copyright ... by Leo H. De Silva. Stamford-in-the-Catskills, N.Y., 1926. 72 p. illus. (incl. map) 19½ x 28 cm. 26-14665.
F127. C3 D4

CATKILLS. The Catskills. An illustrated hand-book and souvenir fully describing and illustrating all summer resort localities in the entire region, lowland or highland ... By (R. Ferris) Profusely illustrated in half tone. Kingston, N.Y., Ferris publication co. (1897) 189 p. illus. 8º. 1-14053-M1.
F127. C3 F3

CATSKILLS. Picturesque Catskill Mountain summer resorts; select list of hotels and boarding houses ... By (William J. Fitchett) New York, United States resort co., 1906. 2, 7-96 p. illus. 23½ cm. 6-24571.
F127. C3 F5

— 1907. 4, 11-112 p. illus. 23½ cm. 7-23953.
F127.C3 F51

CATSKILLS. Picturesque Catskills, by F. A. Gallt. (Catskill, N.Y., Catskill mountain resort co., 1922 (64) p. illus. (incl. maps) 23 cm. 22-13387.
F127. C3 G2

CATSKILLS. Guide to rambles from the Catskill mountain house. By a visitor. Catskill, J. Joesbury, printer, 1863. 8 p. 14½ cm. 17-2406.
F127. C3 G9

CATSKILLS. Our Catskill mountains, by H. A. Haring; with 42 illus. and 2 maps. New York, London, G. P. Putnam's sons (1931) xviii, 350 p. front., plates, maps (1 fold.) 22½ cm. 31-28448.
F127. C3 H2

CATSKILLS. Guide to the Catskill mountains ... By Howard Hendricks. New York (1903) 20½ x 10 cm.
F127. C3 H4

CATSKILLS. The Kaaterskill region. Rip Van Winkle and Sleepy Hollow, by Washington Irving. (New York) The Kaaterskill pub. co., 1884. 46, 16, (2) p. incl. illus., maps. fold. pl. 19 x 22½ cm. Advertising medium of the Hotel Kaaterskill. 3-27736.
F127. C3 I 7

CATSKILLS. The Kaaterskill mountains. An album of mountain scenery together with descriptive text. Philadelphia, The Levytype co., 1890. 6 p. 24 pl. obl. 12º. 1-14054-M1.
F127. G3 K2

CATSKILLS. Kaaterskill park. Scenery, walks, dives, geology, etc., of the principal points in the Kaaterskill region. (Philadelphia) The Kaaterskill pub. co. (1882) 31 p. illus. (incl. maps) double plates. 19½ x 23 cm. 1-21496 Rev.
F127.C3 K22

CATSKILLS. The Catskills, by T. Morris Longstreth ... illus. with photos. and map. New York, The Century co., 1918. 6. 3-321 p. incl. plates. front., fold. map. 21½ cm. Bibliography: p. 316-317. 18-19146.
F127. C3 L8

— Port Washington, N.Y., Ira J. Friedman Division, Kennikat Press (1970) 321 p. illus. 22 cm. (Empire State historical publications series, no. 85) 75-118782.
F127. C3 L8 1970

CATSKILLS. Enjoying the Catskills; a practical guide to the Catskill Mountain region for the motorist, camper, hiker, hunter, fisherman, skier, and vacationer. By Arthur Carlyle Mack. Maps and illus. by Stephen J. Voorhies. New York, Funk & Wagnalls (1950) viii, 88 p. illus., maps. 21 cm. Bibliography: p. viii. 50-8285.
F127. C3 M3

CATSKILLS. Summer in the Catskill mountains, by Kirk Munroe. (New York) Passenger dept., New York, West shore and Buffalo railway co., 1883. 62 p. illus., fold. map. 18 x 14 cm. 1-16271 Rev.
F127. C3 M9

CATSKILLS. Guide to the Catskills, by Eric Posselt and Arthur E. Layman. New York, Arrowhead Press; Storm Publishers, distributors (1949 - 1 v. illus., maps (part fold.) 20 cm. 49-5521 rev.*
F127.C3 P 68

CATSKILLS.   A guide to the Catskills.   By Eric Posselt.   Haines Falls, N.Y., Arrowhead Press, publishers ... (1952 -   1 v.   illus.   21 cm.   52-3381.   F127.S3 P683

CATSKILLS.   Rider's Catskill mountain boarding-house directory and travelers' guide ... 1881. Bushnellsville, N.Y., C. H. Rider, 1881 -   v.   17 cm.   33-38654.   F127. C3 R4

CATSKILLS.   The Catskill Mountains and the region around.   Their scenery, legends, and history; with sketches in prose and verse, by Cooper, Irving, Bryant, Cole, and others.   By Rev. Charles Rockwell ... New York, Taintor brothers & co., 1867.   xii, 351 p.   front., plates.   19 cm.   1-14055.
F127. C3 R6

CATSKILLS.   'Mid the Catskill Mountains, by John W. Rusk.   Portland, Me., L. H. Nelson co., 1907. (32) p.   illus.   20½ x 25 cm.   CA 17-139 Unrev.   F127. C3 R87

CATSKILLS.   An illustrated guide to the Catskill mountains, with maps and plans ... Catskill, N.Y., S. E. Rusk (1879)   4, 7-138 p.   illus., fold. maps.   12º.   1-14056-M1.   F127. C3 R9

CATSKILLS.   "The scenic Catskills."   Haines Falls, N.Y., Rusk & Andrews, 1911.   12 mounted phot. 32 cm.   11-5253.   F127.C3 R93

CATSKILLS.   The scenery of the Catskill mountains as described by Irving, Cooper, Bryant, W. G. Clark, N. P. Willis, Miss Martineau, Tyrone Power, Park Benjamin, Thomas Cole, Bayard Taylor and other eminent writers.   Catskill, N.Y., J. Joesbury, printer, 1864.   49 p.   8º.   1-22591-M1.
F127. C3 S 2

CATSKILLS.   The illustration of the Catskill mountains, sketches from nature ... A special guide. New York, H. Schile, (1881)   3, 80 p.   front. (map) illus., port.   4º.   1-14058-M1.   F127. C3 S3

CATSKILLS.   Catskill mountains.   Romantische und interessante plaetze in den drei counties, Ulster, Delaware und Greene.   New York, H. Schile, 1881.   24 p.   4º.   1-14057-M1.
F127. C3 S 3

CATSKILLS.   The land of Rip Van Winkle; a tour through the romantic parts of the Catskills; its legends and traditions, by A. E. P. Searing; with illus. by Joseph Lauber, Charles Volkmar, and others; engraved by E. Heinemann.   New York & London, G. P. Putnam's sons, 1884.   xii, 147 p.   illus., fold. pl.   31 x 23 cm.   14-1307.   F127. C3 S 4

—   1885.   xii, 147 p.   illus., fold. pl.   22½ x 17½ cm.   14-15496.   F127.C3 S 42

CATSKILLS.   ... Catskill mountains, the most picturesque mountain region on the globe.   (Issued by) Ulster and Delaware railroad.   Matter descriptive of the haunts of Rip Van Winkle and how to reach them ... Rondout, N.Y., General offices, 1894.   96 p. incl. front., illus. fold. map. 23½ cm.   1-14059 Rev.
F127. C3 U4

—   1895.   23 cm.   F127.C3 U42

—   1901.   22½ cm.   F127.C3 U49

—   Rondout, N.Y. (Press of K. Freeman) 1902.   179 p.   front., illus., fold. map.   22½ cm.   2-14868.
F127. C3 U5

—   1903.   F127.C3 U51

—   1905.   184 p.   illus., fold. map.   22½ cm.   8-20374.   F127.C3 U53

—   1906.   192 p.   illus., fold. map.   22½ cm.   18-8804.   F127.C3U532

—   (1912)   131 p.   illus. (part col.) fold. map.   22½ cm.   13-6120.   F127.C3 U54

CATSKILLS.   Van Loan's Catskill mountain guide ... Part first: Greene county.   Part second: Ulster

and Delaware counties.   New York, Printed for W. Van Loan, by the Aldine pub. co., 1882.
110 (i.e. 106) p. incl. fold. front.   illus., fold. pl., fold. maps.   24 cm.   1-14060 Rev.   F127. C3 V2

CATSKILLS.   Van Loan's panoramic view of Catskill on the Hudson, and its magnificent mountains.
By (Walton) Van Loan.   (Catskill, N.Y.) 1882.   1 fold. col. pl.   24½ cm.   2-21277.
F127. C3 V28

CATSKILLS.   Van Loan's wonderful panoramic view from Slide mountain ... By Walton Van Loan.
(Catskill, N.Y., W. Van Loan, 1882)   col. fold. pl.   19 x 16 cm.   On continuous strip, 16½ x 302 cm. folded to form
23 leaves; text on p. (2) of cover.   1-14061.   F127. C3 V3

CATSKILLS.   The Catskill Mountain House (by) Roland Van Zandt.   New Brunswick, N.J., Rutgers
University Press (1966)   xxii, 416 p.   24 cm.   66-18877.   F127. C3 V38

CATSKILLS.   Views of the Catskills.   New York, 1887.   7½ x 12½ cm.   F127. C2 V7

CATTARAUGUS County.   Historical gazetteer and biographical memorial of Cattaraugus County ...
Ed. by William Adams.   Syracuse, N.Y., Lyman, Horton, 1893.   vi, 1164 p.   1 illus., plates (1 fold.) ports.
fold. map.   25½ cm.   2-12853.   F127. C4 A2

CATTARAUGUS County.   Revolutionary soldiers buried in Cattaraugus County; comp. (by Julia G.
Pierce, regent, and Maud D. Brooks, historian) in celebration of the fiftieth anniversary, 1897 - 1947.
D.A.R. New York. Olean Chapter. (Olean, 1947)   (31) l.   27 cm.   Typewritten (carbon copy)   "References":
leaf 2.   48-16470*   F127. C4 D3

CATTARAUGUS County, Historical review of.   By Michael C. Donovan.   (n.p., 1959?)   128 p.   24 cm.
F127. C4 D6

CATTARAUGUS County, History of.   (By Franklin Ellis)   With illus. and biographical sketches of
some of its prominent men and pioneers.   Philadelphia, L.H. Everts, 1879.   512 p.   front., illus., plates
(part double)   ports., map.   31 cm.   1-14062.   F127. C4 E4

CATTARAUGUS County: embracing its agricultural society, newspapers, civil list ... biographies of
the old pioneers ... colonial and state governors of New York; names of towns and post offices, etc.
Comp. by John Manley ... Little Valley, N.Y., J. Manley, 1857.   136 p.   ports.   23½ cm.   1-14063.
F127. C4 M2

— 1857.   140 p.   ports.   23 cm.   1-14064.   F127. C4 M3

CAYUGA County.   The farm journal ... directory of Cayuga County.   v.   F127. C5 A18

CAYUGA County.   An original paper upon early records in Cayuga County clerk's office, prepared ...
by George W. Benham, county clerk.   (Auburn? N.Y., 1903)   20 p. incl. port.   18½ cm.   23-4663.
F127. C5 B4

CAYUGA County historical society.   First annual meeting ... 1878.   Auburn, N.Y., 1878.
23 cm.   F127. C5 C45

CAYUGA County historical society, Collections of the.   no. 1-12.   (Auburn, N.Y., The Society) 1879 -
1906.   12 v. in 4.   illus., plates, maps (part fold.)   24½ cm.   1-14065 Rev.
F127. C5 C5

CAYUGA County historical society, Manual of the.   (Auburn, Knapp, Peck & Thomson, printers, 1893)
30 p.   23½ cm.   18-15725.   F127. C5 C53

CAYUGA County, Gazetteer and business directory of, for 1867-8.   Comp. and pub. by Hamilton
Child ...   Syracuse, Printed at the Journal office, 1868.   298 p. incl. front. (fold. map)   21½ cm.   8-15807.
F127. C5 C6

CAYUGA County.   Owasco River Valley; facts and folklore, 1793 - 1965, compiled by Stanley and

Isabell Clary Crysdale ...   Ithaca, N.Y., DeWitt Historical Soc. of Tompkins County, 1965.
167 p.   23 cm.   F127.C5 C78

CAYUGA County.   An address before the Cayuga County historical soc. ... by ... Rev. Charles Hawley.   (Auburn, N.Y., 1880?)   4 p.   24 cm.   9-28857.   F127.C5 H25

CAYUGA County.   Early chapters of Cayuga history: Jesuit missions in Goi-o-gouen, 1656-1684. Also an account of the Sulpitian mission among the emigrant Cayugas, about Quinte Bay, in 1668, By Charles Hawley ... With an introd. by John Gilmary Shea ... Auburn, N.Y., Knapp & Peck, print., 1879.   viii, (9) - 106 p.   front. (fold. map)   24 ½ cm.   1-14067.   F127. C5 H3

CAYUGA County.   Fourth and fifth annual addresses, 1881 and 1882, before the Cayuga Co. historical soc., by Charles Hawley, president of the Society.   Auburn, N.Y. (Knapp & Peck, printers) 1882.
41 p.   24 cm.   Reprinted from Collections of C. C. H. S., no. 2.   10-31669.   F127.C5 H35

CAYUGA County.   In memoriam.   The Rev. Charles Hawley, founder and first president of the Cayuga County historical soc.   The proceedings of a special meeting of the Society ... and a memorial ... by Rev. Willis J. Beecher.   With appendix.   Auburn, N.Y., Knapp, Peck & Thomson, printers, 1886.   72 p.   24 cm.   9-34995.   F127.C5 H38

CAYUGA County.   1789.   History of Cayuga County, with illustrations and biographical sketches of some of its promient men and pioneers.   By Elliot G. Storke.   Assisted by Jas. H. Smith.   Syracuse, D. Mason, 1879.   viii, (9) - 518, xxxviii p.   front., illus., plates, ports.   30 cm.   9-30357.
F127. C5 S 8

CAYUGA County.   The inventors and inventions of Cayuga County, by Cyrenus Wheeler, jr., with a supplement by David M. Osborne.   Read before the Cayuga County historical society ... 1880, and forming a part of their publications, "no. 2."   Illus. by Frank R. Rathbun.   Auburn, N.Y., The author, 1882.   102 p. incl. illus., plates.   24 cm.   2-22460.   F127. C5 W5

CAYUGA Lake.   The Sheldrake Springs Cayuga Lake house, Sheldrake-on-Cayuga, New York. (Sheldrake-on-Cayuga, N.Y? 1908)   (17) p.   illus.   19 x 16 cm.   F127.C52 S 5

CHAMPLAIN.   The book of the play of Hiawatha, the Mohawk, depicting the siege of Hochelaga and the Battle of Lake Champlain.   By Louis Olivier Armstrong.   (n.p.) 1909.   24 p.   23 cm.   Based on W. D. Lighthall's The master of life.   48-41091*.   F127. C6 A7

CHAMPLAIN.   Views of Lake Champlain   By G. W. Baldwin ... Boston, 1888.   13 ½ x 19 cm.
F127. C6 B 2

CHAMPLAIN   ... La Mission Champlain aux États-Unis et au Canada, avril-mai 1912.   Avec 23 portrait hors texte de Cormon, etc.   Paris, Editions France-Amérique, 1913.   2, v, 244 p. front., illus., pl., 23 port.   22 ½ cm.   16-25480.   F127. C6 C7

CHAMPLAIN.   Lake Champlain; a guide and story handbook.   By Fred Copeland.   Tokyo, Rutland, Vt., C. E. Tuttle Co. (1958)   88 p.   illus.   21 cm.   58-12286.   F127.C6 C73

CHAMPLAIN.   A history of Lake Champlain; the record of three centuries, 1609 - 1909, by Walter Hill Crockett.   Burlington, Vt., H. J. Shanley (1909)   335 p.   illus., plates.   19 cm.   9-20252.
F127. C6 C9

— Burlington, Vt., McAuliffe paper co. (1937)   xvi, 320 p.   plates, port., double map.   20 ½ cm.   37-22065.
F127. C6 C92

CHAMPLAIN.   La grande semaine; fêtes du troisième centenaire de la découverte du lac Champlain, récit complet, avec poèmes inédits etc., etc.   redige par J. Arthur Favreau ... Worcester, Mass., Compagnie de publication Belisle, 1909.   4, (11) - 194, (2) p.   illus., maps.   23 cm.   9-28144.   F127. C6 F2

CHAMPLAIN.   Glimpses of lake Champlain.   Glens Falls, N.Y., C. H. Possons, 1896.   (34) p. illus.
16 x 23 ½ cm.   1-14068.   F127. C6 G5

CHAMPLAIN. Address by Senator Henry W. Hill, in accepting the bronze bust "La France," by the sculptor Rodin, the gift of the people of France to the New York and Vermont Lake Champlain tercentenary commissions at the Waldorf-Astoria hotel, New York city ... 1912. (New York? 1912)
(7) p.   23 cm.   12-24564.   F127. C6 H6

CHAMPLAIN. Interestate Commission on the Lake Champlain Basin. Report. (Albany) 1958-
Cover title: The Champlain Valley 350th Anniversary Festival.   A 58-9637.   F127. C6 I 5

CHAMPLAIN. The Lake Champlain and Lake George valleys, by Wallace E. Lamb ... New York, The American historical company, inc. (1940)   3 v. fronts., illus. (incl. maps) ports. 27½ cm. Vols. 1 and 2 paged continuously. Vol. 3 consists of biographies.   40-9204.   F127. C6 L3

CHAMPLAIN. The northern gateway, a history of lake Champlain and guide to interesting places in the great valley, by Carroll Vincent Lonergan ... (Burlington, Vt., Free press printing co., 1941)
40, (2) p.   front. (map) illus. (incl. ports., map)   20 cm.   "List of references": p. 40.   44-33296.   F127. C6 L6

CHAMPLAIN. The seigneurie of Alainville on lake Champlain; address read at the annual meeting of the New York branch of the Order of colonial lords of manors in America, held in the city of New York ... 1929, by A. de Lery Macdonald. Baltimore, 1929.   36 p. col. front., illus. (incl. ports., map) 23½ cm.
(Publication no. 20)   34-5029.   F127. C6 M2

CHAMPLAIN. Lake Champlain and its shores. By William H. H. Murray ... Boston, De Wolfe, Fiske & co. (1890)   3, 261 p.   front. (port.)   20 cm.   1-16268.   F127. C6 M9

CHAMPLAIN. The Champlain tercentenary. Report of the New York Lake Champlain tercentenary commission. Prepared by Henry Wayland Hill, secretary of the commission. Albany, J. B. Lyon co., state printers, 1911.   xiii, 534 p. front., plates (partly fold.) ports., fold. map, fold. plan, 27 cm.   12-33070.
F127.C6 N51

— 2d ed. Albany, J. B. Lyon co., 1913.   xiii, 534 p. front., plates (2 fold.) ports., fold. map, fold. plan, facsim.
26½ cm.   22-736.   F127. C6N515

— Albany, J. B. Lyon co., 1913.   xv, 325 p. front., plates, ports.   27 cm.   14-31033.   F127. C6 N52

CHAMPLAIN. ... Financial report of the New York-Lake Champlain tercentenary commission ... Albany, The Argus co., printers, 1912.   6 p.   23 cm.   F127. C6 N53

CHAMPLAIN. ... Lake Champlain tercentenary ... Dates and places of formal exercises ... Albany, New York state education dept., 1909.   32 p.   illus. (partly col.) fold. map.   25½ cm.   "Lake Champlain: a select reading list.": p. 9.   E9-1154.   F127. C6 N6

CHAMPLAIN. ... Papers relating to the French seigniories on Lake Champlain.   (In The documentary history of the state of New-York ... v. 1.   8-27635.   F127. C6 O15

CHAMPLAIN. History of Lake Champlain, from its first exploration by the French, in 1609, to the close of the year 1814. By Peter S. Palmer. Plattsburgh, J. W. Tuttle, book and job printer, 1853.
223 p.   23½ cm.   8-34780.   F127. C6 P 18

— Albany, J. Munsell, 1866.   2, 276 p. incl. maps.   22 cm.   (Munsell's series of local American history. v. 4)
1-14069.   F127. C6 P 2

CHAMPLAIN. Lake George and Lake Champlain; the war trail of the Mohawk and the battle-ground of France and England in their contest for the control of North America, by W. Max Reid; with 84 illus. from photos. by John Arthur Maney and two maps. New York and London, G. P. Putnam's sons, 1910.
xviii, 381 p.   front., plates, fold. maps, plans.   25 cm.   10-13165.   F127. C6 R3

CHAMPLAIN. The first century of Lake Champlain, by Caroline Halstead Royce. New York, The Miller press, 1909.   (26) p. front. 21 cm.   Imprint in manuscript.   9-30187.   F127. C6 R8

CHAMPLAIN. Scenes on Lakes Champlain ... Glens Falls, N. Y. (1904)   15½ x 24 cm.   F127. C6 S 2

CHAMPLAIN.   Souvenir views of Lake Champlain.   New York, 1909.   1 v.   15 x 19 ½ cm.
F127. C6 S 7

— New York, 1909.   3 pts.   15 x 19 ½ cm.
F127.C6 S 72

CHAMPLAIN.   Behold, the splendor of Champlain!   By John Spargo ... (Burlington, Vt., The Lane press, inc., 1938)   13 p.   23 ½ cm.   39-4727.
F127.C6 S 75

CHAMPLAIN.   Historic Lake Champlain.   By Seneca Ray Stoddard.   (Albany, Albany Engraving Co., 1898)   12 plates.   16 x 22 cm.   1-14070 rev.*
F127. C6 S 8

CHAMPLAIN.   Guide to lake George, lake Champlain, Montreal and Quebec, with ... tables of routes and distances from Albany, Burlington, Montreal, etc.   By Z. Thompson ... Burlington (Vt.) C. Goodrich, 1845.   48 p.   front. (fold. map)   illus.   13 cm.   Also pub., 1854 under title: Northern guide, lake George, lake Champlain, etc.   1-11955.
F127. C6 T4

CHAMPLAIN.   Northern guide.   Lake George, Lake Champlain, Montreal and Quebec, Green and White mountains, etc.   (By Zadock Thompson)   Pub. by S. B. Nichols.   Burlington (Vt.) Stacy & Jameson, 1854.   56 p.   front. (map) illus.   14 ½ cm.   Also pub. under title: Guide to Lake George, etc.   20-2084.
F127.C6 T42

CHAMPLAIN.   ... Tercentenary celebration of discovery of Lake Champlain ... Report.   (To accompany H. J. res.   257)   (Washington, Govt. print. off., 1909)   9 p.   23 cm.   (60th Cong., 2d sess. House. Rept. 2169)   9-35299.
F127. C6 U5

CHAMPLAIN.   Lake Champlain and lake George (by) Frederic F. Van de Water ... Indianapolis, New York, The Bobbs-Merrill co. (1946)   9, 17-381 p.   plates, ports., facsim.   22 cm.   (The American lakes series, ed. by M. M. Quaife)   "First edition."   "Bibliographical note": p. 358-362.   46-8118.
F127. C6 V3

— Port Washington, N.Y., I. J. Friedman (1969)   381 p.   illus.   22 cm.   (Empire State historical publications series no. 68)   79-83478.
F127. C6 V3 1969

CHAMPLAIN.   ... Celebration of three hundredth anniversary of discovery of Lake Champlain. Message from the President ... transmitting a report of the secretary of state, submitting a communications from the states of Vermont and New York relating to the celebration ... (Washington, Gov't print. off., 1908)   14 p.   23 cm.   (U. S. 60th Cong., 1st sess. Senate. Doc. 456)   8-35479.
F127. C6 V5

CHAMPLAIN.   The tercentenary celebration of the discovery of Lake Champlain and Vermont, a report to the General assembly of the state of Vermont, by the Lake Champlain tercentenary commission ... (Montpelier, Vt.) Issued by the Lake Champlain tercentenary commission of Vermont, 1910.   167 p.   front., plates, ports.. map.   26 ½ cm.   10-33414.
F127. C6 V6

CHAMPLAIN.   Letter XXXI.   Arthur Middleton to his brother Edwin.   (By Mrs. Priscilla (Bell) Wakefield)   (London, Darton and Harvey, 1806)   265-270 p.   17 ½ cm.   Separate from the author's "Excursion in North America."   1-27972-M2.
F127. C6 W1

CHAMPLAIN.   A descriptive and historical guide to the Valley of Lake Champlain and the Adirondacks. (By Winslow Cossoul Watson) Burlington, Vt., R. S. Styles' Steam Print., 1871.   144. xxiv p.   plates, fold. map.   20 cm.   1-14040 rev.*
F127. C6 W2

CHAMPLAIN.   Three centuries in Champlain Valley; a collection of historical facts and incidents. Tercentenary ed.   Comp. and ed. by Mrs. George Fuller Tuttle ... Plattsburgh, N. Y., Saranac chapter, D. A. R., 1909.   485 p.   front., illus., plates, ports.   23 ½ cm.   10-13926.
F127.C62 T9

CHAUTAUQUA County.   ... The Grape belt rural directory 1914.   Irving, Silver Creek, Forestville, Dunkirk, Fredonia, Brocton, Westfield, Ripley, N.Y.; North East and Harbor Creek, Pa.   (Jamestown, N.Y., The Jamestown pub. co.,   v.   22 cm.   14-9154.
Directories

NEW YORK

CHAUTAUQUA County. ... American agriculturist farm directory and reference book of Chautauqua County, New York 1918. ... including a road map. New York, N.Y., Minneapolis (etc.) Orange Judd co.,   v. illus., fold. map.   23 ½ cm.   18-11073.   Directories

CHAUTAUQUA County. Twentieth annual conference. American library association. Lakewood-on-Chautauqua. Jamestown, N.Y., 1898.   20 ½ cm.   F127. G7 A5

CHAUTAUQUA County. The churches and clergy of the pioneer period in Chautauqua County by Rev. Chalon Burgess ... (n.p., 1902)   24 p. incl. illus., ports.   27 ½ cm. x 20 cm.   6-13948.   F127. C7 B 9

CHAUTAUQUA County. Proceedings of the Chautauqua society of history and natural science ... July 1883 -   Jamestown, N.Y., The Chautauqua society of history and natural science (1908)
1 v.   pl., ports.   23 cm.   9-13121.   F127. C7 C4

CHAUTAUQUA County. Nineteenth-century houses in western New York, by Jewel Helen Conover. Photos. by the author.   (Albany) State University of New York (1966)   161 p.   66-63788.
                                                                                                                                                F127. C7 C6

CHAUTAUQUA County. Soldiers of the American revolution who at one time were residents of, or whose graves are located in Chautauqua County. Issued by Chautauqua County, N.Y., chapters, National society D.A.R. ... (n.p.) 1925.   78. (7) p.   illus.   25 ½ cm.   26-13614.   F127. C7 D2

CHAUTAUQUA County. Biographical and portrait cyclopedia of Chautauqua County. With a historical sketch of the county by Hon. Obed Edson ... Ed. by Butler F. Dilley. Philadelphia, J. M. Gresham, 1891.   5-14, 17-1730 p. incl. plates, ports.   28 ½ x 22 ½ cm.   15-14710.   F127.C7 D57

CHAUTAUQUA County. A century of commerce and finance in Chautauqua county; historical address by Charles M. Dow ... reprinted from the "Centennial history of Chautauqua county." (Jamestown, N.Y., Journal printing co., 1905)   84 p.   22 cm.   5-41659 Rev.   F127. C7 D7

CHAUTAUQUA County, History of and its people. John P. Downs, editor-in-charge and others. Boston, New York (etc.) American historical society, inc., 1921.   3 v. fronts., plates, ports., maps, col. coats of arms.   27 ½ cm.   21-11927.   F127.C7 D75

CHAUTAUQUA County, History of ... Hon Obed Edson, historian. Georgia Drew Merrill, editor. Boston, Mass., W. A. Fergusson, 1894.   xi, (17) - 975 (i.e. 983) p. front., 1 illus., ports. 26 cm. Extra numbered pages (p. 510a - 510 f; 822a - 822 b)   1-14071.   F127. C7 E2

CHAUTAUQUA. Lake Chautauqua illustrated. By "Two Chautauquans." Pittsburgh, S. A. Clarke; Buffalo, P. Paul & brother; (etc.) 1879.   59 p. incl. illus., map.   18 ½ cm.   3-5843.
                                                                                                                                                F127. C7 L2

CHAUTAUQUA County, a history. By Helen Grace McMahon. (1st ed.) Buffalo, H. Stewart (1958)
339 p.   illus.   23 cm.   Includes bibliography.   58-14008.   F127.C7 M23

CHAUTAUQUA County. Politics is people. An authentic look at the great game of politics from the most interesting of all viewpoints, at the grass roots ... New York, Heineman (1962)   116 p. 22 cm.
62-21893.   F127. C7 M5

CHAUTAUQUA. Lake Chautauqua. New York, Lake Erie and western railroad co. Cleveland, O., Ben Franklin print. (1890)   (18) p.   illus.   16 x 23 cm.   1-16278.   F127. C7 N5

CUAUTAUQUA. The Portage trail, by Mable Powers (Yehsennohwehs) East Aurora, N.Y., Printed by the Roycroft shops (1924)   6, 15-95 p. plates.   19 cm.   26-17775.   F127. C7 P 7

CHAUTAUQUA. Legends of Chautauqua, by Susan Blodgett Pulver. Buffalo, The Peter Paul book co., 1895.   64 p. incl. front., 3 pl. illus.   19 cm.   14-7629.   F127. C7 P 9

CHAUTAUQUA County. Where e'er I roam, what e'er I see, my heart, Chautauqua, turns to thee. By

Henry Severance ... Buffalo, N.Y., Art-printing works of Matthews, Northrup, 1891.   67 p. incl.
front. (port.) illus. 23 cm.   In verse.   18-13583.
F127. C7 S 49

CHAUTAUQUA, Lake. The cicernone. A complete guide to Lake Chautauqua and adjacent places of interest. Written by Geo, B. Smith. Comp. and pub. by Guy M. Peterson ... Jamestown, N.Y., The Daily all press, 1897.   100 p.   illus.   21 cm.   10-23179.
F127. C7 S 6

CHAUTAUQUA County. The old portage road, by H. C. Taylor. Read before the Chautauqua county soc. of history and natural sciences, at Greenhurst ... Pub. in the Fredonia Censor. (Fredonia? N.Y., 1891?)   25 p.   24 cm.   2-4674.
F127. C7 T2

CHAUTAUQUA County. Sketches of the history of Chautauqua County. By Emory F. Warren. Jamestown, N.Y., J.W. Fletcher, 1846.   2. (ix) - xiii, (17) - 159 p.   15½ cm.   1-14072.
F127. C7 W2

CHEMUNG County. Abstracts of wills of Chemung county, N.Y. From 1836 - 1850. Copied from the original records at the Court house, Elmira, N.Y. Copied and compiled by Gertrude A. Barber, (New York?) 1941.   47 numb.   27½ cm.   Type-written.   42-7809.
F127.C72 B 3

CHEMUNG County Historical Society Writers' Group. Chemung County ... its history. (Elmira, N.Y., 1961.   108 p.   28 cm.
F127. C72 C5

CHEMUNG County. The Chemung historical journal. Elmira, N.Y. (Chemung County Historical Soc.)   v. in illus.   24 cm.   quarterly.
F127.C72C52

CHEMUNG. Gazetteer and business directory of Chemung and Schuyler counties, N.Y., for 1868-9. Comp. and pub. by Hamilton Child ... Syracuse, Printed at the Journal office, 1868.   254, 16, (255) - 256 p. incl. front. (fold. map)   21½ cm.   7-3383 Rev.
F127.C72C53

CHEMUNG County. ... A brief history of Chemung county, for the use of graded schools, by Ausburn Towner. New York, A. S. Barnes, 1907.   3. ii, 103 p.   front. (port.)   19 cm.   7-16774 Rev.
F127.C72 T7

CHEMUNG. Our county and its people; a history of the valley and county of Chemung; from the closing years of the eighteenth century, by Ausburn Towner ... Syracuse, N.Y., D. Mason, 1892. 702, 160 p.   illus., ports.   25 cm.   1-16756.
F127.C72T73

CHEMUNG Valley. Home in these hills; being a pictorian essay and commentary on time and living in the valley and hills of the Chemung country of New York State. By Burke Carleton. (Elmira? N.Y., 1949)   1 v. (unpaged)   illus.   31 cm.   49-50248*.
F127. C73 B 8

CHEMUNG Valley. Historical sketch of the Chemung Valley, etc., by T. Apoleon Cheney. Watkins, N.Y., 1868.   59 p.   22½ cm.   1-14074.
F127. C73 C5

CHEMUNG Valley. History of Elmira, Horseheads and the Chemung Valley, with sketches of the churches, schools ... etc. Also, directory & business advertiser for 1868 ... Elmira, N.Y., Comp. and pub. by A. B. Galatian, 1868.   4, 280, 36 p.   24 cm.   20-4531.
F127.C73 H6

CHENANGO County. Directory of the New York, Ontario and western railway ... from Norwich to Oswego, and Utica branch ... Newburgh, N.Y., Breed pub. co.   v.   24½ cm.   1-29290 Rev.
F127. C76
F117.5.D 59

CHENANGO County. Williams directory of Broome and Chenango counties ... 18   Binghamton, N.Y., J. E. Williams, 18   v.   front. (port.)   23 cm.   39M262T.   Directories

CHENANGO County. Gazetteer and business directory of Chenango County, for 1869-70. Comp. and

pub. by Hamilton Child ... Syracuse, Printed at the Journal office, 1869. 299 p. incl. front. (map) 21½ cm. 14-19545.
F127.C76C53

CHENANGO County, History of, containing the divisions of the county and sketches of the towns; Indian tribes and titles ... By Hiram C. Clark. Norwich, N.Y., Thompson & Pratt, 1850. 119 p. front., illus., plates, ports. 23 cm. "100 copies printed. Made up from the pages of a newspaper." - Sabin. 1-24060.
F127.C76 C6

CHENANGO County. ... History of Chenango and Madison counties, with illustrations and biographical sketches of some of its prominent men and pioneers. By James H. Smith. Syracuse, N.Y., D. Mason, 1880. viii. (9)-760, xxix p. front., illus., etc. 29 cm. 21-3716. L.C. copy replaced by microfilm.
F127.C76 S65
Microfilm 16943 F

CHENANGO County. Chenango Valley tales. Ed. George William Walter. Sketches by John Mahaffy. (1st ed.) Prospect, N.Y., Prospect Books, 1957. 150 p. illus. 22 cm. 59-30574.
F127.C76 W3

CLINTON County. A new geography and history of Clinton county, New York. Compiled from original manuscripts, surveys, and other reliable sources. 2d ed. rev. and enl. By H. K. Averill, jr. ... Plattsburgh, N.Y., Telegram printing house, 1885. 32 p. front., illus., maps. 29 x 24½ cm. 1-14075.
F127.C77 A9

CLINTON County. Biographical review. This volume contains biographical sketches of leading citizens of Clinton and Essex counties, New York ... Boston, Biographicl review pub. co., 1896. 2. (9) - 543 p. ports. 29 x 23½ cm. 29-27686.
F127.C77 B61

CLINTON County. Pioneer homes of Clinton County, 1790 - 1820. Text and pictures by Allan S. Everest. Plattsburgh, N.Y., Clinton County Historical Assoc., 1966. 96 p. 26 cm.
F127.C77 E85

CLINTON County. History of Clinton and Franklin counties. With illus. and biographical sketches of its prominent men and pioneers. (By Duane Hamilton Hurd) Philadelphia, J. W. Lewis, 1880. 508 p. front., illus. plates (part double) ports., 2 maps. 30½ cm. 1-14076.
F127.C77 H9

CLINTON County, Recollections of Clinton County and the Battle of Plattsburgh, 1800 - 1840; memoirs of early residents from the notebooks of D. S. Kellogg. Ed. by Allan S. Everest. Plattsburgh, N.Y., Clinton County Historical Assoc., 1964. 75 p. 24 cm. "Sesquicentennial memorial edition." 65-55114.
F127.C77 K4

CLINTON County. 1776. 1876. Centennial oration by Hon, Smith M. Weed, at Plattsburgh, Clinton County, New York, July 4th, 1876. (n.p., 1876?) 8 p. 23 cm. 4-24838.
F127.C77 W3

COLUMBIA County. U.S. National Park Service. Master plan (for) Lindenwald National Historic Site, New York. (Washington, 1970?) 31 p. illus. (part col.). col. maps, col. plans. 27 cm. Supt. of Docs. no.: I 29.9/2: L 64. 77-610722 MARC.
F127.C8 A55

COLUMBIA County. Abstract of wills of Columbia county. (Original wills at Surrogate's office, Hudson, Columbia county, New York) ... Copied and compiled by Gertrude A. Barber. (New York) 1934 - 36. 8 v. 28 cm. Type-written. v. 1. 1786-1805. - v.2. 1805-1814. - v.3. 1814-1822. - v.4. 1823-1828. - v.5. 1828-1853. - v.6. 1835-1840. - v.7. 1840-1846. - v.8. 1846-1851. 36-6727 Rev.
F127. C8 B3

COLUMBIA County. Biographical review; this volume contains biographical sketches of the leading citizens of Columbia county ... Boston, Biographical review pub. co., 1894. 3, (9) - 603 p. incl. plates, ports. 29 x 23½ cm. (Atlantic states eries of biographical reviews. v. 4) 11-10260.
F127. C8 B 6

COLUMBIA County. Marriages of Columbia County residents at the Reformed Protestant Dutch church of Chatham, Columbia County, 1843 - 1873, transcribed by Milton Thomas ... Chatham, N.Y., 1921. 6, 14 numb. l., 3 l. 28 cm. "Six copies made." Autographed from type-written copy. 23-2861.
F127. C8 C4

COLUMBIA County. Gazetteer and business directory of Columbia County, N.Y. for 1871-2. Comp.

and pub. by Hamilton Child ... Syracuse, Printed at the Journal office, 1871. 337 p. incl. front. (fold. map) 21 cm. 5-33724.
F127. C8 C5

COLUMBIA County. Columbia in history; an address by Fred'k J. Collier ... delivered on the occasion of the laying of the corner stone of the Columbia County Court house, Hudson, N.Y. ... 1907 ... Chatham, N.Y., Pub. by order of the Board of supervisors of Columbia County (1908) 16 p. incl. pl. 23½ cm. 18-5191.
F127.C8 C69

COLUMBIA County in the world war, by the Home defense committee of Columbia County, New York ... Albany, J. B. Lyon co., printers, 1924. xxxi, 958 p. incl. tables, form. front., plates, ports., fold. diagr. 25½ cm. 26-1665.
F127.C8C696

COLUMBIA County at the end of the century; a historical record of its formation and settlement, its resources, its insitutions, its industries, and its people ... Pub. and ed. under the auspices of the Hudson gazette. Hudson, N.Y., Record printing and pub. co., 1900. 3 pts. in 2 v. fronts., illus. (incl. ports.) map. 26 cm. 1-17036.
F127. C8 C7

COLUMBIA County. Gravestone inscriptions ... Columbia county, New York ... Copied ... by Minne Cowen. (New York?) 1935-39. 9 v. 28 cm. Type-written. 42-7577.
F127. C8 C9

COLUMBIA County, History of. With illustrations and biographical sketches of some of its prominent men and pioneers. By Franklin Ellis. Philadelphia, Everts & Ensign, 1878. 447 (i.e. 451) p. illus. plates, ports., map, facsims. 30½ x 23½ cm. 2-1869 Rev.
F127. C8 E4
Microfilm 16944 F

— Personal name index. (n.p., 1959) Typescript (carbon copy) 1 v. (unpaged) 29 cm.
E127. C8 E4
Suppl.

COLUMBIA County. The Livingston manor; address written for the New York branch of the Order of colonial lords of manors in America, by John Henry Livingston ... (Baltimore? 191-?) 37 p. incl. illus., col. pl., ports., facsim. 23½ cm. 20-16023.
F127.C8 L78

COLUMBIA County. Marriage record of four Reformed congregations in the towns of Germantown, Gallatin, Copake, and Hillsdale, Columbia County, 1736 - 1899. (Transcribed and indexed by Arthur C. M. Kelly. Rhinebeck, N.Y., 1971) iv, 73, 37, 10 p. 28 cm. Includes records of Germantown. 2736-1899; Gallatin, 1755-1899; West Copake, 1784-1899; and Hillsdale, 1781-1792, Reformed Churches. 71-29760 MARC.
F127. C8 M3

COLUMBIA County. A group of great lawyers of Columbia County, by Peyton F. Miller ... (New York) Priv. print. (The De Vinne press) 1904. viii, 264 p. 19 port. 20 cm. 4-35737.
F127. C8 M6

COLUMBIA County. Biographical sketches of the distinguished men of Columbia County,... By William Raymond ... Albany, Weed, Parsons, 1851. 3, (v) - vi. 119 p. 23 cm. 6-2145.
F127. C8 R3

COLUMBIA County. Gravestone inscriptions, Columbia County, New York ... Copied and ed. by Milton Thomas ... Troy, N.Y., 1920 - v. mounted photos., fold. map. 28 x 22 cm. Autographed from type-written copy. Six copies made. 22-22256.
F127. C8 T4
Rare Book Coll.

CORTLAND County. Directory of Cortland county ... 1902 - Elmira, N.Y., G. Hanford, 1902 - v. fold. map. 23 cm. 2-22504.
Directories

CORTLAND County. The Farm journal illustrated rural directory of Cortland County (with a complete road map) Philadelphia, Wilmer Atkinson co., v. illus. 23½ cm. 17-9248.
Directories

CORTLAND County. Book of biographies; this volume contains biographical sketches of leading citizens

of Cortland County ... Buffalo, N.Y., Biographical pub. co., 1898.   iv, (11) - 515 p. inc;. 2 ports. 29 cm.
8-30446.   F127.C85 B 7

CORTLAND County. The geography and history of Cortland county ... by Cornelia Baker Cornish ...
Ann Arbor, Mich., Edwards brothers, inc., 1935.   v, 60 p. illus. (maps) diagrs. 27½ cm. First made for a
thesis (M.S.) ... Cornell university (1929)   Bibliography: p. 59-60.   35-9670.   F127.C85 C6

CORTLAND County. Residents of Cortland County, 1800-1810; a finding list compiled from local records (by Mary Louise Dexter and others) Cortland, N.Y., Cortland County Hist. Soc., 1971.
32 p.   28 cm.   (Cortland County Hist. Soc. Publication no. 10) Includes bibliographical refs. 73-30887 MARC.   F127.C85D48

CORTLAND County. Pioneer history; or, Cortland county and the border wars of New York ...   By
H. C. Goodwin ... New York, A. B. Burdick, 1859.   viii, (9) - 456 p. front., ports. 19 cm.   1-14077 Rev.
                                                                                                F127.C85 G6

CORTLAND County. History of Cortland county, with illustrations and biographical sketches of some
of its prominent men and pioneers, ed. by H. P. Smith. Syracuse, N.Y., D. Mason, 1885.
552 p.   illus., pl., ports., map.   29 cm.   8-18098 Rev.   F127.C85 S6

DELAWARE County. Abstracts of wills of Delaware county ... Copied from the original wills at the
surrogate's office, Delhi ... Compiled by Gertrude A. Barber, (New York?) 1940-41.   6 v. 28 cm.
Typewritten. Contents. - v. 1. 1796-1833. - v.2. 1834-1847. - v.3. 1847-1857. - 1857-1864. - v.5. 1864-1869. - v.6. 1869-1875. 42-8266.
                                                                                                F127. D3 B 3

DELAWARE County. Deaths and marriages taken from the Delaware gazette at Delhi, Delaware
county. From 1880 - 1895. Copied and compiled by Gertrude A. Barber. (Delhi, 1945?)
122 numb. l.   28 x 21½ cm.   Type-written.   46-3277.   F127.D3 B315

DELAWARE County. Letters of administration of Delaware county, New York ... Copied from the
original records at the Court house, Delhi, N.Y. Compiled by Gertrude A. Barber. (New York?)
1939.   4 v.   28 cm. Type-written. Contents. - v.1. 1797-1844. - v.2. 1844-1863. - v.3. 1863-1874. - v.4. 1874-1875. 42-7578.
                                                                                                F127. D3 B 32

DELAWARE County. Biographical review. This volume contains biographical sketches of the leading
citizens of Delaware County ... Boston, Biographical review pub. co., 1895.   (9) - 724 p. incl. ports. pl.,
port.   29 x 24 cm.   (Atlantic states series of biographical reviews, v. 6)   8-16771.   F127. D3 B 6

DELAWARE County. Delhi gazette, pub. in Delhi, Delaware county, N.Y. "Deaths" ... copied and
compiled by Minnie Cowen ... (New York?) 1933-34.   3 v.   28 cm. Type-written. Contents. 1. 1819-1844. -
2. 1844-1868. - 3. 1868-1870.   42-8267.   F127. D3 C9

DELAWARE County. Marriages taken from the Delaware gazette, Delhi, Delaware County ... Compiled by Minnie Cowen ... (New York? 1941.   3 v.   28 cm. Type-written. Contents. - 1. 1819-1844. - 2. 1844-
1868. - 3. 1868-1879.   42-7810.   F127.D3 C92

DELAWARE County, History of Delaware County, and border wars of New York. Containing a sketch
of the early settlements in the county, and a history of the late anti-rent difficulties in Delaware, with
other historical and miscellaneous matter, never before pub. By Jay Gould. Roxbury (N.Y.) Keeny &
Gould, 1856.   xvi. 426 p. front. (port.) 20 cm. 1-14078.   F127. D3 G7
                                                                                            Rare Book Coll.

DELAWARE County. ... History of Delaware County. With illustrations, biographical sketches and
portraits of some pioneers and prominent residents. New York, W. W. Munsell, 1880.   363 p. incl.
front., illus., port. plates (part double, incl. ports., map, facsims.) 36 x 29½ cm. 1-14079. L. C. copy replaced by microfilm.
                                                                                            F127. D3 H6
                                                                                            Microfilm 18342   F

DELAWARE County; history of the century, 1797 - 1897; centennial celebration, June 9 and 10, 1897,
ed. by David Murray. Delhi, N.Y., W. Clark, 1898.   604 p. incl. illus., plates, ports. front., pl. 25½ cm.
Maps and book relating to Delaware County: p. 20-21. 98-2293 Rev.   F127. D 3 M9
                                                                                            Microfilm 24995 F

DUTCHESS County. Vail's Dutchess County business directory ... (v. 1) - 2. 1870/71 - 1876/7. Poughkeepsie city, J. P. A. Vail (1870) - 76. 2 v. 22½ - 23½ cm. 9-16484. Directories

DUTCHESS County. Address delivered before the Dutchess County society in the city of New York ... 1897. (New York, 1897) 6 p. 21½ cm. 9-27146.

F127. D8 A19

DUTCHESS county in colonial days. Paper by Hon. Alfred T. Ackert. Read before "the Dutchess county society in the city of New York" at its second annual banquet ... 1898. (n. p., 1898)
(8) p. 22 cm. 1-14080.

F127. D8 A2

DUTCHESS county in colonial days. Paper by Hon Alfred T. Ackert. Read before the Dutchess county society ... at its third annual banquet ... 1899. (Tarrytown, N.Y., Tarrytown press-record print., 1899) 30 p. 19 cm. 1-14081.

F127. D8 A3

DUTCHESS County. Local tales and historical sketches, by Henry D. B. Bailey. Fishkill Landing (N.Y.) J. W. Spaight, 1874. 431 p. front. (port.) illus. 20½ cm. Contents. - Poetry. - Tales. - Historical sketches. - Essays. 3-28514.

F127. D8 B 2

DUTCHESS County. Abstracts of wills of Dutchess County from Oct., 1834 to Oct., 1839. Copied from the original records at the Surrogate's Court, Poughkeepsie, New York. By Gertrude Audrey Barber. (Poughkeepsie?) 1944. 80 l. 28 cm. 48-35747*.

F127. D8 B 25

DUTCHESS County. County at large, by Martha Collins Bayne ... Poughkeepsie, N. Y., The Women's city and county club with Vassar college, 1937. xi, 194 p. incl. front., illus. (incl. map) 25½ cm. (A Norrie fellowship report (1936 - 37) 37-36906.

F127. D8 B 3

DUTCHESS County. Four days on the Webutuck River, by Charles E. Benton, with an introd. by Sinclair Lewis ... Amenia, N. Y., Priv. print. at the Troutbeck press, 1925. 2, (7) - 19 p. 22½ cm. (Troutbeck leaflets, no. 6) reprinted from the Springfield, Mass. 'Republican' of June 4. 1896. 25-15908.

F127. D8 B 4

DUTCHESS County. 1790, first federal census of all Dutchess county; comprising 12 towns: Amenia, Beekman, Clinton, Fishkill, Frederickstown, Northeast, Pawling, Philipstown, Poughkeepsie, Rinebeck, Southeast, Washington; classified and indexed by Elijah Ellsworth Brownell. Philadelphia, Pa. (The Bertram press) 1938. 94, (33) p. 26 cm. 39-11949.

F127. D8 B 7

DUTCHESS County. Commemorative biographical record of Dutchess County, containing biographical sketches of prominent and representative citizens, and of many of the early settled families ... Chicago, J. H. Beers, 1897. 2, 950 p. ports. 29 x 23½ cm. 8-12286.

F127. D8 C7

DUTCHESS County. Abstracts of wills of Dutchess county ... Compiled by Minnie Cowen. (New York?) 1939-40. 6 v. 28 cm. Type-written. 42-8268.

F127. D8 C9

DUTCHESS County. Points of historical interest in and near Beacon and Fishkill, Dutchess county, compiled by Melzingah chapter, D. A. R. ... (Beacon?) 1931. 16 p. illus. 23 x 10 cm. "Authorities consulted.": p. 16. 32-11063.

F127. D8 D3

DUTCHESS County. Old miscellaneous records of Dutchess County. (The second book of the supervisors and assessors) Poughkeepsie, Vassar brothers' institute, 1909. 2, 80, 91-195 p. illus. 27½ cm. 9-30079.

F127. D8 D7

— (the third book of the supervisors and assessors) Poughkeepsie, N.Y., Vassar brothers' institute, 1911. (16) p. 27½ cm. Accounts copies from lib. C. of Supervisors. 27-14526.

F127. D8 D71

DUTCHESS County. Book of the supervisors of Dutchess County, N. Y., 1718 - 1722. Poughkeepsie, N. Y., Vassar brothers' institute (1907?) 72 p. 27½ cm. Contains besides the tax lists and records of meetings, a number of court records and miscellaneous accounts. 8-31334.

F127. D8 D8

DUTCHESS County Historical Society. Collections. v 1 -   (New York, etc., William-Frederick Press, etc.) 1924 -   v. illus., maps (part fold.) facsims. 23 - 28 cm. 59-22524.

F127. D8 D92

—Poughkeepsie: the origin and meaning of the word, by Helen Wilkinson Reynolds ... 1924.
93 p. front., plates, maps (part fold.) facsims. (Collections, vol. 1) References, bibliography, etc. p. (45) - 82. 24-10197.

— Old gravestones of Dutchess county - nineteen thousand inscriptions collected and ed. by Wilson Poucher and Helen W. Reynolds ... 1924.   xi, 401 p. incl. front. plates. (Collections, vol. 2)   "In general, the editors have omitted stones bearing date in the latter portion of the ninteenth century." 25-18073 Rev.

— Records of the town of Hyde Park, ed. by Franklin D. Roosevelt for the Dutchess County hist. soc. ... Hyde Park, N.Y., 1928.   3-340 p. 28 cm. (Collections, vol. 3) 29-9326.

— Notices of marriages and deaths, about 4,000 in number, pub. in newspapers printed at Poughkeepsie ... 1778 - 1825, comp. and ed. by Helen W. Reynolds.   xii, 140 p. (Collections v. 4) 30-15935.

— The records of the Reformed Dutch church of New Hackensack. ... Ed. by Maria B. Carpenter Tower ... (Poughkeepsie, N.Y., 1932)   vii-xv. 333 p. front. 27½ cm. (Collections vol. 5) 38-29987.

— Eighteenth century records of the portion of Dutchess county, that was included in Rombout precinct and the original town of Fishkill, presenting historical source-material regarding land and people, collected by William Willis Reese ... and ed. by Helen W. Reynolds. (Albany, J. B. Lyon co., printers, 1938)   3, 323 p. 27 cm. (Collections vols. 6) 38-37909.   Contents. - List of tax-payers. - List of deeds. - List of mortgages. - List of estates. - List of roads. - Index to names of persons. - Index to miscellaneous source-material. 38-37909.

— Records of Crum Elbow precint, Dutchess county, 1738-1761, tog. with records of Charlotte precinct, 1762-1785, records of Clinton precinct, 1786-1788, and records of the town of Clinton, 1789-1799, ed. by Franklin D. Roosevelt ... (Poughkeepsie, N.Y.) 1940.   vii, 196 p. front. (fold. map) illus. (map) (Collections, vol. 7) 40-12530.

— Family vista; the memoirs of Margaret Chanler Aldrich. New York, William-Frederick Press, 1958.   233 p. illus., ports., facsims. (Collections vol. 8) 58-11573.

DUTCHESS County Historical Society. Historical monographs. (Poughkeepsie?)1916.
— No. 1: Troutbeck, A Dutchess County homestead, by Charles E. Benton ...   29 p. 4 pl. (incl. front.) 23 cm. Bibliography: p. (30) 16-23388.   F127.D8D925

DUTCHESS County Historical Society. Year book. 1914/15 -   (Poughkeepsie
  v. fronts., illus., plates, ports., fold. maps. 23 cm. Indexes: Vols. 1-12, 1914/15 - 1927, with v. 12. Vols. 13 - 18, 1928 - 33, in v. 18; Vols. 19-24, 1934-39, in v.24; vols. 25-30, 1940-45 in v. 30; vols. 313-36. 1946-51, in v. 36. 20-20174.
                                                                                                F127.D8 D93

DUTCHESS County Planning Board. Landmarks of Dutchess County. 1683 - 1867; architecture worth saving in New York State. (New York) New York State Council on the Arts, 1969.   242 p. illus. 21 cm.
75-628711.   F127.D8 D95

DUTCHESS County. (Federal writers' project) ... Dutchess county ... (Philadelphia) William Penn association of Philadelphia, 1937.   vii, 166 p. illus., plates, maps (part fold.) 23 cm. (American guide series)
Bibliography: p. 154-161. 37-28501.   F127. D8 F4

DUTCHESS County. They all rest together; burial sites of early settlers - southern Dutchess and Putnam Counties .. By Floyd Fisher. (Holmes? N.Y., 1972)   iii, 99 p. 22 cm. 72-177994 MARC.
                                                                                                F127. D8 F5

DUTCHESS County. Insciptions from five New York, Dutchess Co., cemeteries. (By Mrs. Josephine C. Frost) (Brooklyn? 1911)   32, 2 numb. l. 27½ x 21 cm. Autographed from type-written copy. 13-18332 Rev.
                                                                                                F127.D8 F87

DUTCHESS County. Quaker births, Nine Partners Monthly meeting. (By Mrs. Josephine C. Frost) (Brooklyn, 191 -)   55, 3 numb. l. 27 x 21 cm. Autographed from type-written copy. "Quaker deaths ... ": numb. leaves 21 - 55. 12-29735 Rev.   F127. D8 F9

DUTCHESS County. Quaker births and deaths. Oblong, M. M., Dutchess Co., N.Y. (By Mrs. Josephine C. Frost) (Brooklyn, 191 -) 78, 2 numb. l. 27 x 21 cm. Autographed from type-written copy. 12-30324 Rev.
F127. D8 F92

DUTCHESS County. Quaker marriage intentions and marriages. Oblong M. M., Dutchess Co. (By Mrs. Josephine C. Frost) (Brooklyn, 191-) 90, 4 numb. l. 27 cm. Autographed from type-written copy. 12-29743 Rev.
F127. D8 F94

DUTCHESS County. Quaker marriages, births, deaths, slaves. Nine Partners M. M., Dutchess Co. (By Mrs. Josephine C. Frost) (Brooklyn, 191-) 110, 6 numb. l. 27 cm. Autographed from type-written copy. 12-29742 Rev.
F127. D8 F96

DUTCHESS County. Quaker removal certificates from Creek Monthly meeting, Dutchess County, 1787 to 1802 (incl.) (Brooklyn, 191-) 25, 2 numb. l. 26½ cm. Autographed from type-written copy. 13-12781 Rev.
F127. D8 F965

DUTCHESS County. Quaker removal certificates. Nine Partners M. M., Dutchess Co. (By Mrs. Josephine C. Frost) (Brooklyn, 191-) 122, 5 numb. l. 27 cm. Autographed from type-written copy. 12-30325 Rev.
F127. D8 F98

DUTCHESS County. The history of Dutchess County, ed. by Frank Hasbrouck. Poughkeepsie, S. A. Matthieu, 1909. (9) - 791 p. xxxii p. front., plates, ports., maps (partly fold.) 25 cm. 10-10541.
F127. D8 H4

DUTCHESS County. Historical and genealogical record, Dutchess and Putnam counties. Poughkeepsie, N.Y. (Oxford pub. co.) Press of the A. V. Haight co., 1912. xvi. 476 p. illus., plates, ports. 23½ cm. 15-26902.
F127. D8 H64

DUTCHESS County. Anti-Federalism in Dutchess County; a study of democracy and class conflict in the Revolutionary era. By Staughton Lynd. Chicago, Loyola University Press, 1962. ix, 126 p. 24 cm. 62-18101.
F127. D8 L9

DUTCHESS County. Blithe Dutchess; the flowering of an American county from 1812. By Henry Noble MacCracken. New York, Hastings House, 1958. 500 p. illus. 22 cm. Includes bibliography. 1st printing. 58-59900.
F127. D8 M28

DUTCHESS County. Old Dutchess forever! The story of an American county. By Henry Noble Mac-Cracken. New York, Hastings House (1956) viii, 503 p. maps. 22 cm. "Bibliographical notes": p. 484-496. "1st printing" 56-12863.
F127. D8 M 3

DUTCHESS County. Marriage record of the four reformed congregations of Old Rhinebeck, Dutchess County, 1731 - 1899. (Transcribed and indexed by Arthur C. M. Kelly. Rhinebeck, N.Y., 1971) iv, 101, 57, 10 p. 29 cm.
F127. D8 M37

DUTCHESS County. ... History of Duchess County, with ... biographical sketches of some of its prominent men and pioneers. By James H. Smith, and others. Syracuse, N.Y., D. Mason, 1882. 562, xxx p. front., illus., plates (partly double) ports. 29½ cm. 8-18449.
F127. D8 S 5

DUTCHESS County. General history of Duchess county, from 1609 to 1876, inclusive. Illus. with numerous wood-cuts, maps and full-page engravings. By Philip H. Smith. Pawling, N.Y., The author, 1877. 7-507 p. front. (fold. map) illus., plates, diagr. 22 cm. Appendix A. Brief sketches of the towns of Putnam co. (formerly in Dutchess co.)- B. Extracts from the records, incl. rolls of revolutionary soldiers from the county; also list of newspapers, genealogies of a few families, etc. 1-14082 Rev.
F127. D8 S 6

— Index to Philip H. Smith's General history of Duchess county, by Grace M. Pierce. (n.p., 1916?) 69 numb. l. 27 cm. Type-written copy.
F127. D8 S 6 Index

ERIE Canal. Erie Canal; history of the canal that made New York the Empire State from 1817 to the present. (Introductory statement by Louise Broecker. New York, (New York State Council on the Arts 1971) (4) p. 50 plates. Issued in a case.
F127. E5 E74

NEW YORK

ERIE Canal. 40 x 28 x 4, the Erie Canal, 150 years. Ed. by Lionel D. Wyld. Rome, N.Y., Oneida County Erie Canal Commemoration Commission, 1967. 54, x p. 22 x 27 cm.
F127. E5 F6

ERIE Canal. Irish immigrant participation in the construction of the Erie Canal, by George J. Svejda. ( ) Division of History, Office of Archeology and Historic Preservation, National Park Service, U.S. Dept. of the Interior, 1969. ix. 63 l. illus. 27 cm. 77-604341.
F127. E5 S94

ERIE Canal, The; gateway to Empire; selected source materials for college research papers. Ed. by Barbara K. and Warren S. Walker. Boston, Heath (1963) x, 113 p. 24 cm.
F127. E5 W3

ERIE Canal. Low bridge! Folklore and the Erie Canal. By Lionel D. Wyld. (Syracuse, N.Y.) Syracuse University Press, 1962. 212 p. 22 cm. 62-10627.
F127. E5 W9

ERIE County. ... Erie County directory ... 1st - ed., 1924 - Lockport, N.Y., Roberts brothers co., 1924 - v. 23 cm. 24-22051.
Directories

ERIE County Dept. of Parks and Recreation. Annual report. 1965 - (Buffalo) v. illus. 28 cm. 79-617004.
F127. E6 A2

ERIE County. History of Erie County, 1870 - 1970. Ed. by Walter S. Dunn, Jr. Buffalo and Erie County Historical Soc. (1972) 462 p. illus. 28 cm. 72-176247.
F127. E6 D8

ERIE County. Centennial history of Erie County; being its annals from the earliest recorded events to the hundredth year of American independence. By Crisfield Johnson. Buffalo, N.Y., Printing house of Matthews & Warren, 1876. 512 p. 23½ cm. 1-14083.
F127. E6 J 6

ERIE County. Niagara frontier planning board. Annual report. (Buffalo, 1926 - v. illus., plates, fold. maps, tables, diagrs. 25½ cm. 29-27071.
F127. E6 N4

ERIE County. History of the city of Buffalo and Erie county, with ... biographical sketches of some of its prominent men and pioneers ... By H. Perry Smith. Syracuse, N.Y., D. Mason, 1884. 2 v. illus. (incl. plans) ports. 26½ cm. Contents. - 1. History of Erie county. - 2. History of Buffalo. 1-16741 Rev.
F127. E6 S 6

ERIE County. Our county and its people; a descriptive work on Erie County. Ed. by Truman C. White. (Boston) The Boston history co., 1898. 2 v. illus., plates, ports., maps. 25 cm. 1-2592.
F127. E6 W5

ESSEX County. The sticks; a profile of Essex County (by) Burton Bernstein. Drawings by Marcia Erickson. New York, Dodd, Mead (1972) 175 p. illus. 22 cm. 71-39651.
F127. E8 B 4

ESSEX County. The Chasm of the Au Sable, being a set of 22 views ... Plattsburgh, N.Y., H. K. Averill, jr. (1865?) 22 mounted phot. 14½ x 12½ cm. 17-21068.
F127. E8 C4

ESSEX County. Streetroad, its history and its people; facts, folks, and fancies. By Ellen (Adkins) Johnson. Ithaca, N.Y., Linguistica, 1956. 62 l. illus. 28 cm. 58-40066.
F127. E8 J 6

ESSEX County. History of Essex county; with illus. and biographical sketches of some of its prominent men and pioneers; ed. by H. P. Smith. Syracuse, N.Y., D. Mason, 1885. xv, (17) - 754 p. illus., plates, ports., plans. 26 cm. 1-16757 Rev.
F127. E8 S 6

ESSEX County. Souvenir of Ausable chasm. Glens Falls, N.Y., C. H. Possons (1890) 12 pl. 12°. 1-14046-M1.
F127. E8 S 7

ESSEX County.   Souvenir of Ausable Chasm.   (Chicago, C. Teich, 1924)   (14) p. of col. illus. 21½ cm.
CA 25-883 Unrev.
F127.E8 S 73

ESSEX County.   Au Sable Chasm.   By Seneca Ray Stoddard.   (Glens Falls? N.Y., 1888)
22 p.   11 plates.   14 x 16 cm.   1-14045 rev. 2*.
F127. E8 S 8

ESSEX County.   The military and civil history of the county of Essex; and a general survey of its physical geography, its mines and minerals, and industrial pursuits, embracing an account of the northern wilderness; and also the military annals of the fortresses of Crown Point and Ticonderoga. By Winslow C. Watson.   Albany, N.Y., J. Munsell, 1869.   vii, 504 p. front., pl., ports. 23½ cm. 1-14084.
F127. E8 W3

ESSEX County.   A general view ... of the County of Essex ...   Bt Winslow C. Watson.   (Albany, 1852)   p. (651) - 898.   22½ cm.
F127. E8 W39

ESSEX County.   ... A supplement to the Report on the survey of Essex County: by Winslow C. Watson. (Albany, 1843)   39, (1) p.   23 cm.   "From Trans. N. Y. state ag'l society, 1853, vol. 13th"   3-4945.
F127. E8 W4

FINGER Lakes.   Joshua: a man of the Finger Lakes region, a true story taken from life, by Charles Brutcher.   (Syracuse, N.Y., 1927)   xi, 139 p.   illus. (incl. ports.)   22 cm.   27-21777.
F127. F4 B 9

FINGER Lakes.   The beautiful Finger Lakes trails of central New York.   (Watkins, N.Y., The Finger Lakes association, 1923)   sheet. illus.   23 x 30½ cm. fold. to 23 x 10½ cm.   CA 26-301 Unrev.   F127. F4 F4

FINGER Lakes.   The beautiful Finger Lakes call you ... (1923 ed.)   (By Ross W. Kellogg)   (Auburn, N.Y.) Finger Lakes association of central New York (1923)   39 p.   illus. (incl. map) 23 x 20½ cm.
CA 26-300 Unrev.
F127. F4 K2

FINGER Lakes.   Souvenir of the Finger Lakes region.   Written by Harry R. Melone ...   Auburn, N.Y., Cayuga County news co., 1921.   45. (3) p.   illus., fold. map.   21 x 27½ cm.   21-12094.
F127. F4 M5

FINGER Lakes.   The lakes country, by Arch Merrill ... (Rochester, N.Y., Printed by L. Heindl, 1944)   2, 7-154 p. illus., platex. 20 cm.   "Reprinted from the Democrat and chronicle, Rochester, New York."   44-51169.
F127. F4 M52

FINGER Lakes.   The legend of the Finger Lakes, with something of their Indian lore, traditions and present day charms, by Fred Teller ... Seneca Falls, N.Y., Seneca press pub. co. (1920)
(13) p. illus. 21½ cm. 21-21210.
F127. F4 T2

FINGER Lakes.   The Finger Lakes of central New York; the lakes - topography, points of interest and every road with improved highways indicated.   Rochester, N.Y., United States survey co. inc. (1922)   8, (8) p.   maps (1 fold.)   21 cm.   CA 21-215 Unrev.
F127. F4 U5

FISHERS Island.   An island of homes (Fisher's Island)   (By Edmund M. Ferguson.)   (n.p., 189-?)
(24) p. col. illus. 21 cm.   A circular. advertising Fisher's Island as a summer resort.   18-17127.   F127. F5 F3

FISHERS Island.   Abstracts of the title of Edmund M. Ferguson and Walton Ferguson to all that certain island situated in the town of Southold, county of Suffolk, called Fisher's Island, and the several small islands adjacent thereto called the Hommocks and Wicopesset ...   William M. Hoes, attorney ...   1889. (New York, 1889)   iv, 164 p.   27 x 20½ cm.   18-14011.
F127. F5 H6

FISHERS Island.   Munnatawket hotel, Fishers' Island, New York ...   Fishers' Island, N.Y. (1897)
21 cm.
F127. F5 M9

FISHERS Island.   The Winthrop manor of Fishers island; address prepared for the fourteenth annual meeting of the N.Y. branch of the Order of colonial lords of manors in America ... 1926, by the Rev. M. Lloyd Woolsey.   Baltimore, 1927.   26 p. col. front. (coat of arms) illus. (23½ cm. 43-34002.   F127. F5 W 6

NEW YORK

FRANKLIN County. The story of Davis Hill; pioneer life in the Adirondacks. By Darius Alton Davis. (1963) 48 p. 24 cm.
F127. F8 D3

FRANKLIN County. Life on the border, sixty years ago. By William Reed ... Fall River, Mass., R. Adams, 1882. 120 p. 19 ½ cm. 1-16267.
F127. F8 R3

FRANKLIN County. Historical sketches of Franklin county and its several towns, with many short biographies, by Frederick J. Seaver ... Albany, J. B. Lyon co., printers, 1918. xii, 819 p. 24 cm. 19-375 Rev.
F127. F8 S 4

SRANAC Lakes. Saranac Lake in winter. By Seneca Ray Stoddard. Troy, N. Y., Nims & Knight (1889) 11 plates. 15 x 19 cm. 1-14243 rev.*
F127. F8 S 82

— 1889. 15 plates. 15 x 19 cm. 1-14244 rev.*
F127. F8 S 83

FULTON County. Fulton Chain in the Adirondacks. (n. p., n. d.) 15 x 23 ½ cm.
F127. F9 F9

FULTON County. Epistles from the Old man of the hills to the people of the valley ... (By Elisha Judson) Kingsboro (N. Y.) The author, 1859. 46 p. 22 ½ cm. Sketches of places and people in Fulton and Montgomery counties, New York, with chapters on slavery, temperance, etc. 18-6568.
F127. F9 J 9

GENESEE County. The sesquicentennial of Genesee County, 1802 - 1952. (n. p., 1952) 119 p. illus. 23 cm. 54-36143.
F127. G19 A5

GENESEE County. ... Gazetteer and biographical record of Genesee County, 1788 - 1890. Ed. by F. W. Beers ... Syracuse, N. Y., J. W. Vose, 1890. 2 pts. in 1 vol. pl., port. 24 cm. Pt. 2 has title: ... Business directory of Genesee County. 3-5073.
F127. G19 B 4

GENESEE County. Gazetteer and business directory of Genesee County for 1869 - 70. Comp. and pub. by Hamilton Child ... Syracuse, Printed at the Journal office, 1869. 2, (13) - 227 p. incl. tab. front. (fold. map) 21 ½ cm. 3-19773.
F127. G19 C5

GENESEE County. Tombstone inscriptions from the abandoned cemeteries and farm burials of Genesee County. By La Verne C. Cooley. Batavia, N. Y., 1952. 216 p. 24 cm. 56-41928.
F127. G19 C6

GENESEE region. The Indian and his river, being a book of Iroquois Indian songs and legends, and of the river Genessee, by Carleton Burke. (Rochester, N. Y., 1933) 4, 45 p. illus. 23 ½ cm. Illustrations by Jack Bieber. Poems. 33-30821.
F127. G2
PS3503. U6115 I 6

GENESEE region. ... Charles Williamson, Genesee promoter, (by) Helen I. Cowan ... Rochester, N. Y., 1941. xiv, 356 p. front., plates, ports., map, facsim. 24 cm. (Rochester hist. soc. pub. 19) 42-12694.
F127. G2
F129. R7 R58 v. 19

GENESEE region. ... Part I - Foreign travelers' notes on Rochester and the Genesee country before 1840 ... Rochester, 1940. viii p., 4 l., 262 p. front., plates, port., facsim. 24 cm. Rochester hist. soc. publications. 18. 41-25788.
F127. G2
F129. R7R58 vol. 18

GENESEE region. A description of the Genesee country ... (In The documentary history of New York. v. 2) 11-10459.
F127. G2
F122. D63 vol. 2

GENESEE region. Voyage au Kentoukey, et sure les bords du Genesée, précédé de conseils aux libéraux, et à tous ceux qui se proposent de passer aux États-Unis. Paris, M. Sollier, 1821. 243 p. fold. map. 21 ½ cm. 5-9978 Rev.
F127. G2
F455. V97

GENESEE region. An account of the soil, growing timber, and other productions, of the lands in the countries situated in the back parts of the states of New York and Pennsylvania, in North America; and particularly the lands in the county of Ontario, known by the name of the Genesee tract, lately located, and now in the progress of being settled. (London) Printed in the year 1791.   37 p.   2 fold. maps.   25½ cm.   5-6441 Add.
F127.G2 A15
Rare Book Coll.

GENESEE region. Genesee echoes; the upper gorge and falls area from the days of the pioneers. By Mildred Lee Hills Anderson.   Castile, N.Y. (1956)   104 p.   illus.   23 cm.   56-41044.
F127. G2 A6

GENESEE region. The Genesee. By Henry W. Clune. Illus. by Douglas Gorsline. (1st ed.) New York, Holt, Rinehart and Winston (1963)   338 p.   21 cm.   (Rivers of America)   63-12079.
F127. G2 C5

GENESEE region. An instrument agreed upon between commissioners appointed by the states of New-York and Massachusetts, respecting the jurisdiction of the territory therein described. New-York, Printed and sold by S. and J. Loudon, 1787.   12 p.   16½ cm.   9-8972.
F127. G2 C6
Rare Book Coll.

GENESEE region. The Genesee tract. Cessions between New York and Massachusetts. The Phelps and Gorham purchase. Robert Morris. Captain Charles Williamson and the Pulteney estate. By Geo. S. Conover ... Geneva, N.Y., 1889.   16 p. incl. map.   23 cm.   3-28497.
F127. G2 C7

GENESEE region. History of the Genesee country (western New York) comprising the counties of Allegany, Cattaraugus, Chautauqua, Chemung, Erie, Genesee, Livingston, Monroe, Niagara, Ontario, Orleans, Schuyler, Steuben, Wayne, Wyoming and Yates. Ed. by Lockwood R. Doty ... Chicago, The S. J. Clarke pub. co., 1925.   4 v.   front. (v. 1) illus., plates, ports., maps, facsims.   27½ cm.   Vols. 3-4 contain biographical matter.   26-908.
F127. G2 D7

GENESEE region. Power and progress in the Genesee Valley. By Robert Emmett Ginna. Newcomen Society in North America, 1964.   24 p.   23 cm.   (Newcomen address)   "First printing April 1964"   64-18511.
F127. G2 G5

GENESEE region. ... The archeology of the Genesee country, by Frederick Houghton. Rochester, N.Y., Lewis H. Morgan chapter, 1922.   (37) - 66.   plates.   25½ cm.   (Researches and transactions of the New York state archeological assoc. Lewis H. Morgan chapter ... vol. III. no. II)   32-15860.
F127. G2 H8

GENESEE region. The Genesee country & the western New York through which the Genesee so proudly flows, being a brief discourse on an exceedingly fair & gentle land. By Edward Hungerford, & embellished with relief prints by Norman Kent. New York, The Gallery press, 1946.   22, (2) p. incl. front., illus.   18 cm.   46-5818.
F127.G2 H85

GENESEE region. Charles Williamson; a review of his life, ed. by Rev. William Main ... from the official records of the centennial celebration of Bath, U.S., 1893. Perth, Printed for private circution by Cowan & co., ltd., 1899.   xii. 159 p.   front. (port.) illus., maps.   25½ x 19½ cm.   44-31244.
F127. G2 M3

GENESEE region. A river ramble; saga of the Genesee valley, by Arch Merrill ... (Rochester, N.Y., Printed by L. Heindl, 1943)   108 p. incl. illus., pl. plates.   20 cm.   "Reprinted from the Democrat and chronicle, Rochester. N.Y."   44-25013.
F127. G2 M4

GENESEE region. ... Officers and membership list, 1907. Society of the Genesee. New York (1907)   27 p.   20 cm.   8-34775.
F127. G2 S 5

GENESEE region. Society of the Genesee. Year book no. 4. New York, 1905.   1 v. ports.   23½ cm.   CA 6-1738 Unrev.
F127. G2 S 6

NEW YORK

GENESEE region. History of the pioneer settlement of Phelps and Gorham's purchase, and Morris' reserve; embracing the counties of Monroe, Ontario, Livingston, Yates, Steuben, most of Wayne and Allegany, and parts of Orleans, Genesee, and Wyoming. To which is added, a Supplement, or Extension of the pioneer history of Monroe county... By O. Turner... Rochester, W. Alling, 1851.
viii, (9) - 624 p.   23 cm.   1-14230.
F127. G2 T8

— 1852.   xv, (9) - 588 p.   23 cm.   In place of the Monroe Co. supplement (p. 493-624), the present edition contains, (p. 493 - 588) "Supplement. Extension... in the counties of Wayne, Ontario, Yates, Livingston and Allegany, etc."   12-2449.
F127.G2 T82

GENESEE region. Historical sketches of western New York: The Seneca Indians; Phelps and Gorham purchase; Morris reserve and Holland purchase, etc., etc. By E. W. Vanderhoof... Buffalo, N.Y., Printed for private distribution by the Matthews-Northrup works, 1907.   viii, 232 p.   front., ports., fold, map.   25 cm.   7-20750.
F127.G2 V18

— New York, AMS Press (1972)   viii, 232 p.   illus.   22 cm.   71-134434 MARC.
F127.G2 V18
1972

GENESEE region. Réflections offertes aux capitalistes de l'Europe, sur les bénéfices immences que présent l'achat de terres incultes, situées dans les etats-Unis de l'Amérique. (By Pradelles Van) Amsterdam, 1792.   (v(- vi, (5) - 42 p.   fold. map.   fold. tab.   22 cm.   Published anonymously.   Relates principally to the Genesee lands in western New York.   5-40506.
F127. G2 V2
Rare Book Coll.

GENESEE region. Description of the Genesee country, its rapidly progressive population and improvements: in a series of letters from a gentleman to his friend. (By Charles Williamson) Albany, Printed by L. Andrews, 1798.   37 p.   fold. front., 2 fold. maps.   18 x 15 cm.   7-12928.
F127.G2 W65
Rare Book Coll.

— To which is added, an appendix, containing a description of the military lands. By Robert Munro. New-York: Printed for the author, 1804.   16 p.   map.   23 cm.   6-5567 Rev.   Bound with copy 2 of above item.
F127.G2 W65
Rare Book Coll.

GENESEE region. Description of the settlement of the Genesee country, in the state of New-York. In a series of letters from a gentleman to his friend. New-York: Printed by T. & J. Swords, 1799.
63 p.   front. (fold. map)   21½ cm.   2-6527.   One of four editions, with variations, pub. in 1804.   Pub. also under title: A view of the present situation of the western parts of the state of New-York...
F127. G2 W7
Rare Book Coll.

GENESEE region. A view of the present situation of the western parts of the state of New-York, called the Genesee country. In which the situation, dimensions, civil divisions... and other interesting matters, relative to that country are impartially described. (By Charles Williamson) Frederick-town (Md.): Printed at the 'Herald' press for the author. 1804. (Rochester, N.Y., G. P. Humphrey, 1892)   2, (3) - 23 p.   18½ cm.   1-15796 Rev.
F127.C2 W73

GENESEE region. An outline and source book for the archeology and history of western New York to 1800. By Gordon K. Wright. Pittsford, N.Y., 1942.   88 numb. l.   map.   28 x 21½ cm.   Reproduced from type-written copy.   "References" at end of each unit.   42-15544.
F127. G2 W8

LAKE GEORGE. Bits of lake George scenery. Glens Falls, N.Y., C. H. Possons, 1887.
2 p.   20 pl.   13½ x 19½ cm.   1-14085 Rev.
F127. G3 B 6

— (1889)   2 p., 18 pl.   obl. 24°.   1-14086-M1.
F127. G3 B 7

— (1896)   16 l.   illus.   obl. 16°.   1-14087-M1.
F127. G3 B 8

LAKE GEORGE and Lake Champlain, from their first discovery to 1759... By B. C. Butler. Albany, Weed, Parsons, printers, 1868.   240 p.   4 fold. plans.   19 cm.   19-4293.
F127.G3 B 87
Toner Coll.

— 2d ed. New York, G. P. Putnam; Albany, Durkee & Jenkins, 1869.   2, (3) - 240 p.   front. (map) illus., plates, photos., ports., fold, plans. 18½ cm. 1-14088.   F127.G3 B 9

LAKE GEORGE. Father Jogues at the lake of the Holy Sacrament; an episode. By B. F. De Costa ... (New York) "Messenger of the Sacred heart," 1900.   16 p. 27½ cm. Fifty copies reprinted from the Messenger of the Sacred heart. 1-391.   F127.G3 D19

LAKE GEORGE: its scenes and characteristics, with glimpses of the olden times. To which is added some account of Ticonderoga, with a description of the route to Schroon Lake and the Adirondacks. With ... notes on Lake Champlain ... By B. F. De Costa. New York, A. D. F. Randolph, 1868. iv, (7) - 181, xiv p. front., illus., plates, double map. 17 cm. 1-14089.   F127. G3 D2

LAKE GEORGE. A narrative of events at Lake George, from the early colonial times to the close of the revolution. By B. F. De Costa. New York, 1868.   74 p. front. 28 cm. 75 copies printed. 1-16266.   F127. G3 D3

LAKE GEORGE. Andia-ta-roc-te "Where the mountains close in", by Charles Clifford King, jr. (Hudson Falls, N.Y., Swigert press, 1935)   67 p. incl. illus., pl. 24½ cm. Bibliography: p. 66. 36-25755.   F127. G3 K5

LAKE GEORGE and Fort William Henry hotel, 1892. A descriptive and historical sketch. (New York, N.Y. engraving and printing co., 1891?)   (21) p. incl. front., illus., map, plans. 17 cm. 2-17344.   F127. G3 L2

LAKE GEORGE mirror, devoted to the interests of the queen of American lakes. Assembly Point, Lake George (W. H. Tippetts) 18   v. illus. 30½ cm. CA 10-4008 Unrev.   F127. G3 L4

LAKE GEORGE. Historic lake George. Father Jogues edition. By Wallace E. Lamb. (Glens Falls, N.Y., Printed by the Glens Falls post co., 1946)   2, 9-76 p. incl. plates. front., fold. map. 23 cm. 47-204.   F127.G3 L52

LAKE GEORGE; facts and anecdotes, by Wallace E. Lamb. (Glens Falls, N.Y., Glens Falls post company, 1934)   52 p. incl. front., plates, fold. map. 23 cm. 34-13976.   F127.G3 L53 1934

— 1938.   5-52 p. front., plates, fold. map. 23 cm. "Second ed." 38-21311.   F127.G3 L53 1938

LAKE GEORGE. Exploring Lake George, Lake Champlain, 100 years ago. Compiled, edited, and annotated by Stuart D. Ludlum. Utica, N.Y., Brodock & Ludlum (1972)   47 p. illus. 29 cm. 72-84192.   F127.G3 L82

LAKE GEORGE. A complete history of Lake George, embracing a great variety of information. By Henry Marvin. New-York, Sibells & Maigne, printers, 1853.   vi. (7) - 102 p. front. (fold. map) 15 cm. 1-14090.   F127. G3 M3

LAKE GEORGE. Nelson's guide to Lake George and Lake Champlain, with oil-colour views drawn from photographs taken expressly for this work. London, New York (etc.) T. Nelson, 1869. 48 p. col. front., col. plates (1 fold.) map. 14½ cm. 15-4457.   F127. G3 N4

— 1866.   48 p. col. front., 10 col. pl. (1 fold.) map. 15 cm. 17-10097 Rev.   F127.G3 N42

LAKE GEORGE. Posson's guide to Lake George, Lake Champlain and Adirondacks. Embracing that part of the Adirondack Mountains reached from Lake Champlain. 8th ed. Maps and illus. Glens Falls, N.Y., C. H. Possons, 1890.   3. (17) - 262 p. illus., 2 fold. maps (incl. front.) 19 cm. 1-16265.   F127. G3 P 8

LAKE GEORGE. Mohican point on lake George, the summer home of Mr. and Mrs. W. K. Bixby of St. Louis, Mo., with a brief glance at the history of the lake, by W. H. Samson. New York, Priv. print., 1913.   65 p. front., plates, 2 group port. on 1 l. double map. 23½ cm. 46-36298.   F127.G3 S 15

LAKE GEORGE. Scenes on Lake George ... Glens Falls, N.Y. (1904)   15½ x 24 cm.   F127. G3 S 2

LAKE GEORGE. Lake George in history. By Elizabeth Eggleston Seelye ... Together with a historical map of the Lake George region and a guide to battlefields and other points of interest in the eastern part of the Adirondack mountains. ... Lake George, N.Y., E. Seelye, 1896.   106 p.   illus., map. 14½ cm.   2-5472.   F127. G3 S 3

— 2d ed.   Lake George, N.Y., E. Seelye (1897)   iv, 108 p. front. (fold. map) 14 pl.   15½ x 11½ cm. 1-14091 rev. 2.   F127. G3 S 4

— 5th ed.   (1897)   3. 108 (i.e. 121) p. front. (fold. map) 13 illus.   14½ cm.   18-6163 rev.   F127.G3 S 43

LAKE GEORGE. By Seneca Ray Stoddard. Troy, N.Y., Nims & Knight, 1888.   11 plates. 25 x 30 cm. 1-14092 rev. 2*.   F127. G3 S 7

LAKE GEORGE; illustrated. A book of today. By Seneca Ray Stoddard. Albany, Weed, Parsons, 1873. 115 p.   illus. 20 cm.   1-14093 rev.*   F127.G3 S 72

LAKE GEORGE, illustrated, and Lake Champlain. A book of today. 18th ed. Glen Falls, N.Y., 1888.   177 p. illus., maps. 18 cm.   Bound with the author's Saratoga Springs. Glens Falls, N.Y. (1888)   1-14094 rev. 2*   F127.G3 S 73 1888

— 19th ed.   Glen Falls, N.Y., 1889.   155 p. illus., maps. 19 cm.   Bound with the author's Saratoga Springs. 1889. 1-14095 rev. 2*.   F127.G3 S 73 1889

— 21st ed.   Glens Falls, N.Y., 1891.   175 p. illus., maps (1 fold. col.) 19 cm.   Bound with the author's Saratoga Springs (1891)   1-14098 rev.*   F127.G3 S 73 1891

— 22d ed.   Glens Falls, N.Y., 1892.   174 p. illus., maps (1 fold. col.) 18 cm.   Bound with the (1892)   1-14099 rev.*   F127.G3 S 73 1892

— 24th ed.   Glens Falls, N.Y., 1894.   179 p. illus., maps (1 fold. col.) 18 cm.   Bound with the (1894)   1-14104 rev.2*.   F127.G3 S 73 1894

— 25th ed.   Glens Falls, N.Y. 1895.   175 p. illus., maps (1 fold.) 15 cm.   L.C. copy imperfect: fold. map wanting.   Bound with the author's Saratoga Springs. 1895.   1-14105 rev. 2*.   F127.G3 S 73 1895

— 41st annual ed.   Glens Falls, N.Y., 1906.   37 p. illus., maps. 15 cm.   Bound with the author's Lake George, illus., and Lake Champlain. 1895.   1-14103 rev.*   F127.G3 S 73 1906

LAKE GEORGE; snap shots from the steamboat. By Seneca Ray Stoddard. Troy, N.Y., Nims & Knight, 1889.   18 plates. 15 x 19 cm.   1-14106 rev.*   F127.G3 S 79

LAKE GEORGE. Photopanorama of Lake George, with explanatory and historical notes. By Seneca Ray Stoddard. Glens Falls, N.Y., 1892.   (3), 58 plates on 29 l. 29 x 13 cm.   1-14107 rev. 2*.   F127.G3 S 8

LAKE GEORGE camp and canoe-chats; gossip on canoes, camps, religion, social manners, etc. etc. ... Illus. with ten phototypes of beautiful views on the lake. By J. A. Whiteman. New York, Pub. by private subscription (1886?)   v-vi p., 134 p. pl. 15½ cm.   3-8732.   F127. G3 W5

GREENE County. Picturesque Catskills. Greene County. With over 800 illustrations. By R. Lionel De Lisser. Northampton, Mass., Picturesque pub. co. (1894)   160 p. incl. front., illus. 34 cm. 1-14052.   F127. G7 D3

— Republished with the addition of a foreword, by Alf Evers and an index.   Cornwallville, N.Y., Hope Farm Press, 1967.   160 p.   33 cm.

F127. G7 D3 1967

GREENE county historical society, Catskill, N.Y. ... Constitution, by-laws, officers, members ... (Catskill?) 1932.   20 p.   16 x 8½ cm.   CA 32-919 unrev.

F127.G7 G68

GREENE county historical society, Catskill, N.Y.   Publications ... 1932 -   v. 1

F127. G7 G7

GREENE County, history of, with biographical sketches of its prominent men.   New York, J. B. Beers, 1884.   462 p.   front., plates, ports., 2 maps (1 double)   30½ cm.   1-14108.

F127. G7 H6

GREENE County.   Abstract of wills of Greene county ... compiled and ed. by Ray C. Swayer.   (New York) 1933 -   v.   28 cm.   Typewritten.   Contents. - 1. 1800-1860. - 2. 1861-1880.   34-8456.   F127. G7 S 3
Rare Book Coll.

GREENE County; a short history.   By Mabel Parker Smith.   (Catskill? N.Y.) 1963.   17 p.   23 cm.
63-9527.

F127. G7 S 4

— Rev. ed.   1968.   21 p.   illus.   23 cm.

F127. G7 S.4 1968

GREENE County, History of ... (by) J. Van Vechten Vedder, county historian ... (Catskill, 1927 -
1 v.   illus. (incl. ports.)   23½ cm.   32-24478.

F127. G7 V3

GREENE County.   East Kill Valley genealogy; a record of the burials in two Catskill Mountain grave-yards, with genealogical information from 1620 tp 1964, by Olive Newell Woodworth.   Catskill, N.Y., D.A.R., On-Ti-Ora Chapter, 1964.   41 p.   23 cm.

F127. G7 W6

HAMILTON County, The history of (by) Ted Aber and Stella King.   Lake Pleasant, N.Y., Great Wilderness Books, 1965.   xx, 1209 p.   24 cm.

F127. H2 A49

HAMILTON County.   Tales from an Adirondack County (by) Ted Aber and Stella King.   Prospect, Prospect Books, 1961.   208 p.   22 cm.

F127. H2 A5

HAMILTON County.   An Adirondack resort in the Nineteenth Century; Blue Mountain Lake, 1870 - 1900; statecoaches and luxury hotels.   By Harold K. Hochschild.   Blue Mountain Lake, N.Y., Adirondack Museum, 1962.   99 p.   28 cm.

F127. H2 H6

BLUE MOUNTAINS Lake.   By Seneca Ray Stoddard.   Troy, N.Y., Nims & Knight, 1889.   15 plates.
15 x 19 cm.   1-14047 rev.*

F127. H2 S 82

LONG LAKE.   By Seneca Ray Stoddard.   Troy, N.Y., Nims & Knight (1889)   14 plates.   15 x 19 cm.
1-14928 rev.*

F127. H2 S 83

RAQUETTE LAKE.   By Seneca Ray Stoddard.   Troy, N.Y., Nims & Knight (1889)   16 plates.
15 x 19 cm.   1-14237 rev.*

F127. H2 S 84

HELDERBERG Inn ...(New York, 189-?)   20½ cm.

F127. H25 H4

HEMLOCK Lake.   O-neh-da Te-car-ne-o-di; or, Up and down the Hemlock. Including history, commerce, accidents, incidents, guide, etc.   By D. Byron Waite.   Canadice, N.Y., G. E. Colvin & G. P. Waite, printers, 1883.   112 p.   19 cm.   1-21414.

F127. H3 W2

HERKIMER County ... directory, containing the general directories of the villages of Little Falls,

NEW YORK

Herkimer, Mohawk, Ilion, Frankfort, Cold Brook, Dolgeville, Middleville, Newport, Poland, West Winfield ... also, a business directory of ... the county ... 18   Valatie, N. Y., Lant & Silvernail (18   v.   23 ½ cm.   24-30848.   Directories

HERKIMER County. A history of Herkimer county, including the upper Mohawk valley, from the earliest period to the present time: with a brief notice of the Iroquois Indians ... also biographical notices of the most prominent public men of the county ... By Nathaniel S. Benton. Albany, J. Munsell, 1856.   v, (5) - 497 p. front., illus., plates, port., maps (part fold.)   22 cm.   1-14109.   F127. H5 B 4

HERKIMER County in the world war, 1916 - 1918, compiled by Hon. Franklin W. Cristman ... Little Falls, N.Y., Press of the Journal & courier co., 1927.   2, 9-222 p. ports. 27 ½ cm. 28-11847.
F127. H5 C8

HERKIMER County, History of, illustrated with portraits of many of its citizens. Ed. by George A. Hardin, assisted by Frank H. Willard. Syracuse, N.Y., D. Mason, 1893.   550 p., 276 p. illus., port., maps. 25 ½ cm. "Bibliographical": p. 453-550. "Part II. Family sketches". 2-5352.   F127. H5 H2

HERKIMER County. Papers read before the Herkimer County historical society during the years 1896 - 1899/1902. Herkimer and Ilion, N.Y., 1899 - 1902.   2 v.   24 cm.   Papers for 1896-98 comp. by Arthur T. Smith.   7-30379.   F127. H5 H5

HERKIMER County. ... History of Herkimer county ... New York, F. W. Beers, 1879.   289 p. front., illus. (incl. map) plates, ports.   36 ½ x 30 ½ cm.   Includes biographical matter.   3-26853.
F127. H5 H6

HERKIMER County murders. This book contains an accurate account of the capital crimes committed in the county of Herkimer ... 1783 up to the present time. By ... W. H. Tippetts. Herkimer, N.Y., H. P. Witherstine, printers, 1885.   49 p. 22 cm. 11-26677.   F127. H5 T5

HERKIMER County; Federal population census schedules 1800 - 1810 and 1820; transcripts and index (by) Ralph V. Wood, Jr. Cambridge? Mass., 1965.   viii, 186 p.
F127. H5 W6

HOLLAND Purchase. To the Honourable the Senate and House of representatives of the Commonwealth of Pennsylvania, the memorial of Wilhem Willink and others (of the Holland land company presenting their objection to the act of the legislature of Pennsylvania, not permitting them as aliens to hold titles to their lands) (n.p., 182-?)   20 p. 23 ½ cm. 26-5590.   F127. H7 H8

HOLLAND Purchase. A history of the treaty of Big Tree, and an account of the celebration of the 100th anniversary of the making of the treaty, held at Geneseo, N.Y. ... 1897. (Dansville, N.Y.) Livingston County historical soc. (1897?)   103 p. front., plates, ports., map.   23 ½ cm.   4-17873 Rev.
F127. H7 L7

HOLLAND Purchase. Pioneer history of the Holland purchase of western New York: embracing some account of the ancient remains ... and a history of pioneer settlement under the auspices of the Holland company, etc., etc. By Orasumus Turner. Buffalo, Jewett, Thomas, 1849.   xvi, (17) - 666 p. front., plates, ports., maps. 23 ½ cm. The extreme western part of the state, now included in counties of Erie, Chautauqua, Cattaraugus and Niagara, and western portions of Genesee, Allegany, Wyoming and Orleans. 1-14134.   F127. H7 T7

— 1850.   xvi, (17) - 670 p. front., 1 illus., plates, ports., maps. 23 ½ cm. 1-14135.   F127. H7 T8

HOOSIC Valley. The Hoosac Valley, its legends and its history, by Grace Greylock Niles ... With 110 illustrations. New York and London, G. P. Putnam's sons, 1912.   xxv, 584 p. front., illus. 21 ½ cm. 12-23117.   F127.H73 N6

HUDSON. The greatest park in the world, Palisades interstate park; its purpose, history and achievements, by Arthur P. Abbott. (New York, A. T. De La Mare printing & pub. co., 1914)   64 p. plates, map. 19 cm. 14-20357.   F127.H8 A13

HUDSON. The Hudson River today and yesterday, by Arthur P. Abbott. (New York, A. T. De La

Mare print. and pub. co., ltd., 1915) 85 p. incl. illus., plates. fold. map. 19 cm. 15-15049.

F127.H8 A14

HUDSON. Breed publishing company's directory of the West Shore R. R. Kingston to Albany. Embracing the following places: Lake Katrine, Mt. Marion, Saugerties, Malden, West Camp, Catskill, West Athens, Athens, Coxsackie, New Baltimore, Ravena, Selkirk, Wemple ... Newburgh, N.Y., Breed pub. co.,   v. 24 cm. 14-17070.

Directories

HUDSON. Business directory, and mercantile register of Albany, Troy, Schenectady, Kingston, Poughkeepsie, Cohoes, Amsterdam, Saratoga, Hudson, Gloversville, Pittsfield, Mass., North Adams, Mass., Glens Falls, Rensselaer, Catskill, Johnstown, and intermediate towns ... (1st) - Troy, N.Y., 1902 -   v. 24 cm. 17-28126.

Directories

HUDSON. Hudson-Fulton medal. Designed under direction of the American numismatic society. Adopted as its one official medal by the Hudson-Fulton celebration commission ... By Edward D. Adams ... (Boston, T. R. Marvin, printers) 1909.   8 p. front. 27½ cm. Reprinted from the American journal of numismatics, 1909. 9-31974.

F127.H8 A23

HUDSON. The picturesque valley of the lower and upper Hudson, the Rhine of America ... comp. by American journal of commerce. New York (1900?)   72 p. illus. (incl. ports.) 40½ cm. Industrial number of American journal of commerce. v. 9, no. 10. 4-27929.

F127. H8 A5

— ... Saratoga Springs, nature's inexhaustible fountains of health. America's greatest health and pleasure resort. Ballston Spa and Lake George ... comp. by American journal of commerce. New York (190-?)   28 p. illus. (incl. ports.) (With above) 4-27932.

F127. H8 A5

— ... Cohoes, Lansingburgh, Waterford and Amsterdam. A review of their progress ... New York, (1901?)   16 p. illus. (incl. ports.) 40½ cm. (With above) 4-27931. F127. H8 A5

— Mount Vernon, New Rochelle, Mamaroneck, Rye, Portchester, White Plains; a review of ... progress, etc. New York, 1902.   36 p. illus. (incl. ports) (With above) 4-27933.   F127. H8 A5

HUDSON. In the Hudson highlands ... New York, Publication committee, Appalachian mountain club, New York chapter, 1945.   2, ii-ix, 265 p. illus. (incl. maps) plates. 20 cm. A collection of essays, originally distributed in mimeograph form. 45-4710.

F127.H8A515

HUDSON. The Palisades of the Hudson River; the story of their origin, attempted destruction and rescue.   (From American scenic and historic preservations soc. Eleventh annual report, 1906. Appendix D, p. (191) - 212.) New York (State) Legislature. Assembly. Documents. 1906, no. 74. 9-22100 Rev.

F127.H8 A52

HUDSON. The Hudson River from ocean to source, historical - legendary - picturesque, by Edgar Mayhew Bacon ... with 100 illustrations, and with sectional map of the Hudson River. New York and London, G. P. Putnam's sons, 1902.   xii, 590 p. incl. illus., pl. front., fold. map in pocket. 25 cm. 2-29423.

F127. H8 B 2

HUDSON. Report on a survey of the waters of the upper Hudson and Raquette rivers, in the summer of 1874, with reference to increasing the supply of water for the Champlain canal and improving the navigation of the Hudson River ... By Farrand N. Benedict. (Albany, 1874?)   82 p. 4 maps (3 fold.) fold. diagr. 23½ cm. 8-17407.

F127. H8 B 4

HUDSON. Great river of the mountains: the Hudson; photographs and prose by Croswell Bowen, introd. by Carl Carmer ... New York, Hastings house (1941)   94, (2) p. illus. 32 cm. 41-13015.

F127. H8 B 6

HUDSON. The lordly Hudson, by Henry Collins Brown ... New York, C. Scribner's sons; London, C. Scribner;s sons, ltd. (1937)   xiv, 319 p. incl. col. mounted front., illus. (part col. mounted) plates (part col. mounted) col. facsim. 41½ cm. 37-14678.

F127.H8 B 73
Rare Book Coll.

HUDSON. The Hudson, by Wallace Bruce; illustrated by Alfred Fredericks. Boston, Houghton,

NEW YORK
111

Mifflin, (1881) 37 p. incl. front., illus. 19½ x 16 cm. In verse. 14-20035 Rev. F127.H8 B 77

— ... Edinburgh (etc.) Blackwood & sons; New York, Bryant union (1894) 317 p. incl. illus., plates. front., 5 fold. maps., 2 fold. plans. 18 cm. 1-14110. F127.H8 B 8

— ... New York, Bryant union, 1894. 317 p. incl. illus., plates. front., fold. maps. 17 cm. On cover: The Hudson by daylight. 33-7580. F127.H8 B 81

HUDSON. The Hudson; three centuries of history, romance and invention, by Wallace Bruce. Centennial ed. New York, Bryant union co. (1907) 224 p. illus., plates. 19 cm. Pub. 1894 under title: The Hudson, by Wallace Bruce. 7-32834. F127.H8 B812

HUDSON. The Hudson Highlands. By the author of "The Hudson by daylight." (Wallace Bruce) New York, G. Watson (1876) (26) p. 18 cm. 1-14111-M1. F127.H8 B815

HUDSON. The Hudson River by daylight. New York to Albany, Saratoga Springs, Lake George ... New York, J. Featherston, 1873. 135 p. illus., fold. map. 16½ cm. On cover ... By Thursty McQuill. 1-14112. F127.H8 B 82

— New York to Albany and Troy, Catskill Mountains ... Saratoga Springs, Lake Champlain, etc., etc. New York, G. Watson, 1873. 2, 3-114, 114a-114d, 115-165 p. illus., plates, fold. map. 17 cm. 17-31808. F127.H8 B822

— New York, G. Watson (1884) 2, (3)-150 p. illus., fold. map. 17½ cm. 1-14113. F127.H8 B 83

HUDSON. Panorama of the Hudson, showing both sides of the river from New York to Albany as seen from the deck of the Hudson River day line steamers ... 150 miles of continuous scenery accurately represented from 800 consecutive photographs ... (New ed. New York, Bryant union pub. co., 1906) (97) p. of illus. 17 x 28 cm. 6-24569. F127.H8 B 86

— (New ed.) (New York, Bryant union pub. co., 1906) (84) p. illus. 17 x 28 cm. 6-24570. F127.H8 B 88

HUDSON. The Hudson, by Carl Carmer; illus. by Stow Wengenroth. New York, Toronto, Farrar & Rinehart incorporated (1939) xii, 434, (13) p. illus. (incl. map) 21 cm. (The rivers of America) Bibliography: p. 408-421. 39-27579. F127.H8 C3

— (Rev. ed.) New York, Grosset & Dunlap (1968) 342 p. illus. 26 cm. (Illustrated rivers of America) 67-23792. F127.H8 C3

HUDSON. The Hudson River. By Carl Lamson Carmer. Illus. by Rafaello Busoni. (1st ed.) New York, Holt, Rinehart and Winston (1962) 114 p. illus. 23 cm. 62-11172. F127.H8 C32

HUDSON. The Hudson River celebration. Hudson's and Fulton's jubilee ... By Kinahan Cornwallis. (New York, n.d.) sheet. 42 x 28½ cm. F127.H8 C8

HUDSON. The flow of destiny, 1609-1959. In commemoration of the 350th anniversary of the discovery of the valley of the Hudson River, 1609-1959. By Radford Brown De Corday. (Marceline, Mo., Walsworth Pub. Co., 1959) 80 p. illus. 22 cm. "First printing" 59-4226. F127.H8 D4

HUDSON. Palisades interstate park, by Robt. L. Dickinson ... (New York) American geographical soc. of New York, 1921. 44 p. illus., maps (part fold.) 19 cm. 21-20892. F127.H8 D54

HUDSON. Documents relating to the history and settlement of the towns along the Hudson and Mohawk Rivers (with the exception of Albany) from 1630 to 1684. ... Albany, Weed, Parons, 1881. xxxiii, 617 p. plan, facsim. 30 x 24½ cm. (Docs. relating to the colonial history of the state of New York. vol. xiii- old series; vol. ii- new series. 3-20932. F127.H8 D6

HUDSON. Historic houses of the Hudson valley, by Harold Donaldson Eberlein and Cortland Van Dyke Hubbard ... New York, Architectural book pub. co. (1942)   207 p. incl. front., illus., plates. 31½ cm. "Sponsored by the Hudson river conservation soc. inc." 42-14198.   F127.H8 E18

HUDSON. The manors and historic homes of the Hudson Valley, by Harold Donaldson Eberlein ... With a photogravure and 81 doubletone illustrations mostly from phtographs by the author. Philadelphia and London, J. B. Lippincott co., 1924.   3, v-xvi, 327 p. front., plates. 24½ cm. 24-32143.
F127. H8 E2

HUDSON. Echo; magazine of the Hudson river valley. v. 1 -   May 1938 -   (Hudson, N.Y., 1938.   v. illus. 29½ cm. bimonthly (irregular)
F127.H8 E25

HUDSON. Getting to know the Hudson River, by William B. Fink. Illus. by Kiyo Komoda. New York, Coward-McCann (1970)   67 p. illus. 23 cm. 73-105650.   F127. H8 F5
1970

HUDSON. ... Down the Hudson, by Jean Hosford Fretwell; illustrated by Elizabeth K. Blake. New York, T. Nelson, 1935.   viii, 9-77 p. incl. front., illus. 19½ cm. (Our changing world) 35-3999.   F127. H8 F7

HUDSON. ... Champlain et Hudson. - La découverte du lac Champlain, et celle de la rivière Hudson. ... 1609 - 1909. Par M. l'abbé August Gosselin ... Ottawa, Imprimé pour la Société royale du Canada, 1910.   p. 87-110. 25 cm. Reprinted from Meoires de la Société royale du Canada, 3. sér., 1909-1910, vol. iii sec. 1. 10-22020.   F127. H8 G6

HUDSON. History of the valley of the Hudson, river of destiny, 1609 - 1930, ed. by Nelson Greene; covering the sixteen New York state Hudson river counties of New York, Bronx, Westchester, Rockland, Orange, Putnam, Dutchess, Ulster, Greene, Columbia, Albany, Rensselaer, Saratoga, Washington, Warren, Essex ... Chicago, The S. J. Clarke pub. co., 1931.   5 v. fronts. illus., plates, ports., map. 27 cm. Vols. 3-5: Biographical. 32-3333.   F127. H8 G8

HUDSON and Fulton; a brief history of Henry Hudson and Robert Fulton, with suggestions designed to aid the holding of general commemorative exercises and children's festivals during the Hudson-Fulton celebration in 1909, by Edward Hagaman Hall ... (New York, The Hudson-Fulton celebration com - mission) 1909.   799-870 p. illus., pl., port., fold. map. 23½ cm. CA 9-930 Unrev.   F127.H8 H18

— 1909.   74 p. illus., pl., port., fold. map. 22 cm. 9-18985.   F127.H8 H19

HUDSON. The New York and Albany post road, from Kings Bridge to "the ferry at Crawlier, over against Albany", being an account of a jaunt on foot made at sundry convenient times between May and November, 1905, by Charles G. Hine. New York, C. G. Hine, 1905.   4, iii-vi, 109 p. incl. front., plates. 19½ cm. Pub. also as Hine's annual, 1905, book I. 24-15000.   F127.H8 H26
1905

— (Newark? N.J., 1906)   vi, 89 p. 20½ x 17 cm. (Hine's annual, 1905, book I) 6-18977.   F127.H8 H26
1906

HUDSON. ... The west bank of the Hudson River, Albany to Tappan; notes on its history and legends, its ghost stories and romances. Gathered by a wayfaring man who may now and then have erred therein. By C. G. Hine. (Newark? N.J., 1907)   2, iii, 174 p. 21½ x 17½ cm. (Hine's annual, 1906) 7-20977.
F127.H8H265

HUDSON. Obstructions of the Hudson River during the revolution, by W. M. Hornor, jr. Metuchen, N.J., Printed for C. F. Heartman, 1927.   3, 27, vi p. front. (fold. facsim.) illus. 25 cm. Sixty copies printed. First pub. in the American collector, v.2, no. 6, Sept., 1926. Bibliography: p. 26-27. 28-4540.
F127.H8 H35
Rare Book Coll.

HUDSON. The Hudson highlands; William Thompson Howell memorial ... (New York, Printed by Lenz & Riecker, inc., 1933.   4, 191 p. front., plates, ports. 23½ cm. 33-23792.   F127.H8 H38

NEW YORK

HUDSON-FULTON celebration, 1609 - 1909. Portland, Maine, L. H. Nelson co., 1909.
20 x 25 cm.
F127. H8 H4

HUDSON-FULTON celebration commission. A brief statement of the object and plan of the Hudson-Fulton celebration in 1909. (New York, 1909) 13 p. 23 cm. 9-14732.
F127. H8 H5

HUDSON-FULTON celebration commission. Historical pageant. Hudson-Fulton celebration ... 1909. New York, Redfield brothers, inc. (1909) 64 p. illus. (partly col.) 25½ cm. 9-30868.
F127. H8 H52

HUDSON-FULTON celebration. A collection of the catalogues issued by the museums and institutions in New York city and vicinity. ... New York, 1910. (New York, The Trow press, 1910) 4, (629) p. illus., plates, ports. (2 col.) plans, facsims. 23½ cm. The number of pages given in the collation is the sum of the groups of pages given in the table of contents; the actual number of pages differs somewhat. 12-16196.
F127. H8H525

HUDSON-FULTON celebration, 1909, the fourth annual report of the Hudson-Fulton celebration commission to the Legislature of the state of New York. ... Albany, Printed ... by J. B. Lyon co., 1910. 2 v. fronts., plates, ports. 27 cm. 11-19252.
F127. H8 H527

HUDSON-FULTON celebration, souvenir ... (New York? (1909) 24½ cm.
F127. H8H5275

HUDSON-FULTON celebration commission. Hudson ter-centenary joint committee ... Minutes of ... 1906 ... (New York, 1906?) (35) - 55 p. 23½ cm. 22-5734.
F127. H8H528

HUDSON-FULTON celebration commission. Official minutes of the Hudson-Fulton celebration commission ... Albany, J. B. Lyon co., 1905-11. 2 v. illus., plates, ports., fold. map. 23 cm. Paged continuously. 11-26701.
F127. H8H529

HUDSON-FULTON celebration commission. Official program, Hudson-Fulton celebration. New York, Printed ... Redfield bros,, 1909. 32 p. illus. 31 cm. 9-23773.
F127. H8 H53

HUDSON-FULTON celebration commission. Official souvenir Hudson-Fulton celebration carnival pageant. New York, Printed ... Redfield bros., (1909) 64 p. illus. 11½ x 16½ cm. 12-11581.
F127. H8H532

HUDSON-FULTON celebration commission. Testimonials of appreciation to Herman Ridder, acting president and Henry W. Sackett, secretary of the Hudson-Fulton celebration commission. (New York, The De Vinne press, 1910) 25 p. 2 pl. incl. ports.) 24 cm. Printed on one side of leaf only. 10-21780.
F127. H8 H54

HUDSON. The Hudson illustrated with pen and pencil; comprising sketches, local and legendary, of its several places of interest, together with the route to Niagara Falls; forming a companion for the pleasure tourist. New York, T. W. Strong, 1852. (3) - 32 p. illus. 28 cm. 1-16880.
F127, H8 H7

HUDSON. The Hudson River. Portland, Me., 1905. 20 x 25 cm.
F127. H8 H76

— (Portland, Me., L. H. Nelson co,, 1910) (1) p. (31) p. of illus. 20 x 25 cm.
F127. H8 H77

HUDSON River and the Hudson River railroad, with a complete map, and wood cut views of the principal objects of interest upon the line. New York, W. C. Locke; Boston, Bradbury & Guild (1851) (5) - 50 p. front. (fold. map) illus. 22½ cm. 1-14114.
F127. H8 H8

HUDSON River summer excursion routes and Catskill mountain resorts, 1910 ... Issued by the Hudson River day line ... (New York, 1910) 188 p. (incl. plates, map) illus. 19½ x 10 cm. Cover-title: Hudson River by daylight.
F127. H8 H85

HUDSON. Letters about the Hudson River. And its vicinity. Written in 1835 & 1836 ... By a citizen

of New York. (Freeman Hunt) New York, F. Hunt & co.; Boston, Otis, Broaders, 1836.
x, 209 p. 16 cm. 1-14115. F127, H8 H9

— Written in 1835-1837 ... 3d ed., with additions ... New York, F. Hunt, 1837. x, (11) - 252 p.
fold. pl., 3 fold. maps (incl. front.) 15½ cm. 1-14116. F127, H8 H92

HUDSON. A book of the Hudson. Collected from the various works of Diedrich Knickerbocker. Ed. by Geoffrey Crayon (pseud. for Washington Irving) New York, G. P. Putnam, 1849. viii, (11) - 215 p. 15½ cm. Pub. in 1912, with an additional tale, under the title: Stories of the Hudson. 3-19162. F127. H8 I 86
Rare Book Coll.

— New-York, G. P. Putnam, 1849. (4), (7) - 283 p. plates. 16 cm. 48-30270*.
F127, H8 I 86
1849 a
Rare Book Coll.

HUDSON. ... Catalogue of an historical exhibition held by the Free public library of Jersey City ... 1909, comp. by Esther E. Burdick, librarian. Jersey City, The Library, 1909. 38 p. front., plates, 23 cm. Hudson-Fulton celebration. 11-7318. F127. H8 J 45

HUDSON. Sail and steam. An historical sketch showing New Jersey's connection with the events commemorated by the Hudson-Fulton celebration ... 1909. 2d ed. Prepared by the Free public library of Jersey City. (Jersey City, Press of A. J. Doan, 1909) 20 p. 3 pl., 3 port. 23 cm. Compiled from records and documents owned by the library, by Edmund W. Miller, assistant librarian. 9-27673 Rev. F127. H8 J 5

HUDSON. The picturesque Hudson, written and illustrated by Clifton Johnson ... New York, London, The Macmillan co., 1909. xi, (3), 2-227 p. incl. col. front. 46 pl. 18 cm. (Picturesque river series) 9-24935.
F127. H8 J 65

HUDSON. Miniatures of scenes along the Hudson. (By Thomas Wallace Jones) Cincinnati, O., 1904)
8 x 10½ cm. F127. H8 J 7

HUDSON. Juet's journal; the voyage of the Half Moon from 4 April to 9 November, 1607. By Robert Juet. Newark, 1959. x, 37 p. 24 cm. (The collections of the New Jersey Historical Soc., v.12) 59-12939.
F127. H8 J 85

HUDSON. The Hudson River ... By Moses King. New York, 1904. 12½ x 19½ cm.
F127. H8 K5

HUDSON. The picturesque beauties of the Hudson River and its vicinity; illus. in a series of views, from original drawings... With historical and descriptive illus. by Samuel L. Knapp. (pt. I-II) New-York, J. Disturnell, 1835-36. 2 v. in 1. illus., 6 pl. 35 cm. (v.2: 27 cm.) Paged continuously. No more pub. 1-14122 Add. F127. H8 K6

HUDSON. The Hudson-Fulton celebration, MCMIX, by Gustav Kobbé, with a foreword by William Loring Andrews. New York, Soc. of iconophiles, 1910. 63, (5) p. front., illus. 25½ cm. 11-699.
F127, H8 K7

HUDSON. The Hudson from Lake Tear of the Clouds to New York Harbor. Illus. with photos and line drawings. New York, McGraw-Hill (1969) 127 p. illus. 25 cm. 69-16256.
F127. H8 K75

HUDSON. The Hudson by daylight map, showing the prominent residences, historic landmarks, old reaches of the Hudson, Indian names, etc. With descriptive pages. (By William F. Link) New York, W. F. Link (1878) 15 l. illus., fold. map. 16°. 1-14123-M1. F127. H8 L7

HUDSON. On the banks of the Hudson; a view of its history and folklore (by) Beman Lord. Illustrated by Rocco Negri. New York, H. Z. Walck (1971) 63 p. illus. 24 cm. 75-142451.
F127. H8 L75

HUDSON. The Hudson, from the wilderness to the sea. By Benson J. Lossing. Illus. by 306 engravings on wood, from drawings by the author ... Troy, N.Y., H. B. Nims (186-?) vii, 464 p. incl. front., illus. 23 cm. Printed in Great Britain. 46-36856.
F127.H8 L78

— New York, Virtue & Yorston (1866) vii, 464 p. front., illus. 23½ x 18 cm. 1-14124.
F127. H8 L8

HUDSON. The romance of the Hudson. (First paper) (By Benson John Lossing) (New York, 1876) 26 cm.
F127. H8 L9

HUDSON. The Hudson; river of history. By May Yonge McNeer. Champaign, Ill., Garrard Pub. Co. (1962) 96 p. 24 cm. (Rivers of the world, W-6) 62-15313.
F127.H8 M25

HUDSON. ... Guide book of the steamer Mary Powell, describing summer homes along the famous Hudson ... Rondout, N.Y., Mary Powell steamboat co., 1892. 43 p. illus. 17 cm. 2-19333.
F127. H8 M3

HUDSON. Hudson-Fulton pageant of dramatizations; the book of the words. By Norbert John Melville. New York, Hinds, Noble & Eldredge, 1909. 2, 5-32 p. 24 cm.
F127. H8 M5

HUDSON. The story of a young man's tramp across three states, cooking his meals & camping along 360 miles of road in New Hampshire, Vermont and New York ... by William Moore. New York, The Markey press, 1911. 76 p. 17 cm. Across Sullivan Co., N.H., Windsor and Rutland counties, Vt., Washington Co., N.Y. to the Hudson; thence down the river to New York. 11-22352.
F127.H8 M 8

HUDSON. Munsell's guide to the Hudson river by railroad and steamboat. Representing every town, village, landing, railroad station and point of interest on or adjacent to the Hudson river, from Staten island to Troy, with minute descriptions and references, for the convenience of the business man and the traveler. Albany, J. Munsell (1864) 58 p. 8 maps (1 fold.) 14½ cm. 1-14125 Rev.
F127. H8 M9

HUDSON. Biography of a river; the people and legends of the Hudson Valley. By John Mylod. Alec Thomas, editor. New York, Hawthorn Books (1969) 244 p. illus. 27 cm. 78-85437.
F127.H8 M95

HUDSON. New Hudson river guide. New York, J. Disturnell, 1848. 1 p., 1 l. 24°. 1-14126.
F127. H8 N2

HUDSON. ... Preliminary report of the Hudson valley survey commission to the Legislature ... 1938. Albany, J. B. Lyon co., printers, 1938. 21 p. fold. map. 23 cm. Legislative document (1938) no. 98. State of New York. 40-31683.
F127.H8 N37
1938

HUDSON Valley. ... Report of the Hudson valley survey commission to the Legislature, 1939. Albany, J. B. Lyon co., printers, 1939. 80 p. incl. illus., tables. maps (part fold.) 23½ cm. Legislative document (1939) no. 71. State of New York. 39-28286.
F127.H8 N37
1939

HUDSON. ... Report of the Hudson valley survey commission to the Legislature ... 1940. Albany, J. B. Lyon co., printers, 1940. (4) p. 23 cm. Legislative document (1940) no. 63. State of New York. 40-31684.
F127.H8 N37
1940

HUDSON. ... Hudson - Fulton celebration ... 1909; a brochure for the use of schools of the state, comp. and ed. by Harlan Hoyt Horner. Albany, New York state education dept., 1909. 64 p. illus. (part col. and incl. ports., plan, facsims.) fold. map. 25½ cm. Bibliography: p. 60-64. E9-1072 Rev.
F127.H8 N39

HUDSON. ... Hudson-Fulton essay contest ... (Albany, 1909) 10 p. 23 cm. Names of winners of medals in public high schools and academies. 10-2750.
F127.H8N394

116   LOCAL HISTORIES IN THE LIBRARY OF CONGRESS

HUDSON. The Hudson-Fulton celebration in the city of New York and the Edison system ... (New York) 1910. 2 p., 60 pl. 28 x 36 cm. 10-10437. F127.H8 N45

HUDSON. Official Robert Fulton exhibition of the Hudson-Fulton commission; the New York historical society in coöperation with the Colonial dames of America ... 1909. (New York, 1909) 66, (8) p. front. (col. port.) 23 cm. 34-8744. F127.H8 N56

HUDSON. Report of the aboriginal names and geographical terminology of the state of New York. Part I. - Valley of the Hudson. Made to the New York historical society, by the committee appointed to prepare a map, etc. By Henry R. Schoolcraft (chairman) ... New York, The Society, 1845. 43 p. 23 cm. "Pub. from the society's Proceedings for 1844." No more pub. 1-16608. F127. H8 N6

HUDSON. New York State's mid-Hudson area guide to Orange, Dutchess, Ulster, Columbia, Greene counties. Kingston, M. C. Starkman. v. illus. 19 cm. annual. 54-43952. F127.H8N615

HUDSON. New York tribune. Hudson-Fulton celebration number, containing copy of the complete programme. 1909. New York, 1909. (104) p. illus. 46½ cm. Various paging. 10-1801.

                                      F127. H8 N7

HUDSON-FULTON celebration. (By Theodore Newcomb) New York, Newcomb pub. co., 1909. (15) p. incl. col. illus., col. pl., col. ports. 23 cm. 9-23775. F127. H8 N8

HUDSON. Palisades interstate park com. (N.Y.) Annual report. (18 - v.

                                      F127.H8 P 16

HUDSON. Palisades interstate park commission. Annual report. Albany (etc.) v. 23 cm. The New York reports and the New Jersey reports are combined in this entry. 11-30524 Add. F127.H8 P 17

HUDSON. A map of the Bear Mountain-Harriman section of the Palisades interestate park, copyright ... by the Commissioners of the Palisades interestate park. (New York) The Commissioners of the Palisades interstate park, 1920. 16 p. fold. map. 24½ cm. 20-16768.

                                      F127.H8 P 18

HUDSON. Panorama of the Hudson, showing both banks of the river from New York to Poughkeepsie .. Photographed by G. Willard Shear. Palisades, highlands, cities and villages in one continuous view... (New York, Bryant literary union, 1888) 2 p., 1 pl. fold. in 32. 17 x 40 cm. 1-14127.

                                      F127. H8 P 2

— first photo-panorama of any river ever published ... (New York, Bryant literary union, 1888) 1 p. 48 pl. 20½ x 32 cm. Photographed by G. W. Shear. 1-14128. F127.H8 P 21

HUDSON. A descriptive reading on Hudson river ... (By Caryl S. Parrott) Philadelphia, W. H. Rau, 1890. 2, 693-707 p. 12°. One of a number of "readings" forming part of an intended comprehensive work to include lantern slides. The "readings" were never pub. in collective form. 1-14129-M1. F127. H8 P 4

HUDSON. The Picturesque Hudson ... Palisades, Highlands, Catskills ... New York, Bryant literary union (1889) 2 p., 41 pl. on 21 l., 8 maps on 4 l. 10½ x 18½ cm. 1-14130. F127. H8 P6

HUDSON. Rand, McNally & co.'s illustrated guide to the Hudson river and Catskill mountains, by Ernest Ingersoll. Chicago and New York, Rand, McNally, 1893. 243 p. front., plates, fold. maps, plan. 19 cm. 1-14117 Rev. F127. H8 R2

— 1894. 243 p. front., plates, fold. maps. plan. 18½ cm. 1-14118 Rev. F127.H8 R21

— 1895. 249 p. front., plates, fold. maps, plan. 18½ cm. 1-14119 Rev. F127.H8 R22

— 4th ed. 1896. 245 p. front., plates, fold. maps, plan. 18 cm. 1-14120 Rev. F127.H8 R23

— 5th ed. - rev. for 1897. 245 p. front., plates, fold. maps. plan. 17 cm. 1-14121 Rev. F127.H8 R24

NEW YORK 117

— 7th ed. 1899. 251 p. front., plates, fold. maps, plan. 17½ cm. 99-3148 Rev. F127.H8 R26

— 8th ed. 1900. (3) - 251 p. front., plates, fold. maps, plan. 17 cm. 0-3213 Rev. F127.H8 R27

— 9th ed. 1901. 246 p. incl. front. plates, fold. maps, plan. 17½ cm. 1-10748 Add. F127.H8 R28

— 10th ed. 1902. 245 p. incl. front. plates, fold. maps, plan. 17½ cm. 2-19283 Add. F127.H8 R29

— 13th ed. 1905 (5) - 245 p. plates, fold. maps, plan. 19 cm. 5-21061 Add. F127.H8 R32

HUDSON. Rand McNally Hudson River guide, with maps and illus., incl. reference list of hotels, places of amusement, etc. in New York city. New York, Chicago, Rand McNally (1915) 60 p. illus., fold. maps. 19½ cm. 15-15911. F127.H8 R34

— (1916) 60 p. illus., fold. maps. 19½ cm. 16-12263. F127.H8R342

— (1919) 59 p. illus., fold. maps. 19½ cm. 19-14292. F127.H8R343

— (1920) 59 p. illus., fold. maps. 19½ cm. 20-12883. F127.H8R344

HUDSON. The Hudson river valley. By John Reed. (1st ed.) New York, C. N. Potter (1960) 239 p. 32 cm. 60-8925. F127. H8 R4

HUDSON. The river Hudson, together with descriptions and illustrations of the city of New York, Catskill Mountains, Lake George, Lake Champlain, Saratoga. Illus. with 50 engravings. New York, Ross & Tousey (etc., 1859) 63 p. illus. (incl. map) 23 cm. CA 25-254 Unrev.
F127. H8 R6
1859

— New York, A. Harthill (1860) 63 p. illus. 23 cm. 1-22593.
F127. H8 R6
1860

HUDSON. Historic resources of the Hudson; a preliminary inventory, Jan., 1969. Study prepared by Lewis C. Rubenstein. (Tarrytown, N.Y.) Hudson River Valley Commission (1969) 96 p. illus., maps. 28 cm. 75-631530. F127.H8 R87

HUDSON. "De Halve Maen" en de Hudson-Fulton feesten te New-York, door E. Ruempol. Amsterdam, Scheltema & Holkema (1909) 18 p. incl. front., illus., pl. 18 cm. 20-17066.
F127. H8 R9

HUDSON. A report on historic sites and buildings in the Hudson River Valley. By Russell D. Bailey and Associates. (Bear Mountain, N.Y., Hudson River Valley Commission, 1966) iv, 105 a (i.e. iv, 247 p. illus., maps. 28 cm. F127.H8 R96

HUDSON. Historic map of the picturesque Hudson from New York to Albany, 143 miles, most beautiful river scenery in the world ... (New York, Printed by M. P. E. Saltzman, 1914) map. 62 x 59½ cm. fold. to 17 x 9 cm. 14-13666. F127. H8 S 2

— Rev. ed. ... (Washington, D.C., M. P. E. Saltzman) 1915. map. 62½ x 60 cm. fold. to 16 x 17½ cm. Accompanied by historical and descriptive notes. 22-19761. F127.H8 S 22

HUDSON. The river of renown: the Hudson; the river, its valley, its cities and people, its role in the history of America. By Otto Louis Schreiber. (1st ed.) New York, Greenwich Book Publishers (1959) 195 p. 21 cm. 59-8078. F127.H8 S 32

HUDSON. Sketches of the North river ... New York, Wm. H. Colyer, 1838. 119 p. front. (fold. map) 16 cm. 1-14131. F127. H8 S 6

HUDSON. Souvenir of the Hudson river. (New York, Wittemann bros., 1881) 20 pl. 8½ x 13 cm.

851

A continuous strip (7½ x 230 cm) folded, accordion fashion, to form 20 leaves; end paper attached to stiff covers.   1-14132.

F127. H8 S 7

HUDSON.   Souvenir views of the Hudson River.   (New York, Souvenir post card co., (1909)
1 v.   14½ x 19 cm.

F127. H8 S 72

— (1909)   3 parts.   14½ x 19½ cm.

F127. H8 S73

HUDSON.   The Hudson River.   By Seneca Ray Stoddard.   Troy, N. Y., Nims & Knight (1888)
(1) 1, 9 plates.   25 x 30 cm.   1-14133 rev.*

F127. H8 S 9

HUDSON.   Constitution, rules, and list of officers and members of the Storm King club, Cornwall-on-Hudson.   New York,   v.   fold. pl., fold. plans.   17½ cm.   CA 17-114 Unrev.

F127. H8 S 94

HUDSON.   The Hudson River, from New York to Albany, as seen from the "Day line" and other steamers, with descriptive sketches of cities ... and objects of interest along the route ... New York, Taintor brothers (1876)   (112) p.   illus. (incl. maps)   fold. map.   17½ cm.   Paging irregular.   (Taintor's route and city guides)   4-28339.

F127. H8 T18

HUDSON.   ... Hudson River railway route.   New York, Albany, Troy, Saratoga ... New York, Taintor brothers (1871)   34 p.   illus., maps (1 fold.)   16 cm.   (Taintor's route and city guides)   Contains also "The New York central railway and its branches."   5-33171.

F127. H8 T19

HUDSON.   The New York central railway and its branches.   With descriptive sketches of the cities, villages, stations, and scenes and objects of interest along the route ... New York, Taintor brothers (1867)   1, 5-54 p. incl. front., maps.   16 cm.   (With above item)   5-33172.

F127. H8 T19

HUDSON.   The traveller's steamboat and railroad guide to the Hudson River ... New York, (1857)
22½ cm.

F127. H8 T7

— New York, H. Phelps (1857)   2, (7) - 50 p.   illus. (incl. map)   fold. map.   23 cm.   1-14136.   F127. H8 T8

HUDSON-Fulton celebration; historical explanation of the Dutch floats in the All-nations' division of the Hudson-Fulton parade, Albany, N. Y., Oct. 8, 1909.   (By Arnold Johan Ferdinand Van Laer)   Issued by the Holland Hudson-Fulton society of Albany and vicinity.   (Albany? 1909)   10 p.   pl.   18 cm.
26-23742.

F127. H8 V2

HUDSON.   Chronicles of the Hudson; three centuries of travelers' accounts.   Comp. Roland Van Zandt.   New Brunswick, N. J., Rutgers University Press (1971)   xiii, 369 p.   illus.   27 cm.   73-152722 MARC

F127. H8 V23

HUDSON.   Views of the Hudson river route.   (New York, A. Wittemann, 1886)   12 pl.   8½ x 13 cm.
A continuous strip (7½ x 138 cm.) folded, accordian fashion, to form 12 leaves; end paper attached to stiff covers.   1-14137.

F127. H8 V6

HUDSON.   Vivid panorama of the flood ... (Albany, Printed by J. B. Lyon co., 1913)   (32) p.   illus.
11 x 14½ cm.   Text on p. (2) of cover.   Views of the flood of the Mohawk and Hudson River valleys.   13-8633.   F127. H8 V85

HUDSON.   ... Hudson river.   New York, Albany, Troy, Saratoga.   Maps and descriptions by Henry F. Walling.   New York, Taintor brothers, 1867.   2, 3-26 p., 27-34 numb. l., (2) p.   illus. (maps)   15½ cm.
(Walling's route and city guides)   1-21443.

F127. H8 W3

HUDSON.   Historic Wallkill and Hudson River valleys ... (18   Walden, N. Y., Wallkill Valley pub. assoc., (18 - 19   v.   illus., plates, ports.   20 x 25½ - 25 cm.   Title varies.   24-3032.

F127. H8 W4

HUDSON.   Ter-centenary of the Hudson and centennial of the steamboat ... Walden, N. Y., The Wallkill Valley publishing assoc. (1909)   65 p.   illus.   25 cm.   24-18909.

F127. H8 W47

NEW YORK

HUDSON. Forest, rock, and stream; a series of twenty steel line-engravings by W. H. Bartlett and others; with descriptive text by N. P. Willis and others, including poems by American and foreign authors. Boston, Estes and Lauriat, 1886. 84 p. front., 19 pl. 32½ cm. Selections from the author's American scenery. 1840. ed. by George H. Coues. Principally views and description of places on or near the Hudson River. 1-26580.   F127. H8 W6

HUDSON. The discovery of the Hudson River, by James Grant Wilson ... (From New York (State) Legislature. Assembly. Docs. Albany, 1906. v. 12 no. 74. p. 143-171) 9-22098.   F127. H8 W7

HUDSON. Wilson's illustrated guide to the Hudson river. 1st ed. of 2000 copies. New-York, H. Wilson, 1848. 112 p. incl. maps. 15 cm. 2-20090.   F127. H8 W72 1848

— 8th ed. New York, H. Wilson, 1850. 2, 7-61, 27, 86-91 p. front. (fold. plan) illus. (incl. maps) 15 cm. Includes description and street directory of New York city. 6-10178.   F127. H8 W72 1850

HUDSON. Hudson river landings, by Paul Wilstach ... Indianapolis, The Bobbs-Merrill co. (1933) 311 p. incl. front., illus. plates. ports. 24 cm. "First edition." 33-25057.   F127. H8 W75

— Port Washington, N.Y., I. J. Friedman (1969) 311 p. illus. 22 cm. (Empire State historical publications series no. 67) 77-83480.   F127. H8 W75 1969

HUDSON. Summer days on the Hudson: the story of a pleasure tour from Sandy Hook to the Saranac lakes, including incidents of travel, legends, historical anecdotes, sketches of scenery, etc., by Daniel Wise. Illus. by 109 engravings. New York, Nelson & Phillips; Cincinnati, Hitchcock & Walden, 1875. 288 p. incl. front., illus. 19½ cm. 1-14138.   F127. H8 W8

— 1876. 288 p. incl. front., illus. 19 cm. 1-14139.   F127. H8 W9

HUDSON River. Pamphlets, broadsides, clippings, and other miscellaneous matter on this subject, not separately cataloged, are classified in: F127. H8 Z9

JEFFERSON County. ... American agriculturist farm directory and reference book of Jefferson and Lewis counties, New York ... including a road map ... New York, N.Y., Minneapolis (etc.) Orange Judd co. v. illus., fold. map. 23½ cm. 18-17857.   Directories

JEFFERSON County. Kimball's Jefferson county directory ... 1879. Watertown, N.Y., Hungerford & Coates, 1879 - v. 23½ cm. CA 33-685 Unrev.   Directories

JEFFERSON County. ... Gazetteer and business directory, of Jefferson County, for 1866-7. Comp. and pub. by Hamilton Child ... Watertown (N.Y.) Printed at the New York reformer office, 1866. 208 p. illus. (incl. map) 21½ cm. 17-7697.   F127. J 4 C4

JEFFERSON County. ... Geographical gazetteer of Jefferson county. 1684-1890. Ed. by William H. Horton. Compiled and pub. by Hamilton Child ... Syracuse, N.Y., The Syracuse journal co., printers and binders, 1890. 2 pt. in 1 v. illus., ports., fold. maps. 23½ cm. Part 2 has title: ... Business directory of Jefferson county, N.Y. 1890. 2-7160.   F127. J 4 C5

JEFFERSON County. Our county and its people. A descriptive work on Jefferson County, ed. by Edgar C. Emerson. (Boston) The Boston history co., 1898. xiii, 936, 318 p. illus., plates, ports., plan. 26 cm. Pt. II. Biographical: p. (877) - 936. Pt. III. Personal references: p. (1) - 276. L.C. copy replaced by microfilm. 1-22618.   F127. J 4 E5 Microfilm 18435 F

JEFFERSON County. The growth of a century: as illustrated in the history of Jefferson County, from 1793 to 1894 ... Comp. from state, county and town records, with many original articles upon interesting subjects, by John A. Haddock. Albany, N.Y., Weed-Parsons, 1895. 824 (i.e. 920) p. incl. illus., pl., ports., plan, facsim. front., plates (1 fold.) port., fold. maps, facsim. 27½ cm. Paging irregular. Imperfect: p. 203-232 b wanting. Binder's title: Haddock's centennial history of Jefferson County. Includes biographical sketches. 3-6078.   F127. J 4 H2

JEFFERSON County. ... History of Jefferson County. With illustrations and biographical sketches of some of its prominent men and pioneers. Philadelphia, L. H. Everts, 1878.   593 p. front., illus., plates, ports., map. 31 x 22 cm. Introd. signed: Samuel W. Durant and Henry B. Peirce. 9-27672.   F127. J 4 H6

JEFFERSON County. A history of Jefferson County ... from the earliest period to the present time. By Franklin B. Hough ... Albany, J. Munsell; Watertown, N.Y., Sterling & Riddell, 1854. 601 p. incl. illus., pl., ports. front. 23 cm. "Biographical notices": p. 419-457. 1-14140.   F127. J 4 H8

JEFFERSON County. ... Outline of the object, work, condition and needs of the society. Some historic facts and pictures of Jefferson county and the city of Watertown. (Watertown, A. W. Munk press, 1928)   (16) p. illus. (incl. port.) 23 cm. Jefferson county historical society. 32-3335.
F127. J 4 J 37

JEFFERSON County historical society. Transactions. (vol. I -   1886/87 - Watertown, N.Y., 1887 -   v. fronts., illus., ports., double map. 23 cm. 1-14141.   F127. J 4 J 4

JEFFERSON County prior to 1797, by Robert Lansing. (Watertown, N.Y., 1905?) 37-74 p. 23½ cm. (Reprint from the pub. proceedings issued by the Jefferson Co. centennial committee) "References": p. 71-74. 15-842.   F127. J 4 L29

JEFFERSON County. The history of Penet square and herein a brief sketch of the life character and operations of Peter Penet. An address delivered on the occasion of the observance of the centennial of Jefferson County ... 1905, by Irvin W. Near ... Hornell, N.Y., W. H. Greenhow, printer, 1906. 15 p. 23½ cm. 7-20.   F127. J 4 N3

JEFFERSON County. Genealogical and family history of the county of Jefferson; a record of the achievements of her people and the phenomenal growth of her agricultural and mechanical industries, comp. under the supervision of the late R. A. Oakes ... New York, Chicago, The Lewis pub. co., 1905.   2 v. front., plates, ports. 28 cm. 9-12046.   F127. J4 O11

JEFFERSON County. Folk-stories of the northern border. By Frank D. Rogers. Clayton, N.Y., Thousand Islands pub. co., 1897.   3, (11) - 273 p. 5 pl., 2 port. 21 x 16½ cm. 15-12398.
F127. J 4 R73

KEENE valley. "In the heart of the mountains." By Katherine Elizabeth McClellan. Saranac Lake, N.Y., The author (1898)   (26) p. illus. (incl. map) 17½ x 23 cm. (Her The Adirondack series) 98-380.
F127. K2 M2

KEUKA Lake memories; the champagne country. By William Reed Gordon. Rochester, N.Y. (1967) 240 p. 28 cm. 67-29817.   F127. K4 G6

KEUKA Lake. Lake Keuka. Buffalo, N.Y. The Matthews-Northrup co. (1891)   31 p. illus. obl. 16°. 1-14144-M1.   F127. K4 L2

KINGS County. The Ferry road on Long Island, by Eugene L. Armbruster; with 6 illus. and three maps ... New York (Printed by G. Quattlander) 1919.   40 p. illus. (incl. maps) 27 cm. 19-7329.
F127. K5 A7

KINGS County. Register in alphabetical order, of the early settlers of Kings County, Long Island, from its first settlement by Europeans to 1700; with contributions to their biographies and genealogies, comp. from various sources. By Teunis G. Bergen ... New York, S. W. Green's son, printer, 1881. 452 p. 24½ cm. 1-14142.   F127. K5 B 4

KINGS County. A synoptical history of the towns of Kings County from 1525 to modern times. Containing the origin of the names of the streets, avenues and lanes. Comp. from the manuscripts of Stiles, Ostrander, Furnam, and other historians by E. A. Custer. (New York, Sherwood'd incorporated, 1911)   36 p. 17½ cm. Cover-title: Cradle days of Brooklyn and Kings County, N.Y. 16-7120.
F127. K5 C9

KINGS County. Historic homesteads of Kings County ... (by) Charles Andrew Ditmas ... Brooklyn, N.Y., The compiler, 1909.   120 p. incl. col. illus., etc. 32 cm. Bibliography: p. 113. 9-29348.   F127. K5 D6

NEW YORK

KINGS County. ... Cemeteries in Kings and Queens counties, Long Island, New York, 1753 - 1913. William Applebie Eardeley ... Brooklyn, N.Y., 1916. 2 v. 28½ cm. Type-written copy. 23-14852.
F127. K5 E2

KINGS County. ... Assessment rolls of the five Dutch towns in King's County, L.I. 1675. Tr. from the original Dutch ms. (From The documentary history of the state of New-York ... v.4 (1851) p. (139) - 161) 7-34368.
F127. K5 K4

KINGS County. Report of Samuel McElroy, superintendent of survey. Brooklyn, Rome brothers, printers, 1874. 28 p. incl. tables. 22 cm. Town survey commission of Kings county. 1-14143 Rev.
F127. K5 K5

KINGS County. Report of the commissioner of records Kings County. 1910. (New York, M. B. Brown printing & binding co., 1911?) 131 p. incl. plates, maps, facsims. 28 cm. 11-23160.
F127.K5 K55

KINGS County genealogical club. Collections. v.1, no. I-VI. (New York, E. W. Nash, 1882-94) 5 pts. in 1 v. 24 cm. No more pub. This club existed only in names, the publisher of the Collections being Edward W. Nash. Contents. - v.1, no. I. Inscriptions on tombstones in cemetery of Reformed Dutch church, New Utrecht, L.I. 1882. - no. II. Inscriptions on tombstones in cemetery of Reformed Dutch church, Flatlands, L.I. 1882. - no. III. Inscriptions on tombstones in cemetery of Reformed Dutch church, Gravesend, L.I. 1882. - no. IV. Inscriptions on tombstones in Old Bushwick graveyard and Brooklyn baptismal records from 1660. 1888. - no. V - VI. Brooklyn baptismal records, from 1679 to end of 1719. Marriages from Oct. 1660 to June 1696. 1894. 5-6251.
F127. K5 K6

KINGS County historical society, Brooklyn. Contributions to American history. Brooklyn, N.Y., 1920 -   1 v. 23 cm.
F127.K5 K64

— ... The life and service of Major-General William Alexander also called the Earl of Stirling, by Charles Andrew Ditmas ... 15 p. front. (port.) 23 cm. (no. 1) Bibliography: p. 15 20-20630.

KINGS County historical society magazine ... (Brooklyn, N.Y.) 19   illus., fold. map. 23 cm.
F127.K5 K65

KINGS County. The civil, political, professional and ecclesiastical history, and commercial and industrial record of the county of Kings and the city of Brooklyn from 1683 to 1884, by Henry R. Stiles and others. New York, W. W. Munsell, (1884) 7, (9) - 1408 p. incl. front., illus. plates, ports., maps (1 fold.) fold. tab. 30½ cm. Many extra pages inserted. Includes biographical sketches. 1-14145.
F127. K5 S 8

KINGS County. Index to the wills, administrations and guardianships of Kings County, 1650 to 1850, compiled and edited by Milton Halsey Thomas ... in collaboration with Charles Shepard II ... Washington, D.C., C. Shepard II, 1926. 93 p. 24 cm. (Shepard genealogical series, no. 18) One hundred copies. 27-3244.
F127. K5 T4

LEWIS County. History of Lewis County, 1880 - 1965. Ed. by G. Byron Bowen. (Lowville, N.Y., Board of Legislators of Lewis County, 1970) 563 p. illus. 1 fold. col. map (in pocket) 24 cm.
F127. L6 B 6

LEWIS County. Tales from little Lewis. By Hazel C. Drew. Lyons Falls, N.Y. 56 p. 20 cm.
F127. L6 D7

LEWIS County. A history of Lewis County ... from the beginning of its settlement to the present time. By Franklin B. Hough ... Albany, Munsell & Rowland, 1860. iv, 319 p. front., illus., pl., ports. 22 cm. 1-14146.
F127. L6 H8

LEWIS County. 1805. History of Lewis county, with illustrations and biographical sketches of some of its prominent men and pioneers. By Franklin B. Hough. Syracuse, N.Y., D. Mason, 1883. viii, (11) - 606, xxxvii p. illus., pl., port., diagr. 29 cm. 1-28341-M2.
F127. L6 H82

LEWIS County. By Franklin Benjamin Hough. (Albany? 1872) 47½ x 29 cm. broadside.
F127. L6 H84

LEWIS County. Pamphlets, broadsides, clippings, and other miscellaneous matter on this subject, not separately cataloged, are classified in: F127. L6 Z9

LIVINGSTON County. New gazetteer and business directory for Livingston county ... 18 - Geneva, N.Y., G. E. Stetson, 18   v. fold. tab. 22 cm. 38M3102T.   Directories

LIVINGSTON County. Biographical review; this volume contains biographical sketches of Livingston and Wyoming counties ... Boston, Biographical review pub. co., 1895.   2, (9) - 683 p. incl. ports. 29 cm. (Atlantic states series of biographical reviews. v. 7)   6-34773 Rev.   F127. L7 B 6

LIVINGSTON County. A history of Livingston County; from its earliest traditions, to its part in the war for our Union: with an account of the Seneca nation of Indians, and biographical sketches of earliest settlers and prominent public men: by Lockwood L. Doty. Illus. by portraits on steel, and engravings on wood. To which is prefixed a biographical introduction, by A. J. H. Duganne. Geneseo (N.Y.) E. E. Doty, 1876.   xxvi, 685 p. front., illus., pl., ports. 22½ cm. 1-14147.   F127. L7 D7

LIVINGSTON County. History of Livingston County, from its earliest traditions to the present time, tog. with early town sketches; ed. by Lockwood R. Doty ... Jackson, Mich., W. J. Van Deusen, 1905. 1016, lxxix, 142 p. front., illus., plates, ports., maps, facsims. 25 x 19 cm. 2 parts in 1 vol. Through chapter 19 the present work follows L. L. Doty's History of Livingston County, pub. in 1876.   12-2455.   F127. L7 D75

LIVINGSTON County historical society. 2d-4th, 7th-8th, 10th-11th, 16th-29th, 33d annual meeting ... Dansville, N.Y., 1879 - 1904.   21 v.   22½ cm.   F127. L7 L7

LIVINGSTON County. The annual address: The judges and lawyers of Livingston County and their relation to the history of western New York. By L. B. Proctor.   (In Livingston County historical sociey. Third annual meeting. Dansville, N.Y., 1879. p. (7) - 26)   3-20270.   F127. L7 L7

LIVINGSTON County. 1687. History of Livingston County, with illustrations and biographical sketches of some of its prominent men and pioneers. By James H. Smith ... Syracuse, N.Y., D. Mason & co., 1881.   490, xxiv p. front., illus., plates (partly fold.) ports. 29 cm. 12-2444.   F127. L7 S 6

LONG ISLAND. Curtin's directory of ... Long Island, with a business directory of patrons of the work, 1864/5 - 1865/66, 1868/9,   New York, D. Curtin (etc., 1864) -   v. 19-21 cm. 18-16812.   Directories

LONG ISLAND. ... The Montauk business directory of Long Island; Queens, Nassau and Suffolk counties, 1913.   New York city, Mort F. Levy pub. co.   v. 26 cm. 13-5572.   Directories

LONG ISLAND society register ... Brooklyn, N.Y., Rugby press, inc., 19   v. 20½ cm. Preceded by Brooklyn blue book and Long Island society register.   CA 27-82 Unrev.   Directories

LONG ISLAND landmarks. Prepared by the Metropolitan New York District Office of the State Office of Planning Coordination. Albany, (1969)   122 p. 21 cm. 71-633167.   F127. L8 A5

LONG ISLAND. Guide to the noted places on Long Island, historical and otherwise ... By Eugene L. Armbruster. Brooklyn, N.Y. (E. L. Armbruster) 1925 -   1 v. illus., fold. map. 19 cm. 26-11518.   F127. L8 A68

LONG ISLAND. ... Long Island, its early days and development ... By Eugene L. Armbruster ... Brooklyn-New York, The Brooklyn daily eagle, 1914.   96 p. illus. (incl. maps) 28½ cm. (The Eagle library, vol. xxix, no. 7, serial no. 182) Biographical sketches: p. 49-68.   14-12554.   F127. L8 A7

LONG ISLAND. Long island landmarks, by Eugene L. Armbruster ... New York, 1923 -   pts. 28 cm.   Contents. - pt. 1. The town of Newtown, including Long Island City.   A 24-767.   F127. L8 A72

LONG ISLAND. Colonial Long Island. By Paul Bailey. Amityville, N.Y., Long Island Forum, 1958.   58 p. illus. 19 cm. 58-42541.   F127. L8 B 15

NEW YORK 123

LONG ISLAND. Early Long Island, its Indians, whalers and folklore rhymes. Westhampton Beach, N.Y., Long Island Forum, 1962. 128 p. 23 cm. F127.L8 B155

LONG ISLAND. Historic Long Island in pictures, prose, and poetry. By Paul Bailey. Amityville, N.Y., Long Island Forum, 1956. 168 p. illus. 23 cm. 56-57455. F127.L8 B 16

LONG ISLAND; a history of two great counties, Nassau and Suffolk. By Paul Bailey. New York, Lewis Hist. Pub. Co. (1949) 3 v. illus., ports., maps. 28 cm. Vol. 3: Personal and family history. 49-48187*. F127.L8 B 17

LONG ISLAND. Physical Long Island; its glacial origin, historic storms, beaches, prairies and archaeology. By Paul Bailey. Amityville, N.Y., Pub. by the Long Island Forum (1959) 130 p. illus. 20 cm. 59-3718. F127.L8 B173

LONG ISLAND. ... Road-book of Long island, containing, also, best riding of New York and New Jersey, within fifty miles of New York city, and through routes to New Haven, Hartford, Springfield, Boston, Albany, Philadelphia, etc. ... Compiled by Albert B. Barkman ... Pub. under the auspices of the Brooklyn bicycle club. 1st ed. ... Philadelphia, Franklin printing house, 1886. (94) p. maps (1 fold. in pocket) 8½ x 17½ cm. League of American wheelmen. 1-14148 Rev. F127. L8 B 2

LONG ISLAND. Bayles' Long Island hand book. 1885. By Richard Mather Bayles. Middle Island, Suffolk co., N.Y., R. M. Bayles, 1885. 120 p. illus., fold. map. 8°. 1-16309-M1. F127. L8 B 3

LONG ISLAND Sound. By Fessenden Seaver Blanchard. Princeton, N.J., Van Nostrand (1958) 222 p. illus. 27 cm. 58-14052. F127.L8 B 55

LONG ISLAND genealogies. Families of Albertson, Andrews, Bedell, Birdsall ... Willets, Williams, Willis, Wright, and other families. Being kindred descendants of Thomas Powell of Bethpage, L.I., 1688. Comp. by Mary Powell Bunker. Albany, J. Munsell's sons, 1895. 350 p. fold. map. 22½ x 18½ cm. (Munsell's historical series, no. 24) 3-13311. F127. L8 B 9

LONG ISLAND. The heritage of Long Island. Woodcuts and text by W. Oakley Cagney. Ed. with an introd. by Joan D. Berbrich. Port Washington, N.Y., I. J. Friedman Division, Kennikat Press (1970) 1 v. (unpaged) 28 cm. (Empire state historical publications series, no. 90) 74-134274. F127.L8 C27

LONG ISLAND. Homes on the South Side railroad of Long Island. A sketch of the region traversed by the South Side railroad of Long Island, between Brooklyn and Moriches, tog. with a statement of the inducements offered by property owners along the line, for the purchase of homes for New York business men ... By George L. Catlin. Brooklyn, The South Side railroad co. of Long Island, 1873. 92 p. illus. 17½ cm. 4-6466. F127. L8 C3

LONG ISLAND. Central and eastern Long Island and its attractions, embracing Bay Shore, Patchogue, Sayville, Bellport, Blue Point, Bayport, East and Centre Moriches, Islip, Huntington, Northport, Port Jefferson and Riverhead ... New York, G. W. Richardson, 1911. 44 p. illus. 35 cm. The text is devoted to advertising sketches of business houses. 11-23039. F127. L8 C4

LONG ISLAND. The hurricane of 1938 on eastern Long island, written and compiled by Ernest S. Clowes. Bridgehampton, L.I., Hampton press, 1939. 3, 66 p. plates. 23 cm. 39-3068. F127. L8 C6

— 1939. 3, 67 p. plates, diagr. 23½ cm. 41-9951. F127.L8 C62

LONG ISLAND. The commodities of the iland called Manati ore Long Ile which is in the continent of Virginia. (Albany) Imprinted by J. M. for J. G. S., ... (1865?) 16 p. 25 cm. Printed by J. Munsell for J. G. Shea. Written about 1632. The original is in the Public record office, London, Colonial papers, v. 6, no. 61. 3-15637. F127. L8 C7

LONG ISLAND. Photographed and described by C. Manley De Bevoise. Ed. by Richard N. Powdrell. Port Washington, N.Y., Kennikat Press (1963) 168 p. 28 cm. 63-22606. F127. L8 D4

LONG ISLAND. Documents relating to the conveyance of land, etc., on Long Island. New York, Print. Bell & Gould, 1850. 24p. 23 cm. Deeds and patents from Aug. 1660 to March, 1702/3 24-555. F127. L8 D5
Rare Book Coll.

LONG ISLAND. Documents relating to the history of the early colonial settlements principally on Long Island, with a map of its western part, made in 1666. Tr. and comp. and ed. from the original records in the office of the secretary of state and the State library ... by B. Fernow ... Albany, Weed, Parsons, 1883. 2, xxxiii, 800 p. fold. map. 30 x 24 ½ cm. (Documents rel. to the colonial history of the state of New York. vol. xiv - old series; vol. iii - new series) 3-20931. F127. L8 D6

LONG ISLAND; an unconventional excursion with a camera around New York's neighboring isle. 100 photographs and a little text by Russell Doubleday. New York, Doubleday, Doran, 1939. 80 p. incl. front., illus. 19 ½ cm. "First ed." 39-11065 Rev. F127. L8 D7

LONG ISLAND. Anecdotes and events in Long Island history (by) Verne Dyson. Port Washington, N.Y., I. J. Friedman, 1969. 140 p. 22 cm. (Empire state historical publications series, no. 79)
F127. L8 D9

LONG ISLAND. The human story of Long Island (by) Verne Dyson. Port Washington, N.Y., I. J. Friedman, 1969. 139 p. 22 cm. (Empire State historical publications, series no. 78)
F127. L8 D92

LONG ISLAND. Manor houses and historic homes of Long Island and Staten Island, by Harold Donaldson Eberlein; with a frontispiece in photogravure and 75 illus. in doubletone. Philadelphia & London, J. B. Lippincott, 1928. 4, vii-x, (1), 318 p. front., plates. 24 ½ cm. 28-30240.
F127. L8 E2

— Port Washington, N.Y., I. J. Friedman (1966) x, 318 p. 22 cm. (Empire State historical publications series, 40) 66-21378. F127. L8 E2 1966

LONG ISLAND. Early Long Island, a colonial study. By Martha Bockée Flint. New York, London, G. P. Putnam's sons, 1896. ix, 549 p. front. (map) 20 ½ cm. "List of books consulted": p. 530-538. 1-28287-M2.
F127. L8 F6

LONG ISLAND. Long Island before the revolution; a colonial study, by Martha Bockée Flint. Port Washington, N.Y., I. J. Friedman (1967) ix, 549 p. 23 cm. (Empire state historical publication 15) 67-16257.
F127. L8 F6 1967

LONG ISLAND. Antiquities of Long Island; by Gabriel Furman. To which is added a Bibliography by Henry Onderdonk, jr. Ed. by Frank Moore. New York, J. W. Bouton, 1875. viii, (9) - 478 p. 22 cm. 1-14149. F127. L8 F9

— Microfilm. Ann Arbor, Mich, University Microfilms, 1963. 1 reel. 35 mm. (American culture series, 230:8) Microfilm 01271 reel 230 no. 8E

— Port Washington, N.Y., I. J. Friedman (1968) 271 p. 21 cm. (Empire state historical publications series, no. 32) Reprinted from 1875 ed. which includes other material. 68-18358. F127. L8 F9 1968

LONG ISLAND. Notes geographical and historical, relating to the town of Brooklyn in Kings county, on Long island ... By Gabriel Furman. Brooklyn, A. Spooner, 1824. (In his Antiquities of Long island ... N.Y., 1875, p. 273-434) 1-14150. F127. L8 F9

LONG ISLAND. Bibliography of Long island. By Henry Onderdonk, jr. "Printed from a manuscript, prepared ... in 1866, and presented to the N.Y. historical society." 1-14152. F127. L8 F9

LONG ISLAND. The evolution of Long Island; a story of land and sea, by Ralph Henry Gabriel ...

NEW YORK

New Haven, Yale university press; (etc.) 1921. 194 p., front. (fold. map) 23 cm. (Yale historical publications. Miscellany. ix) "Bibliographical note": p. (187) - 189. 22-1376.
F127.L8 G12

— Port Washington, N.Y., I. J. Friedman, 1960. 194 p. illus. 22 cm. A revision of the author's thesis, Yale University. Includes bibliography. "2d printing, Jan. 1960" 60-51433.
F127.L8 G12 1960

— Port Washington, N.Y., I. J. Friedman (1968) 194 p. 23 cm. (Empire State historical publications, no. 1)
F127.L8 G12 1968

LONG ISLAND. The Sagtikos manor, 1697; an address read before the annual meeting of the Order of colonial lords of manors in America ... 1934, by Miss Sarah D. Gardiner. New York, 1935. 31 p. illus. (incl. ports., facsims.) 23½ cm. (Publications of the Order of colonial lords of manors in America. no. 26) 36-15043.
F127.L8 G37

LONG ISLAND. Early Long Island; an address by Hon. William Winton Goodrich delivered before the New York society of the Order of the founders and patriots of America ... 1904. (New York, 1904) 22 p. 23 cm. (Order of the founders and patriots of America. N.Y. soc. Pubs. no. 7) 4-33478.
F127. L8 G6

LONG ISLAND. The beauties of Long island ... (By Herbert Foster Gunnison) New York, Press of American bank note co.) 1895. 94 p. illus., fold. map. 23½ cm. "Issued by the Traffic department of the Long island railroad." 1-14156 Rev.
F127. L8 G9

LONG ISLAND. Sketches from local history, written and compiled by William Donaldson Halsey. Bridgehampton, N.Y. (Harry Lee pub. co.) 1935. 2, 7-204 (i.e. 233) p. incl. illus., double maps. 28½ cm. 36-345.
F127.L8 H26

— Southampton, N.Y., Yankee Peddler Book Co. (1966) 189 p. 29 cm.
F127.L8 H26 1966

LONG ISLAND. The boroughs of Brooklyn and Queens, counties of Nassau and Suffolk, Long Island, 1609-1924. By Henry Isham Hazelton. New York, Chicago, Lewis historical pub. co., 1925. 5 v. fronts., plates, etc. 27½ cm. vols. 1-3 paged continuously. Vols. 4 & 5 contain biographical matl. 25-10750.
F127. L8 H3

LONG ISLAND. Two travellers on Long island, by Ettie C. Hedges ... East Hampton, L.I., Priv. print., 1934. (5) - 11 p. 22 cm. "A paper read at the meeting of the Westhampton woman's club ... 1934" 34-38739.
F127. L8 H4

LONG ISLAND. The inland sea, by Morton M. Hunt. (1st ed.) Garden City, N.Y., Doubleday, 1965. 144 p. 22 cm. 65-13983.
F127.L8 H85

LONG ISLAND. Long Island's domestic architecture: old churches, mills; special exhibition ... 1920. Huntington, N.Y., Huntington hist. soc. (1920) (8) p. illus. 23½ cm. 20-9589.
F127. L8 H9

LONG ISLAND. A silver gray's r.r. reminiscences. (By Inglis Stuart) (Fishkill Landing, N.Y., Fishkill Standard print, 1908) (20) p. illus., 2 pl., ports. 23 cm. 10-2002 Add.
F127. L8 I 5

LONG ISLAND. How they lived, as disclosed by old Long island tales and chronicles, by Birdsall Jackson ... Rockville Centre, N.Y., Paumanok press (1941) viii, 222 p. 21 cm. Bibliography: p. 221-222. 42-2302.
F127.L8 J 28

LONG ISLAND. Stories of old Long island, by Birdsall Jackson ... Long island ed. Rockville Centre, N.Y., Paumanok press (1934) viii, 230 p. 21 cm. "Acknowledgments": p. 229-230. 34-42833.
F127. L8 J 3

— Port Washington, N.Y., I. J. Friedman, 1963. 227 p. 23 cm. (Empire State historical publication 26) 63-1462.
F127. L8 J 3 1963

LONG ISLAND. The mills of Long Island. Comp. Cornell Jaray. Port Washington, I. J. Friedman, 1962. 44 p. 25 cm. (Empire State historical publicaion 10) 62-15664. F127.L8 J 34

LONG ISLAND. By W. Alfred Jones ... Read before the Long island historical soc. ... 1863. New York, Baker & Godwin, printers, 1863. 23 p. 23 cm. 1-14153. F127. L8 J 7

LONG ISLAND. The Journal of Long Island history. v.1 - Spring 1961 - (Brooklyn) Long Island Historical Society. v. in 23 cm. F127.L8 J 75

LONG ISLAND. The new Long island; a hand book of summer travel. Designed for the use and information of visitors to Long island and its watering places. (By William Mackay Laffan) New York, Rogers & Sherwood, 1879. 96 p. incl. front., illus. 25 cm. 1-14154 Rev. F127. L8 L2

— 1880. 110 p. incl. front., illus. 24½ cm. 2-13853 Rev. F127.L8 L22

LONG ISLAND. ... Lawrence, Oakley & Fleury, general auctioneers, and real estate agents. Long Island property a speciality. Jamaica, N.Y., Long Island farmer print. 1870. 8 p. 8°. 1-22616-M1. F127. L8 L4

LONG ISLAND. Exploring Long Island. By John J. Leitch. Illus. by Inez Heine. New York, Noble and Noble (1961) 138 p. 28 cm. F127.L8 L45

— (1964) 138 p. 28 cm. F127.L8 L45 1964

LONG ISLAND. The Long Island almanac and year book ... a book of information respecting Nassau and Suffolk counties ... 1927 - Brooklyn, N.Y., The Brooklyn daily eagle, 1927 - v. illus. (maps) 22½ cm. 27-2024. F127.L8 L65

LONG ISLAND, an island empire of the Empire State, New York's sunrise homeland. Island-wide survey of boroughs, counties, cities, towns, villages and communities which make up this remarkable island lying at New York City's doorstep. With island-wide governmental information ... New York, Long Island Assoc. v. illus., maps. 23-26 cm. 37-18575 rev.* F127.L8 L67

LONG ISLAND calendar for 1902; legends, myths, stories and historical sketches of Long Island ... pub. for the mid-winter fête, "From colonial America to the United States, its colonies and protectorates". Brooklyn, N.Y. (1901) 7-151, (3) p. illus. (incl. ports.) fold. map. 24½ cm. 2-1766. F127. L8 L7

LONG ISLAND forum. (Amityville, N.Y., etc.) v. in illus. 29 cm. monthly. Began publication with Jan. 1938 issue. 52-34737. F127.L8 L73

LONG ISLAND historical bulletin, 1913. v. F127.L8 L75

LONG ISLAND home journal, the village life magazine, illustrated monthly ... v.1 - Mar. 1914 - Jamaica, N.Y., Long Island home journal, inc. (1914 - v. illus. 31 cm. 15-25657. F127.L8 L78

LONG ISLAND .. (New York) The Long island railway company, 1882. 3, 50 p. front., illus., map. 25 cm. 1-14155 Rev. F127. L8 L8

LONG ISLAND, illustrated. Long Island railroad co. (New York 1901) 22½ cm. F127.L8L808

— 1904. 23 cm. F127.L8 L81

LONG ISLAND, "where cooling breezes blow" ... Issued by the Passenger dept., Long Island railroad ... (New York, Isaac H. Blanchard co.) 1913. 112 p. illus. (incl. map) 22½ cm. 13-9842. F127.L8L813

NEW YORK 127

LONG ISLAND and real life,, Long Island railroad. (New York, Issued by the Passenger department, Long Island railraod, 1915)   104 p. illus. 22 x 17 cm. 15-11464.   F127.L8L814

— (1916)   104 p. illus. (incl. map) 22 x 17 cm. 16-12902.   F127.L8L815

LONG ISLAND illustrated; issued by the Passenger department, Long Island railroad. 1903. Long Island City, N.Y., H.M. Smith, gen'l passenger agent (1903)   134 p. illus., fold. map. 22½ cm.
17-19463.   F127.L8L817

LONG ISLAND. Summer resorts in Long Island   Long Island railroad co., (1908)
F127.L8L819

LONG ISLAND. Unique Long Island ... Long Island railroad co. (New York, 1901)   14 x 19 cm.
F127.L8 L82

LONG ISLAND. Unique Long Island camera sketches. (Long Island railroad co.) (New York, The Powers press, 1904)   (2) p. 38 pl., map. 20½ x 15½ cm. 6-27973.   F127.L8L83

LONG ISLAND. Out on Long Island ... Issued by the Traffic department of the Long Island railroad co. (New York, Press of C.K. Alley) 1890.   65 p. illus., fold. map. 21½ cm. By Herbert F. Gunnison.
2-18874.   F127.L8 L85

— (New York, American bank note co.) 1892.   82 p. illus., map. 22 cm. 1-21445 Rev.
F127.L8 L87

— (New York, American bank note co.) 1894.   82 p. illus., fold. map. 23½ cm. 1-16264 Rev.
F127.L8 L89

LONG ISLAND. Summer homes on Long Island. Long Island railroad co. (New York) 1898.
13 x 19½ cm.   F127. L8 L9

LONG ISLAND. The Long Island tourist. v. 1, no. 2. Feb. 1902. Long Island City, N.Y., Tourist pub. co., 1902.   1 no. illus. 30½ cm.   F127.L8 L93

LONG ISLAND. Salts of the sound, by Roger Williams McAdam; a story of steamboating on Long Island sound from 1815 to the present. Brattleboro, Ct., Stephen Daye press (1939)   247 p. plates,
ports. 24½ cm. 40-661.   F127.L8 M14

LONG ISLAND. Salts of the Sound; an informal history of steamboat days and the famous skippers who sailed Long Island Sound. Rev. and enl. By Roger Williams McAdam. New York, Stephen Daye Press (1957)   240 p. illus. 24 cm. 57-13348.   F127.L8 M14

LONG ISLAND. ... Long island gazetteer, a guide to historic places, compiled and ed. by Arthur R. Macoskey. Brooklyn, N.Y., The Eagle library, inc., 1939.   144 p. illus. (incl. maps) 21½ cm.
(Eagle library, no. 342, vol. 54) 39-7071.   F127. L8 M2

LONG ISLAND. Long Island discovery; an adventure into the history, manners, and mores of America's front porch (by) Seon Manley. (1st ed.) Garden City, N.Y., Doubleday, 1966.
x, 318 p. 24 cm. 66-15669.   F127.L8 M24

LONG ISLAND. Our island. By George Mannello. (Woodmere? N.Y.) 1949.   iii, 99 l. 30 cm.
"Sources consulted": leaves 98-99. 49-29539*.   F127.L8 M25

LONG ISLAND. Our Long Island. By George Mannello. New York, Noble and Noble (1951)
150 p. illus. 27 cm. 51-14106.   F127.L8 M26

— (1960)   150 p. 26 cm.   F127.L8 M26 1960

— (1964)   iv, 150 p. 27 cm.   F127.L8 M26 1964

861

LONG ISLAND. Witches, whales, petticoats & sails; adventures and misadventures from three centuries of Long Island history. By Barbara Marhoefer. Illus. by Fred Guardineer. Port Washington, N.Y., I. J. Friedman Division of Kennikat Press (1971) xiii, 206 p. illus. 24 cm. (Empire State historical publication series, no. 92) "These stories and their illustrations first appeared in the Suffolk sun, a daily newspaper pub. on Long Island by Cowles Communications, Inc. from Nov. 1966 to Oct. 1969." 74-151807 MARC.
 F127. L8 M28

LONG ISLAND. Fish-shape Paumanok; nature and man on Long Island. By Robert Cushman Murphy. Philadelphia, American Philosophical Society, 1964. ix, 67 p. 24 cm. (Memoirs of the American Philosophical Society ... v. 58) Penrose memorial lecture for 1962. 63-22603.
 F127. L8 M8

LONG ISLAND. Bethpage State Park. (Babylon? N.Y.) Long Island State Park Commission, Bethpage Park Authority, 1958. (8) p. illus. 28 cm. A 58-9556.
 F127. L8 N47

LONG ISLAND. (Long Island family cemetery inscriptions from the following names cemeteries: the Lawrence cemetery, Steinway, Long Island City; the Riker and Luyster cemeteries, North Beach; and the Moore cemetery, Woodside. New York, New York genealogical and biographical society, 1923) 19 numb. l. 28 cm. 24-6101.
 F127. L8 N5

LONG ISLAND. ... Papers relating to Long Island. (From the documentary history of the state of New-York ... v. 1. Contains names of inhabitants of Hempstead, 1673, Flushing, Southampton, 1698, etc., etc. 8-27633.
 F127. L8 O15

LONG ISLAND. On the sound. (Byram, Conn., Seascape Publications) v. illus. (part col.) 29 cm. monthly. Began in 1971. 70-618682.
 F127. L8 O5

LONG ISLAND. Long Island's story, by Jacqueline Overton; illus. with reproductions from old prints and decorations by Edw. A. Wilson. Garden City, Doubleday, Doran, 1929. 4, vii-x p., 348 p. front., illus., plates, ports., double map, facsims. 24 cm. Bibliography: p. 323-325. 29-17844.
 F127. L8 O96

— (2d ed.) With a sequel. The rest of the story, 1929 - 1961, by Bernice Marshall (1st ed.) Port Washington, L.I., N.Y., I. J. Friedman (1961) 348, 44 p. 24 cm. 61-15755.
 F127. L8 O96 1961

LONG ISLAND. A history of Long Island, from its first settlement by Europeans, to the year 1845, with special reference to its ecclesiastical concerns ... By Nathaniel S. Prime. New York and Pittsburg, R. Carter, 1845. xii, 420 p. fold. front. (map) 20 cm. 1-14157.
 F127. L8 P 9

LONG ISLAND. Long-Island of to-day ... (By Julian Ralph) (New York, American bank note co., 1884) 105 p. illus., fold. map. 8°. 1-14158-M1.
 F127. L8 R2

LONG ISLAND. Ship ashore! A record of maritime disasters off Montauk and eastern Long Island, 1640-1955. By Jeannette (Edwards) Rattray. New York, Coward-McCann (1955) 256 p. illus. 22 cm. 55-6141.
 F127. L8 R3

— Southampton, N.Y., Yankee Peddler Book Co. (1955) vii, 256 p. illus. 21 cm.
 F127. L8 R3 1966

LONG ISLAND. Long Island behind the British lines during the Revolution. By John Reynolds. Setauket, Long Island, Society for the Preservation of Long Island Antiquities. 1960. 40 p. 23 cm.
 F127. L8 R4

LONG ISLAND. Pioneers and patriots of Long island, 1640-1840, by W. Willard Roberts ... (Bridgeport, Conn., Columbia printing co.) 1936. (20) p. 22 cm. "(A) guide for descendants in the United States of certain families of Puritan, colonial, or revolutionary background ..." 36-7465.
 F127. L8 R7

LONG ISLAND. A history of Long Island, from its earliest settlement to the present time, by Peter Ross ... New York and Chicago, The Lewis pub. co., 1902. 3 v. front., illus., pl., port. 27½ cm. Vol. 2-3 biographies. 2-14589.
 F127. L8 R8

NEW YORK

LONG ISLAND. A history of Long island, from its earliest settlement to the present time, by Peter Ross ... New York and Chicago, The Lewis pub. co., 1905. 3 v. fronts. (v.1-2) illus. (incl. plans) plates, ports., maps, facsims. 27½ cm. Vol. 3: biographies. A revision of the 1902 edition, with v.2-3 rewritten by William S. Pelletreau. 44-29413.
F127. L8 R6
1905

LONG ISLAND. Long Island to-day; consisting of sketches on the political, industrial, topographical and geological history of Long Island and Long Island towns and villages, but more particularly of general views illustrating Long Island scenes of to-day. By Frederick Ruther. 610 illustrations. Hicksville, N.Y., The author (1909) (9)-271 p. front., illus. 26 cm. 10-871.
F127. L8 R9

LONG ISLAND. Marriages published in the Christian intelligencer of the Reformed Dutch church from 1830 - 1871 which took place in Brooklyn and Long island, also marriages of Brooklyn and Long island residents which occured (!) elsewhere. Comp. and ed. by Ray C. Sawyer (New York?) 1933. 196 numb., 19 l. 29 cm. Typewritten. CA 33-709 Unrev.
F127. L8 S 3

LONG ISLAND. Colonel John Scott of Long Island, 1634 (?) - 1696, by Wilbur C. Abbott ... New Haven, Yale university press (etc.) 1918. 4, 93 p. 22½ cm. Also pub., 1918, as no. 30 of the Publications of the Society of colonial wars in the state of New York. 19-12626.
F127. L8 S 4

LONG ISLAND. The indomitable John Scott: citizen of Long Island 1632 - 1704. By Lilian (Thomson) Mowrer. Pref. by Harold Hume. New York, Farrar, Straus and Cudahy (1960) 438 p. 22 cm. 60-12983.
F127. L8 S 42

LONG ISLAND. The Tangier Smith manor of St. George, address delivered at the 8th annual meeting of the New York branch of the Order of colonial lords of manors in America ... by Rev. Howard Duffield. Baltimore, 1921. 32 p. incl. illus., facsim. 23 cm. 21-11773.
F127. L8 S 66

LONG ISLAND; or, New York City's necessity, by Warren L. Starkey. New York, Jackson bros. realty co., 1910. 16½ x 25½ cm.
F127. L8 S79

LONG ISLAND. Discovering Long island, by William Oliver Stevens; illus. by the author. New York, Dodd, Mead, 1939. xvii, 349 p. col. front., illus., plates. 22½ cm. 39-27412.
F127. L8 S 85

— Port Washington, N.Y., I.J. Friedman (1969) xvii, 349 p. illus. 23 cm. (Empire State historical publications series no. 77) 76-101022.
F127. L8 S 85
1969

LONG ISLAND. True tales from the early days of Long island, as told by Kate W. Strong. Bay Shore, N.Y., Long island forum (1940) 16 p. illus. 19 cm. 41-5250.
F127. L8 S 88

LONG ISLAND. The Long Island story, by Alexander M. Swaab. Designed by Tamara Koral. Illus. by Ruth Altman. (Phoenix? N.Y., 1966) 106 p. 28 cm.
F127. L8 S 93

LONG ISLAND. Rhymes of the sunrise trail, by Si Tanhauser, illus. by Senator Ford. New York, N.Y., Parnassus, 1929. 47 p. illus. 21 cm. 29-16257.
F127. L8 T16

LONG ISLAND. History of Long Island; containing an account of the discovery and settlement; with other important and interesting matters to the present time. By Benjamin F. Thompson ... New-York, E. French, 1839. x, (11)-536 p. front. 24 cm. p. 142 - 481 devoted to histories of the counties and towns. 1-22567.
F127. L8 T39

— 2d ed. 1843. 2 v.
F127. L8 T4

— The 3d ed., rev. and greatly enl., with additions and a biography of the author by Charles J. Werner ... New York, R.H. Dodd, 1918. 4 v. fronts. (3 col.) plates (1 double) ports., fold. maps, facsims. 25½ cm. Biography and genealogy: v.4, p. 99-457. 18-7130.
F127. L8 T42

— Port Washington, N.Y., I. J. Friedman, 1962 (1918)   3 v.   23 cm.   61-18270.
F127.L8 T42
1962

LONG ISLAND.   The Indian place-names on Long Island and islands adjacent, with their probable significations, by William Wallace Tooker, Algonkinist, ed., with an introd. by Alexander F. Chamberlain ... pub. for the John Jermain memorial library ... New York and London, G. P. Putnam's sons, 1911.   xxviii, 314 p.   22½ cm.   Bibliography: p. 303-314.   11-27486.
F127. L8 T6

— Port Washington, N.Y., I. J. Friedman, 1962.   314 p.   23 cm.   (Empire State historical publications, 6) 62-13522.
F127. L8 T6
1962
G & M

LONG ISLAND.   Loafing down Long Island, by Charles Hanson Towne; with drawings by Thomas Fogarty.   New York, The Century co., 1921.   6, 3-212 p. incl. plates.   front.   21½ cm.   21-9059.
F127.L8 T64

LONG ISLAND.   Personal reminiscences of men and things on Long Island ... By Daniel M. Tredwell ... Brooklyn, C. A. Ditmas, 1912-17.   2 v.   mounted fronts., illus., plates, ports. (part mounted) maps, facsim.   26½ cm.   Paged continuously.   12-26762 Rev.
F127. L8 T7

LONG ISLAND.   History of Long Island; containing an account of the discovery and settlement; with other important and interesting matters to the present time.   By Benjamin Franklin Thompson.   New York, E. French, 1839.   x, 11-536 p.   front. (pl.)   8º.   1-22567-M1.
F127.L8 T39

— ... including notices of numerous individuals and families ...   2d ed. rev. and greatly enl ...   New York, Gould, Banks, 1843.   2 v.   fronts. (v.1: port) plates, fold. map.   23 cm.   1-16540.
F127. L8 T4

LONG ISLAND.   The early history of Long Island Sound and its approaches, by Charles Hervey Townshend ... New Haven, Tuttle, Morehouse & Taylor, printers, 1894.   31 p.   2 fold. maps.   23½ cm.   17-24779.
F127.L8 T65

LONG ISLAND.   Heritage roads on Long Island, by Vincent R. Turner.   1st ed.   Mineola, N.Y.   Mineola Lithographer (1965)   60 p.   22 cm.
F127. L8 T8

LONG ISLAND.   Vacation guide to eastern Long Island.   Southampton, Countrytown Associates.   v. illus., maps.   22 cm.   57-45874.
F127.L8 V27

LONG ISLAND.   Keskachauge, or the first white settlement on Long Island, by Frederick Van Wyck ... New York & London, G. P. Putnam's sons, 1924.   xlv, 778 p.   fold. front., plates (part fold.) ports., fold. maps, plans (part fold.) facsims.   24 cm.   25-1025.
F127. L8 V3

LONG ISLAND.   Long island colonial patents, by Frederick Van Wyck ... Boston, A. A. Beauchamp, 1935.   xvi, 175 p.   front., plates, ports.   24 cm.   100 copies printed.   35-22341.
F127.L8 V33
Rare Book Coll.

LONG ISLAND.   History of Eaton's Neck, Long Island, by Mary Voyse; tog. with its geological background, by Sydney Bevin.   (n. p.) 1955.   42 p.   illus.   22 cm.   56-22627.
F127. L8 V6

LONG ISLAND.   The plains of Long island.   By Winslow C. Watson ... Albany, Printed by C. Van Benthuysen, 1860.   23 p.   23 cm.   From the Transactions of the New York state agricultural society, 1859.   1-14159.
F127. L8 W3

LONG ISLAND.   Isle of shells, Long Island, by George L. Weeks, Jr.   (1st ed.)   Islip, New York, Printed by Buys Bros., 1965.   vi, 313 p.   24 cm.
F127. L8 W4

LONG ISLAND.   Genealogies of Long Island families; a collection of genealogies relating to the following Long Island families: Dickerson, Mitchill, Wickham, Carman, Raynor, Rushmore, Satterly,

NEW YORK

Hawkins, Arthur Smith, Mills, Howard, Lush, Greene; comp. by Charles J. Werner ... Mainly from records left by Benjamin F. Thompson ... New York, C. J. Werner, 1919. 170 p., front., plates, ports. 23½ cm. 19-15263. F127. L8 W48

LONG ISLAND. Historical miscellanies relating to Long Island, by Charles J. Werner ... Huntington, L. I., Priv. print. (New York, Tobins A. Wright press) 1917. 6, 11-71 p. plates, 2 port. (incl. front.) 21 cm. 100 copies printed. 17-21950. F127. L8 W49

LONG ISLAND. Where to go, what to do, how to do it on Long Island Sound, by Julius M. Wilensky. Ed. by Albert J. Forman. Stamford, Conn., Snug Harbor Pub. Co., (1968) 211 p. illus. 29 cm. 68-26398. F127. L8 W66

LONG ISLAND. Historic Long Island, by Rufus Rockwell Wilson ... New York, The Berkeley press, 1902. 364 p. incl. front., pl. 23½ cm. 2-30085. F127. L8 W7

— Port Washington, N. Y., I. J. Friedman (1969) 364 p. illus. 23 cm. (Empire State historical publications series, no. 66) 72-83479. F127. L8 W7 1969

LONG ISLAND. A sketch of the first settlement of the several towns on Long-Island; with their political condition, to the end of the American revolution. By Silas Wood. Brooklyn, N. Y., Printed by A. Spooner, 1824. 66 p. 21 cm. 21-4356. F127. L8 W79 Rare Book Coll.

— Rev. ed. Brooklyn, N. Y., A. Spooner, 1826. 111 p. 8°. 1-14160-M1. F127. L8 W8

— A new ed. Brooklyn, N. Y., Print. A. Spooner, 1828. 181, (2) p. 22 cm. 1-14161. F127. L8 W9

MADISON County. The Farm journal illustrated rural directory of Madison County (with a complete road map) Philadelphia, Wilmer Atkinson co. v. illus. 23½ cm. 17-14104. Directories

MADISON County historical society, Charter, constitution and by-laws of the. Incorporated ... 1900. Oneida, Baker & Maxon, printers, 1900. 18 p. 18½ cm. 9-27143. F127. M2 M1

MADISON County. Our country and its people; a descriptive and biographical record of Madison county; ed. by John E. Smtih. (Boston) The Boston history co., 1899. x, 649, 239 p. illus., ports., maps (1 fold.) 24½ cm. 1-22619. F127. M2 S6

MADISON County. 1806 - 1906. Biographical sketches of the Madison County bench and bar; an address by B. Fitch Tompkins ... delivered before the Madison County historical soc. ... 1911. Oneida, N. Y., The Madison County hist. soc., 1911. 41 p. 23 cm. 13-1118. F127. M2 T6

MADISON County. History of Madison County. By Mrs. L. M. Hammond. Whitney. Syracuse (N. Y.) Truair, Smith, printers, 1872. 774 p. plates, ports. 21½ cm. 1-14163. F127. M2 W6

— Syracuse, Truair, Smith, (1900) 774 p. pl., port. 8°. Jan 31, 1901-239. F127. M2 W7

MOUNT MEENAHGA, a quiet summer home ... (n. p.) 1887. 26½ cm. F127. M4 M4

MOUNT MEENAHGA a summer home in the Shawangunk Mountains ... Ellenville, N. Y., 1897. 13½ x 21½ cm. F127. M4 M44

MOUNT MEENAHGA. Ellenville, N. Y., 1903. 13½ x 21 cm. F127. M4 M45

MINISINK region. The Old Mine Road. By Charles Gilbert Hine. Introd. by Henry Charlton Beck. New Brunswick, N. J., Rutgers University Press (1963) 171 p. 21 cm. 63-15524. F127. M5 H 5 1963

MINISINK region.   Addresses delivered and papers read before the Minisink Valley historical soc., 1896.   Port Jervis, N.Y., Gazette book & job print, 1897.   (27) p.   23 cm.   7-4498.
F127. M5 M5

MINISINK region.   Minisink Valley historical society, Port Jervis. ... Collections., (Port Jervis, N.Y., Gazette job print, 1895)   45 p.   20 ½ cm.   A catalog of the deeds, papers, vols., relics, etc., in the possession of the Society.   7-30328.
F127. M5 M52

MINISINK Valley historical society.   An appeal ... (Port Jervis, N.Y., 1889)   20 ½ x 18 ½ cm.
F127. M5 M54

MINNEWASKA. Lake.   Cliff house, on Lake Minnewaska.   A. H. Smiley, proprietor ... (New York, J. J. Little) 1890.   4 l.   illus.   8°.   1-21479-M1.
F127. M53 C6

— 1894.   Minnewaska, 1894.   28 x 19 cm.
F127. M53C61

MINNEWASKA Lake.   Minnewaska, "Frozen waters"; the intimate story of the origin and growth of the Lake Minnewaska mountain houses, by Nan L. Knickerbocker.   New York, The author, 1937.
87 p.   front., plates, ports.   19 cm.   37-12255.
F127. M53 K6

MINNEWASKA mountain houses.   (Fulton, N.Y., 1887?)   14 x 19 ½ cm.
F127. M53M48

— (Minnewaska P.O.? N.Y.) 1898.   14 x 19 ½ cm.
F127. M53 M5

— 1900.   19 ½ cm.
F127. M53M52

MOHAWK Valley.directory for Canajoharie, Fonda, Fort Plain, Fultonville, Nelliston, Palatine Bridge, St. Johnsville, Sprakers (New York) ... v.1 -   1928 -   Schenectady, N.Y., H. A. Manning co., 1928 -   v.   23 ½ cm.   CA 29-327 Unrev.
Directories

MOHAWK Valley.   The bloody Mohawk, by T. Wood Clarke.   New York, The Macmillan co., 1940.
xviii, 372 p. incl. front., illus. (incl. ports., maps) 24 ½ cm.   "First printing."   Bibliography: p. 353-360.   40-7305.   F127. M55 C6

— Port Washington, N.Y., I. J. Friedman (1968)   xviii, 372 p.   illus.   24 cm.   (Empire State historical publications series, no. 53)   68-18361.
F127. M55 C6 1968

MOHAWK Valley.   The historic Mohawk, by Mary Riggs Diefendorf, with 24 illustrations.   New York and London, G. P. Putnam's sons, 1910.   xiv, 331 p.   front., plates.   21 cm.   "Principal authorities consulted": p. xiii-xiv.   10-28359.
F127. M55 D5

MOHAWK Valley.   Lure of the valley.   (1st ed.)   By Anson Getman.   New York, Pageant Press (1956)
284 p.   21 cm.   56-13120.
F127. M55 G4

MOHAWK Valley.   The old Mohawk turnpike book, by Nelson Greene ... A historical and present-day description of the Mohawk Valley, from Schenectady to Rome, traversed by this historic road ...   Fort Plain, N.Y., N. Greene, 1924.   291 p. incl. front., illus.   23 cm.   "The first ed. of this book was issued for the Mohawk Valley historic assoc."   25-15882.
F127.M55G78

MOHAWK Valley.   The story of old Fort Plain and the middle Mohawk Valley (with five maps); a review of Mohawk Valley history from 1609 ... Written, comp., and ed. by Nelson Greene.   Fort Plain, N.Y., O'Connor brothers, 1915.   xv, 399 p.   maps.   23 ½ cm.   15-20597.
F127. M55 G8

MOHAWK River.   The Mohawk, by Codman Hislop, illus. by Letterio Calapai.   New York, Rinehart (1948)   xv, 367 p.   illus., maps.   21 cm.   (Rivers of America)   Bibliography: p.339-350.   48-9184*.   F127.M55H57

MOHAWK Valley.   History of the Mohawk Valley, gateway to the West, 1614-1925; covering the six counties of Schenectady, Schoharie, Montgomery, Fulton, Herkimer and Oneida.   Ed. by Nelson

NEW YORK 133

Greene ... Chicago, The S. J. Clarke pub. co., 1925. 4 v. front., illus. (incl. maps, facsims.) ports. 28 cm.
Vols. 3-4: Biographical. 28-12480. F127.M55 H6

MOHAWK Valley. ... The Mohawk Valley and Lake Ontario, by Edward Payson Morton. Chicago, Ainsworth & co. (1913) 99 p. incl. front. (map) illus. 19 cm. (The Great Lakes series) 13-7865.
F127.M55 M8

MOHAWK Valley. The Mohawk Valley, New York, at the beginning of the 20th century. Showing its superior advantages on account of its shipping facilities and natural resources ... (New York) The New York industrial recorder, 1901. 55 p. illus. 41½ cm. Special number of the New York industrial recorder.
10-23120. F127.M55N35

MOHAWK Valley. ... Ann Lear, by L. Nelson Nichols. St. Johnsville, N.Y., Enterprise & news, 1933. 24 p. illus. 23 cm. (Tales of the early Mohawk region. no. 2) 34-1155. F127.M55 N4

MOHAWK Valley. ... Bony of Wilmurt, by L. Nelson Nichols; drawings by Calvin Ashley, jr. St. Johnsville, N.Y., Enterprise and news, 1934. 19 p. illus. 23 cm. (Tales of the early Mohawk region, no. 3) A story of the Mohawk valley of the early 19th century. 35-1793. F127.M55N42

MOHAWK Valley. ... Nick Spencer, mighty hunter, by L. Nelson Nichols. St. Johnsville, N.Y., Enterprise & News, 1932. 24 p. illus. 23 cm. (Tales of the early Mohawk region, no. 1) 35-13978.
F127.M55N43

MOHAWK Valley. ... Percival Brooder; a musical ritual in the Ilion gulf, by L. Nelson Nichols. St. Johnsville, N.Y., Enterprise and news, 1935. 28 p., illus. 23 cm. (Tales of the early Mohawk region. no. 4)
36-25880. F127.M55N44

MOHAWK Valley. The Wagner re-interment, at Fort Plain ... (Utica, 1881?) 16 p. 25½ cm.
13-18450. F127.M55 O5

— (In Transactions of Oneida historical soc., 1881-1884) 7-38332. F127.M55O52

MOHAWK Valley. The Mohawk valley, its legends and its history, by W. Max Reid; with illus. from photographs by J. Arthur Maney. New York and London, G. P. Putnam's sons, 1901. xii, 455 p. incl. pl., port. front. 25 cm. 1-26927-M2. F127.M55 R3

MOHAWK Valley. The story of old Fort Johnson, by W. Max Reid ... illus. by John Arthur Maney. New York and London, G. P. Putnam's sons, 1906. xii, 240 p. front., plates, ports. 23 cm. 6-34695.
F127.M55 R4

MOHAWK Valley. At the gateway of the Mohawk ... Schenectady railway co. (Schenectady? N.Y.) 1905. 15½ x 26 cm. F127.M55 S3

MOHAWK Valley. The upper Mohawk Valley, a land of industry; an outline of the present commercial conditions and a presentation of the future industrial possibilities of that part of the Empire state which is commonly known as the "Gateway of the West". Compiled and arranged by members of the staff ... Utica, N.Y., Utica gas & electric co., 1923. (3) - 142 p. illus. (incl. ports., plans, facsims.) 30½ cm.
23-17886. F127.M55 U8

MOHAWK Valley. Prehistoric man in the Mohawk region, by Percy M. Van Epps ... (Schenectady? N.Y.) Van Epps-Hartley chapter, New York state archeological assoc., 1935. 2 p., 9 numb. l.
27 cm. 38M5897T. F127.M55 V3

MOHAWK Valley. Stories and legends of our Indian paths. By Percy M. Van Epps ... Glenville, N.Y., Town board, 1940. 4, 50 p. front., plates. 28 cm. Reproduced from type-written copy. "Sources quoted":
4th prelim. leaf. 44-36701. F127.M55V32

MOHAWK Valley. Forts and firesides of the Mohawk country, New York; the stories and pictures of landmarks of the pre-revolutionary war period throughout the Mohawk valley and the surrounding country side, including some historic and genealogical mention during the post-war period, written by John J. Vrooman. Comp. and pub. by Elijah Ellsworth Brownell. Philadelphia, Pa., 1943. 2, vii, (4), 266 p. illus. (facsims.) plates, maps. 27½ cm. 43-18540.　　　F127.M55 V7

— (Rev. ed.) Johnstown, N.Y., Baronet Litho Co., 1951.　xv, 320 p. illus., maps. 24 cm.　Bibliography: p. 307-308.　52-137.　　　F127.M55 V7 1951

MOHAWK Valley. The romance of the valley, by Josephine Wilhelm Wickser, presented at the Family theatre, Rome, N.Y. ... 1926... (Rome? 1026)　16 p. 23 cm.　CA 26-748 Unrev.　　　F127.M55 W5

MOHONK Lake mountain house. A. K. Smiley, proprietor. New Paltz, Ulster co., New York. (n.p., 1886)　(12) p. illus. 4°. 2-5358.　　　F127.M57 M5

— (New York, Press of J. J. Little, 1893?)　15 p. illus. 27½ cm. 2-17362.　　　F127.M57M52

— (Fulton, N.Y.) 1897.　14 x 19½ cm.　　　F127.M57M53

— (Fulton, N.Y.) 1898.　19½ cm.　　　F127.M57M54

— (Fulton, N.Y., 1900?)　19½ cm.　　　F127.M57M56

MONROE County. American agriculturist farm directory and reference book, Monroe and Livingston counties, a rural directory and reference book including a road map. New York, Minneapolis (etc.) Orange Judd co.　v. illus., fold. map. 23½ cm. 17-24426.　　　Directories

MONROE county directory ...　　Rochester, Darrow, 18　v. map. 22-23cm. 39M5005T.　　　Directories

MONROE County. Abstracts of wills of Monroe county ... Copied from the original records at the surrogate's office, Rochester, N.Y. Copied and compiled by Gertrude A. Barber. (New York?) 1940-41.　2 v. 28 cm. Type-written. Contents. - v.1. 1821-1841. - v.2. 1839-1847.　42-7811.　　　F127. M6 B3

MONROE County. Moral, "Third Bull Run battle": or, The boys in blue's 1882 manual for defence of their political rights, under section 1754 and 1755 of the revised statutes of the U. S., etc. title ... (By John J. Bowen) (Rochester, N.Y., G. F. Flannery's print, 1883)　10 p. 23 cm. Reprint of three articles which appeared in the Sunday morning Tribune, of Rochester, N.Y., Feb. - March, 1883. 12-26361.　　　F127. M6 B7

MONROE County. Gazetteer and business directory of Monroe County for 1869-70. Comp. and pub. by Hamilton Child ... Syracuse, Printed at the Journal office, 1869.　419 p. 21½ cm. 9-27665.　　　F127. M6 C5

MONROE County. ... On the origin of the names of places in Monroe County. By Franklin Hanford. Scottsville, N.Y., I. Van Hooser, printer, 1911.　54 p. 17½ cm. (Publications of the Scottsville literary society. no. 5) 11-22355.　　　F127. M6 H2

MONROE County, 1821 - 1971; the sesquicentennial account of the history of Monroe County, by Howard C. Hosmer. (1st ed. Rochester, N.Y.) Rochester Museum and Science Center, 1971. 327 p. illus. 23 cm. Bibliography: p. 302. 78-31924. MARC.　　　F127. M6 H6

MONROE County. Landmarks of Monroe County ... Boston, Mass., The Boston history co., 1895. xi, 492, 103, 339 p. ports. 25½ cm. Contents. - pt. 1. A sketch of Monroe County. A sketch of Rochester. The geology of Monroe County. The bench and bar. The medical profession. The towns of Monroe County. Judges and attorneys - pt. 2. Biographical. - pt. 3. Family sketches. 1-14165.　　　F127. M6 L3

MONROE County. Pleasant Valley; an early history of Monroe County and Region, 1650 - 1850. By Florence Lee. New York, Carlton Press (1970)　321 p. 21 cm. (A Hearthstone book)　　　F127. M6 L4

MONROE County. ... History of Monroe County, New York; with illustrations descriptive of its scenery, palatial residences, public buildings, fine blocks, and important manufactories ... Philadelphia, Everts, Ensign & Everts, 1877. vi, (7) - 320 p. illus., cxxxvi pl. (part double; incl. front., ports., maps) 36 x 30 cm. 1-14166.
F127. M6 M2

MONROE County. The struggle for Monroe county, by Howard L. Osgood. Read before the Rochester historical society ... 1892. (Rochester, 1892) (4) p. 24 cm. CA 34-1582 Unrev. F127. M6 O8

MONROE County. History of Rochester and Monroe County, from the earliest historic times to the beginning of 1907, by William F. Peck ... also biographical sketches of some of the more prominent citizens of Rochester and Monroe County. New York and Chicago, The Pioneer pub. co., 1908. 2 v. front., plates, ports., maps. 29½ x 23½ cm. Paged continuously. v. 1: viii, (5) - 706 p.; v. 2: xi, (711) - 1433 p. 8-19288. L. C. copy replaced by microfilm.
F127. M6 P3
Microfilm 22826 F

MONTGOMERY County. A descriptive geography of Montgomery county, with historical explanations and notes ... Amsterdam, N.Y., Daily democrat print, 1892. 63 p. 16°. 1-14167-M1.
F127. M7 B2

MONTGOMERY County. Gazetteer and business directory of Montgomery and Fulton counties, for 1869-70. Comp. and pub. by Hamilton Child ... Syracuse, Printed at the Journal office, 1870. 315 p. incl. front. (fold. map) 21½ cm. 15-23155.
F127. M7 C5

MONTGOMERY County. The Rev. James Dempster's record of marriages and baptisms in vicinity of Tryon County, 1778 - 1803. By James Dempster. (Albany? 1918?) 3, 35 numb. l. 27 cm. Type-written copy. 18-20066.
F127. M7 D3

MONTGOMERY County. ... History of Montgomery and Fulton counties, with illus. ... and portraits of old pioneers and prominent residents. New York, F. W. Beers, 1878. 252 p. illus. (incl. maps) plates, ports. 36 x 30½ cm. 1-14168. L. C. copy replaced by microfilm.
F127. M7 H6
Microfilm 21172 F

MONTGOMERY County Historical Society. Transactions. Amsterdam, N.Y. v. illus. 23 cm. annual. 57-54514.
F127. M7 M7

MONTGOMERY County Historical Society. Year book. 1904 - (Amsterdam, N.Y.) v. 15 cm. 57-53569.
F127. M7M713

MONTGOMERY County. The minute book of the Committee of safety of Tryon County, the old New York frontier, now printed verbatim for the first time; with an introd. by J. Howard Hanson, and notes by Samuel Ludlow Frey. New York, Dodd, Mead, 1905. 4, vii-xv p., 2 l., 151 p. front., 14 pl. map, facsim. 25 cm. 5-40356.
F127. M7 T8

NASSAU County. Non-whites in suburbia; an analysis of population changes in Nassau County, 1960-1965. New York (1966?) iv, 46 l. 29 cm. 78-633698.
F127.N2 A53

NASSAU County. 1930 commercial survey of metropolitan Long Island, compiled expressly for the Nassau daily review, Rockville Centre, New York, by Harry G. Hall ... (Mineola, L. I., Printed by the Davenport press, 1930) 63, (9) p. incl. front. (port.) illus., maps, diagrs. 20½ cm. On cover: Metropolitan Long Island, prophets and profits. 30-4541.
F127. N2 H2

NASSAU County. The family guide to Long Island. By Louis Kruh. Garden City, N.Y., Context Pub. Corp. (1967) 90 p. 21 cm.
F127. N2 K7

NASSAU County. The Nassau County historical journal. (Uniondale, etc., N.Y., Nassau County Historical and Genealogical Society) v. in illus., ports. 23 - 27 cm. Semiannual. Began publication in 1937. 58-30748.
F127. N2 N3

NASSAU County.   The story of the five towns: Inwood, Lawrence, Cedarhurst, Woodmere, and Hewlett, Nassau county, Long island.   Compiled by workers of the W.P.A. ...   (Rockville Centre, N.Y.) The Nassau daily review-star (1941)   2, 3-70 p.   illus.   23½ cm.   (American guide series)   42-9285.
F127. N2 W7

NIAGARA County.   The Niagara County directory for 1895/6   Newburgh, N.Y., L. P. Waite, 1895.   1 v.   24 cm.   8-25421.
Directories

NIAGARA County.   The Niagara County directory and real estate record ... 3d ed.   Lockport, N.Y., Roberts brothers co., 1908.   1 v.   fold. map.   24½ cm.   8-21943.
Directories

NIAGARA County Historical Society.   Occasional contributions.   no. 1 -   Lockport, N.Y., 1948 -   illus.   26 cm.
F127. N5 N5

NIAGARA County.   Outpost of empires; a short history of Niagara County, by John Aiken (and others) Maps by Robert Wilhelms, etc., etc.   Phoenix, N.Y., F. E. Richards, 1961.   152 p.   23 x 29 cm.
F127. N5 A6

NIAGARA County.   ... History of Niagara county, with illustrations descriptive of its scenery, private residences, public buildings, fine blocks, and important manufactories, and portraits of old pioneers and prominent residents.   New York, Sanford & co., 1878.   397 p.   illus., plates (part double) ports.   30½ x 24 cm.   1-14169.
F127. N5 H6
Microfilm 21049 F

NIAGARA County.   News of the day - yesterday (by) Donald E. Loker.   Original drawings by Barbara Whitman Torrence.   Special pref. by John and Michael Walsh.   (Lockport, N.Y.) Niagara County Hist. Soc., 1971.   xi, 94 p.   illus.   26 cm.   (Occasional contributions of the Niagara County Historical Society, no. 20) 77-31207 MARC.
F127. N5 N5 no. 20

NIAGARA County.   Landmarks of Niagara County; ed. by William Pool.   (Syracuse) D. Mason, 1897. vi, 447, 254 p. front., ports. 25½ cm.   "Part II. Biographical. Part III. Family sketches"   1-2540.
F127. N5 P 8

NIAGARA County.   Biographical and portrait cyclopedia of Niagara county.   Ed. by Samuel T. Wiley and W. Scott Garner.   Illus.   Philadelphia, Richmond, Ind. (etc.) Gresham pub. co., 1892. (v) - xiii, (7)-640 (i.e. 632) p. incl. illus., plates, ports.   plates, ports.   28 cm.   Errors in paging: numbers 173-4, 333-4, 373-4, 511-12 omitted.   2-19055 Rev.
F127. N5 W6

NIAGARA County ... a concise record of her progress and people, 1821 - 1921, pub. during its centennial year.   Written by ... Edward T. Williams ... Chicago, J. H. Beers (1921)   2 v.   front., plates, ports.   28 cm.   Paged continuously.   Contents. - I. Historical. - II. Biographical.   22-8324.
F127. N5 W7

NIAGARA River.   ... The river Niagara.   Descriptive and historical.   Pan-American ed.   By Barton Atkins.   Buffalo, N.Y. (Matthews-Northrup co., printers) 1899.   44 p. incl. front., illus. 16½ cm.   19-13704.
F127. N6 A8

NIAGARA Valley.   Address on the early reminiscences of western New-York and the lake region of country.   Delivered before the Young men's association of Buffalo ... By James L. Barton.   Buffalo, Press of Jewett, Thomas, 1848.   69 p.   23½ cm.   17-22191.
F127.N6 B 28
Toner Coll.

— (2d ed.)   1848.   69 p.   23½ cm.   3-5059.
F127. N6 B 3
Rare Book Coll.

NIAGARA River.   The Niagara.   By Donald Braider.   (1st ed.)   New York, Holt, Rinehart, and Winston (1972)   xvii, 294 p.   illus.   21 cm.   (Rivers of America)   Bibliography: p. 277-278.   76-155505 MARC.   F127. N6 B 7

NIAGARA River.   Sketches of Niagara falls and river.   By Cousin George (pseud. for George William Clinton)   Illus. with numerous engravings and correct maps.   Buffalo, W.B. & C.E. Peck, 1846. viii, (9) - 142 p. incl. front., illus.   plates.   16 x 13 cm.   (Cousin George's series)   Issued without maps.   Buffalo historical society, Publications, v. 6, p. 595.   46-41028.
F127. N6 C5
Rare Book Coll.

NIAGARA frontier. Niagara's frontier, without a soldier and without a gun. By Sir Angus Fletcher. New York, Newcomen Society of England, American Branch, 1948. 28 p. illus. 23 cm. Newcomen address delivered at New York, Jan. 8, 1948. "First printing." 49-3381*
F127.N6 F58

NIAGARA frontier. Someone has been here before you, by Emma Gibbons. (Buffalo, 1938) 3, 11-134 p. front., illus. 19½ cm. 38-14746.
F127. N6 G5

NIAGARA frontier. Niagara country. By Lloyd Graham. New York, Duell, Sloan & Pearce (1949) xiii, 321 p. map. 22 cm. (American folkways) "1st printing." 49-9928*.
F127. N6 G7

NIAGARA frontier. Thundergate; the forts of Niagara. By Robert West Howard. Englewood Cliffs, N.J., Prentice-Hall (1968) xiii, 241 p. illus. 24 cm. (The American forts series) 68-16321.
F127. N6 H6 1968

NIAGARA River. The Niagara River, by Archer Butler Hulbert ... With maps and illustrations. New York and London, G. P. Putnam's sons, 1908. xiii, 319 p. front., plates, ports., maps (1 fold.) plans. 25 cm. 8-29355.
F127. N6 H8

NIAGARA Valley. Stories of old Niagara; being a reprint of a series of articles recently published in newspapers and designed to familiarize the public, particularly school children, with the romantic struggles of those early pioneers whose untiring efforts laid the foundation for the Niagara frontier and the America which we know today. By Claud H. Hultzen, sr ... pub. by Old Fort Niagara assoc., inc. ... (Niagara Falls, N.Y., Power city press) 1928. 31 p. incl. front., illus. 23 cm. 28-17736.
F127.N6 H85

NIAGARA River. The river Niagara, by Donald Lashelle. Limited ed. Buffalo, N.Y., Hammond press, 1938. 2, (3) - 64 p. illus. (incl. map) 20 cm. "The river Niagara" (poem): p. 14-46. 38-17337.
F127. N6 L3

NIAGARA Valley. Bressani - Tonti - Busti, three Italians in the history of Niagara frontier. (By Ferdinand Magnani) Buffalo, N.Y., 1931. 15 p. incl. illus., ports., map. 21 cm. 31-11350.
F127.N6 M19

NIAGARA Valley. The Niagara frontier: embracing sketches of its early history, and Indian, French and English local names. Read before the Buffalo historical club ... by Orsamus H. Marshall. (Buffalo, J. Warren, printers, 1865) 46 p. 23 cm. L. C. copy replaced by microfilm. 1-14170.
F127. N6 M3
Microfilm 27600 F

— (Buffalo) 1881. 37 p. 24 cm. "Reprinted .. from the Pubs. of the Buffalo hist. soc." 17-14600. F127.N6M314

NIAGARA River. Historical sketches and local names of the Niagara frontier. By O. H. Marshall. (Albany, J. Munsell's sons, 1887?) 46 p. 22 x 18 cm. First ed., Buffalo, 1865, pub. under title: The Niagara frontier. 8-27833.
F127.N6 M32

NIAGARA River. For all girls and boys who ask "Is it really true?" ... by Lou Harriet Metz. Buffalo, N.Y., Otto Ulbrich co., 1938. (95) p. illus. 19½ x 24½ cm. 38-13381.
F127. N6 M5

NIAGARA County. Souvenir history of Niagara County, commemorative of the 25th anniversary of the Pioneer association of Niagara County. (Lockport, The Lockport journal) 1902. 228 p. illus. 34 cm. 12-24153.
F127.N6 N57

NIAGARA frontier. The Niagara frontier landmarks association; a record of its work; ed. by George Douglas Emerson. Buffalo, N.Y., The Association, 1906. 4, 153 p. front., plates, ports. 25½ cm. 6-27345.
F127. N6 N6

NIAGARA Valley. The Niagara frontier; data compiled and arranged for the Niagara frontier society of New York, and presented to the members of the society, by William P. Mahoney ... Albany, N.Y., Boyd printing co. (1923) v, 95 p. front., illus., maps (part fold.) 25½ cm. Bibliography: p. 82-91. 24-4780.
F127.N6 N65

NIAGARA Valley. American Niagara frontier in war of 1812 ... Public and private property damaged by the British from Buffalo to Fort Niagara. By Peter A. Porter ... (n.p., 1915?)   (4) p. 23 cm.
18-8369.   F127.N6 P 75

NIAGARA River. How lake commerce began. La Salle's visits to the Niagara. By Peter A. Porter ... Niagara Falls, N.Y. (1914?)   31 p. illus. 24 cm. 33-17564.   F127.N6 P 78
Rare Book Coll.

NIAGARA Valley. Landmarks on the Niagara frontier; a chronology, by Peter A. Porter. Niagara Falls, 1914.   69 p. illus. (incl. plans) fold. map. 23½ cm. 14-14158.   F127. N6 P 8

NIAGARA Valley. A short history of the Niagara portage. By Josiah Boardman Scovell. (Lewiston, N.Y.) Rotary Club of Lewiston, New York (and) Queenston, Ontario, 1951.   21 p. illus., port. 22 cm.
51-30011.   F127. N6 S 4

NIAGARA Valley. An old frontier of France; the Niagara region and adjacent lakes under French control, by Frank H. Severance ... New York, Dodd, Mead, 1917.   2 v. fronts., illus., plates, ports., maps, plans, facsims. 24 cm. 17-13293.   F127.N6 S 49

NIAGARA frontier. An old frontier of France; (the Niagara region and adjacent lakes under French control. By Frank Hayward Severance. New York) Arno Press (1971)   xvii, 436, x, 485 p. illus. 23 cm. (The First American frontier) Reprint of the 1917 ed. Includes bibliographical references. 77-146421 MARC.   F127.N6 S 49

NIAGARA Valley. Old trails on the Niagara frontier, by Frank H. Severance. Buffalo, N.Y. (The Matthews-Northrup co.) 1899.   xii p., 321 p. incl. front. 20½ cm. 99-4771 Rev.   F127. N6 S 5

— 2d ed. Cleveland, The Burrows brothers co., 1903.   xii, 270 p. front. (fold. map) 23 cm. 3-4991.   F127. N6 S 51

NIAGARA, Fort. The story of Joncaire, his life and times on the Niagara, by Frank H. Severance. Buffalo, 1906.   viii, 135 p. 25½ cm. 50 copies printed. 6-25622.   F127.N6 S 53

NIAGARA, Fort. A short history and description of Fort Niagara, with an account of its importance to Great Britain. Written by an English prisoner, 1758. With a view of the fort. Ed. by Paul Leicester Ford. Brooklyn, Historical printing club, 1890.   18 p. pl. 17½ cm. (Winnowings in American history. New York colonial series. no. 1) Reprinted from the Royal magazine, Sept., 1759. 3-27393.   F127. N6 S 6

NIAGARA Valley. A child's story of the Niagara frontier, by Alice C. A. Williams. (Buffalo and New York city) Priv. print. (The Whitney-Graham co., inc.) 1932.   172 p. incl. front. (map) illus. 21½ cm.
32-10946.   F127. N6 W6

NIAGARA Valley. Niagara frontier; a narrative and documentary history, by Merton M. Wilner ... Chicago, The S. J. Clarke pub. co., 1931.   4 v. front., illus., plates, ports., maps, plans. 27 cm. Vols. I-II paged continuously. "The narrative portion is expanded from The story of Buffalo, pub. in daily installments during 1929-30 by the Buffalo evening news." Vols. III-IV are biographical. "Authorities" at end of each chapter of vol. I-II. 31-11472.   F127.N6 W 74

NIAGARA, Fort. Historic forts. By David H. Young. (1895)   F127. N6 Y6

NIAGARA FALLS. Album of the table rock, Niagara falls and sketches of the falls and scenery adjacent. Buffalo, Press of Jewett, Thomas & co., 1848.   v, (7) - 85, 22 p. 19 cm. Also pub. with the title: Table rock album, and sketches of the falls and scenery adjacent. 1-14286.   F127. N8 A4
Rare Book Coll.

NIAGARA FALLS. Table rock album, and sketches of the falls ... 3d ed., with additions. Buffalo, Jewett, Thomas, 1850.   v, (7) - 108 p. 18½ cm. 1-14292. See above item.   F127.N8 A43

NIAGARA FALLS. Allen's illustrated guide to Niagara ... Buffalo, 1883.   18½ cm.
  F127.N8 A47

NIAGARA FALLS. American library association. ... 25th annual conference.... 1903. (Niagara

NEW YORK

Falls? 1903)   (50) p. illus. (incl. ports., plan) 27 cm.   4-33410.   F127. N8 A5

NIAGARA FALLS from uncommon points of view. (By William Cushing Bamburgh) New York, The Phoenix art pub. co., 1893.   18 l.   18 phot.   sq. 16º.   1-14172-M1.   F127. N8 B 1

NIAGARA FALLS. Descriptions of Niagara; selected from various travellers; with original additions by William Barham ... Gravesend (Eng.) The compiler (1847)   180 p. illus. (map) 2 pl. (incl. front.) 23 cm.
1-14287.   F127. N8 B 3

NIAGARA FALLS. The red book of Niagara; a comprehensive guide to the scientific, historical and scenic aspects of Niagara for the use of travellers, by Irving P. Bishop ... with many illustrations, index and maps. Buffalo, N.Y., The Wenborne-Sumner co., 1901.   117, (3) p. incl. front., illus. fold. map.
20 cm.   "References": p. 115. 1-23746.   F127. N8 B 6

— Rev. and enl. ed. ... Buffalo, N.Y., C. A. Wenborne, 1907.   119, (5) p. incl. front., illus. 18½ cm.
"References": p. 119. 7-27372.   F127. N8 B 7

NIAGARA FALLS. Blondin; hero of Niagara (by) Richard A. Boning. Illus. by Jim Sharpe. Baldwin, N.Y., Dexter & Westbrook (1972)   47 p. col. illus. 24 cm. (The incredible series) 70-185887 MARC.
                                                                                                                     F127. N8 B 74

NIAGARA FALLS. Niagara, the unconquered ... Buffalo, Niagara & eastern power corporation. (Buffalo, N.Y., Baker, Jones, Hausauer, inc., 1929)   (27) p. illus. 21 cm. 37M918T.
                                                                                                                     F127. N8 B 76

NIAGARA FALLS. Description of a view of the falls of Niagara, now exhibiting at the Panorama, Leicester square. Painted by the proprietor Robert Burford, from drawings taken by him in the autumn of 1832. London, Printed by T. Brettell, 1833.   12 p. fold. front. (plan) 21 cm. 1-14288 Rev.
                                                                                                                     F127. N8 B 8
                                                                                                                     Rare Book Coll.

— 1834.   12 p. fold. front. 22½ cm. 4-27007.   F127. N8 B 82
                                                                                                                     Rare Book Coll.

NIAGARA FALLS. Burke's descriptive guide; or, The visitors' companion to Niagara Falls: its strange and wonderful localities. By an old resident ... Buffalo, A. Burke, 1850.   (2), 107 p. front.,
illus., fold. map. 15 cm. 3-23022.   F127. N8 B 88
                                                                                                                     Rare Book Coll.

— (1856)   128 (i.e. 126) p. front., illus., fold. plates, fold. map. 15 cm. "Enlarged edition." Error in paging: numbers 35-36 omitted. 1-14173.   F127. N8 B 9
                                                                                                                     Rare Book Coll.

NIAGARA FALLS. ... The Falls of Niagara, their evolution and varying relations to the Great Lakes; characteristics of the power, and the effects of its diversion, by Joseph William Winthrop Spencer ... 1905-6. Ottawa, Printed by S. E. Dawson, 1907.   xxxi, 490, 4 p. incl. front., illus., plates, maps (partly fold.) fold. map. 25 cm. Canada, Department of mines, Geological survey branch ... GS 8-254.
                                                                                                                     F127. N8 C2

NIAGARA FALLS. Convention and protocol between Canada and the United States regarding the Niagara Falls and the Niagara River. Signed at Ottawa, Jan. 2, 1929. Ottawa, F. A. Acland, printer, 1929.   19 p. incl. tables. fold. pl., 2 fold. diagr. 25 cm. 29-10281.   F127. N8 C26

NIAGARA FALLS. The reservation of Niagara. An address delivered at the celebration of the opening of the Niagara reservation at Niagara Falls ... 1885, by James C. Carter. (n.p.) 1885.
16 p. 28½ cm. 3-28496.   F127. N8 C3

NIAGARA FALLS. ... The menace to Niagara, by Dr. John M. Clarke ... (New York? 1905?)
p. (489) - 504. illus. 23½ cm. Reprinted from the Popular science monthly, April 1905.   F127. N8 C6

NIAGARA FALLS.   Falls of Niagara, as seen from the Table Rock, Oct., 1834.   A poem ... By William H. Coyle)   Jacksonville, Printed by C. Goudy, 1835.   16 p.   22½ cm.   16-20059.

    F127. N8 C8
    Toner Coll.

NIAGARA FALLS.   Cutter's Guide to Niagara falls, and adjacent points of interest ... (Charles Cutter)   (Niagara Falls? N.Y.) Cutter's guide pub. co. (1897)   98, (2) p. incl. illus., plates.   15 x 23 cm.   44-30427.

    F127. N8 C85

NIAGARA FALLS.   A guide to the falls of Niagara.   By J. De Tevoli.   With a splendid lithographic view by A. Vaudricourt...   New York, Burgess, Stringer, 1846.   15 p. pl.   8°.   1-14174-M1.

    F127. N8 D37
    Rare Book Coll.

NIAGARA FALLS.   The falls of Niagara, or Tourist's guide to this wonder of nature, including notices of the whirlpool, island, etc. and a complete guide thro' the Canadas ... By S. De Veaux.   Buffalo, W. B. Hayden, 1839.   viii, (17) - 168 p. front. (map) plates.   16 cm.   1-14175 Rev.   F127. N8 D4

NIAGARA FALLS.   Anthology and bibliography of Niagara Falls, by Charles Mason Dow ... Pub. by the state of New York.   Albany, J. B. Lyon co., printers, 1921.   2 v. fronts. (v.1, port.) plates (3 col.) maps, fold. chart. 23 cm.   "List of bibliographies": v.1, p. 11-13.   21-27296.   F127. N8 D55

NIAGARA FALLS.   The state reservation at Niagara, a history, by Charles M. Dow, commissioner State reservation at Niagara, 1898-1914, president of the Commission, 1903-1914.   Albany, J. B. Lyon co., printers, 1914.   202 p.   23 cm.   GS 14-817.   F127. N8 D7

NIAGARA FALLS.   Niagara, the picture book of the Falls.   By Joseph P. Driscoll.   Buffalo, Birchwood Books, 1954.   64 p. (chiefly illus.)   28 cm.   55-18657.   F127. N8 D75

NIAGARA FALLS.   New guide and key to Niagara Falls, pub. for the convenience and guidance of tourists and visitors.   The information conveyed in this guide is authentic and taken from official sources and is therefore accurate and reliable.   Niagara Falls, N.Y., Buffalo, N.Y., John Edbauer, 1920.   72 p. illus. (incl. map) 18½ cm.   20-14448.   F127. N8 E2

— Buffalo, N.Y., 1926.   80 p. illus. (incl. plan) fold. col. pl.   19 cm.   29-14024.

    F127. N8 E2
    1926

NIAGARA FALLS.   The falls of Niagara: being a complete guide to all the points of interest around and in the immediate neighbourhood of the great cataract.   With views taken from sketches by Washington Friend, and from photographs.   London, New York (etc.) T. Nelson, (etc., etc.) 1858.   (v) - vi, (7) - 64 p. illus., 12 col. pl. (incl. front.) map. 14½ cm.   7-18008.   F127. N8 F1

— New York, T. Nelson and sons; Toronto, J. Campbell (187-?)   40 p. illus., 12 pl. 11 x 16½ cm.   16-17956.   F127. N8 F16

NIAGARA FALLS.   The falls of Niagara, by Glenn C. Forrester.   New York, D. Van Nostrand, (1928)   xiii, 155 p. front., illus. (incl. maps) plates, fold. tab. 23 cm.   "Reading references": p. 155.   28-16220.   F127. N8 F7

NIAGARA FALLS.   The history of the Niagara River, by Grove Karl Gilbert.   Extracted from the sixth annual report of the Commissioners of the state reservation at Niagara, for the year 1889.   Albany, J. B. Lyon, printer, 1890.   (61) - 84 p. plates. 23 cm.   "... the substance of a lecture read to the American assoc. for the advancement of science at its Toronto meeting, Aug. 1889."   4-36326.   F127. N8 G4

NIAGARA FALLS.   Niagara Falls and their history.   By G. K. Gilbert.   1895.   1 v.

    F127. N8 G45

NIAGARA FALLS.   ... Rate of recession of Niagara Falls, by Grove Karl Gilbert, accompanied by a report on the survey of the crest, by W. Carvel Hall.   Washington, Gov't print. off., 1907.   31, v p.   illus, xi pl. (partly fold.) diagrs. 23½ cm. (U.S. Geological survey. Bulletin no. 306) Issued also as House doc. no. 59, 59th Cont., 2d sess.   GS 7-163.   F127. N8 G46

NEW YORK 141

NIAGARA FALLS. A little guide to Niagara falls containing a brief description of the principal points of interest ... and a program for a two weeks' visit, by an old resident (James Fraser Gluck) ... Buffalo and New York, Matthews, Northrup, 1890. 44 p. incl. front., illus. (map) plates. 18 cm. 1-14176 Rev.
F127. N8 G5

NIAGARA FALLS. ... Greater Niagara. (Tourist's ed.) Niagara Falls, N. Y., and Niagara Falls, Ont., Mrs. S. D. Morse, 1896. 40 p. illus. (incl. ports.) 23 cm. 1-14289 Rev.
F127. N8 G7

NIAGARA FALLS in 1907; a paper read before the American civic association at the annual convention, Providence, R. I. ... by Francis V. Greene ... Niagara Falls, Ontario power co. of Niagara Falls (1907) 5 - 59 p. illus. 26 cm. 8-1470.
F127.N8 G88

NIAGARA FALLS. Free Niagara. By James W. Greene. Buffalo, N. Y., Matthews, Northrup (1885) 26 p. incl. front., illus., map. 4°. 1-14177-M1.
F127. N8 G9

NIAGARA FALLS. Niagara (by) Ralph Greenhill and Thomas D. Mahoney. Toronto, University of Toronto Press, 1969. 184 p. 29 cm.
F127.N8 G93

NIAGARA FALLS. ... Hackstaff's new guide book of Niagara Falls ... Niagara Falls, W. E. Tunis, 1853. 80 p. incl. illus., 5 pl. front. (fold. map) 16½ cm. 17-12324.
F127.B8 H14

NIAGARA FALLS: their physical changes, and the geology and topography of the surrounding country. By James Hall ... Boston (1844) 30 p. diagrs. 24 cm. (From the Boston journal of natural history) 1-22668.
F127. N8 H2

NIAGARA FALLS. The condition of Niagara Falls, and the measures needed to preserve them. Eight letters published in the New York Evening post, the New York tribune, and the Boston daily advertiser, during the summer of 1882. By J. B. Harrison. New York (Cambridge, J. Wilson) 1882. 62 p. 23 cm. Appendix: Extracts from Harper's weekly, N. Y. herald, N. Y. tribune and the Nation. 3-6083.
F127. N8 H3

NIAGARA FALLS. The falls of Niagara, with supplementary chapters on the other famous cataracts of the world. By George W. Holley ... New-York, A. C. Armstrong, 1883. xv, 183 p. front., illus., plates, port., map. 22 x 16 cm. First pub. 1872 under title: Niagara: its history and geology, etc. 1-14178 Rev.
F127. N8 H7

NIAGARA FALLS. Niagara: its history and geology, incidents and poetry ... By George W. Holley. New York city, Sheldon and co. (etc.) 1872. xii, (13) - 165 p. plates, fold. map. 18 cm. Enlarged edition pub. 1883 under title: The falls of Niagara, with supplementary chapters ... 1-14179 Rev.
F127. N8 H8

— 2d ed. New York city, Sheldon and co. (etc.) 1872. xii, (13) - 165 p. plates, fold. map. 17½ cm. 39-32922.
F127. N8 H8
1872 a

NIAGARA FALLS. How to see Niagara ... (Buffalo & New York, Matthews, Northrup, 1889) (42) p. illus. 15 x 23 cm. 5-32161.
F127. N8 H81

NIAGARA FALLS. By Robert West Howard. New York, F. Watts (1969) 90 p. illus. 23 cm. (A First book) 78-80012.
F127.N8H812

NIAGARA FALLS. Every man his own guide to the falls of Niagara, or The whole story in a few words ... To which is added a chronological table, containing the principal events of the late war between the United States and Great Britain. By (T. G. Hulett, a resident at the falls. 4th ed. Buffalo, Printed by Faxon & co., 1844. viii, (9) - 128 p. illus., 4 pl. (incl. front.) 2 maps (1 fold.) 18-7514.
F127. H8H817
Rare Book Coll.

NIAGARA FALLS. Every stranger his own guide to Niagara Falls ... By W. Hulett. Buffalo, Steele's press, 1845. 35 p. pl. 24°. 1-14181-M1.
F127.N8 H82
Rare Book Coll.

NIAGARA FALLS. Immortal Niagara, official guide book. (Buffalo, 1950) 48 p. illus., maps. 22 cm. "Sponsored by Niagara Falls Chamber of Commerce." 50-55696.
F127. N8 I 5

875

142   LOCAL HISTORIES IN THE LIBRARY OF CONGRESS

NIAGARA FALLS.   They dared Niagara.   By Adi-Kent Thomas Jeffrey.   Illus. by Jack Breslow. Chicago, Follett Pub. Co. (1968)   58 p.   illus.   23 cm.   (Interesting reading series)   68-14101.
                                                                                                                                                                                              F127. N8 J 43

NIGARAR FALLS.   A guide for every visitor to Niagara falls.   Including the sources of Niagara, and all places of interest, both on the American and Canada side ... Also a description of several routes ..
By Frederick H. Johnson.   Rochester, D. M. Dewey (1852)   viii, (9)-144 p.   8 pl. (incl. front.)   map.
14 cm.   1-14183 Rev.   F127. N8 J 7
                                                                                                                                                                            Rare Book Coll.

NIAGARA FALLS.   Guide to Niagara falls and its scenery, including all the points of interest, etc. Geology and recession of the falls by Sir Charles Lyell ... By Frederick H. Johnson ... Philadelphia, G. W. Childs, 1863.   65 p.   front., plates.   15 cm.   1-14184 Rev.   F127. N8 J 8
                                                                                                                                                                           Rare Book Coll.

— (Buffalo, 1868)   80 p.   pl.   16°.   1-14185-M1.   F127. N8 J 9

NIAGARA FALLS.   Niagara; its history, incidents and poetry.   By R. L. Johnson.   1898.
1 v.   8°.   F127. N8 J 91

NIAGARA FALLS.   Miniatures of Niagara Falls.   (By Tom Jones)   (Cincinnati, O., 1904)
8 x 10 ½ cm.   F127. N8 J 94

NIAGARA FALLS.   Pleasure travel made easy.   A better way to see old sights or new ... By J. Addison Kingsbury.   Pittsburgh, Pa.   (Allegheny Valley railroad company) 1884.   . v. 6 ½ x 10 ½ cm.
1-23626 Add.   F127. N8 K5

— Pittsburgh, Pa. (Allegheny Valley railroad co.) 1885.   v. 1 illus., maps.   7 x 10 ½ cm.   1-23627 Add.
                                                                                                                                                                   F127. N8 K51

NIAGARA FALLS.   Niagara - river of fame.   Stamford, Ont., Kiwanis Club.   Toronto, Printed by Ryerson Press, 1968.   231-388 p.   illus.   25 cm.   "Consists of 160 p. with 262 pictures from the River section of 'Niagara Falls, Canada - a history.'"   72-178529 MARC.   F127. N8 K54

NIAGARA FALLS.   Reports upon the existing water-power situation at Niagara Falls, so far as concerns the diversion of water on the American side, by the American members of the International waterways commission and Captain Charles W. Kutz, corps of engineers, U. S. army.   Washington, Gov't print. off., 1906.   28 p.   23 cm.   6-35029.   F127. N8 K9

NIAGARA FALLS.   The great cataract illustrated.   And complete guide to all points of interest at and in the vicinity of the falls of Niagara ... (Ed. R. Lespinasse)   Chicago, R. Lespinasse, 1884.
96 p. inlc. front., illus. (incl. ports., maps) 20 cm.   1-14186 Rev.   F127. N8 L6

NIAGARA FALLS.   Notes on Niagara.   Illustrated.   Pub. R. Lespinasse.   Chicago, R. Lespinasse, 1883.   184 p. incl. front., illus., maps, daigrs. pl. 32 cm. Excerpts from Houghton's "Niagara and other poems", Hardy's "Through cities and prairie lands", Dickens' "American notes", etc.   1-14187.   F127. N8 L7

NIAGARA FALLS.   Niagara power.   Niagara shore real estate.   Long & Long.   *(1891)
1 v.   F127. N8 L8

NIAGARA FALLS.   Maid of the mist, and famous Niagara news stories (by) C. O. Lewis (and others) Niagara Falls, Ont., Kiwanis Club of Stamford, 1971.   28 p.   illus.   25 cm.   71-884537 MARC.
                                                                                                                                                              F127. N8 M35

NIAGARA FALLS.   Visit to the falls of Niagara in 1800.   (By John Maude)   London, Longman, Rees, Orme, Brown & Green, 1826.   viii, v, 313, xxvi p.   plates.   24 cm.   Comprising a journey from New York city to Niagara Falls, Kingston, Montreal, and Quebec.   1-14188 Rev.   F127. N8 M 4

NIAGARA FALLS.   Album of the Table rock, Niagara Falls, C. W., and sketches of the falls, etc.

NEW YORK

Ed. by Geo. Menzies. Niagara, Printed at the Chronicle office, 1846. v, (7) - 79, iv, (5) - 24 p. 18 cm.
17-10084.
F127.N8 M55
Toner Coll.

NIAGARA FALLS. From city to surf. Compliments Passenger department, Michigan central railroad. "The Niagara Falls route." Chicago, Rand, McNally & co., printers, 1888. 104 p. front. (fold. map) illus. 26 cm. 1-16823.
F127. N8 M6

NIAGARA FALLS. The fairy isle of Mackinac ... Compliments of the Passenger dept., Michigan central railroad ... Chicago, Rand, McNally, printers (1888) 48 p. incl. illus., maps. 26 cm. (With above item) 1-16822.
F127. N8 M6

NIAGARA FALLS in miniature ... (Michigan central railroad co.) Chicago, Rand, McNally, 1896. (28) p. incl. col. front., col. illus. (incl. map) 16 cm. 1-14290.
F127.N8 M62

— Chicago, 1903. 16½ cm.
F127.N8 M67

NIAGARA FALLS. Historic Niagara falls, corroborated by information gleaned from various sources. By James C. Morden ... Pub. under the direction of the Lundy's lane historical soc. ... Niagara Falls, Can., Lindsay press, ltd., 1932. 2, 117 p. front., plates, ports., map. 23½ cm. 33-11595.
F127. N8 M8

NIAGARA FALLS. ... Preservation of Niagara Falls ... Petition from the National society of colonial dames of America in the District of Columbia, praying for the preservation of Niagara Falls, with indorsements from several states. (Washington, Gov't print. off., 1906) 8 p. 23 cm. (U.S. 59th Cong., 1st sess. Senate. Doc. 217) 6-16721 Add.
F127. N8 N27

NIAGARA FALLS. Niagara and Chautauqua. (By Samuel B. Newton) Compliments of Western New York and Pennsylvania railroad. Buffalo, N.Y., Wenborne-Sumner co. (1891) (106) p. incl. pl., map. front. obl. 24°. 1-21499-M1.
F127. N8 N4

NIAGARA FALLS. What can I see? and how much will it cost me in two days at Niagara Falls. New York, New York central & Hudson river R. R. co. (1894) folder (4 l.) 2-7217.
F127.N8 N48

NIAGARA FALLS. New York (State) Commissioners of the state reservation of Niagara. Annual report. (1st - (1883/4) - 19 Albany, (1885) - 19 v. in illus., plates, maps (part fold.) plans. 22½ - 23½ cm. "A partial bibliography of Niagara falls, compiled by Daniel C. Haskell ...": 29th report (1911/12) p. 49-98. 1-14189.
F127. N8 N5

NIAGARA FALLS. New York (State) Special report of New York State survey on the preservation of the scenery of Niagara Falls, and Fourth annual report on the triangulation of the state. For the year 1879. Albany, C. Van Benthuysen, 1880. 4, (7) - 96 p. xi pl. (1 fold.) 5 fold. maps, facsim. (3 l., double pl.) 24½ cm. (its Fourth report) 1-22121.
F127.N8 N51

NIAGARA FALLS. Supplemental report of the Commissioners of the state reservation at Niagara. Albany, The Argus co., printers, 1887. 50 p. fold. map. 23½ cm. 3-29139 Rev.
F127.N8 N52

NIAGARA FALLS. Niagara. (Portland, Maine, L. H. Nelson co., 1909) (48) p. illus. 20 x 25 cm.
F127.N8 N57

NIAGARA FALLS. The Niagara book; a complete souvenir of Niagara falls, containing sketches, stories and essays ... By W. D. Howells, Mark Twain (pseud.) and others. Fully illus. by Harry Fenn. Buffalo, Underhill and Nichols, 1893. 3, 225 p. incl. illus., maps. front., plates. 18 cm. 1-14180 Rev.
F127.N8 N59

— New and rev. ed., with remarkable photographic illustrations. New York, Doubleday, Page, 1901. viii, 353 p. front., illus. (incl. maps) plates. 21 cm. 1-7129.
F127. N8 N6

NIAGARA FALLS.   (Buffalo and New York, Matthews, Northrup, 1890)   82, (2) p. incl. front., plates.
pl. 18 cm. 1-14190.   F127. N8 N7

— (New York? 190?)   20 mounted pl. 24½ x 32 cm.   F127. N8 N72

NIAGARA FALLS.   Report of the Executive committee of the Niagara Falls association. Jan., 1885.
(New York) 1885.   43 p. front. (map) 19 x 16½ cm. 1-14191 Rev.   F127. N8 N8

NIAGARA FALLS. ... The Niagara falls guide.   With full instructions to direct the traveller to all
the points of interest at the falls and vicinity.   With a map and engravings.   Buffalo, A. Burke, 1849.
iv, (5) - 112 p. incl. illus., plates. front. (fold. map) 14½ cm. 1-14192.   F127. N8 N81
                                                                                                             Rare Book Coll.

NIAGARA FALLS, nature's throne; pub. by the Williamson-Haffner co., Denver, for J. Whitney Vogt,
Niagara Falls ... Denver, 1907.   20 mounted col. pl. 24½ x 30 cm. CA 28-885 Unrev.
                                                                                                             F127. N8N835

NIAGARA FALLS.   Niagara in summer and winter.   (n. p., n. d.)   (32) p. illus. 19½ x 25 cm.
CA 17-142 Unrev.   F127. N8 N85

— Niagara Falls, N. Y. (190-)   (54) p. of pl. 23 x 30½ cm.   F127. N8N855

NIAGARA FALLS.   Niagara, its falls and scenery: together with Genesee Falls, Trenton Falls,
Montmorenci Falls, River Ottawa, River Saguenay, the city of Quebec, and route down the St. Lawrence.   The whole described and illus. with thirty engravings.   New York, A. Harthill, (186 -)
55 p. illus. 23½ cm. 7-18009.   F127. N8 N86

NIAGARA FALLS sketch book.   Buffalo, N. Y., C. W. Sumner, 1888.   (24) p. front., illus. obl. 24º.
1-14291-M1.   F127. N8 N87

NIAGARA FALLS.   Niagara the majestic ... Buffalo, N. Y., C. D. Arnold, 1901.   52 pl. 13 x 16½ cm.
1-10751.   F127. N8 N91

NIAGARA FALLS.   Daredevils of Niagara.   By Andy O'Brien.   Toronto, Ryerson Press (1964)
xviii, 134 p. 21 cm.   F127. N8 O2

NIAGARA FALLS.   A descriptive reading on Niagara Falls ... (By Caryl S. Parrott)   Philadelphia,
W. H. Rau, 1890.   2, 839 - 851 p. 12º. On of a number of "readings" forming part of an intended comprehensive work, to
accompany lantern slides. The collective vol. never appeared. 1-14194-M1.   F127. N8 P 2

NIAGARA FALLS.   A guide to travelers visiting the falls of Niagara, containing much interesting and
important information respecting the Falls and vicinity ... By Horatio A. Parsons.   2d ed. greatly
enl. Buffalo, O. G. Steele, 1835.   96 p. front. (2 maps on fold. l.) 14½ cm. Later editions pub. under title: The book
of Niagara Falls and Steele's book of Niagara Falls. 1-14195 Rev.   F127. N8 P 29

NIAGARA FALLS.   The book of Niagara Falls.   By Horatio A. Parsons.   3d ed.   Carefully rev. and
enl. ... Buffalo, O. G. Steele, 1836.   8, (13) - 111 p. 2 maps on 1 fold. l. 14½ cm. See above item. 16-9501 Rev.
                                                                                                             F127. N8 P 3
                                                                                                             Rare Book Coll.

— Buffalo, Steele & Peck; New-York, Wiley & Putnam, 1838.   8, (13) - 111 p. 2 maps on fold. l. 15 cm.
See above item. 17-10090 Rev.   F127. N8 P 33
                                                                                                             Toner Coll.

— Steele's book of Niagara Falls.   7th ed., carefully rev. and improved.   Buffalo, O. G. Steele,
1840.   2, (13) - 109 p. front. (2 maps on fold. l.) 6 pl. 15 cm. See above item. 1-14204 Rev.   F127. N8 P339
                                                                                                             Rare Book Coll.

— 8th ed. Buffalo, O. G. Steele, 1840.   2, (13)-109 p. etc. 18-18251. See above item.   F127. N8 P 34
                                                                                                             Rare Book Coll.

NIAGARA FALLS. Peck's tourist's companion to Niagara falls, Saratoga springs, the lakes, Canada, etc. Containing, in addition to full directions for visiting the cataract and vicinity, the springs, etc., full tables of routes and distances, etc. Buffalo, W. B. & C. E. Peck, 1845.   176, 179-194 p. front., illus., plates, maps. 15½ cm. 20-6165 Rev.
F127. N8 P 4
Rare Book Coll.

— Another issue. 1850. Typographical differences.
F127.N8 P 42
Rare Book Coll.

NIAGARA FALLS. Pictorial guide to the falls of Niagara: a manual for visiters, giving an account of this stupendous natural wonder; and all the objects of curiosity in its vicinity, etc., etc. The illustrations designed and engraved by J. W. Orr. Buffalo, Press of Salisbury and Clapp, 1842. xiv, (15) - 232 p. front., illus., 3 pl., 3 maps. 15 cm. 1-14196.
F127. N8 P 6
Rare Book Coll.

— Buffalo, Salisbury and Clapp, 1845.   xiv, (15) - 232 p. front., pl., maps. 24°. 1-14197-M1.
F127.N8 P 61

NIAGARA FALLS. The falls of Niagara. Our school of sublimity ... By Chester E. Pond. Topeka, Kan., 1888.   14 p. 12°. 1-14198-M1.
F127. N8 P 7

NIAGARA FALLS. Historical sketch of Niagara from 1678 to 1876. (By Albert H. Porter) (Buffalo, N. Y., 1876)   51 p. front. (map) 8°. 1-14199-M1.
F127. N8 P 8

NIAGARA FALLS. The first reference to Niagara Falls in literature. (By Peter Augustus Porter) (Niagara Falls, N.Y., Gazette pub. co., 1899)   15 p. 27 cm. Cover-title: Champlain not Cartier. Oct. 12, 99-103 Add. 2.
F127.N8 P 83

NIAGARA FALLS. Champlain not Cartier made the first reference to Niagara Falls in literature; by Peter A. Porter. (Niagara Falls, N. Y., The Gazette press, 1899)   15 p. 27 cm. 99-4451 Rev.
F127.N8 P 83

NIAGARA FALLS. The complete illustrated guide to Niagara Falls and vicinity. (By Peter Augustus Porter) (Niagara Falls, N. Y., "Gazette print., 1883)   68 p. illus., map. 12° 1-14200-M1.
F127.N8 P 84

NIAGARA FALLS. Goat island ... By Peter A. Porter. (Niagara Falls, N. Y.) 1900.   54 p. front., plates, maps, fold. facsim., diagrs. 25 cm. 0-6058 Rev.
F127.N8 P 85

NIAGARA FALLS. Niagara, an aboriginal center of trade, by Peter A. Porter. Niagara Falls, 1906. 74 p. col. front., plates. 16½ cm. 8-19767.
F127.N8 P858

NIAGARA FALLS. The Niagara region in history. By Peter A. Porter ... New York and London, 1895.   24 p. incl. illus., port. 25½ cm. "Repr. from the Niagara power no. of Cassier's magazine. 6-1125.
F127.N8 P 86

NIAGARA FALLS. Official guide, Niagara: falls, river, frontier; scenic, botanic, electric, historic, geologic, hydraulic. By Peter A. Porter; with illustrations by Charles D. Arnold. (Buffalo, N. Y., The Matthews-Northrup works, 1901)   4-311 p. incl. front., illus., map. 17 cm. 1-21796.
F127.N8 P 87

NIAGARA FALLS. Poetry of Niagara ... comp. by M. T. Pritchard. Boston, Lothrop pub. co. (1901) 128 p. front., pl. 12°. 1-22901-M2 Oct. 24.
F128.N8 P 95

NIAGARA FALLS. The collapse at Niagara; pictorial story of the titanic rock fall which destroyed Prospect Point! Regular Veterans Assoc. (n. p., 1954)   unpaged. illus. 28 cm. 55-25444.
F127. N8 R4

NIAGARA FALLS. Scenic gems of Niagara Falls ... (19-?)   1 v.
F127. N8 S 2

NIAGARA FALLS. A new guide to Niagara Falls and vicinity ... (By Frank Hayward Severance)

Chicago and New York, Rand McNally, 1892.   159 p. front., pl., map. 12°. 1-14202-M1.

F127. N8 S 4

NIAGARA FALLS.   The international temple of Niagara.   Reprinted from Modern thought for March, 1882.   London, The modern press (1882)   8 p.   16°.   1-22665-M1.

F127. N8 S 5

NIAGARA FALLS.   Niagara park illustrated.   Original and selected.   Descriptions, poems and adventures.   Ed. by Alice Hyneman Rhine.   New York, W. T. Hunter, 1888.   3, (2), 17-58, (30) p. front., illus. (incl. map)   25½ cm.   1-14201 Rev.

F127. N8 S 7

NIAGARA FALLS.   A souvenir of Niagara Falls, with a series of views in oil colors, from photographs taken on the spot.   Buffalo, Sage, sons & co., 1864.   39 p.   4 col. pl.   obl. 8°.   1-14203-M1.

F127. N8 S 74

NIAGARA FALLS.   The preservation of Niagara Falls.   Interim report of the Special international Niagara board ... Ottawa, F. A. Acland, printer, 1928.   25 p.   illus., fold. pl.   25 cm.   28-24391.

F127. N8 S 78

NIAGARA FALLS.   The preservation of Niagara falls.   Final report of the Special international Niagara board ... Ottawa, F. A. Acland, printer to the King, 1930.   xiv, 394 p. incl. illus., tables, diagrs. charts. plates (1 fold.) maps (1art fold.)   25½ cm.   31-18579.

F127. N8 S781

NIAGARA FALLS.   ... Preservation and improvement of the scenic beauty of the Niagara falls and rapids.   Message from the President of the U.S. transmitting the final report of the Special international Niagara board ... Washington, U.S. Govt. print. off., 1931.   354 p. incl. illus., tables. pl., maps (1 fold.) diagrs. (1 fold.)   30 cm.   (U.S. 71st Cong., 2d sess. Senate. Doc. 128)   31-26516.

F127. N8 S782

NIAGARA FALLS.   Spoliation of the falls of Niagara, by Dr. J. W. Spencer ... (Washington? 1908) (289) - 305. illus. 23 cm.   Reprinted from the Popular science monthly, Oct. 1908.   12-9119.

F127. N8 S803

NIAGARA FALLS.   Steele's Niagara falls port-folio, containing eight new views of Niagara falls. Taking (!) from the most striking points.   By Oliver Gray Steele.   Lithographed by Hall & Mooney. Buffalo, Steele's press, 1842.   2 p., 8 pl.   22 x 17½ cm.   46-40573.

F127. N8 S806
Rare Book Coll.

—   1843.   2 p., 9 pl.   21½ x 17 cm.   17-13774.

F127. N8 S808
Rare Book Coll.

—   1844.   2 p., front., 8 pl.   21½ x 17 cm.   17-16293.

F127. N8 S809
Rare Book Coll.

NIAGARA FALLS.   Steele's Niagara guide book: being a synopsis of Steele's book of Niagara falls ... Buffalo, O. G. Steele, 1840.   35 p.   maps.   24°.   1-22669-M1.

F127. N8 S 83

NIAGARA FALLS.   Through the gorge of Niagara.   Photo-gravures.   New York, The Albertype co., 1896.   1 p., 16 pl.   obl. 24°.   Copyright by A. Wittemann.   1-14205-M1.

F127. N8 T5

NIAGARA FALLS.   The Tower hotel, Niagara, N.Y.   Niagara Falls, N.Y. (190?)   13½ x 17½ cm.

F127. N8 T73

NIAGARA FALLS.   Tunis' illustrated guide to Niagara.   Rev. and pub. by H. T. Allen.   Buffalo, The Courier co., printers, 1879.   72 p.   2 front. (maps, 1 fold.) illus., pl.   18 cm.   1-14206.

F127. N8 T84

NIAGARA FALLS.   Tunis's topographical and pictorial guide to Niagara; containing also, a description of the route through Canada, etc., etc.   Niagara Falls (N.Y.) W. E. Tunis, 1855.   2, (9) - 137 p. illus., plates (part fold.) 3 fold. maps (incl. front.)   14½ cm.   18-11599.

F127. N8 T85

—   1856.   2, (9) - 138 p.   illus., plates, maps.   16½ cm.   18-11600.

F127. N8 T86

NEW YORK 147

NIAGARA FALLS. Diversion of water from the Niagara River. Hearings before the Committee on foreign affairs, House of representatives, Jan. 23 and 24, 1913, on bill proposed by the subcommittee on Niagara Falls legislation, dated Jan. 15, 1913. Washington, Govt. print. off., 1913. 113 p. 23 cm.
CA 16-344 Unrev.
F127. N8 U3

NIAGARA FALLS. Preservation of Niagara Falls. Hearings before the Committee on foreign affairs, House of representatives, Jan. 16, 18, 19, 20, 23, 26 and 27, 1912, on H. R. 6746 ... and H. R. 7694 ... Washington, Govt. print. off., 1912. iii, 399 p. 23 ½ cm. 12-35219.
F127.N8 U36

—
F127.N8 U36
1912a

NIAGARA FALLS and River. Hearings before the Committee on Public Works, House of Representatives, 81st Congress 2d session, on H. R. 8343, a bill to preserve the scenic beauty of the Niagara Falls and River ... Washington, U. S. Govt. Print. Off., 1950. iv, 89 p. 24 cm.
"No 81-16." 50-61365.
F127.N8 U42

NIAGARA FALLS. Preservation of Niagara Falls (H. R. 18024) Hearings ... 59th Congress, first session ... Washington, Govt' print. off., 1906. iv, 325 p. 23 cm. 6-35275.
F127.N8 U45

NIAGARA FALLS. Preservation of Niagara Falls (H. R. 16086 and H. R. 16748) Hearings ... (Feb. 17, 1908, and Appendix) Washington, Govt. print. off., 1908) 19 - 50 p. 23 cm. CA 9-2573 Unrev.
F127.N8 U46

NIAGARA FALLS. Preservation of Niagara Falls. Hearings on the subject of H. R. 26688, 61st Congress, second session, relating to the control and regulation of the waters of Niagara River, etc. Washington, Govt. print. off., 1911. iii, p. 537-624. illus., plates. 23 cm. 11-16312.
F127.N8 U47

NIAGARA FALLS. ... Preservation of Niagara Falls ... Hearings before the Committee on foreign relations ... Washington, Gov't print. off., 1906) 22 p. 23 cm. (59th Cong., 1st sess. Senate. Doc. 393)
6-35099.
F127. N8 U5

NIAGARA FALLS. ... Preservation of Niagara Falls. Message from the President ... transmitting the report of the American members of the International waterways commission ... (Washington, Gov't print. off., 1906) 22 p. 23 cm. (59th Con., 1st sess. Senate. Doc. 242) 6-35088.
F127.N8 U58

NIAGARA FALLS. Hearings in the matter of the granting of permits for the transmission from the Dominion of Canada into the United States of power from the Niagara River, before the secretary of war, at Washington, D. C. Washington, Gov't print. off., 1906. 152 p. 23 cm. 6-35030.
F127. N8 U6

NIAGARA FALLS. Hearings upon applications for permits for the diversion of water from Niagara River or its tributaries for the creation of power, and for the transmission of power from the Dominion of Canada to the U. S., before the secretary of war at Niagara Falls ... Washington, Govt. print. off., 1906. 54 p. 23 cm. 24-12696.
F127.N8 U61

NIAGARA FALLS. ... National park at Niagara Falls. Letter from the secretary of war, submitting ... a recommendation for the establishment of a national park at Niagara Falls ... (Washington, Govt. print. off., 1909) 10 p. 5 fold. pl. 23 cm. (61st Cong., 2d sess. House. Doc. 431) 10-35110.
F127.N8 U62

NIAGARA FALLS. ... Preservation of Niagara Falls. Message from the President of the U. S. ... for the preservation of Niagara Falls ... Washington (Govt. print. off.) 1911. 173 p. incl. tables. front., fold. plates, fold, maps, diagrs. (partly fold.) 29 ½ cm. (62d Cong., 1st sess. Senate. Doc.105) 11-35911.
F127.N8 U63

NIAGARA FALLS. ... Preservation of Niagara Falls. Message from the President ... submitting additional information concerning the operation of the U.S. Lake survey ... Washington, (Govt. print. off., 1911)   22 p.   plates (partly fold.)   29½ cm.   (62d Cong., 2d sess. House. Doc. 246) 12-35068.

F127.N8U632

NIAGARA FALLS.   Views of Niagara Falls.   (Columbus, O., Ward brothers, 1890)   18 pl. obl. 16°.
1-14208-M1.
F127. N8 V5

— (Niagara Falls, N.Y., 1905)   20 x 25 cm.   F127.N8 V52

— (85th thousand.   Portland, Me., L. H. Nelson, 1907)   (48) p. illus. 20 x 25 cm.   F127.N8 V54

NIAGARA FALLS in half-tone.   Text by Holman D. Waldron ... Portland, Me., Chisholm bros., 1901.   16 l.   (30 illus. with descriptive text) 21½ x 30 cm. 2-4713.   F127. N8 W2

NIAGARA FALLS.   With pen and camera at Niagara falls; text by Holman D. Waldron.   Portland, Me., Chisholm bros., 1898.   (48) p. illus. 23 x 30½ cm. 98-112.   F127.N8 W24

NIAGARA FALLS.   Niagara, queen of wonders; a graphic history of the big events in three centuries along the Niagara frontier, one of the most famous regions in the world ...   By Edward Theodore Williams ... Boston, Chapple pub. co., ltd., 1916.   iv, 188 p.   front., plates, ports. 23½ cm. 16-12903.

F127.N8 W68

NIAGARA FALLS.   Scenic and historic Niagara Falls, river, rapids, whirlpool and frontier; written and compiled by ... Edward T. Williams ... (Niagara Falls, 1925)   168 p. illus. (incl. ports.)   23 cm.
"This book contains more than 150 fine engravings ... the greatest coll. of regional pictures ever published. 25-17588.   F127. N8 W69

NIAGARA FALLS.   The foresters: a poem, descriptive of a pedestrian journey to the falls of Niagara, in the autumn of 1804.   By the author of American ornithology.   (Alexander Wilson)   Newtown, Pa., S. Siegfried & J. Wilson, 1818.   106 p.   18 cm. 5-18361.   F127. N8 W7

NIAGARA FALLS ... Copyright ... by A. Wittemann ... New York, The Albertype co., 1888.
2 p., 12 pl. fold. map. 12½ x 18½ cm. Folded map attached to inside of back cover. 1-14193 Rev.   F127.N8 W75

NIAGARA FALLS.   The Niagara story.   By Raymond Francis Yates.   Buffalo, Foster and Stewart Pub. Corp. (1947)   56 p. illus. 31½ cm. 47-26283*.   F127. N8 Y3

— (4th ed.   Buffalo) Foster and Stewart Pub. Corp. (1950)   56 p. illus., ports., map. 30 cm. 50-4166.
F127. N8 Y3
1950

NIAGARA FALLS.   The humbugs of Niagara Falls exposed.   With a complete tourists' guide, giving hints that will enable the visitor to avoid imposition.   By David Young.   Suspension Bridge, N.Y. (1884)   36 p.   16°.   1-14209-M1.   F127. N8 Y6

NIAGARA FALLS.   Thrilling incidents in real life and other items of interest at Niagara Falls and vicinity.   Being remarkable historical facts, gathered from authentic sources and personal recollections by David Young.   Suspension Bridge, N.Y., 1889.   46 p.   14½ cm. 17-22213.
F127.N8 Y62

ONEIDA County   American agriculturist farm directory and reference book of Oneida County, inc. a road map.   New York, Minneapolis (etc.) Orange Judd co.,   v. illus., fold. map. 23½ cm. 17-6236.
Directories

ONEIDA county gazetteer and business directory ... c.1902.   v.   Directories

ONEIDA County.   The early bar of Oneida; a lecture, delivered at the request of the members of the bar of Oneida County, at the court house in the city of Utica ... by William Johnson Bacon ... Utica, N.Y., T. J. Griffiths, printer, 1876.   48 p.   22 cm. 10-22409.   F127. O5 B2

ONEIDA County.   Abstracts of wills of Oneida county ... Copied from the original records at surro-

NEW YORK

gate's office, Utica. Copied and compiled by Gertrude A. Barber. (New York?) 1939 - 45.
6 v. 28 x 21½ cm. Type-written. Contents. - v.1. 1798 to 1822. - v.2. 1822 to 1832. - v.3. 1832 to 1839. - v.4. Feb. 1840 to Oct., 1843. - v.5. Oct., 1843 to March, 1847. - v.6. Mar., 1847 to Sept. 1848. 42-7579 Rev.
F127. O5 B 3

ONEIDA County. Index of wills of Oneida county ... Copied from the original records of the Court house, Utica, N.Y. Copied and compiled by Gertrude A. Barber. (New York) 1940 -
1 v. 28 x 21½ cm. Type-written. 46-36621.
F127.O5 B 32

ONEIDA County. Sheriffs of Oneida County, by Isaac P. Bielby. Utica, N.Y., P. E. Kelly, printer, 1890. 44 p. 24 cm. In double columns. 4-20173.
F127. O5 B 5

ONEIDA County. Things worth knowing about Oneida County, by W. W. Canfield and J. E. Clark. Utica, N.Y., T. J. Griffiths, 1909. 5, (9) - 148 p. front., plates. 21 cm. 10-25853.
F127. O5 C2

ONEIDA County. Gazetteer and business directory of Oneida County for 1869. Comp. and pub. by Hamilton Child ... Syracuse, Printed at the Journal office, 1869. 418, 16, 435-436 p. incl. front. (fold. map) 21½ cm. The Gazetteer includes historical notes. 15-2711.
F127. O5 C5

ONEIDA County. History of Oneida County, from 1700 to the present time, by Henry J. Cookinham ... Chicago, The S. J. Clarke pub. co., 1912. 2 v. plates, ports., maps. 27 cm. 12-9175.
F127.O5 C77

ONEIDA County. ... History of Oneida County. (By Samuel W. Durant) Philadelphia, Everts & Fariss, 1878. 678 p. front., illus., plates, ports., maps. 20½ cm. 1-14210.
F127. O5 D9

ONEIDA County. ... Commerce, manufactures and resources, of Oneida co. A historical, statistical & descriptive review. (Ed. I. J. Isaacs) (Utica, N.Y.) National pub. co. (1883) 2, (9) - 176 (i.e. 160) p. illus. 25 cm. 1-14211 Rev.
F127. O5 I 7

ONEIDA County. Annals and recollections of Oneida County ... By Pomroy Jones. Rome (N.Y.) The author, 1851. xvi, 893 p. 23 cm. 1-14212.
F127. O5 J 7

ONEIDA County. Articles of incorporation, constitution, by-laws, officers and members of the Oneida historical society at Utica, with the annual reports of the officers for 1878, and some account of the collections of the society and its needs and purposes ... Utica, N.Y., E. H. Roberts, printers, 1879.
38 p. 23½ cm. 10-25271.
F127. O5O36

ONEIDA County. Constitution and by-laws of the Oneida historical soc., Utica, etc. Utica, E. H. Roberts, book and job print., 1887. 29 p. 23 cm. 10-31409.
F127.O5O365

ONEIDA County. Charter, constitution and by-laws of the Oneida historical soc. at Utica. (Utica, N.Y., Press of T. J. Griffiths) 1901. 56 p. front. 21 cm. 4-1127 Rev.
F127.O5O37

ONEIDA historical soc. at Utica. Officers and standing committees. (Utica, N.Y.) v. 15½ cm.
F127.O5O377

ONEIDA County. The Oneida historical society. (Utica? 1902) 28 cm.
F127.O5 O38

ONEIDA County. Oneida historical society. Publications ... no. 2, 5. Utica (etc.) 1879-80.
2 v. 23 cm.
F127. O5 O4
— Historical fallacies regarding colonial New York ... By Douglas Campbell. New York, F. J. Ficker, printer, 1879. 32 p. 23 cm. (no. 2) 3-5826 Rev.
— ... Men, events, lawyers, politics and politicians of early Rome. By D. E. Wager. Utica, N.Y., E. H. Roberts, printers, 1879. 47 p. 22½ cm. (no. 3) 1-14971 Rev.
— A long lost point in history. An address ... by L. W. Ledyard ... Utica, N.Y., T.H. Floyd, printer, 1883. 16 p. 22½ cm. (No. 8) 3-8084 Rev.

— Catalogue of the library of the Oneida historical society at Utica ... Utica, N.Y., E. H. Roberts, printers, 1890.   2, (3) - 127 p.   23½ cm.   (no. 15)   9-389 Rev.
— Col. Marinus Willett.   The hero of Mohawk Valley.   By Daniel E. Wager.   Utica, Utica Herald pub. co., 1891.   50 p.   23 cm.   (no. 16)   10-31934 Rev.

ONEIDA County.   Year book ... of the Oneida historical soc. ... (no. 1) -   1881 -   Utica, N.Y., 1881 - 1905.   10 v. in 6.   illus., etc.   22½ x 24 cm.   Nos. 1-9 have title: Transactions.   1-14213.   F127. O5 O5
— The historical address (at the centennial celebration of the settlement of Whitestown) By Hon. Charles Tracy.   (In Transactions ... 1881-4)   Also pub. separately, Utica, 1885.   7-38297.
— "The Whitestown country." 1784-1884.   Centennial celebration of the settlement of Whitestown ...   (In Transactions, 1881-4)   7-38298.
— Whitesboro's golden age.   By D. E. Wager.   (In Transactions ... 1881-4)   7-38299.
— The Wagner re-interment, at Fort Plain ...   (In Transactions ... 1881-4)   7-38332.
— Dedication of the site of old Fort Schuyler ...   (In Transactions ... 1881-4)   7-38331.
— Dedication of the Oriskany monument ...   (In its Transactions ... 1881-4)   7-38330.
— The Mohawks.   An enquiry into their origin, migrations and influence upon the white settlers.   by S. L. Frey.   41 p.   front. (port.)   25 cm.   (Transactions, no. 8)   4-31158.

ONEIDA County.   ... Historical society.   The colonial newspaper press described by Colonel Stone. A communication from President Roberts - the Steuben monument - new members elected - the address.   (Utica, 1890)   (3) p.   25½ cm.   From Utica herald, Oct. 28, 1890.   12-24131.
F127. O5 O6

ONEIDA County.   Presentation of the battle flags of the Oneida County regiments to the Oneida historical society, Utica, N.Y.   (Utica, 1898)   90 p.   pl., ports.   23 cm.   "Largely copied from the Utica daily newspapers - the Observer, the Herald and the Press."   2-14959 Rev.
F127. O5 P 93

ONEIDA County.   Notices of men and events connected with the early history of Oneida County.   Two lectures, delivered before the Young mens' association, by William Tracy ... Utica, R. Northway, jr., printer, 1838.   45 p.   22½ cm.   1-14214.
F127. O5 T7

ONEIDA County.   ... Second annual address before the society, by William Tracy ...   New York, W. S. Gottsberger, printer (1880)   34 p.   23 cm.   (Oneida hist. soc. Pub. no. 5)   2-1365-M2)
F127. O5 T73

ONEIDA County.   Utica herald year book of Oneida County for 1884 - 86.   (1st year) -   Comp. by S. N. D. North ... Utica, N.Y., 1884 - 86.   3 v. in 1.   19 cm.   10-31408.
F127. O5 U8

ONEIDA County.   Our country and its people; a descriptive work on Oneida county; ed. by Daniel E. Wager.   (Boston) The Boston history co., 1896.   xi, 636, 180, 411 p.   illus., port.   25½ cm.   pt. 1. Historical. - pt. 2. Biographical. - pt. 3. Family sketches.   2-19060 Rev.
F127. O5 W2

ONEIDA Lake.   Oneida Lake, past and present; an historical sketch by Harmon C. Landgraff.   Cleveland, N.Y., The Lakeside press, 1926.   4, 66, ii p.   pl.   22½ cm.   26-20716.
F127. O52 L2

ONONDAGA County.   The Farm journal illus. dir. of Onondaga Co.   v.
Directories

ONONDAGA County.   Architecture worth saving in Onondaga County.   (Syracuse? Syracuse University School of Architecture (1964)   201 p.   21 cm.   Publ. with Syracuse Univ. School of Architecture.
F127. O6 A5

ONONDAGA County.   Pioneer Irish of Onondaga (about 1776 - 1847) by Theresa Bannan.   New York and London, G. P. Putnam's sons, 1911.   xii, 333 p.   21½ cm.   Bibliography: p. xi-xii.   11-25968.
F127. O6 B 17

ONONDAGA County.   A brief geography of Onondaga county, prepared for the use of public schools,

NEW YORK

by C. W. Bardeen ... Syracuse, N.Y.. Davis, Bardeen, 1879. viii, (9) - 48 p. front. (fold. map) 15 cm.
1-14215. F127. O6 B 2

ONONDAGA County. Past and present of Syracuse and Onondaga County, from prehistoric times to the beginning of 1908, by the Rev. William M. Beauchamp ... Also biographical sketches of some prominent citizens of Syracuse and Onondaga County. New York and Chicago, The S. J. Clarke pub. co. 1908.   2 v. fronts., plates, ports. 26½ cm. 12-24877. F127. O6 B 37

ONONDAGA County. Revolutionary soldiers resident or dying in Onondaga County, N.Y.; with supplementary list of possible veterans, based on a pension list of Franklin H, Chase, Syracuse, N.Y. Prepared by Rev. William M. Beauchamp ... for the Onondaga historical association. Syracuse, N.Y., The McDonnell co., 1913.   1, 307 p. 24½ cm. (Onondaga hist. assoc. Pubs. vol. 1 no. 2) 13-17269.
F127. O6 B375

ONONDAGA County. Onondaga's centennial. Gleanings of a century. Ed. by Dwight H. Bruce ... (Boston) The Boston history co., 1896.   2 v. front., illus., pl., ports., maps. 26 cm. Vol. 1 and (pt. 1) of vol. 2 paged continuously. "Bibliographical": v. 2, pt. 2, 233 p.; "Family sketches": v. 2, pt. 3, 493 p. 2-23212. F127. O6 B 8

ONONDAGA County. Onondaga's soldiers of the revolution. Official records, compiled by Frank H. Chase ... Syracuse, N.Y., The Onondaga historical assoc., 1895.   47 p. 23½ cm. L. C. copy replaced by microfilm. 4-8798 Rev.
F127. O6 C3
Microfilm 9485   F

ONONDAGA County. Lights and lines of Indian character, and scenes of pioneer life. By Joshua V. H. Clark ... Syracuse, E. H. Babcock; New York, J. C. Derby; (etc.) 1854.   vi, (7) - 375 p. front. (port.) 19½ cm. "Some few of these pieces have previously appeared in the New York 'Commercial advertiser,' and other papers. Some of them may be found in the 'History of Onondaga.'" 2-12851 Rev. F127. O6 C4

ONONDAGA County. Onondaga; or, Reminiscences of earlier and later times; being a series of historical sketches relative to Onondaga; with notes on the several towns in the county, and Oswego. By Joshua V. H. Clark. ... Syracuse, Stoddar and Babcock, 1849.   2 v. illus., 10 port. (incl. front.) fold. map. 22½ cm. 1-14216 Rev. F127. O6 C5

ONONDAGA County. Gazetteer and business directory of Onondaga County, N.Y., for 1868-9. Comp. and pub. by Hamilton Child ... Syracuse, Printed at the Journal office, 1868.   435 p. incl. front. (fold. map) 21½ cm. 8-15806. F127. O6 C6

ONONDAGA County. ... History of Onondaga county, New York. With illus. and biographical sketches of some of the prominent men and pioneers ... By W. Woodford Clayton ... Syracuse, N.Y., D. Mason, 1878.   iv, 430 p. front., pl., port., map. fol. 1-14217-M1. F127. O6 C7

ONONDAGA. Report on the agriculture and industry of the county of Onondaga, state of New York, with an introductory account of the aborigines ... From the Transactions of the N.Y. state agricultural soc., 1859 . By George Geddes. Albany, C. Van Benthuysen, 1860.   140 p. illus., pl., fold. map. 8°. 1-16522-M1. F127. O6 G3

ONONDAGA. Early Onondaga in letters to young students, by "an old lady," ed. by Mary Josephine Hasbrouck ... Syracuse, N.Y.. Bardeen's inc., 1942.   66 p. illus. (map) 17½ x 13 cm. "Sources": p. 63-66. 42-24885. F127. O6 H3

ONONDAGA. Foreign policy and Onondaga County. By Gerard J. Mangone. Syracuse, N.Y., Maxwell Graduate School of Citizenship and Public Affairs, Syracuse University, 1964.   75 p. 23 cm.
64-18433. F127. O6 M3

ONONDAGA County. Onondaga historical assoc. Annual volume. 1914 -   Syracuse, N.Y.
(1914 -   v. ports. 23 - 24½ cm. 16-23643. F127. O6 O63
— Notes of other days in Skaneateles, ... by Rev. Wm. M. Beauchamp ...   (In Annual vol. 1914. 16-23641.
— Reminiscences of Syracuse, by Timothy C. Cheney. Comp. by Parish B. Johnson from personal recollections of the author ...   (In Annual vol. 1914) 16-23642.

— ... Onondaga's part in the civil war, by Mrs. Sarah Sumner Teall ... Arranged for publication by Dr. E. P. Tanner ...   (Syracuse, N.Y.) The Dehler press (1915)   85 (3) p.   (In Annual vol. 1915)   16-21590.

ONONDAGA County.   ... Catalogue of historical objects, portraits, relics, etc. from nos. 1 to 1000 in the Onondaga historical assoc. building ... Syracuse, N.Y.   Catalogued with notes by Franklin H. Chase, secretary.   Syracuse, N.Y., The Dehler press, 1930.   132 p.   24 cm.   32-23042.   F127.O6 O66

ONONDAGA County.   Onondaga historical association leaflet.   (1st ser.) no. 1-22, Jan. 1896 - Jan. 1904; 2d ser. no. 1-3   (Syracuse, Onondaga hist. assoc.) 1896 - (1904)   26 vols. in 1.   illus.   23½ cm. Title varies.   21-6186.   F127. O6 O7

ONONDAGA County.   Manual of the Onondaga historical association.   Pub. by direction of the board of directors.   Syracuse (Press of E. M. Grover) 1895.   36 p.   23 cm.   10-7238.   F127.O6 O71

— 1906.   42 p.   23 cm.   9-13990.   F127.O6 O72

ONONDAGA historical association.   Publications ... v. 1   (Syracuse, N.Y.) 1912 - v.   24½ cm.   13-17270.   F127.O6 O73

— Revolutionary soldiers resident or dying in Onondaga County ...   by Rev. W. M. Beauchamp ... 1913.   307 p.   (vol. 1, no. 2)   13-17269.

— ... An act to incorporate the village of Syracuse ...   74, (6) p.   (vol. 1 no. 1)   16-2291.

— ... Catalogue of portraits, relics, etc. in Historical building, Syracuse ... by Leonora Goodrich.   47 p.   23½ cm.   (vol. 1 no. 2)   16-2290.

ONONDAGA historical association (Its officers, history, charter, etc.)   Syracuse, N.Y., H. P. Winsor, printer, 1865.   24 p.   20½ cm.   8-31725.   F127.O6 O74

ONONDAGA County.   Pioneer times in the Onondaga country, by Carroll E. Smith ... Syracuse, N.Y., C. W. Bardeen, 1904.   415 p. incl. front. (port.) illus.   24 cm.   "Originally published in the Syracuse Sunday Herald in the year 1899."   4-12784.   F127. O6 S 6

ONONDAGA County.   A vanished world.   By Anne Gertrude Sneller.   Illus. by Nancy B. Perkins. (Syracuse, N.Y.) Syracuse University Press, 1964.   x, 365 p.   22 cm.   64-16923.   F127.O6 S 63

ONONDAGA County.   The Lesley E. Voorhees records.   Copied and compiled by Lesley E. Voorhees. Ed. by Alice Laughlin Arneson.   Syracuse, N.Y., History's People, 1965 -   1 v.   28 cm. (History's people, inc., publication no. 1)   F127.O6 V65

ONONDAGA County.   Tryphena Ely White's journal; being a record, written 100 years ago, of the daily life of a young lady of Puritan heritage.   1805 - 1905.   Pub. by her only remaining granddaughter, Fanny Kellogg.   (New York, The Grafton press, 1904)   40 p. incl. facsims. plates, geneal. tab.   20 cm. Pioneer life in the town of Camillus.   The journal extends from June 15 to Sept. 20, 1805.   4-33235.   F127.O6 W 5

ONTARIO County.   ... directory, containing the general directories of Canandaigua and Geneva, tog. with the business directories of all other villages in Ontario county ... 18   Rochester, E. Darrow, 18   v.   22½ - 23½ cm.   40M150T.   Directories

ONTARIO County.   History of Ontario County, with illus. and family sketches of some of the prominent men and families; ed. by George S. Conover, comp. by Lewis Cass Aldrich.   Syracuse, N.Y., D. Mason, 1893.   (11) - 518 p.   396 p. illus (incl. plans, facsim.) plates, ports.   25 cm.   "Biographical": p. 464-518.   Part II: Family sketches.   4-5213.   F127. O7 A3

ONTARIO County.   Gazetteer and business directory of Ontario County, for 1867-8.   Comp. and pub. by Hamilton Child ... Syracuse, Printed at the Journal office, 1867.   240 p.   front. (fold. map)   21½ cm. Includes historical sketches.   16-8174.   F127. O7 C5

ONTARIO County.   ... History of Ontario co., with illus. descriptive of its scenery, palatial residences,

NEW YORK

public buildings ... and important manufactories ... Philadelphia, Everts, Ensign & Everts, 1876. iv, 7-276 p. xcvi pl. (incl. front., ports., maps; part double) 35½ x 29 cm. Plate xli omitted. 1-14218.
F127. O7 M2

ONTARIO County. A history of Ontario County and its people, by Charles F. Milliken ... New York, Lewis historical pub. co., 1911. 2 v. front., illus., ports. 27½ cm. Vol. 2, Genealogical and biographical. 11-28849.
F127. O7 M6

ONTARIO County. ... A contact period Seneca site situated at Factory Hollow, by Arthur C. Parker ... With a map by Walter H. Cassebeer and report of a field survey by H. C. Follett. Rochester, N.Y., Lewis H. Morgan chapter, 1919. 36 p. illus. (incl. maps) 25½ cm. (Researches and transactions of the New York state archeological association, Lewis H. Morgan chapter ... v. 1, no. 2) 32-15849.
F127. O7 P 3

ONTARIO County, 1810 Federal population census schedule, transcript and index. (by) Ralph V. Wood, Jr. Cambridge, Mass., 1964. iv, 162 p. 28 cm. "Data ... were taken from a positive microfilm copy ... from the National Archives in Washington, D.C.
F127.O7 W 6

OQUAGA Lake farm. (Deposit, N.Y. 19 -) 13½ x 17 cm.
F127.O75 O7

ORANGE County. Vail's Orange county farmers and business directory ... 1871/2. Poughkeepsie city, J. P. A. Vail (1871) (1) v. 22 cm.
Directories

ORANGE County. Outposts of history in Orange county (by) Dwight Akers; drawing by Hector St. John de Crevecoeur; wodcuts by Fiske Boyd. Washingtonville, N.Y., Blooming Grove chapter, D.A.R. 1937. 3, 114 p. front., plates. 21½ cm. "The book is the outgrowth of a series of articles on Orange county history pub. in the Washingtonville times in 1935 and 1936." 37-1822.
F127. O8 A3

ORANGE County. Bethlehem Presbyterian church records, Cornwall. (In Historical soc. of Newburgh Bay and the Highlands ... Historical papers no. 6) 8-19315.
F127. O8 C8

ORANGE County. Abstracts of wills of Orange and Rockland counties ... Compiled by Minnie Cowen. (New York?) 1937-39. 3 v. 28 cm. Type-written. 42-7580.
F127. O8 C9

ORANGE County. Survey of Orange County. By Goldsmith Denniston. From Transactions, N.Y. state agricultural society, 1862. Albany, Steam press of C. Van Benthuysen, 1863. 103 p. illus., pl., 2 fold. maps. 23 cm. 1-14219 Add.
F127. O8 D4

ORANGE County. An outline history of Orange county ... tog. with local traditions and short biographical sketches of early settlers, etc. By Sam'l W. Eager ... Newburgh, S. T. Callahan, 1846-7. 3, (5) - 652 p. 21 cm.
F127. O8 E2

— Index to Eager's History of Orange county by Lillian O. Estabrook; prepared for publication by Marguerite Estabrook. Rutland, Vt., The Tuttle pub. co., (1940) 48 p. 22½ cm. 1-14220 Rev.
F127. O8 E2 Index

ORANGE County. Orange County ... By Emmet Van Rensselaer Gardiner. (Middletown? N.Y., 1904) 25 cm.
F127. O8 G2

ORANGE County. The history of Orange County, ed. by Russel Headley. Middleton, N.Y., Van Deusen and Elms, 1908. 10, (17) - 997 p. xviii p. incl. front. plates, ports. 24½ x 17 cm. 9-8885.
F127. O8 H4

ORANGE County. Historical society of Newburgh Bay and the Highlands. Publication. (no. 1, Newburgh, N.Y., 1884-19 v. fronts., illus., plates, ports., map, plans. 23 cm. 16-4771.
F127. O8 H6

— First annual meeting of the Historical society of Newburgh Bay and the Highlands ... 20 p. 23 cm. (no. 1) 5-42471.
— Address by Hon, Erastus Brooks. (In no. 1, p. 6-19) 8-19326.
— Unveiling of the statue of George Clinton ... 49 p. incl. front., illus. (ports.) fold. pl. 23 cm. (no. 4) 5-16548.

— A record of the inscriptions in the old town burying ground of Newburgh ...   2, (5) - 180 p. pl., plan. 23 cm. 5-6278.   (no. 5)

— Bethlehem Presbyterian church records, Cornwall.   (no. 6, p. 9-23)   8-19315.

— Colonel Thomas DeKay, a pioneer of western Orange County. By David Barclay ... (No. 6, p. 35-44) 8-18968.

— Account of the unveiling of the tablet on the site of the old Palatine church, 1899. (No. 6, p. 52-54) 8-19317.

— Major Patrick MacGregorie. By Adelaide Skeel and David Barclay.   (No. 6, p. 55-62) 8-18967.

— ... Centennial number. May 8, 1900.   78 p. front., illus., plates, ports., plan. 22½ cm. (No. 7)

— Record of baptisms and marriages. Copied from and compated with the original entries in stewards' book, Newburgh ... 1789-1835. By Augusta Leslie.   No. 8 p. 7-30) 8-19318.

— Marriages performed by Rev. James I. Ostram, copied from note book kept by himself, by Mrs, William Vanamee.   (In no. 8 p. 31-35) 8-19309.

— Balmville. From the first settlement to 1860. By David Barclay.   (No. 8 p. 45-58) 8-18969.

— The valley of the Moodna in history... by E. M. Ruttenber ...   (No. 8 p. 59-62) 8-19321.

— ... Inscriptions on gravestones in New Windsor cemetery.   (No. 9, p. 11-23) 8-19316 rev.

— Inscriptions in Balmville burying ground.   (No. 9, p. 25-30) 8-19322.

— ... Lauchlin Campbell, of Campbell Hall, and his family.   (No. 9, p. 31-36) 8-18970.

— Location of New fort. A visit to Shawangunk's ancient battle-field.   (No. 9, p. 51-54) 8-19320.

— Gardnertown cemetery. Inscriptions in the Gardnertown M. E. church cemetery, 1902. (No. 10, p. 11-19) 8-19319.

— The King's highway. Its early road districts and the residents or owners of lands thereon.   (No. 10, p. 21-33) 8-18966.

— Wawayanda vs. Cheesek-ook. Notes of testimony in a hearing at Chester, in 1785, to determine boundary lines.   (In no. 11, p. 61-67) 8-19310.

— Tom Quick and Claudius Smith ... By Theo. D. Schoonmaker ...   (No. 11, p. 74-90. 8-19324.

— Gen. John Hathorn, a revolutionary soldier, patriot and statesman. By Ferdinand V. Sanford ...   (no. 11, p. 91-98) 8-19323 Rev.

— The Fullerton family.   By Hon, Walter C. Anthony.   (no. 13, p. 199-200) 17-9561.

— ... Old houses and historic places in the vicinity of Newburgh.   3, 135-211 p. incl. plates, map. 22½ cm. (No. 15) 11-4013.

ORANGE County. (Scrap-book: historical and genealogical articles relating to Orange co., including court records; clippings from the Independent Republican, Sept. 1, 1908 - Oct. 15, 1912. Goshen, N.Y., 1912)   100 l. 1 illus. 23½ cm. 39M4286T.   F127. O8 I 6

ORANGE County; a narrative history ... Compiled by Almet S. Moffat. Washingtonville, N.Y., 1928. 87 p. illus., plates, ports. 23½ cm.   "List of authorities": p. 7.   29-15897.   F127. O8 M6

ORANGE County; a history. Goshen, N.Y., The National bank of Orange County (1922) 23 p.   21½ cm. 22-9577.   F127. O8 N3

ORANGE County historical magazine. By E. M. Ruttenber. Vol. 1, no. 1-3, 8, 10. Newburgh, N.Y., 1875 -   5 nos. 25 cm.   F127. O8 O8

ORANGE County. Portrait and biographical record of Orange county. Containing portraits and biographical sketches of prominent and representative citizens of the county. Tog. with biographies and portraits of all the presidents of the U.S. New York and Chicago, Chapman pub. co., 1895. 4, (19) - 1547 (i.e. 1517) p. incl. illus., plates, ports. ports. 27½ cm. Some pages omitted in paging. 1-14221 Rev.   F127. O8 P 8

ORANGE County. The origin of Orange County, from 1683 to 1847, by Mildred F. Roberts. Orange, Calif., 1970.   31, 19 l. 30 cm.   F127. O8 R6

ORANGE County. History of the county of Orange: with a history of the town and city of Newburgh: general, analytical and biographical by E. M. Ruttenber. Newburgh, N.Y., E. M. Ruttenber, printers, 1875.   424 p. front., illus., plates, ports., maps. 23½ cm. 1-14222.   F127. O8 R9

NEW YORK

ORANGE County. History of Orange County, with illustrations and biographical sketches of many of its pioneers and prominent men. Comp. by E. M. Ruttenber and L. H. Clark, and a corps of biographical writers. Philadelphia, Everts & Peck, 1881. xii, 9-820 p. illus., plates, ports., maps (part col.) 28½ cm. 16-20351. F127. O8 R91

ORANGE County. A history of the Minisink region: which includes the present towns of Minisink, Deerpark, Mount Hope, Greenville and Wawayanda, in Orange County, from their organization and first settlement to the present time; also, including a general history of the first settlement of the county. By Charles E. Stickney ... Middletown, N.Y., C. Finch and I. F. Guiwits, 1867. 2, (vii) - viii p. (11) - 211 p. 19½ cm. 1-14164. F127. O8 S 8

ORANGE County. History of the Minisink country, by Horace E. Twichell. (New York, Printed by the Schilling press, 1912) 207 p. front., plates. 24 cm. 12-18534. F127. O8 T9

ORANGE County. Old Orange houses ... by Mildred Parker Seese. (Middletown, N.Y., The Whitlock press, 1941 - v. illus. 22 x 28 cm. Reproduced from type-written copy. "First edition." 42-3763.
F127.O8
NA7235.N7S4

ORLEANS County directory (1910 - v.1 - including a complete directory of the villages of Albion, Medina, Holley, and a complete directory of the rural delivery routes of the county ... Lockport, N.Y., Roberts bros. co. (1910 - 1 v. fold. map. 24 cm. 10-26930. Directories

ORLEANS County. Swart's Orleans county directory ... Albion, Holley and Medina separate ... (1894 - (Albion, N.Y., A. M. Eddy, printer, 1894 - v. map. 23 cm. 33-38653.
Directories

ORLEANS County. ... Historical album of Orleans county, with illustrations descriptive of its scenery ... and portraits of old pioneers and prominent residents. New York, Sanford & co., 1879. 320 p. front., illus., plates, ports., map, plan. 36 x 30 cm. 1-14223. F127. O9 H6

ORLEANS County. Record of the Orleans county pioneer association; original minutes, 1858 to 1905 ... Albion, N.Y., Orleans chapter, D.A.R., 1939. 316 p. 23½ cm. 45-45239.
F127. O9 O7

ORLEANS County. Landmarks of Orleans county ... ed. by Hon. Isaac S. Signor ... Syracuse, D. Mason, 1894. viii, 688, 48, 242 p. fold. pl., port. 25 x 19½ cm. pt. II. Biographical. - pt. III. Family sketches. 3-11789.
F127. O9 S 5

ORLEANS County. Pioneer history of Orleans County. Containing some account of the civil divisions of western New York, with brief biographical notices of early settlers, etc., etc., by Arad Thomas. Albion, N.Y., H. A. Bruner, Orleans American steam press print, 1871. xii, (13) - 463 p. ports. 23 cm. 1-14224* Cancel. F127. O9 T4

ORISKANY Creek. Along the Oriskany. By David Harold Beetle. (Utica, N.Y., Utica Observer-Dispatch, 1947) 189 p. illus., ports. 20 cm. 48-12919*. F127.O905 B4

OSWEGO County. Directory of the New York, Ontario and western railway ... from Norwich to Oswego, and Utica branch ... Newburgh, N.Y., Breed pub. co. v. 24½ cm. 1-29290 Rev.
F127.O91
F117.5.D 59

OSWEGO County. The north country; a history, embracing Jefferson, St. Lawrence, Oswego, Lewis and Franklin counties, by Harry F. Landon ... Indianapolis, Ind., Historical pub. co., 1932. 3 v. plates, ports., map. 27½ cm. Paged continuously. Vols. 2 and 3 contain biographical material. 32-10390. F127.O91
F119.L 28

OSWEGO County. American agriculturist farm directory and reference book of Oswego County, a rural directory and reference book including a road map of Oswego County. Minneapolis, Chicago (etc.) Orange Judd co. v. fold. map. 23½ cm. 18-287. Directories

OSWEGO County. Kimball's Oswego County directory ... 1878 -   Oswego, N.Y., R. J. Oliphant, printer, 1878-   1 v.   23 cm.   10-3170.
Directories

OSWEGO County. Perkins' rural directory, containing a general directory of the people living in the villages and on rural free delivery routes adjacent to Fulton and Oswego ... (v. 1 - (1909/10 -   Oswego, N.Y., A. K. Perkins, sr., 1909 -   1 v.   23 cm.   9-28570.
Directories

OSWEGO County. Gazetteer and business directory of Oswego County, for 1866-7. Compiled and pub. by Hamilton Child ... Oswego, Printed at the Daily commercial advertiser office, 1866. iv, 224 p.   20½ cm.   25-5892.
F127.O91 C5

OSWEGO County. Landmarks of Oswego county; ed. by John C. Churchill, and others. Syracuse, N.Y., D. Mason, 1895.   xi, 843, 72, 348 p.   illus., plates, ports., maps (part fold.) facsims.   25 cm.   Pt. II. Biographical. - pt. III. Family sketches; indexes.   1-2737.
F127.O91C56

OSWEGO County. ... History of Oswego County. With illus. and biographical sketches of some of its prominent men and pioneers. (By Crisfield Johnson) Philadelphia, L. H. Everts, 1877. 449 p. incl. illus., map.   front., plates (part double) ports.   31 cm.   1-14225.
F127.O91 J 6

OSWEGO County. Oswego Historical Society. Publication. 1st - 3d; 1899 - 1904; (n. s.) Oswego, N.Y., Palladium-Times, printers (etc.)   v.   illus., ports.   23 - 25 cm.   annual.   New series began publication in 1937. Vol. nos. ireegular. no. 11 repeated. 1-14226 rev. 2*.
F127.O91 O9

OSWEGO County. History of the various projects, reports, discussions and estimates for reaching the Great Lakes from tidewater. 1768 - 1901. By Wm. Pierson Judson. (Oswego? N.Y., 1901) 22 p.   fold. map.   23 cm.   (Oswego hist. soc. Publication no. 2)   6-286.
F127.O91 O9

OSWEGO County. ... Certified copies of ancient field notes and maps: Totten and Crossfield's purchase, 1772; Macomb's purchase, 1796; Old military tract, 1787 - 1797. (Albany, O. A. Quayle, 1904)   (5) - 83 p.   4 fold. maps.   23½ cm.   (Oswego hist. soc. Publication no. 3)   Report of state engineer.   8-30438.
F127.O91 O9

OSWEGO County fifty years ago. Address delivered by Hon. R. H. Tyler, before the Old settlers' association ... 1879. Fulton, N.Y., Morrill bros., printers, 1880.   18 p.   23 cm.   20-18475.
F127.O91T98

OTSEGO County. ... American agriculturist farm directory and reference book of Otsego and Herkimer counties, New York, a rural directory and reference book including a road map of Otsego and Herkimer counties. New York, Minneapolis (etc.) Orange Judd co.   v.   illus., fold. map.   23½ cm. 17-29769.
Directories

OTSEGO County. Directory of the business and progessional men of Otsego co. ... (1895)   Afton, N.Y., Enterprise steam print (1895 -   v.   19½ cm.   33-33143.
Directories

OTSEGO County; geographical and historical, from the earliest settlement to the present time, with county and township maps from original drawings, by Edwin F. Bacon. Oneonta, N.Y., The Oneonta herald, 1902.   85 p. incl. front., illus.   maps.   23½ cm.   2-23429.
F127.O93 B 2

OTSEGO County. Abstracts of wills of Otsego county ... Copied and compiled by Gertrude A. Barber. (New York) 1941 -   5 v.   28 cm.   Typewritten.   Contents. - v. 1. 1794-1824. - v.2. 1817-1829. - v.3. 1829-1838. - v.4. 1838-1845. - v.5. 1845-1850.   42-7812 Rev.
F127.O93 B28

OTSEGO County. Deaths taken from the Otsego herald & western advertiser & Freeman's journal ... Copied and compiled by Gertude A. Barber. (Cooperstown? N.Y., 1942 -   1 v.   28 cm.   Typewritten (carbon) copy.   Contents. - v.1. 1795-1840. - v.2. Jan. 1841 - Sept. 5, 1862. - v.3. Sept. 19, 1842 (i.e.1862) - Dec. 30, 1875. A 47-1225.
F127.O93B285

OTSEGO County. Marriages taken from the Otsego herald and western advertiser and Freeman's journal, Otsego county newspapers, from 1795 - 1840 ... Copied and compiled by Gertrude A. Barber. (New York? 194 -   1 v.   28 cm.   Type-written.   47-33430.   F127.O93 B29

OTSEGO County.   Reminiscences; personal and other incidents; early settlement of Otsego County; notices and anecdotes of public men; judicial, legal, and legislative matters; field sports; dissertations and discussions.   By Levi Beardsley ... New-York, Printed by C. Vinten, 1852.   x, 575 p. front. (port.) 22 ½ cm.   1-14227.   F127.O93 B 3

OTSEGO County.   Biographical review.   This volume contains biographical sketches of the leading citizens of Otsego County ... Boston, Biographical review pub. co., 1893.   2, (9) - 857 p. incl. ports. port. 28 ½ x 24 cm.   21-11747.   F127.O93 B 6

OTSEGO County.   Gazetteer and business directory of Otsego County, for 1872-3.   Comp. and pub. by Hamilton Child ... Syracuse, Printed at the Journal office, 1872.   273 p. incl. front. (fold. map)   21 cm. 5-33723.   F127.O93 C5

OTSEGO County.   The legends and traditions of a northern county (by) James Fenimore Cooper ... New York and London, G. P. Putnam's sons, 1921.   4, vii-xi, 263 p.   20 ½ cm.   21-14065.
F127.O93C77

OTSEGO County.   ... History of Otsego County.   (By Duane Hamilton Hurd) With illus. and biographical sketches of some of its prominent men and pioneers.   Philadelphia, Everts & Fariss, 1878, 378 p.   plates, ports., map.   31 cm.   8-19464.   F127.O93 H9

OTSEGO County.   Growing up in the Cooper country; boyhood recollections of the New York frontier, ed. by Louis C. Jones.   (Syracuse, N.Y., Syracuse University Press, 1965.   198 p.   22 cm. 64-23343.
F127.O93 J 6

OTSEGO County historical society.   Publications.   Cooperstown, N.Y., 1936 -   v. 23 cm. 38M3442T.   F127.O93 O9

— Reminiscences of mid-Victorian Cooperstown and a sketch of William Cooper (by) James Fenimore Cooper ... Cooperstown, N.Y., 1936.   56 p.   23 cm.   (No. 1)   "Series of sketches ... which first appeared in the Cooperstown newspapers during the winter of 1935 and 1936."   37-18835.   F127.O93 O9

OTSEGO County: 1800 federal population census schedule, transcript and index, by Ralph V. Wood, Jr. (Cambridge, Mass.) 1965.   vii, 68 p.   28 cm.   Data for this transcript were taken from a positive microfilm copy of the original census schedule now held by the National Archives.   D127.O93 W6

OWAHGENA, Lake.   Shells and pebbles from lake Owahgena.   (By Albert Guvera Marshall)   Cazenovia, N.Y., Marshall bros., 1888.   (1) p.   xiv pl.   25 x 20 ½ cm.   "From the original drawings in charcoal ... Edition de luxe, limited to 50 copies."   1-14228.   F127.O97 M3
Rare Book Coll.

PALISADES.   The Palisades of the Hudson; their formation, tradition, romance, historical associations, natural wonders and preservation, by Arthur C. Mack.   Edgewater, N.J.. The Palisade press (1909)   2, 58 p.   front., illus., fold. map.   24 cm.   9-25288.   F127. P2 M2

PALISADES.   New York (State) Commissioners of Palisades interstate park.   Annual report. Albany,   v. 23 cm.   11-30524.   F127. P2 N 4

PALISADES.   Message of the governor of the state of New York.   Transmitted to the Legislature. Albany, J. B, Lyon co., printers, 1910.   1 v.   23 cm. Annual message. 9-33883.
F127. P2 N 5

PALISADES.   Summer in the Palisades.   A description of the Northern railroad of New Jersey and the Palisades.   (By Edward G. Tuckerman)   New York, Lange, Little, 1875.   49 p.   5 l. incl. pl. 16º. 1-14229-M1.   F127. P2 T 8

PUTNAM County.   The history of Putnam County; with an enumeration of its towns, villages, rivers, creeks, lakes, ponds, mountains, hills, and geological features; local traditions; and short biographical sketches of early settlers, etc. By William J. Blake ... New York, Baker & Scribner, 1849.   iv, (13) - 368 p.   18½ cm.   1-14232.   F127. P9 B6

PUTNAM County.   Inscriptions from 13 old cemeteries in Putnam Co.   (Copied by Josephine C. Frost (Mrs. Samuel Knapp Frost) Brooklyn, 1912?)   107, 4 numb. 1.   27 x 21 cm.   Autographed from type-written copy. Contents. - Ellis cemetery near Brewster - Cemetery in orchard near Brewster. - Cemetery, north end of Ellis farm. - Hughson, near Lake Mahopac. - Barrett Hill, near Carmel, N. Y. - Bailey, at Kent, N. Y. - Williams, near Carmel. - Crane, near Carmel. - Cole, near Carmel. - Carver, near Carmel. - Towners, at Towners, - Old Patterson (a pasture) - Patterson villages.   13-5139 Rev.

F127. P9 F 9

PUTNAM County cemetery inscriptions, copied by Josephine C. Frost.   (Brooklyn, 191 -)   154, 6 numb. 1.   27½ cm.   Autographed from type-written copy.   Contents. - Back of Baptist church, Carmel. - Baptist cemetery, Kent Cliffs. - Halstead cemetery, Carmel. - Baptist cemetery, Ludingtonville, N. Y. - Small cemetery west of Ludingtonville. - Raymond cemetery, Carmel. - Gilead cemetery, Carmel. - Kelley cemetery, Carmel.   13-13690 Rev.

F127. P9 F 94

PUTNAM County.   Early settlers of Putnam County.   By Frederick C. Haacker.   (New York) 1946. 51 l.   maps.   28 cm.   Tyepscript (carbon copy)   52-34001.   F127. P9 H 3

PUTNAM County historical society.   Calendar, 1911.   New York, 1910 -   16½ x 31½ cm.
F127. P9 P9

PUTNAM County.   ... In commemoration of the visit of the New York state historical association to West Point ... 1915 ... (New York, Print. E. S. Forham, 1915)   (8) p.   22½ cm.   34-25061.
F127. P9 P93

QUEENS County.   ... Papers relating to the churches in Queens County.   (By Edmund Bailey O'Callaghan.   (In The documentary history of the state of New-York.   v. 3, p. 187-340)   11-10996.   F127. Q
F122. D63 v. 3

QUEENS County.   Papers of the Lloyd family of the manor of Queens Village, Lloyd's Neck, Long Island, 1654 - 1826.   (Ed. Dorothy C. Barck)   2 v.   2 maps.   24½ cm.   (Collections of the New-York historical society for the year 1926-27.   Paged continuously.   v. 2 has genealogical appendix.   28-6973.   F127.Q3
F116. N63 vol. 59-60

QUEENS County.   ... The Montauk business directory of Queens County, Long Island ... 1912 - Jamaica, N. Y., The Montauk directory co., 1911 -   v. 26 cm. 11-30058.   Directories

QUEENS County.   Art work of Queens County ... Chicago, The W. H. Parish pub. co., 1895. 17 numb. 1.   1 illus., 69 pl.   35 cm.   Pub. in 12 parts.   20-9265.   F127. Q3 A7

QUEENS County.   ... Cemetery inscriptions ... from manuscripts in the possession of Mr. William F. Wyckoff, of Jamaica, Long Island ... Copied ... by Josephine C. Frost (Mrs. Samuel Knapp Frost) March, 1912.   3 v.   27 x 21 cm.   Autographed from type-written copy. 12-23351 Rev.   F127. Q3 F9

QUEENS County.   ... History of Queens County, with illustrations, portraits, & sketches of prominent families and individuals.   New York, W. W. Munsell, 1882.   476 (i. e. 472) p. incl. illus., plates (1 double) ports. front., plates, ports., fold. map.   30½ x 24 cm.   Some errors in paging.   1-14233.   F127. Q3 H6

QUEENS County.   Documents and letters intended to illustrate the revolutionary incidents of Queens county; with connecting narratives, explanatory notes, and additions.   By Henry Onderdonk, jr. New-York, Leavitt, Trow, 1846.   264 p.   20 cm.   1-14234 Rev.   F127.Q3 O55
Toner Coll.

QUEENS County in olden times: being a supplement to the several histories thereof.   By Henry Onderdonk ... Jamaica, N. Y., C. Welling, 1865.   2, (3) - 122 p.   30 x 23 cm.   Items extracted from newspapers and other sources, arranged chronologically, 1639-1832.   1-14235.   F127. Q3 O6

QUEENS County.   Portrait and biographical record of Queens county (Long Island) Containing portraits and biographical sketches of ... citizens of the county.   Together with biographies and portraits

NEW YORK

of all the presidents of the U.S.   New York, and Chicago, Chapman pub. co., 1896.   4, (19) - 1204
(i.e.1194) p. incl. illus., pl., ports.   port.   30 x 22½ cm.   Several pages omitted in paging. 1-14236. Rev.   F127. Q3 P 8

QUEENS County Surrogate records at Jamaica, New York, 1787 per 1835 (with some records of a later date) ... copies by William Applebie Daniel Eardeley ... Brooklyn, N.Y., 1905-18.   2 v.   28½ cm.
Type-written copy.   v. 1. Indexes of wills and abstracts. - v.2. Abstracts of wills and administrations. 24-177.   F127. Q3 Q3

QUEENS County.   Abstracts of wills for Queens county, compiled and ed. by Ray C. Sawyer.   (New York?) 1934.   2 v.   28 cm.   Type-written.   vol. 1, 1787-1813. - v.2. 1813-1828. 34-32602.   F127. Q3 S 3

RENSSELAER County.   ... Farmers' and country merchants' almanac and ready reference book. 1870.   Containing historical sketches of the counties of Albany, Rensselaer Washington, Warren, Schenectady, Saratoga, Rutland and Bennington; tog. with farmers; names, etc.   (1870)
207 p.   23 cm.   10-5637.   F127. R
F127. A3 F2

RENSSELAER County.directory, 18   ... together with a business directory of ... Troy, Lansingburgh and Greenbush ... Troy, 18   v.   22½ - 23 cm.   CA 6-1293 Unrev.   Directories

RENSSELAER County.   Landmarks of Rensselaer County, by George Baker Anderson ... Syracuse, N.Y., D. Mason, 1897.   xi, 735, 460 p.   ports.   25½ cm.   pt. II Biographical. - pt. III. Family sketches.   1-16740.
F127. R3 A5

RENSSELAER.   Gazetteer and business directory of Rensselaer County for 1870-71.   Comp. and pub. by Hamilton Child ... Syracuse, Printed at the Journal office, 1870.   349 p. incl. front. (fold. map)
21½ cm.   8-15804.   F127. R3 C5

RENSSELAER.   Our yesterdays, a history of Rensselaer County, by Stephanie Hicks Craib and Roderick Hull Craib.   (Troy? N.Y.) 1948.   121 l.   maps, diagrs.   29 cm.   48-11131*.   F127. R3 C7

RENSSELAER County pioneers ...   D.A.R., New York, Philip Schuyler chapter.   (Excerpt from the Troy Record, Dec. 31, 1919 p. 5)   F127.R3 D23

RENSSELAER County.   Taconic trails, being a partial guide to Rensselaer County rambles by auto and afoot.   By Edward Thornton Heald.   Albany, J. B. Lyon Co., 1929.   xii, 202 p.   front., plates, fold. map.   21 cm.   29-10698 rev.*   F127. R3 H4

RENSSELAER County.   In memoriam.   Isaac McConihe ... Troy, N.Y., The Daily press (1867?)
97 p.   front. (port.)   8°.   1-13603-M1.   F127. R3 I 3

RENSSELAER County.   Abstracts of wills proved in the Court of common pleas of Rensselaer County, from 1794 to 1822, together with one will from Washington County, by Charles Shepard.   Troy, N.Y., C. Shepard, 1921.   20 l.   28 x 22 cm.   Type-written copy.   Six copies made.   22-4155 Rev.   F127. R3 S 5

RENSSELAER County.   Some Rensselaer County gravestone inscriptions, by Charles Shepard II ... and Milton Thomas ... Washington, D.C., C. Shepard, 1923.   27 numb. l.   28 x 21½ cm.   (Shepard genealogical series. no. 15)   Mimeographed copy.   Contents. - Preface. - Groesbeck cemetery. - Read cemetery. - Barberville cemetery. - Peck cemetery. - Slouter cemetery. - Barringer-Sharp cemetery. - Myers cemetery. - East Poestenkill cemetery. - Index.   24-5131.
F127. R3 S 56

RENSSELAER County.   History of Rensselaer Co.   With illustrations and biographical sketches of its prominent men and pioneers.   By Nathaniel Bartlett Sylvester ... Philadelphia, Everts & Peck, 1880.
564 p.   illus., plates (1 double) ports., maps.   31 cm.   2-1296.   F127. R3 S 9

RENSSELAER County.   A souvenir of the founding of Rensselaer county, 1791.   Compiled by workers of the W.P.A.   (Troy, N.Y., The Whitehurst printing and binding co., 1941?)   31 p.   illus. (incl. ports., map)   23 cm.   43-7978.   F127. R3 W7

RENSSELAERSWYCK.   Inventory of the Rensselaerswyck manuscripts, ed. from the original manuscript in the N.Y. public library, by Victor Hugo Paltsits ... New York (Printed at the N.Y. public

library) 1924.   54 p.   25 ½ cm.   "Reprinted Sept. 1924 from the Bulletin of the New York public library of May, June, July, 1924."
25-16960.
F127. R 32
CD3409.5.V3N4 1924a

RENSSELAERSWYCK.   Old Hellebergh; historical sketches of the West manor of Rensselaerswyck, incl. an account of the anti-rent wars, the glass house, and Henry R. Schoolcraft, by Arthur B. Gregg. With a foreword by Dr. Alexander C. Flick ... (Altamont, N. Y., The Altamont enterprise, 1936)
viii, 188, (4) p.   illus. (incl. ports., facsims.)   23 cm.   38-18747.
F127. R32 G7

RENSSELAERSWYCK.   By Torstein Knutsson Torstensen Jahr.   (Bratt-aetten)   (In Symra ... 1909.
v. 5, p. 65-79)   10-31401 Rev.
F127. R32 J 2

RENSSELAERSWYCK.   Van Rensselaer Bowier manuscripts, being the letters of Kiliaen Van Rensselaer, 1630 - 1643, and other documents relating to the colony of Rensselaerswyck.   R. and ed. by A. J. F. van Laer, archivist. ...   Albany, University of the state of New York, 1908.   909 p.
facsims.   23 cm.   (History bulletin. 7)   Folded facsim. map in pocket at end.   "Settlers of Rensselaerswyck, 1630-1658": p. 805-846.
8-29380 Rev.
F127. R32 N5

RENSSELAERSWYCK.   Settlers of Rensselaerswyck, 1630 - 1658.   Ed. by A. J. F. Van Laer. Baltimore, Genealogical Pub. Co., 1965.   54 p.   25 cm.
F127. R32N53

RENSSELAERSWYCK.   Redres van de abuysen en de faulten in de colonie van Rensselaers-wijck. (By Kiliaen van Rensselaer)   t'Amsterdam ... Thunis Iacobsz ... 1643.   (Boston, 1928)
facsim.: (15) p.   22 ½ cm.   (Americana series: photostats by the Mass. historical soc. no. 205)   33-18716.
F127. R32R284
Rare Book Coll.

RENSSELAERSWYCK.   Waerschovwinge, verboth, ende, toe-latinghe, weghens de colonie van Renselaers-wyck.   t'Amsterdam ... Theunis Jacobsz ... (1643)   (Boston, 1922)   sheet.   42 ½ x 28 ½ cm. fold. and mounted in cover 23 ½ x 17 ½ cm.   (Americana series. Photostats by Mass. hist. soc. no. 59) 23-4651 Rev.
F127. R32R288
Rare Book Coll.

RENSSELAERSWYCK.   Insinuatie, protestatie, ende presentatie van weghen den patroon van de colonie van Rensselaers-wijck: (Amsterdam, 1643)   (Boston, 1922)   sheet.   40 x 28 ½ cm.   mounted in cover 23 ½ x 17 ½ cm.   (Americana series: photostats by the Mass. hist. soc. no. 59) 23-4652 Rev.
F127. R32R288
Rare Book Coll.

RENSSELAERSWYCK.   Kiliaen van Rensselaer van 1623 tot 1636, door dr J. Spinoza Catella Jessurun. 's-Gravenhage, M. Nijhoff, 1917.   3, 213, xxv p.   25 cm.   18-20596 Rev.
F127. R32R293

RENSSELAERSWYCK.   Kiliaen van Rensselaer, first patroon of the colony of Rensselaerswyck (by) Dunkin H. Sill.   (New York, 1926)   13 p.   26 cm.   "Reprinted from the New York genealogical and biographical record, July, 1926."   CA 26-804 Unrev.
F127. R32R296

RENSSELAERSWYCK.   Minutes of the court of Rensselaerswyck, 1648 - 1652, trans. and ed. by A. J. F. van Laer, archivist ...   Albany, The University of the state of New York, 1922.
5-236 p.   3 facsim.   23 cm.   23-27332.
F127. R32R32

RENSSELAERSWYCK.   Decision of the Supreme court of the U. S. in the suit of Jeremiah Van Rensselaer, appellant, vs. Philip Kearney and Frederick de Peyster ...   Hudson (N. Y.) P. D. Carrique's print, 1851.   8 p.   24 cm.   11-26993.
F127. R32 U5

RENSSELAERSWYCK.   Correspondence of Jeremias Van Rensselaer, 1651-1674, trans. and ed. by A. J. F. van Laer, archivist ...   Albany, The University of the state of New York, 1932.
494 p.   23 ½ cm.   "Pub. as a supplement to the Van Rensselaer Bowler mss., issued ... in 1908."   32-27659.
F127. R32V14

RENSSELAERSWYCK.   The Van Rensselaer manor.   By K. Van Rensselaer.   1917.   1 v.
F127. R32V27

NEW YORK

RENSSELAERSWYCK. The Van Rensselaer manor, address delivered at the third annual meeting of the New York branch of the Order of colonial lords of manors in America ... 1815, by Kiliaen Van Rensselaer. Repr. in 1929, with some additions by Florence Van Rensselaer and others. Baltimore, 1929. 100 p. col. front., illus. (incl. ports.) 23½ cm. (Publication no. 21) 34-5928.
F127.R32V27

RENSSELAERSWYCK. Correspondence of Maria van Rensselaer, 1669-1689; translated and ed. by A. J. F. van Laer ... Albany, The University of the state of New York, 1935. 206 p. 23 cm. 35-28190.
F127.R32V29

ROCKLAND County. Now and then and long ago in Rockland county, compiled by Cornelia F. Bedell. (Duffern, N. Y.) Priv. print. (The Ramapo valley independent) 1941. xvii, 3-368 p. 2 maps on fold. 1. (in pocket) 23½ cm. 42-3487.
F127. R6 B 4

— (Orangeburg? N. Y. 1968) xvii, 399 p. 24 cm.
F127. R6 B 4 1968

ROCKLAND County. Arnold, the American traitor; Andre, the British spy; Washington, the defender of constitutional liberty, the father of his country ... Address ... by Hon. Erastus Brooks ... New York, The Burr print., 1881. 34 p. front. 23½ cm. 9-16681.
F127. R6 B 8

ROCKLAND County. History of Rockland County, with biographical sketches of its prominent men. Ed. by Rev. David Cole. New York, J. B. Beers, 1884. ii, (3)-344, 75 p. front., illus., plates (2 double) ports., 3 maps (1 double) plan. 30½ cm. "Appendix. Baptisms at Tappan (1694-1816) and Clarkstown (1749-1795)": p. 1-75 at end. 1-14238.
F127. R6 C6

ROCKLAND County. The history of Rockland County, by Frank Bertangue Green. New York, A.S. Barnes, 1886. vi, 444 p. double map. 25½ cm. 1-14239.
F127. R6 G7

ROCKLAND County. The Rockland record, being the proceedings and historical collections of the Rockland county society of the state of N.Y. inc. for the years 1921 and 1922. ... Nyack, N.Y., The Rockland county soc...(1921 -
F127.R6 R75

ROCKLAND County. To the Republicans of the state of New York, and especially those of Rockland County. (Hempstead, N.Y., 1925) 22½ cm.
F127. R6 T6

ROCKLAND County. Historical record ot the close of the nineteenth century of Rockland County ... Ed. by Arthur S. Tompkins. Nyack, N. Y., Van Deusen & Joyce, 1902. 4, (17) - 577 p. 192, (6) p. front., plates, ports., maps. 25½ cm. Contents. - pt. I. Historical. - pt. II. Biographical. 20-16034.
F127. R6 T66

ST LAWRENCE County. ... American agriculturist farm directory and reference book of St. Lawrence County ... including a road map ... New York, N. Y., Minneapolis (etc.) Orange Judd co., v. fold. map. 23½ cm. Map detached. 18-14521.
Directories

ST. LAWRENCE County. Gazetteer and business directory of St. Lawrence County, N.Y., for 1873-4. Comp. and pub. by Hamilton Child ... Syracuse, Printed at the Journal office, 1873. 433 p. fold. map. 21½ cm. 6-9505.
F127. S2 C 5

ST. LAWRENCE County. The forest Arcadia of northern New York. Embracing a view of its mineral, agricultural, and timber resources. Boston, T. O. H. P. Burnham; New York, O. S. Felt, 1864. 224 p. 16½ cm. "That portion of the great wilderness of northern New York visited by the writer, lies in St. Lawrence County, on the western slope of the Adirondack Mountains," 1-14240.
F127. S 2 C6

ST. LAWRENCE County. ... History of St. Lawrence county, New York. (By Samuel W. Durant) With illus. and biographical sketches of some of its prominent men and pioneers. Philadelphia, L. H. Everts, 1878. 521 p. front., illus., plates (part double) ports., map, 2 facsim. 30½ x 23 cm. 1-14241.
F127. S 2 D9

ST. LAWRENCE County. Fortune's wheel, by Martha Gray ... New York, London (etc.) The Abbey press (1901) 2, vii-viii, 275 p. 20½ cm. Autobiographical sketch depicting life in northern New York before and during the civil war. 2-4-M2.
F127. S 2 G7

ST. LAWRENCE County. A history of St. Lawrence and Franklin counties, from the earliest period to the present time. By Franklin B. Hough ... Albany, Little & co., 1853.   xv, (17) - 719 p. incl. illus., plates, ports. front., plates (1 fold.) ports., fold. maps. 22 cm. 1-14242.
F127. S2 H 8

— Baltimore, Regional Pub. Co., 1970. xv, 719 p. illus. 24 cm. Facsim. reproduction, with an added foreword, of the edition pub. in Albany, 1853. 78-938871.
F127. S2 H 8 1970

ST. LAWRENCE County. Souvenir of Black Lake, a story of the past and present, by Florence Earle Payne. (Gouverneur, N.Y., Print. Frank L. Cox, 1917) 16 p. 24½ cm. 17-13930.
F127. S2 P34

ST. LAWRENCE County society of New York city. List of members of St. Lawrence county soc. of New York city. (New York? 1913-?) 43 p. 16½ x 8½ cm. 38M4273T.
F127. S2 S24

ST. LAWRENCE River. St. Lawrence power; recreation, housing, highways, and related matters. Power authority of the State of New York. (New York?) 1954. 7 p. illus. 28 cm. A55-9244.
F127.S23 P 6

ST LAWRENCE River. St. Lawrence reforestation, parks and recreation. Power Authority of the State of New York. (New York?) 1955. 20 p. illus. 28 cm. A 56-9320.
F127.S23 P62

SARANAC Lakes. The story of Saranac; a chapter in Adirondack history, by Henry W. Raymond. New York, The Grafton press (1909) 78 p. incl. front., illus., double pl. 21 cm. 9-3193.
F127.S24 R 2

SARATOGA County. Our county and its people: a descriptive and biographical record of Saratoga County, New York. Prepared and pub. under the auspices of the Saratogian. (comp. George Baker Anderson) (Boston) The Boston history co., 1899. xi, 584, 203 p. ports. 25½ cm. 1-3066* Cancel.
F127.S26 A 5

SARATOGA County. Gazetteer and business directory of Saratoga County, N.Y., and Queensbury, Warren County, for 1871. Comp. and pub. by Hamilton Child ... Syracuse, Print. at the Journal office, 1871. 307 p. incl. front. (fold. map) 21½ cm. 8-15805.
F127.S26 C 5

SARATOGA County. Sweetman and West Charlton cemeteries, Saratoga county. Collected and compiled by Federal writers' project, W.P.A., state of New York. (Albany, N.Y.) 1938. 2, 75 p. 26½ cm. Mimeographed. 39-26068.
F127.S26 F44

SARATOGA County. Quaker records from Saratoga County. (By Mrs. Josephine C. Frost) (72) l. 27½ cm. Autographed from type-written copy. 12-20274 Rev.
F127.S26 F 9

SARATOGA County. A geography of Saratoga County, by Adelbert A. Lavery ... (Ballston Spa, N.Y., Journal print) 1905. 36 p. fold. map. 23 cm. 6-22871.
F127.S26 L39

SARATOGA County. Abstracts of wills, Saratoga county, N.Y., 1791-1815, copied by Elizabeth MacCormick. Jackson Heights, N.Y. (1938?) 2, 2-78 numb. l. 29 cm. Type-written. 41-5816.
F127.S26 M2

SARATOGA County, an historical address, by Geo. G. Scott. And a centennial address, by J. S. L'Amoreaux. Delivered at Ballston Spa, N.Y., July 4, 1876 ... Ballston Spa, N.Y., Waterbury & Inman, 1876. 47 p. 23 cm. 1-14245 Rev.
F127.S26 S 4

SARATOGA County. A poem on the mineral waters of Ballston and Saratoga, with notes illustrating the history of the springs and adjacent country. By Reuben Sears. Ballston Spa (New York): Pub. by the author, J. Comstock, printer, 1819. 108 p. 15 cm. 10-31668.
F127.S26 S43

SARATOGA County. ... History of Saratoga County. With illustrations and biographical sketches of some of its prominent men and pioneers. By Nathaniel Bartlett Sylvester ... Philadelphia, Everts & Ensign, 1878. 514 p. front., illus., plates (part double) ports., maps, plans. 30½ cm. 1-14246.
F127.S26 S 8

NEW YORK 163

SARATOGA County. Saratoga and Kay-ad-ros-se-ra: an historical address, by N. B. Sylvester, delivered at Saratoga Springs ... 1876. 52 p. 23½ cm. 1-1640. F127.S26 S 9

SARATOGA County. Early days in eastern Saratoga county, book 1, by Mrs. J. B. Vanderwerker. (Schuylerville? N. Y., 1938) 23 p. illus. 23 cm. 43-39030. F127.S26 V 3

SCHENECTADY County. History of the county of Schenectady, from 1662 to 1886 ... (by) Howell (and) Munsell. Assisted by local writers. New York, W. W. Munsell, 1886. 2, vi, 218 p. front., illus. (incl. plans, facsims.) ports. 29 cm. (With Howell, George R. Bi-centennial history of Albany. New York, 1886) Includes biographical sketches. 1-14042. F127.S27
F127. A3 H8

SCHENECTADY County. Abstracts of wills of Schenectady county ... copied and compiled by Gertrude A. Barber. (n.p., 1941-43?) 2 v. 28 x 21½ cm. Type-written. 45-13865. F127.S27 B 3

SCHENECTADY County. Biographical review ... containing life sketches of leading citizens of Schenectady, Schoharie and Greene counties ... Boston, Biographical review pub. co., 1899. 2, (9) - 441 p. incl. ports. ports. 29 x 23½ cm. (Atlantic states series of biographical reviews) vol. xxxiii) 22-10736.
F127.S27 B 6

SCHENECTADY County. Private burial grounds in Schenectady county. Collected and compiled by Federal writers' project, W.P.A., state of New York. Albany, 1938. 43 p. 27½ cm. Mimeographed. 39-26072. F127.S27 F45

SCHENECTADY. The Historical record, devoted to the promotion of historical research, and to the diffusion of useful knowledge. Ed. by the Historical society. v. I, no. 1-4; Jan.-Apr. 1872. Schenectady, N.Y., E. Z. Carpenter (1872) 80 p. 28½ cm. monthly. No more pub. 4-13407.
F127.S27 H 6

SCHENECTADY County. Copies of Schenectady County family Bible records. Typewritten and arranged by Charlotte Taylor Luckhurst. Albany, 1921. 41 l. 28½ x 22 cm. Reproduced from type-written copy. 21-11333. F127.S27 L 9

SCHENECTADY County. Family Bible records. From Schenectady Co., N. Y., 1925. ... Arranged by Charlotte Taylor Luckhurst, (Albany, 1925) 53 l. 28 cm. Type-written. 25-13359.
F127.S27 L93

SCHENECTADY County. Contributions for the genealogies of the descendants of the first settlers of the patent and city of Schenectady, from 1662 to 1800. By Jonathan Pearson. Albany, J. Munsell, 1873. iv, 324 p. 1 illus. (coat of arms) pl. 22 x 19 cm. 4-11466. F127.S27 P 3
Rare Book Coll.

SCHENECTADY County. Year book of the Schenectady County historical society, Schenectady, N. Y. 1905/06 - 1906/08. (Schenectady, 1907) - 1908. 2 v. pl., port. 23½ cm. 8-22435.
F127.S27 S 2

SCHENECTADY County. A history of the county of Schenectady. (Schenectady County teachers' association) Schenectady, Barhyte & Birch, 1887. 54 p. front. (fold. map) 17½ cm. 5-11267.
F127.S27 S 3

SCHENECTADY County. History of the city and county of Schenectady; originally prepared in 1887 for use in the public schools of the city, now rev. and brought down to date. (Schenectady County teachers' association) Schenectady, N.Y., 1913. 46 p. 26 cm. First ed. appeared under title: History of the county of Schenectady. 13-24512. F127.S27 S32

SCHOHARIE County. The frontiersmen of New York: showing customs of the Indians, vicissitudes of the pioneer white settlers, and border strife in two wars ... By Jeptha R. Simms ... Albany, N. Y., G. C. Riggs, 1882-83. 2 v. front. (port.) illus. (incl. facsims.) 23½ cm. Greatly enlarged from the author's "History of Schoharie County and the border wars of New York," 1845. The larger part of the work is devoted to the revolutionary period. 1-15827.
F127.S3
E263. N6 S 5

897

SCHOHARIE County. Abstracts of wills, letters of administration and guardianship. Schoharie county. From original records at surrogate's office, Schoharie, New York ... Copied and compiled by Gertrude A. Barber. (New York? 1938)   5 v.   28 cm.   Type-written.   Contents. - v.1. 1795-1820. - v.2. 1820-1832. - v.3. 1832-1848. - v.4. 1848-1860. - v.5. 1860-Jan. 1863.   42-7813.
F127. S3 B 3

SCHOHARIE County. A brief sketch of the first settlement of the county of Schoharie, by the Germans: being an answer to a circular letter, addressed to the author, by "The historical and philosophical society of the state of New-York." By John M. Brown. Schoharie (N.Y.) Printed for the author, by L. Cuthbert, 1823.   23 p.   23 ½ cm.   1-14247 Rev.
F127. S3 B 8

SCHOHARIE County. To-wos-scho-hor, the land of the unforgotten Indian; a true story of the Schoharie Creek. By Dorwin W. Bulson.   1961.   vi, 35 l.   30 cm.
F127.S3 B 85

SCHOHARIE County. Deaths and burials in Schoharie County. Comp. (H. Cady) (1921)   1 v.
F127.S3 C 12

SCHOHARIE County. A history of Schoharie County (by) Marion F. Noyes, editor. (Richmondville, N.Y.) Printed by the Richmondville Phoenix, 1964.   184 p.   22 cm.
F127. S3 N 6

SCHOHARIE County. 1713. History of Schoharie County, with illustrations and biographical sketches of some of its prominent men and pioneers. By William E. Roscoe. Syracuse, N.Y., D. Mason, 1882.   470, xxviii p.   front., illus., plates, ports.   29 ½ cm.   L.C. copy replaced by microfilm.   5-33169.
F127. S3 R 8
Microfilm 8822 F

SCHOHARIE County. Constitution and by-laws of the Schoharie County historical society, etc. Schoharie, N.Y., Printed at the Republican office, 1889.   16 p.   22 ½ cm.   8-7798.
F127. S3 S 3

SCHOHARIE. A summary of Schoharie County, giving the organization, geography, geology, history. Prepared at the request of the County teachers' association by Solomon Sias ... Middleburgh, N.Y., Press of P. W. Danforth, 1904.   ii, (5), 14-154 p.   front. (port.) illus., fold. map.   15 ½ cm.   4-29811.
F127.S3 S 48

SCHOHARIE County. History of Schoharie County, and border wars of New York; containing also a sketch of the causes which led to the American revolution; and interesting memoranda of the Mohawk Valley ... By Jeptha R. Simms ... Albany, Munsell & Tanner, printers, 1845.   xix, (21) - 672 p.   incl. illus., plates, fold. facsim.   front.   22 ½ cm.   1-14248.
F127. S3 S 5

SCHOHARIE. Military records of Schoharie County veterans of four wars; comp. by George H. Warner ... Albany, N.Y., Weed, Parsons, printers, 1891.   428 p.   24 cm.   1-14249.
F127. S3 W2

SCHUYLER County. More tales from little Schuyler. By Barbara Bell. Pub. for the Author for Schuyler County Historical Society, 1967.   89 p.   23 cm.
F127.S34 B 4

SCHUYLER County. A biographical record of Schuyler County ... New York and Chicago, The S. J. Clarke pub. co., 1903.   5, (17) - 546 p. incl. ports.   ports.   28 x 23 cm.   17-16288.
F127.S34 B 6

SCHUYLER County. Reference business directory of Schuyler County, 1893-'94. With map. Comp. by Hamilton Child ... Syracuse, N.Y., D. Mason, 1893.   448 p.   fold. map.   24 cm.   9-10317.
F127.S34 C 5

SCHUYLER County. Descriptive and illustrated guide book of the famous Watkins Glen, a New York state reservation, located at Watkins, Schuyler Co. (head of Seneca Lake) 1st ed., 1916. Pub. for the Hope souvenir shop; comp. by J. D. Hope, agent. (Buffalo, New York, etc., The Matthews-Northrup works, 1916)   39 p.   illus., diagr.   23 cm.   16-13375.
F127.S34 H 8

NEW YORK

WATKINS GLEN. Board of commissioners of Watkins Glen reservation. Annual report. Albany, 1912 - v. 23 cm. 12-33551. F127.S34 N 5

SENECA County. Early chapters of Seneca history: Jesuit missions in Sonnontouan, 1656 - 1684. By Charles Hawley ... Auburn, N.Y., Knapp, Peck & Thomson, printers, 1884. 4, (9) - 89 p. fold. map. 24½ cm. "Reprinted from Collections of C.C.H.S. no. 3." 9-27653. F127.S4 F1030.8.H39

SENECA County directory, giving name and address of owner and tenant of every house in the county (outside villages) with number of acres and how to find the house on the new map ... Syracuse, N.Y., C. C. Ferris (1909) 1 v. 19½ cm. map wanting. Directories

SENECA County. Reference business directory of Seneca County, 1894-'95 ... Comp. by Hamilton Child ... E. M. Child, publisher, Syracuse, N.Y. Seneca Falls, N.Y., Courier printing co., 1894. 626 p. fold. map. 24 cm. 11-13674. F127. S4 C 5

SENECA County. Address of Geo. S. Conover, before the Waterloo library and historical society, at the Academy of music, Waterloo, 1879. (Waterloo, N.Y., 1879?) 12 p. 24½ cm. Title of the address: Echoes of Seneca Lake: or Reminiscences of a centenarian (!) (i.e. John Widner) 3-6507. F127. S4 C 7

SENECA County. ... History of Seneca County, with illustrations descriptive of its scenery, palatial residences, public buildings ... and important manufactories ... Philadelphia, Everts, Ensign & Everts, 1876. iv, (3) - 170 p. incl. 1 illus., plates, ports, etc. 37 x 30 cm. 1-14250. F127. S4 H 6

SENECA County. Portrait and biographical record of Seneca and Schuyler counties, containing portraits and biographical sketches of prominent and representative citizens of the counties. Together with biographies and portraits of all the presidents of the U.S. New York and Chicago, Chapman pub. co., 1895. 5, (19) - 508 p. incl. ports. 27½ cm. 1-14251 Rev. F127. S4 P 8

SENECA County. Centennial anniversary of Seneca County, and auxiliary papers pub. by the Seneca Falls historical soc. 2d annual, 1904. (Seneca Falls?) 1904. 4, 80 p. 23 cm. (Its Papers, no. 2) 5-5540. F127. S4 S 4

SEWARD. Mount. ... Ascent and barometrical measurement of mount Seward. By Verplanck Colvin ... Albany, The Argus company, printers, 1872. 12 p. pl. 23 cm. "From the 24th annual report on the New York State museum of natural history, for the year 1870 ..." 1-16316. F127.S45 C 7

SHAWANGUNKS. A climber's guide to the Shawangunks, by Arthur Gran. (New York) The American Alpine Club, 1964. ix, 155 p. 17 cm. On spine: The Shawagunks. F127. S 5 G7

SHAWANGUNKS. Legends of the Shawangunk (Shon-Gum) and its environs, including historical sketches, biographical notices, and thrilling border incidents and adventures relating to those portions of the counties of Orange, Ulster and Sullivan lying in the Shawangunk region. Illus. by numerous engravings and pen sketches by the author. By Philip H. Smith ... Pawling, N.Y., Smith & co., 1887. viii, 168 p. front., illus., plates. 26½ cm. 6-15856. F127. S5 S 6

SHELTER Island. The history of Shelter island, from its settlement in 1652 to the present time, 1932, by Ralph G. Duvall. Shelter Island Heights, N.Y., 1932. x p., 229 p. front., plates. 21 cm. 32-14954. F127.S54 D 9

SHELTER Island. The history of Shelter Island, 1652 - 1932; with a supplement, 1932-1952, by Jean L. Schladermundt. (2d ed., rev. and enl.) Shelter Island Heights, N.Y., 1952. 270 p. illus. 21 cm. 52-41632. F127.S54 D 9

SHELTER Island. The manor of Shelter island; an address read before the annual meeting of the Order of colonial lords of manors in America, 1931, by Miss Cornelia Horsford. New York, 1934. 27 p. illus. (incl. ports.) 23½ cm. (Publications, no. 25) 35-9797. F127.S54 H 6

SHELTER Island. Historical papers on Shelter Island and its Presbyterian church, with genealogical

166   LOCAL HISTORIES IN THE LIBRARY OF CONGRESS

tables ... By the Rev. Jacob E. Mallmann ... New York, Printed for the author by the A. M. Bustard co., 1899.   332 p. front., plates, ports., facsims. (1 fold.) 23½ cm.   99-4263 Rev.   F127.S54 M3

STATEN Island.   Polk's Staten island (borough of Richmond) directory.   v. 1 -   1933/34 -
New York city, R. L. Polk, 1933 -   v. illus.   27½ cm.   CA 33-331 Unrev.   Directories

STATEN Island advance 1921/11 -   business and telephone directory ... of Staten Island, Richmond borough, New York city.   (Staten Island) Richmond County advance pub. co., 1921 -
    v. fold. map.   23 cm.   21-9892.   Directories

STATEN Island.   Polk's official street guide of Staten island ... including a complete list of Staten island bus lines ... New York, R. L. Polk, 19   v.   15½ cm.   CA 34-505 Unrev.   F127. S7 A2

STATEN Island. . ... Staten Island, one vast city, one million inhabitants, one hour to New York; a dream with his eyes full-opened by George Batchelor.   Tottenville, 1869.   12 p.   17½ cm.
12-5133.   F127.S7 B 29

STATEN Island.   History of Richmond County (Staten Island) New York, from its discovery to the present time.   Ed. by Richard M. Bayles ... New York, L. E. Preston, 1887.   ix, 741 p. illus., plates, ports., maps, plan, facsim.   27 x 21 cm.   1-14252.   L.C. copy replaced by microfilm.   F127. S7 B 7
                                                                                                                                                             Microfilm 21048 F

STATEN Island.   Records of the Reformed Protestant Dutch church in Tompkinsville, Staten Island, Richmond County, in the former town of Castleton, and now the Reformed church, Brighton Heights, in the borough of Richmond, city of New York.   Trans. and ed. by Royden Woodward Vosburgh.   New York city, 1922.   2, v, 152 numb. 1.   front.   36 x 29 cm.   Autographed from type-written copy.   Partial contents. - baps. and births, 1823-1871.- Marriages, 1824-1871 ... Gravestone inscriptions.   22-19775.   F127. S7 B67

STATEN Island.   Historical records of Staten Island, centennial and bicentennial, for 200 years and more.   Delivered at Staten Island ... 1883, by Hon. Erastus Brooks.   (New York? 1883)
39 p.   22 cm.   20-3038.   F127. S7 B79

STATEN Island.   Commercial development of Staten Island, or Richmond borough of the city of New York.   By John Dunwell Brown.   (New York?) 1901.   11 p.   map.   8º.   1-24669-M1.   F127. D7
                                                                                                                                                             HF3163. N7B7

STATEN Island.   Rides and rambles on Staten island, by Reau Campbell ... Pub. for Staten island rapid transit railroad.   New York, C. G. Crawford, 1889.   23 p.   col. illus. (incl. map) 20½ cm.   1-14253.
                                                                                                                                      F127. S7 C 2

STATEN Island.   Annals of Staten island, from its discovery to the present time.   By J. J. Clute ...
New York, Press of C. Vogt, 1877.   xii, 464 p. incl. plan. front., pl.   25 cm.   1-14254 Rev.   F127. S7 C 6

STATEN Island.   The Conference or Billopp house, Staten Island, New York, by William T. Davis, chairman, Committee on history, Conference house assoc. ... (Lancaster, Pa., The Science press printing co.) 1926.   3, 3-200, (3) p.   front., illus.   23½ cm.   "Pub. under the auspices of the Staten Island hist. soc. ..."   28-5758.
                                                                                                                        F127.S7 D 18

STATEN Island.   History of the Staten island historical society, by William T. Davis ... (Staten Island, N.Y.) Staten island historical society, 1936.   15 p.   illus.   23½ cm.   37-38797.
                                                                                                                               F127.S7 D185

STATEN Island.   Staten island names; ye olde names and nicknames.   By William T. Davis, with map by Charles W. Leng ... New Brighton, N.Y., Natural science assoc., 1896.   (20)-76 p.   fold. map.   24 cm.
(Proceedings of the Natural science assoc. of Staten Island. vol. v, no. 5 Special no. 21)   1-14255.   F127. S7 D 2
        — Supplement to Staten island names ... New Brighton, N.Y., Natural science assoc., 1903.
(71)-91 p. incl. map.   23½ cm.   (Proceedings... vol. viii, no. 25. Special no. 23)   1-14255.   F127. S7 D 2
                                                                                                                             Suppl.

STATEN Island.   Colonel Francis Lovelace and his plantation on Staten island, by Edward C. Delavan,

                                                                         900

NEW YORK

jun'r. New Brighton, N.Y., Natural science assoc. of Staten island, 1902. (47) - 79. map, diagrs. (part fold.) 23½ cm. (Proceedings ... vol. vii, no. 15. Special no. 22) 3-2962 Rev.
 F127. S7 D 3

STATEN Island patroons, by Theodore DuBois and Dorothy Valentine Smith. (New York) Staten Island Historical Society, John Frederick Smith Publication Fund, 1961. 34 p. 19 cm.
 F127. S7 D 8

STATEN Island. The great bronze column of Staten Island, vertiably the eighth wonder of the world, 580 feet high. Erected in memory of the North American Indian ... (New York? 1909?) (9) p. pl. 26 cm. 9-27666.
 F127. S7 G 7

STATEN Island. Staten Island's claim to fame, "the garden spot of New York harbor", by Vernon B. Hampton ... Staten Island, N.Y., Richmond borough pub. and print. co. (1925) 187 p. 23½ cm. "Associations with famous personages": p. 29-187. 25-12521.
 F127. S7 H 2

STATEN Island. History and legend of Howard avenue and the Serpentine road, Grymes Hill, Staten Island, gathered by Charles Gilbert Hine from real estate records and long memories ... (New York? Priv. print., Hine brothers printers, 1914) 3, 80 p. front., plates, maps. 23½ cm. (Hine's annual, 1914) 15-23141.
 F127.S7 H 66

STATEN Island. Legends, stories and folklore of old Staten Island, by Charles Gilbert Hine and William T. Davis. (New York) Staten Island Historical Society (1947 - 1 v. illus. 24 cm. Contents. - pt. I. The North Shore. 48-13129*.
 F127.S7 H 67

STATEN Island. The story and documentary history of the Perine house, Dongan Hills, Staten Island, headquarters of the Staten Island antiquarian society, by Charles Gilbert Hine. (New York?) Staten Island antiquarian soc. inc., 1915. 7 - 88, (3) p. front., plates (part col.) 26½ cm. 17-12073.
 F127.S7 H 68

STATEN Island. The Melyn patroonship of Staten island; address delivered at the ninth annual meeting of the New York branch of the Order of colonial lords of manors in America, held in the city of New York ... 1921, by William Churchill Houston ... (n. p.) 1923. 17 p. incl. illus., port. 23½ cm. (Publications. no. 9) 23-12561.
 F127.S7 H 84

STATEN Island. Illustrated sketch book of Staten island, New York, its industries and commerce. (By Selden C. Judson) New York, S. C. Judson, 1886. 160 p. incl. front., illus. (incl. ports., map, plans) 24 cm. 1-14256 Rev.
 F127. S7 J 9

STATEN Island. A guide book ... New York, G. Kobbé (1890) 59 p. incl. front., pl. map. 16º. 1-14257-M1.
 F127. S7 K 7

STATEN Island. Early history of Staten Island, by Cornelius G. Kolff. (Rosebank? N.Y., 1918) (32) p. 22 cm. 19-3750.
 F127. S7 K 8

STATEN Island. Staten island fairies, by Cornelius G. Kolff; illus. by Alice Sargent Johnson ... New York city, Richmond borough pub. and print. co., 1939. 48 p. illus. (incl. map) 22 cm. 40-2911.
 F127. S7 K83

STATEN Island. A condensed history of Staten Island (borough of Richmond, New York city) by Charles W. Leng and Edward C. Delavan, jr. (New York) The Staten Island Edison corp., 1924. 33 p. illus., pl. 23 cm. 24-24846.
 F127. S7 L 5

STATEN Island and its people, a history, 1609 - 1929, by Charles W. Leng ... New York, Lewis historical pub. co., inc., 1930. 4 v. fronts., plates, ports., maps. 27½ cm. Vols. I-II and III-IV paged continuously. Contents. - I-II. Historical. - III-IV. Biographical. 31-24453.
 F127. S7 L 53

STATEN Island. Melyn papers, 1640 - 1699. (In New York historical society. Collections. v. 46) 14-21919.
 F127.S7
 F116.N63 v. 46

STATEN Island. English crown grants, by Stephen L. Mershon ... The foundation of colonial land titles under English common law. New York, The Law and history club (1918) 5, 266 p. 19 cm. 25-11798.
F127.S7 M54

STATEN Island. The major and the queen; or, A royal grant to a gallant soldier, by Stephen L. Mershon ... A Staten Island record of historic import. New York, R. R. Beam (1915) 5, 98 p. plates, double map, 2 port. (incl. front.) 19½ cm. 15-12832.
F127.S7 M57

STATEN Island. Morris's memorial history of Staten Island, New York ... (by) Ira K. Morris. New York (etc.) Memorial publishing co. (etc., 1898 - 1900) 2 v. fronts., illus., ports. 27 cm. Vol. 2 pub. by the author, West New Brighton, Staten Island. 1-27538.
F127. S7 M8

STATEN Island. The National American Indian memorial at Fort Wadsworth, harbor of New York. (Philadelphia, J. Wanamaker) 1913. (12) p. illus. 23 cm. 13-9464.
F127.S7 N 25

STATEN Island. National Prohibition Park Co. Prohibition Park. Port Richmond (1899) 23½ cm.
F127.S7 N 27

STATEN Island. Records of the Asbury Methodist Episcopal church at New Springville, Staten Island, in Richmond County, N.Y., in the former town of Northfield and now in the borough of Richmond, city of New York. Trans. and ed. by Royden W. Vosburgh. New York city, 1922. 3, ii-iii, 90 numb. l. front., photos. 35½ x 28½ cm. Autographed from type-written copy. Partial contents. - Baps. and births, 1857-1881. - Marriages, 1856-1881. - Deaths, 1858-1881 ... Gravestone inscriptions. 23-1912.
F127.S7 N 53
Microfilm 2349 F

STATEN Island. Records of Saint Andrew's Protestant Episcopal church at Richmond, Staten Island, in Richmond County, N.Y., in the former town of Northfield, etc. Vols. 2 and 3. Trans. and ed. by Royden Woodward Vosburgh. New York city, 1923. 2, v, 207 numb. l. 36 x 29 cm. Autographed from type-written copy. 23-14438. (In 1909, the N.Y. genealogical and biographical soc. pub. the first vol.)
F127.S7 N55

STATEN Island. Staten Island; a resource manual for school and community. New York (1964) 297 p. 23 cm. (Its Curriculum research report)
F127.S7 N 57

STATEN Island. Records of the Reformed Protestant Dutch church on Staten Island, Richmond County, etc. Vol. 2. Trans. and ed. by Royden Woodward Vosburgh. New York city, 1923. 2 p., iv, 255 numb. l. 36 x 28½ cm. Autographed from type-written copy. Covers years 1790-1870. The 1st vol. was pub. in Historical and genealogical miscellany by John E. Stillwell, v.1 and also in Collections of the N.Y. Geneal. and biographical soc. v. iv. 23-14439.
F127. S7 P85

STATEN Island. ... The earliest volume of Staten island records, 1678 - 1813. Sponsored by Fiorello H. La Guardia, mayor, city of New York. Prepared by the Historical records survey ... W.P.A. New York, N.Y., 1942. 1 v. maps (part fold. incl. front.) 27½ cm. (Transcriptions of early town records of N.Y.) Various pagings. Bibliography: p. xiii-xliv. 42-18983.
F127.S7 R 39

STATEN Island. Proceedings of the bi-centennial celebration of Richmond county, Staten island, New York. ... 1883. (New York, 1883) 23, 54 p. 23½ cm. On cover "Aquehonga." Contains Historical records of Staten island ... by Hon. Erastus Brooks. Also pub. separately. 1-14258 Rev.
F127. S7 R 4

STATEN Island. Borough of Richmond's solution of housing problem. (New York? 1920) 32 p. incl. illus., port. 25 cm. "Foreword" signed: Calvin D. Van Name. 22-735.
F127. S7 R 5

STATEN Island and Staten Islanders, comp. by the Richmond borough association of women teachers; cover designed by Josephine Thorne; editor, Margaret Louise Lynd ... New York, The Grafton press, 1909. 76 p. front. (map) illus., plates, port. 18½ cm. 9-20757.
F127.S7 R 57

STATEN Island; gateway to New York. By Dorothy Valentine Smith. (1st ed.) Philadelphia, Chilton Book Co. (1970) 238 p. illus. 21 cm. 76-128869.
F127.S7 S 59
1970

STATEN Island. This was Staten Island. By Dorothy Valentine Smith. (Staten Island, N.Y.) Staten Island Historical Soc., 1968. 131 p. illus. "1st printing 1968"
F127. S7 S 6

STATEN Island. ... History - story - legend, of the old King's highway, now the Richmond road,

NEW YORK

Staten Island, N.Y. ... (New York, Hine bros., printers) 1916.   3, 3-27 p. illus. (maps) 18 cm. Publications of the Staten Island antiquarian soc.... 16-16327.
F127.S7 S 67

STATEN Island.   Report on a proposed park system for the borough of Richmond, New York city, prepared and submitted by the Committee on parks of the Staten island chamber of commerce, with map of the borough of Richmond.   (St. George? 1902)   24 p.   map.   23 cm.   CA 10-4083 Unrev.
F127.S7 S675

STATEN Island.   The Staten Island historian   v.1 -   (no. 1 -   Jan. 1938 - (Richmond, N.Y.) Staten Island Historical Society.   v. in   illus., maps.   31 cm.   quarterly.   53-39391.
F127.S7 S 68

STATEN Island.   The Staten Island magazine (A new local literary monthly) v.1, no. 1 - Aug. 1888 -   Stapleton, Staten Island, F. Fagen, 1888 -   1 no.   21½ cm.
F127. S7 S 7

STATEN Island, New York, 50th anniversary.   Staten Island Chamber of Commerce (1945) (Richmond? N.Y.)   100 p.   illus. (incl. ports., map)   30½ cm.   46-5875.
F127. S7 S 75

STATEN Island tercentenial series.   Monograph.
F127.S7 S 76

STATEN Island.   Staten Island's first permanent settlement.   By Vernon Boyce Hampton.   (Staten Island, N.Y.) Staten Island Historical Soc. (1960)   20 p.   23 cm.   (Staten Island tercentennial series, monograph 1)
F127.S7 S 76

STATEN Island, 1524 - 1898.   By Henry George Steinmeyer.   Foreword by Loring McMillen.   Staten Island, N.Y., Staten Island Historical Society, 1950.   x, 134 p.   illus., port., maps.   24 cm.   Bibliography: p. 81-83.   50-4753.
F127.S7 S 78

— (1961)   x, 134 p.   24 cm.   "Second printing."
F127.S7 S 78
1961

STATEN Island under British rule.   By Henry George Steinmeyer.   (Staten Island, N.Y.)   Staten Island Historical Society, 1949.   18 p.   23 cm.   49-17252*.
F127. S7 S 8

STATEN Island.   Records of Saint Paul's Protestant Episcopal church at Tompkinsville, Staten Island, in Richmond County, etc.   Trans. and ed. by Royden Woodward Vosburgh.   New York city, 1923. 2 p., x, 156 numb. l.   front.   36 x 28½ cm.   Autographed from type-written copy.   Partial contents. - Baps. and births, 1833-1876 ... Marriages, 1835-1876. - Burials, 1834-1876.   24-5647.
F127. S7 T 6

STATEN Island gravestone inscriptions from the Sylvan Grove, Merrell and Hillside cemeteries in the former town of Northfield ... (v.1 -   ) New York city, 1924 -   1 v.   36 x 29 cm.
F127. S7 V 8
Rare Book Coll.

STATEN Island.   Records of the Woodrow Methodist Episcopal church at Woodrow, Staten Island ... Trans. and ed. by Royden Woodward Vosburgh.   New York city, 1922.   2 p., iv, 141 numb. l. 36 x 28½ cm.   Autographed from type-written copy.   Partial contents. - Baps. and births, 1798-1841, 1860-1876. - Marriages, 1829-1839, 1858-1875. - Gravestone inscriptions.   22-13928.
F127.S7 W 8

STEUBEN County.   History of Steuben county, with illustrations and biographical sketches of some of the prominent men and pioneers.   By Prof. W. W. Clayton.   Philadelphia, Lewis, Peck, 1879. 460 p.   illus., plates, ports., 2 maps.   20½ cm.   1-14259 Rev.
F127. S8 C 6

STEUBEN County.   Landmarks of Steuben County.   Ed. by Hon. Harlo Hakes and others.   Syracuse, N.Y., D. Mason, 1896.   vii, 379, 80, 530 p.   ports.   25½ cm.   1-2553 Add.
F127. S8 H 2

STEUBEN County.   History of the settlement of Steuben County, including notices of the old pioneer settlers and their adventures.   By Guy H. McMaster.   Bath (N.Y.) R. S. Underhill, 1853.   iv. 318 p. incl. pl.   19 cm.   1-14260.
F127.S 8 M 2

STEUBEN County.   History of the settlement of Steuben County, including notices of the old pioneer settlers and their adventures.   By Guy H. McMaster.   Bath (N.Y.) R. S. Underhill, 1853.   (Rochester, 1893)   iv, 207 p.   24 cm.   14-4847.   F127.S8 M22

STEUBEN County.   A history of Steuben County, and its people, by Irvin W. Near ... Chicago, The Lewis pub. co., 1911.   2 v.   front., pl., ports.   27½ cm.   Paged continuously.   Vol. 2 contains biographical sketches.   15-10343.   F127.S8 N 35

STEUBEN County.   Over my shoulder; a backward look at life in a Steuben County rural community before the 20th century's changes, by Genieva B. Pawling.   Limited ed.   Cameron Mills, N.Y., 1969.   vi, 198 p.   23 cm.   F127. S8 P 3

STEUBEN County.   ... Historical gazetteer of Steuben County, with memoirs and illustrations.   Comp. and ed. by Millard F. Roberts ... Syracuse, N.Y., M. F. Roberts, 1891.   2 v. in 1.   illus.   2 pl., 34 port., fold. map.   24 cm.   Pt. 2 has title ... Directory of Steuben County ...   6-15857.   F127. S8 R 6

STEUBEN County.   Who's who in Steuben; a biographical record of many of the prominent residents of Steuben county, together with an introductory chapter entitled Steuben's place in history, by William M. Stuart.   (Dansville, N.Y., F. A. Owen pub. co., 1935)   294 p.   23½ cm.   35-4000.   F127. S8 S 7

STEUBEN County.   Pioneer history & atlas of Steuben county, compiled from historical, statistical & official records by W. B, Thrall ... author and publisher.   (Perry, N.Y.) 1942.   (3) - 98 p.   illus. (maps)   28½ x 22½ cm.   43-9652.   F127. S8 T 5

SUFFOLK County.   The Montauk business directory of Long Island, Suffolk County ...   Far Rockaway, N.Y., Montauk directory co., 1909 -   1 v.   23½ cm.   9-4953.   Directories

SUFFOLK County.   ... Suffolk County Surrogate records at Riverhead, 1787 per 1829 (with some records of a later date) ... (copied by) William Applebie Daniel Eardeley ... Brooklyn, N.Y., 1905-18.   2 v.   28½ cm.   Type-written copy.   Contents. - v.1. Indexes of wills and abstracts. - v.2. Abstracts of administrations and wills.   24-176.   F127. S9 A4

SUFFOLK County.   Suffolk county's ten great townships of Long island.   (Riverhead? 1939)   222 p. incl. illus. (incl. maps) tables.   34 cm.   41-4388.   F127. S9 A 5 1939

SUFFOLK County.   Historical and descriptive sketches of Suffolk County ... with a historical outline of Long Island, from its first settlement by Europeans.   By Richard M. Bayles.   Port Jefferson, L.I., The author, 1874.   (v) - xii, (13) - 424, ix p.   19 cm.   1-14261.   F127. S9 B 3

— Port Washington, N.Y., I. J. Friedman, 1962.   424, ix p.   22 cm.   (Empire State historical publication 17)   62-20153.   F127. S9 B 3 1962

SUFFOLK County.   Ancient Long Island epitaphs, from the towns of Southold, Shelter Island and Easthampton, New York.   By Edward Doubleday Harris.   Boston, Press of D. Clapp, 1903.   vi, 106 p.   25½ cm.   "An ed. of 50 copies ... reprint from the N.E. hist. and geneal. reg., with additions."   8-31735.   F127. S9 H 3

SUFFOLK County.   Between bay and ocean, by Edith (Wardell) Hildreth.   (1st ed.)   New York, Vantage Press (1960)   92 p.   Autobiographical.   21 cm.   F127. S9 H 5

SUFFOLK County.   ... History of Suffolk County, with illustrations, portraits, & sketches of prominent families and individuals.   New York, W. W. Munsell, 1882.   (488) p. front., illus., plates, ports., fold. map, plan, facsim.   30½ cm.   Contains histories of Babylon, Brookhaven, East Hampton, Huntington, Islip, Riverhead, Shelter Island, Smithtown, Southampton and Southold.   1-14262.   F127. S9 H 6

SUFFOLK County.   Know Suffolk, the Sunrise County, then and now.   By Nathaniel Robinson Howell.   Islip, N.Y., Buys Bros., 1952.   181 p.   illus.   24 cm.   52-33606.   F127.S9 H 68

NEW YORK

SUFFOLK County, by Charles J. McDermott with an introd. by Jeannette E. Rattray. New York, J. H. Heineman (1965) viii, 86 p. 23 cm. "First printing 1965" (Format for America series) 64-23158. F127. S9 M2

FIRE ISLAND. Commissioners of Fire Island state park. Annual report. Albany, 1910.
1 v. 22½ cm. Second annual report ... 11-4732. F127. S9 N 4

FIRE ISLAND. Report on plan to restore and protect Fire Island. W. Earle Andrews, engineer. New York (Lithographed by Acme photo offset corporation) 1938. 72 l. incl. illus., plates (part fold.) maps (part fold.) tables, diagrs., form. 28 cm. Issued by the Long island state park commission. 38-28766. F127. S9 N 45

SUFFOLK County. Early history of Suffolk county, L. I. By Hon. Henry Nicoll. A paper read before the Long island historical society, 1865. Brooklyn, Printed for the Society, 1866. 18 p. 23½ cm. 1-14263. F127. S9 N 6

SUFFOLK County. Revolutionary incidents of Suffolk and Kings counties; with an account of the battle of Long Island, and the British prisons and prison-ships at New-York. By Henry Onderdonk, jr. New-York, Leavitt & co., 1849. (5) - 8, (11) - 268 p. front. (fold. map) 19 cm. 1-14264. F127. S9 O 5

SUFFOLK County. Suffolk and Kings counties in the olden times ... By Henry Onderdonk. Jamaica, L. I., 1866. 37 l. 8°. Mounted newspaper cuttings; ms. t-p. notes and indices. 1-14293-M1. F127. S9 O 6

SUFFOLK County. Early Long Island wills of Suffolk County, 1691 - 1703. An unabridged copy of the manuscript volume known as "The Lester wills book;" being the record of the Prerogative court of the county of Suffolk; with genealogical and historical notes, by William S. Pelletreau ... New York, F. P. Harper, 1897. xi, (9) - 301 p. front. (facsim.) 24 cm. 1-14265. F127. S9 P 3

SUFFOLK County. Portrait and biographical record of Suffolk county (Long island) Containing portraits and biographical sketches of prominent and representative citizens of the county. Together with biographies and portraits of all the presidents of the U.S. New York, Chicago, Chapman pub. co., 1896. 4, (19) - 1039, (6) p. incl. 1 illus., ports. port. 27½ cm. 1-14266. F127. S9 P 8

SUFFOLK County. Colonel Rockwell's scrap-book; short histories, dwellings, mills, churches, taverns, township of Smithtown, Suffolk County, Long Island, 1665 - 1845. Ed. by Charlotte Adams Ganz. (Smithtown, N.Y.) Smithtown Historical Society, 1968. 184 p. illus. 29 cm. 68-28908. F127. S9 R 6 1968

FIRE ISLAND. Legends of Fire Island beach and the South Side, by Edward Richard Shaw. New York, Lovell, Coryell & co. (1895) 212 p. incl. front., illus. 19 cm. 12-12216. F127. S9 S 5

— Port Washington, N.Y., I. J. Friedman (1969) 212 p. illus. 19 cm. (Empire State historical publications series, no. 76) 72-101021. F127. S9 S 5 1969

SUFFOLK County. Suffolk County historical society, Riverhead, L.I. Leaflet, no. 1. Sept., 1900. (Brooklyn, N.Y., 1900) 1 pamphlet 18 x 9½ cm. F127. S9 S 87

SUFFOLK County. Suffolk County historical society Year book ... 1896 - 1907, 1909. Riverhead, N.Y., 1902-09. 13 pamphlets. 24½ cm. F127. S9 S 9

SUFFOLK County. To friends of the Suffolk County historical society. (Riverhead? 1892?) 21½ cm. F127. S9 S 93

SUFFOLK County historical society, Sag Harbor, N.Y. List of articles received for preservation ... (Sag Harbor, N.Y?) 1896. 20½ cm. F127. S9 S 98

— during the years 1895 ... (Riverhead, N.Y., Roanoke press, 1895) 14 p. 4-33419. F127. S9 S982

SUFFOLK County historical society. (Officers constitution and by-laws. Riverhead? 1892?)
21 cm. F127.S9 S 99

— 1886. 16 cm. F127.S9S 995

SUFFOLK County. ... History of Suffolk county, comprising the addresses delivered at the celebration of the bi-centennial of Suffolk county, ... 1883. Babylon, N.Y., Budget steam print, 1885.
125 p. 24 cm. 1-14267 Rev. F127. S9 T 6

SULLIVAN County. Gravestone inscriptions ... Sullivan county ... copied and ed. by Gertrude A. Barber. (New York?) 1929-34. 10 v. 28 x 21½ cm. Type-written. 45-30814. F127.S91 B 3

SULLIVAN County. Gazetteer and business directory of Sullivan County for 1872-3. Comp. and pub. by Hamilton Child ... Syracuse, Printed at the Journal office, 1872. 351 (i.e. 371) p. incl. front. (fold. map)
21½ cm. 6-10826. F127.S91 C 5

SULLIVAN County. History of Sullivan County: embracing an account of its geology, climate, aborigines, early settlement, organization ... with biographical sketches ... by James Eldridge Quinlan. Liberty, N.Y., G. M. Beebe & W. T. Morgans, 1873. 700 p. 23½ cm. 1-14268.
F127.S91 Q 7

SULLIVAN County. Brass buttons and leather boots; Sullivan County and the Civil War. Sullivan County hist. soc. Sullivan County Civil War Centennial Commission. South Fallsburg, N.Y., 1963.
84 p. 63-22714. F127.S91 S 9

SUSQUEHANNA stories. By Lu B. Cake. New York city, 1912. 15½ cm. F127.S96 C 2

SUSQUEHANNA Valley. Life on the Upper Susquehanna, 1783 - 1860. New York, King's Crown Press, 1951. ix, 172 p. maps. 21 cm. Thesis - Columbia University. Bibliography: p. (151) - 166. 51-9991.
F127.S96 F 7

SUSQUEHANNA Valley. The old New York frontier; its wars with Indians and Tories; its missionary schools, pioneers and land titles, 1614 - 1800, by Francis Whiting Halsey ... New York, C. Scribner's sons, 1901. xiii, 432 p. front., plates, ports., 2 fold. maps. 21½ cm. Largely a history of the upper Susquehanna Valley. Bibliography: p. (401) - 411. 1-31627/5 Rev. F127.S96
F119. H 19

SUSQUEHANNA Valley. ... Papers relating to the Susquehannah River. 1683 - 1757. By Edmund Bailey O'Callaghan. (From the documentary history of the state of New-York ... v. 1) 8-27638.
F127.S96 O15

THOUSAND Islands. Alexandria Bay and the Thousand Islands. A summer resort for pleasure seekers. Watertown, N.Y., Post job print., 1874. 22 p. front. 12°. 1-22543-M1.
F127. T5 A3

— 1874. 32 p. front., illus., fold. map. 22½ cm. 18-15038. F127.T5 A32
Toner Coll.

THOUSAND Islands. Extension view card five feet long, 19 views of The Thousand Islands ... Portland, Me., 1908. 1 v. 15½ x 20½ cm. F127. T5 E9

— 1908. 15½ x 21 cm. no. 2. F127.T5 E91

THOUSAND Islands. The Frontenac ... (Fulton, N.Y., 19 -) 18½ cm. F127. T5 F9

THOUSAND Islands. 'Round the islands with Capt. "Dud" Gould ... Horace Graeme Gould. (Syracuse, N.Y.) 1928. 19 p. illus., fold. map. 18 cm. 29-8550. F127. T5 G7

THOUSAND Islands. A souvenir. The Thousand Islands of the St. Lawrence River from Kingston

NEW YORK

and Cape Vincent to Morristown and Brockville. With their recorded history from the earliest times ... Profusely illustrated ... Pub. by Jno. A. Haddock ... Albany, N.Y., Weed-Parsons print., 1895. 416 p. incl. illus., plates, ports. front., 4 pl. (1 fold.) ports., fold. map. 28 cm. 1-14269.   F127. T5 H2

— Alexandria Bay. N.Y., Print, Weed-Parsons, 1896. 256 p. front., illus., plates, ports., fold. map. 25½ cm. Second edition - revised and corrected. 1-21419.   F127. T5 H3

THOUSAND Islands. Hints for pleasure seekers. The Thousand Islands of the St. Lawrence. Alexandria Bay and the Crossmon house. By one who has been there. Dansville, N.Y., A. O. Bunnell, printer, 1874. 24 p. 14½ x 11½ cm. 17-23195.   F127.T5 H66 Toner Coll.

THOUSAND Islands. The Thousand Islands of the river St. Lawrence, with descriptions of their scenery, as given by travellers from different countries, at various periods since their first exploration, and historical notices of events with which they are associated. Ed. by Franklin B. Hough. Syracuse, N.Y., Davis, Bardeen, 1880. vi p., (9) - 307 p. incl. front. (plan) illus. 17 cm. 1-14270.   F127. T5 H8

THOUSAND Islands. The Thousand islands of the St. Lawrence river; with descriptions of the scenery, and historical quotations of events, and reminiscences, with which they are associated, by Captain Henry S. Johnston. Boston, The Christopher pub. house (1937) 142 p. incl. front. (port.) illus. fold. map. 24½ cm. 37-30352 rev. 2.   F127. T5 J 6

THOUSAND Islands. The Thousand Islands ... By Albert G. Marshall. (Syracuse, N.Y.) 1912. 16 x 23½ cm.   F127. T5 M3

THOUSAND Islands. Picturesque Thousand islands of the St. Lawrence. With historical introduction by A. Grosvenor Hopkins. Copyright ... by A. Wittemann ... New York, The Albertype co. (1891) 37 pl., (10) p. 20½ x 25 cm. 1-14271 Rev.   F127. T5 P 6

THOUSAND Islands. The story of Grenell, written in 1945 by Alice Olivia Pratt ... drawings by Margret Ogden McElfresh. Watertown, N.Y., Hungerford-Holbrook co., 1946. 108 p. illus., plates, ports. 20 cm. 46-21119.   F127, T5 P 7

THOUSAND Islands. Meandering among a thousand islands; or, An account of Capt. Visger's daily trip on the St. Lawrence. (By George Rockwell) Watertown, N.Y., Times and reformer print. and pub. house, 1881. 37 p. illus. 8°. Cover title: The steamer Island Wanderer. 1-14272-M1.   F127. T5 R6

— 1882. 39 p. illus. 23 cm. 2-19049.   F127. T5R61

THOUSAND Islands. Sunlight pictures of the Thousand Islands. Half-tones from photographs by McIntyre. New York, The Artotype pub. co. (1895) 5 p. 34 pl., fold. map. obl. 12°. 31 of these plates also issued under title: Views and vistas of the Thousand Islands. (1895) 1-14273-M1.   F127. T5 S 9

THOUSAND Islands. Estes' standard guide to the Thousand islands and voyage down the rapids to Montreal, Quebec, lake St. John and the Saguenay river ... Written and illus. by Frank H. Taylor. Clayton (N.Y.) E. W. Estes (1893) 63 p. illus. (incl. maps) 21 cm. 1-14274 Rev.   F127. T5 T2

THOUSAND Islands. Guide book of the Thousand island house on the St. Lawrence river, Alexandria Bay, New York. R. H. Southgate, proprietor. N.Y., Leve & Alden (1884) 29 (4) p. incl. illus., diagr. 8°. 1-26400-M2.   F127.T5 T47

THOUSAND Islands. Thousand Islands and St. Lawrence River, "the Venice of America." 121 photographic views of the island region. Reproduced in sepia and natures own colors. Automobile road map of northern New York. Toronto, Ont., Pub. expressly for the Canada railway news co., (1917) (67) p. illus. (part col., incl. maps) 18½ x 24 cm. 17-21709.   F127.T5 T49

THOUSAND Islands. The Thousand Islands red book ... Alexandria Bay, N.Y., T. L. James (1895) 32 p. nar. 24°. 1-14275-M1.   F127. T5 T5

THOUSAND Islands. Views and vistas of the Thousand islands. From photos. by McIntyre. New York, The Artotpye pub. co. (1895) 62 pl. on 31 l. 16 x 22 cm. Also issued, with additions, under title: Sunlight pictured of the Thousand Islands. 1-14276.
 F127. T5 V6

THOUSAND Islands. Place-names in the Thousand Islands, St. Lawrence River, by James White ... Pub. by order of Honourable L. P. Brodeur, minister of marine and fisheries of Canada, for the Geographic board of Canada. Ottawa, Government printing bureau, 1910. 7 p. 25 cm. 10-31402.
 F127. T5 W5

TIOGA County. An outline history of Tioga and Bradford counties in Pennsylvania, Chemung, Steuben, Tioga, Tompkins, and Schuyler in New York ... (By John L. Sexton, jr.) (Elmira, N.Y., The Gazette co., 1885) 283 p. 18 cm. 1-10526.
 F127. T6
 F157. T5 S 5
 F157.B76 S 5

TIOGA County. Journey to day before yesterday. By Edward Roe Eastman. Drawings by Paul Frame. Englewood Cliffs, N.J., Prentice-Hall (1963) xiii, 254 p. 16 x 24 cm. 63-18603.
 F127. T6 E2

TIOGA County. ... Historical gazetteer of Tioga County, 1785 - 1888. Comp. and ed. by William B. Gay. ... Syracuse, N.Y., W. B. Gay & co. (etc., 1887?) 2 v. in 1. 21 port., fold. map. 24 cm. Map attached to back cover. Pt. 2 has title ... Directory of Tioga County ... 1887-'88. 6-15855 Rev.
 F127. T6 G2

TIOGA County. 1820 federal census Tioga County. Compiled by Nellie C. Hiday. Typed by: Maryan R. Gill. Danville, Ill., Heritage House, 1970. 25 p. 28 cm.
 F127. T6 H5

TIOGA County. History of Tioga, Chemung, Tompkins and Schuyler counties, New York. With illus. and biographical sketches of some of its prominent men and pioneers. (By Henry B. Peirce) Philadelphia, Everts & Ensign, 1879. 687 p. illus., plates (part double) ports., maps. 31 cm. 1-15073.
 F127. T6 P 3

— Name index. Alphabetized by Nellie M. Sheldon. (n.p.) 1965. 1 v. (unpaged) 28 cm.
 F127. T6 P 3
 Index

TIOGA County. À l'abri, or The tent pitch'd. By Nathaniel P. Willis. New York, S. Colman, 1839. 172 p. 19 cm. Consists of a series of letters describing the valley of the Susquehanna, near Owego, in Tioga County. 14-3402 Rev.
 F127. T6 W9
 Rare Book Coll.

TOMPKINS County. Abstracts of wills of Tompkins county ... From 1817 - 1833. Copied from the original records at the Court house, Ithaca, N.Y. Compiled by Gertrude A. Barber. (New York?) 1941. 47 numb. l. 28 cm. Type-written. 42-7814.
 F127. T7 B 3

TOMPKINS County. Gazetteer and business directory of Tompkins County, for 1868. Comp. and pub. by Hamilton Child ... Syracuse, Printed at the Journal office, 1868. (5) - 240 p. front. (fold. map) 21½ cm. 6-10145.
 F127. T7 C5

TOMPKINS County. De Witt historical society of Tompkins County ... Publications. Ithaca, N.Y., 1905 - 1 v. 22½ cm. 6-9618.
 F127. T7 D5

TOMPKINS County. Two pioneers of Tompkins County. By Albert Benjamin Genung. (Freeville? N.Y., 1954) 27 p. 23 cm. 54-41742.
 F127. T7 G4

TOMPKINS County. This way to Podunk; tales from "Far above Cayuga's waters." By Harold Jansen. New York, Vantage press (1954) 76 p. 22 cm. 54-9133.
 F127. T7 J 3

TOMPKINS County. Early explorers and travelers in Tompkins County. By W. Glenn Norris. DeWitt Historical Soc. of Tompkins County, 1961. Ithaca, N.Y. 68 p. illus. 23 cm.
 F127.T7 N59

NEW YORK

TOMPKINS County. Old Indian trails in Tompkins county, by W. Glenn Norris ... Ithaca, N.Y., Pub. under the auspices of the De Witt hist. soc. of Tompkins county, 1944. 32 p. illus. (incl. maps) 23 cm. Bibliography and "Reference maps": p. 32. 45-13753.
F127. T7 N6

TOMPKINS County. Landmarks of Tompkins county: incl. a history of Cornell University by Prof. W. T. Hewitt; ed. by John H. Selkreg ... Syracuse, D. Mason, 1894. viii, 704, 71, 276 p. illus., port., maps. 25½ cm. Contents. - pt. 1. Historical. - pt. 2, Biographical. - pt. 3, Family sketches. 2-19056.
F127. T7 S 4

TOMPKINS County. Notes from the diary of Abner H. Thomas, Town of Ulysses, Tompkins Co., 1863 - 1864 - 1865. Transcribed by his daughter Eva A. Thomas, 1948. Pub. for DeWitt hist. soc. of Tompkins County. Ithaca, N.Y., 1960. 46 p. 23 cm.
F127. T7 T47

TRYON County. Col. Jacob Klock's regiment, second reg., Tryon County militia, 1775-84. Proposed monument to Col. Klock and his regiment ... Compiled by L. D. MacWorthy ... St. Johnsville, N.Y., Enterprise and news (1929) 14 p. illus. 24 cm. A 30-1073.
F127. T8
E263. N6M17

TRYON County. Annals of Tryon County; or, The border warfare of New York, during the revolution. By William W. Campbell ... New York, J. & J. Harper, 1831. 191, 78 p. front. (fold. map) fold. facsim. 20½ cm. Tryon county comprised all of the province west of the tier of counties on the west bank of the Hudson. Its name was later changed to Montgomery and the county has been many times subdivided. A later edition, N.Y., 1849, pub. under title: The border warfare of N.Y., during the revolution; or, The annals of Tryon County. For other titles see F127. M7. 1-14277.
F127. T8 C2

TUG HILL country; tales from the big woods (by) Harold E. Samson. Lakemont, N.Y., North Country Books, 1971. 227 p. illus. 24 cm.
F127. T83 S 2

ULSTER County. ... Papers relating to Ulster and Dutchess counties. (1660-1782) (By Edmund Bailey O'Callaghan) (In The documentary history of the state of New-York v. 3) 11-10986.
F127. U
F122. D63 v. 3

ULSTER County. ... Breed pub. co.'s directory of the New York, Ontario & western railroad, from Cornwall to Sidney, embracing ... Middletown, Meadowbrook, Little Britain (etc.) ... Newburgh, N.Y., Breed pub. co., v. 24½ cm. No vols. pub. for 1906. 0-3415 Rev.
F127. U4
F117.5. B 83

ULSTER County. The Ulster County business directory, for 1874, containing the names, business and address of all merchants, etc. in the county. Pub. by O. H. Bame, Kingston, N.Y., 1874. 2 p, 25-110 p. 19½ cm. 11-24285.
Directories

ULSTER County probate records in the office of the surrogate, etc. A careful abstract and translation of the Dutch and English wills ... with genealogical and historical notes ... by Gustave Anjou ... with introd. by Judge A. T. Clearwater. v. 1-2. 2 v. fronts., plates, map, facsims. 25 cm. (American record series A.:- Wills. vol. 1-2) 6-13408.
F127. U4 A5

ULSTER County. Art work of Ulster County. Chicago, The W. H. Parish pub. co., 1893. (19) l. illus., (72) pl. 34½ x 27½ cm. Pub. in 12 parts. Text has caption: History of Ulster Co. by Marius Schoonmaker. 11-6062.
F127. U4 A7

ULSTER County. Shawangunk Mountain stories, by Wilhelm Benignus. (Altoona, Pa., Printed by Altoona tribune co.) 1916. 36 p. front. (port.) plates. 19½ cm. 16-16924.
F127. U4 B46

ULSTER County. In days of yore. By L. W. Botsford. Cragsmoor, N.Y. (1902) (32) p. 11 pl. 15½ x 25 cm. 2-20483.
F127. U4 B 7

ULSTER County. Gazetteer and business directory of Ulster County, for 1871-2. Comp. and pub. by Hamilton Child ... Syracuse, Print. at the Journal office, 1871. 333 p. incl. front. (fold. map) 21 cm. 8-18452.
F127. U4 C5

LOCAL HISTORIES IN THE LIBRARY OF CONGRESS

ULSTER County. The history of Ulster County; ed. by Alphonso T. Clearwater ... Kingston, N.Y., W. J. Van Deusen, 1907. (5)-10, (17)-712 p., xii p. front., plates, ports. 24½ x 19 cm. The different chapters are by various local writers. 8-17379.
F127. U4 C6

ULSTER County. Picturesque Ulster; a pictorial work on the County of Ulster, containing over one thousand original illus. By Richard Lionel De Lisser. Republished with a foreword by Alf Evers. Cornwallville, N.Y., Hope Farm Press, 1968. viii, 286 p. illus. "Originally pub. in 8 numbered parts, Kingston, 1896 to 1905." 33 cm.
F127.U4 D28 1968

ULSTER County. Old mine road, trail for Indians and early settlers (by) Amelia Stickney Decker. Sussex, N.J., Wantage recorder press, 1932. 39 p. illus. (incl. map) 23½ cm. "References": p. 38. 33-5630.
F127. U4 D3

ULSTER County. That ancient trail (the Old mine road) first road of any length built in America, by Amelia Stickney Decker, 1942. With more than 75 engravings and illustrations. (Trenton, Petty printing co., 1942) 151 p. illus. (incl. maps) 24 cm. 42-22437.
F127.U4 D32

ULSTER County. Quaker marriage certificates from Marlboro, Ulster County, New York. 2 p. 17 numb. l. 20, 2 numb. l. 27½ x 21 cm. Autographed from type-written copy. 12-24139.
F127. U4 F8

ULSTER County. Quaker records from Plains Monthly meeting, Ulster Co. Births by families and some deaths. (By Mrs. Josephine C. Frost) (71) l. 27 cm. Autographed from type-written copy. 12-20273 Rev.
F127. U4 F9

ULSTER County. History and legend, fact, fancy and romance of the Old mine road, Kingston, N.Y. to the mine holes of Pahaquarry ... (By Charles Gilbert Hine) (New York?) 1908. vi, 176, xiv, (15)-79, (3) p. 21 cm. (Hine's annual, 1908) Road traverses Ulster, Sullivan and Orange counties, N.Y. and Sussex Co., N.J. Contains a reprint; of "The Indians: or, Narratives of massacres ... in Wawasink and its vicinity ... N.Y., 1846" 9-23229.
F127. U4 H6

ULSTER County. The old court houses of Ulster County, and interesting incidents connected with their history. An historical discourse delivered by Chaplain Roswell Randall Hoes ... 1918, to commemorate the centenary of the erection of the present edifice. Kingston, N.Y., Freeman pub. co., 1918. 32 p. 24½ cm. 19-10891.
F127. U4 H7

ULSTER County. Lake Minnewaska mountain houses ... Minnewaska, Ulster County. (Fulton, N.Y., The Morrill press, 1918) (20) p. illus. 20 cm.
F127. U4 L2

ULSTER County. Picturesque Ulster ... By R. Lionel de Lisser. Kingston, N.Y., 1896. pt. 1-2. 34 cm.
F127. U4 L7

ULSTER County. ... Names of the male inhabitants of Ulster County, 1689. A roll of the names and surnames of them that have takin the oath of allegiance in ye county of Ulster ... 1689. (From the documentary history of the state of New-York ... v. 1.) 8-27642.
F127. U4 N5

ULSTER County. ... Old Ulster; an historical and genealogical magazine. v. 1-10; Jan. 1905 - Dec. 1914. Kingston, N.Y., B.M. Brink, 1905-14. 10 v. illus. 24½ cm. monthly. No more pub. 6-13599 Rev.
F127. U4 O4

ULSTER County. The story of Mohonk, by Frederick E. Partington. (Fulton, N.Y., The Morrill press) 1911. 4, 33 p. front. (port.) plates. 17½ cm. 12-22799.
F127. U4 P 2

— (1932) 6, 85 p. front., plates, ports. 18 cm. "Second edition." This edition contains a second part with special t.-p. (p. 35-85) compiled by Daniel Smiley, jr. and Albert K. Smiley, jr., covering the period, 1911-1931. 32-20401.
F127. U4 P 2 1932

ULSTER County. Banners and bugles; a record of Ulster County and the Mid-Hudson region in the Civil War. "compiled with the cooperation of the Ulster County Board of Supervisors." Marlborough, N.Y., Centennial Press (1963) 164, (4) p. 27 cm. 63-20099.
F127.U4 P 55

NEW YORK

ULSTER County. Old gravestons of Ulster county ... By John Wilson Poucher. v.1 - 1931.
F127.U4 U42
— Copy 2 in Rare Book Coll. F127. U4 P 6

ULSTER County. Gravestone inscriptions of Ulster County ... copied & ed. by Lila James Roney.
(n.p.) 2924 -   v. 27 cm.   Autographed from type-written copy.   24-24433.   F127. U4 R7

ULSTER County. Lake Minnewaska ... Minnewaska, N.Y., George A. Smiley, 1933. (24) p. incl. front.,
illus. 22 ½ cm.   F127. U4 S 5

ULSTER County. Legends of the Shawangunk (shon-gum) and its environs; including historical sketches, biographical notices, and thrilling border incidents and adventures relating to those portions of the counties of Orange, Ulster and Sullivan, lying in the Shawangunk region, by Philip H. Smith. Foreword by Carl Carmer. (New ed. Syracuse, N.Y.) Syracuse University Press (1965)
xiv, 212 p. 22 cm. 65-15850.   F127.U4 S 53

ULSTER County. History of Ulster County, with illustrations and biographical sketches of its prominent men and pioneers. By Nathaniel Bartlett Sylvester ... Philadelphia, Everts & Peck, 1880.
311, 339 p. illus., plates (1 double) ports. map. 30 ½ cm. Includes lists of Ulster County men who served in the civil war. Contents. - pt. 1. General history of Ulster County and ... Kingston. - pt. 2. History of the towns of Ulster County. 1-14279 Rev.   F127. U4 S 9

ULSTER County. Collections of the Ulster historical society. Volume I. Kingston, Hommel & Lounsbery, printers (etc.) 1860-62.   260 p. illus. 25 ½ cm. Issued in 4 parts. No more pub. 1-14280 Rev.
F127. U4 U4

ULSTER County. Collections of the Ulster county historical society ... vol. I. 1931. Kingston,
N.Y., 1931 -   (1) v. 28 cm.   F127.U4 U42

ULSTER County. Old gravestones of Ulster County; 22 thousand inscriptions collected and ed. by J. Wilson Poucher and Byron J. Terwilliger. (Kingston, N.Y., 1931.   xii, 407 p. 28 cm. (Collections of the Ulster County hist. soc. vol. 1) 33-8498.   F127.U4 U42
— Index (by) Ruth P. Heidgerd. New Paltz, N.Y., 1958.   28 l. 29 cm.
F127.U4 U42
Index

ULSTER County. Ulster county historical society. Proceedings ... 1930/31 - Kingston,
N.Y., The Society (1931 -   v. plates. 23 cm. 32-20369.   F127.U4 U43

ULSTER County. A history of Ulster County under the dominion of the Dutch, by Augustus H. Van Buren. Kingston, N.Y., 1923.   3, (5) - 146 p. 23 ½ cm. 23-18097.   F127. U4 V2

ULSTER County. Earliest English deeds of Ulster county ... Transcribed in condensed form from deed books in the County clerk's office, Kingston, N.Y., by Louis Hasbrouck Zimm. Woodstock, N.Y. (1936)   2 v. in 1. 28 x 21 ½ cm. Paged continuously. Type-written. 1694 - 1704. With name index. 36-19469 rev.
F127. U4 Z5

UNADILLA Valley historical society. Transactions., v. 1 - (New Berlin, N.Y.) 1907 -
v. front., pl. 18 cm. 16-13887.   F127.U54U54
— Historical sketches of old New Berlin ... by John Hyde, first pub. in 1876.   vii, 108 p. front. (port.) pl. 18 cm. (Transactions ... v.1) 16-13888.

WARREN County. Abstracts of deeds of Warren county, from 1813 to 1825 ... Copied from the original records at the Court house, Lake George, New York. ... by Gertrude A. Barber. (Lake George, 1941?)   85 numb. l. 28 x 21 ½ cm. Type-written. 45-46032.   F127. W2 B28

WARREN County. Abstracts of wills of Warren county ... 1813-1850. Copied from the original records ... by Gertrude A. Barber. (New York?) 1937.   44 numb. l. 28 cm. Type-written. 42-7815.
F127. W2 B3

WARREN County. History of Warren County. Ed. William Howard Brown. (n.p.) Board of Supervisors of Warren County, 1963.   302 p. 24 cm.   F127. W2 B7

WARREN County. Bears, Bibles and a boy; memories of the Adirondacks. By Jesse David Roberts. Illus. by Gil Walker. (1st ed.) New York, W. W. Norton (1961)   256 p.   22 cm.   61-7482.
F127. W2 R6

WARREN County. Luzerne and Schroon Lake. By Seneca Ray Stoddard. Troy, N. Y., Nims & Knight (1889)   1 l. 14 plates. 15 x 19 cm. 1-14929 rev.*
F127. W2 S8

WARREN County; a history and guide. Compiled by workers of the W. P. A ... Pub. by the Warren county board of supervisors. (New York) Printed by the Glens Falls post co., 1942.   275 p. incl. tab.   plates, 2 fold. maps (in pocket)   20 cm.   (American guide series)   Bibliography: p. (257)-258.   43-7977.
F127. W2 W7

WASHINGTON County. Abstracts of wills of Washington county ... Copied from the original records ... by Gertrude A. Barber. (New York?) 1937.   3 v.   28 cm.   Type-written.   Contents. - v. 1. 1788-1806 - v. 2. 1806-1814. - v. 3. 1814-1825.   42-7816.
F127. W3 B3

WASHINGTON County. Index of wills. From 1825-1850. Copied and compiled by Gertrude A. Barber. (New York?) 1937.   25 numb. l.   28 cm.   Type-written.   42-7817.
F127. W3 B33

WASHINGTON County. Gazetteer of the county of Washington, comprising a correct statistical and miscellaneous history of the county and several towns from their organization to the present time. By Allen Corey. Schuylerville, N.Y., 1850.   2 p, 200, (227) - 264 p. incl. maps.   maps.   22 cm.   1-14294.
F127. W3 C8

WASHINGTON County. A historical, topographical & agricultural survey of the county of Washington. Taken under the direction of the New York state agricultural society, by Asa Fitch ...   (In New York state agricultural soc.   Transactions ... v. 8, p. (875)-975; v. 9, p. (753)-944.   illus., maps.   17-12072.
F127. W3 F5

WASHINGTON County. Address of the Hon. James Gibson at the laying of the corner stone of the new court house at Sandy Hill ... "The bench and bar of Washington County for 100 years." (Albany? 1872)   8 p.   25 ½ cm.   12-11582.
F127. W3 G4

WASHINGTON County. History and biography of Washington County and the town of Queensbury, with historical notes on the various towns. Arranged and ed. by the Gresham pub. co. Illustrated. Chicago, Ill., New York, (etc.) Gresham pub. co., 1894.   xii, 17-436 p. incl. front., plates, ports.   2 pl., port.   28 cm.   Imperfect: 2 port. (p. 237-8 and 299-30) wanting.   8-32957.
F127. W3 G8

WASHINGTON County. History of Washington county. The Gibson papers. The history of Washington academy. The bench and bar of Washington county for a century. Compiled by William H. Hill. Fort Edward, N.Y., Honeywood press, 1932.   298 p. incl. front. (mounted port.)   26 ½ cm.   A33-2762.
F127. W3 H4

WASHINGTON County. History of Washington County. With illus. and biographical sketches of some of its prominent men and pioneers. (By Crisfield Johnson) Philadelphia, Everts & Ensign, 1878.   504 p. incl. front., ports.   plates (part fold.)   ports., fold. map.   31 ½ cm.   6-21553 Rev.
F127. W3 J 66

WASHINGTON County. The argyle patent and accompanying documents, by Jennie M. Patten. With notes on Washington County families. Baltimore, Genealogical Pub. Co., 1965.   68 p.   23 cm.   65-29271.
F127. W3 P3

WASHINGTON County; its history to the close of the nineteenth century. Historian and editor-in-chief, William L. Stone ... (New York) New York history co., 1901.   xiii, 570, 318 p.   34 ports., port. gr.   26 cm.   Part 2: Biographical.   4-5212.
F127. W3 S8

WAYNE County. Gazetteer and business directory of Wayne County, for 1867-8. Comp. and pub. by Hamilton Child ... Syracuse, Printed at the Journal office, 1867.   264 p. front. (fold. map)   21 ½ cm.   6-15854.
F127. W4 C4

WAYNE County. Military history of Wayne County. The county in the civil war. By Lewis H. Clark. Sodus, N.Y., L. H. Clark, Hulett & Gaylord (1883)   (933) p.   23 cm.   Various paging.   2-2204.
F127. W4 C5

WAYNE County. Landmarks of Wayne county ... ed. by Hon. George W. Cowles ... Syracuse, N.Y., D. Mason, 1895. viii, 437, 41, 343 p. illus. (incl. maps) ports., fold. map. 25 cm. Contains biographies and family sketches.
1-16736 Rev.
F127.W4 C 8

WAYNE County. History, reminiscences, anecdotes and legends of Great Sodus bay, Sodus Point, Sloop Landing, Sodus village, Pultneyville, Maxwell and the environing regions, the Ridge road and the 4-horse post coaches, by Walter Henry Green. Sodus, N.Y., 1945. x, 308 p. incl. front., illus. (incl. ports.) 20½ cm. 45-19038.
F127. W4 G7

— Sodus, N.Y., 1947. x, 308, (8) p. incl. front., illus. (incl. ports.) 21 cm. "Second edition." 47-22285.
F127. W4 G7
1947

WAYNE County. ... History of Wayne County; with illus. descriptive of its scenery, palatial residences, public buildings, fine blocks, and important manufactories ... (By W. McIntosh) Philadelphia, Everts, Ensign & Everts, 1877. vi, 7-216 p. incl. front., illus. plates (2 double) ports., 2 maps. 36 x 29 cm.
1-14281.
F127. W4 M2

WEST CANADA Creek, by David H. Beetle ... (Utica, N.Y., Utica observer-dispatch, 1946)
5, 158 p. incl. front. plates, port. 19½ cm. "Reprinted from the Utica observer-dispatch ..." 47-15598.
F127.W48 B4

WESTCHESTER County. Boyd's Westchester county directory ... 18(84/85, 1887/88. New York and Yonkers, W. A. Boyd, 18(84-87) (2) v. 24½ cm.
Directories

WESTCHESTER County. Gopsill's Westchester County directory, containing a general directory of names in the towns of Peekskill, Sing Sing, Tarrytown, White Plains & Yonkers, tog. with a business directory of the whole county ... Jersey City, N.J., J. Gopsill (1866) xi, (25) - 283 p. 19½ cm.
11-25536.
Directories

WESTCHESTER County. Curtin's Westchester County directory for 1869-70-(1873-4) ... New York, D. Curtin, 1869-73. 2 v. 22 cm. 11-24289.
Directories

WESTCHESTER. ... Smaw's Westchester directory ... for Yonkers, Peekskill, Sing-Sing, Tarrytown, Mount Vernon, Port Chester, New Rochelle, Rye, White Plains, Irvington ... Yonkers, N.Y., Smaw & co., 1879 - 1 v. 23½ cm. 11-24282.
Directories

WESTCHESTER County. ... Turner's Hudson river directory, 1889, 92, 1902/3, 1904/5, 1906/7, 1910/11, 1911/12, containing a general and classified business directory of Tarrytown, North Tarrytown, Irvington, Dobbs Ferry, Ardsley and Hastings, tog. with a business directory of Yonkers ... Yonkers, W. L. Richmond, 1889-1911. 3 v. 24 cm. 2-3595-M2.
Directories

WESTCHESTER County. Countryside social list. Greenwich, Conn., Countryside pub. co. (1923-
v. 23 cm. 23-12686.
Directories

WESTCHESTER County. The Social list of Westchester County and adjacent territroy, 1913 - White Plains, N.Y., G. O. Bloodgood (1913 - v. 23½ cm. 13-20565.
Directories

WESTCHESTER County social record, including Greenwich, Conn., 19   (Newark, N.J., Reporter pub. co., 19   v. 20 cm. CA 30-752 Unrev.
Directories

WESTCHESTER County. Richmond's classified business directory of Westchester County, N.Y., 1915/16 - Yonkers, N.Y., W. L. Richmond, 1915 - v. front. (fold. map) 24 cm. 15-9451.
Directories

WESTCHESTER County. The attack on Young's house (or Four Corners) ... 1780; an episode of the neutral ground, with a map, and illus. from original photographs, by William Abbatt. Tarrytown, N.Y., W. Abbatt, 1926. 4 p., (7) - 21 numb. l. front., plates, fold. map. 25½ cm. "The scene was in the extreme southeastern corner of the ... township of Mount Pleasant, about six miles east of Tarrytown." Bibliography: l. 21. 27-12594.
F127. W5 A2

WESTCHESTER County. American journal of commerce. Industrial number. N.Y. (1902) 40 cm.
F127. W5 A5

WESTCHESTER County.   Art work of Westchester County.   Pub. in twelve parts.   Chicago, The W. H. Parish pub. co., 1894.   12 pt. illus., plates. 35 cm.   10-21689.
F127. W5 A7

WESTCHESTER County.   The manor of Philipsburgh.   A paper read before the New York historical soc.   By T. Astley Atkins ...   (Yonkers, N.Y.) The Yonkers historical and library assoc., 1894.   23 p.   23½ cm.   2-21287.
F127. W5 A8

WESTCHESTER County.   Biographical history of Westchester County ... Chicago, The Lewis pub. co., 1899.   2 v.   fronts., ports.   27½ x 21 cm.   Paged continuously; v.1, 480 p.; v.2. (481)-992 p.   6-6457.
F127. W5 B5

WESTCHESTER County.   I remember; a short and intimate sketch of the dignified seventies, the elegant eighties and the gay nineties in or near the Hudson valley in the vicinity of Sunnyside, the home of Washington Irving, in the land of Sleepy hollow.   Also a few episodes in the young life of the author. By Jennie Prince Black.   (New York, Thomas Claydon printing co. inc.) 1938.   5, 112 p.   plates, ports. 18½ cm.   "First ed."   39-22919.
F127. W5 B55

WESTCHESTER County.   A history of the county of Westchester, from its first settlement to the present time.   By Robert Bolton, jr. ...   New-York, Printed by A. S. Gould, 1848.   2 v.   front. (port.) illus., plates, maps (partly fold.)   fold. geneal. tables.   22 cm.   Appendix (p. 499-557): Pedigrees of the families of the county of Westchester. 1-14282.
F127. W5 B6

— Carefully revised by the author ... N.Y., C. F. Roper, 1881.   2 v. illus., plates, plans, maps (part fold.) fold. tables (incl. geneal. tab.)   23½ cm.   Appendix A.   Pedigrees of the families of the county of Westchester: v.2, p. 707-766. 1-14283.
F127. W5 B7

WESTCHESTER County magazine ... Devoted to the county and the borough of the Bronx ...   White Plains, N.Y., 1908 - 10.   2 v.   illus.   25½ cm.   monthly.   CA 11-168 Unrev.
F127. W5 B8

WESTCHESTER County.   Van Cortlandt Manor, by Charles H. Brown.   Tarrytown, N.Y., Sleep Hollow Restorations, 1965.   (36) p.   illus., coat of arms, facsim., geneal. table, map, ports.   22 cm.
F127. W5 B83

WESTCHESTER County.   (Cemetery inscriptions from towns in Westchester County, N.Y.)   (n. p., 1922?)   142 numb. l.   31 cm.   Type-written copy.   22-17155.
F127. W5 C5

WESTCHESTER County.   Some of the beginnings of Westchester County history; a paper read before the Westchester County historical society, at the annual meeting at White Plains ... by Ex-Governor Alonzo B. Cornell, with notes and illus.   (White Plains?) Printed for the Westchester County hist. soc., 1890.   38 p.   illus. (incl. ports., map)   27½ cm.   6-1401 Rev.
F127. W5 C8

WESTCHESTER County.   This is Westchester; a study of suburban living.   By Richard F. Crandell. New York, Sterling Pub. Co. (1954)   240 p.   illus., ports., maos, facsims.   29 cm.   Bibliography: p. 238.   54-13488.
F127. W5 C85

— (Rev. and enl. ed.)   New York, Sterling Pub. Co. (1961)   244 p.   29 cm.   61-15868.
F127. W5 C85 1961

WESTCHESTER County.   Biographical sketches of the deceased physicians of Westchester County. Being the annual address before the Westchester County medical soc.   By George J. Fisher ... Pub. by order of the society.   New York, Hall, Clayton, printers, 1861.   52 p.   23 cm.   5-3023.
F127. W5 F5

WESTCHESTER County.   History of Westchester County, editor-in-chief, Alvah P. French ... New York and Chicago, Lewis historical pub. co. inc., 1925.   4 v.   fronts., plates, ports., maps.   27½ cm.   Vols. 2-3 contain biographical material.   25-18271.
F127. W5 F8

WESTCHESTER County.   Births of members, Chappaqua monthly meeting, Westchester County, from

1719. (Copied by Mrs. Josephine C. (Stillman) Frost. Brooklyn, 1912?) 106, 3 numb. l. 27 x 21½ cm. Autographed from type-written copy. 13-6131.
F127. W5 F9

WESTCHESTER County. Quaker marriages, Purchase monthly meeting, Westchester County. (Copied by Mrs. Josephine C. Stillman Frost. Brooklyn, 1912?) 73, 3 numb. l. 27 cm. Autographed from type-written copy. 13-6132.
F127. W5 F92

WESTCHESTER County. Quaker deaths, Purchase monthly meeting, Westchester County. (Copied by Mrs. Josephine C. Stillman Frost. Brooklyn, 1912?) 43, 2 numb. l. 27 cm. Autographed from type-written copy. 13-6133.
F127. W5 F93

WESTCHESTER County. Quaker births, Purchase Monthly meeting, Westchester County, New York. (Brooklyn, 1912?) 68, 2 numb. l. 27 cm. Copied by Mrs. Josephine C. Stillman Frost. Autographed from type-written copy. 13-7168.
F127. W5 F94

WESTCHESTER County. Marriage intentions and dealings relating to marriage, Chappaqua Monthly meeting. Extracts from the first volume of Women's minutes, 1785 to 1797. (By Mrs. Josephine C. Frost. Brooklyn, 191 -) 27, 2 numb. l. 26½ cm. Autographed from type-written copy. 13-12782 Rev.
F127. W5 F95

WESTCHESTER County. Quaker deaths, Chappaqua Monthly meeting, Westchester County. (By Mrs. Josephine C. Frost. Brooklyn, 191-) 60, 3 numb. l. 27½ cm. Autographed from type-written copy. 13-13693 Rev.
F127. W5 F96

WESTCHESTER County. Quaker removal certificates from Chappaqua Monthly meeting, Westchester County. (By Mrs. Josephine C. Frost, Brooklyn, 191 -) 57, 3 numb. l. 26½ cm. Autographed from type-written copy. 13-13691 Rev.
F127. W5 F97

WESTCHESTER County and its people, a record. Under the editorial direction of Ernest Freeland Griffin ... New York, Lewis historical pub. co. (1946) 3 v. fronts., illus. (incl. map, facsims.) ports. 27 cm. Vol. 3 contains biographies. Bibliography: v.2, p. (554)-560. 47-2135.
F127. W5 G7

WESTCHESTER County. The manor of Philipsborough; address written for the New York branch of the Order of colonial lords of manors in America, by Edward Hagaman Hall. Baltimore, 1920. 35 p. incl. front., illus. (incl. ports., coat of arms) fold. pl. 23½ cm. 20-16025.
F127. W5 H17

WESTCHESTER County. Poverty and patriotism of the neutral grounds; a paper read before the Westchester County historical soc. upon the 123d anniversary of the battle of White Plains. By John C. L. Hamilton. Elmsford, 1900. 39 p. front. (port.) pl. 25½ cm. 1-29322 Rev.
F127. W5 H2

WESTCHESTER County. North of Manhattan; persons and places of old Westchester. By Harry Hansen. With fifty-four photos. by Samuel Chamberlain. New York, Hastings House (1950) xi, 181 p. illus. 21 cm. 50-10905.
F127. W5 H22

WESTCHESTER County, America's most impressive suburban section ... (By) Derrill W. Hart. (White Plains, N.Y., Westchester County realty board, 1929?) (16) p. 36 x 26 cm.
F127. W5 H3

WESTCHESTER County. Historic Westchester, 1683-1933. Glimpses of county history, by Elisabeth Cushman ... Historic sites, by Herbert B. Nichols ... (Tarrytown, N.Y., 1933) viii, (9) - 135 p. incl. front., illus., fold. map. 23½ cm. Folded map mounted on lining paper. ... the revised series of Mrs. Cushman's articles, which appeared in Oct., 1933, with additions, in this booklet. 34-1545.
F127. W5 H5

WESTCHESTER County. Sixteen nine to eighteen seventy; glimpses from the past in connection with the early history of the manor of Cortlandt, and more especially of the town of Cortlandt and the village of Peekskill ... By Stephen D. Horton. (Peekskill? 1912) 205 p. 22 cm. 12-24132.
F127. W5 H8

WESTCHESTER County. ... Westchester County during the American revolution, 1775-1783, by Otto

Hufeland ... White Plains, N. Y., Pub. for Westchester County by the Westchester County historical society, 1926. xxvii, 473 p. 4 fold. maps (incl. front.) 23½ cm. (Publications of the Westchester Co. hist. soc. vol. III) 26-12559.
F127. W5 H89

WESTCHESTER County. Incidents from Westchester's history, by Helen L. Hultz ... White Plains, N. Y., Westchester county publications committee (1934) 2, 34 p. illus. (incl. maps) 25 cm. "This is the second of a series of pamphlets designed to help the children of Westchester county" 34-42113.
F127. W5 H93

WESTCHESTER County. ... "Incidents of the revolution in Westchester preceding the battle of White Plains." Address ... By Frederick Wendell Jackson (White Plains? 1897) 34 p. 23½ cm. Westchester County hist. soc. 6-1118.
F127. W5 J14

WESTCHESTER County. Little visits to historical points in Westchester co. ... v. 1, no. 1-5; Jan.-May 1902. Mamaroneck, N. Y., The Richbell press, 1902. 149 (i.e. 157) p. front., 4 pl. 19½ cm. monthly. No more pub. Contents. - 1. White Plains. - 2. New Rochelle. - 3. Tarrytown. - 4. The manors. - 5. Ossining and Crofton. 7-20575.
F127. W5 L7

WESTCHESTER County. ... The McDonald papers ... ed. by William S. Hadaway. White Plains, N. Y., Pub. for Westchester County by the Westchester County historical society, 1926-7. 2 v. 23 cm. (Publications of the Westchester co. hist. soc. vol. iv-v) The 'McDonald papers were prepared by John M. McDonald, a native of Westchester county, and read before the New York historical soc. 27-5414 Rev.
F127. W5 M14

WESTCHESTER County. Greenburgh mansions of the Misses Masters, Washington Irving, T. Coleman Dupont, Professor Draper, Cyrus Field, J. P. Morgan (and) Jay Gould, by Rives Matthews. Hastings-upon-Hudson, N. Y., The Half moon press, 1934. 37 p. 22½ cm. 34-41285.
F127. W5 M26

WESTCHESTER County. The manor of Fordham and its founder. By Harry C. W. Melick. New York, Fordham University Press; (1950) xx, 191 p. illus., fold. maps, facsims. 23 cm. Bibliographical footnotes. 50-11879.
F127. W5 M4

WESTCHESTER County. ... Mount Kisco, Pleasantville, Hawthorne, Katonah, Chappaqua, Brewster, Pawling, Patterson and sections of Westchester Co. Special midsummer ed., 1908. New York, American suburbs co., 1908. 25 p. illus. 40½ cm. (American suburbs illustrated. (v. 3, no. 3) 11-30220.
F127. W5 M9

WESTCHESTER County. The book of the words. (By Violet Oakley) Westchester County historical pageant. 1614. 1846. (Philadelphia? 1909) 2, 3-128 p. 25½ cm. 9-19071.
F127. W5 O2

WESTCHESTER County. Early wills of Westchester County, from 1664 to 1784. ... also the genealogy of "The Havilands" of Westchester County, and descendants of Hon. James Graham (Watkinson and Ackerley families) with genealogical and historical notes; by William S. Pelletreau ... New York, F. P. Harper, 1898. xii, 488 p. front. (port.) pl. 24 x 19 cm. 98-2007 Rev. 98-2007 Rev.
F127. W5 P3

WESTCHESTER County. Records of the Manor of Philipsburgh, Westchester County, transcribed by F. C. Haacker. (n. p.) 1951. 1 v. 28 cm. 54-24621.
F127. W5 P5

WESTCHESTER County. Poundridge Presbyterian church. Marriages performed by Rev. William Patterson, 1837 - 1886. (White Plains, N. Y., 1939) 46 numb. l. 28 cm. Mimeographed. 42-31533 Rev.
F127. W5 P7

WESTCHESTER County. ... The "Neutral ground," by Charles Pryer. New York, London, G. P. Putnam's sons, 1898. 409-443 p. 21½ cm. (Half moon series ... vol. ii, no. 12) 98-1640 Rev.
F127. W5 P9

WESTCHESTER County. The story of present-day Westchester county, by Mary S. Roder ... White Plains, N. Y., Westchester county publications committee (1934) 2, 60 p. illus., diagr. 25 cm. ... designed to help the children of Westchester county. Bibliography at end of each chapter except last. 34-42114.
F127. W5 R6

WESTCHESTER County. History of Westchester County, including Morrisania, Kings Bridge, and

NEW YORK

West Farms, which have been annexed to New York city; by J. Thomas Scharf ... Philadelphia, L. E. Preston, 1886.   2 v.   front., illus., plates, ports., maps (partly fold.)   28 cm.   1-14295.   F127. W5 S3

WESTCHESTER County.and the town of Rye; an address, by A. Outram Sherman. (Rye, N.Y., The Westchester press, 1909)   32 p.   22 cm.   9-19569 Rev.   F127.W5 S47

WESTCHESTER County. History of Westchester County, from its earliest settlement to the year 1900. By Frederic Shonnard and W. W. Spooner. New York, The New York history co., 1900.
vi, 638 p.   front., illus. (incl. maps) pl., ports., double plan, 2 double facsims.   28 cm.   0-6960 Rev.   F127. W5 S5

WESTCHESTER County. Sleepy Hollow Restorations, Tarrytown, N.Y. Phillipsburg manor. Tarrytown, N.Y., 1969.   56 p.   illus.   22 cm.   72-89495.   F127. W5 S55

WESTCHESTER County. Manual of Westchester county. Past and present. Civil list to date. 1898 ... (Comp. Henry Townsend Smith) White Plains, N.Y., H. T. Smith, 1898.   300 p. plates, ports.   24 cm.   99-94 Rev.   F127. W5 S6

WESTCHESTER County. The spirit of Westchester, an explanatory volume, representative of America's most beautiful suburban residential district ... (White Plains, N.Y., Building and realty news inc., 1928)   xxiv, 80, xxv-xlviii p.   illus.   31 cm.   28-14252.   F127. W5 S7

WESTCHESTER County. Where to recuperate; or, Glimpses of Westchester and Putnam counties, as seen along the line of the New York city and northern railroad. (By Edwin A. Studwell) (New York, 1886)   (32) p.   front., illus.   12°.   1-22588-M1.   F127. W5 S9

WESTCHESTER County. The Van Cortlandt manor; anonymous address read by the late Mrs. James Marsland Lawton ... Baltimore, 1920.   27 p. incl. front., illus., plates, ports.   23½ cm. (Order of colonial lords of manors in America. New York branch. Publications)   20-16024.   F127.W5 V22

WESTCHESTER County. Huguenots of Westchester and parish of Fordham. By William Watson Waldron ... Introd. by Rev. Stephen H. Tyng, jr. ... New-York, W. H. Kelley, 1864.   126 p. incl. front.   16½ cm.   18-14447.   F127. W5W17

WESTCHESTER County. Around Westchester with children, by Florence Weiner. (New York) Umbrella Press (1970)   xii, 174 p.   illus.   21 cm.   F127. W5 W53

WESTCHESTER County fair. v. 1 -   Jan. 1927 -   (New York, J. P. Neff ... 1927 -
v.   illus. (incl. ports.)   30½ cm.   monthly. Vol. 1, no. 1 has title: Westchester monthly magazine. 31-2218.   F127, W5 W58

WESTCHESTER County. The Westchester historian. v. 1 -   Jan. 1925 -   (White Plains, N.Y.)   v. in   illus., ports., maps (part fold.)   23 cm.   quarterly. Title varies. Pub. by the Westchester County Historical Soc. Indexes: Vols. 1-18, 1925-42, with v. 17-19.   31-7245 rev.*   F127.W5W594

WESTCHESTER County Historical Society. Officers and members. White Plains, N.Y.
v.   18-23 cm.   55-54849.   F127.W5W595

WESTCHESTER County Historical Society. Constitution and by-laws. (White Plains, N.Y., 188-)
8 p.   23 cm.   8-31340 rev.*   F127. W5 W6

WESTCHESTER County Historical Society. Publications. v. 2-8. White Plains, N.Y., 1924-30.
7 v.   illus., ports., maps (part fold.)   24 cm.   "All pubs. ... to 1924 constitute v.1 of this series." 56-49900.   F127. W5 W7

WESTCHESTER County. ... The minutes of the Court of sessions (1657-1696) ... ed. by Dixon Ryan Fox.   L, 138 p.   23 cm. (Pubs. vol. II) "Source series, vol. I."   25-12439.
— ... Westchester County during the American revolution ... by Otto Hufeland.
xxvii, 473 p.   4 fold. maps (incl. front.)   23½ cm. (Pubs. vol. iii)   26-12559.
— ... The McDonald papers ... ed. Wm. S. Hadaway.   2 v. (Pubs. vol. iv - v) See F127. W5M14.
27-5414 Rev.
— ... A check list of books, maps, pictures, and other printed matter relating to the

counties of Westchester and Bronx, by Otto Hufeland ... White Plains, N.Y. ... 1929.   xvi, 320 p.
23½ cm. (Pubs. vol. vi)   29-15863.

— Anne Hutchinson and other papers ... 1929.   xiv, 3-114 p.   (Pubs. vol. vii)   30-944 rev.

— ... Letters of a Westchester farmer (1774-1775) by the Rev. Samuel Seabury (1729-1796) ed. with an introd. essay by Clarence H. Vance.   White Plains, N.Y. ... 1930.   ix, 162 p. incl. facsims. front. (port.)   23½ cm.   (Pubs. no. viii)   31-23939.

WESTCHESTER County historical society ... Publications of the.   Fiftieth anniversary number. White Plains, N.Y., 1924.   58 p.   front., ports.   23 cm.   26-399 rev.   F127.W5 W73

WESTCHESTER County.   The charm of Westchester. ... (White Plains, N.Y.) Westchester County realty board, 1929.   (62) p.   24 cm.   F127.W5 W74

WESTCHESTER County.   Westchester life.   v.1 (no. 1-26); Jan. 1 - July 16, 1910.   (New York, Westchester life co., 1910)   1 v. illus.   34 cm.   weekly.   No numbers were issued from May 21 to June 4, inclusive. No more published.   29-13335.   F127.W5 W76

WESTCHESTER County.   What to do in Westchester and Putnam;   how - when - what it costs, with road map.   1934 -   Chappaqua, N.Y., C. J. Nuttall (1934 -   v.   illus., fold. map.   21½ cm. annual.   34-8997.   F127.W5W775

WESTCHESTER County.   ... White Plains, New Rochelle, Peekskill, Ossining, Tarrytown, Irvington, Dobbs Ferry, Larchmont and Scarsdale.   Westchester County ed., 1908.   New York, American suburbs co., 1908.   53 p.   illus.   40½ cm.   (American suburbs illus. (v.3, no. 2)   11-30221.   F127. W5 W5

WESTCHESTER County.   The Purchase meeting.   By James Wood ... Quaker Hill, N.Y., Pub. by the Quaker Hill conference association, 1905.   19 p.   20 cm.   (Quaker Hill (local history) series.   xiv   8-1144.
      F127. W5 W8

WYOMING County.   Historical Wyoming.   v.1-   1947 -   Arcade, N.Y.
   v. in   illus.   28 cm.   Bimonthly. 1947-July 1952; quarterly, Oct. 1952 -   56-24949.   F127. W9 H58

WYOMING County.   ... History of Wyoming County.   With illus., biographical sketches and portraits of some pioneers and prominent residents.   New York, F. W. Beers, 1880.   310 p. incl. front., illus. plates, ports., map.   36½ x 30½ cm.   Error in paging.   p. 69 incorrectly numbered 96.   L.C. copy replaced by microfilm.   1-14296.
      F127. W9 H6
      Microfilm 21281 F

YATES County.   History of Yates County.   With illus. and biographical sketches of some of the prominent men and pioneers.   Ed. by Lewis Cass Aldrich.   Syracuse, N.Y., D. Mason, 1892.
(9) - 671 p.   ports.   25½ x 19½ cm.   Several chapters contributed by local writers.   5-6444.   F127. Y3 A3

YATES County.   Some Bible records of Ball, Bootes, Dean, Green, Guthrie, Lafler, Newlove (and) Warner, with index.   Copied by Mrs. Fenton E. Bootes.   (Middlesex? N.Y.) 1955.   10 l.   28 cm.
56-16528.   F127. Y3 B6

YATES County.   History and directory of Yates County ... Including church, school and civil history, and a narrative of the Universal Friend, her society and doctrine.   By Stafford Canning Cleveland. Penn Yan, N.Y., 1873 -   v. illus., ports., fold. map.   23 cm.   1-14284 rev.*   F127. Y3 C8
— Index of family histories, vol. 2.   Compiled by Mrs. Fenton E. Bootes.   Middlesex, N.Y., 1954.   1 v. (unpaged)   28 cm.   F127. Y3 C6
      Index

YATES County.   Inscriptions from three abandoned cemeteries in Yates County: Friends Burying Ground, Stoddard Family Cemetery, Thomas Family Cemetery.   With index and family history ... Copied from History of Yates County, by S.C. Cleveland, 1873, by Thelma Burton Bootes (Mrs. Fenton E.)   (Middlesex? N.Y.) 1955.   11, 3 l.   illus.   28 cm.   56-16529.   F127.Y3 C65

YATES County.   Yates County's "boys in blue", 1861-1865; who they were - what they did; compiled by Robert H. Graham.   Penn Yan, N.Y. (1926)   204 p.   22 cm.   26-19589.   F127. Y3 G8

NEW YORK CITY

YATES County in the world war, 1917-1918, comp. and pub. by E. D. Harrison. Penn Yan, N. Y.,
1921.   120 p.   illus. (incl. ports., 1 col.)   31 cm.   21-7813.   F127. Y3 H3

YATES County.   The military history of Yates county ... By Walter Wolcott ... Penn Yan, N. Y.,
Express book and job print. 1895.   viii, 157 p.   24 cm.   1-14285.   F127. Y3 W8

YATES County chronicle.   Holiday number.   (Penn Yan, N. Y.) 1899.   (14) p.   illus.   61 cm.   8-9297.
                                                                                                                                                F127. Y3 Y3

YONKERS.   Dolph-Stewart official street directory and information guide of Yonkers, N.Y., incl. detailed street map ... New York city, Dolph & Stewart, 1935 -   v.   fold. map.   16 cm.   CA 35-115 Unrev.
                                                                                                                                                F127. Y6 A2

NEW YORK CITY.   NEW YORK COUNTY.

BOTKIN, Benjamin Albert.   New York City folklore: legends, tall tales, anecdotes, stories, sagas,
heroes and characters, customs, traditions, and savings; New York, Random House (1956)
492 p.   illus.   22 cm.   "1st printing."   56-8815.   F128. B 6

WERNER, Morris Robert.   It happened in New York.   New York, Coward-McCann (1957)
256 p.   22 cm.   57-7065.   F128. W 4

NEW YORK CITY.   PERIODICALS. SOCIETIES. COLLECTIONS.

ALCOLM, The, a magazine of the metropolis.   v. 1-4, v. 5, no. 1 - 11; June 1905 - May 1910.   (New
York) The Alcolm co. (etc.) 1905-10.   5 v. in 10.   26½ cm.   monthly.   Title varies.   No more published.
9-25083 Rev.   F128.1. A35

APPLETON's dictionary of greater New York and its neighborhood ... 1879 -   D. Appleton (1879)
- 1905.   v.   fronts., illus., maps (part fold.)   17 cm.   Title varies.   99-3451 Rev.   F128.1. A 65

CITY history club.   Annual report ... 1897/98, 1904/05, 1905/06.   (New York, 1898-1906)
3 pamphlets.   pl.   21 cm.   F128.1. C 5

(CITY history club of New York)   Are you a good citizen?   (New York? 1912?)   (6) p.   15½ cm.
                                                                                                                                       F128.1. C502

CITY history club of New York.   Bulletin ...   (New York, 1901-1910)   15 cm.   F128.1. C504

CITY history club of New York.   (Prospectus)   New York, n. d.   23½ cm.   F128.1. C506

CITY history club of New York.   (Officers, etc.) New York, n. d.   15 x 19½ cm.   F128.1. C508

— (New York, 1906)   21½ cm.   F128.1. C509

CITY history club of New York.   ... Specimen program of class course..   New York, n. d.
14 x 9 cm.   F128.1. C 53

CITY history club of New York.   Bulletin no.   (New York, 1907)   7 pamphlets.   24 cm.   F128.1. C532

CITY history club of New York.   Historical excursion leaflets.   (New York? 1908)
                                                                                                                     16½ cm.   F128.1. C534

CITY history club of New York.   ... Program.   F128.1. C535

CITY history club of N. Y.   Songs used by the City history club.   1908.   1 v.   F128.1. C536

CITY history club of N. Y.   Summary of work. 1906/7 - 1908/9 (New York? 1906-09)
                                                                                                                     20½ cm.   F128.1. C537

CITY history club of New York.   City history leaflets ... (New York, 1897) - 1909.   2 no.   19 cm.

F128.1.C 58

— ... Henry Hudson's third voyage. By Robert Juet.   (1909)   22 p.   19½ cm.   City history leaflets. 1st ser. no. 2) 12-31061.

CITY history club of New York.   ... General organization rules ... (New York, 1909)   8 p.   19½ cm.   10-6831.

F128.1.C 59

CITY history club of New York.   ... Teacher's handbook of the City history club ... pt. 1 -   2d revision, 1908.   (New York, 1908)   19½ cm.

F128.1.C 61

DIRECTORY of agencies in New York City providing community services for international students and sponsored visitors.   1962 -   New York, Institute of International Education.   v.   28 cm.   62-19069.

F128.1.D 57

GRAND street boys' association, inc., Year book of the.   1925 -   New York, (192-
v. illus., col. pl., ports., facsims.   30 x 23 cm.   Formerly pub. as Banquet journal.   30-17011.

F128.1.G 75

HISTORIC New York; being the first (and second) series of the Half Moon papers, ed. by Maud Wilder Goodwin, and others ... New York and London, G. P. Putnam's sons, 1897-99.   2v. fronts., plates, ports., maps (partly fold.) fold. plan, facsims.   21 cm.   Monographs also separately issued, as orig. pub. in (24) monthly parts.   Contents. - 1st ser. 1. Fort Amsterdam in the days of the Dutch, by M. W. Goodwin. - 2. The Stadthuys of New Amsterdam, by Alice M. Earle. - 3. The early history of Wall street, 1653-1789, by O. G. Villard. - 4. Annetje Jans' farm, by R. Putnam. - 5. The city chest of New Amsterdam, by E. D. Durand. - 6-7. Old wells and water-courses of the island of Manhattan, by G. E. Hill and G. E. Waring, jr. - 8. Old Greenwich, by Elizabeth Bisland. - 9. The fourteen miles round, by A. M. Mason and Mary M. Mason. - 10. King's college; now Columbia university, by J. B. Pine. - 11. The Bowery, by F. R. Hewitt and Mary A. Hewitt. - 12. Governor's Island, by Blanche W. Bellamy - Index.   2d ser. 1. Slavery in New York, by E. V. Morgan. - 2. Tammany hall, by T. Williams. - 3. Old prisons and punishments, by Elizabeth D. Lewis. - 4. The New York press and its makers in the eighteenth century, by Charlotte M. Martin and B. E. Martin. - 5. Bowling Green, by S. Trask. - 6. New Amsterdam family names and their origin, by B. Fernow. 7. Old taverns and posting inns, by Elisabeth B. Cutting. - 8. The doctor in old New York, by F. H. Bosworth. - 9. Early schools and schoolmaster of New Amsterdam, by Emma Van Vechten. - 10. The battle of Harlem Heights, by W. R. Shepherd. - 11. Breuckelen, by H, Putnam. - 12. The "neutral ground." by C. Pryer. - Index.   1-14661.

F128.1.H 16

HALF MOON series; papers on historic New York.   New York and London, G. P. Putnam's sons, 1897-98.   2 v.   19½ cm.   Ed. by M. W. Goodwin and others. Pub. in the interest of the New York city history club.   Reprinted under title: Historic New York (above)   L. C. copy replaced by microfilm.   10-27777.

F128.1.H17
Microfilm 18541 F

KLEIN, Alexander.   The Empire City; a treasury of New York.   Coll. and ed. by Alexander Klein. Freeport, N.Y., Books for Libraries Press (1971) (c. 1955)   xxvii, 475 p.   24 cm.   (Essay index reprint series)   75-152184.

F128.1.K 55
1971

NEW AMSTERDAM gazette.   v. 1 -   July 21, 1883 -   New York (M. Coster) 1883 -
v.   illus.   30½ cm.   monthly (irregular)   "Extra edition."   Includes the official proceedings of the Society of the Cincinnati, of the Sons of the revolution, of the Holland society of New York, etc.   27-14520.

F128.1.N 23

NEW AMSTERDAM year book.   New York, 18   v. illus., ports.   25½ cm.

F128.1.N 25

NEW YORK.   v. 1 -   Apr. 8, 1968 -   New York.   v. in illus. (part col.) 28 cm. weekly.

F128.1. N 4

NEW YORK (City) Common council.   Manual of the corporation of the city of New York ... New York, 1841/2 - 1870.   28 v. illus., plates (part fold., part col.) ports., fold. maps, fold. plans. fold. facsims., fold. tables. 13 - 23 cm. annual.   None issued for 1867.   10-6227-8 Rev.

F128.1.N 53

— Historical index to the Manuals of the corporation of the city of New York ("Valentine's manuals") 1841 to 1870, consisting of 2,325 references.   New York, F. P. Harper, 1900. 95 p.   22½ cm.   10-6227-8 Rev.

F128.1.N 53
Index

NEW YORK CITY

NEW YORK Museum of the city of New York.   Annual report of the trustees, 1932 -   New York,
1933 -   (1) v.   plates.   23 cm.   F128.1.N 64

NEW YORK.   Museum of the city of New York.   ... Bulletin ... v. 1 -   Dec. 1937 -   (New
York, 1937 -   v. illus.   24 ½ cm.   Monthly, Nov. or Dec. to April or May.   42-29260.   F128.1.N 65

NEW YORK.   Museum of the city of New York.   ... Special bulletin series no. 1 -   Feb.,
1932 -   (New York city, 1932 -   v.   24 cm.   33-9173.
                                                                                                                                F128.1.N654

NEW YORK.   Museum of the city of New York, its collections and activities.   New York, 1935.
5 - 66 p.   front., plates.   23 cm.   42-46216.   F128.1.N 66

NEW YORK politics.   v. 1, no. 1-4; May - Nov., 1937.   (New York, Politics magazine, inc., 1937)
1 v.   illus.   31 cm.   monthly.   No more pub.   44-33081.   F128.1. N 7

OLD New York; a journal relating to the history and antiquities of New York City.   v.1-2; Aug. 1889-
Mar. 1891.   New York, W. W. Pasko (1889-91)   2 v.   illus., ports.   26 ½ cm.   monthly.   No more pub.
5-9985.   F128.1. O 4

YE OLDE settlers' association of ye West side, New York.   ... History, by-laws, list of members,
and historical papers ...   New York, Priv. print, for the Association, 1914.   4-27, 30-82 (i.e. 81) numb.
l. incl. groups of ports.   front. pl., group of ports.   26 cm.   Leaf 81 incorrectly numbered 82.   14-11076.
                                                                                                                                F128.1.O 43

YE OLDE settlers' association of ye West Side, New York.   Miscellaneous printed matter pub. by this
body is classified in: F128.1.O 45

SAINT NICHOLAS society of the city of New York.   Charter, constitution and by-laws of the St.
Nicholas society ...   New York, Printed by order of the Society, 1854.   43 p.   18 ½ cm.   14-18171.
                                                                                                                                F128.1. S 12

— 1901.   95 p.   front., illus., pl.   18 cm.   4-15763.   F122.1. S 12
                                                                                                                                1901

— 1862.   55 p.   17 ½ cm.   14-18170.   F128.1. S 13

— 1870.   60 p.   17 ½ cm.   14-18169.   F128.1. S 14

— 1881.   64 p.   17 ½ cm.   14-18168.   F128.1.S 145

— 1895.   84 p.   18 cm.   F128.1.S 147

— 1899.   93 p.   front., 1 illus.   18 cm.   F128.1.S 148

— 1904.   96 p.   front. (port.) 1 pl.   18 cm.   4-22373.   F128.1. S 16

— 1907.   98 p.   front. (port.) plates (part col.)   17 ½ cm.   14-18167.   F128.1.S1605

— 1910.   99 p.   front., illus., plates.   18 cm.   10-30094.   F128.1.S 161

— 1913.   113 p.   front., illus., pltes, port., facsims.   18 cm.   13-25652.   F128.1.S 164

SAINT Nicholas Society of the City of New York; history, customs, record of events, constitution,
certain genealogies, and other matters of interest.   New York, 1905 -   v.   24-27 cm.   6-4206.
                                                                                                                                F128.1. S 19

SAINT NICHOLAS society of the city of New York, Historical description of the certificate of membership of the.   New York, Printed by order of the Society, 1893.   29 p.   front.   23 ½ cm.   18-4633.
                                                                                                                                F128.1.S196

— (Reprinted) 1893.   1 v.   F128.1.S197

SAINT NICHOLAS society of the city of New York. ... Portraits of the presidents of the society, 1835-1914 ... (New York) Pub. by order of the society, 1914.   95 p. illus. (ports.) 26½ cm. Includes brief biographical sketches. 14-5805.   F128.1. S 2

SAINT NICHOLAS society of the city of New York; an hundred year record, 1835-1935. (Garden City, N.Y.) Printed for the Saint Nicholas soc. (The Country life press) 1935.   4, v-vi p., xi-xii, 132 p. col. front., illus., plates (incl. music) ports., facsim. 24½ cm. 35-2949.   F128.1. S 25

TOWN TALK. v. 1, no. 1-6; May 1 - Dec. 1902.   1 v.   F128.1.T 74

UPTOWN New York. (New York, 19   v. illus. (incl. ports.) 30 cm. monthly. Official publication of the Uptown chamber of commerce. 43-22443.   F128.1. U 6

VALENTINE'S manual of old New York, 1916/17 - 1917/18, 1919 - 19   New York, Valentine's manual, inc. (etc., 1916 -   v. col. fronts., illus. (incl. facsims.) plates (part col., part fold.) ports. 19½ cm. 16-14583.   F128.1.V 16
— In the golden nineties, by Henry Collins Brown ... Hastings-on-Hudson, Valentine's manual, inc., 1928.   3, 11-422 p. incl. illus., plates (part col.; part double) ports., facsim. col. front. 21 cm. (Valentine's manual no. 12, 1928) 27-20444.

WATSON, John Fanning. Historic tales of olden time: concerning the early settlement and advancement of New-York city and state. For the use of families and schools.
New-York, Collins and Hannay, 1832.   v, (9) - 214 p. front., plates. 18 cm. 1-14317.
F128.1.W 33

WATSON, John Fanning. Annals and occurrences of New York city and state, in the olden time; being a collection of memoirs, anecdotes, and incidents concerning the city, country, and inhabitants, from the days of the founders ... Embellished with pictorial illustrations ... Philadelphia, H. F. Anners, 1846.   iv, 9-390 p. illus., plates, ports., plan. 22½ cm. Enlarged from the author's "Historic tales of olden time ... of New York city and state." 1832. 2-8916.   F128.1.W 34

NEW YORK CITY.   MUSEUMS. EXHIBITIONS, EXHIBITS.

MUSEUMS in New York; a descriptive reference guide to seventy-nine fine arts museums, local history museums, natural history and science museums, libraries, botanical and zoological parks, commercial collections, and historic houses and mansions open to the public within the five boroughs of New York City. Text and 200 photos. by Fred W. McDarrah. Foreword by Thomas P. F. Hoving. (1st ed.) New York, 1967. 66-25127.   F128.15.M 3

NEW YORK CITY.   GUIDEBOOKS.

NEW YORK. City Commission to the United Nations. New York, your host, a New York handbook prepared for members of the United Nations Community. Rev. ed. New York (1969)   vi, 70 p. illus. 23 cm.   F128.18.A 5
1969

AMERICAN Automobile Association. New York City tour book; what to see, where to stay, where to dine; a catalog of complete travel information. World's Fair ed. (Washington, 1964)   52 p. 24 cm.
F128.18.A 7

ARIS, George. Businessman's New York. Maps by Meridian Airmaps. Chicago, Follett Pub. Co. (1969)   127 p. illus. 20 cm. 68-17742.   F128.18.A85

BERMAN, Claire. A great city for kids; parent's guide to a child's New York. Illus. by Shelly

NEW YORK CITY

Sacks. Indianapolis, Bobbs-Merrill, (1969)　　360 p.　illus.　22 cm.　69-13086.

F128.18. B 4

BRYN, Gerd Corall.　New York.　(Stockholm) Bonniers (1964)　　142 p.　20 cm.　(Bonniers reseguider)

F128.18. B 7

CLARK, Kay (pseud.)　New York is for newlyweds; the guidebook for honeymooners of all ages no matter how long married.　(1st ed.)　New York, Exposition Press (1963)　　155 p.　21 cm.

F128.18. C55

DENHOLTZ, Richard, ed.　New York on the house; your guide to free entertainment in New York City.　With illus. by Alan E. Cober.　(1st ed.)　New York, Doubleday, 1962.　　134 p.　21 cm.　62-11306.

F128.18 D 4

FARRELL, Frank.　New York day by day; a columnist's guide to the city.　Foreword by Lowell Thomas.　(World's Fair ed.)　Rudder Pub. Co. (1964)　　229 p.　21 cm.　64-18918.

F128.18. F 3

FEDERAL Writers' Project.　New York (City)　　(Rev. ed.)

F128.18. F37
1972

FELDMAN, Joan M.　New York on 5 dollars a day ...　(New York, Trade distributors: Crown Publishers, 1960 -　　v.　21 cm.

F128.18. F 4

FROMMER, Arthur.　New York; a practical guide ... in cooperation with First National City Bank. (New York.　Frommer/Pasmantier Pub. Corp., 1964)　　192 p.　18 cm.　(Pocket books)　64-18810.

F128.18. F 7

GROSS, Alexander.　Famous guide to New York; pictorial and descriptive.　New York, Geographia Map Co., 1961.　　96 p.　19 cm.

F128.18. G 7
1961

HAGSTROM Company, inc.　Welcome to New York, a new general information and picture guide. (1st ed.)　New York, 1960.　　96 p.　21 cm.

F128.18. H 3

HAMILTON, Seena.　New York on the Family plan.　New York, Random House (1965)　　iv, 252 p. 21 cm.　"First printing"　64-20027.

F128.18. H35

HANNAU, Hans W.　New York City.　Garden City, N.Y., (Munich, W. Andermann) (1968) 60 p.　17 cm.　(Panorama-books)　68-11163.

F128.18.H355

—　Traduction par David Rosset.　Paris, Biblioteque des arts (1967)　　61 p.　col. plates.　17 cm. (Collection Panorama)

F128.18. H3553

HART, Harold H.　Hart's guide to New York City.　Illus. by Ruby Davidson.　Maps by Hilda Simon. New York, Hart Pub. Co. (1964)　　1331 p.　illus., col. maps.　21 cm.　64-23948.

F128.18. H36

HART, Harold H.　New York at your fingertips.　Illus. by Ruby Davidson.　New York, Hart Pub. Co. (1965)　　766 p.　21 cm.

F128.18. H37
1965

HEISS, Karl William.　New York.　(Mit) 32 Bildseiten, etc.　Pforzheim, Goldstadtverlag (1963) 244 p.　17 cm.　(Ferien im Ausland, Bd. 29)

F128.18. H39

HEPBURN, Andrew.　Complete guide to New York City.　New rev. ed.　Garden City, N.Y., Doubleday, 1961.　　192 p.　21 cm.　(American travel series)　61-8889.

F128.18. H 4
1961

—　New rev. ed.　Garden City, N.Y., Doubleday, 1964.　　192 p.　21 cm.　64-14273.

F128.18. H 4
1964

— Garden City, Doubleday, (1966) 192 p. 21 cm. 65-26215. F128.18.H 4 1966

HEPBURN, Andrew. Rand McNally guide: New York City. Chicago, Rand McNally (1970) 184 p. illus. 23 cm. (Rand McNally guides) 69-19964. F128.18.H43

HILLMAN, Howard. Howard Hillman's New York at a glance. New York, D. McKay (1971) 192 p. 18 cm. (Howard Hillman At-A-Glance guidebooks) 77-157939. F128.18.H54

HOOYKASS, Else Madelon. New York. Amsterdam, Kosmos, (1971) 78 p. with illus. 15 cm. (Kosmos reisgidsen) 77-867808. F128.18.H64

IVY league guide to New York, The. (New York, Ivy League Guides) v. illus. 19 cm. annual. 61-986. F128.18. I 8

KARLSTRÖM, Birgitta. New York, en ö i USA. Intryck och praktiaka råd. Stockholm, Almquist & Wiksell, 1970. 167 p. (16) plates. 22 cm. F128.18.K36

KOUWENHOVEN, John Atlee. The New York guidebook. Illus. by Jay Robinson. (New York, Dell Pub. Co., 1964) 447 p. 19 cm. (Laurel edition) F128.18. K6

LANDI, Lando. Guida di New York. Communicazioni, alberghi, ritrovi, cose da vedere, musei e monumenti, spettacoli, sport, negozi, indirizzi, curiosità, dizionarietto. Novara Istituto geografico De Agostini, 1968. 126 p. illus. 18½ cm. F128.18.L 3

LEVINSON, Sandee. Where to go and what to do with the kids in New York. Los Angeles, Price/Stern/Sloan (1972) 126 p. illus. 14 x 22 cm. 72-76344. F128.18.L45

LEWIS, Emory. Cue's New York. Illus. by Charles Kowalski. (1st ed.) New York, Duell, Sloan and Pearce (1963) 306 p. 22 cm. 63-10348. F128.18.L46

— World's Fair ed. New York, Duell, Sloan and Pearce (1964) x, 340 p. 22 cm. F128.18.L46 1964

LINDAHL, Mac. Första gången i New York. Stockholm, Aldus/Bonnier, 1971. 95 p. illus. 19 cm. (Sesam. En Aldus handbok) F128.18.L55

LÓPEZ, Lucretia. New York City and the Fair, 1964-1965. Photos. by Thomas Henion. New York, C. Frank Publications (1964) 264 p. 19 cm. (Frank's modern travel guide) 64-22539. F128.18.L 6

MICHELIN Tyre Co. New York City. 1st ed. (Paris?) Michelin, The Corporation, 1968. 144 (5) p. 26 cm. (Green guide) Bibliography: p. (149) F128.18.M 5

COMPLETE travel guide to New York City, The. New York, Simon and Schuster (1971) 157 p. 19 cm. F128.18.M 6

NEW YORK and environs. Niagara Falls. Paris, Hachette, 1965. 177 p. 16 cm. (Hachette world guides) F128.18.N38

NEW YORK et ses environs. Les Chutes du Niagara. Paris, Hachette, 1964. 189 p. 16 cm. (Les Guides bleus illustrés) F128.18.N39

— 1969. 207 p. obl. plans (fold.) plates. 16 cm. (Les Guides bleus) F128.18.N39 1969

NEW YORK hackmen's and chauffeur's guide. (New York, B. Thurston) v. 16 cm. F128.18.N 4

NIGHT people's guide to New York, The; a Darien House project. Introd. by Jean Shepherd. New

NEW YORK CITY

York, Bantam Books (1965)   160 p.   18 cm.   (A Bantam extra.)   65-15736.   F128.18.N 5

NULL, Gary. Surviving and settling in New York on a shoestring.   New York, Pilot Books (1971)
47 p.   22 cm.   76-160361.   F128.18.N85

PETRONIUS (pseud.)   New York unexpurgated; an amoral guide for the jaded, tired, evil, non-conforming, currupt, condemned and the curious humans and otherwise to under underground Manhattan.
New York, Matrix House (1966)   246 p.   22 cm.   F128.18. P 4

— New York, Grove Press (1969)   viii, 374 p.   19 cm.   (Zebra books)
F128.18. P 4
1969

POLNER, Murray.   Where shall we take the kids? a parent's and teacher's guide to New York City (by) Murray Polmer (and) Arthur Barron.   (1st ed.) Garden City, N.Y., Doubleday, 1961.
238 p.   21 cm.   61-12570.   F128.18. P 6

RINZLER, Alan.   The New York spy.   Illus. by Kaffe Fassett.   New York, D. White Co. (1967)
viii, 440 p.   22 cm.   67-13249.   F128.18. R 5

— London, Blond, 1967.   viii, 440 p.   illus.   22 ½ cm.
F128.18. R 5
1967 b
MRR Alc.

ROBOTTI, Frances Diane.   Key to New York: empire city.   With an introd. by Paul R. Scevans.
Tricentennial ed.   New York, Fountainhead Publishers (1964)   xxv, 626 p.   21 cm.   "First printing."
61-18368.   F128.18. R 6

SHAW, Ray.   New York for children; an unusual guide for parents, teachers and tourists.   New York, Outerbridge & Lazard; (1972)   167 p.   illus.   18 cm.   78-190640.   F128.18. S 45
1972

SIMON, Kate.   New York places & pleasures, an uncommon guidebook.   Drawings by Bob Gill.   Rev. ed.   Cleveland, World Pub. Co. (1962)   381 p.   21 cm.   (Meridian books)   62-13387.
F128.18. S 5
1962

— 3d ed.   Cleveland, Meridian Books (1964)   413 p.   21 cm.   64-23001.   F128.18. S 5
1964

— 4th ed. rev.   New York, Harper & Row (1971)   xxiii, 417 p.   illus.   22 cm.   70-138761 MARC.
F128.18. S 5
1971

STRELOCKE, Hans.   New York.   (Traduit de l'allemand par Marie-Henriette Dervieu ...)   Paris, Éditions Marcus, 1966.   64 p.   illus.   19 cm.   (Poche-voyage Marcus)   F128.18.S714

STRELOCKE, Hans.   Nueva York ...   New York, Las Americas Pub. Co. (1966)   64 p.   20 cm.
F128.18.S718

TAUBER, Gilbert.   The New York City handbook; a comprehensive, practical guide for natives and newcomers living and working in New York, to the ins and outs of the five boroughs' assets, systems, neighborhoods, services and opportunities.   (1st ed.) Garden City, N.Y., Doubleday, 1966.
xxiii, 621 p.   65-21425.   F128.18. T 3

— Rev. ed.   Garden City, N.Y., Doubleday, 1968.   xxiii, 622 p.   21 cm.   67-23822.
F128.18. T 3
1968

THOMSEN, Mogens.   Turen går til New York.   2. rev. udg.   ... København, Politiken, 1968.

64 p. illus. 17 cm. (Politikens Rejsehåndbøger, 28) F128.18.T47
1968

VALLEJO, Frank C. Nueva York y au Feria Mundial, 1964-1965. New York, C. Frank Publications
(1964)   191 p. 20 cm. (Frank's modern travel guide) 64-7969. F128.18.V 3

WEINER, Florence. How to survive in New York with children. Illus. by Isadore Saltzer. (New York) Corinthian Editions, ...1969. 286 p. illus. 24 cm. 76-775-96.
F128.18.W37

WOODSTONE, Art. A fortnight in New York and its seaboard ... London, P. Marshall (1965)
viii, 122 p. 19 cm. (The Fortnight holday series) F128.18. W6

NEW YORK CITY. DIRECTORIES.

The Great metropolis; or, New-York almanac ... v. 1 -   1845 - 18   New-York, H. Wilson
(etc.) 1844 -   v. illus., fold. maps. 14 cm. 33-14363.
F128.2.A
Rare Book Coll.

ELLIOT and Crissy's New York directory ... New York, Elliot and Crissy.   v. 14 cm. 13-24927.
Directories

... The New York directory for 1786, illus. with a plan of the city, prefaced by a general description of New York by Noah Webster, also with an appendix consisting of Annals of New York city 1786 ... New York, The Trow city directory co. (1889)   xxii, facsim. (82p.) (83) - 215 p. front. (fold. map) 19 cm.
Fac-simile reprint of first directory. 100 copies printed. 5-5878 Rev. F128.2.A
1786
Rare Book Coll.

— New York, H. J. Sachs (1905)   107 p. fold. plan. 19½ cm. 11-4000 Rev.   R F128.2.A
1786
Rare Book Coll.

POLK, R. L. and co. Trow general directory of New York city embracing the boroughs of Manhattan and the Bronx ... (v. 128   )   (New York) R.L. Polk (1915 -   (1) v. 34 cm.
Directories

POLK'S New York city directory (borough of Queens and Richmond) v. 1 -   1933/4 -   (New York) R.L. Polk, 1933 -   v. illus. 35½ cm. CA 33-254 Unrev.
Directories

MANHATTAN and Bronx residential directory ... containing an alphabetical list of ... names, addresses and ... business or occupation of Manhattan and Bronx residents ... New York city, Manhattan and Bronx directory pub. co., 1931 -   v. 32 cm. 31-23239.   Directories

TROW'S business and residential directory of the borough of Richmond, city of New York ... vol. I
1898 -   New York, Trow directory, printing and bookbinding co. (1898) -   v. fold. maps.
20½ cm. 99-2697 Rev.   Directories

CITIZEN and strangers' pictorial and business directory for the city of New-York and its vicinity.
1853 -   New York, C. Spalding.   v. illus. 19 cm. 55-2320.   F128.2.C 5

GOULDING'S manual of New York and general statistical guide. 1875 -   New York, L. G. Goulding.   v. 24 cm. annual. 58-52705.   F128.2. G 5

LONGWORTH'S American almanac, New-York register and city directory. New York, T. Longworth.
(1818/19)   v. 19 cm. 55-53723.   F128.2. L 6
Rare Book Coll.

926

NEW YORK CITY

NEW YORK CITY.   SOCIETY DIRECTORIES.

CAFE society register.   19   New York, N.Y., C.S.R. pub. co. inc. (19   v. 22 cm. annual.
41-24877.   Directories

DAU's New York social blue book ... 19   New York city, Dau's blue books, 19   v. 21½ cm.
Title varies.   6-34377 Rev.   Directories

DAU'S New York blue book ... 19   New York city, Dau's blue books inc., 19   v. 21½ cm.
6-34377.   Directories

DIRECTORY of American society, New York state and the metropolitan district.   1st -   ed.,
v. 1 -   1929 -   New York, Town topics (1928 -   1 v.   18½ cm. 28-30434.
                                                                                                                   Directories

THE ÉLITE of New York; society list and club register, 1886/87 -   New York, 1886 - 19
    v.   17½ - 21 cm. . 1-29393 Rev.   F128. 22. E

THE 400 (offically supervised) 1889. (New York) Melville pub. co. (1889 -   v. 16½ cm.
CA 33-1160 Unrev.   Directories
                                                                                                                Rare Book Coll.

LAIN'S New York and Brooklyn élite directory and ladies'. visiting and shopping guide, classified by
streets ... 1882/83 -   New York, Brooklyn. G. T. Lane (1882 -   v. 20 cm.
CA 33-855 Unrev.   Directories

THE LIST, a visiting and shopping directory ... 1879 -   New York, The List pub. so. (1878-86)
    v.   14½ - 18 x 14 cm. Superseded by Society-list & club register.   CA 33-840 Unrev.   Directories

MANHATTAN visiting list.   Comp. by Miss E. D. Bininger.   New York, Evening post job print
(1899)   v.   15½ x 8 cm.   Title varies slightly.   99-5687 Rev.   F128.22.M

NEW YORK-Long island social record, the exclusive registry ... New York city, Social record assoc.
inc. (19   v.   19½ cm.   CA 32-586 Unrev.   Directories

SOCIETY ... a list of New York society ... 18(86 -   )   New York, 18(86 -
(1) v.   18 x 14½ cm.   Superseded by Society-list and club register.   Directories

VISITING index of Social register 1915 -   limited to those families in the Social register who
have city residences.   New York, Social register assoc.   1 v.   diagr.   17½ x 9½ cm.   Alternate pages
blank.   15-14087.   Directories

NEW YORK CITY.   BUSINESS DIRECTORIES.

The ALCOLM, a magazine of the metropolis.   v. 1-4, v.5, no. 1-11; June 1905-May 1910.   (New
York) The Alcolm co. (etc.) 1905-10.   5 v. in 10.   26½ cm. monthly. No more pub. 9-25083 Rev.
                                                                                                              F128.4
                                                                                                              F128.1.A35

NEW-ENGLAND mercantile union business directory.   Part 5 - Rhode Island ...   New York, Pratt &
co.; Boston, L. C. & H. Pratt, etc., 1949.   3, (9)-11, (14)-90, (18), 15 p. incl. tables. fold. map. 14 cm. No
more pub? "Business register. - New York": 15 p. at end.   35-30106.   F128.24
                                                                                                              F77.7.N 28

NEW YORK business directory for 184   - 46/7.   (v.   - 4)   New-York, J. Doggett, jr.,
184   - (46)   v. 19 cm. 16-11527.   Directories

BANKET'S official society directory of the cities of New York, Brooklyn, Jersey City and Newark ...

927

1892 -　　　　New York, F. Banket, 1892 -　　　1 v.　14 cm.　annual.　"This directory is especially for societies, lodges, clubs, hospitals, churches, Grand army post, etc. and colored institutions."
　　　Directories

BOYD'S New York (boroughs of Manhattan and the Bronx) co-partnership and residence-business directory ... (New York) The Boyd New York directory co.　　v.　24 cm.　2-738.　　Directories

BOYD'S New York (boroughs of Manhattan and the Bronx) co-partnership and residence-business directory ... to which is added a complete classified business directory ... 1898 - 19　　(1st -　　year) (New York) The Boyd New York directory co., 1898-19　　v.　24 cm.　0-4009 (rev. '29)
　　　Directories

BRANTON business directory (of New York, New Brunswick, Newark, Perth Amboy); progressive business places, classified and commercial laws　　New York, Branton directory co.
　　v.　25½ cm.　13-25481.　　　　　　　　　　　　　　　　　　　　　　Directories

DIRECTORIO hispano-americano y guia de compradores de Nueva York ... Spanish-American directory and buyers' guide of New York in Spanish, Portuguese and English ...　(New York) 1907 -
　　v. illus., fold. map.　19 cm.　7-20885 (rev. '30)　　　　　　　　　　Directories

RAND'S (improved) New York city business directory ... 1876/77 -　　New York (1876) -
　　v.　15 cm.　CA 11-1705 Unrev.　　　　　　　　　　　　　　　　　Directories

NEW YORK city business directory ... 1912.　37th ed.　　New York, Puritan pub. co.
1 v.　17½ cm.　12-13234.　　　　　　　　　　　　　　　　　　　　　Directories

MERCANTILE business directory of New York, Philadelphia, Boston and Newark, and the states of Maine, New Hampshire, Vermont, Massachusetts, Rhode Island and Connecticut, 1910.　v. 24. ... New York, Puritan pub. co., 1910.　　1 v.　23½ cm.　10-24176.　　Directories

TROW business directory of the boroughs of Manhattan and the Bronx, city of New York ... (1848) v. (1) -　　New York, Trow directory, printing & bookbinding co., 1848 - 19　　v. fold. maps. 14½ x 24 cm.　1-15252 Rev. 2.　　　　　　　　　　　　　　　　Directories

THE GEM, or Fashionable business directory ... 1844.　　1 v.　　　　　F128.24.G 4

GOULDING'S business directory of New York, Brooklyn, Newark, Paterson, Jersey City and Hoboken ...　v.　18　　New York, L. G. Goulding (18　　v.　24 cm.　39M4074T.
　　　　　　　　　　　　　　　　　　　　　　　　　　　　　　　　　　Directories

JONES'S New-York mercantile and general directory, for the 30th year of American independence, and of Our Lord, 1805-6 ...　New-York ... (1805)　　xi, (19), (33)-420 p.　18½ cm.　37-9992.
　　　　　　　　　　　　　　　　　　　　　　　　　　　　　　　　F128.24.J 66
　　　　　　　　　　　　　　　　　　　　　　　　　　　　　　　　Rare Book Coll.

ALCOLM red book.　Export ed. ...　New York, Alcolm pub. co., 1905-06.　　1 v., pt. 1-2.　2 v. 26½ cm.　Contains also Spanish section.　9-3194.　　　　　　　　　　Directories

NEW YORK city mercantile and manufacturers' business directory ... 1856/57 -　　New York, Mason brothers (1857) -　　v.　23½ cm.　24-16071.　　　　　　　　Directories

NEW YORK and surrounding territory classified business directory ... 192　　New York, New York directory co. (192　　v.　23½ cm.　21-12278 Rev.　　　　　　　Directories

NEW YORK classified business directory (Metropolitan area) incl. representative firms in greater New York - Westchester, Nassau and Suffolk counties - northern New Jersey ... New York city, New York pub. co., 19　　v.　23 cm.　CA 33-997 Unrev.　　　　　　　Directories

PHILLIPS' business directory of New York city ... and representative houses of Long Island, Brooklyn, Jersey City, Hoboken and Newark ... 18　　-19　　New York, J. F. White (etc.) 18 -　　(19
　　v.　18½ - 25 cm.　99-202 Rev.　　　　　　　　　　　　　　　　　Directories

NEW YORK CITY   195

QUARTO. The Quarto guide to New York shops and services (on the East Side, 16th to 96th Street. Elizabeth Dunn, editor. New York, Quarto) 1963.   144 p.   16 cm.
 F128.24.Q 3

REFERENCE Register; The; a compendium for general business reference, comprising the financial, commercial, industrial and legal interests of the cities of New York, Philadelphia, Baltimore, Boston and Newark, N.J.   New York city (etc.) White, Orr & co., 1931.   v.   26 cm.   19-871 Rev.
 Directories

TROW Alcolm blue book, The; a desk manual designed to meet the buying needs of 300,000 executives in New York city and the surrounding metropolitan area.   New York city, R. L. Polk, (19
 v.   26½ cm.   25-6833.
 Directories

BIOGRAPHY (COLLECTIVE). GENEALOGY (COLLECTIVE).

BANK of the Manhattan co.   A collection of more than four hundred autographs of leading citizens of New York at the close of the 18th century, reproduced in facsimile ...   New York, Bank of the Manhattan co., 1919.   3 p., facsims.: 16 l.   44 cm.   19-8746.
 F128.25
 Z42.B25 no.1294

LEONARD, John William.   History of the city of New York, 1609-1909 ... tog. with brief biographies of men representative of the business interests of the city ...   N.Y., The Journal of commerce and commercial bulletin, 1910.   2, vii-viii, 954 p.   illus. (incl. ports., maps, facsim.)   pl.   28½ cm.   10-26180.
 F128.25
 F128.3.L 58

BARBER, Gertrude Audrey.   Deaths taken from the New York evening post ...   (New York?) 1939-40.
17 v. in 9.   28½ x 22½ cm.   Type-written.   vols. 13-29 covering years 1835 to 1853.   46-36389.
 F128.25.B 27

(BEACH, Moses Yale) ed.   Present value of real estate in New York city (by wards), compared with that of 1842.   Also a list of the wealthy citizens of New York city forty odd years ago.   Arranged in alphabetical order, with amount attached to each name ...   New York (Evening post job print. off.) 1884.   8 p.   8°.   From his Wealth and biography of the wealthy citizens of New York city, with corrections by Peter F. Daly.   The biographical notices are omitted.   1-14297.
 F128.25.B 34

(BEACH, Moses Yale)   Wealth and wealthy citizens of New York City.   Comprising an alphabetical arrangement of persons estimated to be worth $100,000, and upwards.   With the sums appended to each name.   Being useful to banks, merchants, and others.   New York, The Sun office, 1842.
8 p.   21 cm.   First ed.   3-8091.
 F128.25.B 35

(BEACH, Moses Yale)   Wealth and pedigree of the wealthy citizens of New York city, comprising an alphabetical arrangement of persons estimated to be worth $100,000 and upwards ...   New York, The Sun office, 1842.   24 p.   23 cm.   4th ed. of above title.
 F128.25.B355

 — 6th ed.   1845.   32 p.   22½ cm.   1-14298.
 F128.25.B 36

 — 10th ed.   1846.   32 p.   22½ cm.   4-33431.
 F128.25.B369

 — 13th.ed.   1855.   80 p.   18½ cm.   1-14299.
 F128.25.B 37

BROWN book, The; a biographical record of public officials of the city of New York for 1898-9.   New York, Martin B. Brown co., 1899.   314 p.   col. front., illus. (ports.)   maps.   23 cm.   99-685 Rev.   F128.25.B 87

CONNABLE, Alfred.   Tigers of Tammany; nine men who ran New York.   (1st ed.)   New York, Holt, Rinehart and Winston (1967)   384 p.   22 cm.   66-21623.
 F128.25.C 6

ELIOT, Maud Stoutenburgh.   The Knickerbocker jingles by (Judith Stuyvesant)   New York, The Knickerbocker press, 1927.   ix, 105 p.   illus. (coats of arms)   22½ cm.   27-23963.
 F128.25.E 4

(GRIM, Charles Frederic) An essay towards an improved register of deeds. City and county of New-York. To Dec. 31, 1799, inclusive. New-York, Gould, Banks, & co., 1832. 371 p. 22½ cm.
8-23025.
    F128.25
    HD268.N5 G8

HAMBURGER, Philip Paul. Mayor watching and other pleasures. New York, Rinehart (1958)
276 p. 21 cm. "First pub. in 1958." 58-8684.
    F128.25.H 3

HERRINGSHAW'S city blue book of biography; New Yorker's of 1917 - Chicago, C. J. Herringshaw (1917) - v. 25 cm. 17-30129.
    F128.25.H56

HERSHKOWITZ, Leo, comp. Wills of early New York Jews, 1704 - 1799. With a foreword by Isidore S. Meyer. New York, American Jewish Historical Soc., 1967. xvi, 220 p. 27 cm. (Studies in American jewish history, no. 4)
    F128.25.H58

(KING, Moses) Notable New Yorkers of 1896-1899; a companion volume to King's handbook of New York city. New York, N.Y., Boston, Mass., M. King, 1899. 616 p. illus. (ports.) 22 cm. 2,336 names and portraits, classified and indexed. 99-945 Rev.
    F128.25.K52

— Another copy printed on larger paper.
    F128.25.K521

KING, Moses. King's views of the New York stock exchange; a history and description, with articles on financial topics, illustrated with more than 400 portraits and 65 views of the exchange and vicinity. New York, Boston, M. King (1898) 96 p. illus., ports. 38½ cm. In double columns. "The ... title page ... announces 400 ports. and 65 views ... should now read 93 views and 968 ports." 3-21400.
    F128.25.K53

LEADERS of the twentieth century, New York city, 1918. New York, Unico news service (1918)
272 p. incl. front., ports. 23½ cm. Portraits. 18-9766.
    F128.25.L43

MORRIS, Charles. Makers of New York; an historical work, giving portraits and sketches of the most eminent citizens of New York. Philadelphia, Pa., L. R. Hamersly, 1895. 348 p. illus. (ports.) 32 x 24½ cm. 3-19137.
    F128.25.M87

(MORRIS, Charles) Men of affairs in New York; an historical work giving portraits and sketches of the most eminent citizens of New York. New York, L. R. Hamersly, 1906. 2, 294 p. illus. (ports.) 31½ cm. "Practically a second edition of 'The makers of New York' pub. 1895." 6-18068.
    F128.25.M88

NEW YORK (City) A copy of the poll list, of the election for representatives for the city and county of New-York ... 1761. Alphabetically made (by S. Whitney Phoenix) (New York, Print. F. Hart, 1880) 2, 42 p. 21 x 17½ cm. 50 copies printed. 1-14300.
    F128.25.N51

NEW YORK (City) A copy of the poll list ... 1768. (New York, Print. F. Hart, 1880) 2, 56 p. 21½ x 17½ cm. Fifty copies printed. 1-14301.
    F128.25.N52

NEW YORK (City) A copy of the poll list ... 1769. (New York, F. Hart, print. 1880) 3, 43 p. 21 x 17½ cm. Fifty copies printed. 1-14302.
    F128.25.N53

NEW YORK. Personal records of the Brick Presbyterian church in the city of New York, 1809 - 1908, including births, baptisms, marriages, admissions to membership, dismissions, deaths, etc., arranged in alphabetical order; ed. by Shepherd Knapp. New York, Trustees of the Brick Presbyterian church, 1909. 2, 262 p. 24½ cm. 9-4182.
    F128.25.N55

NEW YORK (City) Tax lists of the city of New York, Dec. 1695 - July, 1699. (In New York Hist. Soc. Collections v. 43 and 44. 14-19867.
    F128.25.N56

NOTABLE New Yorkers, 1942. New York, N.Y., Empire city pub. co., 1942. 132 p. incl. ports. pl. 24 cm. Portraits: p. 17-132. 42-16350.
    F128.25.N 7

POST, John J., comp. Index of wills ... on file in the office of the clerk of the Court of appeals. New York, S. V. Constant, 1899. (49) p. 26 cm. 99-2327.
    F128.25.P75

PURPLE. Contributions to the history of ancient families of New Amsterdam and New York. By Edwin R. Purple ... and additions and emendations to the work, by Samuel S. Purple. New York, Priv. print., 1881. xii, (5)-138 p. front., port. 27½ cm. 100 copies printed. 3-17361. F128.25.P97

PURPLE, Samuel Smith. ... Index to the marriage records from 1639 to 1801 of the Reformed Dutch church in New Amsterdam and New York ... New York, Priv. print., 1890. 2, xii, 9-87 p. port., facsim. 28½ cm. Ed. of 50 copies. Repr. from the "Records of the Reformed Dutch church in New Amsterdam ..." 1890. 3-17743. F128.25.P98

SAWYER, Ray Cowen. Abstracts of wills for New York county ... (New York) 1934-41. 13 v. 28 x 21½ cm. Type-written. v.1. 1801-1808. - v.2. 18-08-1814. 35-14598. F128.25.S27

SAWYER, Ray Cowen. Index of wills of New York County (New York City) from 1662 to 1850. (New York) 1930. 3 v. (497 l.) 26 cm. Typescript (carbon copy) F128.25.S277

SAWYER, Ray Cowen. Marriages performed by the various mayors and aldermen of the city of New York, as well as justices of the peace, etc., 1830-1854. (n. p.) 1936. 2 p., 63 numb. l., 6 l. 28 cm. Type-written. 44-25546. F128.25.S28

SPRAGUE, John Franklin. New York, the metropolis. Its noted business and professional men ... (New York) The New York recorder, 1893. 3 pt. in 1 v. front., illus. (incl. ports.) 30 x 23½ cm. Contents. - pt. 1. Historical. - pt. 2. Biographical. - pt. 3. Commercial. 1-14303. F128.25.S76

TALESE, Cay. The overreachers. With illus. by Stanislav Zagorski. (1st ed.) New York, Harper & Row (1965) 190 p. 22 cm. 64-20542. F128.25.T13 1965

TAMMANY times, The. 4th of July souvenir, Tammany times, vol. I -   New York, 1894 - 1 v. illus., ports. 25½ cm. 6-10176. F128.25.T15

TOLER, Henry Pennington. The New Harlem register; a genealogy of the descendants of the 23 original patentees of the town of New Harlem, containing proofs of births, baptisms and marriages from the year 1630 to date. New York, New Harlem pub. co., 1903. 5, 617, xlviii p. 46 x 34½ cm. 3-31008. F128.25.T64

TUTTLE, Henry Croswell. Abstracts of farm titles in the city of New York, between 39th and 75th streets, east of the common lands. With maps. ... New York, The Spectator co., printers, 1877. 3, (3)-390, iii, (2) p. fold. maps. 25 cm. 5-16857. F128.25.T92

TUTTLE, Henry Croswell. Abstracts of farm titles in the city of New York, East side, between 75th and 120th streets. With maps. ... New York, The Spectator co., printers, 1878. 2, (3)-456 p. fold. maps. 25½ cm. 5-16856. F128.25.T924

TUTTLE, Henry Croswell. Abstracts of farm titles in the city of New York, between 39th and 73rd streets, west of the common lands, excepting the Glass house farm. With maps. ... New York, The Spectator co., printers, 1881. 3, (3) - 573 p. fold. maps. 25½ cm. 5-16855. F128.25.T926

ULMANN, Albert. New Yorkers, from Stuyvesant to Roosevelt, by Albert Ulmann ... New York, Chaucer head book shop, 1928. 7, 267 p. front., illus., plates, ports., facsims. 23 cm. Contents. - Peter Minuit. - Peter Stuyvesant. - Thomas Dongan. - John Peter Zenger. - Thomas Paine. - Alexander Hamilton. - Robert Fulton. - De Witt Clinton. - Washington Irving. - Samuel F. B. Morse. - Peter Cooper. - Edgar Allan Poe. - Theodore Roosevelt. 28-28398. F128.25.U43

— With a new introd. by Ralph Adams Brown. Port Washington, N.Y., Ira J. Friedman (1969) 267 p. illus. 24 cm. (Empire State historical publications series no. 62) 68-58929. F128.25.U43 1969

VAN RENSSELAER, May (King) "Mrs. J. K. Van Rensselaer" New Yorkers of the xix. century. ... New York and London, F. T. Neely (1897) x, 56 p. 49 x 39 cm. Contains pedigrees of the Bard, Barclay, Bronson, Buchanan, Delafield, Duer, Emmet, Fish, Glover, Hoffman, Jay, King, Lynch, McVickar, Morton, Renwick, Rutherford, Schuyler, Stuyvesant and Van Rensselaer families. 99-4482 Rev. F128.25.V27

(WEEKS, Lyman Horace) ed.   Prominent families of New York; being an account in biographical form of individuals and families distinguished as representatives of the social, professional and civic life of New York city.   New York, The Historical co., 1897.   7-641 p.   31 cm.   3-19140 Rev.

          F128.25.W38

— Rev. ed.   New York, The Historical co., 1898.   7-688 p.   29½ x 23½ cm.   34-38761.

          F128.25.W38
          1898

NEW YORK CITY.   GENERAL WORKS. HISTORIES.

FISHER, Nath'l, & co.   Seventy-five years in leather; a brief history of the house of Nath'l Fisher & co., 1838-1913.   New York, Priv. print. (The Trow press, 1913)   24, (2) p.   illus. (incl. port., facsims.) fold. pl.   24 cm.   14-1382.

          F128.3
          HD9787.U45F5

NEW YORK city corporation celebration, commemorating the 250th anniversary of the installation of the first mayor and Board of aldermen and the adoption of the official city flag.   June 24, 1915.   (In American scenic and historic preservations soc. 21st annual report, 1916. p. 443-486)   17-16272.

          F128.3
          E151.A51 vol. 21

WATSON, John Fanning.   Annals of Philadelphia ... To which is added an appendix, containing olden time researches and reminiscences of New York city ...   Philadelphia, E. L. Carey & A. Hart; New York, G. & C. & H. Carvill, 1830.   xii, 740, 78 p.   plates, port.   23 cm.   "Appendix: containing olden time researches & reminiscences of New York city ..." 78 p. was enlarged and pub. separately in 1832 as "Historic tales of the olden time."   1-10546.

          F158.3. W 2

BALDWIN, Orrel T.   New York; past and present.   Ed. by Benjamin E. Strumpf.   New York, Noble and Noble (1961)   125 p.   illus.   28 cm.

          F128.3. B 3

BLIVEN, Bruce.   New York; the story of the world's most exciting city.   New York, Random House (1969)   130 p.   illus.   29 cm.   (Landmark giant)   78-85820.

          F128.3.B 55

BONNER, William Thompson.   New York, the world's metropolis, 1623-4 — 1923-4, a presentation of the greater city at the beginning of its second quarter century of amalgamated government and the 300th anniversary of its founding ...   Commemorative ed., New York city directory.   New York, R. I. Polk & co., 1924.   xvi, 17-958 p. incl. front., illus.   33 cm.   Bibliography: p. 893-896.   25-6038.

          F128.3. B 7

BOOTH, Mary Louise.   History of the city of New York, from its earliest settlement to the present time.   Illus. with over 100 engravings.   New York, W. R. C. Clark & Meeker, 1859.   xix, (21)-846 p. incl. illus., plates, ports. front.   23½ cm.   1-14304.

          F128.3. B 72

— New York, W. R. C. Clark, 1867.   2 v.   front., illus., plates, ports.   24½ cm.   Paged continuously.   1-14305.

          F128.3. B 73

— New York, E. P. Dutton, 1880.   2, 3-920 p. incl. illus., plates, ports.   26 cm.   1-14306.   F128.3. B 74

BOWE, Richard J.   The New York City story.   Official ed.   (New York, Historical Publications 1963)   64 p.   22 x 28 cm.

          F128.3. B 78

(BROWN, Henry Collins) comp.   Book of New York.   New York, Priv. print. for American bankers assoc., 1922.   (76) p. col. front., illus. (part col., incl. facsim.) double pl., ports.   31½ x 24 cm.   22-24418.

          F128.3. B 86

BROWN, Henry Collins.   Book of old New-York; the rare old prints are from the private collections of Mr. Robert Goelet and others.   New York, Priv. print. for the subscribers (The Lent & Graff co.) 1913.   xix, 392 p. incl. col. front., illus., plates (part col.) port. group, 32½ cm.   14-470.

          F128.3. B 87
          Rare Book Coll.

NEW YORK CITY

BROWN, Henry Collins. The city of New York, New York, Old colony press (1915)   287 p. illus.
9 cm.   "This is number one of a series of tarry-at-home travels, in which an intimate glimpse is given of the chief cities in our country, including the wonders of the West."   15-3048.
F128.3. B 88

— 65th thousand. New York, J. M. Ruston, 1917.   287 p. illus. 9 cm.   17-25750.
F128.3.B883

BROWN, Henry Collins. The story of old New York; illus. by Frank Rennie. New York, E. P. Dutton (1934)   xix, (3), 23-373 p. front., illus. (incl. maps) 22½ cm.   "First ed."   34-35661.
F128.3.B 886

CITY history club of New York. ... Free lectures to the people: syllabus of a general lecture and a course of three lectures on the history and development of the city of New York. (New York, Press of the J. W. Pratt co., 1903?)   80 p. 23 cm.   Dept. of Education, the city of New York.   4-28330.
F128.3.C 58

CITY history Club of New York. Know your city; a school broadcast manual for teachers and parents, by Edith McGinnis, Manhattan Borough historian and executive secretary. (2d ed. New York, 1954)
136 p. illus. 23 cm.   54-31327.
F128.3.C585
1954

CITY history club of New York. Teacher's handbook of the City history club of New York ... (New York, 1899)   24 p. 23 cm.   4-28329.
F128.3.C 59

— Revised, 1905. (New York? 1905)   31 p. 19½ cm.   6-38862.
F128.3. C 6

COLLINS, Frederick Lewis. Money town, the story of Manhattan toe: that golden mile which lies between the Battery and the fields, by Frederick L. Collins. (New York) G. P. Putnam's sons (1946)
viii, 327 p. col. front., plates. 22 cm.   46-8328.
F128.3. C 7

(CURRY, Daniel) New York: a historical sketch of the rise and progress of the metropolitan city of America. By a New Yorker ... New-York, Carlton & Phillips, 1853.   339 p. incl. front., 6 pl. 3 pl.,
2 plans. 18½ cm.   5-10329.
F128.3.C 97

DELANEY, Edmund T. New York's Turtle Bay old & new. (Barre, Mass., Barre Publishers, 1965)
85 p. 25 cm.   65-16658.
F128.3. D 4

DIETZ, Robert Edwin. 1913. A leaf from the past; Dietz, then and now; origin of the late Robert Edwin Dietz - his business career, and some interesting facts about New York, comp. by his eldest son Fred. Dietz ... New York, Chicago (etc.) R. E. Dietz co. (1914)   2, 194 p. front., illus. (incl. facsims.)
col. pl., ports., col. coat of arms. 23½ cm.   14-3423.
F128.3. D 56

ELLIS, Edward Robb. The epic of New York City. Drawings by Jeanyee Wong. New York, Coward-McCann (1966)   640 p. 22 cm.   66-20148.
F128.3. E 65

EMERSON, Caroline Dwight. Old New York for young New Yorkers ... illus. by Alida Conover.
New York, E. P. Dutton (1932)   xvi, 311 p. col. front., illus. (incl. maps) 22½ cm.   "First edition." "Further material on the city's history to use with children": p. 299-302.   32-26644 Rev.
F128.3. E 73

— (1st ed.) New York, Dutton (1953)   261 p. illus. 21 cm.   "New and fully revised ed. of 'Old New York for young New Yorkers.'"   53-6071.
F128.3. E 73
1953

FEININGER, Andreas. The face of New York; the city as it was and as it is. Photos. by Andreas Feeninger; text by Susan E. Lyman. New York, Crown Publishers (1954)   1 v. (unpaged) illus. 32 cm.
54-11181.
F128.3. F 4

— (Rev. ed.) New York, Crown Publishers (1964)   1 v. (unpaged)
F128.3. F 4
1964

GUIREMAND, Harry Arthur. Practical facts about New York. New York city, The Knickerbocker information bureau (1917)   47 p.   21 cm.   17-1601.   F128.3.G 96

HARDIE, James. The description of the city of New-York ... to which is prefixed, a brief account of its first settlement by the Dutch, in the year 1629 ... New York, S. Marks, 1827.   3, 360 p.   front. (fold. plan)   18 cm.   1-14363.   F128.3.H 26

HART, Smith. The New Yorkers; the story of a people and their city. New York, Sheridan house (1938)   viii, 11-253 p.   21 cm.   Bibliography: p. 249-253.   39-1030.   F128.3.H 28

HEADLEY, Joel Tyler. The great riots of New York, 1712 ro 1873. Including a full and complete account of the four days' draft riot of 1863. By Hon, J. T. Headley ... New York, E. B. Trent, 1873.   2, (7) - 306, (331) - 359 p.   front., plates.   21 cm.   11-10447.   F128.3.H 43

— New York, E. B. Treat, 1873. Miami, Fla., Reprinted by Mnemosyne Pub. Co. (1969)   359 p.   illus.   23 cm.   70-89407.   F128.3.H 43 1969

— Introd. by Thomas Rose and James Rodgers. Indianapolis, Bobbs-Merrill (1970)   xxx, 312 p.   21 cm.   78-98275.   F182.3.H 43 1970

— With a new introd. by James McCague. New York, Dover Publications (1971)   335 p. (The Dover anarchy library)   21 cm.   76-138390.   F128.3.H 43 1971

HEMSTREET, Charles. The story of Manhattan. New York, C. Scribner's sons, 1901.   xvi, 249 p.   incl. illus., plates.   double pl.   18 ½ x 15 cm.   1-25416.   F128.3. H 5

(HERRMANN, Friedrich) Die Stadt Newyork. Mit einer abbildung nach der natur gezneichnet. (In Kronos; genealogisch-historisches taschenbuch auf das jahr 1820.)   9-8986.   F128.3.H 56

HOLT, Solomon. New York City, State, and nation. New York, Noble and Noble (1955)   198 p.   illus.   27 cm.   55-844.   F128.3.H 64

— (1961)   246 p.   27 cm.   F128.3.H 64 1961

KLEIN, Alexander. The Empire City; a treasury of New York. New York, Rinehart (1955)   475 p.   24 cm.   55-7728.   F128.3.K 53

KOUWENHOVEN, John Atlee. The Columbia historical portrait of New York; an essay in graphic history in honor of the tricentennial of New York City and the bicentennial of Columbia University. With a foreword by Grayson L. Kirk. (1st ed.) Garden City, N.Y., Doubleday, 1953.   550 p.   (chiefly illus. (part col.) ports., maps)   28 cm.   53-8181.   F128.3. K 6 L H & G

LAMB, Mrs. Martha Joanna Reade (Nash) History of the city of New York: its origin, rise, and progress. By Mrs. Martha J. Lamb ... New York and Chicago, A. S. Barnes, 1877 - (96)   3 v.   illus. 43 pl. (incl. front., v.3) 2 maps, 3 plans.   26 ½ cm.   (v.3: 27 cm.)   2 pl. wanting in vol. 2.   Vol. 3 is paged continuously with v.2. 1-1942.

F128.3.L 21

LEHNARTZ, Klaus. New York. Mit einer Einleitung von Fred Ruck. Berlin, Stapp Verlag (1969)   iv, chiefly illus.   28 cm.   F128.3.L 53

LEONARD, John William. History of the city of New York, 1609-1909, from the earliest discoveries to the Hudson-Fulton celebration; together with brief biographies of men representative of the business interests of the city ... New York, The Journal of commerce and commercial bulletin, 1910.   2, vii-viii, 954 p.   illus. (incl. ports., maps, facsim.) pl.   28 ½ cm.   10-26180.   F128.3.L 58

NEW YORK CITY

LESLIE'S history of the greater New York, by Daniel Van Pelt ... New York, Arkell pub. co. (1898) 3 v. fronts., illus. (incl. facsims.) plates (part fold.) ports., map, plans (1 double) 27½ cm. Contents. - v.1. New York to the consolidation. - v.2. Brooklyn and other boroughs. - v.3. Encyclopedia of New York biography and genealogy. 1-14316.   F128.3. L 63

LOCKWOOD, Sarah (McNeil) New York, not so little and not so old; illus. by Ilonka Karasz. Garden City, N.Y., Doubleday, Page, 1926. viii, 197 p. incl. illus., maps. 25½ cm. Bibliography: p. 189. 27-1284 Rev.   F128.3. L 82

LOSSING, Benson John. History of New York City, embracing an outline sketch of events from 1609 to 1830, and a full account of its development from 1830 to 1884. Illus. ... by Perine. New York, G. E. Perine (1884) vi, 881 p. front., 11 pl., 90 port., plan. 30½ cm. 3-18894.   F128.3. L 88

LYMAN, Susan Elizabeth. The story of New York; an informal history of the city. New York, Crown Publishers (1964) vi, 282 p. 24 cm. 64-17843.   F128.3. L 9

McATAMNEY, Hugh Entwistle. Cradle days of New York (1609-1825) New York, Drew & Lewis, 1909. iv, (2) p., iv. 11-230 p. front., illus. 23 cm. "... in its amended form, the series of articles which appeared in the New York tribune under the title 'Little old New York.'" 9-29782 Rev.   F128.3. M 11

MANHATTAN company. "Manna-hatin": the story of New York. New York, The Manhattan co. (1929) 2, vii-xvii, (1), 269 p. incl. front., illus. 20½ cm. 30-1915.   F128.3. M 27

— Port Washington, N.Y., I. J. Friedman (1968) xvii, 269 p. illus. 21 cm. (Empire state historical publications, series no. 55) 68-18364.   F128.3. M 27 1968

MARCUSE, Maxwell F. This was New York; a nostalgic picture of Gotham in the gaslight era, New York, Carlton Press (1965) 447 p. 24 cm. (A Reflection book)   F128.3. M 3

— Rev. and enl. ed. New York, LIM Press (1969) 452 p. illus. 24 cm. 69-18328.   F128.3. M 3 1969

MINES, John Flavel. A tour around New York, and My summer acre; being the recreations of Mr. Felix Oldboy. ... New York, Harper & bros., 1893. xviii, 518 p. incl. front., illus., plates, maps. 22 cm. 1-14307.   F128.3. M 66

MORRIS, Lloyd R. Incredible New York; high life and low life of the last hundred years. New York, Random House (1951) 370 p. illus. 24 cm. "1st printing." 51-14524.   F128.3. M 87

MOSS, Frank. The American metropolis, from Knickerbocker days to the present time; New York city life in all its various phases ... with an introd. by Rev. Charles H. Parkhurst ... New York, P. F. Collier, 1897. 3 v. front., illus., plates, ports. 22 cm. 1-14308.   F128.3. M 91

NAKAUCHI, Masatoshi. Amerika fubutsushi. (In Japanese) 422 p. illus. 20 cm.   F128.3. N 3 Orien. Japan

NEW YORK (City) Report of the Special committee of the Board of aldermen on the 250th anniversary of the installation of the first mayor ... (New York, 1915) 58 p. front., plates (1 col.) facsims. 26 cm. 20-7978.   F128.3. N 56

NEW YORK (City) New York, the city that belongs to the world. (Donald Beggs, compiler. New York, 1956) 48 p. illus. 23 cm. 58-1346.   F128.3. N 58

O'CONNOR, Richard. Hell's kitchen; the roaring days of New York's wild West Side. (1st ed.) Philadelphia, Lippincott (1958) 249 p. illus. 22 cm. Includes bibliography. 58-9536.   F128.3. O 3 1958

OLD NEW YORK. (From Munsey's magazine, v.19, 1898) p. 43-56. 25 cm.   F128.3. O 44

PATTERSON, Samuel White. A fourth grade history and geographical reader for the New York city public schools,   New York, Noble and Noble (1923)   xi, 3-245 p. illus. 21½ cm. 23-7843.
F128.3. P 31

PERINE, Edward Ten Broeck. Here's to Broadway! ... with 17 illus. New York, London, G. P. Putnam's sons, 1930.   xii, 321 p. front., plates, facsims. 24 cm. "First edition." 30-9122.
F128.3. P 44

RICHMOND, John Francis. New York and its institutions, 1609-1871. A library of information, pertaining to the great metropolis, past and present ... New York, E. B. Treat; Chicago, W. T. Keener ... 1871.   (vii)-xvi, (17)-608 (i.e. 526) p. front., illus., plates. 22 cm. Paged irregularly, 221-280 being omitted, and the last page, following p. "585, being numbered 608. 1-14309.
F128.3. R 53

RODGERS, Cleveland. New York: the world's capital city, its development and contributions to progress. New York, Harper (1948)   xviii, 398 p. illus., ports., map. 25 cm. Bibliography: p. 373-383. 48-7417*.
F128.3. R 65

ROOSEVELT, Theodore, pres. U.S. ... New York ... London and New York, Longmans, Green, 1891.   xvii, 232 p. incl. front. 2 fold. plans. 19 cm. (Historic towns, ed. by E. A. Freeman) 1-14310.
F128.3. R 78

— New ed. with postscript, 1890-1895. New York and London, Longmans, Green, 1895.   xvii, 226, (217)-232 p. incl. front. 2 fold. plans. 19 cm. (Historic towns) 1-14311/3.
F128.3. R 79

SHIPPEN, Katherine Binney. I know a city, the story of New York's growth; illus. by Robin King. New York, Viking Press, 1954.   192 p. illus. 22 cm. "1st publ. Mar. 1954" 54-8450.
F128.3. S 5

SMART, Mary F. Historical handbook of the city of New York ... (New York) City history club of New York (1934)   61 p. 19 cm. Bibliography: p. 60-61. 34-6082.
F128.3. S 57

STEVENS, John Austin. Progress of New York in a century. 1776 - 1876. An address delivered before the New York historical soc. New York, Printed for the Society, 1876.   66 p. 24 cm. 1-14312.
F128.3. S 84

STILL, Bayrd. Mirror for Gotham: New York as seen by contemporaries from Dutch days to the present. New York, University Press, 1956.   417 p. illus. 25 cm. Includes bibliography. 56-11979.
F128.3. S 85

STILL, Bayrd. New York City: a student's guide to localized history. New York, Teachers College Press, Teachers College, Columbia University, 1965.   x, 52 p. 23 cm. (Localized history series) 65-15967.
F128.3. S 852

STOKES, Isaac Newton Phelps. The iconography of Manhattan Island, 1498-1909. (New York) Arno Press (1967)   6 v. 27 cm. 67-13560.
F128.3. S 856

STOKES, Isaac Newton Phelps. New York past and present, its history and landmarks 1524 - 1939; one hundred views reproduced and described from old prints, etc., and modern photographs ... (New York, Plantin press, 1939)   xvi, 96 p. illus. (incl. maps, plans) 21½ cm. 39-21438.
F128.3. S 86

STONE, William Leete. History of New York city from the discovery to the present day ... New York, E. Cleave, 1868.   252, (84) p. illus., plates (1 fold.) facsim. 23½ cm. 1-14345.
F128.3. S 88

— New York, Virtue & Yorston, 1872.   xx, (3), (9)-658 p., 136 p. front., illus., plates, ports., maps, facsims. 25 cm. 1-14346.
F128.3. S 89

STONE, William Leete. The centennial history of New York city, from the discovery to the present day ... New York, R. D. Cooke, 1876.   (5)-252 p. pl. 23 cm. First ed., N.Y., 1868, pub. under title: History of New York city. 19-7550.
F128.3. S 90
Toner Coll.

NEW YORK CITY

STRAUBENMÜLLER, Gustave. A home geography of New York city ... Boston, New York (etc.) Ginn & co. (1905)   xv, 229 p. front., illus., maps. 20 cm. 5-36485.   F128.3. S 91

— Rev. ed. Boston, New York, Ginn & co. (1924)   xv, 229 p. double front., illus., maps (1 double) 20 cm. 24-8901.   F128.3. S 92

SUMMARY historical, geographical, and statistical view of the city of New York; tog. with some notices of Brooklyn, Williamsburgh, etc. ... Prepared to accompany the Topographical map of the city and county of New York. New York, J. H. Colton, 1836.   46 p. front. 16 cm. 1-14313.   F128.3. S 95

SWAN, Robert W. New York from village to metropolis ... illus. by James Lewicki. New York, Grosset & Dunlap (1939)   (24) p. fol. illus. 23 ½ x 26 cm. 39-12315.   F128.3. S 973

TAFT, Henry Waters. A century and a half at the New York bar, being the annals of a law firm and sketches of its members, with brief references to collateral events of historical interest . New York, Priv. print., 1938.   xv p., 3-305 p. pl., ports., fold. facsim. 24 cm. In case. 39-11788.   F128.3. T 25

TODD, Charles Burr. A brief history of the city of New York ... New York, Cincinnati (etc.) American book co. (1899)   299 p. front. (double map) illus. 19 cm. 99-5759 Rev.   F128.3. T 63

TODD, Charles Burr. The story of the city of New York ... New York, G. P. Putnam's sons ... 1888. xvi, 478 p. front., illus., 2 fold. pl., 2 fold. maps, 2 facsims. 20 cm. 9-8976.   F128.3. T635

— New York, G. P. Putnam's sons, 1890.   xiv, 478 p. front., illus., 2 fold. pl., 2 fold. plans, 2 fold. facsim. 20 cm. (Great cities of the republic) 1-14314.   F128.3. T 64

URELL, Catherine. The Big City and how it grew. Chicago, Follett Pub. Co. (1958)   127 p. illus. 24 cm. (The Big City series)   F128.3. U 7

VANAMEE, Mrs. Mary de Peyster Rutgers McCrea (Conger) New York's making seen through the eyes of my ancestors,... with nine illus. London, Methuen (1938)   xi, 119 p. front., plates, ports. 19 cm. "First pub. in 1938." 39-17564.   F128.3. V 28

WHITMAN, Walt. Walt Whitman's New York; from Manhattan to Montauk. Ed. by Henry M. Christman. New York, Macmillan (1963)   xiv, 188 p. 22 cm. 63-14529.   F128.3. W 5

— Freeport, N.Y., Books for Libraries Press (1972)   xiv, 188 p. illus. 23 cm. 74-39704.   F128.3. W 5 1972

WILSON, James Grant. The memorial history of the city of New York, from its first settlement to the year 1892. (New York) New-York History Co., 1892-93.   4 v. illus., ports., maps (part fold.) facsims. 27 cm. "A directory for the city of New-York in 1665": v. 1 p. 338-340. v. iv imperfect: p. lxxvii to end wanting. 1-14318 rev.*   F128.3. W 74

WILSON, James Grant. Old New York. (from Cosmopolitan v. 32, 1902) New York, 1902. 25 ½ cm.   F128.3. W 75

WILSON, Rufus Rockwell. New York: old & new; its story, streets, and landmarks ... with many illustrations from prints and photos. and with decorations by Edward Stratton Holloway. Philadelphia and London, J. B. Lippincott co., 1902.   2 v. front., pl. 21 cm. 2-26088.   F128.3. W 76

ZERBO, Jerome. The art of social climbing. (1st ed.) Garden City, N.Y., Doubleday, 1965. 186 p. 22 cm. 64-11747.   F128.3. Z 4

NEW YORK CITY.   JUVENILE WORKS.

FAXON, Lavinia. A young explorer's New York; maps of Manhattan. Maps. by Alan Price. Greenwich, Conn., New York Graphic Society, 1962.   59 p. col. illus. maps. 33 cm.
F128.33.F 3
Rare Book Coll.

FLEMING, Alice (Mulcahey) The key to New York. (1st ed.) Lippincott (1960)   128 p. (Keys to the cities series) 60-13862.
F128.33.F55

GLOGAU, Lillian. You and New York City. Photos. by Michael Chassid. Westchester, Ill., Benefic Press (1968)   192 p. 24 cm. (Learning for living in today's world. Basic social studies series) 68-18773.
F128.33.G54

HOLT, Solomon. Our city, State and nation. Ed. by Thomas F. Nevins. New York, Noble and Noble. (1964)   v, 246 p. 27 cm.
F128.33.H 6
1964

SZASZ, Suzanne. Young folks' New York. New York, Crown Publishers (1960)   124 p. 60-15396.
F128.33.S95

— Rev. ed. New York, Crown Publishers (1968)   144 p. illus. 29 cm. 68-20477.
F128.33.S95
1968

THOMAS, Katrina. My skyscraper city; a child's view of New York. Photos. by Katrina Thomas. Verses by Penny Hamond. (1st ed.) Garden City, N.Y., Doubleday (1963)   60 p. 32 cm. 63-13854.
F128.33.T5

NEW YORK CITY.   MINOR WORKS. PAMPHLETS, ADDRESSES, ESSAYS, ETC.

DALEY, Robert. The world beneath the city. (1st ed.) Philadelphia, Lippincott (1959)   223 p. illus. 21 cm. 59-13081.
F128.35.D 3

NEW YORK, N.Y. (New York, American Heritage Pub. Co. 1968)   144 p. illus. 29 cm. "An American heritage extra,"
F128.35.N 4

NEW YORK CITY.   HISTORIC MONUMENTS (GENERAL). ILLUSTRATIVE MATERIAL.

ANDREWS, George Henry. Twelve letters on the future of New York. New York, M. B. Brown, printer, 1877.   48 p. 23 cm. 6-1694.
F128.37.A53

(ANDREWS, William Loring) The journey of the iconophiles around New York in search of the historical and picturesque. ... New York (The Gillis press) 1897.   ix, 47, p. front. 24½ cm. 3-8083.
"87 copies on Imperial Japan paper"; six copies on American hand-made paper." This copy on Imperial Japan paper.
F128.37.A55
Rare Book Coll.

ANDREWS, William Loring. New Amsterdam, New Orange, New York: a chronologically arranged account of engraved views of the city from the first picture pub. in MDCLI until the year MDCCC. New York, Dodd, Mead, 1897.   xxx, 131 p., a-f, 135-142 p. front., illus., plates (part col.) ports., maps, plans, facsims. 23½ cm. One of 30 copies on Japan paper. Bibliography: p. xxvii - (xxxi) 2-9556.
F128.37.A57

ASBURY, Herbert. ... All around the town. New York, A. A. Knopf, 1934.   7, 3-280, (2) p. illus. 21½ cm. "First ed." 34-36215.
F128.37.A74

BEARD, John. Blue water views of old New York incl. Long Island and the Jersey shore. Embellished with commentary of the time selected by John Beard from out-of-print sources. (Centerville, Mass.) Scrimshaw Press (1970)   127 p. illus. 28 cm. (Scrimshaw illus. Americana.) 69-18952.
F128.37.B48

NEW YORK CITY

BETTS, William. The causes of the prosperity of New-York. An anniversary address, delivered before the St. Nicholas soc. of New-York ... 1850. ... New-York, Stanford and Swords, 1851. 27 p. 22½ cm. 1-14319.   F128.37. B 56

BROWN, Henry Collins. Glimpses of old New-York; the rare old prints are from the private collections of Mr. Robert Gould and others. New York, Priv. print. (Lent & Graff co.) 1917. xviii, 381 p. incl. col. front., col. illus., plates (part col.) map, col. plans. 33 cm. 17-103.   F128.37.B 87

BROWN, Henry Collins. Old New York yesterday & today. New York, Priv. print. for Valentine's manual and to be sold at the sign of the Dog and duck, 1922. (74) p. front., illus. (part col. incl. ports., facsim.) 31½ x 23½ cm. A 30-360.   F128.37.B 89   Rare Book Coll.

CHOURGNOZ, Jean Marie. Ça, c'est New York. Lyon, 1967?   1 v. illus., maps, plates (part col.) 27 cm.   F128.37.C45

CITY history club of New York. Escursion(s) planned for the City history club of New York ... (New York) 1897-1916. 12 v. illus. (incl. maps) 18½ - 20 cm. Nos. 1-8, 11 by Frank Bergen Kelley, no. 9 by Randall Comfort and George W. Nash, no. 10, 12 by George W. Nash. Contents. - no. 1. City hall to Wall street. (Rev.) 1902. - no. 2. Greenwich village and Lispenard's meadows. (Rev. 1902) - no. 3. The Bowery and East side. 1902. - no. 4. Central park to Van Cortlandt park. (Rev) 1897. - No. 4. Central Park to Kingsbridge. (Rev.) 1916. - no. 5. The nineteenth century city: 14th street to 110th street. 1905. 1905. - no. 5. The nineteenth century city: Tenth to One hundred and twenty-fifth street. (Rev.) 1912. - no. 6. Fraunces tavern. 1898. - no. 7. New York city, south of Wall street. 1898. -No. 8. Historic Brooklyn, pt. 1. 1908. No. 9. Historic Bronx. 1906. No. 10. Historic Richmond. 1908. No. 11 Historic Queens. 9-17538 Rev.   F128.37.C5

— Excursion supplement A. Additions and corrections ... (excursions 1-8) New York, 1905. 15 p. 19 cm.

— Excursion supplement B. Additions and corrections ... (excursions 1-4, 6-10) New York) 1907. 4 p. 19 cm.

— Excursion supplement C. Additions and corrections to excursion no. 5 ... (New York) 1907. 6 p. 20 cm.

CITY history club of New York. (Illustrations, reproducted from historical works. New York, 1899?) 45 pl. incl. 9 ports., plan. 16 x 21 cm. 4-7995.   F128.37.C51

CITY history club of New York. Bicycle excurions no. 2. (New York?) 1897. 14 cm.   F128.37.C55

CITY history club of New York. ... The milestones and the old Post road, by George W. Nash ... Reprinted from the Historical guide to the city of New York ... Rev. 1915. (New York, 1915) 371-377 p. illus. 19½ cm. 17-12317.   F128.37.C57

CITY history club of New York. Teachers' handbook of the City history club of New York. Revised, 1905. (New York? 1905) 31 p. 19½ cm. 6-38862.   F128.37.C 6

CRIES of New-York. New York, S. Wood; Baltimore, S. S. Wood, 1882. (Chicago, T. Rubovits, inc., 1936) facsim.: 45 p. illus. 14½ cm. First ed. pub. N. Y. 1808. Leaf of bibliogr. notes. 38-24821.   F128.37.C84   Rare Book Coll.

— New York, Printed and sold by the Harbor press, 1931. 4, 62 p. illus. 16 x 9½ cm. 32-30650.   F128.37.C85

DAVIES, J. C. Some old views of New York city ... (1927) 1 v.   F128.37.D 2

(DEAN, Bashford) The Dyckman house; built about 1783, restored and presented to the ctiy of New York in MCMXVI. (New York? The Gillis press, 1916?) 47 p. incl. illus. (incl. ports.) plate. 22½ cm. 34-15322.   F128.37.D23

DE CASSERES, Benjamin. Mirrors of New York, New York, J. Lawren (1925) 221 p. 24 cm. 25-21896.   F128.37.D26

(DOLAN, Hugh F.) comp. Record and guide index of ten years' conveyances. (New York, 1885)

2, 95 p.   maps.   fol.   Containing "All transfers recorded in the office of the register of the city of New York affecting property from north side of 59th street to south side 125th street, and west of Eighth avenue to Hudson river, for a period of ten years to June 30, 1884, with an addenda comprising conveyances recorded and affecting same property from last-named date to Jan. 1, 1885." 1-14320-M1.

F128.37.D65

FEININGER, Andreas.   New York.   Texte von Kate Simon.   (Wien, Econ-Verlag (1964)   159 p.

F128.37.F455

(FERRIS, Mary Lanman (Douw) "Mrs. Morris P. Ferris")   Van Cortlandt mansion, erected 1748, now in the custody of the Colonial dames of the state of New York.   (New York, The De Vinne press, 1897)   xxiii p.   plates, fold. map.   23 cm.   38-24839.

F128.37.F48

FLOYD, Thomas.   Backward glances; reminiscences of an old New-Yorker.   New York, Brooklyn, Long Island.   (Somerville, N.J., Printed by the Unionist gazette assoc., 1914)   3, iii-xxi, 275 p.   front. (port.) plates, facsims.   23½ cm.   Enlarged from a series of articles which appeared weekly in the Trotter and pacer ... 1908. 14-16972.

F128.37.F64

GERARD, James Watson.   The impress of nationalities upon the city of New York.   A paper read before the New York hist. soc.   New York, Columbia spectator pub. co., 1883.   32 p.   25 cm.

F128.37.G35

GIRDNER, John Harvey.   Newyorkitis ... New York, The Grafton press (1901)   164 p.   18½ cm. 1-15786.

F128.37.G52

GUZMAN, Joseph P.   Series of diagrams for plot and lot out, any block of the city of New York from north of 14th st.   New York, J. P. Guzman (1877)   8 l.   obl. 24°.   1-14321-M1.   F128.37.G93

HEMSTREET, Charles.   Nooks and corners of old New York; illus. by E. C. Peixotto.   New York, Charles Scribner's sons, 1899.   viii, 228 p.   illus.   21½ cm.   99-5415 Rev.   F128.37.H49

HEMSTREET, Charles.   When old New York was young ... New York, C. Scribner's sons, 1902. xi, 354 p. incl. illus., plates, plans.   21½ cm.   2-12293.

F128.37.H52

HISTORIC New York.   Ed. by Maud Wilder Goodwin and others.   Port Washington, N.Y., I. J. Friedman (1969)   2 v. in 4.   illus.   21 cm.   74-83482.

F128.37.H57

HOLLAND society of New York.   Report to the Holland society of New-York by Alexander T. Van Nest, chairman of the special committee on "tablets" to be placed on sites of historic interest in the city of New York.   New York (The De Vinne press) 1889.   24 p.   front.   36½ cm.   3-18807.

F128.37.H73

HOUGH, David.   Improvements in and about the city of New-York, proposed by D. Hough, junr. ... New-York, Oliver & bro., printers, 1851.   16 p.   8°.   1-22566-M1.

F128.37.H83

(JORDAN, Joshua Hawkins)   Catalogue of a loan exhibition of rare views of old New York, exhibited by Lawyers title insurance and trust co. ... New York, 1909.   (New Rochelle? N.Y., 1909)   53 p. plates (1 fold.)   23 cm.   9-14196.

F128.37.J 82

KNICKERBOCKER, Jacob, pseud.   Then and now, by Jacob Knickerbocker, a New Yorker.   Boston, B. Humphries, inc. (1939)   474 p.   front., plates, ports., diagr.   20½ cm.   40-4749.   F128.37.K55

LANDAUER, Bella Clara.   My city, 'tis of thee; New York City on sheet-music covers.   Selections from the music collection of Bella C. Landauer at the New York Historical Society.   New York, New-York Historical Society, 1951.   25 p.   (69) p. of facsims.   23 cm.   52-2489.   F128.37. L3

LEONE Carlo.   Walks through the Fifth avenue.   A New Year's gift to the Grace church congregation. (Part 1. No. 1)   New York, For the author, 1853.   20 p.   12°.   1-22610-M1.   F128.37.L58

LITTLE old New York ... Poughkeepsie, N.Y., Oxford pub. co., 1910.   32 p.   illus., fold. plan.   17½ cm. 10-22959.

F128.37.L77

NEW YORK CITY

LYON, Denny. The destruction of Lower Manhattan. (New York) Macmillan Co. (1969) 75 plates.
28 cm. "1st printing." 69-17103. F128.37.L96

MABLE, Hamilton Wright. The genius of the cosmopolitan city; an address delivered before the New York historical soc. on its 99th anniversary ... 1903. New York, The Society, 1904. 42 p. 25 cm.
4-18838. F128.37.M11

McDARRAH, Fred W. New York, N.Y.; a photographic tour of Manhattan Island from Battery Park to Spuyten Duyvil. New York, Corinth Books (1964) 1 v. (unpaged) 24 cm. 64-19518.
F128.37.M15

MAYER, Grace M. Once upon a city; New York from 1890 to 1910 as photographed by Byron and described by Grace M. Mayer. With a foreword by Edward Steichen. New York, Macmillan, 1958.
xii, 511 p. illus., ports. 29 cm. "The photographs ... are from the ... Museum of the City of New York." 57-10777 rev. F128.37.M3

(MINES, John Flavel) The island of Manhattan, a bit of earth, by Felix Oldboy (pseud.) New York, 1890. 5-20 p. 18 cm. 12-5128 F128.37.M66

(MOREAU, John Bostwick) Events in the history of New York city, with illustrations from Shakespeare, by a New Yorker ... (Priv. print.) 1881. (100) p. 19 cm. "Only a few copies privately reprinted from Block calendars."
21-1999. F128.37.M83

NEW YORK. Bern, Hallwag (1962) 143 p. (chiefly illus., part col.) 12 cm. (Gold-leaf travel photo book)
F128.37.N5

NEW-YORK cries in rhyme, The. Copy-right secured ... New-York. Mahlon Day ... 1836 ... (New York, Grosset & Dunlap, 1939) 4-17 p. col. illus. 18½ cm. 40-5438. F128.37.N54
Rare Book Coll.

NEW YORK Edison co. Thirty years of New York, 1882-1912; being a history of electrical development in Manhattan and the Bronx. (New York) Press of the New York Edison co. (1913) ix, 264 p.
front., illus. (incl. ports., plans, facsim.) plates. 24 cm. Bibliography: p. (vii) 13-17691. F128.37.N 6

NEW YORK herald. The New York market, comp. by the Research department of the New York herald. (New York) 1922. 134 p. maps (1 fold.) diagrs. 29 cm. 22-18520.
F128.37.N65

NEW YORK historical society. New York city, then and now, 1626-1942; a series of views to illustrate the great development of a cosmopolitan city from the Dutch period to the present. Issued by the New York historical soc. from original pictures in its collection ... New York, 1942. 31 p. illus.
19 cm. 42-23986 Rev. F128.37.N 7

OLTARZHEVSKII, Viacheslav K. Contemporary Babylon in pencil drawings by W. K. Oltar-Jevsky; with introd. by Harvey Wiley Corbett. New York, N.Y., Architectural book pub. co., (1933)
4 p. 21 mounted pl. 37½ cm. 33-36890. F128.37.O 4
Rare Book Coll.

PALMER, Elizabeth Story. My memories of old New York, New York, E. S. Gorham, 1923.
2, 44 p. 21 cm. 24-1714. F128.37.P15

PALMER, Robert M. Palmer's views of New York, past and present ... (New York?) 16 x 25½ cm.
F128.37.P17

PATTERSON, Samuel White. Famous men and places in the history of New York city, .. New York, Noble and Noble (1923) ix-xi, 3-245 p. illus. (incl. ports.) 21½ cm. 23-12013. F128.37. P 3

PENNELL, Joseph. The glory of New York; with an introd. by Elizabeth Robins Pennell. New York, W. E. Rudge, 1926. (16) p. 24 col. pl. 46½ cm. Reproduction of 24 water-colors. 27-11823. F128.37. P 4
Rare Book Coll.

(PIERREPONT, Henry Evelyn) Historical sketch of the Fulton ferry, and its associated ferries. By a director. Printed for the private use of the (Union ferry) co. Brooklyn, Eagle job and book print., 1879.   162, 158 p. incl. plates, plans. front. (port.)   26 cm.   L.C. copy replaced by microfilm. 4-19499.   F128.37.P62 Microfilm 15056 F

PRICE, Joseph Henry. An historical sketch, delivered at the closing services in St. Stephen's Church ... 1866. New York, Vinten, 1866.   23 cm.   1-24166-M1.   F128.37.P94

PYNE, Percy Rivington. Illustrated catalogue of the ... collection of views of New York and other American cities, historical china and book relating to New York, formed by Mr. Percy R. Pyne, 2d; to be sold ... (New York, Lent & Graff co., printers, 1917)   (142) p. col. mounted front., plates (part col. 1 fold.) maps.   28 cm.   36-23119.   F128.37.P99

(REMINISCENCES of the city of New York and its vicinity. New York, 1855)   (5) - 326 p. illus., 3 pl. fold. map, fold. facsim. 20½ cm.   Repr. from Valentine's Manuals of the corporation of the city of New York for 1855 and 1856. Fifty copies printed for the authors. Title page, p. 4 and p. 327-350 wanting. 1-14323.   F128.37.R38

RESTORING the century-old residential glories of the East River. New York, H. C. Brown, 1925. 41 p. incl. front., illus. 19 cm. Bibliography: p. 40-41. 25-10433.   F128.37.R43

RIZZUTO, Angelo. New York: "In little old New York, by Anthony Angel."   F128.37.R 5

SARG, Tony. Tony Sarg's New York ... New York, Greenberg, 1926.   (60) p. 24 col. pl. 33 cm. 27-1449.   F128.37.S 24

SCHERMAN, Bernardine (Kielty) The sidewalks of New York, Pub. for the Bowman hotels, John McEntee Bowman, president. New York, Little leather library corporation (1924)   2, (7) - 124 p. illus. (incl. plans)   10½ cm.   24-28567.   F128.37. S 3

SHAW, Charles Green. New York - oddly enough. New York, Toronto, Farrar & Rinehart, inc. (1938)   6. 212 p. illus. (incl. facsim.) pl. 24 cm. 38-11587.   F128.37.S 48

SILVER, Nathan. Lost New York. (Boston) Houghton Mifflin, 1967.   xiii, 242 p.   29 cm.   "1st printing" 66-11220.   F128.37.S 55

STOKES, Isaac Newton Phelps. The iconography of Manhattan Island, 1498-1909, compiled from original sources and illus. by photo-intaglio reproduction of important maps, plans, views and documents in public and private collections. New York, R. H. Dodd, 1915-28.   6 v. fronts. (part col., part double) incl. ports., maps, plans, facsims. 29 cm.   16-765 Rev. 2.

F128.37.S 87
Map Div.

— New York, R. H. Dodd, 1915 -   double col. front., illus. etc. 16-765.   F128.37.S 88 Rare Book Coll.

THOMAS, Guy. New York, 8 (i.e. huit) millions de visages. Paris, l'École des loisirs, 1968. 119 p. illus. (part col.) 19 x 21 cm. (Collection Visages de l'homme) 78-358162.   F128.37.T55

TITLE guarantee and trust co. Key to the block index. New York, 1891.   3, 30 (4) p. obl. 8°. 1-14324-M1.   F128.37.T62

ULMANN, Albert. A landmark history of New York; also the origin of street names and a bibliography ... New York, D. Appleton, 1901.   v-viii, 285 p. front., illus. 19½ cm. 1-31386 Rev.

F128.37.U41

— New ed., with an introd. containing an account of the establishemnt in 1653 of a popular form of government in New Amsterdam ... New York, D. Appleton, 1903.   xxx, 285 p. front., illus. (incl. maps) 19½ cm. Bibliography: p. 267-279. 3-11301.   F128.37.U42

— New York, London, D. Appleton-Century co., 1939.   xviii, 440 p. incl. front., illus. 21 cm. Map. 39-10856.   F128.37.U425

NEW YORK CITY

— Port Washington, N.Y., I. J. Friedman (1969) xvi, 285 p. illus. 18 cm. (Empire State historical publications series, no. 70) 70-101023.
F128.37.U42 1969

VAN RENSSELAER, May (King) The social ladder, by Mrs. John King Van Rensselaer in collaboration with Frederick Van de Water. New York, H. Holt, 1924. 5, 3-309 p. front., plates, ports. 23 cm. 24-12009.
F128.37.V27

YOORE, Jan. Only one New York. Photos. by Jan Yoore. Text by Charles Samuels. New York, Simon and Schuster (1965) 136 p. 31 cm. 64-25192.
F128.37.Y6

NEW YORK (City) Pamphlets, broadsides, clippings, and other miscellaneous matter on this subject, not separatley cataloged, are classified in:
F128.37.Z9

NEW YORK CITY. ANTIQUITIES.

BOLTON, Reginald Pelham. ... Indian paths in the great metropolis. New York, Museum of the American Indian, Heye foundation, 1922. 280 p. illus., xxviii pl., 6 maps (part fold.) and portfolio of 12 fold. maps. 17½ cm. (Indian notes and monographs ... (Miscellaneous, no. 23) Bibliography, etc.: p. 207-219. 22-19522.
F128.39.B69

SKINNER, Alanson Buck. The Indians of Manhattan Island and vicinity ... A guide to the Hudson-Fulton exhibit at the American museum of natural history ... New York, The Museum, 1909. 54 p. incl. front., illus. 25 cm. 10-8053 Rev.
F128.39
E78. N7 S 6

NEW YORK CITY. EARLY TO 1775.

ANDREWS, William Loring. The Bradford map. The city of New York at the time of the granting of the Montgomerie charter: a description thereof comp. by William Loring Andrews, to accompany a facsimile of an actual survey made by James Lyne and printed by William Bradford in 1731. New York, The De Vinne press, 1893. xv, (2), 19-115 p. incl. illus., plan. front., 9 pl. (facsim.) fold. map. (facsim.) 22 cm. 3-6362.
F128.4.A56

BANTA, Theodore Melvin. Dutch records in the City clerk's office, New York ... Collated by Theodore M. Banta ... New York, The Knickerbocker press (1901) 2 v. in 1. 28 cm. Paged continuously. 18 copies only pub. Reprinted from the Year-book of the Holland soc. of New York for 1900-01. Contents. - pt. I. Calendar of the Orphans' court. Synopsis of books of notaries public. List of autographs in the early records. - pt. II. Grants of land from the Indians, from the West India company, and from the burgomasters. Indexes of conveyances and mortgages, powers of attorneys, etc. 16-9883.
F128.4. B 22
Rare Book Coll.

BARTRAM, Ferdinand S. Retrographs: comprising a history of New York city prior to the revolution; biographies of George Washington, Alexander Hamilton, etc., etc. ... Embodying more than a hundred letters and signatures of famous persons ... including a fac-simile of an original official map of the city of New York, made in 1728 ... New York, Yale pub. co. (1888) v-x p. 196 p. illus. (incl. facsims.) fold. map. 26 cm. 1-16261.
F128.4.B29

BOGARDUS. The Anneke Jans delusions, by Torstein Jahr. (Grand Forks, N.D., 1924) 4 p. 25½ cm. Reprinted from "Scandinavia", Grand Forks, N.D., Feb. 1924. 24-8615.
F128.4. B 65

BOGARDUS. ... Anneke Jans fra Marstrand, hennes farm og hennes slekt. (By Torstein Knutsson Torstensen Jahr) (Decorah, Ia., 1913) 28 p. 24½ cm. 13-25480 Rev.
F128.4. B 66

BOGARDUS. Anneke Jans Bogardus; her farm, and how it became the property of Trinity church. An historic inquiry, by Stephen P. Nash. New York, Prepared and printed for the use of the church, 1896. vii, 105 p. 22 cm. 4-20143.
F128.4. B 67

BOGARDUS. Anneke Jans Bogardus and her New Amsterdam estate, past and present; romance of a Dutch maiden and its present day new world sequel; historical, legal, genealogical. Compiled by Thomas Bentley Wikoff. Indianapolis, Ind., 1924.   276 p.   23½ cm.   24-23715.
   F128.4. B 69

CITY history club. Syllabus of a course on I. The English period. II. The revolutionary period. (New York?) 1896.   17 p.   23½ cm.   3-27387.
   F128.4.C 58

COLONIAL order of the acorn. Views of early New York, with illustrative sketches, prepared for the New York chapter of the Colonial order of the acorn. New York, Privately printed (by the De Vinne press) 1904.   142 p.   plates.   23½ cm.   4-15553.
   F128.4. C 71

COLTON, Julia Maria. Annals of old Manhattan, 1609-1664. ... New York, Brentano's (1901) x, 238 p.   front., pl.   maps.   21½ cm.   2-25052.
   F128.4.C 72

DARLING, Charles William. New Amsterdam, New Orange, New York, with chronological data ... (n. p.) Priv. print., 1889.   43 p.   front. (2 ports.)   24 cm.   1-14326.
   F128.4. D 22

DAVIS, Asahel. History of New Amsterdam; or New York as it was in the days of the Dutch governors. Tog. with papers on events connected with the American revolution; and on Philadelphia in the times of William Penn. ... Six fine illus. New York, R. T. Young, 1854.   viii, (9) - 240 p. front., plates.   17½ cm.   Papers on American history.   1-14327.
   F128.4. D 25

DAVIS, John Walter. Four New York boys. New York in aboriginal and colonial days ... Boston, New York (etc.) Educational pub. co. (1903)   244 p.   illus. (incl. maps, plans) fold. map.   20 cm.   6-712.
   F128.4. D 26

DECKER, Malcolm. Brink of revolution; New York in crises, 1765 - 1776. New York, Argosy Antiquarian ltd. (1964)   xi, 290 p., maps (2 in pocket)   24 cm.   64-7580.
   F128.4. D 27

DE FOREST, Louis Effingham. The settlement of Manhattan in 1624. Albany, N.Y., The Argus press, 1935.   48 p.   23 cm.   Bibliography: p. 37-48.   36-1649.
   F128.4. D285

DE FOREST, Louis Effingham. The tercentenary of New York city in 1924; a consideration of conflicting claims ... New York, The National Huguenot-Walloon New Netherland tercentenary commission, 1923.   26 p.   23 cm.   Bibliography: p. 25-26.   33-12184.
   F128.4. D 29

(DE FOREST, T. R.) Olden time in New York. By those who knew. New York, Anderson and Smith, 1833.   54 p.   18 cm.   1-14328.
   F128.4. D 31

EMERSON, Caroline Dwight. New Amsterdam; old Holland in the new world. Illus. by Harvey Kidder. Champagin, Ill., Garrard Pub. Co. (1967)   96 p.   24 cm.   (How they lived series)   67-10035.
   F128.4. E 4

GERARD, James Watson. The old stadt huys of New Amsterdam. A paper read before the New York historical soc. ... 1875. New York, F. B. Patterson, 1875.   2, (3)-59 p.   24½ cm.   1-14791.
   F128.4.G 35

GOODWIN, Mrs. Maud (Wilder) ... Fort Amsterdam in the days of the Dutch   (New York, The Knickerbocker press, 1897)   p. 239-274.   21 cm.   (Half moon series. v.1 no. 8)   Pub. also in "Historic New York," 1897. 1st ser., no. 1.   10-5333.
   F128.4.G 65

HAXTUN, Annie Arnoux. Early settlers of New Amsterdam. New York, 1903.   29½ cm.
   F128.4. H 41

(HORSMANDEN, Daniel) A journal of the proceedings in the detection of the conspiracy formed by some white people, in conjunction with negro and other slaves, for burning the city of New-York in America, and murdering the inhabitants ... By the recorder of the city of New-York ... New York, Printed by J. Parker, 1744.   vi, 205, 16 p.   24½ cm. x 18 cm.   Reprinted, London, 1747, with title "The New-York conspiracy, or a history of the negro plot ... "   New York, Southwick & Pelsue, 1810.   2-19355.
   F128.4. H 81
   Rare Book Coll.

NEW YORK CITY 211

— The charters of the following provinces of North America; viz. Virginia, Maryland, Connecticut, Rhode Island, Pennsylvania, Massachusett's Bay, and Georgia. To which is prefixed, a faithful narrative of the proceedings of the North American colonies, in consequence of the late stamp-act. London, Printed for W. Owen (etc.) 1766.   1, 18, 15, 5, 4, 6, 5, 9, 7 p. front. (fold. map) 24 cm. Title-page slightly mutilated. "Collected from the Daily gazetteer..."   Bound with preceding.   5-20882.

F128.4.H 81
Rare Book Coll.

HORSMANDEN, Daniel. The New-York conspiracy, or A history of the negro plot, with the journal of the proceedings against the conspirators at New-York in the year 1741-2... New-York: Printed pub. by Southwick & Pelsue... 1810.   385, (7) p. incl. tables. 21 cm. Second ed. 1-14322.

F128.4.H 82

HORSMANDEN, Daniel. The trial of John Ury "for being an ecclesiastical person, made by authority pretended from the See of Rome, and coming into the abiding in the province of New York." and with being one of the conspirators in the negro plot to burn the city of New York, 1741. ... (Philadelphia, M. I. J. Griffin, 1899.   58 p. 23 cm. "Abridged from 'The New York conspiracy... New York (2d ed.) 1810.'"
2-9589.

F128.4.H 83

HOY, William Alexander. Syllabus of a course of study in the history of the city of New York. (New York) 1897.   15 p. 23 cm. 4-28328.

F128.4.H 86

HULTS, Dorothy Niebrugge. New Amsterdam days and ways; the Dutch settlers of New York. Illus. by Jane Niebrugge. (1st ed.) New York, Harcourt, Brace & World (1963)   224 p. 21 cm. 63-15400.

F128.4. H 9

INNES, John H. New Amsterdam and its people; studies, social and topographical, of the town under Dutch and early English rule. With maps, plans, views, etc. ... New York, C. Scribner's sons, 1902.   xiv, 365 p. fold. front., plates, ports., plans (partly fold.) 22 cm. 2-25626/3.

F128.4. I 58

— With a new introd. by Sidney I. Pomerantz. Port Washington, N.Y., I. J. Friedman (1969)
2 v. (365 p.) illus., plans, ports.   Reissued in 1969. 24 cm.   (Empire State hist. pubs. series, no. 63) 68-58927.

F128.4. I 58
1969

INNES, John H. The old Bark mill; or, First house of religious worship in New York, and its surroundings. The ministry of Dominie Jonas Michaelis - Some notes respecting the site of the first Jewish synagogue in New York. By J. H. Innes ... (In "Federation," vol. III, no. 5. (New York, 1905)   25½ cm. p. (5) - 16. 5-35749.

F128.4. I 59

JANVIER, Thomas Allibone. In old New York ... New York, Harper & bros., 1894.   x, 285 p. front., illus., 1 port., maps. 12º. 1-14329-M1.

F128.4. J 35

— (New York) Garrett Press (1969)   x, 285 p. illus. 20 cm. (The American short story series v.23) 68-55682.

F128.4. J 35
1969

LYDON, James Gavin. Pirates, privateers, and profits, Introd. by Richard B. Morris. Upper Saddle River, N.J., Gregg Press 1970.   303 p. illus. 23 cm. 74-111659.

F128.4. L 93

MANSFIELD, Blanche (McManus) "Mrs. M. F. Mansfield." ... How the Dutch came to Manhattan: penned and pictured by Blanche McManus. New York, E. R. Herrick (1897)   82 p. illus. 21½ cm. (Colonial monographs) 1-14330.

F128.4. M 16

MOULTON, Joseph White. View of the city of New-Orange, (now New York,) as it was in the year 1673. With explanatory notes. New York, Printed by C. S. Van Winkle, 1825.   40 p. fold. pl. 23 cm. 3-30657.

F128.4. M 91

MOULTON, Joseph White. New York 170 years ago: with a view, and explanatory notes. New York, W. G. Boggs, printer, 1843.   24 p. fold. front. 23½ cm. 1-14331.

F128.4. M 92

LOCAL HISTORIES IN THE LIBRARY OF CONGRESS

NEW YORK (City) Minutes of the executive boards of the burgomasters of New Amsterdam. Berthold Fernow, editor. New York, Arno Press, 1970. 75 - 197 p. 23 cm. (The Rise of urban America) 71-112544.
F128.4.N 49

NEW YORK (City) Original book of N. Y. deeds ... 1914. 1 v.
F128.4. N 5

NEW YORK (City) Records of the city of New Amsterdam, in New Netherland. Ed. by Henry B. Dawson, and pub. by permission of the Common council of New York. vol. I. Morrisania, N.Y. (Bradstreet press) 1867. x, 79 p. 24½ cm. 100 copies printed. Reprinted from Historical magazine, and notes and queries vo.11, 1867. No more pub. of this edition. L.C. copy replaced by microfilm. 1-14332 Rev.
F128.4.N 52
Microfilm 8823 F

NEW YORK (City) The records of New Amsterdam from 1653 to 1674 ... ed. by Berthold Fernow ... New York, Pub. under the authority of the city by the Knickerbocker press, 1897. 7 v. 25 cm. The original in the Dutch language is contained in 6 folio vols. The first of these was translated by a Mr. Westbrook and the remaining five by E. B. O'Callaghan, about 1848. The present editor has retranslated the part trans. by Mr. Westbrook. 1-14333 Add.
F128.4.N 53
L H & G

NEW YORK (City) The minutes of the orphanmasters of New Amsterdam, 1655 to 1663; tr. and ed. under the auspices of the Committee on history and tradition of the Colonial dames of the state of New York by Berthold Fernow ... New York, F. P. Harper, 1902-07. 2 v. 24 x 19½ cm. (Publications of the Committee on histroy and tradition of the Colonial dames of the state of N. Y. no. 1-2) 2-10131 Add.
F128.4.N 56

O'CALLAGHAN. Edmund Bailey, comp. ... Papers relating to the city of New-York. (From the documentary history of the state of New-York ... v. 1. "Census of the city of New-York (about the year 1703)" p. 611-624. 8-27413.
F128.4.O 15

ORDER of the founders and patriots of America. New York soc. ... Proceedings on the dedication of the tablet erected by the New York society ... on the site of Fort Amsterdam, at the U.S. custom house. ... (New York? 1909?) 27 p. incl. facsim., pl. 23 cm. (Pubs. of the N.Y. society of the order of founders and patriots of America) no. 26) 11-9654.
F128.4.O 65

PAST and present religious and racial conditions of oldest New York, The. (In Federation. (New York) 1904. v.3, no. 4, p.10-67, incl. illus., maps) 6-38493.
F128.4. P 29

PAULDING, J. Affairs and men of New Amsterdam, in the time of Governor Peter Stuyvesant. Compiled drom Dutch manuscript records of the period. New York, C. C. Childs, printer, 1843. 161 (2) p. 17½ cm. "A directory for the city of New Amsterdam, in 1665": p. 103-113. 1-14334 Rev.
F128.4. P 32
Rare Book Coll.

PERRY, Arthur Cecil. The Dutch in New York; pictures by Hildegard Woodward. New York, T. Nelson, 1935. vi, 84 p. front., illus. 19½ cm. Maps. "This book is written to conform with the 4A grade requirements ... for the public schools of the city of New York." 35-8079.
F128.4. P 47

PUTNAM, Ruth. ... Annetje Jans' farm. (New York, 1897) (61)- 98 p. 19½ cm. (Half moon series. v.1, no. 3) Pub. also in "Historic New York," 1897. 1st ser. (no.4) 10-6832.
F128.4. P 98

REYNOLDS, James J. When the Dutch ruled New York ... New York, Noble and Noble (1930) v. 54 p. illus. 19 cm. Pub. also under the title: Required history in the N.Y. city public schools, grade 4A. "Books for reference": p. 52. CA 30-1507 Unrev.
F128.4. R 46

ROOSEVELT, Robert Barnwell. Early New York; an address ... delivered before the New York soc. of the Order of the founders and patriots of America ... 1904. (New York, 1904) 16 p. 23 cm. (Order of the founders and patriots of America. New York soc. Publications. no. 5) 4-33477.
F128.4. R 78

SCHAGEN, Pieter Jamsz. The foundation of New York. De stichting van New York. (Amsterdam, P. N. van Kempen, 1946.) (4) l. illus., col. plates (laid in) facsim. 32 cm. A 49-290*.
F128.4. S 35

SEYMANN, Jerrold. Colonial charters, patents and grants to the communities comprising the city of

NEW YORK CITY

New York ... (New York) The Board of statutory consolidation of the city of New York, 1939. xxiv, 612 p. front. (facsim.) maps (part fold.) fold. diagr. 26½ cm. "List of sources of material": p. 585-612. 40-5441. F128.4. S 48

SHEPARD, William Robert. The story of New Amsterdam ... New York, 1917. vii, 111 p. 28 cm. "Reprinted from the ... Year book of the Holland society of New York," 1917. 17-24184. F128.4. S 54

— New York & London, A. A. Knopf, 1926. xiv, 208 p. front., plates (1 fold.) port., maps (part fold.) facsims. 21½ cm. "Reprinted with certain changes from the ... Yearbook for 1917 of the Holland soc. of N. Y." 26-16917. F128.4. S 54 1926

— Port Washington, N.Y., Kennikat Press (1970) xiv, 208 p. illus. 21 cm. (Empire State historical publications series, no. 88) 75-118790. F128.4. S 54 1970

SINGLETON, Esther. Dutch New York ... with numerous illustrations. New York, Dodd, Mead, 1909. xxiii, 360 p. front. (port.) 48 pl. 23 cm. 9-24462. F128.4.S605

— New York, B. Blom, 1968. xxiii, 360 p. illus. 24 cm. 68-20248. F128.4.S605

SINGLETON, Esther. Social New York under the Georges 1714 - 1776; houses, streets and country homes, with chapters on fashions, furniture, china, plate and manners ... New York, D. Appleton, 1902. xix, 407 p. incl. front., illus. 24 cm. 2-28275. F128.4. S 61

— New York, B. Blom (1968) xix, 407 p. illus. 24 cm. 68-26018. F128.4. S 61 1968

— Port Washington, N.Y., I. J. Friedman (1969) 2 v. in 1. (xix, 407 p.) illus. 24 cm. (Empire State historical publications series no. 60) 68-58928. F128.4. S 61 1969

STUYVESANT. Peter Stuyvesant and his New York, by Henry H. Kessler and Eugene Rachlis. New York, Random House (1959) 309 p. illus. 22 cm. Includes bibliography. "First printing." 59-5711. F128.4.S8K4

ULMANN, Albert. Tales of old New York ... New York and London, D. Appleton, 1914 - v. front., illus. 19½ cm. 14-19124. F128.4.U 43

VALENTINE, David Thomas. History of the city of New-York ... New York, G. P. Putnam, 1853. vi, (7) - 404 p. front., plates (partly fold.) plans (partly fold.) fold. maps. 21½ cm. This work brings the history down to the middle of the 18th century. The author planned a continuation. 1-14315. F128.4.V 15

VAN RENSSELAER, Mariana (Griswold) History of the city of New York in the 17th century, by Mrs. Schuyler Van Rensselaer ... New York, The Macmillan co., 1909. 2 v. fronts. 23 cm. "Reference notes" at end of chapters. "List of books and articles of value to the student of the history of New York": v. 2, p. 571-607. 9-14587. F128.4.V 26

VAN RENSSELAER, May (King) The goede vrouw of Mana-ha-ta at home and in society, 1609-1760, by Mrs. John King Van Rensselaer. New York, C. Scribner's sons, 1898. xxii, 418 p. 21 cm. 98-672 Rev. F128.4.V 27

— 1972. F128.4.V 27 1972

VAN WINKLE, Edward. Manhattan, 1624-1639 ... New York city, 1916. vii, 47 p. illus., fold. maps, facsim. 28 cm. 16-20567. F128.4.V 28

VIRLET D'Aoust, Pierre Théodore. ... Fondation de la ville de New-York en 1623 par une colonie de Flamands avesnois et Wallons. (Paris, Lib. imp. réunies, 1891?) 6 p. 22½ cm. 4-33440. F128.4.V 81

WERSTEIN, Irving.   The plotters; the New York conspiracy of 1741.   New York, Charles Scribner's Sons (1967)   viii, 120 p.   24 cm.   67-15495.   F128.4. W 4

WHALEN, Frank Daniel.   New York yesterday.   New York, Noble and Noble (1949)   v, 196 p. illus. map. 20 cm.   A companion book to New York today, by Frank D. Whalen and Orrel Baldwin. 49-48051*.   F128.4.W 48

WILLETT, Thomas.   Pamphlets, broadsides, clippings, and other miscellaneous matter on this subject, not separately cataloged, are classified in: F128.4.W5Z9

NEW YORK CITY.   1775 - 1865.

ABBOTT, Wilbur Cortez.   New York in the American revolution ... illus. selected by Victor H. Paltsits ... New York, London, C. Scribner's sons, 1929.   xiii, 302 p. front., 1 illus., plates, facsims. 23 cm. Maps.   Bibliography: p. 287-292.   29-29220.   F128.44.A13

— Port Washington, N.Y., I. J. Friedman, 1962.   xii, 302 p. 23 cm. 62-13523.
F128.44.A13
1962

— 1972.   F128.4.A13
1972

ACCOUNT of the terrific and fatal riot at the New-York Astor place opera house, on the night of May 10th 1849 ...   New-York, H. M. Ranney, 1849.   32 p. incl. front. 23½ cm. 2-9014.
F128.44.A16
Rare Book Coll.

AIKMAN, William.   Government and administration: a sermon preached on the Sabbath succeeding the secession riots in New York city, July 19, 1863 ... Wilmington (Del.) H. Eckel, printer, 1863.
12 p. 19 cm. 15-3863.   F128.44.A29

ALVAREZ, Raphael.   Guía de Nueva York, para uso de los Españoles e Hispano-americanos ... Nueva York, J. A. Gray, 1863.   166 p. front., plates, fold. plan. 19½ cm. 1-14335.
F128.44.A47

AMERICAN Antiquarian Soc.   Index of marriages and deaths in New York weekly museum, 1788-1817. (Worcester) 1952.   1 v. (unpaged) 26 cm. Typescript (carbon copy) 56-51531.   F128.44.A52
Rare Book Coll.

ANDREWS, William Loring.   New York as Washington knew it after the revolution.   New York, C. Scribner's sons, 1905.   xv, 91 p. incl. front., illus., plan, facsims. 23½ cm. 6-3120.
F128.44.A56
Rare Book Coll.

(BACON, David Francis) The mystery of iniquity: a passage of the secret history of American politics, illus. by a view of metropolitan society ... (New York) 1845.   36 p. 23 cm. 10-1519.
F128.44. B12

BARCK, Oscar Theodore.   New York city during the war for independence, with special reference to the period of British occupation.   New York, Columbia university press; London, P. S. King, 1931. 267 p. incl. map. 23 cm. (Studies in history, economics and public law ... no. 357)   Bibliography: p. 254-262. 32-1742. F128.44. B23

— New York, 1931.   5-269 p. incl. map. 23 cm. Thesis (PH. D.) Columbia university. 32-1267.   F128.44.B232

— Port Washington, N.Y., I. J. Friedman (1966)   267 p. 22 cm. (Empire state historical publications seris, 39) 66-21379.   F128.44.B232
1966

NEW YORK CITY

BARNES, David M. The draft riots in New York, July, 1863. The metropolitan police: their services during riot week. Their honorable record. New York, Baker & Godwin, 1863.   117 p.   23½ cm.   1-16825.
    F128.44.B26

BELDEN, Ezekiel Porter. New-York; past, present, and future; comprising a history of the city of New-York, a description of its present condition, and an estimate of its future increase ... New-York, G. P. Putnam; Boston, B. B, Mussey, etc. 1849.   4. (vii) - viii p., (11)-125 p., front., illus., plates, fold. plan.   19½ cm.   Appended: The author's "New-York - as it is" ... ; The American advertiser ... 1849. 1-14336.
    F128.44.B42

— New-York - as it is; being the counterpart of the metropolis of America. New-York, J. P. Prall, 1849.   24 p.   1 pl.   12°.   (With above) 1-14338-M1.
    F128.44.B42

— The American advertiser; designed for the cards and advertisements of the leading business establishments of the U.S. New York, J. P. Prall, 1849.   180 p.   12°.   (With above) 1-14339.
    F128.44.B42

BELDEN, Ezekiel Porter. New-York: past, present, and future, etc. 2d ed. New-York, Prall, Lewis; Boston, B. B. Mussey, etc. 1850.   4, (vii)-viii p. (11) - 125 p. front., illus., pl., fold. plan.   20 cm.   Appended: The author's "New-York - as it is ..." The American advertiser ... 1849. 1-14337.
    F128.44.B43

— 3d ed. New York, Prall, Lewis; Philadelphia, G. S. Appleton, etc., 1850.   viii, (11) - 141 p. illus., 19 pl. (incl. front.) fold. plan.   19½ cm.   8-1166.
    F128.44.B432

— The American advertiser ... 3d ed. 1850.   vii, 8-203 p.   19½ cm.   (With above) 8-1167. 8-1167.
    F128.44.B432

— 5th ed. rev. and brought up to Sept., 1851. New-York, Prall, Lewis; Boston, Redding & co., 1851.   4, (vii) - viii p., (11)-153 p. front., illus., 2 pl., fold. map.   19½ cm.   With this is bound the author's "New York - as it is." N. Y. 1851. 1-14342.
    F128.44.B44

— The American advertiser. 5th ed.   vii, 8-332 p.   12°   (With above) 1-14340-M1.
    F128.44.B44

The BLOODY week! Riot, murder & arson, containing a full account of this wholesale outrage on life and property, accurately prepared from official sources, by eye witnesses, with portraits of "Andrews," the leader and "Rosa," his Eleventh street mistress ... New York, Contant & Baker (1863)   32 p.   23 cm. 12-5129.
    F128.44.B63
    Rare Book Coll.

DE BLOEDIGE week! Oproer, moord, en brandstichting ... Zierikzee, P. de Looze, 1864.   2, 36 p.   8°.   1-14341-M1.
    F128.44.B64

BLUNT'S stranger's guide to the city of New-York ... To which is prefixed, an historical sketch, general description, plan and extent of the city ... Embellished with a plan of the city, and engravings of public buildings. New-York: Printed for, and pub. by Edmund M. Blunt, At the quadrant, 1817.   xv. (13)-306 p.   front. (plan)   3 pl.   14½ cm. 5-36896.
    F128.44.B65
    Rare Book Coll.

(BOBO, William M.) Glimpses of New York city. By a South Carolinian (who had nothing else to do) Charleston, J. J. McCarter, 1852.   215 p.   12°.   1-14344-M1.
    F128.44.B66

BURFORD, Robert. Description of a view of the city of New York, now exhibiting at the Panorama, Leicester square. London, T. Brettell, 1834.   12 p.   front. (fold. pl.)   8°.   1-14347-M1.
    F128.44.B95
    Map div.

CALLENDER, James Hodge. Yesterdays in little old New York ... New York, Dorland press, 1929.   3, 298 p.   front. (port.)   illus., plates.   24 cm. 29-27669.
    F128.44.C15

CHILD, Mrs. Lydia Maria (Francis) Letters from New-York. ... New-York, C. S. Francis and co., Boston, J. Munroe, 1843.   ix, 276 p.   19½ cm. 19-6724.
    F128.44.C53
    Toner Coll.

— London, R. Bentley, 1843. xii, 310 p. 20 cm. First series, Aug. 19, 1841, to May 1, 1843. 19-15064. F128.44.C532

— 3d ed. New York, C. S. Francis; Boston, J. H. Francis, 1845. 3, (ix)-xii, (13)-288 p. 19½ cm. 33-5222. F128.44.C533

— 3d ed. Freeport, N. Y., Books for Libraries Press, 1970. 288 p. 23 cm. (American fiction reprint series) 79-137726. F128.44.C533 1970

CHILD, Mrs. Lydia Maria (Francis) Letters from New York. Second series. ... New York, C. S. Francis; Boston, J. H. Francis, 1845. 3, (ix)-xii. (13)-287 p. 19½ cm. 28-559. F128.44.C534

CHILD, Mrs. Lydia Maria (Francis) Letters from New York. By L. Maria Child ... 9th ed. New-York, C. S. Francis; Boston, J. H. Francis, 1848. xii, (13)-288 p. 19½ cm. 19-8597. F128.44.C535

— 11th ed. New York, C. S. Francis; Boston, J. H. Francis, 1852. 2 v. 19 x 12 cm. Vol. 2: "Second series." 21-21176. F128.44.C536

CHILD, Mrs. Lydia Maria (Francis) Letters from New York. 1st and 2d series. London, F. Pitman, etc. 1879. xvi, 429 p. 19 cm. 19-15065. F128.44.C538

CLARKE & Stephenson's New York city guide. For August, 1862. (5th ed.) ... New York, French & Wheat, printers (1862) 32 p. fold. mpa. 15 cm. 36M45. F128.44.C 56 Toner coll.

COLYER, Vincent. ... Report of Vincent Colyer on the reception and care of the soldiers returning from the war. Presented Sept. 14, 1865. New York, Union league club, 1865. 56 p. 25 cm. 3-6520. F128.44.C 72

COLYER, Vincent. To the memory of the martyrs: Abraham Franklin, Peter Heuston, William Jones, James Costello, slain in the riots of July, in the city of New York. Funeral services held in Shiloh church, N. Y. ... New York (1863) 8 p. 22½ cm. 5-3872. F128.44.C 74

COOPER, James Fenimore. New York; being an introduction to an unpublished manuscript, by the author, entitled The towns of Manhattan. New York, Printed by S. A. Jacobs for the publisher W. F. Payson, 1930. x, (2), 63 p. incl. front. 21½ cm. Originally pub. April 1864, in "The Spirit of the fair", a daily magazine issued by the U. S. sanitary commission in connection with the Metropolitan fair held in New York. 30-23875. F128.44.C 77

DAY, Bejamin H. and Delano, Joseph C. Two New-Yorkers, editor and sea captain, 1833.(by) Francis B. Whitlock ... New York, The Newcomen soc. of England, American branch, 1945. 28 p. incl. mounted front., illus. 23 cm. "1st printing: Dec. 1945. 2d printing: Dec. 1945." 46-15412. F128.44.D25W5

DAYTON, Abram Child. Last days of Knickerbocker life in New York. By Abram C. Dayton. New York, G. W. Harlan, 1882. 275 p. front. (port.) 18 cm. 1-14404 Rev. F128.44.D 27

— Illus. ed. New York and London, G. P. Putnam's sons, 1897. xxx, 386 p. front., plates, ports. 22½ cm. 1-14405 Rev. F128.44.D 28

DEWEY, Orville. A sermon, on occasion of the late fire, in the city of New York ... New York, D. Felt & co., 1836. 17 p. 24 cm. 15-12400. F128.44.D 5

(DISTURNELL, John) Guide to the city of New York; containing an alphabetical list of streets, etc. .. New York, J. Disturnell, 1836. 14, (2) p. front., fold. map. 12½ cm. 16-9499. F128.44.D 58 Rare Book Coll.

(DIX, John Adams) Sketch of the resources of the city of New-York. With a view of its municipal government, population, etc. from the foundation of the city of the date of the latest statistical accounts. New York, G. & C. Carvill, 1827. 104 p. 23 cm. 1-21403. F128.44.D 61

NEW YORK CITY 217

DODGE, William Earl. Old New York. A lecture. New York, Dodd, Mead, 1880. 59 p. front. (port.) 23½ cm. 1-14351.
F128.44.D64

DOGGETT, John, jr. The great metropolis; or Guide to New-York for 1846. Second publication. New-York, Directory establishment (1846?) 165 p. front. (fold. map) illus. 14½ cm. 10-31405.
F128.44.D65

DUER, William Alexander. New-York as it was, during the latter part of the last century. An anniversary address ... New-York, Stanford and Swords, 1849. 48 p. 21½ cm. 8-33581* Cancel.
F128.44.D83
Rare Book Coll.

DUER, William Alexander. Reminiscences of an old Yorker. New York, W. L. Andrews, 1867. 102 p. 30½ cm. Reprinted from the American mail, 1847. 1-14352.
F128.44.D85
Rare Book Coll.

DUNSHEE, Kenneth Holcomb. As you pass by. New York, Hastings House (1952) 270 p. illus. (part col.) ports., maps. 29 cm. 52-6691.
F128.44.D88

FAY, Theodore Sedgwick. Views in New-York and its environs from accurate, characteristic, & picturesque drawings, taken on the spot, expressly for this work, by Dakin, architect; with historical, topographical, & critical illustrations, by Theodore S. Fay ... assisted by several distinguished literary gentlemen. New York, Peabody & co.; London, O. Rich, 1831. iv, (5)-58, (43)-46 p. plates, fold. map. 28 cm. Bound with the Watering places of Great Britain and fashionable directory of London, 1831. 1-14353.
F128.44.F28
Rare Book Coll.

— The watering places of Great Britain and fahionable directory, illus. with views. London, Pub. for the proprietors by I. T. Hinton, 1831. 200, 40 p., pl. 29 cm. (With above item) 1-14354.
F128.44.F28
Rare Book Coll.

FLOY, Michael. The diary of Michael Floy, Jr., Bowery village, 1833-1837, ed. Richard Albert Edward Brooks, with an introd. note, annotations, and postscript by Margaret Floy Washburn. New Haven, Yale university press; London, H. Milford, Oxford university press, 1941. xi, 269 p. 25 cm. 41-20685.
F128.44.F55

FONER, Philip Sheldon. Business and slavery; the New York merchants & the irrepressible conflict (by) Philip S. Foner ... Chapel Hill, The University of North Carolina press, 1941. ix, 356 p. 24 cm. Bibliography: p. 323-336. 41-6679 Rev.
F128.44.F67

— ix, 356 p. 23 cm. Thesis (PH.D.) Columbia university, 1940. 41-10890.
F128.44.F67
1941 a

— New York, Russell & Russell (1968) ix, 356 p. 25 cm. 68-15122.
F128.44.F67
1968

FOSTER, C. An account of the conflagration of the principal part of the first ward of the city of New-York. Illus. with numerous etchings, etc., etc. (New York, 1835?) 54 p. front. (map) plates. 20 cm. 10-25270.
F128.44.F73
Rare Book Coll.

FOSTER, George G. Fifteen minutes around New York. New York, De Witt & Davenport (1854) v, (7) - 111 p. 22½ cm. 1-14355.
F128.44.F75

(FOSTER, George G.) New York in slices; by an experienced carver, being the original slices pub. in the N.Y. tribune. Rev., enl., and cor, by the author ... New York, W. F. Burgess, 1849. 128 p. illus. 23 cm. Published anonymously. 7-42526.
F128.44.F76
Rare Book Coll.

— Spindler, Karl. The bastard; or, The brother's revenge. A romantic tale. Tr. by Alphonce Braunfels. New-York, E. Winchester, 1845. 234 p. 23 cm. (With above item) 7-42525.

FOSTER, George G.   New York naked. ...   New York, De Witt & Davenport (185-)   (11) - 168 p.
25 cm.   8-10498.   F128.44.F77
Rare Book Coll.

FRANCIS, John Wakefield.   New York during the last half century: a discourse in commemoration of the fifty-third anniversary of the New York historical society ... New York, J. F. Trow, printer, 1857.   3, (5) - 232 p.   24½ cm.   1-14356.   F128.44.F82

FRANCIS, John Wakefield.   Old New York; or, Reminiscences of the past sixty years.   Being an enlarged and revised ed. of the anniversary discourse delivered before the N.Y. Historical Society ... New York, B. Blom, 1971.   cxxxvi, 400 p.   69-16318.   F128.44.F82 1971

— ... New York, C. Roe, 1858.   384 p.   19 cm.   1-14358.   F128.44.F83

— New York, W. J. Widdleton, 1866.   cxxxvi, 400 p.   front.   21½ cm.   Enl. & rev. ed. of F128.44.F82   F128.44.F84

FRANCIS'S New guide to the cities of New-York and Brooklyn, and the vicinity ... New York, C.S. Francis & co., 1853.   vii p., 2 l. (13) - 148 p.   front., illus., plates, fold. map.   15½ cm.   1-14360.   F128.44.F87

— 1854.   vii, (8) - 148 p.   front., pl., fold. map.   16 cm.   2-18825.   F128.44.F88

— 1856.   vii, (13) - 148 p.   front., illus., plates, fold. map, double tabl.   15½ cm.   Imperfect.   17-10091.   F128.44.F89 Toner Coll.

— 1857.   vii, (13)-148 p.   illus., plates, fold. map.   15½ cm.   5-36859.   F128.44.F91

— 1859.   vii, (13)-148 p.   front., illus., plates, fold. map, double tab.   15½ cm.   14-15981.   F128.44.F913

FROTHINGHAM, Octavius Brooks.   The morality of the riot.   Sermon at Ebbitt hall ...   New York, D. G. Francis, 1863.   20 p.   14½ cm.   19-14869.   F128.44.F93

— 2d ed.   (New York) D. G. Francis, 1864.   23 p.   13 cm.   20-17065.   F128.44.P931

(GREENE, Asa)   A glance at New York: embracing the city government, theaters, hotels, churches, mobs, monopolies, learned professions, newspapers, rogues, dandies, fires and firemen, water and other liquids, etc., etc. ...   New-York, A. Greene, 1837.   vi, 264 p.   15 cm.   1-14361 rev.   F128.44.G79

DIE GROSSE feuersbrunst zu New-York, am 19. juli 1845. ...   Hamburg, B. C. Berendsohn.   1845.
27 p.   front.   19 cm.   24-6803.   F128.44.G85

The GROWTH of New York ... New York, G. W. Wood, 1865.   49 p.   22½ cm.   1-14362.   F128.44.G88

GUIDE of the city of New-York, with views of the most interesting points of the city, (printed in oil colors) and a map of Manhattan Island & the Central Park.   New-York, J. H. Kleefish (1859)
28 p.   13 col. pl. (1 fold.) fold. map.   16 cm.   17-24892.   F128.44.G94

HARDIE, James.   A census of the new buildings erected in this city, in the year 1824, arranged in distinct classes, according to their materials and number of stories.   Also, a number of statistical documents ...   New-York, Printed by S. Marks, 1825.   48 p.   20 x 11½ cm.   4-11123 Rev.   F128.44.H25
Rare Book Coll.

HART, Eli.   A sketch of the life and times of Eli Hart, including the report on the title to his famous old alley in Washington street, New York city, by L. Harding Rogers, jr.   (New York, Pandick press, inc., 1931)   51 p. incl. mounted map.   25½ cm.   The title to the alley or "Yard in common" of the block originally owned by Eli Hart and Goold Hoyt is traced through their descendants and successors in interest.   32-11902.   F128.44.H28

NEW YORK CITY

HASWELL, Charles Haynes. Reminiscences of an octogenarian of the city of New York (1816 to 1860) ... New York, Harper & bros., 1896. xii, 581 p. incl. illus., plates. front. (port.) fold. map. 21½ cm. L.C. copy replaced by microfilm. 1-14364.
F128.44.H35
Microfilm 10077 F

HAVEMEYER. William Frederick Havemeyer: a political biography. (1st ed.) New York, American Press (1965) 232 p. 23 cm. 65-11379.
F128.44.H37F8

HAVENS, Catherine Elizabeth. Diary of a little girl in old New York. New York, H. C. Brown (1919) 5, 101, (2) p. incl. front., illus., plates, ports. 18 cm. Also printed in Valentine's manual of old New York, no. 4 new series, 1920. 19-18715.
F128.44.H38

HOLLEY, Orville Luther. A description of the city of New York: with a brief account of the cities, towns, villages and places of resort within thirty miles; designed as a guide for citizens and strangers ... New York, J. Disturnell, 1847. 114 p. front., pl., fold. map, fold. plan. 15 cm. 1-14365.
F128.44.H74

HONE, Philip. The diary of Philip Hone, 1828-1851. Ed., with an introd. by Bayard Tuckerman ... New York, Dodd, Mead, 1889. 2 v. front. (port.) 23 cm. 11-23190.
F128.44.H77

— Allan Nevins, editor, with a pref. by Churchill Rodgers. New York, Arno Press, 1970. xxvii, 962 p. 2 v. in 1. 23 cm. (The Rise of urban America) 77-112559.
F128.44.H77 1970

— New York, Dodd, Mead, 1927. 2 v. front. (ports.) 24 cm. 28-26080.
F128.44.H78

HUBBARD, Nathaniel Tuthill. Autobiography of N. T. Hubbard, with personal reminiscences of New York city from 1798 to 1875. New York, J. F. Trow, 1875. xi, 245 p. front. (port.) 19½ cm. 11-24793.
F128.44.H87

(JACKSON, Lewis Evens) Walks about New York. Facts and figures gathered from various sources. By the secretary of the city mission. New York, Pub, for the society, 1865. 120 p. 12º. 1-14366-M1.
F128.44.J13

JOHNSTON. John Johnston of New York, merchant, by Emily Johnston De Forest ... New York, Priv. print. (The Gilliss press) 1909. xv, 195 p., 2 l. front., illus., plates (1 col.) ports., fold. geneal. tab. 25 cm. 9-21822.
F128.44.J73

JOSEPH (pseud.) New-York aristocracy; or, Gems of japonica-dom. ... New York, C. B. Norton; Philadelphia, W. P. Hazard, etc., 1851. 152 p. front., 12 pl. 18 cm. 1-21614 Rev.
F128.44.J83

KENNEDY. Proceedings of the Democratic republican general committee of the city of New York relative to the death of Colonel William D. Kennedy ... New York, 1861. 6 p. 23 cm. 4-146.
F128.44.K35

KING, Charles. Progress of the city of New-York, during the last fifty years; with notices of the principal changes and important events. A lecture delivered before the Mechanic's society ... 1851. New-York, D. Appleton, 1852. 80 p. 23 cm. 1-14367.
F128.44.K52

KURZGEFASSTE beschreibung der stadt New-York. ... New York, J. Uhl, 1853. viii, 84 p. front. (pl.) fold. map. 16º. 1-14368-M1.
F128.44.K96

LEE, Basil Leo, brother. ... Discontent in New York city, 1861-1865. Washington, D.C., The Catholic university of America press, 1943. x, 306 p. 23 cm. Thesis (PH. D.) Catholic university of America, 1944. Bibliography: p. 296-299. A 44-4238.
F128.44.L54

(LEONARD, Ellen) ... Three days reign of terror, or The July riots in 1863, in New York. (New York? 1867?) 24 p. 22 cm. "From Harper's magazine, Jan., 1867." 3-33157.
F128.44.L58

— From Harper's magazine, Jan. 1867. 25 p. 23 cm. 4-30128.
F128.44.L582

LYON, Isaac S. Recollections of an old cartman, by I. S. Lyon, ex-cartman, Boonton, New Jersey... Newark, N.J., Printed at the Daily journal office, 1872.   (3) - 125 p. 23 cm. "From the Newark journal."
Sketches, mainly descriptive of life and customs in N. Y. city.   14-18161.
F128.44.L99

McCAGUE, James. The second rebellion; the story of the New York City draft riots of 1863. New York, Dial Press, 1968.   viii, 210 p. illus. 68-18636.
F128.44.M 3

MASON, Alfred Bishop. ... "The fourteen miles round," (New York, The Knickerbocker press, 1897)   183-208 p. 19½ cm. (Half moon series. v. 1 no. 6) Pub. also in "Historic New-York." 1897. 1st ser. no. 9) 10-6835.
F128.44.M39

MATHEWS, Cornelius. A pen-and-ink panorama of New-York city. New York, J. S. Taylor, 1853.
iv, (5) - 209 p. 14½ cm. 1-14369.
F128.44.M42
Rare Book Coll.

MATHEWS, James McFarlane. Recollections of persons and events, chiefly in the city of New York: being selections from his journal, by J. M. Mathews ... New York, Sheldon and co., 1865.   368 p.
24 cm. 12-30040.
F128.44.M43

— Microfilm. Ann Arbor, Mich., University Microfilms, 1965.   1 reel. 35 mm. (American culture series, 237:8)
Microfilm 01291 reel 237, no. 8 E

MILLER'S New York as it is; or, Stranger's guide-book to the cities of New York, Brooklyn, and adjacent places ... New York, J. Miller, 1859.   129 p. front., illus., plates (part fold.) fold. map. 16 cm.
1-14370.
F128.44.M65
Rare Book Coll.

— 1860.   74, 75* - 75**, 75-129 p. front., illus., plates. etc. 16 cm. 1-14371.
F128.44.M651
Rare Book Coll.

— 1862.   123, (133)-137 (i. e. 132) p. front., illus., plates, etc. paging irregular. 1-14372.
F128.44.M653

— 1863.   123 (i. e. 131) (5) p. front., illus., plates, etc. 15½ cm. Paging irregular. 1-14373.
F128.44.M654

— 1864.   123 (i. e. 131) (5) p. front., illus., plates, etc. Paging irregular. 1-14374.
F128.44.M655

— 1865.   141 p. front., illus., plates, etc. 15½ cm. Folded map wanting. 1-14375.
F128.44.M656

— 1867.   141 p. front., plates (part fold.) fold. map. 16½ cm. 16-12298.
F128.44.M6563

— 1872.   134 p. front., illus., plates (part fold.) fol. d facsim. 16 cm. 16-27464.
F128.44.M6566

— 1878.   134 p. front., illus., pl. (partly fold.) map. 16°. Map wanting. 1-14376-M1.
F128.44.M657

(MITCHELL, Samuel Latham) The picture of New-York; or, The traveller's guide through the commercial metropolis of the United States. By a gentleman residing in this city. New-York: Pub. by I. Riley and co. ... 1807.   viii, 223 p. front. (fold. plan) 15½ cm. 1-14377.
F128.44.M68
Rare Book Coll.

MONAGHAN, Frank. This was New York, the nation's capital in 1789. Garden City, New York, Doubleday, Doran, 1943.   xi, 308 p. front. (port.) plates, facsims. 22 cm. "First ed." Bibliography: p. 289-291.
43-7106.
F128.44.M86

— Freeport, N.Y., Books for Libraries Press (1970)   xi, 308 p. 23 cm. 70-117884.
F128.44.M86
1970

(MORROW, John) A voice from the newsboys. (New York?) 1860.   2, 7-xiv, 15-135 p. incl. front. (port.)
20 cm. 13-2637.
F128.44.M88

NEW YORK CITY

NELSON'S guide to the city of New York and its neighborhood ... London, New York (etc.) T. Nelson, 1858.   iv, (5)-64 p.   front. (map) illus., col. plates (partly fold.)   15½ cm.   3-29012.   F128.44.N43

— 1859.   iv, (5) - 64 p.   front., illus., col. plates (partly fold.)   map.   15 cm.   4-1136.   F128.44.N44

NEW YORK (City) Report of the Special committee appointed by the Common council of the city of New York, relative to the catastrophe in Hague street ... Presented by Alderman Griffin. New York, McSpedon & Baker, printers to the Common council, 1850.   116 p. incl. tables.   23 cm.   8-19478.   F128.44.N45

NEW YORK (City) Communication from His Honor the mayor, in relation to the precautionary measures adopted by him to secure the public peace at the recent election in this city ... New York, Printed by order of the Common council, 1839.   (293) - 350 p.   22 cm.   12-32395.   F128.44.N47

NEW YORK (County) ... Report of the Committee on substitutes and relief of the Board of supervisors, appointed under ordinance adopted Aug. 28, 1863. New York, W. L. S. Harrison, printer, 1863.   91 p.   22 cm.   2-18423.   F128.44.N51

NEW YORK (County) Reports of the Special committee on volunteering of the county of New York, relative to operations under call dated Dec. 19, 1864. 1864 - 1865 - 1866. Board of supervisors, 1866. New York, The N.Y. printing co., 1866.   258 p.   22 cm.   2-18424.   F128.44.N545

NEW YORK and its vicinity. New York, Bourne, etc., 1831-34.   30 illus. on 18 pl.   15 x 24 cm.   F128.44.N62

NEW-YORK as it is, in (1833-1835) 1837; containing a general description of the city of New-York, list of officers, public institutions, and other useful information.... (1st)- 4th years of publication. New-York, J. Disturnell, 1833-37.   4 v. fronts., fold. maps.   12-15 cm.   Title varies.   12-24133 Rev.   F128.44.N63

NEW YORK. Citizens. Gratitude to Gen. Grant. Mass assemblage of loyal citizens of New York in honor of Lieut.-General Grant, and to celebrate the triumphs of the Union armies, Union Square, June 4, 1864. New York, G. F. Nesbitt, 1864.   23 p.   21½ cm.   23-13240.   F128.44.N642

NEW YORK. Citizens. Proceedings at the mass meeting of loyal citizens ... under the auspices of the chamber of commerce ... the union defence committee ... the Common council, etc. Letters and speeches. New-York, G. F. Nesbitt, printers, 1862.   116 p.   23 cm.   2-14958 Rev.   F128.44.N644

NEW YORK. Report of the Committee of merchants for the relief of colored people, suffering from the late riots in the city of New York. New York, G. A. Whitehorne, printer, 1863.   48 p.   22½ cm.   4-1125 Rev.   F128.44.N646

NEW YORK hand book, and merchants' guide, The. Being a reliable directory, for visiting merchants, to the prominent objects of interest in New-York. Presented by Henry Levy. New-York, 1859.   43 p.   front., pl.   12º.   1-11662-M1.   F128.44.N65

NEW YORK. Reports, resolutions and documents, of the Union defense committee of the citizens of New York. New York, Baptist & Taylor, printers, 1862.   134 p.   22½ cm.   18-341.   F128.44.N66

NEW YORK. The Union defence committee of the city of New York. Minutes, reports, and correspondence; with an historical introd. by John Austin Stevens. (New York) The Union defence committee, 1885.   3, 286 p.   26½ cm.   1-16817 Rev.   F128.44.N664

(O'RIELLY, Henry) First connected account of the efforts of the people of New York for defending the union during the late civil war. (New York, 1875)   25½ x 19 cm.   12-31616 Rev.   F128.44.O66

OSGOOD, Samuel. New York in the nineteenth century. A discourse delivered before the New York hist. soc. New York ... 1867.   127 p. incl. tables.   25 cm.   1-14378.   F128.44.O82

PHELPS, H.   The lions of New York, being a guide to objects of interest in and around the great metropolis. ... New York, Phelps, Fanning, 1853.   2, (7) - 50 p.   illus., fold. map.   20 cm.   Pages 29-48 wanting.   1-14379.   F128.44. P53

PHELPS' New York city guide; being a pocket directory for strangers and citizens to the prominent objects of interest in the great commercial metropolis, and conductor to its environs ... New York, T. C. Fanning, 1852.   vi, (7) - 95 p. incl. front., illus. fold. map.   15 cm.   1-14380.   F128.44. P55
Rare Book Coll.

— New York, Ensign, Bridgman, & Fanning, 1854.   vi, (7) - 96 p. incl. front., illus. fold. map.   14½ cm.   1-14381.   F128.44. P56

PHILLIPS, Stephen Clarendon.   Speech of Mr. Phillips, of Massachusetts, upon the bill for the relief of the sufferers by the fire at New York ...   Washington, National intelligence office, 1836.
16 p.   24½ cm.   18-4784.   F128.44. P57

PICTURE of New-York, and stranger's guide to the commercial metropolis of the U.S.   New-York, A. T. Goodrich (1828)   viii, 492 p.   front., illus., plates, fold. plan.   16 cm.   1-14382 Rev.   F128.44.P61

PINTARD, John.   Letters from John Pintard to his daughter, Eliza Noel Pintard Davidson, 1816-1833 ... New York, Printed for the New-York historical soc., 1940-41.   4 v.   fronts. (ports.)   24½ cm.
(Collections of the N.Y. historical soc. for the year 1937-1940.   lxx-lxxiii)   40-30954 Rev.   F128.44.P635

PINTARD.   John Pintard, founder of the New York historical society; an address delivered before the N.Y. historical soc ... by General James Grant Wilson.   New York, Printed for the Society, 1902.
37 p.   front. (port.) illus., fold. facsim.   24½ cm.   2-11389.   F128.44. P65

POMERANTZ, Sidney Irving.   New York, an American city, 1783-1803; a study of urban life ...
New York, 1938.   531 p. incl. front.   double map.   22½ cm.   Thesis (PH.D.) Columbia university, 1938.   Bibliography:
p. 505-519; bibliographical foot-notes.   39-1230.   F128.44. P75

— New York, Columbia university press; London, P. S. King, 1938.   531 p. front., double map.   23 cm.
(Studies in history, economics and public law   No. 442)   39-1229.   F128.44.P752

— (2d ed.)   Port Washington, N.Y., I. J. Friedman (1965)   531 p.   22 cm.   64-11483.
F128.44. P75
1965

(RANDEL, John)   City of New York, north of Canal street, in 1808 to 1821.   (In Valentine, D.T. Manual of the corporation of the city of New York.   New York, 1864.   18½ cm.   p. (847) - 856)   4-20400.   F128.44. R18

REISS, N.   Excursion à New-York, en 1850, par le docteur N. Reis.   Bruxelles, N. J. Gregoir, 1851.
96 p.   18 cm.   16-20034.   F128.44. R37

A rejoinder to "The replies from England, etc. to certain statements circulated in this country respecting Mr. Macready."   Tog. with an impartial history and review of the lamentable occurrences at the Astor place opera house ...   By an American citizen.   New York, Stringer and Townsend, 1849.
119 p.   23 cm.   10-21798.   F128.44. R38

REPUBLICAN party.   Proceedings of the Republican and Union convention for the 6th congressional district, held at Bleecker buildings ... 1862.   New-York, Chatterton & Parker, printers, 1862.
16 p.   20½ cm.   4-1363.   F128.44. R42

REUBEN Vose's guide to New York city.   A monthly publication.   Jan. 1, 1860.   (New York) R. Vose, 1860.   1 v.   48°.   1-14663-M1.   F128.44. R44

ROSS, Joel H.   What I saw in New-York; or, A bird's eye view of city life.   ... Auburn, N.Y., Derby & Miller, 1851.   x, (11) - 326 p. front., illus.   18½ cm.   7-42514.   F128.44. R82

(RUGGLES, Edward)   A picture of New-York in 1846; with a short account of places in its vicinity;

designed as a guide to citizens and strangers ... New-York, Homans & Ellis, 1846. iv, 172, 3 p. front., plates, fold. map. 16 cm. 1-14383.
 F128.44.R93

— New-York, C. S. Francis, 1846.   iv, 172, 3 p. front., plates, fold. map. 15 cm. 1-14384. F128.44.R94

— in 1848. New-York, C. S. Francis, 1848.   iv, 172, 3 p. front., plates, map. 14 cm. Imperfect; map wanting. 1-14385.
 F128.44.R95

RUGGLES. Ruggles of New York, a life of Samuel B. Ruggles, by D. G. Brinton Thompson. New York, Columbia university press; London, P. S. King & Staples, 1946.   222 p. front., ports., fold. map. 23 cm. (Studies in history, economics and public law ... No. 524) Bibliography: p. 207-214. A 47-345.
 F128.44.R955T5

— New York, 1946.   2, 7-222 p. front., ports, etc. Thesis (PH.D.) - Columbia university. A 47-955. F128.44.R955T5 1946 a

— New York, AMS Press (1968)   222 p. fold. map, ports. 23 cm. 76-76651 MARC.
 F128.44.R955T5 1968

RUTGERS, Elizabeth (Benson) plaintiff. Arguments and judgement of the Mayor's court of the city of New-York, in a cause between Elizabeth Rutgers and Joshua Waddington. New-York: Printed by Samuel Loudon. 1784.   47 p. 20½ cm. An action of trespass. 42-43390.
 F128.44.R96
 Rare Book Coll.

(SAUNDERS, Frederick) New-York in a nutshell, or, Visitors' handbook to the city ... New York, T. W. Strong, 1853.   144 p. incl. front., illus. 15½ cm. 1-14386.
 F128.44.S25

SCHAUKIRK, Ewald Gustav. Occupation of New York City by the British. (New York) New York Times (1969)   28 p. 24 cm. (Eyewitness accounts of the American Revolution) 70-77112. F128.44.S3

(SEARS, Edward Isidore) The Central park under ring-leader rule. New York, E. I. Sears, 1871. 24 p. 22½ cm. Reprinted from the National quarterly review (no. xliv, March, 1871) 9-27139.
 F128.44.S43

SMITH, Thomas Edward Vermilye. The city of New York in the year of Washington's inauguration, 1789 ... New York, Printed for the author, 1889.   iv, (5) - 244 p. front. (fold. map) 24½ cm. 1-14388 rev.
 F128.44.S66

— New York, A. D. F. Randolph, 1889.   iv, (5)-244 p. front. (fold. map) 24½ cm. 1-14389. F128.44.S67

SPANN, Edward K. Ideals and politics; New York intellectual and liberal democracy, 1820-1880.
 F128.44.S73

SPENCER, Ichabod Smith. The conflagration in the city of New-York; a discourse delivered in the Second Presbyterian church in Brooklyn ... New York, J. Post's press, 1836.   30 p. 23 cm. 17-17361.
 F128.44.S74

(STANFORD, Thomas N.) A concise description of the city of New York, giving an account of its early history, public buildings, amusements, exhibitions, benevolent and literary institutions; tog. with other interesting information. New York. Printed by G. Long ... 1814.   (5)-69 p. 14 cm. 12-11034.
 F128.44.S78
 Rare Book Coll.

STEPHEN H. Branch's alligator. v.1; Apr. 24 - Sept. 25, 1858, (New York) 1858.   (92) p. 31 cm. Various paging. weekly. CA 7-61 Unrev.
 F128.44.S82

STEPHEN H. Branch's weekly star. New York, 1860 -   v. 31 cm. (With above item) CA 7-60 Unrev.
 F128.44.S82

THAYER, George Augustine. The draft riots of 1863; a historical study, read at the meeting of the

Ohio commandery, Military order of the loyal legion of the U.S. ... (Cincinnati? 1916) 13 p. 22 cm.
16-20776.
          F128.44.T37

THORBURN, Grant. Fifty years' reminiscences of New-York; or, Flowers from the garden of Laurie Todd: being a collection of fugitive pieces which appeared in the newspapers and periodicals of the day, for the last thirty years ... New-York, D. Fanshaw (1845) 287 p. front. (port.) 15½ cm.
1-14390.
          F128.44.T49

TRES grandes ciudades. Su industria, comercio y artes, su historia, datos estadisticos y noticias de interés general para todo el mundo y especialmente para el comercio ... Nueva-York, J. Russell, 1862. 3 pts. in 1 v. illus. 8°. Contents. - pte. 1. Nueva-York. - pte. 2. Filadelfia. - pte. 3. Boston. 1-21372-M1.
          F128.44.T79

TRUMBULL, Harriet. A season in New York, 1801; letters of Harriet and Maria Trumbull. Ed. with an introd. by Helen M. Morgan. (Pittsburgh) University of Pittsburgh Press (1969) ix, 189 p. 22 cm. 69-12333.
          F128.44.T84
          1969

UNCONDITIONAL union central committee for the city and county of New York. Address, constitution and by-laws ... New York, W. C. Bryant, printers, 1864. 13 p. 8°. 1-21481-M1.
          F128.44.U54

VIELÉ, Egbert Ludovickus. The topography and hydrology of New York. New York, R. Craighead, printer, 1865. 13 p. fold. map. 24 cm. 20-11957.
          F128.44.V65

WALLYS, Philip. About New York: an account of what a boy saw in his visit to the city. New York, Dix, Edwards, 1857. 102 p. 12°. 1-14391-M1.
          F128.44.W21

WERSTEIN, Irving. July, 1863. New York, Messner (1957) 252 p. illus. 22 cm. 57-10511.
          F128.44.W38

WERSTEIN, Irving. The draft riots, July 1863. New York, J. Messner (1971) 255 p. 22 cm.
1957 ed. pub. under title: July, 1863 (above) 70-140678.
          F128.44.W38

WERTENBAKER, Thomas Jefferson. Father Knickerbocker rebels: New York City during the Revolution. New York, C. Scribner's Sons, 1948. xv, 308 p. illus., ports., maps. 25 cm. "Footnotes" (bibliographical): p. 271-294. 48-11329*.
          F128.44.W4

— New York, Cooper Square Publishers, 1969. xv, 308 p. illus., ports. 24 cm. 68-57282.
          F128.44.W4
          1969

WHITMAN, Walt. New York dissected; a sheaf of recently discovered newspaper articles by the author of Leaves of grass; introd. and notes by Emory Holloway and Ralph Adimari; illus. from old prints and photos. New York, R. R. Wilson, inc., 1936. xiii, 257 p. front., illus., pl., ports. 23½ cm.
A collection of articles ... which were pub. in various issues of "Life illustrated" during 1855-1856. 36-10323.
          F128.44.W56

WILLIAMS, Wellington. Appleton's New York city and vicinity guide ... Illus. with maps and engravings. New York, D. Appleton; Philadelphia, G. S. Appleton, 1849. 91 p. front. (fold. map) plates. 14½ cm. 1-14393 Add.
          F128.44.W73

WOOD. A condensed biography of a candidate for speaker! Fernando Wood, his forgeries and other crimes. (New York? 1875) 24 p. 23 cm. Signed: Sentinel. 17-6915.
          F128.44.W85
          Rare Book Coll.

WOOD. ... A condensed biography of Fernando Wood. Comp. from the original documents, by a veteran Democrat ... New York, 1866. 16 p. 22½ cm. 15-3570.
          F128.44.W86

WOOD. A model mayor. Early life, congressional career, and triumphant municipal administration of Hon. Fernando Wood ... By a citizen of New York, (E. Hutchinson) American family publication establishment, 1855. xii (13) - 126 p. incl. front. (port.) 20½ cm. 15-6005.
          F128.44.W862

WOOD. A biography of Fernando Wood. A history of the forgeries, perjuries, and other crimes of our "model" mayor. No. 1 ... (By Abijah Ingraham) (New York, 1856) 32 p. 23 cm. No more pub? 7-30367 Rev.
    F128.44.W863

WOOD. A history of the private, political and official misdeeds and offences of Fernando Wood. To Brown brothers & co., George Douglas, Schuyler Livingston (and others) ... (By Abijah Ingraham) 58 p. 23½ cm. "... originally comp. and pub. in pamphlet form in ... 1854 (i.e. 1856?)" 7-7096 Add.
    F128.44.W865
    Rare Book Coll.

WOOD. Biography of Hon. Ferdnando Wood, mayor of the city of New-York. By Donald MacLeod ... New-York, O. F. Parsons; Boston, Fetridge, etc., 1856. 2. (iii)-v, (11)-335 p. front. (port.) 17½ cm. 14-4018.
    F128.44.W87

WOOD. Fernando Wood of New York. By Samuel Augustus Pleasants. New York, 1948. 216 p. 23 cm. Thesis - Columbia university. Bibliography: p. 207-214. A 48-6854*.
    F128.44.W872
    1948

— New York, Columbia Univ. Press, 1948. 216 p. 23 cm. (Columbia University. Studies in history, economics and public law, no. 536) 48-7608*.
    F128.44.W872
    1948a

— New York, AMS Press, 1966. 216 p. 24 cm. 79-29912 MARC.
    F128.44.W872
    1966

WOOD. Memorial addresses on the life and character of Fernando Wood (a representative from New York), delivered in the House of representatives, Feb. 28, 1881 ... Washington, Govt. print. off., 1882. 40 p. front. (port.) 27 cm. 16-21925.
    F128.44.W875

NEW YORK(City) - Hist. - Revolution. Pamphlets, broadsides, clippings, and other miscellaneous matter on this subject, not separately cataloged, are classified in:
    F128.44.Z 5

NEW YORK CITY. 1865 - 1900.

BROWN, Henry Collins. From Alley pond to Rockfeller center ... New York, E. P. Dutton, 1936. xvi, 299 p. front., illus., plates. 25 cm. "First ed." 36-30914.
    F128.47
    F128.5.B887

DE KOVEN, Anna (Farwell) A musician and his wife, by Mrs. Reginald De Koven ... New York and London, Harper & bros., 1926. viii, 259 p. front., plates, ports. 24½ cm. "First ed." 26-17686.
    F128.47.
    ML410.D432

KELLEY, Frank Bergen. ... Graphic views of government in the U.S., New York state, New York city. For the classes of the City history club of New York (by) Frank Bergen Kelley ... (New York) City history club of New York, 1897. 16 p. diagrs. 19½ cm. 22-9717.
    F128.47.
    JK 38. K4

LEHR, Mrs. Elizabeth (Drexel) "King Lehr" and the gilded age; with extracts from the locked diary of Harry Lehr; with 32 illus. Philadelphia, London, J. B. Lippincott co., 1935. 332 p. front., plates, ports. 22½ cm. "Second impression." 35-13644.
    F128.47.
    CT275.L355L4 1935a

LEWIS, Lloyd. Oscar Wilde discovers America (1882) New York, Harcourt, Brace (1936) xiv, 462 p. front., illus., plates, ports. 24 cm. "First ed." "Notes and bibliography": p. 447-453. 36-12206.
    F128.47.
    PR5823. L 4

TOWNE, Charles Hanson. This New York of mine. New York, Cosmopolitan book corporation, 1931. xii, 289 p. front., plates. 23 cm. "First ed." 31-6994.
F128.47
F128.5.T75

(ABRAHAM, Henry Augustus) Newer York; a centennial offering. By Lunarian (pseud.) New York, O. Jarvis, 1876. 56 p. illus. 8°. 1-14394 Rev.
F128.47.A16

BALES, William Alan. Tiger in the streets. New York, Dodd, Mead, 1962. 212 p. 22 cm. 62-17352.
F128.47.B3

BLAIR, James Lawrence. The first municipal election in greater New York. An address delivered before St. Louis council, Legion of honor ... St. Louis, Nixon-Jones printing co., 1898. 28 p. 23 cm. 45-27372.
F128.47.B56

BOLITHO, Edwin, comp. The Columbus historical guide and map of New York city, from official records and the latest government surveys ... New York, Real estate record and builders' guide, 1891. 83 p. incl. maps. fold. map. nar. 8°. 1-14395-M1.
F128.47.B68

BREEN, Matthew Patrick. Thirty years of New York politics up-to-date ... New York, The author, 1899. xxvi, 843 p. front., plates, ports. 21 cm. 99-4163 Rev.
F128.47.B83

BROWN, Henry Collins. Brownstone fronts and Saratoga trunks ... illus. by old prints and photos. New York, E. P. Dutton, 1935. 4, vii-xxii, 25-412 p. illus. 22½ cm. "First ed." 35-18992.
F128.47.B86

BROWN, Henry Collins. In the golden nineties. New York, Books for Libraries Press (1970) 422 p. illus. 23 cm. "Repr. 1970" 71-133516.
F128.47.B87
1970

BROWNE, Junius Henri. The great metropolis; a mirror of New York. A complete history of metropolitan life and society, with sketches of prominent places, persons, and things in the city, as they actually exist. Hartford, American pub. co.; San Francisco, Cal., H. H. Bancroft, etc. 1869. 4, (7) - 700 p. front., illus., plates. 23 cm. 1-14724.
F128.47.B88

CALLOW, Alexander B. The Tweed Ring. New York, Oxford University Press, 1966. xi, 351 p. 22 cm. 66-24440.
F128.47.C25

CARPENTER, Hugh Smith. Understanding of the times: a sermon in relation to the recent riot, preached ... at the Polytechnic institute, Brooklyn. Brooklyn, Eagle print, 1871. 24 p. 23 cm. 19-18703.
F128.47.C29

CASILL, Peter. New York memories of yesteryear, life and times at the turn of the century (1890-1910) New York, Exposition Press (1964) 276 p. 21 cm. (An Exposition-Lochinvar book)
F128.47.C3

CHURCHILL, Allen. The upper crust; an informal history of New York's highest society. Englewood Cliffs, N.J., Prentice-Hall (1970) 290 p. illus. 32 cm. 78-96270.
F128.47.C47

CITIZENS' association of New York. Reform in New-York city. Address to the people of the city of New-York. Tog. with resolutions of confidence and thanks tendered to the officers of the Citizens' assoc. ... New York, The Citizens' assoc., 1870. 19 p. 27 cm. 1-16326 Add.
F128.47.C526

CITY of New York, The ... New York, 1867. 16½ cm.
F128.47.C55
1867

CITY of New York, The. A complete guide ... and a complete new street directory ... New York, Taintor brothers, Merrill & co., 1876. 82 (i.e. 118), (26) p. illus., plates, fold. map. 17 cm. Comp. by Charles Barnard. 2-5457.
F128.47.C55
1876

— New York, Taintor brothers & co., 1876.   82 (28) p. illus., fold. map. 16°. 1-14669-M1.

F128.47.C55 1876a

— New York, Taintor bros., Merrill & co., 1884.   86, 25 p. illus., fold. map. 12°. 1-14670-M1.

F128.47.C55 1884

— 1886.   2, 9-86, 25 p. illus. 18 cm. 18-16789.

F128.47.C55 1886

— 1887.   2, 9-111 (i.e. 153) p. illus., fold. map. 18 cm. 4-11117.

F128.47.C55 1887

— 1895.   7-126 (i.e. 168) p. illus., plates, fold. map. 17 cm. 1-14671 Rev.

F128.47.C55 1895

CIVIL rights. The Hibernian riot and the "Insurrection of the capitalists." A history of important events in New York, in the midsummer of 1871 ... New York, Baker & Goodwin, printers, 1871. 74 p. plates (part fold.) facsim. 23 cm. 1-14664 Rev.

F128.47.C58

CLINTON, Henry Lauren. Removal of County Clerk Gumbleton. Views of Henry L. Clinton, in regard to the action of Gov. Lucius Robinson ... (New York, 1879)   10 p. 23½ cm. 12-8203.

F128.47.C64

COSTALES, José de J. Guia del viajero en Nueva York, para el uso de los españoles é hispano-americanos. Ed. de bolsillo. Nueva York, Imprenta de E. Perez, 1878.   119, (7) p. front. (fold. map) 14 cm. 1-14666.

F128.47.C83

— 2. ed. 1879-80.   84, (12), 85-119, (7) p. front. (fold. map) illus. (plans) 14 cm. 1-14667.

F128.47.C84

— Nueva York, Vanden Houten, 1885.   63 p. fold. map. 16°   1-14665-M1.

F128.47.C85

CRANDALL, Charles Henry. The season, an annual record of society in New York, Brooklyn, and vicinity. First year, 1882-1883 ... New York, White, Stokes, & Allen, 1883.   427 p. 18½ cm. No more pub. 33-38655.

F128.47.C88

CROCKETT, Albert Stevens. Peacocks on parade; a narrative of a unique period in American social history and its most colorful fugures, ... New York, Sears pub. co. (1931)   xv, 314 p. front., plates, ports. 22½ cm. Descriptive of life in New York from 1890 to 1914, when the Peacock alley of the Waldorf-Astoria was at its height. 31-22625.

F128.47.C91

CROKER. Boss Croker's career. A review of the pugilistic and political activity of Bill Tweed's pupil and successor. With an appendix. Comparing the Croker ring with the Tweed ring and urging a union of all factions against Tammany hall. By Otto Kempner. (New York, The author, 1894) 29 p. illus. 19½ cm. 14-9069.

F128.47.C93

CROKER. Richard Croker, by Alfred Henry Lewis ... New York, Life pub. co., 1901. xv, 372 p. incl. front. 8 pl., 7 port. 21 cm. 1-20242 Rev.

F128.47.C94

CROKER. Master of Manhattan, the life of Richard Croker, by Lothrop Stoddard ... New York, Toronto, Longmans, Green, 1931.   vii, 279 p. plates, ports. (incl. front.) 22 cm. "First ed." Bibliography: p. 271-276. 31-6849.

F128.47.C95

DANA, Ethel Nathalie (Smith) Young in New York, a memoir of a Victorian girlhood. (1st ed.) Garden City, N.Y., Doubleday, 1963.   205 p. 22 cm. 63-16632.

F128.47.D3

DEUTSCHER wegweiser durch New-York und umgegend ... (New York) Tamsen & Dethlefs, 1873. 61, (3) p. fold. map. 16°. 1-14668-M1.

F128.47.D48

DISTURNELL, John. New York as it was and as it is; giving an account of the city from its settlement to the present time; forming a complete guide to the great metropolis of the nation, inc. the city of Brooklyn and the surrounding cities and villages; tog. with a classified business directory ... New York, D. Van Nostrand, 1876.   viii, (ix) - xii, 13-296 p. front., plates, maps (part fold.) 19 cm. 1-14672.
F128.47.D61

EUREKA lozenge manual, The. For 1876. (New York, C. L. Gunn, 1875)   36 p. 16°. A guide to N. Y. city combined with advertisements of Eureka lozenges. 1-14673-M1.
F128.47.E91

FANNING, B. How to get there. An instantaneous city guide. (New York, J. Polhemus) 1883. 3 p. fol. 1-14674-M1.
F128.47.F19

FERNÁNDEZ Juncos, Manuel. De Puerto-Rico a Madrid por la Habana y Nueva-York. Estudios de viaje. 2. ed. Puerto Rico, Tip, de J. G. Font, 1887.   2 p. (vii)-xiv p., 125 p. 18 cm. L. C. copy replaced by microfilm.
F128.47.F36
Microfilm 9461 F

— Puerto-Rico, Bibl. de "El Buscapie," 1886.   202 p. 18 cm. (With above.) 4-5125
F128.47.F36

FIFTY glimpses of New York. Fifty illus. from recent photos. New York, Mercantile illustrating co., 1893.   47 pl. 16½ x 22½ cm. 1-14675.
F128.47.F46

— Chicago and New York, Rand, McNally, 1896 (1895)   48 p. illus. obl. 16° 1-14676-M1.
F128.47.F47

5 CENT city railroad, stage, & ferry guide, The. Lists of hotels, places of amusement, depots, and map of New York city. New York, F. W. Bacon, 1868.   16 p. on verso, map on recto, of sheet. (21½ x 48 cm.) fold. to 11 cm. 2-25015.
F128.47.F52

GENUINE albertypes of rare photographs, New York city, 1885-1900, from the Leonard Hassam Bogart collection of Adolph Wittemann (1845-1938) original negatives; museum specimens. (Brooklyn, The Albertype co.) 1939.   37 pl. mounted on 36 l. 29 x 36 cm. 39-11284.
F128.47.G46
Rare Book Coll.

GOICOECHEA, Rafael de. Guia compendiada de la ciuded de New York y cercanias ... Ed de 1889 i 90. Nueva York, Wynkoop, Hallenbeck y ca. (1889)   207 p. fold. map. 24°. 1-14677-M1.
F128.47.G61

GOODNOW, Frank Johnson. The Tweed ring in New York city. London and New York, Macmillan, 1888.   p. 17-34. 20½ cm. 17-3665.
F128.47.G65

GREAT Empire city, The; or, High and low life in New York ... New York, F. M. Lupton, 1883. 64 p. illus., port. 4°. 1-14678-M1.
F128.47.G76

GREAT sound money parade in New York. New York, Republic press, 1897.   (5) - 243 p. illus., pl., ports. 25½ cm. 1-14679.
F128.47.G78

GREATER New York album. One hundred selected views. New York city, Brooklyn, Staten island, etc. From recent photos. Chicago and New York, Rand, McNally, 1895 (1894)   104 p. illus. 17 x 22 cm. 1-14740.
F128.47.G783

— 1895.   104 p. iillus. 17 x 22 cm. 1-14741.
F128.47.G784

GREATOREX, Eliza (Pratt) "Mrs. H. W. Greatorex" illus. Old New York, from the Battery to Bloomingdale. Etchings by Eliza Greatorex ... Text by M. Despard ... New York, G. P. Putnam's sons, 1875.   247 p. plates. 36½ cm. Issued in 10 parts. 1-14680.
F128.47.G79

GREEN, Andrew Haswell. Communication to the commissioners of the Central park, relative to the improvement of the Sixth and Seventh avenues, from the Central park to the Harlem river; the laying out of the island above 155th street; the drive from 59th st. to 155th st., and other subjects ... New York, W. C. Bryant, 1866.   75 p. 8°. 1-26412-M2.
F128.47.G795

FOLEY, John, of New York. Andrew H. Green & Thomas C. Fields. Secret management of the Central park commission. Extraordinary revelations. John Foley's letters to Mayor Havemeyer and the taxpayers of New York. New York, J. Polhemus, printer, 1874.   40 p.   23½ cm.   46-42064.
F128.47.G799

FOORD, John. The life and public services of Andrew Haswell Green ... Garden City, N.Y., Doubleday, Page, 1913.   x, 322 p., pl., 2 port. (incl. front.) 24 cm.   13-20569.
F128.47.G 8

GRIFFITH, E. T. Griffith's pocket directory and book of ready reference of New York city, with map in compartments and marginal guide to streets ... New York, J. Polhemus, printer, 1877.
iv, 72 p.   fold. map.   15½ cm.   11-13677.
F128.47.G85

... The GUESTS' handy-book and guide to prominent points of interest in New York ... New York, 1886.   1 v.   17½ x 10 cm.   Monthly.
F128.47.G93

GUIDE to Havana, Mexico and New York. A description of the principal cities of the island of Cuba and of Mexico ... Also Guia de Nueva York y los Estados Unidos ... By W. F. Smith & co.   New York, W. F. Smith & co., 1885.   78 p.   23½ cm.   Guide to Cuba and Mexico in English; guide to the U.S. in Spanish.   1-21494.
F128.47.G946

GUIDE to New York: its public buildings, places of amuseument, churches, hotels, etc. ... Also, a guide to the Hudson River, (with map) Saratoga and Lake George. New York, T. E. Zell, 1868.
9-159 p.   plates, fold. map.   15½ cm.   6-15416.
F128.47.G948

GUIDE to New York & vicinity. Containing banks, insurance companies, express offices, lines of steamboats, places of amusement, etc. ... Spring ed. (New York) J. D. Sheldon (1873)
(64) p.   24°.   1-22615-M1.
F128.47.G95

— (1873)   64 p.   24°.   1-22614-M1.
F128.47.G96

GUNNISON, Herbert Foster. A visitor's guide to the greater New York, Jersey City and suburbs; prepared for general circulation and especially for the members of the Young people's Christian union who will attend the annual convention in Jersey City in July, 1896. ... (Brooklyn, N.Y., Eagle press) 1896.   96 p.   illus. (incl. maps)   23 cm.   Cover title: The gate to the sea.   18-17138.
F128.47.G963

— (Brooklyn, N.Y., Eagle press) 1896.   88 p.   illus. (incl. maps)   23½ cm.   1-14743.
F128.47.G97

HALL, Abraham Oakey. The elegant Oakey. By Croswell Bowen. New York, Oxford University Press, 1956.   292 p.   illus.   22 cm.   Includes bibliography.   56-10456.
F128.47.H19B6

HAND-BOOK to New York city ... New York, Hunt & Eaton, 1891.   24 p.   fold. map.   nar. 8°.   1-14681-M1
F128.47.H22

HANDY information about New York. (New York, McKay & co., 1886)   10 p.   32°.   2-6822.
F128.47.H23

HARRIS, Charles Townsend. Memories of Manhattan in the sixties and seventies. New York, The Derrydale press, 1928.   xiv, 125 p.   front., plates, ports.   24 cm.   28-16219.
F128.47.H29

HARRISON, Constance (Cary) "Mrs. Burton Harrison" History of the city of New York: externals of modern New York ... Being chapter xxi, vol. ii, of Mrs. Martha J. Lamb's History of the city of New York. New York, A. S. Barnes (1896)   2, 789-874 p.   front. (map) illus., plates.   27 cm.   1-14682.
F128.47.H31

(HARRISON, Frank) How to have a good time in and about New York. A complete alphabetically arranged guide to all places of interest, amusements, resorts, etc., in and about New York city ... Summer ed. Revised every three months. New York, N.Y. cheap pub. co. (1885)   46, (14) p.   13 cm.   1-22565 Rev.
F128.47.H34

HAYES, M. Vincent. Nostalgic New York. F128.47.H37

HEWITT. Unveiling of the statue of Abram S. Hewitt in the Chamber of commerce of the state of New York. Address by Charles Stewart Smith. New-York, Press of the Chamber of commerce, 1905.
65 p. front., pl., port. 25½ cm. 10-7629. F128.47.H59

(HOBBS, Charles W.) Illustrated New York city and surroundings. A descriptive guide to places of interest. With map. New York, C. W. Hobbs, 1889. 125, (4) p. front., illus., fold. plan. 17½ cm.
1-14683. F128.47.H68

HOW New York is governed. Frauds of the Tammany Democrats. New York, New York daily Times, 1871. 16 p. 26 cm. 12-4239. F128.47.H84

HOW to see New York city, Central park, Coney Island, Rockaway beach. With street directory, list of churches, hotels, theatres, etc. (New York) 1882. 39, (3), 78 p. 32°. Copyright by C. W. Hobbs.
1-14684-M1. F128.47.H85

HOWELLS, William Dean. Letters of an Altrurian traveller, 1893-94. A facsimile reproduction with an introd. by Clara M. Kirk and Rudolph Kirk. Gainesville, Fla., Scholars' Facsimiles & Reprints, 1961. 127 p. (p. 13-127 facsim.) 23 cm. 61-5081. F128.47.H86 1961a

INGERSOLL, Ernest. A week in New York. Illus. by Geo. Spiel and others. New York, Chicago, Rand, McNally, 1891. 328 p. illus., plates. 17½ x 14 cm. 1-14685. F128.47.I 47

— Rand, McNally, 1892. 328 p. illus., plates, fold. map. 17½ x 13½ cm. 1-14686. F128.47.I 48

JENNINGS, Napoleon Augustus, comp. New York in the blizzard; being an authentic and comprehensive recital of the circumstances and conditions which surrounded the metropolis in the great storm of March 12, 1888. ... New York, Rogers & Sherwood (1888) (39) p. 23 cm. 1-14687.
F128.47.J 54

KENNY'S guide, containing full information as to railroads, steamboats and their time tables; hotels and their charges; art galleries; theatres ... public institutions, etc. New York, F. H. Kenny, 1889.
2 v. v. 1, no. 1, 3. 4°. 1-14688-M1. F128.47.K34

KING, Moses. King's handbook of New York city; an outline history and description of the American metropolis; with over 800 illus. ... Boston, Mass. (1892) 928 p. illus. (incl. plans) 20½ cm. 1-14689.
F128.47.K51

— Boston, Mass. (1893) 1008 p. illus. (incl. plans) 20½ cm. 1-14690. F128.47.K52

KING, Moses. ... King's New York views ... Boston, M. King, 1895. 24 illus. p. fol. "Supplementary to King's handbook of New York city." 1-14691-M1. F128.47.K53

KING, Moses. ... King's photographic views of New York. 450 illustrations. A souvenir companion to King's handbook of New York city. Boston, M. King, 1895. 720 p. illus., fold. map. 19 cm.
1-14692. F128.47.K54

(KING, Moses) New York; the metropolis of the American continent, the foremost city of the world.
Boston, M. King (1894) 56 p. illus. 26 cm. 1-16798. F128.47.K56

(KING, Moses) New York; the American cosmopolis, the foremost city of the world. Boston, M. King (1894) 80 p. illus. 25½ cm. 1-16799. F128.47.K57

KOBBÉ, Gustav. New York and its environs ... New York, Harper & bros., 1891. 282 p. incl. front., plates, 3 fold. maps, plans. 16 cm. 1-14693. F128.47.K75

LEO, Emil. Was findet der auswanderer in Amerika? Wahrheitsgetreue schilderungen nach eigener erfahrung, Essen a. d. Ruhr, C. Erdmann, 1883.   45 p.   18½ cm.   Advice to emigrants, based on the personal experiences of the author in New York city. 18-880.   F128.47.L57

(LINTON, William James) The house that Tweed built; dedicated to every true reformer (Republican or Democrat) ... (Cambridge, Mass., The author, 1871)   23 p. illus. 21 cm. In verse. 17-22841 Rev.
F128.47.L76
Rare Book Coll.

LLOYD, Thomas. Lloyd's pocket companion and guide through New York city, for 1866-67. Pub. by Thomas Lloyd ... New York, Torrey bros., printers, 1866.   v, 6-150 p. front., 1 illus., plates. 19 cm. 1-14694.   F128.47.L79

(LONGCHAMP, Ferdinand) Asmodeus in New York ... New York, Longchamp & co., 1868.
vii, (9) - 378 p.   18 cm.   4-12731.   F128.47.L85

(LONGCHAMP, Ferdinand) Asmodée à New-York: revue critique des institutions politiques et civiles de l'Amérique, vie publique et privée, moeurs, coutumes, anecdotes romanesques, etc. ... Paris, H. Plon, 1868.   2, 503 p.   24 cm.   4-12732.   F128.47.L86

LOW, Seth. New York in 1850 and in 1890. A political study. An address delivered before the New York historical soc. on its 87th anniversary ... New York, Printed for the Society, 1892.
32 p.   24½ cm.   1-14695.   F128.47.L91

M, A. B. Guia de la ciudad de Nueva York ... Nueva York, N. Ponce de Leon, 1872.   viii, 236 p.
pl., fold. map.   16°.   1-14696-M1.   F128.47.M11

McCABE, James Dabney. Lights and shadows of New York life; or, The sights and sensations of the great city. A work descriptive of the city of New York in all its various phases ... illus. with numerous fine engravings of notes places, life and scenes in New York ... Philadelphia, Chicago (etc.) National pub. co. (1872)   13-850 p.   front., illus., plates, ports. 22½ cm. 1-14697.   F128.47.M13
Rare Book Coll.

— London, Deutsch, 1971.   (2), 11-856 p. 7 plates. illus., ports. 22 cm. Facsimile of 1st ed. 72-882831 MARC.
F128.47.M13
1872a

— Facsimile ed. New York, Farrar, Straus and Giroux (1970)   850 p. illus. 22 cm. 76-130325.
F128.47.M13
1970

McCABE, James Dabney. New York by sunlight and gaslight. A work descriptive of the great American metropolis ... Philadelphia, Douglass bros; Chicago, H. N. Hinckley, etc., 1882.
xviii, 33-672 p. front., illus. (incl. ports.) plates. 22 cm. 1-14698.   F128.47.M14

(McCABE, James Dabney) The secrets of the great city; a work descriptive of the virtues and the vices, the mysteries, miseries, and crimes of New York city. By Edward Winslow Martin (pseud.) Philadelphia, Chicago (etc.) Jones bros. & co. (1868)   2, 15-552 p. plates (part fold.) 22½ cm. 1-14699.
F128.47.M15

— Microfilm. Ann Arbor, Mich., University Microfilms, 1965.   1 reel. 35 mm. (American culture series 289:5)   Microfilm 01291 reel 289, no. 5 E

MACOY, Robert. Centennial. Illustrated. How to see New York and its environs 1776 ... 1876. A complete guide and hand-book of useful information, collected from the latest reliable resources. New York, R. Macoy (1875)   108 p. illus., fold. map. 12°. 1-14700-M1.   F128.47.M17

MALGÁ Victor. Guia de Nueva York, para el uso de los viajeros españoles é hispano-americanos ... New York, 1880.   220 p. fold. map. 16°. 1-14701-M1.   F128.47.M24

MANDELBAUM, Seymour J. Boss Tweed's New York. (New York, J. Wiley, 1965)   ix, 196 p. 22 cm.
(New dimensions in history: historical cities) 65-16417.   F128.47.M28

MANHATTAN steamboat guide and manual of New York harbor. N.Y., 1889.   4th year.
F128.47.M3

MARKS, Harry Hananel. Small change; or, Lights and shades of New York. New York, The Standard pub. co., 1882.   96 p. 19½ cm. "The sketches... depict... phases of life in New York, as seen by a newspaper reporter... consists literally of leaves from a reporter's note book." 1-14702 Rev.
F128.47.M34

MAURICE, Arthur Bartlett. New York in fiction ... New York, Dodd, Mead, 1901.   xviii, 231 p. incl. front., illus., pl. 21 cm. 2-22452.
F128.47.M45

MAURICE, Arthur Bartlett. The New York of the novelists ... New York, Dodd, Mead, 1916. xxii, 366 p. front., plates. 22 cm. 16-22308.
F128.47.M454

The METROPOLIS explained and illustrated in familiar form, with a map. New York, Devlin and co., 1871.   viii, (9)-61 p. incl. front., illus., fold. map. 16 cm. Map in pocket. 1-14703.
F128.47.M59

MISCHKE, H. New-Yorker Bädeker. Führer durch New-York und umgegend. (New York, 1880) 199, (iv) p. pl., fold. map. 24°. 1-14704-M1.
F128.47.M67

MORFORD, Henry. The practical guide to New York city and Brooklyn ... New York, Union news co. (etc.) London, Trübner & co. (1877)   51 p. 12°. 1-14705-M1.
F128.47.M84

MURDOCH, Augustus, comp. Ladies' shopping guide. Alphabetically arranged and compiled by Aug. Murdoch ... New York, Wynkoop & Hallenbeck, 1872.   64 p. 10½ cm. Includes lists of public buildings, churches, etc. 22-15630.
F128.47.M95

NATIONAL co-operative exchange, New York (City) Daily routes. How to see New York ... New York (National co-operative exchange) 1887.   33 p. 8 x 14½ cm. Copyrighted by Ashby & Van De Carr. 3-5259.
F128.47.N27

NEW YORK. (New York, A. Wittemann, 1886)   20 pl. (fold.) 16°. 1-14707-M1.
F128.47.N52

NEW YORK City, and how to see it: being a compilation of the principal places of interest in the city ... New York, American news co., 1869.   28 p. 24°. 1-14709-M1.
F128.47.N55

NEW YORK city council of political reform. Five reports. 1. - Surface street railroads: value of their franchises; profits; taxation. 2. - A Tammany permit bureau. 3. - Sectarian appropriations of public money. 4. - The exposure of the Tammany frauds, and 5. - Duty of the state to protect the free common schools by amendments to the Constitution. New York, Evening post steam presses (1873)   24, 16, 10, 7 p. 22½ cm. Reports signed: Dexter A. Hawkins. 12-10061.
F128.47.N553

NEW YORK city council of political reform. ... Official document on extravagance of the Tammany ring. Over $50,000,000 a year spent and no accounts rendered. (New York, 1871)   10 p. 22½ cm. 12-7864.
F128.47.N554

NEW YORK city in your vest pocket. Directory of notable features ... Roxbury, Mass., O. Schumm, 1890.   76 p. fold. map. 48° 1-14710-M1.
F128.47.N56
Map div.

NEW YORK. Commercial travelers' club. Progress and prospects of New York, the first city of the world. 1492-1893. New York, Commercial travelers' club, 1893.   4, 200 p. illus., port. fol. 1-14711-M1.
F128.47.N57

NEW YORK illustrated. New York, D. Appleton, 1869.   52 p. illus., fold. map. 25½ cm. 1-14745.
F128.47.N575

— (New ed., with revisions and new illus.) New York, D. Appleton (1872?)   67 p. illus., fold. map. 25½ cm. 1-14746.
F128.47.N576

— (1874)   74 p. illus., fold. map. 25 cm. 1-14747.
F128.47.N577

NEW YORK CITY

— (1875)   72 p.   illus., fold. map.   25½ cm.   1-14748   F128.47.N578

— (Revised to date, with new illus.) 1877.   70 p.   illus., fold. map.   25½ cm. 1-14749 Rev.
     F128.47.N579

— 1878.   86 p.   illus., fold. map.   25½ cm.   1-14750 Rev.   F128.47.N58

NEW YORK illustrated: a pictorial delineation of street scenes, buildings, river views, and other features of the great metropolis. New York, D. Appleton, 1881.   iv, (5) - 156 p.   front. (fold. plan) illus. 26 cm. 1-14751.   F128.47.N581

— 1885.   iv, (5) - 144 p.   2 front. (fold. maps) illus.   26½ cm.   1-14752 Rev.   F128.47.N582

— 1890.   120 p.   illus., fold. maps.   26 cm.   1-14753.   F128.47.N583

NEW YORK illustrated. (New York, D. Appleton, 1872)   56 p.   illus., fold. map.   25½ cm.   Issued also in English. 1-14754.   F128.47.N585

NUEVA YORK illustrada. Nueva York, D. Appleton, 1874.   76p. illus., fold. map.   26½ cm.   Issued also in English. 1-14755.   F128.47.N587

NUEVA YORK ilustrada; descripción de lo más notable que hay en la ciudad de Nueva York y en sus alrededores. Ed. española arreglada según la última ed. de Appleton por Eduardo Molina ... Nueva York, D. Appleton, 1886.   166 p.   fronts. (fold. maps) illus.   26½ cm.   1-14756.   F128.47.N588

— 1900.   162 p.   fronts. (fold. maps) illus., plates.   26½ cm.   Issued also in English.   0-4848 Rev.   F128.47.N589

NEW YORK und Philadelphia. Ein führer für alle diejenigen, welche die weltausstellung zu Philadelphia besuchen und auch New York berühren ... New York, S. Zickel (1876)   136 p. incl. front., illus. map, plans. 16°. 1-23468-M1.   F128.47.N5897

NEWBERRY, John Strong. Geography of New York city and vicinity, a supplement to the Eclectic series of geographies ... (Cincinnati, Van Antwerp, Bragg & co., 1878)   14 p. incl. illus., map. fol. 1-16877-M1.   F128.47.N59

NICHOLS, Francis H., comp. Nichols' pocket guide of the New York elevated railroad, Broadway, Fifth ave., etc., 1891 ... Brooklyn, N.Y. (F. H. Nichols) 1890-91.   68 p.   16°.   1-14712-M1.   F128.47.N67

The NIGHT side of New York. A picture of the great metropolis after nightfall. By members of the New York press. Illus. by Frank Beard. New York, J. C. Haney, 1866.   121 p, incl. illus., pl. 18½ cm. 1-14739 Rev.   F128.47.N68

OBER, Mrs. Corolyn Faville. Manhattan: historic and artistic; a six day tour of New York city. New York, Lovell, Coryell (1892)   x, 232 p. front., illus., 4 plans (1 fold.) 18 cm.   Pub. in 1897 under title: The Greater New York guide book. 1-14759.   F128.47.O12

OBER, Corlyn Faville. The Greater New York guide book. Manhattan historic and artistic; a six-day tour. (Rev. ed.) New York, Boston (etc.) The Morse co. (1897)   275 p. illus., maps. 12°. 1-14760-M1.   F128.47.O13

(OGDEN, Robert Curtis) New York city and how to see it; a complete pocket guide to all places of interest, with much other valuable information for strangers and residents. New York, Hurd & Houghton, 1876.   vi, (7) - 69 p. incl. front., illus., double plan) 1-14713 Rev.   F128.47.O34

PANORAMA of New York, Brooklyn, and vicinity. New York, Wittemann bros. (1879)   1 pl. fold. in 12. obl. 32°. 1-14714-M1.   F128.47.P18

PARTON, James. How New York city is governed. ... Boston, Ticknor and Fields, 1866. 48 p. 17½ cm. "Reprinted from the North American review." 11-32021.   F128.47.P27

PEOPLES free guide to New York city ... New York, Peoples advertising and publishing co. (1894)
94 p.   19½ cm.   2d ed.   1-14715 Rev.
F128.47.P41

(PERCY, Randolph T.) ... "Who was G. W?" being a truthful tale of the Seventh regiment in the armory, during the railroad strikes in July, 1877. Reprinted from "The World." New-York, 1879.
86 p.   18 cm.   ("Out of the World" series, no. iv)   5-37655.
F128.47.P47

PICTORIAL New York and Brooklyn; a guide to the same, and vicinity ... New York, Smith, Bleakley, (1892)   175 p. incl. front., illus. maps (part fold.)   26½ cm.   Text by Charles Lotin Hildreth and Frederic Lyster. Illus. mostly by George Smith.   1-14716.
F128.47.P61

(PIERSON, Frank W.) Business and pleasure; an illus. description of the chief points of interest in New York city and vicinity ... Newark, N.J., Illustro engr. co., 1891.   48 p. illus. 16°. 1-14717-M1.
F128.47.P62

POMEROY, Mark M. Here we are! In New York city. By Brick Pomeroy (pseud.) Recitative, descriptive, suggestive, remunerative, and preservative ... New York, L. E. Adams, 1887.
75 p.   2 pl.   8°.   1-14718-M1.
F128.47.P75

PORTER, Fitz-John. Fitz John Porter, commissioner of public works, to Andrew H. Green, comptroller of the city of New York. (New York) 1875.   35 p.   23 cm.   A criticism of the work of Green as comptroller.   20-2082.
F128.47.P84

(POST, Eugene J.) The wig and the jimmy: or, A leaf in the political history of New York ... New York, The author, 1869.   32 p.   ports.   23 cm.   6-27397.
F128.47.P85

POST, Louis Freeland. An account of the George-Hewitt campaign in the New York municipal election of 1886. New York, John W. Lovell co. (1886)   ix, (3) - 193 p. 18½ cm. 13-22182.
F128.47.P87

(PRESCOTT, Charles Edwin) ed. The hotel guests' guide for the city of New York. 1871-2. New York, W. P. Cleary, 1871.   xii, (2), 5-187 p. 23½ cm. 1-14719.
F128.47.P91

— 2d ed. New York, G. W. Averell, 1872.   12 p.   19 - 165 p.   23½ cm.   1-14720.
F128.47.P92

PRESCOTT, Charles Edwin. New York; its past and present, compiled for the exclusive use of the traveling public. New York, Mercantile pub. co., 1874.   174 p. 23 cm. 1-14721.
F128.47.P93

RAND, McNally & co.'s complete city railway and street number guide of New York city. Chicago and New York, Rand, McNally & co. (1896)   2, 107 p. fold. map. 24°. 1-14722-M1.
F128.47.R18

RAWSON, A. L. A bygone Bohemia ... (1896)   1 v.
F128.47.R23

REDFIED, J. S. Redfield Traveler's guide to the city of New York ... New York, J. S. Redfield, 1871.
108 p.   front. (fold. map)   16 cm.   1-14723 Rev.
F128.47.R25

RITTIG, Johann. Federzeichnungen aus dem amerikanischen stadtleben. 2. aufl. New York, E. Steiger, 1885.   viii, 249 p. 20½ cm. 3-681.
F128.47.R61

ROGERS, Ebenezer Platt. The glory of New York: a discourse delivered in the South reformed church ... New York, U.S. publishing co., 1874.   18 p.   23 cm.   1-14725.
F128.47.R72

ROOSEVELT, Robert Barnwell. Is Democracy dishonest? Are four men to rule New York with a rod of iron? Is the popular voice to be stifled at the ballot-box? ... A Democrat defends Democracy. New York, Journeymen printers' co-operative assoc., 1871.   4 p.   23½ cm.   12-9120.
F128.47.R78

ROOSEVELT. Theodore Roosevelt, senior, a tribute; the proceedings at a meeting of the Union league club ... New York, Pub. by request, 1902.   2 2 p., 9-27 p. front. (port.) 22 cm. Reprint, with preface by William E. Dodge. 3-940 Rev.

F128.47.R79

ROSS, Ishbel. Crusades and crinolines; the life and times of Ellen Curtis Demorest and William Jennings Demorest. (1st ed.) New York, Harper & Row (1963)   x, 290 p. 22 cm. 62-20116.

F128.47.R83

RUGGLES, Samuel Bulkley. The rise and growth of the metropolis. (Letters on rapid transit ...) New York, J. W. Amerman, 1875.   16 p. 8°. 1-20002-M1.

F128.47.R93

(ST. JOHN, Oliver Starr) The downfall of Tammany hall no fall at all. Not by A. Oakey Hall. New-York, St. John & Coffin, 1871.   24 p. 19 cm. In verse. Cartoon on cover by Thomas Nast. 18-13606.

F128.47.S14

(SCHADE van Westrum, Adriaan) New York. New York (etc.) Brentano's (1890)   25 l. 25 pl. 20½ x 25½ cm. (Views of American cities) 1-14706 Add.

F128.47.S29

SELECT New York. Illustrated in albertype. New York, A. Wittemann (1889)   1 p., 55 pl. obl. 12°. 1-14761.

F128.47.S443

SELECT New York. One hundred albertype illustrations. New York, A. Wittemann (1890)   100 pl. obl. 8°. 1-14762-M1.

F128.47.S444

— Brooklyn, N.Y., A. Wittemann, 1898.   102 pl. 20 x 25½ cm. 1-14763.

F128.47.S448

SHEPP, James W. Shepp's New York city illustrated. Scene and story in the metropolis of the western world ... Chicago, Ill., Philadelphia, Pa., Globe Bible pub. co. (1894)   528 p. illus. (incl. ports., map) 22½ x 27 cm. 1-14726.

F128.47.S49

SMITH, Matthew Hale. Sunshine and shadow in New York. (Burleigh.) ... Hartford, J. B. Burr, 1868.   712 p. front., plates. 22½ cm. 1-14387. L. C. copy replaced by microfilm.

F128.47.S65
Microfilm 21707 F

— 1869.   718 p. front., plates. 23 cm. 29-15908.

F128.47.S65
1869

— Microfilm. Ann Arbor, Mich., University Microfilms, 1965.   1 reel, 35 mm. (American culture series, 289-6)

Microfilm 01291 reel 289 no.6 E

— 1879.   854 p. plates. 23 cm. 50-46411.

F128.47.S65
1879

SMITH, Matthew Hale. Wonders of a great city; or, The sights, secrets and sins of New York, being a wonderful portrayal of the varied phases of life in the greatest city of America ...

F128.47.S67

(STIRLING, Edmund) A descriptive reading on New York city, illus. by twelve lantern slides. Philadelphia, W. H. Rau, 1889.   95 - 105 p. 18½ cm. One of a number of "readings forming part of an intended comprehensive work, to accompany lantern slides ... 1-22589 Rev.

F128.47.S84

(STODDARD, William Osborn) The royal decress of Scanderoon. Dedicated by the author to the sachems of Tammany, and to the other grand magnorums of Manhattan. New York, Russells' American steam print., 1869.   45 p. 5 pl. (incl. front.) 18 cm. 15-4527.

F128.47.S85

(STODDARD, William Osborn) The volcano under the city, by a volunteer special ... with map showing New York police precincts. New York, Fords, Howard & Hulbert, 1887.   350 p. front. (fold. map) 17½ cm. An account of the draft-riot of 1863, New York. L. C. copy replaced by microfilm. 1-14727.

F128.47.S86
Microfilm 22636 F

The STRANGERS' guide; and complete hand-book through the city of New York ... New York, Brown & Forster, 1865.   42 p.   fold. map.   14 cm.   2-19054.   F128.47.S88

— New York, D. W. Sisson, 1871.   46 p.   24°.   1-14728-M1.   F128.47.S89

STRONG, Samuel Meredith, comp.   The great blizzard of 1888 ... arrangement by Marion Overton. (Brooklyn, 1938)   xi, 99 p. incl. front., illus.   23 cm.   A collection of "interesting memories of men and women who survived the storm."   38-7546.   F128.47.S897

The SUN'S guide to New York.   Replies to questions asked every day by the guests and citizens of the American metropolis ... (Jersey City, The Jersey City printing co.) 1892.   3, 386 p.   illus. (incl. facsims.) double plans.   20 cm.   Compiled by Colin H. Livingstone.   1-14730.   F128.47.S93

SUVOROV, princess.   ... Quarante jours à New-York; impressions de voyage.   Paris, E. Dentu, 1878.   3, 170 p.   18 cm.   5-13234.   F128.47.S96

SVENSK illustrerad vägvisare öfver New York, Brooklyn, och dess omgifningar.   New York, Wretlind & Kassman, 1881.   133, (13) p.   illus.   8°.   1-14729-M1.   F128.47.S963

SWEETSER, Moses Foster.   ... How to know New York city.   A serviceable and trustworthy guide ... 3d ed.   Boston, Rand, Avery (1887)   (5) - 122 p.   fold. map.   15 x 11 ½ cm.   1-14731.   F128.47.S97

— 7th ed.   New York, 1889.   14 ½ cm.   F128.47.S972

TAMMANY society, or Columbian order.   Address of Tammany hall to the electors of the country. (New York, 1875)   8 p.   17 ½ cm.   12-9121.   F128.47.T15

TELLER, Alfred H.   Nueva York.   Descripción completa de la gran metrópoli americana y guía á sus numerosos lugares de interés ...   Nueva York, Vanden Houten, 1891.   160 p.   plates.   18 x 14 cm.   1-14732.   F128.47.T27

TOBIN, M. F.   A day in New York and where to spend it ... (New York, Vernon & son, 1883)   (46) p.   obl. 48°.   1-14733-M1.   F128.47.T62

(TOMLINSON, Theodore E.)   The United States party.   The United States democracy; its religion: "Peace and good will towards men," Its platform: "The Union, the Constitution, and the laws." Its motto: "Not for ourselves, but for our country."   New-York, E. S. Kellett, printer, 1866. 19 p.   17 ½ cm.   12-9122.   F128.47.T65

TREAT's illustrated New York, Brooklyn, and surroundings.   New York, E. B. Treat, 1874. 100 p.   illus.,   map.   8°.   1-14734-M1.   F128.47.T78

TWEED.   "Boss" Tweed; the story of a grim generation, by Denis Tilden Lynch.   New York, Boni and Liveright, 1927.   ix, 13-433 p.   front., plates, ports.   22 ½ cm.   Bibliography: p. 419-423.   27-20559.   F128.47.T96

(TYLER, Daniel F.)   Why vote at all in '72? ...   New York, Printed for the author, G. P. Putnam, 1872.   60 p.   18 ½ cm.   12-9123.   F128.47.T98

(VALENTINE, Ferdinand Charles)   Gotham and the Gothamites, by Heinrich Oscar von Karlstein (pseud.)   Tr. by F. C. Valentine ...   Chicago, Laird & Lee (1886)   10, (17) - 179 p.   20 cm.   1-21582 Add. L. C. copy replaced by microfilm.   F128.47.V15
                                                                                  Microfilm 15466 F

VAN WYCK.   Recollections of an old New Yorker, Frederick Van Wyck; illus. by Matilda Browne. New York, Liveright, inc. (1932)   xvi, 421 p. incl. front. (port.) illus.   24 ½ cm.   Covers the period from 1860. 32-34827.   F128.47.V18

VIEWS of New York.   (New York. Photo-gravure co., 1887)   12 p.   obl. 48°.   1-14735-M1.
                                                                                     F128.47.V67

NEW YORK CITY

VISITOR'S guide to the city of New York. For the use of the guests of the Fifth avenue hotel. New York, J. F. Trow, printers (1866) 36 p. fold. map. 15½ cm. 18-6577. F128.47.V83

WALLING, Henry Francis. The city of New York. A complete guide. With descriptive sketches of objects and places of interest. With map ... New York, Taintor bros., 1867. 2, 34 p. fold. map. 16 cm. 1-22202. F128.47.W21

(WEIDEMEYER, John William) New York city. Philadelphia, J. B. Lippincott, 1891. 13 p. 12°. Appears as article "New York city" in Chambers's encyclopedia. London, etc. 1891-93. v.7. 1-14736-M1. F128.47.W41

WEINSTEIN, Gregory. Reminiscences of an interesting decade, the ardent eighties ... with a foreword by Lillian D. Wald ... New York, The International press (1928) xiv, (2), 182 p. front., plates, ports. 21 cm. 28-29977. F128.47.W43

— (3d ed.) New York, International Press (1947) xix, 242 p. illus., ports. 21 cm. First pub. in 1928 under title: Reminiscences of an interesting decade, the ardent eighties. 48-424*. F128.47.W43 1947

WEISS, Nancy Joan. Charles Francis Murphy, 1858-1924: respectability and responsibility in Tammany politics. Northampton, Mass., Smith College, 1968. x, 139 p. 24 cm. (The Edwin H. Land prize essays) 67-21037. F128.47.W45

WEITENKAMPT, Frank. ... Manhattan kaleidoscope ... New York, C. Scribner's sons; London, C. Scribner's sons, 1947. 7, 3-290 p. 21½ cm. 47-30088. F128.47.W46

WERSTEIN, Irving. The blizzard of '88. New York, Crowell (1960) 157 p. 22 cm. 60-11544. F128.47.W48

(WHITE, Richard Grant) The chronicles of Gotham. By the author of "The new gospel of peace" ... New York, G. W. Carleton; London, S. Low, 1871-72. 2 v. 18½ cm. Paged continuously. in Biblical language. 1-14325. F128.47.W58

WOHLMUTH, Alois. Newyorker kunst-und strassenbilder. Neue folge der Streifzüge eines deutschen comödianten." Wien, Wallishausser, 1883. 2, 86 p. 8°. 1-14737-M1. F128.47.W84

WOOD'S illustrated hand-book to New York and environs. A guide for the traveller or resident ... New York, G. W. Carleton, etc., 1873. ix, (2), (13)-215 p. incl. front., illus., plans. 16½ cm. 1-14738. F128.47.W87

WRIGHT, Mrs. Mable (Osgood) My New York; illus. by Ivin Sickels, 2d. New York, The Macmillan co., 1926. vii, 276 p. illus. 19½ cm. 26-7079. F128.47.W93

NEW YORK CITY. 1901 - 1950. GREATER NEW YORK.

BAILEY, Vernon Howe. Skyscrapers of New York, with an introd. by Cass Gilbert. New York, W. E. Rudge, 1928. (6) p. front., 23 pl. 42½ cm. 28-13459. F128.5 NA735.N5 B2

BERNARD, Marius. Au pays des dollars, ... Paris, C. Lévy, 1893. 3, 308 p. 18 cm. 11-34229. F128.5 E168. B 52

(CARTER, John Franklin) La Guardia: a biography by Jay Franklin (pseud.) research by Joseph C. Bailey. New York, Modern age books (1937) 3, 176 p. 20 cm. "Owing to objections made by Mayor La Guardia, a portion of the text on paged 58 and 74 has been excised." 37-34605. F128.5 E748. L23 C3

CASCABEL, Cesar.   ... Broadway.   Santiaco (!) Chile (etc.) Nascimento, 1927.   3, (9) - 168 p.
19 cm. (Colección Millaray)   29-1777.
F128.5
E169. C 33

(CRANSTON, Mrs. Ruth)   The meccas of the world; the play of modern life in New York, Paris, Vienna, Madrid and London, by Anne Warwick (pseud.) ... New York, John Lane co., 1913.
7, 3-259 p. front., plates. 22 ½ cm.   English ed. pub. under title: My cosmopolitan years...   13-25637 Rev.
F128.5
D429. C 7

(CRANSTON, Mrs. Ruth)   My cosmopolitan year, by the author of "Mastering flame": with nineteen illustrations.   London, Mills & Boon (1913)   xi, 289 p. front., plates. 22 ½ cm.   See above item.   13-22519 Rev. 2.
F128.5
D429. C 72

CROCOMBE, Leonard Cecil.   An editor goes west; a holiday notebook.   London (etc.) G. G. Harrap (1938)   255 p. front. (port.) 22 ½ cm.   "First pub. 1938."   39-6912.
F128.5
F1015. C 93

DREISER, Theodore.   My city; illus. with eight etchings in color by Max Pollak.   New York, H. Liveright (1929)   18 l. incl. col. illus., col. plates (1 double) 39 cm.   30-709.
F128.5
PS3507. R55M8 1929

FITCH, George Hamlin.   The critic in the Occident ...   Illus. from photos.   San Francisco, P. Elder (1913)   3, v-xx, 177 p. mounted front., plates (part mounted) 21 cm.   "Most of the chapters of this book appeared originally in the Sunday supplement of the San Francisco chronicle."   (Contains a chapter on N. Y.)   13-21732.
F128.5
D921. F 65

FRAU MARSAL, Lorenzo E.   ... La Babel de hierro.   New York-Habana, Graphic press of Cuba, 1918.   216 p. 20 cm.   20-12290.
F128.5
F169. F 84

GORDON, H. Panmure.   The land of the almighty dollar; the illus. by Irving Montagu.   London and New York, F. Warne (pref. 1892)   4, 215 p. incl. illus., plates. front. (port.) 21 cm.   2-1382.
F128.5
E168. G 66

HUMPHREYS, Mrs. Eliza M. J. (Gollan)   America - through English eyes; by "Rita" (Mrs. Desmond Humphreys) ... London, S. Paul (1910)   246 p. front. (port.) 19 ½ cm.   11-24691.
F128.5
E168. H 927

HUNGERFORD, Edward.   Pathway of empire; with an introd. by Dixon Ryan Fox ... New York, R. M. McBride (1935)   xv, 325 p. front., plates. 22 ½ cm.   "First edition."   "A picture of New York state of today ..."   35-27410.
F128.5
F124. H 92

(JEANNERET-GRIS, Charles Édouard)   ... Quand les cathédrales étaient blanches, voyages au pays des timides; avec 45 croquis dans le texte.   Paris, Plon (1937)   4, 11, 325 p. incl. illus., plates. 20½ cm.
Author's pseud., Le Corbusier, at head of title.   37-18573 Rev.
F128.5
E169.1. J 43

KLEIN, Henry H.   Politics, government and the public utilities in New York city ... (New York, Isaac Goldmann, 1933)   195 p. 21 cm.   "Articles, letters, statemenst and leaflets written by the author and speeches delivered by him ... between 1914 and 1932."   33-9694.
F128.5
HD2767. N75N56

LAUZANNE, Stéphane Joseph Vincent.   ... Instantannes d'Amérique.   Paris, F. Juven (1908)
vi, 268 p. 19 cm.   9-10315.
F128.5
E168. L 36

NEW YORK CITY

LEITICH, Ann Tizia. ... Amerika, du hast es besser. Wien, Steyrermühl, 1926.   192 p. 19 cm.
27-21177.   F128.5
   E169. L 53

LIMPUS, Lowell M. This man La Guardia. New York, E. P. Dutton, 1938.   429 p. front., ports.
22½ cm. "First edition." 38-31192.   F128.5
   E748. L23L5

LOW. ... The death of Seth Low; with biographical sketch, an account of his funeral, and a report of the memorial exercises in the City hall of New York.   (In American scenic and historic preservation society.
22d annual report, 1917. 18-5180.   F128.5.L
   E151.A 51 vol. 22

MULLER, Hans Alexander. Woodcuts of New York; pages from a diary. New York city, J. J. Augustine (1938)   lxix, (2) p. incl. illus., plates. 24 cm. "Translation by Paul Standard." 38-34577.   F128.5
   NE1217. M8A33

(NEWLIN, Mrs. Ruth (Cranston) The meccas of the world; the play of modern life in New York, Paris, Vienna, Madrid and London, by Anne Warwick (pseud.) ... New York, John Lane co., 1913.
7, 3-259 p. front., plates. 22½ cm. English ed. pub. under title: My cosmopolitan year. 13-25637.   F128.5
   D429. N 4

(NEWLIN, Mrs. Ruth (Cranston) My cosmopolitan year, by the author of "Mastering flame"; with nineteen illus. London, Mills & Boon (1913)   xi, 289 p. front., plates. 22½ cm. See above item. 13-22519 Rev.
   F128.5
   D429. N 5

SWAHN, Waldemar. Med de blågula färgerna över Atlanten ... Stockholm, P. A. Norstedt (1916)
viii, 185 p. illus. 20 cm. 38-25010.   F128.5
   G540. S 9

PENNELL, Joseph. The great New York. Boston, Le Roy Phillips (1912)   2 p., mounted illus., xxiv mounted pl. 20½ cm. Imperfect: pl. xxiv wanting. 33-176.   F128.5
   NE2210. P4 A25

PERRIN, Henriette. ... Nos alliés les Américains ... 14 gravures. Paris, Larousse (1917)
32 p. illus. (incl. ports.) 17½ cm. (Les livres roses pour la jeunesse, no. 207) 20-1725.   F128.5
   E168. P 45

SCHUTZ, Anton. New York in etchings; introd. and notes by Richard M. Baum ... New York, Bard brothers (1939)   108 p. incl. front., plates. 32 cm. 39-9637.   F128.5
   NE2210.S3 B3

(SIMÓN, Raul) ... Broadway. Sanitaco (!) Chile (etc.) Nascimento, 1927.   3, (9)-168 p. 19 cm.
Author's pseud., Cesar Cascabel, at head of title. 29-1777 Rev.   F128.5
   E169.S594

SWEENY, Peter B. The political situation, resulting from the late state election. (Herald interview with Peter B. Sweeny) (New York) The Jackson assoc. (1869)   43 p. 23 cm. From the New York herald of
Nov. 26th, 1869. Reported by Stephen Hoyes. 12-9131.   F128.5
   F129.N6 S97

THOMAS E. Dewey committee for presidential nomination, New York. Why Dewey wins; the career of Thomas E. Dewey as seen by the American press. New York city ... (1940)   189 p. incl. illus.,
plates. 19½ cm. 40-29767.   F128.5
   E748.D48 T5

ULMAN, Albert. A landmark history of New York, including a guide to commemorative sites and monuments ... New York, London, D. Appleton-Century co., 1939.   xviii, 440 p. incl. front., illus. 21 cm.
Map. 39-10856.   F128.5
   F128.3. U 57

LOCAL HISTORIES IN THE LIBRARY OF CONGRESS

WALKER, Stanley. Mrs. Astor's horse ... with a foreword by Nunnally Johnson; with fifteen reproductions from photos. and an index. New York, Frederick A. Stokes, 1935. xiii, 320 p. front., plates, ports. 22½ cm. 35-20708.
F128.5
E169.1.W26

WRANGEL, Fredrik Ulrik. Ströftåg i New York och annorstädes i U.S.A. Stockholm, Wahlström & Widstrand (1907) xii, 217 p. illus., pl., 3 port., 20 cm. 8-9827.
F128.5
E168.W 94

ABBOTT, Bérénice, illus. Changing New York; photos. by Berenice Abbott, text by Elizabeth McCausland; a publication of the Federal art project of the W.P.A. ... New York, E. P. Dutton, 1939. xiv, (15) - 206, (2) p. incl. front., plates. 30 cm. "First edition." 39-9016.
F128.5.A22

AFFLECK, Thaddeus S. Affleck's handy New York guide ... Brooklyn, N.Y., 1912. 20 cm.
F128.5.A25

An ALBUM of selected views of greater New York ... New York, Isaac H. Blanchard co., 1905. 1 p., (62) p. of illus. 17½ x 25½ cm.
F128.5.A34

ALARCÓN, Mariano. Impresiones de un viaje a New York ... Madrid, V. Rico, 1918. 53 p. 23 cm. Impressions of N.Y. and the U.S. during the world war. 21-8434.
F128.5.A42

ALLEN, William Harvey. Why Tammanies revive: La Guardias mis-guard ... New York, Institute for public service, 1937. vi, 144 p. illus., diagrs. 20½ cm. 39-7388.
F128.5.A45

AMERICAN journal of commerce. New York city, borough of Manhattan; New York the trade centre; comp. by American journal of commerce. New York, 1902. 20 p. illus. (incl. ports.) 40½ cm. Industrial number of American journal of commerce. v. 16, no. 22. 4-27934.
F128.5.A51

AMERICAN journal of commerce. Borough of Brooklyn, the city of churches, Greater New York ... New York (190-?) 24p. illus. (incl. ports.) 40½ cm. (With above item) 4-27937 & 4-27938.
F128.5.A51

AMERICAN journal of commerce. The borough of Bronx, Greater New York ... New York (190-?) 24 p. illus. (incl. ports.) 20½ cm. (with above item) 4-27939.
F128.5.A51

AMERICAN journal of commerce. ... Borough of Queens ... New York (1901?) 24 p. illus. (incl. ports.) 40½ cm. (With above item) 4-27935.
F128.5.A51

AMERICAN journal of commerce. Borough of Richmond, gateway of the nation, Greater New York ... New York (190 ?) 24 p. illus. (incl. ports.) 40½ cm. (With above item) 4-27936.
F128.5.A51

AMERICAN journal of commerce. Pan-American souvenir. New York city, Pan-American metropolis ... New York (1901?) 20 p. illus. (incl. ports. (With above item) 4-27940.
F128.5.A51

ARMSTRONG, Hamilton Fish. Those days. (1st ed.) New York, Harper & Row (1963) 151 p. 22 cm. 63-16502.
F128.5.A 7

ATKINSON, Justin Brooks. East of the Hudson. New York, A. A. Knopf, 1931. 5, (3) - 217 p. 19½ cm. Essays. 31-1373.
F128.5.A87

ATKINSON, Oriana (Torrey) Manhattan and me. Drawings by Hirschfeld. (1st ed.) Indianapolis, Bobbs-Merrill (1954) 267 p. illus. 23 cm. 54-6501.
F128.5.A88

BAILEY, Vernon Howe. Magical city; intimate sketches of New York; pictures by Vernon Howe Bailey; notes by Arthur Bartlett Maurice. New York, London, C. Scribner's sons, 1935. 254, (2) p. incl. front., illus. 27 cm. 35-8544.
F128.5.B25
Rare Book Coll.

NEW YORK CITY

BANKERS trust company. New York and the future. New York ... (1946)   51 p. illus. 26 cm.
46-8212.   F128.5. B 26

(BARTHOLOMEW, Ralph I.) New York in 3 days and three glamorous nights. (New York, R. I. Bartholomew, 1939)   (16) p. illus. 30 ½ x 23 cm. 42-44032.   F128.5. B 27

BARZINI, Luigi Giorgia. Nuova York, di Luigi Barzini junior, prefazione di Luigi Barzini. Milano, G. Agnelli, 1931.   274 p. plates. 18 ½ cm. (Half-title: "Metropoli") 31-8028.   F128.5. B 29

BEATON, Cecil Walter Hardy. Cecil Beaton's New York. Illus. from drawings by the author and from photos. by the author and others. Philadelphia & New York, J. B. Lippincott co. (1938)   viii, 216 p. incl. illus., plates, ports. col. front. 23 cm. "First pub. Oct., 1938." Printed in G. B. 39-8296.   F128.5. B 34

BEATON, Cecil Walter Hardy. Portrait of New York. London, New York, B. T. Batsford (1948)   viii, 135 p. illus. 23 cm. A revision of the author's Cecil Beaton's New York, 1938. 49-906*.   F128.5. B 34 1948

BELDA, Joaquin. ... En el pais del bluff; veinte dias en Nueva York. Madrid, Biblioteca Hispania, 1926.   257 p. 19 ½ cm. 28-15959.   F128.5. B 4

BELDAD, Henry Garcia. Guia ilustrada de Nueva York y sus alrededores; comprende una descripcion ... de Nueva York v poblciones limitrofes de Brooklyn, Bronx y Staten Island ... Nueva York, L. Weiss, 1903.   224 p. illus., fold. map. 19 cm. 3-13391.   F128.5. B 42

— 2. año. Nueva York, L. Weiss, 1904.   256 p. incl. front., illus. fold. map. 19 cm. 4-11514.   F128.5. B 43

— 3. año. Nueva York ... 1905.   247 p. illus., fold. map. 19 cm. 5-13949.   F128.5. B431

BELOUS, Charles. Faith in fusion. New York, Vantage Press (1951)   111 p. 23 cm. 51-4107.   F128.5. B 44

BERCOVICKI, Konrad. Manhattan side-show; illus. by Norman Borchardt. New York, London, The Century co. (1931)   4. 3-354 p. front., illus. 23 cm. "First printing." 31-30924.   F128.5. B 46

BERGER, Meyer. The eight million, journal of a New York correspondent ... illus. by Henry Berger. New York, Simon and Schuster, 1942.   xi, 334 p. illus. 21 ½ cm. 42-15707.   F128.5. B 48

BERNARD, Sid. Your guide to New York. New York, Bernard Publications, 1951.   96 p. illus., maps. 21 cm. 51-3317.   F128.5. B 49

BLANCHARD'S new pocket guide to Manhattan, Bronx, Brooklyn and Queens boroughs ... New York, L. Lipkind (1910)   153 p. fold. map. 15 ½ cm. 10-31406.   F128.5. B 63

BOSSUE, Léon. ... Taches d'encre; chroniques new-yorkaises. Articles de journaux. Éd. intime. New-York, Imprimerie polyglotte lyonnais, 1912.   4. 208 p. 20 ½ cm. 22-14867.   F128.5. B 74

BRITT, Albert. Turn of the century. Barre, Mass., Barre Publishers, 1966.   x, 138 p. 24 cm.
66-23205.   F128.5. B 8

BROCK, Henry Irving. New York is like this. New York, Dodd, Mead, 1929.   3, 236 p. front., illus. 26 ½ cm. 29-29704.   F128.5. B 84

BROOKLYN eagle. A visitor's guide to the city of New York; prepared by the Brooklyn daily eagle on the occasion of the return of Admiral Dewey ... 3d ed. (Brooklyn, N.Y., Brooklyn daily eagle) 1899.   102 p. maps. 16 cm. 99-4789 rev.   F128.5. B 87

BROOKS, Walter Rollin. New York; an intimate guide. New York, A. A. Knopf, 1931.   6, 3-348, xxii p. 19 ½ cm. 31-11192.   F128.5. B 88

BROWN, Henry Collins.   From Alley pond to Rockefeller center ... New York, E. P. Dutton, 1936.
xvi, 299 p.   front., illus., plates.   25 cm.   "First edition."   36-30914.
F128.5.B887

BROWN, Henry Collins.   New York of to-day ... New York, The Old colony press, 1917.   287 p.
incl. plates. α col. front., plates (part col., 1 fold.) map.   16½ cm.   17-24998.
F128.5. B 89

BROWN, Henry Collins.   Valentine's city of New York; a guide book, with six maps and 160 full page pictures ... New York, Valentine's manual (1920)   viii, 384 p.   illus. (incl. ports., maps)   15 cm.   20-5206.
F128.5. B 9

BUCOVICH, Marius von.   Manhattan magic; a collection of 85 photos. by (Philadelphia, Beck engraving co., 1937)   93, (2) p.   illus.   30½ cm.   Illustrations: p. 9-93.   37-21244.
F128.5.B923

BUTLER, Richard Joseph.   Dock walloper; the story of "Big Dick" Butler.   New York, G. P. Putnam's sons (1933)   ix, 276 p. incl. front. (port.)   21 cm.   33-28718.
F128.5.B93

CALZINI, Raffaele.   ... Trionfini e disfatte di Nuova York.   Milano, Ceschina (1937)   5, (13)-232, (4) p.   xx pl.   21 cm.   A 42-767.
F128.5.C 25

CAMBA, Julio.   ... La ciudad automática.   Madrid (etc.) Espasa-Calpe, 1932.   255 p.   19 cm.
33-24032.
F128.5.C 26

— 2. ed.   1934.   255 p.   19 cm.   35-12490.
F128.5.C 26
1934

— Buenos Aires, México, Espasa-Calpe argentina, (1942)   3, (9) - 152 p.   18 cm.   43-14376.
F128.5.C 26
1942

CARPENTER, Frederick Valentine.   A sketch book of New York,   Pelham, N.Y., Bridgman (1927)
62 p.   illus.   22½ cm.   28-1876 Rev.
F128.5.C 29

CATHOLIC central union of America.   Souvenir-programm der 61. general-versammlung des D. R. K. Central-vereins von New York und der 21. jahresversammlung des D. R. K. Staatsverbandes von New York abgehalten ... 1916 in New York.   (Brooklyn, N.Y., The Albertype co., 1916)   16 p.   mounted plates, mounted ports.   21 x 26½ cm.   22-13938 rev. 2.
F128.5.C 34

GEDERSCHIÖLD, Gunnar.   Infödingarna pa Manhattan; studier och stämningar från New York. Stockholm, Aktiebolaget Ljus (1916)   3, 276 p.   illus.   22½ cm.   17-5427.
F128.5.C 38

CHAMBERS, Julius.   The book of New York; forty years' recollections of the American metropolis ... New York city, The Book of New York company (1912)   448 p. incl. illus., ports.   29 cm.   12-14701.
F128.5.C 44

CHAMBERS, Walter.   Samuel Seabury; a challenge ... New York & London, The Century co. (1932)
xii, 389 p. incl. front. plates, ports.   21 cm.   32-6329.
F128.5.C 45

CHASE, William Parker, comp.   New York, the wonder city; an illus. story of New York with statistics and general data concerning New York's vastness, New York's people, New York's activities and New York's intimate inside life in the year 1932 ...   New York city, Wonder city publishing co., 1931.   288 p.   illus.   20½ cm.   32-792.
F128.5.C 48

CHIANG, Yee.   The silent traveller in New York, written and illus. by Chiang Yee.   With a pref. by Van Wyck Brooks.   London, Methuen (1950)   xv, 281 p.   illus. (part col.) map (on lining papers)   23 cm.   Includes Chines poems by the author with English translations.   50-11083.
F128.5.C 52

— New York, John Day Co. (1953?)   xv, 281 p.   illus. (part col.) map.   22 cm.   53-1708.
F128.5.C 52
1953

NEW YORK CITY

CHILDE, Cromwell. New York; a guide in comprehensive chapters ... (Brooklyn) Brooklyn daily eagle, 1903.   80 p. illus. (incl. maps) 15 cm. (Brooklyn eagle library, v. 18 no. 4, serial no. 76) 12-31308.   F128.5.C 53

(CHILDE, Cromwell) comp. Old New York down town. New York, The Broun-Green co. (1901?)
60 p. illus. 25 cm. 10-28025.   F128.5.C 54

CHILDREN'S guide to New York. (New York, Circle Pub. Co.)   v. maps. 19 cm. annual. 50-56721.
F128.5.C 55

CITIZENS' Union, New York. N. Y. City campaign, Nov. 1903. (New York, 1903)   2 v. illus., ports. 55 cm. Includes pamphlets, broadsides, leaflets and posters. 56-53112.   F128.5.C563

CITY bank farmer trust co., New York. New York city ... (1919)   v.
F128.5.C 57

— (1920)   v.   F128.5.C572

CITY history club of New York. Historical guide to the city of New York, comp. by Frank Bergen Kelley from original observations and contributions made by members and friends of the City history club of New York; with 70 maps and diagrams and 46 illus. New York, F. A. Stokes co. (1909)
xvii, 420 p. front., illus. (incl. maps, diagrs.) plates. 17½ cm. Contains bibliographies. A consolidation of the series of "Excursions" issued by the club. 9-25287.   F128.5.C 58

— Rev. ed. New York, Frederick A. Stokes co. (1913)   xix, 421 p. front., illus. (incl. maps) plates, diagrs. 17½ cm. 13-35738 Rev.   F128.5.C 59

— Tercentenary supplement to the Historical guide to the city of New York. The New York commercial tercentenary, 1614 - 1914, by Edward Hagaman Hall, and Additions and corrections to itineraries, by Frank Bergen Kelley. Nov. 1914 ... (New York, 1914)   vi* - vi* p. 17½ cm.
The "additions and corrections" apply to the 1913 edition. 13-35738 Rev.   F128.5.C592

CITY history club of New York. Landmarks of New York; an historical guide to the metropolis, ed. by Everett Peterson. (New York) The City history club, 1923.   261 p. fold. front., illus., maps. 17½ cm.
A consolidation of a series of "Excursion leaflets". Pub. in 1909 and 1913 under title of C 59 and C592. 23-16580.   F128.5.C595

COBB, Irvin Shrewsbury. New York; with illus. by John T. McCutcheon. New York, George H. Doran (1924)   vii, 11-59 p. incl. front., plates. 19 cm. (Cobb's America guyed books) 24-9447.   F128.5.C 64

COBURN, Alvin Langdon. New York; with a foreword by H. G. Wells. London, Duckworth & co.; New York, Brentano's (1911?)   10 p. 20 mounted pl. 41 x 32 cm. 11-24845.   F128.5.C 65

COHEN, Caryl Ernest. New York today and tomorrow ... New York, College entrance book co., 1943.   xi, (1), 546 p. incl. front., illus. (incl. maps) diagrs. 21½ cm. "For further information" at end of most of the chapters. Bibliography: p. 483 - 487. 43-4190.   F128.5.C 72

— Rev. ed. New York ... 1948.   xi, 540 p. illud., mspd. 22 cm. Incl. bibliographies. 48-1278*.   F128.5.C 72
1948

COMMERCE and industry association of New York. ... Pocket guide to New York ... (New York) 1906.   vi, 210 p. fold. maps. 21½ x 10 cm. 6-18327 Rev.   F128.5.C 77

CORNISH, Hubert Ray. Metropolitan New York; its geography, history and civics ... Boston, New York (etc.) D. C. Heath (1925)   xi, 158 p. illus. (incl. maps) 20 x 16½ cm. 25-8862.
F128.5. C 8

CORTÉS DURÁN, Saturnino. Impresiones de un viajero. (San Salvador, Tip. "La Union," 1906)
2, iv, (3) - 240 p. 18 cm. 9-16680.   F128.5.C 82

CUMMINGS, Patricia. New York on a modest income. (New York) Simon and Schuster, 1952.
172 p. 20 cm. "1st printing." 52-3769.   F128.5.C 88

CURRAN, Henry Hastings.   Pillar to post ... New York, C. Scribner's sons, 1941.   viii, 387 p.
front. (port.) illus.   23½ cm.   Autobiography.   41-6107.   F128.5.C 93

CURTIS, Olga.   East of Third; memories of old Manhattan.   (Limited ed.) Berkeley Heights, N.J.,
Pub. and print. privately by the Oriole Press, 1955.   18 p.   20 cm.   55-28164.
                                                                                            F128.5.C 96

DAILY attractions in New York.   Advance information of art exhibitions, lectures, concerts,
churches, theatres, railroads, Pullman accomodations, points of interest, where to dine, etc...
v. 1 - 11, 13-14.   Apr. 2, 1906 - 09.   (New York) Daily attractions in New York (inc.) 1906-10.
13 v. in 9.   illus. (incl. maps)   20 cm.   weekly.   Supersedes the Week in New York.   8-10801.   F128.5.D13

DAYTON, Helena Smith.   New York in seven days ... with one large map and six sectional maps.
New York, R. M. McBride, 1925.   4, 167 p. incl. front., plans.   18½ cm.   Folded plan in pocket.   25-18265.
                                                                                            F128.5.D 27

DENKSCHRIFT der General Slocum katastrophe.   New York, W. W. Wilson (1904?)   48 p. front.,
plates, ports.   15 cm.   43-26926.   F128.5.D 45

DREISER, Theodore.   The color of a great city; illus. by C. B. Falls.   New York, Boni and Liveright
(1928)   xiv, 287 p.   front., illus., plates.   23 cm.   Brief descriptive sketches of New York as it was between 1900 and 1914 or '15.
23-18232.   F128.5.D 77

— (English ed.)   London, Constable (1930)   xiv, 287 p.   21 cm.
                                                                                            F128.5.D 77
                                                                                            1930
                                                                                            Rare Book Coll.

DRUMMOND, Muriel Jean.   New York, our city of progress; a textbook on life in New York city ...
with an introd. by Harold G. Campbell ... Boston, New York (etc.) Allyn and Bacon (1940)   xx, 292 p.
4 p. front., illus., maps (1 double)   diagrs.   20½ cm.   Maps.   41-1766.   F128.5. D 8

EARLY, Eleanor.   New York holiday.   New York, Rinehart (1950)   376 p.   21 cm.   50-10517.
                                                                                            F128.5.E 13

EATON, Walter Prichard.   New York; a series of wood engravings in colour and a note on colour
printing by Rudolph Ruzicka, with prose impressions of the city by Walter Prichard Eaton.   New York,
The Grolier club, 1915.   xxi, 120 p. incl. col. illus., col. plates.   29½ cm.   15-9843.
                                                                                            F128.5.E 14
                                                                                            Rare Book Coll.

EBERHARD, Kurt von.   Respektlosigkeiten über New York.   Umschlag-zeichnung von Carl Josef.
Wien und Leipzig, M. Perles (1910)   vii, 238 p.   21½ cm.   10-26249.
                                                                                            F128.5.E 16

EISENSTEIN, Louis.   A stripe of Tammany's tiger.   (1st ed.) New York, R. Speller (1966)
xii, 300 p.   23 cm.   66-29504.   F128.5.E 38

ENDE, Amelia (Kremper) ... New York; mit zweiundzwanzig vollbildern in tondruck.   Berlin,
Marquardt & co. (1909)   2, 131 p.   front., plates.   16½ cm.   9-31261.   F128.5.E 56

ERSKINE, Helen (Worden)   Discover New York with Helen Worden; sketches by Helen Worden; cover
by Leonebel Jacobs.   (New York) American women's voluntary services (1943)   128 p.   illus. 21 cm.
A guide for the men and women of the armed forces and the general public.   44-606 rev.   F128.5. E 7

ERSKINE, Helen (Worden)   Here is New York; illustrations by author.   New York, Doubleday, Doran,
1939.   xv, 411 p. incl. front., illus.   21 cm.   "First ed."   39-27478 rev.   F128.5.E713

ERSKINE, Helen (Worden)   The real New York; a guide for the adventurous shopper, the exploratory

eater and the know-it-all sightseer who ain't seen nothin' yet.   Indianapolis, The Bobbs-Merrill co.
(1932)   8, 19-401 p.   illus.   22 cm.   32-34645 rev.   F128.5.E717
1932

— (1933)   8, 19-401 p.   illus.   22 cm.   33-6912 rev.   F128.5.E717
1933

ERSKINE, Helen (Worden)   Round Manhattan's rim ... illus. by the author.   Indianapolis, The Bobbs-Merrill co. (1934)   302 p. incl. front., illus.   22½ cm.   "First ed."   34-10070 rev.   F128.5.E718

ERSKINE, Helen (Worden)   Society circus; from ring to ring with a large cast.   New York, Covici, Friede (1936)   321 p. incl. front. plates, ports.   22½ cm.   36-33689 rev.   F128.5.E719

FAY, Edgar Stewart.   Londoner's New York; with 24 plates and endpaper maps ...   London, Methuen (1936)   xii, 235 p.   front., plates.   19 cm.   Maps.   "First pub. in 1936."   37-2563.   F128.5.F 29

FEDERAL writers' project.   ... New York city guide; a comprehensive guide to the five boroughs of the metropolis - Manhattan, Brooklyn, the Bronx, Queens, and Richmond - prepared by the Federal writers' project of the W.P.A ...   New York, Random house (1939)   xx, 708 p. illus., plates, maps (2 fold. on 1 l. in pocket)   21 cm.   (American guide series)   "Books about New York": p. (649)-659.   39-27593 Rev.   F128.5.F376

— New York, Random house (1939)   xx, 680 p., etc.   "Companion volume to New York panorama ...   "Books about New York": p. (625) - 635.   47-33778.   F128.5.F376
1939a

— (Rev. ed.)   New York, Random House (1939)   xx, 680 p. illus., maps, etc.   "Books about New York": p. 627 - 635.   56-51512.   F128.5.F376
1939 b

— With a new introd. by John V. Lindsay.   New York, Octagon Books, 1970.   xx, 708 p. illus., etc. 24 cm.   75-124406.   F128.5.F376
1970

FEDERAL writers' project.   Almanac for New Yorkers ...   New York, Simon and Schuster, 1937 -
v. illus.   25 cm.   37-3974.   F128.5.F 37
Rare Book Coll.

FEDERAL writers' project.   ... New York panorama; a comprehensive view of the metropolis in a series of articles ...   New York, Random house (1938)   xii, 526 p. plates.   21 cm.   (American guide series) "The present volume, although complete in itself ... constitutes in effect the general introduction for a detailed guide book to New York city. 38-27618.   F128.5.F 38
Geneal. Sect. Ref.

— 1972.   F128.5.F38
1972

FEININGER, Andreas.   New York; photos by Andreas Feininger, with an introd. by John Erskine. Picture text by Jacquelyn Judge.   Chicago, New York, Ziff-Davis pub. co. (1945)   viii, 103 p. illus. 37 cm.   Maps.   45-101514.   F128.5.F385

(FELLIG, Arthur)   Naked city, by Weegee (pseud.)   New York, Essential books (1945)   216 p. illus. (incl. ports.)   24 cm.   45-35132.   F128.5.F387

(FELLIG, Arthur)   Weegee's people.   New York, Essential books, Duell, Sloan and Pearce (1946) (242) p. incl. front., illus.   25 cm.   Photos of New York life.   46-8265.   F128.5.F388

FERRAZ, Wanda.   ... Rosinha vai a Nova-York (para classes juvenis) ...   Rio de Janeiro (Bedeschi) 1942.   94 p. illus. (incl. map)   23½ cm.   43-8771.   F128.5. F 4

FINDAHL, Theodore.   ... Manhattan Babylon; en bok om New York idag.   Oslo, Gyldendal, Norsk forlag, 1928.   205 p. plates, ports.   24 cm.   29-12434.   F128.5. F 49

A FINE collection of albertypes of New York city. The historical pictures of New York contained in this album are from the Leonard Hassam Bogart collection. These pictures were reproduced from the original photographic plates made by Adolf Wittemann ... (Brooklyn, The Albertype co., 1938)
2 p., 82 mounted pl. 26 x 33 cm. 41-14730 Rev.
F128.5. F 5

FLEMING, Ethel. New York; with illus. by Herbert S. Kates. New York, The Macmillan co., 1929.
3 p. ix-xii, 139 p. illus., xxiv pl. (incl. front.) 28 cm. Printed in G.B. 30-6281.
F128.5. F 58
Rare Book Coll.

FLYNN, Edward Joseph. You're the boss. (Autobiography) New York, Viking Press, 1947.
x, 244 p. 22 cm. 47-30772*.
F128.5. F 6

— With a new introd. by Eleanor Roosevelt. New York, Collier Books (1962) 255 p. 18 cm.
(Collier books) 62-12296.
F128.5. F 6
1962

FOOTNER, Hulbert. New York, city of cities, by Hulbert Footner; with 45 illus in aquatone from photos. by John J. Floherty. Philadelphia & New York (etc.) J. B. Lippincott co., 1937. 338 p. front., plates, port. 23½ cm. 37-37569.
F128.5. F 65

FORD, Ford Madox. New York is not America ... London, Duckworth (1927) 244 p. 20½ cm.
27-17925.
F128.5. F 73
Rare Book Coll.

— New York, A. & C. Boni, 1927. xiii, 17-292 p. 19½ cm. A vignon edition. 27-24545.
F128.5. F732

FRACCAROLI, Arnaldo. ... New York, ciclone di genti. Milano, Fratelli Treves, 1928.
2, 211 p. 19 cm. 28-14251.
F128.5. F 79

FREDERICK, Justus George. Adventuring in New York ... with ten etchings. N.Y., N. I. Brown, 1923. 127 p. illus. 19 cm. 23-7837.
F128.5. F 85

FREEDMAN, Samuel, comp. Illustrated souvenir of New York; a visible story of New York and a view-guide of what there is best to see. Shown in a remarkable selection of 277 latest photos. Compiled and edited by Samuel Freedman ... New York city, Supervue map and guide co., 1935.
(64) p. illus. 24½ cm. 35-8940.
F128.5. F 87

FULTON trust company of New York. A guide book to the city of New York, with historical, descriptive and statistical facts. New York ... (1945) 99 p. illus. (incl. maps) 15 cm. 45-4972.
F128.5. F 94

GARRETT, Charles. The La Guardia years; machine and reform politics in New York City. New Brunswick, N.J., Rutgers University Press (1961) 423 p. 24 cm. 61-10262.
F128.5.G 25

GAYNOR, William Jay. Some of Mayor Gaynor's letters and speeches. New York, Greaves pub. co. (1913) 320 p. front. (port.) 23½ cm. 13-20398.
F128.5.G 28

GAYNOR, the Tammany mayor who swallowed the tiger; lawyer, judge, philosopher, by Louis Heaton Pink. New York, N.Y., The International press (1931) 5, 3-256 p. incl. plates. front., ports. 23 cm.
31-29400.
F128.5.G293

— Freeport, N.Y., Books for Libraries Press (1970) 256 p. 23 cm. 77-124251.
F128.5.G293
1970

GAYNOR. William Jay Gaynor, mayor of New York. By Mortimer Brewster Smith. Chicago, H. Regnery Co., 1951. 192 p. illus. 22 cm. 51-12724.
F128.5.G294

GAYNOR. The Mayor who mastered New York; the life and opinions of William J. Gaynor, by Lately Thomas. New York, W. Morrow, 1969.   516 p.   illus.   25 cm.   70-83690.   F128.5.G295

GOODWIN, Ida B. ... Hennes höghet av New York. Stockholm, P. A. Norstedt (1925)   4, 136 p. front., illus., plates, ports. 23½ cm.   31-3131.   F128.5.G 65

GRAHAM, Mildred Seymour. New York, "the unfinished city" ... photography and art direction, H. C. A. Schoenfeldt; text and research, Mildred Seymour Graham ... New York city, Visitours, inc., 1935.   (48) p.   illus. (incl. map)   26½ cm.   36-8188.   F128.5.G 72

GRAHAM, Stephen. New York nights ... illus. by Kurt Wiese. New York, George H. Doran (1927) ix, 13-288 p.   front., plates, port.   22½ cm.   27-22649.   F128.5.G 74

GREATER New York and one hundred miles around it, how reached. New York, Crawford & Hyatt (1902)   98 numb. l.   fold. maps.   17½ cm.   Printed on one side of leaf only.   2-10355.   F128.5.G783

GRIFFITHS, Catharine. The children's New York. New York, Chicago (etc.) Rand, McNally, 1939. 34 p.   illus.   23 cm.   39-16992.   F128.5.G795

GROSS, Alexander, ed. Famous guide to New York, pictorial and descriptive, with 12 maps and 60 illus. ... New York city, Manhattan post card pub. co., 1937.   143 p.   illus. (incl. maps)   18½ cm.   37-10643.
    F128.5.G 82

— New York, N.Y., "Geographia" map co., 1944.   128 p.   illus. (incl. maps)   18½ cm.   45-12580.
    F128.5.G 82
    1944

— New York, Geographia Map Co., 1950.   96 p.   illus., maps.   19 cm.   50-3279.
    F128.5.G 82
    1950

GROSS, Alexander. Pictorial souvenir of New York for New Yorkers and visitors, containing over 160 magnificent photos ... New York City, "Geographia map co., 1944.   63 p.   illus. (incl. maps)   28 cm. 45-12578.   F128.5.G826

GUARANTY trust co. of New York. For the visitor in New York city ... (New York) London (etc.) Guaranty trust co. of New York, 1939.   88 p.   illus. (incl. maps)   18½ cm.   39-6008.   F128.5.G 86

GUIA de New York para los touristas hispano-americanos ... 1 - ed. ... 1916 -   New York, M. Hadida (1916) -   v.   illus.   18½ cm.   16-9184.   F128.5.G 88

GUIA de turismo y compras en Nueva York. New York, American International Advertising Corp. v.   illus.   19 cm.   51-37607.   F128.5.G883

GUIA ilustrada de Nueva York ... New York, Spanish American bureau, 1910.   116 p.   illus.   17 cm. 10-18009.   F128.5.G 89

GUIDE to Greater New York. Boston, Mass., G. H. Walker, 1900.   125 p. incl. front., illus.   fold. maps. 17½ cm.   0-5418 Rev.   F128.5.G 94

(HALL, Edward Hagaman) A volume commemorating the creation of the second city of the world, by the consolidation of the communities adjacent to New York harbor under the new charter of the city of New York. New York, The Republic press, 1898.   vi, (2), (9) - 418 p. incl. illus., plates (1 double) ports. col. front., plates.   30½ cm.   99-3132 Rev.   F128.5.H 17

HANSON, John Wesley, ed. ... New York's awful excursion boat horror, told by survivors and rescuers ... (Chicago? 1904)   326 p.   front., plates.   23½ cm.   4-22002.   F128.5.H 25

HARTLEY. Marcellus Hartley, a brief memoir. New York (The DeVinne press) 1903.   xi, 149 p. front., pl., ports.   25½ cm.   Preface signed: J. W. H.   5-16561 Rev.   F128.5.H 33

HAWTHORNE, Hildegarde. ... New York. With twelve full-page illus. in colour, by Martin Lewis. London, A. and C. Black, 1911.   vii, 86 p., 11 col. plates (incl. front.)   20 cm.   (Peeps at great cities)   CA 12-589 D.
F128.5.H 39

HENDERSON, Helen Weston. A loiterer in New York; discoveries made by a rambler through obvious yet unsought highways and byways ... with a preface by Paul W. Bartlett.   New York, George H. Doran (1917)   xvii, 15-454 p.   front., plates, ports., plan.   24½ cm.   17-30247.
F128.5.H 49

HEPBURN, Andrew. A complete guide to New York City, including Westchester County and Long Island.   New York, Travel Enterprises, 1952.   114 p.   illus.   28 cm.   (The American travel series, 4)   52-11802.
F128.5. H 5

HERBCO'S souvenir guide to New York City; illustrations and important facts about New York.   (New York, Herbco Card Co., 1952)   96 p.   illus.   18 cm.   Text by George K. Borkow.   52-68598.
F128.5.H 52

HIDALGO, Diego. Nueva York, impresiones de un español del siglo xix que no sabé ingles.   Madrid, M. Aguilar (1947)   350 p.   22 cm.   48-1727*.
F128.5.H 54

HOGNER, Nils. ... Cartoon guide of New York city.   New York city, J. J. Augustine (1938)   2. 124 p.   illus., fold. map (in pocket)   18½ cm.   (Augustin's cartoon guides of America. 2)   38-17841.
F128.5.H 65

HONAN, William Holmes. Another LaGuardia; how he did it and how we can do it again.   Illus. by Joseph Papin.   New York, Citizen Press, 1960.   16 p.   22 cm.
F128.5.H 67

HORN, Jack. "And on the right ..." The original arm-chair lectured sight-seeing tour of New York with cartoons, restaurant guide, and hotels.   (New York? 1954)   109 p.   illus.   22 cm.   54-3929.
F128.5.H 69

HOROWITZ, Max. A tour of New York city, a workbook for the pupil; study plans prepared by Max Horowitz ...   Meadville, Penna., Keystone view co. (1941)   iv, 83 p.   illus., diagrs.   28 cm.   For use with stereographs and lantern slides.   41-10891.
F128.5. H 7

HOWE, Wirt. New York at the turn of the century, 1899-1916.   Toronto, Can., Priv. print. (by the Ryerson press) 1946.   viii, 155 p.   front. (port.)   20½ cm.   The second portion of an unpublished autobiography presented as a memorial by the author's sister, Bessy Howe Heward.   47-15508.
F128.5.H 75

HRASTNIK, Franz. Das New York-Buch für alle, die dort waren oder hin möchten. ...   Wien, E. Wancura Verlag (1953)   152 p.   col. illus.   26 cm.   54-21253.
F128.5. H 8

HUARD, Charles. New York comme je l'ai vu; texte et dessins par Charles Huard.   Paris, E. Rey, 1906.   3, xi-(xii), 9-202 p., 2 l. incl. illus., plates.   front.   20½ cm.   7-36706.
F128.5.H 87

HUEFFER, Oliver Madox. A vagabond in New York ... 8 illus. by Roy E. Hallings.   New York, John Lane co.; London, John Lane; (etc.) 1913.   229 p.   front., plates.   19½ cm.   A collection of sketches based upon the experiences of a young Englishman in N. Y. city. Some of the sketches first appeared in Truth.   13-20782.
F128.5.H 88

HUGHES, Rupert. The real New York; drawings by Hy. Mayer ...   New York, London, The Smart set publishing co., 1904.   384 p.   front., illus., 22 pl. (partly col.)   19½ cm.   4-16232.
F128.5.H 89

HUMPHREY, Grace. Father takes us to New York.   Philadelphia, The Penn pub. co. (1927)   3, v-viii, 9-243 p. incl. illus., plates.   col. front., plates.   19½ cm.   Maps.   27-24544.
F128.5.H 92

HUNEKER, James Gibbons. New cosmopolis; a book of images. Intimate New York. Certain European cities before the war: Vienna, Prague, little Holland, Belgian etchings, Madrid, Dublin, Marienbad. Atlantic City and Newport.   New York, Scribner, 1915.   ix, 344 p.   15-5694.
F128.5.H 93

HYLAN, John Francis. Autobiography of John Francis Hylan, mayor of New York. Authorized ed.

New York, The Rotary press (1922) 45 p. illus. (incl. ports.) 16 cm. 22-15052. F128.5.H 99

IRWIN, William Henry. Highlights of Manhattan; illus. by E. H. Suydam. New York, London, The Century co. (1927) x, 381 p. col. front., plates. 23½ cm. 27-23036. F128.5. I 7

— Rev. ed. illus. by E. H. Suydam. New York, London, D. Appleton-Century co., 1937.
xii, 432 p. col. front., plates. 23½ cm. 37-4123. F128.5. I 72

ISAACS, Edith S. Love affair with a city; the story of Stanley M. Isaacs. New York, Random House (1967) 167 p. "2d printing" 67-12756. F128.5.I78I8

JAMES, Rian. All about New York; an intimate guide; with a foreword by Ogden Nash and decorations by Jay. New York, The John Day co. (1931) 3, v-ix, 11-316 p. illus., fold. map. 20 cm. Maps. 31-12493. F128.5. J 28

JENNISON, Keith Warren. New York and the State it's in; stories and pictures arranged by Keith Jennison. New York, Sloane Associates (1949) 111 p. (chiefly illus.) 24 cm. "1st printing." 49-11859*. F128.5. J 4

JESUS CASTRO, Tomas de. Nueva York. Santurce, P.R., Impr. Ahora (cover 1950) 34 p. 22 cm. 52-31762. F128.5. J 43

JOHNSTON, George Henry. Skyscrapers in the mist, illus. by Jack Hanna ... Sydney, London, Angus & Robertson, 1946. vii, 222 p. illus. 22 cm. 47-15134. F128.5. J 7

(JONES, Thomas Wallace) Miniatures of New York city. (Cincinnati, O., 1904) 8 x 10½ cm. F128.5. J 73

JOSEPH-RENAUD, Jean. ... New-York flamboie; préface d'André Tardieu. Paris, Fasquelle (1931) 200 p. 19 cm. 32-7875. F128.5. J 82

JOSEPHY, Helen. New York is everybody's town; drawings by Margaret Freeman. New York and London, G. P. Putnam's sons, 1931. viii, 307 p. illus. 21½ cm. 31-11191. F128.5. J 83

JOURNAL of history and biography. Describing and illustrating Greater New York ... New York, The Historical and biographical pub. co., 1899. (3) - 46 p. illus. 35 cm. Souvenir edition. May 25, 99-73. F128.5. J 86

KAERGEL, Hans Christoph. ... Wolkenkratzer. Breslau, Ostdeutsche verlagsanstalt g.m.b.h., 1926. 182 p. 20 cm. 29-4742. F128.5.K 13

KARAKA, Dosoo Framjee. New York with its pants down. Bombay, Thacker (1946) 99 p. 22 cm. "2d impression 1946." 49-41201 rev.* F128.5. K 2

KASHKIN, Ivan Aleksandrovich. New York (an outline) planned and compiled by John Kashkeen; illus. and maps arranged by F. Tahirof; supplement: vocabulary and explanatory notes, by M. Lorie. Moscow, Co-operative pub. soc. of foreign workers in the U.S.S.R., 1933. 157, (3) p. illus., col. plates, plans. 21 cm. Preface in Russian. The supplement is lacking in this ed. Selections from the works of John Dos Passos, Theodore Dreiser and others. CA 34-1410 Unrev. F128.5.K 22

KELLEY, Frank Bergen. ... Excursion planned for the City history club of New York ... No. iv - Central park to Van Cortlandt park (revised) ... (New York) 1897. 9, (3) p. illus. (maps) 18 cm. (City history club of New York. Excursions, no. 4) 17-19483. F128.5.K 27

KELLEY, Frank Bergen. Excursion planned for the City history club of New York ... (New York?) 1902. 19½ cm. F128.5.K 28

KELLEY, Frank Bergen. Excursion planned for the City history club of New York ... The nineteenth century city, 14th street to 110th street. (New York?) 1905. 19½ cm. F128.5.K 29

KELLEY, Frank Bergen. ... Excursion planned for the City history club of New York; no. v - The nineteenth century city: Tenth to One hundred and twenty-fifth street ... Revised, 1909 and 1912 ... (New York, 1912)   p. (103) - 139.   plans.   19 ½ cm.   (City history club ... Excursions ... no. v)   12-31053.   F128.5. K 3

KERR, Alfred.   Newyork und London, stätten des geschicks ...   Berlin, S. Fischer, 1923.   8, 9-201 p.   19 ½ cm.   24-19367.   F128.5.K 42

KING, Moses.   King's color-graphs of New York city.   (New York city, M. King, inc., 1910)   26, (2) p. incl. col. plates.   37 ½ cm.   13-5620.   F128.5.K 53

KING, Moses.   King's views of New York city.   New York, 1903.   37 ½ cm.   F128.5.K 54

— 1905.   37 ½ cm.   F128.5.K542

— 1908, 1909, four hundred illustrations ... (New York, Printed by C. Francis press) 1908.   96 p. of illus.   37 ½ cm.   9-1995.   F128.5.K544

— 1911, 1912; four hundred illus. ... (New York) Moses King, inc., 1911.   96 p. of illus.   37 cm.   11-23042.   F128.5.K545

— (1912)   viii, 96 p. of illus.   38 ½ cm.   12-14101.   F128.5.K546

— (1914)   96 p. of illus.   37 ½ x 26 cm.   On cover: Double number.   14-18313.   F128.5.K5462

— (1915)   viii, 96 p. illus.   38 x 26 ½ cm.   16-355.   F128.5.K5463

KING, Moses, inc.   King's how to see New York; a complete trustworthy guide book; 100 illus., the latest map, complete index.   Planned, ed. and pub. by Moses King inc.   (New York) 1914.   192 p.   illus., fold. map.   16 cm.   14-3991.   F128.5.K547

KLEIN, Henry H.   My last fifty years (an autobiographical history of "inside" New York) ... (New York, Printed by Isaac Goldmann co., 1935)   460 p.   front., plates, ports.   23 ½ cm.   35-2166.   F128.5.K 63

LAIT, Jack.   New York: confidential!   Chicago, Ziff-Davis Pub. Co. (1948)   xi, 316 p.   21 cm.   48-7631*.   F128.5.L 22

LAMUS, G. Ramón, ed.   Guia descriptiva de la ciudad de Nueva York.   2, ed. rev.   New York, Advertising abroad pub. co. (1929)   192 p.   illus.   18 cm.   30-4276.   F128.5.L 24

LANSING, Elisabeth Carleton (Hubbard)   Seeing New York.   New York, Thomas Y. Crowell co. (1938)   4, 7-237 p.   illus. (incl. maps)   23 cm.   38-36023 Rev.   F128.5.L 26

LANUX, Pierre Combret de.   New York, 1939-1945.   (Paris) Hachette (1947)   223 p.   19 cm.   47-6778*.   F128.5.L 27

LAPAQUELLERIE, Yvon.   ... New-York aux sept couleurs.   Paris, Valois, 1930.   159 p. front., plates.   19 cm.   (Capitales du Monde nouveau. II)   30-16978.   F128.5.L 28

LARA, Javier.   En la metropoli del dollar,   New York, The Spanish-American pub. co. (1919)   188, (3) p. incl. illus., plates, ports.   23 ½ cm.   19-3221.   F128.5. L 3

LAUBER, Hedwig.   Manhattan, mit einer Titelzeichnung von Justine Fuller.   Basel, Vineta-Verlag (1951)   54 p.   21 cm.   52-22612.   F128.5.L 36

LAUGHLIN, Clara Elizabeth.   So you're visiting New York city! ... Boston, Houghton Mifflin co., 1939.   5, 84 p.   plates.   19 ½ cm.   39-27550.   F128.5.L 38

LEAVERS, Claude E.   Sloane house guide to New York city ...   Maps by Mary G. Thomas.   New

NEW YORK CITY

York, N.Y., William Sloane house, YMCA (1944) 5 - 46 p. illus. (maps) 17½ cm. 44-35712.
F128.5. L 4

LEITICH, Ann Tizia. New York; mit 69 abbildungen. Bielefeld und Leipzig, Velhagen & Klasing, 1932. 10 p. 64 p. of illus. 25½ cm. 32-31740.
F128.5.L 48

LENSKI, Lois. The wonder city; a picture book of New York. New York, Coward-McCann, 1929. (32) p. of illus. (part col.) 22½ x 28½ cm. Maps. 29-16106.
F128.5. L 57

LEWIS, Harold MacLean. Physical conditions and public services ... incl. a review of earlier planning efforts, by Henry James, and Some concluding observations on the Regional survey, by Thomas Adams. New York, Regional plan of New York and its environs, 1929. 3, 5-209 p. front., illus., maps (2 fold.) diagrs. 28½ cm. (Regional survey of N.Y. and its environs, vol. viii) 29-12433.
F128.5. L 63

LIEBLING, Abbott Joseph. Back where I came from. New York, Sheridan house (1938) 303 p. 21 cm. 38-39406.
F128.5. L66

LIEBLING, Abbott Joseph. The jollity building. New York, Ballantine Books (1962) 184 p. 18 cm.
F128.5. L664

LIEBLING, Abbott Joseph. The telephone booth Indian. Garden City, N.Y., Doubleday, Doran, 1942. 3, v-ix p. 266 p. 20 cm. 42-11062.
F128.5. L 67

(LONG, Solomon Levy) A Texan in New York, by Col. Cactus (pseud.) (Alton, Ill., Melling & Gaskins print. co.) 1914. 54 p. 19½ cm. 15-4954.
F128.5. L 84

LÓPEZ, José Heriberto. ... Senderos de luz y sombra. Habana, La Moderna poesia, 1925. 2, (3)-400 p. 20 cm. 26-19576.
F128.5. L 86

LOUD, Ruth McAneny. New York! New York! A Knickerbocker holiday for you and your children ... illus. by Eileen Evans. New York, Duell, Sloan and Pearce (1946) 78 p. incl. front., illus. (incl. maps) 21 cm. "Some of the drawings and text ... were first pub. under the title All yours, as a supplement to the Brearley school Bulletin, Dec., 1944." Bibliography: p. 73-74. 46-25182.
F128.5. L 88

LOW. Seth Low: the reformer in an urban and industrial age. By Gerald Kurland. New York, Twayne (1971) 415 p. 22 cm. Originally presented as the author's thesis, City University of New York, 1968. Bibliography: p. 397-407. 76-125816 MARC.
F128.5. L 89
1971

LOW. Seth Low, by Benjamin R. C. Low. New York & London, G. P. Putnam's sons, 1925. 7, 92 p., xiii-xix p. front. (port.) 22 cm. 25-8687.
F128.5. L 9

— New York, AMS Press (1971) xi, 92, xix p. 19 cm. 70-137256.
F128.5. L 9
1971

LOW. ... New York (City) Board of estimate and apportionment. ... Joint session in memory of Hon. Seth Low ... (New York, 1916) p. (5349) - 5358. 25½ cm.
F128.5. L 92

— Minutes of the special joint meeting ... (New York, Press of C. S. Nathan, 1916) (23) p. front. (port.) 31½ x 24 cm. 17-19095.
F128.5. L 93

LUBSCHEZ, Ben Jehudah. Manhattan, the magical island, 108 pictures of Manhattan, with prelude and descriptive notes, by Ben Judah Lubschez ... New York, Press of the American institute of architects, inc., 1927. 3, 3-24 p. mounted front., 107 pl. 31½ cm. 27-12858.
F128.5. L935

MAAS, Carl. How to know and enjoy New York. (New York) New American Library (1949) 143 p. port., map (on lining papers) 19 cm. (N.A.L. Mentor books. A Mentor guide, 2) "1st printing April, 1949." 49-8937*
F128.5.M117

— (2d ed. New York) New American Library (1950) 156 p. port. 19 cm. 50-4165.
F128.5.M117
1950

McADOO, Eva T.   How do you like New York? An informal guide.   New York, The Macmillan co., 1936.   viii, 182 p.   front., plates, fold. map.   18½ cm.   "First printing."   Bibliography: p. 173.   36-18190.   F128.5.M125

— Rev. ed.   New York, The Macmillan co., 1939.   viii, 198 p.   front., plates, fold. map.   18½ cm. Bibliography: p. 189.   39-9235.   F128.5.M125 1939

McINTYRE, Oscar Odd.   The big town; New York day by day.   New York, Dodd, Mead, 1935. 5, 3-204 p.   front. (port.)   19½ cm.   "A collection of fifty-one favorite columns."   35-8251.   F128.5.M 13

McINTYRE, Oscar Odd.   White light nights.   New York, Cosmopolitan book corp., 1924.   5, 274 p. 19½ cm.   24-12442.   F128.5.M 15

NEW YORK (1954)   (In Hebrew)   124 p.   illus.   20 cm.   55-46039.
F128.5.M 18
Hebraic Sect.

MARCUS, Peter.   New York, the nation's metropolis; with an appreciation by J. Monroe Hewlett ... New York, Brentano's (1921)   64 p. incl. mounted front., mounted illus.   24½ cm.   21-6058.
F128.5.M 32

MARKEY, Morris.   Manhattan reporter.   New York, Dodge pub. co. (1935)   x, 320 p.   21 cm. "Most of the stories ... are about N.Y. ... and all ... were written for the New Yorker magazine."   35-27412.   F128.5.M 34

MARKEY, Morris.   That's New York!   (New York) Macy-Masius, 1927.   4, 5-204 p.   illus.   23½ cm. 27-8160.   F128.5.M 35

MARSHALL, Francis.   An Englishman in New York, written and illus. by Francis Marshall.   (London) G. B. Publications ... (1949)   96 p.   illus.   26 cm.   50-19035.   F128.5.M 36

MATSCH, Hans von.   8 original colored linoleum prints.   (New York, 1934)   8 col. pl.   51½ x 37 cm.   Issued in portfolio.   35-730.   F128.5.M 37

(MILLS, William Wirt)   ... New York, the capital of a continent ...   (New York, 1908)   1 v. 13 x 19½ cm.   F128.5.M 65

MILLS, William Wirt.   Guía alfabética de Nueva York.   (New York) 1911.   17½ cm.
F128.5.M 66

MIQUELARENA, Jacinto.   ... Pero ellos no tienen bananas (el viaje a Nueva York)   1. ed. Madrid (etc.) Espasa-Calpe, s.a., 1930.   168 p.   19½ cm.   32-566.   F128.5.M 69

MITCHEL.   John Purroy Mitchel, the boy mayor of New York, by Edwin R. Lewinson.   (1st ed., New York, Astra Books, 1965.   299 p.   22 cm.   65-15010.   F128.5.M7L4

MITCHELL, Mrs. Lucy (Sprague)   Manhattan; now and long ago; illus. with photos collected by the authors ...   New York, The Macmillan co., 1934.   viii p., 2 l., 312 p.   front., illus., maps (2 double) 24 cm. Bibliography: p. 311-312.   34-8996.   F128.5.M 72

MOCH, Andrée.   Bocetos de mi viaje a Norte América.   Buenos Aires, "La Baskonia", 1923. 2, (7) - 215 p.   illus., port.   19 cm.   Chiefly describing New York city.   24-4516.   F128.5.M 75

MONAGHAN, Frank.   New York, the World's fair city; a comprehensive collection of brilliant photos. of the world's greatest city at work and at play ... tog. with official plans and photographs of the New York World's fair of 1939.   Garden City, N.Y., Garden City pub. co. (1937)   (89) p.   illus.   25½ cm. 37-30354.   F128.5.M 78

MORAND, Paul.   ... New York.   (Paris) E. Flammarion (1930)   3, (5) - 281 p.   2 l.   front. (map)   18½ cm. 30-9604.   F128.5.M 82

NEW YORK CITY

— (1931)   2, 152 p., 2 l. front., illus., plates. 33 cm.   A cheaper ed., without other illus. than frontispiece, was pub. in 1930.   31-16885.   F128.5.M822 Rare Book Coll.

— (New York) H. Holt (1930)   7, (3) - 322 p. incl. front., platex. 20 cm.   "Translated by Hamish Miles with illus. by Joaquin Vaquero."   "First printing."   30-31141.   F128.5.M825

MORENO, Santiago M. Guía de Nueva York ... 1903.   F128.5.M 84

MORRIS, Newbold. Let the chips fall: my battles against corruption. New York, Appleton-Century-Crofts (1955)   308 p. 21 cm. 55-6071.   F128.5.M 87

MOSCOW, Warren. What have you done for me lately? the ins and outs of New York City politics. Englewood Cliffs, N.J., Prentice-Hall (1967)   xii, 241 p. 22 cm. 67-15177.   F128.5.M885

MUÑOZ AZPIRI, Francisco José. Nueva York; intromisión y testimonio. (Buenos Aires?) ... (1952)   95 p. 21 cm. 54-36256.   F128.5. M 9

MYERS, Willard Gilman. The unbelievable city. New York, 1926.   26 p. front., illus. 23½ cm. 26-11816.   F128.5.M 97

NADEN, Corinne J. The Triangle Shirtwaist fire, March 25, 1911; the blaze that changed an industry. New York, F. Watts (1971)   58 p. illus. 23 cm. (A franklin Watts lib. ed.) 70-137153.   F128.5. N 2

NESTERMAN, Lewis J. New York handy guide. New York city, Manhattan post card pub. co. (1943) 95 p. incl. front., illus. (incl. maps) 20 cm. 43-10646.   F128.5.N 29

— New York City, Progressive Pubs. (1955)   96 p. illus. 20 cm. 56-17663.   F128.5.N 29 1955

NEW YORK. (Brooklyn, N.Y., The Albertype co., 1908?)   24 mounted pl. 24 x 28½ cm.   F128.5. N 3

NEW YORK. Chamber of commerce of the state of New York. ... The city of New York ... A few ... facts of an economic ... character about the city of New York ... 19 -   v.   F128.5.N 33

NEVINS, Allan. The greater city: New York, 1898 - 1948. New York, Columbia Univ. Press, 1948. vii, 260 p. illus., ports. 21 cm. 48-8678*.   F128.5. N 4

NEW ENGLAND water works assoc. Notes on New York city and vicinity, describing engineering works and places of general interst ... New York, McGraw pub. co., 1905.   5, 88 p. front., illus., 2 fold. maps (in pocket) 23 cm. 5-29523.   F128.5.N 44

The NEW "red book" information guide to New York city, Manhattan and Bronx; borough; with new sectional maps, also large folded map ... New York, Newark, N.J., Interstate map co. (1919) 148, (2) p. maps (1 fold.) 15½ cm. 21-1609.   F128.5.N442

NEW YORK. (Portland, Me., 1909)   (2) p. 23 pl. 20 x 25 cm.   F128.5.N443

NEW YORK. A guide book to the city of New York, with historical, descriptive and statistical facts. (New York) The Chamber of commerce of the state of New York, 1947.   99 p. illus. (incl. maps) 15½ x 12 cm. 47-5056.   F128.5.N 45

NEW YORK (City) Mayor's Committee for the Commemoration of the Golden Anniversary of the City of New York. New York at work, 1898-1948; a report. (New York 1948)   51 p. 36 cm.   F128.5.N458

NEW YORK (City) Mayor's committee on celebration of 25th anniversary of the greater city of New

York. Official book of the silver jubilee of Greater New York ... 1923. ... (New York, M. B. Brown print. and binding co., 1923)   284 p. incl. illus., ports., plans, tables, diagr. 30½ cm. 23-18610. 23-18610.

    F128.5.N 46

NEW YORK (City) Mayor's committee on celebration of 25th anniversary of the greater city of New York. ... Parade order. (2d ed.) ... (New York, M. B. Brown print., 1923)   71 p. 23 x 11½ cm. 23-18609.

    F128.5.N463
    1923a

NEW YORK. National bank of North America. Souvenir 30th annual convention American bankers assoc., New York ... 1904 ... New York, 1904.   31 x 15½ cm.

    F128.5.N467

NEW YORK. Recreation training school. Let's go! A guide to places of interest in and around the city of New York. New York city ... (1940?)   3, 66, 4 numb. l. illus. 27 x 21½ cm. Reproduced from typewritten copy. Bibliography: leaves 64-66. 45-40082.

    F128.5.N 47

NEW YORK. Vanderbilt hotel. Two weeks vacation in New York, the nation's best summer resort. Presented by the Vanderbilt hotel, New York. (New York, Press of the Kalkhoff co., 1918)   29 p. illus. (incl. maps) 23 x 11½ cm. 18-10769.

    F128.5.N475

NEW YORK. (1903)   22½ x 28½ cm.

    F128.5.N 48

NEW YORK American. 100,000,000 America. New York American ... Dedicated to the vital forces in the leadership of New York and the supremacy of America. New York, 1911.   48, 36, 32, 24 p. illus. 42½ cm. CA 12-1235 Unrev.

    F128.5.N 49

NEW YORK city calendar, The. 1941 -   New York, Hastings house (1940 -   v. illus. 21 cm. Publication suspended with 1942 issue. 44-32015.

    F128.5.N513

The NEW YORK city (Manhattan and Bronx) vest-pocket guide; corrected semiannually ... June to Dec., 1899. (New York, M. F. Donovan) 1899 -   1 v. 13 x 6½ cm. 99-3395 Rev.

    F128.5.N516

... NEW YORK city standard guide; a new and complete handbook for visitors to New York, and for New Yorkers; with 90 illus. from photos. New York, Foster & Reynolds (1901)   156 p. incl. front., illus., fold. pl., fold. map. 20½ cm. (The standard guide series) Imperfect: map wanting. 1-23950.

    F128.5.N 52

The NEW YORK Edison co. Glimpses of New York; an illustrated handbook of the city, tog. with notes on the electric industry therein and thereabout ... (New York? 1911)   3, 152, (3) p. incl. illus., plates. col. plates. 19 cm. 11-14185.

    F128.5.N533

NEW YORK Edison co. New York in MCMXXIII; an illus. book of the city, compiled in honor of the 46th convention of the National electric light assoc. New York, The New York Edison co., 1923.   3, (125) p. of illus. 29 cm. 23-9632.

    F128.5.N535

NEW YORK Edison co. Towers of Manhattan. (New York) The New York Edison co., 1928.   3 l., 50 pl. (incl. front.) 31 cm. 30-9124.

    F128.5.N 54
    Rare Book Coll.

NEW YORK, greetings from the great metropolis beautiful. (New York, Home life pub. co., 19 -)   (40) p. of illus. 26 x 38½ cm. CA 28-887 Unrev.

    F128.5.N548

NEW YORK, historic and picturesque, a calendar for 1905. New York, 1904.   35 x 27½ cm.

    F128.5.N 55

NEW YORK illustrated. New York 1911.   26 cm.

    F128.5.N558

NEW YORK illustrated ... New York, Success postal card co., 1914.   (64) p. of illus. 26 cm. 14-12095.

    F128.5.N559

NEW YORK of to-day. 300th thousand. (Portland, Me., 1909)   (2) p.   23 pl.   20 x 25 cm.
F128.5.N 56

NEW YORK. (Portland, Me., L. H. Nelson co., 1908)   (24) p. illus. 20 x 25 cm. CA 26-486 Unrev.
F128.5.N562

... NEW YORK, the metropolis of the western world, with 90 illus. from photos. New York, The Foster & Reynolds co. (191-?)   146, (12) p. incl. front., illus. 21 cm. 18-4010.
F128.5.N564

— (1917)   133, 32 p. illus. 21 cm.
F128.5.N564
1917

— Revision of 1937. New York, The Foster & Reynolds co. (1937)   134, (21) p. incl. front., illus. fold. map. 20 cm. 41-11421.
F128.5.N564
1937

NEW YORK, the wonder city ... designed by R. Teising, Chicago. New York city, American art pub. co., 1914.   (64) p. of illus. 25 cm. 14-12426.
F128.5.N 57

— 1914.   (64) p. of illus. 25 cm. 14-17490.
F128.5.N573

— 1915.   (64) p. of illus. 14 x 20 ½ cm. 15-3047.
F128.5.N574

— 1918.   (64) p. of illus. 25 cm. 18-8691.
F128.5.N576

NEW YORK, the wonder city, illustrating in colors the amazing structures and scenic views of the worlds greatest city ... New York, American art pub. co., 1919.   2 p., 24 mounted col. pl. 23 ½ x 30 cm. 20-5735.
F128.5.N577

— Rev. ed. (Chicago, C. Teich, 1946)   (64) p. of illus. 24 cm. 46-20962.
F128.5.N578

NEW YORK fremdenführer ... New York city (1908)   1 v. 23 ½ cm.
F128.5.N 58

(NICHOLS, George Herbert Fosdike) New York, by "Quex" (pseud.) ... with a preface by Jeffery Farnol. London, S. Paul (1927)   v, 7-157 p. incl. front. 20 cm. 28-4905.
F128.5.N 72

— Philadelphia, David McKay co. (1928)   v, 7-157 p. incl. front. 19 ½ cm. 28-9292.
F128.5.N722

NILSSON, Selma. Kort skildring av min resa till U.S.A. ... (Kalmar, Barometerns tryckeri, 1940)   36 p. illus. 18 ½ cm. 43-50414.
F128.5.N 74

NORDIN, Vilhälm. Ur en emigrants anteckningsbok. Några sanningar om Amerika. Stockholm, G. Lindstrom (1902)   56 p. incl. plates. 24 cm. 40-25530.
F128.5.N 78

NORTH American A B C manual and blue book association. The Great New York A B C manual for natives and foreigners ... in five ... languages, English, Spanish, German, French, Italian and Portuguese ... comp. and ed. under the direction of Victor D. Vanderburgh ... New York ... (1923) 304 p. incl. front., illus. 26 cm. 23-12184.
F128.5.N 83

NORTHROP, Henry Davenport. ... New York's awful steamboat horror ... containing thrilling stories of this most overwhelming catastrophe of modern times ... (Memorial ed.) Philadelphia, Pa., National pub. co. (1904)   7, 17-432 p. front., plates, ports. 23 ½ cm. 4-26220.
F128.5.N 87

OGILVIE, John Stuart. History of the General Slocum disaster by which nearly 1200 lives were lost by the burning of the steamer General Slocum in Hell gate, New York harbor, June 15, 1904 ... New York, J. S. Ogilvie pub. co., 1904.   251 p. incl. plates, port., diagr. 18 ½ cm. 4-16790 Rev.
F128.5.O 34

ONE HUNDRED and sixty glimpses of greater New York from the latest and best photographs ... Boston, Mass., 1904.   (72) p. of pl. (1 fold.)   16½ x 23½ cm.   F128.5. O58

OVER one hundred selected views of Greater New York, reproduced from the best and latest photos. New York, I. H. Blanchard co. (1900)   (62) p. of illus.   18½ x 25½ cm.   Dec. 27, 1900-89.   F128.5. O 96

PANASSIÉ, Hughes.   Cinq mois à New-York.   (Paris) Éditions Corrêa (1947)   163 p.   19 cm.   57-46178.   F128.5. P 33

PARTON, Mary Field.   Metropolis; a study of New York.   New York, Toronto, Longmans, Green, 1939.   x, 191 p.   plates.   21 cm.   "First edition."   39-22994.   F128.5. P 37

PECK, John Sanford.   Science and New York city ...   New York city, Teachers college, Columbia university, 1940.   76 numb. l.   27½ x 21½ cm.   40-13195.   F128.5. P 43

PHILLIPS, Constance.   So you want to see New York!   Photos. and text by Constance Phillips.   Chicago, Rand McNally (1938)   (48) p.   illus.   24 cm.   41-5665.   F128.5. P 5

PICTORIAL truth, portraying who's who and why in New York.   New York, 1910.   35½ x 26½ cm.   F128.5. P 61

O SHEEL, Shaemas.   The dear old lady of Eighty-sixth street; a memoir of Laura Skeel Pomeroy, obiit., Aug. 23, 1911.   New York city, S. O Sheel (1912)   (9) p.   23½ cm.   One hundred copies made.   12-7878 Rev.   F128.5. P 78

PORTOR, Laura Spencer.   New York, the giant city; an introd. to New York ... illus. by Alida Conover.   Garrison-on-Hudson, N. Y., The Treasure tower pub. co. (1939)   48 p. incl. front., illus. (map) plates.   25½ cm.   39-13857.   F128.5. P 82

PORTOR, Laura Spencer.   Story of New York, the giant city ...   (1953)   47 p.   illus.   25 cm.   Pub. in 1939 under title: New York, the giant city.   53-36248.   F128.5. P 82 1953

PULSIFER, Susan Farley (Nichols)   A house in time.   Illus. by Edward C. Caswell.   New York, Citadel Press (1959, c.1958)   200 p.   illus.   27 cm.   Reminiscences of the author's childhood.   58-13336.   F128.5. P 87

RAND, McNally.   Greater New York illustrated.   Over 150 photographic views of the foremost city of the western hemisphere.   Chicago and New York, Rand, McNally, 1898.   249 p. incl. plates.   20 x 27 cm. Plates: p. 5-249.   1-14742 Rev.   F128.5. R 17

— 1899.   255 p. of illus.   19½ x 26½ cm.   99-2328 Rev.   F128.5. R 18

RAND, McNally guide to New York city and environs ...   New York, Chicago, Rand, McNally, (1895 - 1905)   16 v.   illus., fold. maps.   19½ cm.   Title varies.   18-14383 Rev.   F128.5. R 2

RAND, McNally New York guide to the city and environs, with map and illus.   New York, Chicago, Rand, McNally, 1917.   3 p., (3) - 139 p.   illus. (incl. plans, maps)   19½ cm.   17-10226.   F128.5. R233

— 1918.   3, (3) - 137 p.   illus. (incl. plans, maps)   19½ cm.   18-14383.   F128.5. R 2 1918

REGIONAL plan of New York and its environs.   The committee on a regional plan for New York and its environs; purposes and methods.   (New York, 1923?)   (4) p.   illus. (map)   28 x 21½ cm.   25-13897.   F128.5. R245

REGIONAL plan of New York and its environs.   Maps and diagrams showing present conditions, New York and its environs, March, 1923.   Prepared by the Physical survey ...   (New York ... 1923.   39 p.   illus. (maps, diagrs.)   30½ cm.   25-15063.   F128.5. R247

NEW YORK CITY

REGIONAL plan of New York and its environs. Plan of New York and its environs; the meeting of May 10, 1922. New York (1922) (25) p. 24 cm. 22-25225 Rev.   F128.5.R 35

REGIONAL plan of New York and its environs. ... Report of progress. (1st) - May 1922 - New York city ... 1923 -   v. 23 cm. 23-14444 Rev.   F128.5.R352

RIDER, Fremont, ed. Rider's New York city and vicinity, including Newark, Yonkers and Jersey City; a guide-book for travelers, with 16 maps and 18 plans, ... New York, H. Holt, 1916. xlii p. 506 p. maps (part fold.) plans (part fold.) 16 cm. Bibliography: p. 99-103. 16-22765 Rev.   F128.5.R 54 1916

RIDER, Fremont. Rider's New York city; a guide-book for travelers, with 13 maps and 20 plans ... 2d ed. New York, H. Holt, 1923. xlvi, 670 p. illus., maps (part fold.) plans. 16½ cm. "Supplementary material relating to Yonkers and to ... the environs of N.Y. in the state of New Jersey" omitted. 23-26861 Rev.   F128.5.R 54 1923

— 2d ed. New York, The Macmillan co., 1924. xlvi, 670 p. maps (part fold.) plans. 16½ cm. "This ed. omits material relating to Yonkers, etc." Bibliography: p. 128-133. 26-9258.   F128.5.R 54 1924

RIESENBERG, Felix. Portrait of New York. New York, The Macmillan co., 1939. xiii, 213 p. incl. front., plates. 26 x 20 cm. "First printing." 39-11281.   F128.5.R 56

ROGERS, Agnes. Metropolis; an American city in photographs ... with running comment by Frederick Lewis Allen ... Edward M. Weyer, photographer. New York and London, Harper & bros., 1934. (192) p. of illus. 31 cm. Photos. of life in N.Y. City. "First ed." 34-38343.   F128.5.R 72

ROTHENHÄUSLER, Paul. New York; ein Skizzenbuch mit Zeichnungen von Rodolf Steiger. (1 Aufl.) Zurich, Origo Verlag (1953) 95 p. illus. 21 cm. 54-23333.   F128.5.R815

ROTHERY, Agnes Edwards. New York today. Illus. by Norman Nisbet. (1st ed.) New York, Prentice Hall (1951) 279 p. illus. 21 cm. 51-14843.   F128.5.R 82

ROTOGRAVURE album of New York. (New York, Williamsburg post card co., 1921) (64) p. of views. 23½ x 30½ cm. 21-12092.   F128.5.R 84

ROULSTON, Marjorie (Hillis) New York, fair or no fair; a guide for the woman vacationist, ... drawings by Cipé Pineles. Indianapolis, New York, The Bobbs-Merrill co. (1939) 206 p. illus. 21 cm. "First ed." 39-12976 rev.   F128.5.R 86

RYDELIUS, Ellen Victoria. New York på 8 dagar, av Ellen Rydelius. Stockholm, A. Bonnier (1939) 199 p. plates (1 fold.) fold. maps, plans (part fold.) 15½ cm. 40-12917 Rev.   F128.5.R 97

ST. THOMAS, Jean. Marvelous New York, a metropolis portrayed. (Philadelphia, David McKay, 1937) 64 p. illus. 30 cm. Includes 59 p. of illus. (p. 6-64) 38-1111.   F128.5.S 17

HASCHID, Democritus. A mole's-eye view of New York. Boston, Charles T. Branford co. (1941) 4, 3-340 p. illus., diagrs. 23½ cm. 41-12187.   F128.5.S 2

SANTAMARÍA, Francisco Javier. ... Crónicas del destierro: Desde la ciudad de hierro. Diario de un desterrado mejicano en Nueva York. Recordaciones del destierro. Méjico, Editorial "Cultura," 1933. 225 p., 3 l. 18½ cm. 41-33071.   F128.5.S 23

SCENES of modern New York. (Portland, Me., 1905) 20½ x 25 cm.   F128.5.S 28

SCENES of modern New York. (160th thousand) Portland, Me., L. H. Nelson (1905) (46) p. of illus. 20 x 25 cm.   F128.5.S282

— 198th thousand. (Portland, Me., L. H. Nelson, 1907) (46) p. of illus. 20 x 23 cm.   F128.5.S284

— 219th thousand. (New York, J. Koehler, 1907) (46) p. of illus. 20 x 25 cm.
F128.5.S285

— 240th thousand. (Portland, Me., W. H. Nelson, 1907) (50) p. of illus. 20 x 25 cm.
F128.5.S286

— (260th thousand. Portland, Me. 1908) 20 x 25 cm.
F128.5. S 29

SCHERMAN, Bernardine (Kielty) Girl from Fitchburg. New York, Random House (1964) 189 p. 22 cm. "1st printing." 64-21275.
F128.5. S 35

SCHULTZE-ALTENWALDE, H. W. Illustrierter führer durch New York. . Oldenburg i. Gr. und New York, G. Stalling (1908) 4. 160 p. fold. front., illus., fold. pl. 21½ cm. 8-19137.
F128.5. S 38

SCHUMACHER, Jack. ... Wolkenkratzermenschen, die schatten selten einer millionenstadt. Bern, H. Peuz (1941) 181 p. 20½ cm.
F128.5. S 39

SEATON, George Whiting. Cue's guide to New York city ... New York, Prentice-Hall, inc., 1940. x, 141 p. plates. 21 cm. Map. 40-10872 Rev.
F128.5. S 42

SEEING New York ... New York, 1906. 23½ cm.
F128.5. S 43

SEGURA, Pedro. ... New York 1935; impresiones de un viaje a los Estados Unidos. Barcelona, Imprenta A. Núñez (1935) 175 p. 18½ cm. 35-22258.
F128.5. S 44

SELDES, Gilbert Vivian. This is New York; the first modern photographic book of New York. New York, D. Kemp, 1934. (64) p. of illus. 25 cm. 34-40667.
F128.5. S 46

SHACKLETON, Robert. The book of New York ... Illus. with photos. and with drawings by R. L. Boyer. Philadelphia, The Penn pub. co., 1917. 4, 377 p. col. front., illus., plates. 20½ cm. 18-87.
F128.5. S 49

— 1920. 4. 377 p. col. front., illus., plates. 20½ cm. 22-8345.
F128.5.S 492

SHALLOW, Edward. Geography of New York city ... (New York) 1904. 23 x 19 cm.
F128.5. S 52

SHISHKO, H. & A. New York illustrated. New York, Manhattan post card co. (1924) (48) p. of illus. 25½ cm. CA 25-681 Unrev.
F128.5. S 54

SIMON, Belle. Peg and Pete see New York. Indianpolis, New York, The Bobbs-Merrill co. (1939) (63) p. illus. 28½ cm. Map. In verse. "First ed." 39-7069.
F128.5. S 58

SINGLETON, Esther. The children's city ... New York, Sturgis & Walton, 1910. 8, 277 p. front., plates, plans, fold. map. 18½ cm. Map. 11-1260.
F128.5. S 61

SKAL, Georg von. Flashlights; momentaufnahmen aus dem leben einer armerikanischen grosstadt. Berlin, E. Fleischel, 1905. 3. 232 p. 20½ cm. 7-10582.
F128.5. S 62

SLOCUM, Rosalie. A key to New York. New York and London, Harper & bros., 1939. viii, 312 p. illus. (incl. maps, plans) 22 cm. "First ed." "Books to read": p. 247-248. 39-21134.
F128.5.S 623

— New York, Modern age books, inc.,(1939) viii. 312 p. illus. (incl. maps, plans) 20½ cm. "Books to read": p. 247-248. 39-27281.
F128.5.S 625

SMITH, Edward Garstin. ... New York politics ... New York (1898) 28 p. 17 cm. "Extract from the National weekly." 19-4951.
F128.5. S 63

SMITH, Francis Hopkinson. Charcoals of new and old New York; pictures and text by F. Hopkinson

NEW YORK CITY

Smith. Garden City, N.Y., Doubleday, Page, 1912.   8, 3-142, (2) p. incl. mounted illus., mounted plates. 29½ cm. 12-29488.   F128.5. S 64

SMITH, Francis Hopkinson. Charcoals of old New York; ... Garden City, N.Y., Doubleday, Doran, 1928.   6, 3-142 p. incl. plates.   26 cm.   Pub. 1912 with title: Charcoals of new and old New York.   29-7218.   F128.5.S 642 Rare Book Coll.

... SOUVENIR guide book of New York city; more than 115 important pictures ... Selected by the Chamber of commerce of the state of New York as the approved guide book of New York ... New York, N.Y., Supervue map & guide organization, 1939.   160 p.   illus. (incl. maps, plan)   17½ cm.   39-11426.   F128.5. S 68

STALEY'S views of New York, 1909 ... New York, F. W. Staley (1909)   (48) p.   illus.   26 cm. CA 17-147 Unrev.   F128.5. S 77

— New York, M. King, 1911.   48 p.   illus.   26 cm.   12-38897.   F128.5. S 78

STANTON, Gerritt Smith. Renting a gurnished apartment; a narrative setting forth the experiences of an out-of-town family in the metropolis ... New York, J. S. Ogilvie pub. co. (1916)   120 p. incl. front., illus.   20 cm.   16-8368.   F128.5. S 8

STEIN, Leon. The triangle fire. (1st ed.) Philadelphia, Lippincott (1962)   224 p.   21 cm.   62-10546.   F128.5. S 83

STOPPELMAN, Joseph Willem Ferdinand. Zo is New York! Amsterdam, Arbeiderspers, 1953. 184 p.   21 cm.   54-25555.   F128.5. S 86

STREET, Julian Leonard. Welcome to our city ... illustrations by James Montgomery Flagg and Wallace Morgan. New York, John Lane co. (1913)   175 p.   front., plates.   19½ cm.   Reprinted from Everybody's magazine and Collier's weekly.   13-11528.   F128.5. S 91

STRUNSKY, Simeon. Belshazzar court; or, Village life in New York city. New York, H. Holt, 1914. 4, 3-190 p.   1 illus., pl.   19½ cm.   Reprinted in part from various periodicals.   14-20792.   F128.5. S 93

— (1922)   3, 3-300 p.   front., plates.   20 cm.   22-14580.   F128.5.S932

STRUNSKY, Simeon. No mean city. New York, E. P. Dutton (1944)   285 p.   22½ cm.   "First ed."   F128.5.S933

The SUN, New York. New York in pictures, with an introd. by James J. Walker, mayor of New York ... (New York, The Sun print. and pub. assoc.) 1928 -   v.   illus.   23 cm.   "Reprinted from the Sun, New York, 1928."   29-8381.   F128.5. S 95

SUPERVUE map and guide corporation. ... The Supervue guide book of New York city ... New York, N.Y., Supervue map and guide organization, 1941.   128 p.   illus. (incl. maps)   17½ cm.   41-12322 rev.   F128.5.S953

— 12 ed. 1945.   128 p.   illus. (incl. maps)   17½ cm.   46-12432 rev.   F128.5.S953 1945

— New York, 1955.   128 p.   illus.   18 cm.   55-25900.   F128.5.S953 1955

(SWEETSSON, Henry, Inc.) Visiting New York city; buyers manual. (New York, Henry Sweetsson, inc., 1921)   2, 60 p.   illus. (incl. map)   23½ cm.   21-19781.   F128.5. S 97

TARR, Ralph Stockman. Georgraphy of the city of New York ... 1903.   F128.5.T 19

THOMAS, Lowell Jackson. A trip to New York with Bobby and Betty. New York, Dodge pub. co. (1936)   4, (11)-89, (3) p.   illus.   28 cm.   "First ed."   36-10320.   F128.5.T 45

THOMPSON, Cecil Vincent Raymond.   Trousers will be worn ... drawings by Margaret Freeman.
New York, G. P. Putnam's sons (1941)   4, 3-243 p. incl. plates.   19½ cm.   41-7623 rev.
F128.5.T 46

The TOURISTS' guide to New York ... Student guide pub. co., 19   New York,   v. illus. (incl. plans)
20½ cm.   quarterly.   28-11326.
F128.5.T 68

The TOURIST'S hand-book of New York ... New York (1905)   20½ x 12 cm.
F128.5.T 72

TOWN taxi co. inc.   New York sight-seeing taxicab tours ... New York, Town taxi co., inc. (1917)
3 v.   illus.   20½ cm.   17-16865.
F128.5.T 74

TOWNE, Charles Hanson.   This New York of mine.   New York, Cosmopolitan book corporation,
1931.   xii, 289 p.   front., plates.   23 cm.   "First ed."   31-6994.
F128.5.T 75

TULLY, Andrew.   Era of elegance.   (New York) Funk & Wagnalls Co., 1947.   xii, 232 p.   illus.
21 cm.   47-11719*
F128.5.T 85

U. S. Bureau of naval personnel.   New York city.   (Washington) Pub. by Bureau of navigation under
authority of the secretary of the navy (1920)   85 p. incl. front., illus.   fold. plan.   13½ x 18 cm.   (Ditty box
guide book series)   Cover-title: Ports of the world.   New York.   21-26473 Rev.
F128.5.U 53

VAN DYKE, John Charles.   The new New York; a commentary on the place and the people; illus. by
Joseph Pennell.   New York, The Macmillan co., 1909.   xv, 425 p.   98 pl.   xxv col. pl. (incl. front.)   22 cm.
9-24461.
F128.5.V 24

VENZMER, Gerhard.   New Yorker spaziergänge, eindrücke und betrachtungen aus der metropole der
neuen welt.   Hamburg, Weltbund-verlag (1925)   301 p.   23 cm.
F128.5.V 4
1925

VENZMER, Gerhard.   New York ohne schminke.   VI bis VIII vollständing neugestaltete aufl. der
"New Yorker spaziergänge."   Hamburg, Weltbundverlag (1930)   215 p.   plates.   22½ cm.   42-35891.
F128.5. V 4
1930

VIEWS of New York.   (160th thousand)   (Portland, Me., 1905)   (2) p.   23 pl.   20 x 25 cm.
F128.5.V 65

— 1911.   20½ x 25 cm.
F128.5.V 67

— 1913.   (48) p.   illus.   20 x 25 cm.   13-8635.
F128.5.V 68

WALKER.   Beau James; the life & times of Jimmy Walker.   By Gene Fowler.   New York, Viking
Press, 1949.   x, 389 p.   ports.   22 cm.   49-8418*.
F128.5.W217
1949

WALKER.   Abroad with Mayor Walker, by Hector Fuller.   New York, Shields pub. co. (1928)
264 p. incl. front.   plates, ports., facsim.   24½ cm.   28-15181.
F128.5. W 22

WALKER.   Jimmie Walker, the story of a personality, by Louis J. Gribetz and Joseph Kaye.   New
York, L. MacVeagh, Dial press, inc., 1932.   5, 3-353 p.   front., plates, ports., facsims.   22½ cm.   32-35512.
F128.5.W223

WARD, Cabot.   List of places and institutions of a public and semi-public character in New York city
comp. ... for the ... delegates to the Second Pan American scientific congress ...   New York, The
Pan American soc. of the U. S. (1915)   (7) p.   20 x 16½ cm.   18-17112.
F128.5.W 26

The WAYFARER in New York; introd. by Edward S. Martin.   New York, The Macmillan co., 1909.
xxii, 266 p.   17 cm.   Consists of extracts from various writers.   9-35849.
F128.5.W 35

NEW YORK CITY

The WEEK in New York. v. 1-4; Oct. 16, 1904 - Mar. 24, 1906. New York, Information pub. co., 1904-6.   4 v. maps. 20½ cm. Laura Skinner, editor. Superseded by Daily attractions in N. Y. 6-13604 Add.   F128.5.W39

WERSTEIN, Irving. The General Slocum incident; story of an ill-fated ship. New York, J. Day Co. 1965.   159 p. 21 cm. 64-14210.   F128.5.W4

WHALEN, Frank Daniel. New York today. New York, Noble and Noble, 1948.   vii, 151 p. illus., maps. 20 cm. A companion book to New York yesterday ... 49-166.*   F128.5.W53

WHALEN, Grover Aloysius. Mr. New York; the autobiography of Grover A. Whalen. New York, Putnam (1955)   321 p. illus. 22 cm. 55-10103.   F128.5.W54

WHAT to see in New York. New York, J. Wanamaker, 1912.   44 p. illus., fold. map. 18½ cm. 24-17740.   F128.5.W55

WHITE, Elwyn Brooks. Here is New York. (1st ed.) New York, Harper (1949)   54 p. illus. 20 cm. "First pub. in Holiday." 49-50146*.   F128.5.W58

WHITING, Alice. Guia practica para visitar a New York ... Habana, P. Fernandez y ca. (1937) xviii, 209 p. illus. (incl. map) fold. pl., fold. plan. 20 cm. 38-16422.   F128.5.W62

WILLIAMS, Jesse Lynch. New York sketches ... New York, C. Scribner's sons, 1902. xii, 133 p. col. front., illus. 26 x 18½ cm. 2-27728.   F128.5.W72

(WILSON, Latimer J.) comp. My trip to New York; New York, F. M. Buckles (1906) 131 p. incl. front., illus. 19 cm. 6-28413.   F128.5.W78

WRONECKI, Daniel. New-York. (Paris) F. Nathan (1949)   187 p. (p. 49-176 illus.) 24 cm. (Merveilles de la France et du monde) Text in French. 49-26963*.   F128.5.W93

ZEISLOFT, E. Idell, ed. The new metropolis; 1600 - memorable events of three centuries - 1900; from the island of Mana-hat-ta to Greater New York at the close of the nineteenth century. Illus. with one thousand engravings. New York, D. Appleton (1899)   2, iii - xxii, 639 (32) p. incl. illus., plates. ports., maps, plans. plates (part double, part col.) 29 x 37 cm. "Edition de luxe ...) 99-4348 Rev.   F128.5.Z47

NEW YORK CITY.   1951 TO DATE.

ALBERT-LEVIN, Marc. Un printemps à New-York. Paris, Pauvert, 1969.   94 p. illus. 28 cm.   F128.52.A4

AŠKENAZY, Ludvik. Indiáneké léto. (Vyd. 3) Praha, Československý spisovatel, 1962. 191 p. illus. 21 cm.   F128.52.A8 1962

AŠKENAZY, Ludvik. Indianischer Sommer. (Deutsch von Anna Wirthová. Prag) Artia (1958) 209 p. illus. 21 cm. 58-42016.   F128.52.A815

AVISHAI, Stela Bokhor. Glasovete na Niu Iork. 1966.   188 p. illus. 21 cm.   F128.52.A9

BEHAN, Brendan. Brendan Behan's New York. Wtih drawings by Paul Hogarth. London, Hutchinson (1964)   159 p. 25 cm. "First publ. 1964."   F128.52.B43 1964

— (New York) B. Geis Associates ... (1964)   159 p. 25 cm. First printing. 64-19592.   F128.52.B43 1964a

BERGER, Meyer. Meyer Berger's New York. N. Y., Random House (1960)   322 p. 24 cm. "1st printing." 60-5556.   F128.52.B45

BJÖRKSTÉN, Ingmar.   Dagar i New York.   Anteckningar 1 maj - 10 juli 1965.   ... Stockholm, Geber, 1966.   168 p.   (6) leaves of plates.   illus.   22 cm.   F128.52. B 5

BOLDIZSÁR, Iván.   New York percröl perore.   Budapest, Magvetö Könyvkiado, (1971)
497 p.   19 cm.   F128.52. B 6

BOL'SHAK, Vasyl' Hryhoriĭovych.   Husak na Brodvei.   333 p.   17 cm.   USSR 71-9974.
F128.52. B63

BOURGEADE, Pierre.   New York Party.   Avec un ... (dessin) de Man Ray.   (Paris,) Gallimard, 1959.   192 p.   plate.   18 cm.   F128.52. B67

BRAUNBURG, Rudolph.   Logbuch New York.   Hamburg, Baken-Verlag (1968)   103 p.   19 cm.
F128.52. B 7

BUCKLEY, William Frank.   The unmaking of a mayor.   New York, Viking Press (1966)
ix, 341 p.   25 cm.   "First pub. 1966."   66-20339.   F128.52. B 8

BULHÕES, Antonio.   Outubro 65 (i.e. sessenta e cinco)   Rio de Janeiro, Editôra Pongetti, 1966.
83 p.   20 cm.   F128.52. B 84

CARNICER, Ramón.   Nueva York, nivel de vida, nivel de muerte.   Barcelona, Editorial Taber (1970)   295 p.   illus.   22 cm.   F128.52. C37

CHABRIER, Agnès.   Mémoires du proche avenir.   Paris, Flammarion (1965)   252 p.   19 cm.   (Le Meilleur des mondes)   F128.52. C45

CHU, Hsiu-chüan.   (Niu-yüeh chien wen.   (61 i.e. 1972)   3, 6, 205 p.   19 cm.
F128.52. C47
Orien, China

CHUECA, Goitia, Fernando.   Nueva York, forma y sociedad.   Madrid, Instituto de Estudios de Administracion Local, 1953.   197 p.   illus., maps, diagrs.   25 cm.   54-39593.
F128.52. C48

COHEN, Mortimer Theodore.   Negroes, Jews and justice in New York City, by J. Frumious Bandersnatch. (pseud.)   (New York, Paragon Publications, 1963?)   68 p.   22 cm.   63-23312.
F128.52. C54

COLE, William.   New York in photographs.   New York, Simon and Schuster, 1961.   28 cm.   "first printing."   61-15118.   F128.52. C58

COPP, Harry Dewitt.   Guide to New York City: hotels, restaurants, night clubs, sightseeing, tours, planned trips.   (New York, Visitors Guide Books, 1955)   192 p.   illus.   16 cm.   Pub. in 1939 under title: New York, day and night.   56-40824.
F128.52. C 6
1955

— 1957.   192 p.   illus., maps (2 fold.)   16 cm.   57-41636.
F128.52. C 6
1957

CRILLEY, Joseph J.   New York: island of islands.   Photos. by Joseph J. Crilley.   Text by Arthur Carduner. ...   (Limited ed.)   Buffalo, W. J. Keller (1965)   124 p.   24 x 32 cm.
F128.52. C 7

DANIEL, Anita.   Je vais à New-York (-) traduit de l'allemand par Eugène Bestaux.   Illustrations de J. Marianne Moll Simons,   Paris, Calmann-Lévy (1952)   268 p.   illus.   18 cm.   53-17686.
F128.52. D 3

DANIEL, Anita.   You'll love New York.   Illus. by J. Marianne Moll.   Basel, Birkhäuser (1964)
163 p.   18 cm.   F128.52. D33

NEW YORK CITY 263

ESQUIRE. New York; a selective guide to its enjoyment. (New York, 1960) 176 p.
F128.52.E 8

ESTOL, Horacio. Nueva York de cerca. Buenos Aires, Compañia General Fabril (1959)
403 p. F128.52.E82

FEININGER, Andreas. New York. Photos. by Andreas Feininger. Text by Kate Simon. New York, Viking Press (1964) 159 p. 31 cm. (A Studio book) 64-11203. F128.52.F 4

FEUERSTEIN, Herbert. New York fur Anfänger. Ein heiterer Leitfaden. (Zurich,) Diogenes-Verlag, (1969) 84 p. illus. 19 cm. F128.52.F44

FLAHERTY, Joe. Managing Mailer. New York, Coward-McCann (1970) 222 p. illus. 22 cm.
71-104682. F128.52.F55

FREDERICKS, Pierce G. All around New York. Photos. by Leonard Stern. New York, Putnam (1961) unpaged. 1 v. 16 cm. 61-15076. F128.52.F 7

FREEMAN, David. U. S. Grant in the city; and other true stories of jugglers and pluggers, swatters and whores. New York, Viking Press (1971) 150 p. 22 cm. 77-148268.
F128.52.F73

FUKOVÁ, Eva. New York. ... Praha, Mlada fronta, 1966) 165 p. illus. 20 cm.
F128.52.F 8

GÁL, Zsuzsanna. Feleség voltam New Yorkban. Budapest (Táncsics Konyvkiado) 1966.
226 p. (Utikalandok, 60) F128.52.G25

GARDNER, Hy. Hy Gardner's offbeat guide to New York. Photos. by Walter Vecchio. New York, Grosset & Dunlap (1964) 192 p. 25 cm. F128.52.G28

GARELICK, May. Manhattan Island. Woodcuts by John Ross and Clare Romano Ross. New York, Crowell (1957) 53 p. illus. 26 cm. 56-9801. F128.52.G 3

GOLDSTON, Robert. New York: civic exploitation. Illus. By Donald Carrick. (New York) Macmillan Co. (1970) 186 p. illus. 24 cm. 72-89586. F128.52.G 6

GOODMAN, Walter. A percentage of the take. New York, Farrar, Strauss and Giroux (1971)
xiii, 225 p. illus. 23 cm. "1st printing, 1971." 72-137751. F128.52.G66

HAMMEL, Faye. The Mademoiselle career girl's guide to New York. New York, Dial Press, 1962.
250 p. 22 cm. 61-15503. F128.52.H257

HAPGOOD, David. The purge that failed: Tammany v. Powell. (New York) Holt (1959)
15 p. 28 cm. (Case studies in practical politics) 59-12379. F128.52.H26

HAWKINS, Stuart. New York, New York. New York, W. Funk (1957) 302 p. illus. 24 cm. 57-6511.
F128.52.H 3

HAYES, Helen. Twice over lightly; New York then and now. (1st ed.) New York, Harcourt Brace Jovanovich (1972) 343 p. illus. 21 cm. 72-75417. F128.52.H33

HENTOFF, Nat. A political life; the education of John V. Lindsay. (1st ed.) New York, A. A. Knopf, 1969. 354 p. 22 cm. 78-88743. F128.52.H38

HEPBURN, Andrew. New York City; (complete guide. Rev. Boston) Houghton Mifflin, 1957.
168 p. illus. 22 cm. (The Amer. travel series, no. 4) Pub. in 1953 under title: A complete guide to N. Y. City. 57-1904. F128.52.H 4
1957

HOLUB, Miroslav. Die explodierende Metropole New York. ... (Mit) 130 Fotografien von Karol

997

Kallay. Berlin, Verlag Volk und Welt, 1967.   123 p.   31 cm.

F128.52.H55

HOLUB, Miroslav. Žit v New Yorku. 1. vyd. P., Melantrich, t. Tisk 2, Brno 1969.   8º.   169, (1) s. 25000 výt. Váz. 15 Kčs. - Obulka a vazba: Miroslav Váša.

F128.52.H56

HONDA, Ichiji. Uesuto saido no Nihonjin.   Ōsaka, Rokugatsusha, 1963.   258 p.   18 cm.

F128.52.H57
Orien. Japan

HORN, Jack. "And on the right - " A New York City guide. (New York? 1956)   140 p. illus.
22 cm.   "3d printing."   56-45725.

F128.52.H 6
1956

IRVING Trust Co. Impressions of New York; a photographic essay designed to recall pleasant memories of your visit to our city. New York (1956)   48 p. (chiefly illus.)   29 cm.   56-26160.

F128.52. I 7

JOTTERAND, Franck. New York. Lausanne. Editions Rencontre, 1968.   192 p.   27 cm. (L'atlas des voyages)

F128.52. J 6

KLEIN, Woody. Lindsay's promise: the dream that failed; a personal account.   (New York) Macmillan Co. (1970)   xv, 349 p.   21 cm.   "First prtg."   73-114327.

F128.52.K55

KUBLITSKII, Georgiy Ivanovich.   Inostranet͡s v N'i͡u-Yorke. 1965.   238 p.   21 cm.

F128.52.K78

KUBLITSKII, Georgiy Ivanovich. Tri n'i͡u-York - skikh oseni.   1964.   268 p.   21 cm.

F128.52.K 8

KURODA, Hiroko. Watakushi wa Nyūyōku o aishita.   Tōkyō, Hakuó Sha (1964)   235 p.   19 cm.

F128.52.K87
Orien Japan

LACHTERMAN, David. New York, l'humanité au mètre cube.   Paris, Casterman, 1966.
205 p.   illus. (part col.)   19 cm.   (Collection Horizon 2000)   "Reprinted

F128.52.L28

LAVINE, David. Under the city. Photos. by Ira Mandelbaum. (1st ed.) Garden City, N.Y., Doubleday, 1967.   128 p.   25 cm.   67-10680.

F128.52.L 3

LOVE, Edmund G. Subways are for sleeping. (1st ed.) New York, Harcourt, Brace (1957)
185 p.   21 cm.   57-10069.

F128.52.L 6

MANNES, Marya. The New York I know. With photos by Herb Snitzer. (1st ed.) Philadelphia, Lippincott (1961)   159 p.   26 cm.   61-12195.

F128.52.M 3

MANSO, Peter. Running against the machine; the Mailer-Breslin campaign. Ed. by Peter Manso. (1st ed.) Garden City, N.Y., Doubleday, 1969.   xiii, 313 p.   illus.   22 cm.   78-93201.

F128.52.M33

MILLSTEIN, Gilbert. New York: true north. Photos. by Sam Falk. (1st ed.) Garden City, N.Y., Doubleday 1964.   288 p.   29 cm.   63-16640.

F128.52.M55

MOOKERJEE, Sivatosh. Myanahatana o martini.   204 p.   22 cm.

F128.52.M 6
Orien Ben

NEW YORK City. (Prepared with the cooperation of the American Geographical Soc.) Garden City, N.Y., Doubleday (1968)   64 p.   illus.   21 cm.   (Know your America program)   1958 - 1963 editions by Alice Taylor.

F128.52.N29
1968

NEW YORK CITY

NEW YORK City guide and almanac. 1957-58 -   (New York) New York University Press.
v. illus., ports., maps. 21 cm. 57-10348.   F128.52.N 3

NEW YORK et ses environs. (1. éd.) Paris, Hachette, 1954.   382 p. maps (part fold. col.) plans. 17 cm.
(Les Guides bleus)   Bibliography: p. (79) - 81. 55-15745.   F128.52.N 4

NEW YORK herald tribune. New York Herald Tribune presents New York, New York, by Tom Wolfe (and others) New York, Dial Press, 1964.   190 p. 21 cm. "First printing." (A Delta book) 64-21096.
F128.52.N43

NOTHOMB, Pierre. Dieu à New-York. (Paris) Dutilleul (1957)   44 p. illus. 19 cm. A 57-7074.
F128.52.N65

OLIVA, Felix M. Nueva York para el perfecto turista. (1 ed.) Barcelona, Ediciones Martes, 1970)
298 p. illus., maps (on lining papers) 21 cm. (Novela y documento) 76-286939.   F128.52.O 4

PASSAVANT, Peggy. Buntes New York; gesammelte Skizzen. Winterthur, Gemsberg-Verlag (1962)
165 p. 19 cm.   F128.52. P 3

PERSSON, Hasse. New York, kontrasternas stad. En bildberättalse. Halmstad, Spektra; (Solna, Seelig, 1969)   (156) p. illus. 29 cm.   F128.52. P38

PETERSON, Joyce. The New York I love. Introd. by Robert F. Wagner. Photography by Peter Fink. New York, Tudor Pub. Co., 1964.   125 p. 27 cm.   F128.52. P 4

PLA, José. Week-end (d'estiu) a New York; tercera serie de "Cartes de lluny." (1. ed.) Barcelona, Editorial Selecta (1955)   248 p. illus. 15 cm. (Biblioteca Selecta. 180.) 59-20366.
F128.52.P55

POLLAK, Betty. Manhattan transplant. Illus. by Ed Fisher. New York, Crowell (1959)
198 p. illus. 21 cm. An account of the author's family's experiences on a sabbatical year in N.Y. city. 59-11384.   F128.52. P 6

PRITCHETT, Victor Sawdon. New York proclaimed. Photos, by Evelyn Hofer. (1st ed. London) Chatto & Windus (1965)   116 p. 29 cm.   F128.52.P73

— (1st Amer. ed.) New York, Harcourt, Brace & World (1965)   116 p. illus. (part col.) 29 cm.
65-11986.   F128.52.P73
                                                                1965a

PROVINS, LeRoy G. So you want to be a New Yorker. (1st ed.) New York, Harper (1958)
192 p. 21 cm. 58-8878.   F128.52.P75

RANDÉ, Jenő. New Yorkból jelentem. (Budapest) Móra Ferenc Könyvkiado (1958)   204 p. 20 cm.
F128.52.R 3

RANDÉ, Jenő. Szputnyik New York felett. Budapest, Móra Ferenc Könyvkiadó, 1960.   199 p.
21 cm.   F128.52.R32

RICH, Joan. How to be a New Yorker. (1st ed.) Garden City, N.Y., Doubleday, 1964.   v, 180 p.
22 cm. 64-19292.   F128.52.R 5
                                                                1964

SCHARPENBERG, Margot. Einladung nach New York. Mit Fotos von Klaus Wellmann. (München) Langen Muller (1972)   246 p. plates (part col.) 24 cm.   F128.52. S 3

SEITLIN, Percy. New York; people and places. Photos. by Victor Laredo. New York, Reinhold Pub. Corp. (1964)   188 p. 27 cm. 64-13645.   F128.52. S 4

SHAPIRO, Fred C. Race riots New York 1964. New York, Crowell (1964)   222 p. 21 cm. 64-8479.
F128.52.S 48

SIMON, Kate. New York places & pleasures; an uncommon guidebook. Drawings by Bob Gill. New York, Meridian Books (1959)   352 p. illus. 22 cm. (Meridian books, MG 18) "First publ. June, 1959" "First printing, Apr. 1959.   59-7186.
 F128.52. S 5

SURBEK, Victor. New York; Impressionen. Zurich, Orell Füssli (1961)   (60) p. 25 illus. 32 cm.
 F128.52. S 8

SYLVESTER, Robert. Notes of a guilty bystander. Englewood Cliffs, N.J., Prentice-Hall (1970) x, 305 p. illus. 25 cm. 75-110670.
 F128.52. S 9

TAK, Max. Hier is New York. Utrecht, A. W. Bruna (1960)   80 p. 18 cm. (Zwarte beertjes 289/290)
 F128.52. T26

TALESE, Gay. Fame and obscurity, portraits. New York, World Pub. Co. (1970)   x, 357 p. 24 cm. "1st printing 1970" 72-112433.
 F128.52. T27

TALESE, Gay. New York; a serendipiter's journey. With photos. by Marvin Lichtner. (1st ed.) New York, Harper (1961)   141 p. 24 cm. 61-6443.
 F128.52. T28

TAYLOR, Alice. New York City. (Prepared with the cooperation of the American Geographical Soc.) Garden City, N.Y., N. Doubleday (1958)   64 p. illus. 21 cm. 58-3932.
 F128.52. T 3

— (1963)   64 p. (American Geographic Soc. Know your America program)
 F128.52. T 3 1963

TOFANELLI, Arturo. Il cielo di Nuova York. (Milano) Edizioni della Meridiana (1955) 54 p. 17 cm. 58-24520.
 F128.52. T 6

TRESS, Arthur. Open space in the inner city; ecology and the urban environment. Photos. by Arthur Tress. New York State Council on the Arts, 1971.   (4) p., 50 plates. 37 cm.
 F128.52. T73

UP against New York; a handbook for survival in the city, by John Berenyi. New York, Morrow, 1971.   290 p. 21 cm. 77-142394.
 F128.52. U 6

VASILIU, Mircea. Which way to the melting pot? With illus. by the author. (1st ed.) Garden City, N.Y., Doubleday, 1963.   309 p. 22 cm. 63-11229.
 F128.52. V 3

WELTSTADTE. Wolfgang Koeppen: New York. Maximilian Braun: Moskau. Reinhold Schneider: Liszabon. Mit 96 Bildtafeln, darunter 12 farbig. Munchen u. Ahrbeck/Hannover, Knorr u. Hirth (1965)   (74) l. 18 cm. (Das kleine Kunstbuch. Sammelband)
 F128.52. W 4

WHALEN, Richard J. A city destroying itself; an angry view of New York. Illus. by Feliks Topolski. New York, W. Morrow, 1965.   127 p. 20 cm. 65-26936.
 F128.52.W47

WILSON, Earl. Earl Wilson's New York. Drawings by Lawrence Ratzkin. New York, Simon and Schuster, 1964.   384 p. 21 cm. "First printing." 64-14428.
 F128.52. W 5

NEW YORK CITY - SECTIONS. LOCALITIES. DISTRICTS, etc.

NEW YORK CITY. CEMETERIES.

FAIRCHILD sons. Fairchild cemetery manual; a reliable guide to the cemeteries of Greater New York and vicinity. Brooklyn, N.Y., Fairchild sons (1910)   v, 6-298 p. front., illus. (map) 20 cm. 10-15633.
 F128.61.A1F3

(JUDSON, Selden C.) The cemeteries of New York, and how to reach them. New York, G. H. Burton, printer (1881)   62 p. 2 fold. maps.   15 x 12 cm.   11-23144.   F128.61.A1 J9

LEONARD, John Henry, comp. The Leonard manual of the cemeteries of New York and vicinity. A hand guide; embodying a brief history and description of all the regular New York and neighboring cemeteries ... New York, J. H. Leonard, 1895.   126 p. illus. 15 cm.   11-23143.
     F128.61.A1L5

— New York, J. H. Leonard (1901)   3, 9-143 p. illus. 16½ cm.   2-1126-M2.   F128.61.A1L52

MINES, John Flavel. Walks in our churchyards; old New York, Trinity Parish. By Felix Oldboy (John Flavel Mines) New York, G. G. Peck, 1896.   181 p. illus. 19 cm.   Originally pub. in the Trinity record during 1890-1892.   1-14764 rev.*   F128.61.A1M6

NEW YORK. Trinity Church. Churchyards of Trinity Parish in the City of New York, 1697-1947. Pub. in observance of the 250th anniversary of the founding of Trinity Church. (New York, 1948) 77 p. illus., maps. 22 cm.   49-13711*.   F128.61.T7N4

— Enl. ed. (New York, 1955)   85 p. illus., maps. 22 cm.   55-59586.   F128.61.T7N4 1955

WOODLAWN cemetery. (New York, Designed and executed by the Kalkhoff co.) 1910.   (8) p. plates. 21 x 26 cm.   F128.61.W8W8

WOODLAWN. 1915.   1 v.   F128.61.W8W82

WOODLAWN. (New York, Press of the Kalkhoff co.) 1916.   (14) p. front., illus. 24½ cm.   16-25269.   F128.61.W8W84

— 1917.   (14) p. front., illus. 24½ cm.   17-15086.   F128.61.W8W85

NEW YORK CITY.   CHURCHES.

A FAMILIAR conversation history of the evangelical churches of New-York. New York, R. Carter, 1838.   222 p. front. 15½ cm.   6-13607.   F128.62.A1F2

BENNETT, William Harper. Handbook to Catholic historical New York city ... New York, Schwartz, Kirwin & Fauss (1927)   3, 154 p. 16 cm.   27-17350.   F128.62.A13 B47

BRICK Presbyterian church in the city of New York, A history of the, by Shepherd Knapp ... New York, Trustees of the Brick Presbyterian church, 1909.   xxii, 566 p. front., plates, ports., plans, facsim. 24 cm.   Bibliography: p. (495)-510.   9-4285.   F128.62.B8K6

CHRIST Protestant Episcopal church in New York city, Records of ... New York city, 1919.   v. 36 x 28½ cm.   F128.62.C5N47

CHURCH of the Puritans, The British mission of the. Its true origin and prosecution under the policy of Dr. H. A. Hartt. (By Elizabeth Johnstone) Pub. by the author. New-York, J. A. Gray, printer, 1861.   36 p. 23 cm.   34-19821.   F128.62.C54J6

CHURCH of the transfiguration. The Little church around the corner, by George MacAdam ... New York & London, G. P. Putnam's sons, 1925.   x, 347 p. front., plates, ports., facsims. (1 fold.) diagr. 22½ cm. 25-5621.   F128.62.C56M12

CHURCH of the transfiguration. Through the lich-gate; a biography of the Little church around the corner, by Ishbel Ross; sixteen illus. from dry points by Ralph L. Boyer. New York, W. F. Payson, 1931.   2, iii-v, 164 p. front., plates, ports. 28 cm.   31-30853 rev.   F128.62.C56R8

COLLEGIATE Church. ... A monograph to commemorate the 300th anniversary of the organization,

in 1628, of the Reformed Protestant Dutch church of the city of New York. Collated and ed. by Wm. Leverich Brower ... New York, The Consistory of the Collegiate Reformed Dutch church, 1928.
113 p.   illus. (facsims.)   plates.   23 cm.   Also pub. under title: ...   A tribute to the settlement of Manhattan Island ...   28-29678.
F128.62.C6B76

COLLEGIATE church. ... A tribute to the settlement of Manhattan Island, now New York, by the Dutch, early in the 17th century. This monograph issued to commemorate the 300th anniversary of the purchase of the island by Peter Minuit. New York, The Consistory of the Collegiate Reformed Dutch church, 1926.   111 p.   illus. (facsims.)   plates.   23 cm.   See above item.   26-15441.   F128.62.C6B8

COLLEGIATE church. The celebration of the quarter millennial anniversary of the Reformed Protestant Dutch church, of the city of New York ... 1878. In the church, Fifth ave. and 29th st. (New York, C. H. Jones, printers, 1878)   104 p.   23 cm.   1-2554 Add.   F128.62.C6N43

COLLEGIATE church. Historical sketch of the origin and organization of the Reformed church in American and of the Collegiate church of the city of New York. (New York) The Consistory (of the Collegiate reformed church, 1899)   54 p.   illus. (incl. ports.)   18 cm.   8-32772.
F128.62.C6N48

— 3d ed. 1904.   1 v.   F128.62.C6N482

FRENCH Protestant church, Difficulties in the.   (From Documentary history of the state of New York ... Albany, 1850.   22 cm.   v. 3, p. (1157) - 1177)   2-5714-5.   F128.62.E3R8

FIFTH Avenue Presbyterian church, A brief history of the, from its organization in Cedar street, in 1808, with a list of the present officers and members. Nov. 1877. Pub. by the session. New York, A. D. F. Randolph (1878?)   67 p.   front., pl., plans.   18 cm.   2-1854-M2.   F128.62.F4N5

MADISON avenue Reformed church. Records of the Madison avenue Reformed church. Trans. by the New York genealogical and biographical society. Ed. by Royden Woodward Vosburgh. New York city, 1921.   2 v. in 1.   36 x 28 cm.   Autographed from type-written copy. Partial contents. - v.1. Births and baptisms, 1808 - 1850. - v.2. Marriages, 1808 - 1850.   21-6313.   F128.62.M18N5

ST. PAUL'S chapel. (Erected A.D. 1766) The oldest public building and the only colonial church edifice in New York city. By Charles F. Wingate ... (11th thousand) New York, A. B. King (1901)
43 p.   18½ cm.   (Historical handbook no. 1)   5-34083.   F128.62.S3W5

SOUTH Dutch church. Records of the South Reformed Dutch church in Garden street. Transcribed by Royden Woodward Vosburgh. New York city. 1921.   2 p., 121 numb. l.   36 x 28½ cm.   Autographed from type-written copy. Located in Garden street until 1835, from 1837-1848 in Murray street, in 1848 removed to Fifth avenue and 21st street, and later to Madison ave. and 38th street. Contains births, baps. and marriages, 1812 - 1853.   21-21028.   F128.62.S7N5

TRINITY parish. Sheep without a shepherd; or, The rector's cure of souls. A contribution to the Trinity church question. By one of the disfranchised. New-York, 1857.   41 p.   8°.   1-21402-M1.
F128.62.T8S5

NEW YORK CITY.   HOTELS, TAVERNS, ETC.

BAYLES, William Harrison. Old taverns of New York. New York, Frank Allaben genealogical co. (1915)   xvi, 489 p.   illus. (incl. ports.)   20 cm.   16-10690.   F128.625.B25

CHAPPELL, George Shepard. The restaurants of New York. ... New York, Greenberg, inc., 1925.
3, 169 p.   19½ cm.   25-22871.   F128.625.C46

CUTTING, Elisabeth Brown. ... Old taverns and posting inns. New York, London, G. P. Putnam's sons (1898)   241 - 276 p.   20½ cm.   (Half moon series. vol. II, no. 7)   Also pub. in Historic New York, series 2, no. 7.
4-33414.   F128.625.C98

NEW YORK CITY

DROWNE, Henry Russell. The story of Fraunces Tavern. (6th ed.) New York, Fraunces Tavern, 1966.   40 p.   21 cm.
F128.625.F7D7 1966

JAMES, Rian. Dining in New York. New York, The John Day co. (1930)   viii p., 2 l., 3-266 p. 20 cm. 30-34234.
F128.625.J 28

—— Rev. ed. New York, The John Day co. (1931)   viii, 266 p. 19½ cm. "Second ed., Jan. 1931." 45-44206.
F128.625.J 28 1931
Rare Book Coll.

—— Repeal ed., completely rev. New York, The John Day co. (1934)   271 p. 20 cm. "Fourth ed., revised, 1934." 34-28491.
F128.625.J 28 1934

KELLER, Julius. Inns and outs; ed. by James R. Crowell. New York, G. P. Putnam's sons, 1939.   vi, 250 p. front. (port.) 22 cm. Autobiography. 39-8102.
F128.625.K45

The PLAZA; its life and times, by Eve Brown. (1st ed.) New York, Meredith Press (1967)   xii, 244 p. 24 cm. (A Duell, Sloan and Pearce Book) 67-12634.
F128.625.P55 B7

WHERE and how to dine in New York; the principal hotels, restaurants and cafes of various kinds and nationalities which have added to the gastronomic fame of New York and its suburbs. New York, Lewis, Scribner & co., 1903.   5, 214 p. front., pl. 18½ cm. 3-7190.
F128.625.W56

NEW YORK CITY.   PLACES OF AMUSEMENT.

DURANTE, Jimmy. ... Night clubs. New York, A. A. Knopf, 1931.   5, 3-246 p. front., plates, ports. 21 cm. 31-7190.
F128.627.D85

FREEDOMLAND; official guide to more than 200 exhibits and 40 fabulous rides. (New York? 1962)   (16) p. ports., col. maps. 21 x 30 cm.
F128.627.F 7

HEIMER, Melvin Leighton. The big drag; illus. by Peggy Bacon. New York, Whittlesey House (1947)   201 p. plates. 21 cm. 47-30390*.
F128.627.H 4

SHAW, Charles Green. Nightlife; decorated by Raymond Bret-Koch. Vanity fair's intimate guide to New York after dark. New York, The John Day co. (1931)   vi, 182 p. illus. 19½ cm. 31-31001.
F128.627.S38

SYLVESTER, Robert. No cover charge; a backward look at the night clubs. New York, Dial Press, 1956.   301 p. 21 cm. 56-5433.
F128.627.S 9

WALKER, Stanley. The night club era ... with an introd. by Alva Johnston; with an index. New York, Frederick A. Stokes co., 1933.   xi, 327 p. 22½ cm. 33-33675.
F128.627.W26

ZERBE, Jerome. John Perona's El Morocco family album with photos. by Jerome Zerbe and an introd. by Lucius Beebe. (New York city, Priv. print., Federal printing service, 1937.   3 p. 62, (3) p. illus. (incl. ports.) 37 cm. 40M.1804T.
F128.627.Z47

NEW YORK CITY.   HARBOR.

BARNARD, John Gross. The dangers and defences of New York. Addressed to the Hon. J. B. Floyd, secretary of war, by Major J. G. Barnard ... Pub. by order of the Chamber of commerce, by permission of the secretary of war.   New York, D. Van Nostrand, 1859.   62 p.   22½ cm.   8-4994.

F128.63. B 25

BRADLEY, David L.   Bradley's reminiscences of New York harbor, and complete water front directory of New York, Brooklyn, and Jersey City.   1881, 1896.   ... (New York) 1896.   3, 5-61 p. illus. (maps) 27½ cm.   1-14765.

F128.63. B 81

COCHRANE.   Further remarks (1880) on Cochrane's proposal.

F128.63. C 66

KINSCELLA, Hazel Gertrude.   Liberty's Island; stories of the harbor of New York, Bedloe's Island and the Statue of Liberty.   Illus. by Kevin Royt.   Lincoln, University Pub. Co. (1947)   96 p.   illus. 20 cm.   48-2458*.

F128.63. K 5

MITCHELL, Joseph.   The bottom of the harbor.   Boston, Little, Brown (1959)   243 p.   22 cm. 60-6523.

F128.63. M 5

PHOTOGRAPHIC views of the statue of Liberty and New York harbor ... Chicago and New York, Rand, McNally, 1896.   (28) p. illus.   obl. 16°.   1-14766.

F128.63. P 57

SPERR, Percy Loomis.   Tall ships and tall buildings; the harbor of New York in photographs ... (Staten Island., N.Y.) 1932.   (1) v.   mounted photos.   23 x 39½ cm.   Loose-leaf.

F128.63. S 75
Rare Book Coll.

NEW YORK CITY.   MONUMENTS. STATUES.

SALTUS, John Sanford.   Statues of New York; with 82 full-page illustrations.   New York & London, G. P. Putnam's sons, 1922.   xxii, 164 p.   plates, ports.   23½ cm.   23-233.

F128.64.A1 S1

BOLIVAR statue.   Discurso pronunciado por el doctor Esteben Gil Borges, ministro de relaciones exteriores de los Estados Unidos de Venezuela en el acto de la dedicatión de la estatua del Libertador a la cuidad de New York...   (New York, Madison square press, inc., 1921)   8 p.   22½ cm.   21-18390.

F128.64.B7B73

BOLIVAR statue.   ... El Libertador Simón Bolívar; discursos pronunciados con motivo de la inauguración del monumento del Libertador, regalado por el gobierno de Venezuela a la cuidad de Nueva York ...   Washington, D.C., 1921.   3-50 p.   2 pl.   20 cm.   21-17510.

F128.64.B7 P2

GEORGE III.   The equestrian statue of George III, and the pedestrian statue of William Pitt, erected in the city of New York, 1770, by Alexander J. Wall ... (New York) The New York historical society, 1920.   (37) - 57.   illus.   24 cm.   "Reprinted from the Quarterly bulletin, July, 1920."   22-10764.

F128.64.G3W18

GRANT monument.   King's views of Grant's tomb; dedication, 27 April, 1897.   New York, M. King, 1897.   16 p. of illus. (incl. ports.)   41 cm.   8-18432.

F128.64.G7K5

JOAN OF ARC.   The dedication of the statue of Joan of Arc in the city of the New York ... 1915, by George Frederick Kunz ... New York, N.Y., 1916.   53 p.   front., plates (1 fold.) port.   23½ cm.   "Reprinted ... from the 21st annual report of the American scenic & historic preservation soc."   33-8478.

F128.64.J 7K8

LIBERTY.   Inauguration of the statue of Liberty enlightening the world by the President of the United State on Bedlow's island, 1886.   Issued under the authority of the committee.   New York, D. Appleton, 1887.   62 p.   front. (facsim.)   22½ cm.   2-11300 Rev.

F128.64.L6A5

LIBERTY.   An appeal to the people of the U.S. in behalf of the great statue, Liberty enlightening the world.   New York, 1882 (1884)   10 p.   front.   27½ x 22½ cm.   2-18686.

F128.64.L6A6

LIBERTY enlightening the world. (By Herbert Filmer) (New York, Illustrative press bureau, 1886) (8) p. illus. (incl. port.) 18 x 14 cm. 36-3749. F128.64.L6F56

LIBERTY. Statue of Liberty enlightening the world, by Rodman Gilder. (New York) The New York trust co. (1943) 40 p. front., illus. (incl. ports.) 23½ cm. 43-10610. F128.64.L6G5

LIBERTY. Statue of Liberty, by Oscar Handlin and the editors of the Newsweek Book Division. New York, Newsweek (1971) 172 p. illus. 30 cm. (Wonders of man) 77-136435. F128.64.L6H3

LIBERTY. The Statue of Liberty comes to America, by Robert Kraske. Illus. by Victor Mays. Champaign, Ill., Garrard Pub. co. (1972) 95 p. illus. 23 cm. 74-171412. F128.64.L6K7

LIBERTY. Statue of Liberty, national monument, Bedloe's Island, New York, by Benjamin Levine and Isabelle F. Story. Washington, 1952. 35 p. illus. 23 cm. (National Park Service historical handbook series, no. 11) 52-61019. F128.64.L6L48

— Rev. Washington, 1957. 34 p. illus. 24 cm. 57-60529. F128.64.L6L48

LIBERTY. The story of the Statue of Liberty, by Natalie Miller. Illus. by Lucy and John Hawkinson. Chicago, Childrens Press 1965. 30 p. 25 cm. (Cornerstones of freedom) 65-12216. F128.64.L6M5

LIBERTY. Our Statue of Liberty (by) Thelma Nason. Illus. by Adolph Le Moult. Chicago, Follett Pub. Co., 1969. 32 p. illus. 21 cm. 69-10260. F128.64.L6N3

LIBERTY. Meet Miss Liberty. By Lillie Patterson. Illus. with historic engravings and photos. New York, Macmillan, 1962. 162 p. illus. 22 cm. "1st printing." 62-10645. F128.64.L6P28

LIBERTY. Gateway to America; Miss Liberty's first hundred years, by Hertha Pauli. Illus. by Leonard Vosburgh. New York, D. McKay Co. 1965. 70 p. 22 cm. 65-23833. F128.64.L6P29

LIBERTY. I lift my lamp: the way of a symbol, by Hertha Pauli and E. B. Ashton (pseud.) New York, Appleton-Century Crofts (1948) ix, 368 p. 22 cm. 48-6534*. F128.64.L6P3

— Port Washington, N.Y., I. J. Friedman (1969) ix, 368 p. 22 cm. (Empire state historical publications series, no. 65) 70-83481. F128.64.L6P3 1969

LIBERTY. Biografiia statui Svobody. (Title romanized from Russian) By Arnol'd Shlepakov. 1969. 116 p. 20 cm. F128.64.L6S5

LIBERTY. The tallest lady in the world: the Statue of Liberty, by Norah Smaridge. Illus. by Leonard Vosburgh. (1st ed.) New York, Hawthorne Books (1967) 94 p. 21 cm. "First ed.: March 1967" AC 67-10374. F128.64.L6S6

NEW YORK state Theodore Roosevelt memorial, dedicated Jan. 19, 1936. Prepared under the direction of the board of trustees by George N. Pindar, secretary. (Albany, J. B. Lyon co., printers, 1936) 16, (6), 17 - 53 p. front. (port.) plates. 26 cm. 37-27575. F128.64.N4N4

PILGRIM statue. Unveiling of the Pilgrim statue, by the New England society in the city of New York, at Central Park, June 6, 1885. (New York, 1885?) 33 p. 23½ cm. 3-4948. F128.64.P63N5

WASHINGTON. An address at the unveiling of the statue of Washington, upon the spot where he took the oath as first president of the U.S. ... by George William Curtis. New York, Harper & bros., 1883. 35 p. front. 25 cm. 12-11574. F128.64.W31C9

WASHINGTON. The equestrian statue of Washington. (By James Lee) New York, J. F. Trow, printer, 1864. 15 p. front. 19½ cm. 19-20251. F128.64.W31L4
Rare Book Coll.

WASHINGTON statue. Report of the Committee on arts and sciences, on communication from His Honor the mayor, recommending the purchase of Hubard's duplicate copy of the statue of Washington, by Houdon. New York, C. W. Baker, printer, 1860. 24 p. 22 cm. 18-24613 Rev.

F128.64.W31N5

WEBSTER statue. Proceedings at the inauguration of the statue of Daniel Webster, erected in the Central park, New York ... 1876, by Gordon W. Burnham, and by him presented to the city ... New York, D. Appleton, 1876. 56 p. front. 37 x 29 cm. 13-24930.

F128.64.W4B9

NEW YORK CITY.   PARKS. SQUARES. CIRCLES.

BATTERY. The inconography of the Battery and Castle garden, by William Loring Andrews. New York, C. Scribner's sons, 1901. xvi p., 3-43 p. incl. col. front., illus., plates, plans. fold. plan. 22 cm. 1-10172.

F128.65.B3 A6

BATTERY, The; the story of the adventurers, artists, statesmen, grafters, songsters, mariners, pirates, guzzlers, Indians, thieves, stuffed-shirts, turn-coats, millionaires, inventors, etc., etc. who played their parts during full four centuries on Manhattan island's tip, by Rodman Gilder ... Boston, Houghton Mifflin, 1936. xiii, 304 p. front., plates. 24½ cm. Maps. 36-35939.

F128.65.B3 G5

... BOWLING Green, by Spencer Trask. New York (etc.) G. P. Putnam's sons, 1898. p. 163-208. (Half moon series. vol. II, no. 5) References: p. 208. Pub. also in "Historic New York," 2d ser. no. 5) 1-14767.

F128.65.B7 T7

BRONX. Report of the Bronx River parkway commission appointed under chapter 669 of the laws of 1906. Madison Grant, chairman ... (New York, The Trow press, 1907?) 15 p. plates (1 fold.) 2 fold. maps. 25½ cm. 10-3155 Rev.

F128.65.B8 N5

BRONX. Report of the Bronx parkway commission ... Albany, J. B. Lyon co., 1907. 21 p., plates, (1 fold.) fold. maps (in pocket) 23 cm. 19-4295.

F128.65.B8N51

BRONX. Report(s and Final report) of the Bronx parkway commission ... 1909, 1911/12, 1913/14-1918, 1822, 1925. Albany (etc.) J. B. Lyon co.... 1909 - (26) 9 v. illus., plates (part fold.) ports., map, tables (part fold.) diagr. 23-25½ cm. 16-11142 Rev.

F128.65.B8N53

CENTRAL park. Asher & Adams' New map and guide of Central park, with directory to prominent places of interest in New York & vicinity ... New York, Asher & Adams, 1876. 64 p. fold. map. 14 cm. 1-14768 Rev.

F128.65.C3A8

CENTRAL park. Baldwin's handbook of Central park. (New York, H. A. Baldwin, 1866) 64 p. incl. illus., plates. 19 cm. 37-18079.

F128.65.C3 B3
Rare Book Coll.

CENTRAL park (by) the Central park association. New York, T. Seltzer, 1926. 174 p. incl. front., illus. 21 cm. 26-10709.

F128.65.C3C3

CENTRAL park. Complete guide to Central park ... (New York, E. S. Dodge print. co.) 1877. 39 p. fold. map. 16°. 1-14769-M1.

F128.65.C3C7

CENTRAL park. A description of the New York Central park. (By Clarence Chatham Cook) New York, F. J. Huntington, 1869. x, (9) - 206 p. incl. front., illus., plan. 23½ cm. Published anonymously. 1-14770.

F128.65.C3C8

— New York, B. Blom, 1972. x, 206 p. illus. 26 cm. Reprint of 1869 ed. 70-174831 MARC.

F128.65.C3C8
1972

CENTRAL park. The Egyptian obelisk in Central park. (By Charles William Darling) (Utica? N.Y., 1887?) 6 p. 23½ cm. In verse. 17-23284.

F128.65.C3D22

NEW YORK CITY

CENTRAL park. Tree trails in Central Park, by M. M. Graff. Illus. by Jacques Hnizdovsky. New York, Greensward Foundation, 1970. x, 189 p. illus., col. map. 22 cm. 73-125006.
F128.65.C3G7

CENTRAL park. A guide to the Central park. With a map of the proposed improvements. By an officer of the park. New York, A. P. Moore, 1859. 24 p. fold. map. 12°. 1-14771-M1.
F128.65.C3G9

— (Skating pond ed.) New York, C. M. Saxton, Barker, 1859. 30 p. fold. map. 12°. 1-14772-M1.
F128.65.C3G91

CENTRAL park. A guide book to the Central park; containing a description of the park as far as completed, and of work yet to be done. New York, C. M. Saxton & Barker, 1860. 50 p. front., 2 maps 1 fold.) 12°. L. C. copy replaced by microfilm.
F128.65.C3G92
Microfilm 21544 F

CENTRAL park. McGown's Pass and vicinity; a sketch of the most interesting scenic and historic section of Central Park in the city of New York, by Edward Hagaman Hall. New York, Pub. under the auspices of the American scenic and historic preservation soc., 1905. 48 p. 7 pl., 2 maps (1 fold.) 18½ cm. 6-3491.
F128.65.C3H2

CENTRAL park. Guide to the Central park, by Oscar Hinrichs... New York, J. Polhemus, printer, 1875. iv numb. l., 6-22 numb. l. 16 cm. 1-14774 Rev.
F128.65.C3H6

CENTRAL park. Illustrated souvenir of the Plaza and Central park. New York, J. L. Babe (1892) (42) p. illus., fold. map. obl. 32°. 1-14775-M1.
F128.65.C3 I2

CENTRAL Park country; a tune within us. Photos. by Nancy and Retta Johnston. Ed. with a foreword, by David Brower. Text by Mireille Johnston. Introd. by Marianne Moore. San Francisco, Sierra Club (1968) 151 p. illus. 36 cm. (Sierra Club exhibit format Series, v.18) 68-28667.
F128.65.C3J6

— New York, Sierra Club - Ballantine Books (1970) 157 p. 24 cm. (A Sierra Club-Ballantine book)
F128.65.C3J6
1970

CENTRAL park. The park. By Richard Lewis. Photos. by Helen Buttfield. New York, Simon & Schuster (1968) 1 v. (chiefly illus.) 16 x 23 cm. 68-28917.
F128.65.C3L4

CENTRAL park. Report of Special committee appointed to examine into condition, affairs and progress of the New York Central park. Transmitted to the Legislature Jan. 25, 1861. Albany, C. Van Benthuysen, printer, 1861. 56 p. 23 cm. 12-20469.
F128.65.C3N5

CENTRAL park. Description of a plan for the improvement of the Central park. "Greensward." (by F. L. Olmstead and Calvert Vaux) New York, 1858; Reprinted (by Sutton, Bowne) 1868. 36 p. fold. map. 23 cm. 4-33420.
F128.65.C3O5

CENTRAL park; a history and a guide, by Henry Hope Reed and Sophia Duckworth. With an introd. by Thomas P. F. Hoving. (1st ed.) New York, C. N. Potter (1967) xv, 165 p. 22 cm. 66-22407.
F128.65.C3R4

CENTRAL park. Guide to the Central park... By T. Addison Richards. New York, J. Miller, 1866. ii, (3) - 101 p. front., illus., plates, fold. plan. 17 cm. 1-14776.
F128.65.C3R5

— 1870. ii, (3) - 101 p. mounted col. front., illus., plates, fold. map. 17 cm. 46-41900.
F128.65.C3R5
1870

CITY hall park. An appeal for the preservation of City hall park, with a brief history of the park. New York, The American scenic and historic preservation soc., 1910. 40 p. incl. plan. front. 23 cm. 10-13756.
F128.65.C5A5

CITY hall park. Reminiscences of the Park and its vicinity. (By Henry Barton Dawson) New York, 1855. 64 p. front., plates, ports. 21 cm. Originally written for Valentine's 'Manual'. 25 copies printed. 33-24049. F128.65.C5D19
Rare Book Coll.

CITY hall park. The Park and its vicinity, in the city of New York. By Henry B. Dawson ... Morrisania, N.Y., 1867. viii, 95 p. incl. front. port. 26½ cm. (Gleanings from the harvest-field of American history ... pt. 1) First printed in the Manual of the corporation of the city of New York, for 1855. 12-32392 Rev. F128.65.C5D2

CITY hall. Outline of a new city hall, requiring no tax or expenditure by the city ... By D. Hough, jr. ... New York, I. J. Oliver, printer, 1856. 19 p. illus. (incl. plans) 22 cm. 1-22667 Rev. F128.65.C5H8

Dreamland. Again the city pays. How William H. Reynolds, the mayor's friend, turns his Dreamland failure into a $1,360,000 success at the taxpayers' expense. (New York) Bureau of city inquiry, 1917. 32 p. 23 cm. 17-18811. F128.65.D7B9

GOUVERNEUR Morris park, Proposed ... New York, Bronx board of trade, 1905. 23 cm. F128.65.G7B75

HARRIMAN state park, ... The proposed. (By Ernest Stagg Whitin) (New York) 1910. 12 p. illus. 25 cm. Reprinted from the Survey April 2, 1910. F128.65.H3W6

JOSEPH Rodman Drake park; address of James L. Wells, representing the North side board of trade at the public hearing by the Board of estimate and apportionment of the city of New York ... (New York, Press of Kiesling bros., 1904?) 15 p. illus. (incl. plans) 23½ cm. 5-24717. F128.65.J8W4

MADISON square. ... A historical sketch of Madison square. (By Marcus Benjamin) New York, Meriden Britannia co., 1894. 47 p. incl. front., illus. 18 cm. (Meriden monographs, no. 1) 12-5130.
F128.65.M18B4

RIVERSIDE park. Ceremonies commemorating the tercentenary of the landing, May 4th, 1626, of Peter Minuet ... Women's league for the protection of Riverside park, (New York, 1926) 8 p., 13 l. illus., fold., ap. 29½ x 23 cm. F128.65.R5W8

TIMES Square. Carnival crossroads: the story of Times Square by Wm. G. Rogers and Mildred Weston. Drawings by O. Soglow. (1st ed.) Garden City, N.Y., Doubleday, 1960. 183 p. 22 cm. 60-9489. F128.65.T5R6

WASHINGTON square. Washinton Hiroba no kae; Face of Washington Square. By Sumiharu Watanabe. (Tokyo, Yuyudo, 1965) 1 v. (chiefly illus.) 26 cm. F128.65.W3W3
Orien Japan

ZOOLOGICAL park. Views in the New York zoological park (New York) The New York zoological soc., 1903. 20 pl. 13½ x 19½ cm. 6-15400. F128.65.Z6N5

NEW YORK CITY.   STREETS. BRIDGES. RAILROADS, ETC.

BROOKLYN and New York street directory, 1882/1883 ... Brooklyn, A. L. Wood, 1882. 252 p. incl. map. 18 cm. 24-14361. F128.67.A1A2

COMPLETE guide to New York city, Manhattan and Bronx ... New York city, "Geographia" map co. (1934 - v. 16 cm. CA 34-287 Unrev. F128.67.A1A2

GUIDE of Guides, The. Up-to-date handbook. Especially adapted in the interest of the citizens and visitors of New York city. Guides the stranger from any part to any other part of the city by the easiest and best routes of transportation. ... (New York city, Davis & Hopp bros.) 1896. 97 p. 17 cm. 11-10264. F128.67.A1A2
(1896)

NEW YORK city new street number guide and map, with complete subway-elevated street car line

NEW YORK CITY 275

directory. (Chicago and New York, Rand McNally, 1920) 128 p. fold. map. 16 cm. 21-5357.
F128.67.A1A2

RAND, McNally & co.'s complete street number guide of New York city ... Chicago and New York, Rand McNally, 1899. 2, 96 p. fold. map. 15½ cm. 98-1878 Rev. F128.67.A1A2 1899

RAND McNally street number guide and complete transit directory of Manhattan ... Chicago, New York, Rand, McNally v. fold. map. 16½ cm. 24-30055. F128.67.A1A2

RAND McNally street number guide and indexed map of Manhattan ... Chicago, New York, Rand, McNally, 19 v. fold. map. 16 x 8 cm. 24-23637. F128.67.A1A2

TROW street and avenue directory of the borough of Manhattan ... 18 New York city, The Trow directory, print. and bookbinding co., 18 -19 v. 11½ x 18½ x 10½ cm. 1-29842 Rev.
F128.67.A1A2

"UP-to-date" street directory and guide to Greater New York, boroughs of the Manhattan and Bronx ... New York, Gregory bros., 1898. 94 p. 16½ x 7½ cm. 98-110 Rev. F128.67.A1A2

BRIERLY, J. Ernest. The streets of old New York; a pictorial rebirth of a vanished city. New York, Hastings House (1953) 127 p. illus. 22 cm. 53-6147. F128.67.A1B75

CITY history club of New York. ... Milestones of old New York. New York, 19-) 24 cm.
F128.67.A1C5

COMPLETE guide to New York City, Manhattan and Bronx. With detailed street and transportation map attached. An entirely new ed. Compiled under the direction of Alexander Gross. (New York) Geographia Map Co., 1962. 192 p. maps (part fold.) 16 cm. F128.67.A1C6

GERARD, James Watson. The old streets of New York under the Dutch. A paper read before the New York historical soc. ... 1874. New York, D. Taylor, printer, 1874. 65 p. 24½ cm. 16-8888.
F128.67.A1G3

HOW-to-get-there (Barkan system) street directory of New York city (Manhattan and the Bronx) compiled from the latest official map of the city of New York ... Brooklyn, N.Y., The Barkan system street directory co., 19 v. fold. map. 16 x 8½ cm. 41-13259. F128.67.A1H6

NEW YORK (City) Colonial highways of Greater New York, a discussion of the present interest of the city therein, reports of Herman A. Metz, comptroller to the Commissioners of the sinking fund, 1907-1908. New York, Bureau for the examination of claims, Dept. of finanace (1908?) 164 p. incl. pl., maps. 27½ cm. 10-31404. F128.67.A1N5

OSBORN, Gardner. The streets of old New York; an historical picture book. New York and London, Harper & bros., 1939. 49 p. illus. (incl. ports.) 30½ cm. 39-19291. F128.67.A1O7

POST, John J. Old streets, roads, lanes, piers and wharves of New York. Showing the former and present names, tog. with a list of alterations of streets ... New York, R. D. Cooke, 1882.
2, (3) - 76 p. 25½ cm. 1-14777. F128.67.A1 P8

BOWERY. The Bowery men. By Elmer Bendiner. New York, T. Nelson (1961) 187 p. 22 cm.
61-7865. F128.67.B6 B4

BOWERY. Old Bowery days; the chronicles of a famous street, by Alvin F. Harlow. New York & London, D. Appleton, 1931. xi, 564 p. front., illus., plates, ports., facsim. 23 cm. Bibliography: p. 545 - (553)
31-16766. F128.67.B6 H3

BOWERY. ... The Bowery, by Edward Ringwood and Mary Ashley Hewitt. (New York, The Knickerbocker press, 1897) p. i-iv, 371-406. 19½ cm. (Half moon series. v. 1, no. 12) Pub. also in "Historic New York."
1st ser. no. 11) 10-6836. F128.67.B6 H6

1009

BOWERY. The Bowery on 75¢ a day, by Harold Rand and Robert Saffron. Drawings by Donald Silverstein. New York, Pocket Books (1966) 53 p. 22 cm. (A Pocket book special) F128.67.B6 R3

BROADWAY. The path of progress, by Reginald Pelham Bolton. (New York) Central savings bank in the city of New York (1928) 38 p. illus. (incl. maps) 23½ cm. 29-6041. "A story of the growth of modern Broadway between the Bouwery of Stuyvesant and the farm of Jacob Harsen." 29-6041. F128.67.B7 B5

BROADWAY; the Grand Canyon of American business ... New York, Broadway association, 1926. 169 p. illus. (incl. ports.) 23½ cm. Addresses on the occasion of the 300th anniversary of the founding of New York. 27-24508.
F128.67.B7 B6

BROADWAY. Both sides of Broadway, from Bowling green to Central park ... (Comp. by Rudolph M. De Leeuw) New York city, The De Leeuw Riehl pub. co. (1910) 504 p. illus. 24½ x 31½ cm. 10-16635 Rev. F128.67.B7 D4

BROADWAY. The Broadway of yesterday; a collection of 20 prints of old Broadway, tog. with a full description, by Charles Hemstreet ... (New York, Issued by the Cadwallader pub. co. under the direction of the National soc. for historical research) 1905. (4) p. illus., 20 pl. 30½ x 26 cm. 6-19692.
F128.67.B7 H4

BROADWAY. The greatest street in the world; the story of Broadway, old and new, from the Bowling Green to Albany, by Stephen Jenkins ... 160 illus. and 6 maps. New York and London, G. P. Putnam's sons, 1911. xxii, 509 p. front., illus., plates, fold. maps., fold. plans. 23½ cm. Bibliography: p. 469 - 473. 11-26982.
F128.67.B86J5

BROADWAY, by J. B. Kerfoot; drawings by Lester F. Hornby. Boston and New York, Houghton Mifflin co., 1911. vii, 188, (4) p. incl. plates. front. 22½ cm. 11-27481. F128.67.B7 K3

EXCHANGE place. From sheep pasture to skyscraper, by Reginald Pelham Bolton. (New York) The Equitable trust co. of New York (1926) 38 p. incl. illus., plates, maps. 23½ cm. 27-10316.
F128.67.E9B69

FIFTH avenue old and new, 1824 - 1924, by Henry Collins Brown ... official publication of the Fifth avenue assoc. in commemoration of the 100th anniversary of the founding of Fifth ave. (New York, 1924) 3, 13-126 p. incl. illus. (part col.) maps, col. front., col. pl. 31 cm. 24-29537. F128.67.F4B8

FIFTH avenue. Collins' both sides of Fifth Avenue ... New York, J. F. Collins, 1910. 21½ cm.
F128.67.F4C7

FIFTH avenue, New York, from start to finish. New York, Welles & co., 1911. (114) p. incl. illus. plates. 20½ x 56 cm. 11-13548. F128.67.F4F5

FIFTH Avenue Fifty years on Fifth, 1907 - 1957. Fifth Avenue Assoc. (New York, 1957) 162 p. illus. 30 cm. Includes bibliography. 58-1462. F128.67.F4F52

FIFTH avenue; glances at the vicissitudes and romance of a world-renowned thoroughfare, tog. with many rare illustrations that bring back an interesting past. (New York) Printed for the Fifth avenue bank of New York, 1915. 77 p. front., illus. (incl. maps) 23½ cm. "Authorities": (1) p. at end. 15-21164.
F128.67.F4F53

FIFTH avenue events, a brief account of some of the most interesting events which have occurred on the avenue. (New York) The Fifth avenue bank of New York, 1916. 76 p. front., illus. (incl. ports.) 23½ cm. 17-2033. F128.67.F4F54

FIFTH avenue. By Theodore James. With photos. by Elizabeth Baker. New York, Walker (1971) 310 p. illus. 35 cm. 76-161109. F128.67.F4 J3
1971

FIFTH avenue, by Arthur Barlett Maurice ... drawings by Allan G. Cram. New York, Dodd, Mead, 1918. x, 331 p. front., plates. 23 cm. 18-18520. F128.67.F4M4

FIFTH avenue. The history of a great thoroughfare; a few facts concerning Fifth avenue and its adjacent streets. New York, The Thoroughfare pub. co. (1916)   (64) p. illus. (part col.)   29 ½ cm.   16-10816.
                                                                                                                                                         F128.67.F4R46

FIFTH avenue. 5th ave.; 100 photographs by Fred Stein, picture text by Andy Logan ... (New York) Pantheon (1947)   4, 99 (i.e. 100) pl. on 50 l.   25 cm.   47-2717.   F128.67.F4S7

FIFTY-second street. The street that never slept; New York's fabled 52d St. by Arnold Shaw. Foreword by Abel Green. New York, Coward, McCann & Geoghegan (1971)   xiv, 378 p.   illus.   25 cm.   76-154776 MARC.   F128.67.F5S5 1971

FORTY-second street. The world's greatest thoroughfare, Forty-second street, the centre of New York. (New York, Forty-second street property owners and merchants assoc., 1919)   3-30 p.   illus.   31 ½ x 23 ½ cm.   20-6156.   F128.67.F7F74

FORTY-second street. Yesterday and today on Forty-Second Street. (New York, 1922)   48 p.   illus., port.   21 cm.   Reminiscences.   48-31850*.   F128.67.F7S3

MAIDEN lane; the story of a single street, by Albert Ulmann ... New York, The Maiden lane hist. soc., 1931.   5, 172 p.   front., illus., plates.   23 cm.   "A brief story of Maiden lane was pub. originally in the Manufacturing jeweler in 1884. In 1910 the narrative was brought up to date in a series of articles printed in the Jewelers' circular-weekly. The present volume is a further up-to-date revision..."   31-25245.   F128.67.M2U7

NORTH River bridge at New York city. (n.p., 1895?)   19 p.   front., fold. maps.   17 cm.   2-17349.   F128.67.N8N8

ONE hundredth street. East 100th Street (by) Bruce Davidson. Cambridge, Mass., Harvard University Press, 1970.   1 v. (unpaged)   illus.   32 cm.   76-120714.   F128.67.O5D3

PAISLEY place. Paisley: a local sketch, from Valentine's manual for 1863. By Prosper Montgomery Wetmore)   6 p.   col. front., 1 port.   23 cm.   An account of Paisley place, a weavers' settlement in old Greenwich Village.   4-9992.   F128.67.P2W5

PARK avenue. The romance of Park avenue, by F. A. Collins; under the auspices of the Park avenue assoc. (New York, Park avenue assoc., 1930)   107 p.   plates.   19 ½ cm.   30-15345.   F128.67.P3C69

RIVERSIDE drive. By Clarence True. (New York) New York, Unz & co. (1899)   26 p.   illus. pl.   obl.   16°.   June 1, 99-127.   F128.67.R6T8

TENTH street. (By) Bill Binsen. New York, Paragraphic Books (1968)   (95) p.   18 cm.   "1st printing."   68-55658.   F128.67.T4B5 1968

TIMES Square. Crossroads of the world, the story of Times Square, by William Leas. New York, Popular Library (1965)   159 p.   18 cm.   F128.67.T5L3

— With exclusive photos by Boris Erwitt. New York, Living Books (1965)   114, (2) p.   23 cm.   65-28005.   F128.67.T5P3

TIMES Square. (Prepared by Sam Minskoff & Sons and a Lehman Brothers group. Newport? 1969)   1 v. (unpaged)   illus.   41 cm.   F128.67.T5S2

WALL street. A history of fifty feet in New York at Wall & William streets, told in pictures & text which show its development from 1644 to 1926. New York, The Bank of America (1926)   5, 13-90 p.   incl. front., illus. (incl. ports., plans, facsims.)   19 cm.   46-36297.   F128.67.W2B3

WALL street. The story of a street; a narrative history of Wall street from 1644 to 1908, by

Frederick Trevor Hill. New York and London, Harper & brothers, 1908.   xiii, 170 p. front., plates, maps, facsims. 21½ cm. 8-31816.
F128.67.W2H6

WALL Street; a pictorial history. By Leonard Louis Levinson. New York, Ziff-Davis Pub. Co. (1961)   vi, 376 p. 31 cm. 61-8465.
F128.67.W2L4

WALL Street. The site of the Assay office on Wall street, an illustrated historical sketch of the successive public buildings and men in public life connected with the site; interspersed with some family history, by William E. Verplanck. (Princeton, Princeton university press) 1921.   42 p. incl. front., plates, ports. 23½ cm. 22-3085.
F128.67.W2V5

WALL street. ... The early history of Wall street; 1653 - 1789, by Oswald Garrison Villard ... (New York) G. P. Putnam's sons (1897)   99-140 p. 20 cm. (Half moon series. vol. 1, no. iv) "References": p. 139-140. 1-15031.
F128.67.W2V7

NEW YORK CITY. SUBURBS. SECTIONS OF THE CITY. RIVERS.

DAU's New York suburban blue book ... (v.1) - 1917 -   New York city, Dau's blue books, inc., 1917 -   1 v. 21½ cm. 17-16740.
Directories

ATLEE, William Yorke, comp. Suburban homes for city business men. A description of the country adjacent to the Eastern division and branches of the Erie railway and Northern railroad of New Jersey ... (5th ed.) New York, Erie railway co., 1873.   98 p. illus., maps. 12º. 1-14778-M1.
F128.68.A1A8

CATLIN, George L. Homes on the Midland for New York business men. A description of the region traversed by the New Jersey division of the New York midland railway, between New York city and Ellenville, Ulster co., N.Y. ... New York, J. W. Pratt, 1872.   111 p. illus., map. 16º. 1-14779-M1.
F128.68.A1C3

COMSTOCK, Sarah. Old roads from the heart of New York; journeys today by ways of yesterday, within thirty miles around the Battery. With 100 illus. by the author and others. New York and London, G. P. Putnam's sons, 1915.   xxiv, 401 p. front., plates, 2 fold. maps. 22 cm. "Itineraries": p. 373-384. Bibliography: p. 385-392. 15-19989.
F128.68.A1C73

HOMES in the country (east) and summer resorts on the Sound, via New York, New Haven & Hartford railroad. ... (New York, R. W. Grout) 1882.   32 p. illus. 12º. 1-14780-M1.   F128.68.A1H6

HOMES on the Sound for New York business men: a description of the region contiguous to the shore of Long Island sound, between New York and New Haven ... New York, G. L. Catlin, 1875.   88 p. illus., 2 maps (1 fold.) 16º. 1-14781-M1.
F128.68.A1H7

JOHNSON, Jeremiah, jr. Building a nation. (New York) 1891.   28 x 21 cm.   F128.68.A1 J6

LEAGUE of American wheelmen. Fifty miles around New York; a book of maps and descriptions of the best roads, streets, and routes for cyclists and horesmen. Prepared under direction of the League of American wheelmen (New York state division) 20th thousand ... (New York) ... 1896.   (212) p. illus. (maps) 20 x 10½ cm. Also issued under title: Fifty miles around Brooklyn. 1-14782.
F128.68.A1L4

(MOTTELAY, Paul Fleury) One hundred miles around New York and how reached ... Time tables, maps and diagrams. 2d ed. ... New York, C. T. Dillingham, 1883.   2, 90 p. fold. maps. 17 cm. 1-16274.
F128.68.A1M91

— 3d ed. ... New York, The J. H. Brown pub. co., 1884.   2, 76 p. fold. maps. 17 cm. 1-16275.
F128.68.A1M92

— 4th annual ed. ... Boston, Lee & Shepard; N.Y., Dillingham, 1885.   3, 100 p. fold. front., fold. maps. 17 cm. p. 71-78 wanting. 1-16276.
F128.68.A1M93

NEW YORK CITY

— 5th annual ed. (1886) 4, 56 p. incl. maps. front. (fold. plan) 17½ cm. 4-28326 Rev. F128.68.A1M94

NEW YORK suburbs, The. v. 1 - 1959 - (New York, Magabooks) v. maps. 28 cm.
(A Magabook) 59-2848. F128.68.A1N4

NEW YORK walk book. 4th ed., completely rev. under the sponsorship of the New York-New Jersey Trail Conference and the American Geographical Society. Pen sketches by Robert L. Dickinson and Richard Edes Harrison. With an introd. to the geology of the region by Christopher J. Schuberth. Garden City, N.Y., Doubleday, 1971. x, 326 p. illus., col. maps. 22 cm. Bibliography: p. (307) - 311.
70-150876 MARC. F128.68.A1N44

POPULAR places of resort around New York. Coney Island, Rockaway, Long Branch, Long Beach, Far Rockaway, Fire Island, Fort Lee, High Bridge, Glen Island, etc. Descriptive guide. Summer season, 1881. New York, J. Williams, 1881. 31 p. 16°. 1-14783-M1. F128.68.A1 P8

RAND, McNally & co's handy guide to the country around New York, for the wheelman, driver, and excursionist. With original maps and illus. Chicago and New York, Rand, McNally, 1896.
3, 5-182 p. front., illus., plates, fold. map. 18 cm. Map wanting. 1-14784. F128.68.A1R1

SPECTORSKY, Auguste C. The exurbanites. With drawings by Robert Osborn. (1st ed.) Philadelphia, Lippincott (1955) 278 p. illus. 22 cm. 55-10462. F128.68.A1 S6

SUBURBAN New York. The Globe and Commercial advertiser, 1911. 32½ cm.
F128.68.A1 S9

— 1912. 126 p. illus. 33 cm. 12-10466. F128.68.A1S91

TORREY, Raymond H. ... New York walk book; suggestions for excursions afoot within a radius of fifty to one hundred miles of the city and including Westchester County, the Highlands of the Hudson and the Ramapo, northern and central New Jersey and the New Jersey pine barrens, Long Island, the Shawangunk Range, the Catskills, and the Toconics ... Pocket ed. New York, American geographical soc. 1923. xvi, 217 p. incl. front., illus. maps, (part fold.) 19½ cm. (Outing series no. 2) 23-18234. F128.68.A1T63

— Special ed. New York, American geographical soc. 1923. xvi, 217 p. 34 p. incl. front., illus. plates, maps (part fold.) 22 cm. "Maps and guidebooks": p. 209-210. 24-2921. F128.68.A1T64

— New and rev. ed. New York, Dodd, Mead, 1934. xvi, 332 p. incl. front., illus. maps (part fold.) 19 cm.
"Guide books and maps of special regions": p. 318-319; "Nucleus for a tramper's library": p. 320-321; "Books": p. 322-323. 34-38342.
F128.68.A1T64
1934

— Raye R. Platt, editor. New York, American Geographical Soc., 1951. xxiv, 336 p. illus., maps (part col., 1 fold. col. in pocket) 20 cm. Bibliography: p. 319-323. 51-4829. F128.68.A1T64
1951

AUDUBON park; the history of the site of the Hispanic society of American and neighbouring institutions, by George Bird Grinnell. New York, Printed by order of the trustees, 1927. v, 25 p. front., plates, ports., maps. 16½ cm. 27-15112. F128.68.A92G7

BLOOMINGDALE. The New York of yesterday; a descriptive narrative of old Bloomingdale, its topographical features, its early families and their genealogies, its old homesteads and country-seats, its French invasion, and its war experiences considered in their relation to its first relgious society, the Bloomingdale Reformed church, organized in 1805. Incorporated in 1806 as the church at Harsenville, by Hopper Striker Mott ... with 78 illus., diagrams, and maps. New York and London, G. P. Putnam's sons, 1908. 2, iii-xxvi, 597 p. front., illus., plates, ports., fold. maps, fold. plans, fold. chart, diagrs. 24 cm. "Authorities cited": p. xvii-xix. 8-16917. F128.68.B6M9

BRONX. Henry's directory of Morrisania and vicinity ... 1853/4 Morrisania, Spratley's Westchester gazette print., 1853 - v. fold. map. 19 cm. 32-34845. Directories

BRONX. Morrisania and Tremont directory. 1871/2   Morrisania, Times print, 1871 -
v.   20½ cm.   18-2192 Rev. Directories

QUEENSBORO street directory for all parts of Queens.   Long Island City, Long Island beobachter
v.   16 cm.   16-14618. F128.68.B8 A2

MORRISANIA. The Morris manor; address delivered at the fifth annual meeting of the New York branch of the Order of colonial lords of manors in America, Dec. 9, 1916, by Lucy D. Akerly ... (Baltimore? 1916?)   29 p. incl. col. front., illus. (ports.)   23½ cm.   20-16020.
F128.68.B8 A3

BRONX. The great north side; or, Borough of the Bronx.   New York, North side board of trade, 1897.   vi, 249, xv, 32 p. incl. plates. illus., ports., fold. map. 19½ cm.   1-14785 Rev.   F128.68.B8B75

BRONX. The Bronx, New York city's fastest growing borough ... (New York) The Bronx board of trade, 1921 -   v.   21 cm.   21-17633. F128.68.B8 B8

BRONXBORO; official monthly magazine of the Bronx board of trade. v. 1 -   May 1923 - (New York, 1923 -   v. illus. 27 cm. 30-9192. F128.68.B8 B85

BRONX. ... Excursion planned for the City history club of New York by Randall Comfort; no. ix. - Historic Bronx ... Rev. 1910 ... (New York, 1910)   p. (176) - 215. illus., diagrs.   19½ cm. "Reprinted from the Historical guide to the city of New York." 12-31037. F128.68.B8 C68

BRONX. History of Bronx borough, city of New York; compiled for the North side news, by Randall Comfort ... with collaboration of Charles D. Steurer, Charles A. D. Meyerhoff.   New York, North side news press, 1906.   xi, 422 p.   front., illus., ports.   31½ cm.   6-29984. F128.68.B8 C7

BRONX. The borough of the Bronx, 1639-1913; its marvelous development and historical surroundings, by Harry T. Cook ...   New York, The author, 1913.   5, 198 p. front., illus. (incl. ports., facsims.) 26 cm.   14-1375. F128.68.B8C77

BRONX. The borough beautiful. By Albert E. Davis. (New York, 1904)   23½ cm.   F128.68.B8 D2

BRONX. The Bronx through the years; a geo-graphy and history.   By George J. Fluhr.   Bronx, Aidan Press (1964)   51, (16) p. 22 cm. F128.68.B8F54

BRONX. The historical geography of the West Bronx.   New York, Aidan Press, 1960.   14 l.
F128.68.B8F55

BRONX. Guide to the Bronx ... New York, 1905.   15 cm.
F128.68.B8G9

BRONX. The Home news directory and guide of the Bronx.   (New York)Bronx home news, 1918.
165 p. fold. maps.   18½ x 8½ cm.   19-14621. F128.68.B8 H7

BRONX. The story of the Bronx from the purchase made by the Dutch from the Indians in 1639 to the present day, by Stephen Jenkins ... with 110 illus. and maps.   New York and London, G. P. Putnam's sons, 1912.   xix, 451 p.   front., plates, maps (1 fold.) 23½ cm.   12-23119. F128.68.B8 J5

BRONX. The Pell manor; address prepared for the New York branch of the Order of colonial lords of manors in America, by Captain Howland Pell ... Baltimore, 1917.   20 p. incl. illus., pl. 23½ cm.
20-16022. F128.68.B8P38

BRONX. Rand, McNally new street number guide and complete transit directory of the Bronx, showing the location of any given corner number on any street or avenue ... New York, Chicago, Rand, McNally (1918)   2, (3)-163 p. illus. (map) 16½ cm. 19-15088. F128.68.B8 R2

BRONX. The new north end, Bronx borough, issued by the Taxpayers' alliance ... New York, Diagram pub. co. (1910)   (102) p. illus. 25½ cm. 10-10808. F128.68.B8 T2

NEW YORK CITY

BRONX. Riverdale, Kingsbridge, Spuyten Duyvil, New York City; a historical epitome of the Northwest Bronx (by) William A. Tieck. Old Tappan, N.J., F. H. Revell Co. (1968) xix, 230 p. illus. 29 cm. 68-25827.
F128.68.B8 T5

BRONX. The Bronx and its people; a history, 1609 - 1927, board of editors: James L. Wells and others ... New York, The Lewis historical pub. co., 1927. 3 v. fronts., plates, ports., map. 27½ cm. Vols. 1-2 paged continuously; v.3 contains biographical material. 27-24588.
F128.68.B8W4

BRONX. Autobiography: the Bronx, 1928 - 1938 (by) Israel G. Young. Photos. by David Gahr. Introd. by Moses Asch. New York, Folklore Center Press, 1969. 42 p. illus. 14 x 22 cm.
F128.68.B8 Y68

CHELSEA. Turn west on 23rd; a toast to New York's Old Chelsea, by Robert Baral. New York, Fleet Pub. Corp. (1965) 128 p. 24 cm. 65-24028.
F128.68.C45B3

CITY ISLAND; history, legend and tradition, yachting. (By Allen Flood and Robert Mullen) City Island, N.Y. (1949) 92 p. illus., ports., map. 23 cm. 50-1277.
F128.68.C5F5

CITY ISLAND; tales of the clam diggers. By Alice Payne. Illus. by Dorothy Payne. (1st ed. Floral Park, N.Y., Printed by Graphicopy, 1969) 88 p. illus. 22 cm.
F128.68.C5 P3

FAIRVIEW, Yonkers ... New York, The Manhattan & Yonkers land co. (1900) 32 p. incl. diagr. fold. map. 19½ cm. 0-5472 Rev.
F128.68.F1M2

FORDHAM. Records of the Reformed church of Fordham in the Borough of Bronx. Formerly the Reformed Protestant Dutch church of Fordham, in the town of West Farms, Westchester county. Transcribed by the New York genealogical and biographical soc.; ed. by Royden Woodward Vosburgh. New York city, 1921. 2, vii, 138 numb. l. 36 x 28½ cm. Reproduced from type-written copy. Contains baps. and births, 1793-1912; marriages, 1836-1888, members, etc. 21-12122 rev.
F128.68.F6N4

FORT CLINTON. History of the southwest fort known as Fort Clinton (Castle Clinton) (Castle Garden) on the Battery, New York City, New York, and its eventful past. (n.p.) 1950. 18, 6, v l. 28 cm. 51-713.
F128.68.F7C8

GOVERNORS Island. Three centuries under three flags; the story of Governors Island from 1637. By Anastasio Carlos Mariano Azoy. Governors Island, N.Y., Headquarters First Army, 1951. 110 p. illus., port. 24 cm. 52-34907.
F128.68.G7A9

... GOVERNOR'S island, by Blanche Wilder Bellamy. (New York) G. P. Putnam's sons (1897) p. 141-181. 19½ cm. (Half moon series. v. 1, no. 5) Pub. also in "Historic New York". 1897. 1st ser. (no.12) 10-6834 Rev.
F128.68.G7 B4

GOVERNORS island, its history and development, 1637 - 1937. New York, The Governors island club, 1937. 64 p. incl. illus. (incl. ports.) pl. fold. map. 23½ cm. Bibliography: p. 63-64. 37-20747.
F128.68.G7G6

GOVERNOR'S Island; its military history under three flags, 1637-1913, by the Reverend Edmund Banks Smith ... New York, The author, 1913. 178 p. front., illus., plates, facsim. 24½ cm. "Authorities consulted": p. 9-10. 13-17128.
F128.68.G9 S6

— New York, Valentine's manual, inc., 1923. 5, 7-243 p. illus. (1 mounted) plates (part col.) ports., facsims. 26 cm. "Authorities consulted": p. (4) - 5. 22-23562.
F128.68.G7S62

GOVERNOR'S Island. Record of medical history of post medical department U.S.A.: instructions for keeping the medical history of the post, May 14, 1868. Washington (19 -) 29 l. 27 cm. 56-48296.
F128.68.G7U5

GREENWICH Village historic designation report. (New York) Landmarks Preservation Commission 1969. 2 v. (420 p.) illus. 36 cm. 73-289242.
F128.68.G8A5

GREENWICH Village. The little book of Greenwich Village; a handbook of information concerning New York's Bohemia, with which is incorporated a map and directory. (By Egmont Arens) (2d ed.) ... New York, E. Arens (1918)   32 p.   illus. (map)   9 x 19½ cm.   19-16308.   F128.68.G8A68

— (3d ed.) ... New York, E. Arens (1919)   24, (8) p.   illus. (map)   9 x 19 cm.   19-16309.
F128.68.G8A69

GREENWICH Village. The inside guide to Greenwich Village, winter-spring, 1964-1965, by Beth Bryant. (New York) Oak Publications, 1964)   52 p.   22 cm.
F128.68.G8B7

GREENWICH Village. The new inside guide to Greenwich Village, by Beth Bryant. (New York, Oak Publications) 1965.   65 p.   22 cm.   F128.68.G8B7 1965

GREENWICH Village, and landmarks in its vicinity ... (By) T. J. Burton. (New York?) 1894. (7)-20 p.   illus.   30 x 24 cm.   "A portion of this article ... originally pub. in ... the 'Greenwich landmark,' in 1883."   3-2489.
F128.68.G8B9
Rare Book Coll.

GREENWICH Village, by Anna Alice Chapin ... with illustrations by Alan Gilbert Cram. New York, Dodd, Mead, 1917.   5, ix-x p., 2 l., 3-301 p.   front., plates, fold. plan.   22 cm.   17-30045.   F128.68.C8C4

GREENWICH Village. The improper Bohemians; a re-creation of Greenwich Village in its heyday. By Allen Churchill. (1st ed.) New York, Dutton, 1959.   349 p.   illus.   21 cm.   Includes bibliography. 58-9604 rev.   F128.68.G8C45

GREENWICH Village. New York's Greenwich Village (by) Edmund T. Delaney. Barre, Mass., Barre Publishers, 1968.   144 p.   illus.   30 x 27 cm.   67-23657.   F128.68.G8D4

GREENWICH Village. Rambling through Greenwich Village, Washington square, lower 5th ave. (by) Grand Pierre; a guide to the most interesting section of New York ... New York, The Greenwich Village weekly news, 1935.   5-111 p.   fold. plan.   19½ cm.   39-1232.   F128.68.G8G7

GREENWICH Village. Records of the Reformed Dutch church at Greenwich in the city of New York. Transcribed by the New York genealogical and biographical soc. Ed. by Roden Woodward Vosburgh. New York city, 1920.   2, iii, 298 numb. l.   36 x 28½ cm.   Autographed from type-written copy.   20-16612.
F128.68.G8G8

GREENWICH Village. ... Excursion planned for the City history club of New York, by Frank Bergen Kelley ... No. II - Greenwich village and Lispenard's meadows (revised) (15th street to Chambers street, west of Broadway) ... (New York, 1902)   12 p.   illus. (maps)   19 cm.   17-19485.
F128.68.G8K3

GREENWICH Village. Off Washington Square; a reporter looks at Greenwich Village. By Jane Kramer. (1st ed.) New York, Duell, Sloan and Pearce (1963)   viii, 128 p.   21 cm.   63-16826.
F128.68.G8K7

GREENWICH Village, today & yesterday. By Henry Wysham Lanier. Photos. by Berenice Abbott. (1st ed.) New York, Harper (1949)   xi, 161 p.   illus., ports.   24 cm.   "Books to read": p. 155.   49-11616*.
F128.68.G8L3

GREENWICH Village. Poor Richard's guide to non-tourist Greenwich Village. By Richard Lewis. Art by Phoebe McKay. New York, Cricket Press (1959)   46 p.   18 cm.   "First printing - 1959"
F128.68.G8L4

GREENWICH Village. By Fred W. McDarrah. With an introd. by David Boroff. New York, Corinth Books, 1963.   96 p.   23 cm.   62-17663.   F128.68.G8M2

GREENWICH Village. My heart's in Greenwich Village (by) Seon Manley. New York, Funk & Wagnalls (1969)   221 p.   22 cm.   75-80704.   F128.68.G8M25

NEW YORK CITY

GREENWICH Village. Saloon society; (the diary of a year beyond aspirin. By William H. Manville. Photos. by David Attie. Design by Alexey Brodovitch. 1st ed. New York, Duell, Sloan and Pearce, 1960) 124 p. 26 cm. 60-12838.
F128.68.G8M3

GREENWICH Village. The New guide to Greenwich Village. New York, Corinth Books (1959) 64 p. illus. 21 cm. 59-3806.
F128.68.G8N45

GREENWICH Village. Old New York: our neighborhood, by Arthur Kneerim. (New York, The New York savings bank (1932) 16 p. illus. 20 cm.
F128.68.G8N5

GREENWICH Village. Where to go in Greenwich Village, by Rosetta Reitz & Joan Geisler. Drawings by Robert Reitz. (New York) ... (1961) 95 p. 22 x 10 cm. 61-11986.
F128.68.G8R9

GREENWICH Village. The Village freen. v. (1)-2, no. 7; Feb. 15, 1936 - July/Aug. 1937. (New York) Greenwich avenue committee, inc. (1936-37) 2 v. illus. 28 cm. Semimonthly, Feb.-Apr. 1936; monthly, May 1936-1937. No more pub? L.C. set incomplete: v.2, no. 3,5 wanting. 45-28109.
F128.68.G8V5

GREENWICH Village. The Village voice reader; a mixed bag from the Greenwich Village newspaper. Ed. by Daniel Wolf and Edwin Fancher. With line drawings by Muriel Jacobs (and others. 1st ed.) Garden City, N.Y., Doubleday, 1962. 349 p. 22 cm. 61-12596.
F128.68.G8V52

GREENWICH Village. The Greenwich Village guide, compiled under the auspices of the Villager, the community newspaper. (Ed. by Clementene Wheeler) New York, Bryan Publications (1947) 128 p. illus., map. 20 cm. 47-5455*.
F128.68.G8V53

GREENWICH Village. The Greenwich Village guide. Ed. by William H. Honan. Illus. by Joseph Papin. New York, Bryan Publications, 1959. iv, 140 p. illus. 18 cm.
F128.68.G8V53 1959

... GREENWICH Village, 1920 - 1930; a comment on American civilization in the post-war years. Boston, Houghton Mifflin co., 1935. xii, 21., (3) - 496 p. maps (1 fold.) diagrs. 22½ cm. Prepared under the auspices of Columbia university council for research in the social sciences in collaboration with Greenwich house. 35-6370.
F128.68.G8W25

GREENWICH Village, 1920 - 1930; a comment on American civilization in the post-war years (by) Caroline F. Ware. New York, Harper & Row (1965) xii, 496 p. 21 cm. (Harper colophon books) First pub. in 1935.
F128.68.G8W25 1965

GREENWICH Village. ... Old Greenwich, by Elizabeth Bisland ... Mrs. Elizabeth (Bisland) Wetmore. (New York) The Knickerbocker press, 1897) p. 275-301. 19½ cm. (Half moon series. v. 1, no. ix) Pub. also in "Historic New York", 1897. 1st ser. (no. 8) 10-5324.
F128.68.G8W3

GREENWICH Village. The village square. By John Wilcock. (1st ed.) New York, L. Stuart (1961) 192 p. 22 cm. 60-11143.
F128.68.G8W5

HARLEM River. Haarlem River; its use previous to and since the revolutionary war, and suggestions relative to present contemplated improvement. New York, Printed by J. D. Torrey, 1857. iv, (5) - 161 p. 22 cm. 12-5131.
F128.68.H28H2

HARLEM. The complete report of Mayor LaGuardia's Commission on the Harlem Riot of March 19, 1935. New York, Arno Press, 1969. 136 p. 24 cm. (Mass violence in America) 76-90204.
F128.68.H3A53

HARLEM. It was fun while it lasted. By Frederic Alexander Birmingham. (1st ed.) Philadelphia, Lippincott (1960) 224 p. 21 cm. Autobiographical. 60-7850.
F128.68.H3B5

HARLEM. The black Jews of Harlem; Negro nationalism and the dilemmas of Negro leadership. By Howard Brotz. (New York) Free Press of Glencoe (1964)   144 p. 21 cm. 64-13240.
                                            F128.68.H3 B7

— New York, Schocken Books (1970)   xi, 144 p. 21 cm. (Sourcebook in Negro history) 74-111301.
                                            F128.68.H3 B7
                                            1970

HARLEM; a community in transition. Ed. by John Henrik Clarke. (1st ed.) New York, Citadel Press (1965)   223 p. 21 cm. Publ. also under title: Harlem, U.S.A. 64-21891.   F128.68.H3C55

HARLEM, U.S.A. Ed. and with an introd. by John Henrik Clarke. Rev. ed. New York, Collier Books (1971)   xxvi, 388 p. illus., ports. 20 cm. "The contents of this book, in part, have been taken from various issues of Freedomways." 72-151162.
                                            F128.68.H3C55
                                            1971

HARLEM. Win progress for Harlem, by James W. Ford ... (New York, The Harlem division of the Communist party, 1939)   31 p. 2 illus. (ports.) 19 cm. 47-3081.
                                            F128.68.H3F6

HARLEM. Minutes and proceedings of the town meeting of ... New Harlem ... (1903)   23½ cm.
                                            F128.68.H3H3

HARLEM. Sea island to city; a study of St. Helena Islanders in Harlem and other urban centers. By Clyde Vernon Kiser. New York, AMS Press, 1967.   272 p. maps. 23 cm. (Studies in history, economics and public law, no. 368) Reprint of the 1932 ed. ... thesis, Columbia. Bibliography: p. 265-267. 70-29898 MARC.   F128.68.H3K5
                                            1967

— With a new pref. by Joseph S. Himes. New York, Atheneum, 1969.   272 p. 22 cm. (Studies in American Negro life) 69-15525.
                                            F128.68.H3K5
                                            1969

HARLEM: Negro metropolis, by Claude McKay; illus. with photos. New York, E. P. Dutton, (1940) xi, 15-262 p. front., illus. (facsim.) plates, ports. 22½ cm. "First edition." 40-32205.   F128.68.H3M3

HARLEM. New Harlem past and present; the story of an amazing civic wrong, now at last to be righted. By Carl Horton Pierce. With a review of the principles of law invovled in the recovery of the Harlem lands, by William Pennington Toler and Harmon De Pau Nutting ... New York, New Harlem pub. co., 1903.   (vii) - xiv p. 332 p. front., illus., plates, ports., maps (partly fold.) 23 cm. 3-19704.
                                            F128.68.H3 P6

HARLEM. Poverty and politics in Harlem; report on project uplift 1965, by Alphonso Pinkney and Roger R. Woock. New Haven, Conn., College & University Press (1970)   191 p. 21 cm. 79-116379.
                                            F128.68.H3P65

HARLEM (city of New York): its origin and early annals. Prefaced by home scenes in the fatherlands; or, notices of its founders before emigration. Also, sketches of numerous families, and the recovered history of the land-titles. ... By James Riker ... New York, Printed for the author, 1881.
xii, (2), 636 p. illus., fold. map., facsims. 24 cm. 1-16796.
                                            F128.68.H3R5
                                            Rare Book Coll.

— ... New York, New Harlem publishing co., 1904.   xiv, (2), 908 p. front. (port.) illus., fold. map. 24 cm. "Revised from the author's notes and enlarged by Henry Pennington Toler. Ed. Sterling Potter." 4-10895.   F128.68.H3R6

— Upper Saddle River, N.J., Literature House (1970)   xiv, 908 p. 22 cm. 78-104551.
                                            F128.68.H3R6
                                            1970

HARLEM on my mind; cultural capital of black America, 1900-1968. Comp. Allon Schoener. Pref.

by Thomas P. F. Hoving. Introd. by Candice Van Ellison. New York, Random House (1969) 255 p. illus. 29 cm. "1st printing." 68-28558. F128.68.H3 S3

HARLEM. Who's who in Harlem. 1st - ed.; 1949/50 - New York, Magazine & Periodical Print. & Pub. Co. v. illus., ports. 24 cm. 51-30549. F128.68.H3W5

HARLEM; the story of a changing community. By Bernice Elizabeth Young. New York, Messner (1972) 64 p. illus. 23 cm. 79-180535 MARC. F128.68.H3Y6

HELL'S Kitchen. Angels in Hell's Kitchen. By Tom McConnon. (1st ed.) Garden City, N.Y., Doubleday, 1959. 281 p. 22 cm. Reminiscences of the author's childhood. 59-13978. F128.68.H4M2

HELL Gate Hill section of New York; a brief sketch of an interesting part of the island of Manhattan, by Abner I. Weisman. New York (1965) (8) l. map. 30 cm. F128.68.H43W4

... KLEY homeseeker's survey and guide, designed to present in standard form useful data concerning residential and industrial communitites within the suburbs of New York city ... New York city, Kley pub. corporation, 1925. 118 p. 24½ x 12 cm. "Spring 1925, first ed." 25-10434. F128.68.K6K6

LOWER East Side, The; a portrait in time, by Diana Cavallo. With photos. by Leo Stashin. New York, Crowell-Collier Press (1971) 134 p. illus. 29 cm. 75-127459. F128.68.L6C3

MANHATTAN. ... Excursion planned for the City history club of New York by Frank Bergen Kelley; no. vii. - New York city south of Wall street ... Rev. 1912 ... (New York, 1912) p. 12-39. illus., plans. 19½ cm. "Reprinted from the Historical guide to the city of New York." 12-31039. F128.68.M27K27

QUEENS. ... Norwood's guide, first and second wards, Queen best street directory, Corona, L.I. City, Woodside, Elmhurst, East Elmhurst, Jackson Heights, Maspeth, Glendale, Ridgewood, Forest Hills, Kew Gardens, Middle Village ... Woodside, N.Y., C.W. Norwood, 19 v. illus. (maps) 15½ cm. Successor to the "X" book. CA 31-122 Unrev. F128.68.Q4A2

QUEENS. Polk's official street directory, car line and information guide of New York city, borough of Queens. New York, Detroit (etc.) R. L. Polk (1922) v. 15½ cm. 22-14136. F128.68.Q4A2

QUEENS. The "Red book' information and street guide of Queens borough, New York city ... New York, Interstate map company (1929 - v. fold. map. 15½ cm. CA 30-1201 Unrev. F128.68.Q4A2

QUEENS. Plan for permanent world capitol at Flushing Meadow Park. Mayor's Committee on Plan and Scope. (New York) 1946. 26 p. illus. 45 cm. 53-34312. F128.68.Q4N42

QUEENS (Borough) Historian. Report. 1st - 1944 - Jamaica, N.Y. v. 28 cm. annual. Report for 1944 includes a supplement: The origin of community names in Queens Borough. 52-15307. F128.68.Q4Q25

QUEENS. ... Description of private and family cemeteries in the borough of Queens, compiled by the Topographical bureau ... Jamaica, N.Y., Long island collection, The Queens borough public library, 1932. 81 p. incl. illus., plates, maps. 28½ x 22 cm. "The Queens borough pub. library ... records are, in several places, fuller than those of the Topographical bureau. The two files have been combined." 34-3534. F128.68.Q4Q33

QUEENS Borough; being a descriptive and illustrated book of the boroughs of Queens, city of Greater New York, setting forth its many advantages and possibilities as a section wherein to live, work and succeed ... Issued by the Manufacturing and industrial committee of the Chamber of commerce of the borough of Queens; ... (Brooklyn, Brooklyn eagle press, 1913) 110 p. illus. 26 cm. 14-12558. F128.68.Q4Q4

QUEENS Borough, the borough of homes and industry; a descriptive and illus. book setting forth its wonderful growth and development in commerce, industry and homes during the past few years .... (Brooklyn, Brooklyn eagle press) 1915. 126 p. illus., fold. map (in pocket) 26 cm. 16-17975. F128.68.Q4Q45

QUEENS Borough, 1910 - 1920; the borough of homes and industry, etc. etc. (New York, Presses of the L. I. star pub. co.) 1920.   240 p. incl. front., illus., double plan. 26 cm. 20-12286.   F128.68.Q4Q46

QUEENS. Illustrated history of the borough of Queens, by George von Skal, comp. by F. T. Smiley pub. co., New York city, for the Flushing journal. (Flushing, N.Y.) 1908.   167, (2) p. incl. front., illus., plates, ports. 29 cm. 10-8903.   F128.68.Q4 S6

QUEENS. Who's who in Queens ... (Jamaica, N.Y., 1936 -   v. 20½ cm. 37-2451.
F128.68.Q4W5

STUYVESANT Village. The evolution of Stuyvesant Village. Tenth to Bleecker streets, Broadway to Second avenue and around there, by A. A. Rikeman. Mamaroneck (N.Y.) (Press of C. G. Peck) 1899.   88 p. 23 cm. 3-15266.   F128.68.S9 R5

WASHINGTON Heights, Manhattan, its eventful past, by Reginald Pelham Bolton ... Pub. by Dyckman institute. New York, Printed for the author ... 1924.   xii, 366 p. front., illus., plates, maps. 23 cm. In 6 parts ... "Book references" at end of each part. 25-10436.   F128.68.W2B6

NEW YORK CITY.   BUILDINGS, COLLECTIVE.

CHASE Manhattan Bank. Historic buildings now standing in New York, which were erected prior to 1800. New York (1914)   45 p. 24 cm. Pub. by the bank under its earlier name: Bank of the Manhattan Co. 14-8251 rev.*
F128.7.C 46

DIAGRAMS of the leading New York theatres. (New York) T. J. McBride (1879)   40 p. 24°. 1-14786-M1.   F128.7.D 53

(HAMILTON, Isabel) Palatial homes in the city of New York and dwellers therein ... arr. for the convenience of the passer-by. New York, 1910.   64 p. illus. 20½ cm. 10-10806.
F128.7.H 21

HERITAGE of New York, The; historic-landmark plaques of the New York Community Trust. Pref. by Whitney North Seymour. New York, Fordham University Press, 1970.   xxi, 402 p. illus. 26 cm. "1st publ. 1970." 69-13762.   F128.7.H 47

(KRESS, S. H., & co.) Old New York. (New York?) 1935.   (19) p. of col. illus. 17 x 25½ cm. "Contains reproductions in miniature of ... original sketches ... (by Edward Trumbull and Maurice Gautier for) mural paintings (which) decorate the walls of the cafeteria of the new Kress store at 444 Fifth ave." 36-1650.
F128.7.K 57
Rare Book Coll.

NEW YORK Edison co. Towers of Manhattan. (New York) The New York Edison co., 1928. 3 l., 50 pl. (incl. front.) 31 cm. 30-9124.
F128.5.N 39
Rare Book Coll.

OLD buildings of New York city, with some notes regarding their origin and occupants. New York, Brentano's, 1907.   179 p. incl. illus., plates. 23 cm. 8-1762.   F128.7.O 44

PELLETREAU, William Smith. Early New York houses, with historical and genealogical notes by William S. Pelletreau; photos of old houses and original illustrations by C. G. Moller, jr. ... New York, F. P. Harper, 1900.   viii, 243 p. incl. illus., 50 pl. 28 cm. In 10 parts, paged continuously. 1-30804 Rev.
F128.7. P 38

PETERSON, Arthur Everett. Thirty historic places in greater New York ... Pub. by the City history club of New York in cooperation with the New York World's fair, 1939. (New York, 1939)   68 p. incl. front., illus. (incl. map) 23½ cm. 39-14036.   F128.7. P 43

SOUVENIR of places of amusement of N.Y. city. (New York) Annunciator press, 1874.   (25) p. 16° 1-14787-M.   F128.7. S 72

NEW YORK CITY.   BUILDINGS, INDIVIDUAL.

ABIGAIL Adams Smith house.   Colonial Dames of America.   New York (1968)   16 p.   illus.   21 cm.
68-29091.
F128.8. A2 C6

ABIGAIL Adams Smith Mations and the Mount Vernon estate, The story of the.   By Katherine Metcalf Roof.   (New York, Colonial Dames of America, 1949)   12 p.   22 cm.   49-26223*.
F128.8. A2 R66

B & O station.   The new Baltimore and Ohio station in the heart of New York city.   (New York, Baltimore and Ohio railroad co., 1929)   31 p.   illus. (incl. maps)   21½ x 25½ cm.   CA 30-1267 Unrev.
F128.8. B17 B 4

BARNUM'S museum.   Sights and wonders in New York; incl. a description of ... Barnum's museum; also a memoir of Barnum himself ... New York, J. S. Redfield, 1849.   24 p.   illus.   12°.   1-14788-M1.
F128.8. B 2 S 5

BUCKINGHAM hotel, Fifth Ave.   (New York, 1877)   22½ cm.
F128.8. B92 B 9

CAFÉ boulevard.   Boulevard reminiscences, by Vilma M. Goodman.   (New York, Printed by the Amerikai Magyar népszava, 1922)   29 p.   illus.   23½ cm.   22-22630.
F128.8. C2 G6

CITY hall.   The preservation of the historic City hall of New York.   Letter of Hon. Andrew H. Green to the commissioners, appointed to locate the site for a new municipal building.   (New York) Printed under the auspices of the New York State society, Sons of the American revolution, 1894.
14 p.   front.   23½ cm.   9-23623.
F128.8. C5 G7

CITY hall.   The renascence of City Hall; commemorative presentation, rededication of City Hall, the City of New York, July 12, 1956.   Pub. with the cooperation of the co-sponsor Downtown Manhattan Assoc., inc.   (New York, 1956.   94 p.   illus., ports., maps.   28 cm.   "2d printing. Nov.1956"   A 57-8604.
F128.8. C5 N4

The CITY investing building.   Broadway-Courtlandt co., (New York, 1907)   31 cm.
F128.8. C52 B 8

CLAREMONT inn.   Claremont of history and to-day; illustrating various incidents and places round about historic Claremont, Claremont Heights, Riverside drive.   (New York? Chasmar-Winchell press, 1907)   (30) p. incl. front., illus.   31½ cm.   7-26027.
F128.8. C59 C5

CUSTOM-house building.   General description and specifications of the alterations and repairs required to be made in the present customhouse building, in the city of New York ... New York, J. Clarke, printer, 1862.   16 p.   8°.   2-6377.
F128.8. C9 Y7

SUPREME court.   The first homes of the Supreme court of the U. S. (by) Robert P. Reeder.   (Lancaster, Pa., Lancaster press, inc., 1936)   p. 543-596.   10 pl. (incl. plans)   25½ cm.   "Describes its homes in New York and Philadelphia."   "Reprinted from the Proceedings of the Amer. philosophical soc. v. 76, no. 4."   37-2494.
F128.8. E9 R4

FEDERAL Hall Memorial; seat of the founding of the government.   (New York, 194-)   (16) p.   28 cm.
F128.8. F4 F4

FRAUNCES tavern.   A sketch of Fraunces tavern and those connected with its history, by Henry Russell Drowne, secretary of the Sons of the revolution in the state of New York ... New York, Fraunces tavern, 1919.   2, 23, (2) p.   illus. (incl. map)   20 cm.   "In 1904 Fraunces tavern was purchased by the Sons of the revolution."   19-4338.
F128.8. F7 D7

— 2d ed. ... New York, Fraunces tavern, 1925.   35, (3) p.   front. (port.) illus.   20 cm.   26-412.
F128.8. F7 D7
1925

— 4th ed.   N. Y., Sons of the Revolution in the State of New York) 1949.   35 p.   illus., ports.   20 cm.
49-51314*.
F128.8. F7 D7
1949

FRAUNCES tavern. ... Excursion planned for the City history club of New York by Frank Bergen Kelley ... No. vi - Fraunces tavern (rev.) ... (New York, 1908)   2-8 p. illus., plan. 19½ cm. 12-31051.

F128.8. F7 K33

FRAUNCES' tavern. The landmark of Fraunces' tavern; a retrospect, read ... in the long room of the Tavern, on 117th anniversary of the famous "farewell" of 1783, at the first patriotic reunion of the Women's auxiliary to the Society for the preservation of scenic and historic places and objects ... by Mrs. Melusina Fay Peirce ... (New York) Printed for distribution by the Women's auxiliary (1901) 44 p. front., illus., map. 20 cm. 2d ed. 5-33358.

F128.8. F7 P 4

GRANGE. Mr. Daniels and the Grange, by Eric Sloane and Edward Anthony. New York, Funk & Wagnalls (1968)   viii, 119 p. illus. 29 cm. 68-12006.

F128.8.G7 S 55

HALL of records. The old martyr's prison, New York; an historical sketch of the oldest municipal building in New York city: used as a British prison during the war for American independence: built about 1756 and known at different times as "the New gaol," "the Debtors' prison," "the Provost," "the Hall of records" and "the Register's office" Presented to the Board of Aldermen of the city of New York by the American scenic and historic preservation soc. (New York, 1902?)   16 p. 24 cm. "Reprinted from "The City record" of Oct. 23, 1902." "By Edward Hagaman Hall." 7-24909.

F128.8.H17 A5

HIPPODROME. The mighty hippodrome. By Norman Clarke. South Brunswick (N.J.) A. S. Barnes (1968)   144 p. 29 cm. 67-19466.

F128.8.H5 C55

HOLLAND house, Fifth avenue and Thirtieth street, New York. New York, H. M. Kinsley & Baumann, 1891.   (33) p. front., illus. 12º. 1-14792-M1.

F128.8. H7 H7

MERCHANTS coffee house. ... The birthplace of our union - 140th anniversary, the Merchants coffee house, southeast corner of Wall and Water streets. Erected about 1737; destroyed by fire Dec. 18th, 1804. (New York, J. D. McGuire, printer, 1914)   (3) p. 30½ cm.

F128.8.M55W2

MORRIS mansion. Washington's headquarters, New York. A sketch of the history of the Morris mansion (or Jumel mansion) in the city of New York, used by Washington as his headquarters in 1776, by Reginald Pelham Bolton. New York, The American scenic and historic preservation soc., 1903. 40 p. incl. plan. front. (port.) pl. 18½ cm. 3-28200.

F128.8. M8 B6

MORRIS mansion. The Jumel mansion, being a full history of the house on Harlem Heights built by Roger Morris before the revolution. Tog. with some account of its more notable occupants ... By William Henry Shelton. Boston & New York, Houghton Mifflin, 1916.   xii, 257 p. front., plates, ports., maps, plans, facsim., fold. geneal. tab. 28½ cm. 17-216.

F128.8. M8 S5

MORRIS mansion. Historic events connected with the Roger Morris mansion, Washington's headquarters, 160th st. and Jumel place, New York city. (By Mrs. Emma Adelia Flint Smith) (New York? 1907)   (6) p. 23 cm. 8-991 Rev.

F128.8. M8 S6

MORRIS mansion. Historical sketch of Washington's headquarters, prepared under the auspices of the Washington headquarters assoc., New York, by Emma A. F. Smith ... (New York) 1908. xviii p. plates. 25 cm. 8-30583.

F128.8. M8 S62

— (Rev. ed.) (New York, George Harjes co.) 1908 (1910)   xix p. plates. 25½ cm. 10-12418 Rev.

F128.8. M8S63

— (Rev. ed.) (New York, Press of George Harjes co.) 1908 (1913)   xix p. plates. 25½ cm. 13-9167.

F128.8. M8 S64

NEW YORK university. Castle Solitude in the metropolis; a study in social science, by Karl Kron (pseud. for Lyman Hotchkiss Bagg) ... New York, K. Kron, 1888.   4, 48, (142) p. incl. col. port. 19½ cm. An account of University building, of New York university, on Washington square. The 142 unnumbered pages contain extracts from the author's "Ten thousand miles on a bicycle," and press notices relating to the same work. 8-25397.

F128.8.N5 B 14

NEW YORK CITY

PENNSYLVANIA station in New York city. ... (Philadelphia?) Pennsylvania R.R., 1910. (36) p. incl. front., illus. fold. pl. 19½ cm. 10-27726.
F128.8. P4 P4

ROCKEFELLER Center; a photographic narrative. By Samuel Chamberlain. New York, Hastings House (1951) 72 p. (chiefly illus.) 21 cm. 51-2633.
F128.8. R7 C5 1951

— (Rev. ed.) New York, Hastings House (1956) 72 p. illus. 21 cm. 56-11968 rev.
F128.8. R7 C5 1956

— (1961) 48 p. 26 cm. 61-9291.
F128.8. R7 C5 1961

— 1972.
F128.8. R7 C5 1972

ROCKEFELLER center. The city within a city; the romance of Rockefeller center (by) David Loth. New York, W. Morrow, 1966. 214 p. 22 cm. 66-17182.
F128.8. R7 L6

ROCKEFELLER center. ... The last rivet; the story of Rockefeller center, a city within a city, as told at the ceremony in which John D. Rockefeller, jr., drove the last rivet of the last building ... 1939. New York, Columbia university press, 1940. (5)-45 p. front., illus., ports. 28½ cm. "This book was prepared for publication under the direction of Merle Crowell." 40-31940.
F128.8. R7 R65

ROCKEFELLER center. The story of Rockefeller center ... (New York) Rockefeller center, inc., 1939. (24) p. illus. 29 cm. 39-22759.
F128.8. R7 R7

— New York, Printed by Select printing co., 1942. (20) p. illus. 29½ cm. 42-12129.
F128.8. R7 R7 1942

ST. PATRICK'S cathedral. A full description of the exterior and interior of the new cathedral, the altars and windows: with biographical sketches of Cardinal McCloskey, and the Most Rev. Archbishop Hughes. Westchester (N.Y.) The New York Catholic protectory print, 1879. 56 p. front., port. 12°. 1-14793 Rev.
F128.8. S1 S1

SHERMAN square hotel, Grand Boulevard, West 71st street. E. N. Wilson. (New York, New York art pub. co., 1893) (28) p. front., illus. sq. fol. Prospectus. 1-14794-M1.
F128.8. S5 S5

STADT HUYS. The Stadt huys of New Amsterdam, by Alice Morse Earle. 2d ed. (New York, Press of J. J. Little, 1896) 29 p. 19½ cm. (Half moon series. v. 1. no. 1) Pub. also in "Historic New York." 1897. 1st ser. (no. 2) 10-6833 rev.
F128.8. S7 E1

TRINITY church. History of Trinity church and its grave yard ... By Allan Pollock. New York, A. Pollock, 1880. 32 p. front., illus. 16½ cm. 1-14795.
F128.8. T8 P7

TURTLE BAY. The brownstones of Turtle Bay Gardens, by Mable Detmold. New York, East 49th Street Assoc. (1964) 77 p. map. 22 cm. 64-8538.
F128.8. T85 D4

VAN CORTLANDT mansion. Frederick Van Cortlandt mansion, Van Cortlandt park, where Washington was guest of one brother while the other served King George (by) Mabel Lorenz Ives ... (Upper Montclair, N.J., Lucy Fortune, 1932) 4, 16 p. incl. front., illus. 23 cm. "Pre-print series" of Washington's headquarters series, no. 6. 32-9941.
F128.8. V2 I8

VAN CORTLANDT house. Historical sketch of the Van Cortlandt house ... by Catharine Van Cortlandt. New York, 1903. 23 cm.
F128.8. V2 M4

VAN NEST homestead, Reminiscences of the, by Mrs. Ann Van Nest Bussing, also an historical sketch. N.Y. ... (The Gilliss press) 1897. (16) p. illus. 22 x 17 cm. 12-5132.
F128.8. V26 B9

The WALDORF. (By George C. Boldt) (New York, 1893)   43 p.   illus.   15 x 20 ½ cm.   George C. Boldt
was the proprietor of the Waldorf hotel, and later of the Waldorf-Astoria.   1-14796 Rev.
          F128.8. W2 B7
          Rare Book Coll.

The WALDORF-Astoria, New York.   By George C. Boldt.   Ed. de luxe.   (New York, American lithographic co.) 1903.   (72) p. incl. illus., double map.   20 x 23 ½ cm.   31-31245.
          F128.8. W22 B7
          Rare Book Coll.

WALDORF.   Old Waldorf bar days; with the cognomina and composition of 491 appealing appetizers and salutary potations long known, admired and served at the famous big brass rail; also, a glossary for the use of antiquarians and students of American mores; by Albert Stevens Crockett; with illus. by Leighton Budd.   New York, Aventine press, 1931.   6, 5-242 p., 3 l.   illus.   23 ½ cm.   "First ed."   31-32316.
          F128.8. W22 C8

WALDORF-Astoria, The story of the (by) Edward Hungerford ... New York and London, G. P. Putnam's sons, 1925.   vi, 283 p.   front., plates, ports., facsims.   22 ½ cm.   25-13987.
          F128.8. W22 H8

WALDORF-Astoria.   Peacock alley; the romance of the Waldorf-Astoria, by James Remington McCarthy ... New York and London, Harper & bros., 1931.   x, 213 p.   front., plates, ports.   23 cm.   "First ed." Bibliography included in foreword.   31-30404.
          F128.8. W22 M3

WOOLWORTH building.   Above the clouds and old New York; an historical sketch of the site and a description of the many wonders of the Woolworth building, by H. Addington Bruce.   Pub. for distribution among the visitors to the Woolworth tower.   (Baltimore-New York, Munder-Thomsen press, 1913) (30) p.   col. front., illus. (part col.)   26 cm.   13-9562.
          F128.8. W82 B8

NEW YORK CITY.   ELEMENTS IN THE POPULATION.

BERCOVICI, Konrad.   Around the world in New York; illus. by Norman Borchardt.   New York & London, The Century co. (1924)   5, 3-416 p.   front., illus.   23 cm.   24-26898.
          F128.9. A1 B 4

BLACK, Algernon David, and others.   The city's children and the challenge of racial discrimination. (New York, Society for Ethical Culture, 1958)   29 p.   21 cm.   (Ethical frontiers)   58-26539.
          F128.9. A1 B 5

CAROLINE Zachry Institute of Human Development.   Around the world in New York; a guide to the city's nationality groups ...   New York, Common Council for American Unity, 1950.   112 p.   24 cm. 50-11557.
          F128.9. A1 C3

ERNST, Robert.   Immigrant life in New York City, 1825 - 1863.   New York, King's Crown Press, 1949.   xvi, 331 p.   24 cm.   Issued also as thesis, Columbia University.   Bibliography: p.(297)-319.   49-9759*.
          F128.9. A1 E7
          1949

— 1949.   xvi, 331 p.   24 cm.   Thesis - Columbia university.   A 49-8191*.
          F128.9. A1 E7
          1949 a

— Port Washington, N.Y., I. J. Friedman (1965)   xvi, 331 p.   22 cm.   (Empire State Historical publications, 37)   64-8789.
          F128.9. A1 E7
          1965

GLAZER, Nathan.   Beyond the melting pot; the Negroes, Puerto Ricans, Jews, Italians and Irish of New York City.   Cambridge, Mass., M. I. T. Press, 1963.   vii, 360 p.   21 cm.   63-18005.
          F128.9. A1 G55

— 2d ed.   Cambridge, Mass., M. I. T. Press (1970)   xcviii, 363 p.   (Publications of the Joint Center for Urban Studies)   22 cm.   78-118346.
          F128.9. A1 G55
          1970

NEW YORK CITY

HANDLIN, Oscar. The newcomers; Negroes and Puerto Ricans in a changing metropolis. Cambridge, Harvard University Press, 1959. 171 p. 22 cm. (New York metropolitan region study) 59-14737.
F128.9. A1 H3

The LOWER East Side; immigrant portal to American from 1875 to 1925. New York. State Council on the Arts. Visual Arts Program. (Introd. statement by Allon Schoener. New York, 1971) (4) p. 50 plates. 37 cm.
F128.9. A1 L68
Spec format

NEW YORK Borad of Education. Community in action; a report on a social integration project in School Districts 12, 13, and 14, Manhattan, 1950 - 1958. New York (1958) 27 p. 27 cm.
F128.9. A1 N4

ARABS. The immigrant Arab community in New York. By Ishag T. Qutub. (East Lansing? Mich., 1962) 24 l. 29 cm. 62-63849.
F128.9. A65 Q8

BOHEMIANS. The Čech (Bohemian) community of New York, with introductory remarks on the Čechoslovaks in the U.S., by Thoms Čapek ... New York, The Czechoslovak section of America's making, inc., 1921. 93 p. 20 cm. 22-2714.
F128.9. B67 C 3

— Photo-offest. San Francisco, R. & E. Research Associates, 1969.
F128.9. B67 C 3
1969

CANADIANS. The kinship of two countries; a history of the Canadian Club of New York, 1903-1963, by Hugh A. Anderson. With an introd. by Thomas B. Costain and a foreword by W. Boyd O'Connor. (New York) Canadian Club of New York (1964) xv, 190 p. 23 cm. 64-24730.
F128.9. C2 A7

CANADIAN club of New York. Annual banquet. The speeches. (New York? v. illus. (ports.) 26 cm. CA 10-5233 Unrev'd.
F128.9. C2 C2

CANADIAN club of New York. Canadian leaves; history, art, science, literature, commerce; a series of new papers read before the Canadian club of New York ... Ed. by G. M. Fairchild, jr. ... illus. by Thomson Willing. New York, N. Thompson, 1887. viii, 289 p. illus., ports. 24 x 18½ cm.
F128.9. C2 C24

CANADIAN club of New York. ... Year book. 19 v. 20 cm. 34-11013.
F128.9. C2 C28

— (New York, Printed by F. H, Hitchcock, v. 18½ cm. 14-17065.
F128.9. C23 C2

CANADIAN society of New York. Annual dinner. (New York, 19 v. illus., ports. 17 cm. 15-3590.
F128.9. C23 C3

CATHOLICS. ... Catholic footsteps in old New York, a chronicle of Catholicity in the city from 1524 to 1808. By William Harper Bennett. New York, Schwartz, Kirwin and Fauss, 1909. viii, 499 p. front., plates, ports. 21½ cm. "Bibliography, etc.": p. (465) - 470. 9-6272.
F128.9. C3 B 4

CATHOLICS. A letter on the moral causes that have produced the evil spirit of the times; addressed to the Hon. James Harper, mayor of New-York ... By the Right Rev. Dr. Hughes ... New-York, J. Winchester (1844) 23 p. 24 cm. 11-21768.
F128.9. C3 H8

CHINESE. New York's Chinatown; an historical presentation of its people and places. By Louis J. Beck ... New York, Bohemia pub. co. (1898) xi, 332 p. incl. front., illus., ports. 23 cm. 1-14797 Rev.
F128.9. C5 B 3

CHINESE. Official Chinatown guide book ... ed. T'ien-ên Ch'ên. New York, N.Y., (Henin & co.) 1939. 96 p. illus. (incl. ports., plan) 19½ cm. James Boyle, joint editor. 41-25349 rev.
F128.9. C5 C48

CHINESE. Welcome to Chinatown; official China-town guide book, New York, 1964-65; official guide book for World's Fair visitors, year of dragon. (Henin Chin) T'ien-ên Ch'ên, editor.
64 p.   23 cm.   64-22586. F128.9. C5 C49

CHINESE. The Chinese annual. v.1 -   Aug. 1911 -   New York, New York Chinese students' club, 1911 -   illus. 26 cm. 12-4616. F128.9. C5 C5

CHINESE. Chinatown handy guide, New York City. By John T. C. Fang. New York, 1958.
96 p. illus. 19 cm. 59-29174. F128.9. C5 F3

CHINESE. ... Shake hands with the dragon, by Carl Glick, illus. by Donald McKay. New York, London, Whittlesey house, McGraw-Hill book co, (1941)   vii, 327 p. incl. front., illus. 22 cm. 41-15603.
F128.9. C5 G5

— London, H. Jenkins (1946)   220, (2) p. illus. 22½ cm. "First (London) printing." 46-20454. F128.9. C5 G5 1946

— New York, Whittlesey House. Ann Arbor, Mich., Gryphon Books, 1971.   vii, 327 p. illus. 22 cm. 75-162513 MARC. F128.9. C5 G5 1971

CHINESE. Chinatown and her mother country, by George L. Hsiong and others. (New York city, New China co.) 1939.   127 p. illus. 20½ cm. 42-31364. F128.9. C5 H8

CHINESE. New York Chinatown. By William Wirt Mills. (New York, 1908)   13 x 20 cm. F128.9. C5 M6

CHINESE. Chinatown as I saw it. (By Charles Rose) New York, A. W. Knox, 1895.   (16) p.
14½ cm. Signed "Pilgrim". 1-14798. F128.9. C5 R7

CHINESE. Who's who of the Chinese in New York, by Warner M. Van Norden. New York, 1918.
2, (3) - 148 p. illus. (incl. ports., map) pl. 18½ cm. 18-2692. F128.9. C5 V26

CHINESE. Shêng huo tsai Niu-yüeh T'ang jên chieh, 1959. By Yang-ch'êng Wu.   190 p. 19 cm.
F128.9. C5 W8
Orien China

JEWS. A Bintel brief; sixty years of letters from the Lower East Side to the Jewish Daily Forward. Comp. ed. and with an introd. by Isaac Metzker. Foreword and notes by Harry Golden. (1st ed.) Garden City, N.Y., Doubleday, 1971.   214 p. illus. 22 cm. 71-139047.
F128.9. F5 M4

FINNS. Suur-New Yorkin suomalaisten osoiteopas sekä hyödyllisia teitoja. Greater New York Finnish directory and useful information. 1932 -   New York, N.Y., U. S. Finnish directory ass'n, 1931 -   v. 23 cm. annual. Finnish and English. CA 33-355 Unrev. F128.9. F5 S 8

FRENCH. France in New York; a directory. New York, French Cultural Services (195)
35 p. 23 cm. 56-43788. F128.9. F8 F7

— prepared by the French-American Bureau for Educational Research in cooperation with the French Cultural Services. New York (1950)   27 p. 22 cm. 50-37575. F128.9. F8 F8

FRENCH. ... Hier et aujourd'hui. 75ème anniversaire Société St. Jean-Baptiste de bienfaisance de N.Y. 1850 - 1925. By Antonio Fitzpatrick. New-York (Fenn & Fenn, printers) 1925.   136 p.
illus. (incl. ports.) 23½ cm. 25-22363. F128.9. F85 F5

GERMANS. Denkschrift zum 150, jahrestag der Deutschen gesellschaft der stadt New York, 1784 - 1934, von Rudolf Cronau. (New York, 1934)   54 p. 2 l., 57-97 p. incl. front. plates, ports. 23½ cm.
German text followed by an English translation. 34-39237. F128.9. G3 C78

NEW YORK CITY

GERMANS. Die Deutschen als gründer von New Amsterdam-New York und als urheber und träger der amerkanischen freiheitsbestrebungen; eine denkschrift zur erinnerung an die vor 300 jahren erfolgte erwerbung der insel Manhattan durch Peter Minuit, und an die 150 jährige feier des amerikanischen unabhängigkeitskerieges, von Rudolf Cronau. New York, Heiss, 1926. 70 p. illus. (incl. ports.) 26 cm. 26-13626.
F128.9. G3 C8

GERMANS. Das deutsche element der stadt New York; biographisches jahrbuch der Deutsch-Amerikaner New Yorks und umgebung ... New York city, v. front., illus., ports. 25½ cm. 14-2318.
F128.9. G3 D2

GERMANS. Geschichte des deutschthums von New York von 1848 bis auf die gegenwart. Von Theodor Lemke, 1891-92. 2 v. ports. 27 x 21 cm. Vol. 2 wanting. 5-36847 Rev.
F128.9. G3 L3

GERMANS. Geschichte des Plattdutschen volksfest-vereen von New York un umgegend, nebst adressbuch ... Bernhard Meyborg ... New York, Druck der "N.Y. Platt-dütsche post," 1892. 227 p. front., ports. 20 cm. 17-10761.
F128.9. G3 M6

GERMANS. 1859. 1900. Zur feier des funfzigjährigen jubilaums des New York turn vereins in der New York turn-halle, 3. bis 6. juni 1900. New York (1900) 52 p. illus. (incl. ports.) 28½ x 21 cm. 10-14032.
F128.9. G3 N4

GERMANS. New Yorker vereins-kalender für das jahr 1884 ... Hrsg. von H. A. Dittrich. New York (1883 - 1 v. illus. (ports.) 25½ cm. 10-6857.
F128.9. G3 N5

GERMANS. Die deutschen vereine von New York und umgegend. Jubiläums-ausgabe der "N.Y. staats-zeitung" zum 75. jahrestage der gründung. 24. april 1910. (New York, 1910) 32 p. 43½ cm. 10-23118.
F128.9. G3 N6

GERMANS. Klein-Deutschland: bilder aus dem New Yorker alltagsleben, von C. Stürenburg. New York, E. Steiger, 1886. viii, 225 p. 20½ cm. 1-14799.
F128.9. G3 S 9

GERMANS. ... Feier des Deutschen tages, sonntag den 21. oktober 1923 ... (New York, Buchdr. J. Seeke, 1923) (82) p. illus. (incl. facsims.) plates, ports. 25 cm. 25-25197.
F128.9.G3 V37

GERMANS. ... Festschrift der Vereinigte deutschen gesellschaften der stadt New York zum Deutschen tag. (New York, 1902 - v. illus. (ports.) 25½ cm. 9-12808.
F128.9. G3 V4

HUGUENOTS. Registers of the births, marriages, and deaths of the "Eglise François a la Nouvelle York." from 1688 to 1804. Ed. by Alfred V. Wittmeyer. Baltimore, Genealogical Pub. Co., 1968. 324 p. 24 cm. 68-20805.
F128.9. H9 N4 1968

IRISH. The attitudes of the New York Irish toward state and national affairs, 1848 - 1892. By Florence Elizabeth Gibson. New York, 1951. 480 p. 22 cm. Thesis - Columbia university. Bibliography: p. 453 - 464. A 51-1642.
F128.9. I 6 G5

— New York, Columbia University Press, 1951. 480 p. 23 cm. (Columbia University ... Studies in history, economics and public law, no. 563) 51-9425.
F128.9. I 6 G 5 1951 a

— (1st AMS ed.) New York, AMS Press (1968) 480 p. 23 cm. Reprint. 68-58578 MARC.
F128.9. I 6 G 5 1968

IRISH. The history of the Society of the Friendly Sons of Saint Patrick in the City of New York, 1784 to 1955, by Richard C. Murphy. New York, 1962. 566 p. 27 cm. 63-13775.
F128.9. I 6 M8

IRISH. In old New York; the Irish dead in Trinity and St. Paul's churchyards, by Michael J. O'Brien

... New York, The American Irish historical soc., 1928.   4, 262 p.   front., plates, facsim.   24½ cm.
Marriage, baptism and other testamentary records of N. Y. county: p. 154-247.   28-9549.
                         F128.9.I 6 O14
                         F128.9.I 6O141

IRISH.   Addresses of Alfred E. Smith delivered at the meetings of the Society of the friendly sons of St. Patrick, 1922-1944.   ... (New York) ... 1945.   129 p.   port., col. facsim.   23½ cm.   46-21331.
                         F128.9.I 6 S 37

IRISH.   Charter, constitution, by-laws, officers, committees, roll of members, etc. of the Society of the friendly sons of St. Patrick in the city of New York ... 1894.   New York, Print. Dempsey & Carroll (1894)   58 p.   16½ cm.   7-32887.
                         F128.9. I 6 S 4

—   (1905)   83, (5) p.   plates.   20 cm.   5-17858.
                         F128.9. I 6 S 5

IRISH.   Anniversary dinner ... Society of the friendly sons of St. Patrick in the city of New York. 18   -19   (New York, 18 - 19   v.   fronts., illus., plates, ports.   21-32 cm.   12-40494 Rev.
                         I 6 S 6

IRISH.   Proceedings at the banquet to Hon. James A. O'Gorman.   Reported and pub. by order of the soc. of the friendly sons of St. Patrick ... (New York, Press of W. P. Mitchell) 1903.   48 p. port. 20½ cm.   4-24201 Add.
                         F128.9. I 6 S62

IRISH.   Proceedings at the dinner to the Rochambeau special mission given by the Friendly sons of St. Patrick ... (New York, Press of W. P. Mitchell, 1903?)   2, 79 p.   illus. (incl. ports.)   pl.   20 cm. 6-21.
                         F128.9.I 6 S63

IRISH.   Dinner to Honorable James Fitzgerald, given by the Soc. of the friendly sons of St. Patrick ... Chicago and New York, Rogers & co., 1908.   46 p. incl. front. (port.)   23½ cm.   9-13997.
                         F128.9. I6 S 64

IRISH.   Ulster-Irish society of New York ... Year book ... list of members, committees and reports of the proceedings ... (New York) 19   v.   illus. (incl. ports.)   23½ cm.   38-4594.
                         F128.9. I 6 U 6

ITALIANS.   The Italians of New York; a survey prepared by workers of the Federal writers' project, W. P. A.   ... New York, Random house (1938)   xx, 241 p.   front., plates.   21 cm.   (The American guide series) Maps.   Bibliography: p. 227-230.   38-27087.
                         F128.9. I 8 F4

—   New York, Arno Press, 1969.   xx, 241 p. illus. 22 cm. (The Amer. immigration collection)
                         F128.9. I 8 F4
                         1969

ITALIANS.   Gli italiani di New York ... W. P. A.   New York, Labor press, 1939.   xiv, 242 p. plates, port.   22 cm.   (The American guide series)   "Bibliografia": p. 225-227.   42-4919.
                         F128.9.I 8 F44

ITALIANS.   The Italian contribution to American democracy, by John Horace Mariano ... with an introd. by Hon. F. H. La Guardia.   Boston, The Christopher pub. house (1921)   x, 317 p.   front. (map)   19½ cm.   Pub. also as thesis (PH. D.) New York university under title: The second generation of Italians in New York city. Bibliography: p. 311 - 317.   21-5772.
                         F128.9.I 8 M33

ITALIANS.   The second generation if Italians in New York city, by John Horace Mariano.   Boston, The Christopher pub. house (1921)   x, 317 p. incl. front. (map)   19½ cm.   See above item.   21-5773.
                         F128.9.I 8 M332

JAPANESE.   Japan in New York ... (New York, Anraku pub. co.) 1908.   3, 5-48 p., 46 p.   plates, ports. 23 cm.   Text in English and Japanese, each separately paged.   8-4356.
                         F128.9. J 2 J 3

JAPANESE.   Kuwayama Senzō Ō monogatari.   By Wasataku Kamide.   Kyōto, tankō Shinsha (1963) 331 p.   22 cm.
                         F128.9. J 2 K3

JAPANESE.   New York Japanese address book, 1921 ... Pub. by Nippon-Jin Sha.   (New York city, 1921)   69 p.   15 cm.   Text in Japanese and English.   21-15118.
                         F128.9. J 2 N7

NEW YORK CITY

JAPANESE. A social study of the Japanese population in the greater New York area, by the Survey committee... New York city, April 24, 1942 - June, 26, 1942. (New York, 1942) 2, (vii)-x, (2), 29 p. incl. tables. 21½ cm. Reproduced from type-written copy. 46-36388. F128.9. J 2 S 8

JEWS. "Our crowd": the great Jewish families of New York (by) Stephen Birmingham. (1st ed.) New York, Harper & Row (1967) xi, 404 p. 25 cm. 66-20725. F128.9. J 5 B 5

JEWS. Jewish communal survey of Greater New York ... New York, Bureau of Jewish social research, 1928 - v. fold. maps. tables (part fold.) diagrs. 23½ cm. 28-10387. F128.9. J 5 B 9

JEWS. Jewish communal survey of Greater New York; report of Executive committee. (New York, Herald-Nathan press) 1929. 80 p. fold. maps, 4 diagr. on 1 fold. 1. 23 cm. 31-21617. F128.9.J5 C 63

JEWS. Dorothy and David explore Jewish life, by Michael Conovitz. Cincinnati, The Union of American Hebrew congregations, 1938. xviii, 206 p. illus. 22 cm. 38-23721. F128.9. J 5 C7

JEWS. The Jews of New York. By Charles P. Daly. New York, 1883. 16½ cm. F128.9. J 5 D2

JEWS. Points in the first chapter of New York Jewish history. By Albion Morris Dyer. (From American Jewish hist. soc. Publications. (Baltimore, 1895) v.3, p. 41-60) CA 9-2563 Unrev. F128.9. J 5 D9

JEWS. Site of the first synagogue of the Congregation Shearith Israel of New York. By Albion Morris Dyer. With two maps. (From American Jewish hist. soc. Publications. Baltimore... 1893 - v. 8 (1900) p. 25-41) 10-5368. F128.9.J 5 D92

JEWS. Jewish families and family circles of New York, by the Yiddish writers' group of the Federal writers' project, W.P.A. (New York ... 1939) 206, (2) p. 22 cm. In Yiddish. 44-18093. F128.9.J 5 F48

JEWS. The Jewish landsmanschaften of New York. Prepared by the Yiddish writers' group of the Federal writers' project, W.P.A. 397, (3) p. illus. (incl. facsims.) 28½ cm. In Yiddish. 40-30609 Rev. F128.9. J 5 F5

JEWS. Juden ohne Geld. (Autorisierte Übertragung aus dem Englischen von Paul Baudisch) By Michael Gold. Berlin, Universum-Bucherei für Alle, 1931. 305 p. 19 cm. Autobiography. 51-53241. F128.9.J5 G613

JEWS. ... Judíos sin diner; traducción del inglés por Márgara Villega. By Michael Gold. 1. ed. ... Madrid, Editorial Cenit, s.a., 1930. 305 p. 3 l. 19½ cm. Autobiography. 44-38526. F128.9.J5 G615

JEWS. New York Jews and the quest for community; the Kehellah experiment, 1908 - 1922 (by) Arthur A. Goren. New York, Columbia University Press, 1970. x, 361 p. 24 cm. 76-129961. F128.9.J 5 G63

JEWS. The Jews settle in New Amsterdam, 1654. By Samuel Grand. New York, Union of American Hebrew Congregations, 1954. unpaged. illus. 22 cm. 54-31951. F128.9.J 5 G67

JEWS. The rise of the Jewish community of New York, 1654 - 1860, by Hyman B. Grinstein. Philadelphia, The Jewish publication soc. of America, 5705 - 1945. xiii, 645 p. front., plates, 2 port. on 1 l., facsims. 22 cm. Issued also as thesis (PH.D.) Columbia university. Maps. Bibliography: p. 597-607. 45-9927. F128.9. J 5 G7

— 1945. xiii, 645 p. front., plates, 2 port., facsims. 22 cm. Thesis (PH.D.) A 46-755. F128.9. J 5 G7 1945 a

1029

JEWS. The spirit of the Ghetto; studies of the Jewish quarter in New York, by Hutchins Hapgood; with drawings from life by Jacob Epstein. New York and London, Funk & Wagnalls, 1902.
311 p. front., illus. 20½ cm. 2-27222.   F128.9. J 5 H2

— (1965)   xiv, 300 p. 24 cm. 65-15317.   F128.9. J 5 H2 1965

— New ed., pref. and notes by Harry Golden. New York, Schocken Books (1966)   xiv, 300 p.
21 cm. (Schocken paperbacks, 128) 66-26729.   F128.9. J 5 H2 1966

— Cambridge, Mass., Belknap Press of Harvard University Press, 1967.   xi, 315 p. 22 cm. (A John Harvard Library book) 67-12099.   F128.9. J 5 H2 1967

JEWS. The old East Side; an anthology. Ed. and with an introd. by Milton Hindus. (1st ed.) Philadelphia, Jewish Publication Soc. of America, 1969.   xxvi, 301 p. illus. 22 cm. 69-19040.
     F128.9. J 5 H5

JEWS. Whence came the first Jewish settlers of New York? By Leon Huhner ... From the Publications of the American Jewish historical soc., no. 9, 1901. (Baltimore, 1901)   (75) - 85 p. 25 cm. 4-19251.
     F128.9. J 5 H9

JEWS. Jewish calendar, lodge and soc. direct. (1905)   1 v.   F128.9. J 5 J 45

JEWS. The Jewish center annual. v. 1, no. 1 -   Brooklyn, N.Y., The Brooklyn Jewish Center (1925 -   1 v. illus. 30 cm.   F128.9. J 5 J 47

JEWS. Jewish community directory of Greater New York; a guide to central organizations and institutions: relief, welfare, religious, cultural, educational and other leading agencies. 1947 - (New York) Jewish Information Bureau.   v. 21 cm. 48-11333*.   F128.9. J 5 J 48

JEWS. Jewish communal directory, a classified guide book to the congregations, fraternal orders, lodges, mutual benefit societies, educational organizations, etc. in the five boroughs of Greater New York. 1st ed. issued Jan. 1912. (Shebat, 5672) New York city, The Jewish community (Kehillah) of New York city, 1912.   xiii, 143 p. 20½ cm. 12-24134.   F128.9. J 5 J 5

JEWS. The Jewish communal register of New York city, 1917 - 1918 ... 2d ed. Ed. and pub. by the Kehillah (Jewish community) of New York city. New York city (1919)   vi, 17 p. 19 - 1597 p. incl. plates, diagrs. fold. maps (incl. front.) fold. plan, fold. tables. 19 cm. "A list of books and articles on the Jews of New York, by S. Margoshes": p. 1503-1524. 19-4545.   F128.9. J5 J 52

JEWS. Proceedings of the ... annual convention. 4th - 1913 -   New York, The Jewish community (Kehillah) of New York city (1913 -   v. 20 cm. 16-21358.
     F128.9. J 5 J 55

JEWS. Report of the executive committee, presented at the annual convention. 1st - 1910 - New York, The Jewish communtiy (Kehillah) of New York city (1910 -   v. 19½ - 21 cm. 16-21359.
     F128.9. J 5 J57

JEWS. The Lower East Side: portal to American life, 1870 - 1924; (exhibition) ... 1966, the Jewish Museum, New York. Ed. by Allon Schoener. (New York, 1966)   68 p. 25 cm. 66-28528.
     F128.9. J5 J 58

JEWS. The mirrors of the East Side, by Jacob Magidoff. Illus. by S. Raskin. New York, The author, 1923.   218 p. illus. 20½ cm. 23-11113.   F128.9. J5 M17 Hebraic Sect.

JEWS. The Jewish community of New York city, by J. L. Magnes. New York, 1909.   13 p. 20½ cm. 18-19943.   F128.9. J5 M 19

JEWS. ... Investigation of anti-American and anti-Semitic vandalism.   New York.Dept. of investigation.   Report.   New York, 1944.   2, 170 numb. l.   3 diagr.   35½ cm.   Reproduced from type-written copy.
A 44-2775.
 F128.9. J 5 N4
 1944

JEWS.   The early history of the Jews in New York, 1654 - 1664.   Some new matter on the subject. By Samuel Oppenheim.   Printed for the author and for the publications of the American Jewish historical soc., no. 18 (1909)   (New York?) 1909.   96 p.   24½ cm.   9-16447.
 F128.9. J 5 O6

JEWS.   More about Jacob Barsimson, the first Jewish settler in New York.   By Samuel Oppenheim. (New York, 1925)   p. 39-52.   24½ cm.   "Reprinted from Publications of the American Jewish hist. soc., no. 29, 1925."
25-24199.
 F128.9.J 5 O63

JEWS.   Portraits etched in stone; early Jewish settlers, 1681 - 1831.   By David de Sola Pool.   New York, Columbia University Press, 1952.   xiv, 543 p.   illus., ports., maps, geneal. tables.   26 cm.   Bibliography: p. (513) - 517.   52-14151.
 F128.9. J 5 P 6

JEWS.   Jewish landmarks in New York; an informal history and guide, by Bernard Postal and Lionel Koppman.   Illus. by Lynette Logan.   (1st ed.)   New York, Hill and Wang (1964)   vii, 277 p.   21 cm.
64-15383.
 F128.9.J 5 P 63

JEWS.   The other Jews; portraits in poverty.   By Dorothy Rabinowitz.   New York, Institute of Human Relations Press, American Jewish Committee (1972)   63 p.   23 cm.   (Paperback series)
77-183251 MARC.
 F128.9.J 5 R23

JEWS.   The city of many nations.   1.   About the Hebrews.   Foreign New York.   Talk about the Jews ... (New York, 1885)   1 l.   folio.   1-14800-M1.
 F128.9. J 5 R3

JEWS.   The promised city; New York's Jews.   1870 - 1914.   Cambridge, Harvard University Press, 1962.   342 p.   22 cm.   62-11402.
 F128.9. J 5 R5

JEWS.   The time that was then; the Lower East Side, 1900 - 1914, an intimate chronicle, by Harry Roskolenko.   New York, Dial Press, 1971.   218 p.   24 cm.   76-131180.
 F128.9. J 5 R 6

JEWS.   The downtown Jews; portraits of an immigrant generation, (by) Ronald Sanders.   (1st ed.) New York, Harper & Row (1969)   x, 477 p.   illus.   22 cm.   70-83620.
 F128.9. J 5 S 2

JEWS.   Portal to America: the Lower East Side, 1870 - 1925.   comp. Allen Schoener.   (1st ed.) New York, Holt, Rinehart and Winston (1967)   256 p.   27 cm.   67-19055.
 F128.9. J 5 S 3

JEWS.   So talently my children (by) Edna Sheklow.   Illus. by Eugene Samuelson.   Cleveland, World Pub. Co. (1966)   xiii, 160 p.   21 cm.   "First printing 1966."   66-22549.
 F128.9. J 5 S 5

JEWS.   Jews and Judaism in New York.   (New York, 1887)   xii, 124 p.   20 cm.   No more pub.   51-50500.
 F128.9. J 5 W4
 Hebraic Sect.

LITHUANIANS.   Lietuviu demonstracija Didžianjame New Yorke, liepos 4d., 1918. ...   Brooklyn, N.Y., 1918.   64 p.   illus. (incl. ports., music) 23 cm.   19-489.
 F128.9. L7 L7

NEGROES.   Mann's Afro-American Business directory Jan., 1914 -   New York, E. M. Mann, 1913 -   1 v.   illus.   21 cm.   quarterly.
 F128.9.N3 A18

NEGROES.   Harlem on review; exhibition of printed materials from the Harold Jackman collection. ... Atlanta university library ...   (Atlanta, 1943)   (7) p.   21½ cm.   Reproduced from type-written copy.
 F128.9. N3 A8

NEGROES.   Black portfolio.   1st -   ed.; 1970 -   White Plains, N.Y., Robert Mayhawk Associates.   v.   illus.   25 cm.
 F128.9.N3 B 55

NEGROES. Story of the riot, pub. by the Citizens' protective league. (New York, 1900)
79 p.   22 ½ cm.   "Persecution of negroes by roughs and policemen, in the city of N. Y., Aug. 1900.   Statement and proofs written and compiled by Frank Moss and issued by the Citizens' protective league."   5-42437.
F128.9. N3 C6

— New York, Arno Press, 1969.   79 p.   23 cm.   (Mass violence in America)   Reprint of the 1900 ed. with a new editorial note.   73-90186.
F128.9. N3 C6
1969

NEGROES. Dark ghetto; dilemmas of social power, by Kenneth B, Clark.   Foreword by Gunnar Myrdal.   (1st ed.)   New York, Harper & Row (1965)   xxix, 251 p.   22 cm.   64-7834.
F128.9.N3 C65

NEGROES. The sweet fly paper of life (by) Roy De Carava and Langston Hughes.   (New York, Simon and Schuster, 1955)   98 p.   illus.   19 cm.   "1st printing."   55-10048.
F128.9. N3 D4

— New York, Hill and Wang (1967)   96 p.   22 cm.   67-26855.
F128.9. N3 D4
1967

NEGROES. The Black North in 1901; a social study.   By William Edward Burghardt Du Bois.   New York, Arno Press, 1969.   xii, 46 p.   23 cm.   (The American Negro, his history and literature)   "A series of articles originally appearing in the New York times, Nov. - Dec. 1901."   70-92229.
F128.9. N3 D8
1969

NEGROES. Harlem, ville noire (par) Michel Fabre (et) Paul Oren.   Paris, A. Colin (1971)
288 p.   illus., maps.   16 cm.   72-307398.
F128.9. N3 F3

NEGROES. Federation of Negro Civil Service Organizations.   Journal.   1961 -   (New York?)
v.   28 cm.
F128.9. N3 F4

NEGROES. Hunger and terror in Harlem, by James W. Ford ... (New York, Harlem section, Communist party, 1935)   23, 14 p.   17 ½ cm.   45-46484.
F128.9. N3 F6

NEGROES. Aspects of Negro life in the Borough of Queens: an analysis of population trends, employment patterns and opportunities, housing, health and recreation for the Negro population, prepared by Olivia P. Frost and others.   New York, Urban League of Greater New York, 1947.
xiii, 106 p.   diagrs.   27 cm.   47-7018*.
F128.9. N3 F7

NEGROES. Harlem stirs.   Prologue: John O. Killens.   Text: Fred Halstead.   Photography: Anthony Aviles (and) Don Charles.   (1st ed.)   New York, Marzani & Munsell (1966)   128 p.   illus., facsims., ports.   29 cm.   Includes bibliographical references.   67-4073.
F128.9. N3 H3

NEGROES. Black-Jewish relations in New York City (by) Louis Harris (and) Bert E. S. Swanson.   New York, Praegar (1970)   xxiii, 234 p.   25 cm.   (Praeger special studies in U.S. economic and social development)
71-124862.
F128.9.N3 H33
1970

NEGROES. Negro history tour of Manhattan, by Uncle Spike, the Negro history detective.   (M. A. Harris)   1st ed.   New York, Negro History Associates, 1967.   i, 65 l.   28 cm.
F128.9.N3 H35

— New York, Greenwood Pub. Corp. (1968)   xiii, 113 p.   illus.   22 cm.   68-54217.
F128.9.N3 H35
1968

— Teacher's guide (by M. A. Harris and Morris Levitt.   Westport, Conn., Greenwood Pub. Corp. (1969)   18 p.   21 cm.
F128.9.N3 H35
Teacher's guide

NEGROES.   ... Black Manhattan.   By James Weldon Johnson.   New York, A. A. Knopf, 1930.
xvii p., 2 l., (3) - 284, (xxi) - xxxiv p.   front., pl., ports., 2 maps on 1 pl., facsim.   19 ½ cm.   30-18832.
F128.9.N3 J 67

NEW YORK CITY

— New York, Arno Press, 1968. xxxiv, 284 p. illus. 21 cm. (The American Negro; his history and literature)
68-29003.
F128.9.N3 J 67
1968

— With a new pref. by Allan H. Spear. New York, Atheneum, 1972. xviii, 284 p. illus. 21 cm.
(Atheneum Studies in American Negro life) 68-9823.
F128.9.N3 J 67
1972

NEGROES. Often back: the tales of Harlem, by Samuel M. Johnson. (1st ed.) New York, Vantage Press (1971) 281 p. illus. 22 cm. 72-176082.
F128.9.N3 J 69

NEGROES. Sea island to city; a study of St. Helena islanders in Harlem and other urban centers, by Clyde Vernon Kiser ... New York, Columbia university press; London, P. S. King, 1932.
272 p. illus. (maps) 23 cm. (Studies in history, economics and public law ... no. 368) Issued also as thesis. 32-34112.
F128.9. N3 K5

— 2, 7-273 p. illus. (maps) 22½ cm. Thesis (PH.D.) Columbia university, 1932. 32-34113.
F128.9.N3 K52

NEGROES. ... Auprès de ma noire ... By Jean Lassette. Paris, Les Editions de France, 1930.
3, ii, 218 p., 2 l. 19 cm. 30-24868.
F128.9.N3 L34

NEGROES. The torture of mothers, by Truman Nelson. Introd. by Maxwell Geismar. Newburyport, Mass., Garrison Press (1965) 121 p. 21 cm.
F128.9.N3 N37

— Boston, Beacon Press (1968) 121 p. illus. 21 cm. 68-17428.
F128.9.N3 N37
1968

NEGROES. New York State Commission against Discrimination. Research Division. Trend reports.
Until bound and cataloged, issues of the above will be found in the Government Publications Reading Room.
F128.9. N3 N4

NEGROES. New York State Commission for Human Rights. Research Division. Nonwhites in New York's four "suburban" counties, an analysis of trends. New York, 1959. 19 b (i.e. 27) l. tables.
29 cm. (Its Trench reports, no. 3) A 59-9690.
F128.9. N3 N4
no. 3

NEGROES. The Harlem riot, a study in mass frustration, by Harold Orlansky ... (New York, 1943)
29 p. 23 cm. (Social analysis. Report no. 1) Bibliographical foot-notes. 44-32017 rev.
F128.9. N3 O7

NEGROES. Harlem: the making of a ghetto; Negro New York, 1890-1930, by Gilbert Osofsky. (1st ed.) New York, Harper & Row (1966) xi, 259 p. 22 cm. 66-10913.
F128.9.N3 O73

— 2d ed. New York, Harper & Row (1971) xiv, 276, 8 p. illus. 21 cm. (Harper torchbooks. TB 1572)
F128.9.N3 O73

NEGROES. The Negro in New York; an informal social history. Roi Ottley & William J. Weatherby, editors. New York, New York Public Library, 1967. xix, 328 p. 24 cm. 67-21389.
F128.9.N3 O74

— New York, Praeger Publishers (1969) xix, 328 p. 21 cm. (Praeger paperbacks, P-262) 72-98461.
F128.9.N3 O74
1969

NEGROES. 'New world a-coming'; inside black America, by Roi Ottley ... Boston, Houghton Mifflin, 1943. vi, (2), 364 p. incl. front., illus. 21½ cm. Bibliography: p. (349) - 354. 43-11506.
F128.9.N3 O75

NEGROES. New world a-coming. By Roi Ottley. New York, Arno Press, 1968. vi, 364 p. illus.
23 cm. (The American Negro; his history and literature) Reprint of 1943 ed. 68-29014.
F128.9.N3 O75
1968

NEGROES. ... Negros da América ... By Roi Ottley. Tradução de Isaac Paschoal ... Rio de Janeiro, Brasil, "Seção de livros," da emprésa gráfica "O Cruzeiro," s.a., 1945.   4, (11)-384 p.   illus.   21 cm.   Translation of 'New world a-comin'."   47-17236.
F128.9.N3O755

NEGROES.   Half a man; the status of the Negro in New York, by Mary White Ovington.   With a foreword by Franz Boas.   New York, Negro Universities Press (1969)   xi, 236 p.   23 cm.   "Repr. of the 1911 ed."   "Originally publ. 1911."   79-84692.
F128.9. N3 O9 1969

— New York, Schocken Books (1969)   xvii, 236 p.   21 cm.   (Sourcebooks in Negro history)   75-91548.
F128.9. N3 O9 1969 b

— With an introd. by Charles Flint Kellogg.   New York, Hill & Wang (1969)   xxiii, 128 p.   21 cm.   (American century series)   74-86819.
F128.9. N3 O9 1969 c

NEGROES.   Negro Mecca; a history of the Negro in New York City, 1865 - 1920, by Seth M. Scheiner. (New York) New York University Press, 1965.   ix, 246 p.   25 cm.   65-19521.
F128.9. N3 S 3

NEGROES.   I wish I had an Afro, by John Shearer.   (1st ed.)   New York, Cowles Book Co. (1970)   (50) p.   illus.   27 cm.   71-108003.
F128.9. N3 S 5 1970

NEGROES.   One family.   Text and photos. by Nancy Sirkis.   Introd. by Julian Bond.   (1st ed.) Boston, Little, Brown (1970)   123 p.   illus.   26 cm.   73-121425.
F128.9.N3 S 53

NEGROES.   My people is the enemy; an autobiographical polemic.   By William Stringfellow.   (1st ed.) New York, Holt, Rinehart and Winston (1964)   vii, 149 p.   22 cm.   64-14361.
F128.9. N3 S 8

NEGROES.   Harlem, Harlem.   Av Lars Ulvenstam.   Stockholm, Bonnier, 1971.   253 p.   illus.   22 cm.   76-880357.
F128.9.N3 U38

NEGROES.   At the edge of Harlem; portrait of a middle-class Negro family.   By Edward Wakin.   Photos. by Edward Lettau.   New York, W. Morrow, 1965.   127 p.   26 cm.   64-23581.
F128.9. N3 W3

NEGROES.   It's wings that make birds fly; the story of a boy.   By Sandra Weiner.   (New York) Pantheon Books (1968)   55 p.   illus.   29 cm.   68-12658.
F128.9. N3 W4

POLES.   Polacy w New Yorku.   By Joseph Mierzynski.   (Toledo, A. A. Paryski, 1910)   135 p.   illus., ports.   27 cm.   L.C. copy imperfect: t. p. wanting.   52-55638.
F128.9. P6 M54

POLES.   Na nowojorskich szańcach Skarbu Narodowego.   New York, 1953.   80 p.   illus. 28 cm.   57-23193.
F128.9. P6 S 5

PUERTO RICANS.   80 Puerto Rican families in New York City; health and disease studies in context.   By Beatrice (Bishop) Berle.   New York, Columbia University Press, 1958.   331 p.   illus.   21 cm.   Includes bibliography.   58-8226.
F128.9. P8 B 4

PUERTO RICANS.   The Puerto Rican migrant in New York city, by Lawrence R. Chenault ... New York, Columbia university press, 1938.   xii, 190 p. incl. illus. (maps) tables, diagrs.   23 cm.   Thesis (PH. D.) Columbia university, 1938.   Bibliography: p. (173) - 180.   39-1416.
F128.9. P8 C 5

— 1938.   xii, 190 p. incl. illus., etc.   39-1415.
F128.9. P8 C 52

— With a foreword by Francesco Cordasco.   New York, Russell & Russell (1970)   190 p.   25 cm.   74-102477.
F128.9. S8 C 5

PUERTO RICANS. A Puerto Rican in New York, and other sketches. By Jesus Colon. New York, Mainstream Publishers, 1961. 202 p. 21 cm. F128.9. P8 C 6

PUERTO RICANS. The Puerto Ricans in New York City. By Patricia Aran Gosnell. New York, New York Univ., 1949. 15 p. 23 cm. Abridgement of thesis - New York Univ. 49-5255*. F128.9. P8 G 68

PUERTO RICANS. Los viajeros de la cuidad. By David Lagmanovich. (La Plata) Departamento de Filosofia, Instituto de Historia de la Folosofia y el Pensamiento Argentino, 1961. 47 p. 22 cm. (Cuaderno de sociologia, 3) F128.9. P8 L 3

PUERTO RICANS. A study of slum culture; backgrounds for la vida. By Oscar Lewis. New York, Random House (1968) xiv, 240 p. 21 cm. "First printing." 68-11969. F128.9.P8 L 38

PUERTO RICANS. La vida; a Puerto Rican family in the culture of poverty - San Juan and New York. New York, Random House (1966) lix, 669 p. 25 cm. "First printing." 66-11983. F128.9. P8 L 4

PUERTO RICANS. The Puerto Rican journey; New York's newest migrants, by C. Wright Mills and others. (1st ed.) New York, Harper (1950) xi, 238 p. tables. 22 cm. (Publications of the Bureau of Applied Social Research, Columbia University) "Notes and sources": p. 171-204. 50-9532. F128.9. P8 M5

— New York, Russell & Russell (1967) xi, 238 p. 22 cm. 66-27125.
F128.9. P8 M5 1967

PUERTO RICANS. Up from Puerto Rico. By Elena Padilla. New York, Columbia University Press, 1958. 317 p. illus. 23 cm. 58-7171. F128.9. P 8 P 3

PUERTO RICANS. The Puerto Ricans. By Christopher Rand. New York, Oxford University Press, 1958. 178 p. 21 cm. 58-10733. F128.9. P 8 R 3
M R R Alc.

PUERTO RICANS. The Puerto Ricans of New York City. By Clarence Ollson Senior. Washington, Office of Puerto Rico (1948) 102 p. 28 cm. "References" at end of each chapter. 48-47632*.
F128.9.P8 S45

— New York, New York Office, Employment and Migration Bureau, Puerto Rico Dept. of Labor (1948?) 102 p. 28 cm. Includes bibliographies. 50-62761. F128.9.P8 S 45
1948 a

PUERTO RICANS. Spanish Harlem; anatomy of poverty (by) Patricia Cayo Sexton. (1st ed.) New York, Harper & Row (1965) xiii, 208 p. 22 cm. 65-11717. F128.9.P8 S 48

PUERTO RICANS. Down these mean streets, by Piri Thomas. (1st ed.) New York, A.A. Knopf, 1967. xiii, 333 p. 22 cm. 66-19402. F128.9. P8 T 5

PUERTO RICANS. Island in the city; the world of Spanish Harlem. By Dan Wakefield. Boston, Houghton Mifflin, 1959. 278 p. 22 cm. "First printing." 59-5396. F128.9. P8 W3

PUERTO RICANS in New York City; the report of the Committee ... (New York, Welfare Council of New York City, 1948) 60 p. 23 cm. "First printing." 48-18368*. F128.9. P8 W4

PUERTO RICANS. Puerto Rico en Nueva York; sociologia de una immigracion (por) Jesus de Galindez. Prologo de Dardo Cuneo. (Buenos Aires) Editorial Tiempo Contemporaneo (1968, c.1969) 106 p. 20 cm. (Coleccion Mundo actual) 69-3371. F128.9. P85 G3

PUERTO RICANS. Puerto Rican population of New York City; a series of papers (by A. J. Jaffe and others) ... (New York) Bureau of Applied Social Research, Columbia University, 1954. 61 l. illus. 28 cm. Bibliographical footnotes. A 55-6610. F128.9.P85 J 3

PUERTO RICANS. A week in Henry's world: El Barrio. Photos. and text by Inger McCabe. New

York, Crowell-Collier Press (1971)   (47) p.   illus.   28 cm.   78-146609.

    F128.9.P85 M3

PUERTO RICANS.   A study of povery conditions in the New York Puerto Rican community.   Puerto Rican Forum.   (3d ed.)   New York (1970)   iv, 85, viii p.   24 cm.

    F128.9.P85 P 8

PUERTO RICANS.   Savior, Savior, hold my hand (by) Piri Thomas.   (1st ed.)   Garden City, N.Y., Doubleday, 1972.   xii, 372 p.   22 cm.   77-175401.

    F128.9.P85 T 5

PUERTO RICANS.   Palante: Young Lords Party.   Photos. by Michael Abramson.   Text by the Young Lords Party and Michael Abramson.   (1st ed.)   New York, McGraw-Hill (1971)   160 p.   illus.   29 cm.   70-158054 MARC.

    F128.9.P85 Y 6

RUSSIANS.   Moscow-on-the-Hudson, by M. K. Argus (pseud. for Mikhail K. Jeleznov.   With illus. by the author.   (1st ed.)   New York, Harper (1951)   182 p.   illus.   20 cm.   51-9240 rev.

    F128.9. R8 J 4

RUSSIANS.   Russkiĭ émigrantskiĭ dom.   Russian Orthodox Christian Immigrant Society in North America.   (1909)   46 p.   illus.   22 cm.   58-54894.

    F128.9.R8 R83

SCANDINAVIANS.   Skandinavernas blåa bok ... Upplagsbok för Greater New York, jämte almanacka ... (no. 1 -   1916 -   New York, W. J. Adams, 1915 -   v.   17 cm.   18-2259.

    F128.9. S2 S6

SCANDINAVIANS.   40 aar i Amerika;   oplevelser og hændelser, af Victor Bancke.   Ringkøbing, Danmark.   A Rsumussens bogtrykkeri;   Brooklyn, N.Y., Udgivet af V. Bancke, 1935.   388, (2) p.   front. (port.)   23½ cm.   37-19271.

    F128.9.S21 B 3

SCANDINAVIANS.   Norwegians in New York, 1825-1925, by A. N. Rygg ... Brooklyn, N.Y., The Norwegian news co. (pref. 1941)   4, 296 p.   1 illus., plates, ports.   23 cm.   Bibliographical foot-notes.   42-25805.

    F128.9.S22 R 9

SWEDES.   Svenskarne i New York, af V. Berger.   New York, W. J. Adams, 1918.   plates.   22 cm.   17-29816.

    F128.9.S23 B 4

SWEDES.   Souvenir program of our centennial celebration, commemorating 100 years of service, benevolence, progress ... (New York, East End printing co.) 1936.   (96) p.   illus. (incl. ports.)   25 cm.   36-29799.

    F128.9.S23 S 9

SLAVS.   Slovenci v New Yorku.   By John A. Arnez.   New York, Studia Slovenica, 1966.   268 p.   23 cm.   (Studia Slovenica. Special series, no. 1)

    F128.9.S65 A 7

SPANISH Americans.   New York: Infierno gris; el fracaso de los Latinoamericanos en los Estados Unidos de Norteamerica.   La Habana, Cuba.   (1961)   By Juan Aquilar Derpich.   180 p.   19 cm.

    F128.9.S7 A 36

SPANISH Americans.   Broadway habla espanol.   By Aldana B. Fernandez.   Mexico, Ediciones Radio-Prensa, 1947.   236 p.   illus.   23 cm.   48-19923*.

    F128.9. S7 F 4

SYRIANS.   A study of the Syrian population of Greater New York, by Lucius Hopkins Miller.   (New York? 1904?)   48 p.   illus.   25½ cm.   4-22376.

    F128.9. S9 M6

SYRIANS.   The Syrian American directory almanac.   1930 -   New York city, Arida & Andria (1929 -   v.   illus.   23 cm.   30-6385.

    F128.9. S9 S 9

SYRIANS.   Our Syrian population; a study of the Syrian communities of greater New York, by Lucius Hopkins Miller.   San Francisco, Calif., 1969.   48 p.   illus.   28 cm.   Previously publ. under title: A study of the Syrian population of greater New York.   79-79418.

    F128.9.S98 M5
    1969

NEW YORK 303

UKRAINIANS. V Novomu Sviti. By Platon Stasiuk. 1958. 158 p. 24 cm. 59-18474.
F128.9. U4 S 8

UKRAINIANS. Statut. Tovarystvo "Vil'nist' v Amerytsi," New York. New York, 1912.
17 p. 14 cm. 59-47889.
F128.9. U4 T6

UKRAINIANS. Zolota iuvileĭna knyha. United American Ukrainian Organizations Committee of New York. Alexander Sokolyshyn, ed. 192 p. illus. 24 cm. 56-39125.
F128.9. U4 U5

OTHER CITIES, TOWNS, ETC., A - Z

ALBANY and Rensselaer, N.Y., directory ... v. (1) - 1813 - (Boston) Sampson & Murdock co., 1813 - 19   v. illus., plates, fold. maps. 17½ - 28 x 22 cm. 99-2747 rev.   Directories

ALBANY. Tri-city suburban (Albany-Schenectady-Troy) directory for towns of Bethlehem, Brunswick, Colonie, East Greenbush, Glenville, Guilderland, Niskayuna, Rotterdam, Schaghticoke and villages of Alplaus, Altamont, Aqueduct, Carman, Delmar, Elsmere, Hoffmans, Lathams, Loudonville, Pattersonville, Slingerlands, South Bethlehem, South Schenectady, Valley Falls ... Schenectady, N.Y., H.A. Manning co., 19   v. 23 cm. CA 27-286 unrev.   Directories

ALBANY. The Argus house directory of the city of Albany ... (1895) Albany, The Argus co., printers, 1895. 2, 224 p. 24½ cm. 9-14003.   Directories

ALBANY. The Albany and Troy blue book of selected names for Albany, Troy, Cohoes, Lansingburgh, Waterford, Bath, Greenbush, East Albany, West Troy, Green Island, Menands, Loudonville and Newtonville ... Albany, Tory, Sampson, Murdock, 1894.   307 p. 20 cm. 10-1804.   Directories

ALBANY. Albany society directory. 1896. Albany, N.Y., The Argus company, printers, 1896.
205, (2), xl p. 18½ cm. 10-1805.   Directories

ALBANY. The Albany, Troy and Schenectady blue book ... 1899, 1903, 1910. New York, Dau pub. co., 1899-1910.   3 v. 17½ - 21 cm. Nov. 30, 99-3 Add.   Directories

ALBANY. Society directory of Albany and Troy, 2889, 1890/91. Albany, N.Y., F. C. Manning, 1889 -   2 v. 15½ cm. 10-3166.   Directories

ALBANY. Hunt's Albany commercial directory, for 1848-9 ... Comp. and pub. by William Hunt ... Albany, J. Munsell, printer, 1848.   136, 32 p. incl. front., illus. plates, ports. 19½ cm. 18-15151.   Directories

ALBANY. City guide to Albany and Rensselaer, with map; a complete guide to the streets and avenues, incl. lists of blocks and buildings ... Albany parks ... etc. ... Albany, N.Y., Sampson & Murdock co., inc., 19   v. fold. maps. 12-15½ cm. 18-16004 Rev.
F129. A3 A2

ALBANY. Italian contributions to Albany in the nineteenth century, by Leonard Accardi; preface by James A. Pisarri ... Schenectady, N.Y., Franklin print shop (1941)   107 p. 20 cm. 41-8229.
F129. A3 A 25

ALBANY and the New York state capitol from original negatives by the Albertype co. New York, 1891.
36 pl. 12°. 1-14811-M1.
F129. .A3 A3

ALBANY. Albany army letter, v.1, no. 1, Tuesday, April 14, 1863. (Albany, N.Y., 1863)
1 pam. 20 cm. Daily edition.
F129. A3 A35

— v. 1, no. 1-2 ... (Albany, 1863)   2 pams. 28½ cm. Bi-weekly ed.
F129. A3A351

ALBANY. Catalogue of Albany's Bicentennial loan exhibition, at the Albany academy ... 1886. Albany, Weed, Parsons, printers, 1886.   xxii, (5) - 155 p. 27½ cm. 3-18816.
F129. A3 A4

1037

ALBANY. ... Albany, New York, a beautiful and attractive city in which to live, a most advantageous city in which to do business; pub. by the Albany chamber of commerce. (Albany, 190-)
(24) p. illus. 15½ x 25 cm. 7-30333.
F129.A3 A45

— (Albany, 190-) (32) p. illus. 16½ x 25½ cm. 9-27097 Rev.
F129.A3 A46

— (Albany, N.Y., Chamber of commerce, 1912?) 47 p. illus., map. 23 cm. 12-18478.
F129.A3A462

— (Albany, N.Y., The Argus co., 1918) 46 p. front. (diagr.) illus. 23 cm. CA 26-520 unrev.
F129.A3A463

ALBANY. Facts: Albany, issued by the Chamber of commerce. (Albany, 1907) 15½ cm.
F129.A3 A47

ALBANY. Proceedings of the Common council, and the various religious corporations of the city of Albany, relative to the State street burial grounds. Albany, Weed, Parsons, printers, 1867.
87 p. 23½ cm. 11-27443.
F129.A3 A48

ALBANY. ... Early records of the city and county of Albany, and colony of Rensselaerswyck ... Tr. from the original Dutch by Jonathan Pearson ... v.3. Albany, The University of the state of New York, 1869-19 10-209.
F129.A3A484

ALBANY. Records of the First Lutheran church in the city of Albany. Transcribed by the New York genealogical and biographical society. Ed. by Royden Woodward Vosburgh. New York city, 1917.
2 v. 36 x 28½ cm. Autographed from type-written copy. Contents. - Births and baps, 1784-1900. - Marriages, 1794-1900 ... Deaths and funerals, 1872-1900. 17-6652 Rev.
F129.A3 A49

ALBANY. Records of the First Presbyterian church in the city of Albany. Transcribed by the New York genealogical and biographical soc. Ed. by Royden Woodward Vosburgh. New York city, 1917.
2, ii, 220 numb. l. 36 x 28½ cm. Autographed from type-written copy. Covers period 1785-1870. 17-24796.
F129.A3A495

ALBANY. Register of the Albany historical and art soc. (Albany, Weed-Parsons printing co., 1899)
46 p. front. 26 x 19½ cm. 1-14802.
F129.A3 A5

ALBANY. Proposed erection of local historical monuments. Report of special committee on archaeology ... Albany institute. Albany, Weed, Parsons, 1881. p. (137) - 144. 23½ cm. From Transactions of Albany institute, vol. x. 11-28996.
F129.A3 A55

ALBANY. Albany Institute of History and Art. Bulletin. v. 1 - Oct. 1958 - (Albany, N.Y.)
v. in illus. 29 cm. bimonthly (Oct.-Apr.) Supersedes ... Magazine of art. 59-40469.
F129.A3A553

ALBANY Institute of History and Art. Report. (Albany) v. 29 cm. annual. 57-15949.
F129.A3A555

ALBANY. The Albany institute of history and art, and its future. (Albany, 1941) 27 p. 21½ cm.
45-40401.
F129.A3A557

ALBANY. Historic State street. (Albany) Albany institute of history and art, 1943. 3 p., 15 numb. l.
28 x 21½ cm. Reproduced from type-written copy. 43-18079.
F129.A3 A56

ALBANY. Albany's tercentenary. America's oldest city, 1624 - 1924; historical narrative, souvenir. (Albany, J. B. Lyon co., printers, 1924) 2 l. 7-185 p. incl. illus., pl., ports. 25½ cm. "Books relating to the history of Albany": p. (186) 24-18326.
F129.A3 A58

ALBANY. Special number, the Argus, descriptive of and illustrating Albany, N.Y., and vicinity. (Albany, The Argus, 1902?) 39 p. illus. 21 cm. 18-15873.
F129.A3 A69

ALBANY. ... Albany bi-centennial. Historical memoirs. A. Bleecker Banks, chairman printing committee. Albany and New York, Banks & bros., 1888. viii, 461 p. front., plates (part col., 1 double) ports. 24 cm. 1-14803 Rev.
F129.A3 B 16

ALBANY. Souvenir of the Albany bi-centennial celebration, July, 1886, containing the official programme with the only authorized descriptive and illuminated lithographs of the great historical pageant, tog. with an account of the settlement and early history of Albany ... Ed. Thurlow Weed Barnes. Albany, N.Y., The Journal co., 1886. 67 p. illus. (partly col.) 35 cm. 7-29680. F129.A3 B 18

ALBANY. The settlement and early history of Albany; a prize essay, delivered before the Young men's assoc ... 1850. By William Barnes. Albany, Gould, Banks & Gould, 1851. 25 p. fold. map. 23 cm. 1-14804 Rev. F129. A3 B 2

— Albany, N.Y., J. Munsell, 1864. 3, (5) - 100 p. incl. pl., 2 plans. front. 23 cm. 1-14805. F129. A3 B 3

ALBANY. Studies for Albany (by) Arnold W. Brunner, architect ... (New York, Bartlett-Orr press) 1914. 7-101 p. front., illus., plans (3 fold., 1 col.) 27½ cm. 14-14430. F129. A3 B 8

ALBANY. The new Capitol. A criticism ... By Benjamin Clapp Butler. Albany, N.Y., 1881. 9 p. 22 cm. F129. A3 B 9

ALBANY. The capitol at Albany. New York, Judson & Gordon (1889) 15 pl. 16º. 1-14807-M1. F129. A3 C2

ALBANY. The capitol at Albany. Photographs in black. Waterbury, Conn., Adt & bros., 1889. 12 pl. 24º. 1-14806-M1. F129. A3 C3

ALBANY. A discourse commemorative of the heroes of Albany, who have fallen during the present war ... by Rufus W. Clark. Albany, Steam press of C. Van Benthuysen, 1864. 50 p. 23 cm. 4-33451 F129. A3 C5

ALBANY'S part in the world war; comp. under the direction of Harry Cohen ... Albany, N.Y., The General publishing co., 1919. 148 p. illus. (incl. ports.) 30½ cm. 19-13003. F129.A3 C67

ALBANY. St. Agnes' cemetery; its past and present associations; ed. by Myron A. Cooney. Albany, N.Y., F. S. Hills, 1899. 249 p. incl. front., pl., ports. 31½ cm. Dec. 21, 99-52. F129. A3 C7

ALBANY. Early Irish in old Albany, with special mention of Jan Andriessen "De Iersman van Dublingh". By Hon, Franklin M. Danaher ... Boston, The American-Irish hist. soc., 1903. 44 p. front. (port.) 22 cm. 4-31135 Rev. F129.A3 D17

ALBANY. The Friendly sons of St. Patrick in Albany; an historical sketch of some celebrations of St. Patrick's day in Albany, in the early part of the 19th century ... by Hon. Franklin M. Danaher ... (Albany, N.Y., 1905) (7) p. 23 cm. "From the Argus, Albany, March 26, 1905." 6-22942. F129.A3 D18

ALBANY. Dutch settlers society of Albany ... Year book, 1924/25 - Albany, N.Y. (1924 - v. fold. facsim. 24 cm. 26-2490. F129. A3 D8

ALBANY. The House of Peace. By Louise A. Dyer. Illus. by Larry Toschik. (1st ed.) New York, Longmans, Green, 1956 (1955) 191 p. illus. 22 cm. Includes bibliography. 55-8737. F129. A3 D9

ALBANY - past and present. (Federal writers' project. New York (State) (Albany? 1938?) 27 p. illus. (incl. map) 25½ cm. (American guide series) 38-26487. F129.A3 F43

ALBANY. ... Albany and its place in the history of the U.S. A memorial sketch written for the 200th anniversary of its birthday as a city. By Berthold Fernow ... Albany (N.Y.) C. Van Benthuysen, 1886. 98 p. 21 cm. 1-14808. F129.A3 F47

ALBANY. A hand book for the Albany rural cemetery, with an appendix on emblems. By Edward Fitzgerald. Albany, Van Benthuysen printing house, 1871. 141 p. front., plates (partly fold.) fold. plan. 20 cm. 12-9124. F129. A3 F55

ALBANY. Old Albany. By Morris Gerber. (1st ed. Albany, 1961-65) 2 v. F129. A3 G4

ALBANY. "Old Albany" A picture book from the Morris Gerber collection. Albany, 1970 - 71.
v. 1. (chiefly illus.) 29 cm. F129.A3 G42

ALBANY. (By Charles Warren Greene) Philadelphia, J. B. Lippincott co., 1888. 5 p. 12º.
Reprint from "Chamber's encyclopaedia. New ed. 1888." 1-14809-M1. F129. A3 G7

ALBANY. In loving memory of William Stormont Hackett, 67th mayor of Albany ... 1866 - 1926 ... Compiled by David M. Kinnear ... (Albany, Designed and printed by the Argus co., 1926)
33 p. incl. front. (port.) 32½ cm. 27-4703. F129.A3 H12

ALBANY. Noted living Albanians and state officials. A series of biographical sketches, by David Addison Harsha ... Albany, N.Y., Weed, Parsons, printers, 1891. xiv, 524 p. front., plates, ports.
24½ cm. Edition de luxe. 5-34058. F129. A3 H2

ALBANY. The Albany institute of history and art; a sketch of its early forerunners, by John Davis Hatch, jr. (Albany) Albany institute of history and art, 1944. (16) p. pl. 23 cm. "Reprinted from New York history, July 1944." 45-1859. F129.A3 H23

ALBANY. Reminiscences of Albany. By John J. Hill ... New York, Printed by J. Medole & son, 1884.
41 p. 23 cm. 5-33704. F129. A3 H6

ALBANY: Dutch, English, and American, by Codman Hislop ... with a foreword by Dixon Ryan Fox ... Albany, N.Y., The Argus press, 1936. xv, 413 p. illus. (incl. ports., maps) 20 cm. Bibliography: p. 383-396.
37-12265. F129.A3 H67

ALBANY, a cradle of America, founded 1614, chartered 1686. Pub. by the Committee on the celebration of the 250th anniversary of the granting of the Dongan charter ... (Albany, Printed by the Argus co.) 1936. 62 p. illus. (incl. ports., map) 22½ cm. 36-14889. F129.A3 K53

ALBANY. At State and Pearl, by David Mitchell Kinnear. Albany, N.Y. (1916) (28) p. illus. (incl. ports.) 25½ cm. In verse. 17-3605. F129.A3 K55

ALBANY. Symbols of the capital; or, Civilization in New York. By Amory D. Mayo. New York, Thatcher & Hutchinson, 1859. vi, 7-368 p. 19 cm. 1-14810. F129. A3 M4

ALBANY. The annals of Albany. By Joel Munsell. Albany, J. Munsell, 1850-59. 10 v. front., illus., plates, ports., maps (partly fold.) plans (partly fold.) 18½ cm. 1-14812. F129. A8 M9

ALBANY. Collections on the history of Albany, from its discovery to the present time. With notices of its public institutions, and biographical sketches of citizens deceased ... Albany, N.Y., J. Munsell, 1865-71. 4 v. fronts., illus., plates, ports., fold. maps, facsims., tables. 26 cm. 1-14813. F129.A3 M91

ALBANY County records ... (1654 - 1678) (In previous item, v.3 p. 1-224; v.4, p. 225-510) 11-11660.
F129.A3 M91
vol. 3-4

ALBANY. Contributions for the genealogies of the first settlers of Albany. (In Collections on the history of Albany ... v.4 p. 84-184z. Reprinted ... By Prof. Jonathan Pearson. Albany, 1872. 11-11652. F129.A3 M91
vol. 4

ALBANY. Men and things in Albany two centuries ago. By Joel Munsell. (Albany, 1876)
(5) - 32 p. front., illus. (incl. port., plan) 23½ cm. 1-14814. F129.A3 M92

ALBANY, birthplace of the Union; commemorating America's oldest community, the growth of an idea, and an institution dedicated to the advancement of each. (Albany) The National savings bank of the city of Albany, 1940. xi, 66 p. incl. front., illus. 27 cm. "First ed." Bibliography: p. 64-65. 40-8027.
F129.A3 N26

ALBANY'S historic street; a collection of some of the historic facts and interesting traditions relating

1040

NEW YORK 307

to State street & its neighborhood; pub. in commemoration of its fiftieth anniversary, by the National savings bank of the city of Albany. (Albany) 1918. xiv, (4), 43, (2) p. incl. front., illus., ports. 23 cm. Bibliography: p. xiv-xv. 18-21547. F129. A3 N27

ALBANY. The New Albany. A record of the city's progress. v. 1 - May 1891 - Albany, Brandow printing co., 1892 - v. illus. (incl. ports.) 21 cm. bimonthly (monthly, Jan.-Oct. 10-22929. F129. A3 N5

ALBANY. (The attorney general's answer; to the reflections upon him in the votes of the 19th June last. New York, Printed by William Bradford, 1729. Boston, 1929) facsim: 3 p. 29½ cm. (Americana series: photostat reproductions by the Mass. historical soc. no. 237) 41-2929. F129. A3 N58

ALBANY. The New York State capitol. (Albany, 1951) 16 p. illus. 18 cm. A 51-9633.
F129. A3N584

ALBANY. Proceedings of the Legislature of the state of New York in commemoration of its removal from the old to the new Capitol. Albany, Weed, Parsons, printers, 1879. 65 p. 23 cm. 11-4730.
F129. A3 N6

ALBANY. Race relations in the Albany-Troy area; a profile for 1957 by Eunice and George Grier. (Albany) 1957. 51 l. illus. 29 cm. Includes bibliography. A 58-9356. F129.A3N618

ALBANY. The Schuyler mansion, Albany, New York. (Albany, 1964) 1 v. (unpaged) ports. 22 cm. (Historic sites of New York State) A 66-7011. F129. A3 N62

ALBANY. Margaret Schuyler. The story of her heroic deed. An historical ballad with an account of the old Schuyler house at Albany, by Charles C. Nott. Washington, 1889. (iii) - vi p., 3 l., p.(441) - 529. illus., port. 24 cm. CA 12-919 Unrev. F129. A3 N9

ALBANY. The Albany hand-book for 1881. A strangers' guide and residents' Manual... Comp. and alphabetically arranged by H. P. Phelps... Albany, N.Y. (C. van Benthuysen, printers) 1880. 146 p. front., illus., plates, maps (1 double) 17½ cm. 1-14815 Rev. F129. A3 P 5

— Albany, N.Y., Brandow & Barton, 1884. 178 p. front., illus., plates, ports., maps (1 double) 18 cm. 1-14816 Rev. F129. A3 P 53

ALBANY. The Albany rural cemetery, its beauties, its memoires, by Henry P. Phelps. Albany and Chicago, Phelps and Kellogg, 1893. 9, (17) - 223 p. incl. front., illus. plates, ports., fold. plan. 25 x 21½ cm. Bibliography: p. 215. 12-9125 Rev. F129. A3 P 54

ALBANY. ... The Capitol at Albany. (By Henry Pitt Phelps) 5th ed. Albany, N.Y., Press of Brandow printing co., 1889. 16 p. pl. 18 cm. "From the Albany hand book. 1-14818 Rev.
F129. A3 P 56

ALBANY. History and description of the Capitol at Albany... Albany, N.Y., 1880. 15 p. fold. front. 17 cm. 1-14817 Rev. F129. A3 P 58

ALBANY. The King memorial. By Henry P. Phelps. Albany, Phelps and Kellogg, 1893. 46 p. front., plates, ports. 25 cm. A fountain... in memory of... Rufus H. King. 11-23142 Rev. F129. A3 P 63

ALBANY. Rectors of St. Peter's church, Albany. (From the documentary history of the state of New-York. Albany, 1850. vol. 3, p. 1151-1155) 2-5716. F129. A3 R3

ALBANY chronicles, a history of the city arranged chronologically, from the earliest settlement to the present time; illus. with many historical pictures of rarity and reproductions of the Robert C. Pruyn collection... comp. by Cuyler Reynolds. Albany, N.Y., J. B. Lyon co., printers, 1906. xxiv, 817 p. front., plates, ports., maps, plans, facsims. 24½ cm. 7-19559. F129. A3 R4

ALBANY. A historical discourse on the Reformed Prot. Dutch church of Albany... by ... Rev.

E. P. Rogers ... New York, Board of publication of the Reformed Protestant Dutch church, 1858.
120 p.   front., plates.   22½ cm.   6-37982.
F129. A3 R7

ALBANY.   Capitol story, by Cecil R. Roseberry.   With photos. by Arthur John Daley.   (Albany)
State of New York, 1964.   128 p.   29 cm.   64-63030.
F129.A3 R73

ALBANY.   The Executive Mansion in Albany, an informal history, 1856 - 1960.   By Isabelle K. Savell.
(Albany, 1960)   47 p.   27 cm.
F129. A3 S 3

ALBANY.   The Governor's Mansion in Albany.   By Isabelle K. Savell.   (Albany, 1962)   32 p. illus.
(part col.) group ports.   26 cm.   62-64238.
F129.A3 S 32

ALBANY.   The Schuyler mansion at Albany, residence of Major-General Philip Schuyler, 1762 - 1804,
by the Spirit of '76 (Georgina Schuyler)   New York, The De Vinne press, 1911.   4, (3) - 43 p.   col.
front., plates, ports., facsims.   23 cm.   Also pub. as Appendix K in Annual report of American scenic and historic preservation soc., 1912.
12-23451 Rev.
F129.A3 S 39

ALBANY.   Unveiling of the equestrian statue of General Philip H. Sheridan, Capitol park, Albany,
New York, Oct. 7, 1916, by the citizens of Albany and the state of New York.   (Albany, Press of J. B.
Lyon co., 1916)   124 p.   front., plates, ports.   26 cm.   20-23891.
F129.A3 S 55

ALBANY.   Souvenir of Albany ...   (37th thousand.   Portland, Me., L. H. Nelson co., 1909)
(32) p.   illus.   20 x 25 cm.   CA 17-132 Unrev.
F129.A3 S 67

ALBANY.   Souvenir of Albany.   (Portland, Me., 1912)   20 x 25 cm.
F129.A3 S 68

ALBANY.   "Sparks" from the New York state capitol fire, Albany, March 29, 1911.   Over 50 souvenir views.   (Albany, N.Y. Coulson & Wendt, 1911)   20 x 25 cm.
F129. A3 S 7

ALBANY.   Albany's bicentennial of the past 200 years ... 1686 - 1886 ... By A. O. Springer.   (Albany,
N.Y., 1886)   48 p.   illus.   fol.   1-14819-M1.
F129.A3 S 76

ALBANY.   Fort Crailo, the Greenbush manor house.   By S. de L. Van Rensselaer Strong.   (n. p.,
1898?)   31 p.   22½ cm.   41-36267.
F129. A3 S 8

ALBANY.   New England in Albany.   By Jonathan Tenney.   Boston, Crocker & co., 1883.
126 p.   15½ x 12 cm.   "Biographical notes": p. 65-123.   13-23463.
F129. A3 T2

ALBANY.   This guide to Albany.   (Albany, Cyrene Temple No. 18, Daughters of the Nile)
v.   illus.   22 cm.   annual.   55-25439.
F129. A3 T5

ALBANY.   Times-Union.   250th anniversary edition.   Albany, 1936.   1 v.   illus.   54 cm.   40M1010T.
F129.A3 T55

ALBANY.   Our ancient landmarks.   The sermon delivered in St. Paul's church, Albany, on the bi-
centennial commemoration of the city's charter ...   By the Rev. Maunsell Van Rensselaer ... Albany,
The Argus co., printers, 1886.   32 p.   24½ cm.   10-3152.
F129. A3 V2

ALBANY.   Views of Albany.   (Portland, Me., 1905)   19½ x 25 cm.
F129. A3 V6

ALBANY.   Views of Albany.   (Albany, 1908)   1 v.   20½ x 25½ cm.
F129.A3 V62

ALBANY.   Views of Albany.   (Portland, Me., L. H. Nelson co. 1908)   1 v.   20½ x 25½ cm.
F129.A3 V63

ALBANY street directory, and city guide, containing a list of public buildings, post office, arrival and
departure of mails, etc., etc.   Comp. and pub. by Joseph C. Wallace ... 1869.   Albany, N.Y., C.
Van Benthuysen, print., 1869.   64 p.   14½ cm.   9-14865.
F129. A3 W1

ALBANY.   Wallace's street and city guide.   Albany, 1870.   14 cm.
F129. A3 W2

NEW YORK

ALBANY. The history of the city of Albany, from the discovery of the great river in 1524, by Verrazzano, to the present time, by Arthur James Weise. Albany, E. H. Bender, 1884. viii, 520 p. front., illus., plates, maps (1 fold.) plans (1 fold.) 24 cm. 1-14820. F129. A3 W4

ALBANY. ... Albany tourist's handy guide ... (By John D. Whish) Albany, N.Y., Brandow printing co. (1900) 73 p. plates. 14½ cm. Nov. 8, 1900-220. F129. A3 W5

ALBANY. ... Albany guide book ... (By John D. Whish) Albany, J. B. Lyon co., printers, 1917. 224 p. front., plates, fold. plan. 15½ cm. 17-16209. F129. A3 W57

ALBANY. ... Albany city guide: being a general description of the public buildings, literary, charitable, and benevolent institutions, etc. with numerous useful tables and statistics, relating to the city. Comp. by S. Wilson ... Albany, Print. C. Wendell, 1844. 144 p. front., illus., plates (1 fold.) plan. 24 cm. 16-20031. F129. A3 W69

— Comp. and pub. by S. Wilson. Albany, 1845. 33, 112 p. illus., 2 pl. (1 fold.) fold. map, plan. 14 cm. 8-30443. F129. A3 W7

ALBANY. Random recollections of Albany, from 1800 to 1808: by Gorham A. Worth. 3d ed., with notes by the publisher. Albany, N.Y., J. Munsell, 1866. vi, (17) - 144 p. incl. front., illus. plates, ports. 22½ cm. The earlier editions appeared under the speud. Ignatius Jones. 1-14821. F129. A3 W9

ALBION. An alphabetical list of the residents of the village of Albion ... Lockport, N.Y., Roberts bros., v. 22 cm. 26-6458. Directories

ALBION. Boyd's directory of Albion, Attica, Batavia, Le Roy and Warsaw ... 18(93/94 Philadelphia, Pa., C. E. Howe, co., 18(93 - (1) v. 24½ cm. Directories

ALBION. Sketches of the village of Albion: containing incidents of its history and progress, from its first settlement, and a statistical account of its trade, schools, societies, manufactures, etc. By Arad Thomas. Albion, N.Y., Willsea & Beach, 1853. iv, (5) - 40 p. 22½ cm. 20-20185. Directories

ALLEGHANY city. Articles of association for the Allegany city company, tog. with a description of the property, etc. New York, J. Narine, 1837. 20 p. 8°. 1-14822-M1. F129. A4 A4

ALMOND. The Almond story; the early years. By John P. Reynolds. Hornell, N.Y., 1962. 120 p. 22 cm. F129. A43 R4

AMENIA. Troutbeck, A Dutchess County homestead. By C. E. Benton. 1916. v. F129. A45 B 4

AMENIA. Early history of Amenia, by Newton Reed. Amenia, N.Y., De Lacey & Wiley, printers, 1875. vi, (3) - 151 p. 20½ cm. 3-24073. F129. A45 R3

AMHERST. A history of the town of Amherst, 1818 - 1965, by Sue Miller Young. New York, Town Board of Amherst, 1965. xx, 306 p. 24 cm. F129. A46 Y6

AMITYVILLE. Seven cemeteries, village of Amityville, town of Babylon, Long Island, 1813 - 1913. William Applebie Eardeley ... Brooklyn, N.Y., 1913. 82 numb. l. 28½ cm. Type-written copy. 24-15753. F129. A47 E2

AMITYVILLE. A brief history of Amityville, by William T. Lauder. Amityville, N.Y., 1970. iii, 31, v p. 22 cm. 79-129663. F129. A47 L3

AMSTERDAM. Williams' Amsterdam city directory ... Amsterdam, N.Y., Press of the Daily Democrat and recorder, 18 v. fold. map. 23 cm. 12-11040. Directories

AMSTERDAM. General and business directory of Amsterdam and Hagaman's and Harrower's Mills, for 1888-'89. Tog. with a street directory and a miscellaneous department of useful information ... Lyons, N.Y., The Globe directory pub. co., 1888. (1)-24, 33-159 p. 23½ cm. 12-11042. Directories

AMSTERDAM. ... New York, 1893. 27 cm. F129. A5 A6

AMSTERDAM. A poem. By Horace Sprague ... Amsterdam, N.Y., Printed at the "Recorder" offic, 1860. 45 p. 23½ cm. 8-31346. F129. A5 S 7

ARCADE, New York. 1912. (By Darwin Grant Hodge) (Arcade, D. G. Hodge, 1912) (68) p. illus. (incl. ports.) 13½ x 27½ cm. 12-26758. F129. A66 H6

AUBURN daily advertiser city directory. Auburn, Knapp & Peck, Daily advertiser office, 1862 -
1 v. fold. map. 19½ cm. 9-12010. Directories

AUBURN. Brigham's general directory of Auburn, Weedsport, Port Byron, Union Springs, Aurora, Moravia and Cayuga, and business directory of Auburn, 1863 and 1864. Tog. with histories of the towns, from their first settlement. Comp. and pub. by A. De Lancey Brigham. Auburn, W. J. Moses' pub. house, 1863. 288 p. fold. map. 21½ cm. 12-7447. Directories

AUBURN directory for 1869 - Syracuse, 1869 - 1 v. 22½ cm. 9-14847. Directories

AUBRUN directory. Auburn, N.Y., J. W. Burroughs, 1878 - 1909. 21 v. plans (partly fold.) 23-24 cm. 9-12012. Directories

AUBURN city directory! 1880-81. Containing ... a map of the city, also a business directory of the villages, a farmers' register, and a map of Cayuga County. Comp. ... by N. H. Potter. Auburn, N.Y., N. H. Potter, 1880. 2-392 p. maps. 22½ cm. Maps wanting. 9-14848. Directories

AUBURN. J. E. Williams' Auburn city directory for 1882 - ... v.1 - Auburn, N.Y., J. E. Williams, 1882 - 1 v. 23 cm. 9-14849. Directories

AUBURN. City directory, Auburn, 1921 - (Watertown, N.Y.) Watertown directory co., inc., 1921 - v. 23½ cm. 21-6953. Directories

AUBURN. The story of Auburn to August 1935, by Henry M. Allen ... (Auburn? N.Y., 1935)
14 l. 28 cm. "Books for additional reading": 1st leaf. 44-35607. F129. A7 A1832

AUBURN. ... Anthony's standard business directory, guide and reference book of Auburn, Skaneateles, Moravia, Seneca Falls, Geneva, New York ... Comp. and pub. by the Anthony pub. co. ... (New Bedford, Mass.) ... 1893. 138 p. 23½ cm. 9-14850. Directories

AUBURN. Map of Auburn with street directory, buildings, halls and fire alarms ... Syracuse, N.Y., Sampson & Murdock co., inc. (1922 - v. fold. map. 15½ cm. 23-5682. F129. A7 A2

AUBURN sketches, being a series of studies of Auburn history and life, a supplement of The story of Auburn. By Henry M. Allen. Auburn, N.Y., 1939. 1 v. (various pagings) 28 cm. 48-37613*.
F129. A7 A4

AUBURN. A chronicle of Auburn, 1870 to 1935, by Henry M. Allen. Auburn, N.Y. (1940-46?)
1 v. (various pagings) 28 cm. 44-6577. F129. A7 A42

AUBURN. A chronicle of early Auburn 1793 to 1860. By Henry M. Allen. Auburn, 1953.
1 v. illus. 28 cm. 55-17747. F129. A7 A43

AUBURN. A narrative of Auburn from 1861 to 1950, formerly presented as Auburn history notes, being in part an enlargement of the Auburn chronicle, by Henry M. Allen. (Auburn, N.Y.) 1951 (i.e. 1944-53) 1 v. (various pagings) 29 cm. Typescript (carbon copy) 72-204966. F129. A7 A45

AUBURN. ... Centennial demonstration, at Auburn. A report of the proceedings, including ... the remarks of President Myers, and the address of Judge Hall ... Auburn, W. J. Moses' pub. house, 1876. 48 p. 22½ cm. 1-14823 Rev. F129. A7 A7

AUBURN. A souvenir. City of Auburn in the state of New York. (Auburn, N.Y.) Auburn business men's association, 1900.   (96) p. incl. illus., plates, ports.   17½ x 26½ cm.   1-14824 Rev.   F129. A7 B9

AUBURN.   The Seward House.   Foundation Historical Association, Auburn, N.Y., 1955.   31 p. illus., ports., facsim.   27 cm.   55-56774.   F129. A7 F6

AUBURN.   The history of Auburn, by Henry Hall ... Auburn (N.Y.) Dennis bros., 1869.
xvi, 579 p.   18½ cm.   1-14825.   F129. A7 H32

AUBURN, its facilities and resources, by D. Morris Kurtz ... (Auburn, N.Y.) The Kurtz pub. co., 1884.   viii, (9) - 152 p. illus.   23 cm.   1-14826.   F129. A7 K9

AUBURN.   Historical records of a hundred and twenty years, Auburn, N.Y., by Jowel H. Monroe. (Geneva, N.Y., W. F. Humphrey, printer) 1913.   278 p. plates, ports.   19½ cm.   24-9648.
F129. A7 M7

AVON.   Genealogical records of the pioneer families of Avon, N.Y.   Pierson, Waterous, Hosmer, Martin, etc., and their descendants.   Committee: Judge John Pierson and others ... Rochester, N.Y., Express printing house, 1871.   32 p.   22½ cm.   Includes reports of annual meetings of descendants of early settlers, 1864-1870.
7-22428.   F129. A96 G3

BABYLON.   Babylon reminiscences, by Benjamin P. Field, sketch of the author by James B. Cooper; historical sketch of Babylon, by James W. Eaton.   Babylon, N.Y., Babylon pub. co., 1911.
viii, 80 p. plates, port.   23½ cm.   19-4215.   F129.B18 F 4

BALLSTON SPA.   Manning's Ballston Spa, Corinth and Schuylerville, village of Victory Mills directory ... v.   19   Schenectady, N.Y., H. A. Manning co., 19   v.   23 cm.   CA 31-83 Unrev.
Directories

BALLSTON SPA.   Directory of Ballston Spa, Mechanicville, and Stillwater ... 1898/99 -
Albany, 18   v.   23 cm.   Directories

BALLSTON.   Records of the First Presbyterian church at Ballston in Ballston Center, Saratoga County, N.Y.   Transcribed by the New York genealogical and biographical society.   Ed. by Royden Woodward Vosburgh.   New York city, 1916.   2, vii, 242 numb. l.   36 x 28 cm.   Autographed from type-written copy.   Includes records of the Presbyterian church of Freehold, in Charlton, N.Y., 1786 - 1788.   16-11137.   F129. B 2 B 2

BALLSTON.   The first book of Chronicles.   The political war in Ballston.   By Nuel Bostwick.   (Ballston? N.Y.) 1799.   4 p.   23½ cm.   A satire relating to Ballston, N.Y. written in Biblical style.   16-3758.
F129. B 2 B 7
Rare Book Coll.

BALLSTON SPA.   Centennial history of the village of Ballston Spa, including the towns of Ballston and Milton, by Edward F. Grose; incl. an unpubl. history by the late John C. Booth.   ... (Ballston Spa, N.Y.) The Ballston journal, 1907.   258 p. incl. front., illus., ports.   27½ cm.   8-15500.
F129. B 2 G8

BANGALL.   Historical sketch of the First Stanford (Baptist) church at Bangall, Dutchess County, N.Y., by Mr. Evelyn Briggs Baldwin.   (New York? New York genealogical and biographical soc., 191 -)
12 numb. l.   27½ cm.   Type-written copy.   22-7827.   F129.B23 B 2

BATAVIA (New York) directory ... incl. Batavia town directory, East Pembroke village and country road ... Springfield, Mass., H. A. Manning co., 19   v.   23 cm.   23-16581.   Directories

BATAVIA.   Kirwin's Batavia and Genesee County directory (v. 1 -   1888/89 -   ... directories of the villages of Le Roy, Alexander, Bergen, Corfu and Oakfield ... Lockport, N.Y., W. H. Kirwin, 1888 -   1 v.   23 cm.   12-37144.   Directories

BATAVIA.   A historical sketch of the village of Batavia, by William Seaver.   Batavia, Printed by W. Seaver, 1849.   56 p.   22 cm.   10-21697.   F129. B 3 S 6

BATAVIA.   Souvenir of Batavia.   Photogravures.   New York, The Albertype co. (1897)   2 p., 16 pl.
24°.   1-14827-M1.   F129. B3 S9

BATAVIA.   ... Batavia, New York, the past and present, arranged and photographed by W. S. Wakeman; over 400 photographs.   Batavia, N.Y., J. J. Patterson, 1902.   2 p., 18 pl.   26½ x 31 cm.   2-20485.
F129. B3 W2

BATAVIA.   Outline history of Batavia, by Clara L. T. Williams.   Batavia, N.Y., Deo-on-go-wa chapter, D.A.R., 1934.   17 p.   illus.   19 cm.   34-13734.   F129. B3 W6

BATH.   ... The official records of the centennial celebration, Bath, Steuben county ... 1893.   Nora Hull, ed.   Authorized by the general committee.   (Bath, N.Y., Press of the Courier co., 1893)
280 p.   front. (port.)   fold. map, plan.   23 cm.   1-14828.   F129.B32 B3

BATH directory, 19   Binghamton, N.Y., The Calkin-Kelly directory co., 19
v.   24 cm.   CA 31-243 Unrev.   Directories

BAY RIDGE.   The community in which you live; highlights and sidelights of the story of Bay Ridge, proud survivor of the old Dutch town of New Utrecht, in the Borough of Brooklyn, New York City.
Brooklyn, 1950.   49 p.   illus., ports., maps (1 fold.)   23 cm.   51-23862.   F129.B34 B7

BAY RIDGE.   Old Bay Ridge.   Brooklyn, Library Associates of Brooklyn College, 1962.   15 p.   21 cm.
F129.B34 G5

BEACON.   Waite's Beacon city directory incl. Glenham and Fishkill for 1910/11 -   Newburgh, N.Y.,
L. P. Waite, 1909 -   v.   24½ cm.   10-653 (rev. '15)   Directories

BEDFORD.   Historical records.   Bedford, 1966-72.   4 v.   28 cm.   67-58349.   F129.B37 A55

BEDFORD.   A short historical tour of the town of Bedford.   (2d ed.)   Bedford Historical Society,
Bedford, N.Y. (1971)   iv, 36 p.   illus.   23 cm.   F129.B37 B4
1971

BEDFORD.   A brief history of the Presbyterian church, at Bedford, N.Y., from the year 1680.   With an account of the laying of the corner-stone, and the services at the dedication of the present edifice in the year 1872.   By Rev. P. B. Heroy.   New York, Printed by E. O. Jenkins, 1874.   34 p.   23 cm.
3-31341.   F129.B37 H5

BEDFORD.   Old Bedford days; recollections.   By Eloise Payne Luquer.   Bedford Village, N.Y.
(1953)   39p.   illus., ports., map.   24 cm.   54-16596.   F129.B37 L8

BEDFORD; heritage survives in a modern world.   Text and photos. by Edgar B. Van Winkle.   Bedford, N.Y., Coleraine Press (1972)   112 p.   illus.   29 cm.   73-190620.   F129.B37 V3

BELLE TERRE, Long Island; its whereabouts - its purpose, its plans and its attractions described with pictures.   Dean Alvord co., managers ... New York city.   (New York, Chasmar-Winchel press,
1910)   6 l.   front., illus., plates.   31½ cm.   10-1961.   F129.B385 A4

BELLPORT and Brookhaven; a saga of the Sibling hamlets at Old Purchase South, compiled by Stephanie S. Bigelow.   (1st ed.)   Bellport, N.Y.) Bellport-Brookhaven Historical Soc., 1968.   iv, 126 p.   illus.
24 cm.   68-55991.   F129.B387 B5

BERNE.   Records of St. Paul's Evangelical Lutheran church in the town of Berne, Albany County.
Transcribed by the New York genealogical and biographical soc ... Ed. by Royden Woodward Vosburgh.
New York city, 1916.   2 v.   map, facsim.   36 x 28 cm.   Autographed from type-written copy.   The records extend from 1790 to
1875.   16-7853.   F129.B39 B5

BERNE.   Records of the Reformed Dutch church of the Beaver Dam in the town of Berne, Albany County.   Transcribed by the N.Y. genealogical and biographical soc. Ed. Royden W. Vosburgh.   N.Y.,
1918.   2 p., xvii, 172 numb. l. incl. map.   36 x 28½ cm.   Autographed from type-written copy.   18-19394.   F129.B39 B52

NEW YORK 313

BETHLEHEM. Town of Bethlehem, Albany County; a brief history, by Allison P. Bannett. (Bethlehem? N.Y.) 1968. 28 p. 23 cm. 68-24800. F129.B392 B4

BETHPAGE bygones, by Iris & Alonzo Gibbs. (Bethpage, N.Y., 1962) 54 p. 22 cm.
F129.B394 G5

BINGHAMTON. The Anthony pub. co.'s standard city directory of Binghamton, Port Dickinson and Lestershire, 1893/94. (Binghamton, N.Y.) The Anthony pub. co., 18   1 v. 24 cm. 13-22562.
Directories

BINGHAMTON, Lestershire, Union, Endicott, Port Dickinson, East Union, Hooper, Vestal, Westover and R. D. routes directory 1905 -   (Binghamton, N.Y.) Bingham chamber of commerce (etc.) 1905 -   v. 24½ cm. 5-21467 Rev.   Directories

BINGHAMTON and Port Dickinson alphabetical directory. Household ed. (Binghamton) Binghamton chamber of commerce (inc.)   v. 23 cm. 12-20572.   Directories

...BINGHAMTON city directory, incl. Johnson City, Endicott, Union, Port Dickinson, Oakdale, East Union, Hooper, Stella, Westover and r.d. routes ... 1914. Binghamton, N.Y., Calkin-Kelly directory co.   v. 24 cm. 16-14142.   Directories

BINGHAMTON directory, 1870/71. Albany, N.Y., Weed, Parsons and co., printers, 1875 -
1 v. 22½ cm.   Directories

BINGHAMTON. Boyd's Binghamton city and Susquehanna railroad directory ... Binghamton, N.Y. (etc.) A. Boyd, 1869-73. 2 v. 23½ cm. 13-22568.   Directories

BINGHAMTON. ... Directory of Binghamton, including Endicott, Lestershire, Union, Port Dickinson, East Union, Hooper, Oakdale, Stella, Vestal, Westover and R.F.D. routes ... Binghamton, N.Y., C. E. Hewitt.   v. 24 cm. 39M2689T.   Directories

BINGHAMTON. Empire directory co.'s Binghamton city directory, 1909 -   (v. 1 -
... directory of the citizens of Binghamton, Lestershire and Endicott ... Binghamton, N.Y., Empire directory co. (1909 -   1 v. 24½ cm. 9-26170.   Directories

BINGHAMTON. Williams' Binghamton city directory ... 18   Binghamton, N.Y., J. E. Williams, 1887 - 1908   18 v. fold. maps. 23½ cm. 13-22567.   Directories

BINGHAMTON. Wilson's Binghamton directory for 1857 ... by H. Wilson. Binghamton, Preston & Sears; New York, H. Wilson, 1856.   88 p. 19½ cm. 9-14005.   Directories

BINGHAMTON. Winfield's Binghamton directory, also Lestershire, Port Dickinson and Union ... 1902 ... v. 2 ... Binghamton, N.Y., F. R. Keough, 1902.   24½ cm. 2-18768.   Directories

BINGHAMTON. ... Anthony's standard business directory, guide and reference book of Binghamton and Lester-shire ... Binghamton, N.Y., Anthony pub. co., 1872.   1 v. 23½ cm. 13-22563.
Directories

BINGHAMTON. ... A classified business directory of Binghamton, N.Y. (Binghamton) Walker bros., print. (1912)   (44) p. 24 cm. 12-26359.   Directories

BINGHAMTON. Pruden's business directory of Binghamton, Elmira, Ithaca, Cortland, Corning, Owego, Bath, Waverly, Penn Yan, Sayre, Athens, Hammondsport, Chenango Forks, Lestershire, Horseheads, Union, etc. ... 1900/01 -   (v. 1) -   Cincinnati, O., The Pruden directory co. (1900) -
v. 22½ cm. 24-17084.   Directories

BINGHAMTON. Saltzman & Haskell's pocket business directory, for cities. Binghamton ed. ... (Binghamton, N.Y.) Saltzman & Haskell, 1888.   20 p. fold. map. 14½ cm. 13-21571.
Directories

1047

BINGHAMTON street directory ... including streets in Johnson City, Endicott, Port Dickinson, Parkview and Belmont. Binghamton, N.Y., Calkin-Kelly directory co., 1929 - v. 15 cm.
CA 30-1238 Unrev.   F129. B4 A 2

BINGHAMTON. Commemorating the centennial of the incorporation of Binghamton as a village in the state of New York, 1834 - 1934 ... (Johnson City, N.Y., Johnson City pub. co., 1934) (32) p. illus. (incl. ports.) 23 cm. 34-38726.   F129. B4 B 38

BINGHAMTON. Board of trade review of Binghamton, the great manufacturing city of southern New York. Its magical growth, rapid development, wonderful beauty, and natural attractions, tog. with an account of its representative business enterprises. Binghamton, N.Y., J. P. McKinney, 1892.
160 p. illus. (incl. ports., map) 23 ½ cm. CA 30-1266 Unrev.   F129. B4 B 42

BINGHAMTON. City of Binghamton; the great manufacturing center of southern New York. Its growth, wonderful beauty, repid develpment and natural advantages, together with an account of its representative enterprises. (Binghamton) Board of trade, 1901.   (39) p. illus., port. 18 x 20 ½ cm.
2-11305.   F129. B4 B 43

BINGHAMTON. City of Binghamton ... Its growth, wonderful beauty ... and natural advantages ...
(Binghamton, N.Y., 1903)   17 ½ x 20 ½ cm.   F129. B4 B 44

BINGHAMTON. First Presbyterian church of Chenango Point, Broome county, New York, now known as Binghamton, Broome county, New York. Compiled and ed. by Ray C. Sawyer. (New York?) 1941.
2 p., 72 numb. l., 5 l. 28 cm. Type-written. Contains Marriages, 1827-1835, baptisms, deaths, 1828-1833. 42-10167.
                                                                                                                          F129. B4 B 45

BINGHAMTON. Illustrated Binghamton and vicinity. (Binghamton, N.Y.) Binghamton daily republican, 1905.   44 p. incl. illus., ports. 41 ½ cm. 5-32212.   F129. B4 B 46

BINGHAMTON, past and present: its commerce, trade and industries, descriptive and historical. (Binghamton, N.Y.) Evening herald co., 1894.   (11) - 120 p. front., illus., pl. 31 cm. 8-29255.
                                                                                                                          F129. B4 B 48

BINGHAMTON press. ... Twenty-fifth anniversary number. 1929. (Issued April 11, 1929)
1 v.   F129. B4 B485

BINGHAMTON. Guide to Binghamton. United States census of 1900 ... Binghamton, N.Y., Independent print, 1901.   40 p. 24º. 1-16288-M1.   F129. B4 B 5

BINGHAMTON. The Dwight house, Binghamton. (Binghamton, N.Y., 1874) 27 ½ x 21 ½ cm.
                                                                                                                          F129. B4 D 9

BINGHAMTON. A journal of some of the leading professional, commercial, and manufacturing interests of Binghamton, in 1882. (Binghamton, N.Y.)? Republican office (1882)   24 p. 8º. 1-14830-M1.
                                                                                                                          F129. B4 J 8

BINGHAMTON, its settlement, growth and development, and the factors in its history, 1800 - 1900. By William S. Lawyer, editor. (Boston) Century memorial pub. co., 1900.   xiii, 1035 p. illus., plates, ports. 25 ½ cm. 1-24521.   F129. B4 L 4

BINGHAMTON. Historical sketch of the First Presbyterian church of Binghamton, New York, with an unfinished introduction, by G. Parsons Nichols. (n.p.) 1909.   iv, (5) - 24 p. 18 cm. 10-15884.
                                                                                                                          F129. B4 N 6

BINGHAMTON. Better Binghamton; a report to the Mercantile-press club of Binghamton, N.Y. ... 1911, by Charles Mulford Robinson. (Cleveland, O., Printed by The J. B. Savage co., 1911)
5-105, (35) p. incl. front. (facsim.) illus. pl., 2 maps (1 fold.) 26 cm. 12-2266.   F129. B4 R65

BINGHAMTON. Chronology of the main events in the history of Binghamton, Broome county. 1783 - 1930. (By) Ray C. Sawyer. (N.Y?) 1941.   6 numb. l. 28 cm. Type-written. 42-10168.   F129. B 4 S 3

NEW YORK 315

BINGHAMTON. Death notices publ. in the Broome county republican, a weekly newspaper of Binghamton, from 1831 - 1870, comp. and ed. by Ray C. Sawyer. (New York?) 1942. 185 numb. l., 10 l. 29 x 22 ½ cm. Type-written. 46-41788. F129.B4 S313

BINGHAMTON. Marriage announcements publ. in the Broome county republican, a weekly newspaper of Binghamton, N.Y. ... Comp. and ed. by Ray C. Sawyer. (New York?) 1941. 2 v. 28½ cm. Type-written. Contents. - 1. 1831-1857. - 2. 1858-1870. 42-16078. F129.B4 S 32

BINGHAMTON and Broome County; a history, editor-in-chief, William Foote Seward ... historical and biographical ... New York and Chicago, Lewis historical publ. co., inc., 1924. 3 v. fronts., plates, ports., maps, facsims. 27½ cm. Vols. 1-2 paged continuously; v. 3 contains biographical material. 24-7521. F129. B4 S 5

BINGHAMTON. The annals of Binghamton, and of the country connected with it, from the earliest settlement. By J. B. Wilkinson ... Binghamton, Cooke & Davis, printers, 1840. vi, (7) - 256 p. 18 ½ cm. 1-14829. F129. B4 W6

— Reprinted, with notes and appendix, from the original ed. pub. in 1840. Binghamton, The Times association, 1872. v, (7) - 312 p. pl., map. 18 cm. 3-684. F129.B4 W61

BINGHAMTON. J. B. Wilkinson's The annals of Binghamton of 1840, with an appraisal, 1840 - 1967, by Tom Cawley. Illus. by John Hart. (Binghamton, N.Y.) The Broome County Historical Soc., 1967. x, 254 p. 21 cm. 67-22264. F129.B4 W63

BLOOMING GROVE. Inscriptions of ancient cemeteries at Greycourt and Washingtonville, Orange county,. copied and compiled by Lila James Roney ... (New York?) 1925. 36 numb. l. 3 l. 29 x 22 cm. Type-written. 32-9743. F129.B43 R 7

BLOOMING GROVE. Graveyard inscriptions of Greycourt cemetery, Bloomingrove and the Reformed Dutch church cemetery, Montgomery, both located in Orange county, compiled and ed. by Ray C. Sawyer ... (New York) 1931. 54 (i.e. 56) numb. l. 29 x 22 cm. Error in paging: nos. 15 and 16 repeated. Type-written. 32-9742. F129.B43 S 3

BLOOMINGBURG. Records of the Reformed Dutch church at Bloomingburgh, Sullivan county. Copied from the original church records ... by Gertrude A. Barber. (Bloomingburg, 1945?) 81 numb. l. 28 x 21 ½ cm. Type-written. 45-19819. F129.B44 B 5

BOLIVAR, New York, pioneer oil town. By John P. Herrick. Los Angeles, W. Ritchie Press, 1952. x, 150 p. map. 25 cm. 53-17026. F129.B46 H 4

BOONVILLE and its beighbors, the chronicle of an American community. By Tharratt Gilbert Best. (Boonville, N.Y.) 1960 (c. 1961) 198 p. 23 cm. F129.B47 B 4

BOONVILLE. Black cotton stockings. Compilation and comments by Don Ryder. Photographic collaboration by Jim Fynmore. Boonville, N.Y., Country Books (1954) 1 v. (unpaged, chiefly illus., ports.) 32 cm. 54-39487. F129.B47 R 9

BRIARCLIFF Manor. Briarcliff outlook ... for promotion of country life. v. 1-5; June 1902 - Sept. 1906. Briarcliff Manor, N.Y., 1902-06. 5 v. in 4. illus., plates (partly col.) port. 23 cm. (v.1-2: 35 cm.) monthly. Superseded by "Briarcliff once-a-week." 7-20574. F129.B48 B 5

BRIARCLIFF once-a-week, telling of a new hotel and residential resort, its characteristics and locale with other matters. v. 1 - Oct. 14, 1906 - Briarcliff Manor, N.Y., 1906 - 1 v. in 2. plates (partly col.) 21 cm. Supersedes Briarcliff outlook. 8-20405. F129.B48 B 5

BRIARCLIFF outlook, for the promotion of country life, v. 3-4. Briarcliff Manor, N.Y., 1904 - 06. 2 v. illus., plates, port. 23 cm. monthly. CA 6-1263 Unrev. F129.B48 B 5

BRIDGEHAMPTON. Memorials of old Bridgehampton, by James Truslow Adams. Bridgehampton, L.I., Priv. print. (at the press of the Bridgehampton news) 1916. vi, 399 p. 23 cm. "References": p. (v) - vi. "Gravestones": p. (312) - 383. 16-23613. F129. B5 A 2

1049

— Port Washington, N.Y., I. J. Friedman, 1962.   399 p.   24 cm.   (Empire State historical publications 13)
62-20908.
F129. B5 A 6

BRIDGEHAMPTON.   ... Historical address and appendix, by Elder H. P. Hedges ...   Sag-Harbor, N.Y., Express steam print (1886?)   34, vii p., 2 l., (3) p.   23½ cm.   5-5544.
F129. B8 B 6

BRIDGEHAMPTON.   Wayfarings; a collection chosen from pieces which appeared under that title in the Bridgehampton news, 1941 - 1953.   By Ernest Seabury Clowes.   Bridgehampton, N.Y. (1953)
346 p.   23 cm.   54-32435.
F129. B5 C 6

BRIDGEHAMPTON'S three hundred years; historic material from many sources selected by a special committee on the occasion of Bridgehampton's tercentenary celebration in 1956.   Co-chairmen: Mrs. Albert W. Topping (and) Everett C. Foster.   Bridgehampton, N.Y., Hampton Press, 1956.
169 p.   illus.   24 cm.   56-38459.
F129. B5 C 8

BRIDGEHAMPTON.   A centennial and historical address, delivered at Bridge-Hampton, L.I., by Hon. Henry P. Hedges ... 1876.   Sag-Harbor, J. H. Hunt, printer, 1876.   3, 24, vi p.   fold. facsim.   23 cm.
2-13917 Rev.
F129. B5 H 4

BRIDGEHAMPTON.   The hurricane; an account of the disastrous hurricane which swept New England on Sept. 21, 1938; as witnessed at Bridgehampton, by Olga L. Lafrentz.   New York, G. P. Putnam's sons, 1939.   12 p.   23 cm.   39-13859.
F129. B5 L 2

BRIDGEWATER.   Historical sketches of Bridgewater, Oneida County, New York; with papers and anecdotes relating to pioneers and events, comp. and pub. by Eleanor Louise Porter ...   Oxford, N.Y., The Oxford times print, 1914.   115 p., plates, groups of ports.   23½ cm.   "Descendants of early settlers": p. 77-91.
15-3046.
F129. B52 P 8

BRIGHTON.   Sesquicentennial history of the Town of Brighton, Monroe County, 1814 - 1964.   Planned and ed. by Helen Reynolds Williams, illus. Douglas Howland, history William S. Akin.   (Brighton? N.Y.) Sesqicentennial Committee (1964)   56 p.   23 cm.   64-23372.
F129. B53 W5

BROADALBIN in history; being a brief and concise narrative of the principal events in the settlement and development of Broadalbin Township from the earliest date to the present time.   By R. J. Honeywell.   Illus. by D. G. Fordes ...   Amsterdam, N.Y., Evening recorder job print, 1907.   24 p.   front., pl.   22 cm.   7-28164.
F129. B56 H 7

BRONXVILLE.   Polk's Bronxville and Tuckahoe directory ... including that part of Yonkers covered by Bronxville and Tackahoe post offices ... v. 1 -   1929/30   New York, N.Y., R. L. Polk, 1929 -   v.   24 cm.   CA 29-232 Unrev.
Directories

BRONXVILLE.   Pathway to a village; a history of Bronxville, by Victor Mays.   Illus. with drawings by the author and photos.   (2d ed.)   Bronxville, N.Y., Nebko Press (1962, c.1961)   xix, 153 p.   23 cm.
F129. B58 M3
1962

BRONXVILLE.   The Bronxville portfolio; a collection of pictorial photographs.   Photos. ... by James Owen.   Bronxville, N.Y., The Bronxville review, 1927 -   1 v.   plates.   35 x 26½ cm.
44-12050.
F129. B58 O 9

BROOKHAVEN town records ... 1662 -   Pub. by order of the Trustees of the freeholders and commonalty of the town ... Copied, annotated and compiled by Archibald C. Weeks.   New York, T. A. Wright, 1924 -   v.   2 facsim. (incl. front.)   24 cm.   25-11520.
F129. B6 B 6

BROOKHAVEN.   Records.   Town of Brookhaven up to 1800 ...   Patchogue, Office of the "Advance," 1880.   viii p., 2 l., 219 p.   8°.   1-14831-M1.
F129. B6 B 8

BROOKHAVEN.   Records of the town of Brookhaven, Suffolk County ... Copied from the original

NEW YORK

records, in their order, under the direction of the supervisor and justices of the peace, and pub. by the authority of the town. Patchogue (N.Y.) Printed at the office of the "Advance": (etc., etc.) 1880-93. 3 v. 23 cm. Contents. - v.1. 1655-1798. - v.2. 1798-1856. - v.3. 1856-1885. 1-14832 Rev. F129. B6 B 9

BROOKHAVEN. Records of the town of Brookhaven ... Pub. by order of the trustees of the freeholders and commonality of the town ... Transcription copy by William J. Weeks (and others) ... Compared and corrected with the original by Osborn Shaw. New York, The Derrydale press, 1930-32. 3 v. pl., maps (1 fold.) facsims. 24 cm. Contents. - book A. 1657-1679 (i.e. 1797) - book. B. 1679-1756. - Book c. 1687-1789. 34-29495. F129.B6 B 93

BROOKHAVEN. The diary of Captain Daniel Roe, an officer of the French and Indian war and of the revolution: Brookhaven, Long Island, during portion of 1806-7-8; with introduction and notes by Alfred Seelye Roe ... Worcester, The Blanchard press, 1904. (5) - 64 p. incl. illus., ports., facsims. front. 26 cm. 4-30123. F129.B6 R 6

BROOKLYN. The Brooklyn city directory. ... 18   Brooklyn, Brooklyn directory co., 18 -1912. v. fold. maps. 17½ - 27 cm. 1-15253 (rev. '29) Directories

BROOKLYN directory for the years 1838-39. Pub. by A. G. Stevens & Wm. H. Marschalk. Brooklyn, Arnold & Van Anden, printers, 1838. 147 p. 18½ cm. 9-14009. Directories

BROOKLYN. Polk's Brooklyn city directory ... 1933/34 - (New York) R. L. Polk, 1933 - v. 36 cm. CA 33-238 Unrev. Directories

BROOKLYN. Upington's elite directory of the borough of Brooklyn, city of New York ... 1877/78 - 1885/86, 1887 - Brooklyn, G. Upington (1877) - 19 v. fold. map. 18 - 20½ cm. 1-26514 (rev. '32) Directories

BROOKLYN. Blue book of Brooklyn. 19 Brooklyn, N.Y., Brooklyn blue book assoc. (19 v. illus. (ports.) 20 cm. 42-21466. Directories

BROOKLYN Heights blue book, 1940 - v. 1 - no. 1 - June 1940 - Brooklyn, N.Y., Brooklyn Heights blue book assoc. (1940 - v. 19½ cm. 40-14247. Directories

BROOKLYN. Branton's business directory (of Brooklyn) containing a list of the progressive business places, also commercial laws. Classified. New York, Branton directory co., 1912 - v. 24 cm. 12-21169. Directories

BROOKLYN. Lain & Healy's Brooklyn and Long Island business directory ... Brooklyn, Lain & Healy (etc.) 18 v. fold. maps. 24 cm. 30-17022. Directories

BROOKLYN. Polk's ... New York copartnership and corporation directory, boroughs of Brooklyn and Queens ... (1922 - v. 1 - (New York) R. L. Polk, 1922 - v. 23½ cm. 22-3194. Directories

BROOKLYN. Trow business directory of the boroughs of Brooklyn and Queens, city of New York ... also ... a Brooklyn street directory ... vol. I 1898 New York, Trow directory, printing & bookbinding co. (1898) - 19 v. fold. maps. 20 - 23½ cm. 99-1769 Rev. Directories

BROOKLYN. Whittier's business directory of the city of Brooklyn, incl. Brooklyn, Gowanus, Williamsburg and Greenpoint ... (1867) G. E. Whitten, 1867. 1 v. 15½ cm. Directories

BROOKLYN. Lain's Brooklyn street directory and buyer's guide ... (18 Brooklyn, Lain & Healy, 18 v. 15½ cm. 20-12174. Directories

BROOKLYN. Upington's Brooklyn street directory and buyers' guide ... 1904 - Brooklyn, N.Y., 19 v. 18 cm. Directories

BROOKLYN. The complete guide to Brooklyn ... New York city, "Geographia" map co. (1934 - v. fold. map. 16 cm. CA 34-286 Unrev. F129. B7 A 2

BROOKLYN.   Street directory of Brooklyn.   By E. T. Griffith ... New York, J. F. Oltrogge, printers, 1881.   54 p.   22½ cm.   F129. B7 A 2

BROOKLYN.   Lain & Healy's Brooklyn street directory and guide ... 18   -1900.   Brooklyn (etc.) Lain & Healy etc., 18 - 1900.   v.   13½ - 17½ cm.   99-3376 Rev.   F129. B7 A 2

BROOKLYN.   Street ward directory, borough of Brooklyn, compiled from records in the Department of taxes and assessments, ward maps in the Bureau of elections, and from the Department of highways. (New York, 1899)   52 numb. l.   28 cm.   99-1172 Rev. 2.   F129.B7 A 2

BROOKLYN.   Polk's official street directory, car line and information guide of New York city, borough of Brooklyn.   New York, Detroit (etc.) R. L. Polk (1922)   v.   15½ cm.   22-14135.   F129. B7 A 2

BROOKLYN.   ... Street number guide and complete transit directory of Brooklyn ... Chicago, New York, Rand, McNally (19   v.   fold. map.   16½ cm.   CA 25-968 Unrev.   F129. B7 A 2

BROOKLYN.   History of Brooklyn Jewry, by Samuel P. Abelow ... Brooklyn, N.Y., Scheba pub. co. (1937)   4, 344 p.   plates, ports., map.   24 cm.   37-10936.   F129.B7 A 32

BROOKLYN.   Souvenir of Brooklyn.   Descriptive, historical and statistical review.   (By Thomas J. Anderson)   New York, Anderson & Gillette, 1890.   129 (2) p.   front., illus. obl. 4°.   1-14833-M1.
F129. B7 A 5

BROOKLYN.   What's past is prologue, by Mrs. Reginald Angus.   With Reflections in the River Raisin, by Marian Palmer Greene.   Photos. from the Paul Totten collection.   (Brooklyn, Mich., Exponent Press, pref. 1962?)   223 p.   23 cm.   F129.B7 A 53

BROOKLYN'S Eastern district (by) Eugene L. Armbruster.   Brooklyn, N.Y., 1942.   5, 400 p.   illus. (incl. maps)   plates.   23½ cm.   42-17982.   F129.B7 A 68

BROOKLYN.   Bruijkleen Colonie (Borough of Brooklyn) 1638-1918, by Eugene L. Armbruster ... New York, 1918.   12 p.   illus. (map) 23 cm.   19-481.   F129. B7 A 7

BROOKLYN.   The Eastern district of Brooklyn; with illus. and maps, by Eugene L. Armbruster ... New York (Printed by G. Quattlander) 1912.   205 p.   illus., maps (2 fold.)   18 cm.   12-12937.
F129.B7 A 72

BROOKLYN.   The Olympia settlement in early Brooklyn, by Eugene L. Armbruster ... New York, 1929.   35 p.   27½ cm.   29-24169.   F129. B7 A 73

BROOKLYN.   An historical sketch of the city of Brooklyn, and the surrounding neighborhood, including the village of Williamsburgh, and the towns of Bushwick, Flatbush. Flatlands, New Utrecht, and Gravesend.   To which is added, an interesting account of the battle of Long Island.   Comp. from the best authorities.   By J. T. Bailey.   Brooklyn, The author, 1840.   iv, (5) - 72 p.   fold. map. 18 cm.   1-14834.
F129. B7 B 1

BROOKLYN.   The "Bayside review" souvenir album; Bath Beach, Bensonhurst and vicinity.   Brooklyn, New York ... (Brooklyn? 1905)   17 x 25½ cm.   F129.B7 B 28

BROOKLYN.   History of the corporation of the Reformed Dutch church of the town of Brooklyn. (Known as the First Reformed Dutch church) By Abraham J. Beekman.   Compiled from the original records.   (Brooklyn) Press of Brooklyn eagle, 1886.   20 p. incl. front.   21½ cm.   2-11290.
F129. B7 B 4

BROOKLYN.   Bits of old Brooklyn ... (Brooklyn, J. A. Davidson) 1881.   14 p.   24°.   1-14835-M1.
F129. B7 B 6

BROOKLYN.   Official Brooklyn guide book ... (ed. James Boyle)   Endorsed by Brooklyn chamber of commerce.   Brooklyn, N.Y. (Henin & co.) 1939.   96 p.   illus. (incl. port.)   20½ cm.   42-5168.
F129.B7 B 62

NEW YORK 319

BROOKLYN. The future of Brooklyn. The city's promised growth and increase, with comments on the building statistics for the year 1888. Message of the Hon. Alfred C. Chapin, mayor. (Brooklyn, 1888) 30 p. 22½ cm. 8-31262. F129.B7 B 63

BROOKLYN. (Brooklyn, N.Y., 1904) 24 x 28½ cm. F129.B7 B 65

(BROOKLYN) 19 v. in illus. (incl. ports.) 28 - 30½ cm. Weekly - May 1929; monthly, July 1929 - Official organ of the Brooklyn chamber of commerce. 44-10156. F129.B7 B652

BROOKLYN and Long island. (Whitestone, N.Y., etc., Chapman publications, 19 illus. 31½ cm. monthly. Ceased publication with v.21, no. 8, Mar. 1940? 43-44841. Library has: v.18, no. 10 - 12. May - July, 1937; v.19, no. 1, 3, 9-10, 12, Aug., Oct., 1937, Apr. - May, July, 1938; v. 20, no. 2, Sept. 1938. F129.B7 B653

BROOKLYN. The Brooklyn Catholic historical society records. no. 1 - April 1901 - (Brooklyn) The Brooklyn Catholic historical soc., 1901 - v. 23½ cm. 14-22884. F129.B7 B655

BROOKLYN. The Brooklyn daily eagle souvenir pictorial, 1841 - 1926. (Brooklyn, 1926) (12) p. incl. illus. (part col.) double map. 42 cm. F129.B7 B658

BROOKLYN. ... The Eagle and Brooklyn: the record of the progress of the Brooklyn daily eagle, issued in commemoration of its semi-centennial and occupancy of its new building; together with the history of the city of Brooklyn ... ed. by Henry W. B. Howard ... With nearly 1300 illus. (Proof ed. Brooklyn) The Brooklyn daily eagle, 1893. 2, (xvii) - xxxi, (33) - 1195 p. front., illus. (incl. ports.) 33½ cm. Includes biographical sketches. 1-14839 rev. F129.B7 B 66

BROOKLYN. ... The pictorial history of Brooklyn, issued by the Brooklyn daily eagle on its 75th anniversary ... Comp. and ed. by Martin H. Weyrauch ... (Brooklyn) The Brooklyn daily eagle, 1916. 96 p. illus. 36 cm. 20-22585 rev. F129.B7 B665

BROOKLYN. The Brooklyn city and Kings county record: a budget of general information; with a map of the city, an almanac, and an appendix, containing the new city charter. Compiled ... by William H. Smith. Brooklyn, W. H. Smith, 1855. 216, 71 p. front. (fold. map) 19½ cm. Map wanting in L.C. copy. 3-489. F129.B7 B 67

BROOKLYN. History of the First Reformed Protestant Dutch church of Breuckelen, now known as the First Reformed church of Brooklyn, 1654 to 1896. Comp. by order of the Consistory. (Brooklyn?) 1896. 93 p. front., illus., 7 pl., 3 port. 29½ cm. x 24 cm. 15-20701. F129.B7 B 68

BROOKLYN. From original negatives by The Albertype co. New York, A. Wittemann (1891) 14 pl. obl. 8º. 1-14836-M1. F129. B7 B 7

BROOKLYN Heights; yesterday, today, tomorrow ... 1937 - (Brooklyn) 1937 - v. front., illus. 23 cm. 39-21907. F129.B7 B715

BROOKLYN. Jubilee book of the Brooklyn Jewish center, pub. in commemoration of the 25th anniversary of its founding. Brooklyn, 1946. 96 p. illus. (incl. ports.) 24 cm. 46-18432. F129.B7 B717

BROOKLYN. Photographs in black. New York, The Albertype co. (1891) 39 pl. obl. 24º. 1-14837-M1. F129.B7 B 72

BROOKLYN. Old Brooklyn Heights, 1827 - 1927. Originally printed 1927 to commemorate the 100th anniversary of the founding of the Brooklyn savings bank. (Brooklyn) 1937. 2, 7-48 p. incl. col. front., illus., (part col..; incl. ports.) col. plates. 23 cm. 47-33432. F129.B7 B 75

BROOKLYN. Historic Brooklyn; a collection of the facts, legends, traditions and reminiscences that time has gathered about the historic homesteads and landmarks of Brooklyn. Issued in commemoration of the 75th anniversary of the Brooklyn trust co. Brooklyn, N.Y. (Boston, Mass., Printed by

Walton advertising & printing co.) 1941. vii, 59, (3) p. incl. front., illus. 23 ½ cm. 41-8230.

F129.B7 B 77

BROOKLYN. Rambles about historic Brooklyn; a collection of the facts, legends, traditions and reminiscences that time has gathered about the historic homesteads and landmarks of Brooklyn; illus. by reproductions of rare prints and old photos. Brooklyn, N.Y., Printed for the Brooklyn trust co., 1916. vii, 54 p. incl. front., illus. 23 ½ cm. "Authorities": p. vii. 16-23456. F129. B7 B 8

BROOKLYN. Yesterdays on Brooklyn Heights, by James H. Callender. New York, The Dorland press, 1927. 296 p. front., illus., plates, ports., facsim. 24 cm. 30-28430. F129.B7 C 15

BROOKLYN. The visitor's guide to Calvary cemetery, with map and illustrations. 1876 ... New York, J. J. Foster (1876) 80 p. front. (fold. map) plates. 23 ½ cm. 12-9129 rev. F129. B7 C 2

BROOKLYN. Atlas and directory to the plots and grounds of Calvary cemetery. By W. H. McDonough ... (Brooklyn, N.Y., 1886) 2 p., 14 double plans. 17 ½ cm. 23-3766.

F129. B7 C 6

BROOKLYN. The Citizen almanac; a compendium of statistics concerning Brooklyn, its people, its institutitons and its island neighbors. (Brooklyn) Brooklyn citizen. v. maps (part fold.) 23 cm. 58-54454. F129.B7 C 65

BROOKLYN. The city of Brooklyn. With map. New York, J. H. and C. M. Goodsell, 1871. v, (6) - 163 p. front. (fold. map) plates (partly fold.) 16 ½ cm. 11-13675. F129. B7 C 7

BROOKLYN. The Brooklyn compendium, compiled by the late John Dikeman, jr., showing the opening, closing, and alterations in the lines of the various streets, avenues, etc. in the city of Brooklyn ... from the year 1819 down, to the date of the close of the compilation ... Pub. by order of the Brooklyn common council. Brooklyn, Brooklyn daily times print, 1870. 322 p. 2 l. 23 cm. 1-14838.

F129. B7 D 5

BROOKLYN. Old Dutch houses of Brooklyn, by Maud Esther Dilliard. New York, R. R. Smith, 1945. 3, (vi) - viii, (119) p. incl. front., illus. (incl. maps) 24 ½ cm. 45-6223. F129. B7 D 53

BROOKLYN. Good old east New York; commemorating the 75th anniversary of the East New York savings bank, Brooklyn, N.Y. (Brooklyn, Printed by E. C. Lampe, inc.) 1943. (48) p. illus. (incl. ports. facsims.) 31 cm. "Sources": p. (4) of cover. 44-120. F129. B7 E 2

BROOKLYN. Ghetto crisis, riots or reconciliation? by Henry Etzkowitz and Gerald M. Schaflander. (1st ed.) Boston, Little, Brown (1969) x, 212 p. illus. 21 cm. 69-15062.

F129. B7 E 8

BROOKLYN. Historic and antiquarian scenes in Brooklyn and its vicinity, with illustrations of some of its antiquities, by T. W. Field. Brooklyn, 1868. iv, 96 p. plates (part col., 1 fold.) fold. map. 29 cm. 1-14840 Rev. F129. B7 F 4

BROOKLYN. St. Ann's church, (Brooklyn) from the year 1784 to the year 1845, with a memorial of the Sunday schools. To which is added, an appendix, containing a brief notice of the other Episcopal churches in Brooklyn. By a Sunday school teacher. (Francis G. Fish) Brooklyn, F. G. Fish, 1845. v, (3), (9) - 200 p. front., 1 illus. 19 cm. 1-659. F129. B7 F 5

BROOKLYN. Notes geographical and historical, relating to the town of Brooklyn, in Kings County on Long-Island. By Gabriel Furman ... Brooklyn, Printed by A. Spooner, 1824. 3, (5) - 116 p. 20 cm. 7 views and a portrait of Washington are inserted in this copy. 1-14841. F129. B7 F 9
Rare Book Coll.

— Brooklyn, Reprinted for the Faust club, 1865. xxxiv, 116 p., xxxix p. 27 ½ cm x 20 cm. The only publication of the Faust club. 1-14842. F129.B7 F 91

BROOKLYN. Glimpses of Brooklyn ... New York, Mercantile illustrating co., 1894. 23 pl. 8°. 1-14843-M1. F129. B7 G 5

NEW YORK

BROOKLYN. Rambling reflections in Greenwood (cemetery), with a description of the same, in 1853. By Campeador (pseud.) New York, Printed by G. W. Wood, 1853.   60 p.   18 cm.   52-52857.
F129.B7 G72

BROOKLYN. Green-wood (cemetery): a directory for visitors.   By N. Cleaveland ... New York, 1850.   vii, (3) - 271 p. incl. plates.   front., fold. plan.   17 cm.   11-19264.
F129.B7 G 75

BROOKLYN. Green-wood (cemetery) illustrated. In highly finished line engraving, from drawings taken on the spot, by James Smillie. With descriptive notices, by Nehemiah Cleaveland. New York, R. Martin, 1847.   4, 93 p.   front. (map)   20 pl.   27 x 21 cm.   (The rural cemeteries of America. Greenwood)   11-30521.
F129.B7 G756

BROOKLYN. Mount Auburn (cemetery) illustrated. In highly finished line engraving, from drawings taken on the spot, by James Smillie. With descriptive notices, by Cornelia W. Walter. New York, R. Martin, 1847.   3, (5) - 119 p.   front. (map)   19 pl.   37 x 28½ cm.   (The rural cemeteries of America. Mount Auburn)   With above title.   25-18628.
F129.B7 G756

BROOKLYN. Hints concerning Green-wood; its monuments and improvements. By N. Cleaveland. New York, Pudney & Russell, printers, 1853.   44 p.   21½ cm.   12-9126.
F129.B7 G 76

BROOKLYN. Rules and regulations of the Green-wood cemetery; with a catalogue of proprietors. And Mr. Cleaveland's descriptive notices of "Green-wood illustrated ... " New York (Printed by Pudney & Russell) 1848.   29, 64 p.   23 cm.   12-9127.
F129.B7 G 79
1848

— New York, 1851.   31, 64, 46 p.   23 cm.   12-9128.
F129.B7 G 79
1851

— New York, printed for the cemetery, 1853.   46 p.   67 p.   23 cm.
F129.B7 G 79
1853

BROOKLYN. Greenwood cemetery. ... Supplemental catalogue of proprietors, to May 12, 1873. Brooklyn, Eagle print, 1873.   112 p.   23 cm.   17-22200.
F129.B7 G795

BROOKLYN. ... Guide ... Greenwod (cemetery) as it is. (By Louisa Richardson) (New York, F. Richardson & co., 1901)   176 p.   illus.   14½ cm.   1-25838.
F129.B7 G 83

BROOKLYN. Souvenir. Greenwood cemetery. (New York, Wittemann bros., 1882)   1 pl. fold. in 18.   48º.   1-14844-M1.
F129.B7 G 85

BROOKLYN. Old days and old ways in East New York, an historical narrative. By Frederick J. Heidenreich. (Brooklyn? 1948)   79 p.   illus., port.   24 cm.   49-1366*.
F129.B7 H 45

BROOKLYN. Elevated railroad and rapid transit guide of Brooklyn (N.Y.) ... by George A. Humbert. (Brooklyn, Advance-record print, 1890)   61 p.   24º.   1-14845-M1.
F129.B7 H 9

BROOKLYN. Historical markers and monuments in Brooklyn, a list. By Edna Huntington. Brooklyn, Long Island Historical Soc., 1952.   56 p.   23 cm.   52-66012.
F129.B7 H 93

BROOKLYN. Excursion planned for the City history club of New York by Frank Bergen Kelley ... No. 8 - Historic Brooklyn - Part I (New York) 1905.   19½ cm.
F129.B7 K 3

BROOKLYN. King's views of Brooklyn ... 300 views.   1904 ...   (New York, M. King, 1904)   72 p. of illus.   38cm.   8-14525.
F129.B7 K 5

BROOKLYN. Williamsburg: a Jewish community in transition; a study of the factors and patterns of change in the organization and structure of a community in transition. New York, F. Feldheim (1961)   310 p.   24 cm.   The author's thesis, first issued on microfilm in 1954 ...
F129.B7 K 7
1961

BROOKLYN. Brownsville; the birth, development and passing of a Jewish community in New York (by) Alter F. Landesman. New York, Bloch Pub. Co. (1969)   x, 418 p.   24 cm.   68-57434.
F129.B7 L 3

— 2d ed. with a foreword by Louis Finkelstein. New York, Bloch Pub. Co. (1971)   xiv, 418 p. 24 cm.   72-15029.
F129. B7 L 3

BROOKLYN. By Robert F. Leighton. Philadelphia, J. B. Lippincott co., 1888.   6 p.   12º.   Appears as article "Brooklyn" in Chamber's encyclopedia.   1-14846-M1.
F129. B7 L 5

BROOKLYN. The Citizens guide to Brooklyn and Long Island. The city's resources and residences, the island's retreats and resorts ... Brooklyn (Printed by The Jersey City printing co.) 1893.
4, 320 p.   illus. (incl. maps)   18½ cm.   Published anonymously.   3-18825.
F129. B7 L 7

BROOKLYN. The wealthy men and women of Brooklyn and Williamsburgh; embracing a complete list of all whose estimated possessions (in real and personal property) amount to the sum of ten thousand dollars and upwards; tog. with brief biographical sketches of many meritorious and eminent persons. By John Lomas and Alfred S. Peace. Brooklyn, Printed for the proprietors by A. S. Peace, 1847.
48 p.   15½ cm.   11-4729.
F129. B7 L 8

BROOKLYN. Historical and descriptive sketch of the Church of the pilgrims, Brooklyn, N.Y. ... By (Henry H. McFarland) Brooklyn, H. M. Gardner, jr., printer, 1871.   19 p.   pl., plan.   8º.   "Reprinted from the Congregational quarterly, Jan. 1871."   1-16302-M1.
F129. B7 M2

BROOKLYN. Looking through life's window; personal reminiscences, by Henry A. Meyer. New York, Coward-McCann, inc., 1930.   7, 3-236 p.   front., plat;es, ports., maps., facsim.   22½ cm.   The author tells of his part in various real estate developments in Brooklyn and on the shore of Jamaica bay.   31-209.
F129.B7 M61

BROOKLYN, the home borough of New York city; its family life, educational advantages, civic virtues, physical attractions and varied industries, prepared by the Municipal club of Brooklyn. (Brooklyn, 1912)   128 p.   illus.   25½ cm.   12-23452.
F129. B7 M9

BROOKLYN. A treasury of Brooklyn; ed. by Mary Ellen and Mark Murphy, and Ralph Foster Weld. New York, W. Sloane Associates (1949)   xi, 435 p.   22 cm.   "1st printing 1949"   49-9553*.
F129.B7 M93
1949

BROOKLYN. The New "red book" information and trolley guide to Brooklyn borough, New York city ... Newark, N.J., New York (etc.) Interstate map co., 19   v.   fold. map.   15½ cm.   22-15671.
F129. B7 N 5

BROOKLYN. ... Bedford Corners, Brooklyn ... Albany, The University of the state of New York, 1917.   6 p.   pl., ports., 2 maps.   23 cm.   "Repr. from the annual report of the State historian.   19-10886 rev. 2.   F129.B7 N 55

BROOKLYN. A history of the city of Brooklyn and Kings County, by Stephen M. Ostrander ... Ed. with introd. and notes, by Alexander Black ... Brooklyn, Pub. by subscription, 1894.   2 v.   front., plates, 2 plans, 2 facsim. (1 fold.) chart.   23½ cm.   Pub. in part ... in the Brooklyn "Eagle" 1870-80.   1-14847.   F129. B7 O 8

BROOKLYN. Zlota ksiega Zjednoczenia Polsko Narodowego. Polish National Alliance of Brooklyn. New York, 1953 (i.e. 1954)   336 p.   illus.   29 cm.   55-43359.
F129. B 7 P 6

BROOKLYN. ... Origin of Breuckelen, by Harrington Putnam. New York, London (etc.) G. P. Putnam's son, 1898.   387-405 p.   illus. (incl. maps) 20½ cm.   (Half moon series ... v.2, no.11) 98-1641 Rev.   F129. B 7 P 9

BROOKLYN, U.S.A.; text (by) John Richmond, layout and design (by) Abril Lamarque. New York, Creative age press, inc. (1946)   2, 138, (2) p.   illus. (incl. ports.)   28 x 22 cm.   46-7553.
F129. B 7 R 5

BROOKLYN. Reflections on a teapot; the personal history of a time (by) Ronald Sanders. (1st ed.) New York, Harper & Row (1972)   xi, 385 p.   22 cm.   78-181643.
F129.B7 S 25
1972

BROOKLYN. Services and addresses at the unveiling of the statue of Abraham Lincoln, Brooklyn, N.Y. Pub. by the War fund committee. Brooklyn (H. M. Gardner, jr., printer) 1869. 32 p. 23½ cm.
12-18990.   F129. B7 S 4

BROOKLYN. Jan: a tale of the early history of Brooklyn. By A. L. O. B. (Miss E. W. Simonson) Brooklyn, N.Y., Orphans' press, 1883.   153 p.   18 cm.   2-10410.   F129. B7 S 6

BROOKLYN. ... Tombstone inscriptions in the burial ground of the old Bushwick church, (Brooklyn, N.Y.) copied ... by George Sparrow. (From Kings County genealogical club collections. v.1, no. iv (1888) p. 45-52)
7-23565.   F129.B7 S 73

BROOKLYN. The civil, political, professional and ecclesiastical hist. ... By H. R. Stiles. (1884)
1 v.   F129.B7 S 78

BROOKLYN. A history of the city of Brooklyn. Including the old town and village of Brooklyn, the town of Bushwick, and the village and city of Williamsburgh. By Henry R. Stiles ... Brooklyn, N.Y., Pub. by subscription, 1867-70.   3 v. fronts., illus., plates, ports., plans (partly fold.) 24½ cm. 7-23810.
                                                                                                                                           F129.B7 S 79

— Albany, J. Munsell; ... 1869-70.   3 v. fronts., illus., plates, ports., maps (partly fold.) 25½ cm. Edition of 80 copies printed on thick tinted paper.   1-14848.   F129. B7 S 8

BROOKLYN. An account of the dinner by the Hamilton club to Hon. James S. T. Stranahan ... Brooklyn, N.Y. (Eagle press) 1889.   84 p. front. (port.) 23 cm.   14-22120.   F129. B7 S 83

BROOKLYN. In memoriam. Mrs. Mariamne Fitch Stranahan. By Rev. Samuel T. Spear ... New York, Print. C. A. Alvord, 1867.   vi, (7) - 112 p. incl. front. (port.) 21½ cm. 15-2712.   F129.B7 S 85

BROOKLYN. A thrilling personal experience! Brooklyn's horror. Wholesale holocaust at the Brooklyn, New York, theatre, on the night of Dec. 5th, 1876 ... Philadelphia, Barclay & co. (1876)
19 - 62 p. incl. 5 pl. (2 port. on 1 pl.) 25 cm. 7-38312.   F129. B7 T 5

BROOKLYN. ... Names of persons, enrolled as liable to military duty (under the act of Congress, approved March 3, 1863) in the Third congressional district, New York. Eleventh ward. (New York? 1863)   143 p. 22 cm. 13-24912.   F129. B7 U 5

BROOKLYN. Views of Brooklyn. (Portland, Me., L. H. Nelson co., 1905)   (48) p. illus. 20½ x 25 cm.
CA 17-131 Unrev.   F129. B7 V 6

BROOKLYN. Vrouw Knickerbocker; the romance of the building of Brooklyn, by Maude Stewart Welch. Philadelphia, Dorrance and co. (1926)   271 p. front. 21 cm. 26-22545.   F129. B7 W4

BROOKLYN is America. By Ralph Foster Weld. New York, Columbia University Press, 1950.
viii, 266 p. illus. 23 cm. Bibliography: p. (249) - 254. 50-8082.   F129.B7 W42
                                                                                                                                1950

BROOKLYN village, 1816 - 1834, by Ralph Foster Weld. New York, Columbia university press, 1938.
xviii p., 2 l., (3) - 362 p. front. (port.) pl. map. 23½ cm. (New York state historical association series ... no. vii) Bibliography: p.333-346. 39-1231.   F129.B7 W43

— xviii, (3) - 362 p., etc. Thesis (PH.D.) Columbia university, 1938. 39-9019.   F129.B7 W44

— New York, AMS Press (1970)   xviii, 362 p. 24 cm. 78-112945.   F129.B7 W44
                                                                                                                             1970

BROOKLYN. Our Brooklyn, by Ralph Foster Weld ... Brooklyn, N.Y., The Brooklyn institute of arts and sciences, 1940.   vi, 42 p. illus. (incl. maps) 19 cm. "Bibliography for teachers": p.42. 40-32947. F129.B7 W46

BROOKLYN. Building up greater Brooklyn, with sketches of men instrumental in Brooklyn's amazing development, by Leon Wexelstein ... Brooklyn, N.Y., Brooklyn biographical soc. (1925)
2, iii-xxii p., 244 p. front., ports. 23½ cm. 26-8477.   F129. B7 W5

BROOKLYN. The pageant of Brooklyn, by Martin H. Weyrauch. (n.p.) 1915. (4) p. 33 x 26 cm.
15-9574. F129.B7 W54

BROOKLYN. Pamphlets, broadsides, clippings, and other miscellaneous matter on this subject, not separately cataloged, are classified in F129. B7 Z 5

BRUNSWICK. Records of the Gilead Evangelical Lutheran church at Center Brunswick, in the town of Brunswick, Rensselaer County. Transcribed by the N.Y. genealogical and biographical soc. Ed. by Royden Woodward Vosburgh ... New York, 1913. 2 v. 36 cm. Autographed from typewritten copy.
Paged continuously. 13-22935. F129.B74 B 9

BUFFALO. The Buffalo directory, 1832, 18   Buffalo, 1832 - 1916. 5 v. fold. maps.
17 - 24 cm. 9-14006 (rev. '17)
Directories

BUFFALO. Polk's Buffalo city directory ... including Kenmore ... 18   Buffalo, N.Y. Polk-Clement directory co., inc., 18   -19   v. fold. maps. 17 - 24 cm. The issue for 1876 includes a reprint of the first directory of Buffalo. "Buffalo's first directory (was pub. in 1828) The second did not appears until 1832. No Buffalo directories were issued in the years 1829, 30, 31, 33, 34, 43, 45 or 46." Historical papers are prefixed to several issues, as follows: 1862, A sketch of the early history of Buffalo, by G. W. Clinton in 1847; A glance at its progress down to the present time, by S. B. Hunt. - 1863, Buffalo, past and present, by G. H. Salisbury. - 1864. The physiognomy of Buffalo ... by G. W. Hosmer; The history of our lake commerce, by E. P. Dorr. - 1865, The old ferry at Black Rock, by C. D. Norton; A sketch of the life and character of the late Henry Daw, by H. W. Rogers. - 1866. Buffalo: its manufacuring, commercial and business position, by G. H. Salisbury; A sketch relative to the early residents of Buffalo. - 1867. Sewerage and sanitary science, by O. G. Steele; History of grain elevators, by J. Dart; Early history of Grant Island and the city of Ararat, by L. F. Allen. Title varies: 1828, A directory for the village of Buffalo.
Directories

BUFFALO. The Buffalo address book and family directory ... (1901) Buffalo, N.Y., Stoddard and Seward (1901)   vii - xxiv, 643 p. front., illus., port. 18 cm. 1-27289 Rev.   Directories

BUFFALO. The Buffalo elite directory; or, Ladies' visiting list ... also lists of clubs and societies. Compiled by Sidney G. Sherwood and John W. Bosche. Buffalo, Baker, Jones, 1883. 2, (9) - 81 p.
17 cm. CA 33-579 Unrev.   Directories

BUFFALO. The Buffalo standard society directory and ladies' visiting guide ... also, a list of the members of the principal clubs and societies, including the residents of Grand Island, Lancaster and Tonawanda. Compiled by S. G. Sherwood (and) Geo. Forrester. Buffalo, Ulbrich & Kingsley, 1880.
2, (9) - 88 p. 17 cm. CA 33-580 Unrev.   Directories

BUFFALO. Dau's blue book, Buffalo ... 1900, 1909, 1910, 1914. New York city, Dau pub. co.,
1900 - 1914. 4 v. 18 x 21½ cm. 0-1243 (rev. '14)   Directories

BUFFALO. Social register, Buffalo ... v.   New York city, Social register association, 19
v. 17½ cm. 2-26497.   Directories

BUFFALO. ... The Buffalo courier classified directory ... of business concerns, institutions and professional people of Buffalo and vicinity ... Cleveland, O., P. Goering & co.,   v. 27 cm.
Directories

BUFFALO. The Buffalo business directory, 1900 -   Buffalo, The Courier co., 1900 -
v. 24 cm.   Directories

BUFFALO. Niagara area pioneers established 1776 to 1882. Buffalo Chamber of commerce.
(Buffalo? 1931)   3-31 p. 23½ cm. Lists of firms, etc. established 1882 or before.   32-5810.
Directories

BUFFALO. Official arrow street guide of Buffalo and suburbs ... (Buffalo) The Polk-Clement directory co., inc., 19   v. fold. map. 17 cm. CA 31-183 unrev.   F129. B8 A 2

BUFFALO. Pilkey's street and street railway service guide, Buffalo, N.Y. 18   Buffalo, C. J. Pilkey, 18   v. 13 cm. 1-14863 Rev.   F129. B8 A 2

BUFFALO. Street guide of Buffalo. M. Endres (1896-97) 2 v. 11½ cm.
F129. B8 A 2

BUFFALO. From Ararat to Suburbia, the history of the Jewish community of Buffalo, by Selig Adler and Thomas E. Connolly. (1st ed.) Philadelphia, Jewish Publication Soc. of America, 1960-5721. 498 p. 24 cm. (The Jacob R. Schiff library of Jewish contributions to American democracy no. 12) 60-15834.
F129.B8 A 38

BUFFALO. All about the Pan-American city and vicinity ... Buffalo, N.Y., The Baldwin pub. co., 1901. 111 p. illus. 17 cm. 1-21791.
F129.B8 A 4

BUFFALO. Modern antiquities: comprising sketches of early Buffalo and the Great Lakes, also sketches of Alaska, by Barton Atkins. Buffalo, N.Y., The Courier co., printers, 1898. 190 p. incl. front., illus. 17½ cm. 98-556 Rev.
F129. B8 A 8

BUFFALO, 1893, a descriptive and statistical sketch of the city of Buffalo and its suburbs, by George M. Bailey ... (Buffalo) Rowland & co., 1893. 2-104 p. illus. 19½ cm. 1-14849 Rev.
F129.B8 B 18

BUFFALO. Illustrated Buffalo: the queen city of the lakes. Its past, present and future ... Historical description by George M. Bailey ... New York, Acme pub. and engr. co., 1890. xi, 33-234 p. illus. 27 x 21½ cm. 1-14850 Rev.
F129. B8 B 2

BUFFALO. Buffalo's text book; adopted by the Department of education for use in the public schools of Buffalo. Ed. by John F. Barry and Robert W. Elmes. 1st ed. Buffalo, N.Y., R. W. Elmes, 1924. 223 p. incl. illus., ports., maps. 23 cm. E 25-210.
F129. B8 B27

BUFFALO. Buffalo's text book; authorized by the Council of the city of Buffalo and adopted by the Department of education for use in the public schools ... 2d impression. Buffalo, N.Y., R. W. Elmes, 1927. 4, (11) - 223 p. illus. 23 cm. 27-14511.
F129.B8 B 27
1927

— reissued, R. W. Elmes, 1929. 4, (11) - 223 p. illus. (incl. ports., maps) 23 cm. 33-16491.
F129.B8 B 27

BUFFALO. Beautiful Buffalo; a New year's greeting. Compliments of the Buffalo express (Buffalo? 1910) (36) p. illus. 12½ x 20½ cm.
F129.B8 B 38

BUFFALO. Statistics relating to the government of the city of Buffalo and early history of Buffalo Creek, compiled and pub. under the direction of Philip Becker ... Buffalo, E. W. Beach, printer (1896) 50 p. 23½ x 40½ cm. 4-4917.
F129.B8 B 39

BUFFALO. Sketches of early Buffalo and the Niagara region. By Sophie C. Becker ... Buffalo, N.Y., 1904. 2, 9-168 p. front. (port.) 19½ cm. Bibliography: 1 l. following p. 168. 5-1159.
F129. B8 B 4

BUFFALO. Anatomy of a riot; Buffalo '67, by Frank P. Besag. (Buffalo, University Press, 1967) 210 p. 22 cm.
F129.B8 B 45

— Rev. ed. Buffalo, University Press (1970) 225 p. 22 cm.
F129.B8 B 45
1970

BUFFALO. ... The projected park and parkways on the south side of Buffalo. Two reports by the landscape architects. 1888. (Buffalo) Printed by order of the Commission, 1888. 49 p. front. (fold. map) illus. 23 cm. 4-7252.
F129.B8 B 48

BUFFALO. Historic sites within the Queen city & A century of progress, by Robert W. Bingham. (Buffalo) Buffalo historical society, 1932. 27 p. 18½ x 9½ cm. In commemoration of the centennial of the incorporation of the city of Buffalo. CA 33-285 Unrev.
F129.B8 B 56

BUFFALO. The city of Buffalo and its surroundings; its business facilities and its advantages as a

place of residence and summer resort ... Buffalo, W. Thurstone, 1880. 24 p. 23 cm. 6-1147.
F129. B8 B 6

BUFFALO. Greater Buffalo & Niagara frontier, Niagara Falls, the Tonawandas, Lockport and Depew, commercial and industrial ... (Buffalo) Pub. under the supervision of the Publicity committee, Buffalo chamber of commerce, 1914. 76 p. incl. front., illus. 26½ cm. 14-9397.
F129. B8 B64

BUFFALO, America's gateway to and from the great north west, 1920 -   year book of industrial, commercial, financial, educational, civic Buffalo. Buffalo, N.Y., J. W. Clement co. (1920 -
v. illus., fold. map. 23½ cm. 21-2838.
F129.B8 B 67

BUFFALO city views. (n. p., 1875?) 11 pl. 17½ x 13½ cm. 4-25023.
F129.B8 B 68

BUFFALO old and new; supplement Buffalo courier. no. 1-18; Nov. 11, 1900 - July 14, 1901. (Buffalo, N.Y., 1900-01) 144 p. illus. (incl. ports.) 31 x 45 cm. No more pub. 5-10317.
F129.B8 B 69

BUFFALO. A history of the city of Buffalo, its men and institutions; biographical sketches of leading citizens ... Buffalo, The Buffalo evening news, 1908. 252 p. incl. front., illus. (incl. ports.) pl. 31 x 25 cm. 44-21378.
F129. B8 B 7

BUFFALO express album of the year past. A new year's greeting ... Buffalo, The Buffalo express, 18   v. illus. (incl. ports.) 16 x 24½ cm. 18-12892.
F129. B8 B71

BUFFALO. ... The city of Buffalo: its history and institutions, with illustrated sketches of its industries and commerce and some of tis citizens ... Buffalo, N.Y., Matthews, Northrup, 1888.
60 p. incl. front., illus. (incl. ports., maps, plans) 62½ cm. 1-23460 Rev.
F129.B8 B 72

BUFFALO. ... Forest Lawn (cemetery): its history, dedications, progress, regulations, names of lot holders, etc. Buffalo, Thomas, Howard & Johnson, 1867. iv, (9) - 170 p. 22½ cm. 18-8939.
F129. B8 B75

BUFFALO. Constitution and by-laws of the Buffalo historical society ... Buffalo, Franklin steam print., 1863. 7 p. 22½ cm. 18-7650.
F129.B8 B 79

BUFFALO. Certificate of incorporation and constitution and by-laws of the Buffalo historical society ... Buffalo, Thomas, Howard & Johnson, 1868. 19 p. 22½ cm. 2-23958.
F129.B8 B 79
1868

— Buffalo, Courier co., printers, 1875. 31 p. 22½ cm. 2-23959.
F129.B8 B 79
1875

— (Buffalo) 1935. 7 p. 22½ cm. 37-18061.
F129.B8 B 79
1935

BUFFALO. Address of the president and report of the director submitted at the annual meeting. 9th -   Buffalo Historical society. 1871 -   (Buffalo) v. in 24 cm. 52-35577.
F129. B8 B84

BUFFALO Historical Society. Museum notes. v. 1 -   Apr./May 1930 -   (Buffalo)
v. in   illus., ports. 23 cm. irregular. Publication suspended May 1937 - June 1945. 53-24467.
F129.B8 B 87

BUFFALO historical society. Publications. v. 1 -   Buffalo, N.Y., The Buffalo hist. soc., 1879
- 19   v. fronts., illus., plates, ports., maps, facsims. 23-24½ cm. 12-31045.
F129. B8 B88

— Niagara frontier. v. 1 - winter 1953 -   (Buffalo) Buffalo hist. soc.   v. in illus., ports., maps, facsims. 26 cm. quarterly. 58-47557.

— Inaugural address of the Hon. Millard Fillmore. 1862. In v. 1 p. 1-15. 14-10648.

— The origin of the name of Buffalo. By William Ketchum. v. 1, p.17-42. 14-21250.

1060

NEW YORK

— Buffalo cemeteries. By William Hodge. v. 1 p. 49-75. 3-7913. Reprinted the same year with additions and corrections.
— The old Black Rock ferry. By Charles D. Norton. v.1, p. 91-112. 14-10649.
— Annual address by the Rev. John C. Lord. v.1, p. 113-129. 14-10650.
— Buffalo in 1825. By Sheldon Ball. v. 1, p. 139-152. 14-10651.
— Early reminiscences of Buffalo and vicinity. By James L. Barton. v. 1, p. 153-178. 14-10652.
— The village of Buffalo during the war of 1812. By William Dorsheimer. v.1, p. 185-209. 14-10653.
— Major Norris' journal of Sullivan's expedition. v.1, p.217-252. 14-10654.
— The building and voyage of the Griffon in 1679. By Orsamus H. Marshall. v.1, p.253-288. 14-10655.
— A history of the Israelites in Buffalo. By Sampson Falk. v.1, p. 289-304. 14-10656.
— Founding of the city of Ararat on Grant Island - by Mordecai M. Noah. By Hon. Lewis F. Allen. v.1, p. 305-328. 14-10657.
— Orlando Allen. Glimpses of life in the village of Buffalo. By William C. Bryant. v.1, p. 329-371. 12-10658.
— The life and public services of Oliver Forward. By Hon. James Sheldon. v.1, p.373-390. 14-10659.
— The grain elevators of Buffalo. By Joseph Dart. v.1, p.391-404. 14-10660.
— The Buffalo common schools. By O. G. Steele. v.1, p. 405-436. 14-10661.
— Physiognomy of Buffalo. By Rev. George W. Hosmer. v.2, p. 1-16. 14-10662.
— New York state early transportation. By Col. William A. Bird. v.2, p. 17-32. 14-10663.
— Extracts from the Vanderkemp papers. From the Hudson to Lake Ontario in 1792. v.2, p. 33-116. 14-10664 Rev.
— An historical essay. The Germans of Buffalo. By Ismar S. Ellison. v.2, p. 117-144. 14-10665.
— Oliver Gray Steele. By Rev. George W. Hosmer. v.2, p. 145-156. 14-10666.
— The Inland lock navigation co. First report of the directors and engineer. v.2, p. 157-180. 14-10667.
— Reminiscences of Joseph Ellicott. By Ellicott Evans. v.2, p. 181-198. 14-10668.
— Early history of the press of Erie County. By Guy H. Salisbury. v.2, p. 199-217. 14-10669.
— The portrait of Red Jacket ... By O. G. Steele. v.2, p. 219-226. 22-13955.
— Origin of the Erie canal. By Merwin S. Hawley. v.2, p.227-261. 14-10670.
— The Erie canal. Origin and history of the measures that led to its construction. By George Geddes. v.2, p. 263 - 304. 14-10671.
— The Erie canal. Its origin, its resources and its necessity. By Merwin S. Hawley. v.2, p. 305-334. 14-10672.
— The Erie canal ... By Merwin S. Hawley. v.2, p. 335-349. 14-10673 Rev.
— Fifty years ago. By Hon. James Sheldon. v.2, p. 357-374. 14-10674.
— The early history of Hon. Millard Fillmore. Written by himself. v.2, p. 375-387. 14-10675.
— The Niagara frontier. By Orsamus H. Marshall. v.2, p. 395-429. 14-10676.
— ... Red Jacket. By order of the Society 1885. 117 p. v.3. 2-25014.
— Reminiscences of the boundary survey between the U. S. and British provinces. By William A. Bird. v.4, p. 1-14. 14-10677.
— Captain Brant and the Old King. The tragedy of Wyoming. By William C. Bryant. v.4, p. 15-34. 14-10678.
— The adventures and enterprises of Elijah D. Efner. An autobiographical memoir. v.4, p. 35-54. 14-10679.
— Buffalo's first mayor, Dr. Ebenezer Johnson. By F. M. Inglehart. v.4, p. 55-69. 14-10680.
— ... Samuel Wilkeson. By Rev. John C. Lord. v.4, p. 71-91. 14-10681.
— The early firm of Juba Storrs & co. By the Rev. Albert Bigelow. v.4, p. 93-124. 14-10682.
— The journeys and journals of an early Buffalo merchant (John Lay) By Frank H. Severance. v.4, p. 125-145. 14-10683.
— The National Free soil convention of '48. By John Hubbell. v.4, p. 147-162. 14-10684.

— Development of constitutional law in New York state and the Constitutional convention of 1894. By Hon. Henry Wayland Hill ... v.4, p. 163-201. 14-10685.
— An address commemorative of George W. Clinton. By David F. Day. v.4, p. 203-225. 14-10686.
— A forgotten people: the flint workers. By the Very Rev. William R. Harris ... v.4, p. 227-244. 14-10804.
— First appearance, in 1832, of the cholera in Buffalo. By Lewis F. Allen. v.4, p. 245-256. 14-10766.
— Roswell Willson Haskins. By Laurentius F. Sellstedt. v.4, p. 357-284. 14-10767.
— Nathan Kelsey Hall. By Hon, James O. Putnam. v.4, p. 285-298. 14-10768.
— The postal service of the U.S. in connection with the local history of Buffalo. v.4, p.299-316. 14-10769.
— The speculative craze of '36. By Guy H. Salisbury. v.4, p.317-337. 14-10770.
— Random notes on the authors of Buffalo. By France K. Severance. v.4, p.339-379. 14-21248.
— Public speeches ... by Hon, Erastus Granger ... and Red Jacket ... respecting the part the Six nations would take in the present war against Great Britain. v.4, p. 385-414. 14-10771. Facsimile reprint.
— The achievements of Captain John Montresor on the Niagara ... By Frank H. Severance. v.5, p. 1-19. 14-10772.
— Papers relating to the war of 1812 on the Niagara frontier. (By Frank H. Severance) v.5, p. 21-109. 14-10773.
— A Niagara Falls tourist of the year 1817. Being the journal of Capt. Richard Langslow ... v.5, p. 111-133. 14-10774.
— Historical writings of Judge Samuel Wilkeson. v.5, p. 135-214. 14-10778.
— Early trade routes. Adventures and recollections of a pioneer trader, with an account of his share in the building of Buffalo harbor. By Capt. James Sloan. v.5, p. 215-237. 14-10775.
— History of Buffalo harbor ... by Major Thomas W. Symons ... and John C. Quintus ... v.5, p. 239-285. 14-10776.
— Early days on the Lakes, with an account of the cholera visitation of 1832. From manuscript records of Capt. Augustus Walker. v.5, p. 287-318. 14-10777.
— How Niagara was made free. By the Hon. Thomas V. Welch. v.5, p. 325-359. 14-10779.
— An historical sketch of the Buffalo library ... By J.N. Larned. v.5, p.361-376. 14-10780.
— The Buffalo free library movement in the year 1897. By Henry L. Elmendorf. v.5, p.377-384. 14-10781.
— The new home of the historical soc. in Delaware park. v.5, p. 385-404. 14-10782.
— The Niagara frontier landmarks association. v.5, p. 409-425. 14-10783.
— Contributions towards a bibliography of the Niagara region. The Upper Canada rebellion of 1837-38. (69) p. v.5, p. 427-495. 3-19205.
— From Lake Erie to Morocco. The diplomatic controversy occasioned by the visit of a vessel from the Great Lakes ... to Mediterranean ports in 1859. By George V. Brown ... v.6, p. 1-14. 14-21249.
— ... Navy Island and the first successors to the Griffon. (By Henry Raymond Howland) v.6, p. 17-33. 14-21244.
— ... The Niagara portage and its first attempted settlement under British rule. (By Henry Raymond Howland) v.6, p. 35-45. 14-10784.
— ... A British privateer in the American revolution. (By Henry Raymond Howland) v.6, p.47-71. 14-21245.
— ... Robert Hamilton, the founder of Queenston. (By Henry Raymond Howland) v.6, p. 73-95. 14-10785.
— ... Old Caneadea council house and its last council fire. (By Henry Raymond Howland) v.6, p. 97-123. 14-10786.
— ... The Seneca mission at Buffalo Creek. (By Henry Raymond Howland) v.6, p. 125-161. 14-10787.
— Narratives of early mission work on the Niagara frontier and Buffalo Creek. (By Frank Hayward Severance) v.6, p. 163-380. 14-10788.
— The life of Horatio Jones. By George H. Harris. v.6, p. 381-526. 14-10789.
— The story of Captain Jasper Parrish, captive, interpreter ... v.6, p. 527-538. 14-10790.
— Personal recollections of Captains Jones and Parrish and of the payment of Indian annuities in Buffalo. By Hon. Orlando Allen. v.6, p. 539-546. 14-10791.

NEW YORK

— ... Contributions towards a bibliography of the Niagara region. Pamphlets and books printed in Buffalo prior to 1850. (By Frank H. Severance) (58) p. v. 6, p. 547-605. 4-8759.

— A bundle of Thomas Jefferson's letters, now first pub. Ed. by Frank H. Severance. v. 7, p. 1-32. 14-10792.

— Journals of Henry A. S. Dearborn. v. 7, p. 33-225. 14-21247.

— The life of Judge Augustus Porter, by Charles Mulford Robinson. v. 7, p. 229-276. 14-10793.

— Narrative of early years in the life of Judge Augustus Porter. v. 7, p. 277-330. 14-10794.

— Judah Colt's narrative ... v. 7, p. 331-359. 14-10795.

— Journal of a survey of the south shore of Lake Erie, made in 1789. v. 7, p. 364-376. 14-21246.

— The life and adventures of Matthew Bunn. v. 7, p. 377-436. 14-10796.

— The story of David Ramsay ... v. 7, p. 437-451. 14-10797.

— Life and public services of John Jay. By George A. Stringer. v. 7, p. 465-479. 14-10798.

— The relations of the U. S. to the Canadian rebellion of 1837-38. By Orrin E. Tiffany. v. 8, p. 1-147. Bibliography: p. 115-118. 14-10799.

— History of the abolition of railroad grade crossings in the city of Buffalo. v. 8, p. 149-254. 14-10800.

— The Dobbins papers. (By William W. Dobbins) v. 8, p. 255-379. 14-10801.

— Life of Stephen Champlin ... by Hon. George W. Clinton. v. 8, p. 381-399. 14-10802.

— Narrative of Col. Samuel Blakeslee ... v. 8, p. 419-438. 14-10803.

— Social life in earlier Buffalo, by Martha Fitch Poole. v. 8, p. 439-493. 14-11432.

— Writings of General Parker. v. 8, p. 520-536. 14-11433 rev.

— The Johnson's Island plot ... By Frederick J. Shepard. v. 9, p. 1-51. 14-11434.

— Millard Fillmore and his part in the opening of Japan ... by Wm. Elliot Griffis ... v. 9, p. 53-79. 14-11435.

— The story of Joncaire ... by Frank H. Severance ... v. 9, p. 81-219. 14-11436.

— The tale of captives at Fort Niagara, by Frank H. Severance. v. 9, p. 221-307. 14-11437.

— Papers relating to the burning of Buffalo ... v. 9, p. 309-406. 14-11438.

— "The Charles Lamb of Buffalo." Memoir of Guy H. Salisbury ... By David Gray. v. 9, p. 407-429. 14-11439.

— Memoir of Stephen Louis Le Couteulx de Caumont, by Martha J. F. Murray. v. 9, p. 431-483. 14-11440.

— ... Millard Fillmore papers ... Ed. by Frank H. Severance ... 2 v. vol. x - xi. Bibliography; some publications by Millard Fillmore ... v. 2, p. 455-463. 8-10420.

— A narrative of the singular sufferings of John Fillmore and others, on board the noted pirate vessel commanded by Captain Phillips ... v. 10, p. 27-39. 8-10421.

— An examination of the question, 'Is it right to require any religious test as a qualification to be a witness in a court of justice?' (By Millard Fillmore) v. 10, p. 69-82. 8-10900.

— Mr. Fillmore's views relating to slavery ... v. 10, p. 311-324. 8-10898.

— An historical review of waterways and canal construction in New York state, by Henry Wayland Hill ... xiv, 3-549 p. v. 12. 9-13607.

— Canal enlargement in New York state. xvii, 446 p. v. 13. 10-2880.

— The Holland land co., and canal construction, in western New York; Buffalo-Black Rock harbor papers, journals and documents. Buffalo, N. Y., The Buffalo hist. soc., 1910. xiv, 496 p. front., illus. v. 14. 10-23257.

— The Erie canal and the settlement of the West, by Lois Kimball Mathews ... v. 14, p. 187-203. 10-23152 Rev.

— Studies of the Niagara frontier, by Frank H. Severance. 3, 437 p. v. 15. 12-12859.

— The picture book of earlier Buffalo ... By Frank H. Severance. xx, 508 p. v. 16. "... relates, mostly, to the town ... during the decades from 1820 to 1870." 13-15944.

— William Pryor Letchworth. By J. N. Larned. v. 17, p. 1-36. 14-11441.

— Lars Gustav Sellstedt. By Henry Ware Sprague. v. 17, p. 37-74. 14-11442.

— The semi-centennial of the Buffalo hist. soc. v. 17, p. 75-126. 14-11443.

— Early recollections of Buffalo. By Mrs. Julia F. Snow. v. 17, p. 127-164. 14-11444.

— Some early Buffalo characters. By Frank M. Hollister. v. 17, p. 165-190. 14-11445 Rev.

— Memories of early days in Buffalo. By Sylvester J. Mathews. v. 17, p. 191-226. 14-11446.

— The case of Benjamin Rathbun ... v. 17, p. 227-270. 14-11447.

330   LOCAL HISTORIES IN THE LIBRARY OF CONGRESS

— Documents relating to the war of 1812; the letter-book of Gen. Sir Rogers Hale Sheaffe. v. 17, p. 271-381. 14-11448.

— Peace episodes on the Niagara.   x, 382 p. v. 18.   15-10348.

— The Peace conference at Niagara Falls in 1914. (By Frank H. Severance)   v. 18, p. 1-75. 15-10349.

— The Peace conference at Niagara Falls in 1864. (By Frank H. Severance)   v. 18, p. 77-94.   15-10350.

— The consecration of Niagara to peace. (By Frank H. Severance)   v. 18, p. 95-112. 15-10351.

— The peace mission to Niagara of Ephraim Douglass in 1783. (By Frank H. Severance) v. 18, p. 113-142.   15-10352.

— The peace centenary on the Great Lakes and the Niagara frontier. (By Frank H. Severance)   v. 18, p. 143-166.   15-10353.

— The Quaker mission among the Indians of New York state. (By Joseph Elkinton) v. 18, p. 167-189.   15-10354.

— Notes on the literature of the war of 1812. (By Frank H. Severance)   v. 18, p. 191-212. 15-10355.

— The case of Brig. Gen. Alexander Smyth ...   v. 18, p. 213-255.   15-10356.

— "Le pour et le contre," ... (By Jean Louis Bridel)   v. 18, p. 357-321.   15-10357.

— Josephus N. Larned, by Hon. John B. Olmsted.   v. 19, p. 133-136.   16-16818.

— Selected papers and addresses, by J. N. Larned.   v. 19, p. 35-132.   16-16816.

— Henry A. Richmond; a tribute, by Henry R. Howland.   v. 19, p. 137-151.   16-16817.

— The periodical press of Buffalo; a few reminiscences ...   v. 19, p. 153-175.   16-16814.

— Contributions towards a bibliography of Buffalo and the Niagara region. By Frank H. Severance.   v. 19, p. 177-312.   16-16815.

— An old frontier of France; the Niagara region and adjacent lakes under French control, by Frank H. Severance.   2 v.   v. 20-21.   18-17860.

— A history of the University of Buffalo, 1846-1917, by Julian Park ...   v. 22, p. 1-87.   18-15011.

— Roswell Park: a memoir, by Charles G. Stockton.   v. 22, p. 89-123.   18-15010.

— Ernest Wende: a memoir, by Adelbert Moot.   v. 22, p. 124-144.   18-15009.

— The Women's educational and industrial union of Buffalo; comp. by Mrs. Frederick J. Shepard.   v. 22, p. 147-200.   18-14603.

— Historical sketch of Niagara ship canal projects, by Hon. Henry W. Hill. v. 22, p. 201-266.   18-15004.

— Participation of the Buffalo hist. soc. in the Erie canal centenary ...   v. 22, p. 267-295.   18-15008.

— Frank M. Hollister, by Charles P. Norton.   v. 22, p. 297-310.   18-15007.

— Our neighbors the Tuscaroras, by Frank H. Severance.   v. 22, p 311-331.   18-15006.

— Where is Buffalo? (The determination of its latitude and longitude in 1861) v. 22, p. 333-342.   18-15005.

— The life of General Ely S. Parker ... by Arthur Caswell Parker.   vii-xiv. 346 p. 19-17502 rev.

— The history of the Buffalo Creek reservation, by Frederick Houghton.   v. 24, p. 1-181. 21-11741.

— Gen. Brown's inspection tour up the lakes in 1819. (By Roger Jones)   v. 24, p. 295-323. 27-25111.

— Service of Capt. Samuel D. Harris ...   v. 24, p. 327-342.   21-11740.

— The story of Phinney's Western almanack ... by Frank H. Severance. v. 24, p. 343-358.   21-11739.

— William F. Sheehan. (By John Woodward)   v. 24, p. 359-369.   21-11738.

— ... The book of the museum, ed. by Frank H. Severance ...   412 p.   v. 25.   22-12431.

— A Ku Klux uniform, by Elizabeth M. Howe.   v. 25, p. 9-41.   Bibliography: p. 39-41.   22-12430.

— Carrier's addresses. (By Frank H. Severance)   v. 25, p. 84-112.   22-12429.

— The story of the tablet of the city of Ararat, by Hon. Lewis F. Allen.   v. 25, p. 113-144. 22-12428.

— Historic figure-heads. (By Frank H. Severance)   v. 25, p. 191-200.   23-14435.

— The Red Jacket relics. (By Frank H. Severance)   v. 25, p. 233-242.   22-12427.

— The Fenian raid of '66. (By Frank H. Severance)   v. 25, p. 263-285.   22-12426.

1064

NEW YORK 331

— ... Recalling pioneer days, ed. by Frank H. Severance ...   ix, 473 p.   v.26.   23-13532.
— Andrew and Joseph Ellicott ... By Dr. G. Hunter Bartlett.   v.26, p.3-48.   23-13738.
— Extracts from Jos. Ellicott's letter books and early correspondence.   v.26, p.49-166.   23-13736.
— The William Hodge papers ...   v.26, p.167-314.   23-13533.
— The changing town. (By Frank H. Severance)   v.26, p.412-422.   23-13737.
— Seneca myths and folk tales, by Arthur C. Parker ...   xxviii, 465 p.   v.27.   24-17122.
— The Holland land company, by Paul Demund Evans ...   xiv, (3)-469 p.   v.28.   26-9257.
— The war of 1812 on the Niagara frontier, by Louis L. Babcock.   (3)-385 p.   v.29.   27-27567.
— War losses on the Niagara frontier. (By Frank H. Severance)   v.29, p.249-319.   28-9130.
— The Peter A. Porter collection. (By Frank H. Severance)   v.29, p.321-330.   28-9131.
— The changing town (pictures of old Buffalo) (By Frank H. Severance)   v.29, p.33--366.   28-9129.
— Dedication of the historical building as enlarged, 1929 ...   v.30, p.25-292.   30-28453.
— The cradle of the Queen city, a history of Buffalo to the incorporation of the city, by Robert W. Bingham.   8, 41, 43-504 p.   vol. xxxi.   32-19207.
— ... Reports of Joseph Ellicott as chief of survey ... Ed. Robert W. Bingham ,.. 2 v.   v.32 ½ 33.   38-23729 rev.
— Niagara frontier miscellany; ed. by Robert W. Bingham.   177 p.   v.34.   48-2100*
— Millard Fillmore; biography of a President.   xiv, 470 p.   v.40.   58-14009.

BUFFALO.   1832 - 1882.   Semi-centennial celebration of the city of Buffalo. ... (Buffalo, Press of E. H. Hutchinson) 1882.   59 p.   front., pl., port.   24 ½ cm.   2-23957.   F129.B8 B 89

BUFFALO.   Seventy-fifth anniversary of the founding of the Buffalo historical soc.   Buffalo, N.Y., Printed for the members, 1937.   45 p. incl. mounted front., illus., mounted ports.   pl.   23 ½ cm.   37-15581.
F129.B8 B893

BUFFALO.   Buffalo historical soc.   Miscellaneous printed matter published by this body is classified in   F129.B8 B895

BUFFALO.   Addresses of Henry Wayland Hill ... in accepting ... the Lincoln statue ... in presenting ... a gold key to Hon. Andrew Langdon ... (Buffalo, Press Union and times, 1903)   11 p.   23 ½ cm.   18-4301.   F129. B8 B 9

BUFFALO illustrated.   Commerce, trade and industries of Buffalo.   Buffalo, Anderson & Gillette, 1890.   188 p.   front., illus.   28 x 35 ½ cm.   1-15963.   F129. B8 B91

BUFFALO.   "Where rail and water meet."   Achievement number of the Buffalo times, July 23 ...1911.   (20) p.   illus.   37 cm.   12-11528.   F129.B8 B 95

BUFFALO's amusement guide and Pan-American bulletin...   Buffalo, N.Y., 1901 - 1 v.   no. 1.   8°.   F129.B8 B 96

BUFFALO.   Queen of the lakes, Buffalo, the electric city of the future.   Souvenir of the tenth convention of the National assoc. of builders.   (Buffalo, The Courier co., printers, 1896)   205 p. incl. front., plates.   17 ½ cm.   5-33692.   F129.B8 B 97

BUFFALO.   The city of Buffalo, comprising its commercial and financial resources.   A souvenir of the Buffalo evening news.   (By Edward Hubert Butler) (Buffalo, The C. L. Sherrill co., 1887)   122 p.   illus., map.   obl. fol.   1-14851 Rev.   F129.B8 B 98

BUFFALO.   ... A study of acculturization in the Polish group of Buffalo, 1926 - 1928, by Niles Carpenter ...   (Buffalo, 1929)   p. (103) - 133.   23 cm.   (Buffalo. University. Monographs in sociology: mo. 3)   University of Buffalo studies.   vol. vii, no.4.   29-22532.   F129.B8 C 29

BUFFALO.   The city of Buffalo and its surroundings.   Its business facilities and its advantages as a place of residence and summer resort ... Buffalo, W. Thurstone, 1880.   48 p.   8°.   1-14852-M1.
F129. B8 C 5

BUFFALO.   Half century discourse.   The first church in Buffalo.   Delivered ... 1862.   By Walter

1065

Clarke. Buffalo, T. Butler, 1862. vii, (11) - 92 p. 23 cm. 3-7947. F129. B8 C 6

BUFFALO. ... Commerce, manufactures & resources of Buffalo and environs. A descriptive, historical and statistical review ... (Buffalo) Commercial publishing co. (1880) 2. 141, (3), 153-196 p. incl. illus., map. 25½ cm. 1-14853. F129. B8 C 7

BUFFALO. A directory for the city of Buffalo; containing the names and residence of the heads of families, householders, and other inhabitants ... 1837. Buffalo, Pub. by S. Crary, printed by C. Faxon, 1837. 143 p. 17 cm. 55-54865. F129. B8 D 5
Rare Book Coll.

BUFFALO. It happened here; a presentation of people and events that made history on the Niagara frontier. (Buffalo, N.Y., Erie County Savings Bank, 1969) 80 p. illus. 23 cm.
F129. B8 E 7

BUFFALO. Memorial of the city and county hall opening ceremonies. Ed. and pub. by F. F. Fargo. Buffalo, N.Y., The Courier co,, printers, 1876. 156 p. fold. front., illus. (plans) plates. 23 cm. 1-14854 Rev.
F129. B8 F 2

BUFFALO. ... The index guide to Buffalo and Niagara Falls, arranged alphabetically, by Frederik Atherton Fernald ... with map and illus. ... Buffalo, N.Y., F. A. Fernald, 1910. 224 p. illus., fold. map. 20 cm. 10-12419. F129. B8 F 3

BUFFALO. The life and public services of Oliver Forward ... By Hon. James Sheldon. Buffalo, Press of Warren, Johnson, 1875. 8 p. 22½ cm. 6-19813. F129. B8 F 7

BUFFALO. When Buffalo was young; some incidents of local history retold for your people, with drawings and maps, by Myrtilla Constantine Fosdick. Buffalo, N.Y., Otto Ulbrich co. (1925) 3, 9-118, (2) p. illus. (incl. maps) 18½ cm. Bibliography: p. (119) 27-3959. F129.B8 F 74

BUFFALO. Geschichte der Deutschen in Buffalo und Erie County, mit Biographien und Illustrationen hervorragender Deutsch-Amerikaner, welche zur Entwickelung der Stadt Buffalo beigetragen haben. Buffalo, Reinecke & Zesch, 1898 (1897) 337, 121 p. illus., ports., maps. 25 x 32 cm. The historical section is in German and English; the biographical, in German only. 52-51409. F129. B8 G 4

BUFFALO, your city, by Alice Ennis Glazier and Edwin F. Rundell. Pen and ink illus. by Victor Aures. Buffalo, Foster & Stewart Pub. Corp. (1947) vii, 255 p. illus., map. 23 cm. Includes bibliographies. 48-2052*. F129.B8 G 55

BUFFALO. Greater Buffalo; a monthly journal of twentieth century Americanism ... v. 1 - 3. Buffalo, The Greater Buffalo pub. co., 1897 - 1900. 3 v. in 7. illus. (incl. maps) ports., plan. 28½ cm. 7-18600. F129. B8 G 7

BUFFALO. Pioneers of Buffalo; its growth and development, by Stephen Gredel. Buffalo, Commission on Human Relations (1966) 48 p. 26 cm. 66-25385. F129.B8 G 74

BUFFALO. The industries of Buffalo. A résumé of the mercantile and manufacturing progress of the queen city of the lakes ... Buffalo, N.Y., The Elstner pub. co., 1887. 276 p. illus. 8°. 1-14855-M1.
F129. B8 H 3

BUFFALO, her present, her future. By Wesley G. Hartwell. Buffalo, N.Y., W. G. Hartwell, 1889. 3 l. 24°. 2-6554. F129.B8 H 34

BUFFALO. Buffalo fifty years ago. A paper read before the Buffalo historical soc ... by Lucy Williams Hawes. Buffalo, The Courier co., printers, 1886. 10 p. 23½ cm. 1-14856.
F129. B8 H 5

BUFFALO. The Buffalo hist. soc. building. (Dedicatory ode, by Henry W. Hill ... (Buffalo, 1929) (3) p. 19 cm. 30-1670. F129.B8 H 53

NEW YORK

BUFFALO. Municipality of Buffalo, New York; a history, 1720 - 1923; editor-in-chief, Henry Wayland Hill ... New York and Chicago, Lewis historical pub. co., 1923.   4 v. fronts., plates, ports., maps, facsim. 27½ cm.   Vols. iii-iv contain biographical material. "Principal authorities": v. 1, p. (xi) - xiii.   24-31496.
F129.B8 H 54

BUFFALO. Buffalo greets the South with a synopsis of her history.   By Richmond C. Hill.   Buffalo, (1895?)   23 cm.
F129.B8 H 56

BUFFALO. ... Twentieth century Buffalo; an illus. compendium of her municipal financial, industrial, commercial, and general public interests.   Prepared by Richmond C, Hill.   Buffalo ... J. N. Matthews co., 1902.   iv, 160, viii, 248 p. incl. front., illus. ports., maps. 27 cm.   6-1858.
F129.B8 H 57

BUFFALO. Buffalo cemeteries; an account of the burial-places of Buffalo ...   By William Hodge. Buffalo ... Bigelow bros.   iv, 24 p. 22½ cm.   Reprinted, with additions and corrections, from v. 1 of the Publications of the Buffalo historical soc.   3-7914.
F129. B8 H 6

BUFFALO. A memoir of the late William Hodge, sen., ... By his son, William Hodge ... Buffalo, Bigelow bros., 1885.   vii, 160 p. 2 port. (incl. front.) 23 cm.   6-868.
F129.B8 H 65

BUFFALO. Horner's Buffalo and Niagara Falls guide and encyclopedia of useful knowledge.   Buffalo, W. T. Horner, 1874.   127 p. illus. 16º.   1-14857-M1.
F129. B8 H 8

BUFFALO. The physiognomy of Buffalo: the annual address delivered before the Buffalo historical soc.   By George W. Hosmer.   (Buffalo? 1864?)   9 p.   23 cm.   2-14725.
F129.B8 H 83

BUFFALO. Hotel Iroquois. (New York, Exhibit pub. co., 1890)   (70) p.   illus.   8º.   1-16018-M1.
F129.B8 H 85

BUFFALO. A little journey to Buffalo, by Elbert Hubbard.   East Aurora, N.Y., The Roycrofters, 1914.   16 p. 20½ cm.
F129.B8 H 88

BUFFALO. Edward Howard Hutchinson; eighty years of activity. (By Charles Edwin Knowles) Buffalo 1932?)   8, 181 p.   front. (port.) plates. 23½ cm.   Consists for the most part of newspaper articles   S 33-240.
F129.B8 H 93
Rare Book Coll.

BUFFALO. ... Ins and outs of Buffalo, the queen city of the Lakes; a thoroughly authentic and profusely illustrated guide ... Buffalo, A. B. Floyd, 1899.   3, (11) - 199 p. illus. (incl. port.) 2 fold. plans. 17½ x 14 cm.   1-31320 Rev.
F129. B6 I 6

BUFFALO. Miniatures of Buffalo. (By Thomas Wallace Jones) (Cincinnati, O., 1904) 8 x 10½ cm.
F129. B8 J 7

BUFFALO. An authentic and comprehensive history of Buffalo, with some account of its early inhabitants, both savage and civilized ...   By William Ketchum ... Buffalo, N.Y., Rockwell, Baker & Hill, printers, 1864-65.   2 v.   2 fold. plans. 23 cm.   1-14859.
F129. B8 K 4

— St. Clair Shores, Mich., Scholarly Press, 1970.   71-108500.
F129.B8 K 42

BUFFALO ... (By John P. Lamberton) Philadelphia, J. B. Lippincott co., 1888.   6 p. 12º. Appears as article "Buffalo" in Chambers's encyclopedia. 1-14860-M1.
F129. B8 L 2

BUFFALO. A history of Buffalo, delineating the evolution of the city, by J. N. Larned; with sketches of the city of Rochester by the Hon. Charles E. Fitch and the city of Utica by the Hon. Ellis H. Roberts ... New York, The Progress of the Empire state co., 1911.   2 v. fronts., plates, ports. 28 cm. 11-26983.
F129. B8 L 3

BUFFALO. The dead of the present war, a funeral discourse ... By Rev. John C. Lord. Buffalo, M. Taylor, 1862.   40 p. 21½ cm. 4-28331.
F129. B8 L 8

BUFFALO. "The valiant man." A discourse on the death of the Hon. Samuel Wilkeson, of Buffalo. By John C. Lord ... Buffalo, Steam press of Jewett, Thomas, 1848. 46 p. 23½ cm. 14-5930.
F129.B8 L 83

BUFFALO. The past and future of Buffalo. A paper read before the American bankers' assoc ... by Henry Martin ... Buffalo, The Courier co., printers, 1881. 11 p. 22½ cm. 5-36559.
F129. B8 M3

BUFFALO. Men of Buffalo; a collection of portraits of men who deserve to rank as typical representatives of the best citizenship, foremost activities and highest aspirations of the city of Buffalo. Chicago, A. N. Marquis, 1902. (5)-416 p. incl. ports. 22½ cm. "Portraits": p. (15)-416. 2-16759.
F129. B8 M4

BUFFALO, the city of the Pan-American exposition. Chicago, General passenger dept., Michigan central, 1901. 32 p. illus. 15 cm. 2-12068.
F129. B8 M6

BUFFALO. Buffalo to-day, industrial and commercial; the 36th annual National conference of charities and correction ... (Buffalo and New York, The Matthews-Northrup works, 1909) 61 p. incl. front., illus. 21½ x 17½ cm. 21-2814 rev.
F129.B8 N 27

BUFFALO. Great citizens of Buffalo, the individuals to whom the University of Buffalo has awarded the Chancellor's medal ... Buffalo, The University of Buffalo, 1944. 69 p. 23½ cm. 45-2772.
F129. B8 N 4

BUFFALO. A concise view of Black Rock, including a map and schedule of property, belonging to the Niagara city association ... Black Rock (Buffalo, Steele's press) 1836. 92 p. map. 16½ cm. Map wanting. 8-15363.
F129. B8 N 5

BUFFALO. Journal in jail, kept during a four month's imprisonment for libel, in the jail of Erie county. By Thomas L. Nichols. Buffalo, A. Dinsmore, 1840. 248 p. 19½ cm. Containing an account of the author's connection with the Buffalonian and his defense of Benjamin Rathbun. 13-5290 Rev.
F129. B8 N 6
Rare Book Coll.

— (New York) Arno (1970) 247 p. 23 cm. (The American journalists) 71-125709.
F129. B8 N 6
1970

BUFFALO. The old ferry at the Black Rock. By Charles D. Norton. (Buffalo? 1863?) (9)-19 p. 23½ cm. Pub. in v.1 of the Publications of the Buffalo hist. soc. 4-25033 Rev.
F129. B8 N 8

BUFFALO. The old settlers' festival held in Buffalo ... 1867 ... Buffalo, Express printing co. (186-) 20 p. 8°. 1-14861-M1.
F129. B8 O 4

BUFFALO. Palmer's view of Buffalo ... By Robert M. Palmer. (New York?) 1911. 18½ x 27 cm.
F129.B8 P 17

BUFFALO. Paul's dictionary of Buffalo, Niagara falls, Tonawanda and vicinity ... a descriptive index and guide to the various institutions, public buildings, societies, amusements, resorts, etc., in and about the city of Buffalo. Buffalo, The Peter Paul book co. (1896) 2, 256 p. front. (fold. map) illus., plates (1 double) 18½ x 13½ cm. 1-14862.
F129. B 8 P 3

BUFFALO. Pictorial history of the Superior court of Buffalo; its records and traditions - its judges from the beginning - reminiscences ... (Buffalo, Art-printing works of Mathews-Northrup, 1886) 2, (7)-13 p. incl. front., illus., ports. 30½ x 24 cm. "Repr. from the Buffalo Sunday morning express, Jan. 31" 7-13445. F129. B 8 P 5

BUFFALO. The city of Buffalo ... (By Frank Spencer Presbrey) (New York, Forum pub. co., 1895) (32) p. illus. 23 cm. Reprinted from the Forum of March, 1895, for the Buffalo merchants' exchange. 2-19334 Rev. F129. B 8 P 9

BUFFALO. Program. Independence day. (Buffalo ...) 1915. 21 p. 23½ cm.
F129.B8 P 96

BUFFALO. The new wonder of the world. Buffalo, the electric city. Buffalo, N. Y., The Matthews-

NEW YORK

Northrup co. (1892)　　40 p.　illus.　8º.　　　　　　　　　　　　　　　　F129. B8 R 5

BUFFALO.　Buffalo & Niagara frontier from the air.　Buffalo, N.Y., Ronne & Washburn, 1924.
23 p. incl. front., illus.　21½ x 25½ cm.　24-23640.　　　　　　　　　　　F129. B8 R 7

BUFFALO.　The city of Buffalo and its charitable and correctional institutions, 1888.　(Buffalo, N.Y., Matthews, Northrup, 1888)　　2, 9-45 p.　front., illus., fold. map.　16 x 14 cm.　1-14865.
　　　　　　　　　　　　　　　　　　　　　　　　　　　　　　　　　　　F129. B8 R 8

BUFFALO.　Buffalo, your city.　By Edwin F. Rundell.　Pen and ink illus. by Victor Aures.　(3d. ed., completely rev. and rewritten by the author)　Buffalo, H. Stewart (1955)　　343 p.　illus.　23 cm.　Includes bibliographies.　55-42154.　　　　　　　　　　　　　　　　　　F129.B8 R 84
　　　　　　　　　　　　　　　　　　　　　　　　　　　　　　　　　　　1955

BUFFALO.　Souvenir of Buffalo.　(Portland, Me., S. H. Nelson co. (1913)　　(32) p.　illus.　20 x 25 cm.
　　　　　　　　　　　　　　　　　　　　　　　　　　　　　　　　　　　F129. B 8 S 7

BUFFALO.　An inkling of Buffalo, illus. by Charles W. Sumner.　Buffalo (1886)　　(49) p. (p.3 - 37 illus.)
map.　18 x 14 cm.　1-14858 rev.*　　　　　　　　　　　　　　　　　　　　F129. B 8 S 8

BUFFALO.　History of Buffalo and Erie County, 1914-1919, comp. by Daniel J. Sweeny ...　pub. ... under authority of the city of Buffalo.　(Buffalo, 1920)　　2, 3-5, 11-733 p.　front., illus., ports., maps.　28 cm.
20-5913.　　　　　　　　　　　　　　　　　　　　　　　　　　　　　　　F129.B8 S 97

BUFFALO.　A sketch of the commerce, industries and resources of Buffalo, by William Thurstone ...
Buffalo, Buffalo merchants' exchange, 1883.　　24 p.　23 cm.　6-1702.　　　F129.B8 T 48

BUFFALO.　Some things in and about Buffalo; a souvenir of the annual convention of the American society of civil engineers held at Buffalo ... 1884.　By William Thurstone.　(Buffalo, People's press, 1884)　　33 l.　14 pl.　19 x 24 cm.　1-14866-M1.　　　　　　　　　　　　　F129. B8 T 5

BUFFALO.　Sheldon K. Viele, a biographical sketch, together with a small portfolio of his drawings, compiled and annotated by Henry C. F. Stewart and James F. Foster.　(Buffalo) Airport publishers, inc., 1935.　　(32) p. incl. illus., plates.　31½ cm.　35-8570.　　　　　　　　F129.B8 V 54

BUFFALO.　Views of Buffalo ... (40th thousand.　Buffalo, N.Y., S. H. Knox, 1909)　　(48) p.　illus.
20 x 25 cm.　CA 17-141 Unrev.　　　　　　　　　　　　　　　　　　　　　F129.B8 V 58

— (Portland, Me., L. H. Nelson, 1910)　　20 x 25 cm.　　　　　　　　　　　F129. B8 V 6

— (1911)　　20 x 25 cm.　　　　　　　　　　　　　　　　　　　　　　　　F129.B8 V 61

BUFFALO.　Home history.　Recollections of Buffalo during the decade from 1830 to 1840, or fifty years since.　Descriptive and illustrative, with incidents and anecdotes.　By Samuel M. Welch.
Buffalo, P. Paul, 1891 (1890)　　viii p., 2 l., 423 p.　front., illus., plates, ports., plan.　23½ cm.　1-14867 Rev.
　　　　　　　　　　　　　　　　　　　　　　　　　　　　　　　　　　　F129. B8 W4

BUSHWICK.　Early settlers of Bushwick, Long Island, New York, and their descendants.　By Andrew Jackson Provost.　(Darien? Conn.) 1952. - 60.　　3 v.　28 cm.　Vol. 3, rev. 1960, includes indexes to v.1-3.　Vols. 1-2, typescript (carbon copy)　55-21608.　　　　　　　　　　　　　　　　　　　F129. B9 P 7

BUSHWICK.　A history of the town of Bushwick and of the town, village and city of Williamsburgh, by John M. Stearns.　Reprinted from "The illustrated history of Kings county," ed. by Dr. H. R. Stiles ... Brooklyn, N.Y., 1884.　　37 p.　illus., fol.　1-14868-M1.　　　　　　　　F129. B 9 S 7

BUTTERNUTS.　Quaker records from Duanesburgh, later called Butternuts.　Births, 1778 to 1861.
Deaths, 1809 to 1869.　(By Mrs. Josephine C. Frost) (Brooklyn, 191 -)　　24 l.　28½ cm.
Autographed from type-written copy.　12-29738 Rev.　　　　　　　　　　　F129.B97 F 9

CAMBRIDGE.　Proceedings of the centennial anniversary of the old town of Cambridge.　Comp. by

Smart & Noble. Cambridge, N.Y., Washington County post, 1874. 111 p. 21½ cm. 20-9606.
F129.C16C14

CAMBRIDGE. Records of the First united Presbyterian congregation in Cambridge in the village of Cambridge. Transcribed by the New York genealogical and biographical society. Ed. by Roden Woodward Vosburgh. New York city, 1917. 2, vii, 141 numb. l. 36 x 28 cm. Autographed from type-written copy. 17-12297.
F129.C16C15
L H & G

— Records of the Congregational church of Sandgate in the town of Sandgate ... Vermont.
2 p., 35 numb. l. 36 x 28 cm. (With above item) 17-12298. F129.C16C15

CAMBRIDGE. Records of the Protestant Presbyterian congregation of Cambridge in the village of Cambridge. Transcribed by the New York genealogical and biographical soc. Ed. by Royden W. Vosburgh. New York city, 1916. 2 p., vi, 105 numb. l. incl. 2 facsim. 36 x 28 cm. Autographed from type-written copy. 16-7854.
F129.C16C16

CAMDEN. Pioneer history of Camden ... (By Mrs. Elizabeth T. Pike) Utica, N.Y., Press of T. J. Griffiths, 1897. 559 p. front., illus. (incl. ports.) plates. 24 cm. 1-14869. F129.C17 P 6

CAMDEN. "Grip's" historical souvenir of Camden. (By Edgar L. Welch) (Camden? N.Y., 1902) (3) - 149 p. front. (map) illus. 27 cm. 2-20487. F129.C17 W4

CAMILLUS. Among the hills of Camillus; the story of a small town. By Mary Ellis Maxwell. (Syracuse? N.Y., 1952) 137 p. illus. 30 cm. 52-66461. F129.C18 M3

CANAAN. Records of the Congregational church and society of New Canaan at Canaan Four Corners in the town of Canaan, Columbia County. Transcribed by the N.Y. genealogical and biographical soc.; ed. by Royden W. Vosburgh. New York, 1919. 2 p., iii, 136 numb. l. 2 facsim. 36 x 28½ cm. Autographed from type-written copy. 19-17761.
F129. C19 C2

CANANDAIGUA. Boyd's directory of Canandaigua and Geneva, with farmers' and business men's names in Ontario County ... 1890/91. Syracuse, N.Y., Central city pub. house, 1890.
1 v. 24 cm. 11-4059. Directories

CANANDAIGUA city directory ... 1911. Canandaigua, N.Y., J. C. Smith, 1911
1 v. 23 cm. 11-13014. Directories

... CANANDAIGUA directory ... 19   Binghamton, N.Y., The Calkin-Kelly directory co., 19
v. 24½ cm. CA 30-1092 Unrev. Directories

CARDIFF. The American goliah, a wonderful geological discovery. A petrified giant, ten and one-half feet high, discovered in Onondaga County, N.Y. ... Syracuse, N.Y., Printed at the Journal office, 1869. 15 p. 22 cm. 9-14750.
F129. C2 A5
Rare Book Coll.

CANANDAIGUA. Diary of Caroline Cowles Richard, 1852 - 1872, Canandaigua ... (Rochester? 1908) 85 p. front., illus. 20 cm. A later ed., 1913 pub. under title: Village life in America ... 9-2760. F129. C2 C6

CANANDAIGUA. Village life in America, 1852 - 1872, including the period of the American Civil War, as told in the diary of a schoolgirl. By Caroline Cowles (Richards) Clarke. With an introd. by Margaret E. Sangster. London, T. F. Unwin, 1912. 207 p. plates, ports. 20 cm. See above itme. W12-66*.
F129.C2 C62

— New and enl. ed. New York, H. Holt, 1913. xv, 225 p. front., plates, ports. 20 cm. 13-17134.
F129.C2 C63

CANANDAIGUA. The history of Canandaigua. An address delivered at the centennial celebration, July 4, 1876. By J. Albert Granger. Canandaigua, N.Y., Ontario repository and messenger, 1876.
16 p. 8°. 1-14870-M1. F129. C2 G7

NEW YORK

CANANDAIGUA. A history of early Canandaigua, by J. Albert Granger. Read before the Ontario County hist. soc. (Canandaigua, N.Y., Journal print., 1905?) 25 p. 21 cm. 9-23292.
F129. C2 G8

CANANDAIGUA. An historical statement concerning the "Old cemetery" at Canandaigua. Tog. with a recommendation relating thereto by the Board of public works, and a few suggestions for its permanent care and maintenance. Canandaigua, N.Y., The Ontario county times presses, 1918. 30 p. front., illus. 11 x 15½ cm.
F129. C2 H5

CANANDAIGUA. Picturesque Canandaigua ... Canandaigua, N.Y., Finley, Crandall & Brace (1899) 13¼ x 18 cm.
F129. C2 P 6

CANTON. Souvenir of Canton. From recent photos. Philadelphia, Press of the F. Gutekunst co. (1895) 2 p., 17 pl. obl. 24°. 1-14871-M1.
F129. C22 S 7

CAPE VINCENT. Cape Vincent and its history, comp. by Nelie Horton Casler. Watertown, N.Y., Hungerford-Holbrook co., 1906. 240 p. incl. front. (port.) illus., plates, maps, facsims. 21 cm. 7-5086.
F129. C24 C3

CAPE VINCENT. A historical sketch of the town of Cape Vincent. Read at the centennial celebration of the township ... by Elizur H. Pratt. ... Cape Vincent, N.Y., W. W. Ames, printer, 1876. 48 p. 24 cm. 1-21411.
F129. C24 P 7

CARDIFF. The Cardiff giant (by) Richard A. Boning. Illus. by Joseph Forte. Baldwin, N.Y., Dexter & Westbrook (1972) 47 p. col. illus. 24 cm. (The Incredible series) 74-184888 MARC.
F129. C27 B 6

CARDIFF See also F129.C2 A5

CARMEL. Inscriptions from old Baptist cemetery at Carmel. (By Mrs. Josephine C. Frost) 9 numb. l. 27 cm. Autographed from type-written copy. 12-6957 Rev.
F129. C28 F9

CARTHAGE and West Carthage directory ... Schenectady, N.Y., H. A. Manning co., 19 v. 23 cm. 23-17251.
Directories

CARTHAGE, Natural Bridge, Harrisville and Jayville directory ... 1888/9 - Carthage, N.Y., W. H. Waite, 1888 - v. 24 cm. CA 33-606 Unrev.
Directories

CASTLE CREEK. Annals of Castle Creek and vicinity, tog. with genealogies of some of the early families. By Julius W. Lilly ... Whitney's Point, N.Y., Printed by the Whitney's Point reporter (1903) 32 p. 22½ cm. 19-4216.
F129. C282L7

CASTLETON. A discourse in commemoration of James P. Bell ... and other volunteers from Castleton, who have died in the national army during the present war. Preached ... by Rev. Edgar L. Heermance, pastor. Albany, Van Benthuysen's steam print., 1864. 47 p. 23 cm. 17-16988.
F129. C29 H4

CASTORLAND. Translation of a memorial of Rodolphe Tillier's justification of the administration of Castorland, county of Oneida, Rome (N.Y.): Printed by Thomas Walker. 1800. 16 p. 20½ cm. 1-15886.
F129. C3 T5
Rare Book Coll.

CATHARINE. The history of the town of Catharine. Compiled by Mrs. Robert Cleaver (Mary Louise Catlin Cleaver) ... Rutland, Vt., The Tuttle pub. co., (1945) xx, (4), 686 p. front., plates, ports., maps. 23½ cm. A 45-4686.
F129. C32C56

CATSKILL. Manning's Catskill, Coxsackie, Cairo and Athens directory ... incl. Acra, Freehold, Gayhead, Purling, Round Top, So. Cairo and Urlton, Leeds, Jefferson Heights ... v. 19 Schenectady, N.Y., H. A. Manning co., 19 v. 23½ cm. CA 31-82 Unrev.
Directories

... CATSKILL and Saugerties. With illustrations, 1909. New York, American suburbs co., 1909. 9 p. illus. 41 cm. (American suburbs illus. v.3, no.5) 11-30222.
F129. C36C19

CATSKILL association, formed for the purpose of improving the town of Catskill ... New York ... 1836. New York, Mitchell & Turner, 1837.   47 p.   map.   16°.   1-14872.   F129.C36 C2

CATSKILL. Record of the Presbyterian church of Catskill. Comp. and ed. by Ray C. Sawyer. (New York?) 1945.   2 p., 68 numb. l.   28½ x 22 cm.   Type-written (carbon copy)   46-17558.   F129.C36C28

CATSKILL. Records of the Reformed Dutch church of Catskill in the town of Catskill. Transcribed by the N.Y. genealogical and biographical soc. Ed. by Royden W. Vosburgh. New York city, 1919. x, 239 numb. l. incl. 4 facsim.   36 x 28 cm.   Autographed from type-written copy.   20-2052.   F129.C36 C3
Rare Book Coll.

CATSKILL. Recollections of an octogenarian, by Henry Hill. Boston, D. Lothrop (1884) 195 p.   17 cm.   The author gives reminiscences of his early life in Catskill, N.Y., travels in Europe 1815 - 1816, residence in South America 1817 - 1821, with biographical sketches of men he had met.   11-30893.   F129.C36 H6

CATSKILL. Reminiscences of Catskill. Local sketches, by the late James D. Pinckney, tog. with interesting articles by Thurlow Weed and others. Catskill (N.Y.) J.B. Hall, 1868.   79 p.   24 cm. 1-14873.   F129.C36 P 6

CATSKILL. Historic Catskill, by Mrs. Jessie Van Vechten Vedder ... (Catskill, 1922) 98 p.   illus.   23½ cm.   Includes several small towns on Catskill creek.   32-24481.   F129.C36 V3

CATSKILL. History of Cayuga village, compiled and written by Florence Pharis McIntosh ... Syracuse and New York, Mason printing corp., 1927.   2, 7-112 p. fold. front., illus. (incl. ports., map) 23½ cm. "Genealogy record of the first families, 1798-1927": p. (89) - 112.   27-13339.   F129.C37 M2

CAZENOVIA, past and present; a descriptive and historical record of the village, by Christine O. Atwell. (Orlando, Fla., Printed by Florida press, inc., 1928)   v-xii, 64 p. front., pl. 24 cm. 28-18795.
F129.C38 A8

CAZENOVIA. Souvenir of. (Cazenovia, Marshall bros., 1887)   15 phot.   32°.   1-14874-M1.
F129.C38 S 7

CENTER BRUNSWICK. (Cemetery inscriptions from the towns of Center Brunswick, Cropseyville and Eagle Mills, Rensselaer County. (n.p., 1920?)   17 numb. l.   28½ cm.   Type-written copy.   22-17153 Rev.
F129.C392C7

CENTRAL ISLIP. The history of Central Islip. By Verne Dyson. Sponsored by the First Methodist Men's Club ("Methodist Men") Brentwood, N.Y., Brentwood Village Press, 1954.   104 p.   illus. 22 cm.   55-1902.   F129.C394D9

CERES. The history of Ceres and its near vicinity, from its early settlement in 1798 to the present. The early part written by M. W. Mann, and the latter part by Maria King. Olean, N.Y., Gillett & Weston, 1896.   150 p.   23 cm.   55-46561.   F129.C396M3

CHAMPLAIN. A memoir of the life of the Rev. Amos Pettengill ... By Rev. Luther Hart ... Boston, Mass., Sabbath school soc., 1834.   viii, 264 p.   14½ cm.   Most of Mr. Pettengill's career was spent in three parishes: Champlain, N.Y., Litchfield, Conn., and Salem parish, Waterbury, Conn.   12-16488.   F129. C4 H3

CHAMPLAIN. Historical oration, delivered at Champlain ... By Daniel T. Taylor ... Boston, Repository press, 1880.   31 p.   12°.   1-14875-M1.   F129. C4 T2

CHAPPAQUA deaths, Westchester County, New York. (By Mrs. Josephine C. Frost) (Brooklyn, 191-) 2 v.   27½ cm.   13-13692 rev.   F129.C45 F9

CHARLESTON. Marriages by Rev. Elijah Herrick, and Rev. Calvin Herrick, of Charleston, Montgomery County, 1796 - 1876. (m.p., 1917)   28 l.   28 x 21½ cm.   Type-written copy.   18-8815.
F129. C46 C4

CHARLOTTE. Celebration of the 100th anniversary of American independence, at Sinclairville ...

With an appendix. (Sinclairville) Pub. by direction of the Committee of arrangements (1876)
73 p. 22 ½ cm. 1-14876 Rev. F129.C47C18

CHARLTON. Stories and pictures of Charlton, by W. Bronson Taylor and others. Pictures by Alexander Crane. Middle Grove, N.Y. (1959) 122 p. illus. 24 cm. 59-12780. F129.C47 T3

CHARLTON. Records of the (Freehold) Presbyterian church in Charlton, Saratoga County. Transcribed by the New York genealogical and biographical soc.; ed. by Royden W. Vosburgh. New York city, 1921. 2, iii, 93 numb. l. 36 x 28 ½ cm. Autographed from type-written copy. 21-10661. F129.C473C4

CHATHAM directory for 1893. (v.1, no.1) Chatham, N.Y., M. J. McCann (1893) v. 17 cm.
13-11859. Directories

CHATHAM. Quaker records, Chatham, Columbia County & Queensbury, Warren County. (By Mrs. Josephine C. Frost) (Brooklyn, 191 -) 35, 2 numb. l. 27 cm. Autographed from type-written copy.
12-29740 Rev. F129.C48 F9

CHAUTAUQUA. The conquest of Chautauqua; Jamestown and vicinity in the pioneer and later periods as told by pioneer newspapers and persons, by Arthur Wellington Anderson ... Jamestown, N.Y. (Printed by Journal press) 1932 - v. illus. (incl. ports.) 24 cm. 33-728. F129.C49 A8

CHAUTAUQUA as a convention center, a summer city. (Buffalo, 18 -) 16 ½ x 24 ½ cm.
F129.C45 C4

CHAUTAUQUA. Pen and picture. A Chautauqua sketch-book, by J. T. Edwards,... Meadville, Pa., Flood & Vincent, 1896. vii, 9-92 p. front., illus. 15 ½ x 23 ½ cm. 1-14877. F129.C49 E2

CHAUTAUQUA. Special excursions to Chautauqua. Erie railroad co. (New York) 1904.
23 ½ cm. F129.C49 E9

CHAUTAUQUA impressions. By Helen P. Strong. (New York. Photo engraving co., 1890)
31 p. illus. 16°. 1-14878-M1. F129.C49 S 9

CHAUTAUQUA. (By George Edgar Vincent) Philadelphia, J. B. Lippincott co., 1889. 4 p. 19 cm.
Appears as article "Chautauqua" in Chambers's encyclopedia. 1-23428. F129.C49 V7

CHAZY. ... A book of views of Heart's delight farm. By William H. Miner. Chazy, New York. Clinton County. (Chicago, The Lammers Shilling co., 1909) (5) - 156 p. incl. illus., mounted col. plates.
front. 35 x 28 cm. 10-4611. F129.C493M5

CHAZY. Heart's delight farm, Chazy ... (By William H. Miner. (Chicago, Lammers Shilling, 1911)
60 p. incl. illus. (partly col.) fold. mounted map. 33 ½ x 27 ½ cm. 11-19630. F129.C493M6

— (1915) 114 p. illus. (part col.) fold. map. 33 x 26 ½ cm. 15-14794. F129.C493M62

CHAZY, A history of the town of Chazy, Clinton County (by) Nell Jane Barnett Sullivan and David K. Martin. (Burlington, Vt. Printed by G. Little 1970) iv, 360 p. illus., facsims., maps, ports. 29 cm.
79-140387. F129.C493 S9

CHERRY CREEK. Historical and biographical sketch of Cherry Creek, Chautauqua County. With views of business places and residences, tog. with sketches of prominent citizens of various professions and occupations, past and present. Ed. and pub. by Chas. J. Shults ... (Buffalo, G. M. Hausauer, printer) 1900. 3, 9-175, (5) p. illus. (incl. ports.) 26 ½ cm. 16-8883. F129.C498 S6

CHERRY VALLEY. The centennial celebration at Cherry Valley, Otsego co. The addresses of William W. Campbell and Gov. W. H. Seward ... New York, Taylor & Clement, 1840. 59 p. 17 ½ cm.
1-14879. F129. C5 C5

CHERRY VALLEY. Records of the First Presbyterian church of Cherry Valley. Transcribed by the

New York genealogical and biographical soc.; ed. by Royden W. Vosburgh. New York city, 1920.
2 p., viii, 136 numb. 1.   36 x 28 ½ cm.   Autographed from type-written copy.   20-9790.   F129.C5 C54

CHERRY VALLEY. History of Cherry Valley from 1740 to 1898. By John Sawyer. Cherry Valley, N.Y., Gazette print, 1898.   2, 156 p.   21 ½ cm.   1-14880.   F129. C5 S 2

CHERRY VALLEY. The story of Cherry Valley, by Henry U. Swinnerton. Cherry Valley, N.Y. (1908)   (22) p.   22 ½ cm.   Reprinted from Proceedings of the N.Y. state hist. assoc. v. 7.   45-51628.   F129. C5 S 9

CHESTER, a history. By Samuel Jacob Levy. Chester, Chamber of Commerce, 1947.   122 p. 22 cm.
Bibliography: p. 10.   47-28866*.   F129.C52 L4

CHURCHTOWN. Baptismal record of St. Thomas Lutheran Church, Churchtown; Lutheran Church of Claverack, 1760 - 1899. Trans. and indexed by: Arthur C. M. Kelly. (Rhinebeck, N.Y., 1969)
iv, 288, 44, 30 p.   29 cm.   F129.C525C5

CLARKSTOWN. Reformed Dutch church at Clarkstown, Rockland County. Births and baptisms, 1795-1849. (n. p., 1924?)   84 numb. 1.   27 ½ cm.   Type-written copy.   25 - 12661.
F129. C53 C6

CLARENDON. History of Clarendon from 1810 to 1888; by David Sturges Copeland. Buffalo, The Courier co,, printers, 1889.   x, 382 p.   19 ½ cm.   3-5248.   F129.C56 C7

CLAVERACK. Baptismal record of Reformed Church, Claverack, 1727 - 1899. (Transcribed and indexed by Arthur C. M. Kelly. Rhinebeck, N.Y., 1970)   iv, 320, 73, 50 p.   29 cm.
F129.C58C55

CLAVERACK. Marriage record of Reformed Church, Claverack, 1727 - 1899. (Transcibed by Arthur C. M. Kelly. Rhinebeck, N.Y., 1970.)   iv, 116, 69, 13 p.   29 cm.
F129.C58C56

CLAVERACK. The parsonage between two manors; annals of Clover-Reach, by Elizabeth L. Gebhard. Hudson, N.Y., Bryan print., 1909.   xxiii, 315 p. incl. front. plates, ports.   20 cm.   9-30188.
F129.C58 G3

CLAYTON. Historical sketch of the village of Clayton and a complete history of St. Mary's parish, by Rev. P. S. Garand. Clayton, N.Y., G. H. Bates, printer, 1902.   2, 216 p. incl. plates, ports. pl.
19 cm.   11-25532.   F129.C59 G2

CLERMONT. A biographical history of Clermont, or Livingston manor, before and during the war for independence, with a sketch of the first steam navigation of Fulton and Livingston. By Thomas Streatfield Clarkson ... Clermont, N.Y., 1869.   vii, (2), (11)-319 p.   5 phot. (incl. front.)   23 ½ cm.
Frontispiece wanting. 1-246* Cancel.   F129. C6 C6

CLERMONT. A historical sketch of the town of Clermont, by Thomas Hunt. Hudson, N.Y., Priv, print., The Hudson press, 1928.   7, 149 p. front., plates, ports., maps (1 double, 1 fold.) 23 ½ cm.   30-8664.
F129. C6 H94

CLIFTON SPRINGS. Indelible photos. New York, The Albertype co., 1890.   (8) p., 16 pl.   13 x 18 cm.
1-16259.   F129. C63 C6

CLIFTON SPRINGS. The sanitarium, Clifton Springs, New York. (Boston, Mass., 1899)
13 ½ x 17 ½ cm.   F129.C63C68

CLIFTON SPRINGS. Souvenir of Clifton Springs, N.Y. By John Wentworth Sanborn. The sanitarium and environs ... (Boston, 1889)   8 l.   pl.   24⁰.   1-14881-M1.   F129. C63 S 1

CLIFTON SPRINGS. Souvenir and autograph book of the village of Clifton Springs, New York ... By John Wentworth Sanborn ... (n. p., 1894)   8 l. plates, port. 15 x 20 ½ cm.   7-29231.
F129. C63 S18

CLINTON. Clinton Historical Society. Publication. no. 1 -   Clinton, N.Y., 1964 -
no. illus. (ports.) 22 cm.   F129.C65C56

— A century of schools in Clinton, by Helen Neilson Rudd.   Clinton, N.Y., Clinton Hist. Soc., 1964.   27 p.   22 cm.   (Clinton Historical Society publication no. 1)

CLINTON. The talking trees of Clinton.   From Prof. Edward North's half-century letter.   Hamilton college, 1891. With illus. by Margaret Landers Randolph ... (n.p., 1891)   9 l.   illus.   21 cm.
1-14882.   F129.C65 N8
Rare Book Coll.

CLINTON. The early history of Clinton.   A lecture before the Young men's lyceum, of Clinton. By Othniel S. Williams.   Clinton (N.Y.) L.W. Payne, 1848.   28 p.   8º.   1-14883-M1.   F129.C65 W7
Rare Book Coll.

CLYDE. History of Clyde, Wayne County, 1722 - 1955; with illustrations descriptive of its scenery, buildings, prominent men, etc.   By Aretta J. and Wayne E. Morrison.   Williamson, N.Y., Printed by Bel-Gra Print, 1955.   48 p.   illus.   28 cm.   55-34882.   F129.C654M6

CLYDE. ... "Grip's" historical souvenir of Clyde.   (By Edgar Luderne Welch)   (Syracuse? N.Y.) 1905.   68 p.   illus. (incl. ports.)   26½ cm.   (Historical souvenir series, no. 19)   5-11063 Rev.   F129.C654W4

COBLESKILL. Records of Zion's evangelical Lutheran church of Cobleskill in Schoharie County. Transcribed by the N.Y. genealogical and biographical soc.   Ed. by Royden Woodward Vosburgh. New York city, 1916.   3, ii-xlii, 189 numb. l.   36 x 28½ cm.   covers period 1795-1871.   16-25921.   F129.C66 C6
L H & G

COBLESKILL. ... Historical souvenir of Cobleskill ...   (By Edgar Luderne Welch)   Albany, 1895. 48 p. incl. illus., pl. (ports.)   27 cm.   (Historical souvenir series no. 2)   Map.   4-21099* Cancel.
F129.C66 W4

COEYMANS. Quaker records, Coeymans, Albany County & New Baltimore, Green Co.   (By Mrs. Josephine C. Frost) (Brooklyn, 191 -)   2 p., 53, 3 numb. l.   27 cm.   Autographed from type-written copy.
12-29741 Rev.   F129.C665F9

COEYMANS. The Hudson River overslagh, and Coeyman bouwery.   (By Joel Munsell) (Albany, 1875) 8 p.   illus.   19½ cm.   7-22.   F129.C665M9

COHOES. Le guide français de la Nouvell-Angleterre.   Et de l'état de New-York ....   Suivi d'une foule d'autres statistiques et renseignements précieux, sur tous les centres canadiens des États-Unis et du guide de Cohoes.   Lowell, Mass., La Société de publications françaises des États-Unis (18
v.   illus.   22½ cm.   8-15352.   F129.C67
F15. F8 G92

COHOES. ... Where Hudson's voyage ended, an inquiry; Cohoes, and the origin of the name, by Harry Montford Sweet ... Albany, J. B. Lyon co., printers, 1909.   28 p.   illus. (incl. port., map., facsims.)
25½ cm.   11-15755.   F129.C67
E129.H8 S 9

COHOES. The city of Cohoes, its history, growth and prospects, its great manufactures.   Albany, C. Van Benthuysen, 1869.   56 p.   front.   19 cm.   48-41721*.   F129.C67 C5

COHOES. The history of Cohoes, from its earliest settlement to the present time.   (By Arthur Haynsworth Masten)   Albany, J. Munsell, 1877.   viii, 327 p.   front., 1 illus.   21½ cm.   "Necrological record," 1834-1876: p. (265) - 294.   1-14884 Rev.   F129.C67 M4

COLD SPRING HARBOR. Out of the wilderness; being an account of aspects of the settlement of Cold Spring Harbor, Long Island, and the activities of some of the settlers, from the beginning to the Civil War, by Walter K. Earle.   (Cold Spring Harbor) Whaling Museum Soc. (1966)   63 p.   27 cm.
F129.C68 E3

342 LOCAL HISTORIES IN THE LIBRARY OF CONGRESS

COLD SPRING HARBOR. Main Street, Cold Spring Harbor, by Harriet G. Valentine and others. Long Island, N.Y., Huntington Hist. Soc., 1960.   28 p.   illus.   23 cm.
F129.C68 V3

COLLINS. Quaker records, Collins, Erie Co., & Western, Oneida Co. (By Mrs. Josephine C. Frost) 20, 2 numb. l.   27 cm.   Autographed from type-written copy.   12-29745.
F129.C69 F9

CONCORD. History of the original town of Concord, being the present towns of Concord, Collins, N. Collins and Sardinia, Erie County. By Erasmus Briggs, Rochester, N.Y., Union and advertiser co.'s print, 1883.   xiv, (3) - 977 p.   illus. (incl. ports., plan)   24 cm.   1-14885.
F129. C7 B 8

CONESUS. History of the town of Conesus, Livingston County, from its first settlement in 1793, to 1887, with a brief genealogical record of the Conesus families, by William P. Boyd ... Conesus, N.Y., Boyd's job print., 1887.   176 p.   front., plates, ports.   22½ x 19 cm.   1-14886* Cancel.
F129.C73 B 7

CONEY ISLAND. Albert' Coney Island. A compendium of useful information and a complete descriptive guide ... New York, 1883.   37 p.   pl., maps.   24º.   (Cicerone and souvenir series)   1-14887-M1.
F129.C75 A3

CONEY ISLAND. Bell's picturesque guide to American watering places. Coney Island and what is to be seen there ... New York, C. J. Macdonald 1880.   (45) p.   illus.   12º.   1-14888-M1.
F129.C75 B 4

CONEY ISLAND. Complete guide to the great watering place of New York. How to reach and enjoy Manhattan beach, Brighton beach, West Brighton beach, and Coney Island, by boat and rail ... New York, The American news co., 1879.   24 p.   illus., maps.   16º.   1-15967-M1.
F129.C75C37

CONEY ISLAND. An illustrated guide to the sea. With official time tables. Season of 1883. Containing an account of a ramble on the beach by a pleasure party ... Brooklyn, Truax & co. (1883) 88 p.   front., illus., maps.   12º.   1-15968-M1.
F129.C75 C4

... CONEY ISLAND and the Jews. A history of the development and success of this famous seaside resort, together with a full account of the recent Jewish controversy. New York, G. W. Carleton, 1879.   42 p.   19 cm.   6-28956.
F129.C75 C5

CONEY ISLAND. The Coney Island souvenir: for the season of 1881. An accurate and reliable directory and travellers' guide of the township of Gravesend, Kings co., including its hotels, stores, trades and tradesmen ... New York, W. P. Griffith (1881)   127 p.   illus.   16º.   1-14889-M1.
F129.C75 C6

— (1883)   (64) p.   illus., maps (part fold.)   15½ cm.   1-21564.
F129.C75C65

CONEY ISLAND to-day. The only authorized publication on the world's greatest playground. v.1, no. 1) June 1911. (New York, 1911)   1 no.   illus.   30½ cm.
F129.C75C67

CONEY ISLAND. The history of Coney Island from its first discovery in 4, 11, 44, down to last night, in rhyme. Adapted for all children under 85 ... (By I. F. Eaton) New York, Morrison, Richardson, 1878.   47 p.   illus.   22½ cm.   20-12695 Rev.
F129.C75E15

— 1879.   48 p.   illus.   23 cm.   12-16740 Rev.
F129.C75E16

CONEY ISLAND. History of Coney Island ... (New York) 1904.   23½ x 18½ cm.
F129.C75 H6

CONEY ISLAND. Good old Coney Island, a sentimental journey into the past; the most rambunctious, scandalous, rapscallion, splendiferous, pugnacious, spectacular, illustrious, prodigious, frolicsome island on earth. By Edo McCullough. New York, Scribner (1957)   344 p.   illus.   24 cm.   57-7582.
F129.C75 M3

CONEY ISLAND. Percy's Pocket dictionary of Coney island. An index and guide to railroad and steamboat routes, hotels, amusements, restaurants ... ed. and comp. by Townsend Percy ... Season of 1880. New York, F. Leypoldt, 1880.   120 p. incl. front., illus., maps, plan, tables. 13 cm. 1-15966.
F129.C75 P 4

CONEY ISLAND. ... Sodom by the sea; an affectionate history of Coney island. By Oliver Ramsay Pilat. Garden City, N.Y., Doubleday, Doran, 1941.   ix, 334 p. illus. (map) plates. 22 cm. 41-12188.
F129.C75 P 5

CONEY ISLAND. Seeing Coney Island of today ... New York, 1904.   24 x 18½ cm.   F129.C75 S 4

CONEY ISLAND. ... Souvenir guide to Coney Island ... Brooklyn, N.Y., 1905.   20½ cm.
F129.C75 S 7

CONEY ISLAND. Staley's views of Coney Island ... New York, F. W. Staley, 1907.   31 pl. 24 cm.
F129.C75 S78

— New York, 1908.   24 cm.   F129.C75 S79

CONEY ISLAND. Thompson's Coney island, guide ... Ed. by Thos. L. Russell. Edition of 1884. (New York) J. P. Tracy (1884)   32 p. front. 15 cm. 1-16015.   F129.C75 T4

— (New York, 1885)   14½ cm.   F129.C75T42

CONEY ISLAND. The tourists companion and guide to Coney Island, Fort Hamilton, Bath Beach, Sheepshead Bay, Rockaway Beach and Far Rockaway, to which is added a description of public buildings ... and other matters of interest ... in the city New York and vicinity. Ed. by J. Perkins Tracy. A select business directory of each place noticed in ... this guide. New York, Austin pub. co., 1887. iv, (5) - 68 p. illus. 20½ cm. 1-21542.   F129.C75 T7

CONEY ISLAND frolics. How New York's gay girls and jolly boys enjoy themselves by the sea! (3d ed.) New York, R. K. Fox (1883?)   67 p. pl. 8°. 1-14890-M1.   F129.C75 T8

CONEY ISLAND. Views of Coney Island. (Portland, Me., 1905)   20 x 25 cm.   F129.C75 V6

— 1909.   (32) p. illus. 20 x 25 cm. CA 17-130 Unrev.   F129.C75V65

CONSTITUTION ISLAND. The fort that never was; a discussion of the Revolutionary War fortifications built on Constitution Island, 1775 - 1783 (by) Merle G. Sheffield. West Point, N.Y., Constitution Island Assoc., 1969.   vi, 29, (36) p. illus., maps, plans, port. 26 cm. Bibliog. p.29. 70-24946 MARC.   F129.C76 S 5

COOPERSTOWN. Complete directory of the village of Cooperstown, Otsego County, Jan. 1915 - no. 1 - Cooperstown, N.Y., E. J. Bailey (1915)   v. illus. (incl. port.) 19½ cm. 15-5435.
F Directories

COOPERSTOWN directory ... 1928 - v. 1 - Schenectady, N.Y., H. A. Manning co., 1928 -
v. illus. 23 cm. CA 29-148 Unrev.   Directories

COOPERSTOWN. Attractions of Cooperstown, Otsego lake. Being a descriptive sketch of the picturesque village ... etc. Glens Falls, N.Y., C. H. Possons, 1889.   16 p. front. (fold. map) illus. (incl. plan) 15 x 12 cm. 1-16290.   F129.C77 A8

COOPERSTOWN. Fenimore Cooper's grave and Christ churchyard, by Ralph Birdsall ... illus. from photos by A. J. Telfer, and others ... New York, F. H. Hitchcock, 1911.   74 p. incl. front., illus. pl. 21 cm. 11-16284.   F129.C77 B 6

COOPERSTOWN. The story of Cooperstown, by Ralph Birdsall ... with seventy illus. from photos. Cooperstown, N.Y., Arthur H. Crist co. (1917)   4, 425 p. front., illus. (incl. ports., maps) 18 cm. 17-18707.
F129.C77 B62

— N.Y., Augur's Book Store, 1948.   433 p. illus., ports., map. 19 cm. 48-22684*.   F129.C77 B62 1948

COOPERSTOWN. Full harvest, by Charlotte Prentiss Browning, with an introd. by Henry W. Anderson; ... Philadelphia, Dorrance & co., (1932)　　6, 9 - 301 p.　front., plat;s, ports.　22 cm.　Reminiscences of the author's life in Cooperstown, N.Y.　32-18921.　　　　F129.C77 B86

COOPERSTOWN. The home of Cooper and the haunts of Leatherstocking. By Barry Gray (pseud. for Robert Barry Coffin) New York, Russell bros., 1872.　　38 p.　front. (port.)　illus., 2 pl. (1 double) 24 cm.　1-15964.　　　　F129.C77 C6

COOPERSTOWN. The chronicles of Cooperstown ... (By James Fenimore Cooper) Cooperstown (N.Y.) H. & E. Phinney, 1838.　　100 p.　19 cm.　Published anonymously.　6-12298.　　　F129.C77C65
　　　　Rare Book Coll.

COOPERSTOWN. To commemorate the foundation of the village of Cooperstown and its corporate existence of one hundred years, this memorial celebration was held ... Cooperstown, N.Y., Print. by the Otsego republican (1907)　　180 p. incl. front. (port.) plates.　23½ cm.　8-29102.　　F129.C77C68

COOPERSTOWN. Records of the Presbyterian church of Cooperstown, in Otsego County. Transcribed by the New York genealogical and biographical soc.; ed. by Royden W. Vosburgh. New York city, 1920.　　2, iii, 127 numb. l.　36 x 28½ cm.　Autographed from type-written copy.　20-12201.　　F129.C77C69

COOPERSTOWN and Otsego Lake; descriptive sketch of the village made famous by J. Fenimore Cooper, in his Leather-stocking tales, with views of village and lake. (Cooperstown, N.Y., The Otsego republican, 1900.　　32 p. incl. illus., pl.　obl. 16°.　Nov. 1, 1900-82.　　　F129.C77 C7

COOPERSTOWN. A history of Cooperstown; incl. "The chronicles of Cooperstown", by James Fenimore Cooper; "The history of Cooperstown", 1839-1886, by Samuel M. Shaw; "The history of Cooperstown", 1886-1929, by Walter R. Littell. (Cooperstown, N.Y., The Freeman's journal co.) 1929.　　5, 3-259 p.　26 cm.　29-22927.　　　F129.C77H67

COOPERSTOWN. By Louis Clark Jones. Cooperstown, N.Y., Otsego Co. Historical Soc. (1949)　66 p. illus., ports.　26 cm.　Bibliography: p. 86.　49-10686*.　　　F129.C77 J 6

— (4th ed. rev.) Cooperstown, N.Y., New York State Historical Assoc. (1965)　　90 p.　26 cm.
　　　　F129.C77 J 6
　　　　1965

COOPERSTOWN. A visit to Cooperstown. By Walter Ricks Littell. (Cooperstown, N.Y.) 1946.　40 p.　illus., fold. map, ports.　23 cm.　Bibliography: p. 13-14.　47-27314*.　　　F129.C77 L5

COOPERSTOWN. A condensed history of Cooperstown, with a biographical sketch of J. Fenimore Cooper. By Rev. S. T. Livermore ... Albany, J. Munsell, 1862.　　vii, (9) - 276 p.　18½ cm.　1-14891.
　　　　F129.C77 L7

COOPERSTOWN. A centennial offering; being a brief history of Cooperstown with a biographical sketch of James Fenimore Cooper, by Hon. I. N. Arnold. ... Ed. by Samuel M. Shaw. Cooperstown, N.Y., Printed at the Freeman's journal office, 1886.　　240 p.　17½ cm.　1-14892 Rev.　F129.C77 S 5

CORINTH. Directory of Corinth, with telephone subscribers and census ... (1915 - Corinth, N.Y., The Corinthian, 1915 -　　1 v.　illus.　21½ cm.　15-19460.　　　Directories

CORNING. Pioneer days and later times in Corning and vicinity, 1789 - 1920, by Uri Mulford. Corning, N.Y., U. Mulford (1922)　　3, 3-528 p.　port.　25½ cm.　22-2113.　　　F129. C8 M9

CORNWALL. By Lewis Beach. Newburgh, N.Y., E. M. Ruttenber, 1873.　　200 p.　8°.　1-14893-M1
　　　　F129.C82 B 3

CORTLAND. Manning's Cortland, Homer and McGraw directory ... 189　　Schenectady, N.Y., A. A. Manning, 189 -　　v.　fold. maps.　23-24 cm.　38M762T.　　　Directories

CORTLAND. Past and present. A historical and descriptive sketch of Cortland, and its manufacturing and commercial interests. By D. Morris Kurtz. Showing its attractions as a place of residence and advantages as a location for manufacturing enterprises. Binghamton, Republican book and job print, 1883. 53 p. illus. 22 cm. 1-14894 Rev. F129.C83 K9

CORTLAND. "Grip's" historical souvenir of Cortland. (n.7) (Cortland, N.Y., Standard press, 1899) (comp. Edgar L. Welch) 234 p. illus. 4°. May 31, 1900-110. F129.C83 W4

CORTLANDT. A country village as affected by the war. An address delivered before Middleton post, no. 500, Grand army of the republic, dep't N.Y. ... by A. H. Clark. New York, 1902. 12 p. 22 cm. 3-32508. F129.C85 C5

COVENTRY. History of the town of Coventry from the first white man's log hut, with all the most important events, down to the present time. By Oliver P. Judd ... (Oxford, N.Y., The Oxford review, 1912) 99 p. port. 24 cm. 16-1749. F129.C87 J9

COXSACKIE. Ye olden time, as compiled from the Coxsackie news of 1889, written by Robert Henry Van Bergen ... (Coxsackie, N.Y., Printed by the Coxsackie union-news, 1935) 16 p. 118 p. 21½ cm. 37-18834. F129.C88 V3

CREEK. Quaker mattiates recorded on Creek records (1786 - 1802) in the custody of the Friends at the 15th st. meeting house, N.Y. city. (1911?) 4 numb. l. 27 cm. Autographed from type-written copy. 12-6958 Rev. F129.C91F 9

CROWN POINT, New York, in the Civil War. By Elmer Eugene Barker. (Albany?) Reproduced by the New York Civil War Centennial Commission, 1961. 133 p. 31 cm. 63-64423. F129.C95 B3

CROWN POINT. Historic Crown Point, the story of the forts and of the village, by Carroll Vincent Lonergan ... (Burlington, Vt., Free press printing corporation, 1942) 79 p. front., illus. (incl. ports., maps) 23½ cm. 42-24199. F129.C95 L6

CROWN POINT. Spaulding's history of Crown Point, from 1800 - 1874. (By Samuel S. Spaulding) (Port Henry, N.Y., Herald print, 1875) 42 p. 8°. 1-14895-M1. F129.C95 S7

CRUM ELBOW. Records of Crum Elbow precinct, Dutchess county, 1738 - 1761, tog. with records of Charlotte precinct, 1762 - 1785, records of Clinton precinct, 1786 - 1788, and records of the town of Clinton, 1789 - 1799, ed. by Franklin D. Roosevelt ... (Poughkeepsie, N.Y., 1940. vii, 196 p. front. fold. map) illus. (map) 27½ cm. (Colls. of the Dutchess county hist. soc. vol. vii) 40-12530. F129.C96 R6
Rare Book Coll.

CRYSTAL SPRING ... Crystal Springs, N.Y., 1880. 23½ cm. F129.C97 C9

CUBA. The Cuba of New York state; a study in Hispanic toponymy of the Empire state, by Grace D. Alvarex. Littel Valley, N.Y., Straight Pub. Co. (1970) 48 p. illus. 22 cm. F129.C976A76

CUTCHOGUE, Southold's first colony, by Wayland Jefferson; decorations by James Van Alst. New York, 1940. 6, 3-166 p. illus. 24 cm. 40-30614. F129.C98 J4

DANSVILLE-Wayland directory for 19 Lockport, N.Y., Roberts brothers co., 19 v. 23½ cm. 40-16146. Directories

DANSVILLE. ... Dansville; historical, biographical, descriptive, ed. by A. O. Bunnell, compiled by F. I. Quick. Dansville, N.Y., Instructor pub. co. (1902?) 270 p., (5) - 267 p. incl. illus., plates, ports., maps. 26½ cm. 10-13970. F129.D2 B9

DANSVILLE. Miniature of Dansville village: humbly inscribed to the first settlers, and their immediate descendants. By J. W. Clark. Dansville, N.Y., J. W. Clark, 1844. 5, (7) - 72 p. 21 cm. 20-3605. F129.D2 C5

DANSVILLE. Boyhood reminiscences. Dansville, 1855 - 1865. By Hermon Wells De Long.

Dansville, N.Y., F.A.Owen pub. co., 1913.　　67 p.　illus. (port.)　20 cm.　22-25772.　　　F129. D2 D3

DANSVILLE.　The Jackson health resort ... (Buffalo, 1903?)　15½ x 23 cm.　　F129. D2 J 17

DANSVILLE.　The Jackson sanatorium ... (Dansville)　Buffalo, N.Y., 189-?)　15 x 23 cm.
F129. S2 J 2

DEER PARK.　A history of Deerpark in Orange County.　By Peter E. Gumaer ...　Pub. by the Minisink Valley hist. soc.　(Port. Jervis, N.Y.) Port Gervis union print., 1890.　(7) - 204, (2) p. front. (port.)　pl.　19 cm.　1-14896.　　F129. D3 G9

DELHI.　... Historical souvenir of Delhi, N.Y. ...　(By Edgar Luderne Welch)　(Albany, N.Y., 1897)　62 p.　illus. (incl. ports.)　26½ cm.　(Historical souvenir, series no. 4)　"Grip's" valley gazette, v.5.　4-28342*.　F129. D36 W4

DE PEYSTER.　U.S. census records, 1850, De Peyster, St. Lawrence co., copied by Doris Wolcott Strong.　Washington, D.C., 1941.　10 numb. l.　27½ cm.　Type-written (carbon copy)　43-236.
F129. D37 S 8

... DE RUYTER and vicinity ... By Edgar Luderne Welch.　(De Ruyter? 1900)　64 p.　illus. (incl. ports.)　27½ cm.　("Grip's! historical souvenir no. 8)　Grip's gazette, v. 8, no. 3.　4-27743* Cancel.　F129. D38 W4

DE RUYTER.　History of De Ruyter and vicinity, from time of Indians to 1964, by Walter R. Wood. (De Ruyter, N.Y., 1964?)　152 p.　28 cm.　　F129. D38 W6

DIX HILLS.　Cemetery inscriptions in the Buffet burying-ground, Dix Hills, L.I., copied by Mr. Evelyn Briggs Baldwin.　(n.p., 1922?)　18 numb. l.　27½ cm.　Type-written copy.　22-22250.
F129. D6 B 2

DOVER.　Records of the First Baptist church of Dover, Dutchess Count (now located in Wingdale, New York)　Copied from the original records by Miss Martha Taber ...　(Brooklyn, N.Y., 1915)
117 numb. l.　27 cm.　Autographed from type-written copy.　Earliest records are dated 1757.　16-7141.　F129. D7 D7

DRYDEN.　The centennial history of the town of Dryden.　1797 - 1897.　Comp. and ed. by Geo. E. Goodrich, with the aid of the Centennial executive committee and many others.　Dryden, N.Y., J. G. Ford, printer, 1898.　vi, 272 p.　front., illus. (inck. music) ports., 3 fold. maps., fold, tab.　24 cm.　One folded map in pocket.　20-3057.　F129. D79 G6

DRYDEN.　Ellis Hollow lore; pioneer days, yesteryear, today.　By Zella (Middaugh)Pritchard. Ithaca, N.Y., Ladies' Circle, Ellis Hollow Community Church, 1962.　54 p.　22 cm.　F129. D79 P 7

DUANESBURGH.　A memorial census for Duanesburgh, with supplement for the bordering towns. Comp. by Clarence Foote ...　Delanson, N.Y., The author (1935)　159 p.　illus. (map)　22 cm.
F129. D86 F6

— Supplement to A memorial census for Duanesburgh ...　Delanson, N.Y. ... 1935.
(161) - 244 p.　23 cm.　37-68.　"Includes a census of the Esperance cemetery recording nearly 1800 names ...　Bibliography: p. 232.
F129. D86F62

DUNKIRK.　Polk's Dunkirk-Fredonia directory ... 1925 -　Pittsburgh, Pa., R. L. Polk, 1925 -
v.　23½ cm.　25-8866.　　Directories

DUNKIRK.　Historical and descriptive review of Dunkirk, Chautauqua county.　Compiled under the auspices of the Commercial assoc. of Dunkirk ...　Dunkirk, N.Y., 1889.　95 p.　1 illus.　21½ cm.
1-14897 Rev.　　F129. D9 C6

DURHAM.　Records of the First Presbyterian church in the village of Durham, town of Durham, Greene County.　Transcribed by the New York genealogical and biographical soc.　Ed. by Royden Woodward Vosburgh.　New York city, 1920.　2, 87 numb. L.　36 x 28½ cm.　20-18586.
F129. D96 D9

— A short historical sketch of the Second Presbyterian church of West Durham, Greene

County. Comp. by Rev. L. H. Fellows ... Winton, Ia., Printed at the Eagle office, 1871. facsim.: 29 p. mounted on 8 l. 35½ x 28 cm. 20-20517. F129.D96 D9

DURHAM. Records of the Reformed Dutch church in Oak Hill in the town of Durham, Greene County. Transcribed by the N.Y. genealogical and biographical soc. Ed. by Royden W. Vosburgh. New York city, 1920. 2 p., 87 numb. l. 36 x 28½ cm. Autographed from type-written copy. 20-23479. F129.D96D95

EAST AURORA. Pictorial and historical review, East Aurora and vicinity ... biographical sketches of prominent business, progessional and civic leaders. Copyright ... (by) History recording association, Holland, N.Y. ... (East Aurora, N.Y., East Aurora advertiser print) 1940. (84) p. illus. (incl. ports.) 23 cm. 41-1767. F129.E114H5

EASTCHESTER. Records of the town of Eastchester, Westchester County (compiled by) Fred C. Haacker. (n.p.) 1952. 118 l. 28 cm. 54-36611. F129.E117E17

EAST GREENBUSH. Records of the Reformed Protestant Dutch church of Greenbush, at East Greenbush, Rensselaer County. Transcribed by the New York genealogical and biographical soc. ... Ed. by Royden W. Vosburgh. New York city, 1914. 2 v. illus. (maps) 35½ cm. Autographed from type-written copy. 14-5806. F129.E12E12

EAST HAMPTON social guide ... (East Hampton, N.Y., The East Hampton star, 19   v. 22 cm. CA 32-631 Unrev. Directories

EAST HAMPTON. A sermon, containing a general history of the town of East-Hampton, (L.I.) from its first settlement to the present time. ... By Lyman Beecher, pastor of the church ... Sag-Harbor, N.Y. Printed by Alden Spooner. 1806. 40 p. 21 cm. 10-207. F129.E13 B 4
Rare Book Coll.

EAST HAMPTON. Records of the town of East Hampton, Long Island, Suffolk Co., with other ancient documents of historic value ... Sag-Harbor, J. H. Hunt, printer, 1887 - 1905. 5 v. 2 plans (1 fold.) 24 cm. Vol. 5 includes the records of the church at East Hampton, 1696-1881. 1-14898 Add. F129.E13 E1

EAST HAMPTON. Chronicles of the town of Easthampton, county of Suffolk. By David Gardiner. New York (Bowne & co., printers) 1871. 4. 121 p. 24½ cm. 1-14899. F129.E13 G2

EAST HAMPTON. The papers and biography of Lion Gardiner. 1599 - 1663. With an appendix ... Ed., with notes critical and illustrative, by Curtiss C. Gardiner. St. Louis (Press of Levison & Blythe stationery co.) 1883. 106 p. front., illus., map, facsim. 27 x 21½ cm. 9-14000. F129.E13G25

EAST HAMPTON. Early memories of Gardiner's Island (the Isle of Wight, New York) Chronology by Abigail Fithian Halsey. (East Hampton, N.Y., East Hampton Star, 1947) 123 p. plates, ports., map. 24 cm. "References": p. 120-121. 48-22289*. F129.E13 G3

EAST HAMPTON. An address, delivered on the 26th Dec., 1849, on the occasion of the celebration of the 200th anniversary of the settlement of the town of East-Hampton, tog. with an appendix containing a general history of the town from its first settlement to the year 1800: by Henry P. Hedges. Sag-Harbor, L.I., Corrector office, 1850. 2, (iii)-iv, 100 p. 22½ cm. "Family history and genealogy": p. (52) - 71. 16-8177. F129.E13 H3

EAST HAMPTON. A history of the town of East-Hampton, N.Y., including an address delivered at the celebration of the bi-centennial anniversary of it settlement in 1849, introductions to the four printed vols. of its records, with other historic material, an appendix and genealogical notes. By Henry P. Hedges ... Sag-Harbor, J. H. Hunt, printer, 1897. 4, 344 p., 10 p. front. (port.) plates. 22½ cm. 1-14900 Rev. F129.E13 H4

EAST HAMPTON. The island: being the story of the fortunes & vicissitudes & triumphs of the island, once known as Monchonake ... now known as Gardiner's Island ... Now faithfully related from original documents and presented to the public. By Pierre Stephen Robert Payne. (1st ed.) New York, Harcourt, Brace (1958)   248 p.   illus.   22 cm.   58-5479.   F129.E13 P 3

EAST HAMPTON history, including genealogies of early families. By Jeannette (Edwards) Rattray. East Hampton, N.Y. (1953)   xv, 619 p.   illus., ports., maps.   24 cm.   53-2765.   F129.E13R25

EAST HAMPTON. The old Hook mill and other old English windmills of East Hampton, Long island, and vicinity, by Jeannette Edwards Rattray ... Issued by the Board of trustees of the village of East Hampton. (East Hampton, 1942)   28 p.   illus. (incl. port.)   24 cm.   42-15898.   F129.E13 R3

EAST HAMPTON. Three centuries in East Hampton, Long Island, by Jeannette Edwards Rattray. (East Hampton) East Hampton star press (1937)   43 p.   illus., fold. map.   17½ x 21 cm.   Map.   43-1403.
F129.E13R33

EAST HAMPTON. Up and down Main Street; an informal history of East Hampton and its old houses. By Jeannette (Edwards) Rattray. (East Hampton, N.Y., East Hampton star, 1968)   152 p.   illus., map.
F129.E13R34

EAST HAMPTON. Two hundred and seventy-five years of East Hampton, Long Island; a historical sketch, by Samuel Seabury, tog. with the book of the pageant celebrating the 275th anniversary of the founding of the town written by Miss Abigail Halsey.   East Hampton, N.Y., Pub. for the community, 1926.   140 p, incl. front., illus.   28 cm.   26-20113.   F129.E13 S 3

EAST HAMPTON. Indian place-names in East-Hampton Town, with their probably significations, by Wm. Wallace Tooker. Written for the East-Hamtpon town records, vol. iv.   Sag-Harbor (N.Y.) J. H. Hunt, printer, 1889.   x p.   22½ cm.   5-5548.   F129.E13 T6

EAST HAMPTON. The Gardiner manor; address delivered at the third annual meeting of the colonial lords of manors in America, held in the city of New York ... by Sarah Gardiner Tyler.   Baltimore, 1916.   24 p. incl. illus., plates, ports.   23½ cm.   20-18276.   F129.E13T98

EAST WILLISTON history, 1663 - 1970 (by) Nicholas A. Meyer ... East Williston, N.Y., Incorporated Village of East Williston (1970)   65 p.   illus.   23 cm.   77-100604.   F129.E14 M4

EASTON. Records of the Reformed Protestant Dutch church in the town of Easton, Washington County. Transcribed by the New York genealogical and biographical soc.; ed. by Royden W. Vosburgh.   New York city, 1917.   2, 103 numb. l.   35½ x 28½ cm.   Autographed from type-written copy.   17-21142.   F129.E15E15

EASTON. Graveyard inscriptions from the towns of Easton and Greenwich. (n. p., 1922?)
4 p., 77 numb. l.   28½ cm.   Type-written copy.   22-22254.   F129.E15 G7

EASTVIEW. The Hammond house at Eastview, near Tarrytown, the home of Captain William Hammond, etc., owned and restored by Westchester County Historical Society, 1926. Its story.   White Plains, 1927.   21 p.   plates.   23 cm.   49-34523*.   F129.E18 B 6

EDEN. An informal history of Eden, by Doris Anderson. (Eden, N.Y., 1946)   72 p.   illus. (incl. group ports.)   26½ cm.   Reproduced from type-written copy.   46-3451.   F129.E25 A7

EDEN. Sketches of Eden history, commemorating Eden's sesquicentennial, 1812 - 1962. By Doris Marguerite (Lyon) Anderson. (Eden? N.Y.)   32 p.   22 cm.   F129.E25A73

ELIZABETHTOWN. Pleasant Valley; a history of Elizabethtown, Essex County, by George Levi Brown. (Elizabethtown, N.Y.) Post and gazette print,, 1905.   xiv, 474, (6) p. incl. plates, ports., maps. plates, ports.   21½ cm.   8-30963.   F129.E3 B 8

ELLENVILLE days and ways, until 1897. By Dorothy Hurlbut Sanderson. Ellenville, N.Y., Rondout Valley Pub. Co., 1968.   166 p.   illus.   21 cm.   F129.E37 S3

NEW YORK

ELLICOTT. The early history of the town of Ellicott, Chautauqua county. Compiled largely from the personal recollections of the author, by Gilbert W. Hazeltine. Jamestown, N.Y., Journal print. co., 1887.   xv, 556 p.   23 cm.   Includes the early history of Jamestown and Chautauqua county. 1-14901 Rev.   F129. E4 H4

ELMA. History of the town of Elma, Erie county, N.Y., 1620 to 1901, by Warren Jackman. Buffalo, Printed by G. M. Hausauer, 1902.   4, 11-331 p.   plan.   23½ cm.   2-12291.   F129. E5 J 2

ELMHURST. Baptismal record of the Reformed Dutch church at Newtown, L.I., 1736 to 1846. Marriages by Rev. Garretson at Newtown from 1835 to 1846. Copied by Josephine C. Frost (Mrs. Samuel Knapp Frost) Brooklyn, N.Y., 1913.   2 p., 92 numb. l.   26½ cm.   Autographed from type-written copy.   The name of Newtown was changed to Elmhurst. 14-12730.   F129. E55 E4

ELMIRA. Manning's Elmira, Elmira Heights and Horseheads (New York) directory ... 18 Schenectady, N.Y., H. A. Manning co., 18   -19   v.   fold. maps.   19 - 23½ cm.   12-18197 Rev.
Directories

ELMIRA; a news magazine of the Elmira district. (Elmira, N.Y. Elmira pub. co., 19
v.   illus.   30 cm.   monthly.   44-42807.   F129. E6 E45

ELMIRA gazette. In memoriam ... (1876)   1 v.   F129. E6 E48

ELMIRA star-gazette. Diamond jubilee edition, marking Elmira's 75th anniversary. Elmira, N.Y. (1939)   1 v.   illus.   58 cm.   Consits of regular news section of Elmira star-gazette (v. 32, no. 277, June 27, 1939) followed by special sections A - C.   40M2185T.   F129. E6 E53

ELMIRA. A short history of Elmira, prepared for the Steele memorial library, by Eva Taylor, Elmira, N.Y., Steele memorial library, 1937.   68 p. incl. front., illus. (incl. ports., facsims.) 23½ cm. 39-3638.   F129. E6 T38

... ENDICOTT directory, including Endwell, Vestal, Twin Orchards and Vestal Gardens. Binghamton, N.Y., The Calkin-Kelly directory co., 19   v.   24 cm.   CA 36-544 Unrev.   Directories

ERIEVILLE, history and pictures (by) Louise M. Isbell. Hamilton, N.Y., Printed by Mid-York Press (1971)   (27) p.   illus., map, ports.   26 cm.   76-291795 MARC.   F129. E8 I 8

FAIR HAVEN folks and folklore, by Raymond T. Sant. (Red Creek, N.Y., F. H. Hosmer, 1941) 145 p.   plates, ports.   23 cm.   42-11298.   F129. F15 S 3

FARMINGTON. Quaker records from Farmington Monthly meeting, Ontario County. (By Mrs. Josephine C. Frost) (Brooklyn, 191 -)   49, 3 numb. l.   27 x 21 cm.   Autgographed from type-written copy. 12-30323 Rev.   F129. F18 F9

FAYETTE. Centennial historical sketch of the town of Fayette, Seneca County. Prepared by Diedrich Willers. Geneva, N.Y., Press of W. F. Humphrey, 1900.   157 p.   23 cm.   Biographical sketches: p. (90) - 136. 1-14902.   F129. F2 W7

FAYETTEVILLE. An Archer directory of Fayetteville and vicinity, including Highbridge, Homewood development and Sunrise Terrace, with a guide map of general information, 19   Fayetteville, N.Y., The Archer directory service (19   v.   illus. (plan)   23½ cm.   CA 36-305 Unrev.
Directories

FISHKILL. Historical sketch and directory of the town of Fishkill, with an appendix ... Fishkill landing (N.Y.) Dean and Spaight, 1866.   3, (9) - 10, (50) - 152 p.   illus.   20 cm.   20-3055.
F129. F4 H6

FISHKILL. The homestead of a colonial dame; a monograph by Alice Crary Sutcliffe ... Poughkeepsie, N.Y., Press of the A. V. Haight co., 1909.   57 p.   front., illus., plates, ports., facsims.   23 cm.   9-31667.
F129. F4 S 9

FISHKILL. Tombstone inscriptions from the churchyard of the First Reformed Dutch church of Fishkill village, Dutchess County. Comp. by E. W. Van Voorhis ... For private distribution only. (New York, Press of G. P. Putnam's sons, 1882. viii, 229 p. front. 21½ cm. 1-14903 Rev.

 F129. F4 V2

FLATBUSH. Brooklyn's garden; views of picturesque Flatbush. (Brooklyn, N.Y., C. A. Ditmas, 1908) 24 col. pl. 21½ x 26 cm. 8-37335. F129. F5 B 8

FLATBUSH, past and present. By Edmund D. Fisher; illus. from drawings by Allen B. Doggett ... Brooklyn, N.Y., Flatbush trust co., 1901. 90, (5) p. incl. front., illus., plates. 21 cm. "Authorities consulted.": p. (8). 1-30575 Rev. F129. F5 F5

FLATBUSH. ... Flatbush of to-day ... Pub. on the occasion of the tri-centennial celebration of the coming of the Dutch to Flatbush and the Dutch festival held the week of April 27 to May 2. (By Herbert Foster Gunnison) Brooklyn - New York, 1908. 168 p. illus. 25½ cm. 8-14523.

 F129. F5 G9

FLATBUSH. The history of the town of Flatbush, in Kings County, Long-Island, by Thomas M. Strong ... New-York, T. R. Mercein, jr., printer, 1842. 178 p. plates. 19 cm. 1-14904 Add.

 F129. F5 S 2

— (Brooklyn, F. Loeser, 1908) 188 p. front. (port.) 7 pl., double map. 19 cm. 9-771. F129. F5 S 3

FLATBUSH. Tales of old Flatbush, by John J. Snyder ("Snyder of Flatbush") Flatbush, Brooklyn, city of New York, 1945. vii, 231 p. illus. (incl. facsim.) 19½ cm. 45-2576. F129. F5 S 6

FLATBUSH. The social history of Flatbush, and manners and customs of the Dutch settlers in Kings County. By Gertrude Lefferts Vanderbilt ... New York, D. Appleton, 1881. 351 p. fold. map. 19½ cm. 1-14905 Rev. F129. F5 V2

FLATLANDS. A history of the town of Flatlands, Kings county. By Rev. Anson Dubois. Reprinted from "The illustrated history of Kings county", ed. by Dr. H.R. Stiles ... Brooklyn, N.Y. (W.W. Munsell) 1884. 16 p. illus. (facsims.) 31½ x 23½ cm. "30 copies printed." 1-14906. F129.F51 D8

FLEMING. Mohr's directory of the town of Fleming, Cayuga County. (Auburn, N.Y? 1904) 1 v. 24 cm. Directories

FLEMING. Records of the Reformed Protestant Dutch church at the Owasco Outlet in the town of Fleming, Cayuga County. Transcribed by the New York genealogical and biographical soc.; ed. by Royden Woodward Vosburgh. New York city, 1919. 2, viii, 61 numb. l. 36 x 28½ cm. With this is bound: Records of the Reformed Dutch church of Owasco. Autographed from type-written copy. 19-19374. F129. F53 F5

— Records of the Reformed Dutch church of Owasco ... 1919. 2 p., 33 numb. l. 36 x 28½ cm. With above item. 19-19608. F129. F53 F5

FLORAL PARK Golden Anniversary, 1908 - 1958, Incorporated Village of Floral Park, Nassau County, Long Island, New York. 35 p. 36 cm. F129. F56 F5

FLORAL PARK. Robinson's Floral Park, Stewart Manor, Bellerose, red book resident directory ... Hempstead, N.Y., Resident directory service, 19 v. fold. map. 23 cm. Includes "Robinson's Floral Park, Stewart Manor, Bellerose, directory of householders, etc." 38M4146T. Directories

FLORAL PARK. Across the year; the story of Floral Park, written for the fiftieth anniversary of the incorporation of the village ... By Edith M. Purcell. Uniondale, L.I., Salisbury Printers, 1958. 160 p. 24 cm. 58-14215. F129. F56 P 8

FLUSHING directory ... 18 (Flushing) Boyd's directory co., 18 v. 24 cm. 24-28109.

 Directories

FLUSHING. Famous men of Flushing; a series of biographies written by members of the Flushing historical soc. 1st - 8th. (Flushing, 1943-44) 8 nos. in 1 vol. 21½ cm. No more pub. 44-6898.

 F129. F6 F5

NEW YORK

FLUSHING, Queens County, L. I., monthly meeting of Friends, intentions of marriage, 1704 - 1776. William Applebie Eardeley ... Brooklyn, N. Y., 1913. 18 numb. l. 28½ cm. Type-written copy.
24-16059. F129. F6 F9

FLUSHING. Address; reminiscences of Flushing, 1847 to 1864. (By) Harry R. Gelwicks, 1907. (Flushing? 1907?) 16 p. 23 cm. Flushing historical soc. 10-31403. F129. F6 G3

FLUSHING. Olde Flushing. By Harriet (Dondero) Lawson. (1st ed. Flushing? N. Y., 1952)
207 p. illus. 24 cm. 53-31333. F129. F6 L3

FLUSHING, past and present: a historical sketch, by Rev. G. Henry Mandeville ... Flushing, L. I., Home lecture commmittee of 1857-8, 1860. 180 p. mounted front., mounted plates. 16 cm. 1-14907 Rev.
F129. F6 M2

FLUSHING. The story of Flushing cemetery, by Schuyler Brandon Stuart. Pub. for the tri-centennial of Flushing, 1645-1945 ... (Flushing, N. Y., 1945) 24 p. 23 cm. 46-1545.
F129. F6 S 8

FLUSHING. Colonial Flushing, a brief history of the town of Flushing, called by the Dutch Vlissingen. Founded in 1645 ... By Haynes Trébor. (Flushing) Flushing federal savings and loan assoc., 1945.
64 p. illus. 21½ cm. 45-5847. F129. F6 T7

FLUSHING. History of the town of Flushing, Long Island, by Henry D. Waller. Flushing, J. H. Ridenour, 1899. 3 p. (v) - viii, 287 p. 21½ cm. "Titles of books quoted, or referred to, in this history": p. (273) - 276.
99-1006 Rev. F129. F6 W1

FONDA. Records of the Reformed Protestant Dutch church of Caughnawaga, now the Reformed church of Fonda, in the village of Fonda, Montgomery County. Transcribed by the New York genealogical and biographical soc.; ed. by Royden W. Vosburgh. New York city, 1917. 3 v. front., facsims.
36 x 28½ cm. 17-21143 Rev. F129. F67 F6

FORT EDWARD. Old Fort Edward before 1800; an account of the historic ground now occupied by the village of Fort Edward, (by) William H. Hill. Fort Edward, N. Y. ... 1929. 383 p. front.
(facsim.) plates, maps (1 fold.) plans, diagrs. 26 cm. A 31-410. F129. F67 H5

FOREST HILLS. Why we have chosen Forest Hills Gardens for our home. (By Frederic W. Goudy) Forest Hills Gardens, N. Y., 1915. (26) p. front., illus. 23 cm. 15-15328. F129. F68 G6

FORT COVINGTON and her neighbors, a history of three towns. By Herbert D. A. Donovan. New York, O'Hare Books (1963) 447 p. 22 cm. 63-21001. F129. F69 D6

FORT EDWARD. The Fort Edward book, containing some historical sketches, with illustrations, and family records. By Robert O. Bascom ... Fort Edward, N. Y., J. D. Keating, 1903. 274 p. front.,
4 pl. 2 maps. 23½ cm. 3-31446. F129. F7 B 3

FORT HERKIMER church, erected in 1765. A historical discourse! delivered ... by Rev. Wm. Johns. (n. p., 1874?) 7 p. 22½ cm. 10-3154. F129. F75 J 6

FORT MILLER, N. Y. burial records. (By Daniel Veile) (Albany, N. Y., 1923) 30 l. 28 x 22 cm.
Type-written. Covers years 1832-1880, with some burials from Bacon Hill and other cemeteries. 24-5652. F129. F77 V6

FORT PLAIN. Records of the Reformed Dutch church ... v. 1. New York city, 1918.
1 v. pl., map. 36 x 28½ cm. F129. F79 F7

FORT PLAIN. - Nelliston Historical Society. Publication. Fort Plain, N. Y., 194 v. illus. 24 cm.
Began publication in 1943. 53-26338. F129. F79F73

FRANKLINVILLE, in pictures and story, by Roy W. Van Hoesen ... (Hornell, N. Y., Hornell printing co., 1914) 184 p. front., illus. (incl. ports.) 16 x 24 cm. "Biographical sketches": p. 44-168. 15-1492. F129. F83 V2

FREDONIA. The Mullin-Kille and Censor, Fredonia, consurvey city directory ... v.1 - Hebron, Neb., Parsons, Kan (etc.) Mullin-Kille co.; (Fredonia) The Fredonia censor, 1942 -
    v. illus. 23½ cm. 42-22085. Directories

FREEPORT. An authentic classified directory of the incorporated village of Freeport, Nassau County, for the year   ; cyclopedia and hand book of facts ... Freeport, L.I., The Long Island directory co., 1914 1 v. fold. map. 22½ cm. 14-6691. Directories

FREEPORT. R. L. Polk & co.'s Freeport village directory. New York city, R. L. Polk, 19
    v. 24½ cm. 23-8352. Directories

FREEPORT. Village of Freeport, town of Hempstead, county of Nassau, Presbyterian church cemetery, 1818 to 1911. William Applebie Eardeley ... Brooklyn, N.Y., 1913. 20 numb. l. 28½ cm.
24-15752. F129. F85 E2

FULTON city directory ... Elmira N.Y., M. P. Goodhue, 1909 - 1 v. fold. map. 23 cm.
9-4106. Directories

GALWAY. Stories and pictures of Galway, Saratoga County, by W. Bronson Taylor. Middle Grove, N.Y. (1966) 144 p. 24 cm. F129.G126T3

GANSEVOORT. Early days in Gansevoort and vicinity, book 3, by Mrs. J. B. Vanderwerker. (Schuylerville? N.Y., 1938?) 23 p. illus. 23½ cm. Book 3 of the author's Early days series. 43-39031. F129.G13 V3

GARDEN CITY. Robinson's Garden City red book resident directory ... Hempstead, N.Y., Resident directory service, inc., 193   v. fold. map. 23 cm. Includes "Robinson's Garden City directory of householders, occupants of office buildings, etc." 38M4147T. Directories

GARDEN CITY. History of Garden City. By Mildred H. Smith. Manhasset, N.Y., Channel Press (1963) 144 p. illus. 24 cm. 63-14160. F129.G15 S 5

GARDINER. History of the township of Gardiner. By Kenneth Edward Hasbrouck. Centennial, 1853 - 1953. (New Paltz? N.Y., 1953) 68 p. illus. 24 cm. 54-26896. F129.G17 H3

GENESEO. Village memories of twenty years; or, Geneseo between 1848 and 1863. An address ... by F. De W. Ward ... Geneseo, N.Y., J. W. Clement, printer, 1869. 26 p. 23 cm. 13-5269.
F129. G2 W2

GENEVA city directory ... Geneva, N.Y., W. F. Humphrey, 18   -19   v. 23 cm. 18-8215.
Directories

GENEVA. The Mullin-Kille and Humphrey Geneva, New York, consurvey city directory ... v.1 - 1942 -   Hebron, Neb., Parsons, Kan. (etc.) Mullin-Kille co., 1942 -   v. illus. 24 cm.
42-21704. Directories

GENEVA. Four centennials, by Charles D. Bean ... 3d ed. Geneva, N.Y., The Delphian historical soc. (1927?) 85 p. incl. illus., plates, ports. 23½ cm. 36-11404. F129.G3 B 43

GENEVA, the lakeside city; its industrial, social, educational and residential advantages, ed. by Charles H. Congdon. (Geneva) The Geneva Chamber of commerce (1905?) 53 p. (59) - 96, (4) p. incl. illus., plates. plates. 26½ cm. 16-21930. F129.G3 C67

GENEVA. Early history of Geneva (formerly called Kanadesaga) - by George S. Conover ... Geneva, N.Y., Courier steam presses (1880) 47, xii p. 21½ cm. From the Geneva courier, March, 1879. 1-297 Rev.
F129.G3 C73

— Supplement to Early history of Geneva. (Geneva, N.Y.) 1881) 3 p. 21½ cm. with above.

GENEVA. Delphian historical soc., Geneva, N.Y. Miscellaneous documents ... v. no.
F129. G3 D3

NEW YORK 353

GENEVA. Early history of Geneva. Address by George S. Conover ... Geneva, N.Y., 1877.
8 p. 21½ cm. 23-14449.
                                           F129.G3 C75
                                           Rare Book Coll.

GENEVA on Seneca lake, prepared by Frank H. Taylor ... Geneva, Chamber of commerce, 1902.
108 p. incl. illus., ports., map, plan, facsim. pl. 16½ x 26 cm. 3-9010.
                                          F129.G3 G25

... GENEVA historical. By Zcyhzawrvlteqsdubietkayn. Nasr-ed-din. Descriptive of its scenery, palatial residences, public buildings, fine blocks and important industries. Pub. under the auspices of the Delphian literary soc. Geneva, N.Y., 1887. (39) p. illus. 23½ cm. 3-18812.
                                           F129.G3 G28

— 3d ed. Geneva, N.Y., 1896. (34) p. front., etc. 24 cm. Delphian historical soc.   F129.G3 G3

GENEVA. An elegant but salubrious village, a portrait of Geneva, New York ... by Warren Hunting Smith, with linocuts by the author, assisted by Helen Sholes Smith. Geneva, N.Y. (Press of W. F. Humphrey) 1931. 4, 146, (3) p. front., plates. 23½ cm. Bibliography: p. (147) 31-34110.   F129.G3 S 75

GEORGE, Fort. Notes on the history of Fort George during the colonial and revolutionary periods, with contemporaneous documents and an appendix. By B. F. De Costa ... New York (etc.) J. Sabin, 1871. 3, 78 p. front. (plan) illus. (map) 24½ cm. 4-18821.   F129. G4 D2

GERMAN FLATS. History of the old Fort Herkimer Flatts Reformed church, 1723, by W. N. P. Dailey ... St. Johnsville, N.Y., St. Johnsville enterprise and news (1929?) 32 p. illus. 23 cm.
Bibliography: p. 30-31. 29-23856 Rev.   F129.G42 D2

GERMAN FLATS. Records of the Reformed Protestant Dutch church of German Flatts in Fort Herkimer, town of German Flats, Herkimer County. Transcribed by the New York genealogical and biographical soc. Ed. by Royden W. Vosburgh. New York, 1918. v. front. 36 x 28 cm. Autographed from type-written copy. 18-13628.   F129.G42 G3

GERMANTOWN. Records of Christ's evangelical Lutheran church of Germantown, Columbia County. Transcribed by the New York genealogical and biographical soc. Ed. by Royden W. Vosburgh. New York, 1913. 2, xvi, 252 numb. l. 36 cm. Autographed from type-written copy. 13-12767.   F129.G45 G3

GERMANTOWN. Baptismal record of Reformed Church of Germantown, New York, 1729 - 1898. (Transcribed and indexed by Arthur C. M. Kelly, Rhinebeck, N.Y. (A.C.M. Kelly, 1969.
iv, 243, 55, 44 p. 30 cm.   F129.G45G33

GERMANTOWN, Columbia County, graveyard inscriptions from the following named graveyards: - Reformed church cemetery, Lutheran church cemeteries, Methodist Episcopal church cemetery, New Methodist Episcopal cemetery on old Winans farm, North Germantown, Cheviot cemetery. Copied by Henry Oscar Rockefeller ... New York city (New York (genealogical and biographical soc.) 1920.
2 p., 68 numb. l. 32 x 26 cm. 20-22892.   F129.G45R68

GHENT. Records of Christ's Evangelical Lutheran church, in the town of Ghent, Columbia County. Transcribed by the N.Y. genealogical and biographical soc. Ed. by Royden W. Vosburgh. New York, 1912. 3, ii-iii, 244 (i.e. 243) numb. l. 36 cm. Autographed from type-written copy. 13-16528. F129.G48 G4

GHENT. Records of the Reformed Dutch church, called Christ church, in the town of Ghent, Columbia County. Transcribed by the N.Y. genealogical and biographical soc.; ed. by Royden W. Vosburgh, New York city, 1920. 2, vii, 150 numb. l. 36 x 28 cm. Autographed from type-written copy. With this is bound: Records of the Congregational church of New Concord in the town of Chatham, Columbia County. 20-4649.   F129.G48G45

GILBERTSVILLE. Reminiscences of early days; Abijah Gilbert, 1747-1811; Joseph T. Gilbert, 1783-1867, Compiled by Helen Gilbert Ecob, 1927. (n.p., 1927) 68 p. plates, ports. 21 cm. 28-531.
                                           F129. G5 E2

GILBOA. Records of the Reformed church in the village of Gilboa, Schoharie County, formerly the reformed Dutch church in Dyse's Manor, in the town of Broome. And records of the Reformed Dutch church in Blenheim in the old village of Blenheim, Schoharie County. Transcribed by the New York

1087

genealogical and biographical soc.; ed. by Royden W. Vosburgh. New York city, 1918.
xx, 179 numb. l. 36 x 38½ cm. Autographed from type-written copy. 18-9081.   F129.G53 G4

GLEN. Records of the First Reformed Protestant Dutch church at Glen in the town of Glen, Montgomery County, formerly the First Reformed Protestant Dutch church at Charleston. Transcribed by the New York genealogical and biographical soc. Ed. by Royden W. Vosburgh. New York city, 1918.
2, iv, 121 numb. l. 36 x 28½ cm. Autographed from type-written copy. 18-19958.   F129.G55 G5

GLEN COVE. Polk's Glen Cove directory, including Locust Valley ... New York, R. L. Polk, 19
  v.   24 cm.   24-990.   Directories

GLEN COVE. A history of Glen Cove, by Robert Reed Coles ... Glen Cove, N.Y., 1967.
82 p.   28 cm.   F129.G57 C6

GLEN COVE. An address delivered at Glen Cove, L.I., at the celebration of the second centennial anniversary of the settlement of that village, by Henry J. Scudder .. 1868. With an appendix. Glen Cove, Printed for the Committee, 1868.   2, (3) - 195 p.   20 cm.   1-14908 Rev.
                                                                                           F129.G57 S 4

GLENS FALLS. Directory of Glens Falls, South Glens Falls, Sandy Hill, Fort Edward, Caldwell, and Saratoga ... 18   (Glens Falls, N.Y.) The J. Rowen co. (18   v. illus., fold. map. 23½ cm.
CA 25-249 Unrev.   Directories

GLENS FALLS. ... Stoddard & Spencer's directory and map of Glen's Fall ... Ed. by A. L. Stoddard. Glen's Falls, Stoddard & Spencer, 1874.   94, (2) p. front. (fold. plan) 19 cm. 7-38087.   Directories

GLENS FALLS, Sandy Hill and Fort Edward directory, for the years 1879 and 1880 ... Dwyer & co., Sandy Hill, N.Y. ... 1879.   216 p.   22½ cm.   7-38085.   Directories

GLENS FALLS. Kirwin's Glens Falls, Sandy Hill and Fort Edward directory ... Wm. H. Kirwin, comp. ... v.2,3,5   Lockport, N.Y., Journal book and job printing house, 1885 - 91.
3 v.   23 cm.   7-38086.   Directories

GLENS FALLS. Waite's directory of Glens Falls, South Glens Falls, Sandy Hill, and Fort Edward, for 1901 -   ... (v.1) -v.5.   (Newburgh, N.Y.) L. P. Waite, 1901 - 1909/10.   map. 23½ cm.
1-25735.   Directories

GLENS FALLS. ... Anthony's standard business directory, guide and reference book for Glens Falls, South Glens Falls, Sandy Hill and Fort Edward, N.Y ...   (Glens Falls, N.Y.) Glens Falls printing co., 1892.   127 p.   23½ cm.   7-41348.   Directories

GLENS FALLS. In memoriam. Orange Ferriss, 1814 - 1894. (By James Austin Holden) (Glens Falls, N.Y., C. H. Parsons, 1894)   5-39 p. port. 19 cm. 4-30101 Add.   F129. G6 F3

GLENS FALLS, "the Empire city"; our part and place in history. A descriptive and illustrative edition introducing to the readers the Empire city of the state and her citizens, past and present ... Glens Falls, N.Y., Glens Falls pub. co., 1908.   3, (5) - 16 p., (32) l. illus., ports. 33 x 24 cm. 9-10993.
                                                                                           F129. G6 H7

GLENS FALLS. History of Glens Falls and its settlement, by Louis Fiske Hyde. Glens Falls, N.Y., Priv. print. (Glens Falls post co.) 1936.   347 p. incl. front. (mounted port.) plans, facsims. 26 cm. 38-10286.
                                                                                           F129. G6 H9
                                                                                           Rare Book Coll.

GLENS FALLS. A short talk about Glens Falls. By Charles H. Possons. (Glens Falls, 1893)
12 x 18 cm.   F129. G6 P 8

GLENS FALLS. ... Glens Falls centennial edition ... The Post-star. (1839)- 1939. Glens Falls, N.Y., 1939.   1 v. illus. 57½ cm. Forms v. 35, whole no. 10,009 of the Post-star, issued Apt. 24, 1939. 40M379T.
                                                                                           F129. G6 P 84

NEW YORK

GLENS FALLS. By Seneca Ray Stoddard. Troy, N.Y., Nims & Knight, 1889. 1 l., 17 pl.
15 x 19 cm. 1-14909 rev.* F129. G6 S 8

GLENVILLE. A complete copy of the church records of Glenville, Schenectady County, 1814 - 1920, members, marriages, baptisms, deaths. Copied by Charlotte Tayler(!) Luckhurst ... Albany, N.Y., 1922. 101 l. 28½ x 22 cm. Type-written copy. 22-7131. F129.G62 L9

GLENVILLE, N.Y., cemetery records. (Comp. Mrs. Charlotte (Taylor) Luckhurst) (Albany? N.Y., 1923) 68 l. 28½ x 22 cm. Type-written copy. 24-5651. F129.G62L92

GLENVILLE. The Schenectady patent of 1684 and the common land of Glenville. By Percy Myers Van Epps. (Glenville, Town Board) 1948. 15 p. illus. 25 cm. 49-15352*. F129.G62V28

GLENVILLE. Wolf hollow, Glenville's notable scenic feature, by Percy M. Van Epps ... Glenville, N.Y., The Town board, 1939. 3, 18 p. front., plates. 28 cm. Mimeographed. Bibliography: leaf at end. 41-7350.
F129.G62 V3

GLOVERSVILLE and Johnstown directory ... vol. - 36. - 1909. Gloversville and Johnstown, O. H. Bame pub. co., 18 - 1909. v. fold. maps. 21½ cm. 1-21976 Rev. Directories

GLOVERSVILLE. The Mullin-Kille and Credit bureau Gloversville, including Johnstown, consurvey city directory ... v. 1 - 1942 - Hebron, Neb., Parsons, Kan (etc.) Mullin-Kille co; (Gloversville) Gloversville credit bureau, 1942 - v. illus. 24 cm. 42-21703.
F129.G64A18

GLOVERSVILLE. Littauer day, Gloversville ... (Gloversville? 1927) 75 p. illus., port. 23 cm.
CA 28-452 Unrev. F129.G64 G6

GLOVERSVILLE: or, The model village. A poem. With an appendix, containing a succinct history of the same; also, biographical sketches of prominent persons and notices of influential families whose history is connected with its foundation and progress. By Horace Sprague ... Gloversville, N.Y., Printed by W. H. Case, 1859. vi, (7) - 131 p. 19 cm. 1-6087. F129.G64 S 7

GOSHEN. The First Presbyterian church, Goshen, 1720 - 1895. Robert Bruce Clark, pastor. New York, A. D. F. Randolph, 1895. 6 p. 13-79 numb. l. front., plates, etc. 25½ x 20 cm. 6-38849. F129.G66 C5

GOSHEN. The early records of the First Presbyterian church at Goshen, from 1767 to 1885, comp. by Charles C. Coleman. Goshen, N.Y. (The Democrat printing co., 1934) 3, (9) - 215 p. 24 cm.
34-5888. F129.G66 G7

GOSHEN. Land o' Goshen; then and now. By Elizabeth Sharts. Ed. by Mildred Parker Sesse ... Goshen, N.Y., The Bookmill, 1960. 147 p. 24 cm. First printing. 60-9809. F129.G60 S 5

GOWANDA. Historical sketch of the village of Gowanda, in commemoration of the fiftieth anniversary of its incorporation. Comp. by I. R. Leonard. Buffalo, N.Y., The Art-printing works of the Matthews-Northrup co. (1898) 116, (2), 117-147 p. illus., plates. 24 cm. 22-13272. F129.G67 L5

GOWANDA. Address delivered at Gowanda ... by Albert H. Plumb, in commemoration of the fiftieth anniversary of the incorporation of the village. (n. p., 1898) (12) p. port. 23 cm. 22-13923 Rev.
F129.G67 P 7

GRAND ISLAND. Cinderella Island. By Rob Roy Macleod. Grand Island, N.Y., 1950.
52 p. port., map. 24 cm. 50-988. F129.G68 M3

GRANVILLE directory including Pawlet, Rupert, Wells, Vt., Cambridge and White Creek, N.Y. ... v. 5. Springfield, Mass., H. A. Manning co., 1912. 1 v. 23½ cm. v. 5 does not contain separate directories of Cambridge and White Creek, but does contain directories of Shushan and Salem. 12-26029. Directories

GRANVILLE. U.S. census, Washington county, 1800 and 1810, also the town of Fair Haven, Vt.,

1800 and 1810. St. Johnsville, N.Y., Enterprise and News, (n.d.)   15 p.   23 cm.   39M2798T.
F129.G69 E5

GRAVESEND. ... The 250th anniversary of the Reformed (Dutch) church of Gravesend ... (Brooklyn, N.Y., Eagle press, 1905)   80 p.   front. (port.)   plates.   23½ cm.   22-19777.   F129.G693G6

GREAT NECK. Robinson's Great Neck (Nassau county) red book resident directory ... (Hempstead, N.Y., Resident directory service, inc., 19   v.   illus.   23 cm.   38-4617.   Directories

GREEN POINT. Historic Green Point; a brief account of the beginning and development of the northerly section of the borough of Brooklyn, locally known as Green Point, by William L. Felter ... Issued in connection with the semicentennial of the Green Point savings bank and by that institution. (Brooklyn, 1918?)   61 p. incl. front., illus. 24 cm.   19-10156.   F129.G695F3

GREENE. From raft to railroad; a history of the town of Greene, Chenango County, 1792 - 1867. By Mildred English Cochrane. (Ithaca, N.Y., Cayuga Press, 1967)   viii, 357, xxxii, 22 cm.
F129. G7 C6

GREENE. Echoes of the past; or, Annals of the town of Greene, Chenango County, 1867 - 1967. By Mildred English Cochrane Folsom. (Binghamton, N.Y., Hall Print. Co., 1971)   vii, 386 p. illus. 22 cm.   71-30656 MARC.   F129. G7 F6

GREENE. Views of Greene. Indelible photographs. (Greene, N.Y., E. L. Page, 1892) 16 pl.   12°.   1-14910-M1.   F129. G7 V6

GREENFIELD. Historical sketch of the town of Greenfield, Saratoga county, read ... before the Greenfield total abstinence soc. by R. E. Cronkhite ... (Saratoga Springs, 1876)   3 l. fol. Mounted newspaper clippings.   1-15940-M1.   F129.G71 C5

GREENPORT, yesterday and today, and The diary of a country newspaper, by Elise Knapp Corwin in collaboration with her husband, Frederick Langton Corwin. (Greenport, N.Y., Printed by The Suffolk Times, 1972.)   284 p. illus. 21 cm. Part 1 consists of articles sent by readers to the Suffolk Weekly Times: part 2 of articles by the authors.   72-181187 MARC.   F129.G714C6

GREENVILLE. Records of the Presbyterian church in the town of Greenville, Greene County. Transcribed by the New York genealogical and biographical soc. Ed. by Royden W. Vosburgh. New York city, 1920.   2 p., vi, 69 numb. l.   36 x 28½ cm.   Autographed from type-written copy.   20-17988.   F129.G715G7

GREENWICH. The Directory of Greenwich, Schuylerville, Victory Mills and Cambridge, incl. Centre Falls, Battenkill, Middle Falls, Bald Mountain, East Greenwich and North Greenwich ... (v.1 - 1892 -   Albany, N.Y., R. S. Dillon (1892) -   v. 23 cm.   22-13247.   Directories

GREENWICH. The story of Union Village as gathered from the files of the Greenwich journal ... by Grant J. Tefft ... Greenwich, N.Y., The Greenwich journal, 1942 -   1 v.   20 cm.   42-23749.
F129.G72 T4

GREENWICH. History of the town of Greenwich, from the earliest settlement, to the centennial anniversary of our national independence ... Compiled by Elisha P. Thurston. Salem, N.Y., H. D. Morris, printer, 1876.   iv, (5) - 78, xvii p.   front.   19½ cm.   1-14911.   F129.G72 T5

GROTON. Historical sketch of the town of Groton, Tompkins county, being a lecture delivered before the Groton literary assoc. by Prof. M. M. Baldwin ... Pub. by the association. Groton, N.Y., H. C. Marsh, printer, 1868.   40 p.   22½ cm.   1-14912.   F129.G75 B1

HAMILTON. Progressive Hamilton. A description of the village of Hamilton, New York; its scenery, material development, institutions of learning, and business enterprises. Utica, N.Y., J. P. Gomph, 1896.   109 p. incl. front., illus. (incl. ports.) 25 cm.   1-14913.   F129. H2 P9

HAMMONDSPORT. A history of Hammondsport, pt. 1 -   (Hammondsport, N.Y., Arranged and print. ... Hammondsport herald, 190) -   1 v.   illus. (incl. ports.)   32 x 25½ cm.   8-18597.   F129.H24 H6

NEW YORK

HANNIBAL. Hannibal's historical highlights. By Gordon W. Sturge. (Hannibal? N.Y., 1949) 280 p. illus., group ports. 24 cm. 50-13491.   F129.H25 S 8

HARPERSFIELD. Records of the Presbyterian congregation of Harpersfield, in the town of Harpersfield, Delaware County. Transcribed by the N.Y. genealogical and biographical soc. Ed. by Royden W. Vosburgh. New York city, 1921. iii, 36 numb. l. 36 x 28 ½ cm. Autographed from type-written copy. 21-19749.   F129.H26 H2

STAMFORD. Records of the First Presbyterian church of Stamford in the village and town of Stamford, Delaware County. Transcribed by the N.Y. genealogical and biographical soc. Ed. by Royden W. Vosburgh. New York city, 1921. 2, iii, 51 numb. l. 36 x 28 ½ cm. (With above item) 21-19748.   F129.H26 H2

STAMFORD. Private records of the Rev. L. E. Richards, while pastor of the First Presbyterian church of Stamford. Transcribed by the New York genealogical and biographical soc. Ed. by Royden W. Vosburgh. New York city, 1921. 2 p., iii, 25 numb. l. 36 x 28 ½ cm. (With above item) 21-19747.   F129.H26 H2

HARRISON. Record of Births, marriages and deaths in Harrison, Westchester Co. (n. p., 1922?) 3 numb. l. 27 ½ cm. Type-written copy. 22-22255.   F129.H27 R3

HARTFORD. The story of Hartford, a history, compiled by Mrs. Isabella Brayton ... Hartford, N.Y. (Glens Falls, N.Y., The Bullard press) 1929. xi, 212 p. front. (fold. map) plates, ports. 24 cm. "A genealogical study of a few Hartford families": p. 161 - 200. Bibliography: p. 202. 29-24631.   F129.H276 B8

HARTLAND. Quaker births, marriages and deaths, from Hartland Monthly meeting, Niagara County. (By Mrs. Josephine C. Frost) (Brooklyn, 191 -) 41 (i.e. 42) numb. l. 27 cm. Autographed from type-written copy. 12-29736 Rev.   F129.H28 F9

HARTLAND. Quaker records, Hartland Monthly meeting, Niagara Co. (By Mrs. Josephine C. Frost) (Brooklyn, 191 -) 2, 43 (i.e. 45) 2 numb. l. 27 cm. 12-29737 Rev.   F129.H28F92

HARTWICK. History of Hartwick (village and town) by Pearl Almyra Weeks ... Hartwick, N.Y., Hartwick reporter, 1934. 3, 89 p. illus., pl. 22 ½ cm. 35-845.   F129. H3 W4

HAUPPAUGE. A history of Hauppauge, Long Island, tog. with genealogies of the following families: Wheeler, Smith, Bull Smith, Blydenburgh, Wood, Rolph, Hubbs, Price, McCrone, by Simeon Wood; ed. by Charles J. Werner. New York, N.Y., C. J. Werner, 1920. 92 p. front. (port.) 20 cm. One hundred copies printed. 21-12140.   F129.H37 W8

HAVANA GLEN. 2 dozen selected stereoscopic views, with sketch of Havana glen ... Havana, N.Y. (1872) 10 x 18 cm.   F129.H38 M6

HAVANA GLEN, Views of ... (n.p., 18 - 9 ½ cm.   F129.H38 V6

HAVANA. Glen sketches at Havana, with descriptive poems. By H. C. Winton. Ithaca, N.Y., Andrus, McChain, 1868. 80 pp. 12o 1-14914-M1.   F129.H38 W7

HAVERSTRAW. - my home town, by James A. Farley ... address at the laying of the cornerstone for the new post-office building at Haverstraw... Washington, U. S. Govt. print. off., 1935. 11 p. 23 cm. 35-18230.   F129.H39F25

HEMPSTEAD. R. L. Polk & co.'s Hempstead ... directory ... New York city, R. L. Polk, 19 v. 23 ½ cm. 23-3190.   Directories

HEMPSTEAD. Robinson's Hempstead, West Hempstead, red book resident directory ... Hempstead, N.Y., Resident directory service, inc., 19 v. illus., fold. map. 23 cm. 37-33495.   Directories

HEMPSTEAD. Cemetery inscriptions from Hempstead, Long Island ... (Copied by) Josephine C.

Frost ...   Brooklyn, (191-?)   2, 91, 4 numb. l.   27 cm.   Autographed from type-written copy.   12-32394 Rev.
F129. H4 F9

HEMPSTEAD.   Records of the towns of North and South Hempstead, Long island.   (1654 - 1880)   Ed. by Benjamin D. Hicks ...   Jamaica, N.Y., Long island farmer print, 1896-1904.   8 v. 24 cm.
No more pub?   7-21514 Rev.
F129.H4 H36

HEMPSTEAD.   Souvenir of the 250th anniversary of Christ's first Presbyterian church, Hempstead, L.I.   Hempstead, N.Y., Inquirer power press print, 1895.   72 p.   front., plates, facsim.   23½ cm.   7-6493.
F129. H4 H4

HEMPSTEAD.   Colonial Hempstead, by Bernice S. Marshall; blockprints by Mary I. Oman; photos. by Historic American buildings survey and Irving B. Schwartz.   Lynbrook, N.Y., The Review-star press, 1937.   x, 392 p. incl. front., illus.   plates.   24 cm.   Maps.   Bibliography: p. 369-374.   38-3545.
F129. H4 M3
1937

— 2d ed.   Port Washington, L.I., I. J. Friedman, 1962.   392 p.   24 cm.   (Empire State historical publication, 9)
F129. H4 M3
1962

HEMPSTEAD.   The early history of Hempstead (L.I.)   By Charles Benjamin Moore)   New York, Trow's Print. and Bookbinding Co., 1879.   14 p.   25 cm.   "Reprinted from the New York genealogical and biographical record, vol. x, no. 1, Jan., 1870."   4-19253 rev.*
F129. H4 M8

HEMPSTEAD.   The annals of Hempstead; 1643 to 1832; also, the rise and growth of the Soc. of Friends on Long Island and in New York, 1657 to 1826; by Henry Onderdonk, jr.   Hempstead, N.Y., L. Van de Water, 1878.   107 p.   24 cm.   1-14915.
F129. H4 O5

HEMPSTEAD.   Antiquities of the parish church, Hempstead, incl. Oysterbay and the churches in Suffolk County, illus. from letters of the missionaries and other authentic documents.   By Henry Onderdonk, jr. ...   Hempstead, N.Y., L. Van de Water, 1880.   iv, 33 p. front.   23½ cm.   6-42568.
F129.H4 O52

HEMPSTEAD.   An historical sketch, of ancient agriculture, stock breeding and manufactures, in Hempstead, (Queens Co., N.Y.) by Henry Onderdonk, jr.   Jamaica (N.Y.) 1867.   (41) - 63 p.   front. 23 cm.   Reissue of part of the 26th annual report of the Queens County agricultural soc., 1867.   3-33160.
F129.H4 O54

HERKIMER.   Steber directory of the villages of Herkimer, Mohawk, Ilion and Frankfort in Herkimer County ...   1904, 1909/10.   Utica, N.Y., Utica directory pub. co.   2 v.   23½ cm.   4-24521 Add.
Directories

HERKIMER.   Records of the Reformed Protestant Dutch church of Herkimer in the town of Herkimer, Herkimer County.   Transcribed by the N.Y. genealogical and biographical soc. ...   Ed. by Royden W. Vosburgh.   New York city, 1918-20.   3 v.   facsims. (incl. maps)   36 x 28½ cm.   Autographed from type-written copy.   19-777 Rev.
F129. H5 H5

HICKSVILLE.   Robert Williams plain purchase, 1648.   Photostatic reproduction of the original division records prepared under the supervision of Jesse Merritt by the Nassau Co. Dept. of Photostat. Mineola, N.Y., 1948.   (2) p., facsim.: 157 p.   40 cm.   One of 15 copies authorized for the tercentenary, 1948.   50-31940.
F129.H57 R6
1746 a

HILLSDALE.   A history of Hillsdale, Columbia County; a memorabilia of persons and things of interest, passed, and passing, by the Hon. John Francis Collin ...   Philmont, N.Y., Printed by E. J. Beardsley, 1883.   (iii) - xiii, 143, 195 p.   22 cm.   The appendix (p. 1 - 195) includes biographical sketches, and speeches of the author.   3-18826.
F129. H6 C7

HILLSDALE.   Baptismal record of Reformed Dutch Church, Hillsdale, New York (Krum Church) (Dutch Church of New Claverack) 1776 - 1849.   (Transcribed and indexed by Arthur C. M. Kelly, Rhinebeck, N.Y., 1970.   iv, 37, 14, 10 p.
F129. H6 H5

NEW YORK 359

HOBART. Records of St. Peter's Episcopal church in the village of Hobart, town of Stamford, Delaware County. Transcribed by the New York genealogical and biographical soc. Ed. by Royden W. Vosburgh. New York city, 1921. 2 v. in 1. illus. 36 x 28½ cm. Paged continuously. Autographed from type-written copy. 21-9898 F129.H68 H6

— Supplement. New York city, 1921. 2 p., ii, 68 numb. l. 28½ x 36 cm. 21-9898 Rev. F129.H68H62

HOLLEY. An alphabetical list of the residents of the village of Holley ... Lockport, N.Y., Roberts bros. co. v. 22 cm. 26-6376. Directories

HOOSICK directory ... embracing the residents of Hoosick Falls, Hoosick, North Hoosick, Eagle Bridge, Buskirks Bridge, Walloomsac, West Hoosick, and Potter Hill ... 18 Albany, N.Y., R. S. Dillon, 18 v. 23½ cm. 24-28110. Directories

HOOSICK FALLS directory incl. the suburban villages of Hoosick, North Hoosick, Buskirk, Walloomsac, West Hoosick, Potter Hill, and R. F. D. routes nos. 1, 2 and 3. v. 9 ..... Springfield, Mass., H. A. Manning co., 1903 - 1 v. 23 cm. 8-27158. Directories

HOOSICK FALLS. Resources and attractions of Hoosick Falls. Its location, surroundings ... Hoosick Falls, Board of trade, 1890. 68 p. incl. front., pl. 8°. 1-14916-M1. F129. H7 P 8

HOPKINTON. Early history of the town of Hopkinton, history of East Village (Nicholville) and vicinity, diaries of Elisha Risdon and Artemas Kent, soldiers of the civil war, genealogical record of sixty of the pioneer families; with two maps and a hundred and forty illus. By Carlton E. Sanford. Boston, The Bartlett press, 1903. xiv, 604 p. incl. facsims. front., plates, ports., port., groups. 25 cm. 4-7984.
F129.H72 S 2

HORNELL city directory ... including Almond, Arkport and Canisteo with rural free delivery routes ... compiled and pub. by J. N. Schenck ... Hornell, N.Y., Schenck printer, 1937 - v. 24½ cm. Loose-leaf. 38-20437. Directories

HORNELL. Manning's Hornell and Canisteo directory, incl. villages of Almond, Arkport, North Hornell and rural delivery routes ... Schenectady, N.Y., H. A. Manning co. 19 v. 23½ cm. 39M4864T. Directories

HORNELL. ... Moore's standard directory of Hornell ... 19 New York city, The S. H. Moore co. (19 v. 23½ cm. 24-30844. Directories

HORNELLSVILLE city directory (1896 M'Connellsville, N.Y., F. R. Keough, 1896. 1 v. 23½ cm. 11-10207. Directories

HORNELLSVILLE, Canisteo and Arkport, Directory of for 1900. Binghamton, N.Y., C. A. Williams, 1900 - 1 v. fold. map. 24 cm. 0-6617 Rev. Directories

HORNELL, Williams' duplex directory of Hornell ... Binghamton, N.Y., J. E. Williams, 1911. 1 v. 23½ cm. 11-8153. Directories

HORNELL. Latham's Hornell city quadruple directory, 1914 ... also Canisteo village directory ... Almond village ... and Arkport village ... Bradford, Pa., C. H. Latham. v. 24½ cm. 15-1255. Directories

HORNELLSVILLE. The early history of Hornellsville, Steuben County. An address made at the centennial of the first settlement of Hornellsville ... By Irvin W. Near. Hornellsville, N.Y., The Evening tribune printing house, 1890. 29 p. 23 cm. 7-21. F129.H73 N3

HOWES CAVE. Story of Howe caverns ... comp. and ed. by Virgil H. Clymer. Cobleskill, N.Y., Howe caverns, inc., 1937. 72 p. incl. front., illus. col. pl., fold. map. 18½ cm. 37-12554.
F129.H75 C6

— 1941. 72 p. incl. front., illus. plates (part col.) fold. map. 18½ cm. 41-15233. F129.H75 C6
1941

HOWE'S CAVE. A description of Howe's Cave; with a popular treatise on the formation of caves in lime rock ... Illus. with numerous engravings. Albany, Weed, Parsons, printers, 1865.
28 p. fold. front. 23 cm. 9-23614.   F129.H75 D4

HOWES CAVE. A summer home. The Pavilion hotel, Howe's Cave, Schoharie County. Howes Cave assoc ... Albany, N.Y., Van Bentuysen printing house, 1889. 24 p. illus. (incl. map) 19½ cm.
1-14917 Rev.   F129.H75 H8

— 1885.   24 p. incl. illus., map. 17 cm. 2-6759 Rev.   F129.H75H85

HOWES CAVE. By Seneca Ray Stoddard. Troy, N.Y., Nims & Knight, 1889. 15 plates. 15 x 19 cm.
55-52917.   F129.H75 S 8

HUDSON. The Hudson city and Columbia County directory, for the year 1862-3, with an appendix, containing a record of the soldiers of the city and county, and a variety of useful information. W. V. Hackett ... comp. and pub. Albany, J. Munsell, 1862. 208 p. 20 cm. 9-16482.
     Directories

HUDSON city, Claverack and Stottville directory ... 18   Hudson, N.Y., J. H. Lant, 18 - (19
     v. fold. maps. 19½ - 22 cm. 1-12827 Rev.   Directories

HUDSON. Directory of the city of Hudson, for the years 1851 - 52. By Parmenter & Van Antwerp. Hudson, Parmenter & Van Antwerp, 1851. 70 p. 16½ cm. 9-16481.   Directories

HUDSON. Richmond's directory of Hudson, incl. Claverack and Stottville ... Yonkers, N.Y., Richmond directory co., 19   v. fold. map. 23½ cm. 26-795.   Directories

HUDSON. History of the city of Hudson, with biographical sketches of Henry Hudson and Robert Fulton, by Mrs. Anna R. Bradbury. Hudson, N.Y., Record printing and pub. co., 1908.
3 p., (ix) - x;ii, 223 p. 20 cm. 9-2761.   F129. H8 B 7

HUDSON. A travelers' directory of the city of Hudson, 1880. By H. R. Bryan.   v.
     F129. H8 B 9

HUDSON. Quaker marriage records from Hudson, Columbia County. (By Mrs. Josephine C. Frost)
2 p., 16 numb. l. 11, 2 numb. l. 27 x 21 cm. Autographed from type-written copy. 12-19129 Rev.   F129. H8 F9

HUDSON. Historical sketches of Hudson; embracing the settlement of the city, city government, business enterprises, etc., etc. By Stephen B. Miller. Hudson (N.Y.) Bryan & Webb, printers, 1862.   120 p. 23½ cm. 1-14918.   F129. H8 M6

HUDSON. The "Hudsonian," old times and new. By Robert M. Terry. Hudson, N.Y., E. C. Rowley, 1895.   9 p., 23 - 264 p. 8°. 1-16002-M1.   F129. H8 T3

HUDSON. A traveler's directory of the city of Hudson, containing railroad, steamboat, cab & ferry time tables ... Hudson, N.Y., H. R. Bryan, 1880.   10 cm.   F129. H8 T7

HUDSON FALLS. Some facts concerning our local history, by Willoughby Lord Sawyer. Hudson Falls, N.Y., Swigert press (1930)   62 p. illus. (plan) map. 22½ cm. 30-18639.   F129.H81 S27

HUNTINGTON directory, incl. Huntington Station, Northport, East Northport. Binghamton, N.Y., The Calkin-Kelly directory co., 19   v. 24 cm. CA 29-753 Unrev.   Directories

HUNTINGTON, Northport, Centreport, Cold Spring Harbor, Long Island ... New York, American photograph co., 1909.   96 p. illus. 23½ cm. (Illustrated America series) 9-7418.   F129. H9 A5

HUNTINGTON. Rural cemetery, Huntington, Suffolk County, Long Island, 1728 - 1913. William Applebie Eardeley ... Brooklyn, N.Y., 1914. 66 numb. l. 28½ cm. Type-written copy. 23-14853.
     F129. H9 E2

NEW YORK 361

HUNTINGTON. Cemetery inscriptions from Huntington, Long Island; copied by Josephine C. Frost
... Aug. 1911.   2, p.   87 numb. l.   27 x 21 cm.   Autographed from type-written copy.   CA 13-353 Unrev.   F129. H9 F9

HUNTINGTON town records, including Babylon, Long Island ... With introd., notes and index, by Charles R. Street ... Transcribed, comp. and pub. by authority and at the expense of the two towns. (Huntington, L. I., The "Long Islander" print) 1887-89.   3 v.   24 cm.   Babylon formed a part of Huntington until made a separate town in 1872.   1-14919.   F129. H9 H9

HUNTINGTON. ... The records of Huntington, Suffolk County, Romanah Sammis, local historian. Albany, The University of the state of New York, 1921.   17 p.   3 pl.   23 cm.   (New York state local history, town records, prepared by the Division of archives and history)   22-7160.   F129.H9 H92

HUNTINGTON. Records of the First church in Huntington, Long island, 1723 - 1779. Being the record kept by the Rev. Ebenzer Prime, the pastor during those years. Containing lists of members of the church, and of baptisms and of marriages, etc. Huntington, N. Y., Printed for M. L. Scudder, 1899.   144 p.   26½ cm.   2-2943.   F129.H7 H73

HUNTINGTON. Constitution and by-laws of the Huntington hist. soc. ... (Huntington, 1927)
4 p.   20 cm.   28-29659.   F129.H9 H94

HUNTINGTON hist. soc. Year book, 19 (Huntington, 19   v.   illus.   22 cm.   4-22091.   F129.H9 H95

HUNTINGTON. A handbook of Huntington, containing map, history and general information on the village of Huntington ... by Leonard M. Leonard. Huntington, N. Y., L. M. Leonard, 1931.
40 p.   illus. (incl. map)   23 cm.   49-31385.   F129.H9 L38

HUNTINGTON. Old times in Huntington. An historical address, by Hon. Henry C. Platt, delivered at the centennial celebration ... (With additional notes and family sketches) ... Huntington (N. Y.) Long islander print, 1876.   83 p.   19½ cm.   1-16115 Rev.   F129. H7 P 7

HUNTINGTON-Babylon town history. (By Romanah Sammis) (Huntington, N. Y.) Huntington hist. soc., 1937.   xi, 296 p. incl. front., illus.   21 cm.   38-5844.   F129. H9 S 3

HUNTINGTON. A sketch of the geography of the town of Huntington; with a brief history of its first settlement and political condition to the end of the revolution, by Silas Wood. Washington, Printed by Davis & Force, 1824.   30 p.   21½ cm.   46-37457.   F129. H9 W8
1824
Rare Book Coll.

HUNTINGTON. Silas Wood's sketch of the town of Huntington, L. I., from its first settlement to the end of the American revolution. Ed. with genealogical and historical notes by William S. Pelletreau. New York, F. P. Harper. 1898.   x, 63 p.   front. (port.)   23½ cm.   With facsim. t-p. of original ed.; A sketch of the geography of the town of Huntington ... Washington, 1824.   98-1173 Rev.   F129. H 9 W8
1898

HYDE PARK. Our local heritage; a short history of the town of Hyde Park. By Beatrice Fredrikson. (Hyde Park? 1962)   56 p.   22 cm.   F129.H99 F7

HYDE PARK, Dutchess County, Hudson-Champlain 350th anniversary celebration, 1609 - 1959. (1st ed. Hyde Park, N. Y., 1959)   (16) p.   23 cm.   F129.H99 H9

HYDE PARK. Historical notes of Saint James parish, Hyde-Park-on-Hudson, in commemoration of the belated centenary anniversary of the consecration of the first parish church. (By Edward Pearsons Newton) Poughkeepsie, N. Y., The A. V. Haight co., 1913.   2, (3) - 88 p.   front., plates, ports., facsims.   25 cm.   16-9882.   F129.H99 N5

HYDE PARK. Franklin D. Roosevelt's Hyde Park, by Lili Réthi and Frederick L. Rath, Jr. New York, H. Holt (1947)   (3) l., 21 plates.   2z x 28 cm.   47-31295*.   F129.H99 R4

HYDE PARK. Vanderbilt mansion, national historic site, New York. By Charles W. Snell.

Washington, 1960.   52 p.   24 cm.   (National Park service historical handbook series no. 32)   60-64527.   F129.H99 S 5

HYDE PARK.   Vanderbilt mansion national historic site, New York ...   (Washington, U.S. Govt. print. off., 1942)   15 p. illus. (incl. ports., maps) 26½ cm.   42-38172.   F129.H99 U6

— 1946.   folder (6 p.) illus. (incl. map) 21½ cm.   46-7103.   F129.H99U62

HYDE PARK.   Home of Franklin D. Roosevelt national historic site, Hyde Park.   (Washington, U.S. Govt. print. off., 1946)   folder (8 p.) illus. (incl. map) 22 cm.   46-7730.   F129.H99U63

— 1947.   folder (8p.) illus. (incl. map) 22 cm.   47-32377.   F129.H99U64

ILION.   Steber complete street directory and up-to-date map of the village of Ilion, Herkimer County, New York state ... Utica, N.Y., Utica directory pub. co.,   v. fold. map. 23 cm.   16-14617.
                                                                                                                                     Directories

IRONDEQUOIT story; a history of the town of Irondequoit (suburb of Rochester, county of Monroe) covering the years 1839 - 1957.   By Maude I. West.   (Irondequoit? N.Y.) Town of Irondequoit (1957) 149 p.   illus.   23 cm.   Includes bibliography.   57-12431.   F129.I 68 W4

    — 2d ed.   Town of Irondequoit, (1967)   x, 188 p.   illus.   22 cm.   68-23434.   F129.I 68 W4 1967

IRVINGTON.   Wolfert's Roost, Irvington-on-Hudson; portrait of a village.   Irvington-on-Hudson, N.Y., Washington Irving Press (1971)   151 p.   illus.   24 cm.   77-180730 MARC.   F129.I 72 W6

ISLIP town almanac.   Islip, Islip Pub. Co.)   v. fold. maps. 23 cm.   55-17246.   F129.I 75 I 8

ISLIP.   Some of town of Islip's early history; by George Lewis Weeks; illus. by the author.   (1st ed.) Bay Shore (N.Y.) Consolidated Press, 1955.   160 p.   illus.   27 cm.   55-3060.   F129.I 75 W4

ITHACA.   Manning's Ithaca directory ... 1883/84,   Schenectady, N.Y., H. A. Manning co., 1883 - 19   v. fold. maps. 22½ - 23½ cm.   1-17635 Rev.   Directories

ITHACA.   Norton & Goodhue's Ithaca city directory ... 1888/9, 1899 - 1910 ...   (Ithaca) M. P. Goodhue, 1888 - 1910.   7 v. fold. maps. 23 cm.   Nov. 16, 99-108.   Directories

ITHACA, by Henry Edward Abt.   Ithaca, N.Y., R. W. Kellogg, 1926.   7, 251 p. front., plates (2 fold.) ports., maps (1 fold.) 24 cm.   Bibliography: p. (231) - 238.   36-32621.   F129.I 8 A23

ITHACA.   Views around Ithaca; being a description of the waterfalls and ravines of this remarkable locality, by F. W. Clarke ... Ithaca, N.Y., Andrus, McChain (1869)   155 p. photos. 18½ cm. 16-7139.   F129. I 8 C5

ITHACA.   A history of the Jews in Ithaca.   Prepared by Anita Shafer Goodstein under the auspices of the Ithaca Jewish Tercentenary Committee.   (n.p.) 1955.   10 l.   27 cm.   56-23134.
                                                                        F129. I 8 G58

ITHACA as it was, and Ithaca as it is; with thoughts suggestive of the future.   By H. C. Goodwin. Ithaca, N.Y., Andrus, Gauntlett, printers, 1853.   64 p.   21½ cm.   8-34781 Rev.   F129. I 8 G6

ITHACA.   A guide book to Cornell university and Ithaca ... New York, Boston (etc., 1904) 17½ x 14 cm.   F129. I 8 G9

ITHACA in a nut shell.   (Ithaca, N.Y., 1904)   9½ x 12½ cm.   F129.I 8 I 83

ITHACA.   The Ithaca journal.   Anniversary edition.   Ithaca, 1938.   1 v.   illus.   58 cm.   Forms no. 128 of the 123d year of the Ithaca journal, issued June 1, 1938.   41M2384T.   F129.I 8 I 84

    ITHACA.   The Ithaca journal.   Ithaca's 150 years, 1789 - 1939 ...   Anniversary edition.   Ithaca,

NEW YORK 363

N. Y., 1939.   12, 20 p.   illus.   58 cm.   Issued Oct. 28, 1939.   41M2385T.   F129.I 8 I 85

ITHACA. Early history of Ithaca: a lecture, delivered ...   By Horace King.   Ithaca, N. Y., Mack, Andrus & co., 1847.   21 p.   23 cm.   1-14920 Rev.   F129.I 8 K5
Rare Book Coll.

ITHACA and its resources. Being an historical and descriptive sketch of the "Forest city" and its magnificent scenery ... By D. Morris Kurtz ... Ithaca, N. Y., Journal assoc. book and job print., 1883.   vi, (7) - 122 p.   illus.   23 cm.   1-14921.   F129. I 8 K6

ITHACA, past and present; written for the Ithaca Public Schools. By Virginia W. Mayer. (Ithaca, 1956)   92 p.   illus.   28 cm.   Includes bibliography.   57-30591.   F129. I 8 M3

ITHACA. Picturesque Ithaca. Photogravures.   Ithaca, N. Y., Taylor & Preswick (1896)
20 pl.   13 ½ x 18 ½ cm.   1-14922 rev.   F129. I 8 P 6

ITHACA. Views of Ithaca and its environs. By an impartial observer. (Solomon Southwick) Ithaca (N. Y.) Printed by D. D. & A. Spencer, 1835.   44 p.   23 ½ cm.   1-16014.   F129. I 8 S7
Rare Book Coll.

ITHACA. The scenery of Ithaca and the head waters of the Cayuga Lake, as portrayed by different writers, and edited by the publisher.   Ithaca, N. Y., S. Spencer, 1866.   150 p. incl. front., illus., plates. fold. pl. 18 cm. 1-16291.   F129. I 8 S 8

ITHACA. In and out of Ithaca. A description of the village, the surrounding scenery, and Cornell university, by C. H. Thurber ... Ithaca, N. Y., Andrus & Church, 1887.   vi, 104 p. front., plates.
20 x 15 ½ cm. 1-16013.   F129. I 8 T5

JAMAICA. Allen's Jamaica village and Richmond Hill directory ... 18   New York, G. E. Allen,
18   v.   23 ½ cm.   CA 33-692 Unrev.   Directories

JAMAICA. Morris' directory of Jamaica, 1921/22 - including Hollis and Queens village ... (New York) The Metropolitan directory co., 1921 -   v.   23 ½ cm.   22-2318.   Directories

JAMAICA. Inscriptions from Prospect cemetery at Jamaica, L. I., copied by Josephine C. Frost ...
Sept. 1910.   (2), 134, 5 numb. l.   27 x 21 cm.   Type-written.   12-16487 Rev.   F129. J 2 F9

JAMAICA. Inscriptions from Methodist cemetery at Jamaica; copied by Josephine C. Frost ... Aug., 1911.   7 numb. l., 76, 4 numb. l.   27 ½ x 21 cm.   Autographed from type-written copy.   CA 13-354 Unrev.   F129.J 2 F91

JAMAICA. Records of the town of Jamaica, L. I., 1656 - 1751; ed. by Josephine C. Frost ... Brooklyn, N. Y., The Long Island hist. soc., 1914.   3 v.   24 ½ cm.   15-5533.   F129. J 2J 15

JAMAICA. Baptismal record of the First Reformed Dutch church at Jamaica, L. I. ... 1702 to ... (1851) Copied from the original record by Josephine C. Frost. Brooklyn, N. Y., 1912-13.
4 v.   27 cm.   Autographed from type-written copy.   14-5776.   F129. J 2 J 2

JAMAICA. Marriages at Jamaica, L. I., by Rev. Jacob Schoonmaker, pastor of the Reformed Dutch church, 1803 - 1851. Copied by Josephine C. Frost ... Brooklyn, N. Y., 1913.   62 numb. l.   27 cm.
Autographed from type-written copy.   15-10367.   F129. J 2J 24

JAMAICA. Account book of Aaron Van Nostrand (chairmaker, 1767) sexton ... at the Grace Episcopal church of Jamaica, L. I., 1883 - 1820. Copied by Josephine C. Frost. Brooklyn, N. Y., 1913.
60 numb. l.   27 cm.   Autographed from type-written copy.   14-4610.   F129. J 2J 26

JAMAICA. Baptisms, marriages, funerals, recorded at Grace Episcopal church, Jamaica, L. I., 1769 - 1853. Copied from the original records in the early sixties by Henry Onderdonk, jr. ...
Copied from the above by Josephine C. Frost ... Brooklyn, N. Y., 1913.   2 p., 108 numb. l.   27 cm.
Autographed from type-written copy.   14-7376.   F129. J2 J 27

JAMAICA. The origin and history of Grace church, Jamaica, by Horatio Oliver Ladd ... New York,

The Shakespeare press) 1914. 441 p. front., illus., plates, ports., facsims. 24½ cm. 14-12549.
F129. J 2L15

JAMAICA. The history of the Jamaica estates, 1929 - 1969, by Thomas J. Lovely. (Jamaica, N.Y., Jamaica Estates Assoc., 1969) 55 p. illus. 28 cm. F129. J 2L 6

JAMAICA. A sketch of the history of the Presbyterian church, in Jamaica, L.I. By James M. Macdonald ... New York, Leavitt, Trow & co., printers, 1847. 138 p. 19 cm. 3-19774 Rev.
F129. J 2 M2

JAMAICA. Two centuries in the history of the Presbyterian church, Jamaica, L.I.; the oldest existing church, of the Presbyterian name, in America. By James M. Macdonald ... New York, R. Carter & bros., 1862. 329 p. front. 19½ cm. 6-42198 Rev. 2. F129. J 2 M3

JAMAICA. History of the First Reformed Dutch church of Jamaica, L.I., by Henry Onderdonk, jr. ... With an appendix by Rev. Wm. H. De Hart, the pastor. (Jamaica) The Consistory, 1884. 207 p. 7 pl. (incl. front.) 6 port., plan. 22½ cm. 16-9475. F129. J2 O46

JAMAICA centennial ... Also, recollections of school and college life. By Henry Onderdonk. Jamaica, L.I., 1876. 75 l. front., pl. 8°. Mounted newspaper clippings. 1-14923-M1. F129. J 2 O5

JAMAICA. The Dongan charter to Jamaica of 1686, its antecedents and implications; historical address, by the Hon. Victor Hugo Paltsits ... Jamaica, N.Y., B. Gertz, inc., 1940. 11 p. 20½ cm. 40-34520. F129. J 2 P 3

JAMAICA. Record kept by Rev. Thomas Poyer, rector of Episcopal churches at Jamaica, Newtown & Flushing, L.I. Copied in the early sixties by Henry Onderdonk, jr. ... copied from the above ms by Josephine C. Frost ... Brooklyn, N.Y., 1913. 2 p., 57 numb. l. 27 cm. Autographed from typewritten copy. 14-13121. F129. J 2 P 8

JAMAICA. First Presbyterian church of Jamaica, 1662 - 1942; a narrative history of its 280 years of continuous service, by George Woodruff Winans. Jamaica, L.I., The Church, 1943. xxi, 248 p. front., plates, 9 port. on 1 l. 22 cm. "List of principal sources consulted": p. 211-220. 43-6119. F129. J 2 W5

JAMESTOWN. White brothers' Jamestown directory ... 1888 - Jamestown, N.Y. (18 v. 23½ cm.
Directories

JAMESTOWN. The Journal's directory of Jamestown, Falconer, Lakewood, Celoron and rural free delivery routes of Jamestown ... 1899/1900 - Jamestown, N.Y., Journal printing co., 1899 - 19 v. fold. maps. 24 cm. 0-895 Rev.
Directories

JAMESTOWN. R. L. Polk & co.'s Jamestown city directory. (Pittsburgh) R. L. Polk, 19 v. 23½ cm. 20-8250.
Directories

JAMESTOWN. Autobiography by Samuel A. Carlson, mayor emeritus, and comments on his fifty years of public service. Jamestown, N.Y., Liberty print. (1943) 4, 71 p. plates, 2 port. on 1 l. 23 cm. 44-2767. F129. J 3 C3

JAMESTOWN, in Chautauqua County; a history, with selections from original sources. By Helen Grace McMahon. Jamestown, N.Y., 1952. 52 p. illus. 28 cm. 52-41630. F129. J3 M25

JAMESTOWN. Who's who in Jamestown. (Jamestown, N.Y., Economy service print., 1922 - v. 15½ cm. 22-13917. F129. J 3 W 6

JERICHO. Quaker records. Jericho, Long Island. (By Mrs. Josephine C. Frost) (Brooklyn, 191 -) 1 p., 87, 3 numb. l. 27 cm. Autographed from type-written copy. 12-29744 Rev. F129. J 5 F9

JERUSALEM. History of Jerusalem ... by Miles A. Davis. (Penn Yan, N.Y., Printed by H. C. Earles) 1912. 103 p. front., plates. 22½ cm. 12-28672. F129.J53 D 2

NEW YORK 365

JOHNSTOWN. Directory of Johnstown ... 18   Johnstown, A. E. Blunck, printer, 18
    v. 22 cm.   CA 33-924 Unrev.   Directories

JOHNSTOWN. Records of the Presbyterian church of Johnstown in Fulton County. Transcribed by the New York genealogical and biographical soc. Ed. by Royden W. Vosburgh. New York city, 1916.
2, vii, 190 numb. l. 36 x 28 cm. Autographed from type-written copy. 17-3606.   F129. J 7 J 7

JOHNSTOWN. Records of St. John's Episcopal church in the village of Johnstown, Fulton County. Transcribed by the New York genealogical and biographical soc. Ed. by Royden W. Vosburgh. New York city, 1919.   2, viii, 123 numb. l. 36 x 28 ½ cm. Autographed from type-written copy. 19-17760 . With this is bound: Records of the United Presbyterian church in Florida ...   19-19173.   F129. J 7 J 74

JOHNSTOWN. Johnstown in New York state's Mohawk valley, a friendly American community surrounded by scenic beauty, rich in historic tradition; comp. and written by workers of the Writers' program, W. P. A. ... (Johnstown, 1941)   89, (7) p. illus. (part col., incl. maps) 11 ½ x 15 ½ cm. 43-12.
                                                                                    F129. J 7 W7

KINGSTON. ... Historical account and inventory of records of the city of Kingston. Albany, The University of the state of New York, 1918.   48 p. plates. 23 cm. (Its New York state local history. City records)
19-27020 Rev.   F129. K5 A5
                                                                                    1918

KATONAH. ... Katonah, Westchester Co., N.Y. (By George Ancestry) (Brooklyn, 1907)
24 p. 20 cm. (Ancestry's genealogical series. A: Cemeteries. 1) Gravestone records from cemeteries in Kathonah, N. Y. and neighboring villages in Westchester Co., N. Y., and Fairfield Co., Conn. 8-34532.   F129. K2 A5

KATONAH. Historical sketch of Katonah, Westchester co., and its public institutions. Katonah, N. Y., S. S. Deacon, printer, 1896.   (26) p. illus., plates. 26 ½ cm. By various authors. 1-16188 Rev.
                                                                                    F129. K2 H6

KATONAH. Judge Wm. H. Robertson - the Katonah post-office - the Willett swindle - and the Harlem bridge. (By John Jay) (New York, 1863)   16 p. 23 cm. Letter from John Jay to the editor of the Eastern state journal.
11-19265.   F129. K2 J 4

KATONAH; the history of a New York village and its people by Frances R. Duncombe and other members of the Historical Committee, Katonah Village Improvement Soc. Katonah, N. Y., The Society, 1961.   xvii, 515 p. 24 cm.   F129. K2 K3

KATSBAAN. Gravestone inscriptions of Katsbaan, Ulster county. Comp. and ed. by Lila James Roney ... (New York?) 1927.   37 numb. l. 2 l. 29 x 22 cm. Type-written. 32-9741.
                                                                                    F129. K22 R8

KENMORE. History of Kenmore, Erie county, New York, 1926 (by) Frederick S. Parkhurst, local historian. (Kenmore, N. Y., 1926)   5 - 96 p. plates. 23 ½ cm. 32-32242.
                                                                                    F129. K32 P15

KENSICO ... New York, Press of the Kalkhoff co., 1910.   (48) p. incl. 41 pl., map. 25 ½ x 31 cm. 10-10809.
                                                                                    F129. K36 K4

KINDERHOOK. A history of old Kinderhook from aboriginal days to the present time; incl the story of the early settlers, their homesteads, their traditions, and their descendants; with an account of their civic, social, political, educational, and religious life, by Edward A. Collier ... New York and London, G. P. Putnam's sons, 1914.   xiv p., 572 p. front., plates, ports., plans (2 fold.) facsims. 23 ½ cm. 14-22607.
                                                                                    F129. K4 C69

KINDERHOOK. The village beauriful, Kinderhook, N. Y. (Kinderhook, N. Y., Fellowcraft shop, 1910)   3 l. plates, photos. 24 ½ x 29 ½ cm. 10-21041.   F129. K4 F3

KINDERHOOK. Records of the Reformed Dutch church of Kinderhook in Kinderhook, Columbia

County. Transcribed by the New York genealogical and biographical soc. ... Ed. by Royden W. Vosburgh. New York city, 1920-21.   3 v.   36 x 28 cm.   Autographed from type-written copy.   21-1970.

F129. K4 K5
L H & G

KINDERHOOK. Inscriptions of the historic stones, Kinderhook, copied and compiled by Lila James Roney. (n. p.) 1925.   4 p., 81 numb. l., 3 l.   phot.   28 cm.   Type-written copy.   25-16136.   F129. K4 R5

KINDERHOOK. An old Kinderhook mansion, by Henry C. Van Schaack ... (New York, 1878)
16 p.   pl.   24 x 18½ cm.   "100 copies printed."   Repr. from the Magazine of American history, Sept. 1878.   5-41573.   F129.K4 V27

KINGSBRIDGE. History of the town of Kings Bridge, now part of the 24th ward New York city; with map and index, by Thomas H. Edsall ... New York, Priv. print., 1887.   102 p.   front. (fold. map)
25½ cm.   9-10334.   F129.K45 E2

KING'S LANDING; a history of the first white settlement west of the Genesee River in the State of New York, 1797. By Helen Edson Slocum. Rochester, N. Y., Special Committee of the Rochester Historical Soc., 1948.   24 p.   illus., maps.   23 cm.   Bibliographical references in "Acknowledgments and notes" 9 p. 22-24)
48-2837*.   F129.K46 S55

KINGSBOROUGH. The addresses and other papers connected with the dedication of the Parsons memorials to Rev. Elisha Yale, pastor of the Kingsborough church ... Gloversville, N. Y., 1932.
90 p.   illus. (incl. ports.)   23½ cm.   33-25754.   F129.K47 M6

KINGSTON. The Dutch records of Kingston, Ulster County (Esopus, Wildwyck, Swanenburgh, Kingston) 1658 - 1684, with some later dates ... by Samuel Oppenheim ...   (In New York state historical assoc. Proceedings ... vol. xi - 1912-)   13-33600.   F129.K5 K49

KINGSTON. The Kingston and Rondout directory ... Comp. by William H. Boyd ... 1858. Kingston, F. S. Wynkoop (etc.) Rondout, A. Winter, 1858.   2, (25) - 140 p.   19½ cm.   Contains also Wiltwyck directory, 1858.
9-28873.   Directories

KINGSTON. The Kingston and Rondout directory: containing the names of the inhabitants, with an Ulster county business directory, and an appendix of much useful information. By J. H. Lant & co., Albany, N. Y. Kingston, F. S. Wynkoop, jr., 1864.   144 p.   19½ cm.   9-28871 Rev.
Directories

KINGSTON & Rondout directory for 1866. Also business directory, and Wiltwyck directory. New York, Fitzgerald, Webb & co. (1866)   xi - xii, (13) - 124, 16 p.   22½ cm.   7-40130.   Directories

KINGSTON. Directory of the city of Kingston, 1880. Kingston, Kraft & Childs.   1 v.   23 cm.
9-28867.   Directories

KINGSTON. Thompson & Breed's annual directory of the city of Kingston for the years 1888/89 -
(v. 1 - Newburgh, N. Y., Thompson & Breed (1888) -   1 v.   23½ cm.   8-25431.
Directories

KINGSTON. Breed publishing co.'s ... directory of the city of Kingston ... no. 4-5 Newburgh, N.Y., Breed pub. co. (1890 - 94.   2 v.   24 cm.   7-3386.   Directories

KINGSTON. The Freeman's 1st - 3d, 5 - 7 directory of the city of Kingston for the years (1895) - 1906. Kingston, N. Y., The Daily freeman staff (1895) - 1906.   6 v.   fold. plan.   23½ cm.   8-19446.
Directories

KINGSTON. Carle's annual directory of the city of Kingston for the years 1899/1900 -   (Kingston, N. Y.) S. B. Carle (1899 -   1 v.   24 cm.   8-19447.   Directories

KINGSTON directory ... 1907 - 09. Kingston, N. Y., The Price & Lee co., 1907 - 09.
3 v.   fold. map.   24 cm.   7-38038.   Directories

NEW YORK

KINGSTON. Kingston and Rondout, their representative business men and points of interest. By Geo. F. Bacon. Newark, N.J., Mercantile pub. co., 1892. 86, (2) p. 26½ cm. 3-27747.
F129.K5 B 12

KINGSTON. People's history of Kingston, Rondout and vicinity, the first capital of New York state (1820 to 1943) ... by William C. De Witt, city historian of Kingston, New York. New Haven, Conn. (Printed by Tuttle, Morehouse & Taylor co.) 1943 (i.e. 1944) 7, 445 p. front., plates. 24 cm. 44-47400.
F129. K5 D4

KINGSTON. Old Kingston, New York's first capital. By Mary Isabella Forsyth. 1893. 25½ cm.
F129. K5 F7

KINGSTON. The founding and early development of Kingston, with a description and views of old houses standing at the time Kingston was burned by British troops Oct. 16, 1777 ... (Kingston, N.Y., Freeman pub. co.) 1924. 47 p. incl. plates. 23 x 31 cm. 25-1028.
F129.K5 F78

KINGSTON. The city of Kingston, birth place of New York state. By Howard Hendricks. A bit of its early history, its rare native attractions, and its modern advantages for business and home life. (Kingston, N. Y.) The Kingston board of trade (1902) 70, (2) p. incl. illus., map. 23 cm. 2-20486.
F129. K5 H4

KINGSTON. The story of Kingston, first capitol (sic) of New York State, 1609-1952. New York, Stratford House, 1952. 233 p. illus. 24 cm. (American heritage series) Includes bibliography. 52-12097.
F129. K5 H5

KINGSTON. The Dutch records of Kingston, Ulster County (Esopus, Wildwyck, Swanenburgh, Kingston) 1658 - 1684, with some later dates ... Rev. translation for New York state historical assoc., by Samuel Oppenheim ... (New York?) 1912. v. 21½ cm. 13-22127.
F129.K5 K49

KINGSTON. ... report of the city historian for the year ending Dec. 31st, 1930, Alphonso T. Clearwater, city historican. (Kingston, 1931) (11) p. 22½ cm. CA 33-465 Unrev.
F129.K5K493

KINGSTON, ... (on the Hudson): city of civic pride and industrial growth. Pub. by authority of the Publicity committee of the Chamber of commerce, Kingston, New York ... (Kingston) 1913. (56) p. of illus. 23½ x 12 cm. 13-24433.
F129.K5K495

KINGSTON. Baptismal and marriage registers of the old Dutch church of Kingston, Ulster County (formerly named Wiltwyck, and often familiarly called Esopus or 'Sopus), for 150 years from their commencement in 1660. Trans. and ed. by Roswell Randall Hoes ... New York, Printed for the editor by the De Vinne press, 1891. 6, 797 p. 31½ cm. 1-24523 Rev.
F129. K5 K5

KINGSTON. Historical address delivered at the city of Kingston by William Lounsbery, at the centennial anniversary of American independence, July 4, 1876 ... Kingston, N.Y., W. H. & J. C. Romeyn, 1876. 31 p. 8°. 1-21540-M1.
F128. K5 L6

KINGSTON. The history of Kingston. From its early settlement to the year 1820. By Marius Schoonmaker ... New York, Burr printing house, 1888. ix, 558 p. front., illus., (incl. ports., plans, facsims.) 26 cm. "Ancestral notes": p. (472) - 495. 1-14924.
F129. K5 S 3

KINGSTON. The 200th anniversary of the erection of the building occupied as the Senate house of the state of New York in 1777 ... with sketches of old prominent citizens of Kingston, etc. etc. By Frederick Edward Westbrook ... Kingston, N.Y., Journal & freeman branch office print, 1883. 48 p. 24 cm. 1-14925.
F129. K5 W5

KIRKLAND. History of the town of Kirkland. By Rev. A. D. Gridley. New York, Hurd and Houghton, 1874. xiv, 232 p. incl. front. (map) plates, port. 19½ cm. 1-14926.
F129. K6 G8

LACKAWANNA. Directory ... Lackawanna ... Blasdell, Gardenville ... Ebenezer, Winchester. Buffalo, N.Y., Lackawanna, N.Y., Journal directory pub. co. v. illus, etc. 23½ cm. 14-13366. Directories

LAKE PLACID, its early history and developments, from the time of the civil war to the present time, as told by Arthur W. Hayes, a citizen, guide and building contractor of the Adirondack mountains. (Lake George, N.Y., Adirondack resorts press, inc.) 1946.   52 p. incl. illus., plates.   21½ cm.   47-17240.
 F129.L18 H3

LAKE PLACID club. circular. (Morningside? N.Y., 1906)   7½ x 12½ cm.   F129.L18L14

LAKE PLACID. Placid Park club; houses, rooms and prices. (Morningside, Lake Placid, N.Y., 1900)   24 p. incl. plans.   12½ x 7½ cm.   F129.L18 L2

LAKE PLACID club news. v. 1-4; Aug. 12, 1927 - Sept. 12, 1930. Lake Placid club, N.Y. (Forest pres, 1927-30)   4 v. in 1. illus.   27 cm. "Publisht weekly 5 months a year, July thru Sept., mid Dec. thru Feb. "Simpler spelling." Vol. 2, no. 22, incorrectly numbered v.2, no. 6. No more pub? 36-29802.
 F129.L18L33

LAKE PLACID and an experiment in intelligence ... By T. Morris Longstreth ... New York, The Century co. (1918?)   231-257 p.   20 cm. Reprinted from the "Adirondacks." 21-1995.   F129.L18 L9

LAKE PLACID. Picturesque Lake Placid ... Lake Placid, N.Y., 1904.   18½ cm.
 F129.L18 P 5

LAKE PLACID. By Seneca Ray Stoddard. Troy, N.Y., Nims & Knight, 1889.   1 l.   15 pl.   15 x 19 cm.   1-14231 rev.*
 F129.L18 S 8

LAKESIDE PARK hotel... (New York, 1899?)   13½ x 17 cm.
 F129. L2 L3

LAKE SUCCESS. History of the village of Lake Success. By Kate Van Bloem. (1st ed. Lake Success, N.Y.) Incorporated Village of Lake Success (1968)   ii, 56 p.   illus.   23 cm.
 F129.L24 V3

LAKEWOOD. The Kent house and cottages ... the Waldmere and cottages, Lakewood, on Lake Chautauqua. (Buffalo, 1897)   12½ x 17 cm.   F129. L3 K5

LANSINGBURGH, 1771 - 1971. (Prepared under the direction of Jane S. Lord with the assistance of the following contributors: Frances D. Broderick and others. Lansingburgh, N.Y., Lansingburgh Hist. Soc., 1971)   48 p. illus., coat of arms, map, etc. 28 cm. Bibliography: p. 48.   71-174720 MARC.   F129. L3 L3

LANSINGBURGH. History of Lansingburgh from the year 1670 to 1877. By Arthur James Weise. Troy, N.Y., W. H. Young, 1877.   44 p.   24 cm.   With this is bound his "History of the city of Troy." 6-13949.
 F129. L3 W4

LARCHMONT. By Rita Grunbaum. Larchmont, N.Y., J. P. Hackett (1961)   unpaged (chiefly illus.)   18 x 23 cm.
 F129.L35 G7

LARCHMONT. The story of Larchmont manor park, by Edward H. Tatum for Larchmont manor park society. (New York, Printed by F. Hubner, 1946)   48 p. incl. illus., mounted fold. maps.   23½ cm.   47-15630.
 F129.L35 T3

LAWYERSVILLE. Records of the German reformed church in New Rhinebeck, near Dorlach (or Sharon). Now the Reformed church of Lawyersville, in the town of Cobleskill, Schoharie County. Also, Record of the Union reformed Dutch church o Cobleskill. 1827 - 1855. Transcribed by the New York genealogical and biographical soc.; ed. by Royden Woodward Vosburgh. New York city, 1915.   2 p., xxi, 202 numb. l.   35½ x 28 cm. Autographed from type-written copy. 16-4774.   F129.L38L38

LEBANON. A sketch of Lebanon springs ... Pub. by Daniel Gale ... Pittsfield (N.Y.) Chickering & Axtell, printers (1872)   31 p.   fold. map.   17 cm.   1-14927.   F129. L4 G1

LEBANON SPRINGS. A sketch of Lebanon Springs ... (By Daniel Gale) 1881.   17½ cm.
 F129. L4 G3

NEW YORK

LEEDS. Records of the Protestant Reformed Dutch church of Leeds in the town of Catskill, Green County. Transcribed by the N.Y. genealogical and biographical soc. Ed. by Royden W. Vosburgh. New York city, 1920.   2, ii, 141 numb. l. incl. 2 maps (facsims.)   front.   36 x 28½ cm.   Autographed from type-written copy. With this is bound: Records of the Reformed Protestant Dutch church of Kiskatom in the town of Catskill. 20-4224.   F129.L48 L4

LEEDSVILLE burying round (near Amenia, New York. By Mary H. Reed. n.p., 1948) 3, 6 l.   map.   28 cm.   A photocopy of tombstone inscriptions ... 50-32393.   F129. L5 R4

LEON. History of the town of Leon. By Bert J. Dorsey. Leon, N.Y., 1958.   131 p.   23 cm.   58-40202.   F129.L56 D6

LEVITTOWN. A legacy for Levittown (by) Clarie T. Ellis. (Levittown? N.Y., 1965)   ix, 92, A68, 93-106 p.   28 cm.   F129.L58 E4

LEWISTON. The Devil's Hole, with an account of a visit made to it in 1679, by Robert Cavelier de La Salle. ... By Nelson Colt. 4th ed. Niagara City (N.Y.) Printed by N. T. Hackstaff, 1859.   16 p.   15½ cm.   2-10411.   F129. L6 C7

LEWISTON. Under the mountain. By Margaret D. Robson. Buffalo, H. Stewart (1958)   140 p.   illus.   23 cm.   Includes bibliography.   58-14007.   F129. L6 R7

LEWISTON. A back number town. Test and illus. by Frank Raymond Rosseel ... Buffalo, The Courier co., printers, 1891.   (28) p.   12 pl.   28 x 36 cm.   6-27420.   F129. L6 R8

LIBERTY. Souvenir of Liberty and vicinity ... By Otto Hillig. Liberty, N.Y., (1903)   (32) p. of illus.   16 x 20½ cm.   F129.L63 H6

LIBERTY, Sullivan County ... By Theodore Winthrop Weston. Liberty, N.Y., 1903.   16 p.   illus.   21 cm.   F129.L63 W5

LISLE. La Fayette and Lisle, by Frank P. Lewis ... Seattle (1924?)   12 p.   illus. (ports.)   22½ cm.   25-13928.   F129.L68 L4

LITTLE FALLS. Carter's directory of Litte Falls, Herkimer, Mohawk and Ilion ... 188 New York, Carter & co., 188   v.   23½ cm.   33-33144.   Directories

LITTLE FALLS. Directory of the city of Little Falls and the village of Dolgeville (Herkimer county) ... 1897, 1899/1900, 1903, 1905   Utica, N.Y., Utica dir. pub. co., 1897-19   v. plates, ports., fold. maps.   24½ cm.   0-904 Rev.   Directories

LITTLE FALLS. Williams' Little Falls and Dolgeville directory ... 1893/94   Utica, N.Y., J. E. Williams, 1893 -   v.   23½ cm.   33-33145.   Directories

LITTLE NECK. Robinson's Little Neck-Douglaston red book resident directory ... Hempstead, N.Y., Resident directory service, 19   v.   fold. map.   28 cm.   41-36268.   Directories

LIVERPOOL. Directory of Liverpool and vicinity ... (1924) -   (Liverpool, N.Y.) G. W. Freeman, 1924 -   v.   fold. maps.   23½ cm.   24-22914.   Directories

LIVINGSTON. Baptismal record of Linlithgo Reformed Church, Livingston, New York, 1722 - 1899. (Transcribed and indexed by Arthur C. M. Kelly. Rhinebeck, N.Y.)   iv, 152, 44, 33 p.   29 cm.   F129.L73 L5

LIVINGSTON. Marriage record of Linlithgo Reformed Church, Livingston, New York, 1723 - 1899. (Transcribed and indexed by: Arthur C. M. Kelly. Rhinebeck, N.Y., 1970)   iv, 39, 24, 4 p.   30 cm.   73-15395 MARC.   F129.L73L53

LOCKPORT. Boyd's Lockport city directory, with a business directory of Niagara County, and an appendix. By Andrew Boyd. 1866-7. Comp. by Andrew Boyd. Lockport, N.Y., 1866.   2, (25) - 160 p.   20 cm.   7-40104.   Directories

LOCKPORT city directory. (1908) Directories

LOCKPORT. The Lockport city and Niagara County directory for the year (1884, 87) v. iv-v.
Comp. by Wm. H. Kirwin ... Lockport, N.Y., Journal book and job print. (1884-87) 2 v. 23½ cm.
7-40102. Directories

LOCUST VALLEY. The Underhill burying ground, an account of a parcel of land situate at Locust Valley. Long Island, New York, deeded by the Matinecock Indians ... compiled by David Harris Underhill ... New York, Printed by the Hine pub. co., 1826 (i.e. 1926) 6, (3) - 79 p. front. (map)
plates, fold. map (in pocket) facsims. 29 cm. 28-1550. F129.L76 U5

LONG BEACH. The Estates of Long Beach. Long Beach, (N.Y? 1911) 19½ x 25½ cm.
F129.L77 E7

LONG ISLAND City. ... The Star directory of Long Island City, embracing Hunter's Point, Blissville, Dutch Kills, Ravenswood, Astoria, Steinway and the German Settlement ... 188 v.
Long Island City, T. H. Todd (188 v. 23 cm. 24-30843. Directories

LONG ISLAND City. History of Long Island City, New York. A record of its early settlement and corporate progress. Sketches of the villages that were absorbed in the growth of the present municipality. Its business, finance, manufactures, etc. ... Written by J. S. Kelsey. (New York) Issued by the Long Island star pub. co., 1896. 202, (2) p. incl. illus., ports. front., ports. 30 cm. 11-25202.
F129.L78 K3

LOWVILLE. General and business directory of Lowville, Croghan, Copenhagen, Constableville, Turin, Port Leyden, Boonville, Glendale, Forestport, Prospect, Trenton, Holland Patent ... 18
Lyons, N.Y., The Globe directory pub. co., 18 v. 24 cm. 22-15636.
Directories

LOWVILLE. Williams' directory of Lowville, Carthage, Copenhagen, Boonville, Black River, West Carthage, Croghan, Evans Mills, Felts Mills, Great Bend, Jerdon Falls, and Philadelphia. 18
Binghamton, N.Y., J. E. Williams, 18 v. 23½ cm. 22-15635. Directories

LUZERNE. ... From home-spun to calico. A centennial address delivered at Luzerne ... by B. C. Butler ... Albany, Weed, Parsons, 1877. 52 p. 23½ cm. 5-18342. F129.L96 B 9

LYNBROOK. Polk's Lynbrook village directory, including East Rockaway and Malverne ... New York city, R. L. Polk, 19 v. 24 cm. 23-12685. Directories

LYNDONVILLE. An alphabetical list of the residents of the village of Lyndonville ... Lockport, N.Y., Roberts bros. co. v. 22 cm. 26-6375. Directories

LYONS. ..."Grip's "historical souvenir of Lyons. (By Edgar Luderne Welch) Lyons, N.Y., The Lyons Republican print, 1904. 108 p. illus. (incl. ports.) 26 cm. (Historical souvenir series no. 18) 4-35801* Cancel.
F129.L98 W4

LYSANDER. Historical review of the town of Lysander. Comp. L. Pearl Palmer, (Baldwinsville? N.Y., 1947?) 1 v. (unpaged) 29 cm. "Printed serially in the Baldwinsville messenger from 1941 to 1946." Bibliography:
leaf 1. 50-38244. F129.L99 P 3

MALONE. The Mullin-Kille and Chamber of commerce Malone, New York, consurvey. Master ed. ... v. 1 - 1942 - Hebron, Neb., and Parsons, Kan., The Mullin-Kille co.; (Malone) Malone chamber of commerce, 1942 - v. illus. 24 cm. 42-14914. Directories

MALONE. Sesqui-centennial of Malone, 1802 - 1952. (Malone, N.Y., 1952) 102 p. illus. 28 cm.
55-58665. F129.M168 S4

MAMARONECK. Polk's Mamaroneck & Harrison directory ... New York, R. L. Polk, 19
v. 24 cm. 24-335. Directories

NEW YORK

MAMARONECK. Turner's annual directory, embracing the residents of Mamaroneck, Harrison, Rye and Port Chester, New York, and Greenwich and Rockyneck, Conn., along the line of the New York, New Haven & Hartford railroad ... 18   Yonkers, N.Y., E. F. Turner & co., 18
  v.   23½ cm.   CA 31-233 Unrev. Directories

MAMARONECK. "Mamaroneck through the years," by William Gershom Fulcher ... (Larchmont, N.Y.) The Larchmont times (1936)   64 p. fold. front., illus. (incl. ports., facsims.) maps (part fold.)   28 cm.
39-31745. F129.M17 F8

MANHASSET. Robinson's Manhasset-Plandome, Munsey Park, Flower Hill, North Hills, Roslyn estates (Nassau county) red book resident directory ...   Hempstead, N.Y., Resident directory service, inc., 19   v. illus., fold. map. 23 cm.   Includes "Robinson's Manhasset-Plandome, Munsey Park, Flower Hill, North Hills, Roslyn estates directory ..."   38M4148T. Directories

MANHASSET. Robinson's Manhasset-Plandome, Munsey Park, Flower Hill, North Hills, Roslyn estates (Nassau) red book resident directory ... Hempstead, N.Y., Resident directory service, inc., 19   v. illus., fold. map. 23 cm.   Includes "Street and avenue guide ..."   38M4144T. Directories

MANHASSET. Baptisms from Reformed Dutch church at Success, Long Island (now Manhasset), 1742 - 1793. Copied from the original books (which cannot now be found) by Henry Onderdonk, jr. Copied from the above ... by Josephine C. Frost. Brooklyn, N.Y., 1913.   2 p., 66 (i.e. 68) numb. l. 27 cm.
Autographed from type-written copy.   14-5938. F129.M19M18

MANHASSET. Deaths from Reformed Dutch church at Manhasset ... Josephine C. Frost ... Brooklyn, N.Y., 1913.   69 numb. l.   27 cm.   14-4171. F129.M19M185

MANHASSET. Marriages recorded at Reformed Dutch church, Manhasset ... 1785-1878, 1826-1859, also a few deaths, 1841-1878 ... Josephine C. Frost. Brooklyn, N.Y., 1913.   69, 70-88 numb. l.
27 cm.   Autographed from type-written copy.   14-5937. F129.M19M19

MANHATTAN BEACH. The village color-bearer. Tog. with a story of a U.S. life-saving service keeper. By Capt. Richard H. Ryder ... Brooklyn, N.Y., G. S. Patton, 1891.   200 p. incl. front. (port.)
illus., pl.   21 cm.   13-6011. E601. R 99

MANHATTAN BEACH. The story of Manhattan beach; a practical and picturesque delineation of its history, development and attractions ... Also, an account of Coney Island from the earliest times ... New York, F. Hart, 1879.   61 p. incl. front., map. 12º.   1-14930-M1. F129. M2 D4

MANLIUS. History of Fayetteville-Manlius area. By Lena Putnam Anguish. Manlius, N.Y., Fayetteville-Manlius Central School District, 1966.   96 p.   23 cm.
F129.M22 A7

MANLIUS. Church records 1805 - 1910 in the Township of Manlius, Onondaga County, copied by the Mediceans Club. (Manlius) 1960.   457 p.   22 x 29 cm.   Typescript (carbon copy) F129.M22 M4

MANLIUS. A history of Manlius village, in a course of lectures read before the Manlius literary assoc., by Henty C. Van Schaack ... Rev. and enl. Fayetteville, N.Y., Printed at the Recorder office, 1873.   82 p.   22½ cm.   10-6839. F129.M22 V2

MANORTON. Baptismal record of St. John's Lutheran Church, Manorton, (Lutheran Church of Livingston) 1765 - 1872. (Transcribed and indexed by Arthur C. M. Kelly. Rhinebeck? N.Y., 1971)
iv, 215, 29, 23 p.   28 cm.   72-177996 MARC. F129.M223M3

MANORTON. Records of St. John's Evangelical Lutheran church at Manorton, in the town of Livingston, Columbia County. Transcribed by the New York genealogical and biographical soc. Ed. by Royden Woodward Vosburgh, New York, 1913.   2 v.   36 cm.   Autographed from typewritten copy.   13-16527.
F129.M223M33

MARATHON. ...Marathon and vicinity... comp. Edgar Luderne Welch. (Fayetteville, N.Y., Bulletin pub. co., 1901.   87 p. illus. (incl. ports.) 27 cm.   "Grip's" historical souvenir .. no. 9) 1-21788 Rev. F129.M23 W4

MARCELLUS. The centennial history, of the town of Marcellus ... By Israel Parsons. Marcellus (N.Y., Reed's printing house) 1878.   2, 108 p.   23 cm.   1-21497.

F129.M25 P2

MARLBOROUGH. The history of the town of Marlborough, Ulster County, New York: from the first settlement in 1712, by Capt. Wm. Bond, to 1887. By Charles H. Cochrane ... Poughkeepsie, Print. W. F. Boshart, 1887.   2, 202 p. front., plates (1 fold.) fold. map. 23½ cm.   10-13006.

F129.M34 C6

MARLBOROUGH. Marriages performed by Rev. James I. Ostrom, copied from note book kept by himself, by Mrs. William Vanamee.   (From Historical soc. of Newburgh Bay and the Highlands. Historical papers. Newburgh, 1901. no. 8.   8-19309.

F129.M34 O8

MARLBOROUGH. History of the town of Marlborough, Ulster County, from its earliest discovery, by C. M. Woolsey ... Albany, J. B. Lyon co., printers, 1908.   471 p. front., plates, ports., maps (1 fold. in pocket) facsims. (2 fold.) 24 cm.   8-30965.

F129.M34 W8

MASSAPEQUA welcomes you. Chamber of Commerce (Massapequa? 1950)   72 p. illus., fold. map (inserted) 22 cm.   51-21349.

F129.M36 M3

MASSENA and Potsdam directory ... Schenectady, N.Y., H. A. Manning co., 1919   v. 23½ cm. 20-346.

Directories

MASSENA. The Mullin-Kille Massena, consurvey city directory. Master ed. ... v.1 - 1941 -   Hebron, Neb., and Parsons, Kan., Mullin Kille co., 1941 -   v. illus. 23½ cm. 42-4198.

Directories

MASSENA. Souvenir of Massena. From recent photos. (Camden, N.J., Moebius, phototype, 1900) (5) l. 25 pl., map. 16½ x 24½ cm. ... the Ladies' auxiliary, St. John's church, Massena, N.Y.   CA 25-1525 Unrev.

F129.M38 M4

MATTITUCK. A history of Mattituck, Long Island, by Rev. Charles E. Craven. (Mattituck? N.Y.) For the author (1906)   400 p. incl. front. (port.) illus. fold. map. 21 cm.   7-426.

F129. M4 C8

MAYFIELD. Records of the Reformed Dutch church of Mayfield, formerly in the town of Mayfield, Montgomery County; the First Presbyterian church of Broadalbin in the village and town of Broadalbin, Fulton County; the United Presbyterian church of Broadalbin in the town of Perth, Fulton County. Transcribed by the New York genealogical and biographical soc. Ed. by Roden W. Vosburgh.   New York city, 1918.   2 p., viii, 197 numb. l. 36 x 28½ cm.   Autographed from type-written copy. 19-873.   F129.M46 B8

MECHANICVILLE and Stillwater directory. Springfield, Mass., H. A. Manning co.   1 v. 23½ cm. 11-3271.

Directories

MEDINA. An alphabetical list of the residents of the village of Medina ... Lockport, N.Y., Roberts Bros. co.   v. 22 cm.   26-6373.

Directories

MENANDS; the garden suburb of Albany and Troy. By Henry P. Phelps. Albany, N.Y., Brandow, Barton, 1886.   16 p.   8°.   1-14931-M1.

F129. M5 P5

MERRICK. An historical sketch of Merrick, Long Island, 1643 - 1900. Written for the Merrick library, by Chas. N. Kent. Merrick, N.Y., The Merrick library, 1900.   79 p. 22½ cm. 1-1852.

F129. M6 K3

MEXICO. The old Pratham church. With incidents in the early history of Mexico. A sermon delivered by Rev. A. Parke Burgess ... Syracuse, N.Y., Printed at 45 Jefferson st., 1877. 56 p. 22 cm. 32-8225.

F129.M63 B9

MEXICO, mother of towns; fragments of local history. By Elizabeth Mary Simpson. (Buffalo, J. W. Clement Co., 1949)   551 p. illus., port., maps, facsim. 24 cm. Bibliography: p. 529-533. 49-5746*.   F129.M63S55

NEW YORK 373

MEXICO. "Grip's" historical souvenir of Mexico. (By Edgar Luderne Welch) (Syracuse? 1904)
92 p. illus. (incl. ports.) 26½ cm. (Historical souvenir seris, no. 15) 4-14327* Cancel. F129.M63 W4

MIDDLEBURG. Records. Transcribed by the New York Genealogical and Biographical Soc., ed. by
Royden W. Vosburgh. New York, 1918. ii, 150 l. front., 9 facsim. 36 cm. 18-10881 rev.*
F129.M67M67
L H & G

MIDDLEBURGH. Picturesque Middleburgh and vicinity. Middleburgh, N.Y., P. W. Danforth (19 -)
1 v. (unpaged) illus., ports., map. 16 x 26 cm. 49-30104*. F129.M67 P5

MIDDLEBURGH. ... Historical sourvenir of Middleburgh ... (By Edgar Ludern Welch) (Albany,
N.Y., 1894) 16 p. illus. (incl. ports.) 27 cm. ("Grip's" illustrated souvenir, historical series no. 1) "Grip's valley gazette, v.2,
no. 4, Nov., 1894. 4-28344 Cancel. F129.M67 W4

MIDDLETOWN directory including Goshen, 19   New Haven, The Price & Lee co., 19
v. fold. front. (map) 23½ cm. 21-16027. Directories

MIDDLETOWN, its representative business men, and points of interest. New York, Mercantile pub.
co., 1893. 68 p. illus. 4°. 1-14932-M1. F129. M7 B1

MIDDLETOWN. Fifty years commemorating the fiftieth anniversary of Middletown, as a city ...
Program; history of Middletown; committees; pictures and maps old and new ... (Middletown, N.Y.,
The Whitlock press, inc., 1938) 38 p. illus. (incl. ports., maps) 26 cm. 38-31156. F129. M7 F5

MIDDLETOWN, the metropolis of Orange County. (Middletown) Business men's association of Middletown, 1910. 48 p. illus. 25½ cm. 11-1056. F129. M7 M8

MIDDLETOWN times herald. (Firemen's edition) Middletown, N.Y., 1936. 1 v. illus. 58 cm.
With the regular news section, forms v.85, no. 147 of the Middleton times herald, June 23, 1936. 39M4866T. F129. M7 M87

MIDDLETOWN. Souvenir of the city of Middletown, N.Y. Photogravures. Middletown, Southwell &
Rifenbary (1895) 15 pl. obl. 24°. 1-14933-M1. F129. M7 S7

MIDDLETOWN; a biography, by Franklin B. Williams ... Middletown, N.Y., L. A. Toepp, 1928.
3, 5-201 p. front., illus. (incl. ports., plans) 22½ cm. Bibliography: p. 189. 28-29978. F129. M7 W7

MIDWAY PARK (Orange co.) souvenir. (Middleton, N.Y., Press of L. S. & J. D. Stivers) 1894.
(20) p. illus. obl. 24°. 1-16296-M1. F129. M72 M7

MILLER'S PLACE. History of Miller's place, by Margaret Davis Cass. (n.p.) St. Gerard Print.
1971. 70 p. illus. 22 cm. F129.M725G3

MINAVILLE. Records of the Reformed Protestant Dutch church of Florida, in the village of Minaville, town of Florida, Montgomery County. Preceded by the records of the Reformed Protestant
Dutch church of Duanesburgh, 1798-1804. Transcribed by the N.Y. genealogical and biographical
soc.; ed. by Royden W. Vosburgh. New York city, 1919. 2, viii, 189 numb. l. 36 x 28½ cm. Autographed
from type-written copy. 19-3092. F129.M73M73

MINDEN. Records of the Lutheran St. Paul's church in the town of Minden, otherwise known as the
Geisenberg church, formerly at Hallsville, in the town of Minden, Montgomery County. Transcribed
by the New York genealogical and biographical soc. Ed. by Royden W. Vosburgh. New York, 1914.
3 p., ii-xxv, 277 numb. l. (incl. maps) 35½ cm. Autographed from type-written copy. 14-12722. F129.M735M6

MINEOLA. Robinson's Mineola, East Williston-Williston Park red book resident directory ...
Hempstead, N.Y., Resident directory service, 19   v. illus., fold. map. 28 cm. 40-19853.
Directories

MINEOLA, Long Island. Mineola, L.I., 1908. 16 x 23½ cm. F129.M74 M7

1107

MODENA. History of Modena. By Kenneth Edward Hasbrouck. (New Paltz? N. Y.) 1949.
20 p. illus., map. 23 cm. 49-22652*.
F129.M746H3

MONROE. Chronicles of Monroe in the olden time; town and village, Orange County, by Rev. Daniel Niles Freeland. New York, The De Vinne press, 1898. v-x, 249 p. front. (map) 24 cm. 98-2257 Rev.
F129.M75 F8

MONTAUK, by Eugene L. Armbruster ... New York, 1923. 8 p. 27½ cm. 23-10429.
F129.M76A72

MONTAUK: three centuries of romance, sport and adventure, by Jeannette Edwards Rattray ... (East Hampton, L. I., The Star press) 1938. 94 p. incl. illus., facsim. 18 x 21 cm. 38-17845.
F129.M76 R3

MONTAUK. A romantic tale of high American life; or, Excursion to Montauk. First and last time. By Ned Stratton ... Providence, J. F. Moore, printer, 1847. 32 p. incl. plates. 22 cm. 24-7431.
F129.M76 S8

MORAVIA. Historical sketches of early Moravia and St. Matthew's Church. By Henry Gregory. Moravia, N. Y, 1956) (11) l. 28 cm.
F129.M767G7

MORAVIA and its past, and adjoining townships (by) Leslie L. Luther. Indianapolis, F. Luther (1966) xvii, 534 p. 23 cm. 66-29143.
F129.M767L8

MORAVIA. Historical sketches of the town of Moravia, from 1791 to 1873, by James A. Wright. Auburn, N. Y., Benton & Reynolds, printers, 1874. 289 p. 21½ cm. A 32-10.
F129.M767W8

MORICHES. Pictorial history of the Moriches. By August Stout. Center Moriches, N. Y., Central Press (1964) 1 v. unpaged. 28 cm.
F129.M77 S8

MORRIS, New York, 1773 - 1923 (by) Joyce Foote. (Morris? N. Y. 1970) 108 p. illus. 23 cm.
F129.M78 F6

MOUNT KISCO. History of Mount Kisco. By E. Clarence Hyatt. (Mount Kisco, N. Y.) 1893. 32 p. illus. 23 cm. 1-15965.
F129. M8 H9

MOUNT MORRIS. A discourse embodying facts connected with the early settlement and growth of Mount Morris, delivered at the dedication of the Presbyterian church edifice. By Darwin Chichester. Geneseo, J. T. Norton, printer, 1855. 21 p. 22½ cm. 9-13995.
F129.M92 C5

MOUNT VERNON. Dolph-Stewart official street directory and information guide of Mt. Vernon, Bronxville, Tuckahoe, Pelham's, town of Eastchester, N. Y. ... compiled and pub. by Dolph & Stewart. New York, N. Y., 1935 - v. fold. map. 16 cm. CA 35-809 Unrev.
F129.M94 A2

MOUNT VERNON. Polk's Mt. Vernon directory of householders, occupants of office buildings and other business places, incl. a complete street and avenue guide ... incl. the Pelhams ... New York, N. Y.. R. L. Polk, 19 v. 24 cm. Folded map laid in. 37-33517.
F129.M94 A2

MOUNT VERNON. Billy Crawford's tavern, a historic landmark, Mount Vernon; Pell, Crawford, Grigg and Fay, by Minnie Hicks Fay. (Rutland, Vt., The Tuttle pub. co., 1944) 67 p. front., plates, ports., facsim. 19½ cm. 44-43483.
F129.M94F28

MOUNT VERNON. The historic Fay homestead, formerly Billy Crawford's tavern. (By Minnie (Hicks) Fay) (Rutland, Vt., The Tuttle pub. co., 1941) 37 p. incl. front., illus. (incl. ports., coat of arms) 23½ cm. 42-7818.
F129.M94 F3

MOUNT VERNON. The social and cultural development of Mount Vernon. Mount Vernon, Mount Vernon Public Library, 1951. 34 p. illus., ports. 24 cm. (Mount Vernon Public Library. Historical pamphlet no. 4) 51-5375.
F129.M94 G6

NEW YORK

MOUNT VERNON. Early Mount Vernon, by Otto Hufeland. Mount Vernon, N.Y., Mount Vernon public library, 1940. 3, 35 p. front., illus. 23½ cm. 40-32707. F129.M94 H8

MOUNT VERNON. Story of the Stevens house, 1851 - 1882. By Louise Stevens Miller. Mount Vernon, Mount Vernon Public Library, 1951. 43 p. illus., ports. 24 cm. (Mount Vernon, N.Y. Public Library Historical pamphlet no. 5) 51-11647. F129.M94 M5

MOUNT VERNON. The village of Mount Vernon, from 1851 to 1891, by John G. Wintjen ... Mount Vernon, N.Y., Mount Vernon public library, 1940. 3, 37 p. front., illus. 23½ cm. (Mount Vernon Public library. Historical pamphlet no. 2) 41-37490. F129.M94 W5

MOUNT VERNON. Along the road to Bedford and Vermont; a colonial highway through Mount Vernon. By Julia Treacy Wintjen. Mount Vernon, N.Y., Mount Vernon Public Library, 1949. 28 p. mounted illus., map. 24 cm. (Mount Vernon pub. library. Historical pamphlets) "Reprinted ... from 'The Columbian of April and May 1949, pub. by the Westchester Woman's Club." Bibliography: p. 27-28. 50-2. F129.M94W53

MOUNT VERNON. The restoration of Saint Paul's church, cemetery and rectory at Eastchester in New York. (Mount Vernon, N.Y., Printed by W.E. Rudge) 1930. (24) p. incl. front., illus. (incl. port.) 31 cm. Two folded facsimiles inserted. 42-44885. NA5235.M6A35

MOUNT VERNON. Village green fair, commemorating the 275th anniversary of the founding of Historic St. Paul's church Eastchester, South Third avenue, Mount Vernon, N.Y., 1665 - 1940 ... (New York, Pandick press) 1940. 23 p. illus. (incl. ports., facsim.) 30 cm. 42-45401. NA5235.M6A4

MOUNTAIN VIEW. Water over the dam at Mountain View in the Adirondacks; early resort days in the Great North Woods, by Floy S. Hyde. (Mountain View, N.Y., 1970) xx, 371 p. illus. 24 cm. 73-126350. F129.M944H9

MUITZESKILL. Records of the Reformed Dutch church of Schodack, Muitzeskill in the town of Schodack, Rensselaer County. Transcribed by the New York genealogical and biographical soc. ... Ed. by Royden W. Vosburgh. New York city, 1920. 2 v. in 1. facsims. 36 x 28½ cm. Autographed from type-written copy. 20-9739. F129.M95 M9

NASSAU. Records of the Reformed Protestant Dutch church in the town of Nassau, Rensselaer County. Transcribed by the New York genealogical and biographical soc.; ed. by Royden W. Vosburgh. New York city, 1919. 2 p., iii, 144 numb. l. 36 x 28½ cm. Autographed from type-written copy. 19-14063. F129.N2 N5

NEPONSIT. Letterette ... Neponsit. Brooklyn, New York city, H.L. Simpson (1919) 1 sheet of illus. 29½ x 29½ cm. folded to 9 x 15 cm. F129.N44 L6

NEW BRIGHTON. Description of New Brighton, on Staten island, opposite the city of New York. (New York, 1836) 8 p. fold. pl., fold. map. 19½ cm. 1-14934. F129.N5 W2
Rare Book Coll.

NEW HARTFORD. Records of the Presbyterian church in New Hartford (formerly the First religious soc. in Whitestown) in the town of New Hartford, Oneida County, N.Y. Transcribed by the New York genealogical and biographical soc.; ed. by Royden W. Vosburgh. New York city, 1921. 2, v. 163 p. 36 x 28½ cm. Autographed from type-written copy. 21-11171. F129.N515N5

NEW HURLEY. History of New Hurley, the Flint, Plains Road, Sherwood Corners, St. Elmo. By Kenneth Edward Hasbrouck. (New Paltz? N.Y.) 1949. 25 p. illus., fold. map. 23 cm. Bibliography: p. 24. 51-2863. F129.N517H3

NEW LOTS. Hamilton's hand book of the town of New Lots, Long Island, with descriptive sketches of its villages, business, public buildings, etc. 1874-5. East New York, Vansicklen & Pickering, printers (1874) iv, (2), (7), 82 p. 16½ cm. 15-14745. F129.N52H2

NEW LEBANON. ... Marriages in New Lebanon, New York (recorded by) Rev. Silas Churchill, 1795 - 1851 (and) Ira Hand, justice of the peace, 1832 - 1852 ... (By Elmer Irwin Shepard) Williamstown, Mass., 1943) 2 p., 49 numb. l. 27½ x 21½ cm. (Berkshire genealogical notes, No.4) 45-45727. F129.N525 S5

NEW PALTZ. The story of the Paltz; being a brief history of New Paltz. A compilation. (By Cornelia Eltinge Du Bois) (n. p.) 1915. 46 p. front., plates. 20 cm. 28-12496. F129.N53 B8

NEW PALTZ. The Huguenot, with emphasis upon the Huguenots of New Paltz (by) Kenneth E. Hasbrouck. New Paltz, N. Y., Huguenot Historical Soc., 1970. 14 p. 23 cm. 72-30529 MARC. F129.N53 H3

NEW PALTZ. The street of the Huguenots, a registered historic landmark, by Kenneth E. Hasbrouck, text, and Erma R. De Witt, photos. (New Paltz, N. Y., Pub. for the authors by the Franklin Print. Co., 1970) 46 p. illus. 16 x 24 cm. 77-30530 MARC. F129.N53H33 1970

NEW PALTZ. A history of New Paltz. By William Heidgerd. Elting Memorial Library (19) v. 21 cm. (Elting Memorial Library, Haviland Collection. Bulletin no. 1/2, 4-6) F129.N53 H4

NEW PALTZ and its old families (from 1678 to 1820) including the Huguenot pioneers and others who settled in New Paltz previous to the revolution, by Ralph Lefevre ... Albany, N. Y., Fort Orange press, 1903. xiv, 593 p. front., illus. (incl. facsims.) ports. 24 cm. 4-7856 Rev. F129.N53 L4

— 2d ed. Albany, N. Y., Brandow printing co., 1909. xiv, 593, (8), (v) - vi, 208 p. front., illus. (incl. maps, facsims.) ports. 24 cm. 11-15199. F129.N53 L5

NEW PALTZ. ... Records of the Reformed Dutch church of New Paltz, containing an account of the organization of the church and the registers of consistories, members, marriages, and baptisms. (New York) The Society, 1896. viii, 269 p. 25 cm. (Collections of the Holland soc. of New York, vol. III) Copied ... by D. Versteeg. The records cover 1683-1816, but are missing between 1702 and 1730. 5-19364 Rev. F129.N53 N5

NEW PALTZ. See also F129.N73

NEW PROSPECT. Records of the Reformed Protestant Dutch church at New Prospect, Shawangunk, Ulster co., N. Y., copied from the original church records. Copied and compiled by Gertrude A. Barber. (New Prospect, 1945?) 45 numb. l. 28 x 21½ cm. Type-written. 45-19820. F129.N54 N4

NEW ROCHELLE. Richmond's annual directory of New Rochelle, Larchmont and Pelham (Westchester County, N. Y.) 18   Yonkers, N. Y., W. L. Richmond, 18   - 19   v. fold. maps. 24 cm. 12-26030 Rev. Directories

NEW ROCHELLE through seven generations ... By C. H. Augur. (New Rochelle, National city bank, 1908) 63 p. illus. 19½ cm. 8-16526. F129.N55 A9

NEW ROCHELLE. A guide to New Rochelle and its vicinity. (By Robert Bolton) New York, Printed by A. Hanford, 1842. 67 p. front. 16 cm. (Frontispiece removed from L. C. copy, mounted, and transferred to Prints and Photographs Division.) F129.N55 B6 Rare Book Coll.

NEW ROCHELLE tombstone inscriptions, a record of all inscriptions in the old cemeteries; with supplementary information ... New Rochelle, N. Y., New Rochelle chapter, D. A. R., 1941. 165 numb. l. incl. plates, plans. 29½ cm. Reproduced from type-written copy. 41-19146 Rev. F129.N55D27

NEW ROCHELLE. The Davis annual, containing a complete list of the deaths in the town of New Rochelle, with short biographical sketches of the most prominent. Also a church and society directory with the town and village officers ... comp. and arranged by George T. Davis, 1889 - New Rochelle, N. Y., Pioneer book and job print., 1889 -   v. illus. 21½ cm. 19-13177. F129.N85 D3

NEW ROCHELLE, two hundred and fifty years; official historical program, 250th anniversary of the founding of New Rochelle, June 12 to 18, 1938 (by) Robert Lucas Forbes, editor and publisher ... New York city, 1938. 64 p. incl. front., illus. (part col. incl. ports., map, facsims.) diagr. 35½ cm. 38-17840. F129.N55 F6

NEW ROCHELLE. A good humored traveler in New Rochelle one hundred years ago, by Otto Hufeland.

NEW YORK

... (New Rochelle, N.Y.) The Huguenot and historical assoc. of New Rochelle, N.Y., 1929.
10 p.   23 cm.   James Stuart's "Three years in N. America" is the source from which most of the matter ... has been taken.   30-6886.
F129.N55H88

NEW ROCHELLE.   Huguenot and historical assoc. of New Rochelle ... Constitution and by-laws; officers and standing committees. (New Rochelle) 1909.   8, (4) p.   illus.   15 cm.   30-9786.
F129.N55H92
1909

— 1913.   7, (5) p.   illus.   15 cm.   30-9787.
F129.N55H92
1913

NEW ROCHELLE'S historical society.   (New Rochelle) The Huguenot and historical assoc. of New Rochelle, N.Y., 1929.   (12) p.   illus.   16½ cm.   30-9788.
F129.N55H925

NEW ROCHELLE.   Huguenot and historical assoc. of New Rochelle.   Publications.   (New Rochelle) 1924 -   v.   plates.   23 cm.   30-9179.
F129.N55H93

NEW ROCHELLE.   Thomas Paine cottage and grounds, New Rochelle, prepared by Committee on local history, Morgan H. Seacord, chairman ... (New Rochelle) The Huguenot and hist. assoc. of New Rochelle, N.Y. (1931)   45 p. incl. illus. (map) plates, port.   front.   23 cm.   Includes biographical sketch of Paine.   31-35656.
F129.N55H97

NEW ROCHELLE.   ... Through fifty years ... an account of the founding and development of the Huguenot and historical assoc. of New Rochelle.   Compiled by William S. Hadaway ...   New Rochelle, N.Y., The Association, 1936.   4, 50 p.   front. (port.)   23 cm.   38-529.
F129.N55H99

NEW ROCHELLE.   ... Modern New Rochelle and the National city bank; a tenth anniversary memento with articles contributed by the chief executives of three city administrations.   (1899 - 1909) (New York, Augur, Swyers & Machold, 1909)   63 p. incl. illus., col. pl., ports.   19½ cm.   9-18984.
F129.N55 N3

NEW ROCHELLE.   Records of the town of New Rochelle, 1699 - 1828, transcribed, translated and pub. by Jeanne A. Forbes ... with introd. by Caryl Coleman.   By authority of the Board of estimates of the city of New Rochelle.   New Rochelle, N.Y., The Paragraph press, 1916.   xvi, 525 p.   pl., fold. maps, facsims.   24 cm.   16-18628.
F129.N55N48

NEW ROCHELLE, the city of the Huguenots, compiled and pub. for the city of New Rochelle by the Chamber of commerce.   (New Rochelle, N.Y., The Knickerbocker press, 1926)   (36) p. incl. col. front., illus. (part col.)   25½ cm.   Map.   26-19487.
F129.N55N49

NEW ROCHELLE, the city beautiful ... (New Rochelle, N.Y., R. L. Forbes, 1912)   64 p.   illus.   35½ cm.   12-6710.
F129.N55 N5

NEW ROCHELLE.   Historic New Rochelle, by Herbert B. Nichols.   New Rochelle, N.Y., The Board of education, 1938.   2, vii-xv, 212 p. incl. front., illus. (incl. ports., facsims.)   diagr.   maps (1 fold.)   23½ cm.   Maps. "References:" p. 190-195.   39-221.
F129.N55N63

NEW ROCHELLE, her part in the great war; historical and biographical sketches of individuals and organizations who rendered valuable service to their country during the great world war.   Ed. by Condé B. Pallen ... (New Rochelle?) W. C. Tindall, 1920.   viii, 411 p.   front., plates, ports.   23½ cm.   21-19944.
F129.N55 P16

NEW ROCHELLE.   Today and yesterday in New Rochelle, by Gaylord Joel Pettit.   New York, William R. Jenkins co. (1913)   5, 106 p.   front., plates.   18½ cm.   13-14784.
F129.N55 P 5

NEW ROCHELLE.   The Sutton Manor story in historic New Rochelle.   By Ruth (Sutton) Reynolds. (New Rochelle, 1963)   53 p.   27 cm.
F129.N55 R6

NEW ROCHELLE.   Historical landmarks of New Rochelle, by Morgan H. Seacord ...   Pub. under

auspices of the Huguenot and historical assoc.　New Rochelle, N.Y., New Rochelle trust co., 1938.
vii-xiv, 135 p.　plates, maps.　23½ cm.　38-36021.　　　　　　　　　　　　　　F129.N55 S 4

NEW ROCHELLE.　One fatt calfe, being an account of the New Rochelle half-dollar and of the celebration marking the 250th anniversary of the founding & settlement of the city of New Rochelle, by Amy C. Skipton.　(New Rochelle) New Rochelle commemorative coin committee, 1939.　4, 123 p.　plates, ports.　22½ cm.　39-21844.　　　　　　　　　　　　　　　　　　　　　　F129.N55 S 6

NEW ROCHELLE.　Biographical sketches and index of the Huguenot settlers of New Rochelle 1687 - 1776, by Morgan H. Seacord...　New Rochelle, N.Y., The Huguenot and historical assoc. of New Rochelle, 1941.　2, 54 p.　front., pl.　23 cm.　"References in the text": p. 54.　42-18984.　F129. N6 S 4

NEW SCOTLAND.　Records of the Presbyterian church of New Scotland in the town of New Scotland, Albany County, N.Y.　Transcribed by the New York genealogical and biographical soc.　Ed. by Royden W. Vosburgh.　New York city, 1919.　2, iii, 108 numb. l.　36 x 28 cm.　Autographed from type-written copy. 19-6090.　　　　　　　　　　　　　　　　　　　　　　　　　　　　　　F129.N56 N5

NEW SPRINGVILLE.　Gravestone inscriptions in the Asbury Methodist Cemetery; first transcribed in 1922 (by William T. Davis, Charles W. Lang and Royden W. Vosburgh)　Rev. and map added by James A. McKimm.　(New Springville? N.Y.) 1971.　59 l.　illus.　28 cm.　77-31491 MARC.　F129.N59 D3 1971

NEW UTRECHT.　Reminiscences of old New Utrecht and Gowanus, by Mrs. Bleecker Bangs.　(Brooklyn, Brooklyn eagle press, 1912)　194 p.　illus., group of ports.　25 cm.　12-6526.
　　　　　　　　　　　　　　　　　　　　　　　　　　　　　　　　　F129.N58 B 2

NEW WINDSOR.　... Inscriptions on gravestones in New Windsor cemetery.　Copied by A. G. Barratt.
(From Hist. soc. of Newburgh Bay and the Highlands.　Historical papers, no. 9, 1902) 8-19316.　F129. N6 B 2

NEW WINDSOR.　18th century homes in New Windsor and its vicinity as depicted by Simeon De Witt, geographer to the Army, on his map of the Cantonment 1783, by Marion MacKenzie Mailler and Janet Dempsey.　(Vails Gate, N.Y.) National Temple Hill Assoc. (1968)　112 p.　illus., maps, ports.　23 cm.
　　　　　　　　　　　　　　　　　　　　　　　　　　　　　　　　　F127. N6 M3

NEW WINDSOR.　History of the town of New Windsor, Orange County, by Edward M. Ruttenber.　Newburgh, N.Y., Printed for the Historical soc. of Newburgh Bay and the Highlands, 1911.　2, (3) - 213 p. plates, ports., map.　24 cm.　13-1822.　　　　　　　　　　　　　　　F129. N6 R9

NEW WINDSOR.　The old Falls house, located at New Windsor, near Newburgh; a collection of pen sketches made in and around the old building ...　Drawn by Sid Turner ...　Newburgh, N.Y., W. M. Stanbrough, 1915.　8 l.　illus., plates (1 fold.)　16½ x 26½ cm.　16-5987.　F129. N6 T9

NEWARK. . . Directory of Newark, New York, and vicinity ... Newark, N.Y., The Newark union gazette, 1919 -　v.　fold. map.　19-14790.　　　　　　　　　　　　　Directories

NEWARK.　Old-time days in Newark and a half-century of St. Mark's parish, by Imogen Russell. Newark, N.Y., J. H. Teller, 1902.　64 p.　front., pl.　22 cm.　2-20484.　F129.N65 R9

NEWBURGH.　Breed publishing co.'s Newburgh city directory ... 1868 -　1920.　Spring Valley, N.Y. ... Breed pub. co., 1867 - 1920.　v.　fold. maps.　20 - 23½ cm.　99-2984 (rev. '30)　Directories

NEWBURGH.　The Newburgh directory for 1858/59 ... Comp. by Turnbull & Mears ... Newburgh, T. S. Quackenbush (1859)　2, (25) - 120 p.　19½ cm.　23-4058.　　　　　Directories

NEWBURGH directory, 1921 -　New Haven, Conn., The Price & Lee co., 1921 -
　　v.　fold. map.　23½ cm.　21-9062.　　　　　　　　　　　　　　　Directories

NEWBURGH.　Reference and general guide book for the city of Newburgh, established to guide purchasers to the most prominent business firms ... 1872　Newburgh, N.Y., Carter & Sutherland pub. co., 1872 -　v.　19 cm.　33-33156.　　　　　　　　　　　　　　Directories

1112

NEW YORK 379

NEWBURGH. Balmville. From the first settlement to 1860. By David Barclay. (In Historical soc. of Newburgh Bay and the Highlands. Historical papers. no. 8, 1901) 8-18969.
F129. N7 B 2
F129. N7 B 3

NEWBURGH. History and guide to Newburgh and Washington's headquarters, and a catalogue of manuscripts and relics in Washington's headquarters. By John Baldwin. New York, N. Tibballs (1883) 52 p. illus. 12°. 1-14936-M1.
F129. N7 B 8

NEWBURGH. A true history of the acquisition of Washington's headquarters at Newburgh, by the state of New York. By Richard Caldwell ... (Middletown, N.Y., Stivers, Slauson & Boyd, 1887) 2, (7) - 46 p. incl. illus. (ports.) plan) 23 cm. 3-27745.
F129. N7 C2

NEWBURGH. Unveling of the statue of George Clinton, Newburgh, ... (Newburgh, Newburgh journal print, 1896?) 49 p. incl. front., illus. (ports.) fold. pl. 23 cm. (Historical society of Newburgh Bay and the Highlands, Historical papers, no. 4) 5-16548.
F129. N7 C5

NEWBURGH. Hartwood politician ... a series of pamphlets intended to illustrate the principles of political economy and public law ... by William J. Clowes ... Presbyterian "Daily press" print, 1853. 2 v. 21-23½ cm. 10-22026.
F129. N7 C6

NEWBURGH. The story of the Hasbrouck House, Washington's headquarters, Newburgh. By Amos Elwood Corning. (n.p., Board of Trustees, State of New York of Washington's Headquarters) 1950. 68 p. illus. 23 cm. 53-24466.
F129. N7 C67

NEWBURGH. General guide to Newburgh and vicinity, with sketch of Washington's headquarters. Comp. Fletcher De Bois. New York, F. Du Bois (1883) 24 p. 24°. 1-22558-M1.
F129. N7 D8

NEWBURGH in the world war; a review of the part played by residents of the city of Newburgh and the towns of Newburgh, New Windsor and vicinity in the great conflict, produced under the supervision of John Deyo ... Text matter written and research work by Edward P. Dunphy ... (Newburgh, N.Y.) Newburgh world war pub. co., 1924. 185 p. incl. front. plates, ports. 23½ cm. 25-106.
F129. N7 D9

NEWBURGH. A record of the inscriptions in the old town burying ground of Newburgh ... Newburgh, N.Y., The Historical soc. of Newburgh Bay and the Highlands, 1898. 180 p. front. (plan) pl. 23 cm. (Historical soc. of Newburgh Bay and the Highlands. Historical papers. no. 5) 5-6278.
F129. N7 E5

NEWBURGH. 1784 - 1884. Centennial celebration of the First Presbyterian church, Newburgh. Newburgh, N.Y., Journal printing house and book bindery, 1884. 47 p. front. 27½ cm. 9-10335.
F129. N7 F5

NEWBURGH. Reasons for the centennial at Washington's headquarters. Prepared by J. T. Headley ... Newburgh, N.Y., Journal book and job print., 1881. 16 p. incl. pl. 24½ cm. 2-3073.
F129. N7 H4

— 1881. 20 p. incl. front. 24 cm. 42-7437.
F129. N7 H42

NEWBURGH. ... Centennial number. May 8, 1900. (Newburgh, N.Y., Newburgh journal print. (1900) 78 p. front., illus., plates, ports., plan. 22½ cm. (Historical society, Newburgh Bay and the Highlands. Historical papers, no. vii) 7-30352.
F129. N7 H6

NEWBURGH. Inscriptions in Balmville burying ground. Copied by Miss Anna Hulett. (From Historical society of Newburgh Bay and the Highlands. Historical papers. Newburgh, 1902. no. 9) 8-19322.
F129. N7 H9

NEWBURGH. Record of baptisms and marriages. Copied from and compared with the original entries in stewards' book ... 1789 to 1835. By Miss Augusta Leslie. (From Historical society of Newburgh Bay and the Highlands. Historical papers. 1901. no. 8. 8-19318.
F129. N7 L6

NEWBURGH. Historical sketches. Washington's head-quarters, Newburgh, and adjacent localities,

1113

by J. J. Monell ... Newburgh, N. Y., E. M. Ruttenber, 1872.   iv, (5) - 98 p.   illus. (incl. port.)   plates, plan.
20 ½ cm.   1-14937 Rev. 2.   F129. N7 M7

NEWBURGH.   ... Report of the Select committee on the petition of Washington Irving, and others
(Albany, 1839)   5 p.   25 cm.   Petition of citizens of New York city and Orange County for an act of incorporation to enable them to
preserve and perpetuate Washington's headquarters in Newburgh.   21-20779.   F129. N7 N55
                                                                                           Toner Coll.

NEWBURGH.   ... 20th century special edition of the Newburgh daily news, 16th anniversary number.
Newburgh, N. Y. ... (1901)   49 p.   illus. (incl. ports.)   34 ½ cm.   4-35095.   F129. N7 N7

NEWBURGH; her institutions, industries and leading citizens.   Historical, descriptive and biographical ... Compiled by John J. Nutt.   Newburgh, N. Y., Pub. by Ritchie & Hull, 1891.   335 p.   front.
(fold. map) illus. (incl. ports.)   30 ½ cm.   1-14938.   F129. N7 N9

NEWBURGH.   Account of the unveiling of the tablet on the site of the old Palatine church.   By Cornelia
W. Rankin ...   (From Historical society of Newburgh Bay and the Highlands. Historical papers. Newburgh, 1900. no. 6.   8-19317.
                                                                                           F129. N7 R2

NEWBURGH.   Catalogue of manuscripts and relics in Washington's head-quarters, Newburgh.   With
historical sketch.   Prepared ... by E. M. Ruttenber.   Newburgh, N. Y., E. M. Ruttenber, printer,
1874.   74 p.   front., illus.   22 cm.   18-20070.   F129.N7 R82

— 1879.   75 p.   front., illus.   22 ½ cm.   20-13493.   F129.N7 R84

— Newburgh, N. Y., Journal printing house ... 1890.   77 p.   front., illus., pl.   22 ½ cm.   25-19254.   F129.N7 R86

NEWBURGH.   Historical sketch (of Newburgh)   (By Edward Manning Ruttenber)   (From Carter's centennial
city, general and business directory. Newburgh, 1876.   8º.   p. 9-56)   1-14939-M1.   F129. N7 R9

NEWBURGH.   History of the town of Newburgh, by E. M. Ruttenber ... Illustrations by Chas, W. Tice
... Newburgh (N. Y.) E. M. Ruttenber, printers, 1859.   vi, (9) - 322, (2), viii, xi p.   front., illus. (incl. ports.,
plans, facsims.)   plates.   26 cm.   1-14940.   F129.N7 R91
                                                                                           Microfilm 22504 F

NEWBURGH.   The centennial celebration and Washington monument at Newburgh.   Report of the Joint
select committee.   Washington, Govt. print. off., 1889.   105 p.   front. (map)   plates.   27 cm.   24-5655.
                                                                                           F129. N7 U8

NEWBURGH.   George Washington's headquarters.   Pamphlets, broadsides, clippings, and other
miscellaneous matter on this subject, not separately cataloged, are classified in   F129.N7 W35

NEWBURGH.   Gardnertown cemetery.   Inscriptions in the Gardnertown M. E. church cemetery, 1902.
Copied ... by Jonathan N. Weed.   (From Historical society of Newburgh Bay and the Highlands. Historical papers. no. 10.
1903.   8-19319.   F129.N 7 W4

NEWBURGH.   Bobby and Jean of Newburgh, by Irene E. Wegle.   Newburgh, N. Y., Printed by Grayson
print. (1937)   5, 63, (5) p.   plates, ports., fold. map.   18 cm.   Bibliography: 1 leaf at end.   38-14163.   F129. N7 W5

NEWBURGH.   Pamphlets, broadsides, clippings, and other miscellaneous matter on this subject, not
separately cataloged are classified in: F129.N7 Z27

NEW PALTZ.   The street of the Huguenots, by Kenneth E. Hasbrouck and Erma R. De Witt.   (Goshen,
N. Y., Bookmill on Windy Hill, 1952)   41 p.   illus.   16 x 24 cm.   52-40970.   F129.N73H38

NEW PALTZ.   The Huguenots of New Paltz.   By Edward Walmsley Stitt.   (n. p., 1947?)   22 l.   fold.
map.   29 cm.   Typewritten (carbon copy)   50-21828.   F129.N73 S75

NEW PALTZ.   See also F129.N53

NEWTOWN.   ... Minutes of the town courts of Newtown, 1656 - 1690.   New York city, N. Y., The

NEW YORK

Historical records survey, 1940. 2, ix, 314 (i.e. 317) numb. l. facsims. 27½ cm. (Transcriptions of early town records of New York) Reproduced from type-written copy. Prepared by ... W.P.A. Bibliography: leaf ix. 42-13575.   F129.N75 N4

NEWTOWN. ... Town minutes of Newtown ... New York city, N.Y., The Historical records survey, 1940-41. 2 v. in 3. maps, facsims. 27½ cm. (Transcriptions of early town records of New York) Reproduced from type-written copy. "Prepared by ... W.P.A." Bibliography: v.1, p.189-190. 40-29275 Rev.   F129.N75N43

NEWTOWN. The annals of Newtown, in Queens County: containing its history from its first settlement, tog. with many interesting facts concerning the adjacent towns; also, a particular account of numerous Long Island families now spread over this and various other states of the Union. By James Riker, jr. ... New-York, D. Fanshaw, 1852. 3, (3) - 437 p. illus. (coats of arms) 2 fold. maps (incl. front.) 22 cm. 1-14941.   F129.N75 R5
Rare Book Coll.

NIAGARA FALLS city directory ... 1886/87 - 1900/91, 1892-1920, 1921/22 - 1931/32, 1933 Lockport, N.Y. (etc.) Roberts bros. co., 1886 - 19 v. msps (part fold.) 24 cm. 8-27428 (rev. '33)
Directories

NIAGARA FALLS city directory ... Niagara Falls, N.Y., Wahl print. and W.N. Schneider, 19 v. 24 cm. 38-11793.   Directories

NIAGARA FALLS. The story of the 'old stone chimney," by Peter A. Porter. Niagara Falls, N.Y., 1915. 16 p. illus., pl. 19½ cm. 15-21983.   F129.N78 P84

NIAGARA FALLS. Niagara portage from past to present. By Theodora Vinal. Buffalo, Foster & Stewart (1949) v, 157 p. illus., ports., maps. 23 cm. Bibliography: p. (145)-150. 50-8171.
F129.N78 V5

NIAGARA, Fort. A brief history of old Fort Niagara, by Peter A. Porter, photos. by Orrin E. Dunlap. Niagara Falls (Buffalo, N.Y., Mathews-Northrup co.) 1896. 84 p. incl. front., illus. 25 cm. 1-15941.
F129.N79 P 7

NIAGARA, Fort. Old Fort Niagara, by Peter A. Porter ... Albany, The Argus co., printers, 1903. (125) - 227 p. plates, plans. 23 cm. "From the nineteenth annual report of the commissioners of the state reservation at Niagara." A new edition of his "Brief history of old Fort Niagara." 1896. 3-18486.   F129.N79 P 8

NISKAYUNA. Records of the Protestant Reformed Dutch church of Niskayuna, in the town of Niskayuna, Schenectady County. Transcribed by the New York genealogical and biographical soc. Ed. by Royden W. Vosburgh. New York city, 1919. 2, vi, 112 numb. l. 36 x 28½ cm. Autographed from type-written copy. With this is bound: Records of the Reformed Dutch church of Amity in the village of Visscher's Ferry. 19-16561.   F129.N797N7

NILES. Mohr's directory of the town of Niles, Cayuga County. (Auburn? 1904) 1 v. 24 cm.
Directories

NORTH ELBA and beyond. By Seneca Ray Stoddard. Troy, N.Y., Nims & Knight, 1889. 1 l., 15 plates. 15 x 19 cm. 1-14942 rev.*   F129. N8 S 8

NORTH GUILFORD pioneers, by Ida Palen. New York, N.Y., The Hobson book press, 1946. 2, vii-viii p. 165 p. plates, ports., facsims. 22 cm. Reproduced from type-written copy. 46-15824.   F129.N813 P3

NORTH SALEM. When our town was young; stories of North Salem's yesterday, collected and written by boys and girls of today. Ed. by Frances Eichner and Helen F. Tibbets; photos. ... by Fred C. Warner. ... (Garden City, N.Y., The Country life press, 1945) xxi, 170 p. incl. front., illus. (incl. ports.) 20½ cm. Map. "First edition." 45-18831.   F129.N815N6

NORTH TARRYTOWN. First record book of the "Old Dutch church of Sleepy Hollow," organized in 1697 and now the First Reformed church of Tarrytown ... by Rev. David Cole ... (Yonkers, N.Y.) The Yonkers historical and library assoc., 1901. vii p., 2 l., 252 p. plates, facsim. 27 cm. L. C. copy replaced by microfilm. 1-30715 Rev. 2.   F129.N22 N7
Microfilm 21485 F

NORTH TARRYTOWN. First English record book of the Dutch Reformed church in Sleepy Hollow, formerly the Manor church of Philipsburgh, now the First Reformed church of Tarrytown ... prepared for publication by Edgar Mayhew Bacon. (Tarrytown, N.Y.) Tarrytown hist. soc., 1931) 122 p. 23 cm. 35-2953 Rev. F129.N82N72

NORTH TARRYTOWN. The old Dutch burying ground of Sleepy Hollow in North Tarrytown; a record of the early gravestones and their inscriptions. (Boston, Rand Press) 1953. 175 p. illus., fold. map. 23 cm. A 55-4374 Rev. F129.N82 P 4

NORTH TARRYTOWN. Sleepy Hollow cemetery at Tarrytown. Tarrytown, N.Y., Sleepy Hollow cemetery, 1925. 35 p. illus. 23 cm. 25-14657. F129.N82S53

NORTH TARRYTOWN. The old Dutch burying ground of Sleepy Hollow. (New York) History research soc. of the Tappan Zee, 1926. 4, 7-87 p. illus., fold. map. 23½ cm. 26-17835. F129.N82S56

NORTH TARRYTOWN. Sleepy Hollow cemetery, at Tarrytown, on the Hudson river ... New York, C. S. Westcott & co.'s union printing-house, 1866. 29 p. front., plates. 23½ cm. 1-16312. F129.N82S58

NORTHAMPTON. Old Northampton in western New York, by Albert Hazen Wright ... (Rochester, N.Y., 1928) p. (235) - 424. front., illus. (plans) facsim. 23½ cm. vol. vii of publications of the Rochester historical soc.) Northampton town records (1797 - 1809): p. 328-424. 29-12017. F129.N83 W9

NORTHFIELD. An account of the centennial celebration of the 4th of July, 1876, by the citizens of the town of Northfield, Richmond county ... New York, C. Vogt, printer, 1876. 23 p. 23½ cm. 1-21498. F129.N85 N8

NORTHUMBERLAND. Early days in the vicinity of Northumberland and Bacon Hill, book 2, by Mrs. J. B. Vanderwerker. (Schuylerville? N.Y., 1938) 21 p. illus. 23½ cm. Book 2 of the author's Early days series. 43-39032. F129.N855V3

NORTHVILLE, Broadalbin and Mayfield directory ... vol. I 1896. Gloversville and Johnstown, N.Y., O. H. Bame, 1896 - v. 22½ cm. CA 33-483 Unrev. Directories

NORWICH. ... Norwich, Oxford and Sherburne directory ... 19 Binghamton, N.Y., The Calkin-Kelly directory co., 1930 - v. 24½ cm. CA 30-726 Unrev. Directories

NORWICH. Williams directory of Norwich. Binghamton, N.Y., J. E. Williams, 1908. 1 v. 23½ cm. 8-31662. Directories

NUNDA. 1808 - 1908. Centennial history of the town of Nunda, with a preliminary recital of the winning of western New York, from the fort builders age to the last conquest by our revolutionary forefathers, ed. by H. Wells Hand. (Rochester, N.Y.) Rochester Herald press, 1908. 636 p. incl. illus., plates, ports., maps. 26 cm. 10-9295. F129.N95 H3

NYACK. Richmond's directory of Nyack, Upper Nyack, South Nyack, Central Nyack, Grand View, Piermont and Sparkill (Rockland County) 1914/15 - v. 1 - Yonkers, N.Y., W. L. Richmond, 1914 - 1 v. 23½ cm. 14-21035.

NYACK. The Lincoln memorial boulder ... dedicated ... 1908. Nyack-on-Hudson (N.Y.) C. M. Montgomery (1908) 36 p. 5 pl. (incl. col. front.) 4 port. 17½ x 13½ cm. 18-16089. F129.N99 M7

OGDENSBURG. Kimball's Ogdensburg city directory ... 1900 - 1901. Watertown, N.Y., Kimball, 1900. 8°. Sept. 20, 1900-67. Directories

OGDENSBURG. ... Kimball's Ogdensburg city directory... 18 Watertown, N.Y., Kimball. 18 -19 v. fold. map. 23 cm. 10-1806 Rev. Directories

OGDENSBURG city directory ... 1898/99 - (v.1) - Binghamton, N.Y., C. A. Williams, 1898 - v. 24 cm. 24-28107. Directories

NEW YORK 383

OGDENSBURG directory ... Schenectady, N.Y., H. A. Manning co., 19   v. 23 cm. 26-553.
Directories

OGDENSBURG. Reminiscences of Ogdensburg, 1749 - 1907. Ed. by Swekat-si-chapter, D. A. R. New York, Boston (etc.) Silver, Burdett, 1907. 6, 183 p. 2 pl., 4 port. (incl. front.) 23 cm. 7-42467.
F129. O3 D3

OGDENSBURG. The history of the city of Ogdensburg, by Rt. Rev. P. S. Garand ... relating the life of Father Picquet and his Indians, etc., etc. Ogdensburg, N. Y., 1927. 3, (ix) - xv, 469 p. front., plates, ports., maps. 24 cm. 27-13028.
F129.O3 G17

OGDENSBURG. ... Papers relating to the early settlement at Ogdensburgh, New-York. 1749. By Edmund Bailey O'Callaghan. (From the documentary history of the state of New York ... v. 1 (1849) 8-27637.
F129.O3 O15

OGDENSBURG. Souvenir of Ogdensburg, N. Y. in heliotype. (Ogdensburg, N. Y., E. N. Crane, 1895) 2 p., 48 pl. obl. 24º. 1-14943-M1.
F129. O3 S 7

OLD FORGE. Adirondack development corporation, Old Forge. ... Old Forge, New York ... Old Forge, N. Y. (1917)   folder (16 p.) 25 ½ x 11 ½ cm.
F129.O4 A23

OLD FORGE. Photographic views of Fourth Lake and vicinity. (Herkimer? N.Y., 1905) 13 x 17 ½ cm.
F129. O4 P 5

OLEAN. Duplex directory of Olean. Olean, N.Y., Morris and Van Campen, 1904 -   v. 24 cm. 3-25753 Rev.
Directories

OLEAN directory, 18   Olean, N.Y., Olean directory co., 18   v. fold. map. 24 cm. 24-28105.
Directories

OLEAN. Williams' duplex directory of Olean, N.Y. for 1911/12 -   (v.1 -   containing Allegany, Portville, Westons Mills, Hinsdale, Pleasant Valley ... Binghamton, N.Y., J. E. Williams, 1911 -   1 v. 24 cm. 11-27501.
Directories

OLEAN. R. L. Polk & co.'s Olean, N. Y., directory 1916 -   including directories of Allegany, Hinsdale, Portville, Westons Mills and the Olean rural routes ... vol. I -   Pittsburgh, Pa., R. L. Polk, 1915 -   1 v. 24 cm. 16-1680.
Directories

OLEAN duplex directory ... including Allegany, Portville and Westons Mills ... 1897 - 1901. vol.1 - 3.   ... Oil City, Pa., Derrick pub. co., 1897-1900. 3 v, fold. maps. 24 cm. 13-6110.
Directories

OLEAN. Sketches: the Olean rock city; historic glimpses of Olean; the Bradford oil district; historic glimpses of Bradford, Pa. (by) Katherine Eaton Bradley. (Olean, N. Y.) 1920. 2, (7) - 54 p. pl. 18 ½ x 11 cm. 20-4644.
F129.O45 B76

OLEAN. A sketch of the early settlement of Olean and its founder, Major Adam Hoops, by Maud D. Brooks. Olean, N. Y., Priv. print., 1898. 32 p. 20 ½ cm. 16-27481.
F129.O45 B 8

OLEAN. The Times-herald. 1860 - Diamond jubilee number - 1935 ... vol. lxxv, May 15, 1935. Olean, N.Y. (1935) 20, 20, 20, 20, 16, 12, 24 p. illus. (incl. ports., map) 58 cm. 38M5186T.
F129.O45 T5

ONEIDA. Hayne's Oneida and Canastota directory ... incl. Oneida Castle and Kenwood ... 18 Albany, N.Y., C. S. Hayne (18   v. front. (fold. map) 23 ½ cm. 24-28108.
Directories

ONEIDA. Manning's Oneida, Oneida Castle, Wampsville, Durhamville, Kenwood and Sherrill directory   Schenectady, N.Y., H. A. Manning co., 19   v. fold. map. 23 ½ cm. 23-1670 Rev.
Directories

ONEIDA and Canastota directory. Including Oneida Castle and Durhamville ... 1887/88   Ilion,

384 LOCAL HISTORIES IN THE LIBRARY OF CONGRESS

N.Y., "The Globe" directory co., 1887 -   v. 23½ cm. 33-34841.
                                                                    Directories

ONEONTA.   Directory of Oneonta and vicinity ...   18   Oneonta, N.Y., H. B. Hawkins, 18
    v. 22½ cm.   39M2690T.   Directories

ONEONTA.   Manning's Oneonta, including Oneonta Plains, East End, South Side and West Oneonta, and Cooperstown (New York) directory, incl. Laurens, Mt. Vision, Hartwick, Milford, Portlandville, Colliers and Hartwick Seminary ... Schenectady, N.Y., H. A. Manning co., 19   v. fold. maps.
23½ cm. 38-4602.   Directories

ONEONTA.   A sketch of the history of Oneonta.   By Dudley M. Campbell.   Oneonta, N.Y., Herald and Democrat office, 1883.   67 p. 16½ cm. 1-14944.   F129. O5 C19

ONEONTA.   A history of Oneonta from its earliest settlement to the present time.   By Dudley M. Campbell.   Oneonta, N.Y., G. W. Fairchild, 1906.   190 p. incl. front. (port.) 11 pl. 19 cm. Much enlarged from his Sketch of the history of Oneonta, 1883. 6-3550.   F129. O5 C2

ONEONTA memories and sundry personal recollections of the author.   By Willard V. Huntington.   San Francisco, The Bancroft co., 1891.   vi, (9) - 219 p. front. (port.) 20½ cm. 11-21022.
                                                                    F129. O5 H9

ONEONTA.   Seven acres of history; the story of Riverside Cemetery in Oneonta, by Edwin R. Moore.   (n. p.) 1970.   14 p. 21 cm.   F129. O5 M6

ONEONTA.   The official blue book, Oneonta and Otsego Co ... 1907 - 8.   Oneonta, 1907 -
1 v. 12 cm.   F129. O5 O3

ONEONTA.   ... Historical souvenir of Oneonta, N.Y. ... comp. (Edgar Luderne Welch) (Albany, N.Y., 1896)   85 p. illus. (incl. ports.) fold. pl. 26½ cm. (Historical souvenir, series no. 3) "Grip's" valley Gazette, v.4, no. 12, Dec. 1896. 1-14945 Rev.   F129. O5 W4

ORANGEBURG.   Disposal of Shanks Village.   Hearing before a subcommittee of the Committee on Banking and Currency, U.S.Senate ... on the disposal of Shanks Village, Orangetown, by the Public Housing Administration.   Washington, U.S.Govt. Print. Off., 1955.   iii, 30 p. tables. 24 cm. 55-60715.
                                                                    F129.O57 U5

ORCHARD PARK before we remember, a compiled history of Orchard Park, by John N. Printy.   (Orchard Park, N.Y.) Orchard Park Historical Soc. (1969)   66 p. 24 cm.
                                                                    F129.O58 P 7

OSSINING.   Breed publishing co.'s directory of the village of Ossining ... Newburgh, N.Y., Breed pub. co. (1889 -   19   v. 24 cm. 11-12578 Add.   Directories

OSSINING.   Polk's Ossining directory ... 1924/25 -   v.1 -   New York, R. L. Polk & co.
1924 -   v. 24½ cm. 24-2364.   Directories

OSSINING.   (Cemetery inscriptions from Ossining, Sleepy Hollow cemetery, and White Plains, in Westchester County; Lake Mahopac in Putnam County; Middle Bush and Clinton Corners in Dutchess County; and the Carpenter family Bible record, Brattleboro, Vt.) (n.p., 1922?)   64 p. 21 cm.
Type-written copy. 22-17154.   F129. O6 C4

OSSINING.   ... Centennial anniversary of American independence at Sing Sing. ... Compiled by C. B. Palmer ...   Scarborough (N.Y.) Sunny Side printing co., 1876.   46 p. 23½ cm. 1-21500 Rev.
                                                                    F129. O6 O6

OWASCO.   Mohr's directory of the town of Owasco, Cayuga County.   (Auburn, N.Y? 1904)
1 v. 24 cm.   Directories

OSWEGO city and county directory & gazetteer ... 1859, 1861, 1864/5, 1866/7, 70/1.   Oswego,

1118

NEW YORK 385

R. J. Oliphant, printer (etc.) 1859 - 1870.   8 v. 19½ - 23 cm. 10-1790.
Directories

OSWEGO. Brigham's Oswego and Fulton directory and history, for 1862 and 1863. Comp. and pub. by A. DeLancey Brigham. Oswego, N.Y., J. N. Brown, printer, 1862.   viii, 208, iv, 84 p. 22 cm. 10-1788 Add.
Directories

OSWEGO. Boyd's Oswego directory ... v. (1   1872/73, 73/4, 74/5, 75/6, 77/8 Oswego, N.Y., A. Boyd, 1872 - 77.   5 v. 22½ cm. 10-1789.
Directories

OSWEGO city directory ... 1880, 88, 99, 1902, 04, 06. Oswego, N.Y., R. J. Oliphant (1880-1906) 6 v. fold. map. 23½ cm. Oct. 12. 99-99 Additions.
Directories

OSWEGO. ... Hall's standard business directory, guide and reference book of Oswego, Fulton and Oswego Falls ... (1894 - 1895) Comp. and pub. by the Hall pub. co. Oswego, N.Y., Times book and job print., 1894.   100 p. 23 cm. 10-1537.
Directories

OSWEGO. ... Kimball's Oswego city business directory and pocket memorandum combined. comp. J. C. Kimball. Watertown, N.Y., M.M.Kimball, 1881.   33 numb. l. 9 x 15 cm. 10-1536.
Directories

OSWEGO: an historical address, delivered ... at the centennial celebration of the evacuation by the British of Fort Ontario, Oswego, and their surrender of the military posts of the northern frontier to the U.S.; by George T. Clark. (Oswego? N.Y., 1896?)   26 p. 23½ cm. 3-4885.
F129. O7 C5

OSWEGO. The story of Oswego; with notes about the several towns in the county. (By Ralph Milligan Faust) (Oswego, N.Y., R. M. Faust, 1934)   3, 107, (4) p. illus. 18½ cm. 35-4761.
F129. O7 F3

OSWEGO. ... Papers relating to the first settlement and capture of Fort Oswego. 1727 - 1756. (From The documentary history of the state of New-York ... v.1) 8-27636.
F129.O7 O15

OSWEGO. Indelible photographs. New York, The Albertype co., 1889.   1 p. l., 16 pl. obl. 24°. 1-14946-M1.
F129. O7 O7

OSWEGO. Oswego, the industrial and commercial city ... Oswego, N.Y., 1913.   (32) p. illus. 56½ cm. Commercial and industrial supplement. Special number, Jan.1913. 13-9640.
F129.O7 O75

OSWEGO. Stories of Oswego; tales of the early days told to the children of the Oswego normal training school. by Lida Scovil Penfield. (Oswego, N.Y.) Made in the Normal print shop by the students, 1919.   26 p. incl. illus., plates. 22 cm. 19-16310.
F129. O7 P 3

OSWEGO, from buckskin to bustles, by Charles M. Snyder. Port Washington, N.Y., I. J. Friedman (1968)   xiii, 286 p. illus. 23 cm. (Empire State historical pubs. series 56) 68-18352.
F129. O7 S65

OSWEGO. Pamphlets, broadsides, clippings, and other miscellaneous matter on the subject not separately cataloged are classified in:
F129. O7 Z5

OSWEGO. Souvenir booklet of the Oswego Town sesqui-centennial, 1818 - 1968. (Oswego? 1968) 1 v. (unpaged) illus. 22 cm.
F129.O72 S 68

OTEGO. A history of Otego, by Stuart Banyar Blakely. (Cooperstown, N.Y., Crist, Scott & Parshall, 1907)   xii, (13) - 152 p. incl. map. 20½ cm. Bibliography: p. 152. 8-18111.
F129. O8 B 6

OWEGO. ... Owego directory ... 18   Binghamton, N.Y., J. E. Williams, 18 v. 24 cm. 24-20953.
Directories

OWEGO directory ... Binghamton, N.Y., Calkin-Kelly, 19   v. 24 cm. 26-157.
Directories

OWEGO. Some account of the early settlement of the village in Tioga County, N.Y., called Ah-wa-ga by the Indians ... By Le Roy Wilson Kingman. Owego, Owego gazette office, 1907. 2, 673, (3) p.
1 illus., plates, ports. 23½ cm. Only 50 copies printed. 10-2007. F129. O9 K5

OWEGO. Souvenir of Owego. Indelible photos. ... New York, The Albertype co., 1892.
1 l., 16 pl. 12 x 17½ cm. 1-16301 Rev. F129. O9 S 7

OXFORD. Directory of the village of Oxford ... Oxford, N.Y., The Men's class of the Methodist Episcopal church (1935 -   v. illus. (map) 23 cm. CA 35-152 Unrev. Directories

OXFORD. Annals of Oxford, with illustrations and biographical sketches of some of its prominent men and early pioneers. Comp., ed. and pub. by Henry J. Galpin. Oxford, N.Y., Times book and job print., 1906. 568 p. front., illus., plates, ports., facsim. 23½ cm. 7-6738. F129.O95 G2

OXFORD. ... Historical souvenir of Oxford, N.Y. ... (By Edgar Luderne Welch) ... (Albany, N.Y., 1897) 76 p. illus. (incl. ports.) 25 cm. ("Grip's" valley gazette, v.5, no. 11. 4-28343 * Cancel. F129.O95 W4

OYSTER BAY. Inscriptions ... copied by Josephine C. Frost ... Aug., 1911. (44) type-written sheets.
27½ cm. Various paging. CA 12-670 Unrev. F129.O98 F9

OYSTER BAY. Historic Oyster Bay (by) Frances Irvin. (East Norwich, Long Island, N.Y., 1926)
12 p. 1 illus. 15 cm. 26-15731. F129.O98 I 5

OYSTER BAY. The village of Oyster Bay, its founding and growth from 1653 to 1700. By Van Santvoord Merle-Smith. Garden City, N.Y., Priv. print.; distributed by Doubleday, 1953.
xv, 104 p. msp. 24 cm. 53-10751 rev. F129.O98 M4

OYSTER BAY town records, 1653 - 1763 ... Pub. by order of the town by Frederick E. Willits, Daniel Underhill, Edward T. Payne, committee. Compared, annotated and indexed by John Cox, jr. New York, T. A. Wright, 1916 - '31. 6 v. front. 24 cm. 17-8383.
F129.O98O85

OYSTER BAY. Baptismal record of the Reformed Dutch church at Oyster Bay, Long Island, 1741-1846. Copied by Josephine C. Frost ... 1913. (Brooklyn? 1913?) 2 p, 129, 9 numb. l. 27 cm. 14-5936.
F129.O98O9

OYSTER BAY. Records of the Reformed Dutch church of Oyster Bay, L.I., 1741 - 1835: the Wolver Hollow church. Taken from a copy made by the Holland soc. of New York. Transcribed by the New York genealogical and biographical soc., Oct. 1912. (New York, 1912) 2 p., 113 numb. l. 28½ cm.
Autographed from type-written copy. 16-2288. F129.O98O97

OYSTER BAY. A documentary history of het (the) Nederdvytsche gemeente, Dutch congregation, of Oyster Bay, Queens County, island of Nassau, now Long Island, by Henry A. Stoutenburgh. (New York, 1902-07) 10 v. 3 port. 22 cm. 3-10793 Add. F129.O98 S 8

PALATINE. Following "the old Mohawk turnpike" ... (By Lou D. MacWethy) Saint Johnsville, N.Y., Press of the Enterprise and news, 1927. 27 p. incl. illus., map. 23½ cm. CA 31-22 Unrev.
F129.P15M17

PALATINE. Records of the Lutheran Trinity church of Stone Arabia in the town of Palatine, Montgomery County. Transcribed by the New York genealogical and biographical soc ... Ed. by Royden W. Vosburgh. New York city, 1914. 3 v. in 4. illus., facsims. 35½ cm. Autographed from type-written copy.
14-22167. F129.P15 S 8

PALATINE. Records of the Reformed Dutch church of Stone Arabia in the town of Palatine, Montgomery County. Transcribed by the New York genealogical and biographical soc ... Ed. by Royden W. Vosburgh. New York city, 1916. 3 v. 36 cm. Autographed from type-written copy. 16-23646. F129.P15 S83

PALISADES. The story of the Ferry. Being an account of the ferry, between Dobbs Ferry, West-

NEW YORK

chester Co. and Snedens Landing, Rockland Co. on the Hudson River established about the year 1698. Also Nicholas Gesner's diary, and other papers relating more or less to the history of Palisades. Comp. by Winthrop S. Gilman ... (Palisades, N.Y., 1903) 2 v. 71 phot. (incl. 4 ports., 5 maps) 2 maps, 2 plans. 23½ x 18½ cm. v. 1, 105 numb. l. vl. 2, 106-159 numb. l. 4 copies only. 4-4893. F129. P2 G 4
Rare Book Coll.

PALMYRA. The early history of Palmyra: a Thanksgiving sermon ... by Horace Easton ... Rochester, Press of A. Strong, 1858. 26 p. 22½ cm. 25-4517. F129. P3 E 2

PALMYRA. A memorial of the celebration at Palmyra, of the centennial Fourth of July, incl. the oration by Theodore Bacon, and a sketch of the early history of Palmyra, by Rev. Horace Eaton. Rochester, N.Y., E. R. Andrews, printer, 1876. 34 p. 23 cm. 16-8152.
F129. P3 M35

PALMYRA, Wayne County ... Comp. by the Woman's society of the Western Presbyterian church. (Rochester, N.Y., The Herald press) 1907. 76, (4) p. incl. front., illus. 18 x 14½ cm. 7-41771.
F129. P3 P3

PARIS. Records of the Paris religious society (a Congregational church) in the town of Paris, Oneida County. Transcribed by the New York genealogical and biographical soc. Ed. By Royden W. Vosburgh. New York city, 1921. 2, iii, 106 numb. l. 36 x 28 cm. 22-1678. F129. P34 P 3

PARIS. History of the town of Paris, and the valley of the Sauquoit; pioneers and early settlers ... anecdotes and reminiscences. To which is added, an account of the ceremonies attending the reinterment of Col. Isaac Paris. By Henry C. Rogers ... Utica, N.Y., White & Floyd, printers, 1881. 398, vi (i.e. iv) p. front. (port.) illus. 23½ cm. 16-27487. F129. P34 R 7

PATCHOGUE. The Argus business and residential directory of Patchogue, with historical sketch. 1904 -   Patchogue, N.Y., L. B. Green (1904 -   v. illus. (incl. ports.) map. 21½ cm. 34-15330.
Directories

PATCHOGUE. The Patchogue advance. 65th anniversary ed. Patchogue, N.Y., 1936. 1 v. illus. 56½ cm. Forms v. 66, no. 6, of the Patchogue advance, Oct. 16, 1936. 40M232T. F129. P36 P35

PATCHOGUE. Reminiscenees of Patchogue, by the Rev. Barnabas F. Reeve, at the centennial celebration ... Riverhead, N.Y., Priv. print., 1906. 1, 7 p. 20½ cm. 8-18596.
F129. P36 R 3
Rare Book Coll.

PAVILION. The Pavilion community of New York state, 1800 - 1941. Pub. by the Pavilion rotary club, ed. by J. L. Broughton. LeRoy, N.Y., Printed by the Gazette-news co. (1941?) 155 p. plates, ports. 23½ cm. 43-26930. F129. P367 B7

A rose of the nineties. Drawings by R. C. N. Rosalind (Case) Newell. (Southold? N.Y.. 1962) 115 p. 24 cm. Autobiographical. F129. P369 N4

PEEKSKILL. Breed pub. co.'s ... directory of Peekskill ... 188   N.Y. (etc.) Breed pub. co., 1888   -19   v. 24½ cm. 0-4164 Rev. Directories

PEEKSKILL. Polk's Peekskill (Westchester county) directory ... 1924 -   New York, N.Y., R. L. Polk, 1924 -   v. 23½ - 24 cm. 24-4781 (rev. '38) Directories

PEEKSKILL. Around Peekskill since 1882; recollections of the olden days, and the ways we lived and did things. By Clinton Seaman Acker. Brooklyn, T. Gaus' Sons (1961) 116 p. 24 cm.
F129. P37 A 2

PEEKSKILL. This and that about here and there around old Peek's Kill; and recollections about some of our older citizens in Peekskill, of people, places and events during the 18th, 19th and 20th centuries. Ed. Clinton S. Acker. Peekskill-on-Hudson, N.Y., Monument Printers ... (1963) 124 p. 24 cm. 63-20333. F129. P37 A22

PEEKSKILL. Centennial celebration ... commemorative of the 100th anniversary of the granting of the first charter ... to the village of Peekskill; comp, and ed. by Geo. E. Briggs, assisted by Leverett F. Crumb and Karl M. Sherman ... (Peekskill, N.Y.) The Highland Democrat co. (1916) 54 p. illus., ports. 23 cm. 16-16342.
F129. P37 B8

PEEKSKILL. The story of early Peekskill, 1609 - 1876. By Joseph M. Fox. Peekskill, N.Y., Print. by the Enterprise Press, 1947. 180 p. illus., ports., maps. 22 cm. 47-7182*.
F129.P37 F 6

PEEKSKILL. Pioneers, patriots, and people, past and present; a history of Peekskill. By William Tompkins Horton. (Peekskill, N.Y.) 1953 (i.e.1954) 355 p. illus. 24 cm. 54-8751.
F129.P37 H 6

PEEKSKILL. Lincoln in Peekskill; the Lincoln exedra, the Lincoln memorial in books, exercises at the Lincoln memorial in Peekskill ... (Peekskill) The Lincoln society in Peekskill (1926) 22 p. illus. (incl. ports.) 23 cm. 27-1137.
F129.P37 L 5

PEEKSKILL. Civil War days in a country village. By Colin T. Naylor. Peekskill, N.Y., Highland Press, 1961. 122 p. 29 cm.
F129.P37 N 3

PEEKSKILL. Peekskill in the American revolution, by Emma L. Patterson; illust. by A. Marie Doherty, with an introd. by Hon. George McAneny. Peekskill, N.Y., The Friendly town assoc. 1944. 5, 183 p. plates, map. 24 cm. "First edition." Bibliography: p. 173-175. 45-1632.
F129.P37 P 3

PEEKSKILL. Who's who in Peekskill. By Chester Allen Smith. (1st ed.) Peekskill, N.Y., Friendly Town Assoc., 1954 (1955) 289 p. illus. 24 cm. 54-11946.
F129.P37 S 5

PEEKSKILL, a friendly town, its historic sites and shrines; a pictorial history of the city from 1654 to 1952. By Chester Allen Smith. With an introd. by Albert B. Corey. Peekskill, Friendly Town Assoc., 1952. 456 p. illus. 29 cm. 54-4299.
F129.P37 S 6

PEEKSKILL. Gems of the Hudson; Peekskill and vicinity, compiled by G. M. Vescelius. (Newburgh, N.Y., The News co., 1914?) 108 p. illus., plates (1 fold.) 15 x 23 cm.
F129.P37 V 3

PELHAM. A brief, but most complete & true account of the settlement of the ancient town of Pelham, Westchester county ... compiled by Lockwood Barr ... Richmond, Va., The Dietz press, 1946 (i.e. 1947) 4, (vii) - xv, 28 p., (29) - 190 p. front., illus. (incl. coats of arms) plates, etc. 23½ cm. 47-3441.
F129.P38 B 3

PENFIELD'S past, 1810 - 1960. By Katherine Wilcox Thompson. Publ. in observance of its 150th anniversary by the town of Penfield. (Penfield) 1960. 213 p. 24 cm.
F129.P385 T5

PENN YAN directory. Binghamton, N.Y., Calkin-Kelly directory co. v. 24 cm. 12-29319.
Directories

PENN YAN directory ... v.1 -   1927 -   Schenectady, N.Y., H. A. Manning co., 1927. v. 23 cm. CA 28-50 Unrev.
Directories

PENN YANN. Stark's Penn Yan directory, July 1, 1941 -   ... Compiled by John V. Stark ... (Penn Yan, N.Y.) Printed by Penn Yan printing co. (1941 -   v. fold. map. 23½ cm. 42-13579.
Directories

PERU. Quaker records, Peru, Clinton Co. (By Mrs. Josephine C. Frost) (Brooklyn, 191 -   38, 2 numb. l. 27 cm. 12-29739 Rev.
F129. P4 F 9

PETERBORO. The borough of Peter, by Raymond P. Ernenwein. Sherburne, N.Y., Heritage Press (1970) 150 p. illus. ports. 22 cm.
F129.P43 E 7

PHILMONT. ... Philmont and Mellenville directory ... with a brief history ... v.1 - 1895 -   Philmont, N.Y., The author, 1895. v. 23 cm. 34-2724.
Directories

PHOENIX. Historical souvenir of Phoenix and vicinity. (By Edgar Luderne Welch) (Pulaski, N.Y., The Seamans press, 1902) 92 p. illus. (incl. ports.) 27 cm. (Historical souvenir series, no. 14) 4-9576* Cancel.
                                                                                          F129. P5 W4

PINE PLAINS. History of Little Nine Partners, of North East precint, and Pine Plains, New York, Duchess county. By Isaac Huntting. ... Vol. I Amenia, N.Y., C. Walsh, printers, 1897.
3, (3) - 411 p. illus. (incl. ports., facsims.) fold. map. 23½ cm. No more pub? 1-14947 Rev.   F129. P6 H9

— Index to Huntting's History of Little Nine Partners ... (n. p.) 1921. 102 numb. l.
26½ x 21 cm. Type-written (carbon copy) 1-14947 Rev.   F129. P6 H9
                                                                                          Index

PINE PLAINS. Record of the Round top Lutheran church in the town of Pine Plains, Dutchess County. Transcribed by the New York genealogical and biographical soc. Ed. by Royden W. Vosburgh. New York city, 1921.   3, 47 numb. l. 36 x 28½ cm. Autographed from type-written copy. 21-21004.   F129. P6 P6

— Records of the United Presbyterian church at West Charlton ... Transcribed by the New York genealogical and biographical soc. Ed. by Royden W. Vosburgh. New York city, 1921.
2 p., 47 numb. l. 36 x 28½ cm. Bound with above. 21-21520.

— Records of the Society of Clinton, A congregational church in the village of Clinton, in the town of Kirkland, Oneida County. Transcribed by the New York genealogical and biographical soc. Ed. by Royden W. Vosburgh. New York city, 1921.   2, ii, 81 numb. l. 36 x 28½ cm. Bound with above.
21-21521.

PLATTSBURGH. Manning's Plattsburgh directory ... (vol. I -   1886/7, 1889/90 - 1891/92, 1892/93 - 1904/05, 1907 - 1917, 1919 -   Schenectady, N.Y. (etc.) H. A. Manning co., 1886 -   v. fold. maps. 33½ cm. 0-6052 (rev. '33)   Directories

PLATTSBURGH and vicinity ... Plattsburgh, N.Y., The Adirondack bureau, 1924. 32 p. 19½ cm.
24-29762.   F129. P7 A2

PLATTSBURGH. Independence day celebration, given to the American legion, Plattsburgh post, no. 20. (Plattsburgh, N.Y., Clinton press, inc., 1921) 96 p. illus. (incl. ports.) 31 cm. 21-20784.
                                                                                          F129. P7 A5

PLATTSBURGH. Tombstone inscriptions from Riverside Cemetery, Riverside near Broad Street, Plattsburgh, New York, Clinton County. Compiled by Margaret Lunt. (Toledo? 1967) 52 l. 32 cm.
                                                                                          F129. P7 L8

PLATTSBURGH. Kent Delord house. (By William Henry Miner) (Chicago, 1924) (40) p. illus.
17 x 24 cm. 24-23810.   F129. P7 M6

PLATTSBURGH. History of Plattsburgh from its first settlement to Jan. 1, 1876. (By Peter Sailly Palmer) Plattsburgh, N.Y., 1877. 2, (3) - 83 p. 22½ cm. 1-14948.   F129. P7 P1

PLATTSBURGH, 1785 - 1815 - 1902: Plattsburgh barracks, 1814. By Marjorie Lansing Porter. (Anniversary ed. 1814 - 1964. n. p.) G. Little Press, 1964. 122 p. 23 cm.
                                                                                          F129. P7 P6

POMFRET. Yesterdays, in and around Pomfret. By Elizabeth L. Crocker. Fredonia, N.Y., 1960 - 64. 22 cm. 4 v.   F129. P78 C7

POMPEY. Re-union of the sons and daughters of the old town of Pompey ... Also, a history of the town, reminiscenees and biographical sketches of its early inhabitants ... Pompey, By direction of the Re-union meeting, 1875. 431 p. front., plates, ports. 23 cm. 1-14949.   F129. P8 P8

POUNDRIDGE. God's country; a history of Pound Ridge. By Jay Harris. (Chester) Conn., Pequot Press, 1971. xvii, 541 p. illus., maps. 28 cm. Bibliography: p. (191) - 208. 78-166178 MARC.   F129. P83 H3

PORT CHESTER. Walker's red book for Port Chester ... May, 1903. New Rochelle, N.Y., 1903.
14½ x 7 cm.   F129. P85 W2

390   LOCAL HISTORIES IN THE LIBRARY OF CONGRESS

PORT HENRY. History of Port Henry, by Dr. Charles B. Warner, Rutland, Vt., The Tuttle co., 1931. 182 p. incl. front. (plrt.) illus. 24 cm. 32-6552.   F129.P86 W2

PORT JERVIS. Breed pub. co.'s ... directory of Port Jervis and Monticello, N. Y. and Matamoras and Milford, Pa.; also the New York, Ontario & western railway from Port Jervis to Monticello. Newburgh, N.Y., Breed pub. co. v. 24½ cm. 12-21736.   Directories

PORT JERVIS. ... Port Jervis directory, including Sparrowbush, N. Y., Matamoras and Milford, Pa. ... 19   Binghamton, N.Y., The Calkin-Kelly directory co., 19 v. 24 cm.
CA 30-1097 Unrev.   Directories

PORT JERVIS, by John P. Fritts, illus. by Wm. H. Allerton, ed. by W. H. Nearpass & James Bennett. (New York, Printed by the Abbott press, 1908) (47) p. illus. 26 cm. 8-23286.
                                  F129.P87 F 9

PORT JERVIS. Machackemeck gravestone inscriptions, Port Jervis, Orange Co. Contributed by Royden W. Vosburgh ... New York (Tobias A. Wright press) 1913. 7 p. front., fold. plan. 26½ cm.
Ed. of 100 copies. Reprinted from the New York genealogical and biographical record, Oct. 1913. 23-2859. F129.P87 V 8

PORT WASHINGTON. Robinson's Port Washington-Plandome (Nassau county) red book resident directory ... Hempstead, N.Y., Resident directory service, inc., 19 v. illus. 23 cm.
37-33528.   Directories

PORT WASHINGTON. Tales of Sint Sink, by Charlotte E. Merriman ... illus. by Lyman A. Langdon ... Port Washington, N.Y. (1935) 6, 258 p. incl. front. plates, maps. 28 cm. Bibliography: 1 leaf at end.
35-17055.   F129.P876 M4

— (Port Washington? N.Y., 1965) 258 p. 65-25999.   F129.P876M4
                                  1965

PORTLAND. Historical sketches of the town of Portland, comprising also the pioneer history of Chautauqua County, with biographical sketches of the early settlers. By H. C. Taylor ... Fredonia, N.Y., W. McKinstry, printers, 1873. (v) - xiv, (15) - 446 p. front., ports. 22 cm. 9-30071.
                                  F129.P88 T 2

POTSDAM. The Mullin-Kille and Courier & freeman Potsdam consurvey city directory. Master ed. ... v. 1 - 1941 - Hebron, Neb., and Parsons, Kan., Mullin-Kille co.; (Potsdam, N.Y.) The Courier & freeman, 1941 - v. illus. 23½ cm. 42-4199. Directories

POTSDAM. Potsdupinni; a history of Potsdam, by Charles H. Leete. With a foreword by his son, Edward H. Leete. (Hartsdale? N.Y., 1967) iii, 98 p. 28 cm. Transcription of the author's unpublished ms. with additions. 67-30553.   F129.P89 L 4

POUGHKEEPSIE. C. P. Luyster's directory for the village of Pougkeepsie. July, 1843. (June, 1845) Comprising a complete list of all the business men and regular residents of the corporation, alphabetically arranged. Poughkeepsie, Printed by I. Platt (1843-45) 2 v. 22 cm. 11-4171. Directories
                                  Rare Book Coll.

POUGHKEEPSIE. The Poughkeepsie directory for 1859 - 1860. Containing the names of the inhabitants, a business directory, with the various progessions, trades, etc., classed under their respective headings. ... Comp. by David B. Lent, jr. Poughkeepsie, Osborne & Killey, printers (1859)
234 p. illus. 19½ cm. 11-4173.   Directories

POUGHKEEPSIE. Boyd's Poughkeepsie and Fishkill Landing directory, with a business directory and gazetteer of Dutchess County ... Poughkeepsie, A. Wilson, J. H. Hickok (etc., 1862 - 64.
2 v. 19½ cm. 11-4172.   Directories

POUGHKEEPSIE. Vail's Poughkeepsie city directory ... with a classified business directory ... 1870/71 - 1880/81. Poughkeepsie, J. P. A. Vail (1974 - 11 v. 22 cm. 11-4056.
                                  Directories

NEW YORK

POUGHKEEPSIE. The A. V. Haight company's Poughkeepsie directory ... 1910/11. (Poughkeepsie) The A. V. Haight co., 1910. 1 v. fold. map. 23½ cm. 10-15651. Directories

POUGHKEEPSIE. Account book of a country store keeper in the 18th century at Poughkeepsie; records in Dutch and English, preserved among the papers in the office of the clerk of Dutchess County, N. Y. (By Francis Filkin) (Poughkeepsie) Vassar Brothers' institute, 1911. 2, 122 p. 31 x 18 cm. 12-8973.
F129. P9 F 4

POUGHKEEPSIE. The Eagle's history of Poughkeepsie from the earliest settlements 1683 to 1905, by Edmund Platt. Poughkeepsie, Platt & Platt, 1905. 328 p. incl. illus., plates, ports., maps. 21½ x 25 cm. In double columns. 5-26897.
F129. P9 P 7

POUGHKEEPSIE. The records of Christ church, Poughkeepsie, ed. by Helen Wilkinson Reynolds ... Poughkeepsie, F. B. Howard, 1911 - 19? 2 v. front. (port.) illus., plates, ports., map. 25 cm. Contents. - v. 1 History. - v. 2. Parish register. 11-5392 Rev.
F129. P9 P75

POUGHKEEPSIE. The city of Poughkeepsie; historical and descriptive, with illustrated sketches of its institutions, its industries and trade, and its leading citizens ... (Poughkeepsie, Platt & Platt, 1889) 44 p. incl. front. map. fol. 1-14950-M1.
F129. P9 P 8

POUGHKEEPSIE, present & past; a half century of progress, 1861. 1911. Poughkeepsie eagle anniversary number (June 1911) (Poughkeepsie, N. Y., Poughkeepsie eagle, 1911) 44 p. illus. 55½ cm. 11-13549.
F129. P9 P 82

POUGHKEEPSIE eagle-news. Apr. 25, 1939. (Poughkeepsie, 1939) 1 v. illus. 57½ cm. Includes reprint of the 50th anniversary ed. of the Poughkeepsie evening star, Apr. 24, 1939. 40M386T.
F129. P9 P825

POUGHKEEPSIE through the camera ... 1903. 15½ x 23½ cm.
F129. P9 P 85

POUGHKEEPSIE; the origin and meaning of the word, by Helen Wilkinson Reynolds ... Poughkeepsie, N. Y., 1924. 3, 93 p. front., plates, maps (part fold.) facsims. 27 cm. (Collections of the Dutchess County hist. soc. vol. I) Bibliography, etc. p. (45) - 82. 24-10197.
F129. P9 R 3

POUGHKEEPSIE. Main street, by Lucy M. Salmon. Poughkeepsie, N. Y. (Printed by Lansing & Broas) 1915. 28 p. front. 24½ cm. 15-23032.
F129. P9 S27

POUGHKEEPSIE. Anniversary discourse and history of the First Reformed church of Poughkeepsie. By the pastor, Rev. A. P. Van Gieson ... Poughkeepsie, Pub. by request of the Consistory, 1893. iv, (5) - 128 p. 23½ cm. 3-14071.
F129. P9 V 2

POUNDRIDGE. Tombstone records of eighteen cemeteries in Poundridge, Westchester county. Fully indexed. Compiled by Mrs. Sterling B. Jordan and Mrs. Frank W. Seth. White Plains, N. Y., 1941. 2 p., 52, 12 numb. l. map. 28 x 21½ cm. Reproduced from type-written copy. 41-18030 Rev.
F129. P915 J 6

POUNDRIDGE. Burials in and around Pound Ridge, 1860 - 1871; accounts of an undertaker, name unknown ... copied ... by Mildred E. Struble... (n. p.) 1947. 16 l. 29 cm. 47-27886*.
F129. P915 S 7

PRATTSVILLE. Records of the Reformed Dutch church in Prattsville, Greene County, and of the Reformed Dutch church in Moresville, in the town of Roxbury, Delaware County. Transcribed by the New York genealogical and biographical soc. Ed. by Royden W. Vosburgh. New York city, 1921. 3, xxvi, 148, vi numb. l. 36 x 28½ cm. Autographed from type-written copy. 21-13636. L. C. copy replaced by microfilm.
F129. P93 P 9
Microfilm 10078 F

PROSPECT. The life of a village; a history of Prospect. By Howard Thomas. Prospect, Prospect Books, 1950. 151 p. illus., map. 23 cm. 50-10693.
F129. P94 T 5

PULASKI. Historical souvenir of Pulaski. and vicinity. (By Edgar Luderne Welch) (n. p., 1902?) 75 p. illus. (incl. ports.) 27 cm. (Historical souvenir series, no. 13) 5-17839.
F129. P95 W4

QUAKER HILL. Hiram B. Jones and his school, by Rev. Edward L. Chichester ... Quaker Hill, N.Y., Pub. by the Quaker Hill conference assoc., 1902.   5-17 p.   front. (port.)   pl.   19½ cm.   (Quaker Hill (local history) series. vii)   8-1139.
 F129.Q12 C5

QUAKER HILL. Cemetery inscriptions, Haviland Hollow & Quaker Hill. (By Mrs. Josephine C. Frost) (Brooklyn, 1912)   32, 2 numb. l.   27 x 21 cm.   Autographed from type-written copy.   13-1256 Rev.
 F129.Q12 F9

QUAKER HILL. Richard Osborn: a reminiscence. 2d ed. By Margaret B. Monahan ... Quaker Hill, N.Y., Pub. by the Quaker Hill conference assoc., 1902.   26 p. incl. front.   19 cm.   (Quaker Hill (local history) series. viii)   8-1140.
 F129.Q12 M7

QUAKER HILL. Thomas Taber and Edward Shove. A reminiscence. By Rev. Benjamin Shove ... Quaker Hill, N.Y., Pub. by the Quaker Hill conference assoc., 1903.   33 p. incl. front. (port.)   19½ cm.   (Quaker Hill (local history) series.   xi)   8-1142.
 F129.Q12 S 5

QUAKER HILL. Ancient homes and early days of Quaker Hill, by Amanda Akin Stearns; read at the fifth annual meeting of the Quaker Hill conference ... 2d ed. Quaker Hill, N.Y., Pub. for the Akin free library by the Akin hall assoc., 1913.   44 p.   front. (fold. map)   plates.   20 cm.   (Quaker Hill (local history) series, x)   14-11077.
 F129.Q12 S 7

QUAKER HILL. Some glimpses of the past. By Alicia Hopkins Taber ... Quaker Hill, N.Y., Pub. by the Quaker Hill conference assoc., 1905.   30 p.   19 cm.   (Quaker Hill (local history) series.   xiii)   8-1143.
 F129.Q12T11

QUAKER HILL. David Irish: a memoir; by Mrs. Phoebe T. Wanzer ... Quaker Hill, N.Y., Pub. by the Quaker Hill conference assoc., 1902.   15 p. incl. front. (port.)   18½ cm.   (Quaker Hill (local history) series   ii)   8-1136.
 F129.Q12 W2

QUAKER HILL. Albert J. Akin; a tribute, by Rev. Warren H. Wilson ... Quaker Hill, N.Y., Pub. by the Quaker Hill conference assoc., 1903.   35 p.   front. (port.(19 cm.   (Quaker Hill local history) series.   ix)   8-1141.
 F129.Q12 W7

QUAKER HILL; a sociological study ... By Warren Hugh Wilson. New York, 1907.   2, 168 p. 2 maps (1 fold.)   23½ cm.   Thesis (PH.D.) - Columbia university.   "Sources": p. (5-7)   8-8833.
 F129.Q12W72

QUAKER HILL in the eighteenth century. 2d ed. By Rev. Warren H. Wilson ... Quaker Hill, N.Y., Pub. by the Quaker Hill conference assoc., 1905.   68 p.   front. (double map)   20½ cm.   (Quaker Hill (local history) series.   iii)   8-1137 rev.
 F129.Q12W74

QUAKER HILL in the nineteenth century. 2d ed. By Rev. Warren H. Wilson ... Quaker Hill, N.Y., Pub. by the Quaker Hill conference assoc., 1907.   36p.   front. (double map)   18½ cm.   Quaker Hill (local history) series. iv)   8-1138 Rev.
 F129.Q12W76

QUAKER HILL conference association. Publications. Quaker Hill, N.Y., 1901 - 07.   17 v.   plates, ports., maps, facsim.   18½ - 20 cm.   Divided into 2 subseries: Quaker Hill series (no. 1, 5, 6, 12) and Quaker Hill (local history) series (no. 2-4, 7-11, 13-17)   Assoc. dissolved permanently July, 1908. Nos. x and xii wanting in L.C. set.   10-13009.
 F129.Q12W76

QUAKER HILL. In loving remembrance of Ann Hayes, by Mrs. Warren H. Wilson ... Quaker Hill, N.Y., Pub. by the Quaker Hill conference assoc., 1906.   18 p.   front. (port.)   pl.   20 cm.   (Quaker Hill (local history) series, xv)   8-1145 Rev.
 F129.Q12 W8

QUEENS. Trow business directory of the borough of Queens, city of New York, also residential directory of Flushing, Jamaica, Long Island City and Richmond Hill (1898) - 19 (v. 1) -   New York, Trow directory,.. co. (1898) - 19   v. fold. maps.   20½ - 24 cm. 1-31573 Rev.
 Directories

QUEENS. Papers of the Lloyd family of the manor of Queens Village, Lloyd's Neck, Long Island, 1654 - 1826. (Ed. Dorothy C. Barck) N.Y.... 1927.   2 v.   2 maps.   24½ cm.   (Collections of the N.Y. hist. soc. for 1926-27.   vol. 2 has genealogical appendix.   28-6973.
 F129.Q27 B 3

NEW YORK

QUEENS. The Lloyd manor of Queens Village; address ... by the Rev. Melancthon Lloyd Woolsey. Baltimore, 1925. 37 p. incl. illus., pl., ports., facsims. 23½ cm. (Order of colonial lords of manors in America. New York branch. Publications. no. 14) 28-6860.   F129.Q27 W9

RANDOLPH. Memorial address at the dedication of the Soldiers; monument, Maple Grove cemetery, Randolph. Written by Hon. James T. Edwards. Read by Mrs. J. T. Edwards. (Randolph? N.Y., 1906) (16) p. front., plates. 26½ x 20 cm. 6-21548.   F129. R2 E2

RED HOOK. Address delivered ... by Brevet Maj.-Gen. J. Watts De Peyster ... upon the occasion of the inauguration of a monument by "this immediate neighborhood, (Tivoli-Madalin,) to her defenders who lost their lives in suppressing the slaveholders' rebellion" ... New York, 1867. 122, lx p. 22½ cm. 3-31542.   F129. R3 D4

RED HOOK. Baptismal record of St. Paul's (Zion's) Lutheran Church 1730 - 1899. (Transcribed and indexed by Arthur C. M. Kelly. Rhinebeck, N.Y., 1971. iv, 211, 50, 40 p. 29 cm.   F129. R3 R4

REMSEN. A narrative history of Remsen, including parts of adjoining townships of Steuben and Trenton, 1789 - 1898, by Millard F. Roberts ... (Syracuse, N.Y.) The author, 1914. 4, (v) - xviii, 398 p. front. (coat of arms) 22½ cm. 14-13365.   F129.R35 R6

RENSSELAERVILLE. Quaker records from Rensselaerville, Albany Co. ... 28 l. 27 x 20½ cm. Autographed from type-written copy. CA 13-355 Unrev.   F129.R37 F8

RENSSELAERVILLE. The story of old Rensselaerville, based on old documents, early publications, public records, family letters, etc., etc. By Mary Fisher Torrance. New York, Priv. print., 1939. 2, 7-72 p. front., 1 illus., plates, ports., maps (part fold.) fold. facsism. 25 cm. "Bibliography": p. 72. 40-34521.   F129.R37 T7

RHINEBECK. The marriage record of the three Lutheran congregations, Rhinebeck, 1746 - 1899: St. Peter's Lutheran Church, 1746 - 1899; St. Paul's Lutheran Church, 1766 - 1899; Third Lutheran Church, 1843 - 1899. (Transcribed and indexed by Arthur C. M. Kelly. Rhinebeck? N.Y., 1969) iv, 93, 42, 15 p. 30 cm. 77-16665 MARC.   F129. R4 M3

RHINEBECK. Historic old Rhinebeck, echoes of two centuries; a Hudson River and post road colonial town. When; where; by whom settled and named, the whys and the wherefores, who's who and was; historical; genealogical; biographical; traditional ... By Howard H. Morse ... (1st ed.) Rhinebeck, N.Y., The author, 1908. 4, 448 p. front., illus., plates, ports., fold. map. 19 cm. 8-36777.   F129. R4 M8

RHINEBECK. Baptismal record of Reformed Church, Rhinebeck (also called) Reformed Church of Rhinebeck Flatts (and) Church of Christ at Rhinebeck Flatts, 1731 - 1899. (Transcribed and indexed by: Arthur C. M. Kelly. Rhinebeck, N.Y., 1970) 1 v. (various pagings) 30 cm.   F129.R4 R37

RHINEBECK. Baptismal record of St. Peter's Lutheran Church, Rhinebeck (called Stone Church) 1733 - 1899. (Transcribed and indexed by Arthur C. M. Kelley Rhinebeck, N.Y., 1968) 1 v. (various pagings) 30 cm.   F129. R4 R4

RHINEBECK. Documentary history of Rhinebeck, in Dutchess county, embracing biographical sketches and genealogical records of our first families and first settlers, with a history of its churches and other public institutions. By Edward M. Smith. Rhinebeck, N.Y., 1881. v, (7) - 239 p. front. (map) 23 cm. 2-7929.   F129. R4 S 6

RICHFIELD. Annals of Richfield. By Dr. Henry A. Ward. Utica, N.Y., Fierstine print., 1898. 102 p. 19½ cm. C 394 Rev.   F129.R48 W2

RICHFIELD.SPRINGS and vicinity. Historical, biographical, and descriptive. By W. T. Bailey. New York and Chicago, A. S. Barnes, 1874. viii, (9) - 227 p. incl. front., illus., plates, port. 19½ cm. 1-14952 Rev.   F129. R5 B 1

RICHFIELD SPRINGS illustrated. Historical and descriptive. By Dr. W. T. Bailey. Richfield,

Springs, N. Y., Mercury office, 1886.   4, (8) - 106 p.   front., illus. (incl. map) plates.   16 x 13 cm.   1-14953 Rev.
F129. K5 B 2

RICHFIELD SPRINGS, Otsego co. and the New American.   New York, Pub. for U. Welch by Dempsey
& Carroll (1883)   37 p.   illus. (incl. map, plans)   16 cm.   1-21503 Rev.   F129. R5 N38

RICHFIELD SPRINGS.   The new American hotel, Richfield Springs, Otsego County.   New York, 1882.
18 cm.   F129. R5 N4

RICHFIELD SPRINGS.   1881.   1 v.   F129. R5 R48

RICHFIELD SPRINGS visitors' list, Spring house.   (Utica, N.Y., 1877)   22 cm.
F129. R5 R6

RICHMOND HILL.   Metropolitan directory co.'s 1922/23 -   directory of Richmond Hill and
Woodhaven, N.Y., including Kew Gardens, Forest Hills and Ozone Park ... Brooklyn, N.Y., The
Metropolitan directory co., 1922 -   v.   23½ cm.   22-20892.   Directories

RIDGEWOOD.   Long island tercentenary edition.   Ridgewood times.   Ridgewood, N.Y., 1936.
1 v.   illus.   57 cm.   Forms v. 27, no. 1448 of the Ridgewood times, June 5, 1936.   40M598T.   F129. R56R57

RIPLEY, New York, sesquicentennial, 1816 - 1966.   July 4 - 8, 1966.   (Ripley, 1966)   88 p.   illus.,
ports.   29 cm.   71-294639 MARC.   F129. R57 R5

RIVERDALE.   Yesterday in Riverdale, Spuyten Duyvil.   Prepared for the celebration of the 75th
anniversary of the Riverdale Library.   (New York? 1947)   (5), 42 p.   illus., fold. map.   23 cm.   "Books and
materials .. consulted": 5th prelim. page.   49-20202*.   F129. R58 K3

RIVERHEAD town records, 1792 - 1886.   Arthur Channing Downs, Jr., ed.   Huntington, N.Y., Printed
by the Long-Islander, 1967.   xxiii, 846 p.   67-24324.   F129. R6 A57

RIVERHEAD.   History of the town of Riverhead, Suffolk county.   Written by Hon. George Miller ...
(n. p., 1876)   8 p.   20½ cm.   1-14954.   F129. R6 M6

RIVERHEAD.   Celebration of the 100th anniversary of the organization of the town of Riverhead,
Suffolk County, at Riverhead, July 4, 1892.   New York, The Republic press, 1894.   52 p.   23½ cm.
4-33847.   F129. R6 R6

ROCHESTER.   Description and memorandums of the county of Monroe and its envirions.   (By Jesse
Hawley)   (In the Rochester directory ... 1827)   11-21093.   Directories

ROCHESTER.   The Rochester directory ... v. 1 -   Rochester, Drew, Allis co., 18
v.   fronts. (fold. plans)   18 x 24 cm.   1-15255 Add.   Directories

ROCHESTER suburban directory ... including the towns of Brighton, Gates, Greece and Irondequoit ...
v. 1 -   1930 -   Rochester, N.Y., Sampson & Murdock co., inc., 1930 -
v.   illus.   24 cm.   CA 30-728 Unrev.   Directories

ROCHESTER.   Dau's blue book, Rochester, including Albion, Avon, Brighton, Canandaigua, Churchville, Clifton Springs, Dansville, Fairport, Geneseo, Geneva, Mount Morris, Newark, Pittsford,
Scottsville, Sodus, Spencerport, Victor and Webster ...   19   v.   New York
city, Dau's blue books, inc., 19   v.   21½ cm.   8-18571 Rev.
Directories

ROCHESTER and Monroe county business directory ... no. 1   1885   Rochester, The
Drew Allis co., 1885 -   v.   24½ cm.   Directories

ROCHESTER.   Progressive business places classified (Rochester, Syracuse and Rome)   Brooklyn,
Branton directory co.   v.   25½ cm.   12-27855.   Directories

NEW YORK

ROCHESTER and suburbs street guide; completely indexed, including official map; Rochester, Irondequoit, Brighton, Pittsford, Greece, Gates, Chili, etc. (Rochester, N.Y., W. P. Munger,
v. mounted fold. map. 18 x 10 ½ cm. 38M4155 T. F129. R7 A2

ROCHESTER. Sampson & Murdock co., inc. city guide and street directory of Rochester, with map. Rochester, N.Y., Sampson & Murdock, 1921 - v. fold. map. 14½ cm. 21-9523.
F129. R7 A2

ROCHESTER. George W. Aldridge, big boss, small city, by Clement G. Lanni. Rochester, N.Y., Rochester alliance press, 1939. x, 158 p. front. (port.) 22½ cm. Bibliography: p. 152-153. 39-25459.
F129. R7 A45

ROCHESTER. A guide or hand-book for Mount Hope cemetery, with photo-engravings and diagram. By Edward Angevine ... Rochester, N.Y., Democrat and chronicle print, 1885. 72 p. front., plates, fold. map. 17 cm. 12-9132.
F129. R7 A5

ROCHESTER. Moses Atwater of Canandaigua to Samuel R. Andrews of Derby, Conn. A packet of letters relating to the early history of Rochester. 1812 - 14. (Rochester, N.Y.) Rochester herald press, 1914. 31 l. 23 cm. 42-51312.
F129. R7 A8

ROCHESTER. The semi-centennial souvenir. An account of the great celebration ... Together with a chronological history of Rochester, by William Mill Butler ... Rochester, N.Y., Post-express printing co., 1884. (5) - 75 p. incl. plates, ports., map. 25½ cm. 1-14955.
F129. R7 B9

ROCHESTER. Ye citie of Rochester; illus. by C. K. Darrow. Buffalo, N.Y., C. L. Sherrill co., 1888. (62) p. illus. 24°. 1-14967-M1.
F129. R7 C5

ROCHESTER. City of Rochester illustrated. Descriptive, historical and statistical review. Rochester, N.Y., The Post-express printing co., 1890. 16, iii, 17-104, ii p. front., illus. (incl. ports.) 28 x 35½ cm. 1-14956.
F129. R7 C55

ROCHESTER. George Halford Clark ... Rochester, N.Y., Rochester athenaeum and mechanics institute, 1942. 3, 25 p. mounted illus. (port.) 21½ cm. (Its Our master builders) 43-4853 Rev.
F129. R7 C6

ROCHESTER. Commerce, manufactures & resources of Rochester. A descriptive review. (Buffalo) Commercial pub. co. (1881) 136 p. illus. 25 cm. 1-14957.
F129. R7 C7

ROCHESTER. Every Friday; an illus. weekly magazine of special features and comment. v. 1, no. 1-8; Sept. 6 - Oct. 25, 1907. Rochester, N.Y. (Every Friday pub. co.) 1907. (212) p. illus. 31 cm. No more published. 8-18109.
F129. R7 E9

ROCHESTER. Extension view card five feet long; 21 views of Rochester. ... Portland, Me., 1908. 15½ x 21 cm.
F129. R7 E95

ROCHESTER. ... Rochester and Monroe county (by) Federal writers' project, W. P. A. Rochester, N.Y., Scrantom's, 1937. 9, 24-460 p. incl. front. (port.) illus. maps (part fold.) 20 - cm. (American guide series) Bibliography: p. 443-447. 38-1950.
F129. R7 F43

ROCHESTER. How Rochester grows; compliments of Garfield real estate co ... (Rochester, N.Y., 1930) folder. 22 x 25½ cm. fold. to 22 x 8½ cm.
F129. R7 G2

ROCHESTER. Genessee country scrapbook. v. 1 - 1950 - Rochester, N.Y., Rochester Historical Soc. v. illus. 26 cm. Supersedes Rochester Hist. Soc. Publications. 52-42733.
F129. R7 G34

ROCHESTER. Good enough for grandpa. By Curt Gerling. (1st ed.) Webster, N.Y., Plaza Publishers (1958) 237 p. 21 cm. 59-17812.
F129. R7 G39

ROCHESTER. Smugtown, U.S.A. By Curt Gerling. Webster, N.Y., Plaza Publishers (1957) 201 p. 22 cm. 58-16149.
F129. R7 G4

ROCHESTER. (Memorial) General Jacob Gould. (Rochester, 1867) 15 p. 23½ cm. 9-23642.
F129. R7 G6

ROCHESTER. The industries of the city of Rochester. A resume of her past history and progress ... (By John F. Hart) Rochester, N.Y., The Elstner pub. co., 1888. 280 p. front. (port.) illus. 8°. 1-14960-M1.
F129. R7 H5

ROCHESTER, a good town to live in, by Edward Hungerford. 1st ed. Rochester, N.Y., University of Rochester (1923) 5 - 118 p. illus. (maps, plan) plates. 20 cm. 23-12560.
F129. R7 H9

ROCHESTER. The pioneer days of Rochester ... (By Mosher Story Hutchins) Rochester, N.Y., The Paine drug co. (1925) 34, (2) p. illus. (incl. ports.) 18½ cm. CA 25-791 Unrev.
F129. R7 H95

ROCHESTER. The grandest playground in the world, delivered before the Rochester historical soc. by Rossiter Johnson ... Rochester, N.Y., The Society, 1918. 23 p. front. (port., facsim.) 23 cm. 18-19976.
F129. R7 J 4

ROCHESTER. ... Historical collections of the Junior pioneer association of the city of Rochester and Monroe County ... Rochester, Pub. ... by D. M. Dewey; New York, C. B. Norton, 1860 48 p. 22 cm. No more pub. 16-7871.
F129. R7 J 4

ROCHESTER. Desultory notes and reminiscences of the city of Rochester; its early history, remarkable men and events, etc., etc. for the last 50 years. By an octogenarian. Rochester, N.Y., 1868. 36 p. 22 cm. 23-6160.
F129. R7 L2

ROCHESTER. Carl Ferdinand Lomb ... Rochester, N.Y., Rochester athenaeum and mechanics institute, 1944. 2, 27 p. incl. front. 22 cm. (Its Our master builders) 45-2445.
F129. R7 L6

ROCHESTER. History of the Polish people in Rochester (by) Norman T. Lyon. (Buffalo, Printed by the Polish everybody's daily) 1935. 3, vi, (5) - 180, vii-xiii p. illus. (incl. maps) ports. 22½ cm. 35-13619.
F129. R7 L9

ROCHESTER: an emerging metropolis, 1925 - 1961. By Blake McKelvey. Rochester, N.Y., Christopher Press, 1961. 404 p. 24 cm. (Rochester Public Library ... Publication 4) 61-18763.
F129.R7M228

ROCHESTER, the flower city, 1855 - 1890. By Blake McKelvey. Cambridge, Harvard Univ. Press, 1949. xvii, 407 p. illus., ports. maps. 24 cm. (Rochester Public Library ... Publication 2) Bibliographical footnotes. 49-10783*.
F129. R7 M23

ROCHESTER: the quest for quality, 1890 - 1925. By Blake McKelvey. Cambridge, Harvard University Press, 1956. xiv, 432 p. illus., ports. 24 cm. (Rochester Public Library. ... Publication 3) 56-11284.
F129.R7M238

ROCHESTER. ... Rochester, the water-power city, 1812 - 1854, by Blake McKelvey ... Cambridge, Mass., Harvard university press, 1945. xvi, 383 p. front., plates, ports., maps, facsims. 23½ cm. (Rochester public library ... Publication 1) Bibliographical foot-notes. A 45-4785.
F129. R7 M24

ROCHESTER. A story of Rochester, by Blake McKelvey; compiled under the supervision of Dexter Perkins, city historian ... Rochester, N.Y., The Board of education, 1938. 3, 223 p. front., illus. 19½ cm. 38-37218.
F129. R7 M25

ROCHESTER. Mr. & Mrs. Ezra R. Andrews. By Arch Merrill. Rochester, N.Y., Rochester Institute of Technology, 1953. 21 p. illus. 23 cm. (Our master builders) 55-32235.
F129. R7 M4

ROCHESTER'S story. By Evelyn L. Moore. Illus. by Patricia M. Bryce. Rochester, N.Y., Board of Education (1960) 144 p. 26 cm.
F129. R7 M6

ROCHESTER in 1835. Brief sketches of the present condition of the city of Rochester. Furnished

NEW YORK

originally, as communications, for the Rochester newspapers, by Henry O'Reilly. Rochester, Republished for a committee of citizens. L. Tucker, printer, 1835.   14 p.   23 cm.   24-552.
F129.R7 O57

ROCHESTER. Settlement in the West. Sketches of Rochester; with incidental notices of western New-York ... Arranged by Henry O'Reilly ... Rochester, W. Alling, 1838.   2. (xvii) - xxii, (23) - 416 (i.e. 468) p.   front., illus., plates, ports., fold. plan.   19 cm.   1-14961 Rev.
F129. R7 O6

ROCHESTER. Sketches of Rochester, with incidental notices of western New York, by Henry O'Reilly; index, compiled by Florence Fischer Van Slyke.   Rochester, N.Y., Rochester public library, 1934.
1 p., 50 numb. l.   29 cm.   Mimeographed.   35-23908.
F129.R7 O62

ROCHESTER; its founders and founding, by Howard L. Osgood ... (Rochester? N.Y., 1894?)
(8) p.   illus. (maps, facsim.)   23 ½ cm.   30-1668.
F129. R7 O8

ROCHESTER. Backward glances at old Rochester, by Katharine Rochester Montgomery Osgood. Buffalo, N.Y., Foster & Stewart publishing corp., 1937.   3, 56 p.   front. (facsim.)   20 cm.   38-2884.
F129.R7 O84

ROCHESTER; a story historical, by Jenny Marsh Parker ... Rochester, N.Y., Scranton, Wetmore, 1884.   viii, 412 p.   front., illus., plates, ports., plans (part double)   22 ½ cm.   1-14962 Rev.
F129. R7 P 2

ROCHESTER. Semi-centennial history of the city of Rochester, with illustrations and biographical sketches of some of its prominent men and pioneers, by William F. Peck.   Syracuse, N.Y., D. Mason, 1884.   736 p.   illus. (incl. facsim.) pl., 36 port. (incl. front.)   3 plans (1 double)   26 ½ x 20 cm.   5-11039.
F129. R7 P 4

ROCHESTER. Das deutschthum Rochester's, historische skizze, seinen deutschen mitburgern zum 50-jährigen jubiläum der stadt Rochester. Gewidmet von Hermann Pfäfflin.   Rochester, N.Y., 1884.
69 p.   20 cm.   1-14963 Rev.
F129. R7 P 5

ROCHESTER ways, by Charles Mulford Robinson.   Rochester, N.Y., Scrantom, Wetmore (1900)
70 p.   15 ½ cm.   Jan. 17, 1901-124* Cancel.
F129. R7 R4

ROCHESTER. Third ward traits. By Charles Mulford Robinson.   Rochester, N.Y., The Genesee press, 1899.   39 p.   16º.   Mar. 8, 1900-56.
F129. R7 R5

ROCHESTER, the power city, 1900 - 1901; Rochester Chamber of commerce, publishers.   (Rochester, N.Y.) Press of Union and advertiser co. (1901)   167 p.   front., illus. (incl. ports.)   fold. map.   24 ½ cm.   7-9634.
F129. R7 R52

ROCHESTER in 1904 ... (Rochester) Rochester chamber of commerce (1903)   158, (2) p.   illus., ports. 25 cm.   5-4118.
F129. R7 R54

ROCHESTER, 1906. Rochester Chamber of commerce, publishers.   (Rochester, N.Y., Press of Union and advertiser co., 1906)   178 p.   fold. front., illus. (incl. ports.)   25 cm.   6-20101.
F129. R7R543

ROCHESTER, N.Y., U.S.A., The convention city.   (Rochester, N.Y., 1909)   1 sheet fold. to 16 x 12 cm. illus.
F129. R7 R55

ROCHESTER. 1834. Centennial almanac. 1934. Commemorating the 100th anniversary of the charter of Rochester; text by Arthur C. Parker; (Rochester, N.Y.) The Municipal museum commission, Rochester museum of arts and sciences, 1934.   (29) p.   illus.   20 ½ x 30 cm.   34-11227.
F129. R7R556

ROCHESTER. Proceedings at the annual festivals of the pioneers of Rochester, held at Blossom hall ... 1848. Rochester, N.Y., Butts & Merrell, 1848.   23 p.   8º.   1-14965-M1.
F129. R7R558

ROCHESTER. Studies of metropolitan Rochester.   no. 1 -   Rochester University.
no.   illus., maps.   23 cm.   50-56244.
F129. R7R559

ROCHESTER. The book of the Rochester centennial ... officially authorized by the Rochester centennial ... (Rochester, N.Y.) Rochester centennial, inc., 1934. 108 p. incl. illus., ports. (1 col.) 30 cm. CA 34-550 Unrev.
F129. R7R562

ROCHESTER. Rochester guidebook ... (Rochester, N.Y.) Adams & Ellsworth, 1911 -
v. front. (fold. plan) illus. 17½ cm. 11-17837.
F129. R7R564

ROCHESTER. ... Handbook, comp. and ed. by the president and printed by authority of the Board of managers. Rochester, N.Y., Rochester historical soc., 1916. 140 p. incl. front. 21 x 11 cm. 16-23389.
F129. R7R566

ROCHESTER historical society. Publications ... v. 1 - 2. Rochester, N.Y., 1892 -
2 v. 24 cm.
F129. R7 R57
... Sketch of the public and private life of Samuel Miles Hopkins, of Salem, Conn., written by himself ... Tog. with reminiscences by his children, and a genealogy of the Hopkins family. Rochester, N.Y., The Society, 1898. iv, 56 p. 24½ cm. (Publications no. II) 4-7514.

ROCHESTER historical society. Publications. Publication fund series, v. 1 - 24. Rochester, N.Y., The Society, 1922 - 1948. 24 vols. front., illus., ports., facsim. 23½ cm. 24-5653.
F129. R7 R58

— Centennial history of Rochester ... Comp. and ed. by Edward R. Foreman, city historian ... Rochester, N.Y., 1931 - 34. 4 v. fronts., illus, plates, etc. vols. x - xiii. 32-15854 Rev.

— ... The history of Rochester libraries, Blake McKelvey, editor ... 1937. xiv, 416 p. front., plates, ports., etc. vol. xvi. 38-5854.

— ... Part I - The history of education in Rochester. Part II - Selected articles on Rochester history. 1939. viii, 384 p. front., plates, ports., etc. vol. xvii. 39-24959.

— Part I - Foreign travelers' notes on Rochester and the Genesee country before 1840. Part II - Nurseries, farm papers, and selected Rochester episodes. 1940. viii, 262 p. front., plates, ports., etc. vol. xviii. 41-25788.

— ... Charles Williamson, Genesee promoter, friend of Anglo-American rapprochement (by) Helen I. Cowan. Rochester, N.Y., The Society, 1941. xiv, 356 p. front., plates, ports., etc. vol. xix. 42-12694.

— ... Reminiscences of Rochester in the nineties ... William Berczy's Williamsburg documents. 1942. 8, 278 (i.e. 280) p. front., plates. 24 cm. vol. xx. A 44-4709.

— ... Rochester in the civil war. 1944. 9, 5-266 p. front., plates, etc. vol. xxii. A 45-3095.

— The life and work of Jane Marsh Parker, by Marcelle Le Menager Lane. ... 1946. 166 p. plates, ports, map. vol. 23. 48-1337*.

— Henry A. Ward. museum builder to America. By Roswell Howell Ward. Rochester, N.Y., 1948. xxiv, 297 p. illus., ports. vol. 24. A 49-9847*.

ROCHESTER. Rochester history ... v. 1 - Jan. 1932 - (Rochester, N.Y., The Rochester pub. lib. (1939 - v. 23 cm. quarterly.
F129. R7 R59

ROCHESTER in 1827. With a map of the village. Rochester, Printed by E. Peck & co., 1828. iv, (71) - 155 p. front. (map) 18½ cm. First pub. without the appendix (p. (131) - 150) in the Rochester directory, 1827. 1-14964.
F129. R7 R6

ROCHESTER. ... Early history of Rochester. 1810 to 1827, with comparisons of its growth and progress to 1860. Rochester, N.Y., G.W. Fisher, 1860. 24 p. illus. (incl. map) 23½ cm. First pub. as an appendix to the Rochester directory, 1827. Also issued separately under previous title. 1-14958.
F129. R7 R62

ROCHESTER, the flower city. (Philadelphia, J. M. Jordan, 1905) (32) p. (p. 2-32 illus.) 20 x 26 cm. 49-31841*.
F129. R7 R76

ROCHESTER. The Jewish community in Rochester, 1843 - 1925. New York, Columbia University Press, 1954. xv, 325 p. 25 cm. (American Jewish communal histories, no. 1) Thesis - Columbia University. Bibliography: p. (301) - 312. 54-6713.
F129. R7 R8
1954

ROCHESTER. Boys grown tall, a story of American initiative ... (By Roy Rutherford) Rochester,

NEW YORK

N.Y.) Rochester Democrat and chronicle, 1946. 115 p. illus. (ports.) 25 cm. "A reprint of 32 biographical sketches of Rochester industrialists pub. in the daily and Sunday Democrat and chronicle during ... 1945" 47-3735. F129.R7 R87

ROCHESTER. Reminiscences of early Rochester; a paper read ... by Augustus Hopkins Strong ... (Rochester) The Rochester historical soc., 1916. 18 p. 23½ cm. 16-18056. F129.R7 S 92

ROCHESTER. "Rochester in tabloid" ... The Union and advertiser, Apr. 22 - May 13, 1911. Rochester, N.Y., 1911. 36, 16, 16 p. illus. 41½ cm. 13-9639. F129.R7 U5

ROCHESTER. Views of Rochester. (Portland, Me., L. H. Nelson co., 1908) 1 v. 20½ x 25 cm. F129.R7 V6
F129.R7 V62

ROCHESTER. Views of Rochester. (Portland, Me., L. H. Nelson co., 1910) (32) p. illus. 20 x 25 cm. F129.R7V602

ROCHESTER. The new court house of Monroe County; its architecture, construction and cost, with a brief history of the erection of Monroe County and its first and second court houses. (By Charles Ketcham Watkyns) Rochester, N.Y. (The Rochester pub. co.) 1896. (66) p. front., illus. 17½ x 27 cm. 1-14966 Add. F129.R7 W3

ROCHESTER. The city of Rochester and vicinity; where to go, how to go, and what to see in and about the flower city ... (By Charles Ketcham Watkyns) Rochester, N.Y., Watkyns pub. co., 1911. 96 p. illus. 23 cm. 11-22353 Rev. F129.R7 W31

ROCKAWAY. Far Rockaway, Rockaway Beach, Rockaway Park, Long Island. New York, American photograph co., 1910. 23½ cm. F129.R8 A5

ROCKAWAY. History of the Rockaways ... 1685 - 1917 ... By A. H. Bellot. (1918) 1 v. F129.R8 B 4

ROCKAWAY. History of the Rockaways; sponsored by the Exchange club of Far Rockaway and written by the students of Far Rockaway high school ... (Far Rockaway, N.Y.) 1932. 56 p. incl. front., illus. plates. 23½ cm. Maps. Bibliography: p. 53-54. 32-35030. F129.R8 F3

ROCKAWAY park, Long Island. New York, The Rockaway park improvement co., 1890. (6) p. front., illus., pl., maps. obl. 32°. 1-14968-M1. F129.R8 R8

ROCKAWAY and Rockaway Beach. Descriptions of the progress of popular favor to the sea ... By Augustus St. Clair. New York, Garland & co. (1880) 28 p. maps. 16°. 1-14969-M1. F129.R8 S 1

ROCKAWAY. Far Rockaway in reminiscence, by Valentine W. Smith; an address ... Jamaica, N.Y. The Queens borough public library, 1936. 30, (6) p. front. (port.) 1 illus., pl. 27½ cm. Multigraphed. CA 36-373 Unrev. F129.R8 S 6

ROCKVILLE CENTRE. ... Bettye Gorindar's yellow book, Rockville Centre (Lakeview) Oceanside telephone & non-telephone complete village directory with street guide and map ... a complete village and street directory with home owners guide ... Rockville Centre, Merchants advertising service inc., 19   v. fold. map. 23½ cm. Also issued without "A complete village ... directory" 39-2512. Directories

ROCKVILLE. R. L. Polk & co.'s Rockville Centre (incorporated village) directory, including Oceanside and East Rockaway ... New York city, R. L. Polk, 19   v. 24½ cm. 23-11095. Directories

ROCKVILLE CENTRE. Robinson's Rockville Centre and Oceanside red book resident directory ... v. 1 - 1937 -   ... Hempstead, N.Y., Resident directory service, inc., 1937 -   v. illus., fold. map. 23 cm. 38M4149T. Directories

ROCKVILLE CENTRE. The history of Rockville Centre (by) Preston R. Bassett and Arthur L. Hodges. Uniondale, N.Y., Salisbury Printers, 1969.   x, 244 p. illus. 24 cm. 71-88168.
F129.R81 B3

ROCKVILLE CENTRE. Rockville Centre illustrated; pub. by the American photograph co. ... New York, under the direction of the Board of trade of Rockville Centre. New York, American photograph co., 1908.   72 p. illus. 22 cm. 8-29862.
F129.R81 R8

ROGERS ROCKS on Lake George. (n. p., 190-?)   11 p. 12 plates. 20 cm.
F129.R818R7

ROME directory, tog. with a business directory of Oneida county ... 18   Rome, E. H. Shelley; Utica, N. Hollister (18   v. 19 cm. 33-34844.
Directories

ROME. The construction and military history of Fort Stanwix, by John F. Luzader. Division of History, Office of Archaeology and Historic Preservation, National Park Service, U.S. Dept. of the Interior, 1969.   v, 169 l. 70-607979.
F129.R82 L8

ROME. A souvenir of Rome. By William E. Ninde. Rome, N.Y., W. E. Ninde, 1894. 40 pl. obl. 24°. 1-14970-M1.
F129.R82 N7

ROME centennial history, 1870 - 1970. Compiled by Rome Historical Society for the celebration of the centennial of the city of Rome. (Rome, N.Y., 1970)   vii, 88 p. illus. 28 cm. 73-134168.
F129.R82 R6

ROME, a short history ... (By John Albert Scott) (Rome) Rome historical society (1945) 35 p. incl. illus., ports. 23 cm. 45-7689.
F129.R82 S3

ROME. Our city and its people; a descriptive work on the city of Rome. Ed. by Daniel E. Wager. (Boston) The Boston history co., 1896.   vii, 247, 54 p. port., plans. 25 cm. 2-19061.
F129.R82 W2

ROME. ... Men, events, lawyers, politics and politicians of early Rome. By Daniel E. Wager. An address delivered before the Oneida historical society, at Utica, N.Y. Utica, N.Y., E. H, Roberts, printers, 1879.   47 p. 22½ cm. (Oneida historical soc. ... Publications, no. 3) 1-14971 Rev.
F129.R82 W3

ROMULUS. Centennial celebration of the official organization of the town of Romulus, Seneca county. (Geneva, N.Y., Courier job department) ... 1894.   142 p. 23 cm. 1-14972.
F129.R84 R7

ROMULUS. Historical address, delivered by Diedrich Willers ... (Geneva, N.Y., Courier job dept., 1894)   87 (i.e. 69) p. 23 cm. 1-14973.
F129.R84 W7

ROSE neighborhood sketches, Wayne County; with glimpses of the adjacent towns: Butler, Wolcott, Huron, Sodus, Lyons and Savannah. By Alfred S. Roe ... Worcester, Mass., The author, 1893. xvi, 443 p. front., plates, ports., maps. 26½ cm. 1-16303.
F129.R85 R6

ROSLYN. The story of Roslyn Grist Mill. New ed., rev. by Marion Willetts Brower ... Roslyn, (N.Y.) Board of Trustees, Roslyn Grist Mill, 1953.   16 p. illus. 24 cm. 54-25706.
F129.R86 B7

ROSLYN Harbor. The story of Sycamore Lodge, Roslyn Harbor, Long Island, by Catherine B. Fahnestock. Port Washington, N.Y., Printed by Port Printing Service, 1964.   viii, 72 p. 22 cm. 64-66260.
F129.R86 R3

ROSLYN. Old Roslyn, by Peggy and Roger Gerry, Foreword by Abbott Cummings. Photos. by John Parrott and Morton Russin. (Roslyn, N.Y.) Bryant Library, 1954.   40 p. illus. 23 cm. Includes bibliography. 54-29652.
F129.R86 G4

ROSLYN. Our town Roslyn; a brief history of the Roslyn area to serve the staff in guiding their

NEW YORK

students on trips around Roslyn. By Roy W. Moger. Illus. by Frank Walter. Roslyn, N.Y., Roslyn Public Schools, 1960. 31 l. 28 cm.
F129.P86 M6

— 2d ed., enl. Roslyn, N.Y. Roslyn Public Schools (1965) x, 185 p. 64-23957.
F129.R86 M6 1965

ROSLYN and North Hempstead in olden times. By Henry Onderdonk. Jamaica (L.I.) 1879. (44) p. 8°. Mounted newspaper clippings. 1-14974.
F129.R86 O5
Rare Book Coll.

ROSSVILLE. Records of Saint Luke's Protestant Episcopal church at Rossville, Staten Island, in Richmond County, in the former town of Westfield and now in the borough of Richmond. Transcribed and ed. by Royden W. Vosburgh. New York city, 1923. 2, viii, 74 numb. l. front., 5 pl. 36 x 28½ cm. Autographed from type-written copy. 24-4227.
F129.R87 R7

— Records of the Reformed Protestant Dutch church at Richmond, Staten Island, in Richmond County ... 2 p., iii, 50 numb. l. 36 x 28½ cm. With above item. 24-4229.

— Records of the Reformed Protestant Dutch church, Westfield, Staten Island, at Huguenot, State Island, in Richmond County, in the former town of Westfield ... 2 p., vii, 24 numb. l. With above item. 24-4228.

ROTTERDAM. Schenectady County cemetery records ... arranged and typewritten by Charlotte Taylor Luckhurst. (Schenectady?) 1919. 61 l. 28 x 22 cm. Autographed from type-written copy. 20-9616.
F129.R88 R8

ROUND LAKE. History of Round Lake, Saratoga county, by Arthur James Weise ... (New York, Press of D. Taylor, 1887) 103 p. incl. front., illus. 24 cm. 1-14975.
F129.R9 W4

RUSH. Rush in retrospect ...; town of river, reeds and rushes 1788 - 1808, 1818-1968, by Bessie A. Hallock. Rush (N.Y.) Printed by O'Brien Bros. Print. Co., 1968. 84 p. illus. 23 cm.
F129.R94 H3

RUSHFORD and Rushford people, planned, ed. and pub. by Helen Josephine White Gilbert ... (Rushford, N.Y.) H.J.W. Gilbert, 1910. 6, 572 p. illus. (incl. ports.) double map. 20½ cm. Books consulted: 2d prelim. leaf. 11-1873.
F129.R95 G4

RUSSELL. U.S. census records, 1850, Russell, St. Lawrence co., copied by Doris Wolcott Strong. Washington, D.C., 1941. 38 numb. l. 27½ cm. Type-written (carbon copy) 43-337.
F129.R96 S8

RYE. Chronicles of a border town. History of Rye, Westchester County, 1660 - 1870, including Harrison and the White Plains till 1788, by Charles W. Baird; illus. by Baram Hosier. New York, A.D.F. Randolph, 1871. xvi, 570 p. illus., maps (1 fold.) fold. facsim. 23½ cm. Contains families of Rye. 1-14976.
F129.R98 B1

RYE. Fifty years of Rye, 1904 - 1954. By Marcia Dalphin. Rye, N.Y., City of Rye, 1955. 162 p. illus. 21 cm. 55-4450.
F129.R98 D3

RYE. Views of Rye ... By Blakeman Quintard Meyer. (New York) B.Q. Meyer, 1917. 94, (2) p. illus. 20½ x 26 cm. 18-1579.
F129.R98 M6

RYE. Services in commemoration of the 200th anniversary of the first election of wardens and vestrymen of the parish of Rye ... New York, The Evening post job print., 1895. 6, (2) p., (2), (9) - 89 p. illus., pl. 23 cm. 16-7867.
F129.R98 R9

RYE. The bar of Rye Township, Westchester County; an historical and biographical record, 1660 - 1918 (by) Arthur Russell Wilcox ... (New York, The Knickerbocker press, 1918) 2, iii-xv, 347 p. front., plates, ports. 25 cm. 20-11944.
F129.R98 W6

SAG-HARBOR. Early Sag-Harbor. An address delivered before the Sag-Harbor historical society ...

by H. P. Hedges. Sag-Harbor, J. H. Hunt, printer, 1902. 2, 51 p. 23 cm. 24-3059. F129.S12 H 4
Rare Book Coll.

SAG HARBOR. Sleights of Sag Harbor; a biographical, genealogical and historical record of 17th, 18th, and 19th century settlers of eastern Long Island and the Hudson valley in the state of New York ... By Harry D. Sleight. Sag Harbor, N.Y., 1929. (7)-306 p., xii p. 24 cm. 100 copies printed. 32-34117. F129.S12 S 6

ST. HELENA, ghost town of the Genesee, 1797-1954. Written for the Castile Historical Society by Mildred Lee Anderson ... Castile, N.Y., 1954. 42 p. illus. 23 cm. 54-33390 rev.
F129.S13 A 7

ST. JOHNSVILLE. Record of the Dutch reformed Saint John's church in the town of St. Johnsville, Montgomery County. Transcribed by the New York genealogical and biographical soc. ... Ed. by Royden W. Vosburgh. New York city, 1914. 2 v. maps, facsims. 36 cm. Autographed from type-written copy. 14-13120. F129.S14 S14

SALAMANCA, including Little Valley and Killbuck directory, 19   Binghamton, N.Y., The Calkin-Kelly directory co., 19   v. 24 cm. CA 31-240 Unrev.   Directories

SALEM. Early history of the town of Salem, from its first settlement in 1761 to the close of the revolutionary war, tog. with incidents of pioneer days in other towns of Washington county. By Dr. Asa Fitch ... (Salem? N.Y.) 1927. 20 p. 20½ cm. 46-41790.
F129. S3 F 5

SALEM. The Salem book; records of the past and glimpses of the present, prepared for publication by a group of Salem's sons and daughters. Salem, N.Y., The Salem review-press, 1896.
250 p. front. (port.) 5 pl. 24 cm. 4-377. F129.S2 S 23

SALEM. Anniversary souvenir; to keep in memory the proceedings of the 25th and 27th Oct., 1896. New York, Press of T. A. Wright. viii, 100 p. incl. front. 18 cm. 2-11299. F129.S2 S 24

SALEM. 1797-1897. Centennial celebration of the United Presbyterian (the Old white) church building, Salem, Washington county ... New York, Printed by T. A. Wright, 1898. 91, (2) p. pl., port., facsim. (loose) 23½ cm. 2-11304. F129.S2 S 25

SALEM. The Woody Hill meadow, by Harriet Martin Williams ... Salem, N.Y., Priv. print., 1912.
29 p. mounted front., illus. 18½ cm. 43-44041. F129.S2 W 5

SANGERFIELD. The first white man that owned the town of Sangerfield. By Willis H. Weller. (Waterville, N.Y.) 1944. 11 p. 23½ cm. 44-47572. F129.S22 W4

SARANAC LAKES. Picturesque Saranac Lake, in the heart of the Adirondack Mountains. (By Kenneth W. Goldthwaite) (Saranac Lake, N.Y., K. W. Goldthwaite, 1915) (31) p. of illus. 21½ x 27½ cm. 24-17729. F129.S26 G 6

SARATOGA. History of Saratoga; an address by Gen. Edward F. Bullard ... Ballston Spa, N.Y., Waterbury & Inman, 1876. 22 p. 22½ cm. 1-27501-M2. F129.S28 B 9

SARATOGA, Ballston and Waterford directory, for 1872-3 ... tog. with a business directory of Mechanicville, Schuylerville and Stillwater, and much other miscellaneous information. By J. H. Lant. Saratoga (N.Y.) 1872. 2, (49)-248 p. 19½ cm. 11-12621. Directories

SARATOGA SPRINGS. Manning's Saratoga Springs and Ballston Spa directory ...   Schenectady, N.Y., H. A. Manning, 19   v. front. (fold. map) illus. 23½ cm. CA 35-31 Unrev.   Directories

SARATOGA SPRINGS. An analysis of the principal mineral fountains at Saratoga Springs, embracing an account of their history; their chemical and curative properties, etc., etc. New York, Ross & Tousey, 1858. 113 p. plates. 15½ cm. 8-11333. F129.S3 A 39

NEW YORK

SARATOGA SPRINGS. Hand-book of Saratoga, and strangers' guide. By R. L. Allen ... New-York, W. H. Arthur, printers and stationers, 1859.   131 p. plates. 19½ cm. A new issue ... of his "An analysis of the principal mineral fountains," etc. See above item. 1-15942* Cancel.   F129. S 3 A4

SARATOGA SPRINGS. Hand-book of Saratoga, and strangers' guide. By R. L. Allen ... Albany, N. Y., J. Munsell, 1866.   2, (3) - 147 p. incl. 4 pl. 2 pl. (incl. front.) 20 cm. See above item. 1-16298 Rev. 2.
   F129. S3 A 41

SARATOGA SPRINGS. ... Such was Saratoga. By Hugh Bradley. New York, Doubleday, Doran, 1940.   viii, 386 p. 21½ cm. Map. "First edition." Bibliography: p. 359 - 367. 40-30167.   F129. S 3 B 7

SARATOGA SPRINGS. Chronicles of Saratoga; a series of articles, pub. since 1947 in the Saratogian, daily newspaper of Saratoga Springs and Saratoga County, and including the radio series, Down memory lane. ... Saratoga Springs, N. Y. (1959)   620 p. illus. 24 cm. 59-14475.
   F129. S3 B 72

SARATOGA. History of Saratoga; an address by Gen. Edward F. Bullard ... Ballston Spa, N. Y., Waterbury & Inman, 1876.   22 p. 22½ cm. 1-27501 Rev.   F129. S3 B 9

SARATOGA SPRINGS. Saratoga, and how to see it; containing a full account of its celebrated springs, mammoth hotels, health institution, beautiful drives and walks, various objects of interest and amusement ... Saratoga, N. Y., R. F. Dearborn, 1871.   70 p. illus. 15 x 11½ cm. 1-14983 Rev.
   F129. S3 D 18

— 3d rev. and enl. ed. Saratoga, N.Y., R.F. Dearborn, 1871.   80 p. illus., fold. map. 13½ x 11 cm. 2-19066 Rev.   F129. S3 D 19

SARATOGA SPRINGS. Saratoga, and how to see it. Containing a description of the watering place, with a treatise on its mineral springs, by Dr. R. F. Dearborn ... Published annually. Albany, Weed, Parsons, print., 1873.   181 p. fold. front., illus., plates, ports., maps. 15½ cm. 19-10855.   F129. S3 D 2

SARATOGA SPRINGS. Reminiscences of Saratoga, compiled by Cornelius E. Durkee ... (Saratoga, N. Y., 1929?)   316 p. front. (port.) illus. 23 cm. "Reprinted from the Saratogian, 1927-28." 46-38564.   F129. S3 D 8

SARATOGA SPRINGS. Gollner's pocket guide of Saratoga Springs, With a condensed history of Saratoga Springs, a description of the village, the springs ... New York, E. G. Gollner, 1881. 67 p. fold. map. 17 cm. 2-19328.   F129. S3 G 6

SARATOGA SPRINGS. Fabulous bawd; the story of Saratoga. By Melvin Leighton Heimer. (1st ed.) New York, Holt (1952)   244 p. illus. 22 cm. 52-6626.   F129. S3 H 4

SARATOGA. Historical views, Saratoga battleground and vicinity. (Schuylerville, N. Y., 1884?) 15½ x 24 cm.   F129. S3 H 5

SARATOGA SPRINGS. Lee's guide to Saratoga, the queen of spas ... Ed. Henry Lee. New York, C. R. Parker, printer, 1883.   3, (5) - 227 p. fold. front. (plan) illus., fold. map. 17½ cm. 1-21567.
   F129. S3 L 4

SARATOGA SPRINGS. Death notices, 1840 - 1843; 1870-1875, Saratoga Springs and vicinity ... taken from early Saratoga papers, the Saratoga Whig, the Sentinal, and the Daily Saratogian ... copied ... by Elisabeth Janet MacCormick. Jamaica, N. Y. (1944)   73 (i.e. 74) numb. l. 28½ x 22 cm. Type-written. 45-7586.   F129. S3 M15

SARATOGA SPRINGS. A concise history of High Rock Spring, by Henry McGuier. Saratoga Springs, Presses of G. M. Davison, 1867.   38 p. 17 cm. 3-27744.   F129. S3 M2

— Albany, Printing house of C. Van Benthuysen, 1868.   42 p. 16 cm. 7-29230.   F129. S3 M22

SARATOGA SPRINGS. Confessions of Congress Park, Saratoga Springs; a scrapbook history. By Arthur A. Merrill. (Schenectady?) 1955.   unpaged. illus. 28 cm. 55-41647.   F129. S3 M4

SARATOGA SPRINGS. Preliminary report of the commissioners of the state reservation at Saratoga Springs 1910 ... Transmitted to the Legislature Jan. 13, 1910. Albany, J. B. Lyon co., printers, 1910.   50 p.   23 cm.   (Assembly doc. no. 13)   11-3989.   F129. S3 N 4

SARATOGA SPRINGS. New York (State) Commissioners of state reservation at Saratoga Springs. Annual report. (1909) - 19   Albany, 1910 -   v. illus., plates, ports., fold. maps. 23 cm.
13-19554 (rev. '17)   F129. S3 N 42
F129. S3 N422

SARATOGA SPRINGS. Miller's guide to Saratoga Springs and vicinity. By Thomas Addison Richards. Illustrated. New York, J. Miller, 1867.   91 p.   pl. 16°. 1-14978-M1.   F129. S3 R 4

SARATOGA SPRINGS. Saratoga album. (New York, Wittemann bros., 1883)   20 pl. 8½ x 13 cm.
A continuous strip (7½ x 230 cm.) of illustrations folded to form 20 leaves. 1-14979 Rev.   F129. S3 S 3

SARATOGA's daily hotel reporter. v. 1, no. 4, July 10, 1902. Saratoga Springs, N.Y., 1902.
1 no.   31 cm.   Daily.   F129. S3 S 68

SARATOGA SPRINGS: camera slivers from the famous spa ... Glens Falls, N.Y., C. H. Possons, 1887.   2 p., 19 pl.   13½ x 18½ cm. 1-14980.   F129. S3 S 7

— 1888.   2 p., 18 pl.   13½ x 18 cm. 1-14981.   F129. S3 S 72

SARATOGA SPRINGS souvenir. (Saratoga Springs? 1906)   (63) p. of illus. 20 x 28 cm. 6-23060.
F129. S3 S 78

SARATOGA SPRINGS. Souvenir, 50th anniversary, the Saratogian, 1855-1905. (Saratoga Springs, 1905)   unpaged. illus. 48 cm. 54-55053.   F129. S3 S 8

SARATOGA SPRINGS. Saratoga and Lake Champlain in history. By Elizabeth Eggleston Seelye ... 1st ed. Lake George, N.Y., E. Seelye (1898)   1 v. 111 p. plates, maps (1 fold.) 15½ cm. 1-14984 Rev.
F129. S3 S 91

SARATOGA SPRINGS. Reminiscences of Saratoga; or, Twelve seasons at the "States", by Joseph Smith ... New York, The Knickerbocker press, 1897.   vi, 326 p. front., pl., ports. 20½ cm. 1-14985.
F129. S3 S 93

SARATOGA. Souvenir view book of Saratoga ... Portland, 1908.   1 v.   20½ x 25½ cm.
F129. S3 S932

— 4th ed. Portland, 1905.   20 x 25 cm.   F129. S3 S 934

SARATOGA and Mount McGregor. By Seneca Ray Stoddard. Troy, N.Y., Nims & Knight, 1889.
(1) l., 19 plates.   15 x 19 cm.   1-14986 rev.*   F129. S3 S 94

SARATOGA SPRINGS. Reminiscences of Saratoga and Ballston. By William L. Stone ... New York, Virtue & Yorston, 1875.   2. 451 p. front., illus, plates. 19½ cm. Bibliography: p. 439-448. 1-14987.   F129. S3 S 95

— New York, R. Wrothington, 1880.   2, 451 p. front. (plan) illus., plates. 19½ cm. 16-9885.   F129. S3 S953

SARATOGA SPRINGS. Souvenir of Saratoga Springs. (By Walter M. Stroup) (Saratoga Springs, N.Y., W. M. Stroup, 1910)   (64) p. illus. 19½ x 27½ cm. CA 16-353 Unrev.   F129. S3 S 96

SARATOGA SPRINGS. Saratoga illustrated; the visitor's guide to Saratoga Springs. Containing descriptions of the routes of approach, hotels, institutions and boarding-houses, mineral springs, walks, drives, etc. Illus. with maps. New York, Taintor bros., 1875.   iv, (5) - 118 p. illus. (incl. tables) plates, port., map, fold. plan. 17½ cm. 1-14982.   F129. S3 T 13

— New York, Taintor bros., Merrill & co., 1884.   124 (i.e. 152) p. front., illus., 2 fold. maps. 17 cm.
5-3868 Add.   F129. S3 T 17

NEW YORK

— New York, Taintor bros., 1887. 124 p. illus., fold. maps. 12°. 1-21541-M1. F129. S3 T 2

— 1900. 133 (i. e. 206) p. incl. front., illus. plates, 2 fold. maps. 17 cm. 7-6745. F129. S3 T 3

SARATOGA SPRINGS. Visitors' and automobilists' guide book of Saratoga Springs, with map of village and vicinity map for automobilists. ... Saratoga Springs, N. Y., The Saratogian co., 1910. 127 p. 2 fold. maps (incl. front.) 17 cm. 10-15492. F129. S3 V 8

SARATOGA. Seeing Saratoga; a scenic and historic guide in twenty-two trips (by) Marjorie Peabody Waite ... (Saratoga Springs, N. Y., Business and professional women's club, 1935) 64 p. fold. map. 20 cm. 35-21894. F129.S3 W23

SARATOGA SPRINGS. Yaddo, yesterday and today (by) Marjorie Peabody Waite; with illustrations by Penina Kishore. Saratoga Springs, N. Y., 1933. 5, 3-91 p. front., illus. 20½ cm. "References": p. (95) 34-1803. F129.S3 W24

SARATOGA; saga of an impious era, by George Waller. Englewood Cliffs, N. J., Prentice-Hall (1966) xxi, 392 p. 32 cm. 66-26229. F129.S3 W26

SARATOGA SPRINGS. A Saratoga boyhood; By Robert Sloane Wickham. illus. by Anne E. Allaben. (Binghamton? N. Y., 1948) 242 p. illus., map. 23 cm. Includes bibliographical footnotes. 48-23621*. F129. S3 W5

SAUGERTIES. Polk's Saugerties directory ... incl. Glasco and Malden ... New York city, Baltimore (etc.) R. L. Polk, 19 v. 24 cm. CA 28-241 Unrev. Directories

SAUGERTIES. The early history of Saugerties, 1660-1825, by Benjamin Myer Brink ... Kingston, N. Y., R. W. Anderson, 1902. viii, 365 p. pl., port. 18 cm. 2-17064. F129. S4 B 8

SAUGERTIES. The Pearl. v. 1, no. 1 - 9; Jan. - Sept. 1875. Saugerties (N. Y., L. Barritt and E. Jernegan) 1875. 72 p. illus. (partly mounted) 22 cm. monthly. No more pub? 11-32002. F129.S4 P 35

SAYVILLE. A history of early Sayville, by Clarissa Edwards. Sayville, N. Y., Suffolk county news press, 1935. 38, (2) p. front., illus. (2 coats of arms) plates, 6 port. on 1 pl., map. 26½ cm. Bibliography: p. (2) at end. "The old families": p. (25) - 30. 35-37737. F129.S44 E 4

SCARSDALE, from Colonial manor to modern community. (1st ed.) By Harry Hansen. New York, Harper (1954) 340 p. illus. 22 cm. 54-8955. F129.S48 H 3

SCARSDALE. A history of Scarsdale, by a sixth grade, Edgewood school; Aliced M. Hoben, teacher. (Scarsdale, N. Y.) Edgewood school of the Scarsdale public schools (1935) 2, (iii) - ix, 34, (2) p. illus. (incl. map) plates. 23½ cm. 35-6527. F129.S48 S35

SCARSDALE. The Heathcote manor of Scarsdale; address ... by Hon. Charles B. Wheeler ... Baltimore, Williams & Wilkins co., 1923. 20 p. incl. illus., ports., facsim. 23½ cm. (Order of colonial lords of manors in America. New York branch. Publications) 23-12563. F129.S48 W5

SCHAGHTICOKE. Centennial day; an oration, delivered at Schaghticoke ... by Joseph Foster Knickerbacker ... Troy, N. Y., E. Green, printer, 1876. 24 p. 23 cm. 2-6545. F129.S49 K 6

SCHENECTADY. A report on the present alarming state of national affairs. (Federal party) (Schenectady, 1808) 15 p. 21 cm. Signed by Alex. Kelly and eight others. 9-20477. F129. S5 E336. F29

SCHENECTADY city and county directory, for 1862-3 ... Comp. by Henry Y. Bradt. Schenectady, Young & Graham, 1862. 141 p. 30 cm. 7-38081. Directories

SCHENECTADY city and county directory, containing the names of the inhabitants of Schenectady city

and Ballston Spa, with a business directory and gazetteer of Schenectady County. Comp. by Andrew Boyd. 1864 - 5. Schenectady, Young & Graham (1864)   2, (21) - 171 p.   19 cm.   7-38091.
Directories

SCHENECTADY. The Schenectady directory for 1865 ... Comp. by Henry Y. Bradt. Schenectady, W. D. Davis, printer (1865)   92 p.   23½ cm.   7-38082.
Directories

SCHENECTADY. ... Marlette's Schenectady directory ... incl. village of Scotia ... Schenectady, N.Y., W. C. Marlette, 1883 - 1910.   21 v.   fold. plans.   23½ cm.   Some vols. include Alplaus, Aqueduct, Ballston Lake, Burnt Hills, Bellevue, Edison Park, Delanson, Haynes Junction, Mariaville, Mohawkville, Mont Pleasant, Pattersonville, Quaker Street, Rexford Flats, Rotterdam Junction, Scotia and South Schenectady.   2-18958 Add.
Directories

SCHENECTADY directory and city register for the years 1841/42 ... Schenectady, Printed by J. & W. H. Riggs, 1841.   46 p.   18½ cm.   23-2871.
Directories

SCHENECTADY city directory for the year 1866, 1867/8. Schenectady, Bradt & Truax (1866-67 2 v.   24 cm.   7-39272.
Directories

SCHENECTADY and Amsterdam city directory ... 1873/4, 1875/6. Albany, J. H. Fitzgerald, 1873-75.   2 v.   23½ cm.   7-3381.
Directories

SCHENECTADY directory ... incl. Carman, (Athens Junction), Mohawkville, Scotia and South Schenectady ... Schenectady, N.Y., G. W. Marlette, 1883 -   1 v.   fold. map.   23 cm.   2-18958.
Directories

SCHENECTADY. Many Mohawk moons, by C. E. Bennett ... 1638 - 1938. (Schenectady, The Gazette press, 1938)   2, 27, (2) p.   illus. (incl. maps, plans)   24 cm.   39-8106.
F129. S5 B 5

SCHENECTADY. The markers speak; an informal history of the Schenectady area. By John Joseph Birch. Schenectady, N.Y., Schenectady County Historical Society (1962)   179 p.   24 cm.   62-22308.
F129.S5 B 57

SCHENECTADY. Complete street directory and map of the city of Schenectady and environs; comp. from new surveys and latest official data by E. S. Cullings ... Schenectady, Saratoga (etc.) Robson & Adee (1906)   (28) p. incl. maps.   front. (fold. map)   21 cm.   6-24565.
F129. S5 C 9

SCHENECTADY. A story of Schenectady and the Mohawk Valley, by Frederick Dales and Marion D. Dales ... (Schenectady, N.Y., Printed by the Maqua co., 1926)   15 p., col. illus.   21 cm.   CA 26-664 Unrev.
F129. S5 D 2

SCHENECTADY. Greater Schenectady. (Schenectady, N.Y., 1909)   1 v.   20 x 25½ cm.
F129. S5 G 7

— (Portland, Me., 1912)   20 x 25 cm.
F129.S5 G 72

SCHENECTADY. A history of Schenectady during the revolution, to which is appended a contribution to the individual records of the inhabitants of the Schenectady District during that period, by Willis T. Hanson, jr. (Brattleboro, Vt.) Priv. print. (E. L. Hildreth) 1916.   ix, 304 p.   25 cm.   Bibliography: p. (281) - 284.   16-17933.
F129. S5 H 24

SCHENECTADY. Miniatures of Schenectady. By Thomas W. Jones. 1909.   8½ x 11 cm.
F129.S 5 J 7

SCHENECTADY. Why Schenectady was destroyed in 1690. A paper read before the Fortnightly club of Schenectady ... by Judson S. Landon. (Schenectady, N.Y., 1897)   16 p.   23 cm.   4-22388.
F129. S5 L 2

SCHENECTADY. The pageant of Schenectady, in celebration of thet 250th anniversary of the founding of Schenectady ... Pageant director, Constance D'Arcy Mackay ... (Schenectady, Gazette press, 1912)   64 p.   illus. (incl. ports.)   20½ x 16 cm.   12-18535.
F129. S5 M2

SCHENECTADY. Schenectady, ancient and modern; a complete and connected history of Schenectady from the granting of the first patent in 1661 to 1914, presenting also many historic pictures and portraits of those who have been conspicuous figures in its history. By Joel Henry Monroe. (Geneva, N.Y., Press of W. F. Humphrey) 1914.   285 p. plates (part double) ports., map, plans. 19½ cm. 14-9550.
F129.S5 M75

SCHENECTADY. A history of the Schenectady patent in the Dutch and English times; being contributions toward a history of the lower Mohawk Valley by Prof. Jonathan Pearson and others. Ed. by J. W. MacMurray ... Albany, N.Y. (J. Munsell's sons, printers) 1883.   xvii, 466 p. front. (port.) illus., plates, maps (partly fold.) plans, fold, facsim. 22 x 18 cm. 2-2230.
F129. S5 P 3

SCHENECTADY. Propositions made by the sachems of the three Maquas castles, to the mayor, aldermen, and commnanalty (!) of the city of Albany ... Boston, Printed by S. Green. (Boston, 1941) facsim.: 12 p. 23 x 17½ cm. (Photostat Americana. 2d series. Photostated at the Mass. histocical soc. No. 126) Subsequently published under title: The destruction of Schenectady. 41-17208.
F129.S5 P 72
1690 a

SCHENECTADY. Old Schenectady, by George S. Roberts. Schenectady, N.Y., Robson & Adee (1904)   5, (17) - 296 p. front., illus., pl. 22½ cm. 5-1157.
F129. S5 R 6

SCHENECTADY. (Views ...) Schenectady, (Robson & Adee) (19 -?)   1 v.
F129. S5 R 7

SCHENECTADY. Centennial address relating to the early history of Schenectady, and its first settlers. Delivered at Schenectady ... by Hon, John Sanders ... Albany, N.Y., Van Benthuysen printing house, 1879.   xiv, 346 p. front., ports. 24 cm. 1-16287.
F129. S5 S 2

SCHENECTADY Genealogical Society. Publication. (Schenectady, 19   v. 28 cm. 49-31842*.
F129.S5 S 35

SCHENECTADY. ... The Schenectadian, portraying the advantages, attractions and opportunites of the electric city. Issued for the Board of trade, Schenectady, N.Y. (Schenectady, N.Y., The Gasette press) 1914.   56 p. illus. (incl. ports.) 30½ cm. 15-1495.
F129. S5 S 5

SCHENECTADY and the Great western gateway, past and present, published under the auspices of the Schenectady chamber of commerce ... Schenectady, 1926.   4, 65, (3) p. front., illus. 24 cm. "List of books": p. (66)   26-12263.
F129. S5 S 6

SCHENECTADY. Early Schenectady cemetery records. (Schenectady? N.Y.) 1914.   56 l. 28 x 22 cm. Autographed from type-written copy. Records of the cemetery of the First Reformed church. 20-9354.
F129. S5 S74

SCHENECTADY. Extracts from the doop-boek, or baptismal register of the Reformed Protestant Dutch church of Schenectady (1694 - 1704) Albany, J. Munsell, 1864.   14 p. 25 cm. 17-16973 Rev.
F129. S5 S76

SCHENECTADY. Marriage records of the Reformed Protestant Dutch church of Schenectady. Copied by Charlotte Taylor Luckhurst. (Albany?) 1917.   206 l. 28 cm. Autographed from type-written copy. 18-16264.
F129.S5 S 78

SCHENECTADY ... Two hundredth anniversary of the First Reformed Protestant Dutch church ... 1880. (Schenectady, Daily and weekly union steam printing house, 1880)   264 p. front. 23 cm. 15-9182.
F129. S5 S 8

SCHENECTADY. Six belts of wampum; a guide to the Schenectady stockade. (Schenectady 1964) (48) p. 14 x 22 cm.
F129. S5 S85

— "2nd printing, Apr., 1965."   (3), 45 p.
F129. S5 S852

SCHENECTADY. The story of the Schenectady massacre; pub. under the auspices of the Schenectady

Chamber of commerce and the Schenectady county historical soc. (Schenectady, N.Y., 1940)
24 p.   1 illus.   23 cm.   "List of books": p. 23-24.   40-4555. F129. S5 S 9

SCHENECTADY. A narrative, embracing the history of two or three of the first settlers and their families, of Schenectady. ...   By Dan'l J. Toll ...   (Schenectady) 1847.   57 p.   21½ cm.   20-20186.
F129.S5 T 65

SCHENECTADY. Walls have ears including the Stockade story and Samuel Fuller, master builder of the Mohawk, by Giles Yates Van der Bogert. Drawings by Werner L. Feibes. (Schenectady, N.Y., Printed by the Schenectady Herald Print. Co., 1966)   iii, 113 p.   21 cm.
F129. S5 V 3

SCHENECTADY. Door to the Mohawk Valley; a history of Schenectady for young people. By Millicent Winton Veeder. Albany, Cromwell Printery (1947)   156, (6) p.   illus., ports., maps.   23 cm.
Bibliography: p. (157) - (158)   48-13195*. F129. S5 V 4

SCHENECTADY. Schenectady, past and present, historical papers ed. by Myron F. Westover. Strasburg, Va., Shenandoah publishing house, 1931.   5, 73, (2) p.   illus. (incl. ports., map)   23½ cm.   "List of books": p. 71.   31-14482. F129.S5 W38

SCHODACK. Vital records of the town of Schodack, Rensselaer county, prior to 1880. Compiled by Lauretta P. Harris. Baltimore, Gateway Press, 1970.   139, 96 p.   24 cm.   77-146823.
F129.S53 H 3

SCHOHARIE. Burials in the Old stone fort cemetery at Schoharie; copied from the gravestones ... by Frank D. Andrews ... Vineland, N.J., Priv. print., 1917.   32 p.   23½ cm.   "Fifty-two copies only."
17-10370. F129.S55 A 5

SCHOHARIE. An account of Knoepfel's Schoharie cave, Schoharie county: with the history of its discovery, subterranean lake, minerals and natural curiositites. By William H. Knoepfel. New-York, W. E. & J. Sibell, 1853.   16 p.   fold. front., fold. plan.   23½ cm.   1-14988 Rev. F129.S55 K 7

SCHOHARIE. Records of the High and Low Dutch Reformed congregation at Schoharie, now the Reformed church in the town of Schoharie, Schoharie County. Transcribed by the New York genealogical and biographical soc. ... Ed. by Royden W. Vosburgh. New York city, 1917-18.   3 v. in 2.   4 pl.
3 facsim., map.   36 x 28½ cm.   Map.   Autographed from type-written copy.   18-6887. F129.S55 S48

SCHOHARIE. Records of St. Paul's Evangelical Lutheran church in the town of Schoharie, Schoharie County. Transcribed by the New York genealogical and biographical soc. ... Ed. by Royden W. Vosburgh. New York city, 1914.   v.   facsims.   35½ cm.   15-63. F129.S55 S 5

SCHUYLERVILLE. The story of old Saratoga and history of Schuylerville, by John Henry Brandow ... Albany, N.Y., Brandow printing co., 1900.   xxiii, 396 p.   front., illus., pl., fold. maps.   21 cm.   "Sources and literature": p. 381-382.   1-15048. F129.S57 B 7

SCHUYLERVILLE. The story of old Saratoga; the Burgoyne campaign, to which is added New York's share in the revolution, by John Henry Brandow ... 2d ed. Albany, N.Y., The Brandow print., 1919.
3, xi-xxiii, 528 p.   front., illus., plates, ports., fold. maps.   23 cm.   "Sources and literature": p, 515-517.   20-5214. F129.S57 B 7

SCHUYLERVILLE. Records of the Reformed Protestant Dutch church of Saratoga, at Schuylerville, Saratoga County. Transcribed by the New York genealogical and biographical soc. Ed. by Royden W. Vosburgh. New York city, 1913.   3, ii-xiii, 189 numb. 1.   35 cm.   Autographed from type-written copy.
14-12720. F129.S57 S 3
L H & G

SCIPIO. Mohr's directory of the town of Scipio, Cayuga county.   1904 -   (Auburn? N.Y.,
1904 -   v.   24 cm.   CA 33-617 Unrev. Directories

SCOTIA. Scotia-Glenville cemetery records ... Copy made by Charlotte Taylor Luckhurst ...

(Albany? N.Y., 1924) 52 l. 28 x 22 cm. Type-written copy. 24-15721. F129. S6 L 9

SCOTIA. Story of the Maalwyck. Its settlers; its house, long a famous landmark, and of its school, the first north of the Mohawk river. By Percy M. Van Epps ... Glenville, N.Y., Town board, 1937. 231 - 243 p. pl. 28 cm. 44-37303. F129. S6 V 3

SCOTTSVILLE. ... The first house in Scottsville. By George E. Slocum. Scottsville, N.Y., I. Van Hooser, printer, 1904. 13 p. 17½ cm. 100 copies. 10-23254. F129.S61 S 7

SOMERS. Glimpses of Somers Village, 1908 - 1958, by Alice E. Scott. (1969) 59 l. 30 cm. Typescript (carbon copy) F129.S613S35

SEA CLIFF. One square mile; a Sea Cliff sketch-book, by Frank O. Braynard. (Ann Arbor, Priv. print. by Edwards Bros, Press, 1967) 144 p. 23 x 29 cm. 67-20405.
F129.S615 B7

SENECA FALLS and Waterloo directory ... v.1 - 1927 - Schenectady, N.Y., Springfield, Mass., H.A. Manning co., 1927 - v. 23 cm. CA 28-49 Unrev.
Directories

SENECA FALLS. Papers read before the Seneca Falls historical society ... (1903) - 08. Seneca Falls? N.Y., 1903 - 08 6 v. illus. 23 - 23½ cm. 8-2667. F129.S62 S 6

SENECA FALLS. "Grip's" historical souvenir of Seneca Falls. (By Edgar Luderne Welch) (Syracuse? 1904) 144 p. illus. (incl. ports.) 26½ cm. (Historical souvenir series, no. 17) 4-9575. F129.S62 W4

SHAWANGUNK. Gravestone inscriptions of historic Bruynswyck churchyard, Shawangunk; comp. and ed. by Lila James Roney. (Brooklyn, N.Y.) 1924. 4 p., 53 numb. l. 3 l. 26½ cm. Type-written copy. 25-2341. F129. S634 R7
Rare Book Coll.

SHERBURNE. Reminiscences, anecdotes and statistics of the early settlers and the 'olden time' in the town of Sherburne, Chenango county. By Joel Hatch, jr. Utica, N.Y., Curtiss & White, printers, 1862. 104 p. 19 cm. 1-14989. F129.S66 H 3

SHERBURNE. Souvenir of the Sherburne centennial celebration and dedication of monument to the proprietors and early settlers. Also sketches of families and other historical data. Pub. by Marcius D. Raymond. Tarrytown, N.Y., 1893. 111 p. illus., plates, ports., facsim. 25½ cm. 4-20373.
F129.S66 S 7

SHERRILL. 50th anniversary celebration. Sherrill, smallest city in New York State, 1916 - 1966. (Sherrill? N.Y., 1966) 122 p. 28 cm. F129.S662 F5

SILVER CREEK. Steiran's Silver Creek (Chautauqua county) directory ... Including the villages of Forestville, Irving and Sheridan ... Dunkirk, N.Y., Steiran directories, 19 v. illus. (incl. port.) 23 cm. 39-14763. Directories

SINCLAIRVILLE. History of Evergreen cemetery, Sinclairville, Chaut. Co., and other burial gounds in its vicinity, with its laws, rules, regulations, names of lot-owners, and map. Prepared by Obed Edson ... Sinclairville, N.Y., Press of the Commercial, 1890. 3, (5) - 42 p. front. (fold. plan) 23½ cm. 12-9133. F129.S663 S6

SKANEATELES. A peep at Skaneateles, containing descriptions of various localities on and around the Skaneateles Lake: - to which is added a map of the lake, and eight views in illustration of the scenery. (By William Martin Beauchamp) Skaneateles, 1850. 28 p. front. (fold. map) illus., 7 pl. 13½ cm. 19-8789. F129.S68 B 3
Rare Book Coll.

SKANEATELES. History of Skaneateles and vicinity. 1781 - 1881. Comp. by E. Norman Leslie. Auburn, N.Y., C.P. Cornell (1882) 142 p. incl. front. 17½ cm. 9-15734. F129.S68 L 6

SKANEATELES; history of its earliest settlement and reminiscences of later times; disconnected sketches of the earliest settlement of this town and villages, not chronologically arranged ... With notes of the individuality of prominent citizens, by Edmund Norman Leslie ... New York, Press of A. H. Kellogg, 1902.   (vii) - xxii, 477 (i.e. 483) p.   front., illus., plates (1 fold.)   ports. 26½ cm. Originally pub., in part, in the Skaneateles Democrat.   2-21266.

F129.S68 L 7

SMALLWOOD. Civic Association of Smallwood. (Yearbook and directory) 1950 -   (Smallwood)   v.   23 cm.   52-42146.

F129.S685 C5

SMITHTOWN. A chronicle of the Head of the River, Smithtown, Long Island, 1700 - 1900, by Charlotte Adams Ganz. (Smithtown, N.Y., 1966)   18, (3) p. 28 cm.

F129.S69 G 3

SMITHTOWN. Records of the town of Smithtown, Long Island, with other ancient documents of historic value. Transcribed from the originals ... with notes and introd. by William S. Pelletreau, and pub. by authority of the town. (Huntington, N.Y., Long-Islander print) 1898.   xvi, 503 p. front., illus., pl., port., plans., facsim. 23½ cm.   2-2229.

F129.S69 S 6

SMYRNA. Early years in Smyrna and our first Old home week, by George A. Munson. (Norwich, N.Y.) Chenango union presses, 1905.   208 p. plates, ports. 21½ cm.   6-38545.

F129.S693M9

SOLVAY, Onondaga County. Phoenix, N.Y., Pub. by F. E. Richards for the Solvay Public School System, 1959.   73 p.   23 x 29 cm.

F129.S694 C6

SOMERS. Cemetery inscriptions from the towns of Somers and Somers Centre, Westchester Co. (By Mrs. Josephine C. Frost) (n.p.) 1922?)   2 p., 58 numb. l. 31 cm. Type-written copy. 22-22252 Rev.

F129.S695 F9

SOMERS. Somers Historical Society. The Elephant Hotel, its architecture and history. Somers, N.Y., 1962.   20 p. 20 cm.

F129.S695 S6

SOUTH SALEM. Sesqui-centennial celebration of the Presbyterian church of South Salem ... (Elizabeth, N.J., Press of Elizabeth daily journal, 1902)   (6) p. 18½ cm. 8-36492.

F129.S697 S6

SOUTH SALEM. South Salem gravestone inscriptions (compiled by) Theodore Langdon Van Norden. South Salem, N.Y., The Horse and hound, 1926.   iv, 98 p. 21 cm. A new ed. of the compiler's "Old churchyard inscriptions, South Salem, Westchester County" pub. in 1908 to which the inscriptions upon the older stones in the Keeler and Mead street burying grounds and in the cemetery have been added. 26-23119.

F129.S697 V3

SOUTH SALEM soldiers and sailors (by) Theodore Langdon Van Norden. South Salem, N.Y., The Horse and hound, 1927.   vii, 172 p. 21 cm. Contains Benedict, Bouton, Gilbert, Howe, Hoyt, Keeler, Lawrence, Mead, Rockwell, Rusco-Ruscoe and Wood genealogical tables. 27-8154.

F129.S697V33

SOUTH SALEM. A brief history of the Presbyterian church of South Salem, 1752 - 1902. By Joseph A. Webster ... (Elizabeth, N.J., Journal printing house, 1902)   74 p. incl. front., illus., pl. plates, port. 22 cm. 8-29218.

F129.S697W3

SOUTHAMPTON. Southampton directory ... (Southampton, N.Y.) Southampton times, 19   v. illus. (incl. ports.) 23 cm. Folded map laid in. 38-24854.

Directories

SOUTHAMPTON. History of the town of Southampton (east of Canoe place) by James Truslow Adams. Bridgehampton, L.I., Hampton press, 1918.   xx, 424 p. front., plates, ports., maps, facsims. 23½ cm. "References": p. (ix) - xvii. 18-3261.

F129. S7 A 2

— Port Washington, N.Y., I. J. Friedman, 1962.   424 p. 22 cm. (Empire State historical publications 14) 62-20909.

F129. S7 A 2
1962

NEW YORK

SOUTHAMPTON. Celebration of the 275th anniversary of the founding of the town of Southampton. Southampton, the first English settlement in the state of New York ... 1640 - 1915. Colonial society. Sag Harbor, N.Y., J. H. Hunt (1915)   8, 9-90 p., 8 l.   front., plates, ports.   23 cm.   24-17119.
 F129. S7 C 6

SOUTHAMPTON. Documents relating to the early settlement of the town of Southampton, L.I. Sag-Harbor, Office of the Sag-Harbor express, 1863.   2, 8 p.   8°.   Introd. signed W.S. Pelletreau.   1-14990-M1.
 F123. S7 D 6

SOUTHAMPTON. In old Southampton, by Abigail Fithian Halsey; with a foreword by Nicholas Murray Butler. New York, Columbia university press, 1940.   ix p., 3 l., 3-143 p. incl. front., illus. (incl. port., map) 21½ cm.   "Acknowledgment": p. ix-x.   40-5233.
 F129. S7 H 2

SOUTHAMPTON. An address ... by Hon. H.P. Hedges. (Sag-Harbor, N.Y., J. H. Hunt, printer, 1889)   14 p.   22 cm.   On the priority of settlement of Southold, against claim of Southampton.   1-24517 Rev.
 F129. S7 H 4

SOUTHAMPTON. The early history of Southampton, L.I., with genealogies. By George Rogers Howell ... New York, J. N. Hallock, 1866.   4, (13) - 318 p.   19 cm.   1-14991.
 F129. S7 H 8

— 2d ed. Albany, Weed, Parsons, 1887.   viii, (9) - 473 p. illus., pl. 23 cm.   9-30076.
 F129. S7 H 85

— Rev., corr. and enl. 2d ed. Southampton, N.Y., Yankee Peddler Book Co. (1969) 473 p.   illus.   23 cm.
 F129. S7 H 85 1969

SOUTHAMPTON. When Southampton and Southold, on Long Island, were settled. By Geo. R. Howell. Albany, Weed, Parsons, 1882.   14 p.   24 cm.   1-14992.
 F129. S7 H 9

SOUTHAMPTON. Patent of the town of Southampton. Pub. by authority of the town. Sag-Harbor (N.Y.) Corrector office, 1835.   12 p.   8°.   1-14994-M1.
 F129. S7 N 5

SOUTHAMPTON. ... Records of the town of Southampton, with other ancient documents of historic value ... Sag-Harbor, N.Y., J. H. Hunt, printer, 1874 - 1915.   6 v.   front., plates, facsims. (part fold.) fold. maps. 23½ cm.   Vols. 2, 4 include lists of births, marriages and deaths.   "List of soldiers and sailots ... in the war of the rebellion, from the town of Southampton": v. 4, (16) p. at end.   5-4100 Rev.
 F129. S7 S 65

SOUTHAMPTON. ... Addresses delivered at the celebration of the 250th anniversary of the village and town of Southampton ... by Hon. Henry P. Hedges and others ... Printed by order of the committee. Sag-Harbor, N.Y., J. H. Hunt, 1890.   (4) - 104 p. 2 port. 24 cm.   1-14993.
 F129. S7 S 7

SOUTHOLD. History of the colony of New Haven, before and after the union with Connecticut. Containing a particular description of the towns which composed that government, viz., New Haven, Milford, Guildford, Branford, Stamford, & Southold, L.I. ... By Edward R. Lambert. New Haven, Hitchcock & Stafford, 1838.   216 p.   front. (map) illus., plates, plans.   19 cm.   Contains genealogical sketch of the Lambert family.   1-Rc-3184.
 F98. L 2

SOUTHOLD. Study of the 1658 and 1686 depositions of Thomas Osman and early history of Hashamomuck in the town of Southold, Long Island, by Wesley L. Baker, in collaboration with Arthur Channing Downs, Jr. (N.p., 1969)   43, (38) l. illus. 29 cm.   Carbon copy typescript.
 F129. S74 B 3

SOUTHOLD. Historical sketch of Southold town ... by ... Albertson Case ... Carefully revised and corrected. Greenport, D. O. Crawford, printer, 1876.   16 p. 20 cm.   1-16284 rev.
 F129. S74 C 3

SOUTHOLD. ... Diary of Col. Benjamin Case, justice of the peace in Southold, Long Island, and

postmaster of Cutchogue, Long Island ...   Loaned by Teunis Bergen Burr ... to be copied for the
Long Island historical soc., 1906.   (n.p., 1906?)   39 l.   27 cm.   Type-written.   26-3082.

F129.S74 C 4

SOUTHOLD.   Old Southold town's tercentenary, by Ann Hallock Currie-Bell; photos. by professionals
and amateurs of the town ...   Garden City, Long island, Country life press, 1940.   xii, 161 p.   illus.,
plates.   23½ cm.   Bibliographical references in "Acknowledgments" (p. ix)   41-67.

F129.S74 C87

SOUTHOLD.   Griffin's journal.   First settlers of Southold; the names of the heads of those families,
being only thirteen at the time of their landing; first proprietors of Orient; biographical sketches, etc.,
etc., by Augustus Griffin.   Orient, L.I., A. Griffin, 1857.   (3) - 312 p.   front. (port.)   19 cm.   2-17683.

F129.S74 G 8
Rare Book Coll.

SOUTHOLD.   The story of the 275th anniversary celebration of the founding of Southold town ... by
Ella B. Hallock. ...   Garden City, N.Y., Doubleday, Page, 1915.   4, 3-85 p.   front., plates, ports.
23½ cm.   16-1489.

F129.S74 H 2

SOUTHOLD.   The settlement of Southold.   By George Rogers Howell.   (Babylon, N.Y., The Signal
steam print, 1894)   (4) p.   24 cm.   In double columns.   2-13808.

F129.S74 H 8

SOUTHOLD and its people in the revolutionary days, by Wayland Jefferson.   Southold, N.Y., L.I.
traveler print., 1932.   35 p.   21½ cm.   33-29102.

F129.S74 J 3

SOUTHOLD.   Town of Southold, Long Island; personal index prior to 1698, and index of 1698.   By
Charles Benjamin Moore.   New York, J. Medole, printer, 1868.   145 p.   22 x 29 cm.   1-16310 rev*.

F129.S74 M8

SOUTHOLD.   The Salmon records; a private register of marriages and deaths of the residents of the
town of Southold, Suffolk County, and of persons more or less closely associated with that place,
1696 - 1811; commenced by William Salmon and continued by members of the Salmon family; ed. by
William A. Robbins ...   (New York) New York genealogical and biographical soc., 1918.   115 p.
26 cm.   100 copies.   Reprinted from the New York genealogical and biographical record.   19-4159.

F129.S74 S 2

SOUTHOLD.   Southold town records, copied, and explanatory notes added, by J. Wickham Case.
Printed by order of the towns of Southold and Riverhead.   (New York, S. W. Green's son, printer,
etc.) 1882-84.   2 v.   fold. plan.   24½ cm.   1-16297.

F129.S74 S 7

SOUTHOLD.   Southold town, Suffolk county, Long island ...   (Mattituck, N.Y., Mattituck press, 1938)
104 p.   illus. (incl. maps)   31 cm.   "Genealogies of the founding families of Southold": p. 25-33.   39-5462.

F129.S74 S 8

SOUTHOLD.   Guide to historic markers; first list of historic markers placed in Southold, Peconic and
Arshamomaque.   Southold Historical Society.   (Southold, N.Y., 1960)   59 p.   23 cm.

F129.S74 S84

SOUTHOLD.   Celebration of the 250th anniversary of the formation of the town and the church of
Southold, L.I.   (By Epher Whitaker)   Southold, Printed for the town, 1890.   220 p.   23½ cm.
16-9490.

F129.S74W45

SOUTHOLD.   History of Southold, L.I., its first century.   By the Rev. Epher Whitaker ... Southold,
Printed for the author, 1881.   viii, 354 p.   front., plates.   19½ cm.   1-16295.

F129.S74 W5

SOUTHOLD.   Whitaker's Southold; being a substantial reproduction of the History of Southold, L.I.,
its first century, by the Rev. Epher Whitaker; ed. with additions by the Rev. Charles E. Craven ...
Princeton, Princeton university press, 1931.   viii, 194 p.   front. (port.)   plates.   22 cm.   Maps.   32-2758.

F129.S74W53

SPAFFORD.   Mortuary records with genealogical notes of the town of Spafford, Onondaga County, by

Captain George Knapp Collins. (Syracuse, N.Y.) Onondaga historical assoc., 1917.   280, (4) p. 2 pl.
24½ cm.   18-19959.   F129.S742 C7

SPAFFORD, Onondaga County, by Captain George Knapp Collins. 1902. (Syracuse, N.Y.) Onondaga historical assoc., 1917.   112 p. plates, ports. 24½ cm. Includes biographical sketches. 18-19960.
F129.S742C72

SPARKHILL. Rockland cemetery: illustrated suggestions and associations connected with it ... by William Wales. New York, A.D.F. Randolph (1881)   157 p. incl. front., plates. 19 cm. 11-19481.
(Concerns Sparkhill and Piermont)   F129.S743W1

SPENCER. Some Spencer history. By Floyd I. Ferris. Ithaca, N.Y., Pub. by the author for De Witt Historical Soc. of Tompkins Co., 1958.   113 p. 18 cm. 58-45417.   F129.S746 F4

SPENCER. Cemetery inscriptions, town of Spencer, New York, 1795 - 1906. Copies by Mary F. Hall. Pub. by Mary F. Hall and Ida Hallock Fisher ... Ithaca, N.Y., I.P.C. press (1906)
(53) p.   3 pl.   22½ cm.   7-3930.   F129.S746 H2

SPENCER. Book of remembrance, Presbyterian church, Spencer, 1815 - 1915 ... Spencer, N.Y., The Needle press, 1915.   (34) p. 20½ cm. 22-16584.   F129.S746 S7

SPENCERTOWN. Proceedings of the independence jubilee, celebrated at Spencertown, July 4, 1846. Albany, Press of Carroll & Cook, 1846.   48 p. 23 cm. 2-6546.   F129.S75 S7

SPRINGFIELD. ... History of Springfield, town of Jamacia, Long island. (Compiled by) William Applebie Eardeley ... Brooklyn, N.Y., 1914 -   v. 28½ cm. Type-written. Includes biographical material and genealogies of the Higbie and Mills families. 23-14854.   F129.S754 E2

SPRINGFIELD. The history of Springfield, by Kate M. Gray ... (East Springfield, N.Y.) Pub. by General James Clinton chapter, D.A.R., 1935.   5, 3-251 p. fold. map. 24 cm. Includes short genealogies.
36-13989.   F129.S754 G7

SPRINGFIELD. A history of the First Presbyterian church, of Springfield, N.Y. Presented in a memorial discourse... By Rev. P.F. Sanborne. Cherry Valley, N.Y., Gazette print, 1876.
22 p.   23½ cm.   3-7946.   F129.S754 S2

SPRINGFIELD. Records of the First Baptist church of Springfield in Springfield Center, Otsego County, N.Y. Transcribed by the New York genealogical and biographical soc.; ed. by Royden W. Vosburgh. New York city, 1920.   2 p., 39 numb. l. 36 x 28½ cm. 20-23481.   F129.S756 S7
— Records of the First Presbyterian church of Canaan at Canaan Center in the town of Canaan ...   2 p., 27 numb. l. 36 x 28½ cm. With above item. 20-23480.

STAMFORD. Souvenir of Stamford, "Queen of the Catskills." Middleburgh, N.Y., P.W. Danforth (1905)   (95) p. illus. 16 x 26 cm. 5-26905 * Cancel.   F129.S758 S7

STAMFORD. See also F129.H26 H2

STARKEY. Starkey Township of Bonnie Dundee; honey recipes and illustrated tales of Starkey, past and present. Adelaide Eddy Sunderlin. (n.p.) 1960)   unpaged. 22 cm.   F129.S7585S8

STILLWATER. Records of the First Congregational church of Stillwater in the town of Stillwater, Saratoga County, and the First Presbyterian church of Stillwater ... Transcribed by the New York genealogical and biographical soc; ed. by Royden W. Vosburgh. New York city, 1919.
2 p., viii, 129 numb. l. front. 36 x 28½ cm. Autographed from type-written copy. 19-4212.   F129.S759 S8

STONEY BROOK. Our heritage; a community of early American homes, churches and places. By Kathleen Fullam. (Stony Brook, N.Y., Bank of Suffolk County, 19 -)   unpaged. 23 cm.
F129.S7595 F8

STONY BROOK. Stony Brook secrets, by Edward A. Lapham. New York, The Gotham bookmart press (1942)   146 p. plates, ports. 23½ cm. "First edition." 42-19572.   F129.S7595L3

STONY POINT. Stony Point illustrated. An account of the early settlements on the Hudson, with traditions and relics of the revolution, and some genealogical records of the present inhabitants ... Ed. and pub. by Rev. W. R. Kiefer. New York, Z. R. Bennett, printer, 1888. 166 p. front. (map) illus., port. 23½ cm. 1-16299. F129.S76 K 4

SUFFERN. Romantic Suffern; the history of Suffern, from the earliest times to the incorporation of the village in 1896. By Saxby Vouler Penfold. Tallman, N. Y., Rockland County Historical Committee (1955) 106 p. 24 cm. 56-16644. F129.S77 P 4

SULLIVAN. Sullivan in history; interesting people and events contributing to the development of the township of Sullivan, Madison county, by Claude A. Nichols. 1st ed., 1939. 95 p. illus. 23 cm. A 41-1617. F129.S78 N 5

SYRACUSE. Winsor's Syracuse city directory for 18 -   Syracuse, H. P. Winsor (18
  v. 20 cm. 16-11525. Directories

SYRACUSE. Daily journal city register and directory ... (of Syracuse, N. Y.) 1851/52 - Syracuse, The Journal office, 1851 - 1 v. 19 cm. 23-2872. Directories

SYRACUSE. The Syracuse directory, including Solvay ... 1851/52   v. 1 -   Syracuse, N. Y., Sampson & Murdock, 1851 - 19   v. fold. maps. 19 - 24 cm. 1-17682 Rev.
  Directories

SYRACUSE. The Syracuse and central New York blue book ... New York city, Dau pub. co.
  v. 21½ cm. 10-19932. Directories

SYRACUSE. Sampson & Murdock city guide and street directory of Syracuse; a complete guide to the streets, avenues, church, schools, etc., with map. Syracuse, Sampson & Murdock (1920 -
  v. fold. map. 15½ cm. 21-9522. F129. S8 A 2

SYRACUSE. A history of old Syracuse, 1654 - 1899, by Anne Kathleen Baker. Fayetteville, N. Y., Manlius pub. co., 1941. 5, 182 p. 20½ cm. 42-23753. F129. S8 B 3

SYRACUSE. Memorial history of Syracuse, from its settlement to the present time. Ed. by Dwight H. Bruce. Syracuse, N. Y., H. P. Smith, 1891. (5) - 718 p. illus. (incl. maps) ports. 25 cm. 36-6730.
  F129. S8 B 7

SYRACUSE and its environs; a history, by Franklin H. Chase ... New York and Chicago, Lewis historical publishing co., 1924. 3 v. fronts., plates, ports. 27½ cm. Biographical material comprises last part of v. 2 and all of v. 3. 24-29538. F129. S8 C 4

SYRACUSE, a study in urban geography (by) Eric Henry Faigle ... (Ann Arbor? Mich., 1936)
4 p., 36 numb. l., 25 l. plates, maps, plans (1 fold.) diagr. 30½ x 23 cm. Thesis (PH. D.) - University of Michigan, 1935. Mimeographed. Bibliography: 5 leaves at end. 37-15583. F129.S8 F 23

SYRACUSE. From a forest to a city. Personal reminiscences of Syracuse. By M. C. Hand. Syracuse, Masters & Stone, printers, 1889. 203 p. front., illus., plates. 18½ cm. 1-16294 Additions.
  F129. S8 H 2

SYRACUSE. Census tract address key and street guide for Syracuse, prepared by Dr. William C. Lehmann ... (Syracuse, N. Y.) Syracuse council of social agencies, 1942. iv, 53 p. double map. 20½ cm. Reproduced from type-written copy. 42-13581. F129. S8 L 4

SYRACUSE. Picturesque Oakwood: its past and present associations. Ed. by Mrs. Annie C. Maltbie. Syracuse, N. Y., F. S. Hills, 1894. 284 p. incl. front., plates, ports. 26 x 24 cm. 11-19482 Rev.
  F129. S8 M2

SYRACUSE; the city that salt built, by Lilian Steele Munson. New York, Pageant Press International Corp. (1969) 328 p. 21 cm. 68-58935. F129. S8 M9

NEW YORK

SYRACUSE. Race relations in Syracuse; a profile by Eunice and George Grier. Rev. ed. (Albany) 1958.   36 l.   illus.   29 cm.   Includes bibliography.   A 58-9876.   F129.S8 N 45 1958

SYRACUSE. Syracuse of to-day, with a brief review of its wonderful progress of a century. ... (New York) The New York industrial recorder, 1898.   40 p.   illus.   41½ cm.   Special number of the New York industrial recorder.   10-23119.   F129. S8 N 5

SYRACUSE. Gone are the days, by E. Alexander Powell. Boston, Little, Brown, 1938. 6, 3-293 p.   21 cm.   "First edition."   38-19808.   F129. S8 P 7

SYRACUSE. From a minyan to a community; a history of the Jews of Syracuse (by) B. G. Rudolph. (1st ed. Syracuse, Syracuse University (1970)   xix, 314 p.   illus.   24 cm.   F129. S8 R 8

SYRACUSE. Souvenir of Syracuse. (Philadelphia, 1905)   19½ x 25½ cm.   F129. S8 S 72

SYRACUSE. Souvenir of Syracuse. (Portland, Me., 1908)   1 v.   20½ x 25½ cm.   F129.S8 S 74

SYRACUSE. Early landmarks of Syracuse. By Gurney S. Strong ... With an introd. by George J. Gardner ... Syracuse, N.Y., Printed by the Times pub. co., 1894.   xviii, 19-393 p.   front., pl., ports., map.   22 cm.   1-16300.   F129. S8 S 8

SYRACUSE. When Syracuse was a village; snap shots of early days, taken from village records in the city clerk's offic. (Syracuse?) 1915.   41 p.   23 cm.   Comp. by John N. Alsever, city clerk.   16-10507.   F129.S8 S 82

SYRACUSE and its surroundings illustrated. Buffalo, N.Y., C. L. Sherrill co., 1888. (46) p. incl. illus., pl.   obl. 24°.   1-16293-M1.   F129.S8 S 83

SYRACUSE. The city of Syracuse, its location, surroundings and ... attractive features ... (Syracuse, Chamber of commerce) 1899.   52 p.   illus.   obl. 16°.   Pub. as a souvenir for the 86th annual conclave of the Grand commandery Knights templar ... 1899.   1-16286-M1.   F129.S8 S 85

SYRACUSE. Early records of the First Presbyterian church of Syracuse. From the date of establishment in 1826 to the end of the first pastorate in 1850 ... Ed. A. J. Northrup ... Syracuse (N.Y.) The Genealogical soc. of central New York, 1902.   53 p.   20½ cm.   (Bulletin of the Genealogical soc. of central New York, no. 1)   3-8741.   F129. S 8 S 9

SYRACUSE. The history, incorporation, rules and regulations of Oakwood cemetery ... Syracuse, J. G. K. Truair, printers, 1860.   79 p.   22 cm.   CA 25-252 Unrev.   F129.S8 S 92

SYRACUSE. Geschichte der Deutschen in Syracuse und Onondaga County, nebst kurzen biographien von beamten und hervorragenden buergern ... hrsg. von der "Syracuse union." Syracuse, N.Y., Druck von J. P. Pinzer, 1897.   304 p.   illus. (incl. ports.)   23 cm.   9-13989.   F129.S8 S 95

SYRACUSE. Business directory, and mercantile register of Albany, Troy, Schenectady, Kingston, Poughkeepsie, Cohoes, Amsterdam, Saratoga, Hudson, Gloversville, Pittsfield, Mass., North Adams, Mass., Glens Falls, Rensselaer, Catskill, Johnstown, and intermediate towns ... (1st) - Troy, N.Y., 1902 -   v.   24 cm.   17-28126.   Directories

TAPPAN. The Washington masonic shrine at Tappan. (New York) The Washington masonic shrine committee, Grand lodge, F. & A. M., New York (1934)   4, 11-86 p.   front., plates, ports., map.   19 cm. The Amos De Wint house at Tappan.   34-16879.   F129.T17 F83

TAPPAN. Washington's Tappan headquarters, the oldest headquarters of the revolution (by) Mable Lorenz Ives ... (Upper Montclair, N.J., Lucy Fortune, 1932)   3, 17 p. incl. front., illus.   23½ cm. "Pre-print series" of Washington's headquarters series, no. 17.   32-17252.   F129.T17 I 9

TAPPAN.   Record of marriages (1699 - 1824) from the Protestant Reformed Dutch church at Tappan, Rockland County.   Translated from the Dutch by Dr. D. S. Cole.   (n.p., 1924?)   2 p., 55 numb. l.   28 x 21 ½ cm.   Autographed from type-written copy.   25-25166.
 F129.T17 T2

TARRYTOWN.   ... Richmond's directory of Tarrytown, North Tarrytown, Irvington, Dobbs Ferry, Ardsley and Hastings (Westchester County, N.Y.) 18 Yonkers, N.Y., W. L. Richmond,   v.   24 cm.   Some vols. have title: Turner's New York central and Hudson river railroad directory, embracing the following stations: Peekskill, Verplanck's Point, Montrose, Crugers, Oscawana, Croton, Sing Sing, Scarborough, Tarrytown, Dobbs Ferry, Irvington, Hastings, Yonkers, city business ... 2-3595 (rev. '14)
 Directories

TARRYTOWN.   Chronicles of Tarrytown and Sleepy Hollow.   By Edgar Mayhew Bacon ... New York and London, G. P. Putnam's sons, 1897.   x, 163 p.   front., plates, fold. map.   17 ½ cm.   1-16311.
 F129.T19 B14

— 1902. x, 163 p. front., plates, fold. map. 17 ½ cm. 39-32905.
 F129.T19 B14 1902

TARRYTOWN.   A "centennial souvenir," A brief history of Tarrytown, from 1680 to ... 1880. With a map of Tarrytown as it was 100 years ago ... Tarrytown, G. L. Wiley, 1880.   24 p. fold. map. 22 ½ cm. 9-24124.
 F129.T19 C3

TARRYTOWN.   Historical Tarrytown and North Tarrytown (a guide).   (By Margaret Swancott Conklin) (Tarrytown, N.Y., The Tarrytown historical soc., 1939)   58 p. illus. (incl. ports.) 23 cm. 30-32993.
 F129.T19 C6

TARRYTOWN.   Fourteen of them, by John Hersey (and others) ... With a foreword by Mary Roberts Rinehart.   New York, Toronto, Farrar & Rinehart, inc. (1944)   x, 85 p. front. (ports.) 23 ½ cm.   "Originally appeared in the Tarrytown Daily news, Nov. 5-20, 1943." 44-3102.
 F129.T19 F6

TARRYTOWN.   Pocantico Hills, 1609 - 1959.   By William A. Owens.   Tarrytown, N.Y., Sleepy Hollow Restorations (1960)   53 p. 23 cm. 60-9169.
 F129.T19 O9

TARRYTOWN.   Philipse Castle restoration, 1683.   (n.p., 194-?)   (16) p. illus. 24 cm.   "(No) 2 of a series of historical restorations pub. through the courtesy of Scalamandré Silks, inc." 48-43500.
 F129.T19 P45

TARRYTOWN.   Washington at Tarrytown. ... By M. D. Raymond.   1893.   1 v.
 F129.T19 R27

TARRYTOWN.   Souvenir of the revolutionary soldiers' monument dedication ...   Comp. by Marcius D. Raymond ... (New York, Rogers & Sherwood, printers) 1894.   207 p., 2 l., front., illus., plates, ports.   26 ½ cm.   Edition limited to 100 copies.   9-10368.
 F129.T19 T2
 Rare Book Coll.

TAUGHANNOCK.   The falls of Taughannock: containing a complete description of this the highest fall in the state of New York.   With historical and descriptive sketches.   By Lewis Halsey ... New York, J. A. Gray & Green, printers, 1866.   95 p. incl. front., 1 illus. 14 ½ x 11 cm. 1-14995.
 F129.T2 H17

TAUGHANNOCK.   ... Taughannock Falls ...   Ithaca, N.Y., Taughannock development corporation, (1922)   (8) p. illus. 21 ½ x 9 cm.
 F129.T2 T22

TICONDEROGA.   The taking of Ticonderoga in 1775: the British story; a study of captors and captives, by Allen French, based upon material hitherto unpublished.   Cambridge, Harvard university press, 1928.   89 p. front. (facsim.) 21 cm. Bibliography: p. 71- (74) 28-21231.
 E241.T5 F8

TICONDEROGA.   Manning's Ticonderoga, Port Henry, Crown Point, Westport (New York) directory, for townships and villages of Ticonderoga, Moriah, Crown Point, Westport, Chilson, Montcalm Landing, Fort Ticonderoga, Streetroad, Moriah Center, Mineville, Witherbee, Wadhams, Crown Point Center, Factoryville and Ironville. v.1 - 1929 - Schenectady, N.Y., H. A. Manning, 1929 - v. illus. 23 ½ cm. CA 30-171 Unrev.
 Directories

NEW YORK

TICONDEROGA. The restoration of Fort Ticonderoga, by Alfred C. Bossom. The German redoubt, by Howland Pell. (In American scenic and historic preservation soc. 18th annual report. 1913) 14-4409. F129. T5 B 7

TICONDEROGA. An historical address, by Joseph Cook, delivered at the first centennial anniversary of the settlement of Ticonderoga ... Ticonderoga, N.Y., Ticonderoga hist. soc. (1909) 109 p. col. front., plates, ports. 21 cm. 9-27023. F129. T5 C6

TICONDEROGA. Home sketches of Essex county. First number. Ticonderoga: 1. What it is; 2. What it does; 3. What it enjoys; 4. What it needs. By Flavius J. Cook. Keeseville, N.Y., W. Lansing, printers, 1858. vii, (8) - 139 p. 23½ cm. No more pub? 1-23703 Rev. F129. T5 C7

TICONDEROGA. Liberty monument unveiling ... Ticonderoga, N.Y. (n. p.) 1924. (11) p. illus. 21 cm. 25-2955. F129. T5 L6

TICONDEROGA; historic portage. Ticonderoga, N.Y., Port Mount Hope Soc. Press (1959) 248 p. 59-12781. F129. T5 L65

TICONDEROGA. Ticonderoga: past and present. "Mixed." A companion to "Lake George, illustrated." Being a history of Ticonderoga. By Seneca Ray Stoddard. Albany, Weed, Parsons, printers, 1873. 68 p. illus. 20 cm. 1-14996 rev.* F129. T5 S 8

TICONDEROGA. A memorial tablet at Ticonderoga, a corporation's gift to history. Reprinted by the Ticonderoga pulp and paper co., by permission of Ticonderoga hist. soc. (Cambridge, Mass., The University press, 1911) 29 p. incl. front., illus. 23½ cm. 11-3267. F129. T5 T6

TONAWANDA. A directory of the twin cities of Tonawanda and North Tonawanda for 1895 - Comp. and pub. by Edwin Curtiss ... Tonawanda, N.Y., 1896 - 1 v. 24 cm. 7-38355. Directories

TONAWANDA. R. L. Polk & co.'s North Tonawanda city directory, 1905/6 - ... Chicago, Detroit (etc.) R. L. Polk, 1905 - 23 cm. (With their Tonawanda (N.Y.) city directory. ...) 7-38093. Directories

TONAWANDA. North Tonawanda city directory ... 1900/01, 1903, 1905/06, 1907/08, 1909. Lockport, N.Y., Roberts bros. co., 1900 - 19 v. fold. maps. 22½ - 24½ cm. (With Tonawanda city directory ... 9-5695 (rev. '32) Directories

TONAWANDA city directory ... 1900/01, 1903, 1905/6, 1907/8, 1909. Lockport, N.Y., Roberts bros. 1900 - 9-5694 (rev. '32) v. fold. maps. 22½ - 24½ cm. Directories

TONAWANDA directory for the year 1887 - Pub. by Wm. H. Kirwin ... Lockport, N.Y., Journal book and job print., 1887 - 1 v. 22 cm. 7-38095. Directories

TONAWANDA. Historical Society of the Tonawandas. (Publications) Until bound and cataloged, will be found in the Periodical Reading Room. F129. T6 H5
— Recollections of the Erie Canal, by Richard G. Garrity. 1966. 36 p. 23 cm. (Publication no. 2)

TONAWANDA. History of the town of Tonawanda, Erie county, 1805 - 1930 (by) Frederick S. Parkhurst, local historian ... (Kenmore, N.Y., 1930) vii - xiv, 126 p. incl. illus., pl., ports. front., fold. map. 23½ cm. 32-32243. F129. T6 P 15

TONAWANDA. North Tonawanda and Tonawanda, located in Niagara and Erie counties, the "lumber city" ... Tonawanda, N.Y., Herald printing house, 1891. 96 p. 8°. 1-14997-M1. F129. T6 R6

TONAWANDA-Kenmore historical soc. Publication ... no. 1 v. F129. T6 T65

TONAWANDA. School houses and cemeteries, town of Tonawanda, 1932 (by) Frederick S. Parkhurst,

local historian. (Kenmore, N.Y., 1932) 24 p. 1 illus. 23 cm. (Publication no. 3-4. Tonawanda-Kenmore hist. soc.) 32-33144.
F129.T6 T65

TRENTON. Centennial address delivered at Trenton ... by John Seymour, with letters from Francis Adrian van der Kemp, written in 1792, and other documents relating to the first settlement of Trenton and central New York. Utica, N.Y., White & Floyd, printers, 1877. 149 p. 22 cm. 9-12001.
F129.T69 S 5

TRENTON FALLS. The golden era of Trenton Falls, by Charlotte A. Pitcher ... Utica, N.Y. (Fierstine printing house) 1915. 5, (9) - 103 p. front., plates. 21 cm. 15-15251.
F129.T7 P 68

TRENTON FALLS. A description of Trenton Falls, Oneida county. By John Sherman ... Utica, W. Williams, 1838. 23 p. 16°. 1-14998-M1.
F129.T7 S 5

— New York, W. H. Colyer, 1847. 23 p. 16½ cm. 1-14999.
F129.T7 S 6

TRENTON FALLS. (By John Sherman) (Oldenbarneveld (i.e. Trenton Falls) N.Y., 1822.
(6) p. 12°. 1-22590-M1.
F129.T7 S 63

TRENTON FALLS. Trenton Falls, yesterday & today. By Howard Thomas. (1st ed.) Prospect, N.Y., Prospect Books, 1951. 177 p. illus. 21 cm. 51-11632.
F129.T7 T5

TRENTON FALLS. Trenton Falls, picturesque and descriptive: ed. by N. Parker Willis; embracing the original essay of John Sherman, the first proprietor and resident. ... New York, G. P. Putnam, 1851. 90 p. front., illus., plates. 15½ x 11 cm. 1-15000.
F129.T7 W7

— New York, Pub. for the proprietor by N. Orr, 1868. 96 p. illus., 14 pl. (incl. front.) 17½ x 13½ cm.
17-10092.
F129.T7 W8
Toner Coll.

TROY. The Troy directory ... 1839/40. (Troy) Kellogg & Cook (1839? 1 v. 18 x 10 cm.
Directories

TROY. Kneelands' Troy directory, 1847/8 - vol. 1 - Troy, J. C. Kneeland, 1847 -
v. front. (fold. map) 19 cm. 16-4793.
Directories

TROY. The Troy directory, also Cohoes and Waterford, Watervliet and Green Island ... (vol. 1) - 1829 - 1831, 1832/3 - 1856/7, 1857 - 19 (Albany, N.Y.) Sampson & Murdock co., 1829 - 19 v. fold. maps. 17½ - 28 x 21 cm. annual. 1-13971 (rev. '33)
Directories

TROY. Troy and Albany County business directory ... (1852) - (v.1) - Troy, Merriam, Moore, 1852 v. 15 cm. 19-7553.
Directories

TROY street directory, and city guide, containing a list of public buildings ... 1869 Troy, N.Y., J. C. Wallace, 1869 - v. 14½ cm. CA 33-1171 Unrev.
F129.T8 A2

TROY pocket guide of Troy ... Troy, N.Y., Beck printing co., 19 v. 14½ cm. CA 35-61 Unrev.
F129.T8 B 4

TROY. Troy for fifty years: a lecture ... By David Buel, jun. ... Troy, N.Y., N. Tuttle, printer, 1841. 35 p. 21 cm. 1-22548.
F129.T8 B 9

TROY. Troy and Rensselaer County; a history, by Rutherford Hayner ... New York and Chicago, Lewis historical pub. co., 1925. 3 v. fronts., plates, ports., facsim., coat of arms. 27½ cm. Vol. III: Biographical. Bibliography: v.1, p. (vii) - ix. 25-7308.
F129.T8 H4

TROY. Second Presbyterian church of Troy; historical sketch prepared and read at the reopening of the auditorium ... by William H. Hollister, jr., clerk of the session; rev. and extended to April, 1916. (Troy, N.Y.) By direction of the session (1917) 69 p. incl. front. 4 port. 23½ cm. 24-6095.
F129.T8 H7

NEW YORK

TROY. Miniatures of Troy. (By Thomas Wallace Jones) (Cincinnati, O., 1904) 8 x 10 ½ cm.
F129. T8 J 7

TROY. Mt. Ida cemetery inscriptions, Troy, N.Y. ... Work of the Philip Schuyler chapter, D.A.R. (Troy?) 1923. 92 p. 23 ½ cm. 25-5888.
F129. T8 M9

TROY. Profiles out of the past of Troy, since 1789, by Samuel Rezneck. Troy, N.Y., 1970. 231 p. illus. 23 cm.
F129. T8 R4

TROY. A martyr of to-day. The life of Robert Toss, sacrificed to municipal misrule, a story of patriotism calling for municipal reforms. By Rev. James H. Ross. With an introd. by Rev. Josiah Strong ... Boston, J. H. Earle, 1894. 180 p. incl. plates. front., plates, ports. 19 cm. 1-14427.
F129. T8 R8

TROY. A live city in the Hudson Valley; eastern terminal great barge canal system, New York state; situated at the head of navigation on the Hudson River: Troy, N.Y. (Troy, Troy times art press, 191-?) 12 p. illus., 2 pl. 18 ½ x 26 cm. 19-3115.
F129. T8T765

TROY. New Troy; a joint report presented by the Municipal affairs and Civic arts committees of the Troy chamber of commerce to the citizens of Troy ... issued by the Chamber of commerce, Troy. Troy, N.Y. ... (1913) 120 p. incl. front., illus., ports. 17 ½ cm. 13-23913.
F129. T8 T77

TROY. Supplement to the Troy daily times ... Tuesday, June 25, 1901. (Troy, N.Y., 1901) 20 p. illus. (incl. ports., facsims.) 34 ½ cm. 4-33546.
F129. T8 T8

TROY. Records of the First Presbyterian church of Troy and ... of the First Presbyterian church of Lansingburgh in Rensselaer County. Transcribed by the New York genealogical and biographical soc. Ed. by Royden W. Vosburgh. New York city, 1915. 2 v. 36 x 28 cm. Autographed from typewritten copy. 15-6389.
F129. T8 T85

TROY. Records of the Second street Presbyterian church in the city of Troy, Rensselaer County. Transcribed by the N.Y. genealogical and biographical soc. Ed. by Royden W. Vosburgh. New York, 1915. 2, iii-vi, 90 numb. l. 36 x 28 cm. Autographed from type-written copy. 15-10271.
F129. T8 T87

TORY. Views of Troy and Cohoes. Portland, Me., L. H. Nelson co. (190-) (31) p. of illus. 20 x 25 cm. CA 28-999 Unrev.
F129. T8 V6

TROY. The city of Troy and its vicinity, by Arthur James Weise. Troy, E. Green, 1886. 3, 376 p. fold. front. (map) illus. 18 x 14 ½ cm. 1-15001.
F129. T8 W4

TROY. History of the city of Troy, from the expulsion of the Mohegan Indians to the present centennial year ... By A. J. Weise. ... Troy, N.Y., W. H. Young, 1876. 400 p. front., illus., plates, fold. maps, fold. plans, facsims. 23 ½ cm. 1-15002.
F129. T8 W6

TROY'S one hundred years. 1789 - 1889. By Arthur James Weise. Troy, N.Y., W. H. Young, 1891. vii, 453 p. incl. front., illus. fold. pl. 28 ½ cm. 1-15003.
F129. T8 W7

TROY. Reminiscences of Troy, from its settlement in 1790, to 1807, with remarks on its commerce, enterprise, improvements, etc. ... by the Hon. John Woodworth ... Albany, J. Munsell, 1853. 39 p. 23 cm. 1-15004.
F129. T8 W9

— 2d ed. with notes, explanatory, biographical, historical, and antiquarian. Albany, N.Y., J. Munsell, 1860. iv, 112 p. illus. 22 x 17 ½ cm. 1-15005.
F129. T8W91

TRUMANSBURG; incorporation centennial, 1872 - 1972, by Carolyn A. Martin. Trumansburg, N.Y., Trumansburg Centennial Assoc. (1972) 130 p. illus. 25 cm.
F129. T83 M3

TUPPER LAKE. Tupper Lake region. By Seneca Ray Stoddard. Troy, N.Y., Nims & Knight (1889) (1) l., 14 plates. 15 x 19 cm. 1-15006 rev.*
F129. T9 S 8

TUSTEN.   ... and they called it Tusten; by Arthur N. Meyers.   Narrowsburg, N.Y., 1967.
65 p.   23 cm.
F129.T94 M4

TUXEDO PARK.   The story of Tuxedo Park, by Edwin C. Kent.   Rhinebeck, N.Y., Priv. pub., 1937.
30 p.   24 cm.   37-5817.
F129.T96 K5

TUXEDO PARK.   The world with a fence around it; Tuxedo Park, the early days.   By George M. Rushmore.   (1st ed.) New York, Pageant Press (1957)   232 p.   illus.   21 cm.   57-9744.
F129.T96 R8

TUXEDO PARK.   Report to the Executive Committee of the Tuxedo Club, from the committee appointed to examine into the original historical names of the Tuxedo region ...   New York, 1888.
7 p.   fold. map.   17 cm.   55-49915.
F129.T96 T8

UNADILLA.   The pioneers of Unadilla village, 1784 - 1840, by Francis Whiting Halsey ... Reminiscences of village life and of Panama and California from 1840 - 1850, by Gaius Leonard Halsey ... Unadilla, N.Y. ... 1902.   xv, 323 p.   front., plates, ports.   fold. plan.   19½ cm.   2-18369.
F129. U5 H2

UNADILLA.   Unadilla in its first century (by Ralph Dewey Morse. n.p., 1964)   18 p.   illus.   22 cm.
F129. U5 M6

UNADILLA.   The village beautiful, being a compilation of local history of Unadilla in the last 50 years. Rotary Club. Unadilla, 1957.   255 p.   illus.   21 cm.   58-17280.
F129. U5 R6

UTICA.   The enemies of the Constitution discovered, or, An inquiry into the origin and tendency of popular violence.   Containing a complete and circumstantial account of the unlawful proceedings at the city of Utica ...   By Defensor (pseud. for William Thomas) New-York, Leavitt, Lord; Utica, G. Tracy, 1835.   xii, (9) - 183 p.   18 cm.   11-12651.
E449. T 459

UTICA city directory ... 1828 - 1890   (no. 1 - 61) Utica, N.Y., C. N. Gaffney, etc., 1828-90.
v.   fold. plans.   17 - 23½ cm.   1-13999.
Directories
1828-1829 in Rare Book Coll.

UTICA.   Williams' Utica city directory ... for the year (1891) - 95.   Also containing the names of residents of the villages of New Hartford, New York Mills, Whitesboro and Yorkville ... Utica, N.Y., J. E. Williams (1891) - 95.   5 v.   fold. plans.   23½ cm.   8-29251.
Directories

UTICA.   Boyd's business directory of Utica, Rome, Camden, Lowville, Washington Mills, Oriskany Falls, Clayville, Richfield Springs, Little Falls, Herkimer, Sherburne, Norwich and intermediate railroad villages.   Comp. by Andrew Boyd ... Utica, N.Y., Gilbert & Salisbury, booksellers, 1871-72.
(vii) - viii, 9-208 p.   23½ cm.   11-16715.
Directories

UTICA.   Batchelor's pictorial business directory of Utica, 1874-5 ... Comp. by Berk Batchelor. Utica, N.Y., Curtiss & Childs, (1874)   82 p.   illus. (photos.)   17½ x 23 cm.   8-29406.
Directories

UTICA.   ... The Utica observer 1916 classified directory ... of business concerns, institutions and professional people of Utica and vicinity ... Cleveland, O., P. Goering,   v.   23 cm.   17-5860.
Directories

UTICA.   ... Map, street directory and guide of Utica, comp. and pub. by the Utica directory pub. co., Utica, N.Y. (Utica, 1921)   48 p.   illus., fold. map.   19½ x 10 cm.   CA 24-161 Unrev.
F129. U8 A2

UTICA.   Arrow street guide of Utica ... (Utica, N.Y.) R. L. Polk, 1938 -   v.   fold. map.   17 cm.
38-34417.
F129. U8 A2

UTICA.   Picturesque Utica, in photo-gravure, from recent negatives.   The Albertype co. Utica, N.Y., W. A. Semple, 1898.   18 pl.   23 x 18½ cm.   Dec. 14, 98-4.
F129. U8 A3

NEW YORK 421

UTICA. The pioneers of Utica; being sketches of its inhabitants and its institutions, with the civil history of the place, from the earliest settlement to the year 1825, - the era of the opening of the Erie canal, by M. M. Bagg ... Utica, N.Y., Curtiss & Childs, 1877.   ii, (5) - 665 p. illus., pl., ports. 24½ cm.
1-15007 Rev.   F129. U8 B 1

UTICA. Republican political records ... (By Frederick W. Bean) Utica, N.Y., 1903.
F129.U8 B 3

UTICA. Outline history of Utica and vicinity, prepared by a committee of the New century club. Utica, N.Y., L. C. Childs, 1900.   iv p., 2 l., 201 p. plates. 23½ x 18 cm. Bibliography: p. (181) - 190.
0-2383 Rev.   F129. U8 B 8

UTICA. Utica, for a century and a half. By Thomas Wood Clarke. Utica, N.Y., Widtman Press, 1952.   332 p. illus. 25 cm. Includes bibliography. 53-3759.   F129. U8 C5

UTICA. Confession and execution of Horace B. Conklin, tried at Utica ... 1851. For arson in the first degree. New York, Printed for W. Conklin, 1851.   16 p. 21 cm. 7-21572.
F129. U8 C7

UTICA. Utica, the heart of the Empire state. By T. Harvey Ferris. (Boonville, N.Y., Printed by the Willard press, 1913)   (32) p. illus. 18½ cm.   F129.U8 F38

UTICA. A city reborn. Fusco Advertising Agency. (Utica, N.Y., 1960?)   53 p. 22 x 28 cm.
F129. U8 F8

UTICA. Address at the dedication of the Soldiers' and sailors' monument, Utica. By J. R. Hawley. Hartford, Conn., Press of the Case, Lockwood & Brainard co., 1891.   18 p. 24½ cm. 20-20158.
D129.U8 H39

UTICA. ... Guide book of Utica, and key to the city, with a general directory of New Hartford, New York Mills and Whitesboro. By H. C. Kilian. (Utica, N.Y.) 1887.   62, (18) p. illus. 23 cm.
8-29800.   F129. U8 K4

UTICA. The Jewish community of Utica, 1847 - 1948. By Solomon Joshua Kohn. New York, American Jewish Historical Soc., 1959.   221 p. illus. 24 cm. (American Jewish communal histories, no. 2) Includes bibliography. 59-7832.   F129. U8 K6

UTICA. Social studies program, New York state education dept., Utica and Oneida county. 1. Community life ... Compiled by C. Irene Martin ... (Utica, N.Y., Thomas J. Griffith) 1942.
iv, 90 p. illus., diagrs. 24½ cm. "For use in the Utica schools ... 7th grade..." Bibliography: p. iv. 42-23751.   F129.U8 M35

UTICA. A sketch of old Utica. (By Blandina Dudley Miller) (Utica, N.Y., L. C. Childs, 1895)
64 p. illus. 26½ x 21 cm. 1-15008.   F129. U8 M6

— (2d ed.) (Utica, N.Y., Fierstine printing house) 1913.   92 p. incl. front. (port.) illus. plates.
18½ cm. 13-1813.   F129. U8 M6

— (3d ed.) (Utica, N.Y., Fierstine printing house) 1909 (i.e. 1919)   91 p. incl. front. (port.) illus.
plates. 19 cm. 20-3319.   F129.U8 M62

UTICA. Dedication of the site of old Fort Schuyler, Utica ...   (From Transactions of the Oneida historical soc. ...
7-38331.   F129. U8 O5

UTICA. Semi-centennial of the city of Utica ... Pub. by the Oneida hist. soc. Utica, N.Y., Curtiss & Childs, printers, 1882.   196 p. front., ports. 23½ cm. The Half century club: p. (153) - 191.
10-19542.   F129. U8 O6

UTICA. Americans by choice (history of the Italians in Utica) by George Schiro ... (Utica, N.Y., Thomas J. Griffiths sons, 1940)   183 p. plates, port., geneal. tab. 19½ cm. "Sources of information": p. 171.
41-2193.   F129. U8 S 3

UTICA. Utica and its Savings bank, 1839 - 1939. Savings bank of Utica. (New York) 1939.
46 p. incl. illus. (1 col. incl. ports., map, facsims.)   col. plates.   23 cm.   39-31438.
F129.U8 S36

UTICA. Souvenir of Utica. Portland, Maine, L. H. Nelson co. (190?)   (32) p.   illus.   20½ x 25 cm.
F129. U8 S7

UTICA. Rules and regulations of the Utica cemetery association ... Utica, N.Y., 1849.
2, (3) - 35 p.   22 cm.
F129. U8 U7

UTICA. The tale of the treasure chest, being somewhat the story of old Fort Schuyler and its people (issued by the) First bank trust co. (Utica, Moser & Cotins, 1926)   (3) - 45 p.   illus.   23 cm.
27-12485.
F129.U8 U72

UTICA. Records of the First Presbyterian church of Utica in Oneida County. Transcribed by the New York genealogical and biographical soc.; ed. by Royden W. Vosburgh. New York city, 1920.
2, x, 196 numb. l. incl. facsims.   36 x 28 cm.   20-14630.
F129.U8 U75

UTICA. The Utica commercial blue-book. Utica, N.Y., Utica publicity co., 1920 -
v.   illus.   23 cm.   20-9736.
F129. U8 U8

UTICA. Views of Utica, N.Y. (Portland, Me., 1904)   20 x 25 cm.
F129. U8 V6

VALLEY STREAM. R. L. Polk & co.'s Valley Stream village directory incl. Hewlett, Woodmere, Cedarhurst, Lawrence and Inwood ... New York city, R. L. Polk, 19   v.   24 cm.   23-16054.
Directories

VERONA Town history, by Raymond P. Ernenwein. Verona, N.Y., Verona Town Board (1970)
95 p.   illus., group ports.   22 cm.
F129. V4 E7

VICTOR. Historical sketch of the First Presbyterian church of Victor, incl. an introductory sketch of Victor and its early history, etc., etc. By Rev. Clarence W. Backus ... (Rochester, N.Y., A. A. Gillies, print., 1888)   122 p.   22½ cm.   "... Sources": p. (2)   29-6053.
F129.V6 B14

VIRGIL. Festive gathering of the early settlers and present inhabitants of the town of Virgil, Cortland County. ... Embracing a historic sketch of the town, by Nathan Bouton. Cortland, N.Y., H. G. Crouch, printer, 1855.   47 p.   22 cm.   3-29114.
F129. V8 F4

VISSCHER'S FERRY. Records of the Reformed Dutch church of Amity, in the village of Visscher's Ferry, town of Clifton Park. Transcribed by the N.Y. genealogical and biographical soc. Ed. by Royden W. Vosburgh. New York city, 1919.   2, ii, 71 numb. l.   36 x 28½ cm.   (With Records of the Protestant Reformed Dutch church of Niskayuna ...   19-16897.
F129.N797N7

WAINSCOTT. The bringing of the mill (1942 - 1943); a documentary history from wartime in Wainscott. By George Wilson Pierson. New Haven, 1962.   50 p.   22 cm.
F129.W12 P5

WALTON. The founders and the founding of Walton; being an intimate historical sketch of the making of an American settlement in the critical period immediately preceding the adoption of the federal Constitution, by Arthur W. North ... (Walton, N.Y., Printed by Walton reporter co., 1924)
51 p.   front., pl., ports., map.   23 cm.   Bibliography: p. 51.   25-1475.
F129.W13 N7

WARRENSBURG. Report of the Warrensburgh war committee, 1861 - 65. Warrensburgh, N.Y., The News press, 1913.   45 p.   19 cm.   15-27904.
F129.W18W2

WARSAW. History of the town of Warsaw, from its first settlement to the present time; with numerous family sketches and biographical notes. By Andrew W. Young ... Buffalo, Press of Sage, sons & co., 1869.   xiv, 17-400 p.   front., plates, ports.   22½ cm.   T.p. and front. wanting, replaced by photostat copy.
1-15009.
F129. W2 Y7

WARWICK. Trail sketches from Honey Ranch. By George W. Hansen. (Ed. by Mildred Parker

NEW YORK

Seese. 1st ed. Goshen, N.Y., The Bookmill, 1963. 140 p. 23 cm. 63-17932.
F129.W24 H3

WARWICK. Historical society of the town of Warwick. Historical papers. no. 1 - Warwick, N.Y., 1914 - v. front., plates, ports. 23 cm. 14-11772.
F129.W24 H6

WARWICK. Under old rooftrees (by) Mrs. E. B. Hornby. Jersey City, N.J., 1908. 4, (11) - 271 p. 20 cm. 8-23872.
F129.W24 H8

WATERFORD. J. W. Williams' Waterford village and town of Waterford directory ... 1884. (Waterford, N.Y.) Auburn pub. co., printers (1844) 1 v. 23 cm. 11-24290.
Directories

WATERFORD. The history of Waterford. By Sydney Ernest Hammersley. Waterford, N.Y., 1957. 399 p. illus. 24 cm. Includes bibliography. 57-7758.
F129.W25 H3

WATERLOO. A history of the village of Waterloo, and thesaurus of related facts. By John E. Becker. Waterloo, Waterloo Library and Historical Soc., 1949. 576 p. illus., ports., maps. 24 cm. "Sources of information": p. 525-529. 49-49297*.
F129.W27 B4

WATERLOO. "Grip's" historical souvenir of Waterloo. (By Edgar Luderne Welch) (Syracuse? N.Y.) 1903. 104 p. illus. (incl. ports.) 26½ cm. (Historical souvenir series, no. 16) 4-9574.
F129.W27 W4

WATERTOWN. City directory of Watertown ... (New York) Watertown directory co., 19 v. 24 cm. 20-3910.
Directories

WATERTOWN. Kimball's Watertown (Jefferson county) city directory ... (1877 Watertown, N.Y. (etc.) Kimball directory pub. co., 1877 - 19 v. plans. 24 cm. 2-2059 Rev.
Directories

WATERTOWN. Kimball's Watertown City business directory and pocket memorandum combined ... Watertown, N.Y., M. M. Kimball, 1881. 8½ x 15 cm.
Directories

WATERTOWN. ... Anthony's standard business directory, guide and reference book of Watertown, and vicinity ... (Watertown) The Anthony pub. co., 1894. 120 p. 23½ cm. 8-31699.
Directories

WATERTOWN. The park picturesque, Watertown, N.Y. 1909.
F129. W3 P3

WATERTOWN. Picturesque Watertown. (Watertown, N.Y., 1905) 20½ x 25 cm.
F129. W3 P6

WATERTOWN. Watertown, N.Y. A history of its settlement and progress, with a description of its commercial advantages, as a manufacturing point ... (By Charles Rufus Skinner) Watertown, N.Y., Watertown manufacturers aid assoc., 1876. 2, (7) - 128 p. front., illus., plates, ports., maps (2 fold.) diagr. 23 cm. 1-15010.
F129. W3 S6

WATERTOWN. Views of Watertown and vicinity. Compiled by George D. Treadwell. ... (Watertown, N.Y., Hungerford-Holbrook co.) 1901. (30) p. of illus. fold. pl. 13½ x 17½ cm. 1-18719.
F129. W3 T8

WATERTOWN. Views of Watertown and its picturesque park. (Watertown, N.Y., 1905) 15½ x 23 cm.
F129. W3 V5

WATERTOWN. The city of Watertown; containing a brief description of the city and its envirions, with numerous illustrations, and a list of the officers and members of the Watertown Chamber of commerce. (Watertown) The Chamber of commerce, 1908. 31 p. illus. 23 cm. 8-18592.
F129. W3 W3

WATERVILLE. Social change in a central New York rural community. By Walfred Albin Anderson.

(Ithaca, New York State College of Agriculture) 1954.   56 p. illus., map. 23 cm. (Cornell Experiment Station bulletin 907)   55-62193.
F129.W35 A6

WATERVILLE.   Souvenir of Waterville.   Waterville, G. W. Irving and W. P. Doyle (1908)
5 - 32 p.   illus.   23½ cm.   Pub. for the Annual convention of the Oneida County firemen's assoc.   9-27668.
F129.W35 S7

WATERVILLE.   Waterville, New York, Centennial history, 1871 - 1971.   72 p. illus. 28 cm.
F129.W35 W3

WATERVLIET.   Inscriptions from the grave stones in the cemetery on Eighth street, Watervliet, adjoining the United States arsenal on the south west.   (By C. P. Evans)   Albany, New York State library, 1913.   3, 2 - 42 numb. l.   25 x 20 cm.   Autographed from type-written copy.   15-9307.
F129.W37 E9

WATERVLIET.   History of the city of Watervliet, 1630 to 1910, comp. by James T. Myers ... Troy, N.Y., Press of H. Stowell (1910?)   124 p.   front., illus., ports.   22½ cm.   13-3032.
F129.W37 M9

WATERVLIET.   Record of marriages performed, 1814 - 36, in the Reformed Protestant Dutch church of Gibbonsville, a place variously known as Washington, Port Schuyler, West Troy, and Watervliet. Albany, New York State library, 1915.   17 l.   10 numb. l.   25½ cm.   Autographed from type-written copy.   16-9884.
F129.W37 W37

WATKINS GLEN.   Illustrated and descriptive guide book of the Watkins glen, (located at Watkins - head of Seneca lake - Schuyler co., N.Y.,) and its romantic surroundings ... By M. Ells.   Syracuse, N.Y., Hitchcock & co., 1871.   65 (i.e. 66) p.   mounted photos.   21 cm.   1-15011.
F129. W4 E2

— 3d ed., rev. and cor. by J. J. Lytle.   Philadelphia, Culbertson & Bache, printers, 1872.
72 p.   mounted photos.   20 cm.   1-15012 Rev.
F129. W4 E4

— 4th ed., rev. and cor. by J. J. Lytle.   Philadelphia, Culbertson & Bache, printers, 1874.
64 p. incl. front., illus.   20 cm.   2-19332.
F129.W4 E45

— 6th ed., corr. and rev. by A. J. Michener.   Philadelphia, Culbertson & Bache, printers, 1879.
44 p. incl. front., illus.   21 cm.   1-15013 Rev.
F129. W4 E5

— 8th ed., cor. and rev. by A. J. Michener.   New York, Leve & Alden, 1884.   43 p. incl. front., illus.   8°.   1-15014-5-M1.
F129. W4 E6

— 9th ed., cor. and rev. by A. J. Michener.   Philadelphia, Press of American printing house (1886)
43 p. incl. front., illus.   8°.   1-15014-5-M1.
F129. W4 E7

WATKINS GLEN.   Glen mountain house.   Watkins Glen, N. Y.   A. J. Michener, prop'r. (Philadelphia, American printing house, 1886)   6 l. incl. illus. on recto.   obl. 48°.   1-22540-M1.
F129.W4 G 5

WATKINS GLEN.   The Glen Springs, Watkins Glen, New York ... (Buffalo and New York) 1903.
18½ cm.
F129. W4 G6

WATKINS GLEN.   ... The physiographic history of Watkins Glen.   By Ralph S. Tarr ...
(In American scenic and historic preservation soc. ... 1906. 9-22097 Rev.
F129.W4 T19

WATKINS GLEN.   Guide book of the Watkins glen, near the village of Watkins, head of Seneca lake, Schuyler co. and its romantic surroundings.   (Watkins) W. E. Robinson, 1901.   38 p. illus. 12°.
1-15212-M1 Aug. 15
F129.W4 T 2

WATKINS GLEN.   Views of Watkins glen ... (n. p., 18 -   9½ cm.
F129. W4 V6

WATKINS GLEN.   (Watkins glen.   New York, Wittemann bros., 1882)   11 phot.   48°.   1-15016-M1.
F129. W4 W4

NEW YORK

WATSON. Historical notes of the settlement on no. 4, Browns' tract, in Watson, Lewis county. With notices of the early settlers ... Utica, N.Y., Roberts, printer, 1864.   27 p. front. (mounted port.)   18½ cm.   1-15017.   F129. W5 S9

WAVERLY. Waverly, New York, and Sayre and Athens, Pennsylvania directory ... Elmira, N.Y., M. P. Goodhue, 1908.   1 v. fold. plans. 23 cm. 8-37651.   Directories

WAVERY. Picturesque views of Waverly and vicinity. Waverly, N.Y., 1904)   13 x 18½ cm.   F129. W54 P6

WAWARSING. The Indians: or, Narratives of massacres and depredations on the frontier, in Wawasink and its vicinity. During the American revolution ... By a descendants of the Huguenots (Abraham Garret Bevier) Rondout, N.Y. ... 1846.   xiv, (15)-79 p. 20 cm. 2-3374 Rev.   F129. W55 B5   Rare Book Coll.

WELLSVILLE. Wellsville directory ... 19   Binghamton, N.Y., The Calkin-Kelly directory co., 19   v. 24½ cm. CA 30-686 Unrev.   Directories

WELLSVILLE. Manning's Wellsville, Andover, Belmont and Scio directory ... Schenectady, N.Y., H. A. Manning co., 1940-   1 v. 23½ cm. 41-36269.   Directories

WELLSVILLE. A history of the Town of Wellsville. By Martha Elston Howe. Wellsville, N.Y., 1963.   224 p. 23 cm.   F129. W59 H6

WEST COPAKE. Baptismal record of Reformed Church of West Copake. (Transcribed and indexed by Arthur C. M. Kelly. Rhinebeck, N.Y., 1969)   iv, 133, 32, 24 p. 30 cm. 78-10936.   F129.W62W57

WEST COPAKE. Records of the Reformed church of West Copake (formerly Taghkanick) at West Copake, Columbia County. Transcribed by the New York genealogical and biographical soc.; ed. by Walter Kenneth Griffin ... New York, 1912.   2 p., iv, 184 numb. l. 36½ cm. Autographed from type-written copy. 13-18341.   F129. W62 W6   L H & G

WEST COXSACKIE. Records of the First Reformed church of Coxsackie in West Coxsackie, Greene County. Transcribed by the N.Y. genealogical and biographical soc. Ed. by Royden W. Vosburgh. New York city, 1919.   3 v. fronts. (v.1: facsim.) 36 x 28 cm. 19-12262.   F129. W63 R3

WEST GALWAY. Records of the First Presbyterian church of West Galway in the town of Perth, Fulton County, originally the First Presbyterian church in Galloway. Transcribed by the N.Y. genealogical and biographical soc. Ed. by Royden W. Vosburgh. New York city, 1916.   2 p., v, 148 numb. l. 36 x 28 cm. Autographed from type-written copy. 16-23645.   F129. W64 W6

WESTHAMPTON. Historical sketch of the incorporated village of Westhampton Beach, 1640-1951. By Beatrice G. Rogers. Islip, N.Y., Buys Bros. (1953)   151 p. illus. 24 cm. 54-15952.   F129. W65 R6

WEST HAMPTON. Letters from the sea-side, by George B. Warren, jr. Troy, N.Y., W. H. Young, 1876.   25 p. 23½ cm. 9-20151 Rev.   F129. W65 W2

WEST NEW HEMPSTEAD. Records of the Reformed Dutch church of Kakiat, Rockland Co., 1774-1864 ... Being, in most part, a copy of the translation of the records made by Rev. David Cole, with additions and corrections by Walter Kenneth Griffin. New York, 1909.   2 p., 118 numb. l. 28½ cm. 16-2289.   F129. W68 W6

WEST SENECA. Just for old times sake, by Frank J. Lankes. West Seneca, N.Y., West Seneca Historical Soc., 1968.   80 p. illus. 22 cm.   F129. W67 L3

WEST POINT. The West Point guide book. 29th annual ed. Accurate information - copiously illustrated. 155 pictures, ten in natural colors - text, 18,000 words ... By William H. Tripp. West Point, N. Y., W. H. Tripp, 1928.   56 p. illus. (part col.) 20½ x 24 cm. 28-17153.   F129. W7
U410. Pl T 7

WEST POINT. Three rivers, the James, the Potomac, the Hudson; a retrospect of peace and war, by Joseph Pearson Farley ... New York and Washington, The Neale pub. co., 1910.   277 p. col. front., 9 col. pl. 21 cm. 10-2665.   F227. F 23

WEST POINT. West Point battle monument: history of the project to the dedication of the site ... Oration of Maj.-Gen. McClellan. New York, Sheldon & co., 1864.   35 p., (2) p. 19 cm. 20-15300.   F129. W7 B3

WEST POINT. Guide to West Point, and the U.S. Military academy ... (By Edward Carlisle Boynton) New York, D. Van Nostrand, 1867.   105 p. front., 2 fold. maps, fold. plan. 15 cm. 1-15020* Cancel.   F129. W7 B65

WEST POINT. History of West Point, and its military importance during the American revolution: and the origin and progress of the U.S. military academy. By Captain Edward C. Boynton ... New York, D. Van Nostrand; (etc.) 1863.   xviii, (9)-408 p. fold. front., illus., plates (1 col.) maps, fold. plans, facsim. 24 cm. 1-15021.   F129. W7 B7
Rare Book Coll.

— Freeport, N.Y., Books for Libraries Press (1970)   xviii, 408 p. illus. 23 cm. 71-126233.   F129. W7 B7 1970

— 2d ed. New York, D. Van Nostrand, 1871.   xviii, (7)-416 p. illus., 2 pl., 7 maps (incl. front.) 23½ cm. "List of authorities": p. (vii)-viii. 4-18969.   F129. W7 B72

WEST POINT. West Point in literature, by General William H. Carter ... Baltimore, Lord Baltimore press, 1909.   12 p. 23 cm. Reprinted from Journal of the Military service institution. 9-28859.   F129. W7 C3

WEST POINT. A guide book to West Point and vicinity. New York, J. H. Colton, 1844. vi, 7-112 p. front. (fold. map) 16 cm. 1-15019 Rev.   F129. W7 G8

WEST POINT. The river and the rock; the history of Fortress West Point, 1775-1783, by Dave Richard Palmer. New York, Greenwood Pub. Corp. (1969)   xii, 395 p. 32 cm. (The West Point military library) 77-79061.   F129. W7 P17

WEST POINT. A sketch of the history and topography of West Point and the U.S. Military academy ... By Roswell Park. Philadelphia, H. Perkins, 1840.   140 p. 16 cm. 1-15022.   F129. W7 P2

WEST SANDLAKE. Inscriptions from the second cemetery of Zion's Lutheran church, West Sandlake, Rensselaer County. (By William Solyman Coons) (n. p., 1920?)   2 p., 2-39 numb. l. 31 cm. Typewritten copy. 22-17156 Rev.   F129.W702C6

WEST SAND LAKE. Records of the Zion evangelical Lutheran church in Rensselaerwyck and Greenbush. Now the First evangelical Luthern church, in West Sandlake, Rensselaer County. Transcribed by the N.Y. genealogical and biographical soc. Ed. by Royden W. Vosburgh. New York, 1913. 2 p., xxx, 331 numb. l. 35½ x 28 cm. Autographed from type-written copy. 1785 to 1868. 14-12712.   F129.W702W5
L H & G

WESTCHESTER. The borough town of Westchester. An address ... before the Westchester County historical soc. ... by Morris Fordham. (White Plains, N.Y., The Eastern state journal, 1896?) 22 p. 22½ cm. 6-4470.   F129. W706M8

WESTFIELD. Mrs. Clara Utley Drake and Westfield as she knew it. (Washington, D.C., 1938) facsim. 19 p. 27½ cm. Photostat made by the Library of Congress, 1938. 41M3119T.   F129.W707L4 1938a

NEW YORK 427

WESTMORELAND. Records of the First Congregational church of Westmoreland, Oneida County, New York ... (n.p., 1927?) 33 numb. 1. 28 cm. Autographed from type-written copy. Text runs parallel with back of cover. 28-537. F129.W708W7

WESTPORT. Bessboro: a history of Westport, Essex Co., by Caroline Halstead Royce. (n.p., 1902) 7 p., vi-xviii, 611, (4) p. incl. maps. 20½ cm. 7-41860. F129.W71 R8

WESTPORT. The Westport inn ... (n.p., 19 -) 20½ cm. F129.W71 W4

WHEATLAND. History of the town of Wheatland: Scottsville, Mumford, Garbutt, Belcoda, Beulah, Wheatland Center. By Carl Frederick Schmidt. Rochester, N.Y., 1953. 296 p. illus. 23 cm. Includes bibliography. 54-20773. F129.W716S4

WHEATLAND, Monroe county. A brief sketch of its history, by George E. Slocum. Scottsville, N.Y., Printed by I. Van Hooser, 1908. 138 p. 2 port. (incl. front.) 22½ cm. 8-29099.
F129.W716S6

WHITE PLAINS. ... Richmond's directory of White Plains and towns along the Harlem railroad between Bronxville and Brewster (Westchester County, N.Y.) Yonkers, N.Y., W. L. Richmond, 1903. v. fold. maps. 24 cm. 3-2159 Rev. 2. Directories

WHITE PLAINS. ... Richmond's directory of White Plains, Hartsdale and Scarsdale (Westchester County, N.Y.) Yonkers, N.Y., W. L. Richmond, 1905. v. fold. maps. 24 cm. 14-22347.
Directories

WHITE PLAINS. Dolph-Stewart official street directory and information guide of White Plains, Scarsdale, Hartsdale, Elmsford (and) Ardsley ... comp. and pub. by Dolph & Stewart. New York city, 1935 - v. fold. maps 16 cm. CA 35-808 Unrev. F129.W72 A2

WHITE PLAINS. Historical sketch of the Washington headquarters, prepared under the auspices of the White Plains chapter, D.A.R., by Elizabeth G. H. Coles ... (White Plains, N.Y., 1923) 2, 9-58 p. illus. (incl. map) pl. 22 cm. Bibliography: p. 58. 23-17790. F129.W72 C6

WHITE PLAINS. Historic White Plains (by) John Rösch. (White Plains, N.Y., Printed by Balletto-Sweetman, inc., 1939) xvi, 395 p. incl. front., illus., plates, ports. 23½ cm. 39-14445. F129.W72R67

WHITE PLAINS. Picturesque White Plains. By John Rösch. (1902) 1 v. fol. F129.W72 R7

— (White Plains, N.Y., J. Rösch, 1906) 47 p. illus. 30½ x 26 cm. 6-27343. F129.W72R72

WHITE PLAINS. ... Anne Hutchinson and other papers; with illustrations and maps. White Plains, N.Y., Pub. for Westchester county by the Westchester county hist. soc., 1929. xiv p., 3 l., 3-114 p. double front., plates, maps. 23½ cm. (Pubs. of the Westchester county historical soc., vol. vii) 30-944 rev. F129.W72 W5

WHITEHALL. A sketch of the history of Whitehall, civil and religious. A discourse delivered on the 27th of June, 1847. By Rev. Lewis Kellogg ... Whitehall, S. B. Fairman, printer, 1847. 16 p. 22½ cm. 1-15023 Rev. F129.W73 K2

WHITEHALL. Philip Skene of Skenesborough. ... Granville, N.Y., Grastorf Press, 1959. 84 p. 24 cm. F129.W73 M6

WHITEHALL, Washington County; excerpt of the commercial history of the state of New York ... New York city (1912) 34½ cm. F129.W73 W7

WHITESBORO. Here's Whitesboro; an informal history. By D. Gordon Rohman. New York, Stratford House, 1949. 110 p. illus., map. 21 cm. 49-5347*. F129.W737R6

WHITESBORO. Whitesboro's golden age. By Daniel E. Wager. (From Oneida hist. soc. Transactions ... 1885. 7-38299. F129.W737W13

WHITESBORO. A few stray leaves in the history of Whitesboro. By M. Whitcher. (Clinton? N.Y.) Clinton Courier, 1957. 27 p. 26 cm. F129.W737W68

WHITESBORO. Records of the First Presbyterian church of Whitesboro in the town of Whitestown, Oneida County. Transcribed by the New York genealogical and biographical soc; ed. by Royden W. Vosburgh. New York city, 1920. 2,p. 137 numb. 1. 36 x 28½ cm. Autographed from type-written copy. 20-7047.
F129.W737W7

WHITESTONE. The scene from Powell's Hill, from Francis Lewis to Capt. Merritt; a story of Whitestone. By Harry J. Lucas. (n.p.) 1962. 44 p. 24 cm.
F129.W739L8

WHITESTOWN. "The Whitestown country." 1784 - 1884. Centennial celebration of the settlement of Whitestown ... From Oneida historical soc. Transactions ... 1885. 7-38298. F129.W74 O5

WHITESTOWN. Historical discourse ... By Charles Tracy. Utica, N.Y., E. H. Roberts, printers, 1885. 16 p. 23 cm. 3-31540. F129.W74 T7

WILLIAMSBURG. Reynolds' Williamsburgh directory ... Williamsburgh, L. Darbee, printers.
v. double front. (plan) illus. 19 cm. 11-24286. Directories

WILLIAMSBURG. A history of the city of Williamsburgh containing a succinct account of its early settlement, rapid growth and prosperous condition; with many other important and interesting facts connected with the same. By Samuel Reynolds ... Williamsburgh, J. C. Gandar, 1852. viii, 9-137, iv p. 19 cm. 1-15024 Rev. F129.W75 R4

WILLIAMSON. A directory and brief history of the town of Williamson (with map) as compiled by members of Williamson post, no. 394, the American legion. Williamson, N.Y., Cooper & Cooper, printers (1928) 4, (11) - 100 p. fold. map. 22½ x 17 cm. 28-15333. F129.W76 A5

WILLSBORO. Pioneer history of the Champlain Valley; being an account of the settlement of the town of Willsborough by William Gilliland, tog. with his journal and other papers, and a memoir, and historical and illustrative notes, by Winslow C. Watson. Albany, N.Y., J. Munsell, 1863.
viii, (9) - 231 p. 22½ cm. (Munsell's local American history. 1) 1-15025. F129.W77 W3

WINDHAM. Old times in Windham, by Henry Hedges Prout. Transcribed by Olive N. Woodworth. Cornwallville, N.Y., Hope Farm Press, 1970. x, 178 p. illus. 24 cm.
F129. W8 P7

WOLCOTT. ... "Grip's: historical souvenir of Wolcott. (By Edgar Luderne Welch) (Lyons, N.Y., Republican print) 1905. 2, 3-84 p. incl. front., illus. 26 cm. (Hist. souvenir series, no. 20) 5-26899. F129.W84 W4

WOODSTOCK. It happened in Woodstock. (Woodstock, N.Y.) Stonecrop, (1972) xviii, 165 p. illus. 22 cm. Based on Woodstock: history and hearsay, by A. M. Smith. 77-172442 MARC. F129.W85 I 8

WOODSTOCK. The vanishing village. By Will Rose. New York, Citadel Press (1963) 350 p. 22 cm. 63-11759 F129.W85 R6

WOODSTOCK. Woodstock; history and hearsay. By Anita M. Smith. (Saugerties, N.Y.) Catskill Mountains Pub. Corp. (1959) 209 p. illus. 29 cm. 59-27331. F129.W85 S5

WURTEMBURG. St. Paul's Lutheran Church. Baptismal record, 1760 - 1899. (Transcribed and indexed by Arthur C. M. Kelly. Rhinebeck, N.Y., 1969.) iv, 88, 14, 10 p. 29 cm.
F129. W9 W 8

WYNANTSKILL. Records of the Reformed Protestant Dutch church of Wynantskill, at Wynantskill, in the town of North Greenbush, Rensselaer County. Transcribed by the New York genealogical and biographical soc. Ed. by Royden W. Vosburgh. New York, 1914. 2, xxxii. 259 p. 25½ cm. Autographed from type-written copy. 14-12721. F129.W98 W9

NEW YORK 429

YAPHANK. Yaphank as it is, and was, and will be. Containing biographical sketches of all its prominent men, the characteristic proclivities of its "funny" people, etc. ... By L. Beecher Homan ... (New York, J. Polhemus, printer, 1875) xviii, (21) - 220 p. incl. front., ports. pl. 23 cm. 5-34807.
F129. Y2 H7

YONKERS. Boyd's Yonkers city directory. 1887/88. New York and Yonkers, W. A. Boyd.
1 v. 23½ cm. 12-7265. Directories

YONKERS. Polk's Yonkers city directory ... 18   New York, R. L. Polk, 18   - 19
v. fold. maps. 24 - 27 cm. 1-22020 Rev. Directories

YONKERS. Richmond's ... annual directory of Yonkers (Westchester County) 1912 - Yonkers, N.Y., W. L. Richmond, 1912   1 v. fold. map. 24 cm. 12-26031.   Directories

YONKERS. Thompson & Fowler's ... directory of the city of Yonkers ... 1885/6 -   v. 1 - Newburgh, N.Y., Thompson & Fowler, 1885 -   v. fold. map. 23½ cm. 31-4346.   Directories

YONKERS. Polk's Yonkers directory of householders, occupants of office buildings and other business places, including a complete street and avenue guide ... New York, N.Y., R. L. Polk, 19
v. 27 cm. 37-33491. F129. Y5 A2

YONKERS. The history of Yonkers from the earliest times to the present ... finely illustrated with views ... and with portraits of many of its citizens. By the Rev. Charles Elmer Allison ... Issued under the auspices of the Yonkers board of trade. New York, W. B. Ketchum (1896)   4, 454 p. front., illus. (incl. ports.) 33 x 24 cm. 1-15026.
F129. Y5 A4

YONKERS. Park Hill. Yonkers on the Hudson. New York's most delightful suburb ... American investment union. (New York) 1892.   46 p. incl. pl. maps, tab. obl. 12°. 1-15027-M1.
F129. Y5 A5

YONKERS. Indian wars and the uprising of 1655 - Yonkers depopulated. A paper read before the Yonkers historical and library assoc. by Hon. T. Astley Atkins ... Yonkers, The Society, 1892.
14 p. 23½ cm. 2-14108. F129. Y5 A7

YONKERS. Yonkers in the rebellion of 1861 - 1865. Incl. a history of the erection of the monument to honor the men of Yonkers who fought to save the Union. By Thomas Astley Atkins ... (Yonkers) The Yonkers Soldiers' and sailors' monument association, 1892.   262 p. incl. plates, port. front. 25 cm.
1-16114 Rev. F129. Y5 A8

YONKERS. Yonkers through three centuries. (Central national bank of Yonkers) (Yonkers, N.Y., 1946)   16 (2) p. illus. (incl. ports., plans) 28 x 21½ cm. 47-18647.   F129. Y5 C4

YONKERS. Philipse manor hall at Yonkers; the site, the building and its occupants, by Edward Hagaman Hall. New York, N.Y., The American scenic and historic preservation soc., 1912.
255 p. xiv pl. (2 fold.; incl. ports., plan) 19 cm. Enlarged from an article pub. as an appendix to the 13th annual report of the American scenic and historic preservation soc., 1908. 12-11737. F129. Y5 H17

YONKERS. Richmond's guide to the city of Yonkers ... Yonkers, N.Y., W. L. Richmond, 1919.
32 p. fold. map. 16 cm. 19-10818. F129. Y5 R49

YONKERS. Views of Yonkers. (Portland, Me., 1904)   20½ x 25 cm.   F129. Y5 V5

YONKERS. Pillars of Yonkers. By Frank Ledyard Walton. New York, Stratford House, 1951.
xiv, 347 p. illus., map. 22 cm. (American heritage series) 51-2962. F129. Y5 W3

YONKERS. Yonkers illustrated; issued by the Dept. of publicity of the Yonkers Board of trade ... (Yonkers, 1903?)   3, 192 p. illus., plates. 29 cm. CA 26-407 Unrev.   F129. Y5 Y45

YONKERS. ... Yonkers historical and library assoc. bulletin. v. 1, no. 1 (-2); 1895 (-96) (New York, W. B. Ketcham, printer, 1895-96)   2 no. 25½ cm. 9-4684   F129. Y5 Y5

1163

YORK. History of the town of York, Livingston county (by) Mary R. Root. Caledonia, N.Y., Big Springs historical soc., 1940. vii, (9) - 205 p. incl. front., illus. plates. 23 ½ cm. 42-41686.
F129.Y56 R6

YORKTOWN. Cemetery inscriptions from the towns of Yorktown, Yorktown Heights and Amawalk, Westchester County. (n.p., 1922?) 2 p., 91 numb. l. 31 cm. Type-written copy. 22-22251.
F129. Y6 C4

YORKTOWN. The journal of the Reverend Silas Constant, pastor of the Presbyterian church at Yorktown: with some of the records of the church and a list of his marriages, 1784 - 1825, tog. with notes on the Nelson, Van Cortlandt, Warren, and some other families ... by Emily Warren Roebling; ed. by Josiah Granville Leach. Philadelphia, Printed for private circulation by J. B. Lippincott co., 1903. xv, 561 p. front., illus., pl., port., maps, facsim., geneal. tab. 25 cm. 3-4213.
F129. Y6 C7

YORKTOWN. Vital records of Yorktown (in Cortland manor), Westchester Co., kept by Louis D. Pomeroy, town clerk. (n.p., 1922?) 4 numb. l. 27 cm. "Not complete" 22-22253.
F129. Y6 Y6

YOUNGSTOWN. Record of the Presbyterian cemetery, Youngstown. Collected by Emily Halson Rowland ... Greenwich, Ct., 1921. 23, 9 numb. l. 28 x 21 ½ cm. Type-written copy. 22-4172.
F129. Y8 R8

ELEMENTS IN THE POPULATION.

NEW YORK State Commission for Human Rights. Public equality; an explanation of your rights of access to places of public accommodation, resort or amuseument, under the New York State law against discrimination. (New York, 1954?) (8) p. 11 x 18 cm. A 54-9490.
F130. A1 A5

(ISSERMAN, A. J.) Everybody's business, a summary of New York state anti-discrimination laws and how to use them. (New York, National federation for constitutional liberties, 1946) 64 p. illus. 15 x 12 cm. 46-5764.
F130. A1 I 8

BELGIANS. ... La part des Belges dans la fondation de l'état de New-York, par le baron de Borchgrave ... Buxelles, Hayez, 1913. 48 p. illus. 24 ½ cm. Publications de la Société belge d'études coloniales. Bulletin no. 12. 15-7714.
F130. B4 B 7

COLUMBIANS. Proceedings of the reception given in honr of His Excellency Dr. Enrique Olaya Herrera, president-elect of Columbia ... in co-operation with the Committee of the Colombian colony, New York, Roerich museum (1930) 23 p. front. 23 cm. 34-40402 Rev.
F130. C
E183.8.C7R6

CATHOLICS. Letters of the Reverend Adelbert Inama; translated from the German ... (Evansville, Wis., The Antes press, 1928?) 127 p. 26 cm. 29-27252.
F130. C3
BX4705.I5A3

DANES. De første danske i New York. By Carlo Christensen. Kjøbenhavn, Nyt nordisk forlag, 1953. 249 p. plates, maps. 25 cm. Bibliography: p. 228 - (236) A 54-1806.
F130. D3 C5

GERMANS. ... Der Deutsch-Amerikaner im spansich-amerikanischen kriege. (In German American annals. 1904. v.6) 11-14848.
F130. G
E184. G3 G3

GERMANS. The first Germans in North America and the German element of New-Netherland, by Otto Lohr. New York (etc.) G. E. Stechert, 1912. 15 p. 22 ½ cm. 13-1110.
F130. G4
E184.G3 L84

GERMANS. ... Über's meer! Über's meer! By Edmund Sabott. Berlin, Buchmeister-verlag g m b h. (1936) 316 p. incl. map. 19 ½ cm. Bibliography: p. 315-316. 37-7479.
F130. G4
PT2637.S35U4 1936

NEW YORK

GERMANS. Charter und statuten der Deutschen gesellschaft der stadt New-York ... New-York, Druck von G. B. Teuber, 1869. 12 p. 22 cm. Charter in English; statutes in German. 10-3714. F130.G4 D34

GERMANS. Charter and by-laws of the German society of the city of New-York. With a list of the members. New-York: Printed for E. Sargent by D. & G. Bruce, 1808. iv, (5)-24 p. 19½ cm.
1-3963 Rev. F130.G4 D35

GERMANS. Charter und statuten der Deutschen gesellschaft der stadt New York. New York, Druck von J. Oehler, 1900. 16 p. 18½ cm. Charter in English; statutes in German. 5-42442. F130.G4 D36

GERMANS. Freibrief und nebengesetze der Deutschen gesellschaft der stadt New-York. New York, Gedruckt bei G. B. Teubner, 1852. 31 p. 22 cm. 10-1516. F130.G4 D37

GERMANS. Mitglieder-verzeichniss der Deutschen gesellschaft der stadt New-York, für 1863. New-York, Druck von G. B. Teubner, 1863. 24 p. 22½ cm. Interleaved. 10-3715. F130.G4 D375

GERMANS. Verzeichniss der mitglieder der Deutschen gesellschaft in New-York. New York, 1846-1849. 2 v. 22 cm. CA 9-6293 Unrev. F130.G4 D38

GERMANS. Die Deutsche gesellschaft der stadt New York. Jahresberieht fur 1856, 1859, 1865, 1866-71. 1872-1900, 1901-3, 1904-6, 1907, 1908, 1910. Vols. 83-88, 89-117, 118-120, 121-123, 124, 125 - 14 v. 23 cm. F130.G 4 D4

GERMANS. Kassen-bericht und mitglieder-verzeichniss der Deutschen gesellschaft der stadt New-York. New York, 1857. 1 v. 21½ cm. CA 9-6292 Unrev. F130.G4 D42

GERMANS. Deutsche gesellschaft der stadt New York. Annual report. 100th - 101st. 1883-84. New York, 1884-1885. 22½ cm. 2 v. F130.G4 D45

GERMANS. Bericht über das festessen zur feier des 118-jährigen bestchens der Deutschen gesellschaft der stadt New York ... (New York, Press of Lauter & Lauterjung, 1902) 46, (8) p. incl. facsim. 23 cm. 4-11132. F130.G4 D48

GERMANS. Banquet of the German Republican central committee of the city and county of New York ... New York, H. A. Rost, printer, 1876. 15 p. 23 cm. 12-8204. F130. G4 G3

GERMANS. Geschichte der Deutschen im staate New York bis zum anfange des neunzehnten jahrhunderts. Von Friedrich Kapp. Mit einer karte. New York, E. Steiger, 1867. vii, 410 p. fold. map.
The greater part of this work was pub. at N.Y., 1884, with title "Die Deutschen im staate New York wahrend des achtzehnten jahrhunderts", as v. 1 of "Geschichtsblatter, bilder und mittheilungen aus dem leben der Deutsche in America." L.C. copy replaced by microfilm. 22-1115.
F130.G4 K19
Microfilm 15057 F

GERMANS. Geschichte der deutschen einwanderung in Amerika. Von Friedrich Kapp. Erster band. New York, E. Steidger, 1867. vii, 410 p. fold. map. 23 cm. No more pub. L.C. copy replaced by microfilm.
1-16526 Rev. F130.G4 K19
Microfilm 15057 F

GERMANS. Die Deutschen im staate New York wahrend des achtzehnten jahrhunderts, von Friedrich Kapp. New York, E. Steiger, 1884. 2, iv p., 2 l., 229 p. Contains the greater part of the material in F130.G4K19.
1-15028. F130. G4 K2

GERMANS. Geschichte der deutschen einwanderung in Amerika. Von Friedrich Kapp. 1. bd. 3. aufl. New York, E. Steiger, 1869. 2, xxviii p., 416 p. 18½ cm. No more pub. 22-12456. F130.G4 K22

GERMANS. See also F127.H5 B4

HUGUENOTS. The Huguenot element among the Dutch. By Ashbel G. Vermilye ... (Schenectady, N.Y., 1877?) 23 p. 23½ cm. Reprinted from "Reformed church in America ... 1-23435. F130. H8 V5

HUGUENOTS. See also F129.N6 S4; F122.D63 vol. 3

IRISH. My Irish colleagues of New York; reminiscences and experiences of a journalist, 1861 to 1901 ... by Thomas J. Cummins. In memory of the dead. In compliment of the living. In argument for the right. In exposure of the wrong. Souvenir copy. (New York) 1901. 19 p. front. (port.) 23½ cm. 6-12282.
F130. I 6 C9

IRISH. Irish colonists in New York; a lecture delivered before the New York state historical association at Lake George ... by Michael J. O'Brien. (New York) The Shamrock literary soc. of New York (1906) 20 p. incl. ports. 22 cm. 7-14892 Rev.
F130.I 6 O12

JEWS. Ein besuch beim judentum in New-York und umgebung; drei vortrage von dr. Joseph S. Bloch ... nebst einem anhang. Wien, Verlag der "Oesterreichischen wochenschrift", 1912. 3, (5) - 96 p. 16½ cm. 26-12061.
F130. J 5 B 6

JEWS. Wills of early Jewish settlers in New York. Contributed by Lee M. Friedman. (Baltimore, 1915) p. 147-161. 25 cm. Reprinted from Publications of the American Jewish historical soc. no. 23, 1915. 20-22894.
F130. J 5 F8

JEWS. The Jews of New York in the arts, sciences and professions. By Leon Huhner. New York, 1905. 16 cm.
F130. J 5 H7

JEWS. Naturalization of Jews in New York under the act of 1740. By Leon Hühner ... (New York, 1905) 5 p. 25 cm. Reprinted from Publications of the American Jewish historical soc. no. 13. 9-30072.
F130. J 5 H8

MORAVIANS. A memorial of the dedication of monuments erected by the Moravian historical soc., to mark the sites of ancient missionary stations in New York and Connecticut. New York, C. B. Richardson; Philadelphia, J. B. Lippincott, 1860. viii, (5) - 184 p. illus. (incl. plan, music) 4 pl. 24 cm.
F130. M
E99. M9 M8

NEW ENGLANDERS. The expansion of New England, the spread of New England settlement and institutions to the Mississippi River, 1620 - 1865, by Lois Kimball Mathews ... Boston and New York, Houghton Mifflin, 1909. xiv, 303 p. front., maps. 23 cm. Bibliographical notes at end of most chaps. 9-29148.
F5. M 42
F4. R 81

PALATINES. Auswanderung und koloniegründungen der Pfalzer im 18, jahrhundert ... Von dr. phil. nat. Daniel Häberle ... Kaiserslautern, H. Kayser, 1909. xix, 263 p. front., illus. (incl. ports., facsim.) maps (1 fold.) 23½ cm. "Allgemeine literatur." p. (xiv) 9-24190.
F130. P
E184. G3 H2

PALATINES. ... Papers relating to the manor of Livingston, including the first settlement of Schoharie. 1680 - 1795. (By Edmund Bailey O'Callaghan) (In the documentary history of the state of New-York. v.3) 11-10991.
F130. P
F122. D 63 vol. 3

PALATINES. The Palatine, or German immigration to New York and Pennsylvania. A paper read before the Wyoming historical and geological soc. by Rev. Sanford H. Cobb ... Wilkes Barré, Pa., Printed for the Society, 1897. 30 p. 24 cm. 4-384.
F130. P2 C 58

PALATINES. The story of the Palatines. An episode in colonial history, by Sanford H. Cobb. New York & London, G. P. Putnam's sons, 1897. ix, 319 p. maps. 20½ cm. 1-16285.
F130. P2 C 6

PALATINES. The early eighteenth century Palatine emigration; a British government redemptioner project to manufacture naval stores ... (by) Walter Allen Knittle. Philadelphia, 1936. xix, 320 p. front., illus (incl. ports., maps, facsims.) 23 cm. Thesis (PH.D.) University of Pennsylvania, 1931. Bibliography: p. (229) - 241. 37-16677.
F130. P2 K 59

— ... with a foreword by Dixon Ryan Fox. Philadelphia, Dorrance (1937) xix, 320 p. front. (port.) illus. 23½ cm. Bibliography: p. (229) - 241; bibliographical foot-notes. 37-522.
F130. P2 K 6

NEW YORK

— Baltimore, Genealogical Pub. Co., 1965.   xix, 320 p.   23 cm.   65-21924.   F130. P2 K 6 1965

— Baltimore, Genealogical Pub. Co., 1970.   xix, 320 p. illus. 23 cm.   F130. P2 K 6 1970

PALATINES. ... Papers relating to the palatines ...   (From The documentary history of the state of New York, v. 3)   F130. P 2 P3

PALATINES. True and authentic register of persons still living ... who in the year 1709 ... journeyed from Germany to America ... by Ulrich Simmendinger ... Reutlingen, printed by John G. Fuesing ... St. Johnsville, N.Y., Reprinted by the Enterprise and news, 1934.   x, 11-20 p. 23 cm. 35-14005.   F130. P2 S 5

— Baltimore, Genealogical Pub. Co., 1962.   F130. P2 S513 1968   Rare Book Coll.

PALATINES. Palatines along the Mohawk and their church in the wilderness. By Ada Laura Fonda Snell. Drawings by Sybil Clark Fonda. (South Hadley, Mass., 1948)   57 p. illus. 24 cm. 48-3413*.   F130. P2 S 6

POLES. ... Poles in New York in the 17th and 18th centuries, by Meicislaus Haiman. Chicago, Ill., Polish R. C. union of America, 1938.   64 p. fold. plan. 22½ cm.   (Annals of the Polish Rom. Cath. union archives and museum. vol. III)   Bibliography: p. 59-64. 38-19810.   F130. P6 H 3

— Photo-offset. San Francisco, R. and E. Research Associates, 1970.   63 (13) p.   F130. P6 H 3 1970

PUERTO RICANS. Puerto Ricans in New York States (Puertorriqueños en el Estado de Nueva York) 1960 - 1969. New York (1969)   xi, 67 l. 29 cm. Bibliography: leaf 67. 76-629257 MARC.   F130. P85 A 5

SCANDINAVIANS. Scandinavian immigrants in New York, 1630 - 1674 ... By John Oluf Evjen. Baltimore, Genealogical Pub. Co., 1972.   xxiv, 438 p. illus. 22 cm. Reprint of the 1916 ed. 76-39383 MARC.   F130. S18 E 9 1972

— Minneapolis, Minn., K. C. Holter pub. co., 1916.   xxiv, 438 p. front. (map) illus., plates (part double) ports., facsim. 24 cm. 16-6157.   F130. S2 E 9

SCOTS. Biographical register of Saint Andrew's society of the state of New York ... by William M. MacBean. New York, Printed for the society, 1922-25.   2 v. fronts. (ports.) facsims. 27 cm. 22-20893 Rev.   F130. S4 M2

SCOTS. Roster of Saint Andrew's society of the state of New York, with biographical data ... comp. by William M. MacBean ... pt. I -   New York (D. Taylor & co.) 1911 -   v. 24½ cm. 12-5449.   F130. S4 S 2

— Another ed,   1 v.   F130. S4 S 21

SCOTS. Register of Saint Andrew's soc. of the state of New York ... 2d - 3d series. comp. by Wm. M. MacBean ... (New York) Printed for the soc., 1922-23.   4 v. 23½ cm. 23-2277.   F130. S4 S 24

WALLOONS. The Belgians, first settlers in New York and in the middle states ... by Henry G. Bayer ... New York, The Devin-Adair co., 1925.   xviii, 373 p. plates, ports., maps, facsim. 21 cm. 25-6831.   F130. S2 B3

WALLOONS. ... De Pierre Minuit aux Roosevelt, l'epopee belge aux Etats-Unis. (N.Y.) Brentano's (1943)   3, (9)-284 p. illus., plates, etc. 18 cm. "Sources bibliographiques: p. (1277)-280. 43-3880.   F130. W2 G6

NEW YORK
SUPPLEMENTARY INDEX OF PLACES

ACRA. 1071
ADIRONDACK MTNS. 840
ALASKA. 1059
ALBANY. 746, 766, 774, 786, 795, 806, 816, 844, 852, 897, 1106, 1149, 1152
ALBANY Co. 751, 755, 765, 808, 846, 893
ALBION. 889, 1128
ALEXANDER. 1045
ALEXANDRIA BAY. 906
ALLEGANY. 1117
ALLEGANY Co. 838, 839, 843
ALMOND. 1093
ALPLAUS. 1037, 1140
ALTAMONT. 1037
AMAWALK. 1164
AMENIA. 832, 1103
AMSTERDAM. 844, 1140, 1149
ANDOVER. 1159
AQUEDUCT. 1037, 1140
ARARAT. 1061, 1064
ARDSLEY. 913, 1150, 1161
ARKPORT. 1093
ARSHAMOMAQUE. 1146
ASTORIA. 1104
ATHENS. 844, 1047, 1071
ATHENS JCT. 1140
ATTICA. 1043
AUBURN. 750
AURORA. 1044
AUSABLE CHASM. 815, 835
AUSABLE LAKES. 812
AVON. 1128
BABYLON. 904, 1043, 1095
BACON HILL. 1116
BALD MOUNTAIN. 1090
BALLSTON (SPA) 795, 844, 896, 1136, 1138, 1140
BALLSTON LAKE. 1140
BALMVILLE. 888
BATAVIA. 1043
BATH. 1037, 1047
BATH BEACH. 1052, 1077
BATTENKILL. 1090
BAY SHORE 857
BAYPORT. 857
BEACON. 832
BEDFORD CORNERS. 1056
BEEKMAN. 832
BELCODA. 1161

BELLEROSE. 1084
BELLEVUE. 1140
BELLPORT. 857
BELMONT. 1048, 1159
BERGEN. 1045
BENSONHURST. 1052
BETHLEHEM. 816, 1037
BEULAH. 1161
BINGHAMTON. 746, 819
BLACK RIVER. 1104
BLACK RIVER CANAL. 760
BLASDELL. 1101.
BLENHEIM. 1087
BLISSVILLE. 1104
BLUE MOUNTAIN LAKE. 812, 813, 814, 842
BLUE POINT. 857
BOONVILLE. 1104
BREWSTER. 892, 916, 1161
BRIGHTON. 1128, 1129
BRIGHTON HEIGHTS. 900
BROADALBIN. 1106, 1116
BROCTON. 826
BRONX Co. 846, 918, 975, 979, 988, 1008, 1009
BRONXVILLE. 1108, 1161
BROOKHAVEN. 904, 1046
BROOKLYN. 845, 855 928, 935, 937, 952, 954, 962, 966, 967 968, 970, 974, 975, 979, 1004, 1008, 1012
BROOME. 1087
BROOME Co. 828
BROWNSVILLE. 1056
BRUNSWICK. 1037
BUFFALO. 786, 795, 835, 872
BURNT HILLS. 1140
BUSHWICK. 1052
BUSKIRK. 1093
BUSKIRKS BRIDGE. 1093
BUTLER. 1134
CAIRO. 1071
CALDWELL. 1088
CAMBRIDGE. 1089, 1090
CAMDEN. 1154
CAMILLUS. 886
CANAAN. 1147
CANAJOHARIE. 866
CANANDAIGUA. 886, 1128
CANASTOTA. 1117
CANISTEO. 1093

CARMAN. 1037, 1140
CARMEL. 892
CARTHAGE. 817, 1104
CATSKILL. 844, 1103, 1149
CATSKILL FALLS. 785
CATSKILLS. 841, 1013
CATTARAUGUS Co. 838, 843
CAYUGA. 1044.
CAYUGA Co. 808
CAYUGA LAKE. 1097
CEDARHURST. 870, 1156
CELORON. 1098
CENTREPORT. 1094
CENTRAL NYACK. 1116
CENTRE FALLS. 1090
CHAPPAQUA. 916
CHARLESTON. 1088
CHARLOTTE. 1079
CHARLOTTE PRECINCT. 833
CHARLTON. 1045
CHATHAM. 1087
CHAUTAUQUA. 877
CHAUTAUQUA Co. 838, 843, 1083, 1124
CHEMUNG Co. 808, 838, 908
CHENANGO Co. 808, 819
CHENANGO FORK. 1047
CHENANGO POINT. 1048
CHILI. 1129
CHILSON. 1150
CHURCHVILLE. 1128
CLARKSTOWN. 895
CLAVERACK. 1094
CLAYVILLE. 1154
CLIFTON PARK. 1156
CLIFTON SPRINGS. 1128
CLINTON. 832, 833, 1079, 1123
CLINTON CORNERS. 1118
COBLESKILL. 1102
COHOES. 844, 1037, 1149, 1152
COLD BROOK. 843
COLD SPRING HARBOR. 1094
COLLIERS. 1118
COLLINS. 1076
COLONIE. 1037
COLUMBIA Co. 751, 755, 846, 850, 1094
CONEY ISLAND. 798, 1013
CONKLIN. 819
CONSTABLEVILLE. 1104
COOPERSTOWN. 798, 891, 1118
COPAKE. 830
COPENHAGEN. 1104
CORFU. 1045

CORINTH. 1045
CORNING. 1047
CORNWALL. 746, 887, 888
CORNWALL-ON-THE-HUDSON. 747
CORTLAND. 1041
CORTLAND Co. 808
CORTLANDT. 915
COXSACKIE. 844, 1071
CRANBERRY LAKE. 816
CROFTON. 916
CROGHAM. 1104
CROPSEYVILLE. 1072
CROTON. 1150
CROWN POINT. 836, 1150
CRUGERS. 1150
CRUM ELBOW PRECINCT. 833
CUTCHOGUE. 1145
DANSVILLE. 1128
DEERPARK. 889
DELANSON. 1140
DELAWARE Co. 823
DELMAR. 1037
DEPEW. 1060 1060
DOBBS FERRY. 913, 918, 1120, 1150
DOLGEVILLE. 843, 1103
DORLACH. 1102
DOUGLASTON. 1103
DUANESBURGH. 1069, 1107
DUNKIRK. 788, 826
DURHAMVILLE. 1117
DUTCH KILLS. 1104
DUTCHESS Co. 765, 766, 808, 846, 850
DYSE'S MANOR. 1087
EAGLE BRIDGE. 1093
EAGLE MILLS. 1072
EAST ALBANY. 1037
EAST END. 1118
EAST GREENBUSH. 1037
EAST GREENWICH. 1090
EAST NORTHPORT. 1094
EAST PEMBROKE. 1045
EAST ROCKAWAY. 1104, 1133
EAST UNION. 1047
EAST VILLAGE. 1093
EAST WILLISTON. 1107
EASTCHESTER. 1108, 1109
EASTHAMPTON. 904
EDISON PARK. 1140
ELIZABETHTOWN. 812
ELMHURST. 738
ELMIRA. 828, 1047
ELMSFORD. 1161

ELSMERE. 1037
ENDICOTT. 819, 1048
ENDWELL. 1083
ERIE CANAL. 760, 786
ERIE Co. 755, 838, 843, 1061, 1063, 1069
ESOPUS. 743, 1100
ESSEX Co. 829, 846
EVANS MILLS. 1104
FACTORY HOLLOW. 887
FACTORYVILLE. 1150
FAIRPORT. 1128
FALCONER. 1098
FAR ROCKAWAY. 1013, 1077
FAYETTEVILLE. 1105
FELTS MILLS. 1104
FIRE ISLAND. 1013
FISHKILL. 832, 833, 1040
FISHKILL LANDING. 1124
FLATBUSH. 1052
FLATLANDS. 855, 1052
FLORIDA. 1099, 1107
FLOWER HILL. 1105
FLUSHING. 798, 862, 1098, 1126
FORDHAM. 916, 917
FOREST HILLS. 1128
FORESTPORT. 1104
FORESTVILLE. 826, 1143
FORT EDWARD. 1088
FORT HAMILTON. 1077
FORT LEE. 1013
FORT PLAIN. 866
FORT SCHUYLER. 884
FORT TICONDEROGA. 1150
FRANKFORT. 843, 1092
FRANKLIN Co. 755, 829, 889, 896
FREDERICKSTOWN. 832
FREDONIA. 826, 1080
FREEHOLD. 1045, 1071
FULTON. 750, 1119
FULTON CHAIN. 814
FULTON Co. 751, 755, 866, 869, 890
FULTONVILLE. 866
GALLATIN. 830
GALLOWAY. 1159
GARBUTT. 1161
GARDENVILLE. 1101
GARDINER'S ISLAND. 1082
GARDNERTOWN. 888, 1114
GATES. 1128, 1129
GAYHEAD. 1071
GENESEE Co. 755, 843
GENESEE FALLS. 878

GENESEE VALLEY CANAL. 760
GENESEO. 1128
GENEVA. 886, 1044, 1070, 1128
GERMANTOWN. 830
GIBBONSVILLE. 1158
GLASCO. 1139
GLEN ISLAND. 1013
GLENDALE. 1104
GLENHAM. 1046
GLENS FALLS. 844, 1149
GLENVILLE. 1037
GLOVERSVILLE. 844, 1149
GOAT ISLAND. 879
GORHAM. 839
GOSHEN. 1107
GOTHAM. 762
GOWANUS. 1051, 1112
GRAND ISLAND. 1058
GRAND VIEW. 1116
GRAVESEND. 855, 1076
GREAT BEND. 1104
GREAT LAKES. 1059
GREECE. 1128, 1129
GREEN ISLAND. 1037, 1152
GREEN MOUNTAIN. 826
GREENBUSH. 893, 1037, 1160
GREENE. 751
GREENE Co. 755, 822, 846, 850, 897
GREENPOINT. 1051
GREENVILLE. 889
GREENWICH. 1082
GREYCOURT. 1049
GUILDERLAND. 816, 1037
HAGAMAN'S MILLS. 1043
HALLSVILLE. 1107
HAMMONDSPORT. 1047
HARRISON. 1104, 1105, 1135
HARRISONVILLE. 1071
HARROWER'S MILLS. 1043
HARTSDALE. 1161
HARTWICK. 1118
HARTWICK SEMINARY. 1118
HASHAMOMUCK. 1145
HASTINGS. 913, 1150
HAVANA GLEN. 799
HAVILAND HOLLOW. 1126
HAWTHORNE. 916
HAYNES JUNCTION. 1140
HEATHCOTE MANOR. 1139
HEMPSTEAD. 862
HERKIMER. 1103, 1154
HERKIMER Co. 755, 866, 890

HEWLETT. 870, 1156
HIGH BRIDGE. 1013
HIGHBRIDGE. 1083
HIGHLANDS OF THE HUDSON. 1013
HILLSDALE. 830
HINSDALE. 1117
HOFFMANS. 1037
HOLLAND PATENT. 1104
HOLLEY. 889
HOLLIS. 1097
HOMER. 1078
HOMEWOOD. 1083
HOMMOCKS. 836
HOOPER. 1047
HOOSICK FALLS. 1093
HORSEHEADS. 828, 1047, 1083
HUDSON. 844, 1149
HUNTER'S POINT. 1104
HUNTINGTON. 857, 904
HURON. 1134
HYDE PARK. 833
ILION. 843, 1092, 1103
INWOOD. 870, 1156
IRONDEQUOIT. 1128, 1129
IRONVILLE. 1150
IRVING. 826, 1143
IRVINGTON. 913, 918, 1150
ISLIP. 857, 904
ITHACA. 1047
JAMAICA. 893, 1126
JAMAICA BAY. 1056
JAMESTOWN. 1073, 1083
JAYVILLE. 1071
JEFFERSON Co. 755, 889
JEFFERSON HEIGHTS. 1071
JERDON FALLS. 1104
JOHNSON CITY. 819, 1047, 1048
JOHNSTOWN. 844, 1089, 1149
KAKIAT. 1159
KANADESAGA. 1086
KATONAH. 916
KENT. 892
KENWOOD. 1117
KESKACHAUGE. 864
KEW GARDENS. 1128
KILLAWOG. 820
KILLBUCK. 1136
KINGS Co. 766, 905
KINGS BRIDGE. 916
KINGSBRIDGE. 1015
KINGSTON. 743, 767, 844, 910, 1149
KIRKLAND. 1123

KIRKWOOD. 819
KISKATOM. 1103
LAKE CANANDAIGUA. 799
LAKE CHAMPLAIN. 745, 774, 786, 792, 799, 806,
    811, 815, 839, 840, 845, 851, 1138
LAKE CAYUGA. 799
LAKE ERIE. 1063
LAKE GEORGE. 745, 774, 785, 786, 793, 809, 811,
    815, 825, 826, 798, 799, 806, 844, 851, 1151
LAKE KATRINE. 844
LAKE KEUKA. 799
LAKE LUZERNE. 815
LAKE MAHOPAC. 892, 1118
LAKE MINNEWASKA. 910
LAKE ONTARIO. 762
LAKE PLACID. 809
LAKE ST. REGIS. 809
LAKE SARANAC. 809
LAKE SENECA. 799
LAKEWOOD. 1098
LANCASTER. 735, 1058
LANSINGBURGH. 844, 893, 1034
LARCHMONT. 918, 1110
LAURENS. 1118
LAWRENCE. 870, 1156
LEBANON. 795
LEEDS. 1071
LESTERSHIRE. 1047
LEWIS Co. 755, 853, 889
LISLE. 820
LITTLE FALLS. 750, 842, 1154
LIVINGSTON. 1105
LIVINGSTON Co. 838, 839, 868
LIVINGSTON MANOR. 1074, 1166
LLOYDS NECK. 892
LOCKPORT. 735, 1060
LOCUST VALLEY. 1088
LONG BEACH. 1013
LONG ISLAND. 928, 938, 982, 1013, 1051, 1052
LONG ISLAND CITY. 856, 862, 1126
LONG LAKE. 814, 842
LOON LAKE. 809
LOUDONVILLE. 1037
LOWVILLE. 1154
LUDINGTONVILLE. 892
LUZERNE. 912
LYNDONVILLE. 1104
LYONS. 1134
MADISON Co. 808, 829
MALDEN. 844, 1139
MAMARONECK. 844
MARIAVILLE. 1140

MARLBORO. 910
MASSENA SPRINGS. 815
MAXWELL. 913
McGRAW. 1078
MAYFIELD. 1116
MECHANICVILLE. 1045, 1136
MEDINA. 889
MELLENVILLE. 1122
MENANDS. 1037
MIDDLE BUSH. 1118
MIDDLE FALLS. 1090
MIDDLEVILLE. 843
MILFORD. 1118
MILTON. 1045
MINEVILLE. 1150
MINISINK. 889
MOHAWK. 842, 1092, 1103
MOHAWKVILLE. 1140
MOHONK. 910
MONROE Co. 838, 839, 1128, 1130
MONT PLEASANT. 1140
MONTAUK. 862, 892, 904
MONTCALM LANDING. 1150
MONTGOMERY. 1049
MONTGOMERY Co. 751, 755, 837, 866, 909
MONTICELLO. 1124
MONTMORENCI FALLS. 878
MOODNA. 888
MORAVIA. 1044
MORESVILLE. 1125
MORIAH. 1150
MORIAH CENTER. 1150
MORICHES (East and Center) 857
MORRISANIA. 916
MOUNT HOPE. 889
MOUNT KISCO. 916
MOUNT McGREGOR. 1138
MOUNT MORRIS. 1128
MOUNT PLEASANT. 913
MOUNT VERNON. 844, 913
MT. VISION. 1118
MUMFORD. 1161
MUNSEY PARK. 1105
NASSAU Co. 856, 857, 859, 860, 928
NATURAL BRIDGE. 1071
NELLISTON. 866
NEW BALTIMORE. 844, 1075
NEW CONCORD. 1087
NEW HARLEM. 931
NEW HARTFORD. 1154, 1155
NEW RHINEBECK. 1102
NEW ROCHELLE. 844, 913, 916, 918

NEW SCOTLAND. 816
NEW SPRINGVILLE. 902
NEW UTRECHT. 855, 1046, 1052
NEW WINDSOR. 888, 1113
NEW YORK CITY. 786, 787, 796, 800, 851, 852, 853, 1114
NEW YORK Co. 931
NEW YORK MILLS. 1154, 1155
NEWARK. 1128
NEWBURGH. 766, 820, 887, 888
NEWBURGH BAY. 887
NEWPORT. 843
NEWTOWN. 856, 1083, 1098
NEWTONVILLE 1037
NIAGARA. 762, 768, 785
NIAGARA Co. 755, 838, 843, 1103, 1104
NIAGARA FALLS. 783, 784, 786, 792, 793, 794, 796, 800, 806, 924, 1060, 1062, 1064, 1066, 1067, 1068
NISKAYUNA. 1037, 1156
NORTH BEACH. 862
NORTH COLLINS. 1076
NORTH GREENBUSH. 1162
NORTH GREENWICH. 1090
NORTH HEMPSTEAD. 1135
NORTH HILLS. 1105
NORTH HOOSICK. 1093
NORTH HORNELL. 1093
NORTH TARRYTON. 913, 1150
NORTHEAST. 832
NORTHFIELD. 902, 903
NORTHPORT. 857, 1094
NORWICH. 746, 1154
OAKDALE. 1047
OAKFIELD. 1045
OCEANSIDE. 1133.
OGDENSBURG(H) 746, 765
ONE THOUSAND ISLANDS. 800, 815
ONEIDA. 750
ONEIDA CASTLE. 1117
ONEIDA Co. 808, 866, 1134, 1155
ONEONTA PLAINS. 1118
ONONDAGA Co. 762, 808
ONTARIO Co. 808, 838, 839
ORANGE Co. 765, 808, 846, 850, 899
ORANGETOWN. 1118
ORIENT. 1146
ORISKANY. 884
ORISKANY FALLS. 1154
ORLEANS Co. 755, 838, 839, 843
OSCAWANA. 1150
OSSINING. 916, 918

OSWEGO. 746, 747, 750, 762, 885
OSWEGO Co. 755
OSWEGO FALLS. 1119
OTSEGO Co. 755, 1118
OTSEGO LAKE. 1077, 1078
OWEGO. 908, 1047
OXFORD. 1116
OZONE PARK. 1128
PAHAQUARRY. 910
PALATINE BRIDGE. 866
PARKVIEW. 1048
PATCHOGUE. 857
PATTERSON. 892, 916
PATTERSONVILLE. 1037, 1140
PAWLING. 832, 916
PECONIC. 1146
PEEKSKILL. 913, 915, 918, 1150
PELHAM. 1108, 1110
PENN YAN. 1047
PERTH. 1106, 1159
PHELPS. 839
PHILADELPHIA. 1104
PHILIPSBOROUGH. 915
PHILIPSBURG(H). 914, 916, 917
PHILIPSTOWN. 832
PIERMONT. 788, 1116
PINE HILL & SUMMIT MOUNTAIN. 820
PITTSFORD. 1128, 1129
PLAINS. 910
PLANDOME. 1124
PLEASANT VALLEY. 1117
PLEASANTVILLE. 916
POLAND. 843
PORT BYRON. 1044
PORT CHESTER. 844, 913
PORT DICKINSON. 1047, 1048
PORT HENRY. 1150
PORT JEFFERSON. 857
PORT LEYDEN. 817, 1104
PORT RICHMOND, S.I. 737
PORT SCHUYLER. 1158
PORTLANDVILLE. 1118
PORTVILLE. 1117
POTSDAM. 1106
POTTER HILL. 1093
POUGHKEEPSIE. 832, 833, 844, 850, 1149
PROSPECT. 1104
PULTNEYVILLE. 913
PURLING. 1071
PUTNAM Co. 808, 833, 834, 846, 917, 918
QUAKER STREET. 1140
QUEENS. 974, 975, 979, 1051

QUEENS Co. 766, 856
QUEENS VILLAGE. 1097
QUEENSBURY. 896, 912, 1073
RAMAPO. 1013
RAQUETTE LAKE. 814, 842
RAVENA. 844
RAVENSWOOD. 1104
RENSSELAER. 844, 1037, 1149
RENSSELAER Co. 751, 755, 816, 817, 846, 1152
RENSSELAERSWYCK. 1038, 1160
REXFORD FLATS. 1140
RHINEBECK. 832, 834
RICHFIELD SPRINGS. 1154
RICHMOND. 902, 974, 979, 1135
RICHMOND Co. 700
RICHMOND HILL. 1097, 1126
RIPLEY. 826
RIVERDALE. 1015
RIVERHEAD. 857, 904, 1146
ROCHESTER. 760, 868, 869, 1067
ROCKAWAY. 1013
ROCKAWAY BEACH. 798, 1077
ROCKLAND Co. 808, 846, 887
ROME. 746, 750, 883, 1128, 1154
RONDOUT. 1100
ROSLYN ESTATES. 1105
ROTTERDAM. 1037
ROTTERDAM JUNCTION. 1140
ROUND TOP. 1071
ROXBURY. 1125
RYE. 844, 913, 917, 1105
ST. JOHNSVILLE. 866
ST. LAWRENCE Co. 755, 889
SALEM. 1089
SANDGATE. 1070
SANDY HILL. 1088
SARATOGA. 798, 799, 844, 851, 852, 1088, 1142, 1149
SARATOGA Co. 751, 816, 817, 846, 893
SARATOGA SPRINGS. 786, 792, 793, 795, 806, 815, 841, 844, 845, 879
SARDINIA. 1076
SAUGERTIES. 844, 1071
SAVANNAH. 1134
SAYRE. 1047
SAYVILLE. 857
SCARBOROUGH. 1150
SCARSDALE. 918, 1161
SCHAGHTICOKE. 1037
SCHENECTADY. 740, 765, 844, 897, 1149
SCHENECTADY Co. 755, 816, 817, 866, 893, 1140

SCHOHARIE.   766, 1166
SCHOHARIE Co.   755, 866, 897
SCHROON LAKE.   815, 840, 912
SCHUYLER Co.   808, 828, 838, 899, 908
SCHUYLERVILLE.   1045, 1090, 1136
SCIO.   1159
SCOTIE.   1140
SCOTTSVILLE.   1128, 1161
SELKIRK.   844
SENECA Co.   808
SENECA FALLS.   1044
SHANKS VILLAGE.   1118
SHARON SPRINGS.   798, 1102
SHAWANGUNK.   1110
SHAWANGUNK MTS.   865
SHEEPSHEAD BAY.   1077
SHELTER ISLAND.   904
SHERBURNE.   1116, 1154
SHERIDAN.   1143
SHERRILL.   1117
SHUSHAN.   1089
SIDNEY.   746
SILVER CREEK.   826
SINCLAIRVILLE.   1072
SING SING.   913, 1150
SKANEATALES.   1044
SLEEPY HOLLOW.   1150
SLIDE MOUNTAIN.   823
SLINGERLANDS.   1037
SLOOP LANDING.   913
SNEDENS LANDING.   1120
SODUX.   913, 1128, 1134
SOLVAY.   1148
SONNONTOUAN.   899
SOUTH BETHLEHEM.   1037
SOUTH CAIRO.   1071
SOUTH GLENS FALLS.   1088
SOUTH NYACK.   1116
SOUTH SCHENECTADY.   1037, 1140
SOUTHAMPTON.   862, 904
SOUTHEAST.   832
SOUTHOLD.   836, 904, 1145
SPARKHILL.   1116
SPARROWBUSH.   1124
SPENCERPORT.   1128
SPRAKERS.   866
SPUYTEN DUYVIL.   1015
STATEN ISLAND.   798, 849, 857, 962
STEINWAY.   1104
STELLA.   1047
STEUBEN.   808, 838, 839, 908, 1127
STEWART MANOR.   1084

STILLWATER.   1045, 1106, 1136
STOTTVILLE.   1094
STREETROAD.   1150
SUCCESS.   1105
SUFFOLK Co.   766, 856, 857, 859, 860, 928
SULLIVAN Co.   899
SUNNYSIDE.   914
SUNRISE TERRACE.   1083
SWANENBURGH.   743, 1100, 1101
SYRACUSE.   750, 885, 886, 1128
TAGHKANICK.   1159
TAPPAN.   895
TARRYTOWN.   913, 916, 918
TICONDEROGA.   836, 840
TIOGA Co.   808, 908
TICONICS.   1013
TOMPKINS Co.   808, 908
TOMPKINSVILLE.   900, 903
TONAWANDA.   1058, 1068
TONAWANDAS (The)   1060
TOWNERS.   892
TRENTON.   1104
TRENTON FALLS.   815, 878, 1127
TROY.   786, 844, 849, 852, 893, 1037, 1106, 1149
TRYON Co.   869
TUCKAHOE.   1050, 1108
TURIN.   1104
TWIN ORCHARDS.   1083
ULSTER Co.   765, 766, 808, 822, 846, 850, 899,
        1100, 1101
ULYSSES.   909
UNION SPRINGS.   1044
UPPER NYACK.   1116
URLTON.   1071
UTICA.   746, 750, 882, 883, 884, 1067
VALLEY FALLS.   1037
VAN CORTLAND MANOR.   917
VERPLANCK'S POINT.   1150
VESTAL.   819, 1047, 1083
VESTAL GARDENS.   1083
VICTOR.   1128
VICTORY MILLS.   1045, 1090
VISSCHER'S FERRY.   1115
WADHAMS.   1150
WALLKILL VALLEY.   852
WALLOOMSAC.   1093
WAMPSVILLE.   1117
WARREN Co.   817, 846, 893
WARSAW.   1043
WASHINGTON.   832
WASHINGTON Co.   751, 817, 846, 849, 893
WASHINGTON MILLS.   1154

WASHINGTONVILLE. 1049
WATERFORD. 844, 1037, 1136, 1152
WATERLOO. 1143
WATERVLIET. 1152
WATKINS GLEN. 799, 898, 899
WAVERLY. 1047
WAWASINK. 1159
WAWAYANDA. 889
WAYLAND. 1079
WAYNE Co. 808, 838, 839
WEBSTER. 1128
WEEDSPORT. 1044
WEMPLE. 844
WEST ATHENS. 844
WEST CARTHAGE. 1104
WEST CAMP. 844
WEST CHARLTON. 1123
WEST DURHAM. 1080
WEST FARMS. 917, 1015
WEST HOOSICK. 1093
WEST NEW BRIGHTON. 902
WEST ONEONTA. 1118
WEST POINT. 892
WEST TROY. 1037, 1158
WEST WINFIELD. 843
WESTCHESTER Co. 766, 846, 928, 982, 1013

WESTFIELD. 826, 1135
WESTONS MILLS. 1117
WESTOVER. 1047
WESTPORT. 1150
WHEATLAND CENTER. 1161
WHITE CREEK. 1089
WHITE MOUNTAIN. 826
WHITE PLAINS. 844, 913, 916, 918, 1118, 1135
WHITESBORO. 884, 1154, 1155
WHITESTOWN. 884, 1109
WHITNEY'S POINT. 820
WICOPESSET. 836
WILTWYCK. 743, 1100, 1101
WILLIAMSBURG(H). 937, 1051, 1052, 1056, 1069
WILLISTON PARK. 1107
WINGDALE. 1080
WITHERBEE. 1150
WOLCOTT. 1134
WOODHAVEN. 1128
WOODMERE. 870, 1156
WOODROW. 903
WOODSIDE. 862
WYOMING Co. 755, 838, 839, 843, 856
YATES Co. 808, 838, 839
YONKERS. 913, 991, 1050, 1150
YORKTOWN HEIGHTS. 1164
YORKVILLE. 1154

ADDITIONS TO INDEX

LATHAMS. 1037
LEROY. 1043, 1045
MONTROSE. 1159

SMITHTOWN. 904, 905
UNION. 819, 1047
WATERTOWN. 746, 750, 854